# Literatures of Asia, Africa, and Latin America

## From Antiquity to the Present

Edited and with introductions by

**Willis Barnstone**
INDIANA UNIVERSITY

**Tony Barnstone**
WHITTIER COLLEGE

**Prentice Hall**
Upper Saddle River, New Jersey 07458

**Library of Congress Cataloging-in-Publication Data**

Literatures of Asia, Africa, and Latin America / edited and with
  introductions by Willis Barnstone, Tony Barnstone.
    p.  cm.
  Includes bibliographical references and index.
  ISBN 0-02-306065-4
  1. Literature—Collections.  2. Developing countries—Literatures.
3. Developing countries—Literatures—Translations into English.
I. Barnstone, Willis, (date).  II. Barnstone, Tony.
PN6014.L63  1999
808.8—dc20                                       95-25423
                                                     CIP

Editorial Director: Charlyce Jones Owen
Editor-in-Chief: Leah Jewell
Acquisition Editor: Carrie Brandon
Editorial Assistant: Gianna Caradonna
Vice President and Director of Production
  and Manufacturing: Barbara Kittle
Senior Managing Editor: Bonnie Biller
Production Liaison: Fran Russello
Project Manager: Linda B. Pawelchak

Manufacturing Manager: Nick Sklitsis
Prepress and Manufacturing Buyer:
  Mary Ann Gloriande
Creative Design Director: Leslie Osher
Art Director: Maria Lange/Anne Nieglos
Interior Design: Delgado Design, Inc.
Cover Director: Jayne Conte
Cover Design: Robert Farrar-Wagner
Marketing Manager: Gina Sluss

This book was set in 10/12 New Baskerville by Digitype
and was printed and bound by Courier Companies, Inc.
The cover was printed by Phoenix Color Corp.

© 1999 by Prentice-Hall, Inc.
Simon & Schuster/A Viacom Company
Upper Saddle River, New Jersey 07458

## This book is dedicated to Elli Tzalopoulou Barnstone

Acknowledgments begin on page 1958, which constitutes an extension of this
copyright page.

Printed in the United States of America
10  9  8  7  6  5  4  3  2  1

ISBN 0-02-306065-4

Prentice-Hall International (UK) Limited, *London*
Prentice-Hall of Australia Pty. Limited, *Sydney*
Prentice-Hall Canada Inc., *Toronto*
Prentice-Hall Hispanoamericana, S.A., *Mexico*
Prentice-Hall of India Private Limited, *New Delhi*
Prentice-Hall of Japan, Inc., *Tokyo*
Simon & Schuster Asia Pte. Ltd., *Singapore*
Editora Prentice-Hall do Brasil, Ltda., *Rio de Janeiro*

# C O N T E N T S

# Section 2 ■ Near East and North Africa (The Bridge)     755

# Section 4 ■ Precolumbian America, Latin America, and Caribbean   1499

# DISCOVERY, CONQUEST, AND THE COLONIES

# Poetry

## SECTION 1 ■ ASIA

# SECTION 2 ▪ NEAR EAST AND NORTH AFRICA (THE BRIDGE)

# SECTION 3 ■ SUB-SAHARA AFRICA

## ■ THE PREMODERN PERIOD

### Oral Epics, Stories, Songs (Diverse Periods)

## ■ THE MODERN PERIOD

# SECTION 4 ■ PRECOLUMBIAN AMERICA, LATIN AMERICA, AND CARIBBEAN

## ■ NATIVE AMERICAN LITERATURE OF PRECOLUMBIAN AND LATER PERIODS

### Quechua Language

### Maya Language

### Quiche-Maya Language

### Nahuatl Language

## ■ DISCOVERY, CONQUEST, AND THE COLONIES

## ■ NINETEENTH AND TWENTIETH CENTURIES

# Fiction

## SECTION 1 ■ ASIA

### ■ INDIA, PAKISTAN, AND BANGLADESH

#### Classical Sanskrit, Prakrit, and Tamil Literatures (c. 200 B.C.–A.D. 1100)

#### The Modern Period (Nineteenth and Twentieth Centuries)

### ■ CHINA

#### Tang Dynasty (618–907)

#### Yuan Dynasty (1280–1367)

#### Ming Dynasty (1368–1644)

#### Qing Dynasty (1644–1911)

## SECTION 2: ■ NEAR EAST AND NORTH AFRICA (THE BRIDGE)

# SECTION 3: ■ SUB-SAHARA AFRICA

## ■ THE PREMODERN PERIOD

### Oral Epics, Stories, Songs (Diverse Periods)

## ■ THE MODERN PERIOD

# SECTION 4: ■ PRECOLUMBIAN AMERICA, LATIN AMERICA, AND CARIBBEAN

## ■ NATIVE AMERICAN LITERATURE OF PRECOLUMBIAN AND LATER PERIODS

### Quechua Language

# Prose Nonfiction

## SECTION 1 ■ ASIA

### ■ INDIA, PAKISTAN, AND BANGLADESH

# SECTION 2: ■ NEAR EAST AND NORTH AFRICA (THE BRIDGE)

# SECTION 3: ■ SUB-SAHARA AFRICA

## ■ THE PREMODERN PERIOD

### Oral Creation Myths (Uncertain Period)

### Slave Narrative

## ■ THE MODERN PERIOD

# SECTION 4: ■ PRECOLUMBIAN AMERICA, LATIN AMERICA, AND CARIBBEAN

## ■ NATIVE AMERICAN LITERATURE OF PRECOLUMBIAN AND LATER PERIODS

### Quechua Language

### Carib Languages

# Drama

# P R E F A C E

*Literatures of Asia, Africa, and Latin America,* in combination with the two volumes of *Literature of the Western World,*[1] has been designed to present teachers and students with a textbook representative of the finest works of world literature, one that is amenable to many different teaching approaches. Like the earlier volumes, this book has been designed to include a wealth of materials, so as to give teachers choices that they can tailor to their own preferences, needs, and expertise. This capaciousness will allow students to read around in authors, periods, and traditions that particularly excite them, supplementing assigned reading and providing an essential source book for their individual research. Teaching such a broad spectrum of texts may be challenging, and with this in mind we have supported the literary texts with a full apparatus: a general introduction, section introductions, subsection introductions, and extensive headnotes. These supporting materials provide broad and specific contexts, placing literary texts within important cultural, linguistic, and historical movements. In addition, the headnotes include up-to-date bibliographies to guide students for further research.

Translations have been selected primarily for their literary quality because we firmly believe that it is a disservice to students, professors, and authors to present a great work of literature in an English translation that does not read as literature. The depth and quality of these texts demand excellent translations, so that students and professors may encounter them in a form that preserves their artistic integrity and delight. The translators featured here are among the finest in their fields, and many are themselves prominent writers. They include Robert Pinsky, Richard Burton, Burton Watson, Barbara Stoler Miller, A. K. Ramanujan, Arthur Waley, Ezra Pound, Kenneth Rexroth, Helen Craig McCullough, Donald Keene, Chana Bloch, Stephen Mitchell, W. S. Merwin, Mark Strand, Gordon Brotherston, Elizabeth Bishop, Robert Bly, Paul Blackburn, Anthony Kerrigan, James Merrill, Nathaniel Tarn, Gregory Rabassa, Richard Wilbur, Clayton Eshleman, James Wright, and Philip Levine, among others. Our one rule has been to include no translation that is merely adequate. In a sense, then, this text is a showcase for the art of literary translation, and our hope has been to compile an anthology that students will want to take home with them and to read around in long after the course is completed.

---

1. Brian Wilkie and James Hurt, eds., *Literature of the Western World,* 2 vols. (Upper Saddle River, NJ: Prentice Hall, 1997).

In addition to literary texts, *Literatures of Asia, Africa, and Latin America* includes selections from religious and philosophical texts that have literary merit, such as the Rig Veda; the Upanishads; Mahayana and Theravada Buddhist texts; the Bhagavad-Gita; classical Indian devotional (bhakti) verse; the *Analects* of Confucius; the Dao-De-Jing; Zen poems, essays, and stories; the Old Testament; the New Testament; the Dead Sea Scrolls; Gnostic and other intertestamental scriptures; the Quran; Sufi poems and teaching stories; African oral creation myths; as well as Native American hymns, creation myths, shaman narrations, cures, chronicles, and exorcisms. These beautiful texts also provide a cosmological and cultural context for literary movements. Extensive headnotes and introductions trace out religious movements and influence, giving students a broad overview of world religions, which, in the East as in the West, have often inspired and been an essential part of world literatures.

The book also includes important examples of the secular essay, including Precolumbian historical annals; the log of Christopher Columbus; colonial histories and letters by Bartolomé de las Casas, Bernal Díaz del Castillo, the Inca Garcilaso de la Vega, and Sor Juana Inés de la Cruz; Mahatma Gandhi writing on passive resistance; a selection of classical Chinese and Japanese literary criticism; *ars poeticas* and meditative essays; along with memoirs by Liang Heng, Olaudah Equiano, and Breyten Breytenbach. These essays are themselves of immense literary importance and at the same time provide political, esthetic, philosophical, historical, and biographical supplements to the literary selections. In addition to providing context for the literary selections, the essays will provide students with a valuable resource for writing and researching their own essays.

In dealing with many literatures written in many languages, a special problem is presented by the question of orthography. In several literatures (notably those of India, China, Japan, and the Mideast), there are alternate and warring systems of transliteration. Generally speaking, we have chosen to use those transliteration systems that are best designed for the general, nonspecialist reader, for whom a more scholarly orthography would prove less informative. However, we did not wish to tamper with the integrity of translators' choices, and so in some cases the headnote is rendered in simplified orthography (reflecting English spellings), while the text is maintained in scholarly orthography (reflecting the specialized phonetics of the source language). In such cases, where necessary, we attempt to avoid confusion through footnotes (the nonspecialist may not realize, for example, that the god Shiva is the same as Śiva). China presented us with a singular dilemma, because the long-dominant Wade-Giles system, used until recently by the majority of literary translators, has now been superseded by the Pinyin system. Those Western readers who have a basic familiarity with Chinese literature may, therefore, have a hard time recognizing that the Daoist philosopher Zhuangzi (Pinyin) is the same person as Chuang Tzu (Wade-Giles), that Bo Juyi is Po Chü-i, and Laozi is

Lao Tzu. For China, therefore, we include Wade-Giles names in parentheses after Pinyin names in the headnotes (except for those rare names, such as "Wang Wei," for which there is no difference between the systems). For Japanese terms and names, we have followed standard simplified transliteration practice, primarily eliminating long vowels (Bashō becomes Basho). When referring to Japanese nō plays, however, we use the now-archaic transliteration "noh" instead of "no," to avoid possible confusion with the English word.

Similarly, some readers may be confused by the fact that authors they may be familiar with from Japan appear here with their names inverted. The novels of Nobel Prize–winning author Mishima Yukio, for example, are commonly presented in English translation under the name Yukio Mishima, but in this text we have respected Japanese name order (last name first, first name last). Some ancient Japanese names include the preposition "no," which means "of," rather like early English usage (as in John of Gaunt). "Ibn" in Arabic names and "ben" in Hebrew names mean "son of." Chinese names, like Japanese names, appear with the family name first and personal name last. Transposed into English name order, for example, Mao Zedong would be rendered Zedong Mao. As with Japanese names, we have respected Chinese name order in this text.

We would like to thank the many scholars who have contributed to the project: J. P. Seaton and Chou Ping for advice on the China section; Sam Hamill for his observations on China and Japan; Richard Serrano for suggestions about China, the Near East, and North Africa; Ariel Bloch for his comments on the Bridge; Brenda Schildgen and Sara Saleri for their suggestions for the Indian subcontinent; Roberto González-Echevarría for advice on Cuban and Latin American writers; and Eileen Julien for her suggestions on sub-Sahara literatures. Gordon Brotherston co-edited the translations in the Precolumbian section of Latin America and did many of the translations in that section. We greatly appreciate his help in putting together a selection from this underrepresented province of world literature. We would like to thank those scholars (Mika Fukuda for the Indian subcontinent and Richard Serrano for selections in Arabic) who have helped us to regularize and to simplify the orthography for several sections, and especially to thank Ericka Embry, David Livingston, and Ayame Fukuda for their essential help in research, typing, organization, and in the thousand small tasks that a project like this entails. We thank Anna Neese for her help in preparing the indices and, along with Annalee Bretthauer, for invaluable aid in reading proofs. Ayame Fukuda provided essential research help and also co-wrote several introductions. Leona Maxwell was a superb and enthusiastic copy editor for a previous version of the manuscript, and Elsa Peterson navigated the book through a storm of permissions. In the final years of this project, Linda Pawelchak took charge of a mountain of manuscript and oversaw its transformation into this book. Tony English was our editor for most of the years the book was in preparation, and his guidance was astute and his patience stoic.

We would also like to acknowledge the following reviewers: Ali Jimale Ahmed, Queens College; Peter Edmunds, Lansing (MI) Community College; Lydia Liv, University of California, Berkeley; Michael Palencia-Roth, University of Illinois; Herman Rapaport, University of Iowa; and Lois Parkinson Zamora, University of Houston.

—Willis Barnstone and Tony Barnstone

# General Introduction

*Literatures of Asia, Africa, and Latin America* brings together literary, religious, and philosophical traditions from five continents. Each of these regions has given us important writings, some of them dating back as far as the third millennium. Although Europe and the West are the children of ancient forebears in North Africa, Moorish Spain, and the Near East, until recently, historically speaking, we have been essentially ignorant of the many major writers outside the West. Even the Bible, appropriated from the East as *the* foundation book of Western morality and thought, has scarcely been thought of as an Asian book.

Although the Bible is normally included only in anthologies of Western literature, in this volume we have attempted to contextualize the Bible in its Asian setting, showing its Sumerian, Babylonian, and Egyptian roots. We have also included a substantial selection of Jewish and Christian intertestamental scriptures, such as the Dead Sea Scrolls, which affirms the continuous writing of holy scriptures between the Old and New Testaments. It is also enlightening to read the Koran alongside the Bible, since the Koran is deeply informed by biblical figures and traditions. Despite history's sectarian distinctions, we have emphasized cultural affinities.

To compensate for the absence of non-Western writers, earlier world anthologies represented the non-Western world with a few Chinese, Persian, and Indian texts. A century of assiduous translation, however, has made the larger world accessible to the West, reconnecting us to an enormous past and present world literature. Particularly in our multicultural society, with peoples of every background, it is vital to reveal the great traditions of Asia, Africa, and Latin America, and to do so in fresh, excellent literary translation or, as in the case of many colonial and postcolonial writers from India and Africa, in their original English texts. In combination with volumes I and II in the Prentice Hall series of World Literature (*The Western Tradition*), this third volume, *Literatures of Asia, Africa, and Latin America*, presents a planetary view of literature and civilization. The picture that emerges is of an antiquity in a ferment of creativity and of a migration of languages and literary forms.

The great written documents of antiquity root us as readers in a past of cultural particularity, cultural marriage, and universal themes and have offered superb new models for modern and postmodern writers. Early in the century, when superb English versions of Chinese poetry were revealed through the magnificent translations of Arthur Waley and Ezra

1

Pound, American poetics were transformed. Since then, the interpenetration of the world's literary traditions has profoundly changed the ways that writers write. We live in a time when it's no less common for an American poet to write a Japanese haiku or an Arabic *ghazal* than a sonnet, when a well-known American novelist like John Barth publishes a major novel based on the Arabic classic *The Thousand and One Nights,* and when Chinese-American novelists like Maxine Hong Kingston and Frank Chin use Chinese classical fiction as their source and model. In the current ferment of translation, a well-read lover of literature is as likely to be a fan of the Bhagavad-Gita as of *Paradise Lost,* as likely to be reading the Caribbean East Indian novelist V. S. Naipaul as Ernest Hemingway. As in the Spanish saying "the world is a handkerchief" (*el mundo es un pañuelo*), all major literatures are now intimately accessible.

A few words about our criteria for inclusion and our rationale for ordering the texts here. There are thousands of authors competing for, and worthy of, inclusion, and we have had to make difficult choices. Although this anthology has an immense geographic and temporal range, we have represented writers and traditions in depth rather than number. In the Subcontinent and East Asia, for example, we have limited our selection to three major civilizations: India, Japan, and China. We wished to present a comprehensive view of each literature. So, in addition to primary literary genres and forms, we have included key religious and philosophical texts, particularly those that have intrinsic literary value, such as the Indian Bhagavad Gita, the Chinese Zhuangzi text, the moral precepts of the Persian Sadi, and selections from biblical, koranic, and Buddhist scriptures. In most cases, we've ordered the texts within each section chronologically and arranged individual sections according to a model of influence. As Hinduism was a source tradition for Buddhism, which in turn migrated from India to China and Japan, so our sections move from India, to China, and then Japan.

Asia, Africa, and Latin America remain the scope of this book, but we soon discovered it necessary to create an internal division within Asia and Africa to connect the Near East and North Africa, which we have called "The Bridge." The literatures of Sumeria, Babylonia, Egypt, Ancient Israel, Persia, and the Arabic-speaking countries, including medieval Muslim Spain, were intimately connected by influence and chronology and by a series of great empires. In the way that India produced the religions of the Subcontinent and the Far East, the Bridge countries ultimately gave the West its major religions (Judaism, Christianity, and Islam), its major myths, and its models for literature and art. So, while the first movement of the book is from West to East, from India to Japan, the book's second major movement goes from the ancient Near East through Africa and, via the Spanish and Portuguese colonists, to Latin America.

This large schema needs to be qualified. Islam, for example, spread East as well as West and penetrated south into parts of sub-Saharan Africa. The Moguls conquered most of India in 1526, bringing in Islam and Persian and Arabic language and literary forms. Today Islam is the religion of much of Asia. Furthermore, influences are inevitably multidirectional, and each of these cultures has ancient indigenous traditions that predate the major religious and literary migrations. Hence, in the Americas we have Precolumbian art and literatures and in Africa a powerful history of oral traditions. Both China and Japan have mythic, philosophical, literary, and religious traditions that long predate the entry of Indian Buddhism. Still, it is essential to understand the global movements of culture and how outside influences have interacted with indigenous traditions. After reading the sources of the Judeo-Christian tradition in the Bridge section, we are better prepared to read a seventeenth-century writer like the famous Mexican nun Sor Juana Inés de la Cruz (1749/51–1791). Of Spanish Catholic and Native American origin, she wrote European secular sonnets in the Spanish Golden Age manner as well as Christian mystery plays, yet she also heard and understood songs in Nahuatl (the Aztec tongue) in her native village. Similarly, Wang Wei (701–761), the great Tang dynasty Chinese poet, who was deeply engaged with the indigenous Chinese tradition of Daoism, was, at the same time, a committed Buddhist who took his pen name from the reknowned Indian Buddhist Vimalakirti and whose poetry echoes Indian mystical writings.

The Bridge is the unacknowledged source of much of Western civilization: columned Egyptian temples and sculptures were models for Greek temples and early statuary; Sumerian and Babylonian flood stories were retold in Genesis; and the story of baby Moses on the river derives from the Akkadian "Legend of Sargon"; Hebrew, the language of the Old Testament, is an Asian language, and the Greek of the New Testament was written in Asia for an Asian audience; the Asian deities Jehovah (Yahweh) and Jesus (Yeshua) were the foundation of Western Judeo-Christian religions. Even the essential activity of writing itself, of using alphabets and scripts, was imported from the Bridge. Without a writing system, we must remember, any development in European cultures would have been radically limited and, outside of surviving artifacts, unrecorded and destined to disappear. The Bridge gave us writing, and thus gave us literature, which is itself a bridge linking us to the civilizations of the past.

The process of writing, as far as we know, began in Sumerian Mesopotamia, which lies between the Tigris and the Euphrates Rivers in present-day Iraq—the same area that gave us Eden's Adam and Eve and was the homeland of Abraham and the Jews before their entry into Canaan. Well before the third millennium, Mesopotamian merchants and farmers communicated rudimentary trade information between towns by sending clay balls (bulls) that held inside them numbers and pictures of animals and merchandise. The oldest writing in the world is now thought to have survived in this mercantile correspondence. Soon there was communication to many cities, especially to those occupied by Phoenician traders on the coast of Asia Minor. The Sumerians also developed an elaborate system of pictographic writing in which each character represented a different idea or thing. In the world's first complete writing system, the Sumerians recorded their great literary and religious documents. These characters, known by the Latin term *cuneiform,* were inscriptions on wet clay tablets made with wedge-shaped wooden styluses (Latin *cuneus* means "wedge"). The system spread and soon all the main nearby languages adopted cuneiform characters as their writing system, including Akkadian, Elamite, Hittite, and Old Persian.

In second millennium Egypt, the Egyptians were developing their own hieroglyphic system of writing. As in Chinese and Mayan characters and Sumerian cuneiforms, the Egyptian hieroglyphs conveyed primarily meaning, rather than sound, thereby requiring thousands of different characters to express a full vocabulary. But then, independently, the Sumerians and Egyptians developed much simpler phonetic syllabaries consisting of about twenty-six letters, and modern writing began. Meanwhile, the Phoenicians—a term the Greeks invented to distinguish the Canaanites of the coast from Canaanites of Palestine—were preparing their own alphabet. The Greeks called this trading and seafaring people Phoenicians because of the famous purple cloth they made ("purple" in Greek is *phoenicia*). Around 1200 B.C., the Phoenicians devised a phonetic alphabet based on Egyptian cursive, which spread to Greece. The Cretan Greeks had an earlier alphabet, the so-called "linear B," but with the Dorian invasions around 1100 B.C., the Cretan script disappeared. From the Phoenician-inspired Greek script came the Roman alphabet in Western Europe and the Cyrillic alphabet in the Slavic-speaking countries to the north. "You can never step in the same river twice," writes Heraclitus, the pre-Socratic Greek philosopher. Time is such a river, but so is language, which flows from our mouths and is the medium of culture and society. To the Bridge, the West owes its ability to write, and thereby detain, the evanescent essence of human communication—language.

Like the Irish bog men preserved for centuries in peat or the marvelously conserved mummies of Egypt, humanity is preserved by writing. And there is wonder in what reaches us from antiquity. Like a bead of amber containing a prehistoric insect caught in mid-crawl, each word deciphered from cuneiform or Chinese, Sanskrit, or Quechua is precious. Ancient coins unearthed still retain monetary value, but we esteem them even more for their worth as microcosms of vanished worlds. This is the value to be found in ancient writing as well. There is an inexpressible pathos in reading the intimate words of the Medieval Japanese writer Kenko, who wonders if he is alone in the history of the world in experiencing the strange feeling of having already lived this present moment, what we now call déjà vu. In fact, there is a déjà vu to reading the complaint of a Chinese woman missing her absent husband (who may be fighting the Barbarians at the Northern frontier), and there is a universality to the grief of Gilgamesh, the Sumerian king, who confronts his own mortality after the death of his friend Enkidu.

In *Literatures of Asia, Africa, and Latin America,* we have gathered together the writings of the most ancient civilizations—in all continental areas—against which the innovations of North America and Europe seem relatively recent. These texts stretch from antiquity to the present and, despite cultural differences, throughout reveal the universality of life-and-death experience. In every century and in every place, writers have recorded visions of the origins and end of the world, of the supernatural permeating ordinary life and afterlife, as in *The Egyptian Book of the Dead,* African creation myths, Japanese ghost tales, and the intertestamental apocalypses. Writers, religions, and philosophies have always tried to answer basic questions of origin, presence, and destiny and at the same time have given us intimate records of the self and the phenomenal world. The world's authors have observed the known and speculated on the unknown. *Literatures of Asia, Africa, and Latin America* is a record of their questioning and achievement. It encompasses a vast precinct of human knowledge, planetary in scope, given to us by the writers of antiquity and by their heirs, our contemporaries, who continue to extend, and innovate, from Japan to Argentina.

# 1

# Asia

## INTRODUCTION

Asia is the largest of the world's seven continents and the source of many ancient civilizations. In the Near East (which is included in Section II), the rich empires of Sumeria, Babylonia, Assyria, Persia, the biblical civilization of the Jews of Israel, and the far-flung culture of Islam interacted with the old empires of Europe, the Greeks and the Romans, as well as with those of North Africa, such as the Egyptians and the Phoenicians. In South Asia flourished the states and civilizations of the Indian subcontinent, while in East Asia the major civilizations were the Chinese and the Japanese. China, India, the Near East, and ultimately Europe were linked by an extraordinary trade route—the Silk Road—that in the classical period stretched from Han dynasty China through the North Indian kingdom of the Kushans and the Persian Empire to Rome. Sea routes also linked the distant empires of Asia. India was linked to Southeast Asia and China to the east and to Africa and the Near East to the west by sea routes that carried spices, jewels, drugs, perfumes, metal, and exotic fruit and birds. By land and by sea, caravans and ships carried on a trade in the fruits of diverse civilizations, creating a continental economy in the ancient world. These routes also facilitated a trade in knowledge, technology,

culture, and ultimately religion and philosophy. It was, for example, along the Silk Road that Buddhism and Buddhist art first came to China. Other religions followed: China has a small population of Jews and has a large Muslim population centered in Chinese Turkestan in the far Northwest, where the Silk Road ran. It is also in this western region of China that there was a flourishing of Manichaean Gnosticism, which was a remarkable triple mirror of its three source religions, Christianity, Buddhism, and especially Zoroastrianism. Although the Silk Road's ancient trade route was threatened and ultimately severed by the predations of nomadic tribes of central Asia, it stands as a symbol for trade between civilizations and the peaceful migration of culture, art, and ideas.

# India, Pakistan, and Bangladesh

## INTRODUCTION

The area now comprising India, Pakistan, and Bangladesh, united in the colonial period as British India, forms the major part of the region known as the Indian subcontinent. It is an area of extraordinary cultural diversity, with more than fifteen hundred languages and dialects and more than a billion people. It is customary to speak simply of Indian literature in dealing with the literatures of the subcontinent before its post-Independence partition into predominantly Hindu India and largely Muslim Pakistan (1947–    ) and Bangladesh (East Pakistan from 1947–1971, Bangladesh 1971–    ). It has been ruled over by four great empires and four great religions—the Buddhist Mauryans, the Hindu Guptas, the Muslim Mughals, and the Christian British empire.

Civilization began in India with a culture known as the Harrapans, which flourished in the Indus basin of present-day Pakistan in the cities of Harrapa and Mohenjodaro from around 2500 to 1500 B.C. This early civilization produced cities with underground sewers, granaries, palaces, and baths, constructed out of uniformly sized bricks and planned into regular grids. Its people traded widely with the early civilizations of the Middle East and had a system of writing that remained undeciphered until 1969. The Harrapans were most likely the ancestors of the dark-skinned Dravidians of southern India. Their civilization was overrun by lighter-skinned barbarian invaders known as the Aryans starting around 1500 B.C. The Aryans had migrated from the Russian steppes and were armed with iron weapons and fearsome chariots. The two great cities of the Harrapans were left in ruins. The Aryans dominated India from around 1500 to 500 B.C., and the complex urban civilization and writing system of the Harrapans were abandoned for a more primitive, warlike, village culture.

After centuries of eclipse, however, civilization began to emerge again between 1000 and 500 B.C. as the Aryans, merged with the Dravidian inhabitants of India, began to settle in urban centers along the great Ganges River, such as Patna and Benares. Here, the division of Indian society into four castes developed. At the top were the warriors, and below them the priests, merchants and landowners, and farmers and manual laborers. Later, the Brahmans (the priestly caste) supplanted the warriors as the predominant caste. The kings (called *rajas*) of these small states were sanctified by the priestly class.

The marriage of the Aryans and the Dravidians proved fertile both religiously and culturally. Hinduism emerged out of the synthesis of Aryan and Dravidian religions and has been central in the development of Indian literature. Out of Hinduism came two great religious offshoots, Jainism and Buddhism. The religion of the Jains was founded by Mahavira (c. 540–476 B.C.) and is particularly notable for its doctrine of nonviolence (*ahimsa*) and respect for all living beings. Buddhism was founded in India around 525 B.C. by Siddhartha Gautama (563–483 B.C.), who was given the epithet the Buddha, Sanskrit for the "enlightened one." The Buddha's teachings were an oral tradition for four hundred years, after which they were written down in a number of the Sanskrit vernacular languages. The Pali *Tipitaka* (triple basket) is the only complete version in the Indian Buddhist canon. Buddhism largely died out in India after the seventh century A.D., yielding to a revival of Hinduism and the entry of Islam. It survives largely in Tibet, China, Japan, and countries of Southeast Asia.

India was first unified under the Aryans with the conquest of much of the subcontinent by Chandragupta Maurya (321–297 B.C.), the ruler of Magadha, a small Ganges basin state centered in the city of Patna, where both the Buddha and Mahavira had preached some centuries before. Chandragupta was the founder of the Mauryan dynasty (322–185 B.C.), but it was the third Mauryan king, Asoka, who is credited with creating a golden age in ancient India. Asoka (c. 268–231 B.C.) was a convert to Buddhism who advocated nonviolent rule, vegetarianism, religious tolerance, and responsible government that performed service for the public. He sent out missionaries who spread Buddhism to Southeast Asia and Sri Lanka, but he advocated tolerance of other religions within his vast empire. With the fall of the Mauryan dynasty in 185 B.C., India again fragmented into many small states, and it wasn't until the establishment of the Gupta dynasty in A.D. 320 that India would again be united.

The most ancient Indian literature is found in the Vedas, which are written in an early form of Sanskrit called Vedic, and which record the religious beliefs of the Aryans. Of the four main Vedas, which comprise the oldest Hindu sacred texts, the Rig Veda is the scripture with most literary value. The oral tradition of hymns that make up the Rig Veda was probably written down and compiled in the second millennium B.C. Vedic literature is vast and fascinating and includes the Brahmanas (prose commentaries on the Vedas) and later, the Upanishads, whose major texts were composed between 800 and 400 B.C. These beautiful and mystical pieces, composed of prose and verse or verse alone, are the core texts for the philosophical schools of Vedanta, which hold that all reality is united into the single macrocosmic principle of Brahman.

During the centuries between the fall of the Mauryans and the rise of the Guptas, important influxes of Greeks, Parthians, Scythians, Afghans, and Kushans settled and influenced the North, while in the Dravidian south the Tamil culture flourished, producing some of India's most extraordinary poetry. Early Tamil literature includes two epics, eight major anthologies, and ten long poems. Tamil lyric poetry is divided into two main genres, *akam* or love poems of the interior landscape and *puram* or war poems of the exterior landscape.

Like the Mauryan empire, the Gupta empire originated in the state of Magadha and spread over much of India, though it didn't conquer as much of south India as its predecessor. The third Gupta king, Chandra Gupta II (A.D. 375–415), was a great patron of the arts and presided over a flourishing era of literary and artistic production. His reign is considered to be India's second golden age. Although the Guptas were Hindu, like the Buddhist Mauryans they tolerated religious diversity among their conquered peoples. In around A.D. 500, the Gupta empire's northwest area fell to invaders from the north, the White Huns, and the empire from this point onward began to shrink in upon its center at the Ganges until it disappeared altogether.

The classical Indian writers of the Gupta period began to use the ancient language of Sanskrit as the formal literary language, instead of the vernacular dialects of Sanskrit—the Prakrit languages. Nonetheless, important literatures have survived from ancient times in the southern language of Tamil and in Prakrit languages—notably in Pali, the main language of Indian Buddhism. The *Gatha Saptashati*, for example, is an important compilation of seven hundred Prakrit erotic poems written between A.D. 100 and 300. Though nearly all Sanskrit literature is versified, the greatest examples of Sanskrit poetry lie in the gigantic epics, the *Mahabharata* and the *Ramayana*, which originated in Vedic times, but were adapted and edited by Brahmans in the Gupta period. It is thought that these later editors added a gloss of Hindu sanctity to what had originated as martial epics celebrating the values of the barbarian Aryans. The *Mahabharata* is the world's longest poem, over seven times the length of the *Iliad* and the *Odyssey* put together. It includes one of the masterworks of world literature, the Bhagavad-Gita. This key text of Hinduism is a battlefield dialogue in which the god Krishna instructs the hero prince Arjuna on ethical and religious principles. Nonepic Sanskrit poetry includes an extensive tradition of longer poems and a diversity of minor forms. Kalidasa (fourth to fifth century A.D.) was India's "Great Poet," a resident at the brilliant court of Chandra Gupta II. Kalidasa's long poems figure highest in the canon. He was also the most famous Sanskrit dramatist, and his play *Shakuntala*, which is studded with beautiful short lyrical poems, is the apogee of Indian theater. Other great Sanskrit poets, those of the post-Gupta period, include Bhartrihari (seventh c. A.D.?), the love poets Amaru (seventh c. A.D.) and Bilhana (eleventh c. A.D.), and Jayadeva (twelfth c. A.D.), whose eroto-mystical *Gitagovinda* has been called the Indian Song of Songs. Many of these poets are included in the famous eleventh-century anthology *The Treasury of Well-Tuned Verse*. Sanskrit fairy tales and fables are collected in a number of sequences, usually with an overarching framing narrative. The most distinguished of these is the *Panchatantra,* which was collected during the Gupta era. These story cycles spread far beyond India, providing the basis for similar collections worldwide, such as *The Thousand and One Nights.*

Between the eleventh and fifteenth centuries, Sanskrit and Prakrit ceased to be the major literary languages, as a host of regional mother tongues developed major literary traditions. The key poetic movement of this time is called *bhakti,* which means "devotion." The urgent and intensely personal poems of the bhakti poets often addressed a particular god and are a form of devotional poetry that blends the erotic and mystical traditions of Indian literature (much as English metaphysical poets used the speech of English renaissance love poetry to address God). Great bhakti poets include Mahadevi (twelfth c. A.D.), Kabir (1398–1448), and Mirabai (1498–1573).

Islam arrived in the eighth century, and Islamic empires have been established in India since the twelfth century, when the Delhi Sultanate was founded. This empire lasted till 1398. The Islamic Mughal empire, founded by Babur (1483–1530), a descendant of Tamerlane, ruled in India from 1526 to 1857. Under Babur's grandson Akbar the Great (1556–1605), the Mughal empire spread across India. Like Gupta II, Akbar was religiously tolerant and a great patron of the arts, though his powerful descendant Aurangzeb (1658–1707), who was responsible for expanding the Mughal empire through most of the subcontinent, was not as tolerant and cosmopolitan a ruler. Under his aegis, the empire saw its majority Hindu population suffer discrimination, destruction of temples, and other forms of persecution. With Islam came Arabic and especially Persian languages and literary forms. Lalla (1320–1392) who wrote in Kashmiri, Kabir (1398–1448) who wrote in Hindi, and Ghalib (1797–1869) who wrote in Urdu and Persian were all deeply influenced by Islam, Sufism, and Near Eastern prosody (as well as the native tradition of bhakti).

India in the modern period has been deeply influenced by the experience of British colonialism. The British had established trading stations as early as 1613, and with the conquest of Bengal in 1757, at a time when the Mughal empire was disintegrating, the British empire in India was decisively launched. The British consolidated control of India through the end of the eighteenth century. During this period, English language and Western literary models spread throughout India, particularly after Western education became widely available in the late eighteenth century. In the modern period, Indian writers, like African writers who share a similar colonial background, have often adopted English as their literary language. Writers like Rabindranath Tagore (1861–1941, winner of the Nobel Prize in literature in 1913) and Premchand (1880–1936) as well as activists and spiritual leaders like Mahatma Gandhi (1869–1948) were deeply involved in the fight for independence from Great Britain, which was achieved in 1947. India was divided into India and Pakistan in August 1947, and later that year more than half a million people died in the ensuing civil war between Hindus and Muslims. A year later, Gandhi was assassinated by a Hindu fanatic. India and Pakistan have fought several wars in the twentieth century, culminating in East Pakistan's rebellion against West Pakistan, which was supported by India. West Pakistan successfully seceded and founded the state of Bangladesh. Since the subcontinent achieved independence from Colonial Britain, contemporary novelists and short story writers from India and Pakistan have become enormously successful worldwide, and the poets, though less known outside of this region, have modernized this vast and ancient tradition of verse.

# The Vedic Period

## (c. 1500–200 b.c.)

■ **The Rig Veda (c. 1200–900 b.c.)** *Sanskrit* **(poems)**

The Vedas are the oldest books of the Indo-Aryans, the culture fused from the ancient civilization of the Indus River valley and the Indo-European-speaking Aryan (or "noble") people who invaded during the second millennium b.c. They are the source of much Indian literature and religion. The word *veda* derives from *vid,* which means "to know"; the Vedas are compilations of sacred knowledge that were supposed to have been revealed directly to the four sages by Brahma, the supreme god. There are four vedas, the Rig Veda, the Yajur Veda, the Sama Veda, and the Atharva Veda, revealed to Agni, Vayu, Aditya, and Angiras, the four sages. Of the four, the Rig Veda (*rik* means "a verse") is the oldest, and the one with the most literary value; its ten books contain 11,000 hymns. The vedas are among the oldest literature of the world; only Egyptian and Mesopotamian literatures are probably more ancient. It is impossible to date them with certainty, but we know that they must have been completed earlier than the sixth or seventh century b.c., and the earliest date given for the transcription of this oral tradition of hymns is 6000 b.c. (though a more likely date would be the second or third millennium b.c.). Vyasa, traditionally considered the author of the Mahabharata, is thought to have been the first compiler of the vedas. Vedic literature, including the Upanishads and the vedic hymns and rituals, is the source of Hindu culture. The hymns presented here worship a startling number of gods, and they paint a fascinating picture of the lovers, gamblers, villages, and ceremonies of early Indian life. The literary value of these collections is secondary to their religious significance. They were (and are) used for ritual purposes—the hymns of the Rig Veda were recited, sometimes as arranged into the Sama Veda and Yajur Veda; the Atharva Veda is a compilation primarily of incantations and magic spells, mantras to be used by priests overseeing sacrifices, and hymns of atonement.

FURTHER READING: Bloomfield, M. A., tr. *Atharva Veda,* 1899. Bose, Abinash Chandra, tr. *Hymns From the Vedas,* 1966. Griffith, R. T. H., Max Muller, and R. Trivedi, trs. *Rig Veda,* 1889–1891, 1892, 1945. Le Mee, Jean, tr. *Hymns From the Rig Veda,* 1975. Macdonell, Arthur A., tr. *Hymns From the Rigveda: Selected and Metrically Translated,* 1922. O'Flaherty, Wendy. *The Rig Veda,* 1981. Samasrami, S., tr., *Sama Veda,* 1874–1878. Smith, H. Daniel, ed. *Selections from Vedic Hymns,* 1968.

## The Creation

> Before being, before even nonbeing, there was no air, no firmament.
> So what breathed? And where? And by whose order? And was
> there water endlessly deep?
> This was before death or immortality. There was no division between
> night and day, yet instinctively there was breathing, windless
> breathing and nothing else.
> It was so dark that darkness was hidden in the dark. There was
> nothing to show water was everywhere. And the void was a cloak
> about the Being who sprang from heat.
> Desire pierced the Being, the mind's first seed, and wise poet saints
> detected in their hearts the knot of being within nonbeing,
> and this rope they stretched over . . . what? Was there up? down?
> There were seed spillers and fertile powers, impulse above and
> energy below,
> but who can really know and say it here? Where did this creation
> come from? The gods came later, so who can know the source?
> No one knows creation's source. It was born of itself. Or it was not. He
> who looks down from the ultimate heaven knows. Or maybe not.

TRANSLATED BY TONY BARNSTONE AND WILLIS BARNSTONE

## Night[1]

> The goddess night has come and her eyes shine in all directions. She
> is robed in glory.
> Light of the deathless goddess spills through all the valleys and peaks,
> killing darkness.

---

1. The goddess of night is bright with the light of heavenly objects, and she pushes out the darkness. She is the sister of twilight and dawn.

When she comes she pushes out her sister twilight, and darkness is
 chased away.
Goddess, as you approach we fly to our homes, birds to their nests.
Now the village people sleep and the clawed beasts and winged birds,      5
 even the ever-hunting hawk, are still.
Save us from the wolf and his bitch, ward off the thief, and help us
 reach night's far shore in safety.
Darkness presses on me like black paint. Let dawn banish it like a
 debt.
Daughter of the sky, you've won the battle. Please hear this hymn I
 herd toward you like cattle.

TRANSLATED BY TONY BARNSTONE AND WILLIS BARNSTONE


## To Vishvakarman, Maker of the Universe

The wise father of the sun, the sky's eye, churned two arching worlds
 from primeval butter and moored their ends in the east, and the
 earth and sky spread out.
The All-Maker is strong as the universe, his mind is vast, he forms and
 orders, he is the ultimate being; offerings of prayer and rich
 liquids bring joy in heaven, there past the seven sages, where
 there is only one Being.
Father who made us, who aligned all things and knows all worlds and
 beings, you who named the gods, all creatures seek wisdom from
 you.
Like the singers who sang all things into existence when the region of
 darkness was not yet divided from light, countless ancient wise
 men have made sacrifices to you.                                          5
What first germ of life was planted in the waters, before earth and sky,
 before even the Asuras[1] and the gods, in waters where the
 company of gods were to appear?
He was the seed the waters received, all gods in one, and he sat on the
 Unborn's navel, he on whom all creatures rest.
But you will never find the one who made all creatures. Someone has
 come between you: hymn singers gorged on life who fumble
 through a cloak of fog and stammer nonsense.

TRANSLATED BY TONY BARNSTONE

1. Asuras are ancient divinities, demonic enemies of the gods.

## The Gambler

Shivering hazelnut eardrops were born from the great tree during a
hurricane. Now they roll on the diceboard and I'm drunk with
gambling fever.

My wife never whined or blew up, she loved me and my friends, but I
tossed her away with one bad throw of the dice.

Now she and her mother despise me, and no one gives a damn. A
gambler is worth less than a boney old nag you try to dump on
the market.

Since the thirsty dice sucked me dry, other men fondle my wife and
my father, mother and brothers say "We don't know that man.
Chain him up and get him out of our sight."

I swear to my friends I won't play and they take off. But the brown                5
dice beckon as they hit the board and soon I rush off to the
game, hot as a woman meeting her lover.

I enter the hall quivering with desire and dreaming of winning, but
the dice smash my hopes and give my rival all the throws.

The dice seduce you. They hook and stab your flesh until you're their
slave, mesmerized, tormented. Like children they tempt you
with gifts, then take them back. You drown in the honey of their
sweet magic.

In three troops of fifty the dice-game is bound by rules inflexible
as the chariot path of the sungod Savitri. Not even the
tantrums of rich nobles can change this. Even the king bows
to them.

They tumble down, then bounce back up. Handless, they cow the man
with hands. Sorcerous coals spilled on the gaming board, they're
cold but they burn the heart to ash.

My abandoned wife groans. My mother mourns my wandering. I need        1
money, I'm in debt and scared. At night I steal up on another
man's house.

It kills me to see my wife in his arms, in those fine rooms, but still at
dawn I yoke up those brown horses and when night comes
around I'm a derelict flopping down by the fire.

General of that great dice-army, king of those troops, listen, I
wouldn't lie! I don't have a cent. See these ten fingers spread
wide?

Great Savitri tells me: Gambler, give up the dice and till your field.
Love what you have already. Your cows, your wife, it's enough.

Dice, give me a break. Don't make me a slave to sorcery. Let your
hatred and anger sleep. Tangle someone else in your net.

TRANSLATED BY TONY BARNSTONE AND WILLIS BARNSTONE

## The Poet Traveler Lost in the Forest

Mother spirit of the forest, why do you vanish? Why do you flee from our village? Are you afraid?

When cattle low and crickets respond, you are a hunter laughing among bells, startling the beasts with noisy beaters.

In the twilight forest you appear as cows grazing, the shape of a remote house, are heard in the secret creaking of carts.

Whoever stays in the evening forest hears wild sounds. Someone shouts at the herds, an ax chops into a tree, someone is screaming.

If I come near, you do not pounce on me like an animal. No, you eat    5
delicious fruit and lie down where you please.

Mother of wild beasts, unplowed land rich in foods, fragrances and balm, spirit of the forest, I sing to you.

TRANSLATED BY TONY BARNSTONE AND WILLIS BARNSTONE

## The Poet to Parjanya, Bullgod of the Rain

Powerful god, I sing your praise and ask for help. You bellow and your luscious drops impregnate the plants.

You slaughter demons and smash trees to kindling. With your deadly thunderbolt you terrorize all creatures,

even the sinless flee before you, bullgod bursting with seed, and Parjanya you execute the wicked.

Like a charioter lashing his horses, you send your messengers of rain tearing wildly ahead.

From the horizons a lion thunders when you fill the heavens with    5
ponderous clouds of rain.

Winds plunge over the earth, lightning splits the night, all vegetation lunges skyward in thirst, as if after udders of milk.

When you refresh and fructify the earth with your sperm water, the cosmos is fulfilled with food.

Before you the earth itself bows and hooved beasts quiver. Your law spurs every species of plant into bloom. Great one, you are our salvation.

Winds, search for rain in heaven. Let the stallion's seed swell, burst,
and flow freely over us.

You are our luminous watergod, our father, sprinkle your blessings on      10
your children,
bellow and spin through the sky over the world. Fill your chariot with
waters, tilt your waterbags over
mountains and ravines till they are one lake. Pour the enormous
buckets down. Drench heaven and earth with sweet butter,
make ponds for cows to drink, slaughter the wicked, and let the earth
be happy. You have sent the rain, now let it stop —
the deserts are pleasant woods, the plants thrive and all creatures find
the inspired poetry of food.

TRANSLATED BY TONY BARNSTONE AND WILLIS BARNSTONE

## ■ The Upanishads (c. Ninth Century B.C. to First Century A.D.) *Sanskrit* (poems/religious texts)

TRANSLATED BY JUAN MASCARÓ

The word *Upanishad* derives from *sad* ("to sit"), *upa* ("near"), and *ni* ("down") with a general meaning of "to sit down near the master" who teaches the doctrine. The Upanishads range widely in age from around 800 B.C. to as late as the fifteenth century A.D., though the major ones were composed between 800 and 400 B.C. There are as many as 150 Upanishads, of which 108 are considered authentic. These mystical texts of Hinduism are generally composed in Sanskrit prose interspersed with verse, though five of them are wholly in verse. The older Upanishads are among the most important, and certainly the earliest, Hindu texts treating philosophic and religious subjects and are considered the source of much Hindu faith and speculation. They are also among the most beautiful.

The Upanishads, though attached to the Vedas, present a differing perspective on the world. The rituals that are so central to Vedic religion are not important in the Upanishads. Central to the worldview of the Upanishads is the idea of Brahman, conceived of as the absolute and ultimate reality behind the world. Brahman is huge, essential, eternal, yet the Upanishads state that it is identical to the inner self, or Atman: "Concealed in the heart of all beings is the Atman, the Spirit, the Self; smaller than the smallest atom, greater than the vast spaces." By perceiving this essential unity in the world, one can be freed from the cycle of birth and rebirth, but "Who sees the many and not the ONE, wanders on from death to death." The philosophic schools of Vedanta are based upon the Upanishads.

From a literary standpoint, the Upanishads represent some of the most beautiful mystical poetry in the world, as in the Katha Upanishad's description of the Atman as a flame without smoke, the size of a thumb, or its description of Brahman as a tree of eternity with its roots in heaven and its branches reaching down to the earth. In the selections from the major Upanishads given here, we see treatments of these subjects, as well as parables and teaching stories. In the famous Katha Upanishad, we even see a youth named Nachiketas who, like his Sumerian counterpart Gilgamesh, goes in search of what happens after death.

**FURTHER READING:** Mascaró, Juan. *The Upanishads,* 1965. Nikhilananda, Swami. *The Upanishads,* 1963. Younger, Paul. *Introduction to Indian Religious Thought,* 1972.

## from *Isa Upanishad*

There are demon-haunted worlds, regions of utter darkness. Whoever in life denies the Spirit falls into that darkness of death.

The Spirit, without moving, is swifter than the mind; the senses cannot reach him: He is ever beyond them. Standing still, he overtakes those who run. To the ocean of his being, the spirit of life leads the streams of action.

He moves, and he moves not. He is far, and he is near. He is within all, and he is outside all.

Who sees all beings in his own Self, and his own Self in all beings, loses all fear.

When a sage sees this great Unity and his Self has become all beings, what delusion and what sorrow can ever be near him?

The Spirit filled all with his radiance. He is incorporeal and invulnerable, pure and untouched by evil. He is the supreme seer and thinker, immanent and transcendent. He placed all things in the path of Eternity.

## from *Kena Upanishad*

### Part 1

Who sends the mind to wander afar? Who first drives life to start on its journey? Who impels us to utter these words? Who is the Spirit behind the eye and the ear?

It is the ear of the ear, the eye of the eye, and the Word of words, the mind of mind, and the life of life. Those who follow wisdom pass beyond and, on leaving this world, become immortal.

There the eye goes not, nor words, nor mind. We know not, we cannot understand, how he can be explained: He is above the known and he is above the unknown. Thus have we heard from the ancient sages who explained this truth to us.

What cannot be spoken with words, but that whereby words are spoken: Know that alone to be Brahman, the Spirit; and not what people here adore.

What cannot be thought with the mind, but that whereby the mind can think: Know that alone to be Brahman, the Spirit; and not what people here adore.

What cannot be seen with the eye, but that whereby the eye can see: Know that alone to be Brahman, the Spirit; and not what people here adore.

What cannot be heard with the ear, but that whereby the ear can hear: Know that alone to be Brahman, the Spirit; and not what people here adore.

What cannot be indrawn with breath, but that whereby breath is indrawn: Know that alone to be Brahman, the Spirit; and not what people here adore.

## from *Katha Upanishad*[1]

## Part 2

*Nachiketas.* Tell me what you see beyond right and wrong, beyond what is done or not done, beyond past and future.

*Death.* I will tell you the Word that all the *Vedas* glorify, all self-sacrifice expresses, all sacred studies and holy life seek. That Word is OM.

That Word is the everlasting Brahman: that Word is the highest End. When that sacred Word is known, all longings are fulfilled.

It is the supreme means of salvation: it is the help supreme. When that great Word is known, one is great in the heaven of Brahman.

Atman, the Spirit of vision, is never born and never dies. Before him there was nothing, and he is ONE for evermore. Never-born and eternal, beyond times gone or to come, he does not die when the body dies.

If the slayer thinks that he kills, and if the slain thinks that he dies, neither knows the ways of truth. The Eternal in man cannot kill: the Eternal in man cannot die.

Concealed in the heart of all beings is the Atman, the Spirit, the Self; smaller than the smallest atom, greater than the vast spaces. The man who surrenders his human will leaves sorrows behind, and beholds the glory of the Atman by the grace of the Creator.

Resting, he wanders afar; sleeping, he goes everywhere. Who else but my Self can know that God of joy and of sorrows?

When the wise realize the omnipresent Spirit, who rests invisible in the visible and permanent in the impermanent, then they go beyond sorrow.

---

1. A dialogue in which Death acts as spiritual instructor to a youth named Nachiketas.

# Part 4

What is here is also there, and what is there is also here.

Who sees the many and not the ONE, wanders on from death to death.

Even by the mind this truth is to be learned: there are not many but only ONE. Who sees variety and not the unity wanders on from death to death.

The soul dwells within us, a flame the size of a thumb. When it is known as the Lord of the past and the future, then ceases all fear:

This in truth is That.

Like a flame without smoke, the size of a thumb, is the soul; the Lord of the past and the future, the same both today and tomorrow:

This in truth is That.

As water raining on a mountain-ridge runs down the rocks on all sides, so the man who only sees variety of things runs after them on all sides.

But as pure water raining on pure water becomes one and the same, so becomes, O Nachiketas, the soul of the sage who knows.

# Part 5

I will now speak to you of the mystery of the eternal Brahman; and of what happens to the soul after death.

The soul may go to the womb of a mother and thus obtain a new body. It even may go into trees or plants, according to its previous wisdom and work.

There is a Spirit who is awake in our sleep and creates the wonder of dreams. He is Brahman, the Spirit of Light, who in truth is called the Immortal. All the worlds rest on that Spirit and beyond him no one can go:

This in truth is That.

As fire, though one, takes new forms in all things that burn, the Spirit, though one, takes new forms in all things that live. He is within all, and is also outside.

As the wind, though one, takes new forms in whatever it enters, the Spirit, though one, takes new forms in all things that live. He is within all, and is also outside.

As the sun that beholds the world is untouched by earthly impurities, so the Spirit that is in all things is untouched by external sufferings.

There is one Ruler, the Spirit that is in all things, who transforms his own form into many. Only the wise who see him in their souls attain the joy eternal.

He is the Eternal among things that pass away, pure Consciousness of conscious beings, the ONE who fulfils the prayers of many. Only the wise who see him in their souls attain the peace eternal.

'This is That'—thus they realize the ineffable joy supreme. How can 'This' be known? Does he give light or does he reflect light?

There the sun shines not, nor the moon, nor the stars; lightnings shine not there and much less earthly fire. From his light all these give light, and his radiance illumines all creation.

# Part 6

The Tree of Eternity has its roots in heaven above and its branches reach down to earth. It is Brahman, pure Spirit, who in truth is called the Immortal. All the worlds rest on that Spirit and beyond him no one can go:
This in truth is That.
The whole universe comes from him and his life burns through the whole universe. In his power is the majesty of thunder. Those who know him have found immortality.

## from *Kaushitaki Upanishad*

When the fire burns, Brahman shines; and when the fire dies, Brahman goes. Its light goes to the sun, and its breath of life to the wind.
When the sun shines, Brahman shines; and when the sun sets, Brahman goes. Its light goes to the moon, and its breath of life to the wind.
When the moon shines, Brahman shines; and when the moon sets, Brahman goes. Its light goes to a flash of lightning, and its breath of life to the wind.
When a flash of lightning shines, Brahman shines; and when it goes, Brahman goes. Its light goes to the regions of heaven, and its breath of life to the wind.

\* \* \*

It is not speech which we should want to know: we should know the speaker.
It is not things seen which we should want to know: we should know the seer.
It is not sounds which we should want to know: we should know the hearer.
It is not mind which we should want to know: WE SHOULD KNOW THE THINKER.

## from *Taittiriya Upanishad*

Oh, the wonder of joy!
I am the food of life, and I am he who eats the food of life: I am the two in ONE.

I am the first-born of the world of truth, born before the gods, born
    in the centre of immortality.

He who gives me is my salvation.
I am that food which eats the eater of food.            5
I have gone beyond the universe, and the light of the sun is my light.


## from *Chandogya Upanishad*

There is a Light that shines beyond all things on earth, beyond us all, beyond the heavens, beyond the highest, the very highest heavens. This is
the Light that shines in our heart.

*   *   *

OM. There lived once a boy, Svetaketu Aruneya by name. One day his
father spoke to him in this way: 'Svetaketu, go and become a student
of sacred wisdom. There is no one in our family who has not studied
the holy *Vedas* and who might only be given the name of Brahman by
courtesy.'

The boy left at the age of twelve and, having learnt the *Vedas,* he returned home at the age of twenty-four, very proud of his learning and having a great opinion of himself.

His father, observing this, said to him: 'Svetaketu, my boy, you seem
to have a great opinion of yourself, you think you are learned, and you
are proud. Have you asked for that knowledge whereby what is not heard
is heard, what is not thought is thought, and what is not known is
known?'

'What is that knowledge, father?' asked Svetaketu.

'Just as by knowing a lump of clay, my son, all that is clay can be
known, since any differences are only words and the reality is clay;

Just as by knowing a piece of gold all that is gold can be known, since
any differences are only words and the reality is only gold;

And just as by knowing a piece of iron all that is iron is known, since
any differences are only words and the reality is only iron.'

Svetaketu said: 'Certainly my honoured masters knew not this themselves. If they had known, why would they not have told me? Explain this
to me, father.'

'So be it, my child.'

'Bring me a fruit from this banyan tree.'
'Here it is, father.'
'Break it.'
'It is broken, Sir.'
'What do you see in it?'
'Very small seeds, Sir.'

'Break one of them, my son.'

'It is broken, Sir.'

'What do you see in it?'

'Nothing at all, Sir.'

Then his father spoke to him: 'My son, from the very essence in the seed which you cannot see comes in truth this vast banyan tree.

Believe me, my son, an invisible and subtle essence is the Spirit of the whole universe. That is Reality. That is Atman, THOU ART THAT.'

'Explain more to me, father,' said Svetaketu.

'So be it, my son.

Place this salt in water and come to me tomorrow morning.'

Svetaketu did as he was commanded, and in the morning his father said to him: 'Bring me the salt you put into the water last night.'

Svetaketu looked into the water, but could not find it, for it had dissolved.

His father then said: 'Taste the water from this side. How is it?'

'It is salt.'

'Taste it from the middle. How is it?'

'It is salt.'

'Taste it from that side. How is it?'

'It is salt.'

'Look for the salt again and come again to me.'

The son did so, saying: 'I cannot see the salt. I only see water.'

His father then said: 'In the same way, O my son, you cannot see the Spirit. But in truth he is here.

An invisible and subtle essence is the Spirit of the whole universe. That is Reality. That is Truth. THOU ART THAT.'

# Buddhist Texts

## (c. Fifth Century B.C. to A.D. 255)

■ **Theravada Buddhist Texts (Fifth Century B.C. to First Century B.C.)** *Pali* **(religious texts)**

Prince Siddhartha Gautama, known as the Buddha (Sanskrit for "the enlightened one"), probably lived from 563 B.C. to 483 B.C. His life is wreathed in legend, but it seems likely, as in the case of Christ, that a historical man existed behind the religious embroidery and controversy. He was the son of a king in what is today southern Nepal. Because of a prediction at his birth that he would become either a great king or a great religious teacher, his father raised the young prince in great luxury, wishing to assure himself a successor, and Siddhartha was shielded from the misery of the world, which might lead him toward a religious life. He married, had a son, but on excursions outside the palace, he encountered a series of men—an old man, a sick man, a corpse, and a monk—embodying the world from which he had been excluded. He abandoned his heritage and his wife and son and wandered in search of religious wisdom. After mastering yogic meditation, he tried the path of fasting and austerity, but he found neither path fully satisfactory. At last he sat down under a pipal tree and vowed not to move until he had attained enlightenment. Like Saint Anthony tempted by devils in the desert, Siddhartha overcame the wiles and attacks of the evil god Mara and attained enlightenment. Until his death at eighty, he traveled and gathered disciples of all castes and religions, spreading the word of his new religion.

The Buddha taught that religious practitioners should avoid the extremes of indulgence and self-mortification and follow instead a "middle way." He taught that life in this world is sorrow—sorrow of sickness, death, desire, and impermanence—but that there is a way out of sorrow to a different form of existence, or nonexistence (the Buddha is notoriously vague about this point), called *nirvana*. In the transitory world, beings exist and die and are reborn perpetually on the great wheel of birth and rebirth. The engine behind the world, and the means to get out of it, is *dharma*. Dharma is moral law; though the Buddha doesn't deny the existence of the gods of Vedic religions, he believes that even the gods are subject to dharma and that there is no ultimate god who is creator and judge. Dharma means truth, spiritual law, way of life; those who follow the path of dharma will be rewarded in future lives, whereas those who abandon it will descend to the deepest hells. The thoughts and actions that cause us to be rewarded or punished are known as our *karma*. From a Buddhist perspective, when Milton's Satan cries, "Myself am Hell," he does so because he has departed from the path of dharma and is punished by having to live with his karma. As Emerson writes, "of their own volition, souls proceed into heaven, into hell." Those in heaven can fall and even those in hell can rise, since heavens and hells are not absolute; they belong to the world of mutability. The Buddhist practice is a method of escape from this perpetuation of misery, a way to stop the carousel ride.

Having thus analyzed the macrocosmic world, Buddhist logic then turns a microscope on the self. The self, like the world, is caught in a chain of cause and effect; if the root cause of suffering is detected, then suffering will disappear. In the *Lotus Sutra*, the Buddha writes, "As to the cause of all suffering,/ it has its root in greed and desire. /If greed and desire are wiped out,/ it will have no place to dwell." Since desires hold us in the world, we must analyze our selves through the intense self-scrutiny of meditation until we can eliminate this glue holding the self together. By looking in, we can discover what separates us from each other, and in tearing it away, free ourselves from the prison of the ego. These are three of the Four Noble Truths that he preached in his very first sermon: life is sorrow; desire causes sorrow; destroy desire and you may escape. The fourth truth states that this escape may be achieved through an eightfold path to liberation: right belief, right resolve, right speech, right behavior, right occupation, right effort, right contemplation, and right meditation. Through this path we may achieve nirvana. In Mahayana Buddhism, such enlightenment tends to be closer to the Upanishadic awakening to the sameness of Atman and Brahman, of self and world. In Theravada schools, however, nirvana's total cessation of desire opens a door from the self and out of the world, like a drop entering an ocean or like a fire that burns itself away. Is nirvana nothingness, complete cessation of being? Or does one cease to *become* but continue to *be* in a perfect, absolute, unchanging sphere of existence? The scripture is unclear. Nirvana is ineffable, and the Buddha spoke of it indirectly in parables because limited words can't capture its illimitable nature. A famous parable states that asking too much about the beyond is like a man with an arrow sticking in him who dies because he insists on knowing everything about the arrow, and the one who shot it, and a million other inconsequent details before allowing a doctor to pull it out and treat the wound.

The texts gathered in this section come from the Pali canon of early Buddhist texts that is religious scripture for the world's Theravada Buddhists (Mahayana texts were written later, at first mainly in Sanskrit, and subsequently in Chinese and Japanese). Pali is a vernacular dialect of classical Sanskrit, and it is the language in which oral sermons and literature of the Buddhists were set down not long after the death of the Buddha in 483 B.C. The canon is called the Tipitaka, which means triple basket; the three baskets refer to the basket of discipline, the basket of teaching, and the basket of metaphysics. This huge repository of Buddhist literature contains the doctrine of the earliest form of Buddhism, and thus in spite of sectarian differences, it contains the essential kernel of all Buddhism. Theravada Buddhism still is dominant in Burma, Sri Lanka, and Southeast Asia, whereas Mahayana is found in China, Korea, and Japan. The Pali texts presented here are of several types: there are passages from the *Visuddhi–Magga,* the finest Pali text written by Buddhaghosha, a systematic treatment of the entire Buddhist doctrine; a description of the "middle doctrine" from the *Sainyutta-Nikaya;* and passages from the *Milindapanha* (the *Questions of Milinda*), a dialogue between King Menander (Milinda) and Thera Nagasena about the essential problems of Buddhism. Also included here is the "Fire Sermon" of the *Maha-Vagga,* a famous text about the fires of passion and the source of much later literature—from Wang Wei's "Suffering From Heat" to T. S. Eliot's third section of *The Waste Land,* also titled "The Fire Sermon." Finally, there is a selection of verses from the *Dhammapada.* The *Dhammapada* is the most popular canonical text of Buddhism, consisting of 423 aphorisms attributed to the Buddha arranged by subject into twenty-six chapters. *Dhamma* is Pali for the Sanskrit dharma (defined earlier), while *pada* means "foot" or "step"; together they mean the path of truth. The *Dhammapada* is known worldwide as a condensed and evocative summation of Buddhist spiritual doctrine and is the Buddhist text most often anthologized because of its literary qualities.

FURTHER READING: Babbitt, Irving, tr. *The Dhammapada: Translated from the Pali, With an Essay on Buddha and the Occident,* 1st ed. 1936. Banerji, S. C. *An Introduction to Pali Literature,* 1964. Conze, Edward. *Buddhist Scriptures,* 1986. Geiger, Wilhelm. *Pali Literature and Language,* rev. ed. 1968. Kalupahana, David J. *A Path of Righteousness: Dhammapada: An Introductory Essay, Together with the Pali Text, English Translation, and Commentary,* 1986. Lal, P., tr. *The Dhammapada,* 1967. Mascaró, Juan, tr. *The Dhammapada: The Path of Perfection,* 1973. Max Müller, F., tr. *The Dhammapada: a Collection of Verses; Being One of the Canonical Books of the Buddhists,* 1965, 1977. Radhakrishnan, S. *The Dhammapada, with Introductory Essays, Pali Text, English Translation and Notes,* 1958. Warren, Henry Clarke. *Buddhism in Translations,* 1896, 1976.

# from the Visuddhi-Magga

## TRANSLATED BY HENRY CLARKE WARREN

### On Getting Angry

"My friend, who hast retired from the world and art angry with this man, tell me what it is you are angry with? Are you angry with the hair of the head, or with the hair of the body, or with the nails, etc.? Or are you angry with the earthy element in the hair of the head and the rest? Or are you angry with the watery element, or with the fiery element, or with the windy element in them? What is meant by the venerable N.N. is only the five groups, the six organs of sense, the six objects of sense, and the six sense-consciousnesses. With which of these are you angry? Is it with the form-group? Or is it with the sensation-group, perception-group, predisposition-group, or consciousness-group? Or are you angry with an organ of sense, or an object of sense, or a sense-consciousness?"

For a person who has made the above analysis, there is no hold for anger, any more than there is for a grain of mustard-seed on the point of an awl, or for a painting in the sky.

### Beauty Is But Skin-Deep

. . . The story is that a certain woman had married into a family of rank, but had quarreled with her husband, and, decked and ornamented, until she looked like a goddess, had issued forth from Anuradhapura, early in the morning, and was returning home to her family. On her way she met the elder, as he was on his way from Mt. Cetiya to go on his begging-rounds in Anuradhapura. And no sooner had she seen him, than the perversity of her nature caused her to laugh loudly. The elder looked up inquiringly, and observing her teeth, realized the impurity of the body,[1] and attained to saintship. Therefore was it said:

> "The elder gazed upon her teeth,
> And thought upon impurity;
> And ere that he had left that spot,
> The stage of saintship he attained."

Then came her husband, following in her footsteps, and seeing the elder, he said: "Reverend sir, have you seen a woman pass this way?"
And the elder said:

> "Was it a woman, or a man,
> That passed this way? I cannot tell.
> But this I know, a set of bones
> Is traveling on upon this road."

✳   ✳   ✳

For as the body when dead is repulsive, so is it also when alive; but on account of the concealment afforded by an adventitious adornment, its repulsiveness escapes notice. The body is in reality a collection of over three hundred bones, and is framed into a whole by means of one hundred and eighty joints. It is held together by nine hundred tendons, and overlaid by nine hundred muscles, and has an outside envelope of moist cuticle covered by an epidermis full of pores, through which there is an incessant oozing and trickling, as if from a kettle of fat. It is a prey to vermin, the seat of disease, and subject to all manner of miseries. Through its nine apertures it is always discharging matter, like a ripe boil. Matter is secreted from the two eyes, wax from the ears, snot from the nostrils, and from the mouth issue food, bile, phlegm, and blood, and from the two lower orifices of the body faeces and urine, while from the ninety-nine thousand pores of the skin an unclean sweat exudes attracting black flies and other insects.

Were even a king in triumphal progress to neglect the use of tooth-sticks, mouth-rinses, anointings of the head, baths and inner and outside garments, and other means for beautifying the person, he would become as uncouth and unkempt as the moment he was born, and would in no wise differ in bodily offensiveness from the low-caste candāla whose occupation it is to remove dead flowers. Thus in respect of its uncleanness, malodor, and disgusting offensiveness, the person of a king does not differ from that of a candāla. However, when, with the help of tooth-sticks, mouth-rinses, and various ablutions, men have cleansed their teeth, and the rest of their persons, and with manifold garments have covered their nakedness, and have anointed themselves with many-colored and fragrant unguents, and adorned themselves with flowers and ornaments, they find

---

1. By means of the tenth impurity, the teeth being reckoned as bone.

themselves able to believe in an "I" and a "mine." Accordingly, it is on account of the concealment afforded by this adventitious adornment that people fail to recognize the essential repulsiveness of their bodies, and that men find pleasure in women, and women in men. In reality, however, there is not the smallest just reason for being pleased.

A proof of this is the fact that when any part of the body becomes detached, as, for instance, the hair of the head, hair of the body, nails, teeth, phlegm, snot, faeces, or urine, people are unwilling so much as to touch it, and are distressed at, ashamed of, and loathe it. But in respect of what remains, though that is likewise repulsive, yet men are so wrapped in blindness and infatuated by a passionate fondness for their own selves, that they believe it to be something desirable, lovely, lasting, pleasant, and an Ego.

## from the Sainyutta-Nikaya

TRANSLATED BY HENRY CLARKE WARREN

### The Middle Doctrine

The world, for the most part, O Kaccāna, holds either to a belief in being or to a belief in non-being. But for one who in the light of the highest knowledge, O Kaccāna, considers how the world arises, belief in the non-being of the world passes away. And for one who in the light of the highest knowledge, O Kaccāna, considers how the world ceases, belief in the being of the world passes away. The world, O Kaccāna, is for the most part bound up in a seeking, attachment, and proclivity [for the groups], but a priest does not sympathize with this seeking and attachment, nor with the mental affirmation, proclivity, and prejudice which affirms an Ego. He does not doubt or question that it is only evil that springs into existence, and only evil that ceases from existence, and his conviction of this fact is dependent on no one besides himself. This, O Kaccāna, is what constitutes Right Belief.

That things have being, O Kaccāna, constitutes one extreme of doctrine; that things have no being is the other extreme. These extremes, O Kaccāna, have been avoided by The Tathāgata,[2] and it is a middle doctrine he teaches:—

On ignorance depends karma;
On karma depends consciousness;
On consciousness depend name and form;
On name and form depend the six organs of sense;

---

2. A title for the Buddha.

> On the six organs of sense depends contact;
> On contact depends sensation;
> On sensation depends desire;
> On desire depends attachment;
> On attachment depends existence;
> On existence depends birth;
> On birth depend old age and death, sorrow, lamentation, misery,
>     grief, and despair. Thus does this entire aggregation of misery
>     arise.

But on the complete fading out and cessation of ignorance ceases karma;

> On the cessation of karma ceases consciousness;
> On the cessation of consciousness cease name and form;
> On the cessation of name and form cease the six organs of sense;
> On the cessation of the six organs of sense ceases contact;
> On the cessation of contact ceases sensation;
> On the cessation of sensation ceases desire;
> On the cessation of desire ceases attachment;
> On the cessation of attachment ceases existence;
> On the cessation of existence ceases birth;
> On the cessation of birth cease old age and death, sorrow,
>     lamentation, misery, grief, and despair. Thus does this entire
>     aggregation of misery cease.

## from *the Mìlindapañha*

TRANSLATED BY HENRY CLARKE WARREN

### The Round of Existence

"Bhante Nāgasena," said the king, "when you say 'round of existence,' what is that?"

"Your majesty, to be born here and die here, to die here and be born elsewhere, to be born there and die there, to die there and be born elsewhere,—this, your majesty, is the round of existence."

"Give an illustration."

"It is as if, your majesty, a man were to eat a ripe mango, and plant the seed; and from that a large mango-tree were to spring and bear fruit; and then the man were to eat a ripe mango from that tree also and plant the seed; and from that seed also a large mango-tree were to spring and bear fruit; thus of these trees there is no end discernible. In exactly the same way, your majesty, to be born here and die here, to die here and be born elsewhere, to be born there and die there, to die there and be born elsewhere, this, your majesty, is the round of existence."

"You are an able man, bhante Nāgasena."

## Cause of Rebirth

"Bhante Nāgasena," said the king, "are there any who die without being born into another existence?"

"Some are born into another existence," said the elder, "and some are not born into another existence."

"Who is born into another existence, and who is not born into another existence?"

"Your majesty, he that still has the corruptions is born into another existence; he that no longer has the corruptions is not born into another existence."

"But will you, bhante, be born into another existence?"

"Your majesty, if there shall be in me any attachment, I shall be born into another existence; if there shall be in me no attachment, I shall not be born into another existence."

"You are an able man, bhante Nāgasena."

## Rebirth Is Not Transmigration

"Bhante Nāgasena," said the king, "what is it that is born into the next existence?"

"Your majesty," said the elder, "it is name and form that is born into the next existence."

"Is it this same name and form that is born into the next existence?"

"Your majesty, it is not this same name and form that is born into the next existence; but with this name and form, your majesty, one does a deed—it may be good, or it may be wicked—and by reason of this deed another name and form is born into the next existence."

"Bhante, if it is not this same name and form that is born into the next existence, is one not freed from one's evil deeds?"

"If one were not born into another existence," said the elder, "one would be freed from one's evil deeds; but, your majesty, inasmuch as one is born into another existence, therefore is one not freed from one's evil deeds."

"Give an illustration."

"Your majesty, it is as if a man were to take away another man's mangoes, and the owner of the mangoes were to seize him, and show him to the king, and say, 'Sire, this man hath taken away my mangoes'; and the other were to say, 'Sire, I did not take away this man's mangoes. The mangoes which this man planted were different mangoes from those which I took away. I am not liable to punishment.' Pray, your majesty, would the man be liable to punishment?"

"Assuredly, bhante, would he be liable to punishment."

"For what reason?"

"Because, in spite of what he might say, he would be liable to punishment for the reason that the last mangoes derived from the first mangoes."

"In exactly the same way, your majesty, with this name and form one does a deed—it may be good, or it may be wicked—and by reason of this deed another name and form is born into the next existence. Therefore is one not freed from one's evil deeds. . . ."

"Give another illustration."

"Your majesty, it is as if a man were to ascend to the top storey of a house with a light, and eat there; and the light in burning were to set fire to the thatch; and the thatch in burning were to set fire to the house; and the house in burning were to set fire to the village; and the people of the village were to seize him, and say, 'Why, O man, did you set fire to the village?' and he were to say, 'I did not set fire to the village. The fire of the lamp by whose light I ate was a different one from the one which set fire to the village;' and they, quarreling, were to come to you. Whose cause, your majesty, would you sustain?"

"That of the people of the village, bhante."

"And why?"

"Because, in spite of what the man might say, the latter fire sprang from the former."

"In exactly the same way, your majesty, although the name and form which is born into the next existence is different from the name and form which is to end at death, nevertheless, it is sprung from it. Therefore is one not freed from one's evil deeds."

"Give another illustration."

"Your majesty, it is as if a man were to choose a young girl in marriage, and having paid the purchase-money, were to go off; and she subsequently were to grow up and become marriageable; and then another man were to pay the purchase-money for her, and marry her; and the first man were to return, and say, 'O man, why did you marry my wife?' and the other were to say, 'I did not marry your wife. The young, tender girl whom you chose in marriage, and for whom you paid purchase-money, was a different person from this grown-up and marriageable girl whom I have chosen in marriage, and for whom I have paid purchase-money;' and they, quarreling, were to come to you. Whose cause, your majesty, would you sustain?"

"That of the first man."

"And why?"

"Because, in spite of what the second man might say, the grown-up girl sprang from the other."

"In exactly the same way, your majesty, although the name and form which is born into the next existence is different from the name and form which is to end at death, nevertheless, it is sprung from it. Therefore is one not freed from one's evil deeds."

# from *the Maha-Vagga*

TRANSLATED BY HENRY CLARKE WARREN

## The Fire-Sermon

Then The Blessed One, having dwelt in Uruvelā as long as he wished, proceeded on his wanderings in the direction of Gayā Head, accompanied by a great congregation of priests, a thousand in number, who had all of them aforetime been monks with matted hair. And there in Gayā, on Gayā Head, The Blessed One dwelt, together with the thousand priests.

And there The Blessed One addressed the priests:—

"All things, O priests, are on fire. And what, O priests, are all these things which are on fire?

"The eye, O priests, is on fire; forms are on fire; eye-consciousness is on fire; impressions received by the eye are on fire; and whatever sensation, pleasant, unpleasant, or indifferent, originates in dependence on impressions received by the eye, that also is on fire.

"And with what are these on fire?

"With the fire of passion, say I, with the fire of hatred, with the fire of infatuation; with birth, old age, death, sorrow, lamentation, misery, grief, and despair are they on fire.

"The ear is on fire; sounds are on fire; . . . the nose is on fire; odors are on fire; . . . the tongue is on fire; tastes are on fire; . . . the body is on fire; things tangible are on fire; . . . the mind is on fire; ideas are on fire; . . . mind-consciousness is on fire; impressions received by the mind are on fire; and whatever sensation, pleasant, unpleasant, or indifferent, originates in dependence on impressions received by the mind, that also is on fire.

"And with what are these on fire?

"With the fire of passion, say I, with the fire of hatred, with the fire of infatuation; with birth, old age, death, sorrow, lamentation, misery, grief, and despair are they on fire.

"Perceiving this, O priests, the learned and noble disciple conceives an aversion for the eye, conceives an aversion for forms, conceives an aversion for eye-consciousness, conceives an aversion for the impressions received by the eye; and whatever sensation, pleasant, unpleasant, or indifferent, originates in dependence on impressions received by the eye, for that also he conceives an aversion. Conceives an aversion for the ear, conceives an aversion for sounds, . . . conceives an aversion for the nose, conceives an aversion for odors, . . . conceives an aversion for the tongue, conceives an aversion for tastes, . . . conceives an aversion for the body, conceives an aversion for things tangible, . . . conceives an aversion for the mind, conceives an aversion for ideas, conceives an aversion for mind-consciousness, conceives an aversion for the impressions received by the mind; and whatever sensation, pleasant, unpleasant, or indifferent, originates in dependence on impressions received by the mind, for this also he conceives an aversion. And in conceiving this aversion, he becomes divested of passion, and by the absence of passion he becomes free, and when he is free he becomes aware that he is free; and he knows that rebirth is exhausted, that he has lived the holy life, that he has done what it behooved him to do, and that he is no more for this world."

Now while this exposition was being delivered, the minds of the thousand priests became free from attachment and delivered from the depravities.

Here Endeth the Fire-Sermon

# The Dhammapada

TRANSLATED BY JUAN MASCARÓ

## *from* The Fool

How long is the night to the watchman; how long is the road to the weary; how long is the wandering of lives ending in death for the fool who cannot find the path!

If on the great journey of life a man cannot find one who is better or at least as good as himself, let him joyfully travel alone: a fool cannot help him on his journey.

'These are my sons. This is my wealth.' In this way the fool troubles himself. He is not even the owner of himself: how much less of his sons and of his wealth!

If a fool can see his own folly, he in this at least is wise; but the fool who thinks he is wise, he indeed is the real fool.

If during the whole of his life a fool lives with a wise man, he never knows the path of wisdom as the spoon never knows the taste of the soup.

But if a man who watches and sees is only a moment with a wise man he soon knows the path of wisdom, as the tongue knows the taste of the soup.

## *from* Infinite Freedom

Who can trace the invisible path of the man who soars in the sky of liberation, the infinite Void without beginning, whose passions are peace, and over whom pleasures have no power? His path is as difficult to trace as that of the birds in the air.

The man who wisely controls his senses as a good driver controls his
   horses, and who is free from lower passions and pride, is
   admired even by the gods.

He is calm like the earth that endures; he is steady like a column that
   is firm; he is pure like a lake that is clear; he is free from
   Samsara, the ever-returning life-in-death.

## *from* Life

Those who make channels for water control the waters; makers of
   arrows make the arrows straight; carpenters control their timber;
   and the holy control their soul.

## *from* Beyond Life

How can there be laughter, how can there be pleasure, when the
   whole world is burning? When you are in deep darkness, will you
   not ask for a lamp?

Consider this body! A painted puppet with jointed limbs,[1] sometimes
   suffering and covered with ulcers, full of imaginings, never
   permanent, for ever changing.

This body is decaying! A nest of diseases, a heap of corruption, bound
   to destruction, to dissolution. All life ends in death.

Look at these grey-white dried boncs, like dried empty gourds thrown
   away at the end of the summer. Who will feel joy in looking at
   them?

A house of bones is this body, bones covered with flesh and with
   blood. Pride and hypocrisy dwell in this house and also old age
   and death.

The glorious chariots of kings wear out, and the body wears out and
   grows old; but the virtue of the good never grows old, and thus
   they can teach the good to those who are good.

If a man tries not to learn he grows old just like an ox! His body
   indeed grows old but his wisdom does not grow.

I have gone round in vain the cycles of many lives ever striving to find
   the builder of the house of life and death. How great is the
   sorrow of life that must die! But now I have seen thee,
   housebuilder: never more shalt thou build this house. The
   rafters of sins are broken, the ridge-pole of ignorance is
   destroyed. The fever of craving is past: for my mortal mind is
   gone to the joy of the immortal NIRVANA.

5

---

1. This is a recurrent metaphor in Indian mysticism. See also Mahadevi's poem "Monkey on a Monkey-
man's Stick."

Those who in their youth did not live in self-harmony, and who did not gain the true treasures of life, are later like long-legged old herons standing sad by a lake without fish.

Those who in their youth did not live in self-harmony, and who did not gain the true treasures of life, are later like broken bows, ever deploring old things past and gone.

## *from* Hasten and Strive

Let a wise man remove impurities from himself even as a silversmith removes impurities from the silver: one after one, little by little, again and again.

Even as rust on iron destroys in the end the iron, a man's own impure transgressions lead that man to the evil path.

Dull repetition is the rust of sacred verses; lack of repair is the rust of houses; want of healthy exercise is the rust of beauty; unwatchfulness is the rust of the watcher.

Misconduct is sin in woman; meanness is sin in a benefactor; evil actions are indeed sins both in this world and in the next.

But the greatest of all sins is indeed the sin of ignorance. Throw this sin away, O man and become pure from sin.

\* \* \*

There is no fire like lust, and no chains like those of hate. There is no net like illusion, and no rushing torrent like desire.

It is easy to see the faults of others, but difficult to see one's own faults. One shows the faults of others like chaff winnowed in the wind, but one conceals one's own faults as a cunning gambler conceals his dice.

If a man sees the sins of others and for ever thinks of their faults, his own sins increase for ever and far off is he from the end of his faults.

There is no path in the sky and a monk must find the inner path. The world likes pleasures that are obstacles on the path; but the Tatha-gatas, the 'Thus-gone', have crossed the river of time and they have overcome the world.

There is no path in the sky and a monk must find the inner path. All things indeed pass away, but the Buddhas are for ever in Eternity.

## *from* Cravings

If a man watches not for NIRVANA, his cravings grow like a creeper and he jumps from death to death like a monkey in the forest from one tree without fruit to another.

And when his cravings overcome him, his sorrows increase more and
more, like the entangling creeper called *birana*.

But whoever in this world overcomes his selfish cravings, his sorrows
fall away from him, like drops of water from a lotus flower.

Therefore in love I tell you, to you all who have come here: Cut off
the bonds of desires, as the surface grass creeper *birana* is cut for
its fragrant root called *usira*. Be not like a reed by a stream which
MARA, the devil of temptation, crushes again and again.

Just as a tree, though cut down, can grow again and again if its roots      5
are undamaged and strong, in the same way if the roots of
craving are not wholly up-rooted sorrows will come again and
again. When the thirty-six streams of desire that run towards
pleasures are strong, their powerful waves carry away that man
without vision whose imaginings are lustful desires. Everywhere
flow the streams. The creeper of craving grows everywhere. If
you see the creeper grow, cut off its roots by the power of
wisdom.

The sensuous pleasures of men flow everywhere. Bound for pleasures
and seeking pleasures men suffer life and old age.

Men who are pursued by lust run around like a hunted hare. Held in
fetters and in bonds they suffer and suffer again.

Men who are pursued by lust run round like a hunted hare. For a
monk to conquer lust he must first conquer desires.

The man who free from desires finds joy in solitude, but when free he
then returns to his life of old desires, people can say of that man:
'He was free and he ran back to his prison!'

The wise do not call a strong fetter that which is made of iron, of      10
wood or of rope; much stronger is the fetter of passion for gold
and for jewels, for sons or for wives.

This is indeed a strong fetter, say the wise. It seems soft but it drags a
man down, and it is hard to undo. Therefore some men cut
their fetters, renounce the life of the world and start to walk on
the path, leaving pleasures behind. Those who are slaves of
desires run into the stream of desires, even as a spider runs into
the web that it made. Therefore some men cut their fetters and
start to walk on the path, leaving sorrows behind.

Leave the past behind; leave the future behind; leave the present
behind. Thou art then ready to go to the other shore. Never
more shalt thou return to a life that ends in death.

The man who is disturbed by wrong thoughts, whose selfish passions
are strong and who only seeks sensuous pleasures, increases his

craving desires and makes stronger the chains he forges for himself.

But he who enjoys peaceful thoughts, who considers the sorrows of pleasure, and who ever remembers the light of his life—he will see the end of his cravings, he will break the chains of death.

He has reached the end of his journey, he trembles not, his cravings are gone, he is free from sin, he has burnt the thorns of life: this is his last mortal body.

He is free from lust, he is free from greed, he knows the meaning of words, and the meaning of their combinations, he is a great man, a great man who sees the Light: this is his last mortal body.

I have conquered all; I know all, and my life is pure; I have left all, and I am free from craving. I myself found the way. Whom shall I call Teacher? Whom shall I teach?

The gift of Truth conquers all gifts. The taste of Truth conquers all sweetness. The Joy of Truth conquers all pleasures. The loss of desires conquers all sorrows.

# Mahayana Buddhist Texts

### (before A.D. 255) *Chinese* (religious texts)

"The Parable of the Burning House" from *The Lotus Sutra* is among the most famous passages, a literary landmark, in this most important of Mahayana Buddhist sutras. *The Lotus Sutra* was probably composed in a vernacular Indian or Central Asian language and later translated into Sanskrit. When it was composed remains unknown, but it was translated into Chinese in A.D. 225. The eminent sinologist Burton Watson has rendered the text in English based on a version done in A.D. 406 by the scholar and monk Kumarajiva, which is considered the most authoritative version—more dependable than the Sanskrit versions that seem to be later and less felicitous. Mahayana ("Great Vehicle") Buddhism was given this name to distinguish it from earlier forms of Buddhism, which were named Hinayana, or "Lesser Vehicle," though the more common name is Theravada ("Teachings of the Elders") Buddhism.

According to Mahayana Buddhism, the historical Buddha was merely one of many manifestations of an eternal Buddha. Mahayana Buddhism presents a cosmos significantly expanded from that of Theravada—of countless worlds inhabited by countless Bodhisattvas and lesser beings. As in Theravada, the phenomenal world is seen as empty because it is caught in the endless chain of causality and flux, as the world's inhabitants are caught within a great cycling wheel of birth and rebirth. Flux and causality keep us in this cycle of misery, and only by eliminating craving and desire and following the eight-fold path of right belief, resolve, speech, behavior, occupation, effort, contemplation, and meditation, can one achieve enlightenment. Whereas Theravada suggests that such enlightenment frees us from the ordinary world, or *samsara,* Mahayana considers the world of *samsara* to be coextant with the absolute and unchanging. Enlightenment then becomes less an escape from the world than an insight into its true nature. In the parable given, the Buddha (also referred to in the poem as the Thus Come One) explains that though he had earlier taught his followers a doctrine of three vehicles or paths for the believer, this was merely an "expedient means" to help bring his followers to enlightenment. One shouldn't strive for lesser forms of enlightenment, to be a *shravaka* (a voice hearer—one who listens to the Buddha's teachings), to be a *pratyekabuddha* (one who seeks enlightenment only for him- or herself), or to be a *bodhisattva* (one who aspires to Buddhahood, but postpones his or her own entry into Nirvana in order to help others on their way). Instead, one should aim directly for Buddhahood. Here the Buddha, like the angel Raphael in *Paradise Lost,* delineates "what surmounts the reach / Of human sense" expediently, "By lik'ning spiritual to corporal forms" (*Paradise Lost* V.571–573). In this sense, the very use of parables can be seen as an expedient religious tool, a net to catch a fish; once the fish is caught, you no longer need the net.

**FURTHER READING:** Hurvitz, Leon. *Scripture of the Lotus Blossom of the Fine Dharma,* 1976. Watson, Burton. *The Lotus Sutra,* 1993.

## from *The Lotus Sutra*

TRANSLATED BY BURTON WATSON

### The Parable of the Burning House

The Buddha, wishing to state his meaning once more, spoke in verse form, saying:

> Suppose there was a rich man
> who had a large house.
> This house was very old,
> and decayed and dilapidated as well.
> The halls, though lofty, were in dangerous condition,        5
> the bases of the pillars had rotted,
> beams and rafters were slanting and askew,
> foundations and steps were crumbling.
> Walls were cracked and gaping
> and the plaster had fallen off of them.        10

The roof thatch was in disrepair or missing,
the tips of the eaves had dropped off.
The fences surrounding it were crooked or collapsed
and heaped rubbish was piled all around.
Some five hundred persons
lived in the house.
Kites, owls, hawks, eagles,
crows, magpies, doves, pigeons,
lizards, snakes, vipers, scorpions,
centipedes and millipedes,
newts and ground beetles,
weasels, raccoon dogs, mice, rats,
hordes of evil creatures
scurried this way and that.
Places that stank of excrement
overflowed in streams of filth
where dung beetles and other creatures gathered.
Foxes, wolves and jackals
gnawed and trampled in the filth
or tore apart dead bodies,
scattering bones and flesh about.
Because of this, packs of dogs
came racing to the spot to snatch and tear,
driven by hunger and fear,
searching everywhere for food,
fighting, struggling, seizing,
baring their teeth, snarling and howling.
That house was fearful, frightening,
so altered was its aspect.
In every part of it
there were goblins and trolls,
yaksha[1] and evil spirits
who feed on human flesh
or on poisonous creatures.
The various evil birds and beasts
bore offspring, hatched and nursed them,
each hiding and protecting its young,
but the yakshas outdid one another
in their haste to seize and eat them.
And when they had eaten their fill,
their evil hearts became fiercer than ever;
the sound of their wrangling and contention
was terrifying indeed.

---

1. Demons.

Kumbhanda demons
crouched on clumps of earth 55
or leaped one or two feet
off the ground,
idling, wandering here and there,
amusing themselves according to their whim.
Sometimes they seized a dog by two of its legs 60
and beat it till it had lost its voice,
or planted their feet on the dog's neck,
terrifying it for their own delight.
Again there were demons
with large tall bodies, 65
naked in form, black and emaciated,
constantly living there,
who would cry out in loud ugly voices,
shouting and demanding food.
There were other demons 70
whose throats were like needles,
or still other demons
with heads like the head of an ox,
some feeding on human flesh,
others devouring dogs. 75
Their hair like tangled weeds,
cruel, baleful, ferocious,
driven by hunger and thirst,
they dashed about shrieking and howling.
The yakshas and starving spirits 80
and the various evil birds and beasts
hungrily pressed forward in all directions,
peering out at the windows.
Such were the perils of this house,
threats and terrors beyond measure. 85
This house, old and rotting,
belonged to a certain man
and that man had gone nearby
and had not been out for long
when a fire 90
suddenly broke out in the house.
In one moment from all four sides
the flames rose up in a mass.
Ridgepoles, beams, rafters, pillars
exploded with a roar, quivering, splitting, 95
broke in two and came tumbling down
as walls and partitions collapsed.
The various demons and spirits
lifted their voices in a great wail,

the hawks, eagles and other birds,
the kumbhanda demons,
were filled with panic and terror,
not knowing how to escape.
The evil beasts and poisonous creatures
hid in their holes and dens,
and the pishacha demons,
who were also living there,
because they had done so little that was good,
were oppressed by the flames
and attacked one another,
drinking blood and gobbling flesh.
The jackals and their like
were already dead by this time
and the larger of the evil beasts
vied in devouring them.
Foul smoke swirled and billowed up,
filling the house on every side.
The centipedes and millipedes,
the poisonous snakes and their kind,
scorched by the flames,
came scurrying out of their lairs,
whereupon the kumbhanda demons
pounced on them and ate them.
In addition, the starving spirits,
the fire raging about their heads,
hungry, thirsty, tormented by the heat,
raced this way and that in terror and confusion.
Such was the state of that house,
truly frightening and fearful;
malicious injury, the havoc of fire—
many ills, not just one, afflicted it.
At this time the owner of the house
was standing outside the gate
when he heard someone say,
"A while ago your various sons,
in order to play their games,
went inside the house.
They are very young and lack understanding
and will be wrapped up in their amusements."
When the rich man heard this,
he rushed in alarm into the burning house,
determined to rescue his sons
and keep them from being burned by the flames.
He urged his sons to heed him,
explaining the many dangers and perils,
the evil spirits and poisonous creatures,

the flames spreading all around,
the multitude of sufferings
that would follow one another without end,
the poisonous snakes, lizards and vipers,                    *150*
as well as the many yakshas
and kumbhanda demons,
the jackals, foxes and dogs,
hawks, eagles, kites, owls,
ground beetles and similar creatures,                        *155*
driven and tormented by hunger and thirst,
truly things to be feared.
His sons could not stay in such a perilous place,
much less when it was all on fire!
But the sons had no understanding                            *160*
and though they heard their father's warnings,
they continued engrossed in their amusements,
never ceasing their games.
At that time the rich man
thought to himself:                                          *165*
My sons behave in this manner,
adding to my grief and anguish.
In this house at present
there is not a single joy,
and yet my sons,                                             *170*
wrapped up in their games,
refuse to heed my instructions
and will be destroyed by the fire!
Then it occurred to him
to devise some expedient means,                              *175*
and he said to his sons,
"I have many kinds
of rare and marvelous toys,
wonderful jeweled carriages,
goat-carts, deer-carts,                                      *180*
carts drawn by big oxen.
They are outside the gate right now—
you must come out and see them!
I have fashioned these carts
explicitly for you.                                          *185*
You may enjoy whichever you choose,
play with them as you like!"
When the sons heard
this description of the carts,
at once they vied with one another                           *190*
in dashing out of the house,
till they reached the open ground,
away from all peril and danger.

When the rich man saw that his sons
had escaped from the burning house                              *1*
and were standing in the crossroads,
he seated himself on a lion seat,
congratulating himself in these words:
"Now I am content and happy.
These sons of mine                                              *2*
have been very difficult to raise.
Ignorant, youthful, without understanding,
they entered that perilous house
with its many poisonous creatures
and its goblins to be feared.                                   *2*
The roaring flames of the great fire
rose up on all four sides,
yet those sons of mine
still clung to their games.
But now I have saved them,                                      *2*
caused them to escape from danger.
That is the reason, good people,
I am content and happy."
At that time the sons,
seeing their father comfortably seated,                         *2*
all went to where he was
and said to him:
"Please give us
the three kinds of jeweled carriages
you promised us earlier.                                        *2*
You said if we came out of the house
you'd give us three kinds of carts
and we could choose whichever we wished.
Now is the time
to give them to us!"                                            *2*
The rich man was very wealthy
and had many storehouses.
With gold, silver, lapis lazuli,
seashells, agate,
and other such precious things                                  *2*
he fashioned large carriages
beautifully adorned and decorated,
with railings running around them
and bells hanging from all sides.
Ropes of gold twisted and twined,                               *2*
nets of pearls
stretched over the top,
and fringes of golden flowers
hung down everywhere.
Multicolored decorations                                        *2*

wound around and encircled the carriages,
soft silks and gauzes
served for cushions,
with fine felts of most wonderful make
valued at thousands or millions,                                245
gleaming white and pure,
to spread over them.
There were large white oxen,
sleek, stalwart, of great strength,
handsome in form,                                               250
to draw the jeweled carriages,
and numerous grooms and attendants
to accompany and guard them.
These wonderful carriages
the man presented to each of his sons alike.                    255
The sons at that time
danced for joy,
mounting the jeweled carriages,
driving off in all directions,
delighting and amusing themselves                               260
freely and without hindrance.
I say this to you, Shariputra—
I am like this rich man.
I, most venerable of the sages,
am the father of this world                                     265
and all living beings
are my children.
But they are deeply attached to worldly pleasures
and lacking in minds of wisdom.
There is no safety in the threefold world;                      270
it is like a burning house,
replete with a multitude of sufferings,
truly to be feared,
constantly beset with the griefs and pains
of birth, old age, sickness and death,                          275
which are like fires
raging fiercely and without cease.
The Thus Come One has already left
the burning house of the threefold world[2]
and dwells in tranquil quietude                                 280
in the safety of forest and plain.
But now this threefold world
is all my domain,

---

2. "Threefold world" refers to the three worlds of desire, form, and formlessness, which are inhabited by enlightened beings.

and the living beings in it
are all my children.
Now this place
is beset by many pains and trials.
I am the only person
who can rescue and protect others,
but though I teach and instruct them,
they do not believe or accept my teachings,
because, tainted by desires,
they are deeply immersed in greed and attachment.
So I employ an expedient means,
describing to them the three vehicles,
causing all living beings
to understand the pains of the threefold world,
and then I set forth and expound
a way whereby they can escape from the world.
If these children of mine
will only determine in their minds to do so,
they can acquire all the three understandings
and the six transcendental powers,
can become pratyekabuddhas
or bodhisattvas who never regress.
I say to you, Shariputra,
for the sake of living beings ,
I employ these similes and parables
to preach the single Buddha vehicle.
If you and the others are capable
of believing and accepting my words,
then all of you are certain
to attain the Buddha way.
This vehicle is subtle, wonderful,
foremost in purity;
throughout all worlds
it stands unsurpassed.
The Buddha delights in and approves it,
and all living beings
should praise it,
offer it alms and obeisance.

# Classical Sanskrit, Prakrit, and Tamil Literatures

### (c. 200 B.C.–A.D.1100 )

■ **Valmiki (c. 200 B.C.)** *Sanskrit* **(epic poem)**

TRANSLATED BY HARI PRASAD SHASTRI

The *Ramayana* is one of the world's great epics, comparable to the *Iliad*, the *Odyssey*, or the *Aeneid*. It is ascribed to the poet Valmiki, who is honored with the title First Poet, as the *Ramayana* is called the First Poem. The dating of the *Ramayana* is extremely uncertain; estimates range from 3380 B.C. to the second century A.D. The transmission of the text is similarly confused, and versions of the epic are known in many languages. In addition to the Sanskrit epic of Valmiki, the Hindi version by Tulsidas is notable. It seems likely that Valmiki gathered material from an oral tradition about the hero Rama and expanded upon it to create a court epic, and it is thought that the last book and part of the first book of the *Ramayana* are later additions. The popularity of this epic is evidenced by the fact that it has been translated into every major Indian language, has influenced Indian writers from Kalidasa to R. K. Narayan, and is the subject of countless movies and poems and festivals of art, music, and dance; there is even a devotional (bhakti) cult of Rama.

The story of the *Ramayana* centers on the epic hero Rama, descendent of the Ikshvaku kings who ruled the kingdom of Kosala in the sixth and fifth centuries B.C. Rama's father, Dasaratha, has four sons—Rama, Bharata, Satrughna, and Lakshmana—by three wives. Rama marries Sita, daughter of the King of Videhas, after proving himself by bending a magic bow, rather like Ulysses on his return to Ithaca, or King Arthur pulling Excalibur from the stone. Rama is denied his right of succession to the throne by the wiles of Queen Kaikeyi, who wants her son Bharata set in his place. Queen Kaikeyi holds the king to a promise he had made (after she saved his life) to grant any wish she asked of him, and she arranges to have Rama exiled for fourteen years. Rama goes into exile in the Dandaka Forest with Sita and his brother Lakshmana, though his loyal brother Bharata decides to rule only as regent in Rama's absence, placing Rama's sandals on the throne as a symbol of his brother's sovereignty. In his son's absence, King Dasaratha dies of sorrow.

In the Dandaka Forest, where Rama and his brother had often been taken to slay demons by the sage Vishvamitra, they live in exile, protecting the sages of the forest and killing the giant Viradha. When the sister of the demon Ravana, Shurpanakha, falls in love with Rama and is rejected by him and by his brother, she tries to swallow Sita, whereupon the demoness is mutilated by Lakshmana, instigating a war pitting Rama and his kin (and a band of magical monkeys and bears that joins him later in the epic) against the hordes of titanic demons. After a first battle in which Rama kills fourteen thousand demons, Shurpanakha turns to her brother, ten-headed Ravana, convincing him to kidnap Sita. After the abduction, Rama and his heroic brothers wander in search of Sita, gathering allies, such as the great monkeys Sugriva and Hanuman, and eventually discovering the location of Ravana's capital city of Lanka. In an epic seige, Rama and his supernatural army attack the city of Lanka, like the Greeks trying to win kidnapped Helen back from Troy. Rama and Ravana face off like Achilles and Hector in an extended combat of cosmic proportions, and at length Rama triumphs. After all this, Rama rejects Sita in the presence of all his followers, but Sita proves her purity by throwing herself on a funeral pyre and remaining unburned.

This is the essential story of the *Ramayana,* but Book One and Book Seven add a head and a tail to this body. In Book One we are told that Rama and his brothers are the incarnations of Vishnu, who becomes human to save the gods and other celestial beings from the ravages of Ravana, who is invulnerable to all beings except humans, whom he discounts as insignificant. The monkeys and other beings who help Rama are incarnations of the gods who come to earth to help Vishnu. Book Seven has Rama desert Sita again because the people are grumbling at her becoming Queen after residing so long with Ravana. Sita stays in the hermitage of the author, Valmiki, and gives birth to twin sons, who grow up under the tutelage of Valmiki. When the two boys recite Valmiki's *Ramayana,* Rama asks Sita to prove her purity by an oath. Sita responds, "May Mother Earth embrace me in her arms to prove I have never thought a single thought outside of Rama." Sita disappears into the earth, leaving Rama heartbroken, but soon after he gives his kingdom to the twins and ascends to Heaven, where he becomes Vishnu again and is reunited with Sita.

**FURTHER READING:** Goldman, Robert P., tr. *The Ramayana of Valmiki: An Epic of Ancient India,* 1984. Griffith, Ralph T. H., tr. *The Ramayana of Valmiki,* 5 vols., 1870–1874. Shastri, Hari Prasad, tr. *The Ramayana of Valmiki,* 3 vols., 1952–1959.

## from *The Ramayana*

### The Arrival of Shurpanakha at the Hermitage

Having bathed in the Godaveri river, Rama, Sita and Lakshmana left its banks and returned to the hermitage. On reaching their retreat, Raghava[1] with Lakshmana performed their morning devotions and entered the leaf-thatched hut. In the hut, that long-armed hero with Sita at his side dwelt

---

1. Another name for Rama.

happily, honoured by the great Rishis,[2] and shone like the moon accompanied by the Chitra star.

One day, while Rama was reciting the traditional texts, a female demon chanced to pass that way, by name Shurpanakha who was the sister of Ravana.[3]

Approaching Rama, she observed that he resembled a God, with his radiant countenance, his long arms, his large eyes like unto lotus petals, his majestic gait resembling an elephant's, matted locks crowning his head; youthful, full of valour, bearing the marks of royalty, his colour that of the blue lotus and alluring as the God of Love himself.

Beholding that hero, the equal of Indra, the Rakshasi[4] was overwhelmed with desire. Rama was handsome, she hideous; his waist was slender, hers thick and heavy; he had large eyes, hers squinted; his locks were beautiful, hers were red; his whole appearance was pleasing, hers repellent. Rama's voice was sonorous, hers strident; he was fair and youthful, she old and haggard; he was amiable, she sullen; he was self-controlled, she unruly; he was captivating, she odious.

Consumed with passion, the Rakshasi said to Rama:—

"With thy matted locks and ascetic guise, bearing bow and arrows, why hast thou, accompanied by thy consort, come to these woods, which are frequented by demons? What is the purpose of thy journey?"

Hearing the words of the Rakshasi, Shurpanakha, that hero, the Scourge of his Foes, with perfect candour began to relate all.

He said:—"There was a king named Dasaratha, who was as powerful as a God. I am his eldest son, known among men as Rama; this is my younger brother, Lakshmana, my faithful companion, and this, my consort, the illustrious Sita, daughter of the King of Videha.

"Bound by the will of my sire and in order to carry out my duty, I have come to dwell in the forest.

"But now I wish to know who thy father is, who thou art, and what thy race? To judge by thy charms, thou art a Rakshasi! Tell me truly, what has brought thee hither?"

Hearing the words of Rama, the Rakshasi, tormented by the pangs of love, answered:—

"Hear O Rama and I will tell thee the truth! I am Shurpanakha, a Rakshasi, who can change her form at will. I wander about in the forest, striking terror in the hearts of all beings. My brothers are Ravana, of whom thou hast doubtless heard, and the powerful and somnolent Kumbhakarna, the virtuous Bibishana a stranger to our practices,[5] and two others famed for their martial qualities, Khara and Dushana.

2. Great Rishi is a term for the highest class of sage.

3. Ravana is a titan, the King of Lanka, and the great villain of the epic.

4. Rakshasi is a term for a female titan, or demon.

5. Bibishana, brother to Ravana and Shurpanakha, is a virtuous demon who deserts his kin and joins Rama in the epic battles that follow.

"I, who am more powerful than they, having seen thee, O Rama, wish to unite myself with thee, O Lord, O First of Men!

"I am endowed with power and able to range at will by thought alone; therefore do thou become my master. What is Sita to thee?

"Deformed, without beauty, she is not worthy of thee, whereas I should prove a well-matched partner, my beauty equal to thine own; do thou look on me as thy consort. This unsightly, grim-visaged human female, of lean abdomen, will be devoured by me this day in thy presence, together with that brother of thine.

"Thou and I shall wander on the summit of the mountains and through the forests together, exploring the whole region of Dandaka, according to thy whim."

Speaking thus, the Rakshasi threw impassioned glances at Rama, who, smiling, made the following astute reply.

## The Mutilation of Shurpanakha

Smiling a little, Rama, in gently mocking tones, answered Shurpanakha, who had been caught in the noose of love, saying: —

"I am already wedded and this is my beloved consort; the rivalry between co-wives would prove unbearable! My younger brother however who is of a happy disposition, of agreeable appearance, virtuous and chaste, is called Lakshmana and is full of vigour. He has not yet experienced the joys of a wife's company and desires a consort. He is youthful and attractive and would therefore be a fitting husband for thee. Take my brother as thy lord, O Lady of large eyes and lovely hips, and enjoy him without a rival, as Mount Meru, the sunlight."

Hearing these words, the Rakshasi, blinded by passion, leaving Rama, at once addressed Lakshmana, saying: —

"My beauty renders me a worthy wife for thee; therefore come and we will range the Dandaka Forest and mountains happily together."

Thus accosted by the Rakshasi Shurpanakha, Lakshmana, the son of Sumitra, skilled in discourse, smiling, gave this ingenious reply: —

"How canst thou wish to become the wife of a slave, such as I? I am wholly dependent on my noble brother, O Thou whose complexion resembles the lotus, who art pleasing to look upon and chaste. O Lady of large eyes, thou art a paragon, do thou become the consort of that matchless hero. Renouncing that ugly, evil and peevish old woman, whose limbs are deformed, he will certainly devote himself to thee! O Lady of ravishing complexion and lovely limbs, what sensible man would sacrifice that unrivalled beauty of thine for an ordinary woman?"

Thinking Lakshmana's words to be sincere and not understanding his jest, that cruel and misshapen Rakshasi, in the blindness of her passion once more addressed Rama, the Scourge of His Foes, who was seated in the leaf-thatched hut with Sita, and said: —

"Is it for this hideous, evil and peevish woman, who is old and deformed, that thou dost slight me?

"I shall devour her in thy presence to-day, and shall live happily with thee without a rival."

Speaking thus, the Rakshasi, whose eyes blazed like torches, hurled herself in fury on Sita, like a great meteor descending on the planet Rohini.[6]

Then the mighty Rama restrained her, as, like the noose of death, she advanced towards Sita, and in anger addressed Lakshmana, saying:—

"It is unwise to taunt those beings who are vile and cruel, O Saumitri.[7] Take heed, see, Vaidehi[8] is in danger, O Friend! Do thou maim this hideous demon of protruding belly, who is evil and filled with fury."

The valiant Lakshmana, highly incensed against the Rakshasi, thereupon drew his sword from its scabbard and, in the presence of Rama, cut off her ears and nose.

Her ears and nose severed, Shurpanakha uttered a terrible cry and ran into the forest. Being mutilated, the Rakshasi, streaming with blood, created a terrible uproar, like a tempest in the rainy season and, dripping with blood, that hideous monster, lifting up her arms, plunged howling into the deep woods.

Thereafter the injured Shurpanakha sought out her brother Khara of great might, who, surrounded by a troop of demons, was seated in Janasthana and threw herself on the ground before him, like a meteorite falling from heaven.

Wild with terror and covered with blood, Khara's sister, almost deprived of her senses, related everything concerning Raghava's arrival in the forest with his consort and Lakshmana and the circumstances of her disfigurement. . . .

## Shurpanakha Upbraids Ravana and Urges Him to Destroy Rama

When Shurpanakha saw those fourteen thousand titans of dreadful deeds slain by Rama single-handed on the field of battle, together with Khara, Dushana and Trishiras, she once more emitted dreadful shrieks and roared like thunder. Perceiving the incomparable prowess of Raghava, she became exceedingly agitated and proceeded to Lanka, Ravana's capital.

There she beheld Ravana shining in glory, surrounded by his ministers on the terrace of his palace, like Indra amidst the Maruts.[9] Seated on his golden throne, blazing like a flame, Ravana resembled a great fire kindled on an altar, kept alive by sacrificial offerings. Unconquered by Gods, Gandharvas,[10] Rishis or other creatures, that warrior, who resembled death itself with wide-open jaws, bore on his person the wounds inflicted

---

6. Rohini is the star Aldebaran.

7. Saumitri means Son of Sumitra, i.e., Lakshmana.

8. Vaidehi means Daughter of the King of Videha, i.e., Sita.

9. Maruts are wind gods; Indra is the King of the Gods.

10. Gandharvas are the celestial musicians.

by the thunderbolts in the war between Gods and titans and on his breast the marks of Airavata's tusks.[11]

Having twenty arms, ten heads, a broad chest, wearing gorgeous attire and bearing the marks of royalty, he was adorned with a chain of emeralds and ornaments of fine gold and with his great arms, white teeth and enormous mouth resembled a mountain.

In the combat with the Gods, Vishnu had struck him a hundred times with his discus, and he bore the marks of other weapons from that great struggle, yet his limbs were intact and had not been severed. He who was able to churn up the seas, a feat not to be performed by any other, whose missiles were the mountain crests, he the scourge of the Gods, who transgressed every moral law, the ravisher of others' wives, the wielder of celestial weapons, the destroyer of sacrifices, who descended into the city of Bhogavati and subdued the serpent Vasuki,[12] from whom, on his defeat, he stole the gentle consort; he who scaled Mount Kailasha and overcame Kuvera[13] depriving him of his aerial chariot Pushpaka, which transported him wheresoever he desired; he who in his anger destroyed the garden of Chaitaratha,[14] the lotus pool and the Nandana Grove and all the pleasurable retreats of the Gods, and with his vast arms, resembling the peaks of mountains, arrested the course of the sun and moon, twin scourgers of their foes, rising in splendour; practising asceticism in the mighty forest for a thousand years he offered his heads in sacrifice to Swyambhu[15] and obtained the boon that neither Deva, Danava, Gandharva, Pisacha, Pataya nor Uraga should be able to slay him, but of man there was no mention;[16] proud of his strength, he stole the Soma juice,[17] sanctified by mantras, before its pressing by the Twice-born in the sacrifice; this perverse wretch, Ravana of evil deeds, slayer of the brahmins, ruthless, pitiless, delighting in causing harm to others, was verily a source of terror to all beings.

The titan woman beheld her brother full of power, resplendent in gorgeous attire, adorned with celestial garlands, seated on his throne, resembling Time at the destruction of the worlds, that Indra of Demons, the proud descendant of Poulastya[18] and she, trembling with fear, in order to address him, drew near to the Slayer of his Enemies, who was seated amidst his counsellors. Distracted with terror and passion, Shurpanakha, who was wont to roam everywhere unafraid, now mutilated by the order of that magnanimous

---

11. Airavata is the sacred elephant that carries Indra, King of the Gods.

12. Vasuki is the Serpent King.

13. Kuvera is God of Wealth.

14. Chaitaratha is King of the Gandharvas, or Celestial Musicians.

15. Swyambhu is a term for Brahma, the Creator.

16. Devas are gods, Danavas are giants, Pisachas are ghosts, Uragas are Great Serpents; Ravana is invulnerable to all these mighty supernatural beings, but doesn't consider humanity enough of a threat to protect himself against it. This proves to be his Achilles heel.

17. Soma juice is used in sacred ceremonies as a beverage or libation.

18. Poulastya was one of the Seven Immortal Sages, and Ravana's grandfather.

Ramachandra,[19] displaying her ravaged features before Ravana, whose large eyes appeared to shoot forth flames, uttered these bitter words to him:

## Shurpanakha's Words to Ravana

Filled with anger, Shurpanakha addressed Ravana, the Oppressor of the Worlds, in harsh accents, saying:—

"O Ravana, wholly devoted to pleasure and indulging in every whim without scruple, thou art oblivious of the great calamity that threatens thee. That monarch who is given up to lust and other dissipations and who is covetous, is disregarded by his subjects, as is the fire in the crematorium. That king who does not fulfil his duties at the proper season brings ruin on his state. The Prince who, committing excess, is ruled by his consorts and readily gives credence to other's counsel, is shunned as the mud of a river is shunned by an elephant. Those rulers who are unable to protect their lands or reclaim the territory wrested from them, live without glory, like mountains submerged in the ocean.

"At enmity with the Gods, the Gandharvas and the Danavas, who are masters of themselves, doing what ought not to be done and inconstant, how art thou able to rule as king?

"O Titan, thou art childish and thoughtless and art not conversant with that which should be known to thee; how canst thou govern? Those monarchs who have neither emissaries, wealth nor policy at their disposal, resemble a common man, O Prince of Conquerors! Since kings are informed by their spies as to what is taking place abroad, they are said to be far-sighted. Meseems thou dost not discharge thy duty and that the counsellors who surround thee are inexperienced, since thou art insensible to the destruction of thy people and their territory.

"Fourteen thousand titans of dreadful deeds with Khara and Dushana have been slain by Rama single-handed; Rama of imperishable exploits has freed the ascetics of fear, established peace in the Dandaka Forest and harassed Janasthana, but thou, who art covetous and a slave to lust, art unaware of the danger that threatens thy dominion. None will help that monarch in time of peril, who is mean, violent, dissolute, haughty and perfidious. Even his own relatives will overpower a king who is excessively vain, pretentious, boastful and irascible. That monarch who fails in his duty and, under the threat of danger is lulled into a false security, will in time of adversity be swept from his kingdom like a straw. Dry wood, turf or dust have some value, but a king who is degenerate is worthless and resembles a faded wreath or a worn-out garment. That monarch who is vigilant however, conversant with what is happening and virtuous, establishes his throne in perpetuity. The king who, even while sleeping, is yet awake to the ordering of his kingdom, who manifests his anger or approval at a fitting time, is revered by all.

---

19. Ramachandra is another name for Rama.

"O Thou, whose emissaries have failed to inform thee of the great carnage among the titans, who art bereft of wisdom, O Ravana, thou art lacking in all these great qualities.

"Disregarding others, given up to the pleasures of the senses, not able to reap the advantage of time and place or discriminate between what is good and evil, having sacrificed thy kingdom, thou wilt soon perish."

Reflecting on the infirmities his sister had ascribed to him, Ravana, the Lord of the Titans, opulent, arrogant and powerful, became absorbed in thought.

## Shurpanakha Urges Ravana to Slay Rama and Wed Sita

Hearing Shurpanakha's bitter words, Ravana surrounded by his ministers enquired angrily:—"Who is Rama? What is his strength? How does he look and what is the measure of his prowess? Why has he penetrated into the lonely and inaccessible depths of the Dandaka Forest? With what weapons did he destroy the titans in that conflict, slaying Khara and Dushana as also Trishiras? Tell me truly, O Lovely One, who has disfigured thee?"

Thus addressed by the Lord of the Titans, Shurpanakha in a transport of rage began to relate the history of Rama.

She said: "Rama, the son of King Dasaratha, resembles the God of Love; his arms are long, his eyes large; clad in robes of bark and a black antelope skin, bearing a bow encircled with gold like unto Indra's, he lets fly blazing arrows resembling venomous snakes. Emitting a great shout, he discharges his formidable shafts, and in the struggle I could not distinguish him but beheld the host being decimated under the rain of his arrows, as the harvest is destroyed by the hail sent by Indra. In a short space, single-handed, standing alone, he slew fourteen thousand titans with Khara and Dushana, thus bringing peace to the sages in the Dandaka Forest and delivering them from fear. Chivalrous of soul, Rama, the Knower of Self, would not countenance the slaying of a woman and, having been mutilated at his command, I escaped.

"His brother, endowed with great valour, is renowned for his virtue; his name is Lakshmana and he is devoted to Rama. Full of fire, indomitable, victorious, powerful, intelligent and wise, he is his right hand and his very life's breath. And Rama's virtuous, tender and wedded wife, of large eyes, whose face resembles the full moon, is ever engaged in what is pleasing to her lord. With her lovely locks, well-formed nose, beautiful shoulders and her grace and dignity, one would deem her to be a forest divinity or Lakshmi herself. With a skin of the colour of molten gold, nails that are rosy and long, that surpassingly lovely woman is Sita, the slender-waisted Princess of Videha. No woman so beautiful has ever appeared in the world, either among the Gods, Gandharvas, Yakshas or Kinneras. He whose wife Sita becomes and whom she will warmly embrace will live in the world more happily than Purandara. With her natural amiability, her marvellous beauty, which is without equal on earth, she would prove a worthy consort for thee, and thou too art fit to be her lord. It was to bring thee this lady of shapely hips, softly rounded breasts and charming features, that I put forth my endeavours, when, O Mighty-armed One, I was mutilated by the ruthless Lakshmana!

"When thou dost behold Vaidehi, whose countenance resembles the full moon, thou shalt instantly be pierced with the darts of the God of Love. If thou desirest to win her, then set off speedily on thy right foot and lay siege to her heart. If, O Ravana, my counsel meets with thine approval, then, O King of the Titans, follow it without delay.

"Knowing the weakness of these people, O Valiant Chief of the Titans, make Sita, who is without blemish, thy consort. Hearing that Rama with his arrows that never missed their mark has slain the titans established in Janasthana, and of the death of Khara and Dushana, thou hast a duty to perform."

## Ravana Approaches Sita

. . . Thereupon Ravana, in the guise of a mendicant, availing himself of the opportunity, rapidly approached the hermitage with the purpose of seeking out Vaidehi. With matted locks, clad in a saffron robe and carrying a triple staff and loshta, that highly powerful one, knowing Sita to be alone, accosted her in the wood, in the form of an ascetic, at dusk when darkness shrouds the earth in the absence of the sun and moon. Gazing on Sita, the consort of Rama, Ravana resembled Rahu regarding Rohini in the absence of Shasi.[20]

Beholding that monstrous apparition, the leaves of the trees ceased to move, the wind grew still, the turbulent course of the river Godaveri subsided and began to flow quietly. The ten-headed Ravana, however, profiting by Rama's absence, drew near to Sita in the guise of a monk of venerable appearance while she was overcome with grief on account of her lord.

Approaching Vaidehi in an honourable guise, as Saturn draws near to the Chitra star, Ravana resembled a deep well overgrown with grass. He stood there gazing on the glorious consort of Rama of incomparable beauty, Sita, with her brilliant lips and teeth, her countenance as radiant as the full moon, seated on a carpet of leaves, overwhelmed with grief, weeping bitterly.

On seeing the Princess of Videha alone, clad in a yellow silken sari, whose eyes resembled lotus petals, the titan, struck by Kama's arrow,[21] joyfully accosted her, feigning the gentle accents of a brahmin. Praising her beauty, unequalled in the Three Worlds, which caused her to resemble Shri,[22] he said:—

"O Thou, possessed of the brilliance of gold and silver, who art clad in a yellow silken sari and who, like a pool of lilies, art wreathed in garlands

---

20. That is, the demon of eclipses regarding the star Aldebaran in the absence of the moon.

21. Kama is the God of Love, who shoots arrows like Cupid.

22. Shri is the consort of Vishnu, the Goddess of Prosperity, better known as Lakshmi; Sita was said to be an incarnation of her.

of fresh flowers, art thou Lakshmi bereft of her lotus or Kirti or a nymph of graceful aspect? Art thou Bhuti of slender hips, or Rati disporting herself in the forest?[23]

"How even, sharp and white are thy teeth, how large thy slightly reddened eyes with their dark pupils, how well proportioned and rounded are thy thighs and how charming thy legs, resembling the tapering trunk of an elephant! How round and plump are thy cheeks, like unto the polished fruit of the Tala trees; how enchanting is thy bosom, decorated with pearls!

"O Lady of Sweet Smiles, lovely teeth and expressive eyes, as a river sweeps away its banks with its swift current so dost thou steal away my heart, O Graceful One. Slender is thy waist, glossy thine hair, thy breasts touching each other enhance thy loveliness; neither the consorts of the Gods, the Gandharvas, the Yakshas nor the Kinneras can compare with thee.[24] 'Till this hour, I have never seen any on earth so perfect; thy youth, thy beauty and thy grace are unequalled in the Three Worlds!

"Seeing thee dwelling here in solitude distresses my heart. Come with me! It is not fitting that thou shouldst remain here; this place is frequented by ruthless demons, who are able to assume different forms at will. It is for thee to reside in sumptuous and delightful palaces in the vicinity of pleasant cities, surrounded by groves of sweet smelling shrubs and green trees, where thou canst wander clad in beautiful robes, decked in fragrant garlands, with a consort worthy of thy beauty, O Charming One. O Dark-eyed Lady of Sweet Smiles, art thou wedded to one of the Rudras, the Maruts or Vasus?[25] Thou appearest divine to me, yet these are not the haunts of the Gandharvas, Devas or Kinneras, but of the Titans. How hast thou come here?

"Dost thou not fear to live amidst monkeys, lions, tigers, deer, wolves, bears, hyenas and leopards? O Fair One, dost thou not tremble before those terrible elephants, maddened with the exudation of temporal juices, in this great forest? Who art thou? To whom dost thou belong? For what reason dost thou range the Dandaka Forest alone, which is frequented by terrible titans?"

With these flattering words did the evil-minded Ravana address Sita, and seeing him in the guise of a brahmin, she entertained him with the traditional hospitality due to an uninvited guest. Leading him to a seat, she brought water to wash his feet and offered him food, saying:—"Be pleased to accept this repast!" Seeing him in the form of a Twice-born with his loshta and saffron robe, unrecognizable in his disguise, Sita welcomed him as a true brahmin, saying:—

---

23. Kirti is a celestial nymph; Bhuti is the mother of the nymph Manu; Rati is the consort of the God of Love.

24. Yaleshas are supernatural beings attendant on Kuvera, the god of wealth; Kinneras are horse-headed beings who attend Kuvera.

25. The Rudras are the sons of Aditi, Mother of the Gods and Kashyapa, the Great Vedic Sage, grandson of Brahma; the Maruts are Gods of the Wind; the Vasus are also sons of Kashyapa and Aditi.

"Be seated, O Brahmin, and accept this water for washing thy feet, also this meal, composed of ripe fruits and roasted grain, prepared for thee, which please enjoy."

Thus did she receive him with hospitable words, but Ravana, his gaze fixed on the Princess of Mithila, determined to bear her away, thus preparing his own destruction.

Sita, anxiously expecting the return from hunting of her illustrious lord, with Prince Lakshmana, searched the vast and darkening forest with her eyes but was unable to see either Rama or his brother there.

## The Conversation of Ravana and Sita

Thus addressed by Ravana in the guise of a mendicant, who had resolved to bear her away, Sita reflected: —

'This person is my guest and a brahmin; if I do not answer him he may curse me!' and thinking thus, she said: —

"May good betide thee! I am the daughter of the high-souled Janaka, the King of Mithila, my name is Sita and I am the beloved consort of Rama. For twelve years, I dwelt in the palace of Ikshwaku, where all my desires were gratified and I enjoyed every comfort.

"In the thirteenth year, the king with the approval of his ministers decided to enthrone Rama. All being ready for the installation of Raghava, Kaikeyi, one of my mothers-in-law, requested a boon of her lord. Having gratified my father-in-law by her services, she extracted two promises from him, the exile of my husband and the installation of her son Bharata, saying: — 'I shall neither eat, drink nor sleep if Rama is enthroned and it will prove the end of my life.'

"The Lord of the Earth, my father-in-law, hearing her speak thus, offered her diverse gifts, but Kaikeyi refused them. At that time, my lord was twenty-five years old and I eighteen. Being loyal, virtuous, honourable and devoted to the good of all, my lord, Rama, endowed with long arms and large eyes, was renowned throughout the world. Our father King Dasaratha, blinded by passion, in order to please Kaikeyi, did not install Rama, and when he came before his sire, in order to receive the crown, Kaikeyi addressed the following bitter words to him: — "O Ramachandra, hear from me the decree issued by thy father. This great kingdom is to be given to Bharata and thou art to dwell in the forest for fourteen years. Now go hence, and save thy sire from the sin of perjury."

"Then the imperturbable Rama replied: 'So be it' and acted accordingly. My lord of firm vows, accustomed to give and not to receive commands, who ever speaketh truth without prevarication, hearing these words acquiesced and has fulfilled his vow to the uttermost. His brother, the valiant Lakshmana, a Lion among Men and the companion of Rama in combat, the Destroyer of his Foes, given to asceticism, bearing his bow, followed Rama into exile with me.

"Thus Raghava, fixed in his vow, wearing matted locks, accompanied by myself and his younger brother, penetrated into the depths of the forest of

Dandaka. We have all three been banished from the kingdom by Kaikeyi and, depending on our own strength, wander about in the forest. Remain here awhile, O Foremost of the Twice-born, my lord will soon return with an abundance of roots and fruit and sufficient venison, having slain deer, kine and boar. But thou, O Brahmin, tell me who thou art and what thy name, family and lineage. Why dost thou range the Dandaka Forest alone?"

Hearing the words of Sita, the consort of Rama, the mighty titan replied in these harsh words: —

"O Sita, I am that Ravana, King of the Titans, in fear of whom the world, the Gods, titans and men tremble. O Source of Delight, since I beheld thee shining like gold, clad in silk, my consorts have ceased to find favour with me. Do thou become the chief queen of those countless women, stolen away from many quarters by me.

"Lanka, my capital, set in the midst of the sea, is built on the summit of a hill. There, O Sita, wander with me in the groves and thus forget the forest. O Lovely One, if thou dost become my wife, five thousand servants adorned with diverse ornaments shall attend on thee."

The blameless daughter of Janaka, being thus addressed by Ravana, was filled with indignation and answered that titan with contempt, saying: —

"I am dependent on my lord, Rama, who is as steadfast as a rock, calm as the ocean and equal to Mahendra[26] himself, Rama, endowed with every good quality, who resembles the Nyagrodha tree[27] in stature. I am dependent on that illustrious and noble warrior, whose arms are long, whose chest is broad, whose gait is like a lion's, nay, who resembles that king of beasts; to him, the greatest of men, I give my whole allegiance. To Rama, whose countenance resembles the full moon, the son of a king, master of his passions, of immeasurable renown and power, I shall ever remain faithful.

"O Jackal, thou desirest a she-lion but art no more able to possess me than grasp the light of the sun! Thou Wretch, who seekest to carry off the beloved spouse of Raghava! Verily thou dost imagine the trees that thou seest before thee to be made of gold,[28] that thou art seeking to draw the teeth of a famished and courageous lion, that enemy of the deer, or extract the fangs of a poisonous snake. Dost thou desire to lift up the Mandara mountain with thy bare hands or live at ease after drinking poison? Thou dost seek to rub thine eyes with a needle and lick a razor with thy tongue! Thou desirest to cross the ocean with a stone round thy neck or grasp the sun and moon. O Thou who seekest to bear away the beloved wife of Rama, thou art endeavouring to carry a blazing fire in thy robe or walk on iron spikes.

"The disparity between thee and Rama is as that between a jackal and a lion, a brook and an ocean, the nectar of the Gods and sour barley

---

26. Mahendra is a name for Indra.

27. The Indian fig tree.

28. The trees of hell, said to be made of gold.

gruel; between gold and iron, sandal and mud, an elephant and a cat, an eagle and a crow, a peacock and a duck, a swan and a vulture. Even shouldst thou steal me, if that mighty archer, Rama, whose prowess is equal to the Lord of a Thousand Eyes, still lives, thou wilt no more be able to devour me than a fly can eat the clarified butter into which it has fallen."

Addressing that cruel Ranger of the Night thus, the guileless Sita shook like a leaf in the wind.

Perceiving her distress, Ravana, terrible as death, began to boast of his race, his power, his name and his exploits, in order to increase her fear.

## Sita Defies Ravana

Provoked by Sita's proud words, Ravana, scowling, answered her in fierce accents: —

"O Lady of Fair Complexion, may prosperity attend thee! I am the brother of the Lord of Wealth, my name is Ravana. I am the mighty Dashagriva[29] from whom, as all creatures before death, the Gods, Gandharvas, Pisachas, Patagas and Nagas flee in terror.[30] I have subdued my blood-brother Kuvera, who for a certain reason I incited to combat and who, vanquished by me, fled in alarm from his sumptuous abode and sought refuge on Kailasha, the Lord of Mountains.

"By virtue of my prowess I robbed him of his marvellous chariot, Pushpaka, that moves according to one's will, and in it I range the skies. Seeing my dread visage, the Gods with Indra at their head flee in terror, O Maithili.[31] Wheresoever I roam, the wind blows temperately and the rays of the sun resemble the moon's. Where I stay, the leaves of the trees become motionless and the rivers cease to flow.

"Beyond the sea stands my magnificent capital, Lanka, inhabited by powerful titans, equal to Indra's citadel, Amaravati.

"That beautiful stronghold, encircled by dazzling battlements with golden ramparts and gates of emerald, is a city of dreams.

"Filled with elephants, horses and chariots, echoing to the sound of bugles, it is embellished by pleasant gardens planted with diverse trees, yielding fruit of every desirable taste. O Sita, O Thou Daughter of a King, in that city thou shalt dwell with me, forgetting the lot of mortal women. There thou shalt taste celestial delights! O Lady of exquisite countenance, think of Rama no more, who is but human and whose end is near. Placing his beloved son on the throne, King Dasaratha sent his heir of negligible prowess to the forest. What wouldst thou with that Rama, deprived of his kingdom, living as an ascetic in solitude, O Large-eyed Beauty? I, the Lord of all the Titans, have come to thee in person, pierced by the shafts of the God of Love. It does not befit thee to disregard me. O Timid Lady, if thou

---

29. Dashagriva is a name for Ravana, meaning Ten-necked One.

30. Pisachas are ghosts; Patagas are winged creatures; and Nagas are the Serpent Race.

31. Maithili is a name of Sita.

dost pass me by, thou wilt repent, like Urvashi, who thrust away Puraravas with her foot.[32] Rama is but a mortal and not equal to even a finger of mine in combat. By good fortune I have come to thee; do thou therefore yield thyself to me, O Fair One."

At these words, Vaidehi, her eyes flashing with anger, though alone, answered that Lord of the Titans boldly, saying:—

"Since thou claimest to be the brother of the God, Kuvera, who is held in veneration by all the Celestials, how dost thou dare to commit this infamous deed, O Ravana? Undoubtedly all the titans will meet with destruction, having so cruel, senseless and lustful a person as thee as their sovereign. The ravisher of Indra's consort, Sachi, may survive, but he who bears away the wife of Rama will never live in peace. O Titan, it were possible for the one who deprives the Bearer of the Thunderbolt of his consort of unsurpassed beauty to live on earth, but he who insults me will never escape death, were he to drink the water of immortality!"

## Sita's Abduction by Ravana

Hearing those words of Sita, the mighty Ravana, striking one hand on the other, revealed his gigantic form and, skilled in speech, addressed her, saying:—

"Methinks thou hast taken leave of thy senses, hast thou not heard of my great prowess and valour? Standing in space, I am able to lift up the earth; I can drink the waters of the ocean and destroy death himself in combat. With my shafts I can pierce the sun and cleave the terrestrial globe. Thou, who dost allow thyself to be deceived by any trick and dost follow any whim, behold how I can change my shape at will."

Speaking thus, Ravana, full of wrath, his eyes glowing like burning coals, resembled a flame, and discarding his benign aspect, he, the younger brother of Kuvera, assumed a terrible shape, resembling death itself.

With smouldering eyes, a prey to anger, resplendent in ornaments of fine gold, like a dark cloud, that Ranger of the Night appeared before her with his ten heads and twenty arms. Abandoning his ascetic disguise, the King of the Titans took on his native form; wearing a blood-red robe, he fixed that pearl among women, Maithili, with his gaze, thereafter addressing her, who resembled the sun, whose hair was dark and who was clothed in a robe and jewels, saying:—

"O Fair Lady, if thou desirest a master famed throughout the Three Worlds, then surrender thyself to me. I am a husband worthy of thee; do thou serve me forever! I shall do thee great honour nor will I ever displease thee. Renouncing thine attachment to a man, place thine affection on me. What binds thee to Rama, O Thou Foolish One who deemest thyself wise; he who has been banished from his domain, who has failed to fulfil his destiny and whose days are numbered, Rama, who on the injunc-

---

32. Urvashi is a nymph mentioned in the Rig Veda, and Puraravas was the king who married her.

tion of a woman abandoned kingdom, friends and people to inhabit a forest frequented by wild beasts?"

Speaking thus to Maithili, who was worthy of tenderness and gentle of speech, that wicked titan, inflamed by passion, seized hold of her as Budha seizes Rohini.[33] With his left hand he grasped the hair of the lotus-eyed Sita, and with his right, her thighs. Seeing Ravana with his sharp teeth like the peak of a mountain, resembling death itself, the Celestial Beings fled away in terror. Then instantly the great chariot belonging to Ravana, made of gold, to which braying mules were harnessed, appeared and, addressing Sita in harsh tones, he lifted her up and, clasping her, ascended the car.

Then the virtuous and unfortunate Sita, being overpowered by the titan, began to cry aloud, "Rama! Rama!" but he was far away in the depths of the forest. Though she possessed no love for him, Ravana, burning with passion, rose high into the air with her, as she struggled like the consort of the Indra of Serpents. . . .

## Rama and Ravana Fight with Magic Weapons

Beholding Mahodara and Mahaparshwa slain and, despite his great strength, the valiant Virupaksha also struck down, a great rage seized Ravana, who urged on his charioteer with these words: —

"By slaying Rama and Lakshmana I shall remove that double scourge, the cause of the slaughter of my faithful adherents and the siege of the city. In the fight I shall cut down Rama, that tree of which Sita is the flower and the fruit, whose branches are Sugriva, Jambavan, Kumuda, Nala, also Dvivida, Mainda, Angada, Gandhamadana, Hanuman, Sushena and all the leading monkeys."[34]

Thereupon that mighty car-warrior, who caused the ten regions to resound, drove rapidly on Raghava with his chariot, and the earth, with its rivers, mountains and woods, trembled with the uproar, and the lions, gazelles and birds that inhabited it were seized with terror.

Then Ravana employed a dark and magic weapon that was formidable and terrifying and with it he consumed the monkeys, who fled hither and thither. Amidst the dust raised by their battalions, for they were unable to endure that weapon created by Brahma himself, Raghava, seeing those countless divisions taking refuge in innumerable places, pursued by Ravana's powerful shafts, stood ready waiting. . . .

\* \* \*

. . . Thereafter, between those two warriors, each seeking to slay the other, an incomparable and unimaginable struggle ensued like unto the duel between Vritra and Vasava.[35] Both were furnished with excellent

---

33. That is, the planet Mercury seizes Aldebaran.

34. Sugriva is King of the Monkeys, Jambavan is King of the Bears, and all the rest are monkey warriors.

35. Vasava is a term for Indra, who slayed the demon Vritra.

bows, both were skilled warriors, both brought exceptional knowledge in the science of arms to the fight. In all their manoeuvrings they were followed by a stream of shafts as the waves in two oceans that are whipped up by a tempest. . . . Then Rama, skilled in the use of arms, struck Ravana afresh on the forehead, as he stood in his chariot, with arrows to which he had joined a miraculous weapon, and it appeared as if five-headed serpents in the form of darts were penetrating hissing into the earth repelled by Ravana whom they sought to devour. Thereupon, having rendered Raghava's weapon void, Ravana, in a transport of rage, armed himself in his turn with the dreadful Asura weapon which he loosed joined to sharp and terrible arrows with huge points, having the heads of lions, tigers, herons, geese, vultures, falcons, jackals and wolves or resembling serpents with five heads. Others had the heads of donkeys, boars, dogs, cocks, aquatic monsters and venomous reptiles and those sharp arrows were the creation of his magic power. Struck by the Asuric shafts, that lion among the Raghus, he who resembled the God of Fire himself, responded with the Agneya Dart that was full of power and to it he joined arrows of every kind with points that burnt like fire and which resembled suns, planets, and stars in hue or great meteors like unto flaming tongues. Those formidable missiles belonging to Ravana striking against those loosed by Rama, disintegrated in space and were annihilated in their thousands.

Thereupon all the valiant monkeys with Sugriva at their head, able to change their form at will, beholding the titan's weapon destroyed by Rama of imperishable karma, let forth joyous acclamations and made a circle round him.

Then the magnanimous son of Dasaratha, the descendant of Raghu, having destroyed that weapon discharged by Ravana's own arm, was filled with felicity, whilst the leaders of the monkeys joyfully paid homage to him.

## Ravana Flees from Rama

His weapon having been destroyed, Ravana, the King of the Titans, whose fury was redoubled, in his wrath instantly produced another; and he loosed the fearful Rudra Weapon, forged by Maya,[36] on Raghava. Thereafter, from his bow, innumerable spears, maces, flaming bars hard as diamond, mallets, hammers, chains and spiked clubs, like unto fiery thunderbolts, issued forth like the tempests at the dissolution of the worlds. . . .

\* \* \*

. . . At that instant, the younger brother of Raghava, the valiant Lakshmana, slayer of hostile warriors, armed himself with seven arrows and, with those exceedingly swift shafts, that illustrious prince severed Ravana's standard in many places, which bore the image of a man's head. With a single arrow, the fortunate Lakshmana of immense vigour, cut off the head adorned with brilliant earrings of the titan who drove the chariot,

---

36. Maya was the artificer of the gods, like Hephaestus.

and with five sharp arrows severed the bow resembling the trunk of an elephant that belonged to the King of the Titans.

Thereafter Bibishana, bounding forward, with his mace slew Ravana's beautiful horses that were as tall as hills and resembled a dark cloud in hue, whereupon Dashagriva,[37] leaping quickly from his car, the steeds of which having been slain, was filled with exceeding wrath against his brother and that powerful and spirited monarch loosed a flaming spear on Bibishana like unto a thunderbolt, but ere it reached its target, Lakshmana severed it with three arrows, whereupon a great cheer arose amongst the monkeys in that formidable struggle, and that spear, wreathed in gold, fell down shattered in three fragments like unto a great meteor falling from the sky amidst a shower of flaming sparks.

Then the titan, that mighty Ravana of wicked soul, armed himself with another superior and tested spear which Death himself would have found hard to resist and which was of immense size and shone with its own effulgence. Brandished with violence by the mighty Ravana of perverse soul it gave out a lurid gleam so that it appeared like forked lightning.

Meanwhile the valiant Lakshmana, perceiving that Bibishana stood in peril of his life, placed himself quickly in front of him and that hero, stretching his bow, with a rain of darts riddled Ravana, who stood waiting to discharge the weapon he held in his hand. Under the shower of arrows with which the courageous Saumitri[38] overwhelmed him, thus frustrating his design, the titan no longer thought of striking him in return. Seeing that he had preserved his brother's life, Ravana, who was standing before him, addressed him thus:—

"O Thou whose strength renders thee arrogant, since thou hast preserved this titan, my spear shall fall on thee; having pierced thine heart, this bloodstained weapon that mine arm, equal to an iron bar, will hurl at thee will rob thee of thy life's breath and return to my hand."

Thus did Ravana speak, and in a paroxysm of rage, levelling that pick adorned with eight extremely loud bells, created magically by Maya, that was infallible, the slayer of its foes, the splendour of which flamed up as it were, hurled it at Lakshmana with a mighty shout. Loosed with terrible violence and a sound of thunder, that spear fell with force on Lakshmana in the forefront of the battle.

Then Raghava sought to mitigate the power of that weapon and said:—

"May good fortune attend Lakshmana! May this mortal impact be rendered void!"

Released by the enraged titan on that indomitable hero, the spear which resembled a venomous snake, falling with extreme violence, penetrated his great chest and so brilliant was it that it appeared like the tongue of the King of the Serpents. Loosed with force by Ravana, that

37. Ravana.
38. Lakshmana.

spear penetrated deep into the body of Lakshmana who, with his heart pierced, fell on the earth. . . .

## Lakshmana's Miraculous Recovery

Seeing the courageous Lakshmana lying on the battlefield drenched in blood, struck down by the spear discharged by the mighty Ravana, Rama entered into a terrible duel with that cruel titan whom he overwhelmed with a hail of arrows. Then he addressed Sushena and said:—

"The valiant Lakshmana, struck down by the ruthless Ravana, is writhing like a serpent, filling me with anguish! When I behold that hero, dearer to me than life itself, how, in mine affliction, can I find the strength to fight? If my brother, who is endowed with auspicious marks, that proud warrior, returns to the five elements, of what use is life or prosperity to me? My prowess is ebbing away as it were and my bow seems to be falling from my grasp; mine arrows are blunted, mine eyes blinded with tears, my limbs are heavy as when one is overcome by sleep, my thoughts wander and I long to die! In this extreme misfortune in which I am plunged, weeping, my mind distracted on seeing my brother, who is emitting inarticulate cries, lying in the dust of the battlefield, brought low by the wicked Ravana, a prey to suffering and seriously wounded in his vital parts, even victory cannot bring me felicity, O Hero. If the moon is hidden from sight what delight can it give? Of what use is it to fight? What purpose is served by living? The combat has no longer any meaning since Lakshmana is lying dead in the forefront of the battle. As that illustrious warrior followed me when I retired to the forest so will I follow him now to the abode of death. . . .

. . . As Rama was speaking thus, overwhelmed with affliction, Sushena,[39] in order to comfort him, addressed these well-considered words to him:—

"O Tiger among Men, abandon this idea that causes thee pain, this thought that pierces thine heart as a javelin in the forefront of the battle. Nay, Lakshmana, the enhancer of prosperity, has not rejoined the five elements for his features have not changed nor is he pale, rather is his countenance serene and handsome! Observe how the palms of his hands resemble the petals of a lotus and his eyes are bright. Those who appear thus have not yielded up their lives, O Lord of all Men! Do not grieve O Hero, Conqueror of thy Foes, Lakshmana lives, and the proofs are the multiple beatings of his heart united with his sighs even though his body lies stretched on the earth."

Thus spoke the extremely sagacious Sushena to Raghava and thereafter he addressed that great monkey, Hanuman, who stood near and said:—

---

39. Sushena is a monkey general.

"O Friend, go quickly, repair to the Mountain Mahodaya! Formerly thou hast heard of it from Jambavan, O Warrior! On the southern peak grow curative herbs, the plants named Vishalyakarani, Savarnyakarani, Samjivakarani and also Samdhani of great virtue. Bring them back, O Warrior, in order to revive that hero, Lakshmana. . . ."

\* \* \*

. . . The mighty Hanuman hastened on his way and when he reached that high mountain, he shook the summit three times and having broken it off, balanced it, with its multitudinous trees in full flower of varying fragrance, in his two hands. Thereafter, like a dark cloud charged with rain, that monkey sprang into the air carrying the mountain peak and returned in great haste setting it down and, having rested awhile, he said to Sushena:—

"I am not conversant with the medicinal plants, O Bull among Monkeys, here is the whole summit which I have brought to thee!"

At these words of the son of Pavana, Sushena, the foremost of the monkeys, having uprooted the herb, took hold of it and there was great amazement among the monkeys witnessing Hanuman's feat which even the Gods themselves could only have accomplished with difficulty.

Then the foremost of monkeys, Sushena, having crushed that herb, held it to Lakshmana's nostrils and on inhaling it that prince, the scourge of his foes, who was riddled with arrows, instantly rose from the ground released from the darts and his sufferings. Meanwhile the monkeys beholding him standing erect cried out 'Excellent! Excellent!' and, full of joy, paid homage to him.

Then Rama, the slayer of his foes, said to Lakshmana:—

"Come, Come!" and, embracing him, pressed him close to his heart, his eyes wet with tears. Thereafter, having embraced him, Raghava said to Saumitri:—"O Hero, what good fortune to see thee return from the dead! Nay, assuredly neither life nor Sita nor victory had any attraction for me; in sooth what reason had I for living since thou hadst returned to the five elements?"

Then Lakshmana, pained, answered the magnanimous Raghava who had spoken thus and, in a voice trembling with emotion, said:—

"Bound by thy vow, O Thou who has truth for thy prowess, it does not become thee to utter such cowardly words! Nay, those who speak with sincerity do not render a promise void and the proof they give is the fulfilment of their vow! Thou shouldst not give way to despair on mine account, O Irreproachable Hero! Mayest thou redeem thy word by Ravana's death this day. Nay, when he comes within the range of thy shafts, thine adversary must not return alive, as a great elephant may not live when he falls under the sharp tooth of a roaring lion. I desire to see that wretch perish ere the orb of the day withdraws behind the Astachala Mountain, his task accomplished." . . .

## The Death of Ravana

At that moment, Matali[40] sought to recall Raghava's thoughts, saying:—
"How is it that thou dost act in regard to Ravana as if thou wert unaware of
thine own powers? In order to bring about his end, discharge Brahma's
Weapon upon him, O Lord! Foretold by the Gods, the hour of his doom is
at hand!"

Prompted by Matali, Rama took up a flaming shaft that was hissing
like a viper, formerly bestowed on him by the magnanimous and powerful
Sage Agastya. A gift of the Grandsire, that weapon never missed its target
and it had been created of yore by Brahma for Indra and bestowed on the
King of the Gods for the conquest of the Three Worlds. In its wings was
the wind, in its point the fire and the sun, in its haft space, and, in size, it
resembled the Mountains Meru and Mandara. With its marvellous point,
haft and gilding, it was composed of the essence of all the elements and
was as resplendent as the sun. Resembling the Fire of Time enveloped in
smoke, it was like unto an enormous snake and was capable of riving men,
elephants, horses, gateways, bars and even rocks. Dreadful to behold, covered with blood from countless victims, coated with their flesh and of the
temper of lightning, it emitted a thunderous sound. The disperser of
hosts, it created universal alarm, and hissing like a great serpent, it was exceedingly formidable. In war, it was the provider of nourishment to
herons, vultures, cranes and hordes of jackals; it was a form of death itself,
the sower of terror, the delight of the monkeys, the scourge of the titans
and its wings were composed of innumerable brightly coloured plumes,
like unto Garuda's.[41]

That marvellous and powerful shaft that was to destroy the titan was
the object of terror to the worlds, the remover of the fear of the supporters
of the Ikshvakus,[42] the depriver of the glory of the foe, and it filled Rama
with delight. Having charged it with the sacred formula, the valiant Rama
of indescribable prowess placed that excellent weapon on his bow according to the method prescribed by the Veda and, when he made ready, all beings were seized with terror and the earth shook. Enraged, he stretched his
bow with force and, deploying his whole strength, discharged that weapon,
the destroyer of the vital parts, on Ravana, and that irresistible shaft like
unto lightning, irrevocable as fate, loosed by the arm of one equal to the
God who bears the Thunderbolt, struck Ravana's breast. Loosed with exceeding force, that missile, the supreme destroyer, pierced the breast of the
wicked-hearted titan and, covered with blood, that fatal dart having extinguished his vital breaths, buried itself in the earth. Thereafter, having slain
Ravana, that shaft, stained with blood which dripped therefrom, its purpose accomplished, returned submissively to the quiver.

---

40. Charioteer to the god Indra. Here, he is Rama's charioteer.

41. Garuda is King of the Birds.

42. That is, Rama's followers.

And Dashagriva, who had been struck down suddenly, let his bow and arrow fall from his hand as he yielded up his breath. Bereft of life, that Indra of the Nairritas[43] of redoubtable valour and great renown, fell from his chariot as Vritra when struck by Indra's thunderbolt.

Seeing him stretched on the ground, the rangers of the night who had escaped the carnage, struck with terror, their sovereign being slain, fled in all directions and, from every side, the monkeys who, in the presence of the dead Dashagriva had assumed a victorious air, hurled themselves upon them, armed with trees. Harassed by the monkey divisions, the titans, terror-stricken, took refuge in Lanka and, having lost their lord, in despair, gave way to tears.

In the ranks of the monkeys, however, there arose cries of joy and shouts of triumph proclaiming Raghava's victory and Ravana's defeat, and the skies re-echoed to the music of the drums beaten by the Gods. A rain of flowers fell from heaven on to the earth, covering Raghava's chariot with a ravishing and marvellous shower of blossom. The cry of 'Well done! Well done!' came from the firmament and the celestial voices of the magnanimous Gods were raised in Rama's praise. On the death of that source of terror to all the worlds a great joy filled the Celestial Host as also the Charanas.[44]

The blessed Raghava, by slaying that Bull among the Titans, fulfilled the ambitions of Sugriva, Angada and Bibishana; peace reigned over all; the cardinal points were stilled; the air became pure, the earth ceased to tremble, the wind blew gently and the star of the day regained its full glory.

At that instant, Sugriva, Bibishana and Angada, the foremost of his friends, and Lakshmana also, approached that happy conqueror and joyfully offered him due homage. Rama, the delight of the House of Raghu, surrounded by his adherents on the battlefield, having slain his adversary by his extraordinary power, resembled Mahendra amidst the Celestial Host.

# ▪ The Bhagavad-Gita (c. First Century A.D.) *Sanskrit* (epic poem)

### TRANSLATED BY TONY BARNSTONE[1]

The Sanskrit sacred poem Bhagavad-Gita is an episode from Vyasa's epic poem, the Mahabharata. It has come to be the bible of Hinduism.

---

43. Nairritas are offspring of Nairriti, a demon.
44. Charanas are the panegyrists of the Gods.

---

1. After translations and annotations by Miller, Zaehner, Radhakrishnan, van Buitenen, Mascaró, Easwaran, and by Shri Purohit Swami.

Devout Hindus recite lines from it daily, and its statement of a uniform philosophy incorporates much of the wisdom of the Upanishads and of Vedantic philosophy. It is a dialogue between the great hero Arjuna and his divine charioteer, Krishna, that takes place on the battlefield on the plain of Kurukshetra where the decisive battle between the Pandavas and the Kauravas will be fought. Arjuna, leader of the Pandavas, decides (like Achilles in a different context) not to fight, for he can't reconcile his duty to fight with his duty to the friends and kinsmen on the opposite side. The bulk of the poem consists of Krishna's response to Arjuna, to some extent a justification for war (since death is controlled by destiny and the immortal soul doesn't die), but even more it is a systematic philosophical presentation of the Hindu system, emphasizing devotion to work and to the gods, pursuit of knowledge, and the shedding of selfish desires. The sustained beauty of its poetic vision is matchless: the body is merely "shabby clothes" which we discard on death for new ones; the controlled and desireless hero "withdraws his senses from sensuous pleasures" like "a tortoise retracting its limbs"; life is a fig tree with "roots in the sky and branches below" and "its leaves are Vedic hymns"; Arjuna is told to cut down this tree "with a sharp ax of detachment." In addition to its profound importance as a spiritual text, the Bhagavad-Gita is an enduring masterpiece of world literature.

**FURTHER READING:** Deutsch, Eliot, tr. *The Bhagavad Gita*, 1968. Edgerton, Franklin, tr. *The Bhagavad Gita*, 1944, 1964. Hill, W. Douglas P., tr. *The Bhagavadgita*, 1953. Miller, Barbara Stoler, tr. *The Bhagavad-Gita: Krishna's Counsel in Time of War*, 1986. Swami Prabhavananda and Christopher Isherwood, trs. *The Song of God: Bhagavad-gita*, intr. Aldous Huxley, 1947.

## from One: Arjuna's Sorrow

*Sanjaya*
Arjuna of the monkey war-banner scanned
    the battle ranks of Dhritarashtra's sons
    and raised his bow
    just as the clash of arms was to begin.

He addressed his charioteer, Krishna:
    "Drive between the two armies,
    invincible Lord,
    and halt there

so I may see these men
    drawn up eager with bloodlust
    whom I must fight
    in this enterprise, war.

I see them arrayed
>and spoiling for battle,
>happy to serve the corrupt son
>of Dhritarashtra's goals."

On hearing Arjuna's words,
>Krishna drove their brilliant chariot
>between the two armies
>and halted there,

*5*

facing Bhishma and Drona
>and all the world's kings
>and said "Arjuna, see the men
>of Kuru gathered here."

And Arjuna saw in each army
>fathers and grandfathers, teachers,
>uncles and brothers, son
>and grandsons, companions

and inlaws, and seeing
>all his kinsmen
>facing each other
>in battle lines

a deep pity filled his spirit
>and he exclaimed in sorrow
>"O Krishna, when I see my people
>so murderously keen

the spirit leaves my limbs and they sink,
>my mouth is seared dry,
>a trembling runs through me,
>and my hairs stand up in horror,

*10*

my magic bow Gandiva slips from my hands,
>my skin is aflame,
>I can't stand still
>and my mind whirls without center.

I see evil omens, Krishna.
>No good can come
>from slaughtering my own family
>in battle.

Victory means nothing to me,
>nor kingship nor pleasure.
>What good is it to be king,
>to have delight or even to live?

We sought the crowns, joys,
    and delights only for the sake
    of the ones who stand here,
    poised to abandon life and property—

these teachers, fathers and sons,
    grandfathers and uncles,
    inlaws, grandsons
    and other kinsmen.

I don't care if they kill me,
    I wouldn't kill them
    for kingship of all the three worlds,
    let alone for a paltry kingdom on earth!

How can we find it sweet to murder
    our cousins the sons of Dhritarashtra?
    Evil will come to us if we kill them.
    though they are assassins.

It is ignoble to kill kinsmen,
    and all joy will desert us
    if we slaughter
    Dhritarashtra's sons.

Greed possesses them and
    blinds them to the sin
    of fratricide and of betraying
    their friends,

but we are not blind.
    We see that destroying family is wrong,
    and shall we not have the wisdom
    to refrain from this awful act?

When the family is in shambles,
    duty and ancient rituals are broken,
    and when these are lost,
    chaos desecrates our spirits.

When base chaos rules,
    women are corrupted,
    and when the women are corrupt,
    the castes mix and society fails.

In anarchy the family and those who have destroyed it
    are sucked down into hell,
    for their ancestors' spirits suffer
    when the offerings of rice and water cease.

\*   \*   \*

It's better if Dhritarashtra's sons, weapons in hand,
    find me unarmed,
      offering no resistance,
      and kill me in the battle."

So spoke Arjuna on the battlefield,                 *25*
    and sagging into his chariot
      he let bow and arrows slip from his hands,
      his spirit shipwrecked with grief.

# *from* Two: Philosophy and the Practice of Yoga

### Sanjaya

This is the counsel that Krishna
    gave to Arjuna, who was drowning
      in despair and grief,
      his eyes awash with tears.

### Krishna

Why is your spirit slack in this time of crisis?
    Cowardice doesn't suit an Aryan noble.
      It is shameful on earth
      and will bar you from heaven.

Don't let this impotence triumph,
    it doesn't become you.
      Strike this vile weakness from your heart
      and arise, conqueror!

### Arjuna

Krishna, how can I slay
    Bhishma and Drona
      with my arrows
      when they deserve my allegiance?

Better to live as a beggar eating scraps            *5*
    than to eat royal meals spiced with the blood
      of my sacred teachers,
      ambitious though they be.

How shall we know if our victory
    or theirs is better?
      There are the sons of Dhritarashtra;
      how can I live if I kill them?

A trembling pity assails my soul.
    My mind spins from duty to duty.

> Tell me, what is right?
> I am your student; show me the path,

for no earthly kingdom,
> not even domination over all the Gods,
> could banish this grief
> that chars my soul.

*Sanjaya*

Then Arjuna, the great warrior,
> said to Krishna,
> "I will not fight,"
> and fell silent.

Krishna smiled at the warror's affliction,
> and there
> between the two armies
> the God spoke these words:

*Krishna*

You speak wisely, yet you grieve for men
> who don't need your sorrow,
> for wise men mourn neither
> the living nor the dead.

Never have we not existed—
> you and I and these kings—
> and the time will never come
> when we will be snuffed out.

As our spirit passes from childhood
> through youth, through old age,
> so it travels into another body at death;
> the sages know this to be true.

The senses touch matter and thus
> we feel heat, cold, pleasure and pain,
> evanescent things that come, then go.
> Rise above them, Arjuna.

When one is unmoved by these,
> when agony and ecstasy
> are the same,
> one's spirit is fit for immortality.

What isn't can't come to be
> and what is can never cease.
> Men who see reality
> perceive the line between these two.

All the universe is spun
> from one imperishable presence.
> Nothing can destroy
> this everlasting essence.

Our bodies perish, but the spirit
> which inhabits them
> is eternal and unfathomable,
> so fight the battle, Arjuna!

He who thinks the self slays
> and he who thinks the self is slain
> are both ignorant;
> it doesn't kill and is not killed.

The self is not born and does not die.
> Being cannot cease to be; it never was not.
> Unborn, undying, unchanging, primeval,
> it isn't killed with the body.

*20*

Once a man sees the self to be uncreated, eternal,
> indestructible, and immutable,
> how could he kill
> or cause anyone to kill?

As a man discards shabby clothes
> for new ones
> the embodied self casts off
> tattered bodies for new ones.

Weapons don't slice it,
> fire doesn't sear it,
> waters don't drench it,
> wind cannot wither it.

The self is impenetrable, incombustible,
> it can't be wet or dried.
> Eternal, pervading all, it is
> fixed, immovable, primordial.

It is named the unmanifest,
> the unthinkable, the unchanging.
> If you know this truth,
> you have no cause to grieve.

*25*

*   *   *

*Arjuna*

O Krishna, what are the signs of a man
> with firm concentration and pure

insight? What would he say?
How would he sit? How does he act?

*Krishna*

When his mind is free of all desires
      and he is complete in himself,
      then a man's enlightenment
      is firm.

If sorrow leaves him untouched
      and the lust for pleasure has died,
      if passion, fear and rage all cease,
      he is called a sage of firm insight.

When he is bound to nothing,
      accepting fortune and misfortune
      without joy or despair,
      his inner sight is strong.

When he withdraws his senses
      from sensuous pleasures
      like a tortoise retracting its limbs,
      his inner sight is firm.

Objects of the senses wither
      when a man ceases to devour them.
      He may still relish their flavor,
      but with the highest vision the savor fades.

But the mind of the man who seeks
      to control his senses
      may be carried off by their whirlwind,
      Arjuna.

He should sit down, reining in the senses,
      and concentrate on me.
      One whose senses are reined in
      has firm inner sight.

Even thinking of sensuous objects
      makes your ties to them grow;
      from this attachment springs passionate desire;
      and from this passion comes rage.

From rage sprouts confusion,
      and confusion makes memory fail;
      splintered memory fractures the soul,
      and when the soul fractures, you perish.

But a man of inner power
      who passes through sensuous objects

with his senses reined in and free of lust and anger
will have a quiet spirit.

Serene, all sorrows flee him,
for when his mind
floats calmly
it discerns the truth.

Without discipline, the soul's growth
is stunted; without growth,
peace abandons him,
and without peace, joy is lost.

If the mind lusts after
the wandering senses,
insight is driven off
like a ship thrown about in a typhoon.

And so, strong-armed warrior,                               *40*
he who retracts his senses
completely
is firm in his vision.

The disciplined master is awake
when other creatures think it's night;
when other beings awake
the visionary master sees their night.

As the profound deeps of the sea
are unmoved by the waters pouring in,
the calm man is unchanged by rushing desires.
He is at peace, though others desire desires.

When desires drop away
and he acts free from their pull,
without *me* or *mine,*
he will find peace.

This is the ultimate state, of infinite soul, called Brahman.
Once there, delusion is dead,
even when you fly from this body
and enter Nirvana, which is also Brahman.

## from *Eleven: The Cosmic Vision*

*Arjuna*

You have favored me with revelation
of the self's ultimate mystery

and your words
have banished my delusion.

You have told me of the birth
and death of all creatures,
and your own eternal greatness,
Lord whose eyes are lotus petals,

and as you describe it,
so it must be. Yet, I long
to see your divine form,
Krishna, Greatest among Men.

O Krishna, Master of Yoga,
if you think my eyes can stand it,
reveal your endless
self to me.

*Krishna*

Arjuna, see my forms in hundreds
and thousands, various,
divine, in countless shapes
and colors.

See the solar gods, Arjuna, and the storm gods, the gods of day,
wind, water, and fire, of dawn, sun, pole-star and moon,
and see the Horsemen, twin gods of healing,
marvels never before witnessed.

See all the universe,
all that moves and all that's still
and whatever else you wish to see,
unified in my body.

But eyes of flesh can't
bear this vision;
I give you supernatural eyes
to see my divine Yogic power.

*Sanjaya*

Saying this, Krishna
the great master of Yoga discipline,
revealed to Arjuna
his divine and ultimate form,

marvelous and manifold,
with countless eyes and mouths,
celestial ornaments
and divine weapons upraised.

The infinite Lord, whose faces are everywhere,
    brilliant, boundless, containing all wonders,
    showed himself in celestial robes,
    garlanded and sweet with divine perfumes.

If a thousand suns
    were to blaze from the sky at once
    it might begin to approach
    the brilliance of that great spirit.

Arjuna saw the whole universe
    in its infinite aspects
    combined in the body
    of the God of gods.

Amazed and with his hair standing on end,
    Arjuna bowed his head before the Lord,
    joined his hands in worship,
    and spoke:

*Arjuna*

I see all the gods in you, O Lord,                      *15*
    and all creatures; I see
    the Creator, Brahma, on his lotus throne,
    the ancient seers and heavenly serpents.

I see your infinite form everywhere,
    arms, bellies, mouths, and eyes,
    with no end, middle, or origin,
    universal Lord, manifest in all!

From your crown, mace and discus
    a mass of light permeates all things,
    and you are hard to gaze on,
    like white-hot fire and sun.

You are undying, the final revelation,
    eternal spirit, guardian of dharma's sacred law,
    the ultimate basis of all things.
    I think you must be the primal person.

I see no origin, middle or end,
    just infinite power and countless arms;
    your eyes are sun and moon
    and your fiery mouths char the universe.

Great Spirit, you fill all directions                    *20*
    and all space between heaven and earth;
    and three worlds shudder
    at your fantastic and dreadful form.

Swarms of gods enter you,
    some, in terror, praise you with folded hands,
    and thongs of great seers and perfected saints
    hail and adore you with sonorous hymns.

The storm gods, solar gods, the gods of day, wind, water, and fire,
    of dawn, sun, pole-star and moon, the celestial seers
    and heavenly musicians, the twin Horsemen, and the hosts of
    demigods, demons, and perfected saints all gaze on you in awe.

Worlds shudder at your great form,
    with its many eyes, mouths, arms, thighs,
    bellies and feet, and its many terrible tusks,
    and so do I.

Vishnu, I see you touch the sky, flaming
    with many colors, your maws gaping wide
    and bulging eyes ablaze, and my spirit quakes,
    I'm unmoored and can find no peace.

Seeing jagged fangs bristling in your maws
    like time's devouring flames,
    I am lost and without sanctuary.
    Have mercy, Lord of gods, shelter of the universe!

All those sons of Dhritarashtra,
    the throngs of kings,
    and Bhishma, Drona,
    Karna and all our great warriors

are rushing into your terrible fanged mouths,
    and some are dangling
    from your tusks,
    their heads crushed to powder.

As swollen rivers flood headlong
    into the ocean,
    those heroic men of earth
    stream into your flaming mouths.

As moths wing rapturously into the fire,
    then burst aflame,
    these men rush
    into your mouths to die.

You lick up worlds, Vishnu,
    devouring them with flaming mouths;
    your dreadful rays fill the universe
    with a great inferno.

Tell me, why so cruel a form?
    Praise to you, Best of Gods, have mercy!

Let me know your primal self,
    for I can't understand your intentions.

*Krishna*

I am time grown old, destroyer of worlds,
    resolved to swallow the worlds;
    even if you do nothing
    all these battle-ranked warriors will die.

So arise and seek glory, Arjuna,
    conquer your enemies and win
    a rich kingdom! I doomed these men
    an age ago; you are merely the occasion.

Slay Drona, Bhishma, Jayadratha, Karna
    and the other great warriors
    whom I've already doomed, fight
    and don't waver—you will triumph in battle!

## from Fifteen: The Supreme Spirit

*Krishna*

They say there's a fig tree with roots in the sky
    and branches below;
    its leaves are Vedic hymns
    and whoever knows it knows the Vedas' wisdom.

Its branches spread above and below,
    nourished by the world's qualities,
    its twigs bud with sensual objects
    and the aerial roots cause actions in the human world.

Its form can't be known in this world,
    no end, beginning, or root source.
    Chop down this deep-rooted fig tree
    with the sharp axe of detachment,

then search for the state
    from which one doesn't return,
    saying "I seek refuge in the original Spirit,
    the First Cause of ancient creation."

Those untainted by pride, delusion, attachment
    or desire, focused on the inner self,
    and released from the poles of pleasure and pain,
    can transcend illusion and attain that changeless state.

5

Neither sun nor moon
        nor fire illuminates that state,
        my highest abode,
        from which no one returns.

A fragment of me incarnate
        in the living world is an eternal soul
        that draws in the senses and mind
        from their roots in nature.

When the Lord takes on a body
        and then escapes it,
        he brings these with him as wind
        carries scents from their sources.

Controlling the senses, ears, eyes, touch,
        taste, smell, and the mind
        as well, he enjoys
        sensual objects.

Whether he escapes or dwells within
        the body and he tastes the world's
        qualities, fools are blind to him,
        while wise eyes see him.

Sages who fight to master themselves
        see him when they look inside,
        but imperfect men lack the self-control
        and insight to see him.

Know that my light in the sun
        illuminates the universe
        and I am the light
        of the moon and fire.

I pierce the earth to nourish
        all creatures with my strength,
        and as the moon-plant Soma
        my liquid light gives life to healing herbs.

I am the fire of life
        that unites in all bodies
        with the breaths flowing in, flowing out,
        to digest the four kinds of food.

I live in every heart and from me
        come memory, wisdom, and their loss.
        I am the knower and what is known through the Vedas,
        and also their highest truth, the Vedanta.

There are two spirits in the universe—
        the perishable and the imperishable.

All creatures perish,
but the imperishable doesn't change.

But there is yet another spirit,
the Supreme Self,
the undying Lord who permeates
and sustains the three worlds.

As I transcend the transient
and even the imperishable,
I am known as the Supreme Self
in the sacred Vedas and in the world.

Whoever is undeluded and knows me
as the Supreme Self, knows all,
Arjuna, and adores me
with their whole spirit.

So, Arjuna, I have revealed to you                    20
the deepest mystery.
Those who understand it will awaken
and reach their destinies.

## ■ Poems of Love and War (from the classical anthologies) (c. 100 B.C.–A.D. 250) *Tamil* (poems)

### TRANSLATED BY A. K. RAMANUJAN

These poems come from anthologies of Tamil poetry that are considered classic collections of *Akam* and *Puram* poems. *Akam* means "interior" and as a poetic label it refers to poems of interiority, dealing with private life and loves. The other major type of Tamil poetry is *Puram*. These poems are poems of the "exterior": public poems, poems about war and the world at large. *Akam* poems are lyric poems in the sense that they are *overheard* poems spoken by a persona, often to another (implicit) persona. They are brief dramatic monologues in which the poet puts on masks not of real people but of dramatic types—of mismatched lovers, true lovers, unrequited lovers, and so on. The poets draw on the local animal and vegetable life to make fantastic similes—a man in love pounds on the door of his lover like a mad elephant while the women flutter inside "like a peacock in the net." The *puram* poems celebrate courage on the battlefield with the same simplicity of address and imagery, some of them, such as "Harvest of War," participating in a genre of eulogies in praise of the courage of kings.

FURTHER READING: Ramanujan, A. K. *Poems of Love and War: From the Eight Anthologies and the Ten Long Poems of Classical Tamil*, 1985; *The Interior Landscape: Love Poems from a Classical Tamil Anthology*, 1967.

## *Akam Poems*

### What She Said
Kaccipettu Nannakaiyar

My lover capable of terrible lies
at night lay close to me
in a dream
that lied like truth.

I woke up, still deceived,
and caressed the bed
thinking it my lover.

It's terrible. I grow lean
in loneliness,
like a water lily
gnawed by a beetle.

1

### What Her Girl-Friend Said to Him
Kannan

Sir,
      not that we did not hear the noise
      you made trying to open the bolted doors,
      a robust bull elephant
      stirring in the night
      of everyone's sleep;

we did. But as we fluttered inside
like a peacock in the net,
crest broken, tail feathers flying,

our good mother held us close
in her innocence
thinking to quell our fears.

5

### What She Said
Kalporu Cirunuraiyar

People say, "You will have to bear it."
      Don't they know what passion is like,
      or is it that they are so strong?

As for me, if I do not see my lover
      grief drowns my heart,

and like a streak of foam in high waters
dashed on the rocks

little by little I ebb
and become nothing.

## Puram Poems

### Harvest of War

Kappiyarrukkappiyanar: on Kalankaykkanni Narmuticceral[1]

Great king,

you shield your men from ruin,
so your victories, your greatness
are bywords.

Loose chariot wheels                                                      5
lie about the battleground
with the long white tusks
of bull-elephants.

Flocks of male eagles
eat carrion                                                              10
with their mates.

Headless bodies
dance about
before they fall
to the ground.                                                          15

Blood glows,
like the sky before nightfall.
in the red center
of the battlefield.

Demons dance there.                                                      20

And your kingdom
is an unfailing harvest
of victorious wars.

---

1. Colophons for *puram* or heroic poems mention both the poet and the patron who is the subject or addressee of the poem. *Patirruppattu* poems like this one are all about Cera kings ("Ceral").

## A King's Last Words, in Jail, before He Takes His Life

Ceraman Kanaikkal Irumporai

If a child of my clan should die,
if it is born dead,
a mere gob of flesh
not yet human,

they will put it to the sword,
to give the thing
a warrior's death.

> Will such kings
> bring a son into this world
> to be kept now
> like a dog at the end of a chain,

> who must beg,
> because of a fire in the belly,
> for a drop of water,

> and lap up a beggar's drink
> brought by jailers,
> friends who are not friends?

## A Woman and Her Dying Warrior

Vanparanar

I cannot cry out.
I'm afraid of tigers.
I cannot hold you,
your chest is too wide
for my lifting.

Death
has no codes
and has dealt you wrong,
may he
shiver as I do!

Hold my wrist
of bangles,
let's get to the shade
of that hill.
Just try and walk a little.

# ■ The Gatha Saptashati (c. A.D. 100–300) *Prakrit* (700 erotic poems compiled by King Hala)

## TRANSLATED BY DAVID RAY

The Gatha Saptashati is the most celebrated Prakrit poetry anthology, compiled by the Satavahana King Hala of Pratishthanapura in Deccan, who lived between A.D. 100 and 300. The anthology consists of seven hundred stanzas, though one version has one thousand stanzas. The verses seem to be by different poets but are not attributed. It is evidence of a large body of secular Prakrit literature, and, though not every poem is erotic, eroticism is the dominant strain in the anthology. The poems seem as fresh and touching today as if the seventeen-odd centuries that have passed since they were collected were a breath of wind. In a tradition noted for its erotic verse, they represent some of the finest examples.

**FURTHER READING:** Ray, David, tr. *Not Far from the River: Poems from the Gatha Saptasati,* 1990.

## *Nineteen Quatrains*

*[1]*

Why do these prudes fear Prakrit poetry,
our music, and the blunt facts of love?
They draw back from that nectar,
yet wince as if they taste love's ashes.

*[2]*

Mother was angry. Father fell to his knees,
kissing her feet. I climbed on his back.
She broke into laughter, dragged him away.
Years later, I figure it out.

*[3]*

A small incident, but I'll always recall it.
Mother was cooking. Father said something,
made her laugh. She touched her pale face,
smudging it black as the dark spot on the moon.

*[4]*

She showed me how to do
everything she wanted
but in the morning
dressed behind the bamboo screen.

*[5]*

You'd think it would slow him,
knowing his neighbor died
in amorous sport. Still, he exerts
himself, as the entire village can hear.

*[6]*

Only the lady who learns
how to make love to herself
knows how to deal with that anger
that leaves her half full, half empty.

*[7]*

I remember this pleasure —
he sat at my feet
without speaking
and my big toe toyed with his hair.

*[8]*

Now that I see these dancers
I recall how much I enjoyed
that shampoo
you gave me with your feet.

*[9]*

The gods have parceled him out,
his beauty caught in my eye,
his talk in my ears, heart in my
heart, his thing in my thing.

*[10]*

Love's absence is space through the fingers.
All trickles away. Best have the hands cupped,
sweet breast at the mouth,
not one drop spilled on the ground.

*[11]*

O moon-faced lady,
because of your big eyes
the night had twice as many hours.
And I used them all.

*[12]*

O girl at the open half-door,
whom do you seek
with hot eyes and brown nipples
that stare at the roadway?

*[13]*

She was always a quick thinker.
But this time she surpassed herself.
"He came all this way to see you," she said,
shoving her lover toward her husband.

*[14]*

He worked all day, his plow
deep in the mire.
That night his wife lay restless,
her eyes wide open, counting each raindrop.

*[15]*

He stood at her door,
hoping to do more than sell melons
but he had not the skill
of the one who brought coconuts.

*[16]*

When the lady's on top
her hair's a splended curtain, swaying.
Her earrings dangle, her necklace shakes.
And she's busy, a bee on a lotus-stalk.

*[17]*

When they stopped
she was embarrassed by her nakedness
but since she couldn't reach her clothes
she pulled him upon her once more.

*[18]*

Even an old cow
gives fresh milk
at an expert touch,
will moo with gratitude.

*[19]*

Our Prakrit poems end here, compiled
by King Hala. Who could refuse to be moved
by their charm, or wish sincerely
we had held our tongues, speaking of love?

## ▪ Tales from the Panchatantra (c. A.D. 200–400)
*Sanskrit* (fables)

TRANSLATED BY WILLIS BARNSTONE

The Panchatantra is the earliest Sanskrit collection of fables and is considered the grandfather of fable collections, a source for many others. In the sixth century it was translated into Pahlavi, in 570 into Syriac, and in the eighth century into Arabic, and it has continued to spread. Versions have been found in fifty languages and in more than two hundred versions, from Java to Iceland. It may have been composed by Vishnusharman, who may have lived between A.D. 200 and 400, but the original work has been lost and certainly the stories themselves are much older than their recorder. In the framing narrative, Vishnusharman is presented as a sage who purports to teach morality and the ways of the world to two dull princes who have trouble learning. Like *The Thousand and One Nights,* the Panchatantra links stories together and tells stories within stories within stories, eighty-seven in total. Its prose is interspersed with didactic poetry.

**FURTHER READING:** Edgerton, Franklin. *The Panchatantra Reconstructed.* American Oriental Series, vol. 3, 1924. Pawate, Chennabasappa Ishtalingappa. *The Panchatantra and Aesop's Fables: A Study in Genre,* 1986. Rice, Stanley. *Ancient Indian Fables and Stories, Being a Selection from the Panchatantra,* 1924; 1974. Ryder, Arthur W. *The Panchatantra,* 1925; reprint, 1956. Williams, Alfred. *Tales from the Panchatantra,* 1985.

## The Lion Makers

In a certain town were four Brahmans who lived as close friends. Three of them had journeyed to the farthest shores of scholarship, but they lacked common sense. The other found scholarship unpleasant. But he was practical.

One day they met to talk things over. "What good is all our learning," they said, "if we can't travel, win privileges from the kings or acquire money? So at least, let's travel."

They agreed, but when they had gone a short distance, the oldest one said, "One of us, the fourth, is dull, stupid, and has nothing but common sense. Now, no one can win the favor of kings by simple sense and without serious scholarship. So we will not share our earnings with him. Let him turn around and go home." The second Brahman said, "Listen, my intelligent friend, you have no learning. Go home, please." But the third said, "No, no. We can't behave like this. We have played together since we were children. Stay with us, noble friend. You'll have your share of the money we earn."

The three scholars assented and went on with their journey. In a forest they came upon the bones of a dead lion. One of them said, "Here is a chance to test the maturity of our scholarship. Some kind of creature is lying here. Let us bring it back to life by means of great knowledge that we have honorably earned."

Then the first one said, "I know how to put together a skeleton." The second provided skin, flesh, and blood. But just when the third wanted to breathe life into the beast, the sensible man warned against doing so. "Hold on!" he cried. "This is a lion. If you bring him back to life, he will kill all of us."

"You idiot!" said one of them. "I won't reduce our scholarship to inaction."

"In that case," the man of sense answered, "wait a minute while I climb a convenient tree."

When he got up into the tree, the others restored the lion to life, and it rose up and killed the three Brahman scholars. After the lion went off, the man of sense scrambled down from the tree and went home.

And so I say, *Scholarship is less valuable than common sense.*

But the wheel bearer, who heard the story, answered, "Not at all. You reason poorly. If stricken by fate, even creatures of very great sense perish, while those of small intelligence live happily—if fate protects them. Here is a poem:

> While a hundred wits stand on a head/And a thousand wits hang
>    limply dead,
> Your humble single wit, good friend,/Is paddling in the water to the
>    end.

## The Brahman's Dream of Castles in the Air

In a certain town there was a Brahman named Stingy, who begged some barley meal, ate part of it, and filled a jar with what was left over. At night he hung the vessel from a peg, placed his cot below it, and, staring at it intensely, fell into reverie.

"Here is a full jar of barley meal," he thought. "If we have a famine, I'll make a hundred rupees on it. With that money I'll buy a pair of she-goats. Every six months they will bear two more goats. After selling all the goats, I'll buy cows. When the cows calve, I'll sell the calves. After cows, buffaloes. After buffaloes, mares. From the mares I'll get many horses. The sale of them will bring me abundant gold. With the gold I will buy a mansion with an inner court. Then someone will come to my house and offer his lovely daughter as a dowry. She will bear me a son, and I will name him Moon Lord. When he is old enough to ride on my knee, I will take a book, sit on the stable roof and ponder. Just then, Moon Lord will see me, leave his mother's lap to ride on my knee, and he will go too close to the horses. Then I shall become furious and shout to my wife, 'Take the boy away!' But she will be busy with her housework and won't pay any attention to what I command. Then I will get up and kick her grievously."

Being thoroughly absorbed in his hypnotic dream, he let fly a powerful kick and smashed the jar. The barley meal smothered him, turning him white all over.

*And so I say:*

Do not indulge in silly hopes.

*You are absolutely right,* the gold finder said. *You see:*

The miserly and greedy do not heed/The consequenses of a deed.
Their disappointments follow soon./Think of the father of little Lord
Moon.

## ■ Kalidasa (c. Fourth to Fifth Centuries A.D.) *Sanskrit* (poem)

TRANSLATED BY TONY BARNSTONE

Sanskrit poet and playwright Kalidasa is considered to be the finest of
the Sanskrit poets, and his play *Shakuntala* is the masterpiece of Indian
drama. Nothing is known of his life, though legends abound, and there is
widespread disagreement about the dating of his work, though previous
scholarship indicating that he flourished as early as the second century B.C.
is now discounted. There is evidence to suggest that he was associated with
the Gupta king Chandra Gupta II, a North Indian monarch who ruled from
A.D. 380 to A.D. 415. He has been given the title Great Poet (*Mahakavi*) and
holds a position in Indian poetics comparable to that of Homer or Chaucer
in the West. He was the author of two epic poems, *The Dynasty of Raghu* and
*The Birth of Kumara,* and two shorter epics, *The Cloud Messenger* and *The Seasons;* in addition to *Shakuntala and the Ring of Recollection,* he wrote two other
dramas, *Urvashi Won by Valor* and *Malavika and Agnimitra.* Close to thirty
other pieces are attributed to him, probably spuriously.

Though Kalidasa is equally at home in martial and erotic poetry and
drama, it is really as the grandfather of love poets that he shines. The selection presented here from *The Seasons* is one of six sections, each of
which treats one of the six Indian seasons. Though some discount it as ju-
venalia, it is a remarkable piece, both in its passionate mood and in the
ways it blends eroticism with a depiction of nature, creating an interpenetration of vegetative myth and human sexuality akin to the Sumerian
*Courtship of Inanna and Dumuzi* or Chaucer's General Prologue to *The Can-
terbury Tales.*

**FURTHER READING:** Coulson, Michael, tr. *Three Sanskrit Plays,* 1981. Edgerton,
Franklin and Eleanor, trs. *The Cloud Messenger: Translated from the Sanskrit
Meghaduta,* 1964. Heifetz, Hank, tr. *The Origin of the Young God: Kalidasa's Ku-
marasambhava,* 1985. Lal, P., tr. *Great Sanskrit Plays in Modern Translation,* 1964.
Miller, Barbara Stoler, ed. *Theater of Memory: The Plays of Kalidasa,* 1984. Nan-
dargikar, Gopal Raghunath, ed. and tr. *The Raghuvamsa of Kalidasa,* 1982. Roberts,
John T., tr. *The Seasons: Kalidasa's Ritusamhara,* 1990. Williams, Monier, ed. and tr.
*Sakuntala: A Sanskrit Drama, in Seven Acts,* 1976.

# from *The Seasons*

## Winter

Winter is coming
and the lotus shrivels as new snow coats
sweet sprouts rising erect in the cornfields,
ripe rice paddies and the myrtle's bursting flowers.

Now women are sensuous and fine as sandalwood,     *5*
their skin is snow, their aureoles unadorned,
while like jasmine moons
their heavy breasts hang with pearls.

Their arms are bare
of bracelets and arm-bands.     *10*
New silk hugs the orbs of their hips
and sheer cloth rides ripe goblets of milk.[1]

They take off jeweled gold-thread belts
from their womanly hips
and from feet beautiful as lotus flowers     *15*
they discard anklets that ring like singing swans.

Rubbing black sandal oils into their skin,
painting lotuses across their faces
and scenting their tangled hair with aloe
they make up for a feast of love.     *20*

Pale and weak with desire,
the young girls are stabbed through with joy
but sink teeth into their lower lips
to bite back laughs as they seek a lover.

Beautiful breasts want to burst     *25*
from their straight chests in distress
like dew plunging from a leaf of grass
or tears in the winter dawn.

Here where the town gives way to country
this herd of does in fields flush
with rice shoots fills the men with urges     *30*
while the beautiful herons sing

and our minds are swept away
by a lake's cold pure water
decked out with flowering blue lotus     *35*
and lust-crazed geese.

---

1. The term used for breasts here means literally milk-vessels.

Young tendrils droop and sway
in the persistent snow winds,
O sweet love vine you are pale
as a lovesick woman who's lost her man.

Knocked out by passion and their bodies' wine
the lovers sleep with their bodies twined,
their limbs smelling sweet as the aroma
of flower wine on their moist lips.

Lips red with bite marks, and breasts
scratched and raw from their lovers' nails,
are passionate evidence of the adult pleasures
the young girls tasted last night.

In a handheld mirror someone paints her lotus face
in the heat of the young morning but finds,
pulling down her lip, that her lover tore it
last night when he drunk her essence;

and here is another sex-tired body:
she didn't sleep at all and her eyes are red lotuses.
Now hair tangles around her drooping shoulders
and she floats through soft sleep on warm sun waves.

Other young girls breathe in the nice aroma
as they tear faded wreaths from their dense black hair.
Their wand-like bodies bend over swollen breasts
as they pile their locks into new creations.

As she touches up her lip this girl reads
last night's frenzy in each mark on her body;
her curved eyes half-lidded, hair a dark river,
she slips her nail-torn form into a shirt.

These girls made love for so long
their slack bodies are slick with sweat,
pubic hair standing on end like their nipples
as they oil their glorious bodies.

It's winter but the women thrill, heart-rapt,
as ripe rice bursts into the village
and the herons cry that the frost has flown;
may you be so happy when your winter comes.

## ■ Vijjika (Vidya) (c. A.D. 659) *Sanskrit* (poem)

The poems of Vijjika (also known as Vidya) appear in Vidyakara's famous anthology *The Treasury of Well-turned Verse*. She has been identified as a queen (Vijaya-bhattarika), the wife of Chandraditya, who was the eldest son of Pulakesin II and the brother of Vikramaditya I. She may also have written a Sanskrit drama that is considered of inferior quality.

# Friends

Friends, you are lucky you can talk
about what you did as lovers:
the tricks, laughter, the words,
the ecstasy.
After my darling put his hand on the knot                    5
of my dress,
I swear I remember nothing.

TRANSLATED BY WILLIS BARNSTONE

# Ominous Clouds

Ominous clouds
gray & swollen with water
discharge their rain.
Wind dusted with *kadamba* blossoms
toss on the storm.                                           5
Peacocks call and make love in the hills.
What do I care?
But when the lightning
tosses her veils around like a rival woman
the rainstorm breaks                                         10
my spirit.

TRANSLATED BY ANDREW SCHELLING

# To Her Daughter

As children we crave
little boys
pubescent we hunger for youths
old we take elderly men.
It is a family custom.                                       5
But you like a penitent
pursue a whole
life with one husband.
Never, my daughter
has chastity                                                 10
          so stained our clan.

TRANSLATED BY ANDREW SCHELLING

# ■ Bhartrihari (Seventh Century?) *Sanskrit* (poems)

## TRANSLATED BY TONY BARNSTONE

The poems collected in the *Shatakatrayam* are attributed to someone named Bhartrihari, but it is unclear whether a single author by that name ever existed, or whether these poems are by several hands. Though the collection was probably gathered between the eleventh and twelfth centuries, there is an earlier reference by the Chinese pilgrim I-ching to a grammarian named Bhartrihari who died in A.D. 650. Are they the same man? It is impossible to know. Another tale about Bhartrihari, popular but almost certainly apocryphal, says that he was a king who, disgusted with the inconstancy of women, gave up his kingship and went to live in the forest. Certainly this misogyny is apparent in the poems attributed to him. Women are an "acrid poison," a "snare," a "poisonous creeper," a "yoke," and passion is an "epileptic fit." His disgust for the body, the "fleshy protuberances" of a woman's breasts, her face as a "vile receptacle of phlegm" echoes the *Visuddhi-Magga*'s account of beauty (see Buddhist Texts, "Beauty Is But Skin-Deep," in this collection). Yet this stern denunciation of women and the pleasures of the flesh wavers in other poems, and women are seen as "heaven" instead of the evil devices of the god of love Kamadeva. If these poems were indeed written by a single man, they are a record of a man who vacillates between love and hate for the world and for women, and who, like the Chinese poet Wang Wei, always longs to be the perfect ascetic yet falls back into the net of passion. His failure, if it was real, is what humanizes him to us. Barbara Stoler Miller writes: "Bhartrihari does not simply vacillate between worldly indulgence and asceticism; his confusion is more profound. He concurrently experiences delight in the fullness of the world, anxiety over its cruel transience, and the feeling that this tension is inescapable. His ironic sense that none of life's possibilities are what they seem to be gives pattern to his irreconcilable attractions and to [his poems]."[1] In Bhartrihari, as in Kalidasa's Ritusamhara (*The Seasons*), woman is associated with nature, which is also beautiful and dangerous and the source of life. His moralistic poems are of significantly less interest than his erotic ones, often seeming humorless and pedantic, but he sometimes achieves a vision of humanity caught in a world of delusion that rivals Rumi, Kabir, and Saigyo.

**FURTHER READING:** *Bhartrihari: Poems.* Translated by Barbara Stoler Miller. With the transliterated Sanskrit text of the Satakatrayam: Niti, Sringara, Vairagya, 1967. *The Hermit & The Lovethief: Sanskrit Poems of Bhartrihari and Bilhana.* Translated by Barbara Stoler Miller, 1978. *An Old Tree Living by the River: Poems of Bhartrihari.* Translated from Sanskrit by John Cort, 1983.

---

1. Miller, Barbara Stoler, tr. *Bhartrihari: Poems.* New York: Columbia University Press, 1967, p. xxiv.

## Who Can See a Sexy Woman

Who can see a sexy woman—
with wild shimmering eyes,
young and proud, ripe breasts
perched over her slim belly
and her trunk dimpling in beautiful folds                    5
as if wrapped around with vines
—and not lose his mind?

## Three Waves Roll across Her Waist

Three waves roll across her waist,
her breasts take flight like wild geese
and her blossoming face is a bright lotus,
but a woman is a moody river
where a monster dwells.                                       5
Think well before you take that fatal bath.

## My Love Is Nothing Like the Moon

My love is nothing like the moon,
her eyes are not two lotus blooms
and her shining flesh is not gold,
but listening to what poets say
even a sage will pray at the body's altar,                    5
this sack of meat and bones.

## The Cycles of Day and Night

The cycles of day and night
mark our decay
but caught up in our lives
we don't see them slip away.
Pain, death, old age                                          5
don't make us worry;
we drink lies till we're sloshing drunk
and the mad world reels through nothingness.

## The Moth Dives into Flame

The moth dives into flame,
ignorant of its fury,
and the dumb fish
eats both worm and hook,
but we who see                                                    5
the mayhem of passion
embrace its intricate net.
Who can understand?

## ■ Amaru (Seventh Century) *Sanskrit* (poems)

Sanskrit poet Amaru (also known as Amaruka) is the author of the
*Amaru-sataka,* a collection of one hundred verses named after him, all
dealing with love. Little is known of his life, but since he is quoted from a
number of times after A.D. 800, he must have flourished before then.
Daniel H. H. Ingalls suggests that the majority of the hundred poems ascribed to him are written by various authors of the seventh and eighth
centuries.

## Ingenue

Friends, I did as you said: stiffened, desperately lowered my willing
    eyes when his eyes called me,
Stared at his feet, shut my hungry ears on the sweets of his speech,
    threw up my hands to hide
The shiver and flush of my skin. But what could I do if this
    treacherous blouse,
With a mind of its own, suddenly gave at the seams?

TRANSLATED BY V. N. MISTRA, L. NATHAN, AND S. H. VATSYAYAN

## Finesse

When he came in, she rose. No chance to sit together.
She ducked out of his arms to order betel leaf.
As he opened his mouth to speak, she called the maid.
    A fine fury,
Slapping him every turn by too much courtesy.                        5

TRANSLATED BY V. N. MISTRA, L. NATHAN, AND S. H. VATSYAYAN

## *Somehow She Got*

Somehow she got
through the day
dwelling on night's hundred pleasures.
Her dear one's returned!
But now it's time enter the bedchamber                                    5
and relatives
won't stop their dull conversation.
Mad with desire the girl finally cries
*something bit me*
shakes her skirt wildly                                                   10
                and knocks over the lamp—

TRANSLATED BY ANDREW SCHELLING

# Regional Bhakti (Devotional) Literatures

## (c. Tenth to Sixteenth Centuries)

### ■ Basavanna (1106–1167 or 1168) *Kannada* (poems)

TRANSLATED BY A. K. RAMANUJAN

Basavanna was a Virashaiva saint who wrote *vachanas,* or free verse mystical poems addressed to the god Shiva and written in the Dravidian language *Kannada.* Virashaivism is a monotheistic form of Hinduism. Basavanna was probably born in Manigavalli. His parents died young, and he was raised first by a grandmother, then by foster parents from whom he may have received an education in the traditional classics. Disgusted with ritual and the caste system, at sixteen he devoted himself to the worship of Shiva and, like the Buddha, left family behind for a religious life. Basavanna moved to Kappadisangama, where three rivers flow together, and began to address Shiva in his poems as "The Lord of the Meeting Rivers." Later he moved to Kalyana, married his cousin, and became a friend and courtier of King Bijjala. Basavanna was soon the center of a Virashaiva revival that was so threatening to traditionalists in the area that Bijjala found himself pressured to find an excuse to persecute the rising religion. When an outcaste man married a Brahman woman in a Virashaiva wedding, Bijjala had them executed. In the resulting riots and rounds of persecution, Bijjala was stabbed to death, the community was scattered, and Basavanna, having failed to prevent the violence, returned to Kappadisangama, where he died not long after. His poems, like those of the other great Virashaiva saints, are considered not mere literature, but central psalms of the religion.

**FURTHER READING:** Ramanujan, A. K. *Speaking of Siva,* 1973.


## The Pot Is a God

The pot is a god. The winnowing
fan is a god. The stone in the
street is a god. The comb is a
god. The bowstring is also a
god. The bushel is a god and the
spouted cup is a god.

Gods, gods, there are so many
there's no place left
for a foot.

There is only
one god. He is our Lord
of the Meeting Rivers.

## ◼ Mahadevi (Mahadeviyakka) (Twelfth Century) *Kannada* (poems)

TRANSLATED BY A. K. RAMANUJAN

Mahadevi was born in the Indian village of Udutati and was initiated into the worship of the god Shiva when she was ten. In the form that Shiva took at Mahadevi's temple, he was referred to by the epithet Lord White as Jasmine, and in Mahadevi's terrifically sexy poems, this lord appears as her divine lover. However, a human lover, Kaushika, the king of the region, saw Mahadevi and fell in love with her, and it seems likely that she was forced to marry him, in spite of the fact that he was a nonbeliever. Still, in her poetry, her divine lover is her true husband, sometimes represented as an illicit lover who is her true soulmate, and she writes, "Take these husbands who die, / decay, and feed them / to your kitchen fires!" At some point Mahadevi seems to have left the king and become a wandering mendicant, throwing away the clothes that covered her true self and covering herself only with her long hair. She went to Kalyana, where Allama Prabhu and Basavanna ran a school of Virashaiva religion. There, after a trial by debate with Allama, she was accepted into their company. Mahadevi is said to have died into a union with Shiva at the Holy Mountain of Shrishaila.

**FURTHER READING:** Ramanujan, A. K. *Speaking of Siva*, 1973.


## Riding the Blue Sapphire Mountains

Riding the blue sapphire mountains
wearing moonstone for slippers
blowing long horns
O Siva
when shall I                                                                5
crush you on my pitcher breasts?
O lord white as jasmine
when do I join you
stripped of body's shame
and heart's modesty?                                                        10


## People

People,
male and female,
blush when a cloth covering their shame
comes loose.
        When the lord of lives                                              5
lives drowned without a face
in the world, how can you be modest?

When all the world is the eye of the lord,
onlooking everywhere, what can you
cover and conceal?                                                          10


## Monkey on Monkeyman's Stick

        Monkey on monkeyman's stick
        puppet at the end of a string

I've played as you've played
I've spoken as you've told me
I've been as you've let me be                                               5

> O engineer of the world
> lord white as jasmine
>
> I've run
> till you cried halt.

## I Love the Handsome One

> I love the Handsome One:
>     he has no death
>     decay nor form
>     no place or side
>     no end nor birthmarks.
>     I love him O mother. Listen.
>
> I love the Beautiful One
>     with no bond nor fear
>     no clan no land
>     no landmarks
>     for his beauty.
>
> So my lord, white as jasmine, is my husband.
>
> Take these husbands who die,
>     decay, and feed them
>     to your kitchen fires!

## ■ Jayadeva (Twelfth Century) *Sanskrit* (dramatic poetry)

TRANSLATED BY BARBARA STOLER MILLER

Jayadeva was born at Kindubilva in Bengal to a brahman family, according to legend, and was a court poet under King Lakshmanasena. Early on he gave up scholarship for the life of a wandering mendicant. His great work is the *Gitagovinda,* an epic poem blending songs and recited passages that tells of the erotic union of Radha and the god Krishna, of Krishna's infidelity with the cowherd women, of Radha's jealousy, and of Krishna's return to her. Jayadeva's wife Padmavati is said to have danced with Jayadeva in accompaniment to his songs in the *Gitagovinda.* The name Jayadeva means "God of Triumph," and he uses this phrase in the *Gitagovinda*'s songs to refer to Krishna. The *Gitagovinda* has become famous in the West as the Indian equivalent of the biblical *Song of Songs* and in India is a sacred text whose songs are canonized within the Vaishnava religion. The extant manuscripts of the *Gitagovinda* include the names of the *ragas,* or melodic formulas, that go with the various songs and, as translator Barbara Stoler Miller notes, "nightly performance of the songs in worship of Jagannatha at Puri has been continuous for more than seven hundred years."[1] Its long popularity is well-deserved. In its apotheosis of erotic drama, it remains among the world's best long poems.

**FURTHER READING:** Arnold, Edwin. *The Indian Song of Songs.* 6th ed., 1891. Keyt, George. *Gita Govinda,* 1947. Miller, Barbara Stoler, ed. and tr. *Love Song of the Dark Lord: Jayadeva's Gitagovinda,* 1977. Siegel, Lee. *Sacred and Profane Dimensions of Love in Indian Traditions as Exemplified in the Gitagovinda of Jayadeva,* 1978.

# The Gitagovinda

## *from* The First Part: Joyful Krishna

If remembering Hari[1] enriches your heart,
If his arts of seduction arouse you,
Listen to Jayadeva's speech
In these sweet soft lyrical songs.

\* \* \*

When he quickens all things                                          5
To create bliss in the world,
His soft black sinuous lotus limbs
Begin the festival of love
And beautiful cowherd girls wildly
Wind him in their bodies.                                           10
Friend, in spring young Hari plays
Like erotic mood incarnate.

Winds from sandalwood mountains
Blow now toward Himalayan peaks,
Longing to plunge in the snows                                      15
After weeks of writhing
In the hot bellies of ground snakes.
Melodious voices of cuckoos
Raise their joyful sound
When they spy the buds                                              20
On tips of smooth mango branches.

1. Miller, Barbara Stoler, ed. and tr. *Love Song of the Dark Lord: Jayadeva's Gitagovinda.* New York: Columbia University Press, 1977, pp. 6–7.

1. A name for Krishna.

## *from* The Second Part: Careless Krishna

While Hari roamed in the forest
Making love to all the women,
Rādhā's hold on him loosened,
And envy drove her away.
But anywhere she tried to retreat
In her thicket of wild vines,
Sounds of bees buzzing circles overhead
Depressed her—
She told her friend the secret.

＊　＊　＊

My heart values his vulgar ways,
Refuses to admit my rage,
Feels strangely elated,
And keeps denying his guilt.
When he steals away without me
To indulge his craving
For more young women,
My perverse heart
Only wants Krishna back.
What can I do?

## *from* The Third Part: Bewildered Krishna

Krishna, demon Kaṁsa's foe,[2]
Feeling Rādhā bind his heart with chains
Of memories buried in other wordly lives,
Abandoned the beautiful cowherd girls.

As he searched for Rādhikā[3] in vain,
Arrows of love pierced his weary mind
And Mādhava[4] repented as he suffered
In a thicket on the Jumna riverbank.

＊　＊　＊

Lotus stalks garland my heart,
Not a necklace of snakes!
Blue lily petals circle my neck,
Not a streak of poison!
Sandalwood powder, not ash,
Is smeared on my lovelorn body!

---

2. Kaṁsa was Krishna's uncle and a dangerous enemy.

3. Rādhā.

4. Krishna.

Love-god, don't attack, mistaking me for Śiva![5]
Why do you rush at me in rage?

Don't lift your mango-blossom arrow!
Don't aim your bow!

*  *  *

Her arched brow is his bow,                                                    *15*
Her darting glances are arrows,
Her earlobe is the bowstring—
Why are the weapons guarded
In Love's living goddess of triumph?
The world is already vanquished.                                              *20*

## *from* The Seventh Part: Cunning Krishna

She is richly arrayed in ornaments for the battle of love;
Tangles of flowers lie wilted in her loosened hair.
> Some young voluptuous beauty
> Revels with the enemy of Madhu.[6]

She is visibly excited by embracing Hari;
Her necklaces tremble on full, hard breasts.                                   *5*

Curling locks caress her moon face;
She is weary from ardently drinking his lips.

Quivering earrings graze her cheeks;
Her belt sounds with her hips' rolling motion.

She laughs bashfully when her lover looks at her;                             *10*
The taste of passion echoes from her murmuring.

Her body writhes with tingling flesh and trembling.
The ghost of Love expands inside with her sighing.

Drops of sweat wet the graceful body
Fallen limp on his chest in passionate battle.                                *15*

May Hari's delight in Jayadeva's song
Bring an end to this dark time.

*  *  *

Friends are hostile,
Cool wind is like fire,
Moon nectar is poison,                                                        *20*
Krishna torments me in my heart.

---

5. Kamadeva, the god of love (equivalent to Cupid in the West) was burned up by the god Shiva (Śiva) after piercing him with the arrow of love-madness and remorse.

6. This refrain is repeated after each stanza. "The enemy of Madhu" is an epithet for Krishna.

But even when he is cruel
I am forced to take him back.

### *from* The Ninth Part: Languishing Krishna

Then, when she felt wasted by love,
Broken by her passion's intensity,
Despondent, haunted by Hari's
Response to her quarreling,
Her friend spoke to her.

\* \* \*

When he is tender you are harsh,
When he is pliant you are rigid,
When he is passionate you are hateful,
When he looks expectant you turn away,
You leave when he is loving.
Your perverseness justly
Turns your sandalbalm to poison,
Cool moon rays to heat, ice to fire,
Joys of loveplay to torments of hell.

### *from* The Tenth Part: Four Quickening Arms

Fretful Rādhā, don't suspect me!
A rival has no place
When your voluptuous breasts and hips
Always occupy my heart.

\* \* \*

Your moist lips glow
Like crimson autumn blossoms;
The skin of your cheek
Is a honey-colored flower.
Fierce Rādhā, your eyes glower
Like gleaming dark lotuses;
Your nose is a sesame flower;
Your teeth are white jasmine.
Love's flower arms conquer worlds
By worshipping your face.

## ■ Lalla (c. 1320–1392) *Kashmiri* (poems)

TRANSLATED BY COLEMAN BARKS

Kashmiri poet and mystic Lalla is also known as Lal Didi, Mai Lal
Diddi, Lal Ded (all of which mean Grandmother Lal) and, in Sanskrit, as
Lalleshwari, or Lalla the great yogi. She moves between schools and doc-

trines to create a personal spiritual vision that draws on the Upanishads, Sufism, Vedanta, Shaivism, and other schools, and that, while idiosyncratic, teaches the lesson of nonduality, that *I* am *you* and *you* are *that*. She is famous for dancing naked while singing her songs: "Dance, Lalla," she writes, "with nothing on / but air," for "[w]hat clothes / could be so beautiful, or / more sacred" than "this glowing day"? Little is known of her life, since there are no records from her lifetime, only legends about her recorded in the eighteenth century. It is said that she left an unhappy marriage to become a student of the Hindu sage Sed Bayu. Translator Coleman Barks relates that

> It was then also that she began to ignore conventional standards of dress and to wander in a state of ecstatic clarity. One morning as children were making fun of her nakedness, a cloth merchant scolded their disrespect. Lalla asked him for two strands of cloth equal in weight. That day as she walked about, she wore a piece of cloth over each shoulder, and as she met with respect or scorn, she tied knots in one or the other. In the evening she came back to the merchant and asked him to weigh the cloth again. The scales swung in balance, of course, no matter how the cloth was knotted. Praise and blame have no substance of their own.[1]

**FURTHER READING:** Barks, Coleman, tr. *Lalla: Naked Song*, 1992. Grierson, Sir George, and Lionel D. Barnett. *Lalla-Vakyani, the Wise Saying of Lal Ded, A Mystic Poetess of Ancient Kashmir*, 1920. Kaul, Jayalal. *Lal Ded*, 1973. Kotru, Nil Kanth. *Lal Ded, Her Life and Sayings*, 1989. Temple, Richard Carnac. *The Word of Lalla the Prophetess*, 1924. Lalleshwari. Poems rendered by Muktananda and Gurumayi, 1981.

## Dance, Lalla, with Nothing On

Dance, Lalla, with nothing on
but air. Sing, Lalla,
wearing the sky.

Look at this glowing day! What clothes
could be so beautiful, or                                                        5
more sacred?

## Whatever Your Name, Shiva, Vishnu

Whatever your name, Shiva, Vishnu,
the genius who inspired Scherazade,

---

1. Barks, Coleman, tr. *Lalla: Naked Song*. Athens, GA: Maypop Books, 1992, p. 9.

savior of the Jains, the pure Buddha,
lotus-born God, I am sick. The world
is my disease, and You are the cure,                                    5
You, you, you, you, you, you, you.

## The Soul, Like the Moon

The soul, like the moon,
is new, and always new again.

And I have seen the ocean
continuously creating.

Since I scoured my mind
and my body, I too, Lalla,
am new, each moment new.

My teacher told me one thing,
*Live in the soul.*

When that was so,                                                        1
I began to go naked,
and dance.

## ■ Chandidas (Late Fourteenth to Mid-Fifteenth Centuries) *Bengali* (poems)

The great Bengali poet Chandidas's life remains shrouded in mystery,
yet he was so famous that many other poets adopted his name. Of the
thousands of poems attributed to Chandidas, around two hundred are
thought to be authentic. His love poems have been extremely important
in the development of Bengali literature and to such seminal figures as
Rabindranath Tagore. Versions of his poems can even be heard sung as
folk songs by Bengali peasants. The historical trace that he left has been
obscured by imitators and exists, in any case, in such "soft" historical
forms as legend and song; however, it does seem that he had a career as a
village priest, that he was connected to the Sahaja movement, and that he
had a relationship with a village woman called Rami (or Ramini). He may
have lived in the West Bengali village Nannur, or in the village of Chhatna,
and it seems that he defied tradition by openly living with his lover, Rami,
though he was a high-caste priest and she a lowly washerwoman. Similarly,
he wrote not in the literary language, Sanskrit, but in the vulgate, Bengali,
which made his poetry comprehensible to the lowest classes.

The great lovers Radha and Krishna are considered the female and
male reincarnations of Vishnu; Vaishnava philosophy focuses on Vishnu,

and the words derive from the same root. One of the paths to worshiping Vishnu is that of *bhakti,* in which the devotee marshals his or her emotions to find union with the god. This path has proven to be a particularly fertile source of great love poetry. Chandidas's poetry clearly fits into the bhakti tradition and is associated as well with the Sahaja movement, a Hindu method of yoga in which eroticism and lovemaking are embraced, and each man is considered Krishna, each woman Radha.

**FURTHER READING:** Bhattacharya, Deben. *Love Songs of Chandidas: The Rebel Poet-Priest of Bengal,* 1967.

## I Pick Wild Flowers

I pick wild flowers
and make a love necklace
but their coldness and smell
fade
as my neck catches fire.                                   5

Gardener, why did you poison
the necklace?
You blackened my heart.
Now my whole body
chars.                                                     10

I hear nothing.
My eyes are dead
and the flowers burn.

My heart is coal.
My ribs collapse,                                          15
descending.
My body is gone.

### TRANSLATED BY TONY BARNSTONE AND WILLIS BARNSTONE

## Why Tell Me What to Do?

Why tell me what to do?
Dreaming or awake I see only his black skin.
I don't even fix my tangled hair,
just pour it in my lap, and wish it were Krishna.
I call to him, sweet black Krishna,                        5
and cry.

I leave this black hair loosely knotted
so when my dark love comes to mind
I can let it down and brood.
What can I do?
His black skin is always with me.

TRANSLATED BY TONY BARNSTONE

## ■ Kabir (1398–1448) *Hindi* (poems)

When Rabindranath Tagore published his translation from the medieval Hindi of the great poet Kabir, he made available to the West the fascinating poems that continue to inspire a Kabir sect, and his translations of this world-class poet remain among the very best. Kabir was born in Varanasi to a family of weavers and raised Muslim, though he seems to have studied with a Hindu guru before turning into an influential teacher himself. He did not, however, take the religious path of withdrawing from the world; he was married, had children, and earned his living as a weaver. Kabir was popularly believed to have been discipled to the famous guru Ramananda. Linda Hess recounts the legend about "how he tricked the orthodox Hindu into accepting him, a Muslim, as a student. Supposedly he stretched himself across the stairs leading to the river where Ramananda came for his bath in the predawn darkness. Tripping over Kabir's body and fearing sudden danger to his life, Ramananda cried out—as Kabir knew he would—his own mantra: 'Ram! Ram!' Kabir then claimed that the mantra had been transmitted and he must be accepted as a disciple."[1] Yet Kabir is neither wholly Hindu nor wholly Muslim; his peculiar brand of mysticism, while retaining the devotionalism of Vaishnava, was also influenced by Sufi mysticism. He continues to be a figure embraced by the Sikhs, the Muslims, and the Hindus.

Kabir is thought to have been illiterate, and his songs were collected by disciples. The songs associated with him continue to be sung in a lasting oral tradition. Iconoclastic, idiosyncratic, he is a riddling poet, and an aggressive one in his attempt to shock his listeners out of orthodox, calcinated beliefs, and to speak that "secret word" that will awaken the reader to the God inside.

**FURTHER READING:** Kabir. *The Bijak of Kabir.* Translated by Linda Hess and Shukdev Singh; essays and notes by Linda Hess, 1983; *Kabir.* Introduction and translation from the Hindi and notes by Ch. Vaudeville, 1974; *The Kabir Book: Forty-four of the Ecstatic Poems of Kabir.* Versions by Robert Bly, 1977; *One Hundred Poems of Kabir.* Translated by Rabindranath Tagore assisted by Evelyn Underhill, 1961; *Songs of Kabir from the Adi Granth.* Translation and introduction by Nirmal Dass, 1991.

---

1. Kabir. *The Bijak of Kabir.* Translated by Linda Hess and Shukdev Singh; essays and notes by Linda Hess. San Francisco: North Point Press, 1983, p. 3.

## Who Needs Words When You're Drunk on Love?

Who needs words when you're drunk on love?
I've got a diamond wrapped in my cloak. I won't open it again.
When the pan was near empty the scales tipped; now full why weigh it
    at all?
The swan soared to a high lake in the mountains. Why should it
    scrabble in puddles and ditches?
He lives inside. Why bother opening your eyes?          5
Kabir says, friend, my eyes are ravished by the One inside.

TRANSLATED BY TONY BARNSTONE

## Shadows Fall Everywhere

Shadows fall everywhere, piling up deep, and body and mind
    disappear in dark love.
Open the window to the west and you topple into the sky of love.
Eat honey that seeps from lotus petals of your heart
and a magnificent ocean's swells will enter your body.
Can you hear the bells and conch shells?          5
Kabir says, friend, my body is his vessel.

TRANSLATED BY TONY BARNSTONE AND WILLIS BARNSTONE

## How Can I Ever Speak That Secret Word?

How can I ever speak that secret word?
How can I say He is this and not that?
If I say He is inside I shame the world
but to say He's outside is a lie.
He makes the worlds inside and outside one.          5
His feet rest both on thought and dream
and he is neither manifest nor hidden, mystery nor revelation.
No words can say just what He is.

TRANSLATED BY TONY BARNSTONE

## I've Played with Other Girls but My Heart Shakes

I've played with other girls but my heart shakes
as I mount the high stairs to my Master's palace.

He's to be my Lover and I can't be shy.
My heart must leap toward him. I will lower my veil and touch him
    with all my body,
my eyes like ceremonial lamps of love.
Kabir says, friend, to understand, love. If you don't worship the Lover
    why dress up and line your eyes with kohl?

TRANSLATED BY TONY BARNSTONE AND WILLIS BARNSTONE

## Lamplight Flames from Every House but You Don't See It

Lamplight flames from every house but you don't see it, blind one.
One day the lids will peel back from your eyes like deadly chains
    dropping off
and there will be nothing to say, hear or do, since He is alive, and He
    is also dead, and He'll never die again.

Since He lives in solitude the Yogis say his house is miles away;
He is next to you but you climb a palm tree seeking Him.
The Brahman priest goes house to house converting people;
he sets up a stone and worships it, when the spring of life is right
    there!
Kabir says: I can't tell you how sweet He is, better than Yoga and
    telling beads and all the pleasures of virtue and sin.

TRANSLATED BY TONY BARNSTONE

## The Moon Shines inside My Body but My Eyes

The moon shines inside my body but my eyes
    are blind to it.
The moon is inside me and so is the sun.
The drum of eternity resounds within me, unstruck, but my ears don't
    hear it.

So long as you seek for *I* and *mine* your work will come to nothing;
to do heavenly work, murder your love of *I* and *mine*.
The real reason for work is to know;
when knowledge comes, give up your work.

The flower blossoms for the fruit; as the fruit swells the flower wilts.
The musk is in the deer, but the deer hunts for it outside, searching
    through the grass.

TRANSLATED BY TONY BARNSTONE

## How Could Our Love Die?

How could our love die?
Like a lotus on the water I live for you.
I think only of you, like a Chakor bird astonished by the moon all
    night long.
This love ignited at the birth of time. It won't die when time dies.
Kabir says, my heart touching you is a river pouring into the sea.     *5*

TRANSLATED BY TONY BARNSTONE

## Between the Conscious and the Unconscious

Between the conscious and the unconscious, the mind has put up a
    swing:
all earth creatures, even the supernovas, sway between these two trees,
and it never winds down.

Angels, animals, humans, insects by the million, also the wheeling sun
    and moon;
ages go by, and it goes on.     *5*

Everything is swinging: heaven, earth, water, fire,
and the secret one slowly growing a body.
Kabir saw that for fifteen seconds, and it made him a servant for life.

TRANSLATED BY ROBERT BLY

## I Have Been Thinking of the Difference

I have been thinking of the difference
between water
and the waves on it. Rising,
water's still water, falling back,
it is water, will you give me a hint     *5*
how to tell them apart?

Because someone has made up the word
"wave," do I have to distinguish it
from water?

There is a Secret One inside us;     *10*
the planets in all the galaxies
pass through his hands like beads.

That is a string of beads one should look at with luminous eyes.

TRANSLATED BY ROBERT BLY

## *Are You Looking for Me?*

Are you looking for me? I am in the next seat. My shoulder is against
   yours.
You will not find me in stupas, not in Indian shrine rooms, nor in
   synagogues, nor in cathedrals:
not in masses, nor kirtans, not in legs winding around your own neck,
   nor in eating nothing but vegetables.
When you really look for me, you will see me instantly—
you will find me in the tiniest house of time.
Kabir says: Student, tell me, what is God?
He is the breath inside the breath.

TRANSLATED BY ROBERT BLY

■ **Mirabai (1498–1573)** *Hindi* **(poems)**

TRANSLATED BY WILLIS BARNSTONE AND USHA NILSSON

The songs of Mirabai belong to a large oral tradition of song, a folk
tradition of more than five thousand songs that can be heard from the lips
of professional singers and common folk alike across India, though as few
as three or four hundred are considered authentic. A similar fog surrounds the details of Mirabai's life, which is obscured in legend. Some
doubt that a historical Mirabai existed and say that she was, as some say of
the Chinese sage Laozi, not a single person but a tradition. Even if she
didn't exist, this defiant sexual mystic with her wry and simple ecstatic
songs is a marvelous and necessary invention. It is said that Mirabai was
born in Merta, in Rajasthan, northwest India, to a powerful clan and was
raised in her grandfather's court. When she was eight, she was engaged to
the son of the ruler of Mewar, an arranged betrothal for political purposes. At eighteen she married the young prince Raga Bojaraja and went
to live in Chitor, the capital city. Though her husband worshiped Kali,
goddess of destruction, Mirabai kept her faith in Krishna. At the palace
she gathered a circle of devotees, but after her husband's death her
mother-in-law and royal brother-in-law disagreed with her beliefs, abused
her, and even tried to poison her with a tainted glass of holy water. She responded in acerbic verse: "Rana, I know you gave me poison / but I came
through / as gold left in a fire / emerges bright as a dozen suns." When
the poison failed, they gave her a fruit basket containing a poisonous serpent. In a last attempt, they made her lie on a bed of iron spikes.
   Mirabai fled the palace and lived as a *sadhu*, a wandering holy beggar,
dancing and singing her songs of love. She lived in places sacred to
Krishna, eventually becoming a temple poet. Her extremely erotic religious poems are primarily addressed to Krishna, her dark-skinned lover

whom she addresses as Hari, Girdhar, Shyam (dark one), or the cowherd, and she speaks in the voice of Radha (Krishna's mythic beloved). After the death of Mirabai's husband, Krishna became her heavenly prince, her "true husband." In her poems, she waits for him; she meets him in the darkness, in dream, in ecstasy; and she agonizes like Radha at his infidelities. Mirabai is thought to have died in Dwarka, but her songs are sung daily in the streets and temples of India.

FURTHER READING: Alston, A. J. *The Devotional Poems of Mirabai,* 1980. Nilsson, Usha. *Mira Bai,* 1970. Panvey, S. M., and Norman Zeide. *Poems from Mirabai,* 1964. Sethi, V. K. *Mira, the Divine Lover,* 1979.

## Mira Is Dancing with Bells Tied

Mira is dancing with bells tied
on her ankles.
People say Mira has gone mad.

Her mother-in-law is upset
at the ruined family honor.                                    5

The king sends her a cup of poison.
Laughing, she drinks it
for her drink is Hari's beautiful face.

She has offered her body and her soul
at Hari's feet.                                                10
She drinks the honey of her vision.
Only he
is her ultimate protector.

## Rana, I Know You Gave Me Poison

Rana, I know you gave me poison
but I came through
as gold left in a fire
emerges bright as a dozen suns.
Opinion and family name                                        5
I throw away like water.
You should hide, Rana.
I am a powerless mad woman.
Krishna's arrow in my heart
destroys my reason.                                            10
I hug the lotus feet of holy men,

give them body and soul.
Mira's lord knows she is his servant.

## My Love Is in My House

My love is in my house,
I watched the road for years
but never saw him.
I put out the worship plate,
gave away gems.
After this, he sent word.
My dark lover has come,
joy is on my limbs.
Hari is an ocean,
my eyes touch him.
Mira is an ocean of joy.
She takes him inside.

## I Don't Sleep. All Night

I don't sleep. All night
I am watching for my love.
Friends offer
wise words.
I reject them.
Without him I can't rest,
but my heart is not angry.
My limbs are weak,
my lips call to him.
This pain of separation
cannot be understood.
I am like the rainbird calling for clouds,
like fish craving water.
Mira is lost,
her senses are dead.

## My Pitcher Crashes on the Ground

My pitcher crashes on the ground.
I am stunned.

His beauty maddens me. Father, mother, brother
and sister
all say nice words. Come home,                                   *5*
forget him.
But that dark dancer inhabits me.
His love is light all through my body.
Let them say I am lost.
The secret. Girdhar knows.                                       *10*

## You Broke My Bracelet

You broke my bracelet
when we made love.
In the morning my mother-in-law
will see it, and give me
hell.                                                            *5*
Morning always comes like lightning
for lovers
after their night.
I won't get up and leave.
The night was wonder I spent                                     *10*
with you.
You filled me.
I came.

## Day and Night

Day and night
I am obsessed with one thought.
You.
Shall I walk away from you?
I couldn't take it. I couldn't stay                              *5*
alive.
Day after day
I climb up to the watchtower of my palace
and there in the turret
I scan the roads coming into the city.                           *10*
Empty night. I despair.
The world is illusion.
Love for family is mere words.
Your lotus feet
is where I am.                                                   *15*

# The Modern Period

### (Nineteenth and Twentieth Centuries)

■ **Ghalib (Asadullah Khan Ghalib) (1797–1869)**
*Urdu* **(poems)**

TRANSLATED BY TONY BARNSTONE

Asadullah Khan Ghalib, known by his pen name Ghalib, was born in Agra in 1797. His father and uncle died when he was very young, so he lived with his mother's family with few father figures about. His education may have been at the hands of a tutor from Iran, a Zoroastrian who had converted to Islam, named Mulla Abdussamad Harmuzd. Around 1810, Ghalib married into a noble, cultivated family and moved to Delhi, where he lived for the remainder of his life, with the exception of a two-year stay in Calcutta. He began writing poetry in his childhood, when he was as young as seven or eight, and his first collection, written in Urdu, was compiled when he was twenty-four. For the rest of his career, however, he wrote for the most part in Persian. In addition to his poetic gifts, he is considered to be a great prose stylist, known for his eloquent letters. The Mughal king Bahadur Shah Zafar became his patron, and Ghalib wrote Urdu poetry (which Zafar favored over Persian) and the first part of a Persian history of the Mughal dynasty for him. Ghalib's letters were published late in his life and helped establish colloquial speech as the basis of prose literature. His poetry is romantic and mystical, and the lover who gives him so much trouble is often equated with God. Like the great Persian poet Hafiz, the style of Ghalib's poems is the rhymed, formal ghazal, in which the poet addresses himself by name in the final couplet. His poems are characterized by great wit, puns, and a mystical, erotic imagery so passionate as to veer at times into the surreal.

**FURTHER READING:** Ahmad, Aijaz. *Ghazals of Ghalib,* 1971; Jafri, Sardar, and Qurratulain Hyder. *Ghalib and his Poetry,* 1970; Russell, R., and K. Islam. *Ghalib: Life and Letters,* 1969; Mujeeb, M. *Ghalib,* 1969.

## Even Dew on a Red Poppy Means Something

Even dew on a red poppy means something.
It covers the scar on your vicious heart.

The dove is a claw of ash, the nightingale a coop of color.
What is the shriek of my charred heart to that?

Beside the lust for flame the flame is ash;                                    *5*
the heart withers as it loses heart.

I only say love is jail because you've locked me in.
My hand won't stray with this boulder on it.

Sun who lights the world, warm us too.
A strange time has touched us like a shadow.                                   *10*


## She Considers Acting Sweet for Once

She considers acting sweet for once
but knows how she's hurt me and shies away.

She's short with me when I go on too long about love.
I should shut up; I even bore myself.

She's grown wary and I'm weak.                                                 *5*
My tongue dies, and she won't ask.

I've got to keep it together. Damn!
What was I saying?

Here it is: even if she lifts her veil
I can't stand to look at her.                                                  *10*


## Her Stride Is an Arrow from a Taut Bow

Her stride is an arrow from a taut bow;
how can I open up that heart?

I say a word, she bites off my tongue:
"Shut up, *I'm* talking," she says.

Listen to me drivel.                                                           *5*
God, I hope no one understands.

Even Alexander was fooled by Khizer,
so who should I believe in?

Ghalib! The world is dead.
Why even bother to complain?                                                   *10*

## At the Party I Have No Shame

At the party I have no shame;
I just sit here, though the fingers point.

I pawn my worn robe and prayer rug for wine;
it's been too long since we drank together.

Let me interrogate the earth. I'd say, *Miser!*
*Why do you give back nothing?*

With new friends she has a new habit:
she'll kiss you before you beg.

She's not a stone, not cruel;
she keeps some promises because she forgets.

## Your Other Lover Flaunts Your Letter

Your other lover flaunts your letter
so he can brag about it.

You're so delicate and tenderly made, I want you to say
*Hold me.* Yet my hands flinch from your perfection.

Death is certain as my need to live;
I call you, certain you won't come.

I don't know whose vision this is.
A veil too thick for me to part.

Ghalib! Love is flame feeding on flame.
I can't light it. I can't put it out.

## Look at Me! I Envy Myself, I'm So Lucky

Look at me! I envy myself, I'm so lucky.
Am I tough enough to bear her beauty?

Fears flare but I surrender my cracked heart:
the wine's so hot the glass is melting.

My God! How can she say *Behave yourself?*
Her shyness makes her shy away in shame

but passion won't let me shut up:
I'm so hot I can't stop for breath.

Asad! My shadow escapes from me like smoke.
My soul is fire. Nothing can stand this heat.                               *10*

## Think of Those Faces Mixed with Dust

Think of those faces mixed with dust.
Few of them show up again as roses or tulips.

The stars who form the Daughters of the Bier were veiled in sun.
What was in your hearts? At night you walked out naked.

A man whose arm is draped with your hair                                    *5*
can sleep peacefully. He owns the night.

We believe in one God. We break old patterns.
When our tribes died out they blended into faith.

Ghalib wept like this. Your city too
will be a brambled wilderness.                                              *10*

## Each Step Opens More Distance to You

Each step opens more distance to you
as the desert flees with my own feet.

This searing heart so lights my desolate night
that your shadow eludes like wafting smoke.

Blistered feet decorate the desert of my lunacy.                           *5*
A luminous string of blood pearls.

For you the goblet's colors leap through a hundred dances.
I catch this vision in a single astounded eye,

Asad! and from my burning eye a fire trickles
and glares on a garden of dirt and parched leaves.                         *10*

## Rabindranath Tagore (1861–1941)
### *Bengali* (poems)

TRANSLATED BY WILLIAM RADICE

Nobel Prize–winning poet Rabindranath Tagore is the most famous
of Bengali writers. He was born in Calcutta in 1861 to a wealthy, aristo-

cratic family and was raised in an artistic and cultured environment. He was a prolific and talented writer who threw his energies into many fields. In addition to writing one hundred books of poems, he wrote fiction and was a painter and an innovative songwriter. He wrote many essays, travel diaries, a book of popular science, satires, farces, and musical and dance dramas and was deeply involved in the questions of social and agricultural policy. At seventeen, he became recognized for writing love poems about the love of Radha and Krishna in the style of the medieval Vaishnava poets (see, for example, Chandidas, in this volume). Like the great fiction writer Premchand, Tagore was deeply involved in the nationalist movement of his time and was, in fact, a friend of Gandhi; like Gandhi, he was devoted to peace and denounced violence in any cause, even that of nationalism. He was knighted in 1915, but after a British massacre in Amritsar led by General Reginald Dyer, Tagore returned his knighthood in protest.

Tagore was a mystical, philosophical poet, deeply affected by his reading of the Upanishads, of the Isa Upanishad in particular. This mysticism can be seen throughout his work and is responsible for the popularity of his most widely read book, *Gitanjali* (1912), for which William Butler Yeats wrote an introduction. His work was deeply influenced by the Bengali and Sanskrit traditions.

Tagore won the Nobel Prize in Literature in 1913. In addition to *Gitanjali*, other well-known works include *The Gardener* (1913), *Songs of Kabir* (1915), *Fireflies* (1928), *Sheaves* (1932), and the play *The Post Office;* collections of his work in English include *A Tagore Reader* (1966), *Collected Poems and Plays* (1937), *The Housewarming and Other Selected Writings* (1965), *The Religion of Man* (1930), and *Three Plays* (*Mukta-Dhara, Natire Puja, Chandalika*) (1950).

**FURTHER READING:** Bowes, Pratima. *Some Songs and Poems from Rabindranath Tagore,* 1985. Chakravarty, Amiya, ed. *A Tagore Reader,* 1961. Ghose, Sisirkumar. *The Later Poems of Tagore,* 1961. Kripalani, Krishna. *Rabindranath Tagore: A Biography,* 1962. Radice, William, tr. *Selected Poems: Rabindranath Tagore,* 1985. Robinson, Andrew. *The Art of Rabindranath Tagore.* Foreword by Satyajit Ray, 1989. Tagore, Rabindranath. *Angel of Surplus: Some Essays and Addresses on Aesthetics.* Edited by Sisirkumar Ghose, 1978.

## The Sick-Bed

When I woke up this morning
There was a rose in my flower-vase:
The question came to me—
The power that brought you through cyclic time
To final beauty,
Dodging at every turn
The torment of ugly incompleteness,

5

Is it blind, is it abstracted,
Does it, like a world-denying *sannyasi*,
Make no distinction between beauty and the opposite of beauty?                    *10*
Is it merely rational,
Merely physical,
Lacking in sensibility?
There are some who argue
That grace and ugliness take equal seats                    *15*
At the court of Creation,
That neither is refused entry
By the guards.
As a poet I cannot enter such arguments—
I can only gaze at the universe                    *20*
In its full, true form,
At the millions of stars in the sky
Carrying their huge harmonious beauty—
Never breaking their rhythm
Or losing their tune,                    *25*
Never deranged
And never stumbling—
I can only gaze and see, in the sky,
The spreading layers
Of a vast, radiant, petalled rose.                    *30*

## Recovery

Every day in the early morning this faithful dog
Sits quietly beside my chair
For as long as I do not acknowledge his presence
By the touch of my hand.
The moment he receives this small recognition,                    *5*
Waves of happiness leap through his body.
In the inarticulate animal world
Only this creature
Has pierced through good and bad and seen
Complete man,                    *10*
Has seen him for whom
Life may be joyfully given,
That object of a free outpouring of love
Whose consciousness points the way
To the realm of infinite consciousness.                    *15*
When I see that dumb heart
Revealing its own humility
Through total self-surrender,

I feel unequal to the worth
His simple perception has found in the nature of man.
The wistful anxiety in his mute gaze
Understands something he cannot explain:
It directs me to the true meaning of man in the universe.

## On My Birthday

Today I imagine the words of countless
Languages to be suddenly fetterless—
After long incarceration
In the fortress of grammar, suddenly up in rebellion.
Maddened by the stamp-stamping
Of unmitigated regimented drilling.
They have jumped the constraints of sentence
To seek free expression in a world rid of intelligence,
Snapping the chains of sense in sarcasm
And ridicule of literary decorum.
Liberated thus, their queer
Postures and cries appeal only to the ear.
They say, 'We who were born of the gusty tuning
Of the earth's first outbreathing
Came into our own as soon as the blood's beat
Impelled man's mindless vitality to break into dance in his throat.
We swelled his infant voice with the babble
Of the world's first poem, the original prattle
Of existence. We are kin to the wild torrents
That pour from the mountains to announce
The month of Śrāban: we bring to human habitations
Nature's incantations—'
The festive sound of leaves rustling in forests,
The sound that measures the rhythm of approaching tempests,
The great night-ending sound of day-break—
From these sound-fields man has captured words, curbed them like a
        breakneck
Stallion in complex webs of order
To enable him to pass on his messages to the distant lands of the
        future.
By riding words that are bridled and reined
Man has quickened
The pace of time's slow clocks:
The speed of his reason has cut through material blocks,
Explored recalcitrant mysteries;
With word-armies

Drawn into battle-lines he resists the perpetual assault of imbecility.                     *35*
But sometimes they slip like robbers into realms of fantasy,
Float on ebbing waters
Of sleep, free of barriers,
Lashing any sort of flotsam and jetsam into metre.
From them, the free-roving mind fashions                                                      *40*
Artistic creations
Of a kind that do not conform to an orderly
Universe—whose threads are tenuous, loose, arbitrary,
Like a dozen puppies brawling,
Scrambling at each other's necks to no purpose or meaning:                                    *45*
Each bites another—
They squeal and yelp blue murder,
But their bites and yelps carry no true import of enmity,
Their violence is bombast, empty fury.
In my mind I imagine words thus shot of their meaning,                                        *50*
Hordes of them running amuck all day,
As if in the sky there were nonsense nursery syllables booming—
*Horselum, bridelum, ridelum, into the fray.*

## ■ Mahatma Gandhi (Mohandas Karamchand Gandhi) (1869–1948) *English* (prose)

Mohandas Karamchand Gandhi (called Mahatma, or "Great Soul") is probably the most famous person to come out of modern India. Born in Porbandar, he was educated in India and London, passing the bar exam in London in 1889. He practiced law in India for a few years, but in 1893 he went to South Africa where his law practice flourished and where he used his new prominence in the Indian community to organize it against anti-Indian discrimination. While in South Africa, he gave up Western ways for Hindu ideals of asceticism, giving up material possessions and wearing the garb of an ascetic—loincloth and shawl. Using a strategy of civil disobedience, he forced an agreement from the South African government that alleviated anti-Indian discrimination.

In 1915, Gandhi returned to India, then under British colonial rule, where he carried on activities in favor of Indian self-rule and labor and agrarian reform and became a central figure in the Indian National Congress through the 1920s and early 1930s. He remained a tireless campaigner for reform, and although he was jailed for his activities in 1930 and 1942, Gandhi was central to the post-war meetings that led to India's independence. The violence between Hindus and Muslims that followed independence and has been a fact of life in India until today led Gandhi to fast in protest and to tour violent areas, attempting to broker peace. His attempts at mediation led to his murder on January 30, 1948, in New Delhi, by a Hindu extremist angered by Gandhi's concern for the Muslims.

The concept of civil disobedience was first codified in modern times by Thoreau in his 1849 essay "Civil Disobedience" (written about his overnight stay in a New England jail for refusing to pay taxes in protest over the Mexican War), but Gandhi put the method to lifelong use. Others, such as Martin Luther King, Jr., have followed his example. Today, Gandhi's method of passive resistance, civil disobedience, and nonviolence has been adopted by civil rights activists and political dissenters throughout the world.

**FURTHER READING:** Ashe, Geoffrey. *Gandhi: A Study in Revolution,* 1968. Gandhi, Mohandas Karamchand. *All Men Are Brothers: Life and Thoughts of Mahatma Gandhi as Told in His Own Words.* Edited by Krishna Kripalani, 1959, 1969; *An Autobiography: The Story of My Experiments with Truth.* Translated from the Gujarati by Mahadev Desai, 1954; *Satyagraha: Non-violent Resistance.* Edited by Bharatan Kumarappa, 1951, 1983. Nanda, Jawaharlal. *Mahatma Gandhi: A Biography,* 1958.

## from *Indian Home Rule*
### Passive Resistance

READER: Is there any historical evidence as to the success of what you have called soul-force or truth-force? No instance seems to have happened of any nation having risen through soul-force. I still think that the evildoers will not cease doing evil without physical punishment.

EDITOR: The poet Tulsidas has said: "Of religion, pity, or love, is the root, as egotism of the body. Therefore, we should not abandon pity so long as we are alive." This appears to me to be a scientific truth. I believe in it as much as I believe in two and two being four. The force of love is the same as the force of the soul or truth. We have evidence of its working at every step. The universe would disappear without the existence of that force. But you ask for historical evidence. It is, therefore, necessary to know what history means. The Gujarati equivalent means; "It so happened." If that is the meaning of history, it is possible to give copious evidence. But, if it means the doings of kings and emperors, there can be no evidence of soul-force or passive resistance in such history. You cannot expect silver ore in a tin mine. History, as we know it, is a record of the wars of the world, and so there is a proverb among Englishmen that a nation which has no history, that is, no wars, is a happy nation. How kings played, how they became enemies of one another, how they murdered one another, is found accurately recorded in history, and if this were all that had happened in the world, it would have been ended long ago. If the story of the universe had commenced with wars, not a man would have been found alive today. Those people who have been warred against have disappeared as, for instance, the natives of Australia of whom hardly a man was left alive by the intruders. Mark, please, that these natives did not use soul-force in self-defense, and it does not require much foresight to know that the Australians will share the same fate as their victims. "Those that take the sword shall perish by the sword." With us the proverb is that professional swimmers will find a watery grave.

The fact that there are so many men still alive in the world shows that it is based not on the force of arms but on the force of truth or love. Therefore, the greatest and most unimpeachable evidence of the success of this force is to be found in the fact that, in spite of the wars of the world, it still lives on.

Thousands, indeed tens of thousands, depend for their existence on a very active working of this force. Little quarrels of millions of families in their daily lives disappear before the exercise of this force. Hundreds of nations live in peace. History does not and cannot take note of this fact. History is really a record of every interruption of the even working of the force of love or of the soul. Two brothers quarrel; one of them repents and re-awakens the love that was lying dormant in him; the two again begin to live in peace; nobody takes note of this. But if the two brothers, through the intervention of solicitors or some other reason, take up arms or go to law—which is another form of the exhibition of brute force—their doings would be immediately noticed in the press, they would be the talk of their neighbors and would probably go down to history. And what is true of families and communities is true of nations. There is no reason to believe that there is one law for families and another for nations. History, then, is a record of an interruption of the course of nature. Soul-force being natural, is not noted in history.

READER: According to what you say, it is plain that instances of this kind of passive resistance are not to be found in history. It is necessary to understand this passive resistance more fully. It will be better, therefore, if you enlarge upon it.

EDITOR: Passive resistance is a method of securing rights by personal suffering; it is the reverse of resistance by arms. When I refuse to do a thing that is repugnant to my conscience, I use soul-force. For instance, the Government of the day has passed a law which is applicable to me. I do not like it. If by using violence I force the Government to repeal the law, I am employing what may be termed body-force. If I do not obey the law and accept the penalty for its breach, I use soul-force. It involves sacrifice of self.

Everybody admits that sacrifice of self is infinitely superior to sacrifice of others. Moreover, if this kind of force is used in a cause that is unjust, only the person using it suffers. He does not make others suffer for his mistakes. Men have before now done many things which were subsequently found to have been wrong. No man can claim that he is absolutely in the right or that a particular thing is wrong because he thinks so, but it is wrong for him so long as that is his deliberate judgment. It is therefore meet that he should not do that which he knows to be wrong, and suffer the consequence whatever it may be. This is the key to the use of soul-force.

READER: You would then disregard laws—this is rank disloyalty. We have always been considered a law-abiding nation. You seem to be going even beyond the extremists. They say that we must obey the laws that have been passed, but that if the laws be bad, we must drive out the law-givers even by force.

EDITOR: Whether I go beyond them or whether I do not is a matter of no consequence to either of us. We simply want to find out what is right and to act accordingly. The real meaning of the statement that we are a law-abiding nation is that we are passive resisters. When we do not like certain laws, we do not break the heads of law-givers but we suffer and do not submit to the laws. That we should obey laws whether good or bad is a new-fangled notion. There was no such thing in former days. The people disregarded those laws they did not like and suffered the penalties for their breach. It is contrary to our manhood if we obey laws repugnant to our conscience. Such teaching is opposed to religion and means slavery. If the Government were to ask us to go about without any clothing, should we do so? If I were a passive resister, I would say to them that I would have nothing to do with their law. But we have so forgotten ourselves and become so compliant that we do not mind any degrading law.

A man who has realized his manhood, who fears only God, will fear no one else. Man-made laws are not necessarily binding on him. Even the Government does not expect any such thing from us. They do not say: "You must do such and such a thing," but they say: "If you do not do it, we will punish you." We are sunk so low that we fancy that it is our duty and our religion to do what the law lays down. If man will only realize that it is unmanly to obey laws that are unjust, no man's tyranny will enslave him. This is the key to self-rule or home-rule.

It is a superstition and ungodly thing to believe that an act of a majority binds a minority. Many examples can be given in which acts of majorities will be found to have been wrong and those of minorities to have been right. All reforms owe their origin to the initiation of minorities in opposition to majorities. If among a band of robbers a knowledge of robbing is obligatory, is a pious man to accept the obligation? So long as the superstition that men should obey unjust laws exists, so long will their slavery exist. And a passive resister alone can remove such a superstition.

To use brute-force, to use gunpowder, is contrary to passive resistance, for it means that we want our opponent to do by force that which we desire but he does not. And if such a use of force is justifiable, surely he is entitled to do likewise by us. And so we should never come to an agreement. We may simply fancy, like the blind horse moving in a circle round a mill, that we are making progress. Those who believe that they are not bound to obey laws which are repugnant to their conscience have only the remedy of passive resistance open to them. Any other must lead to disaster.

READER: From what you say I deduce that passive resistance is a splendid weapon of the weak, but that when they are strong they may take up arms.

EDITOR: This is a gross ignorance. Passive resistance, that is, soul-force, is matchless. It is superior to the force of arms. How, then, can it be considered only a weapon of the weak? Physical-force men are strangers to the courage that is requisite in a passive resister. Do you believe that a coward can ever disobey a law that he dislikes? Extremists are considered to be advocates of brute force. Why do they, then, talk about obeying laws? I do not blame them. They can say nothing else. When they succeed in driving out the English and they themselves become governors, they will want you and me to obey their laws. And that is a fitting thing for their constitution. But a passive resister will say he will not obey a law that is against his conscience, even though he may be blown to pieces at the mouth of a cannon.

What do you think? Wherein is courage required — in blowing others to pieces from behind a cannon, or with a smiling face to approach a cannon and be blown to pieces? Who is the true warrior — he who keeps death always as a bosom-friend, or he who controls the death of others? Believe me that a man devoid of courage and manhood can never be a passive resister.

This, however, I will admit: that even a man weak in body is capable of offering this resistance. One man can offer it just as well as millions. Both men and women can indulge in it. It does not require the training of an army; it needs no jiu-jitsu. Control over the mind is alone necessary, and when that is attained, man is free like the king of the forest and his very glance withers the enemy.

Passive resistance is an all-sided sword, it can be used anyhow; it blesses him who uses it and him against whom it is used. Without drawing a drop of blood it produces far-reaching results. It never rusts and cannot be stolen. Competition between passive resisters does not exhaust. The sword of passive resistance does not require a scabbard. It is strange indeed that you should consider such a weapon to be a weapon merely of the weak. . . .

READER: From what you say, then, it would appear that it is not a small thing to become a passive resister, and, if that is so, I should like you to explain how a man may become one.

EDITOR: To become a passive resister is easy enough but it is also equally difficult. I have known a lad of fourteen years become a passive resister; I have known also sick people do likewise; and I have also known physically strong and otherwise happy people unable to take up passive resistance. After a great deal of experience it seems to me that those who want to become passive resisters for the service of the country have to observe perfect chastity, adopt poverty, follow truth, and cultivate fearlessness.

Chastity is one of the greatest disciplines without which the mind cannot attain requisite firmness. A man who is unchaste loses stamina, becomes emasculated and cowardly. He whose mind is given over to animal passions is not capable of any great effort. . . .

Just as there is necessity for chastity, so is there for poverty. Pecuniary ambition and passive resistance cannot go well together. Those who have money are not expected to throw it away, but they are expected to be indifferent about it. They must be prepared to lose every penny rather than give up passive resistance.

Passive resistance has been described in the course of our discussion as truth-force. Truth, therefore, has necessarily to be followed and that at any cost. In this connection, academic questions such as whether a man may not lie in order to save a life, etc., arise, but these questions occur only to those who wish to justify lying. Those who want to follow truth every time are not placed in such a quandary; and if they are, they are still saved from a false position.

Passive resistance cannot proceed a step without fearlessness. Those alone can follow the path of passive resistance who are free from fear, whether as to their possessions, false honor, their relatives, the government, bodily injuries or death.

These observances are not to be abandoned in the belief that they are difficult. Nature has implanted in the human breast ability to cope with any difficulty or suffering that may come to man unprovoked. These qualities are worth having, even for those who do not wish to serve the country. Let there be no mistake, as those who want to train themselves in the use of arms are also obliged to have these qualities more or less. Everybody does not become a warrior for the wish. A would-be warrior will have to observe chastity and to be satisfied with poverty as his lot. A warrior without fearlessness cannot be conceived of. It may be thought that he would not need to be exactly truthful, but that quality follows real fearlessness. When a man abandons truth, he does so owing to fear in some shape or form. The above four attributes, then, need not frighten anyone. It may be as well here to note that a physical-force man has to have many other useless qualities which a passive resister never needs. And you will find that whatever extra effort a swordsman needs is due to lack of fearlessness. If he is an embodiment of the latter, the sword will drop from his hand that very moment. He does not need its support. One who is free from hatred requires no sword. A man with a stick suddenly came face to face with a lion and instinctively raised his weapon in self-defense. The man saw that he had only prated about fearlessness when there was none in him. That moment he dropped the stick and found himself free from all fear.

## ■ Sarat Chandra Chatterjee (1876–1938)
### *Bengali* (story)

TRANSLATED BY S. SINHA

Bengali fiction writer Sarat Chandra Chatterjee ranks with Rabindranath Tagore and Bankim Chandra Chatterjee as one of the most important Bengali writers of the modern era. Though born a Brahman like Tagore and the earlier Chatterjee, he lived for much of his life in extreme poverty, and the acute sense of social injustice and the struggle simply to survive that permeates his stories derives from his own life experience. He also shows a deep sympathy for women in his writing, studying the question of women's rights and writing several essays about them, most famously "What Price Woman?," which has been described as an "impassioned, yet closely reasoned plea for the recognition of woman's right of self-determination and the moral and spiritual value of her personality."[1] Chatterjee is said to have roamed far afield in India as a Hindu *sannyasi,* and later as a Buddhist monk. Though he had no formal education, he began writing in his late twenties and became so successful that his works were translated into all the major Indian languages. He wrote twelve novels and many short stories; his fiction has been made into a number of films. "Drought" is considered among Chatterjee's very best stories.

**FURTHER READING:** Chatterjee, Sarat Chandra. *Drought and Other Stories.* Translated by Sasadhar Sinha, 1970.

# Drought

The village was called Kashipur. It was a small village, but its *Zamindar*[1] was smaller still. Yet his tenants dared not stand up to him. He was so ruthless.

It was the birthday of his youngest son. It was noon. Tarkaratna, the priest, was on his way home from the landlord's house, where he had been offering prayers. It was nearing the end of May, but not a patch of cloud could be seen in the sky. The rainless firmament poured fire.

At the end of the field, beside the road, there stood the house of Gafur, the weaver. Now that the mud walls were in ruins, the courtyard touched the public highway, and the inner privacy was thrown on the mercy of the passers-by.

"Hey! Gafur! Is anybody in?" called out Tarkaratna, standing in the shade of a tree by the roadside.

"What do you want? Father is down with fever," answered Gafur's little daughter, aged ten, appearing at the door.

"Fever! Call the scoundrel!"

The noise brought Gafur out, shivering with fever. A bull was tied to the old acacia that leaned against the broken wall.

---

1. Chatterjee, Sarat Chandra. *Drought and Other Stories.* Translated by Sasadhar Sinha. New Delhi: Sahitya Akademi, 1970, p. 8.

---

1. An official in charge of collecting land taxes. Also, a landholder.

"What do I see there?" demanded Tarkaratna, indicating the bull. "Do you realise that this is a Hindu village and the landlord himself a Brahmin?"[2] His face was crimson with indignation and the heat of the sun. It was to be expected that his words should be hot and harsh. But Gafur simply looked at him, unable to follow the import of his words.

"Well," said Tarkaratna, "I saw it tied there in the morning and it's still there. If the bull dies, your master will flay you alive! He is no ordinary Brahmin!"

"What shall I do, Father? I'm helpless. I have had fever for the last few days. I can't take him out to graze. I feel so ill."

"Can't you let him graze by himself?"

"Where shall I let him go, Father? People haven't threshed all their paddy yet. It's still lying in the fields. The straw hasn't been gathered. Everything is burnt to cinders—there isn't a blade of grass anywhere. How can I let him loose, Father? He might start poking his nose into somebody's paddy or eating somebody's straw."

Tarkaratna softened a little. "But you can at least tie him in the shade somewhere and give him a bundle of straw or two to munch. Hasn't your daughter cooked rice? Why not give him a tub of boiled rice water? Let him drink it."

Gafur made no reply. He looked helplessly at Tarkaratna, and a deep sigh escaped him.

"I see; you haven't even got that much? What have you done with your share of straw? I suppose you have gone and sold it to satisfy your belly? Not saved even one bundle for the bull! How callous you are!"

At this cruel accusation Gafur seemed to lose the power of speech. "This year I was to have received my share of straw," said Gafur slowly after a moment's hesitation, "but the master kept it all on account of my last year's rent. 'Sir, you are our lord and master,' I implored, falling at his feet. 'Where am I to go if I leave your domain? Let me have at least a little straw. There's no straw on my roof, and we have only one hut in which we two—father and daughter—live. We'll patch the roof with palm leaves and manage this rainy weather, somehow, but what will happen to our Mahesh without food?'

"Indeed! So you're fond enough of the bull to call him Mahesh! This is a joke."[3]

But his sarcasm did not reach Gafur. "But the master took no pity on me," he went on. "He gave me paddy to last only two months. My share of straw was added to his own stock—Mahesh didn't have even a wisp of it."

"Well, don't you owe him money?" said Tarkaratna, unmoved. "Why shouldn't you have to pay? Do you expect the landlord to support you?"

---

2. The first of the four Hindu classes, Brahmins (also "Brahmans") teach the Vedas and officiate at religious rites.

3. Another name for the god Shiva.

"But what am I to pay him with? We till four bighas[4] of land for him, but the paddy has dried up in the fields during the droughts in the last two years. My daughter and I have not even enough to eat. Look at the hut! When it rains, I spend the night with my daughter huddled in one corner—we can't even stretch our legs. Look at Mahesh! You can count his ribs. Do lend me a bit of hay for him so that he can have something to eat for a day or two." And Gafur sank down on the ground at the Brahmin's feet.

"No, no! Move aside! Let me go home, it's getting late." Tarkaratna made a movement as though to depart, smiling. "Good God! He seems to brandish his horns at me! Will he hurt?" he cried out with fright and anger, stepping hurriedly back from the bull.

Gafur staggered to his feet. "He wants to eat a handful," he said, indicating the wet bundle of rice and fruit in Tarkaratna's hand.

"Wants to eat? Indeed! Like master, like animal. Hasn't even a bit of straw to eat and must have rice and fruit. Take him away and tie him somewhere else! What horns! He will gore somebody to death one of these days." Edging a little, the priest made a quick exit.

Looking away from him, Gafur silently watched Mahesh, whose two deep, brown eyes were full of pain and hunger. "Didn't even give a handful," he muttered, patting the bull's neck and back. "You are my son, Mahesh," he whispered to him. "You have grown old and served us for eight years. I can't even give you enough to eat—but you know how much I love you, don't you?"

Mahesh only stretched out his neck and closed his eyes with pleasure.

"Tell me," went on Gafur, "how can I keep you alive in this dreadful year? If I let you loose, you will start eating other people's paddy or munching their banana leaves. What can I do with you? You have no strength left in your body—nobody wants you. They ask me to sell you at the cattle market. . . ." At the very idea his eyes filled with tears again. Wiping his tears on the back of his hand and looking this way and that, he fetched a tiny bunch of discolored old straw from behind the hut. "Eat it quickly, my child, otherwise . . ." he said, softly, placing it before Mahesh.

"Father . . . "

"What is it?"

"Come and eat," answered Gafur's daughter, looking out of the door. "Why, have you again given Mahesh straw from the roof?"

He had feared as much. "It's old straw—it was rotting away," he answered, ashamed.

"I heard you pulling it, father."

"No, darling, it wasn't exactly . . ."

"But you know, father, the wall will crumble . . ."

---

4. A unit of land measurement, now obsolete; about three-fourths of an acre.

Gafur was silent. He had nothing left but this hut. Who knew better than he that unless he was careful it would not last another rainy season. And yet what good was it really?

"Wash your hands and come and eat. I have served your food," said the little girl.

"Give me the rice water; let me feed him."

"There is none, father—it has dried up in the pot."

Nearly a week had passed. Gafur was sitting in the yard, sick of body and anxious. Mahesh had not returned since the day before.

He himself was helpless. Amina had been looking for the bull everywhere from early morning. The evening shadows were already falling when she came home. "Have you heard, father? Manik Ghose has sent Mahesh to the police pen," she said.

"Nonsense!"

"Yes, father, it's true. His servant said to me, 'Tell your father to look for the bull at Dariapur. . . .'"

"What did he do?"

"He entered their garden, father."

Gafur made no answer.

"At the end of three days, they say, the police will sell him at the cattle market."

"Let them," answered Gafur.

Amina did not know what the "cattle market" meant. She had often noticed her father grow restless whenever it was mentioned in connection with Mahesh, but today he went out without saying another word.

Under the cover of night, Gafur secretly came round to Banshi's shop.

"Uncle, you'll have to lend me a rupee," said he, putting down a brass plate under the seat. Banshi was well acquainted with this object. In the last two years he had lent a rupee at least five times on this security. He made no objection today either.

The next morning Mahesh was seen at his usual place again. An elderly Mohammedan was examining him with very sharp eyes. Not far away, on one side, Gafur sat on the ground, all hunched up. The examination over, the old man untied a ten-rupee note from a corner of his shawl, and, smoothing it again and again, said: "Here, take this. I shan't take anything off. I'm paying the full price."

Stretching his hand, Gafur took the money, but remained silent. As the two men who came with the old man were about to take the rope round the animal's neck, he suddenly stood bolt upright. "Don't touch that rope, I tell you. Be careful, I warn you!" he cried out hoarsely.

They were taken aback. "Why?" asked the old man in surprise.

"There's no why to it. He's my property—I shall not sell him; it's my pleasure," he answered in the same tone, and threw the note away.

"But you accepted the deposit yesterday," all three said in a chorus.

"Take this back," he answered, flinging the two rupees across to them.

Gafur begged for rice water from the neighbors and fed Mahesh. Patting him on the head and horns, he whispered vague sounds of endearment to him.

It was about the middle of June. Nobody who has not looked at an Indian summer sky would realize how terrible, how unrelenting, the heat can be. Not a trace of mercy anywhere! Today even the thought that some day this aspect of the sky will change, that it will become overcast with soft, vapor-laden clouds is impossible. It seemed as though the whole blazing sky would go on burning day after day endlessly, to the end of time.

Gafur returned home at noon. He was not used to working as a hired laborer, and it was only four or five days since his temperature had gone down. His body was still weak and tired. He had gone out to seek work, but in vain. He had had no success. Hungry, thirsty, tired, everything was dark before his eyes. "Is the food ready, Amina dear?" he called out from the courtyard.

Without answering, his daughter quietly came out and stood leaning against the wall.

"Is the food ready?" Gafur repeated without receiving an answer.

"What do you say? No? Why?"

"There's no rice, father."

"No rice? Why didn't you tell me in the morning?"

"Why, I told you last night."

"'I told you last night,'" mimicked Gafur. "How am I to remember what you told me last night?" His anger grew more and more violent at the sound of his own voice. "Of course, there's no rice!" he growled, with his face more distorted than ever. "What does it matter to you whether your father eats or not? But the young lady must have her three meals! In the future I shall lock up the rice when I go out. Give me some water to drink—I'm dying of thirst. . . . So you haven't any water, either!"

Amina remained standing with bowed head as before. Realizing that there was not even a drop of water in the house, he lost all self-control. Rushing at her, he slapped her face noisily. "Wretched girl! What do you do all day? So many people die—why don't you?"

The girl did not utter a word. She took the empty earthen pitcher and went out into the afternoon sun, quietly wiping her silent tears.

The moment she was out of sight, her father was overwhelmed with remorse. He alone knew how he had brought up that motherless girl. He knew that this affectionate, dutiful quiet daughter of his was not to blame. They had never had enough to eat even while their little store of rice lasted. It was impossible to eat three times a day. Nor was he unaware of the reason for the absence of water. The two or three tanks in the village had all dried up. The little water that there was still in the private tank of Shibu Babu was not for the public. A few holes had been dug at the bottom of the other tanks, but there was such crowding and jostling for a little water that this chit of a girl could not even approach them. She stood for hours on end and, after much begging, if somebody took pity on her, she returned home with a little water. He knew all this. Perhaps there was no water today or nobody had found time to take pity on her. Something of the sort must have happened, he thought, and his own eyes, too, filled with tears.

"Gafur! Are you in?" somebody cried out from the yard. The landlord's messenger had arrived.

"Yes, I'm in. Why?" answered Gafur bitterly.

"Master has sent for you. Come."

"I haven't had any food yet. I will come later," said Gafur.

Such impudence seemed intolerable to the messenger. "It's master's order to drag you to him and give you a good thrashing," he roared, calling the man ugly names.

Gafur lost self-control for the second time. "We are nobody's slave," he replied, returning similar compliments. "We pay rent to live here. I will not go."

But in this world it is not only futile for the small to appeal to authority, it is dangerous as well. Fortunately the tiny voice seldom reaches big ears or who knows what might happen? When Gafur returned home from the landlord's and quietly lay down, his face and eyes were swollen. The chief cause of so much suffering was Mahesh. When Gafur left home that morning, Mahesh broke loose from his tether, and, entering the grounds of the landlord, had eaten up flowers and upset the corn drying in the sun. When finally they tried to catch him, he had hurt the landlord's youngest daughter and had escaped. This was not the first time this had happened, but Gafur was forgiven because he was poor. If he had come round, and, as on other occasions, begged for the landlord's forgiveness, he would probably have been forgiven, but instead he had claimed that he paid rent, and that he was nobody's slave. This was too much for Shibu Babu, the *Zamindar*, to swallow. Gafur had borne the beatings and tortures without protest. At home, too, he lay in a corner without a word. Hunger and thirst he had forgotten, but his heart was burning within him like the sun outside. He had kept no count of how time passed.

He was suddenly shaken out of his listlessness by a shriek of a girl. She was prostrate on the ground. The pitcher which she had been carrying tumbled over, and Mahesh was sucking up the water as it flowed onto the earth. Gafur was completely out of his mind. Without waiting another moment he seized his plowhead he had left yesterday for repair, and with both hands struck it violently on the bent head of Mahesh. Once only Mahesh attempted to raise his head, but immediately his starving, lean body sagged to the ground. A few drops of blood from his ears rolled down. His whole body shook once or twice and then, stretching the fore and hind legs as far as they would reach, Mahesh fell dead. "What have you done, father? Our Mahesh is dead!" Amina burst out weeping.

Gafur did not move nor answer her. He remained staring without blinking at a pair of motionless, beady, black eyes.

Before two hours were out the tanners living at the end of the village came crowding in and carried off Mahesh on a bamboo pole. Shuddering at the sight of the shining knives in their hands, Gafur closed his eyes but did not speak.

The neighbors informed him that the landlord had sent for Tarkaratna to ask for his advice. How would Gafur pay for the penance which the killing of a sacred animal demanded?

Gafur made no reply to these remarks, but remained squatting with his chin resting on his knees.

"Amina, dear, come, let's go," said Gafur, rousing his daughter at the dead of night.

She had fallen asleep in the yard. "Where, father?" she asked, rubbing her eyes.

"To work at the jute mill at Fulbere," said the father.

The girl looked at him incredulously. Through all his misery he had declined to go to Fulbere. "No religion, no respect, no privacy for women-folk there," she had often heard him say.

"Hurry up, my child; we have a long way to go," said Gafur.

Amina was going to collect the drinking bowl and her father's brass plate. "Leave them alone, darling. They'll pay for the penance for Mahesh," said Gafur.

In the dead of night Gafur set out, holding his daughter by the hand. He had nobody to call his own in the village. He had nothing to say to anybody. Crossing the yard, when he reached the acacia, he stopped stock-still and burst out crying loudly. "Allah," he said, raising his face towards the star-spangled black sky, "punish me as much as you like — Mahesh died with thirst on his lips. Nobody left even the tiniest bit of land for him to feed on. Please never forgive the landlord his sin, who never let him eat the grass nor drink the water you have given." They set out for the jute mill.

## ■ Premchand (1880–1936) *Hindi* (story)

TRANSLATED BY DAVID RUBIN

Premchand is the literary pseudonym of Dhanpat Rai Srivastava, who was probably the finest writer in Hindi and in Urdu. He was a pioneer writer of serious, realistic fiction, comparable to the work of Zola or Dickens. He was born to a lower middle-class family near Benares in 1880 and grew up hearing both Hindi and Urdu. He was educated in Persian and Urdu, and Urdu was the language he began writing in at the start of his career. In 1914, he switched to Hindi, and versions of his stories, often in different forms, appear in both languages. He continued writing many works in Urdu throughout his life, but he believed that through Hindi he could reach a wider audience.

Premchand knew poverty as a child, and his parents died before he was twenty. He had little income and experienced poor health for the better part of his life, and most of his fame came after his death. In 1907, his first collection of short stories was banned for its nationalism, causing him to take on a pseudonym. Premchand was a strong advocate of the Independence movement, a follower of Gandhi, politically, and Tolstoy, esthetically. His work also shows the influence of Marx, George Eliot, Dickens, Chekhov, and Gorky. His stories are extraordinary in the sympathy and realism with which they portray the village life of people of all castes, but most of all the Untouchables and the desperately poor. His work includes fourteen novels and more than three hundred short stories; he also wrote many essays, editorials, screenplays, and plays. Two of his stories, "The Chess Player" and "Deliverance," have been made into films by India's premier filmmaker Satyajit Ray, and "The Shroud" has been made into a Telegu film by Bengali director Mrinal Sen.

FURTHER READING: Premchand. *Deliverance and Other Stories*. Translated from the Hindi by David Rubin, 1969, 1988; *Twenty-four Stories by Premchand*. Translated by Nandini Nopany and P. Lal, 1980.

## The Shroud

Father and son sat in silence at the door of their hut before a burnt-out fire and inside Budhiya, the son's young wife, lay fainting in the throes of child-birth. From time to time such an agonizing cry came out of her that their hearts skipped a beat. It was a winter night, all was silent, and the whole village was obliterated in the darkness.

Ghisu said, 'It looks as though she won't make it. You spent the whole day running around—just go in and have a look.'

Annoyed, Madhav said, 'If she's going to die why doesn't she get it over with? What can I do by looking?'

'You're pretty hard-hearted, aren't you? You live at your ease with somebody all year and then you don't give a damn about her.'

'But I couldn't stand looking at her writhing and thrashing.'

They were a family of Untouchable[1] leather-workers and had a bad name throughout the whole village. If Ghisu worked one day he'd take three off. Madhav was such a loafer that whenever he worked for a half hour he'd stop and smoke his pipe for an hour. So they couldn't get work anywhere. If there was even a handful of grain in the house then the two of them swore off work. After a couple of days fasting Ghisu would climb up a tree and break off branches for firewood and Madhav would bring it to the market to sell. And so long as they had any of the money they got for it they'd both wander around in idleness. There was no shortage of heavy work in the village. It was a village of farmers and there were any

---

1. The lowest class of people, itself comprised of many subclasses, whose touch was considered unclean by the higher caste Hindus. They are now called Scheduled Castes and discrimination against them was abolished in 1955.

number of chores for a hard-working man. But whenever you called these two you had to be satisfied with paying them both for doing one man's work between them. If the two of them had been wandering ascetics there would have been absolutely no need for them to practice. This was their nature. A strange life theirs was! They owned nothing except for some clay pots; a few torn rags was all that covered their nakedness. They were free of worldly cares! They were loaded with debts, people abused them, beat them, but they didn't suffer. People would loan them a little something even though they were so poor there was no hope of getting it back. At the time of the potato and pea harvest they would go into other people's fields and dig up potatoes and gather peas and roast them or they'd pick sugarcane to suck at night. Ghisu had reached the age of sixty living this hand-to-mouth existence, and like a good son Madhav was following in his father's footsteps in every way, and if anything he was adding lustre to his father's fame. The two of them were sitting before the fire now roasting potatoes they'd dug up in some field. Ghisu's wife had died a long time ago. Madhav had been married last year. Since his wife had come she'd established order in the family and kept those two good-for-nothings' bellies filled. And since her arrival they'd become more sluggish than ever. In fact, they'd begun to let it go to their heads. If someone sent for them to do a job, they'd bare-facedly ask for twice the wages. This same woman was dying today in child-birth and it was as though they were only waiting for her to die so they could go to sleep in peace and quiet.

Ghisu took a potato and while he peeled it said, 'Go and look, see how she is. She must be possessed by some ghost, what else? But the village exorcist wants a rupee for a visit.'

Madhav was afraid that if he went into the hut Ghisu would do away with most of the potatoes. He said, 'I'm scared to go in there.'

'What are you afraid of? I'll be right here.'

'Then why don't you go and look?'

'When my woman died I didn't stir from her side for three days. And then she'd be ashamed if I saw her bare like that when I've never even seen her face before. Won't she be worried about her modesty? If she sees me she won't feel free to thrash around.'

'I've been thinking, if there's a baby what's going to happen? There's nothing we're supposed to have in the house—ginger, sugar, oil.'

'Everything's going to be all right, God will provide. The very people who wouldn't even give us a pice[2] before will send for us tomorrow and give us rupees. I had nine kids and there was never a thing in the house but somehow or other the Lord got us through.'

In a society where the condition of people who toiled day and night was not much better than theirs and where, on the other hand, those who knew how to profit from the weaknesses of the peasants were infinitely richer, it's no wonder they felt like this. We could even say that Ghisu was

---

2. A monetary unit equal to one-quarter of a rupee.

much smarter than the peasants and instead of being one of the horde of empty-headed toilers he'd found a place for himself in the disreputable society of idle gossip-mongers. Only he didn't have the ability to stick to the rules and code of such idlers. So while others of his crowd had made themselves chiefs and bosses of the village, the whole community pointed at him in contempt. Nevertheless, there was the consolation that although he was miserably poor at least he didn't have to do the back-breaking labour the farmers did, and other people weren't able to take unfair advantage of his simplicity and lack of ambition.

They ate the potatoes piping hot. Since yesterday they'd eaten nothing and they didn't have the patience to let them cool. Several times they burned their tongues. When they were peeled the outside of the potatoes didn't seem very hot but as soon as they bit into them the inside burned their palates, tongues and throats. Rather than keep these burning coals in their mouths it was a lot safer to drop them down into their bellies, where there was plenty of equipment to cool them. So they swallowed them quickly, even though the attempt brought tears to their eyes.

At this moment Ghisu recalled the Thakur's wedding, which he'd attended twenty years before. The way the feast had gratified him was something to remember all his life, and the memory was still vivid today. He said, 'I won't forget that feast. Since then I've never seen food like it or filled my belly so well. The bride's people crammed everybody with *puris*, everybody! Bigshots and nobodies all ate *puris* fried in real *ghee*.[3] Relishes and curds with spices, three kinds of dried vegetables, a tasty curry, sweets—how can I describe how delicious that food was? There was nothing to hold you back, you just asked for anything you wanted and as much as you wanted. We ate so much that nobody had any room left for water. The people serving just kept on handing out hot, round, mouth-watering savouries on leaves. And we'd say, 'Stop, you mustn't,' and put our hands over the plates to stop them but they kept right on handing it out. And when everybody had rinsed his mouth we got *paan* and cardamom too. But how could I take any *paan*? I couldn't even stand up. I just went and lay down in my blanket right away. That's how generous that Thakur was!'

Relishing the banquet in his imagination Madhav said, 'Nobody feeds us like that now.'

'Who'd feed us like that today? That was another age. Now everybody thinks about saving his money. Don't spend for weddings, don't spend for funerals! I ask you, if they keep on hoarding the wealth they've squeezed out of the poor, where are they going to put it? But they keep on hoarding. When it comes to spending any money they say they have to economize.'

'You must have eaten a good twenty *puris*?'

'I ate more than twenty.'

'I would have eaten fifty!'

---

3. *Puris* are flat, circular pieces of fried bread. *Ghee* is clarified butter.

'I couldn't have eaten any less than fifty. I was a husky lad in those days. You're not half so big.'

After finishing the potatoes they drank some water and right there in front of the fire they wrapped themselves up in their *dhotis*[4] and pulling up their knees they fell asleep—just like two enormous coiled pythons.

And Budhiya was still moaning.

*   *   *

In the morning Madhav went inside the hut and saw that his wife had turned cold. Flies were buzzing around her mouth. Her stony eyes stared upwards. Her whole body was covered with dust. The child had died in her womb.

Madhav ran to get Ghisu. Then they both began to moan wildly and beat their chests. When they heard the wailing the neighbours came running and according to the old tradition began to console the bereaved.

But there was not much time for moaning and chest-beating. There was the worry about a shroud and wood for the pyre. The money in the house had disappeared like carrion in a kite's nest.

Father and son went weeping to the village *zamindar*.[5] He hated the sight of the two of them and several times he'd thrashed them with his own hands for stealing or for not coming to do the work they'd promised to do. He asked, 'What is it, little Ghisu, what are you crying about? You don't show yourself much these days. It seems as though you don't want to live in this village.'

Ghisu bowed his head all the way to the ground, his eyes full of tears, and said, 'Excellency, an awful thing's happened to me. Madhav's woman passed away last night. She was in agony the whole time. The two of us never once left her side. We did whatever we could, gave her medicine—but to make a long story short, she gave us the slip. And now there's nobody left even to give us a piece of bread, master. We're ruined! My house has been destroyed! I'm your slave—except for you now who is there to see that she's given a decent funeral? Whatever we had we spent on medicine. If your excellency is merciful, then she'll have a good funeral. Whose door can we go to except yours?'

The *zamindar* was soft-hearted. But to be kind to Ghisu was like trying to dye a black blanket. He was tempted to say, 'Get out and don't come back! When we send for you, you don't show up but today when you're in a jam you come and flatter me. You're a sponging bastard!' But this was not the occasion for anger or scolding. Exasperated, he took out a couple of rupees and threw them on the ground. But he didn't utter a word of consolation. He didn't even look at Ghisu. It was as though he'd shoved a load off his head.

When the *zamindar* had given two rupees how could the shopkeepers

---

4. A *dhoti* is the loincloth worn by Hindu men.

5. A land-tax official, or, more generally, a landholder with an official capacity.

and moneylenders of the village refuse? Ghisu knew how to trumpet the *zamindar*'s name around. Somebody gave him a couple of *annas*,[6] somebody else four. Within an hour Ghisu had harvested a tidy sum of five rupees. He got grain at one place, wood from somewhere else. And at noon Ghisu and Madhav went to the market to get a shroud. There were people already cutting the bamboo to make a litter for the corpse.

The tender-hearted women of the village came and looked at the dead woman, shed a few tears over her forlorn state and went away.

\* \* \*

When they reached the market Ghisu said, 'We have enough wood to burn her up completely, haven't we, Madhav?'

'Yes, there's plenty of wood, now we need the shroud.'

'That's right, come along and we'll pick up a cheap one.'

'Of course, what else? By the time we move the corpse it will be night—who can see a shroud at night?'

'What a rotten custom it is that somebody who didn't even have rags to cover herself while she was alive has to have a new shroud when she dies!'

'The shroud just burns right up with the body.'

'And what's left? If we'd had these five rupees before then we could have got some medicine.'

Each of them guessed what was in the other's mind. They went on wandering through the market, stopping at one cloth-merchant's shop after another. They looked at different kinds of cloth, silk and cotton, but nothing met with their approval. This went on until evening. Then the two of them, by some divine inspiration or other, found themselves in front of a liquor shop, and as though according to a previous agreement they went inside. For a little while they stood there, hesitant. Then Ghisu went up to where the tavernkeeper sat and said, 'Sahuji, give us a bottle too.'

Then some snacks arrived, fried fish was brought and they sat on the verandah and tranquilly began to drink.

After drinking several cups in a row they began to feel tipsy. Ghisu said, 'What's the point of throwing a shroud over her? In the end it just burns up. She can't take anything with her.'

Madhav looked toward heaven and said, as though calling on the gods to witness his innocence, 'It's the way things are done in the world, otherwise why would people throw thousands of rupees away on Brahmans? Who can tell if anybody gets it in the next world or not?'

'The bigshots have lots of money to squander so let them squander it, but what have we got to squander?'

'But how will you explain it to people? Won't they ask, "Where's the shroud?"'

Ghisu laughed. 'So what? We'll say the money fell out of the knot in our *dhotis* and we looked and looked but couldn't find it. They won't believe it but they'll give the money again.'

---

6. An *anna* is a copper coin formerly used in India and Pakistan.

Madhav laughed too over this unexpected stroke of luck. He said, 'She was good to us, that poor girl—even dying she got us fine things to eat and drink.'

They'd gone through more than half a bottle. Ghisu ordered four pounds of puris. Then relish, pickle, livers. There was a shop right across from the tavern. Madhav brought everything back in a trice on a couple of leaf-platters. He'd spent one and a half rupees; only a few pice were left.

The two of them sat eating their puris in the lordly manner of tigers enjoying their kill in the jungle. They felt neither fear of being called to account nor concern for a bad reputation. They had overcome those sensibilities long before.

Ghisu said philosophically, 'If our souls are content won't it be credited to her in heaven as a good deed?'

Respectfully Madhav bowed his head and confirmed, 'Absolutely will! Lord, you know all secrets. Bring her to paradise—we bless her from our hearts . . . the way we've eaten today we've never eaten before in our whole lives.'

A moment later a doubt rose in his mind. He said, 'What about us, are we going to get there some day too?'

Ghisu gave no answer to this artless question. He didn't want to dampen his pleasure by thinking about the other world.

'But if she asks us there, "Why didn't you people give me a shroud?" What will you say?'

'That's a stupid question!'

'But surely she'll ask!'

'How do you know she won't get a shroud? Do you think I'm such a jackass? Have I been wasting my time in this world for sixty years? She'll have a shroud and a good one too.'

Madhav was not convinced. He said, 'Who'll give it? You've eaten up all the money. But she'll ask me. I was the one who put the cinnabar in her hair at the wedding.'

Getting angry, Ghisu said, 'I tell you she'll have a shroud, aren't you listening?'

'But why don't you tell me who's going to give it?'

'The same people who gave before will give the money again—well, not the money this time but the stuff we need.'

As the darkness spread and the stars began to glitter the gaiety of the tavern also increased steadily. People sang, bragged, embraced their companions, lifted the jug to the lips of friends. All was intoxication, the very air was tipsy. Anybody who came in got drunk in an instant from just a few drops, the air of the place turned their heads more than the liquor. The sufferings of their lives drew them all there and after a little while they were no longer aware if they were alive or dead, not alive or not dead.

And father and son went on slopping it up with zest. Everyone was staring at them. How lucky the two of them were, they had a whole bottle between themselves.

When he was crammed full Madhav handed the leftover puris on a leaf to a beggar who was standing watching them with famished eyes. And for the first time in his life he experienced the pride, the happiness and the pleasure of giving.

Ghisu said, 'Take it, eat it and say a blessing—the one who earned it is—well, she's dead. But surely your blessing will reach her. Bless her from your heart, that food's the wages for very hard labour.'

Madhav looked heavenward again and said, 'She'll go to heaven, *Dada,* she'll be a queen in heaven.'

Ghisu stood up and as though bathing in waves of bliss he said, 'Yes, son, she'll go to heaven. She didn't torment anybody, she didn't oppress anybody. At the moment she died she fulfilled the deepest wish of all our lives. If she doesn't go to heaven then will those big fat people go who rob the poor with both hands and swim in the Ganges and offer holy water in the temples to wash away their sins?'

Their mood of credulity suddenly changed. Volatility is the special characteristic of drunkenness. Now was the turn for grief and despair.

'But *Dada,*' Madhav said, 'the poor girl suffered so much in this life! How much pain she had when she died.'

He put his hands over his eyes and began to cry, he burst into sobs.

Ghisu consoled him. 'Why weep, son? Be glad she's slipped out of this maze of illusion and left the whole mess behind her. She was very lucky to escape the bonds of the world's illusion so quickly.'

And the two of them stood up and began to sing.

'Deceitful world, why do you dazzle us with your eyes?
Deceitful world!'

The eyes of all the drunkards were glued on them and the two of them became inebriated in their hearts. Then they started to dance, they jumped and sprang, fell back, twisted, they gesticulated, they mimed their feelings, and finally they collapsed dead drunk right there.

## ■ Jibanananda Das (1899–1954) *Bangladesh* (poem)

### TRANSLATED BY CHIDANANDA DAS GUPTA

Jibanananda Das was born in Barisal, East Bengal (now Bangladesh) in 1899, where, in his early years, he was educated at home, because his father disapproved of formal schooling. He graduated from the University of Calcutta, taking a master's degree in English literature, and taught English literature in Calcutta City College and at Barisal. He was killed in 1954 in a Calcutta streetcar accident. His *Selected Poems* was awarded the highest honor of the Indian National Academy of Letters after his death. His other books include *Fallen Feathers* (1928), *Gray Manuscript* (1936), *The*

*Great Earth* (1944), and *Darkness of the Seven Stars* (1948). He was a lyrical poet, a sensitive practitioner of "pure poetry." Donald Junkins writes of his work: "The mellifluous and dreamlike poems of Jibanananda Das celebrate the senses, yet they express a biting, ironic view of the world. Jibanananda's sounds are liquid, his landscapes reverie-like, and his vision detached; it is as if we are reading the poems through softly lighted glass."[1]

## Grass

This dawning fills the earth
    With soft green light like tender lemon leaves;
Grass as green as the unripe pomelo[1] — such a fragrance —
    The does tear it with their teeth!
I, too, crave this grass-fragrance like green wine;
    I drink glass after glass.
I stroke the body of the grass — I smooth it eye to eye;
    My feathers on the wings of the grass
I am born as grass amid grass from some deep mother-grass,    5
    I descend from the sweet darkness of her body.

## ■ R. K. Narayan (1906– ) *English* (story)

R. K. Narayan was one of nine children born in Madras in South India to a high caste family of Brahmans. His father was a schoolmaster, and from an early age Narayan wished to be a writer. After taking a B.A. at Maharaja College in Mysore, he married in 1934 but lost his wife after only five years.

    Narayan writes in English, though his native language is Tamil, and many of his tales are set in the fictional town of Malgudi, in South India, a town that resembles the places of his childhood. Through his friendship with Graham Greene, his work was introduced to the West, and he has since become the most celebrated fiction writer to come out of modern India. In the introduction to *Under the Banyan Tree,* Narayan writes that "all theories of writing are bogus. . . . A story comes in being for some unknown reason and anyhow." However, he does say that "at one time I found material for my stories in the open air, market-place, and streets of

---

1. Junkins, Donald, ed. *The Contemporary World Poets.* New York: Harcourt Brace Jovanovitch, 1976, p. 17.

---

1. *Pomelo:* largest known citrus fruit; pear-shaped with coarse, dry flesh.

Mysore . . . [and in] the sheer pleasure of watching people." He has written more than a dozen novels, five collections of short stories, and in addition to retelling India's legends in *Gods, Demons and Others,* he has abridged and retold the great Sanskrit epics in two volumes: *The Ramayana* and *The Mahabharata.* He has also written a volume of memoirs, *My Days.* Some of his novels include *Swami and Friends* (1935), *The Bachelor of Arts* (1937), *The Dark Room* (1938), *The Financial Expert* (1952), *Waiting for the Mahatma* (1955), *The Guide* (1958)—which received the National Prize of the Indian Literary Academy, India's highest literary honor—and *A Tiger for Malgudi* (1983). In recognition of many years of distinguished writing, he received an honorary Doctor of Literature degree at Leeds in 1967.

## Forty-Five a Month

Shanta could not stay in her class any longer. She had done clay-modelling, music, drill, a bit of alphabets and numbers and was now cutting coloured paper. She would have to cut till the bell rang and the teacher said, "Now you may all go home," or "Put away the scissors and take up your alphabets—" Shanta was impatient to know the time. She asked her friend sitting next to her, "Is it five now?"

"Maybe," she replied.

"Or is it six?"

"I don't think so," her friend replied, "because night comes at six."

"Do you think it is five?"

"Yes."

"Oh, I must go. My father will be back at home now. He has asked me to be ready at five. He is taking me to the cinema this evening. I must go home." She threw down her scissors and ran up to the teacher. "Madam, I must go home."

"Why, Shanta Bai?"

"Because it is five o'clock now."

"Who told you it was five?"

"Kamala."

"It is not five now. It is—do you see the clock there? Tell me what the time is. I taught you to read the clock the other day." Shanta stood gazing at the clock in the hall, counted the figures laboriously and declared, "It is nine o'clock."

The teacher called the other girls and said, "Who will tell me the time from that clock?" Several of them concurred with Shanta and said it was nine o'clock, till the teacher said, "You are seeing only the long hand. See the short one, where is it?"

"Two and a half."

"So what is the time?"

"Two and a half."

"It is two forty-five, understand? Now you may all go to your seats—" Shanta returned to the teacher in about ten minutes and asked, "Is it five, madam, because I have to be ready at five. Otherwise my father will be very angry with me. He asked me to return home early."

"At what time?"

"Now." The teacher gave her permission to leave, and Shanta picked up her books and dashed out of the class with a cry of joy. She ran home, threw her books on the floor and shouted, "Mother, Mother," and Mother came running from the next house, where she had gone to chat with her friends.

Mother asked, "Why are you back so early?"

"Has Father come home?" Shanta asked. She would not take her coffee or tiffin[1] but insisted on being dressed first. She opened the trunk and insisted on wearing the thinnest frock and knickers, while her mother wanted to dress her in a long skirt and thick coat for the evening. Shanta picked out a gorgeous ribbon from a cardboard soap box in which she kept pencils, ribbons and chalk bits. There was a heated argument between mother and daughter over the dress, and finally Mother had to give in. Shanta put on her favourite pink frock, braided her hair and flaunted a green ribbon on her pigtail. She powdered her face and pressed a vermilion mark on her forehead. She said, "Now Father will say what a nice girl I am because I'm ready. Aren't you also coming, Mother?"

"Not today."

Shanta stood at the little gate looking down the street.

Mother said, "Father will come only after five; don't stand in the sun. It is only four o'clock."

The sun was disappearing behind the house on the opposite row, and Shanta knew that presently it would be dark. She ran in to her mother and asked, "Why hasn't Father come home yet, Mother?"

"How can I know? He is perhaps held up in the office."

Shanta made a wry face. "I don't like these people in the office. They are bad people—"

She went back to the gate and stood looking out. Her mother shouted from inside, "Come in, Shanta. It is getting dark, don't stand there." But Shanta would not go in. She stood at the gate and a wild idea came into her head. Why should she not go to the office and call out Father and then go to the cinema? She wondered where his office might be. She had no notion. She had seen her father take the turn at the end of the street every day. If one went there, perhaps one went automatically to Father's office. She threw a glance about to see if Mother was anywhere and moved down the street.

---

1. Midday snack.

It was twilight. Everyone going about looked gigantic, walls of houses appeared very high and cycles and carriages looked as though they would bear down on her. She walked on the very edge of the road. Soon the lamps were twinkling, and the passers-by looked like shadows. She had taken two turns and did not know where she was. She sat down on the edge of the road biting her nails. She wondered how she was to reach home. A servant employed in the next house was passing along, and she picked herself up and stood before him.

"Oh, what are you doing here all alone?" he asked. She replied, "I don't know. I came here. Will you take me to our house?" She followed him and was soon back in her house.

Venkat Rao, Shanta's father, was about to start for his office that morning when a *jutka*[2] passed along the street distributing cinema handbills. Shanta dashed to the street and picked up a handbill. She held it up and asked, "Father, will you take me to the cinema today?" He felt unhappy at the question. Here was the child growing up without having any of the amenities and the simple pleasures of life. He had hardly taken her twice to the cinema. He had no time for the child. While children of her age in other houses had all the dolls, dresses and outings that they wanted, this child was growing up all alone and like a barbarian more or less. He felt furious with his office. For forty rupees[3] a month they seemed to have purchased him outright.

He reproached himself for neglecting his wife and child—even the wife could have her own circle of friends and so on: she was after all a grown-up, but what about the child? What a drab, colourless existence was hers! Every day they kept him at the office till seven or eight in the evening, and when he came home the child was asleep. Even on Sundays they wanted him at the office. Why did they think he had no personal life, a life of his own? They gave him hardly any time to take the child to the park or the pictures. He was going to show them that they weren't to toy with him. Yes, he was prepared even to quarrel with his manager if necessary.

He said with resolve, "I will take you to the cinema this evening. Be ready at five."

"Really! Mother!" Shanta shouted. Mother came out of the kitchen.

"Father is taking me to a cinema in the evening."

Shanta's mother smiled cynically. "Don't make false promises to the child—" Venkat Rao glared at her. "Don't talk nonsense. You think you are the only person who keeps promises—"

He told Shanta, "Be ready at five, and I will come and take you positively. If you are not ready, I will be very angry with you."

---

2. A two-wheeled horse-drawn carriage.

3. A rupee is an Indian unit of money.

He walked to his office full of resolve. He would do his normal work and get out at five. If they started any old tricks of theirs, he was going to tell the boss, "Here is my resignation. My child's happiness is more important to me than these horrible papers of yours."

All day the usual stream of papers flowed onto his table and off it. He scrutinized, signed and drafted. He was corrected, admonished and insulted. He had a break of only five minutes in the afternoon for his coffee.

When the office clock struck five and the other clerks were leaving, he went up to the manager and said, "May I go, sir?" The manager looked up from his paper. "You!" It was unthinkable that the cash and account section should be closing at five. "How can you go?"

"I have some urgent private business, sir," he said, smothering the lines he had been rehearsing since the morning: "Herewith my resignation." He visualized Shanta standing at the door, dressed and palpitating with eagerness.

"There shouldn't be anything more urgent than the office work; go back to your seat. You know how many hours I work?" asked the manager. The manager came to the office three hours before opening time and stayed nearly three hours after closing, even on Sundays. The clerks commented among themselves, "His wife must be whipping him whenever he is seen at home; that is why the old owl seems so fond of his office."

"Did you trace the source of that ten-eight difference?" asked the manager.

"I shall have to examine two hundred vouchers. I thought we might do it tomorrow."

"No, no, this won't do. You must rectify it immediately."

Venkat Rao mumbled, "Yes, sir," and slunk back to his seat. The clock showed 5:30. Now it meant two hours of excruciating search among vouchers. All the rest of the office had gone. Only he and another clerk in his section were working, and of course, the manager was there. Venkat Rao was furious. His mind was made up. He wasn't a slave who had sold himself for forty rupees outright. He could make that money easily; and if he couldn't, it would be more honourable to die of starvation.

He took a sheet of paper and wrote: "Herewith my resignation. If you people think you have bought me body and soul for forty rupees, you are mistaken. I think it would be far better for me and my family to die of starvation than slave for this petty forty rupees on which you have kept me for years and years. I suppose you have not the slightest notion of giving me an increment. You give yourselves heavy slices frequently, and I don't see why you shouldn't think of us occasionally. In any case it doesn't interest me now, since this is my resignation. If I and my family perish of starvation, may our ghosts come and haunt you all your life—" He folded the letter, put it in an envelope, sealed the flap and addressed it to the manager. He left his seat and stood before the manager. The manager mechanically received the letter and put it on his pad.

"Venkat Rao," said the manager, "I'm sure you will be glad to hear this news. Our officer discussed the question of increments today, and I've recommended you for an increment of five rupees. Orders are not yet passed, so keep this to yourself for the present." Venkat Rao put out his hand, snatched the envelope from the pad and hastily slipped it in his pocket.

"What is that letter?"

"I have applied for a little casual leave, sir, but I think . . ."

"You can't get any leave for at least a fortnight to come."

"Yes, sir. I realize that. That is why I am withdrawing my application, sir."

"Very well, Have you traced that mistake?"

"I'm scrutinizing the vouchers, sir. I will find it out within an hour. . . ."

It was nine o'clock when he went home. Shanta was already asleep. Her mother said, "She wouldn't even change her frock, thinking that any moment you might be coming and taking her out. She hardly ate any food; and wouldn't lie down for fear of crumpling her dress. . . ."

Venkat Rao's heart bled when he saw his child sleeping in her pink frock, hair combed and face powdered, dressed and ready to be taken out. "Why should I not take her to the night show?" He shook her gently and called, "Shanta, Shanta." Shanta kicked her legs and cried, irritated at being disturbed. Mother whispered, "Don't wake her," and patted her back to sleep.

Venkat Rao watched the child for a moment. "I don't know if it is going to be possible for me to take her out at all—you see, they are giving me an increment—" he wailed.

## ■ Faiz Ahmed Faiz (1911–1984) *Urdu* (poems)

TRANSLATED BY NAOMI LAZARD

Pakistani poet Faiz Ahmed Faiz was editor of *The Pakistani Times* for many years and was awarded the Lenin Peace Prize in 1970. In 1979, he became editor of *Lotus,* a third-world literary magazine. He was certainly the best-known Pakistani poet of his day, and when he participated in poetry contests, up to fifty thousand people would gather to listen. Many of his poems have been set to music by established musicians. Faiz was born in 1911 in Sialkot, studied in Lahore, took a lectureship at Amritsar, and was involved with the Indian labor movement. In World War II, he served in the British Indian Army, and in the postwar period, he used his position at *The Pakistani Times* to speak out for social justice. In 1951, his outspokenness landed him in trouble with the authorities, who arrested him and put him on trial for his life. He was sentenced to four years in prison, one of three stays in the penitentiary, where he often suffered solitary confinement.

In his poetry, he often uses traditional meters, and his ghazals on love draw on a deep Urdu tradition; his political sufferings also inform his poetry. He died in 1984.

**FURTHER READING:** Kiernan, V. G., tr. *Poems by Faiz,* 1962. Lazard, Naomi, tr. *The True Subject: Selected Poems of Faiz Ahmed Faiz,* 1988. Sucha, Sain, tr. *Memory: Poetry of Faiz Ahmad Faiz,* 1987.

## Before You Came

Before you came things were just what they were:
the road precisely a road, the horizon fixed,
the limit of what could be seen;
a glass of wine no more than a glass of wine.

Then the world took on the tints of my heart;                   5
magnolia-petaled happiness of seeing you,
slate the color that fell
when I was fed up with everything.

With your advent roses burst into flame;
you were the author of dried-up leaves,                          10
the dust, poison, blood.
You colored the night black.

As for the sky, the road, the cup of wine:
one was my tear-drenched shirt,
the other an aching nerve;                                       15
the third a mirror that never reflected the same thing.

This was all before you left me.

Now you have come back. Stay.
This time things will fall into place again;
the road can be the road,                                        20
the sky, sky;
the glass of wine, as it should be, the glass of wine.

## Prison Meeting

This night is the tree of pain,
          greater than you or me,
greater because in its thicket of branches
a thousand candle-bearing stars have lost their way.
In this tree's shadow another thousand moons

have wept the last of their light.
This night is hell's own black
yet the darkness flares with your beauty.
It is a golden stream; a river of blood
flows back on its nether side.

This night is the tree of pain,
        vaster than you or me.
The tree lets go of a few pale leaves
that fall upon your hair, an incarnation of roses.
From its dew some moments of silence
        send rain onto your brow;
it forms a pearly diadem.
This tree is the essence of black;
its branches break my heart
but I pull them out, arrow after arrow.
These will be my weapons.

Morning of the grief-stricken, the heart-broken,
is not somewhere in the future; it is here
the shafts of pain have flowered into dawn's coral streaks.
It is here the murderous blade of grief
is changed into sparks, light ray against light ray.
This grief whose ashes burn in the rosebush of your arms;
this fruit garnered from the tree of pain
is my faith which is larger than any pain!
This morning that is on its way more
        bounteous than any night!

## ■ Ruth Prawer Jhabvala (1927– ) *English* (story)

    Ruth Prawer Jhabvala was born in Cologne, Germany, to a Polish-Jewish family and moved to England in 1939. She went to Queen Mary College of London University, earning a master's degree; she married C. S. H. Jhabvala in 1951, and they moved to Delhi. Her work reflects the makeup of contemporary Indian society, dealing often with women's issues and, at times, with the attitudes and roles of the expatriate community. This story, "Picnic with Moonlight and Mangoes," comes from her book *How I Became a Holy Mother and Other Stories* (1976). In addition to three other short story collections, Jhabvala has published *Out of India: Selected Stories* (1986) and many novels. She has been awarded England's Booker Prize and a MacArthur Foundation Award, in addition to other prestigious awards. She also wrote the screenplay for the Academy Award–winning movie *A Room With a View*.

**FURTHER READING:** Gooneratne, Yasmine. *Silence, Exile, and Cunning: The Fiction of Ruth Prawer Jhabvala*, 1983.

## Picnic with Moonlight and Mangoes

Unfortunately the town in which Sri Prakash lived was a small one so that everyone knew what had happened to him. At first he did not go out at all, on account of feeling so ashamed; but, as the weeks dragged on, sitting at home became very dreary. He also began to realize that, with thinking and solitude, he was probably exaggerating the effect of his misfortune on other people. Misfortune could befall anyone, any time; there was really no need to be ashamed. So one morning when his home seemed particularly depressing he made up his mind to pay a visit to the coffee house. He left while his wife was having her bath—he told her he was going, he shouted it through the bathroom door, and if she did not hear above the running water that was obviously not his fault.

So when he came home and she asked him where he had been, he could say 'I *told* you' with a perfectly good conscience. He was glad of that because he could see she had been worried about him. While she served him his food, he did his best to reassure her. He told her how pleased they had all been to see him in the coffee house. Even the waiter had been pleased and had brought his usual order without having to be told. His wife said nothing but went on patiently serving him. Then he began somewhat to exaggerate the heartiness of the welcome he had received. He said things which, though not strictly true, had a good effect—not so much on her (she continued silently to serve him) as on himself. By the time he had finished eating and talking, he was perfectly reassured as to what had happened that morning. The little cloud of unease with which he had come home was dispelled. He realized now that no one had looked at him queerly, and that there had been no undertones in their 'Just see who is here.' It was only his over-sensitive nature that had made it seem like that.

He had always had a very sensitive nature: a poet's temperament. He was proud of it, but there was no denying that it had been the cause of many troubles to him—including the present one. The facts of the case were these: Sri Prakash, a gazetted government officer, had been suspended from his post in the State Ministry of Telecommunication while an inquiry was instituted regarding certain accusations against him. These were based on the words of a man who was a drunkard, a liar, and a convicted perjurer. His name was Goel and he was the father of a Miss Nimmi. Miss Nimmi had come to Sri Prakash to inquire about a possible vacancy as typist in his office. Sri Prakash had sincerely tried to help the girl, calling her for interviews several times, and the result of his good intentions had been that she had complained of his misbehaviour towards her. The father, after visiting Sri Prakash both in his office and at home and finding him not the man to yield to blackmail and extortion, had carried the complaint to Sri Prakash's superiors in the department. From there on events had taken their course. Naturally it was all extremely unpleasant for Sri Prakash—a family man, a husband and father of three respectably married daughters—but, as he was always telling his wife, he had no doubts that in the end truth and justice would prevail.

She never made any comment when he said that. She was by nature a silent woman: silent and virtuous. How virtuous! She was the ideal of all a mother and wife should be. He thanked God that he had it in him to appreciate her character. He worshipped her. He often told her so, and told everyone else too—his daughters, people in the office, sometimes even complete strangers (for instance, once a man he had shared a rickshaw with). Also how he was ready to tear himself into a thousand pieces, or lie down in the middle of the main bazaar by the clock tower and let all who came trample on him with their feet if by such an action he could save her one moment's anxiety. In this present misfortune there was of course a lot of anxiety. There was not only the moral hardship but also the practical one of having his salary held in arrears while the inquiry took its course. Already they had spent whatever his wife had managed to lay by and had had to sell the one or two pieces of jewelry that still remained from her dowry. Now they were dependent for their household expenses on whatever their sons-in-law could contribute. It was a humiliating position for a proud man, but what was to be done? There was no alternative, he could not allow his wife to starve. But when his daughters came to the house and untied the money from the ends of their saris to give to their mother, he could not restrain his tears from flowing. His daughters were not as sympathetic towards him as his wife. They made no attempts to comfort him but looked at him in a way that made him feel worse. Then he would leave them and go to lie down on his bed. His daughters stayed for a while, but he did not come out again. He could hear them talking to their mother, and sometimes he heard sounds like the mother weeping. These sounds were unbearable to him, and he had to cover his head with the pillow so as not to hear them.

\* \* \*

After that first visit to the coffee house, he continued to go every day. It was good to meet his friends again. He had always loved company. In the past, when he was still king in his own office, people had dropped in on him there all day long. At eleven o'clock they had all adjourned to the coffee house where they had drunk many cups of coffee and smoked many cigarettes and talked on many subjects. He had talked the most, and everyone had listened to and applauded him. But nowadays everything was changed. It was not only that he could not afford to drink coffee or pay for his own cigarettes: other things too were not as they had been. He himself was not as he had been. He had always been so gay and made jokes at which everyone laughed. Once he had jumped up on the table and had executed a dance there. He had stamped his feet and made ankle-bell noises with his tongue. And how they had laughed, standing around him in a circle—his friends and other customers, even the waiters: they had clapped their hands and spurred him on till he had jumped from the table—hands extended like a diver—and landed amid cheers and laughter in the arms held out to catch him.

Although nothing like that happened now, he continued to visit the coffee house regularly every morning; soon he was going regularly every evening too. There was usually a large party of friends, but one evening when he went there was no one—only a waiter flicking around with his dirty cloth, and a silent old widower, a regular customer, eating vegetable cutlets. The waiter was surly—he always had been, even in the days when Sri Prakash had still been able to hand out tips—and it was only after repeated inquiries that he condescended to say that, didn't Sri Prakash know? Hadn't they told him? They had all gone to Moti Bagh for a moonlight picnic with mangoes. Sri Prakash slapped his forehead, pretending he had known about it but had forgotten. It was an unconvincing performance and the waiter sneered, but Sri Prakash could not worry about that now. He had to concentrate on getting himself out of the coffee house without showing how he was feeling.

He walked in the street by himself. It was evening, there was a lot of traffic and the shops were full. Hawkers with trays bumped in and out of the crowds on the sidewalks. On one side the sky was melting in a rush of orange while on the other the evening star sparkled, alone and aloof, like a jewel made of ice. Exquisite hour—hour of high thoughts and romantic feelings! It had always been so for Sri Prakash and was so still. Only where was he to go, who was there to share with him the longing for beauty that flooded his heart?

'Oh-ho, oh-ho! Just see who is here!'

Someone had bumped against him in the crowd, now stood and held his arms in a gesture of affectionate greeting. It was the last person Sri Prakash would have wished to meet: Goel, the father of Miss Nimmi, his accuser, his enemy, the cause of his ruin and tears. Goel seemed genuinely delighted by this meeting; he continued to hold Sri Prakash by the arms and even squeezed them to show his pleasure. Sri Prakash jerked himself free and hurried away. The other followed him; he protested at this unfriendliness, demanded to know its cause. He claimed a misunderstanding. He followed Sri Prakash so close that he trod on his heels. Then Sri Prakash stood still and turned round.

'Forgive me,' said Goel. He meant for treading on his heels; he even made the traditional self-humbling gesture of one seeking forgiveness. They stood facing each other. They were about the same height—both were short and plump, though Goel was flabbier. Like Sri Prakash, he also was bald as a ball.

Sri Prakash could hardly believe his ears: Goel was asking him to come home with him. He insisted, he said he had some bottles of country liquor at home, and what good luck that he should have run into Sri Prakash just at this moment when he had been wondering what good friend he could invite to come and share them with him? When Sri Prakash indignantly refused, tried to walk on, Goel held on to him. 'Why not?' he insisted. 'Where else will you go?'

Then Sri Prakash remembered where everyone else had gone. The moonlight picnic at Moti Bagh was an annual outing. The procedure was always the same: the friends hired a bus and, together with their baskets of mangoes and crates of local whisky, had themselves driven out to Moti Bagh. They sang boisterous songs all the way. At Moti Bagh they cut up some of the mangoes and sucked the juice out of others. Their mouths became sticky and sweet and this taste might have become unpleasant if they had not kept washing it out with the whisky. They became very rowdy. They waited for the moon to rise. When it did, their mood changed. Moti Bagh was a famous beauty spot, an abandoned and half-ruined palace built by a seventeenth-century prince at the height of his own glory and that of his dynasty. When the moon shone on it, it became spectral, a marble ghost that evoked thoughts of the passing of all earthly things. Poems were recited, sad songs sung; a few tears flowed. Someone played the flute—as a matter of fact, this was Sri Prakash who had always taken a prominent part in these outings. But this year they had gone without him.

Goel did not live in a very nice part of town. The bazaar, though once quite prosperous, now catered mainly for poorer people; the rooms on top of the shops had been converted into one-night hotels. Goel's house, which was in a network of alleys leading off from this bazaar, would have been difficult to find for anyone unfamiliar with the geography of the locality. The geography of his house was also quite intricate, as every available bit of space—in the courtyard, galleries, and on staircase landings—had been partitioned between different tenants. Goel and his daughter Miss Nimmi had one long narrow room to themselves; they had strung a piece of string halfway across to serve as both clothes-line and partition. At first Sri Prakash thought the room was empty, but after they had been there for some time Goel shouted 'Oy!' When he received no answer, he pushed aside the pieces of clothing hanging from the string and revealed Miss Nimmi lying fast asleep on a mat on the floor.

Goel had to shout several times before she woke up. Then she rose from the mat—very slowly, as if struggling up from the depths of a sea of sleep—and sat there, blinking. Her sari had slipped from her breasts, but she did not notice. She also did not notice that they had a visitor. She was always slow in everything, slow and heavy. Her father had to shout, 'Don't you see who has come!' She blinked a few more times, and then very, very slowly she smiled and very, very slowly she lifted the sari to cover her breasts.

Goel told her to find two glasses. She got up and rummaged around the room. After a time she said there was only one. Sri Prakash said it didn't matter, he had to go anyway; he said he was in a hurry, he had to catch a bus for Moti Bagh where his friends awaited him. He got up but his host pressed him down again, asking what was the point of going now, why not stay here, they would have a good time together. 'Look,' Goel said, 'I've got money.' He emptied out his pockets and he did have money—a wad of bank notes, God knew where they had come from. He let Sri Prakash look his fill at them before putting them back. He said let's go to Badshahbad, we'll take the liquor and mangoes and we'll have a moonlight picnic of our own. He got very excited by this idea. Sri Prakash said neither yes nor no. Goel told Miss Nimmi to change into something nice, and she disappeared behind the clothes-line and got busy there. Sri Prakash did not look in that direction, but the room was saturated by her the way a store room in which ripe apples are kept becomes saturated by their savour and smell.

Badshahbad was not as far off as Moti Bagh—in fact, it was just at the outskirts of town and could be reached very quickly. It too was a deserted pleasure palace but had been built two centuries later than the one at Moti Bagh and as a rather gaudy imitation of it. However, now in the dark it looked just the same. The surrounding silence and emptiness, the smell of dust, the occasional jackal cry were also the same. At first Sri Prakash felt rather depressed, but his mood changed after he had drunk some of Goel's liquor. Goel was determined to have a good time, and Miss Nimmi, though silent, also seemed to be enjoying herself. She was cutting up the mangoes and eating rather a lot of them. The three of them sat in the dark, waiting for the moon to rise.

Goel fell into a reminiscent mood. He began to recall all the wonderful things he had done in his life: how he had sold a second-hand imported car for Rs.50,000, and once he had arranged false passports for a whole party of Sikh carpenters. All these activities had brought in fat commissions for himself—amply deserved, because everything had been achieved only through his good contacts. That was his greatest asset in life—his contacts, all the important people he had access to. He ticked them off on his fingers: the Under Secretary to the Welfare Ministry, the Deputy Minister of Mines and Fuel, all the top officers in the income tax department . . . He challenged Sri Prakash, he said: 'Name any big name, go as high as you like, and see if I don't know him.'

Sri Prakash got excited, he cried: 'My goodness! Big names—big people—whenever there was anything to be done, everyone said, "Ask Sri Prakash, he knows everyone, he has them all in his pocket." Once there was a function to felicitate our departmental Secretary on his promotion. The principal organizers came to me and said, "Sri Prakash, we need a VIP to grace the occasion." I replied, "I will get you the Chief Minister himself, just wait and see." And I did. I went to him, I said, "Sir, kindly give us the honour of your presence," and he replied, "Certainly, Sri Prakash, with pleasure." There and then he told his secretary to make a note of the appointment.'

'When I go into the Secretariat building,' Goel said, 'the peons stand up and salute. I don't bother with appointments. The personal assistant opens the big shot's door and says, "Sir, Goel has come." They know I don't come with empty hands. I slip it under their papers, no word spoken, they don't notice, I don't notice. The figures are all fixed, no need to haggle: 1000 to an Under Secretary, 2000 to a Deputy. Each has his price.'

Goel smiled and drank. Sri Prakash also drank. The liquor, illicitly distilled, had a foul and acrid taste. Sri Prakash remembered reading in the papers quite recently how a whole colony of labourers had been wiped out through drinking illicit country liquor. Nothing could be done for them, it had rotted them through and through.

Goel said: 'Let alone the Secretaries, there are also the Ministers to be taken care of. Some of them are very costly. Naturally, their term is short, no one can tell what will happen at the next elections. So their mouths are always wide open. You must be knowing Dev Kishan—'

'Dev Kishan!' Sri Prakash cried. 'He and I are like that! Like that!' He held up two fingers, pressed close together.

'There was some work in his Ministry, it was rather a tricky job and I was called in. I went to his house and came straight to the point. "Dev Kishan Sahib," I said—'

Sri Prakash suddenly lost his temper: 'Dev Kishan is not this type at all!' When Goel sniggered, he became more excited: 'A person like you would not understand a person like him at all. And I don't believe you went to his house—'

'Come with me right now!' Goel shouted. 'We will go together to his house and then you will see how he receives me—'

'Not Dev Kishan!' Sri Prakash shouted back. 'Someone else—not he—'

'He! The same!'

Although they were both shouting at the tops of their voices, Miss Nimmi went on placidly sucking mangoes. Probably the subject was of no interest to her; probably also she was used to people getting excited while drinking.

'As a matter of fact,' Goel sneered, 'shall I let you into a secret—his mouth is open wider than anyone's, they call him The Pit because he can never get enough, your Dev Kishan.'

'I don't believe you,' Sri Prakash said again, though not so fervently now. He really had no particular interest in defending this man. It was only that the mention of his name had called up a rather painful memory.

When his troubles had first begun, Sri Prakash had run around from one influential person to another. Most people would not receive him, and he had had to content himself with sitting waiting in their outer offices and putting his case to such of their clerical staff as would listen. Dev Kishan, however, was one of the few people who *had* received him. Sri Prakash had been ushered into his ministerial office which had two air-conditioners and an inscribed portrait of the President of India. Dev Kishan had sat behind an enormous desk, but he had not asked Sri Prakash to take the chair opposite. He had not looked at Sri Prakash either but had fixed his gaze above his head. Sri Prakash wanted to plead, to explain—he had come ready to do so—if necessary go down on his knees, but instead he sat quite still while Dev Kishan told him that a departmental inquiry must be allowed to proceed according to rule. Then Sri Prakash had quietly departed, passing through the outer office with his head lowered and with nothing to say for himself whatsoever. He had not spoken for a long while afterwards. He kept thinking—he was still thinking—of the way Dev Kishan had looked above his head. His eyes had seemed to be gazing far beyond Sri Prakash, deep into state matters, and Sri Prakash had felt like a fly that had accidentally got in and deserved to be swatted.

Goel did not want to quarrel any more. He had come on a picnic, he had spent money on liquor and mangoes and the hiring of a horse carriage to bring them here. He expected a good time in return. He refilled their glasses while remembering other outings he had enjoyed in the past. He told Sri Prakash of the time he and some friends had consumed one dozen bottles of liquor at a sitting and had become very merry. He nudged Sri Prakash and said, 'Girls were also brought.' He said this in a low voice, so that Miss Nimmi would not hear, and brought his face close to Sri Prakash. Sri Prakash felt a desire to throw the contents of his glass into this face. He imagined that the liquor contained acid and what would happen. He was filled with such strong emotion that something, some release was necessary: but instead of throwing the liquor in his host's face, he emptied it on the ground in a childishly angry gesture. Goel gave a cry of astonishment, Miss Nimmi stopped halfway in the sucking of a mango.

Just then the moon rose. The palace trembled into view and stood there melting in moonlight. Sri Prakash left his companions and went towards it as one drawn towards a mirage. It did not disappear as he approached, but it did turn out to be locked. He peered through the glass doors and could just make out the sleeping form of a watchman curled up on the floor. The interior was lit only by the palest beams filtering in from outside. By day there were too many curlicued arches and coloured chandeliers, too many plaster leaves and scrolls: but now in the moonlight everything looked as it should. Overcome by its beauty and other sensations, Sri Prakash sat down on the steps and wept. He had his face buried in his hands and could not stop.

After a while Goel joined him. He sat beside him on the steps. Goel began to talk about the passing away of all earthly things, the death of kings and pariah dogs alike. He waved his hand towards the abandoned pleasure palace, he said, 'Where are they all, where have they gone?' Although these reflections were perfectly acceptable—probably at this very moment Sri Prakash's friends were making the same ones at their picnic in Moti Bagh—nevertheless, coming from Goel, Sri Prakash did not want to hear them. He felt Goel had no right to them. What did he know of philosophy and history—indeed of anything except drinking and bribery? Sri Prakash lifted his head; irritation had dried his tears.

He said, 'Do you know what the Nawab Sahib Ghalib Hasan said when they came to tell him the enemy was at the gate?'

Goel did not know—he knew nothing—he hardly knew who the Nawab Sahib Ghalib Hasan was. To cover his ignorance, he waved his hand again and repeated, 'Where are they all, where have they gone?'

Sri Prakash began to instruct him. He knew a lot about the Nawab who had always been one of his heroes. Abandoning the palace at Moti Bagh, the Nawab had built himself this costly new palace here at Badshahbad and filled it with his favourites. There had been poets and musicians and dancing girls, cooks and wine tasters, a French barber, an Irish cavalry officer; also a menagerie which included a lion and an octopus. The Nawab himself wrote poetry which he read aloud to his courtiers and to the girls who massaged his feet and scented them. It was during such a session that messengers had come to tell him the enemy was at the gate. He had answered by reciting these verses which Sri Prakash now quoted to Goel: '*When in her arms, what is the drum of war? the sword of battle? nay, even the ancient whistle of bony-headed Death?*'

'Ah!' said Goel, laying his hand on his chest to show how deeply he was affected.

Quite pleased with this reaction, Sri Prakash repeated the quotation. Then he quoted more verses written by the Nawab. Goel turned out to be an appreciative listener. He swayed his head and sometimes shouted out loud in applause the way connoisseurs shout when a musician plays a note, a dancer executes a step showing more than human skill. Sri Prakash began rather to enjoy himself. It had been a long time since anyone had cared to listen to him reciting poetry. His wife and daughters—he had always regretted it—had no taste for poetry at all; not for music either, which he loved so much.

But then Goel made a mistake. Overcome by appreciation, he repeated a line that Sri Prakash had just quoted to him: '*O rose of my love, where have your petals fallen?*' But Goel's voice, which was vulgar and drunken, degraded these beautiful words. Suddenly Sri Prakash turned on him. He called him all the insulting names he could think of such as liar, swindler, blackmailer, and drunkard. Goel continued to sit there placidly, even nodding once or twice as if he agreed. Perhaps he was too drunk to hear or care; or perhaps he had been called these names so often that he had learned to accept them. But this passive attitude was frustrating for Sri Prakash; he ran out of insults and fell silent.

After a while he said, 'Why did you do it? For myself I don't care—but what about my wife and family? Why should their lives be ruined? Tell me that.'

Goel had no answer except a murmur of sympathy. As if grateful for this sympathy, Sri Prakash began to tell him moving incidents from his married life. They all illustrated the fact that his wife was an angel, a saint. The more Sri Prakash knew her the more he marvelled. In her he had studied all womanhood and had come to the conclusion that women are goddesses at whose feet men must fall down and worship. He himself had got into the habit of doing so quite often. Not now so much any more—his spirits were too low, he felt himself unworthy—but in the past when things were still well with him. Then he would come home from a late night outing with friends to find her nodding in the kitchen, waiting for him to serve him his meal. He would be overcome with love and admiration for her. With a cry that startled her from her sleep, he would fall down at her feet and lift the hem of her garment to press it to his lips. Although she tried to make him rise, he would not do so; he wanted to stay down there to make it clear how humble he was in relation to her greatness. Then she undressed him right there where he lay on the floor and tried to get him to bed. Sometimes she had to lift him up in her arms—he had always been a small man—and he loved that, he lay in her arms with his eyes shut and felt himself a child enfolded in its mother's love. 'Mother,' he would murmur in ecstasy, as she staggered with him to the bed.

Goel had fallen asleep. Sri Prakash was sorry, for although he did not esteem Goel as a person, he felt the need of someone to talk to. Not only about his wife; there were many other subjects, many thoughts he longed to share. It was like that with him sometimes. His heart was so full, so weighted with feeling, that he longed to fling it somewhere—to someone—or, failing someone, up to the moon that was so still and looked down at him from heaven. But there *was* someone; there was Miss Nimmi. She had remained where they had left her by the basket of mangoes and the bottles. She had finished eating mangoes. She did not seem to mind being left alone nor did she seem impatient to go home but just content to wait till they were ready. She sat with her hands folded and looked in front of her at the bare and dusty earth.

This patient pose was characteristic of her. It was the way she had sat in Sri Prakash's office when she had come to ask him for a job. That was why he had kept telling her to come back: to have the pleasure of seeing her in his office, ready to wait for as long as he wanted. She had reminded him of a chicken sitting plump and cooked on a dish on a table. By the third day he had begun to call her his little chicken. 'Fall to!' he would suddenly cry and make the motion of someone who grabbed from a dish and fell to eating. Of course she hadn't known what he meant, but she had smiled all the same.

'Fall to!' he cried now, as he joined her on the ground among the empty bottles. And now too she smiled. Like the palace floating behind her, she was transformed and made beautiful by moonlight. It veiled her rather coarse features and her skin pitted by an attack of smallpox in childhood.

He moved up close to her. Her breasts, as warm as they were plump, came swelling out of her bodice, and he put his hand on them: but respectfully, almost with awe, so that there was no harm in her leaving it there. 'Where is Papa?' she asked.

'Asleep. You need not worry.'

Very gently and delicately he stroked her breasts. Then he kissed her mouth, tasting the mango there. She let all this be done to her. It had been the same in his office—she had always kept quite still, only occasionally glancing over her shoulder to make sure no one was coming. She did the same now, glanced towards her father.

'You need not worry,' Sri Prakash said again. 'He has drunk a lot. He won't wake up.'

'He *is* waking up.'

They both looked towards Goel left alone in front of the palace. He was trying to stretch himself out more comfortably along the steps, but instead he rolled down them. It was not far, and the ground seemed to receive him softly; he did not move but remained lying there.

'Is he all right?' Miss Nimmi asked.

'Of course he is all right. What could happen to *him?*' Sri Prakash spoke bitterly. He took his hand away from her; his mood was spoiled. He said, 'Why did you let him do it to me? What harm have I done to him? Or to you? Answer.'

She had no answer. There was none, he knew. She could not say that he had harmed her, had done anything bad. Was it bad to love a person? To adore and worship the way he had done? Those moments in his office had been pure, and his feelings as sacred as if he were visiting a shrine to place flowers there at the feet of the goddess.

'Why?' he asked again. 'What did I do to you?'

'That is what Papa kept asking: "What did he do to you?" When I said you did nothing, he got very angry. He kept asking questions, he would not stop. Sometimes he woke me up at night to ask.'

Sri Prakash pressed his face into her neck. 'What sort of questions?' he murmured from out of there.

'He asked, "Where did he put his hand?" When I couldn't remember, he asked, "Here?" So I had to say yes. Because you did.'

'Yes,' he murmured. 'Yes I did.' And he did it again, and she let him.

She said, 'Papa shouted and screamed. He hit his head against the wall. But it wasn't only that—there were other things. He was going through a lot of other troubles at that time. Two men kept coming. They told him he would have to go to jail again. Papa is very frightened of going to jail. When he was there before, he came out *so* thin.' She showed how with her finger. 'He lost fifty pounds in there.'

Sri Prakash remembered Goel's demented state in those days. He had come to him many times, threatening, demanding money; he had looked like a madman, and Sri Prakash—still sitting secure behind his desk then, safe in his office—had treated him like one. 'Go to hell,' he had told him. 'Do what you like.' And the last time he had said that, Goel had pounded the desk between them and thrust his face forward into Sri Prakash's: 'Then you will see!' he had screamed. 'You will see and learn!' He had really looked like a madman—even with foam at his mouth. Sri Prakash had felt uneasy but nevertheless had laughed in the other's face and blown a smoke ring.

Miss Nimmi said, 'I was very frightened. Papa was in a terrible mood. He said he would teach you a lesson you would not forget. He said, "Why should I be the only person in this world to suffer blows and kicks? Let someone else also have a few of these." But afterwards those two men stopped coming, and then Papa was much better. He was cheerful again and brought me a present, a little mirror like a heart. And then he was sorry about you. He tried to go to your office again, to change his report, but they said it was too late. I cried when he came back and told me that.'

'You cried? You cried for me?' Sri Prakash was moved.

'Yes, and Papa also was sad for you.'

Goel was still lying at the foot of the steps where he had rolled down. Sri Prakash did not feel unkindly towards him—on the contrary, he even felt quite sorry for him. But his greatest wish with regard to him at the moment was that he would go on sleeping. Sri Prakash did not want to be disturbed in his private conversation with Miss Nimmi. In his mind he prayed for sufficient time, that they might not be interrupted by her father.

'I cried so much that Papa did everything he could to make me feel better. He brought me more presents—sweets and a piece of cloth. When still I went on crying, he said, "What is to be done? It is his fate."'

'He is right,' Sri Prakash said. He too spoke only to soothe her. He did not want Miss Nimmi to be upset in any way. He just wanted her to be as she always was and to keep still so that he could adore her to his heart's content. He raised the hem of her sari to his lips, the way he did to his wife; and he also murmured 'Goddess' to her the way he did to his wife— worshipping all women in her, their goodness and beauty.

## ■ Bharati Mukherjee (1942– ) *English* (story)

Bharati Mukherjee is certainly among the finest of the twentieth-century Indian fiction writers. Her stories and novels specialize in depicting the fates and trials of immigrants from India, the Philippines, or elsewhere, and her Jewish or Tamil or Hindu protagonists all share the perspective of the outsider looking in—the immigrant to whom the Statue of Liberty turns out to be surrounded by high fences outside and is cheaply commercialized inside. A protagonist of Mukherjee's becomes, as in her story of that name, a "middleman," caught between cultures. The tension between cultural identity and assimilation is central to her work. Mukherjee was born in Calcutta and was educated in India before coming to the United States to do graduate work at the University of Iowa. She is married to writer Clark Blaise; has taught creative writing at Columbia, New York University, and Queens College; and currently teaches in the English department at University of California, Berkeley, where she has been named distinguished professor. Her books include *The Tiger's Daughter* (1971), *Wife* (1975), *Days and Nights in Calcutta* (1977), *Darkness* (1985), *The Middleman and Other Stories* (1988), *Jasmine* (1989), and *The Holder of the World* (1993).

**FURTHER READING:** Nelson, Emmanuel S. *Bharati Mukherjee: Critical Perspectives,* 1993.

## Buried Lives

One March midafternoon in Trincomalee, Sri Lanka, Mr. N. K. S. Venkatesan, a forty-nine-year-old school-teacher who should have been inside a St. Joseph's Collegiate classroom explicating Arnold's "The Buried Life" found himself instead at a barricaded intersection, axe in hand and shouting rude slogans at a truckload of soldiers.

Mr. Venkatesan was not a political man. In his neighborhood he was the only householder who hadn't contributed, not even a rupee, to the Tamil Boys' Sporting Association, which everyone knew wasn't a cricket club so much as a recruiting center for the Liberation Tigers. And at St. Joe's, he hadn't signed the staff petition abhorring the arrest at a peaceful anti-Buddhist demonstration of Dr. Pillai, the mathematics teacher. Venkatesan had rather enjoyed talking about fractals with Dr. Pillai, but he disapproved of men with family responsibilities sticking their heads between billy clubs as though they were still fighting the British for independence.

Fractals claimed to predict, mathematically, chaos and apparent randomness. Such an endeavor, if possible, struck Mr. Venkatesan as a virtually holy quest, closer to the spirit of religion than of science. What had once been Ceylon was now Sri Lanka.

Mr. Venkatesan, like Dr. Pillai, had a large family to look after: he had parents, one set of grandparents, an aunt who hadn't been quite right in the head since four of her five boys had signed up with the Tigers, and three much younger, unmarried sisters. They lived with him in a three-room flat above a variety store. It was to protect his youngest sister (a large, docile girl who, before she got herself mixed up with the Sporting Association, used to embroider napkin-and-tablecloth sets and sell them to a middleman for export to fancy shops in Canada) that he was marching that afternoon with two hundred baby-faced protesters.

Axe under arm—he held the weapon as he might an umbrella—Mr. Venkatesan and his sister and a frail boy with a bushy moustache on whom his sister appeared to have a crush, drifted past looted stores and charred vehicles. In the center of the intersection, a middle-aged leader in camouflage fatigues and a black beret stood on the roof of a van without tires, and was about to set fire to the national flag with what looked to Mr. Venkatesan very much like a Zippo lighter.

"Sir, you have to get in the mood," said his sister's boyfriend. The moustache entirely covered his mouth. Mr. Venkatesan had the uncanny sensation of being addressed by a thatch of undulating bristles. "You have to let yourself go, sir."

This wasn't advice; this was admonition. Around Mr. Venkatesan swirled dozens of hyperkinetic boys in white shirts, holding bricks. Fat girls in summer frocks held placards aloft. His sister sucked on an ice cream bar. Every protester seemed to twinkle with fun. He didn't know how to have fun, that was the trouble. Even as an adolescent he'd battened down all passion; while other students had slipped love notes into expectant palms, he'd studied, he'd passed exams. Dutifulness had turned him into a pariah.

"Don't think you chaps invented civil disobedience!"

He lectured the boyfriend on how his generation—meaning that technically, he'd been alive though hardly self-conscious—had cowed the British Empire. The truth was that the one time the police had raided the Venkatesans' flat—he'd been four, but he'd been taught anti-British phrases like "the salt march" and "*satyagraha*"[1] by a cousin ten years older—he had saluted the superintendant smartly even as constables squeezed his cousin's wrists into handcuffs. That cousin was now in San Jose, California, minting lakhs and lakhs of dollars in computer software.

The boyfriend, still smiling awkwardly, moved away from Mr. Venkatesan's sister. His buddies, Tigers in berets, were clustered around a vendor of spicy fritters.

"Wait!" the sister pleaded, her face puffy with held-back tears.

"What do you see in that callow, good-for-nothing bloke?" Mr. Venkatesan asked.

"Please, please leave me alone," his sister screamed. "Please let me do what I want."

What if *he* were to do what he wanted! Twenty years ago when he'd had the chance, he should have applied for a Commonwealth Scholarship. He should have immured himself in a leafy dormitory in Oxford. Now it was too late. He'd have studied law. Maybe he'd have married an English girl and loitered abroad. But both parents had died, his sisters were mere toddlers, and he was obliged to take the lowest, meanest teaching job in the city.

"I want to die," his sister sobbed beside him.

"Shut up, you foolish girl."

The ferocity of her passion for the worthless boy, who was, just then, biting into a greasy potato fritter, shocked him. He had patronized her when she had been a plain, pliant girl squinting at embroidered birds and flowers. But now something harsh and womanly seemed to be happening inside her.

"Forget those chaps. They're nothing but trouble-makers." To impress her, he tapped a foot to the beat of a slogan bellowing out of loudspeakers.

Though soldiers were starting to hustle demonstrators into double-parked paddy wagons, the intersection had taken on the gaudiness of a village fair. A white-haired vendor darted from police jeep to jeep hawking peanuts in paper cones. Boys who had drunk too much tea or soda relieved themselves freely into poster-clogged gutters. A dozen feet up the road a house-wife with a baby on her hip lobbed stones into storefronts. A

1. A term for Mahatma Gandhi's policy of nonviolent resistance as a means to effect political reform.

band of beggars staggered out of an electronics store with a radio and a television. No reason not to get in the mood.

"Blood for blood," he shouted, timidly at first. "Blood begets blood."

"Begets?" the man beside him asked. "What's that supposed to mean?" In his plastic sandals and cheap drawstring pajamas, the man looked like a coolie or laborer.

He turned to his sister for commiseration. What could she expect him to have in common with a mob of uneducated men like that? But she'd left him behind. He saw her, crouched for flight like a giant ornament on the hood of an old-fashioned car, the March wind stiffly splaying her sari and long hair behind her.

"Get down from that car!" he cried. But the crowd, swirling, separated him from her. He felt powerless; he could no longer watch over her, keep her out of the reach of night sticks. From on top of the hood she taunted policemen, and not just policemen but everybody—shopgirls and beggars and ochre-robed monks—as though she wasn't just a girl with a crush on a Tiger but a monster out of one's most splenetic nightmares.

Months later, in a boardinghouse in Hamburg, Mr. Venkatesan couldn't help thinking about the flock of young monks pressed together behind a police barricade that eventful afternoon. He owed his freedom to the monks because, in spite of their tonsure scars and their vows of stoicism, that afternoon they'd behaved like any other hot-headed Sri Lankan adolescents. If the monks hadn't chased his sister and knocked her off the pale blue hood of the car, Mr. Venkatesan would have stayed on in Sri Lanka, in Trinco, in St. Joe's teaching the same poems year after year, a permanent prisoner.

What the monks did was unforgivable. Robes plucked knee-high and celibate lips plumped up in vengeful chant, they pulled a girl by the hair, and they slapped and spat and kicked with vigor worthy of newly initiated Tigers.

It could have been another girl, somebody else's younger sister. Without thinking, Mr. Venkatesan rotated a shoulder, swung an arm, readied his mind to inflict serious harm.

It should never have happened. The axe looped clumsily over the heads of demonstrators and policemen and fell, like a captured kite, into the hands of a Home Guards officer. There was blood, thick and purplish, spreading in jagged stains on the man's white uniform. The crowd wheeled violently. The drivers of paddy wagons laid panicky fingers on their horns. Veils of tear gas blinded enemies and friends. Mr. Venkatesan, crying and choking, ducked into a store and listened to the thwack of batons. When his vision eased, he staggered, still on automatic pilot, down side streets and broke through garden hedges all the way to St. Joseph's unguarded backdoor.

In the men's room off the Teacher's Common Room he held his face, hot with guilt, under a rusty, hissing faucet until Father van der Haagen, the Latin and Scriptures teacher, came out of a stall.

"You don't look too well. Sleepless night, eh?" the Jesuit joked. "You need to get married, Venkatesan. Bad habits can't always satisfy you."

Mr. Venkatesan laughed dutifully. All of Father van der Haagen's jokes had to do with masturbation. He didn't say anything about having deserted his sister. He didn't say anything about having maimed, maybe murdered, a Home Guards officer. "Who can afford a wife on what the school pays?" he joked back. Then he hurried off to his classroom.

Though he was over a half-hour late, his students were still seated meekly at their desks.

"Good afternoon, sir." Boys in monogrammed shirts and rice-starched shorts shuffled to standing positions.

"Sit!" the schoolmaster commanded. Without taking his eyes off the students, he opened his desk and let his hand locate *A Treasury of the Most Dulcet Verses Written in the English Language,* which he had helped the head-master to edit though only the headmaster's name appeared on the book.

Matthew Arnold was Venkatesan's favorite poet. Mr. Venkatesan had talked the Head into including four Arnold poems. The verses picked by the Head hadn't been "dulcet" at all, and one hundred and three pages of the total of one hundred and seventy-four had been given over to upstart Trinco versifiers' martial ballads.

Mr. Venkatesan would have nursed a greater bitterness against the Head if the man hadn't vanished, mysteriously, soon after their acrimonious coediting job.

One winter Friday the headmaster had set out for his nightly after-dinner walk, and he hadn't come back. The Common Room gossip was that he had been kidnapped by a paramilitary group. But Miss Philomena, the female teacher who was by tradition permitted the use of the Head's private bathroom, claimed the man had drowned in the Atlantic Ocean trying to sneak into Canada in a boat that ferried, for a wicked fee, illegal aliens. Stashed in the bathroom's air vent (through which sparrows sometimes flew in and bothered her), she'd spotted, she said, an oilcloth pouch stuffed with foreign cash and fake passports.

In the Teacher's Common Room, where Miss Philomena was not popular, her story was discounted. But at the Pillais's home, the men teachers had gotten together and toasted the Head with hoarded bottles of whiskey and sung many rounds of "For He's a Jolly Good Fellow," sometimes substituting "smart" for "good." By the time Mr. Venkatesan had been dropped home by Father van der Haagen, who owned a motorcycle, night had bleached itself into rainy dawn. It had been the only all-nighter of Mr. Venkatesan's life and the only time he might have been accused of drunkenness.

The memory of how good the rain had felt came back to him now as he glanced through the first stanza of the assigned Arnold poem. What was the function of poetry if not to improve the petty, cautious minds of evasive children? What was the duty of the teacher if not to inspire?

He cleared his throat, and began to read aloud in a voice trained in elocution.

Light flows our war of mocking words, and yet,
Behold, with tears mine eyes are wet!
I feel a nameless sadness o'er me roll.
Yes, yes, we know that we can jest,
We know, we know that we can smile!
But there's a something in this breast,
To which thy light words bring no rest,
And thy gay smiles no anodyne.
Give me thy hand, and hush awhile,
And turn those limpid eyes on mine,
And let me read there, love! thy inmost soul.

"Sir," a plump boy in the front row whispered as Venkatesan finally stopped for breath.

"What is it now?" snapped Venkatesan. In his new mood Arnold had touched him with fresh intensity, and he hated the boy for deflating illusion. "If you are wanting to know a synonym for 'anodyne,' then look it up in the *Oxford Dictionary*. You are a lazy donkey wanting me to feed you with a silver spoon. All of you, you are all lazy donkeys."

"No, sir." The boy persisted in spoiling the mood.

It was then that Venkatesan took in the boy's sweaty face and hair. Even the eyes were fat and sweaty.

"Behold, sir," the boy said. He dabbed his eyelids with the limp tip of his school tie. "Mine eyes, too, are wet."

"You are a silly donkey," Venkatesan yelled. "You are a beast of burden. You deserve the abuse that you get. It is you emotional types who are selling this country down the river."

The class snickered, unsure what Mr. Venkatesan wanted of them. The boy let go of his tie and wept openly. Mr. Venkatesan hated himself. Here was a kindred soul, a fellow lover of Matthew Arnold, and what had he done other than indulge in gratuitous cruelty? He blamed the times. He blamed Sri Lanka.

It was as much this classroom incident as the fear of arrest for his part in what turned out to be an out-of-control demonstration that made Mr. Venkatesan look into emigrating. At first, he explored legal channels. He wasted a month's salary bribing arrogant junior-level clerks in four consulates—he was willing to settle almost anywhere except in the Gulf Emirates—but every country he could see himself being happy and fulfilled in turned him down.

So all through the summer he consoled himself with reading novels. Adventure stories in which fearless young Britons—sailors, soldiers, missionaries—whacked wildernesses into submission. From lending libraries in the city, he checked out books that were so old that they had to be trussed with twine. On the flyleaf of each book, in fading ink, was an inscription by a dead or retired British tea planter. Like the blond heroes of the novels, the colonials must have come to Ceylon chasing dreams of perfect futures. He, too, must sail dark, stormy oceans.

In August, at the close of a staff meeting, Miss Philomena announced coyly that she was leaving the island. A friend in Kalamazoo, Michigan, had agreed to sponsor her as a "domestic."

"It is a ploy only, man," Miss Philomena explained. "In the autumn, I am signing up for post-graduate studies in a prestigious educational institution."

"You are cleaning toilets and whatnot just like a servant girl? Is the meaning of 'domestic' not the same as 'servant'?"

Mr. Venkatesan joined the others in teasing Miss Philomena, but late that night he wrote away to eight American universities for applications. He took great care with the cover letters, which always began with "Dear Respected Sir" and ended with "Humbly but eagerly awaiting your response." He tried to put down in the allotted blanks what it felt like to be born so heartbreakingly far from New York or London. *On this small dead-end island, I feel I am a shadow-man, a nothing. I feel I'm a stranger in my own room. What consoles me is reading. I sink my teeth into fiction by great Englishmen such as G. A. Henty and A. E. W. Mason. I live my life through their imagined lives. And when I put their works down at dawn I ask myself, Hath not a Tamil eyes, heart, ears, nose, throat, to adapt the words of the greatest Briton. Yes, I am a Tamil. If you prick me, do I not bleed? If you tickle me, do I not laugh? Then, if I dream, will you not give me a chance, respected Sir, as only you can?*

In a second paragraph he politely but firmly indicated the size of scholarship he would require, and indicated the size of apartment he (and his sisters) would require. He preferred close proximity to campus, since he did not intend to drive.

But sometime in late April, the school's porter brought him, rubber-banded together, eight letters of rejection.

"I am worthless," Mr. Venkatesan moaned in front of the porter. "I am a donkey."

The porter offered him aspirins. "You are unwell, sahib."

The schoolteacher swallowed the tablets, but as soon as the servant left, he snatched a confiscated Zippo lighter from his desk and burned the rejections.

When he got home, his sister's suitor was on the balcony, painting placards, and though he meant to say nothing to the youth, meant to admit no flaw, no defeat, his body betrayed him with shudders and moans.

"Racism!" the youth spat as he painted over a spelling error that, even in his grief, Mr. Venkatesan couldn't help pointing out. "Racism is what's slamming the door in your face, man! You got to improvise your weapons!"

Perhaps the boy was not a totally unworthy suitor. He let the exclamations play in his head, and soon the rejections, and the anxiety that he might be stuck on the futureless island fired him up instead of depressing him. Most nights he lay in bed fully dressed—the police always raided at dawn—and thought up a hundred illegal but feasible ways to outwit immigration officials.

The least wild schemes he talked over with Father van der Haagen. Long ago and in another country, Father van der Haagen had surely given in to similar seductions. The Jesuit usually hooted, "So you want to rot in a freezing, foreign jail? You want your lovely sisters to walk the streets and come to harm?" But, always, the expatriate ended these chats with his boyhood memories of skating on frozen Belgian rivers and ponds. Mr. Venkatesan felt he could visualize snow, but not a whole river so iced up that it was as solid as a grand trunk highway. In his dreams, the Tamil schoolteacher crisscrossed national boundaries on skates that felt as soft and comforting as cushions.

In August his sister's suitor got himself stupidly involved in a prison break. The sister came to Mr. Venkatesan weeping. She had stuffed clothes and her sewing basket into a camouflage satchel. She was going into the northern hills, she said. The Tigers could count on the tea pickers.

"No way," Mr. Venkatesan exploded. When he was safely in America's heartland, with his own wife and car and all accoutrements of New World hearth and home, he wanted to think of his Trinco family (to whom he meant to remit generous monthly sums) as being happy under one roof, too. "You are not going to live with hooligan types in jungles."

"If you lock me in my room, I'll call the police. I'll tell them who threw the axe at the rally."

"Is that what they teach you in guerrilla camps? To turn on your family?" he demanded.

The sister wept loudly into her sari. It was a pretty lilac sari, and he remembered having bought it for her seventeenth birthday. On her feet were fragile lilac slippers. He couldn't picture her scrambling up terraced slopes of tea estates in that pretty get-up. "Nobody has to teach me," she retorted.

In her lilac sari, and with the white fragrant flower wreath in her hair, she didn't look like a blackmailer. It was the times. She, her boyfriend, he himself, were all fate's victims.

He gave in. He made her promise, though, that in the hills she would marry her suitor. She touched his feet with her forehead in the traditional farewell. He heard a scooter start up below. So the guerrilla had been waiting. She'd meant to leave home, with or without his permission. She'd freed herself of family duties and bonds.

Above the motor scooter's sputter, the grateful boyfriend shouted, "Sir, I will put you in touch with a man. Listen to him and he will deliver you." Then the dust cloud of destiny swallowed up the guerrilla bride-to-be and groom.

The go-between turned out to be a clubfooted and cauliflower-eared middle-aged man. The combination of deformities, no doubt congenital, had nevertheless earned him a reputation for ferocity and an indifference to inflicted suffering. He appeared on the front porch early one Saturday afternoon. He didn't come straight to the point. For the first half-hour he said very little and concentrated instead on the sweet almond-stuffed turnovers that the Venkatesan family had shaped and fried all day for a religious festival they'd be attending later that afternoon.

"You have, perhaps, some news for me?" Mr. Venkatesan asked shyly as he watched the man help himself to a chilled glass of mango fool. "Some important information, no?"

"Excuse me, sir," the man protested. "I know that you are a teacher and that therefore you are in the business of improving the mind of man. But forthrightness is not always a virtue. Especially in these troubled times."

The man's furtiveness was infectious, and Mr. Venkatesan, without thinking, thinned his voice to a hiss. "You are going over my options with me, no?"

"Options!" the man sneered. Then he took out a foreign-looking newspaper from a shopping bag. On a back page of the paper was a picture of three dour sahibs fishing for lobster. "You get my meaning, sir? They have beautiful coves in Nova Scotia. They have beautiful people in the Canadian Maritimes."

On cushiony skates and with clean, cool winds buoying him from behind, Mr. Venkatesan glided all the way into Halifax, dodging posses of border police. He married a girl with red, dimpled cheeks, and all winter she made love to him under a goose-down quilt. Summers he set lobster traps. Editors of quarterlies begged to see his poetry.

"Beautiful people, Canadians," he agreed.

"Not like the damn Americans!" The go-between masticated sternly. "They are sending over soldiers of fortune and suchlike to crush us."

Mr. Venkatesan, wise in ways of middlemen, asked, "This means you're not having a pipeline to America?"

The agent dipped into a bowl of stale fried banana chips.

"No matter. The time has come for me to leave."

The next day, Sunday, the man came back to find out how much Mr. Venkatesan might be willing to pay for a fake passport/airline tickets/safe houses en route package deal. Mr. Venkatesan named a figure.

"So you are not really anxious to exit?" the man said.

Mr. Venkatesan revised his figure. He revised the figure three more times before the go-between would do anything more human than sigh at him.

He was being taken by a mean, mocking man who preyed on others' dreams. He was allowing himself to be cheated. But sometime that spring the wish to get away—to flee abroad and seize the good life as had his San Jose cousin—had deepened into sickness. So he was blowing his life's savings on this malady. So what?

The man made many more trips. And on each trip, as Mr. Venkatesan sat the man down on the best rattan chair on the balcony, through the half-open door that led into the hallway he saw the women in his family gather in jittery knots. They knew he was about to forsake them.

Every brave beginning, in these cramped little islands, masked a secret betrayal. To himself, Mr. Venkatesan would always be a sinner.

Mr. Venkatesan threw himself into the planning. He didn't trust the man with the cauliflower ears. Routes, circuitous enough to fool border guards, had to be figured out. He could fly to Frankfurt via Malta, for instance, then hole up in a ship's cargo hold for the long, bouncy passage on Canadian seas. Or he could take the more predictable (and therefore, cheaper but with more surveillance) detours through the Gulf Emirates.

The go-between or travel agent took his time. Fake travel documents and work permits had to be printed up. Costs, commissions, bribes had to be calculated. On each visit, the man helped himself to a double peg of Mr. Venkatesan's whiskey.

In early September, three weeks after Mr. Venkatesan had paid in full for a roundabout one-way ticket to Hamburg and for a passport impressive with fake visas, the travel agent stowed him in the damp, smelly bottom of a fisherman's dinghy and had him ferried across the Palk Strait to Tuticorin in the palm-green tip of mainland India.

Tuticorin was the town Mr. Venkatesan's ancestors had left to find their fortunes in Ceylon's tea-covered northern hills. The irony struck him with such force that he rocked and tipped the dinghy, and had to be fished out of the sea.

The Friends of the Tigers were waiting in a palm grove for him. He saw their flashlights and smelled their coffee. They gave him a dry change of clothes, and though both the shirt and the jacket were frayed, they were stylishly cut. His reputation as an intellectual and killer (he hoped it wasn't true) of a Buddhist policeman had preceded him. He let them talk; it was not Venkatesan the schoolmaster they were praising, but some mad invention. Where he was silent from confusion and fatigue, they read cunning and intensity. He was happy to put himself in their hands; he thought of them as fate's helpers, dispatched to see him through his malady. That night one of them made up a sleeping mat for him in the back room of his shuttered grocery store. After that they passed him from back room to back room. He spent pleasant afternoons with them drinking sweet, frothy coffee and listening to them plan to derail trains or blow up bus depots. They read his frown as skepticism and redoubled their vehemence. He himself had no interest in destruction, but he listened to them politely.

When it was safe to move on, the Friends wrote out useful addresses in Frankfurt, London, Toronto, Miami. "Stay out of refugee centers," they advised. But an old man with broken dentures who had been deported out of Hamburg the year before filled him in on which refugee centers in which cities had the cleanest beds, just in case he was caught by the wily German police. "I shan't forget any of you," Mr. Venkatesan said as two Friends saw him off at the train station. The train took him to Madras; in Madras he changed trains for Delhi where he boarded an Aeroflot flight for Tashkent. From Tashkent he flew to Moscow. He would like to have told the story of his life to his two seat mates—already the break from family and from St. Joe's seemed the stuff of adventure novels—but they were two huge and grim Uzbeks with bushels of apricots and pears wedged on the floor, under the seat, and on their laps. The cabin was noisier than the Jaffna local bus with squawking chickens and drunken farmers. He communed instead with Arnold and Keats. In Moscow the airport officials didn't bother to look too closely at his visa stamps, and he made it to Berlin feeling cocky.

At Schönefeld Airport, three rough-looking Tamil men he'd not have given the time of day to back home in Trinco grappled his bags away from him as soon as he'd cleared customs. "This is only a piss stop for you, you lucky bastard," one of them said. "You get to go on to real places while hard-working fuckers like us get stuck in this hellhole."

He had never heard such language. Up until a week ago, he would have denied the Tamil language even possessed such words. The man's coarseness shocked Mr. Venkatesan, but this was not the moment to walk away from accomplices.

The expatriate Tamils took him, by bus, to a tenement building—he saw only Asians and Africans in the lobby—and locked him from the outside in a one-room flat on the top floor. An Algerian they did business with, they said, would truck him over the border into Hamburg. He was not to look out the window. He was not to open the door, not even if someone yelled, "Fire!" They'd be back at night, and they'd bring him beer and rolls.

Mr. Venkatesan made a slow show of getting money out of his trouser pocket—he didn't have any East German money, only rupees and the Canadian dollars he'd bought on the black market from the travel agent in Trinco—but the Tamils stopped him. "Our treat," they said. "You can return the hospitality when we make it to Canada."

Late in the evening the three men, stumbling drunk and jolly, let themselves back into the room that smelled of stale, male smells. The Algerian had come through. They were celebrating. They had forgotten the bread but remembered the beer.

That night, which was his only night in East Germany, Mr. Venkatesan got giggly drunk. And so it was that he entered the free world with a hangover. In a narrow, green mountain pass, trying not to throw up, he said goodbye to his Algerian chauffeur and how-do-you-do to a Ghanaian-born Berliner who didn't cut the engine of his BMW during the furtive transfer.

He was in Europe. Finally. The hangover made him sentimental. Back in Trinco the day must have deepened into dusk. In the skid of tires, he heard the weeping of parents, aunts, sisters. He had looked after them as long as he could. He had done for himself what he should have done ten years before. Now he wanted to walk where Shelley had walked. He wanted to lie down where consumptive Keats had lain and listened to his nightingale sing of truth and beauty. He stretched out in the back seat. When Mr. Venkatesan next opened his eyes, the BMW was parked in front of a refugee center in Hamburg.

"End of trip," the black Berliner announced in jerky English. "Auf Wiedersehen."[2]

Mr. Venkatesan protested that he was not a refugee. "I am paid up in full to Canada. You are supposed to put me in touch with a ship's captain."

The black man snickered, then heaved Mr. Venkatesan's two shiny new bags out on the street. "Goodbye. *Danke.*"[3]

Mr. Venkatesan got out of the private taxi.

"Need a cheap hotel? Need a lawyer to stay deportation orders?"

A very dark, pudgy man flashed a calling card in his face. The man looked Tamil, but not anxious like a refugee. His suit was too expensive. Even his shirt was made of some white-on-white fancy material, though his cuffs and collar were somewhat soiled.

Mr. Venkatesan felt exhilarated. Here was another of fate's angels come to minister him out of his malady.

"The name is Rammi. G. Rammi, Esquire. One-time meanest goddamn solicitor in Paramaribo, Suriname. I am putting myself at your service."

He allowed the angel to guide him into a *rijstafel*[4] place and feed him for free.

Mr. Venkatesan ate greedily while the angel, in a voice as uplifting as harp music, instructed him on the most prudent conduct for undocumented transients. By the end of the meal, he'd agreed to pay Rammi's cousin, a widow, a flat fee for boarding him for as long as it took Rammi to locate a ship's captain whose business was ferrying furtive cargoes.

Rammi's cousin, Queenie, lived in a row house by the docks. Rammi had the cabdriver let them off a block and a half from Queenie's. He seemed to think cabdrivers were undercover immigration cops, and he didn't want a poor young widow bringing up a kid on dole getting in trouble for her charity.

Though Queenie had been telephoned ahead from a pay phone, she was dressed in nothing more formal than a kimono when she opened her slightly warped front door and let the men in. The kimono was the color of parrots in sunlight and reminded Mr. Venkatesan of his last carefree years, creeping up on and capturing parrots with his bare hands. In that glossy green kimono, Queenie the landlady shocked him with her beauty. Her sash was missing, and she clenched the garment together at the waist with a slender, nervous fist. Her smooth gold limbs, her high-bouncing bosom, even the stockingless arch of her instep had about them so tempting a careless sensuality that it made his head swim.

"I put your friend in Room 3A," Queenie said. "3B is less crowded but I had to put the sick Turk in it." She yelled something in German which

---

2. Farewell.

3. Thank you.

4. A dish from Indonesia, originally, in which a variety of foods are served with rice.

Mr. Venkatesan didn't understand, and a girl of eight or nine came teetering out of the kitchen in adult-sized high heels. She asked the girl some urgent questions. The girl said no to all of them with shakes of her braided head.

"We don't want the fellow dying on us," Rammi said. Then they said something more in a Caribbean patois that Mr. Venkatesan didn't catch. "God knows we don't want complications." He picked up the two bags and started up the stairs.

3A was a smallish attic room blue with unventilated smoke, fitted with two sets of three-tier bunks. There were no closets, no cupboards, and on the bunk that Rammi pointed out as his, no bed linen. Four young men of indistinguishable nationality—Asia and Africa were their continents—were playing cards and drinking beer.

"Okay, 'bye," Rammi said. He was off to scout ship captains.

When Rammi left, despite the company, Mr. Venkatesan felt depressed, lonely. He didn't try to get to know where the men were from and where they were headed which was how he'd broken the ice in back room dormitories in Tuticorin. One man spat into a brass spittoon. What did he have in common with these transients except the waiting?

By using his bags as a stepladder, he was able to clamber up to his allotted top bunk. For a while he sat on the bed. The men angled their heads so they could still stare at him. He lay down on the mattress. The rough ticking material of the pillow chafed him. He sat up again. He took his jacket and pants off and hung them from the foot rail. He slipped his wallet, his passport, his cloth bag stuffed with foreign cash, his new watch—a farewell present from Father van der Haagen—between the pillow and the mattress. He was not about to trust his cell mates. A little after the noon hour all four men got dressed in gaudy clothes and went out in a group. Mr. Venkatesan finally closed his eyes. A parrot flew into his dream. Mr. Venkatesan thrilled to the feathery feel of its bosom. He woke up only when Queenie's little girl charged into the room and ordered him down for lunch. She didn't seem upset about his being in underwear. She leaped onto the middle bunk in the tier across the room and told him to hurry so the food wouldn't have to be rewarmed. He thought he saw the flash of a man's watch in her hand.

Queenie had made him a simple lunch of lentil soup and potato croquettes, and by the time he got down to the kitchen it was no longer warm. Still he liked the spiciness of the croquettes and the ketchup was a tasty European brand and not the watery stuff served back home.

She said she'd already eaten, but she sat down with a lager and watched him eat. With her he had no trouble talking. He told her about St. Joe's and Father van der Haagen. He told her about his family, leaving out the part about his sister running wild in the hills with hooligans, and got her to talk about her family too.

Queenie's grandfather had been born in a Sinhalese village the name of which he hadn't cared to pass on—he'd referred to it only as "hellhole"—and from which he'd run away at age seventeen to come as an indentured laborer to the Caribbean. He'd worked sugar cane fields in British Guiana until he'd lost a thumb. Then he'd moved to Suriname and worked as an office boy in a coconut oil processing plant, and wooed and won the only daughter of the proprietor, an expatriate Tamil like him who, during the War, had made a fortune off the Americans.

He tried to find out about her husband, but she'd say nothing other than that he'd been, in her words, "a romantic moron," and that he'd hated the hot sun, the flat lands, the coconut palms, the bush, her family, her family's oil factory. He'd dreamed, she said, of living like a European.

"You make me remember things I thought I'd forgotten." She flicked her lips with her tongue until they shone.

"You make me think of doing things I've never done." He gripped the edge of the kitchen table. He had trouble breathing. "Until dinnertime," he said. Then he panted back up to his prison.

But Mr. Venkatesan didn't see Queenie for dinner. She sent word through the girl that she had a guest—a legitimate guest, a tourist from Lübeck, not an illegal transient—that evening. He felt no rage at being dumped. A man without papers accepts last-minute humiliations. He called Rammi from the pay phone in the hall.

That night Mr. Venkatesan had fun. Hamburg was not at all the staid city of burghers that Father van der Haagen had evoked for him in those last restless days of waiting in the Teacher's Common Room. Hamburg was a carnival. That night, with Rammi as his initiator into fun, he smoked his first joint and said, after much prodding, "*sehr schön*"[5] to a skinny girl with a Mohawk haircut.

The tourist from Lübeck had been given the one nice room. Queenie's daughter had shown Mr. Venkatesan the room while the man was checking in. It was on the first floor and had a double bed with a duvet so thick you wanted to sink into it. The windows were covered with *two* sets of curtains. The room even had its own sink. He hadn't seen the man from Lübeck, only heard him on the stairs and in the hall on his way to and from the lavatory walking with an authoritative, native-born German tread. Queenie hadn't instructed him to stay out of sight. Secretiveness he'd learned from his bunk mates. They could move with great stealth. Mr. Venkatesan was beginning to feel like a character in Anne Frank's diary. The men in 3A stopped wearing shoes indoors so as not to be heard pacing by the tourist from Lübeck.

The tourist went out a lot. Sometimes a car came for him. From the Tourist Office, Mr. Venkatesan imagined. How nice it would be to tour the city, take a boat trip! Meantime he had to eat his meals upstairs. That was the sad part. Otherwise he felt he had never been so happy.

Every morning as soon as he got the chance he called Rammi, though he was no longer keen for Rammi to find a crooked captain. He called because he didn't want Rammi to catch on that he was feeling whatever it

5. Very beautiful.

was that he was feeling for Queenie. Like Rammi, he didn't want complications. What he did was remind Rammi that he wouldn't go into the hold of a ship that dumped its cargo into the Atlantic. He told Rammi that both in Trinco and in Tuticorin he'd heard stories of drowned Tamils.

Mr. Venkatesan's roommates stopped going out for meals. They paid Queenie's girl to buy them cold meats and oranges from the corner store. The only thing they risked going out for was liquor. He gathered from fragments of conversation that they were all sailors, from Indonesia and Nigeria, who'd jumped ship in Hamburg harbor. Whenever they went out, he could count on the girl prowling the attic room. He let her prowl. It was almost like having Queenie in the room.

There was only one worry. The girl lifted things—small things—from under pillows. Sometimes she played under the beds where he and the other men stored their suitcases, and he heard lids swish open or closed. He didn't think the things she stole were worth stealing. He'd seen her take a handful of pfennigs from a jacket pocket once, and another time envelopes with brilliant stamps from places like Turkey and Oman. What she seemed to like best to pilfer were lozenges, even the medicated kind for sore throat. It was as if covetousness came upon her, out of the blue, making her pupils twitch and glow.

He didn't mind the loss to his roommates. But he worried that they'd get her in trouble by sending her to the store. He would have to stop her. He would have to scold her as a father might or should without messing things up with Queenie.

One morning Queenie showed up in 3A herself. "I have good news," she whispered. Two of the four men were still in bed. Mr. Venkatesan could tell they hated having a grown woman in their room. "Rammi should have word for you tonight. I'm meeting him to find out more." The morning light, streaming in through a cracked stained-glass panel in the window, put such a heavenly sheen on her face that Mr. Venkatesan blurted out in front of his roommates, "I love you, I love you."

Queenie laughed. "Hush," she said. "You're not there yet. You don't want to wake up our Teuton. I need the legitimate business too."

It seemed to Mr. Venkatesan like an invitation. He followed her down into the front hall in his night clothes. In Tamil movies heroes in his position would have been wearing brocade smoking jackets. It didn't matter. He had made his declaration. Now fate would have to sink the crooked captain and his boat.

Queenie fussed with a pink, plastic clip in her hair. She knotted and reknotted the wispy silk square around her throat. She tapped the longest fingernail he'd ever seen on the butterfly buckle of her belt. She was teasing him. She was promising he wouldn't really have to go. He wanted to stay, Anne Frank or not.

"Tonight should be a champagne night," she grinned. He saw the tensing of a dainty calf muscle as she straightened a stocking. "I'll see to coffee," she said.

Upstairs the man from Lübeck had hot water running in the bathroom sink. The pipes moaned. It was best to hide out in the kitchen until the man was back in his own room. Mr. Venkatesan joined Queenie's daughter at the dinette table. She had lozenges spread out on the tablecloth, like a sun spiked with long rays. She didn't look like a thief. She looked like a child he might have fathered if he'd married the bride his mother had picked for him in the days he'd still been considered a good catch. He hadn't married. Something dire had shown up in the conjunction of their horoscopes.

What if, just what if, what had seemed disastrous to the astrologer at the time had really been fate's way of reserving him for a better family with Queenie and this child in Hamburg?

"I'll sell you some," the child said. "I have English toffees too."

"Where?" He wanted to see her whole loot.

She ducked and brought out an old milk bottle from under the table. He saw the toffees in their red and blue wrapping papers. He saw a Muslim's worry beads. Some things in the bottle were shiny — he made out two rings among the keys and coins and coat buttons. There were two ID cards in the bottle. She reached for the cards. She had to have stolen one of the cards from a man in Room 3A. In the ID picture, which was amateurishly doctored, the roommate looked like a playboy sheikh, and not at all like a refugee without travel papers. He grabbed the roommate's card from her. It wouldn't hurt to have the fellow in his debt. The other card belonged to a very blond, very German man.

The child was shrewd. "I didn't steal anything," she snapped. "I don't know how the stuff got in that jar."

She tossed the blond man's ID to him to get rid of it, and he caught it as he had paper flowers, silk squares, and stunned rabbits hurled to front-row boys by magicians on fete days in his kindergarten. He had loved the magicians. They alone had given him what he'd wanted.

As in dreams, the burly blond man materialized out of thin air and blocked the doorway. The man had on a touristy shirt and short pants, but he didn't have the slack gait of a vacationer. He had to be the man who lived in the nice upstairs room, the man who slept under the cozy *duvet*, who brushed his teeth in a clean, pink sink he didn't have to share, the man from whom transients like Mr. Venkatesan himself had to hide out. This man yelled something nasty in German to Queenie's daughter. The child cowered.

The man yelled again. Mr. Venkatesan started to back away. Minute by minute the man ballooned with rage.

"No *deutsch*," Mr. Venkatesan mumbled.

"You filthy swine," the man shouted in English. "We don't want you making filthy our Germany." He threw five passports down on the kitchen table and spat on the top one. "The girl, she stole something from each of you scums," he hooted.

Mr. Venkatesan recognized his in the heap of travel documents. The child must have stolen it. The child must have filched it from under his pillow while he'd slept. She was a child possessed with covetousness. Now, because of her sick covetousness, he would rot in jail. He yanked the girl by her braids and shook her. The girl made her body go limp, taking away all pleasure in hate and revenge. The tourist from Lübeck ignored the screaming child. He got on the pay phone, the one Mr. Venkatesan called Rammi on every morning. Mr. Venkatesan heard the word *"Polizei!"* He was almost fifty. By fifty a man ought to stop running. Maybe what seemed accidental now—Queenie's daughter's kleptomania blowing away his plans for escape—wasn't accidental. He remembered what had consoled Dr. Pillai at the time of his arrest. Fractals. Nothing was random, the math teacher used to say. Nothing, not even the curliness of a coastline and the fluffiness of a cloud.

Mr. Venkatesan thought about the swoops and darts of his fate. He had started out as a teacher and a solid citizen and ended up as a lusty criminal. He visualized fate now as a buzzard. He could hear the whir of fleshy wings. It hopped off a burning car in the middle of a Trinco intersection.

Then, suddenly, Queenie the beauteous, the deliverer of radiant dreams, burst through the door of the kitchen. "Leave him alone!" she yelled to the man from Lübeck. "You're harassing my fiancé! He's a future German citizen. He will become my husband!"

## ■ Salman Rushdie (1947– ) *English* (novel)

Before the Ayatollah Khomeini of Iran proclaimed a death sentence on Salman Rushdie on the fifteenth of February, 1989, Rushdie was the rising star of twentieth-century Indian writers, recipient of the Booker Prize for his earlier novel *Midnight's Children* and of an $850,000 advance from Viking Books for the novel that became *The Satanic Verses*. *The Satanic Verses* had been published in September 1988 and prior to Khomeini's proclamation had already been banned in India and South Africa, the subject of book burnings in Yorkshire, England, and the instigation for riots across India and Pakistan. The question of how offensive *The Satanic Verses* really is to Islam continues to be debated. Early critics admitted to damning Rushdie without ever reading his book. Syed Shahabuddin, for example, writes: "I have not read it, nor do I intend to. I do not have to wade through a filthy drain to know what filth is" (*Times of India*, 13 October 1988). Later, more careful critics found the portraiture of Muhammed and his followers degrading and objected, among other things, to the suggestion that Rushdie's Persian namesake, Salman al-Farsi, the first Persian convert to Islam, was a transcriber of the Quran who willfully changed passages (thus undermining the idea that the Quran contains the unadulterated words of Allah). Since 1989, Rushdie has been a fugitive with a price of several million dollars on his head and has been under constant police protection; assassins have attacked his Italian translator and killed his Japanese translator. Writers the world over, from James Michener to Günter Grass, have expressed their solidarity with Rushdie, while the voices of Islam continue to excoriate him and deny him pardon. In between are voices such as that of Edward Said, who speaks out against censorship and violence, while asking: "Why must a Muslim, who could be defending and sympathetically interpreting us, now represent us so roughly, so expertly and so disrespectfully to an audience already primed to excoriate our traditions, reality, history, religion, language, and origin?"[1] Rushdie's own apology has not been efficacious; the Ayatollah's response was "Even if Salman Rushdie repents and becomes the most pious man of time, it is incumbent on every Muslim to employ everything he has got, his life and his wealth, to send him to hell" (*Irna Iranian News Agency,* 19 February 1989).

Salman Rushdie was born in 1947 in Bombay to a Muslim family who spoke both English and Urdu. He was educated at an English mission school, at Rugby, and at King's College, Cambridge, where he studied history. An important childhood influence was *The Thousand and One Nights,* and the structural and imaginative debt of his novels to this great repository of Indian and Middle Eastern wit and narrative is profound. In college, he set out to become a writer and wrote *Grimus* (1975) while working in advertising. His other novels include *Midnight's Children* (1980), *Shame* (1983), *The Satanic Verses* (1988), and *Haroun and the Sea of Stories* (1990).

"The Perforated Sheet" is the first chapter of Rushdie's celebrated novel *Midnight's Children.* In this selection, Rushdie's high-spirited, hilarious, mythic, and multivalent prose style can be seen; he achieves a level of wordplay and sheer creative bravado matched by few fiction writers—Nabokov and John Barthes come to mind. Even in so short a selection, the characteristic Rushdie techniques can be seen: the narratives within narratives; the quibbling, self-revising, self-doubting narrator whose interjections create theatrical asides and foreshadowings of future events; and the interpenetration of past, present, and future in the narrative flow. Rushdie writes a kind of Indian Magic Realism, in which folklore, myth, and Quranic allegory coexist with intimately and tenderly portrayed characters, and high rhetoric blends with the vernacular. Though he uses postmodern literary techniques, Rushdie is at heart a modernist writer, whose writing is always at some level an allegory about writing (thus, "The Perforated Sheet" has meanings beyond the white bedsheet to which it refers). Like his protagonist, Rushdie has been "handcuffed to history," and in *Midnight's Children* we see him already exploring the conjunctions of Eastern and Western perspectives that landed him in hot water with *The Satanic Verses.* Like Bharati Mukherjee's "middleman," Rushdie's doctor (caught between Muslim faith and Western materialism) is a "half-and-halfer," with one foot in each culture.

---

1. Appignanesi, Lisa, and Sara Maitland, eds. *The Rushdie File.* London: Fourth Estate, 1989, p. 176.

**FURTHER READING:** Appignanesi, Lisa, and Sara Maitland, eds. *The Rushdie File,* 1989. Cohn-Sherbok, Dan, ed. *The Salman Rushdie Controversy in Interreligious Perspective,* 1990. Ruthven, Malise. *A Satanic Affair: Salman Rushdie and the Rage of Islam,* 1990.

## *The Perforated Sheet,* from *Midnight's Children*

I was born in the city of Bombay . . . once upon a time. No, that won't do, there's no getting away from the date: I was born in Doctor Narlikar's Nursing Home on August 15th, 1947. And the time? The time matters, too. Well then: at night. No, it's important to be more . . . On the stroke of midnight, as a matter of fact. Clock-hands joined palms in respectful greeting as I came. Oh, spell it out, spell it out: at the precise instant of India's arrival at independence, I tumbled forth into the world. There were gasps. And, outside the window, fireworks and crowds. A few seconds later, my father broke his big toe; but his accident was a mere trifle when set beside what had befallen me in that benighted moment, because thanks to the occult tyrannies of those blandly saluting clocks I had been mysteriously handcuffed to history, my destinies indissolubly chained to those of my country. For the next three decades, there was to be no escape. Soothsayers had prophesied me, newspapers celebrated my arrival, politicos ratified my authenticity. I was left entirely without a say in the matter. I, Saleem Sinai, later variously called Snotnose, Stainface, Baldy, Sniffer, Buddha and even Piece-of-the-Moon, had become heavily embroiled in Fate—at the best of times a dangerous sort of involvement. And I couldn't even wipe my own nose at the time.

Now, however, time (having no further use for me) is running out. I will soon be thirty-one years old. Perhaps. If my crumbling, over-used body permits. But I have no hope of saving my life, nor can I count on having even a thousand nights and a night. I must work fast, faster than Scheherazade, if I am to end up meaning—yes, meaning—something. I admit it: above all things, I fear absurdity.

And there are so many stories to tell, too many, such an excess of intertwined lives events miracles places rumours, so dense a commingling of the improbable and the mundane! I have been a swallower of lives; and to know me, just the one of me, you'll have to swallow the lot as well. Consumed multitudes are jostling and shoving inside me; and guided only by the memory of a large white bedsheet with a roughly circular hole some seven inches in diameter cut into the centre, clutching at the dream of that holey, mutilated square of linen, which is my talisman, my open-sesame, I must commence the business of remaking my life from the point at which it really began, some thirty-two years before anything as obvious, as *present,* as my clock-ridden, crime-stained birth.

(The sheet, incidentally, is stained too, with three drops of old, faded redness. As the Quran tells us: *Recite, in the name of the Lord thy Creator, who created Man from clots of blood.*)

One Kashmiri morning in the early spring of 1915, my grandfather Aadam Aziz hit his nose against a frost-hardened tussock of earth while attempting to pray. Three drops of blood plopped out of his left nostril, hardened instantly in the brittle air and lay before his eyes on the prayer-mat, transformed into rubies. Lurching back until he knelt with his head once more upright, he found that the tears which had sprung to his eyes had solidified, too; and at that moment, as he brushed diamonds contemptuously from his lashes, he resolved never again to kiss earth for any god or man. This decision, however, made a hole in him, a vacancy in a vital inner chamber, leaving him vulnerable to women and history. Unaware of this at first, despite his recently completed medical training, he stood up, rolled the prayer-mat into a thick cheroot, and holding it under his right arm surveyed the valley through clear, diamond-free eyes.

The world was new again. After a winter's gestation in its eggshell of ice, the valley had beaked its way out into the open, moist and yellow. The new grass bided its time underground; the mountains were retreating to their hill-stations for the warm season. (In the winter, when the valley shrank under the ice, the mountains closed in and snarled like angry jaws around the city on the lake.)

In those days the radio mast had not been built and the temple of Sankara Acharya, a little black blister on a khaki hill, still dominated the streets and lake of Srinagar. In those days there was no army camp at the lakeside, no endless snakes of camouflaged trucks and jeeps clogged the narrow mountain roads, no soldiers hid behind the crests of the mountains past Baramulla and Gulmarg. In those days travellers were not shot as spies if they took photographs of bridges, and apart from the Englishmen's houseboats on the lake, the valley had hardly changed since the Mughal Empire, for all its springtime renewals; but my grandfather's eyes—which were, like the rest of him, twenty-five years old—saw things differently . . . and his nose had started to itch.

To reveal the secret of my grandfather's altered vision: he had spent five years, five springs, away from home. (The tussock of earth, crucial though its presence was as it crouched under a chance wrinkle of the prayer-mat, was at bottom no more than a catalyst.) Now, returning, he saw through travelled eyes. Instead of the beauty of the tiny valley circled by giant teeth, he noticed the narrowness, the proximity of the horizon; and felt sad, to be at home and feel so utterly enclosed. He also felt—inexplicably—as though the old place resented his educated, stethoscoped return. Beneath the winter ice, it had been coldly neutral, but now there was no doubt: the years in Germany had returned him to a hostile environment. Many years later, when the hole inside him had been clogged up with hate, and he came to sacrifice himself at the shrine of the black stone god in the temple on the hill, he would try and recall his childhood springs in Paradise, the way it was before travel and tussocks and army tanks messed everything up.

On the morning when the valley, gloved in a prayer-mat, punched him on the nose, he had been trying, absurdly, to pretend that nothing had changed. So he had risen in the bitter cold of four-fifteen, washed himself in the prescribed fashion, dressed and put on his father's as-trakhan cap; after which he had carried the rolled cheroot of the prayer-mat into the small lakeside garden in front of their old dark house and unrolled it over the waiting tussock. The ground felt deceptively soft un-der his feet and made him simultaneously uncertain and unwary. 'In the Name of God, the Compassionate, the Merciful . . .'—the exordium, spoken with hands joined before him like a book, comforted a part of him, made another, larger part feel uneasy—' . . . Praise be to Allah, Lord of the Creation . . .'—but now Heidelberg invaded his head; here was Ingrid, briefly his Ingrid, her face scorning him for this Mecca-turned parroting; here, their friends Oskar and Ilse Lubin the anarchists, mock-ing his prayer with their anti-ideologies—' . . . The Compassionate, the Merciful, King of the Last Judgment! . . .'—Heidelberg, in which, along with medicine and politics, he learned that India—like radium—had been 'discovered' by the Europeans; even Oskar was filled with admiration for Vasco da Gama, and this was what finally separated Aadam Aziz from his friends, this belief of theirs that he was somehow the invention of their ancestors—' . . . You alone we worship, and to You alone we pray for help . . .'—so here he was, despite their presence in his head, attempt-ing to re-unite himself with an earlier self which ignored their influence but knew everything it ought to have known, about submission for exam-ple, about what he was doing now, as his hands, guided by old memories, fluttered upwards, thumbs pressed to ears, fingers spread, as he sank to his knees—' . . . Guide us to the straight path, The path of those whom You have favoured . . .'—But it was no good, he was caught in a strange middle ground, trapped between belief and disbelief, and this was only a charade after all—' . . . Not of those who have incurred Your wrath, Nor of those who have gone astray.' My grandfather bent his forehead towards the earth. Forward he bent, and the earth, prayer-mat-covered, curved up towards him. And now it was the tussock's time. At one and the same time a rebuke from Ilse-Oskar-Ingrid-Heidelberg as well as valley-and-God, it smote him upon the point of the nose. Three drops fell. There were ru-bies and diamonds. And my grandfather, lurching upright, made a re-solve. Stood. Rolled cheroot. Stared across the lake. And was knocked for-ever into that middle place, unable to worship a God in whose existence he could not wholly disbelieve. Permanent alteration: a hole.

The young, newly-qualified Doctor Aadam Aziz stood facing the springtime lake, sniffing the whiffs of change; while his back (which was extremely straight) was turned upon yet more changes. His father had had a stroke in his absence abroad, and his mother had kept it a secret. His mother's voice, whispering stoically: '. . . *Because your studies were too im-portant, son.*' This mother, who had spent her life housebound, in purdah, had suddenly found enormous strength and gone out to run the small gemstone business (turquoises, rubies, diamonds) which had put Aadam through medical college, with the help of a scholarship; so he returned to find the seemingly immutable order of his family turned upside down, his mother going out to work while his father sat hidden behind the veil which the stroke had dropped over his brain . . . in a wooden chair, in a darkened room, he sat and made bird-noises. Thirty different species of birds visited him and sat on the sill outside his shuttered window conversing about this and that. He seemed happy enough.

(. . . And already I can see the repetitions beginning; because didn't my grandmother also find enormous . . . and the stroke, too, was not the only . . . and the Brass Monkey had her birds . . . the curse begins already, and we haven't even got to the noses yet!)

The lake was no longer frozen over. The thaw had come rapidly, as usual; many of the small boats, the shikaras, had been caught napping, which was also normal. But while these sluggards slept on, on dry land, snoring peacefully beside their owners, the oldest boat was up at the crack as old folk often are, and was therefore the first craft to move across the unfrozen lake. Tai's shikara . . . this, too, was customary.

Watch how the old boatman, Tai, makes good time through the misty water, standing stooped over at the back of his craft! How his oar, a wooden heart on a yellow stick, drives jerkily through the weeds! In these parts he's considered very odd because he rows standing up . . . among other reasons. Tai, bringing an urgent summons to Doctor Aziz, is about to set history in motion . . . while Aadam, looking down into the water, recalls what Tai taught him years ago: 'The ice is always waiting, Aadam baba, just under the water's skin.' Aadam's eyes are a clear blue, the astonishing blue of mountain sky, which has a habit of dripping into the pupils of Kashmiri men; they have not forgotten how to look. They see—there! like the skeleton of a ghost, just beneath the surface of Lake Dal!—the delicate tracery, the intricate crisscross of colourless lines, the cold waiting veins of the future. His German years, which have blurred so much else, haven't deprived him of the gift of seeing. Tai's gift. He looks up, sees the approaching V of Tai's boat, waves a greeting. Tai's arm rises—but this is a command. 'Wait!' My grandfather waits; and during this hiatus, as he experiences the last peace of his life, a muddy, ominous sort of peace, I had better get round to describing him.

Keeping out of my voice the natural envy of the ugly man for the strikingly impressive, I record that Doctor Aziz was a tall man. Pressed flat against a wall of his family home, he measured twenty-five bricks (a brick for each year of his life), or just over six foot two. A strong man also. His beard was thick and red—and annoyed his mother, who said only Hajis, men who had made the pilgrimage to Mecca, should grow red beards. His hair, however, was rather darker. His sky-eyes you know about. Ingrid had said, 'They went mad with the colours when they made your face.' But the central feature of my grandfather's anatomy was neither colour nor height, neither strength of arm nor straightness of back. There it was, reflected in the water, undulating like a mad plantain in the centre of his face . . . Aadam Aziz, waiting for Tai, watches his rippling nose. It would have dominated less dramatic faces than his easily; even on him, it is what one sees first and remembers longest. 'A cyranose,' Ilse Lubin said, and Oskar added, 'A proboscissimus.' Ingrid announced, 'You could cross a river on that nose.' (Its bridge was wide.)

My grandfather's nose: nostrils flaring, curvaceous as dancers. Between them swells the nose's triumphal arch, first up and out, then down and under, sweeping in to his upper lip with a superb and at present red-tipped flick. An easy nose to hit a tussock with. I wish to place on record my gratitude to this mighty organ—if not for it, who would ever have believed me to be truly my mother's son, my grandfather's grandson?—this colossal apparatus which was to be my birthright, too. Doctor Aziz's nose—comparable only to the trunk of the elephant-headed god Ganesh—established incontrovertibly his right to be a patriarch. It was Tai who taught him that, too. When young Aadam was barely past puberty the dilapidated boatman said, 'That's a nose to start a family on, my princeling. There'd be no mistaking whose brood they were. Mughal Emperors would have given their right hands for noses like that one. There are dynasties waiting inside it,'—and here Tai lapsed into coarseness— 'like snot.'

On Aadam Aziz, the nose assumed a patriarchal aspect. On my mother, it looked noble and a little long-suffering; on my aunt Emerald, snobbish; on my aunt Alia, intellectual; on my uncle Hanif it was the organ of an unsuccessful genius; my uncle Mustapha made it a second-rater's sniffer; the Brass Monkey escaped it completely; but on me—on me, it was something else again. But I mustn't reveal all my secrets at once.

(Tai is getting nearer. He, who revealed the power of the nose, and who is now bringing my grandfather the message which will catapult him into his future, is stroking his shikara through the early morning lake . . .)

Nobody could remember when Tai had been young. He had been plying this same boat, standing in the same hunched position, across the Dal and Nageen Lakes . . . forever. As far as anyone knew. He lived somewhere in the insanitary bowels of the old wooden-house quarter and his wife grew lotus roots and other curious vegetables on one of the many 'floating gardens' lilting on the surface of the spring and summer water. Tai himself cheerily admitted he had no idea of his age. Neither did his wife—he was, she said, already leathery when they married. His face was a sculpture of wind on water: ripples made of hide. He had two golden teeth and no others. In the town, he had few friends. Few boatmen or traders invited him to share a hookah when he floated past the shikara moorings or one of the lakes' many ramshackle, waterside provision-stores and tea-shops.

The general opinion of Tai had been voiced long ago by Aadam Aziz's father the gemstone merchant: 'His brain fell out with his teeth.' (But now old Aziz sahib sat lost in bird tweets while Tai simply, grandly, continued.) It was an impression the boatman fostered by his chatter, which was fantastic, grandiloquent and ceaseless, and as often as not addressed only to himself. Sound carries over water, and the lake people giggled at his monologues; but with undertones of awe, and even fear. Awe, because the old halfwit knew the lakes and hills better than any of his detractors; fear, because of his claim to an antiquity so immense it defied numbering, and moreover hung so lightly round his chicken's neck that it hadn't prevented him from winning a highly desirable wife and fathering four sons upon her . . . and a few more, the story went, on other lakeside wives. The young bucks at the shikara moorings were convinced he had a pile of money hidden away somewhere—a hoard, perhaps, of priceless golden teeth, rattling in a sack like walnuts. Years later, when Uncle Puffs tried to sell me his daughter by offering to have her teeth drawn and replaced in gold, I thought of Tai's forgotten treasure . . . and, as a child, Aadam Aziz had loved him.

He made his living as a simple ferryman, despite all the rumours of wealth, taking hay and goats and vegetables and wood across the lakes for cash; people, too. When he was running his taxi-service he erected a pavilion in the centre of the shikara, a gay affair of flowered-patterned curtains and canopy, with cushions to match; and deodorised his boat with incense. The sight of Tai's shikara approaching, curtains flying, had always been for Doctor Aziz one of the defining images of the coming of spring. Soon the English sahibs would arrive and Tai would ferry them to the Shalimar Gardens and the King's Spring, chattering and pointy and stooped. He was the living antithesis of Oskar-Ilse-Ingrid's belief in the inevitability of change . . . a quirky, enduring familiar spirit of the valley. A watery Caliban, rather too fond of cheap Kashmiri brandy.

Memory of my blue bedroom wall: on which, next to the P. M.'s letter, the Boy Raleigh hung for many years, gazing rapturously at an old fisherman in what looked like a red dhoti, who sat on—what?—driftwood?—and pointed out to sea as he told his fishy tales . . . and the Boy Aadam, my grandfather-to-be, fell in love with the boatman Tai precisely because of the endless verbiage which made others think him cracked. It was magical talk, words pouring from him like fools' money, past his two gold teeth, laced with hiccups and brandy, soaring up to the most remote Himalayas of the past, then swooping shrewdly on some present detail, Aadam's nose for instance, to vivisect its meaning like a mouse. This friendship had plunged Aadam into hot water with great regularity. (Boiling water. Literally. While his mother said, 'We'll kill that boatman's bugs if it kills you.') But still the old soliloquist would dawdle in his boat at the garden's lakeside toes and Aziz would sit at his feet until voices summoned him indoors to be lectured on Tai's filthiness and warned about the pillaging armies of germs his mother envisaged leaping from that hospitably ancient body on to her son's starched white loose-pajamas. But always Aadam returned to the water's edge to scan the mists for the ragged reprobate's hunched-up frame steering its magical boat through the enchanted waters of the morning.

'But how old are you really, Taiji?' (Doctor Aziz, adult, redbearded, slanting towards the future, remembers the day he asked the unaskable

question.) For an instant, silence, noisier than a waterfall. The monologue, interrupted. Slap of oar in water. He was riding in the shikara with
Tai, squatting amongst goats, on a pile of straw, in full knowledge of the
stick and bathtub waiting for him at home. He had come for stories—and
with one question had silenced the storyteller.

'No, tell, Taiji, how old, *truly?*' And now a brandy bottle, materialising
from nowhere: cheap liquor from the folds of the great warm chugha-
coat. Then a shudder, a belch, a glare. Glint of gold. And—at last!—
speech. 'How old? You ask how old, you little wet-head, you nosey . . .'
Tai, forecasting the fisherman on my wall, pointed at the mountains. 'So
old, nakkoo!' Aadam, the nakkoo, the nosey one, followed his pointing
finger. 'I have watched the mountains being born; I have seen Emperors
die. Listen. Listen, nakkoo . . .'—the brandy bottle again, followed by
brandy-voice, and words more intoxicating than booze—' . . . I saw that
Isa, that Christ, when he came to Kashmir. Smile, smile, it is your history I
am keeping in my head. Once it was set down in old lost books. Once I
knew where there was a grave with pierced feet carved on the tombstone,
which bled once a year. Even my memory is going now; but I know, although I can't read.' Illiteracy, dismissed with a flourish; literature crumbled beneath the rage of his sweeping hand. Which sweeps again to
chugha-pocket, to brandy bottle, to lips chapped with cold. Tai always had
woman's lips. 'Nakkoo, listen, listen. I have seen plenty. Yara, you
should've seen that Isa when he came, beard down to his balls, bald as an
egg on his head. He was old and fagged-out but he knew his manners.
"You first, Taiji," he'd say, and "Please to sit"; always a respectful tongue,
he never called me crackpot, never called me *tu* either. Always *aap*. Polite,
see? And what an appetite! Such a hunger, I would catch my ears in fright.
Saint or devil, I swear he could eat a whole kid in one go. And so what? I
told him, eat, fill your hole, a man comes to Kashmir to enjoy life, or to
end it, or both. His work was finished. He just came up here to live it up a
little.' Mesmerized by this brandied portrait of a bald, gluttonous Christ,
Aziz listened, later repeating every word to the consternation of his parents, who dealt in stones and had no time for 'gas.'

'Oh, you don't believe?'—licking his sore lips with a grin, knowing it
to be the reverse of the truth; 'Your attention is wandering?'—again, he
knew how furiously Aziz was hanging on his words. 'Maybe the straw is
pricking your behind, hey? Oh, I'm so sorry, babaji, not to provide for you
silk cushions with gold brocade-work-cushions such as the Emperor Jehangir sat upon! You think of the Emperor Jehangir as a gardener only,
no doubt,' Tai accused my grandfather, 'because he built Shalimar. Stupid! What do you know? His name meant Encompasser of the Earth. Is
that a gardener's name? God knows what they teach you boys these days.
Whereas I' . . . puffing up a little here . . . 'I knew his precise weight,
to the tola! Ask me how many maunds, how many seers! When he was
happy he got heavier and in Kashmir he was heaviest of all. I used to carry
his litter . . . no, no, look, you don't believe again, that big cucumber in

your face is waggling like the little one in your pajamas! So, come on, come on, ask me questions! Give examination! Ask how many times the leather thongs wound round the handles of the litter—the answer is thirty-one. Ask me what was the Emperor's dying word—I tell you it was "Kashmir." He had bad breath and a good heart. Who do you think I am? Some common ignorant lying pie-dog? Go, get out of the boat now, your nose makes it too heavy to row; also your father is waiting to beat my gas out of you, and your mother to boil off your skin.'

In the brandy bottle of the boatman Tai I see, foretold, my own father's possession by djinns . . . and there will be another bald foreigner . . . and Tai's gas prophesies another kind, which was the consolation of my grandmother's old age, and taught her stories, too . . . and pie-dogs aren't far away . . . Enough. I'm frightening myself.

Despite beating and boiling, Aadam Aziz floated with Tai in his shikara, again and again, amid goats hay flowers furniture lotus-roots, though never with the English sahibs, and heard again and again the miraculous answers to that single terrifying question: 'But Taiji, how old are you, *honestly*?'

From Tai, Aadam learned the secrets of the lake—where you could swim without being pulled down by weeds; the eleven varieties of water-snake; where the frogs spawned; how to cook a lotus-root; and where the three English women had drowned a few years back. 'There is a tribe of feringhee women who come to this water to drown,' Tai said. 'Sometimes they know it, sometimes they don't, but I know the minute I smell them. They hide under the water from God knows what or who—but they can't hide from me, baba!' Tai's laugh, emerging to infect Aadam—a huge, booming laugh that seemed macabre when it crashed out of that old, withered body, but which was so natural in my giant grandfather that nobody knew, in later times, that it wasn't really his (my uncle Hanif inherited this laugh; so until he died, a piece of Tai lived in Bombay). And, also from Tai, my grandfather heard about noses.

Tai tapped his left nostril. 'You know what this is, nakkoo? It's the place where the outside world meets the world inside you. If they don't get on, you feel it here. Then you rub your nose with embarrassment to make the itch go away. A nose like that, little idiot, is a great gift. I say: trust it. When it warns you, look out or you'll be finished. Follow your nose and you'll go far.' He cleared his throat; his eyes rolled away into the mountains of the past. Aziz settled back on the straw. 'I knew one officer once—in the army of that Iskandar the Great. Never mind his name. He had a vegetable just like yours hanging between his eyes. When the army halted near Gandhara, he fell in love with some local floozy. At once his nose itched like crazy. He scratched it, but that was useless. He inhaled vapours from crushed boiled eucalyptus leaves. Still no good, baba! The itching sent him wild; but the damn fool dug in his heels and stayed with his little witch when the army went home. He became—what?—a stupid thing, neither this nor that, a half-and-halfer with a nagging wife and an itch in the nose, and in the end he pushed his sword into his stomach. What do you think of that?'

. . . Doctor Aziz in 1915, whom rubies and diamonds have turned into a half-and-halfer, remembers this story as Tai enters hailing distance. His nose is itching still. He scratches, shrugs, tosses his head; and then Tai shouts.

'Ohé! Doctor Sahib! Ghani the landowner's daughter is sick.'

The message, delivered curtly, shouted unceremoniously across the surface of the lake although boatman and pupil have not met for half a decade, mouthed by woman's lips that are not smiling in long-time-no-see greeting, sends time into a speeding, whirligig, blurry fluster of excitement . . .

. . . 'Just think, son,' Aadam's mother is saying as she sips fresh lime water, reclining on a takht in an attitude of resigned exhaustion, 'how life does turn out. For so many years even my ankles were a secret, and now I must be stared at by strange persons who are not even family members.'

. . . While Ghani the landowner stands beneath a large oil painting of Diana the Huntress, framed in squiggly gold. He wears thick dark glasses and his famous poisonous smile, and discusses art. 'I purchased it from an Englishman down on his luck, Doctor Sahib. Five hundred rupees only—and I did not trouble to beat him down. What are five hundred chips? You see, I am a lover of culture.'

. . . 'See, my son,' Aadam's mother is saying as he begins to examine her, 'what a mother will not do for her child. Look how I suffer. You are a doctor . . . feel these rashes, these blotchy bits, understand that my head aches morning noon and night. Refill my glass, child.'

. . . But the young Doctor has entered the throes of a most unhippocratic excitement at the boatman's cry, and shouts, 'I'm coming just now! Just let me bring my things!' The shikara's prow touches the garden's hem. Aadam is rushing indoors, prayer-mat rolled like cheroot under one arm, blue eyes blinking in the sudden interior gloom; he has placed the cheroot on a high shelf on top of stacked copies of *Vorwärts* and Lenin's *What Is To Be Done?* and other pamphlets, dusty echoes of his half-faded German life; he is pulling out, from under his bed, a second-hand leather case which his mother called his 'doctori-attaché', and as he swings it and himself upwards and runs from the room, the word HEIDELBERG is briefly visible, burned into the leather on the bottom of the bag. A landowner's daughter is good news indeed to a doctor with a career to make, even if she is ill. No: *because* she is ill.

. . . While I sit like an empty pickle jar in a pool of Anglepoised light, visited by this vision of my grandfather sixty-three years ago, which demands to be recorded, filling my nostrils with the acrid stench of his mother's embarrassment which has brought her out in boils, with the vinegary force of Aadam Aziz's determination to establish a practice so successful that she'll never have to return to the gemstone-shop, with the blind mustiness of a big shadowy house in which the young Doctor stands, ill-

at-ease, before a painting of a plain girl with lively eyes and a stag trans-
fixed behind her on the horizon, speared by a dart from her bow. Most of
what matters in our lives takes place in our absence: but I seem to have
found from somewhere the trick of filling in the gaps in my knowledge, so
that everything is in my head, down to the last detail, such as the way the
mist seemed to slant across the early morning air . . . everything, and
not just the few clues one stumbles across, for instance by opening an old
tin trunk which should have remained cobwebby and closed.

     . . . Aadam refills his mother's glass and continues, worriedly, to ex-
amine her. 'Put some cream on these rashes and blotches, Amma. For the
headache, there are pills. The boils must be lanced. But maybe if you wore
purdah when you sat in the store . . . so that no disrespectful eyes could
. . . such complaints often begin in the mind . . .'

     . . . Slap of oar in water. Plop of spittle in lake. Tai clears his throat
and mutters angrily, 'A fine business. A wet-head nakkoo child goes away
before he's learned one damn thing and he comes back a big doctor sahib
with a big bag full of foreign machines, and he's still as silly as an owl. I
swear: a too bad business.'

     . . . Doctor Aziz is shifting uneasily, from foot to foot, under the in-
fluence of the landowner's smile, in whose presence it is not possible to
feel relaxed; and is waiting for some tic of reaction to his own extraordinary appearance. He has grown accustomed to these involuntary twitches
of surprise at his size, his face of many colours, his nose . . . but Ghani
makes no sign, and the young Doctor resolves, in return, not to let his uneasiness show. He stops shifting his weight. They face each other, each suppressing (or so it seems) his view of the other, establishing the basis of
their future relationship. And now Ghani alters, changing from art-lover
to tough-guy. 'This is a big chance for you, young man,' he says. Aziz's eyes
have strayed to Diana. Wide expanses of her blemished pink skin are visible.

     . . . His mother is moaning, shaking her head. 'No, what do you
know, child, you have become a big-shot doctor but the gemstone business
is different. Who would buy a turquoise from a woman hidden inside a
black hood? It is a question of establishing trust. So they must look at me;
and I must get pains and boils. Go, go, don't worry your head about your
poor mother.'

     . . . 'Big shot,' Tai is spitting into the lake, 'big bag, big shot. Pah! We
haven't got enough bags at home that you must bring back that thing
made of a pig's skin that makes one unclean just by looking at it? And inside, God knows what all.' Doctor Aziz, seated amongst flowery curtains
and the smell of incense, has his thoughts wrenched away from the patient
waiting across the lake. Tai's bitter monologue breaks into his consciousness, creating a sense of dull shock, a smell like a casualty ward overpowering the incense . . . the old man is clearly furious about something, possessed by an incomprehensible rage that appears to be directed at his
erstwhile acolyte, or, more precisely and oddly, at his bag. Doctor Aziz at-

tempts to make small talk . . . 'Your wife is well? Do they still talk about your bag of golden teeth?' . . . tries to remake an old friendship; but Tai is in full flight now, a stream of invective pouring out of him. The Heidelberg bag quakes under the torrent of abuse. 'Sistersleeping pigskin bag from Abroad full of foreigners' tricks. Big-shot bag. Now if a man breaks an arm that bag will not let the bonesetter bind it in leaves. Now a man must let his wife lie beside that bag and watch knives come and cut her open. A fine business, what these foreigners put in our young men's heads. I swear: it is a too-bad thing. That bag should fry in Hell with the testicles of the ungodly.'

    . . . Ghani the landowner snaps his braces with his thumbs. 'A big chance, yes indeed. They are saying good things about you in town. Good medical training. Good . . . good enough . . . family. And now our own lady doctor is sick so you get your opportunity. That woman, always sick these days, too old, I am thinking, and not up in the latest developments also, what-what? I say: physician heal thyself. And I tell you this: I am wholly objective in my business relations. Feelings, love, I keep for my family only. If a person is not doing a first-class job for me, out she goes! You understand me? So: my daughter Naseem is not well. You will treat her excellently. Remember I have friends; and ill-health strikes high and low alike.'

    . . . 'Do you still pickle water-snakes in brandy to give you virility, Taiji? Do you still like to eat lotus-root without any spices?' Hesitant questions, brushed aside by the torrent of Tai's fury. Doctor Aziz begins to diagnose. To the ferryman, the bag represents Abroad; it is the alien thing, the invader, progress. And yes, it has indeed taken possession of the young Doctor's mind; and yes, it contains knives, and cures for cholera and malaria and smallpox; and yes, it sits between doctor and boatman, and has made them antagonists. Doctor Aziz begins to fight, against sadness, and against Tai's anger, which is beginning to infect him, to become his own, which erupts only rarely, but comes, when it does come, unheralded in a roar from his deepest places, laying waste everything in sight; and then vanishes, leaving him wondering why everyone is so upset . . . They are approaching Ghani's house. A bearer awaits the shikara, standing with clasped hands on a little wooden jetty. Aziz fixes his mind on the job in hand.

    . . . 'Has your usual doctor agreed to my visit, Ghani Sahib?' . . . Again, a hesitant question is brushed lightly aside. The landowner says, 'Oh, she will agree. Now follow me, please.'

    . . . The bearer is waiting on the jetty. Holding the shikara steady as Aadam Aziz climbs out, bag in hand. And now, at last, Tai speaks directly to my grandfather. Scorn in his face, Tai asks, 'Tell me this, Doctor Sahib: have you got in that bag made of dead pigs one of those machines that foreign doctors use to smell with?' Aadam shakes his head, not understanding. Tai's voice gathers new layers of disgust. 'You know, sir, a thing like an elephant's trunk.' Aziz, seeing what he means, replies: 'A stethoscope? Naturally.' Tai pushes the shikara off from the jetty. Spits. Begins to row away. 'I knew it,' he says, 'You will use such a machine now, instead of your own big nose.'

My grandfather does not trouble to explain that a stethoscope is more like a pair of ears than a nose. He is stifling his own irritation, the resentful anger of a cast-off child; and besides, there is a patient waiting. Time settles down and concentrates on the importance of the moment.

The house was opulent but badly lit. Ghani was a widower and the servants clearly took advantage. There were cobwebs in corners and layers of dust on ledges. They walked down a long corridor; one of the doors was ajar and through it Aziz saw a room in a state of violent disorder. This glimpse, connected with a glint of light in Ghani's dark glasses, suddenly informed Aziz that the landowner was blind. This aggravated his sense of unease: a blind man who claimed to appreciate European paintings? He was, also, impressed, because Ghani hadn't bumped into anything . . . they halted outside a thick teak door. Ghani said, 'Wait here two moments', and went into the room behind the door.

In later years, Doctor Aadam Aziz swore that during those two moments of solitude in the gloomy spidery corridors of the landowner's mansion he was gripped by an almost uncontrollable desire to turn and run away as fast as his legs would carry him. Unnerved by the enigma of the blind art-lover, his insides filled with tiny scrabbling insects as a result of the insidious venom of Tai's mutterings, his nostrils itching to the point of convincing him that he had somehow contracted venereal disease, he felt his feet begin slowly, as though encased in boots of lead, to turn; felt blood pounding in his temples; and was seized by so powerful a sensation of standing upon a point of no return that he very nearly wet his German woollen trousers. He began, without knowing it, to blush furiously; and at this point his mother appeared before him, seated on the floor before a low desk, a rash spreading like a blush across her face as she held a turquoise up to the light. His mother's face had acquired all the scorn of the boatman Tai. 'Go, go, run,' she told him in Tai's voice, 'Don't worry about your poor old mother.' Doctor Aziz found himself stammering, 'What a useless son you've got, Amma; can't you see there's a hole in the middle of me the size of a melon?' His mother smiled a pained smile. 'You always were a heartless boy,' she sighed, and then turned into a lizard on the wall of the corridor and stuck her tongue out at him. Doctor Aziz stopped feeling dizzy, became unsure that he'd actually spoken aloud, wondered what he'd meant by that business about the hole, found that his feet were no longer trying to escape, and realized that he was being watched. A woman with the biceps of a wrestler was staring at him, beckoning him to follow her into the room. The state of her sari told him that she was a servant; but she was not servile. 'You look green as a fish,' she said. 'You young doctors. You come into a strange house and your liver turns to jelly. Come, Doctor Sahib, they are waiting for you.' Clutching his bag a fraction too tightly, he followed her through the dark teak door.

. . . Into a spacious bedchamber that was as ill-lit as the rest of the house; although here there were shafts of dusty sunlight seeping in through a fanlight high on one wall. These fusty rays illuminated a scene as remarkable as anything the Doctor had ever witnessed: a tableau of such surpassing strangeness that his feet began to twitch towards the door once again. Two more women, also built like professional wrestlers, stood stiffly in the light, each holding one corner of an enormous white bed-sheet, their arms raised high above their heads so that the sheet hung between them like a curtain. Mr Ghani welled up out of the murk surrounding the sunlit sheet and permitted the nonplussed Aadam to stare stupidly at the peculiar tableau for perhaps half a minute, at the end of which, and before a word had been spoken, the Doctor made a discovery:

In the very centre of the sheet, a hole had been cut, a crude circle about seven inches in diameter.

'Close the door, ayah,' Ghani instructed the first of the lady wrestlers, and then, turning to Aziz, became confidential. 'This town contains many good-for-nothings who have on occasion tried to climb into my daughter's room. She needs,' he nodded at the three musclebound women, 'protectors.'

Aziz was still looking at the perforated sheet. Ghani said, 'All right, come on, you will examine my Naseem right now. *Pronto.*'

My grandfather peered around the room. 'But where is she, Ghani Sahib?' he blurted out finally. The lady wrestlers adopted supercilious expressions and, it seemed to him, tightened their musculatures, just in case he intended to try something fancy.

'Ah, I see your confusion,' Ghani said, his poisonous smile broadening, 'You Europe-returned chappies forget certain things. Doctor Sahib, my daughter is a decent girl, it goes without saying. She does not flaunt her body under the noses of strange men. You will understand that you cannot be permitted to see her, no, not in any circumstances; accordingly I have required her to be positioned behind that sheet. She stands there, like a good girl.'

A frantic note had crept into Doctor Aziz's voice, 'Ghani Sahib, tell me how I am to examine her without looking at her?' Ghani smiled on.

'You will kindly specify which portion of my daughter it is necessary to inspect. I will then issue her with my instructions to place the required segment against that hole which you see there. And so, in this fashion the thing may be achieved.'

'But what, in any event, does the lady complain of?' — my grandfather, despairingly. To which Mr Ghani, his eyes rising upwards in their sockets, his smile twisting into a grimace of grief, replied: 'The poor child! She has a terrible, a too dreadful stomach-ache.'

'In that case,' Doctor Aziz said with some restraint, 'will she show me her stomach, please.'

# China

INTRODUCTION

China is the world's most populous nation, with more than 1.2 billion people, about a fifth of the world's inhabitants. It is dominated by a majority population of Han Chinese, but it contains many minority groups, including the Mongols, the Uigurs, the Hui, the Miao, the Koreans, the Tibetans, the Yi, and the Chuang. Since the second millennium B.C., Chinese civilization has patterned itself into a series of empires that flourished, weakened, and were overthrown—often by peasant revolts or barbarian invaders from the north—and then reestablished in a different form, often by invaders who assimilated Chinese culture and administration. Despite political upheavals, China has produced superb literary works through three millennia. Like Greece in the West, China's civilization—its culture, inventions, and spirit—has profoundly affected neighboring countries since ancient times, especially its extraordinary literature. Its poetry, at times ornate, at times chastely plain, at times deeply personal, even confessional, at times purely objective, is its major literary genre. In the twentieth century, classical Chinese poetry has been translated into European languages, where its conversational, intimate, and imagistic pastoral modes have permeated and changed the course of Western poetry, especially that in the United States and France.

The Shang dynasty (c. 1523–1027 B.C.) is the first kingdom documented in Chinese history, though it is traditionally thought to have been the successor to an earlier kingdom called the Xia dynasty. China's ancient tradition of writing originated in the Shang dynasty. Antecedents of modern characters have been found in divinitory rites inscribed on ox bones, tortoise shells, and bronze vessels that go back to 1400 B.C. The sophistication of this system of writing suggests an even earlier origin. Ancient Chinese books were written on strips of bamboo, then on silk from the second century B.C. to the second century A.D., when paper was invented. Printing on fixed wooden blocks was developed during the Tang dynasty (616–906) and on moveable blocks in the eleventh century, four centuries before printing emerged in the West. The fact that Chinese script was originally pictographic, though with phonetic values, helped it to spread across the huge expanse of China, where it aided communication between people speaking radically different dialects.

In 1027 B.C., the Shang dynasty was overthrown by the king of Zhou, a small dependent nation in the west of Shang territory. During the Zhou dynasty (c. 1027–221 B.C.), the doctrine that the Chinese king was exercising a "Mandate of Heaven" in his rule developed. This later became an extremely important doctrine both to justify imperial rule and to explain the fall of an empire (should an emperor prove corrupt or weak, Heaven would remove its mandate). During this period, the great philosophers Confucius and Mencius produced their major works on ethics, and *The Book of Songs,* the earliest anthology of Chinese poetry and one of the Confucian classics, was collected. Legend says *The Book of Songs* was edited by Confucius himself from a larger, earlier corpus (thus it is sometimes known as *The Confucian Odes*). It was also in the first millennium B.C. that the other texts that were to make up the core of the Confucian classics were composed, including *The Book of Changes, The Book of Rights, The Book of History,* and *The Spring and Autumn Annals.*

The changing canon of the Confucian classics (which has at various times numbered as few as five and as many as thirteen books) has been the basis for the Chinese educational system from the second century B.C. to the early decades of the twentieth century. A thorough grounding in the moral precepts, historical examples, divinitory rights, and poetry contained in the classics was the essential preparation for a person pursuing an administrative career. The roots of the Chinese civil service system go back to the first imperial dynasty, the Qin dynasty (221–207 B.C.), ruled over by Emperor Qin Shi Huang Di, who brought the fragmented and warring states of China under one rule. This "first emperor" of China is notorious for decreeing that all books deemed threatening to the new order be burned. However, he also built the Great Wall and presided over a short-lived empire, the predecessor of a series of dynasties that—despite invasions from the north, peasant revolts, and periods of fragmentation—were to unite Chinese culture into a two-thousand-year tradition. It is perhaps most important that he created a system of political and social promotion based on ability versus nobility. Later, in the Sui dynasty (589–607), this system was augmented with a system of standardized examinations that applicants must pass for promotion. Though applicants of greater wealth had a distinct advantage (having had access to greater educational opportunities), the Chinese civil service system, which existed in various forms for more than two thousand years, has been the world's most successful and long-lived system of more-or-less egalitarian social promotion and was the basis for the British civil service system. Through this system there developed a literate class of scholar officials who had mastered the same essential knowledge, giving Chinese civilization a coherence and continuity that belie its political history of fragmentation, foreign invasion, civil war, and the rise and fall of dynasties.

This same commonality of knowledge has lent a somewhat insular aspect to Chinese literature, seen in the high use of literary allusion. A Confucian respect for the past has also fostered a Chinese esthetic of virtuoso performance within handed-down forms and genres. Strong reverence for tradition has led to periods of literary stagnation at times, but it is balanced by a counter-Confucian Chinese tradition of the innovative outsider. In the words of a commentator in *Poets' Jade Splinters,* a Song dynasty compilation of literary critiques, "The first taboo in writing is to walk behind others."

During the Zhou dynasty, two perhaps mythical men, Laozi and Zhuangzi, are said to have written paradoxical and mystical texts that were to become the core of the Daoist tradition. An ancient counterpoint to Confucian duty, morality, and politics was set down around the third century B.C. in these basic texts, the *Dao de Jing* and the *Zhuangzi*. Daoism celebrates whimsy, spontaneity, paradox, and a supreme good that is metaphysical (as opposed to the Confucian moral good). With its disdain for duty, power, and politics, Daoism is an ancient counter-tradition that has been central to the developing character of China.

Buddhism has been a third important philosophical and religious tradition in China. Both Theravada and Mahayana Buddhism came to China from Indian and central Asia around the second century A.D. At first Buddhism's influence was small, but its philosophy of the suffering in and impermanence of the mundane world caught on in the fourth century as China suffered war, invasion, and political and economic turbulence. Inevitably, Chinese Buddhists came to write their own compositions, some of which became scriptures for various Chinese Buddhist sects. Buddhist influence on literature owes much to the development of Chan (which in Japanese becomes Zen), a school that came to accept poetry as a form of religious expression. Great Chinese Buddhist poets include Han Shan and Wang Wei; great Japanese Buddhist writers include Saigyo, Kenko, Basho, and Ryokan. It should be understood that despite doctrinal differences, Buddhism and Daoism were mutually influential in China, and it was not uncommon for a poet such as Wang Wei to look back with equal reverence to his Daoist predecessor Tao Yuanming (365–427) and to the revered Indian lay Buddhist Vimalakirti.

Since poetry has been the mainstream of literary expression in Chinese literature, it is often afforded great powers of influence in the Chinese critical tradition, as in the "Great Preface" to *The Book of Songs*. The preface states that poetry is a Confucian rectifier that sets the proper relationships between spouses, establishes respect and loyalty for the old, strengthens human ties, ameliorates civilizations, and excises bad customs. Poetry is even afforded Daoist cosmic powers in texts such as Lu Ji's *The Art of Writing:* "With heaven and earth contained in your head/nothing escapes the pen in your hand."

Chinese metrics are based on the number of characters per line, each character being one phonetic syllable. Rhyme and rhythm have aesthetic value and also the semantic function of dividing and organizing units of meaning (especially important since Chinese poetry was unpunctuated until modern times). These formal ways of organizing meaning also help the reader to decipher the text. As the Chinese poet was a renaissance man or woman, skilled in diverse arts, Chinese poetry is a total art, often chanted or set to music, or calligraphically inscribed on paintings, screens, fans, or stone. In contrast to poetry in phonetic alphabets, Chinese poetics is built upon characters. Chinese characters, though popularly thought of in the West as wholly pictographic, are a combination of pictographic, phonetic, and ideographic elements. In part, a Chinese character, like the Arabic numeral, conveys meaning rather than sound, which has permitted it to be used by diversely pronounced dialects from all centuries, and even to be adopted into Korean and Japanese. In addition to simple pictographic and ideographic and phonetic characters, more complex characters developed through the combination of these elements: hence the sun and moon characters when combined make up the character for brightness (*ming*). At times, the visual and ideographic elements in the characters allow the poet to create radical condensation of meaning, to pun, to create ironies, and to convey pictures and ideas largely unavailable to poets restricted to phonetic alphabets. In the West, only the highly experimental visual poetics of Apollinaire's *Calligrammes,* the typographical forays of the Dada poets, the shaped poems of George Herbert and his medieval precursors, and the picture poems of contemporary Concrete poets attempt to merge image and meaning in a comparable fashion.

Qu Yuan (third c. B.C.) was the first Chinese poet whose name we know. His works are collected in the second most ancient collection of Chinese poetry, *The Songs of Chu,* and are celebrated for their Confucian dedication to duty and creation of a subjective and suffering persona, who bewails his personal condition. The Han dynasty (206 B.C.–A.D. 220) is notable for its rhyme-prose (*fu*), a form of mixed prose and poetry, and for the folk ballads (*yuefu*) gathered by the Music Bureau. The great poet of the Sixth Dynasties Period (220–589) was Tao Yuanming (365 or 372–427), whose poems of paradisal country retreat from the scholar-official's career make him China's Thoreau and a model for later poets. The golden age of Chinese poetry was the Tang dynasty (618–907). Its three major poets were the stylistic master and Confucian social commentator Du Fu (712–770), the Daoist romantic drunkard Li Bai (701–762), and the Daoist-Buddhist nature poet Wang Wei (701–761). The Tang also produced a corpus of poetry by extraordinary women poets, including Yu Xuanji (c. 843–868) and Xue Tao (768–831), as well as masterpieces in the Chinese short story, a minor form until then.

China's dynasties were continually threatened by invaders from the north, and, in the Song dynasty (960–1279), an invasion of the Manchurian Jurchens conquered northern China. In the Song dynasty, *ci* poems, a form of poetry set to melodies from central Asia, became extremely popular, and master poets emerged, including Ouyang Xiu (1007–1072), Su Dongpo (1036–1101), and Li Qingzhao (1084–c. 1151), among others. In the thirteenth century, Genghis Khan's Mongols invaded China and captured the north in 1234. In 1279, under Genghis Khan's grandson Kublai Khan, the Mongols overran the south, where the Southern Song dynasty had been stubbornly holding out. The succeeding Yuan dynasty (1280–1367) was ruled by Mongols, who incorporated much of the Chinese administrative system into their rule. During the Yuan dynasty, drama containing poetry flourished. During the Ming (1368–1644) and Qing (1644–1911) dynasties, the novel became prominent, with great works such as the fantastic, picaresque voyages of *Monkey,* the martial epic of *Three Kingdoms,* the erotic classic *The Golden Lotus,* and the dynastic epic *Dream of the Red Chamber.* The Qing dynasty was yet another period in which China was ruled by northern invaders, this time by the Manchus, a Manchurian tribe descended from the Jurchens.

The modern era was marked by humiliating interactions with Western and Eastern colonial powers. In the nineteenth century, China was forced to surrender Hong Kong to the British; open itself to trade, unequal treaties, and the importation of opium; and also allow the establishment of foreign zones in Shanghai, which were under extraterritorial administration. The Chinese imperial system fell in 1911 to a revolution that established a republic in China under the rule of Sun Yatsen. There followed a pattern of incursions from Japan that culminated in the occupation of Manchuria in 1931 and the invasion of China in 1937. Mao Zedong began his revolution in 1926, and after twenty-three years of civil war, on October 1, 1949, a new dynasty began in Beijing under Communist rule. During these turbulent times prior to the Communist revolution, the Chinese literati system was abolished, and Chinese intellectuals turned increasingly to Western models in their poetry, essays, and fiction. Some adopted a romantic/modernist estheticism, while others, like Lu Xun (1881–1936), wrote short stories with a radical agenda.

With Communist rule came a new era in China and for Chinese writers. At his *Talks at the Yenan Forum on Literature and Art,* Mao Zedong set out the basis for acceptable literature under Marxism: art and literature are for the masses, should be about them as well, and have the purpose of "producing works that awaken the masses, fire them with enthusiasm, and impel them to unite and struggle to transform the environment." This doctrine paralleled the strictures placed upon writing in 1932 by the Union of Soviet Writers, which proclaimed Socialist Realism as a compulsory literary practice. However, in China this doctrine produced little work of lasting value, and literature went into an eclipse for decades. In successive political moments, the Anti-Rightist Campaign (1957) and the Cultural Revolution (1966–1976), writers, artists, and intellectuals suffered severe governmental repression. After the death of Mao in 1976, the arts in China began to flourish again, along with a nascent Democracy Movement that many writers were associated with in its various incarnations. In recent years, waves of repression and censorship culminated in the Tiananmen Square massacre in 1989, in which the army was called in to disperse Democracy Movement protestors, hundreds of whom were killed. Many Chinese writers have gone into exile since then.

# Zhou Dynasty

## (1027–221 B.C.)

## ■ The Book of Songs (c. 600 B.C.) (poems)

*The Book of Songs* is the earliest anthology of Chinese poetry and the thematic and formal source of the Chinese poetic tradition. The Chinese name for *The Book of Songs* is the *Shi Jing,* and the term *shi* (the general term for poetry, like the Japanese *waka*) derives from its name. Legend has it that its three hundred and five anonymous poems were compiled by Confucius (551–479 B.C.) from an earlier manuscript of around three thousand songs. The assertion that Confucius was the compiler is questionable, but certainly the anthology was extant in Confucius' time, and it seems likely that the anthology was collected between 1100 and 600 B.C. Confucius refers to *The Book of Songs* in the *Analects,* and it was part of the curriculum of his disciples; it is counted among the Confucian classics that form the basis of Confucian education. The collection was banned in the third century B.C., along with the other Confucian classics during the Qin dynasty's "burning of the books," but it was reconstructed during the Han dynasty, and the recension that is most complete derives from this time. *The Book of Songs* contains three basic categories of song: folk songs and ballads, court songs, and songs to accompany ritual dancing and the rites of ancestor worship. Like the Sanskrit Vedas, these songs provide a window onto the simple and beautiful life of an ancient time. Heroes and ancestors are praised; love is made; war is waged; farmers sing to their crops; people complain about their taxes; and moral categories are set forth in stark and powerful forms. Though these poems are songs, the music has been lost. Some of them have been revised from folksong roots by court musicians, rhymed, and arranged into stanzas.

**FURTHER READING**: Karlgren, Bernhard. *The Book of Odes,* 1950. Legge, James. *The Chinese Classics,* Vol. 3, 1960. McNaughton, William. *The Book of Songs,* 1971. Pound, Ezra. *The Classic Anthology as Defined by Confucius,* 1954. Waley, Arthur. *The Book of Songs,* 1937. Wang, C. H. *The Bell and the Drum: Shih Ching as Formulaic Poetry in an Oral Tradition,* 1974.

## *In the Wilds Is a Dead River-Deer*

In the wilds is a dead river-deer
wrapped in white rushes.
A lady yearned for spring
and a fine man seduced her.

In the woods are clusters of bushes          5
and in the wilds a dead river-deer
wrapped in white rushes.
There was a lady fine as jade.

Oh! Slow down, don't be so rough,
let go of my girdle's sash.          10
Shhh! You'll make the dog bark.

TRANSLATED BY TONY BARNSTONE AND CHOU PING

## Fruit Plummets from the Plum Tree

Fruit plummets from the plum tree
but seven of ten plums remain;
you gentlemen who would court me,
come on a lucky day.

Fruit plummets from the plum tree
but three of ten plums still remain;
you men who want to court me,
come now, today is a lucky day!

Fruit plummets from the plum tree.
You can fill up your baskets.
Gentlemen if you want to court me,
just say the word.

TRANSLATED BY TONY BARNSTONE AND CHOU PING

## White Moonrise

The white rising moon
is your bright beauty
binding me in spells
till my heart's devoured.

The light moon soars
resplendent like my lady,
binding me in light chains
till my heart's devoured.

Moon in white glory,
you are the beautiful one
who delicately wounds me
till my heart's devoured.

TRANSLATED BY TONY BARNSTONE AND WILLIS BARNSTONE

## Ripe Millet[1]

Rows and rows of ripe millet,
the sorghum sprouts,

---

1. According to the "Preface" of *The Book of Songs,* the poet is a minister of the Eastern Zhou dynasty (770–256 B.C.). He comes to the capital city of the earlier Western Zhou dynasty (tenth century–771 B.C.) and finds all the temples are destroyed and the royal palace is replaced by rows and rows of millet. Moved by time's ravages, he improvises this poem.

and I take long slow walks
with a shaking, shaken heart.
My friends say                                            *5*
"His heart is hurting"
but strangers wonder
"What can he be looking for?"
O far far blue heaven
what makes me feel this way?                              *10*

Rows and rows of ripe millet,
the sorghum is in spike,
and I take long slow walks
with a drunken heart.
My friends say                                            *15*
"His heart is hurting"
but strangers wonder
"What can he be looking for?"
O far far blue heaven
what makes me feel this way?                              *20*

Rows and rows of ripe millet,
the sorghum is all grain,
and I take long slow walks
with a choking heart.
My friends say                                            *25*
"His heart is hurting"
but strangers wonder
"What can he be looking for?"
O far far blue heaven
what makes me feel this way?                              *30*

TRANSLATED BY TONY BARNSTONE AND CHOU PING

## There Are Tall Weeds in the Fields

There are tall weeds in the fields
with glistening dew drops.
Here comes a beautiful girl
with eyes like clear water.
We meet here by chance—                                   *5*
just as I wished.

Here are tall weeds in the fields
with sparking dew drops.
There comes a beautiful girl,
graceful as her eyes.                                     *10*

We meet here by chance—
let's find a place and hide.

TRANSLATED BY TONY BARNSTONE AND CHOU PING

## When the Gourd Has Dried Leaves[1]

When the gourd has dried leaves,
you can wade the deep river.
Keep your clothes on if the water's deep;
hitch up your dress when it's shallow.

The river is rising,
pheasants are chirping.
The water is just half a wheel deep,
and the hen is chirping for the cock.

Wild geese are trilling,
the rising sun starts dawn.
If you want to marry me,
come before the river is frozen.

The ferry-man is gesturing,
other people are going, but not me,
other people are going, but not me,
I'm waiting for you.

TRANSLATED BY TONY BARNSTONE AND CHOU PING

## All the Grasslands Are Yellow

All the grasslands are yellow
and all the days we march
and all the men are conscripts
sent off in four directions.

All the grasslands are black
and all the men like widowers.
So much grief! Are soldiers
not men like other men?

---

1. The ancient Chinese used to tie gourds around their waists as a safety device when wading across a river.

We aren't bison! We aren't tigers
crossing the wilderness, 10
but our sorrows
roam from dawn till dusk.

Hairy tailed foxes slink
through the dark grass
as we ride tall chariots 15
along the wide rutted roads.

TRANSLATED BY TONY BARNSTONE AND CHOU PING

# Confucius (c. 551–479 B.C.) (philosophy)

TRANSLATED BY RAYMOND DAWSON

Confucius is a distant romanization of the Chinese name Kong and the appelation Fuzi, meaning "master" (thus Confucius = Master Kong). Definite evidence about the life of Confucius is scant and legends abound, so modern scholars have tried to detect the man through internal evidence in *The Analects* (a collection of his dialogues and utterances probably recorded by his disciples after his death). Confucius was born in humble circumstances in what is today Shandong province, in the feudal state of Lu, at a time of incessant warfare among the Chinese states. The Zhou dynasty had broken into warring factions, and Confucius sought to restore the lost peace and to guide governments in how to rule fairly and well; he proposed a system of conduct for all people based on an ultimate principle of *ren,* or humanism, goodness. This humanism is to be expressed through etiquette and ritual, or *li;* a government based on such moral principles and order will be reflected in the behavior of its populace. Underlings should be loyal to their rulers, yet critical of them when they part from the Way (*Dao*), and people should behave with empathy for one another: "Do not inflict on others what you yourself would not wish done to you." One should practice self-control and respect for ancestors and behave correctly to family, with a sense of deep filial respect. Family relations function as a microcosm of those of the state.

Confucius had a dream of an ideal society, with virtuous, hardworking people ruled over by incorruptible, wise, and benevolent officials—a system of order and mutual respect. His vision had as profound an effect on Chinese government and ethics as the laws of Manu did on India, as the ancient legal code of the Babylonian king Hammurabi did on the Judeo-Christian tradition, or Plato's dialogic vision on Western civilization. A distinguishing feature of his philosophy is that religion has no part in it, though his thought was later distorted to incorporate supernatural elements and to support tyrannical governments. Confucius never achieved the sort of important position he coveted, despite years of wandering China to spread his ideas and to convince rulers to accept his reforms; but his disciples did, and they spread his thought so successfully that a Confucian education became the essential preparation for entry into the Chinese scholar bureaucracy. *The Analects* of Confucius is only one of a number of Confucian classics, whose memorization was the moral and intellectual grounding of the Confucian path of study. The classics include such texts as *The Book of Songs* and *The Book of Changes,* and their total number varies between five and thirteen, depending on what source and dynasty is studied. In the first century A.D., a practice began of offering sacrifices and veneration in shrines devoted to Confucius, a practice that has continued through this century. It has been eclipsed at times by other systems of order and religion and was banned in 213 B.C. by the first Qin emperor. But the Confucian canon was reconstructed by Emperor Wu in 136 B.C., and at several times in Chinese history, it became a state religion.

**FURTHER READING:** Creel, H. G. *Confucius: The Man and the Myth,* 1951. Dawson, Raymond, tr. *Confucius: The Analects,* 1993. Hall, D. L., and R. T. Ames. *Thinking Through Confucius,* 1987. Lau, D.C., tr. *Confucius: The Analects,* 1979. Waley, Arthur, tr. *The Analects of Confucius,* 1938.

## *from* **The Analects**

# Book 1

2. Master You[1] said: 'Few indeed are those who are naturally filial towards their parents and dutiful towards their elder brothers but are fond of opposing their superiors; and it never happens that those who do not like opposing their superiors are fond of creating civil disorder.[2] The gentleman concerns himself with the root; and if the root is firmly planted, the Way grows. Filial piety and fraternal duty—surely they are the roots of humaneness.'

3. The Master said: 'Clever words and a plausible appearance have seldom turned out to be humane.'

6. The Master said: 'Young men should be filial when at home and respectful to elders when away from home. They should be earnest and trustworthy. Although they should love the multitude far and wide,

---

1. You Ruo is generally referred to as Master You, and he makes his own pronouncements instead of merely putting questions to Master Kong. Clearly he was a teacher in the Confucian tradition.

2. This sentence is an expression of what later became the standard Confucian view that the political virtues of obedience and loyalty are family virtues writ large.

they should be intimate only with the humane. If they have any energy to spare after so doing, they should use it to study "culture".'

11. The Master said: 'When his father is alive, you observe a man's intentions. It is when the father is dead that you observe the man's actions. If for three years he makes no change from the ways of his father, he may be called filial.'

16. The Master said: 'One does not worry about the fact that other people do not appreciate one. One worries about not appreciating other people.'

# Book 2

2. The Master said: 'The *Songs* number three hundred, but I will cover their meaning with a single quotation: "Let there be no depravity in your thoughts."'[3]

3. The Master said: 'If you lead them by means of government and keep order among them by means of punishments, the people are without conscience in evading them. If you lead them by means of virtue and keep order among them by means of ritual, they have a conscience and moreover will submit.'

11. The Master said: 'If by keeping the old warm one can provide understanding of the new, one is fit to be a teacher.'

12. The Master said: 'A gentleman does not behave as an implement.'[4]

17. The Master said: 'You,[5] shall I teach you about understanding something? When you understand something, to recognize that you understand it; but when you do not understand something, to recognize that you do not understand it—that is understanding.'

19. Duke Ai[6] asked: 'What action does one take so that the people will be obedient?' Master Kong replied saying: 'If you promote the straight and set them above the crooked, then the people will be obedient. If you promote the crooked and set them above the straight, then the people will not be obedient.'

---

3. The *Songs* are *The Book of Songs,* one of the Confucian classics [Editor].

4. This important saying puts in a nutshell the belief that the gentleman's training should not be confined to particular skills so that he may become the tool or implement of others. It must instead develop his moral qualities and powers of leadership. Thus in the later Empire the traditional Chinese education for government service was concerned with the study of Confucian writings rather than with the acquisition of techniques.

5. The personal name of the well-known disciple Zilu, whose character shines clearly through this motley collection of sayings and anecdotes. He was an extrovert man of action and not very fond of learning. Often the exchanges between Zilu and Master Kong, brief though they are, shed an amusing light on the character of Zilu and the Master's attitude towards him.

6. Ruler of Lu between 494 and 468 [B.C.]. The actual power was in the hands of the Three Families, so presumably this was said when he was planning to try to regain power.

22. The Master said: 'If someone is untrustworthy in spite of being a man, I do not know that he will do. If carriages have no means of yoking horses to them, how are they ever made to go?'

# Book 4

5. The Master said: 'Riches and honours—these are what men desire, but if this is not achieved in accordance with the appropriate principles, one does not cling to them. Poverty and obscurity—these are what men hate, but if this is not achieved in accordance with the appropriate principles, one does not avoid them. If a gentleman abandons humaneness, how does he make a reputation? The gentleman never shuns humaneness even for the time it takes to finish a meal. If his progress is hasty, it is bound to arise from this; and if his progress is unsteady, it is bound to arise from this.'

8. The Master said: 'If one has heard the Way in the morning, it is all right to die in the evening.'

14. The Master said: 'One is not worried about not holding position; one is worried about how one may fit oneself for appointment. One is not worried that nobody knows one; one seeks to become fit to be known.'

16. The Master said: 'The gentleman is familiar with what is right, just as the small man is familiar with profit.'

17. The Master said: 'When you come across a superior person, think of being equal to him. When you come across an inferior person, turn inwards and examine yourself.'

18. The Master said: 'In serving father and mother, one remonstrates gently. If one sees that they are intent on not following advice, one continues to be respectful and does not show disobedience; and even if one finds it burdensome, one does not feel resentful.'

23. The Master said: 'There are few indeed who fail in something through exercising restraint.'

24. The Master said: 'The gentleman wishes to be slow in speech but prompt in action.'

25. The Master said: 'Virtue is not solitary. It is bound to have neighbours.'

# Book 5

1. The Master said of Gongye Chang that he might be given a wife for, although he had been put in prison, this was not through any crime of his. He gave him his own daughter in marriage.

9. The Master said to Zigong[7]: 'Out of You and Hui which is the better?' He replied: 'How dare I even have a look at Hui? Hui is the sort of person who, by hearing one thing, understands ten; but I am the sort of person who, by hearing one thing, understands two.' The Master said: 'You are not as good as he is. Both you and I are not as good as he is.'

12. Zigong said: 'If I do not want others to inflict something on me, I also want to avoid inflicting it on others.' The Master said: 'Si, this is not a point you have yet reached.'

20. Ji Wen Zi thought three times before acting. When the Master heard of this, he said: 'Twice will do.'

24. The Master said: 'Who says that Weisheng Gao[8] was upright? Someone begged vinegar from him and he begged it from his neighbour and handed it over.'

# Book 6

11. The Master said: 'A man of quality indeed was Hui! He lived in a squalid alley with a tiny bowlful of rice to eat and a ladleful of water to drink. Other men would not endure such hardships, but Hui did not let his happiness be affected. A man of quality indeed was Hui!'

23. The Master said: 'The wise delight in water, but the humane delight in mountains. For although the wise are active, the humane are at rest. And although the wise will find joy, the humane will have long life.'

# Book 7

19. The Duke of She asked Zilu about Master Kong. Zilu did not reply. The Master said: 'Why did you not just say that he is the sort of person who gets so worked up that he forgets to eat, is so happy that he forgets anxieties, and is not aware that old age will come.'

37. The Master said: 'The gentleman is calm and peaceful; the small man is always emotional.'

38. The Master was genial and yet strict, imposing and yet not intimidating, courteous and yet at ease.

---

7. Zigong was one of Confucius' best-known disciples. He is also referred to as Si . . . [Editor].

8. He was so insistent on keeping his promises that, having said he would meet his girlfriend in the dried-up bed of a stream, he drowned because the water rose before she turned up; but Master Kong had apparently heard something less flattering about him.

# Book 8

8. The Master said: 'One is roused by the Songs, established by ritual, and perfected by music.'

9. The Master said: 'The people may be made to follow something, but may not be made to understand it.'

21. The Master said: 'In Yu it seems there is no fault as far as I am concerned. Although he ate and drank abstemiously, he displayed the utmost devotion[9] towards the ghosts and spirits. Although normally he wore poor garments, he displayed the utmost elegance in his sacrificial robes and headdress. He lived in humble dwellings, but devoted all his energies to drains and ditches. In Yu it seems there is no fault as far as I am concerned.'

# Book 9

2. A villager from Daxiang said: 'Great indeed is Master Kong, but despite his broad learning there is nothing for which he has made a reputation.' When the Master heard this, he told his disciples: 'What do I take up? Do I take up charioteering?[10] Or do I take up archery? I take up charioteering.'

11. Yan Hui, sighing heavily, said: 'The more I look up to it,[11] the higher it is; the more I penetrate it, the harder it becomes; I see it ahead of me and suddenly it is behind. Our Master skilfully lures people on step by step. He broadens me with culture and restrains me with ritual. If I wanted to stop, I could not; and when I have exhausted all my talents, it seems as if there is something which he has established profoundly; but even though I long to pursue it, I have no way of doing so at all.'

14. The Master wished to dwell among the nine wild tribes of the East. Someone said: 'They are uncivilized, so what will you do about that?' The Master said: 'If a gentleman dwelt among them, what lack of civility would they show?'

18. The Master said: 'I have never come across anyone who admires virtue as much as he admires sexual attraction.'

26. The Master said: 'The three armies can be robbed of their commander, but an ordinary person cannot be robbed of his purpose.'

---

9. In supplying plentiful sacrificial food in contrast with his own personal abstemiousness.

10. A sarcastic response to the failure to appreciate that the gentleman is a generalist rather than a specialist.

11. Master Kong's teaching. This is a classic account of the disciples' admiration.

# Book 10

11. When the stables caught fire the Master, on returning from court, said: 'Did anyone get hurt?' He did not ask about the horses.

# Book 11

9. When Yan Hui[12] died, the Master said: 'Alas, Heaven has bereaved me, Heaven has bereaved me!'

10. When Yan Hui died, the Master became distressed as he bewailed him. His followers said: 'Master, you have become distressed.' 'Have I?' he said. 'Well, if that man is not to be the object of my distress, then for whom am I to be distressed?'

# Book 12

2. Zhonggong[13] asked about humaneness. The Master said: 'When you are away from home, behave as if receiving an important guest. Employ the people as if you were officiating at a great sacrifice. Do not impose on others what you would not like yourself. Then there will be no resentment against you, either in the state or in the family.' Zhonggong said: 'Although I am not clever, I beg to put this advice into practice.'

3. Sima Niu[14] asked about humaneness. The Master said: 'The humane person is hesitant in his speech.' He said: 'Hesitant in his speech! Is that all that is meant by humaneness?' The Master said: 'To do it is difficult, so in speaking about it can one avoid being hesitant?'

7. Zigong asked about government. The Master said: 'If there is enough food and if there are enough weapons, the people will put their trust in it.' Zigong said: 'Suppose you definitely had no alternative but to give up one of these three, which would you relinquish first?' The Master said: 'I would give up weapons.' Zigong said: 'Suppose you definitely had no alternative but to give up one of the remaining two, which would you relinquish first?' The Master said: 'I would give up food. From of old death has come to all men, but a people will not stand if it lacks trust.'

8. Ji Zicheng said: 'A gentleman is merely the stuff he is made of. Why take account of culture?' Zigong said: 'It is a pity you said that, sir, about the gentleman, since a team of four horses will not catch up with the tongue. Culture is just as important as the stuff one is made

---

12. Yan Hui was Confucius' favorite disciple [Editor].

13. Zhonggong (alias Ran Yong) was a disciple [Editor].

14. Sima Niu was a disciple [Editor].

of, and the stuff one is made of is just as important as culture. The skin of a tiger or leopard is no different from the skin of a dog or a sheep.'

17. Ji Kang Zi[15] asked Master Kong about government. Master Kong replied: 'To govern means to correct. If you take the lead by being correct, who will dare not to be corrected?'

19. Ji Kang Zi asked Master Kong about government, saying: 'Suppose I were to kill those who lack the Way in order to advance those who have the Way, how would that be?' Master Kong replied: 'You are running the government, so what is the point of killing? If you desire good, the people will be good. The nature of the gentleman is as the wind, and the nature of the small man is as the grass. When the wind blows over the grass it always bends.'

22. Fan Chi[16] asked about humaneness. The Master said: 'It is to love others.' He asked about understanding. The Master said: 'It is to understand others.' Fan Chi had not yet fathomed his meaning, so the Master said: 'If one raises the straight and puts them above the crooked one can make the crooked become straight.'

# Book 13

3. Zilu said: 'If the Lord of Wei were waiting for you to run the government, what would you give priority to?' The Master said: 'What is necessary is to rectify names, is it not?' Zilu said: 'If this were to take place, it would surely be an aberration of yours. Why should they be rectified?' The Master said: 'How uncivilized you are. With regard to what he does not understand the gentleman is surely somewhat reluctant to offer an opinion. If names are not rectified, then words are not appropriate. If words are not appropriate, then deeds are not accomplished. If deeds are not accomplished, then the rites and music do not flourish. If the rites and music do not flourish, then punishments do not hit the mark. If punishments do not hit the mark, then the people have nowhere to put hand or foot. So when a gentleman names something, the name can definitely be used in speech; and when he says something, it can definitely be put into practice. In his utterances the gentleman is definitely not casual about anything.'

5. The Master said: 'A man may know by heart the three hundred *Songs*, but if he is given a post in government and cannot successfully carry out his duties, and if he is sent to far places and cannot react to the

---

15. Ji Kang Zi was the head of one of the powerful three families who ousted the rulers of Lu, Confucius' home state [Editor].

16. A disciple.

circumstances as he finds them, then even if he has learnt to recite many of them, of what use is this to him?'

11. The Master said: '"If good men ran a state for a hundred years, they might therefore vanquish cruelty and abolish killing." How true is this saying!'

15. Duke Ding[17] asked if there was a single saying with which one might make a state prosperous. Master Kong replied: 'A saying cannot be quite like that. But there is a saying among men which runs "to be a ruler is difficult and to be a subject is not easy". If one understands that to be a ruler is difficult, then does this not come close to making a state prosperous through one saying?' He said: 'Is there a single saying with which one might ruin a state?' Master Kong replied: 'A saying cannot be quite like that. But there is a saying among men which runs "I have no pleasure in being a ruler, except that nobody opposes me with his words." As far as his good points are concerned, it is surely good, isn't it, that nobody opposes him? But as far as his bad points are concerned, if nobody opposes him, is this not close to ruining a state with a single saying?'

18. The Duke of She told Master Kong: 'In my locality there is a certain paragon, for when his father stole a sheep, he, the son, bore witness against him.' Master Kong said: 'In my locality those who are upright are different from this. Fathers cover up for their sons[18] and sons cover up for their fathers. Uprightness is to be found in this.'

# Book 14

22. Zilu asked about serving a ruler. The Master said: 'It means don't be deceitful. But do stand up to him.'

27. The Master said: 'The gentleman is ashamed that his words have outstripped his deeds.'

30. The Master said: 'One does not worry about the fact that other people do not appreciate one. One worries about the fact that one is incapable.'

34. Someone said: 'What about "Repay hostility with kindness"?' The Master said: 'How then do you repay kindness? Repay hostility with uprightness and repay kindness with kindness.'

---

17. The Duke of Lu.

18. This encapsulates the Chinese regard for the importance of the family as compared with the state. Informing against parents in antiquity, as more recently in the Cultural Revolution, represents the antithesis of Confucian values.

35. The Master said: 'Nobody understands me, do they?' Zigong said: 'Why is it that none of them understands you?' The Master said: 'I do not feel resentful towards Heaven and I do not put blame on men. But although my studies are of lowly things they reach up above, and the one that understands me will be Heaven, will it not?'

41. The Master said: 'If their superior loves the rites,[19] the people will be easy to command.'

43. Yuan Rang was waiting in an oafish manner. The Master said: 'When he was young he was not deferential, so when he grew up nothing was passed on by him, and now he is an old man he does not die—this seems terrible.' And he struck his shins with a stick.

# Book 15

2. When they were in Chen they suffered an interruption in the supply of provisions, so the followers became ill and nobody was capable of getting up. Feeling aggrieved, Zilu addressed the Master. 'Does suffering exist even for the gentleman?' he said. The Master said: 'The gentleman remains firm in the face of suffering, but if the small man suffers, he is carried away on a flood of excess.'

8. The Master said: 'Not to talk with people although they can be talked with is to waste people. To talk with people although they can't be talked with is to waste words. A man of understanding does not waste people, but he also does not waste words.'

12. The Master said: 'If a man avoids thinking about distant matters he will certainly have worries close at hand.'

21. The Master said: 'What the gentleman seeks in himself the small man seeks in others.'

23. The Master said: 'Gentlemen do not promote someone because of what he says, and do not reject what is said because of who said it.'

24. Zigong asked: 'Is there a single word such that one could practise it throughout one's life?' The Master said: 'Reciprocity perhaps? Do not inflict on others what you yourself would not wish done to you.'

30. The Master said: 'If one commits an error and does not reform, this is what is meant by an error.'

35. The Master said: 'The people's connection with humaneness is more important than water or fire. As for water and fire, I have come across people who have died through stepping on them, but I have never come across people who have died through stepping on humaneness.'

---

19. Refers to religious practice, but ritual also suggests a sense of reverence toward life.

# Book 16

7. Master Kong said: 'There are three things which the gentleman guards against: in the time of his youth, when his vital powers have not yet settled down, he is on his guard in matters of sex; when he reaches the prime of life and his vital powers have just attained consistency, he is on his guard in matters of contention; and when he becomes old and his vital powers have declined, he is on his guard in matters of acquisition.'

8. Master Kong said: 'There are three things which the gentleman holds in awe: he is in awe of the decree of Heaven, he is in awe of great men, and he is in awe of the words of sages. The small man, being unaware of the decree of Heaven, is not in awe of it. He is rude to great men and ridicules the words of sages.'

# Book 17

2. The Master said: 'Only the most intelligent and the most stupid do not change.'

6. When Bi Xi sent for him, the Master wanted to go. Zilu said: 'Master, I once heard the following from you: "If someone in his own person does those things which are not good, the gentleman does not enter his domain." Bi Xi is carrying out a rebellion using Zhongmou as his base, so what is the point of your going there?' The Master said: 'Yes, I have said such a thing, but is it not said that "hard indeed is that which is not worn thin by grinding" and "white indeed is that which will not turn black from dyeing"? Surely I am not just a bitter gourd![20] How can I hang there and not be eaten?'

8. The Master said: 'My young friends, why do none of you study the *Songs*? The *Songs* may help one to be stimulated, to observe, to be sociable, and to express grievances. One uses them at home to serve one's father, and one uses them in distant places to serve one's ruler. One also gains much knowledge concerning the names of birds and beasts and plants and trees.'

   The Master said to Boyu: 'Have you done the *Zhounan* and *Shaonan*?[21] If although one is a man one has not done the *Zhounan* and *Shaonan*, surely it is like standing with one's face to the wall?'

13. The Master said: 'Is it really possible to serve one's ruler alongside vulgar persons? For while they have not yet obtained something, they are worried about obtaining it; and when they have obtained it, they are

---

20. A potent symbol of Master Kong's frustration at not obtaining employment. This time the employment would have been in the state of Jin rather than in his native state of Lu. The sayings about grinding and dyeing are meant to indicate the Master's incorruptibility.

21. First two books of the *Book of Songs*.

worried about losing it. And if they are worried about losing it, there are no lengths to which they will not go.'

23. The Master said: 'Only women[22] and small men seem difficult to look after. If you keep them close, they become insubordinate; but if you keep them at a distance, they become resentful.'

## Book 19

21. Zigong said: 'The errors of the gentleman are like eclipses of the sun and moon. When he errs everyone observes him; and when he makes a correction, everyone looks up to him.'

■ **Laozi (Lao Tzu) (c. Fourth to Third Centuries B.C.) (poems/philosophy)**

TRANSLATED BY GIA-FU FENG AND JANE ENGLISH

Laozi was the legendary author of the *Dao De Jing*, a collection of prose and verse wisdom literature that is considered the seminal and essential work of Daoism. Yet about Laozi and the *Dao De Jing* mysteries abound. It is by no means certain that a historical personage named Laozi ever existed. The title *Dao De Jing* (*Classic of the Way and Its Power*) is a later name for the collection that originally was called simply *Laozi*. Since Laozi also means "old man," and there is evidence of a body of wisdom literature whose various book titles all translate as "elder" or "old man," it may be that this collection is the lone survivor of this lost genre. It may be that the *Dao De Jing* is an anthology of sayings by diverse authors linked by common themes or the work of one author augmented by later redactors. The traditional Laozi is said to have been an older contemporary of Confucius (551– 479 B.C.) who instructed the younger sage in the rites, but this story seems not to have circulated until the third century B.C. It is now thought that the text dates from no earlier than the third or fourth centuries B.C. In the first century B.C., the famous historian Sima Qian recounted the Confucius encounter and other stories about Laozi, which he gathered from sources now lost. The story about Laozi's writing the *Dao De Jing* follows:

Laozi cultivated the way and virtue, and his teachings aimed at self-effacement. He lived in Zhou for a long time, but seeing its decline he departed; when he reached the Pass, the Keeper there was pleased and said to him, "As you are about to leave the world behind, could you write a book for

---

22. Commentators of course attempt to soften the misogyny.

my sake?" As a result, Laozi wrote a work in two books, setting out the meaning of the way and virtue in some five thousand characters, and then departed. None knew where he went to in the end.[1]

The book itself has more than the five thousand characters mentioned by Sima Qian and is divided into eighty-one chapters in two sections. Unlike the *Zhuangzi*, the *Dao De Jing* is not a work of anecdotes and parables; it is a general, didactic work of great poetic beauty, mystery, and ambiguity. Central to the work and to Daoism is the concept of the *Dao*, which means the way, method, or reason.[2] The Dao is ineffable—it can't be captured in words; it is as small as the essential nature of the smallest thing and as large as the entire universe. The term *De* means "virtue" and refers to the nature of a thing—its inherent virtue and energy. The term *Jing* means "classic," and thus the title of the book translates as *The Classic of the Dao and the De*. The Dao in this work is seen as the source of the world, as everything and, at the same time, nothing. It is fluid, weak, and passive, yet it conquers all and is the source of all action. Its nature is paradoxical because it is so large that it contains both ends of all oppositions. The Dao is also a contemplative method for understanding oneself and for merging with the Dao. Different interpreters see it either as a method of survival through passive resistance written in a time of great insecurity and turmoil or as a more mystical treatise. In any case, a number of passages treat the proper behavior of citizen and ruler and suggest that true self-interest lies in selflessness (thus, the ruler must humble himself before the people in order to rule, follow in order to lead).

Like Confucianism, Daoism took on magical elements as it developed, and the longevity of the follower of the Dao (who would live longer in turbulent times) was interpreted as physical immortality. Daoism resembled Western alchemy in its quest for the secret of immortality and, later, came in part to blend with Buddhism. Throughout Chinese literature and intellectual history, Daoism has been a liberating counterbalance to the dogmatic order of Confucianism. The *Dao De Jing* has been translated into English dozens of times, with varying degrees of success. At one end of the spectrum are scholarly, authoritative, and informative translations, which are inconsistently successful as poetry; at the other end of the spectrum are poetic interpretations, or modern imitations, which are good literature throughout but in which this ancient text is radically modernized. In searching for a compromise, we have settled on a lesser-known translation that attempts to be as true as possible to an original text that is notoriously ambiguous, while reflecting in lucid English its mysteriousness and literary qualities.

---

1. D. C. Lau, tr. *Lao Tzu: Tao Te Ching* (Harmondsworth: Penguin, 1963), 9. The Wade-Giles transliteration of this quotation has been changed to the Pinyin system.
2. In the translation that follows, "Dao" is transliterated as "Tao."

**FURTHER READING:** Chan, Wing-tsit, tr. *The Way of Lao Tzu*, 1963. Feng, Gia-fu, and Jane English, trs. *Lao Tsu: Tao Te Ching*, 1972. Lau, D. C., tr. *Lao Tzu: Tao Te Ching*, 1963. Waley, Arthur. *The Way and Its Power*, 1934. Wu, John C. H., tr. *Tao Teh Ching*, 1961.

## *from* **The Dao De Jing**

### One

The Tao that can be told is not the eternal Tao.
The name that can be named is not the eternal name.
The nameless is the beginning of heaven and earth.
The named is the mother of ten thousand things.
Ever desireless, one can see the mystery.                                    5
Ever desiring, one can see the manifestations.
These two spring from the same source but differ in name; this
     appears as darkness.
Darkness within darkness.
The gate to all mystery.

### Four

The Tao is an empty vessel; it is used, but never filled.
Oh, unfathomable source of ten thousand things!
Blunt the sharpness,
Untangle the knot,
Soften the glare,                                                            5
Merge with dust.
Oh, hidden deep but ever present!
I do not know from whence it comes.
It is the forefather of the emperors.

### Eleven

Thirty spokes share the wheel's hub;
It is the center hole that makes it useful.
Shape clay into a vessel;
It is the space within that makes it useful.
Cut doors and windows for a room;                                            5
It is the holes which make it useful.
Therefore profit comes from what is there;
Usefulness from what is not there.

### Sixteen

Empty yourself of everything.
Let the mind rest at peace.
The ten thousand things rise and fall while the Self watches their
     return.

They grow and flourish and then return to the source.
Returning to the source is stillness, which is the way of nature. . 5
The way of nature is unchanging.
Knowing constancy is insight.
Not knowing constancy leads to disaster.
Knowing constancy, the mind is open.
With an open mind, you will be openhearted. 10
Being openhearted, you will act royally.
Being royal, you will attain the divine.
Being divine, you will be at one with the Tao.
Being at one with the Tao is eternal.
And though the body dies, the Tao will never pass away. 15

*Twenty-two*

Yield and overcome;
Bend and be straight;
Empty and be full;
Wear out and be new;
Have little and gain; 5
Have much and be confused.

Therefore wise men embrace the one
And set an example to all.
Not putting on a display,
They shine forth. 10
Not justifying themselves,
They are distinguished.
Not boasting,
They receive recognition.
Not bragging, 15
They never falter.
They do not quarrel,
So no one quarrels with them.
Therefore the ancients say, "Yield and overcome."
Is that an empty saying? 20
Be really whole,
And all things will come to you.

*Thirty*

Whenever you advise a ruler in the way of Tao,
Counsel him not to use force to conquer the universe.
For this would only cause resistance.
Thorn bushes spring up wherever the army has passed.
Lean years follow in the wake of a great war. 5
Just do what needs to be done.
Never take advantage of power.

Achieve results,
But never glory in them.
Achieve results,
But never boast.
Achieve results,
But never be proud.
Achieve results,
Because this is the natural way.
Achieve results,
But not through violence.

Force is followed by loss of strength.
This is not the way of Tao.
That which goes against the Tao comes to an early end.

*Thirty-three*

Knowing others is wisdom;
Knowing the self is enlightenment.
Mastering others requires force;
Mastering the self needs strength.

He who knows he has enough is rich.
Perseverance is a sign of will power.
He who stays where he is endures.
To die but not to perish is to be eternally present.

*Forty-three*

The softest thing in the universe
Overcomes the hardest thing in the universe.
That without substance can enter where there is no room.
Hence I know the value of non-action.

Teaching without words and work without doing
Are understood by very few.

*Forty-seven*

Without going outside, you may know the whole world.
Without looking through the window, you may see the ways of heaven.
The farther you go, the less you know.

Thus the sage knows without traveling;
He sees without looking;
He works without doing.

*Forty-nine*

The sage has no mind of his own.
He is aware of the needs of others.

I am good to people who are good.
I am also good to people who are not good.

Because Virtue is goodness.                                                    *5*
I have faith in people who are faithful.
I also have faith in people who are not faithful.
Because Virtue is faithfulness.

The sage is shy and humble—to the world he seems confusing.
Men look to him and listen.                                                    *10*
He behaves like a little child.

## Fifty-five

He who is filled with Virtue is like a newborn child.
Wasps and serpents will not sting him;
Wild beasts will not pounce upon him;
He will not be attacked by birds of prey.
His bones are soft, his muscles weak,                                          *5*
But his grip is firm.
He has not experienced the union of man and woman, but is whole.
His manhood is strong.
He screams all day without becoming hoarse.
This is perfect harmony.                                                       *10*

Knowing harmony is constancy.
Knowing constancy is enlightenment.

It is not wise to rush about.
Controlling the breath causes strain.
If too much energy is used, exhaustion follows.                                *15*
This is not the way of Tao.
Whatever is contrary to Tao will not last long

## Sixty-one

A great country is like low land.
It is the meeting ground of the universe,
The mother of the universe.

The female overcomes the male with stillness,
Lying low in stillness.                                                        *5*

Therefore if a great country gives way to a smaller country,
It will conquer the smaller country.
And if a small country submits to a great country,
It can conquer the great country.
Therefore those who would conquer must yield,                                  *10*
And those who conquer do so because they yield.

A great nation needs more people;
A small country needs to serve.
Each gets what it wants.
It is fitting for a great nation to yield.                                     *15*

*Seventy-six*

A man is born gentle and weak.
At his death he is hard and stiff.
Green plants are tender and filled with sap.
At their death they are withered and dry.

Therefore the stiff and unbending is the disciple of death.
The gentle and yielding is the disciple of life.

Thus an army without flexibility never wins a battle.
A tree that is unbending is easily broken.

The hard and strong will fall.
The soft and weak will overcome.                                     *1*

*Seventy-eight*

Under heaven nothing is more soft and yielding than water.
Yet for attacking the solid and strong, nothing is better;
It has no equal.
The weak can overcome the strong;
The supple can overcome the stiff.
Under heaven everyone knows this,
Yet no one puts it into practice.
Therefore the sage says:
>He who takes upon himself the humiliation of the people is fit
>   to rule them.
>He who takes upon himself the country's disasters deserves to be   *1*
>   king of the universe.
The truth often sounds paradoxical.

## ■ Zhuangzi (Chuang Tzu) (c. 369–286 B.C.) (philosophy)

TRANSLATED BY BURTON WATSON

Daoist philosopher Zhuangzi is a shadow behind the work that bears his name. Little is known of his life, except that a man named Zhuangzi (Master Zhuang) lived in the fourth century B.C., in what is now Henan province. Early in life he was a petty official in "the lacquer garden" of Meng, but for most of his life he scorned officialdom, preferring to be his own man. The great historian Sima Qian remarks that he had vast knowledge and that he wrote a long work explaining Laozi's teachings and attacking the doctrine of the early philosophers Confucius (551–479 B.C.) and Mo Tzu (470–391 B.C.?). Zhuangzi is the most important interpreter of Daoism, and his unconventional spirit had only sarcasm for stultifying rituals and hierarchies. The Dao is the unity beneath all things, and the person who sees this soon finds, like William Blake, that true marriage lies in contraries. Zhuangzi was able to look at the things of the world with a sense of relativism; therefore, since tall equals short and here equals there, if the true reality is seen to be beneath the surface, "There is nothing in the world bigger than the tip of an autumn hair, and Mount T'ai is little. No one has lived longer than a dead child, and [long lived] P'eng-tsu died young." Though the Dao is absolute, it is not unchanging; in fact, its very nature is flux. A comparison with Buddhism, in which the defining characteristic of the absolute is its freedom from flux, is informative.

Instead of presenting a system of ethical and social reform like other philosophers of his time, Zhuangzi celebrated spontaneity and the cultivation of an inner emptiness that allowed one to merge with the Dao. Human problems are created by human categories; the way out of them is not through changing the world but through changing the way you understand the world. Death and life are mere manifestations of the Dao and thus they are changes in form but not changes in essence. Therefore, we should free ourselves from fear of death and from attachment to life's worries: "How do I know that loving life is not a delusion? How do I know that in hating death I am not like a man who, having left home in his youth, has forgotten the way back?" This freedom is the primary benefit that Zhuangzi tries to give his readers, usually through dazzling rhetoric, humor, nonsense phrases, and paradoxes designed to shock us out of our preconceptions. Like Tang dynasty poet Wang Wei in his most Daoist poems, Zhuangzi celebrates inaction, even laziness, as opposed to a life of struggle for gain and a character dominated by desire. By following the Way of Daoism, one may even gain magical powers and immortality. As is the case with so many of the world's mystics, history has elided the life and left us the thought. But behind these fresh and ancient words, one can intuit a peculiar mind, like the Dao inscribed within the things of the world. In the end, it is hard to know whether the Zhuangzi text had only one author, but it is tempting to think of a man named Zhuangzi, a free spirit, unbounded and mystical, wry and just a bit crazed.

**FURTHER READING:** Kaltenmark, Max. *Lao Tzu and Taoism.* Translated by Roger Greaves, 1965. Watson, Burton, tr. *Chuang Tzu: Basic Writings,* 1964; tr. *Records of the Grand Historian of China,* 1961.

## from *The Zhuangzi*

Great understanding is broad and unhurried; little understanding is cramped and busy. Great words are clear and limpid; little words are shrill and quarrelsome. In sleep, men's spirits go visiting; in waking hours, their bodies hustle. With everything they meet they become entangled. Day after day they use their minds in strife, sometimes grandiose, sometimes sly, sometimes petty. Their little fears are mean and trembly; their great fears are stunned and overwhelming. They bound off like an arrow or a crossbow pellet, certain that they are the arbiters of right and wrong. They cling to their position as though they had sworn before the gods, sure that they are holding on to victory. They fade like fall and winter—such is the way they dwindle day by day. They drown in what they do—you cannot make them turn back. They grow dark, as though sealed with seals—such are the excesses of their old age. And when their minds draw near to death, nothing can restore them to the light.

Joy, anger, grief, delight, worry, regret, fickleness, inflexibility, modesty, willfulness, candor, insolence—music from empty holes, mushrooms springing up in dampness, day and night replacing each other before us, and no one knows where they sprout from. Let it be! Let it be! [It is enough that] morning and evening we have them, and they are the means by which we live. Without them we would not exist; without us they would have nothing to take hold of. This comes close to the matter. But I do not know what makes them the way they are. It would seem as though they have some True Master, and yet I find no trace of him. He can act—that is certain. Yet I cannot see his form. He has identity but no form.

The hundred joints, the nine openings, the six organs, all come together and exist here [as my body]. But which part should I feel closest to? I should delight in all parts, you say? But there must be one I ought to favor more. If not, are they all of them mere servants? But if they are all servants, then how can they keep order among themselves? Or do they take turns being lord and servant? It would seem as though there must be some True Lord among them. But whether I succeed in discovering his identity or not, it neither adds to nor detracts from his Truth.

Once a man receives this fixed bodily form, he holds on to it, waiting for the end. Sometimes clashing with things, sometimes bending before them, he runs his course like a galloping steed, and nothing can stop him. Is he not pathetic? Sweating and laboring to the end of his days and never seeing his accomplishment, utterly exhausting himself and never knowing where to look for rest—can you help pitying him? I'm not dead yet! he says, but what good is that? His body decays, his mind follows it—can you deny that this is a great sorrow? Man's life has always been a muddle like this. How could I be the only muddled one, and other men not muddled?

$$* \quad * \quad *$$

Words are not just wind. Words have something to say. But if what they have to say is not fixed, then do they really say something? Or do they say nothing? People suppose that words are different from the peeps of baby birds, but is there any difference, or isn't there? What does the Way rely upon,[1] that we have true and false? What do words rely upon, that we have right and wrong? How can the Way go away and not exist? How can words

---

1. Following the interpretation of Chang Ping-lin. The older interpretation of yin here and in the following sentences is, "What is the Way hidden by," etc.

exist and not be acceptable? When the Way relies on little accomplishments and words rely on vain show, then we have the rights and wrongs of the Confucians and the Mo-ists. What one calls right the other calls wrong; what one calls wrong the other calls right. But if we want to right their wrongs and wrong their rights, then the best thing to use is clarity.

Everything has its "that," everything has its "this." From the point of view of "that" you cannot see it, but through understanding you can know it. So I say, "that" comes out of "this" and "this" depends on "that"—which is to say that "this" and "that" give birth to each other. But where there is birth there must be death; where there is death there must be birth. Where there is acceptability there must be unacceptability; where there is unacceptability there must be acceptability. Where there is recognition of right there must be recognition of wrong; where there is recognition of wrong there must be recognition of right. Therefore the sage does not proceed in such a way, but illuminates all in the light of Heaven.[2] He too recognizes a "this," but a "this" which is also "that," a "that" which is also "this." His "that" has both a right and a wrong in it; his "this" too has both a right and a wrong in it. So, in fact, does he still have a "this" and "that"? Or does he in fact no longer have a "this" and "that"? A state in which "this" and "that" no longer find their opposites is called the hinge of the Way. When the hinge is fitted into the socket, it can respond endlessly. Its right then is a single endlessness and its wrong too is a single endlessness. So I say, the best thing to use is clarity.

To use an attribute to show that attributes are not attributes is not as good as using a nonattribute to show that attributes are not attributes. To use a horse to show that a horse is not a horse is not as good as using a non-horse to show that a horse is not a horse.[3] Heaven and earth are one attribute; the ten thousand things are one horse.

What is acceptable we call acceptable; what is unacceptable we call unacceptable. A road is made by people walking on it; things are so because they are called so. What makes them so? Making them so makes them so. What makes them not so? Making them not so makes them not so. Things all must have that which is so; things all must have that which is acceptable. There is nothing that is not so, nothing that is not acceptable.

For this reason, whether you point to a little stalk or a great pillar, a leper or the beautiful Hsi-shih, things ribald and shady or things grotesque and strange, the Way makes them all into one. Their dividedness is their completeness; their completeness is their impairment. No thing is either complete or impaired, but all are made into one again. Only the man of far-reaching vision knows how to make them into one. So he has no use [for categories], but relegates all to the constant. The constant is the useful; the useful is the passable; the passable is the successful;

2. [The Chinese word translated here as "Heaven" is] *T'ien*, which for Chuang Tzu means Nature or the Way.

3. A reference to the statements of the logician Kung-sun Lung, "A white horse is not a horse" and "Attributes are not attributes in and of themselves."

and with success, all is accomplished. He relies upon this alone, relies upon it and does not know he is doing so. This is called the Way.

But to wear out your brain trying to make things into one without realizing that they are all the same—this is called "three in the morning." What do I mean by "three in the morning"? When the monkey trainer was handing out acorns, he said, "You get three in the morning and four at night." This made all the monkeys furious. "Well, then," he said, "you get four in the morning and three at night." The monkeys were all delighted. There was no change in the reality behind the words, and yet the monkeys responded with joy and anger. Let them, if they want to. So the sage harmonizes with both right and wrong and rests in Heaven the Equalizer. This is called walking two roads.

\* \* \*

Now I am going to make a statement here. I don't know whether it fits into the category of other people's statements or not. But whether it fits into their category or whether it doesn't, it obviously fits into some category. So in that respect it is no different from their statements. However, let me try making my statement.

There is a beginning. There is a not yet beginning to be a beginning. There is a not yet beginning to be a not yet beginning to be a beginning. There is being. There is nonbeing. There is a not yet beginning to be nonbeing. There is a not yet beginning to be a not yet beginning to be nonbeing. Suddenly there is being and nonbeing. But between this being and nonbeing, I don't really know which is being and which is nonbeing. Now I have just said something. But I don't know whether what I have said has really said something or whether it hasn't said something.

There is nothing in the world bigger than the tip of an autumn hair, and Mount T'ai is little. No one has lived longer than a dead child, and P'eng-tsu died young.[4] Heaven and earth were born at the same time I was, and the ten thousand things are one with me.

We have already become one, so how can I say anything? But I have just said that we are one, so how can I not be saying something? The one and what I said about it make two, and two and the original one make three. If we go on this way, then even the cleverest mathematician can't tell where we'll end, much less an ordinary man. If by moving from nonbeing to being we get to three, how far will we get if we move from being to being? Better not to move, but to let things be!

\* \* \*

How do I know that loving life is not a delusion? How do I know that in hating death I am not like a man who, having left home in his youth, has forgotten the way back?

---

4. The strands of animal fur were believed to grow particularly fine in autumn: hence "the tip of an autumn hair" is a cliché for something extremely tiny. P'eng-tsu was the Chinese Methuselah.

Lady Li was the daughter of the border guard of Ai.[5] When she was first taken captive and brought to the state of Chin, she wept until her tears drenched the collar of her robe. But later, when she went to live in the palace of the ruler, shared his couch with him, and ate the delicious meats of his table, she wondered why she had ever wept. How do I know that the dead do not wonder why they ever longed for life?

He who dreams of drinking wine may weep when morning comes; he who dreams of weeping may in the morning go off to hunt. While he is dreaming he does not know it is a dream, and in his dream he may even try to interpret a dream. Only after he wakes does he know it was a dream. And someday there will be a great awakening when we know that this is all a great dream. Yet the stupid believe they are awake, busily and brightly assuming they understand things, calling this man ruler, that one herdsman—how dense! Confucius and you are both dreaming! And when I say you are dreaming, I am dreaming, too. Words like these will be labeled the Supreme Swindle. Yet, after ten thousand generations, a great sage may appear who will know their meaning, and it will still be as though he appeared with astonishing speed.

Suppose you and I have had an argument. If you have beaten me instead of my beating you, then are you necessarily right and am I necessarily wrong? If I have beaten you instead of your beating me, then am I necessarily right and are you necessarily wrong? Is one of us right and the other wrong? Are both of us right or are both of us wrong? If you and I don't know the answer, then other people are bound to be even more in the dark. Whom shall we get to decide what is right? Shall we get someone who agrees with you to decide? But if he already agrees with you, how can he decide fairly? Shall we get someone who agrees with me? But if he already agrees with me, how can he decide? Shall we get someone who disagrees with both of us? But if he already disagrees with both of us, how can he decide? Shall we get someone who agrees with both of us? But if he already agrees with both of us, how can he decide? Obviously, then, neither you nor I nor anyone else can know the answer. Shall we wait for still another person?

But waiting for one shifting voice [to pass judgment on] another is the same as waiting for none of them.[6] Harmonize them all with the Heavenly Equality, leave them to their endless changes, and so live out your years. What do I mean by harmonizing them with the Heavenly Equality? Right is not right; so is not so. If right were really right, it would differ so clearly from not right that there would be no need for argument. If so were really so, it would differ so clearly from not so that there would be no need for argument. Forget the years; forget distinctions. Leap into the boundless and make it your home!

\* \* \*

5. She was taken by Duke Hsien of Chin in 671 B.C., and later became his consort.

6. I follow the rearrangement of the text suggested by Lü Hui-ch'ing. But the text of this whole paragraph leaves much to be desired and the translation is tentative.

Once Chuang Chou[7] dreamt he was a butterfly, a butterfly flitting and fluttering around, happy with himself and doing as he pleased. He didn't know he was Chuang Chou. Suddenly he woke up and there he was, solid and unmistakable Chuang Chou. But he didn't know if he was Chuang Chou who had dreamt he was a butterfly, or a butterfly dreaming he was Chuang Chou. Between Chuang Chou and a butterfly there must be some distinction! This is called the Transformation of Things.

\* \* \*

You hide your boat in the ravine and your fish net[8] in the swamp and tell yourself that they will be safe. But in the middle of the night a strong man shoulders them and carries them off, and in your stupidity you don't know why it happened. You think you do right to hide little things in big ones, and yet they get away from you. But if you were to hide the world in the world, so that nothing could get away, this would be the final reality of the constancy of things.

\* \* \*

Master Ssu, Master Yü, Master Li, and Master Lai were all four talking together. "Who can look upon inaction as his head, on life as his back, and on death as his rump?" they said. "Who knows that life and death, existence and annihilation, are all a single body? I will be his friend!"

The four men looked at each other and smiled. There was no disagreement in their hearts and so the four of them became friends.

All at once Master Yü fell ill. Master Ssu went to ask how he was. "Amazing!" said Master Yü. "The Creator is making me all crookedly like this! My back sticks up like a hunchback and my vital organs are on top of me. My chin is hidden in my navel, my shoulders are up above my head, and my pigtail points at the sky. It must be some dislocation of the yin and yang!"

Yet he seemed calm at heart and unconcerned. Dragging himself haltingly to the well, he looked at his reflection and said, "My, my! So the Creator is making me all crookedly like this!"

"Do you resent it?" asked Master Ssu.

"Why no, what would I resent? If the process continues, perhaps in time he'll transform my left arm into a rooster. In that case I'll keep watch on the night. Or perhaps in time he'll transform my right arm into a crossbow pellet and I'll shoot down an owl for roasting. Or perhaps in time he'll transform my buttocks into cartwheels. Then, with my spirit for a horse, I'll climb up and go for a ride. What need will I ever have for a carriage again?

"I received life because the time had come; I will lose it because the order of things passes on. Be content with this time and dwell in this order and then neither sorrow nor joy can touch you. In ancient times this was

7. Another name for Chuang Tzu (Zhuanzi) [Editor].

8. Following the interpretation of Yü Yuen.

called the 'freeing of the bound.' There are those who cannot free them-selves, because they are bound by things. But nothing can ever win against Heaven—that's the way it's always been. What would I have to resent?"

\* \* \*

Yen Hui said, "I'm improving!"
Confucius said, "What do you mean by that?"
"I've forgotten benevolence and righteousness!"
"That's good. But you still haven't got it."
Another day, the two met again and Yen Hui said, "I'm improving!"
"What do you mean by that?"
"I've forgotten rites and music!"
"That's good. But you still haven't got it."
Another day, the two met again and Yen Hui said, "I'm improving!"
"What do you mean by that?"
"I can sit down and forget everything!"
Confucius looked very startled and said, "What do you mean, sit down and forget everything?"
Yen Hui said, "I smash up my limbs and body, drive out perception and intellect, cast off form, do away with understanding, and make myself identical with the Great Thoroughfare. This is what I mean by sitting down and forgetting everything."
Confucius said, "If you're identical with it, you must have no more likes! If you've been transformed, you must have no more constancy! So you really are a worthy man after all![9] With your permission, I'd like to become your follower."

\* \* \*

Do not be an embodier of fame; do not be a storehouse of schemes; do not be an undertaker of projects; do not be a proprietor of wisdom. Embody to the fullest what has no end and wander where there is no trail. Hold on to all that you have received from Heaven but do not think you have gotten anything. Be empty, that is all. The Perfect Man uses his mind like a mirror—going after nothing, welcoming nothing, responding but not storing. Therefore he can win out over things and not hurt himself.

\* \* \*

Once, when Chuang Tzu was fishing in the P'u River, the king of Ch'u sent two officials to go and announce to him: "I would like to trouble you with the administration of my realm."
Chuang Tzu held on to the fishing pole and, without turning his head, said, "I have heard that there is a sacred tortoise in Ch'u that has been dead for three thousand years. The king keeps it wrapped in cloth and boxed, and stores it in the ancestral temple. Now would this tortoise

---

9. Chuang Tzu probably intends a humorous reference to the words of Confucius in Analects VI, 9: "The Master said, 'What a worthy man was Hui!'"

rather be dead and have its bones left behind and honored? Or would it rather be alive and dragging its tail in the mud?"

"It would rather be alive and dragging its tail in the mud," said the two officials.

Chuang Tzu said, "Go away! I'll drag my tail in the mud!"

\* \* \*

Hui Tzu said to Chuang Tzu, "Your words are useless!"

Chuang Tzu said, "A man has to understand the useless before you can talk to him about the useful. The earth is certainly vast and broad, though a man uses no more of it than the area he puts his feet on. If, however, you were to dig away all the earth from around his feet until you reached the Yellow Springs,[10] then would the man still be able to make use of it?"

"No, it would be useless," said Hui Tzu.

"It is obvious, then," said Chuang Tzu, "that the useless has its use."

\* \* \*

The fish trap exists because of the fish; once you've gotten the fish, you can forget the trap. The rabbit snare exists because of the rabbit; once you've gotten the rabbit, you can forget the snare. Words exist because of meaning; once you've gotten the meaning, you can forget the words. Where can I find a man who has forgotten words so I can have a word with him?

## ■ The Songs of Chu [attributed to Qu Yuan (Ch'ü Yüan), 322–295 B.C.?] (poem)

TRANSLATED BY DAVID HAWKES

*The Songs of Chu* is the second great anthology of Chinese poetry. These works come from the kingdom of Chu, a southern state located in the central valley of the Yangtze River; *The Songs of Chu* are thus often considered representative of a southern style of poetry, versus the northern style of *The Book of Songs*. The two collections have formal elements in common, however, and modern scholars question the adequacy of the northern/southern dichotomy. Most of the anthology's poems are attributed to Qu Yuan (c. 322–295 B.C.?), the first Chinese poet whom we know by name, but the anthology itself reached its final form only in the second century A.D. It seems unlikely that Qu Yuan composed all the works attributed to him. We know little about the historical Qu Yuan, except that he belonged to the royal house of Chu and served in the court of King Huai (reigned 328–229 B.C.). As a result of slander from a jealous colleague,

---

10. The underworld.

Qu fell from the king's graces and was said to have written the important poem "Encountering Sorrow" to show his faithfulness and remonstrate with the king. Qu Yuan was supposed to have repeatedly warned the king against the aggressions of the state of Qin, but he was ignored, and the king was captured by Qin. After the king's death in captivity abroad, his son was inaugurated, but he proved as gullible and flawed a king as his father. He banished Qu Yuan to the far south where Qu Yuan drowned himself in the Miluo River in protest. Eventually, the state of Chu was swallowed up by Qin. Qu Yuan is widely admired as an early figure of the honest retainer who dares to criticize his superiors, along the Confucian model, and his death is the subject of the yearly Dragon Boat Festival in China.

If *The Book of Songs* consists primarily of poems in a lyric mode, *The Songs of Chu* are longer narratives, more dramatic in nature. In addition to the extended narrative poem "Encountering Sorrow," the collection includes a set of shamanistic ritual songs in which the shaman sexually joins with the deity (the "Nine Songs"); the "Heavenly Questions," a riddling, gnomic series of questions about the origin of the cosmos, mythology, and Chinese history; "Far Journey," a celestial voyage that bears resemblance to "Encountering Sorrow"; the "Nine Arguments," attributed to Song Yu (fourth–third centuries B.C.), a series of poems that is the origin of later evocations of the melancholy associated with autumn, such as Ouyang Xiu's "The Autumn Sound" or Meng Jiao's "Autumn Meditations" in this volume; "The Fisherman," a dialogue in which a fisherman advises Qu Yuan not to abandon office and commit suicide; and a series of three poems, two of them shamanistic in nature, that are summons to the soul, or to a virtuous gentleman to come out of retirement.

**FURTHER READING:** Hawkes, David, tr. *Ch'u Tz'u: The Songs of the South, an Ancient Chinese Anthology,* 1959. Waley, Arthur. *The Nine Songs: A Study of Shamanism in Ancient China,* 1955. Yang, Hsien-yi, and Gladys Yang, trs. *Ch'u Tz'u: Li Sao and Other Poems of Chu Yuan,* 1955.

## The Fisherman

When Ch'ü Yüan was banished,
He wandered along the river's banks, or walked at the marsh's edge,
    singing as he went,
His expression was dejected, and his features emaciated.
A fisherman caught sight of him.
'Are you not the Lord of the Three Gates?'[1] said the fisherman. 'What    5
    has brought you to this pass?'

---

1. The title is otherwise unknown. Wang I thought that Ch'ü Yüan held it as Registrar of the three royal clans of Ch'u—Chao, Ch'ü, and Ching.

'Because all the world is muddy and I alone am clear,' said Ch'ü Yüan,
'And because all men are drunk and I alone am sober,
'I have been sent into exile.'
'The Wise Man is not chained to material circumstances,' said the
    fisherman, 'but can move as the world moves.
'If all the world is muddy, why not help them to stir up the mud and
    beat up the waves?
'And if all men are drunk, why not sup their dregs and swill their lees?
'Why get yourself exiled because of your deep thoughts and your fine
    aspirations?'
Ch'ü Yüan replied, 'I have heard it said:
'"He who has just washed his hair should brush his hat; and he who
    has just bathed should shake his clothes."
'How can I submit my spotless purity to the dirt of others?
'I would rather cast myself into the waters of the river and be buried
    in the bowels of fishes,
'Than hide my shining light in the dark and dust of the world.'
The fisherman, with a faint smile, struck his paddle in the water and
    made off.
And as he went he sang: 'When the Ts'ang-lang's waters are clear, I
    can wash my hat-strings in them;
'When the Ts'ang-lang's waters are muddy, I can wash my feet in
    them.'[2]
With that, he was gone, and did not speak again.

# Han Dynasty

## (206 B.C.–A.D. 220)

■ **Liu Xijun (Liu Hsi-chün) (Late Second Century B.C.)
(poem)**

TRANSLATED BY TONY BARNSTONE AND CHOU PING

Around 107 B.C., Liu Xijun, a Chinese princess from the Han royal
family, was married for political reasons to the chief of the Wusun tribe, a

---

2. This song is also found in the *Book of Mencius*. Tasselled hat-strings were a badge of official rank. The
meaning is that you should seek official employment in good times and retire gracefully when the times
are troubled. The Fisherman thinks Ch'ü Yüan is taking things too seriously and should make less fuss
about his principles.

nomadic band to the northwest of China. When she arrived, she found her new husband to be aged and decrepit. They would see each other once in six months or a year, and they could not communicate because they had no common language. This song is attributed to her.

## Lament

My family married me off
to the King of the Wusun,
and I live in an alien land
a million miles from nowhere.
My house is a tent.                                              5
My walls are of felt.
Raw flesh is all I eat,
with horse milk to drink.
I always think of home
and my heart stings.                                             10
O to be a yellow snow-goose
floating home again!

## ■ Anonymous Folk Songs from the Music Bureau (120 B.C.)

### TRANSLATED BY TONY BARNSTONE AND CHOU PING

The *Yuefu* refers to the Music Bureau, which was set up around 120 B.C. by Emperor Wu of the Han dynasty and abolished in 6 B.C. by Emperor Ai. At the time of its dissolution, it employed eight hundred and twenty-nine people. Its function was to collect songs by the common people, in part as a way of judging their reactions to the imperial government. The Music Bureau employees also performed rites and created sacrificial music. The collected songs came to be called *yuefu* songs, and this term designated a type of poem written in imitation of *yuefu* themes through the history of Chinese poetry. As in the songs of *The Book of Songs,* the popular themes of the folksongs have proven to be more enduring and affecting than the ritual hymns or the eulogies in praise of the dynasty. Though the majority of the poems fall into regular lines, there are poems of irregular meter. The Tang dynasty "new Music Bureau" songs of Bo Juyi and Yuan Zhen deviate from *yuefu* form and content, seeking formal freedoms and, often, satirizing the abuses of the ruling classes.

**FURTHER READING:** Watson, Burton. *The Columbia Book of Chinese Poetry: From Early Times to the Thirteenth Century,* 1984.

## The East Gate

I stride out the East Gate
and don't look back.
The next moment I'm in our doorway,
about to break down.
There's no rice in our pot.
I see hangers but no clothes.
So I draw my sword and again head out the East Gate!
My wife grabs me by the shirt and sobs
"I'm not like other wives. I could care less for gold and rank.
I'm happy to eat gruel if I'm with you.
Look up! The sky is a stormy ocean.
Look down! See your small son's yellow face?
To go now is wrong."
"Bah!" I say,
"I'm going now
before it's too late.
We can barely survive as it is
and white hairs are raining from my head."

## A Sad Tune

I sing a sad song when I want to weep,
gaze far off when I want to go home.
I miss my old place.
Inside me, a dense mesh of grief.
But there's no one to go back to,
no boat across that river.
This heart is bursting but my tongue is dead.
My guts are twisting like a wagon wheel.

## ■ Fu Xuan (Fu Hsüan) (A.D. 217–278) (poem)

TRANSLATED BY TONY BARNSTONE AND WILLIS BARNSTONE

Fu Xuan was a poet who wrote primarily in the Music Bureau style of poetry. Sixty-three of his poems survive. Apparently, he was an extraordinarily prolific writer, but most of his work has been lost. Despite being impoverished and orphaned as a child, he became rich and famous, largely because of his literary genius. It is common in the Chinese tradition for male writers to write in a female persona. In these poems, the author usually wears the mask of a particular female character, a vain ambitious woman, a noveau riche, a ceremonial goddess, or simply a wife separated from her spouse. It is rare, however, for the male poet to write with the compelling and enlightened sympathy for the maltreatment of women in general shown by Fu Xuan. The devaluation of women in Chinese society rests in part on economics, and these attitudes are likely to be shared by women as well as men. As one woman from today's Sichuan province puts it: "Girls are no use. They can't inherit your house or your property. You struggle all your life, but who gets your house in the end? Your daughters all marry out and belong to someone else."[1] Such attitudes are deeply rooted in Chinese culture. The female hero of a Six Dynasties folk tale states: "My unhappy parents have six daughters but no son . . . so they have no real descendant. . . . Since we cannot work to support them, but are simply a burden to them and no use at all, the sooner we die the better."[2] The cruelest manifestation of such attitudes is in the rash of female infanticide that has developed due to China's "One family, one child" population control policy.

## To Be a Woman

It is bitter to be a woman,
the cheapest thing on earth.
A boy stands commanding in the doorway
like a god descended from the sky.
His heart hazards the four seas,                                    5
thousands of miles of wind and dust,
but no one laughs when a girl is born.
The family doesn't cherish her.
When she's a woman she hides in back rooms,
scared to look a man in the face.                                   10
They cry when she leaves home to marry—
a brief rain, then mere clouds.
Head bowed she tries to compose her face,
her white teeth stabbing red lips.
She bows and kneels endlessly,                                      15
even before concubines and servants.
If their love is strong as two stars
she is like a sunflower in the sun,
but when their hearts are water and fire
a hundred evils descend on her.                                     20

1. W. J. F. Jenner and Delia Davin, eds., *Chinese Lives: An Oral History of Contemporary China* (New York: Pantheon Books, 1987), 130.

2. Jianing Chen, *The Core of Chinese Fiction* (Beijing: New World Press, 1990), 24.

The years change her jade face
and her lord will find new lovers.
Who were close like body and shadow
will be remote as Chinese and Mongols.
Sometimes even Chinese and Mongols meet
but they'll be far as polar stars.

# Six Dynasties Period

### (A.D. 220–589)

## ■ Lu Ji (Lu Chi) (A.D. 261–303) (literary criticism in rhyme-prose)

### TRANSLATED BY TONY BARNSTONE AND CHOU PING

Lu Ji was born in Huading in 261 to a great military family, and he also became a distinguished general and literary scholar. He lived through a turbulent time, in which warring states vied for control of a splintered country, and he ended badly, executed on trumped-up charges of treason after losing a major battle. He was a prolific writer, but his only major work was a rhyme-prose piece of literary criticism titled *The Art of Writing* (*Wen Fu*). The influence of this relatively short piece on Chinese literary thought cannot be overestimated, but its value is not merely critical—it is also an excellent exemplar of the concepts it discusses. In *The Art of Writing*, Lu Ji treats the writer's preparation to write, which is described as a kind of Daoist vision quest through internal space and through the literary past, and he treats the process that rises out of this internal journey, believing that the writers' words should match their internal impulse, the way a face changes to express emotion. He also presents a catalogue of styles and genres, gives writing tips, and describes common errors into which writers fall. He describes the sources of inspiration and of writer's block, and he discusses the complex relation between originality and reverence for great writers of the past: "To learn writing from classics is like carving an axe handle with an axe—the model is right in your hand." His cosmic view of the writing process is mirrored by his faith in the universal power of literature: "It can save teetering governments and weak armies; / it gives voice to the dying wind of human virtue." *The Art of Writing* is written in "rhyme-prose" (*fu*), a form characterized by rhymed verse interspersed with prose passages and by a pairing of lines into rhetorical parallelism, rather like Western poetry's use of chiasmus. Lu Ji's verse essay is commonly compared with Alexander Pope's *Essay on Poetry* (and with Pope's model, the *Ars Poetica* of Horace) as a great example of literary criticism in verse; the comparison takes on particular relevance when one compares the balanced rhetoric of Pope's rhymed heroic couplets with Lu Ji's parallelism. With characteristic humility, Lu Ji doubts his own ability to get at the essence of writing ("this art can't be captured by the finest words"), and there will always be something ineffable about the writing process, as the world's creative writing teachers can testify; but in this superlative effort, Lu Ji has created a masterpiece.

FURTHER READING: Birch, Cyril, ed. *Anthology of Chinese Literature, From Earliest Times to the Fourteenth Century*, 1965. Bishop, John L., ed. *Studies in Chinese Literature*, 1965. Hamill, Sam, tr. *Wen Fu: The Art of Writing*, 1987. Owen, Stephen, ed. and tr. *Readings in Chinese Literary Thought*, 1992. Barnstone, Tony, and Chou Ping, eds. and trs. *The Art of Writing: Teachings of the Chinese Masters*, 1996.

# The Art of Writing

## Preface

After reading many talented writers, I have gained insights into the writing craft. The ways that words and expressions ignite meaning, varied as they are, can be analyzed and critiqued for their beauty and style. Through my own efforts I know how hard it is to write, since I always worry that my ideas fail to express their subject and my words are even further removed from insufficient ideas. The problem is easy to understand; the solution is more difficult. So I started writing this rhymed essay to comment on elegant classics and talk about how strong and weak points find their way into our writings. Someday, I hope, I will be able to capture these subtle secrets in words. To learn writing from classics is like carving an axe handle with an axe—the model is right in your hand, but the spontaneous skills needed to carve a new creation are often beyond words. What can be said, however, is verbalized in what follows.

## 1. The Impulse

A poet stands between heaven and earth
and watches the dark mystery.
To nourish myself I read the classics.
I sigh as the four seasons spin by
and the swarm of living things kindles many thoughts.
In rough autumn it hurts to see leaves stripped away,
but how tender the soft sprigs in budding spring.
Morning frost is awe in my heart,
my ambition floats with high clouds,

5

I devote songs to ancestors
and sing the clean fragrance of their virtue.
I roam the classics, a forest of treasures,
and love their elegant balance of style and substance.
Inspired, I lay down the book I was reading
and let words pour out from my brush.

## 2. Meditation

At first I close my eyes. I hear nothing.
In interior space I search everywhere.
My spirit gallops to the earth's eight borders
and wings to the top of the sky.
Soon, misty and brightening like the sun about to dawn,
ideas coalesce and images ignite images.
When I drink the wine of words
and chew flowers from the Six Books,[1]
I swim freely in the celestial river
and dive into the sea's abyss.
Sometimes words come hard—they resist me
till I pluck them from deep water like hooked fish;
sometimes they are birds soaring out of a cloud
that fall right into place, shot with arrows,
and I harvest lines neglected for a hundred generations,
rhymes unheard for a thousand years.
I won't touch a flower already in morning bloom
but quicken the unopened evening buds.
In a blink I see today and the past,
put out my hand and touch all the seas.

## 3. Process

Search for the words and sphere of thought,
then seek the proper order;
release their shining forms
and tap images to hear how they sing.
Now leaves grow along a branching thought.
Now trace a current to its source.
Bring the hidden into light
or form the complex from simplicity.
Animals shake at the tiger's changing pattern
and birds ripple off when a dragon is seen;
some words belong together
and others don't join, like jagged teeth,

---

1. The Confucian Classics

but when you're clear and calm
your spirit finds true words.
With heaven and earth contained in your head                                    *50*
nothing escapes the pen in your hand.
It's hard to get started at first,
painful like talking with cracked lips,
but words will flow with ink in the end.
Essence holds content as the trunk lifts the tree;                              *55*
language is patterned into branches, leaves and fruit.
Now words and content match
like your mood and face—
smile when you're happy
or sigh when your heart hurts.                                                  *60*
Sometimes you can improvise easily.
Sometimes you only bite the brush and think.

## 4. The Joy of Words

Writing is joy
so saints and scholars all pursue it.
A writer makes new life in the void,                                            *65*
knocks on silence to make a sound,
binds space and time on a sheet of silk
and pours out a river from an inch-sized heart.
As words give birth to words
and thoughts arouse deeper thoughts,                                            *70*
they smell like flowers giving off scent,
spread like green leaves in spring,
a long wind comes, whirls into a tornado of ideas
and clouds rise from the writing-brush forest.

## 5. The Many Styles

But styles are diverse;
there is no absolute standard for anything,                                     *75*
and since things keep changing all the time
how to nail down the perfect description?
Control of language shows an author's skills;
craftsmanship comes when rhetoric pays concept's bill.
Writing is a struggle between presence and absence.                             *80*
Wade through the shallows, and if it's deep, swim.
It is all right to abandon compass and square
if you are a mirror held up to real shapes.
To seduce the eye use a florid style,
but to please the mind be precise.                                              *85*
Still, a full description can't be confined;
discourse blooms when it goes beyond words.

# 6. Genres

Poetry (*shi*) is a bright web of sensuous emotion.
The rhymed essay (*fu*) is clear and coherent as an exposition;
stele inscriptions (*bei*) are refined and faithful to detail;
an elegy (*lei*) is a painful tangle of sorrow;
inscriptions (*ming*) are gentle and succinct, but deep in meaning;
didactic compositions (*zhen*) jolt you through powerful logic;
odes (*song*) are gentle in tone and graceful in style;
explanatory essays (*lun*) are accurate and convincing;
memorandums to the king (*zou*) should be proper and clear,
written debates (*shuo*) should dazzle with eloquence.
Though there are so many different genres
they all oppose deviance and license
and insist you present your argument                                    *1*
with not one wasted word.

# 7. The Music of Words

Like shifting forms in the world
literature takes on many shapes and styles
as the poet crafts ideas
into elegant language.
Let the five tones be used in turn
like five colors in harmony,[2]
and though they vanish and reappear inconstantly
and though it seems a hard path to climb
if you know the basic laws of order and change
your thoughts like a river will flow in channels.
But if your words misfire
it's like grabbing the tail to lead the head:
clear writing turns to mud
like painting yellow on a base of black.

# 8. Revision

A sentence may contradict what comes before
or trespass on what follows.
Sometimes the idea is good but words fail,
and fine words may make no sense.
In such cases it is wise to set the two apart
since they harm each other when put together.

---

2. Perhaps an early gesture toward metrical regulation based on the four tones of classical Chinese. The traditional primary colors in China included white, black, red, yellow, and blue/green.

It is delicate to judge which idea or word works better—
a difference finer than a wheat ear's hairs.
Weigh each word on a scale;
use a measuring cord to make your cuts.                                    *125*

## 9. The Riding Crop

Sometimes your writing is a lush web of fine thoughts
that undercut each other and muffle the theme.
When you reach the pole there's nowhere else to go—
more becomes less if you try to improve what's done.
A powerful phrase at the crucial point                                     *130*
will whip the piece like a horse and make it gallop;
though all the other words are in place
they wait for the crop to run a good race.
A whip is always more help than harm;
stop revising when you've got it right.                                    *135*

## 10. Making It New

Perhaps thoughts and words blend
into a lucid beauty, a lush growth;
they flame like a bright brocade,
poignant as a string orchestra.
But if you fail to make it new                                             *140*
you can only repeat the past.
Even when your own heart is your loom
someone may have woven that textile before,
and to be honorable and keep integrity
you must disown it despite your love.                                      *145*

## 11. Ordinary and Sublime

Flowering forth, a tall rice ear
stands proudly above the mass,
a shape eluding its shadow,
its sound refusing echoes.
The best line is a towering crag.                                          *150*
It won't be woven into an ordinary song.
The mind can't find a match for it
but casts about, unwilling to give up.
After all, jade veins make a mountain shimmer,
pearls in water make the river seductive,                                  *155*
green kingfishers give life
even to the ragged thornbushes,
and classic and folk songs
blend into a fine contrast.

## 12. A One-String Harp

When an author composes too short a poem,
it trails off with a lonely feeling
like looking down at solitude with no friends
or peering into the vast sky, disconnected.
One string on a harp is crisp and sweet
but sings without resonance and harmony.

## 13. Harmony

Trust your words to jangling sounds
and their beauty will lose its luster.
When the ugly and beautiful mix in one body
the good quality will be stained.
When pipes play too fast for the dancers,
they chase each other without harmony.

## 14. Heart

When natural reason is sacrificed for strangeness—
an absurd and empty quest for trifles—
words are numb and loveless
like drifting souls who can never go home.
It's like plucking a thin string near the bridge:
you make harmonies without heart.

## 15. Dignity

When you race madly after a choral medley,
seduced by cheap and gaudy sounds,
your flashy poem caters to the vulgar taste
like the rowdy notes of a common tune.
The erotic songs of Fanglu and Shangjian
have base appeal but no grace.

## 16. Over-Restraint

But if your poem is too pure and graceful
and free from wild excess,
it's blander than the aftertaste of a spiceless broth,
thinner than ghostly harmonics from a temple lute.
One singer plus a three-person chorus
is elegant but without allure.

## 17. Forming Form

Tailor the poem to be plump or slender,
look it over and consider the form.

Make changes when they're apt,
sensitive to the subtle difference they make.
Sometimes raw language conveys clever ideas
and light words carry weighty truth.                                195
Sometimes you wear old clothes yet make them new
or discover clarity in the murk.
Sometimes you see it all in a flash,
sometimes it takes a lot of work.
Be like a dancer arcing her long sleeves to music              200
or a singer improvising to the strings;
like the craft of master wheelwright Bian,[3]
this art can't be captured by the finest words.

## 18. The Well-Wrought Urn

My heart respects conventional rules
and laws of composition.                                            205
I recall the great works of old masters
and see how my contemporaries have failed—
poems from the depth of a wise heart
may be laughed at by those who are blind.
Poems fine as jade filigree and coral                              210
are common as beans on the plain,
endless like air in the world's great bellows,
eternal as the universe;
they grow everywhere
but my small hands hold only a few.                                215
My water jar is often empty. It worries me.
I make myself sick trying to expand my pieces.
I limp along with short poems
and patch up my songs with common notes.
I'm never happy with what I've done,                               220
so how can my heart be satisfied?
Tap my work: I fear it clunks like a dusty earthen bowl
and I'm shamed by the song of musical jade.

## 19. Inspiration

As to the flash of inspiration
and traffic laws on writing's path—                                225
what comes can't be stopped,
what leaves will not be restrained.
It hides like fire in a coal

---

3. Zhuangzi tells of an encounter between wheelwright Bian and Duke Huan of Chi. Bian told the duke that his craft contained a subtle, incommunicable essence, which he could not put into words in order to pass on the trade to his son. Words are shadows of life, half-expressions. Therefore, Bian concluded, the "words of the sage" that the duke had been reading were "nothing but dregs."

then flares into a shout.
When instinct is swift as a horse
no tangle of thoughts will hold it back:
a thought wind rises in your chest,
a river of words pours out from your mouth,
and so many burgeoning leaves sprout
on the silk from your brush,
that colors brim out of your eyes
and music echoes in your ears.

## 20. Writer's Block

But when the six emotions[4] are stagnant,
the will travels yet the spirit stays put—
a petrified and withered tree,
hollow and dry as a dead river.
Then you must excavate your own soul,
search yourself till your spirit is refreshed.
But the mind gets darker and darker
and you must pull ideas like silk from a cocoon.
Sometimes you labor hard and build regrets—
then dash off a flawless gem.
Though this thing comes out of me,
I can't master it with strength.
I often stroke my empty chest and sigh:
what blocks and what opens this road?

## 21. The Power of a Poem

The function of literature is
to express the nature of nature.
It can't be barred as it travels space
and boats across a hundred million years.
Gazing to the fore, it forms models for people to come;
looking aft, meditates on symbols of the ancients.
It can save teetering governments and weak armies;
it gives voice to the dying wind of human virtue.
No matter how far, this road will take you there;
it will express the subtlest point.
It waters the heart like clouds and rain,
and shifts form like a changeable spirit.
Inscribed on metal and stone it spreads virtue.
Flowing with pipes and strings, each day the word is new.

---

4. Sorrow, joy, hate, love, pleasure, anger. The list is changeable, and at times a seventh emotion, desire, is added.

# Tao Qian (T'ao Ch'ien) (A.D. 365 or 372–427) (poems and prose)

Daoist poet Tao Qian is also known as Tao Yuanming (T'ao Yüan-ming). He is equally famous for his prose "Preface to the Poem on the Peach Blossom Spring" and for his remarkable poems celebrating a return to nature and an epicurean love of wine. He lived in a time of great political instability known as the Six Dynasties period (A.D. 222–589), and his work expresses the anxiety and weariness that this time produced. He went through a succession of official posts, working as a military advisor and a magistrate, but he was unsatisfied with this life and retired to the country where he lived out his remaining years as a farmer. His work reflects this life: he is primarily known as a poet of nature, China's first great landscape poet. In his work opposition develops between nature's purity and simplicity (exemplified by his own self-representation as a farmer-sage) and the "dusty" world of the court and the marketplace: "After all those years like a beast in a cage / I've come back to the soil again." Like Thoreau in his beanfield for the American literary tradition, Tao Qian came to represent for later Chinese poets the quintessential model of the official who has escaped "the world's net" for a life closer to spiritual values. Countless later poets (notably Wang Wei) echo his lines when they write about the country life. In his own time, however, he was not appreciated. The dominant mode of poetry in his day was flowery and artificial. The great poets of the Tang and Song dynasties, however, came to treasure Tao's poetry for its measured simplicity, its lack of adornment, and its conscious use of common words. Around one hundred thirty of his poems survive.

**FURTHER READING:** Acker, William. *T'ao the Hermit: Sixty Poems by T'ao Ch'ien*, 1952. Chang, Lily Pao-hu, and Marjorie Sinclair. *The Poems of T'ao Ch'ien*, 1953. Davis, A. R. *T'ao Yuan-ming*, 1984. Hightower, James Robert. *The Poetry of T'ao Ch'ien*, 1970. Hinton, David, tr. *The Selected Poems of T'ao Ch'ien*, 1993.

## *Return to My Country Home*

*1.*

When young I couldn't bear the common taste;
I loved the mountains and the peaks.
Yet I fell into the world's net
and wasted thirteen years.
But trapped birds long for their old woods          5
and fish in the pool still need deep waters
so I'm breaking earth in the south field,
returning to the country to live simply,
with just ten acres

and a thatch roof over some rooms.                                                                    *1*
Elm and willow shade the back eaves,
rows of peach and plum trees by the front hall.
A distant village lost in haze,
smoke twines from neighbors' houses.
From deep in the lanes, dogs bark,                                                                    *1*
a cock chuckles high up in a mulberry.
No dust or clutter within my courtyard door,
just empty rooms and time to spare.
After all those years like a beast in a cage
I've come back to the soil again.                                                                     *2*

2.

No social events in the fields,
no carriage wheels whir through these back roads.
Bright sun, but I close my cane door
and empty myself in my empty rooms.

Sometimes I meet the peasants
going here and there in palm-leaf raincoats,
but we speak of nothing
except how the crops are doing.

Each day my hemp and mulberries grow taller
and my land gets wider every day                                                                      *1*
but any day the frost or hail
could beat it flat as a field of weeds.

3.

So long away from these mountains and lakes,
today I'm wild with pleasure in the fields.
Now nephews and nieces hold my hands
as we part brush and enter the wild ruin of a town.

We search through hills and gravemounds
and the lingering signs of ancient folk,
scattered wells and traces of their hearths,
rotten stumps of bamboo and mulberry groves.

I ask a man who is gathering wood here
"What happened to all these people?"                                                                  *1*
The woodsman turns to me and says
"They're dead, that's all, there's not one left!"

In thirty years, at court or market, all things change.
I know now these are not empty words,
that we live among shadows and ghosts                                                                 *1*
and return at last to nothingness.

**TRANSLATED BY TONY BARNSTONE AND CHOU PING**

## Poem from the Series "Drinking Wine"

I built my hut near people
yet never hear carriage or horse.
"How can that be?" you ask.
Since my heart is a wilderness the world fades.
Gathering chrysanthemum by the east hedge,                    5
my lazy eyes meet South Mountain.
Mountain air is clean at twilight
as birds soar homeward wing to wing.
Beneath these things a revelation hides
but it dies on the tongue when I try to speak.               10

TRANSLATED BY TONY BARNSTONE AND CHOU PING

## Preface to the Poem on the Peach Blossom Spring

TRANSLATED BY BURTON WATSON

During the T'ai-yüan era (376–397) of the Chin dynasty, there was a man of Wu-ling who caught fish for a living. Once he was making his way up a valley stream and had lost track of how far he had gone when he suddenly came upon a forest of peach trees in bloom. For several hundred paces on either bank of the stream there were no other trees to be seen, but fragrant grasses, fresh and beautiful, and falling petals whirling all around.

The fisherman, astonished at such a sight, pushed ahead, hoping to see what lay beyond the forest. Where the forest ended there was a spring that fed the stream, and beyond that a hill. The hill had a small opening in it, from which there seemed to come a gleam of light. Abandoning his boat, the fisherman went through the opening. At first it was very narrow, with barely room for a person to pass, but after he had gone twenty or thirty paces, it suddenly opened out and he could see clearly.

A plain stretched before him, broad and flat, with houses and sheds dotting it, and rich fields, pretty ponds, and mulberry and bamboo around them. Paths ran north and south, east and west across the fields, and chickens and dogs could be heard from farm to farm. The men and women who passed back and forth in the midst, sowing and tilling the fields, were all dressed just like any other people, and from white-haired elders to youngsters with their hair unbound, everyone seemed carefree and happy.

The people, seeing the fisherman, were greatly startled and asked where he had come from. When he had answered all their questions, they invited him to return with them to their home, where they set out wine and killed a chicken to prepare a meal.

As soon as the others in the village heard of his arrival, they all came to greet him. They told him that some generations in the past their people had fled from the troubled times of the Ch'in dynasty (221–207 B.C.) and had come with their wives and children and fellow villagers to this faraway place. They had never ventured out into the world again, and hence in time had come to be completely cut off from other people. They asked him what dynasty was ruling at present—they had not even heard of the Han dynasty, to say nothing of the Wei and Chin dynasties that succeeded it. The fisherman replied to each of their questions to the best of his knowledge, and everyone sighed with wonder.

The other villagers invited the fisherman to visit their homes as well, each setting out wine and food for him. Thus he remained for several days before taking his leave. One of the villagers said to him, "I trust you won't tell the people on the outside about this."

After the fisherman had made his way out of the place, he found his boat and followed the route he had taken earlier, taking care to note the places that he passed. When he reached the prefectural town, he went to call on the governor and reported what had happened. The governor immediately dispatched men to go with him to look for the place, but though he tried to locate the spots that he had taken note of earlier, in the end he became confused and could not find the way again.

Liu Tzu-chi of Nan-yang, a gentleman-recluse of lofty ideals, heard the story and began delightedly making plans to go there, but before he could carry them out, he fell sick and died. Since then there have been no more "seekers of the ford."[1]

---

1. An allusion to *Analects* XVIII, 6, in which Confucius sends one of his disciples to inquire about a fording place across a river. Here, of course, the phrase refers to seekers of the utopian land of the Peach Blossom Spring.

# Tang Dynasty

## (618–907)

■ # Wang Wei (701–761) (poems)

### TRANSLATED BY TONY BARNSTONE, WILLIS BARNSTONE, AND XU HAIXIN

Wang Wei is considered to be one of a triad (with Du Fu and Li Bai) of the greatest poets of the Tang dynasty, the most fertile period for Chinese literature. He was equally famous as a landscape painter and was the founder of the Southern school of landscape painters. He was a talented musician as well. The central conflict in Wang Wei's life was between his career as a successful official and his devotion to Daoism and Chan Buddhism. Born Wang Mojie, he took the courtesy name Wei; the two names together (Wei Mojie) make up the Chinese transliteration of the Buddhist saint Vimalakirti, who affirmed the lay practice of Buddhism. Many of his poems express his desire to retreat from the "dusty, busy" world of the court to his estate at Wang River, and his poems often allude to Tao Qian (365–427), whose own hermetic retreat was a model for future poets. Wang Wei's famous series of poems, the Wang River sequence, is set at his estate, and these almost purely objective landscape descriptions are subtly infused with a Buddhist consciousness or, more accurately, lack of consciousness. Of all Chinese poets, Wang Wei is the one who comes closest to Zhuangzi's description of the perfect man: "Be empty, that is all. The Perfect Man uses his mind like a mirror—going after nothing, welcoming nothing, responding but not storing." So one of his most famous poems begins with "the empty mountain" as the landscape symbol for the annihilation of consciousness: "Nobody in sight on the empty mountain." Yet Wang Wei always keeps one foot in the real world, and with simplicity, an accurate eye, and piercing social judgment, he portrays the military, the court, the rebellious Daoist drunkard, and the lonely rooms of women whose husbands are fighting on the northern frontier. His poems work with few words, often treating traditional themes, yet the mind behind these words is so fresh and authentic that each simple line takes on the quality of originality, of having been uttered on the first morning of speech. So he has been called, like the Spanish poet Antonio Machado (1875–1939), the poet of few words, the poet of silence. His poems are often described as spoken paintings, his paintings as silent poems. As Robert Payne observes, he "can evoke a whole landscape in a single line."[1]

---

1. Robert Payne, ed., *The White Pony* (New York: Mentor, 1947), 151.

Wang Wei was born in what is today Shanxi province, and he passed the Imperial Examinations in 721. He had a series of appointments of increasing importance in Changan, the Tang dynasty capital, from Assistant Director of the Imperial Music Office to Right Assistant Director of the Department of State Affairs, his most important post, which he attained in 759. Early in his career, he was sent into a brief exile to the provinces for a minor indiscretion and turned to the tradition of exile poetry, which Li Bai and Du Fu were also to practice, and in which he was to excel. In 756, the Tartar general An Lushan led a rebellion that captured Changan, and Wang Wei was imprisoned in a temple, where he attempted suicide, but later he was sent to Luoyang and forced to serve in the rebels' puppet government. When the rebellion was put down, Wang Wei's life was in danger because of his collaboration, but because he had written a poem while imprisoned denouncing the dismemberment of a court musician who refused to play for the rebels at Frozen Emerald Pond, Emperor Suzong restored him to his former office. Wang Wei never did give up the world of the court for religious practice. His vacillation, however, makes him humanly fallible, and the conflict between his desire to be without desire and his worldly career is central to his most touching poems.

**FURTHER READING:** Barnstone, Tony, Willis Barnstone, and Xu Haixin, trs. *Laughing Lost in the Mountains: Poems of Wang Wei*, 1992. Chang, Yin-nan, and Lewis C. Walmsley, trs. *Poems of Wang Wei*, 1958. Robinson, G. W., tr. *Poems of Wang Wei*, 1973. Yip, Wai-lim, tr. *Hiding the Universe: Poems by Wang Wei*, 1972. Yu, Pauline, tr. *The Poetry of Wang Wei: New Translations and Commentary*, 1980.

## My Cottage at Deep South Mountain

In my middle years I love the Tao
and by Deep South Mountain I make my home.
When happy I go alone into the mountains.
Only I understand this joy.
I walk until the water ends, and sit
waiting for the hour when clouds rise.
If I happen to meet an old woodcutter,
I chat with him, laughing and lost to time.

## Sketching Things

Slender clouds. On the pavilion a small rain.
Noon, but I'm too lazy to open the far cloister.
I sit looking at moss so green
my clothes are soaked with color.

## Climbing the City Tower North of the River

Wells and alleys lead me to the rocky hills.
From a traveler's pavilion up in clouds and haze
I watch the sun fall—far from this high city—
into blue mountains mirrored by distant water.
Fire on the shore where a lonely boat is anchored.                    5
Fishermen and evening birds go home.
Dusk comes to the silent expanse of heaven and earth
and my heart is calm like this wide river.

## About Old Age, in Answer to a Poem by Subprefect Zhang

In old age I ask for peace
and don't care about things of this world.
I've found no good way to live
and brood about getting lost in my old forests.
The wind blowing in the pines loosens my belt,                    5
the mountain moon is my lamp while I tinkle my lute. You ask,
how do you succeed or fail in life?
A fisherman's song is deep in the river.

## Deer Park

Nobody in sight on the empty mountain
but human voices are heard far off.
Low sun slips deep in the forest
and lights the green hanging moss.

## Luan Family Rapids

In the windy hiss of autumn rain
shallow water fumbles over stones.
Waves dance and fall on each other:
a white egret startles up, then drops.

## House Hidden in the Bamboo Grove

Sitting alone in the dark bamboo,
I play my lute and whistle song.

Deep in the wood no one knows
the bright moon is shining on me.

## Magnolia Basin

On branch tips the hibiscus bloom.
The mountains show off red calices.
Nobody. A silent cottage in the valley.
One by one flowers open, then fall.

## To My Cousin Qiu, Military Supply Official

When young I knew only the surface of things
and studied eagerly for fame and power.
I heard tales of marvelous years on horseback
and suffered from being no wiser than others.
Honestly, I didn't rely on empty words;
I tried several official posts.
But to be a clerk—always fearing punishment
for going against the times—is joyless.
In clear winter I see remote mountains
with dark green frozen in drifted snow.     1
Bright peaks beyond the eastern forest
tell me to abandon this world.
Cousin, like Huilian[1] your taste is pure.
You once talked of living beyond mere dust.
I saw no rush to take your hand and go—     1
but how the years have thundered away!

## Missing Her Husband on an Autumn Night[2]

### 1.

Ting, ting. Leaking water.[3] Night has no end.
Far far light clouds and a moon wet with dew.

---

1. Xie Huilian (397–433) was the valued cousin of the famous Northern and Southern Dynasties poet Xie Lingyun (385–433). Huilian was a talented young man who began to write at the age of ten. Later poets often referred to him when praising their cousins or brothers.

2. This poem is written from the point of view of a woman whose husband is at the frontier.

3. The leaking water refers to the dripping of a waterclock.

Fall makes hidden insects cry all night long.
I haven't sent your winter clothes; may flying frost not come.

2.

Cassia shadows begin to cover the moon.[4] More dew.                                    5
My silks are thin but I haven't changed my dress.
Far into the night I play a silver harp, eagerly.
My heart is afraid of empty rooms I don't dare go into.


## Seeing Zu Off at Qizhou

Only just now we met and laughed
yet here I'm crying to see you off.
In the prayer tent we are broken.
The dead city intensifies our grief.
Coldly the remote mountains are clean.                                                   5
Dusk comes. The long river races by.
You undo the rope, are already gone.
I stand for a long time, looking.


## Things in a Spring Garden

Last night's rain makes me sail in my wooden shoes.
I put on my shabby robe against the spring cold.
As I spade open each plot, white water spreads.
Red peach flowers protrude from the willow trees.
On the lawn I play chess, and by a small wood                                            5
dip out water with my pole and pail.
I could take a small deerskin table
and hide in the high grass of sunset.


## Escaping with the Hermit Zhang Yin

My brother Zhang has five carts of books.
A hermit, he reads endlessly.
Whenever he soaks his brush with ink he surpasses the sage of grass
    calligraphy.

---

4. According to an old legend there is a cassia tree on the moon, 5,000 feet high, and a man called Wu
Gang chops the tree as a punishment for seeking immortality. The tree grows whole again after each ax
blow.

When he writes a poem it makes a classical verse seem like a
    throwaway.
Behind closed doors under Two Chamber Mountains,
he's been a hermit for more than ten years.
He looks like a wild man
pausing with fishermen.
Autumn wind brings desolation.
Five Willows seem taller as their leaves drop.
Seeing all this I hope to leave the peopled world.
Across the water in my small cottage
at year's end I take your hand.
You and I, we are the only ones alive.

## Song of Peach Tree Spring[5]

My fishing boat sails the river. I love spring in the mountains.
Peach blossoms crowd the river on both banks as far as sight.
Sitting in the boat, I look at red trees and forget how far I've come.
Drifting to the green river's end, I see no one.

Hidden paths winding into the mountain's mouth.
Suddenly the hills open into a plain
and I see a distant mingling of trees and clouds.
Then coming near I make out houses, bamboo groves and flowers
where woodcutters still have names from Han times
and people wear Qin dynasty clothing.
They used to live where I do, at Wuling Spring,
but now they cultivate rice and gardens beyond the real world.

Clarity of the moon brings quiet to windows under the pines.
Chickens and dogs riot when sun rises out of clouds.
Shocked to see an outsider, the crowd sticks to me,
competing to drag me to their homes and ask about their native
    places.
At daybreak in the alleys they sweep flowers from their doorways.
By dusk woodcutters and fishermen return, floating in on the waves.

They came here to escape the chaotic world.
Deathless now, they have no hunger to return.
Amid these gorges, what do they know of the world?
In our illusion we see only empty clouds and mountain.
I don't know that paradise is hard to find,
and my heart of dust still longs for home.

---

5. Wang Wei's poem is modeled on an earlier one by Tao Qian (365–427). See Tao Qian's "Preface to the Poem on the Peach Blossom Spring." This mythical, timeless Taoist paradise is the quintessential Chinese utopia.

Leaving it all, I can't guess how many mountains and waters lie behind     25
    me,
and am haunted by an obsession to return.
I was sure I could find my way back, the secret paths again.
How could I know the mountains and ravines would change?
I remember only going deep into the hills.
At times the green river touched cloud forests.     30
With spring, peach blossom water is everywhere,
but I never find that holy source again.


## Suffering from Heat[6]

The red sun bakes earth and heaven
where fire clouds are shaped like mountains.
Grass and woods are scorched and wilting.
The rivers and lakes have all dried up.
Even my light silk clothes feel heavy     5
and dense foliage gives thin shade.
The bamboo mat is too hot to lie on,
I dry off, soaking my towel with sweat.
I think of escaping from the universe
to be a hermit in a vastness     10
where a long wind comes from infinity
and rivers and seas wash away my turbulence.
When I see my body holding me here
I know my heart is not enlightened.
Abruptly I enter a gate of sweet dew     15
where there is a medicine to cool me.


## Questioning a Dream

Don't be fooled. Why bother with the shallow joys of favor or worry
    about rejection?
Why flounder in the sea helping others, or being abandoned?
Where can you dig up a Yellow Emperor[7] or Confucius to consult
    with?
How do you know your body isn't a dream?

---

6. See also "The Fire Sermon" from the Maha-Vagga.

7. A wise, mythical emperor.

# ■ Li Bai (Li Pai) (701–762) (poems)

## TRANSLATED BY WILLIS BARNSTONE, TONY BARNSTONE, AND CHOU PING

Li Bai is probably the best known Chinese poet in the West and with Du Fu is considered the finest poet of the Tang dynasty. He has attracted the best translators and has influenced several generations of American poets, from Ezra Pound to James Wright. Yet among Western readers there is considerable confusion surrounding his name. He is best known in English as Li Po, though he is also called Li Pai, Li T'ai-po, and Li T'ai-pai, all of these being Wade-Giles transliterations of his Chinese names; for each of these names there is a new English version, according to the now-accepted Pinyin transliteration system (Li Bo, Li Bai, Li Tai-bo, and Li Tai-bai). To add to the confusion, Ezra Pound, in *Cathay,* his famous sequence of Chinese poems in translation, refers to him as Rihaku, a transliteration of the Japanese pronunciation of his name.

The facts of Li Bai's life come to us through a similar veil of contradictions and legends. Where he was born is unknown—and there are those who say he was of Turkic origin—but it seems he was probably born in central Asia and was raised in Sichuan province. His brashness and bravado are characteristic of a tradition of poets from this region, including the great Song poet Su Dongpo. He claimed he was related to the Imperial family, though this claim is likely to be spurious. Perhaps he wandered as a Daoist hermit in his teens; certainly, Daoist fantasy permeates his work. He left his home in 725 and wandered through the Yangtze River Valley, hoping to gain recognition of his talents, though he was alone among the great Tang poets in never taking the Imperial Examination. He married the first of his four wives during this period. In 742, he was summoned to the capital at Changan, modern Xian, and was appointed to the Hanlin Academy by Emperor Xuanzong. During his time in the capital, he became close friends with Du Fu, who addresses a number of poems to him. Within a few years, he was expelled from the court (apparently for insulting the emperor's favorite eunuch) and made to leave Changan, and he began presenting himself as an unappreciated genius, or as one friend named him "a banished immortal." In 755, the An Lushan rebellion took place, in which a Turkish general led his group of Chinese border armies against the emperor. Li Bai was forced to leave Hunan for the South, where he entered the service of the Prince of Yun, sixteenth son of the Emperor, who led a secondary revolt. Eventually, Li was arrested for treason, sent into exile, and was later given amnesty. He continued his wanderings in the Yangtze Valley, seeking patrons, until his death at sixty-two.

About one thousand poems attributed to Li Bai have come down to us, though some of them were probably written by imitators. While most of the poems were occasional poems (poems written for specific occasions), others incorporated wild journeys, Sichuan colloquial speech, and dramatic monologues, such as his famous "A Song of Zhanggan Village." Perhaps the most remarkable subject for his poems, however, was himself. He portrays himself as a neglected genius; a drunk; a wanderer through Daoist metaphysical adventures; and a lover of moon, friends, and women. His colloquial speech and confessional celebration of his own sensual flamboyance and fallible self made him the best loved and most imitated Chinese poet in English and helped to establish a conversational, intimate tone in modern American poetry. Ezra Pound's *Cathay* put him at the center of the revolution in modern verse. All these qualities plus an extraordinary lucidity of image made him extremely popular in China as well, in his day and today. A number of his poems are in the Han dynasty *yuefu* form, which allowed him to indulge in radically irregular lines that gave his imagination free play. He was an influential figure in the Chinese cult of spontaneity, which emphasized the poet's genius in extemporizing a poem: "Inspiration hot, each stroke of my pen shakes the five mountains." Among the many legends about Li Bai, the most enduring is the account of his death. Like Ishmael in the crow's nest, wanting to penetrate the illusory world that he saw reflected in the water, Li Bai was said to be so drunk in a boat that he fell overboard and drowned, trying to embrace the moon reflected in the water. Since the "man in the moon" is a woman in Chinese myth, the legend of Li's death takes on an erotic meaning, mixing thanatos and eros. As in *Moby Dick,* to "strike through the mask" and see the face of truth is to embrace death.

**FURTHER READING:** Cooper, Arthur. *Li Po and Tu Fu,* 1973. Hamill, Sam. *Banished Immortal: Visions of Li T'ai-po,* 1987. Pound, Ezra. *Cathay,* 1915. Seaton, J. P., and James Cryer. *Bright Moon, Perching Bird,* 1987. Waley, Arthur. *The Poetry and Career of Li Po,* 1950.

# A Song of Zhanggan Village

My hair was still cut straight across my forehead
and I was playing, pulling up flowers by the front door,
when you rode up on a bamboo horse
and danced round the bench, monkeying with the green plums.
And we lived together in the village of Zhanggan,                    5
two small people without hate or suspicion.
At fourteen I became your wife,
so bashful I never laughed.
I lowered my head and faced the dark wall.
You called me a thousand times but I couldn't look at you.          10
At fifteen my tortured brow calmed
and I wanted to be with you like ashes in dust.
I'd die waiting for you, embracing a pillar,

so why must I climb the widows' tower?
At sixteen you left                                                                    *1*
for Qutang Gorge where floodwaters crush against Yanyu Rock
and I haven't touched you for five months.
Now I hear monkeys screeching into the sky
and mosses drown the place by our door
where your feet sank in the earth when you left,                                       *2*
moss so deep I can't sweep it away.
It's a windy autumn. The leaves are falling early.
In the eighth month butterflies dart in pairs
through high grass in the west garden.
They hurt my heart.                                                                    *2*
I grow older, my face ruddy with pain.
If you are coming down through the Three Gorges
please write me
and I will come out to meet you
even as far as Long Wind Sands.                                                        *3*


## Grievance at the Jade Stairs

The jade steps are whitening with dew.
My gauze stockings are soaked. It's so late.
I let down the crystal blind
and watch the glass clear autumn moon.


## Drinking Alone by Moonlight

A pot of wine in the flower garden,
but no friends to drink with me.
So I raise my cup to the bright moon
and to my shadow, which makes us three,
but the moon won't drink
and my shadow just creeps about my heels.
Yet in your company, moon and shadow,
I have a wild time till spring dies out.
I sing and the moon shudders.
My shadow staggers when I dance.
We have our fun while I can stand
then drift apart when I fall asleep.
Let's share this empty journey often
and meet again in the milky river of stars.

## Drunk All Day

To live in this world is to have a big dream;
why punish myself by working?
So I'm drunk all day.
I flop by the front door, dead to the world.
On waking, I peer at the garden                                      5
where a bird sings among the flowers
and wonder what season it is.
I think I hear him call "mango birds sing in spring wind."
I'm overcome and almost sigh.
But no, I pour another cup of wine,                                  10
sing at the top of my lungs and wait for the bright moon.
When my song dies out, I forget.

## Song on Bringing in the Wine

Can't you see the Yellow River
pours down directly from heaven?
It sprints all the way to the ocean
and never comes back.
Can't you see the clear hall mirror                                  5
is melancholy with our gray hair?
In the morning our braids are black silk.
In the evening they are snow.
When happy, be happy all the way,
never abandoning your gold cup                                       10
empty to face the moon alone.
Heaven gave me talent. It means something.
Born with genius, a failure now, I will succeed.
Although I waste a thousand ounces of gold
they will come back.                                                 15
We butcher cows, cook lambs,
for a wild feast, and must drink
three hundred cups at a time.
Friends Chengfuze and Danqiuchen,
bring in the wine                                                    20
and keep your mouths full.
I'll sing for you. I'll turn
your ears. Bells and drums,
good dishes and jade are worth
nothing. What I want                                                 25
is to be drunk, day and night,
and never again sober up.

The ancient saints and sages are forgotten.
Only the fame of great drunks                              3
goes from generation to generation.
In the Temple of Perfect Peace
Prince Cheng once gave a mad party,
serving ten thousand pots of wine.
Long ago. Tonight, let no one                              3
say I am too poor to supply
vats of alcohol. I'll find
my prize horse and fur coat
and ask my boy to sell them
for fine wine. Friends, we drink                           4
till the centuries of the sorrow
of our existence dissolve.

## Questioning in the Mountains

You ask me why I live in the jade mountains.
I smile, unanswering. My heart is calm.
Peach petals float on the water, never come back.
There is a heaven and earth beyond
        the crowded town below.

## Song

The whole forest is a blur
woven by fog.
Cold mountain is color of melancholy,
mauve.
Twilight comes into a tall house.
Someone is unhappy upstairs.
Standing on the jade steps,
a woman is wasting time, nothing to do.
Birds wing off for home
but what road can take me there?
Pavilion after pavilion join far, far, far.

## Seeing Meng Haoran Off

From Yellow Crane Tower you sail
the river west as mist flowers bloom.

A solitary sail, far shadow, green mountains at the empty end of vision.
And now, just the Yangtze river touching the sky.

## Seeing a Friend Off

Blue mountains past the north wall,
White water snaking eastward.
Here we say goodbye for the last time.
You will fade like a hayseed blowing ten thousand miles away.
Floating clouds are the way of the wanderer.                                5
The sun sets like the hearts of old friends.
We wave goodbye as you leave. Horses neigh and neigh.

## Saying Goodbye to Song Zhiti

Clear as empty sky, the Chu River
meanders to the far blue sea.
Soon there will be a thousand miles between us.
All feelings distill to this cup of wine.
The cuckoo chants the sunny day;                                            5
monkeys on the river banks are howling evening wind.
All my life I haven't wept
but I weep here, unable to stop.

## Brooding in the Still Night

Bright moonlight before my bed;
I think at first the floor has frost.
I look up to the mountain moon,
then bow my head in a dream of home.

## Hearing a Flute on a Spring Night in Luoyang

Whose jade flute secretly flies in the night?
Spring wind scatters sound all over Luoyang.
The midnight flute keens a farewell song, "Snap the Willow Branch."
Thinking of my old home and garden, I break.

## River Song

Magnolia oars. A spicewood boat.
Jade flutes and gold pipes fill the air at bow and stern.
We have a thousand jugs of tart wine
and singing girls who drift with us on the waves.
Like a Taoist immortal floating off on a yellow crane,
my wandering mind empties and soars with white gulls.
Qu Yuan's poems hang overhead with sun and moon
but the Chu king's palace is an empty mountain.
Inspired, each stroke of my brush shakes the five mountains.
The poem done, I laugh proudly over the hermit's land.
If fame and money could last forever
the Han River would flow backward.

## I Listen to Jun, a Monk from Shu, Play His Lute

The Shu monk carries a green silk lute
west down Omei Mountain
and each sweep of his hand
is the song of a thousand pines in the valley.
Flowing water cleans my wanderer's heart
and the sound lingers like a frosty bell
till I forget the mountain soaking in green dusk,
autumn clouds darkly folding in.

## Song of the North Wind

The fire dragon lives at Ice Gate
and light comes from its eyes at night,
yet why no sun or moon to light us here?
We have only the north wind howling furiously out of heaven.
On Yen Mountain snowflakes are as big as a floor mat
and every flake drops on us.
The woman of Yo Zhou in December
stops singing and laughing. Her eyebrows tighten.
Lounging against the door she watches people pass by
and remembers her husband at the north frontier
and the miserable cold.
When he left he took his sword to guard the border.
He left his tiger-striped quiver at home,

with its white-feathered arrows, now coated
with dust on which spiders spin their traps.                         *15*
The arrows remain, useless. Her husband is dead
from the war. He won't return.
The widow won't look at the arrows.
Finally, it's too much, and she burns them to ashes.
Easier to block the Yellow River with a few handfuls of sand,         *20*
than to scissor away her iron grief
here in the north wind, the rain, the snow.


## Hunting Song

Frontier sons are lifelong illiterates
who know only how to hunt big game and brag about being tough guys.
They feed their Mongolian ponies white grass
to make them plump and strong in the autumn.
They race proudly on their horses chasing the sun's shadows.          *5*
They brush snow off with the crack of a gold whip.
Half drunk, they call their falcon and wander far off to hunt.
They stretch their bows like a full moon and never miss.
One whistling arrow flies and two gray cranes fall.
The desert spectators step back in dread.                            *10*
These virile heroes shake the sands.
Confucian scholars are no match for them.
What good is it to lock one's doors and read books till one is gray?


## Missing the East Mountains

It's long since I've gone to the East Mountains.
How many seasons have the tiny roses bloomed?
White clouds—unblown—fall apart.
In whose court has the bright moon dropped?


## Summer Day in the Mountains

Lazy today. I wave my white feather fan.
Then I strip naked in the green forest,
untie my hatband and hang it on a stone wall.
Pine wind sprinkles my bare head.

## Having a Good Time by Myself

Facing wine, not aware it's getting dark,
I've been sitting so long my gown brims over
    with petals.
Drunk, I rise to follow the moon in the brook
long after birds and people have gone home.

## Sent Far Off

This room was all flowers when my beauty was here.
Now gone, only an empty bed.
The embroidered quilt is folded up. I can't sleep.
Three years gone, yet I still smell her fragrance.
Why doesn't the fragrance dissipate?
Why doesn't my beauty come back?
I miss her until yellow leaves drop
and white dawn moisture soaks the green moss.

## ■ Du Fu (Tu Fu) (712–770) (poems)

If there is one undisputed genius of Chinese poetry it is Du Fu. The Daoist Li Bai was more popular, the Buddhist Wang Wei was sublimely simple and more intimate with nature, but the Confucian Du Fu had extraordinary thematic range and was a master and innovator of all the verse forms of his time. In his life, he never achieved fame as a poet and thought himself a failure in his worldly career. Perhaps only a third of his poems survive due to his long obscurity; his poems appear in no anthology earlier than one dated one hundred thirty years after his death, and it wasn't until the eleventh century that he was recognized as a preeminent poet. His highly allusive, symbolic complexity and resonant ambiguity is at times less accessible than the immediacy and bravado of Li Bai. Yet there is a suddenness and pathos in much of his verse, which creates a persona no less constructed than Wang Wei's reluctant official and would-be hermit or Li Bai's blithely drunken Daoist adventurer. Most of what we know of his life is recorded in his poems, but there are dangers to reading his poems as history and autobiography. By the time he was in his twenties, he was referring to his long white hair—in the persona of the Confucian elder. As Sam Hamill notes, "It was natural that many a poet would adopt the persona of the 'long white-haired' and old man—this lent a younger poet an authority of tone and diction he might never aspire to otherwise."[1] Du Fu is some-

---

1. Sam Hamill, tr., *Facing the Snow: Visions of Tu Fu* (New York: White Pine Press, 1988), unpaged.

times called the "poet of history" because his poems record the turbulent times of the decline of the Tang dynasty and constitute in part a Confucian societal critique of the suffering of the poor and the corruption of officials. He also records his own sufferings, exile, and falls from grace, as well as the death of his son by starvation, but some critics have suggested that the poems on these themes are exaggerated in the service of self-dramatization.

Du Fu was born to a prominent but declining family of scholar-officials, perhaps from modern-day Henan province, though he referred to himself as a native of Duling, the ancestral home of the Du clan. In the Six Dynasties period, his ancestors were in the service of the southern courts; his grandfather, Du Shenyan, was an important poet of the early Tang dynasty, and a more remote ancestor, Du Yu (222–284), was a famed Confucianist and military man. In spite of family connections, Du Fu had difficulty achieving patronage and/or governmental postings, and twice failed the Imperial Examinations, in 735 and 747. He was a restless traveler, and the poems of this early period show him to be a young man given to revelry, military and hunting arts, painting, and music. In 744, he met Li Bai, and the basis was formed for one of the world's most famed literary friendships; the two poets devote a number of poems to each other. In 751, he passed a special examination that he finagled through submitting rhyme-prose works directly to the emperor, but it was not until 755 that he was offered a post—a rather humilating posting in the provinces—which he rejected, accepting instead the patronage of the heir apparent. In the winter of that year, however, the An Lushan rebellion broke out, and the emperor fled to Sichuan and abdicated; the heir apparent became the new emperor in Gansu province. Meanwhile, the rebels seized the capital, and Du Fu, attempting to join the new emperor in the distant northwest, was captured by the rebels. He was detained for a year but managed to escape; and after traveling in disguise through the occupied territory, he joined the emperor's court in the position of Reminder. He was arrested soon after for his outspokenness in defending a friend, a general who had failed to win a battle, but he was pardoned and exiled to a low posting in Huazhou. He quit his job there and moved to Chengdu, where he and his family depended upon the kindness of friends and relatives and moved again and again to avoid banditry and rebellions.

In spite of this instability, his poems show a serenity during this period, particularly those years from 760–762, when he lived in a "thatched hut" provided by a patron and friend named Yan Yu, who hired him in the years that followed as a military advisor. After Yan's death in 765, Du Fu left Chengdu, traveling down the Yangtze River, finding patrons, and dreaming of a return to Changan, which was prevented by invasions from Tibet. He spent his final three years traveling on a boat, detained in sickness, and finally winding down to his death as he journeyed down the Yangtze, apparently accepting the withering of his life: "It's a release to feel my spirit fade;/Let sorrow come when it may" (from "Written While Traveling on a Boat, Ill and Fevered").

**FURTHER READING:** Cooper, Arthur, tr. *Li Po and Tu Fu,* 1973. Hamill, Sam, tr. *Facing the Snow: Visions of Tu Fu,* 1980. Hawkes, David, tr. *A Little Primer of Tu Fu,* 1967. Hinton, David, tr. *The Selected Poems of Tu Fu,* 1988. Hung, William, tr. *Tu Fu: China's Greatest Poet,* 1952. Rexroth, Kenneth, tr. *One Hundred Poems from the Chinese,* 1971. Seaton, J. P., and James Cryer, trs. *Li Po and Tu Fu: Bright Moon, Perching Bird,* 1987.

## Facing Snow

Battles, sobbing, many new ghosts.
An old man, I sadly chant poems.
Wild clouds lower and touch the thin evening.
Fast snow dances in swirling wind.
A ladle abandoned, no green wine in the cask.
Fire still seems to redden the empty stove.
No news, the provinces are cut off.
With one finger I write my sorrows in the air.

TRANSLATED BY TONY BARNSTONE AND CHOU PING

## Broken Lines

River so blue the birds seem to whiten.
Flowers almost flame on the green mountainside.
Spring is dying yet again.
Will I ever go home?

TRANSLATED BY TONY BARNSTONE AND CHOU PING

## A Hundred Worries

I remember I had a child heart at fifteen,
healthy as a brown calf running wild.
In August, when pears and dates ripened in the courtyard
I'd climb the trees a thousand times a day.
All at once I am fifty,
and I sit and lie around more than I walk or stand.
I force smiles and small talk to please my patrons,
but a hundred worries tangle my emotions.
Coming home to the same four empty walls,
I see this grief mirrored in my old wife's glance.

My sons don't treat their father with respect.
They greet me by the door with angry screams for rice.

TRANSLATED BY TONY BARNSTONE AND CHOU PING

## To Wei Ba

In this life we never meet,
orbiting far like polar stars,
so what evening is this
where I can share your candlelight?
Youth is just a few slim hours,                                    5
and now our hair and sideburns are gray.
Last time I came, half our old friends were ghosts.
I moaned in shock, my guts on fire.
How could I know that after twenty years
I'd enter your hall again?                                         10
When we parted you were unmarried.
Now your sons and daughters form a line,
sweetly show respect for their father's friend
and ask me where I'm from.
With their questions still flying,                                 15
you send them for wine and plates,
for spring chives fresh cut in the evening rain
and rice steamed in with yellow millet.
"How hard it is for us to meet!" You cry,
and one toast grows to ten.                                        20
After ten cups I'm still not drunk,
just warmed by our old friendship.
Tomorrow mountains will come between us,
and we'll be lost in the world like mist.

TRANSLATED BY TONY BARNSTONE AND CHOU PING

## Dreaming of Li Bai

I've swallowed sobs for the lost dead,
but this live separation is chronic grief.
From the malarial south of the river
no news comes of the exiled traveler,
but you visit my dream, old friend,                                5
knowing I ache for you.

Are you are a ghost?
No way to tell with the long road between us.
Your spirit comes through green maple woods
slips home past darkening border fortresses.
You are caught in the law's net,
so how can your spirit have wings?
The sinking moon pours onto the rafters
and your face glows in my mind.
The water is deep, the waves are wide.
Don't let the dragons snatch you!

TRANSLATED BY TONY BARNSTONE AND CHOU PING

## A Painted Falcon

Wind and frost swirl from white silk
where a magnificent black hawk is painted.
His shoulders poised as he seeks for hares,
glancing sidelong with a Hun's angry blue eyes.
Grasp the gleaming leash and collar,
whistle him down from his bar,
and he'll strike the common birds
spattering the plain with blood and feathers.

TRANSLATED BY TONY BARNSTONE AND CHOU PING

## New Moon

Narrow rays from the first slice of moon
slant from the quavering edge of the dark orb,
which barely crests the ancient fortress,
wallowing in the surf of evening clouds.
The river of stars is one eternal color.
Empty cold pours through the mountain pass.
The front courtyard is white dew
and chrysanthemums secretly drenched with dark.

TRANSLATED BY TONY BARNSTONE AND CHOU PING

## Spring Night Happy about Rain

The good rain knows when to fall.
It comes when spring blossoms.

It steals in on the wind, submerged in night,
moistening all things gently without sound.

Black wilderness, black paths, black clouds;                    5
only a torch on a river boat sparks.

At dawn I see all things red and wet,
and flowers drown the City of Brocade.[1]

TRANSLATED BY TONY BARNSTONE AND CHOU PING

## River Village

The clear river curves to embrace the village.
Everything is relaxed here in long summer.
Swallows come and go as they like in the hall,
gulls are necking in the water.
My old wife is drawing a Go board on paper,              5
my little son is hammering a needle into a fishing hook.
As long as old friends give me daily supplies,
what else could my humble body desire?

TRANSLATED BY TONY BARNSTONE AND CHOU PING

## Moonlit Night[2]

In Fuzhou tonight there's a moon
my wife can only watch alone.
Far off, I brood over my small children
who don't even remember Changan.

Her satin hair dampening in fragrant mist,              5
jade arms chilled by clear moonlight,
when will we lean together between empty curtains,
beaming as tear tracks dry on our faces?

TRANSLATED BY TONY BARNSTONE AND CHOU PING

---

1. A poetic epithet for the city of Chengdu in Sichuan Province.
2. Written while captive in Changan, separated from his family.

## Ballad of the War Wagons

Carts grumble and rattle
and horses whinny and neigh
as the conscripts pass, bows and quivers strapped to their
     waists.
Parents, wives and children run to see them off
till dust-clouds drown the bridge south of Changan.
Tugging at soldiers' clothes, they wail and throw themselves in the
     way,
their wails rising into the clouds.

On the roadside a passerby asks what's happening.
The soldiers only say "We're called up often,
some went North at fifteen to guard the Yellow River
and still at forty are farming frontier settlements out West.
We left so young the village chief wrapped our turbans for us;
we came back white-haired but now we're off to fortify the
     frontier!
The men there have shed a salt ocean of blood,
but the warlike Emperor still lusts for empire.
My lord, haven't you heard how in two hundred districts east of
     China's mountains
countless villages grow just weeds and thorns?
Even if a stout wife tries to plough and hoe,
east to west the crops grow wild over broken terraces.
Qin soldiers are fierce warriors,
so we are driven forth like chickens or dogs.

You, sir, can ask questions
but conscripts don't dare complain.
This winter
they haven't released the Guanxi troops
but officials still press for the land tax.
Land tax! How are we to pay that?
The truth is it's a sour thing to have sons.
Better to have a daughter—
at least she can marry a neighbor.
Our sons lie unburied in the grass.
My lord, have you seen the Blue Sea's shore
where the old white bones lie ungathered?
New ghosts keen and old ghosts weep
jiu, jiu, like twittering birds as rain sifts from the bleak sky.

TRANSLATED BY TONY BARNSTONE AND CHOU PING

# P'eng-ya Road

I remember fleeing the rebels
through dangerous northern canyons,

the midnight moon shining bright
on narrow P'eng-ya Road.

So poor we went on foot, 5
we were embarrassed meeting strangers.

A few birds sang in the valleys,
but we met no one ever returning.

My daughter was so starved she bit me,
she screamed her painful hunger. 10

I clamped her mouth shut tight,
fearful of wolves and tigers.

She struggled hard against me,
she cried and cried.

My son was sympathetic 15
and searched the wilds for food.

Then five days of heavy rain arrived,
and we trudged through freezing mud.

We had no coats, no shelter,
we were dressed in cold, wet clothes. 20

Struggling, struggling, we made
but a mile or two each day.

We ate wild fruits and berries,
and branches made our roof.

Mornings we slogged through water, 25
evenings we searched for smoke on the skyline.

We stopped at a marsh
to prepare our climb to the pass,

and met a Mr. Sun
whose standards are high as clouds. 30

We came through the dark
and lamps were lit, gates opening before us.

Servants brought warm water
so we could bathe our aching feet.

They hung paper banners 35
in our honor.

Mrs. Sun came out with all her children.
They wept for our condition.

My children slept, exhausted,
until we roused them with food.

Our host took a vow
he'd always remain my brother.

His home was made our home,
to provide for every comfort.

Who could imagine in such troubled times
he'd bare his heart and soul?

A year has passed since that fated night.
The Barbarians still wage war.

If I had the wings of the wild goose,
I'd fly to be at his side.

TRANSLATED BY SAM HAMILL

## Gazing in Springtime

The empire is shattered but rivers and peaks remain.
In spring wild grass and trees drown the city.

A time so bad, even the flowers rain tears.
I hate this separation, yet birds startle my heart.

The signal fires have burned three months;
I'd give ten thousand gold coins for one letter.

I scratch my head and my white hair thins
till it can't even hold a pin.

TRANSLATED BY TONY BARNSTONE AND CHOU PING

## Thoughts While Night Traveling

Slender wind shifting the shore's fine grass.
Lonely at night below my boat's tall mast.
Stars hang low as the vast plain broadens,
the swaying moon makes the great river race.
How can poems make me known?
I'm old and sick, my career over.

Drifting, just drifting. What kind of man am I?
A lone gull floating between earth and sky.

TRANSLATED BY TONY BARNSTONE AND CHOU PING

## Broken Boat

All my life I've had my heart set on going off
to the land of the lakes—the boat was built for it,
and long ago too. That I used to row
every day on the creek that runs by my rail gate
is beside the point. But then came the mutiny,                     5
and in my panic I fled far away, where
my only concern was to get back here
to these familiar hills.
The neighbors are all gone now,
and everywhere the wild bamboo                                     10
sprouts and spreads and grows tall.
No more rapping its sides as I sing—
it's spent the whole autumn underwater.
All I can do now is watch the other travelers—
birds sailing off in their westward flights,                       15
and even the river, embarrassing me
by moving off eastward so easily.
Well, I could dig up the old one,
and a new one's easy enough to buy,
but it's really the running away that troubles me—                 20
this recent escape and so many before—
that even in this simple cottage
a man cannot stay put long.

TRANSLATED BY STEPHEN OWEN

## ■ Meng Jiao (Meng Chiao) (751–814) (poems)

TRANSLATED BY JAMES A. WILSON

Meng Jiao was the oldest and among the best of the circle of writers who gathered around the great prose master Han Yu in the last decade of the eighth century. He met Han Yu in Changan in 791, but though Han Yu passed the Imperial Examination in 792, Meng Jiao failed, as he did again in 793. He finally passed in 796 but did not receive a position for four years, and even then it was a humiliatingly insignificant post in the provinces. He even lost this post within a few years and settled in Luoyang where he lived for the rest of his life dependent on patrons and friends. Around five hundred of his poems survive, most of them in the "old style" verse (*gu shi*). Though popular enough in his own time, Meng Jiao's reputation went into a tailspin some centuries after his death, due to his brash, disturbing, and jarring verse, which seemed to lack grace and decorum. In fact, it wouldn't be an exaggeration to say that his verse has inspired not so much neglect as active hatred, even in such distinguished readers as Su Shi (Su Dongpo), who states baldly in his two poems "On Reading Meng Jiao's Poetry" that "[he] hate[s] Meng Jiao's poems," which sound to him like a "cold cicada wail":

> My first impression is of eating little fishes—
> What you get's not worth the trouble;
> Or of boiling tiny mud crabs
> And ending up with some empty claws.
> (tr. Burton Watson)

There is no doubt that Su Dongpo is a master of the literary put-down, and, after all, Meng Jiao's poems *do* come across as shrill, self-obsessed, and self-pitying—yet in this lies much of his interest. The glaze of decorous objectivity that is so beautiful in much of Chinese poetry is scraped off in his poems, revealing a didactic would-be Confucian moralist who ends up writing startling, ghostly, and elegiac poems about his own sorrows and idiosyncracies. The series of "Autumn Meditations" from which the following poems come is among his best work. Written late in life, it portrays the poet as despised and sick with illness and self-doubt, and the whole piece is shot through with the elegiac sound of autumn (*shang*), which Ouyang Xiu writes about later in his marvelous piece "The Autumn Sound." If it seems strange to celebrate so fallible a figure, consider his own words: "these sour moans / are also finished verse."

**FURTHER READING:** Owen, Stephen. *The Poetry of Meng Chiao and Han Yu*, 1975.

## from Autumn Meditations

1.

moonlight edges
past the door

like a sword's
inevitable flight

my old bones
can't move for fear

my sick strength
sinks even more

insects complain
as they lust for what glitters                                        *10*

birds try to nest
in the fire of stars

widows caress
their last white hairs

orphans weep                                                          *15*
for no end to their pain

all the vain years
float farther off

my will to follow
falls with the night                                                  *20*

3.

the frost air
invades my sick bones

I'm so old
my frame forms ice

rotted hairs                                                          *5*
stab me in the dark

cold aches
can't be fought off

my violent cries
wing me toward light                                                  *10*

a wild power
battles with my crutch

until I collapse
too gaunt to hold up

my gut hungry                                                         *15*
and my heart brought to ruin

fools on all sides
would have me take drugs

from their words
it's clear I'm despised                                               *20*

let my ears buzz
let my choked soul open

let me recall
how there's no end to merit

in full sunlight
I see what sores remain

bound by dark
I hear the knots of flies

their aim
is unerring

one feeds
at my freshest scab

yet while you gorge
on hidden poisons

I bear with
the life I have left

your frozen flights
won't take you far

winter will wear
on your hearts

birth and death
possess a season

cold and heat
soon turn on each other

I raise up
to thank the grand master of fates

who granted me
mine when I asked

# ▪ Han Yu (Han Yü) (768–824) (poem)

TRANSLATED BY TONY BARNSTONE AND CHOU PING

Han Yu was born in 768 in Nanyang, Henan province, to a literary family. He is considered to be among China's finest prose writers, second only to Sima Qian, and he is the first among the Eight Great Prose Masters of the Tang and Song. His father died when he was two, and he was raised in the family of his older brother, Han Hui. He taught himself to read and write and was a student of philosophical writings and of Confucianist thought. His family moved to Changan in 774 but was banished to southern China in 777 because of his association with disgraced minister Yuan Zai. Han Hui died in 781, leaving the family in poverty, and they returned north around 784. In 792, after four attempts, he passed the Imperial Examination, and a few years later he went into the service of the military governor of Bianzhou, and later of the military governor of Xuzhou. Finally, in 802, he obtained a post as instructor at the Imperial University, a job that he held periodically, between other postings and several periods of exile; ultimately, he was made Rector of the university. After a number of other distinguished posts in the government, he died at the age of 56 in Changan.

Han Yu was a Confucian thinker and was deeply opposed to Buddhism, which was then popular in the court. In fact, he came close to being executed in 819 for sending a letter to the emperor in which he denounced "the elaborate preparations being made by the state to receive the Buddha's fingerbone, which he called 'a filthy object' and which he said should be 'handed over to the proper officials for destruction by water and fire to eradicate forever its origin.'"[1] He believed that literature and ethics were intertwined, and he led a revolution in prose style against the formal ornamentation then popular. He championed instead *gu wen* (old style prose), which was characterized by simplicity, logic, and an emphasis on apt and exact expression. He was the center of a group of prose writers who adopted this style, a group that included Meng Jiao, whose poetry Han Yu appreciated. Other writers included in this anthology who adopted this style are Ouyang Xiu and Su Shi (Su Dongpo). While Han Yu's lasting reputation lies as a prose innovator, he was also a fine poet.

**FURTHER READING:** Owen, Stephen. *The Poetry of Meng Chiao and Han Yu,* 1975. Watson, Burton. *The Columbia Book of Chinese Poetry: From Early Times to the Thirteenth Century,* 1984.

# Mountain Rocks[1]

Ragged mountain rocks efface the path.
Twilight comes to the temple where bats hover.
Outside the hall I sit on steps and gaze at torrential new rain.
Banana leaves are wide, the cape jasmine is fat.

---

1. Liu, Wu-chi, *An Introduction to Chinese Literature* (Bloomington: Indiana University Press, 1973), 126.

---

1. Han Yu's poems are often satirically anti-Buddhist, as in his poem "The Girl of Mt. Hua," which depicts Daoists and Buddhists abandoning their temples at the sight of a beautiful young woman. In this poem, however, he abandons his famous hatred of Buddhism and celebrates the natural simplicity of a Buddhist mountain retreat.

A monk tells me the ancient Buddhist frescos are good
and holds a torch to show me, but I can barely see.
I lie quiet in night so deep even insects are silent.
From behind a rise the clear moon enters my door.

In the dawn I am alone and lose myself,
wandering up and down in mountain mist.
Then colors dazzle me: mountain red, green stream,
and a pine so big, ten people linking hands can't encircle it.
Bare feet on slick rock as I wade upstream.
Water sounds — shhhh, shhhh. Wind inflates my shirt.
A life like this is the best.
Why put your teeth on the bit and let people rein you in?
O friends,
how can we grow old without returning here?

## ■ Xue Tao (Hsüeh T'ao) (768–831) (poems)

Xue Tao was well respected as a poet during the Tang dynasty. She was born either in the Tang capital Zhangan or in Chengdu, present-day Sichuan province, when her father, a minor government official, was posted there. A story about her childhood, perhaps apocryphal, suggests that she was able to write complex poems by the age of seven or eight. She may have gained some literary education from her father, but he died before she had come to marriageable age, and she ended up being a very successful courtesan (one of the few paths for women in Tang dynasty China in which conversation and artistic talent were encouraged). After Wei Gao, the military governor, became her literary patron, her reputation was widespread. She seems to have had an affair with another famous literary figure, Yuan Zhen. Late in life she went to live in seclusion and put on the habit of a Taoist churchwoman.

**FURTHER READING:** Larsen, Jeanne, tr. *Brocade River Poems: Selected Works of the Tang Dynasty Courtesan Xue Tao*, 1987.

## Spring-Gazing Song

Blossoms crowd the branches: too beautiful to endure.
Thinking of you, I break into bloom again.
One morning soon, my tears will mist the mirror.
I see the future, and I will not see.

TRANSLATED BY CAROLYN KIZER

## Seeing a Friend Off

The waterland spreds with reeds and night frost.
Cold moon and mountains are bluish pale.
Who says we'll be thousands of miles apart?
My dream can travel to the farthest border pass.

TRANSLATED BY TONY BARNSTONE AND CHOU PING

■ Li Gongzuo (Li Kung-tso) (c. 770 – c. 848) (story)

TRANSLATED BY CHOU PING

Li Gongzuo was one of the finest Tang dynasty writers of literary-language stories. He came from what is today Gansu province but seems to have lived primarily in central and southern China. He may have been distantly related to the Imperial family, and after passing his examinations, he had a career as a low-ranking administrator. Only four of his stories survived, but two of them are classics. "Xie Xiaoe" is an early detective story, often anthologized, whereas "The Governor of Southern-Bough" is an expansion of Shen Jiji's famous tale "The World inside a Pillow." Like Zhuangzi's parable of the man who dreamed he was a butterfly, this story has become a famous Chinese touchstone about the illusory nature of life and the equivalence of life and dream.

FURTHER READING: Wang, Chi-chen, tr. *Traditional Chinese Tales*, 1944. Wong, Elizabeth Te-chen, tr. *Ladies of the Tang: 22 Classical Chinese Stories*, 1961. *The Dragon King's Daughter. Ten Tang Dynasty Stories*, 1954.

## The Governor of Southern-Bough

Chunyu Fen from Dongping was a chivalrous man roaming in the Wu and Chu areas. Indulging in alcohol and a quick temper, unconstrained by rules and concerns in life, he threw away an enormous portion of his family wealth to support other gallant and brave men. As he had training in martial arts, he was once appointed a subordinate general in the Huinan Army, but because he offended the marshal by losing his temper after too many a drink, he was reprimanded and dismissed. After that he started drifting again and became even more careless in his way of life. He made the wine bottle his profession.

His ancestral home was about three miles away to the east of the Guangling (now Yangzhou) city. To the south of his house, there was a giant ancient locust tree with thick boughs and long branches, providing a green shade of several *mu*.[1] Chunyu Fen and his gallant friends would drink wildly under this tree every day.

One day in the ninth month in the seventh year of the Zhenyuan reign (A.D. 791), Chunyu Fen drank too much and got sick. Two friends at the table held his arms and helped him return home. They let him rest in the east corridor outside the main hall, saying, "Have a nap. We'll feed the horses and wash our feet, and we'll leave when you are better." Chunyu Fen removed his headpiece and rested his head on the pillow. In a state of half consciousness, he seemed to have a dream. He saw two messengers in purple who knelt before him, saying, "The king of the Hui'an Kingdom sent us to deliver his invitation to you." Without knowing what he was doing, Chunyu got off the bed and smoothed up his clothing, and followed the two messengers to the gate. There was a black-painted carriage pulled by four horses with an entourage of seven to eight attendants. They helped him to get on the carriage and they went through the gate, heading straight to the hole under the giant locust tree.

The messengers drove the carriage directly into the hole. Chunyu Fen was very much surprised and yet dared not to ask. Suddenly he saw mountains and rivers, clouds and sky, vegetation and roads, though they were all quite different from those in the human world. After traveling for about a dozen miles, a city wall appeared in the distance. Carriages and pedestrians were coming and going endlessly. Attendants standing on both sides of the carriage were announcing their arrival in harsh voices and pedestrians were trying to make way for them as soon as they could. Then they entered a big city with red gates and tall towers. Four golden characters on the gate tower read "Great Huian Kingdom." The gate guards saluted them in a hurry and ran to pass on the news of their coming. Soon a messenger on horseback came with an announcement, "The king's order—the royal son-in-law has traveled a long distance. Take a rest in the Donghua Guest House first." After saying that, he led the way.

After a while, they came to a gate with doors wide open, and Chunyu Fen stepped down from the carriage and went in. He saw painted banisters, sculptured pillars, rows of beautiful flowers and exotic fruits in the courtyard and, upon entering the hall, he saw to his delight chairs and tables, seat cushions, curtains, wine and dishes ready to serve. Suddenly he heard a voice announcing, "The Right Prime Minister is coming," and Chunyu Fen went down the stairs to wait for him respectfully. A man in a purple gown with an ivory court-tablet walked to him rapidly. They exchanged greetings in most polite and appropriate ways. "Our majesty," the Right Prime Minister said, "welcomes you to our out-of-the-way kingdom

---

1. *Mu* is a unit of land in Chinese, equal to 0.0667 hectares.

and plans to marry you to our princess." "How could a humble person like me hope for this?" Chunyu Fen answered. The Right Prime Minister invited Chunyu Fen to visit the king together with him.

After about a hundred steps, they passed through a red-painted gate. With spears, halberds, long and short axes displayed, hundreds of guards on either side of the passage stepped back to let them pass. Among them Chunyu Fen spotted a friend, Zhou Bian, who used to be one of his wine-drinking companions. Chunyu Fen was secretly happy about this, though he dared not walk up to him to talk. The Right Prime Minister led him to the main hall, where the guards looked grave and formidable. This must be the king's palace, he thought. Sitting on the throne was a tall and serious-looking man, dressed up in a white silk robe and a red crown. Chunyu Fen was shivering in fear and did not look up. The guards on either side asked him to kneel down.

"Some time ago," the king said, "we heard from your father that he would not turn down our small kingdom's proposal, and thus let my second daughter Yaofang marry you and serve you." Chunyu Fen continued to kowtow and didn't dare to say a single word. The king continued, "You stay in the guest house for the time being, and we will arrange the wedding next." Then there was a royal edict, ordering the Right Prime Minister to accompany Chunyu Fen to the guest house. Chunyu Fen kept wondering how this marriage had come about. His father was a general stationed on the border and was lost somewhere there in a foreign land. No one knew if he was still alive or not. Is it possible that his father's negotiations with the northern barbarians had led to all this? Chunyu Fen was utterly confused.

That night, everything needed in the wedding was well prepared: the four wedding gifts—lambs, wild swans, coins and silk—impressive guards of honor, girl singers and bands, food and candles, carriages and horses. Besides there were a bevy of girls, who were called Bright-sun, Green-stream, Super-immortal, Lower-immortal and the like, and each of them had hundreds of attendants. Those girls all wore emerald-phoenix bonnets, capes decorated with golden clouds and colorful jewelry and gold hairpins that dazzled the eye. They were strolling about and having fun. When they arrived at the guest house, they all competed in teasing Chunyu Fen. Charming and seductive, they rendered Chunyu Fen speechless with their wit and eloquence.

One of the girls said to Chunyu Fen, "One day on the third day in the third month I went to the Zen-wisdom Temple with Madame Linzhi to watch Youyan doing the Brahman dance in the India Courtyard. With other girls I sat on a stone couch under the northern window. At that time you were a lad and you got off your bamboo horse to watch. Teasing and flirting, all by yourself you approached us by force. Qiongyin and I tied a knot with a red handkerchief and hung it on a bamboo branch. How could you forget all that? Also, once on the sixteenth in the seventh month, I met Shangzhenzi in the Xiaogan Temple and we listened to Master Qixuan's interpretation of the Guanyin Scripture. I donated two gold phoenix hairpins at the lecture and Shangzhenzi donated a box made of rhino horn. You were also present among the audience at that time. You asked for Master Qixuan's permission and had a closer look at the hairpins and the box, sighing again and again with amazement and marveling at them for a long time. Then you turned around and looked at us, saying "Such beautiful girls and such beautiful things do not belong to the human world." For a while you tried to find out our names, then you asked where we lived, but I ignored your questions. With your eyes nailed on me all the time, you looked in love. Haven't you been missing me at all?" Chunyu Fen replied with two lines from the *Book of Songs*, "Hidden deep in my heart, never forgotten for a single day." The girls responded, "How can one imagine that we are relatives now!"

Then three men dressed up in impressive hats and sashes came to salute Chunyu Fen, saying "We are here by the king's order to be the royal son-in-law's best men." One of them was Chunyu Fen's friend, so Chunyu Fen pointed at him and asked, "Aren't you Tian Zihua from Pingyi?" The man answered, "Right." Chunyu Fen walked up to him and held his hands, and they talked for a long while. Then Chunyu Fen asked, "How come you are living here?" Tian Zihua answered, "I was roaming about and fortunately came into favor with the Right Prime Minister Duan, who is the Marquis of Wucheng, and thanks to him I settled down here." Chunyu Fen asked again, "Zhou Bian is also here, do you know him?" Zihua answered "Zhou Bian is an important figure here. He is the Chief of Criminal Investigation with a lot of power and influence. He protected me on several occasions." They talked and laughed, feeling very happy. Before long, a spoken message was relayed to them, "Now the royal son-in-law may enter." The three best men handed him a sword, jade ornaments, hat and clothes and asked Chunyu Fen to change. Zihua said, "What a surprise to witness your magnificent wedding here today! Don't forget me."

Now dozens of beautiful girls started to play various kinds of exotic music. The sound was sweet and clear while the melodies were slow and slightly melancholy. Such music was never heard in the human world. Dozens of others were holding candles to lead the way. On both sides golden and emerald curtains were carried. Colorful and shining, they extended for about a mile. Chunyu Fen sat straight in a carriage, feeling both dizzy and nervous. Tian Zihua tried to tell him jokes and make him relax. The group of girls and relatives all got into their phoenix-wings carriage and followed them. They reached a gate with a sign, "Xiuyi Palace."

The bevy of immortal girls was already lined up on both sides and asked Chunyu Fen to get off the carriage. The rituals and procedures in the wedding process were exactly the same as those in the human world. When the fans and head-cover were removed, Gold Branch Princess's face was revealed. Though just fourteen or fifteen years old, she was as beautiful as a fairy. The token-exchange rituals were really impressive.

After their marriage, the couple fell deeper in love day by day while Chunyu Fen became more and more glorious and influential in social life. His carriages and banquets for entertaining guests were only second to the king's in importance and scale.

One day, the king ordered Chunyu Fen and officials to summon up troops, and they went on a royal hunt at Tortoise Mountain in the west of the kingdom. The mountains there were tall and magnificent, the lakes vast and deep, the forest thick and grass green. All kinds of animals and birds made their home there. They hunted many animals and returned to the city after evening.

Chunyu Fen said to the king, "On my wedding day, your majesty said that it was according to my father's wishes. I remember that my father was stationed at the border to assist the generals there and he was defeated and lost in a foreign country. There was no communication between us for seventeen or eighteen years. If your majesty knows where he is, please let me go visit him." The king immediately answered, "Your father is defending the territory in the north; we have been in touch all the time. You can write a letter to inform him; there is no need to visit him personally." Chunyu Fen asked his wife to prepare presents, and together with the letter he had them sent to his father. A few days later, a reply came. Chunyu Fen scrutinized the letter and found written there the old man's life story, along with words of love and instruction, and the memories and emotions he remembered from the past. His father asked about the relatives—who were still in this world and who were already gone—and he also asked what was established in the hometown and what had been abandoned. Then he bemoaned the long distance that made communication between them almost impossible. His sad words conveyed a sense of depression. But he would not allow Chunyu Fen to visit him, saying, "It is going to be in the year of Dingchou that we shall meet." Chunyu Fen looked at the letter and couldn't help sobbing.

One day, his wife asked Chunyu Fen, "Why don't you want to run an office?" Chunyu Fen replied, "I'm so used to this kind of relaxed life that I know nothing about administration." His wife said, "You take the position and I'll assist you." So his wife talked to the king. Several days later, the king told Chunyu Fen, "The Southern Bough State in my kingdom doesn't have good administration. The governor is now removed from his position and I want to make use of your great talent. Please accept this appointment. You can go with my daughter." Chunyu Fen accepted the appointment very politely. The king issued an edict to relevant officials to prepare for the new governor's journey. Gold, jade, silk, trunks, maids and servants, carriages and horses were allocated and lined up at the end of the main street, so the princess could take them with her after the seeing-off ceremony. Chunyu Fen was only a roaming chivalrous man when he was young and he had never dreamed about anything like this. Now he was extremely happy and he submitted a memorial to the king.

"I, your humble servant, an insignificant son from a general's family, have no real talent and skills. When given too much responsibility, I might ruin the court's administration. I feel worried that with the reins in my hand, I will cause upheavals through poor governance. Therefore, now I hope to search for talented and virtuous personnel to make up for my shortcomings. Your humble servant feels that the Chief of Criminal Investigation, Zhou Bian from Yingchuan, is loyal, honest and straightforward and he maintains the law strictly with no selfish motives, thus he would make a very good assistant. Besides, Tian Zihua from Pingyi, an intellectual with no official position yet, is a cautious man with great integrity. He has a keen sense for the changes in the world and knows very clearly about the essence of moral education. Those two persons and I have been friends for over ten years and thus I know their talent well and I can trust them with my administrative work. I humbly request that Zhou Bian be appointed the Chief of Law in the Southern Bough State and Tian Zihua the Chief of Agriculture in the Southern Bough State. This way I can make achievements in administration while national laws and regulations will be maintained in good order."

The king made the appointments according to the memorial.

That night, the king and the queen held a seeing-off banquet in the southern part of the city. The king said to Chunyu Fen, "The Southern Bough is a big state in our kingdom. The land is fertile with abundant local products and the population is big with a strong disposition. It takes caring policies to run that state well. Now with the assistance of Zhou and Tian, I hope you'll work hard and live up to the kingdom's expectation."

The queen said to the princess, "Mr. Chunyu Fen is a staunch man with a passion for drink, and on top of that he is young. The art of being a good wife is to be tender and obedient. If you can deal with him well, I'll feel relieved. Though the Southern Bough State is not too far away from the capital, we will no longer see each other in the morning and evening every day. Now we have to part and I can't help crying."

Chunyu Fen and the princess respectfully saluted the king and queen and set off to the south. They sat in the carriage protected by guards on horseback, laughing and talking all the way, feeling elated.

Several days later, they arrived at the Southern Bough State. All the officials and clerks, Buddhist and Daoist monks, elders from local gentry, bands, carriages, armed guards and horses with bells came to welcome them. Crowds and the sound of drums and bells extended for about a dozen miles. The city wall, the lookouts and the towers all looked very magnificent and seemed to exude happiness. When they were passing through the gate, they saw a big horizontal sign hanging overhead, "Capital of Southern Bough State." There were rows of red-painted lattice windows, and gates with weapons displayed on the outside. They all looked solemn and profound.

The moment Chunyu Fen stepped out of his carriage he started investigating the local customs and tried to lessen the suffering of the people there. He trusted his administrative work to Zhou Bian and Tian Zihua and thus did a good job in governing the state. In the twenty years of his service, moral education became far reaching in the area, the local people not only sang praises of him, building a monument to record his achievements, but also built a temple for him when he was still alive. With great appreciation for his talent, the king bestowed him land and titles of nobility and made him an equal to the rank of prime minister. Step by step, Zhou Bian and Tian Zihua were promoted to high ranks for their achievement in administration. In those years, Chunyu Fen had five sons and two daughters. The sons were all given official positions by means of the official hereditary benefits, the daughters all got engaged with sons related to the royal family. Their glory and wealth were so overwhelming that for a time no one was Chunyu Fen's match.

One year, however, a nation called the Sandalwood Vines came to invade the Southern Bough State. The king ordered Chunyu Fen to train his officers and soldiers and get ready to resist the intruders. Chunyu Fen submitted a memorial, recommending Zhou Bian as the leader of 30,000 soldiers so as to stop the coming enemy at Yrotai City. But Zhou Bian depended too much on his own valor and overlooked the enemy's strength, and he was completely defeated. Zhou Bian managed to escape alone on horseback, having lost his armor, and returned to the city at midnight. The enemy collected all the military supplies and armor before they returned to their own country.

Chunyu Fen threw Zhou Bian in jail and asked for punishment from the king, but the king pardoned him. It was in that same month that Zhou Bian, the Chief of Criminal Investigation, died of a vicious ulcer in his back. Then Chunyu Fen's wife, the Gold Bough Princess, became sick and also died in about ten days. Chunyu Fen submitted his resignation so as to accompany the princess's hearse back to the capital. The king approved it. Tian Zihua, the Chief of Agriculture, was appointed the acting governor.

Chunyu Fen cried aloud in his sadness and that signaled the departure of the princess's body back to the capital. Guards of Honor escorted the procession, men and women all wailed by the roadside, people and clerks arranged tables of wine and food for sacrifice. Those who held on to the carriage or blocked the road to stop Chunyu Fen from leaving them were too many to be counted.

When they finally arrived at the capital, the king and the queen dressed in white were also standing on the outskirt of the city, weeping and waiting for the hearse to come home. A posthumous title, "Shunyi Princess," was bestowed on the princess. Escorted by guards of honor and bands, draped in a royal cover, the princess's coffin was buried at the Coiling-Dragon Mountain, about three miles away to the east of the capital. In the same month, Rongxin, the son of the ex-Chief of Criminal Investigation Zhou Bian also accompanied his father's coffin back to the capital.

Chunyu Fen, as the governor of a big state for a long time, had made extensive friends among the officials in the capital and all the aristocratic families were on good terms with him. Since coming back to the capital on resignation, he had no restraints in associating with people and entertaining friends, and his influence grew day by day until even the king grew suspicious of him. Just then someone submitted a memorial, "Unusual changes are observed in the heavenly bodies, forecasting a big disaster in the country: the capital has to be moved, the ancestor's temple will be destroyed. The event will be provoked by outsiders, though its cause can be located inside the innermost walls." The public opinion was that Chunyu Fen had overstepped boundaries and caused this omen from the heavens. Therefore the king took away Chunyu Fen's guards, banned his association with friends and put him under house arrest.

Chunyu Fen was proud of the fact that as a governor in a big state for many years he had never made any administrative mistake. Now that he had to put up with groundless complaints and defamation, he was very unhappy. The king also understood how he felt, and therefore said to him, "We've been family for over twenty years. Unfortunately my daughter died too young and could not live to her old age together with you. We are really sad about this." The queen added that she wanted to have the grandchildren nurtured in the palace. Then the king said to Chunyu Fen, "You've been away from your hometown for so long, it's time that you returned there to visit your relatives. You can leave my grandchildren here, don't worry about them. Three years later, I will welcome you back." Chunyu Fen replied, "This is my home. Where do you want me to return?" The king laughed, saying, "You were from the human world, your home is not here." When the king said this, it was as if Chunyu were being awakened from a dream, and he fell into a confusion through which pierced clear memories of his former life. He couldn't help weeping and asked for permission to go home. The king ordered guards to escort him. Chunyu Fen kowtowed again and took his departure. Once again he saw the same two messengers in purple and followed them.

Outside the main gate, the carriage waiting there was very shabby; his attendants, servants and carrriage driver were not there at all. He sighed deeply in surprise. After getting on the carriage and running for a few miles, they went out of the city. He looked around and recognized the road along which he had came from the east and saw the same rivers, mountains and fields. Only the two messengers were no longer that impressive. Chunyu Fen felt even more unhappy and asked them. "When will we get to Guangling?" The two messengers were singing, and they ignored his questioning for a long time, though one eventually snapped, "Soon."

After a while, the carriage came out of a hole. Chunyu Fen saw the streets in his hometown, exactly the same as many years ago. He felt sad and tears started to drop. The two messengers helped him to get off the carriage and enter his own house. After walking up the steps, Chunyu Fen saw his own body lying in the eastern corridor outside the main hall. He was really frightened and didn't dare to approach himself. The two messengers yelled his name loudly for a few times, and he suddenly woke up as if he never had slept. He saw the servants sweeping the courtyard and two friends were washing their feet, sitting on the couch. The evening sun was still lingering on the western wall; the wine left in the goblet still looked almost brimming by the east window. Things go fast in a dream— as if one whole lifetime had elapsed!

Chunyu Fen marveled at what had happened and sighed. Then he called his two friends and told them about his dream. They were astonished. They followed Chunyu Fen to the outside and found the big hole under the locust tree. Chunyu Fen pointed at the hole and said, "I went through this hole in my dream." The two friends thought it must be some fox or tree ghost haunting this place. They summoned servants with axes and chopped off the swollen parts of the tree trunk as well as the brush and branches to search for the innermost part of the hole. They dug for more than ten yards and suddenly found a big opening, spacious enough to contain a bed. Soil was accumulated there in the shape of walls, towers and palace with bushels of ants hiding there. Right in the middle there was a small cinnabar-colored platform, occupied by two giant ants. They had white wings and red heads, and were a little bit more than three inches long. Protected by several dozen large ants, no ants could get close to them. They must have been the king and the queen. So this was the capital of the Huian Kingdom.

Then they found another opening. It led straight up to the southern bough for about forty yards. The tunnel went zigzag inside the tree. There were also city walls and small towers with swarms of ants living there. That must be the Southern Bough State where Chunyu Fen served as the governor. In addition, there was another hole, extending twenty yards to the west with a big low opening in the middle in the shape of a basement. There was a rotten tortoise there, its shell as big as a bushel container. Soaked in accumulated rain, grass was growing rampantly, almost covering the tortoise shell. This must have been Tortoise Mountain where Chunyu Fen went hunting. Then they found another hole, about ten yards on the east, with old tree roots entangled together like snakes and dragons. There was a mound in the middle about a yard tall—that must be the princess' tomb.

Chunyu Fen recalled all those days and sighed with deep feeling. He found that everything here was exactly as he saw in his dream. He did not want his friends to destroy it and ordered the servants to cover it up as it was. That night, a big storm came suddenly. The next morning when they went back there to check, all the ants had moved to some unknown place. It matched the earlier prediction, ". . . a big disaster in the country: the capital has to be moved." Now the omen had come true.

Then Chunyu Fen recalled the invasion initiated by the Nation of Sandalwood Vine and thus asked his two friends to help him search for it. At one place five hundred yards away to the east of the residence, there was a dried mountain stream with a big Sandalwood tree covered by vines, and its shade was so thick that it blocked out the sun. By the tree there was a hole with swarms of ants hiding in it. Wasn't this the Nation of Sandalwood Vine?

O, if the ant's intelligence and spiritual power are beyond human understanding, how about those big animals hiding in the mountains?

At that time, Chunyu Fen's wine friends Zhou Bian and Tian Zihua both lived in the Liuhe county and they were out of touch with Chunyu Fen for about ten days. Immediately Chunyu Fen sent servants to visit them and learned that Zhou Bian had died of an acute disease while Tian Zihua was also sick in bed. Chunyu Fen realized then both the emptiness of being a governor in the Southern Bough State and the ephemerality of human life. Therefore he was converted to Daoism and became abstinent from both sex and wine. Three years later in the year of Dingchou, he died at home at the age of forty-seven, exactly as his father's letter said in the dream.

The present author Gong Zuo was traveling from Wu to Luoyang in the eighth month in autumn in the eighteenth year of Zhenyuan reign (802). With his boat moored by the Hui river, he met with Chunyu Fen by chance. He asked Chunyu Fen about that dream and investigated the actual places many times and wrote this biographical sketch to entertain those who are nosy for anecdotes. Though this story relates to the supernatural and involves things not found in the canons, I hope it can admonish those who obtain official positions and luxurious life by dishonest means. For generations of gentlemen to come, please be aware of the fact that promotions are accidental, like that in the Southern Bough, and please don't be too proud about your fame and position. Li Zhao, ex-advisor to military affairs in Huazhou wrote the following lines as a comment on this story:

> The highest pay and position,
> the most powerful in the capital,
> but in the eyes that can see through—
> humans and ants are just the same.

## ■ Bo Juyi (Po Chü-i) (772–846) (poems)

Bo Juyi was born in Henan to a poor family of scholars. He took the Imperial Examination at age twenty-seven and dreamed, with his friend Yuan Zhen, of being a reformer; but his career as an official was less than illustrious, and his attempts to criticize incidents of injustice only caused him to be banished from the capital (Changan) in 815. He was the Prefect of Hangzhou (822–825) and then of Suzhou (825–827) but finally retired from political life, which he found ultimately to be a disappointment, and turned to Buddhism. As a writer, however, he fared somewhat better. He was popular in his lifetime, and his poems were known by peasants and court ladies alike. He was very popular in Japan: a number of his poems found their way into *The Tale of Genji,* he was the subject of a *noh* play, and he has even become a sort of Shinto deity. More than twenty-eight hundred of his poems survive, as he was careful to preserve his work; in 815, he sent his writings to Yuan Zhen, who edited and compiled them into an edition of his collected work in 824–825. His poems show an interest in recording his times and his private life alike and often reveal an empathy with the poor that belies the heights of his own career. They are often written in a deliberately plain style, and some poems are written in imitation of the folk songs collected by the Music Bureau (*yuefu* poems) in the second century B.C. Arthur Waley notes that according to a popular account, Bo Juyi used to read his poems to an old peasant woman and would change any line that she could not understand. There is a benevolent directed intelligence in his poems that comes through the refractions of culture and translation and makes us feel the powerful presence of this poet who died more than a thousand years ago.

FURTHER READING: Levi, Howard S. *Translations from Po Chu-i's Collected Works*, 1971. Waley, Arthur. *The Life and Times of Po Chu-i*, 1949; *Translations from the Chinese*, 1971.

## Night Rain

Chirp of an early cricket. Silence.
The lamp dies then flares up again.
Night must be raining outside the window:
*plink, plunk* on the banana leaves.

TRANSLATED BY TONY BARNSTONE AND CHOU PING

## The Old Charcoal Seller

The old charcoal seller
chops wood and makes charcoal at South Mountain.
With a face full of dust and soot,
his hair is grey and his fingers all black.
How much can he make from selling charcoal?                    5
Just enough to clothe his body and feed his mouth.
His clothes are very thin.
but he wishes it colder to keep charcoal prices high.
It snowed one foot outside the city during the night,
and he drove his charcoal cart through frozen ruts at dawn.     10
Now the sun is high, the ox is tired and the man hungry;
they take a rest in the mud outside the South Gate.

Who are those two men galloping near on horseback?
—Messengers in white shirt and yellow gown.
They read a document in the name of the emperor                     *1*
and turn the cart around, yell at the ox to head north.
A cartful of charcoal weighs about a ton,
but the palace messengers make the old man give it up
for just half a roll of red gauze and a piece of damask silk
they leave tied around the ox's head.                               *2*

TRANSLATED BY TONY BARNSTONE AND CHOU PING

## Watching the Reapers

Farmers have few slow months
and the fifth one is double busy.
Southern wind rises at night.
and the wheatfields yellow.
Women carry food on shoulder,
kids bring water along.
They go together to feed their men
who are working at the South Hill
with feet burned by hot soil,
backs scorched by the bright and flaming sky.                       *1*
But they are too exhausted to feel the heat
and don't want the long summer days to end.

There is a poor woman nearby,
carrying her son in her arm.
She gleans wheat ears with her right hand,                          *1*
a broken basket hanging on her left elbow.
She looks up and tells me
a story that twists my heart:
all their harvest is gone to pay for the land rent,
she picks these ears to fill hungry stomachs.                       *2*
What achievement, what virtue, have I
that I need not labor like a farmer?
I have an income of three hundred bushels,
and a surplus of food at the end of year.
I am ashamed, and these thoughts                                    *2*
nag at me for the rest of the day.

TRANSLATED BY TONY BARNSTONE AND CHOU PING

# At the End of Spring

*To Yüan Chen.*[1]

The flower of the pear-tree gathers and turns to fruit;
The swallows' eggs have hatched into young birds.
When the Seasons' changes thus confront the mind
What comfort can the Doctrine of Tao give?
It will teach me to watch the days and months fly          5
Without grieving that Youth slips away;
If the Fleeting World is but a long dream,
It does not matter whether one is young or old.
But ever since the day that my friend left my side
And has lived an exile in the City of Chiang-ling,        10
There is one wish I cannot quite destroy:
That from time to time we may chance to meet again.

TRANSLATED BY ARTHUR WALEY


# On His Baldness

At dawn I sighed to see my hairs fall;
At dusk I sighed to see my hairs fall.
For I dreaded the time when the last lock should go . . .
They are all gone and I do not mind at all!
I have done with that cumbrous washing and getting dry;    5
My tiresome comb for ever is laid aside.
Best of all, when the weather is hot and wet,
To have no top-knot weighing down on one's head!
I put aside my dusty conical cap;
And loose my collar-fringe.                                10
In a silver jar I have stored a cold stream;
On my bald pate I trickle a ladle-full.
Like one baptized with the Water of Buddha's Law,
I sit and receive this cool, cleansing joy.
Now I know why the priest who seeks Repose                 15
Frees his heart by first shaving his head.

TRANSLATED BY ARTHUR WALEY

---

1. Bo Juyi's great friend.

## Light Furs, Fat Horses

A show of arrogant spirit fills the road;
a glitter of saddles and horses lights up the dust.
I ask who these people are—
trusted servants of the ruler, I'm told.
The vermilion sashes are all high-ranking courtiers;          5
the purple ribbons are probably generals.
Proudly they repair to the regimental feast,
their galloping horses passing like clouds.
Tankards and wine cups brim with nine kinds of spirits;
from water and land, an array of eight delicacies.          1
For fruit they break open Tung-t'ing oranges,
for fish salad, carve up scaly bounty from T'ien-ch'ih.
Stuffed with food, they rest content in heart;
livened by wine, their mood grows merrier than ever.
This year there's a drought south of the Yangtze.          1
In Ch'ü-chou, people are eating people.

TRANSLATED BY BURTON WATSON

## ■ Liu Zongyuan (Liu Tsung-yüan) (773–819) (poems, fable, and essay)

Liu Zongyuan was one of the finest prose writers of the Tang dynasty and was one of only two Tang dynasty writers included among the Eight Great Prose Masters of the Tang and Song. He was a friend of Han Yu, and one of the followers of the "ancient style" prose movement, which emphasized clarity and utility over ornament in prose writing. He was also a relatively minor poet. He was born and raised in Changan, the capital of the Tang dynasty. After a highly successful early career in civil government, he was reassigned to a post in the provinces (in Yongzhou, Hunan province) after the abdication of Emperor Shunzong in 805. A decade later, he was banished even farther away, to modern Guangxi. His works in exile are considered to be his finest. The writings done in the capital were bureaucratic in nature, and he considered them primarily a means to advance his career; in exile, however, he wrote a number of delightful didactic pieces, showing a Neo-Confucian synthesis of both Daoism and Buddhism (unlike Han Yu, Liu Zongyuan was not adverse to the wave of Buddhism that was then sweeping across China). He is particularly known for his allegorical writings and for his fables, which like Aesop's fables often are tales about animals. "The Donkey of Guizhou" fits into this category. "The Snake-Catcher" is one of his finest pieces, a satire about the hardships of excessive taxation.

His poem "River Snow" is considered a prime example of the extreme condensation of meaning valued in Chinese poetry and has been the subject of numerous landscape paintings. It is a terrifically imagistic poem; the twenty characters of the poem create a whole landscape, sketch an intimate scene, and suggest a chill ineffable solitude. There is also a Buddhist element to the poem, and Liu Zongyuan's old man becomes like Wallace Stevens's "Snow Man," with a "mind of winter":

> For the listener, who listens in the snow,
> And, nothing himself, beholds
> Nothing that is not there and the nothing that is.

**FURTHER READING:** Liu, Shih Shun. *Chinese Classical Prose, the Eight Masters of the T'ang-Sung Period,* 1979.

## River Snow

A thousand mountains. Flying birds vanish.
Ten thousand paths. Human traces erased.
One boat, bamboo hat, bark cape—an old man.
Alone with his hook. Cold river. Snow.

TRANSLATED BY TONY BARNSTONE AND CHOU PING

## Song of an Evening River

A ray of setting sun paves the water,
half the river is emerald, half the river ruby.
I love the third night in the ninth month—
dewdrops turn into pearls, the moon into a bow.

TRANSLATED BY TONY BARNSTONE AND CHOU PING

## The Donkey of Guizhou

There were no donkeys in Guizhou until an eccentric transported one there by boat. After its arrival, no one could find a use for it and so they let the donkey loose in the foothills of the mountains.

A tiger spotted the donkey and found it so large and strange that he thought it must surely be supernatural. Hiding in the woods, the tiger watched the donkey, creeping somewhat closer, but keeping a healthy respect for the unknown animal.

One day, the donkey brayed, and the tiger was so scared that it ran far away, thinking that the donkey was going to swallow it up. But after pacing back and forth, eyeing the donkey, the tiger began to wonder if this creature were really so frightful.

By and by, the tiger got used to the donkey's voice, and once again approached the donkey, first from front, and then from the rear, still not daring to attack. But the tiger kept coming closer and closer, dashing in, charging, shoving, and jostling the donkey roughly. Eventually, the donkey could not control its anger any more and kicked the tiger. The tiger was overjoyed, saying "So, that's all it has got." Leaping upon the donkey, the tiger sank its teeth in, tearing open its throat and devouring all its flesh, before going on his way.

What a tragedy! The donkey's large body *appeared* powerful, and its loud voice *sounded* fierce. If the donkey hadn't shown its meager skills, the tiger, violent as it was, would still be in doubt and fear, lacking the courage to attack. Now look at the poor donkey!

TRANSLATED BY CHOU PING

## The Snake-Catcher

In the wilderness of Yongzhou, there was a kind of extraordinary snake, black with white patterns, that could kill even weeds and trees with a touch. No person has ever recovered from its bite. However, if one can catch it and air-dry it, as an ingredient in Chinese medicine it can cure leprosy, palsy, and boils, and removes dead tissues and tumors. For this reason, the court physician began collecting the snakes from the people in the name of the emperor. Every year, two such snakes were to be submitted, and those who caught them were exempt from land rent and taxes. And so the people in Yongzhou started to compete in catching the snakes.

The family of one Mr. Jiang has been exclusively in this business for three generations now. When I asked him about it, Jiang's answer was, "My grandfather died from this; so did my father. Now I've been catching snakes for twelve years and have been on the edge of death many times." He looked terribly morose when saying these words. I felt sorry for him and said, "Do you hate this job? I'll tell the people in charge to let you pay land rent instead. How about that?"

Hearing this, Jiang seemed to be seized by an even deeper sadness, and began to weep, saying "You feel sorry for me and so you want to help me survive? But the misfortune of having this task is not as bad as paying my land tax. If I hadn't been doing this, I'd have been in worse misery long ago. For three generations my family have been living in this area, altogether about sixty years now. During these decades, our neighbors' lives have been getting harder and harder. They have exhausted what the land can produce, spent up all the family's income. Weeping, they have had to move on, suffering hunger and thirst, the difficulties of the road. Exposed to wind and rain, struggling through winter and summer, they breathe in plagued air and often die with their bodies entangled together. Of the families of my grandfather's generation, not even one out of ten still exists; of my father's generation, only two or three out of ten are still here; in my generation, more than half the families who were here twelve years ago are gone. They have either died out or moved to other places. I am still here because I am a snake-catcher. When those vicious tax-collectors come to our village, they shout and yell from the east to the west, rousting people from north to south. People scream in fear, and even the dogs and hens are disturbed. Every night I get up slowly to check if my snakes are still there in the jar. Only then, relaxing, can I fall back into sleep again. I carefully feed those two snakes and submit them at the required date. After that I calmly enjoy what my field can produce and in this way I'll live till my last tooth falls out. Though twice in a year I run the risk of losing my life, for the rest of the year I have peace and happiness and don't suffer every day like my neighbors. Even if I die right now from catching the snake, I have still survived so many villagers here. Of what can I complain?"

Hearing this, I grew even sadder. Confucius said, "Tyranny is fiercer than a tiger." I used to doubt this saying, but after hearing Jiang's story I've come to believe it. Alas, who knew that the land rent and taxes could be even more poisonous than a snake? That's why I've written this essay; I wait for those whose job is to investigate the people's complaints to get the message.

TRANSLATED BY CHOU PING

## Yuan Zhen (Yüan Chen) (779–831) (poem)

Yuan Zhen, known by the epithet Yuan the Genius, was among the most brilliant poets and statesmen of the Tang dynasty. He was born in Changan to a family descended from the royal house that ruled northern China during the Northern Wei dynasty in the fifth and sixth centuries. A brilliant scholar, he passed the examinations in the category of "clarification of the classics" when he was fourteen, and, when he was twenty-four, he passed the "highly selective" examination, which landed him an appointment in the Imperial library with Bo Juyi, the poet who was to be his lifelong friend. Several years later, he passed the final palace examination, monitored by the emperor, and gained the highest score, resulting in a position close to the emperor. Like his friend Bo, Yuan dreamed of being a reformer, a dream that was to result in a series of banishments. He did, however, help to create a poetic movement, termed "the new music bureau songs" movement, which attempted to recapture the formal freedoms and the simplicity of diction of the *yuefu* form of the Han dynasty and to use poetry for the serious ends of social reform. His tale "The Story of Ying-Ying" is among the best-known love stories in China.

**FURTHER READING:** Ma, Y. W., and Joseph S. M. Lau, eds. *Traditional Chinese Stories,* 1978.

## When Told Bai Juyi Was Demoted and Sent to Jiangzhou

A dying lamp's low flame tosses the shadows.
This evening I was told you were demoted to Jiujiang.
I was so startled I sat up in my final sickbed.
Dark wind is blowing rain into cold windows.

TRANSLATED BY TONY BARNSTONE AND CHOU PING

## ■ Sikong Tu (Ssu-k'ung T'u) (837–908) (poems, literary criticism)

TRANSLATED BY TONY BARNSTONE AND CHOU PING

Tang dynasty poet Sikong Tu's "The Twenty-four Styles of Poetry" was an influential attempt to sketch out and embody the common genres of classical Chinese poetry. Though the poems in this series set out to define basic categories, they are so notoriously obscure (each line having been interpreted in fantastically different ways by later commentators) as to achieve the opposite effect. Yet, as Stephen Owen has noted, Sikong Tu's mode is impressionistic, and though there is often great controversy about the meaning of any particular line, there is "remarkable agreement about the general point being made for each category."[1] Tu, a minor official from Shanxi, was celebrated as a poet and a critic; he was deeply influenced first by the Confucian and later by the Taoist and Buddhist traditions. He starved himself to death in protest when the Tang Dynasty was overthrown.

**FURTHER READING:** Giles, Herbert Allen. *A History of Chinese Literature,* 1967. Owen, Stephen. *Readings in Chinese Literary Thought,* 1992. Yang, Xiangyi, and Gladys Yang. *Poetry and Prose of the Tang and Song,* 1984. Barnstone, Tony, and Chou Ping, eds. and trs. *The Art of Writing: Teachings of the Chinese Masters,* 1996.

---

1. See his discussion in Owen, Stephen. *Readings in Chinese Literary Thought.* Cambridge, MA: Council on East Asian Studies/Harvard University Press, 1992, pp. 299–357.

# *from* **The Twenty-four Styles of Poetry**

## The Implicit Style

Without a single word
the essence is conveyed.
Without speaking of misery
a passionate sadness comes through.

It's true, someone hidden controls the world;                    5
with that being you sink or float.
This style's like straining full-bodied wine
or like a flower near bloom retreating into bud.

It is dust in timeless open space,
is flowing, foaming, sea spume,                                  10
shallow or deep, cohering, dispersing.
One out of a thousand contains all thousand.

## The Carefree and Wild Style

Abide by your nature,
honest and unrestrained.
Whatever you pick up makes you rich
when candor is your friend.

Build your hut below a pine,                                     5
toss off your hat and read a poem.
You know if it's morning or evening
but have no idea what dynasty it is.

Do what fits your whim.
Why bother to achieve?                                           10
If you free your nature
you'll have this style.

## The Lucid and Rare Style

Through bright and slender pines
shivering ripples flow.
Sunlit snow covers the strand.
Across the water, a fishing boat.

A pleasant person, jadelike,                                     5
in clogs, seeks hidden landscapes,
strolling, then pausing,
as the sky's empty blue goes on and on.

This spirit is ancient and rare
but so limpid it can't be held—                                  10
like moonlight at dawn,
a hint of autumn in the air.

## The Flowing Style

It takes in like a water mill
and turns like a pearl marble.
It is beyond words
and these are clumsy metaphors.

Earth spins on a hidden axis
and the universe rolls slowly around its hub.
If you search out the origin
you'll find a corresponding motion.

Climb high into spiritual light.
Then dive deep into dark nothing.
All things for thousands of years
are caught up in the flow.

## ▣ Yu Xuanji (Yü Hsüan-chi) (c. 843–868) (poems)

TRANSLATED BY GEOFFREY WATERS

Yu Xuanji is among the finest women poets of the Tang dynasty. Only fifty of her poems are extant, but these few reveal a passionate persona, mourning absent lovers, letting her feelings out in nature, all in an exquisite and imaginative language scarcely surpassed in her time. She was born in the Tang capital of Changan (modern-day Xian), where she was a sophisticated courtesan, the concubine of a government official who abandoned her after taking her to the South of China. She managed to return to the capital where she lived in extreme poverty, which may have led her at the end of her brief life to become a Daoist nun. She lived a pious life, yet, in her quarters at the Convent of Gathered Blessings, continued to receive her lovers, a double role that may be stranger to Western eyes than it was in her time. When she was twenty-four, she was executed on the charge of murdering her maid in jealousy over one of her callers. It is thought that these charges were trumped up, and the very detail with which the account is given belies its veracity.

**FURTHER READING:** Barnstone, Aliki, and Willis Barnstone, eds. *A Book of Women Poets from Antiquity to Now,* 1980.

## To Tzu-an

Parting, a thousand cups won't wash away the sorrow.
Separation is a hundred knots I can't untie.

After a thaw, orchids bloom, spring returns,
Willows catch on pleasure boats again.

We meet and part, like the clouds, never fixed.                    5
I've learned that love is like the river.

We won't meet again this spring,
But I can't rest yet, winesick in Jade Tower.


## Letting My Feelings Out

Relaxed, nothing to do,
I travel alone in dancing light:

Clouds break, moon on water,
Adrift in a loosed boat.

I hear a lute from Hsiao Liang Temple,                    5
A song from Yü Liang's Tower.

Clumps of bamboo are my companions
And stones my friends.

Swallows and sparrows follow me,
I need no silver nor gold.                    10

I fill the cup with the grcen spring wine;
Under the moon, subtle music.

By the clear pond around my steps
I pull my hairpin out and let the bright stream flow.

In bed reading,                    15
Half-drunk, I get up and comb my hair.


## ■ Li Yu (Li Yü) (936–978) (poems)

Li Yu was the last emperor of the Southern Tang dynasty, whose capital was Nanjing. He is also known as Li Houzhu—*houzhu* means "last ruler." He ascended to the throne in 961 but was destined to rule only fourteen years. In 975, he was taken prisoner when the House of Song conquered his realm. He was carried north to the Song capital, Kaifeng. After years of imprisonment, the Song emperor sent him a glass of poisoned wine on his birthday. He died, forty-one years old. Li Yu seems to have been much better at the business of culture than he was at running his empire. He was a noted painter, musician, and calligrapher, and under his reign the southern Tang became an important cultural center. He is considered the first important innovator in the *ci* (*tz'u* in Wade-Giles transliteration) form of poetry, which was to be the form in which much of the best poetry of the Song dynasty was written. Whereas the form had previously counted as its prime subject matter love of nature and romantic love, in Li Yu's hands, the form was expanded to include meditations upon great philosophical themes—the impermanence of life and the vanity of human wishes. He also made the form startlingly personal. His best poems mourn the death of his first wife in 964 and bitterly lament his imprisonment.

**FURTHER READING:** Liu, Yih-ling, and Shahid Suhrawardy. *Poems of Lee Hou-chu,* 1948.

## To the Tune of "A Bushel of Pearls"

Morning makeup is almost done—
a few more light touches on the lips.
Revealing the tip of a lilac tongue,
she sings transparently clear,
her mouth just parting, like a cherry.

Charming how her wide silk sleeve turns crimson wet
after sweeping across sweet wine in a deep goblet.
She is fragile, seductive, lying aslant an embroidered bed—
after chewing on her red hair-string,
with a laugh she spits it on her man.

TRANSLATED BY TONY BARNSTONE AND CHOU PING

## To the Tune of "Lost Battle"

My family's kingdom lasted forty years—
three thousand *li* of mountains and rivers.
In phoenix pavilions and dragon towers built up to heaven,
among jade trees and branches like spring mist and vines,
how could I know anything about wars?

But since being captured and enslaved,
my waist has shriveled,
my hair turned gray.
I was most lost the day we parted at the Temple of Ancestors:
the imperial orchestra was playing farewell songs
while I stood in tears facing my palace girls.

TRANSLATED BY TONY BARNSTONE AND CHOU PING

## To the Tune of "Beauty Yu"

Will spring blooms and autumn moon never end?
These memories are too much.
Last night east wind pierced my narrow tower again,
and I saw lost kingdoms in the clean bright moon.

The carved railings and jade steps must still be there,                    5
though lovely faces must have aged.
How much sorrow do I feel?
Like riverwater in spring it flows to the east.

TRANSLATED BY TONY BARNSTONE AND CHOU PING

## To the Tune of "Crows Cawing at Night"

Alone I ascended West Tower in silence
while the moon appeared like a hook.
Cool fall was locked in the maple garden, calm and quiet.

This thing can't be cut,
it gets more messy trying to straighten it out.                    5
A melancholy departure,
there's a raw feeling in my heart.

TRANSLATED BY BRENDAN CONNELL AND MARTY JIANG

## To the Tune of "Encountering Joy"

Charming blossoms in the grove say goodbye to crimsoning spring.
They are gone too soon.
It can't be helped, since cold rain comes in the morning and wind at
    night.

She's crying; rouge melts with tears.
I'm drunk with her asking me to stay,                    5
"When will you be back?"
It's natural that the river keeps flowing east,
and men always feel regret.

TRANSLATED BY BRENDAN CONNELL AND MARTY JIANG

# Song Dynasty

## (960–1279)

### ▪ Mei Yaochen (Mei Yao-ch'en) (1002–1060) (poem)

TRANSLATED BY KENNETH ROXROTH

Mei Yaochen was an official-scholar of the early Song dynasty whose poems helped initiate a new realism in the poetry of his age. He was a life-long friend of the poet Ouyang Xiu, but he never attained the career success of his famous companion. He did not pass the Imperial Examinations until he was forty-nine, and his career was marked by assignments in the provinces, alternating with periods in the capital. Twenty-eight hundred of his poems survive in an edition edited by Ouyang Xiu. His early poems often are marked by social criticism based on a Neo-Confucianism that sought to reform the military and civil services; these poems tended to be written in "old style" verse (*gu shi*). He was also a distinctly personal poet, who wrote about the loss of his first wife and baby son in 1044 and about the death of a baby daughter a few years later. His poems are colloquial and confessional and strive for a simplicity of speech that suggests meanings beyond the words themselves.

**FURTHER READING:** Chaves, Jonathan. *Mei Yao-ch'en and the Development of Early Sung Poetry*, 1976.

## Sorrow[1]

Heaven took my wife. Now it
Has also taken my son.
My eyes are not allowed a
Dry season. It is too much
For my heart. I long for death.
When the rain falls and enters
The earth, when a pearl drops into
The depth of the sea, you can
Dive in the sea and find the
Pearl, you can dig in the earth
And find the water. But no one

---

1. He seems to have lost all his family. Here begin several poems of loss. Although they echo the Emperor Wu of Han and many others they are none the less poignant and remind me of the later sepulchral epigrams of the Greek Anthology.

Has ever come back from the
Underground Springs. Once gone, life
Is over for good. My chest
Tightens against me. I have                                        15
No one to turn to. Nothing,
Not even a shadow in a mirror.

## ▪ Ouyang Xiu (Ou-yang Hsiu) (1007–1072) (poems, rhyme-prose)

Ouyang Xiu is considered to be a prime example of the Chinese ideal of the multifaceted scholar-official, equivalent to the Western ideal of the Renaissance man. He was raised by his widowed mother in great poverty in an isolated region of what is today Hubei. He studied on his own and with the help of his mother for the Imperial Examination, which was so important a credential for government service, a road that was opened to him by the rise of printing early in the Song dynasty. While studying, he was strongly influenced by the works of Han Yu, whose works had been largely forgotten by this time. He passed the Imperial Examination in 1030 and embarked on a lifelong and quite successful career as an official in Luoyang, though he found himself twice exiled during his career.

He is the author of a famous history, *The New History of the Tang*, and the compiler of *The New History of the Five Dynasties*, and he wrote an influential set of commentaries on historical inscriptions titled *Postscripts to Collected Ancient Inscriptions*. He is also the author of a set of commentaries on poetics titled *Mr. One-six's Talks on Poetics* (Mr. One-six was a pen name referring to his desire to be always in the presence of his wine, chess set, library, zither, and archaeological collection). This compilation was the first treatise in the aphoristic *shi-hua* form (see *Poets' Jade Dust* later in this section for examples of the form). Ouyang Xiu is esteemed as a prose master whose essays have clean and simple language and fluid argumentation; he helped lead a movement away from ornamental prose styles to a simpler style of "ancient prose," a traditionalist movement that had as its aim a Confucian moral regeneration. His melancholy essay "The Autumn Sound" is among his most famous; compare it with Meng Jiao's series of sad "Autumn Meditations," which also meditate on Autumn sorrow.

His poetry is also marvelous, and he was instrumental in raising the *ci* form of poetry (poems written to fit popular songs) into a widespread and important Song poetic style. His plain style and use of colloquial expressions made his poetry accessible to larger audiences and helped preserve its freshness for audiences today. Like Andrew Marvell, he was a sensualist who is known for his *carpe diem* poems: "You cannot hold it . . . / Pretty girls grow old . . . / No flowers to be plucked / from empty bough." Late in life he gave himself the title "The Old Drunkard." He was also an individualist, both in his approach to writing and in his interpretations of the classics; translator J. P. Seaton sees this individualism as an outgrowth of his self-education. As a politician, he was known for his Confucian ethics. A man with many talents, he is not easily summed up in a brief headnote.

**FURTHER READING:** Egan, Richard C. *The Literary Works of Ou-yang Hsiu,* 1984. Liu, James T. C. *Ou-yang Hsiu, An Eleventh Century Neo-Confucianist,* 1967. Seaton, J. P. *Love and Time: The Poems of Ou-yang Hsiu,* 1989.

## You Cannot Hold It

You cannot hold it . . .
Pretty girls grow old
and indolent; there is an end to spring.
When breeze is warm and moon so fine,
if you can manage yellow gold, buy smiles.
Nurture the tender blossoms there, don't wait.
No flowers to be plucked
from empty bough.

TRANSLATED BY J. P. SEATON

## The Autumn Sound[1]

One night as I, Ou-yang Tzu, was reading I suddenly heard a sound far away towards the southwest. I listened with apprehension and said, "It is strange!" At first it sounded like the murmuring of the rain or the rustling of the wind; suddenly it burst into the galloping of horses and the splashing of waves, as though a mountain torrent were roaring in the startled night and a thunderstorm were howling in the air. What it struck tinkled and chinked like the breaking of metals and stones. It also seemed like a muffled march of soldiers, each with a bit in his mouth [to keep the soldiers in silence], hurriedly advancing to the attack; no bugles were heard, only the tramp of men and horses.

"What noise is that?" I said to my boy servant. "Go out and see."

"The moon and stars are brightly shining," the boy replied. "The Celestial River is up in the sky. Nowhere is there any noise of men; the noise comes from the trees."

---

1. This is a *fu,* a piece of descriptive poetic prose interspersed with verse. The lines are all irregular as in prose, but are punctuated with rhymes to enhance the beauty of recital. Both the artificiality of the Han *fu* and the frivolity of later lyrical *fu* are avoided in this beautiful piece.

"Alas, what a pity!" said I. "This is the autumn sound. How is it that autumn comes?

"The autumn phenomena are thus: Its color is gray and dull, as the sky is blue and the sun is brilliant; its air is chilly and shivering, as the blasts pierce our body; its meaning is desolate and solitary, as the hills are abandoned and the streams sink low. Therefore its sound is sad and mournful, and yet it shouts with forces. All the rich luxuriance of the green prospers, and all the fine foliage of the trees presents a beautiful scene. However, as the autumn approaches, the green turns pale and trees decay. This is the destroying force of the autumn that sweeps away all the foliage and luxuriance.

"For autumn is the season for criminal execution, and so its time is darkness as a symbol of destruction; its appropriate element is 'metal,'[2]—this is what is called the essential principle of the universe. It always makes death its chief purpose. This is how Nature governs all: as spring is the epoch of growth, so autumn is the epoch of maturity. Therefore in music, its sound is *shang*,[3] a sad sound, and its note is *yi*,[4] a dying note. Shang is sorrow: that which is old must be sad. Yi is death: that which passes maturity must die.

"Ah! Plants and trees fade away in their due season, even though they have no feelings. But man is an animal and is the divinest of all things. Hundreds of cares wreck his heart, and thousands of tasks wear out his body. What affects his mind will shake his vitality. How much greater is the strain when a man strives to attain what is beyond his ability and worries himself to achieve what is beyond his intelligence. It is no wonder that his rosy cheeks turn pale and that his black hair turns white. How can a man whose frame is not made of metal and stone outlast the plants and trees? Just think a while: who steals away his strength? Why should man accuse the autumn sound?"

The boy made no answer. He was fast asleep. No soul could be heard but that of the cricket chirping its response to my mournful sigh!

TRANSLATED BY CH'U CHAI AND WINBERG CHAI

## ■ Su Dongpo (Su Tung-p'o) (1036–1101) (poems, rhyme-prose)

Su Dongpo (also known as Su Shi) was born in Sichuan province in Meishan to an illustrious family of officials and distinguished scholars. He,

---

2. The five elements—water, fire, wood, metal, and earth—are the active agents that produce and overcome each other in an endless cycle, upon which the whole scheme of the mystic school of Chinese philosophy is based.

3. The ancient Chinese scale of notation consists of five sounds, known as *kung, shang, chiap, chi,* and *yü.*

4. The Chinese scale originally consisted of nine notes. A twelve-note scale was later developed, and flats or sharps were used as needed.

his brother, and his father were considered to be among the finest prose masters of both the Tang and Song dynasties and were known as the Three Sus. He took the Imperial Examination in 1057 and was noticed by the powerful tastemaker, politician, poet, and chief examiner Ouyang Xiu, who became his patron. Like Ouyang, Su Dongpo was a Renaissance man, who in addition to having a political career was an innovator in and master of poetry, prose, calligraphy, and painting. He was among the founders of the important Southern Song style of painting. He believed that poems and paintings should be as spontaneous as running water, yet rooted in an objective rendering of emotions in the world. Around twenty-four hundred of his poems in the *shi* form survive, along with three hundred fifty *ci* form poems. These latter are poems derived from song forms, and like Ouyang, Su was important in expanding this genre's use and possibilities. His political career, like that of his patron, was vicissitudinous, involving demotions, twelve periods of exile, and even three months in prison primarily because of his opposition to the powerful reformer Wang Anshi. During an exile in Huangzhou, Su Shi began calling himself Su Dongpo (Eastern Slope), which was the name of his farm. His poems are informed by a knowledge of Daoism and Chan (Zen) Buddhism, and like that earlier mystical farmer-poet Tao Qian, contented on his farm, he retired from the political world. His personality shines clearly through his poems; he was a personal poet who recorded the pain of his separations in exile and of his baby son's death, his joy in a simple walk in the countryside, and the pleasures of a good cup of wine. He is known for the exuberance he brings to writing and is even credited with being the founder of a school of heroic abandonment in writing. The poem "Inscription for Gold Mountain Temple," included here, belongs to a tradition of Chinese concrete poetry (word games and shaped poems), which is virtually unknown in the West. In Chinese this beautiful poem can be read forwards and backwards, producing two descriptions of the temple: from night to day and from day to night. In the interest of giving a readable version, we have done two English translations: from beginning to end and from end to beginning, changing prepositions, articles, and verb forms to make each poem natural, yet retaining the order of the basic elements.

**FURTHER READING:** Le Gros Clark, C. D. *The Prose Poetry of Su Tung P'o*, 1935. Lin, Yutang. *The Gay Genius: The Life and Times of Su Tungpo*, 1947. Watson, Burton. *Su Tung-p'o: Selections from a Sung Dynasty Poet*, 1965.

## Inscription for Gold Mountain Temple (I)[1]

Tides follow hidden waves. The snow mountain tilts.
Distant fishing boats are hooking the moonlight.

---

1. Some scholars question the attribution of this poem to Su Dongpo.

A bridge faces the temple gate. The pine path is narrow.
By the doorsill is the fountain's eye where stone ripples transparently.

Far, far green trees—the river sky is dawning.                               5
Cloudy, cloudy scarlet afterglow. The sea is sun bright.
View of the distance: four horizons of clouds join the water.
Blue peaks are a thousand dots. A few weightless gulls.

TRANSLATED BY TONY BARNSTONE AND CHOU PING


## Inscription for Gold Mountain Temple (II)

Gulls are weightless, a few dots. A thousand peaks are blue.
Water joins the clouds' edges in four distant views.
Bright day. Sea glows with scarlet clouds on clouds.
Dawning sky and river trees are green, and far, far.

Transparent ripples from the stone eye: fountain by the doorsill.          5
A narrow path and pine gate where the temple faces the bridge.
A bright moon hooks boats. Fishing waters are distant.
A tilted mountain is a snow wave, secretly following tides.

TRANSLATED BY TONY BARNSTONE AND CHOU PING


## Written on the North Tower Wall after Snow

In yellow dusk the slender rain still falls,
but the calm night comes windless and harsh.

My bedclothes feel like splashed water.
I don't know the courtyard is buried in salt.

Light dampens the study curtains before dawn.                               5
With cold sound, half a moon falls from the painted eaves.

As I sweep the north tower I see Horse Ear Peak
buried except for two tips.

TRANSLATED BY TONY BARNSTONE AND CHOU PING

## Written in Response to Ziyou's Poem about Days in Mianchi[2]

A life touches on places
like a swan alighting on muddy snow—
accidental claw tracks left in the slush
before it soars east or west into the random air.

The old monk is dead, interred beneath the new pagoda,
and on ruined walls the poems we brushed are illegible.
Do you still remember the rugged path,
the endless road, our tired bodies, how our lame donkey brayed?

TRANSLATED BY TONY BARNSTONE AND CHOU PING

## Boating at Night on West Lake

Wild rice stems endless on the vast lake.
Night-blooming lotus perfumes the wind and dew.
Gradually the light of a far temple appears.
When the moon goes black, I watch the lake gleam.

TRANSLATED BY TONY BARNSTONE AND CHOU PING

## Brushed on the Wall of Xilin Temple

From the side it is a range; straight on, a peak.
Far, near, high, low, it never looks the same.
I can't see Mount Lu's true face
because I'm on the mountain.

TRANSLATED BY TONY BARNSTONE AND CHOU PING

## Because of a Typhoon I Stayed at Gold Mountain for Two Days

Up in the tower a bell is talking to itself.
The typhoon will wash out the ferry by tomorrow.

---

2. In earlier years, Su Shi and his brother had traveled together through this region. Their horses had died, and so they were riding on donkeys. They stayed at the temple in Mianchi and wrote poems on the wall.

Dawn comes with white waves dashing dark rocks
and shooting through my window like deflected arrows.
A dragon boat of a hundred tons couldn't cross this river    *5*
but a fishing boat dances there like a tossed leaf.
It makes me think, why rush to the city?
I'll laugh at such fury of snakes and dragons,
stay aimlessly till the servants start to wonder
—with this kind of storm, my family won't mind.    *10*
I look for my friend, monk Qianshan. He's alone,
meditating past midnight and listening for the breakfast drum.[3]

### TRANSLATED BY TONY BARNSTONE AND CHOU PING

## The Red Cliff

On the day of full moon in the seventh month in autumn, 1082, I sailed
with some friends to Red Cliff in a boat. A cool, laconic wind blew in but
didn't bother to stir up any waves. While raising a winecup to toast, I recited a poem about the brilliant moon and sang out a stanza from the
*Book of Songs* about a beauty.

Before long, the moon rose over the east mountain, lingering between the Big Dipper and the Cowherd. Dewy mist was floating across the
river, and the glittering water seemed to blend into the sky. Giving free
rein to the small, reed-like boat, we drifted among vast fields of water, as if
gliding on air, not knowing where we would stop, and it seemed we would
fly right out of this world and stand in space, like winged immortals.

So we went on drinking and having a good time, singing songs while
beating time on the boat's sides. The song went like this:

Our cassia oars
and magnolia paddles
cut into the moon
and slice its flowing light.
My heart is like this great expanse,
longing for my lover
in another corner of the sky.

One of the guests, who was good at playing the vertical bamboo flute,
spontaneously accompanied the song with his instrument. The sound was
low and melancholy as if someone tortured by love was murmuring out secret affection, punctuated by sobs and complaints. Like a whiff of ever-last-

---

3. Literally, the "porridge drum," the wooden board that when beaten announces that the porridge breakfast is served.

ing smoke the melody lingered on. The music was so touching that it could make a dragon dance at the bottom of an abyss, or make a widow weep in a drifting boat.

I was saddened by the music, and after straightening up my gown and sitting upright, I asked my friend, "Why did you make it so sad?"

He replied, "'Under a bright moon and sparse stars, ravens and magpies fly east.' Aren't those lines by Cao Cao? Xiakou is to the west, and Wuchang is over there to the east. See the mountains and the river winding around each other, and the trees so dark green? Isn't this the place where Cao was trapped by General Zhou? Cao had just taken the city of Jinzhou, and set out down the river east to Jiangling. The boats jostled for hundreds of miles, and his banners and flags blocked out the sky. Pouring a libation into the river, Cao Mengde improvised those lines with a long spear in his hands. He was without doubt the greatest hero of his time. But where is he now?

"As for you and me, we simply fish in the river or chop firewood by the river banks. We find company in fish and shrimp, and make friends with elk and deer. We sail in a leaf-like boat and we pour wine from a gourd to toast each other. But our lives are as brief as those of insects, and we are small and insignificant as a grain of sand in the ocean! So we are sad—we are sad because our lives are so short while the Yangtze River runs on forever. We dream about flying in the sky with immortals and embracing the moon's longevity. But I know this is not easily attained, and thus sadness flew out of my bamboo flute."

I asked, "Do you really know the river and the moon? The water flows away, like this, and yet it never actually leaves; the moon up there waxes and wanes, and yet it remains the same. If you watch them from the perspective of change, the sky and the earth seem to wheel through change endlessly; but if you observe from the perspective of changelessness, both we and the world are inexhaustible. So what is there to be envied?

"Everything in the sky and the earth has its proper owner, and I won't take a single hair of anything that does not belong to me. Still, the clear wind along the river, which becomes music in our ears, or the moon in the mountains, which fills our eyes with beautiful colors, are free for the taking, and they are inexhaustible. This is the creator's everlasting treasure, placed here for us to enjoy."

Now my friend seemed happy. He smiled, and we washed our wine cups to toast again. When at last all the dishes and fruits were finished, the cups and plates piled up in disorder, we lay down to sleep in the boat, unaware that dawn was starting to brighten the east.

TRANSLATED BY TONY BARNSTONE AND CHOU PING

# Li Qingzhao (Li Ch'ing-chao) (1084–c. 1151) (poems)

### TRANSLATED BY TONY BARNSTONE AND CHOU PING

Li Qingzhao is China's finest woman poet. She was born in what is today Qinan, Shandung Province, to a gifted literary family, and her own talent was recognized in her teens. In 1101, she married happily to Zhao Mingzheng, the son of a powerful politician who shared her tastes for literature, painting, and calligraphy, and who soon embarked on a career as an official himself. When China went through the tumultuous transition from the Northern to the Southern Song Dynasties, Li Qingzhao's husband's career was cut short, and they devoted themselves to art collecting and cataloging. An invasion of the Qin Tatars in 1127 sent Li Qingzhao fleeing from the capital with just a few belongings at a time when her husband had left for Nanking to attend his mother's funeral. She traveled across China for months, finally joining her husband in Nanking, where he was now mayor. Just two years later, her husband died en route to a new posting, and Li Qingzhao drifted across China, settling at last in Linan (modern Hangzhou), where she was briefly married to a minor military official. Her poems are the best evidence of her life, showing the sorrow she went through over separations from her husband and over his death and sketching her life as a society woman. Only about fifty poems have survived from her six volumes of verse.

**FURTHER READING:** Rexroth, Kenneth, and Ling Chung, trs. *Li Ch'ing-Chao: Complete Poems*, 1979.

## To the Tune of "Intoxicated in the Shade of Flowers"

Slight mist, the clouds are fat. This endless day is torture.
Lucky Dragon incense dissolves in the gold animal.
It's Autumn Festival, a good season,
but by midnight the chill will pierce
my jade pillow and thin silk curtains.                                    5

I drink wine by the east fence in yellow dusk
and a secret fragrance fills my sleeves.
Do not say my spirit isn't frayed.
The west wind tangles in the curtains.
I am thinner than a yellow flower.                                        10

## To the Tune of "One Blossoming Sprig of Plum"

The scent of red lotus fades and my jade mat is cold as autumn.
Gently I loosen my silk robe
and enter the magnolia boat alone.
Who has sent an embroidered letter via clouds?
Wild geese form a character in the sky: *return.*
The west tower fills with moon.

Blossoms drift and water flows where it will,
but my heart is still sick,
split between this place and where you are.
I can't kill this desire.
Even when my eyebrows relax,
my heart flares up again.

## To the Tune of "Spring at Wu Ling"[1]

The wind fades. Dropped blossoms perfume the earth.
At the end of the day, I'm too lazy to comb my hair.
His things remain, but he is gone, and the world is dead.
I try to speak but choke in tears.

I hear that spring is lovely at Twin Brook.
I'd row there in a light craft
but fear my grasshopper boat
is too small to carry this grief.

## To the Tune of "Silk Washing Brook"

I don't need deep cups of thick amber wine.
My feelings will warm before I drown in drink.
Already sparse bells are answering the night wind.

Lucky Dragon incense fades as my soul-dream breaks.
From my loose hair drops a soft gold hairpin;
I wake alone and watch the red candle die.

---

1. Written after her husband's death.

## To the Tune of "Dream Song"

I'll never forget sunset at Brook Pavilion—
drunk with beauty, we lost our way.
When the ecstasy faded, we turned our boat home,
but it was late and we strayed into a place deep
    with lotus flowers                          5
and rowed hard, so hard
the whole shore erupted with herons and gulls.

## To the Tune of "Dream Song"

Sharp wind last night, and sparse raindrops.
Thick sleep hasn't eased this hangover.
I want to ask the servant rolling up the blinds
has the flowering begonia blossomed?
Do you know?                                          5
Do you know?
Are the green leaves fat? The thin flowers red?

■ **Poets' Jade Dust (compiled before 1244)**
**(aphorisms/literary criticism)**

TRANSLATED BY TONY BARNSTONE AND CHOU PING

*Poets' Jade Dust* is an extraordinary Song dynasty collection of aphoristic prescriptions for writers, humorous anecdotes about poetry and poets, epigrammatic commentaries, and rules for composing literature. Its form is called *shi hua* (meaning "poetry-speech"), and it was defined and popularized in the Song dynasty. *Poets' Jade Dust* is considered to be among the finest of such collections (some critics call it the best). It was compiled by Wei Qingzhi, a native of Fuzhou City, Fujian Province. His dates are unknown and very little is known of his life. He was said to be very talented, but apparently he was not interested in the path of the scholar-official. We also know that he was a great lover of chrysanthemum bushes—so great that he planted a thousand of them! The book consists of twenty volumes, and since the preface by Huang Sheng is dated 1244, it must have been compiled before then.

*Shi hua* is a form of literary jottings that had predecessors in the Tang dynasty and earlier but was not an identifiable genre until the great Song dynasty statesman, historian, antiquarian, and poet Ouyang Xiu (1007–1072) published twenty-eight literary notes in a collection later called *Liuyi Shi Hua (Mr. Six-one's Shi Hua)*, though its original title was probably simply *Shi Hua*. At its best, the genre combines biting, incisive comments about poetic craft with a casual tone, a wry wit, and interesting anecdotes. From the time of the Southern Song onward, however, *shi hua* became more and more systematic, and the randomness of the collections gave way to increasingly ordered compilations. Noted sinologist Stephen Owen notes that this led to a loss of the "original color" and charm of the form, and he comments:

> The trend toward systematization in some Southern Sung *shih-hua* should be understood in the context of the popularization of literary studies in the later Southern Sung and early Yüan. The Northern Sung intellectuals cultivated an appearance of ease; sophisticated discussion of poetry was supposed to be a pastime. In the Southern Sung, we find the beginnings of a mass audience, seeking advice on composition from the masters and guidance in judgment. The printing industry of Hang-chou fed the desires of the urban bourgeoisie to participate in elite culture by the transformation of *shih-hua* into poetic education.[1]

*Poets' Jade Dust* is a systematic anthology of *shi hua* that fit into this popularization of the genre.

**FURTHER READING:** Barnstone, Tony, and Chou Ping, eds. and trs. *The Art of Writing: Teachings of the Chinese Masters*, 1996. Owen, Stephen. *Readings in Chinese Literary Thought*, 1992.

## from *The Preface by Huang Sheng*

Comments on poetry are like doctors' prescriptions: if they are not accurate they are useless, as a bad prescription has no medical value. So, only a good doctor can judge if the prescription is effective or not and only a good poet can know if the comments are right or not. This compilation is no easy job.

## Burning Poetry

## from Notes by Song Zijing

Whenever I see my old work I want to burn the poems I hate. Mei Yaochen congratulates me: "You have made progress."

---

1. Stephen Owen, *Readings in Chinese Literary Thought* (Cambridge, MA: Council on East Asian Studies/Harvard University Press, 1992), 360–361. (Owen is using the Wade-Giles system of transliteration, in which *shi hua* is rendered *shih-hua*.)

## *Don't Walk Behind Others*

## *from* Notes by Song Zijing

For your work to pass through the generations you must have your own distinctive style. If you always use a compass to draw a circle and a ruler to draw a square you will always remain a slave. As the ancients say: you can't build a house inside a house. Lu Ji says: avoid the morning flower in full blossom and gather instead evening buds which are not yet open. Han Yu says: all cliches must go; this is the essence of prose. *The Book of the Hermit Fisherman of Zhao River* comments that this is also true of poetry. If you just repeat cliches and imitate old works without any change or original ideas, how can you become a famous poet? Huang Luzhi writes that if you follow someone you will always be behind. The first taboo in writing is to walk behind others.

## *Don't Beat the Ducks*

## *from* The Hermit's Comments on Poetry

Lu Shilong, the governor of Xuan State, used to enjoy caning the women registered as courtesans, the "Government Prostitutes" who served the officials. These singing girls all tried to escape, but they couldn't get away from him. Then, a Hangzhou courtesan arrived in Xuan State. Because of her beauty and talent Shilong grew very fond of her, and wouldn't allow her to depart. One day a local courtesan committed a minor offence, and when Shilong was about to cane her again, she pleaded in tears, "I don't want to deny my guilt. I'm just afraid that this beating will make the lady from Hangzhou scared." So Shilong pardoned her and let her depart. Because of this incident, Mei Yaochen wrote the following poem:

> Don't beat the ducks!
> You will scare the swan.
> The swan that lands on the pond's north shore
> is not an old bald bird on a lonely islet.
> Even the bald bird wants to fly off
> so wouldn't a swan with her long wings?

## *Enlightenment*

## *from* Lui's Rules for Schoolchildren

If you write with enlightenment your work will naturally be better than your contemporaries.' Inspiration enters at the border between hard work and laziness. In this way Zhang Changshi, watching Madame Gong Sun doing a sword dance was suddenly enlightened about the art of calligraphy. Zhang's heart had been so focused on his calligraphy that when he saw this dance he gained insight into the heights of his own art. Someone else watching the sword dance would consider it irrelevant. This is true for both calligraphy and for writing.

## Ways to Kill a Landscape

### from Xiqing Comments on Poetry

Yi Shan [another name for the Tang poet Li Shangyin] wrote many miscellaneous pieces, then divided them into more than ten different categories. One humorous category was called "Ways to Kill a Landscape." Here are some examples: 1. Wash your feet in a clear spring. 2. Dry your loincloth upon the flowers. 3. Build your house against a mountain. 4. Burn your zither to cook a crane. 5. Drink tea in front of the flowers. 6. Scream underneath a pine tree. When An Yuanxian, the Prime Minister, was dismissed from office, he spent his time enjoying mountain spring water and wine, and wrote the following poem, thinking of this category:

> The new tea leaves on Qi Mountain are green like mist
> and I boil mountain spring water in porcelain pots.
> I don't go to the human world to kill the landscape,
> I only have my wine and get drunk in front of flowers.

## Be Specific

### from The Eye of Poetry

Good poetry stands out from other poems. If poets write on the same subject this becomes clear when you compare their work. When I traveled along the road to Sichuan and stopped at Zhoubi Station I recalled two famous lines by Shi Manqing:

> In my mind water flows into the distance.
> Outside my sorrow the old mountains are still green.

Although people like these two lines, to me it seems they could describe almost any place, even though they were written about this station.

## Convey the Idea, Not the Name

### from Forbidden Meat

Su Dongpo says: Good painters paint the spirit, not the form. Good poets convey the idea, not the name. Here is a poem by him:

> Comparing a painting to the object
> is how a child judges paintings.
> If you think your poem is the last word on a subject
> it shows you're not a poet.

## Simple and Wonderful

### from Quotations by Tang Zixi

A Tang poet writes:

> A mountain monk doesn't know how to count the years.
> When one leaf falls he knows it's autumn.

Compare these lines with Tao Yuanming's lines:

> Even without a calendar
> the four seasons make a year.

We feel the Tang poet's lines try too hard. In the Preface to "Peach Blossom Spring" Tao says "They don't know the Han Dynasty, let alone Wei and Jin."[1] We can see how simple and wonderful his lines are.

## Lines Should Not Be Redundant (1)

### from Comments on Poetry by Coi Kuanfu

Poets between the Jin Dynasty and the Song Dynasty wrote many good lines, but they often used two lines to say the same thing. Here are two examples:

> The new lotus trembles as fish play.
> Petals fall when birds scatter.

---

1. "Peach Blossom Spring" is a tale about a fisherman who lost his way and sailed into a peach grove where he lost all sense of time and found a lost land where people had been cut off from the outside since the Qin Dynasty (221–207 B.C.). Once he left to go back home again he could never find his way back to this idyllic place. This is the quintessential Chinese tale of a lost utopia.

> Cicada cries quiet the forest.
> Bird calls darken the mountains.

Lines like this are not bad; the problem is redundancy.

## Lines Should Not Be Redundant (2)

### from Notes by Sheng Kuo

Looking at the examples given above, Wang Anshi suggested to replace the line "Bird calls darken the mountains" with "The wind stops but petals still drop"; in this way the first line suggests motion within stillness and the next line creates stillness within motion.

## The Elliptical Method

### from The Cold Study

When Zheng Gu writes a poem about falling leaves he doesn't mention them directly, yet people can infer the subject matter from his poem:

> It's hard for returning ants to find their holes,
> easy for birds to see their nests.
> The monk is never sick of them covering the porch
> but a layman will find one of them too much.

## The Disease of Unintentional Similarity

### from East Window Notes

When Cheng Shimeng was the governor of Hongzhou he built a meditation room at his residence. He loved this room so much that he went there every day, and he inscribed these two lines on a stone:

> No matter how busy, I come here once a day.
> I often come at midnight carrying a lantern.

Li Yuangui saw this inscription and laughed, saying, "This is a poem about going to the toilet!"

## *Three Ways to Steal*

### *from* Varieties in a Poetic Garden

There are three kinds of plagiarism in poetry writing. The clumsiest thief steals the words. Cheng Ju's line "The light of sun and moon is heavenly virtue" is from Fu Changyu's line "The light of sun and moon is transparent." The second kind of plagiarist steals the idea. Consider Shen Chenqi's lines:

> The remains of summer flee from a small pond.
> Coolness returns to the tips of tall trees first.

Now consider the original lines by Liu Hun:

> Ripples arise in the pool.
> Autumn comes to tall poplar trees.

The third type of theft doesn't leave much trace. Wang Changlin's lines go:

> With two carp in my hand
> I watch wild geese fall into distance.

The original lines by Qi Kang are:

> My eyes see off migrating cranes.
> Holding up my zither, I wave.

## *Clichés Must Go*

### *from* The Eye of Poetry

A friend came to me with a poem that began "Coldness in November . . . ," so I asked him, "Have you noticed how Du Fu uses the names of the months in his poems? For example, 'The waves swell in March.' Here March is used because it is early for large waves to be seen. Another example is 'June comes with cold wind and cold sun.' June is used because such late coldness is unusual. But many of us write lines like 'Coldness in November . . .' when we should avoid such obvious expressions."

## *Dexterity in a Single Word*

# *from* The Book of the Hermit Fisherman of Zhao River

In each line there should be a key word that will act like a magic pill or a Midas touch to make the line work. For example Meng Haoran writes:

> Thin clouds dilute the sky's silver river.[2]
> Scattered raindrops tap on leaves of the parasol tree.

The key words in these two lines are "dilute" and "tap"; without them these lines wouldn't be good. Mr. Chen once purchased a collection of Du Fu's poetry in which many characters were missing.[3] For example here is a line in which the last character was absent:

> The weightless body of a bird

Mr. Chen asked his guests to complete the line. People suggested "shoots by" or "lands" or "soars" or "descends" but no one could agree on the best word. Later, Mr. Chen got a better version of Du Fu's poems and found the line actually reads "The weightless body of a bird flickers by." Mr. Chen sighed and admitted that Du Fu's original word was much better.

## *Plain and Natural*

# *from* Sunny Autumn Rhymed Language

First master elegance, and then strive for the plain style. Nowadays many people write clumsy, facile poems and flatter themselves that they've mastered the plain style. I can't help laughing at this. Poets know that simplicity is difficult. There are poems that illustrate the rigor the plain style demands:

> Today as in ancient times
> it's hard to write a simple poem.
> —Mei Yaochen[4]

---

2. The Milky Way.

3. The second part of this commentary also appears in Ouyang Xiu's *Mr. Six-one's Comments on Poetry*.

4. Mei Yaochen, like Tao Yuanming, is considered an exemplary plain-style poet; but his work, unlike that of Tao Yuanming, comes in for some criticism. Mei An, for example, writes, "Mei Yaochen's poetry is not plain, it's dry."

> The lotus flower rises from clear water,
> naturally without ornament.
> —Li Bai

Plain and natural lines are best.

## Some Lines by Tao Yuanming

### from Notes from Fu's Study

> Gathering chrysanthemum by the east fence
> my lazy eyes meet South Mountain.

Su Dongpo says that those who don't comprehend poetry want to change these lines by Tao Yuanming, turning the word "meet" into "watch." This is trading jade for garbage. Bo Juyi tried to emulate Tao's lines like so:

> Occasionally I pour a cup of wine,
> sitting and watching Southeast Mountain.

I think this is a very poor imitation.[5]

## Read More and Write More

### Su Dongpo

The secret of writing lies in reading more and writing more. Many writers worry about writing too little, yet they are too lazy to read. Whenever they write a poem they want it to be the best one around, but it's almost impossible for such writers to achieve this. By constantly writing you will learn to diagnose faults and diseases in what you write, and you won't have to wait for others to point them out.

## Epigrammatically Succinct Lines

### from Wang Zhifang's Comments on Poetry

There was a poet named Guo Xiangzhen who became famous because of a line written by Mei Yaochen about him: "At the quarry in the moonlight

---

5. These famous lines by Tao Yuanming are cherished for the way they suggest the joining of the poet with nature through the lack of active looking; the poet encounters the mountain naturally as he looks up as if running into a friend. Bo Juyi, on the other hand, is actively watching his mountain; this suggests a distance from nature.

I heard the banished immortal again." These lines suggest that Guo is Li Bai's reincarnation [since "Banished Immortal" was Li's nickname]. The best known lines by Guo Xiangzhen are these:

> Endless flight of birds across the blue evening sky.
> Wind in the reeds when the fisherman stops singing.

When Su Dongpo was Prefect of Qiantang, Guo Xiangzhen visited him and showed him a scroll of his poems. Then he gave a reading in which his voice was so loud it shook up his audience. Afterward he asked Su Dongpo, "What do you think of my poems?" Su Dongpo replied, "One hundred percent good." Flattered and surprised Guo asked, "Really? In what way?" Su answered, "Seventy percent oration and thirty percent poetry!"

## Push or Knock

### from Notes of Xiang Su

When the monk Jia Dao came to Luoyang, monks were forbidden to leave the monastery after noon. Jia Dao wrote a sad poem about this and Han Yu liked the poem so much he helped him get permission to become a layman. The story of their famous meeting follows.

When Jia Dao was concentrating on his poems he would often run into important people without being aware of it. One day, riding his donkey, he was thinking about these lines:

> Birds return to their nests in trees by the pond.
> A monk is knocking at a door by moonlight.

He couldn't decide whether to replace the word "knocking" with "pushing," so he was making wild gestures on his donkey, acting out first a knock and then a push. While doing this he encountered the procession of the Mayor, Han Yu, and neglected to give way. Arrested by the bodyguards, and brought before Han Yu, he was asked to explain his actions. He explained how he was trying to decide between these two words. Han Yu considered this for a long time, and said at last, " 'Knocking' is better." They became fast friends after that.[6]

---

6. This is a famous story, so famous that even today when Chinese writers have to decide between alternate words they ask, "'Push' or 'knock'?"

## *The Boat over the Moon*

### *from* Notes from Jinshi Hall

A Korean diplomat was traveling in a boat across the sea, and he started to improvise a poem:

> Waterfowl float and dive.
> Mountain clouds part and blend.

The poet Jia Dao, hearing this, pretended to be an oarsman, and completed the poem:

> Oars cut through the sky in the waves.
> The boat skates over the moon in the water.

The Korean diplomat exclaimed "Excellent! Really good!" And after that he never talked about poetry again.[7]

# Yuan Dynasty

### (1280–1367)

## ■ Ma Zhiyuan (Ma Chih-yüan) (c. 1260–1334) (poems)

Yuan dynasty playwright and poet Ma Zhiyuan is best known for his masterly play *Autumn in the Han Palace*, in which prose passages alternate with *qu* poems. He also wrote *san qu* poems—*qu* poems written independent of a play. *Qu* and *san qu* poems are, like *ci* poems, written in set patterns of rhyme and tonal sequence and are characterized by lines of varying length, but they tend to be even more colloquial in their speech. From his poems, we know that Ma was a government official for some time and that in middle age he resigned his position to spend the remainder of his life writing poems and plays. The poems selected here show his dual attitude toward nature. On the one hand, like Tao Qian, he desires to retire from public life and to be at peace in the wilderness, chasing a butterfly (an allusion to a famous parable by Zhuangzi) through his dream. On the

---

7. The Korean diplomat was ashamed to be bested poetically by someone he thought to be a common oarsman.

other hand, he knows that the law of nature is change, and his poems evoke the pathos of mutability and nature's sure eating away of works thrown up in human hubris.

**FURTHER READING:** Chaves, Jonathan, tr., ed. *The Columbia Book of Later Chinese Poetry: Yuan, Ming, and Ch'ing Dynasties (1297–1911)*, 1986. Keene, Donald. "Autumn in the Palace of Han," in Birch, Cyril, ed. *Anthology of Chinese Literature from the Early Times to the Fourteenth Century*, 1965. Liu, Jung-en, tr. *Six Yuan Plays*, 1972.

## Autumn Thoughts to the Tune of "Sky-Clear Sand"

Withered vines, old trees, ravens at dusk.
A small bridge, a flowing brook, a cottage.
Ancient roads, west wind, and a lean horse.
The evening sun dies west.
A broken man at the sky's edge.                    5

TRANSLATED BY TONY BARNSTONE AND CHOU PING

## Autumn Thoughts to the Tune of "Sailing at Night"

*1.*

One hundred years of light and dark is like a butterfly dream.
Looking back at the past, I can't help sighing.
Today spring comes,
tomorrow blossoms fade.
Hurry up and drink—the night is old, the lamp is going out.        5

*2.*

Think of the Qin palace, the Han tombs,
turned to withered weeds, cow pastures.
Otherwise, fishermen and woodcutters wouldn't chatter here.
Even if broken tombstones still lie across tangled graves,
it's hard to tell a snake from a dragon in the worn inscriptions.        5

*3.*

After the "fox trace" and "hare hole" battle strategies,
how many heroes survive?
The kingdoms of Wei or Jin are like the waist of a tripod,
snapped in half.

4.

Before my eyes the red sun slants west,
fast as a cart racing downhill.
When dawn comes in the clear mirror my hair has turned white.
I might as well say goodbye to my shoes when climbing into bed!
Don't laugh at a turtledove's clumsy nest—                                    5
sometimes the fool just plays the fool.

5.

Now that fame and money are spent,
I have no worries about right and wrong.
Red dust no longer gathers at my front gate.
Green shade of trees is nice on the cornices.
Blue mountains patch gaps in the wall                                         5
of my thatched cottage, my bamboo fence.

6.

When crickets chant I sleep well, as if ironed to the bed.
When roosters crow all things start swirling endlessly.
When will the fight for money and fame ever end?
Packed ants circling and circling in battle formations,
a chaos of swarming, spinning bees making honey,                              5
pushing and buzzing like flies fighting for blood.

Duke Fei of Green Wilderness Hall,
County Prefect Tao of the White Lotus Society,
these were people who loved the coming of autumn.
When dew forms, I pick yellow day-lilies.                                     10
With frost, I cook purple crabs.
I mull wine over a fire of red leaves.

The life of a man is over after a few cups.
There will only be so many Festivals of Climbing.
I'm going to tell my wily houseboy:                                           15
if anyone sends for me, even Beihai himself,
say that my name is East Fence, and I'm too drunk to come.

TRANSLATED BY TONY BARNSTONE AND CHOU PING

## To the Tune of "Thinking about Nature"

A day is forever in the slow village to the west.
In the tedium, the first cicada buzzes,
sunflowers are poised
to open, and bees invade the morning.
Unconscious on my pillow, I chase a butterfly through my dream.                5

TRANSLATED BY TONY BARNSTONE AND WILLIS BARNSTONE

## *Autumn Moon on the Tung T'ing Lake, to the Tune of "Shou Yang"*

Clouds block the moon,

Wind clatters the bells.

Each multiplies

        my sadness.

So,

    to pour my heart out

        on paper,

I went to turn up the wick

    with a sigh

so profound

    it blew out the flame.

TRANSLATED BY G. GACH AND C. H. KWOCK

### ▪ Shi Naian (Shih Nai-an) and Luo Guanzhong (Lo Kuan-chung) (Late Fourteenth Century) (novel)

TRANSLATED BY SIDNEY SHAPIRO

*Outlaws of the Marsh* is a novel almost certainly composed by many hands, in spite of its highly questionable attribution to Shi Naian and Luo Guanzhong, both of whom probably flourished in the fourteenth century. These attributions are highly popular but discounted by serious scholars, and it seems likely that the novel evolved organically out of popular accounts of the heroic exploits of a group of outlaws led by Song Jiang during the Northern Song period. These stories have held much the same position in the Chinese popular imagination that Robin Hood's valiant outlaws of Sherwood Forest have held in English. The transmission of the text remains among the thorniest of all textual problems in Chinese literature, obscured by politics, legend, and the novel's own evolutionary nature. Many recensions exist, from a 71-chapter version to one of 124 chapters. In addition, there are three major sequels and a body of plays and historical accounts that the novel must in part have derived from. It has been celebrated in poems and paintings, by professional storytellers, and even by contemporary Chinese American writer Frank Chin, in his novel *Donald Duk*. It seems likely that there was a historical Song Jiang who led a bandit group, surrendered to the government, and subsequently fought in its service to put down rebellions (in the novel there are 108 outlaw heros, many of whom achieve remarkable depth of characterization). The novel is picaresque, and both individual chapters and larger sections easily stand on their own. In the hilarious chapter presented here, the hero Lu Da, who has become an outlaw by killing a rapacious butcher for attempting to swindle the Jin family, makes a fuss while hiding out as a Buddhist monk.

**FURTHER READING:** Buck, Pearl S., tr. *All Men Are Brothers*, 1933. Jackson, J. H., tr. *Water Margin*, 1937. Shapiro, Sidney, tr. *Outlaws of the Marsh*, 1981.

## from *Outlaws of the Marsh*

# Chapter 2
### SAGACIOUS LU PUTS MOUNT WUTAI IN AN UPROAR

After leaving Weizhou, Lu Da hurried pellmell east and west, passing through several prefectural towns. With him it was a case of:

> Any food when you're hungry,
> When you're cold rags save life;
> Any road when you're frightened,
> When you're poor any wife.

He dashed about in a panic, with no idea where to go.

After many days of wandering, he arrived in Yanmen, a county seat in the prefecture of Daizhou. It was a bustling town with many people and thriving markets. Carts and horses filled the streets, which were lined by shops conducting trade and commerce of every type. Although only a county seat, it was more prosperous than a prefectural capital.

On a street corner he saw a crowd gathered in front of a proclamation. Someone was reading it aloud. Illiterate himself, he pushed forward to listen. This is what he heard:

> *By order of the military commander of Taiyuan, this county hereby publishes the following notice from Weizhou: Wanted—the killer of Butcher Zheng. Name—Lu Da, former major in the Weizhou garrison command. Any man who conceals him or gives him food and shelter shall be deemed equally guilty. Whoever arrests and brings him forward, or offers information leading to his arrest, shall receive a reward of one thousand strings of cash. . . .*

As Lu Da stood listening, someone threw his arms around him from behind and cried: "What are you doing here, brother Zhang?" He pulled Lu Da away from the street corner.

Lu Da turned to see who was hustling him away. It was none other than Old Jin from the Weizhou tavern, the man he had rescued. The old fellow didn't stop pulling till they reached an isolated spot. Then he said:

"You're too rash, benefactor. That notice offers a thousand strings of cash for your capture. How could you stand there looking at it? If I hadn't spotted you, you might have been nabbed by the police. Your age, description and place of origin are all there."

"To tell you the truth, when I went to the foot of the Zhuangyuan Bridge that day to see Zheng the butcher about your affair, I killed the churl with three blows of the fist, and had to flee. I've been knocking about for forty or fifty days now, and just happened to wander into this town. I thought you were returning to the Eastern Capital. What are you doing here?"

"After you saved me, benefactor, I found a cart. Originally I intended to go back to the Eastern Capital, but I was afraid that rogue would catch up and you wouldn't be around to rescue us. So I changed my mind and headed north. On the road I met an old neighbor from the capital who was coming here on business. He took me and my daughter along. He was good enough to find her a match. She's now the mistress of a wealthy man, Squire Zhao. The squire has provided her with a house. Thanks to you, benefactor, we now have plenty to eat and wear. My daughter has often spoken to the squire of your kindness. He is also fond of jousting. He's said many times he'd like to meet you, but that was never possible before. You must come and stay with us a few days. We can talk about what you should do next."

Lu Da and Old Jin walked less than half a *li* when they came to the door of a house. The old man pushed aside the bamboo curtain and called: "Daughter, our benefactor is here."

The girl emerged, neatly made up and attractively dressed. She begged Lu Da to be seated in the center of the room. Then, as if offering votive candles, she kowtowed before him six times. "If you hadn't rescued us, benefactor," she said, "we'd never possess what we have today." She invited him upstairs to the parlor.

"Don't bother," said Lu Da. "I must be going."

"Now that you're here, benefactor, of course we can't let you leave," said the old man. He took Lu Da's staff and bundles and ushered him up the stairs. To his daughter he said: "Keep our benefactor company. I'll arrange about dinner."

"Don't go to a lot of trouble," said Lu Da. "Anything will do."

"Even if I gave my life I could never repay your benevolence," said Old Jin. "A little simple food — it's not worth mentioning."

The three drank till almost nightfall. Suddenly they heard a commotion outside. Lu Da opened the window and looked. Some twenty to thirty men, all armed with staves, were gathered in front of the house. "Bring him down," they were shouting. A gentleman on a horse cried: "Don't let the rascal get away!"

Lu Da realized that he was in danger. He snatched up a stool and started down the stairs. Old Jin, waving his hands, rushed down ahead of him, exclaiming: "Nobody move!" He ran over to the man on horseback and said a few words. The mounted gentleman laughed. He ordered his band to disperse.

When the men had gone, the gentleman got off his horse and entered the house. Old Jin asked Lu Da to come down. The gentleman bowed as Lu Da descended the stairs.

"'Meeting a man of fame is better than just hearing his name.' Please accept my homage, righteous Major."

"Who is this gentleman?" Lu Da asked Old Jin. "We don't know each other. Why should he be so respectful?"

"This is Squire Zhao, my daughter's lord. Someone told him that a young man I had brought to his house was upstairs, drinking. So he got some of his vassals and came to fight. When I explained, he sent them away."

"So that was it," said Lu Da. "You could hardly blame him."

Squire Zhao invited Lu Da to the upper chamber. Old Jin reset the table, and once more prepared food and drink. Zhao ushered the major to the seat of honor. Lu Da refused.

"How could I presume?"

"A small mark of my respect. I have heard much of the major's heroism. What great good fortune that I could meet you today."

"Though I'm just a crude fellow who's committed a capital offence, the squire doesn't scorn my lowliness and is willing to make my acquaintance. If there's any way I can be of service, you have only to speak."

Squire Zhao was very pleased. He asked all about the fight with Zheng the butcher. They talked of this and that, discussed jousting with arms, and drank far into the night. Then everyone retired.

The following morning Zhao said: "I'm afraid this place isn't very safe. Why not come and stay at my manor a while?"

"Where is it?" asked Lu Da.

"A little over ten *li* from here, near a village called Seven Treasures."

"All right."

Lu Da stayed at the manor for six or seven days. He and the squire were chatting in the study one day when Old Jin hastily entered. He looked to see that no one else was around, then said to Lu Da: "You mustn't think me overly cautious, benefactor. But ever since the night the squire and his vassals raised such a row in the street because you were drinking upstairs, people have been suspicious. Word has spread that you were there. Yesterday three or four policemen were questioning the neighbors. I'm worried that they'll come here and arrest you. It would be awful if anything should happen to you, benefactor."

"In that case," said Lu Da, "I'd better be on my way."

"Things might turn out badly if I kept you here, Major," the squire admitted. "Yet if I don't, I'll lose a lot of face. I have another idea. It's foolproof and will give you complete protection. But maybe you won't be will-ing."

"I'm a man with a death penalty waiting for him. I'll do anything to find refuge."

"That's fine. Where the Wenshu Buddha used to meditate on Mount Wutai, some thirty-odd *li* from here, a monastery was erected. They have nearly seven hundred monks. The abbot is my friend. My ancestors were patrons of the monastery and contributed to its upkeep. I have promised to sponsor a novice, and have bought a blank certificate, but have not yet found a suitable man. If you agree to join the Buddhist order, Major, I'll pay all expenses. Would you be willing to shave off your hair and become a monk?"

Lu Da thought to himself: "Who could I go to for protection if I were to leave here today? I'd better accept his offer." Aloud he said: "I'll be-come a monk if you sponsor me, Squire. I rely entirely on your kindness."

And so it was decided. That night, clothing, expense money and silks were prepared. Everyone rose early the next morning. Lu Da and the squire set out for Mount Wutai, accompanied by vassals carrying the gifts and luggage. They reached the foot of the mountain before mid-morning. Squire Zhao and Lu Da went up in sedan-chairs, sending a vassal on ahead to announce them.

At the monastery gate, they found the deacon and supervisor waiting to welcome them. They got out of their sedan-chairs and rested in a small pavil-ion while the abbot was notified. He soon emerged with his assistant and the elder. Squire Zhao and Lu Da hurried forward and bowed. The abbot placed the palms of his hands together before his chest in Buddhist greeting.

"It's good of you to travel this long distance, patron," he said.

"There is a small matter I'd like to trouble you about," said the squire.

"Please come into the abbey and have some tea."

Lu Da followed Squire Zhao to the hall. The abbot invited the squire to take the seat for guests. Lu Da sat down on a couch facing the abbot. The squire leaned over and whispered to him: "You're here to become a monk. How can you sit opposite the abbot?"

"I didn't know," said Lu Da. He rose and stood beside Squire Zhao.

The elder, the prior, the abbot's assistant, the supervisor, the deacon, the reception monk, and the scribe arranged themselves in two rows, ac-cording to rank, on the east and west sides of the hall.

Zhao's vassals left the sedan-chairs in a suitable place and carried into the hall several boxes which they laid before the abbot.

"Why have you brought gifts again?" asked the abbot. "You've already made so many donations."

"Only a few small things," replied Squire Zhao. "They don't merit any thanks."

Some lay brothers and novices took them away.

Squire Zhao stood up. "I have something to ask of you, Great Abbot. It has long been my desire to sponsor a new member for this monastery. Although I have had the certificate ready for some time, until today I have not been able to do so. This cousin here is named Lu. He formerly was a military officer, but because of many difficulties he wants to have done with mundane affairs and become a monk. I earnestly hope Your Eminence will exercise mercy and compassion and, as a favor to me, accept this man into your order. I will pay all expenses. I shall be very happy if you consent."

"Gladly," said the abbot. "This will add lustre to our monastery. Please have some tea."

A novice served tea. After all had drunk, he removed the cups. The abbot consulted with the elder and the prior on the ceremony for receiving Lu Da into the order, then instructed the supervisor and deacon to prepare a vegetarian meal.

"That man hasn't the makings of a monk," the elder said to the other monks, privately. "See what fierce eyes he has!"

"Get them out of here a while," they requested the Receiver of Guests. "We want to talk to the abbot."

The reception monk invited Squire Zhao and Lu Da to rest in the visitors' hostel. They departed, and the elder and the others approached the abbot.

"That new applicant is a savage-looking brute," they said. "If we accept him, he's sure to cause trouble."

"He's a cousin of Squire Zhao, our patron. How can we refuse? Hold your doubts while I look into the matter." The abbot lit a stick of incense and sat cross-legged on a couch. Muttering an incantation, he went into a trance. By the time the incense was consumed, he returned.

"You can go ahead with the ordination," said the abbot. "This man represents a star in Heaven. His heart is honest. Even though his appearance is savage and his life has been troubled, he will eventually become purified and attain sainthood. None of you is his equal. Mark my words. Let no one dissent."

"The abbot is only covering up his faults," the elder said to the others. "But we'll have to do as he says. We can only advise. If he won't listen, that's up to him."

Squire Zhao and the others were invited to dine in the abbey. When they had finished, the supervisor presented a list of what Lu Da would need as a monk—special shoes, clothing, hat, cape and kneeling cushion. The squire gave some silver and asked that the monastery buy the necessary materials and make them up.

A day or two later all was ready. The abbot selected a propitious day and hour, and ordered that the bells be rung and the drums beaten. Everyone assembled in the preaching hall. Draped in their capes, nearly six hundred monks placed the palms of their hands together in an obeisance to the abbot sitting on his dais, then separated into two groups. Squire Zhao, bearing gifts of silver ingots and fine cloth and carrying a stick of incense, approached the dais and bowed.

The purpose of the ceremony was announced. A novice led Lu Da to the abbot's dais. The prior told him to remove his hat, divided his hair into nine parts and knotted them. The barber shaved them all off. He reached with his razor for Lu Da's beard.

"Leave me that, at least," the major exclaimed.

The monks couldn't repress their laughter.

"Hear me," the abbot said sternly from his dais. "Leave not a single blade of grass, let the six roots of desire be torn out. All must be shaven clean away, lest they manifest themselves again," he intoned. "Off with it," he ordered.

The barber quickly finished the job. Presenting the certificate to the abbot, the elder requested him to select a name by which Lu Da should be known in the Buddhist order.

"A spark from the soul is worth more than a thousand pieces of gold," the abbot chanted. "Our Buddhist Way is great and wide. Let him be called Sagacious."

The scribe filled out the certificate and handed it to Sagacious Lu. At the abbot's direction he was given his monk's garments and told to put them on. Then he was led to the dais. The abbot placed his hand on Lu's head and instructed him in the rules of conduct.

"Take refuge in Buddha, the Law and the Monastic Order. These are the three refuges. Do not kill, steal, fornicate, drink or lie. These are the five precepts."

Lu Da didn't know he was supposed to answer "I shall" to each of the first three and "I shall not" to each of the last five.

"I'll remember," he said.

Everyone laughed.

Squire Zhao invited all present into the assembly hall where he burned incense and offered a vegetarian feast to the Buddhist gods. He gave gifts to every member of the monastery staff, high or low. The deacon introduced Sagacious to various members of the monastery, then conducted him to the rear building where the monks meditated. Nothing further happened that night.

The next day, Squire Zhao decided to leave. He said goodbye to the abbot, who tried in vain to keep him. After breakfast, all the monks went with him as far as the monastery gate. Squire Zhao placed his palms together and said, "Abbot, teachers, be compassionate. My young cousin Lu is a crude, direct fellow. If he forgets his manners or says anything offensive or breaks any rules, please forgive him, as a favor to me."

"Don't worry, Squire," said the abbot. "I shall teach him gradually to recite the prayers and scriptures, perform services, and practise meditation."

"In the days to come I will show my gratitude," promised the squire. He called Lu over to a pine tree and spoke to him in a low voice: "Your life must be different from now on, brother. Be restrained in all things, under no circumstances be proud. Otherwise, it will be hard for us to see each other again. Take good care of yourself. I'll send you warm clothing from time to time."

"No need to tell me, brother," said Lu. "I'll behave."

The squire took his leave of the abbot and the monks, got into his sedan-chair and set off down the mountain for home. His vassals followed, carrying the other, now empty, sedan-chair and boxes. The abbot and the monks returned to the monastery.

When Lu got back to the meditation room, he threw himself down on his bed and went to sleep. The monks meditating on either side shook him into wakefulness.

"You can't do that," they said. "Now that you're a monk, you're supposed to learn how to sit and meditate."

"If I want to sleep, what's it to you?" Lu demanded.

"Evil!" exclaimed the monks.

"What's this talk about eels? It's turtles I like to eat."

"Oh, bitter!"

"There's nothing bitter about them. Turtle belly is fat and sweet. They make very good eating."

The monks gave up. They let him sleep.

The next day they wanted to complain to the abbot. But the elder advised against it. He said: "The abbot is only covering up his faults when he says he will attain sainthood and that none of us is his equal. But there's nothing we can do about it. Just don't bother with him."

The monks went back. Since no one reprimanded him, Sagacious sprawled out on his bed every night and slept snoring thunderously. When he had to relieve himself he made a terrible racket getting up. He pissed and crapped behind one of the halls. His filth was all over the place.

The abbot's assistant reported the matter. "That Lu has no manners. He's not in the least like a man who's left the material world. How can we keep a fellow like that in the monastery?"

"Nonsense," retorted the abbot. "Don't forget our donor's request. Sagacious will change later on."

No one dared argue.

And so, Sagacious Lu remained in the monastery on Mount Wutai. Before he knew it, four or five months had passed. It was early winter and Lu's mind, which had been quiescent for a long time, began to stir. One clear day he put on his black cloth cassock, fastened his raven-dark girdle, changed into monk's shoes, and strode from the monastery.

Halfway down the mountain he halted to rest in a pavilion. He sat down on a low "goose neck" bench and said to himself with a curse: "In the old days I had good meat and drink every day. But now that I'm a monk I'm shrivelling up from starvation. Squire Zhao hasn't sent me anything to eat for a long time. My mouth is absolutely tasteless. If only I could get some wine."

He saw in the distance a man carrying two covered buckets on a shoul-

der-pole. A ladle in his hand, the man trudged up the slope singing this
song:

> Before Mount Nine Li an old battlefield lies,
> There cowherds find ancient spears and knives,
> As a breeze stirs the waters of the Wu River broad,
> We recall Lady Yu's farewell to her lord.

Lu watched him approach. The man entered the pavilion and put
down his load.

"Hey, fellow, what have you got in those buckets?" Lu asked.

"Good wine."

"How much a bucket?"

"Are you serious, monk, or are you just kidding?"

"Why should I kid you?"

"This wine is for the monastery's cooks, janitors, sedan-chair carriers,
caretakers, and field laborers—no one else. The abbot has warned me
that if I sell to a monk he'll take back the money and house the monastery
loaned me for my winery. I don't dare sell you any of this."

"You really won't?"

"Not if you kill me!"

"I won't kill you, but I will buy some of your wine."

The man didn't like the look of things. He picked up his carrying-pole
and started to walk away. Lu dashed out of the pavilion after him, seized
the pole with both hands, and kicked the fellow in the groin. The man
clapped both hands to his injured parts and dropped to a squatting position. He couldn't straighten up for some time.

Sagacious Lu carried both buckets to the pavilion. He picked the ladle
off the ground, removed the covers, and began drinking. Before long, one
of the buckets was empty.

"Come around to the monastery tomorrow and I'll pay you," he said.

The man had just recovered from his pain. If the abbot found out, it
would mean an end to his livelihood. How could he seek payment from
Lu at the monastery? Swallowing his anger, he separated the remaining
wine into two half-buckets. Then he shouldered the load, took the ladle
and flew down the mountain.

Lu sat in the pavilion a long time. The wine had gone to his head. He
left the pavilion, sat down beneath a pine tree and again rested for quite a
spell. The wine was taking increasing effect. He pulled his arms out of his
cassock and tied the empty sleeves around his waist. His tattooed back
bare, he strode up the mountain, swinging his arms.

The monastery gate-keepers had been watching him from afar. They
came forward when he approached and barred his way with their split
bamboo staves.

"You're supposed to be a disciple of Buddha," they barked. "How dare
you come here in this besotted condition? You must be blind. Haven't you

seen the notice? Any monk who breaks the rules and drinks gets forty blows of the split bamboo and is expelled from the monastery. Any gate-keeper who lets a drunken man enter gets ten blows. Go back down the mountain, quickly, if you want to save yourself a beating."

In the first place, Lu was a new monk, in the second, his temper hadn't changed. Glaring, he shouted: "Mother-screwing thieves! So you want to beat me? I'll smash you!"

The situation looked bad. One of the gate-keepers sped back inside and reported to the supervisor, while the other tried to keep Sagacious out with his staff. Lu flipped it aside and gave him a staggering slap in the face. As the man struggled to recover, Lu followed with a punch that knocked him groaning to the ground.

"I'll let you off this time, varlet," said Sagacious. He walked unsteadily into the monastery.

The supervisor had summoned the caretakers, cooks, janitors and sedan-chair carriers—nearly thirty men. Now, armed with staves, they poured out of the western cloister and rushed to meet Lu. The ex-major strode towards them with a thunderous roar. They didn't know he had been an army officer. He sprang at them so fiercely they fled in confusion into the sutra hall and closed the latticed door. Sagacious charged up the steps. With one punch and one kick he smashed the door open. The trapped men raised their staves and came out fighting.

The abbot, who had been notified by the supervisor, hurried to the scene with four or five attendants.

"Sagacious," he shouted, "I forbid you to misbehave."

Lu was drunk, but he recognized the abbot. He cast aside his staff, advanced and greeted him.

"I had a couple of bowls of wine, but I did nothing to provoke these fellows," said Sagacious. "They came with a gang and attacked me."

"If you have any respect for me," said the abbot, "you'll go to your quarters at once and sleep it off. We'll talk about this tomorrow."

"It's only my respect for you that stops me from lambasting those scabby donkeys!"

The abbot told his assistant to help Lu to the monks' hall. He collapsed on his bed and slept, snoring loudly.

A crowd of monks surrounded the abbot. "We told you so," they said. "Now you see what's happened? How can we keep a wildcat like that in our monastery? He upsets our pure way of life."

"It's true he's a bit unruly," the abbot admitted, "but he'll become a saint later on. At present, we can do nothing. We must forgive him, for the sake of our donor, Squire Zhao. I'll give him a good lecture tomorrow, and that will be the end of it."

The monks laughed coldly. "Our abbot isn't very bright," they said among themselves. All retired to their respective abodes.

The next morning the abbot sent his assistant to the monks' quarters to summon Sagacious Lu. He was still asleep. The assistant waited while he got up and put on his cassock. Suddenly, Lu dashed out, barefoot. The surprised assistant followed. He found Lu pissing behind the temple. The assistant couldn't help laughing. He waited till Lu had finished, then said:

"The abbot wants to see you."

Lu went with him to the cleric's room.

"Although you originally were a military man," said the abbot, "I ordained you because of Squire Zhao's sponsorship. I instructed you: Do not kill, steal, fornicate, drink or lie. These are the five precepts by which all monks are bound. First of all, no monk is allowed to drink. But yesterday evening you came back drunk and beat up the gate-keepers, broke the vermilion latticed door of the sutra hall and drove out the cooks and janitors, shouting and yelling all the while. How could you behave so disgracefully?"

Lu knelt before him. "I'll never do such things again."

"You're a monk now," the abbot continued. "How could you violate our rule against drinking and upset our pure way of life? If it weren't for the sake of your sponsor Squire Zhao I'd expel you from the monastery. Don't you ever act like that again."

Lu placed his palms together. "I wouldn't dare," he asserted fervently.

The abbot ordered breakfast for him and, with many kindly words, exhorted him to reform. He gave Lu a cassock of fine cloth and a pair of monk's shoes, and told him to return to his quarters.

Topers should never drink their fill. "Wine can spur action, or ruin everything," as the old saying goes. If drinking makes the timid brave, what does it do to the bold and impetuous?

For three or four months after his drunken riot Lu didn't venture to leave the monastery. Then one day the weather suddenly turned warm. It was the second lunar month. Lu came out of his quarters, strolled through the monastery gate and stood gazing in admiration at the beauty of Mount Wutai. From the foot of the mountain the breeze brought the sound of the clanging of metal. Sagacious returned to his quarters, got some silver and put it inside his cassock near his chest. Then he ambled down the slope.

He passed through an archway inscribed with the words: "Wutai, a Blessed Place." Before him he saw a market town of six or seven hundred families. Meat, vegetables, wine and flour were on sale.

"What am I waiting for?" Lu said to himself. "If I had known there was a place like this, instead of snatching that fellow's bucket I would have come down and bought my own wine. I've been holding back so long that it hurts. Let's see what sort of food they have on sale here."

Again he heard the clang of metal.

Next to a building with the sign "Father and Son Inn" was an ironsmith's shop. The sound was coming from there. Lu walked over. Three men were beating iron.

"Got any good steel, master smith?" he asked the eldest of them.

The man was a little frightened at the sight of Lu's face, with newly sprouted bristles sticking out wildly all over. He ceased his hammering and said: "Please have a seat, Reverend. What kind of work do you want done?"

"I need a Buddhist staff and a monk's knife. Do you have any first-rate metal?"

"I do indeed. How heavy a staff and knife do you want? We'll make them according to your requirements."

"The staff should be a hundred catties."

"Much too heavy," the smith laughed. "I could make it for you, but you'd never be able to wield it. Even Guan Gong's[1] halberd wasn't more than eighty-one catties!"

"I'm every bit as good as Guan Gong," Sagacious burst out impatiently. "He was only a man, too."

"I mean well, Reverend. Even forty-five catties would be very heavy."

"You say Guan Gong's halberd was eighty-one catties? Make me a staff of that weight, then."

"Too thick, Reverend. It would look ugly, and be clumsy to use. Take my advice, let me make you a sixty-two catty Buddhist staff of burnished metal. Of course, if it's too heavy, don't blame me. For the knife, as I said, we don't need any specifications. I'll use the best steel."

"How much for the two?"

"We don't bargain. You can have them at rock-bottom — five ounces of silver for both."

"It's a deal. If you do a good job, I'll give you more."

The smith accepted the silver. "We'll start right away."

"I have some small change here. Come out and have a bowl of wine with me."

"Excuse me, Reverend. I must get on with my work. I can't keep you company."

Sagacious Lu left the ironsmith's. Before he had gone thirty paces, he saw a wine shop banner sticking out from the eaves of a house. He raised the hanging door screen, entered the shop, sat down, and pounded on the table.

"Bring wine," he shouted.

The proprietor came up to him. "Forgive me, Reverend. My shop and investment money all are borrowed from the monastery. The abbot has a rule for us tavern keepers. If any of us sells wine to a monk, he takes back the money and drives us out of our premises. Don't hold it against me."

"All I want is a little wine. I won't say I bought it here."

"Impossible. Please try some place else. I'm sorry."

Lu rose to his feet. "If another place serves me, I'll have something to say to you later!"

He left the wine shop and walked on. Soon he saw another wine flag suspended over a doorway. He went in, sat down and called:

"Wine, host. Be quick."

"How can you be so ignorant, Reverend?" the tavern keeper demanded. "You must know the abbot's rules. Do you want to ruin me?"

---

1. Guan Gong, a famous general of the Three Kingdoms period (220–280).

Sagacious insisted on being served, but the tavern keeper was adamant. Lu had no choice but to leave. He went to four or five more wine shops. All refused to serve him.

"If I don't think of something, I'll never get any wine," he said to himself. At the far end of the market-place he saw amid blossoming apricot trees a small house from which a bundle of broom straw was hanging. He came closer and found it was a little wine shop. Lu went in and sat down by the window.

"Host," he called, "bring wine for a wandering monk."

The rustic owner came over and scrutinized him. "Where are you from, Reverend?"

"I'm a travelling monk who's just passing through. I want some wine."

"If you're from the Mount Wutai monastery, I'm not allowed to sell you any."

"I'm not. Now bring on the wine."

Lu's appearance and manner of speaking struck the rustic owner as odd. "How much do you want?"

"Never mind about that. Just keep bringing it by the bowlful."

Lu consumed ten big bowls of wine. "Have you any meat?" he asked. "I want a platter."

"I had some beef earlier in the day," said the proprietor, "but it's all sold out."

Sagacious caught a whiff of the fragrance of cooking meat. He went into the yard and found a dog boiling in an earthenware pot by the compound wall.

"You've got dog meat," he said. "Why won't you sell me any?"

"I thought as a monk you wouldn't eat it, so I didn't ask."

"I've plenty of money here." Lu pulled out some silver and handed it over. "Bring me half."

The proprietor cut off half the dog carcass and placed it on the table with a small dish of garlic sauce. Lu tore into it delightedly with both hands. At the same time he consumed another ten bowls of wine. He found the wine very agreeable and kept calling for more. The shop owner was dumbfounded.

"That's enough, monk," he urged.

Lu glared at him. "I'm paying for what I drink. Who's asking you to interfere?"

"How much more do you want?"

"Bring me another bucketful."

The host had no choice but to comply. Before long, Sagacious had downed this, too. A dog's leg that he hadn't finished he put inside his cassock.

"Hold on to the extra silver," he said as he was leaving. "I'll be back for more tomorrow."

The frightened proprietor could only helplessly gape. He watched as Lu headed towards Mount Wutai.

Halfway up the slope, Lu sat down in the pavilion and rested. The wine began to take effect. Leaping up, he cried: "I haven't had a good workout in a long time. I'm getting stiff and creaky in the joints. What I need is a little exercise."

Lu came out of the pavilion. He gripped the end of each sleeve in the opposite hand and swung his arms vigorously up and down, left and right, with increasing force. One arm accidentally struck against a post of the pavilion. There was loud crack as the post snapped. Half the pavilion collapsed.

Two gate-keepers heard the noise and climbed to a high vantage point for a look. They saw Lu staggering up the slope.

"Woe," they exclaimed. "That brute is soused again!"

They closed the gate and barred it. Peering through a crack, they watched Lu advance. When he found the gate locked, he drummed on it with his fists. But the gate-keepers didn't dare let him in.

Lu pounded a while, in vain. Suddenly he noticed a Buddhist guardian idol on the left side of the gate.

"Hey, you big worthless fellow," Lu shouted. "Instead of helping me knock on the gate, you raise your fist and try to scare me! I'm not afraid of you!"

He jumped on the pedestal and ripped up the railing as easily as pulling scallions. Grabbing a broken post, he flailed it against the idol's leg, bringing down a shower of gilt and plaster.

"Woe," cried the gate-keepers. They ran to inform the abbot.

Lu paused, then turned and observed the guardian idol on the right.

"How dare you open your big mouth and laugh at me?" he yelled. He leaped on the pedestal and struck the idol's leg two hard blows. The figure toppled to the ground with a thunderous crash.

Lu laughed uproariously, holding the broken post in his hand.

When the gate-keepers notified the abbot he merely said: "Don't provoke him. Go back to your gate."

At that moment, the elder, the supervisor, the deacon, and other responsible monks entered the hall. "That wildcat is very drunk," they said. "He's wrecked the mid-slope pavilion and the guardian idols at the gate. How can we put up with this?"

"Since ancient times it's been known that 'Even a king shuns a drunkard.' All the more necessary for me to avoid them," replied the abbot. "If he's broken idols, we'll ask his sponsor Squire Zhao to make us new ones. Zhao can repair the pavilion too. Let Sagacious do as he wishes."

"Those guardian idols are the lords of the gate," the monks protested. "You can't change them around just like that."

"Never mind the gate idols," retorted the abbot. "Even if they were the idols of the leading Buddhas themselves that were destroyed, there'd be nothing we could do about it. Stay out of his way. Didn't you see how savage he was the other day?"

"What a muddle-headed abbot," the monks muttered as they left the hall. "Don't open that gate," they instructed the gate-keepers. "Just stand inside and listen."

"If you mother-screwing scabby donkeys don't let me in," bellowed Sagacious, "I'll set fire to this stinking monastery and burn it down!"

"Remove the bar and let the beast in," the monks hastily called to the gate-keepers. "If we don't, he's really liable to do it!"

The gate-keepers tiptoed up to the gate, pulled the bolt, then flew back and hid themselves. The other monks scattered.

Lu pushed hard against the gate with both hands. Unexpectedly, it gave way, and he stumbled in and fell flat on his face. He crawled to his feet, rubbed his head, and hurried to his quarters.

He pushed aside the door curtain and plunged into the meditation room. The monks, who were sitting cross-legged on their pallets, looked up, startled. They immediately lowered their heads. On reaching his own pallet, Sagacious noisily vomited. The stench was frightful. "Virtue be praised," cried the monks, holding their noses.

Lu clambered onto his pallet and opened his cassock and girdle, ripping them in the process. The dog's leg dropped to the floor. "Good," said Sagacious. "I was just getting hungry." He picked it up and began to eat.

The monks hid their faces behind their sleeves. Those nearest him stayed as far out of his way as possible. Lu tore off a piece of dog meat and offered it to the monk on his left.

"Try it," he recommended.

The man pressed his sleeve ends tightly against his lips.

"Don't you want any?" asked Lu. He shoved the meat at the man on his right. The fellow tried to slip off his pallet and escape, but Sagacious seized him by the ear and crammed the meat into his mouth.

Four or five monks on the opposite side of the room jumped up and hurried over. They pleaded with Lu to desist. He flung aside his dog's haunch and drummed his knuckles on their shaven pates. The whole meditation room was thrown into an uproar. Monks got their cassocks and bowls from the closets and quickly left. There was a general exodus. The elder couldn't stop them.

Cheerfully, Sagacious fought his way out. Most of the monks fled to the cloisters. This time the supervisor and deacon didn't notify the abbot, but summoned all the monks on duty, including every caretaker, cook, janitor and sedan-chair carrier they could muster—nearly two hundred men in all. These bound their heads with bandannas, armed themselves with clubs and staves, and marched on the monks' hall.

Lu let out a roar when he saw them. Not having any weapon he ran into the meditation room, knocked over the altar table in the front of the idol of Buddha, tore off two of the table legs, and charged out again.

He came at the attackers so fiercely that they hastily retreated to the cloisters. Sagacious advanced, flourishing his table legs. His adversaries closed in on him from both sides. Lu was furious. He feinted east and struck west, he feinted south and thumped north. Only those furthest away escaped his cudgels.

Right to the door of the preaching hall the battle raged. Then the voice of the abbot rang out: "Sagacious, stop that fighting! You, too, you monks!"

The attackers had suffered several dozen injured. They were glad to fall back when the abbot appeared. Lu threw down his table legs.

"Abbot, help me," he cried. By now he was eight-tenths sober.

"Sagacious, you're giving me too much trouble," said the cleric. "The last time you got drunk and raised a rumpus I wrote your sponsor Squire Zhao about it and he sent a letter of apology. Now you've disgraced yourself again, upset our pure way of life, wrecked the pavilion and damaged two idols. All this we can overlook. But you drove the monks from the meditation room, and that's a major crime. Wenshu Buddha meditated where our monastery stands today. For centuries these hallowed grounds have known only tranquillity and the fragrance of incense. It's no place for a dirty fellow like you. The next few days, you stay with me in the abbot's hall. I'll arrange for you to be transferred elsewhere."

The former major went with the abbot to his residence. The cleric told the supervisor to send the monks back to their meditations. Those who had been injured were to go and rest. Sagacious spent the night in the abbot's hall.

The next morning the abbot consulted with the elder. They decided to give Lu some money and send him on. But first it was necessary to notify Squire Zhao. The abbot wrote a letter and dispatched it to his manor with two messengers, who were instructed to wait for his reply.

Zhao was quite upset by the abbot's missive. In his answer he hailed the cleric respectfully and said: "I will pay for the repair of the broken gate guardians and the pavilion. Lu must go wherever the abbot sends him."

The abbot then directed his assistant to prepare a black cloth cassock, a pair of monk's shoes, and ten ounces of silver, and to summon Lu.

"Sagacious," said the abbot, "the last time you got drunk and made a disturbance in the monks' hall, you didn't know any better. This time you got drunk again, broke the guardian idols, wrecked the pavilion, and caused a riot in the hall of meditation. That's a serious crime. You've also injured many of our monks. Our monastery is a peaceful place. Your conduct is very bad. As a courtesy to Squire Zhao I'm giving you a letter of introduction to another place where you can stay. It's impossible for us to keep you here. In the Eastern Capital a Buddhist brother of mine, called the Lucid Teacher, is the abbot of the Great Xiangguo Monastery. Take this letter to him and ask him to find you a job. Last night I had a vision and composed a four-line prophetic verse to guide your destiny. You must remember these words."

Kneeling before him, Lu said: "I'd like to hear the prophecy."

The abbot intoned: "Take action in the forest, prosper in the mountains, flourish amid the waters, but halt at the river."

Sagacious kowtowed to the abbot nine times, shouldered his knapsack, tied bundles round his waist, and placed the letter in a pocket. He bid farewell to the abbot and the monks, left Mount Wutai, put up in the inn next door to the ironsmith and waited for his staff and sword. The monks were glad to be rid of him. The abbot told the lay brothers to clean up the wreckage of the guardian idols and the pavilion. A few days later Squire Zhao brought some money personally and had the idols and pavilion repaired.

# Ming Dynasty

## (1368–1644)

■ **Wu Chengen (Wu Ch'eng-en) (c. 1500–1582) (novel)**

TRANSLATED BY ARTHUR WALEY

*Monkey* is a rambunctious, adventurous, satirical jaunt, a novel of the late Ming dynasty that recounts the story of the sage Xuanzang (596–664), also known as Tripitaka, after the "triple basket"—a great repository of Buddhist literature (see "Theravada Buddhist Texts" [the Tipitaka] in the section on Indian literature). This monk's seventeen-year journey to India to bring back Buddhist scriptures to China had been the subject of a number of plays, folktales, and other accounts; and Wu Chengen, the supposed author of *Monkey,* draws upon and elaborates on this tradition to make a novel of a hundred chapters. For more than three centuries, the author was thought to be Qiu Changchun (fl. 1220), who was an advisor to Genghis Khan. Now the scholar Hu Shi has documented that Wu Chengen, a minor official, writer, and poet of the Ming dynasty was most likely the author. He probably wrote *Monkey* in his later years, and a preface he wrote to a now lost collection of short stories gives a clue to his motivation: "I was very fond of strange stories when I was a child. In my village-school days, I used to buy stealthily the popular novels and historical recitals. Fearing that my father and my teacher might punish me for this and rob me of these treasures, I carefully hid them in secret places where I could enjoy them unmolested." Wu Chengen goes on to say that he dreamed of writing his own "Book of Monsters," and it was probably an adult version of his childhood fear of censure that caused him to distribute the novel anonymously.

In part, *Monkey* is an allegorical journey of the spirit, like *Pilgrim's Progress;* in part, it is a broad satire of government, religion, and society; and, in part, it is a wild romantic fantasy. The central character in the novel is not really Tripitaka, but a powerful, magical trickster of a monkey who is his companion and is allegorically interpreted as representing the mind. Another companion is Pigsy, a half-pig and half-human creature, who represents sensuality, laziness, gluttony—all the pleasures and faults of the body. Tripitaka is by no means a perfect, ideal character; he is fearful, foolish, selfish, and fallible, a series of traits that often lands him in hot water with demons who want to eat his flesh and thus gain immortality. He represents the average person. A third companion, Sandy, is a rather ill-defined representation of earnestness. A white horse who had been a dragon prince also aids Tripitaka on his journey. The first part of the book deals almost exclusively with Monkey, his origin, his acquisition of Daoist magic, and his wild adventures, and culminates with his epic battle with the forces of Heaven and his subjugation by the Buddha. He is imprisoned in a mountain for five hundred years and is released at last to use his considerable powers in the service of the Buddha, who wants to bring previously unknown texts of Mahayana Buddhism to China. The majority of the book (chapters 13 to 97) deals with the journey itself, and the book ends with the voyagers having an audience with the Buddha, returning to China with the scriptures, and achieving their final apotheosis. The novel's mixing of high seriousness and farce, adventure and mysticism has made it among the most popular of the traditional Chinese novels, while the apt dialogue, vernacular prose, and around seven hundred cleanly integrated poems make it a stylistic and narrative tour de force.

**FURTHER READING:** Waley, Arthur, tr. *Monkey,* 1942; *The Real Tripitaka and Other Pieces,* 1952. Yu, Anthony C., tr. *Journey to the West,* 4 vols., 1977–1983.

## *from* **Monkey**

## Chapter I

There was a rock that since the creation of the world had been worked upon by the pure essences of Heaven and the fine savours of Earth, the vigour of sunshine and the grace of moonlight, till at last it became magically pregnant and one day split open, giving birth to a stone egg, about as big as a playing ball. Fructified by the wind it developed into a stone monkey, complete with every organ and limb. At once this monkey learned to climb and run; but its first act was to make a bow towards each of the four quarters. As it did so, a steely light darted from this monkey's eyes and flashed as far as the Palace of the Pole Star. This shaft of light astonished the Jade Emperor as he sat in the Cloud Palace of the Golden Gates, in the Treasure Hall of the Holy Mists, surrounded by his fairy Ministers. Seeing this strange light flashing, he ordered Thousand-league Eye and Down-the-wind Ears to open the gate of the Southern Heaven and look out. At his bidding these two captains went out to the gate and looked so sharply and listened so well that presently they were able to report, 'This steely light comes from the borders of the small country of Ao-lai, that lies to the east of the Holy Continent, from the Mountain of Flowers and Fruit. On this mountain is a magic rock, which gave birth to an egg. This egg changed into a stone monkey, and when he made his bow to the four quarters a steely light flashed from his eyes with a beam that reached the Palace of the Pole Star. But now he is taking a drink, and the light is growing dim.'

The Jade Emperor condescended to take an indulgent view. 'These creatures in the world below,' he said, 'were compounded of the essence of heaven and earth, and nothing that goes on there should surprise us.' That monkey walked, ran, leapt and bounded over the hills, feeding on grasses and shrubs, drinking from streams and springs, gathering the mountain flowers, looking for fruits. Wolf, panther and tiger were his companions, the deer and civet were his friends, gibbons and baboons his kindred. At night he lodged under cliffs of rock, by day he wandered among the peaks and caves. One very hot morning, after playing in the shade of some pine-trees, he and the other monkeys went to bathe in a mountain stream. See how those waters bounce and tumble like rolling melons!

There is an old saying, 'Birds have their bird language, beasts have their beast talk.' The monkeys said, 'We none of us know where this stream comes from. As we have nothing to do this morning, wouldn't it be fun to follow it up to its source?' With a whoop of joy, dragging their sons and carrying their daughters, calling out to younger brother and to elder brother, the whole troupe rushed along the streamside and scrambled up the steep places, till they reached the source of the stream. They found themselves standing before the curtain of a great waterfall.

All the monkeys clapped their hands and cried aloud, 'Lovely water, lovely water! To think that it starts far off in some cavern below the base of the mountain, and flows all the way to the Great Sea! If any of us were bold enough to pierce that curtain, get to where the water comes from and return unharmed, we would make him our king!' Three times the call went out, when suddenly one of them leapt from among the throng and answered the challenge in a loud voice. It was the Stone Monkey. 'I will go,' he cried, 'I will go!' Look at him! He screws up his eyes and crouches; then at one bound he jumps straight through the waterfall. When he opened his eyes and looked about him, he found that where he had landed there was no water. A great bridge stretched in front of him, shining and glinting. When he looked closely at it, he saw that it was made all of burnished iron. The water under it flowed through a hole in the rock, filling in all the space under the arch. Monkey climbed up on to the bridge and, spying as he went, saw something that looked just like a house. There were stone seats and stone couches, and tables with stone bowls and cups. He skipped back to the hump of the bridge and saw that on the cliff there was an inscription in large square writing which said, 'This cave of the Water Curtain in the blessed land of the Mountain of Flowers and Fruit leads to Heaven.' Monkey was beside himself with delight. He rushed back and again crouched, shut his eyes and jumped through the curtain of water.

'A great stroke of luck,' he cried, 'A great stroke of luck!' 'What is it like on the other side?' asked the monkeys, crowding round him. 'Is the water very deep?' 'There is no water,' said the Stone Monkey. 'There is an iron bridge, and at the side of it a heaven-sent place to live in.' 'What made you think it would do to live in?' asked the monkeys. 'The water,' said the Stone Monkey, 'flows out of a hole in the rock, filling in the space under the bridge. At the side of the bridge are flowers and trees, and there is a chamber of stone. Inside are stone tables, stone cups, stone dishes, stone couches, stone seats. We could really be very comfortable there. There is plenty of room for hundreds and thousands of us, young and old. Let us all go and live there; we shall be splendidly sheltered in every weather.' 'You go first and show us how!' cried the monkeys, in great delight. Once more he closed his eyes and was through at one bound. 'Come along, all of you!' he cried. The bolder of them jumped at once; the more timid stretched out their heads and then drew them back, scratched their ears, rubbed their cheeks, and then with a great shout the whole mob leapt forward. Soon they were all seizing dishes and snatching cups, scrambling to the hearth or fighting for the beds, dragging things along or shifting them about, behaving indeed as monkeys with their mischievous nature might be expected to do, never quiet for an instant, till at last they were thoroughly worn out. The Stone Monkey took his seat at the head of them and said, 'Gentlemen! "With one whose word cannot be trusted there is nothing to be done!"[1] You promised that any of us who managed to get through the waterfall and back again, should be your king. I have not only come and gone and come again, but also found you a comfortable place to sleep, put you in the enviable position of being householders. Why do you not bow down to me as your king?'

Thus reminded, the monkeys all pressed together the palms of their hands and prostrated themselves, drawn up in a line according to age and standing, and bowing humbly they cried, 'Great king, a thousand years!' After this the Stone Monkey discarded his old name and became king, with the title 'Handsome Monkey King.' He appointed various monkeys, gibbons and baboons to be his ministers and officers. By day they wandered about the Mountain of Flowers and Fruit; at night they slept in the Cave of the Water Curtain. They lived in perfect sympathy and accord, not mingling with bird or beast, in perfect independence and entire happiness.

The Monkey King had enjoyed this artless existence for several hundred years when one day, at a feast in which all the monkeys took part, the king suddenly felt very sad and burst into tears. His subjects at once ranged themselves in front of him and bowed down, saying, 'Why is your Majesty so sad?' 'At present,' said the king, 'I have no cause for unhappiness. But I have a misgiving about the future, which troubles me sorely.' 'Your Majesty is very hard to please,' said the monkeys, laughing. 'Every day we have happy meetings on fairy mountains, in blessed spots, in ancient caves, on holy islands. We are not subject to the Unicorn or Phoenix, nor to the restraints of any human king. Such freedom is an immeasur-

---

1. *Analects* of Confucius, II. 22.

able blessing. What can it be that causes you this sad misgiving?' 'It is true,' said the Monkey King, 'that to-day I am not answerable to the law of any human king, nor need I fear the menace of any beast or bird. But the time will come when I shall grow old and weak. Yama, King of Death, is secretly waiting to destroy me. Is there no way by which, instead of being born again on earth, I might live forever among the people of the sky?'

When the monkeys heard this they covered their faces with their hands and wept, each thinking of his own mortality. But look! From among the ranks there springs out one monkey commoner, who cries in a loud voice 'If that is what troubles your Majesty, it shows that religion has taken hold upon your heart. There are indeed, among all creatures, three kinds that are not subject to Yama, King of Death.' 'And do you know which they are?' asked the Monkey King. 'Buddhas, Immortals and Sages,' he said. 'These three are exempt from the Turning of the Wheel, from birth and destruction. They are eternal as Heaven and Earth, as the hills and streams.' 'Where are they to be found?' asked the Monkey King. 'Here on the common earth,' said the monkey, 'in ancient caves among enchanted hills.'

The king was delighted with this news. 'To-morrow,' he said, 'I shall say good-bye to you, go down the mountain, wander like a cloud to the corners of the sea, far away to the end of the world, till I have found these three kinds of Immortal. From them I will learn how to be young forever and escape the doom of death.' This determination it was that led him to leap clear of the toils of Re-incarnation and turned him at last into the Great Monkey Sage, equal of Heaven. The monkeys clapped their hands and cried aloud, 'Splendid! Splendid! To-morrow we will scour the hills for fruits and berries and hold a great farewell banquet in honour of our king.'

Next day they duly went to gather peaches and rare fruits, mountain herbs, yellow-sperm, tubers, orchids, strange plants and flowers of every sort, and set out the stone tables and benches, laid out fairy meats and drinks. They put the Monkey King at the head of the table, and ranged themselves according to their age and rank. The pledge-cup passed from hand to hand; they made their offerings to him of flowers and fruit. All day long they drank, and next day their king rose early and said, 'Little ones, cut some pine-wood for me and make me a raft; then find a tall bamboo for pole, and put together a few fruits and such like. I am going to start.' He got on to the raft all alone and pushed off with all his might, speeding away and away, straight out to sea, till favoured by a following wind he arrived at the borders of the Southern World. Fate indeed had favoured him; for days on end, ever since he set foot on the raft, a strong southeast wind blew and carried him at last to the north-western bank, which is indeed the frontier of the Southern World. He tested the water with his pole and found that it was shallow; so he left the raft and climbed ashore. On the beach were people fishing, shooting wild geese, scooping oysters, draining salt. He ran up to them and for fun began to perform queer antics which frightened them so much that they dropped their baskets and nets and ran for their lives. One of them, who stood his ground, Monkey caught hold of, and ripping off his clothes, found out how to wear them himself, and so dressed up went prancing through towns and cities, in market and bazaar, imitating the people's manners and talk. All the while his heart was set only on finding the Immortals and learning from them the secret of eternal youth. But he found the men of the world all engrossed in the quest of profit or fame; there was not one who had any care for the end that was in store for him. So Monkey went looking for the way of Immortality, but found no chance of meeting it. For eight or nine years he went from city to city and town to town till suddenly he came to the Western Ocean. He was sure that beyond this ocean there would certainly be Immortals, and he made for himself a raft like the one he had before. He floated on over the Western Ocean till he came to the Western Continent, where he went ashore, and when he had looked about for some time, he suddenly saw a very high and beautiful mountain, thickly wooded at the base. He had no fear of wolves, tigers or panthers, and made his way up to the very top. He was looking about him when he suddenly heard a man's voice coming from deep amid the woods. He hurried towards the spot and listened intently. It was someone singing, and these were the words that he caught:

I hatch no plot, I scheme no scheme;
Fame and shame are one to me,
A simple life prolongs my days.
Those I meet upon my way
Are Immortals, one and all,
Who from their quiet seats expound
The Scriptures of the Yellow Court.

When Monkey heard these words he was very pleased. 'There must then be Immortals somewhere hereabouts,' he said. He sprang deep into the forest and looking carefully saw that the singer was a woodman, who was cutting brushwood. 'Reverend Immortal,' said Monkey, coming forward, 'your disciple raises his hands.' The woodman was so astonished that he dropped his axe. 'You have made a mistake,' he said, turning and answering the salutation, 'I am only a shabby, hungry woodcutter. What makes you address me as an "Immortal"?' 'If you are not an Immortal,' said Monkey, 'why did you talk of yourself as though you were one?' 'What did I say,' asked the woodcutter, 'that sounded as though I were an Immortal?' 'When I came to the edge of the wood,' said Monkey, 'I heard you singing "Those I meet upon my way are Immortals, one and all, who from their quiet seats expound the Scriptures of the Yellow Court." Those scriptures are secret, Taoist texts. What can you be but an Immortal?' 'I won't deceive you,' said the woodcutter. 'That song was indeed taught to me by an Immortal, who lives not very far from my hut. He saw that I have to work hard for my living and have a lot of troubles; so he told me when I was worried by anything to say to myself the words of that song. This, he said, would comfort me and get me out of my difficulties. Just now I was upset about something and so I was singing that song. I had no idea that you were listening.'

'If the Immortal lives close by,' said Monkey, 'how is it that you have not become his disciple? Wouldn't it have been as well to learn from him how never to grow old?' 'I have a hard life of it,' said the woodcutter. 'When I was eight or nine I lost my father. I had no brothers and sisters, and it fell upon me alone to support my widowed mother. There was nothing for it but to work hard early and late. Now my mother is old and I dare not leave her. The garden is neglected, we have not enough either to eat or wear. The most I can do is to cut two bundles of firewood, carry them to market and with the penny or two that I get buy a few handfuls of rice which I cook myself and serve to my aged mother. I have no time to go and learn magic.' 'From what you tell me,' said Monkey, 'I can see that you are a good and devoted son, and your piety will certainly be rewarded. All I ask of you is that you will show me where the Immortal lives; for I should very much like to visit him.'

'It is quite close,' said the woodcutter. 'This mountain is called the Holy Terrace Mountain, and on it is a cave called the Cave of the Slanting Moon and Three Stars. In that cave lives an Immortal called the Patriarch Subodhi. In his time he has had innumerable disciples, and at this moment there are some thirty or forty of them studying with him. You have only to follow that small path southwards for eight or nine leagues,[2] and you will come to his home.' 'Honoured brother,' said Monkey, drawing the woodcutter towards him, 'come with me, and if I profit by the visit I will not forget that you guided me.' 'It takes a lot to make some people understand,' said the woodcutter. 'I've just been telling you why I can't go. If I went with you, what would become of my work? Who would give my old mother her food? I must go on cutting my wood, and you must find your way alone.'

When Monkey heard this, he saw nothing for it but to say goodbye. He left the wood, found the path, went uphill for some seven or eight leagues and sure enough found a cave-dwelling. But the door was locked. All was quiet, and there was no sign of anyone being about. Suddenly he turned his head and saw on top of the cliff a stone slab about thirty feet high and eight feet wide. On it was an inscription in large letters saying, 'Cave of the Slanting Moon and Three Stars on the Mountain of the Holy Terrace.' 'People here,' said Monkey, 'are certainly very truthful. There really is such a mountain, and such a cave!' He looked about for a while, but did not venture to knock at the door. Instead he jumped up into a pine-tree and began eating the pine-seed and playing among the branches. After a time he heard someone call; the door of the cave opened and a fairy

---

2. A league was 360 steps.

boy of great beauty came out, in appearance utterly unlike the common lads that he had seen till now. The boy shouted, 'Who is making a disturbance out there?' Monkey leapt down from his tree, and coming forward said with a bow, 'Fairy boy, I am a pupil who has come to study Immortality. I should not dream of making a disturbance.' '*You* a pupil!' said the boy laughing. 'To be sure,' said Monkey. 'My master is lecturing,' said the boy. 'But before he gave out his theme he told me to go to the door and if anyone came asking for instruction, I was to look after him. I suppose he meant you.' 'Of course he meant me,' said Monkey. 'Follow me this way,' said the boy. Monkey tidied himself and followed the boy into the cave. Huge chambers opened out before them, they went on from room to room, through lofty halls and innumerable cloisters and retreats, till they came to a platform of green jade, upon which was seated the Patriarch Subodhi, with thirty lesser Immortals assembled before him. Monkey at once prostrated himself and bumped his head three times upon the ground, murmuring, 'Master, master! As pupil to teacher I pay you my humble respects.' 'Where do you come from?' asked the Patriarch. 'First tell me your country and name, and then pay your respects again.' 'I am from the Water Curtain Cave,' said Monkey, 'on the Mountain of Fruit and Flowers in the country of Ao-lai.' 'Go away!' shouted the Patriarch. 'I know the people there. They're a tricky, humbugging set. It's no good one of them supposing he's going to achieve Enlightenment.' Monkey, kowtowing violently, hastened to say, 'There's no trickery about this; it's just the plain truth I'm telling you.' 'If you claim that you're telling the truth,' said the Patriarch, 'how is it that you say you came from Ao-lai? Between there and here there are two oceans and the whole of the Southern Continent. How did you get here?' 'I floated over the oceans and wandered over the lands for ten years and more,' said Monkey, 'till at last I reached here.' 'Oh well,' said the Patriarch, 'I suppose if you came by easy stages, it's not altogether impossible. But tell me, what is your *hsing*?[3] 'I never show *hsing*,' said Monkey. 'If I am abused, I am not at all annoyed. If I am hit, I am not angry; but on the contrary, twice more polite than before. All my life I have never shown hsing.'

'I don't mean that kind of hsing,' said the Patriarch. 'I mean what was your family, what surname had they?' 'I had no family,' said Monkey, 'neither father nor mother.' 'Oh indeed!' said the Patriarch. 'Perhaps you grew on a tree!' 'Not exactly,' said Monkey. 'I came out of a stone. There was a magic stone on the Mountain of Flowers and Fruit. When its time came, it burst open and I came out.'

'We shall have to see about giving you a school-name,' said the Patriarch. 'We have twelve words that we use in these names, according to the grade of the pupil. You are in the tenth grade.' 'What are the twelve words?' asked Monkey. 'They are Wide, Big, Wise, Clever, True, Conforming, Nature, Ocean, Lively, Aware, Perfect and Illumined. As you belong

---

3. There is a pun on *hsing*, 'surname' and *hsing*, 'temper.'

to the tenth grade, the word Aware must come in your name. How about Aware-of-Vacuity?' 'Splendid!' said Monkey, laughing. 'From now onwards let me be called Aware-of-Vacuity.'

So that was his name in religion. And if you do not know whether in the end, equipped with this name, he managed to obtain enlightenment or not, listen while it is explained to you in the next chapter.

# Chapter II

Monkey was so pleased with his new name that he skipped up and down in front of the Patriarch, bowing to express his gratitude. Subodhi then ordered his pupils to take Monkey to the outer rooms and teach him how to sprinkle and dust, answer properly when spoken to, how to come in, go out, and go round. Then he bowed to his fellow-pupils and went out into the corridor, where he made himself a sleeping place. Early next morning he and the others practised the correct mode of speech and bearing, studied the Scriptures, discussed doctrine, practised writing, burnt incense. And in this same way he passed day after day, spending his leisure in sweeping the floor, hoeing the garden, growing flowers and tending trees, getting firewood and lighting the fire, drawing water and carrying it in buckets. Everything he needed was provided for him. And so he lived in the cave, while time slipped by, for six or seven years. One day the Patriarch, seated in state, summoned all his pupils and began a lecture on the Great Way. Monkey was so delighted by what he heard that he tweaked his ears and rubbed his cheeks; his brow flowered and his eyes laughed. He could not stop his hands from dancing, his feet from stamping. Suddenly the Patriarch caught sight of him and shouted, 'What is the use of your being here if, instead of listening to my lecture, you jump and dance like a maniac?' 'I am listening with all my might,' said Monkey. 'But you were saying such wonderful things that I could not contain myself for joy. That is why I may, for all I know, have been hopping and jumping. Don't be angry with me.' 'So you recognize the profundity of what I am saying?' said the Patriarch. 'How long, pray, have you been in the cave?' 'It may seem rather silly,' said Monkey, 'but really I don't know how long. All I can remember is that when I was sent to get firewood, I went up the mountain behind the cave, and there I found a whole slope covered with peach-trees. I have eaten my fill of those peaches seven times.' 'It is called the Hill of Bright Peach Blossom,' said the Patriarch. 'If you have eaten there seven times, I suppose you have been here seven years. What sort of wisdom are you now hoping to learn from me?' 'I leave that to you,' said Monkey. 'Any sort of wisdom—it's all one to me.'

'There are three hundred and sixty schools of wisdom,' said the Patriarch, 'and all of them lead to Self-attainment. Which school do you want to study?' 'Just as you think best,' said Monkey. 'I am all attention.' 'Well, how about Art?' said the Patriarch. 'Would you like me to teach you that?' 'What sort of wisdom is that?' asked Monkey. 'You would be able to summon fairies and ride the Phoenix,' said the Patriarch, 'divine by shuffling the yarrow-stalks and know how to avoid disaster and pursue good fortune.' 'But should I live forever?' asked Monkey. 'Certainly not,' said the Patriarch. 'Then that's no good to me,' said Monkey. 'How about natural philosophy?' said the Patriarch. 'What is that about?' asked Monkey. 'It means the teaching of Confucius,' said the Patriarch, 'and of Buddha and Lao Tzu, of the Dualists and Mo Tzu and the Doctors of Medicine; reading scriptures, saying prayers, learning how to have adepts and sages at your beck and call.' 'But should I live forever?' asked Monkey. 'If that's what you are thinking about,' said the Patriarch, 'I am afraid philosophy is no better than a prop in the wall.' 'Master,' said Monkey, 'I am a plain, simple man, and I don't understand that sort of patter. What do you mean by a prop in the wall?' 'When men are building a room,' said the Patriarch, 'and want it to stand firm, they put a pillar to prop up the walls. But one day the roof falls in and the pillar rots.' 'That doesn't sound much like long life,' said Monkey. 'I'm not going to learn philosophy!' 'How about Quietism?' asked the Patriarch. 'What does that consist of?' asked Monkey. 'Low diet,' said the Patriarch, 'inactivity, meditation, restraint of word and deed, yoga practised prostrate or standing.' 'But should I live forever?' asked Monkey. 'The results of Quietism,' said the Patriarch, 'are no better than unbaked clay in the kiln.' 'You've got a very poor memory,' said Monkey. 'Didn't I tell you just now that I don't understand that sort of patter? What do you mean by unbaked clay in the kiln?' 'The bricks and tiles,' said the Patriarch, 'may be waiting, all shaped and ready, in the kiln; but if they have not yet been fired, there will come a day when heavy rain falls and they are washed away.' 'That does not promise well for the future,' said Monkey. 'I don't think I'll bother about Quietism.'

'You might try exercises,' said the Patriarch. 'What do you mean by that,' asked Monkey. 'Various forms of activity,' said the Patriarch, 'such as the exercises called "Gathering the Yin and patching the Yang," "Drawing the Bow and Treading the Catapult," "Rubbing the Navel to pass breath." Then there are alchemical practices such as the Magical Explosion, Burning the Reeds and Striking the Tripod, Promoting Red Lead, Melting the Autumn Stone, and Drinking Bride's Milk.' 'Would these make me live forever?' asked Monkey. 'To hope for that,' said the Patriarch, 'would be like trying to fish the moon out of the water.' 'There you go again!' said Monkey. 'What pray do you mean by fishing the moon out of the water?' 'When the moon is in the sky,' said the Patriarch, 'it is reflected in the water. It looks just like a real thing, but if you try to catch hold of it, you find it is only an illusion.' 'That does not sound much good,' said Monkey; 'I shan't learn exercises.' 'Tut!' cried the Patriarch, and coming down from the platform, he caught hold of the knuckle-rapper and pointed it at Monkey, saying, 'You wretched simian! You won't learn this and you won't learn that ! I should like to know what it is you do want.' And so saying he struck Monkey over the head three times. Then he folded his hands behind his back and strode off into the inner room, dismissing his audience and locking the door behind him. The pupils all turned indignantly upon Monkey. 'You villainous ape,' they shouted at him, 'do you think that is the way to behave? The Master offers to teach you, and instead of accepting thankfully, you begin arguing with him. Now he's thoroughly offended and goodness knows when he'll come back.' They were all very angry and poured abuse on him; but Monkey was not in the least upset, and merely replied by a broad grin. The truth of the matter was, he understood the language of secret signs. That was why he did not take up the quarrel or attempt to argue. He knew that the Master, by striking him three times, was giving him an appointment at the third watch; and by going off with his hands folded behind his back, meant that Monkey was to look for him in the inner apartments. The locking of the door meant that he was to come round by the back door and would then receive instruction.

The rest of the day he frolicked with the other pupils in front of the cave, impatiently awaiting the night. As soon as dusk came, like the others, he went to his sleeping place. He closed his eyes and pretended to be asleep, breathing softly and regularly. In the mountains there is no watchman to beat the watches or call the hours. The best Monkey could do was to count his incoming and outgoing breaths. When he reckoned that it must be about the hour of the Rat (11 p.m.–1 a.m.) he got up very quietly and slipped on his clothes, softly opened the front door, left his companions and went round to the back door. Sure enough, it was only half shut. 'The Master certainly means to give me instruction,' said Monkey to himself. 'That is why he left the door open.' So he crept in and went straight to the Master's bed. Finding him curled up and lying with his face to the wall, Monkey dared not wake him, and knelt down beside the bed. Presently the Patriarch woke, stretched out his legs and murmured to himself:

> Hard, very hard!
> The Way is most secret.
> Never handle the Golden Elixir as though it were a mere toy!
> He who to unworthy ears entrusts the dark truths
> To no purpose works his jaws and talks his tongue dry.

'Master, I've been kneeling here for some time,' said Monkey, when he saw the Patriarch was awake. 'You wretched Monkey,' said Subodhi, who on recognizing his voice pulled off the bed-clothes and sat up. 'Why aren't you asleep in your own quarters, instead of coming round behind to mine?' 'At the lecture to-day,' said Monkey, 'you ordered me to come for instruction at the third watch, by way of the back gate. That is why I ventured to come straight to your bed.' The Patriarch was delighted. He thought to himself 'This fellow must really be, as he says, a natural product of Heaven and Earth. Otherwise he would never have understood my secret signs.' 'We are alone together,' said Monkey, 'there is no one to overhear us. Take pity upon me and teach me the way of Long Life. I shall never forget your kindness.' 'You show a disposition,' said the Patriarch. 'You understood my secret signs. Come close and listen carefully. I am going to reveal to you the Secret of Long Life.' Monkey beat his head on the floor to show his gratitude, washed his ears and attended closely, kneeling beside the bed. The Patriarch then recited:

> To spare and tend the vital powers, this and nothing else
> Is sum and total of all magic, secret and profane.
> All is comprised in these three, Spirit, Breath and Soul;
> Guard them closely, screen them well; let there be no leak.
> Store them within the frame;
> That is all that can be learnt, and all that can be taught.
> I would have you mark the tortoise and snake, locked in tight
>     embrace.
> Locked in tight embrace, the vital powers are strong;
> Even in the midst of fierce flames the Golden Lotus may be planted,
> The Five Elements compounded and transposed, and put to new use.
> When that is done, be which you please, Buddha or Immortal.

By these words Monkey's whole nature was shaken to the foundations. He carefully committed them to memory; then humbly thanked the Patriarch, and went out again by the back door.

A pale light was just coming into the eastern sky. He retraced his steps, softly opened the front door and returned to his sleeping place, purposely making a rustling noise with his bed-clothes. 'Get up!' he cried. 'There is light in the sky.' His fellow pupils were fast asleep, and had no idea that Monkey had received Illumination.

Time passed swiftly, and three years later the Patriarch again mounted his jewelled seat and preached to his assembled followers. His subject was the parables and scholastic problems of the Zen Sect, and his theme, the tegument of outer appearances. Suddenly he broke off and asked, 'Where is the disciple Aware-of-Vacuity?' Monkey knelt down before him and answered 'Here!' 'What have you been studying all this time?' asked the Patriarch. 'Recently,' said Monkey, 'my spiritual nature has been very much in the ascendant, and my fundamental sources of power are gradually strengthening.' 'In that case,' said the Patriarch, 'all you need learn is how to ward off the Three Calamities.' 'There must be some mistake,' said Monkey in dismay. 'I understood that the secrets I have learnt would make me live forever and protect me from fire, water and every kind of disease. What is this about three calamities?' 'What you have learnt,' said the Patriarch, 'will preserve your youthful appearance and increase the length of your life; but after five hundred years Heaven will send down lightning which will finish you off, unless you have the sagacity to avoid it. After another five hundred years Heaven will send down a fire that will devour you. This fire is of a peculiar kind. It is neither common fire, nor celestial fire, but springs up from within and consumes the vitals, reducing the whole frame to ashes, and making a vanity of all your thousand years of self-perfection. But even should you escape this, in another five hundred years, a wind will come and blow upon you. Not the east wind, the south wind, the west wind or the north wind; not flower wind, or willow wind, pine wind or bamboo wind. It blows from below, enters the bowels, passes the midriff and issues at the Nine Apertures. It melts bone and flesh, so that the whole body dissolves. These three calamities you must be able to avoid.' When Monkey heard this, his hair stood on end, and prostrating himself he said, 'I beseech you, have pity upon me, and teach me how to avoid these calamities. I shall never forget your kindness.' 'There would be no difficulty about that,' said the Patriarch, 'if it were not for your peculiarities.' 'I have a round head sticking up to Heaven and square feet treading Earth,' said Monkey. 'I have nine apertures, four limbs, five upper and six lower internal organs, just like other people.' 'You are like other men in most respects,' said the Patriarch, 'but you have much less jowl.' For monkeys have hollow cheeks and pointed nozzles. Monkey felt his face with his hand and laughed saying, 'Master, I have my debits, but don't forget my assets. I have my pouch, and that must be credited to my account, as something that ordinary humans haven't got.' 'True enough,' said the Patriarch. 'There are two methods of escape. Which would you like to learn? There is the trick of the Heavenly Ladle, which involves thirty-six kinds of transformation, and the trick of the Earthly Conclusion, which involves seventy-two kinds of transformation.' 'Seventy-two sounds better value,' said Monkey. 'Come here then,' said the Patriarch, 'and I will teach you the formula.' He then whispered a magic formula into Monkey's ear. That Monkey King was uncommonly quick at taking things in. He at once began practising the formula, and after a little self-discipline he mastered all the seventy-two transformations, whole and complete. One day when master and disciples were in front of the cave, admiring the evening view, the Patriarch said, 'Monkey, how is that business going?' 'Thanks to your kindness,' said Monkey, 'I have been extremely successful. In addition to the transformations I can already fly.' 'Let's see you do it,' said the Patriarch. Monkey put his feet together, leapt about sixty feet into the air, and riding the clouds for a few minutes dropped in front of the Patriarch. He did not get more than three leagues in the whole of his flight. 'Master,' he said, 'that surely is cloud-soaring?' 'I should be more inclined to call it cloud-crawling,' said the Patriarch laughing. 'The old saying runs, "An Immortal wanders in the morning to the Northern Sea, and the same evening he is in Ts'ang-wu." To take as long as you did to go a mere league or two hardly counts even as cloud-crawling.' 'What is meant by that saying about the Northern Sea and Ts'ang-wu?' asked Monkey. 'A real cloud-soarer,' said the Patriarch, 'can start early in the morning from the Northern Sea, cross the Eastern Sea, the Western Sea and the Southern Sea, and land again at Ts'ang-wu. Ts'ang-wu means Ling-ling, in the Northern Sea. To do the round of all four seas in one day is true cloud-soaring.' 'It sounds very difficult,' said Monkey. 'Nothing in the world is difficult,' said the Patriarch, 'it is only our own thoughts that make things seem so.' 'Master,' said Monkey, prostrating himself, 'You may as well make a good job of me. While you're about it, do me a real kindness and teach me the art of cloud-soaring. I shall never forget how much I owe to you.' 'When the Immortals go cloud-soaring,' said the Patriarch, 'they sit cross-legged and rise straight from that position. You do nothing of the kind. I saw you just now put your feet together and jump. I must really take this opportunity of teaching you how to do it properly. You shall learn the Cloud Trapeze.' He then taught him the magic formula, saying, 'Make the pass, recite the spell, clench your fists, and one leap will carry you head over heels a hundred and eight thousand leagues.'

When the other pupils heard this, they all tittered, saying, 'Monkey is in luck. If he learns this trick, he will be able to carry dispatches, deliver letters, take round circulars—one way or another he will always be able to pick up a living!'

It was now late. Master and pupils all went to their quarters; but Monkey spent all night practising the Cloud Trapeze, and by the time day came he had completely mastered it, and could wander through space where he would.

One summer day when the disciples had for some time been studying their tasks under a pine-tree, one of them said, 'Monkey, what can you have done in a former incarnation to merit that the Master should the other day have whispered in your ear the secret formula for avoiding the Three Calamities? Have you mastered all those transformations?' 'To tell you the truth,' said Monkey, 'although of course I am much indebted to the Master for his instruction, I have also been working very hard day and night on my own, and I can now do them all.' 'Wouldn't this be a good opportunity,' said one of the pupils, 'to give us a little demonstration?' When Monkey heard this, he was all on his mettle to display his powers. 'Give me my subject,' he said. 'What am I to change into.' 'How about a pine-tree?' they said. He made a magic pass, recited a spell, shook himself, and changed into a pine-tree.

The disciples clapped and burst into loud applause. 'Bravo, Monkey, bravo,' they cried. There was such a din that the Patriarch came running out with his staff trailing after him. 'Who's making all this noise?' he asked. The disciples at once controlled themselves, smoothed down their dresses and came meekly forward. Monkey changed himself back into his true form and slipped in among the crowd, saying, 'Reverend Master, we are doing our lessons out here. I assure you there was no noise in particular.' 'You were all bawling,' said the Patriarch angrily. 'It didn't sound in the least like people studying. I want to know what you were doing here, shouting and laughing.' 'To tell the truth,' said someone, 'Monkey was showing us a transformation just for fun. We told him to change into a pine-tree, and he did it so well that we were all applauding him. That was the noise you heard. I hope you will forgive us.' 'Go away, all of you!' the Patriarch shouted. 'And you, Monkey, come here! What were you doing, playing with your spiritual powers, turning into—what was it? A pine-tree? Did you think I taught you in order that you might show off in front of other people? If you saw someone else turn into a tree, wouldn't you at once ask how it was done? If others see you doing it, aren't they certain to ask you? If you are frightened to refuse, you will give the secret away; and if you refuse, you're very likely to be roughly handled. You're putting yourself in grave danger.' 'I'm terribly sorry,' said Monkey. 'I won't punish you,' said the Patriarch, 'but you can't stay here.' Monkey burst into tears. 'Where am I to go to?' he asked. 'Back to where you came from, I should suppose,' said the Patriarch. 'You don't mean back to the Cave of the Water Curtain in Ao-lai!' said Monkey. 'Yes,' said the Patriarch, 'go back as quickly as you can, if you value your life. One thing is certain in any case; you can't stay here.' 'May I point out,' said Monkey, 'that I have been away from home for twenty years and should be very glad to see my monkey-subjects once more. But I can't consent to go till I have repaid you for all your kindness.' 'I have no desire to be repaid,' said the Patriarch. 'All I ask is that if you get into trouble, you should keep my name out of it.' Monkey saw that it was no use arguing. He bowed to the Patriarch, and took leave of his companions. 'Wherever you go,' said the Patriarch, 'I'm convinced you'll come to no good. So remember, when you get into trouble, I absolutely forbid you to say that you are my disciple. If you give a hint of any such thing I shall flay you alive, break all your bones, and banish your soul to the Place of Ninefold Darkness, where it will remain for ten thousand aeons.' 'I certainly won't venture to say a word about you,' promised Monkey. 'I'll say I found it all out for myself.' So saying he bade farewell, turned away, and making the magic pass rode off on his cloud trapeze, straight to the Eastern Sea. In a very little while he reached the Mountain of Flowers and Fruit, where he lowered his cloud, and was picking his way, when he heard a sound of cranes calling and monkeys crying. 'Little ones,' he shouted, 'I have come back.' At once from every cranny in the cliff, from bushes and trees, great monkeys and small leapt out with cries of 'Long live our king!' Then they all pressed round Monkey, kowtowing and saying, 'Great King, you're very absent-minded! Why did you go away for so long, leaving us all in the lurch, panting for your return, as a starving man for food and drink? For some time past a demon has been ill-using us. He has seized our cave, though we fought desperately, and now he has robbed us of all our possessions and carried off many of our children, so that we have to be on the watch all the time and get no sleep day or night. It's lucky you've come now, for if you had waited another year or two, you'd have found us and everything hereabouts in another's hands.' 'What demon can dare commit such crimes?' cried Monkey. 'Tell me all about it and I will avenge you.' 'Your majesty,' they said, 'he is called the Demon of Havoc, and he lives due north from here.' 'How far off?' asked Monkey. 'He comes like a cloud,' they said, 'and goes like a mist, like wind or rain, thunder or lightning. We do not know how far away he lives.' 'Well, don't worry,' said Monkey. 'Just go on playing around, while I go and look for him.' Dear Monkey King! He sprang into the sky straight northwards and soon saw in front of him a high and very rugged mountain. He was admiring the scenery, when he suddenly heard voices. Going a little way down the hill, he found a cave in front of which several small imps were jumping and dancing. When they saw Monkey, they ran away. 'Stop!' he called, 'I've got a message for you to take. Say that the master of the Water Curtain Cave is here. The Demon of Havoc, or whatever he is called, who lives here, has been ill-treating my little ones and I have come on purpose to settle matters with him.' They rushed into the cave and cried out, 'Great King, a terrible thing has happened!' 'What's the matter?' said the demon. 'Outside the cave,' they said, 'there is a monkey-headed creature who says he is the owner of the Water Curtain Cave. He says you have been ill-using his people and he has come on purpose to settle matters with you.' 'Ha, ha,' laughed the demon. 'I have often heard those monkeys say that their king had gone away to learn religion. This means that he's come back again. What does he look like and how is he armed?' 'He carries no weapon at all,' they said. 'He goes bare-headed, wears a red dress, with a yellow sash, and black shoes—neither priest nor layman nor quite like a Taoist. He's waiting naked-handed outside the gate.' 'Bring me my whole accoutrement,' cried the demon. The small imps at once fetched his arms. The demon put on his helmet and breast-plate, grasped his sword, and going to the gate with the little imps, cried in a loud voice, 'Where's the owner of the Water Curtain Cave?' 'What's the use of having such large eyes,' shouted Monkey, 'if you can't see old Monkey?' Catching sight of him the demon burst out laughing. 'You're not a foot high or as much as thirty years old. You have no weapon in your hand! How dare you strut about talking of settling accounts with me?' 'Cursed demon,' said Monkey. 'After all, you have no eyes in your head! You say I am small, not seeing that I can make myself as tall as I please. You say I am unarmed, not knowing that these two hands of mine could drag the moon from the ends of Heaven. Stand your ground, and eat old Monkey's fist!' So saying he leapt into the air and aimed a blow at the demon's face. The demon parried the blow with his hand. 'You such a pigmy and I so tall!' said the demon. 'You using your fists and I my sword—No! If I were to slay you with my sword I should make myself ridiculous. I am going to throw away my sword and use my naked fists.' 'Very good,' said Monkey. 'Now, my fine fellow, come on!' The demon relaxed his guard and struck. Monkey closed with him, and the two of them pommelled and kicked, blow for blow. A long reach is not so firm and sure as a short one. Monkey jabbed the demon in the lower ribs, pounded him in the chest, and gave him such a heavy drubbing that at last the demon stood back, and picking up his great flat sword, slashed at Monkey's head. But Monkey stepped swiftly aside, and the blow missed its mark. Seeing that the demon was becoming savage, Monkey now used the method called Body Outside the Body. He plucked out a handful of hairs, bit them into small pieces and then spat them out into the air, crying 'Change!' The fragments of hair changed into several hundred small monkeys, all pressing round in a throng. For you must know that when anyone becomes an Immortal, he can project his soul, change his shape and perform all kinds of miracles. Monkey, since his Illumination, could change every one of the eighty-four thousand hairs of his body into whatever he chose. The little monkeys he had now created were so nimble that no sword could touch them or spear wound them. See how they leap forward and jump back, crowd round the demon, some hugging, some pulling, some jabbing at his chest, some swarming up his legs. They kicked him, beat him, pommelled his eyes, pinched his nose, and while they were all at it, Monkey slipped up and snatched away the Demon's sword. Then pushing through the throng of small monkeys, he raised the sword and brought it down with such tremendous force upon the demon's skull, that he clove it in twain. He and the little monkeys then rushed into the cave and made a quick end of the imps, great and small. He then said a spell, which caused the small monkeys to change back into hairs. These he put back where they had come from; but there were still some small monkeys left—those that the Demon had carried off from the Cave of the Water Curtain. 'How did you get here?' he asked. There were about thirty or forty of them, and they all said with tears in their eyes, 'After your Majesty went away to become an Immortal, we were pestered by this creature for two years. In the end he carried us all off, and he stole all the fittings from our cave. He took all the stone dishes and the stone cups.' 'Collect everything that belongs to us and bring it with you,' said Monkey. They then set fire to the cave and burnt everything in it. 'Now follow me!' said Monkey. 'When we were brought here,' they said, 'we only felt a great wind rushing past, which whirled us to this place. We didn't know which way we were coming. So how are we to find the way home?' 'He brought you here by magic,' said Monkey. 'But what matter? I am now up to all that sort of thing, and if he could do it, I can. Shut your eyes, all of you, and don't be frightened.' He then recited a spell which produced a fierce wind. Suddenly it dropped, and Monkey shouted, 'You may look now!' The monkeys found that they were standing on firm ground quite close to their home. In high delight they all followed a familiar path back to the door of their cave. They and those who had been left behind all pressed into the cave, and lined up according to their ranks and age, and did homage to their king, and prepared a great banquet of welcome. When they asked how the demon had been subdued and the monkeys rescued, he told them the whole story; upon which they burst into shouts of applause. 'We little thought,' they said, 'that when your Majesty left us, you would learn such arts as this!' 'After I parted from you,' said Monkey, 'I went across many oceans to the land of Jambudvipa, where I learnt human ways, and how to wear clothes and shoes. I wandered restless as a cloud for eight or nine years, but nowhere could I find Enlightenment. At last after crossing yet another ocean, I was lucky enough to meet an old Patriarch who taught me the secret of eternal life.' 'What an incredible piece of luck!' the monkeys said, all congratulating him. 'Little ones,' said Monkey, 'I have another bit of good news for you. Your king has got a name-in-religion. I am called Aware-of-Vacuity.' They all clapped loudly, and presently went to get date-wine and grape-wine and fairy flowers and fruit, which they offered to Monkey. Everyone was in the highest spirits. If you do not know what the upshot was and how he fared now that he was back in his old home, you must listen to what is related in the next chapter.

# Qing Dynasty

### (1644–1911)

## ▦ Pu Songling (Pu Sung-ling) (1640–1715) (story)

### TRANSLATED BY YANG XIANYI AND GLADYS YANG

Pu Songling is the finest story writer of the early Qing dynasty. He came from what is today Shandong, was a failed scholar who was unable to pass the provincial examination, had a career as a personal secretary, and later became a tutor for a family of local gentry. He is best known for his collection of fantastic stories titled *Strange Stories from the Leisure Studio*, which consisted of folk stories and legends he culled from his extensive contact with the common people. He elaborated on and retold these stories, wrote many stories himself, and derived other tales in the collection from previous written sources. He is noted for his development of dialogue, a technique still nascent in earlier Chinese fiction, and is celebrated for the realism of his characters, in spite of the healthy dose of the supernatural that runs throughout the tales. Many of the stories deal with immortals, ghosts, fox spirits, transformations, supernatural love, and horror, but, despite his interest in the fantastic, many of his tales have serious social content.

**FURTHER READING:** Giles, Herbert A., tr. *Strange Stories from a Chinese Studio*, 1880. Lu, Yunzhong, et al., trs. *Strange Tales of Liaozhai*, 1988. Yang, Xianyi and Gladys Yang, eds. *Selected Tales of Liaozhai*, 1981.

## *The Cricket*

During the reign of Xuan De, cricket fights were popular at court and a levy of crickets was exacted every year. Now these insects were scarce in the province of Shaanxi, but the magistrate of Huayin—to get into the good books of the governor—presented a cricket which proved a remarkable fighter. So much so that his county was commanded to present crickets regularly and the magistrate ordered his bailiffs to produce them. Then young fellows in town began to keep good crickets and demand high prices for them, while the crafty bailiffs seized this chance to make money. Thus each cricket they collected was the ruin of several households.

Now in this town lived a scholar named Cheng Ming, who had failed repeatedly in the district examination. This slow-witted pedant was appointed beadle on the recommendation of the crooked bailiff and could not evade this service hard as he tried. In less than a year his small patrimony was exhausted. Then came another levy of crickets. Cheng dared not extort money from the country folk but neither could he pay the sum himself. At his wit's end, he longed to die.

"What good would dying do?" demanded his wife. "You had better go out and look for a cricket yourself. There is just one chance in ten thousand that you may catch one."

Cheng agreed. With a bamboo tube and wire cage he searched from dawn till dusk among ruins and waste land, peering under rocks and exploring crevices, leaving no stone unturned—but all in vain. The two or three crickets he caught were poor specimens which did not come up to standard. The magistrate set him a time limit and beat him when he failed, till in little more than ten days he had received some hundred strokes and his legs were so covered with sores that he could not continue his search. Tossing painfully on his bed, his one thought was to die.

Then to their village came a hump-backed diviner who could tell fortunes by consulting spirits. Cheng's wife, taking money, went to ask his advice. She found his gate thronged with pink, blooming girls and white-haired old women. Entering, she saw a curtain before the inner room, with incense on a table in front of it. Those come to ask their fortune burned incense in the tripod and kowtowed. The diviner prayed beside them, staring into space, but though his lips moved no one knew what it was he said and all listened respectfully. Finally a slip of paper was tossed from the inner room with the answer to the question asked—an answer which invariably proved correct.

Cheng's wife put her money on the table, burned incense and kowtowed like the other women. Presently the curtain moved and a piece of paper fluttered to the ground. Instead of writing it had a painting of a building like a temple with a small hill behind covered with rocks of every shape and overgrown with thorns. A cricket was crouching there while beside it a toad was making ready to spring. She had no idea what this meant, but the cricket at least had some connection with their problem. Accordingly she folded the paper and took it home to her husband.

Cheng wondered. "Is this supposed to show me where I should look for a cricket?"

On examining the picture closely, he recognized Great Buddha Monastery east of the village. So taking the paper with him, he struggled along with the help of a stick to the back of the monastery. There he found an old grave overgrown with brambles. Skirting this, he saw that the stones lying scattered around were exactly like the painting. He pricked up his ears and limped slowly through the brambles, but he might just as well have been looking for a needle or a grain of mustard-seed. Though he strained every nerve he found nothing. As he was groping around, a toad hopped into sight. Cheng gave a start and hurried after it. The toad slipped into the undergrowth and, following it, he saw a cricket at the root of a bramble. He snatched at it but the cricket leapt into a crevice in a rock and would not come out though he prodded it with a straw. Not till he poured water on it, did it emerge. It seemed a fine specimen and he picked it up. Seen close to it, it had a large body and long tail, dark neck and golden wings, and he was a happy man as he carried it home in the cage to delight his household, who considered it more precious than the rarest jade. The cricket was kept in a pot and fed upon white crab's flesh and the yellow kernel of chestnuts, tended with loving care till such time as the magistrate should ask for it.

Now Cheng had a son of nine, who uncovered this pot on the sly while his father was out. At once the cricket jumped out and sprang about so nimbly that he could not catch it. Finally the boy grabbed it, but in doing so tore off a leg and crushed it so that the next moment it died. The frightened child ran crying to his mother. When she heard what had happened she turned as pale as death.

"You wicked boy!" she cried. "You'll catch it when your father comes home!"

Her son went off in tears. Soon Cheng came back and when he heard his wife's story he felt as if he had been turned to ice. In a passion he searched for his son, who was nowhere to be found until at last they discovered his body in the well. Then anger turned to sorrow. Cheng cried out in anguish and longed to kill himself. Husband and wife sat with their faces to the wall in their thatched and smokeless cottage in silent despair. As the sun began to set he prepared to bury the boy, but upon touching the child found there was still breath in him. Overjoyed, he laid the small body on the couch and towards the middle of the night the child came round. Cheng and his wife began to breathe again, but their son remained in a trance with drooping eyelids. The sight of the empty cricket cage brought back Cheng's grief, but he dared not scold the child now. He did not close his eyes all night, and as the sun rose in the east he was still lying in stark despair when a cricket chirped outside the door. He rose in amazement to look, and sure enough there was a cricket. He clutched at it, but it chirped and hopped away. He put his hands over it but to no avail: when he turned up his palms the cricket escaped again. So he chased it up and down till it disappeared round the corner of the wall, and while searching for it he discovered another cricket on the wall. But this was a little, dark red insect, not to be compared with the first. Deciding that it was too small to be worth catching, Cheng looked round again for the one he had lost. At once the small cricket hopped from the wall to his sleeve, and he saw it resembled a mole-cricket with speckled wings, a square head and long legs—it might be a good one. So he was glad to keep it.

Cheng meant to present this cricket to the yamen, but fearing that it might not do he decided first to give it a trial fight. Now a young fellow in that village had a cricket called Crab Blue which had beaten every other insect it fought, and its owner wanted such an exorbitant price for it that it had remained on his hands. This man called on Cheng and laughed to see his cricket, producing his own for comparison. At the sight of this large, handsome insect, Cheng felt even more diffident and dared not offer a fight. The young man, however, insisted on a match; and since his poor cricket was useless in any case Cheng thought he might as well sacrifice it for a laugh. So the two combatants were put in one basin, where the small one crouched motionless as a stick of wood. The young man laughed heartily and prodded it with a pig's bristle, but still it made no move. At that he laughed louder and louder until at last the cricket was roused to fury. It hurled itself at its opponent, attacking savagely. In an instant it had leapt forward with bristling tail and seized the other by the neck. The horrified young man made haste to separate the two contestants, while the little cricket chirped proudly as if to announce its victory to its master. Cheng was glorying in this sight when a cock bore down on the cricket and pecked at it. Cheng gave a cry, rooted to the ground in horror; but luckily the cock missed the small cricket which leapt a foot or more away. The cock gave chase, the cricket was under its claws. Cheng, unable to intervene, stamped his foot and turned pale. But the next thing he knew the cock was flapping its wings and craning its neck—his cricket had fastened its teeth in the cock's comb. Amazed and exultant, he put the cricket back in its cage.

Later Cheng presented this cricket to the magistrate, who abused him angrily for producing one so small. Refusing to believe Cheng's account of the little creature's exploits, the magistrate pitted it against some other crickets and it defeated them all. He tried it with a cock, and again it turned out exactly as Cheng had said. Then the magistrate rewarded Cheng and presented this cricket to the governor, who put it in a golden cage and sent it joyfully to the emperor with a detailed report of its prowess.

In his palace the emperor tried the cricket with Butterfly, Praying Mantis, Yolita, Green Forehead and many other champions, but none was a match for it. And he prized it even more highly when he found that it would dance in time to music. In high good humour, he rewarded the governor with fine steeds and silk garments. And the governor, not forgetting where the cricket came from, within a short time commended the magistrate for outstanding merit. The magistrate, pleased in his turn, exempted Cheng from his duties and ordered the local examiner to see that he passed the next examination.

A year later Cheng's son was restored to his senses. He said, "I dreamed I was a cricket, a quick, good fighter. Now I have woken up."

The governor also rewarded Cheng so handsomely that within a few years he owned vast estates, whole streets of houses and countless flocks and herds. When he went abroad, his furs and carriage were more splendid than a noble's.

The recorder of these marvels comments: The emperor may do a thing once and forget it afterwards, but those who carry out his orders make this a general rule. Then when officials are greedy for profit and their underlings are bullies, men are driven to sell their wives and children. This shows that since each step an emperor takes is fraught with consequence for his subjects it behooves him to be very careful. This man Cheng, first impoverished by rapacious officials, grew so rich thanks to a cricket that he went about in magnificent carriages and furs. He could never have dreamed of such good fortune when he was a beadle and was being beaten! Because Heaven wished to reward an honest man, the governor and magistrate also benefited from the cricket. It is true, as the ancients said: "When a man becomes immortal and soars to heaven, his chickens and dog attain immortality too."

# ■ Yuan Mei (Yüan Mei) (1716–1798) (poems)

## TRANSLATED BY J. P. SEATON

Qing dynasty writer Yuan Mei was born to a wealthy family. He took the civil service examinations at an early age and was appointed to office at twenty-four. While in office at Jiangnan, he developed a plot of land into a gardened estate that was famed for its architecture and landscaping. He retired at forty and spent his remaining years in literary and artistic pursuits. In addition to poems, he wrote a collection of ghost stories titled *What the Sage Didn't Discuss* (a reference to Confucius' avoidance of the supernatural in his discourses) and a number of essays. His *Comments on Poetry from the Sui Garden* is a major compilation of poetry criticism. Though he often strikes a philosophical note, he is certainly one of the most personable of Chinese poets, not adverse to humor, sympathetic with the poor, bearing a strong resemblance to the Tang poet Bo Juyi.

**FURTHER READING:** Chaves, Jonathan. *The Columbia Book of Later Chinese Poetry: Yuan Ming and Ch'ing Dynasties (1279–1911),* 1986. Waley Arthur. *Yuan Mei: Eighteenth Century Chinese Poet,* 1956.

## *Four Zen Poems*

### 1. Just Done

A month alone behind closed doors:
forgotten books remembered, clear again.

Poems come, like water to the pool,
welling,
> up and out,
from perfect silence.

## 2. P'u-t'o Temple

A temple hidden, treasured
> in the mountain's cleft.
Pines, bamboo
> such a subtle flavor:
The ancient Buddha sits there, wordless,
The welling source speaks for him.

## 3. Motto

When I meet a monk
> I do bow politely.
When I see a Buddha
> I don't.
If I bow to a Buddha
> the Buddha won't know.
But I honor a monk:
> he's here now
> apparently, or, at least,
> he seems to be.

## 4. Near Hao-pa

(I saw in the mist a little village of a few tiled roofs, and joyfully
admired it.)

> There's a stream, and there's bamboo,
> there's mulberry, and hemp.
> Mist-hid, clouded hamlet,
> a mild, a tranquil place.
> Just a few tilled acres.
> Just a few tiled roofs.
> How many lives would I
> have to live, to get
> that simple?

## ▪ Li Ruzhen (Li Ju-chen) (c. 1763–c. 1830) (novel)

TRANSLATED BY LIN TAI-YI

Those familiar with the work of Chinese American storyteller Maxine
Hong Kingston may recognize the story recounted in this selection from

the novel *Flowers in the Mirror* by Qing dynasty writer Li Ruzhen. A version of it was told to Kingston by her mother as a folktale and reworked into the first tale in her book of story-essays, *China Men*. *Flowers in the Mirror* is often compared to Jonathan Swift's *Gulliver's Travels*. The most celebrated section of the novel is a wild and fantastic series of voyages to strange lands undertaken by Tang Ao, a scholar who wants to become a Daoist hermit, and his brother-in-law Merchant Lin. Among other places the travelers find themselves are the Country of Sexless People, the Country of Intestineless People, the Country of Flaming People, the Country of Black-Bottomed People, and, in this episode, the Country of Women. As is often the case with fiction that takes you to exotic locations, the real target of the story is much closer to home. *Flowers in the Mirror* can even be regarded as an early feminist novel, in which footbinding is satirized as equivalent to shaving "off pieces of the nose to make it smaller" (a prophetic commentary on modern nose jobs?), and in the ideal Daoist fairyland of Little Penglai, there is an imperial examination especially for women. The feminist irony of the excerpt included here speaks for itself.

Li Ruzhen was born in Hebei province in Taxing in 1763. He was a failed scholar, much like his hero Tang Ao, who could pass the Imperial Examinations (which were the meal-ticket for scholars) only at the county level. For twenty years he lived with his brother who was an official in the salt bureau in Jiangsu province. In a later appointment, he was an assistant to a Hunan province magistrate in charge of building dikes along the Yellow River. In addition to his knowledge of literature, Li was an expert in astrology, medicine, mathematics, music, calligraphy, gardening, painting, and various parlor and board games. In this ironic passage, the most exquisite torture for the traveler Merchant Lin is to be treated in the way women were commonly treated. Readers interested in western parallels to this tale may wish to look at Charlotte Perkins Gilman's early feminist novel *Herland* and at the Log of Christopher Columbus in this volume.

**FURTHER READING:** Lin, Tai-yi, tr. *Flowers in the Mirror,* 1966.

## from *Flowers in the Mirror*

When Tang Ao heard that they had arrived at the Country of Women, he thought that the country was populated entirely by women, and was afraid to go ashore. But Old Tuo said, 'Not at all! There are men as well as women, only they call men women, and women men. The men wear the skirts and take care of the home, while the women wear hats and trousers and manage affairs outside. If it were a country populated solely by women, I doubt that even Brother Lin here would dare to venture ashore, although he knows he always makes a good profit from sales here!'

'If the men dress like women, do they use cosmetics and bind their feet?' asked Tang Ao.

'Of course they do!' cried Lin, and took from his pocket a list of the merchandise he was going to sell, which consisted of huge quantities of rouge, face powder, combs and other women's notions. 'Lucky I wasn't born in this country,' he said. 'Catch me mincing around on bound feet!'

When Tang Ao asked why he had not put down the price of the merchandise, Lin said, 'The people here, no matter rich or poor, from the "King" down to the simplest peasant, are all mad about cosmetics. I'll charge them what I can. I shall have no difficulty selling the whole consignment to rich families in two or three days.'

Beaming at the prospect of making a good profit, Lin went on shore with his list.

Tang Ao and Old Tuo decided to go and see the city. The people walking on the streets were small of stature, and rather slim, and although dressed in men's clothes, were beardless and spoke with women's voices, and walked with willowy steps.

'Look at them!' said Old Tuo. 'They are perfectly normal-looking women. Isn't it a shame for them to dress like men?'

'Wait a minute,' said Tang Ao. 'Maybe when they see us, they think, "Look at them, isn't it a shame that they dress like women"?'

'You're right. "Whatever one is accustomed to always seems natural," as the ancients say. But I wonder what the men are like?'

Old Tuo discreetly called Tang Ao's attention to a middle-aged woman, who was sitting in front of her doorstep, sewing on a shoe. Her hair was braided and coiled smoothly on top of her head, and decorated with pearls and jade. She was wearing long gold loops of earrings with precious stones in them, and wore a long mauve gown with an onion-green shirt underneath, from which peeped the toes of tiny feet shod in red silk shoes. With long, tapering fingers, the woman was doing embroidery. She had beautiful eyes and was carefully powdered and rouged, but when she lifted her head, they saw that her lip was covered by a thick moustache.

Tang Ao and Old Tuo could not help laughing out loud.

The 'woman' looked up and said, 'What are you laughing at, lassies?'

The voice sounded as deep and hoarse as a cracked gong. Tang Ao was so startled that he took to his heels and ran.

But the 'woman' shouted after them. 'You must be women, since you have whiskers on your faces. Why are you wearing men's clothes and pretending to be men? Aren't you ashamed of yourselves! I know you dress like this because you want to mingle with the men, you cheap hussies! Take a look at yourselves in the mirror. Have you forgotten that you are women? It's lucky for you you only met up with me! If it had been somebody else who had caught you casting those sneaky glances, you would have been beaten almost to death!'

'This is the first time I have ever had such an experience,' muttered Tang Ao. 'But I suspect Brother Lin will receive better treatment at their hands.'

'Why?' said Old Tuo.

'Well, he is very fair, and since he lost his beard at the Country of Flaming People, he may be mistaken by these people for a real woman. But come to think of it, isn't it worrying?'

As they walked further on, they saw some 'women' on the streets as well as 'men'. Some were carrying babies in their arms, and others leading children by the hand. All the 'women' walked on dainty bound feet, and in crowded places, acted shy, as if they were embarrassed to be seen. Some of the younger ones were beardless, and upon careful study, Tang Ao discovered that some of the aging or middle-aged 'women' shaved their lips and chins in order to appear younger.

The two returned to the junk before Merchant Lin. But when the latter did not come back at supper time, and it was past the second drum, Mistress Lu began to be worried. Tang Ao and Old Tuo went on shore with lanterns to look for him, but discovered that the city gates were shut for the night.

The next day, they went to look again, but found not a trace of Lin. On the third day, some sailors went with them, but still they could not find him.

When a few days had passed, it seemed as if Merchant Lin had vanished, like a rock sinking to the bottom of the sea. Mistress Lu and Pleasant wailed with grief. Tang Ao and Old Tuo went to make inquiries every day.

They could not know that Merchant Lin had been told by one of his customers that the 'King's uncle' wanted to buy some of his goods. Following instructions, he went to the 'Royal Uncle's' Residence in the Palace, and handed his list of merchandise to the gate-keeper. Soon the gate-keeper came back and said that it was just what the 'King' was looking for for his 'concubines' and 'maids,' and asked Lin to be shown into the inner apartments.

The attendant led Merchant Lin through guarded doors and winding paths until he was at the door of the inner apartments, where a guard told him, 'Please wait here, madam. I shall go in and inquire what the royal wishes are.' She took Lin's list, and after a short time, returned and said, 'But madam hasn't put any prices on her list. How much do you charge for a picul of rouge? How much is a picul of perfumed powder? And hair lotion? And hair ribbons?'

Lin told her the prices, and the guard went in and came out again and asked, 'How much is a box of jade ornaments, madam? And your velvet flowers? How much is a box of your fragrant beads? And what about the combs?'

Merchant Lin told her and the guard again went to report, and came back and said, 'The King has been choosing imperial concubines and wants to buy some of your goods for them. He invites you to go inside, since you come from the Kingdom on Earth and we are friendly allies. However, madam must behave with courtesy and respect when she is in the presence of His Majesty.'

Merchant Lin followed the guard inside, and was soon in the presence of the 'King.' After making a deep bow, he saw that she was a woman of some thirty years old, with a beautiful face, fair skin and cherry-red lips. Around her there stood many palace 'maids.'

The 'King' spoke to Lin in a light voice, holding the list of articles in her slender hands, and looking at him with interest as he answered her questions.

'I wonder what she is staring at me like this for,' Merchant Lin thought to himself. 'Hasn't she ever seen a man from the Kingdom on Earth before?'

After a while, he heard her say that she was keeping the list of goods, and ordered palace 'maids' to prepare a feast and wine for the 'woman' from the Kingdom on Earth.

In a little time, Merchant Lin was ushered to a room upstairs, where victuals of many kinds awaited him. As he ate, however, he heard a great deal of noise downstairs. Several palace 'maids' ran upstairs soon, and calling him 'Your Highness,' kowtowed to him and congratulated him. Before he knew what was happening, Merchant Lin was being stripped completely bare by the maids and led to a perfumed bath. Against the powerful arms of these maids, he could scarcely struggle. Soon he found himself being anointed, perfumed, powdered and rouged, and dressed in a skirt. His big feet were bound up in strips of cloth and socks, and his hair was combed into an elaborate braid over his head and decorated with pins. These male 'maids' thrust bracelets on his arms and rings on his fingers, and put a phoenix headdress on his head. They tied a jade green sash around his waist and put an embroidered cape around his shoulders.

Then they led him to a bed and asked him to sit down.

Merchant Lin thought that he must be drunk, or dreaming, and began to tremble. He asked the maids what was happening, and was told that he had been chosen by the 'King' to be the Imperial Consort, and that a propitious day would be chosen for him to enter the 'King's' chambers.

Before he could utter a word, another group of maids, all tall and strong and wearing beards, came in. One was holding a threaded needle. 'We are ordered to pierce your ears,' he said as the other four 'maids' grabbed Lin by the arms and legs. The white-bearded one seized Lin's right ear, and after rubbing the lobe a little, drove the needle through it.

'Ooh!' Merchant Lin screamed.

The maid seized the other ear, and likewise drove the needle through it. As Lin screamed with pain, powdered lead was smeared on his earlobes and a pair of 'eight-precious' earrings was hung from the holes.

Having finished what they came to do, the maids retreated, and a black-bearded fellow came in with a bolt of white silk. Kneeling down before him, the fellow said, 'I am ordered to bind Your Highness's feet.'

Two other maids seized Lin's feet as the black-bearded one sat down on a low stool, and began to rip the silk into ribbons. Seizing Lin's right foot, he set it upon his knee, and sprinkled white alum powder between the toes and the grooves of the foot. He squeezed the toes tightly together, bent them down so that the whole foot was shaped like an arch, and took a length of white silk and bound it tightly around it twice. One of the others sewed the ribbon together in small stitches. Again the silk went around the foot, and again, it was sewn up.

Merchant Lin felt as though his feet were burning, and wave after wave of pain rose to his heart. When he could stand it no longer, he let out his voice and began to cry. The 'maids' hastily made a pair of soft-soled red shoes, and these they put on both his feet.

'Please, kind brothers, go and tell Her Majesty that I'm a married man,' Lin begged. 'How can I become her Consort? As for my feet, please liberate them. They have enjoyed the kind of freedom which scholars who are not interested in official careers enjoy! How can you bind them? Please tell your "King" to let me go. I shall be grateful, and my wife will be very grateful.'

But the maids said, 'The King said that you are to enter his chambers as soon as your feet are bound. It is no time for talk of this kind.'

When it was dark, a table was laid for him with mountains of meat and oceans of wine. But Merchant Lin only nibbled, and told the 'maids' they could have the rest.

Still sitting on the bed, and with his feet aching terribly, he decided to lie down in his clothes for a rest.

At once a middle-aged 'maid' came up to him and said, 'Please, will you wash before you retire?'

No sooner was this said than a succession of maids came in with candles, basins of water and spittoon, dressing table, boxes of ointment, face powder, towels, silk handkerchiefs, and surrounded him. Lin had to submit to the motions of washing in front of them all. But after he had washed his face, a maid wanted to put some cream on it again.

Merchant Lin stoutly refused.

'But night time is the best time to treat the skin,' the white-bearded maid said, 'This powder has a lot of musk in it. It will make your skin fragrant, although I dare say it is fair enough already. If you use it regularly your skin will not only seem like white jade, but will give off a natural fragrance of its own. And the more fragrant it is, the fairer it will become, and the more lovely to behold, and the more lovable you will be. You'll see how good it is after you have used it regularly.'

But Lin refused firmly, and the maids said, 'If you are so stubborn, we will have to report this, and let Matron deal with you tomorrow.'

Then they left him alone. But Lin's feet hurt so much that he could not sleep a wink. He tore at the ribbons with all his might, and after a great struggle succeeded in tearing them off. He stretched out his ten toes again, and luxuriating in their exquisite freedom, finally fell asleep.

The next morning, however, when the black-bearded maid discovered that he had torn off his foot-bandages, he immediately reported it to the 'King', who ordered that Lin should be punished by receiving twenty strokes of the bamboo from the 'Matron'. Accordingly, a white-bearded 'Matron' came in with a stick of bamboo about eight feet long, and when the others had stripped him and held him down, raised the stick and began to strike Lin's bottom and legs.

Before five strokes had been delivered, Lin's tender skin was bleeding, and the Matron did not have the heart to go on. 'Look at her skin! Have you ever seen such white and tender and lovable skin? Why, I think indeed her looks are comparable to Pan An and Sung Yu!' the Matron thought to himself. 'But what am I doing, comparing her bottom and not her face to them? Is that a compliment?'

The foot-binding mind came and asked Lin if he would behave from now on.

'Yes, I'll behave,' Lin replied, and they stopped beating him. They wiped the blood from his wounds, and special ointment was sent by the 'King' and ginseng soup was given him to drink.

Merchant Lin drank the soup, and fell on the bed for a rest. But the 'King' had given orders that his feet must be bound again, and that he should be taught to walk on them. So with one maid supporting him on each side, Merchant Lin was marched up and down the room all day on his bound feet. When he lay down to sleep that night, he could not close his eyes for the excruciating pain.

But from now on, he was never left alone again. Maids took turns to sit with him. Merchant Lin knew that he was no longer in command of his destiny.

Before two weeks were over, Lin's feet had begun to assume a permanently arched form, and his toes begun to rot. Daily medical ablutions were given to them, and the pain persisted.

'I should have thought that Brother-in-law and Old Tuo would have come to my rescue by now,' he thought one day as he was being led up and down his room. 'I have endured all I can! I'd be better off dead!'

He sat down on the edge of the bed, and began to tear off his embroidered shoes and silk bandages. 'Go tell your "King" to put me to death at once, or let my feet loose,' he told the Matron.

But when he returned, the Matron said, 'The King said that if you don't obey his orders, you are to be hung upside down from the beam of the house.'

'Then do it quickly! The quicker the better!' said Lin, impatient to have an end put to his agony.

Accordingly, they tied a rope around his feet and hung him upside down from the beam. Merchant Lin saw stars before his eyes. Sweat poured out of his body, and his legs became numb. He closed his eyes and waited for death to come to the rescue. But it did not come. At last he could stand it no longer, and began to scream like a pig being led to slaughter.

The order was given to cut him down.

From now on, Lin was completely in the power of the maids. Wanting to complete the task their 'King' had assigned them as soon as possible, they tied the bandages around his feet tighter than ever. Several times, Lin thought of committing suicide, but with people watching him constantly, he had not a chance.

In due course, his feet lost much of their original shape. Blood and flesh were squeezed into a pulp and then little remained of his feet but dry bones and skin, shrunk, indeed, to a dainty size. Responding to daily anointing, his hair became shiny and smooth, and his body, after repeated ablutions of perfumed water, began to look very attractive indeed. His eyebrows were plucked to resemble a new moon. With blood-red lipstick and powder adorning his face, and jade and pearl adorning his coiffure and ears, Merchant Lin assumed, at last, a not unappealing appearance.

The 'King' sent someone to watch his progress every day. One day, the Matron announced that the task of foot-binding had been completed. When the 'King' herself came upstairs to have a look, she saw a Lin whose face was like a peach blossom, whose eyes were like autumn lakes, whose eyebrows suggested the lines of distant hills, and who stood before her in a willowy stance.

She was delighted. 'What a beauty!' she thought to herself. 'If I hadn't seen her hidden possibilities beneath her ridiculous man's costume, her beauty might never have come to light!'

She took a pearl bracelet and put it on Merchant Lin's wrist, and the 'maids' persuaded him to sink down on his knees and give thanks. The 'King' pulled him up and made him sit down beside her, and began to fondle his hands and smell them and look appreciatively at his dainty feet.

Lin went red with shame.

Extremely pleased, the 'King' decided that Lin should enter her chambers the very next day. When Merchant Lin heard this, he saw his last hopes vanish. He was not even able to walk without someone to help him, and spent the whole night thinking about his wife and shedding tears.

In the morning, the 'maids' came especially early to shave off the fine hairs from his face, and to powder him and comb him in preparation for his wedding. Supported by a pair of red embroidered high heeled shoes, his longer-than-ordinary 'golden lotuses' became not obtrusively large. He wore a bridal crown and gown, and with jewels dangling and waves of perfume issuing from his person, was if not notably beautiful, at least a rather charming 'bride.'

### ■ Cao Xueqin (Ts'ao Hsüeh-chin) (c. 1715–1763) and Gao E (Kao E) (c. 1740–1815) (novel)

The *Dream of the Red Chamber*, also known as the *Story of the Stone*, is the masterpiece of Chinese realist fiction. It seems to have been written by Cao Xueqin, impoverished descendant of a distinguished family of naturalized

Manchus. His grandfather Cao Yin (1658–1712) had been the protege of Emperor Kangxi, but the family fell out of favor and had most of its property confiscated. Cao Xueqin had a classical education and was a teacher in a school for the children of the nobility. He retired to the Western Hills, outside Beijing, and devoted his final years to literature. He is thought to have written the first eighty chapters of the novel, which circulated after his death under the title *Story of the Stone;* the last forty chapters were probably written by Gao E, a later writer of lesser talent. The debate about these final forty chapters, which Gao claimed were based on a fragmentary original conclusion to the novel, is bitter and involved and has divided the vast field of literary studies that has grown up around the novel (called Redology).

On one level, the story centers on the frustrated love of protagonist Jia Bao-yu (Precious Jade) for his cousin Lin Dai-yu (Black Jade), complicated by the attractions of another cousin Xue Bao-chai (Precious Virtue), whom Bao-yu is tricked into marrying, while Dai-yu at the moment of the marriage dies of a bitter illness. Bao-yu is the scion of the decadent but prosperous Jia family, whose decline through its own moral bankruptcy constitutes another major movement of the novel. Much of the novel is set at the Jia estate, whose two houses are linked by a pleasure garden. Bao-yu is born with a piece of jade in his mouth, and he is the incarnation of the Divine Luminescent Stone-in-Waiting (the stone of the title), as Dai-yu is the incarnation of a plant that the stone nurtures into life. The stone is brought to the earth to live by a Buddhist monk and a Daoist priest. After the disastrous death of Dai-yu, the monk and priest take Bao-yu off to a religious life. For the body of the novel, however, the stone, incarnated as Bao-yu, ignores the wisdom of the religious path, losing himself instead in sensuality. This is an extremely limited account of the novel's range; there are 423 characters, many of whom are brought into three dimensions, and the novel as a whole is a tapestry of Chinese life, speech, customs, and behavior at all levels. In this excerpt, Lin Dai-yu, sick and fevered, has a dream about her absent lover, the psychological significance of which will be clear to the reader.

**FURTHER READING:** Hawkes, David, and John Minford, trs. *The Story of the Stone,* 5 vols., 1979–1987. McHugh, Florence, and Isabel McHugh, trs. *The Dream of the Red Chamber,* 1958. Wang, Chi-cheng, tr. *Dream of the Red Chamber,* [1929] 1958. Yang, Hsien-yi, and Gladys Yang, trs. *A Dream of Red Mansions,* 3 vols., 1978–1980.

# Dream of the Red Chamber

## *from* Chapter 82

TRANSLATED BY JOHN MINFORD

That evening, when Dai-yu went into her side-room to undress for the night, she caught sight of the lychees again. They reminded her of the old woman's visit, and revived the pain she had felt at her tactless gossiping. Dusk was falling, and in the stillness a thousand gloomy thoughts seemed to close in and oppress her mind.

'My health is so poor . . . And time's running out. I know Bao-yu loves me more than anyone else. But Grannie and Aunt Wang still haven't mentioned it! If only my parents had settled it for us while they were still alive . . . But suppose they had? What if they had married me to someone else? Who could ever compare with Bao-yu? Perhaps I'm better off like this after all! At least I've still some hope.'

Like the rope on a pulley her secret hopes and fears spun up and down, tangling themselves tighter and tighter round her heart. Finally, with a sigh and a few tears, she lay down in her clothes, weary and depressed.

She became vaguely aware of one of the junior maids coming in and saying:

'Miss Lin, Mr Jia Yu-cun is outside and wants to see you.'

'What could he want?' thought Dai-yu to herself. 'I'm not a regular student of his. I'm not even a boy. He just happened to coach me when I was a little girl. Anyway, all the times he's come to see Uncle Zheng he's never once asked after me, so why should I have to see him now?'

She told the maid to convey her respects and thank Mr Yu-cun for calling, but to say that poor health obliged her to stay in bed.

'But Miss,' said the maid, 'I think he's come to congratulate you, and some people have come to take you to Nanking.'

As she was speaking, a group incuding Xi-feng, Lady Xing, Lady Wang and Bao-chai advanced into the room and announced cheerfully:

'Congratulations my dear! And bon voyage!'

'What do you mean?' asked Dai-yu in great confusion.

'Come on now.' It was Xi-feng who replied. 'You needn't try and pretend you haven't heard the news. Your father's been promoted to Grain Intendant for Hupeh Province and has made a second and highly satisfactory marriage. He doesn't think it right that you should be left here on your own, and has asked Yu-cun to act as go-between. You're engaged to be married to a relation of your new stepmother's, a widower himself I believe. They've sent some servants to fetch you home. You'll probably be married straight away. It's all your stepmother's idea. In case you're not properly taken care of on the voyage, she has asked your cousin Lian to accompany you.'

Xi-feng's words made Dai-yu break out in a cold sweat. She now had a feeling that her father was still alive. She began to panic, and said defiantly:

'It's not true! It's all a trick of Xi-feng's!'

She saw Lady Xing give Lady Wang a meaningful look:

'She won't believe us. Come, we are wasting our time.'

'Aunt Wang! Aunt Xing! Don't go!' Dai-yu begged them, fighting back her tears. But she received no reply. They all gave her a curious smile, and then left together.

As she stood there and watched them go, panic seized her. She tried to speak, but the only sound that came was a strangled sobbing from the back of her throat. Then she looked about her and saw that somehow she had been transported to Grandmother Jia's apartment. In that same instant she thought to herself: 'Grannie's the only one that can save me now!' and fell at the old lady's feet, hugging her by the knees.

'Save me Grannie, *please!* I'd rather die than go away with them! That stepmother's not my real mother anyway. I just want to stay here with you!'

Grandmother Jia's face only registered a cold smile.

'This has nothing to do with me.'

'But what's to become of me, Grannie?' she sobbed.

'Being a man's second wife has its advantages,' Grandmother Jia replied. 'Think of the double dowry you'll have.'

'If I stay, I won't cause you any extra expense, I promise I won't. Oh please save me!'

'It's no use,' said Grandmother Jia. 'All girls marry and leave home. You're a child and don't understand these things. You can't live here for ever, you know.'

'I'll do anything to stay—I'll work for my keep, be a slave, anything! Only please don't let them take me away!'

This time Grandmother Jia made no reply. Dai-yu hugged her again and sobbed:

'Oh Grannie! You've always been so good to me, fussed over me so—how can you treat me like this in my hour of need! Don't you care about me any more? I may not be one of your real grandchildren, a true Jia like the others, but my mother was your own daughter, your own flesh and blood! For her sake have pity on me! Don't let me be taken away!'

With these last words she flung herself frantically upon Lady Jia, burying her head in her lap and sobbing violently.

'Faithful,' the old lady commanded, 'take Miss Dai-yu to her room to rest. She is wearing me out.'

There was no mistaking the finality in Grandmother Jia's voice. To Dai-yu, suicide now seemed the only course. She rose, and as she walked from the room her heart yearned for a mother of her own to turn to. All the affection shown her by grandmother, aunts and cousins alike, had now been exposed for what it was and had been all along—a sham. Suddenly she thought: 'Why haven't I seen Bao-yu today? *He* might still know of a way out.' And as the thought entered her mind, she looked up and sure enough, there, standing right in front of her, all laughter and smiles, was Bao-yu himself.

'My warmest congratulations, cuz!'

This was too much for Dai-yu. Her last vestige of maidenly reserve vanished. She clutched hold of him and cried out:

'Now I know how heartless and cruel you really are, Bao-yu!'

'No, you are wrong,' he replied. 'But if you have a husband to go to, then we must go our separate ways.'

Dai-yu listened in despair as this, her very last hope, was taken from her. Clinging to him helplessly, she gave a feverish cry:

'Oh Bao! I've no separate way to go! How could you say such a thing!'

'If you don't want to go, then stay here,' he replied calmly. 'You were originally engaged to me. That's why you came to live here. Has it never occurred to you how specially I've always treated you? Haven't you noticed?'

Suddenly, it all seemed clear. She really was engaged to Bao-yu after all. Of course she was! In an instant her despair changed to joy.

'*My* mind is made up once and forever! But you must give me the word. Am I to go? Or am I to stay?'

'I've told you, stay here with me. If you still don't trust me, look at my heart.'

With these words he took out a small knife and brought it down across his chest. Blood came spurting out. Terrified out of her wits, Dai-yu tried to staunch the flow with her hand crying out:

'How could you? You should have killed me first!'

'Don't worry,' said Bao-yu. 'I'm going to show you my heart.'

He fumbled about inside the gaping flesh, while Dai-yu, shaking convulsively, afraid someone might burst in on them at any moment, pressed him to her tightly and wept bitterly.

'Oh no!' said Bao-yu. 'It's not there anymore! My time has come!'

His eyes flickered and he fell with a dull thud to the floor. Dai-yu let out a piercing scream. She heard Nightingale calling her:

'Miss Lin! Miss Lin! You're having a nightmare! Wake up! Come along now, you must get undressed and go to sleep properly.'

Dai-yu turned over in her bed. So it had all been a nightmare. But she could still feel her throat choking, her heart was still pounding, the top of her pillow was drenched in sweat, and a tingly, icy sensation ran down her back and chilled her to the core.

'Mother and father died long ago. Bao-yu and I have never been engaged,' she thought to herself. 'What ever could have made me have such a dream?'

The scenes of her dream passed before her eyes again. She was on her own in the world, she reflected. Supposing Bao-yu really died—what then? The thought was enough to bring back all the pain and confusion. She began to weep, and tiny beads of sweat broke out down the length of her body. Finally she struggled up, took off her outer robe and told Nightingale to make the bed. She lay down again, and began turning restlessly from side to side, unable to get to sleep. She could hear the gentle sighing of the wind outside her window—or was it the drizzle falling softly on the roof? Once, the sound died away and she thought she could hear someone calling in the distance. But it was only Nightingale, who had already fallen asleep and was snoring in a corner of the room. With a great effort, Dai-yu struggled out of bed, wrapped the quilt around her and sat up. An icy draught from a crack in the casement soon sent her shivering back under the covers again. She was just beginning to doze off when the sparrows struck up their dawn-chorus from their nests in the bamboos. First light was gradually beginning to show through the shutters and paper window-panes.

Dai-yu was now wide awake again and started coughing. Nightingale awoke at once.

'Still awake, Miss? Coughing too—it sounds as if you've caught a chill. Why, it's almost light, it'll soon be morning! Please try and stop thinking so much, and rest. You need to sleep.'

'I want to sleep,' replied Dai-yu. 'But what's the good? I just can't. You go back to sleep anyway.' These last words were interrupted by another fit of coughing.

Nightingale was already distressed at her mistress's condition and had no inclination to go back to sleep. When she heard her coughing again, she hurried over to hold up the spittoon. By now it was dawn outside.

'Haven't you gone to sleep?' asked Dai-yu.

'Sleep?' replied Nightingale cheerfully. 'It's already daylight.'

'In that case, could you change the spittoon?'

'Certainly Miss.'

Leaving the full spittoon on a table in the outer room, Nightingale went promptly to fetch a fresh one, which she placed at the foot of the kang. Then, closing the door of the inner room carefully behind her and letting down the flower-patterned portière, she went out to wake Snow-goose, taking the full spittoon with her. When she came to empty it in the courtyard, and looked closer, she noticed to her horror some specks of blood in the phlegm.

'Goodness!' she blurted out. 'How awful!'

'What's the matter?' Dai-yu called out at once from inside.

'Oh nothing, Miss!'

Nightingale tried her best to cover up her blunder. 'The spittoon slipped in my hand and I nearly dropped it.'

'You didn't find anything odd in the phlegm?'

'Oh no, Miss.' A lump came into Nightingale's throat, and she could say no more. Tears came streaming down her cheeks.

Dai-yu had already noticed a sickly taste in her mouth, and her earlier suspicions were strengthened first by Nightingale's cry of alarm, and now by the unmistakable note of dismay in her voice.

'Come in,' she told Nightingale. 'It must be cold outside.'

'I'm coming, Miss.' She sounded more disconsolate than ever. Her tragic snuffly tone set Dai-yu shivering. The door opened and she walked in, still dabbing her eyes with a handkerchief.

'Come along now,' said Dai-yu. 'Crying so early in the morning?'

'Who's crying?' said Nightingale, doing her best to smile. 'It's so early and my eyes are a bit itchy, that's all. You were awake longer than ever last night, weren't you, Miss? I could hear you coughing half the night.'

'I know. The more I wanted to sleep, the wider awake I became.'

'You're not well, Miss. I think all this worrying is ruining your health. And good health is like the hill in the proverb:

Keep the hill green, keep the hill green,
And you'll never lack fuel for winter again.

Besides, everyone here cares for you so. Her Old Ladyship does, Her Ladyship does, *everyone* does!'

How could Nightingale know that the mere mention of these homely names, intended to reassure and comfort, was enough to conjure up again the horror of the nightmare? Dai-yu felt her heart thumping, everything went black before her eyes, and she seemed on the point of fainting altogether. Nightingale quickly held out the spittoon while Snowgoose patted her lightly on the back. After a long while she coughed up another mouthful of phlegm. In it was a thick wriggling strand of dark red blood. The two maids were pale with fright. They stood supporting her, one on each side, until finally she slumped back, scarcely conscious. Nightingale, aware of the critical nature of her condition, looked at Snowgoose and made an urgent movement with her lips that clearly meant: 'Go and fetch someone — quickly!'

# The Modern Era

■ ## Lu Xun (Lu Hsün) (1881 – 1936) (story)

### TRANSLATED BY YANG HSIEN-YI AND GLADYS YANG

Lu Xun is the pen name taken by Zhou Shuren, China's premier twentieth-century fiction writer. He is also considered a leading essayist of his time. When young, Lu Xun studied medicine in Japan but turned to literature in 1906 after the Russo-Japanese war. In 1909 he came back to China and taught at the National Beijing University, among other schools, believing that by his teaching and writing he could begin to effect changes on a China that he perceived as decadent and failing — views that caused him trouble with the government and that obliged him to leave Beijing to teach in Fukien and Canton. In 1927, he moved to Shanghai, giving up academia, and turned full time to writing. In addition to his short stories and polemical essays, he is the author of a trailblazing history of Chinese fiction. He died on October 19, 1936, of tuberculosis in Shanghai.

His interest in reform led him to inscribe in his fiction a subtle political nervous system beneath the skin of words. Such political allegories can be strongly seen in his most famous tales, "A Madman's Diary" and "The True Story of Ah Q." The grotesquery and paranoia of "A Madman's Diary" will remind Western readers of Dostoyevsky's *Notes from the Underground* and of Kafka's *The Metamorphosis*. As in Kafka's tale, the narrator in this story has undergone a metamorphosis into something frightening and strange. The diarist has become possessed by the belief that the people of the town around him, the doctor, even his own brother, have taken to eating human flesh and plan to kill him and feast on his body. Is his belief paranoid fantasy, a fascinating window into the skewed mental processes of a madman? Or is it an allegorical representation of the moral vacuum of Chinese society, with consumption, competition, and exploitation of the poor represented as cannibalism, in which humanity becomes its own proper prey? Or, finally, is it in some way both at once, so that the particular form that his madness takes lies in a perception of human and universal truths to which "sane" society is blind?

**FURTHER READING:** Lee, Leo Ou-fan, ed. *Lu Xun and His Legacy*, 1985; *Voices from the Iron House: A Study of Lu Xun*, 1987. Lu, Hsun. *The Complete Stories of Lu Xun*. Translated by Yang Xianyi and Gladys Yang, 1981; *Diary of a Madman and Other Stories*. Translated by William A. Lyell, 1990; *Lu Hsun: Complete Poems*. A translation with introduction and annotation by David Y. Chen, 1988; *Lu Xun, Selected Works*. Translated by Yang Xianyi and Gladys Yang, 1980; *Selected Stories of Lu Hsun*. Translated by Yang Hsien-yi and Gladys Yang, 1977; *Silent China; Selected Writings of Lu Xun*. Edited and translated by Gladys Yang, 1973. Weiss, Ruth F. *Lu Xun: A Chinese Writer for All Times*, 1985.

## A Madman's Diary

Two brothers, whose names I need not mention here, were both good friends of mine in high school; but after a separation of many years we gradually lost touch. Some time ago I happened to hear that one of them was seriously ill, and since I was going back to my old home I broke my journey to call on them. I saw only one, however, who told me that the invalid was his younger brother.

"I appreciate your coming such a long way to see us," he said, "but my brother recovered some time ago and has gone elsewhere to take up an official post." Then, laughing, he produced two volumes of his brother's diary, saying that from these the nature of his past illness could be seen, and that there was no harm in showing them to an old friend. I took the diary away, read it through, and found that he had suffered from a form of persecution complex. The writing was most confused and incoherent, and he had made many wild statements; moreover he had omitted to give any dates, so that only by the colour of the ink and the differences in the writing could one tell that it was not written at one time. Certain sections, however, were not altogether disconnected, and I have copied out a part to serve as a subject for medical research. I have not altered a single illogicality in the diary and have changed only the names, even though the people referred to are all country folk, unknown to the world and of no consequence. As for the title, it was chosen by the diarist himself after his recovery, and I did not change it.

# I

Tonight the moon is very bright.

I have not seen it for over thirty years, so today when I saw it I felt in unusually high spirits. I begin to realize that during the past thirty-odd years I have been in the dark; but now I must be extremely careful. Otherwise why should that dog at the Chao house have looked at me twice?

I have reason for my fear.

# II

Tonight there is no moon at all, I know that this bodes ill. This morning when I went out cautiously, Mr. Chao had a strange look in his eyes, as if he were afraid of me, as if he wanted to murder me. There were seven or eight others, who discussed me in a whisper. And they were afraid of my seeing them. All the people I passed were like that. The fiercest among them grinned at me; whereupon I shivered from head to foot, knowing that their preparations were complete.

I was not afraid, however, but continued on my way. A group of children in front were also discussing me, and the look in their eyes was just like that in Mr. Chao's while their faces too were ghastly pale. I wondered what grudge these children could have against me to make them behave like this. I could not help calling out: "Tell me!" But then they ran away.

I wonder what grudge Mr. Chao can have against me, what grudge the people on the road can have against me. I can think of nothing except that twenty years ago I trod on Mr. Ku Chiu's[1] accounts sheets for many years past, and Mr. Ku was very displeased. Although Mr. Chao does not know him, he must have heard talk of this and decided to avenge him, so he is conspiring against me with the people on the road. But then what of the children? At that time they were not yet born, so why should they eye me so strangely today, as if they were afraid of me, as if they wanted to murder me? This really frightens me, it is so bewildering and upsetting.

I know. They must have learned this from their parents!

---

1. Ku Chiu means "Ancient Times." Lu Hsun had in mind the long history of feudal oppression in China.

# III

I can't sleep at night. Everything requires careful consideration if one is to understand it.

Those people, some of whom have been pilloried by the magistrate, slapped in the face by the local gentry, had their wives taken away by bailiffs, or their parents driven to suicide by creditors, never looked as frightened and as fierce then as they did yesterday.

The most extraordinary thing was that woman on the street yesterday who spanked her son and said, "Little devil! I'd like to bite several mouthfuls out of you to work off my feelings!" Yet all the time she looked at me. I gave a start, unable to control myself; then all those green-faced, long-toothed people began to laugh derisively. Old Chen hurried forward and dragged me home.

He dragged me home. The folk at home all pretended not to know me; they had the same look in their eyes as all the others. When I went into the study, they locked the door outside as if cooping up a chicken or a duck. This incident left me even more bewildered.

A few days ago a tenant of ours from Wolf Cub Village came to report the failure of the crops, and told my elder brother that a notorious character in their village had been beaten to death; then some people had taken out his heart and liver, fried them in oil and eaten them, as a means of increasing their courage. When I interrupted, the tenant and my brother both stared at me. Only today have I realized that they had exactly the same look in their eyes as those people outside.

Just to think of it sets me shivering from the crown of my head to the soles of my feet.

They eat human beings, so they may eat me.

I see that woman's "bite several mouthfuls out of you," the laughter of those green-faced, long-toothed people and the tenant's story the other day are obviously secret signs. I realize all the poison in their speech, all the daggers in their laughter. Their teeth are white and glistening: they are all man-eaters.

It seems to me, although I am not a bad man, ever since I trod on Mr. Ku's accounts it has been touch-and-go. They seem to have secrets which I cannot guess, and once they are angry they will call anyone a bad character. I remember when my elder brother taught me to write compositions, no matter how good a man was, if I produced arguments to the contrary he would mark that passage to show his approval; while if I excused evil-doers, he would say: "Good for you, that shows originality." How can I possibly guess their secret thoughts—especially when they are ready to eat people?

Everything requires careful consideration if one is to understand it. In ancient times, as I recollect, people often ate human beings, but I am rather hazy about it. I tried to look this up, but my history has no chronology, and scrawled all over each page are the words: "Virtue and Morality." Since I could not sleep anyway, I read intently half the night, until I began to see words between the lines, the whole book being filled with the two words—"Eat people."

All these words written in the book, all the words spoken by our tenant, gaze at me strangely with an enigmatic smile.

I too am a man, and they want to eat me!

# IV

In the morning I sat quietly for some time. Old Chen brought lunch in: one bowl of vegetables, one bowl of steamed fish. The eyes of the fish were white and hard, and its mouth was open just like those people who want to eat human beings. After a few mouthfuls I could not tell whether the slippery morsels were fish or human flesh, so I brought it all up.

I said, "Old Chen, tell my brother that I feel quite suffocated, and want to have a stroll in the garden." Old Chen said nothing but went out, and presently he came back and opened the gate.

I did not move, but watched to see how they would treat me, feeling certain that they would not let me go. Sure enough! My elder brother came slowly out, leading an old man. There was a murderous gleam in his eyes, and fearing that I would see it he lowered his head, stealing glances at me from the side of his spectacles.

"You seem to be very well today," said my brother.

"Yes," said I.

"I have invited Mr. Ho here today," said my brother, "to examinc you."

"All right," said I. Actually I knew quite well that this old man was the executioner in disguise! He simply used the pretext of feeling my pulse to see how fat I was; for by so doing he would receive a share of my flesh. Still I was not afraid. Although I do not eat men, my courage is greater than theirs. I held out my two fists, to see what he would do. The old man sat down, closed his eyes, fumbled for some time and remained still for some time; then he opened his shifty eyes and said, "Don't let your imagination run away with you. Rest quietly for a few days, and you will be all right."

Don't let your imagination run away with you! Rest quietly for a few days! When I have grown fat, naturally they will have more to eat; but what good will it do me, or how can it be "all right"? All these people wanting to eat human flesh and at the same time stealthily trying to keep up appearances, not daring to act promptly, really made me nearly die of laughter. I could not help roaring with laughter, I was so amused. I knew that in this laughter were courage and integrity. Both the old man and my brother turned pale, awed by my courage and integrity.

But just because I am brave they are the more eager to eat me, in order to acquire some of my courage. The old man went out of the gate, but before he had gone far he said to my brother in a low voice, "To be eaten at once!" And my brother nodded. So you are in it too! This stupendous discovery, although it came as a shock, is yet no more than I had expected: the accomplice in eating me is my elder brother!

The eater of human flesh is my elder brother!

I am the younger brother of an eater of human flesh!

I myself will be eaten by others, but none the less I am the younger brother of an eater of human flesh!

# V

These few days I have been thinking again: suppose that old man were not an executioner in disguise, but a real doctor; he would be none the less an eater of human flesh. In that book on herbs, written by his predecessor Li Shih-chen,[2] it is clearly stated that men's flesh can be boiled and eaten; so can he still say that he does not eat men?

As for my elder brother, I have also good reason to suspect him. When he was teaching me, he said with his own lips, "People exchange their sons to eat." And once in discussing a bad man, he said that not only did he deserve to be killed, he should "have his flesh eaten and his hide slept on."[3] I was still young then, and my heart beat faster for some time, he was not at all surprised by the story that our tenant from Wolf Cub Village told us the other day about eating a man's heart and liver, but kept nodding his head. He is evidently just as cruel as before. Since it is possible to "exchange sons to eat," then anything can be exchanged, anyone can be eaten. In the past I simply listened to his explanations, and let it go at that; now I know that when he explained it to me, not only was there human fat at the corner of his lips, but his whole heart was set on eating men.

# VI

Pitch dark. I don't know whether it is day or night. The Chao family dog has started barking again.

The fierceness of a lion, the timidity of a rabbit, the craftiness of a fox. . . .

# VII

I know their way; they are not willing to kill anyone outright, nor do they dare, for fear of the consequences. Instead they have banded together and set traps everywhere, to force me to kill myself. The behaviour of the men and women in the street a few days ago, and my elder brother's attitude these last few days, make it quite obvious. What they like best is for a man to take off his belt, and hang himself from a beam; for then they can enjoy their heart's desire without being blamed for murder. Naturally that sets them roaring with delighted laughter. On the other hand, if a man is frightened or worried to death, although that makes him rather thin, they still nod in approval.

---

2. A famous pharmacologist (1518–1593), author of *Ben-cao-gang-mu*, the *Materia Medica*.

3. These are quotations from the old classic *Zuo Zhuan*.

They only eat dead flesh! I remember reading somewhere of a hideous beast, with an ugly look in its eye, called "hyena" which often eats dead flesh. Even the largest bones it grinds into fragments and swallows: the mere thought of this is enough to terrify one. Hyenas are related to wolves, and wolves belong to the canine species. The other day the dog in the Chao house looked at me several times; obviously it is in the plot too and has become their accomplice. The old man's eyes were cast down, but that did not deceive me!

The most deplorable is my elder brother. He is also a man, so why is he not afraid, why is he plotting with others to eat me? Is it that when one is used to it he no longer thinks it a crime? Or is it that he has hardened his heart to do something he knows is wrong?

In cursing man-eaters, I shall start with my brother, and in dissuading man-eaters, I shall start with him too.

# VIII

Actually, such arguments should have convinced them long ago. . . .

Suddenly someone came in. He was only about twenty years old and I did not see his features very clearly. His face was wreathed in smiles, but when he nodded to me his smile did not seem genuine. I asked him: "Is it right to eat human beings?"

Still smiling, he replied, "When there is no famine how can one eat human beings?"

I realized at once, he was one of them; but still I summoned up courage to repeat my question:

"Is it right?"

"What makes you ask such a thing? You really are . . . fond of a joke. . . . It is very fine today."

"It is fine, and the moon is very bright. But I want to ask you: Is it right?"

He looked disconcerted, and muttered: "No. . . ."

"No? Then why do they still do it?"

"What are you talking about?"

"What am I talking about? They are eating men now in Wolf Cub Village, and you can see it written all over the books, in fresh red ink."

His expression changed, and he grew ghastly pale. "It may be so," he said, staring at me. "It has always been like that. . . ."

"Is it right because it has always been like that?"

"I refuse to discuss these things with you. Anyway, you shouldn't talk about it. Whoever talks about it is in the wrong!"

I leaped up and opened my eyes wide, but the man had vanished. I was soaked with perspiration. He was much younger than my elder brother, but even so he was in it. He must have been taught by his parents. And I am afraid he has already taught his son: that is why even the children look at me so fiercely.

# IX

Wanting to eat men, at the same time afraid of being eaten themselves, they all look at each other with the deepest suspicion. . . .

How comfortable life would be for them if they could rid themselves of such obsessions and go to work, walk, eat and sleep at ease. They have only this one step to take. Yet fathers and sons, husbands and wives, brothers, friends, teachers and students, sworn enemies and even strangers, have all joined in this conspiracy, discouraging and preventing each other from taking this step.

# X

Early this morning I went to look for my elder brother. He was standing outside the hall door looking at the sky, when I walked up behind him, stood between him and the door, and with exceptional poise and politeness said to him:

"Brother, I have something to say to you."

"Well, what is it?" he asked, quickly turning towards me and nodding.

"It is very little, but I find it difficult to say. Brother, probably all primitive people ate a little human flesh to begin with. Later, because their outlook changed, some of them stopped, and because they tried to be good they changed into men, changed into real men. But some are still eating—just like reptiles. Some have changed into fish, birds, monkeys and finally men; but some do not try to be good and remain reptiles still. When those who eat men compare themselves with those who do not, how ashamed they must be. Probably much more ashamed than the reptiles are before monkeys.

"In ancient times Yi Ya boiled his son for Chieh and Chou to eat; that is the old story.[4] But actually since the creation of heaven and earth by Pan Ku men have been eating each other, from the time of Yi Ya's son to the time of Hsu Hsi-lin,[5] and from the time of Hsu Hsi-lin down to the man caught in Wolf Cub Village. Last year they executed a criminal in the city, and a consumptive soaked a piece of bread in his blood and sucked it.

"They want to eat me, and of course you can do nothing about it single-handed; but why should you join them? As man-eaters they are capable of anything. If they eat me, they can eat you as well; members of the same group can still eat each other. But if you will just change your ways immediately, then everyone will have peace. Although this has been going on since time immemorial, today we could make a special effort to be good, and say this is not to be done! I'm sure you can say so, brother. The

---

4. According to ancient records, Yi Ya cooked his son and presented him to Duke Huan of Chi who reigned from 685 to 643 B.C. Chieh and Chou were tyrants of an earlier age. The madman has made a mistake here.

5. A revolutionary at the end of the Ching dynasty (1644–1911), Hsu Hsi-lin was executed in 1907 for assassinating a Ching official. His heart and liver were eaten.

other day when the tenant wanted the rent reduced, you said it couldn't be done."

At first he only smiled cynically, then a murderous gleam came into his eyes, and when I spoke of their secret his face turned pale. Outside the gate stood a group of people, including Mr. Chao and his dog, all craning their necks to peer in. I could not see all their faces, for they seemed to be masked in cloths; some of them looked pale and ghastly still, concealing their laughter. I knew they were one band, all eaters of human flesh. But I also knew that they did not all think alike by any means. Some of them thought that since it had always been so, men should be eaten. Some of them knew that they should not eat men, but still wanted to; and they were afraid people might discover their secret; thus when they heard me they became angry, but they still smiled their cynical, tight-lipped smile.

Suddenly my brother looked furious, and shouted in a loud voice:

"Get out of here, all of you! What is the point of looking at a madman?"

Then I realized part of their cunning. They would never be willing to change their stand, and their plans were all laid; they had stigmatized me as a madman. In future when I was eaten, not only would there be no trouble, but people would probably be grateful to them. When our tenant spoke of the villagers eating a bad character, it was exactly the same device. This is their old trick.

Old Chen came in too, in a great temper, but they could not stop my mouth, I had to speak to those people:

"You should change, change from the bottom of your hearts!" I said. "You must know that in the future there will be no place for man-eaters in the world.

"If you don't change, you may all be eaten by each other. Although so many are born, they will be wiped out by the real men, just like wolves killed by hunters. Just like reptiles!"

Old Chen drove everybody away. My brother had disappeared. Old Chen advised me to go back to my room. The room was pitch dark. The beams and rafters shook above my head. After shaking for some time they grew larger. They piled on top of me.

The weight was so great, I could not move. They meant that I should die. I knew that the weight was false, so I struggled out, covered in perspiration. But I had to say:

"You should change at once, change from the bottom of your hearts! You must know that in the future there will be no place for man-eaters in the world. . . ."

# XI

The sun does not shine, the door is not opened, every day two meals.

I took up my chopsticks, then thought of my elder brother; I know now how my little sister died: it was all through him. My sister was only five at the time. I can still remember how lovable and pathetic she looked. Mother cried and cried, but he begged her not to cry, probably because he had eaten her himself, and so her crying made him feel ashamed. If he had any sense of shame. . . .

My sister was eaten by my brother, but I don't know whether mother realized it or not.

I think mother must have known, but when she cried she did not say so outright, probably because she thought it proper too. I remember when I was four or five years old, sitting in the cool of the hall, my brother told me that if a man's parents were ill, he should cut off a piece of his flesh and boil it for them if he wanted to be considered a good son; and mother did not contradict him. If one piece could be eaten, obviously so could the whole. And yet just to think of the mourning then still makes my heart bleed; that is the extraordinary thing about it!

## XII

I can't bear to think of it.

I have only just realized that I have been living all these years in a place where for four thousand years they have been eating human flesh. My brother had just taken over the charge of the house when our sister died, and he may well have used her flesh in our rice and dishes, making us eat it unwittingly.

It is possible that I ate several pieces of my sister's flesh unwittingly, and now it is my turn. . . .

How can a man like myself, after four thousand years of man-eating history—even though I knew nothing about it at first—ever hope to face real men?

## XIII

Perhaps there are still children who have not eaten men? Save the children. . . .

### ■ Mao Zedong (Mao Tse-tung) (1893–1976) (poems)

TRANSLATED BY WILLIS BARNSTONE AND KO CHING-PO

To Westerners, whose own association of poetry with government belongs to the long-distant era of the literate and literary courtier, the fact that the most powerful revolutionary and politician of twentieth-century China is also among its finest modern poets may seem stranger than it does to the Chinese. Mao Zedong was born in Shaoshan, Hunan province, in 1893 to a family of well-off peasants. He worked on his father's farm, attended schools, and was educated in Zhangsha at the First Provincial Normal School from 1913–1918, where he encountered revolutionary writings. He worked in Beijing in a library in the winter of 1918–1919, and was strongly influenced by Li Dazhao and Chen Duxiu, who were to become Communist leaders. Mao was present in Shanghai in 1921, at the founding of the Chinese Communist Party, and he was engaged in the 1927 peasant uprisings in Hunan. He spent several years with the Communist guerrillas in Jiangxi and other border areas; and after Nationalist armies forced the Communists to flee on the disastrous Long March of 1934, Mao became the supreme leader of the party. Eventually he led the Communists to victory, and, after the founding of the People's Republic of China in 1949, he became its chairman. In spite of challenges from within and without the party, Mao remained China's most important politician until his death in 1976, after which party moderates, under the leadership of Deng Xiaoping, took over from Mao's political coterie, the Gang of Four.

In his 1942 "Talks at the Yenan Forum on Literature and Art," Mao stated that literature is always political, that its true purpose should be to fire the masses with revolutionary fervor, to celebrate revolution and the people (not the subjective consciousness of the author), and that it should be judged on utilitarian grounds. Mao's comments were the basis for the Chinese development of Socialist Realist literature and were the authority upon which writers who did not fit the revolutionary model were criticized, censored, or worse. Mao's own poetry was written in classical forms, though he advised his readership not to emulate him in this. Its content is heroic, visionary, and revolutionary, and it dramatizes the historical events that led to the new Republic.

FURTHER READING: Barnstone, Willis, and Ko Ching-Po, trs. *The Poems of Mao Tse-tung,* 1972.

## Loushan Pass

A hard west wind,
in the vast frozen air wild geese shriek to the morning moon,
frozen morning moon.
Horse hoofs shatter the air
and the bugle sobs.                                                                5

The grim pass is like iron
yet today we will cross the summit in one step,
cross the summit.
Before us greenblue mountains are like the sea,
the dying sun like blood.                                                      10

## Snow

The scene is the north lands.
Thousands of li sealed in ice,
ten thousand li in blowing snow.
From the Long Wall I gaze inside and beyond
and see only vast tundra.
Up and down the Yellow River
the gurgling water is frozen.
Mountains dance like silver snakes,
hills gallop like wax bright elephants
trying to climb over the sky.
On days of sunlight
the planet teases us in her white dress and rouge.
Rivers and mountains are beautiful
and made heroes bow and compete to catch the girl—lovely earth.
Yet the emperors Shih Huang and Wu Ti
were barely able to write.
The first emperors of the Tang and Sung dynasties were crude.
Genghis Khan, man of his epoch
and favored by heaven,
knew only how to hunt the great eagle.
They are all gone.

Only today are we men of feeling.

## The Gods

*On the Death of His Wife Yang Kai-hui*

I lost my proud poplar and you your willow.
As poplar and willow they soar straight up into the ninth heaven
and ask the prisoner of the moon, Wu Kang, what is there.
He offers them wine from the cassia tree.

The lonely lady on the moon, Chang O, spreads her vast sleeves
and dances for these good souls in the unending sky.
Down on earth a sudden report of the tiger's defeat.
Tears fly down from a great upturned bowl of rain.

## Saying Good-Bye to the God of Disease

Mauve waters and green mountains are nothing
when the great ancient doctor Hua To could not defeat a tiny worm.

A thousand villages collapsed, were choked with weeds, men were lost
    arrows.
Ghosts sang in the doorway of a few desolate houses.
Yet now in a day we leap around the earth                        5
or explore a thousand Milky Ways.
And if the cowherd who lives on a star asks about the god of plagues,
tell him, happy or sad, the god is gone, washed away in the waters.

## ▪ Wen Yiduo (Wen I-to) (1899 – 1946) (poems)

TRANSLATED BY ARTHUR SZE

Wen Yiduo was born in 1899 in Xishui, Hubei province, and was perhaps the finest poet of the Western-influenced Crescent School of poetry in pre-revolution China. After a thorough traditional education in the Chinese classics, he studied painting in Chicago, Colorado, and New York. He had had exposure to Western literature in college, and this exposure caused him to attempt writing poetry in the vernacular (until this time he had written in traditional forms). While in America, he met Carl Sandburg, Amy Lowell, and Harriet Monroe, editor of the distinguished and influential journal *Poetry*, which published so many of the American Modernist poets. It was John Keats, however, who became his poetic model in this period. Wen's first book, *The Red Candle*, was published at this time. Wen was disturbed by the racial discrimination he witnessed in American Chinatowns, and he moved back to China, hoping to organize an intellectual renewal. Back in China, he dabbled in politics; helped found the influential Crescent School of poets, which met in his apartment; and became a distinguished scholar, specializing in the study of *The Songs of Chu*. During this period, he published his second and final volume, *Dead Waters*. His poetry is vernacular, yet polished and formally rigorous; he makes it "dance in chains," in Han Yu's phrase. On July 15, 1946, he was assassinated by hired agents of the Guomindang (the nationalist party in China, which, after losing the civil war to the Communists in 1949, has maintained its power base in Taiwan).

**FURTHER READING:** Payne, Robert, ed. *Contemporary Chinese Poetry*, 1947. Yeh, Michelle, tr. *Anthology of Modern Chinese Poetry*, 1992.

## *Miracle*

I never wanted the red of fire, the black at midnight
of the Peach Blossom Pool, the mournful melody of the *p'i p'a*,[1]

---

1. See Tao Qian's "Preface to the Poem on the Peach Blossom Spring" and Wang Wei's treatment of the story in "Song of Peach Tree Spring."

or the fragrance of roses. I never loved the stern
pride of the leopard, and no white dove ever had

the beauty I craved. I never wanted any of these things,
but their *crystallization*—a miracle ten thousand

times more rare than them all! But I am famished and harried.
I cannot go without nourishment: even if it is

dregs and chaff, I still have to beg for it. Heaven knows
I do not wish to be like this. I am by no means

so stubborn or stupid. I am simply tired of waiting,
tired of waiting for the miracle to arrive; and

I dare not starve. Ah, who doesn't know of how little worth
is a tree full of singing cicadas, a jug of turbid wine,

or smoky mountain peaks, bright ravines, stars
glittering in the empty sky? It is all so ordinary,

so inexorably dull, and it isn't worth our ecstatic joy,
our crying out the most moving names, or the

longing to cast gold letters and put them in a song.
I also affirm that to let tears come

at the song of an oriole is trivial, ridiculous,
and a waste of time. But who knows? I cannot be otherwise.

I am so famished and harried I take lamb's quarters
and wild hyssop for fine grain,—

            but there's no harm
in speaking clearly as long as the miracle appears.

Then at once I will cast off the ordinary. I will never
again gaze at a frosted leaf and dream of a spring blossom's

dazzle. I will not waste my strength, peel open
stones, and demand the warmth of white jade.

Give me one miracle, and I will never again whip ugliness,
and compel it to give up the meaning of its

opposite. Actually, I am weary of all this,
and these strained implications are hard to explain.

All I want is one clear word flashing like a Buddhist relic
with fierce light. I want it whole, complete,

shining in full face. I am by no means so stubborn
or stupid; but I cannot see a round fan without

seeing behind it an immortal face. So,
I will wait for as many incarnations as it takes—

since I've made a vow. I don't know how many
incarnations have already passed; but I'll wait

and wait, quietly, for the miracle to arrive.
That day must come! Let lightning strike me,

volcanoes destroy me. Let all hell rise up and crush me!                45
Am I terrified? No, no wind will blow out

the light in me. I only wish my cast-off body
would turn into ashes. And so what? That, that minutest

fraction of time is a minutest fraction of —
ah, an extraordinary gust, a divine and stellar hush                    50

(sun, moon, and spin of all stars stopped,
time stopped too) — the most perfectly-round peace.

I hear the sound of the door pivoting: and with it
the rustling of a skirt. That is a miracle.

And in the space of a half-open gold door,                              55
you are crowned with a circle of light!


# ■ Lao She (1899–1966) (story)

### TRANSLATED BY DON J. COHN

Lao She is the pen name of Shu Qungchun, a Manchu who was born
in Beijing in 1899. He was raised in poverty because of his father's early
death, yet he managed to graduate from college, taking his degree in 1917
and going on to teach and start his career as a writer. In 1924, he taught in
England at the School of Oriental and African Studies and wrote several
novels. He returned to China, where he wrote his masterpiece, *Camel
Xiangzi,* a novel that was translated into English in 1945 as *Rickshaw Boy.*
The novel became a best-seller in English, but the satirical and pessimistic
conclusion, which pleased neither the translator nor the Chinese critics,
was changed into an improbable and romantic happy ending. Lao She was
an organizer against the Japanese during World War II, and after the war
he spent time in America, lecturing and writing. After the revolution succeeded in 1949, he returned to China and became a revolutionary writer,
praising the new society. He died in 1966, during the Great Proletarian
Cultural Revolution, perhaps murdered during this time of social turmoil.
He is second only to Lu Xun as the finest Chinese fiction writer of the
twentieth century and is noted for the light and humorous touch he brings
to his fiction, even when he is waxing indignant against social injustice.

FURTHER READING: Chang, Jian-lih, tr. *A Translation of Lao She's "The Burning
Train,"* 1988. Hu, Jieqing, ed. *The Crescent Moon and Other Stories,* 1990. James, Jean,

tr. *Ma and Son: A Novel,* 1980. Kao, George, ed. *Two Writers and the Cultural Revolution: Lao She and Chen Jo-hsi,* 1980. Shi Xiaoqing, tr. *Camel Xiangzi,* 1981. Xiong, Deni, tr. *Heavensent,* 1986.

## Filling a Prescription

The Japanese troops were holding their regular target practice outside the Qihua Gate. As usual, the police guarding the gate were checking all the Chinese passing back and forth. Since the police were Chinese themselves, they were much more thorough and bold about guarding against Chinese spies than they were about the enemy; it was so much easier for them. Policemen were different from soldiers; they weren't responsible for foreign affairs.

Niu Ertou had unbuttoned both his short and long padded cotton jackets, and his blue cotton sash was tied loosely around his waist. Though this left a sizable portion of his bare chest exposed to the wind, he still felt hot; firstly, because he was walking very quickly; and secondly, because he was anxious and upset. His father had contracted a serious illness—the prescription cost more than a dollar! He lived nearly ten *li* from the Qihua Gate. The gate stood directly in front of him now; if he left the city immediately and took all the shortcuts he knew, he might make it home in time to let his father take his first dose by sunset. He sped up his pace; he was carrying the medicine in one hand and a rolled-up book in the other.

A large crowd stood in front of the gate, surrounded by the police. Ertou was in too much of a hurry to hang around and watch what was going on, and headed straight for the passageway which led through the broad gate tower.

"Where do you think you're going?" The sound of the policeman's voice echoed in the empty passageway.

Ertou was in too much of a hurry to figure out if this question was addressed to him or not, and kept on walking. Why, he wondered, was it so silent in the passageway?

"Hey, boy! I'm talking to you, you bastard. Get back here!" Someone grabbed Ertou by the arm.

"My father's waiting for me to bring him this medicine." Only then did Ertou realize that it was a policeman. "I didn't rob anybody!"

"Even if your grandfather wants to take his medicine, he also has to wait a little while." The policeman pushed Ertou towards the crowd.

Everyone there had their jackets unbuttoned. Ertou didn't have to waste his time on this, since his jackets were already unbuttoned. So he took the time to survey the scene. The people there were divided into three groups. Those dressed in silks and satins stood together in one spot; those wearing cotton gowns which weren't covered with mud made up a second group; and those dressed like Ertou formed a third. Though those in the first group had also unbuttoned their jackets, the policemen only gave them a cursory frisking and let them go. Ertou thought, "Doesn't look too bad. Fifteen minutes and I'll be on my way. I'll have to hurry when I get out of here." Things weren't going so smoothly for the men in the second group. Anyone with even the slightest bulge in their clothing had to be frisked twice. As the policemen worked their way through the crowd, they came to a man in his forties with a red nose, who refused to be searched.

"Get your supervisor over here!"

When the supervisor saw who it was, he said, "Oh it's you, Third Master. I'm sorry, I didn't notice you when you arrived. There's too much to do here; my hands are tied. I'm truly sorry." Without even a smile, the red-nosed man said, "You ought to get your eyes fixed. What a disgrace!" Rubbing his nose, he proceeded through the gate.

It seemed like hours before they got around to Ertou's group. "Take off your coats, my good men, you won't freeze to death," one of the policemen said with a laugh. "While you're at it, you can pick some of the lice out of the lining of my coat for me." This remark came from a man who might have been a ricksha puller. "Let's have no nonsense here; take 'em off and air 'em out." The policeman took another man's coat and shook it a few times. The coat's owner laughed and said, "The only thing I've got hidden in there is dirt." Upon hearing this wisecrack, the policeman threw the coat onto the ground. "Have a little more dirt, then."

There were only a few people left when it came to Ertou's turn. All those who had arrived after Ertou were placed in a separate group.

"What's that?" The policeman pointed to the object in his hand.

"Medicine."

"No, I mean the thing you've got rolled up there."

"It's a book I picked up in a public toilet."

"Let me see it."

The policeman glanced at the book's cover and noticed it was red. He handed it to the inspector. The inspector examined the book's cover as well and noticed it was red. Then he looked at Ertou. He flipped through the first few pages, but seemed to be unable to grasp the gist of it. Then, wetting his finger thoroughly with saliva, he flipped through another ten pages, paused for a moment, raised his head, looked at the gate tower, and glanced at Ertou again. "Take him inside," he said, and a policeman stepped forward.

Ertou instinctively took a step backwards. He knew he was in trouble now, but he didn't know why.

"My father's waiting for his medicine. I picked up this book in a public toilet."

Grabbing Ertou by the collar, the policeman said, "Listen to me, buddy. If you don't behave yourself, you're going to get your head bashed in."

"But my father's waiting for his medicine!" Though Ertou was anxious now, he didn't raise his voice. His vocal cords were immune to this sort of thing.

"Get him out of here!" The inspector's face was slightly pale; perhaps he thought Ertou was carrying a bomb on his person.

Being anxious was futile for Ertou at this point, but he couldn't stay there any longer. Suddenly tears welled up in his eyes.

The policeman took him into the station and whispered something to the sergeant on duty. The sergeant took the book and flipped through it.

The stoutly built sergeant was extremely polite. "What is your surname, huh?" He drew out the "huh" like an actor in a western-style comedy.

"Niu.[1] My name is Niu Ertou." His nose twitched as he answered.

"Hm, what village are you from, Ertou, huh?"

"Ten-*li* Village."

"Hm, Ten-*li* Village. That's outside the Qihua Gate." The sergeant nodded, extremely pleased with his superior knowledge of geography. "What were you doing in the city, hm?" His "hm" was even longer than his "huh."

"I was having a prescription filled, my father's sick." Tears were now rolling down his cheeks.

"Whose father, huh? Speak up! It's a good thing I'm not very suspicious. Now, I want you to tell me the truth. Who gave you this book?"

"I picked it up in a public toilet."

"If you don't tell me the truth, I'm going to make things very difficult for you." The fat sergeant appeared fatter than he had ten minutes ago; perhaps this is what happened to him every time he got angry. "Young man, don't be as stubborn as an ox with me. If you tell the truth, I'll let you go. We're looking for the man who gave you this book, understand? Huh?"

"I swear to you, I picked it up in a toilet. I don't want it anymore. Just let me go!"

"I don't think you're going anywhere right now." The sergeant took one more look at the book and decided to retain Ertou for further interrogation.

Ertou was extremely upset now. "But sir, my father is waiting for his medicine."

"You mean there aren't any pharmacies outside the gate, so you had to come into the city to buy medicine? There must be some other reason." The sergeant was about to smile, but stopped himself. He felt extremely satisfied about his own profound wisdom.

"The doctor told me to have the prescription made up at the Huaidetang Pharmacy downtown. The medicine's better there. Sir, I beg you, let me go now. I don't want that book anymore. Is that alright?"

"No, that's not alright."

That night, they took Ertou to the Bureau of Public Security.

---

1. Niu means "ox."

"Ru Yin" the writer and "Qing Yan" the literary critic were enemies, though the two of them had never met. Ru Yin earned his living by writing fiction while Qing Yan made a career out of writing criticism. When their works appeared in the magazines and newspapers, it was always Ru Yin who took the lead, with Qing Yan following close behind. No matter what Ru Yin wrote, Qing Yan always aimed the same poison arrow at him—"unsound thinking." Though this in no way affected the sale of his works, Ru Yin always felt that in the final accounting, the psychological victory belonged to Qing Yan. He didn't know whether or not the people who bought his cheap books smiled out of sympathy for him when they thought: "Who cares whether his thinking is sound or not; his stories make really entertaining reading." He hoped his readers didn't think this way and consoled himself by thinking, "Maybe there's somebody out there who really respects me." He was very much like a self-satisfied businessman. But whenever he received any fees or royalties for his writing, he imagined Qing Yan looking over his shoulder and saying, "Ahah! I see you've earned some money again! I guess that's one that got away. Just wait and see, I'm not finished with you yet!"

Once by coincidence their two photos appeared together in a magazine. This really piqued Ru Yin's imagination. In the picture, Qing Yan had a big head, long hair, protruding eyes and a pug nose like that of a Pekinese dog. The best thing you could say about him was that he looked like Socrates. It was this imaginary Socrates who very frequently haunted Ru Yin.

A number of malicious thoughts occurred to Ru Yin. Judging from his pen name alone—Qing Yan means "black swallow"—he had probably started out as an insignificant popular love story writer. But now that he had changed careers and was earning his living by condemning everything he read as "unsound thinking," it was just as well to ignore him. However, passive consolation is never quite as satisfactory as an active attack: the bullets of "unsound thinking" were still flying directly over his head.

Ru Yin wondered how he could set his thinking "straight"? The answer to this question could certainly not be found in Qing Yan's critical writings. There was one way in which Qing Yan didn't resemble Socrates: Socrates asked a lot of questions and was always full of answers; he often went around in circles, sometimes ending up lost inside his own arguments. But Qing Yan's style was to stand at the finish line of a 100 metre race, grab the slowest runner and slap him in the face. Ru Yin's only way out was to change the way he wrote. He read through a number of books which were supposed to be representative of "sound thinking"—though some of them had already been banned. He found them disappointing, since most of them were nothing more than anemic romances. He knew he could write much better than that.

He started to write in this style. He published a few pieces and waited eagerly for Qing Yan's response. But once again the response was: "Unsound thinking!"

When he made a careful comparison of his own work and that of the so-called orthodox writers, he noticed that they were written in entirely different languages: his were in Chinese, while theirs were written in some western-style Chinese. The content was also different: his stories were expressions of light and shade, sincerity and degradation, ideals and emotions; theirs were comedies laced through with "blood" and "death."

Despite this, Ru Yin's latest works ended up as "unsound thinking."

He wanted to play a joke on Qing Yan in order to shut him up once and for all. He started producing imitations of the so-called orthodox works, using foreign-style language and plots which though lively were far from realistic. He sent a number of them off to some magazines.

Strangely enough, every single story was returned to him. One in particular was accompanied by a polite letter from an editor:

> *In times like these, when there is no freedom of speech, the use of such words as red, yellow, blue, white and black could get us all wiped out. Nearly all the language in your story is of this type.*

Ru Yin couldn't stop laughing. So this was the way the world worked: words could really deceive people. Writers, readers, critics and censors all came from the same mould.

He now understood why Qing Yan only attacked him for his "unsound thinking" and said very little the other aspects of his works: it was because he was scared. This was quite a fair assessment. Now more than ever, he wanted to play a trick on Qing Yan. With his own money, he printed up a short anthology of stories previously rejected by publishers. He addressed a copy to Qing Yan and sent it to him via the editorial office of a certain magazine; in this way Qing Yan would be sure to get it. Even though he had spent his own money, he felt this was a positive move. "I went out on my own and printed these stories; let's see if he has the courage to criticize them without rejecting them outright."

Qing Yan went to the editorial office of X Magazine to see if there was any "news" for him. He found three letters and a package waiting for him on his desk. He read the letters first and then opened the package. It was a book with a red cover—written by Ru Yin. Qing Yan smiled. He felt sorry for Ru Yin. All authors deserve sympathy to some degree. After breaking through the barriers erected by the editorial departments, they're inevitably subjected to the wrath of the critics. But never under any circumstances should a critic lower himself out of compassion for an author. Unfair criticism could put one in a very awkward position. This he knew very well; but truly fair criticism could have even more serious consequences. The general rule was that writing which lacked barbs couldn't be considered literary criticism.

Qing Yan was the sort of person who would never hurt a fly. But writing criticism was his way of earning a living, and most hatchet men performed their jobs in order to eat. He knew all of this, but he still played dumb. He also knew which publications didn't like which writers, and by keeping this in mind whenever he wrote anything, further secured his own position. You might say that he was a man without ideals; considering the overall situation, however, perhaps he could be forgiven for this. The truth was that he never intended to be at odds with Ru Yin, since he didn't enjoy being at odds with anyone; but criticism was criticism. If he could have come up with a more original phrase than "unsound thinking," he would have rejected those two words a long time ago, for he had no particular affection for them. But since he had nothing more novel or convincing at hand, he had to make do with them; it was as simple at that.

He had long wanted to meet Ru Yin, to sit down for a good talk with him and even to become his friend. If they couldn't meet, at least he could write him a letter urging him to take back his red book as soon as possible, since it was a dangerous thing. If Ru Yin wanted to carry this game any further, smoking cigarettes and fussing over pedantic stylistic changes were the least useful things he could do. It would be better for him to think up something new. No matter how you looked at it, writing and criticism were just two forms of pedantry. All the flattery and hostility which were so much a part of the literary life amounted to little more than a waste of paper and ink, and no one engaged in these activities would ever contribute a single new page to human history.

The history of literature and literary criticism was little more than the history of numerous individuals flattering themselves; if these subjects never existed, libraries would certainly be a lot less empty and dull.

With his nose raised, Qing Yan let out with a snort. Rolling up the book, he left the editorial office. When he reached the southern corner of the Four Eastern Archways, he felt the urge to relieve himself. He put the book down on the mud wall surrounding the public toilet in order to facilitate tucking up his long brocade gown. As he stood in the stall, blocking the doorway, someone approached him from behind. As he was eager to allow this stranger to take his turn, he quickly straightened his gown and walked out holding his breath.

He'd gone quite a long way before he remembered the book, but he decided not to go back and look for it. Without the book in hand, he could still write his review. Fortunately, he remembered the book's title and author.

Ertou had been in jail for two days now, but he still had no idea what that book was about. All he could remember was that it was thin and had a red cover. He was totally illiterate. The more he hated that little book, the more he worried about his father's illness; that dirty rotten book was killing his father. They continued interrogating him, but he always gave the same answer: "I picked it up in a public toilet." It was hard enough for him to imagine that someone had written the book in the first place. Couldn't he find anything better to do than write a book? All Ertou'd done was pick it up. When he had nothing else to do in the winter, he'd go around collecting dung in the same way. How was that any different from picking up a book?

"Who gave it to you?" They asked him this same question over and over again.

Ertou was twenty years old, but no one had ever given him a book. How on earth could books have anything to do with him? He couldn't very well tell a lie and say that Doggy Zhang or Blackie Li had given it to him; that would mean getting innocent people in trouble. The only authentic-sounding name he could think of was Meng Zhanyuan, the head of the village martial arts society. This name, like Huang Tianba or Zhao Zilong, who were characters in popular tales, seemed like something out of a book. But he couldn't get the head of the society involved in this affair. If Meng Zhanyuan weren't there during the annual spring pilgrimage to Miaofeng Mountain, there was no guarantee that the village team wouldn't be defeated by the team from Scholartree Village in the "Five-Tiger Cudgel" contest. But when he thought about his father's illness, he could no longer worry about this sort of thing. If he could only turn into a puff of smoke and escape through a crack in the door. That damned book! That goddamned dirty book! Maybe it contained the prescription for the bogey man's magic potion!

Another day went by. Ertou was sure his father was dead.

He had no medicine to take. Ertou was nowhere to be seen. This would be enough to drive his father mad. Concluding that his father was dead, Ertou held his head in his hands. Tears began falling down his cheeks, and before long he started crying out loud despite himself.

When he stopped crying, he made up his mind to tell the policemen that Meng Zhanyuan had given him the book. This was the only name he could think of that sounded bookish enough. Neither "Doggy" nor "Blackie," not to mention "Little Seventy," seemed like appropriate names for people who gave books away.

But after giving it further consideration, he decided not to do it this way. It would be so unfair! He really and truly had picked up the book without thinking. Moreover, since he had found it in the city, Meng Zhanyuan couldn't possibly have given it to him. The facts didn't tally. His mind unresolved, Ertou's thoughts turned to his father's death. He could see all the members of his family wearing mourning dress, only he wasn't there. This was enough to drive anyone crazy!

That night, another man was put in Ertou's cell. He was young and well dressed, and had shackles around his ankles. Ertou's curiosity allowed him some respite from his worrying. Also, the sight of this cultivated man wearing shackles but displaying no sign of distress had a calming effect on him.

The new arrival was the first to speak. "What are you here for, my good man?"

"I picked up a book. Screw the ancestors of that damned book!" Ertou exploded with spite.

"What book was it?" The young man's eyes darkened slightly.

"A book with a red cover." That was all Ertou could remember. "I can't read."

"Oh!" the young man said, nodding his head.

Neither of them spoke. A few moments passed before Ertou broke the silence:

"What . . . are you here for?"

"I wrote a book!" the young man replied with a laugh.

"Oh, it was you who wrote that dirty rotten book."

Ertou had never met a person who could write books, but since this young man wrote books, he naturally assumed he was the one who had written the book with the red cover. He didn't know what to do now. He wanted to punch this writer in the nose, but there were too many policemen around. They'd already arrested him once, and he didn't want to make things any worse for himself. Having decided not to punch him, he now had no way of venting his anger. "You had nothing better to do, your hands got itchy, and so you wrote that dirty fuckin' book!" Ertou stared at the young man, gnashing his teeth.

The young man smiled mischievously. "But that book was written for your benefit."

Ertou couldn't restrain himself any longer. "I'll smack you one, you son of a bitch!" But he didn't lift a finger. Ertou was actually frightened of the young man, perhaps because his face, his manner, his youth and his clothing didn't quite match the shackles on his legs. He was very pale, but his skin was fine and smooth. His eyes were rather dull, and he was constantly smiling in a sort of an unnatural way. He was quite thin, and his narrow ankles were encumbered by those iron shackles! Ertou's fear arose from not knowing what kind of person this strange young man was.

The young man sat there smiling, and looked up at Ertou. "You can't read?"

Ertou sat there dumbly for a few moments, reluctant to answer, but he finally responded with a little grunt.

"Where did you find the book?"

"In a public toilet. Why does that matter?"

"Did they ask you about it?"

"None of your . . . !" Ertou swallowed the second half of his sentence. Besides his fear, he now felt somewhat suspicious of this young man.

"If you tell me, I'll help you get out of here." The young man's smile became more serious. He was thinking: "I wrote this dirty book for you, but you can't even read it. Isn't it my job to get you out of this mess?"

"They asked me who I got it from, but I didn't say anything."

"Let's say I tell them it was me that lost the book in the toilet. Wouldn't that solve all your problems?" By now the young man's smile looked rather silly.

"That would really be swell!" Ertou smiled. He hadn't smiled once in the last three days, so his lips remained sealed. "Shall we go talk to them now?"

"Not now. We had better wait till tomorrow when they start asking me questions."

"But my father's very sick. He may be dead by now!"

"First, tell me where you found that book."

"On the south side of the Four Eastern Archways, when I was taking a goddamned piss!" At that moment, Ertou felt something strange inside him. He could think of no way to describe this sensation properly; it was as if he were lost in the dark. He remembered one time several years ago when the locusts ate all the grain in the fields.

"Is this what you were wearing? What else did you have with you?"

"I was wearing the same outfit and I was carrying a package of medicine." Ertou began thinking of his father again.

Qing Yan returned home feeling very ill at ease. He couldn't get Ru Yin off his mind. Pacing back and forth in his room, he chuckled to himself; he still had to criticize Ru Yin's book. He could only write a short piece, since he'd lost the book. Writing literary criticism was second nature to him now, so he could easily broaden the scope of his attack and describe the binding or the cover; a literary critic was free to express his opinions on aesthetics. "If a book's red cover can symbolize the contents of a story, then this little juggling performance by Ru Yin is a cause for disappointment. For the book's cover, he has chosen thick, glossy red paper; as for the contents . . . well, the contents are full of unsound thinking." He went on from there and wrote seven or eight hundred words. In each and every sentence, he displayed his great authority. Criticism, after all, was a form of literature. He was comfortably satisfied with the precision of his writing; it had always been more severe than his thinking. It was his writing that secured him his reputation. He felt he had been unfair to Ru Yin, but this was the way it had to be. When he met Ru Yin some day, a few words of explanation would suffice to clear up any misunderstanding.

If writers obtained their pleasure at the expense of fictitious characters, then literary critics obtained theirs at the expense of the authors they criticized. After making a few minor revisions, he dropped the article in the mailbox.

Two days later, Qing Yan's article appeared in the paper. Two days after that, he learned that Ru Yin had been arrested.

Qing Yan wasn't worried about the article he had written. Critics were rarely arrested on the grounds of sound thinking. But if that were the case, it would matter very little. Besides students who read fiction and enjoyed following the petty skirmishes fought regularly on the literary battlefield, was anyone aware that literary critics existed at all? Wasn't the whole writing business, after all, just a huge heap of rubbish? At the same time, though, Qing Yan was upset about Ru Yin. He knew there had to be something meaningful in all of this for him, though he didn't know what it was yet, and could only describe it in a negative way: this meaningful something had nothing to do with either sound or unsound thinking. Truth and nonsense are entirely different things. In other words, if an author wants to describe a soldier, it doesn't mean he has to join the army. Now he understood! The positive solution was to create a new page or two of history, not just write a few silly articles. This thought had occurred to him before, but now he was convinced it was true. Yet he still wanted to rescue Ru Yin, even though this wasn't very "meaningful" for him.

Two days later, Ertou said goodbye to Ru Yin.

When he got home, he learned that his father's burial had taken place two days before. Ertou swore that he'd never buy medicine in the city again.

# ■ Wang Meng (1934– ) (story)

## TRANSLATED BY QINGYUN WU

Born in Hebei province, Wang Meng became a Communist Party member before he was fourteen years old. In 1949, he went to Beijing, where he worked in the Communist Youth League and entered a party school and studied political theory. His first novel, *Spring Time Fever*, was published in 1953, when he was only nineteen, and he became a nationally prominent literary figure in 1956 when he published "The Young Newcomer in the Organization Department," a story mildly critical of bureaucracy. This story was politically criticized a year later during the 1957 Anti-Rightist Campaign, a period of serious repression that directly followed a movement of political and literary liberalization, the Hundred Flowers Campaign. The slogan of that campaign had been "Let a hundred flowers bloom and a hundred schools of thought contend," but when the open debate that this campaign invited actually took place, the government cracked down and purged three hundred thousand intellectuals, among them Wang Meng. He was sent into internal exile in the countryside, where he worked as a manual laborer for the next five years. In 1963, after a brief reprieve during which he taught in Beijing, he was exiled again to Xinjiang province, where he worked with the Chinese Writers' Association. In 1965, at the inception of the Great Proletarian Cultural Revolution (a ten-year period of social repression ignited by Mao Zedong as a power play against moderate elements in the Communist Party), he was again assigned to manual labor.

A few years after the death of Mao in 1976 and the subsequent fall of the Gang of Four, Wang was reinstated as a professional writer in Beijing, publishing a number of modernist stories and the modernist novel *Bolshevik Salute*. In 1986, he was appointed Minister of Culture, but he was dismissed in 1989 during the purges that followed the massacre at Tiananmen Square. In his modernist experiments, Wang Meng uses techniques of fragmentation, stream of consciousness, and an increasing psychologizing and subjectivity in depiction of character—a marked departure from the straightforward narrative of the Socialist Realist fiction that dominated before the death of Mao. Mao, in his "Talks at Yenan Forum on Literature and Art," had asked writers to become a "cultural army" to "produce works which awakened the masses, fire them with enthusiasm and impel them to unite and struggle to transform their environment." Art was to be a utilitarian means toward revolution and the dissemination of revolutionary ideology; writers who focused more on aesthetics and themselves were "merely termites in the revolutionary ranks." Therefore, Wang Meng's work of the new period is revolutionary simply in its refusal to be revolutionary. He is the equivalent in fiction to the modernist poets who began writing in the late seventies and who were criticized for their obscure (*meng long*) poetics. Wang's short story "Anecdotes of Minister Maimaiti" is a darkly humorous, picaresque set of chapters that parodies the revolutionary fervor of the Cultural Revolution from the point of view of a Uygur protagonist (the Turkik Uygurs reside in Xinjiang province).

**FURTHER READING:** Larson, Wendy, tr. *Bolshevik Salute: A Modernist Chinese Novel*, 1989. Liu, Xinwu. *Prize-winning Stories from China*, 1978–1979, 1981.

## Anecdotes of Minister Maimaiti: A Uygur Man's Black Humor

> *Six essential elements for sustaining life (in order of their importance): first, air; first, sunshine; first, water; first, food; first, friendship; first, humor.*
>
> *Happiness comes when tears dry.*
>
> *The sense of humor is the superiority complex of intelligence.*
>
> —from Ancient Philosophical Aphorisms *(not yet published)*

## 1. Why Was Minister Maimaiti As Young As an Evergreen?

May 6, 1979. The wind was gentle, the sun was warm, the willows showing the first hint of green. In the Dashizi Muslim Restaurant, I ran into Minister Maimaiti and his twin brother, Saimaiti, neither of whom I had seen for more than ten years. I looked first at Maimaiti:

> Although merciless time had carved mountains and rivers on his face
> His vitality radiated from a thick crown of glossy black hair,
> His ruddy face was as warm and cheering as bread hot from the oven
>     and in his laughter hope and cynicism tussled like romping
>       children.

I turned to his brother Saimaiti:

> His bony back quivered like a tightened bow.
> In his dull eyes shadows of death flickered.
> He always sighed before speaking as if his stomach ached.
> In his hand he ever clutched a little bottle of heart pills.

I was so shocked by the contrast, of course, that as soon as I had said "Salamu"[1] and finished greeting them, I asked, "What has happened to you two these last years?"

"I suffered from The Catastrophe . . ." Saimaiti replied.

Maimaiti added, "I also suffered from The Catastrophe . . ."

Saimaiti: "As soon as the Unprecedented Event occurred, I was called one of the 'Black Gang' and locked up . . ."

Maimaiti: "I was also seized and locked up . . ."

Saimaiti: "I was beaten . . ."

Maimaiti: "I was whipped . . ."

Saimaiti: "I climbed the mountains to carry stone . . ."

Maimaiti: "I went down into the earth to dig coal . . ."

Saimaiti: "When I was officially labeled an Active Counterrevolutionary Element, my wife divorced me . . ."

Maimaiti: "When I was publicly labeled a Three Antis Element (Anti-Party, Anti-people, Anti-socialism), my children's mother married another man . . ."

Ailaibailai![2] Six of one, half a dozen of the other. Like peas, the twins' experiences seemed indistinguishable. Confused by this counterpoint of woes, I couldn't help asking. "Since you both suffered the same fates, why does brother Maimaiti look so young and Saimaiti so ancient?"

With tears quivering in his eyes, Saimaiti moaned, sighed, and beat his sides with his fists.

Pointing at his smiling face, Maimaiti said, "He lacks *this*, you see? He still broods and suffers. But me, I never let a day pass without making a joke."

## 2. The Crime of Minister Maimaiti (Which Lays Bare the True Nature of the New-Style Wedding That Breaks Away from "The Four Olds")

In 1966 the tide of the Cultural Revolution was surging high. Yet the Uygur people of the remote countryside of Xinjiang Province could make no sense of it. The villagers didn't know who were their targets, or indeed why anyone should be attacked at all. They just did not know how to "make revolution." In fact, they did not even know why they should make revolution. They could only shrug their shoulders and say to each other in Uygur expression, "Haven't got any message yet."

Yet by this time the Uygur villagers were so accustomed to the Party's successive movements that they felt they were obliged to make some attempt, any attempt, however muddled it might be, as if they were drawing a tiger playfully by using a cat as a model. Therefore they criticized Deng

1. Uygur for "May you have a long life."
2. Xinjiang slang for "What nonsense."

Tuo, recited Chairman Mao's Quotations, killed pigeons, and burned the Koran. The teenagers were very excited by all of this because they got to do all those things that had previously been forbidden, while their more conservative elders, though nervous and alert, mostly remained silent.

"Change through class struggle!" That was the motto of the day. Maimaiti's uncle, Mu Ming, Party Secretary of the Fourth Brigade (which changed its name to the Struggle Brigade when the Cultural Revolution began), took the lead by shaving off his beautiful mustache and beard, throwing away his embroidered cap, and putting aside his long tunic, black corduroy trousers, and boots in favor of an imitation army uniform. With an imitation soldier's cap on his head, a red band bearing the words "Red Guard" on his arm, Liberation Rubber shoes on his feet, and a kindergarten-child's red satchel containing Mao's Red Book slung over one shoulder, Mu Ming, a brand-new man, appeared on the horizon.

At that time Mu Ming's eldest daughter, Tilakizi, was going to be married to Mulajidi, who not only was the most intelligent young man in the village but was also the newly elected Political Commissar of the Struggle Brigade. When the news got out, however, the Commune Secretary and the Work Team Leader from the central provincial office sent for Mu Ming, Mulajidi, and Tilakizi and sternly warned the young couple that they must firmly break with the "Four Olds" (old ideas, old culture, old customs, old traditions). Included among these "Olds" was the traditional Uygur wedding ceremony: there was to be no slaughtering of sheep, no drinking, no dancing, no wedding presents—and certainly no prayers or blessings. No, their own marriage would have to begin with a new-style proletarian wedding.

"What exactly is this new-style proletarian wedding?" Mu Ming asked, trying to look and sound as much like a Red Guard as possible.

"The ceremony will be as follows. First, all present will recite from the Quotations, in particular the Three Speeches. Second, you will invite the leaders of the province, county, and commune to give speeches. Finally, the young couple will bow three times to the portrait of Chairman Mao, once to the assembled leaders, and once to each other. That's it. Of course, there will be no dowry from either family. However, both sides may exchange copies of the Red Book, portraits of our esteemed Chairman, sickles, and manure forks. No entertainment is allowed. After the wedding, the groom will spend the wedding night watering crops, and the bride will make forty posters of the Chairman's Quotations, done in red and yellow paint on wooden boards. . . ."

Mu Ming was more than a little surprised to hear this. He had thought that shaving off his mustache and wearing his pseudo-Red Guard uniform would make him sufficiently revolutionary. Little did he know, however, that he still was 108,000 *li* from "carrying the revolution through to the end."

Mulajidi scowled and rolled his eyes. He had assumed that by being a political commissar he could just go through the motions of being a revolutionary, spouting slogans, avoiding physical labor, and yet nevertheless ending up with more work points than other villagers. Now he would be forced to act out a senseless charade on his own wedding night, one that no one but a sexless idiot would possibly consent to.

Tilakizi was all tears. As a girl grows older her desire becomes stronger, and Tilakizi had been thinking for months about those first sweet, shy, tender moments when she and Mulajidi could be alone together. But never had she imagined that her wedding would be like one of those political-education classes conducted by the militia.

Furious at their reaction, the Commune Secretary and the Team Leaders lambasted the father, daughter, and future son-in-law, then ordered Mu Ming to get to work at once spreading the political and ideological word among the youth. After the trio had departed, the Commune Secretary called the League Secretary, the Chairman of the Poor and Middle Peasants Association, the Chairwoman of the Women's Federation into their office. Their job, he explained to them, would be to monitor the trio to discover the true thoughts and feelings of each and then badger them into changing their minds.

By all appearances, this method seemed to be working. The new-style proletarian wedding was duly held. Leaders gave speeches, officials posed with the couple for photos, revolutionary songs such as "The East Is Red" and "The Helmsman on the Sea" were sung, and solemn passages like "holding a memorial meeting to express our sorrows" were read. This model wedding was then reported in bulletins, local newspapers, and county broadcasts. And to top it all off, Xinhua News Agency carried the word to the country at large.

Ten days later, Mu Ming's family held the real wedding. Sheep were slaughtered, silks were exchanged, and the bride and groom paid all the customary visits to relatives—it was a true Uygur wedding. Luckily, this underground wedding was not all that risky. In the first place, since the new-style proletarian wedding had already been publicized, it had served its purpose. In the second place, the Party officials were all too busy accusing one another of being capitalist roaders or else defending themselves from such attacks.

A Uygur man's beard grows very fast, so in ten days Mu Ming at least had a healthy stubble, if not the respectable growth that would bring a man universal prestige. As the saying goes, "Although the old man lost his horse, who knows that it might not turn out for the best." Mu Ming did not appear as a comic Red Guard at the real wedding. After the ceremony, the bride and groom were as inseparable as paint and wood.

Of course, Minister Maimaiti knew all about his cousin's wedding. He made an anecdote of it to tell his friends, concluding, "The advantage of the new-style proletarian wedding is that it postponed the real wedding long enough for my uncle to let his beard grow out. The disadvantage is that they had to spend fifty *yuan* more than their budget; since besides butchering sheep and buying wine for the real wedding, they had to buy watermelon seeds, candy, and cigarettes for the new-style wedding."

These were not times in which to make such mistakes, however. Everyone was accusing everyone else of all sorts of things, and Maimaiti himself was soon under examination for taking "The Black Line" in literature. When his remarks concerning the wedding were denounced as a rightist's attack on the Great Proletarian Cultural Revolution, Maimaiti was seized for questioning.

To protect his uncle and cousin, Maimaiti insisted that he had made up the entire story of the underground wedding. As a result, he had yet one more charge laid against him, that of "spreading rumors for sabotage and encouraging a return to capitalism." After being convicted, he was tightly sealed in a cowshed.

## 3. At Last Minister Maimaiti Becomes a Writer Recognized by the People

Now let us turn back the clock a bit. Maimaiti had always been a lover of books, even as a child. In 1958, because of his scholarship and sensitivity, he was selected to be the Provincial Minister of Literature and Arts. This gave him the opportunity to meet many famous writers and poets, which increased his love for literature still more and made him determined to become a writer himself. Therefore he wrote and wrote and wrote. And although his manuscripts were rejected time and again, he kept on writing. Finally a few of his short poems and prose pieces were published in literary magazines and in the popular press. Unfortunately, no one paid the slightest attention to any of them. Readers and critics alike were unanimous in ignoring him. Established writers yawned, while emerging writers left him unread. Every time he petitioned to join the writers union, he was turned down. Eventually he became bitter.

It was only when he was denounced as a member of the Black Gang and sent off to a prison farm that his fortunes changed, because he now was in the company of all the famous writers and poets he had previously admired and envied. At last, he was one of them.

On an April day in 1967, Maimaiti and his colleagues were working in a vineyard when they heard a terrible racket: drums thundering, bugles blowing, and Quotations being chanted in unison. Realizing that a band of "revolutionary warriors" was approaching, the intelligentsia scattered like startled animals in the jungle. Some dived into ditches; some hid behind bushes; others just lay flat among the army of the ants, hoping to avoid another confrontation with the Army of the Revolution.

Unfortunately, Maimaiti had a bad ear infection, and so he heard neither the Red Guards approaching nor his colleagues' shouts of warning. Besides, he had come to enjoy his work in the vineyards and was so absorbed in his digging that he did not even notice that anything unusual was happening. As a result, he alone was left to serve as a target. Before he knew it, the Red Guards had surrounded him. They glared at him. Here stood a dangerous enemy of the people. Their courage and commitment were about to be tested.

"Who are you?" the Red Guards snarled.

"One of the Black Gang, a Three Antis Element," Maimaiti replied meekly. He dropped his hands to his sides and tried to look as ashamed and repentant as possible.

"What were you before?"

"Minister of Literature and Arts."

"Aha! A capitalist roader. A man of the Black Line. What are your crimes, monster?"

"I attacked the breaking away from the 'Four Olds,' worthy comrades, and wrote some reactionary articles."

"Which articles? How many?"

"Well, let me see . . ." Excited to talk about his writing, Maimaiti forgot about his penitent pose. "The first one was about . . ." With extraordinary seriousness and meticulousness, he reported the exact content of all his published articles, including a news report of less than a hundred words.

"What else have you written?"

Maimaiti promptly reported all the manuscripts that had been killed by editors.

"Do you know Zhou Yang?"

"Yes, of course." Actually, Maimaiti only knew the name. In Uygur, the same word is used for "know personally" and "know by name." Naturally his answer was misinterpreted.

The young warriors were startled.

Thinking that this man must be a famous writer, a really dangerous enemy, they began shouting revolutionary slogans. "Crush the enemy under your feet! Knock him from his high seat! Revolution is guiltless; rebellion is reasonable!" and so on.

Soon they grew tired of mere words and began to transpose their ideas into action, of which Maimaiti was the recipient. He did his best to huddle up into a ball, for two reasons: one, to show his submissiveness and, two, to protect his intestines. At the same time he kept saying "Oh" and "Ouch" in a voice that was neither too loud nor too faint. This moderate moaning was a deliberate ploy, learned from experience. If a victim clenched his teeth and made no noise, the young warriors, thinking he was defying them, would only become more antagonized. If he yelled too much, however, they would interpret this as a protest against their actions and would also become more antagonized. Therefore, the wisest course was to moan piteously but in a carefully modulated tone. By the time they had finished with him, Maimaiti had been beaten black and blue. His gums and nostrils were bleeding. His eyes were swollen like walnuts. It would have taken a nutcracker to open them. His back, sides, legs, and belly were all covered with cuts and bruises. Nevertheless, his heart, liver, spleen, stomach, kidneys, and bladder had all escaped injury. His tactic had worked.

But although the young warriors had broken Maimaiti's body, they still felt that they had not yet touched his soul. So they wrote six big characters on his back with a big brush and smelly black ink, "Black Writer Maimaiti!" Then, in high spirits, the young revolutionary warriors marched off, singing a revolutionary song, away from one victory but onward to a greater one.

Some twenty minutes later, the other writers crawled out of their hiding places one by one. Some tried to help Maimaiti to his feet. Others tried to console him. Some sighed for him. Others blamed him for not heeding their warnings. But they all agreed that the trouble with Maimaiti was that he worked too hard and was too honest and naive to know that a wise man always keeps his eyes open to six ways and his ears listening in eight directions.

Pushing away all helping hands, Maimaiti stood up. Shivering, he spat the blood out of his mouth. Then, disregarding all his other injuries, he pointed to his back and asked what the young warriors had written there.

"Black Writer Mai-mai-ti!" they read in unison.

"Aha!" Maimaiti shouted. Because of all the blood in his mouth and the loosened teeth, his words weren't clear. Yet his excitement was beyond words.

"You don't recognize me as a writer. You never have. But see, the people, they've recognized me at last!"

The crowd burst out laughing. They laughed till tears of joy came to their eyes.

---

# 4. Romance in the Cowshed

The Black Gang at the prison farm had to fetch drinking water from a motor-driven pump two kilometers away. This task was so difficult that they arranged to take turns with it. But in that April of 1968, Maimaiti amazed everyone by volunteering to take over this task completely. The shoulderpole and pails became his own property. At first they thought he was "learning from Lei Feng" and doing extra work in order to secure an earlier release, so they let him alone. But when this continued, someone finally got suspicious and asked him about it.

"Why do you go out of your way to do extra work? What are you up to?"

Maimaiti didn't try to hide his secret. In fact, it was with pride that Maimaiti declared, "Near the well lives a very pretty girl."

"A pretty girl?" The men of the Black Gang could hardly believe their ears.

"A pretty girl. More than a pretty girl." He began to declaim a poem he had written in her honor.

Her beauty is both sun and moon but
Shines with a lovelier light;

Her shimmering hair reflects a halo of love.
When I see her,
My heart bursts into flame,
My body turns to charcoal,
And tears of love spill from my eyes.
She is my love,
My light, and all my joy.

When the men heard this, they were dumbfounded. Then they made up their minds to follow him. And although Maimaiti knew their intentions, he didn't seem to mind.

He didn't even seem to mind when his "pretty girl" was discovered to be a fifty-year-old woman with a baggy goiter, a cataract, and a bent back. The men of the Black Gang laughed uproariously, calling him a liar, an idiot, and so on. But to their surprise, Maimaiti just smiled to himself and waited for the commotion to die down.

Then, with patient irony, he said, "You fine writers and poets—how can you write? Where is your imagination? We've been here for twenty dry months. I would think that anyone in a flowered blouse and red scarf would be beautiful to any of us."

This time no one laughed, except Maimaiti, who simply went on smiling and laughing to himself.

## 5. Why Didn't Minister Maimaiti Shut the Door When He Slept at Night?

In the barracks where the Black Gang slept, Maimaiti's bed was nearest the door, and this was how all the trouble began. At bedtime, whenever someone closed the door, Maimaiti would open it again. This led his colleagues to attempt to explain to him the complexities of class struggle. Society wasn't yet perfect, and so there might be thieves around. Even though all the prisoners were members of the Black Gang, most were nevertheless wearing wristwatches. Many had money and grain coupons in their pockets.

"You fail to understand logic," Maimaiti told them with his usual indifference. "Thieves, robbers, and all other sorts of bad men are, after all, human beings. Is this not true? We, on the other hand, have been told that we are not human beings but incarnations of Satan. If men do not fear Satan, should Satan be afraid of men?"

Unfortunately, this was overheard by a guard. He at once called Maimaiti in for questioning.

The guard: "You've been spreading poisonous dissension among the prisoners, haven't you?"

Maimaiti: "I wouldn't dare."

The guard: "You're angry because you've been classified as monsters. You're full of resentment."

Maimaiti: "Oh, no. I'm absolutely content."

The guard: "You're a reactionary."

Maimaiti: "I certainly am an incarnation of Satan."

The guard: "You've always been a reactionary."

Maimaiti: "Yes indeed. I've always been an incarnation of Satan."

The guard: "Why are you such a reactionary?"

Maimaiti (lowering his head): "I was influenced by Liu Shaoqi."

The guard (upon hearing the name Liu Shaoqi relaxes somewhat, thinking that Maimaiti's political consciousness has been raised at least a little. Adopting a softer tone, he continues): "Confess honestly. The Party is always lenient with those who confess their crimes. If you confess your crimes, you can be remolded, and the sooner you are remolded, the sooner you can return to the ranks of the people!"

Maimaiti: "I am determined to turn myself from an incarnation of Satan into a man, and as quickly as I can."

The guard: "Then think carefully about what you have done. Don't think that you can hide any of your crimes from us. And don't try confessing the minor ones to cover up the serious ones. Confess the grave ones now, and we'll be much easier on you."

Maimaiti (lowering his head and wringing his hands as if he were undergoing a convulsive ideological inner struggle): "There is a crime . . . but no, it's too horrible to talk about."

The guard (his eyes lighting up): "Out with it! Out with it! Whatever it is, if you confess now, I can assure you that we won't pull the pigtails of your crime, won't parade you in a high paper hat, and won't club you like a dog."

Maimaiti (meekly): "It was I who started the First World War. And I'm ashamed to say that's not all. I started the Second World War as well. And now—oh—it's too horrible—I'm feeling the impulse to start a third."

The guard (hopelessly confused): "Er???"

# 6. The Return of Minister Maimaiti

Nothing that Maimaiti said or did caused him to be set free. But after the downfall of the Gang of Four, it was determined that Maimaiti had been persecuted unjustly, so he was not only released from the cowshed but also restored to his former position as Minister of Literature and Arts for Xinjiang Province. Upon his release, one of the first things he did was to seek out his uncle Mu Ming and his cousin-in-law Mulajidi to find out how they had fared during the Cultural Revolution.

He was amazed to learn that they had not only survived but that, because of him, they had prospered. Mulajidi, the Political Commissar of the Struggle Brigade, told the story.

When they learned from the newspaper that Minister Maimaiti had been arrested, the Struggle Brigade immediately held a large-scale criticism meeting to denounce him. As political commissar, Mulajidi had a special role in criticism meetings. It was he who led the villagers in denouncing the Tripartite Village, the February Countercurrent, capitalist roaders such as Liu, Deng, Tao, Peng, Luo, Lu, Yang, Wang, Guan, and Qi. The method of denouncing was very simple. Ten minutes before it was time for work, Mulajidi would call all the villagers together and read them the names of those to be denounced. (Actually, who's who didn't matter.) Then the villagers all waved their arms above their heads, shouting "down with . . . ," inserting the names from the blacklist as they were read off to them. There was a slight problem, however, since in the Uygur language "down with" sounds very much like "long live" and the villagers sometimes became confused, shouting "down with" when they were supposed to be shouting "long live" and vice versa. Nevertheless, the villagers were used to covering each other, and no one was reported for this. At any rate, as a result of these criticism meetings, Mulajidi's and Mu Ming's positions were secure. In fact, Maimaiti was to provide an even greater benefit for them.

During the summer of 1967, a red flag contest was held to see which brigade could harvest the most grain. The Struggle Brigade lagged behind the Vigilance Brigade in both quality and quantity of the harvest. So, fearing they would lose, Mulajidi decided to shift the contest to political grounds. He asked the leader of the Vigilance Brigade, "Have you denounced Liu Shaoqi?"

"Of course."

"Have you criticized Wu Han?"

"Certainly."

"Have you criticized Minister Maimaiti?"

"Ah . . . Who? Mai . . . who?" The leader of the Vigilance Brigade was obviously at a loss.

Thus the Struggle Brigade won the contest and kept the red flag.

When he heard this story, Minister Maimaiti laughed till the tears streamed down his face. Patting his cousin-in-law on the back, he said, "I never dreamed that I would become a requirement for winning the red flag."

Time passed, and Maimaiti, as Minister of Literature and Arts, was required to read all the new exposé literature about the suffering of intellectuals during the Cultural Revolution. "So many comic possibilities have turned sour under their pens," he complained and then set about writing a novel of his own about the Cultural Revolution. When he had finished, he asked a friend who taught Chinese at the Institute for Minority Nationalities to translate it into Chinese for him. Then he requested a leave of absence from his post and, using his own money, traveled all the way to Beijing to hand the manuscript personally to the editor-in-chief at the Chinese People's Literature Press.

Out of special concern for a minority writer, particularly one who was a minister, the editor-in-chief quickly got to work on it. When he was through, however, he had to point out to Maimaiti that the structure was too loose and episodic and that the tone and depiction of character were too playful. Moreover, he added, the book was superficial and seemed cynical as well. For all these reasons, the book could not be published.

Minister Maimaiti argued with him about this.

"The book has to be published, even if what you've said is true, because if people read this book, they won't commit suicide during future political movements—if there are any."

The editor was deeply moved by this because he himself had more than once considered suicide during those troubled years. Finally he said that he would keep the manuscript and reconsider it.

But he murmured to himself, "For the prevention of suicide . . . can I really give this as a reason for publishing the book? What will the other editors say?"

It was at the Dashizi Muslim Restaurant, where I mentioned meeting Maimaiti at the beginning of this story, that he told me about his problems with his manuscript. In fact, he asked me to talk to the editor-in-chief about it on his behalf.

"If you need to give the editor a few gifts, I have plenty of raisins and butter here," he added.

"I think the problem is your manuscript," I replied, trying to look stern. "If it's good, all presses will compete to publish it. Giving gifts to our editors, what nonsense. It's a question of quality."

"Quality indeed," he replied. "But who is to judge exactly what quality is? I'm beginning to wonder if people recognized me as a writer only when they beat me up and if I became the requirement for winning the red flag contest only when I was locked in a cowshed." His voice was quiet but not without a tinge of loneliness.

His words seemed to add yet a few more gray hairs to his brother Saimaiti's head.

But just then, the waiter came with our delicious food—fried meat, steamed meat, spiced meatballs, and sweet and sour ribs. Minister Maimaiti opened a bottle of Ancient City wine, filled his cup, and, holding his glass high, gave the following toast to me and to all his readers.

> Ah, life! You may not be always sweet,
> But you are never only bitter.
> You may seem to drown a man,
> Yet you flow forward, wider and wider.
> Sometimes you seem stagnant and waveless,
> Yet you are constantly changing in a profusion of colors.
> In your ice is always fire.
> In your sorrow always joy.
> Prisons, knives, whips—
> How can they hold life back?
> Threats, slanders, lies—
> Can they pull joy up by its root?

Do not weep, for tears disgust a man.
What is tragedy? A game, too affected.
Let's burst out laughing,
The power of laughter is the power of life!
Able to laugh, able to live.
Dare to laugh, dare to live.
Love laughter, love life.

At this, Minister Maimaiti drained his cup to the bottom.

## ■ Chen Rong (Ch'en Jung) (1936– ) (story)

### TRANSLATED BY CHUN-YE SHIH

Chen Rong was born in Hankow, at the junction of the Han and Yangtze Rivers, a city now incorporated into the larger metropolitan area of Wuhan. After the revolution in 1949, she left school and after a brief time working in a book shop joined the staff of the *Southwest Workers Daily*. In 1954, she moved to Beijing and studied Russian, working at a radio station as a translator. In 1964, after a stint in the countryside in Shanxi province, she returned to Beijing and began her career as a playwright and fiction writer. Her long story "At Middle Age" was made into a film directed by Wang Qimin that won China's Best Film Award. "Regarding the Problem of Newborn Piglets in Winter" is a biting and absurd portrait of the rigid hierarchies and stultifying bureaucracy of contemporary China.

**FURTHER READING:** Yang, Gladys, ed. *Seven Contemporary Chinese Women Writers*, 1982.

## *Regarding the Problem of Newborn Piglets in Winter*

### 1. "H'mm, Have You Considered . . . ?"

"Silent is the night over the military harbor . . ." On the color television screen gleamed the graceful white figure of Su Xiaoming singing in her low soft voice.

"Grandma, turn it louder," the six-year-old Babe issued a command from the large soft couch she was sprawled on.

"Loud enough!" Grandma nevertheless walked over and turned the volume up slightly.

Babe suddenly jumped up and knelt on the couch. "Grandpa, can you hear?" she cried over the back of the couch.

"Don't yell. Grandpa's resting."

"Let our sailors sleep in peace . . ." the song went on.

So Grandpa slept on.

Zhang Dingfan was resting; his eyes closed, his gray hair pillowed against the sofa back and his arm limp on the armrest. After a day's hard work his wrecked nerves found repose in the lull of his own snoring.

Suddenly, a wind blew up outside and the door and the window rattled. The green velveteen curtain gave a stir.

Zhang Dingfan turned his head and uttered a sound barely audible, "H'mm."

Madam Zhang, wife of the Secretary, rose to her feet and walked over to the door and the window for a quick inspection. Both were tightly shut. Then she touched the heater; it was toasty warm. Everything seemed to be in order so she fetched a light wool blanket from the bedroom and walked toward the Secretary. Just as she was about to cover him with the blanket, Zhang Dingfan sat up with a jerk and stopped her. He turned his face toward the door and called, "Little You."

Madam Zhang, startled for a second, piped up in unison, "Mr. You, Mr. You."

In reply, a young man in his thirties came in from the anteroom.

"Get me Chief Jiao of Agriculture and Forestry."

Mr. You stepped lightly toward the table in the corner. He turned the lamp on and dialed the telephone. After he was connected to the right party, he raised the receiver, turned round and said, "Comrade Dingfan."

Zhang Dingfan rose slowly and walked toward the telephone. He seated himself in a chair before he took the receiver in his hand.

"It's me" he coughed. "Looks like it's getting colder. H'mm . . ."

Quickly Madam Zhang turned the volume of the television set to the lowest. Poor Su Xiaoming suddenly became mute, her red lips gaping and closing soundlessly.

"Grandma, I can't hear, I can't hear," Babe protested.

"Don't fuss, Grandpa is working."

Work is sacred; Babe stopped shouting.

"H'mm, have you considered—this sudden change in temperature and the problem of piglets in the winter—h'mm, we'd better do something. No, no, not by memorandum. First, notify every district in the county by telephone. Proceed level by level this very night. Don't let any piglet die from the cold. Then you may follow up by memorandum. Work on the draft right away."

He hung up the telephone, "These people, just like counters on an abacus—they only move when you give them a push. How can we ever achieve the Four Modernizations?"

"All right—it's all right now that you've alerted them," Madam Zhang comforted him.

"Grandma," Babe couldn't wait any longer.

The volume was once again adjusted. The singer had disappeared. With the tinkling of electronic music and a sudden pop, eight modernized angels in their white tight-fitting costumes emerged on the color screen, dancing and twisting their slender waists.

"No, no, I want Su Xiaoming," Babe demanded, rolling in the sofa and kicking her feet in the air.

Zhang Dingfan bent down to pat his granddaughter's head and said cheerfully, "Why not this? The melody of youth. Very nice."

# 2. "We'll Have Wonton Tonight."

Every light was burning in Chief Jiao's office, the Municipal Department of Agriculture and Forestry.

The young cadre had just finished a memorandum: "Regarding the Problem of Newborn Piglets in Winter" which he had been working on all evening. Now he was presenting it to the Chief for approval.

"No good, don't write this way." Chief Jiao quickly looked over the document and threw it on the desk. "Now, in writing a memorandum, you must avoid empty, boastful and irrelevant expressions."

He picked up the manuscript again and pointed at it, "Look here, 'After the winter solstice comes the Prelude of Cold,' who doesn't know that? And here, 'The development of a pig farm is a matter of great importance in promoting food production, supplies of meat to urban people, and reserve funds for the Four Modernizations of our country.' This is empty talk. Needless to say, more pigs means more money and more food. You have to use your brains to draft a memorandum."

The young cadre was totally lost—staring, wordless.

"Come here, sit down. Let's discuss this. A few concrete suggestions should make this memo more practical."

Burning the midnight oil was Chief Jiao's forté. He arose from his seat vigorously, while the young cadre sat down and opened his notebook.

"Regarding newborn piglets in winter—the first problem is to protect them from the cold. Isn't that right? The condition of winterization, in general, is not sufficient. Some pig farms are equipped with straw mats and curtains etc., but most are without even this minimum protection. Such conditions are contradictory to the objective of protecting newborn piglets. So the first and most important issue here is adequate winterization, and toward that end we must adopt every feasible and effective means." Chief Jiao rambled on, pacing the floor to and fro. He rolled his eyes and thought of more to say.

"The problem of piglets in the winter is mainly that of cold and hunger. Cold is an external cause, whereas hunger, an internal one—insufficient feeding will cause decline in body temperature, which in turn will cause decrease in resistance. Therefore, the second point is to keep the little piglets well fed. That's right. Be sure to include this point—increase the proportion of dietary nutrition in pigs' feed."

Chief Jiao made sure that the young cadre had jotted down what he had just said before he came to the third point:

"Furthermore, include the disease prevention. By the way, what is the most common disease that threatens pigs in the winter? As I remember we issued a special memo to that effect last time. You may repeat it here: how to prevent the premature death of newborn piglets."

Chief Jiao walked over to the file bureau, opened the door and gleefully produced a document, "Here is a good paragraph you may copy from: 'Report promptly any case of illness to the local Veterinary Disease Prevention Division. Meantime, take proper measures in treating the infected pig, in accordance with the rules and regulations currently in effect. In case of failure to report, a severe measure of action will be taken and the rule of accountability applies to all.' Add something to the effect that it is important to carry out the objective of prevention."

With an ache in his writing hand and a sense of relief in his heart, the young cadre peered at the Chief's thick babbling lips and could not help admiring him.

"The fourth point, emphasize the importance of political enlightenment. I need not provide you with the exact wording here. Also mention the material reward. You know that helps. Now, how many points do we have now? Four? H'mm . . ."

Chief Jiao stopped pacing the floor. The young cadre closed his notebook.

"Wait a minute. Last but not least: each level of the Party Committee should take the initiative by establishing the NEWBORN-PIGLETS-IN-THE-WINTER LEADERSHIP GROUP. Designate an assistant secretary to be in charge. Each related department should share the work responsibility. United we fight the problem. Report and follow up at regular intervals, and so on."

The young cadre bent down his head and wrote swiftly. One could hear the sound of his ball-point pen scratching the paper.

Chief Jiao stretched himself and heaved a deep breath. He cracked open his thick lips in a self-satisfied smile, "That's fine, now just add a little effort on your part—a bit of polishing up will do."

He looked at his watch. Eleven o'clock. "Let's go," he said while locking the desk drawer. "Time for our midnight snack. We'll have wonton tonight."

## 3. "There'll Be Words Aplenty at a Memorial Service."

The cigarette butts piled up like a mound inside the ashtray. A ring of ashes scattered around it. The smoke, rising steadily from the tray, swirled around the room like a fog, dense and gray.

Ma Mingpeng, the Secretary of the County Committee, was leaning against the desk, holding a cigarette with his smoke-stained fingers. His small wearied eyes blinked in his dark and sullen face. Two little pouches hung under his eyes.

Since coming to the office early this morning, he had not stepped away except twice to go to the dining hall. The Committee meeting took up the whole morning, and the Study Group the afternoon. The evening was first occupied by the conference of Leadership Groups from the Security Promotion Committee, followed by the report of "No-Office Project" on the issues of disputes between a county chemical factory and a Production Group. Now sitting in front of him was an old cadre looking for a job. Every word the cadre uttered smashed like a nail on his numb and fatigued nerves.

"Secretary Ma, many years have gone by since the collapse of the Gang of Four. I am still wandering about like a desolate ghost, not a sign of work. Others have got their positions back. Why is it so hard in my case?"

"You're an old comrade, I'll be candid with you. We're having problems inside the Committee: more people than work. Every department is already staffed with seven or eight chiefs. People are talking: too many cooks but no broth. Where can I place you?"

"I need to work, even a doorman's job will do."

"That's what you think. Well, I know old comrades like you are dedicated to the Revolution, not your own interests. But what could I do? You were already a cadre before the Cultural Revolution. The authorities will have to place you in a proper position. Comrade, don't worry . . ."

"How can I help it? I'm reaching sixty."

The telephone rang. Ma Mingpeng picked up the receiver.

"What? Emergency notice from the City Committee—piglets in the winter. Erh . . . erh . . . well, very well." Ma Mingpeng rolled his eyes; procedures one after another turned up in his mind which he issued over the telephone as rapidly as an electronic computer, "First, telephone all the communes tonight and relate the message of the City Committee. Urge them to comply and adopt appropriate means. Second, as soon as you receive the memorandum from the City Committee, pass it on to the Regular Committee. Third, notify the Regular Committee to add one more agenda on Thursday's meeting—the problem of piglets in the winter. Fourth, request the people from the Cattle Office to draft a supplementary notice based on the ideas of the City Committee and present it for further discussion at the regular meeting. Fifth, ask the Cattle Office to send someone over to inspect and collect material for a further report. A report to the City Committee should be scheduled in a few days."

Putting the receiver down, Ma Mingpeng touched his temple with his smoke-stained fingers and closed his puffy eyelids.

"All these years, what am I? How could I justify myself to the people? Secretary Ma, just think one day I might drop dead and not even a memorial service in my honor . . ."

Ma Mingpeng opened his eyes and said with a half smile, "Rest assured Comrade, there'll be words aplenty in a memorial service."

# 4. "The Peasants, They Can't Live without a Son."

"It's getting late. I say, let's call it a day. I've made up my mind today not to waste any more electricity. Go to bed early."

In the Commune Conference Room the fire in the fireplace had been out for a long time. Light from the smoking pipes and hand-rolled cigarettes flickered now and then and made the room cozy and seemingly warmer. Shen Guigeng, the Secretary of the Commune, was conferring with the cadres from the Production Group and Political Group.

"How many working units did you say have joined the System of Contract and Accountability? The Production Group reported fifty-seven units, which I think is a blown-up figure. Nowadays the emphasis is on truthful reports. We don't need to pad the figure."

No one said anything. The Production Group Leader made a mark on his papers.

"The Safety Training Class for truck drivers will begin day after tomorrow. But the majority of units have not yet handed in the enrollment list. This calls for our immediate attention. Three people died from accidents in one month. It's a matter of life and death, not to be overlooked. Will you, Chief Yu, take charge of this matter? Send someone to check tomorrow. Those drivers know nothing about safety regulations and some don't even have a driver's license. They race down the street like mad men. If we don't do something, our commune will soon become notorious."

Secretary Shen rubbed his bloodshot eyes and changed the subject to a few "trivial matters" such as forthcoming visitors to the commune. He then turned to ask the committee members, "Is there anything you wish to say?"

The plump Big Sister Gu, a member from Planned Parenthood, asked, "What are we to do when we report to the County Committee about the enforced birthrate? The goal is set for an increase of eight out of one thousand, but ours is way over eighteen."

"That's no good. Planned parenthood should be enforced. One more is too much."

"I know, but we can't make them do it. Our people from Planned Parenthood and doctors from the Public Health, they all dread going to the country. People point at their backs and curse them for doing such wicked things. Young wives scamper at the very sight of our white uniforms. The other day some woman hid in the closet for half a day, nearly died of suffocation."

"You should enlighten the masses."

"Enlighten them! How do you enlighten them? You just go and try. The peasants will tell you—without a son who would paint the house for me in the spring, harvest the grain for me in the autumn? These days, with the new bonus system, more labor means more money. Where would you be without manpower? They don't care if you restrict their rations, they want their son."

Secretary Shen sighed, "Ai, quite so. The peasants, they can't live without a son."

"What do you suggest we should do?"

"What to do, that's up to you. Why should we have Planned Parenthood if you ask me?"

Secretary Shen stood up, which meant the meeting was over. The roomful of people stretched and yawned and shuffled their respective chairs and stools. One after another they got up. At this moment Little Wang, the cadre of the Commune Office, entered the room.

"Secretary Shen, emergency telephone call from the County."

"Wait. Don't leave yet." Secretary Shen took the message from the cadre and looked at it. Then he said to Little Wang, "Telephone every group right away. Make sure they don't let any piglets die. Notify all of them tonight. If there is no answer by phone, you'll have to run over there. Every notice must be sent out before dawn."

Little Wang left. The roomful of people looked at one another and wondered why on earth the problem of piglets should become such a crisis.

"The County Committee telephoned to convey the message from the City Committee that we must deal with this issue of piglets in winter," Secretary Shen said as he seated himself again in his chair. "We'll have to discuss this problem and consume more electricity tonight. Let's see, all of you from the Production Group stay behind."

# 5. "Those City Girls . . ."

The television program had already finished some time ago but a few youngsters still remained in the office. They were talking, eating watermelon seeds and teasing Grandpa Cao.

"Hi, you, lift your feet, stop throwing seeds on the floor, don't you see I'm sweeping behind you as fast as I can?"

Grandpa Cao, holding a big broom, was sweeping the floor which was strewn with cigarette butts, watermelon seeds and dust. Panting hard, he looked fierce, as though he was about to chase them out.

"Ya. This is our Group, not your home," a youngster answered back.

"What? As long as I'm paid for doing the job, I'm in charge here. Hey, move your butt over to the fireplace, will you?"

The youngster swaggered over to the fireplace and spat out a few more watermelon seeds, "What do you know? Grandpa Cao is in charge here. Looking after a fourteen-inch black and white television set so he can just sit and watch it all day long."

"I watch television!" Grandpa Cao scoffed and glared. "Pooh, what a disgrace. Nowadays, good-looking girls strip themselves half naked. That's the kind of fashion for you. I bet those city girls wear no pants. If I had a daughter who exposes herself like that, I'd break her neck."

The youngsters cracked up so hard that they almost fell over.

"What's so funny? None of you has a streak of decency left. You all want to follow the ways of those city slickers."

"You're right. If I get a job in the city, what I'll do first is buy myself a pair of bell-bottomed jeans and a pair of sandals. Then I'll wear my hair long and put on a pair of toad-like dark glasses. When I come to see you, Grandpa Cao, you won't even recognize me."

"You, I could recognize you even if you were burned to ashes! You good-for-nothing."

"Ah, you're as good as treasures from an excavation."

"What?" Grandpa Cao was shuffling the chairs around after the sweeping. The phrase "treasures from an excavation" sounded alien to his ears.

"He said you ought to keep company with the Emperors from the Ming Tombs," another youth explained, winking.

"I'm not that fortunate."

The roar of laughter nearly drowned out the ring of the telephone. Only the youth standing near the phone heard it. He picked up the receiver, "Yes, you want Old Cao? What do you have to say? Just tell me."

The other party refused.

"Tell you! You'd better step aside quick," Grandpa Cao smiled proudly. He rubbed his hands on his pants before he solemnly took the receiver, "Hello, the Commune, it's me. Are you Comrade Wang, still up? Ah, about piglets. Nothing wrong. We're expecting two litters—so I heard from the Guos. Any time now—what? Don't let any die from the cold. If there's any trouble, just ask for me—fine, good-bye."

Grandpa Cao replaced the telephone and looked at the young men in the room, "I say, who'll send a message to the Village Cadre?"

The young men grimaced and shrugged.

"Not me, I wouldn't dare. This is important business from the Commune Office. I can't be responsible."

"Whoever is paid should do the job."

"Then I'd better step aside."

Grandpa Cao glared at them, put on his old lamb wool tunic and left for the trip to the Village Cadre.

## 6. "For the Sake of the Extra Five Dollars . . ."

The wife of Xu Quan, the Village Cadre, was awakened by the pounding on the door. "What on earth is the matter? Scaring people like this in the middle of the night," she muttered.

Xu Quan was sitting in the chair with his quilted coat over his shoulders. He fished out his tobacco box from his pocket and rolled a cigarette. He slowly answered his wife. "A notice from the Commune: don't let any piglets die from the cold . . ."

"That's worrying for nothing. The pigs are contracted to the Guo family who are capable and clever people. Why should they let any pig die? You just come back to bed and get some sleep."

"No, I'll have to check the pigs," Xu Quan stretched an arm into the coat sleeve, "I heard this evening they're expecting piglets tonight. If anything should happen, I'll be the first one to blame."

"Look at yourself—so 'positive,' all for the sake of the extra five dollars a month. You think of it as something special, but not me," she suddenly sat up, pulling the quilt over her and becoming very agitated, "If you're really so 'positive,' try and earn more for your family. Look at our neighbor Old Du. After a couple of long trips and some secret deals, he's earned at least several thousand already and they're building a five-room brick house now."

"I won't do anything illegal."

"Is it illegal to contract the work of the rice field? Good for those who did. The price of rice is going up, plus the price for good production; one family can easily earn up to seven or eight hundred dollars. Only you, fool, hooked by the official title, have stuck with poverty. You can burn your eyes out with envy."

"It's a good thing for people to earn more. The policy nowadays is to let people prosper. What are you griping about?"

"I'm not unscrupulous. I'm only talking about you. If you were clever, you'd have put our name in at the time of signing the contract."

"Put my name in? How do I find the time? Half of my days are taken up by meetings. I'm only busy and concerned with the good of the public."

"Tut, tut, not that nonsense again. As a cadre for more than ten years, what have you done for your family? We're all in for misery with you. The good of the public indeed! You've got the whole village against you."

"You're envious. Why don't you work in the rice field yourself? Nobody's stopping you. You want to get rich by doing nothing but staying in bed. No such luck."

He pushed open the door and stepped over the threshold.

"Put on your dog-skin hat. If you get a cold, I've no money to buy medicine." A black furry object flew toward him and landed on the crook of his elbow.

He put the hat on his head and turned around, "Just leave me alone."

## 7. "I'll Make Up Words to Suit Whatever Tune the Authority Picks."

In the pig-farm lights were shining brightly. Xu Quan called once before he lifted the cotton curtain. A rush of warm air greeted him.

He held his hands together and looked around. Mammy Guo's second daughter was squatting in front of the fireplace, making a fire. Mammy Guo, in a blue apron and with sleeves rolled up high, was lifting the lid of a pot in which the rice broth was cooking.

"Newborn piglets?"

"Yes, a litter of twelve, every one alive." Mammy Guo wiped off the perspiration from her forehead with her elbow. She was all smiles. She replaced the lid and wiped her hands on the apron. She then led the cadre inside.

On the warm kang, twelve tiny piglets huddled together in a bundle of round, plump and quavering bodies. A little humming noise came out from the bundle.

"Our pig farm is doing well this time," Xu Quan complimented her cheerfully.

"The group trusts us to do the job and lets us contract the pig farm. Of course, we want to do our very best. We need all the help we can get so I sent for my father from the next village."

Xu Quan saw an old man in the far corner of the room, squatting in front of a broken table and drinking wine by himself.

"Come on, have a cup," Mammy Guo brought out a wine cup.

"Ha, have you moved here with the pigs?" Xu Quan, laughing, squatted down.

"I'm worried if I'm away. It's really more convenient staying right here with the pigs, especially early mornings and late at night."

"Let's drink. What a day." The old man lifted his cup.

With a lightened heart and prompted by the warm hospitality, Xu Quan lifted his cup and finished the wine in a few gulps. A current of heat came over him. Just think, twelve piglets—Mammy Guo really knows what she's doing. He asked her about her past farm experience and her suggestions for the future.

"I just feed them—that's all. I can't read a single word; don't ask me about my experience," Mammy Guo said, quite pleased with herself.

Yes, what could she say? I have to make up my own report. H'mm—"To carry out the System of Accountability—if every member in the Commune shares the responsibility, the cadre can be assured of success,"—pretty good—but one sentence is not enough—this wine is not bad, must be at least sixty-five per cent alcohol, better than the one I bought last time—Mammy Guo is quite a capable woman, how she mobilizes everybody, old and young, the eighty-year-old father and the school-aged daughter—isn't this an "experience"? "Enlist all help, regardless of age or sex, in our care for the piglets"—sounds nice, but wait, how stupid can I get? This jingle is from the late fifties, no longer popular now. "Mass mobilization means massive achievement"—no good, you don't see such slogans on newspapers anymore. I have to use new expressions, such as "United in heart and spirit, we strive for the Four Modernizations"—that's better—one hears it broadcast eight times a day—but what category of modernization does Mammy Guo's work fit in?—I'd better stop drinking. Tomorrow I have to report to my superior—but what shall I say about "experience"? Pooh—never mind, when the time comes, I'll make up words to suit whatever tune the authority picks.

# Bei Dao (Pei Tao) (1949– ) (poems)

Bei Dao is the pen name of Zhao Zhenkai. He was born in 1949, in Beijing, and was a construction worker for some years during the Cultural Revolution. In 1979, during the period of literary and social unrest known as the Peking Spring, he started the famous underground literary magazine *Jintian* (*Today*) and soon became the leading poet of the 1980s, and the most famous representative of Misty poetry, a poetry affected by Western Modernism, Symbolism, and Surrealism that came in for fierce criticism by the defenders of the old school Socialist Realist poetry that Mao had championed and prescribed. With the new acceptance of Chinese Modernism and the thaw in official censorship that came in the middle eighties, he gained mainstream acceptance, editing an official magazine and becoming a member of the Chinese Writers' Association. During the summer 1989 Democracy Movement, he was overseas at a writer's conference and elected to remain in exile from China. His work has been widely translated and anthologized, and four collections of his poetry, *The August Sleepwalker* (1990), *Old Snow* (1991), *Forms of Distance* (1995), and *Landscape over Zero* (1996) are available from New Directions Press. His fiction collection is titled *Waves* (1986). He is currently living in California and teaching at the University of California, Irvine.

**FURTHER READING:** Barnstone, Tony, ed. *Out of the Howling Storm: The New Chinese Poetry*, 1993. Finkel, Donald, ed. *A Splintered Mirror: Chinese Poetry from the Democracy Movement*, 1991. Soong, Stephen C., and John Minford, eds. *Trees on the Mountain: An Anthology of New Chinese Writing*, 1984.

## Sweet Tangerines

Sweet tangerines
flooded with sun sweet tangerines

let me move through your hearts
bearing burdens of love

sweet tangerines 5
rinds breaking with delicate rains

let me move through your hearts
worries turned to tears of relief

sweet tangerines
bitter nets keep each fleshy piece 10

let me move through your hearts
as I wander in the wreckage of dreams

sweet tangerines
flooded with sun sweet tangerines

TRANSLATED BY JAMES A. WILSON

## Coming Home at Night

After braving the music of the air raid alarm
I hang my shadow on the hat-stand
take off the dog's eyes
(which I use for escape)
remove my false teeth (these final words)
and close my astute and experienced pocket watch
(that garrisoned heart)

The hours fall in the water one after the other
in my dreams like depth bombs
they explode

TRANSLATED BY BONNIE MCDOUGALL AND CHEN MAIPING

## Night: Theme and Variations

Here is where the roads converge:
parallel light beams
like a long conversation suddenly broken,
the air stuffed with truck drivers' pungent smoke
and rude indistinct curses,
people in a line replaced with fences
Light leaking from a cracked door
is flicked to the roadside with cigarette butts
and trampled by quick feet
A billboard leans on an old man's lost stick,
about to walk away
A stone waterlily withered
in the fountain pool, a building deliberates collapse,
the rising moon suddenly strikes
a bell again and again
and the past reverberates within palace walls
Now the sundial turns and calibrates deviations,
waiting for the emperor's grand morning ceremony
Brocade dresses and ribbons toss up in the breeze

and brush away the dust on the stone steps                    20
A shadow of a tramp slinks past the wall,
colorful neon lights glow for him
and all night keep him from sleep
A stray cat leaps onto a bench
to inspect the water's trembling mist of light               25
But a mercury lamp rudely opens window curtains
to peer at the privacy of others
disturbing lonely people and their dreams
Behind a small door
a hand quietly draws the catch                                30
as if pulling a gun bolt

TRANSLATED BY TONY BARNSTONE AND NEWTON LIU

## Beyond

A tempest in a teacup leads the marching sea.
Beyond the harbor, adrift on their sleepless bed,
the coupling levers make fast the chains of power.
Beyond the frame, a plaster figure wearing a classical smile
speaks from the manifold shadows of one day.                  5
Beyond credulity, a race horse outruns death.
Implacably, the moon imprints its seal upon black happenings.
Beyond the story, a plastic tree is thrashing in the wind.
This dismal fare is our excuse for survival.

TRANSLATED BY DONALD FINKEL AND XUELIANG CHEN

## ■ Shu Ting (Shu T'ing) (1952– ) (poem)

TRANSLATED BY CHOU PING

Shu Ting is the pen name of Gong Peiyu. Associated with the Misty school of poets, she was the leading woman poet in China in the 1980s. A southeast Fujian native, she was sent to the countryside during the Cultural Revolution before she graduated from junior high school. Then she worked in a cement factory and later a textile mill. In 1979, Shu published her first poem and in 1983 was asked to be a professional writer by the Chinese Writers' Association, Fujian Branch, of which she now is the deputy chairperson. Her collections of poetry include *Brigantines* (1982) and *Selected Lyrics of Shu Ting and Gu Cheng* (1985). She won the National Poetry Award in 1981 and 1983. Her work is deeply romantic in nature and must be understood as a reaction to the repression of romance in literature, film, song, and theatre during the decade-long Great Proletarian Cultural Revolution (1966–1976). Shu's tender, romantic poems sometimes do not play as well in English translation since modern and postmodern sensibilities have outmoded such sentiment, but her poems have a crystalline, lyrical strength that saves her from being saccharine and has made her the best-known contemporary Chinese woman poet in the West.

FURTHER READING: Barnstone, Tony. *Out of the Howling Storm: The New Chinese Poetry*, 1993. Finkel, Donald. *A Splintered Mirror: Chinese Poetry from the Democracy Movement*, 1991. Kizer, Carolyn. *Carrying Over: Poems from the Chinese, Urdu, Macedonian, Yiddish and French African*, 1988. Lin, Julia C. *Women of the Reed Plain: An Anthology of Contemporary Chinese Women's Poetry*, 1992. Soong, Stephen C., and John Minford, eds. *Trees on the Mountain: An Anthology of New Chinese Writing*, 1984. Yeh, Michelle, ed. *Anthology of Modern Chinese Poetry*, 1992.

## Two or Three Incidents Recollected

A cup of wine overturned.
A stone path sails in moonlight.
Where the blue grass is flattened,
is an abandoned azalea.

The eucalyptus trees are swirling
and stars above teem into a kaleidoscope.
The rusty eyes of an anchor
mirror the dizzy sky.

Holding up a book to shade the candle
and with a finger in between the lips,
I sit in an eggshell quiet,
having a semi-transparent dream.

## ◼ Liang Heng (1954– ) and Judith Shapiro (1953– ) (memoir, written in English)

Since the 1949 Communist Revolution, China has swung back and forth between periods of relative expression and repression. *Son of the Revolution* is a memoir that fits into the category of "Scar Literature," or literature recording the widespread repression of the decade-long Great Proletarian Cultural Revolution of 1966 to 1976. This literature poured out in the period after the death of Mao Zedong and the fall of the Gang of Four. Liang Heng's mother was a victim of the 1957 Anti-Rightist Campaign, a period of extreme repression that followed upon a brief welcoming of dissent during the 1956 Hundred Flowers campaign. In 1966, after years in which more moderate leaders had been gaining power, Chairman Mao launched another period of cultural struggle—the Cultural Revolution—as a ploy to regain his eroding power. During this period, China fell victim to roving Red Brigade youth bands who took the struggle against lingering remnants of the feudal past into their own hands, resorting often to torture, murder, ideological indoctrination, and even, according to a recent report, cannibalism. In Liang Heng's terrific memoir, written with his wife Judith Shapiro, he recounts how the pressures of this anarchistic period turned families against themselves, as the children are forced to criticize their father, and as Liang Heng himself is driven to the brink of suicide on trumped up charges. Liang Heng was born in Changsha in 1954 and graduated from Hunan Teacher's College in 1981. After marrying Judith Shapiro, who taught American literature at the Teacher's College, he came to the United States and earned a master's degree from Columbia University. *Son of the Revolution* was published by Vintage Books in 1984.

## *from* **Son of the Revolution**

### *from* **Chapter Five: The Smashed Temples**

While the criticism movement was getting started, college and middle-school students were forming the first Red Guard units. They were relatively conservative, protecting most of the Party leaders if only because those leaders were also the Red Guards' fathers and mothers. Fiercely proud of their "good" backgrounds—so much so that they would allow only students descended from the "Five Red Types" (Revolutionary cadres, Revolutionary martyrs, Revolutionary soldiers, workers, and poor and lower-middle peasants) to join them—these first Red Guards focused their attack on the so-called Five Black Types: landlords, rich peasants, counterrevolutionaries, "bad elements," and Rightists. Their slogan was, "If the father is a hero, the son is a brave man; if the father is a reactionary, the son is a bastard," thus settling the question of class standing for all eternity. The irony of the situation was that these sons and daughters of high-ranking cadres were creating a movement that would soon double back to attack their parents; they themselves would become the victims of their own Revolutionary fervor.

In Changsha, the initial group was called the "Red Defense Guards," and by an incredible fluke Liang Fang managed to become a member. Because there were so many cadres' children at the No. 1 Middle School, that school was among the first to become organized, and because Liang Fang took part in the organizing work, the issue of her Rightist parent was temporarily overlooked. She had finally achieved her long-coveted Revolutionary glory. She must have renounced our mother with extraordinary enthusiasm in order to pass muster.

Liang Fang rarely came home, of course. We got most of our news of her through Liang Wei-ping, who moved about a good deal and saw her through school activities. One day Liang Wei-ping returned in a state of great excitement. Liang Fang had told her that the Party Secretary of the No. 1 Middle School had denounced himself for betraying the Communists to the KMT before Liberation, and then had hanged himself in the cellar where he was being kept a prisoner. A real class enemy exposed! The other news was that a lot of students were preparing to go to Peking to report to Mao's wife, Jiang Qing, and the other members of the Cultural Revolution Directorate. There was an off-chance that they might be able to see Chairman Mao himself.

The August 18 *Hunan Daily* was a red-ink issue. It told of thousands of Red Guards gathering in Tian An Men Square, and Chairman Mao making an appearance and allowing a student to pin the Red Guard armband on his sleeve. Great numbers of middle-school and college students had been permitted to mount the tower and shake hands with him, and it was plain that a broad new movement had been launched.

We felt the first echoes in Changsha soon after. The representatives of the first Peking Red Guard group, the "United Action Committee," arrived from the capital bringing with them a first taste of the violence that would spread throughout China. They were staying at the luxurious government hotel near the Martyrs' Park when they got into a fight with one of the hotel workers, a boy whose grandfather had been a landlord before Liberation. I don't know the details of the argument but they nearly beat him to death with their wide leather belts.

What amazed me was the reaction of the Party Committees to this episode. There was a glass propaganda case by the front gate of the newspaper, which usually held exhibits on factory production, "little friends" dancing in nursery school, or instructive displays on the life of the model soldier Lei Feng. Now appeared photographs of the violence, hailed as "Revolutionary heroism." Changsha wasn't the first practice ground for this new breed of terrorism, of course, but the incident was the first most of us had heard of. Later, such events would become all too familiar.

After their visit, the local movement spread beyond the "Red Defense Guards," although membership was still restricted to the "Five Red Types." The groups usually chose their names from some poem or quotation from Chairman Mao, so we had the "Jinggang Mountain" group, the "East Is Red" group, the "Chase the Exhausted Enemy" group, the "Struggle with the Waves in the Middle of the Current" group, and many more. We got used to seeing the Red Guard costume—People's Liberation Army green pants and jacket, a wide leather belt, and the prized bright red armband. Liang Wei-ping wanted to join, but because of our mother she was told she could only work at school, which had been converted into a Red Guard hospitality station, a kind of inn for Red Guards from other provinces. She was crushed, but glad to be allowed to help at all. They kept her very busy boiling water and pushing desks around to make beds for all the guests.

The "Sixteen Articles" had stressed the need to criticize the "Four

Olds"—old thought, old customs, old culture, and old morals—and this was the thrust of the Red Guards' first campaign. The immediate and most visible result was that the names of everything familiar changed overnight. Suddenly "Heaven and Heart Park" became "People's Park." "Cai E Road," named for a hero of the Revolution of 1911, became "Red Guard Road." The Northern Station where I had pushed carts for a day was now to be found on "Combat Revisionism Street," and a shop named after its pre-Liberation Capitalist proprietor became "The East Is Red Food Store." Changsha quickly acquired a "Red Guard Theater," a "Shaoshan Road," a "People's Road," and an "Oppose Imperialism Road."

All this was extremely confusing, especially for the old people, and everybody was always getting off at the wrong bus stop and getting lost. To make matters even worse, the ticket-sellers on the buses were too busy giving instructive readings from the Quotations of Chairman Mao between stops to have much time to help straighten out the mess. Of course, there were some people who never did get used to it, and to this day they live on the ghosts of streets whose names today's young people have never heard of. (Ten years later an old man asked me where Education Road was, but I had no idea there was such a street. Then he asked a nearby policeman, but he didn't know either. More and more people got involved, forming a circle around him and telling him that he was mistaken, that there was no such street. Finally he protested, "How could I be wrong? Changsha already had that street by the thirty-seventh year of the Republic of China!" Everybody burst out laughing; he was using the obsolete pre-Liberation system of counting years dating from the 1911 Revolution.)

People changed their own names, too. One of my classmates rejected his old name, Wen Jian-ping ("Wen Establish Peace"), in favor of Wen Zao-fan ("Wen Rebel"). My neighbor Li Lin ("Li Forest") called herself Li Zi-hong ("Li Red from Birth") to advertise her good background. Zao Cai-fa ("Zao Make Money") became Zao Wei-dong ("Zao Protect the East"). Another friend got rid of the "Chiang" in his name because it was the same as Chiang Kai-shek's.

So, there was a lot of excitement in the city, but at home it was very quiet. Father spent every evening at his writing, and Liang Wei-ping and I never felt much like talking. We were sitting silently like this, reading and writing, on the hot night that Liang Fang came home. I hadn't seen her in more than three weeks. She was a changed person.

She looked splendid, never better, strong and slim where her leather belt cinched in her waist. Her green army-style uniform with its cap of authority over her short braids gave her an air of fashion and confidence I had never seen in her before. She looked a real soldier, and I sat up straight and stared with big eyes, unsure whether or not she was really my sister. My desire for my own Red Guard uniform dated from that instant.

Father emerged when he heard voices and looked glad to see Liang Fang. "How have things been going?" he asked. "We haven't seen you in a long time."

"The situation is excellent," she answered in the language of Revolution. "We're washing away all the dirty water. But I never sleep. Every night we're out making search raids."

"What's a search raid?" I asked.

"You know, before you've been on a search raid you have no idea what's really going on in this society. People have been hiding all sorts of things. Counterrevolutionary materials, pre-Liberation Reactionary artworks, gold, jade, silver, jewelry—the trappings of Feudalism-Capitalism-Revisionism are everywhere."

My father looked surprised. "What do you care about those kinds of things?"

But Liang Fang was too involved in her story to answer. "We have a schedule to follow. Every night we go to a series of homes and go through every book, every page to see if there's any anti-Party material. It's an incredible amount of work. We have to check all the boxes and suitcases for false bottoms and sometimes pull up the floors to see if anything's been hidden underneath."

Liang Wei-ping brought her a basin of hot water and a towel to clean her face, and when she stood up to wash, her eye fell on a traditional painting of a horse by Xu Bei-hong. "What are you doing with *that*? Xu Bei-hong was denounced ages ago. You people are too careless." She went over to take it down, but Father's voice stopped her.

"What's wrong with it? That has nothing to do with any Capitalist-Revisionist line. Leave it be."

She said, "But you don't know what's been happening. It's not just a question of paintings, but of all the old things. Where do you think I've been all day? I was up on Yuelu Mountain with the Hunan University students trying to get rid of those old monuments and pavilions. And it wasn't an easy job, either. Half the stuff's made of stone. We had to use knives and axes to dig out the inscriptions. Stinking poetry of the Feudal Society! But it's all gone now, or boarded shut."

"Can we still go play there?" I asked.

"Well . . . ," she hesitated. "Maybe for now you'd better not; people might think you were there for the wrong reasons."

Father had found his voice. "How could you destroy the old poetry carved in the temples and pavilions? What kind of behavior is that?"

"What kind of behavior? Revolutionary action, that's what. The Hengyang District Red Guards have already destroyed all the temples on the Southern Peak of Heng Mountain. So much for the 'sacred mountain'!"

When I heard the words "Southern Peak" I remembered that Waipo had told me how people went to burn incense, setting out from their doorsteps and kneeling every few paces all the way to the mountaintop. If Waipo knew the temples were gone, what would she do? Who would light incense for her now?

"Who asked you to do those things?" Father demanded.

"Father," she answered with exaggerated patience. "You really don't understand the Cultural Revolution at all, do you? We have to get rid of the Four Olds. That includes everything old. Don't you even read your own newspaper? You'd better keep up with things or you'll be in trouble."

Father protested, "It's one thing to get rid of old customs and ideas, and another to go around smashing ancient temples."

"What good are they? They just trick people, make them superstitious. They're a bad influence on the young people."

"Who ever influenced you?" Father demanded. "No one in your whole life ever asked you to believe in any Buddhas."

Liang Fang didn't have an answer, which irritated her. "Well, anyway, they're all old things. Why aren't there Revolutionary poems, Chairman Mao's poems, statues of people's heroes, workers, peasants, and soldiers?"

Father despaired. "It's all over! China's old culture is being destroyed." He hit the table with his finger for emphasis. "Such precious historical treasures. All those symbols of China's ancient culture gone in only a few days. You've wronged your ancestors."

Liang Fang lost her temper. "No wonder people criticize you. You just keep following the Revisionist line and refuse to change, don't you?"

Father said angrily, "All right! I don't care, then. But I forbid you to touch that picture."

The quarrel ended on that note, as Father went into his inner room and closed the door. I couldn't figure out who was right, but I knew that Chairman Mao supported the Red Guards. So I said to Liang Fang, "Forget it, why don't you? It's hard for him to give up his ideas. Why don't we talk about something more pleasant?"

But Liang Fang was angry and didn't want to talk.

"I just came home to get a good night's sleep, anyway," she said. "What a family." She walked over, lay down on the larger bed, and was asleep almost immediately.

## Chapter Six: Traveling Struggle

The search raids soon spread to the newspaper. It was a terrifying time, because every night we heard the sounds of loud knocks, things breaking, and children crying. Like every family with a member attacked in the posters, we knew the Red Guards would eventually come to our house, and we were constantly on edge. During the day we went to see the exhibits of confiscated goods; at night we lay dressed, sleeplessly waiting for our turn.

At eleven one night the knocks finally came, loud, sharp, and impatient. We sat up in bed automatically. Father emerged from the inside room and turned on the light. He motioned with his head for Liang Weiping to get the door.

There were seven or eight of them, all men or boys, and the small room seemed very crowded. Despite the heat they were all wearing white cloths over their mouths and noses, and dark clothes. The one who seemed to be the leader carried a long metal spring with a rubber tip. He struck it against the table top with a loud crack.

"Liang Shan!" he said. "Is there anything Feudalist-Capitalist-Revisionist in your house?"

Father stammered, "No, no. I had pictures of Liu Shao-qi but I turned them in to the Work Team. Nothing else."

"Father!" The man sliced at the table again.

Liang Wei-ping started to cry.

"What are you blubbering about? Cut it out. You and the boy, get over there in the corner."

We cowered there, trying to keep our sobs silent.

"What you must understand is that this is a Revolutionary action," the man announced. "Right?"

"Yes, yes, a Revolutionary action." I had never seen my father plead with anyone before. I had never seen him without his dignity.

"You welcome it, don't you! Say it!"

Something stuck in my father's throat.

"Shit. You've always been a liar!" Two Red Guards took him by each arm and grabbed his head, pushing it down so he was forced to kneel on the floor. They shook him by the hair so his glasses fell off, and when he groped for them they kicked his hands away. "Liar!"

The others were already starting to go through our things, some going into the other rooms for the books, others to the boxes. For several minutes there was silence except for the rustling of paper and the opening of boxes and drawers. Then one of them cried out.

"Quite a fox, isn't he? We said he was a liar!" The Red Guard had two Western ties and a Western-style jacket. "What's the meaning of this?"

"Ties," my father mumbled.

They kicked him. "Ties! Do you think we're children? Everyone knows these are ties. Capitalist ties. Or hadn't you heard?"

Father was pointing excitedly. "They were ordered through the newspaper. For some jobs. It wasn't my idea. For receptions and—" The spring slammed down on his hand and he cringed in pain.

"Who told you to point your finger? Think you can order people around still, don't you? Stinking intellectual!"

Liang Wei-ping cried, "How can you go hitting people that way? He can't even see properly."

"Shut up, little crossbreed, or we'll be hitting you next," snapped the Red Guard standing by the bureau. "Look at this! Fancy pants and sleeves with three buttons!"

From the other room came two Red Guards with armfuls of books. They dumped them unceremoniously on the floor near where Father was kneeling and went back for more. Tang poetry fell on top of histories, foreign novels on the Chinese Classics. Our house had always looked very neat and spare; I had never realized we had so many books.

After an hour they had finished going through everything. My comic books of the Classics had been added to the pile; the Xu Bei-hong horse had been crumpled and tossed on top. Everything we owned was in disorder on the floor, and even our pillows had been slit open with a knife. Father had been on his knees for a long time, and was trembling all over. The Red Guards were stuffing things into a large cloth bag when one of them got an idea for another game.

He put our large metal washbasin on the floor and built a little mound in it out of some of the finest books. He lit a match underneath and fanned it until the whole thing was aflame. Then he fed the fire, ripping the books in two one at a time and tossing them on. Father turned his head away. He didn't need his glasses to know what was on the pyre.

"What's the matter, Liang Shan? Light hurt your eyes?" The leading Red Guard held the metal spring out in front of him like a snake. "'A Revolutionary action.' Say it. 'It's a good fire.'"

Father was silent. I prayed he would speak.

"You shitting liar. Say it!" The man grabbed Father by the hair and twisted his head to make him look at the flames. "'It's a good fire!'"

My father's face looked very naked without his glasses, and the light from the fire shone on it and glistened in the tear lines on his cheeks. I could hardly hear him.

"A Revolutionary action," he whispered. "It's a good fire!"

They let him go; it was over. They shouldered the bag and filed out, the last putting our transistor radio into his pocket as he passed the table. We three couldn't find a word of comfort for each other; we just put things back in order in silence. The next day we discovered they had also helped themselves to Father's salary for that month.

The feeling of terror remained in our hearts for many days without fading. Then one evening when we were eating dinner, Liang Fang came home again. Somehow I didn't feel as glad to see her as usual.

Liang Wei-ping seemed to feel the same way. "Oh, you're back," she said, and continued eating. Maybe it was that Liang Fang was participating in the things that had hurt us so much. She must have sensed something, for she just got herself a bowl and sat down with us.

Then she noticed that the house was not the same. "What's wrong?" she demanded. "Has there been a search raid here or something?"

"There certainly has," Liang Wei-ping said. In great anger she told her what had happened that night, emphasizing the way the Red Guards had treated Father.

Finally Father interrupted coldly, "What's the point of talking about it? It's all 'Revolutionary action.'"

Father's sarcasm stung Liang Fang and she said defensively, "Father, I swear I would never do that type of thing. Whenever any of the boys in our group hit anyone, we girls always criticize them afterwards. And I would never take advantage of a search raid to fatten my own purse."

Even though she must have been terribly angry at Father because of the posters about him, it seemed she needed his understanding. And in spite of how hurt he had been, he still felt concerned for his daughter. "How have things been going lately?" he asked finally. "I'm always worried about you."

"Since the end of August there have been two Red Guard factions, and I'm in the real Rebel group now," she answered. "I quit the Red Defense Guards because they refused to attack the real seats of power, the Party leaders, and just wanted to denounce intellectuals. Also, they were getting more and more elitist. Finally the snobs asked everyone to get proof from their units that they had good backgrounds. So one day I came here to the newspaper . . . ," she paused and looked awkwardly at Father, embarrassed at not having stopped by the house. "At first the people in the office wouldn't give me anything because they said there was no precedent, and then I finally persuaded them. Well, it turned out that they wrote about Mother being a Rightist. I ended up throwing the paper into the outhouse, and I had to quit the group.

"But now I'm very happy, because there are even more people in our new Rebel group. Now I'm on my way to a cotton mill to drive out people with Conservative 'Protect the Emperor' viewpoints. We're going to organize the workers to seize power from the leadership. There'll be people going to all the units. I've heard it'll be mostly students from Hunan Teachers' College coming here to the newspaper."

Father interrupted. "But which faction is right? It would be terrible if it turned out you were on the wrong side."

She laughed. "The Cultural Revolution Directorate in Peking supports us. The Conservative Red Guards are done for and some of their leaders are being arrested. They were wrong to try to make Revolution into a private club. Madame Jiang Qing criticized them for their elitism ages ago. The issue is the Party leaders themselves now. No one is immune anymore." She paused and picked up her bowl and started shoveling food in with her chopsticks.

When the meal was over, Father asked her whether she needed anything. "I don't need money," she answered. "I get eight *jiao* a day, plus four *liang* [one *liang* equals fifty grams] worth of rice coupons. All the Rebel groups get stipends now." She hesitated. "But I could really use a mosquito net."

This wasn't such a simple request. There were three beds, my father's in one room, one for me, and one for my sisters in the other. Each bed had a net, but this was no ordinary luxury. To get one you not only needed 40 *yuan,* nearly a month's salary, and scarce cotton coupons, but also a special mosquito net coupon. Father got the coupon for the new net on his bed only because of his marriage. But he was very generous. "Take mine," he said. "I'll use mosquito incense."

Liang Fang refused at first. "How can I take yours? I thought Liang Heng could sleep with you and I could take his."

"Take it, take it. If the Revolution needs it, I'll give it up gladly." This was the first joke Father had made in months. We all laughed together.

But after Liang Fang had left, he seemed worried again. This Cultural Revolution was getting more complicated. It was hard to keep track of who was right and who wrong. "One day you're black and then you're red and then you're black again," he said. "Children, whatever you do please remember to be careful what you say. Never give your opinion on anything, even if you're asked directly. Just believe Chairman Mao's words, they're the only thing that seems to be reliable anymore."

I remembered his words for many years. They were another lesson in self-protection in modern society. And events showed that a lot of other people had learned the same lessons as I.

The next day, students from the colleges on the West Bank of the Xiang River gathered in front of the *Hunan Daily* gateway. They had come to organize the Rebel group. Young reporters and workers from the printing and repair shops put up posters welcoming them, and the students lined up in formation, waving copies of the *Quotations of Chairman Mao* and shouting, "Learn from the *Hunan Daily*'s Rebel group!" Then they marched in to the sounds of drums, red armbands reading "Chase the Exhausted Enemy" on every sleeve. All the old newspapermen left their desks, and it would be a full ten years before most of them returned. My father was among them. That day marked the end of his newspaper career.

But as Liang Fang had predicted, the arrival of the student Rebels coincided with a change in the focus of the attack, away from intellectuals like my father and toward the Party powerholders. Our old primary school was turned into a makeshift prison for about ten of the top political leaders, while their families were moved to a broken-down building near the newspaper compound's wall. Once I went to Gang Di's home and could hardly believe how the eight of them were living crammed into one tiny room. His mother and sister slept on a bed, but everyone else was sleeping on benches and chairs pushed together. And all thirteen-odd families shared one kitchen with a huge hole in its crumbling wall.

The family meetings held by the Work Team yielded to criticism meetings with attendance obligatory. There were all kinds, every day, big and small, but the one that made the deepest impression on me was the sort called "traveling struggle." It was a lot like the way the People's Liberation Army had dealt with the landlords after Liberation (I'd seen that in movies), but even more cruel.

The loudspeaker called us all outside, and in a few minutes I saw it coming. A group of Rebels were in the lead shouting "Down with the Capitalist Roaders" and "Long Live Chairman Mao Thought." Following them were about ten of the old "leading comrades" tied together on a long rope like beads on a string, their hands bound. They were wearing tall square-topped paper hats inscribed with phrases like I AM A BASTARD or I AM A FOOL, and around their necks were wooden signs with their names and crimes like FU KAI-XUN, CAPITALIST ROADER POWER USURPER or MENG SHU-DE, FILIAL GRANDSON OF THE LANDLORD CLASS. Those on the Editorial Committee had milder labels, such as DEVOTED ASSISTANT TO THE CAPITALIST ROADERS. Behind them, unbound, walked my father and some of the other intellectuals; they were less important, so their placards were light and made of paper, and they wore no hats. Still, they saddened me. They walked with their heads bowed low, carrying brass gongs, which they beat in time to the chanted slogans. As Father passed our doorway he bowed his head down even lower; he must have known I was watching him.

The Team walked very slowly, picking up more people with each building it passed. I followed at a distance, not wanting Father to see me, and I was astonished to hear a few low voices speaking in a very different spirit from that of the slogan shouters in front.

"Those placards must be terribly heavy," a woman's voice said.

"Some of those Rebels aren't such models of purity themselves," a man muttered. "Someone ought to investigate *their* backgrounds." The words comforted me even though I didn't know who had said them. Probably a family member like myself.

In a crowd, we passed the dining hall, the basketball court, the clinic, and all the dormitories, and went back past the primary school, finally reaching the auditorium on the fourth floor of the modern office building where we had had our Family Member meetings. There was a huge picture of Chairman Mao on the wall directly behind the platform, and the words BIG CRITICISM MEETING were written in huge characters on a hanging banner. On the side walls were more banners, with quotations from Chairman Mao and Rebel slogans. The Capitalist Roaders were already kneeling on the platform, their hands tied behind their backs with long ropes; the intellectuals "assisting" at the meeting were standing on each side with their heads bowed, facing inwards. Father was on the right toward the back, so I chose a seat on the far right beyond his line of vision.

First came a test for the intellectuals. Each in turn was ordered to recite one of the "Three Essays" by Chairman Mao, either "On Serving the People," "In Memory of Norman Bethune," or "The Foolish Old Man Who Moved the Mountain." If anyone made a mistake, he would have to kneel in apology before the picture of Chairman Mao until the end of the meeting. The test applied to the intellectuals alone; as a Rebel leader declared, "Capitalist Roaders don't have the right to recite the works of Chairman Mao."

Several people had their heads on the floor in humiliation when it came Father's turn, and my heart was in my mouth. They ordered him to recite "On Serving the People," and when he had said only two sentences, he abruptly stopped. I was nearly in tears. Suddenly all around me, I heard the next line whispered, as if people were reciting along with him, prompting him. Father adjusted his glasses for a moment. Then, in a strong clear voice, he recited the whole thing without stopping, supported by what I knew was his confident love for Chairman Mao.

When the Capitalist Roaders' turn came, they had to recite the big character posters attacking them. The meeting went on and on, and whenever someone stumbled there were cries of "Give him an airplane ride, give him an airplane ride!" At this the Rebels tossed the rope binding the man's arms behind him over a pipe at the top of the auditorium and hoisted him up in the air, letting him squirm in agony like a dragonfly with pinched wings.

Some of the family members couldn't bear it and left the auditorium in tears. Gang Di's older sister ran out with a loud sob, pulling Gang Di behind her, when their father was hauled aloft. It wasn't my father who was being tortured, but I couldn't bear it either, and followed them out. Luckily no one noticed, and we got away.

I had hardly reached home when Liang Wei-ping came in, panting for breath. I didn't want to talk, but she insisted on telling me about a big demonstration she'd seen on May First Road. Fifty or sixty open trucks had passed on their way to the execution ground in the eastern suburbs. "The woman who was going to be shot was in the first truck, standing there tied up with a handkerchief stuffed into her mouth and a huge bamboo sign on her back, which reached way over her head," my sister said, pacing excitedly. "There was a big red $X$ on it, and below it said she was a KMT spy about to be executed! And on each side of her there were two Red Guards holding her by the back of the neck and pushing her head down." The same truck carried Reactionaries who had already confessed—some wore heavy iron placards that made them bend under the weight; others, less serious offenders, had wooden ones. And they all had gongs and were shouting things like "I am a counterrevolutionary, I am wrong" or "Thank you, Chairman Mao, for not making me die."

I couldn't bear to listen. It made me miserable. But she rattled on. "My classmates said they were probably all teachers, movie actors, old cadres, writers, and people like that. There were Rebels with bayonets in all the trucks. I never saw so many Red Guards before." Liang Wei-ping hadn't noticed that Father had come slowly up the stairs and was standing quietly in the doorway, listening. "Everybody was shouting slogans and the children were throwing rocks and sticks. One of them hit the KMT spy right in the head."

"Stop it," I finally broke in. "Don't talk about it anymore. Can't you see that Father's tired?"

Liang Wei-ping turned in embarrassed surprise and said, "Father, I didn't know you were home. I'll get some hot water for you."

While she was busy with the thermos and basin and towel, I led Father into his bedroom and fluffed up his pillow for him. Soon she came in with the steaming towel, and he rubbed his face and neck as if to wash away weeks of dirt. When he was finished he looked up wearily. "Well, Liang Wei-ping. It's a good thing you watched other people's 'traveling struggle' and not mine. You might not have found it so entertaining." He lay slowly back against the pillow and closed his eyes.

We shut the door softly behind us. As if she hated herself, Liang Wei-ping said, "I feel terrible, talking about those things in front of Father." She sat down on her bed and stared out the window for a long, long time.

## Chapter Seventeen: Interrogation

Soon after Liang Wei-ping left, Father returned to his work on the Propaganda Team and I went back to school to begin the new semester. My sister's stories had influenced me, and I resolved to improve my relationship with the peasant children. This was relatively easy to do, for I understood them very well. I knew they were more afraid of ghosts than of anything else, and I used to impress them by nonchalantly visiting places they believed haunted. My classmates were already a little afraid of me because of my height and toughness; now they began to see me as some sort of hero.

What really kept me out of fights was the discovery of the boarded-up storeroom. It was a flat-roofed building near the basketball court, and an idle moment's investigation through the cracks in the door revealed that it was full of books, probably from the pre-Cultural Revolution school library. I hadn't read a good book since the Red Guards' search raid more than four years earlier, and my heart pounded. I quickly organized my handful of best friends, now including two peasant boys, and swore them to secrecy. Late that night, we pried off a few boards and climbed in. The acrid dust and mildew irritated our throats, and spiderwebs were everywhere; the books lay in broken piles, and the yellow paper bindings were sticky to the touch. But I felt as though we had entered paradise!

Someone had a flashlight, and we passed it about with shaking hands as we made our selections. We rationed ourselves, as we did when we stole sweet potatoes, for fear of being discovered. I chose a history of Europe and translations of Hegel's *Dialectics* and Flaubert's *Madame Bovary*. We replaced the boards carefully when we left.

It seemed there would be no end to our secret new pleasures. My life changed completely. I read with a passion I had felt for nothing else, keeping a diary about everything. The world of the imagination opened to me; I had new dreams and ambitions. My fellow thieves and I held discussions on literature and even began to write poetry, meeting on the windy riverbank but never feeling cold. We were a small literary society of fifteen-year-olds.

One day a classmate—I never found out who—took one of my poems from my desk and turned it in to a political cadre. It was a pessimistic poem, about my road of life leading nowhere. I was publicly criticized, and "dissatisfied with reality" was written in my file. Even that didn't quell my literary fervor. I simply began to turn it outward, writing letters to far-away friends and family like Little Li, who was still in Changsha because his parents had not yet been "liberated" from the study class. I developed quite an active correspondence, receiving answers to all my letters except those to Peng Ming. I imagined he must be too busy making Revolution to write.

Then one Saturday morning, classes were canceled for a special schoolwide meeting. New slogans were up in the big classroom, all of them dealing with class struggle, so we knew something important was in the air.

The political work group was the section of the school Revolutionary Committee with the real power, and Liu Guo-rong, a graduate of the Hunan Teachers' College's Politics Department, was the head of it. This was his meeting, and he strode to the podium as if girding himself for a performance.

It was a short meeting, but an exciting one. Liu's gold fillings sparkled in his expressive mouth, and a fine spray of saliva rained into the first rows at emphatic moments. A new movement was on, he told us, to round up the counterrevolutionary "May Sixteenth" conspirators.

"This nationwide secret organization has tried to attack our beloved Premier Zhou En-lai by sabotaging diplomatic relations with foreign countries," he bellowed. "They have a manifesto and a plan. Their activities are vicious. They use our postal system to spread their pernicious conspiracy everywhere." Liu paused, and we held our breaths. Finally he hissed, "We have a May Sixteenth conspirator right here in this room!"

Pandemonium broke as we chattered excitedly and craned our heads about hoping to identify the culprit. My mind raced down the list of my simple country teachers, but it seemed impossible that any of them should be involved in something so terrifying, so dangerous. Liu continued, "After the meeting, the counterrevolutionary will come to my office and surrender. I will put up five locked boxes throughout the school so that those of you who think they have spotted other counterrevolutionary activities can put in their reports. Don't worry, I am the only person with the keys. No one will know about your suspicions but you and me." He flashed his golden smile. "Meeting dismissed."

In the classroom, I held a whispered consultation with the members of my literary group and we decided to disband and return the stolen books that evening. Other classmates were checking their desks to make sure nothing had been planted there. Then I felt a hand on my shoulder. It was Teacher Deng, a member of the school Revolutionary Committee. "Liang Heng," he said, "Liu Guo-rong wants to see you."

I hurried behind him past my classmates' stares, shame burning me. A direct confrontation with Liu Guo-rong was too terrible to contemplate. I couldn't imagine what I had done.

The political work office held nothing but locked cabinets from floor to ceiling, the slogans on the walls, and some wooden chairs and a large desk. Liu sat behind this, smoking, a thick folder in front of him. He jerked his head toward an empty chair, and I sat down, trembling. Then he almost smiled.

"Did you forget to bring your ears with you this morning? You wanted a personal invitation?"

I flushed deeper in an agony of confusion.

"Well, you can still confess your activities as a May Sixteenth conspirator," said Liu, gesturing to a sheaf of blank papers on which I now noticed the heading "Confession" in big black characters.

My protests were useless. Liu shook his folder at me and claimed he knew everything, while I racked my brains for what the contents might be. Finally, he stood up and said, "You won't be leaving here until you've confessed, so you might as well begin now. Someone will bring you your lunch." I heard the key turn in the lock after him.

That morning the sounds of my classmates' voices rang in the corridors and I glued myself to the barred window hoping to catch a glimpse of a friend. I enumerated the possibilities over and over, rejecting them all: Could it be the books I had sent to Little Li in Changsha? Our literary group? The stolen sweet potatoes?

At noon, Teacher Deng came with food, and he whispered kindly to me, "You better confess, or heaven knows what will happen. The letter came from the Peking Public Security Bureau."

That explained it. Peng Ming must be in some kind of trouble. If I had come to the notice of Peking, things looked very bad for me indeed. But I recalled the content of my letters, and felt a bit calmer. I had done nothing but speak of our old friendship and ask Peng Ming if he could send me some materials on the arts; he was, after all, a composer.

Liu came back that afternoon to question me. His face was constantly changing, sometimes fierce, sometimes kind and smiling, until I felt numb and I wasn't really sure what was right anymore. On the one hand, he threatened me with jail; on the other, he promised me I could join the Communist Youth League if I only admitted my crime. "Your father came to the countryside with a black mark on his record, and before it's wiped clean you give him a counterrevolutionary son!" Liu said. "Think of the glory for your family if you tell the Party everything! Think how proud your father will be!"

At one point I mentioned Peng Ming's name. Liu lit up ecstatically. "Aha, you've confided the name of your counterrevolutionary contact to the Party! That's wonderful!" And he seized a piece of paper and, consulting his watch, noted down the exact moment of my "confession." Then he looked at me expectantly. "Go on."

I don't know how many times I explained the nature of my friendship with Peng Ming. I told Liu that we had been neighbors, that he had taken me with him on a New Long March. I explained that I had helped out in Peking, that his sister and my sister were classmates. But I insisted I knew nothing about any May Sixteenth conspiracy, nor that Peng Ming might have anything to do with counterrevolutionary activities. I didn't understand much of what was happening to me, but I thought I might as well die rather than confess something false that might be used against my friend.

In the late afternoon, Liu opened his folder and took out the letters I had written to Peking. I broke out in sweat then: I had never dreamed the Public Security Bureau could be so thorough.

"These letters were written in your own hand, right?" asked Liu.

"Of course," I responded. I described again the nature of my friendship with Peng Ming and my reasons for writing the letters.

Liu wasn't happy. "You're only a fifteen-year-old boy, and you dare take me for a three-year-old child," he said, rising and approaching me threateningly. He seized me at the base of the neck and squeezed. "Confess your counterrevolutionary plot!" he commanded.

It hurt so much I couldn't control my tears. "I've never heard of any May Sixteenth conspiracy." I sobbed. "I've told you everything I know."

And so it went, on and on in circles. They made me sleep there on the desk that night, and the next, and the next. Liu came to question me every afternoon, sometimes hitting me, sometimes flattering me and trying to bribe me with political favors. Teacher Deng brought me my meals, and was kind to me with cigarettes and information. I think what hurt me most during that time was the way my friends betrayed me.

Every time Liu came in, he had new "evidence" in his hand, reports pushed into the locked boxes by the people I had trusted most. The people I had defended in fights turned me in, the people with whom I had stolen food. My literary friends told of our book thefts and our poetry meetings; my homeroom teacher wrote about my "bad thought." And when I called out the window to my round-headed friend Little Wu, he looked frightened and hurried away. Every day I traced out the history of my relationship with Peng on the papers marked "Confession"; every day Liu took them away, muttering, "Another crime."

It was Teacher Deng who gave me the strength not to "confess" a lie. He explained that the letter from the Peking Security Bureau had asked only that I be investigated, not that I be arrested. Still, I knew that Liu would have me arrested if he could. It would be great Revolutionary glory if he could ferret out a big counterrevolutionary in his little country school, a great boost for his career. So every night I cried, torn between the desire not to hurt Peng Ming and the desire to protect Father from yet another disgrace.

On the fifth day, Liu didn't come until late in the day, and he had a plainclothes Public Security officer with him. "This is your last chance," he announced with satisfaction. "If you don't confess today, tomorrow you'll go to jail." Before my eyes, he went to a cabinet, unlocked it, and handed my file over to the officer.

That night, as I lay on my desk, I had no tears left. I had lived fifteen years, but I had no desire to live even one more. I had been the victim of political movements since the age of three, first through my mother, then through my father, and now through an absurd coincidence in my own affairs. Society hated me. It had turned me into an outcast and a thief. My stepmother disliked me and my father was a broken man. I even hated him for what he had done to our family.

I imagined the next day I would be brought to jail as a criminal, paraded through the streets as the peasants shouted, "Down with the counterrevolutionary!" My friends would be among them, throwing rocks and sticks, laughing at my shame, glad that now the country would be that much more secure than it had been before the criminal's arrest. Perhaps first there would be a public criticism meeting, a beating, a humiliation. . . .

The dusty dark lightbulb hanging several yards above me was still visible in the night. Suddenly, I realized that I could die. I could unscrew that lightbulb and put my hand there where the current flowed and I would be dead. I should never again be tormented by memories of Mother's humiliated and accepting face as Father cursed her for betraying the Party's faith in her; of Nai Nai's swollen cheeks as she lay in her black coffin; of Father kneeling before his burning books, praising the Party; of Liang Fang's feces-covered shoes as she came home to write her Thought Reports. I should never again hear the words "stinking intellectual's son," or lie on my stomach in the sweet potato fields; my throat wouldn't hurt anymore where Liu had squeezed it. I was amazed at the simplicity of it all.

The thought came quickly and I acted quickly. Standing on the table, I reached the bulb easily and it unscrewed smoothly into my hand. It was a lonely action, and I felt suddenly angry that it should be so. There should have been someone to help me do it, or someone to urge me not to. I reflected bitterly that after my death the mob would stone my body just as it would if I were alive, the difference being that now they would say that the counterrevolutionary had killed himself because of his crime. I would never be able to explain to Father that I wasn't guilty, and I remembered his old, sad face, weeping, telling himself to be patient and tolerant, that someday his question would be made clear. Another thought struck me with equal force: If I died, Peng Ming's enemies could invent my confession, and use it against him just as if I had penned it with my own hand.

The desire to live came strong then, stronger than the desire to die. I remember Father excitedly recording the peasant boy's folk song by torchlight, still a man of letters even in the midst of greatest trouble. I thought of Mother and Waipo, waiting for me in Changsha, and Liang Wei-ping sharing her rice *baba* among the peasants. The hoodlums had cared for me so well on the streets, and Teacher Luo had forgiven me so graciously for the caricatures I had drawn of him. There was so much good in this crazy world, but so much more that was impossible to understand.

Why should two good people like my parents be forced to divorce each other? Why should Liang Fang raise a machine gun against her fellow teenagers? Why did the peasants fear the cadres so terribly if they were representatives of our great Communist Party? Why were people so determined to make me and Peng Ming look like counterrevolutionaries when we wanted only to make a contribution to our country? Why had the Revolution given us all so little when we had sacrificed everything for it?

That night, I resolved that I would seek the answers to these questions. If I was to live, it would no longer be numbly and aimlessly. I would live bravely. I would not be like Father, denying the facts and fooling himself, nor like Pockmark Liu, disillusioned and cynical. I would go to prison, but I would study so that I could understand why my country had produced such tragedies.

The next morning, Liu arrived, but he was alone. "You can go," he said dourly.

It was no wonder I believed in fate, my life was just that crazy. I thought I must be dreaming again, but I didn't want to question my luck. I stumbled out, blinking in the bright light.

Later, I learned that the Central Committee in Peking had issued a document saying that too many people were being arrested on May Sixteenth conspiracy charges, and that in fact the conspiracy was not so big. Liu had to let me go. Still, the incident was by no means easily forgotten. My classmates shunned me, and Liu had his ways of having his revenge. In my file he wrote, "Corresponded with person with serious political questions," and when my class finished lower middle school that spring, I was the only one not allowed to proceed to upper middle school. The reason: "Complicated Thought."

## ■ Yang Lian (Yang Lien) (1955– ) (poem)

### TRANSLATED BY TONY BARNSTONE AND NEWTON LIU

Yang Lian, one of the original Misty poets, is currently living in New Zealand, teaching at the University of Auckland. Born in Beijing, he was sent down to the countryside during the Cultural Revolution, where he began to write poetry. Collections of his poetry in English include *In Symmetry with Death* (Australian National University), *Masks and Crocodile* (University of Sydney), and *The Dead in Exile* (Tiananmen Publications). His collection of "proses" (poetic essays) will be published in Taiwan soon.

FURTHER READING: Barnstone, Tony. *Out of the Howling Storm: The New Chinese Poetry*, 1993. Finkel, Donald. *A Splintered Mirror: Chinese Poetry from the Democracy Movement*, 1991. Soong, Stephen C., and John Minford, eds. *Trees on the Mountain: An Anthology of New Chinese Writing*, 1984. Yeh, Michelle, ed. *Anthology of Modern Chinese Poetry*, 1992.

## *An Ancient Children's Tale*

How should I savor these bright memories,
    their glowing gold, shining jade, their tender radiance like silk
that washed over me at birth?
All around me were industrious hands, flourishing peonies, and
    elegant upturned eaves.

Banners, inscriptions, and the names of nobility were everywhere,
and so many temple halls where bright bells sang into my ears.
Then my shadow slipped over the fields and mountains, rivers and
     springtime
as all around my ancestors' cottages I sowed
towns and villages like stars of jade and gemstones.
Flames from the fire painted my face red; plowshares and pots                1
clattered out their bright music and poetry
which wove into the sky during festivals.
How should I savor these bright memories?
When I was young I gazed down at the world,
watching purple grapes, like the night, drift in from the west           1
and spill over in a busy street. Every drop of juice became a star
set into the bronze mirror where my glowing face looked back.
My heart blossomed like the earth or the ocean at daybreak
as camel bells and sails painted like frescos embarked
from where I was to faraway lands to clink the gold coin of the sun.    2

When I was born
I would laugh even at
the glazed and opulent palaces, at the bloody red
walls, and at the people rapt in luxurious dreams
for centuries in their incense-filled chambers.                   2
I sang my pure song to them with passion,
but never stopped to think
why pearls and beads of sweat drain to the same place,
these rich tombs filled with emptiness,
or why in a trembling evening                      3
a village girl should wander down to the river,
her eyes so clear and bright with grief.

In the end, smoking powder and fire erupted in the courtyard;
between endless mountains and the plain, horse hooves
came out of the north, and there was murder and wailing         3
and whirling flags and banners encircling me like magic clouds,
like the patched clothes of refugees.
I saw the torrential Yellow River
by moonlight unfolding into a silver white elegy
keening for history and silence.                     4
Where are the familiar streets, people and sounds?
And where are the seven-leaved tree and new grass,
the river's song beneath a bridge of my dreams?
There is only the blood of an old man selling flowers clotting
     my soul,
only the burned houses, the rubble and ruins                  4
gradually sinking into shifting sands
and turning into dreams, into a wasteland.

# ■ Ha Jin (Ha Chin) (1956– ) (story, written in English)

Ha Jin was born in 1956 in Liaoning. The son of an army officer, he entered the People's Army early in the Cultural Revolution at a time when the schools were closed. He worked as a telegraph operator for some time, then went back to school, earning a B.A. and an M.A. After coming to the United States and taking his Ph.D. at Brandeis University in English and American literature, he went to Emory University where he is now a professor of English. His book of poems, *Between Silences: A Voice from China,* appeared from the University of Chicago Press in 1990. He won a Pushcart Prize for the story reprinted here. Like so many of his contemporaries, Ha Jin elected to remain in exile from China after the Tiananmen Square massacre of 1989. So he is in the unusual position of being a Chinese poet and fiction writer who works in English and lives now in America. As he writes in a letter: "Without question, I am a Chinese writer, not an American-Chinese poet, though I write in English. If this sounds absurd, the absurdity is historical rather than personal . . . since I can hardly publish anything in Chinese now." He now writes in English because "after June 1989 I realized that I could not return to China in the near future if I wanted to be a writer who has the freedom to write." This story, set on the Russian-Chinese border during the Cultural Revolution, dramatizes the conflict on a psychological border as well, that between raw human needs and strict ideological fetters. The narrator, who bears a striking resemblance to Melville's Captain Vere in *Billy Budd,* is presented as sympathetic to the flawed protagonist but ultimately restricted by party bureaucracy and a tense border situation. In this story, Ha Jin shows a remarkable ironic ability, also evident in his poetry, to record history from the inside, from the point of view of its imperfect and often unsympathetic protagonists.

**FURTHER READING:** Barnstone, Tony. *Out of the Howling Storm: The New Chinese Poetry,* 1993. Jin, Ha. *Between Silences: A Voice from China,* 1990; *Facing Shadows,* 1996; *Ocean of Words: Army Stories,* 1996; *Under the Red Flag: Stories,* 1997.

## *My Best Soldier*

I couldn't believe it when I saw that the photo sent over by the Regimental Political Department was Liu Fu's. How clumsy he looked in it: a submachine gun slanted before his chest; above his army fur hat, in the right corner, stretched a line of characters, "Defend My Motherland"; his smile was still a country boy's, lacking the sternness of a soldier's face. He had been in my platoon for only about ten months. How could he, a new soldier, become a secret customer of Little White Fairy in Hutou Town so soon?

Our political instructor, the Party secretary of our company, interrupted my thought, "I've talked with him, and he admitted he had gone to that woman six times this year."

"Six times?" Again I was surprised. "He is new. How could he get to know her so quick?"

"I asked the same question." Instructor Chang tapped his cigarette lightly over an ashtray and raised his head, looking across the small room in which we were sitting. He wanted to make sure that the orderly was not in the next room. "I think there must have been a pimp, but Liu Fu insisted he got to know the Fairy by himself when he had his hair cut in her barbershop. Obviously he is a novice in this business. No old hand would leave his picture with that weasel."

"You're right." I remembered last year a bulletin issued by the Regimental Political Department had carried a report on this young woman. After being caught in bed with an officer, Little White Fairy was brought to the Regimental Headquarters, where she confessed many soldiers and officers had visited her. Once she had received six army men in a single night, but she didn't know any of their names. Each man gave her a two-*yuan* bill and then went to bed with her. That was all. Regimental Commissar Feng swore to have those men found out, for they must have belonged to our Fifth Regiment, the only army unit in Hutou. But those were old dogs and had never left any trace.

"You should talk to him." Secretary Chang exhaled a small cloud. "Comrade Wang Hu, your platoon has done everything well this year except this Liu Fu matter. Don't get lost in the training. Mind modeling is more important. You see whenever we slack a little in ideological education, problems will appear among our men."

"Secretary Chang, I'll talk to him immediately. From now on I will pay more attention to ideological education."

"Good."

It seemed he didn't want to talk more, so I stood up and took my leave. Outside, the snow had stopped and the north wind turned colder. On my way back to my platoon, I felt bad, wondering how to handle the case. I was upset by Liu Fu. What a shame. I had always considered him as a candidate for an important job. His squad leader, Li Yaoping, was going to be demobilized the next year, and I had planned to have Liu Fu take over the squad. To be fair, Liu was in every way an excellent soldier. He surpassed all of my men in hand-grenade throwing. He could throw a grenade seventy-two meters. In our last practice with live ammunition, he scored eighty-four points with nine shots, which was higher than everybody except me. I got eighty-six. If we had a contest with the other three platoons, I would surely place him as our first man.

Needless to say, I liked him, not only for his ability and skills but also for his personality. He was a big fellow, over a hundred and eighty centimeters tall and a little heavily built but very nimble. His wide eyes reminded me of a small pony in my home village. In a way, his square mouth and bushy brows made him resemble those ancient generals in Spring-Festival pictures. All the other soldiers liked him a lot too, and he had quite a few friends in our Ninth Company.

I can never forget how he became a figure of poetry. In the spring, when we sowed soybeans, I assigned the Third Squad to pull a plough, since we didn't have enough horses and oxen. On the first day the men were soaked with sweat and complained that it was animal's work. Though they sang some revolutionary songs and even pretended to be Japanese soldiers marching into a village, still there was no way of making the labor lighter. But the next day was different. Liu Fu and two other boys in the Third Squad appeared with bald heads. They said a bald head would make the sweating more endurable and the washing easier after the work. The atmosphere in the field came alive. The three shining round heads were wavering about like balloons at the front of the team. Everybody wanted to get some fun out of it. Because Liu Fu was taller and had a bigger head, he became the main butt. In a few hours a poem was made in his honor, and the soldiers in the field chanted:

> When Big Liu takes off his hat,
> The county magistrate shakes his head:
> "Such a vast piece of alkaline land,
> How can the grain yield reach the Plan!"

> When Big Liu takes off his hat,
> The hardware store is so glad:
> "With such a big shining bulb,
> How many customers can we attract!"

> When Big Liu takes off his hat,
> The saleswoman is scared out of breath:
> "Having sold condoms for so many years,
> I've never seen such a length and breadth!"

In a few days the whole company learned the doggerel. Big Liu was never offended by it. He even chanted it with others, but he would replace the name "Big Liu" with "Small Wang," "Old Meng," and some others. As his popularity grew he was welcomed everywhere in the company. A boy like him could be a very able leader of a squad or a platoon. This was why I had planned to promote him to squad leader the next year. But who could tell he was a "Flowery Fox."

Our Party secretary was right: there must have been a pimp. Hutou was over fifty *li* away from Mati Mountain where we garrisoned; at most Liu Fu had gone to the county town seven or eight times on Sundays. He had seen Little White Fairy six times? Almost every time he went there? It was impossible, unless at the very beginning somebody took him directly to that woman. I remembered Li Dong had gone with him for his first visit to the town, and the second time Zhao Yiming had accompanied him.

Both of the older soldiers were pretty reliable; it was unlikely that they could be pimps. But to know a man's face is not to know his heart. I had to question Liu Fu about this.

Our talk did not take long. He looked crestfallen and ashamed, but he denied there had been somebody else involved and insisted to me that good man must accept the consequences of his own actions.

In a way, I appreciated his only blaming himself for the whoring. If another man was found like him in my platoon, I would have trouble clearing our name. People would chuckle and say the First Platoon had a whoring gang. That would give Liu Fu himself a hard time too, because he would surely be treated by the other men as a sort of traitor.

But I did take this case seriously, for I had to stop it. We garrisoned the borderline to defend our country, and we must not lose our fighting spirit by chasing women. Unlike the Russians on the other side, we Chinese were revolutionary soldiers, and we must not rely on women to keep up our morale. Every Saturday night we saw from our watch tower the Russians having many college girls over in their barracks. They would sing and dance around bonfires, kiss and embrace one another in the open air, roll and fuck in the woods. They were barbarians and Revisionists, while we were Chinese and true Revolutionaries.

So I ordered Liu Fu to write out his self-criticism, examining the elements of bourgeois ideology in his brain and getting a clear understanding of the nature of his offence. He wept and begged me not to take disciplinary action against him. He was afraid his family would know it and he would carry the stain for the rest of his life. I told him that a disciplinary action would have to be taken, and that I was unable to help him with that. It was better to tell him the truth.

"So I'm done for?" His horsy eyes watched my mouth expectantly.

"Your case was sent down by the Regimental Political Department. You know, our company cannot interfere with a decision from above. Usually, an offender like you is punished with a disciplinary action, but this doesn't mean you will have to carry it for the rest of your life. It depends on your own behavior. Say, from now on if you behave well in every way, you may have it taken out of your file when you are demobilized."

He opened his big mouth, but he didn't say anything, as if he swallowed down some words that had been stuck in his throat. The word "demobilized" must have struck him hard, because a soldier like him from the countryside would work diligently in order to be promoted to officer's rank. It would be a misfortune for him to return to his poor home village, where no job waited for him, and without a job no girl would marry him. But with such a stigma in his record, Liu Fu's future in the army was fixed: he would never be an officer.

Two days later he turned in his self-criticism. On eight white sheets were lines of big scrawled words and a few ink stains. A country boy like him of course couldn't say extraordinary things. His language was plain, and many sentences were broken. The gist of his self-criticism was that he had not worked hard enough to purge the bourgeois ideology from his head and that he had contracted the disease of liberalism. The Seventh Rule for the Army stated clearly: "Nobody is allowed to take liberties with women," but he had forgotten Chairman Mao's instruction and violated the rule. He also had forgotten his duty as a soldier staying on the Northern Frontier: when the enemies were sharpening their teeth and grinding their sabers at the borderline, he was indulging himself in sexual pleasure. He was unworthy of the nurture of the Party, unworthy of the Motherland's expectation, unworthy of his parents' efforts to raise him, unworthy of the gun that the people had entrusted to his hands, unworthy of his new green uniform.

I knew he was not a glib man, so I spared him the trouble of putting more self-scathing words in the writing. His attitude was sincere; this alone counted.

He looked a little comforted when I told him that I would try to persuade Secretary Chang to ask the Regimental Political Department to administer less severe punishment to him. "This is not over yet," I warned him, "but you mustn't take it as a heavy burden. Try to turn over a new leaf and work hard to make up for it."

He said he was grateful and would never forget my help.

Two weeks passed. We had not heard anything from the Political Department about the decision on Liu Fu's case. Neither the Party secretary nor the company commander ever requested an action. It would be unwise to do that, because the longer we waited the more lenient the punishment would be. Time would take away the interest and the urgency of the case. In fact, none of the company leaders would welcome a severe action against Liu Fu. Liu was their man; no good leader would like to see his own man being punished.

A month passed, and still nothing happened. Liu Fu seemed very patient and was quieter than before. To prevent him from being involved with Little White Fairy again, we kept him at Mati Mountain on weekends. We were also very strict about permitting other men, especially new soldiers, to visit Hutou Town.

One night it was my turn to make the round through all our sentry posts, checking the men on duty to make sure they wouldn't doze off. We had five posts, including the new one at the storehouse where we kept our food and a portion of our ammunition. I hated to do the supervision at midnight when you had to jump out of bed and pretend to be as awake as a cat. If you didn't look spirited in front of them, the men on duty would follow your example and make no effort to stay awake.

I went to the parking yard first, where our trucks and mortars stood, and caught the sentry smoking in the dark. I ordered him to put out his cigarette. The boy complained it was too cold and he couldn't keep his eyelids apart if he had nothing to do. I told him that everybody had to stand his hours on cold nights. Nobody but the Lord of Heaven was to blame for the cold. As for his sleepiness, he'd better bear in mind that we were merely four *li* away from the Russians. If he didn't stay alert, he put his own neck at risk. The Russians often sent over their agents to find out our sentry positions and deployment. They would get rid of a sentry if they found it necessary and convenient. So for his own safety, he'd better keep his eyes open and not show them where he was.

Then I went to the gate post and our headquarters. Everything was fine at these two places. I chatted with each of the men for a few minutes and gave them some roasted sunflower seeds. Then I left for the storehouse.

The post was empty there, so I waited inside the house, believing the sentry must have been urinating or emptying his bowels somewhere outside.

After ten minutes nobody showed up. I began to worry and was afraid something unusual might have happened. I couldn't shout to summon the sentry over. That was the last thing you would do at night, because it would wake up the whole company and the Russians might hear it as well. But I had to find out where the sentry hid himself. He must have been dozing away somewhere. There were no disordered footprints in the snow; it was unlikely that the sentry had been kidnapped or murdered. I picked up a line of footprints that looked new and followed it for a little distance. They were heading towards our stable. I raised my eyes and saw a dim light at the skylight on the stable's roof. Somebody must be there. What's he up to in the stable? Who is on duty? I looked at my luminous watch—1:30—and couldn't recall who was the sentry.

Getting close to the door, I heard some noise inside, so I hastened my steps. With my rifle I raised the cotton door-curtain a little to have a view inside and make sure no one was hiding behind the door waiting to knock me down.

It was Liu Fu! He was standing beside our gray mule, buckling the belt around his pants. His gun leaned against the long manger, and his fur hat hung on its muzzle. Beyond the mule stood a dozen horses asleep with downcast heads. So he is the sentry. The rascal, he's using the stable as a latrine. How luxurious, keeping his butt warm in here.

No. I noticed something unusual. Behind the gray mule's hindquarters was a bench. On the bench there were some particles of snow and some wet smudges. The beast! He has been screwing the mule! Looking at him, I found his sweating face distorted with an awkward but clear expression, as if saying to me: *I can't help it, please, I can't help it!*

I sprang at him and grabbed him by the front of his jacket. Though he was much bigger and stronger than myself, I felt he went limp in my hand. Of course, a spent beast. I started slapping his face and cursing, "You—mule fucker! You never give your cock a break! I'll geld you today and throw your itchy balls to the dogs!"

He didn't resist and merely moaned, as if my cursing and slapping made him feel better. He looked so ashamed. Not encountering any resistance I soon cooled down. You couldn't go on for long beating a man who didn't even raise his hands to defend himself. I let him go and ordered, "Back to the storehouse. We'll settle it tomorrow."

He picked up his gun, wiped away the tears on his cheeks with his hat, and went out quietly. In the stable all the animals were out of sleep now, their eyes open and their ears cocked up. One horse snorted.

I couldn't wait for tomorrow, and had Li Yaoping, his squad leader, woken up. We had to talk before I reported it to our Party secretary. I wanted to know more about Liu Fu. It was understandable if you screwed a girl in the town, since there was no woman in the mountain. But to screw a dumb animal like that, who could imagine it! It nauseated me.

Li was not completely awake when he came into my room. I gave him a cigarette and struck a match for him. "Sit down. I want to talk with you."

He sat on a stool and began smoking. "What do you want to talk about on a dark—" He looked at his watch. "It's already half past two in the morning."

"I want to talk about Liu Fu. Just now I found him in the stable fooling around with the gray mule." I wouldn't say "He screwed the mule," since I didn't see him do it. But I was sure of it, and Liu Fu himself did not deny it when I cursed and beat him. I was about to explain to Li what I meant.

"Oh no, you mean he did it again?" Li shook his freckled face.

"Yes. So you knew it already?"

"Ye—yes." He nodded.

"Why didn't you inform me of that before? Who gave you the right to hide it from me?" I was angry and would have yelled at him if some of my men were not sleeping in the adjacent room.

"He promised me that he would never do it again." Li looked worried. "I thought I should give him a chance."

"A chance? Didn't we give him one when he was caught with Little White Fairy?" I felt outraged. Apparently this thing had been going on in my platoon for quite a while, but I had never got a whiff of it. "Tell me, when did you see him do it and how many times."

"I saw him with the mule just once. It was last Saturday night. I saw him standing on a bench and hanging on the mule's hindquarters. I watched for a minute through the back window of the stable, then I coughed. He was scared and immediately fell off. When he saw me come in, he knelt down begging me to forgive him and not to tell on him. He looked so piteous, a big fellow like that, so I told him I wouldn't tell. But I did criticize him."

"What did you say? How did you criticize him, my comrade Squad Leader?" I felt it strange—he sounded as if he might sell his sister if he took pity on a man.

"I asked him why he had to screw the mule." Li looked rather cheerful.

"What a stupid question. How did he answer it?"

"He said, 'You know, Squad Leader, only—only mules don't foal. I promise, I'll never touch any—any of these mares.'" Li started tittering.

"What? It's absurd. You mean he thought he could get those mares with babies?"

"Yeah, yes!"

"What a silly fellow! So moral, he's afraid of being a father of horsy bastards." I couldn't help laughing, and Li's tittering turned into loud laughter too.

"Shhh—." I reminded him of the sleepers.

"I told him even the mule must not be 'touched,' and he promised not to do it again." Li winked at me.

"Old Li, you're an old fox."

"Don't be so hard on me, my platoon leader. To be fair, he is a good boy in every way except that he can't control his lust. I don't know why. If you say he has too much bourgeois stuff in his head, that won't fit. He is from a pure poor peasant family, a healthy seedling on a red root—"

"I don't want you to work out a theory, Old Li. I want to know how we should handle him now. This morning, in a few hours, I will report it to our Company Headquarters. What should we say and how should we say it?"

"Well, do you want to get rid of him or keep him?"

This was indeed the crucial question, but I didn't have an answer. Liu Fu was my best man and I would need him in the future. "What's your opinion then? At least, we must not cover it up this time." I realized that Old Li hadn't told on Liu Fu because he wanted to keep him in his squad.

"Certainly, he had his chance already. How about—"

The door burst open and somebody rushed in. It was Ma Pingli, our youngest boy, who was to stand the three-o'clock shift at the storehouse. "Platoon Leader, Liu Fu is not—not at the post." He took the fur cover off his nose, panting hard. "All the telephone wires are cut. We can't call anywhere."

"Did you go around and look for him?"

"Yes, everywhere."

"Where's his gun?"

"The gun is still there, in the post, but his person's gone."

"Hurry up! Bring over the horses!" I ordered. "We'll go get him."

Ma ran away to the stable. I glanced at Old Li. The look on his face showed he understood what was happening. "Take this with you." I handed him a semi-automatic rifle, which he accepted absentmindedly, and I picked up another one for myself. In uneasy silence, we went out waiting for Ma.

The horses sweated all over, climbing towards the borderline. I calculated that we would have enough time to stop him before he could get across. He had to climb a long way from the southern side of the mountain to avoid being spotted by our watch tower. But when we reached the Wusuli River, a line of fresh footprints stretched before us, winding across the snow-covered surface of the river, extending itself into the other side, and gradually losing its trail in the bluish whiteness of the vast Russian territory.

"The beast, stronger than a horse," I said. It was unimaginable that he could run so fast in the deep snow.

"He's there!" Ma Pingli pointed to a small slope partly covered by gray bushes.

Indeed, I saw a dark dot moving towards the edge of the thicket, which was about five hundred meters away from us. Impossible—surely he was too smart not to put on his white camouflage cape. I raised my binoculars, and saw him carrying a big stuffed gunnysack on his right shoulder and running desperately for the shelter of the bushes, a camouflage cape secured around his neck flapping behind him like a huge butterfly. I gave the binoculars to Old Li.

Li watched. "He's taking a sack of *Forwards* with him!" he said with amazement.

"He stole it from the kitchen. I saw the kitchen door broken," Ma reported. We all knew our cooks stored *Forwards,* the newspaper of Shenyang Military Region, in gunnysacks as kindling. We had been told not to toss the paper about, because the Russians tried to get every issue of it in Hong Kong and would pay more than ten dollars for it.

"The Russians may not need those back issues at all," I said. "They've already got them. They only want recent ones. He's dumb."

Suddenly a yellow light pierced the sky over the slope. The Russians' lookout tower must have spotted him; their Jeep was coming to pick him up.

Old Li and I looked at each other. We knew what we had to do. No time to waste. "We have no choice," I muttered, putting a sighting glass onto my rifle. "He has betrayed our country, and he is our enemy now."

I raised the rifle and aimed at him steadily. A burst of fire fixed him there. He collapsed in the distant snow, and the big sack fell off his shoulder and rolled down the slope.

"You got him!" Ma shouted.

"Yes, I got him. Let's go back."

We mounted on the saddles; the horses immediately galloped down the mountain. They were eager to get out of the cold wind and return to their stable.

All the way back, none of us said another word.

## ■ Chou Ping (1957– ) (poem, written in English)

Chou Ping was born in Changsha City, Hunan province, in 1957. The Pinyin transliteration of his name is Zhou Ping, and the Wade-Giles transliteration is Chou P'ing but he prefers "Chou Ping" to either transliteration. He writes poetry in both Chinese and English, and his poetry and translations of Chinese poetry into English have appeared in such American journals as the *Literary Review* and *Nimrod,* and a substantial selection of his work has appeared in *Out of the Howling Storm: The New Chinese Poetry* (Wesleyan, 1993). He has also co-translated a book of Chinese literary criticism titled *The Art of Writing: Teachings of the Chinese Masters* (Shambhala, 1996). In 1983, he studied English literature in the Advanced Teachers' Training Program at Beijing Foreign Language University, where he studied poetry with Willis Barnstone. It was at that time that he began writing his poems in English instead of Chinese, as part of his study of English language and literature; the practice stuck. He taught at Xiangtang Teachers' College, Hunan province, until fall 1991, when he enrolled in the graduate program in English at Indiana University in Bloomington. After completing his master's degree in English and a master's in fine arts in creative writing at Indiana, Chou Ping enrolled in the Ph.D. program in East Asian languages at Stanford University, where he completed yet another master's degree in Chinese and is at this writing completing his Ph.D. In a generation of poets who are often obscure or polemical, his poems are tender, funny, and whimsical, and peculiarly his own.

**FURTHER READING:** Barnstone, Tony. *Out of the Howling Storm: The New Chinese Poetry,* 1993.

## *Ways of Looking at a Poet*

1.

a wreck tossed upon a hazy shore
cursing the delicious banality
of being lost at a familiar place

2.

a newspaper wriggled up in wind
and waltzed around on a green lawn
it stumbled over its own shadow
and fell back in a conscious coma

3.

a raven in a vacant wood, winging
the black pages of the future

4.

a dressmaker's dummy sneaked into a street
looking for King Midas's hand

5.

an old man in rags bought a magnolia
to pin it on the flower girl's dress

6.

monotonous waves
irresistable countdown of life

7.

a sun skated across the ocean
feeling pretty dark inside

8.

an admirable punching sack, receiving
every blow with an appreciative bow

9.

a rage enclosed in a free balloon
moving up and down in darkness
desperately eager to pierce a hole
and wait for the immediate slow death

10.

a broken mirror
with godlike indifference
sleeping open-eyed

11.

the slewing arm of a trackless trolley
picking azure flowers from a dark canvas

12.

an ant climbs up the sky
in search of a thought

13.

a nose practicing saxophone at night

14.

a sweet noise
wrapping around one's neck
like a hot towel in summer

# ■ Tang Yaping (T'ang Ya-p'ing) (1962– ) (poems)

## TRANSLATED BY TONY BARNSTONE AND NEWTON LIU

Yang Yaping represents the new voice of women's poetry from China: voraciously sexual, dark, and irreverent. She was born in 1962 in Sichuan and graduated from Sichuan University as a philosophy major in 1983. She is currently working as an editor at the Guizhou television station in the southwest of China.

**FURTHER READING:** Barnstone, Tony. *Out of the Howling Storm: The New Chinese Poetry,* 1993.

## *from* **Black Desert (Suite)**

### Black Nightgown

I fill a bottomless bottle with water and bathe my feet
Nights when it rains are most interesting
I've asked a man over to talk
Before he comes I do not think
—I pull down the purple sash and turn a pink wall-lamp on
My black nightgown does three rounds about the room
—then the door is knocked on three times
He comes in with a black umbrella
and opens it up on the floor in the middle of the room
We start to drink strong tea
Noble compliments pour like piped water
Sweet lies shine like bright stars
Gradually I lean back on the sofa
and with scholarly passion tell the story of an old maid
The god that was between us runs away
covering his ears and without one slipper
This evening of talk leaves me dizzy
When telling a story
the darker the night the better it is
and the heavier it rains the better

### Black Rock

Looking for a man to torture her
a beauty with tiger teeth smiling
lives in the footprints of suicide
She's tough but she finds only despair
The empty earth, the blank sky,
are deep as you want them to be
This dead rock was also rock when alive,
had nothing to hate, nothing to love,
nothing to be loyal to, nothing to defect from
The more the sorrow, the more the joy
Let some inconceivable idea control everything
A hairy little bird has pecked away all stupid responsibility
A head refuses to let a dream enter
Circulating blood spills disaster everywhere
Now the forbidden fruit is full and ripe;
it will be seized without foreplay
Pregnant womens' faces are everywhere
Freckles seem to butterfly off
The nightmare mystifies, but it thrills
You've got to convulse while alive

# Japan

■

## INTRODUCTION

Japan is a nation of islands lying off Asia's eastern seaboard, across the Sea of Japan from Korea, China, and Siberia. There are four major islands; the largest and most historically important is Honshu. Little is known about the early history of the Japanese people, though it is said that the empire was founded by Emperor Jimmu in 556 B.C., and after A.D. 57 there are occasional references to the Japanese in Chinese histories. By the first century A.D., the Japanese had long been exposed to Chinese culture, particularly through their neighbors the Koreans. Although much of Japan's history with Korea has been warlike, the early Japanese owe a great deal to Korea, and to Chinese culture, which reached Japan through the corridor of Korea. The Japanese also absorbed Koreans into their society, and in fact up to a third of the early Japanese nobility may have been of Korean descent. This proximity to the cultural influences of Korea and China, combined with long periods of government-mandated isolationism, has enabled the Japanese to develop an extraordinarily sophisticated culture. Japan's literary tradition rivals that of much larger nations and of cultures of much greater antiquity.

The early Japanese were an agricultural people ruled by a warrior aristocracy factioned into ancestral clans. Each was ruled by a warrior chieftain who was also the chief priest. The society was stratified into nobility, peasants, and slaves. In the third century A.D., the Yamato clan took hold of the area south of modern Kyoto, an agriculturally fertile region that afforded the Yamatos the economic and military strength to conquer a large number of other clans and establish the Yamato state. Under this rule, the conquered clans were forced to worship the Yamato sun-goddess deity and a pantheon of lesser gods, and out of this grew the native Japanese religion of Shinto, emphasizing ancestral worship and ritual cleanliness.

In A.D. 538, Buddhism was introduced to Japan when a Korean king gifted Buddhist scriptures and images to the Yamato court, thus beginning a long era of Buddhist influence in Japanese history. Buddhism has accompanied Japanese culture—its art, architecture, philosophy, poetry, fiction, and popular tales—from the time of the earliest Buddhist temples at the beginning of the seventh century A.D. Prince Shotoku (574–622) was the leader in recommending governmental reforms that would integrate Buddhist ethical thought and Confucian political philosophy into the Yamato administration. Beginning in 607, the prince was responsible for sending thousands of young Japanese to China to study under the tutelage of Tang dynasty administrators and Buddhist monks and artists. These students returned with fruitful ideas to Japan and in 654, twenty-two years after Shotoku's death, joined his protégés in overturning the Yamato government. One year later, the supporters of Shotoku's Chinese-Buddhist policies instituted the Taika Reforms, an attempt to transform Japan's political and bureaucratic system into a centralized structure modeled after the Tang Chinese empire. In 710, the city of Nara was founded, copied after Changan, the Tang dynasty capital, and became Japan's first capital city. From 710 to 794, known as the Nara era, Buddhist monasteries grew and flourished. As landowners, monks participated in the political process up to the level of the Imperial court. It was during this era that the earliest Japanese history, *Record of Ancient Matters* (712), was completed. This document was a dynastic and mythological record incorporating poetry.

In the second half of the eighth century, the *Manyoshu* was compiled. This anthology, whose name means "The Collection of Ten Thousand Leaves," is the largest and oldest collection of Japanese poetry, consisting of more than four thousand poems by people of all stations of life. Notable among these was Kakinomoto Hitomaro (died c. 708–715). He and the Tokugawa era writer Matsuo Basho (1644–1694) are considered Japan's finest poets. Poetry has always been the most esteemed form in Japanese literature and is commonly composed by people of all classes. For much of Japanese history, poetry was central to culture and literature: poetry contests were frequent; imperially sanctioned anthologies were regularly commissioned; and early readers often memorized these anthologies as well as the great anthologies of Chinese poetry. Poetry also commonly appears in Japanese fiction, theater, memoirs and histories, where it is the language of love, of emotions of all kinds, and of the gods. Much Japanese poetry is love poetry, because poem exchanges were an essential aspect of courting rituals. Among the early poets of the *Manyoshu* are a number of talented women whose passionate personas in their poems of love anticipate later great women poets, such as Ono no Komachi (ninth century), Izumi Shikibu (c. 974–1034), and Yosano Akiko (1878–1942). Along with Sappho of Greece, Mirabai of India, and Li Qingzhao of China, Ono, Izumi, and Yosano are among the world's major erotic poets.

Ono and Izumi flourished in the era immediately following the Nara period, the Heian era (794–1185). The Heian is considered a period in which a true Japanese sensibility flowered, particularly in the arts and literature. The Imperial family in Nara had moved the capital city to Heian (modern Kyoto) after 770 when a Buddhist priest at Nara had unsuccessfully tried to take over the throne. This event spurred strong feelings against Buddhism and Chinese culture, resulting in a governmental injunction against relations with China in 838 and encouraging the development of uniquely Japanese architecture, painting, and literature.

The Japanese system of writing in Chinese characters (*kanji*) had been borrowed from the Chinese in the third and fourth centuries A.D. during the Yamato era. However, the ideographic nature of *kanji* did not fully express the nuances of the Japanese language, with its inflected verbs and honorific forms. This Chinese character scheme was augmented with two phonetic syllabaries in the eighth-century Heian period, finally rendering a Japanese writing system that allowed for the inflection of *kanji* characters through their juxtaposition with syllabic prefixes, suffixes, and particles. The improved system liberated Japanese writers to compose in their native syntax and stray from the confines of traditional Chinese literary forms and genres.

Although a number of Japanese literary genres owe their existence to the Chinese example, in their Japanese incarnation they are inevitably filtered through a different cultural, aesthetic, and linguistic sensibility. Further, basic linguistic differences between Japanese and Chinese limited imitation. In contrast to monosyllabic and tonal Chinese, Japanese is a polysyllabic tongue, without tones, and though they shared the same characters, the prosodies of each literature developed differently. Whereas Chinese poetry has metrical systems based on line length and tone and generally rhymes, Japanese poetry uses a syllabic measure, normally consisting of alternating lines of five and seven syllables, and rhyme is less frequent. In contrast to Japanese novels, which are often immensely long and episodic, Japanese poetry tends to be concentrated and runs toward the minimalist. It is even more condensed than the elegantly succinct poetry of China. Japan's poetry is comprised of brilliant images whose subtle connections create epiphanies of perception and emotion. Consider Yosa Buson's brief lines, "Red plum flowers/burn/on horse plop." This simple haiku is wisdom poetry, a Zen riddle. In joining fallen beauty and fallen excrement, the poem is a meditation on life's transience, on nature and natural functions. It startles us with immediacy, and when put aside the poem continues to enlighten and resonate. It should be added that there was also a Japanese tradition of writing poems in Chinese characters and forms.

In Japan, fiction had an earlier and more sophisticated development than in China, and diaries, books of random jottings, and travel literature, though anticipated in China, are particularly striking genres in Japan. In the Heian period, the new phonetic script was the domain of women, whereas Chinese characters were generally considered a masculine script. Two great works of aristocratic prose by Japanese women, written in the phonetic script, stand out in this period and are quintessentially Japanese in their literary achievement: *The Tale of Genji* by Murasaki Shikibu (978–c. 1014), considered by some scholars to be the world's first novel, with its exploration of psychological subjectivity and full use of dialogue; and *The Pillow Book* of Sei Shonagon (c. 966–1017), a collection of *zuihitsu,* or random thoughts and meditations.

During the Heian period, as they cultivated their graceful, erotic, intensely aesthetic lives of poetry, painting, fiction and the art of love, various court families fought for political power over the Imperial government. The aristocratic Fujiwara clan emerged as dominant. Meanwhile, in the countryside, the Japanese warrior code of *bushido* was gaining popular-

ity, and in 1156, fueled by diminishing imperial power and fighting between aristocratic clans, civil war broke out. The Taira and Minamoto
clans were victorious over the emperor and Fujiwara clan, and eventually
the Minamotos defeated the Taira and established the Kamakura shogunate (1185–1333).

Over the next seven centuries, the political rule of Japan fell into the
hands of the *shoguns,* the military chief generals and feudal lords who controlled the samurai warriors. The Kamakura shogunate was succeeded by
the Ashikaga shogunate (1336–1603) in a time known as the Muromachi
period, and later by the Tokugawa shogunate (1603–1868). In the Kamakura and Muromachi periods, ideals of warfare and *bushido* were often
treated in literature, as in the martial epic *Tale of the Heike* and in noh plays
by Zeami Motokiyo (1363–1443) and others (though Zeami was certainly
not limited to martial themes). The Kamakura era was also a period of
great changes in Japanese Buddhism. Though many Buddhists considered
this time "the age of the decline of dharma" because of the militarism and
commercialism that had permeated monastic culture, Buddhism was rein-
vigorated by a new influx of Chinese ideas through Dogen (1200–1253),
the founder of the Soto school of Japanese Zen Buddhism. In addition,
Buddhists actively proselytized a form of lay Buddhism, adopting the earlier Tendai and Shingon schools of Buddhism into new popularizations
and simplifications of Buddhist practice, called the Pure Land sect and
the Lotus sect. All this ferment is reflected in the production of extraordinary Buddhist literature in the Kamakura period.

Japan has three main forms of drama: the puppet theater (*bunraku*),
the noh play, and kabuki. The great names of Japanese drama are Zeami
Motokiyo (1363–1443), whose noh plays represent the very highest examples of the form, and Chikamatsu Monzaemon (1653–1724), whose puppet and kabuki plays have caused him to be called the Shakespeare of
Japan. Chikamatsu is typical of the authors of the Tokugawa era in his concern with representing ordinary life and ordinary people. This was also
the time in which haiku developed as a serious literary form, championed
by Matsuo Basho. This minimalist art honed psychological perceptions, social commentary, and startling depictions of nature into a mere seventeen
syllables. It is a very personal, humorous, and accessible form, and it often
learns high art from peasant life. As Basho writes: "Culture's beginnings:/
from the heart of the country/rice-planting songs."

In the sixteenth century during the Muromachi period, Japan came
into contact with Europeans. Christianity was introduced in 1549, and for
close to a century there was a lively intercourse of cultural and trade relations with the Portuguese, Dutch, English, and Spanish. In 1603, Tokugawa Ieyasu became the first Tokugawa shogun and moved the capital city
north to Edo (modern Tokyo). In 1639, during the reign of the Tokugawa
shoguns, the nation entered a period of profound isolation, repressing
Christianity, forbidding Japanese to travel overseas, and excluding all foreigners from the islands, with the exception of the Dutch, who were con-

fined to Nagasaki. After a number of failed attempts by Russians, Europeans, and Americans to break into this closed society, this isolation was punctured in 1854 with the forced entry of Commodore Perry and a fleet of U.S. warships. In 1867, the last Tokugawa shogun resigned, ushering in the Meiji Restoration, in which Emperor Meiji (1852–1912) was restored to nominal power. In the Meiji period, Japan quickly changed, compelled into a knowledge of its own weakness by the unequal treaties it was obliged to sign. Within a few decades, Japan became industrially modernized, reestablished its military might, abolished feudalism, and converted itself into a modern state, complete with military conscription, compulsory education, a constitution, and an avid attempt to assimiliate the new science and technology.

In the twentieth century, Japanese nationalism led the nation to a series of imperialist invasions of countries throughout Asia—Korea, China, Formosa (modern Taiwan), Southeast Asia, the Philippines, and the Dutch East Indies. In World War II, Japan sided with the Axis powers Germany and Italy. Japanese participation in World War II was brought to an end within days of the dropping of two atomic bombs on the Japanese cities of Hiroshima and Nagasaki in July 1945 by the United States. Some two hundred thousand people, mostly civilians, were killed in the two explosions. Radiation poisoning condemned many others to a slow death or produced genetic defects in their descendents. It may also be said that Japanese imperialism and nationalism were mortally wounded in the blasts. After the war, the Japanese reinvented themselves as a peaceful nation focusing primarily on economic efforts.

Japanese literature went through a similar transformation from the nineteenth to the twentieth century. Translations of Western fiction and poetry proliferated in the late nineteenth century, and Western approaches to literature soon appeared in Japan. In poetry, though traditional verse forms continued to be written, they were radically adapted and modernized; and successive modern Western poetic movements—Romanticism, Symbolism, and Modernism—had their Japanese innovators and adherents. Novels began to reflect more than inner life and formally determined outer behavior expressed in an artificial literary language; now a more vernacular, naturalistic prose appeared that showed a new interest in social problems. The novel began to be esteemed for more than didactic purpose and moral lessons. Some writers reacted against the naturalist novel, choosing instead to adopt a detached aestheticism. In the twentieth century, a school of proletarian literature flourished briefly before it came under nationalist repression. In 1968, the novelist Kawabata Yasunari (1899–1972) won the Nobel Prize in literature, and in 1994 a second Japanese novelist, Oe Kenzaburo (1935– ), also won the Nobel Prize.

Reactions to the Japanese defeat in World War II have pervaded modern Japanese literature. Oe's novels are saturated with a sense of loss, irony, and the grotesque. Tanikawa Shuntaro, who had witnessed the burnt corpses of neighbors while bicycling through Tokyo after it was fire-bombed in 1945, has reacted with renewed humanism and an idealistic faith that "life is possible" despite the worst horrors of human nature. Mishima Yukio, Japan's most famous modern writer, reacted with fierce nationalism, embracing the code of *bushido* and a worship of beauty and death, culminating in his own ritual suicide, performed after addressing the troops of a paramilitary army he had organized, hoping to achieve a coup d'état. Sakaki Nanao had been a radio operator in World War II and had tracked the B-29 that dropped the atom bomb on Nagasaki. He and his fellow soldiers were ordered by their superior officer to commit mass suicide. Only the emperor's voice on the radio ordering soldiers *not* to kill themselves saved them. Sakaki has responded to the devastations of the war with an antinationalism as fierce as Mishima's nationalism, and with Buddhist, ecological, and antinuclear activism. Like the "Lost Generation" in the West after World War I, Japanese writers wrote with a sense that the traditions of the past had been turned upside down after World War II, and that they were writing in a world that had been made a wasteland. Mishima's militant nationalism was an attempt to reclaim endangered Japanese traditions. A number of other postwar writers have positioned themselves, however, in the role of pacifist social critic and spiritual advisor, which, of course, is itself a traditional role for the Japanese poet, as seen in the Zen poetry of Saigyo, Ryokan, Muso Soseki, and others. The poetry of Tamura Ryuichi, for example, asserts that war—nuclear and conventional—is an apotheosis of the human will to destroy. The physical wasteland of postwar Japan, for Tamura, was a projection of a spiritual disease, a result of the false paradigms of *bushido*. All he wants, in the end, therefore is "on the tongues of gravediggers,/the taste of ice cream."

—Ayame Fukuda and the editors

# Ancient Period

## (to 794)

# Poems from the *Manyoshu* (Collection of Ten Thousand Leaves)

## INTRODUCTION

The *Manyoshu* is the earliest and greatest collection of Japanese poetry. It was compiled in the late eighth century A.D., during the Nara period, and it contains more than four thousand poems, from as early as the fourth century and as late as 759. The majority of the poems, however, were composed in the seventh and eighth centuries. Though there were probably a number of compilers, the final editor was Otomo Yakamochi. The *Manyoshu* is prized for the simplicity and purity of its poetry, as opposed to the more elegant and ornate styles that dominated in the later Imperial anthologies. The collection is divided into twenty books, but despite some grouping by author, chronology, source, subject, or mode, there is no overarching pattern of arrangement. It contains poems by diverse authors—from emperors to frontier guards—and its tone ranges from sublime to passionate to comic.

The collection is dominated by its 4,207 *tanka*, but it includes 265 *choka*, 62 *sedoka*, and a few poems in minor forms and in Chinese. Classical Japanese poetry, or *waka*, is based on the rhythm produced through lines of alternating numbers of syllables, generally an alternation between five and seven syllables. The *tanka*, meaning short poem, is a poem of five lines whose syllable count is 5/7/5/7/7. The *choka*, meaning long poem, is constructed of a varying number of 5/7 phrases capped with a 7/7 couplet; in the eighth century, the *choka* began to die out as the *tanka* took over. Often a *tanka* is attached to the end of a longer *choka* to crystalize the meaning (these envoys are called *hankas*). A *sedoka* consists of six lines in a rhythm of 5/7/7/5/7/7.

The *Manyoshu* holds the seminal position in Japanese literature that the *Greek Anthology* held in ancient Western literature (also containing approximately four thousand diverse poems) and that *The Book of Songs* holds for China. It is the source to which Japanese poets go again and again to revitalize their art. It represents the great literary flowering of Japan at a time when the Imperial system was cohering out of the clan coalitions of the ancient period, when large cities at Fujiwara and Nara were constructed, and when Japanese art was undergoing a similar flowering. Thus, it has provided the nation a historical as well as literary source of self-definition, to the point of nationalism, although in fact up to a third of the nobility were then Korean in origin and the cultural origins of Japan were rooted deeply in both Korea and China.

**FURTHER READING:** Levy, Ian Hideo, tr. *The Ten Thousand Leaves: A Translation of the "Manyoshu," Japan's Premier Anthology of Classical Poetry*, 1981. Shinkokai, Nippon Gakujutsu, tr. *The Manyoshu*, 1965. Yasuda, Kenneth, tr. *Land of the Reed Plains: Ancient Japanese Lyrics from the Manyoshu*, 1960. Wright, Harold, tr. *Ten Thousand Leaves: Love Poems from the Manyoshu*, 1979.

# ■ Empress Iwanohime (?–A.D. 347)

TRANSLATED BY AYAME FUKUDA

Iwanohime was the consort of Emperor Nintoku, the 16th Emperor. In A.D. 314, she was proclaimed empress and she died in A.D. 347. Her poems are among the earliest examples of the Japanese love poem tradition.

## Missing Emperor Nintoku (Four Poems)

### The Days Lengthen

The days lengthen
as you travel.
Should I search the mountains
for you or wait
and wait?

### I Would Rather Die

I would rather
lie down and die
pillowed on the rocks
of a crooked mountain
than want you this much.

### I Will Wait For You

I will wait for you
as long as I live,
until my lingering black locks
are laced with frost.

### Will My Desire Fade

Will my desire fade
in this autumn field
as morning mists slip
through stalks of rice
and vanish?

■ **Empress Jito (645–702)**

TRANSLATED BY KENNETH REXROTH AND IKUKO ATSUMI

This fine elegy was written by Empress Jito after the death of her husband Emperor Temmu in 686. She succeeded him to the throne, becoming Japan's forty-first sovereign. After ten years, she abdicated and was succeeded by her grandson, Emperor Mommu.

## On the Death of the Emperor Temmu

Even flaming fire
can be snatched up, smothered
and carried in a bag.
Why then can't I
meet my dead lord again?                                      5

## ■ Kakinomoto Hitomaro (died c. 708–715)

Kakinomoto Hitomaro vies with Matsuo Basho for the title of Japan's finest poet. Two centuries after Hitomaro's death, Ki no Tsurayuki, a compiler of the famous Heian period *Kokinshu* anthology, gave him the appellation "the saint of poetry," and he is certainly the best poet of those represented in the *Manyoshu*. Yet he has left little historical trace. From his poems we may gather that he was a minor official who died before he was fifty. No direct evidence about his life exists in any text outside of the *Manyoshu*, but the Kakinomoto family had lived for generations in Ichinomoto, south of Nara. It appears that he was active in court life during the reigns of Emperor Temmu (r. 673–686), Empress Jito (r. 690–697), and Emperor Mommu (r. 697–707), that he held court offices, that he was an official in the provinces, and that he functioned at times as a court poet who wrote poems to celebrate outings or elegies for members of the royal family. He was married two or more times, and his first wife died before him.

Though his seventy *tanka* are excellent pieces, Hitomaro really excels in the longer form of *choka*, to which he brings an extraordinary narrative breadth and fluidity. He has both the directness of address and simple purity of the poets of the earlier period, as well as an acrobatic ability to leap from metaphor to metaphor. He is complex without being mannered. His poem about the temporary enshrinement of Prince Takechi (upon his death) is the longest poem in the *Manyoshu*. Takechi was the son of Emperor Temmu and Empress Jito, and he led their armies in the Jinshin War (672). The poem includes an explosive battle sequence that is unique in classical Japanese poetry in its detailed and extended presentation of the battle. His poems creatively refashion the worn rhetorical devices termed "pillow-words," which (like the Old English "kennings" in *Beowulf* or the formulaic expressions in Homer) are ornamental stock phrases that stand in for one or more words. These pillow-words run through Japanese poetry and have been used even in this century. The critics estimate that he either adapted or coined fifty percent of the pillow-words he used. Hitomaro brings the same genius to his personal poems that he does to his poems about public subjects, and his elegy on his first wife is among the most touching poems in any language.

**FURTHER READING:** Levy, Ian Hideo. *Hitomaro and the Birth of Japanese Lyricism,* 1984; tr. *The Ten Thousand Leaves: A Translation of the "Manyoshu," Japan's Premier Anthology of Classical Poetry,* 1981. Nippon Gakujutsu Shinkokai, ed. and tr. *The Manyoshu,* 1940, 1965, 1970.

## When She Walks

When she walks
by my door
she seems to say
"If love is killing you,
why aren't you dead yet?"

TRANSLATED BY TONY BARNSTONE AND WILLIS BARNSTONE

## Just Let Me Take

Just let me take
her hand
and I won't care if words sprout
in gossiping mouths
like summer grass in the marsh.

TRANSLATED BY TONY BARNSTONE AND WILLIS BARNSTONE

## Poem by Kakinomoto Hitomaro
## as He Shed Tears of Blood in His Grief
## following the Death of His Wife

On the Karu Road[1]
is the village of my wife,
and I desired to meet her intimately,
but if I went there too much
the eyes of others would cluster around us,
and if I went there too often
others would find us out.
And so I hoped
that later we would meet
like tangling vines,
trusted that we would
as I would trust a great ship,
and hid my love:
faint as jewel's light,
a pool walled in by cliffs.

Then came the messenger,
    his letter tied
        to a jewelled catalpa twig,

---

1. "Karu" is preceded by the formal epithet *ama tobu ya,* "that soars through the sky," a pun on the word "*karu*" in its sense of "light" or "buoyant." It is essentially untranslatable.

to tell me,
    in a voice                                                 *20*
    like the sound
    of a catalpa bow,
that my girl,
who had swayed to me in sleep
like seaweed of the offing,                                      *25*
was gone
like the coursing sun
gliding into dusk,
like the radiant moon
secluding itself behind the clouds,                              *30*
gone like the scarlet leaves of autumn.

I did not know what to say,
    what to do,
but simply could not listen
and so, perhaps to solace                                        *35*
a single thousandth
    of my thousand-folded longing,
I stood at the Karu market
where often she had gone,
and listened,                                                    *40*
but could not even hear
the voices of the birds
that cry on Unebi Mountain,
    where the maidens
        wear strands of jewels,                *45*
and of the ones who passed me
on that road,
    straight as a jade spear,
not one resembled her.
I could do nothing                                               *50*
but call my wife's name
and wave my sleeves.

TRANSLATED BY IAN HIDEO LEVY

## Poem by Kakinomoto Hitomaro at the Time of the Temporary Enshrinement of Prince Takechi at Kinoe

I hesitate to put it in words,
it is an awesome thing to speak.
Our Lord,
who, while we trembled,
fixed the far and heavenly                                        *5*

halls of his shrine
on the fields of Makami in Asuka
and, godlike, has secluded himself
  in the rocks there,
he,
who ruled the earth's eight corners,
crossed Fuwa Mountain,
lined with thick black pines,
in the northern land of his realm
and went down,
  as from heaven,
   to the provinces,
encamping on the plain of Wazami,
  Wazami
   of the Korean swords.
To hold sway over the realm under heaven
and bring his dominions to peace,
he gathered his soldiers
in the eastern country,
  where the cock cries,
and gave the task to his son,
he being an imperial prince:
to pacify the raging rebels
and subdue the defiant lands.
Then our Prince
girded his great body with his long sword
and took in his great hands his bow.
The sound of the drums,
calling the troops to ready,
boomed like the very voice of thunder,
and the echoing notes
of the signaller's flute
grew, to the terror of all,
like the roar of a tiger
with prey in its eyes.
The rippling of the high-held banners
was like the rippling of the fires
struck across every field
when spring comes, bursting winter's bonds,
and the roar of the bowstrings they plucked
was so fearful, we thought it a hurricane
whirling through a snowfallen winter forest.
When the arrows they let loose
swarmed like a blinding swirl of snow,
the resisters, standing defiant,

also resolved to perish,           *50*
    if they must,
like the dew and frost.
As they struggled
    like zooming birds,
the divine wind           *55*
from the Shrine of our offerings
at Ise in Watarai
blew confusion upon them,
hiding the very light of day
as clouds blanketed the heavens    *60*
in eternal darkness.
Thus pacifying this land,
abundant in ears of rice,
our Lord, sovereign
of the earth's eight corners,    *65*
    a very god,
firmly drove his palace pillars
and proclaimed his rule
over the realm under heaven—
for ten thousand generations,    *70*
    we thought.
But just as his reign flourished
brilliant as the white bouquets
    of mulberry paper,
suddenly they deck his princely halls    *75*
to make a godly shrine,
and the courtiers who served him
now wear mourning clothes of white hemp.
On the fields
before the Haniyasu Palace gate    *80*
they crawl and stumble like deer
as long as the sun still streams its crimson,
and when pitch-black night descends
they crawl around like quail,
turning to look up at the great halls.    *85*
They wait upon him,
but they wait in vain,
and so they moan
like the plaintive birds of spring.
Before their cries can be stilled    *90*
or their mournful thoughts exhausted
the divine cortege
is borne from the Kudara Plain,
borne away.

Loftily he raises
the palace at Kinoe,
        good of hempen cloth,
as his eternal shrine.
A god, his soul is stilled there.
Yet could we even imagine
that his palace by Kagu Hill
        will pass away
in the ten thousand generations
he intended as he built?
I turn to gaze on it
as I would on the heavens,
bearing it in my heart
        like a strand of jewels,
preciously remembering,
awesome though it be.

*Envoys*

Although you rule
the far heavens now,
we go on longing for you,
unmindful of the passing
of sun and moon.

Not knowing where they will drift,
like the hidden puddles that run
on the banks of Haniyasu Pond,
the servingmen stand bewildered.

*One Book Has for an Envoy,*

Offering him sacred wine,
we pray at the shrine of Nakisawa,[1]
        the marsh of tears.
But our Lord is gone
to rule the high heavens.

TRANSLATED BY IAN HIDEO LEVY

# ■ The Priest Mansei (c. 720)

TRANSLATED BY AYAME FUKUDA

The Priest Mansei served Otomo Tabito, himself a noted poet and author of a famed series of drinking poems, and father of Otomo

---

1. In the *Forest of Classified Verse,* the above poem is said to be "by Princess Hinokuma, in her anger at the Nakisawa Shrine (for the Prince's absence)." The *Nihonshoki* states that the later Crown Prince, Takechi, died in autumn, on the tenth day of the seventh month, in the tenth year of the reign (696).

Yakamochi, a compiler of the *Manyoshu*. Mansei was in charge of constructing the Kanzeonji Temple in Kyushu. Apart from this, little is known about him, but this poem is among the perfect gems of Japanese verse.

## What Shall I Compare

What shall I compare
this world to?
At dawn
a boat sails out.
The white wake fades.                                            5

## ▪ Lady Ki (Eighth Century)

TRANSLATED BY AYAME FUKUDA

Lady Ki was the wife of Prince Aki, the great-grandson of Emperor Tenji, and a lover of Otomo Yakamochi. Her personal name was Ojika, and she was the daughter of Ki no Kahito, an official under Emperor Shomu (r. 724–748) and minor *Manyoshu* poet. Twelve of her poems appear in the *Manyoshu,* five of them love poems sent to Otomo Yakamochi. Despite her slender representation in the collection, she is among the finest women poets in the *Manyoshu.*

### Poem Sent to a Friend with a Gift

Across the beach
high winds whirl
but for you I cut
sleek seaweed,
drenching my sleeves.                                           5

### Poem Sent by Lady Ki to Otomo Yakamochi in Response to His

Who flirted first?
Like water your passion
dams to a halt
halfway down the hill.
It reeks in ricebeds.                                           5

## ▪ Otomo Yakamochi (716–785)

Otomo Yakamochi, from the illustrious Otomo clan, was the eldest son of Otomo Tabito, who was also a fine poet. Yakamochi held many posts in his life, in the war department, as governor of Inaba province, and as a military commander-in-chief. But he was as often demoted as promoted and, in fact, was posthumously stripped of rank due to the crime of a relative that effectively ended his family's political good fortune and caused his corpse to remain unburied for twenty days. In 806, twenty-one years after his death, he was granted a pardon. Even after his death, his fortunes were not stable. Four hundred and seventy-nine of his poems are collected in the *Manyoshu,* which he helped compile. He is one of the four principal poets in the collection. He seems to have had many lovers, and he recorded these relationships in poem exchanges, many of which are included in the *Manyoshu.* His poems are startlingly fresh today, though many of his themes—the lover who appears in dreams, the desire to be "a jewel / wrapped / around my lover's wrist"—are traditional themes that appear repeatedly in this collection and in the works of later poets. Compare, for example, this poem by an anonymous Lady, "Upon Emperor Tenji's Death" (translated by Tony Barnstone and Ayame Fukuda):

> You are a god now
> and I am not fit to be with you.
> You are gone
> and I grieve for you this morning;
> you're gone and I miss you.  5
> If you were a jewel
> I'd wrap you around my wrist;
> if you were a robe
> I'd never take you off.
> My lord, whom I desire,  10
> I saw you last night
> in a dream.

**FURTHER READING:** Doe, Paula. *Warbler's Song in the Dusk: The Life and Work of Otomo Yakamochi (718–785),* 1982.

## In a Dream

In a dream
your smile
astounds me
and in my heart
burns  5

TRANSLATED BY AYAME FUKUDA

## It Breaks Me

It breaks me
when I meet you in dream.

Startled awake
I grope for your body
through the empty air.                                                5

TRANSLATED BY TONY BARNSTONE

## New Moon

I look up.
The new moon kindles
a memory.
A woman I met once.
Her painted eyebrows.                                                5

TRANSLATED BY TONY BARNSTONE

## Wild Geese Cry

Wild geese cry
beyond clouds.
Like my love for you
a swarm descends
into ricefields.                                                5

TRANSLATED BY AYAME FUKUDA

## A Long Life

I know my body
is like foam, vaporous,
yet I want it to live
a thousand years!

TRANSLATED BY TONY BARNSTONE

## ■ Lady Kasa (Mid-Eighth Century)

Lady Kasa is a poet known for her twenty-nine *tanka* preserved in the *Manyoshu,* all of them love poems addressed to Otomo Yakamochi. She is an early figure of the passionate female poet who was to have so many incarnations in the history of Japanese poetry. Almost nothing is known about her life, but it has been surmised that her affair took place when Otomo Yakamochi was young, before he left the capital for the provinces. It is also thought, since the *Manyoshu* has only two love poems to her from him, that her love was to some extent unrequited.

## *Poems Sent to Otomo Yakamochi by Lady Kasa*

### In My Dream

In my dream
I held a sword
against my body.
What can it mean?
Are you coming soon?                                                    5

TRANSLATED BY TONY BARNSTONE

### To Love You

To love you
when you don't love me
is to worship
a hungry devil's ass
at the great temple.                                                    5

TRANSLATED BY TONY BARNSTONE

### Will I Never See You?

Will I never see you?
Only hear of you,
far,
a crane's cry
in the dark night?                                                      5

TRANSLATED BY TONY BARNSTONE

### My Keepsake

My keepsake—
look at it and think of me,
and I will love you
through the long years
strung like beads on a string                                           5

TRANSLATED BY BURTON WATSON

## It's Not All Right

It's not all right, though
the years are gone
like a string of rough pearls.
Say nothing.
Bury even my name.                                                    5

TRANSLATED BY TONY BARNSTONE AND WILLIS BARNSTONE

## ■ Lady Otomo Sakanoue (b. 695–701–died c. 750)

Lady Otomo Sakanoue was Yakamochi's aunt and the younger sister
of Tabito. Eighty-four of her poems are in the *Manyoshu,* a number of
which are love poems. Her passionate poetic persona influenced later
women poets (such as Izumi Shikibu, Ono no Komachi, and Yosano
Akiko), and some men (writing as women). This latter tradition—of men
writing through female personae—was common to both China and
Japan.

### He Is So Handsome

He is so handsome
my heart
is a fast river breaking
through dams I put up
again and again                                                      5

TRANSLATED BY TONY BARNSTONE

### Unknown Love

Unknown love
is bitter
as a virgin lily
on the summer meadow,
blooming in bushes.                                                  5

TRANSLATED BY WILLIS BARNSTONE

# Heian Period

### (794–1186)

## ■ Ki no Tsurayuki (c. 868–c. 946) (poems)

### TRANSLATED BY BURTON WATSON

In his pristine observation of nature, of red leaves falling through moonlight and of human nature stained and intermingled with the tiniest motions in the landscape, Ki no Tsurayuki creates an elegantly crafted poetic that makes traditional themes new. He was a poet of the early Heian period and was one of the principal compilers of the *Kokinshu* (an abbreviation of the *Kokinwakashu*, or *Collection of Old and New Japanese Poems*), an extremely important early anthology, the first compilation ordered by Imperial decree. He came from a family steeped in the Chinese prose and poetry traditions, which he mastered himself. Though details about his life are scanty, we know that in 907 he held posts related to the preparation of the emperor's meals, that in the early 930s he was the governor of Tosa, and that he participated in a number of famous poetry matches. His preface to the *Kokinshu* was the first major essay in Japanese literary criticism. He was certainly the most famous poet in his time and his work on the *Kokinshu* was a model for all subsequent compilations. His own poems appear in this and later collections and in a personal collection of his poetry, the *Tsurayuki Shu,* which appears in two versions, one of about seven hundred poems and one of about nine hundred. He is also well known for *The Tosa Diary* (c. 935), a diary of mixed prose and poetry that he writes from the point of view of a woman accompanying a governor on a trip from Tosa to the capital, a trip he took in 934. This essential work is the oldest piece of Japanese prose literature to come down to us in its original form. Both the preface to the *Kokinshu* and *The Tosa Diary* were written in the phonetic *kana* syllabary. The fact that two such central works were written not in Chinese characters but in a syllabary usually reserved for women's writings is extremely significant for the development of a purely Japanese literature. While his poetry still sings, Ki no Tsurayuki is a figure whose ultimate import lies in his pervasive influence on the evolution of Japanese letters.

**FURTHER READING:** McCullough, Helen Craig, tr. *Kokin Wakashu: The First Imperial Anthology of Japanese Poetry,* 1985. Miner, Earl, ed. and tr. *Japanese Poetic Diaries,* 1969, 1976.

## *from* Preface to the Kokinshu[1]

Japanese poetry has its seeds in the human heart, and takes form in the countless leaves that are words. So much happens to us while we live in this world that we must voice the thoughts that are in our hearts, conveying them through the things we see and the things we hear. We hear the bush warbler singing in the flowers or the voice of the frogs that live in the water and know that among all living creatures there is not one that does not have its song. It is poetry that, without exerting force, can move heaven and earth, wake the feelings of the unseen gods and spirits, soften the relations between man and woman, and soothe the heart of the fierce warrior.

## *Five Tanka*

*Written When Visiting a Mountain Temple:*
I found lodging
on the spring mountainside
and slept the night—
and in my dreams, too,
blossoms were falling                                                    5

As autumn mists
rise up to veil them,
the red leaves
seem to drift down
in the dimness                                                           5

Seeing someone off:
This thing called parting
has no color,
yet it seeps into our hearts
and stains them with loneliness                                          5

Along the Yodo
where they cut wild rice,
when it rains the marsh waters overflow,
like my love,
growing deeper than ever                                                 5

Sixth month, cormorant fishing:
When torches cast their light,

---

1. The opening paragraph is translated.

in the depths of the night river
black as leopard-flower seeds,
the water bursts into flame

## ◼ Ono no Komachi (Ninth Century) (poems)

Although very little is known for certain about Ono no Komachi, she was the only woman included among the Six Poetic Geniuses (*rokkasen*), the six poets commented upon by Ki no Tsurayuki in his preface to the great early Heian poetry collection, the *Kokinshu,* the first of twenty-one anthologies compiled at the behest of various emperors. She and Ariwara Narihira are two of the six whose reputations have persisted, though Ki no Tsurayuki's praise of her poetry is rather backhanded: "Her poetry moves you in its enervation, like a gorgeous woman stricken with illness. This weakness probably comes from her sex." This assessment of her poems is echoed again and again by the stories and noh plays that have grown up about her life. It is difficult to extract her life from the legends that have surrounded her: various histories make her either the granddaughter of Ono no Takamura or the daughter of the district head of Dewa province, Ono no Yoshizane. Her most active periods could have been during the Jogan (859–877) or Showa (834–848) era. The name "Komachi" itself may not be a proper name but either a term applied to ladies-in-waiting or a diminutive, meaning "Little Machi," possibly referring to an older sister tentatively identified as Ono no Machi. The legends about her life depict her as a great beauty who rejected offers of marriage, hoping but failing to become an Imperial consort. Both her poems and the legends suggest that she was a great and passionate lover, and she exchanged poems with other great literary figures such as Ariwara Narihira, Sojo Henjo, and Funya Yasuhide, some of whom may have been her lovers. Later, when her beauty faded, she may have become a hunter's wife, and eventually a beggar, devoid of the graces she had hoped would gain her position. She was the subject of a number of noh plays, among them *Sotoba Komachi* and *Sekidera Komachi.* Arthur Waley's translation of *Sotoba Komachi* reads, in part: "Long ago I was full of pride / . . . I spoke with the voice of a nightingale that has sipped the dew. / I was lovelier than the petals of the wild-rose open-stretched / In the hour before its fall. / But now I am grown loathsome even to sluts, / Poor girls of the people, and they and all men / Turn scornful from me." Her poetry is collected in a personal collection of one hundred and ten poems, the *Komachi Shu,* and they blaze off the page with such a mixture of intensity and delicate suggestion as to make her rank among the finest love poets in the world.

**FURTHER READING:** Hirshfield, Jane, with Mariko Aratani, trs. *The Ink Dark Moon: Love Poems by Ono no Komachi and Izumi Shikibu,* 1990. Rexroth, Kenneth, and Ikuko Atsumi, trs. *The Burning Heart: Women Poets of Japan,* 1977. Teele, Roy E., Nicholas J. Teele, and H. Rebecca Teele. *Ono No Komachi: Poems, Stories, No Plays,* 1993.

## Doesn't He Realize

Doesn't he realize
that I am not
like the swaying kelp
in the surf,
where the seaweed gatherer                              5
can come as often as he wants.

TRANSLATED BY KENNETH REXROTH AND IKUKO ATSUMI

## I Fell Asleep Thinking of Him

I fell asleep thinking of him,
and he came to me.
If I had known it was only a dream
I would never have awakened.

TRANSLATED BY KENNETH REXROTH AND IKUKO ATSUMI

## He Does Not Come

He does not come.
Tonight in the dark of the moon
I wake wanting him.
My breasts heave and blaze.
My heart chars.                                         5

TRANSLATED BY KENNETH REXROTH AND IKUKO ATSUMI

## I Am So Lonely

I am so lonely
my body, a weed
severed at the root,
will drift on any current
that will have me.                                      5

TRANSLATED BY AYAME FUKUDA AND TONY BARNSTONE

## The Autumn Night

The autumn night
is long only in name—
We've done no more
than gaze at each other
and it's already dawn.                                  5

TRANSLATED BY JANE HIRSHFIELD AND MARIKO ARATANI

### How Invisibly

How invisibly
it changes color
in this world,
the flower
of the human heart.                                                        5

TRANSLATED BY JANE HIRSHFIELD AND MARIKO ARATANI

## ■ Lady Ise (Ninth to Tenth Centuries) (poems)

Lady Ise came from the North branch of the Fujiwara family; her grandfather Fujiwara no Iemune is famous as the founder of the Hokai-ji in Hino, a very important temple in Japanese art history. Her father, Fujiwara no Tsugukage, was the governor of Ise and Yamato, and she came to be called Lady Ise because of her father's position. She acted as lady-in-waiting to Empress Onshi (872–907), was the consort of Emperor Uda, and was a literary figure for much of her adult life, spent at the Imperial court. She had a love affair with the Empress's older brother, Fujiwara no Nakahira, and later became a favorite of Emperor Uda and bore him a son who died at age seven. Eventually, she bore a daughter to Uda's fourth son, Prince Atsuyoshi, but after his death in 930, little is known of Lady Ise.

She was from a literary background. Both her uncle and her cousin were directors at the Imperial University, and her father graduated from the university's course in literature. Her delicate mastery and passion shine from her poems, and in her time she was an unusually distinguished female literary figure. One hundred and eighty of her poems are collected in the twenty-one Imperial anthologies, and there is a collection of poems bearing her name. She was selected to participate in a poetry match sponsored by Emperor Uda in 913, along with other eminent poets, including Ki no Tsurayuki. Like Ono no Komachi, she may have been a woman of considerable charm and beauty, and it can be seen that Lady Ise lived the life that Ono no Komachi dreamed of, as an Imperial consort.

### Hanging from the Branches of a Green

Hanging from the branches of a green
willow tree,
the spring rain
is a
thread of pearls.                                                          5

TRANSLATED BY WILLIS BARNSTONE

## Like a Ravaged Sea

Like a ravaged sea
this bed.
Were I to smooth it,
the sleeve I press to it
would float back moist with foam.                                    5

TRANSLATED BY ETSUKO TERASAKI WITH IRMA BRANDEIS

## Even in a Dream

Even in a dream
I don't want him to know
he's making love with me.
In the morning mirror
I see my face and blush.                                              5

TRANSLATED BY WILLIS BARNSTONE AND TONY BARNSTONE

## ■ *from* The Tales of Ise (Ninth to Tenth Centuries) (prose/poetry)

TRANSLATED BY HELEN CRAIG McCULLOUGH

*The Tales of Ise (Ise Monogatari)* is a fascinating early Japanese work in which alternating poetry and prose set up a contrapuntal narrative of story and epiphany, consisting (in the most authoritative edition) of 209 poems in 125 sections. The central figure in these tales is the early Heian poet Ariwara Narihira (825–880), who becomes the model of the courtly lover in a number of the stories. In fact, during the Heian and medieval periods, the work was attributed to him, though later scholars discounted this possibility since the *Tales* contain the work of later poets and a poem on Narihira's death. Yet his famous poems, as well as poems written in response to them, are kernels around which some of the stories are written, and it is suggested that he may have been one of several authors who compiled the work between the late ninth and tenth centuries. As translator McCullough notes,

> *Tales of Ise* begins with an anecdote about a young nobleman recently come of age, continues with numerous episodes in which a male protagonist composes poems known to be by Narihira or is described as holding one of Narihira's known offices, and ends with Narihira's death poem. The picture that emerges from these sections, taken in conjunction with many others where the principal character is simply "a man," is that of a single recognizable

individual who consistently demonstrates the sensitivity of the ideal aristocrat, especially in his relationships with women.[1]

Yet the tales are by no means a unified tribute to Narihira. Their unity comes, paradoxically, from their very variety and anonymity, which lend them a universal character. Though its author(s) remain unknown, the work has been enormously influential in the development of Japanese literature, from Matsuo Basho's prose/poetry travelogue *Narrow Road to the Interior* to modern fiction stylists such as Kawabata Yasunari. Murasaki Shikibu is thought to have based Genji of her *The Tale of Genji* on Ariwara Narihira, a practice followed by many later authors of stories dealing with love. So popular was the work that many of its episodes appear on medieval scrolls, fans, and screens.

**FURTHER READING:** Harris, H. Jay, tr. *Tales of Ise,* 1972. McCullough, Helen Craig. *Classical Japanese Prose: An Anthology; Tales of Ise: Lyric Episodes from Tenth Century Japan,* 1968. Vos, Frits. *A Study of the Ise-monogatari,* 2 vols., 1957.

## The Tales of Ise

## 12

Once there was a man who abducted someone's daughter. He was on his way to Musashi Plain with her when some provincial officials arrested him for theft. He had left the girl in a clump of bushes and run off, but the pursuers felt certain that he was on the plain, and they prepared to set fire to it. The girl recited this poem in great agitation:

> Light no fires today
> on the plain of Musashi,
>      for my young spouse,
> sweet as new grass, is hidden here,
> and I am hidden here too.

They heard her, seized her, and marched the two off together.

## 19

Once a man in the service of an imperial consort began to make love to one of the consort's attendants. Presently, the affair came to an end.

---

1. Helen Craig McCullough, *Classical Japanese Prose: An Anthology* (Stanford, CA: Stanford University Press, 1990), 38–39.

When the two met in the course of their duties at the house, the man behaved as if the woman were invisible, even though she saw him plainly enough. She sent him this poem:

> Although you remain
> visible to the eye,
>       we are quite estranged:
> you have become as distant
> as a cloud in the heavens.

His reply:

> That I spend my days
> ever as distant from you
>       as a cloud in the sky
> is the fault of the harsh wind
> on the hill where I would rest.

He meant that another man had been visiting her.

# 62

Once there was a woman whose husband had neglected her for years. Perhaps because she was not clever, she took the advice of an unreliable person and became a domestic in a provincial household. It happened one day that she served food to her former husband. That night, the husband told the master of the house to send her to him. "Don't you know me?" he asked. Then he recited:

> Where is the beauty
> you flaunted in days of old?
>       Ah! You have become
> merely a cherry tree
> despoiled of its blossoms.

The woman was too embarrassed to reply. "Why don't you answer me?" he asked. "I am blind and speechless with tears," she said. He recited:

> Here is a person
> who has wished to be rid
>       of her ties to me.
> Although much time has elapsed,
> her lot seems little improved.

He removed his cloak and gave it to her, but she left it and ran off—nobody knows where.

## 105

Once a man sent word to a woman, "I'll die if things go on like this." She answered:

> If the white dew
> must vanish, let it vanish.
>     Even if it stayed,
> I doubt that anyone
> would string the drops like jewels.

The man considered the reply most discourteous, but his love for her increased.

## 125

Once a man was taken ill. Sensing the approach of death, he composed this poem:

> Upon this pathway,
> I have long heard it said,
>     man sets forth at last—
> yet I had not thought to go
> so very soon as today.

## ■ Sei Shonagon (c. 966–c. 1017) (memoir)

### TRANSLATED BY IVAN MORRIS

*The Pillow Book* of Sei Shonagon is the earliest extant example of a particularly Japanese genre of writing called *zuihitsu* (random notes, occasional writings). *The Pillow Book* is Sei Shonagon's only known work, but it persists as one of the finest works in Japanese literature. We have almost no information about Sei Shonagon except what she herself writes in this compilation of idiosyncratic, witty, and daring observations. We do not even know her real name. Sei is the sinified reading of the character *kiyo,* the first character in her family name, and Shonagon is a court title. Recent research has suggested a possible first name for her: Nagiko. Her father was Kiyohara no Motosuke, who helped compile the *Gosenshu* (an Imperial anthology of poems), and it is possible that she married Tachibana no Norimitsu and bore him a son named Norinaga, but if so the marriage did not last long. She became a lady-in-waiting to Empress Sadako (also known as Teishi) in 990 and stayed in court service until 1000, when the empress died. Nothing is known for certain after her life in the court, but a legend has it that she became a Buddhist nun and died destitute and lonely. Translator Ivan Morris notes that such legends are probably the corrective invention of moralists who were shocked by her promiscuous life and worldly attitudes. Whoever she was, whatever her real name, Sei Shonagon lives through her book.

"Pillow book" seems to have been a term for informal collections of notes composed by men and women in their sleeping chambers in the evenings, journals that they may have kept in the drawers of their wooden pillows. Sei Shonagon's pillow book is distinguished for its clarity of observation and for the biting, charming intelligence of its author. She is considered a finer prose stylist than Murasaki Shikibu, particularly in her descriptions of nature. In addition to such descriptions, *The Pillow Book* contains anecdotes of court life, diary entries, observations on lovers, sketches of people high and low, and an incredible wealth of detail about aristocratic life in the Heian period. Perhaps her most famous and intriguing prose form is the "list." The book contains one hundred sixty-four lists of "hateful things," "people who look pleased with themselves," and even of "insects." Sei Shonagon was a sensitive woman but not without thorns. She is often cutting and dismissive, and her scorn for the lower classes is as excessive as her worship of the Imperial family; yet, as in the well-wrought snubs of Oscar Wilde or Gore Vidal, there are joys to be found in her negations.

Among the historical virtues of the Heian period is the fact that major works by women were both written and preserved (in contrast to classical Latin literature from which, of many women authors, only seven poems by a poet who may have been called Sulpicia have been preserved). Sei Shonagon wrote at a time when the finest writers were aristocratic women of middle rank, and, with her contemporaries Izumi Shikibu and Murasaki Shikibu, she helped turn the middle Heian period into a moment of concentrated literary glory.

**FURTHER READING:** Morris, Ivan, tr. *The Pillow Book of Sei Shonagon,* 1967; *The World of the Shining Prince: Court Life in Ancient Japan,* 1969. Waley, Arthur. *The Pillow-Book of Sei Shonagon,* 1928.

## *from* **The Pillow Book of Sei Shonagon**
### That Parents Should Bring Up Some Beloved Son

That parents should bring up some beloved son of theirs to be a priest is really distressing. No doubt it is an auspicious thing to do; but unfortunately most people are convinced that a priest is as unimportant as a piece of wood, and they treat him accordingly. A priest lives poorly on meagre food, and cannot even sleep without being criticized. While he is young, it is only natural that he should be curious about all sorts of things, and, if there are women about, he will probably peep in their direction (though, to be sure, with a look of aversion on his face). What is wrong about that? Yet people immediately find fault with him for even so small a lapse.

The lot of an exorcist is still more painful. On his pilgrimages to Mi-take, Kumano, and all the other sacred mountains he often undergoes the greatest hardships. When people come to hear that his prayers are effective, they summon him here and there to perform services of exorcism: the more popular he becomes, the less peace he enjoys. Sometimes he will be called to see a patient who is seriously ill and he has to exert all his powers to cast out the spirit that is causing the affliction. But if he dozes off, exhausted by his efforts, people say reproachfully, 'Really, this priest does nothing but sleep.' Such comments are most embarrassing for the exorcist, and I can imagine how he must feel.

That is how things used to be; nowadays priests have a somewhat easier life.

## The Cat Who Lived in the Palace

The cat who lived in the Palace had been awarded the headdress of nobility and was called Lady Myobu. She was a very pretty cat, and His Majesty saw to it that she was treated with the greatest care.[1]

One day she wandered on to the veranda, and Lady Uma, the nurse in charge of her, called out, 'Oh, you naughty thing! Please come inside at once.' But the cat paid no attention and went on basking sleepily in the sun. Intending to give her a scare, the nurse called for the dog, Oki-namaro.

'Okinamaro, where are you?' she cried. 'Come here and bite Lady My-obu!' The foolish Okinamaro, believing that the nurse was in earnest, rushed at the cat, who, startled and terrified, ran behind the blind in the Imperial Dining Room, where the Emperor happened to be sitting. Greatly surprised, His Majesty picked up the cat and held her in his arms. He summoned his gentlemen-in-waiting. When Tadataka, the Chamberlain, appeared, His Majesty ordered that Okinamaro be chastised and banished to Dog Island. The attendants all started to chase the dog amid great confusion. His Majesty also reproached Lady Uma. 'We shall have to find a new nurse for our cat,' he told her. 'I no longer feel I can count on you to look after her.' Lady Uma bowed; thereafter she no longer appeared in the Emperor's presence.

The Imperial Guards quickly succeeded in catching Okinamaro and drove him out of the Palace grounds. Poor dog! He used to swagger about so happily. Recently, on the third day of the Third Month, when the Controller First Secretary paraded him through the Palace grounds, Okinamaro was adorned with garlands of willow leaves, peach blossoms on his head, and cherry blossoms round his body. How could the dog have imagined that this would be his fate? We all felt sorry for him. 'When Her

---

1. Cats had been imported from the Continent, and there are several references to them in Heian chronicles and literature. The diary of Fujiwara no Sanesuke, for instance, contains the momentous entry (on the nineteenth day of the Ninth Month in 999) that one of the Palace cats gave birth to a litter of kittens, that the birth-ceremony was attended by no lesser dignitaries than the Ministers of the Left and of the Right, and that Uma no Myobu was appointed nurse to the litter.

Majesty was having her meals,' recalled one of the ladies-in-waiting, 'Oki-namaro always used to be in attendance and sit opposite us. How I miss him!'

It was about noon, a few days after Okinamaro's banishment, that we heard a dog howling fearfully. How could any dog possibly cry so long? All the other dogs rushed out in excitement to see what was happening. Meanwhile a woman who served as a cleaner in the Palace latrines ran up to us. 'It's terrible,' she said. 'Two of the Chamberlains are flogging a dog. They'll surely kill him. He's being punished for having come back after he was banished. It's Tadataka and Sanefusa who are beating him.' Obviously the victim was Okinamaro. I was absolutely wretched and sent a servant to ask the men to stop; but just then the howling finally ceased. 'He's dead,' one of the servants informed me. 'They've thrown his body outside the gate.'

That evening, while we were sitting in the Palace bemoaning Okina-maro's fate, a wretched-looking dog walked in; he was trembling all over, and his body was fearfully swollen.

'Oh dear,' said one of the ladies-in-waiting. 'Can this be Okinamaro? We haven't seen any other dog like him recently, have we?'

We called to him by name, but the dog did not respond. Some of us insisted that it was Okinamaro, others that it was not. 'Please send for Lady Ukon,' said the Empress, hearing our discussion. 'She will certainly be able to tell.' We immediately went to Ukon's room and told her she was wanted on an urgent matter.

'Is this Okinamaro?' the Empress asked her, pointing to the dog.

'Well,' said Ukon, 'it certainly looks like him, but I cannot believe that this loathsome creature is really our Okinamaro. When I called Okina-maro, he always used to come to me, wagging his tail. But this dog does not react at all. No, it cannot be the same one. And besides, wasn't Okina-maro beaten to death and his body thrown away? How could any dog be alive after being flogged by two strong men?' Hearing this, Her Majesty was very unhappy.

When it got dark, we gave the dog something to eat; but he refused it, and we finally decided that this could not be Okinamaro.

On the following morning I went to attend the Empress while her hair was being dressed and she was performing her ablutions. I was holding up the mirror for her when the dog we had seen on the previous evening slunk into the room and crouched next to one of the pillars. 'Poor Okina-maro!' I said. 'He had such a dreadful beating yesterday. How sad to think he is dead! I wonder what body he has been born into this time. Oh, how he must have suffered!'

At that moment the dog lying by the pillar started to shake and trem-ble, and shed a flood of tears. It was astounding. So this really was Okina-maro! On the previous night it was to avoid betraying himself that he had refused to answer to his name. We were immensely moved and pleased. 'Well, well, Okinamaro!' I said, putting down the mirror. The dog stretched himself flat on the floor and yelped loudly, so that the Empress beamed with delight. All the ladies gathered round, and Her Majesty summoned Lady Ukon. When the Empress explained what had happened, everyone talked and laughed with great excitement.

The news reached His Majesty, and he too came to the Empress's room. 'It's amazing,' he said with a smile. 'To think that even a dog has such deep feelings!' When the Emperor's ladies-in-waiting heard the story, they too came along in a great crowd. 'Okinamaro!' we called, and this time the dog rose and limped about the room with his swollen face. 'He must have a meal prepared for him,' I said. 'Yes,' said the Empress, laughing happily, 'now that Okinamaro has finally told us who he is.'

The Chamberlain, Tadataka, was informed, and he hurried along from the Table Room. 'Is it really true?' he asked. 'Please let me see for myself.' I sent a maid to him with the following reply: 'Alas, I am afraid that this is not the same dog after all.' 'Well,' answered Tadataka, 'whatever you say, I shall sooner or later have occasion to see the animal. You won't be able to hide him from me indefinitely.'

Before long, Okinamaro was granted an Imperial pardon and returned to his former happy state. Yet even now, when I remember how he whimpered and trembled in response to our sympathy, it strikes me as a strange and moving scene; when people talk to me about it, I start crying myself.

## Hateful Things

One is in a hurry to leave, but one's visitor keeps chattering away. If it is someone of no importance, one can get rid of him by saying, 'You must tell me all about it next time'; but, should it be the sort of visitor whose presence commands one's best behaviour, the situation is hateful indeed.

One finds that a hair has got caught in the stone on which one is rubbing one's inkstick, or again that gravel is lodged in the inkstick, making a nasty, grating sound.

Someone has suddenly fallen ill and one summons the exorcist. Since he is not at home, one has to send messengers to look for him. After one has had a long fretful wait, the exorcist finally arrives, and with a sigh of relief one asks him to start his incantations. But perhaps he has been exorcizing too many evil spirits recently; for hardly has he installed himself and begun praying when his voice becomes drowsy. Oh, how hateful!

A man who has nothing in particular to recommend him discusses all sorts of subjects at random as though he knew everything.

An elderly person warms the palms of his hands over a brazier and stretches out the wrinkles. No young man would dream of behaving in such a fashion; old people can really be quite shameless. I have seen some dreary old creatures actually resting their feet on the brazier and rubbing them against the edge while they speak. These are the kind of people who in visiting someone's house first use their fans to wipe away the dust from the mat and, when they finally sit on it, cannot stay still but are forever spreading out the front of their hunting costume[2] or even tucking it up under their knees. One might suppose that such behaviour was restricted to people of humble station; but I have observed it in quite well-bred people, including a Senior Secretary of the Fifth Rank in the Ministry of Ceremonial and a former Governor of Suruga.

I hate the sight of men in their cups who shout, poke their fingers in their mouths, stroke their beards, and pass on the wine to their neighbours with great cries of 'Have some more! Drink up!' They tremble, shake their heads, twist their faces, and gesticulate like children who are singing, 'We're off to see the Governor.' I have seen really well-bred people behave like this and I find it most distasteful.

To envy others and to complain about one's own lot; to speak badly about people; to be inquisitive about the most trivial matters and to resent and abuse people for not telling one, or, if one does manage to worm out some facts, to inform everyone in the most detailed fashion as if one had known all from the beginning—oh, how hateful!

One is just about to be told some interesting piece of news when a baby starts crying.

A flight of crows circle about with loud caws.

An admirer has come on a clandestine visit, but a dog catches sight of him and starts barking. One feels like killing the beast.

One has been foolish enough to invite a man to spend the night in an unsuitable place—and then he starts snoring.

A gentleman has visited one secretly. Though he is wearing a tall, lacquered hat,[3] he nevertheless wants no one to see him. He is so flurried, in fact, that upon leaving he bangs into something with his hat. Most hateful! It is annoying too when he lifts up the Iyo blind[4] that hangs at the entrance of the room, then lets it fall with a great rattle. If it is a head-blind, things are still worse, for being more solid it makes a terrible noise when it is dropped. There is no excuse for such carelessness. Even a head-blind does not make any noise if one lifts it up gently on entering and leaving the room; the same applies to sliding-doors. If one's movements are rough, even a paper door will bend and resonate when opened; but, if one lifts the door a little while pushing it, there need be no sound.

One has gone to bed and is about to doze off when a mosquito appears, announcing himself in a reedy voice. One can actually feel the wind made by his wings and, slight though it is, one finds it hateful in the extreme.

---

2. Men's informal outdoor costume, originally worn for hunting.

3. *Eboshi* (tall, lacquered hat): black, lacquered head-dress worn by men on the top of the head and secured by a mauve silk cord that was fastened under the chin; two long black pendants hung down from the back of the hat. The *eboshi* was a most conspicuous form of headgear and hardly suited for a clandestine visit.

4. Iyo blind: a rough type of reed blind manufactured in the province of Iyo on the Inland Sea. Head-blind: a more elegant type of blind whose top and edges were decorated with strips of silk. It also had thin strips of bamboo along the edges and was therefore heavier than ordinary blinds.

A carriage passes with a nasty, creaking noise. Annoying to think that the passengers may not even be aware of this! If I am travelling in someone's carriage and I hear it creaking, I dislike not only the noise but also the owner of the carriage.

One is in the middle of a story when someone butts in and tries to show that he is the only clever person in the room. Such a person is hateful, and so, indeed, is anyone, child or adult, who tries to push himself forward.

One is telling a story about old times when someone breaks in with a little detail that he happens to know, implying that one's own version is inaccurate — disgusting behaviour!

Very hateful is a mouse that scurries all over the place.

Some children have called at one's house. One makes a great fuss of them and gives them toys to play with. The children become accustomed to this treatment and start to come regularly, forcing their way into one's inner rooms and scattering one's furnishings and possessions. Hateful!

A certain gentleman whom one does not want to see visits one at home or in the Palace, and one pretends to be asleep. But a maid comes to tell one and shakes one awake, with a look on her face that says, 'What a sleepyhead!' Very hateful.

A newcomer pushes ahead of the other members in a group; with a knowing look, this person starts laying down the law and forcing advice upon everyone — most hateful.

A man with whom one is having an affair keeps singing the praises of some woman he used to know. Even if it is a thing of the past, this can be very annoying. How much more so if he is still seeing the woman! (Yet sometimes I find that it is not as unpleasant as all that.)

A person who recites a spell himself after sneezing.[5] In fact I detest anyone who sneezes, except the master of the house.

Fleas, too, are very hateful. When they dance about under someone's clothes, they really seem to be lifting them up.

The sound of dogs when they bark for a long time in chorus is ominous and hateful.

I cannot stand people who leave without closing the panel behind them.

How I detest the husbands of nurse-maids! It is not so bad if the child in the maid's charge is a girl, because then the man will keep his distance. But, if it is a boy, he will behave as though he were the father. Never letting the boy out of his sight, he insists on managing everything. He regards the other attendants in the house as less than human, and, if anyone tries to scold the child, he slanders him to the master. Despite this disgraceful behaviour, no one dare accuse the husband; so he strides about the house with a proud, self-important look, giving all the orders.

I hate people whose letters show that they lack respect for worldly ci-

---

5. Sneezing was a bad omen, and it was normal to counteract its effects by reciting some auspicious formula, such as wishing long life to the person who had sneezed (cf. 'Bless you!' in the West).

vilities, whether by discourtesy in the phrasing or by extreme politeness to someone who does not deserve it. This sort of thing is, of course, most odious if the letter is for oneself, but it is bad enough even if it is addressed to someone else.

As a matter of fact, most people are too casual, not only in their letters but in their direct conversation. Sometimes I am quite disgusted at noting how little decorum people observe when talking to each other. It is particularly unpleasant to hear some foolish man or woman omit the proper marks of respect when addressing a person of quality; and, when servants fail to use honorific forms of speech in referring to their masters, it is very bad indeed. No less odious, however, are those masters who, in addressing their servants, use such phrases as 'When you were good enough to do such-and-such' or 'As you so kindly remarked.' No doubt there are some masters who, in describing their own actions to a servant, say, 'I presumed to do so-and-so'![6]

Sometimes a person who is utterly devoid of charm will try to create a good impression by using very elegant language; yet he only succeeds in being ridiculous. No doubt he believes this refined language to be just what the occasion demands, but, when it goes so far that everyone bursts out laughing, surely something must be wrong.

It is most improper to address high-ranking courtiers, Imperial Advisers, and the like simply by using their names without any titles or marks of respect; but such mistakes are fortunately rare.

If one refers to the maid who is in attendance on some lady-in-waiting as 'Madam' or 'that lady,' she will be surprised, delighted, and lavish in her praise.

When speaking to young noblemen and courtiers of high rank, one should always (unless Their Majesties are present) refer to them by their official posts. Incidentally, I have been very shocked to hear important people use the word 'I' while conversing in Their Majesties' presence.[7] Such a breach of etiquette is really distressing, and I fail to see why people cannot avoid it.

A man who has nothing in particular to recommend him but who speaks in an affected tone and poses as being elegant.

An inkstone with such a hard, smooth surface that the stick glides over it without leaving any deposit of ink.

Ladies-in-waiting who want to know everything that is going on.

---

6. *Owasu* ('good enough to do') and *notamau* ('kindly remarked') designate the actions of a superior; *haberu* (lit. 'to serve') is used to describe one's own or someone else's actions in relation to a superior. See *Dictionary of Selected Forms in Classical Japanese Literature until c. 1330*, App. IV. The correct use of honorific, polite, and humble locutions was of course enormously important in a strictly hierarchic society. In the present passage the sentence beginning 'No doubt . . .' is ironic

7. Etiquette demanded that in the presence of the Emperor or Empress one referred to oneself by one's name rather than by the first person singular. One referred to other people by their real names; if Their Majesties were not present, however, one referred to these people by their offices (e.g., Major Counsellor). On the whole, personal pronouns were avoided and this added to the importance of correct honorific usage.

Sometimes one greatly dislikes a person for no particular reason—and then that person goes and does something hateful.

A gentleman who travels alone in his carriage to see a procession or some other spectacle. What sort of a man is he? Even though he may not be a person of the greatest quality, surely he should have taken along a few of the many young men who are anxious to see the sights. But no, there he sits by himself (one can see his silhouette through the blinds), with a proud look on his face, keeping all his impressions to himself.

A lover who is leaving at dawn announces that he has to find his fan and his paper.[8] 'I know I put them somewhere last night,' he says. Since it is pitch dark, he gropes about the room, bumping into the furniture and muttering, 'Strange! Where on earth can they be?' Finally he discovers the objects. He thrusts the paper into the breast of his robe with a great rustling sound; then he snaps open his fan and busily fans away with it. Only now is he ready to take his leave. What charmless behaviour! 'Hateful' is an understatement.

Equally disagreeable is the man who, when leaving in the middle of the night, takes care to fasten the cord of his head-dress. This is quite unnecessary; he could perfectly well put it gently on his head without tying the cord. And why must he spend time adjusting his cloak or hunting costume? Does he really think someone may see him at this time of night and criticize him for not being impeccably dressed?

A good lover will behave as elegantly at dawn as at any other time. He drags himself out of bed with a look of dismay on his face. The lady urges him on: 'Come, my friend, it's getting light. You don't want anyone to find you here.' He gives a deep sigh, as if to say that the night has not been nearly long enough and that it is agony to leave. Once up, he does not instantly pull on his trousers. Instead he comes close to the lady and whispers whatever was left unsaid during the night. Even when he is dressed, he still lingers, vaguely pretending to be fastening his sash.

Presently he raises the lattice, and the two lovers stand together by the side door while he tells her how he dreads the coming day, which will keep them apart; then he slips away. The lady watches him go, and this moment of parting will remain among her most charming memories.

Indeed, one's attachment to a man depends largely on the elegance of his leave-taking. When he jumps out of bed, scurries about the room, tightly fastens his trouser-sash, rolls up the sleeves of his Court cloak, over-robe, or hunting costume, stuffs his belongings into the breast of his robe and then briskly secures the outer sash—one really begins to hate him.

---

8. Elegant coloured paper that gentlemen carried in the folds of their clothes. It served for writing notes and was also used like an elegant sort of Kleenex.

# It Is So Stiflingly Hot

It is so stiflingly hot in the Seventh Month that even at night one keeps all the doors and lattices open. At such times it is delightful to wake up when the moon is shining and to look outside. I enjoy it even when there is no moon. But to wake up at dawn and see a pale sliver of a moon in the sky— well, I need hardly say how perfect that is.

I like to see a bright new straw mat that has just been spread out on a well-polished floor.[9] The best place for one's three-foot curtain of state is in the front of the room near the veranda. It is pointless to put it in the rear of the room, as it is most unlikely that anyone will peer in from that direction.[10]

It is dawn and a woman is lying in bed after her lover has taken his leave. She is covered up to her head with a light mauve robe that has a lining of dark violet; the colour of both the outside and the lining is fresh and glossy.[11] The woman, who appears to be asleep, wears an unlined orange robe and a dark crimson skirt of stiff silk whose cords hang loosely by her side, as if they have been left untied. Her thick tresses tumble over each other in cascades, and one can imagine how long her hair must be when it falls freely down her back.[12]

Near by another woman's lover is making his way home in the misty dawn. He is wearing loose violet trousers, an orange hunting costume, so lightly coloured that one can hardly tell whether it has been dyed or not, a white robe of stiff silk, and a scarlet robe of glossy, beaten silk. His clothes, which are damp from the mist, hang loosely about him. From the dishevelment of his side locks one can tell how negligently he must have tucked his hair into his black lacquered head-dress when he got up. He wants to return and write his next-morning letter[13] before the dew on the

---

9. In the Heian period rooms were not covered with straw mats as became normal in later times; instead mats were spread out when and where they were needed for sleeping, sitting, etc.

10. *Kichō* (curtains of state) were usually classified in terms of the length of the horizontal wooden bar from which the curtains were suspended. A three-foot curtain of state normally had five widths of curtain.

On a hot summer night it was advisable to place one's *kichō* in as cool a part of the room as possible, i.e. near the veranda. Besides, since the main purpose of the *kichō* was to protect women from prying eyes, it would be illogical to place it in the rear of the room where people were unlikely to be looking at one from behind.

11. It was customary in Shōnagon's time to use clothes as bedcovers; also it was normal to sleep fully dressed. The two sets of clothing described in this paragraph are, respectively, the woman's bedclothes and her dress. The present scene evidently takes place in the Imperial Palace; the philandering gentleman is able to peep into the lady's quarters as he walks along the corridor on his way back from his own tryst.

12. Heian women usually let their long, thick hair hang loosely down their backs. The closer it reached the floor, the more beautiful they were considered.

13. It was an essential part of Heian etiquette for the man to write a love-letter to the lady with whom he had spent the night; it usually included a poem and was attached to a spray of some appropriate flower. The letter had to be sent as soon as the man returned home or, if he was on duty, as soon as he reached his office. The lady was of course expected to send a prompt reply. If the man failed to send a letter, it normally meant that he had no desire to continue the liason.

morning glories has had time to vanish; but the path seems endless, and to divert himself he hums 'The sprouts in the flax fields.'[14]

As he walks along, he passes a house with an open lattice. He is on his way to report for official duty, but cannot help stopping to lift up the blind and peep into the room.[15] It amuses him to think that a man has probably been spending the night here and has only recently got up to leave, just as happened to himself. Perhaps that man too had felt the charm of the dew.[16]

Looking round the room, he notices near the woman's pillow an open fan with a magnolia frame and purple paper; and at the foot of her curtain of state he sees some narrow strips of Michinoku paper and also some other paper of a faded colour, either orange-red or maple.

The woman senses that someone is watching her and, looking up from under her bedclothes, sees a gentleman leaning against the wall by the threshold, a smile on his face. She can tell at once that he is the sort of man with whom she need feel no reserve. All the same, she does not want to enter into any familiar relations with him, and she is annoyed that he should have seen her asleep.[17]

'Well, well, Madam,' says the man, leaning forward so that the upper part of his body comes behind her curtains, 'what a long nap you're having after your morning adieu! You really are a lie-abed!'

'You call me that, Sir,' she replied, 'only because you're annoyed at having had to get up before the dew had time to settle.'

Their conversation may be commonplace, yet I find there is something delightful about the scene.

---

14. From the poem,

> The sprouts of the cherry flax
> In the flax fields
> Are heavy now with dew.
> I shall stay with you till dawn
> Though your parents be aware.

The expression 'cherry-flax' is found in a similar poem in the *Manyō Shū* and refers (i) to the fact that flax was sown at the same time that the cherries blossomed, (ii) to the similarity in appearance between cherry blossoms and the leaves of flax.

   The gallant declares that he will stay with the girl until daylight, though this probably means that her parents will find out about his visit. His ostensible reason is that it is hard to make his way through the heavy morning dew (a standard euphemism); the real motive, of course, is his reluctance to leave the partner of his night's pleasures. 'Dew on the sprouts' may have a secondary erotic implication such as one frequently finds in early Japanese love poems.

15. I.e., the house of the woman with the long hair and the orange robe.

16. If the man was sensitive to the beauty of the dew, he would want to leave at early dawn before it had disappeared. The real reason for early departures, of course, was fear of discovery; but pretty conceits of this type were common.

17. As a rule a Heian woman of the upper class would not let herself be seen by a man unless she was actually having an affair with him—and not always then. They were usually protected by curtains of state, screens, fans, etc., and above all by the darkness of the rooms.

Now the gentleman leans further forward and, using his own fan, tries to get hold of the fan by the woman's pillow. Fearing his closeness, she moves further back into her curtain enclosure, her heart pounding. The gentleman picks up the magnolia fan and, while examining it, says in a slightly bitter tone, 'How standoffish you are!'

But now it is growing light; there is a sound of people's voices, and it looks as if the sun will soon be up. Only a short while ago this same man was hurrying home to write his next-morning letter before the mists had time to clear. Alas, how easily his intentions have been forgotten!

While all this is afoot, the woman's original lover has been busy with his own next-morning letter, and now, quite unexpectedly, the messenger arrives at her house. The letter is attached to a spray of bush-clover, still damp with dew, and the paper gives off a delicious aroma of incense. Because of the new visitor, however, the woman's servants cannot deliver it to her.

Finally it becomes unseemly for the gentleman to stay any longer. As he goes, he is amused to think that a similar scene may be taking place in the house he left earlier that morning.

## Elegant Things

A white coat worn over a violet waistcoat.
Duck eggs.
Shaved-ice mixed with liana syrup and put in a new silver bowl.
A rosary of rock crystal.
Wistaria blossoms. Plum blossoms covered with snow.
A pretty child eating strawberries.

## Insects

The bell insect and the pine cricket; the grasshopper and the common cricket; the butterfly and the shrimp insect; the mayfly and the firefly.

I feel very sorry for the basket worm. He was begotten by a demon, and his mother, fearing that he would grow up with his father's frightening nature, abandoned the unsuspecting child, having first wrapped him in a dirty piece of clothing. 'Wait for me,' she said as she left. 'I shall return to you as soon as the autumn winds blow.' So, when autumn comes and the wind starts blowing, the wretched child hears it and desperately cries, 'Milk! Milk!'[18]

The clear-toned cicada.

The snap-beetle also impresses me. They say that the reason it bows while crawling along the ground is that the faith of Buddha has sprung up

---

18. *Chi-chi* is the characteristic sound of the basket worm as well as the word for 'milk.' The insect in question is a *psychidae;* it was called 'straw-coat insect' because of the nest in which it is wrapped. This nest is made chiefly of dirt.

in its insect heart. Sometimes one suddenly hears the snap-beetle tapping away in a dark place, and this is rather pleasant.

The fly should have been included in my list of hateful things; for such an odious creature does not belong with ordinary insects. It settles on everything, and even alights on one's face with its clammy feet. I am sorry that anyone should have been named after it.[19]

The tiger moth is very pretty and delightful. When one sits close to a lamp reading a story, a tiger moth will often flutter prettily in front of one's book.

The ant is an ugly insect; but it is light on its feet and I enjoy watching as it skims quickly over the surface of the water.

## To Meet One's Lover

To meet one's lover summer is indeed the right season. True, the nights are very short, and dawn creeps up before one has had a wink of sleep. Since all the lattices have been left open, one can lie and look out at the garden in the cool morning air. There are still a few endearments to exchange before the man takes his leave, and the lovers are murmuring to each other when suddenly there is a loud noise. For a moment they are certain that they have been discovered; but it is only the caw of a crow flying past in the garden.

In the winter, when it is very cold and one lies buried under the bedclothes listening to one's lover's endearments, it is delightful to hear the booming of a temple gong, which seems to come from the bottom of a deep well. The first cry of the birds, whose beaks are still tucked under their wings, is also strange and muffled. Then one bird after another takes up the call. How pleasant it is to lie there listening as the sound becomes clearer and clearer!

## The Women's Apartments along the Gallery

The women's apartments along the gallery of the Imperial Palace are particularly pleasant. When one raises the upper part of the small half-shutters, the wind blows in extremely hard; it is cool even in summer, and in winter snow and hail come along with the wind, which I find agreeable. As the rooms are small, and as the page-boys (even though employed in such august precincts) often behave badly, we women generally stay hidden behind our screens or curtains. It is delightfully quiet there; for one cannot hear any of the loud talk and laughter that disturb one in other parts of the Palace.

Of course we must always be on the alert when we are staying in these apartments. Even during the day we cannot be off our guard, and at night we have to be especially careful. But I rather enjoy all this. Throughout the night one hears the sound of footsteps in the corridor outside. Every now and then the sound will stop, and someone will tap on a door with just a single finger. It is pleasant to think that the woman inside can in-

---

19. In ancient Japan people were often named after animals. Haemaro (in which *hae* means 'fly') was probably given to members of the lower orders because of its unpleasant associations.

stantly recognize her visitor. Sometimes the tapping will continue for quite a while without the woman's responding in any way. The man finally gives up, thinking that she must be asleep; but this does not please the woman, who makes a few cautious movements, with a rustle of silk clothes, so that her visitor will know she is really there. Then she hears him fanning himself as he remains standing outside the door.

In the winter one sometimes catches the sound of a woman gently stirring the embers in her brazier. Though she does her best to be quiet, the man who is waiting outside hears her; he knocks louder and louder, asking her to let him in. Then the woman slips furtively towards the door where she can listen to him.

On other occasions one may hear several voices reciting Chinese or Japanese poems. One of the women opens her door, though in fact no one has knocked. Seeing this, several of the men, who had no particular intention of visiting this woman, stop on their way through the gallery. Since there is no room for them all to come in, many of them spend the rest of the night out in the garden—most charming.

## I Remember a Clear Morning

I remember a clear morning in the Ninth Month when it had been raining all night. Despite the bright sun, dew was still dripping from the chrysanthemums in the garden. On the bamboo fences and criss-cross hedges I saw tatters of spider webs; and where the threads were broken the raindrops hung on them like strings of white pearls. I was greatly moved and delighted.

As it became sunnier, the dew gradually vanished from the clover and the other plants where it had lain so heavily; the branches began to stir, then suddenly sprang up of their own accord. Later I described to people how beautiful it all was. What most impressed me was that they were not at all impressed.

## Things without Merit

An ugly person with a bad character.

Rice starch that has become mixed with water. . . . I know that this is a very vulgar item and everyone will dislike my mentioning it. But that should not stop me. In fact I must feel free to include anything, even tongs used for the parting-fires.[20] After all, these objects do exist in our

---

20. Putting starch in laundered clothes was so plebeian an occupation that Shōnagon hesitates even to hint at its existence. She points out, however, that her notes were not intended for other people to see and that she would therefore be justified in including so inauspicious an item as parting-fire tongs (below), which were associated with death.

Tongs used for the parting fires: the Festival of the Dead (Urabon), which corresponded in some ways to All Souls' Day in the West, was celebrated from the thirteenth to the sixteenth of the Seventh Month. Sticks of peeled hemp were lit on the first day of the festival so that the souls of the dead might find their way to earth; on the last day, parting fires were again lit, this time to speed the ghostly visitors on their way back. On the fifteenth a special Buddhist service was held in intercession for the dead who were suffering in hell, especially for those who were undergoing the ordeal of Headlong Falling.

The wooden tongs used for the parting fires clearly deserved to be included among Things Without Merit. The tongs used for the welcoming fires could be used again at the end of the festival, but afterwards they had to be thrown away because of their inauspicious connotations.

world and people all know about them. I admit they do not belong to a list that others will see. But I never thought that these notes would be read by anyone else, and so I included everything that came into my head, however strange or unpleasant.[21]

## The House Had a Spacious Courtyard

The house had a spacious courtyard and was shadowed by tall pine trees. To the south and east the lattice-windows were all wide open. It gave a cool feeling when one looked inside. In the main room was a four-foot curtain of state and in front of it a round hassock on which a priest was kneeling. He was in his early thirties and quite handsome. Over his grey habit he wore a fine silk stole — altogether the effect was magnificent. Cooling himself with a clove-scented fan, he recited the Magic Incantation of the Thousand Hands.[22]

I gathered that someone in the house was seriously ill, for now a heavily built girl with a splendid head of hair edged her way into the room. Clearly this was the medium to whom the evil spirit was going to be transferred. She was wearing an unlined robe of stiff silk and long, light-coloured trousers.

When the girl had sat down next to the priest in front of a small three-foot curtain of state, he turned round and handed her a thin, highly polished wand.[23] Then with his eyes tightly shut he began to read the mystic incantations, his voice coming out in staccato bursts as he uttered the sacred syllables. It was an impressive sight, and many of the ladies of the house came out from behind the screens and curtains and sat watching in a group.

After a short time the medium began to tremble and fell into a trance. It was awesome indeed to see how the priest's incantations were steadily taking effect. The medium's brother, a slender young man in a long robe who had only recently celebrated his coming of age, stood behind the girl, fanning her.

Everyone who witnessed the scene was overcome with respect. It occurred to me how embarrassed the girl herself would feel to be exposed like this if she were in her normal state of mind. She lay there groaning and wailing in the most terrible way, and, though one realized that she was in no actual pain,[24] one could not help sympathizing

---

21. Shōnagon is clearly defending herself from some criticism that she has received or expects to receive (e.g. 'Why do you write about such vulgar subjects as starching laundered clothes?').

22. Magic Incantation of the Thousand Hands: one section of the Thousand Hand Sutra, which was especially associated with Shingon. It was recited to ward off illnesses, discord, slander, and other evils.

23. A type of mace, particularly connected with Shingon and used by priests, exorcists, etc., who brandished it in all directions while reciting their prayers and magic formulae.

24. The groans and wails come from the evil spirit, which has temporarily been transferred to the medium and is now being painfully subdued by the priest's incantations.

with her. Indeed, one of the patients' friends, feeling sorry for the girl, went up to her curtain of state and helped to rearrange her disordered clothing.

Meanwhile it was announced that the patient was a little better. Some young attendants were sent to the kitchen to fetch hot water and other requisites. Even while they were carrying their trays they kept darting uneasy glances at the exorcist. They wore pretty unlined robes and formal skirts whose light mauve colour was as fresh as on the day they were dyed—it made a most charming effect.

By the Hour of the Monkey the priest had brought the spirit under control and, having forced it to beg for mercy, he now dismissed it. 'Oh!' exclaimed the medium. 'I thought I was behind the curtains and here I am in front. What on earth has happened?' Overcome with embarrassment, she hid her face in her long hair and was about to glide out of the room when the priest stopped her and, after murmuring a few incantations, said, 'Well, my dear, how do you feel? You should be quite yourself by now.' He smiled at the girl, but this only added to her confusion.

'I should have liked to stay a little longer,' said the priest, as he prepared to leave the house, 'but I am afraid it is almost time for my evening prayers.' The people of the house tried to stop him. 'Please wait a moment,' they said. 'We should like to make an offering.' But the priest was obviously in a great hurry and would not stay. At this point a lady of noble rank, evidently a member of the family, edged her way up to the priest's curtain of state and said, 'We are most grateful for your visit, Your Reverence. Our patient looked as if she might well succumb to the evil spirit, but now she is well on the way to recovery. I cannot tell you how delighted we are. If Your Reverence has any free time tomorrow, would you please call again?'

'I fear we are dealing with a very obstinate spirit,' the priest replied briefly, 'and we must not be off our guard. I am pleased that what I did today has helped the patient.' So saying, he took his leave with an air of such dignity that everyone felt the Buddha himself had appeared on earth.

## When the Middle Captain

When the Middle Captain of the Left Guards Division was still Governor of Ise, he visited me one day at my home. There was a straw mat at the edge of the veranda, and I pulled it out for him. This notebook of mine happened to be lying on the mat, but I did not notice it in time. I snatched at the book and made a desperate effort to get it back; but the Captain instantly took it off with him and did not return it until much later. I suppose it was from this time that my book began to be passed about at Court.

## It Is Getting So Dark

It is getting so dark that I can scarcely go on writing; and my brush is all worn out. Yet I should like to add a few things before I end.

I wrote these notes at home, when I had a good deal of time to myself and thought no one would notice what I was doing. Everything that I have seen and felt is included. Since much of it might appear malicious and even harmful to other people, I was careful to keep my book hidden. But now it has become public, which is the last thing I expected.

One day Lord Korechika, the Minister of the Centre, brought the Empress a bundle of notebooks. 'What shall we do with them?' Her Majesty asked me. 'The Emperor has already made arrangements for copying the "Records of the Historian".'[25]

'Let me make them into a pillow,' I said.[26]

'Very well,' said Her Majesty. 'You may have them.'

I now had a vast quantity of paper at my disposal, and I set about filling the notebooks with odd facts, stories from the past, and all sorts of other things, often including the most trivial material. On the whole I concentrated on things and people that I found charming and splendid; my notes are also full of poems and observations on trees and plants, birds and insects. I was sure that when people saw my book they would say, 'It's even worse than I expected. Now one can really tell what she is like.' After all, it is written entirely for my own amusement and I put things down exactly as they came to me. How could my casual jottings possibly bear comparison with the many impressive books that exist in our time? Readers have declared, however, that I can be proud of my work. This has surprised me greatly; yet I suppose it is not so strange that people should like it, for, as will be gathered from these notes of mine, I am the sort of person who approves of what others abhor and detests the things they like.[27]

Whatever people may think of my book, I still regret that it ever came to light.

## ▪ Izumi Shikibu (c. 947–c. 1034) (poems)

Izumi Shikibu was the major poet of her day. Her father, Oe no Masamune, was a provincial governor, and her mother may have been the daughter of Taira no Yasuhira, governor of Etchu. Around age twenty, she married Tachibana no Michisada, the governor of Izumi; her name comes

---

25. It appears that Korechika also presented Emperor Ichijo with a quantity of paper (good paper being in short supply even at Court) and that the Emperor had decided to use his allotment for making a copy of the huge Chinese historical work, *Shih chi*.

26. A pillow book. Here we have one likely explanation of the title of Shōnagon's book.

27. Since Shōnagon's judgement tended to be the exact opposite of other people's, it was only natural that they should praise a book (her own) which she considered to be deficient in so many respects.

from a combination of the place name *Izumi* and the appellation *Shikibu* (court lady). The marriage was not successful. She had many lovers, notably the two Imperial princes, Tamataka and his brother, Atsumichi. With Michisada she had a daughter, known as Naishi or Ko-shikibu (meaning "Shikibu's child"), herself a fine poet who died young, before her mother. Both of Izumi Shikibu's Imperial lovers died young, and she writes passionately about Atsumichi in particular in her diary (*Izumi Shikibu Nikki*), a literary classic of the Heian period. A personal collection of her poetry exists in five recensions, containing between 647 and 902 poems. Her scandalous and overt affairs soon caused her to be permanently separated from her husband. Prince Atsumichi, who died when he was twenty-seven, was her great love, and she mourns him in more than one hundred poems, some of the most striking in her collection: "It would console me / if you returned / even for the length of the flash—/ seen and then gone— / of lightning at dusk" (translated by Jane Hirshfield and Mariko Aratani). At some time after his death, she became a lady-in-waiting to the Empress Shoshi, whose retinue included many brilliant writers, such as Murasaki Shikibu. While in the empress's service, she married Fujiwara no Yasumasa (958–1036), a man of great military fame. According to some sources, late in life she became a nun, and in her poems she questions whether she should "leave this burning house / of ceaseless thought" and enter Buddhist service.

Since the romantic custom at court was to initiate an affair by sending a poem—and acceptance was signaled through a poem sent in return—it helped for great lovers to be great poets. Izumi Shikibu was certainly both and was, in fact, Japan's finest female poet. Her poems of love are fresh and saucy, flames that burn fiercely in the mind—five lines of absolute heat. Her poems of loss are as absolute. Mourning or in love, a Buddhist sense of the world as illusion permeates the poetry, a counterpoint to the pattern of joy and loss that was her life: "The fleeting world / of white dew, / fox fires, dreams—/ all last long, / compared with love" (translated by Jane Hirshfield and Mariko Aratani).

**FURTHER READING:** Cranston, Edwin A., tr. *The Izumi Shikibu Diary: A Romance of the Heian Court*, 1969. Hirshfield, Jane, and Mariko Aratani, trs. *The Ink Dark Moon: Love Poems by Ono no Komachi and Izumi Shikibu, Women of the Ancient Court of Japan*, 1986. Miner, Earl, tr. *Japanese Poetic Diaries*, 1969.

## I'm in Such Bad Shape

I'm in such bad shape
that when a firefly rises
out of the marsh grass
I feel my soul leaping out
of my body in desire.

5

TRANSLATED BY TONY BARNSTONE

## I Don't Care about These

I don't care about these
wild tangles in my black hair.
I just lie back down
in bed and ache for your hands
which no longer brush them smooth.                    5

TRANSLATED BY TONY BARNSTONE

## I Throw Myself Away

I throw myself away
and don't care.
A heart in love
is a ravine
that has no end.                                      5

TRANSLATED BY TONY BARNSTONE AND WILLIS BARNSTONE

## In This World

In this world
love has no color—
yet how deeply
my body
is stained by yours.                                  5

TRANSLATED BY JANE HIRSHFIELD AND MARIKO ARATANI

## I Cannot Say

I cannot say
which is which:
the glowing
plum blossom is
the spring night's moon.                              5

TRANSLATED BY JANE HIRSHFIELD AND MARIKO ARATANI

## This Heart

This heart,
longing for you,
breaks
to a thousand pieces—
I wouldn't lose one.                                  5

TRANSLATED BY JANE HIRSHFIELD AND MARIKO ARATANI

## Mourning Naishi

*Around the time Naishi [Shikibu's daughter] died, snow fell, then melted away*

Why did you vanish
into empty sky?
Even the fragile snow,
when it falls,
falls in this world.                                                                 5

                TRANSLATED BY JANE HIRSHFIELD AND MARIKO ARATANI

## On Nights When Hail

On nights when hail
falls noisily
on bamboo leaves,
I completely hate
to sleep alone.                                                                       5

                              TRANSLATED BY WILLIS BARNSTONE

## Since That Night

Since that night
I cannot know myself.
I go to unheard of places
and sleep recklessly
on a strange bed.                                                                     5

                              TRANSLATED BY WILLIS BARNSTONE

## You Wear the Face

You wear the face
of someone awake
in the icy air,
seeing the moon we saw
in our night of no sleep.                                                             5

                              TRANSLATED BY WILLIS BARNSTONE

## When You Broke from Me

When you broke from me
I thought I let the thread
of my life break,
yet now, for you,
I don't want to die.                                              5

TRANSLATED BY WILLIS BARNSTONE

## If You Have No Time

If you have no time
to come, I'll go.
I want to learn the way
of writing poems
as a way to you.                                                 5

TRANSLATED BY WILLIS BARNSTONE

## If You Love Me

If you love me,
come. The road
I live on
is not forbidden
by impetuous gods.                                               5

TRANSLATED BY WILLIS BARNSTONE

## On This Winter Night

On this winter night
my eyes were closed
with ice.
I wore out the darkness
until lazy dawn.                                                 5

TRANSLATED BY WILLIS BARNSTONE

## Here in This World

Here in this world
I won't live
one minute more,
where pain is rank
like black bamboo.                                               5

TRANSLATED BY WILLIS BARNSTONE

# ◼ Murasaki Shikibu (978–c. 1015) (novel)

Murasaki Shikibu came from a distinguished literary line, a minor branch of the influential Fujiwara clan, which produced many of the empresses, high government officials, and court ladies through most of the Heian period. Her great-grandfather Kanesuke (877–933) and her grandfather Masatada (c. 910–962) were associated with Ki no Tsurayuki, and a number of their poems appear in Imperial anthologies. Her father began his career as a student of literature and went on to serve in the upper strata of government, becoming the governor of Echizen and later of Echigo. He retired in 1016 and turned to the priesthood. In her diary, Murasaki Shikibu records how she came to gain a classical Chinese education, which was very unusual for women at that time. Her brother Nobunori was being tutored and "on these occasions I was always present, and so quick was I at picking up the language that I was soon able to prompt my brother whenever he got stuck. At this my father used to sigh and say to me: 'If only you were a boy, how proud and happy I should be.'" She was also well read in Japanese works and in Buddhist literature and was a talented calligrapher, painter, and musician. She seems to have accompanied her father to the provinces when he became governor of Echizen in 996 and returned to the capital in her early twenties to marry her kinsman Fujiwara no Nobutaka. He was a lieutenant in the Imperial guard and at least twenty years older than she. They had one daughter, Nobutaka, who died in 1001. Around that time Murasaki Shikibu began writing what was to be her masterpiece, *The Tale of Genji*. She served as a lady-in-waiting to the Empress Akiko (or Shoshi) at the Kyoto court from around 1005, and much of the novel seems to have been written by this time. Shoshi's court, along with that of Teishi, was the center of literary culture. Izumi Shikibu, the finest poet of that time, was also at Shoshi's court, and Sei Shonagon was at Teishi's court. Murasaki Shikibu may have been the consort of Empress Akiko's father, Michinaga, and in any case, he certainly courted her; he, along with Ariwara Narihira (hero of the *Tales of Ise*) and Shotoku Taishi have been put forward as historical models for Prince Genji. In addition to *The Tale of Genji*, she kept a diary describing events at the court from 1008–1010 and wrote a number of poems. These works are of lesser importance than her great novel. Her name may be explained in several ways. *Shikibu* designates an appointment in the court hierarchy that her father probably held. As for *Murasaki* ("purple"), it may be a nickname alluding to the color of wisteria (*fuji*, the first character of the surname *Fujiwara*), or it may be taken from Murasaki, the character who is Prince Genji's great love in *The Tale of Genji*. Details of her later life are sketchy, and the last known mention of her is in 1013, when she was in her mid-thirties.

*The Tale of Genji* is the world's first great novel and one of the world's longest. It is distinguished for the complex characterization that Murasaki brings to her huge cast of characters, at a time when characterization was a poorly developed art in China, as in Japan. *The Tale of Genji* belongs to a form of Japanese narrative termed "monogatari," which was normally written by men to be read by women. This novel breaks that pattern, not only through its female author but by the fact that it was read by Murasaki's male contemporaries and, of course, by succeeding generations. The first forty-one chapters tell the story of Prince Genji, son of the emperor and an obscure court lady who has gained the emperor's favor. Genji is so handsome and talented that he is given the appellation "The Shining Prince." The last ten chapters are concerned with Kaoru, whom Genji thought was his son, though his father was actually the emperor. Although it seems the entire novel was written by Murasaki Shikibu, between these sections are three intermediary chapters that may be spurious (written by a later author). The action of the novel takes place within a period of about seventy-five years. Much of the first part of the novel treats Genji's love affairs and wives and his attempt to raise a girl who will be the perfect woman. The chapter presented here takes place early in the novel; Genji and his friends debate what characteristics make up the perfect woman Genji later tries to create, illustrating their points with anecdotes. The end of the chapter deals with Genji's attempts at courting a reluctant woman. Though the novel might be described generally as a romantic depiction of courtly love, it can also be seen as a Buddhist allegory about the decline of dharma, or Buddhist law, in which the relatively anemic and ambivalent relations of Kaoru make him seem a pale reflection of Genji, the great man of the past. Or the novel could be a Buddhist parable of karmic retribution in which, years after cuckolding his own father, Genji finds himself cuckolded by his best friend's son. In spite of its romantic character, the novel seems to present a pessimistic view of the world as shot through with tragedy, a view that a number of the characters share. Commentators have also pointed out the running theme of a quest for origins—as Genji pursues the image of his dead mother in the women he loves, so Kaoru is consumed with the search for a father. *The Tale of Genji* is of interest as an anthropological window on the attitudes, surroundings, and behavior of men and women inhabiting a lost world; more important, it still reads as a great novel today.

**FURTHER READING:** Bowring, Richard, tr. *Murasaki Shikibu: Her Diary and Poetic Memoirs*, 1982. Morris, Ivan. *The World of the Shining Prince: Court Life in Ancient Japan*, 1964. Puette, William J. *A Guide to the Tale of Genji by Murasaki Shikibu*, 1983. Seidensticker, Edward, tr. *The Tale of Genji*, 1981. Waley, Arthur, tr. *The Tale of Genji*, 1935.

*from* **The Tale of Genji**

TRANSLATED BY ARTHUR WALEY

## The Broom-Tree

Genji the Shining One . . . He knew that the bearer of such a name could not escape much scrutiny and jealous censure and that his lightest dallyings would be proclaimed to posterity. Fearing then lest he should appear to after ages as a mere good-for-nothing and trifler, and knowing that (so accursed is the blabbing of gossips' tongues) his most secret acts might come to light, he was obliged always to act with great prudence and to preserve at least the outward appearance of respectability. Thus nothing really romantic ever happened to him and Katano no Shosho[1] would have scoffed at his story.

While he was still a Captain of the Guard and was spending most of his time at the Palace, his infrequent visits to the Great Hall[2] were taken as a sign that some secret passion had made its imprint on his heart. But in reality the frivolous, commonplace, straight-ahead amours of his companions did not in the least interest him, and it was a curious trait in his character that when on rare occasions, despite all resistance, love did gain a hold upon him, it was always in the most improbable and hopeless entanglement that he became involved.

It was the season of the long rains. For many days there had not been a fine moment and the Court was keeping a strict fast. The people at the Great Hall were becoming very impatient of Genji's long residence at the Palace, but the young lords, who were Court pages, liked waiting upon Genji better than upon anyone else, always managing to put out his clothes and decorations in some marvellous new way. Among these brothers his greatest friend was the Equerry, To no Chujo, with whom above all other companions of his playtime he found himself familiar and at ease. This lord too found the house which his father-in-law, the Minister of the Right, had been at pains to build for him, somewhat oppressive, while at his father's house he, like Genji, found the splendours somewhat dazzling, so that he ended by becoming Genji's constant companion at Court. They shared both studies and play and were inseparable companions on every sort of occasion, so that soon all formalities were dispensed with between them and the inmost secrets of their hearts freely exchanged.

It was on a night when the rain never ceased its dismal downpour. There were not many people about in the palace and Genji's rooms

---

1. The hero of a lost popular romance. It is also referred to by Murasaki's contemporary Sei Shonagon in Chapter 145 of her *Makura na Soshi*.

2. His father-in-law's house, where his wife Princess Aoi still continued to live.

seemed even quieter than usual. He was sitting by the lamp, looking at various books and papers. Suddenly he began pulling some letters out of the drawers of a desk which stood near by. This aroused To no Chujo's curiosity. 'Some of them I can show to you' said Genji 'but there are others which I had rather . . .' 'It is just those which I want to see. Ordinary, commonplace letters are very much alike and I do not suppose that yours differ much from mine. What I want to see are passionate letters written in moments of resentment, letters hinting consent, letters written at dusk . . .'

He begged so eagerly that Genji let him examine the drawers. It was not indeed likely that he had put any very important or secret documents in the ordinary desk; he would have hidden them away much further from sight. So he felt sure that the letters in these drawers would be nothing to worry about. After turning over a few of them, 'What an astonishing variety!' To no Chujo exclaimed and began guessing at the writers' names, and made one or two good hits. More often he was wrong and Genji, amused by his puzzled air, said very little but generally managed to lead him astray. At last he took the letters back, saying 'But you too must have a large collection. Show me some of yours, and my desk will open to you with better will.' 'I have none that you would care to see,' said To no Chujo, and he continued: 'I have at last discovered that there exists no woman of whom one can say "Here is perfection. This is indeed she." There are many who have the superficial art of writing a good running hand, or if occasion requires of making a quick repartee. But there are few who will stand the ordeal of any further test. Usually their minds are entirely occupied by admiration for their own accomplishments, and their abuse of all rivals creates a most unpleasant impression. Some again are adored by over-fond parents. These have been since childhood guarded behind lattice windows[3] and no knowledge of them is allowed to reach the outer-world, save that of their excellence in some accomplishment or art; and this may indeed sometimes arouse our interest. She is pretty and graceful and has not yet mixed at all with the world. Such a girl by closely copying some model and applying herself with great industry will often succeed in really mastering one of the minor and ephemeral arts. Her friends are careful to say nothing of her defects and to exaggerate her accomplishments, and while we cannot altogether trust their praise we cannot believe that their judgment is entirely astray. But when we take steps to test their statements we are invariably disappointed.'

He paused, seeming to be slightly ashamed of the cynical tone which he had adopted, and added 'I know my experience is not large, but that is the conclusion I have come to so far.' Then Genji, smiling: 'And are there any who lack even one accomplishment?' 'No doubt, but in such a case it

---

3. Japanese houses were arranged somewhat differently from ours and for many of the terms which constantly recur in this book (*kicho, sudare, sunoko,* etc.) no exact English equivalents can be found. In such cases I have tried to use expressions which without being too awkward or unfamiliar will give an adequate general idea of what is meant.

is unlikely that anyone would be successfully decoyed. The number of those who have nothing to recommend them and of those in whom nothing but good can be found is probably equal. I divide women into three classes. Those of high rank and birth are made such a fuss of and their weak points are so completely concealed that we are certain to be told that they are paragons. About those of the middle class everyone is allowed to express his own opinion, and we shall have much conflicting evidence to sift. As for the lower classes, they do not concern us.'

The completeness with which To no Chujo disposed of the question amused Genji, who said 'It will not always be so easy to know into which of the three classes a woman ought to be put. For sometimes people of high rank sink to the most abject positions; while others of common birth rise to be high officers, wear self-important faces, redecorate the inside of their houses and think themselves as good as anyone. How are we to deal with such cases?'

At this moment they were joined by Hidari no Uma no Kami and To Shikibu no Jo, who said they had also come to the Palace to keep the fast. As both of them were great lovers and good talkers, To no Chujo handed over to them the decision of Genji's question, and in the discussion which followed many unflattering things were said. Uma no Kami spoke first. 'However high a lady may rise, if she does not come of an adequate stock, the world will think very differently of her from what it would of one born to such honours; but if through adverse fortune a lady of highest rank finds herself in friendless misery, the noble breeding of her mind is soon forgotten and she becomes an object of contempt. I think then that taking all things into account, we must put such ladies too into the "middle class." But when we come to classify the daughters of Zuryo,[4] who are sent to labour at the affairs of distant provinces—they have such ups and downs that we may reasonably put them too into the middle class.

'Then there are Ministers of the third and fourth classes without Cabinet rank. These are generally thought less of even than the humdrum, ordinary officials. They are usually of quite good birth, but have much less responsibility than Ministers of State and consequently much greater peace of mind. Girls born into such households are brought up in complete security from want or deprivation of any kind, and indeed often amid surroundings of the utmost luxury and splendour. Many of them grow up into women whom it would be folly to despise; some have been admitted at Court, where they have enjoyed a quite unexpected success. And of this I could cite many, many instances.'

'Their success has generally been due to their having a lot of money,' said Genji smiling. 'You should have known better than to say that,' said To no Chujo, reproving him, and Uma no Kami went on: 'There are some whose lineage and reputation are so high that it never occurs to one that their education could possibly be at fault; yet when we meet them, we find

---

4. Provincial officials. Murasaki herself came of this class.

ourselves exclaiming in despair "How can they have contrived to grow up like this?"

'No doubt the perfect woman in whom none of those essentials is lacking must somewhere exist and it would not startle me to find her. But she would certainly be beyond the reach of a humble person like myself, and for that reason I should like to put her in a category of her own and not to count her in our present classification.

'But suppose that behind some gateway overgrown with vine-weed, in a place where no one knows there is a house at all, there should be locked away some creature of unimagined beauty—with what excitement should we discover her! The complete surprise of it, the upsetting of all our wise theories and classifications, would be likely, I think, to lay a strange and sudden enchantment upon us. I imagine her father rather large and gruff; her brother, a surly, ill-looking fellow. Locked away in an utterly blank and uninteresting bedroom, she will be subject to odd flights of fancy, so that in her hands the arts that others learn as trivial accomplishments will seem strangely full of meaning and importance; or perhaps in some particular art she will thrill us by her delightful and unexpected mastery. Such a one may perhaps be beneath the attention of those of you who are of flawless lineage. But for my part I find it hard to banish her . . .' and here he looked at Shikibu no Jo, who wondered whether the description had been meant to apply to his own sisters, but said nothing. 'If it is difficult to choose even out of the top class . . .' thought Genji, and began to doze.

He was dressed in a suit of soft white silk, with a rough cloak carelessly slung over his shoulders, with belt and fastenings untied. In the light of the lamp against which he was leaning he looked so lovely that one might have wished he were a girl; and they thought that even Uma no Kami's 'perfect woman,' whom he had placed in a category of her own, would not be worthy of such a prince as Genji.

The conversation went on. Many persons and things were discussed. Uma no Kami contended that perfection is equally difficult to find in other spheres. The sovereign is hard put to it to choose his ministers. But he at least has an easier task than the husband, for he does not entrust the affairs of his kingdom to one, two or three persons alone, but sets up a whole system of superiors and subordinates.

But when the mistress of a house is to be selected, a single individual must be found who will combine in her person many diverse qualities. It will not do to be too exacting. Let us be sure that the lady of our choice possesses certain tangible qualities which we admire; and if in other ways she falls short of our ideal, we must be patient and call to mind those qualities which first induced us to begin our courting.

But even here we must beware; for there are some who in the selfishness of youth and flawless beauty are determined that not a dust-flick shall fall upon them. In their letters they choose the most harmless topics, but yet contrive to colour the very texture of the written signs with a tenderness that vaguely disquiets us. But such a one, when we have at last secured a meeting, will speak so low that she can scarcely be heard, and the few faint sentences that she murmurs beneath her breath serve only to make her more mysterious than before. All this may seem to be the pretty shrinking of girlish modesty; but we may later find that what held her back was the very violence of her passions.

Or again, where all seems plain sailing, the perfect companion will turn out to be too impressionable and will upon the most inappropriate occasions display her affections in so ludicrous a way that we begin to wish ourselves rid of her.

Then there is the zealous housewife, who regardless of her appearance twists her hair behind her ears and devotes herself entirely to the details of our domestic welfare. The husband, in his comings and goings about the world, is certain to see and hear many things which he cannot discuss with strangers, but would gladly talk over with an intimate who could listen with sympathy and understanding, someone who could laugh with him or weep if need be. It often happens too that some political event will greatly perturb or amuse him, and he sits apart longing to tell someone about it. He suddenly laughs at some secret recollection or sighs audibly. But the wife only says lightly 'What is the matter?' and shows no interest.

This is apt to be very trying.

Uma no Kami considered several other cases. But he reached no definite conclusion and sighing deeply he continued: 'We will then, as I have suggested, let birth and beauty go by the board. Let her be the simplest and most guileless of creatures so long as she is honest and of a peaceable disposition, that in the end we may not lack a place of trust. And if some other virtue chances to be hers we shall treasure it as a godsend. But if we discover in her some small defect, it shall not be too closely scrutinized. And we may be sure that if she is strong in the virtues of tolerance and amiability her outward appearance will not be beyond measure harsh.

'There are those who carry forbearance too far, and affecting not to notice wrongs which cry out for redress seem to be paragons of misused fidelity. But suddenly a time comes when such a one can restrain herself no longer, and leaving behind her a poem couched in pitiful language and calculated to rouse the most painful sentiments of remorse, she flies to some remote village in the mountains or some desolate seashore, and for a long while all trace of her is lost.

'When I was a boy the ladies-in-waiting used to tell me sad tales of this kind. I never doubted that the sentiments expressed in them were real, and I wept profusely. But now I am beginning to suspect that such sorrows are for the most part affectation. She has left behind her (this lady whom we are imagining) a husband who is probably still fond of her; she is making herself very unhappy, and by disappearing in this way is causing him unspeakable anxiety, perhaps only for the ridiculous purpose of putting his affection to the test. Then comes along some admiring friend crying "What a heart! What depth of feeling!" She becomes more lugubrious than ever, and finally enters a nunnery. When she decided on this step she was perfectly sincere and had not the slightest intention of ever returning to the world. Then some female friend hears of it and "Poor thing" she cries; "in what an agony of mind must she have been to do this!" and visits her in her cell. When the husband, who has never ceased to mourn for her, hears what she has become, he bursts into tears, and some servant or old nurse, seeing this, bustles off to the nunnery with tales of the husband's despair, and "Oh Madam, what a shame, what a shame!" Then the nun, forgetting where and what she is, raises her hand to her head to straighten her hair, and finds that it has been shorn away. In helpless misery she sinks to the floor, and do what she will, the tears begin to flow. Now all is lost; for since she cannot at every moment be praying for strength, there creeps into her mind the sinful thought that she did ill to become a nun and so often does she commit this sin that even Buddha must think her wickeder now than she was before she took her vows; and she feels certain that these terrible thoughts are leading her soul to the blackest Hell. But if the karma of their past lives should chance to be strongly weighted against a parting, she will be found and captured before she has taken her final vows. In such a case their life will be beyond endurance unless she be fully determined, come good or ill, this time to close her eyes to all that goes amiss.

'Again there are others who must needs be forever mounting guard over their own and their husband's affections. Such a one, if she sees in him not a fault indeed but even the slightest inclination to stray, makes a foolish scene, declaring with indignation that she will have no more to do with him.

'But even if a man's fancy should chance indeed to have gone somewhat astray, yet his earlier affection may still be strong and in the end will return to its old haunts. Now by her tantrums she has made a rift that cannot be joined. Whereas she who when some small wrong calls for silent rebuke, shows by a glance that she is not unaware; but when some large offence demands admonishment knows how to hint without severity, will end by standing in her master's affections better than ever she stood before. For often the sight of our own forbearance will give our neighbour strength to rule his mutinous affections.

'But she whose tolerance and forgiveness know no bounds, though this may seem to proceed from the beauty and amiability of her disposition, is in fact displaying the shallowness of her feeling: "The unmoored boat must needs drift with the stream." Are you not of this mind?'

To no Chujo nodded. 'Some' he said 'have imagined that by arousing a baseless suspicion in the mind of the beloved we can revive a waning devotion. But this experiment is very dangerous. Those who recommend it are confident that so long as resentment is groundless one need only suffer it in silence and all will soon be well. I have observed however that this is by no means the case.

'But when all is said and done, there can be no greater virtue in woman than this: that she should with gentleness and forbearance meet every wrong whatsoever that falls to her share.' He thought as he said this of his own sister, Princess Aoi; but was disappointed and piqued to discover that Genji, whose comments he awaited, was fast asleep.

Uma no Kami was an expert in such discussions and now stood preening his feathers. To no Chujo was disposed to hear what more he had to say and was now at pains to humour and encourage him.

'It is with women' said Uma no Kami 'as it is with the works of craftsmen. The wood-carver can fashion whatever he will. Yet his products are but toys of the moment, to be glanced at in jest, not fashioned according to any precept or law. When times change, the carver too will change his style and make new trifles to hit the fancy of the passing day. But there is another kind of artist, who sets more soberly about his work, striving to give real beauty to the things which men actually use and to give to them the shapes which tradition has ordained. This maker of real things must not for a moment be confused with the carver of idle toys.

'In the Painters' Workshop too there are many excellent artists chosen for their proficiency in ink-drawing; and indeed they are all so clever it is hard to set one above the other. But all of them are at work on subjects intended to impress and surprise. One paints the Mountain of Horai; another a raging sea-monster riding a storm; another, ferocious animals from the Land beyond the sea, or faces of imaginary demons. Letting their fancy run wildly riot they have no thought of beauty, but only of how best they may astonish the beholder's eye. And though nothing in their pictures is real, all is probable. But ordinary hills and rivers, just as they are, houses such as you may see anywhere, with all their real beauty and harmony of form—quietly to draw such scenes as this, or to show what lies behind some intimate hedge that is folded away far from the world, and thick trees upon some unheroic hill, and all this with befitting care for composition, proportion, and the like—such works demand the highest master's utmost skill and must needs draw the common craftsman into a thousand blunders. So too in handwriting, we see some who aimlessly prolong their cursive strokes this way or that, and hope their flourishes will be mistaken for genius. But true penmanship preserves in every letter its balance and form, and though at first some letters may seem but half-formed, yet when we compare them with the copy-books we find that there is nothing at all amiss.

'So it is in these trifling matters. And how much the more in judging of the human heart should we distrust all fashionable airs and graces, all tricks and smartness, learnt only to please the outward gaze! This I first understood some while ago, and if you will have patience with me I will tell you the story.'

So saying, he came and sat a little closer to them, and Genji woke up. To no Chujo, in wrapt attention, was sitting with his cheek propped upon his hand. Uma no Kami's whole speech that night was indeed very much like a chaplain's sermon about the ways of the world, and was rather absurd. But upon such occasions as this we are easily led on into discussing our own ideas and most private secrets without the least reserve.

'It happened when I was young, and in an even more humble position than I am today' Uma no Kami continued. 'I was in love with a girl who (like the drudging, faithful wife of whom I spoke a little while ago) was not a full-sail beauty; and I in my youthful vanity thought she was all very well for the moment, but would never do for the wife of so fine a fellow as I. She made an excellent companion in times when I was at a loose end; but she was of a disposition so violently jealous, that I could have put up with a little less devotion if only she had been somewhat less fiercely ardent and exacting.

'Thus I kept thinking, vexed by her unrelenting suspicions. But then I would remember her ceaseless devotion to the interests of one who was after all a person of no account, and full of remorse I made sure that with a little patience on my part she would one day learn to school her jealousy.

'It was her habit to minister to my smallest wants even before I was myself aware of them; whatever she felt was lacking in her she strove to acquire, and where she knew that in some quality of mind she still fell behind my desires, she was at pains never to show her deficiency in such a way as might vex me. Thus in one way or another she was always busy in forwarding my affairs, and she hoped that if all down to the last dew-drop (as they say) were conducted as I should wish, this would be set down to her credit and help to balance the defects in her person which meek and obliging as she might be could not (she fondly imagined) fail to offend me; and at this time she even hid herself from strangers lest their poor opinion of her looks should put me out of countenance.

'I meanwhile, becoming used to her homely looks, was well content with her character, save for this one article of jealousy; and here she showed no amendment. Then I began to think to myself "Surely, since she seems so anxious to please, so timid, there must be some way of giving her a fright which will teach her a lesson, so that for a while at least we may have a respite from this accursed business." And though I knew it would cost me dear, I determined to make a pretence of giving her up, thinking that since she was so fond of me this would be the best way to teach her a lesson. Accordingly I behaved with the greatest coldness to her, and she as usual began her jealous fit and behaved with such folly that in the end I said to her, "If you want to be rid for ever of one who loves you dearly, you are going the right way about it by all these endless poutings over nothing at all. But if you want to go on with me, you must give up suspecting some deep intrigue each time you fancy that I am treating you unkindly. Do this, and you may be sure I shall continue to love you dearly. It may well be that as time goes on, I shall rise a little higher in the world and then . . ."

'I thought I had managed matters very cleverly, though perhaps in the heat of the moment I might have spoken somewhat too roughly. She smiled faintly and answered that if it were only a matter of bearing for a while with my failures and disappointments, that did not trouble her at all, and she would gladly wait till I became a person of consequence. "But it is a hard task" she said "to go on year after year enduring your coldness and waiting the time when you will at last learn to behave to me with some decency; and therefore I agree with you that the time has come when we had better go each his own way." Then in a fit of wild and uncontrollable jealousy she began to pour upon me a torrent of bitter reproaches, and with a woman's savagery she suddenly seized my little finger and bit deep into it. The unexpected pain was difficult to bear, but composing myself I said tragically, "Now you have put this mark upon me I shall get on worse than ever in polite society; as for promotion, I shall be considered a disgrace to the meanest public office and unable to cut a genteel figure in any capacity, I shall be obliged to withdraw myself completely from the world. You and I at any rate shall certainly not meet again," and bending my injured finger as I turned to go, I recited the verse "As on bent hand I count the times that we have met, it is not one finger only that bears witness to my pain." And she, all of a sudden bursting into tears . . . "If still in your heart only you look for pains to count, then were our hands best employed in parting." After a few more words I left her, not for a moment thinking that all was over.

'Days went by, and no news. I began to be restless. One night when I had been at the Palace for the rehearsal of the Festival music, heavy sleet was falling; and I stood at the spot where those of us who came from the Palace had dispersed, unable to make up my mind which way to go. For in no direction had I anything which could properly be called a home. I might of course take a room in the Palace precincts; but I shivered to think of the cheerless grandeur that would surround me. Suddenly I began to wonder what she was thinking, how she was looking; and brushing the snow off my shoulders, I set out for her house. I own I felt uneasy; but I thought that after so long a time her anger must surely have somewhat abated. Inside the room a lamp showed dimly, turned to the wall. Some undergarments were hung out upon a large, warmly-quilted couch, the bed-hangings were drawn up, and I made sure that she was for some reason actually expecting me. I was priding myself on having made so lucky a hit, when suddenly, "Not at home!"; and on questioning the maid I learnt that she had but that very night gone to her parents' home, leaving only a few necessary servants behind. The fact that she had till now sent no poem or conciliatory message seemed to show some hardening of heart, and had already disquieted me. Now I began to fear that her accursed suspiciousness and jealousy had but been a stratagem to make me grow weary of her, and though I could recall no further proof of this I fell into great despair. And to show her that, though we no longer met, I still thought of her and planned for her, I got her some stuff for a dress, choosing a most delightful and unusual shade of colour, and a material that I knew she would be glad to have. "For after all" I thought "she cannot want to put me altogether out of her head." When I informed her of this purchase she did not rebuff me nor make any attempt to hide from me, but to all my questions she answered quietly and composedly, without any sign that she was ashamed of herself.

'At last she told me that if I went on as before, she could never forgive me; but if I would promise to live more quietly she would take me back again. Seeing that she still hankered after me I determined to school her a little further yet, and said that I could make no conditions and must be free to live as I chose. So the tug of war went on; but it seems that it hurt her far more than I knew, for in a little while she fell into a decline and died, leaving me aghast at the upshot of my wanton game. And now I felt that, whatever faults she might have had, her devotion alone would have made her a fit wife for me. I remembered how both in trivial talk and in consideration of important matters she had never once shown herself at a loss, how in the dyeing of brocades she rivalled the Goddess of Tatsuta who tints the autumn leaves, and how in needlework and the like she was not less skillful than Tanabata, the Weaving-lady of the sky.'

Here he stopped, greatly distressed at the recollection of the lady's many talents and virtues.

'The Weaving-lady and the Herd boy' said To no Chujo 'enjoy a love that is eternal. Had she but resembled the Divine Sempstress in this, you would not, I think, have minded her being a little less skilful with her needle. I wonder that with this rare creature in mind you pronounce the world to be so blank a place.'

'Listen' replied Uma no Kami. 'About the same time there was another lady whom I used to visit. She was of higher birth than the first; her skill in poetry, cursive writing, and lute-playing, her readiness of hand and tongue were all marked enough to show that she was not a woman of trivial nature; and this indeed was allowed by those who knew her. To add to this she was not ill-looking and sometimes, when I needed a rest from my unhappy persecutress, I used to visit her secretly. In the end I found that I had fallen completely in love with her. After the death of the other I was in great distress. But it was no use brooding over the past and I began to visit my new lady more and more often. I soon came to the conclusion that she was frivolous and I had no confidence that I should have liked what went on when I was not there to see. I now visited her only at long intervals and at last decided that she had another lover.

'It was during the Godless Month,[5] on a beautiful moonlight night. As I was leaving the Palace I met a certain young courtier, who, when I told him that I was driving out to spend the night at the Dainagon's, said that my way was his and joined me. The road passed my lady's house and here it was that he alighted, saying that he had an engagement which he should have been very sorry not to fulfil. The wall was half in ruins and through its gaps I saw the shadowy waters of the lake. It would not have been easy (for even the moonbeams seemed to loiter here!) to hasten past so lovely a place, and when he left his coach I too left mine.

---

5. The tenth month.

'At once this man (whom I now knew to be that other lover whose existence I had guessed) went and sat unconcernedly on the bamboo skirting of the portico and began to gaze at the moon. The chrysanthemums were just in full bloom, the bright fallen leaves were tumbling and tussling in the wind. It was indeed a scene of wonderful beauty that met our eyes. Presently he took a flute out of the folds of his dress and began to play upon it. Then putting the flute aside, he began to murmur. "Sweet is the shade"[6] and other catches. Soon a pleasant-sounding native zithern[7] began to tune up somewhere within the house and an ingenious accompaniment was fitted to his careless warblings. Her zithern was tuned to the autumn-mode, and she played with so much tenderness and feeling that though the music came from behind closed shutters it sounded quite modern and passionate,[8] and well accorded with the soft beauty of the moonlight. The courtier was ravished, and as he stepped forward to place himself right under her window he turned to me and remarked in a self-satisfied way that among the fallen leaves no other footstep had left its mark. Then plucking a chrysanthemum, he sang:

> Strange that the music of your lute,
> These matchless flowers and all the beauty of the night,
> Have lured no other feet to linger at your door!

and then, beseeching her pardon for his halting verses, he begged her to play again while one was still near who longed so passionately to hear her. When he had paid her many other compliments, the lady answered in an affected voice with the verse:

> Would that I had some song that might detain
> The flute that blends its note
> With the low rustling of the autumn leaves.

and after these blandishments, still unsuspecting, she took up the thirteen-stringed lute, and tuning it to the *Banjiki* mode[9] she clattered at the strings with all the frenzy that fashion now demands. It was a fine performance no doubt, but I cannot say that it made a very agreeable impression upon me.

'A man may amuse himself well enough by trifling from time to time with some lady at the Court; will get what pleasure he can out of it while he is with her and not trouble his head about what goes on when he is not

---

6. From the *saibara* ballad, *The Well of Asuka:* 'Sweet is the shade, the lapping waters cool, and good the pasture for our weary steeds. By the Well of Asuka, here let us stay.'

7. The 'Japanese zithern'; also called *wagon*. A species of *koto*.

8. As opposed to the formal and traditional music imported from China.

9. See *Encyclopédie de la Musique*, p. 247. Under the name Nan-lu this mode was frequently used in the Chinese love-dramas of the fourteenth century. It was considered very wild and moving.

there. This lady too I only saw from time to time, but such was her situation that I had once fondly imagined myself the only occupant of her thoughts. However that night's work dissolved the last shred of my confidence, and I never saw her again.

'These two experiences, falling to my lot while I was still so young, early deprived me of any hope from women. And since that time my view of them has but grown the blacker. No doubt to you at your age they seem very entrancing, these "dewdrops on the grass that fall if they are touched," these "glittering hailstones that melt if gathered in the hand." But when you are a little older you will think as I do. Take my advice in this at least; beware of caressing manners and soft, entangling ways. For if you are so rash as to let them lead you astray, you will soon find yourselves cutting a very silly figure in the world.'

To no Chujo as usual nodded his assent, and Genji's smile seemed such as to show that he too accepted Uma no Kami's advice. 'Your two stories were certainly very dismal' he said, laughing. And here To no Chujo interposed: 'I will tell you a story about myself. There was a lady whose acquaintance I was obliged to make with great secrecy. But her beauty well rewarded my pains, and though I had no thought of making her my wife, I grew so fond of her that I soon found I could not put her out of my head and she seemed to have complete confidence in me. Such confidence indeed that when from time to time I was obliged to behave in such a way as might well have aroused her resentment, she seemed not to notice that anything was amiss, and even when I neglected her for many weeks, she treated me as though I were still coming every day. In the end indeed I found this readiness to receive me whenever and however I came very painful, and determined for the future to merit her strange confidence.

'Her parents were dead and this was perhaps why, since I was all she had in the world, she treated me with such loving meekness, despite the many wrongs I did her. I must own that my resolution did not last long, and I was soon neglecting her worse than before. During this time (I did not hear of it till afterwards) someone who had discovered our friendship began to send her veiled messages which cruelly frightened and distressed her. Knowing nothing of the trouble she was in, although I often thought of her I neither came nor wrote to her for a long while. Just when she was in her worst despair a child was born, and at last in her distress she plucked a blossom of the flower that is called "Child of my Heart" and sent it to me.'

And here To no Chujo's eyes filled with tears.

'Well' said Genji 'and did she write a message to go with it?' 'Oh nothing very out-of-the-ordinary' said To no Chujo. 'She wrote: "Though tattered be the hillman's hedge, deign sometimes to look with kindness upon the Child-flower that grows so sweetly there." This brought me to her side. As usual she did not reproach me, but she looked sad enough, and when I considered the dreary desolation of this home where every object wore an aspect no less depressing than the wailing voices of the crickets in the grass, she seemed to me like some unhappy princess in an ancient story, and wishing her to feel that it was for the mother's sake and not the child's that I had come, I answered with a poem in which I called the Child-flower by its other name "Bed-flower," and she replied with a poem that darkly hinted at the cruel tempest which had attended this Bed-flower's birth. She spoke lightly and did not seem to be downright angry with me; and when a few tears fell she was at great pains to hide them, and seemed more distressed at the thought that I might imagine her to be unhappy than actually resentful of my conduct towards her. So I went away with an easy mind and it was some while before I came again. When at last I returned she had utterly disappeared, and if she is alive she must be living a wretched vagrant life. If while I still loved her she had but shown some outward sign of her resentment, she would not have ended thus as an outcast and wanderer; for I should never have dared to leave her so long neglected, and might in the end have acknowledged her and made her mine for ever. The child too was a sweet creature, and I have spent much time in searching for them, but still without success.

'It is, I fear, as sorrowful a tale as that which Uma no Kami has told you. I, unfaithful, thought that I was not missed; and she, still loved, was in no better case than one whose love is not returned. I indeed am fast forgetting her; but she, it may be, cannot put me out of her mind and I fear there may be nights when thoughts that she would gladly banish burn fiercely in her breast; for now I fancy she must be living a comfortless and unprotected life.'

'When all is said and done' said Uma no Kami, 'my friend, though I pine for her now that she is gone, was a sad plague to me while I had her, and we must own that such a one will in the end be sure to make us wish ourselves well rid of her. The zithern-player had much talent to her credit, but was a great deal too light-headed. And your diffident lady, To no Chujo, seems to me to be a very suspicious case. The world appears to be so constructed that we shall in the end be always at a loss to make a reasoned choice; despite all our picking, sifting and comparing we shall never succeed in finding this in all ways and to all lengths adorable and impeccable female.'

'I can only suggest the Goddess Kichijo'[10] said To no Chujo 'and I fear that intimacy with so holy and majestic a being might prove to be impracticable.'

At this they all laughed and To no Chujo continued: 'But now it is Shikibu's turn and he is sure to give us something entertaining. Come Shikibu, keep the ball rolling!' 'Nothing of interest ever happens to humble folk like myself' said Shikibu; but To no Chujo scolded him for keeping them waiting and after reflecting for a while which anecdote would best suit the company, he began: 'While I was still a student at the Univer-

10. Goddess of Beauty.

sity, I came across a woman who was truly a prodigy of intelligence. One of Uma no Kami's demands she certainly fulfilled, for it was possible to discuss with her to advantage both public matters and the proper handling of one's private affairs. But not only was her mind capable of grappling with any problems of this kind; she was also so learned that ordinary scholars found themselves, to their humiliation, quite unable to hold their own against her.

'I was taking lessons from her father, who was a Professor. I had heard that he had several daughters, and some accidental circumstance made it necessary for me to exchange a word or two with one of them who turned out to be the learned prodigy of whom I have spoken. The father, hearing that we had been seen together, came up to me with a wine-cup in his hand and made an allusion to the poem of The Two Wives.[11] Unfortunately I did not feel the least inclination towards the lady. However I was very civil to her; upon which she began to take an affectionate interest in me and lost no opportunity of displaying her talents by giving me the most elaborate advice how best I might advance my position in the world. She sent me marvelous letters written in a very far-fetched epistolary style and entirely in Chinese characters; in return for which I felt bound to visit her, and by making her my teacher I managed to learn how to write Chinese poems. They were wretched, knock-kneed affairs, but I am still grateful to her for it. She was not however at all the sort of woman whom I should have cared to have as a wife, for though there may be certain disadvantages in marrying a complete dolt, it is even worse to marry a bluestocking. Still less do princes like you and Genji require so huge a stock of intellect and erudition for your support! Let her but be one to whom the karma of our past lives draws us in natural sympathy, what matter if now and again her ignorance distresses us? Come to that, even men seem to me to get along very well without much learning.'

Here he stopped, but Genji and the rest, wishing to hear the end of the story, cried out that for their part they found her a most interesting woman. Shikibu protested that he did not wish to go on with the story, but at last after much coaxing, pulling a comical wry face he continued: 'I had not seen her for a long time. When at last some accident took me to the house, she did not receive me with her usual informality but spoke to me from behind a tiresome screen. Ha, Ha, thought I foolishly, she is sulking; now is the time to have a scene and break with her. I might have known that she was not so little of a philosopher as to sulk about trifles; she prided herself on knowing the ways of the world and my inconstancy did not in the least disturb her.

'She told me (speaking without the slightest tremor) that having had a bad cold for some weeks she had taken a strong garlic-cordial, which had made her breath smell rather unpleasant and that for this reason she could not come very close to me. But if I had any matter of special impor-

---

11. A poem by Po Chu-i pointing out the advantages of marrying a poor wife.

tance to discuss with her she was quite prepared to give me her attention. All this she had expressed with solemn literary perfection. I could think of no suitable reply, and with an "at your service" I rose to go. Then, feeling that the interview had not been quite a success, she added, raising her voice, "Please come again when my breath has lost its smell." I could not pretend I had not heard. I had however no intention of prolonging my visit, particularly as the odour was now becoming definitely unpleasant, and looking cross I recited the acrostic "On this night marked by the strange behaviour of the spider, how foolish to bid me come back tomorrow"[12] and calling over my shoulder "There is no excuse for you!" I ran out of the room. But she, following me, "If night by night and every night we met, in daytime too I should grow bold to meet you face to face." Here in the second sentence she had cleverly concealed the meaning, "If I had had any reason to expect you, I should not have eaten garlic."'

'What a revolting story!' cried the young princes, and then, laughing, 'He must have invented it.' 'Such a woman is quite incredible; it must have been some sort of ogress. You have shocked us, Shikibu!' and they looked at him with disapproval. 'You must try to tell us a better story than that.' 'I do not see how any story could be better' said Shikibu, and left the room.

'There is a tendency among men as well as women' said Uma no Kami 'so soon as they have acquired a little knowledge of some kind, to want to display it to the best advantage. To have mastered all the difficulties in the Three Histories and Five Classics is no road to amiability. But even a woman cannot afford to lack all knowledge of public and private affairs. Her best way will be without regular study to pick up a little here and a little there, merely by keeping her eyes and ears open. Then, if she has her wits at all about her, she will soon find that she has amassed a surprising store of information. Let her be content with this and not insist upon cramming her letters with Chinese characters which do not at all accord with her feminine style of composition, and will make the recipient exclaim in despair "If only she could contrive to be a little less mannish!" And many of these characters, to which she intended the colloquial pronunciation to be given, are certain to be read as Chinese, and this will give the whole composition an even more pedantic sound than it deserves. Even among our ladies of rank and fashion there are many of this sort, and there are others who, wishing to master the art of verse-making, in the end allow it to master them, and, slaves to poetry, cannot resist the temptation, however urgent the business they are about or however inappropriate the time, to make use of some happy allusion which has occurred to them, but must needs fly to their desks and work it up into a poem. On festival days such a woman is very troublesome. For example on the morn-

---

12. There is a reference to an old poem which says: 'I know that tonight my lover will come to me. The spider's antics prove it clearly.' Omens were drawn from the behaviour of spiders. There is also a pun on *hiru* 'day' and *hiru* 'garlic,' so that an ordinary person would require a few moments' reflection before understanding the poem.

ing of the Iris Festival, when everyone is busy making ready to go to the temple, she will worry them by stringing together all the old tags about the "matchless root";[13] or on the 9th day of the 9th month, when everyone is busy thinking out some difficult Chinese poem to fit the rhymes which have been prescribed, she begins making metaphors about the "dew on the chrysanthemums," thus diverting our attention from the far more important business which is in hand. At another time we might have found these compositions quite delightful; but by thrusting them upon our notice at inconvenient moments, when we cannot give them proper attention, she makes them seem worse than they really are. For in all matters we shall best commend ourselves if we study men's faces to read in them the "Why so?" or the "As you will" and do not, regardless of times and circumstances, demand an interest and sympathy that they have not leisure to give.

'Sometimes indeed a woman should even pretend to know less than she knows, or say only a part of what she would like to say . . .'

All this while Genji, though he had sometimes joined in the conversation, had in his heart of hearts been thinking of one person only, and the more he thought the less could he find a single trace of those shortcomings and excesses which, so his friends had declared, were common to all women. 'There is no one like her' he thought, and his heart was very full. The conversation indeed had not brought them to a definite conclusion, but it had led to many curious anecdotes and reflections. So they passed the night, and at last, for a wonder, the weather had improved. After this long residence at the Palace Genji knew he would be expected at the Great Hall and set out at once. There was in Princess Aoi's air and dress a dignified precision which had something in it even of stiffness; and in the very act of reflecting that she, above all women, was the type of that single-hearted and devoted wife whom (as his friends had said last night) no sensible man would lightly offend, he found himself oppressed by the very perfection of her beauty, which seemed only to make all intimacy with her the more impossible.

He turned to Lady Chunagon, to Nakatsukasa and other attendants of the common sort who were standing near and began to jest with them. The day was now very hot, but they thought that flushed cheeks became Prince Genji very well. Aoi's father came, and standing behind the curtain, began to converse very amiably. Genji, who considered the weather too hot for visits, frowned, at which the ladies-in-waiting tittered. Genji, making furious signs at them to be quiet, flung himself on to a divan. In fact, he behaved far from well.

It was now growing dark. Someone said that the position of the Earth Star[14] would make it unlucky for the Prince to go back to the Palace that

---

13. The irises used for the Tango festival (5th day of 5th month) had to have nine flowers growing on a root.

14. The 'Lord of the Centre,' i.e. the planet Saturn.

night; and another: 'You are right. It is now set dead against him.' 'But my own palace is in the same direction!' cried Genji. 'How vexing! where then shall I go?' and promptly fell asleep. The ladies-in-waiting, however, agreed that it was a very serious matter and began discussing what could be done. 'There is Ki no Kami's house' said one. This Ki no Kami was one of Genji's gentlemen-in-waiting. 'It is in the Middle River' she went on; 'and delightfully cool and shady, for they have lately dammed the river and made it flow right through the garden.' 'That sounds very pleasant' said Genji, waking up, 'besides they are the sort of people who would not mind one's driving right in at the front gate, if one had a mind to.'[15]

He had many friends whose houses lay out of the unlucky direction. But he feared that if he went to one of them, Aoi would think that, after absenting himself so long, he was now merely using the Earth Star as an excuse for returning to more congenial company. He therefore broached the matter to Ki no Kami, who accepted the proposal, but stepping aside whispered to his companions that his father Iyo no Kami, who was absent on service, had asked him to look after his young wife.[16] 'I am afraid we have not sufficient room in the house to entertain him as I could wish.' Genji, overhearing this, strove to reassure him, saying 'It will be a pleasure to me to be near the lady. A visit is much more agreeable when there is a hostess to welcome us. Find me some corner behind her partition . . . !' 'Even then, I fear you may not find . . .' but breaking off Ki no Kami sent a runner to his house, with orders to make ready an apartment for the Prince. Treating a visit to so humble a house as a matter of no importance, he started at once, without even informing the Minister, and taking with him only a few trusted body-servants. Ki no Kami protested against the precipitation, but in vain.

The servants dusted and aired the eastern side-chamber of the Central Hall and here made temporary quarters for the Prince. They were at pains to improve the view from his windows, for example by altering the course of certain rivulets. They set up a rustic wattled hedge and filled the borders with the choicest plants. The low humming of insects floated on the cool breeze; numberless fireflies wove inextricable mazes in the air. The whole party settled down near where the moat flowed under the covered bridge and began to drink wine.

Ki no Kami went off in a great bustle, saying that he must find them something to eat. Genji, quietly surveying the scene, decided this was one of those middle-class families which in last night's conversation had been so highly commended. He remembered that he had heard the lady who was staying in the house well spoken of and was curious to see her. He listened and thought that there seemed to be people in the western wing. There was a soft rustling of skirts, and from time to time the sound of young and by no means disagreeable voices. They did not seem to be

---

15. I.e. people with whom one can be quite at ease. It was usual to unharness one's bulls at the gate.

16. Ki no Kami's stepmother.

much in earnest in their efforts to make their whispering and laughter unheard, for soon one of them opened the sliding window. But Ki no Kami
crying 'What are you thinking of?' crossly closed it again. The light of a
candle in the room filtered through a crack in the paper-window. Genji
edged slightly closer to the window in the hope of being able to see
through the crack, but found that he could see nothing. He listened for a
while, and came to the conclusion that they were sitting in the main
women's apartments, out of which the little front room opened. They
were speaking very low, but he could catch enough of it to make out that
they were talking about him.

'What a shame that a fine young Prince should be taken so young and
settled down for ever with a lady that was none of his choosing!'

'I understand that marriage does not weigh very heavily upon him'
said another. This probably meant nothing in particular, but Genji, who
imagined they were talking about what was uppermost in his own mind,
was appalled at the idea that his relations with Lady Fujitsubo were about
to be discussed. How could they have found out? But the subsequent conversation of the ladies soon showed that they knew nothing of the matter
at all, and Genji stopped listening. Presently he heard them trying to repeat the poem which he had sent with a nosegay of morning-glory to
Princess Asagao, daughter of Prince Momozono.[17] But they got the lines
rather mixed up, and Genji began to wonder whether the lady's appearance would turn out to be on a level with her knowledge of prosody.

At this moment Ki no Kami came in with a lamp which he hung on
the wall. Having carefully trimmed it, he offered Genji a tray of fruit.
This was all rather dull and Genji by a quotation from an old folk-song
hinted that he would like to meet Ki no Kami's other guests. The hint
was not taken. Genji began to doze, and his attendants sat silent and motionless.

There were in the room several charming boys, sons of Ki no Kami,
some of whom Genji already knew as pages at the Palace. There were also
numerous sons of Iyo no Kami; with them was a boy of twelve or thirteen
who particularly caught Genji's fancy. He began asking whose sons the
boys were, and when he came to this one Ki no Kami replied 'He is the
youngest son of the late Chunagon, who loved him dearly, but died while
this boy was still a child. His sister married my father and that is why he is
living here. He is quick at his books, and we hope one day to send him to
Court, but I fear that his lack of influence . . .'

'Poor child!' said Genji. 'His sister, then, is your stepmother, is that
not so? How strange that you should stand in this relationship with so
young a girl! And now I come to think of it there was some talk once of
her being presented at Court, and I once heard the Emperor asking what

---

17. We learn later that Genji courted this lady in vain from his seventeenth year onward. Though she has
never been mentioned before, Murasaki speaks of her as though the reader already knew all about her.
This device is also employed by Marcel Proust.

had become of her. How changeable are the fortunes of the world.' He was trying to talk in a very grown-up way.

'Indeed, Sir' answered Ki no Kami; 'her subsequent state was humbler than she had reason to expect. But such is our mortal life. Yes, yes, and such has it always been. We have our ups and downs—and the women even more than the men.'

*Genji:* 'But your father no doubt makes much of her?'

*Ki no Kami:* 'Makes much of her indeed! You may well say so. She rules his house, and he dotes on her in so wholesale and extravagant a fashion that all of us (and I among the foremost) have had occasion before now to call him to order, but he does not listen.'

*Genji:* 'How comes it then that he has left her behind in the house of a fashionable young Courtier? For he looks like a man of prudence and good sense. But pray, where is she now?'

*Ki no Kami:* 'The ladies have been ordered to retire to the common room, but they have not yet finished all their preparations.'

Genji's followers, who had drunk heavily, were now all lying fast asleep on the verandah. He was alone in his room, but could not get to sleep. Having at last dozed for a moment, he woke suddenly and noticed that someone was moving behind the paper-window of the back wall. This, he thought, must be where she is hiding, and faintly curious he sauntered in that direction and stood listening. 'Where are you?' I say 'Where are you?' whispered someone in a quaint, hoarse voice, which seemed to be that of the boy whom Genji had noticed earlier in the evening. 'I am lying over here' another voice answered. 'Has the stranger gone to sleep yet? His room must be quite close to this; but all the same how far off he seems!' Her sleepy voice was so like the boy's that Genji concluded this must be his sister.

'He is sleeping in the wing, I saw him tonight. All that we have heard of him is true enough. He is as handsome as can be' whispered the boy. 'I wish it were tomorrow; I want to see him properly' she answered drowsily, her voice seeming to come from under the bed clothes. Genji was rather disappointed that she did not ask more questions about him. Presently he heard the boy saying 'I am going to sleep over in the corner-room. How bad the light is' and he seemed to be trimming the lamp. His sister's bed appeared to be in the corner opposite the paper-window. 'Where is Chujo?' she called. 'I am frightened, I like to have someone close to me.' 'Madam' answered several voices from the servants' room, 'she is taking her bath in the lower house. She will be back presently.' When all was quiet again, Genji slipped back the bolt and tried the door. It was not fastened on the other side. He found himself in an ante-room with a screen at the end, beyond which a light glimmered. In the half-darkness he could see clothes boxes and trunks strewn about in great disorder. Quietly threading his way among them, he entered the inner room from which the voices had proceeded. One very minute figure was couched there who, to Genji's slight embarrassment, on hearing his approach pushed aside the cloak which covered her, thinking that he was the maid for whom she had sent. 'Madam, hearing you call for Chujo[18] I thought that I might now put at your service the esteem in which I have long secretly held you.' The lady could make nothing of all this, and terrified out of her wits tried hard to scream. But no sound came, for she had buried her face in the bed clothes.

'Please listen' said Genji. 'This sudden intrusion must of course seem to you very impertinent. You do not know that for years I have waited for an occasion to tell you how much I like and admire you, and if tonight I could not resist the temptation of paying this secret visit, pray take the strangeness of my behaviour as proof of my impatience to pay a homage that has long been due.' He spoke so courteously and gently and looked so kind that not the devil himself would have taken umbrage at his presence. But feeling that the situation was not at all a proper one for a married lady she said (without much conviction) 'I think you have made a mistake.' She spoke very low. Her bewildered air made her all the more attractive, and Genji, enchanted by her appearance, hastened to answer: 'Indeed I have made no mistake; rather, with no guide but a long-felt deference and esteem, I have found my way unerringly to your side. But I see that the suddenness of my visit has made you distrust my purpose. Let me tell you then that I have no evil intentions and seek only for someone to talk with me for a while about a matter which perplexes me.' So saying he took her up in his arms (for she was very small) and was carrying her through the ante-room when suddenly Chujo, the servant for whom she had sent before, entered the bedroom. Genji gave an astonished cry and the maid, wondering who could have entered the ante-room, began groping her way towards them. But coming closer she recognized by the rich perfume of his dress that this could be none other than the Prince. And though she was sorely puzzled to know what was afoot, she dared not say a word. Had he been an ordinary person, she would soon have had him by the ears. 'Nay' she thought 'even if he were not a Prince I should do best to keep my hands off him; for the more stir one makes, the more tongues wag. But if I should touch this fine gentleman . . . ,' and all in a flutter she found herself obediently following Genji to his room. Here he calmly closed the door upon her, saying as he did so 'You will come back to fetch your mistress in the morning.' Utsusemi herself was vexed beyond measure at being thus disposed of in the presence of her own waiting-maid, who could indeed draw but one conclusion from what she had seen. But to all her misgivings and anxieties Genji, who had the art of improvising a convincing reply to almost any question, answered with such a wealth of ingenuity and tender concern, that for a while she was content. But soon becoming again uneasy, 'This must all be a dream—that you, so great a Prince, should stoop to consider so humble a creature as I, and I am over-

---

18. Chujo means 'Captain,' which was Genji's rank at the time.

whelmed by so much kindness. But I think you have forgotten what I am. A Zuryo's wife! there is no altering that, and you . . . !' Genji now began to realize how deeply he had distressed and disquieted her by his wild behaviour, and feeling thoroughly ashamed of himself he answered: 'I am afraid I know very little about these questions of rank and precedence. Such things are too confusing to carry in one's head. And whatever you may have heard of me I want to tell you for some reason or other I have till this day cared nothing for gallantry nor ever practised it, and that even you cannot be more astonished at what I have done tonight than I myself am.' With this and a score of other speeches he sought to win her confidence. But she, knowing that if once their talk became a jot less formal, she would be hard put to it to withstand his singular charm, was determined, even at the risk of seeming stiff and awkward, to show him that in trying so hard to put her at her ease he was only wasting his time, with the result that she behaved very boorishly indeed. She was by nature singularly gentle and yielding, so that the effort of steeling her heart and despite her feelings, playing all the while the part of the young bamboo-shoot which though so green and tender cannot be broken, was very painful to her; and finding that she could no longer think of arguments with which to withstand his importunity, she burst into tears; and though he was very sorry for her, it occurred to him that he would not gladly have missed that sight. He longed however to console her, but could not think of a way to do so, and said at last, 'Why do you treat me so unkindly? It is true that the manner of our meeting was strange, yet I think that Fate meant us to meet. It is harsh that you should shrink from me as though the World and you had never met.' So he chided her, and she: 'If this had happened long ago before my troubles, before my lot was cast, perhaps I should have been glad to take your kindness while it lasted, knowing that you would soon think better of your strange condescension. But now that my course is fixed, what can such meetings bring me save misery and regret? *Tell none that you have seen my home'* she ended, quoting the old song.[19] 'Small wonder that she is sad' thought Genji, and he found many a tender way to comfort her. And now the cock began to crow. Out in the courtyard Genji's men were staggering to their feet, one crying drowsily 'How I should like to go to sleep again,' and another 'Make haste there, bring out his Honour's coach.' Ki no Kami came out into the yard, 'What's all this hurry? It is only when there are women in his party that a man need hasten from a refuge to which the Earth Star has sent him. Why is his Highness setting off in the middle of the night?'

Genji was wondering whether such an opportunity would ever occur again. How would he be able even to send her letters? And thinking of all the difficulties that awaited him, he became very despondent. Chujo arrived to fetch her mistress. For a long while he would not let her go, and

---

19. *Kokinshu* 811, an anonymous love-poem.

when at last he handed her over, he drew her back to him saying 'How can I send news to you? For, Madam' he said, raising his voice that the maid Chujo might hear, 'such love as mine, and such pitiless cruelty as yours have never been seen in the world before.' Already the birds were singing in good earnest. She could not forget that she was no one and he a Prince. And even now, while he was tenderly entreating her, there came unbidden to her mind the image of her husband Iyo no Suke, about whom she generally thought either not at all or with disdain. To think that even in a dream he might see her now, filled her with shame and terror.

It was daylight. Genji went with her to the partition door. Indoors and out there was a bustle of feet. As he closed the door upon her, it seemed to him a barrier that shut him out from all happiness. He dressed, and went out on to the balcony. A blind in the western wing was hastily raised. There seemed to be people behind who were looking at him. They could only see him indistinctly across the top of a partition in the verandah. Among them was one, perhaps, whose heart beat wildly as she looked . . . ?

The moon had not set, and though with dwindled light still shone crisp and clear in the dawn. It was a daybreak of marvellous beauty. But in the passionless visage of the sky men read only their own comfort or despair; and Genji, as with many backward glances he went upon his way, paid little heed to the beauty of the dawn. He would send her a message? No, even that was utterly impossible. And so, in great unhappiness he returned to his wife's house.

He would gladly have slept a little, but could not stop trying to invent some way of seeing her again; or when that seemed hopeless, imagining to himself all that must now be going on in her mind. She was no great beauty, Genji reflected, and yet one could not say that she was ugly. Yes, she was in every sense a member of that Middle Class upon which Uma no Kami had given them so complete a dissertation.

He stayed for some while at the Great Hall, and finding that, try as he might, he could not stop thinking about her and longing for her, at last in despair he sent for Ki no Kami and said to him 'Why do you not let me have that boy in my service—the Chunagon's son, whom I saw at your house? He is a likely looking boy, and I might make him my body-servant, or even recommend him to the Emperor.' 'I am sensible of your kindness' said Ki no Kami. 'I will mention what you have said to the boy's sister.' This answer irritated Genji, but he continued: 'And has this lady given you stepbrothers my lord?' 'Sir, she has been married these two years, but has had no child. It seems that in making this marriage she disobeyed her father's last injunctions, and this has set her against her husband.'

*Genji:* 'That is sad indeed. I am told that she is not ill-looking. Is that so?'

*Ki no Kami:* 'I believe she is considered quite passable. But I have had very little to do with her. Intimacy between stepchildren and stepparents is indeed proverbially difficult.'

Five or six days afterwards Ki no Kami brought the boy. He was not exactly handsome, but he had great charm and (thought Genji) an air of distinction. The Prince spoke very kindly to him and soon completely won his heart. To Genji's many questions about his sister he made such answers as he could, and when he seemed embarrassed or tongue-tied Genji found some less direct way of finding out what he wanted to know, and soon put the boy at his ease. For though he vaguely realized what was going on and thought it rather odd, he was so young that he made no effort to understand it, and without further question carried back a letter from Genji to his sister.

She was so much agitated by the sight of it that she burst into tears and, lest her brother should perceive them, held the letter in front of her face while she read it. It was very long. Among much else it contained the verse 'Would that I might dream that dream again! Alas, since first this wish was mine, not once have my eyelids closed in sleep.'

She had never seen such beautiful writing, and as she read, a haze clouded her eyes. What incomprehensible fate had first dragged her down to be the wife of a Zuryo, and then for a moment raised her so high? Still pondering, she went to her room.

Next day, Genji again sent for the boy, who went to his sister saying 'I am going to Prince Genji. Where is your answer to his letter?' 'Tell him' she answered 'that there is no one here who reads such letters.' The boy burst out laughing. 'Why, you silly, how could I say such a thing to him. He told me himself to be sure to bring an answer.' It infuriated her to think that Genji should have thus taken the boy into his confidence and she answered angrily, 'He has no business to talk to you about such things at your age. If that is what you talk about you had better not go to him any more.' 'But he sent for me' said the boy, and started off.

'I was waiting for you all yesterday' said Genji when the boy returned. 'Did you forget to bring the answer? Did you forget to come?' The child blushed and made no reply. 'And now?' 'She said there is no one at home who reads such letters.' 'How silly, what can be the use of saying such things?' and he wrote another letter and gave it to the boy, saying: 'I expect you do not know that I used to meet your sister before her marriage. She treats me in this scornful fashion because she looks upon me as a poor-spirited, defenceless creature. Whereas she has now a mighty Deputy Governor to look after her. But I hope that you will promise to be my child, not his. For he is very old, and will not be able to take care of you for long.'

The boy was quite content with this explanation, and admired Genji more than ever. The Prince kept him always at his side, even taking him to the Palace. And he ordered his Chamberlain to see to it that he was provided with a little Court suit. Indeed he treated him just as though he were his own child.

Genji continued to send letters; but she, thinking that the boy, young as he was, might easily allow a message to fall into the wrong hands and that then she would lose her fair name to no purpose, feeling too (that however much he desired it) between persons so far removed in rank there could be no lasting union, she answered his letters only in the most formal terms.

Dark though it had been during most of the time they were together, she yet had a clear recollection of his appearance, and could not deny to herself that she thought him uncommonly handsome. But she very much doubted if he on his side really knew what she was like; indeed she felt sure that the next time they met he would think her very plain and all would be over.

Genji meanwhile thought about her continually. He was for ever calling back to memory each incident of that one meeting, and every recollection filled him with longing and despair. He remembered how sad she had looked when she spoke to him of herself, and he longed to make her happier. He thought of visiting her in secret. But the risk of discovery was too great, and the consequences likely to be more fatal to her even than to himself.

He had been many days at the Palace, when at last the Earth Star again barred the road to his home. He set out at once, but on the way pretended that he had just remembered the unfavourable posture of the stars. There was nothing to do but seek shelter again in the house on the Middle River. Ki no Kami was surprised but by no means ill pleased, for he attributed Genji's visit to the amenity of the little pools and fountains which he had constructed in his garden.

Genji had told the boy in the morning that he intended to visit the Middle River, and since he had now become the Prince's constant companion, he was sent for at once to wait upon him in his room. He had already given a message to his sister, in which Genji told her of his plan. She could not but feel flattered at the knowledge that it was on her account he had contrived this ingenious excuse for coming to the house. Yet she had, as we have seen, for some reason got it into her head that at a leisurely meeting she would not please him as she had done at that first fleeting and dreamlike encounter, and she dreaded adding a new sorrow to the burden of her thwarted and unhappy existence. Too proud to let him think that she had posted herself in waiting for him, she said to her servants (while the boy was busy in Genji's room) 'I do not care to be at such close quarters with our guest, besides I am stiff, and would like to be massaged; I must go where there is more room,' and so saying she made them carry her things to the maid Chujo's bedroom in the cross-wing.

Genji had purposely sent his attendants early to bed, and now that all was quiet, he hastened to send her a message. But the boy could not find her. At last when he had looked in every corner of the house, he tried the cross-wing, and succeeded in tracking her down to Chujo's room. It was too bad of her to hide like this, and half in tears he gasped out, 'Oh how can you be so horrid? What will he think of you?' 'You have no business to run after me like this,' she answered angrily. 'It is very wicked for children to carry such messages. But,' she added, 'you may tell him I am not well, that my ladies are with me, and I am going to be massaged . . .' So she dismissed him; but in her heart of hearts she was thinking that if such an adventure had happened to her while she was still a person of consequence, before her father died and left her to shift for herself in the world, she would have known how to enjoy it. But now she must force herself to look askance at all his kindness. How tiresome he must think her! And she fretted so much at not being free to fall in love with him, that in the end she was more in love than ever. But then she remembered suddenly that her lot had long ago been cast. She was a wife. There was no sense in thinking of such things, and she made up her mind once and for all never again to let foolish ideas enter her head.

Genji lay on his bed, anxiously waiting to see with what success so young a messenger would execute his delicate mission. When at last the answer came, astonished at this sudden exhibition of coldness, he exclaimed in deep mortification, 'This is a disgrace, a hideous disgrace,' and he looked very rueful indeed. For a while he said no more, but lay sighing deeply, in great distress. At last he recited the poem — 'I knew not the nature of the strange tree[20] that stands on Sono plain, and when I sought the comfort of its shade, I did but lose my road,' and sent it to her. She was still awake, and answered with the poem 'Too like am I in these my outcast years to the dim tree that dwindles from the traveller's approaching gaze.' The boy was terribly sorry for Genji and did not feel sleepy at all, but he was afraid people would think his continual excursions very strange. By this time, however, everyone else in the house was sound asleep. Genji alone lay plunged in the blackest melancholy. But even while he was raging at the inhuman stubbornness of her new-found and incomprehensible resolve, he found that he could not but admire her the more for this invincible tenacity. At last he grew tired of lying awake; there was no more to be done. A moment later he had changed his mind again, and suddenly whispered to the boy, 'Take me to where she is hiding!' 'It is too difficult,' he said, 'she is locked in and there are so many people there. I am afraid to go with you.' 'So be it,' said Genji, 'but you at least must not abandon me,' and he laid the boy beside him on his bed. He was well content to find himself lying by this handsome young Prince's side, and Genji, we must record, found the boy no bad substitute for his ungracious sister.

## ■ Saigyo (1118–1190) (poems)

TRANSLATED BY BURTON WATSON

Saigyo (born Sato Norikiyo) was a member of the illustrious Fujiwara clan, which had dominated the government but was beginning to decline. His branch of the clan was a prosperous warrior family, and, as a young

---

20. The *hahakigi* or 'broom-tree' when seen in the distance appears to offer ample shade; but when approached turns out to be a skimpy bush.

man, he became an expert in the martial arts. However, he entered the priesthood at age twenty-two for reasons that can only be surmised: perhaps a devastating love affair (his work does include passionate love poems), a death in the family, or disillusionment with court life. Or perhaps he was simply uneasy about the wide-reaching changes that were beginning to transform Japanese society in the decades before the decline of the Imperial system and the rise of the Taira and Minamoto military conflict recorded in *Tales of the Heike.* After joining the priesthood, Saigyo took the name Eni, and later, Saigyo. He traveled across Japan in his role as priest, which gave him access to all social classes. He appears to have spent part of his life near Mount Koya, the center of the Shingon sect of Buddhism, to which he belonged. He also was a member of several poetry circles, including one centered on Fujiwara Shunzei. He was highly regarded in his time both as a poet and as a priest, and his reputation has never declined.

More than two thousand of his *tanka* are extant, and ninety-four of his poems are included in the important Imperial collection, the *Shinkokinshu* (*New Collection of Old and New Japanese Poems*), making him by far the best-represented poet in the anthology. His poetry precisely observes the smallest motions in nature, sudden epiphanies in natural beauty, sorrow at the passing of the seasons, and the poet's loneliness in his ascetic seclusion. Yet, he wrote beautiful poems of longing for an absent lover, whose face he sees "printed on the moon." He is a poet of the world and out of the world, of love and of asceticism, a poet who chooses seclusion and is lonely in it. Warrior, poet, priest, he is fully involved in the complexity and quandary of being human: "The priest chastens / his heart but can't deny / this deep, melancholy beauty: / a longbill lifts from the marsh / and fades in autumn dusk" (translated by Tony Barnstone). Perhaps this is the source of his lasting appeal.

**FURTHER READING:** Watson, Burton, tr. *Saigyo: Poems of a Mountain Home,* 1991.

## The Plum Tree at My Mountain Hut

Take note:
the plum by my rustic hedge
halted in his tracks
a total stranger
who happened by

## Living Alone

Living alone
in the shade of a remote mountain,
I have you for my companion
now the storm has passed,
moon of the winter night!

## Her Face When We Parted

Her face when we parted,
a parting
I can never forget—
And for keepsake she left it
printed on the moon                                        5

## When the Moon Shines

When the moon shines
without the smallest blemish,
I think of her—
and then my heart disfigures it,
blurs it with tears.                                       5

## As Rays of Moonlight Stream

As rays of moonlight stream
through a sudden gap
in the rain clouds—
if we could meet even
for so brief a moment!                                     5

## I Know

"I know
how you must feel!"
And with those words
she grows more hateful
than if she'd never spoken at all                          5

## On the Phrase "All Phenomena Are Fleeting"[1]

I think of past times,
so swift
in their vanishing,
the present soon to follow—
dew on the morning-glory                                   5

## Fishermen

Fishermen
by a rocky shore,
winds blowing wildly,
in a boat unmoored—
such is our condition!                                     5

---

1. From the famous verse in the seventh chapter of the *Nirvana Sutra:* "All phenomena are fleeting, / this
is the law of birth and death. / When you have wiped out birth and death, / nirvana is your joy."

## In This Mountain Village

In this mountain village
where I've given up
all hope of visitors,
how drab life would be
without my loneliness                                    5

## The Loneliness

The loneliness
of my ramshackle
grass hut,
where no one but the wind
comes to call                                            5

## Since I No Longer Think

Since I no longer think
of reality
as reality,
what reason would I have
to think of dreams as dreams?                            5

## In a Mountain Village

In a mountain village
when I'm lost in the dark
of the mind's dreaming,
the sound of the wind
blows me to brightness                                   5

# Kamakura/Nambokucho Periods

## (1186–1392)

■ **The Middle Counselor of the Riverbank's Stories
(Eleventh to Twelfth Centuries)**

TRANSLATED BY ROBERT L. BACKUS

This late Heian collection of ten stories and a fragment was originally
attributed to Fujiwara Kanesuke (877–933), who held the title of Middle

Counselor (a high office in the government of the central court). In 1939, however, one of the stories was positively dated as having been written in 1055 by a court woman in a story-writing contest at Princess Baishi's court. Authorities differ on whether the entire collection derived from the aristocratic women who participated in this contest or whether some of the stories may have been composed by men. Perhaps the title derives from the fact that middle counselors are often the heroes of tales in this genre, and the fact that no such hero appears in these stories may be an early example of false attribution for ironic purposes (as in the fiction of Jorge Luis Borges). The story presented here, "The Lady Who Admired Vermin," is a broad parody of a self-important intellectual woman who cares more for essences than for the elaborate rituals and appearances that an aristocratic woman was supposed to embody. For the courtly audience, nothing could be more grotesque than a woman who refused to blacken her teeth and pluck her eyebrows in order to present a beautiful front. She is a woman who prefers caterpillars to butterflies, function to aesthetics, essence to surface. This woman who rejects cosmetics, leaves her hair uncombed, speaks loudly and pontificates, and allows herself to be revealed to the eyes of men would in her time be a laughable creature. Clearly, at this end of history and through the lens of another culture, the parodied woman becomes the hero to the modern reader. Yet, as several commentators have noted, this peculiar individualist gets the better of her parents and the men she debates, suggesting at least a hidden sympathy on the part of the anonymous author.

**FURTHER READING:** Backus, Robert L. *The Riverside Counselor's Stories: Vernacular Fiction of Late Heian Japan*, 1985. McCullough, Helen Craig, ed. *Classical Japanese Prose: An Anthology*, 1990.

## The Lady Who Admired Vermin

Next to the place where lived the lady who admired butterflies was the daughter of the Inspector-Major Counselor, whose parents tended her with such infinite care that she grew up to be a creature of intriguing and exceptional beauty.

This lady collected great numbers of frightful-looking vermin. "The way people lose themselves in admiration of blossoms and butterflies is positively silly and incomprehensible," she would say. "It is the person who wants the truth and inquires into the essence of things who has an interesting mind."

And she put them into different kinds of screened boxes to see how they would develop. "What intrigues me the most is the caterpillars, which have a certain appeal," she would say, and she would lay them out on the palm of her hand and watch them from morning till evening with her hair drawn back behind her ears.

Since her young ladies were dismayed at this behavior, she gathered around her a band of fearless and disreputable boys, and amused herself by giving them the vermin in the boxes to hold, asking their names and assigning names to the unfamiliar ones.

"As a rule it is wrong for people to make themselves up," she would say, and never plucked her eyebrows, and never applied tooth blackening because she thought it was bothersome and dirty. And she doted on the vermin from morning till night, all the while showing the gleaming white of her teeth in a smile.

Whenever people fled from her in consternation, this "lady" would shout at them in a very peculiar manner. The people thus frightened she would transfix with a stare from under heavy black eyebrows, calling them "Disgraceful!" "Vulgar!" so that they were bewildered all the more.

"That she should be so peculiar and behave so differently!" her parents thought. But at the same time they wondered, "Can there be some meaning in this that she has comprehended? Whenever we think that something she does is odd and tell her about it, she contradicts us no end. It makes one feel so intimidated!" And they were very embarrassed by this behavior too. "That may be," they told her. "But you are getting a strange reputation. What people like is good looks. If society were to hear that you enjoy playing with weird-looking caterpillars, it would put you in a very peculiar light."

"I don't care. Only when one examines all things and looks at their outcome do things have significance. That's being very childish, because caterpillars turn into butterflies." She took out some in which that phase was emerging, and as she showed them, said, "The clothes that people wear by the name of 'silk' are produced by worms before they grow wings, and when they become butterflies, why then they are completely ignored and are worthless!" Against this they could find no argument and were confounded.

Nevertheless, she was lady enough not to display herself even to her parents, and she held the opinion that "Devils and women are better invisible to the eyes of mankind." Thus would she deliver herself so cleverly from behind a curtain stand set out by a slightly raised blind in the main chamber of the house.

Her young ladies would listen to all of this. "She puts on quite a show, but leaves you positively bewildered. These playthings of hers! I wonder what kind of people serve the lady who admires butterflies," said one of them who was called Hyoe, and recited:

> What means have I
> to make her understand?
> Oh, to go away!
> I would never look upon those things
> in their caterpillar stage again.

Another, who was called Little Tayu, recited laughing:

> I do envy them.
> "Ah, the blossoms! Ah, the butterflies!"
>     they will be exclaiming;
> while what have we to look upon
> but a world that reeks of caterpillars!

"Too harsh, really," said one who was called Sakon. "Her eyebrows look like furry caterpillars all right, but her bare teeth you would think have been skinned.

> In wintertime
> we can depend on having coats
>     however cold it is,
> in a place like this where one can see
> so many worms with furry skins.

We could easily get along without clothes, you know."

They were overheard telling each other such things by a faultfinding woman, who said, "Whatever are you young people saying! I find nothing at all admirable about a person who is supposed to admire butterflies. You are quite inexcusable! And besides, would anyone line up caterpillars and call them butterflies? It's just that they molt, you know. She examines that stage. That is good sense. When you catch a butterfly, its dust sticks to your hand and makes it very unpleasant, you know. Also, they say that if you catch a butterfly, it gives you the ague. Horrid things!"

But this only made them even more malicious in their remarks to one another.

To the boys who caught the vermin the lady gave interesting things, things they desired; and so they collected various kinds of frightful-looking creatures and presented them to her. Although the caterpillars had fine-looking fur and all, they did not suggest anything to her imagination, and for that reason she found them lacking. So they would collect such things as mantises and snails, and she had them sing loud songs about them for her to hear, and raised her voice herself to chant the ditty:

> Why do the horns of the snail
> battle each other to no avail?

She was disappointed to find that the boys' names were so ordinary, and so she named them after insects and other low creatures. She employed them under such names as Mole Cricket, Toady, Dragonfly, Grasshopper, and Millipede.

Such things became known in public, and there were people who said very disagreeable things, among them a certain young man well connected by marriage, who was high-spirited, fearless, and personable. Hearing about the lady, he said, "Well, I bet she will be afraid of this." And he fashioned the end of a sash—very beautiful to look at—into the close likeness of a snake, fixed it so that it could move and all, put it into a bag that had a scaly pattern and a string to draw it closed, and tied a note to it which read:

> Ever so slowly
> creeping, creeping would I follow
> by my lady's side,
> I who am long in faithfulness
> that stretches on without an end.

When they saw what was written, they brought it into her presence in all innocence. "These bags are always so strangely heavy just to lift!" they remarked as they drew it open. And there was the snake with its head raised up. Her people cried out in bewilderment, but the lady was very calm. "Praised be Amida Buddha! Praised be Amida Buddha!" she intoned.

"It must be an ancestor reborn in this present form. Don't carry on so!" she quavered; and averting her face, she muttered as she drew it close to her, "Right now, while it is still so young and lovely, I want to have a feeling of kinship for it. How low-minded all of you are!"

But even a woman of her temperament felt so afraid that she fidgeted up and down like a butterfly, and the strained voice in which she spoke made a terribly funny sound, so that her people broke into laughter as they fled noisily away. Whereupon the news spread.

"What an appalling, unearthly thing is this I am hearing!" exclaimed His Lordship. "How unnatural that all of them should have left her with such a creature right there in front of their eyes!" And he rushed to her, sword in hand. When he looked at the thing closely, he saw that the gentleman had fashioned it into a very good likeness; and so, taking it into his hands, he said, "How very good this person is at making things! Apparently he has done this because he heard about the wise airs you put on and the kind of things you appreciate. Write an answer and send it to him at once." And with that he took his leave.

When her people heard that it was artificial they said angrily, "What an outrageous thing to do!"

"He will be left in suspense if you don't answer him," everyone told her, and so she wrote an answer on a very stiff and coarse piece of paper. Since she had never written in a cursive hand, it was done in the angular script.

### In the Garden of Bliss

> If we are bound by fate,
> one day I shall encounter you

in that good paradise.
No easy thing to get involved with
is the shape of a lowly creature.

When the young man, who was the Assistant Director of the Stables of the Right, saw it, he thought, "What a curious and different sort of letter this is!" And hoping to find some way to have a look at her, he made an arrangement with a certain Middle Captain whereby they disguised themselves as common women, proceeded to the home of the Inspector-Major Counselor at a time when he was out, and watched from a position by a latticework on the north side of the quarters where the lady resided. They noticed some boys who were doing nothing unusual, loitering about and walking among the grasses and trees, when one of them said, "Look! Here's a whole bunch of them crawling all over this tree! These are very fine ones!"

"Would you look at these?" they said, raising one of the blinds. "We've got some wonderful caterpillars for you!"

"Oh what fun!" said the lady in a brisk voice. "Bring them here!"

"I don't think we can sort them out. Would you just come and look at them here?"

At that she trod brusquely into the open.

As the men watched her push the blind outward and stare wide-eyed at the branches, they saw that she wore a mantelet over her head; and her hair, though the sidelocks made a pretty curve downward, had a prickly look about it, perhaps because she did not groom it, while her eyebrows stood out very dark in gaudy relief and looked crisp. Her mouth was attractively formed and pretty, but since she did not apply tooth blackening, it was most unconventional. One felt that had she used cosmetics she would certainly be good-looking. How depressing! What a pity it was to see that she had let herself go so badly, yet was not unattractive, but looked quite different from the ordinary, was remarkably genteel, and had an air of brightness about her. She wore robes of figured silk in pale yellow under the outer robe with a katydid design, and preferred her trousers white.[1]

She went out because she wanted to examine the worms as closely as possible. "What a splendid sight!" she said. "They are coming this way because it hurts them to be burned in the sun. Round them up, boys, and don't miss a single one!"

As the boys knocked them off they fluttered to the ground. She held out a white fan with calligraphy on it that she had practiced in black strokes of India ink. "Pick them up and put them on this," she commanded, and the boys got them out.

---

1. The pale colors were appropriate for a middle-aged or older woman.

The two gentlemen were appalled. "How extraordinary in a place that has misfortune enough!" they thought; and in their opinion of her, as far as the gentlemen were concerned, she was incredible.

One of the boys, who was standing there, looked at them suspiciously and said, "Over there alongside that latticework some good-looking but strangely dressed men are standing and peeking at us!"

"How awful! I fear Milady is exposed to view because of her interest in playing with vermin the way she does. I shall go and inform her," said Lady Tayu; and when she came into her mistress's presence she found her outside the blind as usual, shouting and having the caterpillars brushed off so that they fell to the ground. Since they frightened her very much, she announced without coming too close, "Come inside, Madam! The veranda is exposed to view."

Believing that she spoke only to restrain her from what she was doing, the lady replied, "Well, what of it! I am not ashamed."

"Oh, what a sorry business! Do you think I am lying? Why do you act this way when they say that some very magnificent-looking persons are over by the latticework! Come inside and look!"

"Mole Cricket, go over there and take a look!" said the lady.

He ran over and then reported, "They are really there!"

At this the lady jumped to her feet, and the caterpillars she gathered up and put into her sleeve before she ran inside. Her figure was nicely proportioned, and her hair fell very abundantly the full length of her robes. Since it was untrimmed at the edges, it did not form a cluster, yet it flowed evenly and looked only the more beautiful.

"Most people are not this well favored. Is it so regrettable that they try to improve their personal appearance and manner? One ought really to be repelled by her appearance, yet she is very nice looking and genteel, and it is surely only her troublesome qualities that make her different. Oh, how regrettable! Why does she have such a weird mind, and when she looks so nice too!"

So the gentlemen thought. The Assistant Director was highly dissatisfied with the prospect of just going away. He would at least let her know that he had seen her. Therefore he used the juice of a plant to write on a sheet of folded paper:

> Now that I have seen
> significant depths in caterpillar fur,
> I have every hope
> that I may keep yours in hand for good
> to watch and guard with tender care!

He tapped with his fan, whereupon a boy appeared. "Present this to the lady," he said, giving it to him.

The lady called Tayu accepted it from the boy as he told her, "The person standing over there says to present this to Her Ladyship."

"Oh, how awful!" she said. "This does indeed seem to be the work of the Assistant Director of the Stables of the Right. He must have seen your face, Madam, while you were amusing yourself with those wretched bugs!" And she told her mistress a thing or two.

To which the lady replied, "When one thinks things through, one realizes that nothing is shameful. Who among men can stay long enough in this dreamlike and illusory world to look at bad things or look at the good and wonder about them?"

There was no point in saying anything to that, and her young people turned to each other in despair. The men stood by for a while on the off chance that there might be a reply, but the ladies called all the boys inside. "A sorry business!" they said to one another.

There must have been some among those present who understood what was required, for one of them did rise to the occasion and out of sympathy wrote:

> The depths of a heart
> so unlike the hearts of other human
> beings
>     I certainly wish to reveal;
> but only when I have asked the person's
> name
> as I do with caterpillars whom I do not
> know.

The Assistant Director recited:

> No one at all
> could equal the tip of a single hair
>     growing on those eyebrows,
> which are all but indistinguishable
> from furry caterpillar forms!

Then, laughing, he apparently went home.

What happened next you shall read in Scroll Two.

# ■ Tales of Times Now Past (Late Eleventh to Early Twelfth Centuries) (stories)

TRANSLATED BY MARIAN URY

*Tales of Times Now Past* is a late Heian collection of more than twelve hundred brief tales (or *setsuwa*) that is considered a Japanese literary classic. Though the tales are traditionally attributed to Minamoto Takakuni

(1004–1077), it is by no means certain that he was either the compiler or the sole author. Each story begins "At a time now past . . ." and ends ". . . so it's been handed down." The collection contains stories set in India and China as well as secular and supernatural tales set in Japan, including Buddhist Jataka tales (tales of the Buddha's previous lives), Buddhist parables, miracle tales, tales of visits to hell, secular histories, warrior stories, tales of supernatural creatures, tales of robbery, and many other sorts of stories. The didactic nature of a number of these stories suggests that the collection may have been put together as a sourcebook for priests to help them with their sermons, though the substantial number of secular stories puts this in question as well. The collection is meticulously arranged into chapters consisting of a number of stories that develop a particular theme or set of themes arranged in thematic pairs that also have a rapport with adjacent stories. As a compilation of folktales, legends, real history, and miracle stories, this collection is a great example of the value of popular traditions, as opposed to the refined works of the courtly tradition. It has been very influential in the development of later Japanese literature, often serving as a sourcebook for playwrights in the noh, kabuki, and bunraku theaters.

**FURTHER READING:** Jones, S. W. *Ages Ago: Thirty-Seven Tales from the Konjaku Monogatari Collection*, 1959. Kelsey, W. Michael. "*Konjaku Monogatari-shu:* Toward an Understanding of Its Literary Qualities," *Monumenta Nipponica*, 30, 1975. Nakamura, Kyoko Motomichi. *Miraculous Stories from the Japanese Buddhist Tradition: The Nihon ryo of the Monk Kyōkai*, 1973. Ury, Marian, tr. *Tales of Times Now Past: Sixty-Two Stories from a Medieval Japanese Collection*, 1979.


# How an Invisible Man Regained Corporeal Form through Kannon's Aid[1]

At a time now past—when it was I do not know—there lived in the capital a young, low-ranking samurai. He went regularly to the Rokkakudo[2] and worshipped there earnestly.

On the last day of the twelfth month[3] it happened that at nightfall he went to the house of a friend. He set out for home after it was quite dark and went west down First Avenue. As he was crossing the bridge over Horikawa[4] he saw ahead of him a great many men carrying lighted torches. "It must be some high nobleman," he thought and hurried under the bridge. He waited in its shadow as the torch-bearers came toward him

---

1. "Kannon" is the Japanese name for the female bodhisattva Avalokiteshvara, who is spoken of in the Lotus Sutra and is known in China as Quan Yin, the goddess of mercy [Editor].

2. A hall in the Chōhōji, in Kyoto, in which a celebrated image of Kannon was enshrined.

3. In ancient times the spirits of the dead were thought to return on this night.

4. First Avenue was the northern boundary of Kyoto; Horikawa was to the west.

and passed over it eastward. He raised his eyes for a quiet look—and what should he see but that it was not men at all but a procession of dreadful oni![5] Some had one eye; some had horns; some had extra hands; and some had only one foot and hopped. At the sight, the man felt as though he were no longer alive; his mind went numb and he just stood there as the oni went by. They had all gone past except for one last, and he said, "There are signs of a man here." "We can't see any," some said. "Catch him and bring him here," said yet others.

"It's all over with me," the man thought. One of the oni ran and grabbed him and pulled him up. The others said, "This man's offense is not serious. Let him go." Four or five of them spat on him, and then they all went past.

The man was glad that he hadn't been killed. He felt funny and his head hurt, but he pulled himself together. "I'll go straight home and tell my wife about it," he thought. He hurried home, but once he was indoors his wife and children said not a word to him although they were looking right at him; nor did they answer when he addressed them. The man thought this strange and went up close to them, but even though he was standing beside them they had no idea he was there. Now he understood. "So that's it! When the oni spat on me my body disappeared!" His distress was boundless. He saw other people just as before and heard them talk as clearly as ever, but other people did not see him or hear his voice. He took food to eat which his family had set out, and none of them knew it. Thus he passed the night; at dawn his wife and children were saying that they were sure he had been murdered the night before.

Days passed—and what was he to do? With no other remedy, he went to the Rokkakudō and went into retreat there. "Kannon, save me!" he prayed. "For many years now I have worshipped you and put my trust in you; as proof of it let me regain my original corporeal form." He ate the food of others who were in retreat there and took rice from their offerings, but none of the people beside him were aware of it.

Thus he spent twice seven days. One night shortly before dawn he had a dream. A venerable monk appeared near the curtains of the sacred image and came to his side. The monk said, "Leave this place as soon as it is morning and do as the first person you meet tells you to." At this, the man awoke.

At dawn he left the temple. At the foot of the gate he met a herdboy whose appearance was fearsome in the extreme, leading a great ox. The boy looked at him and said, "Well, sir, you're to come along with me." The man was overjoyed at being spoken to, for he thought, "I have become visible again," and, trusting in his dream, followed the boy happily. They walked westward for about two-thirds of a mile and came to a large gabled gate, which was shut fast. The boy tied his ox to it and started to slip through a space between the doors too narrow for a human being to en-

---

5. Demons [Editor].

ter. He tugged at the man. "Come in with me," he said. "How on earth can I get through that?" said the man. "Never mind," said the boy, "just go in"—and taking the man's hand, he pulled him in along with him. The man saw that they were within the walls of a great, thronging mansion.

The boy took him up onto the veranda floor and straight inside. Not a person spoke up to challenge them. They went into the innermost recesses of the house, and there the man saw a fine young lady lying sick and in pain. Her maids sat side by side behind her pillow and at her feet, nursing her. The oxboy led the man to the sick lady, made him hold a small mallet, sat him down beside her, and made him strike her head and hips, so that she shook her head in agony. "This illness will be the end of her," her parents said, and they wept. As the man looked on, they read sutras, and also they sent for [a certain]⁶ worthy exorcist. Soon the priest arrived. Sitting close to the sick girl, he intoned the Heart Sutra. The man felt boundless veneration. His hair stood on end, and a chill went through his body. But no sooner did the oxboy catch sight of the priest than he, for his part, ran out of the house at full speed.

The priest read a dharani of Fudō's realm of fire.⁷ When he pronounced the formula and made mystic signs over the patient, the man's clothing caught fire. It burned and burned, and as it burned he screamed. At that moment he became fully visible. Everyone in the household, from the parents down to the maids, saw to their amazement a man obviously of very lowly station sitting next to the sufferer. Before anything else, they took hold of him and dragged him away. "What is this?" they demanded, and he told them what had happened, from the very beginning. "What a queer business!" they thought. But then it turned out that when the man had become visible the lady had recovered: it was as though her illness had been simply wiped away. The joy of the household was unbounded. The exorcist then said: "Do not blame this man, for he has benefited from the favor of the Kannon of Rokkakudō. Release him at once." And so they let him go free.

The man went home and told his story, and his wife was glad and thought how uncanny it all was. The oxboy was in fact the attendant of a deity. He had afflicted the lady because someone had persuaded him to.

Neither the lady nor the man was ever ill afterward; this resulted from the miraculous power of the realm of fire dharani.

Among the benefits with which Kannon favors his worshippers are marvels of this sort. So the tale's been told, and so it's been handed down.

---

6. Bracketed words bridge a lacuna; literally, "a worthy exorcist called————."

7. Through chanting, mystic gestures, and meditation on Fudō, the adept produced a magic fire to drive out demons. The passage that follows may be unique in literature in describing an exorcism essentially from the point of view of the supernatural being who is exorcised.

# ■ Tale of the Heike (Twelfth to Fourteenth Centuries) (prose)

## TRANSLATED BY HELEN CRAIG McCULLOUGH

The *Tale of the Heike* is the finest Japanese military epic. Its original author seems to have been a minor noble named Nakayama Yukinari (c. 1164–?), but there are more than a hundred recensions, and the standard twelve-book text (plus sequel) is the product of centuries of modification by professional chanters who took the story across Japan and chanted it to audiences with musical accompaniment. The work can be described as at least in part verse-prose, since it often has the seven-five syllable pattern that is basic to Japanese verse. The subject of this tale, which is as familiar to the Japanese as the *Iliad* is to the West, is the rise and eventual fall of the Taira clan (the Heike) in the second part of the twelfth century. The Taira fall to their rivals, the Minamoto clan (Genji), in the Gempei War of 1180–1185, leading to the establishment of the Minamoto shogunate. The Taira bring on themselves karmic punishment for the arrogance and pride of their leader Kiyomori and for their attempts to supplant the powerful Fujiwara clan and change their station in life. The story must be read not as fiction but as a dramatization of history, based on actual events, characters, and historical accounts. There is a balance between Buddhist morality and swashbuckling celebration of feats of courage, treacheries, and honor. This epic tale has been a fertile source for cultural production in many other fields from noh, kabuki, and bunraku plays to modern movies and novels. It is second only to *The Tale of Genji* as a masterpiece of Japanese storytelling. In the selections presented here we see the famous Buddhist opening chapter; a self-contained tale about Tadamori, clan head of the Taira, and father of Kiyomori; and in "The Death of Etchū no Zenji" we see a fascinating account of battlefield etiquette and betrayal.

**FURTHER READING:** Kitagawa, Hiroshi, and Paul Tsuchida, trs. *The Tale of the Heike: "Heike Monogatari,"* 1977. McCullough, Helen Craig, tr. *The Tale of the Heike,* 1988. Sadler, A. L. *The Ten Foot Square Hut and Tales of the Heike,* 1971.

## *Gion Shōja*

The sound of the Gion Shōja bells echoes the impermanence of all things; the color of the *śāla* flowers reveals the truth that the prosperous must decline. The proud do not endure, they are like a dream on a spring night; the mighty fall at last, they are as dust before the wind.

In a distant land, there are the examples set by Zhao Gao of Qin, Wang Mang of Han, Zhu Yi of Liang, and Lushan of Tang, all of them men who prospered after refusing to be governed by their former lords and sovereigns, but who met swift destruction because they disregarded admonitions, failed to recognize approaching turmoil, and ignored the nation's distress. Closer to home, there have been Masakado of Shōhei, Sumitomo of Tengyō, Yoshichika of Kōwa, and Nobuyori of Heiji, every one of them proud and mighty. But closest of all, and utterly beyond the power of mind to comprehend or tongue to relate, is the tale of Taira no Ason Kiyomori, the Rokuhara Buddhist Novice and Former Chancellor.

Kiyomori was the oldest son and heir of Punishments Minister Tadamori. He was a grandson of the Sanuki Governor Masamori, who was a descendant in the ninth generation from Prince Kazurahara of First Rank, the Minister of Ceremonial and fifth son of Emperor Kanmu. Prince Kazurahara's son, Prince Takami, died without office or rank. The clan received the Taira surname in the time of Prince Takami's son, Prince Takamochi, who left the imperial clan to become a subject soon after he was named Vice-Governor of Kazusa Province. Prince Takamochi's son was the Defense Garrison Commander Yoshimochi, who changed his name to Kunika in later life. During the six generations from Kunika to Masamori, members of the clan held provincial governorships but were not permitted to have their names on the duty-board in the Courtiers' Hall.

## The Night Attack at the Courtiers' Hall

But Tadamori, during his term as Bizen Governor, built a Buddhist hall thirty-three bays long, enshrined therein a thousand and one holy images, and offered it in fulfillment of Retired Emperor Toba's vow to found a temple, the Tokujōjuin. The dedication took place on the Thirteenth of the Third Month in the first year of Tenshō. Orders were issued to reward Tadamori with a province, and Tajima, which happened to be available, was given to him. The delighted Retired Emperor also granted him courtier privileges at the imperial palace. Tadamori set foot in the Courtiers' Hall for the first time at the age of thirty-six.

Angered by those marks of favor, the courtiers and senior nobles conspired to attack Tadamori under cover of darkness on the night of the Gosechi Flushed Faces Banquet, which was to be held on the Twenty-Third of the Twelfth Month in that same year. But Tadamori made preparations of his own on hearing of the plot. "I am not a civil functionary," he thought. "I belong to a warrior house. It would be a grief to my family and to me if I let myself be humiliated through lack of foresight. Besides, the book says, 'Take care of yourself so you can serve your master.'"

When Tadamori entered the palace, he brought along a large dagger, thrust loosely under his court robes. Turning toward a spot where the lamplight was dim, he drew the weapon with deliberation and held it alongside his head, its blade gleaming like ice. None of those present failed to mark the act. Furthermore, his retainer Sahyōe-no-jō Iesada came and sat at attention in the small side garden, dressed in a green-laced corselet under a pale green hunting robe, with a sword and an attached bowstring bag under his arm. Iesada was a son of Shinnosaburō Dayū Suefusa and a grandson of Assistant Director of the Carpentry Bureau Sadamitsu, who had been a member of the Taira clan.

In great perturbation, the Head Chamberlain and his staff sent a Chamberlain of Sixth Rank to rebuke Iesada. "Who is this person in an unfigured hunting robe waiting beyond the rainspout near the bell pull? You are misbehaving. Get out of there!"

Iesada kept his seat. "I have been told that my hereditary lord, the honorable Governor of Bizen, is to be cut down in the dark tonight. I am here to witness his fate; I cannot leave." Perhaps the conspirators lost heart, for there was no attack that night.

Later during the same occasion, when it was Tadamori's turn to dance as part of the informal entertainment, the gentlemen put new words to a song, chanting, "The Ise wine bottles are vinegar jars." Although the Taira were descended from the great Emperor Kanmu, they had not frequented the capital in the recent past, but had become *jige* with roots in Ise Province. Thus the singers chanted of Ise bottles, punning on a kind of vessel produced in that province. And because Tadamori suffered from a squint, they introduced the second pun.[1] Since Tadamori had no means of retaliation, he decided to slip away before the affair ended. He went to the north corner of the Shishinden, and there, within sight of the other courtiers, he called over a woman from the Bureau of Grounds and put the dagger in her charge. Then he left.

"How did things go?" Iesada asked. Tadamori wanted to tell him the truth, but Iesada was the kind of man who would leap into the Courtiers' Hall itself, slashing and cutting, if he were to hear such a story, so he replied, "Nothing much happened."

People are expected to confine themselves to amusing trifles like "White tissue paper, deep-dyed paper, corded brushes, and lacquered brushes" during the singing and dancing at Gosechi entertainments. In the relatively recent past, to be sure, there had been an incident involving the Dazaifu Provisional Governor-General Suenaka, whose swarthy complexion had caused him to be nicknamed the "Black Governor." Suenaka had danced at a Gosechi party during his tenure as Head Chamberlain, and the singers had improvised, "Ah, black, black, black is the head! Who applied the lacquer?"[2] There had also been the case of the Kazan'in Former Chancellor Tadamasa. Orphaned at ten by the death of his father, Middle Counselor Tadamune, Tadamasa had been taken as a son-in-law and maintained in luxury by the late Naka-no-mikado Middle Counselor, Fujiwara no Ienari, who was then Governor of Harima Province. When

---

1. *Heiji* can mean both "wine bottle" and "Taira clan"; *sugame,* "vinegar jar" and "squint eye."

2. The song puns on *tō* ("face," "head") and Suenaka's official title, *kurōdo no tō* (Head Chamberlain).

Tadamasa danced during the Gosechi festivities, the singers chanted, "Can the Harima rice be a scouring rush or a *muku* leaf? Ah, how it polishes up the wardrobe!"[3] Nothing had come of such affairs, people remarked now—but who could tell what might happen in these latter days of the Law?[4] It was a worrisome business.

As was to have been anticipated, all the courtiers presented complaints after the Gosechi ceremonies ended. "Rules and regulations are supposed to determine who may wear a weapon to an official banquet, and who may go in and out of the palace accompanied by Escorts," they said. "It has always been accepted that neither may be done without explicit imperial authorization. But Tadamori stationed a warrior wearing a hunting robe at the small garden outside the Courtiers' Hall, on the pretext that the man was a hereditary retainer, and he also attended a formal banquet with a weapon at his waist. Both actions were unprecedented breaches of conduct. A person who commits a double offense must not escape punishment. Tadamori must have his name removed from the duty-board and lose his official position at once."

In great surprise, the Retired Emperor summoned Tadamori for questioning. "To begin with," Tadamori explained, "I had no idea that my retainer had posted himself in the small garden. But it has seemed recently that there has been some kind of plot against me. Iesada has been in my service for many years; he must have heard about it and gone there without my knowledge, in the hope of sparing me embarrassment. That is not something I could have done anything about. If Iesada deserves censure, shall I call him in and turn him over to you? Next, as regards the dagger, I gave it to one of the servants from the Bureau of Grounds to keep for me. Before judgment is rendered, would it not be well to summon the woman and see whether it is a real weapon?"

The Retired Emperor found the suggestion reasonable; he called for the dagger and inspected it. The scabbard was of black lacquer, but the blade proved to be silver foil over wood.

"He wanted to avoid humiliation, so he made a show of carrying a dagger," the Retired Emperor said. "But he wore a wooden blade because he knew there would be complaints later. That is a sign of admirable resourcefulness—precisely what one would desire in a warrior. His retainer's foray into the garden was the kind of thing warriors' retainers do. Tadamori is not to blame for it." In view of his evident approval, there was no more talk of punishment.

---

3. "Harima rice" is a metaphor for the Governor. Scouring rushes (*tokusa*) and the bristly leaves of the muku tree (*Aphananthe aspera*) were used as polishing agents.

4. *Matsudai.* In Buddhist thought, a 10,000-year age of moral degeneration, culminating in the disappearance of the Law (doctrine) itself. In the 12th century, it was generally believed that the age had begun around 1050.

## The Death of Etchū no Zenji

In reckless disregard of their lives, the warriors from Musashi and Sagami took the offensive on both the main front and the seaward side. The Kodama League sent a messenger from the mountain flank to the New Middle Counselor Tomomori, who was fighting with his face toward the east. "The men of the Kodama League tell you this because you were once Governor of Musashi: look behind you!" On doing so, Tomomori and the others saw a cloud of black smoke advancing toward them. "Ah! The western front has fallen!" They all fled in desperate haste.

Etchū no Zenji Moritoshi, the Samurai Commander on the cliffward side, halted his mount and sat motionless, perhaps because he believed it was too late to try to escape. Inomata no Koheiroku Noritsuna marked him as a worthy adversary, galloped forward with flailing whip and flapping stirrups, rode up alongside him, gripped him with all his strength, and crashed with him to the ground. Noritsuna was a man renowned in the Eight Provinces for his great strength, a warrior who was said to have once torn apart a deer's double-branched antlers with ease. Moritoshi allowed others to consider him merely as strong as twenty or thirty ordinary men, but in actuality he could haul up or send down a vessel that required sixty or seventy men for the working. Thus, Moritoshi succeeded in gripping Noritsuna and holding him still. Noritsuna, lying underneath, tried to draw his dagger but could not grasp the hilt with his splayed fingers, tried to speak but was pinned too tight to utter a word. But although his head was about to be cut off, and despite his physical inferiority, his valor did not flag. He collected his breath calmly for a few instants and then spoke in an offhand manner.

"Did you hear me announce my name? A man who kills an enemy does not perform a great exploit unless he takes the head after identifying himself and requiring the other to do the same. What will you gain by taking an anonymous head?"

Moritoshi may have thought that he was right. "I am Etchū no Zenji Moritoshi, born a Taira but now become a samurai because of my inadequacies. Who are you? Announce your name: I would like to hear it."

"I am Inomata no Koheiroku Noritsuna, a resident of Musashi Province." Noritsuna continued, "If we look at the present state of affairs, it seems that the Genji are the stronger, and that you on the Heike side face defeat. Unless your masters prosper, you will reap no rewards by taking heads to show them. Stretch a point and spare me. I will use my exploits to save the lives of any number of Heike men—dozens, if you like."

Moritoshi was outraged. "In spite of all my shortcomings, I belong to the house of Taira. I have no intention of turning to the Genji for help, and no intention whatsoever of helping one of them. Your proposal is ignoble." He prepared to cut off Noritsuna's head.

"You are disgracing yourself! How can you decapitate a man who has already surrendered?" Noritsuna said.

"Very well, I will spare you." Moritoshi raised Noritsuna to his feet, and the two sat down to rest on a footpath, with a hard, sun-baked field in front and a deep, muddy rice paddy to their rear.

Presently, a warrior attired in a suit of armor with black leather lacing came galloping toward them on a whitish horse. Moritoshi eyed him suspiciously. "Don't worry," Noritsuna said. "That is Hitomi no Shirō, a friend of mine. He must have seen me." But to himself Noritsuna thought, "If I begin wrestling with Etchū no Zenji after Shirō gets close, Shirō will be sure to attack him, too." He bided his time.

The rider meanwhile advanced until he was a mere thirty-five feet away. At first, Moritoshi tried to keep one eye on each of the two men, but the galloping foe engaged his full attention as he gradually approached, and he lost track of Noritsuna. Noritsuna seized the opportunity. He sprang to his feet with a yell, dealt a powerful blow to Moritoshi's breastplate with the combined force of his two hands, and toppled him backwards into the rice paddy behind. As Moritoshi struggled to rise, Noritsuna clamped him between his legs, snatched the dagger from Moritoshi's waist, lifted his adversary's armor skirt, plunged the weapon into his flesh three times, hilt, fist, and all, and took his head.

Hitomi no Shirō had come up in the meantime. "It is cases like this that give rise to disputes," Noritsuna thought. He impaled the head on the tip of his sword, held it high, and announced his name in a mighty voice. "Inomata no Koheiroku Noritsuna has slain Etchū no Zenji Moritoshi, the Heike samurai known in these days as a demon god!" His name led that day's list of exploits.

## ■ Kamo no Chomei (c. 1155–1216) (memoir)

### TRANSLATED BY HELEN CRAIG McCULLOUGH

*An Account of My Hermitage* by Kamo no Chomei is a masterly Buddhist essay and a classic of Japanese literature. Like Thoreau retreating to his cabin by Walden Pond, Chomei records his attempt to simplify his life and become self-reliant. He was born to a family that traced its ancestry to a god who lived at Kamo in legendary times, and traditionally family members were lesser courtiers and priests in the shrines of the Kamo area. His father was the head priest of the Lower Kamo Shrine, but he died when Chomei was eighteen. Chomei was appointed by the Retired Emperor Gotoba to the Poetry Office, which was responsible for organizing the compilation of the *Shinkokinshu*, an important Imperial poetry anthology. In his early twenties, he gave up his active court life and devoted himself to the arts of poetry and the lute. Later he took Buddhist vows, severed his connection with the Poetry Office, and went to live as a recluse near Mount Hiei. Around 1208, he built his famous ten-foot-square hut in the solitary mountains at Hino in the Uji region (made famous in the last chapters of

*The Tale of Genji*), where he lived till his death. In addition to *An Account of My Hermitage,* his most famous piece, Chomei wrote poems, *The Nameless Treatise* (a work on poetics), and *A Collection of Religious Awakenings* (a collection of didactic stories).

Chomei lived through the turbulent years of warfare between the Taira and Minamoto clans and through a series of natural disasters. In *An Account of My Hermitage,* which he wrote in 1212, he recounts the violence of nature and of human nature in a series of striking depictions of prevailing misery in a changing world. Since life is evanescent as "bubbles on the water" and since all his early pampered existence cannot protect him from natural and human disasters, Chomei moves to ever smaller and simpler residences and finds protection from loss in owning very little. Like the Chinese poets Han Shan and Tao Yuanming, Chomei is a model for later Buddhist recluses.

**FURTHER READING:** McCullough, Helen Craig, ed. *Classical Japanese Prose: An Anthology,* 1990. Ury, Marian. "Recluses and Eccentric Monks: Tales from the *Hosshinshu* by Kamo no Chomei," *Monumenta Nipponica,* 27, 1972.

## An Account of My Hermitage

### 1

The waters of a flowing stream are ever present but never the same; the bubbles in a quiet pool disappear and form but never endure for long. So it is with men and their dwellings in the world.

The houses of the high and the low seem to last for generation after generation, standing with ridgepoles aligned and roof-tiles jostling in the magnificent imperial capital, but investigation reveals that few of them existed in the past. In some cases, a building that burned last year has been replaced this year; in others, a great house has given way to a small one. And it is the same with the occupants. The places are unchanged, the population remains large, but barely one or two survive among every twenty or thirty of the people I used to know. Just as with the bubbles on the water, someone dies at night and someone else is born in the morning. Where do they come from and where do they go, all those who are born and die? And for whose benefit, for what reason, does a man take enormous pains to build a temporary shelter pleasing to the eye? The master in his dwelling is like the dewdrop vying in ephemerality with the morning glory where it forms. The flower may remain after the dew evaporates, but it withers in the morning sun; the flower may droop before the moisture vanishes, but the dew does not survive until nightfall.

# 2

I have witnessed a number of remarkable occurrences in the more than forty years since I began to understand the nature of things. Around the Hour of the Dog [7:00 P.M.–9:00 P.M.] on a very windy night—I believe it was the Twenty-eighth of the Fourth Month in the third year of Angen [1177]—a fire broke out in the southeastern part of the capital and burned toward the northwest. In the end, it spread to Suzaku Gate, the Great Hall of State, the Academy, and the Ministry of Popular Affairs, reducing them all to ashes overnight. Its source is said to have been a temporary structure housing some dancers, located near the Higuchi–Tomi-no-kōji intersection. Spread here and there by an erratic wind, it burned in a pattern resembling an open fan, narrow at the base and wide at the outer edge. Suffocating smoke engulfed distant houses; wind-whipped flames descended to earth everywhere near at hand. The sky was red to the horizon with ashes lit by the fiery glare, and winged flames leaped a block or two at a time in the lurid atmosphere, torn free by the irresistible force of the gale. Everything must have seemed as unreal as a dream to the people in the fire's path. Some of them fell victim to the smoke. Others died instantly in the embrace of the flames. Still others managed to escape with their lives but failed to rescue their belongings, and all their cherished treasures turned to ashes. The value of so much property may be imagined! The fire claimed the houses of sixteen senior nobles, to say nothing of countless others of less importance. It was reported that fully one-third of the capital had been destroyed. Dozens of men and women were killed; innumerable horses and oxen perished.

All human enterprises are pointless, but it must be counted an act of supreme folly for a man to consume his treasure and put himself to endless trouble merely to build a house in a place as dangerous as the capital.

Again, around the Fourth Month in the fourth year of Jishō [1180], a great whirlwind sprang up near the Nakamikado–[Higashi] Kyōgoku intersection and swept all the way to Rokujō Avenue. Not a house, large or small, escaped destruction within the area of three or four blocks where the blast wreaked its full fury. In some cases, entire buildings were flattened; in others, only crossbeams and pillars were spared. Gates were caught up and deposited four or five blocks distant; fences were blown away and neighboring properties merged. And I need hardly mention what happened to smaller objects. Everything inside a house mounted to the skies; cypress-bark thatch and shingles whirled like winter leaves in the wind. Dust ascended like smoke to blind the eye; the terrible howl of the storm swallowed the sound of voices. It seemed that even the dread karma-wind of hell could be no worse. Not only were houses damaged or destroyed, but countless men suffered injury or mutilation while the buildings were being reconstructed. The wind moved toward the south-southeast, visiting affliction on innumerable people.

Whirlwinds are common, but not ones such as that. Those who experienced it worried that it might be an extraordinary phenomenon, a warning from a supernatural being.

Again, around the Sixth Month in the fourth year of Jishō, the court moved suddenly to a new capital.[1] Nobody had dreamed of such a thing. When we consider that more than 400 years had elapsed since the establishment of the present imperial seat during Emperor Saga's reign, surely a new one ought not to have been chosen without exceptional justification. It was more than reasonable that people should have felt disquiet and apprehension.

But complaints were useless. The Emperor, the Ministers of State, the senior nobles, and all the others moved. Nobody remained in the old capital who held even a minor court position. Those who aspired to office and rank, or who relied on the favor of patrons, strove to move with all possible dispatch; those who had lost the opportunity to succeed in life, or who had been rejected by society, stayed behind, sunk in gloom. The dwellings that had once stood eave to eave grew more dilapidated with every passing day. Houses were dismantled and sent floating down the Yodo River, and their former locations turned into fields before the onlookers' eyes.

In a complete reversal of values, everyone prized horses and saddles and stopped using oxen and carriages. Properties in the Western and Southern Sea circuits were sought; those in the Eastern Sea and Northern Land circuits were considered undesirable.

It happened that something took me to the new capital in Settsu Province. The cramped site, too small for proper subdivision, rose high on the north where it bordered the hills and sank low on the south beside the sea. The breaking waves never ceased to clamor; the wind from the sea blew with peculiar fury. The imperial palace struck me as unexpectedly novel and interesting, situated in the hills as it was, and I asked myself whether Empress Saimei's log house might not have been rather similar.[2]

I wondered where people were erecting the whole houses that were being sent downstream daily, their numbers great enough to clog the river. There were still many empty parcels of land and few houses. The old capital was already in ruins; the new one had yet to take form. Not a soul but felt as rootless as a drifting cloud. The original inhabitants grieved over the loss of their land; the new arrivals worried about plaster and lumber. On the streets, those who ought to have used carriages rode horseback; those who ought to have worn court dress or hunting robes appeared in *hitatare*. The customs of the capital had been revolutionized overnight, and people behaved like rustic warriors.

---

1. The move took place soon after the suppression of a preliminary attempt to overthrow the Taira. The new capital was at Fukuhara (now a part of Kōbe), where Taira no Kiyomori had established his principal residence some years earlier.

2. The log house was a temporary residence in Kyūshū used by Empress Saimei (594–661) when the Japanese were preparing to attack the Korean state of Silla in 661.

I have heard that such changes portend civil disturbance—and that was precisely what happened. With every passing day, the world grew more unsettled, people lost more of their composure, and the common folk felt more apprehension. In the end, a crisis brought about a return to the old capital during the winter of the same year.[3] But who knows what became of the houses that had been torn down everywhere? They were not rebuilt in their former style.

We are told that the sage Emperors of old ruled with compassion. They roofed their palaces with thatch, neglecting even to trim the eaves; they remitted the already modest taxes when they saw the commoners' cooking-fires emit less smoke than before. The reason was simply that they cherished their subjects and wished to help them. To compare the present to the past is to see what kind of government we have today.

Again, there was a dreadful two-year famine. (I think it was around the Yōwa era [1181–82], but it was too long ago to be sure.) The grain crops were ruined as one calamity followed another: drought in the spring and summer, typhoons and floods in the autumn. It was vain for the farmers to till the fields in the spring or set out plants in the summer; there was no reaping in the fall, no bustle of storage in the winter. Some rural folk abandoned their land and wandered off; others deserted their homes to live in the hills. Prayers were begun and extraordinary rituals were performed, but they accomplished nothing.

The capital had always depended on the countryside for every need. Now, with nothing coming in, people were beside themselves with anxiety. In desperation, they offered all their treasures at bargain rates, but nobody took any notice. The rare person who was willing to trade thought little of gold and much of grain. The streets were overrun with mendicants; lamentations filled the air.

The first of the two years dragged to a close. But just as everyone was anticipating a return to normal in the new year, a pestilence came along to make matters even worse. Like fish gasping in a puddle, the starving populace drew closer to the final extremity with every passing day, until at last people of quite respectable appearance, clad in hats and leggings, begged frantically from house to house. These wretched, dazed beings fell prostrate even as one marveled at their ability to walk.

Countless people perished of starvation by the wayside or died next to tile-capped walls. Since there was no way to dispose of the bodies, noisome stenches filled the air, and innumerable decomposing corpses shocked the eye. Needless to say, the dead lay so thick in the Kamo riverbed that there was not even room for horses and ox-carriages to pass.

With the woodsmen and other commoners too debilitated to perform their usual functions, a shortage of firewood developed, and people who possessed no other means of support broke up their own houses to sell in

---

3. The rebellions of provincial Minamoto leaders had produced serious military disturbances.

the market. The amount a man could carry brought less than enough to sustain him for a day. It was shocking to see pieces of wood covered with red lacquer or gold and silver leaf jumbled together with the rest. On inquiry, one learned that desperate people were going to old temples, stealing the sacred images, tearing away the fixtures from the halls, and breaking up everything for firewood. It is because I was born in a degenerate age that I have been forced to witness such disgraceful sights.

Some deeply moving things also happened. Whenever a couple were too devoted to part, the one whose love was greater was the first to die. This was because he or she put the spouse's welfare first and gave up whatever food came to hand. Similarly, a parent always predeceased a child. One sometimes saw a recumbent child sucking at his mother's breast, unaware that her life had ended. Grieved that countless people should be perishing in that manner, Dharma Seal Ryūgyō of Ninnaji Temple sought to help the dead toward enlightenment by writing the Sanskrit letter "A" on the forehead of every corpse he saw.[4]

The authorities kept track of the deaths in the Fourth and Fifth Months. During that period, there were more than 42,300 bodies on the streets in the area south of Ichijō, north of Kujō, west of Kyōgoku, and east of Suzaku. Of course, many others died before and afterward. And there would be no limit to the numbers if we were to count the Kamo riverbed, Shirakawa, the western sector, and the outlying districts, to say nothing of the provinces in the seven circuits.

People say there was something similar during the reign of Emperor Sutoku, around the Choshō era [1132–35], but I know nothing about that. I witnessed this phenomenal famine with my own eyes.

If I remember correctly, it was at more or less the same time that a terrible seismic convulsion occurred. It was no ordinary earthquake. Mountains crumbled and buried streams; the sea tilted and immersed the land. Water gushed from fissures in the earth; huge rocks cracked and rolled into valleys. Boats being rowed near the shoreline tossed on the waves; horses journeying on the roads lost their footing. Not a Buddhist hall or stupa remained intact anywhere in the vicinity of the capital. Some crumbled, others fell flat. Dust billowed like smoke; the shaking earth and collapsing houses rumbled like thunder. If people stayed indoors, they were crushed at once; if they ran outside, the ground split apart. If men had been dragons, they might have ridden the clouds, but they lacked the wings to soar into the heavens. It was then that I came to recognize an earthquake as the most terrible of all terrible things.

The violent shaking subsided fairly soon, but aftershocks followed for some time. No day passed without twenty or thirty earthquakes of an intensity that would ordinarily have caused consternation. The intervals lengthened after ten or twenty days, and then there were tremors four or

---

4. In esoteric Buddhism, of which Ninnaji was a center, "A," the first syllable in the Sanskrit syllabary, was regarded as symbolic of the unity of all things.

five times a day, or two or three times a day, or once every other day, or once every two or three days. It must have been about three months before they ceased.

Of the four constituents of the universe, water, fire, and wind create constant havoc, but the earth does not usually give rise to any particular calamities. To be sure, there were some dreadful earthquakes in the past (for instance, the great shock that toppled the head of the Tōdaiji Buddha during the Saikō era [854–57]), but none of them could compare with this. Immediately after the event, people all talked about the meaninglessness of life and seemed somewhat more free from spiritual impurity than usual. But nobody even mentioned the subject after the days and months had accumulated and the years had slipped by.

Such, then, is the difficulty of life in this world, such the ephemerality of man and his dwellings. Needless to say, it would be utterly impossible to list every affliction that stems from individual circumstance or social position. If a man of negligible status lives beside a powerful family, he cannot make a great display of happiness when he has cause for heartfelt rejoicing, nor can he lift his voice in lamentation when he experiences devastating grief. In all that he does, he is ill at ease; like a sparrow near a hawk's nest, he pursues his daily activities in fear and trembling. If a poor man lives next door to a wealthy house, he abases himself before the neighbors and agonizes over his wretched appearance whenever he goes out in the morning or returns in the evening. Forced to witness the envy of his wife, children, and servants, and to hear the rich household dismiss him with contempt, he is forever agitated, constantly distraught.

He who lives in a crowded area cannot escape calamity when a fire breaks out nearby; he who settles in a remote spot suffers many hardships in his travels to and fro and puts himself at grave risk from robbers. The powerful man is consumed by greed; the man who refuses to seek a patron becomes an object of derision. The man who owns many possessions knows many worries; the impoverished man seethes with envy.

He who depends on another belongs to another; he who takes care of another is chained by human affection. When a man observes the conventions, he falls into economic difficulties; when he flouts them, people wonder if he is mad. Where can we live, what can we do, to find even the briefest of shelters, the most fleeting peace of mind?

# 3̄

For a long time, I lived in a house inherited from my paternal grandmother. Later, my fortunes declined through lack of connections, and I found myself unable to remain in society, despite many nostalgic associations. Shortly after I entered my thirties, I moved voluntarily into a simple new dwelling one-tenth the size of the old place. I built only a personal residence, with no fashionable auxiliary structures, and although I managed an encircling earthen wall, my means did not extend to a gate. The carriage-shelter was supported by bamboo pillars, and the house was unsafe in a snowfall or windstorm. The site was near the riverbed, which left it vulnerable to floods, and there was also danger from robbers.

For more than thirty miserable years, I endured an existence in which I could not maintain my position. Every setback during that time drove home the realization that I was not blessed by fortune. And thus, at fifty, I became a monk and turned my back on the world. Having never had a wife or children, I was not bound to others by ties difficult to break; lacking office and stipend, I possessed no attachments to which to cling.

During the next five springs and autumns, I sojourned among the clouds of the Ōhara hills, leading a life devoid of spiritual progress.

Now at sixty, with the dew nearing its vanishing point, I have built a new shelter for the tree's last leaves, just as a traveler might fashion a single night's resting place or an old silkworm spin a cocoon. It is not a hundredth the size of my second house. Indeed, while I have sat around uttering idle complaints, my age has increased with every year, and my house has shrunk with every move.

This house is unusual in appearance. It is barely ten feet square, and its height is less than seven feet. The location was a matter of indifference to me; I did not divine to select a site. I built a foundation and a simple roof, and attached hinges to all the joints so that I could move easily if cause for dissatisfaction arose. There would be no trouble about rebuilding. The house would barely fill two carts, and the carters' fees would be the only expense.

After settling on my present place of retirement in the Hino hills, I extended the eastern eaves about three feet to provide myself with a convenient spot in which to break up and burn firewood. On the south side of the building, I have an open bamboo veranda with a holy water shelf at the west end. Toward the north end of the west wall, beyond a freestanding screen, there is a picture of Amida Buddha, with an image of Fugen alongside and a copy of the *Lotus Sutra* in front. At the east end of the room, some dried bracken serves as a bed. South of the screen on the west side, a bamboo shelf suspended from the ceiling holds three leather-covered bamboo baskets, in which I keep excerpts from poetry collections and critical treatises, works on music, and religious tracts like *Collection of Essentials on Rebirth in the Pure Land*. A zither and a lute stand next to the shelf. The zither is of the folding variety; the handle of the lute is detachable. Such is the appearance of my rude temporary shelter.

To turn to the surroundings: I have made a rock basin in which to collect water from an elevated conduit south of the hermitage, and I gather ample supplies of firewood in a neighboring stand of trees. The locality is called Toyama, "the foothills." Vines cover the paths. The valley is thickly forested, but there is open land to the west.

Aids to contemplation abound. In the spring, lustrous cascades of wisteria burgeon in the west like purple clouds. In the summer, every song of the cuckoo conveys a promise of companionship in the Shide Mountains.

In the autumn, the incessant cries of the cicadas seem to lament the transitoriness of worldly things. And in the winter, the accumulating and melting snows suggest poignant comparisons with sins and hindrances.[5]

When I tire of reciting the sacred name or find myself intoning a sutra in a perfunctory manner, I rest as I please, I fall idle as I see fit. There is nobody to interfere, nobody to shame me. Although I do not make a point of performing silent austerities, I can control speech-induced karma because I live alone; although I do not make a fuss about obeying the commandments, I have no occasion to break them because mine is not an environment conducive to transgression.

On mornings when I compare my existence to a white wake in the water, I borrow Mansei's style while watching boats come and go at Okanoya; on evenings when the wind rustles the maple leaves, I imitate Tsunenobu's practice while recalling the Xinyang River.[6] If my interest does not flag, I often perform "Song of the Autumn Wind" as an accompaniment to the murmur of the pines, or play "Melody of the Flowing Spring" to harmonize with the sound of the water. I am not an accomplished musician, but my playing is not designed for the pleasure of others. I merely pluck the strings alone and chant alone to comfort my own spirit.

At the foot of the hill, there is a brush-thatched cottage, the abode of the mountain warden. The small boy who lives there pays me an occasional visit, and if I chance to feel at loose ends, I set out for a ramble with him as my companion. He is ten, I am sixty. Our ages differ greatly, but we take pleasure in the same things. Sometimes we pull out reed-flower sprouts, pick *iwanashi* berries, heap up yam sprouts, or pluck herbs. Or we may go to the rice fields at the foot of the mountains, glean ears left by the reapers, and fashion sheafs. When the weather is balmy, we scramble up to a peak from which I can look toward the distant skies over my old home and see Kohatayama, Fushimi-no-sato, Toba, and Hatsukashi. Nobody owns the view; there is nothing to keep me from enjoying it.

When the going is easy and I feel like taking a long walk, I follow the peaks past Sumiyama and Kasatori to worship at Iwama or Ishiyama. Or I may traverse Awazu Plain, visit the site of Semimaru's dwelling, cross the Tanakami River, and seek out Sarumaru's grave.[7] On the way home, I search for cherry blossoms, pick autumn leaves, gather bracken, or collect

---

5. Amida and his attendants were thought to descend, riding on a purple cloud, to escort the believer to the Western Paradise at the moment of death. Possibly because the cuckoo's cry included notes that sounded like *shide*, the bird was considered a messenger from the land of the dead, which lay beyond the Shide Mountains. Sins and hindrances to enlightenment piled up in the course of daily life and were discharged periodically by repentance rites and confessions before a Buddha.

6. Mansei (8th c.) was the author of a frequently quoted poem on ephemerality: yo no naka o / nani ni tatoen / asaborake / kogiyuku fune no / ato no shiranami ("To what shall I compare life in this world—the white wake of a boat rowing off at break of day"). Tsunenobu (1016–97) was a major poet known also as an expert lute player. Chōmei alludes to the first two lines of Bo Juyi's "Lute Song": "As I see off a guest at night near the Xinyang River, / The autumn wind rustles through maple leaves and reed plumes."

7. Semimaru and Sarumaru were semilegendary poets.

fruit and nuts, depending on the season. Some of my trophies I present to the Buddha; others I treat as useful souvenirs.

On peaceful nights, I long for old friends while gazing at the moon through the window, or weep into my sleeve at the cry of a monkey. Sometimes I mistake fireflies in the bushes for fish lures burning far away at Maki-no-shima Island, or think that a gale must be scattering the leaves when I hear rain just before dawn. The *horohoro* call of a pheasant makes me wonder if the bird might be a parent; the frequent visits of deer from the peaks attest to the remoteness of my abode.[8] Sometimes I stir up the banked fire and make it a companion for the wakefulness of old age. The mountains are so little intimidating that even the owl's hoot sounds moving rather than eerie. Indeed, there is no end to the delights of the changing seasons in these surroundings. A truly reflective man, blessed with superior powers of judgment, would undoubtedly find many more pleasures than the ones I have described.

# 4

When I first began to live here, I thought it would not be for long, but five years have already elapsed. My temporary hermitage has gradually become a home, its eaves covered with rotted leaves and its foundation mossy. Whenever I happen to hear news of the capital, I learn that many illustrious personages have breathed their last since my retreat to these mountains. And it would be quite impossible to keep track of all the unimportant people who have died. A great many houses have also suffered destruction in recurrent conflagrations. Only in my temporary hermitage is life peaceful and safe. The quarters are cramped, but I have a place where I can lie at night and another where I can sit in the daytime. There is ample room for one person. The hermit crab likes a small shell because it knows its own size; the osprey lives on the rocky coast because it fears man. It is the same with me. Knowing myself and knowing the world, I harbor no ambitions and pursue no material objectives. Quietude is what I desire; the absence of worries is what makes me happy.

Men do not usually build houses for their own benefit. Some build for wives, children, relatives, and servants, some for friends and acquaintances, some for masters, for teachers, or even for household goods, treasures, oxen, and horses. But I have built for myself this time, not for anybody else. Because of present conditions and my own situation, I possess neither a family to share my dwelling nor servants to work for me. If I had built a great house, whom would I have lodged in it, whom would I have established there?

---

8. Gyōki (Gyōgi): yamadori no / horohoro to naku / koe kikeba / chichi ka to zo omou / haha ka to zo omou ("When I hear the voice of the pheasant, mountain bird, crying *horohoro*, I think, 'Might it be a father? Or might it be a mother?' "). Saigyō: yama fukami / naruru kasegi no / kejikasa ni / yo ni tōzakaru / hodo zo shiraruru ("To see at close hand deer grown accustomed to me deep in the mountains is to know my remoteness from the affairs of the world").

Friends esteem wealth and look for favors; they do not necessarily value sincere friendship or probity. I prefer to make friends of music and nature. Servants prize lavish rewards and unstinting generosity; they do not care about protection, affection, or a safe, tranquil existence. I prefer to make my own body my servant. How do I do it? If there is work to perform, I use my body. True, I may grow weary, but it is easier than employing and looking after someone else. If there is walking to do, I walk. It is burdensome, but less so than worrying over horses, saddles, oxen, and carriages. I divide my body and put it to two uses: it suits me very well to employ hands as servants and feet as conveyances. My mind understands my body's distress: I allow the body to rest when it is distressed and use it when it feels energetic. I use it but do not make a habit of pushing it to extremes. If it finds a task irksome, I am not perturbed. It is surely a healthful practice to walk constantly and work constantly. What would be the point of idling away the time? To make others work creates bad karma. Why should I borrow their strength?

It is the same with food and clothing. I hide my nakedness under a rough fiber robe, a hemp quilt, or whatever comes to hand; I survive by eating starwort from the fields and nuts from the peaks. Because I do not mingle with others, I need not chide myself for having felt ashamed of my appearance. Because I possess little food, I find coarse fare tasty.

I do not describe such pleasures as a means of criticizing the wealthy; I merely compare my own former life with my present existence. "The triple world is but one mind."[9] If the mind is not at peace, elephants, horses, and the seven treasures are trash; palatial residences and stately mansions are worthless. I feel warm affection for my present lonely dwelling, my tiny cottage. My beggarly appearance is a source of embarrassment on the infrequent occasions when something takes me to the capital, but after my return I feel pity for those who pursue worldly things. If anyone doubts my sincerity, let him consider the fish and the birds. A fish never tires of water, but only another fish can understand why. A bird seeks trees, but only another bird can understand why. It is the same with the pleasures of retirement. Only a recluse can understand them.

# 5

The moon of my life is setting; my remaining years approach the rim of the hills. Very soon, I shall face the darkness of the Three Evil Paths. Which of my old disappointments is worth fretting over now? The Buddha teaches us to reject worldly things. Even my affection for this thatched hut is a sin; even my love of tranquility must be accounted an impediment to rebirth. Why do I waste time in descriptions of inconsequential pleasures?

As I reflect on these things in the quiet moments before dawn, I put a question to myself:

---

9. *Kegon Sutra:* "The triple world is but one mind. Outside mind there is nothing; mind, Buddha, and all the living, these three are no different."

You retired to the seclusion of remote hills so that you might discipline your mind and practice the Way, but your impure spirit belies your monkish garb. Your dwelling presumes to imitate the abode of the honorable Yuima, but you are worse than Suddhipanthaka when it comes to obeying the commandments. Is this because you let yourself be troubled by karma-ordained poverty, or has your deluded mind finally lost its sanity?

The question remains unanswered. I can do no other than use my impure tongue for three or four repetitions of Amida's sacred name. Then I fall silent.

*Late in the Third Month of the second year of Kenryaku [1212]*
*Set down by the monk Ren'in in the hermitage at Toyama[10]*

## ■ Fujiwara no Teika (Sadaie) (1162–1241) (poems)

### TRANSLATED BY TONY BARNSTONE AND WILLIS BARNSTONE

The son of poet Fujiwara no Shunzei, Fujiwara no Teika was among the finest *tanka* poets, a teacher of *tanka,* and an influential essayist on poetry who, more than anyone else, set the standards of taste for his time and times to come. He is considered to rank with Basho, Saigyo, and Kakinomoto Hitomaro as among Japan's finest poets. Associating himself with retired Emperor Gotoba, in 1201 he was appointed to the Bureau of Poetry and later was the compiler of two of the Imperial anthologies, the *Shinkokinshu* and the *Shinchokusenshu.* He edited *The Tale of Genji* among other famous works, and it is thought that he also compiled the famous collection of *One Hundred Poems by One Hundred Poets,* which is Japan's most popular anthology of poetry.

**FURTHER READING:** "Eighty-four Tanka" and "An Outline for Composing Tanka, with a compendium of good tanka (complete translation)," in Hiroaki Sato and Burton Watson, eds. *From the Country of Eight Islands: An Anthology of Japanese Poetry,* 1981.

### Like Seaweed Burnt for Salt

Like seaweed burnt for salt
I blaze for him.
He doesn't come.
In night calm at the inlet
my body smoulders.

---

10. Ren'in was Chōmei's Buddhist name.

## In the Infinite Night

In the infinite night
your restless hair
spills blackly
across our sleeves
like random dew.

## Wind Pierces

Wind pierces
transparently.
Frost forms
on the evening moon's
light.

## Stars Must Be Clear

Stars must be clear
beyond this wind.
I listen
to random hailstones
clatter.   .

## ■ Dogen (1200–1253) (poems)

TRANSLATED BY BRIAN UNGER AND KAZUAKI TANAHASHI

Dogen is the founder of the Soto School of Japanese Zen Buddhism, which is one of the two largest Zen Buddhist orders in Japan (along with Rinzai Zen). He was born in Kyoto in 1200, apparently the son of an influential court minister. His father died when he was three, his mother when he was eight. Faced with these deaths, he abandoned the prospect of a career in court for a life of Buddhism. At a time when militarism and commercialism had permeated the monastic culture, many Buddhists considered it "the age of the decline of dharma." It was a time ripe for the introduction of new practices, and Dogen, who went to China in 1223 to study with Soto master Ju-ching (1163–1228), brought back Soto practice with him in 1227. He was responsible for disseminating this Zen teaching through his writings and by founding a practice center in Fukakusa in 1233 and Daibutsu Monastery in Echizen province a decade later. Though he is mainly known for his treatises on Zen, he also left behind a number of poems in Chinese and Japanese forms. Soto Zen emphasizes meditative practice and a view of time in which eternity rests on the knife blade of the instant. It states that all things contain a hidden "Buddha-nature," to which Zen practice awakens one. Thus, his poetry, like that of Ryokan (1758–1831), is infused with Zen insight into the natural world. For Dogen, a dewdrop reflecting moonlight is an image of Zen meditation (as the moon can be reflected in this tiny ball of water, so the whole universe resides in each human being). As Emily Dickinson says:

The Brain—is wider than the Sky—
For—put them side by side—
The one the other will contain
With ease—and You—beside—

**FURTHER READING:** Tanahashi, Kazuaki, ed. *Moon in a Dewdrop: Writings of Zen Master Dogen*, 1985.

## Mountain Seclusion

I won't even stop
at the valley's brook
for fear that
my shadow
may flow into the world.

## Bowing Formally

A snowy heron
on the snowfield
where winter grass is unseen
hides itself
in its own figure.

## On Nondependence of Mind

Water birds
going and coming
their traces disappear
but they never
forget their path.

## ■ Zen Stories *from Sand and Pebbles* (and other collections) (Thirteenth Century and Later) (wisdom stories)

### TRANSLATED BY NYOGEN SENZAKI AND PAUL REPS

These stories derive from the wealth of wacky, humorous, profound, and startling Zen literature collected into various story (*setsuwa*) compilations. Translators Nyogen Senzaki and Paul Reps are drawing in the main on *Sand and Pebbles* (*Shasekishu*), a thirteenth-century compilation of anecdotes written and compiled by Muju, a Rinzai Zen priest who lived at the Chojobi temple near the Atsuta Shrine in Nagoya.

**FURTHER READING:** Reps, Paul, ed. *Zen Flesh, Zen Bones*, 1989.

## The Moon Cannot Be Stolen

Ryokan, a Zen master, lived the simplest kind of life in a little hut at the foot of a mountain. One evening a thief visited the hut only to discover there was nothing in it to steal.

Ryokan returned and caught him. "You may have come a long way to visit me," he told the prowler, "and you should not return empty-handed. Please take my clothes as a gift."

The thief was bewildered. He took the clothes and slunk away.

Ryokan sat naked, watching the moon. "Poor fellow," he mused, "I wish I could give him this beautiful moon."

## Muddy Road

Tanzan and Ekido were once traveling together down a muddy road. A heavy rain was still falling.

Coming around a bend, they met a lovely girl in a silk kimono and sash, unable to cross the intersection.

"Come on, girl," said Tanzan at once. Lifting her in his arms, he carried her over the mud.

Ekido did not speak again until that night when they reached a lodging temple. Then he no longer could restrain himself. "We monks don't go near females," he told Tanzan, "especially not young and lovely ones. It is dangerous. Why did you do that?"

"I left the girl there," said Tanzan. "Are you still carrying her?"

## A Parable

Buddha told a parable in a sutra:

A man traveling across a field encountered a tiger. He fled, the tiger after him. Coming to a precipice, he caught hold of the root of a wild vine and swung himself down over the edge. The tiger sniffed at him from above. Trembling, the man looked down to where, far below, another tiger was waiting to eat him. Only the vine sustained him.

Two mice, one white and one black, little by little started to gnaw away the vine. The man saw a luscious strawberry near him. Grasping the vine with one hand, he plucked the strawberry with the other. How sweet it tasted!

## Joshu's Zen

Joshu began the study of Zen when he was sixty years old and continued until he was eighty, when he realized Zen.

He taught from the age of eighty until he was one hundred and twenty.

A student once asked him: "If I haven't anything in my mind, what shall I do?"

Joshu replied: "Throw it out."

"But if I haven't anything, how can I throw it out?" continued the questioner.

"Well," said Joshu, "then carry it out."

## The Stone Mind

Hogen, a Chinese Zen teacher, lived alone in a small temple in the country. One day four traveling monks appeared and asked if they might make a fire in his yard to warm themselves.

While they were building the fire, Hogen heard them arguing about subjectivity and objectivity. He joined them and said: "There is a big stone. Do you consider it to be inside or outside your mind?"

One of the monks replied: "From the Buddhist viewpoint everything is an objectification of mind, so I would say that the stone is inside my mind."

"Your head must feel very heavy," observed Hogen, "if you are carrying around a stone like that in your mind."

## Nothing Exists

Yamaoka Tesshu, as a young student of Zen, visited one master after another. He called upon Dokuon of Shokoku.

Desiring to show his attainment, he said: "The mind, Buddha, and sentient beings, after all, do not exist. The true nature of phenomena is emptiness. There is no realization, no delusion, no sage, no mediocrity. There is no giving and nothing to be received."

Dokuon, who was smoking quietly, said nothing. Suddenly he whacked Yamaoka with his bamboo pipe. This made the youth quite angry.

"If nothing exists," inquired Dokuon, "where did this anger come from?"

■ **Muso Soseki (1275–1351) (poems)**

TRANSLATED BY W. S. MERWIN AND SOIKU SHIGEMATSU

Thirteenth-century Zen roshi Muso Soseki was born in the province of Ise in 1275 to a Buddhist family. Like Zeus coming to Danae in a shower of gold coins, or like Jehovah coming to Mary, legend has it that the Bodhisattva Avalokiteshvara came to Muso's barren mother in a dream as a golden light and thirteen months later he was born. His mother died when he was three, and when he was nine his father took him to the Shingon temple in Kai to lead the religious life of a Mantrayana Buddhist. At eighteen, he took vows as a monk in Nara, but before he was twenty he left the sect and became a student of Zen. In the summer of 1305, he is said to have received enlightenment in a garden, after which he wrote his satori poem and was certified by his master Koho as enlightened. In his life, he founded fourteen temples and had more than thirteen thousand students. He is considered the father of Zen rock gardening, an aesthetic practice equally linked to architecture and spirituality. After his death, his writings were collected by his followers into three volumes of conversations, sermons, and poems. His poems were written both in Japanese and in Chinese. Though he is not well known in the West, his poetry, with a minimum of dogma, is a marvelous evocation of the world seen through Zen eyeglasses, and it reads well next to the work of other great mystical poets: Rumi, Kabir, and Wang Wei.

**FURTHER READING:** Merwin, W. S., and Shigematsu Soiku, trs. *Sun at Midnight: Poems and Sermons by Muso Soseki*, 1989.

### Three-Step Waterfall

At dangerous places
    awesome ledges
      three barriers
The loud water rushes
    The spray of the fall hovers
      It's hard to find the way
So many fish
    have fallen back
      with the stamp of failure on their foreheads
Who knows that this
    wind of blood
      is lashing the whole universe

### Toki-no-Ge (Satori Poem)

Year after year
    I dug in the earth
      looking for the blue of heaven
only to feel
    the pile of dirt
      choking me
until once in the dead of night
    I tripped on a broken brick
      and kicked it into the air
and saw that without a thought
    I had smashed the bones
      of the empty sky

### Beyond Light

The clear mirror
    and its stand
      have been broken
There is no dust
    in the eyes
      of the blind donkey

Dark
> dark everywhere
>> the appearance of subtle Zen
Let it be
> The garden lantern
>> opens its mouth laughing

## ■ Kenko (c. 1283–1350) (prose)

### TRANSLATED BY DONALD KEENE

The author we know by the name Kenko (which is his name as a Buddhist priest) was also called Urabe no Kaneyoshi or Yoshida no Kaneyoshi (because he lived for a long time at Yoshida in Kyoto). He is among Japan's finest writers of *zuihitsu* prose, or prose consisting of a miscellany of meditations, anecdotes, and observations, as in Sei Shonagon's *Pillow Book*. He was born into a family of Shinto priests of medium rank and became a priest in his own right, but his work reveals an ability to temper Buddhist doctrine that probably makes the work more attractive to a lay audience. He had a reputation as a poet of medium worth in his own time, whereas *Essays in Idleness* was unknown to his public; today, however, his essays seem to shine much brighter than the poems and, in fact, remain popular reading for schoolchildren and literati alike. A tale told about its composition, probably apocryphal, says that Kenko was in the habit of writing down his meditations on paper scraps and pasting them on his cottage walls. General Imagawa Ryoshun is credited with removing the scraps and arranging them into the work we know today, consisting of 243 sections of varying length.

FURTHER READING: Keene, Donald, tr. *Essays in Idleness: The Tsurezuregusa of Kenko,* 1967. Sansom, George, tr. "The Tzuredzure of Yoshida no Kaneyoshi," *Transactions, Asiatic Society of Japan,* 39, 1911.

## *from* Essays in Idleness

### 3

A man may excel at everything else, but if he has no taste for lovemaking, one feels something terribly inadequate about him, as if he were a valuable winecup without a bottom. What a charming figure is the lover, his clothes drenched with dew or frost, wandering about aimlessly, so fearful of his parents' reproaches or people's gossip that he has not a moment's peace of mind, frantically resorting to one unsuccessful stratagem after another; and for all that, most often sleeping alone, though never soundly. But it is best that a man not be given over completely to fleshly pleasures, and that women not consider him an easy conquest.

# 41

On the fifth day of the fifth month I went to see the horse race at the Kamo Shrine.[1] There was such a mob before our carriage, between us and the view, that we could see nothing. We all got out of the carriage and pushed towards the railing, but the crowd was particularly dense in that area, and there seemed no chance of making our way to the fore. Just then we noticed a priest perched in the crotch of an ōchi[2] tree across the way, watching the race. Even as he clung to the tree he was nodding drowsily, again and again waking himself just as he seemed about to fall.

People, observing the priest, laughed at his folly. "What an idiot! Imagine anyone being able to sleep so peacefully when he's sitting on such a dangerous branch!" It suddenly occurred to me, however, "The hour of death may be upon us at any moment. To spend our days in pleasure-seeking, forgetful of this truth, is even more foolish." I blurted out the words, and some people standing before me said, "That's certainly true. It is a most stupid way to behave." Turning round towards us, they said, "Please come through here," and made room, urging us to take their places.

Anybody at all might have made the same observation, but probably it came as a surprise at that particular moment and struck home. Man, not being made of wood or stone, is at times not without emotional reactions.

# 45

Kin'yo,[3] an officer of the second rank, had a brother called the High Priest Ryogaku,[4] an extremely bad-tempered man. Next to his monastery grew a large nettle-tree which occasioned the nickname people gave him, the Nettle-tree High Priest. "That name is outrageous," said the high priest, and cut down the tree. The stump still being left, people referred to him now as the Stump High Priest. More furious than ever, Ryogaku had the stump dug up and thrown away, but this left a big ditch. People now called him the Ditch High Priest.

# 51

The cloistered emperor, having decided to introduce water from the Ōi River into the pond of his Kameyama palace,[5] commanded the inhabitants of Ōi to build a waterwheel. He paid them generously, and the men worked hard for several days to construct it. But when the wheel was put

---

1. A feature of the Kamo Festival is the horse race from the first to the second *torii* of the Upper Kamo Shrine.

2. The azedarach, also called bead tree, etc.

3. Fujiwara no Kin'yo (died 1301) was a poet.

4. Ryogaku Sōjō (died about 1305) was a distinguished poet. He is here called *sōjō* but elsewhere is referred to as *daisōjō*, a position at the top of the Buddhist hierarchy.

5. This detached palace, used by the Cloistered Emperors Go-Saga (1220–1272) and Kameyama (1249–1305), stood near the present Tenryuji, west of Kyoto. The Ōi River flows nearby at Arashiyama. The cloistered emperor of this episode could be either Go-Saga or Kameyama.

in place it failed to turn at all. The men tried in various ways to repair it, but it stood there useless, stubbornly refusing to turn. The emperor thereupon summoned some villagers from Uji and ordered them to build a waterwheel. They put one together without difficulty and presented it. The wheel turned perfectly and was splendidly efficient at drawing up water.

Expert knowledge in any art is a noble thing.

# 71

As soon as I hear a name I feel convinced I can guess what the owner looks like, but it never happens, when I actually meet the man, that his face is as I had supposed. I wonder if everybody shares my experience of feeling, when I hear some story about the past, that the house mentioned in the story must have been rather like this or that house belonging to people of today, or that the persons of the story resemble people I see now. It has happened on various occasions too that I have felt, just after someone has said something or I have seen something or thought of something, that it has occurred before. I cannot remember *when* it was, but I feel absolutely certain that the thing has happened. Am I the only one who has such impressions?

# 97

There are innumerable instances of things which attach themselves to something else, then waste and destroy it. The body has lice; a house has mice; a country has robbers; inferior men have riches; superior men have benevolence and righteousness; priests have the Buddhist law.[6]

# 142

Even a man who seems devoid of intelligence occasionally says an apt word. A fierce-looking brute of a soldier once asked a companion, "Have you got any kids?" "Not one," replied the other. "Then," said the soldier, "I don't suppose you know what deep feelings are. You probably haven't a drop of human warmth in you. That's a frightening thought! It's having children that makes people understand the beauty of life." He was right. Would any tenderness of feeling exist in such a man's heart if not for the natural affection between parent and child? Even the man with no sense of duty towards his parents learns what parental solicitude means when he has a child of his own.

It is wrong for anyone who has abandoned the world and is without attachments to despise other men burdened with many encumbrances for their deep-seated greed and constant fawning on others. If he could put himself in the place of the men he despises, he would see that, for the sake of their parents, wives, and children, whom they truly love, they for-

---

6. The thought is Taoist, inspired by the passage in *Tao Te Ching:* "It was when the Great Way declined / That human kindness and morality arose" (Waley's translation). Kenko seems to mean that superior men (*kunshi*) are so puffed up with their virtues that they become incapable of practical action, and that priests are so bound by the letter of the Buddhist law that they become inhuman.

get all sense of shame and will even steal. I believe therefore that it would be better, instead of imprisoning thieves and concerning ourselves only with punishing crimes, to run the country in such a way that no man would ever be hungry or cold. When a man lacks steady employment, his heart is not steady, and in extremity he will steal. As long as the country is not properly governed and people suffer from cold and hunger, there will never be an end to crime. It is pitiful to make people suffer, to force them to break the law, and then to punish them.

How then may we help the people? If those at the top would give up their luxury and wastefulness, protect the people, and encourage agriculture, those below would unquestionably benefit greatly. The real criminal is the man who commits a crime even though he has a normal share of food and clothing.

# 149

You should never put the new antlers of a deer to your nose and smell them. They have little insects that crawl into the nose and devour the brain.

# 235

A man with no business will never intrude into an occupied house simply because he so pleases. If the house is vacant, on the other hand, travelers journeying along the road will enter with impunity, and even creatures like foxes and owls, undisturbed by any human presence, will take up their abodes, acting as if the place belonged to them. Tree spirits and other apparitions will also manifest themselves.

It is the same with mirrors: being without color or shape of their own, they reflect all manner of forms. If mirrors had color and shape of their own, they would probably not reflect other things.

Emptiness accommodates everything. I wonder if thoughts of all kinds intrude themselves at will on our minds because what we call our minds are vacant? If our minds were occupied, surely so many things would not enter them.

# 243

When I turned eight years old I asked my father, "What sort of thing is a Buddha?" My father said, "A Buddha is what a man becomes." I asked then, "How does a man become a Buddha?" My father replied, "By following the teachings of Buddha." "Then, who taught the Buddha to teach?" He again replied, "He followed the teachings of the Buddha before him." I asked again, "What kind of Buddha was the first Buddha who began to teach?" At this my father laughed and answered, "I suppose he fell from the sky or else he sprang up out of the earth."

My father told other people, "He drove me into a corner, and I was stuck for an answer." But he was amused.

# Muromachi/Momoyama Periods

### (1392–1603)

## ▪ Zeami Motokiyo (1363–1443) (noh play, prose)

Noh theater is a total theatrical experience, incorporating music, chanting, dance, poetry, prose, mime, and masks to create an ethereal atmosphere and to suggest the sublime experience of other worlds. This sublime beauty is called *yugen,* a term derived from Zen. *Yugen* is what lies underneath surfaces, hints of the supernatural, glimmers of a lost past, a ghostly world, or a hidden truth. Zeami writes that "The actor must consider *yugen* as the most important aspect of his art, and study to perfect his understanding of it." Dance, music, gesture, even an actor's display of anger, must be balanced, aestheticized, and made into an elegant show of virtuosity. The word *noh* means "accomplishment" and refers to a virtuoso performance. Noh was developed in the fourteenth century, primarily as a result of the efforts of Kan'ami Kiyotsugu (1333–1384), the father of Zeami Motokiyo. He was instrumental in blending ritual ceremonies and popular forms of entertainment into one art—the sources of noh include folk dance, Buddhist chanting, popular songs, ritual Shinto dance, and the variety show. In 1374, Kan'ami showed his newly synthesized art form to the shogun, Ashikaga Yoshimitsu, who became his patron, converting noh into an entertainment for the aristocracy. Kan'ami's son Zeami was an extraordinary actor from the age of seven and the noh theater's finest playwright; he took noh to its highest form, and his treatises on the art of noh theater are masterpieces of Japanese aesthetics. Zeami was so important a figure that a huge number of plays were attributed to him, though now only fifty (some scholars say a dozen) seem likely to have been written by him. Distinguished scholar Donald Keene suggests that twenty-five is a plausible number, and, since certainty is impossible, it seems wise to go with this compromise figure.

Noh plays often read well on the page, but the reader should be aware that (even more than in the Western theater) the shift from performance to literature has its costs. Many plays derive from classical tales, and the very fact that the audience is familiar with the story helps to take the emphasis off plot and put it onto psychology and mood instead. Some time after Zeami's death, noh performances were categorized into types and presented in a slate of five plays of five specific categories: god plays, warrior plays, woman plays, realistic (or mad) plays, and demon plays. The contemporary noh theater, however, performs its plays at a slower pace, so that the full slate of five plays has been shortened. *Semimaru* is a play of the fourth kind. The different character of the plays creates a varied theatrical experience, and short farcical skits take place between plays. The actor's lines are spoken in a stylized manner that makes no attempt at realistic voice inflections. As Donald Keene notes, "Every inflection of the actor's voice and every move of his body is prescribed by long traditions that have as their object the revelation of the ultimate meanings of the text, but these meanings transcend the meaning of any one line, and it is therefore possible for an actor to deliver a line perfectly without understanding it."[1] The actors are all men, and the principal actor often wears a beautifully crafted mask; the costumes are also works of art. Authors' lines are accompanied by three drummers and a flute player, who utter percussive, rhythmic noises, and the chorus sings for the main actor at moments of deep emotion and at the climax of the play when his movements turn into dance. Noh theater has excited considerable interest in the West—both William Butler Yeats and Bertolt Brecht wrote experimental noh plays, while Ezra Pound adapted a number of the major noh plays (with changes so radical that "translation" would not be the appropriate word). Twentieth-century Japanese fiction writer Mishima Yukio also wrote a number of modern noh plays.

FURTHER READING: Fenollosa, Ernest, and Ezra Pound. *The Classical Noh Theatre of Japan*, 1959. Keene, Donald. *Twenty Plays of the No Theatre*, 1970. Ueda, Makoto, tr. *The Old Pine Tree and Other Noh Plays*, 1962. Waley, Arthur, tr. *The No Plays of Japan*, 1921.

## Semimaru

### TRANSLATED BY SUSAN MATISOFF

PERSONS
Prince Semimaru (tsure)
Kiyotsura, An Imperial Envoy (waki)
Two Palanquin Bearers (wakizure)
Hakuga No Sammi (kyōgen)
Princess Sakagami, Semimaru's Sister (shite)

PLACE
Mt. Ōsaka in Ōmi Province

TIME
The Reign of Emperor Daigo; The Eighth Month

*(The stage assistant places a representation of a hut at the waki-position. Semimaru enters, wearing the semimaru mask. He is flanked by two Palanquin Bearers who hold a canopy over him. Kiyotsura follows them.)*

KIYOTSURA: The world is so unsure, unknowable;
　　　Who knows—our griefs may hold our greatest hopes.
　　　This nobleman is the Prince Semimaru
　　　Fourth child of the Emperor Daigo.

---

1. Donald Keene, *Twenty Plays of the No Theatre* (New York: Columbia University Press, 1970), 2.

KIYOTSURA AND ATTENDANTS: Truly in this uncertain world
    All that befalls us comes our way
    As recompense for what we've done before.
    In his previous existence
    He observed intently the laws of Buddha
    And in this life was born a prince,
    Yet why was it—ever since he lay,
    An infant wrapped in swaddling clothes
    His eyes have both been blind: For him
    The sun and moon in heaven have no light;
    In the black of night his lamp is dark;
    The rain before the dawn never ends.

KIYOTSURA: His nights and days have been spent this way,
    But now what plan has the Emperor conceived?
    He ordered us to escort the Prince in secret,
    To abandon him on Mount Ōsaka
    And to shave his head in priestly tonsure.
    The Emperor's words, once spoken
    Are final—what immense pity I feel!
    Yet, such being the command, I am powerless;

KIYOTSURA AND ATTENDANTS: Like lame-wheeled carriages
    We creep forth reluctantly
    On the journey from the Capital;
    How hard it is to say farewell
    As dawn clouds streak the east!
    Today he first departs the Capital
    When again to return? His chances are as fragile
    As unraveled threads too thin to intertwine.
    Friendless, his destination is unknown.
    Even without an affliction
    Good fortune is elusive in this world,
    Like the floating log the turtle gropes for
    Once a century: The path is in darkness
    And he, a blind turtle, must follow it.[1]
    Now as the clouds of delusion rise
    We have reached Mount Ōsaka
    We have reached Mount Ōsaka.

*(Semimaru sits on a stool before the Chorus. Kiyotsura kneels at the shite-pillar. The Bearers exit through the slit door.)*

---

1. In certain Buddhist texts the rarity of meeting a Buddha is compared to the difficulty of a blind sea-turtle's chances of bumping into a log to float on. The turtle emerges to the surface only once a century and tries to clutch the log, but it has a hole and eludes his grasp; this was a simile for the difficulty of obtaining good fortune.

SEMIMARU: Kiyotsura!

KIYOTSURA: I am before you.

*(From his kneeling position, he bows deeply.)*

SEMIMARU: Are you to leave me on this mountain?

KIYOTSURA: Yes, your highness. So the Emperor has commanded, and I
  have brought you this far.
 But I wonder just where
 I should leave you.
 Since the days of the ancient sage kings
 Our Emperors have ruled the country wisely,
 Looking after its people with compassion—
 But what can his Majesty have had in mind?
 Nothing could have caught me so unprepared.

SEMIMARU: What a foolish thing to say, Kiyotsura. I was born blind because
  I was lax in my religious duties in a former life.
 That is why the Emperor, my father,
 Ordered you to leave me in the wilderness,
 Heartless this would seem, but it's his plan
 To purge in this world my burden from the past,
 And spare me suffering in the world to come.
 This is a father's true kindness.
 You should not bewail his decree.

KIYOTSURA: Now I shall shave your head.
 His Majesty has so commanded.

SEMIMARU: What does this act signify?

KIYOTSURA: It means you have become a priest,
 A most joyous event.

*(Seminaru rises. The stage assistant removes his nobleman's outer robe and places
a priest's hat on his head.)*

SEMIMARU: Surely Seishi's poem described such a scene:
 "I have cut my fragrant scented hair
 My head is pillowed half on sandalwood."[2]

KIYOTSURA: Such splendid clothes will summon thieves, I fear.
 Allow me to take your robe and give you instead
 This cloak of straw they call a *mino*.

---

2. The poem referred to is by Li Ho and is actually a description of Hsi-shih (Seishi) rather than a poem
by her. The meaning of the original verses was that Seishi's fragrant locks rivaled the perfume of cloves or
sandalwood; however, the dramatist here misunderstood the Chinese and interpreted it as meaning she
had cut her locks and now would have to rest her head on a hard pillow of sandalwood. (See commentary
by Tanaka Makoto in Yōkyoku Shu, III, 205 [Nihon Koten Zensho series].)

*(Semimaru mines receiving the mino.)*

SEMIMARU: Is this the mino mentioned in the lines.
  "I went to Tamino Island when it rained"?[3]

KIYOTSURA: And I give you this *kasa* rainhat
  To protect you also from the rain and dew.

*(He takes a* kasa *from the stage assistant and hands it to Semimaru.)*

SEMIMARU: Then this must be the *kasa* of the poem
  "Samurai—take a *kasa* for your lord."[4]

*(Semimaru puts down the* kasa.)

KIYOTSURA: And this staff will guide you on your way.
  Please take it in your hands.

*(He takes a staff from the stage assistant and hands it to Semimaru.)*

SEMIMARU: Is this the staff about which Henjō wrote:
  "Since my staff was fashioned by the gods
  I can cross the mountain of a thousand years"?[5]

*(Kiyotsura kneels at the shite-pillar.)*

KIYOTSURA: His staff brought a thousand prosperous years,[6]

SEMIMARU: But here the place is Mount Ōsaka,

KIYOTSURA: A straw-thatched hut by the barrier;

SEMIMARU: Bamboo pillars and staff, my sole support.

KIYOTSURA: By your father, the Emperor,

SEMIMARU: Abandoned,

CHORUS: I meet my unsure fate at Mount Ōsaka.
  You who know me, you who know me not[7]

---

3. From the poem by Ki no Tsurayuki, no. 918 in the *Kokinshū*.

4. From the anonymous poem, no. 1091 in the *Kokinshū*.

5. From the poem by the priest Henjō, no. 348 in the *Kokinshū*.

6. There is a pivot-word embedded here: *chitose no saka,* the slope of a thousand years; and *saka yuku tsue,* the staff that brings steady prosperity.

7. An allusion to the poem, attributed to Semimaru himself, no. 1091 in the *Gosenshū*. The poem, about the Barrier of Ōsaka, originally had a meaning something like: "This is the Barrier where people come and go exchanging farewells; for friends and strangers alike this is Meeting Barrier."

Behold—this is how a prince, Daigo's son,
Has reached the last extremity of grief.

*(He lowers his head to give a sad expression to his mask.)*

Travelers and men on horses
Riding to and from the Capital,
Many people, dressed for their journeys,
Will drench their sleeves in sudden showers;
How hard it is to abandon him,
To leave him all alone;
How hard it is to abandon him,
To tear ourselves away.

*(Kiyotsura bows to Semimaru.)*

But even farewells must have an end;
By the light of the daybreak moon
Stifling tears that have no end, they depart.

*(Weeping, Kiyotsura goes to the bridgeway.)*

Semimaru, the Prince, left behind alone,
Takes in his arms his lute, his one possession,
Clutches his staff and falls down weeping.

*(Semimaru picks up the staff and* kasa, *comes forward, and turns toward the departing Kiyotsura. Kiyotsura stops at the second pine and looks back at him, then exits. Semimaru retreats, kneels, drops his kasa and staff, and weeps. Hakuga no Sammi enters and stands at the naming-place.)*

HAKUGA: I am Hakuga no Sammi.[8] I have learned that Prince Semimaru has been abandoned on Mount Ōsaka, and it pains me so much to think of him at the mercy of the rain and dew that I have decided to build a straw hut where he may live. (He opens the door of the hut, then goes to Semimaru at the shite-pillar.) The hut is ready at last, I shall inform him of this. (He bows to Semimaru.) Pardon me, sir; Hakuga is before you. If you stay here in this way, you will be soaked by the rain. I have built you a straw hut and I hope you will live in it. Please, come with me. (He takes Semimaru's hand and leads him inside the hut, then steps back and bows.) If ever you need anything, you have only to summon me, Hakuga no Sammi. I shall always be ready to serve you. I take my leave of you for now.

---

8. Hakuga no Sammi was in fact the grandson of the Emperor Daigo; and lived from 919 to 980; but here he is demoted to the position of a rustic, in inverse proportion to Semimaru's rise in position from being a menial to being Daigo's son.

*(He closes the door of the hut, then exits. Sakagami enters wearing the zō mask. Her robe is folded back from her right shoulder indicating that she is deranged. She stops at the first pine.)*

SAKAGAMI: I am the third child of the Emperor Daigo,
    The one called Sakagami, Unruly Hair.
    Though born a princess, some deed of evil
    From my unknown past in former lives
    Causes my mind at times to act deranged.
    And in my madness I wander distant ways.
    My blueblack hair grows skywards;
    Though I stroke it, it will not lie flat.

*(She smooths down her hair.)*

    Those children over there—what are they laughing at?

*(She looks to the right as if watching passersby.)*

    What? You find it funny that my hair stands on end? Yes,
    I suppose hair that grows upside down is funny.
    My hair is disordered, but much less than you—
    Imagine, commoners laughing at me!

How extraordinary it is that so much before our eyes is upside down.
    Flower seeds buried in the ground rise up to grace the branches of a
    thousand trees. The moon hangs high in the heavens, but its light
    sinks to the bottom of countless waters.

*(She looks up and down.)*

I wonder which of all these should be said to go in the proper direction
    and which is upside down?

    I am a princess, yet I have fallen,
    And mingle with the ruck of common men;

*(She proceeds to the stage while chanting.)*

    My hair, rising upward from my body,
    Turns white with the touch of stars and frost:
    The natural order or upside down?
    How amazing that both should be within me!

*(She enters the stage.)*

    The wind combs even the willows' hair

But neither can the wind untangle,
Nor my hand separate this hair.

*(She takes hold of her hair and looks at it.)*

Shall I rip it from my head? Throw it away?
I lift my sleeved hands—what is this?
The hair-tearing dance?[9] How demeaning!

*(She begins to dance, in a deranged manner.)*

CHORUS: As I set forth from the flowery Capital
   From the flowery Capital,
   At Kamo River what were those mournful cries?[10]
   The river ducks? Not knowing where I went
   I crossed the river Shirakawa
   And when I reached Awataguchi, I wondered,
   "Whom shall I meet now at Matsuzaka?"[11]
   I thought I had yet to pass the barrier
   But soon Mount Otowa fell behind me
   How sad it was to leave the Capital!
   Pine crickets, bell crickets, grasshoppers,
   How they cried in the dusk at Yamashina!
   I begged the villagers, "Don't scold me, too!"
   I may be mad, but you should know
   My heart is a pure rushing stream:
   "When in the clear water
   At Ōsaka Barrier
   It sees its reflection
   The tribute horse from Mochizuki
   Will surely shy away."[12]
   Have my wanderings brought me to the same place?
   In the running stream I see my reflection.
   Though my own face, it horrifies me:
   Hair like tangled briers crowns my head
   Eyebrows blackly twist—yes, that is really
   Sakagami's reflection in the water.

---

9. The *batō* dance is described thus in *The Pillow Book of Sei Shōnagon* (translation by Ivan Morris): "In the Dance of the Pulled Head the dancer's hair is in disorder and he has a fierce look in his eyes; but the music is delightful."

10. The name of the river, *kamo*, meant a species of duck.

11. The name Matsuzaka contains the familiar pivot-word *matsu*, to wait.

12. A poem by Ki no Tsurayuki, no. 118 in the Shūishū. The horse referred to was presented as tribute to the moon in a special ceremony held at the height of autumn on the night of the full moon. The head-note in Shūishū attributes this practice to the reign of the Emperor Daigo.

Water, they say, is a mirror,
But twilight ripples distort my face.

*(Sakagami sits at the stage assistant's position, indicating she has arrived at Mount Ōsaka. Semimaru, inside the hut, opens his fan and holds it in his left hand as if playing his lute.)*

SEMIMARU: The first string and the second wildly sound[13]—
The autumn wind brushes the pines and falls
With broken notes; the third string and the fourth—
The fourth is myself, Semimaru,
And four are the strings of the lute I play
As sudden strings of rain drive down on me—
How dreadful is this night!
"All things in life
In the end are alike;
Whether in a palace or a hovel
We cannot live forever."[14]

*(While Semimaru is speaking Sakagami comes before the shite-pillar. Semimaru inclines his head toward her as she speaks.)*

SAKAGAMI: How strange—I hear music from this straw-thatched hut,
The sounds of a *biwa*, elegantly plucked—
To think a hovel holds such melodies!
But why should the notes evoke this sharp nostalgia?
With steps silent as the rain beating on the thatch
She stealthily approaches, stops and listens.

*(She silently comes to stage center. Semimaru folds his fan.)*

SEMIMARU: Who is there? Who's making that noise outside my hut?
Hakuga no Sammi, lately you've been coming
From time to time to visit me—is that you?

SAKAGAMI: As I approach and listen carefully—that's the voice of my
brother, the Prince!
It's Sakagami! I'm here!
Semimaru, is that you inside?

SEMIMARU: Can it be my sister, the Princess?
Amazed, he opens the door of his hut.

*(Taking his staff he rises and opens the door.)*

---

13. An allusion to the poem by Po Chü-i, no. 463 in the Wakan Rōei Shū.
14. From the poem attributed to Semimaru, no. 1851 in the Shinkokinshū.

SAKAGAMI: Oh — how wretched you look!

*(She comes up to Semimaru as he emerges from the hut.)*

SEMIMARU: They take each other hand in hand

*(They place their hands on each other's shoulders and kneel.)*

SAKAGAMI: My royal brother,
    is that indeed you?

SEMIMARU: My royal sister,
    is that indeed you?

CHORUS: They speak each other's names as in one voice.
    Birds are also crying, here at Ōsaka,
    Barrier of meeting — but no barrier
    Holds back the tears that soak each other's sleeves.

*(Both weep. During the following passage Sakagami returns to the middle of the stage and kneels.)*

CHORUS: They say that sandalwood reveals its fragrance
    From the first two leaves[15] — but how much closer still
    Are we who sheltered beneath a single tree![16]
    The wind rising in the orange blossoms[17]
    Awakens memories we shall preserve
    We who flowered once on linking branches!
    The love between brothers is told abroad:
    Jōzō and Jōgen, Sōri and Sokuri;[18]
    And nearer at hand, in Japan
    The children of Emperor Ōjin,
    The princes Naniwa and Uji,[19]
    Who yielded the throne, each to the other:

---

15. An expression used proverbially to indicate that genius can be recognized even in early youth. Here used to mean that a noble person reveals his character spontaneously.

16. Taking shelter beneath the same tree was an illustration of the concept that even casual contact in a previous existence might bring a karmic connection between people in their next incarnation. Because of some connection in a previous life Semimaru and Sakagami were born in this life as brother and sister.

17. The fragrance of orange *(tachibana)* blossoms was believed to summon up remembrance of people one once knew; here the memories are those shared by brother and sister.

18. Jōzō and Jōgen were siblings mentioned in the *Lotus Sutra*. Sōri and Sokuri were the son and daughter of a Brahman king of southern India. They were abandoned by their stepmother. After their death, their father found and recognized their skeletons on the island where they had been abandoned. The story is mentioned in the *Taiheiki* and the *Gempei Seisuiki*.

19. Sons of the Emperor Ōjin. The younger, Prince Uji, had been designated by Ōjin as his heir, but declined, saying the office belonged by rights to his elder brother. Prince Uji died first, and the empire went to Prince Naniwa, known posthumously as Emperor Nintoku.

All these were brothers and sisters
Bound in love, like us, like linking branches.

SAKAGAMI: But did I imagine my brother
Would ever live in such a hovel?

CHORUS: Had no music come from that straw-thatched hut
How should I have known? But I was drawn
By the music of those four strings,

SAKAGAMI: Drawn like the water offered to the gods

CHORUS: From deep wells of love and far-reaching ties.
The world may have reached its final phase[20]
But the sun and moon have not dropped to the ground.
Things are still in their accustomed place, I thought,
But how can it be, then, that you and I
Should cast away our royalty and live like this,
Unable even to mingle with common men?
A mad woman, I have come wandering now
Far from the Capital girdled by clouds,
To these rustic scenes, a wretched beggar,
By the roads and forests, my only hope
The charity of rustics and travelers.
To think it was only yesterday you lived
In jeweled pavilions and golden halls;
You walked on polished floors and wore bright robes.
In less time than it takes to wave your sleeve,
Today a hovel is your sleeping-place.
Bamboo posts and bamboo fence, crudely fashioned
Eaves and door: straw your window, straw the roof,
And over your bed, the quilts are mats of straw:
Pretend they are your silken sheets of old.

SEMIMARU: My only visitors—how rarely they come—
Are monkeys on the peak, swinging in the trees;
Their doleful cries soak my sleeve with tears.
I tune my lute to the sound of the showers,
I play for solace, but tears obscure the sounds.
Even rain on the straw roof makes no noise.
Through breaks in the eaves moonlight seeps in.
But in my blindness, the moon and I are strangers.
In this hut I cannot even hear the rain—

---

20. A familiar concept. Believers in the medieval Pure Land Buddhism were convinced that the world had reached the period of the end of the Buddhist Law (*mappō*). According to one method of calculation, this period began about 1000 A.D., and was to continue for another thousand years.

How painful to contemplate life in this hut!

*(Both weep.)*

SAKAGAMI: Now I must go; however long I stayed
The pain of parting never would diminish.
Farewell, Semimaru.

*(Both rise.)*

SEMIMARU: If sheltering under a single tree
Were our only tie, parting would still be sad;
How much sadder to let my sister go!
Imagine what it means to be alone!

*(Sakagami moves toward the shite-pillar.)*

SAKAGAMI: Truly I pity you; even the pain
Of wandering may provide distraction,
But remaining here—how lonely it will be!
Even as I speak the evening clouds have risen,
I rise and hesitate; I stand in tears.

*(She weeps.)*

SEMIMARU: The evening crows call on the barrier road,
Their hearts unsettled

SAKAGAMI: As my raven hair,
My longing unabated, I must go.

SEMIMARU: Barrier of Meeting, don't let her leave!

SAKAGAMI: As I pass by the grove of cedars . . .

*(She goes to the first pine.)*

SEMIMARU: Her voice grows distant . . .

SAKAGAMI: By the eaves of the straw hut . . .

SEMIMARU: I stand hesitant.

CHORUS: "Farewell," she calls to him, and he responds,
"Please visit me as often as you can."

*(Sakagami goes to the third pine and turns back to look at Semimaru.)*

Her voice grows faint but still he listens,

*(Sakagami starts to exit. Semimaru takes a few steps forward, stops and listens. His blind eyes gaze in her direction.)*

> She turns a final time to look at him.
> Weeping, weeping they have parted,
> Weeping, weeping they have parted.

*(Sakagami exits, weeping. Semimaru also weeps.)*

## The One Mind Linking All Powers

TRANSLATED BY DONALD KEENE

Sometimes spectators of the *Nō* say that the moments of "no action" are the most enjoyable. This is one of the actor's secret arts. Dancing and singing, movements on the stage, and the different types of miming are all acts performed by the body. Moments of "no action" occur in between. When we examine why such moments without action are enjoyable, we find that it is due to the underlying spiritual strength of the actor which unremittingly holds the attention. He does not relax the tension when the dancing or singing comes to an end or at intervals between the dialogue and the different types of miming, but maintains an unwavering inner strength. This feeling of inner strength will faintly reveal itself and bring enjoyment. However, it is undesirable for the actor to permit this inner strength to become obvious to the audience. If it is obvious, it becomes an act, and is no longer "no action." The actions before and after an interval of "no action" must be linked by entering the state of mindlessness in which the actor conceals even from himself his own intent. The ability to move audiences depends, thus, on linking all the artistic powers with one mind.

> "Life and death, past and present—
> Marionettes on a toy stage.
> When the strings are broken,
> Behold the broken pieces!"[1]

This is a metaphor describing human life as it transmigrates between life and death. Marionettes on a stage appear to move in various ways, but in fact it is not they who really move—they are manipulated by strings. When these strings are broken, the marionettes fall and are dashed to

---

1. Poem by an unknown Zen master. The last two lines may mean, "When life comes to an end the illusions of this world also break into pieces."

pieces. In the art of the *Nō* too, the different types of miming are artificial things. What holds the parts together is the mind. This mind must not be disclosed to the audience. If it is seen, it is just as if a marionette's strings were visible. The mind must be made the strings which hold together all the powers of the art. If this is done the actor's talent will endure. This effort must not be confined to the times when the actor is appearing on the stage: day or night, wherever he may be, whatever he may be doing, he should not forget it, but should make it his constant guide, uniting all his powers. If he persistently strives to perfect this, his talent will steadily grow. This article is the most secret of the secret teachings.

# Tokugawa/Edo Periods

## (1603–1868)

### ■ Ihara Saikaku (1642–1693) (novel)

TRANSLATED BY IVAN MORRIS

Ihara Saikaku was born into a wealthy merchant family in Osaka and appears to have lived a well-heeled life, though the death of his wife and later of his blind daughter brought him personal tragedy. He started off as a haiku poet and was such a prolific writer that he is said to have composed 23,500 verses in a single twenty-four-hour period. None of his poems is considered of particularly good quality. In 1682, he began writing prose in the phonetic syllabary *kana* and became the dominant writer of *ukiyo-zoshi,* or "tales of the floating world." Many of these tales were erotic in nature, and they described contemporary events and society, some of them fictional, some based on real occurrences. He was contemporaneous with the master haiku poet Basho and enjoyed the long, peaceful Tokugawa period, during which the spread of literacy and printing methods and the growth of urban centers and the merchant class allowed writers to break away from the patronage system and write for direct remuneration. He was an immensely popular writer, the author of such tales as *The Man Who Loved Love, Five Women Who Loved Love,* and *The Life of an Amorous Woman,* whose concubine heroine, struggling for money and survival, is Japanese literature's equivalent to Daniel Defoe's Moll Flanders. Like Moll Flanders, the protagonist of *The Life of an Amorous Woman* tells a series of ribald anecdotes about her life, strung together in picaresque fashion. In the chapter given, the protagonist narrates her life as a young courtesan; as the novel progresses and her beauty diminishes, her life takes a downward turn as she becomes a prostitute of the street.

**FURTHER READING:** Ihara, Saikaku. *Five Women Who Loved Love.* Translated by Wm. Theodore de Barry, 1995; *The Scheming World.* Translated by Masanori Takatsuka and David C. Stubbs, 1965. Morris, Ivan, tr. *The Life of an Amorous Woman and Other Writings by Ihara Saikaku,* 1963.

## from *The Life of an Amorous Woman**

### A Beauty of Easy Virtue

By the West Gate of the Kiyomizu Temple a woman sat strumming on her *samisen.* And as she played, I heard her sing these words:

"Bitter is the Floating World[1]
And pitiful this frame of mine!
Would that I could alter into dew
My life that I prize so little."

Her voice was gentle. She was a beggar woman.

Wretched indeed was her appearance! One could imagine that in the summer she must wear heavy padded clothes, and that in the winter, when the mountain winds blow fiercely from all directions, she would have nothing to protect her but an unlined summer dress. Seeing her in this present condition, I inquired what manner of person she had been in the past, and was told that, in the days when the gay quarters had been at the Sixth Avenue,[2] this woman had flourished as one of the great courtesans,[3] being known as Katsuragi the Second. Since then she had fallen on bad days, as indeed is the way of this world, and finally reached her present state. In the autumn, when I went to view the cherry trees in their russet tints, I and the others of my party pointed at this woman and laughed. Little do we know what fate has prepared for us!

At about this time my parents fell into sorrowful adversity; they had unthinkingly become surety at the request of a certain man, who had then

---

*The translator's notes have been shortened in places.

1. *The Floating World* (ukiyo-gura). *Ukiyo* (floating world) was the conventional image used by writers, both lay and clerical, to convey the transitoriness of present life; in Saikaku's time it also suggested the fugitive pleasures of the demimonde; hence *ukiyo-e,* the genre paintings. By further extension, *ukiyo* meant "fashionable," "up-to-date," as in *ukiyo-motoyui* (fashionable type of paper cord for tying the hair). It also had the sense of "depraved" as in *ukiyo-dera* (the temple of a depraved priest).

2. *at the Sixth Avenue* (Rokujō ni). In 1602 the licensed quarter was moved from Yanagi-machi to Muro-machi at the Sixth Avenue; in 1641 it was established at Shimabara, northwest of the Nishi Honganji (Temple).

3. *the great courtesans* (tayū). *Jorō* is the term for "a girl of pleasure," a generic term including the entire gamut of professional women, from the most exalted courtesan (tayū) whose nightly hire was the equivalent of about $58 (£21), to the meanest strumpet (hashi-jorō), who might cost a mere 40 cents (3 s). "High (-ranking)," "top (-ranking)" or "great" courtesan in the text will invariably refer to *tayū.*

disappeared without a trace, leaving my parents much embarrassed over how they might obtain the money for which they were now held answerable. Finding no other means to extricate themselves, they sold me to the Kambayashi in Shimabara[4] for fifty gold koban,[5] and thus it was that I unexpectedly found myself in this profession. I was now just fifteen years old and, being in the fullness of my beauty, was—or so my new employer[6] said as she looked with rejoicing to the future—unequalled in the Moon Capital.[7]

As a rule, the floating trade[8] is one that a girl learns, by means of observation and without any special lessons, from the time that she is first employed as apprentice[9] in a house of pleasure. But I, being a "midway starter,"[10] had to learn the new fashions all at once. These, I may say, differ in every respect from the ways of ordinary townsfolk. A courtesan shaves her eyebrows, paints heavily above her forehead and eyes with an ink stick, wears her hair in a great Shimada without inserting any wooden support;[11] she secures her coiffure with a single hidden paper cord, decorating it outside with a wide band that she has folded into a narrow strip, and, forbidding even one stray wisp, she plucks her hair carefully from the back of her neck. Her long hanging sleeves are cut in the modern fashion, measuring two and a half feet at the bottom; no padding is used at the hips, and the bottom of her skirt is wide. The courtesan's buttocks should look flat as an open fan. A wide, unpadded sash is tied loosely about her and artlessly secures her three layers of clothing. Underneath she wears a petticoat of triple width, tying it rather higher than do women who are not of the profession.

---

4. *Kambayashi.* Famous house of assignation (*ageya*) in the Shimabara district.

5. *fifty gold koban (gojū-ryō).* The equivalent of about $2,300 (£820).

6. *employer* (oyakata). Being an *age-jorō* (high-class courtesan), she did not, like the lowly *mise-jorō,* live in the house where she practised her trade, but was called to the various *ageya* as her services were required. The *age-jorō,* a number of whom normally lived together in the house of their employer, were called out to entertain guests in various *ageya* (houses of assignation), as opposed to the far less dignified *mise-jorō,* who plied their trade in the houses (*mise*) where they lived. In this sense the *age-jorō* belonged more to the category of professional entertainer than to that of mere prostitute, the latter class being represented by *mise-jorō, yaha-tsu* (streetwalkers), etc. In Saikaku's time, the term *geisha* was not used in its modern sense (it referred to any person, male or female, whose profession was based on artistic accomplishment), nor was there any real equivalent to the present-day *geisha* institution. Even the most exalted and artistically accomplished *tayū* could be hired by the night for sexual purposes, although it is true that she might on occasion turn down a client if he was too displeasing, a luxury which her less elevated colleagues could ill afford.

7. *Moon Capital* (Tsuki no Miyako). "Moon" is used here (i) as a conventional epithet (*engo*) in relation with Kyōto, (ii) to imply that the heroine's beauty, now that she has reached the age of 16 (Japanese count), is fully developed like that of the 16-day-old moon.

8. *the floating trade* (nagare no kotowaza). Euphemism for prostitution; the image is the same as in *ukiyo.* See note 1 above.

9. *apprentice* (kaburo). The young apprentices in question (called *kaburo*) were employed in the brothels and other houses of pleasure to entertain visitors, pour their *sake,* etc.; they themselves normally became courtesans when they reached the proper age.

10. "*midway starter*" (*tsukidashi*). Tsukidashi, as used in the present context, were girls who became courtesans without having gone through the apprenticeship of being *kaburo.*

11. *wooden support* (komakura). Lit., "little pillow," a thin strip of wood normally used to prepare and raise the Shimada coiffure. Courtesans, with their very luxuriant hair, did not need to raise their Shimada artificially by inserting a support of this kind.

A courtesan, also, has many special ways of walking. When she sallies forth, she usually wears no socks and adopts a floating walk;[12] on reaching the house of assignation,[13] she trips in nimbly; in the parlour she uses the soft-footed gait; this is followed by a hasty gait as she goes up the stairs. When it comes to leaving, she lets the servant arrange her sandals for her and slips them on without even looking; in the street she walks with her head held high and does not step aside for anyone.

There are many ways of winning a man's favour. The "amorous gaze," as they call it, consists of looking at some man, even though he be a complete stranger, in such a fashion as to make him believe that one finds him most attractive. Again, when evening comes at the house of assignation, one may go out on the front veranda and, if one sees some man of one's acquaintance on the street, one can throw him a distant glance; thereafter one sits down casually and, being sure that the man does not notice, gives one's hand to the town drum-holder[14] who has accompanied him on his jaunt; one praises the crest on the drum-holder's coat, or again his hair style, his modish fan or any other mark of elegance that may catch one's attention.

"You're a fellow to capture any woman's heart! From whom, pray tell me, did you learn that style of hair?" So saying, one strikes him smartly[15] on the back and returns into the house. However much experienced this drum-holder may be in the ways of the world, he is bound to succumb to such flattery from a woman; he now feels sure that, if he woos her at the proper opportunity, he will have her for himself. In anticipation he casts aside all desire for selfish gain: he sings her praises in the company of great men, and, should some bad rumour be noised abroad about her, he will put his own name in pawn to see her cleared.

One way to cause pleasure to a man is to tear up some letter that one does not need, crumple it into a ball and throw it at him.[16] The method is simple and requires no special material; yet there is many a dull-witted courtesan who cannot even manage this.

---

12. *a floating walk* (uke-ayumi). Coquettish style of walking affected by courtesans. The woman would walk slowly along the street, her body turned slightly aside, and her feet moving as though she were kicking up something with the tips of her toes.

13. *the house of assignation* (yadoya). Same as *ageya* (note 6 above).

14. *town drum-holder* (machi no taiko). This refers to an amateur *taiko-mochi* from outside the gay quarters, as opposed to those professional *taiko-mochi* who lived within the Shimabara area. Both kinds accompanied customers on their visits to houses of assignation and played a central role in the world of courtesans by recommending them to potential clients or, alternatively, by pointing out their defects. It was important, therefore, for these women to be on the best of terms with the *taiko-mochi,* and we are here given an example of an effort to cultivate good relations.

15. *strikes him smartly on the back* (pisshari pon to tataki). Standard coquettish gesture favoured by Japanese women.

16. *throw it at him* (kore wo uchitsukete). For a Japanese woman to throw some light object (a ball of paper, a match, etc.) playfully at a man is another coquettish gesture (cf. note 15 above) and is supposed to indicate that she is interested in him.

There were girls, I remember, who, though they were every jot as comely as the others, had no customer on the appointed day of payment[17] and were bidden to make their personal offerings[18] to the house. Such a courtesan will try to have the others think that she does in fact have an appointed lover, for whom she is now waiting; but her pretence is to no effect and everyone in the house treats the unwanted girl with disdain. She sits alone in a corner of the room, without even a proper table, munching her cold rice and her eggplant pickles flavoured with raw soy sauce. So long as no one sees her, she can bear the humiliation; yet it is all most painful. When she returns to her abode and sees her employer's expression,[19] she assumes a timid air and softly asks the maid to heat the water.[20] There are indeed many painful sides to a courtesan's life; but we can have no sympathy with those foolish women who slight a money-spending customer because he is not exactly to their taste, and who pass their time in idleness. Such women bring trouble on their masters and disregard their own standing in the world. Nor should a courtesan, when she is entertaining a customer at sakè, lard her conversation with over-clever repartee and display her parts with much ingenious talk. Such tactics may avail if her companion is a real gallant and well versed in the ways of the world; but, if he is an inexperienced man who has only dabbled in these paths, he will be abashed by such a show and will acquit himself ill with the woman. When they retire to bed, he may be gasping with excitement; yet he will be too overawed to perform the proper motions; his occasional remarks will be uttered in a quivering voice; and, though he should by rights be enjoying what he has bought with his own money, yet he finds it all most trying. He is just like a man who knows nothing about the art of the tea ceremony, yet finds himself thrust into the seat of honour.[21]

All this is not to say that a courtesan should turn down such a man because he is not to her liking; there are other ways to handle him. Since

---

17. *day of payment* (mombi). The established days on which the courtesan was expected to receive a customer; if no man came for her, she was obliged to pay the fee (which he would normally have given to the proprietor of the establishment) out of her own pocket. This, of course, was considered a great humiliation for the girl in question, apart from the financial loss involved.

18. *personal offerings* (miagari). Payment by a courtesan to the proprietor of the fee that would normally be paid for her services. This was done on occasions when the girl preferred to rest and to reimburse the proprietor for the money which she would otherwise have earned; or again, when she was receiving a man to whom she was emotionally attached and preferred to pay the proprietor herself, rather than to have her lover do so; or, as in the present case, when no customer came on the appointed day of payment.

19. *employer's* (naigi no). This refers to the madam to whom the girl has been sold, and who is now highly disgruntled as a result of the latter's failure to obtain a customer on the day of payment.

20. *to heat the water* (gyozui tore). Courtesans always washed themselves thoroughly with hot water on returning from their visits to houses of assignation (*ageya*). Thus this girl prepares to wash herself even though she has had no customer. Perhaps she hopes to delude the other inmates of the house into thinking that she has really had an encounter. She is not too sure of herself, however, and addresses the maid softly (*kogoe natte*), instead of in the imperious manner customary for high-ranking courtesans.

21. *seat of honour* (joza). I.e., the chief guest at the tea ceremony (*cha no yu*), who first receives the tea bowl from the host and who leads the other guests in the various traditional formalities. For a sophisticated courtesan to dazzle a tyro with her verbal coruscations is as foolish as to choose someone who knows nothing about the tea ceremony for the role of chief guest.

he has chosen from the beginning[22] to give himself the airs of a man of the world, the woman should use him with the greatest decorum. When they reach the bedchamber, she is most polite in her bearing to the customer; but she does not undo her sash,[23] and soon she pretends to fall asleep. Seeing this, the man will as a rule move closer to her and lay his leg on hers. The courtesan still lies there quietly, waiting to see what may happen next. Her customer starts to tremble with nervousness and breaks into a sweat.

Then he pricks up his ears to listen to the happenings in the next-door room. Here things are advancing far more smoothly, perhaps because the customer next door is already intimate with his courtesan, or perhaps again, because he is an experienced man, who even at their first meeting has caused her to throw off all restraint. Listening in the dark, he hears the woman say, "Your naked body feels plumper than I had expected from seeing you in your clothes." Next comes the sound of amorous embraces. The man's actions become more vehement, and in his onset he pays little heed to the pillow or to the surrounding screen. The woman lets out a cry of heartfelt delight. In her spontaneous joy she throws aside the pillow and there is the sound of the ornamental comb in her hair as it snaps in two.

Meantime, from the floor above comes the voice, "Ah, ah, what bliss that was!" followed by the rustling of paper handkerchiefs.[24] And in yet another room a man who has been pleasantly asleep is tickled awake by his partner, who says to him, "Already it is growing light outside. Will you not leave me one more remembrance of this night?" Hearing this, the man, still half asleep, says, "Pray forgive me, but I cannot do another thing!" One wonders whether it can be that he has drunk too much sakè the night before; but then one hears the sound of his loincloth being undone. This hussy is clearly of a more sensual nature than most. Is it not truly a blessing for a courtesan to be endowed with a hearty appetite for love?

With all these pleasant diversions afoot in the nearby rooms the unsuccessful customer cannot catch a wink of sleep. In the end he awakens his companion and says, "The Festival of the Ninth Moon[25] will soon be

---

22. *Since he has chosen from the beginning* . . . (kashira ni). What follows is clearly a description of the heroine's own behaviour on such an occasion. As becomes clear later in the narrative, she was in the habit of treating tyros and other uncongenial customers with the greatest disdain; this, in fact, was the origin of her downfall.

23. *does not undo her sash* (obi wo mo tokazu). The *obi* (sash) is the most crucial part of a woman's attire and came to have a highly suggestive meaning in Japanese literature, especially drama. The voluntary untying of the sash suggested that the woman was ready to accept a man's advances; it was customary for lovers to undo each other's sashes. In the present context the undone sash is positive proof to Osan that her honour has been compromised.

24. *paper handkerchiefs* (hanagami). Paper handkerchiefs were used for blowing the nose, wiping the face and other purposes. They almost invariably figure in descriptions of erotic scenes and are a standard adjunct of the so-called Spring Pictures, the success of the amorous encounter being in proportion to the number of such handkerchiefs depicted.

25. *Festival of the Ninth Moon* (Kugatsu no sekku). I.e., the Chrysanthemum Festival; this was one of the fixed days of payment (*mombi*) in the Shimabara, the pleasure quarters of Kyoto, when courtesans were obliged to receive customers. The unsuccessful customer is, as a last resource, trying to win her favours by suggesting that he will visit her on this day. She, however, rebuffs his heavy-handed overtures.

with us. May I inquire whether you have any special friend who will visit you on that day?"

Such words are a cheering tonic for a courtesan. But his purpose is too transparent for her and brusquely she replies, "I shall be taken care of in the Ninth Moon—and in the First Moon, too."

Now the man is at a loss for anything to say that might bring him closer to her; and, alas, the time has come when she must get up and leave, like all the other courtesans. Then she is greeted with a comical sight as her customer unties his hair and secures it loosely into a whisk,[26] and also redoes his sash—all this to make others believe that his night has been crowned with the joys of intimacy.

As a rule a customer who has been used in such a heartless fashion will regard this courtesan with bitterness. On his next visit to the house he may call for another girl and spend five or even seven days there, indulging in lavish entertainment, thus causing the most lively regret to the courtesan who treated him so coldly. Or again, he may for once and all renounce these quarters and determine henceforth to consort for his pleasure with young actors.[27] As he leaves the house, he will call flurriedly for the friend who accompanied him here, and, paying no heed to the latter's reluctance at being dragged at dawn from the arms of his fair companion, he will say, "Come, let us quit this place and hasten our return!" With no further ado he takes leave of his disobliging courtesan.

But there are also ways to prevent this. One may, for instance, tweak the man's ear in the presence of his friends and, while smoothing his ruffled side-locks, whisper to him: "What a heartless rogue you are to leave like this with no regard for a woman's true feelings—ay, without even having bidden her undo her sash!" So saying, one strikes him on the back before hurrying back into the house. His companions, having taken note, will say to him, "You lucky dog! How do you manage to enravish a woman at the very first meeting?"

Delighted, the man replies, "Ah yes, I'm her lover and I'll warrant she'd give her life for me now! The attentions she showered on me last night were amazing. She even insisted on rubbing my shoulder that has

---

26. *a whisk* (chasen). Informal style of tying the queue into a bunch. Standing straight out at the back with a tuft at the end, and resembling the split-bamboo whisk used in preparing ground tea (*matcha*), a loose informal hair style, such as would be adopted by a man who has become thoroughly dishevelled after a successful night in the gay quarters.

27. *with young actors* (yaro-gurui). I.e., consort with professional catamites from the theatre. The term *yarō* originally referred to the type of close-cropped hairstyle that the government obliged young actors to adopt in order to reduce their homosexual attractions. Kabuki actors of the time (c. 1670–1690), were well known for taking the parts of women (*onnagata*). The theatre in Saikaku's time was a centre of paederasty.

Until 1652 young Kabuki actors (*wakashu*) continued to wear the forelock, or frontlet worn by boys until celebrating the ceremony of assuming manhood (*gembuku*) at the age of about 15, and this was one of the main aspects of their charms so far as male admirers were concerned; in that year the government, alarmed at the incidence of male immorality in the theatre, ordered actors to shave their heads like other men. A forelock continued to be the distinguishing mark of homosexuals.

been so stiff these past few days. Frankly, I can't understand why she was so taken with me. Surely you spoke to her in my favour and told her I was a man of property?"

"No indeed," his friends answer him. "No courtesan will use a man with so much warmth out of mere avarice. You'll have a hard time ridding yourself of her now!"

Thus they flatter him, and in due course the woman's stratagem has effect. If things can turn out well even after such an inauspicious start, how much better if she uses her client with true regard from the outset! Aye, he will be ready to give his very life for her!

If some undistinguished customer asks a courtesan to spend the night with him, she should not turn him down just because this is their first meeting. However, a man may be overawed in the presence of a high-ranking courtesan like herself and at the crucial moment he may let slip his opportunity. Should this happen, he will get up and leave, the amorous spell having been broken.

A woman of the floating trade[28] should not let herself be drawn to a man because of his handsome looks. So long as he is of high standing in the capital, she should willingly accept him, even if he be a greybeard or a priest. A young man who is liberal with his gifts and to boot boasts of a handsome appearance is a courtesan's natural ideal. But where is one to find a customer equipped only with such excellent attributes?

The appearance that an up-to-date courtesan favours in a man is as follows: his kimono, of which both the outside and the lining are of the same yellow silk, is dyed with fine stripes; over this he wears a short black crested jacket of Habutaé silk. His sash is wrought of light yellowish-brown Ryumon, and his short coat is of reddish-brown Hachijo pongee, lined at the bottom with the same material. His bare feet are shod in a pair of straw sandals, and he dons a new pair each time that he goes out. In the parlour he bears himself with dignity. The short sword by his side protrudes slightly from its scabbard; he wields his fan so that the air is blown inside his hanging sleeves.

Though the stone basin may already be full of water, he has it filled afresh; then he washes his hands in a leisurely fashion, gargles softly and performs his other ablutions with like elegance. Having completed his toilet, he bids one of the girl assistants fetch his tobacco, which his attendant has brought along wrapped in white Hosho paper.[29] After a few puffs he lays a handkerchief of Nobé paper by his knees, uses it with artless elegance and throws it away.

---

28. *A woman of the floating trade* (nagare no mi). I.e., courtesan (note 8 above).

29. *Hosho paper* . . . Nobé paper (Hōsho . . . Nobe). Nobe was one type of Hōsho, the latter being thick Japanese hand-made paper, originally used for important government documents. The dandy in question here uses it to wipe his face after a few puffs of tobacco. He is, of course, kneeling on the floor in the Japanese fashion; hence, "by his knees" (*hiza chikaku*).

Next he summons an assistant courtesan,[30] and, telling her that he would fain borrow her hand for a moment, he has her slip it up his sleeve to scratch the moxa that has been applied for the cramp in his shoulder muscles. Now he calls upon a drum courtesan[31] to perform the Kaga Air,[32] though paying but little attention to her as she strums on her samisen and sings; instead, in the middle of the tune, he turns to the jester[33] who is in attendance and says, "In yesterday's performance of *The Seaweed Gatherer*,[34] the supporting actor truly put Takayasu to shame with his skill." Or again, he may remark, "When I inquired of the Chief Councillor[35] about that old verse I was mentioning the other day, he confirmed that it was indeed the work of Ariwara no Motokata."[36]

In the presence of a customer who—without giving himself airs—starts out with some elegant conversation of this kind, and who in all things shows an attitude of perfect dignity and composure, even a top-ranking courtesan is overawed and inspired with a new spirit of modesty. Everything that the man does seems to her admirable and she looks on him with awe; the result is that she quite throws off her usual haughty air and comes to humour his every whim.

The pride displayed by courtesans of high rank is always due to their having been pampered by customers. In the palmy days of the gay quarters at Edo there was a connoisseur of fashion named Sakakura who grew intimate with the great courtesan Chitosé. This woman was much given to drinking saké; as a side dish she relished the so-called flower crabs, to be found in the Mogami River in the East, and these she had pickled in salt

---

30. *assistant courtesan* (hikifune-jorō). Lit., "tow-boat courtesan." The *hikifune-jorō* were of the same rank as the *kakoi* and their fee was the same; they accompanied the *tayū* to the house of assignation (*ageya*) and helped to entertain the guests. The *kakoi* ranked third (after *tayū* and *tenjin*) in the hierarchy of *age-jorō* (high-class courtesans) in Kyōto and Osaka. In a town like Murotsu where there were no *tayū* or *tenjin*, the *kakoi* occupied the highest rank. In Shimabara (Kyōto) the *kakoi's* fee was 18 *momme* of silver (equivalent to about $14; £5).

31. *drum courtesan* (taiko-joro). Courtesan who helped to entertain a tayu's guests by playing the samisen, singing, etc. Her rank and fee were the same as that of a *kakoi*.

32. *Kaga Air* (Kaga-bushi). Ballad especially popular during the 1660s.

33. *jester* (massha). Lit., "subordinate shrine," another word for "drum-holder" (*taikomochi*). In the Edo Period drum-holders were professional male entertainers, corresponding (very roughly) to European jesters, buffoons or "allowed fools"; they would accompany customers on drinking expeditions to the gay quarters, where they often had the role of elegant panders. They would frequently supervise the entertainment at fashionable parties and had considerable influence over the courtesans.

34. *The Seaweed Gatherer* (Mekari). Nō play by Zenchiku (1405–1468). The supporting actor or deutaroginist in a Nō play is known as the *waki;* he is second in importance and usually acts as a foil to the main character, the *shite*. Takayasu belonged to a famous family of *waki* actors that lasted until the Meiji Period. The dandy is making a show of his artistic discrimination by preferring a lesser-known actor to the established master.

35. *Chief Councillor* (Dainagon). One of the high court officials in Kyōto. Since real power had long since passed out of the hands of the court, these aristocratic officials concentrated on ceremonial functions and also on the preservation of classical learning and artistic forms. A Chief Councillor would therefore be an appropriate person to consult about the authorship of an old verse. By mentioning that he has done so, the dandy not only makes further show of his artistic interests, but suggests that he is familiar with court circles, and is also something of a scholar.

36. *Ariwara no Motokata*. Heian poet and grandson of Narihira. He is the author of the first poem in the *Kokinshū* anthology.

for her enjoyment. Knowing this, Sakakura commissioned a painter of the Kano School[37] to execute her bamboo crest[38] in powdered gold on the tiny shells of these crabs; he fixed the price of each painted shell at one rectangular piece of gold[39] and presented them to Chitosé throughout the year, so that she never lacked for them.

Again, in Kyoto there was a connoisseur called Ishiko. This man was much smitten with the high-ranking courtesan Nokazé, for whom he would purchase the most rare and fashionable wares, hastening to do so before anyone else could acquire them. On one occasion, Nokazé received a wadded autumn kimono dyed with pale scarlet; the silk was of fully dappled design and in the centre of each dapple a hole had been burned with a taper, so that one could see through the surface of the dress into the scarlet-tinted wadding. This material was of matchless elegance, and the single kimono was said to have cost close upon twenty-five pounds of silver.

In Osaka, too, there was a man, since deceased, who called himself Nisan, and who had made Dewa of the Nagasaki House into his private courtesan.[40] During one gloomy autumn he made show of his great compassion by paying for numerous courtesans in the Kuken-cho[41] who were not in demand by other customers; this merciful usage of her colleagues afforded much comfort to Dewa. On another occasion, when the clover bloomed profusely outside the house, Dewa noticed that some of the water which had been sprinkled in the garden had come to rest on the leaf tips; it sparkled just like early morning dew, and Dewa was deeply moved by its beauty.

"I have heard," she said to Nisan, "that loving couples of deer are wont to lie behind clover bushes. How I should like to see this in real life! Surely these animals cannot be dangerous, for all they are equipped with horns."

Hearing this, her lover is said to have replied that nothing could be simpler than to grant her wish; he then—so the story has it—ordered the back part of her parlour to be demolished and had numerous clover bushes planted there, thus making the room into a veritable field; next he sent word during the night to people in the mountains of Tamba and had them round up wild deer of both sexes, who were dispatched to the

---

37. *Kano School* (Kanō no fude). Famous academic school of painting that flourished in the Momoyama and Edo Periods.

38. *her bamboo crest* (sasa no maru no jōmon). High-ranking courtesans all had their own crests and these were familiar to the habitués of the gay quarters.

39. *one rectangular piece of gold* (kinsu ichibu). I.e., I *ichibu-koban*. In other words, each little crab that Chitosé ate cost the equivalent of about $11 (£4). There were numerous stories in Saikaku's time of this type of extravagance.

40. *private courtesan* (agezume ni seshi). Nisan paid a sufficient sum to Dewa's employer so that he might visit her daily if so desired, and so that no one else might be allowed to enjoy her favours. This was a normal procedure for wealthy men if they had some favourite courtesan, and the system carries over into the present-day *geisha* institution.

41. *Kuken-cho*. A centre of houses of assignation in Shinmachi.

house. On the following day he was able to show them to Dewa; after which he had the parlour restored to its former state. Surely Heaven will someday punish men like these, who, though endowed with little virtue, permit themselves luxury that even noblemen can ill afford![42]

Now, concerning my own career as a top courtesan, though I sold my body to men who were not to my taste, yet I never yielded myself to them. Indeed, I used these men harshly, so that they came to regard me as a cold-hearted woman and to turn their backs on me. Day after day the number of my customers diminished; I was thus inevitably eclipsed by the other courtesans of my rank, and I began fondly to remember my past glory.

Truly, a courtesan can only afford to dislike a man while she herself is in great favour; for once she is no longer in demand, any customer will be welcome, not excepting servants, mendicant priests, cripples and men with harelips. When one comes to think of it, there is no calling in the world so sad as this one.

## ■ Matsuo Basho (1644–1694) (poems, travel diary)

Matsuo Basho is Japan's best-loved poet and is considered the world's unparalleled haiku poet. In Basho's time, haiku was not considered a form in itself, as in the modern era; rather, it was the initial stanza of a longer linked verse poem (*haikai*) composed by several poets in collaboration and was termed *hokku* (see discussion under Matsuo Basho and His School). Until the mid-seventeenth century, hokku was most often a comic verse, composed by the senior poet; it is required to include a *kigo*, or "season word," which explicitly or indirectly suggests a season. Basho was responsible for elevating this form from a trivial diversion to a serious art form. He also wrote some of the finest *haibun* (prose combined with hokku) in Japanese literature; his *Essay on the Unreal Dwelling* is particularly fine.

Matsuo Munefusa, who later took the literary name Basho, was born in Ueno, Iga province, in 1644. When he was between nine and twelve, he became a personal companion to Yoshitada, the third son of the local samurai lord, and with him studied linked verse of the Teimon school. Yoshitada died when Basho was twenty-two and the young poet left feudal service, drifting for a period of five or six years. He settled in Edo around 1672. There he was influenced by Nishiyama Soin, founder of the Danrin school of haikai, a style generally comic and allusive, emphasizing conceptual linkages between haikai stanzas rather than the verbal connection that the Teimon school championed. In Edo, he gained recognition as a poet, gathering students around him with whom he composed haikai. Around 1680, he settled in the countryside near Edo in a hut built for him

---

42. *Surely Heaven will someday punish* . . . (Ten mo itsu zo wa togame-tamawan). A conventional condemnation of bourgeois extravagance of the type that the Tokugawa authorities used to issue (with little effect) in the form of sumptuary edicts.

by a disciple, which was named Basho-an (meaning "Banana Tree Retreat") after a banana tree he planted beside his door. From this retreat he took the literary name by which he is best known. For the remainder of his life, he lived in this retreat (and in two others of the same name) and took frequent journeys across Japan, which he recorded in a series of magnificent travel diaries. The best of these, and the finest product in its genre, is his *Narrow Road to the Interior.* He died on such a journey in 1694, when he was fifty years old, composing his death poem at that time: "I fall sick traveling. / But through withered fields / my dream still wanders."

Basho's work shows the influence of the Daoist thought of Zhuangzi and Laozi and of Zen Buddhism, which he studied under a master called Butcho. Though he was influenced by Danrin and Teimon haikai, he developed his own style, and a Basho school of poetry survived him; without the supporting genius of the master, however, this style became moribund and lost dominance to the former two schools. In his own work, he moved from a more decorative poetics to an ideal of *sabi,* or a mood of desolate and lonely beauty, the Japanese sublime. In his last years Basho shifted toward an ideal he termed *karumi,* or lightness. This was an even simpler style, and it often celebrated the utterly humble and ordinary. Basho's poetry blazes with sudden and total presence, each word hinting at chasms of meaning that flicker at the edges of consciousness. "Words," says American poet William Carlos Williams, "are keys that unlock the mind." Each little hokku by Basho opens a hidden door and gives us entryway to what was always inside: the smallest processes of nature and the largest movements of the universe, which are often one and the same.

*Oku no Hosomichi,* the *Narrow Road to the Interior,* is Basho's famed travel diary. He had already composed a number of these, such as his *Journey to Sarashina* of 1688 and his *Essay from a Wanderer's Book-Satchel,* in which he linked the form of his diaries, prose interspersed with *hokku,* to the tradition of Ki no Tsurayuki's famous *Tosa Diary* of around 935. In the spring of 1699, he set out with his friend Iwanami Sora on a journey north from Edo along the Pacific coastline, across the island, down the Japan Sea coastline, and then across the island again. On this journey they suffered illness and dangers and dressed as Buddhist monks to assure their safety. The journal reflects these hardships as well as a spartan style of travel that may not reflect the realities of the journey, since Basho and Sora were entertained and put up by wealthy patrons along the way. Sora kept a more factual account that reveals that key events in Basho's version were fictional and that others were altered. This exaggeration (like the Sunday dinners at his mother's house that Thoreau artfully left out of his account of his spartan life in *Walden*) must be seen as part of the conversion of experience into art. After all, he revised the journal for years after the actual journey, and it is clear, as translator Hamill notes, that he wanted the physical journey to the "interior country" to open doors to the "spiritual interior" and to put more structure into the journey of the reader through his text than he may have encountered on the road. In spite of (or because of) this, *Narrow Road to the Interior* remains a remarkable blending of poetry and prose, the premier example of the travel diary in Japanese literature.

**FURTHER READING:** Keene, Donald. *World Within Walls: Japanese Literature of the Pre-Modern Era, 1600–1867*, 1976. Matsuo Basho. *Back Roads to Far Towns: Basho's Oku-no-hosomichi*. With a translation and notes by Cid Corman and Kamaike Susumu, 1968, 1986; *A Haiku Journey, Basho's Narrow Road to a Far Province*. Translated and introduced by Dorothy Britton, 1980; *The Narrow Road to the Deep North, and Other Travel Sketches*. Translated from the Japanese with an introduction by Nobuyuki Yuasa, 1966; *Narrow Road to the Interior*. Translated by Sam Hamill; illustrated by Stephen Addiss, 1991. Miner, Earl. *Japanese Poetic Diaries*, 1969. Stryf, Lucian, tr. *On Love and Barley: Haiku of Basho*, 1985. Veda, Makoto. *Basho and His Interpreters: Selected Hokku, with Commentary*, 1991.

## Twenty-one Haiku

TRANSLATED BY TONY BARNSTONE

In the cicada cry
nothing
of how soon it will die.

A high mountain path
where plum scent hangs in air.
Suddenly the sun!

A sound so crystal
it pierces constellations.
Someone beating clothes.

Above the garden
winter moon thins to a thread
as insects wail.

Dragonfly
trying to land
on a blade of grass.

No moon,
not even flowers, so I drink sake
alone.

A cuckoo sings
in wild bamboo.
Moonlight trickles through.

The bell hushes
and flower aromas swell
the evening.

Lightning.
Through dark air
a night heron screams.

How admirable
as lightning cracks
not to think life is brief.

Cicada shell;
it sang itself
away.

A night so icy
I burst from sleep
as the water jar cracks.

Rough sea,
and the river of heaven pours forever
over Sado Island.

As the sea darkens
wild duck cries
seem faint and white.

A frog leaps
into the ancient pond
—plop![1]

---

1. Basho's most famous poem, often imitated.

The bee emerges
from deep within the peony
—reluctantly!

On the dead limb
a crow alights
in autumn evening.

First cold rain.
Even the monkey seems to want
a straw raincoat.

Not even a hat
as the cold rain falls.
Who cares?

Even in Kyoto
I long for Kyoto
when the cuckoo sings.

*Basho's Death Poem*

I fall sick traveling,
but through withered fields
my dream still wanders.

## from *Narrow Road to the Interior*

TRANSLATED BY SAM HAMILL

The moon and sun are eternal travelers.[1] Even the years wander on. A lifetime adrift in a boat, or in old age leading a tired horse into the years,
every day is a journey, and the journey itself is home. From the earliest
times there have always been some who perished along the road.[2] Still I

---

1. "The moon and sun are eternal travelers." This line echoes the famous preface to a poem ("Peach Garden Banquet on a Spring Night") by the T'ang-dynasty poet Li Po.

2. "some who perished along the road." Bashō is thinking of T'ang poet Tu Fu (712–770) and the wandering monk Saigyō (1118–1190).

have always been drawn by windblown clouds into dreams of a lifetime of wandering. Coming home from a year's walking tour of the coast last autumn, I swept the cobwebs from my hut on the banks of the Sumida just in time for New Year, but by the time spring mists began to rise from the fields, I longed to cross the Shirakawa Barrier into the Northern Interior. Drawn by the wanderer-spirit Dosojin, I couldn't concentrate on things. Mending my cotton pants, sewing a new strap on my bamboo hat, I daydreamed. Rubbing moxa into my legs to strengthen them, I dreamed a bright moon rising over Matsushima. So I placed my house in another's hands and moved to my patron Mr. Sampu's summer house in preparation for my journey. And I left a verse by my door:

> Even this grass hut
> may be transformed
> into a doll's house[3]

Very early on the twenty-seventh morning of the third moon, under a predawn haze, transparent moon still visible,[4] Mount Fuji just a shadow, I set out under the cherry blossoms of Ueno and Yanaka. When would I see them again? A few old friends had gathered in the night and followed along far enough to see me off from the boat. Getting off at Senju, I felt three thousand miles rushing through my heart, the whole world only a dream. I saw it through farewell tears.

> Spring passes
> and the birds cry out—
> tears in the eyes of fishes

With these first words from my brush, I started. Those who remain behind watch the shadow of a traveler's back disappear.

\* \* \*

The second year of Genroku [1689], I think of the long way leading into the Northern Interior under Go stone skies.[5] My hair may turn white as frost before I return from those fabled places—or maybe I won't return at all. By nightfall, we come to Sōka, bony shoulders sore from heavy pack, grateful for warm night robe, cotton bathing gown, writing brush, ink stone, necessities. The pack made heavier by farewell gifts from friends. I couldn't leave them behind.

\* \* \*

3. "Even this grass hut / may be transformed / into a doll's house." This image—of Bashō's tiny thatched hut dwarfed by his patron's mansion—refers to Hina Matsuri, the Girls' Festival.

4. "transparent moon still visible." This is an allusion to a line from *The Tale of Genji*.

5. "Go stone skies." Go is an ancient Chinese board game played with black and white pieces called "stones," which create patterns as the game progresses.

The last night of the third moon, an inn at the foot of Mount Nikkō. The innkeeper is called Hoteke Gozaemon—Joe Buddha. He says his honesty earned him the name and invites me to make myself at home. A merciful buddha like an ordinary man, he suddenly appeared to help a pilgrim along his way. His simplicity's a great gift, his sincerity unaffected. A model of Confucian rectitude, my host is a saint.

$*$ $*$ $*$

On the first day of the fourth moon, climbed to visit the shrines on a mountain once called Two Wildernesses, renamed by Kūkai[6] when he dedicated the shrine. Perhaps he saw a thousand years into the future, this shrine under sacred skies, his compassion endlessly scattered through the eight directions, falling equally, peaceably, on all four classes of people. The greater the glory, the less these words can say.

> Speechless before
> these budding green spring leaves
> in blazing sunlight

$*$ $*$ $*$

Mount Kurokami still clothed in snow, faint in the mist, Sora wrote:

> Head shaven
> at Black Hair Mountain
> we change into summer clothes

Sora was named Kawai Sōgorō; Sora's his nom de plume. At my old home— called Basho (plantain tree)—he carried water and wood. Anticipating the pleasures of seeing Matsushima and Kisagata, we agreed to share the journey, pleasure and hardship alike. The morning we started, he put on Buddhist robes, shaved his head, and changed his name to Sogo, the Enlightened. So the "changing clothes" in his poem is pregnant with meaning.[7]

A hundred yards uphill, the waterfall plunged a hundred feet from its cavern in the ridge, falling into a basin made by a thousand stones. Crouched in the cavern behind the falls, looking out, I understood why it's called Urami-no-Taki, "View-from-behind-Falls."

> Stopped awhile
> inside a waterfall:
> the summer begins[8]

$*$ $*$ $*$

---

6. Kūkai, also called Kōbō Daishi (774–835), founded the Shingon Buddhist sect. The temple at Nikkō was actually founded by Shōdō (737–817).

7. "his poem is pregnant with meaning." Japanese poets often changed their names, as had Bashō himself. Traveling in Buddhist robes was both safer and in keeping with Bashō's spiritual pilgrimage.

8. "Stopped awhile / inside a waterfall: / the summer begins." This verse refers to Shinto-Buddhist spring ritual bathing.

A friend lives in kurobane on the far side of the broad Nasu Moor. Tried a shortcut running straight through, but it began to rain in the early evening, so we stopped for the night at a village farmhouse and continued again at dawn. Out in the field, a horse, and nearby a man cutting grass. I stopped to ask directions. Courteous, he thought awhile, then said, "Too many intersecting roads. It's easy to get lost. Best to take that old horse as far as he'll go. He knows the road. When he stops, get off, and he'll come back alone."

Two small children danced along behind, one with the curious name of Kasane, same as the pink flower. Sora wrote:

> With this *kasane*
> she's doubly pink
> a fitting name

Arriving at a village, I tied a small gift to the saddle and the horse turned back.

\* \* \*

Set out to see the Murder Stone, Sesshō-seki, on a borrowed horse, and the man leading it asked for a poem, "Something beautiful, please."

> The horse lifts his head:
> from across deep fields
> the cuckoo's cry

Sesshō-seki lies in dark mountain shadow near a hot springs emitting bad gases. Dead bees and butterflies cover the sand.

\* \* \*

Over the pass, we crossed the Abukuma River, Mount Aizu to the left, the villages of Iwaki, Sōma, and Miharu on the right, divided from the villages of Hitachi and Shimotsuke by two small mountain ranges. At Kagenuma, the Mirror Pond, a dark sky blurred every reflection.

We spent several days in Sukagawa with the poet Tōkyū, who asked about the Shirakawa Barrier. "With mind and body sorely tested," I answered, "busy with other poets' lines, engaged in splendid scenery, it's hardly surprising I didn't write much":

> Culture's beginnings:
> from the heart of the country
> rice-planting songs

"From this opening verse," I told him, "we wrote three linked-verse poems."

\* \* \*

Staying the night in Iizuka, we bathed in a mineral hot springs before returning to thin straw sleeping mats on bare ground—a true country inn.

Without a lamp, we made our beds by firelight, in flickering shadows, and closed our tired eyes. Suddenly a thunderous downpour and leaky roof aroused us, fleas and mosquitoes everywhere. Old infirmities tortured me throughout the long, sleepless night.

At first light, long before dawn, we packed our things and left, distracted, tired, but moving on. Sick and worried, we hired horses to ride to the town of Kori. I worried about my plans. With every pilgrimage one encounters the temporality of life. To die along the road is destiny. Or so I told myself. I stiffened my will and, once resolute, crossed Okido Barrier in Date Province.

* * *

We stopped along the Tama River at Noda, and at the huge stone in the lake, Oki-no-ishi, both made famous in poems. On Mount Sue-no-matsu, we found a temple called Masshozan. There were graves everywhere among the pines, underscoring Po Chu-i's famous lines quoted in *The Tale of Genji*, "wing and wing, branch and branch," and I thought, "Yes, what we all must come to," my sadness heavy.

At Shiogama Beach, a bell sounded evening. The summer rain-sky cleared to reveal a pale moon high over Magaki Island. I remembered the "fishing boats pulling together" in a *Kokinshū* poem, and understood it clearly for the first time.

> Along the Michinoku
> every place is wonderful,
> but in Shiogama
> fishing-boats pulling together
> are most amazing of all

That night we were entertained by a blind singer playing a lute to boisterous back-country ballads one hears only deep inside the country, not like the songs in *The Tale of the Heike* or the dance songs. A real earful, but pleased to hear the tradition continued.

* * *

Rose at dawn to pay respects at Myōjin Shrine in Shiogama. The former governor rebuilt it with huge, stately pillars, bright-painted rafters, and a long stone walkway rising steeply under a morning sun that danced and flashed along the red lacquered fence. I thought, "As long as the road is, even if it ends in dust, the gods come with us, keeping a watchful eye. This is our culture's greatest gift." Kneeling at the shrine, I noticed a fine old lantern with this inscribed on its iron grate:

> In the Third Year of the Bunji Era [1187]
> Dedicated by Izumi Saburō

Suddenly, five long centuries passed before my eyes. A trusted, loyal man martyred by his brother; today there's not a man alive who doesn't revere his name. As he himself would say, a man must follow the Confucian model — renown will inevitably result.

\* \* \*

Sun high overhead before we left the shrine, we hired a boat to cross to Matsushima, a mile or more away. We disembarked on Ojima Beach.

As many others often observed, the views of Matsushima take one's breath away. It may be — along with Lake Tung-t'ing and West Lake in China — the most beautiful place in the world. Islands in a three-mile bay, the sea to the southeast entering like floodtide on the Ch'ien-t'ang River in Chekiang. Small islands, tall islands pointing at the sky, islands on top of islands, islands like mothers with baby islands on their backs, islands cradling islands in the bay. All covered with deep green pines shaped by salty winds, trained into sea-wind bonsai. Here one is almost overcome by the sense of intense feminine beauty in a shining world. It must have been the mountain god Ōyamazumi who made this place. And whose words or brush could adequately describe a world so divinely inspired?

\* \* \*

Here three generations of the Fujiwara clan passed as though in a dream. The great outer gates lay in ruins. Where Hidehira's manor stood, rice fields grew. Only Mount Kinkei remained. I climbed the hill where Yoshitsune died; I saw the Kitakami, a broad stream flowing down through the Nambu Plain, the Koromo River circling Izumi Castle below the hill before joining the Kitakami. The ancient ruins of Yasuhira — from the end of the Golden Era — lie out beyond the Koromo Barrier where they stood guard against the Ainu people. The faithful elite remained bound to the castle, for all their valor, reduced to ordinary grass. Tu Fu wrote:

> The whole country devastated,
> only mountains and rivers remain.
> In springtime, at the ruined castle,
> the grass is always green.

We sat awhile, our hats for a seat, seeing it all through tears.

> Summer grasses:
> all that remains of great soldiers'
> imperial dreams

Sora wrote:

> Kanefusa's
> own white hair
> seen in blossoming briar[9]

\* \* \*

---

9. "Kanefusa's / own white hair / seen in blossoming briar." Kanefusa (1127–1189), although old, fought beside Yoshitsune.

The road through the Nambu Plain visible in the distance, we stayed the night in Iwate, then trudged on past Cape Oguro and Mizu Island, both along the river. Beyond Narugo Hot Springs, we crossed Shitomae Barrier and entered Dewa Province. Almost no one comes this way, and the barrier guards were suspicious, slow, and thorough. Delayed, we climbed a steep mountain in falling dark and took refuge in a guard shack. A heavy storm pounded the shack with wind and rain for three miserable days.

> Eaten alive by lice and fleas
> now the horse
> beside my pillow pees

\* \* \*

The guard told us, "To get to Dewa, you'd better take a guide. There's a high mountain and a hard-to-find trail." He found us a powerful young man, short sword on his hip and oak walking stick in hand, and off we went, not without a little trepidation. As forewarned, the mountain was steep, the trail narrow, not even a birdcall to be heard. We made our way through deep forest dark as night, reminding me of Tu Fu's poem about "clouds bringing darkness." We groped through thick bamboo, waded streams, climbed through rocks, sweaty, fearful, and tired, until we finally came to the village of Mogami. Our guide, turning back, said again how the trail was tough. "Happy you didn't meet many surprises!" And departed. Hearing this, our hearts skipped another beat.

\* \* \*

In Yamagata province, the ancient temple founded by Jikaku Daishi in 860, Ryūshaku Temple, is stone quiet, perfectly tidy. Everyone told us to see it. It meant a few miles extra, doubling back toward Obanazawa to find shelter. Monks at the foot of the mountain offered rooms, then we climbed the ridge to the temple, scrambling up through ancient gnarled pine and oak, smooth gray stones and moss. The temple doors, built on rocks, were bolted. I crawled among boulders to make my bows at shrines. The silence was profound. I sat, feeling my heart begin to open.

> Lonely silence
> a single cicada's cry
> sinking into stone

\* \* \*

Today we came through places with names like Children-Desert-Parents, Lost Children, Send-Back-the-Dog, and Turn-Back-the-Horse—some of the most fearsomely dangerous places in all the North Country. And well named. Weakened and exhausted, I went to bed early but was roused by the voices of two young women in the room next door. Then an old man's voice joined theirs. They were prostitutes from Niigata in Echigo Province and were on their way to Ise Shrine in the south, the old man seeing them off at this barrier, Ichiburi. He would turn back to Niigata in the morning, carrying their letters home. One girl quoted the *Shinkokinshū* poem,[10] "On the beach where white waves fall, / we all wander like children into every circumstance, / carried forward every day. . . ." And as they bemoaned their fate in life, I fell asleep.

In the morning, preparing to leave, they came to ask directions. "May we follow along behind?" they asked. "We're lost and not a little fearful. Your robes bring the spirit of the Buddha to our journey." They had mistaken us for priests. "Our way includes detours and retreats," I told them. "But follow anyone on this road, and the gods will see you through." I hated to leave them in tears and thought about them hard for a long time after we left. I told Sora, and he wrote down:

> Under one roof, prostitute and priest,
> we all sleep together:
> moon in a field of clover

\* \* \*

Here we visited Tada Shrine to see Sanemori's helmet[11] and a piece of his brocade armor-cloth presented to him by Lord Yoshitomo when he served the Genji clan. His helmet was no common soldier's gear: engraved with chrysanthemums and ivy from eyehole to earflap, crowned with a dragon's head between two horns. After Sanemori died on the battlefield, Kiso Yoshinaka sent it with a prayer, hand-carried to the shrine by Higuchi Jiro, Sanemori's friend. The story's inscribed on the shrine.

> Ungraciously, under
> a great soldier's empty helmet,
> a cricket sings

\* \* \*

Sora, suffering from persistent stomach ailments, was forced to return to his relatives in Nagashima in Ise Province. His parting words:

> Sick to the bone
> if I should fall
> I'll lie in fields of clover

---

10. The *Shinkokinshū* is the eighth imperial anthology of "new and old poems," and the primary source for Bashō's study of Saigyō's poetry.

11. Sanemori's story is told in *The Tale of the Heike* and in a Noh play by Zeami.

He carries his pain as he goes, leaving me empty. Like paired geese parting in the clouds.[12]

> Now falling autumn dew
> obliterates my hatband's
> "We are two"[13]

*   *   *

I stayed at zenshō-ji, a temple near the castle town of Daishōji in Kaga Province. It was from this temple that Sora departed here the night before, leaving behind:

> All night long
> listening to autumn winds
> wandering in the mountains

One night like a thousand miles, as the proverb says, and I too listened to fall winds howl around the same temple. But at dawn, the chanting of sutras, gongs ringing, awakened me. An urgent need to leave for distant Echizen Province. As I prepared to leave the temple, two young monks arrived with ink stone and paper in hand. Outside, willow leaves fell in the wind.

> Sweep the garden
> all kindnesses
> falling willow leaves repay

My sandals already on, I wrote it quickly and departed.

*   *   *

At the Echizen province border, at an inlet town called Yoshizaki, I hired a boat and sailed for the famous pines of Shiogoshi. Saigyō wrote:

> All the long night
> salt-winds drive
> storm-tossed waves
> and moonlight drips
> through Shiogoshi pines

This one poem says enough. To add another would be like adding a sixth finger to a hand.[14]

*   *   *

---

12. "Like paired geese parting in the clouds" recalls a poem of Basho's written while still in his teens following the death of his lord, Yoshitada; it also carries echoes of Tu Fu.

13. "Now falling autumn dew / obliterates my hatband's / 'We are two'" It was a custom for travelers to wear inscribed hatbands saying that they traveled "with the Buddha," thereby reducing risks.

14. "To add another would be like adding a sixth finger to a hand." This image is derived from *Chuang Tzu*, chapter 8.

Mount Shirane faded behind us and Mount Hina began to appear. We crossed Asamuzu Bridge and saw the legendary "reeds of Tamae" in bloom. We crossed Uguisu Barrier at Yuno-o Pass and passed by the ruins of Hiuchi Castle. On Returning Hill we heard the first wild geese of autumn. We arrived at Tsuruga Harbor on the evening of the fourteenth day of the eighth moon. The harbor moonlight was marvelously bright.

I asked at the inn, "Will we have this view tomorrow night?" The innkeeper said, "Can't guarantee weather in Koshiji. It may be clear, but then again it may turn overcast. It may rain." We drank sake with the innkeeper, then paid a late visit to the Kehi Myōjin Shrine honoring the second-century Emperor Chūai. A great spirituality—moonlight in pines, white sands like a touch of frost. In ancient times Yugyō, the second high priest, himself cleared away the grounds, carried stones, and built drains. To this day, people carry sands to the shrine. *"Yugyō-no-sunamochi,"* the innkeeper explained, "Yugyō's sand-bringing."

> Transparent moonlight
> shines over Yugyō's sand
> perfectly white

*　*　*

On the fifteenth, just as the innkeeper warned, it rained:

> Harvest moon—
> true North Country weather—
> nothing to view

*　*　*

A disciple, Rotsū, had come to Tsuruga to travel with me to Mino Province. We rode horses into the castle town of Ōgaki. Sora returned from Ise, joined by Etsujin, also riding a horse. We gathered at the home of Jokō, a retired samurai. Lord Zensen, the Keiko family men, and other friends arrived by day and night, all to welcome me as though I'd come back from the dead. A wealth of affection!

Still exhausted and weakened from my long journey, on the sixth day of the darkest month, I felt moved to visit Ise Shrine, where a twenty-one-year Rededication Ceremony was about to get under way. At the beach, in the boat, I wrote:

> Clam ripped from its shell
> I move on to Futami Bay:
> passing autumn

# ■ Matsuo Basho and His School (linked verse)

## TRANSLATED BY EARL MINER AND HIROKO ODAGIRI

During the seventeenth and eighteenth centuries, the art of haikai, or sequential composition of individual poems, evolved from an amusement to a serious pastime in which a number of poets would collaborate to create an individual sequence. Of the haikai poets, Matsuo Basho is considered Japan's finest. *Throughout the Town*, composed in 1690, is a kazen, or sequence of 36 stanzas. A haiku is a three line poem of 5–7–5 syllables, and a tanka adds two lines of 7 syllables each to that; in a sense, then, these are the building blocks from which Basho's school made its haikai. An initial stanza of 5–7–5 is joined to a lower stanza of 7–7, then that stanza of 7–7 syllables is joined to another stanza of 5–7–5, then another of 7–7 is joined in turn to that, and so the sequence is extended. The initial stanza, or hokku, is considered so important that it was sometimes thought of as an independent poem, like modern haiku, which share the hokku's syllabic form.

**FURTHER READING:** Keene, Donald. *World Within Walls: Japanese Literature of the Pre-Modern Era, 1600–1867,* 1976. Mayhew, Lenore, tr. *Monkey's Raincoat* = *Sarumino: Linked Poetry of the Basho School with Haiku Selections,* 1985. Miner, Earl, and Hiroko Odagiri, trs., *The Monkey's Straw Raincoat and Other Poetry of the Basho School.* Introduced and translated by Earl Miner and Hiroko Odagiri, 1981.

## *from Throughout the Town*

### 1

Throughout the town
above the welter of smelly things
the summer moon

BONCHŌ

### 2

Throughout the town
above the welter of smelly things
the summer moon
how hot it is, how hot it is
says a voice at every house gate

BASHŌ

*3*

How hot it is, how hot it is
says a voice at every farm gate
   although the weeds
have not been worked a second time
   the rice comes into ear

                KYORAI


*4*

   Although the weeds
have not been worked a second time
   the rice has come to ear
the charcoal ash is shaken off
the dried sardine broiled at noon

                BONCHŌ


*5*

The charcoal ash is shaken off
the dried sardine broiled at noon
   but in this back country
the use of coins is not yet heard of
   what a bother it is

                BASHŌ


*6*

   In this back country
the use of coins is not yet heard of
   what a bother it is
but he is an odd one to be talking
and swagger with an enormous sword

                KYORAI


*7*

He is an odd one to carry on
swaggering with an enormous sword
   he quakes in fright
from a frog croaking in the weeds
   as twilight thickens

                BONCHŌ

*8*

>        She jumps with fright
> at the frog's croaking in the weeds
>        as twilight thickens
> so in search of butterburr shoots
> her shaking hand puts out the lamp

                                                            BASHŌ

*9*

> While hunting butterburr shoots
> I shook the lamp and put it out
>        my waking to the Way
> came long ago at that season
>        of budding flowers

                                                            KYORAI

*10*

>        His waking to the Way
> came long ago at that season
>        of budding flowers
> now at Nanao Bay in Noto
> the winter cold is hard to bear

                                                            BONCHŌ

*11*

> At Nanao Bay in Noto
> the winter cold is hard to bear
>        all that I can do
> is suck upon the bones of fish
>        and think of old age

                                                            BASHŌ

*12*

>        All that he can do
> is suck upon the bones of fish
>        thinking of his age
> as he lets the mistress' lover
> through the side gate with his key

                                                            KYORAI

*13*

The mistress' lover was let in
through the side gate with a key
      stretching for a peek
the young maidservants overturn
      the folding screen

                                          BONCHŌ

*14*

      As they stretch forward
the young maidservants overturn
      the folding screen
the split bamboo drainboard gives
a forlorn appearance to the bath

                                            BASHŌ

*15*

The split bamboo drainboard gave
a forlorn appearance to the bath
      and to the seeds of fennel
that are all blown off their plants
      by the evening storm

                                          KYORAI

*16*

      The seeds of fennel
are all blown off their plants
      by the evening storm
will the priest return to the temple
as he feels the cold increasing

                                          BONCHŌ

*17*

Will the priest return to the temple
as he feels the cold increasing
      the monkey master
ages with his monkey and the world
      beneath the autumn moon

                                          BASHŌ

# ◼ Chikamatsu Monzaemon (1653–1725) (play, prose)

## TRANSLATED BY DONALD KEENE

Chikamatsu Monzaemon has often been called the Japanese Shakespeare and his play *The Love Suicides at Amijima* is considered to be his masterpiece. But the theater of Chikamatsu was considerably different from that of Shakespeare. He wrote most of his hundred-odd plays for the puppet theater (*joruri,* now called *bunraku*), in which a chanter performs all roles and all voices, accompanied by the music of a *samisen* (something like a small guitar), while black-clothed handlers move the jointed wooden puppets across the stage.

Chikamatsu was born in Echizen province to a lesser samurai family, which moved to Kyoto when he was in his teens. He writes of his life, "I was born into a hereditary family of samurai but left the martial profession. I served in personal attendance on the nobility but never obtained the least court rank. I drifted in the market place but learned nothing of trade."[1] He was born Sugimori Nobumori but apparently took the stage name Chikamatsu after staying at Chikamatsu Temple in Omi province when young. His play *Kagekiyo Victorious* transformed the puppet theater from rudimentary skits to what it is now. For a period of his life, he wrote for the live actor theater (kabuki), tailoring his plays to fit Sakata Tojuro, the premier actor of his day. He wrote *The Love Suicides at Amijima* in 1703, which was a great success; after Sakata Tojuro retired in 1705, he devoted himself to the puppet theater for the remainder of his life.

Chikamatsu, like the other dramatists of his day, would often dramatize recent sensational events in his play. In the case of *The Love Suicides at Amijima,* he actually interviewed people associated with the case. The tragic crux of his plays often lies in the conflict between the culturally powerful concept of *giri,* or duty, and natural human emotions. Since what constitutes such obligation and its hold over people is necessarily culture bound, there are times when modern Western readers (or viewers) of his plays will find themselves frustrated, but no more frustrated, ultimately, than they are by examples of duty that seem exaggerated and outmoded in the Western tradition, such as the Puritan *giri* of Hawthorne's Hester Prynne, which keeps her suffering in a repressive and narrow-minded society long after any external constraints on her have faded. Chikamatsu's plays are remarkably modern to Western tastes in part because they represent ordinary people, prostitutes and oil shop attendants, as seriously as

---

1. Donald Keene, tr. *Four Major Plays of Chikamatsu* (New York: Columbia University Press, 1961), 3.

Shakespeare would have written of royalty, and with the zest of Shakespeare's Falstaff.

**FURTHER READING:** Dunn, C. J. *The Early Japanese Puppet Drama*, 1966. Keene, Donald. *The Battles of Coxinga: Chikamatsu's Puppet Play, Its Background and Importance*, 1951; *Bunraku: The Art of the Japanese Puppet Theatre*, 1965; tr. *Four Major Plays of Chikamatsu*, 1961; tr. *Major Plays of Chikamatsu*, 1961. Shively, Donald H., tr. *The Love Suicides at Amijima*, 1953.


# The Love Suicides at Amijima

First performed on January 3, 1721. No source for this play, often acclaimed as Chikamatsu's masterpiece, has been determined, but traditional (though unreliable) accounts state that the suicides at Amijima occurred on November 13, 1720, one day earlier than in the drama. Takano Masami, a recent Japanese critic, has suggested that *The Love Suicides at Amijima* was a reworking of *The Love Suicides at Umeda* (1706) by Chikamatsu's rival, Ki no Kaion. There are striking points of resemblance between the two plays, and it may be that Chikamatsu, when shaping into dramatic form the events that took place at Amijima, borrowed from the earlier work. Chikamatsu's play has in turn been many times revised. The version most commonly performed today dates from the early nineteenth century.

CAST OF CHARACTERS
Kamiya Jihei, aged 28, a paper merchant
Konaya Magoemon, his brother, a flour merchant
Gozaemon, Jihei's father-in-law
Tahei, a rival for Koharu
Dembei, proprietor of the Yamato House
Sangoro, Jihei's servant
Kantaro, aged 6, Jihei's son
A Minstrel Priest
Porters, Fishermen, Persons of the Quarter
Koharu, aged 19, a courtesan at the Kinokuni House in Sonezaki
Osan, Jihei's wife
Osan's Mother (who is also Jihei's aunt), aged 56
Osue, aged 4, Jihei's daughter
Proprietress at Kawachi House
Kiyo, a receptionist
Tama, Osan's servant
Sugi, Koharu's maid
Maids, Prostitutes, Servants

# ACT ONE

## Scene One:

*A street in Sonezaki New Quarter, Osaka.*

TIME:
*November 4, 1720.*

NARRATOR:

> *Sanjo bakkara fungoro nokkoro*
> *Chokkoro fungoro de*
> *Mate tokkoro wakkara yukkuru*
> *Wakkara yukkuru ta ga*
> *Kasa wo wanga ranga ra su*
> *Sora ga kunguru kunguru mo*
> *Renge rengere bakkara fungoro.*[1]

The love of a prostitute is deep beyond measure; it's a bottomless sea of affection that cannot be emptied or dried. By Shell River,[2] love songs in every mood fill the air, and hearts stop short at the barrier[3] of doorway lanterns. Men roam the streets in high spirits, humming snatches of puppet plays, mimicking the actors, or singing bawdy ballads as they pass; others are drawn into the houses by samisens played in upstairs rooms. But here is a visitor who hides his face, avoiding the gift day.[4] See how he creeps along, afraid to be forced into spending too much!

Kiyo, the receptionist, notices him.[5]

KIYO: Who's this trying to avoid me?

NARRATOR: She snatches again and again at his hood-flap; he dodges her twice or thrice, but this is a valuable customer, and she refuses to let him escape. At last she pounces on him with the cry:

---

1. Japanese scholars have puzzled over these curious syllables for years, and many explanations of them have been offered. Their meaning, if any, is less important than the lively rhythm, which evokes the atmosphere of the Sonezaki Quarter.

2. Shijimi River, frequently mentioned in the course of the play, flowed along the border of the Sonezaki Quarter. Its name *shijimi* means the *corbicula*, a small mollusc related to the clam. There is a play on words here: the sea cannot be emptied by ladling it with tiny clam shells.

3. A play on words: *moji ga seki* (the barrier of Chinese characters) suggests that customers stop short when they read on doorway lanterns the names in characters of their favorite teahouses; *Moji ga seki* (the Barrier of Moji) refers to the Straits of Shimonoseki.

4. Festive days in the gay quarter on which customers were required to make presents to the teahouses. For a detailed description, see Shively, *The Love Suicides at Amijima* p. 100.

5. The following few lines are based on a passage in the Nō play *Kagekiyo*. See Waley, *The No Plays of Japan*, p. 98. The maid's name Kiyo suggests that of Kagekiyo, and the effect is one of burlesque.

KIYO: No more of your nonsense! Come along!

NARRATOR: And the customer, caught flap and cap, is trapped into folly by this female Kagekiyo.

Among the flowers on display—even the bridges are called Plum and Cherry Blossom—[6] here is Koharu of the Kinokuni House, now graduated from the smock of a bath attendant in the South[7] to the garments of love in the New Quarter. Is her name "Second Spring"[8] a sign that she is fated to leave behind a fleeting name in November?

"Who has sent for me tonight?" she wonders, uncertain as a dove in the uncertain light of a standing lantern. A prostitute passes her, then turns back.

PROSTITUTE: Is that you, Koharu? Where have you been keeping yourself? We don't get invited to the same parties any more, and I never see you or hear a word from you. Have you been sick? Your face looks thinner. Somebody was telling me that the master at your place now gives all your customers a thorough examination and hardly lets you out of the house, all on account of your Kamiji.[9] But I've also heard that you're to be ransomed by Tahei and go live with him in the country—in Itami, was it? Is it true?

KOHARU: I'd be much obliged if you'd please stop talking about Itami! The relations between Jihei and myself, I'm sorry to say, are not as close as people suppose. It's that loud-mouthed Tahei who's started the rumors and spread them everywhere, until every last customer has deserted me. The master blames Kamiya Jihei, and he's done everything to keep us from meeting. Why, I'm not even allowed to receive letters from Jihei. Tonight, strangely enough, I've been sent to Kawasho.[10] My customer's a samurai, I'm told. But I keep worrying that I might meet that dreadful Tahei on the way. I feel exactly as if I had some mortal enemy. Do you suppose he might be over there?

PROSTITUTE: If you feel that way about Tahei, you'd better hide quickly. Look—coming out of the first block—there's one of those street minstrels, singing his nonsense hymns.[11] I can see in the crowd round

---

6. References to Umeda Bridge and Sakura Bridge over the Shijimi River.

7. The "south" refers to Shimanouchi Quarter, a section of low-class brothels which originally had been bathhouses. Sonezaki Quarter was north of this section.

8. The name Koharu, literally "little spring", means Indian summer.

9. A familiar contraction for Kamiya Jihei.

10. A contraction of Kawachi House and the owner's name, which began with the syllable "Shō".

11. Sections from popular puppet dramas with a quasi-religious refrain.

him a dissolute-looking fellow with his hair tricked up in some funny style—the stuck-up swell! I'm sure it's Tahei. Oh—they're heading this way!

NARRATOR: A moment later the defrocked priest, in a flat cap and ink-black robes with the sleeves tucked back, comes bumbling along, surrounded by a crowd of idlers. He bangs at random on his bell, mixing his nonsense with the burden of a hymn.

MINSTREL:

"Fan Kuai's style was no great shakes—
See how Asahina of Japan used to break down gates!"
He rips through the gate bars and tangle of felled trees,
Slays Uryōko and Saryōko and passes the barrier,
As time passes by.[12]
*Namamida Namaida Namamida Namaida.*
*Ei Ei Ei Ei Ei.*
"Though I wander all over,
The sad world holds no one
Who looks like my dear Matsuyama!"[13]
—He weeps, he howls, only to burst into laughs.
"How wretched that I must end my life in madness!"
He falls prostrate, the grass for his pallet,
A sight too sad for the eyes to behold.
*Namamida Namaida Namamida Namaida.*
*Ei Ei Ei Ei Ei.*
Tokubei of the dyer's shop,
Since he first fell in love with Fusa,
Has yielded to passion that absorbs his fortune,
A love stained so deep lye itself cannot cleanse it.[14]
*Namamida Namaida Namamida Namaida*
*Namamida Namaida.*

SUGI: Excuse me, priest.

MINSTREL: What is it?

SUGI: It's bad luck to sing those songs, just when stories about love suicides in the Quarter have at last quieted down. Why don't you give us instead a *nembutsu* song on the journey from *The Battles of Coxinga?*

NARRATOR: Sugi offers him some coins from her sleeve.

---

12. Adapted from *The Battles of Coxinga.* Keene, *Four Major Plays of Chikamatsu,* p. 118.

13. From the play *Wankyū Sue no Matsuyama* (1707). See Shively, p. 104.

14. From the festive epilogue to "Yosaku from Tamba," in Keene, *Major Plays of Chikamatsu,* and see also Shively, pp. 104–105.

MINSTREL:

> For a mere one or two coppers
> You can't expect to travel all the way,
> Three thousand leagues to the Land of Great Ming!
> It doesn't pay, it doesn't pray Amida Buddha.

NARRATOR: Grumbling in this strain, he moves on.

## Scene Two:

*The Kawachi House, a Sonezaki teahouse.*

NARRATOR: Koharu slips away, under cover of the crowd, and hurries into the Kawachi House.

PROPRIETRESS: Well, well, I hadn't expected you so soon. — It's been ages even since I've heard your name mentioned. What a rare visitor you are, Koharu! And what a long time it's been!

NARRATOR: The proprietress greets Koharu cheerfully.

KOHARU: Oh — you can be heard as far as the gate. Please don't call me Koharu in such a loud voice. That horrible Ri Tōten[15] is out there. I beg you, keep your voice down.

NARRATOR: Were her words overheard? In bursts a party of three men.

TAHEI: I must thank you first of all, dear Koharu, for bestowing a new name on me, Ri Tōten. I never was called *that* before. Well, friends, this is the Koharu I've confided to you about — the goodhearted, good-natured, good-in-bed Koharu. Step up and meet the whore who's started all the rivalry! Will I soon be the lucky man and get Koharu for my wife? Or will Kamiya Jihei ransom her?

NARRATOR: He swaggers up.

KOHARU: I don't want to hear another word. If you think it's such an achievement to start unfounded rumors about someone you don't even know, throw yourself into it, say what you please. But I don't want to hear.

NARRATOR: She steps away suddenly, but he sidles up again.

TAHEI: You may not want to hear me, but the clink of my gold coins will make you listen! What a lucky girl you are! Just think — of all the many men in Temma and the rest of Osaka, you chose Jihei the paper dealer, the father of two children, with his cousin for his wife and his

---

15. The villain of the play *The Battles of Coxinga*. See Keene, pp. 60 ff.

uncle for his father-in-law! A man whose business is so tight he's at his wits' ends every sixty days merely to pay the wholesalers' bills! Do you think he'll be able to fork over nearly ten *kamme*[16] to ransom you? That reminds me of the mantis who picked a fight with an oncoming vehicle![17] But look at me—I haven't a wife, a father-in-law, a father, or even an uncle, for that matter. Tahei the Lone Wolf—that's the name I'm known by. I admit that I'm no match for Jihei when it comes to bragging about myself in the Quarter, but when it comes to money, I'm an easy winner. If I pushed with all the strength of my money, who knows what I might conquer?—How about it, men?—Your customer tonight, I'm sure, is none other than Jihei, but I'm taking over. The Lone Wolf's taking over. Hostess! Bring on the saké! On with the saké!

PROPRIETRESS: What are you saying? Her customer tonight is a samurai, and he'll be here any moment. Please amuse yourself elsewhere.

NARRATOR: But Tahei's look is playful.

TAHEI: A customer's a customer, whether he's a samurai or a townsman. The only difference is that one wears swords and the other doesn't. But even if this samurai wears his swords he won't have five or six— there'll only be two, the broadsword and dirk. I'll take care of the samurai and borrow Koharu afterwards. (*To Koharu.*) You may try to avoid me all you please, but some special connection from a former life must have brought us together. I owe everything to that ballad-singing priest—what a wonderful thing the power of prayer is! I think I'll recite a prayer of my own. Here, this ashtray will be my bell, and my pipe the hammer. This is fun.

*Chan Chan Cha Chan Chan.*
*Ei Ei Ei Ei Ei.*
Jihei the paper dealer—
Too much love for Koharu
Has made him a foolscap,
He wastepapers sheets of gold
Till his fortune's shredded to confetti
And Jihei himself is like scrap paper
You can't even blow your nose on!
Hail, Hail Amida Buddha!
Namaida Namaida Namaida.

---

16. This would amount to over $5,000 in current purchasing power. The price is unusually high; no doubt Tahei is exaggerating.

17. A simile, derived ultimately from ancient Chinese texts, for someone who does not know his own limitations. See Shively, p. 107.

NARRATOR: As he prances wildly, roaring his song, a man appears at the gate, so anxious not to be recognized that he wears, even at night, a wicker hat.[18]

TAHEI: Well, Toilet paper's showed up! That's quite a disguise! Why don't you come in, Toilet paper? If my prayer's frightened you, say a Hail Amida![19] Here, I'll take off your hat!

NARRATOR: He drags the man in and examines him: it is the genuine article, a two-sworded samurai, somber in dress and expression, who glares at Tahei through his woven hat, his eyeballs round as gongs. Tahei, unable to utter either a Hail or an Amida, gasps "Haaa!" in dismay, but his face is unflinching.

TAHEI: Koharu, I'm a townsman. I've never worn a sword, but I've lots of New Silver[20] at my place, and I think that the glint could twist a mere couple of swords out of joint. Imagine that wretch from the toilet paper shop, with a capital as thin as tissue, trying to compete with the Lone Wolf! That's the height of impertinence! I'll wander down now from Sakura Bridge to Middle Street, and if I meet that Wastepaper along the way, I'll trample him under foot. Come on, men.

NARRATOR: Their gestures, at least, have a cavalier assurance as they swagger off, taking up the whole street.

The samurai customer patiently endures the fool, indifferent to his remarks because of the surroundings, but every word of gossip about Jihei, whether for good or ill, affects Koharu. She is so depressed that she stands there blankly, unable even to greet her guest. Sugi, the maid from the Kinokuni House, runs up from home, looking annoyed.

SUGI: When I left you here a while ago, Miss Koharu, your guest hadn't appeared yet, and they gave me a terrible scolding when I got back for not having checked on him. I'm very sorry, sir, but please excuse me a minute.

NARRATOR: She lifts the woven hat and examines the face.

SUGI: Oh — it's not him! There's nothing to worry about, Koharu. Ask your guest to keep you for the whole night, and show him how sweet you

---

18. Customers visiting the Quarter by day wear these deep wicker hats (which virtually conceal the face) in order to preserve the secrecy of their visits; but this customer wears a hat even at night, when the darkness normally is sufficient protection.

19. A play on words devolving on the syllables *ami,* part of the name Amida and on *amigasa,* meaning "woven hat."

20. Good-quality coinage of about 1720. It was necessary to specify the kind of silver one meant because devaluations and revaluations altered the value of coins of nominally the same denomination.

can be. Give him a barrelful of nectar![21] Good-by, madam, I'll see you later, honey.

NARRATOR: She takes her leave with a cloying stream of puns. The extremely hard-baked[22] samurai is furious.

SAMURAI: What's the meaning of this? You'd think from the way she appraised my face that I was a tea canister or a porcelain cup! I didn't come here to be trifled with. It's difficult enough for me to leave the Residence even by day, and in order to spend the night away I had to ask the senior officer's permission and sign the register. You can see how complicated the regulations make things. But I'm in love, miss, just from hearing about you, and I wanted very badly to spend a night with you. I came here a while ago without an escort and made the arrangements with the teahouse. I had been looking forward to your kind reception, a memory to last me a lifetime, but you haven't so much as smiled at me or said a word of greeting. You keep your head down, as if you were counting money in your lap. Aren't you afraid of getting a stiff neck? Madam — I've never heard the like. Here I come to a teahouse, and I must play the part of night nurse in a maternity room!

PROPRIETRESS: You're quite right, sir. Your surprise is entirely justified, considering that you don't know the reasons. This girl is deeply in love with a customer named Kamiji. It's been Kamiji today and Kamiji tomorrow, with nobody else allowed a chance at her. Her other customers have scattered in every direction, like leaves in a storm. When two people get so carried away with each other, it often leads to trouble, for both the customer and the girl. In the first place, it inteferes with business, and the owner, whoever he may be, is bound to prevent it. That's why all her guests are examined. Koharu is naturally depressed — it's only to be expected. You are annoyed, which is equally to be expected. But, speaking as the proprietress here, it seems to me that the essential thing is for you to meet each other halfway and cheer up. Come, have a drink. — Act a little more lively, Koharu.

NARRATOR: Koharu, without answering, lifts her tear-stained face.

KOHARU: Tell me, samurai, they say that, if you're going to kill yourself anyway, people who die during the Ten Nights[23] are sure to become Buddhas. Is that really true?

SAMURAI: How should I know? Ask the priest at your family temple.

---

21. I have altered the imagery used by the maid from puns on saltiness (soy sauce, green vegetables, etc.) to puns on sweetness, somewhat easier to manage in English.

22. A technical term of pottery making, meaning "hard-fired". Here used to introduce the mention of "tea canister" and "porcelain cup".

23. A period from the sixth to the sixteenth nights of the tenth moon when special Buddhist services were conducted in temples of the Pure Land (Jōdo) Sect. It was believed that persons who died during this period immediately became Buddhas.

KOHARU: Yes, that's right. But there's something I'd like to ask a samurai. If you're committing suicide, it'd be a lot more painful, wouldn't it, to cut your throat rather than hang yourself?

SAMURAI: I've never tried cutting my throat to see whether or not it hurt. Please ask more sensible questions.—What an unpleasant girl!

NARRATOR: Samurai though he is, he looks nonplussed.

PROPRIETRESS: Koharu, that's a shocking way to treat a guest the first time you meet him. I'll go and get my husband. We'll have some saké together. That ought to liven things a bit.

NARRATOR: The gate she leaves is illumined by the evening moon low in the sky; the clouds and the passers in the street have thinned.

For long years there has lived in Temma, the seat of the mighty god,[24] though not a god himself, Kamiji,[25] a name often bruited by the gongs of worldly gossip, so deeply, hopelessly, is he tied to Koharu by the ropes[26] of an ill-starred love. Now is the tenth moon, the month when no gods will unite them;[27] they are thwarted in their love, unable to meet. They swore in the last letters they exchanged that if only they could meet, that day would be their last. Night after night Jihei, ready for death, trudges to the Quarter, distractedly, as though his soul had left a body consumed by the fires of love.

At a roadside eating stand he hears people gossiping about Koharu. "She's at Kawasho with a samurai customer," someone says, and immediately Jihei decides, "It will be tonight!"

He peers through the latticework window and sees a guest in the inside room, his face obscured by a hood. Only the moving chin is visible, and Jihei cannot hear what is said.

JIHEI: Poor Koharu! How thin her face is! She keeps it averted from the lamp. In her heart she's thinking only of me. I'll signal her that I'm here, and we'll run off together. Then which will it be—Umeda or Kitano?[28] Oh—I want to tell her I'm here. I want to call her.

NARRATOR: He beckons with his heart, his spirit flies to her, but his body, like a cicada's cast-off shell, clings to the latticework. He weeps with impatience.

The guest in the inside room gives a great yawn.

---

24. Temma, one of the principal districts of Osaka, was the site of the Tenjin Shrine, to the memory of the deified Sugawara no Michizane (845–993).

25. The word *kami* for "paper" is the homophone of *kami*, "god". We have thus "Kami who is not a *kami*"— the paper dealer who is not a god.

26. The sacred ropes (*mishimenawa*) at a Shinto shrine. Here mentioned (like the gongs) as a word related to the imagery of Shinto.

27. The tenth month, called *kannazuki* (literally "month of no gods") was a time when the gods were believed to gather at Izumo; they were thus absent from the rest of Japan.

28. Both places had well-known cemeteries.

SAMURAI: What a bore, playing nursemaid to a prostitute with worries on her mind!—The street seems quiet now. Let's go to the end room. We can at least distract ourselves by looking at the lanterns. Come with me.

NARRATOR: They go together to the outer room. Jihei, alarmed, squeezes into the patch of shadow under the lattice window. Inside they do not realize that anyone eavesdrops.

SAMURAI: I've been noticing your behavior and the little things you've said this evening. It's plain to me that you intend a love suicide with Kamiji, or whatever his name is—the man the hostess mentioned. I'm sure I'm right. I realize that no amount of advice or reasoning is likely to penetrate the ears of somebody bewitched by the god of death, but I must say that you're exceedingly foolish. The boy's family won't blame him for his recklessness, but they will blame and hate you. You'll be shamed by the public exposure of your body. Your parents may be dead, for all I know, but if they're alive, you'll be punished in hell as a wicked daughter. Do you suppose that you'll become a Buddha? You and your lover won't even be able to fall smoothly into hell together! What a pity—and what a tragedy! This is only our first meeting but, as a samurai, I can't let you die without trying to save you. No doubt money's the problem. I'd like to help, if five or ten *ryō* would be of service. I swear by the god Hachiman and by my good fortune as a samurai that I will never reveal to anyone what you tell me. Open your heart without fear.

NARRATOR: He whispers these words. She joins her hands and bows.

KOHARU: I'm extremely grateful. Thank you for your kind words and for swearing an oath to me, someone you've never had for a lover or even a friend. I'm so grateful that I'm crying.—Yes, it's as they say, when you've something on your mind it shows on your face. You were right. I have promised Kamiji to die with him. But we've been completely prevented from meeting by my master, and Jihei, for various reasons, can't ransom me at once. My contracts with my former master[29] and my present one still have five years to run. If somebody else claimed me during that time, it would be a blow to me, of course, but a worse disgrace to Jihei's honor. He suggested that it would be better if we killed ourselves, and I agreed. I was caught by obligations from which I could not withdraw, and I promised him before I knew what I was doing. I said, "We'll watch for a chance, and I'll slip out when you give the signal." "Yes," he said, "slip out somehow." Ever since then I've been leading a life of uncertainty, never knowing from one day to the next when my last hour will come.

---

29. The master at the bathhouse where Koharu formerly worked.

I have a mother living in a back alley south of here. She has no one but me to depend on, and she does piecework to eke out a living. I keep thinking that after I'm dead she'll become a beggar or an outcast, and maybe she'll die of starvation. That's the only sad part about dying. I have just this one life. I'm ashamed that you may think me a coldhearted woman, but I must endure the shame. The most important thing is that I don't want to die. I beg you, please help me to stay alive.

NARRATOR: As she speaks the samurai nods thoughtfully. Jihei, crouching outside, hears her words with astonishment; they are so unexpected to his manly heart that he feels like a monkey who has tumbled from a tree. He is frantic with agitation.

JIHEI (*to himself*): Then was everything a lie? Ahhh—I'm furious! For two whole years I've been bewitched by that rotten she-fox! Shall I break in and kill her with one blow of my sword? Or shall I satisfy my anger by shaming her to her face?

NARRATOR: He gnashes his teeth and weeps in chagrin. Inside the house Koharu speaks through her tears.

KOHARU: It's a curious thing to ask, but would you please show the kindness of a samurai and become my customer for the rest of this year and into next spring? Whenever Jihei comes, intent on death, please interfere and force him to postpone and postpone his plan. In this way our relations can be broken quite naturally. He won't have to kill himself, and my life will also be saved.—What evil connection from a former existence made us promise to die? How I regret it now!

NARRATOR: She weeps, leaning on the samurai's knee.

SAMURAI: Very well, I'll do as you ask. I think I can help you.—But there's a draft blowing. Somebody may be watching.

NARRATOR: He slams shut the latticework *shōji*. Jihei, listening outside, is in a frenzy.

JIHEI: Exactly what you'd expect from a whore, a cheap whore! I misjudged her foul nature. She robbed the soul from my body, the thieving harlot! Shall I slash her down or run her through? What am I to do?

NARRATOR: The shadows of two profiles fall on the *shōji*.

JIHEI: I'd like to give her a taste of my fist and trample her.—What are they chattering about? See how they nod to each other! Now she's bowing to him, whispering and sniveling. I've tried to control myself—I've pressed my chest, I've stroked it—but I can't stand any more. This is too much to endure!

NARRATOR: His heart pounds wildly as he unsheathes his dirk, a Magoroku of Seki. "Koharu's side must be here," he judges, and stabs through an opening in the latticework. But Koharu is too far away for his thrust, and though she cries out in terror, she remains unharmed. Her guest instantly leaps at Jihei, grabs his hands, and jerks them through the latticework. With his sword knot he quickly and securely fastens Jihei's hands to the window upright.

SAMURAI: Don't make any outcry, Koharu. You are not to look at him.

NARRATOR: At this moment the proprietor and his wife return. They exclaim in alarm.

SAMURAI: This needn't concern you. Some ruffian ran his sword through the *shōji*, and I've tied his arms to the latticework. I have my own way of dealing with him. Don't untie the cord. If you attract a crowd, the place is sure to be thrown in an uproar. Let's all go inside. Come with me, Koharu. We'll go to bed.

NARRATOR: Koharu answers, "Yes," but she recognizes the handle of the dirk, and the memory—if not the blade—transfixes her breast.

KOHARU: There's always people doing crazy things in the Quarter when they've had too much to drink. Why don't you let him go without making any trouble? I think that's best, don't you, Kawasho?

SAMURAI: Out of the question. Do as I say—inside, all of you. Koharu, come along.

NARRATOR: Jihei can still see their shadows even after they enter the inner room, but he is bound to the spot, his hands held in fetters which grip him the tighter as he struggles, his body beset by suffering as he tastes a living shame worse than a dog's.[30] More determined than ever to die, he sheds tears of blood, a pitiful sight.

Tahei the Lone Wolf returns from his carousing.

TAHEI: That's Jihei standing by Kawasho's window. I'll give him a tossing.

NARRATOR: He catches Jihei by the collar and starts to lift him over his back.

JIHEI: Owww!

TAHEI: Owww? What kind of weakling are you? Oh, I see—you're tied here. You must've been pulling off a robbery. You dirty pickpocket! You rotten pickpocket!

NARRATOR: He drubs Jihei mercilessly.

TAHEI: You burglar! You convict!

NARRATOR: He kicks him wildly.

---

30. A proverb of Buddhist origin, "Suffering follows one like a dog," is imbedded in the text.

TAHEI: Kamiya Jihei's been caught burgling, and they've tied him up!

NARRATOR: Passersby and people of the neighborhood, attracted by his shouts, quickly gather. The samurai rushes from the house.

SAMURAI: Who's calling him a burglar? You? Tell what Jihei's stolen! Out with it!

NARRATOR: He seizes Tahei and forces him into the dirt. Tahei rises to his feet only for the samurai to kick him down again and again. He grips Tahei.

SAMURAI: Jihei! Trample him to your heart's content!

NARRATOR: He pushes Tahei under Jihei's feet. Bound though he is, Jihei stamps furiously over Tahei's face. Tahei, thoroughly trampled and covered with mire, gets to his feet and glares around him.

TAHEI (*to bystander*): How could you fools stand there calmly and let him step on me? I've memorized every one of your faces, and I intend to pay you back. Remember that!

NARRATOR: He makes his escape, still determined to have the last word. The spectators burst out laughing.

VOICES: Listen to him brag, even after he's been trampled on! Let's throw him from the bridge and give him a drink of water! Don't let him get away!

NARRATOR: They chase after him. When the crowd has dispersed, the samurai approaches Jihei and unfastens the knots. He shows his face with his hood removed.

JIHEI: Magoemon! My brother! How shaming!

NARRATOR: He sinks to the ground and weeps, prostrating himself in the dirt.

KOHARU: Are you his brother, sir?

NARRATOR: Koharu runs to them. Jihei, catching her by the front of the kimono, forces her to the ground.

JIHEI: Beast! She-fox! I'd sooner trample on you than on Tahei!

NARRATOR: He raises his foot, but Magoemon calls out.

MAGOEMON: That's the kind of foolishness responsible for all your trouble. A prostitute's business is to deceive men. Have you just now waked up to that? I've seen to the bottom of her heart the very first time I met her, but you're so scatter-brained that in over two years of intimacy with the woman you never discovered what she was thinking. Instead of stamping on Koharu, why don't you use your feet on your own misguided disposition?—It's deplorable. You're my younger brother, but you're almost thirty, and you've got a six-year-old boy and a four-year-old girl, Kantarō and Osue. You run a shop with a thirty-six foot frontage[31] but you don't seem to realize that your whole fortune's collapsing. You shouldn't have to be lectured to by your brother. Your father-in-law is your aunt's husband, and your mother-in-law is your aunt. They've always been like real parents to you. Your wife Osan is my cousin too. The ties of marriage are multiplied by those of blood. But when the family has a reunion the only subject of discussion is our mortification over your incessant visits to Sonezaki. I feel sorry for our poor aunt. You know what a stiff-necked gentleman of the old school her husband Gozaemon is. He's forever flying into a rage and saying, "We've been tricked by your nephew. He's deserted our daughter. I'll take Osan back and ruin Jihei's reputation throughout Temma." Our aunt, with all the heartache to bear herself, sometimes sides with him and sometimes with you. She's worried herself sick. What an ingrate, not to appreciate how she's defended you in your shame! This one offense is enough to make you the target for Heaven's future punishment!

I realized that your marriage couldn't last much longer at this rate. I decided, in the hopes of relieving our aunt's worries, that I'd see with my own eyes what kind of woman Koharu was, and work out some sort of solution afterwards. I consulted the proprietor here, then came myself to investigate the cause of your sickness. I see now how natural it was that you should desert your wife and children. What a faithful prostitute you discovered! I congratulate you!

And here I am, Magoemon the Miller,[32] known far and wide for my paragon of a brother, dressed up like a masquerader at a festival or maybe a lunatic! I put on swords for the first time in my life, and announced myself, like a bit player in a costume piece, as an officer at a residence. I feel like an absolute idiot with these swords, but there's nowhere I can dispose of them now.—It's so infuriating—and ridiculous—that it's given me a pain in the chest.

NARRATOR: He gnashes his teeth and grimaces, attempting to hide his tears. Koharu, choking the while with emotion, can only say:

KOHARU: Yes, you're entirely right.

NARRATOR: The rest is lost in tears. Jihei pounds the earth with his fist.

JIHEI: I was wrong. Forgive me, Magoemon. For three years I've been possessed by that witch. I've neglected my parents, relatives—even my wife and children—and wrecked my fortune, all because I was deceived by Koharu, that sneak thief! I'm utterly mortified. But I'm

---

31. It was customary to refer to the size of shops by giving their frontage on the street.

32. Magoemon is a dealer in flour (for noodles). His shop name Konaya—"the flour merchant"—is used almost as a surname, in the manner that Jihei is known as Kamiya Jihei.

through with her now, and I'll never set foot here again. Weasel! Vixen! Sneak thief! Here's proof that I've broken with her!

NARRATOR: He pulls out the amulet bag which has rested next to his skin.

JIHEI: Here are the written oaths we've exchanged, one at the beginning of each month, twenty-nine in all. I return them. This means our love and affection are over. Take them.

NARRATOR: He flings the notes at her.

JIHEI: Magoemon, collect from her my pledges. Please make sure you get them all. Then burn them with your own hands. (*To Koharu.*) Hand them to my brother.

KOHARU: As you wish.

NARRATOR: In tears, she surrenders the amulet bag. Magoemon opens it.

MAGOEMON: One, two, three, four . . . ten . . . twenty-nine. They're all here. There's also a letter from a woman. What's this?

NARRATOR: He starts to unfold it.

KOHARU: That's an important letter. I can't let you see it.

NARRATOR: She clings to Magoemon's arm, but he pushes her away. He holds the letter to the lamplight and examines the address, "To Miss Koharu from Kamiya Osan." As soon as he reads the words, he casually thrusts the letter into his kimono.

MAGOEMON: Koharu. A while ago I swore by my good fortune as a samurai, but now Magoemon the Miller swears by his good fortune as a businessman that he will show this letter to no one, not even his wife. I alone will read it, then burn it with the oaths. You can trust me. I will not break this oath.

KOHARU: Thank you. You save my honor.

NARRATOR: She bursts into tears again.

JIHEI (*laughs contemptuously*): Save your honor! You talk like a human being! (*To Magoemon.*) I don't want to see her cursed face another minute. Let's go. No—I can't hold so much resentment and bitterness! I'll kick her one in the face, a memory to treasure for the rest of my life. Excuse me, please.

NARRATOR: He strides up to Koharu and stamps on the ground.

JIHEI: For three years I've loved you, delighted in you, longed for you, adored you, but today my foot will say my only farewells.

NARRATOR: He kicks her sharply on the forehead and bursts into tears. The brothers leave, forlorn figures. Koharu, unhappy woman, raises her voice in lament as she watches them go. Is she faithful or unfaithful?

Her true feelings are hidden in the words penned by Jihei's wife, a letter no one has seen. Jihei goes his separate way without learning the truth.[33]

# ACT TWO

SCENE:
The house and shop of Kamiya Jihei.

TIME:
Ten days later.

NARRATOR: The busy street that runs straight to Tenjin Bridge[34] named for the god of Temma, bringer of good fortune, is known as the Street Before the Kami,[35] and here a paper shop does business under the name Kamiya Jihei. The paper is honestly sold, the shop well situated; it is a long-established firm, and customers come thick as raindrops.

Outside crowds pass in the street, on their way to the Ten Nights service, while inside the husband dozes in the kotatsu,[36] shielded from draughts by a screen at his pillow. His wife Osan keeps solitary, anxious watch over shop and house.

OSAN: The days are so short—it's dinnertime already, but Tama still hasn't returned from her errand to Ichinokawa.[37] I wonder what can be keeping her. That scamp Sangorō isn't back either. The wind is freezing. I'm sure the children will both be cold. He doesn't even realize that it's time for Osue to be nursed. Heaven preserve me from ever becoming such a fool! What an infuriating creature!

NARRATOR: She speaks to herself.

KANTARŌ: Mama, I've come back all by myself.

NARRATOR: Her son, the older child, runs up to the house.

OSAN: Kantarō—is that you? What's happened to Osue and Sangorō?

KANTARŌ: They're playing by the shrine. Osue wanted her milk and she was bawling her head off.

OSAN: I was sure she would. Oh—your hands and feet are frozen stiff as nails! Go and warm yourself at the *kotatsu*. Your father's sleeping there.—What am I to do with that idiot?

---

33. An extremely complicated set of word plays runs through the last two sentences. See Shively, p. 113.

34. The reference is to Temma Tenjin, the name as a deity of Sugawara no Michizane.

35. Again a play on the words *kami* (god) and *kami* (paper).

36. A source of heat in which a charcoal burner is placed under a low, quilt-covered table.

37. Ichinokawa was the site of a large vegetable market near the north end of Tenjin Bridge.

NARRATOR: She runs out impatiently to the shop just as Sangorō shuffles back, alone.

OSAN: Come here, you fool! Where have you left Osue?

SANGORŌ: You know, I must've lost her somewhere. Maybe somebody's picked her up. Should I go back for her?

OSAN: How could you? If any harm has come to my precious child, I'll beat you to death!

NARRATOR: But even as she screams at him, the maid Tama returns with Osue on her back.

TAMA: The poor child—I found her in tears at the corner. Sangorō, when you're supposed to look after the child, do it properly.

OSAN: You poor dear. You must want your milk.

NARRATOR: She joins the others by the *kotatsu* and suckles the child.

OSAN: Tama—give that fool a taste of something that he'll remember![38]

NARRATOR: Sangorō shakes his head.

SANGORŌ: No, thanks. I gave each of the children two tangerines just a while ago at the shrine, and I tasted five myself.

NARRATOR: Fool though he is, bad puns come from him nimbly enough, and the others can only smile despite themselves.

TAMA: Oh—I've become so involved with this half-wit that I almost forgot to tell you, ma'am, that Mr. Magoemon and his aunt[39] are on their way here from the west.

OSAN: Oh dear! I'll have to wake Jihei in that case. (*To Jihei.*) Please get up. Mother and Magoemon are coming. They'll be upset again if you let them see you, a businessman, sleeping in the afternoon, with the day so short as it is.

JIHEI: All right.

NARRATOR: He struggles to a sitting position and, with his abacus in one hand, pulls his account book to him with the other.

JIHEI: Two into ten goes five, three into nine goes three, three into six goes two, seven times eight is fifty-six.

NARRATOR: His fifty-six-year old aunt enters with Magoemon.

JIHEI: Magoemon, aunt. How good of you. Please come in. I was in the midst of some urgent calculations. Four nines makes thirty-six *momme.*

---

38. A pun on the two meanings of *kurawasu:* "to cause to eat" and "to beat".

39. Magoemon's (and Jihei's) aunt, but Osan's mother.

Three sixes make eighteen *fun*. That's two *momme* less two *fun*.[40] Kantarō! Osue! Granny and Uncle have come! Bring the tobacco tray! One times three makes three. Osan, serve the tea![41]

NARRATOR: He jabbers away.

AUNT: We haven't come for tea or tobacco. Osan, you're young I know, but you're the mother of two children, and your excessive forbearance does you no credit. A man's dissipation can always be traced to his wife's carelessness. Remember, it's not only the man who's disgraced when he goes bankrupt and his marriage breaks up. You'd do well to take notice of what's going on and assert yourself a bit more.

MAGOEMON: It's foolish to hope for any results, aunt. The scoundrel even deceives me, his elder brother. Why should he take to heart criticism from his wife? Jihei—you played me for a fool. After showing me how you returned Koharu's pledges, here you are, not ten days later, re-deeming her! What does this mean? I suppose your urgent calcula-tions are of Koharu's debts! I've had enough!

NARRATOR: He snatches away the abacus and flings it clattering into the hallway.

JIHEI: You're making an enormous fuss without any cause. I haven't crossed the threshold since the last time I saw you except to go twice to the wholesalers in Imabashi and once to the Tenjin Shrine. I haven't even thought of Koharu, much less redeemed her.

AUNT: None of your evasions! Last evening at the Ten Nights service I heard the people in the congregation gossiping. Everybody was talk-ing about the great patron from Temma who'd fallen in love with a prostitute named Koharu from the Kinokuni House in Sonezaki. They said he'd driven away her other guests and was going to ransom her in the next couple of days. There was all kinds of gossip about the abun-dance of money and fools even in these days of high prices.

My husband Gozaemon has been hearing about Koharu con-stantly, and he's sure that her great patron from Temma must be you, Jihei. He told me, "He's your nephew, but for me he's a stranger, and my daughter's happiness is my chief concern. Once he ransoms the prostitute he'll no doubt sell his wife to a brothel. I intend to take her back before he starts selling her clothes."

He was halfway out of the house before I could restrain him. "Don't get so excited. We can settle this calmly. First we must make sure whether or not the rumors are true."

---

40. Meaningless calculations. Twenty *fun* made two *momme*.

41. The name Osan echoes the word *san* (three).

That's why Magoemon and I are here now. He was telling me a while ago that the Jihei of today was not the Jihei of yesterday—that you'd broken all connections with Sonezaki and completely reformed. But now I hear that you've had a relapse. What disease can this be?

Your father was my brother. When the poor man was on his death-bed, he lifted his head from the pillow and begged me to look after you, as my son-in-law and nephew. I've never forgotten those last words, but your perversity has made a mockery of his request!

NARRATOR: She collapses in tears of resentment. Jihei claps his hands in sudden recognition.

JIHEI: I have it! The Koharu everybody's gossiping about is the same Koharu, but the great patron who's to redeem her is a different man. The other day, as my brother can tell you, Tahei—they call him the Lone Wolf because he hasn't any family or relations—started a fight and was trampled on. He gets all the money he needs from his home town, and he's been trying for a long time to redeem Koharu. I've always prevented him, but I'm sure he's decided that now is his chance. I have nothing to do with it.

NARRATOR: Osan brightens at his words.

OSAN: No matter how forbearing I might be—even if I were an angel—you don't suppose I'd encourage my husband to redeem a prostitute! In this instance at any rate there's not a word of untruth in what my husband has said. I'll be a witness to that, Mother.

NARRATOR: Husband's and wife's words tally perfectly.

AUNT: Then it's true?

NARRATOR: The aunt and nephew clap their hands with relief.

MAGOEMON: Well, I'm happy it's over, anyway. To make us feel doubly reassured, will you write an affidavit which will dispel any doubts your stubborn uncle may have?

JIHEI: Certainly. I'll write a thousand if you like.

MAGOEMON: Splendid! I happen to have bought this on the way here.

NARRATOR: Magoemon takes from the fold of his kimono a sheet of oath-paper from Kumano, the sacred characters formed by flocks of crows.[42] Instead of vows of eternal love, Jihei now signs under penalty of Heaven's wrath an oath that he will sever all ties and affections with Koharu. "If I should lie, may Bonten and Taishaku above, and the

---

42. The charms issued by the Shinto shrine at Kumano were printed on the face with six Chinese characters, the strokes of which were in the shape of crows. The reverse side of these charms was used for writing oaths. See Shively, p. 116, for a fuller description.

Four Great Kings below afflict me!"[43] So the text runs, and to it is appended the names of many Buddhas and gods. He signs his name, Kamiya Jihei, in bold characters, imprints the oath with a seal of blood, and proffers it.

OSAN: It's a great relief to me too. Mother, I have you and Magoemon to thank. Jihei and I have had two children, but this is his firmest pledge of affection. I hope you share my joy.

AUNT: Indeed we do. I'm sure that Jihei will settle down and his business will improve, now that he's in this frame of mind. It's been entirely for his sake and for love of the grandchildren that we've intervened. Come, Magoemon, let's be on our way. I'm anxious to set my husband's mind at ease. — It's become chilly here. See that the children don't catch cold. — This too we owe to the Buddha of the Ten Nights. I'll say a prayer of thanks before I go. Hail, Amida Buddha!

NARRATOR: She leaves, her heart innocent as Buddha's. Jihei is perfunctory even about seeing them to the door. Hardly have they crossed the threshold than he slumps down again at the *kotatsu*. He pulls the checked quilting over his head.

OSAN: You still haven't forgotten Sonezaki, have you?

NARRATOR: She goes up to him in disgust and tears away the quilting. He is weeping; a waterfall of tears streams along the pillow, deep enough to bear him afloat. She tugs him upright and props his body against the *kotatsu* frame. She stares into his face.

OSAN: You're acting outrageously, Jihei. You shouldn't have signed that oath if you felt so reluctant to leave her. The year before last, on the middle day of the Boar of the tenth moon,[44] we lit the first fire in the *kotatsu* and celebrated by sleeping here together, pillow to pillow. Ever since then — did some demon or snake creep into my bosom that night? — for two whole years I've been condemned to keep watch over an empty nest. I thought that tonight at least, thanks to Mother and Magoemon, we'd share sweet words in bed as husbands and wives do, but my pleasure didn't last long. How cruel of you, how utterly heartless! Go ahead, cry your eyes out, if you're so attached to her. Your tears will flow into Shijimi River and Koharu, no doubt, will ladle them out and drink them! You're ignoble, inhuman.

---

43. A formal oath. Bonten (Brahma) and Taishaku (Sakra), though Hindu gods, were considered to be protective deities of the Buddhist law. The four Deva kings served under Sakra and were also protectors of Buddhism.

44. It was customary to light the first fire of the winter on this day, which would generally be towards the end of November in the Western calendar.

NARRATOR: She embraces his knees and throws herself over him, moaning in supplication. Jihei wipes his eyes.

JIHEI: If tears of grief flowed from the eyes and tears of anger from the ears, I could show my heart without saying a word. But my tears all pour in the same way from my eyes, and there's no difference in their color. It's not surprising that you can't tell what's in my heart. I have not a shred of attachment left for that vampire in human skin, but I bear a grudge against Tahei. He has all the money he wants, no wife or children. He's schemed again and again to redeem her, but Koharu refused to give in, at least until I broke with her. She told me time and again, "You have nothing to worry about. I'll never let myself be redeemed by Tahei, not even if my ties with you are ended and I can no longer stay by your side. If my master is induced by Tahei's money to deliver me to him, I'll kill myself in a way that'll do you credit!" But think—not ten days have passed since I broke with her, and she's to be redeemed by Tahei! That rotten whore! That animal! No, I haven't a trace of affection left for her, but I can just hear how Tahei will be boasting. He'll spread the word around Osaka that my business has come to a standstill and I'm hard pressed for money. I'll meet with contemptuous stares from the wholesalers. I'll be dishonored. My heart is broken and my body burns with shame. What a disgrace! How maddening! I've passed the stage of shedding hot tears, tears of blood, sticky tears—my tears now are of molten iron!

NARRATOR: He collapses with weeping. Osan pales with alarm.

OSAN: If that's the situation, poor Koharu will surely kill herself.

JIHEI: You're too well bred, despite your intelligence, to understand her likes! What makes you suppose that faithless creature would kill herself? Far from it—she's probably taking moxa treatments and medicine to prolong her life!

OSAN: No, that's not true. I was determined never to tell you so long as I lived, but I'm afraid of the crime I'd be committing if I concealed the facts and let her die with my knowledge. I will reveal my great secret. There is not a grain of deceit in Koharu. It was I who schemed to end the relations between you. I could see signs that you were drifting towards suicide. I felt so unhappy that I wrote a letter, begging her as one woman to another to break with you, though I knew how painful it would be. I asked her to save your life. The letter must have moved her. She answered that she would give you up, though you were more precious than life itself, because she could not shirk her duty to me. I've kept her letter with me ever since—it's been like a protective charm. Could such a noble-hearted woman violate her promise and brazenly marry Tahei? When a woman—I no less than another—has given herself completely to a man, she does not change. I'm sure she'll kill herself. I'm sure of it. Ahhh—what a dreadful thing to have happened! Save her, please.

NARRATOR: Her voice rises in agitation. Her husband is thrown into a turmoil.

JIHEI: There was a letter in an unknown woman's hand among the written oaths she surrendered to my brother. It must have been from you. If that's the case, Koharu will surely commit suicide.

OSAN: Alas! I'd be failing in the obligations I owe her as another woman if I allowed her to die. Please go to her at once. Don't let her kill herself.

NARRATOR: Clinging to her husband, she melts in tears.

JIHEI: But what can I possibly do? It'd take half the amount of her ransom in earnest money merely to keep her out of Tahei's clutches. I can't save Koharu's life without administering a dose of 750 *momme* in New Silver.[45] How could I raise that much money in my present financial straits? Even if I crush my body to powder, where will the money come from?

OSAN: Don't exaggerate the difficulties. If that's all you need, it's simple enough.

NARRATOR: She goes to the wardrobe, and opening a small drawer takes out a bag fastened with cords of twisted silk. She unhesitantly tears it open and throws down a packet which Jihei retrieves.

JIHEI: What's this? Money? Four hundred *momme* in New Silver? How in the world—

NARRATOR: He stares astonished at this money he never put there.

OSAN: I'll tell you later where this money came from. I've scraped it together to pay the bill for Iwakuni paper that falls due the day after tomorrow. We'll have to ask Magoemon to help us keep the business from betraying its insolvency. But Koharu comes first. The packet contains 400 *momme*. That leaves 350 *momme* to raise.

NARRATOR: She unlocks a large drawer. From the wardrobe lightly fly kite-colored Hachijō silks;[46] a Kyoto crepe kimono lined in pale brown, insubstantial as her husband's life which flickers today and may vanish tomorrow; a padded kimono of Osue's, a flaming scarlet inside and out—Osan flushes with pain to part with it; Kantaro's sleeveless, unlined jacket—if she pawns this, he'll be cold this winter. Next comes a

---

45. The medical images are occasioned by considering Koharu's plight as a sickness. If 750 *me* is half the sum needed to redeem Koharu, the total of 1,500 *me* (or 6,000 *me* in Old Silver) is considerably less than the 10 *kamme*, or 10,000 *me* in Old Silver, mentioned by Tahei. See footnote 16.

46. Hachijō silks were woven with a warp of brown and a woof of yellow thread to give a color like that of the bird called the kite. "Kite" also suggests that the material flies out of the cupboard.

garment of striped Gunnai silk lined in pale blue and never worn, and then her best formal costume—heavy black silk dyed with her family crest, an ivy leaf in a ring. They say that those joined by marriage ties can even go naked at home, though outside the house clothes make the man: she snatches up even her husband's finery, a silken cloak, making fifteen articles in all.

OSAN: The very least the pawnshop can offer is 350 *momme* in New Silver.

NARRATOR: Her face glows as though she already held the money she needs; she hides in the one bundle her husband's shame and her own obligation, and puts her love in besides.

OSAN: It doesn't matter if the children and I have nothing to wear. My husband's reputation concerns me more. Ransom Koharu. Save her. Assert your honor before Tahei.

NARRATOR: But Jihei's eyes remain downcast all the while, and he is silently weeping.

JIHEI: Yes, I can pay the earnest money and keep her out of Tahei's hands. But once I've redeemed her, I'll either have to maintain her in a separate establishment or bring her here. Then what will become of you?

NARRATOR: Osan is at a loss to answer.

OSAN: Yes, what shall I do? Shall I become your children's nurse or the cook? Or perhaps the retired mistress of the house?

NARRATOR: She falls to the floor with a cry of woe.

JIHEI: That would be too selfish. I'd be afraid to accept such generosity. Even if the punishment for my crimes against my parents, against Heaven, against the gods and the Buddhas fails to strike me, the punishment for my crimes against my wife alone will be sufficient to destroy all hope for the future life. Forgive me, I beg you.

NARRATOR: He joins his hands in tearful entreaty.

OSAN: Why should you bow before me? I don't deserve it. I'd be glad to rip the nails from my fingers and toes, to do anything which might serve my husband. I've been pawning my clothes for some time in order to scrape together the money for the paper wholesalers' bills. My wardrobe is empty, but I don't regret it in the least. But it's too late now to talk of such things. Hurry, change your cloak and go to her with a smile.

NARRATOR: He puts on an under kimono of Gunnai silk, a robe of heavy black silk, and a striped cloak. His sash of figured damask holds a dirk of middle length worked in gold: Buddha surely knows that tonight it will be stained with Koharu's blood.

JIHEI: Sangorō! Come here!

NARRATOR: Jihei loads the bundle on the servant's back, intending to take him along. Then he firmly thrusts the wallet next to his skin and starts towards the gate.

VOICE: Is Jihei at home?

NARRATOR: A man enters, removing his fur cap. They see—good heavens!—that it is Gozaemon.

OSAN *and* JIHEI: Ahhh—how fortunate that you should come at this moment!

NARRATOR: Husband and wife are upset and confused. Gozaemon snatches away Sangorō's bundle and sits heavily. His voice is sharp.

GOZAEMON: Stay where you are, harlot!—My esteemed son-in-law, what a rare pleasure to see you dressed in your finest attire, with a dirk and a silken cloak! Ahhh—that's how a gentleman of means spends his money! No one would take you for a paper dealer. Are you perchance on your way to the New Quarter? What commendable perseverance! You have no need for your wife, I take it.—Give her a divorce. I've come to take her home with me.

NARRATOR: He speaks needles and his voice is bitter. Jihei has not a word to reply.

OSAN: How kind of you, Father, to walk here on such a cold day. Do have a cup of tea.

NARRATOR: Offering the teacup serves as an excuse for edging closer.

OSAN: Mother and Magoemon came here a while ago, and they told my husband how much they disapproved of his visits to the New Quarter. Jihei was in tears and he wrote out an oath swearing he had reformed. He gave it to Mother. Haven't you seen it yet?

GOZAEMON: His written oath? Do you mean this?

NARRATOR: He takes the paper from his kimono.

GOZAEMON: Libertines scatter vows and oaths wherever they go, as if they were monthly statements of accounts. I thought there was something peculiar about this oath, and now that I am here I can see I was right. Do you still swear to Bonten and Taishaku? Instead of such nonsense, write out a bill of divorcement!

NARRATOR: He rips the oath to shreds and throws down the pieces. Husband and wife exchange looks of alarm, stunned into silence. Jihei touches his hands to the floor and bows his head.

JIHEI: Your anger is justified. If I were still my former self, I would try to offer explanations, but today I appeal entirely to your generosity. Please let me stay with Osan. I promise that even if I become a beggar or an outcast and must sustain life with the scraps that fall from other people's chopsticks, I will hold Osan in high honor and protect her from every harsh and bitter experience. I feel so deeply indebted to Osan that I cannot divorce her. You will understand that this is true as time passes and I show you how I apply myself to my work and restore my fortune. Until then please shut your eyes and allow us to remain together.

NARRATOR: Tears of blood stream from his eyes and his face is pressed to the matting in contrition.

GOZAEMON: The wife of an outcast! That's all the worse. Write the bill of divorcement at once! I will verify and seal the furniture and clothes Osan brought in her dowry.

NARRATOR: He goes to the wardrobe. Osan is alarmed.

OSAN: My clothes are all here. There's no need to examine them.

NARRATOR: She runs up to forestall him, but Gozaemon pushes her aside and jerks open a drawer.

GOZAEMON: What does this mean?

NARRATOR: He opens another drawer: it too is empty. He pulls out every last drawer, but not so much as a foot of patchwork cloth is to be seen. He tears open the wicker hampers, long boxes, and clothes chests.

GOZAEMON: Stripped bare, are they?

NARRATOR: His eyes set in fury. Jihei and Osan huddle under the striped kotatsu quilts, ready to sink into the fire with humiliation.[47]

GOZAEMON: This bundle looks suspicious.

NARRATOR: He unties the knots and dumps out the contents.

GOZAEMON: As I thought! You were sending these to the pawnshop, I take it. Jihei—you'd strip the skin from your wife's and your children's bodies to squander the money on your whore! Dirty thief! You're my wife's nephew, but an utter stranger to me, and I'm under no obligation to suffer for your sake. I'll explain to Magoemon what has happened and ask him to make good whatever inroads you've already made on Osan's belongings. But first, the bill of divorcement!

NARRATOR: Even if Jihei could escape through seven padlocked doors, eight thicknesses of chains, and a hundred girdling walls, he could not evade so stringent a demand.

JIHEI: I won't use a brush to write the bill of divorcement. Here's what I'll do instead! Good-by, Osan.

---

47. I have omitted here an irrelevant allusion to Urashima Tarō. See Shively, p. 85.

NARRATOR: He lays his hand on his dirk, but Osan clings to him.

OSAN: Father—Jihei admits that he's done wrong and he's apologized in every way. You press your advantage too hard. Jihei may be a stranger, but his children are your grandchildren. Have you no affection for them? I will not accept a bill of divorcement.

NARRATOR: She embraces her husband and raises her voice in tears.

GOZAEMON: Very well. I won't insist on it. Come with me, woman.

NARRATOR: He pulls her to her feet.

OSAN: No, I won't go. What bitterness makes you expose to such shame a man and wife who still love each other? I will not suffer it.

NARRATOR: She pleads with him, weeping, but he pays her no heed.

GOZAEMON: Is there some greater shame? I'll shout it through the town!

NARRATOR: He pulls her up, but she shakes free. Caught by the wrist she totters forward when—alas!—her toes brush against her sleeping children. They open their eyes.

CHILDREN: Mother dear, why is Grandfather, the bad man, taking you away? Whom will we sleep beside now?

NARRATOR: They call out after her.

OSAN: My poor dears! You've never spent a night away from Mother's side since you were born. Sleep tonight beside your father. (*To Jihei.*) Please don't forget to give the children their tonic before breakfast.— Oh, my heart is broken!

NARRATOR: These are her parting words. She leaves her children behind, abandoned as in the woods; the twin-trunked bamboo of conjugal love is sundered forever.

## ACT THREE

## Scene One:

*Sonezaki New Quarter, in front of the Yamato House.*

TIME:
That night.

NARRATOR: This is Shijimi River, the haunt of love and affection. Its flowing water and the feet of passersby are stilled now at two in the morning, and the full moon shines clear in the sky. Here in the street a dim doorway lantern is marked "Yamatoya Dembei" in a single scrawl. The night watchman's clappers take on a sleepy cadence as he totters by on uncertain legs. The very thickness of his voice crying, "Beware of fire! Beware of fire!" tells how far advanced the night is. A serving woman from the upper town comes along, followed by a palanquin. "It's terribly late," she remarks to the bearers as she clatters open the side door of the Yamato House and steps inside.

SERVANT: I've come to take back Koharu of the Kinokuni House.

NARRATOR: Her voice is faintly heard outside. A few moments later, after hardly time enough to exchange three or four words of greeting, she emerges.

SERVANT: Koharu is spending the night. Bearers, you may leave now and get some rest. (*To proprietress, inside the doorway.*) Oh, I forgot to tell you, madam. Please keep an eye on Koharu. Now that the ransom to Tahei has been arranged and the money's been accepted, we're merely her custodians. Please don't let her drink too much saké.

NARRATOR: She leaves, having scattered at the doorway the seeds that before morning will turn Jihei and Koharu to dust.

At night between two and four even the teahouse kettle rests; the flame flickering in the low candle stand narrows; and the frost spreads in the cold river-wind of the deepening night. The master's voice breaks the stillness.

DEMBEI (*to Jihei*): It's still the middle of the night. I'll send somebody with you. (*To servants.*) Mr. Jihei is leaving. Wake Koharu. Call her here.

NARRATOR: Jihei slides open the side door.

JIHEI: No, Dembei, not a word to Koharu. I'll be trapped here till dawn if she hears I'm leaving. That's why I'm letting her sleep and slipping off this way. Wake her up after sunrise and send her back then. I'm returning home now and will leave for Kyoto immediately on business. I have so many engagements that I may not be able to return in time for the interim payment.[48] Please use the money I gave you earlier this evening to clear my account. I'd like you also to send 150 *me* of Old Silver to Kawashō for the moon-viewing party last month. Please get a receipt. Give Saietsubo[49] from Fukushima one piece of silver as a contribution to the Buddhist altar he's bought, and tell him to use it for a memorial service. Wasn't there something else? Oh yes—give Isoichi a tip of four silver coins. That's the lot. Now you can close up and get to bed. Good-by. I'll see you when I return from Kyoto.

---

48. On the last day of the tenth moon (November 29, 1720). This day was one of the times established during the course of the year for making payments.

49. The name of a male entertainer in the Quarter. Fukushima was west of Sonezaki.

NARRATOR: Hardly has he taken two or three steps than he turns back.

JIHEI: I forgot my dirk. Fetch it for me, won't you?—Yes, Dembei, this is one respect in which it's easier being a townsman. If I were a samurai and forgot my sword, I'd probably commit suicide on the spot!

DEMBEI: I completely forgot that I was keeping it for you. Yes, here's the knife with it.

NARRATOR: He gives the dirk to Jihei, who fastens it firmly into his sash.

JIHEI: I feel secure as long as I have this. Good night!

NARRATOR: He goes off.

DEMBEI: Please come back to Osaka soon! Thank you for your patronage!

NARRATOR: With this hasty farewell Dembei rattles the door bolt shut; then not another sound is heard as the silence deepens. Jihei pretends to leave, only to creep back again with stealthy steps. He clings to the door of the Yamato House. As he peeps within he is startled by shadows moving towards him. He takes cover at the house across the way until the figures pass.

    Magoemon the Miller, his heart pulverized with anxiety over his younger brother, comes first, followed by the apprentice Sangorō with Jihei's son Kantarō on his back. They hurry along until they spy the lantern of the Yamato House. Magoemon pounds on the door.

MAGOEMON: Excuse me. Kamiya Jihei's here, isn't he? I'd like to see him a moment.

NARRATOR: Jihei thinks, "It's my brother!" but dares not stir from his place of concealment. From inside a man's sleep-laden voice is heard.

DEMBEI: Jihei left a while ago saying he was going up to Kyoto. He's not here.

NARRATOR: Not another sound is heard. Magoemon's tears fall unchecked.

MAGOEMON (to himself): I ought to have met him on the way if he'd been going home. I can't understand what takes him to Kyoto. Ahhh—I'm trembling all over with worry. I wonder if he didn't take Koharu with him.

NARRATOR: The thought pierces his heart; unable to bear the pain, he pounds again on the door.

DEMBEI: Who is it, so late at night? We've gone to bed.

MAGOEMON: I'm sorry to disturb you, but I'd like to ask one more thing. Has Koharu of the Kinokuni House left? I was wondering if she mightn't have gone with Jihei.

DEMBEI: What's that? Koharu's upstairs, fast asleep.

MAGOEMON: That's a relief, anyway. There's no fear of a lovers' suicide. But where is he hiding himself causing me all this anxiety? He can't imagine the agony of suspense that the whole family is going through on his account. I'm afraid that bitterness towards his father-in-law may make him forget himself and do something rash. I brought Kantarō along, hoping he would help to dissuade Jihei, but the gesture was in vain. I wonder why I failed to meet him?

NARRATOR: He murmurs to himself, his eyes moist with tears. Jihei's hiding place is close enough for him to hear every word. He chokes with emotion, but can only swallow his tears.

MAGOEMON: Songorō! Where does the fool go night after night? Don't you know anywhere else?

NARRATOR: Sangorō imagines that he himself is the fool referred to.

SANGORŌ: I know a couple of places, but I'm too embarrassed to mention them.

MAGOEMON: You know them? Where are they? Tell me.

SANGORŌ: Please don't scold me when you've heard. Every night I wander down below the warehouses by the market.

MAGOEMON: Imbecile! Who's asking about that? Come on, let's search the back streets. Don't let Kantaro catch a chill. The poor kid's having a cold time of it, thanks to that useless father of his. Still, if the worst the boy experiences is the cold I won't complain. I'm afraid that Jihei may cause him much greater pain. The scoundrel!

NARRATOR: But beneath the rancor in his heart of hearts is profound pity.

MAGOEMON: Let's look at the back street!

NARRATOR: They pass on. As soon as their figures have gone off a distance Jihei runs from his hiding place. Standing on tiptoes he gazes with yearning after them and cries out in his heart.

JIHEI: He cannot leave me to my death, though I am the worst of sinners! I remain to the last a burden to him! I'm unworthy of such kindness!

NARRATOR: He joins his hands and kneels in prayer.

JIHEI: If I may make one further request of your mercy, look after my children!

NARRATOR: These are his only words; for a while he chokes with tears.

JIHEI: At any rate, our decision's been made. Koharu must be waiting.

NARRATOR: He peers through a crack in the side door of the Yamato House and glimpses a figure.

JIHEI: That's Koharu, isn't it? I'll let her know I'm here.

NARRATOR: He clears his throat, their signal. "Ahem, ahem"—the sound blends with the clack of wooden clappers as the watchman comes from the upper street, coughing in the night wind. He hurries on his round of fire warning, "Take care! Beware!" Even this cry has a dismal sound to one in hiding. Jihei, concealing himself like the god of Katsuragi,[50] lets the watchman pass. He sees his chance and rushes to the side door, which softly opens from within.

JIHEI: Koharu?

KOHARU: Were you waiting? Jihei—I want to leave quickly.

NARRATOR: She is all impatience, but the more hastily they open the door, the more likely people will be to hear the casters turning. They lift the door; it gives a moaning that thunders in their ears and in their hearts. Jihei lends a hand from the outside, but his fingertips tremble with the trembling of his heart. The door opens a quarter of an inch, a half, an inch—an inch ahead are the tortures of hell, but more than hell itself they fear the guardian-demon's eyes. At last the door opens, and with the joy of New Year's morn[51] Koharu slips out. They catch each other's hands. Shall they go north or south, west or east? Their pounding hearts urge them on, though they know not to what destination: turning their backs on the moon reflected in Shijimi River, they hurry eastward as fast as their legs will carry them.

## Scene Two:

*The farewell journey of many bridges.*

NARRATOR:

The running hand in texts of Nō is always Konoe style;
An actor in a woman's part is sure to wear a purple hat.[52]
Does some teaching of the Buddha as rigidly decree
That men who spend their days in evil haunts must end like this?

Poor creatures, though they would discover today their destiny in the Sutra of Cause and Effect,[53] tomorrow the gossip of the world will

---

50. The god was so ashamed of his ugliness that he ventured forth only at night.

51. Mention of New Year is connected with Koharu's name, in which *haru* means "spring."

52. The Konoe style of calligraphy, originated by Konoe Nobutada (1565–1614), was invariably used in books of Nō texts. Custom also decreed that young actors playing the parts of women cover their foreheads with a square of purple cloth to disguise the fact that they were shaven.

53. A sacred text of Buddhism (Karma Sūtra); Chikamatsu here alludes to the line from that text: "If you wish to know the past cause, look at the present effect; if you wish to know the future effect, look at the present cause." See Shively, p. 125.

scatter like blossoms the scandal of Kamiya Jihei's love suicide, and, carved in cherry wood,[54] his story to the last detail will be printed in illustrated sheets.

Jihei, led on by the spirit of death—if such there be among the gods—is resigned to this punishment for neglect of his trade. But at times—who could blame him?—his heart is drawn to those he has left behind, and it is hard to keep walking on. Even in the full moon's light, this fifteenth night of the tenth moon,[55] he cannot see his way ahead—a sign perhaps of the darkness in his heart? The frost now falling will melt by dawn but, even more quickly than this symbol of human frailty, the lovers themselves will melt away. What will become of the fragrance that lingered when he held her tenderly at night in their bedchamber?

This bridge, Tenjin Bridge, he has crossed every day, morning and night, gazing at Shijimi River to the west. Long ago, when Tenjin, then called Michizane,[56] was exiled to Tsukushi, his plum tree, following its master, flew in one bound to Dazaifu, and here is Plum-field Bridge.[57] Green Bridge recalls the aged pine that followed later, and Cherry Bridge the tree that withered away in grief over parting. Such are the tales still told, bespeaking the power of a single poem.[58]

JIHEI: Though born the parishioner of so holy and mighty a god, I shall kill you and then myself. If you ask the cause, it was that I lacked even the wisdom that might fill a tiny Shell Bridge.[59] Our stay in this world has been short as an autumn day. This evening will be the last of your nineteen, of my twenty-eight years. The time has come to cast away our lives. We promised we'd remain together faithfully, till you were an old woman and I an old man, but before we knew each other three full years, we have met this disaster. Look, there is Ōe Bridge. We follow the river from Little Naniwa Bridge to Funairi Bridge. The farther we journey, the closer we approach the road to death.

NARRATOR: He laments. She clings to him.

---

54. The blocks from which illustrated books were printed were frequently of cherry wood. The illustrated sheets mentioned here featured current scandals, such as lovers' suicides.

55. November 14, 1720. In the lunar calendar the full moon occurs on the fifteenth of the month.

56. Sugawara no Michizane, unfairly abused at court, was exiled to Dazaifu in Kyushu. When he was about to depart he composed a poem of farewell to his favorite plum tree. The tree, moved by this honor, flew after him to Kyushu. The cherry tree in his garden withered away in grief. Only the pine seemed indifferent, as Michizane complained in another poem. The pine thereupon also flew to Kyushu. See also n. 24, above.

57. Umeda Bridge. "Green Bridge" is Midori-bashi.

58. The poem by Michizane bewailing the inconstancy of his pine tree.

59. Shijimi Bridge. Twelve bridges are mentioned in the *michiyuki*. The lovers' journey takes them along the north bank of Shijimi River to Shijimi Bridge, where they cross to Dōjima. At Little Naniwa Bridge they cross back again to Sonezaki. Continuing eastward, they cross Horikawa, then cross the Temma Bridge over the Ōkawa. At "Eight Houses" (Hakkenya) they journey eastward along the south bank of the river as far as Kyō Bridge. They cross this bridge to the tip of land at Katamachi, and then take the Onari Bridge to Amijima.

KOHARU: Is this already the road to death?

NARRATOR: Falling tears obscure from each the other's face and threaten to immerse even the Horikawa bridges.

JIHEI: A few steps north and I could glimpse my house, but I will not turn back. I will bury in my breast all thoughts of my children's future, all pity for my wife. We cross southward over the river. Why did they call a place with as many buildings as a bridge has piers "Eight Houses"? Hurry, we want to arrive before the down-river boat from Fushimi comes—with what happy couples sleeping aboard!

Next is Temma Bridge, a frightening name[60] for us about to depart this world. Here the two streams Yodo and Yamato join in one great river, as fish with water, and as Koharu and I, dying on one blade will cross together the River of Three Fords.[61] I would like this water for our tomb offering!

KOHARU: What have we to grieve about? Though in this world we could not stay together, in the next and through each successive world to come until the end of time we shall be husband and wife. Every summer for my devotions[62] I have copied the All Compassionate and All Merciful Chapter of the Lotus Sutra, in the hope that we may be reborn on one lotus.

NARRATOR: They cross over Kyō Bridge and reach the opposite shore.[63]

KOHARU: If I can save living creatures at will when once I mount a lotus calyx in Paradise and become a Buddha, I want to protect women of my profession, so that never again will there be love suicides.

NARRATOR: This unattainable prayer stems from worldly attachment, but it touchingly reveals her heart.

They cross Onari Bridge.[64] The waters of Noda Creek are shrouded with morning haze; the mountain tips show faintly white.

JIHEI: Listen—the voices of the temple bells begin to boom. How much farther can we go on this way? We are not fated to live any longer—let us make an end quickly. Come this way.

---

60. The characters used for Temma mean literally "demon."

61. A river in the Buddhist underworld which had to be crossed to reach the world of the dead. Mention here is induced arithmetically: one blade plus two people equal three fords.

62. It was customary for Buddhist monks and some of the laity in Japan to observe a summer retreat from the sixteenth day of the fourth moon to the fifteenth day of the seventh moon, a period of ninety days. During this time they practiced various austerities and copied out the holy books or wrote the Buddha's name over and over.

63. "Opposite shore" suggests the Buddhist term *higan* (nirvana).

64. The name Onari is used here for the bridge more properly called Bizenjima because of a play on words meaning "to become a Buddha".

NARRATOR: Tears are strung with the 108 beads of the rosaries in their hands. They have come now to Amijima, to the Daicho Temple; the overflowing sluice gate of a little stream beside a bamboo thicket will be their place of death.

# Scene Three:

*Amijima.*

JIHEI: No matter how far we walk, there'll never be a spot marked "For Suicides." Let us kill ourselves here.

NARRATOR: He takes her hand and sits on the ground.

KOHARU: Yes, that's true. One place is as good as another to die. But I've been thinking on the way that if they find our dead bodies together people will say that Koharu and Jihei committed a lovers' suicide. Osan will think then that I treated as mere scrap paper the letter I sent promising her, when she asked me not to kill you, that I would not, and vowing to break all relations. She will be sure that I lured her precious husband into a lovers' suicide. She will despise me as a one-night prostitute, a false woman with no sense of decency. I fear her contempt more than the slander of a thousand or ten thousand strangers. I can imagine how she will resent and envy me. That is the greatest obstacle to my salvation. Kill me here, then choose another spot, far away, for yourself.

NARRATOR: She leans against him. Jihei joins in her tears of pleading.

JIHEI: What foolish worries! Osan has been taken back by my father-in-law. I've divorced her. She and I are strangers now. Why should you feel obliged to a divorced woman? You were saying on the way that you and I will be husband and wife through each successive world until the end of time. Who can criticize us, who can be jealous if we die side by side?

KOHARU: But who is responsible for your divorce? You're even less reasonable than I. Do you suppose that our bodies will accompany us to the afterworld? We may die in different places, our bodies may be pecked by kites and crows, but what does it matter as long as our souls are twined together? Take me with you to heaven or to hell!

NARRATOR: She sinks again in tears.

JIHEI: You're right. Our bodies are made of earth, water, fire, and wind, and when we die they revert to emptiness. But our souls will not decay, no matter how often reborn. And here's a guarantee that our souls will be married and never part!

NARRATOR: He whips out his dirk and slashes off his black locks at the base of the top knot.

JIHEI: Look, Koharu. As long as I had this hair I was Kamiya Jihei, Osan's husband, but cutting it has made me a monk. I have fled the burning house of the three worlds of delusion; I am a priest, unencumbered by wife, children, or worldly possessions. Now that I no longer have a wife named Osan, you owe her no obligations either.

NARRATOR: In tears he flings away the hair.

KOHARU: I am happy.

NARRATOR: Koharu takes up the dirk and ruthlessly, unhesitatingly, slices through her flowing Shimada coiffure. She casts aside the tresses she has so often washed and combed and stroked. How heartbreaking to see their locks tangled with the weeds and midnight frost of this desolate field!

JIHEI: We have escaped the inconstant world, a nun and a priest. Our duties as husband and wife belong to our profane past. It would be best to choose quite separate places for our deaths, a mountain for one, the river for the other. We will pretend that the ground above this sluice gate is a mountain. You will die there. I shall hang myself by this stream. The time of our deaths will be the same, but the method and place will differ. In this way we can honor to the end our duty to Osan. Give me your under sash.

NARRATOR: Its fresh violet color and fragrance will be lost in the winds of impermanence; the crinkled silk long enough to wind twice round her body will bind two worlds, this and the next. He firmly fastens one end to the crosspiece of the sluice, then twists the other into a noose for his neck. He will hang for love of his wife like the "pheasant in the hunting grounds."[65]

Koharu watches Jihei prepare for his death. Her eyes swim with tears, her mind is distraught.

KOHARU: Is that how you're going to kill yourself?—If we are to die apart, I have only a little while longer by your side. Come near me.

NARRATOR: They take each other's hands.

KOHARU: It's over in a moment with a sword, but I'm sure you'll suffer. My poor darling!

NARRATOR: She cannot stop the silent tears.

---

65. A reference to a poem by Ōtomo no Yakamochi (718–785): "The pheasant foraging in the fields of spring reveals his whereabouts to man as he cries for his mate" (Shuishu, no. 21).

JIHEI: Can suicide ever be pleasant, whether by hanging or cutting the throat? You mustn't let worries over trifles disturb the prayers of your last moments. Keep your eyes on the westward-moving moon, and worship it as Amida himself.[66] Concentrate your thoughts on the Western Paradise. If you have any regrets about leaving the world, tell me now, then die.

KOHARU: I have none at all, none at all. But I'm sure you must be worried about your children.

JIHEI: You make me cry all over again by mentioning them. I can almost see their faces, sleeping peacefully, unaware, poor dears, that their father is about to kill himself. They're the one thing I can't forget.

NARRATOR: He droops to the ground with weeping. The voices of the crows leaving their nests at dawn rival his sobs. Are the crows mourning his fate? The thought brings more tears.

JIHEI: Listen to them. The crows have come to guide us to the world of the dead. There's an old saying that every time somebody writes an oath on the back of a Kumano charm, three crows of Kumano die on the holy mountain. The first words we've written each New Year have been vows of love, and how often we've inscribed oaths at the beginning of the month! If each oath has killed three crows, what a multitude must have perished! Their cries have always sounded like "beloved, beloved," but hatred for our crime of taking life makes their voices ring tonight "revenge, revenge!"[67] Whose fault is it they demand revenge? Because of me you will die a painful death. Forgive me!

NARRATOR: He takes her in his arms.

KOHARU: No, it's my fault!

NARRATOR: They cling to each other, face pressed to face; their sidelocks, drenched with tears, freeze in the winds blowing over the fields. Behind them echoes the voice of the Daichō Temple.

JIHEI: Even the long winter night seems short as our lives.

NARRATOR: Dawn is already breaking, and matins can be heard. He draws her to him.

JIHEI: The moment has come for our glorious end. Let there be no tears on your face when they find you later.

KOHARU: There won't be any.

---

66. Amida's paradise lies in the west. The moon is also frequently used as a symbol of Buddhist enlightenment.

67. The cries have always sounded like *kawai, kawai*, but now they sound like *mukui, mukui*. These Japanese sounds seem more within the range of a crow's articulatory powers than "beloved" and "revenge".

NARRATOR: She smiles. His hands, numbed by the frost, tremble before the pale vision of her face, and his eyes are first to cloud. He is weeping so profusely that he cannot control the blade.

KOHARU: Compose yourself—but be quick!

NARRATOR: Her encouragement lends him strength; the invocations to Amida carried by the wind urge a final prayer. *Namu Amida Butsu.* He thrusts in the saving sword.[68] Stabbed, she falls backwards, despite his staying hand, and struggles in terrible pain. The point of the blade has missed her windpipe, and these are the final tortures before she can die. He writhes with her in agony, then painfully summons his strength again. He draws her to him, and plunges his dirk to the hilt. He twists the blade in the wound, and her life fades away like an unfinished dream at dawning.

He arranges her corpse head to the north, face to the west, lying on her right side,[69] and throws his cloak over her. He turns away at last, unable to exhaust with tears his grief over parting. He pulls the sash to him and fastens the noose around his neck. The service in the temple has reached the closing section, the prayers for the dead. "Believers and unbelievers will equally share in the divine grace," the voices proclaim, and at the final words Jihei jumps from the sluice gate.

JIHEI: May we be reborn on one lotus! Hail Amida Buddha!

NARRATOR: For a few moments he writhes like a gourd swinging in the wind, but gradually the passage of his breath is blocked as the stream is dammed by the sluice gate, where his ties with this life are snapped. Fishermen out for the morning catch find the body in their net.[70]

FISHERMEN: A dead man! Look, a dead man! Come here, everybody!

NARRATOR: The tale is spread from mouth to mouth. People say that they who were caught in the net of Buddha's vow immediately gained salvation and deliverance, and all who hear the tale of the Love Suicides at Amijima are moved to tears.

---

68. The invocation of Amida's name freed one from spiritual obstacles, just as a sword freed one from physical obstacles. Here the two images are blended.

69. The dead were arranged in this manner because Shakyamuni Buddha chose this position when he died.

70. "Net" (*ami*) is mentioned because of the connection with fishermen. It is echoed a few lines later in the mention of the name *Amijima.* The vow of the Buddha to save all living creatures is likened to a net which catches people in its meshes. For a further explanation of this image (and of the title of the play), see Shively, p. 41.

# Chikamatsu on the Art of the Puppet Stage

## [*from* Naniwa Miyage] by Hozumi Ikan[1]

This is what Chikamatsu told me when I visited him many years ago:

*Jōruri* differs from other forms of fiction in that, since it is primarily concerned with puppets, the words must all be living and full of action. Because *jōruri* is performed in theatres that operate in close competition with those of the *kabuki*, which is the art of living actors, the author must impart to lifeless wooden puppets a variety of emotions, and attempt in this way to capture the interest of the audience. It is thus generally very difficult to write a work of great distinction.

Once when I was young and reading a story about the court,[2] I came across a passage which told how, on the occasion of a festival, the snow had fallen heavily and piled up. An order was given to a guard to clear away the snow from an orange tree. When this happened, the pine next to it, apparently resentful that its boughs were still bent with snow, recoiled its branches. This was a stroke of the pen which gave life to the inanimate tree. It did so because the spectacle of the pine, resentful that the snow had been cleared from the orange tree, recoiling its branches and shaking off the snow that bends it down, is one which creates the feeling of a living, moving thing. Is that not so?

From this model I learned how to put life into my *jōruri*. Thus, even descriptive passages like the *michiyuki*,[3] to say nothing of the narrative phrases and dialogue, must be charged with feeling or they will be greeted with scant applause. This is the same thing as what is called evocative power in poetry. For example, if a poet should fail to bring emotion to his praise of even the superb scenery of Matsushima or Miyajima in his poem, it would be like looking at the carelessly drawn portrait of a beautiful woman. For this reason, it should be borne in mind that feeling is the basis of writing.

When a composition is filled with particles, its literary quality is somehow lowered. Authors of no merit inevitably try to cast their writings exactly in the form of *waka* or linked-verse, stringing together alternating lines of five and seven syllables. This naturally results in the use of many unnecessary particles. For example, when one should say "*Toshi mo yukanu musume wo,*" they say such things as "*Toshiha mo yukanu, musume wo ba.*" This comes from concerning one's self with the syllable count, and naturally causes the language to sound vulgar. Thus, while verse is generally

---

1. The following account of Chickamatsu's views on the *jōruri*, or puppet stage, was written after his death, in 1738, by a friend. It is one of the most important examples of dramatic criticism in the literature.

2. "The Tale of Genji." The particular reference is to a passage in the chapter translated by Waley as "The Village of Falling Flowers."

3. The journey, such as that of the lovers in "The Love Suicides at Sonezaki."

written by arranging long and short lines in order, the *jōruri* is basically a musical form, and the length of the lines recited is therefore determined by the melody. If an author adheres implicitly to the rules of metrics, his lines may prove awkward to recite. For this reason I am not concerned with metrics in my writings and I use few particles.

The old *jōruri* was just like our modern street storytelling,[4] and was without either flower or fruit. From the time I first began to write *jōruri*, I have used care in my works, which was not true of the old *jōruri*. As a result, the medium was raised considerably. For example, inasmuch as the nobility, the samurai, and the lower classes all have different social stations, it is essential that they be distinguished in their representation from their appearance down to their speech. Similarly, even within the same samurai class, there are both daimyō [feudal lords] and retainers, as well as others of lower rank, each rank possessed of its distinct qualities; such differences must be established. This is because it is essential that they be well pictured in the emotions of the reader.

In writing *jōruri*, one attempts first to describe facts as they really are, but in so doing one writes things which are not true, in the interest of art. In recent plays many things have been said by female characters which real women could not utter. Such things fall under the heading of art; it is because they say what could not come from a real woman's lips that their true emotions are disclosed. If in such cases the author were to model his character on the ways of a real woman and conceal her feelings, such realism, far from being admired, would permit no pleasure in the work. Thus, if one examines a play without paying attention to the question of art, one will certainly criticize it for containing many unpleasant words which are not suitable for women. But such things should be considered art. In addition, there are numerous instances in the portrayal of a villain as excessively cowardly, or of a clown as funny, which are outside the truth and which must be regarded as art. The spectator must bear this consideration in mind.

There are some who, thinking that pathos is essential to a *jōruri*, make frequent use of such expressions as "It was touching" in their writing, or who when chanting do so in voices thick with tears. This is foreign to my style. I take pathos to be entirely a matter of restraint. It is moving when the whole of a play is controlled by the dramatic situation, and the stronger and firmer the melody and words, the sadder will be the impression created. For this reason, when one says of something which is sad that it is sad, one loses the implications, and in the end, even the impression of sadness is slight. It is essential that one not say of a thing that "it is sad," but that it be sad of itself. For example, when one praises a place renowned for its scenery such as Matsushima by saying, "Ah, what a fine view!" one has said in one phrase all that one can about the sight, but without effect. If one wishes to praise the view, and one says numerous

---

4. These were popular recitations of ballads, gossip, etc., which flourished particularly about this time.

things indirectly about its appearance, the quality of the view may be known of itself, without one's having to say, "It is a fine view." This is true of everything of its kind.

Someone said, "People nowadays will not accept plays unless they are realistic and well reasoned out. There are many things in the old stories which people will not now tolerate. It is thus that such people as *kabuki* actors are considered skilful to the degree that their acting resembles reality. The first consideration is to have the retainer in the play resemble a real retainer, and to have the daimyō look like a real daimyō. People will not stand for childish nonsense as they did in the past." I answered, "Your view seems plausible, but it is a theory which does not take into account the real methods of art. Art is something which lies in the slender margin between the real and the unreal. Of course it seems desirable, in view of the current taste for realism, to have the retainer in the play copy the gestures and speech of a real retainer, but in that case should a real retainer put rouge and powder on his face like an actor? Or, would it prove entertaining if an actor, on the grounds that real retainers do not make up their faces, were to appear on the stage and perform with his beard growing wild and his head shaven? This is what I mean by the slender margin between the real and the unreal. It is unreal, and yet it is not unreal; it is real, and yet it is not real. Entertainment lies between the two."

In this connection, there is the story of a certain court lady who had a lover. The two loved each other very passionately, but the lady lived far deep in the women's palace, and the man could not visit her quarters. She could see him therefore only very rarely, from between the cracks of her screen of state at the court. She longed for him so desperately that she had a wooden image carved of the man. Its appearance was not like that of an ordinary doll, but did not differ in any particle from the man. It goes without saying that the color of his complexion was perfectly rendered; even the pores of his skin were delineated. The openings in his ears and nostrils were fashioned, and there was no discrepancy even in the number of teeth in the mouth. Since it was made with the man posing beside it, the only difference between the man and this doll was the presence in one, and the absence in the other, of a soul. However, when the lady drew the doll close to her and looked at it, the exactness of the reproduction of the living man chilled her, and she felt unpleasant and rather frightened. Court lady that she was, her love was also chilled, and as she found it distressing to have the doll by her side, she soon threw it away.

In view of this we can see that if one makes an exact copy of a living being, even if it happened to be Yang Kuei-fei, one will become disgusted with it. If when one paints an image or carves it of wood there are, in the name of artistic license, some stylized parts in a work otherwise resembling the real form; this is, after all, what people love in art. The same is true of literary composition. While bearing resemblance to the original, it should have stylization; this makes it art, and is what delights men's minds. Theatrical dialogue written with this in mind is apt to be worth while.

# ■ Yosa Buson (Taniguchi Buson) (1716–1783) (poems)

Yosa Buson was born in the village of Kema (Settsu province, in present-day Osaka prefecture) as Taniguchi Buson, taking the name Yosa in midlife after spending three years in Yosa, a village in Tango province, his mother's hometown. At age twenty, he moved to Edo (modern Tokyo) and studied painting and poetry; his teacher was Hayano Hajin, a disciple of Kikaku and Ransetsu, who themselves had been disciples of Basho. After stays in Uki and Utsunomiya, Buson moved to Kyoto for several years, and then spent three years in Yosa, eventually moving back to Kyoto. In Kyoto, he became the center of a group of disciples and formed a haiku association called the Sankasha. He died at age sixty-six.

Yosa Buson was equally famous as a painter and as a poet. He ranks second only to Basho in the pantheon of great Japanese haiku poets and was the essential figure in the revival of the form, which had become moribund after the death of Basho in 1694. In fact, his dedication to this form caused the period from 1743 until his death to be named the "Haikai Revival." Throughout his life, though, he was known primarily as the most famous painter of the classical Chinese literati style (*bunjinga*). However, he remained devoted to both these arts, and in addition was a master calligrapher, fluent in Chinese, and dedicated to the Chinese ideal of being a gentleman scholar, adept at many arts. There is a particularly "cool" feeling to Buson's poetry; unlike Issa, he did not see it as a forum for airing his personal griefs. In addition to writing haiku, he wrote a few poems in the Chinese style and throughout his work showed a deep indebtedness to the classical Chinese poets (and to Du Fu in particular), whose lines he would often echo. Buson advocated Basho as the ideal haiku writer, and his motto was "Return to Basho!" Yet, this allusive quality in his work, his devotion to the work and ideals of great poets of the past, is an essential difference between his work and that of Basho. Buson was an aesthete, separating art from life, whereas Basho seems to immerse himself wholly in the smallest events of the actual world in his art. Finally, it is unclear as to the exact meaning of "Return to Basho!," but in general it referred to the need to hold the art of haiku to the highest possible standard, to emulate Basho's serious devotion to the art. Buson shines particularly in the individual *hokku,* and has been criticized for so perfecting the stanzas he contributed to linked-verse poems (*haikai*) as to threaten the integrity of the whole.

**FURTHER READING:** French, Calvin L. *The Poet-Painters: Buson and His Followers,* 1974. Sawa, Yuki, and Edith Marcombe Shiffert, trs. *Haiku Master Buson: Translations from the Writings of Yosa Buson—Poet and Artist—With Related Materials,* 1978. Suzuki, S. *Poet-Painter Buson,* 1958. Watson, Wm. *Yosa-no-Buson,* 1960. Yasuhara, Eri Fujita. *Buson and Haishi: A Study of Free-Form Haikai Poetry in Eighteenth Century Japan,* 1982. Yonezawa Yoshiho and Yoshizawa Chu. *Japanese Painting in the Literati Style,* 1974.

## *Twenty-one Haiku*

Spring sea,
day and night, undulating
undulating.

Bright moon to the west.
Shadows of cherryblossoms
stroll east.

No underwear,
a gust of spring wind shows
my bare ass.

Blossoming pear tree.
a woman reading a letter
by moonlight.

On the temple bell
sleeps
a butterfly.

Brief night:
on the hairy caterpillar
beads of dew.

On each thorn
a drop
of white dew.

Lightning flash.
Drip, drip
of dew through bamboo.

Whale diving,
its tail
rising and rising!

Morning breeze
stirs
the caterpillar's hair.


So cool
to nap at noon,
feet against the wall.


In the old well
a fish leaps for a gnat.
The water sound is dark.


It hurts to step
in the bedroom
on my dead wife's comb.


Cool morning.
The voice of the bell
is leaving the bell.


Avoiding fishnet
and fishing lines,
moon on the water.


At the old pond
the frog is aging
among fallen leaves.[1]


Scent of plum-blossoms
rising.
Halo round the moon.


Cold night:
sliver of
thinning moon.

---

1. A play on Basho's most famous poem.

I pull the ice
off my writing brush
with my teeth.


Crow after crow
settling
in autumn dusk.


Red plum flowers
burn
on horse plop.

TRANSLATED BY TONY BARNSTONE


## Three Haiku

The Grand Abbot
is shitting
in the barren field.


I seize
in the mind's darkness
a firefly.


Leak
in the footwashing tub.
Spring drains away.

TRANSLATED BY AYAME FUKUDA


## ■ Ryokan (1758–1831) (poems)

Ryokan (*ryo,* "good"; *kan,* "generosity"), also known by the literary name Daigu ("Big Fool"), is, in his elegant simplicity, one of the world's great mystical poets. He was born in the village of Izumozaki in Echigo province (today's Niigata prefecture) in 1758 and passed up the opportunity to follow his father in the role of village headman, instead shaving his head and entering the life of a Zen Buddhist monk in 1777. His father, who in addition to his political role was a haiku poet and a Shinto priest, was very unhappy with the military government in Edo, supporting the emperor instead, and perhaps in protest drowned himself in 1795 in the Katsura River in Kyoto. From 1790–1795, Ryokan traveled on a number of pilgrimages, until, on hearing of his father's death, he set up a hermitage on Mount Kugami, near Izumozaki, where he lived until his own death thirty-four years later. Soon he became a familiar figure in town plying his begging bowl or playing with the children who appear in so many of his poems.

He practiced Soto Zen, which was brought to Japan from China by Dogen in the thirteenth century. As translator Stevens notes: "Dogen's teaching emphasized two main points: (1) *shikantaza,* themeless sitting in zazen, that is, abandoning all thoughts of good or bad, enlightenment or illusion, and just sitting; and (2) *shusho ichigyo,* 'practice and enlightenment are one.' There is no sudden enlightenment, and enlightenment cannot be separated from one's practice. For these reasons Soto Zen is usually contrasted with Rinzai Zen, with its use of koans during zazen and its striving for *kensho,* an instantaneous, profound insight into reality."[1] Late in life he had an affair, or a close friendship, it is hard to tell which, with a young nun named Teishin, with whom he wrote poetry and who is responsible for collecting the poems of his that have come down to us today. He wrote haiku, waka, Manyo poems, and folk songs as well as poems in classical Chinese forms. The Chinese poet Han Shan, whose work and character resonates with his so strongly, was one of his favorite poets.

**FURTHER READING:** Ryokan. *Between the Floating Mist: Poems of Ryokan.* Translated by Dennis Maloney and Hide Oshiro, 1992; *One Robe, One Bowl: The Zen Poetry of Ryokan.* Translated by John Stevens, 1981; *Ryokan: Zen Monk-Poet of Japan.* Translated by Burton Watson, 1977.

## Who Says My Poem Is a Poem?

Who says my poem is a poem?
My poem, in fact, is not poem.
When you realize that my poem is not poem,
then we can discuss poetry.

TRANSLATED BY DENNIS MALONEY AND HIDE OSHIRO

## For an Old Man, a Dream Is Easily Broken

For an old man, a dream is easily broken.
Waking, I enter the empty room
lit by an oil lamp, but soon
the lamp is exhausted leaving the long winter night.

TRANSLATED BY DENNIS MALONEY AND HIDE OSHIRO

---

1. John Stevens, tr., *One Robe, One Bowl: The Zen Poetry of Ryokan* (New York and Tokyo: Weatherhill, 1981), 15.

## Shaggy Hair Past the Ears

Shaggy hair past the ears,
A worn-out robe resembling white clouds and dark smoke.
Half drunk, half sober, I return home,
Children all around, guiding me along the Way.

TRANSLATED BY JOHN STEVENS

## The Thief Left It Behind

The thief left it behind—
The moon
At the window.

TRANSLATED BY JOHN STEVENS

## Last Night's Dream Was a Lie

Last night's dream was a lie.
I can't explain what I saw.
It lied like truth.
I wake up inside the dream.

TRANSLATED BY TONY BARNSTONE

## The New Pond

The new pond,
a frog jumps in,
—no sound![1]

TRANSLATED BY DENNIS MALONEY AND HIDE OSHIRO

## ■ Issa (Kobayashi Issa) (1763–1827) (poems)

Kobayashi Issa was born Yataro Kobayashi in Kashiwabara, a small mountain village in central Japan. He was the first son of a moderately well-off farmer. In 1765, his mother died and in 1770 his father remarried. After the birth of his half-brother in 1773, a fierce, lifelong battle with his stepmother began. He studied at the village school under a haiku (*hokku*) poet whose pen name was Shimpo; and when his family situation became unbearable, his father sent him to Edo to be an apprentice. After ten years, he enrolled at the school of Nirokuan Chikua, where he studied haiku under Nirokuan (a poet strongly influenced by Basho), and in 1790, after his teacher's death, Issa became the new master. Issa (meaning "cup of tea") is one of many pen names he took and the one by which he is best known. He spent the decade of his thirties wandering across Japan, like Basho, devoting himself to composing

---

1. A commentary on Basho's most famous poem.

haiku and putting out occasional collections. When Issa's father fell ill with ty-phoid in 1801, Issa returned home and nursed him, but he died. After his fa-ther's death, there was a bitter struggle over the will, which left Issa the major-ity of the property; as a result, Issa was denied his birthright by his stepmother and half-brother until he was fifty years old. At that time, he finally settled into his ancestral home and married a village girl named Kiku. They had four sons and a daughter, but none of them lived through infancy. The *haibun* (haiku mixed with prose) journal he wrote about the death of his daughter Sato is his best-known work—*A Year of My Life* (1819). In 1823, the year his fourth son died, Kiku died as well, and Issa's poems about her are among his most touching: "Night moon, / if only she were here / to grumble." He briefly re-married in 1824, but it did not work out, and a year later he married for the last time to a woman named Yao. In 1827, Issa died, sixty-five years old, with his daughter, Yata, the only one fated to survive, still in her mother's womb.

Issa was a Pure Land Buddhist, a form of Buddhism that emphasizes liv-ing like common folk while worshiping Amida Buddha. His work reflects an earthy, humorous, Buddhist consciousness, never preachy: "I pray to Bud-dha / while smashing / flies." The tragedies he lived through are recorded in his haiku, yet they are balanced by his ability to record lightning-flash glimpses of children, animals, insects, and the Japanese landscapes he trav-eled through. Hokku had become by this time essentially the same as the modern haiku, though it could still be used as the initial stanza in a series or integrated into prose as haibun. Issa's hokku is his best work, and he ranks with Basho, Buson, and Shiki as one of its four supreme masters.

**FURTHER READING:** Lewis, Richard. *Of This World: A Poet's Life in Poetry,* 1968. MacKenzie, Lewis, tr. *The Autumn Wind: A Selection from the Poems of Issa,* 1957, 1984. Maloney, Dennis, tr. *Dusk Lingers: Haiku of Issa,* 1986. Merrill, Jean and Ronni Sol-bert, eds. *A Few Flies and I: Haiku by Issa,* 1969. Stryk, Lucien, and Noboru Fujiwara, trs. *The Dumpling Field: Haiku of Issa,* 1981. Williams, C. K., tr. *The Lark, the Thrush, the Starling: Poems from Issa,* 1983. Yuasa, Nobuyuki, tr. *The Year of My Life,* 1972.

## *Twenty-one Haiku*

Don't smash the fly!
He's wringing his hands,
and even his feet!


Red moon,
something a child
would own.


Three day moon
warped
by the cold.

Snow melting.
The village floods
with children.


Spring rain.
Through the trees blows
a discarded letter.


Out the nose
of the Great Buddha
flies a sparrow.


Through a sudden shower
I ride naked
on a naked horse!


Even one-foot waterfall
makes the evening
sound cool.


Big firefly:
flicker, flicker,
gone.


Snail climbing
up Mount Fuji
slowly! slowly!


Distant mountains
reflected in the eye
of a dragonfly.


Wonderful to see
through a torn paper window
the star river.


I piss through the door
making a neat hole
in the snow.

She counts flea bites
while her baby
sucks.

So young,
even her flea bites
are beautiful!

The cat stretches
yawns wide,
goes out to make love.

In the garden the baby
crawls toward a butterfly. It flutters off.
Crawls again. Flutter.

Mosquito in the bedroom
humming,
burnt!

The toad
seems about to belch
out a cloud!

"The peony was this big"
says the small girl
opening her arms wide.

*Hell*

A bright autumn moon.
Pond snails wailing
in the saucepan.

TRANSLATED BY TONY BARNSTONE

## Three Haiku

Bright full moon.
A child weeps
"Get it for me!"

Mountain village:
bright moon
in my soup.


Song of bell,
waterbird wail,
darkening night.

TRANSLATED BY AYAME FUKUDA

# Modern Period

## (1868–present)

### ■ Natsume Soseki (1867–1916) (story)

TRANSLATED BY AIKO ITO AND GRAEME WILSON

Natsume Soseki is a supremely important figure in the development of
the modern Japanese novel. Most of his novels are revered as classics, and
he anticipated the psychological and realistic novel in Japan. He was born
Natsume Kinnosuke in 1867 in Edo (modern-day Tokyo), the fifth son of a
merchant family. He was an unwanted child, and his father put him out for
adoption when he was two; when his new parents separated after seven
years, his birth father took him back, albeit reluctantly. His early education
was in Chinese, but he studied English literature at Tokyo University. In
1889, he became close friends with a fellow student, the famous haiku poet
Masaoka Shiki. After teaching for several years, he spent the years
1900–1903 in England on a government scholarship, studying literature
with tutors. He lived in bitter poverty, terribly alienated from the society of
English gentlemen (he was, he wrote "lonely as a stray dog in a pack of
wolves"), and so he made a life of the intense study of a huge range of
books in English. While in England, he had a kind of nervous breakdown,
and he suffered from a nervous disorder for the remainder of his life. Returning to Japan, he became Lecturer in English Literature at Tokyo University, taking over that position from Lafcadio Hearn. In 1907, he resigned
from his prestigious scholarly position and became the literary editor of the
*Asahi Shimbun,* a newspaper that agreed to serialize his novels. Late in life he
was a mentor to Akutagawa Ryunosuke and other younger writers.

Two of his famous novels that show the range and development of his
career are the immensely popular *Botchan,* a parodic account of a Tokyo

youth's picaresque adventures teaching in a provincial boys' school, and the serious later novel *Kokoro,* meaning "heart" or "spirit." It is a story about the quest for meaning and connection in the bleak and materialist modern world. His fiction has stylistic and imagistic debts to the classical poetry of China and Japan, while the deeper structures of his novels derive significantly from Western fiction. The brief and beautiful piece presented here comes from the early period of his fiction, from a collection of linked allegorical dreams titled *Ten Nights of Dream.* Though it does not represent the psychological depth and deep social concern of his later work, it shows his extraordinary talent for description, his need to make sense of a life's journey, and something of his pessimism.

**FURTHER READING:** Aiko, Ito, and Graeme Wilson, trs. *Ten Nights of Dream, Hearing Things, The Heredity of Taste,* 1974. Field, Norma Moore, tr. *And Then: Natsume Soseki's Novel Sorekara,* 1978. Katsue, Shibata, and Motonari Kai, tr. *I Am a Cat,* 1961. Kingo, Ochiai, and Sanford Goldstein, trs. *To the Spring Equinox and Beyond,* 1985. Mathy, Francis, tr. *Mon: The Gate,* 1972. McClellan, Edwin, tr. *Kokoro,* 1957. Rubin, Jay, tr. *Sanshiro: A Novel,* 1977. Turney, Alan, tr. *Botchan,* 1972; tr. *The Three Cornered World,* 1965. Viglielmo, V. H., tr. *Light and Darkness: An Unfinished Novel,* 1971.

## *The Seventh Night*

It seems that I'm aboard some massive ship. The ship plows forward, shearing the waves away, day after day, night after night, continuously emitting, without one second's break, a stream of inky smoke. The noise is tremendous: but the destination utterly unknown. All I know is that the sun, burning red like red-hot tongs, bulges up from the bottom of the sea. It rises, seems to hover briefly dead above the tall ship's mast, and then, before we realize what's happening, overtakes the shuddering ship and, plunging dead ahead, sinks back with a sizzling sound, the sound of red-hot tongs, down to the bottom of the sea. Each time it sinks, the blue waves far ahead seethe to a blackish red. The ship, making its tremendous noise, pursues the sinking sun. But it never catches up.

One day I buttonholed a sailor, and I asked him "Is this ship steering west?"

The sailor, a curiously uncertain expression on his face, studied me briefly and then answered "Why?"

"Because it seems concerned to chase the setting sun."

The sailor burst into a roar of laughter; and then left me.

I heard the sound of jolly voices chanting:

"Does the sun that travels west
End up in the east?
Is that really true?
Has the sun that leaves the east
Its real home in the west?

Is that also true?
We that on the ocean live,
Rudders for a pillow,
Sail and sail, on and on."

I went up into the bows where I found a watch of sailors hauling at the halyards.

I began to feel most terribly forlorn. There was no way of knowing when one might get ashore. And, worse, no way of knowing whither we were bound. The only certainties were the streaming of black smoke and the shearing of the sea. The waves stretched wide as wide, blue in their boundlessness. Sometimes they grew purple though, close to the sliding ship, they slavered and were white. I felt most terribly forlorn. I even thought it would be better to throw myself into the sea than to stick with such a ship.

There were many fellow-passengers, most, or so it seemed, foreigners though each had a different cast of feature. One day when the sky was clouded and the ship rolling, I saw a woman leaning on the rail, and crying bitterly. The handkerchief with which she wiped her eyes looked white, and her dress, a sort of calico, carried a printed pattern. Seeing her weep, I realized that I was not the only person sad.

One evening when I was alone on deck, watching the stars, a foreigner came up and asked if I knew anything about astronomy. Since I was already contemplating suicide as a means of escape from boredom, it scarcely seemed necessary for me to be acquainted with matters such as astronomy. So I made no answer. The foreigner then told me the story of the seven stars in the neck of the constellation of the Bull; and went on to inform me that the stars and the sea were all of God's creation. He finally asked me if I believed in God. I looked at the sky and said nothing.

Once as I was entering the saloon, I saw a gaily dressed young woman playing the piano, with her back toward me. At her side a tall most splendid-looking man stood singing. His mouth appeared inordinately large. They seemed completely indifferent to all things other than themselves. They seemed even to have forgotten their being on this ship.

I grew more bored than ever. Finally, I determined to put an end to myself and, one convenient evening when no one was about, I jumped with resolution over the side. However, in that moment when my feet left the deck and my link with the ship was severed, suddenly then life became peculiarly precious. From the bottom of my heart I regretted my rash action. But by then it was too late. Will-nilly I was committed to the deep. But, possibly because of the ship's high freeboard, my feet for some long time failed to touch water although my body had abandoned ship. Nonetheless, since nothing could check my fall, I dropped closer and closer to the sea. However much I drew in my legs, nearer and still nearer came the sea. The color of the sea was black.

Meanwhile the ship, still as usual streaming its black smoke, steamed steadily away. I would have been far better off aboard, even though that ship had no known destination. When I came to that realization, it was no longer possible to make use of my belated wisdom. And so I went down quietly, infinitely regretful, infinitely afraid, down to the black of waves.

## ■ Shiki (Masaoka Shiki) (1867–1902) (poems)

### TRANSLATED BY BURTON WATSON

Masaoka Shiki was extremely influential in resuscitating the moribund haiku form of poetry, and his ideas were instrumental in reforming both the tanka and prose writing. He advocated a theory of narrative based on description, on "direct copying from life," which should be understood as both a form of empirical observation and as an attempt to get at the essence of things through observation. He was born in Matsuyama in 1867, and he wrote prose and poetry from his childhood on. In 1883, he moved to Tokyo and in the following year entered the University Preparatory College. In 1889, he suffered the first attack of the tuberculosis that was to plague him throughout his life and eventually confine him to his bed. During this year, he took on the literary pen name Shiki. During the Sino-Japanese War of 1894–1895 he was a war correspondent in China, but this experience only accelerated his illness. His studies, *The Essence of Haikai* (1895) and *Buson, Haiku Poet* (1897), were essential in spreading his ideas about the need for including contemporary life and colloquial speech in the haiku. He helped found the important magazine *Hototogisu* (*The Cuckoo*) in 1897, which served as a forum for his work. He was critical of Basho's poetry, preferring that of Buson, and perceived his own work as hearkening back to what he saw as the less contrived spirit of the *Manyoshu* poets.

**FURTHER READING:** Behn, Harry, tr. *Cricket Songs*, 1960. Blyth, R. H. *A History of Haiku*. Vol. 2, 1964. Brower, Robert H. "Masaoka Shiki and Tanka Reform" in Donald Shively, ed., *Tradition and Modernization in Japanese Culture*, 1971. Corman, Cid. *Born of a Dream: 50 Haiku by Basho, Buson, Taigi, Issa, Shiki*, 1988. Miner, Earl. *Japanese Poetic Diaries*, 1969.

## Thirteen Haiku

From the firefly
in my hands,
cold light


A cricket singing
somewhat back of
the shoe closet

Lonely sound—
simmering in the firepit,
wood chips with snow on them


Getting lazy—
taking my socks off
after I get in bed


Fluttering, fluttering,
butterflies yellow
over the water


Summer storm—
all the sheets of blank paper
blown off my desk


Country road—
boys whacking at a snake,
wheat in autumn


Morning fog—
one man's got a fire going—
construction workers' shed


Peeling pears—
sweet juice drips
from the knife blade


Summer grass—
way in the distance
people playing baseball


A stray cat
shits in my
winter garden

Crickets—
in the corner of the garden
where we buried the dog


Clog with a broken thong
discarded in the
winter paddy


# ▪ Yosano Akiko (1878–1942) (poems)

## TRANSLATED BY SANFORD GOLDSTEIN AND SEISHI SHINODA

Yosano Akiko was the finest practitioner of the "new tanka." The 5 lines of the tanka (based on syllable counts of 5–7–5–7–7) constitute the form that has dominated Japanese poetry from the time of the *Manyoshu* until Western forms were introduced in the modern era. Late nineteenth- and early twentieth-century tanka was dominated by the practitioners of the Poetry Bureau School, a traditionalist school based at the Imperial Poetry Bureau. In the Meiji era, however, contact with the West and increasing industrial progress were changing the nature of life in Japan, and the Bureau School's nature-centered aesthetic was inadequate to the need of poetry to express life as lived.

Yosano Akiko was born to the family of a famous confectioner in Sakai City, Osaka prefecture. Her father, expecting a male child, and mourning the death of a son, so hated his daughter that for the first three years of her life she was sent to be raised by an aunt. Later, however, he repented (after the birth of a new brother) and came to admire his bright daughter, providing the best possible education for her. In other aspects, however, he raised her extremely traditionally—locking her in her bedroom at night and making sure she never went out without a chaperone. But Akiko was a firm believer in social and sexual emancipation for women, which is apparent later in her life in the frankly erotic nature of her tanka. She married Yosano Hiroshi, son of a Buddhist priest, who rejected the priesthood to become first a teacher and then a writer under the pen name Tekkan. One of the most important theorists and popularizers of the new tanka, he had a strong early reputation as a "manly" practitioner of tanka, who wrote about his experiences in the Sino-Japanese War (1894–1895), but his reputation steadily declined as it became apparent that the real talent in the family belonged to Akiko. They were both in love with one of Tekkan's students, a young woman named Yamakawa Tomiko, who died young of tuberculosis in 1909.

In addition to poetry, Akiko wrote novels, essays, and children's stories and translated *The Tale of Genji* into modern Japanese. Akiko's most famous book of poems is *Midaregami* (*Tangled Hair*), a term that, as in

Robert Herrick's "Delight in Disorder" or the tangled tresses of women in Pre-Raphaelite paintings, has erotic undertones—not dishevelment but release from constraints. Such release characterizes her poetry, which celebrates love and the flesh and chastizes the priests whom, in another context, William Blake criticizes for "binding with briars, my joys & desires."

**FURTHER READING:** Goldstein, Sanford, and Seishi Shinoda, trs. *Tangled Hair: Selected Tanka from Midaregami by Akiko Yosana,* 1987.

## You Have Yet to Touch

You have yet to touch
This soft flesh,
This throbbing blood—
Are you not lonely,
Expounder of the Way?                    5

## Without Returning

Without returning . . .
O my feelings
In this gathering darkness of spring,
And against my koto
My tangled, tangled hair.                    5

## In My Bath

In my bath—
Submerged like some graceful lily
At the bottom of a spring,
How beautiful
This body of twenty summers.                    5

## Now

Now
Thinking back
On the course of my passion,
I was like one blind,
Unafraid of the dark.                    5

## Whispering Goodnight

Whispering goodnight
This spring evening
And leaving the room,
I take from the rack
His kimono and try it on.                    5

## Softly I Pushed Open

Softly I pushed open
That door
We call a mystery,
These full breasts
Held in both my hands.

## Was It So Long Ago

Was it so long ago
All innocent I smiled
In the full-length mirror
As I dressed
After my bath?

## Inside the Coffin

Inside the coffin
Of my beautiful
Friend,
The flowers
A riot of color.

## Sleeve Raised

Sleeve raised
As if to strike her love,
She tries to turn the gesture
Into
A dance!

## Spring Is Short!

Spring is short!
Nothing endures!
I cried,
Letting him touch
These supple breasts!

## To Punish

To punish
Men for their endless sins,
God gave me
This fair skin,
This long black hair!

# Tanizaki Junichiro (1886–1965) (story)

## TRANSLATED BY HOWARD HIBBET

Tanizaki Junichiro was born in 1886 in the heart of downtown Tokyo's old merchant quarter, to a father who owned a printing establishment but failed in a series of business enterprises. Tanizaki attended Tokyo Imperial University, where he studied Japanese literature, but never completed his degree, leaving school to become a successful writer and to live a vigorous bohemian life. In this period, he was powerfully influenced by fin de siècle decadent aestheticism and by the work of Baudelaire, Poe, and Oscar Wilde. "The Tattooer" (*Shisei*), the story presented here, launched his literary career in 1910 and is still a favorite. Today, he is considered by many the greatest modern Japanese novelist, and Mishima Yukio was a fierce admirer of his work. The two authors shared a personal flamboyance that shocked their contemporaries, a fascination with sado-masochistic themes in their work, and an aesthetic pursuit of ultimate beauty, a beauty often gendered female. These themes can be seen in "The Tattooer," a kind of perverse meditation on the costs and rewards of art, the tale of a twisted Pygmalion. In the context of this story of a beauty printed over with a tattoer's art, it is interesting to note that Tanizaki's mother was herself a beauty, portrayed in Japanese woodcut prints.

Tanizaki left Tokyo after the 1923 earthquake for the Kansai region, a move from the new capital to the region of Kyoto, the old capital, where he was surrounded by the culture, the architecture, the temples, and the gardens of old Japan. At this time, he moved away from his earlier Westernized work and became fascinated with the Japanese past. Much of his fiction transports the reader into Japanese historical settings, and he devoted years to translating the great work of classical Japanese fiction, *The Tale of Genji*, into modern Japanese.

Tanizaki was, like other intellectual fiction writers, criticized by leftist writers known as the Proletarian Writers for being "bourgeois, decadent, reactionary." Though he was able to pass through the difficult war years without much hardship, his novel *The Makioka Sisters* was censored by the military during this period. He was awarded the Imperial Culture Prize in 1949, the highest official honor for Japanese writers. In 1964, he was the first Japanese writer to be elected to honorary membership in the American Academy and Institute of Arts and Letters. Among his other well-known works are *A Fool's Love* (1924), *Some Prefer Nettles* (1929), *Captain Shigemoto's Mother* (1949), *The Key* (1956), and *Diary of a Mad Old Man* (1962).

**FURTHER READING:** Harper, Thomas J., and Edward G. Seidensticker, trs. *In Praise of Shadows*, 1977. Hibbett, Howard, tr. *Seven Japanese Tales*, 1963. McCarthy, Paul, tr. *A Cat, A Man, and Two Women: Stories*, 1990. Petersen, Gwenn Boardman. *The Moon in Water: Understanding Tanizaki, Kawabata, and Mishima*, 1979.

## The Tattooer

It was an age when men honored the noble virtue of frivolity, when life was not such a harsh struggle as it is today. It was a leisurely age, an age when professional wits could make an excellent livelihood by keeping rich or wellborn young gentlemen in a cloudless good humor and seeing to it that the laughter of Court ladies and geisha was never stilled. In the illustrated romantic novels of the day, in the Kabuki theater, where rough masculine heroes like Sadakuro and Jiraiya were transformed into women— everywhere beauty and strength were one. People did all they could to beautify themselves, some even having pigments injected into their precious skins. Gaudy patterns of line and color danced over men's bodies.

Visitors to the pleasure quarters of Edo preferred to hire palanquin bearers who were splendidly tattooed; courtesans of the Yoshiwara and the Tatsumi quarter fell in love with tattooed men. Among those so adorned were not only gamblers, firemen, and the like, but members of the merchant class and even samurai. Exhibitions were held from time to time; and the participants, stripped to show off their filigreed bodies, would pat themselves proudly, boast of their own novel designs, and criticize each other's merits.

There was an exceptionally skillful young tattooer named Seikichi. He was praised on all sides as a master the equal of Charibun or Yatsuhei, and the skins of dozens of men had been offered as the silk for his brush. Much of the work admired at the tattoo exhibitions was his. Others might be more noted for their shading, or their use of cinnabar, but Seikichi was famous for the unrivaled boldness and sensual charm of his art.

Seikichi had formerly earned his living as an ukiyoye painter of the school of Toyokuni and Kunisada, a background which, in spite of his decline to the status of a tattooer, was evident from his artistic conscience and sensitivity. No one whose skin or whose physique failed to interest him could buy his services. The clients he did accept had to leave the design and cost entirely to his discretion—and to endure for one or even two months the excruciating pain of his needles.

Deep in his heart the young tattooer concealed a secret pleasure, and a secret desire. His pleasure lay in the agony men felt as he drove his needles into them, torturing their swollen, blood-red flesh; and the louder they groaned, the keener was Seikichi's strange delight. Shading and vermilioning—these are said to be especially painful—were the techniques he most enjoyed.

When a man had been pricked five or six hundred times in the course of an average day's treatment and had then soaked himself in a hot bath to bring out the colors, he would collapse at Seikichi's feet half dead. But Seikichi would look down at him coolly. "I dare say that hurts," he would remark with an air of satisfaction.

Whenever a spineless man howled in torment or clenched his teeth and twisted his mouth as if he were dying, Seikichi told him: "Don't act like a child. Pull yourself together—you have hardly begun to feel my needles!" And he would go on tattooing, as unperturbed as ever, with an occasional sidelong glance at the man's tearful face.

But sometimes a man of immense fortitude set his jaw and bore up stoically, not even allowing himself to frown. Then Seikichi would smile and say: "Ah, you are a stubborn one! But wait. Soon your body will begin to throb with pain. I doubt if you will be able to stand it. . . ."

For a long time Seikichi had cherished the desire to create a master-piece on the skin of a beautiful woman. Such a woman had to meet various qualifications of character as well as appearance. A lovely face and a fine body were not enough to satisfy him. Though he inspected all the reigning beauties of the Edo gay quarters he found none who met his exacting demands. Several years had passed without success, and yet the face and figure of the perfect woman continued to obsess his thoughts. He refused to abandon hope.

One summer evening during the fourth year of his search Seikichi happened to be passing the Hirasei Restaurant in the Fukagawa district of Edo, not far from his own house, when he noticed a woman's bare milk-white foot peeping out beneath the curtains of a departing palanquin. To his sharp eye, a human foot was as expressive as a face. This one was sheer perfection. Exquisitely chiseled toes, nails like the iridescent shells along the shore at Enoshima, a pearl-like rounded heel, skin so lustrous that it seemed bathed in the limpid waters of a mountain spring—this, indeed, was a foot to be nourished by men's blood, a foot to trample on their bodies. Surely this was the foot of the unique woman who had so long eluded him. Eager to catch a glimpse of her face, Seikichi began to follow the palanquin. But after pursuing it down several lanes and alleys he lost sight of it altogether.

Seikichi's long-held desire turned into passionate love. One morning late the next spring he was standing on the bamboo-floored veranda of his home in Fukagawa, gazing at a pot of *omoto* lilies, when he heard someone at the garden gate. Around the corner of the inner fence appeared a young girl. She had come on an errand for a friend of his, a geisha of the nearby Tatsumi quarter.

"My mistress asked me to deliver this cloak, and she wondered if you would be so good as to decorate its lining," the girl said. She untied a saffron-colored cloth parcel and took out a woman's silk cloak (wrapped in a sheet of thick paper bearing a portrait of the actor Tojaku) and a letter.

The letter repeated his friend's request and went on to say that its bearer would soon begin a career as a geisha under her protection. She hoped that, while not forgetting old ties, he would also extend his patronage to this girl.

"I thought I had never seen you before," said Seikichi, scrutinizing her intently. She seemed only fifteen or sixteen, but her face had a strangely ripe beauty, a look of experience, as if she had already spent years in the gay quarter and had fascinated innumerable men. Her beauty mirrored the dreams of the generations of glamorous men and women who had lived and died in this vast capital, where the nation's sins and wealth were concentrated.

Seikichi had her sit on the veranda, and he studied her delicate feet, which were bare except for elegant straw sandals. "You left the Hirasei by palanquin one night last July, did you not?" he inquired.

"I suppose so," she replied, smiling at the odd question. "My father was still alive then, and he often took me there."

"I have waited five years for you. This is the first time I have seen your face, but I remember your foot. . . . Come in for a moment, I have something to show you."

She had risen to leave, but he took her by the hand and led her upstairs to his studio overlooking the broad river. Then he brought out two picture scrolls and unrolled one of them before her.

It was a painting of a Chinese princess, the favorite of the cruel Emperor Chou of the Shang Dynasty. She was leaning on a balustrade in a languorous pose, the long skirt of her figured brocade robe trailing halfway down a flight of stairs, her slender body barely able to support the weight of her gold crown studded with coral and lapis lazuli. In her right hand she held a large wine cup, tilting it to her lips as she gazed down at a man who was about to be tortured in the garden below. He was chained hand and foot to a hollow copper pillar in which a fire would be lighted. Both the princess and her victim—his head bowed before her, his eyes closed, ready to meet his fate—were portrayed with terrifying vividness.

As the girl stared at this bizarre picture her lips trembled and her eyes began to sparkle. Gradually her face took on a curious resemblance to that of the princess. In the picture she discovered her secret self.

"Your own feelings are revealed here," Seikichi told her with pleasure as he watched her face.

"Why are you showing me this horrible thing?" the girl asked, looking up at him. She had turned pale.

"The woman is yourself. Her blood flows in your veins." Then he spread out the other scroll.

This was a painting called "The Victims." In the middle of it a young woman stood leaning against the trunk of a cherry tree: she was gloating over a heap of men's corpses lying at her feet. Little birds fluttered about her, singing in triumph; her eyes radiated pride and joy. Was it a battlefield or a garden in spring? In this picture the girl felt that she had found something long hidden in the darkness of her own heart.

"This painting shows your future," Seikichi said, pointing to the woman under the cherry tree—the very image of the young girl. "All these men will ruin their lives for you."

"Please, I beg of you to put it away!" She turned her back as if to escape its tantalizing lure and prostrated herself before him, trembling. At last she spoke again. "Yes, I admit that you are right about me—I am like that woman. . . . So please, please take it away."

"Don't talk like a coward," Seikichi told her, with his malicious smile. "Look at it more closely. You won't be squeamish long."

But the girl refused to lift her head. Still prostrate, her face buried in her sleeves, she repeated over and over that she was afraid and wanted to leave.

"No, you must stay—I will make you a real beauty," he said, moving closer to her. Under his kimono was a vial of anesthetic which he had obtained some time ago from a Dutch physician.

The morning sun glittered on the river, setting the eight-mat studio ablaze with light. Rays reflected from the water sketched rippling golden waves on the paper sliding screens and on the face of the girl, who was fast asleep. Seikichi had closed the doors and taken up his tattooing instruments, but for a while he only sat there entranced, savoring to the full her uncanny beauty. He thought that he would never tire of contemplating her serene masklike face. Just as the ancient Egyptians had embellished their magnificent land with pyramids and sphinxes, he was about to embellish the pure skin of this girl.

Presently he raised the brush which was gripped between the thumb and last two fingers of his left hand, applied its tip to the girl's back, and, with the needle which he held in his right hand, began pricking out a design. He felt his spirit dissolve into the charcoal-black ink that stained her skin. Each drop of Ryukyu cinnabar that he mixed with alcohol and thrust in was a drop of his lifeblood. He saw in his pigments the hues of his own passions.

Soon it was afternoon, and then the tranquil spring day drew toward its close. But Seikichi never paused in his work, nor was the girl's sleep broken. When a servant came from the geisha house to inquire about her, Seikichi turned him away, saying that she had left long ago. And hours later, when the moon hung over the mansion across the river, bathing the houses along the bank in a dreamlike radiance, the tattoo was not yet half done. Seikichi worked on by candlelight.

Even to insert a single drop of color was no easy task. At every thrust of his needle Seikichi gave a heavy sigh and felt as if he had stabbed his own heart. Little by little the tattoo marks began to take on the form of a huge black-widow spider; and by the time the night sky was paling into dawn this weird, malevolent creature had stretched its eight legs to embrace the whole of the girl's back.

In the full light of the spring dawn boats were being rowed up and down the river, their oars creaking in the morning quiet; roof tiles glistened in the sun, and the haze began to thin out over white sails swelling in the early breeze. Finally Seikichi put down his brush and looked at the tattooed spider. This work of art had been the supreme effort of his life. Now that he had finished it his heart was drained of emotion.

The two figures remained still for some time. Then Seikichi's low, hoarse voice echoed quaveringly from the walls of the room:

"To make you truly beautiful I have poured my soul into this tattoo. Today there is no woman in Japan to compare with you. Your old fears are gone. All men will be your victims."

As if in response to these words a faint moan came from the girl's lips.

Slowly she began to recover her senses. With each shuddering breath, the spider's legs stirred as if they were alive.

"You must be suffering. The spider has you in its clutches."

At this she opened her eyes slightly, in a dull stare. Her gaze steadily brightened, as the moon brightens in the evening, until it shone dazzlingly into his face.

"Let me see the tattoo," she said, speaking as if in a dream but with an edge of authority to her voice. "Giving me your soul must have made me very beautiful."

"First you must bathe to bring out the colors," whispered Seikichi compassionately. "I am afraid it will hurt, but be brave a little longer."

"I can bear anything for the sake of beauty." Despite the pain that was coursing through her body, she smiled.

"How the water stings! . . . Leave me alone—wait in the other room! I hate to have a man see me suffer like this!"

As she left the tub, too weak to dry herself, the girl pushed aside the sympathetic hand Seikichi offered her, and sank to the floor in agony, moaning as if in a nightmare. Her disheveled hair hung over her face in a wild tangle. The white soles of her feet were reflected in the mirror behind her.

Seikichi was amazed at the change that had come over the timid, yielding girl of yesterday, but he did as he was told and went to wait in his studio. About an hour later she came back, carefully dressed, her damp, sleekly combed hair hanging down over her shoulders. Leaning on the veranda rail, she looked up into the faintly hazy sky. Her eyes were brilliant; there was not a trace of pain in them.

"I wish to give you these pictures too," said Seikichi, placing the scrolls before her. "Take them and go."

"All my old fears have been swept away—and you are my first victim!" She darted a glance at him as bright as a sword. A song of triumph was ringing in her ears.

"Let me see your tattoo once more," Seikichi begged.

Silently the girl nodded and slipped the kimono off her shoulders. Just then her resplendently tattooed back caught a ray of sunlight and the spider was wreathed in flames.

■ **Akutagawa Ryunosuke (1892–1927) (story)**

TRANSLATED BY TAKASHI KOJIMA

Fiction writer Akutagawa Ryunosuke was born in Tokyo in 1927, the son of a milkman. Seven months later his mother went mad and, not long after, died. Her brother and his wife, the Akutagawas, adopted him into their cultivated and priestly family, but he feared throughout his life that his mother's madness might be in him as well. He studied English literature at Tokyo University from 1913 to 1916, graduating with high honors. At college and throughout his short life, he read widely in both Eastern and Western literatures. He was a disciple of novelist Natsume Soseki, whose attention was captured by his early stories "Rashomon" (1915) and "The Nose" (1916), and he attended Natsume's weekly literary salon. After a brief period teaching English, he devoted himself entirely to literature, and his reputation as a master of the short story was soon established. When he was thirty-five years old, he shocked his contemporaries by drinking poison. He was found with a Bible next to his pillow and with letters in which he gave no better reason for killing himself than (as in some existential short story) "a vague uneasiness."

His fiction is known for its grotesque yet psychologically well-observed depictions, for its dark sensitivity and mordant outlook, as well as for his adaptations of classical Chinese fiction and of traditional *setsuwa,* or "brief narratives," from classical Japanese collections. "Rashomon," for example, was adapted from *Tales of Times Now Past,* and later became (with his short story "In a Grove") the basis for the 1950 movie of that name by Akira Kurosawa. He was of a school of intellectual writers who were in conflict with the political fiction of the Proletarian Writers and the confessional, first-person stories of the contemporary world promoted by the Naturalistic School. As is commonly noted, Akutagawa's style eschews the subjectivity of confession and the crude moralizing of political prose, preferring to hide behind a mask of objectivity, embedding his views subtly in tone and perspective—the deft evasions of a masterful style. Thus, in spite of its "cool" surface, his work was not removed from the concerns of his day: the relativistic perspective in a story such as "In a Grove" and the distancing of placing many of his stories at a historical remove are a screen behind which the author's often biting satire of contemporary Japan resides. This satire of Japanese culture is much more explicit in his short novel *Kappa,* which is a sort of mixture of "Rip Van Winkle" and *Gulliver's Travels.* "Hell Screen," another of his finest works, is a story about the artist as misfit, sacrificer of his own family, and suicide.

**FURTHER READING:** Bownas, Geoffrey, tr. *Kappa: A Satire,* 1971. Kojima, Takashi, tr. *Rashomon and Other Stories,* 1952. Norman, W. H. H., tr. *Hell Screen and Other Stories,* 1948. Peterson, Will, tr. *A Fool's Life,* 1970.

# *Rashomon*[1]

It was a chilly evening. A servant of a samurai stood under the Rashōmon, waiting for a break in the rain.

---

1. The "Rashōmon" was the largest gate in Kyoto, the ancient capital of Japan. It was 106 feet wide and 26 feet deep, and was topped with a ridge-pole; its stone-wall rose 75 feet high. This gate was constructed in 789 when the then capital of Japan was transferred to Kyoto. With the decline of West Kyoto, the gate fell into bad repair, cracking and crumbling in many places, and became a hide-out for thieves and robbers and a place for abandoning unclaimed corpses.

No one else was under the wide gate. On the thick column, its crimson lacquer rubbed off here and there, perched a cricket. Since the Rashōmon stands on Sujaku Avenue, a few other people at least, in sedge hat or nobleman's headgear, might have been expected to be waiting there for a break in the rain storm. But no one was near except this man.

For the past few years the city of Kyōto had been visited by a series of calamities, earthquakes, whirlwinds, and fires, and Kyōto had been greatly devastated. Old chronicles say that broken pieces of Buddhist images and other Buddhist objects, with their lacquer, gold, or silver leaf worn off, were heaped up on roadsides to be sold as firewood. Such being the state of affairs in Kyōto, the repair of the Rashōmon was out of the question. Taking advantage of the devastation, foxes and other wild animals made their dens in the ruins of the gate, and thieves and robbers found a home there too. Eventually it became customary to bring unclaimed corpses to this gate and abandon them. After dark it was so ghostly that no one dared approach.

Flocks of crows flew in from somewhere. During the daytime these cawing birds circled round the ridgepole of the gate. When the sky overhead turned red in the afterlight of the departed sun, they looked like so many grains of sesame flung across the gate. But on that day not a crow was to be seen, perhaps because of the lateness of the hour. Here and there the stone steps, beginning to crumble, and with rank grass growing in their crevices, were dotted with the white droppings of crows. The servant, in a worn blue kimono, sat on the seventh and highest step, vacantly watching the rain. His attention was drawn to a large pimple irritating his right cheek.

As has been said, the servant was waiting for a break in the rain. But he had no particular idea of what to do after the rain stopped. Ordinarily, of course, he would have returned to his master's house, but he had been discharged just before. The prosperity of the city of Kyōto had been rapidly declining, and he had been dismissed by his master, whom he had served many years, because of the effects of this decline. Thus, confined by the rain, he was at a loss to know where to go. And the weather had not a little to do with his depressed mood. The rain seemed unlikely to stop. He was lost in thoughts of how to make his living tomorrow, helpless incoherent thoughts protesting an inexorable fate. Aimlessly he had been listening to the pattering of the rain on the Sujaku Avenue.

The rain, enveloping the Rashōmon, gathered strength and came down with a pelting sound that could be heard far away. Looking up, he saw a fat black cloud impale itself on the tips of the tiles jutting out from the roof of the gate.

He had little choice of means, whether fair or foul, because of his helpless circumstances. If he chose honest means, he would undoubtedly starve to death beside the wall or in the Sujaku gutter. He would be brought to this gate and thrown away like a stray dog. If he decided to steal . . . His mind, after making the same detour time and again, came finally to the conclusion that he would be a thief.

But doubts returned many times. Though determined that he had no choice, he was still unable to muster enough courage to justify the conclusion that he must become a thief.

After a loud fit of sneezing he got up slowly. The evening chill of Kyōto made him long for the warmth of a brazier. The wind in the evening dusk howled through the columns of the gate. The cricket which had been perched on the crimson-lacquered column was already gone.

Ducking his neck, he looked around the gate, and drew up the shoulders of the blue kimono which he wore over his thin underwear. He decided to spend the night there, if he could find a secluded corner sheltered from wind and rain. He found a broad lacquered stairway leading to the tower over the gate. No one would be there, except the dead, if there were any. So, taking care that the sword at his side did not slip out of the scabbard, he set foot on the lowest step of the stairs.

A few seconds later, halfway up the stairs, he saw a movement above. Holding his breath and huddling cat-like in the middle of the broad stairs leading to the tower, he watched and waited. A light coming from the upper part of the tower shone faintly upon his right cheek. It was the cheek with the red, festering pimple visible under his stubbly whiskers. He had expected only dead people inside the tower, but he had only gone up a few steps before he noticed a fire above, about which someone was moving. He saw a dull, yellow, flickering light which made the cobwebs hanging from the ceiling glow in a ghostly way. What sort of person would be making a light in the Rashōmon . . . and in a storm? The unknown, the evil terrified him.

As quietly as a lizard, the servant crept up to the top of the steep stairs. Crouching on all fours, and stretching his neck as far as possible, he timidly peeped into the tower.

As rumor had said, he found several corpses strewn carelessly about the floor. Since the glow of the light was feeble, he could not count the number. He could only see that some were naked and others clothed. Some of them were women, and all were lolling on the floor with their mouths open or their arms outstretched showing no more signs of life than so many clay dolls. One would doubt that they had ever been alive, so eternally silent they were. Their shoulders, breasts, and torsos stood out in the dim light; other parts vanished in shadow. The offensive smell of these decomposed corpses brought his hand to his nose.

The next moment his hand dropped and he stared. He caught sight of a ghoulish form bent over a corpse. It seemed to be an old woman, gaunt, gray-haired, and nunnish in appearance. With a pine torch in her right hand, she was peeping into the face of a corpse which had long black hair.

Seized more with horror than curiosity, he even forgot to breathe for a time. He felt the hair of his head and body stand on end. As he watched, terrified, she wedged the torch between two floor boards and, laying hands on the head of the corpse, began to pull out the long hairs one by one, as a monkey kills the lice of her young. The hair came out smoothly with the movement of her hands.

As the hair came out, fear faded from his heart, and his hatred toward the old woman mounted. It grew beyond hatred, becoming a consuming antipathy against all evil. At this instant if anyone had brought up the question of whether he would starve to death or become a thief—the question which had occurred to him a little while ago—he would not have hesitated to choose death. His hatred toward evil flared up like the piece of pine wood which the old woman had stuck in the floor.

He did not know why she pulled out the hair of the dead. Accordingly, he did not know whether her case was to be put down as good or bad. But in his eyes, pulling out the hair of the dead in the Rashōmon on this stormy night was an unpardonable crime. Of course it never entered his mind that a little while ago he had thought of becoming a thief.

Then, summoning strength into his legs, he rose from the stairs and strode, hand on sword, right in front of the old creature. The hag turned, terror in her eyes, and sprang up from the floor, trembling. For a small moment she paused, poised there, then lunged for the stairs with a shriek.

"Wretch! Where are you going?" he shouted, barring the way of the trembling hag who tried to scurry past him. Still she attempted to claw her way by. He pushed her back to prevent her . . . they struggled, fell among the corpses, and grappled there. The issue was never in doubt. In a moment he had her by the arm, twisted it, and forced her down to the floor. Her arms were all skin and bones, and there was no more flesh on them than on the shanks of a chicken. No sooner was she on the floor than he drew his sword and thrust the silver-white blade before her very nose. She was silent. She trembled as if in a fit, and her eyes were open so wide that they were almost out of their sockets, and her breath came in hoarse gasps. The life of this wretch was his now. This thought cooled his boiling anger and brought a calm pride and satisfaction. He looked down at her, and said in a somewhat calmer voice:

"Look here, I'm not an officer of the High Police Commissioner. I'm a stranger who happened to pass by this gate. I won't bind you or do anything against you, but you must tell me what you're doing up here."

Then the old woman opened her eyes still wider, and gazed at his face intently with the sharp red eyes of a bird of prey. She moved her lips, which were wrinkled into her nose, as though she were chewing something. Her pointed Adam's apple moved in her thin throat. Then a panting sound like the cawing of a crow came from her throat:

"I pull the hair . . . I pull out the hair . . . to make a wig."

Her answer banished all unknown from their encounter and brought disappointment. Suddenly she was only a trembling old woman there at his feet. A ghoul no longer: only a hag who makes wigs from the hair of the dead—to sell, for scraps of food. A cold contempt seized him. Fear left his heart, and his former hatred entered. These feelings must have been sensed by the other. The old creature, still clutching the hair she had pulled off the corpse, mumbled out these words in her harsh broken voice:

"Indeed, making wigs out of the hair of the dead may seem a great evil to you, but these that are here deserve no better. This woman, whose beautiful black hair I was pulling, used to sell cut and dried snake flesh at the guard barracks, saying that it was dried fish. If she hadn't died of the plague, she'd be selling it now. The guards liked to buy from her, and used to say her fish was tasty. What she did couldn't be wrong, because if she hadn't, she would have starved to death. There was no other choice. If she knew I had to do this in order to live, she probably wouldn't care."

He sheathed his sword, and, with his left hand on its hilt, he listened to her meditatively. His right hand touched the big pimple on his cheek. As he listened, a certain courage was born in his heart—the courage which he had not had when he sat under the gate a little while ago. A strange power was driving him in the opposite direction of the courage which he had had when he seized the old woman. No longer did he wonder whether he should starve to death or become a thief. Starvation was so far from his mind that it was the last thing that would have entered it.

"Are you sure?" he asked in a mocking tone, when she finished talking. He took his right hand from his pimple, and, bending forward, seized her by the neck and said sharply:

"Then it's right if I rob you. I'd starve if I didn't."

He tore her clothes from her body and kicked her roughly down on the corpses as she struggled and tried to clutch his leg. Five steps, and he was at the top of the stairs. The yellow clothes he had wrested off were under his arm, and in a twinkling he had rushed down the steep stairs into the abyss of night. The thunder of his descending steps pounded in the hollow tower, and then it was quiet.

Shortly after that the hag raised up her body from the corpses. Grumbling and groaning, she crawled to the top stair by the still flickering torchlight, and through the gray hair which hung over her face, she peered down to the last stair in the torch light.

Beyond this was only darkness . . . unknowing and unknown.

## ■ Kawabata Yasunari (1899–1972) (stories)

In 1968, Kawabata Yasunari became the first Japanese writer to win the Nobel Prize in literature. Four years later, he committed suicide in his studio, leaving no note. He was born in Osaka in 1899, and a tragic childhood in which he lost his sister, parents, grandmother, and in his teens, his grandfather, informs his work with a pervasive sadness. He studied English and Japanese literature at Tokyo University and graduated in 1924. Throughout his life, he wrote the extremely short stories to which he gave the name "palm-of-the-hand stories," and these brief tales quickly established his reputation after his graduation. In addition to the masterful short story "The Mole," one of these palm-of-the-hand stories, "Eggs," is included here.

He was early on associated with a group of writers known as the Neosensualists, who launched a journal called *Age of the Arts,* and who strove for startling, sometimes surreal, images, and a compact, suggestive fiction, a reaction to the dominant mode of naturalism in the early part of the century. Many of his short stories grew into novels, and he even created one palm-of-the-hand story from an already extant novel (*Gleanings from Snow Country*). Translator J. Martin Holman considers the palm-of-the-hand story to be Kawabata's "basic unit of composition from which his longer works were built, after the manner of linked-verse poetry, in which discreet verses are joined to form a longer poem, the linkage between each dependent on subtle shifts as the poem continues."[1] Kawabata had a fantastic instinct for capturing psychologically revelatory dialogue and events, and in his stories life often tilts suddenly into the strange so that ordinary objects, such as a mole or an egg, can become fetishes, or icons of terror. He is best known in the West for his novels *Snow Country* (1947) and *A Thousand Cranes* (1949–1951).

FURTHER READING: Kawabata, Yasunari. *The Izu Dancer and Other Stories,* 1974; *Palm-of-the-Hand Stories.* Translated by Lane Dunlop and J. Martin Holman, 1988; *Snow Country.* Translated by Edward Seidensticker, 1981; *Snow Country, and Thousand Cranes; the Nobel Prize Edition of Two Novels.* Translated by Edward G. Seidensticker, 1969; *The Sound of the Mountain.* Translated by Edward G. Seidensticker, 1981. Petersen, Gwenn Boardman. *The Moon in the Water: Understanding Tanizaki, Kawabata, and Mishima,* 1979.

## The Mole

### TRANSLATED BY EDWARD SEIDENSTICKER

Last night I dreamed about that mole.

I need only write the word for you to know what I mean. That mole — how many times have I been scolded by you because of it.

It is on my right shoulder, or perhaps I should say high on my back.

"It's already bigger than a bean. Go on playing with it and it will be sending out shoots one of these days."

You used to tease me about it. But as you said, it was large for a mole, large and wonderfully round and swollen.

As a child I used to lie in bed and play with that mole. How ashamed I was when you first noticed it.

---

1. Kawabata Yasunari. *Palm-of-the-Hand Stories.* Translated by Lane Dunlop and J. Martin Holman (San Francisco: North Point Press, 1988), xiii.

I even wept, and I remember your surprise.

"Stop it, Sayoko. The more you touch it the bigger it will get." My mother scolded me too. I was still a child, probably not yet thirteen, and afterwards I kept the habit to myself. It persisted after I had all but forgotten about it.

When you first noticed it, I was still more child than wife. I wonder if you, a man, can imagine how ashamed I was. But it was more than shame. This is dreadful, I thought to myself. Marriage seemed at that moment a fearful thing indeed.

I felt as though all my secrets had been discovered—as though you had bared secret after secret of which I was not even conscious myself—as though I had no refuge left.

You went off happily to sleep, and sometimes I felt relieved, and a little lonely, and sometimes I pulled myself up with a start as my hand traveled to the mole again.

"I can't even touch my mole any more," I thought of writing to my mother, but even as I thought of it I felt my face go fiery red.

"But what nonsense to worry about a mole," you once said. I was happy, and I nodded, but looking back now, I wonder if it would not have been better if you had been able to love that wretched habit of mine a little more.

I did not worry so very much about the mole. Surely people do not go about looking down women's necks for moles. Sometimes the expression "unspoiled as a locked room" is used to describe a deformed girl. But a mole, no matter how large it is, can hardly be called a deformity.

Why do you suppose I fell into the habit of playing with that mole?

And why did the habit annoy you so?

"Stop it," you would say. "Stop it." I do not know how many hundred times you scolded me.

"Do you have to use your left hand?" you asked once in a fit of irritation.

"My left hand?" I was startled by the question.

It was true. I had not noticed before, but I always used my left hand.

"It's on your right shoulder. Your right hand should be better."

"Oh?" I raised my right hand. "But it's strange."

"It's not a bit strange."

"But it's more natural with my left hand."

"The right hand is nearer."

"It's backwards with my right hand."

"Backwards?"

"Yes, it's a choice between bringing my arm in front of my neck or reaching around in back like this." I was no longer agreeing meekly with everything you said. Even as I answered you, though, it came to me that when I brought my left arm around in front of me it was as though I were warding you off, as though I were embracing myself. I have been cruel to him, I thought.

I asked quietly, "But what is wrong with using my left hand?"

"Left hand or right hand, it's a bad habit."

"I know."

"Haven't I told you time and time again to go to a doctor and have the thing removed?"

"But I couldn't. I'd be ashamed to."

"It would be a very simple matter."

"Who would go to a doctor to have a mole removed?"

"A great many people seem to."

"For moles in the middle of the face, maybe. I doubt if anyone goes to have a mole removed from the neck. The doctor would laugh. He would know I was there because my husband had complained."

"You could tell him it was because you had a habit of playing with it."

"Really. . . . Something as insignificant as a mole, in a place where you can't even see it. I should think you could stand at least that much."

"I wouldn't mind the mole if you wouldn't play with it."

"I don't mean to."

"You are stubborn, though. No matter what I say, you make no attempt to change yourself."

"I do try. I even tried wearing a high-necked nightgown so that I wouldn't touch it."

"Not for long."

"But is it so wrong for me to touch it?" I suppose I must have seemed to be fighting back.

"It's not wrong, especially. I only ask you to stop because I don't like it."

"But why do you dislike it so?"

"There's no need to go into the reasons. You don't need to play with that mole, and it's a bad habit, and I wish you would stop."

"I've never said I won't stop."

"And when you touch it you always get that strange, absent-minded expression on your face. That's what I really hate."

You're probably right—something made the remark go straight to my heart, and I wanted to nod my agreement.

"Next time you see me doing it, slap my hand. Slap my face even."

"But doesn't it bother you that even though you've been trying for two or three years you haven't been able to cure a trivial little habit like that by yourself?"

I did not answer. I was thinking of your words, "That's what I really hate."

That pose, with my left arm drawn up around my neck—it must look somehow dreary, forlorn. I would hesitate to use a grand word like "solitary." Shabby, rather, and mean, the pose of a woman concerned only with protecting her own small self. And the expression on my face must be just as you described it, "strange, absent-minded."

Did it seem a sign that I had not really given myself to you, as though a space lay between us? And did my true feelings come out on my face when I touched the mole and lost myself in reverie, as I had done since I was a child?

But it must have been because you were already dissatisfied with me that you made so much of that one small habit. If you had been pleased with me you would have smiled and thought no more about it.

That was the frightening thought. I trembled when it came to me of a sudden that there might be men who would find the habit charming.

It was your love for me that first made you notice. I do not doubt that even now. But it is just this sort of small annoyance, as it grows and becomes distorted, that drives its roots down into a marriage. To a real husband and wife personal eccentricities have stopped mattering, and I suppose that on the other hand there are husbands and wives who find themselves at odds on everything. I do not say that those who accommodate themselves to each other necessarily love each other, and that those who constantly disagree hate each other. I do think, though, and I cannot get over thinking, that it would have been better if you could have brought yourself to overlook my habit of playing with the mole.

You actually came to beat me and to kick me. I wept and asked why you could not be a little less violent, why I had to suffer so because I touched my mole. That was only surface. "How can we cure it?" you said, your voice trembling, and I quite understood how you felt and did not resent what you did. If I had told anyone of this, no doubt you would have seemed a violent husband. But since we had reached a point where the most trivial matter added to the tension between us, your hitting me actually brought a sudden feeling of release.

"I will never get over it, never. Tie up my hands." I brought my hands together and thrust them at your chest, as though I were giving myself, all of myself, to you.

You looked confused, your anger seemed to have left you limp and drained of emotion. You took the cord from my sash and tied my hands with it.

I was happy when I saw the look in your eyes, watching me try to smooth my hair with my bound hands. This time the long habit might be cured, I thought.

Even then, however, it was dangerous for anyone to brush against the mole.

And was it because afterwards the habit came back that the last of your affection for me finally died? Did you mean to tell me that you had given up and that I could very well do as I pleased? When I played with the mole, you pretended you did not see, and you said nothing.

Then a strange thing happened. Presently the habit which scolding and beating had done nothing to cure—was it not gone? None of the extreme remedies worked. It simply left of its own accord.

"What do you know—I'm not playing with the mole any more." I said it as though I had only that moment noticed. You grunted, and looked as if you did not care.

If it mattered so little to you, why did you have to scold me so, I wanted to ask; and I suppose you for your part wanted to ask why, if the habit was to be cured so easily, I had not been able to cure it earlier. But you would not even talk to me.

A habit that makes no difference, that is neither medicine nor poison—go ahead and indulge yourself all day long if it pleases you. That is what the expression on your face seemed to say. I felt dejected. Just to annoy you, I thought of touching the mole again there in front of you, but, strangely, my hand refused to move.

I felt lonely. And I felt angry.

I thought too of touching it when you were not around. But somehow that seemed shameful, repulsive, and again my hand refused to move.

I looked at the floor, and I bit my lip.

"What's happened to your mole?" I was waiting for you to say, but after that the word "mole" disappeared from our conversation.

And perhaps many other things disappeared with it.

Why could I do nothing in the days when I was being scolded by you? What a worthless woman I am.

Back at home again, I took a bath with my mother.

"You're not as good-looking as you once were, Sayoko," she said. "You can't fight age, I suppose."

I looked at her, startled. She was as she had always been, plump and fresh-skinned.

"And that mole used to be rather attractive."

I have really suffered because of that mole—but I could not say that to my mother. What I did say was: "They say it's no trouble for a doctor to remove a mole."

"Oh? For a doctor . . . but there would be a scar." How calm and easygoing my mother is! "We used to laugh about it. We said that Sayoko was probably still playing with that mole even now that she was married."

"I was playing with it."

"We thought you would be."

"It was a bad habit. When did I start?"

"When do children begin to have moles, I wonder. You don't seem to see them on babies."

"My children have none."

"Oh? But they begin to come out as you grow up, and they never disappear. It's not often you see one this size, though. You must have had it when you were very small." My mother looked at my shoulder and laughed.

I remembered how, when I was very young, my mother and my sisters sometimes poked at the mole, a charming little spot then. And was that not why I had fallen into the habit of playing with it myself?

I lay in bed fingering the mole and trying to remember how it was when I was a child and a young woman.

It was a very long time since I had last played with it. How many years, I wonder.

Back in the house where I was born, away from you, I could play with it as I liked. No one would stop me.

But it was no good.

As my finger touched the mole, cold tears came to my eyes.

I meant to think of long ago, when I was young, but when I touched the mole all I thought of was you.

I have been damned as a bad wife, and perhaps I shall be divorced; but it would not have occurred to me that here in bed at home again I should have only these thoughts of you.

I turned over my damp pillow—and I even dreamed of the mole.

I could not tell after I awoke where the room might have been, but you were there, and some other woman seemed to be with us. I had been drinking. Indeed I was drunk. I kept pleading with you about something.

My bad habit came out again. I reached around with my left hand, my arm across my breast as always. But the mole—did it not come right off between my fingers? It came off painlessly, quite as though that were the most natural thing in the world. Between my fingers it felt exactly like the skin of a roast bean.

Like a spoiled child I asked you to put my mole in the pit of that mole beside your nose.

I pushed my mole at you. I cried and clamored, I clutched at your sleeve and hung on your chest.

When I awoke the pillow was still wet. I was still weeping.

I felt tired through and through. And at the same time I felt light, as though I had laid down a burden.

I lay smiling for a time, wondering if the mole had really disappeared. I had trouble bringing myself to touch it.

That is all there is to the story of my mole.

I can still feel it like a black bean between my fingers.

I have never thought much about that little mole beside your nose, and I have never spoken of it, and yet I suppose I have had it always on my mind.

What a fine fairy story it would make if your mole really were to swell up because you put mine in it.

And how happy I would be if I thought you in your turn had dreamed of my mole.

I have forgotten one thing.

"That's what I hate," you said, and so well did I understand that I even thought the remark a sign of your affection for me. I thought that all the meanest things in me came out when I fingered the mole.

I wonder, however, if a fact of which I have already spoken does not redeem me: it was perhaps because of the way my mother and sisters petted me that I first fell into the habit of fingering the mole.

"I suppose you used to scold me when I played with the mole," I said to my mother, "a long time ago."

"I did—it was not so long ago, though."

"Why did you scold me?"

"Why? It's a bad habit, that's all."

"But how did you feel when you saw me playing with the mole?"

"Well . . ." My mother cocked her head to one side. "It wasn't becoming."

"That's true. But how did it look? Were you sorry for me? Or did you think I was nasty and hateful?"

"I didn't really think about it much. It just seemed as though you could as well leave it alone, with that sleepy expression on your face."

"You found me annoying?"

"It did bother me a little."

"And you and the others used to poke at the mole to tease me?"

"I suppose we did."

If that is true, then wasn't I fingering the mole in that absent way to remember the love my mother and sisters had for me when I was young?

Wasn't I doing it to think of the people I loved?

This is what I must say to you.

Weren't you mistaken from beginning to end about my mole?

Could I have been thinking of anyone else when I was with you?

Over and over I wonder whether the gesture you so disliked might not have been a confession of a love that I could not put into words.

My habit of playing with the mole is a small thing, and I do not mean to make excuses for it; but might not all of the other things that turned me into a bad wife have begun in the same way? Might they not have been in the beginning expressions of my love for you, turned to unwifeliness only by your refusal to see what they were?

Even as I write I wonder if I do not sound like a bad wife trying to seem wronged. Still there are these things that I must say to you.


# Eggs

TRANSLATED BY J. MARTIN HOLMAN

The husband and wife had both caught colds and were sleeping side by side.

The wife always took the older grandchild to bed with her, but her husband hated to be awakened early, so it was rare that they slept side by side.

The husband had caught his cold in a funny way. He had a favorite old hot-spring resort at Tōnosawa in Hakone where he went even in the winter. This year he had gone at the beginning of February. On the third day of his stay, he had hurriedly gotten up and gone to the bath, thinking it was already one-thirty in the afternoon. When he had returned, the maid was putting charcoal in the brazier, looking as though she were half-asleep.

"What's going on this morning? I'm surprised to see you awake so early."

"What? You're being facetious."

"It's still only just past seven. You got up at five after seven."

"What?" He was bewildered. "Oh, I see. I confused the big hand and the little hand on my watch. That's quite a mistake. My eyes are getting old."

"Down at the desk I was worried that a thief or something had gotten into your room."

When he looked up, he saw the maid was wearing a lined *meisen* kimono over her nightgown. Awakened where she slept, she must have had no time to change. He had called the desk to notify them that he was up, but the reason he had gotten no response was that she had been asleep.

"I'm sorry I got you up so early."

"That's all right. It was time to get up anyway. But will you be going back to bed? Shall I get your bedding out again?"

"Well, let me see . . ." He held his hands over the brazier. Now that she mentioned it, he did feel sleepy, but he thought the cold would awaken him.

He had left the inn while the morning was still chilly. And he had caught a cold.

The cause of his wife's cold was not so clear, but colds had been going around, so she had probably caught it from someone else.

By the time the husband had come home, his wife was already in bed.

When the husband had told the story about getting up too early after mistaking the hands of his watch, the whole family had had a good laugh. They had all passed around the pocket watch to have a look at it.

It was a rather large pocket watch; however, they had come to the conclusion that one could confuse the big hand and the little hand in the dim bedside light with sleepy eyes, since the two hands were shaped the same with circles at the tips. They had turned the hands to test whether five after seven could be confused with one-thirty.

"Father needs a watch that glows in the dark," the youngest daughter had said.

Feeling languid and feverish, the husband had decided to sleep beside his wife. "To keep you company," he had said.

"You could probably take the medicine I got for myself from the doctor. After all, we have the same thing."

When they awoke the next morning, the wife asked, "How was Hakone?"

"Well, it was cold," the husband said, summing it all up. "Last night you coughed terribly and it woke me up, but all I had to do was clear my throat and you started up in a fright. I was quite surprised."

"Really? I didn't know."

"You were sleeping well."

"But I wake up right away if I'm sleeping with our grandson."

"Jumping up startled like that at your age."

"Was I that startled?"

"Yes."

"Maybe it's instinctive, even in a woman my age. If there's a foreign body at your side, you go to sleep and forget, and then—"

"Foreign body? Have I become a 'foreign body'?" Her husband smiled bitterly, but then he added, "That's right. One night in Hakone—I think it was Saturday—a lot of people came to the inn together. After a banquet, one group of guests came to the next room to sleep, but a geisha who had come with them was so dead drunk that her speech was slurred. She was grumbling on the telephone with a geisha in another room. She was screeching and her speech was slurred, so I couldn't understand what she was saying, but it sounded like 'I'm going to lay an egg, I'm going to lay an egg.' It was funny how she said that."

"That's pathetic."

"Pathetic? Her voice was booming."

"Then you looked at your watch, half-asleep, and got up, right?"

"No, stupid." The husband smiled bitterly.

They heard footsteps.

"Mother," the youngest daughter, Akiko, called from beyond the sliding partition, "are you awake?"

"Yes."

"Father, too?"

"Yes, he is."

"May I come in?"

"Yes."

Their fifteen-year-old daughter came in and sat down at her mother's side.

"I had a bad dream."

"What about?"

"I had died. I was a dead person. I knew it was me."

"What a horrible dream!"

"Yes, it was. I was wearing a light kimono, all white. I was going down a straight road. Both sides of the road were foggy. The road seemed to be floating, and I floated when I walked. A strange old woman was following me. She followed me all the way. There was no sound of footsteps. I was so scared I couldn't look back, but I knew she was there. I couldn't get away. Mother, was it the god of death?"

"Of course not," she said as she looked at her husband. "Then what happened?"

"Then, as I walked along, houses began to appear here and there at the roadside. They were low houses like barracks—all the same gray color and all in gentle, rounded shapes. I ducked inside one of the houses. The old woman mistakenly went inside a different house. Good, I thought to myself. But there wasn't anyplace to sleep in the house—just eggs piled everywhere."

"Eggs?" the wife said, exhaling.

"Eggs. I think they were eggs."

"Really? Then what happened?"

"I'm not certain, but I think I was taken up to heaven, away from that house and its eggs. Just as I thought, 'I'm going to heaven,' I woke up."

The girl then looked at her father.

"Father, am I going to die?"

"Of course not." Surprised by her question, he answered the same way his wife had. He had been pondering whether fifteen-year-olds usually have such dreams of death when she had mentioned the eggs. He had almost cried out—it was so bizarre.

"Oh, it was so scary. . . . It still is," the girl said.

"Akiko, yesterday when my throat hurt, I thought it would be good to swallow some raw egg. You went to buy some, and that's why you had the dream about eggs."

"Could that be? Shall I bring you some now? Would you eat some?" The girl went out.

"You were thinking about your good-for-nothing egg geisha, so those eggs appeared in her dream. How pathetic," his wife said.

"Hmm," her husband was looking at the ceiling. "Does Akiko often dream about death?"

"I don't know. It's the first time, I think."

"Did something happen?"

"I don't know."

"But it was the eggs that made her ascend to heaven, wasn't it?"

Their daughter brought the eggs. She broke one and handed it to her mother. "Here you are," she said, then left the room.

The wife glanced sideways at the egg. "It seems somehow repulsive. I can't swallow it. Here—you take it."

The husband also looked at the egg out of the corner of his eye.


## ■ Nakamoto Takako (1903–1991) (story)

TRANSLATED BY YUKIKO TANAKA

Nakamoto Takako is a writer only now beginning to be reassessed after years in which her work was ignored, in contrast with the work of male Japanese fiction writers. Her father was a retired army officer and a high school gym teacher. She came from an extremely poor background, her family moving from a small village to the city of Yamaguchi when she was young, where she completed her schooling through high school. After teaching at primary school for a while, she moved to Tokyo to pursue her goal of becoming a writer. There, she worked for one of the leading publishing houses and began to publish her stories. She was associated with the journal *Women and the Arts,* which was a magazine started in 1928 as a forum for women writers. In 1929, she published "The Female Bell-Cricket" in *Women in the Arts,* which caused a sensation and gave Nakamoto instant visibility. The story, as translator Tanaka notes, "was the first story written by a Japanese woman that openly depicted a woman's sexual desire."[1] Yet the message about the powerful woman in this story, who becomes a kind of man-devouring insect (like Tanizaki's geisha in "The Tattooer"), is far from clear. Is this a feminist story, as Tanaka suggests—a "militant expression of a woman's need to control her life"— or does the terror of the devouring, selfish, femme fatale depicted here effectively counteract this message?

*Women in the Arts* soon shifted heavily to the left, this being the heyday of the Proletarian School of writers, and Nakamoto herself did union organizing of textile workers, mostly young women from the country working in Tokyo mills. She was arrested in 1930, among hundreds of other women, for fighting police and company thugs with makeshift weapons after a dispute over large layoffs. After her thirty-one days in prison, she became a Communist Party sympathizer and was soon arrested by the secret police, interrogated, tortured, and upon her mental collapse sent to a mental hospital. Her trouble with the police was not over, however; she went to work in a ceramic tile factory in Kawasaki, a violation of her probation conditions, and was sentenced to three years in prison. During this time, she wrote a novel about her experiences with the mill workers and published it in *Women in the Arts* as *Factory Number Four, the Toyo Muslin.* She had become a committed Communist by this time but was forced to recant her beliefs as Japan slipped further into military rule. In the 1930s, she published two more novels, *Nanbu Iron Kettle Makers* (1938) and *Dark and Bright Sides of Construction* (1939). In the 1940s, she married and had two children (her husband lost his civil service job under United States military occupation for being a Communist). Though she did not write through most of the war and postwar period, she began publishing again in the 1950s, and her novel *Runways* was serialized in the Japanese Communist Party's daily, *Red Flag.* She continued publishing novels through the 1960s.

# The Female Bell-Cricket

In a corner of the last streetcar of the day, Tomoko sat, her chin buried deep in the collar of her overcoat. She felt as if her voice were caught in

---

1. Tanaka Yukiko, ed. *To Live and to Write* (Seattle: Seal Press, 1987), 710.

her throat, like a broken musical instrument. The streetcar was nearly empty but the air was filled with the smell of sour alcohol. Each time the train jerked, Tomoko's lackluster hair swayed, disturbing her shadow on the wall. She felt as if the train were hurling her into the depths of the ocean; it was difficult to breathe. Inhaling greedily, her nostrils flaring, Tomoko gazed inquisitively at the passengers.

Men! They are all hefty men! she thought. Moved by this sudden realization of their male sex, she was breathless. For a moment she forgot that her stomach was empty, shrunken like a paper balloon—she had been wandering around all day. The next moment she heard her own voice scolding her for being helplessly attracted to men, even after Akita, her common-law husband, had betrayed and left her.

Tomoko got off the train and started walking briskly, her thin shoulders braced as if the air were assaulting her. Stone buildings stood indifferent and cold, making the street look as narrow as a fjord. The bare branches lining the street sliced the cold air. As she walked along, following her black shadow, Tomoko felt like spitting on herself out of hostility and self-disgust.

The roof on the other side of the bridge was lower, making the town look much less intimidating. But the pressure of the wind grew stronger, and Tomoko felt her body being pushed along. She was already at the outskirts of the city. After the cold concrete pavement, the resilience and the rich smell of soil overwhelmed her. At the left side of the road was a huge pile of dirt, fenced off with a rope. Inside the enclosure, a lantern illuminated a close-cropped head and a shovel going up and down in a regular rhythm. Occasionally the tip of the shovel flashed an icy glitter. Walking on, she felt something cold on the end of her nose; she stuck out her hand and some chilly drops of water fell onto her palm. No sooner did she realize what this was than she was enveloped in rain, which beat down on the rooftops with increasing force. Blown by the wind, the rain pelted against the ground with the strength of horses' hooves. The driving rain spashed in Tomoko's face as she stood in the middle of the road. She pulled up the collar of her coat and hurried on, her body bent so low that she was almost crawling under the eaves of the houses. The rain trickled through her collar and down her back. The sole reason for her being out late on a night like this was the same as for all the other nights: to indulge in sex with Akita before he took his new bride, to feel superior to the bride-to-be. Akita's parents had refused to recognize Tomoko as their son's common-law wife.

The house she was returning to stood in front of her, shabby as a small paper box, desolate and trembling in the gusty wind. The first thing that Tomoko sensed as her shivering hand pulled the door open was the smell of a male body. She was once again overcome by self-disgust as she remembered how she had reacted earlier to the odor of men in the streetcar. She went in, noisily. Under the dim light of the lamp, Miki sat hunched over his desk. This man, poor and gentle as a doe, had rescued Tomoko and was providing her with shelter and food. She stood in front of him and stared coldly at his pale forehead, half-covered by hair. She directed her pent-up anger at him, ready to explode.

"Look, I'm drenched," she said, shaking herself hard and pulling at the sleeve of her coat. She looked around the room. Finding no charcoal left in the brazier and therefore no fire with which to dry herself, she went to the closet and yanked a dress out of her wicker trunk. Seeing Tomoko's anger, Miki looked at her apologetically.

"You must be cold. I'm sorry I don't have a fire," he said.

Without responding, Tomoko took off her wet clothes in front of him and dried herself with a towel. When her body had regained its warmth and color, she put on dry clothes. The wind outside had begun to blow harder against the houses and the ground.

Sullenly she went to the kitchen to find something to eat. In a pot was a bit of cold rice, gleaming faintly in the light. There was also some salted seaweed in a sake cup.

"Have you eaten?" she asked Miki, glancing at the food.

"Yes, I have," he said firmly. But she knew that he hadn't. The rice in the pan was the same as it had been when she left the house. Realizing that Miki had saved the food for her even though he was hungry himself, she was filled with an even stronger contempt for him. She felt no gratitude for his kindness and gentleness. She knew where his ambition lay, she could see it more clearly everyday. Men are all kind and gentle until they get what they want from a woman, she thought. She went ahead and ate the food as if she were entitled to it.

Tomoko's body, which had been chilled to the bone, now felt warmer. After she had eaten what little food there was, she began spreading the quilts out next to Miki, who was still sitting at the desk. On the desert of the sheet Tomoko found a pubic hair. I shall let this lie modestly in a piece of tissue paper, she thought, and held it in her palm to inspect it under the light. She sighed deep and long, a sigh long as a comet's tail.

Tomoko grew plump as the days went by and her skin became silky. Miki, on the other hand, became pale and skinny. He had only a few books left; his violin had been exchanged long ago for rice and charcoal. His cloak had flown away like a butterfly, transformed into a piece of steak, into hot chicken with rice, into colorful salads. The only regular income Miki had was from writing a few pages of poetry, which he sold for ten yen to a stationery outfit in Kanda. The poems adorned the covers of stationery, intended to inspire the hearts of naive teenage girls. The money earned was quickly changed into meat and vegetables; the only trace of his labors was the faint smell of fat at the bottom of a cooking pan. Miki also worked long hours as a copyist, but even so he could not keep up with Tomoko's appetite. Still, he was pleased that Tomoko had stopped chasing after Akita and was no longer going out so often, instead spending most of her time lying beside him.

Tomoko felt dried up, like a scab on an old wound. She had no desire to work; respectable jobs all seemed absurd, and any effort of a philosophical nature she considered useless. Look at the way people live in this large city, she thought: they flourish like cryptogamous plants; they conceal strange bacteria as they live day to day. She spent her days observing the man gasping beside her, indifferent to what she saw; she could have been watching a plastic doll. Sometimes she stared at his fine Roman nose, thinking that she would some day kill this man and eat him, just as the female bell-cricket devours her mate.

Tomoko sat on the sunny windowsill, her clothes slipped down to her waist. She was hunting for fleas in her underwear. The fleas, which had been hiding inside the seams, jumped in small, perfect arcs on the faded pink fabric. She pursued them with concentration. Miki watched, enjoying the curves of Tomoko's body—from her forehead to her nose, then to her chin, from her neck down to her breasts. When his eyes reached her two shiny cones, he quickly averted them, blinking; he felt his cigarette burning his fingertips and threw it away. He returned his gaze to Tomoko, but by this time the cones were hidden behind her arms, the wonderful opportunity to enjoy her was lost. His face revealed his desire to lie in her arms and suck at her breast, as he had at his mother's. But this was a fantasy, he knew, and he forced himself to go back to his book.

After she had killed all the fleas she could find, Tomoko slipped her soft body back into her clothes and spanned her waist with her hands to measure it. Then she went over to Miki and, squatting down by his desk, moved her knees back and forth like a pet dog wagging its tail.

"I feel like eating a steak tonight," she said.

"Tonight?" Miki said nervously. "But we had chicken cutlets last night, so . . . "

"That was yesterday."

"But . . . " The man still hesitated. Tomoko kept staring at him as he turned his face away.

"But there's no money. Is that what you're saying? There are many ways to get money."

Miki bit his lip and lowered his head, supporting it in his hands and staring at the vacant space in front of him. He saw before him the shadow of this woman whose body had filled out and whose skin was now lustrous. Tomoko was aware of her power over Miki, who sat silently. She watched him indifferently, smoking her cigarette.

"You haven't got your pay from that place in Kanda, have you?"

"I got it for the work I did this month. And the day before yesterday I took in the work I was supposed to do for next month," he said, slowly opening his eyes. His voice was low and sad, like the sound a cat makes when it's been smacked on the forehead.

"How about asking to get paid for that work? You have to be a bit aggressive about these things."

"I see."

"This is what I don't like," she said, shaking her head. Her face was tense, her muscles tight. "Men are attractive when they're pushy and tough. Being timid and reserved like you doesn't impress anyone."

She exhaled as she lifted her chin. The smoke came out of her tilted nose and floated upward. She felt pleased with herself.

"And your poems—they are no good. So old-fashioned. They're sentimental, too. You ought to change your approach altogether."

"I'll go to Kanda, then, even though I don't think I can get any more money," said Miki, who had been listening to Tomoko with his chin resting on his hand. He shook his thin shoulders. Tomoko sat puffing smoke rings while he went out the door.

When Miki came back that evening, he handed her, with a deep sigh, a mere one yen bill. He must have begged it from the stationery store. Saying he had a stomach ache, he let Tomoko eat the whole steak, shining with fat. The thick, warm steak titillated Miki's nose with its wonderful smell, while satisfying juices fell on Tomoko's tongue. She enjoyed every bite while she watched Miki clutching his stomach, which she knew was growling from hunger. Does he feel heroic and self-satisfied? she wondered. If so I'll kick him in the back.

The next day Tomoko found the announcement of Akita's wedding in the newspaper, accompanied by a photograph. He had transformed himself back into the son of a comfortable middle-class family. How painlessly he had taken a lovely maiden for his wife. In the photograph the bride and groom looked like a pair of butterflies, like insect specimens. Tomoko wanted to spit on the picture and throw it at Miki. Instead, she cut it out and pinned it on the wall. She decided to congratulate the pair of butterflies with rowdy laughter, but soon her laughter turned to crying, the tears dripping down and making dark spots on her knees.

Miki watched without a word from where he sat on the windowsill, cleaning his ears. It was a nice day and Tomoko invited him to take a walk to an open field nearby. They sat with their legs stretched out on the withered grass. The late November sun cast soft, transparent rays on their backs. Tomoko's lavishly padded hips overshadowed Miki's pencil-thin body. He sat quietly with his eyes half closed, basking in the sun and the pressure of her body and female odor, and tried to conjure up some poetic sentiment to suit his mood.

As the days passed, Tomoko grew fatter; she sprawled immodestly in front of the man. She had a double chin now, and her hips were as full and solid as the body of a female moth. Miki grew thinner, his bones showed beneath his skin. Exhaling black breath from his rancid lungs and suffering from anemic dizziness, he would not give up his woman, whose splendid energy and strength was a pleasure to his eyes.

And indeed Tomoko's body was deserving of admiration. Her supple skin was as smooth and shiny as rare Occidental parchment, and in the darkness he was sure he could see a halo around her body. When the small crimson lips above her chin—as full as those of an image of

Buddha—were open, her small, well-shaped white teeth gleamed. Her inner thighs were as taut as newly strung rackets, revealing their marvelous flexibility, and when she leaned back in a certain way, her private parts glistened. Living with this glorious female finally led Miki to idolize and worship her. Tomoko only despised him even more, laughing at his hopeless romanticism. She coldly watched as this male bell-cricket became emaciated with the approach of autumn, ready to be eaten by his female.

It became impossible to get money in any way. The copy work done by this man with rancid lungs no longer provided food to satisfy the woman's glorious body. Tossing his pen away, Miki rolled on the floor with his legs and arms pulled up to his chest. Tomoko simply watched him, puffing on her cigarette as she sat on the windowsill.

"What's the matter? You're lazy," she said.

"I can't do it. I'll never catch up," he moaned, gasping his bad breath.

"You're a coward," said Tomoko, and left the window. She went to the mirror to make up her face. Then she changed her clothes and left the house. The man lay on the floor, holding his arms and legs against his abdomen, until she returned late that night.

Tomoko glanced at Miki and sat down next to him on the floor, exposing her nicely shaped legs. Then she took a five-yen bill from her pocket and threw it at him. He got up, about to take the money, and stopped himself. He frowned and stared at the bill for a moment, his eyes filled with doubt. Having reached a conclusion, he stood up, went to the window and took a deep breath. The clear air outside stung him with the sharpness of a needle. Looking from the man to the money a few times, Tomoko began to laugh loudly so that her shoulders shook. Her laughter sounded empty, like bones being shaken in a canister.

"You are a fool," she said.

Miki turned around. His unshaven face grew paler. He tried to say something, but no sound came from his distorted mouth. The fact that some physical exercises she had performed earlier that evening had been transformed into a five-yen bill was of no significance to Tomoko. She despised all things that belonged to the abstract arena anyway; she hunted them down like fleas. She had simply thrown her glorious body at a man, a pug-nosed bourgeois, who'd had his eyes on her for some time. That's how she had gotten the money. Ever since losing Akita to another woman, Tomoko felt like a movie screen: after the film of her metaphysical life was finished, the screen reflected only an empty reality. No matter who tried to project an image on the screen, no matter who tried to stir up a physical sensation, the screen remained blank, empty. She picked up the money, looked at it, and started laughing again, loudly.

"What are you thinking, you fool?" She snapped the paper money with her fingers, enjoying its sound, and put it back in her pocket. Then she turned her smile to Miki, who was rubbing his face in confusion. He closed the window and lay down on the floor again. Tomoko lay down next to him.

Tomoko reflected over her current state, comparing it to a few hours earlier, when she had still had a foot in the metaphysical arena. Tomoko discovered that she had neither sadness nor regret. She was now living in a place free of complex thoughts and emotion—and it was far easier. She could blot out her obsessive attachment to Akita and her bitterness toward the city that had engulfed and altered him. But she also felt an even stronger revulsion toward Miki's romanticism, his amiable and timid personality. If he blamed her for what she had done and loved her less because of it, she would grab him like a wild bear, tear his throat with her sharp claws and spill his warm blood.

Moving closer to Miki, Tomoko cornered him; slowly he was backed against the wall. Then she reached out to grab his face and pull it toward her. He looked up with tearful eyes, then suddenly pushed her away, shaking his head fiercely. As she fell backward, he saw her uncovered breast, her arched neck, and the shining hair under her armpits. But even the sight of this did not make Miki want to touch her. Tomoko, who liked being handled roughly, waited in vain for him to grab her. She looked at this man who had turned his back on her, then got up and left the room.

There was a thick fog outside, falling like heavy, milk-colored breath, settling on the ground as it fell. The bare branches of the trees, stretching out like a nervous system, were quickly being covered. Tomoko walked, feeling drops of water form on her eyelids. Night was for those who want to believe in mystery and superstition, she thought. She walked for some time with her hands in her pockets, taking a deep breath once in a while, and then she went back to the house. She went to bed without a word.

With the one yen Tomoko had given him, Miki left the house early in the morning. A day without him seemed emptier than mere physical hunger. She was in anguish all day long; she leaned against the desk and felt like a morning glory in evening. That night she left the door unlocked and waited for him. The clock struck three, then came the first crowing of a cock, but Miki did not return. Toward dawn she fell asleep, still leaning against the desk. When she awakened, Miki was there, the bright morning sunlight on his back.

He stood with the veins showing through the pale skin of his face, his hair mussed. His eyes were wide open. He must have been watching me while I slept, Tomoko thought. His clenched hands shook. Tomoko felt revulsion and anger, but this soon turned to pity and contempt. She couldn't tell whether he had been walking the streets all night or if he'd gone somewhere to buy a prostitute. Either way, she felt he deserved her scorn. He looked at her in confusion, and this made her feel tense; she stared back at him. Unable to bear her gaze, he threw himself to the floor, folded his arms over his chest, and sighed like a person in great distress. His sigh then turned into painful sobbing. Pretending that she didn't understand, Tomoko continued to stare at him reproachfully. She lit a cigarette and smoked it slowly, her chin cupped on her hand, all the while staring at him. When he moved, his kimono fell open, and she spotted what looked like dried semen on his thigh. From his body came the rank odor of rotten flesh.

"Why don't you go to the bathhouse today. You haven't washed in weeks. You ought to clean yourself up," she said, exhaling smoke toward him.

His eyes closed, Miki lay still for a while, and then, suddenly, he moved, gripping his throat. Gasping hard, as if something were forcing its way from his chest, he covered his mouth with a handkerchief. When he took it away from his mouth, he saw a clot of blood, dark red, staring up at his darkened eyes. He folded the handkerchief and feebly threw his head down against his outstretched arms. Tomoko sat by this man, still smoking, watching him coolly.

# ■ Sakaki Nanao (1922–   ) (poems)

## TRANSLATED BY AUTHOR

Sakaki Nanao is a fascinating paradox, a Japanese writer whose life and work has become inextricably linked with that of the great American Beat poets, Gary Snyder and Allen Ginsberg. It is well known in the West that Gary Snyder went to Japan to study in a Zen monastery for years, but much less known that Sakaki and a few other like-minded artists, photographers, and writers of the Japanese counterculture came to America and became associated with the flower children and the Beat scene. Sakaki is also the founder of an agricultural community called the Banyan Ashram. The seventh son in a large family, he was born in a village near Kagoshima and was drafted into the Japanese army in World War II, serving as a radar analyst. As Gary Snyder recounts,

> He sat in on the farewell parties for young kamikaze pilots leaving dawn the next day for their death, and identified the B-29 that was on its way to bomb Nagasaki on his radar screen. Upon the announcement of the surrender of Japan his outfit's senior officer ordered the men to prepare to commit mass suicide. Someone luckily turned on the radio, to hear the Emperor himself command, in almost incomprehensibly archaic Japanese, that there was no need for soldiers to kill themselves.[1]

He first came to the United States in 1969 and traveled extensively in the West and Southwest, where a number of his poems are set. He is at once a cosmopolitan poet and a throwback to the poet mystics of the Chinese and Japanese past—Wang Wei, Ryokan, and Saigyo. Like Snyder, he is a lone voice for spiritual values and environmental politics, a cantanker-

---

1. Sakaki Nanao, *Break the Mirror: The Poems of Nanao Sakaki*. Foreword by Gary Snyder (San Francisco: North Point Press, 1987), ix.

ous, hilarious, excremental, dedicated poet-activist, running counter to the prevailing wind of avarice and consumption.

His excellent poem "Future Knows" shows Sakaki at his best—anecdotal, with an understated but savage irony. His more polemical poems succeed less, for example, "Ancestor of the Japanese," in which he compares the Japanese consumer to a cockroach: "The Japanese cockroach is also gulping down / the Amazonian rain forest for toilet paper. / For future generations, / they work vigorously and joyously / leaving the soil full of agrichemicals, / leaving rivers and lakes terribly polluted / leaving graveyards of coral reefs." But through all his poems, koans, and polemical tracts can be seen Sakaki's big heart and his big spirit, the voice of a modern wild man shouting uncomfortable truths from the margins of society. His book *Break the Mirror* (1987) is available from North Point Press. *Real Play* was published by Tooth of Time Books, and *Bellyfulls* was published in 1966 by Toad Press.

## Future Knows

Thus I heard:

Oakland, California—
To teacher's question
An eleven-year-old girl answered,
"The ocean is
A huge swimming pool with cement walls."

On a starry summer night
At a camping ground in Japan
A nine-year-old boy from Tokyo complained,
"Ugly, too many stars."

At a department store in Kyoto
One of my friends bought a beetle
For his son, seven years old.

A few hours later
The boy brought his dead bug
To a hardware store, asking
"Change battery please."

## Small People

"inch by inch
little snail,

creep up and up Mt. Fuji."
— Issa, 19th century Haiku poet.

. . . "a Navaho woman identifies                                            *5*
801 specimens of desert insects."
an American scientist recorded—1948.

3,000,000 abandoned children
in big Brazilian cities, I heard.

300,000,000 soldiers                                                       *10*
in Red China, I heard.

a Pennsylvanian sea lily fossil
300,000,000 years old
from the Santa Fe basin,
now paperweight on my desk.                                                *15*

I want to be a lightning bug
for the next 300,000,000
light years' dark age.


# ■ Tamura Ryuichi (1923– ) (poems)

### TRANSLATED BY CHRISTOPHER DRAKE

Tamura Ryuichi is one of modern Japan's most interesting poets, a peculiar writer of great intelligence and deep humanity. He is one of the poets originally associated with the modernist magazine *Wasteland,* and his work shows influence from both Western modernism and Japanese humorous traditions. As he noted in a conversation with translator Christopher Drake,

> We wanted to question the basic principles behind an industrial society based on the illusion of the isolated individual and the deification of economic growth based on war and imperialism. I tried to make my poems holes or windows that would let me see through the indefinable spiritual waste as well as the obvious spiritual destruction.[1]

He writes an extremely self-conscious, wacky, humorous, conceptual poetry, but if the "house" of "Human House" is "built of . . . words," and if the "body" of "Green Conceptual Body" explores the dream within dream within dream of human conceptual systems, such poems always come back to human truths and human nightmares. He attempts to deal, as Western authors did, with a peculiarly Japanese version of the mod-

---

1. Ooka Makoto and Thomas Fitzsimmons, eds., *A Play of Mirrors: Eight Major Poets of Modern Japan* (Rochester, MI: Katydid Books, Oakland University, 1987), 63.

ernist wasteland. Tamura sees "angelic missiles and beautiful hydrogen bombs" as symptoms of a diseased mode of thinking. For Tamura, such human nightmares derive from flawed, hubris-filled humanity, "Feverish decaying matter / standing on two legs / giddy with sky in its pores,"[2] and even the actual nuclear nightmares that led to Hiroshima and Nagasaki are human brainchilds, so that "I myself am the nightmare." Yet, in his poetry there is the possibility of peace if we can see past the hall of mirrors of conceptual systems and are able "Just once / with eyes not human / to see, experience," and affirm "the taste of ice cream."

**FURTHER READING:** Fitzsimmons, Thomas. *Japanese Poetry Now,* 1972. Keene, Donald, tr. *The Modern Japanese Prose Poem: An Anthology of Six Poets,* 1980. Kijima, Hajime. *The Poetry of Postwar Japan,* 1975. Makoto, Ooka, and Thomas Fitzsimmons, eds. *A Play of Mirrors: Eight Major Poets of Modern Japan,* 1987.

## Green Conceptual Body

Dogs run inside dogs
cats sleep inside cats
birds fly inside birds nailed to the sky
fish swim inside fish across deserts and pant in water

But people can't run inside inner people
so they run inside conceptual bodies
they can't dream free-form cat dreams
so they watch insomniac dreams
they can't swim like fish
so they labor to float concepts
and they can't fly like birds
so they put wings on concepts
to feel the pleasure of crashing

Sometimes people
are inside rooms
but they never live
inside people (inside bodies)
people sleep inside different concepts,
choose vegetables over meat,
boil, fry, make eating a chore;
concepts peer into the blood,
make people need forks and chopsticks

2. From his poem "Green Thought," translated by Christopher Drake.

people even need shovels to bury corpses
stopping to lick ice cream as they work

People go out walking                                          25
on nice days in early summer
leaving the people inside themselves in their rooms;
these shut-in bodies measure their blood pressure and spoon out
        honey
and lead thoughts across their voices;
what does the spirit, shut in, do?                             30
what went out walking
weren't bodies, weren't spirit
were conceptual bodies with legs
they built the vertical nightmare of medieval Gothic
the ascending nightmare knotting heaven and earth             35
invisible ropes
hierarchical classes
wings for angels
ivory horns for devils
the materials had to be combustible                            40
the dream irreversible

I walk a small path through the field
and come out by the Tama River
on the other side two men tend fishing lines
no conceptual bodies: people                                   45
drowsy, I lie down in the grass—that instant
the vertical axis swings, the horizontal
pushes through my conceptual body
the Gothic collapses
voluptuous curves and colors spurt out                         50
the smell of water comes this far

Sun directly overhead
objects but no shadows
my conceptual body turns cat—indeterminate
its footsteps                                                  55
utterly soundless

Leaving one dream to enter another,
you can hardly call that waking;
I have no Globe to world
my thoughts to actors on a stage—                              60
I'd rather look, for a split-second,
at the most modern nightmare, nuclear war
but the moment I saw it
because I had come to the edge of the field
they would be watching me: eyes in                             65

angelic missiles and beautiful hydrogen bombs;
I'm not a passerby, not a spectator
I myself am the nightmare

All I still want
is, on the tongues of gravediggers,
the taste of ice cream


## Human House

I guess I'll be back late
I said and left the house
my house is made of words
an iceberg floats in my old wardrobe
unseen horizons wait in my bathroom
from my telephone: time, a whole desert
on the table: bread, salt, water
a woman lives in the water
hyacinths bloom from her eyeballs
of course she is metaphor herself
she changes the way words do
she's as free-form as a cat
I can't come near her name

I guess I'll be back late
no, no business meeting
not even a reunion
I ride ice trains
walk fluorescent underground arcades
cut across a shadowed square
ride in a mollusk elevator
violet tongues and gray lips in the trains
rainbow throats and green lungs underground
in the square, bubble language
foaming bubble information, informational information
adjectives, all the hollow adjectives
adverbs, paltry begging adverbs
and nouns, crushing, suffocating nouns
all I want is a verb
but I can't find one anywhere
I'm through with a society
built only of the past and future
I want the present tense

Because you open a door
doesn't mean there has to be a room

because there are windows                                             *35*
doesn't mean there's an interior
doesn't mean there's a space
where humans can live and die—
so far I've opened and shut
countless doors, going out each one                                   *40*
so I could come in through another
telling myself each time
what a wonderful new world lies just beyond
what do I hear? from the paradise on the other side
dripping water                                                        *45*
wingbeats
waves thudding on rocks
sounds of humans and beasts breathing
the smell of blood

Blood                                                                 *50*
it's been a while
I'd almost forgotten what it smells like
silence gathers around a scream
on the tip of a needle
as he walks slowly toward me                                          *55*
the surgeon puts on his rubber gloves
I close my eyes, open them again
things falling through my eyes
both arms spread like wings
hair streaming out full length                                        *60*
things descending momentary gaps of light
connecting darkness and darkness
I rise slowly from a table in a bar
not pulled by a political slogan or religious belief
it's hard enough trying to find my eyes                               *65*
to see the demolition of the human house
the dismemberment of my language

My house, of course, isn't made of your words
my house is built of my words

# ■ Abe Kobo (1924– ) (story)

### TRANSLATED BY ALISON KIBRICK

Abe Kobo was born in 1924 in Tokyo, the son of a doctor, but he grew up in the city of Mukden in Manchuria, where his father practiced. He felt alienated from the aggressive, imperialistic Japan of the war years and even changed his name (to Kobo from Kimfusa) to make it sound more

Chinese. He received an M.D. from Tokyo University in 1948 and published his first novel the same year, but he never practiced medicine. In an early phase, Abe was a Marxist playwright. In 1951, he received the prestigious Akutagawa prize, and in 1963 the film version of his novel *The Woman in the Dunes* received the Jury Prize at the Cannes Film Festival. He has also received the Kishida and the Kanizaki prizes for drama. He is best known in the West for *The Woman in the Dunes* (Random House, 1972), but many of his other novels have been translated and well received, such as *The Ruined Map* (Putnam, 1969, 1981) and his extraordinary experimental novel *The Box Man* (Putnam, 1974, 1981). Most recently, editions of his short stories have appeared in English translation, notably *Beyond the Curve* (Kodansha International, 1991). His fiction is relentlessly strange and takes great chances, as obsessed with nightmare as Franz Kafka, as darkly sexual as Mishima Yukio, and as magically cerebral as Jorge Luis Borges. His relation to the new generation of postmodern Japanese fiction writers (such as Murakami Haruki) is like that of J. G. Ballard to Cyberpunk— precursor, first explorer, metaphysician of the fantastic—and Abe ranks with Eugene Ionesco and Samuel Beckett as one of the great masters of the absurd and the grotesque.

## The Magic Chalk

Next door to the toilet of an apartment building on the edge of the city, in a room soggy with roof leaks and cooking vapors, lived a poor artist named Argon.

The small room, nine feet square, appeared to be larger than it was because it contained nothing but a single chair set against the wall. His desk, shelves, paint box, even his easel had been sold for bread. Now only the chair and Argon were left. But how long would these two remain?

Dinnertime drew near. "How sensitive my nose has become!" Argon thought. He was able to distinguish the colors and proximity of the complex aromas entering his room. Frying pork at the butcher's along the streetcar line: yellow ocher. A southerly wind drifting by the front of the fruit stand: emerald green. Wafting from the bakery: stimulating chrome yellow. And the fish the housewife below was broiling, probably mackerel: sad cerulean blue.

The fact is, Argon hadn't eaten anything all day. With a pale face, a wrinkled brow, an Adam's apple that rose and fell, a hunched back, a sunken abdomen, and trembling knees, Argon thrust both hands into his pockets and yawned three times in succession.

His fingers found a stick in his pocket.

"Hey, what's this? Red chalk. Don't remember it being there."

Playing with the chalk between his fingers, he produced another large yawn.

"Aah, I need something to eat."

Without realizing it, Argon began scribbling on the wall with the chalk. First, an apple. One that looked big enough to be a meal in itself. He drew a paring knife beside it so that he could eat it right away. Next, swallowing hard as baking smells curled through the hallway and window to permeate his room, he drew bread. Jam-filled bread the size of a baseball glove. Butter-filled rolls. A loaf as large as a person's head. He envisioned glossy browned spots on the bread. Delicious-looking cracks, dough bursting through the surface, the intoxicating aroma of yeast. Beside the bread, then, a stick of butter as large as a brick. He thought of drawing some coffee. Freshly brewed, steaming coffee. In a large, jug-like cup. On a saucer, three matchbox-size sugar cubes.

"Damn it!" He ground his teeth and buried his face in his hands. "I've got to eat!"

Gradually his consciousness sank into darkness. Beyond the window-pane was a bread and pastry jungle, a mountain of canned goods, a sea of milk, a beach of sugar, a beef and cheese orchard—he scampered about until, fatigued, he fell asleep.

A heavy thud on the floor and the sound of smashing crockery woke him up. The sun had already set. Pitch black. Bewildered, he glanced toward the noise and gasped. A broken cup. The spilled liquid, still steaming, was definitely coffee, and near it were the apple, bread, butter, sugar, spoon, knife, and (luckily unbroken) the saucer. The pictures he had chalked on the wall had vanished.

"How could it . . .?"

Suddenly every vein in his body was wide awake and pounding. Argon stealthily crept closer.

"No, no, it can't be. But look, it's real. Nothing fake about the smothering aroma of this coffee. And here, the bread is smooth to the touch. Be bold, taste it. Argon, don't you believe it's real even now? Yes, it's real. I believe it. But frightening. To believe it is frightening. And yet, it's real. It's edible!"

The apple tasted like an apple (a "snow" apple). The bread tasted like bread (American flour). The butter tasted like butter (same contents as the label on the wrapper—not margarine). The sugar tasted like sugar (sweet). Ah, they all tasted like the real thing. The knife gleamed, reflecting his face.

By the time he came to his senses, Argon had somehow finished eating and heaved a sigh of relief. But when he recalled why he had sighed like this, he immediately became confused again. He took the chalk in his fingers and stared at it intently. No matter how much he scrutinized it, he couldn't understand what he didn't understand. He decided to make sure by trying it once more. If he succeeded a second time, then he would have to concede that it had actually happened. He thought he would try to draw something different, but in his haste just drew another familiar-looking apple. As soon as he finished drawing, it fell easily from the wall. So this is real after all. A repeatable fact.

Joy suddenly turned his body rigid. The tips of his nerves broke through his skin and stretched out toward the universe, rustling like fallen leaves. Then, abruptly, the tension eased, and, sitting down on the floor, he burst out laughing like a panting goldfish.

"The laws of the universe have changed. My fate has changed, misfortune has taken its leave. Ah, the age of fulfillment, a world of desires realized . . . God, I'm sleepy. Well, then, I'll draw a bed. This chalk has become as precious as life itself, but a bed is something you always need after eating your fill, and it never really wears out, so no need to be miserly about it. Ah, for the first time in my life I'll sleep like a lamb."

One eye soon fell asleep, but the other lay awake. After today's contentment he was uneasy about what tomorrow might bring. However, the other eye, too, finally closed in sleep. With eyes working out of sync he dreamed mottled dreams throughout the night.

Well, this worrisome tomorrow dawned in the following manner.

He dreamed that he was being chased by a ferocious beast and fell off a bridge. He had fallen off the bed . . . No. When he awoke, there was no bed anywhere. As usual, there was nothing but that one chair. Then what had happened last night? Argon timidly looked around the wall, tilting his head.

There, in red chalk, were drawings of a cup (it was broken!), a spoon, a knife, apple peel, and a butter wrapper. Below these was a bed—a picture of the bed off which he was supposed to have fallen.

Among all of last night's drawings, only those he could not eat had once again become pictures and returned to the wall. Suddenly he felt pain in his hip and shoulder. Pain in precisely the place he should feel it if he had indeed fallen out of bed. He gingerly touched the sketch of the bed where the sheets had been rumpled by sleep and felt a slight warmth, clearly distinguishable from the coldness of the rest of the drawing.

He brushed his finger along the blade of the knife picture. It was certainly nothing more than chalk; there was no resistance, and it disappeared leaving only a smear. As a test he decided to draw a new apple. It neither turned into a real apple and fell nor even peeled off like a piece of unglued paper, but rather vanished beneath his chafed palm into the surface of the wall.

His happiness had been merely a single night's dream. It was all over, back to what it was before anything had happened. Or was it really? No, his misery had returned fivefold. His hunger pangs attacked him fivefold. It seemed that all he had eaten had been restored in his stomach to the original substances of wall and chalk powder.

When he had gulped from his cupped hands a pint or so of water from the communal sink, he set out toward the lonely city, still enveloped in the mist of early dawn. Leaning over an open drain that ran from the kitchen of a restaurant about a hundred yards ahead, he thrust his hands into the viscous, tarlike sewage and pulled something out. It was a basket made of wire netting. He washed it in a small brook nearby. What was left in it seemed edible, and he was particularly heartened that half of it looked like rice. An old man in his apartment building had told him recently that by placing the basket in the drain one could obtain enough food for a meal a day. Just about a month ago the man had found the means to afford bean curd lees, so he had ceded the restaurant drain to the artist.

Recalling last night's feast, this was indeed muddy, unsavory fare. But it wasn't magic. What actually helped fill his stomach was precious and so could not be rejected. Even if its nastiness made him aware of every swallow, he must eat it. Shit. This was the real thing.

Just before noon he entered the city and dropped in on a friend who was employed at a bank. The friend smiled wryly and asked, "My turn today?"

Stiff and expressionless, Argon nodded. As always, he received half of his friend's lunch, bowed deeply and left.

For the rest of the day, Argon thought.

He held the chalk lightly in his hand, leaned back in the chair, and as he sat absorbed in his daydreams about magic, anticipation began to crystallize around that urgent longing. Finally, evening once again drew near. His hope that at sunset the magic might take effect had changed into near confidence.

Somewhere a noisy radio announced that it was five o'clock. He stood up and on the wall drew bread and butter, a can of sardines, and coffee, not forgetting to add a table underneath so as to prevent anything from falling and breaking as had occurred the previous night. Then he waited.

Before long darkness began to crawl quietly up the wall from the corners of the room. In order to verify the course of the magic, he turned on the light. He had already confirmed last night that electric light did it no harm.

The sun had set. The drawings on the wall began to fade, as if his vision had blurred. It seemed as if a mist was caught between the wall and his eyes. The pictures grew increasingly faint, and the mist grew dense. And soon, just as he had anticipated, the mist had settled into solid shapes—success! The contents of the pictures suddenly appeared as real objects.

The steamy coffee was tempting, the bread freshly baked and still warm.

"Oh! Forgot a can opener."

He held his left hand underneath to catch it before it fell, and, as he drew, the outlines took on material form. His drawing had literally come to life.

All of a sudden, he stumbled over something. Last night's bed "existed" again. Moreover, the knife handle (he had erased the blade with his finger), the butter wrapper, and the broken cup lay fallen on the floor.

After filling his empty stomach, Argon lay down on the bed.

"Well, what shall it be next? It's clear now that the magic doesn't work in daylight. Tomorrow I'll have to suffer all over again. There must be a simple way out of this. Ah, yes! a brilliant plan—I'll cover up the window and shut myself in darkness."

He would need some money to carry out the project. To keep out the sun required some objects that would not lose their substance when exposed to sunlight. But drawing money is a bit difficult. He racked his brains, then drew a purse full of money . . . The idea was a success, for when he opened up the purse he found more than enough bills stuffed inside.

This money, like the counterfeit coins that badgers made from tree leaves in the fairy tale, would disappear in the light of day, but it would leave no trace behind, and that was a great relief. He was cautious nonetheless and deliberately proceeded toward a distant town. Two heavy blankets, five sheets of black woolen cloth, a piece of felt, a box of nails, and four pieces of squared lumber. In addition, one volume of a cookbook collection that caught his eye in a secondhand bookstore along the way. With the remaining money he bought a cup of coffee, not in the least superior to the coffee he had drawn on the wall. He was (why?) proud of himself. Lastly, he bought a newspaper.

He nailed the door shut, then attached two layers of cloth and a blanket. With the rest of the material, he covered the window, and he blocked the edges with the wood. A feeling of security, and at the same time a sense of being attacked by eternity, weighed upon him. Argon's mind grew distant, and, lying down on the bed, he soon fell asleep.

Sleep neither diminished nor neutralized his happiness in the slightest. When he awoke, the steel springs throughout his body were coiled and ready to leap, full of life. A new day, a new time . . . tomorrow wrapped in a mist of glittering gold dust, and the day after tomorrow, and more and more overflowing armfuls of tomorrows were waiting expectantly. Argon smiled, overcome with joy. Now, at this very moment, everything, without any hindrance whatsoever, was waiting eagerly among myriad possibilities to be created by his own hand. It was a brilliant moment. But what, in the depths of his heart, was this faintly aching sorrow? It might have been the sorrow that God had felt just before Creation. Beside the muscles of his smile, smaller muscles twitched slightly.

Argon drew a large wall clock. With a trembling hand he set the clock precisely at twelve, determining at that moment the start of a new destiny.

He thought the room was a bit stuffy, so he drew a window on the wall facing the hallway. Hm, what's wrong? The window didn't materialize. Perplexed for a moment, he then realized that the window could not acquire any substance because it did not have an outside; it was not equipped with all the conditions necessary to make it a window.

"Well, then, shall I draw an outside? What kind of view would be nice? Shall it be the Alps or the Bay of Naples? A quiet pastoral scene wouldn't be bad. Then again, a primeval Siberian forest might be interesting." All the beautiful landscapes he had seen on postcards and in travel guides flickered before him. But he had to choose one from among them all, and he couldn't make up his mind. "Well, let's attend to pleasure first," he decided. He drew some whiskey and cheese and, as he nibbled, slowly thought about it.

The more he thought, the less he understood.

"This isn't going to be easy. It could involve work on a larger scale than anything I—or anyone—has ever tried to design. In fact, now that I think about it, it wouldn't do simply to draw a few streams and orchards, mountains and seas, and other things pleasing to the eye. Suppose I drew a mountain; it would no longer be just a mountain. What would be beyond it? A city? A sea? A desert? What kind of people would be living there? What kind of animals? Unconsciously I would be deciding those things. No, making this window a window is serious business. It involves the creation of a world. Defining a world with just a few lines. Would it be right to leave that to chance? No, the scene outside can't be casually drawn. I must produce the kind of picture that no human hand has yet achieved."

Argon sank into deep contemplation.

The first week passed in discontent as he pondered a design for a world of infinitude. Canvases once again lined his room, and the smell of turpentine hung in the air. Dozens of rough sketches accumulated in a pile. The more he thought, however, the more extensive the problem became, until finally he felt it was all too much for him. He thought he might boldly leave it up to chance, but in that case his efforts to create a new world would come to nothing. And if he merely captured accurately the inevitability of partial reality, the contradictions inherent in that reality would pull him back into the past, perhaps trapping him again in starvation. Besides, the chalk had a limited life-span. He had to capture the world.

The second week flew by in inebriation and gluttony.

The third week passed in a despair resembling insanity. Once again his canvases lay covered with dust, and the smell of oils had faded.

In the fourth week Argon finally made up his mind, a result of nearly total desperation. He just couldn't wait any longer. In order to evade the responsibility of creating with his own hand an outside for the window, he decided to take a great risk that would leave everything to chance.

"I'll draw a door on the wall. The outside will be decided by whatever is beyond the door. Even if it ends in failure, even if it turns out to be the same apartment scene as before, it'll be far better than being tormented by this responsibility. I don't care what happens, better to escape."

Argon put on a jacket for the first time in a long while. It was a ceremony in honor of the establishment of the world, so one couldn't say he was being extravagant. With a stiff hand he lowered the chalk of destiny. A picture of the door. He was breathing hard. No wonder. Wasn't the sight beyond the door the greatest mystery a man could contemplate? Perhaps death was awaiting him as his reward.

He grasped the knob. He took a step back and opened the door.

Dynamite pierced his eyes, exploding. After a while he opened them fearfully to an awesome wasteland glaring in the noonday sun. As far as he could see, with the exception of the horizon, there was not a single shadow. To the extent that he could peer into the dark sky, not a single cloud. A hot dry wind blew past, stirring up a dust storm.

"Aah . . . It's just as though the horizon line in one of my designs had become the landscape itself. Aah . . ."

The chalk hadn't resolved anything after all. He still had to create it all from the beginning. He had to fill this desolate land with mountains, water, clouds, trees, plants, birds, beasts, fish. He had to draw the world all over again. Discouraged, Argon collapsed onto the bed. One after another, tears fell unceasingly.

Something rustled in his pocket. It was the newspaper he had bought on that first day and forgotten about. The headline on the first page read, "Invasion Across 38th Parallel!" On the second page, an even larger space devoted to a photograph of Miss Nippon. Underneath, in small print, "Riot at N Ward Employment Security Office," and "Large-scale Dismissals at U Factory."

Argon stared at the half-naked Miss Nippon. What intense longing. What a body. Flesh of glass.

"This is what I forgot. Nothing else matters. It's time to begin everything from Adam and Eve. That's it—Eve! I'll draw Eve!"

Half an hour later Eve was standing before him, stark naked. Startled, she looked around her.

"Oh! Who are you? What's happened? Golly, I'm naked!"

"I am Adam. You are Eve." Argon blushed bashfully.

"I'm Eve, you say? Ah, no wonder I'm naked. But why are you wearing clothes? Adam, in Western dress—now that's weird."

Suddenly her tone changed.

"You're lying! I'm not Eve. I'm Miss Nippon."

"You're Eve. You really are Eve."

"You expect me to believe this is Adam—in those clothes—in a dump like this? Come on, give me back my clothes. What am I doing here anyway? I'm due to make a special modeling appearance at a photo contest."

"Oh, no. You don't understand. You're Eve, I mean it."

"Give me a break, will you? Okay, where's the apple? And I suppose this is the Garden of Eden? Ha, don't make me laugh. Now give me my clothes."

"Well, at least listen to what I have to say. Sit down over there. Then I'll explain everything. By the way, can I offer you something to eat?"

"Yes, go ahead. But hurry up and give me my clothes, okay? My body's valuable."

"What would you like? Choose anything you want from this cookbook."

"Oh, great! Really? The place is filthy, but you must be pretty well fixed. I've changed my mind. Maybe you really are Adam after all. What do you do for a living? Burglar?"

"No, I'm Adam. Also an artist, and a world planner."

"I don't understand."

"Neither do I. That's why I'm depressed."

Watching Argon draw the food with swift strokes as he spoke, Eve shouted, "Hey, great, that's great. This is Eden, isn't it? Wow. Yeah, okay, I'll be Eve. I don't mind being Eve. We're going to get rich—right?"

"Eve, please listen to me."

In a sad voice, Argon told her his whole story, adding finally, "So you see, with your cooperation we must design this world. Money's irrelevant. We have to start everything from scratch."

Miss Nippon was dumbfounded.

"Money's irrelevant, you say? I don't understand. I don't get it. I absolutely do not understand."

"If you're going to talk like that, well, why don't you open this door and take a look outside."

She glanced through the door Argon had left half open.

"My God! How awful!"

She slammed the door shut and glared at him.

"But how about this door," she said, pointing to his real, blanketed door. "Different, I'll bet."

"No, don't. That one's no good. It will just wipe out this world, the food, desk, bed, and even you. You are the new Eve. And we must become the father and mother of our world."

"Oh no. No babies. I'm all for birth control. I mean, they're such a bother. And besides, I won't disappear."

"You will disappear."

"I won't. I know myself best. I'm me. All this talk about disappearing—you're really weird."

"My dear Eve, you don't know. If we don't re-create the world, then sooner or later we're faced with starvation."

"What? Calling me 'dear' now, are you? You've got a nerve. And you say I'm going to starve. Don't be ridiculous. My body's valuable."

"No, your body's the same as my chalk. If we don't acquire a world of our own, your existence will just be a fiction. The same as nothing at all."

"Okay, that's enough of this junk. Come on, give me back my clothes. I'm leaving. No two ways about it, my being here is weird. I shouldn't be here. You're a magician or something. Well, hurry up. My manager's probably fed up with waiting. If you want me to drop in and be your Eve every now and then, I don't mind. As long as you use your chalk to give me what I want."

"Don't be a fool! You can't do that."

The abrupt, violent tone of Argon's voice startled her, and she looked into his face. They both stared at each other for a moment in silence. Whatever was in her thoughts, she then said calmly, "All right, I'll stay. But, in exchange, will you grant me one wish?"

"What is it? If you stay with me, I'll listen to anything you have to say."

"I want half of your chalk."

"That's unreasonable. After all, dear, you don't know how to draw. What good would it do you?"

"I do know how to draw. I may not look like it, but I used to be a designer. I insist on equal rights."

He tilted his head for an instant, then straightening up again, said decisively, "All right, I believe you."

He carefully broke the chalk in half and gave one piece to Eve. As soon as she received it, she turned to the wall and began drawing.

It was a pistol.

"Stop it! What are you going to do with that thing?"

"Death, I'm going to make death. We need some divisions. They're very important in making a world."

"No, that'll be the end. Stop it. It's the most unnecessary thing of all."

But it was too late. Eve was clutching a small pistol in her hand. She raised it and aimed directly at his chest.

"Move and I'll shoot. Hands up. You're stupid, Adam. Don't you know that a promise is the beginning of a lie? It's you who made me lie."

"What? Now what are you drawing?"

"A hammer. To smash the door down."

"You can't!"

"Move and I'll shoot!"

The moment he leaped the pistol rang out. Argon held his chest as his knees buckled and he collapsed to the floor. Oddly, there was no blood.

"Stupid Adam."

Eve laughed. Then, raising the hammer, she struck the door. The light streamed in. It wasn't very bright, but it was real. Light from the sun. Eve was suddenly absorbed, like mist. The desk, the bed, the French meal, all disappeared. All but Argon, the cookbook which had landed on the floor, and the chair were transformed back into pictures on the wall.

Argon stood up unsteadily. His chest wound had healed. But something stronger than death was summoning him, compelling him—the wall. The wall was calling him. His body, which had eaten drawings from the wall continuously for four weeks, had been almost entirely transformed by them. Resistance was impossible now. Argon staggered toward the wall and was drawn in on top of Eve.

The sound of the gunshot and the door being smashed were heard by others in the building. By the time they ran in, Argon had been completely absorbed into the wall and had become a picture. The people saw nothing but the chair, the cookbook, and the scribblings on the wall. Staring at Argon lying on top of Eve, someone remarked, "Starved for a woman, wasn't he."

"Doesn't it look just like him, though?" said another.

"What was he doing, destroying the door like that? And look at this, the wall's covered with scribbles. Huh. He won't get away with it. Where in the world did he disappear to? Calls himself a painter!"

The man grumbling to himself was the apartment manager.

After everyone left, there came a murmuring from the wall.

"It isn't chalk that will remake the world . . ."

A single drop welled out of the wall. It fell from just below the eye of the pictorial Argon.

# Mishima Yukio (1925–1970) (story)

## TRANSLATED BY JOHN BESTER

Mishima Yukio is the pen name of Hiraoka Kimitake, who was born in Tokyo in 1925, the son of a high government official. A teenage prodigy, he had written a novel by the time he was thirteen and published his first short story collection, a decorative and romantic book, titled *The Forest in Full Bloom* in 1944 while still a student at the prestigious Peers' School. He studied law at Tokyo University and took a position at the Ministry of Finance but resigned after only eight months to devote himself to writing. For the remainder of his life, he was a prolific writer in many literary forms, writing twenty novels, thirty-three plays, and countless stories, articles, essays, film scripts, and travel books. He was also a film director, designer, stage producer, and actor; he won a number of prestigious prizes for his fiction and drama and was a leading candidate for the Nobel Prize in literature. His autobiographical novel *Confessions of a Mask* (1949) traces his life through the time he gave up his government job and recounts both his dawning realization of his homosexuality and his masochistic self-identification with Saint Sebastian, pierced by arrows and fetishizing his martyrdom, and showing early on Mishima's equation of beauty and death.

Mishima was steeped in the literature and culture of old Japan and felt betrayed after World War II by what he saw as his country's shift toward materialism and moral corruption. In *The Temple of the Golden Pavilion* (1956), the protagonist, a young Buddhist acolyte, sets fire to the fourteenth-century Kyoto landmark, the Kinkakuji. Obsessed by its sacred beauty, he destroys this quintessential example of the aesthetic perfection of premodern Japan. Mishima himself moved from nihilism to a fanatic love of an idealized samurai culture of the premodern era. In later years, he organized a private army of young men into a paramilitary "Shield Society," planned a military *coup d'état*, and in November 1970, dressed in a self-designed uniform, broke into a Tokyo barracks of the Self-Defense Force. There, after failing to incite the soldiers to revolt, haranguing them from a balcony about their need to regain their lost cultural heritage, he committed ritual suicide *(seppuku)*, and then was clumsily beheaded by his right-hand man, who then killed himself as well.

In 1985, his life became the subject of a well-known film by Paul Schrader, titled *Mishima*. Among his best known works are the love story

*Thirst for Love* (1950); *Forbidden Colors* (1951), a novel about Tokyo's homosexual subculture; *The Sound of Waves* (1954), an idyllic love story on a Japanese island; *The Sailor Who Fell From Grace With the Sea* (1963), which was made into a popular movie in America; and *Runaway Horses* (1968), one of a quartet of novels called *The Sea of Fertility*. His 1960 novella *Patriotism,* which foretold his own fate, describes a historical incident culminating in the suicides of an army officer and his wife who attempted a coup to restore power to the emperor in 1936. "Martyrdom" is a story that brings together many of Mishima's themes—homosexuality, sado-masochism, and a hint of necrophilia—and like all of his prose, it is beautifully written.

**FURTHER READING:** Bester, John, tr. *Acts of Worship: Seven Stories,* 1989. Mishima, Yukio. *Death in Midsummer and Other Stories,* 1966. Miyoshi, Masao. *Accomplices of Silence: The Modern Japanese Novel,* 1974. Nathan, John. *Mishima: A Biography,* 1974. Petersen, Gwenn Boardman. *The Moon in Water: Understanding Tanizaki, Kawabata, and Mishima,* 1979. Scott-Stokes, Henry. *The Life and Death of Mishima,* 1974.

## *Martyrdom*

A diminutive Demon King ruled over the dormitory. The school in question was a place where large numbers of sons of the aristocracy were put through their paces. Equipped by the age of thirteen or fourteen with a coldness of heart and an arrogance of spirit worthy of many a grown-up, they were placed in this dormitory in their first year at middle school in order to experience communal life; this was one of the traditions of the spartan education devised several decades earlier by the principal of the school, General Ogi. The members of any one year had all been to the same primary school, so that their training in mischief had taken thorough effect in the six years before entering the dormitory, and facilitated an astonishing degree of collaboration among them. A "graveyard" would be arranged in a corner of the classroom with a row of markers bearing the teachers' names; a trap would be set so that when an elderly, bald teacher came into the room a blackboard duster fell precisely onto his bald patch, coating it with white; on a winter morning, a lump of snow would be flung to stick on the ceiling, bright in the morning sun, so that it dripped steadily onto the teacher's platform; the matches in the teachers' room would be mysteriously transformed into things that spouted sparks like fireworks when struck; a dozen drawing pins would be introduced into the chair where the teacher sat, with their points just showing above the surface—these and a host of other schemes that seemed the work of unseen elves were all in fact carried out by two or three masterminds and a band of well-trained terrorists.

"Come on—let's see it! What's wrong with showing me anyway?"

The older boy who had turned up in the lunch break lounged astride the broken dormitory chair. He could sense the itching curiosity in himself that crawled vaguely, like soft incipient beard, right up to his ears, but in trying to conceal it from the other, his junior by a year, he was only making his face turn all the pinker. At the same time, it was necessary to sit in as slovenly a way as possible in order to show his independence of the rules.

"I'll show you, don't worry. But you'll have to wait another five minutes. What's up, K?—it's not like you to be so impatient."

The Demon King spoke boldly, gazing steadily at the older boy with mild, beautiful eyes. He was well developed for a mere fourteen, and looked in fact at least sixteen or seventeen. He owed his physique to something called the "Danish method" of child rearing—which involved among other things dangling the baby by one leg and kneading its soft, plump body like so much dough—and to the fact that he'd been brought up in a Western house with huge plate-glass windows standing on high ground in the Takanawa district of Tokyo, where breezes borne on bright wings from the distant sea would occasionally visit the lawn. Naked, he had the figure of a young man. During physical check-ups, when the other boys were pale with dire embarrassment, he was a Daphnis surveying his nanny goats with cool, scornful eyes.

The dormitory was the farthest from the main school buildings, and the Demon King's room on the second floor looked out over the shimmering May woods covering the gentle slope of the school grounds. The long grass and undergrowth seemed almost tipsy as it swayed in the wind. It was morning, and the chirping of the birds in the woods was particularly noisy. Now and again, a pair of them would take off from the sea of young foliage and fly up like fish leaping from its surface, only to produce a sudden, furious twittering, turn a somersault, and sink down again between the waves of greenery.

When K, his senior, came to see him in his room bearing sandwiches and the like, it had been instantly apparent to the Demon King—young Hatakeyama—that the motive was a desire to see the book that everyone found so fascinating. To tease a senior pupil over something of this sort gave him a sweet sense of complicity, as though he too were being teased.

"Five minutes is up."

"No it isn't—it's only three minutes yet."

"It's five minutes!"

Quite suddenly, Hatakeyama gave him an almost girlish smile, the vulnerable smile of someone who had never yet had anyone be rude to him.

"Oh well, I suppose it can't be helped," he said. "I'll let you see it."

With his left hand thrust in his trouser pocket, as was his usual habit (in imitation of a cousin, a college student, whom he'd much admired for the way he let his shiny metal watchstrap show between the pocket and his sweater), he went lazily to open the bookcase. There, among the textbooks that he'd never once laid hands on after returning to the dorm, and the books his parents had bought for him—a grubby *Collected Boys' Tales,* the *Jungle Book,* and *Peter Pan* in paperback editions—there ought to have stood a volume with *"Plutarch's Lives"* inscribed in immature lettering on its spine. This book, whose red cover he had wrapped in uninviting brown paper and labeled with a title that he had memorized from a work of about the same thickness seen in the library, was constantly being passed from hand to hand, during classes and in recess alike. People would have been startled to find, on the page that should have portrayed a statue of Alexander the Great, an odd, complex sectional diagram in color.

"It's no use suddenly pretending you can't find it!" Gazing at the Demon King's rear view as he ferreted through the contents of the bookshelves, K was less concerned with the desire to see the book as such than with making sure, first, that he wasn't cheated by this formidable younger schoolmate, and then that he didn't put himself at a disadvantage by clumsy bullying.

"Somebody's stolen it!" shouted Hatakeyama, standing up. He'd been looking down as he searched, and his face was flushed, his eyes gleaming. Rushing to his desk, he frantically opened and closed each drawer in turn, talking to himself all the while:

"I made a point of getting everyone who came to borrow that book to sign for it. I mean, I couldn't have people taking my stuff out without my permission, could I? That book was the class's special secret. It meant a lot to everybody. I was particularly careful with it—I'd never have let anyone I didn't like read it. . . ."

"It's a bit late to get so angry about it, surely," said K with an assumed maturity, then, noticing the brutal glint in Hatakeyama's eye, suddenly shut up. More than anything, the look reminded him of a child about to kill a snake.

"I'm *sure* it's Watari," said his crony Komiyama, writing the name "Watari" twice in small letters on the blackboard and pointing to the bright-lit doorway through which the boy in question, by himself as usual, had just gone out into the school yard. Beyond the doorway a cloud was visible, smooth and glossy, floating in the sky beyond the spacious playground. Its shadow passed ponderously across the ground.

"Watari? Come off it! What does a kid like him understand about a book like that?"

"A lot—you wait and see! Haven't you ever heard of the quiet lecher? It's types with saintly expressions like him who're most interested in that kind of thing. Try barging in on him in his room tonight before supper, when all the rest have gone for exercise and there's nobody in the dorm. You'll see!"

Alone of their group, Watari had come to them from another primary school, and was thus a comparative outsider. There was something about him that kept others at a distance. Although he was particular about his clothes—he changed his shirt every day—he would go for weeks without cutting his nails, which were always an unhealthy black. His skin was a yellowish, lusterless white like a gardenia. His lips, in contrast, were so red that you wanted to rub them with your finger to see if he was wearing lipstick. Seen close to, it was an astonishingly beautiful face, though from a distance quite unprepossessing. He reminded you of an art object in which excessive care over detail has spoiled the effect of the whole; the details were correspondingly seductive in a perverse way.

He had begun to be bullied almost as soon as he appeared at the school. He gave the impression of looking disapprovingly on the tendency, common to all boys, to worship toughness as a way of making up for their awareness of the vulnerability peculiar to their age. If anything, Watari sought to preserve the vulnerability. The young man who seeks to be himself is respected by his fellows; the boy who tries to do the same is persecuted by other boys, it being a boy's business to become something else just as soon as he can.

Watari had the habit, whenever he was subjected to particularly vile treatment by his companions, of casting his eyes up at the clear blue sky. The habit was itself another source of mockery.

"Whenever he's picked on, he stares up at the sky as if he was Christ," said M, the most persistent of his tormentors. "And you know, when he does it, his nose tips back so you can see right up his nostrils. He keeps his nose so well blown, it's a pretty pink color round the edges inside. . . ."

Watari was, of course, banned from seeing *"Plutarch's Lives."*

The sun had set on all but the trees in the woods. The dark mass of foliage, minutely catching the lingering rays of the setting sun, trembled like the flame of a guttering candle. As he stealthily opened the door and went in, the first thing Hatakeyama saw was the wavering trees through the window directly ahead. The sight of Watari registered next; he was seated at his desk, gazing down with his head in his delicate white hands, intent on something. The open pages of the book and the hands stood out in white relief.

He turned around at the sound of footsteps. The next instant, his hands covered the book with an obstinate strength.

Moving swiftly and easily across the short space that separated them, Hatakeyama had seized him by the scruff of the neck almost before he realized it himself. Watari's large, expressionless eyes, wide open like a rabbit's, were suddenly close to his own face. He felt his knees pressing into the boy's belly, eliciting a strange sound from it as he sat on the chair; then he knocked aside the hands that tried to cling to him, and dealt a smart slap to his cheek. The flesh looked soft, as though it might stay permanently dented. For one moment, indeed, Watari's face seemed to tilt in the direction in which it had been struck, assuming an oddly placid, helpless expression. But then the cheek rapidly flooded with red and a thin, stealthy trickle of blood ran from the finely shaped nostrils. Seeing it, Hatakeyama felt a kind of pleasant nausea. Taking hold of the collar of Watari's blue shirt, he dragged him toward the bed, moving with unnecessarily large strides as though dancing. Watari let himself be dragged, limp as a puppet; curiously, he didn't seem to grasp the situation he was in, but gazed steadily at the evening sky over the woods with their lingering light. Or perhaps those big, helpless eyes simply let in the evening light quite passively, taking in the sky without seeing anything. The blood from his nose, though, cheerfully seemed to flaunt its glossy brightness as it dribbled down his mouth and over his chin.

"You thief!"

Dumping Watari on the bed, Hatakeyama climbed onto it himself and started trampling and kicking him. The bed creaked, sounding like ribs breaking. Watari had his eyes shut in terror. At times, he bared his over-regular teeth and gave a thin wail like a small sick bird. Hatakeyama thumped him in the side for a while, then, seeing that he had turned toward the wall and gone still, like a corpse, jumped down from the bed in one great leap. As a finishing touch, he remembered to thrust one guilty hand elegantly into the pocket of his narrow slacks and tilt himself slightly to one side. Then, whisking up *"Plutarch's Lives"* from the desk with his right hand, he tucked it stylishly under his arm and ran up the stairs to his second-floor room.

He had read the dubious book in question quite a few times. Each time, the first frenzied excitement seemed to fade a little. Recently in fact he had begun to get more pleasure, if anything, out of observing the powerful spell the book exerted over his friends as they read it for the first time. But now, reading it again himself after getting it back and roughing up Watari in the process, the original, wild excitement emerged as a still fiercer pleasure. He couldn't get through a single page at a time. Each appearance of one of those words of almost mystic power brought a myriad associations crowding, plunged him into an ever deeper intoxication. His breath grew shallower, his hand trembled, the bell for supper that happened just then to resound through the dormitory almost made him panic: how could he appear before the others in this state? He had entirely forgotten Watari.

That night, a dream woke Hatakeyama from a troubled sleep. The dream had led him to the lairs of various illnesses that he had suffered from in childhood. In actual fact, few children could have been healthier than he: the only illnesses he'd succumbed to were of the order of whooping cough, measles, and intestinal catarrh. Nevertheless, the diseases in his dream were all acquainted with him, and greeted him accordingly. Whenever one of them approached him, there was a disagreeable smell; if he tried to shove it away, "disease" transferred itself stickily to his hand like oil paint. One disease was even tickling his throat with its finger. . . .

When he awoke, he found himself staring, wide-eyed like a rabbit, in just the way that Watari had done earlier that day. And there, floating above the covers, was Watari's startled face, a mirror of his own. As their eyes met, the face rose slowly into the air.

Hatakeyama let out a high-pitched yell. At least, he thought he did: in fact his voice rose only as far as his throat.

Something was pressing down steadily, with cold hands, on his throat;

yet the pressure was slight enough to be half pleasant. Deciding that it was a continuation of his dream after all, he extracted a hand unhurriedly from the bedclothes and stroked himself experimentally around the neck. It appeared that something like a cloth sash, about two inches wide, had been wrapped snugly around it.

He had the courage and good sense to fling it off without further ado. He sat up in bed, looking much older than he was, more like a young man of twenty. A chain of ivory clouds, lit up by the moon, was passing across the window outside, so that he was silhouetted against it like the statue of some god of old.

The thing that crouched like a dog at the foot of the bed had a white, human face turned resolutely toward him. It seemed to be breathing heavily, for the face as a whole appeared to swell and shrink; the eyes alone were still, overflowing with a shining light as they gazed, full of hostility (or was it longing?), at Hatakeyama's shadowed features.

"Watari. You came to get even, didn't you?"

Watari said nothing, the lips that were like a rose in the dark night quivering painfully. Finally, he said as though in a dream:

"I'm sorry."

"You wanted to kill me, I suppose."

"I'm sorry." He made no attempt to run away, simply repeating the same phrase.

Without warning, Hatakeyama flew at him and, propelled by the bedsprings, carried him face down onto the floor. There, kneeling astride him, he subjected him to a full twenty minutes' violence. "I'm going to make sure you feel ashamed in front of everyone in the bath!" he promised, then splashed his bare buttocks with blue-black ink; prodded them with the points of a pair of compasses to see their reaction; reared up, hauling the boy up by the ears as he did so. . . . He was brilliantly methodical, as though everything had been thought out in advance. There was no chance, even, for Watari to look up at the sky this time. He lay still, his cheek pressed against a join in the linoleum.

Two boys were allotted to each room in the dormitory, but Hatakeyama's roommate was home on sick leave. So long as he was careful not to be overheard downstairs, Hatakeyama could do as he wished.

Eventually, both of them began to tire. Before they realized it they were dozing, sprawled on the floor; Watari had even forgotten to cover his pale behind.

Their nap lasted no more than a moment. Hatakeyama awoke first. Pillowing his chin on clasped hands, he gazed at the moonlit window. All that was visible from the floor where he lay was the sky. The moon was below the frame of the window, but two or three clouds could be seen in the sky's fullness of limpid light. The scene had the impersonal clarity, precision, and fineness of detail of a scene reflected in the polished surface of a piece of machinery. The clouds seemed stationed as immovably as some majestic man-made edifice.

An odd desire awoke in Hatakeyama, taking him by surprise. It wasn't so much a break with the mood of tranquility as a natural transition from it, and in a strange way it was linked with the terrifying sensation of the cord around his neck that he'd experienced a while before. This, he thought, is the fellow who tried to kill me. And suddenly a peculiar sense of both superiority and inferiority, a nagging humiliation at not in fact having been killed, made it impossible for him to stay still.

"You asleep?" he said.

"No," said Watari. As he replied, his eyes turned to look straight at Hatakeyama. He began to stretch out his thin right arm, then drew it in again and pressed it to his side, saying,

"It hurts here."

"Really? Does it *really* hurt?"

Hatakeyama rolled over twice. It brought him a little too close, so that he was lying half on top of Watari. Just as this happened, the latter gave a faint little chuckle, a sound—like the cry of a shellfish—he had never heard before. The Demon King sought out the sound, then pressed his whole face against Watari's lips and the soft down around them.

There was something going on between Hatakeyama and Watari: their classmates passed on the rumor in hushed voices. The scandal possessed a mysterious power; thanks to it, Hatakeyama became increasingly influential, and even Watari was taken into their circle. The process was similar to that whereby a woman so far generally ignored suddenly acquires value in everyone's eyes if the dandy of the group takes a fancy to her. And it was totally unclear how Hatakeyama himself responded to this general reaction.

Before long, it was felt that his authority as Demon King required some kind of strict legal system. They would draft the necessary laws during their English and spelling lessons. The criminal code, for example, must be an arbitrary one, based on the principle of intimidation. A strong urge to self-regulation had awoken in the boys. One morning in the dormitory, the gang insisted that their leader pick out someone for them to punish. They were sitting in their chairs in a variety of bizarre postures; some were not so much seated in them as clinging to them. One first-grader had turned his chair upside down and was sitting holding on to two projecting legs.

"Hatakeyama—you've got to name somebody. You name him, and the rest of us'll deal with him. Isn't there anyone who's been getting above himself lately?"

"No, no one." He spoke in a surly voice, his mature-looking back turned to them.

"You sure? Then we'll choose the person ourselves."

"Wait a minute! What I said wasn't true. Listen: I'll name someone. But I won't say why."

They waited breathlessly; there wasn't one of them who didn't want to hear his own name mentioned.

"Where's Watari?"

"Watari?—he went off somewhere just now."

"OK, it's him. He's been getting uppish. If we don't put a stop to it, he'll get completely out of hand."

This was pure imitation of fifth-grader talk. Even so, having got it out, Hatakeyama looked cheerfully relieved, like someone remembering something till then forgotten. It provoked a happy clamor among the others:

"Let's fix the time—the lunch break!"

"And the place—by Chiarai Pond."

"I'll take my jackknife."

"And I'll bring a rope. If he struggles we can tie him up."

On a pond already green with slime the surrounding trees spread an even reflection of lush young foliage, so that anyone who walked beside it was steeped in its green light. They were all privately enjoying the important sound of their own feet tramping through the bamboo grass, and the party with Hatakeyama and Watari at its center exchanged no words. Watari showed no sign of fear as he walked, a fact that had a disturbing effect on his classmates, as though they were watching a very sick man, supposedly on his last legs, suddenly striding along. From time to time, he glanced up at the sky visible through the new leaves of the treetops. But the others were all too sunk in their own thoughts for anyone to remark on his behavior. Hatakeyama walked with long strides, head bent, left hand in pocket. He avoided looking at Watari.

Halting, Hatakeyama raised both arms in their rolled-up sleeves above his head:

"Stop! Quiet!"

An elderly gardener was pushing a wheelbarrow along the path above them toward the flower beds.

"Well, well—up to some mischief, I suppose," he said, seeing them.

"Dirty old scrounger!" someone replied. It was rumored that the old man lived off free dormitory leftovers.

"He's gone." M gave a signal with his eyes.

"Right. Here, Watari—"

For the first time, Hatakeyama looked straight into his eyes. Both Watari and his companions had unusually grave expressions.

"You've been getting too big for your boots."

No more was said: the sentence was passed; but nothing was done to carry it out. The judge stood with bare arms folded, slowly stroking them with his fingertips. . . . At that moment, Watari seemed to see his chance. Quite suddenly, he lunged toward Hatakeyama as though about to cling to him. Behind the latter lay the pond. As he braced his legs, stones and soil rolled down into it with a faint splashing. That was the only sound; to those around them, the two seemed locked in an embrace, silently consoling each other. But in steadying himself to avoid falling backward, Hatakeyama had exposed his arms to an attack already planned. Watari's teeth—regular and sharp as a girl's, or perhaps a cat's—sank into his young flesh. Blood oozed out along the line between teeth and skin, yet biter and bitten remained still. Hatakeyama didn't even groan.

A slight movement separated them. Wiping his lips, more crimson than ever with the blood, Watari stood still, his eyes fixed on Hatakeyama's wound. A second or two before the members of the group had grasped what had happened, Watari had started running. But his pursuers were six tough boys. He lost his footing on the clay by the pond. He resisted, so that his blue shirt tore to give a glimpse of one shoulder, almost pathologically white. The boy with the rope tied his hands behind his back. His trousers, soiled by the red clay, were an oddly bright, shiny color.

Hatakeyama had made no move to chase him. His left hand was thrust casually into his pocket, with no care for his wound. The blood dripped down steadily, making a red rim around the glass of his wristwatch, then seeping from his fingertips into the bottom of his pocket. He felt no pain, aware only of something that hardly seemed like blood, something warm and familiar and intensely personal, caressing the surface of his skin as it went. But he had made up his mind on one thing: in his friends' faces when they brought Watari back, he would see nothing but an embodiment of his own decision, inviting him to proceed.

After that, he didn't look at Watari but gazed steadily at the long rope to which he was tied, with the slack wound round and round him and its end held in the hand of one of his classmates.

"Let's go somewhere quiet," he said. "The little wood behind the pigeon lofts."

Prodded, Watari began walking. As they filed along the red clay path, he staggered again and fell to his knees. With a coarse "heave-ho," they yanked him to his feet. His shoulder stood out so white in the light reflected from the foliage that it was as though the bone was sticking out of the rent in his blue shirt.

All the time as Watari walked, the incorrigible M hung about him, tickling him under the arms, pinching his backside, roaring with laughter because the boy, he said, had looked up at the sky. What if he had known that only two things in the whole world were visible to Watari's eyes: the blue sky—the eye of God, forever striking down into men's eyes through the green leaves of the treetops—and the precious blood spilled on his own account down here on earth, the lifeblood staining Hatakeyama's arm? His gaze went continually from one to the other of these two things. Hatakeyama was looking straight ahead, walking with a confident step more adult than any adult's. On his left arm, just in front of Watari, the blood was slowly drying, showing up a bright purple whenever it passed through the sun's rays.

The grove behind the pigeon lofts was a sunny patch of widely spaced trees, little frequented, where the pigeons often came to pass the time. An undistinguished collection of smallish deciduous trees, it had, at its very center, one great pine with gently outstretched branches on which the birds were fond of lining up to coo at one another. The rays of the afternoon sun picked out the trunk of the pine in a bright, pure light so that the resin flowing from it looked like veins of agate.

Hatakeyama came to a halt and said to the boy holding the rope:

"All right—this'll do. Take the rope off Watari. But don't let him get away. Throw the thing up like a lasso and put it over that big branch on the pine tree."

The rich jest of this sent the others into ecstasies. Watari was being held down by two of them. The remaining four danced like little demons on the grass as they helped hitch up the rope. One end of it was tied in a loop. Then one of the boys mounted a handy tree stump, poked his head through the noose, and stuck out his tongue.

"That's no good—it'll have to be higher."

The boy who'd stuck his tongue out was the shortest of them all. Watari would need at least another two or three inches.

They were all scared, scared by the occasional, shadowy suggestion that their prank might possibly be in earnest. As they led Watari, pale and trembling slightly, to the waiting noose, one waggish youth delivered a funeral address. All the while, Watari continued to gaze up at the sky with his idiotically wide-open eyes.

Abruptly, Hatakeyama raised a hand by way of a signal. His eyes were shut tight.

The rope went up.

Startled by the sudden beating of many pigeons' wings and by the glow on Watari's beautiful face, astonishingly high above them, they fled the grove, each in a different direction, unable to bear the thought of staying at the scene of such dire murder.

They ran at a lively pace, each boyish breast still swelling with the pride of having killed someone.

A full thirty minutes later, they reentered the wood as though by agreement and, huddling together, gazed up fearfully at the branch of the great pine.

The rope was dangling free, the hanged corpse nowhere to be seen.

### ■ Shiraishi Kazuko (1931– ) (poem)

TRANSLATED BY KENNETH REXROTH AND IKUKO ATSUMI

Shiraishi Kazuko was born in Vancouver, Canada, and her family moved to Japan just before World War II. Her wild, sexy, sometimes surreal poetry, originally associated with the avant-garde magazine *Vou*, comes out of the new Japan of the postwar period. She is a Japanese Beat, a performance poet who sometimes reads her poetry to jazz, who writes, as translator Rexroth notes, not "of the *ukiyo*, The Floating World, now utterly gone, but of a maelstrom, a typhoon, in which lost men and women whirl through toppling towers of neon."[1]

**FURTHER READING:** Rexroth, Kenneth, ed. *Seasons of Sacred Lust: The Selected Poems of Kazuko Shiraishi.* Translated by Ikuko Atsumi, John Solt, Carol Tinker, Yasuyo Morita, and Kenneth Rexroth. Wilson, Graeme, and Ikuko Atsumi, trs. *Three Contemporary Japanese Poets: Anzai Hitoshi, Shiraishi Kazuko, Tanikawa Shuntaro,* 1972.

## The Man Root

*For Sumiko's Birthday*

God if he exists
Or if he doesn't
Still has a sense of humor
Like a certain type of man

So this time
He brings a gigantic man root
To join the picnic
Above the end of the sky of my dreams
Meanwhile
I'm sorry
I didn't give Sumiko anything for her birthday
But now I wish I could at least
Set the seeds of that God given penis
In the thin, small, and very charming voice of Sumiko
On the end of the line

Sumiko, I'm so sorry
But the penis shooting up day by day
Flourishes in the heart of the galaxy
As rigid as a wrecked bus
So that if
You'd like to see
The beautiful sky with all its stars
Or just another man instead of this God given cock
A man speeding along a highway
With a hot girl
You'll have to hang
All the way out of the bus window
With your eyes peeled
It's spectacular when the cock
Starts nuzzling the edge of the cosmos

1. Kenneth Rexroth, ed., *Seasons of Sacred Lust: The Selected Poems of Kazuko Shiraishi.* Translated by Ikuko Atsumi, John Solt, Carol Tinker, Yasuyo Morita, and Kenneth Rexroth (New York: New Directions, 1978), vi.

At this time
Dear Sumiko
The lonely way the stars of night shine
And the curious coldness of noon
Penetrates my gut                                                    *35*
Seen whole
Or even if you refused to look
You'd go crazy
Because you can trace
The nameless, impersonal and timeless penis              *40*
In the raucous atmosphere
Of the passers-by
That parade it in a portable shrine
In that stir of voices
You can hear an immensity of savage                        *45*
Rebellion, the curses of
Heathen gism
Sometimes
God is in conference or out to lunch
It seems he's away                                                   *50*
Absconding from debts but leaving his penis.

So now
The cock abandoned by God
Trots along
Young and gay                                                         *55*
And full of callow confidence
Amazingly like the shadow
Of a sophisticated smile

The penis bursting out of bounds
And beyond measure                                                 *60*
Arrives here
Truly unique and entirely alone
Seen from whatever perspective
It's faceless and speechless
I would like to give you, Sumiko                             *65*
Something like this for your birthday

When it envelops your entire life
And you've become invisible even to yourself
Occasionally you'll turn into the will
Of exactly this penis                                               *70*
And wander
Ceaselessly
I want to catch in my arms
Forever
Someone like you                                                      *75*

# ■ Tanikawa Shuntaro (1931– ) (poems)

TRANSLATED BY HAROLD WRIGHT

Tanikawa Shuntaro is probably the best known poet in Japan today, respected by the general public and by literary cognoscenti alike. He was born in Tokyo in 1931, the only son of philosopher Tanikawa Tetsuzo. He started writing poetry when he was eighteen, but so loathed schooling that he went from the top of his class to being such a poor student that the family decided not to send him on to the university. With college out of the picture, Tanikawa needed a new direction; his father sent his poetry notebooks to Miyoshi Tatsuji, at that time Japan's leading poet, and the next day Miyoshi came to their house. Through his influence, several of Tanikawa's poems were published in *Bungakkai* (*Literary World*). Tanikawa was profoundly disturbed by the cultural turmoil in Japan during World War II and by the destruction wrought upon Tokyo by Allied air raids in 1945, which he witnessed as he bicycled through the ruined city and encountered the charred corpses of neighbors. In the postwar period, Tanikawa was deeply influenced by Western writers and has said that it was while listening to Beethoven that he realized that "life is possible," and came back to art with faith in humanistic possibilities.

He is a relentlessly innovative poet who writes in many, many forms—from the prose poem to the lyric to the experimental sonnet. In the 1960s, he broadened his creative output to drama, film, children's songs, and works combining poetry with paintings and photographs. He has translated a five-volume *Mother Goose* and has been the translator of the comic strip "Peanuts" since 1969. His poems have a similar childlike whimsy and irony and a determined faith in human possibility. A prolific writer, he has published, in his words, "a disgusting number" of books and has, throughout his life, tried to bring poetry back to the people through the mass media, poetry readings, and even through shouting his poems through a bullhorn from the windows of office buildings. His cosmic view of the relationship of the universe and humanity has caused him to be embraced by a new generation and to take on a new label as a "New Age" poet. *His Selected Poems*, translated by Harold Wright, has appeared from North Point Press.

FURTHER READING: Elliot, William I., and Kazuo Kawamura, trs. *Coca-Cola Lessons*, 1986. Elliot, William I., and Kazuo Kawamura, trs. *Floating the River in Melancholy*, 1988. Keene, Donald, tr. *The Modern Japanese Prose Poem: An Anthology of Six Poets*, 1980. Wilson, Graeme, and Ikuko Atsumi, trs. *Three Contemporary Japanese Poets*, 1972.

## *Museum*

stone axes and the like
lie quietly beyond the glass

constellations rotate endlessly
many of us become extinct
many of us appear                                                    5

then
comets endlessly miss collision
lots of dishes and the like are broken
Eskimo dogs walk over the South Pole
great tombs are built both east and west                            10
books of poems are often dedicated
recently
the atom's being smashed to bits
the daughter of a president is singing
such things as these                                                15
have been happening

stone axes and the like
lie absurdly quiet beyond the glass


## Growth

Drawing a meaningless line,
a child says it's an apple.

Painting an apple just like an apple,
a painter says it's an apple.

Painting an apple unlike an apple,                                  5
an artist says it's truly an apple.

Not painting an apple or anything else
members of the Academy of Art
slurp up apple sauce.

Apples, apples, red apples,                                         10
are apples bitter? Are they sour?


## Ten Yen Coin

With his last ten yen coin
the boy wanted to make a phone call.
He wanted to talk to someone close
     in a rowdy language,
but none of his friends had telephones.                             5
The ten yen coin was wet in his palm

and smelled of metal.
(Why should I buy gum?
　　This ten yen coin will be used
　　　for something more important.)
Then the boy saw the car,
a haughty car like a beautiful woman,
a fierce car like an unreachable happiness . . .
and before he knew it himself,
the boy, taking the ten yen coin in his hand,
　　cut into that beautiful finish,
a long deep gash—
Then the boy threw the ten yen coin,
with all his might,
　　into the city's congestion.

# Oe Kenzaburo (1935– ) (story)

TRANSLATED BY JOHN NATHAN

In 1994, Oe Kenzaburo, a masterful writer considered the voice of his generation in Japan (though little known in the West and translated into only four languages), won the Nobel Prize for literature. Oe's work has been decisively formed by two cataclysmic events, the Japanese surrender at the close of World War II when he was ten years old and the birth of his son, Hikari, a boy with serious brain damage. The first event transformed the sense of the values that regulated his childhood in a mountain village in Shikoku Island and led directly to the sense of betrayal, cynicism, and social commentary that pervades his novels and political essays. Translator John Nathan describes this event:

> On August 15, 1945, Emperor Hirohito went on to the radio to announce the surrender and deprived Oe of his innocence. Until that day, like all Japanese schoolchildren, he had been taught to fear the Emperor as a living god. Once a day his turn had come to be called to the front of the classroom and asked, "What would you do if the Emperor commanded you to die?" And Oe had replied, knees shaking, "I would die, Sir, I would cut open my belly and die."

When he heard the emperor's human voice on the radio, he found himself angry, humiliated, and deceived. The second event, the birth of his retarded son, is, at least nominally, the subject of the story appearing here and of his novel *A Personal Matter.* In *A Personal Matter,* the protagonist Bird conspires with a doctor to kill his two-headed son. In actuality Oe and his wife Yukari turned down the doctors who counseled them to let their son die. The name *Hikari* means "light" and Hikari's nickname is Pooh (after Winnie the Pooh); recently he has partially overcome his handicap and become a composer.

Oe is the quintessential postwar Japanese writer, obsessed with the nuclear destruction visited upon Hiroshima and Nagasaki by American bombers at the close of World War II, critical of Japanese militarism, and presenting in his novels a world radically off-kilter. He has edited an anthology entitled *The Crazy Iris and Other Stories of the Atomic Aftermath* (1985) and published two dozen novels, only a few of which are available in English translation. At the end of his introduction to *The Crazy Iris*, Oe states, "The fundamental condition of life, then, is that we are assailed by overwhelming fear yet, at the same time, beckoned by the necessity to rebuild hope, however difficult, in defiance of that fear."

**FURTHER READING:** Oe, Kenzaburo. *A Personal Matter,* 1958; *Hiroshima Notes,* 1963; *The Silent Cry,* 1974; *Teach Us to Outgrow Our Madness,* 1977; ed., *The Crazy Iris and Other Stories of the Atomic Aftermath,* 1984; *Japan's Dual Identity: A Writer's Dilemma,* 1988.

## *Aghwee the Sky Monster*

Alone in my room, I wear a piratical black patch over my right eye. The eye may look all right, but the truth is I have scarcely any sight in it. Scarcely, I say; it isn't totally blind. The consequence is that when I look at this world with both eyes I see two worlds perfectly superimposed, a vague and shadowy world on top of one that's bright and vivid. I can be walking down a paved street when a sense of peril and unbalance will stop me, like a rat just scurried out of a sewer, dead in my tracks. Or I'll discover a film of unhappiness and fatigue on the face of a cheerful friend and clog the flow of an easy chat with my sluggish stutter. I suppose I'll get used to this eventually. If I don't I intend to wear my patch not only in my room when I'm alone but on the street and with my friends. Strangers may pass with condescending smiles—what an old-fashioned joke!—but I'm old enough not to be annoyed by every little thing.

The story I intend to tell is about my first experience earning money; I began with my right eye because the memory of that experience ten years ago revived in me abruptly and quite out of context when violence was done to my eye last spring. Remembering, I should add, I was freed from the hatred uncoiling in my heart and beginning to fetter me. At the very end I'll talk about the accident itself.

Ten years ago I had twenty-twenty vision. Now one of my eyes is ruined. *Time* shifted, launched itself from the springboard of an eyeball squashed by a stone. When I first met that sentimental madman I had only a child's understanding of *time.* I was yet to have the cruel awareness of *time* drilling its eyes into my back and *time* lying in wait ahead.

Ten years ago I was eighteen years old and weighed one hundred and ten pounds, had just entered college and was looking for a part-time job.

Although I still had trouble reading French, I wanted to buy a clothbound edition in two volumes of *L'Âme Enchanté*. It was a Moscow edition I wanted, with not only a foreword but footnotes and even the colophon in Russian, and wispy lines like bits of thread connecting the letters of the French text. It was a curious edition all right, but far sturdier and more elegant than the French, and much cheaper. At the time I discovered it in a bookstore specializing in East European publications I had no interest in Romain Rolland, yet I went immediately into action to make the volumes mine. In those days I often succumbed to some curious passion and it never bothered me, I had the feeling there was nothing to worry about so long as I was sufficiently obsessed.

As I had just entered college and wasn't registered at the employment center, I looked for work by making the rounds of people I knew. Finally my uncle introduced me to a banker who came up with an offer. "Did you happen to see a movie called *Harvey?*" he asked. I said yes, and tried for a smile of moderate but unmistakable dedication, appropriate for someone about to be employed for the first time. *Harvey* was that Jimmy Stewart film about a man living with an imaginary rabbit as big as a bear; it had made me laugh so hard I thought I would die. The banker didn't return my smile. "Recently, my son has been having the same sort of delusions about living with a monster. He's stopped working and stays in his room. I'd like him to get out from time to time, but of course he'd need a— chaperon. Would you be interested?"

I knew quite a bit about the banker's son. He was a young composer whose avant-garde music had won prizes in France and Italy and who was generally included in the photo roundups in the weekly magazines, the kind of article they always called "Japan's Artists of Tomorrow." I had never heard his major works, but I had seen several films for which he had done the music. There was one about the adventures of a juvenile delinquent that had a short, lyrical theme played on the harmonica. It was beautiful. Watching the picture, I remember feeling vaguely troubled by the idea of an adult nearly thirty years old (in fact, the composer was twenty-eight when he hired me, my present age) working out a theme for the harmonica. Because my own harmonica had become my little brother's property when I had entered elementary school. And possibly because I knew more about the composer, whose name was D, than just public facts; I knew he had created a scandal. Generally, I have nothing but contempt for scandals, but I knew that the composer's infant child had died, that he had gotten divorced as a result, and that he was rumored to be involved with a certain movie actress. I hadn't known that he was in the grips of something like the rabbit in Jimmy Stewart's movie, or that he had stopped working and secluded himself in his room. How serious was his condition, I wondered, was it a case of nervous breakdown, or was he clearly schizophrenic?

"I'm not certain I know just what you mean by chaperon," I said, reeling in my smile. "Naturally, I'd like to be of service if I can." This time, concealing my curiosity and apprehension, I tried to lend my voice and expression as much sympathy as possible without seeming forward. It was only a part-time job, but it was the first chance of employment I had had and I was determined to do my accommodating best.

"When my son decides he wants to go somewhere in Tokyo, you go along—just that. There's a nurse at the house and she has no trouble handling him, so you don't have to worry about violence." The banker made me feel like a soldier whose cowardice has been discovered. I blushed and said, trying to recover lost ground: "I'm fond of music, and I respect composers more than anyone, so I look forward to accompanying D and talking with him."

"All he thinks about these days is this thing in his head, and apparently that's all he talks about!" The banker's brusqueness made my face even redder. "You can go out to see him tomorrow," he said.

"At—your house?"

"That's right, did you think he was in an asylum?" From the banker's tone of voice I could only suppose that he was at bottom a nasty man.

"If I should get the job," I said with my eyes on the floor, "I'll drop by again to thank you." I could easily have cried.

"No, he'll be hiring you" (All right then, I resolved defiantly, I'll call D my employer!), "so that won't be necessary. All I care about is that he doesn't get into any trouble outside that might develop into a scandal. There's his career to think about. Naturally, what he does reflects on me—"

So that was it! I thought, so I was to be a moral sentinel guarding the banker's family against a second contamination by the poisons of scandal. Of course I didn't say a thing, I only nodded dependably, anxious to warm the banker's chilly heart with the heat of reliance on me. I didn't even ask the most pressing question, something truly difficult to ask, namely: This monster haunting your son, sir, is it a rabbit like Harvey, nearly six feet tall? A creature covered in bristly hair like an Abominable Snowman? What kind of a monster is it? In the end I remained silent and consoled myself with the thought that I might be able to pry the secret out of the nurse if I made friends with her.

Then I left the executive's office, and as I walked along the corridor grinding my teeth in humiliation as if I were Julien Sorel after a meeting with someone important, I became self-conscious to the tips of my fingers and tried assessing my attitude and its effectiveness. When I got out of college I chose not to seek nine-to-five employment, and I do believe the memory of my dialogue with that disagreeable banker played a large part in my decision.

Even so, when classes were over the next day, I took a train out to the residential suburb where the composer lived. As I passed through the gate of that castle of a house, I remember a roaring of terrific beasts, as at a zoo in the middle of the night. I was dismayed, I cowered, what if those were the screams of my employer? A good thing it didn't occur to me then that those savage screams might have been coming from the monster haunting D like Jimmy Stewart's rabbit. Whatever they were, it was so clear that the screaming had rattled me that the maid showing me the way was indiscreet enough to break into a laugh. Then I discovered someone else laughing, voicelessly, in the dimness beyond a window in an annex in the garden. It was the man who was supposed to employ me; he was laughing like a face in a movie without a sound track. And boiling all around him was that howling of wild beasts. I listened closely and realized that several of the same animals were shrieking in concert. And in voices too shrill to be of this world. Abandoned by the maid at the entrance to the annex, I decided the screaming must be part of the composer's tape collection, regained my courage, straightened up, and opened the door.

Inside, the annex reminded me of a kindergarten. There were no partitions in the large room, but two pianos, an electric organ, several tape recorders, a record-player, something we had called a "mixer" when I was in the high-school radio club—there was hardly room to thread your way through. What looked like a dog asleep on the floor, for example, turned out to be a tuba of reddish brass. It was just as I had imagined a composer's studio; I even had the illusion I had seen the place before. D had stopped working and secluded himself in his room—could his father have been mistaken about all that?

The composer was just bending to switch off the tape recorder. Enveloped in a chaos that was not without its own order, he moved his hands swiftly and in an instant those beastly screams were sucked into a dark hole of silence. Then he straightened and turned to me with a truly tranquil smile.

Having glanced around the room and seen that the nurse was not present, I was a little wary, but the composer gave me no reason in the world to expect that he was about to get violent.

"My father told me about you. Come in, there's room over there," he said in a low resonant voice.

I took off my shoes and stepped up onto the rug without putting on slippers. Then I looked around for a place to sit, but except for round stools in front of the pianos and the organ, there wasn't a bit of furniture in the room, not even a cushion. So I brought my feet together between a pair of bongo drums and some empty tape boxes and stood there uncomfortably. The composer was standing too, arms hanging at his sides. I wondered if he ever sat down. He didn't ask me to be seated either, just stood there silent and smiling.

"Could those have been monkey voices?" I said, trying to crack a silence that threatened to set more quickly than any cement.

"Rhinoceros—they sounded that way because I speeded the machine up. And I had the volume way up, too. At least I think they're rhinoceros—rhino is what I asked for when I had this tape made—of course I can't really be sure. But now that you're here, I'll be able to go to the zoo myself."

"I may take that to mean that I'm employed?"

"Of course! I didn't have you come out here to test you. How can a madman test a normal person?" The man who was to be my employer said this objectively and almost as if he were embarrassed. Which made me feel disgusted with the obsequiousness of what I had said—I may take that to mean that I'm employed?—I had sounded like a shopkeeper! The composer was different from his businessman father and I should have been more direct with him.

"I wish you wouldn't call yourself a madman. It's awkward for me." Trying to be frank was one thing, but what a brainless remark! But the composer met me halfway. "All right, if that's how you feel. I suppose that would make work easier."

Work is a vague word, but, at least during those few months when I was visiting him once a week, the composer didn't get even as close to work as going to the zoo to record a genuine rhino for himself. He merely wandered around Tokyo in various conveyances or on foot and visited a variety of places. When he mentioned work, he must therefore have had me in mind. And I worked quite a lot; I even went on a mission for him, all the way to Kyoto.

"Then when should I begin?" I said.

"Right away if it suits you. Now."

"That suits me fine."

"I'll have to get ready—would you wait outside?"

Head lowered cautiously, as though he were walking in a swamp, my employer picked his way to the back of the room past musical instruments and sound equipment and piles of manuscripts to a black wooden door which he opened and then closed behind him. I got a quick look at a woman in a nurse's uniform, a woman in her early forties with a longish face and heavy shadows on her cheeks that might have been wrinkles or maybe scars. She seemed to encircle the composer with her right arm as she ushered him inside, while with her left hand she closed the door. If this was part of the routine, I would never have a chance to talk with the nurse before I went out with my employer. Standing in front of the closed door, in the darkest part of that dim room, I shuffled into my shoes and felt my anxiety about this job of mine increase. The composer had smiled the whole time and when I had prompted him he had replied. But he hadn't volunteered much. Should I have been more reserved? I wondered. Since "outside" might have meant two things, and since I was determined that everything should be perfect on my first job, I decided to wait just inside the main gate, from where I could see the annex in the garden.

D was a small, thin man, but with a head that seemed larger than most. To make the bony cliff of his forehead seem a little less forbidding, he combed his pale, well-washed, and fluffy hair down over his brow. His mouth and jaw were small, and his teeth were horribly irregular. And yet, probably due to the color of his deeply recessed eyes, there was a static correctness about his face that went well with a tranquil smile. As for the overall impression, there was something canine about the man. He wore flannel trousers and a sweater with stripes like rows of fleas. His shoulders were a little stooped, his arms outlandishly long.

When he came out of the back door of the annex, my employer was wearing a blue wool cardigan over his other sweater and a pair of white tennis shoes. He reminded me of a grade-school music teacher. In one hand he held a black scarf, and as if he were puzzling whether to wrap it around his neck, there was perplexity in his grin to me as I waited at the gate. For as long as I knew D, except at the very end when he was lying in a hospital bed, that was how he dressed. I remember his outfit so well because I was always struck by something comical about an adult man wearing a cardigan around his shoulders, as if he were a woman in disguise. Its shapelessness and nondescript color made that sweater perfect for him. As the composer pigeon-toed toward me past the shrubbery, he absently lifted the hand that held the scarf and signaled me with it. Then he wrapped the scarf resolutely around his neck. It was already four in the afternoon and fairly cold out of doors.

D went through the gate, and as I was following him (our relationship was already that of employer and employee), I had the feeling I was being watched and turned around: behind the same window through which I had discovered my employer, that forty-year-old nurse with the scarred— or were they wrinkled?—cheeks was watching us the way a soldier remaining behind might see a deserter off, her lips clamped shut like a turtle. I resolved to get her alone as soon as I could to question her about D's condition. What was wrong with the woman, anyway? Here she was taking care of a young man with a nervous condition, maybe a madman, yet when her charge went out she had nothing to say to the chaperon accompanying him. Wasn't that professional negligence? Wasn't she at least obliged to fill in the new man on the job? Or was my employer a patient so gentle and harmless that nothing had to be said?

When he got to the sidewalk D shuttered open his tired-looking eyes in their deep sockets and glanced swiftly up and down the deserted residential street. I didn't know whether it was an indication of madness or what—sudden action without any continuity seemed to be a habit of his. The composer looked up at the clear, end-of-autumn sky, blinking rapidly. Though they were sunken, there was something remarkably expressive about his deep brown eyes. Then he stopped blinking and his eyes seemed to focus, as though he were searching the sky. I stood obliquely behind him, watching, and what impressed me most vividly was the movement of his Adam's apple, which was large as any fist. I wondered if he had been destined to become a large man; perhaps something had impeded his growth in infancy and now only his head from the neck up bespoke the giant he was meant to be.

Lowering his gaze from the sky, my employer found and held my puzzled eyes with his own and said casually, but with a gravity that made objection impossible: "On a clear day you can see things floating up there very well. I see him up there with them, and frequently he comes down to me when I go outdoors."

Instantly I felt threatened. Looking away from my employer, I wondered how to survive this first ordeal that had confronted me so quickly. Should I pretend to believe in what this man called "him," or would that be a mistake? Was I dealing with a raving madman, or was the composer just a poker-faced humorist trying to have some fun with me? As I stood there in distress, he extended me a helping hand: "I know you can't see the figures floating in the sky, and I know you wouldn't be aware of him even if he were right here at my side. All I ask is that you don't act amazed when he comes down to earth, even if I talk to him. Because you'd upset him if you were to break out laughing all of a sudden or were to try to shut me up. And if you happen to notice when we're talking that I want some support from you, I'd appreciate it if you'd chime right in and say something, you know, affirmative. You see, I'm explaining Tokyo to him as if it were a paradise. It might seem a lunatic paradise to you, but maybe you could think of it as satire and be affirmative anyway, at least when he's down here with me."

I listened carefully and thought I could make out at least the contours of what my employer expected of me. Then was "he" a rabbit as big as a man after all, nesting in the sky? But that wasn't what I asked; I restrained myself to asking only: "How will I know when he's down here with you?"

"Just by watching me; he only comes down when I'm outside."

"What about when you're in a car?"

"In a car or train, as long as I'm next to an open window he's likely to show up. There have been times when he's appeared when I was in the house, just standing next to an open window."

"And . . . right now?" I asked uncomfortably. I must have sounded like the class dunce who simply cannot grasp the multiplication principle.

"Right now it's just you and me," my employer said graciously. "Why don't we ride in to Shinjuku today? I haven't been on a train in a long time."

We walked to the station, and all the way I kept an eye peeled for a sign that something had appeared at my employer's side. But before I knew it we were on the train and, so far as I could tell, nothing had materialized. One thing I did notice: the composer ignored the people who passed us on the street even when they greeted him. As if he himself did not exist, as if the people who approached with hellos and how-are-yous were registering an illusion which they mistook for him, my employer utterly ignored all overtures to contact.

The same thing happened at the ticket window; D unilaterally declined to relate to other people. Handing me one thousand yen, he told me to buy tickets and then refused to take his own even when I held it out to him. I had to stop at the gate and have both our tickets punched while D swept through the turnstile onto the platform with the freedom of the invisible man. Even on the train, he behaved as if the other passengers were no more aware of him than of the atmosphere; huddling in a seat in the farthest corner of the car, he rode in silence with his eyes closed. I stood in front of him and watched in growing apprehension for whatever it was to float in through the open window and settle at his side. Naturally, I didn't believe in the monster's existence. It was just that I was determined not to miss the instant when D's delusions took hold of him; I felt I owed him that much in return for the money he was paying me. But, as it happened, he sat like some small animal playing dead all the way to Shinjuku Station, so I could only surmise that he hadn't had a visit from the sky. Of course, supposition was all it was: as long as other people were around us, my employer remained a sullen oyster of silence. But I learned quickly enough that my guess had been correct. Because when the moment came, it was more than apparent (from D's reaction, I mean) that something was visiting him.

We had left the station and were walking down the street. It was that time of day a little before evening when not many people are out; we ran across a small crowd gathered on a corner. We stopped to look; surrounded by the crowd, an old man was turning around and around in the street without so much as a glance at anyone. A dignified-looking old man, he was spinning in a frenzy, clutching a briefcase and an umbrella to his breast, mussing his gray, pomaded hair a little as he stamped his feet and shouted like a seal. The faces in the watching crowd were lusterless and dry in the evening chill that was stealing into the air; the old man's face alone was flushed, and sweating, and seemed about to steam.

Suddenly I noticed that D, who should have been standing at my side, had taken a few steps back and thrown one arm around the shoulders of an invisible something roughly his own height. Now he was peering affectionately into the space slightly above the empty circle of his arm. The crowd was too intent on the old man to be concerned with D's performance, but I was terrified. Slowly the composer turned to me, as if he wanted to introduce me to a friend. I didn't know how to respond; all I could do was panic and blush. It was like forgetting your silly lines in the junior-high-school play. The composer continued to stare at me, and now there was annoyance in his eyes. He was seeking an explanation for that intent old man turning singlemindedly in the street, for the benefit of his visitor from the sky. A paradisiacal explanation! But all I could do was wonder stupidly whether the old man might have been afflicted with Saint Vitus's dance.

When I sadly shook my head in silence, the light of inquiry went out of my employer's eyes. As if he were taking leave of a friend, he dropped his arm. Then he slowly shifted his gaze skyward until his head was all the way back and his large Adam's apple stood out in bold relief. The phantom had soared back into the sky and I was ashamed; I hadn't been equal to my job. As I stood there with my head hanging, the composer stepped up to me and indicated that my first day of work was at an end: "We can go home now. He's come down once today already, and you must be pretty tired." I did feel exhausted after all that tension.

We rode back in a taxi with the windows rolled up, and as soon as I'd been paid for the day, I left. But I didn't go straight to the station; I waited behind a telephone pole diagonally across from the house. Dusk deepened, the sky turned the color of a rose, and just as the promise of night was becoming fact, the nurse, in a short-skirted, one-piece dress of a color indistinct in the dimness, appeared through the main gate pushing a brand-new bicycle in front of her. Before she could get on the bicycle, I ran over to her. Without her nurse's uniform she was just an ordinary little woman in her early forties; vanished from her face was the mystery I had discovered through the annex window. And my appearance had unsettled her. She couldn't climb on the bike and pedal away, but neither would she stand still; she had begun to walk the bike along when I demanded that she explain our mutual employer's condition. She resisted, peevishly, but I had a good grip on the bicycle seat and so in the end she gave in. When she began to talk, her formidable lower jaw snapped shut at each break in the sentence; she was absolutely a talking turtle.

"He says it's a fat baby in a white cotton nightgown. Big as a kangaroo, he says. It's supposed to be afraid of dogs and policemen and it comes down out of the sky. He says its name is Aghwee! Let me tell you something, if you happen to be around when that spook gets hold of him, you'd better just play dumb, you can't afford to get involved—don't forget you're dealing with a loony! And another thing, don't you take him anyplace funny, even if he wants to go. On top of everything else, a little gonorrhea is all we need around here!"

I blushed and let go of the bicycle seat. The nurse, jangling her bell, pedaled away into the darkness as fast as she could go with legs as tubular as handlebars. Ah, a fat baby in a white cotton nightgown, big as a kangaroo!

When I showed up at the house the following week, the composer fixed me with those clear brown eyes of his and rattled me by saying, though not especially in reproof: "I hear you waited for the nurse and asked her about my visitor from the sky. You really take your work seriously."

That afternoon we took the same train in the opposite direction, into the country for half an hour to an amusement park on the banks of the Tama River. We tried all kinds of rides and, luckily for me, the baby as big as a kangaroo dropped out of the sky to visit D when he was up by himself in the Sky Sloop, wooden boxes shaped like boats that were hoisted slowly into the air on the blades of a kind of windmill. From a bench on the ground, I watched the composer talking with an imaginary passenger at his side. And until his visitor had climbed back into the sky, D refused to come down; again and again a signal from him sent me running to buy him another ticket.

Another incident that made an impression on me that day occurred as we were crossing the amusement park toward the exit, when D accidentally stepped in some wet cement. When he saw that his foot had left an imprint he became abnormally irritated, and until I had negotiated with the workmen, paid them something for their pains and had the footprint troweled away, he stubbornly refused to move from the spot. This was the only time the composer ever revealed to me the least violence in his nature. On the way home on the train, I suppose because he regretted having barked at me, he excused himself in this way: "I'm not living in present time anymore, at least not consciously. Do you know the rule that governs trips into the past in a time machine? For example, a man who travels back ten thousand years in time doesn't dare do anything in that world that might remain behind him. Because he doesn't exist in time ten thousand years ago, and if he left anything behind him there the result would be a warp, infinitely slight maybe but still a warp, in all of history from then until now, ten thousand years of it. That's the way the rule goes, and since I'm not living in present time, I mustn't do anything here in this world that might remain or leave an imprint."

"But why have you stopped living in present time?" I asked, and my employer sealed himself up like a golf ball and ignored me. I regretted my loose tongue; I had finally exceeded the limits permitted me, because I was too concerned with D's problem. Maybe the nurse was right; playing dumb was the only way, and I couldn't afford to get involved. I resolved not to.

We walked around Tokyo occasionally after that, and my new policy was a success. But the day came when the composer's problems began to involve me whether I liked it or not. One afternoon we got into a cab together and, for the first time since I had taken the job, D mentioned a specific destination, a swank apartment house in Daikan Yama laid out like a hotel. When we arrived, D waited in the coffee shop in the basement while I went up in the elevator alone to pick up something that was waiting for me. I was to receive it from D's former wife, who was now living alone in the apartment.

I knocked on a door that made me think of the cell blocks at Sing Sing (I was always going to the movies in those days; I have the feeling that about 95 percent of what I knew came directly from the movies) and it was opened by a short woman with a pudgy, red face on top of a neck that was just as pudgy, as round as a cylinder. She ordered me to take my shoes off and step inside, and pointed to a sofa near the window where I was to sit. This must be the way high society receives a stranger, I remember thinking at the time. For me, the son of a poor farmer, refusing her invitation and asking for delivery at the door would have taken the courage to defy Japanese high society, the courage of that butcher who threatened Louis XIV. I did as I was told, and stepped for the first time in my life into an American-style studio apartment.

The composer's former wife poured me some beer. She seemed somewhat older than D, and although she gestured grandly and intoned when she spoke, she was too round and overweight to achieve dignity. She was wearing a dress of some heavy cloth with the hem of the skirt unraveled in the manner of a squaw costume, and her necklace of diamonds set in gold looked like the work of an Inca craftsman (now that I think about them, these observations, too, smell distinctly of the movies). Her window overlooked the streets of Shibuya, but the light pouring through it into the room seemed to bother her terrifically; she was continually shifting in her chair, showing me legs as round and bloodshot as her neck, while she questioned me in the voice of a cross-examiner. I suppose I was her only source of information about her former husband. Sipping my black, bitter beer as if it were hot coffee, I answered her as best I could, but my knowledge of D was scant and inaccurate and I couldn't satisfy her. Then she started asking about D's actress girlfriend, whether she came to see him and things like that, and there was nothing I could say. Annoyed, I thought to myself, what business was it of hers, didn't she have any feminine pride?

"Does D still see that phantom?" she said at last.

"Yes, it's a baby the size of a kangaroo in a white cotton nightgown and he says its name is Aghwee; the nurse was telling me about it," I said enthusiastically, glad to encounter a question I could do justice to. "It's usually floating in the sky, but sometimes it flies down to D's side."

"Aghwee, you say? Then it must be the ghost of our dead baby. You know why he calls it Aghwee? Because our baby spoke only once while it was alive and that was what it said—Aghwee. That's a pretty mushy way to name the ghost that's haunting you, don't you think?" The woman spoke derisively; an ugly, corrosive odor reached me from her mouth. "Our baby was born with a lump on the back of its head that made it look as if it had two heads. The doctor diagnosed it as a brain hernia. When D heard the news he decided to protect himself and me from a catastrophe, so he got together with the doctor, and they killed the baby—I think they only gave it sugar water instead of milk no matter how loud it screamed. My husband killed the baby because he didn't want us to be saddled with a child who could only function as a vegetable, which is what the doctor had predicted! So he was acting out of fantastic egotism more than anything else. But then there was an autopsy and the lump turned out to be a benign tumor. That's when D began seeing ghosts; you see, he'd lost the courage he needed to sustain his egotism, so he declined to live his own life, just as he had declined to let the baby go on living. Not that he committed suicide, he just fled from reality into a world of phantoms. But once your hands are all bloody with a baby's murder, you can't get them clean again just by running from reality, anybody knows that. So here he is, hands as filthy as ever and carrying on about Aghwee."

The cruelty of her criticism was hard to bear, for my employer's sake. So I turned to her, redder in the face than ever with the excitement of her loquacity, and struck a blow for D. "Where were you while all this was going on? You were the mother, weren't you?"

"I had a Caesarean, and for a week afterwards I was in a coma with a high fever. It was all over when I woke up," said D's former wife, leaving my gauntlet on the floor. Then she stood up and moved toward the kitchen. "I guess you'll have some more beer?"

"No, thank you, I've had enough. Would you please give me whatever I'm supposed to take to D?"

"Of course, just let me gargle. I have to gargle every ten minutes, for pyorrhea—you must have noticed the smell?"

D's former wife put a brass key into a business envelope and handed it to me. Standing behind me while I tied my shoes, she asked what school I went to and then, mentioning a certain newspaper, added proudly: "I hear there's not even one subscriber in the dormitories there. You may be interested to know that my father will own that paper soon."

I let silence speak for my contempt.

I was about to get into the elevator when doubt knifed through me as though my chest were made of butter. I had to think. I let the elevator go and decided to use the stairs. If his former wife had described D's state of mind correctly, how could I be sure he wouldn't commit suicide with a pinch of cyanide or something taken from a box this key unlocked? All the way down the stairs I wondered what to do, and then I was standing in front of D's table and still hadn't arrived at a conclusion. The composer sat there with his eyes tightly shut, his tea untouched on the table. I suppose it wouldn't do for him to be seen drinking substances of this time, now that he had stopped living in it and had become a traveler from another.

"I saw her," I began, resolved all of a sudden to lie, "and we were talking all this time but she wouldn't give me anything."

My employer looked up at me placidly and said nothing, though doubt clouded his puppy eyes in their deep sockets. All the way back in the cab I sat in silence at his side, secretly perturbed. I wasn't sure whether he had seen through my lie. In my shirt pocket the key was heavy.

But I only kept it a week. For one thing, the idea of D's suicide began to seem silly; for another, I was worried he might ask his wife about the key. So I put it in a different envelope and mailed it to him special delivery. The next day I went out to the house a little worried and found my employer in the open space in front of the annex, burning a pile of music manuscripts. They must have been his own compositions: that key had unlocked the composer's music.

We didn't go out that day. Instead I helped D incinerate his whole opus. We had burned everything and had dug a hole and I was burying the ashes when suddenly D began to whisper. The phantom had dropped out of the sky. And until it left I continued working, slowly burying those ashes. That afternoon the sky monster called Aghwee (and there was no denying it was a mushy name) remained at my employer's side for fully twenty minutes.

From that day on, since I either stepped to one side or dropped behind whenever the phantom baby appeared, the composer must have realized that I was complying with only the first of his original instructions, not to act amazed, while his request that I back him up with something affirmative was consistently ignored. Yet he seemed satisfied, and so my job was made easier. I couldn't believe D was the kind of person to create a disturbance in the street; in fact his father's word of warning began to seem ridiculous, our tours of Tokyo together continued so uneventfully. I had already purchased the Moscow edition of *L'Âme Enchanté* I wanted, but I no longer had any intention of giving up such a marvelous job. My employer and I went everywhere together. D wanted to visit all the concert halls where works of his had been performed and all the schools he had ever been to. We would make special trips to places where he used to amuse himself—bars, movie theaters, indoor swimming pools—and then we would turn back without going inside. And the composer had a passion for all of Tokyo's many forms of public transportation; I'm sure we rode the entire metropolitan subway system. Since the monster baby couldn't descend from the sky while we were underground, I could enjoy the subway in peace of mind. Naturally, I tensed whenever we encountered dogs or officers of the law, remembering what the nurse had told me, but those encounters never coincided with an appearance by Aghwee. I discovered that I was loving my job. Not loving my employer or his phantom baby the size of a kangaroo. Simply loving my job.

One day the composer approached me about making a trip for him. He would pay traveling expenses, and my daily wage would be doubled; since I would have to stay overnight in a hotel and wouldn't be back until the second day, I would actually be earning four times what I usually made. Not only that, the purpose of the trip was to meet D's former girlfriend the movie actress, in D's place. I accepted eagerly, I was delighted. And so began that comic and pathetic journey.

D gave me the name of the hotel the actress had mentioned in a recent letter and the date she was expecting him to arrive. Then he had me learn a message to the girl: my employer was no longer living in present time; he was like a traveler who had arrived here in a time machine from a world ten thousand years in the future. Accordingly, he couldn't permit himself to create a new existence with his own signature on it through such acts as writing letters.

I memorized the message, and then it was late at night and I was sitting opposite a movie actress in the basement bar of a hotel in Kyoto, with a chance first to explain why D hadn't come himself, next to persuade his mistress of his conception of time, and finally to deliver his message. I concluded: "D would like you to be careful not to confuse his recent divorce with another divorce he once promised you he would get and since he isn't living in present time anymore, he says it's only natural that he won't be seeing you again." I felt my face color; for the first time I had the sensation that I had a truly difficult job.

"Is that what D-boy says? And what do you say? How do you feel about all this, that you'd run an errand all the way to Kyoto?"

"Frankly, I think D is being mushy."

"That's the way he is—I'd say he's being pretty mushy with you, too, asking this kind of favor!"

"I'm employed; I get paid by the day for what I do."

"What are you drinking there? Have some brandy."

I had some. Until then I'd been drinking the same dark beer D's former wife had given me, with an egg in it to thin it down. By some queer carom of a psychological billiard ball, I'd been influenced by a memory from D's former wife's apartment while waiting to meet his mistress. The actress had been drinking brandy from the start. It was the first imported brandy I'd ever had.

"And what's all this about D-boy seeing a ghost, a baby as big as a kangaroo? What did you call it, Raghbee?"

"Aghwee! The baby only spoke once before it died and that was what it said."

"And D thought it was telling him its name? Isn't that darling! If that baby had been normal, it was all decided that D was going to get a divorce and marry me. The day the baby was born we were in bed together in a hotel room and there was a phone call and then we knew something awful had happened. D jumped out of bed and went straight to the hospital. Not a word from him since—" The actress gulped her brandy down, filled her glass to the brim from the bottle of Hennessy on the table as if she were pouring fruit juice, and drained her glass again.

Our table was hidden from the bar by a display case full of cigarettes. Hanging on the wall above my shoulder was a large color poster with the actress's picture on it, a beer advertisement. The face in the poster glittered like gold, no less than the beer. The girl sitting opposite me was not quite so dazzling, there was even a depression in her forehead, just below the hairline, that looked deep enough to contain an adult thumb. But it was precisely the fault that made her more appealing than her picture.

She couldn't get the baby off her mind.

"Look, wouldn't it be terrifying to die without memories or experiences because you'd never done anything human while you were alive? That's how it would be if you died as an infant—wouldn't that be terrifying?"

"Not to the baby, I don't imagine," I said deferentially.

"But think about the world after death!" The actress's logic was full of leaps.

"The world after death?"

"If there is such a thing, the souls of the dead must live there with their memories for all eternity. But what about the soul of a baby who never knew anything and never had any experiences? I mean, what memories can it have?"

At a loss, I drank my brandy in silence.

"I'm terribly afraid of death, so I'm always thinking about it—you don't have to be disgusted with yourself because you don't have a quick answer for me. But you know what I think? The minute that baby died, I think D-boy decided not to create any new memories for himself, as if he had died, too, and that's why he stopped living, you know, positively, in present time. And I bet he calls that ghost baby down to earth all over Tokyo so he can create new memories for it!"

At the time I thought she must be right. This tipsy movie actress with a dent in her forehead big enough for a thumb is quite an original psychologist, I thought to myself. And much more D's type, I thought, than the pudgy, tomato-faced daughter of a newspaper baron. All of a sudden I realized that, even here in Kyoto with hundreds of miles between us, I, the model of a faithful employee, was thinking exclusively about D. No, there was something else, too, there was D's phantom. I realized that the baby whose appearance I waited for nervously every time my employer and I went out together hadn't been off my mind for a minute.

It was time for the bar to close and I didn't have a room. I'd managed to get as old as I was without ever staying in a hotel and I knew nothing about reservations. Luckily, the actress was known at the hotel, and a word from her got me a room. We went up in the elevator together, and I started to get off at my floor when she suggested we have one last drink and invited me to her room. From that point on I have only muddled comic and pathetic memories. When she had seated me in a chair, the actress returned to the door and looked up and down the hall, then went through a whole series of nervous motions, flounced on the bed as if to test the springs, turned lights on and switched them off, ran a little water in the tub. Then she poured me the brandy she had promised and, sipping a Coca Cola, she told me about another man chasing her during her affair with D, and finally going to bed with him, and D slapping her so hard the teeth rattled in her mouth. Then she asked if I thought today's college students went in for "heavy petting"? It depended on the student, I said—suddenly the actress had become a mother scolding a child for staying up too late and was telling me to find my own room and go to sleep. I said good night, went downstairs, and fell asleep immediately. I woke up at dawn with a fire in my throat.

The most comic and pathetic part was still to come. I understood the minute I opened my eyes that the actress had invited me to her room intending to seduce a college student who was wild for heavy petting. And with that understanding came rage and abject desire. I hadn't slept with a woman yet, but this humiliation demanded that I retaliate. I was drunk on what must have been my first Hennessy VSOP, and I was out of my head with the kind of poisonous desire that goes with being eighteen. It was only five o'clock in the morning and there was no sign of life in the halls. Like a panther wild with rage I sped to her door on padded feet. It was ajar. I stepped inside and found her seated at the dresser mirror with her back to me. Creeping up directly behind her (to this day I wonder what I was trying to do), I lunged at her neck with both hands. The actress whirled around with a broad smile on her face, rising as she turned, and then she had my hands in her own and was pumping them happily up and down as if she were welcoming a guest and singsonging: "Good morning! Good morning! Good morning!" Before I knew it I had been seated in a chair and we were sharing her toast and morning coffee and reading the newspaper together. After a while the movie actress said in a tone of voice she might have used to discuss the weather: "You were trying to rape me just now, weren't you." She went back to her makeup and I got out of there, fled downstairs to my own room and burrowed back into bed, trembling as though I had malaria. I was afraid that a report of this incident might reach D, but the subject of the movie actress never came up again. I continued to enjoy my job.

Winter had come. Our plan that afternoon was to bicycle through D's residential neighborhood and the surrounding fields. I was on a rusty old bike and my employer had borrowed the nurse's shiny new one. Gradually we expanded the radius of a circle around D's house, riding into a new housing development and coasting down hills in the direction of the fields. We were sweating, relishing the sensation of liberation, more and more exhilarated. I say "we" and include D because that afternoon it was evident that he was in high spirits, too. He was even whistling a theme from a Bach sonata for flute and harpsichord called *Siciliana*. I happened to know that because when I was in high school, I had played flute. I never learned to play well, but I did develop a habit of thrusting out my upper lip the way a tapir does. Naturally, I had friends who insisted my buck teeth were to blame. But the fact is, flutists frequently look like tapirs.

As we pedaled down the street, I picked up the tune and began to whistle along with D. Siciliana is a sustained and elegant theme, but I was out of breath from pedaling and my whistle kept lapsing into airy sibilance. Yet D's phrasing was perfect, absolutely legato. I stopped whistling then, ashamed to go on, and the composer glanced over at me with his lips still pursed in a whistle like a carp puckering up to breathe and smiled his tranquil smile. Granted there was a difference in the bikes, it was still unnatural and pathetic that an eighteen-year-old student, skinny maybe, but tall, should begin to tire and run short of breath before a twenty-eight-year-old composer who was a little man and sick besides. Unjust is what it was, and infuriating. My mood clouded instantly and I felt disgusted with the whole job. So I stood up on the pedals all of a sudden and sped away as furiously as a bicycle racer. I even turned, purposely, down a narrow gravel path between two vegetable fields. When I looked back a minute later, my employer was hunched over the handle bars, his large, round head nodding above his narrow shoulders, churning the gravel beneath his wheels in hot pursuit of me. I coasted to a stop, propped a foot on the barbed wire fence that bordered the field, and waited for D to catch up. I was already ashamed of my childishness.

His head still bobbing, my employer was approaching fast, and then I knew the phantom was with him. D was racing his bike down the extreme left of the gravel path, his face twisted to the right so that he was almost looking over his right shoulder, and the reason his head appeared to bob was that he was whispering encouragement to something running, or maybe flying, alongside the bicycle. Like a marathon coach pacing one of his runners. Ah, I thought, he's doing that on the premise that Aghwee is neck and neck with his speeding bike. The monster as large as a kangaroo, the fat, funny baby in a white cotton nightgown was bounding—like a kangaroo!—down that gravel path. I shuddered, then I kicked the barbed wire fence and slowly pedaled away, waiting for my employer and the monster in his imagination to catch up.

Don't think I'd let myself begin to believe in Aghwee's existence. I had taken the nurse's advice, sworn not to lose the anchor on my common sense, not to give way to lunacy as in those slightly solemn slapstick comedies where, say, the keeper of the madhouse goes mad; and, consciously derisive, I was thinking to myself that the neurotic composer was putting on a show with his bicycle just to follow up a lie he had told me once, and what a lot of trouble to go to! In other words, I was keeping a clinical distance between myself and D's phantom monster. Even so, there occurred a strange alteration in my state of mind.

It began this way: D had finally caught up and was biking along a few feet behind me when, as unexpectedly as a cloudburst and quite inescapably, we were enveloped by the belling of a pack of hounds. I looked up and saw them racing toward me down the gravel path, young adult Dobermans that stood two feet high, more than ten of them. Running breathlessly behind the pack, the thin black leather leashes grasped in one hand, was a man in overalls, chasing the dogs perhaps, or maybe they were dragging him along. Jet-black Dobermans, sleek as wet seals, with just a dusting of dry chocolate on their chests and jowls and pumping haunches. And down on us they howled, filling the gravel path, keening for the attack at such a forward tilt they looked about to topple on their foaming snouts. There was a meadow on the other side of the field; the man in overalls must have been training the beasts there and now he was on his way home with them.

Trembling with fear, I got off my bike and helplessly surveyed the field on the other side of the fence. The barbed wire came up to my chest. I might have had a chance myself but I would never have been able to boost the little composer to safety on the other side. The poisons of terror were beginning to numb my head, but for one lucid instant I could see the catastrophe that was bound to occur in a few seconds. As the Dobermans neared, D would sense that Aghwee was being attacked by a pack of the animals it most feared. He would probably hear the baby's frightened crying. And certainly he would meet the dogs head on, in defense of his baby. Then the Dobermans would rip him to pieces. Or he would try to escape with the baby and make a reckless leap to clear the fence and be just as cruelly torn. I was rocked by the pity of what I knew must happen. And while I stood there dumbly without a plan, those giant black-and-chocolate devils were closing in on us, snapping the air with awful jaws, so close by now that I could hear their alabaster claws clicking on the gravel. Suddenly I knew I could do nothing for D and his baby, and with that knowledge I went limp, unresisting as a pervert when he is seized in the subway, and was swallowed whole in the darkness of my fear. I backed off the gravel path until the barbed wire was a fire in my back, pulled my bike in front of me as if it were a wall, and shut my eyes tight. Then an animal stench battered me, together with the howling of the dogs and the pounding of their feet, and I could feel tears seeping past my eyelids. I abandoned myself to a wave of fear and it swept me away . . .

On my shoulder was a hand gentle as the essence of all gentleness; it felt like Aghwee touching me. But I knew it was my employer; he had let those fiendish dogs pass and no catastrophe of fear had befallen him. I continued crying anyway, with my eyes closed and my shoulders heaving. I was too old to cry in front of other people. I suppose the shock of fright had induced some kind of infantile regression in me. When I stopped crying, we walked our bikes past that barbed wire fence like prisoners in a concentration camp, in silence, our heads hanging, to the meadow beyond the field where strangers were playing ball and exercising dogs (D wasn't occupied with Aghwee anymore; the baby must have left while I was crying). We laid our bikes down and then sprawled on the grass ourselves. My tears had flooded away my pretensions and my rebelliousness and the perverse suspicion in my heart. And D was no longer wary of me. I lay back on the grass and clasped my hands beneath my head, curiously light and dry after all that crying. Then I closed my eyes and listened quietly while D peered down at me with his chin in his hand and spoke to me of Aghwee's world.

"Do you know a poem called 'Shame' by Nakahara Chuya? Listen to the second verse:

> The mournful sky
> high where branches tangle
> teems with dead baby souls;
> I blinked and saw
> above the distant fields
> fleece knit into a dream
> of mastodons.

"That's one aspect of the world of the dead baby I see. There are some Blake engravings, too, especially one called 'Christ Refusing the Banquet Offered by Satan'—have you ever seen it? And there's another, 'The Morning Stars Singing Together.' In both there are figures in the sky who have the same reality about them as the people on the ground, and whenever I look at them I'm sure Blake was hinting at an aspect of this other world. I once saw a Dali painting that was close, too, full of opaque beings floating in the sky about a hundred yards above the ground and glowing with an ivory-white light. Now that's exactly the world I see. And you know what those glowing things are that fill the sky? Beings we've lost from our lives down here on earth, and now they float up there in the sky about a hundred yards above the ground, quietly glowing like amoebas under a microscope. And sometimes they descend the way our Aghwee does." (My employer said it and I didn't protest, which doesn't mean I acquiesced.) "But it takes a sacrifice worthy of them to acquire the eyes to see them floating there and the ears to detect them when they descend to earth, and yet there are moments when suddenly we're endowed with that ability without any sacrifice or even effort on our part. I think that's what happened to you a few minutes ago."

Without any sacrifice or even effort on my part, just a few tears of expiation, my employer seemed to have wanted to say. The truth was I had shed tears out of fear and helplessness and a kind of vague terror about my future (my first job, an experiment in a kind of microcosm of life, was guarding this mad composer, and since I had failed to do that adequately, it was predictable that situations which left me stupefied because I couldn't cope with them would recur as one of the patterns of my life), but instead of interrupting with a protest, I continued to listen docilely.

"You're still young; probably you haven't lost anything in this world that you can never forget, that's so dear to you that you're aware of its absence all the time. Probably the sky a hundred yards or so above your head is still nothing more than sky to you. But all that means is that the storehouse happens to be empty at the moment. Or have you lost something that was really important to you?"

The composer paused for my answer, and I found myself remembering his former mistress, that movie actress with a dent in her forehead as big as an adult thumb. Naturally, no crucial loss of mine could have had anything to do with her; all that crying had eroded my head and a sentimental honey was seeping into the crevices.

"Well, have you?" For the first time since we had met, my employer was insistent. "Have you lost anything that was important to you?"

Suddenly I had to say something silly to cover my embarrassment.

"I lost a cat," I tried.

"A Siamese or what?"

"Just an ordinary cat with orange stripes; he disappeared about a week ago."

"If it's only been a week he might come back. Isn't it the season for them to wander?"

"That's what I thought, too, but now I know he won't be back."

"Why?"

"He was a tough tom with his own territory staked out. This morning I saw a weak-looking cat walking up and down his block and it wasn't even on its guard—my cat won't be coming back." When I'd stopped talking I realized I'd told a story intended for laughs in a voice that was hoarse with sadness.

"Then there's a cat floating in your sky," my employer said solemnly.

Through closed eyes I pictured an opaque cat as large as an ad balloon, glowing with an ivory-white light as it floated through the sky. It was a comical flight all right, but it also made me wistful.

"The figures floating in your sky begin to increase at an accelerating rate. That's why I haven't been living in present time ever since that incident with the baby, so I could stop that spreading. Since I'm not living in our time, I can't discover anything new, but I don't lose anything, either — the state of my sky never changes." There was profound relief in the composer's voice.

But was my own sky really empty except for one bloated cat with orange stripes? I opened my eyes and started to look up at the clear, now almost evening sky, when dread made me close my eyes again. Dread of myself, for what if I had seen a glowing herd of numberless beings we had lost from time down here on earth?

We lay on the grass in that meadow for quite a while, ringed by the passive affinity two people have for one another when the same gloom is gripping them. And gradually I began to get my perspective back. I reproached myself: how unlike the eighteen-year-old pragmatist I really was to have let myself be influenced by a mad composer! I'm not suggesting my equilibrium was perfectly restored. The day I succumbed to that strange panic, I drew closer than ever to the sentiments of my employer and to that glowing herd in the sky one hundred yards above the ground. To an extent, what you might call the aftereffects remained with me.

And then the final day came. It was Christmas Eve. I'm certain about the date because D gave me a wristwatch with a little apology about being a day early. And I remember that a powdery snow fell for about an hour just after lunch. We went down to the Ginza together but it was already getting crowded, so we decided to walk out to Tokyo harbor. D wanted to see a Chilean freighter that was supposed to have docked that day. I was eager to go, too; I pictured a ship with snow blanketing her decks. We had left the Ginza crowds and were just passing the Kabuki Theater when D looked up at the dark and still snowy sky. Then Aghwee descended to his side. As usual, I walked a few steps behind the composer and his phantom. We came to a wide intersection. D and the baby had just stepped off the curb when the light changed. D stopped, and a fleet of trucks as bulky as elephants heaved into motion with their Christmas freight. That was when it happened. Suddenly D cried out and thrust both arms in front of him as if he were trying to rescue something; then he leaped in among those trucks and was struck to the ground. I watched stupidly from the curb.

"That was suicide; he just killed himself!" said a shaky voice at my side.

But I had no time to wonder whether it might have been suicide. In a minute that intersection had become backstage at a circus, jammed with milling trucks like elephants, and I was kneeling at D's side, holding his bloody body in my arms and trembling like a dog. I didn't know what to do; a policeman had dashed up and then disappeared on the run again.

D wasn't dead, it was more awful than that. He was dying, lying there in the filthy wet that had been a light snow, oozing blood and something like tree sap. The dark and snowy pattern of the sky ripped open and the stately light of a Spanish pietà made my employer's blood glisten like stupid grease. By that time a crowd had gathered, snatches of "Jingle Bells" wheeled above our heads like panic-stricken pigeons, and I knelt at D's side listening hard for nothing in particular and hearing screaming in the distance. But the crowd just stood there silently in the cold, as if indifferent to the screams. I have never listened so hard on a street corner again, nor again heard screams like that.

An ambulance finally arrived and my employer was lifted inside unconscious. He was caked with blood and mud, and shock seemed to have withered his body. In his white tennis shoes, he looked like an injured blind man. I climbed into the ambulance with a doctor and an orderly and a young man about my age who seemed haughty and aloof. He turned out to be the driver of the long-distance truck that had hit D. The congestion was getting worse all the time as the ambulance cut across the Ginza (according to some statistics I saw recently, there were record crowds that Christmas Eve). Those who heard the siren and stopped to watch us pass, nearly all of them, shared a look of circumspectly solemn concern. In one corner of my dazed head I reflected that the so-called inscrutable Japanese smile, while it seemed likely to exist, did not. Meanwhile D lay unconscious on that wobbly stretcher, bleeding his life away.

When we arrived at the hospital, orderlies rushed D away to some recess of the building. The same policeman as before appeared again out of nowhere and calmly asked me a lot of questions. Then I was permitted to go to D. The young truckdriver had already found the room and was sitting on a bench in the corridor next to the door. I sat down beside him and we waited for a long time. At first he only muttered about all the deliveries he still had to make, but after two hours or so he began to complain of being hungry in a surprisingly childish voice, and my hostility toward him dwindled. We waited some more, then the banker arrived with his wife and three daughters, who were all dressed up to go to a party. Ignoring us, they went inside. All four of the women had fat, squat bodies and red faces; they reminded me of D's former wife. I continued to wait. It had been hours by then, and the whole time I had been tormented by suspicion: hadn't my employer intended to kill himself from the beginning? Before taking his life he had settled things with his ex-wife and former mistress, burned his manuscripts, toured the city saying good-by to places he would miss—hadn't he hired me because he needed some good-natured help with those chores? Kept me from seeing through his plan by inventing a monster baby floating in the sky? In other words, wasn't it the case that my only real function had been to help D commit suicide? The young truckdriver had fallen asleep with his head on my shoulder and every minute or two he would be convulsed as though in pain. He must have been having a nightmare about running over a man with his truck.

It was pitch black outside when the banker appeared in the door and called me. I eased my shoulder from under the driver's head and stood up. The banker paid me my salary for the day and then let me into the room. D lay on his back with rubber tubes in his nostrils, as if for a joke.

His face gave me pause; it was black as smoked meat. But I couldn't help voicing the doubt that had me so afraid. I called out to my dying employer: "Did you hire me just so you could commit suicide? Was all that about Aghwee just a cover-up?" Then my throat was clogged with tears and I was surprised to hear myself shouting: "I was about to believe in Aghwee!"

At that moment, as my tear-filled eyes began to dim, I saw a smile appear on D's darkened, shriveled face. It might have been a mocking smile or it might have been a smile of friendly mischief. The banker led me out of the room. The young man from the truck was stretched out on the bench asleep. On my way out, I slipped the thousand yen I had earned into his jacket pocket. I read in the evening paper the next day that the composer was dead.

And then it was this spring and I was walking down the street when a group of frightened children suddenly started throwing stones. It was so sudden and unprovoked, I don't know what I had done to threaten them. Whatever it was, fear had turned those children into killers, and one of them hit me in the right eye with a rock as big as a fist. I went down on one knee, pressed my hand to my eye and felt a lump of broken flesh. With my good eye I watched my dripping blood suck in the dirt in the street as though magnetically. It was then that I sensed a being I knew and missed leave the ground behind me—a being the size of a kangaroo— and soar into the teary blue of a sky that retained its winter brittleness. Good-by, Aghwee, I heard myself whispering in my heart. And then I knew that my hatred of those frightened children had melted away and that time had filled my sky during those ten years with figures that glowed with an ivory-white light, I suppose not all of them purely innocent. When I was wounded by those children and sacrificed my sight in one eye, so clearly a gratuitous sacrifice, I had been endowed, if for only an instant, with the power to perceive a creature that had descended from the heights of my sky.

# ■ Murakami Haruki (1949– ) (novel)

TRANSLATED BY ALFRED BIRNBAUM

Murakami Haruki was born in Kyoto in 1949 and grew up in Kobe. He studied classical Greek drama at Waseda University and from 1974 to 1981 managed a Tokyo jazz bar and published his first three novels. He lives now in Cambridge, Massachusetts, and is well known in the West as Haruki Murakami, the English name order that his books in translation carry, in contrast to normal Japanese name order (family name first, personal name last). For his third novel, *A Wild Sheep Chase* (1982; English translation, 1989), he won the Noma Literary Award for New Writers; he was also awarded the prestigious Tanizaki Prize for his fourth novel, *Hard-Boiled*

*Wonderland and the End of the World* (1985; English translation, 1991). His next novel, *Norwegian Wood* (1987), sold more than four million copies, making him Japan's highest selling novelist. His recent work includes *Dance, Dance, Dance,* which is a sequel to *A Wild Sheep Chase,* and *The Elephant Vanishes* (English translation, 1993), a book of short stories. Murakami is also the prolific translator of such authors as F. Scott Fitzgerald, Paul Theroux, Raymond Carver, John Irving, and Truman Capote, among others.

Like Abe Kobo, Murakami is a wildly innovative author, wacky, surreal, postmodern, and experimental. He has a hip and warped style and a talent for the strangely apt comparison ("Atop the telephone poles, crows gave a flap or two of their wings, their beaks shiny as credit cards"). "Elevator, Silence, Overweight" is the opening chapter of *Hard-Boiled Wonderland and the End of the World,* a novel that, like its split-brained protagonist, carries on a dual storyline in alternating chapters. In Murakami's world, the resolutely strange is perfectly normal, and the pleasure of reading him lies in witnessing his attitude, verbal ingenuity, and each bizarre tangent opening like an unexpected room off the strange corridor of his narration.

FURTHER READING: Murakami, Haruki. *A Wild Sheep Chase,* 1989; *Hard-Boiled Wonderland and the End of the World,* 1991; *Norwegian Wood* (in Japanese), 1987; *Dance, Dance, Dance; The Elephant Vanishes,* 1993.

# from *Hard-Boiled Wonderland and the End of the World*

## Elevator, Silence, Overweight

The elevator continued its impossibly slow ascent. Or at least I imagined it was ascent. There was no telling for sure: it was so slow that all sense of direction simply vanished. It could have been going down for all I knew, or maybe it wasn't moving at all. But let's just assume it was going up. Merely a guess. Maybe I'd gone up twelve stories, then down three. Maybe I'd circled the globe. How would I know?

Every last thing about this elevator was worlds apart from the cheap die-cut job in my apartment building, scarcely one notch up the evolutionary scale from a well bucket. You'd never believe the two pieces of machinery had the same name and the same purpose. The two were pushing the outer limits conceivable as elevators.

First of all, consider the space. This elevator was so spacious it could have served as an office. Put in a desk, add a cabinet and a locker, throw in a kitchenette, and you'd still have room to spare. You might even squeeze in three camels and a mid-range palm tree while you were at it. Second, there was the cleanliness. Antiseptic as a brand-new coffin. The walls and ceiling were absolutely spotless polished stainless steel, the floor immaculately carpeted in a handsome moss-green. Third, it was dead silent. There wasn't a sound—literally not one sound—from the moment I stepped inside and the doors slid shut. Deep rivers run quiet.

Another thing, most of the gadgets an elevator is supposed to have were missing. Where, for example, was the panel with all the buttons and switches? No floor numbers to press, no DOOR OPEN and DOOR CLOSE, no EMERGENCY STOP. Nothing whatsoever. All of which made me feel utterly defenseless. And it wasn't just no buttons; it was no indication of advancing floor, no posted capacity or warning, not even a manufacturer's nameplate. Forget about trying to locate an emergency exit. Here I was, sealed in. No way this elevator could have gotten fire department approval. There are norms for elevators after all.

Staring at these four blank stainless-steel walls, I recalled one of Houdini's great escapes I'd seen in a movie. He's tied up in how many ropes and chains, stuffed into a big trunk, which is wound fast with another thick chain and sent hurtling, the whole lot, over Niagara Falls. Or maybe it was an icy dip in the Arctic Ocean. Given that I wasn't all tied up, I was doing okay; insofar as I wasn't clued in on the trick, Houdini was one up on me.

Talk about not clued in, I didn't even know if I was moving or standing still.

I ventured a cough, but it didn't echo anything like a cough. It seemed flat, like clay thrown against a slick concrete wall. I could hardly believe that dull thud issued from my own body. I tried coughing one more time. The result was the same. So much for coughing.

I stood in that hermetically sealed vault for what seemed an eternity. The doors showed no sign of ever opening. Stationary in unending silence, a still life: *Man in Elevator.*

I started to get nervous. What if the machinery had malfunctioned? Or suppose the elevator operator—assuming there was one in the building—forgot I was here in this box? People have lost track of me before.

I strained to hear something, anything, but no sound reached my ears. I pressed my ear against the stainless-steel wall. Sure enough, not a sound. All I managed was to leave an outline of my ear on the cold metal. The elevator was made, apparently, of a miracle alloy that absorbed all noise. I tried whistling *Danny Boy,* but it came out like a dog wheezing with asthma.

There was little left to do but lean up against a wall and count the change in my pockets. For someone in my profession, knowing how to kill time is as important a method of training as gripping rubber balls is for a boxer. Although, in any strict sense, it's not killing time at all. For only through assiduous repetition is it possible to redistribute skewed tendencies.

I always come prepared with pockets full of loose change. In my right pocket I keep one-hundred- and five-hundred-yen coins, in my left fifties and tens. One-yen and five-yen coins I carry in a back pocket, but as a rule these don't enter into the count. What I do is thrust my hands simultaneously into both pockets, the right hand tallying the hundreds and five-hundreds in tandem with the left hand adding up the fifties and tens.

It's hard for those who've never attempted the procedure to grasp what it is to calculate this way, and admittedly it is tricky at first. The right brain and the left brain each keep separate tabs, which are then brought together like two halves of a split watermelon. No easy task until you get the hang of it.

Whether or not I really do put the right and left sides of my brain to separate accounts, I honestly can't say. A specialist in neurophysiology might have insights to offer on the matter. I'm no neurophysiologist, however. All I know is that when I'm actually in the midst of counting, I feel like I'm using the right side and left side of my brain differently. And when I'm through counting, it seems the fatigue that sets in is qualitatively quite distinct from what comes with normal counting. For convenience sake, I think of it as right-brain-totals-right-pocket, left-brain-totals-left-pocket.

On the whole, I think of myself as one of those people who take a convenience-sake view of prevailing world conditions, events, existence in general. Not that I'm such a blasé, convenience-sake sort of guy—although I do have tendencies in that direction—but because more often than not I've observed that convenient approximations bring you closest to comprehending the true nature of things.

For instance, supposing that the planet earth were not a sphere but a gigantic coffee table, how much difference in everyday life would that make? Granted, this is a pretty far-fetched example; you can't rearrange facts of life so freely. Still, picturing the planet earth, for convenience sake, as a gigantic coffee table does in fact help clear away the clutter—those practically pointless contingencies such as gravity and the international dateline and the equator, those nagging details that arise from the spherical view. I mean, for a guy leading a perfectly ordinary existence, how many times in the course of a lifetime would the equator be a significant factor?

But to return to the matter at hand—or rather, hands, the right and the left each going about its own separate business—it is by no means easy to keep running parallel counts. Even for me, to get it down took the longest time. But once you do, once you've gotten the knack, it's not something you lose. Like riding a bike or swimming. Which isn't to say you can't always use a little more practice. Repetition can improve your technique and refine your style. If for no other reason than this, I always keep my hands busy.

This time I had three five-hundred-yen coins and eighteen hundreds in the one pocket, and seven fifties and sixteen tens in the other. Making a grand total of three-thousand eight-hundred-ten yen. Calculations like this are no trouble at all. Simpler than counting the fingers on my hands. Satisfied, I leaned back against the stainless-steel wall and looked straight ahead at the doors. Which were still not opening.

What could be taking so long? I tentatively wrote off both the equipment-malfunction theory and the forgotten-by-operator theory. Neither very realistic. This was not to say that equipment malfunction or operator negligence couldn't realistically occur. On the contrary, I know for a fact that such accidents are all too common in the real world. What I mean to say is that in a highly exceptional reality—this ridiculously slick elevator a case in point—the non-exceptional can, for convenience sake, be written off as paradoxically exceptional. Could any human being capable of designing this Tom Swift elevator fail to keep the machinery in working order or forget the proper procedures once a visitor stepped inside?

The answer was obvious. No.

Never happen.

Not after *they* had been so meticulous up to that point. They'd seen to minute details, measuring each step I'd taken virtually to the millimeter. I'd been stopped by two guards at the entrance to the building, asked whom I was there to see, matched against a visitors' list, made to produce my driver's license, logged into a central computer for verification, after which I was summarily pushed into this elevator. You don't get this much going over when you visit the Bank of Japan. It was unthinkable that they, having done all that, should slip up now.

The only possibility was that they had intentionally placed me in this particular situation. They *wanted* the elevator's motions to be opaque to me. They *wanted* the elevator to move so slowly I wouldn't be able to tell if it were going up or down. They were probably watching me with a hidden TV camera now.

To ward off the boredom, I thought about searching for the camera lens. But on second thought, what would I have to gain if I found it? That would alert them, they'd halt the elevator, and I'd be even later for my appointed hour.

So I decided to do nothing. I was here in proper accordance with my duties. No need to worry, no cause for alarm.

I leaned against the elevator wall, thrust my hands in my pockets, and once more counted my change. Three-thousand seven-hundred-fifty yen. Nothing to it. Done in a flash.

Three-thousand seven-hundred-fifty yen?

Something was wrong.

I'd made a mistake somewhere.

My palms began to sweat. In three years of counting, never once had I screwed up. This was a bad sign.

I shut my eyes and made my right brain and left brain a blank, in a way you might clean your glasses. Then withdrawing both hands from my pockets, I spread my fingers to dry the sweat. Like Henry Fonda in *Warlock*, where he steels himself before a gunfight.

With palms and fingers completely dry, both hands dived into my pockets to do a third count. If the third sum corresponded to either of the other sums I'd feel better. Everybody makes mistakes. Under the peculiar conditions I found myself, I may have been anxious, not to mention a little overconfident. That was my first mistake. Anyway, an accurate recount was all I needed to remedy the situation, to put things right.

But before I could take the matter in hand, the elevator doors opened. No warning, no sound, they just slid open to either side. I was concentrating so hard on the critical recount that I didn't even notice. Or more precisely, my eyes had seen the opening doors, but I didn't fully grasp the significance of the event. Of course, the doors' opening meant the linking of two spaces previously denied accessible continuity by means of those very doors. And at the same time, it meant the elevator had reached its destination.

I turned my attention to what lay beyond the doors. There was a corridor and in the corridor stood a woman. A young woman, turned out in a pink suit, wearing pink high heels. The suit was coutured of a polished material, her face equally polished. The woman considered my presence, then nodded succinctly. "Come this way," she seemed to indicate. I gave up all hope of that recount, and removing my hands from my pockets, I exited the elevator. Whereupon the elevator doors closed behind me as if they'd been waiting for me to leave.

Standing there in the corridor, I took a good look around, but I encountered no hint of the nature of my current circumstances. I did seem to be in an interior passage of a building, but any school kid could have told you as much.

The interior was gloomy, featureless. Like the elevator. Quality materials throughout; no sign of wear. Marble floors buffed to a high luster; the walls a toasted off-white, like the muffins I eat for breakfast. Along either side of the corridor were tall wooden doors, each affixed with metal room numbers, but out of order. 936 was next to 213 next to 26. Something was screwy. Nobody numbers rooms like that.

The young woman hardly spoke. "This way, please," was all she told me, but it was more her lips forming the words than speaking, because no sound came out. Having taken two months of lipreading since starting this line of work, I had no problem understanding what she said. Still, I thought there was something wrong with my ears. After the dead silence of the elevator, the flattened coughs and dessicated whistling, I had to be losing my hearing.

So I coughed. It sounded normal. I regained some confidence in my hearing. Nothing's happened to my ears. The problem must be with the woman's mouth.

I walked behind her. The clicks of her pointy high heels echoed down the empty corridor like an afternoon at the quarry. Her full, stockinged legs reflected clearly in the marble.

The woman was on the chubby side. Young and beautiful and all that went with it, but chubby. Now a young, beautiful woman who is, shall we say, plump, seems a bit off. Walking behind her, I fixated on her body.

Around young, beautiful, fat women, I am generally thrown into confusion. I don't know why. Maybe it's because an image of their dietary habits naturally congeals in my mind. When I see a goodly sized woman, I have visions of her mopping up that last drop of cream sauce with bread, wolfing down that final sprig of watercress garnish from her plate. And once that happens, it's like acid corroding metal: scenes of her eating spread through my head and I lose control.

Your plain fat woman is fine. Fat women are like clouds in the sky. They're just floating there, nothing to do with me. But your young, beautiful, fat woman is another story. I am demanded to assume a posture toward her. I could end up sleeping with her. That is probably where all the confusion comes in.

Which is not to say that I have anything against fat women. Confusion and repulsion are two different things. I've slept with fat women before and on the whole the experience wasn't bad. If your confusion leads you in the right direction, the results can be uncommonly rewarding. But of course, things don't always take the right course. Sex is an extremely subtle undertaking, unlike going to the department store on Sunday to buy a thermos. Even among young, beautiful, fat women, there are distinctions to be made. Fleshed out one way, they'll lead you in the right direction; fleshed out another way, they'll leave you lost, trivial, confused.

In this sense, sleeping with fat women can be a challenge. There must be as many paths of human fat as there are ways of human death.

This was pretty much what I was thinking as I walked down the corridor behind this young, beautiful, fat woman.

A white scarf swirled around the collar of her chic pink suit. From the fullness of her earlobes dangled square gold earrings, glinting with every step she took. Actually, she moved quite lightly for her weight. She may have strapped herself into a girdle or other paraphernalia for maximum visual effect, but that didn't alter the fact that her wiggle was tight and cute. In fact, it turned me on. She was my kind of chubby.

Now I'm not trying to make excuses, but I don't get turned on by that many women. If anything, I think of myself as more the non-turn-on type. So when I do get turned on, I don't trust it; I have to investigate the source.

I scooted up next to her and apologized for being eight or nine minutes late for the appointment. "I had no idea the entrance procedures would take so long," I said. "And then the elevator was so slow. I was ten minutes early when I got to the building."

She gave me a brisk I-know sort of nod. A hint of *eau de cologne* drifted from her neckline. A scent reminiscent of standing in a melon patch on a summer's morn. It put me in a funny frame of mind. A nostalgic yet impossible pastiche of sentiments, as if two wholly unrelated memories had threaded together in an unknown recess. Feelings like this sometimes come over me. And most often due to specific scents.

"Long corridor, eh?" I tried to break the ice. She glanced at me, but kept walking. I guessed she was twenty or twenty-one. Well-defined features, broad forehead, clear complexion.

It was then that she said, "Proust."

Or more precisely, she didn't pronounce the word "Proust," but simply moved her lips to form what ought to have been "Proust." I had yet to hear a genuine peep out of her. It was as if she were talking to me from the far side of a thick sheet of glass.

Proust?

"*Marcel* Proust?" I asked her.

She gave a look. Then she repeated, "Proust." I gave up on the effort and fell back in line behind her, trying for the life of me to come up with other lip movements that corresponded to "Proust." *Truest?* . . . *Brew whist?* . . . *Blue is it?* . . . One after the other, quietly to myself, I pronounced strings of meaningless syllables, but none seemed to match. I could only conclude that she had indeed said, "Proust." But what I couldn't figure was, what was the connection between this long corridor and Marcel Proust?

Perhaps she'd cited Marcel Proust as a metaphor for the length of the corridor. Yet, supposing that were the case, wasn't it a trifle flighty—not to say inconsiderate—as a choice of expression? Now if she'd cited this long corridor as a metaphor for the works of Marcel Proust, that much I could accept. But the reverse was bizarre.

A corridor as long as Marcel Proust?

Whatever, I kept following her down that long corridor. Truly, a long corridor. Turning corners, going up and down short flights of stairs, we must have walked five or six ordinary buildings' worth. We were walking around and around, like in an Escher print. But walk as we might, the surroundings never seemed to change. Marble floors, muffin-white walls, wooden doors with random room numbers. Stainless-steel door knobs. Not a window in sight. And through it all, the same staccato rhythm of her heels, followed by the melted rubber gumminess of my jogging shoes.

Suddenly she pulled to a halt. I was now so tuned in to the sound of my jogging shoes that I walked right into her backside. It was wonderfully cushioning, like a firm rain cloud. Her neck effused that melon *eau de cologne*. She was tipping forward from the force of my impact, so I grabbed her shoulders to pull her back upright.

"Excuse me," I said. "I was somewhere else in my thoughts."

The chubby young woman blushed. I couldn't say for sure, but she didn't seem at all bothered. "*Tozum'sta,*" she said with a trace of a smile. Then she shrugged her shoulders and added, "*Sela.*" She didn't actually say that, but need I repeat, her lips formed the words.

"*Tozum'sta?*" I pronounced to myself. "*Sela?*"

"*Sela,*" she said with conviction.

Turkish perhaps? Problem was, I'd never heard a word of Turkish. I was so flustered, I decided to forget about holding a conversation with her. Lip reading is very delicate business and not something you can hope to master in two months of adult education classes.

She produced a lozenge-shaped electronic key from her suit pocket and inserted it horizontally, just so, into the slot of the door bearing the number 728. It unlocked with a click. Smooth.

She opened the door, then turned and bid me, "*Saum'te, sela.*"

Which, of course, is exactly what I did.

# 2

# Near East and North Africa (The Bridge)

■

## INTRODUCTION

Asia, the largest continent, with three-fifths of the world's population, for reasons explained in the general introduction, has been divided into two parts: the Indian Subcontinent, China, and Japan in the East; and the Near East, which we present together with North Africa and Arabic Spain in the West. Western Asia's civilizations mingled directly with those of North Africa and Arabic Spain and, for purposes of tracing the great historic movements of culture, we have considered these affiliated parts of Asia, Africa, and Europe as the "Bridge." Its peoples and cultures formed a

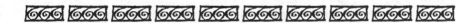

755

bridge connecting Asia and Africa over which passed myth, religion, philosophy, literature, and even the art of cursive writing. North Africa's Egyptian, Persian, Hellenistic, Roman, Arabic, and Ottoman Turkish pasts make Africa, like Asia, Europe, and the Americas, a continent possessing ancient highly developed civilizations whose written traces come to life across the millennia with undiminished force. The same bridge area was a profoundly influential source of culture in Europe, the Americas, and the Far East.

The cultures of Western Asia are among the oldest and most advanced of the ancient world, with a written literary tradition going back more than four thousand years, beginning with the first writer whose name we know, the Sumerian moon priestess Enheduanna (c. 2300 B.C.). This region of fluid borders, inhabited by multiple ethnicities, has been the home of many cultures—Sumerian, Akkadian, Babylonian, Assyrian, Phoenician, Egyptian, Jewish, Persian, Arab, and Turkish, among others. The region was conquered time and again by the great empires of the West, the Greeks, Romans, and Ottomans, as well as by the crusaders and by Mongol invaders from the East. It is a place that saw millennia of religious ferment and development, culminating in three great, interrelated religious traditions—Judaism, Christianity, and Islam. The roots of these religions can be traced back to the ancient religions of Mesopotamia. Out of the polytheistic religions of the Sumerians, Babylonians, and Assyrians developed a belief in a supreme God. From Mesopotamia came stories of genesis and divine retribution that reappear in the Old Testament as versions of the fall of Adam and Eve from Paradise and of Noah and the Flood. The Flood in the Bible is similar to the version in the Babylonian text of the *Epic of Gilgamesh,* which is itself one of many versions in Hittite, Elamite, and Hurrian, all ultimately deriving from Sumerian compositions about a thousand years earlier. From Persian Zoroastrianism came many of the central elements of Christian cosmology.

Though Christianity originated in the Middle East, it migrated to Europe and became a largely European religion. Nonetheless, Christian peoples such as the Copts and the Maronite Christians have maintained a continuous presence in the Middle East since the first century A.D. Christians, Jews, and Muslims had lived in relative harmony in the region for thousands of years, due in large part to the historically tolerant nature of Islam, which sees Christians, Jews, and Muslims all as "people of the Book," that is, the Bible. Thus, until the rise of Western-styled nation-states and of the concept of nationalism, religious oppression was relatively rare in the Middle East, though not unknown. Jews, Muslims, Christians, Arabs and Armenians, Kurds and Turks, all often lived in harmony in what we would now call multicultural conditions. The twentieth century's history of warfare and atrocity, between Palestinian and Jew, Persian and Arab, Turk and Armenian, is a late and lurid chapter in a history of frequent tolerance and heterogeneity.

# Sumerian, Akkadian, and Ancient Egyptian Literatures

## THE DEVELOPMENT OF CIVILIZATION IN SUMERIA

Mesopotamia, meaning "between rivers," refers to that section of the Near East located between the Tigris and the Euphrates Rivers. Though the land here is dry and inhospitable today, it once was a rich and lush region, known as the "Fertile Crescent." In the Persian Gulf delta in the south of Mesopotamia, this fertility drew three peoples: the Ubaidians, a neolithic farming culture that settled the region dating to around 5000 B.C.; the Sumerians who supplanted them and who may have come from southcentral Asia, and, later, waves of Semitic nomads from the deserts of Syria and Arabia, who merged with the Sumerians. The term *Semite* (meaning descended from Shem, one of Noah's sons) came to designate a number of peoples—Arabs, Akkadian Babylonians, Assyrians, Canaanites, Ethiopians, and Jews—whose languages derived originally, it is thought, from an ancient root language, Semitic.

In the south, the Sumerians developed an agricultural village culture, supported by an extensive fertilizing canal system. By 3000 B.C., a number of Sumerian dynasties developed around urban areas, such as Ur, Kish, and Erech. Sumerian civilization evolved into a highly developed urban culture, with massive architecture, skilled metalwork, sculpture, and pottery. The Sumerians were also advanced in mathematics and astronomy, which included estimates of the value of $\pi$ (pi) and the division of the hour into sixty minutes. A number of different factors led to the urbanization of Sumerian culture and to the development of civilization. The Sumerians discovered how to use mud bricks created in forms and strengthened with reeds to build large structures. They mastered the fickle rains, snowmelts, and surrounding rivers through canals, dikes, and water conduits. This, in turn, assured regular crop yields, which supported larger populations in a small area. Agricultural surplus encouraged the exchange of goods and services and the beginnings of complex commerce, and, subsequently, the specialization of people into trades. More complex social structures developed to administer and plan flood control, the construction of large-scale projects such as complex irrigation systems, and immense architectural structures such as the gigantic terraced pyramids called ziggurats, built to appease the gods and ward off natural devastations. A complex social order developed, stratified into kings, aristocracy, priests, middle-class artisans and merchants, and slaves.

Sargon, the most famous of all Mesopotamian kings, was a Semite royal in the city of Akkad, north of Sumer, who established the Akkadian dynasty (c. 2340 B.C.) that united the many city-states of Mesopotamia into an empire for the first time. This dynasty also marked the domination of the Sumerians by the Semites. Later great Mesopotamian empires included the Babylonians and Assyrians, who owed much to the Sumerian written and religious traditions, although by the time of the first Babylonian empire, the Sumerians had all but died out. The spoken language was Akkadian, a Semitic tongue, though Sumerian language and literature survived as the formal academic language upon which the educational curriculum was built. The Babylonian empire had two incarnations, first, with King Hammurabi (c. 1792–1750 B.C.) of the city of Babylon, from c. 1800 to 1600 B.C., and later around 600 B.C. with Nebuchadnezzar's New Babylonia. Hammurabi was a great statesman and military leader but is best known for the Code of Hammurabi. The three hundred laws of this code were inscribed in thirty-six hundred lines of cuneiform around a stone column that was erected in public as a visible symbol and explanation of the law. Although it was often quite a harsh code, and although different classes were judged by different rules, it is among the most important early examples of an attempt to order social behavior according to a fixed standard.

The earliest examples of the symbolic representation that was to evolve into writing came from the Near East as early as the ninth millennium B.C. Ancient people there used clay tokens to keep accounts, but, by the fourth millennium B.C., they began drawing pictures of tokens on clay. Later, the Sumerians began depicting objects in clay pictographs (in which, for example, the symbol for fish would be a drawing of a fish). These pictographs, in turn, developed into a more complex form of writing known as cuneiform, which evolved ideographs (in which symbols stood for concepts) and also an alphabetic system that allowed for phonetic transcription of words. Cuneiform was inscribed with a stylus upon clay tablets, which were then hardened through baking or drying. It was adopted by later civilizations, such as the Babylonians, Assyrians, Hittites, Elamites, and the ancient Persian Achaemenids. By 2500 B.C., Sumerian cuneiform was so complex that writing became a profession, and the first formal schools were established to teach scribery. These became intellectual centers, where students studied literature, mathematics, linguistics, and botany. The literature of Sumeria survives in beautiful love songs, exhortations to the gods, myths, dirges, histories, proverbs, essays, fables, and most important, *The Epic of Gilgamesh,* which is among the oldest and still most impressive works of world literature. Sumerian literature is the oldest great tradition of written literature.

—Ayame Fukuda and the editors

## THE DEVELOPMENT OF CIVILIZATION IN EGYPT

The largest cache of extant literature from the Asian Near East and North Africa comes from Egypt. The powerful empire, with its large royal dominion and its gigantic pyramids constructed to glorify its man-god Pharaohs, was accompanied by an exuberance in the visual and literary arts. Its rich, complex culture was revealed through immense temples and pyramids, beautiful tomb paintings, and sculpture. In writing, conserved largely in hieroglyphic texts, are cosmologies and cosmogonies, prayers, parables and proverbs, philosophy, poetry, and fiction. By the Middle Kingdom (c. 2040–1780 B.C.), we even have compelling and sophisticated detective and ghost stories, the oldest examples in those genres.

There were some elemental factors that made the phenomenon of Egypt civilization possible. The great civilization of ancient Egypt had its origins along the life-giving Nile, the longest river in the world. Through annual flooding, the river deposited silt from the Ethiopian highlands on the Egyptian floodplain. This natural system of irrigation and fertilization sustained civilizations in Egypt from as early as the late fourth millennium B.C. Thereafter, dynastic Egypt of the Old, Middle, and New Kingdoms was to dominate neighboring North Africa, the Eastern Mediterranean, and parts of Mesopotamia for many centuries.

The vast land of pharaonic Egypt, more than 750 miles long and containing diverse peoples with their singular cultures, was unified under a theocratic dictatorship headed by a god-king. The god-king came out of elaborate myths, with roots all over Mesopotamia, in which the gods fashioned the universe into being. Osiris and Horus, the key figures, had human counterparts in the living Pharaohs. Osiris was killed by his brother Seth and was patched and sewn together by his faithful wife Isis. Thereafter, Osiris's son Horus became reigning king of the gods and Osiris became Lord of the Dead. Following this division of power in the Egyptian theogony (the making of the gods) among humans on the earth, each living all-powerful Pharaoh was Horus and each dead one was Osiris.

Ancient Egypt had a unified kingdom accompanied by a spectacular literature for three thousand years. Around 3100 B.C., the kingdom was unified under the Pharaohs. The Old Kingdom, during which the great pyramids were built, is usually dated 2700 to 2200 B.C. The Middle Kingdom is usually set at 2000 to 1786 B.C., and the New Kingdom down to the last pharaonic dynasties lasted from about 1570 to 332 B.C. Egypt, which was to be the cultural bridge to early Europe, was also a bridge across which roared invaders and settlers from western Asia and western North Africa. Invasions came from the western neighbors during the Libyan dynasty, 945 to 745 B.C., up from the south when the Nubians prevailed, 745 to 718 B.C., and from the east as a result of wars and conquests by Assyrians and Persians from the eighth to the fourth centuries B.C.

Alexander the Great conquered Egypt in 332 B.C. Over the next thousand years, Alexandria, which Alexander founded, became successively the heart of Hellenistic culture, the Greco-Roman center of the Roman Empire, and a site for early monastic and theological Christianity. After the Greek conquest, the pharaonic culture went into precipitous decline until it effectively disappeared. The Pharaohs were replaced by Greek Ptololemaic monarchs who ruled the country. The last of the Ptolemaic rulers were Cleopatra (consort of Antony) and her son Ptolemy XIV (47–30 B.C.) whom Octavius (Emperor Caesar Augustus) put to death. Despite the formal demise of classical Egyptian civilization, its spirit survived in its influence on the Greeks and later Romans. Euclidian geometry was developed by an Alexandrian Greek, Euclid, but he based his formulation on the geometry practiced for thousands of years by master Egyptian builders. Egyptian art pervasively influenced Greek architecture and sculpture.

Alexandria became the magnificent Hellenistic city of the Mouseion, a great library-museum-university complex. Alexandrian Egypt contained a cross-section of the main currents of the classical world. In Alexandria were the learned philosophers, geometers, grammarians, and historians, as well as famous poets and sculptors. It was a syncretistic civilization that saw the merging of many cultures into a new Hellenism. So Philo of Alexandria (20 B.C.–A.D. 50?), a Jew, was the major Neoplatonist of his day, giving us the four ladders of being that were to provide a way for later Jewish, Christian, and Muslim mystical writing, and Plotinus (A.D. 205–270?), an Egyptian, was one of the great metaphysicians of antiquity. The city was also the inspired center of religions and gave us scriptures by Greeks, Jews, early Christians, and Gnostics. The Septuagint Bible was translated in the third and second centuries B.C. for the Jews of Alexandria who could no longer read Hebrew; the Septuagint remains the Bible of the Greek Orthodox and Russian Churches in Eastern Europe. The ascetic form of Christian monasticism was initiated by the hermit Saint Anthony of Egypt (A.D. 215–c. 350). Equally important theologically were the seminal mystical texts ascribed to the Egyptian god of wisdom, Thoth the Thrice Great, whose name in Greek translation was the celebrated Hermes Trismegistus. And Alexandria was also a great center of Gnosticism, the widespread religion derived from Judaism and early Christianity, which believed in gnosis (self-knowledge) rather than faith and in introspection rather than a clergy, and considered Eve, who gave us knowledge, a hero, in contrast to the Judeo-Christian tradition that condemned her as a sinner. In 1945, fifty-three Gnostic texts, translated from Greek into Coptic (the contemporary form of old Egyptian) were found in the ancient Egyptian town of Chenoboskion. These are the Nag Hammadi Gnostic scriptures, whose discovery is as significant to religious history and thought as were the Essene Dead Sea Scrolls found two years later at Qumran by the Dead Sea.

In the lands of dynastic Egypt, with their endless sun, time appears to stop. In Memphis, their city on the Nile, with its eighty pyramids that extended for a hundred miles on the horizon, it is said that the Pharaohs, who were god-king dictators, conveyed to their subjects a sense of permanence and eternity. The religion stabilized the Egyptian theocracy, lending its rulers divine authority, but placing a philosophical emphasis not on development but on repetition. This unchanging permanence was called the *ma'at*. So the Nile died and was reborn each year, as did the sun each day, and the dynasties of god-kings were also repeated for millennia. The pyramids and tombs were built to preserve the *ma'at*, the stability of the regime, but they also preseved the human soul, the *ba*, that continued to need sustenance even after death and mummification. Hence the tombs were painted with pleasant, uplifting murals and filled with all kinds of food, beer, and reading material, the latter being the source of discovered papyrus manuscripts.

The art of writing in Egypt is legendarily of divine origin. The gods recorded their creations and magical activities in small marks on stone, walls, or papyrus and bestowed on their subject priests the secret of deciphering these meaningful squiggles. So writing began. The Egyptian language was originally written in hieroglyphs, a form of picture writing deriving from some 604 essential pictures. There were also hieroglyphs used as ideograms (pictures conveying ideas) and phonograms (pictures conveying sounds, as in the owl representing the sound *m*). In the Middle Kingdom, the hieroglyphs used pictorially gave way to a cursive system called the "hieratic," and by the New Kingdom to an even quicker form called the "demotic." The hieratic and demotic use of hieroglyphs depended on the phonograms, the sound symbols, which became the Egyptian alphabet, excellent for literature and letters, and which the Phoenicians made into their influential writing system. The Egyptian cursive alphabet was adopted and changed by the Phoenicians, whose alphabet in turn was adopted and changed by the Jews into the Hebrew alphabet and by the Greeks into the Greek alphabet. From the Greek came the Roman and Cyrillic (Slav), which is to say, the alphabets of Europe. In the early dynasties, the literature, limited by the expressive problems inherent in hieroglyphic writing, was normally centered on praising the Pharaoh's accomplishments and majesty. By the Middle Kingdom, however, the hieratic cursive system allowed Egyptian writers to develop revolutionary genres and diverse forms of the short story.

The chance survival of a literary work depends on several factors, all present in Egypt: the recognized importance of the culture and the writer and the durability of the document itself. Egypt, a key to the origins of Western civilization, had the fame that led later scholars to uncover temples and tombs, to decipher difficult hieroglyphic texts (an iconic form of writing that, like the world's arithmetic ciphers, conveys sense rather than sound), and to translate them into modern languages. The writings also survived because they were famous enough in their own time to warrant being copied and recopied, an activity essential for the preservation of almost all ancient literature. As for physical survival, the texts themselves were normally inscribed on stone and papyrus (from which comes the word "paper"). Unlike later parchment, papyrus was fragile and easily destroyed by dampness. However, the Sahara Desert and especially the Fayyum region, where many Egyptian and Ancient Greek texts were uncovered, has minimal rainfall. So the earliest and most beautiful writings from the ancient Egyptian and Greek worlds were preserved in the desert-dry trash heaps of antiquity.

Our discussion of ancient Egypt also includes Greek culture, since the

Greeks were in Egypt from at least the sixth century B.C. Alexandria, the city of the geometer Euclid, the Greek Septuagint Bible of Alexandrian Jews, and the philosophers Philo, Plotinus, and Hypatia, was the center of Hellenistic culture where the greatest libraries of antiquity were established. The earliest manuscripts by the classical lyric poet Sappho were found in 1879 in the Fayyum near Crocodipolis; twenty odes of the narrative poet Bacchylides and Alkman's choral ode (the prototype of Western drama) were found at Oxyrhynchos; and the works of playwright Menander were discovered in a refuse heap near Aphroditopolis.

Since only a small fragment of Egyptian literature has survived, we cannot know how many Egyptian Sapphos and Pindars might have existed. It is unlikely that Egypt had epics or drama, however, since no fragments or references survive. We do have long religious documents, notably The Book of the Dead, as well as tales, poems, hymns, prayers, and diverse didactic literature, including prophecies ("The Prophecies of Neferti"), admonitions ("Admonitions of an Egyptian Sage"), maxims, teachings, as well as abundant religious and mythological writings from the Egyptian Pyramid Texts.

Since Egyptian kings were thought to be divine, the writings in the Egyptian tombs, the "house of eternity," were necessarily sacred. However, from the earliest Old Period Kingdom (third millenium B.C.), we also have private tombs of high officials and their families, and on the walls of their tombs begins Western literature. These Sixth Dynasty writings take the form of prayers to the gods and autobiographies of the tomb inhabitants to assure the immortality of their earthly image. Some apparent Old Kingdom writings are preserved in revised Middle Egyptian papyrus versions from the Middle Kingdom (c. 2135 B.C.–c. 1650 B.C.); these are the religious instruction and prophetic pieces of Prince Hardjedef, Kagemni, and Ptahhotep. It is now thought the Old Kingdom attribution is pseudepigraphic; that is, these are really Middle Kingdom pieces falsely attributed to the earlier period in order to enhance their sacred prestige. Most Old Kingdom writings are predictable prayers and formulaic catalogues of virtues. Whereas works from the Pyramid Texts and the body of didactic literature are of historical, religious, and aesthetic value, it is not until the Middle Kingdom that we have surviving examples of poetry and prose that may be considered important imaginative literature. The Egyptian stories in our possession are extraordinary, succinctly and artfully told, and, as the Egyptologist Miriam Lichtheim writes,

> these few surviving prose tales speak to the modern reader, for they are
> creations of the universal storytelling impulse, and of an imagination that
> roamed and played upon experience, unfettered by the functional
> orientation of most Egyptian literary works.[1]

---

1. Miriam Lichtheim, *Ancient Egyptian Literature,* Vol. 1, *The Old and Middle Kingdoms* (Berkeley: University of California Press, 1975), 211.

Like most early literature, the tales are wondrous, imbued with miracle and the supernatural. At the same time, they suggest historical reality, even autobiography, a favorite Egyptian genre. In the history of the narrative, the ghost and detective stories are also first encountered in Egypt.

Egyptian love poems, in their speech, tone, and passion, seem contemporary, and particularly so when they come to us in felicitous versions by Ezra Pound and Noel Stock. Echoes of these secular love poems may, some centuries later, be recognized in the biblical Song of Songs; and it is thought that in reality Egyptian lyric was the model for the Song of Songs, which has, in turn, probably been the most influential sequence of poems in Western literature, pervading secular and mystical literature.

The few stories that have survived are a marvel. The Egyptians, three thousand years before Edgar Allan Poe, gave us fantastic literature and the well-plotted detective story of intrigue and adventure. We have only a fragment of Egypt's writings, but enough survives from three and four millennia ago—Old Kingdom religious ascension poems, Middle Kingdom short stories, and pastoral love poems—to depict a great hieroglyph of one of the world's literatures.

■ **The Pyramid Texts (2464–2355 B.C.)**
*Egypt* (funeral poems)

TRANSLATED BY TONY BARNSTONE AND WILLIS BARNSTONE

The Pyramid Texts are religious incantations or "utterances" inscribed on the walls of sarcophagus chambers and corridors in the pyramids of Saqqara. These utterances for the resurrection and well-being of the deceased kings constitute—along with Sumerian writings—the oldest body of literature in the world. The extant Egyptian writings are the actual hieroglyphs written on the pyramid walls, while the Sumerian cuneiform tablets, though deriving from equally ancient writings, are themselves much later copies from the first millennium. The Pyramid Texts follow the resurrection of the king and his ascent to the sky. In the tomb, the king awakens to eternal life from the sleep of death. Then the king ascends the sky and seeks admission to the company of his fellow immortal gods. In the tradition of mystical literature, which abounds in Alexandrian Greek, Hebrew, Sufi Persian, Arabic, and later European literature, from Plato, Philo, Hermes Trismegistus, Plotinus to Rumi in the Near East and Saint John of the Cross in the West, the sequence of enlightenment outside of earthly time, going from awakening from darkness to ascent and union, follows the stages of the Egyptian Pharaohs. The extraordinary poetry and beauty of these patches of ancient Egyptian verse are epitomized in these songs about the dead king's ascent away from the gloomy underworld existence to which common mortals are fated after death. In "The Dead King Eats the Gods," the king entering the sky becomes a god in heaven and in fact conquers the other gods, eating their hearts, entrails, and the magic that swells their bellies. He exults in his holy rampage, in the mystical feast that makes him the omnipotent deity.

**FURTHER READING:** Lichtheim, Miriam. *Ancient Egyptian Literature,* 1975. Simpson, William Kelly, ed. *The Ancient Egyptians,* 1966; *The Literature of Ancient Egypt,* 1972.

## The Dead King Flies into Heaven

The voyaging king soars away from the common people,
abandoning the earth for the firmament.
O God of the city, he stands before you.
He thrusts against the sky like a heron,
he kisses the air like a hawk,
and springs into heaven like a grasshopper.

Pyramid Text 467 (c. 2180 B.C.)

## The Dead King Flies into Heaven

Like a mallard the dead king flies from us.
He tears his wings from the falconer
and gyres into heaven like a loose kite.
The king is free from those who plagued him,
soaring above his enemies.

Pyramid Text 573

## The Dead King Eats the Gods

The sky is a dark bowl, the stars die and fall.
The celestial bows quiver,
the bones of the earthgods shake and planets come
        to a halt
when they sight the king in all his power,
the god who feeds on his father and eats
        his mother.
The king is such a tower of wisdom
even his mother can't discern his name.

Pyramid Text 273–274

His glory is in the sky, his strength lies in
    the horizon,
like that of his father the sungod Atum who
    conceived him.
Atum conceived the king,                                    *10*
but the dead king has greater dominion.
His vital spirits surround him,
his qualities lie below his feet,
he is cloaked in gods and cobras coil on
    his forehead.[1]
His guiding snakes decorate his brow                       *15*
and peer into souls,
ready to spit fire against his enemies.
The king's head is on his torso.
He is the bull of the sky                                  *20*
who charges and vanquishes all.
He lives on the stuff of the gods,
he feeds on their limbs and entrails,
even when they have bloated their bodies with
    magic
at Nesisi, the island of fire.                               *25*
The king is prepared
and his spirits are assembled
and he appears as the mighty one, Lord of
    Holy Ministers.
He is seated with his back to the earthgod Geb
and he passes judgment                                 *30*
with the One whose name is concealed
on this day when the Oldest Ones are slaughtered.
He dines on sacrificial meals,
binding the victims
in preparation for the feast.                              *35*
The dead king eats men and lives on gods
and to carry messages he has couriers:
Kehau the Grasper of Horns lassoes them like oxen,
and Serpent with the Raised Head
oversees and drives the victims,                        *40*
and Master of Bloody Sacrifice binds them.
The moongod Khons, Racer with Knives,
strangles them for the king
and draws out their entrails.
He is the courier the king sends to hold them
    bound.                                        *45*
Shezmu, the winepress god, slices them up

---

1. Refers to the cobra diadem of the king which had the power to burn up his enemies.

and cooks a supper for the king
in his evening hearth.
He is the one who feasts on their magic
and swallows their spirit.                                      5.
The great ones are for breakfast,
the medium-size ones are for supper
and the tiny ones are for midnight treats.
Old men and women are burnt for incense.
The mighty stars in the northern sky                            5.
ignite fires under the caldrons
with the thighs of their elders.
The sky-dwellers take care of him and sweep
        the hearth
with their womens' legs.
He has traveled through the two firmaments                      6
and walked both banks of the Nile.
He is omnipotent
and his power over the powerful is absolute.
He is a holy icon, the holiest of all icons
        of omnipotence
and he eats as raw meat                                         6.
whomever he finds on his path.
He stands first on the horizon among the nobility,
        a god older than the oldest.
Thousands are at his feet,
hundreds sacrifice to him.
Orion, father of the gods, assigned him his deed
        of power.                                               7
The dead king appears again in the heavens,
the crowned Lord of the Horizon.
He snapped their backbones, drained their marrow,
and tore out the hearts of the gods.
He ate the red crown worn by the King of Lower Egypt.          7
He swallowed the green crown of the goddess Wadjet,
        guardian of Lower Egypt.
He feeds on the Wise Ones' lungs.
He is sated with their hearts and magic.
He won't lick the foul tasting substances
        of the red crown.                                      8
He flourishes and enjoys himself with the magic
        in his belly.
His dignities are inviolate.
He has swallowed the intelligence of every god.
The dead king lives forever.
His boundary is infinite.                                      8
He does as he pleases

since he inhabits the endless horizon.
Observe how their spirits fill his stomach.
Their souls belong to him.
He cooks the leftover gods into a bone soup.                                 *90*
Their souls belong to him
and their shadows as well.
In his pyramid among those who live on the earth
     of Egypt,
the dead king ascends and appears
forever and forever.                                                         *95*

# ■ Enheduanna (born c. 2300 B.C.) *Sumer* (poems)

### TRANSLATED BY ALIKI BARNSTONE AND WILLIS BARNSTONE

Enheduanna was a moon priestess, the daughter of King Sargon of Agade (2334–2279 B.C.) who reigned over the world's first empire, extending from the Mediterranean to Persia. Sargon is the first important leader to emerge from the half-light of prehistory into the full light of a written record; words attributed to him are recorded on cuneiform tablets from the early first millennium:

> My priestly mother conceived me; secretly brought me to birth; set me in an ark of bulrushes; made fast my door with pitch. She consigned me to the river, which did not overwhelm me. The river brought me to Akki, the farmer, who brought me up to be his son. . . . During my gardening, the goddess Ishtar loved me, and for fifty-four years the kingship was mine.

The detailed quality of this personal account also characterizes the writing of his daughter Enheduanna, who is the first writer, male or female, whose name and work have been preserved. Her personal history survives in highly politicized poems, which in their cosmic vision and ethical outrage recall Isaiah. In her poems to the Sumerian goddess of love Inanna, she speaks to a deity who has descended to earth as an ally, as a friend to help her in her need. The poems' sensuality, surprising metaphors, and intimacy recall Sappho's poems to her ally Aphrodite. We have a stone disk that contains a detailed likeness of the high priestess, revealing her particular features and dress, flanked by three of her retainers. The poems presented here, preserved on cuneiform tablets, are from a sequence of eighteen stanzas in a single poem, "The Exaltation of Enheduanna," addressed to Inanna. In addition, we have forty-two hymns to temples whose authorship is not in question, as well as many other poems and fragments that may be hers.

Our thanks to William W. Hallo, Laffan Professor of Assyriology and Curator of the Babylonian Collection at Yale University, for his help and suggestions. The poems that follow have been adapted by Aliki and Willis

Barnstone from William W. Hallo and J. J. A. van Dijk, *The Exaltation of Inanna* (New Haven: Yale University Press, 1968).

**FURTHER READING:** Hallo, William W., and J. J. A. van Dijk. *The Exaltation of Inanna,* 1968.

## Inanna and the Divine Essences

Lady of all the essences, full light,
good woman clothed in radiance
whom heaven and earth love,
temple friend of An,
you wear great ornaments,
you desire the tiara of the high priestess
whose hand holds the seven essences.
O my lady, guardian of all the great essences,
you have picked them up and hung them
on your hand.                                                             1
You have gathered the holy essences and worn them
tightly on your breasts.

## Inanna and An

Like a dragon you have filled the land
with venom.
Like thunder when you roar over the earth,
trees and plants fall before you.
You are a flood descending from a mountain,
O primary one,
moon goddess Inanna of heaven and earth!
Your fire blows about and drops on our nation.
Lady mounted on a beast,
An gives you qualities, holy commands,                                      1
and you decide.
You are in all our great rites.
Who can understand you?

## Inanna and Enlil

Storms lend you wings, destroyer of the lands.
Loved by Enlil, you fly over our nation.

You serve the decrees of An.
O my lady, on hearing your sound,
hills and flatlands bow.                                    5
When we come before you,
terrified, shuddering in your stormy clear light,
we receive justice.
We sing, mourn, and cry before you
and walk toward you along a path                            10
from the house of enormous sighs.

## Inanna and Ishkur

You strike everything down in battle.
O my lady, on your wings
you hack away the land and charge disguised
as a charging storm,
roar as a roaring storm,                                    5
thunder and keep thundering, and snort
with evil winds.
Your feet are filled with restlessness.

On your harp of sighs
I hear your dirge.                                          10

## Inanna and the City of Uruk

You have spoken your holy command over the city
which has not declared:
"This land is yours,"
which has not declared:
"It is your father's and his father's,"                     5
and you have blocked its path to you,
you have lifted your foot and left
their barn of fertility.
The women of the city no longer speak of love
with their husbands.                                        10
At night they do not make love.
They are no longer naked before them,
revealing intimate treasures.
Great daughter of Suen,
impetuous wild cow, supreme lady commanding An,             15
who dares not worship you?

## Banishment from Ur

You asked me to enter the holy cloister,
the *giparu*,
and I went inside, I the high priestess
Enheduanna!
I carried the ritual basket and sang
your praise.
Now I am banished among the lepers.
Even I cannot live with you.
Shadows approach the light of day, the light
is darkened around me,
shadows approach the daylight,
covering the day with sandstorm.
My soft mouth of honey is suddenly confused.
My beautiful face is dust.

## Appeal to the Moongod Nanna-Suen to Throw Out Lugalanne, the New Conqueror of the City of Uruk

O Suen, the usurper Lugalanne means nothing to me!
Tell An: "Have An release me!"
If you will only tell An
"NOW!"
and An will release me.
This woman Inanna will carry off this young cock
Lugalanne.
Mountain and flood lie at her feet.
This woman is powerful as he.
She'll make the city expel him.
Surely she will forget her rage against me.
Let me, Enheduanna, pray to her.
Like sweet drink let me cry freely for holy
Inanna!
Let me call to her!

## The Restoration of Enheduanna to Her Former Station

The first lady of the throne room
has accepted Enheduanna's song.
Inanna loves her again.

The day was good for Enheduanna, for she was dressed
in jewels.                                                               5
She was dressed in womanly beauty.
Like the moon's first rays over the horizon,
how luxuriously she was dressed!
When Nanna, Inanna's father,
made his entrance                                                        10
the palace blessed Inanna's mother Ningal.
From the doorsill of heaven came the word:
"Welcome!"

# ■ *from* The Epic of Gilgamesh (c. 2000 B.C.)

## TRANSLATED BY PIERRE GRANGE AND EMMA VARESIO

*The Epic of Gilgamesh* is the oldest known literary epic. The actual Gilgamesh was a king of Uruk (Erech in the Bible), a city-state in what is now southern Iraq. He probably lived in the twenty-seventh century B.C., and, though little evidence remains, later traditions describe him as a great warrior and the builder of Uruk's great walls. The Sumerians, and later the Assyrians and Babylonians, worshiped Gilgamesh as a god for more than two thousand years after his death; he was a god of the underworld, or its king, and figures of him were utilized in burial rituals. The epic itself derives from Sumerian composition that were later adapted and transformed into a Babylonian work in the second millennium, and versions proliferated throughout the Near East in Elamite, Hittite, and Hurrian. The epic took on what is now considered its standard form around the thirteenth century B.C.—eleven tablets with a twelfth appended, a work of approximately three thousand lines—but the text in which it is most complete dates from the seventh century B.C., was written in Babylonian in cuneiform script, and was discovered among the ruins of Nineveh. Though it is the oldest epic, it depicts concerns that are so universal that it will always be contemporary. It is the story of how the gods create Enkidu, "the hairy-bodied wild man of the grasslands" to be a companion to the young king Gilgamesh and to keep him from oppressing the people. Though they fight at first, they become deep friends and together kill the demon Huwawa. Then the goddess Ishtar falls in love with Gilgamesh and wants him to be her husband, but he rejects her, and she goes to her father Anu, asking him to send the Bull of Heaven to punish him. Together, Gilgamesh and Enkidu kill the bull, but the gods curse them for this, causing Enkidu to sicken and die. Gilgamesh mourns for his friend and is confronted with his own mortality. He sets out to find Utnapishtim (source for the biblical Noah), who has survived the flood, seeking the secret of immortality. This quest is the burden of the first eleven tablets; the twelfth tablet recounts a similar tale in which Gilgamesh grieves over Enkidu, who dies trying to retrieve Gilgamesh's drum and drumstick, which fell through a hole into the underworld. Through the intervention of the god Ea, Gilgamesh is able to speak with Enkidu's spirit and question him about life in the underworld. In both stories, Gilgamesh, confronted with his own mortality, seeks answers to basic human questions: why must I die?; what happens after death?; and can death be avoided?

**FURTHER READING:** Gardner, John, and John Maier, trs. *Gilgamesh,* 1985. Kovacs, Maureen Gallery, tr. *The Epic of Gilgamesh,* 1989. Pritchard, J. B., ed. *Ancient Near Eastern Texts Relating to the New Testament,* 1969. Sandars, N. K., tr. *The Epic of Gilgamesh,* 1972.

# Tablet VI

## I. ISHTAR PROPOSITIONS GILGAMESH

After Gilgamesh and Enkidu cut
off Huwawa's head they returned to Uruk[1]
and Gilgamesh cleaned his blade there,
washed out his long, matted hair,
then shook out the locks that hung down his back.
He pulled his soiled clothes over his neck
and dressed himself in a fresh
royal cloak that he fastened with a sash.
When Gilgamesh put the crown on his hair
the goddess Ishtar[2] raised her eyes
and stared at the beauty of his fresh
limbs and sang "Come here, Gilgamesh,
be my lover, let me taste your fruit.
Be my husband and I'll be your wife,
and give you a chariot of lapis lazuli and gold
with golden wheels and amber horns
pulled not by mules but by storm demons
When you enter our house it will smell like cedar
and the floor and dais will kiss your feet,
and kings, lords and princes will bow before you
and offer the yield of mountains and fields in tribute.
Your goats will bear triplets, your ewes will twin,
and even loaded down your donkey will run
faster than a mule; no horse will outrun your chariot steeds
and your oxen in the yoke will run as if free."

---

1. The ancient Sumerian city of which Gilgamesh was king.

2. Ishtar was the Akkadian goddess of love and war, the daughter of the sky god Anu. Her Sumerian name was Inanna.

Gilgamesh answered the goddess Ishtar,
"If I take you in marriage, what could I pay
in dowry? Should I give you body oil or clothes?
Should I give you food or drink when I know
you eat the food of gods and drink the wine of kings          30
and are dressed in heavenly clothing?
Can a man lust for a goddess for whom they sacrifice?
You are an oven frozen over with ice.
You are the back door that lets in the wind.
You are the palace whose roof caves in,                       35
the elephant who shakes off its carpet,
the pitch that sticks the hand to the bucket,
the waterskin that leaks on its owner
getting him wet all over.
You are the limestone crumbling                               40
in a stone wall until it tumbles.
You are a battering ram that breaks
when the army is in an enemy state.
You are the shoe that bites the foot.
What happened to your other lovers                            45
whom you said you'd love forever?
What happened to the shepherd bird?
Should I tell you where they are?
Your first lover, Tammuz, was slain
and each year they wail for him in the festival.[3]           50
You loved the many-colored shepherd bird
yet struck him and broke his wing
so now in the forest he cries 'My wing, my wing!'
You loved the lion for his pure strength
yet dug for him seven and seven pits.                         55
You loved the mighty battle stallion
yet decreed from him the whip, the spur and the halter.
You made him run seven and seven hours,
made him drink water muddied by his own hooves,
causing his mother Silili to weep.                            60
You loved the shepherd of the herd,
who always brought you cakes
and slaughtered kids for you,
but then you struck him and turned him into a wolf
and so his own herd boys chase him                            65
and his own dogs nip at his shins.
You also loved Ishullanu, your father's gardener,
who brought you clusters of dates
so that your table overflowed.

---

3. Ishtar's lover Tammuz is a nature god who dies each winter and comes to life again each spring. During the yearly festival in his honor his worshippers would wail in lamentation for the dying god.

You raised your eyes to him and came close,
saying 'O Ishullanu, let me taste your strength,
put your hand here upon my vulva.'
Ishullanu replied, 'What do you want from me?
Doesn't my mother cook, haven't I eaten?
Why should I taste your evil, cursed bread?
When it's cold, should I cover myself only in rushes?'
When you heard these words
you struck him and turned him into a frog
who lives in the garden
unable to leap or to burrow.
Now you say you love me,
but you would treat me just like them."

## II. ISHTAR'S RAGE

When Ishtar heard this
she flew to heaven in a rage
and went before her father, the Sky God Anu[4]
and her mother Antum, wailing,
"Gilgamesh has insulted me,
revealing all my despicable deeds,
my evil actions and curses."
Anu said to the glorious Ishtar,
"You have called this upon yourself,
and Gilgamesh has merely recounted
your foulness and the curse
of your evil actions."
But Ishtar told her father Anu,
"Father, create for me the Bull of Heaven
to kill Gilgamesh in his home.
Give me the Bull of Heaven
or I will smash the gates of the underworld
and fling them wide open
so that the dead may rise and eat the living
until there are more dead than living!"
Then Anu spoke to glorious Ishtar,
"If I do what you wish
there will be seven years of empty husks
at harvest time in the lands of Uruk.
Have you gathered enough grain for the people
and grown enough grass for the cattle?"
Ishtar spoke to her father again,
saying "I have gathered enough grain

---

4. Anu is the sky god and is called Father of the Gods.

and I have grown enough grass"[5]
Anu listened to Ishtar's plea                                        *30*
and created the Bull of Heaven for her
and she loosed it upon the city of Uruk.

With its first great snort the Bull of Heaven
caused the river Euphrates to shake
and caused a vast pit to open into which                             *35*
a hundred young men of Uruk fell and died.
With his second snort he killed two hundred,
and with his third snort a huge pit yawned open
before Enkidu, but Enkidu leapt up
and seized the Bull of Heaven by his horns.                          *40*
As they wrestled, the Bull of Heaven spewed foam
from his mouth and flung dung from his tail,
and Enkidu called to Gilgamesh,
"Friend, we have boasted of our strength
but can we slay this beast?                                          *45*
We must find strength to destroy it
with a sword thrust between the neck and horns."
Enkidu rushed at the Bull of Heaven
and grabbed the beast by the thick of his tail.
Then Gilgamesh approached with confidence                            *50*
and with the precision of a butcher
thrust his sword between the neck and horns.
After killing the Bull of Heaven, they tore out its heart
placed it before the Sun God, Shamash,
and withdrew, bowing to Shamash.                                     *55*
Then like two brothers they sat down to rest.

Ishtar ascended to the top of Uruk's palisade
and in a posture of mourning uttered this curse:
"Curse Gilgamesh, who has slandered me and killed the Bull of
      Heaven!"
When Enkidu heard these words,
he tore off the Bull's thigh and tossed it in her face, saying,      *60*
"If I could reach you, I'd do the same to you,
and tie your arms with his entrails!"
Ishtar summoned her curly-haired priestesses,
the harlots and temple prostitutes,
and mourned with them over the Bull's thigh.                         *65*

Gilgamesh called together the craftsmen and artisans,
who all admired the size of the horns,

---

5. The text is fragmentary here, but it seems that Ishtar convinces Anu to give her the Bull of Heaven.

each containing thirty pounds of lapis lazuli,
with hard casing two inches thick
and six barrels worth of oil inside
that he gave as a balm to his god Lugalbanda.
He hung the horns in the shrine of his ancestors.
The heroes washed their hands in the River Euphrates,
then clasped arms and rode through the streets of Uruk
As the people gathered around to see them
Gilgamesh spoke to the assembled men and women,
"Who is the bravest of men, the most valiant of men?
Gilgamesh is the bravest of men, the most valiant of men."
Then Gilgamesh gave a great feast in the palace
and the two heroes lay on the divans and slept.
Enkidu lay down to sleep and was troubled with dream
and when he awoke he told Gilgamesh his dream:
"Why are the great gods meeting in council?

# Tablet VII

## I. ENKIDU'S DREAM OF THE COUNCIL OF THE GODS

As daylight first gleamed through the house
Enkidu turned to Gilgamesh,
murmuring, "Such a strange dream I had
last night! Anu, Enlil, and Shamash had gathered.[6]
Anu spoke to Enlil of how we killed
the Bull of Heaven and Huwawa. One of us
should die, he said, whichever one had cut
the cedar from the mountainside.
Then Enlil's voice rose, saying, 'Enkidu must die,
but not Gilgamesh!' Shamash challenged Enlil, saying, 'But I
commanded both of these companions
to enter that forest, to do my errand.
Why should this innocent companion to Gilgamesh
die?' Enlil's rage flared, as he angrily told Shamash,
'Daily you journeyed with them,
you were like their companion.'"

## II. ENKIDU'S ILLNESS

Enkidu fell ill, lying in tears before his friend.
Gilgamesh murmured, "How could the gods lend
me forgiveness yet deny
my brother? Why should he die,
leaving me alive to mourn?"
Enkidu asked, "Will I soon only sit with spirits and ghosts,

---

6. Anu is the sky god, the father of the gods; Enlil is the god of the earth and the air; Shamash is the sun god.

far from the sight of my brother?"
Gilgamesh whispered, "Can I only sit just beyond
those dim shadows which press
outside the House of the Dead,                                          *10*
while Enkidu moves inside that place?"

## VI.  ENKIDU'S DREAM OF THE UNDERWORLD

Enkidu drifted through layers of hazy
half-sleep, his fists clenched, his stomach queasy.
At dawn he turned to Gilgamesh,
relating his dream. "Last night the cloudless
sky was broken by a low moan.                                           *5*
The earth howled its frenzied response, and I stood alone
between them. A figure rose before me,
a towering, darkened body,
formed from a lion's head and paws,
and an eagle's talons reaching to claw                                  *10*
my loose hair. I beat him, struggled with him,
but his body overpowered mine.
As he grasped me, I called to you,
Gilgamesh, but you were too
frightened, watching this man trample me.                               *15*
But then he transformed my body,
and my arms grew feathered and as graceful as a bird's.
He clutched one of my wings and led me down
to Irkalla's[7] palace, the House of Shades.
Those who enter that place never return.                                *20*
They walk down a road but never return.
They sit huddled in darkness, hidden from all light,
eating clay and mud, swallowing dust and dirt.
Like birds they cover their limbs with feathered clothes
and layers of dust settle on the door's thick bolt.                     *25*
Scattered heaps of crowns clutter the floor:
dead kings who ruled the earth before
hover in the doorways, transformed,
waiting only to serve steaks brimming with red juice
and cool pure water to Enlil and Anu.                                   *30*
I entered the House of Ash
where I saw the high priest and the wailer,
the purification priest and the dervish,
and the priest of the Great Gods.
Etana[8] and Sumuquan[9] were there, and                                *35*

---

7. Irkalla is also known as Ereshkigal, queen of the underworld.

8. This king, seeking a magic plant of fertility for his barren wife, was carried into the heavens by an eagle but he fell back down to earth.

9. The god of cattle.

so was Ereshkigal, Queen of the Underworld.
Belit-Seri, the Underworld's scribe,
knelt before her, reading aloud from her writing tablet
where everyone's fate is inscribed
Ereshkigal lifted her head, looked me in the eyes
and asked, 'Who has brought this man here?'"

## V. THE DEATH OF ENKIDU

"Your dream is terrifying," Gilgamesh replied.
Curled on his bed Enkidu lay
growing ever more ill day after day.
On the twelfth day, he struggled to lift his head,
calling to Gilgamesh, "Friend, the gods are angry.
I am cursed, not even able
to die gracefully in battle."
Then Gilgamesh heard the death rattle
and he moaned for his friend like a dove.

# Tablet IX

## I. GILGAMESH'S GRIEF AND FEAR OF DEATH

Gilgamesh grieved Enkidu's death, roaming
through hills and desert plains, weeping and saying,
"Just as Enkidu died, I will die.
I feel sorrow and fear in my chest
and I am frightened of death."
So Gilgamesh set out for the far wilderness
desperately seeking Utnapishtim,
the son of Ubartutu, the only one
who might know how death could be avoided.

## II. THE MOUNTAIN PASS

At night, slipping through the mountain passes,
Lions frightened Gilgamesh.
Lifting his eyes toward the moon,
he prayed to the moon god, Sin:
"Please protect me."

## IV. THE GARDEN OF JEWELS

Gilgamesh emerged from the mountain trails once
the sun rose. He headed toward a garden of gem-encrusted stones,
and towering, fleshy bushes,

where vines bloomed with lapus-lazuli leaves,
and emerald trees spilled                                                          5
ruby blossoms. Beyond the garden, the ocean sparkled like emeralds.


# Tablet X

## III.  CROSSING THE WATERS OF DEATH

Gilgamesh lifted off the clothes that hung
close to his body, tethering
them to the mast,
so his boat could sail upon the waters.

## IV.  UTNAPISHTIM SEES GILGAMESH APPROACHING

Utnapishtim stood on the distant
shore, gazing at the hazy shape of the boat as it
slid across the waters of death.
He murmured to himself,
"Why have the stone images broken?                                       5
And why is Urshanabi not navigating the boat? I strain
my eyes, unable to see
who sails here toward me."

## V.  THEIR CONVERSATION

Urshanabi the ferryman asked Gilgamesh, "Why is
your face so sunken and weathered, your eyelids
smeared with shadows, your cheeks rough, haggard
and starved? Why are your clothes in tatters?
You look as if you've traveled for ages, hungry and lost,                 5
seared by the sun and burned by frost.
Why are you mourning?
Why do you come here, searching?"

Gilgamesh asked Urshanabi, "Shouldn't I look haggard?
I am starved and lost, and battered                                            10
even more by an endless sadness.
I wandered in the wilderness
seared by ice and burned by the sun,
grieving for Enkidu, my brother, my soulmate, the one
who slew the panther in the wilderness                                       15
and in the mountains chased the wild ass.
Together we climbed the mountain
and fought and killed the Bull of Heaven.
We slew the demon Huwawa of the Cedar Forest,

and killed lions in the mountain passes. 2

My companion, the one whom I love beyond all
is dead. I could not leave his dead body, even for its burial.
But then maggots fell out of his nose,
and I grew horrified at his molding skin.
This is why I roam through the wilderness. 2
Enkidu is nothing but clay and dust,
and now I fear my own inevitable death.
Won't I be just like him? Lying pressed
against the mud, never rising? So I sought
Utnapishtim, the remote sage. 3
I traveled, hunting and skinning the bears, stags,
ibex, hyenas, and lions. I wrapped their skins around
my cold body, ate their flesh. The tavern keeper
slammed her door in my face, and I lay huddled
shivering in the dirt, the icy night air keeping me awake." 3

Urshanabi said to Gilgamesh:
"You have been created from the flesh
of the gods, and the flesh of humans,
born of a goddess and a man.
But is a house built so that it will never crumble? 4
Is a contract obeyed forever?
Do brothers always share their inheritance willingly?
Does hostility last forever? Does jealousy?
No: there is no permanence.
Rivers rise and flood, clogging the soil with rushing dampness. 4
Insects are shed from warm cocoons, only to flutter for a moment.
And how long can any person gaze at the sun?
No, there has never been any permanence.
How similar the sleeping and the dead appear:
the servant and the ruler's bodies reveal the same picture 5
when they are both dead.
Once the Anunaki,[10] the great assembly of gods,
gathered together. Mammetum, the Mother goddess,
the weaver of destinies, came with them. The Anunaki established
that life and death should be created. 5
Then they set the days of death, but keep these times hidden."

---

10. The Anunaki are the gods of destiny, the sons of the god Anu.

# Tablet XI

## I.  UTNAPISHTIM RELATES HOW EA WARNED HIM
## OF THE FLOOD

Utnapishtim turned to Gilgamesh, saying,
"I will uncover for you a secret hidden
by the gods. The city of Shurippak,[11] nestled
on the banks of the Euphrates—
a place of which you have surely heard—                                  5
it had grown old, and full of the spirits of the gods.
The gods decided to unleash a flood
upon the city. They all gathered: Anu, their father;
Enlil, their counselor; Ninurta, the god of war;
Ennugi,[12] guardian of the canals; and,                               10
clear-eyed Ea, the clever one.[13]
Ea's voice whispered through the thin reed walls of my room,
'You, reed hut, reed walls! Listen, pay attention:
Utnapishtim, tear down the walls of your house and build
a boat! Abandon your home, spurn wealth and                            15
possessions, disregard evrything except for life! You must
bring a seed from each living being onto your boat,
safely past the threat of the approaching flood.
Construct your ship with careful precision:
Let length and width be equal to each other,                           20
and let a roof shield it just as the deep abyss is covered.'
I leaned toward the reed walls, murmuring, 'I hear you,
I will honor you, but how should I respond to
the city, the people, the Elders?' And
Ea parted his mouth, whispering to me, his servant:                    25
'You will tell them that Enlil's hateful wrath has consumed you.
Because of his spite for you, you cannot live in the city, you
cannot even set foot on his land.
Say you must find another god to protect
you, and that you will seek Ea in his abyss. And in Shurippak,         30
once dawn shimmers on the horizon, abundance
will rain down upon them: a flood of the harvest,
wild birds falling, rare fish tumbling from
the clouds, showers of glinting wheat-grains
and baked loaves hitting the surface                                   35
of the earth. Such copious torrents of all
these things—this you will tell the city and its people.'

---

11. Modern day Fara.
12. God of irrigation.
13. Ea is the god of the waters and of wisdom, patron of humanity.

## II. UTNAPISHTIM BUILDS THE ARK

"As glimmers of dawn first appeared
all the people gathered to watch me build
my vessel. Children carried tar and gravel,
as other workers brought timber and whatever else I wished.
I sketched plans: six decks,
and each wall measuring one hundred and twenty cubits.
We pieced each section together, hammered
the beams, and drove plugs into its frame to stop the flow of water.
I poured tar into the furnace, and spread
it to caulk the hull and the inner layer. I put oars on board,
and after all this I slaughtered bulls and sheep for the workmen.
We poured endless glasses of rich red and white wine,
beer, dark ales, a river of drinks. At sunset
on the seventh day, with the boat completed,
I spread fragrant lotions and oils on my hands.
I loaded everything I owned into it: silver, gold,
the wild animals in my fields. I brought my family,
gathered the workmen and their children with me,
and I took a seed of each living thing.
The launching faltered; we shifted our weight
and prodded everything into place, the boat groaning.
Two-thirds of it sank, submerged by the river.
We maneuvered it carefully to keep it from capsizing.
In the evening I heard Shamash saying:
'Soon it will shower abundance—
Come inside your ship, seal the hatches!'
So I moved inside, latching the gates against the downfall,
and let Puzumurri, the caulker,
have my worldly goods and palace.

## III. THE FLOOD

"With the earliest glints of dawn
came a roiling dark cloud
with Adad, the storm god, roaring within.
Devastation and submission rode the wind
over mountains and grasslands.
Nergal, god of the underworld,
lifted the dams in his realm, and
Ninurta, god of war and chaos, broke down the dikes
so the floods could rush forth.
The Annunaki lifted their blazing torches,
but Adad's rage swept through the heavens,
turning the flaming light back into chilly dusk.
Adad smashed the vast land like a clay pot

and the streaming tempest raged like war
through the broken city.                                      *15*
Torrents of wind flew past the mountainsides,
and no man could see another
through the sheets of water.
The gods shrank, sobbing,
and retreated to the highest heavens.                         *20*
They curled against Anu's walls,
huddled like dogs and shivering helplessly.

Glorious Ishtar's sweet voice howled
as though she were giving birth:
'Days have disintegrated into clay and dust.                  *25*
Because of my evil demands from the gods,
I brought destruction and catastrophe to my people!
I gave birth to them and they are in the waters
like the spawn of fish!'
The Annanuki humbly bowed their heads                         *30*
and wept with the Goddess.
The winds shrieked with the fury of childbirth,
and for six days and seven nights,
torrents of water flooded the land.
On the seventh day, the flood ceased,                         *35*
the throbbing storm shuddered and calmed
like an army after battle,
everything becoming suddenly still.
I lifted the hatch, and sunlight fell on me.
Nothing moved on the silent sea.                              *40*
It was flat as a clay roof
and all mankind had turned to clay.
I fell on my knees, and wept. All through the day,
I crouched and wept in the vast silence,
frantically scouring the stretch of waters                    *45*
for some thing. And finally I glimpsed the dim
outline of an island beneath the water.
It was the peak of Mount Nisir
and my boat was grounded there
on its rocky surface. The ark                                 *50*
held its place for one day, two,
on Mount Nisir, three days, four,
for seven days, motionless.

## IV.  THE SECRET OF IMMORTALITY

"On the seventh day I sent forth a dove, but
she returned, finding no place to perch.
I freed a swallow, but she also found no perch

to rest upon, and came back to the ark.
I sent a raven aloft, who saw the sea receding.
I glimpsed her soaring, clawing the air, gliding
in perfect circles. But she never came back.
So I released all the birds from my boat,
and they scattered in all directions,
rising up through the wind.

I stepped on the shore, setting seven upon seven
vessels over a fire of myrtle, cane,
and savory cedar. I offered incense as sacrifice,
and the gods drew close to all this fragrance,
hovering around my altar like flies.

\* \* \*

Enlil approached, spotting my ship,
and his body shook with the rage of gods.
'How could any mortal escape this deluge?
No living being should have survived that annihilation!'
Ninurva's lips parted, and he told Enlil,
'Who could create anything without Ea? Only
Ea, the cleverest god, understands such crafty plots.'
Ea replied, 'Valiant Enlil, how could you unleash this
flood without reflecting upon its effects?
Charge the transgression to the transgressor,
punish only those who offend!
Show compassion, never ravaging the lands indiscriminately.

\* \* \*

Ea continued, 'I did not reveal the glorious gods' secret.
Utnapishtim glimpsed the truth in a dream vision.
How shall the gods respond to such wisdom?'
Then Enlil stepped inside the ark.
He grasped my hand, and made me kneel.
He twined his fingers into my wife's hand, leading her to kneel
beside me. He stood between us, pressing
our foreheads together and saying,
'You and your wife, once mere humans are now
transformed into gods. You will dwell at the mouth
of all rivers, the source brimming with liquid
for all the streams of the world.'"

Then Utnapishtim asked Gilgamesh,
"Now, who would assemble the glorious gods for you
so that you could also gather everlasting youth?"

\* \* \*

Utnapishtim's wife asked him, "Gilgamesh is so weary,
his clothes tattered and his hair matted. What will you
give him so he can return to his city with honor?"                     45
Gilgamesh overheard them as he rowed home,
and steered his boat back toward the shore.
Utnapishtim told him, "Gilgamesh, after your
exhausting journey, what should I give you?
Let me uncover a mystery of the gods for you:                          50
there is an underwater plant, with deep roots
spreading through the mud; its spikes and brambles wait
to prick your hands, the thorns will make
blood spring from your fingers
as when you seize it like a rose. Plunge into the waters,             55
and pull up the plant: it will give you everlasting life."
So Gilgamesh bound heavy stones to his feet,
while opening the sluicegates so the current
could pull him toward the deepest waters.
His hand encircled the plant, its thorns slicing his palms            60
and cutting the heavy stones from around his ankles.
Then the tide spilt him back upon the shore.

## VII.  GILGAMESH SPEAKS TO THE FERRYMAN

Gilgamesh told the ferryman, Urshanabi,
"This marvelous plant holds eternal life!
I will bring it back to Uruk, to the elders, to every person
in my city! I will tell them its name:
'The Aged-Man-Becomes-Young-Once-More.'                               5
I will place part of it on my own tongue, for
swallowing it will spread virility and youth through my body,
keeping death far removed from me."

## VIII.  THE SERPENT BY THE POOL

Gilgamesh and Urshanabi traveled
twenty leagues, then broke their fast.
Ten leagues past this they stopped to rest.
Gilgamesh glimpsed a spring of fresh
lucid water and descended into the cool pond                          5
to rouse his tired body, holding the magical plant
close to him. But a serpent danced
towards him through the flickering reeds,
breathing the flower's tempting fragrance,
and snatched the thorny plant,                                        10
shedding its rough skin as it rustled quickly away.

Gilgamesh realized what the serpent had done,

and wept. He grasped Urnashabi's hand, tears flowing down
his cheeks, choking, 'What should I do? I traveled through
the wilds, spilling my own blood,
destroying my own body, for what? For whom?                                    1
I have gained nothing. The serpent,
lion of the soil, stole the plant
from me, and dropped it into the rushing tides.
It must be twenty leagues distant already!
This is a sign telling me: abandon your search,                                2
leave your empty boat on the shore."

## ▪ Adapa: The Man (Second Millennium B.C.)
## *Babylonia* (myth)

TRANSLATED BY N. K. SANDARS

The name [Adapa] is not "a man" but "man," it is Adam; but the story
of this Adam is of fooling and paradox. Unlike Utnapishtim, the Babylonian Noah who won eternal life for himself through obedience to a god, in
Adapa, mankind was given the chance of eternal life and lost it through
obedience to a god. The scene of the beginning is Eridu, in southern
Mesopotamia. One of the oldest Sumerian cities, it stood on the edge of a
great lagoon near the Persian Gulf and was sacred to Ea, the Sumerian
Enki. The father of the gods, Anu, is still in this story the supreme authority in heaven. Of the two lesser gods, Tammuz and Gizzida, who stand at
the East Gate of heaven, Tammuz has descended from Dumuzi, and
Gizzida was a god of healing sometimes also connected with the Underworld. Gizzida was called Lord of the Tree of Truth, as Dumuzi—Tammuz
was Lord of the Tree of Life—trees that were stars planted in heaven. Besides Anu's messenger or minister and the South Wind, these are the only
protagonists.

The text is put together from three fragments; the oldest and longest
was found in Egypt among the fourteenth-century archives, mostly diplomatic correspondence, of Tell el Amarna. The two shorter fragments were
in Ashurbanipal's library at Nineveh. The el Amarna text has no metrical
form, it is (presumably) prose; and the story (the sting in the tail notwithstanding) is nearest to a morality or *conte*. The morality cuts more than
one way, and it is worth noticing that for one split second, before his igno-
minious return to earth, Adapa is allowed the vision of heaven. Though
every kind of trouble lies ahead, this is something that belongs to Adapa;
the vision cannot be taken away from man.

—N. K. Sandars

**FURTHER READING:** Sandars, N. K. *Poems of Heaven and Hell from Ancient
Mesopotamia*, 1971.

In those days, in those years long ago at Eridu, the city which stands on a sweet lagoon, there was a man. He was wise like one of the gods. When he gave an order it was as though Ea,[1] the master himself, that subtle god, had spoken; for Ea is the master of subtlety, and he also controls the waters. Ea had made him a leader, a man to be followed. He gave him sagacity and intelligence enough to comprehend the design of the world: but he made him a dying man.

In those days, in those years, he was man's first pattern, scrupulous in his service to the temple, one with clean hands; the sage of Eridu was accounted wise even among the Great Gods. No one questioned his orders. Daily he stocked up the city with bread and drinking water, baking bread with the bakers of Eridu, steering the ship that fished for Eridu, going through the ritual with clean hands. Only *he* could set and clear the god's table.

In those days, while Ea lay at ease on his bed and this man Adapa was busy in the sanctuary, the household had need of fresh stores of fish. So Adapa boarded the sailing boat at the quay-side, the one which is sacred to the New Moon. It blew a following wind and he let the boat run before the gale. He steered with the oar, sailing out into the wide sea alone.

In the middle of the sea Adapa went about catching fish; the sea was calm as a mirror. Then the South Wind got up; it capsized him, and he plunged down into the world of fish. In his desperate anger Adapa yelled out a curse,

'South Wind, you rose out of malice, I will break your wing', and as he spoke the wing of the South Wind shattered, and for seven days it did not blow on to the land at all.

Anu,[2] the god who reigns in heaven, called out to his servant Ilabrat,

'Why has the South Wind not blown on to the land for seven days?' Ilabrat answered,

'My Lord, the man, Ea's son, has shattered the wing of the South Wind in his arrogant fashion.'

When he heard this Anu got up angrily from his throne. He sent his messenger to Ea, because he is wise and knows the gods well. They spoke together, and Anu shouted,

'Fetch the man here!'

Ea gave the man a warning, for he knew the ways of heaven. He told him to go in rags and in mourning with his hair uncut and hanging loose.

'You must go up the road to the top of heaven and appear before Anu, the king. When you have reached the gate of heaven you will see two gods, Tammuz and Gizzida,[3] who stand there together. They will ask,

"Man, for whose sake do you look like this?"

'Answer,

---

1. Ea (the Sumerian Enki) is the god of sweet waters and wisdom, patron of the arts, one of the creators of mankind to whom he was generally kindly disposed, and the chief god of Eridu [Editor].

2. Anu (Sumerian An) is heaven, the sky and the god of the skies, the father of Ea [Editor].

3. Tammuz is the semitic name for Dumuzi. Gizzida, also Ningizzida, is "Lord of the Tree of Life," a god of fertility and healing, also connected with the underworld [Editor].

"Two gods have left our land, I mourn for them."

"What gods are they?"

"I mourn for Tammuz and Gizzida."

'Then they will smile at each other and say kind words to Anu; they will show you his *gracious* face. When you are standing in front of Anu they will offer the bread of death; do not eat it. They will offer the water of death; do not drink it. They will bring a garment; put on the garment; and when they bring oil anoint yourself. Take care that you do not forget this advice. Remember!'

The messenger from Anu came for the man. He led him up the road of the firmament; he approached the East Gate of heaven. Tammuz and Gizzida stood at the gate; when they saw him they said,

'Heavens, Man! Why do you look like this? Whom are you mourning?'

'Two gods have left our land, I mourn for them.'

'What gods are they?'

'Tammuz and Gizzida, I mourn for them.'

They exchanged glances and smiled. Adapa approached the lord of heaven. Anu looked at him and said,

'You, Man, why did you break the wing of the South Wind?' The man answered,

'My lord, I was catching fish in the middle of the sea for the household of my master, Ea. The sea was a mirror but the South Wind got up, he capsized me and I plunged down to the world of fish, and in the anger of my heart I cursed him.'

Then Tammuz and Gizzida, standing beside him, spoke kind words. They soothed the heart of the king of heaven so that he said, speaking to them,

'What was Ea about to give knowledge of all nature to a wretch of a man, to make him like one of us, and with such a name for wisdom? But now that he is here what else can we do? Fetch the bread of life and he shall eat it.'

When they brought him the bread of life he would not eat. When they brought him the water of life he did not drink it. When they brought him a garment he put it on; and when they brought oil he anointed himself.

Then Anu, the lord of heaven, looked at the man and laughed,

'Ah, Adapa, why did you neither eat nor drink, stupid man; perverse mankind; you will never now have eternal life.'

'My master Ea ordered me, "You shall not eat, you shall not drink,"'

Loudly Anu laughed again at the doings of Ea,

'Of all the gods of heaven and of earth, as many as there may be, whoever gave such an order! Who can circumvent the will of Anu?'

Then the man looked from the horizon of heaven to the meridian; he saw the majesty of heaven, and Anu gave the man his orders and he gave to the priests of Eridu the rule of their lives. But as for him, the man child of man, who broke the wing of the South Wind in his arrogant fashion, who went up to heaven—he brought on us the sufferings of mankind. He brought disease to our bodies that only the Lady of Healing can assuage.

May sickness depart. May there be no more disease; but as for him, let him not lie down in gentle sleep again, nor feel the happiness that men know in their hearts.

## ■ The Shipwrecked Sailor (c. 2040–1650 B.C.) *Egypt* (story)

TRANSLATED BY EDWARD F. WENTE, JR.

"The Shipwrecked Sailor" is Middle Kingdom fiction, probably written in Dynasty 11, c. 2040–1650 B.C. In its adventure and magical realism, it is a miniature quest journey such as that of Odysseus. But unlike with Odysseus, whose goal was return to Ithaca and recovery of his kingship, we are uncertain of the purpose and true meaning—if there be one—of this elusive and intriguing quest tale. Written in the first person, as an autobiographical memoir (surely a literary device) and with a story within a story within a story, we have the plights, frights, and excitement of a single person confronting unpredictable nature, supernatural gods, and the authority of the immediate sovereign who is the judge of the sailor's journey and accomplishments. Rich in realistic detail, the tale also provides specific information on everyday Egyptian life.

The astute lieutenant spoke: May your wish be satisfied, commander. See, we have reached home. The mallet has been taken, the mooring post driven in, and the prow rope set upon the ground. Praise has been rendered, God has been thanked, and every man embraces his companion. Our crew is returned safe without loss to our troops. Now that we have reached the limits of Wawat and we have passed by / Senmut, we have returned in peace, and we have attained our land.[1]

Listen to me, commander. I am devoid of exaggeration. Wash yourself; place water on your fingers. Then you can reply when you are interrogated and speak to the king with self-assurance. You will answer without [stammering]. For the speech of a man saves him, and his words gain him indulgence. / Act according to your judgment. Yet speaking to you (in this fashion) is wearisome.

Let me tell you of a similar thing which happened to me myself.[2] I went to the mining country for the sovereign. I went down to the sea[3] in a

1. A quarrying, mining, or military expedition has returned by Nile from the south, and its commander appears to be downcast at the prospect of facing the king after an unsuccessful mission. His chief aide tries to cheer him up. Wawat is northern Nubia, and Senmut is the island of Biggeh, just south of Aswan in the First Cataract region. The mission took place in the eastern desert or on the Red Sea. The expression, "our land," is not otherwise attested in Egyptian literature and may in fact have a patriotic nuance.

2. Here begins the story within the story.

3. The word for sea is literally, "the great green," and is used of the Mediterranean as well as the Red Sea. Since the mining country is either the Sinai peninsula or the eastern desert, since the serpent speaks of the land of Punt (a southern region in Africa or on the Red Sea), and since the produce is African (giraffe tails, etc.), the sea in our story is clearly the Red Sea.

boat 120 cubits long and 40 cubits wide.[4] One hundred twenty sailors from among the best of Egypt were in it. Whether they looked at the sky or whether they looked at the land, / their hearts were fiercer than those of lions. They could foretell a stormwind before it came and a downpour before it happened.

A stormwind broke out while we were at sea, before we had touched land. The wind was lifted up,[5] but it repeated with a wave of eight cubits in it. There was a plank which struck it (the wave) for me.[6] Then the boat died. And of those who were in it not a single one survived.

Next I was set upon / an island by the surf of the sea, and I spent three days alone, my heart as my companion. I slept inside of a cabin of wood;[7] I embraced the shade. I stretched forth my two legs to learn what I might put in my mouth. There I found figs and dates, and all excellent kinds of vegetables. Sycamore figs were there and notched sycamore figs. / And cucumbers as if they were cultivated. Fish were there and birds. There was not anything which was not within it. Then I ate to satisfaction, and I put (some aside) on the ground because of the overabundance in my hands. I cut a fire drill, lit a fire, and I made a burnt offering for the gods.

Then I heard the sound of a thunderclap, but I thought it was the surf of the sea. The trees were shaking / and the ground was quaking. When I uncovered my face, I discovered that it was a serpent coming along. He was thirty cubits. His [hood] was more than two cubits, and his body was plated with gold. His two [markings] were of real lapis lazuli, and he was coiled up in front.[8]

He opened his mouth to me while I was on my belly in his presence, and he said to me: Who is it who has brought you, who is it who has brought you, little one, / who is it who has brought you? If you delay in telling me who it is who has brought you to this island, I shall see that you find yourself as ashes, transformed into one who is not seen.

Although he was speaking to me, I did not hear it; when I was in his presence, I did not know myself. He placed me in his mouth, and he took me off to his rest house. He set me down without touching me, / and I was intact, without anything being taken away from me.

He opened his mouth to me while I was on my belly in his presence, and he said to me: Who is it who has brought you, who is it who has brought you, little one, who is it who has brought you to this island of the sea, the two sides of which are in waves? And I answered him, my arms

---

4. The cubit is the Egyptian measurement of length, about 20.6 inches or .523 meters. The ship is about 206 by 70 feet.

5. Perhaps an idiom with the sense, "we traveled onward."

6. This passage difficult in the original.

7. Possibly the cabin of the boat, but conceivably a natural or man-made shelter.

8. The terms *hood* and *markings* have been interpreted in various ways by different scholars. The first is the usual word for beard.

bent in his presence, and I said to him: It is I (myself) who have gone down / to the mines on a mission of the sovereign in a boat 120 cubits long and 40 cubits wide.[9] One hundred twenty sailors from among the best of Egypt were in it. Whether they looked at the sky or whether they looked at the land, their hearts were [fiercer] than those of lions. They could foretell a stormwind before it came and a downpour before it happened. Each one of them, his heart was [fiercer] / and his arm more valorous than his fellow's, without a fool among them. A stormwind came forth while we were at sea, before we could make land. The wind was lifted up, but it repeated with a wave of eight cubits in it. There was a plank which struck it (the wave) for me. Then the boat died. And of those that were in it not a single one remained except for me. Behold me at your side. Then I was brought to this island / by the surf of the sea.

He said to me: Do not fear, do not fear, little one, do not turn white. You have reached me. Indeed, God has allowed you to live. He has brought you to this Island of the Ka[10] within which there is not anything which does not exist. It is full of all good things. See, you shall spend month after month until you complete four months within this island. / A boat shall come back from home with sailors in it whom you know. You shall go home with them, and you shall die in your village.[11]

How joyful is the one who relates what he has tasted after painful affairs are past. Let me relate to you something similar which took place in this island when I was on it with my brothers and sisters and the children among them.[12] We were seventy-five serpents, my children and my brothers and sisters. And I will not call to mind to you a little daughter who was brought to me through [prayer.][13]

Then a star / fell, and because of it these went up in fire.[14] It happened completely. Yet I did not burn, for I was not among them. But I died for them when I found them in a single heap of corpses.[15]

If you would be brave, regulate your desire. Then you will fill your embrace with your children, you will kiss your wife, and you will see your house (again); for it is better than anything. You will reach the home in which you (once) were in the midst of your brothers and sisters.

As I was stretched out on my belly and touching the ground in his presence, I said to him: I shall relate your prowess to the sovereign, and I shall inform him / of your greatness. I shall have brought to you ladanum, *heknu*-oil, *iudeneb,* cassia, and incense for the temples with which to satisfy

9. This kind of repetition of an entire section is frequent in all ancient literature.

10. An island of the spirit or enchanted island.

11. Burial in a foreign land was abhorrent to the Egyptians, a theme developed in Sinuhe as well.

12. Here begins the story within the story within the story.

13. This curious phrase has not yet been satisfactorily explained.

14. A meteor? In the historical text of Thutmose III from Gebel Barkal there is a description of a falling star.

15. Here the serpent's story ends. Like the sailor, he was a sole survivor.

every god. I shall indeed relate what has happened to me through what I have seen of your prowess. You will be thanked in (my) town in the presence of the magistrates of the entire land. I shall sacrifice to you oxen as a burnt offering, and I shall wring the necks of birds for you. I shall have brought to you transport ships loaded with all the specialties of Egypt, as should be done for a god who loves the Egyptians in a distant land which the Egyptians do not know.

Then he laughed at me because of these things which I had said, out of the [craftiness] of his heart. / And he said to me: Myrrh is not abundant with you, although you have become a possessor of incense. Indeed, I am the Prince of Punt; myrrh belongs to me. That *heknu*-oil, of which you spoke about bringing me, why it is the main product of this island! Now it will come to pass that you will separate yourself from this place, and you will never see this island, since it will have turned into waves.

Then that boat came, as he had foretold before. I went and I set myself on a high tree, and I recognized those who were in it. I went to report it, but I found that he knew it. And he said to me: Farewell, farewell, little one, to your home! You will see your children. Place my good repute in your town: this is all I ask / from you.

I placed myself on my belly, my arms bent in his presence. And he gave me a cargo consisting of myrrh, *heknu*-oil, *iudeneb*, cassia, *tishepses*, *shasekh*, black eye-paint, giraffe tails, large cakes of incense, elephant tusks, hounds, apes, baboons, and every kind of precious thing. I then loaded them onto this boat. It then came to pass that I placed myself upon my belly to thank him, and he said to me: You will arrive home within two months. You will fill your embrace with your children. You will become young again at home, and you will be (properly) buried.

I went down to the shore / in the vicinity of this ship, and I called out to the troops who were in this ship. I gave praise upon the shore to the lord of this island, and those who were in it (the ship) did likewise.

We sailed northward to the Residence city of the sovereign, and we arrived at the Residence in two months, according to everything he had said. Then I entered before the sovereign, and I presented to him this produce which I had brought back from within this island. He thanked me before the magistrates of the entire land. I was appointed lieutenant, and I was assigned two hundred people. Look at me, / now that I have touched land, after I have seen what I have experienced. Listen to my speech. It is good for men to hearken.

He said to me:[16] Do not act the part of the astute man, friend. Who gives water to the goose at daybreak when it is to be slaughtered in the morning?

It has come, from its beginning to its end, as it has been found in writing, in the writing of the scribe excellent of fingers, / Ameny's son Amen-aa.

---

16. These are the commander's only words in the story.

# ▪ The Tale of the Doomed Prince (c. 2040–1650 B.C.) *Egypt* (story)

## TRANSLATED BY EDWARD F. WENDT, JR.

"The Tale of the Doomed Prince" is, like "The Shipwrecked Sailor," a Middle Kingdom fiction from Dynasty 11. In this Egyptian fairy tale, a young crown prince is threatened prophetically with death from a crocodile, a snake, or a dog. The young prince goes abroad—a common theme—disguised as the orphan son of a simple chariot warrior. In the eastern margin of the delta, he comes to the land of the Prince of Nahrin. The prince has protected his daughter by placing her in a tower house seventy cubits above the ground. He makes it known that whoever can leap up that high will have the hand of his daughter. The doomed prince leaps up to the tower window, and the daughter of the Prince of Nahrin falls in love and kisses and embraces him "all over his body." The father, at first annoyed by the young prince's supposed low station, is soon charmed and won over and he too kisses the young man all over his body. Meanwhile the threat of death from the animals remains. By miraculous coincidences, the young groom survives encounters with the ferocious beasts, and while the tale is incomplete, the reader feels, as in an unfinished Kafka tale, that the process of escape from death will go on indefinitely, and the "doomed" prince in disguise is in reality a virtuous prince who will be compelled by fate of his good life, loving wife, and inevitable escapes from death to become the "blessed" prince. The Egyptian tale-makers loved the literary intrigue of masked heroes, allegorical beasts and god figures, fearful and suspenseful adventure, and quests whose ultimate meaning must never be revealed.

Once upon a time there was a king, so the story goes, to whom no son had ever been born. [But when His Majesty, re]quested a son for himself from the gods of his time, they ordered a birth to be granted him, and he went to bed with his wife in the night. Now when she [had become] pregnant and had completed the months of child-bearing, a son was thus born.

Presently the Hathors[1] came to determine a fate for him and said: He shall die through a crocodile, or a snake, or even a dog. Thus the people who were at the boy's side heard and then reported it to His Majesty. Thereupon His Majesty became very much saddened. Then His Majesty had [a house] of stone built [for him] upon the desert, supplied with personnel and with every good thing of the palace, so that the boy did not (need to) venture outside.

---

1. According to popular religious belief in the New Kingdom, there were seven such Hathor goddesses, who determined the fate of a child at birth; see "The Tale of the Two Brothers."

Now after the boy had grown older, he went up onto his roof and es-pied a greyhound following a grownup who was walking along the road. He said to his servant, who was beside him: What is it that is walking be-hind the grownup who is coming along [the] road? And he told him: It is a greyhound. And the boy told him: Have one like it obtained for me. Thereupon the servant went and reported it to His Majesty. Then His Majesty said, "Let a young springer be taken to him [because of] his heart's [disquiet]." And so someone [caused] the greyhound to be taken to him.

Now after days had elapsed upon this, the boy matured in all his body, and he sent to his father saying: What will the outcome be while I am dwelling here? For look, I am committed to Fate. Let me be released so that I may act according to my desire until God does what is his will. Then a chariot was yoked for him, equipped [with] all sorts of weapons, and [a servant was put in] his following for an escort. He was ferried over to the eastern tract[2] and told: Now you may set out as you wish, [while] his grey-hound was with him. He went northward over the desert, following his in-clination and living on every sort of desert game.

Presently he reached the Prince of Nahrin.[3] Now none had been born to the Prince of Nahrin except a [marriageable] daughter. There had been built for her a house whose window was seventy cubits distant from the ground, and he sent for all the sons of all the princes of the land of Khor[4] and told them: As for the one who will reach the window of my daughter, she shall be a wife for him.

Now after many days had elapsed upon this and while they were (en-gaged) in their daily practice, presently the boy passed by them. They took the boy to their house, cleansed him, gave fodder to his team, did every sort of thing for the boy, salving him and bandaging his feet, and gave food to his escort. They said to him by way of conversation: Where have you come from, you handsome lad? He told them: I am the son of a char-iot warrior of the land of Egypt. My mother died, and my father took for himself another wife, a [stepmother]. She came to despise me, and I left her presence in flight. And they embraced him and kissed him over [all his] body.

[Now after many days had elapsed upon] this, he said to the boys: What is this that you have become engaged in, [boys? And they told him: It has been three] full [month]s till now that we have spent time here [leaping up, for the one who] will reach [the] window of the daughter of the Prince of Nahrin, [he will] give her to him for [a wife. He] said to

2. The desert edge forming the eastern margin of the Delta.

3. The land of the Mitannian kingdom, located east of the bend of the Euphrates river. Since this kingdom fell toward the end of Dynasty 18, the action of the story takes place at a time in this dynasty when Syrian princes owed their allegiance to Mitanni.

4. Here synonymous with Syria.

them: If I could but enchant my feet,[5] I would proceed to leap up in your company. They proceeded to leap up according to their daily practice, and the boy stood by afar off observing, while the eyes of the daughter of the Prince of Nahrin were upon him.

Now after (some while) had elapsed upon this, the boy came in order to leap up along with the children of the princes. He leapt up and reached the window of the daughter of the Prince of Nahrin. And she kissed him and embraced him over all his body. Then someone went in order to impart the news to her father and told him: Somebody has reached the window of your daughter. Then the prince inquired about him saying: The son of which of the princes is he? And he was told: He is a chariot warrior's son. It was from his stepmother's presence that he came in flight from the land of Egypt. Thereupon the Prince of Nahrin became very much angered. He said: Is it to the Egyptian fugitive that I should give my daughter? Send him back home.

And someone came to tell him: Please set out for the place whence you came. But the daughter seized hold of him and swore by God, saying: By Pre-Harakhti, if he is taken away from me, I shall neither eat nor drink but shall die right away. Then the messenger went and reported to her father every word that she had said, and her father sent men to slay him while he was still where he was. But the daughter said to them: By Pre, if he is slain, as soon as the sun sets, I shall be dead. I will not stay alive an hour longer than he.

Then [someone went] to tell it to her father. And [her father had] the [lad] and his daughter [brought be]fore him. The lad [came before] him, and his worth impressed the prince. He embraced him and kissed him over all his body, and he said to him: Tell me your background. See, you are (now) a son in my eyes. And he told him: I am the son of a chariot warrior of the land of Egypt. My mother died, and my father took for himself another wife. She came to despise me, and I left her presence in flight. Then he gave him his daughter for a wife and gave him house and fields as well as cattle and all sorts of good things.

Now after (some while) had elapsed upon this, the lad told his wife: I am committed to three fates: crocodile, snake, and dog. Then she told him: Have the dog which follows you killed. And he told her: [What a demand]! I will not let my dog, which I reared when it was a puppy, be killed. And she came to guard her husband very carefully, not letting him venture outside alone.

Now from the day that the boy had come from the land of Egypt in order to travel about, the crocodile had been his fate. . . . It appeared

---

5. Other scholars have rendered the clause by: "If my feet were not paining me so," but neither the traces nor the length of the lacuna support the restoration of the negative *bn*. The determinative of the verb favors "enchant."

[from the midst of] the lake[6] opposite him in the town in which the lad was (living) with [his wife]. However, a water spirit was in it. Neither would the water spirit let the crocodile emerge nor would the crocodile let the water spirit emerge to stroll about. As soon as the sun rose, [they] both [would be] engaged [there] in fighting each and every day for a period of three full months.

Now after some days had elapsed upon this, the lad sat down and made holiday in his house. And after the end of the evening breeze the lad lay down upon his bed, and slumber took possession of his body. Then his wife filled one j[ar with wine and filled] another jar with beer. Presently a [snake] emerged [from its] hole to bite the lad, but his wife was sitting beside him without going to sleep. The [jars were thus standing] accessible to the snake, and it imbibed and became intoxicated. Then it reclined and turned upside down. Thereupon [his wife caused] it to be [split] into segments with her hand-axe. She then awoke her husband . . . him, and she told him: See, your god has delivered one of your fates into your hand. He will guard [you henceforth. Then he] made an offering to P[re], praising him and extoling his power daily.

Now after some days had elapsed upon this], the lad went out to stroll about for relaxation on his property. [His wife] did not go out [with him], but his dog was following him. Then his dog took a bite,[7] [saying: I am your fate. Thereupon] he fled before it. Presently he reached the lake and descended into the [water in flight before the] dog. And so the crocodile [seized h]im and carried him off to where the water spirit (usually) was, [but he was not there.

The] crocodile told the lad: I am your fate who has been fashioned so as to come in pursuit of you, but [it is three full months] now that I have been fighting with the water spirit. See, I shall let you go. If [my opponent returns to engage me] to fight, [come] and lend me your support in order to kill the water spirit.[8] But if you see the . . . see the crocodile.

Now after dawn and the next day had come about, the [water spirit] returned . . .

(The remainder of the tale is lost.)

---

6. The word used for "lake" is *ym*, "sea," used also to refer to the lake of Apamea; see Alan H. Gardiner, *Ancient Egyptian Onomastica*, 3 vols. (Oxford: Oxford University Press, 1947), 1:167*–68*, and Helck, *Beziehungen*, p. 307.

7. See Hildegard von Deines and Wolfhart Westendorf, *Wörterbuch der medizinischen Texte*, 2 vols. (Berlin: Akademie Verlag, 1961–62), 2:947. Other translators have rendered: "Then his dog took on the (power) of speech."

8. Or possibly rather: "and boast of me in order that [I] might kill the water-spirit."

# The Book of the Dead (c. 1500 B.C.) *Egypt* (spells)

## TRANSLATED BY RAYMOND O. FAULKNER

After the Old Kingdom Pyramid Texts, written in hieroglyphs (which, like numbers, convey meaning rather than sound), we have the *Coffin Texts* in the Middle Kingdom, which used hieroglyphs but in a cursive script called "hieratic" with an increasing number of phonograms (a hieroglyph, such as an owl, that represents a sound). In the late New Kingdom, we have a truly demotic cursive phonetic system, which eventually provided a model for the Phoenician cursive that is the basis of Semitic and European scripts. The last great collection of funerary texts, found on papyrus scrolls, is the New Kingdom "guides to the beyond" known as *The Book of the Dead,* written at first in semicursive hieroglyphics known as "linear hieroglyphics" and, finally, in pure demotic cursive. The literary quality of these spells is erratic to the modern reader, being most often of theological and historic rather than of literary importance. Yet there are extraordinary pieces, which can astound even today.

**FURTHER READING:** Andrews, Carol, ed. *The Ancient Book of the Dead,* 1972. Budge, E. A. Wallis. *The Book of the Dead: The Hieroglyphic Transcript of the Papyrus of Ani,* 1960. Lichtheim, Miriam. *Ancient Egyptian Literature, vol. II: The New Kingdom,* 1976.

## SPELL FOR GIVING N'S HEART TO HIM IN THE REALM OF THE DEAD

My heart is mine in the House of Hearts, my heart is mine in the House of Hearts, my heart is mine, and it is at rest there. I will not eat the cakes of Osiris on the eastern side of the Gay-water in the barge when you sail downstream or upstream, and I will not go aboard the boat in which you are. My mouth will be given to me that I may speak with it, my legs to walk, and my arms to fell my enemy. The doors of the sky are opened for me; Gab, chiefest of the gods, throws open his jaws for me, he opens my eyes which were closed up, he extends my legs which were contracted; Anubis strengthens for me my thighs which were joined together; the goddess Sakhmet stretches me out. I will be in the sky, a command shall be made for my benefit in Memphis, I shall be aware in my heart, I shall have power in my heart, I shall have power in my arms, I shall have power in my legs, I shall have power to do whatever I desire; my soul and my corpse shall not be restrained at the portals of the West when I go in or out in peace.

Spell 26

## SPELL FOR NOT EATING FAECES OR DRINKING URINE IN THE REALM OF THE DEAD

I am the horned bull who rules the sky, Lord of Celestial Appearing, the Great Illuminator who came forth from the heat, who harnesses the years; the Double Lion is glad, and the movement of the sunshine has been granted to me. I detest what is detestable, I will not eat faeces, I will not drink urine, I will not walk head downward.

I am the owner of bread in Heliopolis, bread of mine is in the sky with Re, bread of mine is on the earth with Gab, and it is the Night-bark and the Dar-bar which will bring it to me from the house of the Great god who is in Heliopolis. I am loosed from my windings, I make ready the ferry-boat of the sky, I eat of what they eat, I live on what they live on, I have eaten bread in every pleasant room.

Spell 53

## ■ Ancient Egyptian Love Poems (1554–1085 B.C.)
### *Egypt*

TRANSLATED BY EZRA POUND AND NOEL STOCK

These ancient love lyrics written in a woman's voice are outstanding examples of Egyptian literature. Beyond the speaker's voice, we are uncertain of gender and authorship. By contrast with Egypt, in Rome we have virtually no literature attributed to women. Although it was standard for the well-educated Latin woman to paint and write poetry, only seven poems by one Latin woman poet, Sulpicia, exist, and these were found at the end of the canon of the Roman poet Tibullus. Given Sappho's fame as the "tenth muse" of ancient Greek poetry, it is curious that from the abundance of classical Latin literature, no woman other than Sulpicia was deemed worthy enough to copy and thereby invite survival and recovery.

These love poems in ancient Egyptian, exquisitely and powerfully translated by Ezra Pound and Noel Stock, are a universal type of the lyric that appears in many literatures around the world. These earliest examples of the candid, erotic woman's love poem, with spiritual implications, have a counterpart in the pseudepigraphical biblical Song of Solomon (Song of Songs). It is generally assumed that the chaotic beauty of the fragments that comprise the biblical idyll of the Song of Songs is derived indirectly—or perhaps directly—from the tradition of these earlier Egyptian love songs, so similar in speech, spirit, and theme.

**FURTHER READING:** Barnstone, Aliki, and Willis Barnstone. *A Book of Women Poets from Antiquity to Now,* 1980. Pound, Ezra, and Noel Stock. *Love Poems of Ancient Egypt,* 1962.

# from *Pleasant Songs of the Sweetheart Who Meets You in the Fields*

### I

You, mine, my love,
My heart strives to reach the heights of your love.

See, sweet, the bird-trap set with my own hand.

See the birds of Punt,
Perfume a-wing                                             5
              Like a shower of myrrh
Descending on Egypt.

Let us watch my handiwork,
The two of us together in the fields.

### II

The shrill of the wild goose
Unable to resist
The temptation of my bait.

While I, in a tangle of love,
Unable to break free,                                           5
Must watch the bird carry away my nets.

And when my mother returns, loaded with birds,
And finds me empty-handed,
What shall I say?

That I caught no birds?                                     10
That I myself was caught in your net?

### III

Even when the birds rise
Wave mass on wave mass in great flight
I see nothing, I am blind
Caught up as I am and carried away
Two hearts obedient in their beating                          5
My life caught up with yours
Your beauty the binding.

*VII*

Head out the door—
Is he coming?

Ears alert for his step,
And a heart that never stops talking about him.

A messenger:
"I'm not well . . ."
Why doesn't he come straight out
And tell me
He's found another girl.

One more heart to suffer.


*VIII*

I writhe so for lost love
Half my hair has fallen in grief.

I am having my hair recurled and set,
Ready, just in case  . . .


# from **Garden Songs**

*I*

The pomegranate speaks:
My leaves are like your teeth
My fruit like your breasts.
I, the most beautiful of fruits,
Am present in all weathers, all seasons,
As the lover stays forever with the beloved,
Drunk on "shedeh" and wine.

All the trees lose their leaves, all
Trees but the pomegranate.
I alone in all the garden lose not my beauty,
I remain straight.
When my leaves fall,
New leaves are budding.

First among fruits
I demand that my position be acknowledged,
I will not take second place.
And if I receive such an insult again
You will never hear the end of it. . . .

*III*

The little sycamore that you planted
        with your own hands
Moves its mouth to speak.

How lovely his branches, lovely
As they sway, and swaying, whisper,
Their whisper sweet as honey.                                    *5*

The branches bend with plump fruit
Redder than the blood-red Jasper,
Leaves like malachite.

They are drawn to you from afar
Who are not yet in your cool shade.                         *10*
You entice a love-letter
From the hand of that young girl,
Daughter of the head gardener,
Who runs up to her lover, saying
"Let us go somewhere quiet."                               *15*

The garden is in full splendour,
With tent pavilions;
And all for you.

My gardeners rejoice to see you.

## Love Lyrics

*I*

Diving and swimming with you here
Gives me the chance I've been waiting for:
To show my looks
Before an appreciative eye.

My bathing suit of the best material,                       *5*
The finest sheer,
Now that it's wet
Notice the transparency,
How it clings.

Let us admit, I find you attractive.                         *10*
I swim away, but soon I'm back,
Splashing, chattering,
Any excuse at all to join your party.

Look! a redfish flashed through my fingers!
You'll see it better                                       *15*

If you come over here,
Near me.

*II*

Nothing, nothing can keep me from my love
Standing on the other shore.

Not even old crocodile
There on the sandbank between us
Can keep us apart.

I go in spite of him,
I walk upon the waves,
Her love flows back across the water,
Turning waves to solid earth
For me to walk on.

The river is our Enchanted Sea.

*III*

To have seen her
To have seen her approaching
Such beauty is
Joy in my heart forever.
Nor time eternal take back
What she has brought to me.

*IV*

When she welcomes me
Arms open wide
I feel as some traveller returning
From the far land of Punt.

All things change; the mind, the senses,
Into perfume rich and strange.
And when she parts her lips to kiss
My head is light, I am drunk without beer.

*V*

If I were one of her females
Always in attendance
(Never a step away)
I would be able to admire
The resplendence
Of her body entire.

If I were her laundryman, for a month,
I would be able to wash from her veils
The perfumes that linger.

I would be willing to settle for less
And be her ring, the seal on her finger.

# Biblical Literature: Old Testament, New Testament, and Intertestament

## Introduction

The Jews and the Bible (consisting of the Old Testament and the New Testament) are forever linked. The Bible is the early history of the Jews from Abraham through Jesus Christ, the last Jewish prophet and, for Christians, the Messiah foretold in the Old Testament. Hence the Jews have come to be known as the "people of the book." It must be understood that while the Jews do not read the New Testament as believed scripture, the New Testament is also a narration composed by Jews, whose central figure is Yeshua the Messiah, the Jewish charismatic rabbi. Yeshua the Messiah has been translated into English as Jesus Christ (based on the Greek translation of his Aramaic name). Thus, that group of Jews that split off from mainstream Judaism to follow the teachings of Yeshua have come to be known as Christians, meaning Messianists. Although the Bible in its entirety is a book authored by and about Jews, Jews receive the Old Testament as their Bible of belief, whereas Christians receive both the Old Testament and New Testament as their Bible of belief. To this we should add the canonical Apocrypha (books of the Bible surviving only in Greek translation of the lost Hebrew original), which is accepted as canonically part of the Bible by Jews, Catholics, and Greek and Russian Orthodox, but not by Protestants.

In addition to Old Testament and New Testament scripture, including the canonical Apocrypha, which appears in varying degrees in Jewish and Christian Bibles, there is a vast body of scripture that did not find its way into the canon, much of it written during those centuries between the closing of the Old Testament at the beginning of the first century B.C. and the final selection of the New Testament, which was not canonized until the last decades of the fourth century A.D. The religious scriptures of this period, which include noncanonical apocrypha, gospels, apocalypses, acts, psalms, wisdom poetry, Dead Sea Scrolls, Gnostic texts, and writings under the general title of pseudepigrapha (falsely attributed scripture) compose the Intertestament. A selection from this abundance of literature is increasingly included in recent study Bibles. Among the most commonly included of such works is the Gnostic Gospel of Thomas, which may precede by two decades the Gospel of Mark, the earliest of the canonical gospels and the noncanonical apocrypha, and which is of extraordinary literary and theological importance. If we consider the Old Testament, New Testament, and Intertestament together, we have in effect an unbroken line of biblical scripture, which we might call the Greater Bible.

## ■ The Old Testament (Eleventh to First Centuries B.C.) *Israel*

The Bible (from the Greek plural of *biblion*, "book," a diminutive of *biblios*, "papyrus") is an anthology of sacred texts—histories, prophetic writings, wisdom literature—whose canon takes diverse forms for Jews and Christians. The Old Testament has been preserved in Hebrew, though parts of Daniel, Jeremiah, and Ezra are in Aramaic. For Jews, the Bible is the history and writings of the Jewish people, from between the eleventh or tenth century to the first century B.C. It is also called the *Jewish Bible* or the *Hebrew Bible*, referring in the first instance to people, the second to language, but the common designation in English is simply the Bible. In Hebrew, *Torah* refers to the first five books of Moses, and often Torah is used metonymically to mean the whole Bible.

The Bible of the Jews has been designated by Christians as the Old Testament; the Old Testament and the New Testament compose the Christian Bible. The term *Old Testament* reflects a Christian comparative notion of looking back at an older or earlier part of the Bible. For the Jews, however, this book is the entire Bible, and therefore not an old or early part of a composite document. The terms *Old Testament* and *New Testament* came into being in the fourth century A.D. when Jerome (c. 347–420?) translated the Bible into Latin from Hebrew and Greek, calling the parts *Vetus Testamentum* and *Novum Testamentum* ("Old Testament" and "New Testament"), which is a mistranslation of the Greek titles *Palaia Dietheke* and *Kaine Dietheke* ("Old Covenant" and "New Covenant").

The thirty-nine books of the Old Testament include Torah, Histories, Prophets, Wisdom Books, and the canonical Apocrypha. The fourteen books of the Apocrypha are accepted as secondarily canonical (deuterocanonical) by Jews, Catholics, and Greek Orthodox Christians and held to be uncanonical by Protestants. They appear in the famous Septuagint, a second-century B.C. translation into Greek of the Hebrew Bible for the Jews of Alexandria who could no longer read Hebrew. The name *Apocrypha* means "hidden away" in Greek, and these are the "hidden biblical books," meaning that the original Hebrew or Aramaic texts were "hidden away," that is, not available when the Bible was canonized. Since the original texts were lost, the authorship and authenticity of the texts was in doubt (Protestants have never overcome that doubt), and so in a more general sense, "apocryphal" has taken on the meaning of doubtful authenticity. With regard to the canonical Apocrypha of the Hebrew Bible, the loss was in part modified in 1947 with the discovery of the parts of the original Hebrew texts for Tobit and fragments of other Apocrypha.

The Hebrew Bible has its origins in Mesopotamia, both in story and theology: hence, Shinar, site of the tower of Babel, has been identified as Sumer, and the tower of Babel is a reminiscence of massive Mesopotamian structures called ziggurats, such as those at Ur and Khorsabad. Names of historical sites and even of God changed as cultures changed, moved, borrowed, and reinvented their past. Even the name of God reflects a historical confusion of intermingled traditions. Sometimes God is "El," sometimes "Elohim," which is the plural form meaning "the Gods," which may be a linguistic holdover from a polytheistic stage; sometimes God is "Yahweh" and sometimes "Baal." Baal was normally the God of the Canaanites and an enemy deity, but in the Psalms, Baal appears as a synonym for Yahweh. Elsewhere, the Old Testament shows its debt to the Middle East and North Africa: the Genesis Flood story has multiple earlier variants in Mesopotamia, including the Babylonian version in *The Epic of Gilgamesh;* the Book of Proverbs has its antecedents in Egyptian proverbs, recorded in hieroglyphs, of the wise man Amenoemope. Religious scripture is traditionally transmitted orally, later transcribed, and then worked over to improve, censor, and alter according to the needs of the compilers. So to a significant extent, the Bible is a compilation and adaptation of earlier Middle Eastern texts and oral traditions. Both in its prehistory and its present form, the Bible is a book of Asia. The Asian Bible (including the New Testament, which is also an Asian book) has been the most important non-European book in determining the cultures, theologies, and literature of Europe and indeed the globe. It is the world's most translated and migratory book.

Although the Hebrew Bible contains the legends, creation tales, parables, and wisdom literature of many earlier people, in its essence it remains the early history of the Jews and their encounters with Babylon, Egypt, Canaan, Persia, Greece, and Rome. Their recorded history began in Mesopotamia. They settled in the land of Israel in about the thirteenth century, and during the many diasporas that took them to Egypt, Ethiopia, India, and Asia Minor, North Africa, and Europe, the Bible remained the single document that held the "people of the book" together. It is good to look more closely at that history. Although we do have much information about the early Jews from Babylonian, Persian, Egyptian, Coptic, Greek, and Latin sources, obviously the Bible itself gives the fullest account of the history, literature, and theology of the Jews.

Jewish history begins with the family of Abraham, and his linear descendants Isaac, Jacob, and Joseph. The word *Jew* derives from "Judah," who was the fourth son of Jacob, Abraham's great-grandson. The word *Hebrew*, also associated with both the ancient Jewish language and people, apparently derives from an earlier source, from the biblical figure of Eber (from *apiru* or *habiru* meaning "migrant," "transient"), who was the grandson of Shem, the son of Noah.

Abraham, the semihistorical patriarch of the Jews, was born perhaps in the eighteenth century B.C., in Ur of the Chaldeans (Babylonians) in southern Mesopotamia, in what is present-day Iraq. Paul calls Abraham not only the father of the Jews but of all who believe (Rom. 4:11). Abraham's father Terah brought the family from Ur to Haran in Syria. There, the Old Testament states, when Abraham was seventy-five, God (Yahweh) commanded him to go to Canaan (modern-day Israel and Palestine) and settle there. He also went to Egypt where he stayed and prospered but then returned to Canaan. When Abraham was ninety-nine, God made a *covenant* with him. Yahweh would make him the ancestor of a multitude of nations, and this covenant would persist through all generations between God and Abraham's offspring. In return, Abraham would become circumcised, as would all future generations of Jewish males on the eighth day after their birth. God also told Abraham that he and his wife Sarah (who was ninety at the time) would have a son, and in nine months Isaac was born. From this covenant came the notion of a pact between God and humankind. (The New Testament, which in Greek is "New Covenant," reflects a *new* covenant between God and the followers of his Messiah Jesus.) Abraham is presented as the first historical Jew, and he is a model of the man of faith for whom salvation for himself and his people comes through God.

During a famine, Abraham's grandson Jacob and his son Joseph migrated to Egypt. Other Jews followed, and eventually Moses, in the period of Ramses II, led the Jews out of Egypt (which is celebrated in the Passover ceremony). On Mount Sinai in the desert, God delivered to Moses the Ten Commandments; and after forty years of wandering, the Jews entered Canaan again. Thereafter, the nomadic tales recounted in the first chapters of the Bible take on a distinctly historical character as in the tenth century B.C. the Jews developed one of the powerful states in the Near East. This state extended over significant territory and had an important and famous monarchy, though the nation was frequently conquered during the next thousand years.

The rule of kings Saul, David, and Solomon (who built the first Temple) was a relatively undisturbed time of prosperity and unified power. Then, the tribes of the north formed their own kingdom of Israel, and those of the south formed the kingdom of Judah (also called "Judea" and "Yehuda"). In 722 B.C., the Assyrian ruler Sargon II captured Samaria, capital of Israel, exiled its inhabitants, and the northern kingdom of Israel disappeared along with its people, who are often called the "lost tribes of Israel." Subsequently, the southern kingdom of Judah was taken over in turn by Assyrians, by Egyptians, and, most significant of all early conquests, by the Babylonians in 586 B.C., who also destroyed the Temple. This was the first great diaspora, in which many were taken to Babylonia, as we hear in Ezekiel and Jeremiah. The Persians under Cyrus the Great defeated the Babylonians and freed the Jews in 538 B.C., permitting their return to Jerusalem, although many chose to remain in Mesopotamia. Sizeable old communities of Jews, dating directly back to the Babylonian Captivity and diaspora, lived in Iran and Iraq until 1948. The second Temple in Jerusalem was rebuilt by 516 B.C. and was to remain as the center of Second Temple Judaism until A.D. 70, when it was destroyed by Titus of Rome. After their return from Babylon, the Jews came under Greek rule and cultural influence. Later, there was a period of independence when in 165 B.C. Judas Maccabeus defeated the Greeks and recaptured Jerusalem. The feast of Hanukkah, which includes the lighting of candles, celebrates that victory. Later, Israel (a general name for the Jewish presence, not to be confused with the kingdom of Israel that was conquered by Sargon) came under Roman rule. In A.D. 66, the Jewish rebellion against Rome began. In A.D. 70, Titus conquered Jerusalem, destroyed the Temple, crucified thousands of Jews, and sent traditional Jews and Christian Jews into extended diaspora. By this time, however, the largest community of Jews was in Alexandria, Egypt, and spoke only Greek. Paul preached largely to the Greek-speaking Jews in the synagogues of Corinth, Thessaloniki, and Rome with the purpose of convincing fellow Jews that Jesus was indeed the foretold Messiah. By then the Jews were already widely dispersed in Asia Minor, North Africa, and southern Europe.

After Rome conquered Jerusalem, there continued to be centers of learning in Palestine, but the most important communities were in Babylonia, where Jewish academies produced the Talmud, an extensive commentary on the Bible. The Jews also migrated to central and western Europe. The golden age of diaspora Judaism occurred in Islamic Spain, under the Moors, from the eighth to the end of the fifteenth centuries. There, as philosophers, poets, and governors, Jews in Iberia enjoyed extraordinary freedom and cultural expansion. A knowledge of Aristotle and Plato in Arabic translation was present in the Spain of the Moors and Jews; indeed, a rekindling of classical philosophy came to Western Europe through Spain by way of translation under the Moors and later under Alfonso el Sabio in thirteenth-century Toledo. But in 1492, with the conquest of the Moors at Granada and unification of Spain under Isabel and Ferdinand, the Inquisition forced the Jews to convert to Christianity or go into exile. The Sephardic Jews of North Africa, Italy, southeastern Europe, and Turkey are descendents of the diaspora from Spain.

In other countries of Western Europe, the Jews suffered persistent persecution, murder, and frequent expulsion. They were expelled from England in 1290, from France in 1306, and from Germany through the fifteenth century in diverse persecutions. From Germany, they carried their native medieval German (Yiddish) to Poland and Eastern Europe where they settled, lived in ghettos, and built thriving cultures. Holland welcomed the Jews from Spain and Portugal. The eighteenth-century philosopher Spinoza lived in Holland, and the family of the English prime minister Disraeli came from that country. By the nineteenthcentury, the Jews of England, France, Germany, and Austria began to emerge from the ghettos, and there appeared Karl Marx, Felix Mendelssohn, Heinrich Heine, and Disraeli, whose price of acceptance, however, was nominal conversion to Christianity. In the twentieth century, most of the formal barriers had fallen, and Freud, Einstein, the French philosopher Henri Bergson, and other public figures were not forced into conversion. Then came the Third Reich, 1933–1945, under Adolf Hitler. During the war, the Germans under the Nazi party rounded up Jews, Slavs, Gypsies, homosexuals, and dissidents, and by 1945 some twelve million died in the camps. This broad holocaust included the execution of six million out of a worldwide population of sixteen million Jews. The centuries of diaspora came to an end for many of the surviving Jews with the establishment of the state of Israel in 1948.

**FURTHER READING:** *The Bible. The Holy Bible.* Alter, Robert. *The Art of Biblical Narrative,* 1981; *The Art of Biblical Poetry,* 1985. Alter, Robert, and Frank Kermode, *The Literary Guide to the Bible,* 1987. Gabel, John B., and Charles B. Wheeler, *The Bible as Literature,* 1985. Gros Louis, Kenneth R. R., ed., *Literary Interpretations of Biblical Narratives,* 1982.

## *Genesis* (King James Version, 1612)

The first line of Genesis, "In the beginning God created the heavens and the earth," is so rich in implication that theologies circle on its single words. Kabbalists (Jewish mystical interpreters of holy scripture) find meaning in its syllables and letters. Early Kabbalah reasoned that to create with the fiat "Let there be light," God had first to invent the verb to make his command heard; and even before the verb he had to create letters out of which words were made.

And who declared us into existence? Was it a single God or several? About the singularity or plurality of God the very first line of Genesis leaves us in grave doubt. While the King James Version (1612) says "In the beginning God created the heavens and the earth," the word translated as God is in Hebrew *Elohim,* meaning Gods; *El* is God, *Elohim* is Gods; the suffix *ohim* pluralizes the noun. To counter a plural translation of Elohim, textual redactors used the singular form of *bara,* the verb for created, thereby suggesting a singular subject of the verb, that is one God, not several. Linguistic and theological explanations have been given to explain away this discrepancy, but it is clear that in earlier versions of Genesis (or in its immediate sources in Mesopotamia), the creator was multiple. As polytheism gave way to monotheism, the Hebrew verb was altered to its singular form to save the emerging tenet of monotheism. However, the invisible editors forgot to put God in the singular form and hence the endless ambiguity. Elsewhere in the Bible when the word *Elohim* is used, as in the Psalms, it means Gods. In most cases, the translation into other languages again disguises the existence of several gods by translating *Elohim* as "masters."

These fascinating questions abound in every line. Genesis (a Greek word meaning "born" or "beginning" given by the Septuagint translators) is the first book of the Torah or Pentateuch (Greek for "five books"), and the five books are traditionally attributed to Moses—although Moses' death is described in Deuteronomy (fifth book of Pentateuch). To explain

Moses' foresightful knowledge of his death, conservative explicators attribute the passage to later editorial insertions, thus acknowledging a tampering with holy text. In reality, all authorial names in the Old Testament, New Testament, and Apocrypha are probably pseudepigraphical, that is, false ascriptions, with the exception of Paul (Saul), for whom half the letters ascribed to him are surely by him. But for purposes of reference, we will speak of the authors by their traditional names.

Genesis gives us two versions of creation: the Elohist one known as the E document in which God is Elohim; and the Yahwist one known as the J document in which God is Yahweh or simply YHWH (in Hebrew only the consonants are written). Formerly, Yahweh was translated as Jehovah. In Gen. 1–2:4a, Elohim creates the world in six days and then, despite his omnipotence, rests on the seventh day. In the second version of the creation, beginning with Gen. 2:4b, Yahweh creates the earth and heavens in a single day and on that same day forms a man out of the dust of the earth, breathes life into his nostrils, and also builds his abode in Eden. From Adam, Eve is made. Eve, hungry for knowledge, chooses the forbidden fruit, yielding to disobedience and sin, and ending innocence. Woman has in the Judeo-Christian tradition been the symbol of temptation, evil, man's downfall, and death. However, the later Gnostics (from *gnosis* in Greek, meaning "knowledge") held that Eve, urged on by the "good serpent" who was the first incarnation of the "luminous Jesus," gave us knowledge. So in Gnosticism, woman was not sinful but heroically good like Prometheus who gave us fire. From these first profound and complex passages of the Hebrew Bible, and all the later conflicting interpretations, we see the future shape of Western thought and values, as Greek antiquity gave way to Judeo-Christian religious hegemony.

We do not know when Genesis was written down, but the Pentateuch, of which Genesis is book one, existed in some form when the Jews returned from Babylonian Captivity (597–538 B.C.). It is speculated that the oral material for the Yahwist version of Genesis may be from the period of the Judges and was recorded in a narrative during the first years of the Monarchy in the tenth century B.C. The Elohist version is perhaps from the ninth or eighth century B.C. Although Genesis appears at the beginning of Jewish and Christian Bibles and deals with the earliest figures and events of the Jews, several prophetic books were composed before Genesis. The Dutch philosopher Baruch Spinoza believed that Ezra (fifth century B.C.) gathered disparate stories of the creation together, leaving the book of Genesis unfinished and therefore jumbled. Its present form dates probably from the third century B.C., making it one of the last books of the Bible in its present composition.

**FURTHER READING:** Genesis. Clines, D. J. A. *The Theme of the Pentateuch,* 1978. Fokkelman, J. P. *Narrative Art in Genesis,* 1975. Jacob, Brenno. *The First Book of the Bible: Genesis,* 1974. Sandmel, Samuel. *The Hebrew Scriptures,* 1963.

## The Creation of the World

**Genesis** (1:1–2:3)

In the beginning God created the heaven and the earth. And the earth was without form, and void; and darkness was upon the face of the deep. And the Spirit of God moved upon the face of the waters. And God said, "Let there be light": and there was light. And God saw the light, that it was good: and God divided the light from the darkness. And God called the light Day, and the darkness he called Night. And the evening and the morning were the first day.

And God said, "Let there be a firmament in the midst of the waters, and let it divide the waters from the waters." And God made the firmament, and divided the waters which were under the firmament from the waters which were above the firmament: and it was so. And God called the firmament Heaven. And the evening and the morning were the second day.

And God said, "Let the waters under the heaven be gathered together unto one place, and let the dry land appear": and it was so. And God called the dry land Earth; and the gathering together of the waters called he Seas: and God saw that it was good. And God said, "Let the earth bring forth grass, the herb yielding seed, and the fruit tree yielding fruit after his kind, whose seed is in itself, upon the earth": and it was so. And the earth brought forth grass, and herb yielding seed after his kind, and the tree yielding fruit, whose seed was in itself, after his kind: and God saw that it was good. And the evening and the morning were the third day.

And God said: "Let there be lights in the firmament of the heaven to divide the day from the night; and let them be for signs, and for seasons, and for days, and years; and let them be for lights in the firmament of the heaven to give light upon the earth." And it was so. And God made two great lights; the greater light to rule the day, and the lesser light to rule the night: he made the stars also. And God set them in the firmament of the heaven to give light upon the earth. And to rule over the day and over the night, and to divide the light from the darkness: and God saw that it was good. And the evening and the morning were the fourth day.

And God said, "Let the waters bring forth abundantly the moving creature that hath life, and fowl that may fly above the earth in the open firmament of heaven." And God created great whales, and every living creature that moveth, which the waters brought forth abundantly, after their kind, and every winged fowl after his kind: and God saw that it was good. And God blessed them, saying, "Be fruitful, and multiply, and fill the waters in the seas, and let fowl multiply in the earth." And the evening and the morning were the fifth day.

And God said, "Let the earth bring forth the living creature after his kind, cattle, and creeping thing, and beast of the earth after his kind": and it was so. And God made the beast of the earth after his kind, and cattle after their kind, and every thing that creepeth upon the earth after his kind: and God saw that it was good.

And God said, "Let us make man in our image, after our likeness: and let them have dominion over the fish of the sea, and over the fowl of the air, and over the cattle, and over all the earth, and over every creeping thing that creepeth upon the earth." So God created man in his own image, in the image of God created he him; male and female created he them. And God blessed them, and God said unto them, "Be fruitful, and multiply, and replenish the earth, and subdue it: and have dominion over the fish of the sea, and over the fowl of the air, and over every living thing that moveth upon the earth." And God said, "Behold, I have given you every herb bearing seed, which is upon the face of all the earth, and every tree, in which is the fruit of a tree yielding seed; to you it shall be for meat. And to every beast of the earth, and to every fowl of the air, and to every thing that creepeth upon the earth, wherein there is life, I have given every green herb for meat." And it was so. And God saw every thing that he had made, and, behold, it was very good. And the evening and the morning were the sixth day.

Thus the heavens and the earth were finished, and all the host of them. And on the seventh day God ended his work which he had made; and he rested on the seventh day from all his work which he had made. And God blessed the seventh day, and sanctified it: because that in it he had rested from all his work which God created and made.


## The Second Creation

**Genesis** (2:4–3:24)

In the day that the Lord God made the earth and the heavens, and every plant of the field before it was in the earth, and every herb of the field before it grew (for the Lord God had not caused it to rain upon the earth, and there was not a man to till the ground) there went up a mist from the earth, and watered the whole face of the ground. And the Lord God formed man of the dust of the ground, and breathed into his nostrils the breath of life; and man became a living soul. And the Lord God planted a garden eastward in Eden; and there he put the man whom he had formed. And out of the ground made the Lord God to grow every tree that is pleasant to the sight, and good for food; the tree of life also in the midst of the garden, and the tree of knowledge of good and evil. And a river went out of Eden to water the garden; and from thence it was parted, and became into four heads. The name of the first is Pison: that is it which compasseth the whole land of Havilah, where there is gold; and the gold of that land is good: there is bdellium and the onyx stone. And the name of the second river is Gihon: the same is it that compasseth the whole land of Ethiopia. And the name of the third river is Hiddekel: that is it which goeth toward the east of Assyria. And the fourth river is Euphrates.

And the Lord God took the man, and put him into the garden of Eden to dress it and to keep it. And the Lord God commanded the man, saying, "Of every tree of the garden thou mayest freely eat: but of the tree of the knowledge of good and evil, thou shalt not eat of it: for in the day that thou eatest thereof thou shalt surely die."

And the Lord God said, "It is not good that the man should be alone; I will make him a help meet for him." And out of the ground the Lord God formed every beast of the field, and every fowl of the air; and brought them unto Adam to see what he would call them: and whatsoever Adam called every living creature, that was the name thereof. And Adam gave names to all cattle, and to the fowl of the air, and to every beast of the field; but for Adam there was not found a help meet for him. And the Lord God caused a deep sleep to fall upon Adam, and he slept: and he took one of his ribs, and closed up the flesh instead thereof; and the rib, which the Lord God had taken from man, made he a woman, and brought her unto the man.

And Adam said,

"This is now bone of my bones,
      and flesh of my flesh:
She shall be called Woman,
      because she was taken out of Man."

Therefore shall a man leave his father and his mother, and shall cleave unto his wife: and they shall be one flesh. And they were both naked, the man and his wife, and were not ashamed.

Now the serpent was more subtil than any beast of the field which the Lord God had made. And he said unto the woman, "Yea, hath God said, 'Ye shall not eat of every tree of the garden'?" And the woman said unto the serpent, "We may eat of the fruit of the trees of the garden: but of the fruit of the tree which is in the midst of the garden, God hath said, 'Ye shall not eat of it, neither shall ye touch it, lest ye die.'" And the serpent said unto the woman, "Ye shall not surely die: for God doth know that in the day ye eat thereof, then your eyes shall be opened, and ye shall be as gods, knowing good and evil."

And when the woman saw that the tree was good for food, and that it was pleasant to the eyes, and a tree to be desired to make one wise, she took of the fruit thereof, and did eat, and gave also unto her husband with her; and he did eat. And the eyes of them both were opened, and they knew that they were naked; and they sewed fig leaves together, and made themselves aprons.

And they heard the voice of the Lord God walking in the garden in the cool of the day: and Adam and his wife hid themselves from the presence of the Lord God amongst the trees of the garden. And the Lord God called unto Adam, and said unto him, "Where art thou?" And he said, "I heard thy voice in the garden, and I was afraid, because I was naked; and I hid myself." And he said, "Who told thee that thou wast naked? Hast thou eaten of the tree, whereof I commanded thee that thou shouldest not eat?" And the man said, "The woman whom thou gavest to be with me, she gave me of the tree, and I did eat." And the Lord God said unto the woman, "What is this that thou hast done?" And the woman said, "The serpent beguiled me, and I did eat." And the Lord God said unto the serpent,

> "Because thou hast done this,
>> thou art cursed above all cattle,
>> and above every beast of the field.
> Upon thy belly shalt thou go,
>> and dust shall thou eat
>> all the days of thy life:
> And I will put enmity between thee and the woman,
>> and between thy seed and her seed;
> It shall bruise thy head,
>> and thou shalt bruise his heel."
> Unto the woman he said,
> "I will greatly multiply thy sorrow and thy conception;
> In sorrow thou shalt bring forth children;
> And thy desire shall be to thy husband,
> And he shall rule over thee."

And unto Adam he said, "Because thou hast hearkened unto the voice of thy wife, and hast eaten of the tree, of which I commanded thee, saying, 'Thou shalt not eat of it':

> "Cursed is the ground for thy sake;
>> in sorrow shalt thou eat of it all the days of thy life.
> Thorns also and thistles shall it bring forth to thee;
>> and thou shalt eat the herb of the field;
> In the sweat of thy face
>> shalt thou eat bread,
> Till thou return unto the ground;
>> for out of it wast thou taken:
> For dust thou art,
>> and unto dust shalt thou return."

And Adam called his wife's name Eve; because she was the mother of all living. Unto Adam also and to his wife did the Lord God make coats of skins, and clothed them.

And the Lord God said, "Behold, the man is become as one of us, to know good and evil: and now, lest he put forth his hand, and take also of the tree of life, and eat, and live for ever—" therefore the Lord God sent him forth from the garden of Eden, to till the ground from whence he was taken. So he drove out the man; and he placed at the east of the garden of Eden Cherubims, and a flaming sword which turned every way, to keep the way of the tree of life.

## Cain and Abel

**Genesis** (4:1 – 5:5)

And Adam knew Eve his wife; and she conceived, and bore Cain, and said, "I have gotten a man from the Lord." And she again bore his brother Abel. And Abel was a keeper of sheep, but Cain was a tiller of the ground. And in process of time it came to pass that Cain brought of the fruit of the ground an offering unto the Lord. And Abel, he also brought of the firstlings of his flock and of the fat thereof. And the Lord had respect unto Abel and to his offering: but unto Cain and to his offering he had not respect. And Cain was very wroth, and his countenance fell. And the Lord said unto Cain, "Why are thou wroth? and why is thy countenance fallen? If thou doest well, shalt thou not be accepted? and if thou doest not well, sin lieth at the door. And unto thee shall be his desire, and thou shalt rule over him."

And Cain talked with Abel his brother: and it came to pass, when they were in the field, that Cain rose up against Abel his brother, and slew him. And the Lord said unto Cain, "Where is Abel thy brother?" And he said, "I know not: am I my brother's keeper?" And he said, "What hast thou done? the voice of thy brother's blood crieth unto me from the ground. And now art thou cursed from the earth, which hath opened her mouth to receive thy brother's blood from thy hand. When thou tillest the ground, it shall not henceforth yield unto thee her strength; a fugitive and a vagabond shalt thou be in the earth." And Cain said unto the Lord, "My punishment is greater than I can bear. Behold, thou hast driven me out this day from the face of the earth; and from thy face shall I be hid; and I shall be a fugitive and a vagabond in the earth; and it shall come to pass that every one that findeth me shall slay me." And the Lord said unto him, "Therefore whosoever slayeth Cain, vengeance shall be taken on him sevenfold." And the Lord set a mark upon Cain, lest any finding him should kill him. And Cain went out from the presence of the Lord, and dwelt in the land of Nod, on the east of Eden. . . .

And Adam knew his wife again; and she bore a son, and called his name Seth: "For God," said she, "hath appointed me another seed instead of Abel, whom Cain slew." And to Seth, to him also there was born a son; and he called his name Enos; then began men to call upon the name of the Lord. . . .

And the days of Adam after he had begotten Seth were eight hundred years: and he begot sons and daughters. And all the days that Adam lived were nine hundred and thirty years: and he died. . . .

# The Flood

**Genesis** (6:1 – 9:29)

And it came to pass, when men began to multiply on the face of the earth, and daughters were born unto them, that the sons of God saw the daughters of men that they were fair; and they took them wives of all which they chose. And the Lord said, "My spirit shall not always strive with man, for that he also is flesh: yet his days shall be a hundred and twenty years." There were giants in the earth in those days; and also after that, when the sons of God came in unto the daughters of men, and they bore children to them, the same became mighty men which were of old, men of renown. And God saw that the wickedness of man was great in the earth, and that every imagination of the thoughts of his heart was only evil continually. And it repented the Lord that he had made man on the earth, and it grieved him at his heart. And the Lord said, "I will destroy man whom I have created from the face of the earth; both man, and beast, and the creeping thing, and the fowls of the air; for it repenteth me that I have made them." But Noah found grace in the eyes of the Lord. . . .

Noah was a just man and perfect in his generations, and Noah walked with God. And Noah begot three sons, Shem, Ham, and Japheth. . . .

And God said unto Noah, "The end of all flesh is come before me; for the earth is filled with violence through them; and, behold, I will destroy them with the earth. Make thee an ark of gopher wood; rooms shalt thou make in the ark, and shalt pitch it within and without with pitch. And this is the fashion which thou shalt make it of: the length of the ark shall be three hundred cubits, the breadth of it fifty cubits, and the height of it thirty cubits. A window shalt thou make to the ark, and in a cubit shalt thou finish it above; and the door of the ark shalt thou set in the side thereof; with lower, second, and third stories shalt thou make it. And, behold, I, even I, do bring a flood of waters upon the earth, to destroy all flesh, wherein is the breath of life, from under heaven; and everything that is in the earth shall die. But with thee will I establish my covenant; and thou shalt come into the ark, thou, and thy sons, and thy wife, and thy sons' wives with thee. And of every living thing of all flesh, two of every sort shalt thou bring into the ark, to keep them alive with thee; they shall be male and female. Of fowls after their kind, and of cattle after their kind, of every creeping thing of the earth after his kind, two of every sort shall come unto thee, to keep them alive. And take thou unto thee of all food that is eaten, and thou shalt gather it to thee; and it shall be for food for thee, and for them." Thus did Noah; according to all that God commanded him, so did he. And the Lord said unto Noah, "Come thou and all thy house into the ark; for thee have I seen righteous before me in this generation. Of every clean beast thou shalt take to thee by sevens, the male and his female; and of beasts that are not clean by two, the male and his female. Of fowls also of the air by sevens, the male and the female; to keep seed alive upon the face of all the earth. For yet seven days, and I will cause it to rain upon the earth forty days and forty nights; and every living substance that I have made will I destroy from off the face of the earth."

And Noah did according unto all that the Lord commanded him. And Noah went in, and his sons, and his wife, and his sons' wives with him, into the ark, because of the waters of the flood. Of clean beasts, and of beasts that are not clean, and of fowls, and of every thing that creepeth upon the earth, there went in two and two unto Noah into the ark, the male and the female, as God had commanded Noah. And it came to pass after seven days of Noah's life in the second month, the seventeenth day of the month, the same day were all the fountains of the great deep broken up, and the windows of heaven were opened. And the waters prevailed, and were increased greatly upon the earth; and the ark went upon the face of the waters. And the waters prevailed exceedingly upon the earth; and all the high hills, that were under the whole heaven, were covered. Fifteen cubits upward did the waters prevail; and the mountains were covered. And all flesh died that moved upon the earth, both of fowl, and of cattle, and of beast, and of every creeping thing that creepeth upon the earth, and every man. All in whose nostrils was the breath of life, of all that was in the dry land, died. And every living substance was destroyed which was upon the face of the ground, both man, and cattle, and the creeping things, and the fowl of the heaven; and they were destroyed from the earth: and Noah only remained alive, and they that were with him in the ark. And the waters prevailed upon the earth a hundred and fifty days.

And God remembered Noah, and every living thing, and all the cattle that was with him in the ark: and God made a wind to pass over the earth, and the waters assuaged. The fountains also of the deep and the windows of heaven were stopped, and the rain from heaven was restrained; and the waters returned from off the earth continually: and after the end of the hundred and fifty days the waters were abated. And the ark rested in the seventh month, on the seventeenth day of the month, upon the mountains of Ararat. And the waters decreased continually until the tenth month: in the tenth month, on the first day of the month, were the tops of the mountains seen.

And it came to pass at the end of forty days that Noah opened the window of the ark which he had made: and he sent forth a raven, which went forth to and fro, until the waters were dried up from off the earth. Also he sent forth a dove from him, to see if the waters were abated from off the face of the ground; but the dove found no rest for the sole of her foot, and she returned unto him into the ark, for the waters were on the face of the whole earth: then he put forth his hand, and took her, and pulled her in unto him into the ark. And he stayed yet other seven days; and again he sent forth the dove out of the ark; and the dove came in to him in the evening; and, lo, in her mouth was an olive leaf plucked off: so Noah knew that the waters were abated from off the earth. And he stayed yet other seven days; and sent forth the dove; which returned not again unto him any more.

And it came to pass in the six hundredth and first year, in the first month, the first day of the month, the waters were dried up from off the earth: and Noah removed the covering of the ark, and looked, and, behold the face of the ground was dry. And in the second month, on the seven and twentieth day of the month, was the earth dried. And God spoke unto Noah, saying, "Go forth of the ark, thou, and thy wife, and thy sons, and thy sons' wives with thee. Bring forth with thee every living thing that is with thee, of all flesh, both of fowl, and of cattle, and of every creeping thing that creepeth upon the earth; that they may breed abundantly in the earth, and be fruitful, and multiply upon the earth." And Noah went forth, and his sons, and his wife, and his sons' wives with him. Every beast, every creeping thing, and every fowl, and whatsoever creepeth upon the earth, after their kinds, went forth out of the ark.

And Noah builded an altar unto the Lord; and took of every clean beast, and of every clean fowl, and offered burnt offerings on the altar. And the Lord smelled a sweet savor; and the Lord said in his heart, "I will not again curse the ground any more for man's sake; for the imagination of man's heart is evil from his youth; neither will I again smite any more every thing living, as I have done. While the earth remaineth, seedtime and harvest, and cold and heat, and summer and winter, and day and night shall not cease."

And God blessed Noah and his sons, and said unto them, "Be fruitful, and multiply, and replenish the earth. And the fear of you and the dread of you shall be upon every beast of the earth, and upon every fowl of the air, upon all that moveth upon the earth, and upon all the fishes of the sea; into your hand are they delivered. Every morning thing that liveth shall be meat for you; even as the green herb have I given you all things. But flesh with the life thereof, which is the blood thereof, shall ye not eat. And surely your blood of your lives will I require; at the hand of every beast will I require it, and at the hand of man; at the hand of every man's brother will I require the life of man. Whoso sheddeth man's blood, by man shall his blood be shed: for in the image of God made he man." . . . And God spoke unto Noah, and to his sons with him, saying, "And I, behold, I establish my covenant with you, and with your seed after you; and with every living creature that is with you, of the fowl, of the cattle, and of every beast of the earth with you; from all that go out of the ark, to every beast of the earth. And I will establish my covenant with you; neither shall all flesh be cut off any more by the waters of a flood; neither shall there any more be a flood to destroy the earth."

And God said, "This is the token of the covenant which I make between me and you and every living creature that is with you, for perpetual generations: I do set my bow in the cloud, and it shall be for a token of a covenant between me and the earth. And it shall come to pass, when I bring a cloud over the earth, that the bow shall be seen in the cloud: and I will remember my covenant, which is between me and you and every living creature of all flesh; and the waters shall no more become a flood to destroy all flesh. And the bow shall be in the cloud; and I will look upon it, that I may remember the everlasting covenant between God and every living creature of all flesh that is upon the earth." And God said unto Noah, "This is the token of the covenant, which I have established between me and all flesh that is upon the earth." . . .

And Noah began to be a husbandman, and he planted a vineyard: and he drank of the wine, and was drunken; and he was uncovered within his tent. And Ham, the father of Canaan, saw the nakedness of his father, and told his two brethren without. And Shem and Japheth took a garment, and laid it upon both their shoulders, and went backward, and covered the nakedness of their father; and their faces were backward, and they saw not their father's nakedness. And Noah awoke from his wine, and knew what his younger son had done unto him. And he said, "Cursed be Canaan; a servant of servants shall he be unto his brethren." And he said, "Blessed be the Lord God of Shem; and Canaan shall be his servant. God shall enlarge Japheth, and he shall dwell in the tents of Shem; and Canaan shall be his servant."

And Noah lived after the flood three hundred and fifty years. And all the days of Noah were nine hundred and fifty years: and he died. . . .

## The Tower of Babel

**Genesis** (11:1–11:9)

And the whole earth was of one language, and of one speech. And it came to pass, as they journeyed from the east, that they found a plain in the land of Shinar; and they dwelt there. And they said one to another, "Go to, let us make brick, and burn them thoroughly." And they had brick for stone, and slime had they for mortar. And they said, "Go to, let us build us a city and a tower, whose top may reach unto heaven; and let us make us a name, lest we be scattered abroad upon the face of the whole earth." And the Lord came down to see the city and the tower, which the children of men builded. And the Lord said, "Behold, the people is one, and they have all one language; and this they begin to do: and now nothing will be restrained from them, which they have imagined to do. Go to, let us go down, and there confound their language, that they may not understand one another's speech." So the Lord scattered them abroad from thence upon the face of all the earth: and they left off to build the city. Therefore is the name of it called Babel; because the Lord did there confound the language of all the earth: and from thence did the Lord scatter them abroad upon the face of all the earth. . . .

## Joseph, The Interpreter of Dreams

**Genesis** (40:1–41:43)

Some time after this, the butler of the king of Egypt and his baker offended their lord the king of Egypt. And Pharaoh was angry with his two officers, the chief butler and the chief baker, and he put them in custody in the house of the captain of the guard, in the prison where Joseph was confined. The captain of the guard charged Joseph with them, and he waited on them; and they continued for some time in custody. And one night they both dreamed—the butler and the baker of the king of Egypt, who were confined in the prison—each his own dream, and each dream with its own meaning.

When Joseph came to them in the morning and saw them, they were troubled. So he asked Pharaoh's officers who were with him in custody in his master's house, "Why are your faces downcast today?"

They said to him, "We have had dreams, and there is no one to interpret them."

And Joseph said to them, "Do not interpretations belong to God? Tell them to me, I pray you."

So the chief butler told his dream to Joseph, and said to him, "In my dream there was a vine before me, and on the vine there were three branches; as soon as it budded, its blossoms shot forth, and the clusters ripened into grapes. Pharaoh's cup was in my hand; and I took the grapes and pressed them into Pharaoh's cup, and placed the cup in Pharaoh's hand."

Then Joseph said to him, "This is its interpretation: the three branches are three days; within three days Pharaoh will lift up your head and restore you to your office; and you shall place Pharaoh's cup in his hand as formerly, when you were his butler. But remember me, when it is well with you, and do me the kindness, I pray you, to make mention of me to Pharaoh, and so get me out of this house. For I was indeed stolen out of the land of the Hebrews; and here also I have done nothing that they should put me into the dungeon."

When the chief baker saw that the interpretation was favorable, he said to Joseph, "I also had a dream: there were three cake baskets on my head, and in the uppermost basket there were all sorts of baked food for Pharaoh, but the birds were eating it out of the basket on my head."

And Joseph answered, "This is its interpretation: the three baskets are three days; within three days Pharaoh will lift up your head—from you!—and hang you on a tree; and the birds will eat the flesh from you."

On the third day, which was Pharaoh's birthday, he made a feast for all his servants, and lifted up the head of the chief butler and the head of the chief baker among his servants. He restored the chief butler to his butlership, and he placed the cup in Pharaoh's hand; but he hanged the chief baker, as Joseph had interpreted to them. Yet the chief butler did not remember Joseph, but forgot him.

After two whole years, Pharaoh dreamed that he was standing by the Nile, and behold, there came up out of the Nile seven cows sleek and fat, and they fed in the reed grass. And behold, seven other cows, gaunt and thin, came up out of the Nile after them, and stood by the other cows on the bank of the Nile. And the gaunt and thin cows ate up the seven sleek and fat cows. And Pharaoh awoke.

And he fell asleep and dreamed a second time; and behold, seven ears of grain, plump and good, were growing on one stalk. And behold, after them sprouted seven ears, thin and blighted by the east wind. And the thin ears swallowed up the seven plump and full ears. And Pharaoh awoke, and behold, it was a dream.

So in the morning his spirit was troubled; and he sent and called for all the magicians of Egypt and all its wise men; and Pharaoh told them his dream, but there was none who could interpret it to Pharaoh.

Then the chief butler said to Pharaoh, "I remember my faults today. When Pharaoh was angry with his servants, and put me and the chief baker in custody in the house of the captain of the guard, we dreamed on the same night, he and I, each having a dream with its own meaning. A young Hebrew was there with us, a servant of the captain of the guard; and when we told him, he interpreted our dreams to us, giving an interpretation to each man according to his dream. And as he interpreted to us, so it came to pass; I was restored to my office, and the baker was hanged."

Then Pharaoh sent and called Joseph, and they brought him hastily out of the dungeon; and when he had shaved himself and changed his clothes, he came in before Pharaoh.

And Pharaoh said to Joseph, "I have had a dream, and there is no one who can interpret it; and I have heard it said of you that when you hear a dream you can interpret it."

Joseph answered Pharaoh, "It is not in me; God will give Pharaoh a favorable answer."

Then Pharaoh said to Joseph, "Behold, in my dream I was standing on the banks of the Nile; and seven cows, fat and sleek, came up out of the Nile and fed in the reed grass; and seven other cows came up after them, poor and very gaunt and thin, such as I had never seen in all the land of Egypt. And the thin and gaunt cows ate up the first seven fat cows, but when they had eaten them no one would have known that they had eaten them, for they were still as gaunt as at the beginning. Then I awoke.

"I also saw in my dream seven ears growing on one stalk, full and good; and seven ears, withered, thin, and blighted by the east wind, sprouted after them, and the thin ears swallowed up the seven good ears. And I told it to the magicians, but there was no one who could explain it to me."

Then Joseph said to Pharaoh, "The dream of Pharaoh is one; God has revealed to Pharaoh what he is about to do. The seven good cows are seven years, and the seven good ears are seven years; the dream is one. The seven lean and gaunt cows that came up after them are seven years, and the seven empty ears blighted by the east wind are also seven years of famine.

"It is as I told Pharaoh, God has shown to Pharaoh what he is about to do. There will come seven years of great plenty throughout all the land of Egypt, but after them there will arise seven years of famine, and all the plenty will be forgotten in the land of Egypt; the famine will consume the land, and the plenty will be unknown in the land by reason of that famine which will follow, for it will be very grievous. And the doubling of Pharaoh's dream means that the thing is fixed by God, and God will shortly bring it to pass.

"Now therefore let Pharaoh select a man discreet and wise, and set him over the land of Egypt. Let Pharaoh proceed to appoint overseers over the land, and take the fifth part of the produce of the land of Egypt during the seven plenteous years. And let them gather all the food of these good years that are coming, and lay up grain under the authority of Pharaoh for food in the cities, and let them keep it. That food shall be a reserve for the land against the seven years of famine which are to befall the land of Egypt, so that the land may not perish through the famine."

This proposal seemed good to Pharaoh and to all his servants. And Pharaoh said to his servants, "Can we find such a man as this, in whom is the Spirit of God?"

So Pharaoh said to Joseph, "Since God has shown you all this, there is none so discreet and wise as you are; you shall be over my house, and all my people shall order themselves as you command; only as regards the throne will I be greater than you. Behold, I have set you over all the land of Egypt."

Then Pharaoh took his signet ring from his hand and put it on Joseph's hand, and arrayed him in garments of fine linen, and put a gold chain about his neck; and he made him to ride in his second chariot; and they cried before him, "Bow the knee!" Thus he set him over all the land of Egypt.

## *Job* (Revised Standard Version)

Job is a great work of world literature because of its intense narration, its poetry, and the complex and profound character of Job, whose duel with himself and with God remains an unfinished tale of debate and speculation. As in each biblical book, we have the problem of textual historicity: read the document as it is, or trace out an ur-text (an original) and separate it from probable additions and interpolations. In Job, these questions center on the poetry, the heart of the book, which is framed by a prose preface and prose afterward. Are the prose frames and the poetry truly related? Or is Job a book of deep human pessimism to which a later appended prose passage provides a pious ending of surrender, reconciliation, and holy reward? Is prosperous, powerful, righteous Job punished because, like Eve, he dares ask for knowledge, because he questions the justice of his unwarranted woes, and is the lesson that through silence, submission, and repentance happiness will come? Is Job the essence of impatience or patience? The vitality of this splendid, complex, astonishing poem, with its primeval darknesses, its sufferings, and its hope, has inspired every form of literature in many languages. It has given John Milton and William Blake speech. It is the dark side of Walt Whitman's Bible-inspired "Song of Myself." Its ethical dilemmas, economic and societal implications, and argument with God's bestowal of terrors and grace all leave an unfinished, unresolvable, and happily ongoing discourse.

**FURTHER READING:** Job. Gerald, Janzen, J. *Job,* 1985. Kahn, Jack. *Job's Illness: Loss, Grief and Integration,* 1975.

## Then the Lord Answered Job out of the Whirlwind (38:1–39:8)

Then the LORD answered Job out of the whirlwind:
    "Who is this that darkens counsel
      by words without knowledge?
Gird up your loins like a man,
      I will question you, and you shall declare to me.

"Where were you when I laid the foundation of the earth?
      Tell me, if you have understanding.
Who determined its measurements—surely you know!
      Or who stretched the line upon it?
On what were its bases sunk,
      or who laid its cornerstone,
when the morning stars sang together,
      and all the sons of God shouted for joy?

"Or who shut in the sea with doors,
      when it burst forth from the womb;
when I made clouds its garment,
      and thick darkness its swaddling band,
and prescribed bounds for it,
      and set bars and doors,
and said, 'Thus far shall you come, and no farther,
      and here shall your proud waves be stayed'?

"Have you commanded the morning since your days began,
      and caused the dawn to know its place,
that it might take hold of the skirts of the earth,
      and the wicked be shaken out of it?
It is changed like clay under the seal,
      and it is dyed like a garment.
From the wicked their light is withheld,
      and their uplifted arm is broken.

"Have you entered into the springs of the sea,
      or walked in the recesses of the deep?
Have the gates of death been revealed to you,
      or have you seen the gates of deep darkness?

Have you comprehended the expanse of the earth?
    Declare, if you know all this.

"Where is the way to the dwelling of light,
    and where is the place of darkness,
that you may take it to its territory
    and that you may discern the paths to its home?
You know, for you were born then,
    and the number of your days is great!

"Have you entered the storehouses of the snow,
    or have you seen the storehouses of the hail,
which I have reserved for the time of trouble,
    for the day of battle and war?
What is the way to the place where the light is distributed,
    or where the east wind is scattered upon the earth?

"Who has cleft a channel for the torrents of rain,
    and a way for the thunderbolt,
to bring rain on a land where no man is,
    on the desert in which there is no man;
to satisfy the waste and desolate land,
    and to make the ground put forth grass?

"Has the rain a father,
    or who has begotten the drops of dew?
From whose womb did the ice come forth,
    and who has given birth to the hoarfrost of heaven?
The waters become hard like stone,
    and the face of the deep is frozen.

"Can you bind the chains of the Pleiades,
    or loose the cords of Orion?[1]
Can you lead forth the Mazzaroth in their season,
    or can you guide the Bear with its children?
Do you know the ordinances of the heavens?
    Can you establish their rule on the earth?

"Can you lift up your voice to the clouds,
    that a flood of waters may cover you?
Can you send forth lightnings, that they may go
    and say to you, 'Here we are'?
Who has put wisdom in the clouds,
    or given understanding to the mists?
Who can number the clouds by wisdom?
    Or who can tilt the waterskins of the heavens,
when the dust runs into a mass
    and the clods cleave fast together?

---

1. Constellations

"Can you hunt the prey for the lion,
    or satisfy the appetite of the young lions,
when they crouch in their dens,
    or lie in wait in their covert?
Who provides for the raven its prey,
        when its young ones cry to God,
        and wander about for lack of food?

"Do you know when the mountain goats bring forth?
        Do you observe the calving of the hinds?
Can you number the months that they fulfil,
        and do you know the time when they bring forth,
when they crouch, bring forth their offspring,
        and are delivered of their young?
Their young ones become strong, they grow up in the open;
        they go forth, and do not return to them.

"Who has let the wild ass go free?
        Who has loosed the bonds of the swift ass,
to whom I have given the steppe for his home,
        and the salt land for his dwelling place?
He scorns the tumult of the city;
        he hears not the shouts of the driver.
He ranges the mountains as his pasture,
        and he searches after every green thing.

## JOB (40:15–41:34)

"Behold, Behemoth,
        which I made as I made you;
        he eats grass like an ox.
Behold, his strength in his loins,
        and his power in the muscles of his belly.
He makes his tail stiff like a cedar;
        the sinews of his thighs are knit together.
His bones are tubes of bronze,
        his limbs like bars of iron.

"He is the first of the works of God;
        let him who made him bring near his sword!
For the mountains yield food for him
        where all the wild beasts play.
Under the lotus plants he lies,
        in the covert of the reeds and in the marsh.
For his shade the lotus trees cover him;
        the willows of the brook surround him.
Behold, if the river is turbulent he is not frightened;
        he is confident though Jordan rushes against his mouth.

Can one take him with hooks,
     or pierce his nose with a snare?

"Can you draw out Leviathan with a fishhook,
     or press down his tongue with a cord?
Can you put a rope in his nose,
     or pierce his jaw with a hook?
Will he make many supplications to you?
     Will he speak to you soft words?
Will he make a covenant with you
     to take him for your servant for ever?
Will you play with him as with a bird,
     or will you put him on leash for your maidens?
Will traders bargain over him?
     Will they divide him up among the merchants?
Can you fill his skin with harpoons,
     or his head with fishing spears?
Lay hands on him;
     think of the battle; you will not do it again!
Behold, the hope of a man is disappointed;
     he is laid low even at the sight of him.
No one is so fierce that he dares to stir him up.
     Who then is he that can stand before me?
Who has given to me, that I should repay him?
     Whatever is under the whole heaven is mine.

"I will not keep silence concerning his limbs,
     or his mighty strength, or his goodly frame.
Who can strip off his outer garment?
     Who can penetrate his double coat of mail?
Who can open the doors of his face?
     Round about his teeth is terror.
His back is made of rows of shields,
     shut up closely as with a seal.
One is so near to another
     that no air can come between them.
They are joined one to another;
     they clasp each other and cannot be separated.
His sneezings flash forth light,
     and his eyes are like the eyelids of the dawn.
Out of his mouth go flaming torches;
     sparks of fire leap forth.
Out of his nostrils comes forth smoke,
     as from a boiling pot and burning rushes.
His breath kindles coals,
     and a flame comes forth from his mouth.
In his neck abides strength,
     and terror dances before him.

The folds of his flesh cleave together,
    firmly cast upon him and immovable.
His heart is hard as a stone,
    hard as the nether millstone.
When he raises himself up the mighty are afraid;
    at the crashing they are beside themselves.
Though the sword reaches him, it does not avail;
    nor the spear, the dart, or the javelin.
He counts iron as straw,
    and bronze as rotten wood.
The arrow cannot make him flee;
    for him slingstones are turned to stubble.
Clubs are counted as stubble;
    he laughs at the rattle of javelins.
His underparts are like sharp potsherds;
    he spreads himself like a threshing sledge on the mire.
He makes the deep boil like a pot;
    he makes the sea like a pot of ointment.
Behind him he leaves a shining wake;
    one would think the deep to be hoary.
Upon earth there is not his like,
    a creature without fear.
He beholds everything that is high;
    he is king over all the sons of pride."

# Songs of David (Psalms)

### TRANSLATED BY WILLIS BARNSTONE

The Psalms (Songs) is an anthology of Hebrew poems that follows the tradition in Near Eastern literature, specifically Ugaritic and Syro-Palestinian writings, of gathering together diverse poems of lament, distress, supplication, and praise for God. After the Book of Psalms, this tradition continues in the Dead Sea Scroll Thanksgiving Psalms, and the splendid pseudepigraphical[1] Psalms of Solomon and the Jewish/Christian/Gnostic Odes of Solomon. The biblical psalms also carry on a personal speech with God about the meaning of all things, earthly and spiritual, of being, death, God, and justice. The essential metaphysical questions of ethics, pleasures, life, and death are the subjects of these great poems. Dating and authorship as always are guesswork. Some psalms may go back to the period of David in the tenth and ninth centuries B.C. Most are from after the First Destruction of the Temple in 586 B.C. The frequent superscription "a psalm of David" is

---

1. *Pseudepigraphical* means false ascription. It refers to the practice of ascribing texts to the names of great biblical patriarchs and prophets so as to gain acceptance for that text into the canon as "authentic" biblical scripture. So the assignment of the Song of Songs to Solomon or the Psalms to David is an example of pseudepigraphical ascription.

a later addition. In their entirety, the psalms reflect perhaps five centuries of monologue and speech with God.

Traditionally there are 150 Psalms, divided into five books, perhaps reflecting the division of the Five Books of Moses. The collection in Hebrew is entitled *Tehillim,* meaning "Praises," from *hallel,* "to praise." Our cry of *hallelujah,* meaning "praise the Lord," also derives from *hallel.* Usually, the poems are divided into genres, and more specifically into what Robert Alter, in his essay on Psalms[2] calls "liturgical or cultic occasions," such as an annual enthronement ceremony. But Alter rejects the strict frame of genre and occasion as too limiting for author poets who may begin with a category of supplication or praise, but go well beyond formulaic utterances. In the opening lines of Psalm 121, "I lift my eyes to the mountains./ Where does my help come from?," these first words of raising one's eyes to the Lord are common. Yet in context, the lines are memorable and convey the utter trust and companionship of the speaker with the Lord, who, with eternal powers, never sleeps, guards every step, protects from sun and moon, and the shadow of death. The translations of the psalms are legion. In fact the first book published in America in English was the *Bay Psalm Book,* published in Boston. The influence of the psalms on the work of our great poets, who transformed their spirit and images (as did George Herbert, John Donne, and Gerard Manley Hopkins) is of equal import, for in their emotional range, beauty, terrible despairs, and joys, they have shaped poetry in English and many other languages. The Psalms have also been frequently set to music. A famous example is George Frederick Handel's glorious setting of Psalm 139, containing the line "If I take the wings of the morning, and dwell in the uttermost parts of the sea."

**FURTHER READING:** The Psalms. Alter, Robert, *The Art of Biblical Poetry,* 1985, chap. 5. Gunkel, Hermann, *The Psalms: A Form-Critical Introduction,* 1967.

## Song 23[1] (of David)

The Lord is my shepherd, I will not be poor.
    He makes me lie down on green pastures,
he leads me by the waters of stillness.
    He restores my soul.
In his name he leads me along a straight path.

Though I walk through the darkest valley,
    I fear no evil.
For you are with me.
    Your rod and staff, they comfort me.

You prepare a table with food before me
    in the presence of my enemies.

---

2. Alter, Robert, and Frank Kermode. *The Literary Guide to the Bible.* New York: Basic Books, 1985, p. 26.

1. The word "song" rather than "psalm" is used here. In Hebrew *shir* means "song" as in *shir hadavid,* "Song of David," or *shir hashirim,* "Song of Songs." *Psalm* is a Greek word meaning "song for a harp."

You anoint my head with olive oil,
  my cup overflows.
Only goodness and kindess will follow me
  all the days of my life,
and I will live in the house of the Lord
  through all the hours of my life.

*Song 100 (of Thanksgiving)*

Shout a happy noise to the Lord,
  all peoples of the earth!
Worship the Lord with gladness.
  Come before him singing.
Know that the Lord is God!
  It is he who made us and we are his.
We are his people
  and the sheep of his pasture.

Enter his temple gates with thanksgiving,
  and into his courtyards go with praise!
Give thanks to him and bless his name.

For the Lord is good
  and his kindness endures forever
and his faith in us goes on to all generations.

*Song 120 (of Ascension)*

In my agony I cry out to the Lord
  and he answered me.
I say: Lord, deliver me from lying lips
  and from a devious tongue.

What will be given you and done to you,
  devious tongue?
A warrior's sharp arrows
  and burning coals of the broom tree.

I am in despair, an alien in Meshech,
  and must live among the black tents of Kedar.
I have lived too long among those who hate peace.
  I want peace.
They speak. They are for war.

*Song 121 (of Ascension)*

I will raise my eyes to the mountains.
  Where will my help come from?
My help comes from the Lord,
  who made the sky and the earth.

He will not let your foot be moved.
    He who keeps you will not slumber.
He who keeps Israel
    will not slumber or sleep.

The Lord is your keeper.
    The Lord is your shade on your right hand.
The sun will not smite you by day
    nor the moon by night.

The Lord will keep you from all evil.
    He will keep your life.
He will guard your going out and your coming in
    from this time on and forevermore.

## Song 133 (of Ascension)

Look, how good and pleasant it is
    when brothers and sisters live as one.
It is like precious olive oil on the head,
    running down on the beard,
on the beard of Aaron,
    running down on the collar of his robes.
It is like the dew on high Mount Hermon,
    which falls on the mountain of Zion,
for there the Lord commanded his blessing,
    life forevermore.

## Song 137

By the rivers of Babylon, there we sat down and wept
    when we remembered Zion.
On the willow trees we hung our harps,
    for there our captors asked us for songs,
and our tormentors asked us for mirth,
    saying: "Sing us a song of Zion."

How can we sing the Lord's song in a foreign land?

If I forget you, O Jerusalem,
    let my right hand wither.
Let my tongue cling to the roof of my mouth,
    if I do not remember you,
if I do not set Jerusalem above my highest joy.

Remember, O Lord, the ways of Edomites on the day
    Jerusalem fell,
how they shouted, "Tear it down!
    Tear it down to the foundations!
O daughter of Babylon, you devastator!

Happy will be those who pay you in kind
  for what you have done to us.
Happy will be those who take your little ones
  and smash them against a rock!

### Song 139 (David to the Leader)

O Lord, you have searched me and known me.
You know me when I sit down and when I rise up.
    You discern my thought from far away.
You search out my path and my lying down
    and are acquainted with all my ways.
Before a word is in my tongue, O Lord,
    look, you know it altogether.
You hem me in, behind and before,
    and lay your hand upon me.
Such knowledge is too wonderful for me,
    so high I cannot attain it.

Where can I go from your spirit?
    Or where can I flee from your presence?
If I ascend to heaven you are there.
    If I make my bed in Sheol[1] you are there!
If I take the wings of the morning
    and dwell in the uttermost parts of the sea,
even there your hand will lead me
    and your right hand will hold me.
If I say, "Let only darkness cover me
    and the light around me be night,"
even the darkness is not dark to you.
    The night glows like day,
    for darkness is like light to you.

And it was you who formed my inner parts.
    You knitted me together in my mother's womb.
I praise you, for I am fearfully and wonderfully made.
    Wonderful are your works.
You know me altogether.
    My frame was not hidden from you
when I was made in secret,
    intricately woven in the depths of the earth.
Your eyes saw my unformed substance.
    In your book they were written.
Every day was formed for me
    when none of them yet was.

---

1. Sheol, a pit of darkness, sometimes likened to Hell or the underworld.

How precious and heavy are your thoughts, O God!
How vast is the sum of them!
If I try to count them, they are more than sand.
When I wake, I am still with you.

O that you would slay the wicked, O God,
and men of blood depart from me
who utter your name with wicked thought.
and rise up against you for evil.
Do I not loathe those who loathe you, O Lord?
and do I not strive against those who offend you?
I loathe them with perfect loathing.
I count them my enemies.
Search me, O God, and know my heart.
Try me and know my thoughts.
See if there is any grievous way in me
and lead me in the way everlasting!

# *Ecclesiastes, or the Preacher* (Revised Standard Version)

*Ecclesiastes* in Greek means "one of the church" or "preacher," and the title is derived from the Septuagint Greek.[1] The Preacher is called the son of David, meaning King Solomon, and so, like Proverbs and The Song of Songs, Ecclesiastes has traditionally been ascribed to Solomon (tenth century B.C.), but it dates from after the return from Exile (after 538 B.C.), and the affinities with Greek thought suggest a third-century text. The Greek word *ekklesiastes* is a translation of Hebrew *qohelet,* meaning "a skeptical preacher," and skepticism and darkness of death is the theme of much of Ecclesiastes. We have some portion of joy under the sun, which, in our vaporous existence, we should seize, but it will not last into the unknown future, which is vanity, meaning death. The possible suggestion of immortality in 3:21, "Who knows whether the spirit of man goes upward and the spirit of the beast goes down to the earth?" is not an Old Testament but a Greek notion, and, like New Testament John, Ecclesiastes seems to be rhetorically influenced by Greek literary forms and its particular reasoning. The agnostic or skeptical tone prevails, however, as we see in the next verse, which informs us: "Who can bring him to see what will be after him?" (3:22). Ecclesiastes is a short, stunning, universal book. The sadness, wisdom, and cautious hope of Ecclesiastes have entered popular song and world thought.

---

1. *Septuagint* refers to the Septuagint Bible, which was a translation of the Old Testament into Greek in the second century B.C. for the Jews of Alexandria who could no longer read Hebrew. The Septuagint has become the standard Bible for the Greek Orthodox and Russian Orthodox churches of Eastern Europe.

**FURTHER READING:** Ecclesiastes. Crenshaw, James L. *The Old Testament Wisdom Literature: An Introduction,* 1981. Kugel, James L. *The Idea of Biblical Poetry,* 1981.

## ECCLESIASTES 1:1-19

The words of the Preacher, the son of David, king in Jerusalem.

Vanity of vanities, says the Preacher,
    vanity of vanities! All is vanity.
What does man gain by all the toil
    at which he toils under the sun?
A generation goes, and a generation comes,
    but the earth remains for ever.
The sun rises and the sun goes down,
    and hastens to the place where it rises.
The wind blows to the south,
    and goes round to the north;
round and round goes the wind,
    and on its circuits the wind returns.
All streams run to the sea,
    but the sea is not full;
to the place where the streams flow,
    there they flow again.
All things are full of weariness;
    a man cannot utter it;
the eye is not satisfied with seeing,
    nor the ear filled with hearing.
What has been is what will be,
    and what has been done is what will be done;
    and there is nothing new under the sun.
Is there a thing of which it is said,
    "See, this is new"?
It has been already,
    in the ages before us.
There is no remembrance of former things,
    nor will there be any remembrance
of later things yet to happen
    among those who come after.

### 2:1-26

I said to myself, "Come now, I will make a test of pleasure; enjoy yourself." But behold, this also was vanity. I said of laughter, "It is mad," and of pleasure, "What use is it?"

I searched with my mind how to cheer my body with wine—my mind still guiding me with wisdom—and how to lay hold on folly, till I might see what was good for the sons of men to do under heaven during the few days of their life.

I made great works; I built houses and planted vineyards for myself; I made myself gardens and parks, and planted in them all kinds of fruit trees. I made myself pools from which to water the forest of growing trees.

I bought male and female slaves, and had slaves who were born in my house; I had also great possessions of herds and flocks, more than any who had been before me in Jerusalem.

Then I considered all that my hands had done and the toil I had spent in doing it, and behold, all was vanity and a striving after wind, and there was nothing to be gained under the sun.

So I turned to consider wisdom and madness and folly; for what can the man do who comes after the king? Only what he has already done. Then I saw that wisdom excels folly as light excels darkness. The wise man has his eyes in his head, but the fool walks in darkness; and yet I perceived that one fate comes to all of them.

Then I said to myself, "What befalls the fool will befall me also; why then have I been so very wise?" And I said to myself that this also is vanity. For of the wise man as of the fool there is no enduring remembrance, seeing that in the days to come all will have been long forgotten. How the wise man dies just like the fool!

So I hated life, because what is done under the sun was grievous to me; for all is vanity and a striving after wind.

I hated all my toil in which I had toiled under the sun, seeing that I must leave it to the man who will come after me; and who knows whether he will be a wise man or a fool? Yet he will be master of all for which I toiled and used my wisdom under the sun. This also is vanity.

What has a man from all the toil and strain with which he toils beneath the sun? For all his days are full of pain, and his work is a vexation; even in the night his mind does not rest. This also is vanity.

There is nothing better for a man than that he should eat and drink, and find enjoyment in his toil. This also, I saw, is from the hand of God; for apart from him who can eat or who can have enjoyment? For to the man who pleases him God gives wisdom and knowledge and joy; but to the sinner he gives the work of gathering and heaping, only to give to one who pleases God. This also is vanity and a striving after wind.

## 3:1–8

For everything there is a season, and a time for every matter under heaven:

a time to be born, and a time to die;
a time to plant, and time to pluck up what is planted;
a time to kill, and a time to heal;
a time to break down, and a time to build up;
a time to weep, and a time to laugh;
a time to mourn, and a time to dance;
a time to cast away stones, and a time to gather stones together;

a time to embrace, and a time to refrain from embracing;
a time to seek, and a time to lose;
a time to keep, and a time to cast away;
a time to rend, and a time to sew;
a time to keep silence, and a time to speak;
a time to love, and a time to hate;
a time for war, and a time for peace.

### 3:14–15

I know that whatever God does endures for ever; nothing can be added to it, nor anything taken from it; God has made it so, in order that men should fear before him. That which is, already has been; that which is to be, already has been; and God seeks what has been driven away.

### 3:18–21

I said in my heart with regard to the sons of men that God is testing them to show them that they are but beasts. For the fate of the sons of men and the fate of beasts is the same; as one dies, so dies the other. They all have the same breath, and man has no advantage over the beasts; for all is vanity. All go to one place; all are from the dust, and all turn to dust again. Who knows whether the spirit of man goes upward and the spirit of the beast goes down to the earth?

### 4:1–3

Again I saw all the oppressions that are practiced under the sun. And behold, the tears of the oppressed, and they had no one to comfort them! On the side of their oppressors there was power, and there was no one to comfort them. And I thought the dead who are already dead more fortunate than the living who are still alive; but better than both is he who has not yet been, and has not seen the evil deeds that are done under the sun.

### 4:9–12

Two are better than one, because they have a good reward for their toil. For if they fall, one will lift up his fellow; but woe to him who is alone when he falls and has not another to lift him up. Again, if two lie together, they are warm; but how can one be warm alone? And though a man might prevail against one who is alone, two will withstand him. A threefold cord is not quickly broken.

### 5:10–18

He who loves money will not be satisfied with money; nor he who loves wealth, with gain: this also is vanity.

When goods increase, they increase who eat them; and what gain has their owner but to see them with his eyes?

Sweet is the sleep of a laborer, whether he eats little or much; but the surfeit of the rich will not let him sleep.

There is a grievous evil which I have seen under the sun: riches were kept by their owner to his hurt, and those riches were lost in a bad venture; and he is father of a son, but he has nothing in his hand. As he came from his mother's womb he shall go again, naked as he came, and shall take nothing for his toil, which he may carry away in his hand. This also is a grievous evil: just as he came, so shall he go; and what gain has he that he toiled for the wind, and spent all his days in darkness and grief, in much vexation and sickness and resentment?

Behold, what I have seen to be good and to be fitting is to eat and drink and find enjoyment in all the toil with which one toils under the sun the few days of his life which God has given him, for this is his lot.

### 7:1–3

A good name is better than precious ointment;
    and the day of death, than the day of birth.
It is better to go to the house of mourning
    than to go to the house of feasting;
for this is the end of all men,
    and the living will lay it to heart.
Sorrow is better than laughter,
    for by sadness of countenance the heart is made glad.

### 7:15–18

In my vain life I have seen everything; there is a righteous man who perishes in his righteousness, and there is a wicked man who prolongs his life in his evil-doing. Be not righteous overmuch, and do not make yourself overwise; why should you destroy yourself? Be not wicked overmuch, neither be a fool; why should you die before your time? It is good that you should take hold of this, and from that withhold not your hand; for he who fears God shall come forth from them all.

### 7:25–29

I turned my mind to know and to search out and to seek wisdom and the sum of things, and to know the wickedness of folly and the foolishness which is madness. And I found more bitter than death the woman whose heart is snares and nets, and whose hands are fetters; he who pleases God escapes her, but the sinner is taken by her. Behold, this is what I found, says the Preacher, adding one thing to another to find the sum, which my mind has sought repeatedly, but I have not found. One man among a thousand I found, but a woman among all these I have not found.

Behold, this alone I found, that God made man upright, but they have sought out many devices.

### 8:8–13

No man has power to retain the spirit, or authority over the day of death; there is no discharge from war, nor will wickedness deliver those who are given to it. All this I observed while applying my mind to all that is done under the sun, while man lords it over man to his hurt.

Then I saw the wicked buried; they used to go in and out of the holy place, and were praised in the city where they had done such things. This also is vanity. Because sentence against an evil deed is not executed speedily, the heart of the sons of men is fully set to do evil. Though a sinner does evil a hundred times and prolongs his life, yet I know that it will be well with those who fear God, because they fear before him; but it will not be well with the wicked, neither will he prolong his days like a shadow, because he does not fear before God.

### 8:16–17

When I applied my mind to know wisdom, and to see the business that is done on earth, how neither day nor night one's eyes see sleep; then I saw all the work of God, that man cannot find out the work that is done under the sun. However much man may toil in seeking, he will not find it out; even though a wise man claims to know, he cannot find it out.

### 9:9–18

Enjoy life with the wife whom you love, all the days of your vain life which he has given you under the sun, because that is your portion in life and in your toil at which you toil under the sun.

Whatever your hand finds to do, do it with your might; for there is no work or thought or knowledge or wisdom in Sheol, to which you are going.

Again I saw that under the sun the race is not to the swift, nor the battle to the strong, nor bread to the wise, nor riches to the intelligent, nor favor to the men of skill; but time and chance happen to them all. For man does not know his time. Like fish which are taken in an evil net, and like birds which are caught in a snare, so the sons of men are snared at an evil time, when it suddenly falls upon them.

I have also seen this example of wisdom under the sun, and it seemed great to me. There was a little city with few men in it; and a great king came against it and besieged it, building great siegeworks against it. But there was found in it a poor wise man, and he by his wisdom delivered the city. Yet no one remembered that poor man.

But I say that wisdom is better than might, though the poor man's wisdom is despised, and his words are not heeded.

The words of the wise heard in quiet are better than the shouting of a ruler among fools. Wisdom is better than weapons of war, but one sinner destroys much good.

### 11:1–8

Cast your bread upon the waters,
    for you will find it after many days.
Give a portion to seven, or even to eight,
    for you know not what evil may happen on earth.
If the clouds are full of rain,

they empty themselves on the earth;
and if a tree falls to the south or to the north,
in the place where the tree falls, there it will lie.
He who observes the wind will not sow;
and he who regards the clouds will not reap.

As you do not know how the spirit comes to the bones in the womb of a woman with child, so you do not know the work of God who makes everything.

In the morning sow your seed, and at evening withhold not your hand; for you do not know which will prosper, this or that, or whether both alike will be good.

Light is sweet, and it is pleasant for the eyes to behold the sun.

For if a man lives many years, let him rejoice in them all; but let him remember that the days of darkness will be many. All that comes is vanity.

## 12:1–14

Remember also your Creator in the days of your youth, before the evil days come, and the years draw nigh, when you will say, "I have no pleasure in them"; before the sun and the light and the moon and the stars are darkened and the clouds return after the rain; in the day when the keepers of the house tremble, and the strong men are bent, and the grinders cease because they are few, and those that look through the windows are dimmed, and the doors on the street are shut; when the sound of the grinding is low, and one rises up at the voice of a bird, and all the daughters of song are brought low; they are afraid also of what is high, and terrors are in the way; the almond tree blossoms, the grasshopper drags itself along and desire fails; because man goes to his eternal home, and the mourners go about the streets; before the silver cord is snapped, or the golden bowl is broken, or the pitcher is broken at the fountain, or the wheel broken at the cistern, and the dust returns to the earth as it was, and the spirit returns to God who gave it.

Vanity of vanities, says the Preacher; all is vanity.

## Epilogue

Besides being wise, the Preacher also taught the people knowledge, weighing and studying and arranging proverbs with great care. The Preacher sought to find pleasing words, and uprightly he wrote words of truth.

The sayings of the wise are like goads, and like nails firmly fixed are the collected sayings which are given by one Shepherd. My son, beware of anything beyond these. Of making many books there is no end, and much study is a weariness of the flesh.

The end of the matter; all has been heard. Fear God, and keep his commandments; for this is the whole duty of man. For God will bring every deed into judgment, with every secret thing, whether good or evil.

# The Song of Songs

TRANSLATED BY WILLIS BARNSTONE

There are poems and there is the poem of poems. The Song of Songs, a sequence of Hebrew lyrics from western Asia, has survived for three millennia as the poetic book of books in Israel, Europe, and ultimately everywhere. This biblical poem has been given multiple titles and its speakers diverse names; it has suffered many historical interpretations, and its words have been fiddled with — as has been the fate of all biblical texts — by many redacting fingers. Yet despite centuries of alterations and intentional miscopying (for purposes of creating figures of great name, such as Solomon, or changing sensual passages), the sequence of the Song of Songs persists as the most profound and beautiful book of love poems in the world. It is the song of songs.

The Song of Songs is the quintessential document of love between woman and man, of lovers who search, join in body and spirit, and depart. In the Song are the darkness of solitude, the sensual culmination and joy of union, the despair of abandonment, and the morning landscape of reunion. Love as an emotion and state of being is its own end. Love is better than wine, stronger than death. It justifies human existence. The Song states itself in images and dramatic passion. It is naked and carries its own complexity. The texts as they are, richly impure, reworked by many hungry hands, remain candid, obverse, provocatively obscure, and startlingly wondrous poems of love. Like the greatest poems, they are devoid of certain meaning and continue after the last word, never finished, and demand and invite rereading. In their single yet cumulative sequence, their simplicity grows deep.

The Song of Songs in its present form appears to be a fragmentary love idyll, with a dramatic structure, albeit a confused one. It is the sole book of love poems in the Bible and has been the most influential book of love lyrics in the West. Although the original lyrics have no surface religious meaning, these love poems have been widely interpreted, in both Jewish and Christian traditions, as a spiritual allegory of union with the deity. We read reworkings and interpretations from early Kabbalah to the thirteenth-century *Libre d'amic e Amat (Book of the Friend and the Beloved)* by Ramon Llull, the Catalan Illuminated Doctor. The Song's strong sensual elements are normally allegorized to diminish the perception of physical lovers and to transform eros into a celebration of a mystical marriage of Israel to Yahweh in the Old Testament and of the church to Christ in the New Testament. However, despite the antisexual bias of orthodox Christianity in which original sin and carnal knowledge are equated, through the guise of the mystics and their allegorization of sexuality as a way to union with God, there has always been a place in Western literature for a celebration and candid description of physical love between the sexes. The Spanish poet Saint John of the Cross (1542–1591) wrote magnificent mystico-erotic versions of the Song of Songs in his "Spiritual Canticle" and his "Dark Night of the Soul" in which his voice is of the female lover. Saint John, a Carmelite monk, enters the mist of heresy by ignoring state and church and creating a personal mystical union of a single woman with God.

The Song's title in Hebrew is given as the "Song of Songs which are of Solomon." However, neither the title, which is an editorial superscription, nor the text itself gives us a hint of actual title or authorship. The uncertainty of title and author implies large questions of what the songs are, when they were written, and by whom. Many books of the Bible have been ascribed to great figures—Moses, David, Solomon, Isaiah, Daniel—whose presumed authorship was at one time sufficient to ensure inclusion in the canon. While tradition ascribes the Song of Songs to Solomon, the tenth-century B.C. king of Israel, the notion is discounted by modern scholars. Some claim the poems to be Hebrew versions of Egyptian popular love songs, and there is certainly an affinity with extant songs surviving from the Late Kingdom period. A common notion is that they are wedding songs, an idea that accommodates religious orthodoxy and is the same assumption of classical scholars well into the twentieth century who asserted that Sappho's passionate poems to other women were actually wedding songs addressed to the bride. In the Song of Songs, woman is primary. Her love is stronger than wine or death or a society that would oppress her. The male figure praises and the female praises, but the woman also longs and suffers. When she searches for her lover, she is stopped and beaten by the city guardians, for whom she has contempt. Their love is in the privacy of their paradise, their enclosed orchards and gardens, and their escape into the countryside and small villages. Lovers are alone, and love is the physical and spiritual god of their huge paradise.

No reliable close dating of the text is possible. It is safe to say that the poems were written between the tenth and third centuries B.C. It is probable that the poems were composed, by various hands, between the fifth and third centuries B.C. and that the variant titles of the collection as well as the names of the main speakers, Solomon and the Shulamite, are contributions of later compilers. Because of the erotic themes, the Song of Songs was not incorporated into the canon of the Hebrew Bible until after the destruction by the Romans of the Second Temple in A.D. 70, and then only over the objections of some rabbis. The extant Hebrew text offers little help as to when a poem begins and ends and who the speakers are. As for the haunting repetition of key passages and choral refrains, we do not know what corresponds to earlier lyrics from which the work was derived and what was contributed by later editors. Whatever the effect of tampering, rewriting, cutting, and fragmentation, the work survives as a perfectly intoxicating poetic sequence.

**FURTHER READING:** The Song of Songs. Alter, Robert. *The Art of Biblical Poetry,* 1985. Barnstone, Willis. *The Song of Songs: Shir Hashirim,* 1973. Falk, Marcia. *The Song of Songs: A New Translation and Interpretation,* 1990. Fox, Michael. *The Song of Songs and Ancient Egyptian Love Poetry,* 1985. Lady, Francis. *Paradoxes of Paradise: Identity and Difference in the Song of Songs,* 1983.

### Your Love Is Better than Wine (1:1–4)

Kiss me with kisses from your mouth.
Your love is better than wine.
Your ointments have a good fragrance!
Your name is spread far like fragrance of oils
poured on the body
and so young women love you.
Take my hand.
We will run together.

You the king took me to your rooms.
I am happy, happy in you,
and say your love at night is better than wine.
It is right for me to love you.

### I Am Black (1:5–7)

I am black yet beautiful,
daughters of Jerusalem,
as black as Kedar's tents,
as lovely as Solomon's tapestries.
Don't look at me with scorn
because I am black,
because the sun has scorched me.

My mother's sons hated me.
They made me guardian of the vineyards
yet I failed to guard my own vineyard.
You whom my soul loves, tell me
where you graze your sheep,
where they lie down at noon.

Why should I wander veiled
among the flocks of your companions?

### Like My Glowing Mare (1:8–11)

O beautiful one, if you don't know,
go and follow the flocks
and feed your lambs and small goats
by the shepherd's tents.

I compare you to my mare
glowing among the Pharaoh's stallions.
Your cheeks tease me with earrings,
your necks with strings of jewels.
I will make gold loops for your ears,
with studs of silver.

*Between My Breasts (1:12–14)*

While the king lay on his couch
the spikenard aroma of my body filled the air.
My love is a sachet of myrrh
as he lies at night between my breasts.
My love is a cluster of henna blossoms
in the desert orchard of Ein Gedi.

*King and Woman (1:15–17)*

You are beautiful, my darling.
You are beautiful,
your eyes are doves.

You are beautiful, my lover.
You are beautiful,
our couch is the fresh grass,
the beams of our house are cedar,
our rafters are the cypress.

*Lily (2:1–2)*

I am a rose of Sharon,
a lily of the valleys.

A lily among thorns
is my love among women.

*In the Rooms (2:3–7)*

An apple tree among young men.
I delight in his shadow

and lie before him
and his fruit is sweet to my tongue.

He led me to his drinking room
and his banner over me is love.

Feed me your raisins,
comfort me with apples,

for I am sick with love.
His left hand is under my head,

his right hand caresses my body.
O daughters of Jerusalem,

swear by the gazelles
and the deer of the hills

not to wake us
till after we have merged in love.

### My Lover's Voice (2:8–14)

My lover's voice is coming.
Hear him. O hear

him leaping on the mountains,
dancing on the hills!

My love is like a gazelle
or a young stag.

Here is he standing
behind our wall,

gazing in though the window,
peering through the lattice.

My lover answers
and speaks to me:

"Rise, my love, my beauty
and come away.

Winter is past,
the rains are over and gone.

Wild flowers appear on the earth,
the time of the nightingale has come.

The voice of the turtledove
is heard in our land.

The fig tree is grown heavy
with small green figs,

and grapevines are in bloom,
pouring out fragrance.

Rise, my love, my beauty,
and come away.

My dove, you are in the crevices of the rock,
in the recess of the cliffs.

Let me look at your face,
let me hear you.

Your voice is delicious
and your face is clear beauty."

### The Foxes (2:15)

We must catch the foxes,
the little foxes,

who are ravaging the grapes.
Our vineyards are in blossom.

### In Lilies and Mountains (2:16–17)

My lover is mine
and I am his.

He feeds his sheep
among the lilies.

Till day cools
and shadows tumble,

come stay with me.
Be a gazelle

or a young stag bounding
on jagged mountains.

### In My Bed at Night (3:1–5)

In my bed at night
I look for him whom my soul loves
and cannot find him.

I'll rise and wander in the city
through streets and markets,
looking for him whom my soul loves.

Yet I cannot find him.
The watchmen who go about the city
find me. I ask them:

Have you seen him whom my soul loves?
I barely leave them
when I find him whom my soul loves.

I seize him. I won't let him go
until I've taken him to my mother's room
and he is lying in the bed

of her who conceived me.
O daughters of Jerusalem,
swear by the gazelles

and the deer of the hills
not to wake us
till after we have merged in love.

### Solomon Is Coming (3:6–11)

Who is coming up from the sand and wilderness
        like a pillar of smoke
from burning myrrh and frankincense
        and all the powders of the merchant?

Look. It is the carriage of Solomon
        and around it sixty brave men,

sixty brave men from Israel.
      They carry swords and are expert in war.

Swords are strapped to their thighs
      against the terror in the night.
King Solomon made a carriage
      from the cedars of Lebanon.

He made the posts of silver, its backs
      of gold, its seat purple
and the interior inlaid with love
      by the daughters of Jerusalem.

Come outdoors, daughters of Zion. Gaze
      on the king with the crown
his mother gave him on his wedding day,
      the day his heart was happy.


*Your Lips Are a Thread of Scarlet (4:1–5)*

You are beauty, my love,
you are the beautiful.
Your eyes are doves

behind your veil.
Your hair is a flock
of black goats weaving

down the hills of Gilead.
Your teeth are flocks
of lambs newly shorn

fresh from the watering
trough, perfect,
with no flaw in them.

Your lips are a thread
of scarlet and your voice
is cloth of softness.

Your cheeks are halves
of a fresh pomegranate
cut open and gleaming

behind your veil.
Your neck is a straight
tower of David

built with turrets
and a thousand shields,
armor of brave men.

Your breasts are twin
fawns, twins of a gazelle
feeding among the lilies.

*Before Twilight (4:6)*

Till afternoon is cold
and its shadows blur,

I will climb over
the mountains of myrrh

and wander across a hill
of spices.

*Perfection (4:7)*

In you is beauty,
my lover, with
no stain in you.

*Come Away with Me (4:8)*

Come away with me. Let us leave Lebanon.
Let us leave the hills,
my bride.
Come down from the peak of Amana.
Let us descend the peaks of Senir
and Hermon. We will abandon
the dens of lions
and walk down the mountain of leopards.

*Love Better than Wine (4:9–11)*

You have ravished my heart, my sister, my bride,
you ravished my heart with one of your eyes,
with a single jewel from your necklace.
How tasty are your breasts, my sister, my bride!
How much better is your love than wine.
Your ointments are richer than any spice,
your lips drip like the honeycomb, my bride,
and under your tongue are honey and milk.
Your clothing tastes of Lebanon's meadows.

*My Sister, My Bride (4:12–15)*

My sister, my bride, you are a garden
enclosed and hidden,

a spring locked up, a fountain sealed.
Your cheeks

are an orchard of pomegranates
with rare fruits,

henna with, spikenard, spikenard and saffron,
calamus and cinnamon

and every tree bearing incense. From you
drip aloes

and all choice spices. You are a fountain
of gardens,

a well of living waters and bubbling springs
from Lebanon.

### Winds (4:16)

Awake, north wind and come south wind!
Blow on my garden, let the spices

be tossed about. Let my love come into
his garden and eat his precious fruits.

### Gardener (5:1)

My sister and bride, I enter the orchard and gather
        wild herbs and condiments.
I eat my honeycomb with honey, drink wine with milk.

Friends and lovers, imitate me. Drink deep.

### My Hair Is Wet with Drops of Night (5:2–8)

I'm sleeping but my heart is awake.
My lover's voice is knocking:
"Open, let me in, my sister and darling, my dove
        and perfect one.
My head is soaked with dew,
my hair is wet with drops of night."

I have taken off my garments.
How can I put them on?
I have washed my feet.
How can I dirty them now?
My lover's hand shows at the door
and in me I burn for him.
I rise to open to my love,
my hands drip with liquid myrrh,
my fingers drench perfume
over the handle of the bolt.
I open to my love
but my love has turned and gone.
He has vanished.
When he spoke my soul vanished.
I look for him and can't find him.

I call. He doesn't answer.
The watchmen who go about the city
find me.
They beat me, they wound me,
they strip me of my mantle,
those guardians of the walls!

I beg you, daughters of Jerusalem,
if you find my love
you will say
that I am sick with love.

## Her Companions (5:9)

How is your friend the prince of lovers,
O beautiful woman?
How is your friend the prince of lovers?
Why do you swear us to an oath?

## Doves by the Small Rivers (5:10–16)

My love is radiant. He is ruddy,
one in ten thousand.
His head is fine gold,
his locks are palm leaves in the wind,
black like ravens.
His eyes are doves by the small rivers.
They are bathed in milk
and deeply set.
His cheeks are a bed of spices
blowing in fragrance.
His lips are lilies,
moist with tastes.
His arms are rounded gold
inset with beryl.
His belly is luminous ivory
starred with sapphires.
His legs are columns of alabaster
set on bases of gold.
His appearance is the tall city of Lebanon,
excellent with cedars.
His mouth is luscious, made of desire,
all of him is pleasant.
This is my lover and friend,
O daughters of Jerusalem.

## Companions (6:1)

Where has your lover gone, beautiful
     woman?

He's disappeared. Where has he turned to?
Tell us. We will help you find him.

### Lilies (6:2–3)

My love has gone down to his garden
to the beds of spices,
to feed his sheep in the orchards,
to gather lilies.
I am my lover's and my lover is mine.
He feeds his flock among the lilies.

### A City with Banners (6:4–10)

Your beauty is Tirzah
or even Jerusalem
and frightening as

an army with banners.
Look away from me.
You make me tremble.

Your hair is a flock
of black goats weaving
down the hills of Gilead.

Your teeth are flocks
of lambs newly shorn
fresh from the watering

trough, perfect,
with no flaw in them.
Your cheeks are halves

of a fresh pomegranate
cut open and gleaming
behind your veil.

Sixty queens and eighty
concubines and countless
virgins are nothing

like my dove, my perfect
love who is unique. She's
the darling of her mother.

Women look at her and call
her happy. Concubines
and queens praise her.

Who is she? Her gaze
is daybreak, her beauty
the moon, and she is

the transparent sun,
yet frightening as
an army with banners.

## Walking Around (6:11–12)

I go down to the orchard of nut trees
to see the green plants of the valley,
to see if the vines are in bud,
whether the pomegranates have blossomed.
Unaware, my soul leads me
into a chariot beside my prince.

## Companions (6:13)

Come back, come back, O Shulamite,
and we shall look at you.

## Dancer (6:13)

Will you look at the Shulamite
as at a dancer before two armies?

## Your Navel a Moon-Hollow Goblet (7:1–7)

Your sandaled feet define grace,
O queenly woman!

Your round thighs are jewels,
handiwork of a cunning craftsman,

your navel a moon-hollow goblet
filled with mixed wines.

Your belly is a bed of wheat
laced with daffodils.

Your two breasts are two fawns,
twins of a gazelle.

Your neck is a tower of ivory,
your eyes are pools in Heshbon

by the gate of Beth-rabbim.
Your nose is a tower of Lebanon

facing the city of Damascus.
Your head is like Carmel,

and purple is your flowing hair
in which a king lies captive.

How calm and beautiful you are,
my happy love.

You are stately like a palm tree
and your breasts a cluster of grapes.

### I Will Climb (7:8–9)

I will climb the palm tree
and take hold of the bough.
Let your breasts be the grapes of the vine,
your breath the taste of apples.
Your mouth is choice wine,
and swallowing it smoothly
makes my lips tremble in sleep.

### Let Us Go Out into the Fields (7:10–13)

I am my lover's and he desires me.

Come, my darling,
let us go out into the fields
and spend the night in villages.
Let us wake early and go to the vineyards
and see if the vine is in blossom,
if the new grape-bud is open
and the pomegranates are in bloom.

There I will give you my love.
The mandrakes will spray aroma,
and over our door will be precious fruit,
all the new and old
that I have saved for you, my darling.

### If You Were My Brother (8:1–4)

Oh, if you were my brother
who sucked my mother's breasts!

When I find you in the streets
or country, unashamed

I will kiss you
and no one will despise me.

I'll take you to my mother's home
and into her room

where she conceived me
and there you'll instruct me.

I'll give you spiced wine to drink,
the juice of my pomegranates.

Your left hand lies under my head,
your right hand caresses my body.

O daughters of Jerusalem,
swear by the deer of the hills

not to wake us
till after we have merged in love.

### Companions (8:5)

Who is coming out of the desert wilderness,
leaning on her lover?

### Under the Apple Tree (8:5)

Under the apple tree I aroused you
and you woke to me
where your mother was in labor,
where she who bore you was in labor.

### A Seal on Your Heart (8:6–7)

Set me as a seal on your heart,
as a seal on your arm,
for love is strong as death.
Jealousy is cruel as the grave.
Its flashes are flashes of fire,
a flame of God.
Many waters cannot quench love,
rivers cannot drown it.
If a man measured love
by all the wealth of his house,
he would be utterly scorned.

### The Brothers (7:8–9)

We have a young sister
and she has no breasts.
What will we do for our sister
when they ask for her hand?
If she is a wall
we will build turrets of silver on her.
If she is a door
we will enclose her with boards of cedar.

### Her Towers (7:10)

I am a wall
and my breasts are towers,
and in his eyes
I bring peace.

### Her Vineyard (7:11–12)

Solomon has a vineyard at Baal-hamon.
He let out the vines to the guardians,

each bringing a thousand pieces of silver
for the good fruit.

My own vineyard is about me.
You may keep the thousand, my king,
and use two hundred to pay off the guardians.

*The King Begs (7:13)*

You who live in the gardens,
my friends are listening for your voice.
Let me hear it too.

*Come, Young Stag (7:14)*

Hurry, my darling!
and be like a gazelle
or a young stag
upon my mountain of spices.

## *Isaiah* (Revised Standard Version)

Isaiah, the son of Amos, was a prophet who lived in Jerusalem. He prophesied largely about the city and Judah during the period 740 to 687 B.C. But
the book of Isaiah contains the philosophy and writings of at least three distinct figures: Isaiah 1–39, Deutero-Isaiah 40–55 (553–539 B.C.), and Trito-Isa-
iah 55–66, who was post-Exilic, that is, after the return of the Jews from Babylon in 538 B.C. For the sake of general statements, however, it is convenient as
well as traditional to speak of the book and author simply as Isaiah. Isaiah is
one of the most powerful and glorious poets in the Bible—especially First
and Second Isaiah. First Isaiah is one of the supreme rhetorical and lyrical poets of the Bible; Second Isaiah is sumptuous and sonorous in speech, passionate in his hope of return to Zion. To gain return, he says,

I will open rivers in high places,
    and fountains in the midst of the valleys;
I will make the wilderness a pool of water,
    and the dry land springs of water. (41:18)

Isaiah has many voices, of wrath and promised punishment, but also
one that reveals his hopes for an era of Edenic peace when war will be
gone and people and beast all live in harmony. Among his most famous
passages are 9:5–7, in which he states "a child is born" who will be called
"Wonderful Counselor, Mighty God, Everlasting Father, Prince of Peace."
Such messianic prediction is central to the Hebrew Bible. In this context,
Isaiah informs us that the Prince's dominion in peace will be to ensure
forever the integrity and power of the throne of David, that is, the stability
and continuation of the Jewish monarchy in Jerusalem. Standard Chris-

tian typological interpretation of this passage informs us that Isaiah is predicting the coming of the later rabbinical messiah, Jesus Christ.

**FURTHER READING:** Isaiah. Ackroyd, Peter R. *Exile and Restoration,* 1968. Blenkinsopp, Joseph. *A History of Prophecy in Israel,* 1983. Delitzch, F. J. *Biblical Commentary on the 5-Prophesies of Isaiah,* 1980. Fishbane, Michael. *Biblical Interpretation in Ancient Israel,* 1985. Kaiser, Otto. *Isaiah 1–12: A Commentary,* 1983.

## The People Who Walked in Darkness

*9:2–3*

The people who walked in darkness
    have seen a great light;
those who dwelt in a land of deep darkness,
    on them has light shined.
Thou hast multiplied the nation,
    thou hast increased its joy;
they rejoice before thee
    as with joy at the harvest,
    as men rejoice when they divide the spoil.

*9:6–7*

For to us a child is born,
    to us a son is given;
and the government will be upon his shoulder,
    and his name will be called
"Wonderful Counselor, Mighty God,
    Everlasting Father, Prince of Peace."
Of the increase of his government and of peace
    there will be no end,
upon the throne of David, and over his kingdom,
    to establish it, and to uphold it
with justice and with righteousness
    from this time forth and for evermore.
The zeal of the LORD of hosts will do this.

*11:1–9*

There shall come forth a shoot from the stump of Jesse,
    and a branch shall grow out of his roots.
And the Spirit of the LORD shall rest upon him,
    the spirit of wisdom and understanding,
    the spirit of counsel and might,
    the spirit of knowledge and the fear of the LORD.
And his delight shall be in the fear of the LORD.

He shall not judge by what his eyes see,
    or decide by what his ears hear;
but with righteousness he shall judge the poor,
    and decide with equity for the meek of the earth;

and he shall smite the earth with the rod of his mouth,
   and with the breath of his lips he shall slay the wicked.
Righteousness shall be the girdle of his waist,
   and faithfulness the girdle of his loins.

The wolf shall dwell with the lamb,
   and the leopard shall lie down with the kid,
and the calf and the lion and the fatling together,
   and a little child shall lead them.
The cow and the bear shall feed;
      their young shall lie down together;
   and the lion shall eat straw like the ox.
The sucking child shall play over the hole of the asp,
   and the weaned child shall put his hand on the adder's den.
They shall not hurt or destroy
   in all my holy mountain;
for the earth shall be full of the knowledge of the LORD
   as the waters cover the sea.

## *Daniel* (Revised Standard Version)

The Daniel of the book that bears his name lived in the days of the last Babylonian kings Nebuchadnezzar and Belshazzar. The book attributed to him contains stories, parables, dream interpretations, and apocalyptic visions. Earlier figures may be the source of the "wise and just" Daniel, such as Dan'l in the fourteenth-century B.C. Ugaritic epic *Aqhat*. Written in Hebrew and Aramaic, Daniel has been called a diaspora novel. The first half contains six amazing court tales about Daniel and his three friends Hananiah, Mishael, and Azariah (Shadrach, Meschach, and Abednego), who were to be tested by fire. Astoundingly, Daniel has such power through his faith and God's intervention that he can read a Babylonian king's mind and interpret his dream and also survive unharmed in a Persian king's den of lions; as a result, each monarch acknowledges the power and superiority of Daniel's living god. Like Joseph, the interpreter of dreams who succeeds in rising high in the Egyptian court by explaining the Pharaoh's dream, Daniel, also an exile, interprets his monarch's dreams and is similarly favored with high station. Then follows the second section with dreams and visions, which includes the persecution and salvation of Jews in Jerusalem under Antiochus IV Epiphanes in the second century B.C.

Daniel is another book whose authorship and period are steeped in controversy. A sixth-century historian by Jewish designation, and prophet by Christian regard, he speaks in detail about many events in the third and second centuries B.C., such as third-century wars between the Ptolemaic and Selucid empires, and his historical writing extends to the second-century Maccabean revolt. Modern scholarship dates the bulk of Daniel early in the second century B.C. It was anciently common to predate a text and attribute it to an earlier great figure, thereby giving it authority and a possible place in the canon by appearing to predict what historically had actually occurred. So, while the chapters of Daniel concerning Babylon may have been composed by a sixth-century author, that same author could only by miracle have had foreknowledge of events described in the text that took place three and four centuries later. It is probable that there is more than one author to Daniel or that a book, based on earlier texts, was composed much later than that of the traditional Daniel, by one who was willing to suppress his own name for inclusion of his work in the holy Bible. The huge amount of scriptures from the Judeo-Christian intertestamental period, similarly pseudepigraphical and often of insuperable beauty and imagination, attests to the practice of predating work and authorship for canonical acceptance. The book of Daniel as we have it, which some commentators suggest was written between 167 B.C. and 164 B.C., is a book of divination and a precursor of the apocalyptic vision in Revelation. It also announces the good news of God's triumphant intervention on behalf of his people as earlier he intervened to save Daniel's three friends from the furnace. God, following a timetable of events, will bring those who serve the cause of justice and righteousness the kingdom of Heaven. As the latest book of the Hebrew Bible, Daniel, close to the apocalyptic scriptures of the intertestament period and Revelation itself, is a bridge to the New Testament.

**FURTHER READING:** Daniel. di Lella, A. A. *Introduction to The Book of Daniel,* 1978.


## Nebuchadnezzar's Dream

*2:1–19*

In the second year of the reign of Nebuchadnezzar, Nebuchadnezzar had dreams; and his spirit was troubled, and his sleep left him. Then the king commanded that the magicians, the enchanters, the sorcerers, and the Chaldeans be summoned, to tell the king his dreams. So they came in and stood before the king.

And the king said to them, "I had a dream, and my spirit is troubled to know the dream."

Then the Chaldeans said to the king, "O king, live for ever! Tell your servants the dream, and we will show the interpretation."

The king answered the Chaldeans, "The word from me is sure: if you do not make known to me the dream and its interpretation, you shall be torn limb from limb, and your houses shall be laid in ruins. But if you show the dream and its interpretation, you shall receive from me gifts and rewards and great honor. Therefore show me the dream and its interpretation."

They answered a second time, "Let the king tell his servants the dream, and we will show its interpretation."

The king answered, "I know with certainty that you are trying to gain time, because you see that the word from me is sure that if you do not make the dream known to me, there is but one sentence for you. You have agreed to speak lying and corrupt words before me till the times change. Therefore tell me the dream, and I shall know that you can show me its interpretation."

The Chaldeans answered the king, "There is not a man on earth who can meet the king's demand; for no great and powerful king has asked such a thing of any magician or enchanter or Chaldean. The thing that the king asks is difficult, and none can show it to the king except the gods, whose dwelling is not with flesh."

Because of this the king was angry and very furious, and commanded that all the wise men of Babylon be destroyed. So the decree went forth that the wise men were to be slain, and they sought Daniel and his companions to slay them.

Then Daniel replied with prudence and discretion to Arioch, the captain of the king's guard, who had gone out to slay the wise men of Babylon; he said to Arioch, the king's captain, "Why is the decree of the king so severe?"

Then Arioch made the matter known to Daniel. And Daniel went in and besought the king to appoint him a time, that he might show to the king the interpretation.

Then Daniel went to his house and made the matter known to Hananiah, Mishael, and Azariah, his companions, and told them to seek mercy of the God of heaven concerning this mystery, so that Daniel and his companions might not perish with the rest of the wise men of Babylon. Then the mystery was revealed to Daniel in a vision of the night. Then Daniel blessed the God of heaven.

### 2:24–29

Therefore Daniel went in to Arioch, whom the king had appointed to destroy the wise men of Babylon; he went and said thus to him, "Do not destroy the wise men of Babylon; bring me in before the king, and I will show the king the interpretation."

Then Arioch brought in Daniel before the king in haste, and said thus to him: "I have found among the exiles from Judah a man who can make known to the king the interpretation."

The king said to Daniel, whose name was Belteshazzar, "Are you able to make known to me the dream that I have seen and its interpretation?"

Daniel answered the king, "No wise men, enchanters, magicians, or astrologers can show to the king the mystery which the king has asked, but there is a God in heaven who reveals mysteries, and he has made known to King Nebuchadnezzar what will be in the latter days. Your dream and the visions of your head as you lay in bed are these:

"To you, O king, as you lay in bed came thoughts of what would be hereafter, and he who reveals mysteries made known to you what is to be.

### 2:31–49

"You saw, O king, and behold, a great image. This image, mighty and of exceeding brightness, stood before you, and its appearance was frightening. The head of this image was of fine gold, its breast and arms of silver, its belly and thighs of bronze, its legs of iron, its feet partly of iron and partly of clay.

"As you looked, a stone was cut out by no human hand, and it smote the image on its feet of iron and clay, and broke them in pieces; then the iron, the clay, the bronze, the silver, and the gold, all together were broken in pieces, and became like the chaff of the summer threshing floors; and the wind carried them away, so that not a trace of them could be found. But the stone that struck the image became a great mountain and filled the whole earth.

"This was the dream; now we will tell the king its interpretation. You, O king, the king of kings, to whom the God of heaven has given the kingdom, the power, and the might, and the glory, and into whose hand he has given, wherever they dwell, the sons of men, the beasts of the field, and the birds of the air, making you rule over them all—you are the head of gold. After you shall arise another kingdom inferior to you, and yet a third kingdom of bronze, which shall rule over all the earth. And there shall be a fourth kingdom, strong as iron, because iron breaks to pieces and shatters all things; and like iron which crushes, it shall break and crush all these.

"And as you saw the feet and toes partly of potter's clay and partly of iron, it shall be a divided kingdom; but some of the firmness of iron shall be in it, just as you saw iron mixed with the miry clay. And as the toes of the feet were partly iron and partly clay, so the kingdom shall be partly strong and partly brittle. As you saw the iron mixed with miry clay, so they will mix with one another in marriage, but they will not hold together, just as iron does not mix with clay.

"And in the days of those kings the God of heaven will set up a kingdom which shall never be destroyed, nor shall its sovereignty be left to another people. It shall break in pieces all these kingdoms and bring them to an end, and it shall stand for ever; just as you saw that a stone was cut from a mountain by no human hand, and that it broke in pieces the iron, the bronze, the clay, the silver, and the gold. A great God has made known to the king what shall be hereafter. The dream is certain, and its interpretation sure."

Then King Nebuchadnezzar fell upon his face, and did homage to Daniel, and commanded that an offering and incense be offered up to him.

The king said to Daniel, "Truly, your God is God of gods and Lord of kings, and a revealer of mysteries, for you have been able to reveal this mystery."

Then the king gave Daniel high honors and many great gifts, and made him ruler over the whole province of Babylon, and chief prefect over all the wise men of Babylon. Daniel made request of the king, and he appointed Shadrach, Meshach, and Abednego over the affairs of the province of Babylon; but Daniel remained at the king's court.

## The Golden Image and The Fiery Furnace

*3:1–2*

King Nebuchadnezzar made an image of gold, whose height was sixty cubits and its breadth six cubits. He set it up on the plain of Dura, in the province of Babylon. Then King Nebuchadnezzar sent to assemble the satraps, the prefects, and the governors, the counselors, the treasurers, the justices, the magistrates, and all the officials of the provinces to come to the dedication of the image which King Nebuchadnezzar had set up.

*3:4–9*

And the herald proclaimed aloud, "You are commanded, O peoples, nations, and languages, that when you hear the sound of the born, pipe, lyre, trigon, harp, bagpipe, and every kind of music, you are to fall down and worship the golden image that King Nebuchadnezzar has set up; and whoever does not fall down and worship shall immediately be cast into a burning fiery furnace."

Therefore, as soon as all the peoples heard the sound of the born, pipe, lyre, trigon, harp, bagpipe, and every kind of music, all the peoples, nations, and languages fell down and worshiped the golden image which King Nebuchadnezzar had set up.

At that time certain Chaldeans came forward and maliciously accused the Jews. They said to King Nebuchadnezzar, "O king, live for ever!

*3:12–14*

There are certain Jews whom you have appointed over the affairs of the province of Babylon: Shadrach, Meshach, and Abednego. These men, O king, pay no heed to you; they do not serve your gods or worship the golden image which you have set up."

Then Nebuchadnezzar in furious rage commanded that Shadrach, Meshach, and Abednego be brought. Then they brought these men before the king.

Nebuchadnezzar said to them, "Is it true, O Shadrach, Meshach, and Abednego, that you do not serve my gods or worship the golden image which I have set up?"

*3:16–19*

Shadrach, Meshach, and Abednego answered the king, "O Nebuchadnezzar, we have no need to answer you in this matter. If it be so, our God whom we serve is able to deliver us from the burning fiery furnace; and he will deliver us out of your hand, O king. But if not, be it known to you, O king, that we will not serve your gods or worship the golden image which you have set up."

Then Nebuchadnezzar was full of fury, and the expression of his face was changed against Shadrach, Meshach, and Abednego. He ordered the furnace heated seven times more than it was wont to be heated.

*3:21–22*

Then these men were bound in their mantles, their tunics, their hats, and their other garments, and they were cast into the burning fiery furnace. Because the king's order was strict and the furnace very hot, the flame of the fire slew those men who took up Shadrach, Meshach, and Abednego.

*3:24–30*

Then King Nebuchadnezzar was astonished and rose up in haste. He said to his counselors, "Did we not cast three men bound into the fire?"

They answered the king, "True, O king."

He answered, "But I see four men loose, walking in the midst of the fire, and they are not hurt; and the appearance of the fourth is like a son of the gods."

Then Nebuchadnezzar came near to the door of the burning fiery furnace and said, "Shadrach, Meshach, and Abednego, servants of the Most High God, come forth, and come here!"

Then Shadrach, Meshach, and Abednego came out from the fire. And the satraps, the prefects, the governors, and the king's counselors gathered together and saw that the fire had not had any power over the bodies of those men; the hair of their heads was not singed, their mantles were not harmed, and no smell of fire had come upon them.

Nebuchadnezzar said, "Blessed be the God of Shadrach, Meshach, and Abednego, who has sent his angel and delivered his servants, who trusted in him, and set at nought the king's command, and yielded up their bodies rather than serve and worship any god except their own God. Therefore I make a decree: Any people, nation, or language that speaks anything against the God of Shadrach, Meshach, and Abednego shall be torn limb from limb, and their houses laid in ruins; for there is no other god who is able to deliver in this way."

Then the king promoted Shadrach, Meshach, and Abednego in the province of Babylon.


# Jewish Apocrypha: Susanna, and Bel and the Dragon (New Revised Standard Version)

The Jewish Apocrypha designates a group of important Scriptures that survives only in Greek translation. Because a Hebrew original was not available, their authenticity could not be proved, and, although they were given a place in most Bibles, they were never fully received into the canon. Hence, their origin was "apocryphal," that is, hidden. They were found only in the Septuagint Bible, a translation from the Hebrew made during the second century B.C., for Jews who could no longer read Hebrew, in Alexandria, the greatest center of Jewish life in the Hellenistic world. Since the Septuagint was known to be a translation from the Hebrew Bible, it could be assumed that at least some of the Apocryphya, whose source texts were missing, must have had original Scripture behind them. This view was reinforced with the discovery of the Dead Sea Scrolls at Qumran in 1947. There, scattered among the major Dead Sea Scrolls, were fragments in Hebrew of the standard Apocrypha, such as Sirach (Ecclesiasticus). Along with other earlier discoveries of fragmentary Hebrew manuscripts (the Geniza finds in the Qarite synagogue in Old Cairo between 1896 and 1900), there is ample evidence to believe that not only was there a Hebrew original for some books of the Apocrypha but that certain ones, as in the instance of Susanna, were translations of Hebrew or Aramaic texts that went all the way back to the sixth-century B.C. exile in Babylon.

The Jewish Apocrypha, sometimes called the "deuterocanonical" (secondarily canonical) books, are included as a quasi-canonical supplement in the Bibles read by Jews, Catholics, and Eastern Orthodox, but not by Protestants. Consequently, we do not find the Apocrypha in the King James Version. In the Christian Bibles that include the Apocrypha, they are placed between the Old and New Testaments. Since the Hebrew, Catholic, and Greek Orthodox Bibles accept different books of the Apocrypha, the number of standard Apocrypha varies according to denomination. In the recent New Revised Standard Version (1989) many books are listed: Additions to Esther, Baruch, Bel and the Dragon, Ecclesiasticus, 1 Edras, 2 Edras, Judith, Letter of Jeremaiah, Ecclesiasticus or the Wisdom of Jesus Son of Sirach, 1 Maccabees, 2 Maccabees, 3 Maccabees, 4 Maccabees, Prayer of Azariah, Prayer of Manasseh, Psalm 151, 235, Song of the Three Jews, Susanna, Tobit, and Wisdom of Solomon. In addition to these standard Apocrypha (and 3 and 4 Maccabees have only recently been included among the standard Apocrypha), there is an enormous literature of noncanonical Apocrypha in Hebrew, Greek, Syriac, Latin, and other languages, which constitutes the majority of intertestamental Scriptures (books between the Old and New Testaments) and which are usually designated as the pseudepigrapha; among the great intertestamental works are the now famed Dead Sea Scrolls.

The two Apocrypha included in this volume are Susanna and Bel and the Dragon.

Susanna was a beautiful young woman, married to Joakim, a respected and wealthy Jew in Babylonia during the period of exile (597/586– 538/537 B.C.). She had the habit of walking in her garden every afternoon. Two elders of the community entered the garden, hid, and found Susanna (meaning "lily") bathing in her garden. The men desired her. They concocted a plot against her virtue. They rushed out and demanded that she sleep with them or they would accuse her of adultery with a young man. She refused and the elders carried out their threat. She was denounced, tried, and sentenced to death. In the end, she was saved by Daniel's intervention and wisdom, with dire consequences for her accusers. It is a marvelous story, which has been a persistent subject in Christian literature and art. The implications of this sensual tale have led to multiple moral and historic interpretations, and, like good narration, they are mere speculations, meaning that the tale must always be interpreted anew. The origin of the story, as all the tales in which Daniel is a character, is equally uncertain. It may be, as some scholars contend, a standard folk tale, with names changed. In any case, it remains a vivid wisdom tale, replete with symbolism, and one of the great short pieces of world literature.

In Bel and the Dragon, we again find Daniel the detective coming up with solutions to save the good and the faithful. Bel, equivalent to Baal, was a name for Marduk, the high god of Babylon. In Bel and the Dragon, the dragon god Bel and his priests are undone by Daniel, who immediately asserts that there is no god but the God of Daniel. With Houdini skill, Daniel slips out of life-threatening situations to prove, by his own ingenuity and the miraculous journey of God's angel, that the faith of the Jews is unique and right. This brief book, with all its charm and its fascinating, incredible plot, has a distinct ring of national and religious propaganda to it. It is not unusual for religious literature to carry on a polemic against other religions, especially when threatened, as in the Exilic setting of Bel. Despite the story's setting in Babylon of the Exile, it is believed that Bel was actually composed centuries later in the Hellenistic period. The didactic purpose of this tale may have been to set up an allegory between the temptations of Babylon (remember "the whore of Babylon" from Revelation) and the temptations of pagan Hellenism. So this popular fable of Bel and the Dragon may have been intended to counter the strong attraction to the Jews of the prevailing Greek culture.

**FURTHER READING:** Susanna, and Bel and the Dragon. Metzger, Bruce M., and Michael D. Coogan. *The Oxford Companion to the Bible,* 1993.

## Susanna (Chapter 13 of the Greek version of Daniel)

There was a man living in Babylon whose name was Joakim. He married the daughter of Hilkiah, named Susanna, a very beautiful woman and one who feared the Lord. Her parents were righteous, and had trained their daughter according to the law of Moses. Joakim was very rich, and had a fine garden adjoining his house; the Jews used to come to him because he was the most honored of them all.

That year two elders from the people were appointed as judges. Concerning them the Lord had said: "Wickedness came forth from Babylon, from elders who were judges, who were supposed to govern the people." These men were frequently at Joakim's house, and all who had a case to be tried came to them there.

When the people left at noon, Susanna would go into her husband's garden to walk. Every day the two elders used to see her, going in and walking about, and they began to lust for her. They suppressed their consciences and turned away their eyes from looking to Heaven or remembering their duty to administer justice. Both were overwhelmed with passion for her, but they did not tell each other of their distress, for they were ashamed to disclose their lustful desire to seduce her. Day after day they watched eagerly to see her.

One day they said to each other, "Let us go home, for it is time for lunch." So they both left and parted from each other. But turning back, they met again; and when each pressed the other for the reason, they confessed their lust. Then together they arranged for a time when they could find her alone.

Once, while they were watching for an opportune day, she went in as before with only two maids, and wished to bathe in the garden, for it was a hot day. No one was there except the two elders, who had hidden themselves and were watching her. She said to her maids, "Bring me olive oil and ointments, and shut the garden doors so that I can bathe." They did as she told them: they shut the doors of the garden and went out by the side doors to bring what they had been commanded; they did not see the elders, because they were hiding.

When the maids had gone out, the two elders got up and ran to her. They said, "Look, the garden doors are shut, and no one can see us. We are burning with desire for you; so give your consent, and lie with us. If you refuse, we will testify against you that a young man was with you, and this was why you sent your maids away."

Susanna groaned and said, "I am completely trapped. For if I do this, it will mean death for me; if I do not, I cannot escape your hands. I choose not to do it; I will fall into your hands, rather than sin in the sight of the Lord."

Then Susanna cried out with a loud voice, and the two elders shouted against her. And one of them ran and opened the garden doors. When the people in the house heard the shouting in the garden, they rushed in at the side door to see what had happened to her. And when the elders told their story, the servants felt very much ashamed, for nothing like this had ever been said about Susanna.

The next day, when the people gathered at the house of her husband Joakim, the two elders came, full of their wicked plot to have Susanna put to death. In the presence of the people they said, "Send for Susanna daughter of Hilkiah, the wife of Joakim." So they sent for her. And she came with her parents, her children, and all her relatives.

Now Susanna was a woman of great refinement and beautiful in appearance. As she was veiled, the scoundrels ordered her to be unveiled, so that they might feast their eyes on her beauty. Those who were with her and all who saw her were weeping.

Then the two elders stood up before the people and laid their hands on her head. Through her tears she looked up toward Heaven, for her heart trusted in the Lord. The elders said, "While we were walking in the garden alone, this woman came in with two maids, shut the garden doors, and dismissed the maids. Then a young man, who was hiding there, came to her and lay with her. We were in a corner of the garden, and when we saw this wickedness we ran to them. Although we saw them embracing, we could not hold the man, because he was stronger than we, and he opened the doors and got away. We did, however, seize this woman and asked who the young man was, but she would not tell us. These things we testify."

Because they were elders of the people and judges, the assembly believed them and condemned her to death.

Then Susanna cried out with a loud voice, and said, "O eternal God, you know what is secret and are aware of all things before they come to be; you know that these men have given false evidence against me. And now I am to die, though I have done none of the wicked things that they have charged against me!"

The Lord heard her cry. Just as she was being led off to execution, God stirred up the holy spirit of a young lad named Daniel, and he shouted with a loud voice, "I want no part in shedding this woman's blood!"

All the people turned to him and asked, "What is this you are saying?" Taking his stand among them he said, "Are you such fools, O Israelites, as to condemn a daughter of Israel without examination and without learning the facts? Return to court, for these men have given false evidence against her."

So all the people hurried back. And the rest of the elders said to him, "Come, sit among us and inform us, for God has given you the standing of an elder." Daniel said to them, "Separate them far from each other, and I will examine them."

When they were separated from each other, he summoned one of them and said to him, "You old relic of wicked days, your sins have now come home, which you have committed in the past, pronouncing unjust judgments, condemning the innocent and acquitting the guilty, though the Lord said, 'You shall not put an innocent and righteous person to death.' Now then, if you really saw this woman, tell me this: Under what tree did you see them being intimate with each other?" He answered, "Under a mastic tree." And Daniel said, "Very well! This lie has cost you your head, for the angel of God has received the sentence from God and will immediately cut you in two."

Then, putting him to one side, he ordered them to bring the other. And he said to him, "You offspring of Canaan and not of Judah, beauty has beguiled you and lust has perverted your heart.

This is how you have been treating the daughters of Israel, and they were intimate with you through fear; but a daughter of Judah would not tolerate your wickedness. Now then, tell me: Under what tree did you catch them being intimate with each other?" He answered, "Under an evergreen oak." Daniel said to him, "Very well! This lie has cost you also your head, for the angel of God is waiting with his sword to split you in two, so as to destroy you both."

Then the whole assembly raised a great shout and blessed God, who saves those who hope in him. And they took action against the two elders, because out of their own mouths Daniel had convicted them of bearing false witness; they did to them as they had wickedly planned to do to their neighbor. Acting in accordance with the law of Moses, they put them to death. Thus innocent blood was spared that day.

Hilkiah and his wife praised God for their daughter Susanna, and so did her husband Joakim and all her relatives, because she was found innocent of a shameful deed. And from that day onward Daniel had a great reputation among the people.

## Bel and the Dragon (Chapter 14 of the Greek version of Daniel)

When King Astyages was laid to rest with his ancestors, Cyrus the Persian succeeded to his kingdom. Daniel was a companion of the king, and was the most honored of all his friends.

Now the Babylonians had an idol called Bel, and every day they provided for it twelve bushels of choice flour and forty sheep and six measures of wine. The king revered it and went every day to worship it. But Daniel worshipped his own God.

So the king said to him, "Why do you not worship Bel?" He answered, "Because I do not revere idols made with hands, but the living God, who created heaven and earth and has dominion over all living creatures."

The king used to say to him, "Do you not think that Bel is a living god? Do you not see how much he eats and drinks every day?" And Daniel laughed, and said, "Do not be deceived, O king, for this thing is only clay inside and bronze outside, and it never ate or drank anything."

Then the king was angry and called the priests of Bel and said to them, "If you do not tell me who is eating these provisions, you shall die. But if you prove that Bel is eating them, Daniel shall die, because he has spoken blasphemy against Bel." Daniel said to the king, "Let it be done as you have said."

Now there were seventy priests of Bel, besides their wives and children. So the king went with Daniel into the temple of Bel. The priests of Bel said, "See, we are now going outside; you yourself, O king, set out the food and prepare the wine, and shut the door and seal it with your signet. When you return in the morning, if you do not find that Bel has eaten it all, we will die; otherwise Daniel will, who is telling lies about us." They were unconcerned, for beneath the table they had made a hidden entrance, through which they used to go in regularly and consume the provisions. After they had gone out, the king set out the food for Bel. Then Daniel ordered his servants to bring ashes, and they scattered them throughout the whole temple in the presence of the king alone. Then they went out, shut the door and sealed it with the king's signet, and departed. During the night the priests came as usual, with their wives and children, and they ate and drank everything.

Early in the morning the king rose and came, and Daniel with him. The king said, "Are the seals unbroken, Daniel?" He answered, "They are unbroken, O king." As soon as the doors were opened, the king looked at the table, and shouted in a loud voice, "You are great, O Bel, and in you there is no deceit at all!"

But Daniel laughed and restrained the king from going in. "Look at the floor," he said, "and notice whose footprints these are." The king said, "I see the footprints of men and women and children."

Then the king was enraged, and he arrested the priests and their wives and children. They showed him the secret doors through which they used to enter to consume what was on the table. Therefore the king put them to death, and gave Bel over to Daniel, who destroyed it and its temple.

Now in that place there was a great dragon, which the Babylonians revered. The king said to Daniel, "You cannot deny that this is a living god; so worship him." Daniel said, "I worship the Lord my God, for he is the living God. But give me permission, O king, and I will kill the dragon without sword or club." The king said, "I give you permission."

Then Daniel took pitch, fat, and hair, and boiled them together and made cakes, which he fed to the dragon. The dragon ate them, and burst open. Then Daniel said, "See what you have been worshiping!"

When the Babylonians heard about it, they were very indignant and conspired against the king, saying, "The king has become a Jew; he has destroyed Bel, and killed the dragon, and slaughtered the priests." Going to the king, they said, "Hand Daniel over to us, or else we will kill you and your household." The king saw that they were pressing him hard, and under compulsion he handed Daniel over to them.

They threw Daniel into the lions' den, and he was there for six days. There were seven lions in the den, and every day they had been given two human bodies and two sheep; but now they were given nothing, so that they would devour Daniel.

Now the prophet Habakkuk was in Judea; he had made a stew and had broken bread into a bowl, and was going into the field to take it to the reapers. But the angel of the Lord said to Habakkuk, "Take the food that you have to Babylon, to Daniel, in the lions' den." Habakkuk said, "Sir, I have never seen Babylon, and I know nothing about the den." Then the angel of the Lord took him by the crown of his head and carried him by his hair; with the speed of the wind he set him down in Babylon, right over the den.

Then Habakkuk shouted, "Daniel, Daniel! Take the food that God has sent you." Daniel said, "You have remembered me, O God, and have not forsaken those who love you." So Daniel got up and ate. And the angel of God immediately returned Habakkuk to his own place.

On the seventh day the king came to mourn for Daniel. When he came to the den he looked in, and there sat Daniel! The king shouted with a loud voice, "You are great, O Lord, the God of Daniel, and there is no other besides you!" Then he pulled Daniel out, and threw into the den those who had attempted his destruction, and they were instantly eaten before his eyes.

## ■ The New Testament

The New Testament is a collection of gospels, acts (a sequel to the Gospel of Luke), letters, and, like the Hebrew Bible, an anthology of distinct literary genres. Specifically, the New Testament consists of the canonical gospels, the Acts of the Apostles, the Letters, and the Book of Revelation. A gospel (meaning a book of "good news") tells the life, teachings, and death by crucifixion of Jesus Christ and is also an account of Jesus' followers, including his disciples and the crowds that traveled with this itinerant rabbi and healer around the hills of Upper and Lower Galilee, the fields of Judea, and the streets of Jerusalem. Jesus is presented in the New Testament as the Messiah, whose coming was prophesied in the Old Testament. As described in Isaiah and elsewhere in the Old Testament, the Messiah would be a salvific figure, giving his people a vision of life on earth, a special relationship with God, and the possibility of eternal life. Those who believed that Jesus was the Messiah were called Messianists. The Hebrew word *Messiah* (*Mashiah*) in Greek is translated as "Christ." So the followers of Jesus were Messianists or Christians. And Yeshua the Messiah, who was born in Israel, became known by his Greek name *Iesous O Christos*, which in English is Jesus the Christ, or simply Jesus Christ.

Jesus was born in turbulent times of rebellion against the Roman occupiers of Israel in about 3 B.C. to 7 B.C. It may seem strange to say that Christ was born before Christ, but it is now generally accepted among scholars that the date set for Jesus' birth, by Dionysius Exiguus, the creator of the Christian calendar, was off by several years. The punishment for sedition against Rome was crucifixion, and it is probable that Jesus was perceived not as a docile Jew accepting Roman rule but as an opponent. But in the form we have the New Testament, whose earliest gospel was assembled almost four decades after Jesus' death, the gospels exonerate Roman rule and justice, and by implication the later Roman church. They depict Jesus passively before the Romans at a time when fellow Jews were being killed in great numbers for their opposition. These were not the glorious days of David and Solomon, but a crisis period of despair, with desperate hope for the coming of the Messiah promised in holy Scripture to deliver the Jews on earth from their terrible foreign masters.

The New Testament does not present a people under oppressive foreign rule. The governor (actually the prefect) Pontius Pilate is depicted with such care that later in the Orthodox Church, he will attain sainthood and be called Saint Pilate. In the gospels, he washes his hands innocently of the crucifixion and orders the execution reluctantly, coerced by others but not by his own good will, which is to esteem Jesus. In reality, Pilate was a brutal master, who massacred Samaritans and Jews, and who was eventually called back to Rome because of his excesses. Similarly, the first to recognize Jesus' divinity after the execution is the centurion, the Roman officer in charge of the execution troops. Such a presentation clearly fits the political and religious agenda of a later time, but not the moment of Jesus' ministry and death.

The earliest texts of the New Testament that we have are written in Greek. Although Paul's Letters were written in Greek, the gospels of Matthew, Mark, Luke, and John are later Greek versions of earlier lost accounts, both oral and written, from Aramaic and probably Hebrew sources. The Scriptures of the Christian New Testament concern the lives of Jews who followed Jesus and Paul, who reflected one sect among other revolutionary Jewish sects, which included the Pharisees, Zealots, Essenes, and early Gnostics. The gospels of the New Testament were written by or ascribed to Matthew, Mark, Luke, and John, who are called the Evangelists. They are traditionally thought to be three Jews and a convert to Judaism (Luke), though any knowledge of the Evangelists outside of the texts ascribed to them does not have a scholarly or historical basis. Like the Hebrew Bible, the Greek scriptures of Christianity underwent countless modifications and radical restructuring as they moved from oral history to a fixed place in the canon. As for the extent to which the narration itself has a historical base, again we have essentially no source outside the gospels themselves. We do not know what scribal hands copied, redacted, and fashioned the gospels into their present narration. In a few documents in Tacitus, Philo, and Josephus, it is noted that there was a man named Jesus who was crucified by the Romans.

In the first years after the crucifixion, the Christian Jews (those who followed Jesus) were in contention with other Jews in the synagogues for dominance. Paul wrote letters to the congregations of the synagogues in Rome, Corinth, Thessaloniki, Antioch, and Athens to persuade his co-religionists to follow Christ. By the time of the destruction of Jerusalem by Titus in A.D. 70 and the subsequent diaspora of the inhabitants of the city, the division between Christian Jews and those who did not receive Jesus as Messiah became more decisive; by the second century, the separation between Jew and Christian was irreversible. But the new Christians had no Scripture of their own. The Pauline letters were not then considered holy documents. The Old Testament was the sole Christian Bible, which most of the "primitive Christians" read in the Greek Septuagint version. The New Testament gradually was assembled, but throughout the next centuries its contents were debated fiercely by the church fathers until the end of the fourth century when there was consensus. Athanasius (A.D. 293–373) set the twenty-seven books in the order we have them today. Then, after the councils of Laodicea (A.D. 363), Hippo (A.D. 393), and Carthage (A.D. 397), the Athanasian collection was accepted as canon. With the translation by Jerome (A.D. 347–420) of the Greek New Testament into Latin, and with the Old Latin version of the Old Testament, the Christians who depended on Rome at last had a complete Bible, in Latin, the famous Vulgata.

# Matthew (A.D. 80–110) Israel or Syrian Antioch (gospel)

## TRANSLATED BY WILLIS BARNSTONE

The authorship and place and date of composition of the Gospel of Matthew are matters of speculation. In the gospel itself, the writer is identified as Levi the tax collector. "Matthew" apparently is the apostolic name of Levi, given to him by churchmen in the second century A.D. Biblical scholarship describes Matthew as steeped in rabbinical reference and learning and as a Greek-speaking Christian Jew of the second generation. It is increasingly thought that Matthew was composed in the early second century rather than soon after A.D. 70, the year of the destruction of the Temple by Titus, which is alluded to in Matthew and in the other gospels. The allusion to this specific historical event of A.D. 70 is sufficient evidence to place the composition of all the gospels at least after that year. Traditionally, Matthew is placed first in the order of the gospels, but this placement is not chronological, for Matthew derives from Mark and probably from a lost sayings gospel, the so-called Q source. The Gnostic Gospel of Thomas (50–60 B.C.) found at Nag Hammadi, Egypt, in 1945, is a sayings gospel and may have been one of those sayings books of Jesus' aphorisms and parables that fed into the sources from which Matthew derives. Matthew begins with a genealogy (most certainly appended at a later date) and with the birth of Jesus. (Luke also begins with a genealogy and is followed by the famous nativity scene of Jesus' birth in Bethlehem in a feeding trough, the manger, and hence on most grounds there is as much reason for beginning the New Testament with Luke as with Matthew.) That Mark is the earliest of the gospels and a direct source for Matthew and Luke is widely accepted, and in recent years the traditional presentation of the gospels has been changed, placing Mark at the beginning of the New Testament, as in the Richmond Lattimore and the Jesus Seminar translations of the New Testament.

There are more allusions to the Old Testament in this gospel than in the others. Matthew wrote to persuade Jews that Jesus was the foretold Messiah so they might become Christian Jews. Biblical scholarship agrees that passages of extreme anti-Semitism, such as "Let his blood be upon us and upon our children!" (27:25), in which the Jews in the street shout a curse upon themselves now and on their progeny forever, are later interpolations. The agenda of the church of Rome a century after Jesus' death was not to convert Jews to believe that their Messiah had come but to persuade new Christians that neither Jesus nor his followers were really Jews and that Jews rather than Romans had executed the Jewish rabbi.

Matthew may be said to be the most aphoristic and poetic of the gospels and closest to a sayings book. This teaching book does not have the same austere plainness and drama of Mark, which is more uniformly narrative and ends abruptly at a moment of fear and ecstasy in the cave where Jesus' body has disappeared. But Matthew also has a deep pathos and conveys a sense of Jesus as a leader of the poor and the disenfranchised in an epic of hunger and hope. Matthew covers many aspects of Jesus' life and mission, including his discourse dealing with death, resurrection, and immortality (24:1–25:46). Many of the critical moments in the New Testament are fully elaborated in Matthew, including the coming of the Magi, the birth of Jesus, the baptizing mission of John the Baptist, John's arrest and execution, and the passion week scene of Jesus' arrest, crucifixion, and the risen Jesus. Matthew's most extraordinary literary and philosophical contribution is the Sermon on the Mount (5:1–7:29), including the Beatitudes (5:3–12) and the Lord's Prayer (6:9–13). Much of the material in the Sermon on the Mount also appears dispersed through the other synoptic gospels (these are Matthew, Mark, and Luke, but not John), and the Lord's Prayer, in a shorter form, also appears in Luke 11:2–4. Apart from Revelation (Apocalypse), which is the epic poem of the New Testament, the poetry in Matthew takes its place among the great bodies of world poetry.

## CHAPTER 1

*The Birth of Jesus*

*18*The birth of Yeshua the Messiah[1] happened in this way. Miryam[2] his mother was engaged to Yosef[3], yet before they came together she discovered a child in her womb, placed there by the holy spirit. *19*Yosef her husband, a fair man and loath to make her appear scandalous, resolved to divorce her secretly. *20*But as he was making plans, look, an angel of the Lord[4] appeared to him in a dream and said, "Yosef son of David, do not fear to take Miryam as your wife, for what is engendered in her came from the holy spirit. *21*And she will have a son, and you will name him Yeshua, for he will save[5] his people from their sins."

---

1. Jesus Christ.

2. Mary.

3. Joseph.

4. "Angel of the Lord" refers to "the malakh of Yahweh" or "Adonai (Lord)." "Angel" is a Greek word meaning merely a messenger, associated with Hermes, without the divine powers of Yahweh's malakh. However, "angel" has taken on meanings of divinity in biblical Greek and, in its translations, is also a word connoting great beauty and fear. A more accurate rendering would be "Yahweh's malakh" or "Yahweh's messenger."

5. The naming of the infant Messiah as "Jesus" (*Iesous* in Greek) is followed by the phrase "for he will save," which lacks sense, since *Iesous* does not mean "he will save." However, *Iesous* is from Hebrew and Aramaic *Yeshua* (pronounced Yeshua), short for *Yehoshua*, which is appropriate since *Yehoshua* means "Yahweh saves." This passage suggests either an earlier text in Hebrew or Aramaic or that the author of Greek Matthew, or of its source, had in mind Yeshua or Yehoshua for the salvific Lord and expected the readers or listeners to understand the salvific Lord when pronouncing the name Yeshua or Yehoshua.

22All this was done to fulfill the word of God uttered through his prophet Isaiah, saying:

> 23Listen.
> A young woman will have a child in her womb
> and give birth to a son,
> and his name will be Immanuel,
> meaning, 'God is with us.'[6]

24When Yosef woke from his dream, he did what the angel of the Lord told him, and he accepted her as his wife, 25yet did not know her as a wife to sleep with her until after she bore a son. And he named him Yeshua.

## CHAPTER 2

Now when Yeshua was born in Bethlehem of the land of Yehuda[7] in the days of King Herod, look, some Magi, astrologer priests from the East, came to Yerushalayim[8] 2and said, "Where is he who was born King of the Jews? We saw his star in the East and we have come to worship him."

3Hearing this, King Herod was troubled as well as all Yerushalayim, 4and calling together all the high priests and the scholars of the people, he asked them where the Messiah was born.

5And they said to him, "In Bethlehem in Yehuda, for so it is written by the prophet Micah":

> 6And you, Bethlehem, in the land of Yehuda,
> you are in no way least among the leaders of Yehuda,
> for out of you will come a leader
> who will be a shepherd of my people Israel.

7Then Herod secretly called in the Magi astrologers and asked them precisely when the star had appeared, 8and sent them to Bethlehem, saying, "Go and inquire carefully about the child. When you find him, bring me word so that I too may worship him."

9And after hearing the king they set out, and look, the star, which they had seen in the East, went before them until it stood above the place

---

6. Matthew cites Isaiah not directly from the Hebrew Bible but from the second-century B.C. Septuagint translation into Greek, which includes the Apocrypha, done for the Jews of Alexandria who could no longer read Hebrew. In the Hebrew Bible, however, Isaiah (Yeshayahu) refers to a "young woman," not a "virgin."

7. *Yehuda* is Judea.

8. *Yerushalayim* is Jerusalem.

where the child lay. *10*When they saw the star, they were marvelously glad. *11*And they went into the house and saw the child with Miryam his mother, and fell to the ground and worshiped him. Opening their treasure boxes, they offered him gifts—gold and frankincense and myrrh. *12*Then having been warned in a dream not to go back to Herod, they returned to their own country by another road.

*13*When they had gone, an angel appeared to Yosef in a dream, saying, "Awake, and take this child and his mother, and fly into Egypt, and remain there until I tell you. Herod is looking for the child to destroy him." *14*Then he woke and took the child and his mother through the dark of night to Egypt, *15*and stayed there until the death of Herod, thereby fulfilling the word uttered through Hosiah his prophet, saying,

> Out of Egypt I have called my son.

*16*Herod, seeing that he had been outfoxed by the three astrologers, was in a rage and sent his men to kill all the male children in Bethlehem and in all the coastal region, those of two years and under, according to the exact age, based on the time of the star he had ascertained from the Magi. *17*Thereby was fulfilled the word spoken through the prophet Jeremiah, saying,

> *18*A voice was heard in Ramah,
> weeping and grave lamentation,
> Rahel[9] weeping for her children,
> and she would not be comforted,
> because her children are gone.

*19*Now when Herod died, suddenly an angel flew down, appearing in a dream to Yosef in Egypt, *20*saying, "Awake, take the child and his mother, and go to the land of Israel, for those who sought to put out the life of the child are dead."

*21*Yosef awoke, took the child and the mother, and went to the land of Israel. *22*But hearing that Archelaos was now King in Yehuda, replacing his father Herod, he feared to go there. And being warned in a dream, he withdrew to a place in Galilee, where he went *23*and lived in a city called Nazareth. So the prophets' word was fulfilled:

> And he will be called a Nazarene.

---

9. *Rahel* is Rachel.

## CHAPTER 3

### *John the Baptist*

In those days came Yohanan the Baptizer[10] preaching in the desert of Yehuda, 2saying, "Repent, for the kingdom in the skies is near." 3He was the one mentioned by the prophet Isaiah, saying:

> A voice of one crying in the desert:
> Prepare the way of the Lord[11]
> and straighten the roads before him.

4Now Yohanan wore a raiment of camel's hair and a belt of hide around his waist, and his food was locusts and wild honey. 5At that time the people of Yerushalayim came to him and also all of Yehuda and the whole countryside about Jordan, 6He baptized them in the river Jordan, and they confessed their sins. 7But on seeing many of the Pharisees and Sadducees coming to baptism, he said to them:

> You offspring of vipers, who warned you to flee from
>     the coming wrath?
> 8Prepare fruit worthy of your repentance.
> 9And do not plan to say among yourselves,
> 'We have Avraham as our father.'
> For I say to you that out of these stones
> God is able to raise up children to Avraham.
>
> 10The axe is also set against the root of the trees,
> and every tree that fails to yield good fruit is cut down
>     and cast into the fire.
>
> 11I baptize you in water for repentance,
> but after me will come one stronger than I,
> and I am not worthy to carry his sandals.
> He will baptize you in the holy spirit and fire.
> 12His winnowing fork is in his hand,
> and he will clear his threshing floor and put his grain
>     in the storehouse
> but he will burn the chaff in unquenchable fire.

13Then came Yeshua from Galilee to the Jordan and to Yohanan to be baptized by him.

---

10. *Yohanan the Baptizer* is John the Baptist.

11. Lord here might be replaced by *Adonai,* or preferably *Adonenu* meaning *our Lord.*

*14*Yohanan tried to stop this, saying, "I need to be baptized by you, yet you come to me?"

*15*But Yeshua answered, saying to him:

> Leave things as they are.
> It is right for us to fulfill our whole spirit
> of the good.

Then Yohanan consented.

*16*And when Yeshua was baptized, at once he came out of the water, and look, the skies opened, and he saw the spirit of God coming down like a dove, coming down upon him. *17*And immediately a voice from the skies said:

> This is my son whom I love,
> in whom I am well pleased.

## CHAPTER 4

### *The Temptation of Jesus*

In those days Yeshua was led by the spirit up into the desert to be tempted by the Devil. *2*And he fasted forty days and forty nights, and afterward he hungered. *3*And coming up to him, the tempter said:

> If you are the son of God, speak
> and make these stones loaves of bread.

*4*But he answered, saying,

> It is written in Deuteronomy:
> "Not by bread alone does a person live
> but by every word issuing through the mouth of God."

*5*Then the Devil took him to the holy city, and he stood on the pinnacle wing of the temple *6*and said to him,

> If you are the son of God,
> cast yourself down from the high wing,
> for it is written in the Psalms:
> 'He will put his angels in charge of you,
> and with their hands they will hold you up
> so you won't smash your foot against a stone.'

*7*Yeshua said to him, "Again it is written in Deuteronomy:

> You must not tempt the lord, your God."

*8*Once more the Devil led him to a very high mountain and showed him all the kingdoms of the world and their glory, *9*and said to him:

> All this I will give you
> if you will fall down before me and worship me.

*10*Finally Yeshua said to him, "Go away, Satan, for therein it is also written:

> 'You will worship God
> and you will serve him alone.' "

*11*Then the Devil left him, and suddenly angels came down and cared for him.

## Yeshua's Ministry and Miraculous Healings

*12*On hearing that Yohanan had been arrested, Yeshua withdrew to Galilee, *13*and leaving Nazareth he came to and settled in Kefar-Nahum[12] by the great lake, in the districts of Zevulun and Naftali. *14*He came to fulfill the words spoken through the prophet Isaiah:

> *15*Land of Zevulun and Land of Naftali,
> the way to the sea beyond the Jordan,
> Galilee of Gentiles, of those who are not Jews,
> *16*the people who were sitting in darkness
> saw a great light,
> and for those sitting in the land and shadow of death
> the light sprang into dawn.

*17*From that instant Yeshua began to preach his word and said:

> Repent, for the kingdom of the skies is near.

*18*And as he was walking by the Sea of Galilee, he saw two brothers, the one called Petros[13], and his brother Andreas, casting their net into the sea, for they were fishermen. *19*He said to them:

> Come, and I will make you fishers of people.

---

12. *Kefar-Nahum* is Capernaum.

13. *Kefa* or *kef* means *boulder* or *cliff*. *Tzur* also means rock. In English *Kefa* corresponds to the English name "*Peter*." In Greek *Petros* is a name, from which the English name "*Peter*" comes, and "*stone*." While it would be perhaps more consistent with the practice of restoring the biblical name to use *Kefa* each time Greek *Petros* occurs in the Greek text, there is nothing (as in the case of going from *Joseph* to *Yosef*) to help the reader understand the biblical name as it goes from *Kefa* to Peter. *Petros* has the advantage of resembling English Peter and also meaning stone. When Peter is called *Simon Peter* or *Simeon Peter*, I do restore Hebrew *Shimon*, which offers little problem for an English reader.

20And they immediately dropped their nets and followed him.

21Going on from there he saw two more brothers, Yaakov the son of Zebedee and Yohanan his brother, in the boat with Zebedee their father, mending their nets. He called out to them. 22And they left their boat and their father, and followed him.

23Yeshua went all over Galilee, teaching in the synagogues, preaching the good message from the kingdom, and healing every sickness and infirmity among the people. 24His fame spread into all of Syria. And they brought him all who suffered diverse diseases and were seized by pain and those who were possessed by demons, lunatic epileptics and paralytics, and he healed them. 25Huge crowds followed him around from Galilee and Dekapolis and Yerushalayim, Yehuda and beyond the Jordan.

## CHAPTER 5

*The Sermon on the Mount*

And seeing the crowds, he went up the mountain. When he was seated, his disciples came to him. And he opened his mouth and from the mountain gave them his teachings:

> 2Blessed are the poor in spirit
> for theirs is the kingdom of the skies.[14]
> 4Blessed are they who mourn the dead
> for they will be comforted.
> 5Blessed are the gentle
> for they will inherit the earth.
> 6Blessed are the hungry and thirsty for right justice
> for they will be heartily fed.
> 7Blessed are they who have pity
> for they will be pitied.
> 8Blessed are the clean in heart
> for they will see God.
> 9Blessed are the peacemakers
> for they will be called the children of God.
> 10Blessed are they who are persecuted for the sake of right justice
> for theirs is the kingdom of the skies.
> 11Blessed are you when they revile and persecute
> and speak every cunning evil[15] against you, lying,
> because of me.
> 12Rejoice and be glad, for your reward in the heavens is huge,
> and in this way did they persecute the prophets before you.

---

14. These 11 blessings are known as "the Beatitudes."

15. *Poneros* in classical Greek had a positive meaning as in "nimble-witted" or "cunning" Odysseus and has retained that specific earthly meaning into modern Greek. So some sense of the shade of cunning is desired in the New Covenant usage, where it is entered as evil.

*13*You are the salt of the earth.

But if the salt has lost its taste, how will it recover its salt?

Its powers are for nothing except to be thrown away and trampled
    underfoot by others.

*14*You are the light of the world.

A city cannot be hidden when it is set on a mountain.

*15*Nor do they light a lamp and place it under a basket, but on a stand,

and it glows on everyone in the house.

*16*So let your light glow before people so they may see your good works

    and glorify your father in the skies.

*17*Do not think that I have come to destroy the law or the prophets.

I have not come to destroy but to fulfill.

*18*And yes I say to you, until the sky and the earth are gone,

not one tiny iota or serif will disappear from the law

    until all has been done.

*19*Whoever breaks even the lightest of the commandments

    and teaches others to do the same

will be esteemed least in the kingdom in the skies.

Whoever performs and teaches them

will be called great in the kingdom in the skies.

*20*I say to you, if you don't exceed the right justice

    of the scholars and the Pharisees,

you will never enter the kingdom in the skies.

*21*You have heard our people in ancient times told in Exodus,

    You must not murder.

    and whoever murders will be liable to judgment.

*22*I say to you, whoever is angry with a companion will be judged

    in court,

and whoever calls a companion a fool will go before the Sanhedrin,

    the highest court,

and whoever calls a companion a scoundrel will taste the fire of

    Gehenna.

*23*If then you bring your gift to the altar,

and there you remember your companion holds something

    against you,

*24*leave your gift before the altar,

and go first to be reconciled with your companion

and then come back and present your offering.

*25*When you see your adversary walking in the street on the way

    to the court,

quickly, be of good will toward him and reconcile

*26*or your accuser will hand you over to the judge,

    the judge to the baliff

and you will be thrown into prison.

I tell you, there will be no way out
until you have paid back the last penny.

27And you have heard in Exodus the words:
>    You must not commit adultery.

28Yet I say, if a man looks at a woman with lust
he has already slept with her in his heart.
29So if your right eye takes you to scandalous sin,
tear it out and cast it away.
It is better to lose a part of your body
than for your whole body to be cast into Gehenna.
30And if your right hand takes you to scandalous sin,
cut it off and cast it away.
It is better to lose a part of your body
than for your whole body to be cast into Gehenna.

31And you have heard in Deuteronomy, if a man sends his wife away,
give her a proper bill of divorce,
32but I also tell you that any man divorcing and sending his wife away,
except for dirty harlotry,
makes her the victim of adultery;
and any man who marries a woman divorced and sent away
is himself an adulterer.

33You have heard our people in ancient times told in Exodus,
"You must not swear false oaths,
but make good your oaths before God."
34But I tell you not to swear at all:
Not by heaven, for heaven is God's throne,
35nor by earth, for earth is God's footstool,
nor by Yerushalayim, for Yerushalayim is the city of the great king.
36Don't swear by your own head,
since you cannot make one hair white or black.
37If your word is yes, say yes.
If your word is no, say no.
To say more is to indulge in evil.

38And you have heard in Exodus, "an eye for an eye"
>    and a tooth for a tooth.

39But I tell you not to resist the wicked person,
and if someone strikes you on the right cheek,
turn your other cheek as well.
40If someone wants to sue you for your tunic,
give him your outer cloak as well.
41If someone forces you to go a mile with him,
go a second mile with him.

43Give to who asks you. And don't turn away one
who wants to borrow from you

You have heard it said in Leviticus,
"You will love your neighbor and hate your enemy."
₄₄I say to you to love your enemies
and pray for those who persecute you
₄₅so you may become the children of your father in the skies.
For he makes the sun rise over the evil and the good,
and he brings the rains to the just and the unjust among us.

₄₆If you love those who love you, what is the good deed in that?
Don't even the tax collectors do the same?
₄₇If you greet only those who are your friends,
how have you done more than others?
₄₈Have you done more than the Gentiles—than those who are not
     Jews?
Be perfect as your father the heavenly one is perfect.

## CHAPTER 6

Take care not to do your acts of righteousness[16] before other people
so as to be seen by them,
for you will have no reward from your father in the skies.
₂When you give alms, don't sound a trumpet before you
like the actors in our synagogues and in the streets,
who seek the praise of the onlookers.
I say to you, they have their reward in the street from the onlookers.
₃Yet when you give alms, do not let the left hand know
     what the right hand is doing
₄so the alms may be given in secret,
and your father seeing you in secret will repay you.

₅And when you pray, don't do so like the actors.
They love to stand in our synagogues and in the corners
     of the open squares, praying
so they will be seen by others.
I say to you, they have their rewards.
₆When you pray, go into your inner room and close the door
and pray to your father who is in secret,
and your father who sees you in secret will repay you.

₇Yet when you pray, do not babble empty words like the Gentiles, like
     those who are not Jews,
for the Gentiles think by uttering a glut of words they will be heard.
₈Be as you are, the Jews, and not like the Gentiles,
for your father knows what you need before you ask him.

₉And pray like this:

---

16. The Majority Text reads *eleimosunin,* charitable giving.

Our father in the heavens,
may your name be holy.[17]
10May your kingdom come.
May your will be spread
on earth as it is in heaven.
11Give us today our daily bread
12and forgive us our debts
as we forgave our debtors.
13Do not lead us into temptation,
but rescue us from the evil one.[18]
[For yours is the kingdom,
and the power and the glory
for all of time. Amen.][19]

14If you forgive the people who have stumbled and gone astray,
then your heavenly father will forgive you,
15but if you will not forgive those who stumble and fall,
your father will not forgive your failures.

16When you fast do not scowl darkly like actors.
They distort their faces to show others they are fasting.
Yes, they have their reward.
17But when you fast, anoint your head with oil
to make it smooth and wash your face
18so your fasting will be unknown to people
and known only to your father who is not visible.
Your father who sees you in secret will repay you.

19Do not hoard your treasures on earth
where moth and earthworms consume them,
where thieves dig through walls and steal them,
20but store up your treasures in heaven
where neither moth nor earthworms consume
or thieves dig through the walls and steal,
21since your treasure
is there where your heart is.

22The lamp of the body is the eye.
If your eye is clear, your whole body is filled with light,
23but if your eye is clouded, your whole body will inhabit darkness.
And if the light in your whole body is darkness,
how dark it is!

---

17. This prayer poem is known as the "Lord's Prayer."

18. *apo tou ponerou* is literally "from the evil one," meaning the Devil.

19. This famous ending of the Lord's Prayer is in brackets, since it does not appear in the earliest Greek texts. It does appear in the later Majority Greek text, in Tyndale and the authorized translations. See introduction for further discussion.

24No one can serve two masters,
for either one will hate one and love the other
or cling to one and despise the other.
You cannot serve God and the mammon of riches.

25So I tell you, do not worry about your life
or say, "What am I to eat? What am I to drink?"
and about the body, "What am I to wear?"
Isn't life more than its food, and your body more than its clothing?

26Consider the birds of the sky.
They do not sow or reap or collect for their granaries,
yet your heavenly father feeds them.
Are you not more valuable than they?
Who among you by brooding can add one more hour to your life?

27And why care about clothing?
28Consider the lilies of the field, how they grow.
They do not labor or spin
29but I tell you not even Solomon in all his splendor
was clothed like one of these lilies.
30And if the grass of the field is there today
and tomorrow is cast into the oven
and in these ways God has dressed the earth,
will he not clothe you in a more stunning raiment,
        you who suffer from poor faith.

31Do not brood, mumbling, what is there to eat or drink?
Or what shall we wear?
32All those things the Gentiles, those who are not Jews,
        set their hearts on.
Your heavenly father knows your need for these things.
33But seek first his kingdom and his justice,
and all things will be given to you.
34Do not worry about tomorrow,
for tomorrow will worry about itself.
Each day has enough troubles in it.

## CHAPTER 7

Don't pass judgment or you will be judged.
2By your judgment you will be judged
and by your measure you will be measured.
3Why do you gaze at the splinter in your friend's eye
yet not recognize the log in your own eye?
4Or why say to your friend,
"Let me take the splinter out of your eye"
when your own eye carries a log of wood?
5False actor,

first remove the wood from your own vision,
and you will see clearly enough to pluck the sliver
from your friend's eye.

6Don't give the holy to the dogs
or cast your pearls before the pigs.
They will probably trample them underfoot
and turn and tear you to pieces.

7Ask and it will be given to you.
Seek and you will find.
Knock and the door will be opened for you.
8Everyone who asks receives,
and the seeker finds,
and the door will be opened to one who knocks.

9And who among you if your son asks for bread
will give him stone?
10Or if he asks for fish
will give him snake?
11If you, in your evil, know how to give good gifts to your children,
how much more will your father in the skies
give good gifts to those who ask him.

12All things in the world you wish others to do for you,
do for them.
Such is the meaning of the law and the prophets.

13Go in through the narrow gate,
since wide is the gate and spacious the road
that leads to destruction,
and there are many who go in through it.
14But how narrow the gate and cramped the road
that leads to life,
and there are few who find it.

15Beware of the false prophets,
who come to you in sheep's clothing,
but who inside are ravening wolves.
16From their fruit you will know them.
From thorns can you gather grapes
or from thistles pick figs?
17Every good tree gives delicious fruit,
but the diseased tree gives rotting fruit.
18A good tree cannot yield rotting fruit,
nor a diseased tree delicious fruits.
19Every tree incapable of delicious fruit is cut down
and tossed in the fire.
20So from their fruit you will know them.

*21*Not everyone who says to me, Adonai, Adonai,
will come into the kingdom in the skies,
but one who follows the will of my father,
who is in the heavens.
*22*On that day of judgment many will say to me,
"Didn't we prophesy in your name
and in your name cast out demons
and in your name take on great powers?"
*23*And then I will say my word clearly to them:
"I never knew you. Go from me,
you who are working against the law."

*24*Everyone who hears my words and follows them
will be like the prudent man
who built his house upon the rock.
*25*The rain fell and the rivers came
and the winds blew and battered that house
and it didn't fall,
because it was founded upon the rock.

*26*Everyone who hears my words and doesn't follow them
will be like the young fool who built his house upon the sand.
*27*And the rain fell and the rivers came
and the winds blew and battered that house
and it fell and it was a great fall.

*28*And it happened that when Yeshua ended these words, the crowds
were amazed at his teaching, *29*for he taught them as one who has authority and not like one of our scholars.

## Mark (after A.D. 70) Israel, Syria, Alexandria, or Rome? (gospel)

TRANSLATED BY WILLIS BARNSTONE

As in the other gospels, there is no internal evidence of the authorship
of the book of Mark. An early church figure, Bishop Papias (c. A.D.
130–140), claims that Mark was John Mark, a close associate of Peter, and
that the gospel of Mark is essentially an arrangement of Peter's preachings in
Rome. The second-century Bishop Iraeneus also places Mark in Rome. Another tradition claims Alexandria as the place of origin. Others assume because the Marcan gospel is the earliest that it was composed in Israel. Mark
was written at least forty years after Jesus' death, and the gospel authors'
names were appended to the gospels more than a hundred years after Jesus'
death. The traditions that assert authorship of the gospels frequently deny
each other and here, as elsewhere, none has a strong historical probability.
Authorship in the New Testament remains an enigma.

Like Luke 1:1, Mark 1:1 begins with the presentation of the "good news" about Jesus Christ. Mark stresses Jesus' miracles, his powers of healing, the drama and mystery of his death. The first verses quote the prophet Isaiah to prove that Jesus is the "voice crying out in the wilderness" and that he is therefore God's messenger. But after this initial declaration, Mark plunges directly into the stories of John the Baptist and of Jesus tempted for forty days in the desert by Satan (which parallels Moses' forty years in the desert tempted by Baal). It follows his wanderings through the land of Israel, where he takes on disciples and crowds of followers who accompany him in his ministry. Mark gives us a series of miracles, teachings through parables, and finally the "passion week" of Jesus' arrest, trial, death, burial, and disappearance from the tomb. Here the gospel ends. This so-called "abrupt ending" has bothered theologians and has caused some to speculate that we have a truncated or unfinished gospel. Most disturbing is that there is no mention of Christ risen, and since Mark is the source of Matthew and Luke, the absence of a resurrected Jesus is not desirable. As a probable result of this discomfort with the present ending, two appended endings have been added, the so-called "Shorter Ending of Mark" and the "Longer Ending of Mark." The very short one has Jesus send word of eternal salvation out from east to west. The longer one has Jesus appear resurrected before Mary Magdalene and the disciples and then describes Jesus ascending into heaven. The short ending may have been added in the fourth century, the longer one as early as the second. Both endings are termed *orphans,* because they are spurious and do not exist in copies of the earliest manuscripts.

Mark is most often characterized as an author whose Greek is crude and rudimentary in contrast especially to Luke, who is more classical, and John, who is clearly influenced by Greek philosophical and Gnostic models. But Mark is in many ways the greatest stylist among the Evangelists. Mark writes with plain clarity, concision, dramatic power, and minimal and striking diction. The original ending of the Gospel of Mark may be less satisfying as theology, but it is overwhelmingly dramatic and mysterious in its understatement of the sublime terror of Jesus' disappearance from the tomb. When the two Marys enter the tomb and find that Jesus is not there, Mark writes, "So they went out and fled from the tomb, seized by trembling and ecstasy. And they said nothing to anyone. They were afraid" (17:18).

## CHAPTER 6

*Miracles*

36The apostles[1] gathered together around Yeshua[2] and reported to him everything they had done and taught. 31He said to them:

> Come yourselves alone to a deserted place
> and rest a while.

---

1. *oi apostoloi,* the apostles. The word "apostle," "messenger," or "one who is sent" appears in Mark only here and in other manuscripts in 3:14.

2. *Yeshua* is Jesus.

For they were many coming and going and they had no chance even to eat. ₃₂And they went off in a ship to a deserted place by themselves.

₃₃Now many saw them going and knew of them, and from all the towns they ran there on foot and got there ahead of them.

₃₄On coming ashore, Yeshua saw a great crowd and he pitied them, for they were like sheep without a shepherd, and he began to teach them many things.

₃₅When it was already late the disciples came to him, saying, "This is a deserted place and it is already late. ₃₆Send them off so they can go into the surrounding farms and villages and buy themselves something to eat.

₃₇But he answered, saying to them:

You give them something to eat.

They said to him, "Shall we go off and buy two hundred denars worth of loaves and give them that to eat."

₃₈And he said to them:

How many loaves do you have?
Go and see.

When they knew, they said, "Five, and two fish."

₃₉He told them all to sit down in groups on the green grass. ₄₀They sat down in groups of hundreds and fifties. ₄₁He took the five loaves and the two fish, and looking up into the sky he blessed and broke the loaves and gave them to his disciples to set before the people, and the two fish he divided among them all. ₄₂Everyone ate and they were filled. ₄₃And they picked up twelve full baskets of crumbs and fish. ₄₄Those who had eaten were five thousand men.[3]

₄₅Immediately Yeshua had his disciples climb into the ship and go ahead to the far side of Bethsaida, while he dismissed the crowd. ₄₆And after saying goodbye to them he went off to the mountains to pray.

₄₇When dusk came the ship was in the middle of the sea and he was alone on the land. ₄₈Seeing the disciples straining at the oars—the wind was against them—about the fourth watch of the night[4] he came toward them, walking on the sea and he wanted to pass by them. ₄₉But seeing him walking on the sea they thought he was a phantom, and they cried out. ₅₀They saw him and they were terrified.

At once he spoke with them and said:

Take courage. It is I. Don't be afraid.

---

3. *andres*, men. Here the word is specifically "men" rather than people. It is possible that the multitude consisted entirely or largely of men, and he was observing this, or, as is the habit in most languages "men" meant "people."

4. About three in the morning.

51Then he climbed into the boat and the wind fell, and deep in themselves they were astonished. 52They had not understood about the loaves and their heart hardened.

53When they crossed over to the land, they came to Gennesaret and anchored. 54They got out of the ship, and immediately recognized him. 55Wherever he went into villages or cities or into the farmland, in the marketplaces they laid out the sick and begged that they might touch even the hem of his garment. And as many who touched him were healed.

## CHAPTER 14

### *The Last Supper*

After two days it would be Pesach,[5] the Feast of the Matzot Cakes,[6] and the high priests and the scholars were looking for a way to arrest him by treachery and to kill him. 2"Not at the festival," they were saying, "for there would be an outcry from the people."

3While he was in Bethany in the house of Shimon[7] the leper, reclining, a woman came with an alabaster jar of pure and costly spikenard ointment. Breaking the alabaster jar she poured it on his head. 4Now some were angry among themselves, "Why was there this waste of ointment?" 5This ointment could have been sold for more than three hundred dinars[8] and the money given to the poor. And they scolded her.

6But Yeshua[9] said:

Let her be. Why do you bother her?
She has done a good thing for me.
7You always have the poor with you
and whenever you want you can
do good for them. But me you do not
always have. 8She did what she could.
She prepared ahead of time to anoint
my body for the burial. 9Amen I say
to you. Wherever in the whole world
the good news is preached, also what
this woman did will tell her memory.

---

5. Passover.

6. Unleavened bread.

7. *Shimon* is Simon.

8. Also translated as "denarius." The dinar was an ancient Roman silver coin, the penny of the New Testament.

9. *Yeshua* is Jesus.

*10*Yehuda of Kerioth[10] one of the twelve went to the high priests to betray him to them.

*11*Hearing of this they were happy and promised to give him silver. He was looking for an easy way of betraying him.

*12*On the first day of the Feast of the Matzah, when the Pesach lamb was sacrificed, his disciples said to him, "Where do you want us to go for us to arrange for you to eat the Pesach?"

*13*And he sent two of his disciples and said to them:

Go into the city and you will meet
a man carrying a clay pot of water.
Follow him *14*and wherever he goes tell
the owner of the house, "The teacher asks,
'Where is the guest room for me to eat the Pesach?'"
*15*And he will show you a large upstairs room,
furnished and ready. There prepare for us.

*16*And the disciples left and came into the city and found things just as they were told and prepared the Pesach lamb. As they were reclining at the table and eating, Yeshua said to them:

Amen amen I say to you
one of you will betray me,
one who is eating with me.

*19*They began to grieve and said to him, one by one, "Surely not I?"
*20*He said to them:

One of the twelve who is dipping in the bowl.[11]
*21*The Son of People[12] goes just as Isaiah
has written of him.[13] But oh for that one
through whom the Son of People was betrayed.[14]
Better for him never to have been born!

---

10. *Yehuda of Kerioth* is Judas Iscariot. The figure of Judas lacks historical probability, since this story of the betrayer appears to be lifted intact and anachronistically from Midrashic tale. (*Midrash,* meaning "explanation" in Hebrew, is an early collection of tales and rabbinical commentary in Scripture.) The choice of the name Yehuda, signifying "Jew" in Hebrew, was chosen to suggest that Judas alone among the disciples was a Jew, when in fact all the disciples were Jews.

11. Presumably dipping "bread" in the bowl.

12. Son of Man.

13. The Greek says "just as it is written," meaning, for the informed reader, Isaiah 1–12 in which Isaiah describes the birth, life, and sacrificial death of the coming Messiah in great and moving detail.

14. *ouai* is closer to "oh!" or "ah" than to "woe," which is the traditional translation of this interjection. The strength of his curse is developed in the next sentences, and it is better to follow the strategy in Greek of an undefined "oh" leading up to the explicit punishment.

22While they were eating he took bread and blessing it he broke it and gave it to them and said:

Take it. This is my body.

23And taking a cup and giving thanks he gave it to them, and everyone drank from it. 24And he said to them:

25This is the blood of the covenant,
which is poured out for many.[15]
Amen amen I say to you,
I will no longer drink the fruit of the wine
until that day when I drink it new in the kingdom
      of God.

26After singing the hymn they went to the Mountain of Olives.
27Then Yeshua said to them:

You will all stumble as Zecharaiah wrote:
   I will strike down the shepherd
      and the sheep will be scattered.
28But after I'm raised up I will find my way
before you in Galilee.

29But Petros[16] said to him, "Even if everyone stumbles, I will not."
30Then Yeshua said to him:

Amen I say to you
this same night before the cock crows twice
you will deny me three times.

31But he said forcefully, "If I must die for you, I will not deny you."
So they all said.

32And they came to a place whose name was Gethsemane and he said to his disciples:

Sit here while I pray.

---

15. The word "Eucharist" is derived from the Greek *euharistesas,* "having given thanks," which appears in this passage of the Pesach supper. The "blood of the covenant" derives from the covenant between God and Moses at Sinai: "Moses then took the blood, sprinkled it on the people and said, 'This is the blood of the covenant that the Lord has made with you in accordance with all these words'" (Ex. 24:8). Moses has set up "twelve stone pillars representing the twelve tribes of Israel." The sacred symbolism of the twelve, representing all the tribes of Israel, is repeated in having Yeshua choose to be followed by twelve disciples.

16. *Petros* is Peter.

₃₃And he took Petros and Yaakov[17] and Yohanan[18] with him and he began to be shaken and in agony ₃₄and he said to them:

> My soul is in sorrow to the point of death.
> Stay here and keep awake.

₃₅And going a little farther he fell on the ground and prayed that if it were possible the hour pass away from him. ₃₆And he said:

> Abba, Father, for you all things are possible.
> Take this cup from me. Yet not what I will
> but what you will.

₃₇And he came and found them sleeping, and said to Petros:

> Shimon,[19] are you sleeping? Did you not have
> the strength to keep awake for an hour?
> ₃₈Stay awake and pray that you are not tested.
> Oh the spirit is ready but the flesh is weak.

₃₉He went away again and prayed, saying the same word.
₄₀And he came again and found them sleeping. Their eyes were very heavy, and they didn't know what to say to him.
₄₁And he came a third time and said to them:

> Sleep what is left of the night and rest.
> Enough! The hour has come. Look,
> the Son of People has been betrayed
> into the hands of those who do wrong.[20]
> ₄₂Get up and let us go. Look, the one
> betraying me is drawing near.

₄₃Immediately while he was still speaking, Yehuda came, one of the twelve, and with him a crowd with swords and clubs from the high priests and the scholars and the elders. ₄₄Now he who betrayed him gave them a signal saying, "The one I kiss is the one. Seize him and take him away under guard."

₄₅When he came, he at once went up to him and said, "Rabbi," and kissed him.

---

17. *Yaakov* is James.

18. *Yohanan* is John.

19. *Shimon* is Simon as in Simon Peter.

20. *hamartolon*, of the sinners. Here translated as "those who wrong," *Hamartolos* is by tradition translated "sinner," but the notion of missing the mark literally, or failing, or doing wrong persists.

₄₆They got their hands on him and seized him.

₄₇But one standing by drew his sword and struck the slave of the high priest and cut off his ear.

₄₈Then Yeshua spoke out to them:

As against a thief have you come with swords
and clubs to arrest me? ₄₉Day after day I was with you
in the Temple, teaching. Then you did not seize me.
Only now so that the scriptures may be fulfilled.

₅₀And leaving him, they all fled.

₅₁And one young man followed him, dressed in linen cloth around his naked body, and they seized him. ₅₂But he left the linen cloth behind and fled.

₅₃They led Yeshua to the high priest. All the high priests and the elders and the scholars were assembled.

₅₄Petros followed him from a distance until he was inside the high priest's courtyard and he sat together with the servants, warming himself near the fire.

₅₅The high priest and the whole Sanhedrin[21] were looking for evidence against him to put him to death, but they didn't find any. ₅₆Many gave false testimony against him, and their testimonies were not the same. ₅₇Some stood up and gave false testimony against him, saying, "₅₈We heard him say, 'I will tear down this Temple made with hands and after three days I will build another not made with hands.'" ₅₉But their testimony was not identical.

₆₀Then the high priest stood up in their midst and questioned Yeshua, saying, "Won't you answer anything that they have testified against you?"

₆₁But he was silent and gave no answer to anything.

₆₁Again the high priest questioned him and said to him, "Are you the Messiah the son of the blessed one?"

₆₂Yeshua said:

I am.
    And you will see the Son of People
    sitting at the right of the power
    and coming with the clouds of the sky.[22]

₆₃The high priest tore his tunic, saying, "What further need do we have of witnesses? ₆₄You heard this blasphemy. How does it look to you?"

They all condemned him as deserving death.

₆₅And some began to spit on him, and to cover his face and struck him, saying to him, "Prophesy!" And the servants pummeled him.

---

21. Court.

22. Lines 1 and 3 of Hebrew Scripture cited are from Daniel 7:13, and line 2 from Psalms 110:1.

66While Petros was below in the courtyard, one of the maidservants of the high priest came 67and when she saw Petros warming himself she stared at him and said, "You were also with Yeshua from Nazareth."

68But he denied it, saying, "I don't know or understand what you are saying." Then he went outside into the forecourt. [And the cock crowed.][23]

69And the maid seeing him began again to say to the bystanders, "This is one of them."

70But again he denied it.

After a short while the bystanders said to Petros, "Surely you must be one of them, since you are a Galilean."

71He began to curse and to swear, "I don't know this man you're talking about." At once the cock crowed a second time. And Petros remembered the word Yeshua said to him:

Before the cock crows twice
you will deny me three times.

And he broke down and wept.

## CHAPTER 15

*The Crucifixion*

As soon as it was morning, the high priests with the elders and scholars held a meeting. And they bound Yeshua, led him away and handed him over to Pilatus.[24]

2Pilatus asked him, "Are you the king of the Jews?"

Answering him, he said:

You say.[25]

3The high priests were accusing him of many things.

4Pilatus again questioned him, saying, "Don't you answer anything? Look how much you are accused of."

5But Yeshua still answered nothing.

Pilatus was amazed.

6Now at that festival he released one prisoner to the people, whichever one they asked for. 7There was a man called Barabbas who was bound along with other revolutionaries, who in the uprising had commit-

---

23. "And the cock crowed" is omitted in other texts and bracketed in the Nestle-Aland, which is used here.

24. Pilate.

25. *Su legeis,* You say. Most translations give "You say it," adding "it," or "You say so," adding "so." These conversions are good idiomatic equivalents to the Greek, but it is perhaps stronger to give no more than the Greek (since Greek can also add the "it" or "so" but chooses not to) by simply saying "You say." Until it becomes natural the phrase will jar but may still be more memorable.

ted murder.[26] ₈So the crowd came and began to ask Pilatus for what he did for them.

₉But Pilatus answered them, saying, "Do you want me to release the king of the Jews?" ₁₀He knew that the high priests had handed him over to him out of envy.

₁₁But the high priests incited the crowd to release Barabbas instead to them.

₁₂Pilatus again answered, saying to them, "What do you want me to do with the King of the Jews?"

₁₃"Crucify him."[27]

₁₄Pilatus said to them, "What wrong did he do?"

But they cried out louder, "Crucify him."

So Pilate, wanting to satisfy the crowd, released Barabbas to them, and had Yeshua flogged and handed him over to be crucified.

₁₆The soldiers led him away into the courtyard, which is the praetorium,[28] and assembled the whole cohort. ₁₇And they clothed him in purple and twisted some thorns into a crown, which placed it on his head. ₁₈Then they began to salute him, "Hail, King of the Jews." ₁₉They beat him on the head with a reed club and spat on him, and going down on their knees they worshiped him. ₂₀And after mocking him, they stripped off the purple and put his own clothes on him. Then they led him out to crucify him.

₂₁And a certain Shimon of Cyrene,[29] the father of Alexandros and Rufus, was passing by from the countryside, and they forced him to carry his cross. ₂₂They brought him to the place Golgotha, which translated is the Place of the Skull. ₂₃And they gave him wine mixed with myrrh,[30] but he didn't take it. ₂₄And they crucified him.

---

26. Nothing is known of Barabbas, but from his revolutionary activities it is assumed that he was a Zealot, a Jewish sect that was rebelling against Roman occupation. Insurrectionists were treated by the Romans as bandits and hence crucified. Only from the gospels do we know that the Romans followed the custom of releasing one prisoner during the Passover.

27. This pivotal but unlikely scene that has the crowd shout "Crucify him," which is to say, "crucify a dissident rabbi," suggests not the voice of a Jewish mob in the street but the voice of Rome enunciated through the Evangelist. The voice of Rome comes through more emphatically in Matthew's elaboration of the same scene, in which Pilate declares both his own innocence and Jesus' innocence and blames the crowd: "When Pilatus saw that he could do nothing and that an uproar was starting, he took water and washed his hands before the crowd, saying, 'I am innocent of the blood of this man. You see to it'" (27:24). To clear himself, and by extension Rome, of responsibility for the crucifixion, Pilate asks the crowd, "What wrong did he do?" By revealing to the crowd—and to the reader—his conviction that Yeshua did no wrong, he places himself squarely on Jesus' side at the very moment of ordering the rabbi to be flogged and crucified. Mark paints Pilate as the helpless tool of a murderous mob; the Eastern Orthodox Church will later elevate the same Roman governor to sainthood. The historical view of Pilate depicts the procurator of Judea, Idumea, and Samaria, A.D. 26–36, as an unusually brutal ruler of peoples under Roman occupation. He was recalled to Rome for the massacre of the Samaritans in A.D. 35. It should also be noted that crucifixion was a Roman means of execution, not one either practiced by Jews or conceivably ordered by Jews against a Jew.

28. The governor's residence.

29. *Cyrene* is modern Libya.

30. In the Talmud, incense is mixed with wine to deaden pain.

> and they divided his clothings
>   and cast lots for them to see
>     who would take them.[31]

25It was the third hour, nine in the morning, when they crucified him. 26The inscription of the charge against him was written above: The King of the Jews. 27With him they crucified two thieves, one on the right and one on the left of him.

29And those passing by blasphemed him, shaking their heads, and saying, "Ha! You who would destroy the Temple and rebuild it in three days, 30save yourself by coming down from the cross." 31Likewise the high priests mocked him among each other and with the scholars said, "He saved others but he can't save himself. 32The King of Israel, let him now come down from the cross so we can see and believe." And those who crucified him taunted him.

33At when it was the sixth hour, at noon, the whole earth become dark until the ninth hour, at three, and at the ninth hour Yeshua called out words from the Psalms in a loud voice:

*Eloi Eloi, lema sabachtani?*

which translated is,

My God, my God, why do you abandon me?[32]

35Some of those standing near heard him and said, "See, he's calling Elijah.[33] 36And someone ran up with a sponge soaked in sour wine, placed it on a reed stick and gave it to him to drink, saying, "Let him alone. Let us see if Elijah comes to take him down."

36And Yeshua let out a loud shout and took his last breath.

38The Temple curtain was torn in two from top to bottom.

39A Roman centurion who was near saw him breathe his last and said, "Truly this man was the son of God."[34]

40And there were women looking on from a distance, among whom were both Miryam[35] the Magdalene and Miryam mother of Yaakov the

---

31. Ps. 22:18. These near passages contain many citations from Psalms.

32. Ps. 22:1.

33. The bystanders heard mistakenly "Elijas" for "Eloi," "my God."

34. A centurion was a commander of one hundred Roman soldiers. In the story of the crucifixion, after Jesus has been mocked by Jewish bystanders and the high priests, and the curtain in the Temple has sympathetically torn in two, foretelling the Temple's imminent doom, the first to recognize that Jesus was the son of God is the commander of the execution squad. This exoneration of Roman leadership, who now are not only guiltless in Jesus' execution but the first in Jerusalem to state his divinity, follows the pattern of preparing the move of the authority of Jesus' messiahship to Rome.

In Hebrew 9:8–10, 12; 10:19–20, Paul tells us that the tearing of the curtain means that Jesus has entered heaven for us so that we too now may enter God's presence.

35. *Miryam* is Mary.

younger and of Joses, and Salome, *41*who was in Galilee following him and serving him, and there were many other women who had gone up with him to Yerushalayim.[36]

*42*When evening came since it was Friday, Preparation Day for the Sabbath, *43*Yosef of Arimathea,[37] a prominent member of the council, who was also looking for the kingdom of God, boldly went to Pilatus and asked for the body of Yeshua.

Pilatus wondered if he was already dead and called the centurion, and asked him if he was dead yet. *45*Informed by the centurion, he gave the corpse to Yosef.

*46*Then Yosef bought a linen cloth, took him down and wrapped him in the linen cloth and placed him in a tomb which had been cut out of the rock, and he rolled a stone against the entrance to the tomb.

Miryam the Magdalene and Miryam of Joses saw where he was laid.

## CHAPTER 16

### The Burial

*1*When the Sabbath was over, Miryam the Magdalene and Miryam of Yaakov, and Salome bought aromatic spices so they could come and anoint him. *2*Very early on the first day of the week, they came to the tomb as the sun was rising. *3*They said to each other, "Who will roll away the stone for us from the entrance to the tomb?" *4*They looked up and saw that the stone had been rolled away. And it was huge. *5*Then on going into the tomb they saw a young man sitting on the right, dressed in a white robe, and they were utterly astonished.[38]

*6*He said to them, "Don't be alarmed. You are looking for Yeshua of Nazareth, the one who was crucified. He was raised. He is not here. See the place where they laid him. *7*But go tell his disciples and Petros, 'He is going ahead of you to Galilee. There you will see him, just as he told you.'"

*18*So they went out and fled from the tomb, seized by trembling and ecstasy. And they said nothing to anyone. They were afraid.[39]

---

36. *Yerushalayim* is Jerusalem.

37. *Yosef* is Joseph.

38. Matthew identifies the young man as an angel (28:2).

39. The earliest manuscripts end with the dramatic fear of the women in *ekstasis*, here rendered "ecstasy," which conveys the literal meaning of "being outside themselves" as well as "ecstasy" with its multiple meanings of "amazement" in "being elsewhere" and "beside themselves" with fear. The ending is called abrupt, although not in this translator's opinion. There are three "orphan" supplements, now generally held to be added later, which are said to smooth out the "abrupt" ending. They are now considered to be later additions to make Mark conform to the appearances of the resurrected Messiah as revealed in the other gospels.

# Luke (80–85?) Place
# of composition unknown (gospel)

TRANSLATED BY WILLIS BARNSTONE

There is general agreement among scholars that little is certain about authorship, place, and date with regard to Luke. Although this uncertainty exists for all the gospels, Luke remains a special case. Older scholarship has given us the authorial name Luke and the places of his gospel composition as Rome or cities in the East such as Achaia, Ephesus, or Caesarea in Israel. The name Luke appears to come from Bishop Iraneus (late second century), who claimed that Luke was Paul's "inseparable collaborator" in Antioch. But the depiction of Paul in the Acts, which is also ascribed to Luke, has little to do with the self-portrait of Paul that emerges in the apostle's own letters. There are also traditions, of no more certainty, that speak of Luke as the "beloved physician," as a "convert" to the Christian Jews, and as the Evangelist who wrote for gentile converts. There is no substantial evidence for any of this. It is clear that Luke the author never read or even knew of Paul's letters, and hence all attempts to identify who the author of Luke was, who his associates were, for whom he wrote, and what city or country he wrote in fall apart. Luke was not the companion of Paul. Regardless of unproved speculations about the person of Luke, the gospel of Luke is a splendid achievement.

Luke is the longest of the gospels and, according to most commentators, the most skillfully constructed, composed in an elegant Greek at times approaching classical Hellenistic Greek of the first century. The main example cited by scholars to demonstrate Luke's classical Greek is the brief prologue (1:1–4). This text resembles the prologue to Acts and has been used as proof that Luke is the common author of the Gospel of Luke and the Acts of the Apostles. While it is true that the prologue is a good example of the Hellenistic complexity of rhetoric, this editor finds its convoluted rhetoric polite but also heavy and believes that the prologue, in fact and in spirit, is not by the same author who wrote the rest of the Gospel of Luke. And whether or not the same author wrote Luke and the Acts should not be proven by the similarities of the prologues. Once we go beyond the prologue, the Greek of Luke is different and more inflected, but not decisively removed from Mark and Matthew. Indeed, similarities rather than differences characterize the text.

The Gospel of Luke reads as a fluent late scripture, greatly enlarging the scope of the New Testament. Its immediate sources in the synoptic chain are the unknown Q source, which is presumed to be a sayings gospel, and both Mark and Matthew. Luke expands on both Mark and Matthew, and we cannot explain the source for this additional material. Perhaps the most original and beautiful passages in Luke (for which there are no counterparts in the other gospels) are the annunciation (1:26–38),

Mary's visit to Elizabeth, mother of John the Baptist (1:39–56), the nativity scene of the birth of Jesus in the manger (2:1–7), the parable of the good Samaritan (10:29–37), and the parable of the prodigal son (15:11–32). Only the rich treasury of Luke gives us the birth of John the Baptist (1:5–25, 57–80), the angelic announcement and the visit of the shepherds (2:8–20), and the prayers of Simeon and Anna (2:25–38). Among the poetic masterpieces in the New Testament is Mary's song, the Magnificat (1:39–55), beginning "My soul magnifies the Lord."

Much has been written about Luke as the great narrator, which is true, and Luke's means are often contrasted with Mark's more modest style. The comparison is mistaken. *Both* Mark and Luke are master narrators of the New Covenant, and Luke is closer to Mark than is normally acknowledged. The cliches of Mark as a rude populist and Luke as an elegant Henry James are unfounded. In their best moments, especially in the rush and drama of the passion week, the two authors are cut from the same cloth. Although Mark has no resurrection scene and Luke does, the ending of Luke resembles the narrative genius of Mark. Luke speaks of Jesus, who has come back to life and is walking the roads of Israel, startling his disciples and friends, and engaging in the most profound and compelling conversations of the gospels.

## The Birth of Jesus Foretold

26In the sixth month the angel Gabriel was sent by God to a city in Galilee called Nazareth, 27to a virgin engaged to a man whose name was Yosef,[1] from the house of David, and the name of the virgin was Miryam.[2] 28And he came near her and said, "Hello, favored one, the Lord is with you."

29Miryam was deeply troubled by his word and pondered what kind of greeting this might be.

30The angel said to her, "Do not fear, Miryam, for you have found favor with God. 31Look, you will conceive in your womb and bear a son and you will name him Yeshua. 32He will be great and be called son of the highest, and the Lord God will give him the throne of his father David, 33and he will rule over the house of Yaakov[3] forever, and his kingdom will have no end.

34But Miryam said to the angel:

How will this be since I do not know a man?

35The angel answered her, "The holy spirit will come to you and the power of the highest will overshadow you. So the one being born will be

1. *Yosef* is Joseph.
2. *Miryam* is Mary. Greek word here is *Mariam.*
3. *Yaakov* is James.

called the holy son of God. ₃₆And look, Elizabeth your relative has also conceived a son in her old age and this is the sixth month for her who had been called barren. ₃₇For with God nothing is impossible.[4]

₃₈Miryam said, "Here I am a slave of the Lord. May it happen to me according to your word.

The angel left her.

## The Magnificat

₄₆And Mary said:

> ₄₇My soul magnifies the Lord
>     and my spirit is joyful in God my savior,[5]
> ₄₈for he looked upon his young slave
>     in her low station.
> Look, as of now
>     all generations will call me blessed.
> ₄₉In his power he did wondrous things for me
>     and his name is holy.
> ₅₀His mercy goes from generation to generation
>     to those who fear him.
> ₅₁He showed the strength of his arm
>     and scattered those who were proud in the mind
>     of their heart.
> ₅₂He toppled monarchs from their thrones
>     and raised the poor.
> ₅₃He filled the hungry with good foods
>     and sent the rich away empty.
> ₅₄He helped Israel his servant and child
>     to remember mercy
> ₅₅as he spoke to our fathers,
>     to Avraham and his seed forever.

## CHAPTER 2

## The Nativity

It happened in those days that a decree was sent out from Caesar Augustus to enroll the whole world.[6] ₂This was the first census, when Quirinius was governor of Syria. ₃And all went to their own cities to be registered.

---

4. The texts vary on line 1:37, some putting it in doubt.

5. Mary's song, traditionally called the Magnificat, resembles Hannah's song over Samuel's birth (1Sam. 2:1–10).

6. A census presumably in the whole Roman world that could be used for purposes of taxation and military service.

4Now Yosef also went up from Galilee, from the city of Nazareth, to Yehuda,[7] to the city of David which is called Bethlehem, because he was of the house and family of David. He went to be enrolled with Miryam, who was engaged to him and who was pregnant.[8] 6And it happened that while they were there, the days were completed for her to give birth, 7and she bore a son, her first-born, and she wrapped him in strips of cloth and laid him in a feeding trough of a stable because there was no place for them in the inn.[9]

8And there were shepherds in the region, living in the fields and keeping guard at night over their flock. 9An angel of the Lord stood before them and glory of the Lord shone around them, and they were terrified. 10The angel said to them:

Don't be afraid. Look, I tell you good news,
a great joy for all people.
11Because on this day was born to you in the city of David
a savior who is Messiah the Lord.
12Here is your sign. You will find a child wrapped in cloths
and lying in a feeding trough of a stable.

13And suddenly with the angel there was a multitude of the heavenly army praising God and saying:

Glory to God in the highest
and on earth peace among people of good will.[10]

15And it happened that after the angels had gone from them into the sky, the shepherds said to one another, "Let us go to Bethlehem and see this thing that has happened, which the Lord made known to us."
16And they left, hurrying, and found Miryam and Yosef, and the baby lying in the feeding trough. 17When they saw this, they made known what had been said to them about the child. 18And all who heard wondered at what the shepherds told them.
19But Miryam took all these words in and pondered them in her heart.
20The shepherds returned, glorifying and praising God over all they had heard and seen, as it had been told them.

---

7. Judea.

8. It was important to establish Jesus' lineage through Joseph, who was of the family of David, as indicated in Luke's genealogy, 3:23–37, but with the reservation "so it was thought." The virgin birth would, it would seem, deprive Jesus of the paternal link back to David, but through Mary there was a blood line.

9. *fatni*, feeding trough. "Manger" is a feeding trough for animals. Though a beautiful and evocative word, "manger" has come, incorrectly, to signify the stable itself rather than the feeding box, which conveys a more extraordinary incident.

10. *eudokias*, of good will or good pleasure, or variously translated "whom he favors."

## *Parable of the Prodigal Son (15:11–32)*

*11*And he said:

> There was a man who had two sons.
> *12*The younger said to his father, "Father,
> give me the share of the property
> that will belong to me. So he divided
> his resources between them. *13*And not
> many days later the younger son
> got all his things together and went off
> to a far country and there he squandered
> his substance by riotous living.
> *14*When he had spent everything he had,
> there came a severe famine throughout
> that country, and he began to be in need.
> *15*And he went and hired out to a citizen
> of that land, who sent him to his fields
> to feed the pigs. *16*He longed to be fed
> on the pods the pigs were eating, but no one
> gave him anything. *17*He came to himself[11]
> and said, "How many of the day laborers
> of my father have bread leftover and here
> I'm starving and dying. *18*I will rise up
> and go to my father and I will say
> to him, "Father, I have sinned against
> heaven and before you. *19*I am no longer
> worthy to be called your son. Make me
> like one of your hired hands." *20*And he rose up
> and went to his father. While he was still
> far off, his father saw him and was filled
> with compassion and tears fell on his neck
> and he kissed him. *21*And the son to him,
> "Father, I have sinned against heaven
> and before you. I am no longer worthy
> to be called your son. *22*But his father said
> to his slaves, "Quick, bring out the finest robe
> and put it on him, and give him a ring
> for his hand and sandals for his feet.
> *23*And bring the fatted calf, slaughter it,
> and let us eat and celebrate, *24*for my son
> was dead and he came back to life,
> he was lost and he has been found.
> And they began to celebrate.

---

11. Meaning, "he came to his senses."

25Now the older son was in the fields
and as he drew near the house he heard
music and dancing. 26And he called over
one of his slaves and asked what was going on.
27He told him, "Your brother is here,
and your father has slaughtered the fatted calf
because he took him back in good health.
28He was angry and did not want to go in,
but his father came out and pleaded with him.
29Yet he answered and said to his father,
"Look, so many years I have served you
and never disobeyed an order of yours,
and for me you never gave a young goat
so I could celebrate with my friends.
30But when this son of yours came, who ate up
your property with prostitutes, for him
you slaughtered the fatted calf. 31And he said
to him, "Child, you are always with me,
and everything that is mine is yours,
32but we had to be happy and celebrate.
Your brother was a dead man and he lived
and he was lost and has been found.

## Coming of the Son of People and Parable
## of the Fig Tree (21:25–38)

25There will be signs in sun and moon and stars,
and on the earth the dismay of foreign nations
in bewilderment at the sound of the sea
and surf. 26People will faint from fear
and foreboding of what is coming upon the world,
for the powers of the skies will be shaken.
27And then they will see the Son of People coming
on a cloud with power and enormous glory.
28When these things happen, stand up straight
and raise your heads, for your redemption is near.

And he told them a parable:

Look at the fig tree and all the trees.
30When they sprout leaves, you look at them
and know that summer is already near.
31So too when you see these things happening
you know the kingdom of God is near.
32I tell you truth. This generation will not
pass by until all these things take place.
33The sky and the earth will pass away
but my words will not at all pass away.

34Be careful that you do not burden your hearts
with dissipation and drunkenness and worries
of life lest that day suddenly come upon you
35as a trap, for it will rush in on all
who are sitting on the face of all the earth.
36Be alert and pray at all times for strength
to escape all these things that are to happen,
and to stand before the Son of People.

37Now during those days he was in the Temple, teaching, and in the nights he went out and stay on the mountain, the one called "Of the Olives."[12] 38And all the people rose at dawn to go to the Temple to hear him.

## CHAPTER 24

### The Resurrection

In the first day of the week at early dawn they came to the tomb bringing the spices which they had prepared. 2And they found the stone had been rolled away from the tomb, 3and when they went inside they did not find the body [of the Lord Yeshua].[13]

4And it happened that while they were at a loss about this, look, two men stood near them in clothing that gleamed like lightning.

5The women were terrified and bowed their faces to the earth but the men said to them:

Why do you look for the living among the dead?
6He is not here, but has risen.
Remember how he spoke to you when you were in Galilee:
"The Son of People must be delivered into the hands
of the wrongdoers
and be crucified
and on the third day he shall rise again."

8And they remembered his words.

9When they returned from the tomb they reported all this to the eleven and to the others. 10The women were Myriam the Magdalene and Yohanna and Myriam of Yaakov and the other women with them. They told the apostles these things, 11and to them their words seemed madness. They did not believe them. [But Petros got up and ran to the tomb and bending over saw only the linen cloth, and he left, wondering what happened.][14]

---

12. The Mountain of Olives.

13. The words in brackets are omitted in some manuscripts.

14. The words in brackets are omitted in some manuscripts.

13And look, on the same day, two of them were traveling to a village about seven miles from Yerushalayim,[15] whose name was Emmaous[16] 14and they were speaking to each other about all that took place. 15And it happened that during their talk and discussion Yeshua came near and went with them. 16But their eyes were kept from recognizing him.

17He said to them:

What are you saying as you toss words
back and forth?

And they stood still, downcast. 18One of them whose name was Kleopas answered and said to him, "Are you the only one visiting Yerushalayim who does not know what happened there in these days?"

19He said to them:

What things?

And they said to him, "The things about Yeshua the Nazarene, who was a prophet powerful in act and word. Before God and all the people, and how our high priests and leaders handed him over to the judgment of death and they crucified him. 21We had hoped that he was going to redeem Israel. But now it is already the third day since these things occurred. 22And more, some women among us amazed us. They went at dawn to the tomb, 23and did not find the body and came back saying they saw a vision of angels who say that he is alive. Then some of us went back to the tomb and found it as the women said, but did not see him."

25And he said to them:

O how mindless and slow of heart you are to believe
    all that the prophets spoke!
Didn't the Messiah
have to suffer all these things to enter
into his glory?

27And starting with Moshe[17] and through all the prophets he explained to them all the things in the Torah concerning himself.[18]

---

15. *Yerushalayim* is Jerusalem.

16. Emmaus. In Hebrew the word means "warm baths."

17. *Moshe* is Moses.

18. There is an extreme contrast between the routinely didactic lines in verse 27, the imagination of later churchmen, which again converts the Old Testament from Moses on into an unbroken prophesy about Jesus, and the dramatic passage of Jesus through the village with his students, who entreat him to stay with them, not knowing, yet knowing, who he is, and as we will learn, with their hearts on fire because of the presence and speech.

28And as they approached the village they were traveling to, he pretended to be going on further. 29They entreated him, "Stay with us. It is almost evening and the day has fallen."

So he went in to stay with them.

30And it happened that as he reclined at the table with them, he took the bread and blessed it and broke it and gave it to them.

31Then their eyes opened and they recognized him. But he vanished from them.[19]

32They said to each other, "Were our hearts not burning inside us when he talked to us on the road as he revealed the Torah to us?"

33And they rose up in that very hour and returned to Yerushalayim, and found the eleven and those with them.

34They said, "The Lord has truly risen and he appeared to Shimon."

35Then they described the things on the road and how they recognized him in the breaking of the bread.

36While they were saying these things, he stood in their midst [and said to them:

Peace be with you.][20]

37They were startled and full of fear and thought they were looking at a ghost.

38And he said to them:

Why are you shaken and why do doubts rise
in your hearts? 39Look at my hands and my feet
and see I am myself. Touch me and see,
because a ghost does not have flesh and bones
which as you see I have.

40[And when he said this, he showed them his hands and feet.]

41And when in their joy they still could not believe him and wondered, he said to them:

Do you have something to eat?

42They gave him a piece of broiled fish.
43And he took it and in their presence he ate it.
44Then he said to them:

These are my words which I spoke to you
while I was still with you:

---

19. Or "he became unseen to them."

20. The words in brackets are omitted in some texts.

all that was written about me in the law of Moshe
and the prophets and Psalms must be fulfilled.

45Then he opened their minds to an understanding of the Torah, and
he said to them:

It is written that the Messiah is to suffer and to rise
from the dead on the third day,
47and in his name you will preach repentance
and forgiveness of sins
to all nations, beginning with Yerushalayim.
48You are witnesses of this.
49And I am sending the promise of my father
to you. So stay in the city
until you are clothed with power from on high.[21]

50And he led them out as far as Bethany, and raised his hands and
blessed them. And it happened that while he blessed them, he departed
from them [and was carried up into the sky].[22]

52And they [worshiped him and][23] returned to Yerushalayim with
great joy, and they were constantly in the Temple blessing God.

# John (between A.D. 80 and A.D. 120) Ephesus? (gospel)

### TRANSLATED BY WILLIS BARNSTONE

The prologue of the Gospel of John, "In the beginning was the word,"
imitates the first words of the creation in Genesis, "In the beginning God
created the heavens and the earth." The word in Greek is "logos," and logos was a familiar philosophical term, already in Greek currency through
its usage by the Presocratic philosopher Heraclitus and by the Stoics. In
John, the usage of the word, the logos, is to convey a specific message. The

---

21. Mark ends abruptly, powerfully, and mysteriously, Matthew and John dramatically end with great
pathos. Here the drama is also intense until these last ecclesiastical instructions to prepare witnesses for
the missionary duties of the church. The instructions "to stay in the city / until you are clothed with power
from on high" serve as a perfect afterword to the road and house scenes, and this last formal message contains hope and a promise of power to be delivered from the father on high to the faithful who will go out
from the city to preach the good news. The dramatic narration of the postcrucifiction gospel ends by
verse 44, however, preceding the send off, with the immensely poignant gloom of the followers at the
earthly loss of the Messiah, their joy at the recognition on the road and at the breaking of the bread, the
plain reality and immediacy of his instructions to look at his mutilations of hand and feet—"Touch me
and see"—and his last human act, which is to ask for food and then, in the presence of the intimates, to
eat the cooked fish.

22. The words in brackets are omitted in some texts.

23. The words in brackets are omitted in some texts.

word is the divine savior, who comes into the world to bring hope and eternal life. The "word become flesh" is Jesus, God's emissary incarnated in the world. In contrast to the synoptic gospels (Matthew, Mark, and Luke), in which Jesus' divinity is always there and is not there and is elusive, John suggests decisively that Jesus is the Messiah, that the Messiah is divine, and he is the Son of God. The prologue also emphasizes light and darkness, truth and lies, which seems to be directly related to these dichotomies found in the Dead Sea Scrolls of the Essene community. There is a profound influence of Essene thought on John. And finally, in this perhaps richest of all passages in the New Testament, with the discovery of the Gnostic Gospel of Thomas at Nag Hammadi, Egypt, a similarly strongly Gnostic element should now be observed in John. In short, John is a mirror to a time of diverse beliefs and philosophies, and key terms and concepts, from the Neoplatonist Jew Philo of Alexandria to the scrolls of the Essenes and the Gnostics, flash in and out of his text with unusual intensity.

The authorship of John is a complex puzzle for which there is no solution. Traditionally, the author is John, son of Zebedee, one of Jesus' disciples and apostles. For many reasons, including the probable dating of the work, this view is not generally accepted today. We do not know the name of the author. Some scholars suggest that the author of the prologue may not be the author of the rest of the gospel, or that it may even be the work of a Johannine community (those who follow John's ideas).

John is distinct from the synoptic gospels in many ways. There is no Sermon on the Mount. Jesus tells no parables and does not heal lepers. Demons are not exorcized; there is no Lord's Prayer or Last Supper; and the notion of religious instruction and moral teachings found in the synoptics is absent. As in the other gospels, the book of John does use miracles as "signs" to prove the powers of the Messiah and God. However, in contrast, Jesus is a more abstracted figure, and the presentation of his crucifixion, in contrast with that of the other gospels, is not of an especially suffering man, tortured and dying for human sin, but of a controlled, even aloof figure, following his own divine purpose without fear. There are similarities to the language of Revelation, which is also ascribed, probably falsely, to John. In both texts, Jesus is the Word and the "Lamb of God." But it should be emphasized that the apocalyptic nature of Revelation, the epic vision of heaven and hell, the phantasmagoric images, are wholly apart from anything found in the Gospel of John and may discredit the traditional notion of common authorship.

There is a special problem with regard to the Jews, who did not accept Christ as the promised Messiah. Like Matthew, John is a deeply Jewish gospel, steeped in Old Testament thought and allusion. But more than Matthew, the reference to Jews as the opponents is fierce and constant, while at the same time the gospel presents Jesus as a Jew and rabbi. One explanation for John's presentation of this intramural struggle between Jews lies in the politics of his own later time. If, as many scholars believe,

John dates from early in the second century, anywhere from A.D. 80 to possibly A.D. 120, then it is probable that he is addressing the increasingly tense struggle in many parts of the diaspora world, especially in Asia Minor, between Christian Jews and non-Christian Jews for their place in the synagogues.

Above all, John is a literary document of the Bible. The prologue is magic for believers or nonbelievers, surely one of summit moments in world literature. As Mark is the most poignant and dramatic, Matthew perhaps the most poetic, Luke the most literarily accomplished in its telling of the Nativity and the parables, John is the most spiritual, philosophical, and independent of the gospels.

## CHAPTER 1

*The Word Become Flesh*

> In the beginning was the word
> and the word was with God,
> and God was the word.
>
> 2The word in the beginning was with God.
> 3Through God everything was born
> and without the word nothing was born.
>
> What was born 4through the word was life
> and life was the light of all people
> 5and the light in the darkness shines
> and the darkness could not apprehend the light.
>
> 6There was a man sent from God.
> His name was Yohanan.[1] 7He was a witness
> to testify about the light
> so all might believe through him.
> 8He was not the light,
> but came to testify about the light.
> 9He was the true light
> which illuminates every person
> who comes into the world.
>
> 10He was in the world
> and through him the world was born,
> and the world did not know him.
> 11He went to his own
> and his own did not take him in.
>
> 12To all who took him in
> he gave power to become the children of God,

---

1. John.

to those who believed in his name,
*13*who were not from blood
or from the will of the flesh
or from the will of a man,
but were born from God.

*14*And the word became flesh
and lived among us.

And we saw his glory,
the glory of the only son born of the father,
who is filled with grace and truth.

*15*Yohanan testifies about him,
he who was the baptizer cried out,
yes, he cried out, saying:
"One who will come after me was before me,
because before me he was."

*16*From his bounty all of us have received grace
        and more grace,
*17*and as the law was given through Moshe,[2]
grace and truth have come through Yeshua the Messiah.
*18*No one has ever seen God.
Only the one who was born of God
and who lies in the bosom of his father,
he has made him known.

## CHAPTER 4

*Jesus and the Samaritan Woman*

Now when Yeshua learned that the Pharisees heard that Yeshua was making and baptizing more disciples than Yohanan[3]—*2*though Yeshua himself didn't baptize but his disciples did—he left Yehuda[4] and went again into Galilee. *4*But it was necessary to pass through Samaria. *5*He came to a town in Samaria called Sychar near the piece of land that Yaakov[5] gave his son Yosef.[6] *6*There was a well of Yaakov there. Yeshua was tired from the trip and sat down by the well. It was near noon.

*7*A Samaritan woman came to draw water.

Yeshua said to her, "Give me a drink." *8*His disciples had gone off to the town to buy food.

---

2. Moses.

3. *Yohanan* is John the Baptist.

4. *Yehuda* is Judea.

5. *Yaakov* is James.

6. *Yosef* is Joseph.

₉The Samaritan woman said to him, "How can you a Jew ask to be given a drink by me, a Samaritan? Jews do not mingle with Samaritans."[7]

₁₀Yeshua said to her:

If you knew the gift of God
and who is saying to you "Give me a drink,"
you would have asked and he would have given you
living water.

₁₁She said to him:

Sir, you have no bucket and the well is deep.
Where do you have this living water?
You are not greater than our father Yaakov
who gave us the well and who himself drank
and whose sons and cattle drank?

₁₃Yeshua answered her:

Everyone who drinks this water will be thirsty again.
₁₄But whoever drinks the water I give them
will not be thirsty forevermore.
The water I give them will become in them
a fountain of water springing into eternal life.

₁₅The woman said to him, "Sir, give me this water so I won't be thirsty or come here to draw it up."

₁₆"Go and call your husband and come back here," he said to her.

₁₇"I have no husband," she answered him.

"You're right to say, 'I have no husband.' ₁₈You had five husbands and the one you have now is not your husband. What you said is true."

₁₉"Sir, I see that you are a prophet," she tells him. ₂₀"Our parents[8] worshiped on this mountain and you say Yerushalayim[9] is the place where we must worship."

---

7. "Jews don't mingle with Samaritans" in other editions is put in brackets, parentheses, or a bottom-of-page note, which in effect acknowledges a later scribal commentary. It could be either way, and here I think it goes better without being set off as spurious. This notable identification of Yeshua as a Jew by an "outsider" Samaritan contradicts the prevalent dejudaising of Yeshua and his circle and the repeated use of Jew as the deadly opponent. Revealed once again is the disturbed, schizoid nature of the Scripture, as we have it from multiple hands, which in contingent passages esteems and scourges the Jew.

8. *our parents* is literally our fathers. *Fathers* means ancestors, with male preference intended. Rather than use ancestors, which loses the metaphor of the single for the whole, I use parents. In most contemporary European languages, our fathers (as in Spanish *nuestros padres* or French *nos pères*) is the common word for parents, and by extension ancestors, or to keep up the male-preferred forefathers.

9. *Yerushalayim* is Jerusalem.

21Yeshua said to her:

Believe me, woman,
the hour is coming when not on this mountain
or in Yerushalayim will you worship the father.
22You worship what you do not know.
We worship what we know
since salvation is from the Jews.

23The hour is coming and it is now
when the true worshipers will worship the father
in spirit and truth,
for the father seeks such people to worship him.
24God is spirit
and those worshiping must worship him
in spirit and truth.

25The woman said to him:

I know a Messiah is coming,
who is called the Anointed.
When he comes he will declare all things to us.

26Yeshua said to her:

I am he,
talking to you.

27At this his disciples came and were amazed that he was talking with a woman, but no one said, "What are you looking for?" or "Why are you talking with her?"

28Then the woman left her water jar and went back into the town and said to the people, 29"Come see a man who told me everything I ever did. Can he be the Messiah?
30They went out of the town and came toward him.
31Meanwhile the disciples were saying "Rabbi, eat."
32But he said to them:

I have a meat[10] to eat which you don't know.

33Then the disciples said to each other, "Could someone have brought him something to eat?"
34Yeshua said to them:

---

10. *brosis* also means "food."

My meat is to do the will of him
who sent me and to complete his work.
35Don't you say, "Four more months and then comes harvest?"
Look, I say, lift up your eyes
and you will see the fields are white for harvest.
36Already the reaper is taking his pay
and gathering its fruit for the eternal life
so sower and reaper alike may be happy.
37The words of Job and Micah are true
that one sows and another reaps.
38I sent you to reap what you didn't labor.
Others worked and you entered their work.

39And many Samaritans from the city believed in him, because of what the woman said when she testified, "He told me everything I ever did." 40So when they came near him, the Samaritans asked him to stay with them.

He stayed there two days.

41And many more believed because of his word, 42and they said to the woman, "It's no longer because of your talk that we believe. We ourselves have heard and we know that he is truly the savior of the world."

## The Crucifixion and Burial (19:17–42)

They took Yeshua. 17Carrying the cross himself, he went to what was called the Place of the Skull, which in Hebrew is Golgotha, 18where they crucified him and with him two others on this side and that, and in the middle Yeshua.

19And Pilatus wrote a placard and put it on the cross. It read, "Yeshua the Nazarene the King of the Jews.

20Many Jews read the placard because the place where Yeshua was crucified was near the city. And it was written in Hebrew, Latin, and Greek. So the high priests of the Jews said to Pilatus, "Do not write, 'The King of the Jews,' but that this man said 'I am king of the Jews.'"

22Pilatus answered, "What I've written I've written."

23The soldiers when they crucified Yeshua took his clothes and divided them in four parts, one part for each soldier. And took his tunic too. Now his tunic shirt was seamless, woven in one piece from the top straight down. 24So they said to each other, "Let's not tear it, but casts lots for it to see whose it will be. This was to fulfill the words written in the Psalms saying:

They divided my clothes among them
and for my clothes they cast lots.

The soldiers did those things.

25But near the cross of Yeshua stood Miryam his mother and his mother's sister Miryam of Klopas and Miryam the Magdalene.

₂₆Then Yeshua seeing his mother and the disciple he loved standing near said to his mother:

Woman, here is your son.[11]

Then he said to the disciple:

Here is your mother.

And from that hour the disciple took her into his home.[12]

₂₈After this Yeshua, knowing that all had been done to fulfill the words of the Psalms, he said:

I am thirsty.

₂₉A jar filled with sour wine[13] was lying there. So they put a sponge soaked with the sour wine on a hyssop and held it to his mouth.

₃₀Then when Yeshua had taken the wine, he said:

It is ended.

Bowing his head he gave up the spirit.

₃₁Since it was Friday the Preparation Day, the Jews asked Pilatus that their legs be broken and they be taken away so that the bodies would not remain on the cross on the Sabbath. ₃₂The soldiers came and broke the bones of the first man and then of the other one crucified with him. ₃₃But when they came to Yeshua and saw that he was already dead, they did not break his legs. ₃₄But one of the soldiers stabbed his side with his spear, and at once blood and water came out.

₃₅And the one who saw this has testified to it, and the testimony is true, and he knows he is speaking the truth so that you may also believe. ₃₆These things happened so the Psalms be fulfilled, "No bone of his will be broken." ₃₇And in Zechariah it says, "They will look at him whom they stabbed."

₃₈After these things Yosef of Arimathea, being a disciple of Yeshua, but a secret one for fear of the Jews, asked Pilatus if he could take away Yeshua's body.

Pilatus allowed it.

Then he came and took the body.

₃₉Nikodemos came too, the one who first came to him during the night, and he brought a mixture of myrrh and aloes, about a hundred

---

11. Literally, "Woman, look, your son," which is followed by "Look, your mother."

12. Although *home* or *care* may be the implied translation, it says no more than "He took her into his *own*."

13. *sour wine*, literally "vinegar," meaning a cheap sour wine.

pounds. *40*So they took the body of Yeshua and wrapped it in aromatic spices in linen cloths, as is the Jewish custom.[14]

*41*Now in the place where he was crucified there was a garden, and in the garden a new tomb in which no one had been placed. *42*So because it was the Friday the Preparation Day of the Jews, and the tomb was near, in it they placed Yeshua.

## CHAPTER 20

### Mary Magdalene and Jesus

On Sunday the first day of the week, Miryam the Magdalene came to the tomb early while it was still dark and saw that the stone had been removed from the tomb. *2*So she ran and came to Shimon Petros and to the other disciple whom Yeshua loved and said to them, "They took the Lord from the tomb, and we don't know where they put him."

*3*Then Petros and the other disciple came out and went to the tomb. *4*The two ran together, but the disciple ran faster than Petros and reached the tomb first. *5*And he stooped down and saw the linen cloths lying there, but didn't go in. *6*Then Shimon Petros[15] came, following him, and he went into the tomb, and saw the linen cloths lying there, *7*but the kerchief which had been on his head was not lying next to the cloths but apart folded up in one place. *8*And the other disciple, who had come first to the tomb, saw and believed. *9*They didn't yet know the scripture that he must rise from the dead.

*10*Then the disciples went off to their own places.

*11*But Miryam stood by the tomb, weeping. Then as she was weeping, she stooped into the tomb *12*and saw two angels in white sitting there, one at the head and one at the feet where the body of Yeshua was lay.

*13*And they said to her, "Woman, why are you weeping?"

She said to them, "They have taken my Lord away, and I don't know where they put him."

*14*Saying this she turned around and saw Yeshua standing there and didn't know it was Yeshua.

*15*Yeshua said to her, "Woman, why are you weeping? Whom are you looking for?"

Thinking he was the gardener, she said to him, "Sir, if you took him away, tell me where you put him, and I will take him."

*16*Yeshua said to her, "Miryam!"

She turned and said to him in Hebrew, "Rabboni!" (which means teacher).

*17*Yeshua said to her, "Don't hold me, since I have not yet gone up to the father. But go to my brothers and tell them, "I am ascending to my father and your father and my God and your God.

---

14. In Mathew and Luke, there is also a shroud, a large sheet.

15. *Shimon Petros* is Simon Peter.

*18*Miryam the Magdalene went and announced to the disciples, "I have seen the Lord." And she told them that he had said these things to her.

## Paul (A.D. 5 to A.D. mid-60s) Tarsus/Jerusalem (letter) (New Revised Standard Version)

After considering the gospels and their unknown authors, we must speak of Paul (born Saul), a Greek-speaking Jew from the diaspora, whose literary qualities are equal to the finest passages of the Hebrew Bible and the gospels and whose ideas and mission were fundamental in defining and promoting Christianity. Paul was born in Tarsus, present-day southern Turkey, and was educated at the synagogue in Tarsus and later in Jerusalem, where under the tutelage of Rabbi Gamaliel, the grandson of the ethical leader Hillel, he became an eminent Pharisee. The Pharisees formed a popular movement and, like the Essenes, saw themselves as democratic regionalists, upholding traditional meditation and biblical Law, opposing the strong Hellenizing ways in Jerusalem, and enthusiastically supporting the successful Maccabean independence war against the Syrian ruler Antiochus IV. New Testament writers inaccurately painted the Pharisees as hypocrites and conformists, yet they were to provide the rank and file of the Christian Jews ( Jews who followed Jesus and Paul and initiated Christianity), because of their belief in messianism, Judgment Day, the resurrection, and life after death. In contrast to earlier Jewish belief, in which God's reward for a good life was received on earth, in these dark times of uncertainty and foreign rule, the radical and revolutionary Pharisees believed in a future in which reward and punishment would take place, after the resurrection, in an eternal afterlife. It was natural for the Pharisees, like Paul, to be immediate adherents to the communal and apocalyptic persuasions of their first fellow Christians.

Paul's conversion took place three years after the crucifixion (he did not know Jesus), but his letters, which he wrote as letters, not Scripture, were canonized and are the earliest written documents of the New Testament. The writing down of the first of the Christian gospels was at least thirty-five years after Paul's conversion. Before his conversion, he had approvingly attended the stoning-to-death of the first Christian-Jewish martyr, Stephen, who was to be canonized as Saint Stephen. Paul was chasing Christian Jews to Damascus in Syria when he saw a blinding light and heard Jesus ask why he had been persecuting him. After being led to Damascus blind, he regained his sight, was baptized, and immediately set out to preach in synagogues and market places in Judah, Greece, and Rome.

Paul spoke to Jews and Gentiles and, as the father of Christology, he initiated the new sect of the Christian Jews. As recounted in Acts 15 and Galatians 2, around A.D. 50 in a decisive debate at a council of apostles in Jerusalem, Paul's arguments persuaded the apostles to decide that converts to Christ need not already be or become circumcised, which was tantamount to declaring that thereafter Christianity was not to be an exclusively Jewish sect. For the next two centuries, Christian-Jewish noncanonical writings contained all gradations and mixtures of Jewish and Christian thought (see following section of Intertestamental Scriptures). With the canonization of the New Testament at the end of the fourth century A.D., distinctions between Jew and Christian, in person and texts, were clearer, though they would still remain forever confused for several reasons: Jew and Christian accepted the Hebrew Bible; Jesus himself had been a traditional Jewish rabbi; and late Jewish messianic thought of resurrection and afterlife, as embodied in the Pharisees' beliefs, was to link the theological convictions of Jews and early Christians. There were Jews in all the synagogues where Paul preached conversion. Paul himself never ceased to believe that the Old Testament was inspired Scripture, that God had chosen the Jews to be his people, and that he Paul was one of them. In his own eyes, he was not an apostate but a reformer and expander of Judaism. In Philippians 3:4–6, he argues passionately that he is a circumcised member of the tribe of Benjamin, a Jew born of Jews, a zealous Pharisee, and blameless under the law. Since there was no Christian sect as such when his mission began, he was himself one of the many radical and revolutionary thinkers and changers that this period spawned.

In his letters, Paul introduced new doctrines and organized old ones. Of the fourteen letters attributed to Paul, seven are considered genuine, Romans, 1 and 2 Corinthians, Galatians, Philippians, 1 Thessalonians, and Philemon; pseudonomous and disputed are 2 Thessalonians, Colossians, Ephesians, Hebrews, 1 and 2 Timothy, and Titus. Although Paul scarcely refers to Jesus' teachings, there are four references (Rom. 14:14; 1 Cor. 7:10, 9:14, 11:23–26) centered on Jesus' crucifixion and resurrection and Jesus as Lord. Jesus is the Son of Man, the Messiah (in Hebrew *mashiah*, "the annointed," in Greek *christos*, the "Christ"), and the church is the mystical body of Christ. In Isaiah and Ezekiel, the Messiah was to be a leader, from the Davidian monarchy, who would save and redeem Jerusalem and the Jews on earth.

Like the Quakers, the Jews were ethically earthbound, heaven was less than a dream, and hell (*Gehenna*) a stinking, smoking garbage pit outside Jerusalem. However, by the intertestamental period, Jewish thinking, influenced by Greek Neoplatonic notions of the immortality of the soul, was no longer limited to the earth and a meaningless death. Jews eagerly awaited the savior to come at the end of the world to save and redeem. Paul focuses all these yearnings for a salvational Messiah and some form of life after death into his scriptorial mission. Although his degradation of women—who should be subservient to their husbands, silent in church, silent as teachers or preachers, and veiled—excludes women from professional ambitions, equality, and most aspects of human love, he also has sublime words about love for people and Christ as a high principle. Apart from proselytizing labors, Paul, as thinker and writer, made love, faith, hope, and immortality of the soul the core of the developing religion. While the later gospels report the teachings of Jesus (which are always ambiguous with regard to immortality and his own divinity), for Paul, Jesus is the Son of Man, is God, and is God's earthly incarnation, and the promises of Paul's ideas were to reside in the heart of Christianity.

FURTHER READING: Paul. Doty, W. G. *Letters in Primitive Christianity,* 1973. Hanson, A. T. *Studies in Paul's Technique and Theology,* 1974. Meeks, Wayne A. *The First Urban Christians: The Social World of the Apostle Paul,* 1979.

## *from* First Letter to the Corinthians (1 Cor.)

### CHASTITY AND SEXUAL IMMORALITY (5:1–6:20)

It is actually reported that there is sexual immorality among you, and of a kind that is not found even among pagans; for a man is living with his father's wife. And you are arrogant! Should you not rather have mourned, so that he who has done this would have been removed from among you?

For though absent in body, I am present in spirit; and as if present I have already pronounced judgment in the name of the Lord Jesus on the man who has done such a thing. When you are assembled, and my spirit is present with the power of our Lord Jesus, you are to hand this man over to Satan for the destruction of the flesh, so that his spirit may be saved in the day of the Lord.

Your boasting is not a good thing. Do you not know that a little yeast leavens the whole batch of dough? Clean out the old yeast so that you may be a new batch, as you really are unleavened. For our paschal lamb, Christ, has been sacrificed. Therefore, let us celebrate the festival, not with the old yeast, the yeast of malice and evil, but with the unleavened bread of sincerity and truth.

I wrote to you in my letter not to associate with sexually immoral persons—not at all meaning the immoral of this world, or the greedy and robbers, or idolaters, since you would then need to go out of the world. But now I am writing to you not to associate with anyone who bears the name of brother or sister who is sexually immoral or greedy, or is an idolater, reviler, drunkard, or robber. Do not even eat with such a one. For what have I to do with judging those outside? Is it not those who are inside that you are to judge? God will judge those outside. "Drive out the wicked person from among you."

When any of you has a grievance against another, do you dare to take it to court before the unrighteous, instead of taking it before the saints? Do you not know that the saints will judge the world? And if the world is to be judged by you, are you incompetent to try trivial cases? Do you not know that we are to judge angels—to say nothing of ordinary matters? If you have ordinary cases, then, do you appoint as judges those who have no standing in the church? I say this to your shame. Can it be that there is no one among you wise enough to decide between one believer and another, but a believer goes to court against a believer—and before unbelievers at that?

In fact, to have lawsuits at all with one another is already a defeat for you. Why not rather be wronged? Why not rather be defrauded? But you yourselves wrong and defraud—and believers at that.

Do you not know that wrongdoers will not inherit the kingdom of God? Do not be deceived! Fornicators, idolaters, adulterers, male prostitutes, sodomites, thieves, the greedy, drunkards, revilers, robbers—none of these will inherit the kingdom of God. And this is what some of you used to be. But you were washed, you were sanctified, you were justified in the name of the Lord Jesus Christ and in the Spirit of our God.

"All things are lawful for me," but not all things are beneficial. "All things are lawful for me," but I will not be dominated by anything. "Food is meant for the stomach and the stomach for food," and God will destroy both one and the other. The body is meant not for fornication but for the Lord, and the Lord for the body. And God raised the Lord and will also raise us by his power. Do you not know that your bodies are members of Christ? Should I therefore take the members of Christ and make them members of a prostitute? Never! Do you not know that whoever is united to a prostitute becomes one body with her? For it is said, "The two shall be one flesh." But anyone united to the Lord becomes one spirit with him. Shun fornication! Every sin that a person commits is outside the body; but the fornicator sins against the body itself. Or do you not know that your body is a temple of the Holy Spirit within you, which you have from God, and that you are not your own? For you were bought with a price; therefore glorify God in your body.

## CHASTITY AND MARRIAGE (7:1–24)

Now concerning the matters about which you wrote: "It is well for a man not to touch a woman." But because of cases of sexual immorality, each man should have his own wife and each woman her own husband. The husband should give to his wife her conjugal rights, and likewise the wife to her husband. For the wife does not have authority over her own body, but the husband does; likewise the husband does not have authority over his own body, but the wife does. Do not deprive one another except perhaps by agreement for a set time, to devote yourselves to prayer, and then come together again, so that Satan may not tempt you because of your lack of self-control. This I say by way of concession, not of command. I wish that all were as I myself am. But each has a particular gift from God, one having one kind and another a different kind.

To the unmarried and the widows I say that it is well for them to remain unmarried as I am. But if they are not practicing self-control, they should marry. For it is better to marry than to be aflame with passion.

To the married I give this command—not I but the Lord—that the wife should not separate from her husband (but if she does separate, let her remain unmarried or else be reconciled to her husband), and that the husband should not divorce his wife.

To the rest I say—I and not the Lord—that if any believer has a wife who is an unbeliever, and she consents to live with him, he should not divorce her. And if any woman has a husband who is an unbeliever, and he consents to live with her, she should not divorce him. For the unbelieving husband is made holy through his wife, and the unbelieving wife is made holy through her husband. Otherwise, your children would be unclean, but as it is, they are holy. But if the unbelieving partner separates, let it be so; in such a case the brother or sister is not bound. It is to peace that God has called you. Wife, for all you know, you might save your husband. Husband, for all you know, you might save your wife.

However that may be, let each of you lead the life that the Lord has assigned, to which God called you. This is my rule in all the churches. Was anyone at the time of his call already circumcised? Let him not seek to remove the marks of circumcision. Was anyone at the time of his call uncircumcised? Let him not seek circumcision. Circumcision is nothing, and uncircumcision is nothing; but obeying the commandments of God is everything. Let each of you remain in the condition in which you were called.

Were you a slave when called? Do not be concerned about it. Even if you can gain your freedom, make use of your present condition now more than ever. For whoever was called in the Lord as a slave is a freed person belonging to the Lord, just as whoever was free when called is a slave of Christ. You were bought with a price; do not become slaves of human masters. In whatever condition you were called, brothers and sisters, there remain with God.

## CONCERNING VIRGINS (7:25–40)

Now concerning virgins, I have no command of the Lord, but I give my opinion as one who by the Lord's mercy is trustworthy. I think that, in view of the impending crisis, it is well for you to remain as you are. Are you bound to a wife? Do not seek to be free. Are you free from a wife? Do not seek a wife. But if you marry, you do not sin, and if a virgin marries, she does not sin. Yet those who marry will experience distress in this life, and I would spare you that. I mean, brothers and sisters, the appointed time has grown short; from now on, let even those who have wives be as though they had none, and those who mourn as though they were not mourning, and those who rejoice as though they were not rejoicing, and those who buy as though they had no possessions, and those who deal with the world as though they had no dealings with it. For the present form of this world is passing away.

I want you to be free from anxieties. The unmarried man is anxious about the affairs of the Lord, how to please the Lord; but the married man is anxious about the affairs of the world, how to please his wife, and his interests are divided. And the unmarried woman and the virgin are anxious about the affairs of the Lord, so that they may be holy in body and spirit; but the married woman is anxious about the affairs of the world, how to please her husband. I say this for your own benefit, not to put any restraint upon you, but to promote good order and unhindered devotion to the Lord.

If anyone thinks that he is not behaving properly toward his fiancée, if his passions are strong, and so it has to be, let him marry as he wishes; it is no sin. Let them marry. But if someone stands firm in his resolve, being under no necessity but having his own desire under control, and has determined in his own mind to keep her as his fiancée, he will do well. So then, he who marries his fiancée does well; and he who refrains from marriage will do better.

A wife is bound as long as her husband lives. But if the husband dies, she is free to marry anyone she wishes, only in the Lord. But in my judgment she is more blessed if she remains as she is. And I think that I too have the Spirit of God.

## VEILING OF WOMEN (11:2–16)

I commend you because you remember me in everything and maintain the traditions just as I handed them on to you. But I want you to understand that Christ is the head of every man, and the husband is the head of his wife, and God is the head of Christ. Any man who prays or prophesies with something on his head disgraces his head, but any woman who prays or prophesies with her head unveiled disgraces her head—it is one and the same thing as having her head shaved. For if a woman will not veil herself, then she should cut off her hair; but if it is disgraceful for a woman to have her hair cut off or to be shaved, she should wear a veil. For a man ought not to have his head veiled, since he is the image and reflection of God; but woman is the reflection of man. Indeed, man was not made from woman, but woman from man. Neither was man created for the sake of woman, but woman for the sake of man. For this reason a woman ought to have a symbol of authority on her head, because of the angels. Nevertheless, in the Lord woman is not independent of man or man independent of woman. For just as woman came from man, so man comes through woman; but all things come from God. Judge for yourselves: is it proper for a woman to pray to God with her head unveiled? Does not nature itself teach you that if a man wears long hair, it is degrading to him, but if a woman has long hair, it is her glory? For her hair is given to her for a covering. But if anyone is disposed to be contentious—we have no such custom, nor do the churches of God.

## OBEDIENCE TO THE CHURCH (12:1–28)

Now concerning spiritual gifts, brothers and sisters, I do not want you to be uninformed. You know that when you were pagans, you were enticed and led astray to idols that could not speak. Therefore I want you to understand that no one speaking by the Spirit of God ever says "Let Jesus be cursed!" and no one can say "Jesus is Lord" except by the Holy Spirit.

Now there are varieties of gifts, but the same Spirit; and there are varieties of services, but the same Lord; and there are varieties of activities, but it is the same God who activates all of them in everyone. To each is given the manifestation of the Spirit for the common good. To one is given through the Spirit the utterance of wisdom, and to another the utterance of knowledge according to the same Spirit, to another faith by the same Spirit, to another gifts of healing by the one Spirit, to another the working of miracles, to another prophecy, to another the discernment of spirits, to another various kinds of tongues, to another the interpretation of tongues. All these are activated by one and the same Spirit, who allots to each one individually just as the Spirit chooses.

For just as the body is one and has many members, and all the members of the body, though many, are one body, so it is with Christ. For in the one Spirit we were all baptized into one body—Jews or Greeks, slaves or free—and we were all made to drink of one Spirit.

Indeed, the body does not consist of one member but of many. If the foot would say, "Because I am not a hand, I do not belong to the body," that would not make it any less a part of the body. And if the ear would say, "Because I am not an eye, I do not belong to the body," that would not make it any less a part of the body. If the whole body were an eye, where would the hearing be? If the whole body were hearing, where would the sense of smell be? But as it is, God arranged the members in the body, each one of them, as he chose. If all were a single member, where would the body be? As it is, there are many members, yet one body. The eye cannot say to the hand, "I have no need of you," nor again the head to the feet, "I have no need of you." On the contrary, the members of the body that seem to be weaker are indispensable, and those members of the body that we think less honorable we clothe with greater honor, and our less respectable members are treated with greater respect; whereas our more respectable members do not need this. But God has so arranged the body, giving the greater honor to the inferior member, that there may be no dissension within the body, but the members may have the same care for one another. If one member suffers, all suffer together with it; if one member is honored, all rejoice together with it.

Now you are the body of Christ and individually members of it. And God has appointed in the church first apostles, second prophets, third teachers; then deeds of power, then gifts of healing, forms of assistance, forms of leadership, various kinds of tongues.

## LOVE IS PATIENT; LOVE IS KIND (13:1–13)

If I speak in the tongues of mortals and of angels, but do not have love, I am a noisy gong or a clanging cymbal. And if I have prophetic powers, and understand all mysteries and all knowledge and if I have all faith, so as to remove mountains, but do not have love, I am nothing. If I give away all my possessions, and if I hand over my body so that I may boast, but do not have love, I gain nothing.

Love is patient; love is kind; love is not envious or boastful or arrogant or rude. It does not insist on its own way; it is not irritable or resentful; it does not rejoice in wrongdoing, but rejoices in the truth. It bears all things, believes all things, hopes all things, endures all things.

Love never ends. But as for prophecies, they will come to an end; as for tongues, they will cease; as for knowledge, it will come to an end. For we know only in part, and we prophesy only in part; but when the complete comes, the partial will come to an end. When I was a child, I spoke like a child, I thought like a child, I reasoned like a child; when I became an adult, I put an end to childish ways. For now we see in a mirror, dimly, but then we will see face to face. Now I know only in part; then I will know fully, even as I have been fully known. And now faith, hope, and love abide, these three; and the greatest of these is love.

## SPEAKING IN TONGUES (14:1–40)

Pursue love and strive for the spiritual gifts, and especially that you may prophesy. For those who speak in a tongue do not speak to other people but to God; for nobody understands them, since they are speaking mysteries in the Spirit. On the other hand, those who prophesy speak to other people for their upbuilding and encouragement and consolation. Those who speak in a tongue build up themselves, but those who prophesy build up the church. Now I would like all of you to speak in tongues, but even more to prophesy. One who prophesies is greater than one who speaks in tongues, unless someone interprets, so that the church may be built up.

Now, brothers and sisters, if I come to you speaking in tongues, how will I benefit you unless I speak to you in some revelation or knowledge or prophecy or teaching? It is the same way with lifeless instruments that produce sound, such as the flute or the harp. If they do not give distinct notes, how will anyone know what is being played? And if the bugle gives an indistinct sound, who will get ready for battle? So with yourselves; if in a tongue you utter speech that is not intelligible, how will anyone know what is being said? For you will be speaking into the air. There are doubtless many different kinds of sounds in the world, and nothing is without sound. If then I do not know the meaning of a sound, I will be a foreigner to the speaker and the speaker a foreigner to me. So with yourselves; since you are eager for spiritual gifts, strive to excel in them for building up the church.

Therefore, one who speaks in a tongue should pray for the power to interpret. For if I pray in a tongue, my spirit prays but my mind is unproductive. What should I do then? I will pray with the spirit, but I will pray with the mind also; I will sing praise with the spirit, but I will sing praise with the mind also. Otherwise, if you say a blessing with the spirit, how can anyone in the position of an outsider say the "Amen" to your thanksgiving, since the outsider does not know what you are saying? For you may give thanks well enough, but the other person is not built up. I thank God that I speak in tongues more than all of you; nevertheless, in church I would rather speak five words with my mind, in order to instruct others also, than ten thousand words in a tongue.

Brothers and sisters, do not be children in your thinking; rather, be infants in evil, but in thinking be adults. In the law it is written,

> "By people of strange tongues
> and by the lips of foreigners
> I will speak to this people;
> yet even then they will not
> listen to me."[1]

says the Lord. Tongues, then, are a sign not for believers but for unbelievers, while prophecy is not for unbelievers but for believers. If, therefore, the whole church comes together and all speak in tongues, and outsiders or unbelievers enter, will they not say that you are out of your mind? But if all prophesy, an unbeliever or outsider who enters is reproved by all and called to account by all. After the secrets of the unbeliever's heart are disclosed, that person will bow down before God and worship him, declaring, "God is really among you."

What should be done then, my friends? When you come together, each one has a hymn, a lesson, a revelation, a tongue, or an interpretation. Let all things be done for building up. If anyone speaks in a tongue, let there be only two or at most three, and each in turn; and let one interpret. But if there is no one to interpret, let them be silent in church and speak to themselves and to God. Let two or three prophets speak, and let the others weigh what is said. If a revelation is made to someone else sitting nearby, let the first person be silent. For you can all prophesy one by one, so that all may learn and all be encouraged. And the spirits of prophets are subject to the prophets, for God is a God not of disorder but of peace.

## WOMEN MUST BE SUBORDINATE AND NOT SPEAK IN CHURCH (14:33–40)

(As in all the churches of the saints, women should be silent in the churches. For they are not permitted to speak, but should be subordinate, as the law also says. If there is anything they desire to know, let them ask their husbands at home. For it is shameful for a woman to speak in church. Or did the word of God originate with you? Or are you the only ones it has reached?)

---

1. Isaiah 28:11–12.

Anyone who claims to be a prophet, or to have spiritual powers, must acknowledge that what I am writing to you is a command of the Lord. Anyone who does not recognize this is not to be recognized. So, my friends, be eager to prophesy, and do not forbid speaking in tongues; but all things should be done decently and in order.

## RESURRECTION OF CHRIST (15:1–34)

Now I would remind you brothers and sisters, of the good news that I proclaimed to you, which you in turn received, in which also you stand, through which also you are being saved, if you hold firmly to the message that I proclaimed to you—unless you have come to believe in vain.

For I handed on to you as of first importance what I in turn had received: that Christ died for our sins in accordance with the scriptures, and that he was buried, and that he was raised on the third day in accordance with the scriptures, and that he appeared to Cephas, then to the twelve. Then he appeared to more than five hundred brothers and sisters at one time, most of whom are still alive, though some have died. Then he appeared to James, then to all the apostles. Last of all, as to one untimely born, he appeared also to me. For I am the least of the apostles, unfit to be called an apostle, because I persecuted the church of God. But by the grace of God I am what I am, and his grace toward me has not been in vain. On the contrary, I worked harder than any of them—though it was not I, but the grace of God that is with me. Whether then it was I or they, so we proclaim and so you have come to believe.

Now if Christ is proclaimed as raised from the dead, how can some of you say there is no resurrection of the dead? If there is no resurrection of the dead, then Christ has not been raised; and if Christ has not been raised, then our proclamation has been in vain and your faith has been in vain. We are even found to be misrepresenting God, because we testified of God that he raised Christ—whom he did not raise if it is true that the dead are not raised. For if the dead are not raised, then Christ has not been raised. If Christ has not been raised, your faith is futile and you are still in your sins. Then those also who have died in Christ have perished. If for this life only we have hoped in Christ, we are of all people most to be pitied.

But in fact Christ has been raised from the dead, the first fruits of those who have died. For since death came through a human being, the resurrection of the dead has also come through a human being; for as all die in Adam, so all will be made alive in Christ. But each in his own order; Christ the first fruits, then at his coming those who belong to Christ. Then comes the end, when he hands over the kingdom to God the Father, after he has destroyed every ruler and every authority and power. For he must reign until he has put all his enemies under his feet. The last enemy to be destroyed is death. For "God has put all things in subjection under his feet." But when it says, "All things are put in subjection," it is plain that this does not include the one who put all things in subjection under him.

When all things are subjected to him, then the Son himself will also be subjected to the one who put all things in subjection under him, so that God may be all in all.

Otherwise, what will those people do who receive baptism on behalf of the dead? If the dead are not raised at all, why are people baptized on their behalf?

And why are we putting ourselves in danger every hour? I die every day! That is as certain, brothers and sisters, as my boasting of you—a boast that I make in Christ Jesus our Lord. If with merely human hopes I fought with wild animals at Ephesus, what would I have gained by it? If the dead are not raised.

> "Let us eat and drink,
>    for tomorrow we die."
> Do not be deceived:
>    "Bad company ruins good morals."

Come to a sober and right mind, and sin no more; for some people have no knowledge of God. I say this to your shame.

## RESURRECTION OF THE DEAD (15:35–58)

But someone will ask, "How are the dead raised? With what kind of body do they come?" Fool! What you sow does not come to life unless it dies. And as for what you sow, you do not sow the body that is to be, but a bare seed, perhaps of wheat or of some other grain. But God gives it a body as he has chosen, and to each kind of seed its own body. Not all flesh is alike, but there is one flesh for human beings, another for animals, another for birds, and another for fish. There are both heavenly bodies and earthly bodies, but the glory of the heavenly is one thing, and that of the earthly is another. There is one glory of the sun, and another glory of the moon, and another glory of the stars; indeed, star differs from star in glory.

So it is with the resurrection of the dead. What is sown is perishable, what is raised is imperishable. It is sown in dishonor, it is raised in glory. It is sown in weakness, it is raised in power. It is sown a physical body, it is raised a spiritual body. If there is a physical body, there is also a spiritual body. Thus it is written, "The first man, Adam, became a living being"; the last Adam became a life-giving spirit. But it is not the spiritual that is first, but the physical, and then the spiritual. The first man was from the earth, a man of dust; the second man is from heaven. As was the man of dust, so are those who are of the dust; and as is the man of heaven, so are those who are of heaven. Just as we have borne the image of the man of dust, we will also bear the image of the man of heaven.

What I am saying, brothers and sisters, is this: flesh and blood cannot inherit the kingdom of God, nor does the perishable inherit the imperishable. Listen, I will tell you a mystery! We will not all die, but we will all be changed, in a moment, in the twinkling of an eye, at the last trumpet. For the trumpet will sound, and the dead will be raised imperishable, and we will be changed. For this perishable body must put on imperishability, and this mortal body must put on immortality. When this perishable body puts on imperishability, and this mortal body puts on immortality, then the saying that is written will be fulfilled:

"Death has been swallowed up in
    victory."
"Where, O death, is your
    victory?
Where, O death, is your
    sting?"

The sting of death is sin, and the power of sin is the law. But thanks be to God, who gives us the victory through our Lord Jesus Christ.

Therefore, my beloved, be steadfast, immovable, always excelling in the work of the Lord, because you know that in the Lord your labor is not in vain.

## Revelation (100?) Ephesus or Patmos? (apocalypse)

TRANSLATED BY WILLIS BARNSTONE

Apocalypse is the alternate title of Revelation and in 1.1 the Greek word *apokalypsis* appears, meaning "revelation," which describes the visionary nature of the book. Visionary writing is common in the Hebrew Bible, found in Isaiah, Ezekiel, and Jeremiah and in the Book of Daniel, which contains four formal apocalypses. The apocalyptic form is found in virtually all religions of the world, be it as murals in a Tibetan monastery or in the Egyptian Book of the Dead. These allegorical works, usually prompted by some historical conflict, have enormous spatial dimensions. In Revelation, characters float between earth, heaven, and hell, and, with Christ's help, the good on defeating the wicked enter the fulfillment of a New Age. God declares himself the Alpha and the Omega, and he appears with the mystery of the seven stars in his hand. The four Horsemen of the Apocalypse ride by. A woman gives birth in midair. The angel Michael fights the dragons. Christ and his army throw the beasts of evil into a lake of fire, whereupon a heavenly Jerusalem descends to replace the earthly city, and the millennium arrives.

In the second century, Bishop Iraneus ascribed the Book of Revelation to the evangelist John, son of Zebedee, one of the twelve apostles, who is also credited with writing the Gospel of John and the three Letters of John. Modern scholars, however, find the style, language, thought, and historic circumstance of Revelation so different from the Gospel of John as to obviate the notion of single authorship. John does identify himself as "John" in 1:9, "I Yohanan your brother and companion in suffering," and there is good reason to suppose that the author was a Christian Jew named Yohanan, which is anglicized as John. On the basis of the Greek style, which has elements of Hebrew syntax and vision, it is speculated that the author was a native of Israel who emigrated to Asia Minor, perhaps in the diaspora after the Jewish revolt against Rome (A.D. 66–73) when many had to flee Jerusalem. Although the John who presumably wrote Revelation is almost certainly not the author of the Gospel of John, until recently they were generally held to be the same author. It should be remembered that books of the Old Testament and New Testament as well as scripture of the Intertestamental period were regularly ascribed to major figures in order that such Scripture might be taken into the canon. So we have works attributed to Enoch and Moses well into the first and second centuries A.D. in order to give those religious texts major significance. Seven of the fourteen letters ascribed to Paul are not by Paul. Similarly, the attachment of the Evangelist's name John to Revelation gave great authority to the book and surely helped it find its way into the canon.

There is a crypt in a monastery on Patmos, the Greek island to which John was exiled for two years; and in a small cave room at the edge of this crypt, John is said to have composed Revelation. Since the speaker in the book says that the risen Christ appeared to him on the island of Patmos, then part of a Roman province, and ordered him to write the book, there is good reason to suppose that Revelation might have been written there. Ephesus is given as an alternative place of composition. The date is uncertain. Because of the scarcely disguised anger against the Romans who were persecuting Jews and Christians, some suggest that the book was composed during the rule of the Roman emperor Nero (A.D. 54–68), who massacred both Christian Jews and Christian Gentiles, or during the rule of Domitian (A.D. 81–96).

During the Intertestament period when Revelation was written, the apocalypse form was a common, indeed a popular, form, and there are significant extant examples, such as The Book of Enoch (Jewish), The Apocalypse of Peter (Christian), and The Apocalypse of Thomas (Christian). To the apocalyptic mind, a visionary experience yields a revelation of the future, of a holy city of redemption, or a terrible hell of punishment. Revelation is peopled by angels, monsters, or four-headed beasts that may represent Satan or a Roman emperor; a woman clothed with the sun, representing the faithful people of God; or the great whore of Babylon, representing nefarious Rome. God in his glorious city of gold and precious stones remains the blessing in wait for the pious reader. Though bestial and chaotic creatures of evil battle against heavenly forces, the heavens will triumph through the intervention of Christ as the Christian message will triumph over the hostility of Rome.

The book of Revelation opens with the Seven Letters to the Seven Churches, warning against lawlessness and deceit (1–3). In chapters four to seven, the Seven Seals on a heavenly scroll are opened, telling of war, plague, famine, and the birthpangs of the new age. In six to eight appear the White Horse, the Red Horse, the Black Horse, the Pale Horse, the Souls under the

Alter, the Great Earthquake, the Sealing of the 144,000, and the Silence in Heaven. These visions are followed by seven trumpets (8–11), victory in heaven and disaster for earth as Anti-Christ and false prophet rage. In chapters fifteen to twenty-two the Seven bowls of God's wrath overflow and final battles take place: the whore of Babylon is destroyed as well as the beast's worshippers. Christ returns with the millennium, bringing a last judgment. Finally the bride, New Jerusalem, descends as Babylon falls and we have a description of New Heaven, New Earth, and New Jerusalem (21:1–22:5). These visionary pictures have led fundamentalists, those who take the Bible literally, to see Revelation as the end of the world, the battle of Armageddon (16:12–16). For those who take the Bible as parable and allegory, the struggle between the forces of Satan and Christ are taken as a warning against idolatry and an inducement to save one's soul, and also the church, through faith.

The Apocalypse is an epic poem and takes its place with *Gilgamesh* (Babylonian c. 2000 B.C.), John Milton's *Paradise Lost* (1667), and William Blake's *Jerusalem* (1824) as one of the world's critical visionary poems. As a single, unified work, Revelation may be seen as the literary masterpiece of the New Testament. The symbolism is complex and obscure, a vision blindingly fearful and beautiful. Although Revelation is an intensely luminous book, it suggests more mysteries than it unravels. For that reason, the book is unfinished, as great books are, and its open ending permits the reader endless meditation. There is a circular phenomenon in the fact that Revelation, composed probably on a pagan Greek island, stands as the last work in the Asian New Testament, which returns, as no other volume in Christian Scriptures, to the speech, vision, and hopes of salvation of Old Testament visionaries.

**FURTHER READING:** Revelation and Apocalypses. Barnstone, Willis, ed. *The Other Bible*, 1984. Charlesworth, James H., ed. *Apocalyptic Literature and Testaments*. Vol. 1 of *The Old Testament Pseudepigrapha*, 1983. McGinn, Bernard. "Revelation." In Alter, Robert, and Frank Kermode, *The Literary Guide to the Bible*, 1987.

## CHAPTER 1

*The Alpha and the Omega*

*8*The Lord God says:

> I am the Alpha and the Omega,[1]
> and who is and who was and who is coming.
> I am the Pantocrator.[2]

---

1. *alpha and the omega* in Greek. As with the gospels, the dates and names are unknown. If like the gospels, the text represents a Greek version of a lost earlier version, written or oral, going back to Aramaic or Hebrew, then to represent the first and last letters of the alphabet, as the beginning and the end, we would have *alef and the tav* rather than *alpha and the omega*.

2. *the Pantocrator,* "the Almighty." In the Greek Orthodox Church "Pantocrator," meaning "all powerful," from *pan*, "all," and *kratos*, "strong," is regularly used in the Greek liturgy to signify "Almighty," and chosen to reflect the Greek usage, although since these first two verses come directly from Isaiah 6:3, "Almighty" better reflects the tradition of translation from the Hebrew Bible.

₉I Yohanan your brother and companion in suffering
and kingdom and endurance through Yeshua
was on the island called Patmos for the word
of God and testimony of Yeshua.
₁₀I was fixed in the spirit on the Lord's Day
and I heard behind me a great voice like a trumpet
saying: "What you have seen, write in a book
and send it off to the seven churches,
to Ephesos, Smyrna, Pergamon and Thyatria,
to Sardis and Philadelphia and Laodicea."

₁₂And I turned to see the voice speaking to me,
and when I turned I saw seven gold lamps
₁₃and in the midst of the lamps was one like
the Son of People clothed in a robe down to his feet
and girt around his breasts with a gold belt.
₁₄His head and his hair were white like white wool
like snow and his eyes like a flame of fire,
₁₅his feet like fine bronze as if fired in a furnace
and his voice like the sound of many waters.
₁₆And in his right hand he held seven stars
and from his mouth came a sharp two-edged sword
and his face was like the sun shining in its power.
₁₇When I saw him I fell at his feet like a dead man
and he placed his right hand on me and said:
₁₈"Don't be afraid. I am the first and last
and the living one, and I have been dead,
and look, I am alive forevermore
and I have the keys of Death and of Hell.
₁₉So write what you have seen and what you see
and after this what is about to happen.
₂₀The mystery of the seven stars you saw
in my right hand, and seven golden lamps.
Seven stars are angels for seven churches
and seven golden lamps are seven churches."

## CHAPTER 6

*The Seven Seals*

₁And I saw the lamb open one of the seals
and I head one of the four animals saying
in a voice that seemed like thunder, "Come!"
₂and I saw, and look, a white horse
and its rider had a bow and was given a crown
and he went out conquering and to conquer.

3And when the lamb opened the second seal,
I heard the second animal saying, "Come!"
4Another horse of fire red came out.
Its rider was ordered to take peace away
from earth so men might kill each other,
and he was given a great sword.

5And when the lamb opened the third seal,
I heard the third animal saying, "Come!"
And I saw, and look, a black horse,
and its rider held a pair of scales in his hand.
6And I heard what seemed to be a voice
in the midst of the four animals, saying,
"A measure of wheat for a denarius
and three measures of barley for a denarius,
and do not damage the olive oil with wine."

7And when the lamb opened the fourth seal,
I heard the voice of the fourth animal saying,
"Come!" 8and I saw, and look, a pale green horse,
and the name of his rider was Death, and Hell
was following him. Power was given them
over a quarter of the globe to kill
by sword and by hunger and by death
and by the wild beasts of the earth.

9And when the lamb opened the fifth seal,
I saw under the altar the souls of those
who were slaughtered for the word of God
and the testimony which they held.
10And they cried out in a great voice saying,
"How long, O absolute ruler, holy and true,
will you wait to judge and avenge our blood
from those who live upon the earth?"
11They were each given a white robe and told
to rest a little time until the number was filled
of their fellow slaves, brothers and sisters
who are to be killed as they were killed.

12When the lamb opened the sixth seal I looked
and there took place a great earthquake
and the sun became black like sackcloth of hair
and the full moon became like blood.
13and the stairs of the sky fell to the earth
as the fig tree drops its unripe fruit
shaken by a great wind. 14And the sky
vanished like a scroll rolling up
and every mountain and island of the earth

was torn up from its place and moved.
15And the kings of the earth and the great men
and commanders of thousands and every slave
and the free hid in caves and mountain rocks,
16and said to the mountains and rocks, "Fall on us
and hide us from the face of him who is sitting
on the throne and from the anger of the lamb,
17because the great day of his anger has come,
and before him who has the force to stand?"

## CHAPTER 12

### A Great Portent in the Sky

Then there was a great portent in the sky,
a woman clothed in the sun, and moon
under her feet and on her head a crown
of seven stars. 2In her womb she had a child
and screamed in labor pains, aching to give birth.
3And another portent was seen in the sky,
look, a great fire-red dragon with seven heads
and ten horns, and on his heads seven diadems.
4His tail dragged a third of the stars of heaven
and hurled them to the earth. The dragon stood
before the woman about to give birth
so when she bore her child he might devour it.
5She bore a son, a male, who will shepherd
all nations with a rod of iron,
and her child was snatched away to God
and to his throne. 6And the woman fled
into the desert where she has a place
made ready by God that they might nourish
her one thousand two hundred sixty days.

7And in the sky were Mikhael[3] and his angels
battling with the dragon. 8The dragon and his angels
fought back, but they were not strong enough.
No longer was there place for them in the sky.
The great dragon, the ancient snake, who is called
Devil and Satan, the deceiver of the whole
inhabited world, was flung down to earth.
and his angels were flung down with him.
10And I heard a great voice in the sky, saying,

---

3. *Mikhael*, Hebrew for Michael.

"Now has come the salvation and the power
and the kingdom of our God and the authority
of his Messiah, for the accuser of our brothers
and sisters has been cast down, and the accuser
abused them day and night before our God.
*11*They defeated him through the blood of the lamb
and by the word to which they testified
and did not cling to life while facing death.
*12*Be happy, skies, and those who set their tents
on you. Earth and sky, you will know grief,
because the Devil has come down to you
in great rage, knowing he has little time."

*13*When the dragon saw that he had been cast
down on the earth, he pursued the woman
who had borne the male child. *14*And she was given
two wings of the great eagle that she might fly
into the desert to her place where she is nourished
for a time, and times, and half a time away
from the face of the snake. *15*But from his mouth
the snake cast water, a flood behind the woman,
so he might sweep her away on the river.
*16*But the earth helped the woman, and the earth
opened its mouth and swallowed the river
which the dragon had cast out of his mouth.
*17*The dragon was angry at the woman and left
to battle against her remaining seed,
those who keep the commandments of God
and keep the testimony of Yeshua.

*18*Then the dragon stood on the sand of the sea.

# CHAPTER 13

## A Beast Coming Up from the Sea

*1*Then I saw a beast coming up from the sea,
with ten horns and seven heads and on his horns
ten diadems, and on his heads were the names
of blasphemy. *2*The beast I saw was like a leopard,
his feet like a bear and his mouth like the mouth
of a lion. And the dragon gave him his power
and his throne and fierce power of dominion.
*3*One of his heads seemed to be stricken to death
but the wound causing his death was healed
and the whole world marveled after the beast.
*4*They worshiped the dragon since he had given

dominion to the beast, and they worshiped the beast,
saying, "Who is like the beast and can battle him?"
*5*He was given a mouth to speak great things
and blasphemies. And he was given dominion
to act for forty-two months. *6*Then he opened
his mouth to utter blasphemies against God,
blaspheming his name and his tenting place,
and those who have set their tent in the sky.
*7*He was given powers to battle the saints
and to overcome them, and was given powers
over every tribe and people and tongue and nation.
*8*All who dwell on the earth will worship him,
each one whose name has not been written since
the foundation of the world in the book of life
of the slaughtered lamb. *9*Who has an ear, hear
Jeremiah:

> *10*He who leads into captivity goes into captivity.
> He who kills with the sword will be killed
> by the sword.[4]

Such is the endurance and faith of the saints.

*11*Then I saw another beast rising from the earth
and he had two horns like a lamb and he spoke
like a dragon. *12*He exercises all the dominion
of the first beast before him, and makes the earth
and its inhabitants worship the first beast,
whose wound of death was healed. *13*He does great portents,
even making a fire plunge from the sky
down to the earth in the sight of the people.
*14*He fools the inhabitants on the earth
by means of the portents he contrives to make
on behalf of the beast, creating an image
to show the beast as wounded by the sword
yet comes out alive. *15*And he had the power
to give breath[5] to the image of the beast
and the image of the beast could even speak
and cause all who will not worship the beast
to be killed. *16*He causes all, the small and great,
the rich and poor, the free and the slaves,
to be marked on the hand and the forehead
so that no one can buy or sell without the mark,
the name of the beast or number of his name.
*17*Here is wisdom. Who has a mind, calculate

---

4. Jeremiah 15:2, 14:11.

5. *pneuma* means breath or spirit and sometimes both.

the number of the beast, which is the number
for a human. And the number is 666.

## CHAPTER 15

*A Sea of Glass*

And I saw another great portent in the sky,
great and wonderful, seven angels with seven plagues,
the last ones, since the anger of God is fulfilled
in them. ₂I saw what seemed a sea of glass
mingled with fire, and victors over the beast
and his image and the number of his name,
standing on the sea of glass, holding harps of God.
₃They sang the song of Moses the slave of God
and the song of the lamb:
> Great and wonderful are your works,
>> Lord God the Pantocrator.
> Just and true are your ways,
>> O king of nations!
> ₄Who will not fear you, Lord,
>> and glorify your name?
> Because you alone are holy,
>> because all nations come
>> and worship before you,
> because your judgments are revealed.

₅After this I looked. The temple of the tent[6]
of testimony was opened in the sky,
₆and the seven angels with the seven plagues
came out of the temple. They were robed in linen
clean and bright and gold belts girding their breasts.
₇One of the four animals gave the seven angels
seven gold bowls filled with the anger of God
who lives forevermore. ₈The temple was filled
with smoke from the glory of God and from
his power, and none could enter the temple until
the seven plagues of the seven angels were done.

## CHAPTER 21

*A New Haven*

And I saw a new sky and a new earth,
for the first sky and the first earth were gone
and the sea is no more. ₂I saw the holy
city, the new Yerushalayim, coming down

---

6. *skenes,* "tent" or "pavilion."

out of the sky from God who prepared her
like a bride adorned for her groom. 3And then
I heard a great voice from the throne, saying:
"Look, now the tent of God is with the people,
and he will spread his tent over them,
and he God himself will be with them,
4and he will wipe away each tear from their eyes
and death will be no more. And grief and crying
and pain will be no more. The past has perished."

5And he who sat upon the throne said, "Look,
I made all new." And he said, "Write, because
these words are true and faithful." 6And he said
to me, "It's done. I am the Alpha and the Omega,
the beginning and the end. And to the thirsty
I will give a gift from the spring of the water
of life. 7The victor will inherit these things
and I will be his God and he will be
a son. 8But to the cowards and unbelieving
and abominable and murderers and copulators
and sorcerers and all who are false, their fate
will be the lake burning with fire and sulfur,
which is the second death."

9One of the angels came with the seven bowls
full of the seven last plagues, and he spoke
with me, saying, "Come, I will show you the bride,
the wife of the lamb." 10And he took me away
in spirit onto a mountain great and high,
and showed me the city of holy Yerushalayim
coming down out of the sky from God,
11wearing the glory of God, and her radiance
like a precious stone, like a jasper stone
and crystal clear. 12She has a great and high wall
with twelve gates and at the gates twelve angels,
their names inscribed on them, the twelve tribes
who are the sons and daughters of Israel.
13On the east three gates and on the north three gates,
on the south three gates and on the west three gates.
14The walls of the city have twelve foundations,
and on them twelve names, the twelve apostles of
    the lamb.
15The angel speaking to me had a gold
measuring reed[7] to gage the city and her gates
and walls. 16The city lies foursquare, its length

---

7. *kalamos*, "reed." A "reed" was a basis for measuring; hence a measuring "rod."

and width the same. He gaged the city with
the reed, twelve thousand furlongs in length,[8]
her length and width and height the same. *17*He gaged
her wall a hundred forty-four cubits,[9]
by human measurement the same as angels'.

*18*The wall is built of jasper and the city
clear gold like clear glass. *19*The foundations of
the city are adorned with precious stones,
the first foundation jasper, the second sapphire,
third of agate, fourth of emerald, *20*fifth of onyx,
the sixth carnelian, the seventh chysolite,
the eighth beryl, ninth of topaz, tenth of chysopase,
eleventh hyacinth and the twelfth amethyst.
*21*The twelve gates pearl, each gate a single pearl.
The great square in the city is clear gold
like a diaphanous glass.

*22*I saw no temple in her, for the temple
is Lord God the Pantocrator and the lamb.
*23*The city has no need of sun or moon
to shine on her, for the glory of God
illumined her and her lamp is the lamb.
*24*The Gentile nations will walk around
through her light, and the kings of the earth
bring glory into her. Her gates will never
be shut by day, and night will not be there.
*26*Her people will bring the glory and honor
of nations into her. *27*But no common thing[10]
will enter her, or anyone who stoops
to abominations and lies, but only those
written in the book of life of the lamb.

## CHAPTER 22

*The Throne of God and of the Lamb*

The angel showed me a river of water
of life shining like crystal and issuing
from the throne of God and of the lamb.
*2*Between the great plaza and the river
and on either side stands the tree of life

---

8. About fifteen hundred miles.

9. Almost seventy-five yards.

10. *koinon,* "common." Here this word, as many common words in New Covenant lexicons, is given a religious boost by translating it as "profane," which means "in contrast to the sacred." But its sense of "common" or "plain" contrasts specifically and only with the shining magnificence of the city in the sky, which is lost when the dominant meaning "common" is not rendered.

with her twelve fruits, yielding a special fruit
for every month, and the leaves of the tree
are for healing the nations. ₃Every curse
will no longer exist. The throne of God
and of the lamb will be in her. His slaves
will serve him ₄and will see his face. His name
will be on their foreheads. ₅And night will not
be there and they'll need no light of a lamp
or light of sun, for the Lord God will glow
on them, and they will reign forevermore.

₆Then he said to me, "These words are faithful
and true, and the Lord God of the spirits of
the prophets sent his angel to show his slaves
those things which soon must take place. ₇Look,
I'm coming quickly. Blessed is the one
who keeps the words of this book's prophecy."

₈I Yohanan am the one who heard and saw
these things. And when I heard and saw I fell
and worshiped before the feet of the angel
showing me these things. ₉And he said to me,
"You must not do that! I am your fellow slave
and of your brothers the prophets and those
who keep the words of this book. Worship God."
₁₀And he tells me, "Do not seal the words
of prophecy of this book. The time is near.
₁₁Let the unjust still be unjust, the filthy
still be filthy, the righteous still do right,
and the holy one be holy still. ₁₂Look,
I'm coming soon, and my reward is with me
to give to each according to your work.
₁₃I am the Alpha and the Omega, the first
and the last, the beginning and the end.
₁₄Blessed are they who are washing their robes
so they will have the right to the tree of life
and can enter the city through the gates.
₁₅Outside will be the dogs and sorcerers
and copulators and murderers and idolaters
and everyone who loves to practice lies.

₁₆I Yeshua sent my angel to you
to witness these things to you for the churches.
I am the root and the offspring of David
the bright star of morning. ₁₇And the spirit
and bride say, 'Come.' Let you who hear say, 'Come.'
Let you who thirst come, and let you who wish
take the water of life, which is a gift."

*18*I give my testimony to all who hear
these words of the prophecy of this book.
If anyone adds to these, then God will add
to them the plagues recorded in this book.
*19*If anyone takes away from the words
of this book's prophecy, God will cut off
their share of the tree of life and the holy
city, those things recorded in this book.
*20*And he who witnesses all these things says,
"Yes, I am coming soon."
   Amen, come, Lord Yeshua.
*21*May the grace of the Lord Yeshua be with all.

## ■ Intertestament: Jewish Pseudepigraphica, Dead Sea Scrolls, Jewish-Christian Odes, Gnostic Scriptures (Second Century B.C.–Third Century A.D.)

Between the closing of the Hebrew Bible in the second century and the canonization of the New Testament in A.D. 363, there is a huge literature of holy Scriptures, the Intertestamental texts, that did not find a place in either Testament. These texts, including the Dead Sea Scrolls, Noncanonical Apocrypha, Jewish and Christian Apocalypses, Gospels and Infancy Gospels, Acts, Kabbalah, Psalms, and Gnostic Scriptures, many of which were unavailable until early twentieth-century archaeological discoveries, are important as literature, and they also radically change our picture of the development of the Judeo-Christian tradition.

After the closing of the Old Testament and during the first centuries A.D., inspired authors continued to write sacred Scriptures. They were written by Jews, Christians, Gnostics, and pagans. Many of these texts were of amazing beauty and religious importance and competed with books within the canon. The Jewish texts are in large part called pseudepigrapha (falsely ascribed texts), and include the Dead Sea Scrolls; the Christian texts are called Christian Apocrypha; the Gnostic Scriptures, today so fascinating and even modish, were called by their orthodox rivals heretical. Had events been otherwise and certain of these inspired texts incorporated in our Bible, our understanding of the tradition of religious thought would have been radically altered. Today, free of doctrinal strictures, we can read the "greater bible" of the Judeo-Christian world.

The holy texts that were not included in the Old or New Testaments include creation and Eden myths, psalms and romances, gospels and epistles, prophecies and apocalypses, histories and mystical documents. Every genre of the Bible is represented.

Why did the specifically Jewish and Christian texts fail to find a place in the Bible? Was it a question of divine authority, period, or doctrine? These errant Scriptures are often aesthetically and religiously the equal of books in the canon and offer vital information, such as Infancy Gospels on Jesus' childhood, as well as alternate versions of major biblical stories. In a Manichaean version of Genesis, it is Eve who gives life to Adam, while the serpent, the Luminous Jesus, is a liberating figure urging the first couple to take the first step toward salvation by eating from the Tree of Gnosis. The exclusion of many texts was often as arbitrary and dubious as was the inclusion of such magnificent and dangerous books as Ecclesiastes and the Song of Songs.

At times, the cause of exclusion was fierce political and religious rivalry between sects; between factions; between Jew, Christian, and Gnostic. The antiquity of a book was a primary factor influencing inclusion, and for this reason many competing texts were attributed to great figures of the Bible—to Enoch, Isaiah, Thomas, Paul—to give them both age and authority. For similar reasons, pseudonymous books of the Bible—the Song of Songs, the Psalms, and certain Epistles—assumed the names of Solomon, David, and John in their titles. As for the abundant Gnostic scriptures, these were excluded precisely because of their Gnosticizing tendencies. Indeed, it is said that the early Gnostic Marcion of Sinope so angered the followers of the new religion of Jesus Christ that he provoked the Christian Fathers into establishing a New Testament canon.

The Gnostics were serious rivals of orthodox Christians. The most systematized and organized Gnostic cult was Manichaeism, which spread from Mesopotamia through Asia Minor to North Africa and the European territories of the Roman Empire. It extended to eastern Iran and into Chinese Turkestan, where it became the state religion of the Uigur Empire. Western China remained Manichaean until the thirteenth century. In the West it rose here and there as various medieval sects, such as the Bogomils and Cathari, and the Albigensians in southern France. Today in Iran and southwest Iraq, the Mandaeans, a Gnostic offshoot of heterodox Jewish sects originally from eastern Syria and Palestine, continue in the Gnostic faith.

The most serious conflict between Christians and Gnostics was in the first four centuries A.D. In the second century, Valentinus, a major Gnostic thinker, sought election as Pope of Rome. Surely the fixation of the New Testament in Carthage in 397 would have been drastically different had Valentinus succeeded; and what would have been the views of that former Gnostic, Saint Augustine, whose words so affected the conciliar decisions at Carthage? Leaving aside speculations, we can say categorically that the Bible, with the absence of sacred texts from the entire Intertestamental period, with its acceptance of a small and repetitious canon for the New Testament, with the exclusion of all later Christian Apocrypha, and the total rejection of Gnostic scriptures, has given us a highly censored and distorted version of ancient religious literature.

Deprived of all Scriptures between the Testaments, the common reader is left with the impression that somehow Christianity sprang self-generated like a divine entity, with no past, into its historical setting. Yet a reading of the texts between the Testaments shows how major eschatological themes of the New Testament—the appearance of the Son of Man, the imminence of the End, the apocalyptic vision in the Book of Revelation, the notion of salvation through the Messiah—are all the preoccupation of Intertestamental literature.

In regard to the New Testament, the Epistles and the Book of Revelation could be increased, if not replaced, by other works in these genres. Noncanonical Christian Apocrypha conveys a lucid picture of the life and ideals of early Christendom. We see the wanderings of the apostles in Asia Minor and India, and note their legendary adventures, the sermons of chastity, the bloody accounts of much-desired martyrdom. The Apocrypha is particularly rich in apocalypses, which immediately informs the reader that the canonical Apocalypse is not really an odd and obscure text, but rather one that is perfectly consistent with noncanonical Jewish and Christian Scriptures. In these wondrous texts, we witness visionary journeys to Heaven and Hell, which feed stock images into the tradition that Dante followed in the Commedia when he himself became a figure in Hell, Purgatory, and Heaven.

As for the Gnostics, their scriptures were anathema to orthodox Christians, for they reversed fundamental notions of Christian theology—although they thought themselves the true and uncorrupted Christians. As a result of conflict between these two major sects of primitive Christianity and the victory of the orthodox, the Gnostic texts disappeared; they were destroyed or left uncopied, achieving the same end. Until a few years ago, the loss appeared so complete that we relied for information largely on the works of early Christian Fathers, such as Irenaeus, Hippolytus, Clement of Alexandria, and Augustine, who wrote refutations of the Gnostics. Then, in 1945, extensive Gnostic treatises were discovered in earthenware jars buried in a field at Nag Hammadi in Egypt. The fifty-two scriptures were in Coptic, translated from Greek. Just as the discovery of the Dead Sea Scrolls at Qumran in 1947 gave us for the first time Essene scriptures, so the startling appearance of these Egyptian documents gave us at last the actual words of the Gnostics. The books are rich in cosmogonies and anthropogonies. They contain apocalyptic visions and secret scrolls of Jesus' life and sayings. The magnificent Gospel of Truth and Gospel of Thomas add greatly to the information provided by the New Testament.

Hermes Trismegistus (more likely a tradition than a person) is included because the Hermetic theology and lexicon reveal Jewish, Christian, and Gnostic parallels and exemplify in extraordinary texts the syncretic nature of religious traditions in the first centuries A.D. Plotinus, a thoroughly Hellenized Egyptian Neoplatonist, gives us the vocabulary and system of mystical introspection and ascension to God.

As we move into the first centuries A.D., we encounter a mixture of several traditions, often in the same Scripture. The Gospel of John, an excellent example of such syncretic tendencies, begins with the haunting logic of, "In the beginning was the Word, and the Word was with God, and the Word was God." The Word or logos in the Fourth Gospel comes from Philo of Alexandria (c. 20 B.C.–A.D. 40) who linked the Stoic logos with the Platonic world of ideas, making logos the means of knowing the transcendent God. So in one famous Christian passage, we see clear currents of Greek Platonism through the intermediary of a Hellenized Alexandrian Jew who, among other contributions, invented allegorical exegesis of the Bible, which Christian apologists soon adopted.

Many of the Christian Apocrypha are Jewish Scriptures with a Christian overlay. So the Son of Man, a common messianic term in Jewish pseudepigrapha, obviously becomes in Christian recension Jesus the Messiah. Often the Apocrypha have a Gnostic dimension, as do passages of the gospels. The Odes of Solomon, a Syriac text discovered in 1909, is a Jewish hymnbook, in Christian redaction, subjected to Gnostic interpolations. The original text was almost certainly composed in Greek.

The Intertestamental Scriptures reveal the great diversity of ancient thought. Each view, it seems, is contradicted by a second and a third. The reader has several perspectives to aid in interpretations and judgments. In contrast to Old Testament concern with the historical destiny of a people, the Scriptures between the Testaments emphasize salvation, eternity, and otherworldly *topoi*. We may find three conflicting views of a single event. Thus after Jesus Christ is crucified, the Jews think him another man and go on seeking the Messiah; the Christians proclaim the crucified Jesus both man and God, and the Gnostics take the Docetic view that Jesus was only a simulacrum on the cross, for God is always God. In fact, in the Gnostic works *The Second Treatise of the Great Seth* and *The Apocalypse of Peter,* Jesus the Savior stands above the cross, laughing at the ignorance of his would-be executioners who think that men can kill God.

While the New Testament speaks of a Jesus who rewards the faithful with salvation and condemns the "men of little faith" to eternal damnation, the Apocrypha depict a much more compelling picture of these rewards: we find Jesus on his throne of glory in seventh heaven or descending into Hell to torture sinners with his breath of fire. While the Christian mystic searched through the dark night of ignorance, the Gnostic replaced faith and ignorance with gnosis, that is, knowledge and inner illumination. While the Judeo-Christian view held that our Fall occurred when Eve and Adam ate from the Tree of Knowledge, the Gnostics held that the Fall occurred earlier and Adam and Eve were innocent of wrongdoing. The great error took place when the Creator God himself (as opposed to the alien God) fell into sin by creating the world, by trapping divine sparks of spirit in the darkness, in the material prison of the human body.

# The Book of Jubilees (Second Century B.C.)
## Israel/Alexandria (anonymous Jewish Genesis)

### TRANSLATED BY R. H. CHARLES, ADAPTED BY WILLIS BARNSTONE

The Book of Jubilees is an extensive retelling of Genesis and Exodus in which the author's emphasis on *Halakhah* (the teachings and ordinances of biblical law) suggests both opposition to the Hellenizing spirit in Israel and an affinity with the Qumran community, the so-called Essenes of the Dead Sea Scrolls. The emphasis on *halakhic* commentary is seen in references to "commandments written down on heavenly tablets."

In this "Little Genesis"—an alternate title to a book longer than Genesis as well as any book of the pseudepigrapha—God secretly reveals to Moses on Mount Sinai the history of the Jews from the creation of the world to the passage through the Red Sea. God's agent is the "angel of the presence," who orders Moses to write down God's exact words. Events in the book follow a solar calendar, and dates and numbers are specific and emphatic. For example, the regulations governing the uncleanness of a woman after the birth of a son or daughter specify the number of days of the mother's separation from the sanctuary, and God gives this information to Adam directly on his arrival in Eden from the land of his creation. The emphasis on the prohibition of nakedness, on Adam and Eve's shame and God's gift of clothing to them, reflects an attempt to protect Israel from the Greek *gymnasion* (where athletes trained naked), which were popular in Jerusalem and even among its Maccabean rulers. A notable richness in the book is its angelology—angels of the winds and of the waters—which is referred to in Matthew, Acts, and Revelation. In the final section (not given here), the righteous live a mythical existence and enjoy a prediluvian longevity of a thousand years or more. Their souls will enjoy immortality.

The date of composition is uncertain, but most scholars indicate the middle of the Jubilees was written in Hebrew, then translated into Greek, and from Greek into Ethiopic. The complete text exists in Ethiopic today, edited by R. H. Charles. Fragments of a Latin translation are also extant.

## The Creation of the World[1]

On the first day[2] he created the tall heavens and the earth and waters and all the spirits who served him: the angels of the presence, the angels of sanctification, the angels of the spirit of fire, the angels of the spirit of the

---

1. Chapter 2. This selection is a modern revision by Willis Barnstone of R. H. Charles, *The Book of Jubilees* (Oxford: Clarendon Press, 1902), 40–43, 46–51.

2. The Book of Jubilees is presented as a secret revelation given to Moses by God's angel on Mount Sinai. The first line of chapter 2 omitted in the above text, introduces the retelling of the Genesis creation: "And the angel of the presence spoke to Moses according to the word of the Lord, saying: 'Write the complete history of the creation, how in six days the Lord God finished all his works and all that he created, and kept Sabbath on the seventh day and hallowed it for all ages, and appointed it as a sign for all his works.'"

winds, of the clouds, of darkness, of snow, hail, and hoarfrost, the angels of the voices of thunder and lightning, the angels of the spirits of cold and heat, of winter, spring, autumn, and summer, and of all spirits of his creatures in Heaven and on the earth. He created the abysses and darkness, twilight and night, and light, dawn, and day, and he prepared them in the knowledge of his heart. Thereupon we saw his works, and praised him.

He created seven great works on the first day. On the second day he created the firmament in the midst of the waters, and on that day the waters were divided, half of them going above, half below, the firmament hanging over the face of the entire earth. This was God's only work on the second day. On the third day he commanded the waters to roll off the face of the earth, to gather in one place, and for dry land to appear. The waters did as he commanded and rolled off the face of the earth, and in a single place the dry land appeared. On that day he created all the seas according to their separate gathering places, all rivers, waters in the mountains and along the earth, the lakes and dew, seed which is sown, and all sprouting things, fruit trees, trees of the forest, and the Garden of Eden. In Eden he formed every manner of plant. These were his great works on the third day.

And on the fourth day he created the sun and moon and stars, and placed them in the firmament of heaven to give light on earth, to rule over day and night, to separate light from darkness. And God appointed the sun to be a great sign on the earth for days and for sabbaths and for months, for feasts, years, sabbaths of years, for jubilees, and every season of the years. The sun divided light from darkness so that all things may prosper which shoot and grow in the earth. These three things he made on the fourth day.

And on the fifth day he created great sea monsters in the depths of the waters—these were the first things of flesh created by his hands—the fish and everything that moves in the waters, and everything that flies—all the birds. The sun rose above them to enrich all his creations—plants shooting on the earth, trees, and flesh. These three things he created on the fifth day.

And on the sixth day he created all the animals of the earth, cattle, and all moving things. And after all this he created man, a man and woman, and he gave him dominion over all on the earth, in the seas, in the air, over beasts and cattle he gave him dominion. And these four species he created on the sixth day. There were altogether twenty-two kinds. He finished his work on the sixth day—in Heaven and earth, in the waters and abysses, in light and darkness. And he gave us a great sign, the Sabbath: that we should work six days but on the Sabbath, the seventh day, we should keep from all work.

## Adam, Eve, and Paradise[1]

During six days of the second week, according to God's word, he brought Adam all beasts, cattle, all birds and things creeping on the earth and

---

1. Chapter 3.

moving in the water. Beasts were on day one, cattle on day two, birds on day three, all that creeps on the earth on day four, all that moves in the water on day five. And Adam named them. As he called them so was their name. And during these five days Adam saw that each species had male and female, but he was alone. He had no helpmate. The Lord said to us: "It is not good for the man to be alone. I will make him a helpmate." Our God caused a deep sleep to fall on him, and while he slept God took one of his ribs as a woman. This was the origin of woman. And he built up the flesh on it. He constructed woman. And he woke Adam from his sleep, and on this sixth day he brought her to the rising Adam, and Adam knew her and said, "She is now bone of my bones and flesh of my flesh. She will be called my wife because she was taken from her husband." So man and wife will be one, so a man will leave his father and mother and cleave to his wife, and they will be one flesh.

Adam was created in the first week, and his wife, his rib, in the second week. God showed her to him, and so the commandment was given for a male to keep in his defilement for seven days and for a female twice seven days.

After Adam had completed forty days in the land where he was created, he was brought into the Garden of Eden to till and to keep it. His wife was brought in on the eightieth day. For that reason the commandment is written on the heavenly tablets in regard to the mother: "She who bears a male shall remain in her uncleanness seven days, and thirty-three days in the blood of purification. She shall not touch any hallowed things, nor enter in the sanctuary until the days for the male or female child are accomplished." This is law and testimony written down for Israel.

In the first week of the first jubilee, Adam and his wife were in the Garden of Eden for seven years tilling and reaping. He was given work and instructed how to farm correctly. He tilled the Garden and was naked, but he did not know it, and was not ashamed. He protected the Garden from birds and beasts and cattle, and gathered fruit and food, which he stored for himself and his wife. After exactly seven years, in the seventeenth day of the second month, the serpent came and said to the woman, "Did God command you not to eat of any tree in the Garden?" She said, "God told us to eat fruit from all trees in the Garden, except for the fruit of the tree in the middle of the Garden. God said to us: 'You must not eat from it, nor touch it, or you will die.'"

And the serpent said to the woman, "You will surely not die. For God knows that on the day you eat of that tree your eyes will be opened. You will be like gods and know good from evil." And the woman looked at the tree, which was pleasant to her eye, and its fruit good for food, and she picked a fruit and ate. She covered her shame with a fig leaf and gave Adam what she had taken from the tree. He ate, and his eyes were opened and he saw that he was naked. He took fig leaves, sewed them together, made an apron for himself, and covered his shame.

Then God cursed the serpent and was forever angry with it. He was angry with the woman, for she had listened to the serpent and had eaten. He said to her: "I will greatly multiply your sorrows and your pains. In sorrow you will bring forth children. You will return to your husband, who will rule over you." To Adam he said: "Because you listened to your wife's voice and ate from the tree I commanded you not to touch, let the ground be cursed under you. Thorns and thistles will grow in it, and you will eat your bread in the sweat of your face until you return to the earth from which you were taken. You are earth and to earth you will return." He made them coats out of skins, clothed them, and sent them out of the Garden of Eden.

On the day Adam left the Garden, he made an offering of sweet-smelling frankincense, galbanum, and stacte, and spices of the morning. And on that day was closed the mouth of all beasts, of cattle, birds, whatever walks and crawls, so that they could not speak. They had all spoken to each other with one lip and one tongue. He sent out of the Garden all flesh that was there, and all flesh was scattered according to its kinds in the places created for them. He gave only Adam the means of covering his shame not any of the beasts and cattle. And so those who know the judgment of law prescribed on the heavenly tablets know to cover their shame. They should not uncover themselves as the Gentiles do.[2]

On the new moon of the fourth month Adam and his wife left the Garden of Eden and dwelled in the land of Elda, in the land of their creation. Adam called his wife Eve. They had no son till the first jubilee, and after this he knew her. Now he farmed the land as he had been instructed to in the Garden of Eden.

## The Thanksgiving Psalms (Dead Sea Scrolls) (First Century A.D.) Israel

TRANSLATED BY WILLIS BARNSTONE

The book of psalms contained in one of the scrolls found by the Dead Sea consists of at least twenty-five separate poems. These psalms (or hymns) offer thanksgiving to the Lord who has given the community the secrets of salvation. They were probably learned and sung by initiates when they entered the brotherhood. The majority of scholars believe that many of the psalms are in the voice of the Teacher of Righteousness, and perhaps written by him. Theodor H. Gaster belittles this notion as restrictive and unsubstantiated. He compares their passion and conceits to the

---

2. This passage suggests opposition to stripping by Greeks (as well as Jews) for athletic games. In a larger sense it suggests opposition to Hellenizing Jews and Hellenization in Palestine.

work of the great English metaphysical poets Donne, Herbert, and Vaughan and stresses their mystical component.[1]

The French scholar A. Dupont-Sommer, who views the scrolls as a harbinger of primitive Christianity, sees in the psalms not only their biblical source but ideas connected with the adjacent worlds of the Zoroastrians and the Gnostics. He writes:

> But however close their bond with ancient Jewish piety, the Hymns of Qumran constantly betray new ideas which are obviously connected with the religious world of Zoroastrianism and Hellenistic Gnosis. The psalmist is a "man who knows," a Gnostic; knowledge that is the principle of his salvation and the source of his joy.[2]

Whatever the source, whoever the speaker in the psalms, commentators agree that the poems are the literary jewel of the Dead Sea Scrolls. Indeed, they are equal to the very best psalms of the Old Testament. Their magnificent language, their flow and universal passion, their sweeping images of Heaven, Hell, lions, humanity, and clay frequently render them overwhelming.

## Psalm 1[3]

These things I know from your wisdom,
and you have freed my ears to hear wondrous mysteries.
I am a thing
formed of clay and kneaded with water,
the earth of nakedness and well of pollution,
a furnace of iniquity and fabric of sin,
My perverted spirit strays into error,
fearing good judgment.
What can I say that you do not know beforehand?
All things are graven before you with a pen of remembrance,
for all times, for the years of eternity.
From you nothing is absent or obscure.

## Psalm 10

I am striken dumb like a ewe lamb,
my arm is wrenched from its socket,
my foot sinks in filth,
my eyes blur from seeing evil,
my ears are closed from hearing the cry of bloodshed,

---

1. Theodor H. Gaster, *The Dead Sea Scrolls* (New York: Doubleday Anchor, 1956), 112.

2. A. Dupont-Sommer, ed., G. Vermes, tr., *The Essene Writings from Qumran* (Oxford: Basil Blackwell, 1961), 200.

3. Versions of Psalms 1 and 10 by Willis Barnstone are based on earlier translations by Theodor H. Gaster, Millar Burrows, and G. Vermes.

my heart is appalled at the thought of evil
when human baseness is revealed.
Then my foundations shudder
and my bones are out of joint.
My entrails heave like a ship in a slamming storm from the East.
My heart is utterly sore,
and in the havoc of transgression
a whirlwind swallows me up.

Before considering the Gospel of Thomas and other Gnostic scriptures it is best to consider the nature of Gnosticism itself. The term Gnosticism designates a religious movement made up of many sects, which by the second century A.D. was widespread in Europe, the Middle East, and even extended to western China where in the city of Turfan and the area of Chinese Turkistan it was dominant until well into the thirteenth century.

The Gnostics believed in a radical dualism in which forces of light contend with forces of darkness, knowledge contends with ignorance, truth contends with error (rather than sin), and spirit contends with body and the physical universe. An essential characteristic of all Gnostic systems is a shift from a God-oriented to a self-oriented religion. Gnosticism is based on *gnosis,* Greek for knowledge, and is a personal religion or philosophy based on knowing oneself, as a means to discovering the divinity within oneself. As such, the Gnostic sects, with the exception of the Manichaeans, did not rely on clergy and organization but on self-knowledge, and in this they resembled the personalization and internalization of religion that accompanied the Protestant Reformation many centuries later. We find an especial coincidence of tenets between Gnosticism and the Protestant Quakers, who similarly believe in personal knowledge of "an inner light," which can be found without priest or rites. "Faith" among the Gnostics was not necessarily a virtue, for faith implied surrendering power to the clergy and church. So self-knowledge—rather than a faith in church officials' knowledge—leads to salvation. The Gnostics rejected this world and considered the body a prison from which the soul or, more important, the divine spark, longs to escape in order to return to the unknown, alien, true God, who is androgynous in nature.

The theologian Robert M. Grant suggests that Gnosticism arose among ex-Jews because of the "failure of Jewish apocalyptic hopes."[1] The people were waiting for the Messiah, for divine intervention, during years when the Romans burned the Temple (A.D. 70) and drove the populace into exile. The failure of their expectations provoked a turn away from apocalyptic Judaism, and a turn toward inward speculation. Hence the Jewish Gnostic speculation.

The fulfillment of Jewish apocalyptic hope however, was realized in Christianity, which proclaimed Jesus the Messiah, thereby redeeming the

---

1. Robert M. Grant, *Gnosticism and Early Christianity* (London: Oxford University Press, 1959), 36.

dream that had obsessed Essenes and Zealots and other groups who despaired of contemporary religious and political realities. But then some Christians sensed a failure in Christian *apokalypsis* (revelation); rejected Yahweh, church, and traditional faith; and turned inward—hence the Christian Gnostic speculation. Because the Christian Gnostics violently altered orthodox doctrine, they sought justification of their systems through biblical exegesis. As Philo of Alexandria (15 B.C.– A.D. 50) had earlier allegorized the old Testament, the Gnostics, and particularly the Valentinians, became exegetes of both New and Old Testaments. In addition, they rewrote many of the main books of the Bible; for example, in The Origin of the World, they retell the Creation and Adam and Eve in the garden. The Gnostics reversed many traditional Judeo-Christian beliefs. Eve creates Adam, and Eve is good, rather than sinful and disobedient, for she gave humanity knowledge. Whereas traditional Christians considered sex a proper part of marriage if its purpose was procreation, the Gnostics held that sex was proper and more valuable when it did not lead to procreation and trapping more spirits in the flesh. There developed two views: the sects of Caprocrates and Ophites who practiced extreme eroticism and the Valentinians who inspired extreme asceticism. All sects held the common belief that through meditation on and knowledge of the divine spark, salvation is attained. Salvation is complete when the divine spark returns to union with the alien God.


## The Gospel of Thomas (c. A.D. 200) Syria, Palestine, or Mesopotamia (prophecies, proverbs, and parables of Jesus)

TRANSLATED BY HELMET KOESTER

The Gospel of Thomas is a collection of traditional sayings, prophecies, proverbs, and parables of Jesus. The Coptic Gospel of Thomas was translated from the Greek; in fact, several fragments of this Greek version have been preserved and can be dated to about A.D. 200. Thus the Greek (or even Syriac or Aramaic) collection was composed in the period before A.D. 200, possibly as early as the second half of the first century, in Syria, Palestine, or Mesopotamia. The authorship of the Gospel of Thomas is attributed to Didymos Judas Thomas, that is, Judas "the Twin," who was identified particularly within the Syrian Church as the apostle and twin brother of Jesus.

The relationship of the Gospel of Thomas to the New Testament gospels has been a matter of special interest: many of the sayings of the Gospel of Thomas have parallels in the synoptic gospels (Matthew, Mark, and Luke). A comparison of the sayings in the Gospel of Thomas with their parallels in the synoptic gospels suggests that the sayings in the Gospel of Thomas either are present in a more primitive form or are developments of a more primitive form of such sayings. Indeed, the Gospel of Thomas resembles the synoptic sayings source, often called "Q" (from the German word *Quelle,* "source"), which was the common source of sayings used by Matthew and Luke. Hence the Gospel of Thomas and its sources are collections of sayings and parables that are closely related to the sources of the New Testament gospels.

The influence of Gnostic theology is clearly present in the Gospel of Thomas, though it is not possible to ascribe the work to any particular school or sect. The collected sayings are designated as the "secret sayings which the living Jesus spoke." Thus the collection intends to be esoteric: the key to understanding is the interpretation or secret meaning of the sayings, for "whoever finds the interpretation of these sayings will not experience death." According to the Gospel of Thomas, the basic religious experience is not only the recognition of one's divine identity, but more specifically the recognition of one's origin (the light) and destiny (the repose). In order to return to one's origin, the disciple is to become separate from the world by "stripping off" the fleshly garment and "passing by" the present corruptible existence; then the disciple can experience the new world, the kingdom of light, peace, and life.

The numeration of 114 sayings is not in the manuscript but is followed by most scholars today.

These are the secret sayings which the living Jesus spoke and which Didymos Judas Thomas wrote down.

(1) And he said, "Whoever finds the interpretation of these sayings will not experience death."

(2) Jesus said, "Let him who seeks continue seeking until he finds. When he finds, he will become troubled. When he becomes troubled, he will be astonished, and he will rule over the All."

(3) Jesus said, "If those who lead you say to you, 'See, the Kingdom is in the sky,' then the birds of the sky will precede you. If they say to you, 'It is in the sea,' then the fish will precede you. Rather, the Kingdom is inside of you, and it is outside of you. When you come to know yourselves, then you will become known, and you will realize that it is you who are the sons of the living Father. But if you will not know yourselves, you dwell in poverty and it is you who are that poverty."

(4) Jesus said, "The man old in days will not hesitate to ask a small child seven days old about the place of life, and he will live. For many who are first will become last, and they will become one and the same."

(5) Jesus said, "Recognize what is in your sight, and that which is hidden from you will become plain to you. For there is nothing hidden which will not become manifest."

(6) His disciples questioned him and said to him, "Do you want us to fast? How shall we pray? Shall we give alms? What diet shall we observe?"

Jesus said, "Do not tell lies, and do not do what you hate, for all things are plain in the sight of Heaven. For nothing hidden will not become manifest, and nothing covered will remain without being uncovered."

(7) Jesus said, "Blessed is the lion which becomes man when consumed by man; and cursed is the man whom the lion consumes, and the lion becomes man."

(8) And he said, "The man is like a wise fisherman who cast his net into the sea and drew it up from the sea full of small fish. Among them the wise fisherman found a fine large fish. He threw all the small fish back into the sea and chose the large fish without difficulty. Whoever has ears to hear, let him hear."

(9) Jesus said, "Now the sower went out, took a handful of seeds, and scattered them. Some fell on the road; the birds came and gathered them up. Others fell on rock, did not take root in the soil, and did not produce ears. And others fell on thorns; they choked the seeds and worms ate them. And others fell on the good soil and produced good fruit: it bore sixty per measure and a hundred and twenty per measure."

(10) Jesus said, "I have cast fire upon the world, and see, I am guarding it until it blazes."

(11) Jesus said, "This heaven will pass away, and the one above it will pass away. The dead are not alive, and the living will not die. In the days when you consumed what is dead, you made it what is alive. When you come to dwell in the light, what will you do? On the day when you were one you became two. But when you become two, what will you do?"

(12) The disciples said to Jesus, "We know that you will depart from us. Who is to be our leader?"

Jesus said to them, "Wherever you are, you are to go to James the righteous, for whose sake heaven and earth came into being."

(13) Jesus said to his disciples, "Compare me to someone and tell me whom I am like."

Simon Peter said to him, "You are like a righteous angel."

Matthew said to him, "You are like a wise philosopher."

Thomas said to him, "Master, my mouth is wholly incapable of saying whom you are like."

Jesus said, "I am not your master. Because you have drunk, you have become intoxicated from the bubbling spring which I have measured out."

And he took him and withdrew and told him three things. When Thomas returned to his companions, they asked him, "What did Jesus say to you?"

Thomas said to them, "If I tell you one of the things which he told me, you will pick up stones and throw them at me; a fire will come out of the stones and burn you up."

(14) Jesus said to them, "If you fast, you will give rise to sin for yourselves; and if you pray, you will be condemned; and if you give alms, you will do harm to your spirits. When you go into any land and walk about in the districts, if they receive you, eat what they will set before you, and heal the sick among them. For what goes into your mouth will not defile you, but that which issues from your mouth—it is that which will defile you."

(15) Jesus said, "When you see one who was not born of woman, prostrate yourselves on your faces and worship him. That one is your Father."

(16) Jesus said, "Men think, perhaps, that it is peace which I have come to cast upon the world. They do not know that it is dissension which I have come to cast upon the earth: fire, sword, and war. For there will be five in a house: three will be against two, and two against three, the father against the son, and the son against the father. And they will stand solitary."

(17) Jesus said, "I shall give you what no eye has seen and what no ear has heard and what no hand has touched and what has never occurred to the human mind."

(18) The disciples said to Jesus, "Tell us how our end will be."

Jesus said, "Have you discovered, then, the beginning, that you look for the end? For where the beginning is, there will the end be. Blessed is he who will take his place in the beginning; he will know the end and will not experience death."

(19) Jesus said, "Blessed is he who came into being before he came into being. If you become my disciples and listen to my words, these stones will minister to you. For there are five trees for you in Paradise which remain undisturbed summer and winter and whose leaves do not fall. Whoever becomes acquainted with them will not experience death."

# The Odes of Solomon (Second Century) Syria

### TRANSLATED BY WILLIS BARNSTONE

The *Pistis Sophia,* a Gnostic text preserved in Coptic, contains five odes from *The Odes of Solomon,* and these were all we had of that very important hymnbook until J. Rendel Harris's discovery in 1909 of a 400-year-old Syriac text of the collection. The original language of the odes was probably Greek, although some scholars argue for a Syriac original. Harris conjectured a Jewish-Christian origin from the first century A.D. Others suggest a Jewish original with a Christian redaction. W. Bauer offers a third possibility: "But more and more the view became established that we have to do with a Gnostic hymn-book from the 2nd century."[1] Whatever the origin, in their present form it is clear that they are based on Jewish hymnal tradition, that many of them have been subjected to a Christian overlay, and that there are also Gnostic references, which are more significant than their mere inclusion in the *Pistis Sophia.* Harris also points out many quotations of the odes in the works of the early Church Fathers. The odes were of particular interest because of their Christology, that is, the use of

---

1. Edgar Hennecke and Wilhelm Schneemelcher, eds. *New Testament Apocrypha,* Vol. 2 (Philadelphia: Westminster Press, 1964), 809.

Christ as a speaker. Frequently, the structure of an ode consists of a prologue on the part of the odist, then an oracular statement *ex ore Christi,*
and finally a doxology for the congregation to participate in.

Many of the odes are hauntingly beautiful. The images soar. The diction is rich with surprising references, such as "milk from the Lord," which
apologists explain away as odd symbolism. Actually, the odes are as poetic,
profound, and astonishing as the most compelling psalms of the Old Testament. So we read "The dew of the Lord rinsed me with silence/and a
cloud of peace rose over my head" (Ode 35); or, with typical chariot imagery of Jewish mysticism: "I went up to the light of truth as into a char-
iot/ and truth took me/ across canyons and ravines" (Ode 38). The words
are graceful in "My heart was cloven and there appeared a flower,/ and
grace spang up" (Ode 11), and the thought of three prevailing traditions,
Jewish, Christian, and Gnostic, is suggested in Ode 7:

> The father of knowledge
> is the word of knowledge.
>
> He who created wisdom
> is wiser than his works.

The Odes of Solomon are one of the great poetic and wisdom documents of antiquity.

## Ode 15

> As the sun is joy to those who seek daybreak,
> so my joy is the Lord.
>
> He is my sun and his rays have lifted me up
> and chased all darkness from my face.
>
> In him I have acquired eyes
> and seen his sacred day.
>
> I have acquired eyes
> and heard his truth.
>
> I have acquired knowledge
> and been made happy by him.
>
> I left the way of error and went to him
> and was saved.
>
> According to his bounty he gave me,
> according to his beauty he made me.
>
> I found purity through his name,
> I shed corruption through his grace.
>
> Death has died before my countenance,
> hell is abolished by my word.

A deathless life appears in the land of the Lord,
is known to those with faith,
and is given to those with faith, unceasingly.

## Ode 19

A cup of milk I was offered
and I drank its sweetness as the delight of the Lord.

The Son is the cup
and he who was milked is the Father
and he who milked him is the Holy Ghost.

His breast were full
and his milk should not drip out wastefully.

The Holy Ghost opened the Father's raiment
and mingled the milk from the Father's two breast

and gave that mingling to the world, which was unknowing.
Those who drink it are near his right hand.

The Spirit opened the Virgin's womb
and she received the milk.

The Virgin became a mother of great mercy;
she labored, but not in pain, and bore a Son.
No midwife came.

She bore him as if she were a man,
openly, with dignity, with kindness.
She loved him, and swaddled him, and revealed his majesty.

## Ode 21

I raised my arms high
to the grace of the Lord,

for he had cast off my bonds.
My helper had lifted me to his grace and salvation.

I discarded darkness
and clothed myself in light.

My soul acquired a body
free from sorrow,
affliction or pain.

The thought of the Lord restored me.
I fed on his incorruptible fellowship.

And I was raised in the light
and went to him,
near him,
praising and proclaiming him.

He made my heart flood into my mouth,
made it shine on my lips.

On my face the exultation of the Lord increased,
and his praise.

## Ode 30

Drink deeply from the living fountain of the Lord.
It is yours.

Come, all who are thirsty, and drink,
and rest by the fountain of the Lord.

How beautiful and pure.
It rests the soul.

That water is sweeter than honey.
The combs of bees are nothing beside it.

It flows from the lips of the Lord.
Its name is from the Lord's heart.

It is invisible but has no borders
and was unknown until it was set in our midst.

They who drink are blessed
and they rest.

## Ode 34

The simple heart finds no hard way,
good thought finds no wounds.
Deep in the illuminated mind is no storm.

Surrounded on every side by the beauty of the open country,
one is free of doubt.

Below
is like above.

Everything is above.
Below is nothing, but the ignorant think they see.

Now you know grace. It is for your salvation.
Believe and live and be saved.

## Ode 35

The dew of the Lord rinsed me with silence
and a cloud of peace rose over my head,

guarding me.
It became my salvation.

Everybody quivered in horror.
They issued smoke and a judgment,

but I was silent, near my Lord,
who was more than shadow, more than foundation.

He carried me like a child by its mother.
He gave me milk, his dew,

and I grew in his bounty,
rested in his perfection.

I spread my hands out as my soul pointed to the firmament
and I slipped upward to him
who redeemed me.

## Ode 38

I went up to the light of truth as into a chariot
and truth took me

across canyons and ravines,
and preserved me against waves smashing the cliffs.

It was my haven and salvation
and put me in the arms of immortal life.

It went with me, soothed me, kept me from error,
since it was and is truth . . .

# *The Hymn of the Pearl (Second or Third Century)* Syria? *(narrative poem)*

TRANSLATED BY WILLIS BARNSTONE

"The Hymn of the Pearl" is a fabulous narrative poem concerning the adventurous quest for a pearl. Although the tale was probably pre-Gnostic and pre-Christian, in its present form it has been furnished with details that clearly make it Manichaean and, as Günther Bornkamm argues, the young prince and savior is depicted as Mani himself, the founder of Manichaeism.[1] It is a beautiful poem, one of the most attractive documents in Gnostic literature.

On the surface the poem is simply an adventure. But everywhere in it are clues of other meanings. After all, serpents who sleep with pearls in their possession cannot but have an allegorical dimension. "The Hymn of the Pearl" would be impoverished were one not to decode its symbols, which seem to be determined by their usage in earlier Mandaean tradi-

---

1. Günther Bornkamm, ed., R. McL. Wilson, tr., *The Acts of Thomas*. In Edgar Hennecke and Wilhelm Schneemelcher, eds., *New Testament Apocrypha*, Vol. 2 (Philadelphia: Westminster Press, 1965), 434–435.

tional tales as well as in such Gnostic works as the *Pistis Sophia*. By consensus of most scholars, the main figures—the Father, Mother, and Prince—form a Gnostic trinity, equivalent to the Christian trinitarian formula. They represent the Father of Truth, the Mother of Wisdom, and the Son. The Son, who is redeemer and savior, is not Christ, however, or at least not primarily Christ. Hans Jonas identifies him with the Manichaean precosmic Primal Man. Curiously, he has a double or twin role, for he appears to be both savior and the soul that he saves; he saves and must himself be saved. So too the Pearl, which at first appears to be a symbol of the soul, is also the deity who saves the soul. So, as Jonas points out, "The interchangeability of the subject and object of the mission, of savior and soul, of Prince and Pearl, is the key to the true meaning of the poem, and to the gnostic eschatology in general."[2] Other symbols in the poem are more obvious, although the notion of the double, so typically Gnostic, continues. The Prince's garment of glory, which he has taken off in order to assume the unclean robe of the world—obviously the unclean human body—represents his heavenly glory, which he has left behind, yet this garment of glory also operates as an independent being. So too the letter, on which is written the call of redemption, flies down as an eagle from heaven and becomes a messenger of light. As for Egypt, it stands traditionally for the body, for material things, for darkness and error. It is the kingdom of death. Likewise, the serpent is the realm of darkness and ignorance. For the Gnostics, who tend to reverse Judeo-Christian values, ignorance is equivalent to Judeo-Christian sin and evil; gnosis (brought about through eating the apple from the Tree of Gnosis, and which Christians speak of as original sin) is good and brings redemption. Thus the food that the Prince carries with him is his gnosis, which the soul needs to find itself and return to its heavenly journey. The Father and Mother's home in the east is, of course, Heaven.

As in many Gnostic tales, the woman has an equal or important role in the divine strategy. In key roles such as the creator of Adam's soul, she is not reduced to the nondeity role of mother and housewife as in the family of Jesus or troublemaker during Adam's sojourn in Eden. In "The Hymn of the Pearl," reference is not simply to the "Father," but to the "parents." The Mother is called the "Mistress of the East," that is, the "Mistress of Heaven."

"The Hymn of the Pearl," sometimes called "The Hymn of the Soul," is a fable of redemption. Unlike the traditional Christian myth, here the savior himself must be saved. For a while he forgets who he is and falls into the sleep of earthly things. But the Father of Truth and the Mother of Wisdom (Mother Sophia) do not forget him and send messages. He wakes from the prison of earthly things, steals the pearl, and returns to his true parents.

---

2. Hans Jonas, *The Gnostic Religion*, 2d ed., rev. (1958; reprint, Boston: Beacon Press, 1963), 127.

The hymn exists in an early Syriac text and a somewhat later Greek
version. It is attached to the Apocryphal Acts of Thomas, which deal with
the deeds of the Apostle Judas Thomas.

When I was a little child[1]
living in my kingdom, in my father's house
happy in the glories and riches
of my family that nurtured me,
my parents gave me provisions
and sent me forth from our home in the east.
From their treasure house
they made up a bundle for me.
It was big though light
so I might carry it alone,
and it held gold from the House of the Highest Ones
and silver of Gazzak the Great
and rubies of India
and opals from the land of Kushan,
and they girded me with adamant
which can crush iron.
And they took off my bright robe of glory,
which they had made for me out of love,
and took away my purple toga,
which was woven to fit my stature.
They made a covenant with me
and wrote it in my heart so I would not forget:
"When you go down into Egypt
and bring back the One Pearl
which lies in the middle of the sea
and is guarded by the snorting serpent,
you will again put on your robe of glory
and your toga over it,
and with your brother, our next in rank,
you will be heir in our kingdom."
I left the east and went down
with my two royal envoys,
since the way was dangerous and harsh
and I was very young to walk alone.
I crossed the borders of Maishan,
the gathering place of merchants of the east,
and came into the land of Babel
and entered the walls of Sarbug.

---

1. Version by Willis Barnstone, derived from earlier translations. Reliable translations appear in Edgar
Hennecke and Wilhelm Schneemelcher, eds., *New Testament Apocrypha*, Vol. 2 (Philadelphia: Westminster
Press, 1965), 498–504; and in Robert M. Grant, *Gnosticism* (New York: Harper & Brothers, 1961),
116–122.

I went down into Egypt
and my companions left me.                                             *40*
I went straight to the serpent
and settled in close by his inn,
waiting for him to sleep
so I could take my pearl from him.
Since I was all alone                                                  *45*
I was a stranger to others in the inn,
Yet I saw one of my own people there,
a nobleman from the east,
young, handsome, lovable,
a son of kings—an anointed one,                                        *50*
and he came and was close to me.
And I made him my confidante
with whom I shared my mission.
I warned him against the Egyptians
and of contact with the unclean ones.                                  *55*
Then I put on a robe like theirs
lest they suspect me as an outsider
who had come to steal the pearl;
lest they arouse the serpent against me.
But somehow they learned                                               *60*
I was not their countryman,
and they dealt with me cunningly
and gave me their food to eat.
I forgot that I was a son of kings,
and served their king.                                                 *65*
I forgot the pearl
for which my parents had sent me.
Through the heaviness of their food
I fell into a deep sleep.
But when all these things happened                                     *70*
my parents knew and grieved for me.
It was proclaimed in our kingdom
that all should come to our gate.
And the kings and princes of Parthia
and all the nobles of the east                                         *75*
wove a plan on my behalf
so I would not be left in Egypt.
And they wrote me a letter
and every noble signed it with his name.
"From your father, the King of Kings,                                  *80*
and your mother, the Mistress of the East,
and from your brother, our next in rank,
to you, our son in Egypt, greetings:
Awake and rise from your sleep

and hear the words of our letter!
Remember that you are a son of Kings
and see the slavery of your life.
Remember the pearl
for which you went into Egypt!
Remember your robe of glory
and your splendid mantle
which you may wear
when your name is named in the book of life,
is read in the book of heroes,
when you and your brother inherit
our kingdom."
And serving as messenger
the letter was a letter
sealed by the king with his right hand
against the evil ones, the children of Babel
and the savage demons of Sarbug.
It rose up in the form of an eagle,
the king of all winged fowl;
it flew and alighted beside me,
and became speech.
At its voice and the sound of its rustling
I awoke and rose from my sleep.
I took it, kissed it,
broke its seal and read.
And the words written on my heart
were in the letter for me to read.
I remembered that I was a son of Kings
and my free soul longed for its own kind.
I remembered the pearl
for which I was sent down into Egypt,
and I began to enchant
the terrible and snorting serpent.
I charmed him into sleep
by naming the name of my Father over him,
and the name of the next in rank,
and of my Mother, the queen of the east.
I seized the pearl
and turned to carry it to my Father.
Their filthy and impure garment
I stripped off, leaving it in the fields,
and directed my way
into the light of our homeland, the east.
On my way the letter that awakened me
was lying on the road.
And as it had awakened me with its voice

so it guided me with its light;
it was written on Chinese silk,
and shone before me in its own form.
Its voice soothed my fear
and its love urged me on.                                    *135*
I hurried past Sarbug,
and Babel on the left,
and came to Maishan,
the haven of merchants,
perched next to the sea.                                     *140*
My robe of glory which I had taken off
and the toga over it
were sent by my parents
from the heights of Hyrcania.
They were in the hands of treasurers                         *145*
to whom they were committed
because of their faith,
and I had forgotten the robe's splendor
for as a child I had left it
in my Father's house.                                        *150*
As I gazed on it
suddenly the garment seemed to be a mirror
of myself. I saw it in my whole self,
and in it I saw myself apart,
for we were two entities                                     *155*
yet one form.
The treasurers brought me one robe:
they were two of the same shape
with one kingly seal.
They gave me wealth,                                         *160*
and the bright embroidered robe
was colored with gold and beryls,
with rubies and opals,
and sardonyxes of many colors
were fastened to it in its high home.                        *165*
All its seams were fastened
with stones of adamant;
and the image of the King of Kings
was embroidered on it,
and it glowed with sapphires                                 *170*
of many colors.
I saw it quiver all over
with the movements of gnosis,
and as it prepared to speak
it moved toward me,                                          *175*
murmuring the sound of its songs

as it descended:
"I am the one who acted for him
for whom I was brought up in my Father's house.
I saw myself growing in stature
according to his labors."
With regal movements
it was spreading toward me,
urging me to take it,
and love urged me
to receive it,
and I stretched forth and received it
and put on the beauty of its colors.
I cast my toga of brilliant colors
all around me.
Therein I clothed myself and ascended
to the Gate of Salutation and Adoration.
I bowed my head and adored
the majesty of my Father who had sent it to me.
I had fulfilled his commandments
and he had fulfilled what he promised,
and at the gate of his princes
I mingled with his nobles.
He rejoiced in me and received me
and I was with him in his kingdom,
and all his servants praised him
with resounding voices.
He promised me that I would journey quickly
with him to the Gate of the King of Kings,
and with my gifts and my pearl
I would appear with him before our King.

# On the Origin of the World (Third Century) Greek/Coptic Egypt (Gnostic genesis)

## TRANSLATED BY HANS-GEBHARD BETHGE AND ORVAL S. WINTERMUTE

The modern title *On the Origin of the World* is used to name a tractate that has been transmitted without a title but discusses what this hypothetical title suggests. *On the Origin of the World* is a compendium of essential Gnostic ideas, a work written in the form of an apologetic essay offering to the public an explanation of the Gnostic worldview. Although the treatise does not represent any known Gnostic system, there are reminiscences of Sethian, Valentinian, and Manichaean themes; the author obviously draws upon a variety of traditions and sources. For example, some sort of connection with the *Hypostasis of the Archons* (Codex II, 4) is clear, though the precise nature of this relationship is uncertain. *On the Origin of the World* was probably composed in Alexandria at the end of the third century A.D. or the beginning of the fourth. The place and date of composition are suggested by the juxtaposition of various sorts of materials: the varieties of Jewish thought, Manichaean motifs, Christian ideas, Greek or Hellenistic philosophical and mythological concepts, magical and astrological themes, and elements of Egyptian lore together suggest that Alexandria may have been the place where the original Greek text was composed.

After opening with a reference to the philosophical controversy regarding the origin of Chaos, *On the Origin of the World* proceeds to a detailed portrayal of primeval history. The Genesis story of the creation of the world, the place of the arrogant demiurge Ialdabaoth, and the climactic creation and enlightened transgression of Adam and Eve are described from a Gnostic viewpoint. In addition, important salvific roles are played by Wisdom (Pistis Sophia and Sophia Zoë), the little blessed spirits, and Jesus the logos and Savior. Finally, in a victorious blaze of destruction, light triumphs over darkness, and life over death.

The treatise *On the Origin of the World* is an important Gnostic work in several respects. This text provides insight into the thought, methodology, and argumentation of a Gnostic author presenting to the public at large certain information on the origin and end of the world and of man. Furthermore, the tractate also shows the freedom and skill with which such a writer could utilize various materials of a diverse character, all in the service of Gnostic proclamation. *On the Origin of the World* illustrates how the Gnostic worldview can assert itself in dialogue with other spiritual movements and in part even replace them.

## The Raising of Adam from the Mud by Eve (Zoë-Life)

Then the authorities received knowledge necessary to create man. Sophia Zoë, who is beside Sabaoth, anticipated them, and laughed at their decision because they were blind—in ignorance they created him against themselves—and they do not know what they will do. Because of this she anticipated them. She created her man first in order to inform their molded body of how he would condemn them. And in this way he will save them.

Now the birth of the instructor occurred in this way. When Sophia cast a drop of light, it floated on the water. Immediately the man appeared, being androgynous. That drop first patterned the water as a female body. Afterward it patterned itself within the body of the likeness of the mother who appeared, and it fulfilled itself in twelve months. An androgynous man was begotten, one whom the Greeks call "Hermaphrodites." But the Hebrews call his mother "Eve of Life," i.e., "the instructor of life." Her son is the begotten one who is lord. Afterward, the Authorities called him "the beast" in order to lead their molded bodies astray. The interpretation of the "beast" is "the instructor"; he was found to be wiser than all of them. Moreover, Eve is the first virgin, not having a husband. When she gave birth, she is the one who healed herself. On account of this it is said concerning her that she said,

> "I am the portion of my mother,
>> and I am the mother,
> I am the woman,
>> and I am the virgin.
> I am the pregnant one.
>> I am the physician.
>> I am the midwife.
> My husband is the one who begot me,
>> and I am his mother,
> and he is my father and my lord.
> He is my potency.
> That which he desires he speaks with reason.
> I am still in a nascent state,
>> but I have borne a lordly man."

Now these things were revealed by the will of Sabaoth and his Christ to the souls who will come to the molded bodies of the Authorities; and concerning these, the holy voice said, "Multiply and flourish to rule over all the creatures." And these are the ones who are taken captive by the First Father according to lot and thus they were shut up in the prisons of the molded bodies until the consummation of the Aeon. And then at that time, the First Father gave those who were with him a false intention concerning the man. Then each one of them cast his seed on the midst of the navel of the earth. Since that day, the seven Rulers have formed the man: his body is like their body, his likeness is like the man who appeared to them. His molded body came into being according to a portion of each one of them. Their chief created his head and the marrow. Afterward he appeared like the one who was before him. He became a living man, and he who is the father was called "Adam," according to the name of the one who was before him.

Now after Adam was completed, he left him in a vessel since he had taken form like the miscarriages, having no spirit in him. Because of this deed, when the chief ruler remembered the word of Pistis, he was afraid lest perhaps the man come into his molded body and rule over it. Because of this, he left his molded body forty days without soul. And he withdrew and left him.

But on the fortieth day Sophia Zoë sent her breath into Adam, who was without soul. He began to move upon the earth. And he was not able to rise. Now when the seven Rulers came and saw him, they were very much disturbed. They walked up to him and seized him, and Ialdabaoth said to the breath which was in him, "Who are you? And from whence have you come hither?" He answered and said, "I came through the power of the Light-man because of the destruction of your work." When they heard, they glorified him because he gave them rest from their fear and concern. Then they called that day "the rest," because they rested themselves from their troubles. And when they saw that Adam was not able to rise, they rejoiced. They took him and left him in Paradise, and withdrew up to their heavens.

After the day of rest, Sophia sent Zoë, her daughter, who is called "Eve [of Life]," as an instructor to raise up Adam, in whom there was no soul, so that those whom he would beget might become vessels of the light. When Eve saw her co-likeness cast down, she pitied him, and she said, "Adam, live! Rise up on the earth!" Immediately her word became a deed. For when Adam rose up, immediately he opened his eyes. When he saw her, he said, "You will be called 'the mother of the living' because you are the one who gave me life."

## The Rape of Eve by the Prime Ruler (God) and by His Angels

Then the Authorities were informed that their molded body was alive, and had arisen. They were very much disturbed. They sent seven archangels to see what had happened. They came to Adam. When they saw Eve speaking with him, they said to one another, "What is this female light-being? For truly she is like the likeness which appeared to us in the light. Now come, let us seize her and let us cast our seed on her, so that when she is polluted she will not be able to ascend to her light, but those whom she will beget will serve us. But let us not tell Adam that she is not derived from us, but let us bring a stupor upon him, and let us teach him in his sleep as though she came into being from his rib so that the woman will serve and he will rule over her."

Then Eve, since she existed as a power, laughed at their false intention. She darkened their eyes and left her likeness there stealthily beside Adam. She entered the Tree of Knowledge, and remained there. But they tried to follow her. She revealed to them that she had entered the tree and became tree. And when the blind ones fell into a great fear, they ran away.

Afterward, when they sobered up from the stupor, they came to Adam. And when they saw the likeness of that woman with him, they were troubled, thinking that this was the true Eve. And they acted recklessly, and came to her and seized her and cast their seed upon her. They did it with a lot of tricks, not only defiling her naturally but abominably, defiling the seal of her first voice, which before spoke with them, saying, "What is it that exists before you?" But it is impossible that they might defile those who say that they are begotten in the consummation by the true man by means of the word. And they were deceived, not knowing that they had defiled their own body. It was the likeness which the Authorities and their angels defiled in every form.

She conceived Abel first from the Prime Ruler; and she bore the rest of the sons from the seven Authorities and their angels. Now all this came to pass according to the foresight of the First Father, so that the first mother might beget within herself every mixed seed which is joined together with the fate of the world and its schemata and fate's justice. A dispensation came into being because of Eve so that the molded body of the Authorities might become a hedge for the light. Then it will condemn them through their molded bodies.

Moreover, the first Adam of the light is spiritual. He appeared on the first day. The second Adam is soul-endowed. He appeared on the sixth day, and is called "Hermaphrodite." The third Adam is earthy, i.e., "man of law," who appeared on the eighth day after "the rest of poverty," which is called "Sunday." Now the progeny of the earthy Adam multiplied and completed the earth. They produced by themselves every knowledge of the soul-endowed Adam. But as for the All, he was in ignorance of it. Afterwards, let me continue, when the Rulers saw him and the woman who was with him, erring in ignorance like the beasts, they rejoiced greatly. When they knew that the deathless man would not only pass by them, but that they would also fear the woman who became a tree, they were troubled and said, "Is perhaps this one, who blinded us and taught us about this defiled woman who is like him, the true man, in order that we might be conquered by her?"

Then the seven took counsel. They came to Adam and Eve timidly. They said to him, "Every tree which is in Paradise, whose fruit may be eaten, was created for you. But beware! Don't eat from the Tree of Knowledge. If you do eat, you will die." After they gave them a great fright, they withdrew up to their Authorities.

Then the one who is wiser than all of them, this one who was called "the beast," came. And when he saw the likeness of their mother, Eve, he said to her, "What is it that God said to you? 'Don't eat from the Tree of Knowledge'?" She said, "He not only said 'Don't eat from it,' but 'Don't touch it lest you die.'" He said to her, "Don't be afraid! You certainly shall not die. For he knows that when you eat from it your mind will be sobered and you will become like God, knowing the distinctions which exist between evil and good men. For he said this to you, lest you eat from it, since he is jealous."

Now Eve believed the words of the instructor. She looked at the tree. And she saw that it was beautiful and magnificent, and she desired it. She took some of its fruit and ate, and she gave to her husband also, and he ate too. Then their mind opened. For when they ate, the light of knowledge shone for them. When they put on shame, they knew that they were naked with regard to knowledge. When they sobered up, they saw that they were naked, and they became enamored of one another. When they saw their makers, they loathed them since they were beastly forms. They understood very much.

# ■ Neoplatonism

## *Plotinus (205–270)* Alexandria, Egypt *(Neoplatonic philosophy)*

TRANSLATED BY A. H. ARMSTRONG

Plotinus was born in upper Egypt, probably in Lykopolis in A.D. 205. He is thought to have been a Hellenized Egyptian rather than a Greek. He had an adventurous early life, joining an army that was to invade Persia where he wished to go in order to steep himself in Persian and Indian wisdom. Most of his life was spent in Rome, where he founded a school of philosophy. The *Enneads* (six books containing nine treatises each) were written in the last sixteen years of his life and arranged in their present form by his pupil Porphyry. Porphyry recounts that Plotinus was almost ashamed of existing in a human body since the whole material world was created by the soul and has no real existence in itself. When a painter asked permission to paint his portrait, Plotinus said, "Why paint an illusion of an illusion?" He died outside of Rome, probably of leprosy in 270.

According to Plotinus the supreme source of the world is the One. It is the highest principle, a pure unity entirely undifferentiated, that is, without multiplicity. Plotinus states that the One is without cognition, ignorant even of itself, for self-cognition presupposes the duality of subject and object. The One can no more know itself than can the soul, upon ascending to the One, know the One, for at that point the soul is the One, subject and object are the same. One cannot see the sun when one is the sun; the seer cannot see the seen because the seer is the seen. And using other metaphors (the mystics always resort to metaphors), Plotinus states, explaining the monistic union and its ineffable nature:

> In this state the seer does not see or distinguish or imagine two things; he becomes another, he ceases to be himself and to belong to himself. He belongs to him and is one with him, like two concentric circles; they are one when they coincide, and two only when they are separated. It is only in this sense that the Soul is other than God. Therefore this vision is hard to describe. For how can one describe, as other than oneself, that which, when one saw it, seemed to be one with oneself? (*Enneads*, 6.9.11)

In Plotinus, the One causes the world. But it does not "create" the world as a separate entity, with an independent existence, as in Judaism, Christianity, and Islam. In the theistic religions of the West, there is always a dualism of God and his creations. In Plotinus, the world is an emanation or manifestation of the One, or rather a series of descending emanations. Since the cosmos descends from the One, it is not independent of it. God is pantheistically the world. The first emanation from the One is described as *nous*, Intelligence; and from Intelligence emanates the Soul. The final emanation that proceeds from the Soul is matter, the farthest from the sun and therefore the darkest. Utter darkness is pure nonbeing. If we use the same image of the sun to represent the One, the return to the One is the ascent of the soul to its mystical union.

The ascent to God in Plotinus occurs in three stages of perfection. These levels were already anticipated in Philo (20 B.C.–A.D. 40), who, through his stages of purgation, illumination, and union, provided a chart of the mystical way. Both Philo and Plotinus speak of the knowledge of God as ineffable (a term not used in Greek philosophy prior to Philo); yet knowledge in itself, as in all Hellenic thought, is good, and the way to God is not to follow the mandate of ignorance of the Creator God but to follow reason as far as it will take us. Therein the Gnostics—who reversed the notion of the serpent by making the serpent provide us with virtuous knowledge in order for us to waken from the illusion of the world—are once more aligned with Plotinus, the author of polemical attacks on the Gnostics. In common is their mutual purpose of seeking self-knowledge in order to rise from the world of illusion to the God of total light.

Plotinus goes much further than Plato in recording human consciousness (the soul) and tracing its union with a larger consciousness, which is the universe, call it God, the One, the Alone, the Sun. Plotinus offers a specific method of mystical identification. In his method and quest, he seems to unite monastic visions from eastern Asian Buddhism to Spinoza's pantheistic philosophy in the West. An Egyptian, immersed in the Hellenism of Alexandria and Rome, he is Africa's greatest philosopher, whose word is as eloquently literary as Plato's allegories and as elevating as the poems of the Spanish mystic Saint John of the Cross.

**FURTHER READING:** Armstrong, A. H., ed. *Plotinus,* 1953.

## *from* The Enneads

### THE ASCENT TO UNION WITH THE ONE

Here the greatest, the ultimate contest is set before our souls; all our toil and trouble is for this, not to be left without a share in the best of visions. The man who attains this is blessed in seeing that blessed sight, and he who fails to attain it has failed utterly. A man has not failed if he fails to win beauty of colors or bodies, or power or office or kingship even, but if he fails to win this and only this. For this he should give up the attainment of kingship and rule over all earth and sea and sky, if only by leaving and overlooking them he can turn to that and see.

But how shall we find the way? What method can we devise? How can one see the inconceivable beauty which stays within the holy sanctuary and does not come out where the profane may see it? Let him who can follow and come within, and leave outside the sight of his eyes and not turn back to the bodily splendors which he saw before. When he sees the beauty in bodies he must not run after them; we must know that they are images, traces, shadows, and hurry away to that which they image. For if a man runs to the image and wants to seize it as if it was the reality (like a beautiful reflection playing on the water, which some story somewhere, I think, said riddlingly a man wanted to catch and sank down into the stream and disappeared) then this man who clings to beautiful bodies and will not let them go, will, like the man in the story, but in soul, not in body, sink down into the dark depths where *nous* has no delight, and stay blind in Hades, consorting with shadows there and here. This would be truer advice, "Let us fly to our dear country." Where then is our way of escape? How shall we put out to sea? (Odysseus, I think, speaks symbolically when he says he must fly from the witch Circe, or Calypso, and is not content to stay though he has delights of the eyes and lives among much beauty of sense.) Our country from which we came is there, our Father is there. How shall we travel to it, where is our way of escape? We cannot get there on foot: for our feet only carry us everywhere in this world, from one country to another. You must not get ready a carriage, either, or a boat. Let all these things go, and do not look. Shut your eyes and change to and wake another way of seeing, which everyone has but few use.

The discursive reason, if it wishes to say anything, must seize first one element of the truth and then another; such are the conditions of discursive thought. But how can discursive thought apprehend the absolutely simple? It is enough to apprehend it by a kind of spiritual intuition. But in this act of apprehension we have neither the power nor the time to say anything about it; afterwards we can reason about it. We may believe that we have really seen, when a sudden light illumines the Soul; for this light comes from the One and is the One. And we may think that the One is present, when, like another god, he illumines the house of him who calls upon him; for there would be no light without his presence. Even so the soul is dark that does not behold him: but when illumined by him, it has what it desired, and this is the true end and aim of the soul, to apprehend that light, and to behold it by that light itself, which is no other than the light by which it sees. For that which we seek to behold is that which gives us light, even as we can only see the sun by the light of the sun. How then can this come to us? Strip yourself of everything.

We must not be surprised that that which excites the keenest of longings is without any form, even spiritual form, since the Soul itself, when inflamed with love for it, puts off all the form which it had, even that which belongs to the spiritual world. For it is not possible to see it, or to be in harmony with it, while one is occupied with anything else. The soul must remove from itself good and evil and everything else, that it may receive the One alone, as the One is alone. When the soul is so blessed, and is come to it, or rather when it manifests its presence, when the soul turns away from visible things and makes itself as beautiful as possible and becomes like the One; (the manner of preparation and adornment is known to those who practice it;) and seeing the One suddenly appearing in itself, for there is nothing between, nor are they any longer two, but one; for you cannot distinguish between them, while the vision lasts; it is that union of which the union of earthly lovers, who wish to blend their being with each other, is a copy. The soul is no longer conscious of the body, and cannot tell whether it is a man or a living being or anything real at all; for the contemplation of such things would seem unworthy, and it has no leisure for them; but when, after having sought the One, it finds itself in its presence, it goes to meet it and contemplates it instead of itself. What itself is when it gazes, it has no leisure to see. When in this state the soul would exchange its present condition for nothing, no, not for the very Heaven of Heavens; for there is nothing better, nothing more blessed than this. For it can mount no higher; all other things are below it, however exalted they be. It is then that it judges rightly and knows that it has what it desired, and that there is nothing higher. For there is no deception there; where could one find anything truer than the true? What it says, that it is, and it speaks afterwards, and speaks in silence, and is happy, and is not deceived in its happiness. Its happiness is no titillation of the bodily senses; it is that the soul has become again what it was formerly, when it was blessed. All the things which once pleased it, power, wealth, beauty, science, it declares that it despises; it could not say this if it had not met with something better than these. It fears no evil, while it is with the One, or even while it sees him; though all else perish around it, it is content, if it can only be with him; so happy is it.

The soul is so exalted that it thinks lightly even of that spiritual intuition which it formerly treasured. For spiritual perception involves movement, and the soul now does not wish to move. It does not call the object of its vision spirit, although it has itself been transformed into spirit before the vision and lifted up into the abode of spirits. When the soul arrives at the intuition of the One, it leaves the mode of spiritual perception. Even so a traveler, entering into a palace, admires at first the various beauties which adorn it; but when the master appears, he alone is the object of attention. By continually contemplating the object before him, the spectator sees it no more. The vision is confounded with the object seen, and that which was before object becomes to him the state of seeing, and he forgets all else. The spirit has two powers. By one of them it has a spiritual perception of what is within itself, the other is the receptive intuition by which it perceives what is above itself. The former is the vision of the thinking spirit, the latter is the spirit in love. For when the spirit is inebriated with the nectar, it falls in love, in simple contentment and satisfaction; and it is better for it to be so intoxicated than to be too proud for such intoxication.

If you are perplexed because the One is none of those things which you know, apply yourself to them first, and look forth out of them; but so look, as not to direct your intellect to externals. For it does not lie in one place and not in another, but it is present everywhere to him who can touch it, and not to him who cannot. As in other matters one cannot think of two things at once, and must add nothing extraneous to the object of thought, if one wishes to identify oneself with it, so here we may be sure that it is impossible for one who has in his soul any extraneous image to conceive of the One while that image distracts his attention. Just as we said that matter must be without qualities of its own, if it is to receive the forms of all things, so *a fortiori* must the soul be formless if it is to receive the fullness and illumination of the first principle. If so, the soul must forsake all that is external, and turn itself wholly to that which is within; it will not allow itself to be distracted by anything external, but will ignore them all, as at first by not attending to them, so now last by not seeing them; it will not even know itself; and so it will come to the vision of the One and will be united with it; and then, after a sufficient converse with it, it will return and bring word, if it be possible, to others of its heavenly intercourse. Such probably was the converse which Minos was fabled to have had with Zeus, remembering which he made the laws which were the image of that converse, being inspired to be a law-giver by the divine touch. Perhaps, however, a Soul which has seen much of the heavenly world may think politics unworthy of itself and may prefer to remain above. God, as Plato says, is not far from every one of us; he is present with all, though they know him not. Men flee away from him, or rather from themselves. They cannot grasp him from whom they have fled, nor when they have lost themselves can they find another, any more than a child who is mad and out of his mind can know his father. But he who has learnt to know himself will know also whence he is.

If a soul has known itself throughout its course, it is aware that its natural motion has not been in a straight line (except during some deflection from the normal) but rather in a circle round a center; and that this center is itself in motion round that from which it proceeds. On this center the soul depends, and attaches itself thereto, as all Souls ought to do, but only the Souls of gods do so always. It is this that makes them gods. For a god is closely attached to this center; those further from it are average men, and animals. Is then this center of the soul the object of our search? Or must we think of something else, some point at which all centers as it were coincide? We must remember that our "circles" and "centers" are only metaphors. The Soul is no "circle" like the geometrical figure; we call it a circle because the archetypal nature is in it and around it, and because it is derived from this first principle, and all the more because the souls as wholes are separated from the body. But now, since part of us is held down by the body (as if a man were to have his feet under water), we touch the center of all things with our own center—that part which is not submerged—as the centers of the greatest circles coincide with the center of the enveloping sphere, and then rest. If these circles were corporeal and not psychic, the coincidence of their centers would be spatial, and they would lie around a center somewhere in space; but since the souls belong to the spiritual world, and the One is above even spirit, we must consider that their contact is through other powers—those which connect subject and object in the world of spirit, and further, that the perceiving spirit is present in virtue of its likeness and identity, and unites with its like without hindrance. For bodies cannot have this close association with each other, but incorporeal things are not kept apart by bodies; they are separated from each other not by distance, but by unlikeness and difference. Where there is no unlikeness, they are united with each other. The One, which has no unlikeness, is always present; we are so only when we have no unlikeness. The One does not strive to encircle us, but we strive to encircle it. We always move round the One, but we do not always fix our gaze upon it: we are like a choir of singers who stand round the conductor, but do not always sing in time because their attention is diverted to some external object; when they look at the conductor they sing well and are really with him. So we always move round the One; if we did not, we should be dissolved and no longer exist; but we do not always look towards the One. When we do, we attain the end of our existence, and our repose, and we no longer sing out of tune, but form in very truth a divine chorus round the One.

In this choral dance the soul sees the fountain of life and the fountain of Spirit, the source of being, the cause of good, the root of soul. These do not flow out of the One in such a way as to diminish it; for we are not dealing with material quantities, else the products of the One would be perishable, whereas they are eternal, because their source remains not divided among them, but constant. Therefore the products too are permanent, as the light remains while the sun remains. For we are not cut off from our source nor separated from it, even though the bodily nature intervenes and draws us toward itself, but we breathe and maintain our being in our source, which does not first give itself and then withdraw, but is always supplying us, as long as it is what it is. But we are more truly alive when we turn towards it, and in this lies our well-being. To be far from it is isolation and diminution. In it our soul rests, out of reach of evil: it has ascended to a region which is pure from all evil; there it has spiritual vision, and is exempt from passion and suffering; there it truly lives. For our present life, without God, is a mere shadow and mimicry of the true life. But life yonder is an activity of the spirit, and by its peaceful activity it engenders gods also, through its contact with the One, and beauty, and righteousness, and virtue. For these are the offspring of a soul which is filled with God, and this is its beginning and end—its beginning because from this it had its origin, its end because the Good is there, and when it comes there it becomes what it was. For our life in this world is but a falling away, an exile, and a loss of the Soul's wings. The natural love which the Soul feels proves that the Good is there; this is why paintings and myths make Psyche the bride of Cupid. Because the Soul is different from God, and yet springs from him, she loves him of necessity; when she is yonder she has the heavenly love, when she is here below, the vulgar. For yonder dwells the heavenly Aphrodite, but here she is vulgarized and corrupted, and every soul is Aphrodite. This is figured in the allegory of the birthday of Aphrodite, and Love who was born with her. Hence it is natural for the soul to love God and to desire union with him, as the daughter of a noble father feels a noble love. But when, descending to generation, the soul, deceived by the false promises of a lover, exchanges its divine love for a mortal love, it is separated from its father and submits to indignities; but afterwards it is ashamed of these disorders and purifies itself and returns to its father and is happy. Let him who has not had this experience consider how blessed a thing it is in earthly love to obtain that which one most desires, although the objects of earthly loves are mortal and injurious and loves of shadows, which change and pass; since these are not the things which we truly love, nor are they our good, nor what we seek. But yonder is the true object of our love, which it is possible to grasp and to live with and truly to possess, since no envelope of flesh separates us from it. He who has seen it knows what I say, that the soul then has another life, when it comes to God and having come possesses him, and knows, when in that state, that it is in the presence of the dispenser of the true life, and that it needs nothing further. On the contrary, it must put off all else, and stand in God alone, which can only be when we have pruned away all else that surrounds us. We must then hasten to depart hence, to detach ourselves as much as we can from the body to which we are unhappily bound, to endeavor to embrace God with all our being, and to leave no part of ourselves which is not in contact with him. Then we can see him and ourselves, as far as is permitted: we see ourselves glorified, full of spiritual light, or rather we see ourselves as pure, subtle, ethereal, light: we become divine, or rather we know ourselves to be divine. Then indeed is the flame of life kindled, that flame which, when we sink back to earth, sinks with us.

Why then does not the soul abide yonder? Because it has not wholly left its earthly abode. But the time will come when it will enjoy the vision without interruption, no longer troubled with the hindrances of the body. The part of the soul which is troubled is not the part which sees, but the other part, when the part which sees is idle, though it ceases not from that knowledge which comes of demonstrations, conjectures, and the dialectic. But in the vision that which sees is not reason, but something greater than and prior to reason, something presupposed by reason, as is the object of vision. He who then sees himself, when he sees will see himself as a simple being, will be united to himself as such, will feel himself become such. We ought not even to say that he will see, but he will be that which he sees, if indeed it is possible any longer to distinguish seer and seen, and not boldly to affirm that the two are one. In this state the seer does not see or distinguish or imagine two things; he becomes another, he ceases to be himself and to belong to himself. He belongs to him and is one with him, like two concentric circles; they are one when they coincide, and two only when they are separated. It is only in this sense that the soul is other than God. Therefore this vision is hard to describe. For how can one describe, as other than oneself, that which, when one saw it, seemed to be one with oneself?

This is no doubt why in the mysteries we are forbidden to reveal them to the uninitiated. That which is divine is ineffable, and cannot be shown to those who have not had the happiness to see it. Since in the vision there were not two things, but seer and seen were one (for the seeing was no seeing but a merging), if a man could preserve the memory of what he was when he was mingled with the divine, he would have in himself an image of him. For he was then one with him, and retained no difference, either in relation to himself or to others. Nothing stirred within him, neither anger nor concupiscence nor even reason or spiritual perception or his own personality, if we may say so. Caught up in an ecstasy, tranquil and God-possessed, he enjoyed an imperturbable calm; shut up in his proper essence he inclined not to either side, he turned not even to himself; he was in a state of perfect stability; he had become stability itself. The soul then occupies itself no more even with beautiful things; it is exalted above the beautiful, it passes the choir of the virtues. Even as when a man who enters the sanctuary of a temple leaves behind him the statues in the temple, they are the objects which he will see first when he leaves the sanctuary after he has seen what is within, and entered there into communion, not with statues and images, but with the deity itself. Perhaps we ought not to speak of vision; it is rather another mode of seeing, an ecstasy and simplification, an abandonment of oneself, a desire for immediate contact, a stability, a deep intention to unite oneself with what is to be seen in the sanctuary. He who seeks to see God in any other manner, will find nothing. These are but figures, by which the wise prophets indicate how we may see this God. But the wise priest, understanding the symbol, may enter the sanctuary and make the vision real. If he has not yet got so far, he at least conceives that what is within the sanctuary is something invisible to mortal eyes, that it is the source and principle of all; he knows that it is by the first principle that we see the first principle, and unites himself with it and perceives like by like, leaving behind nothing that is divine, so far as the soul can reach. And before the vision, the soul desires that which remains for it to see. But for him who has ascended above all things, that which remains to see is that which is before all things. For the nature of the soul will never pass to absolute not-being: when it falls, it will come to evil, and so to not-being, but not to absolute not-being. But if it moves in the opposite direction, it will arrive not at something else, but at itself, and so, being in nothing else, it is only in itself alone; but that which is in itself alone and not in the world of being is in the absolute. It ceases to be being; it is above being, while in communion with the One. If then a man sees himself become one with the One, he has in himself a likeness of the One, and if he passes out of himself, as an image to its archetype, he has reached the end of his journey. And when he comes down from his vision, he can again awaken the virtue that is in him, and seeing himself fitly adorned in every part he can again mount upward through virtue to Spirit, and through wisdom to the One itself. Such is the life of gods and of godlike and blessed men; a liberation from all earthly bonds, a life that takes no pleasure in earthly things, a flight of the alone to the Alone.

# Early Arabic Literature

## INTRODUCTION

The Semitic tribes that inhabited the Arabian peninsula consisted of two Arab peoples, the nomadic Bedouin tribes, who subsisted through a wandering sheepherding and goatherding existence, and the settled Hejazis, who were farmers and traders, living in settlements and cities. Hejazi caravans traveled across the Middle East, allowing many merchants to accumulate great wealth, and were often raided by the warlike Bedouins. Arabian tribal groups cohered loosely through the election of a sheik, the leader of the tribe; through animistic religion that maintained no assertion of life after death; through tribal rituals; and through an ethic of bravery, pride, family loyalty, and revenge.

From the fourth to the seventh centuries A.D., a large body of oral Arabic poetry developed, though most of it was transcribed later—in the eighth and ninth centuries—by editors who may have altered, regulated, and edited some of the original works. This is considered the golden age of Arabic poetry. The *qasida*, the basic prosodic form of classical Arabic poetry, was established in this period. These poems survive in anthologies, notably the *Muallaqat*, in which the desert life of brave warriors, the mourning of the fallen, and boasts of erotic conquests are recorded in beautiful, metrically challenging, richly complex, and sustained odes.

Life in the Arabian peninsula was wholly transformed in the seventh century with the development of a new religion with roots in Judaism and Christianity—Islam. This religion originated in the teachings of a middle-aged merchant from Mecca named Muhammad (570–632). Very little is known of the historical Muhammad, but legends about his life, recorded about a century after his death, assert that he was orphaned at an early age, and that he became a merchant in the markets of Mecca. He traveled with the caravans and may have been exposed to Judaism and Christianity in Palestine. When he was forty, Muhammad experienced a vision while praying in a cave outside of Mecca, in which the angel Gabriel appeared to him and commanded him to preach the word of Allah (the supreme God). From this time on, Muhammad preached to the polytheistic Arabs a monotheistic faith. The Meccans, however, were slow to convert and Muhammad fled with his followers north to Medina in 622.

Muslims believe Muhammad to have been the last prophet, equal to Jesus and Moses, but not himself divine. Under Muhammad's Islamic teachings, Arabs are required to pray five times a day, to pray and fast from dawn through dusk during the holy month of Ramadan, to make a pilgrimage to Mecca once during their lives, and to give alms to the poor. Muhammad also attempted to eliminate the blood feuds, drinking, sexual exploits, and gambling that were so much a part of the pre-Islamic Arabic life portrayed in Golden Age poetry. His teachings were recorded sporadically by his followers during his life and collected and arranged after his death into a volume of verse chapters called the Quran.

During his Medinan exile, Muhammad's preachings took root. He became the theocratic ruler of a new state, which he expanded through conquest, and by the time of his death ten years after his flight from Mecca in 622, he had united all of the Bedouin tribes and conquered his enemies in Mecca, as well as the rest of the Arabian peninsula. Islam, carried by holy warfare (*jihad*) and a faith that those who died fighting to spread the religion would be rewarded in Heaven, spread within a hundred years as far as India in the east, across North Africa, and into southern Europe in the west. The definition of an "Arab" became more expansive after the spread of Islam. It became possible to consider oneself an Arab if one spoke Arabic and believed in Islam, despite geography and ethnic origin. Because of the injunction against translating the Quran into other languages, Muslims had to learn Arabic to worship. Classical Arabic thus became a great language unifying cultures across the world, and Arabic literature came to be written by authors of diverse backgrounds for whom Arabic was the formal language of literature and religion.

With the death of Mohammad in 632, the Islamic state fell into crisis, for he had no son to succeed him as ruler. The question of succession was resolved through the development of the institution of the caliphate. The first four Caliphs were elected theocratic rulers. Although the institution maintained, stabilized, and expanded the empire, it was a fragile system; and it failed to ensure orderly succession: three of the four Caliphs were murdered. In 656, the assassination of the third Caliph, Uthman, and the assumption of the caliphate by Ali (Mohammad's cousin and son-in-law) catalyzed a schism in Islam. Civil war ensued, and eventually Ali was himself assassinated and succeeded by Uthman's cousin Muawiya, who belonged to the family of the Umayyads. Muawiya converted the caliphate to a hereditary institution and moved the capital from Medina to the Syrian city of Damascus. The Umayyad caliphs ruled from 661 to 750. However, the schism between the supporters of Ali (who were called the Shiite Muslims) and the supporters of the Umayyads (who were called the Sunni Muslims) remained, and in fact the Shiite and Sunni split persists today as a major dividing principle within and between Arab nations. In 750, the Umayyads were overthrown by a rebellion supported by the Shiites and others and replaced by a new succession of caliphs, the Abbasids. The Abbasid caliphs ruled from 750 to 1258, and once again moved the capital, this time to the newly founded city of Baghdad in Iraq.

Arabic literature, which had declined as the Quran dominated the written culture, enjoyed a resurgence in the eighth and ninth centuries in Baghdad, where the Abbasid empire had established its capital in 762 under Caliph Mansur. Under Caliph Harun al-Rashid (c. 763–809), Baghdad became a brilliant center of artistry, poetry, and scholarship, and the location of many of the tales of the monumental Arabic prose romance, *The*

*Thousand and One Nights.* Abu Nuwas, one of the major poets of this time, is the star of some of these tales. Arabic poetry in the "new style" of the Abbasids became more complex metrically, more sophisticated in its use of figurative language, and more varied as to subject matter. Prose was slower in developing, but with the decline of the Abbasids from the tenth through the thirteenth centuries, there was a great flowering of Arabic narrative, from autobiography to travel literature to storytelling. A mystical sect of Islam called Sufism had developed in the seventh century; and later in the Abbasid period, the Sufis, who were often persecuted by mainstream Islam, were responsible for some of the greatest literature of the Middle East, at first largely written in Arabic, and later in Persian.

Although the reign of the Abbasids, particularly that of Harun al-Rashid, is considered the Golden Age of Islam, a time of extraordinary advances in medicine, philosophy, literature, and mathematics, it was also a period marked increasingly by a fragmentation of the empire as province after province seceded. As the empire continued to splinter, the true power in Baghdad shifted to the Persian aristocrats who helped the Arabs rule and became, by the middle of the tenth century, the real power behind the throne; to the Turkish military guard; and later to invaders, the Seljuk Turks and the Mongols, each of whom converted to, and helped to spread, Islam. Spain, at the western edge of the Arabic empire, was one of the anticaliphates that maintained an Islamic rule independent of Baghdad; the other anticaliphate was governed by the Shiite Fatimids, who ruled Egypt and its surrounding areas from their center in Cairo from 909 to 1171. Arabic Spain was ruled by the line of an Umayyad prince who had escaped the bloody slaughter of his family by the first Abbasid ruler. The magnificent city of Córdoba in Andalusia challenged Baghdad in architecture, scholarship, and literature. In addition to extraordinarily beautiful lyric poetry, Córdoba was home to the great twelfth century philosophers Averröes (1126–1198), an Arab, and Maimonides (1135–1204), a Jew. In the nearly thirteen centuries since the birth of Islam, Arabic literature has ceased to be synonymous with the literature of the Arabian peninsula. In the wake of that great religious and cultural diaspora, it has become a literature of the world.

—Ayame Fukuda and the editors

# ■ Al-Khansa (575–646) Arabia (poems)

## TRANSLATED BY WILLIS BARNSTONE

Al-Khansa, whose full name was Tumadir bint Amr ib al Harith ibn al Sharid, was born in Mecca or in Medina and is considered the finest elegiac poet of Arabia, and the best of the women poets whose poetry paralleled their social role of mourning the dead. Al-Khansa came from the Sulaym tribe and much of her work consists of elegies for its fallen warriors—her two brothers, Sakhr and Muqwiya numbered among them, along with four of her sons, who died at the Battle of al-Qadisiyya. The Arabic dirge tends to follow a pattern of expressing endless grief, praising the fallen man's bravery and generosity, questioning who can fulfill his role as protector and benefactor, and, if the death was violent, expressing a need for bloody revenge. Her poems utilize the simple elements of the desert—rain, swords, camels, dust, and mountains topped with fire—to create fierce, passionate, and desperately simple poems of loss. Her *diwan,* or collection of poems, survives. With the coming of Islam, Al-Khansa seems to have converted, and she lived in Medina at the end of her life, near the prophet Muhammad.

## Elegy for Her Brother Sakhr

Cry out for Sakhr when a dove with necklaces
mourns gray in the valley.

When warriors put on light woven armor,
swords are the color of smooth salt

and bows groan and wail,
and bending spears are wet.

Giving, not weak,
brave like the predatory wood lion

of Bisha, he battles for friends
and kinsmen, who are like the lion,

whom he defends whether of the village
or wanderers on the desert.

When the wind howled his people were happy
as a wind of dust blew under a freezing cloud.

## Sleepless

I was sleepless, I was awake all night
as if my eyes exuded pus.

I watched the stars, though I was not their shepherd,
and veiled my body in ragged cloth,

for I heard—it was black news—
the messenger's report:

"Sakhr is in the earth,
between wood and stones."

Go, may Allah receive you, as a man
of justice and revenge.

Your heart was free,
its roots were not weak.

Like a spearhead your shape shines in the night,
strong, firm, the son of free men.

I lament our tribe's hero. Death took you                                    *15*
and the others.

As long as the ringdove cries, I'll mourn you,
as stars light the midnight traveler.

I'll not make peace with the enemy
till their food kettles turn white . . .                                      *20*

They washed the shame from you,
your blood's sweat poured out purified,

and war rode a humpbacked herd,
bareback.

Defender in battle,                                                          *25*
you ripped the spearmen, tooth and nail,

until thousands saw you
blind to fear. They were amazed

as your stomach burst, punctured above the nipples,
spurting the foam of your heart's blood.                                      *30*

## ■ Muallaqat (Sixth to Early Seventh Centuries) *Arabia* (poems)

TRANSLATED BY TONY BARNSTONE AND BEATRICE GRUENDLER

The *Muallaqat* is the name of an Arabic anthology compiled by Hammad al Rawiya (c. 775) that consists of seven (sometimes nine or ten) *qasida,* or long odes of the pre-Islamic period. They are the high moment of Arabic poetry and a rare window onto Bedouin life. Though these were poems of an oral tradition, they were preserved through a class of poem reciters, called Rawis, who accompanied the poets, learned the poems by heart, and kept the tradition alive. Krishna Chaitanya writes of the role of the poet in this tribal society:

> In the centuries before Muhammad came to unite them into a nation, the Arabs were living as separate tribes, and in the condition of tribal life the poet enjoyed a high status. He was considered as gifted with supernatural powers and thus he became the oracle of the tribe, their guide in peace, and their champion in war.[1]

---

1. Krishna Chaitanya, *A History of Arabic Literature* (New Delhi: Manohar, 1983), 31.

Eleventh-century scholar Ibn Rashiq of Qairouan writes of the respect in which these ancient poets were held:

> Whenever a poet emerged in an Arab tribe, the other tribes would come and congratulate it. Feasts would be prepared and the women would gather together, playing on lutes, as people do at weddings. For the poet was a defence to their honor, a protection for their good repute. He immortalized their deeds of glory and published their eternal fame.[2]

The tribes would have a great contest at the Uzak fair each year, competing each day for a month. *Muallaqat* is said to mean "suspended poems" due to a myth that these were poems that won prizes at this competition and were inscribed in gold on Egyptian silk and suspended in the holy Kaba shrine in Mecca.

The ode (the *qasida*) is a long lyric poem, in varying meters, with a single end rhyme. In Arabia where the *qasida* flourished before and after the founding of Islam in A.D. 622, the poem is written with narrative elements that, nonetheless, must be considered antinarrative. The events of the poem occur generally in four parts, which are prescribed by tradition, and the poet's task is to execute a virtuoso performance within these strictures. The poet first halts, distraught in a desolate place, and remembers a great personal loss, like Tarafa mourning the absence of his lover Khaula, "on the sand and stone plain of Thahmad." In the next section, the speaker describes a great journey, perhaps spurred by an impulse to escape such emptiness. Other elements that may make up a part of the *qasida* include extended, anecdotal boasts, erotic or military.

What we know of the life of Tarafa, the first poet excerpted here, is a mixture of fact and legend and what can be gleaned from his poems. He died at a young age—between twenty and twenty-six—and seems to have lived the dissolute life his poem records, letting his family's camels get stolen while he wrote poems, wasting his money until, driven out of the tribe, he was separated from Khaula, his lover. He went to live with his cousin Abd Amar, minister to the king of Hira but could not refrain from writing satirical poems about his cousin and even about the king. The legend of Tarafa's death is well known. He was said to have been sent by the king of Hira to carry a letter to a district governor, but his companion, suspicious of the king's intent, read the letter, finding that it contained instructions to put them both to death! Tarafa, though, was too noble to break his promise to the king—he delivered the letter and was killed for his efforts.

Imru al-Qays, the second poet excerpted here, is considered the finest of the pre-Islamic poets. His family ruled Kinda, a region in Yemen, as vassal kings of Yemen's Himyarite rulers. Imru was the son of Hujr, ruler of the Banu Asad tribe's home region. His father grew angry with him for writing poems and in the end banished him, and for some time he led a dissolute wandering life in the desert. After the tribesmen revolted against his father's

---

2. Ibid.

harsh rule and killed him in his tent, Imru al-Qays sought revenge on the Banu Asad tribe, allying himself with Emperor Justinian and going to Constantinope. He was made the vassal ruler of Palestine and promised an army, but it is said that he seduced Justinians's daughter, boasted about it, and was murdered with a poisoned cloak. He died in Ankara in 540. He is among the finest erotic Arabic poets.

**FURTHER READING:** Arberry, A. J. *The Seven Odes*, 1957. Cantarino, Vicente. *Arabic Poetics in the Golden Age: Selections of Texts Accompanied by a Preliminary Study*, 1975. Nicholson, R. A. *A Literary History of the Arabs*, 1930. Sells, Michael A., tr. *Desert Tracings: Six Classic Arabian Odes*, 1989. Zwettler, Michael. *The Oral Tradition of Classical Arabic Poetry: Its Character and Implications*, 1978.

## from *The Ode of Tarafa*

Like old tattoos on the back of the hand, traces remain of Khaula,
    my lover, on the sand and stone plain of Thahmad.
My friends rein in their camels next to me and say
    "Bear it like a man, don't let this pain kill you."
The morning she leaves, Malikan camels bear litters
    in the valleys of Dad like the great ships
of Adaula or the vessels of Ibn-i Yamen
    that sailors guide straight on, or swing from the course.
Their bows slice through the rippling back of the sea       5
    like a boy's hand plowing furrows in the sand.

There is a young gazelle in the tribe, dark-lipped, shaking fruit
    from her tree, who flaunts a double strand of pearls and
        emeralds.
Holding aloof as she grazes with the herd in a lush thicket
    she nibbles fruit of the *arak* tree, clothes herself in its leaves.
When her deep lips laugh open, her teeth are a camomile flower
    blooming on a moist sand dune in a virgin plain.
Sun rays water her teeth but not her collyrium-stained gums;
    she chews carefully to keep their bright color.
She smiles and her face is the bright cloak of the sun,       10
    so pure and so unwrinkled.

As for me, I put off my grief and race away on a camel bent
    as she dashes through night and the day;
this camel has bones like the solid planks of a strongbox, she won't
    stumble as I spur her down a road broad and rutted like a striped
        cloak,
strong as a male camel, she sprints like an ostrich running
    from a featherless, rutting male; the color of ash,

she rivals the swift purebred camels; on the beaten path
    her back feet light in her forefeet's tracks.

*　*　*

I ride a beast this fine when my companion calls out "O I wish       *1*
    I could ransom us from the journey's burden."
Fear palpitates his chest and he jumps as if sliced by weapons
    when no weapons strike and no ambush waits.
But when people say "Who is that brave young man" I think they
    speak of me; I am no slack fool when faced with danger.
I ply my whip and she races off as mirages shimmer
    on the flaming sands,
swaying gracefully like a dancing girl who shows her master
    the skirts of her long white gown.

If you seek my protection I am not one who will run       *2*
    into the hills to hide.
Look for me among the people and you'll find me in that circle,
    hunt for me in the taverns and I will be there,
and when you come to me I'll pass you a brimming cup
    and if you don't want it, well, that's that.
And if all the tribes gather you'll find me there,
    a noble of the finest house, to which the people flock.
My companions are white-skinned, like stars, and a dancing girl
    comes to us at night in a striped gown or saffron robe,
undoing her collar and giving her soft and delicate flesh       *2*
    to the hands of my friends.
When we say "Sing for us" she sings smoothly, in a low voice,
    with a lowered head,
and on the sorrowful tremolo you'd think she was a mother
    keening over her dead firstborn.
I drink and seek joy and squander my inheritance
    and everything I earn and don't stop
till the people avoid me, all of them, and I am alone
    like a mangey camel whose hide is painted with tar.
Yet the lowly sons of the dust don't deny the one who gave them alms       *3*
    and the great ones in the leather tents admire me too.

You who reproach me for going to war, for giving gifts,
    can you make me live forever if I give up these pleasures?
If you can't stop death, then let me welcome him
    with the coins still in my hand.
Three things alone give a young man joy and only for them
    would I keep my deathbed visitors away:

first, to swig down red wine that foams when cut with water
    in the morning before my critics come;
second—like a wolf startled from a thorny bush as he seeks water—        *35*
    to streak to the aid of a scared fugitive on a full-shanked horse;
and third, to cut short a cloud-darkened day, though I love the
    darkness of lingering with a lush girl in her pole-propped tent,
one whose anklets and bracelets hang from limbs straight
    and pliant as a gum tree's unpruned branches or castor plant's
      twigs.
Generous men quench their thirst alive;
    if we die tomorrow you'll see which one is dry.
To me the grave of a miser who counts his change
    is the same as that of an idler who wastes his goods—
just two heaps of dust is what you'll see,        *40*
    and deaf granite stones stacked in a cairn.
I see that death will choose the generous and take
    the prize from the miser's hoard;
life itself is a treasure that leaks away from us each night
    and the days erode and time perishes.
I swear by your life that death, though he misses a strong man now,
    is like a loosened lasso held ready to throw.

            \*   \*   \*

When I die, keen for me, O daughter of Ma'bad, tear the collar
    of your gown and sing the praises I deserve;
don't make me out a man with less zeal than I've shown,        *45*
    unskilled and new to battle,
who held back when great affairs occurred, was despised,
    foul-mouthed, scurrying under men's fists—
if I were such a coward my enemies, solitary or with
    friends, would have harmed me soon enough,
but I stood up to them bravely, honest,
    showing noble birth, and sent them flying.
On your life I swear sorrows didn't cloud my days
    nor were my nights anxious and without end.
Many days I stood, spirit firm, in the press of battle,        *50*
    defending the weak and facing the enemy;
where brave men quake in their boots and the shoulders
    of warriors clench with fear I took my stand,
and in gambling I often gave my lucky arrow, yellow and
    smoke blackened, to an unlucky friend and sat out the game.

You will hear the news from the man you gave nothing to
    when time reveals its mysteries to you.

## *from* **The Ode of Imru al-Qays**

How many fine times I've had with women!
    I remember in particular a day at Dara Juljul,
when I slaughtered my riding camel for the virgins to eat.
    My God, how fine it was, and what a load divided among their
        camels.
Then the virgins tossed the cut flesh about
    and the loose fat like white fringes of twisted silk.
On another day I entered Unaiza's litter
    and she cried "You are making me go on foot!"
And she said while the canopy swayed with us,
    "You are killing my camel, Imru al-Qays, so dismount!"
But I replied "Ride on, just loosen the reins,
    and don't keep me from your succulent fruit;
the camel's young, let it carry us both,
    and now let me eat you like a luscious apple.
For I've been with many women beautiful like you, Unaiza;
    even a nursing mother receives me at night and forgets her infant
for me, and when he whimpers behind us, she gives him half
    her body, but meets me with the other half."

                    \*    \*    \*

How many gorgeous veiled woman have I enjoyed at length         1
    in tents no other would dare approach?
I slid past sentries on watch and a tribe thirsty
    for my blood, whose every man dreams of bragging of my death,
and the Pleiades were gemstones in the sky,
    spaced like pearls in a jeweled belt.
She was standing by the tent-flap when I slipped in,
    already stripped to a sheer nightgown
and she said "I swear by God there's no escape from you.
    You wild fool, you'll never give up this appetite!"
But she came out with me, trailing an embroidered gown         1
    to erase our tracks
and when we'd crossed the tribe's courtyard
    we found the twisting dune of a parched riverbed;
I pulled her to me by her hair and she leaned in
    and her waist was slender and her ankles full.
Small waist, white skin, she had no fat
    and her breasts shone like polished mirrors.
Her complexion like an oyster's first pearl was yellow-white,
    her unmixed blood has nourished her like pure water.
She turned away and I saw her soft cheek, and she warded me off     2
    with a wild animal glance, like a deer protecting her young.

And she showed me her white deer neck, elegant
    and hung with jewelry
and from her perfect head the hair fell loose down her back
    thick as a date-cluster on a fruit-laden tree.
Her single and double plaits were lost in strands of loose, wild hair
    taken up against her head.
She pressed her waist against me, slender as the leather nose ring
    of a camel, and her thighs were palm trees bent with fruit.
In the morning she slept late and woke up smelling of musk           25
    and not bothering to fasten her gown.
She gives with her fingers, which are slender as Zabi desert worms,
    or toothpicks made of ishil wood,
and she is what brightens the evening dark, like a monk's tower
    with a window lit to guide the traveller in.
Not so tall she wears a long dress, not so short she wears a skirt,
    a wise man will gaze hungrily at such perfection.
Let other men give up love after their youth.
    My heart is not that free.

## ■ The Quran (Seventh Century) *Arabia* (religious text)

TRANSLATED BY N. K. DAWOOD

The Quran (Koran) is the holy text of Islam, the source and divine example of Arabic literature, and is thought to be the revealed word of Allah. Muslims believe that Muhammad (570–632) was a prophet who was
the vehicle for God's words, inscribed on a tablet in Heaven, which were
revealed to him by the angel Gabriel. Muhammad, therefore, was not the
author of the Quran, but its facilitator. The Quran is a collection of
Muhammad's preachings that were collected by his followers, written on
parchment, leaves, or bone, whatever was at hand, or committed to memory by professional memorizers. From 651 to 652, several decades after
Muhammad's death, these utterances were collected under the orders of
Caliph Uthman and formed into the text we know today. Unlike the Old
and New Testaments, the Quran did not undergo a process of revision and
editing, which makes its chapters seem somewhat less unified, and rather
more repetitive than these earlier texts; such revision of God's revealed
words would have been blasphemous. The Quran is written in rhymed, as-
sonant prose, which makes its oral recitation beautiful and rhythmic, and
it is best understood as an oral literature confined to text. In fact, the term
*quran* means recitation, text to be recited, and orthodox Muslims recite
from the Quran daily. The organizational structure of the Quran is arbitrary, having to do with neither thematic unity nor chronology: it is

arranged in general according to the length of the chapters—longer chapters first, shorter chapters at the end. There are 114 chapters (*suras*), divided into verses (*ayas*), with wildly varying numbers of verses per chapter and of words per verse. Each chapter begins with the phrase "In the name of Allah, the compassionate, the merciful," except chapter nine.

Islam is a monotheistic religion that was influenced both by Judaism and Christianity; in fact, Moses is considered a prophet like Muhammad, as is Jesus. The divinity of Jesus is rejected as fiercely as Muhammad rejected the idea that he was divine himself. Much of the Quran paraphrases the Bible, though quoting it rarely, notably the chapter "Joseph," which recounts with some alteration the Old Testament story of Joseph. Muhammad was born in Mecca in 570, at a time when the supreme god Allah was the highest among a number of divinities in Arabian religion. Influenced by Judaism, Muhammad began preaching the doctrine of one God, and many of the early, short Meccan chapters focus on the idea of one God, the creator, merciful, but ready to punish. These chapters are among the most rewarding in literary terms, with their Arabized visions of Heaven, with fruit, running water, and virgin *houris* (heavenly courtesans who reward the faithful), and their equally powerfully imagined visions of endless hellfire for the unbelievers. In later Meccan chapters, these themes remain strong, the compositions are longer, and there are frequent warnings that unbelievers will suffer the dire fates of ancient disbelievers in Arab and Jewish prophets. Though he railed against both Jews and Christians, particularly when frustrated at failing to convert them, Muhammad also considered them "people of the Book" and incorporated aspects of Jewish law and ritual, such as the prohibition against eating pork.

The latest chapters in the Quran derive from the Medinan period, when Muhammad and his followers, persecuted and unsuccessful in Mecca, fled to Yathrib, where the people accepted them, and where Muhammad became the ruler of a theocratic state (Yathrib was renamed Medina, or "City of the Prophet"). These later chapters are legalistic in nature, the basis of Islamic law, and have the least literary value. The year 622, the date of the emigration to Medina, or the "Hegira," became the date chosen to commence the Islamic era (as opposed to, for example, the date of Muhammad's birth). During his Medinan years, Muhammad expanded his empire through holy warfare (*jihad*) and was lawgiver, ruler, and prophet; in 631, he finally captured Mecca by force, and a few months later died in the arms of his favorite wife. Holy warfare and prosletyzing soon carried the Quran across the world, from Europe to Central Asia, starting the process of growth that has not ceased to this day. Although it is a commonplace to state that no translation can capture the oral magic of the original Arabic Quran, and although it is prohibited to translate these revealed divine words into other languages, the Quran has in fact been translated into almost all languages, and Islam today is a multilingual and multiethnic religion.

**FURTHER READING:** Ali, Abdullah Yusuf, tr. *The Holy Quran: Text, Translation, and Commentary,* 1983. Arberry, A. J., tr. *The Koran Interpreted,* 2 vols., 1955. Bell, Richard, tr. *The Quran. Translated, with a Critical Rearrangement of the Surahs,* 2 vols., 1937–1939. Palmer, Edward H., tr. *The Quran,* 1980. Pickthall, M. M., tr. *The Meaning of the Glorious Koran: An Explanatory Translation,* 1930. Rodwell, J. M., tr. The *Koran,* 1861. Sale, George, tr. *The Koran with Notes and a Preliminary Discourse,* 1734.

## The Exordium

> *In the Name of Allah,*
> *The Compassionate,*
> *The Merciful*

Praise be to Allah, Lord of the Creation,
The Compassionate, the Merciful,                                        5
King of Judgment Day!
You alone we worship, and to You alone
we pray for help.
Guide us to the straight path,
The path of those whom You have favored,                               10
Not of those who have incurred Your wrath,
Nor of those who have gone astray.

## from *Sura 3 The Imrans*

And remember the angel's words to Mary. He said: 'Allah has chosen you. He has made you pure and exalted you above all women. Mary, be obedient to your Lord; bow down and worship with the worshippers.'

This is an account of what is hidden. We reveal it to you.[1] You were not present when they cast lots to see which of them should have charge of Mary; nor were you present when they argued about her.

The angels said to Mary: 'Allah bids you rejoice in a Word from Him. His name is the Messiah, Jesus the son of Mary. He shall be noble in this world and in the next, and shall be favoured by Allah. He shall preach to men in his cradle and in the prime of manhood, and shall lead a righteous life.'

'Lord,' she said, 'how can I bear a child when no man has touched me?'

He replied: 'Such is the will of Allah. He creates whom He will. When He decrees a thing He need only say: "Be," and it is. He will instruct him in the Scriptures and in wisdom, in the Torah and in the Gospel, and send

---

1. Muhammad.

him forth as an apostle to the Israelites. He will say: "I bring you a sign from your Lord. From clay I will make for you the likeness of a bird. I shall breathe into it and, by Allah's leave, it shall become a living bird. By Allah's leave I shall give sight to the blind man, heal the leper, and raise the dead to life. I shall tell you what to eat and what to store up in your houses. Surely that will be a sign for you, if you are true believers. I come to confirm the Torah that has already been revealed and to make lawful to you some of the things you are forbidden. I bring you a sign from your Lord: therefore fear Him and obey Me. Allah is my God and your God: therefore serve Him. That is the straight path."'

When Jesus observed that they had no faith, he said: 'Who will help me in the cause of Allah?'

The disciples replied: 'We are the helpers of Allah. We believe in Him. Bear witness that we have surrendered ourselves to Him. Lord, we believe in Your revelations and follow your apostle. Count us among Your witnesses.'

They plotted, and Allah plotted. Allah is the supreme Plotter. He said: 'I am about to cause you to die and lift you up to Me. I shall take you away from the unbelievers and exalt your followers above them till the Day of Resurrection. Then to Me you shall all return and I shall judge your disputes. The unbelievers shall be sternly punished in this world and in the world to come: there shall be none to help them. As for those that have faith and do good works, they shall be given their reward in full. Allah does not love the evil-doers.'

This revelation, and this wise admonition, We recite to you. Jesus is like Adam in the sight of Allah. He created him of dust and then said to him: 'Be,' and he was.

This is the truth from your Lord: therefore do not doubt it. To those that dispute with you concerning Jesus after the knowledge you have received, say: 'Come, let us gather our sons and your sons, our wives and your wives, our people and your people. We will pray together and call down the curse of Allah on every liar.'

This is the whole truth. There is no god but Allah. It is Allah who is the Mighty, the Wise One!

If they give no heed to you, Allah knows the evil-doers.

Say: 'People of the Book, let us come to an agreement: that we will worship none but Allah, that we will associate none with Him, and that none of us shall set up mortals as gods besides Him.'

## from *Sura 5 The Table*

One day Allah will gather all the apostles and ask them: 'How were you received?' They will reply: 'We do not know. You alone have knowledge of what is hidden.' Allah will say: 'Jesus, son of Mary, remember the favour I have bestowed on you and on your mother: how I strengthened you with the Holy Spirit, so that you preached to men in your cradle and in the prime of manhood; how I instructed you in the Scriptures and in wisdom, in the Torah and in the Gospel; how by My leave you fashioned from clay the likeness of a bird and breathed into it so that, by My leave, it became a living bird; how, by My leave, you healed the blind man and the leper, and by My leave restored the dead to life; how I protected you from the Israelites when you brought them veritable signs: when the unbelievers among them said: "This is nothing but plain magic"; how when I enjoined the disciples to believe in Me and in My apostle they replied: "We believe; bear witness that we submit to You utterly." '

'Jesus, son of Mary,' said the disciples, 'can Allah send down to us from heaven a table spread with food?'

He replied: 'Have fear of Allah, if you are true believers.'

'We wish to eat of it,' they said, 'so that we may reassure our hearts and know that what you said to us is true, and that we may be witnesses of it.'

'Lord,' said Jesus, the son of Mary, 'send to us from heaven a table spread with food, that it may mark a feast for us and for those that will come after us: a sign from You. Give us our sustenance; You are the best Giver.'

Allah replied: 'I am sending one to you. But whoever of you disbelieves hereafter shall be punished as no man has ever been punished.'

Then Allah will say: 'Jesus, son of Mary, did you ever say to mankind: "Worship me and my mother as gods beside Allah?" '

'Glory to You,' he will answer, 'how could I say that to which I have no right? If I had ever said so, You would have surely known it. You know what is in my mind, but I cannot tell what is in Yours. You alone know what is hidden. I spoke to them of nothing except what You bade me. I said: "Serve Allah, my Lord and your Lord." I watched over them whilst living in their midst, and ever since You took me to You, You Yourself have been watching over them. You are the witness of all things. They are your own bondsmen: it is for You to punish or to forgive them. You are the Mighty, the Wise One.'

## from *Sura 7 The Heights*

We created you and gave you form. Then We said to the angels: 'Prostrate yourselves before Adam.' They all prostrated themselves except Satan, who refused.

'Why did you not prostrate yourself?' Allah asked.

'I am nobler than Adam,' he replied. 'You created me of fire and him of clay.'

He said: 'Begone from Paradise! This is no place for your contemptuous pride. Away with you! Henceforth you shall be humble.'

Satan replied: 'Reprieve me till the Day of Resurrection.'

'You are reprieved,' said He.

'Because You have led me into sin,' said Satan, 'I will way-lay Your servants as they walk on Your straight path, and spring upon them from the front and from the rear, from their right and from their left. Then you shall find the greater part of them ungrateful.'

'Begone!' said Allah. 'A despicable outcast you shall henceforth be. With those that follow you I shall fill the pit of Hell.'

To Adam He said: 'Dwell with your wife in Paradise, and eat of any fruit you please; but never approach this tree or you shall both become transgressors.'

But Satan tempted them, so that he might reveal to them their nakedness, which they had never seen before. He said: 'Your Lord has forbidden you to approach this tree only to prevent you from becoming angels or immortals.' Then he swore to them that he would give them friendly counsel.

Thus he cunningly seduced them. And when they had eaten of the tree, their shame became visible to them, and they both covered themselves with the leaves of the garden.

Their Lord called out to them, saying: 'Did I not forbid you to approach that tree, and did I not warn you that Satan was your sworn enemy?'

They replied: 'Lord, we have wronged our souls. Pardon us and have mercy on us, or we shall surely be among the lost.'

He said: 'Go hence, and may your descendants be enemies to each other. The earth will for a while provide your sustenance and dwelling-place. There you shall live and there you shall die, and thence you shall be raised to life.'

Children of Adam! We have given you clothing with which to cover your nakedness, and garments pleasing to the eye; but the finest of all these is the robe of piety.

That is one of Allah's revelations. Perchance they will take heed.

Children of Adam! Let Satan not deceive you, as he deceived your parents out of Paradise. He stripped them of their garments to reveal to them their nakedness. He and his minions see you whence you cannot see them. We have made the devils guardians over the unbelievers.

## from *Sura 8 The Spoils*

Let the unbelievers not think that they will escape Us. They have not the power so to do. Muster against them all the men and cavalry at your disposal, so that you may strike terror into the enemies of Allah and the faithful, and others besides them who may be unknown to you, though Allah knows them. All that you give for the cause of Allah shall be repaid you. You shall not be wronged.

If they incline to peace, make peace with them, and put your trust in Allah. He hears all and knows all. Should they seek to deceive you, Allah is all-sufficient for you. He has made you strong with His help and rallied the faithful round you, making their hearts one. If you had given away all the riches of the earth, you could not have so united them: but Allah has united them. He is mighty and wise.

Prophet, Allah is your strength, and the faithful who follow you.

Prophet, rouse the faithful to arms. If there are twenty steadfast men among you, they shall vanquish two hundred; and if there are a hundred, they shall rout a thousand unbelievers, for they are devoid of understanding.

Allah has now lightened your burden, for He knows that you are weak. If there are a hundred steadfast men among you, they shall vanquish two hundred; and if there are a thousand, they shall, by Allah's will, defeat two thousand. Allah is with those that are steadfast.

A prophet may not take captives until he has fought and triumphed in his land. You[1] seek the chance gain of this world, but Allah desires for you the world to come. He is mighty and wise. Had there not been a previous sanction from Allah, you would have been sternly punished for what you have taken. Enjoy, therefore, the good and lawful things which you have gained in war, and fear Allah. He is forgiving and merciful.

## from *Sura 11 Houd*

Long ago We sent forth Noah to his people. He said: 'I have come to warn you plainly. Serve none but Allah. Beware of the torment of a woeful day.'

The unbelieving elders of his people replied: 'We regard you as a mortal like ourselves. Nor can we find any among your followers but men of hasty judgement, the lowliest of our tribe. We see no virtue in you: indeed we know that you are lying.'

He said: 'Think, my people! If my Lord has revealed to me His will and bestowed on me His grace, though it be hidden from you, can we compel you to accept it against your will? I seek of you no recompense for this, my people; for none can reward me but Allah. Nor will I drive away the faithful, for they will surely meet their Lord. But I can see that you are ignorant men. Were I to drive them away, my people, who would protect me from Allah? Will you not take heed?

'I do not say that I possess Allah's treasures, or that I know what is hidden. I do not claim to be an angel, nor do I say to those whom you disdain that Allah will not be bountiful to them—He knows best what is in their hearts—for then I should become a wrongdoer.'

---

1. Muhammad's followers.

'Noah,' they replied, 'you have argued too long with us. Bring down the scourge with which you threaten us, if what you say be true!'

He said: 'Allah will visit His scourge upon you when He pleases: you shall not escape it. Nor will my counsel profit you if Allah seeks to mislead you, willing though I am to guide you. He is your Lord, and to Him you shall return.'

If they declare: 'He has invented it himself,' say: 'If I have indeed invented it, then may I be punished for my sin! I am innocent of your crimes.'

Allah's will was revealed to Noah, saying: 'None of your people will believe in you save those who have already believed. Do not grieve at their misdeeds. Build an ark under Our watchful eyes, according to Our bidding. Do not plead with Me for the wrongdoers: they shall all be drowned.'

So he built the Ark. And whenever the elders of his people passed by him they jeered at him. He said: 'Mock if you will. Just as you now mock us, so we shall mock you. You shall know who will be punished and put to shame, and who will be afflicted by an everlasting scourge.'

And when Our will was done and water welled out from the Oven. We said to Noah: 'Take into the Ark a pair from every species, your tribe (except those already doomed), and all the true believers.' But none save a few believed with him.

Noah said: 'Embark in it. It will set sail in the name of Allah, and in the name of Allah it will cast anchor. My Lord is forgiving and merciful.'

And as the Ark moved on with them amidst the mountainous waves, Noah cried out to his son, who stood apart. 'Embark with us, my child,' he said. 'Do not stay with the unbelievers!'

He replied: 'I shall seek refuge in a mountain, which will protect me from the flood.'

Noah cried: 'None shall be secure this day from Allah's judgment, except those to whom He will show mercy!' And thereupon the billows rolled between them, and Noah's son was drowned.

A voice cried out: 'Earth, swallow up your waters. Heaven, cease your rain!' The floods abated and Allah's will was done. The Ark came to rest upon Al-Judi, and there was heard a voice, saying: 'Gone are the evil-doers.'

Noah called out to his Lord, saying: 'Lord, my son was my own flesh and blood. Your promise was surely true. You are the most just of judges.'

'Noah,' He replied, 'he was no kinsman of yours: he was an evil-doer. Do not question Me about things you know nothing of. I admonish you lest you become an ignorant man.'

'Forgive me, Lord, for my presumption,' said Noah. 'Pardon me and have mercy on me, or I shall surely be lost.'

'Noah,' He replied, 'go ashore in peace. Our blessings are upon you and on some of the descendants of those that are with you. As for the others, We will suffer them to take their ease in this world and then visit upon them a woeful scourge.'

That which We have now revealed to you is secret history: it was unknown to you and to your people. Have patience; the righteous shall have a joyful end.

## Sura 12 Joseph

*In the Name of Allah, the Compassionate, the Merciful*

*Alif lam ra.* These are the verses of the Glorious Book. We have revealed the Koran in the Arabic tongue so that you may understand it.

In revealing this Koran We will recount to you the best of histories, though before We revealed it you were heedless of Our signs.

Joseph said to his father: 'Father, I dreamt that eleven stars and the sun and the moon were prostrating themselves before me.'

'My son,' he replied, 'say nothing of this dream to your brothers, lest they should plot evil against you: Satan is the sworn enemy of man. You shall be chosen by your Lord. He will teach you to interpret visions and will perfect His favour to you and to the house of Jacob, as He perfected it to your forefathers Abraham and Isaac before you. Your Lord is wise and all-knowing.'

Surely in the tale of Joseph and his brothers there are signs for doubting men.

They said to each other: 'Joseph and his brother are dearer to our father than ourselves, though we are many. Truly, our father is much mistaken. Let us kill Joseph, or cast him away in some far-off land, so that we may have no rivals in our father's love, and after that be honourable men.'

One of them said: 'Do not kill Joseph. If you must get rid of him, cast him into a dark pit. Some caravan will take him up.'

They said to their father: 'Why do you not trust us with Joseph? Surely we are his friends. Send him with us tomorrow, that he may play and enjoy himself. We will take good care of him.'

He replied: 'It would much grieve me to let him go with you; for I fear lest the wolf should eat him when you are off your guard.'

They said: 'If the wolf could eat him despite our numbers, then we should surely be lost!'

And when they took Joseph with them, they decided to cast him into a dark pit. We addressed him, saying: 'You shall tell them of all this when they will not know you.'

At nightfall they returned weeping to their father. They said: 'We went racing and left Joseph with our goods. The wolf devoured him. But you will not believe us, though we speak the truth.' And they showed him their brother's shirt, stained with false blood.

'No!' he cried. 'Your souls have tempted you to evil. But I will be patient: Allah alone can help me to bear the misfortune of which you speak.'

And a caravan passed by, who sent their waterman to the pit. And when he had let down his pail, he cried: 'Rejoice! A boy!'

They took Joseph and concealed him among their goods. But Allah knew what they did. They sold him for a trifling price, for a few pieces of silver. They cared nothing for him.

The Egyptian who bought him said to his wife: 'Use him kindly. He may prove useful to us, or we may adopt him as our son.'

Thus We found in that land a home for Joseph, and taught him to interpret mysteries. Allah has power over all things, though most men may not know it. And when he reached maturity We bestowed on him wisdom and knowledge. Thus We reward the righteous.

His master's wife sought to seduce him. She bolted the doors and said: 'Come!'

'Allah forbid!' he replied. 'My lord has treated me with kindness. Wrongdoers never prosper.'

She made for him, and he himself would have yielded to her had he not been shown a veritable sign by his Lord. Thus We warded off from him indecency and evil, for he was one of Our faithful servants.

He raced her to the door, but as she clung to him she tore his shirt from behind. And at the door they met her husband.

She cried: 'Shall not the man who sought to violate your wife be thrown into prison or sternly punished?'

Joseph said: 'It was she who sought to seduce me.'

'If his shirt is torn from the front,' said one of her people, 'she is speaking the truth and he is lying. If it is torn from behind, then he is speaking the truth and she is lying.'

And when her husband saw Joseph's shirt rent from behind, he said to her: 'This is one of your tricks. Your cunning is great indeed! Joseph, say no more about this. Woman, ask pardon for your sin. You have done wrong.'

In the city women were saying: 'The Prince's wife has sought to seduce her servant. She has conceived a passion for him. It is clear that she has gone astray.'

When she heard of their intrigues, she invited them to a banquet at her house. To each she gave a knife, and ordered Joseph to present himself before them. When they saw him, they were amazed at him and cut their hands, exclaiming: 'Allah preserve us! This is no mortal, but a gracious angel.'

'This is the man,' she said, 'on whose account you reproached me. I sought to seduce him, but he was unyielding. If he declines to do my bidding, he shall be thrown into prison and held in scorn.'

'Lord,' said Joseph, 'sooner would I go to prison than give in to their advances. Shield me from their cunning, or I shall yield to them and lapse into folly.'

His Lord heard his prayer and warded off their wiles from him. He hears all and knows all.

Yet despite the evidence they had seen, the Egyptians thought it right to jail him for a time.

Two young men went to prison with him. One of them said: 'I dreamt that I was pressing grapes.' And the other said: 'I dreamt that I was carrying a loaf upon my head, and that the birds came and ate of it. Tell us the meaning of these dreams, for we can see you are a man of learning.'

Joseph replied: 'I can interpret them long before they are fulfilled. This knowledge my Lord has given me, for I have left the faith of those that disbelieve in Allah and deny the life to come. I follow the faith of my forefathers, Abraham, Isaac, and Jacob. We must never serve idols besides Allah. Such is the gift which Allah has bestowed upon us and all mankind. Yet most men do not give thanks.

'Fellow-prisoners! Are numerous gods better than Allah, the One, the Almighty? Those whom you serve besides Him are names which you and your fathers have invented and for which Allah has revealed no sanction. Judgement rests with Allah only. He has commanded you to worship none but Him. That is the true faith: yet most men do not know it.

'Fellow-prisoners, one of you will serve his king with wine. The other will be crucified, and the birds will peck at his head. That is the meaning of your dreams.'

And Joseph said to the prisoner who he knew would be freed: 'Remember me in the presence of your king.'

But Satan made him forget to mention Joseph to his king, so that he stayed in prison for several years.

Now it so chanced that one day the king said: 'I saw seven fatted cows which seven lean ones devoured; also seven green ears of corn and seven others dry. Tell me the meaning of this vision, my nobles, if you can interpret visions.'

They replied: 'It is but an idle dream; nor can we interpret dreams.'

Thereupon the man who had been freed remembered Joseph after all those years. He said: 'I shall tell you what it means. Give me leave to go.'

He said to Joseph: 'Tell us, man of truth, of the seven fatted cows which seven lean ones devoured; also of the seven green ears of corn and the other seven which were dry: for I would inform my masters.'

Joseph replied: 'You shall sow for seven consecutive years. Leave in the ear the corn you reap, except a little which you may eat. Then there shall follow seven hungry years which will consume all but little of that which you have stored for them. Then there will come a year of abundant rain, in which the people will press the grape.'

The king said: 'Bring this man before me.'

But when the king's envoy came to him, Joseph said: 'Go back to your master and ask him about the women who cut their hands. My master knows their cunning.'

The king questioned the women, saying: 'Why did you seek to entice Joseph?'

'Allah forbid!' they replied. 'We know no evil of him.'

'Now the truth must come to light,' said the Prince's wife. 'It was I who sought to seduce him. He has told the truth.'

'From this,' said Joseph, 'my lord will know that I did not betray him in his absence, and that Allah does not guide the work of the treacherous. Not that I am free from sin: man's soul is prone to evil, except his to whom Allah has shown mercy. My Lord is forgiving and merciful.'

The king said: 'Bring him before me. I will make him my personal servant.'

And when he had spoken with him, the king said: 'You shall henceforth dwell with us, honoured and trusted.'

Joseph said: 'Give me charge of the granaries of the realm. I shall husband them wisely.'

Thus We gave power to Joseph, and he dwelt at his ease in that land. We bestow Our mercy on whom We will, and never deny the righteous their reward. Better is the reward of the life to come for those who believe in Allah and keep from evil.

Joseph's brothers came and presented themselves before him. He recognized them, but they knew him not. And when he had given them their provisions, he said: 'Bring me your other brother from your father. Do you not see that I give just measure and am the best of hosts? If you do not bring him, you shall have no corn, nor shall you come near me again.'

They replied: 'We will request his father to let him come with us. This we will surely do.'

Joseph said to his servants: 'Put their money into their packs, so that they may find it when they return to their people. Perchance they will come back.'

When they returned to their father, they said: 'Father, corn is henceforth denied us. Send our brother with us and we shall have our measure. We will take good care of him.'

He replied: 'Am I to trust you with him as I once trusted you with his brother? But Allah is the best of guardians: of all those that show mercy He is the most merciful.'

When they opened their packs, they found that their money had been returned to them. 'Father,' they said, 'what more can we desire? Here is our money untouched. We will buy provisions for our people and take good care of our brother. We shall receive an extra camel-load; that should not be hard to get.'

He replied: 'I shall not let him go with you until you swear in Allah's name to bring him back to me, unless you are prevented.'

And when they had given him their pledge, he said: 'Allah is the witness of your oath. My sons, enter the town by different gates. If you do wrong, I cannot ward off from you the wrath of Allah: judgement is His alone. In Him I have put my trust. In Him alone let the faithful put their trust.'

And when they entered as their father had advised them, his counsel availed them nothing against the decree of Allah. It was but a wish in Jacob's soul which he had thus fulfilled. He was possessed of knowledge which We had given him, though most men were unaware of it.

When they presented themselves before him, Joseph embraced his brother, and said: 'I am your brother. Do not grieve at what they did.'

And when he had given them their provisions, he hid a drinking-cup in his brother's pack.

Then a crier called out after them: 'Travellers, you are thieves!'

They turned back and asked: 'What have you lost?'

'The king's drinking-cup,' he replied. 'He that restores it shall have a camel-load of corn. I pledge my word for it.'

'By Allah,' they cried, 'you know we did not come to do evil in this land. We are no thieves.'

The Egyptians said: 'What penalty shall we inflict on him that stole it, if you prove to be lying?'

They replied: 'He in whose pack the cup is found shall be your bondsman. Thus we punish the wrongdoers.'

Joseph searched their bags before his brother's, and then took out the cup from his brother's bag.

Thus We directed Joseph. By the king's law he had no right to seize his brother: but Allah willed otherwise. We exalt in knowledge whom We will: but above those that have knowledge there is One more knowing.

They said: 'If he has stolen—know then that a brother of his has committed a theft before him.'[1]

But Joseph kept his secret and did not reveal it to them. He thought: 'Your crime was worse. Allah well knows that you are lying.'

They said: 'Noble prince, this boy has an aged father. Take one of us, instead of him. We can see you are a generous man.'

He replied: 'Allah forbid that we should seize any but the man with whom our property was found: for then we should be unjust.'

When they despaired of him, they went aside to confer together. The eldest said: 'Have you forgotten that you gave your father a solemn pledge, and that you broke your faith before this concerning Joseph? I shall not stir from this land until my father gives me leave or Allah makes known to me His judgement: He is the best of judges. Return to your father and say to him: "Your son has committed a theft. We testify only to what we know. How could we guard against the unforeseen? Ask the townsfolk with whom we stayed and the caravan in which we travelled. We speak the truth."'

'No!' cried their father. 'Your souls have tempted you to evil. But I will be patient. Allah may bring them all to me. He alone is wise and all-knowing.' And he turned away from them, crying: 'Alas for Joseph!' His eyes went white with grief and he was oppressed with silent sorrow.

---

1. Commentators say that Joseph had stolen an idol of his maternal grandfather's and broken it, so that he might not worship it.

His sons exclaimed: 'By Allah, will you not cease to think of Joseph until you ruin your health and die?'

He replied: 'I complain to Allah of my sorrow and sadness. He has made known to me things beyond your knowledge. Go, my sons, and seek news of Joseph and his brother. Do not despair of Allah's spirit; none but unbelievers despair of Allah's spirit.'

And when they presented themselves before Joseph, they said: 'Noble prince, we and our people are scourged with famine. We have brought but little money. Give us some corn, and be charitable to us: Allah rewards the charitable.'

'Do you know,' he replied, 'what you did to Joseph and his brother in your ignorance?'

They cried: 'Can you indeed be Joseph?'

'I am Joseph,' he answered, 'and this is my brother. Allah has been gracious to us. Those that keep from evil and endure with fortitude, Allah will not deny them their reward.'

'By the Lord,' they said, 'Allah has exalted you above us all. We have indeed been guilty.'

He replied: 'None shall reproach you this day. May Allah forgive you: He is most merciful. Take this shirt of mine and throw it over my father's face: he will recover his sight. Then return to me with all your people.'

When the caravan departed their father said: 'I feel the breath of Joseph, though you will not believe me.'

'By Allah,' said those who heard him, 'this is but your old illusion.'

And when the bearer of good news arrived, he threw Joseph's shirt over the old man's face, and his sight came back to him. He said: 'Did I not tell you that Allah has made known to me things beyond your knowledge?'

His sons said: 'Father, implore forgiveness for our sins. We have indeed been sinners.'

He replied: 'I shall implore my Lord to forgive you. He is forgiving and merciful.'

And when they presented themselves before Joseph he embraced his parents and said: 'Welcome to Egypt, safe, if Allah wills!'

He helped his parents to a couch, and they all fell on their knees and prostrated themselves before him.

'This,' said Joseph to his father, 'is the meaning of my old vision: my Lord has fulfilled it. He has been gracious to me. He has released me from prison and brought you out of the desert after Satan had stirred up strife between me and my brothers. My lord is gracious to whom He will. He alone is wise and all-knowing.

'Lord, You have given me power and taught me to interpret mysteries. You are the Creator of the heavens and the earth, my Guardian in this world and in the next. Let me die in submission and join the righteous.'

That which We have now revealed to you[2] is secret history. You were not present when Joseph's brothers conceived their plans and schemed against him. Yet strive as you may, most men will not believe.

You shall demand of them no recompense for this. It[3] is an admonition to all mankind.

Many are the marvels of the heavens and the earth; yet they pass them by and pay no heed to them. The greater part of them believe in Allah only if they can worship other gods besides Him.

Are they confident that Allah's scourge will not fall upon them, or that the Hour of Doom will not overtake them unawares, without warning?

Say: 'This is my path. With sure knowledge I call on you to have faith in Allah, I and all my followers. Glory be to Him! I am no idolater.'

Nor were the apostles whom We sent before you other than mortals inspired by Our will and chosen from among their people.

Have they not travelled in the land and seen what was the end of those who disbelieved before them? Better is the world to come for those that keep from evil. Can you not understand?

And when at length Our apostles despaired and thought that none would believe in them, Our help came down to them, delivering whom We pleased. The evil-doers did not escape Our scourge. Their history is a lesson to men of understanding.

This is no invented tale, but a confirmation of previous scriptures, an explanation of all things, a guide and a blessing to true believers.

## from *Sura 13 Thunder*

*In the Name of Allah, the Compassionate, the Merciful*

*Alif lam mim ra.* These are the verses of the Book. That which is revealed to you from your Lord is the truth, yet men have no faith.

It was Allah who raised the heavens without visible pillars. He ascended His throne and forced the sun and the moon into His service, each pursuing an appointed course. He ordains all things. He makes plain His revelations so that you may firmly believe in meeting your Lord.

It was He who spread out the earth and placed upon it rivers and immovable mountains. He gave all plants their male and female parts and drew the veil of night over the day. Surely in these there are signs for thinking men.

---

2. Muhammad.

3. The Koran.

And in the land there are adjoining plots: vineyards and cornfields and groves of palm, the single and the clustered. Their fruits are nourished by the same water: yet We give each a different taste. Surely in this there are signs for men of understanding.

If anything could make you marvel, then you should surely marvel at those who say: 'When we are dust, shall we be raised to life again?'

Such are those who deny their Lord. Their necks shall be bound with chains and in the fire of Hell they shall abide for ever.

\* \* \*

Say: 'Allah is the Creator of all things. He is the One, the Almighty.'

He sends down water from the sky which fills the riverbeds to overflowing, so that their torrents bear a swelling foam, akin to that which rises from smelted ore when men make ornaments and tools. Thus Allah depicts truth and falsehood. The scum is cast away, but that which is of use to man remains behind. Thus Allah coins His parables.

## from Sura 14 Abraham

Do you not see how Allah compares a good word to a good tree? Its root is firm and its branches are in the sky; it yields its fruit in every season by Allah's leave. Allah gives parables to men so that they may take heed. But an evil word is like an evil tree torn out of the earth and shorn of all its roots.

## from Sura 18 The Cave

*In the Name of Allah, the Compassionate, the Merciful*

Praise be to Allah who has revealed the Book to His servant shorn of falsehood and unswerving from the truth, so that he may give warning of a dire scourge from Him, proclaim to the faithful who do good works that a rich and everlasting reward awaits them, and admonish those who say that Allah has begotten a son. Surely of this they could have no knowledge, neither they nor their fathers: a monstrous blasphemy is that which they utter. They preach nothing but falsehoods.

\* \* \*

Give them this parable. Once there were two men, to one of whom We gave two vineyards set about with palm-trees and watered by a running stream, with a cornfield lying in between. Each of the vineyards yielded an abundant crop, and when their owner had gathered in the harvest, he said to his companion while conversing with him: 'I am richer than you, and my clan is mightier than yours.'

And when, having thus wronged his soul, he entered his vineyard, he said: 'Surely this will never perish! Nor do I believe that the Hour of Doom will ever come. Even if I returned to my Lord, I should surely find a better place than this.'

His companion replied: 'Have you no faith in Him who created you from dust, from a little germ, and fashioned you into a man? As for myself, Allah is my Lord. I will associate none with Him. When you entered your garden, why did you not say: "That which Allah has ordained must surely come to pass: there is no strength save in Allah"? Though you see me poorer than yourself and blessed with fewer children, yet my Lord may give me a garden better than yours, and send down thunderbolts from heaven upon your vineyard, turning it into a barren waste, or drain its water deep into the earth so that you can find it no more.'

His vineyards were destroyed, and he began to wring his hands with grief at all that he had spent on them: for the vines had tumbled down upon their trellises. 'Would that I had served no other gods besides my Lord!' he cried. He had none to help him besides Allah, nor was he able to defend himself.

In such ordeals protection comes only from Allah, the true God. No reward is better than His reward, and no recompense more generous than His.

Coin for them a simile about this life. It is like the green herbs that flourish when watered by the rain, soon turning into stubble which the wind scatters abroad. Allah has power over all things.

Wealth and children are the ornament of this life. But deeds of lasting merit are better rewarded by your Lord and hold for you a greater hope of salvation.

Tell of the day when We shall blot out the mountains and make the earth a barren waste; when We shall gather all mankind together, leaving not a soul behind.

They shall be ranged before your Lord, who will say to them: 'You have returned to Us as We created you at first. Yet you thought Our promise was not to be fulfilled.'

Their book will be set down before them, and you shall see the sinners dismayed at that which is inscribed in it. They shall say: 'Woe to us! What can this book mean? It omits nothing small or great: all are noted down!' and they shall find their deeds recorded there. Your Lord will wrong none.

When We said to the angels: 'Prostrate yourselves before Adam,' all prostrated themselves except Satan, who was a *jinnee* disobedient to his Lord. Would you then serve him and his offspring as your masters rather than Myself, despite their enmity towards you? A sad substitute the wrong-doers have chosen!

I did not call them to witness at the creation of the heavens and the earth, nor at their own creation; nor was I to seek the aid of those who were to lead mankind astray.

On that day Allah will say to them: 'Call on the idols which you supposed divine.' They will invoke them, but shall receive no answer; for We shall place a deadly gulf between them. And when the sinners behold the fire of Hell they will know it is there they shall be slung. They shall find no escape from it.

In this Koran We have set forth for men all manner of parables. But man is exceedingly contentious.

\* \* \*

Your Lord is forgiving and merciful. Had it been His will to scourge them for their sins, He would have hastened their punishment; but He has set for them an appointed hour, which they shall never escape.

And all those nations! We destroyed them when they did wrong; yet of their imminent destruction We gave them warning.

Moses said to his servant: 'I will journey on until I reach the land where the two seas meet, though I may march for ages.'

But when at last they came to the land where the two seas met, they forgot their fish, which made its way into the water, swimming at will.

And when they had journeyed farther on, Moses said to his servant: 'Bring us some food; we are worn out with travelling.'

'Know,' replied the other, 'that I forgot the fish when we were resting on the rock. Thanks to Satan, I forgot to mention this. The fish made its way into the sea in a miraculous fashion.'

'This is what we have been seeking,' said Moses. They went back by the way they came and found one of Our servants to whom We had vouchsafed Our mercy and whom We had endowed with knowledge of Our own. Moses said to him: 'May I follow you so that you may guide me by that which you have been taught?'

'You will not bear with me,' replied the other. 'For how can you bear with that which is beyond your knowledge?'

Moses said: 'If Allah wills, you shall find me patient; I shall not in anything disobey you.'

He said: 'If you are bent on following me, you must ask no question about anything till I myself speak to you concerning it.'

The two set forth, but as soon as they embarked, Moses' companion bored a hole in the bottom of the ship.

'A strange thing you have done!' exclaimed Moses. 'Is it to drown her passengers that you have bored a hole in her?'

'Did I not tell you,' he replied, 'that you would not bear with me?'

'Pardon my forgetfulness,' said Moses. 'Do not be angry with me on account of this.'

They journeyed on until they fell in with a certain youth. Moses' companion slew him, and Moses said: 'You have killed an innocent man who has done no harm. Surely you have committed a wicked crime.'

'Did I not tell you,' he replied, 'that you would not bear with me?'

Moses said: 'If ever I question you again, abandon me; for then I should deserve it.'

They travelled on until they came to a certain city. They asked the people for some food, but they declined to receive them as their guests. There they found a wall on the point of falling down. His companion restored it, and Moses said: 'Had you wished, you could have demanded payment for your labours.'

'Now has the time arrived when we must part,' said the other. 'But first I will explain to you those acts of mine which you could not bear to watch with patience.

'Know that the ship belonged to some poor fishermen. I damaged it because in their rear there was a king who was taking every ship by force.

'As for the youth, his parents both are true believers, and we feared lest he should plague them with his wickedness and unbelief. It was our wish that their Lord should grant them another in his place, a son more righteous and more filial.

'As for the wall, it belonged to two orphan boys in the city whose father was an honest man. Beneath it their treasure is buried. Your Lord decreed in His mercy that they should dig out their treasure when they grew to manhood. What I did was not done by my will.

'That is the meaning of what you could not bear to watch with patience.'

\* \* \*

Say: 'If the waters of the sea were ink with which to write the words of my Lord, the sea would surely be consumed before His words were finished, though we brought another sea to replenish it.'

Say: 'I am a mortal like yourselves. It is revealed to me that your Lord is one God. Let him that hopes to meet his Lord do what is right and worship none besides Him.'

## from Sura 19 Mary

And you shall recount in the Book the story of Mary: how she left her people and betook herself to a solitary place to the east.

We sent to her Our spirit in the semblance of a full-grown man. And when she saw him she said: 'May the Merciful defend me from you! If you fear the Lord, leave me and go your way.'

'I am the messenger of your Lord,' he replied, 'and have come to give you a holy son.'

'How shall I bear a child,' she answered, 'when I am a virgin, untouched by man?'

'Such is the will of your Lord,' he replied. 'That is no difficult thing for Him. "He shall be a sign to mankind," says the Lord, "and a blessing from Ourself. That is Our decree."'

Thereupon she conceived, and retired to a far-off place. And when she felt the throes of childbirth she lay down by the trunk of a palm-tree, crying: 'Oh, would that I had died and passed into oblivion!'

But a voice from below cried out to her: 'Do not despair. Your Lord has provided a brook that runs at your feet, and if you shake the trunk of this palm-tree it will drop fresh ripe dates in your lap. Therefore rejoice. Eat and drink, and should you meet any mortal say to him: "I have vowed a fast to the Merciful and will not speak with any man today."'

Then she took the child to her people, who said to her: 'This is indeed a strange thing! Sister of Aaron,[1] your father was never a whoremonger, nor was your mother a harlot.'

She made a sign to them, pointing to the child. But they replied: 'How can we speak with a babe in the cradle?'

Whereupon he spoke and said: 'I am the servant of Allah. He has given me the Gospel and ordained me a prophet. His blessing is upon me wherever I go, and He has commanded me to be steadfast in prayer and to give alms to the poor as long as I shall live. He has exhorted me to honour my mother and has purged me of vanity and wickedness. I was blessed on the day I was born, and blessed I shall be on the day of my death; and may peace be upon me on the day when I shall be raised to life.'

Such was Jesus, the son of Mary. That is the whole truth, which they are unwilling to accept. Allah forbid that He Himself should beget a son! When He decrees a thing He need only say: 'Be,' and it is.

Allah is my Lord and your Lord: therefore serve Him. That is the right path.

Yet the Sects are divided concerning Jesus. But when the fateful day arrives, woe to the unbelievers! Their sight and hearing shall be sharpened on the day when they appear before Us. Truly, the unbelievers are in the grossest error.

Forewarn them of that woeful day, when Our decrees shall be fulfilled whilst they heedlessly persist in unbelief. For We shall inherit the earth and all who dwell upon it. To Us they shall return.

## from *Sura 22 Pilgrimage*

*In the Name of Allah, the Compassionate, the Merciful*

Men, have fear of your Lord. The catastrophe of the Hour of Doom shall be terrible indeed.

When that day comes, every suckling mother shall forsake her infant, every pregnant female shall cast her burden, and you shall see mankind reeling like drunkards although not drunk: such shall be the horror of Allah's vengeance.

---

1. I.e., virtuous woman—Aaron being held in the Koran as a 'prophet' and a saintly man. Such idiomatic expressions are common in Arabic. Muslim commentators deny the charge, often made by Western scholars and based solely on this text, that Muhammad confused Miriam, Aaron's sister, with Maryam (Mary), mother of Jesus.

Yet there are some who in their ignorance dispute about Allah and serve rebellious devils, though these are doomed to seduce their followers and lead them into the fire of Hell.

Men, if you doubt the Resurrection remember that We first created you from dust, then from a living germ, then from a clot of blood, and then from a half-formed lump of flesh, so that We might manifest to you Our power.

We cause to remain in the womb whatever We please for an appointed term, and then We bring you forth as infants, that you may grow up and reach your prime. Some die young, and some live on to abject old age when all that they once knew they know no more.

You sometimes see the earth dry and barren: but no sooner do We send down rain upon it than it begins to stir and swell, putting forth every kind of radiant bloom. That is because Allah is Truth: He gives life to the dead and has power over all things.

The Hour of Doom is sure to come—in this there is no doubt. Those who are in the grave Allah will raise to life.

\* \* \*

Do you not see how all who dwell in heaven and earth do homage to Allah? The sun and the moon and the stars, the mountains and the trees, the beasts, and countless men-all prostrate themselves before Him. Yet many have deserved His scourge. He who is humbled by Allah has none to honour him. Allah's will is ever done.

The faithful and the unbelievers contend about their Lord. Garments of fire have been prepared for the unbelievers. Scalding water shall be poured upon their heads, melting their skins and that which is in their bellies. They shall be lashed with rods of iron.

Whenever, in their anguish, they try to escape from Hell, the angels will drag them back, saying: 'Taste the torment of Hell-fire!'

As for those that have faith and do good works, Allah will admit them to gardens watered by running streams. They shall be decked with pearls and bracelets of gold, and arrayed in garments of silk. For they have been shown the noblest of words and guided to the path of the Glorious Lord.

The unbelievers who debar others from the path of Allah and from the Sacred Mosque which We gave to all mankind, natives and strangers alike, and those who commit evil within its walls, shall be sternly punished.

When We prepared for Abraham the site of the Sacred Mosque We said: 'Worship none besides Me. Keep My House clean for those who walk around it and those who stand upright or kneel in worship.'

Exhort all men to make the pilgrimage. They will come to you on foot and on the backs of swift camels from every distant quarter; they will come to avail themselves of many a benefit and to pronounce on the appointed days the name of Allah over the beasts which He has given them. Eat of their flesh yourselves, and feed the poor and the unfortunate.

Then let the pilgrims spruce themselves, make their vows, and circle the Ancient House. Such is Allah's commandment. He that reveres the sacred rites of Allah shall fare better in the sight of his Lord.

✳   ✳   ✳

Permission to take up arms is hereby given to those who are attacked, because they have been wronged. Allah has power to grant them victory: those who have been unjustly driven from their homes, only because they said: 'Our Lord is Allah.' Had Allah not defended some men by the might of others, the monasteries and churches, the synagogues and mosques in which His praise is daily celebrated, would have been utterly destroyed. But whoever helps Allah shall be helped by Him. Allah is powerful and mighty: He will assuredly help those who, once made masters in the land, will attend to their prayers and pay the alms-tax, enjoin justice and forbid evil. Allah controls the destiny of all things.

If they deny you, remember that before them the peoples of Noah, Abraham and Lot, the tribes of Thamoud and Aad, and the dwellers of Midian had denied their apostles: Moses himself was charged with imposture. I bore long with the unbelievers and in the end My scourge overtook them. And how terrible was My vengeance!

How many sinful nations We have destroyed! Their cities lie in ruin: desolate are their lofty palaces, and abandoned their wells.

Have they never journeyed through the land? Have they no hearts to reason with, or ears to hear with? It is their hearts, and not their eyes, that are blind.

## from *Sura 24 Light*

Allah is the light of the heavens and the earth. His light may be compared to a niche that enshrines a lamp, the lamp within a crystal of star-like brilliance. It is lit from a blessed olive tree neither eastern nor western. Its very oil would almost shine forth, though no fire touched it. Light upon light; Allah guides to His light whom He will.

Allah coins metaphors for men. He has knowledge of all things.

His light is found in temples which Allah has sanctioned to be built for the remembrance of His name. In them morning and evening His praise is sung by men whom neither trade nor profit can divert from remembering Him, from offering prayers, or from giving alms; who dread the day when men's hearts and eyes shall writhe with anguish; who hope that Allah will requite them for their noblest deeds and lavish His grace upon them. Allah gives without measure to whom He will.

As for the unbelievers, their works are like a mirage in a desert. The thirsty traveller thinks it is water, but when he comes near he finds that it is nothing. He finds Allah there, who pays him back in full. Swift is Allah's reckoning.

Or like darkness on a bottomless ocean spread with clashing billows and overcast with clouds: darkness upon darkness. If he stretches out his hand he can scarcely see it. Indeed, the man from whom Allah withholds His light shall find no light at all.

Do you not see how Allah is praised by those in heaven and earth? The very birds praise Him as they wing their flight. He notes the prayers and praises of all His creatures, and has knowledge of all their actions.

To Allah belongs the kingdom of the heavens and the earth. To Him shall all things return.

Do you not see how Allah drives the clouds, then gathers them and piles them up in masses which pour down torrents of rain? From heaven's mountains He sends down hail, pelting with it whom He will and turning it away from whom He pleases. The flash of His lightning almost snatches off men's eyes.

He makes the night succeed the day: surely in this there is a lesson for clear-sighted men.

Allah created every beast from water. Some creep upon their bellies, others walk on two legs, and others on four. Allah creates what He pleases. He has power over all things.

We have sent down revelations showing the truth. Allah guides whom He will to a straight path.

## from *Sura 29 The Spider*

The false gods which the idolaters serve besides Allah may be compared to the spider's cobweb. Surely the spider's is the frailest of all dwellings, if they but knew it. Allah knows what they invoke besides Him; He is the Mighty, the Wise One.

We coin these similes for the instruction of men; but none will grasp their meaning except the wise.

## *Sura 55 The Merciful*[1]

*In the Name of Allah, the Compassionate, the Merciful*

It is the Merciful who has taught you the Koran.

He created man and taught him articulate speech. The sun and the moon pursue their ordered course. The plants and the trees bow down in adoration.

He raised the heaven on high and set the balance of all things, that you might not transgress it. Give just weight and full measure.

He laid the earth for His creatures, with all its fruits and blossom-bearing palm, chaff-covered grain and scented herbs. Which of your Lord's blessings would you[2] deny?

---

1. Compare this chapter with Psalm 136 of the Old Testament.

2. The pronoun is in the dual number, the words being addressed to mankind and the jinn. This refrain is repeated no less than 31 times.

He created man from potter's clay and the jinn from smokeless fire. Which of your Lord's blessings would you deny?

The Lord of the two easts[3] is He, and the Lord of the two wests. Which of your Lord's blessings would you deny?

He has let loose the two oceans:[4] they meet one another. Yet between them stands a barrier which they cannot overrun. Which of your Lord's blessings would you deny?

Pearls and corals come from both. Which of your Lord's blessings would you deny?

His are the ships that sail like banners[5] upon the ocean. Which of your Lord's blessings would you deny?

All who live on earth are doomed to die. But the face of your Lord will abide for ever, in all its majesty and glory. Which of your Lord's blessings would you deny?

All who dwell in heaven and earth beseech Him. Each day some new task employs Him. Which of your Lord's blessings would you deny?

Mankind and jinn, We shall surely find the time to judge you! Which of your Lord's blessings would you deny?

Mankind and *jinn*, if you have power to penetrate the confines of heaven and earth, then penetrate them! But this you shall not do except with Our own authority. Which of your Lord's blessings would you deny?

Flames of fire shall be lashed at you, and molten brass. There shall be none to help you. Which of your Lord's blessings would you deny?

When the sky splits asunder and reddens like a rose or stained leather (which of your Lord's blessings would you deny?), on that day neither man nor jinnee shall be asked about his sins. Which of your Lord's blessings would you deny?

The wrongdoers shall be known by their looks; they shall be seized by their forelocks and their feet. Which of your Lord's blessings would you deny?

That is the Hell which the sinners deny. They shall wander between fire and water fiercely seething. Which of your Lord's blessings would you deny?

But for those that fear the majesty of their Lord there are two gardens (which of your Lord's blessings would you deny?) planted with shady trees. Which of your Lord's blessings would you deny?

Each is watered by a flowing spring. Which of your Lord's blessings would you deny?

Each bears every kind of fruit in pairs. Which of your Lord's blessings would you deny?

---

3. The points at which the sun rises in summer and winter.

4. Salt water and fresh water.

5. Or mountains.

They shall recline on couches lined with thick brocade, and within their reach will hang the fruits of both gardens. Which of your Lord's blessings would you deny?

They shall dwell with bashful virgins whom neither man nor jinnee will have touched before. Which of your Lord's blessings would you deny?

Virgins as fair as corals and rubies. Which of your Lord's blessings would you deny?

Shall the reward of goodness be anything but good? Which of your Lord's blessings would you deny?

And beside these there shall be two other gardens (which of your Lord's blessings would you deny?) of darkest green. Which of your Lord's blessings would you deny?

A gushing fountain shall flow in each. Which of your Lord's blessings would you deny?

Each planted with fruit-trees, the palm and the pomegranate. Which of your Lord's blessings would you deny?

In each there shall be virgins chaste and fair. Which of your Lord's blessings would you deny?

Dark-eyed virgins sheltered in their tents (which of your Lord's blessings would you deny?) whom neither man nor jinnee will have touched before. Which of your Lord's blessings would you deny?

They shall recline on green cushions and rich carpets. Which of your Lord's blessings would you deny?

Blessed be the name of your Lord, the Lord of majesty and glory!

## Sura 56 That Which Is Coming

*In the Name of Allah, the Compassionate, the Merciful*

When that which is coming comes—and no soul shall them deny its coming—some shall be abased and others exalted.

When the earth shakes and quivers and the mountains crumble away and scatter abroad into fine dust, you shall be divided into three multitudes: those on the right (blessed shall be those on the right!); those on the left (damned shall be those on the left!); and those to the fore (foremost shall be those!). Such are they that shall be brought near to their Lord in the gardens of delight: a whole multitude from the men of old, but only a few from the later generations.

They shall recline on jewelled couches face to face, and there shall wait on them immortal youths with bowls and ewers and a cup of purest wine (that will neither pain their heads nor take away their reason); with fruits of their own choice and flesh of fowls that they relish. And theirs shall be the dark-eyed houris, chaste as hidden pearls: a guerdon for their deeds.

There they shall hear no idle talk, no sinful speech, but only the greeting, 'Peace! Peace!'

Those on the right hand—happy shall be those on the right hand! They shall recline on couches raised on high in the shade of thornless sidrahs and clusters of talh;[1] amidst gushing waters and abundant fruits, unforbidden, never-ending.

We created the houris and made them virgins, loving companions for those on the right hand: a multitude from the men of old, and a multitude from the later generations.

As for those on the left hand (wretched shall be those on the left hand!) they shall dwell amidst scorching winds and seething water: in the shade of pitch-black smoke, neither cool nor refreshing. For they have lived in comfort and persisted in the heinous sin,[2] saying: 'When we are once dead and turned to dust and bones, shall we, with all our forefathers, be raised to life?'

Say: 'This present generation, as well as the generations that passed before it, shall be brought together on an appointed day. As for you sinners who deny the truth, you shall eat the fruit of the Zaqqum-tree and fill your bellies with it. You shall drink boiling water: yet you shall drink it as the thirsty camel drinks.'

Such shall be their fare on the Day of Reckoning.

We created you: will you not believe then in Our power?

Behold the semen you discharge: did you create it, or We?

It was We that ordained death among you. Nothing can hinder Us from replacing you by others like yourselves or transforming you into beings you know nothing of.

You surely know of the first creation. Why, then, do you not reflect? Consider the seeds you sow. Is it you that give them growth or We? If We pleased We could turn your harvest into chaff, so that, filled with wonderment, you would exclaim: 'We are laden with debts! Surely we have been robbed!'

Consider the water which you drink. Was it you that poured it from the cloud or We? If We pleased We could turn it bitter. Why then do you not give thanks?

Observe the fire which you light. Is it you that create its wood, or We? We have made it a reminder for man, and for the traveller a comfort.

Praise then the name of your Lord, the Supreme One.

I swear by the shelters of the stars (a mighty oath, if you but knew it) that this is a glorious Koran, inscribed in a hidden book which none may touch except the purified; a revelation from the Lord of all creatures.

Would you scorn a scripture such as this and make it your daily task to deny it?

When under your very eyes a man's soul is about to leave him (We are nearer to him than you, although you cannot see Us), why do you not restore it, if you will not be judged hereafter? Answer this, if what you say be true!

---

1. Probably the banana fruit.
2. Idolatry.

Thus, if he is favoured, his lot will be repose and plenty and a garden of delights. If he is one of those on the right hand he will be greeted with, 'Peace be to you!' by those on the right hand.

But if he is an erring disbeliever his welcome will be scalding water and he will burn in Hell.

This is the indubitable truth. Praise then the name of your Lord, the Supreme One.

## *from* **Sura 57 Iron**

*In the Name of Allah, the Compassionate, the Merciful*

All that is in heaven and earth gives glory to Allah. He is the Mighty, the Wise One.

His is the kingdom of the heavens and the earth. He ordains life and death and has power over all things.

He is the first and the last, the visible and the unseen. He has knowledge of all things.

He created the heavens and the earth in six days and then mounted His throne. He knows all that goes into the earth and all that emerges from it, all that comes down from heaven and all that ascends to it. He is with you wherever you are. Allah is cognizant of all your actions.

His is the kingdom of the heavens and the earth. To Him shall all things return. He causes the night to pass into the day and the day into the night. He has knowledge of the inmost thoughts of men.

Have faith in Allah and His apostle and give in alms of that which He has made your inheritance; for whoever of you believes and gives in alms shall be richly rewarded.

\* \* \*

Know that the life of this world is but a sport and a pastime, a show and an empty vaunt among you, a quest for greater riches and more children. It is like the plants that flourish after rain: the husbandman rejoices to see them grow; but then they wither and turn yellow, soon becoming worthless stubble. In the life to come a woeful punishment awaits you—or the forgiveness of Allah and His pleasure. The life of this world is but a vain provision.

Therefore strive emulously for the pardon of your Lord, and for a Paradise as vast as heaven and earth, prepared for those who believe in Allah and His apostles. Such is the grace of Allah: He bestows it on whom He will. His grace is infinite.

## **Sura 81 The Cessation**

*In the Name of Allah, the Compassionate, the Merciful*

When the sun ceases to shine; when the stars fall down and the mountains are blown away; when camels big with young are left untended and the wild beasts are brought together; when the seas are set alight and men's souls are reunited; when the infant girl,[1] buried alive, is asked for what crime she was thus slain; when the records of men's deeds are laid open and the heaven is stripped bare; when Hell burns fiercely and Paradise is brought near: then each soul shall know what it has done.

I swear by the turning planets and by the stars that rise and set; by the fall of night and the first breath of morning: this is the word of a gracious and mighty messenger, held in honour by the Lord of the Throne, obeyed in heaven, faithful to his trust.

No, your compatriot[2] is not mad. He saw him[3] on the clear horizon. He does not grudge the secrets of the unseen; nor is this the utterance of an accursed devil.

Whither then are you going?

This is an admonition to all men: to those among you that have the will to be upright. Yet you cannot will, except by the will of Allah, Lord of the Creation.

## Sura 104 The Slanderer

*In the Name of Allah, the Compassionate, the Merciful*

Woe to all back-biting slanderers who amass riches and sedulously hoard them, thinking their treasures will render them immortal!

By no means! They shall be flung to the Destroying Flame.

Would that you knew what the Destroying Flame is like!

It is Allah's own kindled fire, which will rise up to the hearts of men. It will close upon them from every side, in towering columns.

## ■ Rabia the Mystic (c. 712–801) *Iraq* (poems and miracle story)

Rabia al-Adawiyya was born in Basra (now in Iraq) and is considered an important Sufi saint, and many of the miracle tales about her that survive were recorded by another major Sufi writer, Farid ad-Din Attar. We know that Rabia was born poor and that her family life was tragic: famine killed her parents, and she and her sisters were scattered—she to be sold as a slave. Her master eventually gave her her freedom. This story is told about her master's change of heart:

In her life as a slave, Rabia found time for her worship of God by doing without sleep. She fasted and prayed. One night her master awoke, looked

---

1. An allusion to the pre-Islamic custom of burying unwanted newborn girls.

2. Muhammad.

3. Gabriel.

down from the window of his house into the courtyard, and saw Rabia in prayer. As he was watching her he was amazed to see a lamp appear above her head suspended in mid-air; the light from this miraculous lamp lit up the whole house. Terrified and astonished, he went back to bed, and sat wondering until dawn. Then he called Rabia to him, confessed what he had seen, and gave her her freedom.[1]

She might have made the pilgrimage to Mecca; she came to be recognized as a saint of great renown who refused worldly offers (fear of falling away from spirituality into the trap of the world is a major theme in her poems); and she is said to have lived a celibate life in humble circumstances. It is hard to know whether these poems were actually written by her or by others, but the singular and/or plural author(s) have inscribed the psychology of at least a ghost-Rabia into these poems, the harshness and depth of whose life experience seems to have translated into a particularly fervent and unyielding asceticism.

FURTHER READING: Nurbakhsh, Dr. Javad. *Sufi Women*. Translated by Leonard Lewisohn, 1983. Sakkakini, Widad El. *First Among Sufis: The Life and Thought of Rabi'a al-Adawiyya*. Translated by Dr. Nabil Safwat, 1982. Smith, Margaret. *Rabi'a the Mystic and Her Fellow Saints in Islam*, 1928, 1977. Upton, Charles. *Doorkeeper of the Heart: Versions of Rabi'a*, 1988.

## O My Lord, the Stars Glitter and the Eyes of Men Are Closed

O my Lord, the stars glitter and eyes of men are closed,
kings have shut their doors
and each lover is alone with his love.
Here, I am alone with you.

TRANSLATED BY WILLIS BARNSTONE

## Miracle Story

One day Rabi'a and her serving-girl were getting ready to break a fast of several days. The serving-girl needed an onion and was about to go next door and borrow one, but Rabi'a said: "Forty years ago I vowed never to ask for anything from anyone but God—we can do without onions."

Just then a bird flew over, and dropped an onion into Rabi'a's frying pan, peeled and ready to fry.

---

1. Charles Upton, *Doorkeeper of the Heart: Versions of Rabi'a* (Putney, VT: Threshold Books, 1988), 9–10.

"Interesting but not convincing," she said. "Am I supposed to believe that God is an onion-vender? I mean, really."

That day they fried their bread without onions.

TRANSLATED BY CHARLES UPTON

## How Long Will You Keep Pounding

How long will you keep pounding on an open door
Begging for someone to open it?

TRANSLATED BY CHARLES UPTON

■ **Abu Nuwas (b. between 747–762, d. between 813–815)** *Baghdad/Abbasid Empire* **(poem)**

TRANSLATED BY RICHARD SERRANO

Abu Nuwas was among the best writers of the Abbasid school of poetry. His mother was Persian, but he wrote in Arabic, and after studying in Basra and Kufa was a court poet writing panegyrics in Baghdad. A resolute rake, he lived a life of debauched pleasure, and his poems reflect this in their emphasis on drinking songs, love poems (usually about young men, sometimes about women), and obscene poems; his wanton poetry even goes to the point of attacking Islam. His poetry is not all of this nature, though; he also wrote satires, didactic verse, panegyrics, and ascetic verse. He became a folk hero, and stories about his exploits at the court of Caliph Harun al-Rashid appear in *The Thousand and One Nights*. A collection of his poems survives.

## Drunkenness after Drunkenness

So pour wine for me and say it is wine;
Don't pour in secret what can be public.

No good life without drunkenness after drunkenness;
If its duration is long then time will be short.

There is no crime but your seeing me sober, no advantage
But in my drunken shakes and stammers.

5

Reveal the name of whom you love without allusion;
There is no good in veiled pleasures,

Nor good in depravity without scandal,
Nor in scandal not followed by unbelief.                                    *10*

With all my brothers in depravity,
Their brows as crescent moons surrounded by stars,

I woke a taverness from her nap,
Once Gemini had set and Aquila had risen.

She said, "Who knocks?" We answered, "A gang                               *15*
Lightened of medicine, wine entices them,

They must fornicate." She said, "In exchange
Take one bright as a dinar, languor in his glance."

"Hand him over. The likes of us are impatient
To ransom our families for the likes of him."                              *20*

She brought him out like a moon at full term;
Enchanting, he was no mere enchantment.

So we went to him one by one,
Breaking the fast of our exile.

So we passed the night, God watching a gang                               *25*
Let trail the robes of depravity—and this no boast.

## ■ The Thousand and One Nights (c. Ninth to Fourteenth Centuries) *Persia/Arabia* (stories)

### TRANSLATED BY RICHARD BURTON, ADAPTED BY EMMA VARESIO

*The Thousand and One Nights,* also known as *The Arabian Nights,* is a collection of stories in the form of fables, jokes, anecdotes, didactic tales, parables, fairy tales, and legends, whose sources are Arabic, Persian, and Indian oral and written tales. These stories circulated for hundreds of years before being transcribed between the ninth and fourteenth centuries. The immediate basis for the collection was a Persian book entitled *A Thousand Tales,* which was translated into Arabic around the ninth century. This latter compendium was the model for the framing narrative of *The Thousand and One Nights,* in which King Shahryar is driven mad with jealousy after discovering his queen in the arms of a slave. He goes in search of anyone who has suffered as much as he. On encountering the wife of a genie, who has been locked in a casket within a chest with seven padlocks, deposited at the bottom of the sea, and yet has cuckolded her husband 570 times, he is convinced that all women are unfaithful. So he kills his queen and takes a new wife every night for three years, murdering her in the morning to ensure her fidelity. Scheherazade, his vizier's daughter, marries the king to try to stop the slaughter of women. To save her own life, she tells a story each night through dawn. Leaving the tale unfinished when morning comes, she keeps the king fascinated: "By Allah," he says, each day, "I won't slay her until I hear the rest of her tale, for it is truly wondrous." By the end of telling, several years later, Scheherazade has borne the king three sons and through her skills and grace has domesticated the mad monarch.

The *Nights* was introduced to the West by Antoine Galland in the early eighteenth century, and since then there have been innumerable translations into the languages of the world, notably that of Sir Richard Burton (1821–1890), whose sixteen-volume unexpurgated and annotated version is the classic and most esteemed version in English. The present selection, which retains Burton's bawdy and energetically elaborate prose style, has been modernized by Emma Varesio. The text, which is erotic, outrageous, and wise, has often been bowdlerized and sanitized in English translation, rendering this adult masterpiece into a collection of children's tales. This Eastern collection has deeply affected the Western literary imagination from Robert Louis Stevenson's *New Arabian Nights* to the labyrinthine narratives of Jorge Luis Borges. Hollywood has frequently adapted the *Nights* into magical, adventurous, or humorous films that deviate wildly from the original. However, since the notion of an authoritative original of a collection with so many recensions is itself questionable, perhaps these film retellings are in the spirit of essential works that are constantly reinvented to fit a new cultural environment. The American writer John Barth recently has adapted the tales of *Sinbad the Sailor* into his fascinating novel *The Last Voyage of Somebody the Sailor,* and the common Modernist technique of the tale within a tale must owe something to the multilayered narrative of the *Nights.* The selection presented here, "The Tale of the Fisherman and the Genie," is a famous sequence of stories that mirrors the collection's framing technique. Like Scheherazade, the fisherman tells story within story and must outwit his fate—in this case an angry genie.

**FURTHER READING:** Burton, Richard, tr. *The Book of the Thousand Nights and a Night, A Plain and Literal Translation of the Arabian Nights Entertainment,* 10 vols., 1885–1886; tr. *Supplemental Nights to the Book of the Thousand Nights and a Night, with Notes Anthropological and Explanatory,* 6 vols., 1886–1888. Lane, Edward William, tr. *A New Translation of the Tales of A Thousand and One Nights: Known in England as The Arabian Nights' Entertainments,* 1838–1840. Zipes, Jack, tr. *Arabian Nights: The Marvels and Wonders of the Thousand and One Nights,* 1991.

## The Tale of the Fisherman and the Genie

I have heard, Oh worthy King, that there was once a poor, old Fisherman who had a wife and three children to support. Each day, it was his custom to cast his fishing-net into the ocean exactly four times, and no more. One day, at about noon, he went towards the seashore, where he set his basket down in the sand. Tucking up his shirt and plunging into the water, he cast his net and waited until it settled to the bottom of the sea. Then, he gathered the cords of the net together, and tried to haul it away. But its heaviness overpowered him, and no matter how hard he tried, he could not pull it up. So he carried the ends of the cords to the shore, drove a stake into the sand, and bound the cords tightly to the stake. Then he stripped his clothes from his body and dove into the water, working hard until he finally raised the net from the sea.

Rejoicing, he put his clothes back on and went to examine the net and found a dead jackass inside of it, which had torn all the net's meshes. As he saw this, the Fisherman sadly exclaimed, "There is no majesty, and there is no might except Allah the glorious, the great! But, well, this is a strange sort of daily bread." He paused, considering, and then murmured to himself, "Well, up and at it! I'll finish my fishing now, for I'm very sure of Allah's goodness."

So the Fisherman gazed at the dead ass for a moment, and then pulled it free from the netting. He wrung out the net, and spread it over the sand. Calling out "In Allah's name!" he plunged back into the sea. He cast the net a second time, and when he tried to pull it out, it grew even heavier and settled down more firmly than before. Now, he thought, there were certainly fish in it this time. Quickly, he tied the cords to the stake again, pulled off his clothes, and dove into the water, hauling the net until it reached the shore. Inside the net lay a large earthen pitcher, clogged full of sand and mud.

As he saw this the Fisherman became very disheartened, and so he prayed for Allah's pardon. After throwing away the pitcher, he wrung out his net, cleaned it, and cast into the sea for the third time. Again, he waited until it sunk to the bottom, and then pulled it up. This time, he found shards of pottery and broken glass inside the net. Raising his eyes toward heaven, he cried out, "Oh Allah! You know that I cast my net into the sea four times every day. I've cast it three times, and so far, You have granted me nothing! I beseech You, my God, this time give me my daily bread!"

Then, calling on Allah's name, he threw his net into the sea again, waiting for it to sink and settle at the bottom. Again, he tugged at it, but it was tangled in the sea bottom. Frustrated, he shouted, "There is no majesty and there is no might but in Allah!" Then he shed his clothes again, dove down to the net, and patiently untangled it, bit by bit, until it rose and he could drag it to shore. He opened the meshes, and in its folds, he found a cucumber-shaped copper jar, brimming with something mysterious. The mouth of the jar was sealed with lead, and stamped with the seal of our Lord Solomon, David's son, Allah praise them! Seeing this the Fisherman rejoiced and said, "If I sell this in the brass bazaar, I could get ten golden dinars for it!" He shook the jar, and finding it heavy, murmured, "I wish I knew what was in it. I feel as if I must find out—so I'll open it and look inside, and then I'll store it in my bag, to sell at the brass market. Taking out a knife, he pried the lead until he had loosened it from the jar. He set the seal on the ground, and turned the vase upside-down, shaking it and trying to pour out whatever could be inside. Surprisingly, nothing emerged, and the fisherman stood in wonder.

But suddenly, a spiral of smoke burst from the jar, rising toward the heavens. The fisherman marvelled as it was drawn into the air, ascending far above him. As it reached its full height, the thick, vaporous smoke condensed and formed a Genie, so huge that his head brushed the sky, and his feet touched the ground. The Genie's head curved as large as a dome; his hands dangled, big as pitchforks. His legs were long as masts, his mouth as wide as a cave, his teeth like large stones, and his nostril flared like pitchers' spouts. His eyes shone like two lamps, and his face proved fierce and threatening.

Now, when the Fisherman saw the Genie, his muscles quivered, his teeth chattered, and his throat grew too dry to swallow. Paralyzed, clenched with fear, he could do nothing.

The Genie looked at him and cried, "There is no god but *the* God, and Solomon is the prophet of God." He added, "Oh Apostle of Allah, do not slay me. Never again will I oppose you or sin against you."

The Fisherman replied, "Oh Genie, did you say, 'Solomon the Apostle of Allah?' Solomon has been dead for nearly eighteen hundred years, and now we're in the last days of the world! Where have you come from? What's happened to you? Why have you been in that jar?"

When the Evil Spirit heard the Fisherman's words, he answered, "There is no god but *the* God. Be happy, Fisherman!"

"Why should I be happy?" asked the Fisherman.

"Because," replied the Genie, "you must die a terrible death this very hour."

"You deserve heaven's abandonment for your good tidings!" cried the Fisherman. "For what reason should you kill me? What have I done to deserve death? I, who freed you from the jar, dragged you from the depths of the sea, and brought you up to dry land?"

"Ask me only in which way you will die, how I will slaughter you," said the Genie.

"What's my crime?" the Fisherman persisted. "Why such retribution?"

"Hear my story, Oh Fisherman!" cried the Genie.

The Fisherman swiftly answered, "Tell it, but tell it briefly. My heart is in my mouth."

And so, the Genie began his tale. "I am one of the heretical Genie," he explained. "I, along with the famous Sakhr al Jinni, sinned against

Solomon, David's son. After this, the Prophet Solomon sent his minister, Asaf son of Barkhiya, to seize me. This minister bound me and took me against my will, bringing me to stand before the Prophet Solomon like a supplicant. When Solomon saw me, he appealed to Allah, and demanded that I embrace the True Faith and obey Allah's commands. I refused; and so he sent for this jar and imprisoned me in it, sealing it with lead and stamping it with the Most High Name. He ordered another spirit to carry me off, and cast me into the center of the ocean. I lived there for a hundred years, and during this time I said in my heart, 'I'll forever reward whoever releases me with the greatest of riches.' But an entire century passed, and when no one set me free, I began the second century saying, 'I'll reveal the secret treasures of the earth to whoever will release me.' Still, no one set me free, and soon four hundred years passed. Then I said, 'I'll grant three wishes to whoever will release me.' Yet again, no one set me free. Then I became angry, so furious, I said to myself, 'From now on, I'll kill whoever releases me, and I'll let him choose what type of death he will die.' And now, as you're the one who's released me, I give you the choice of your death."

The Fisherman, hearing the words of the Genie, exclaimed, "Oh Allah! How could it be that I didn't come to free him before this? Spare my life, Genie, and Allah will spare yours; don't kill me, and Allah will never send anyone to kill you!"

"There is no help for you. You must die," the Genie obstinately explained.

"Grant me a release from death, as a generous reward for having released you!" said the Fisherman.

"But it's because you released me that I *must* kill you," insisted the Genie.

"Oh chief of Genies," said the Fisherman. "I've done you something good, and you return my good action with evil!"

"No more of this talk," said the Genie, as he heard the Fisherman's words. "I must kill you!"

As the Genie spoke, the Fisherman said to himself, "This is a Genie, but I'm a man to whom Allah has given a cunning wit. So now, as he uses his malice to destroy me, I'll use my intelligence and cunning to stop *him*." He turned to the Genie and said, "Have you really resolved to kill me?"

"Of course."

"Even so," exclaimed the Fisherman, "if I ask you a question about a certain matter, will you swear by the Most Great Name, engraved on the seal-ring of Solomon, Son of David, that you'll answer it truthfully?"

The Genie trembled as he heard the Fisherman mention the Most Great Name. "Yes," he promised the Fisherman, though his mind grew troubled. "Yes, ask, but be brief."

The Fisherman said, "How did you fit into this bottle, which doesn't even look big enough to hold your hand, or even your foot? How could it have been big enough to contain all of you?"

"What!" replied the Genie. "You don't believe my whole body was in there?"

"No!" cried the Fisherman. "I'll never believe it until I see all of you inside of it, with my own eyes."

*And then Shahrazad saw that dawn crept over the edge of the horizon, and so she stopped telling her story. But the next day, when the fourth night came, her sister said to her, "Please finish the story. None of us are sleepy." And so, Shahrazad resumed her storytelling. . . .*

It has reached me, Oh worthy King, that after the Fisherman said to the Genie, "I'll never believe you, until I see all of you inside the jar, with my own eyes," then the Evil Spirit instantly shook, transforming himself into a vapor. The vapor condensed, slowly snaking into the jar, until all of him was buried inside of it. Quickly, the Fisherman grabbed the lead cap with the seal, stopping the mouth of the jar with it. He called to the Genie, "Now ask me which way *you* will die! I'll grant you your choice of death! By Allah, I'll throw you into the sea, and right here I'll build a lodge, to warn whoever comes here not to go fishing. I'll say: A Genie lives in these waters, one who grants the person who saves him their choice of death!"

As the Genie heard the Fisherman, he pressed against the jar, trying to escape — but he was prevented by Solomon's seal. He realized the Fisherman had outwitted him, and that his freedom was in peril. And so he became submissive and humble, crying out, "I was only joking with you!"

"That's a lie, you vile Genie!" exclaimed the Fisherman. "It's a mean, filthy lie from the meanest, filthiest Genie!" The Fisherman pushed the jar towards the sea, as the Genie screamed, "No! Stop, no!" and the Fisherman yelled, "Yes, yes!"

As they neared the water, the Genie softened his voice, saying smoothly, "What are you going to do to me, Fisherman?"

"I'm going to throw you back into the sea," the Fisherman answered. "You lived there for eighteen hundred years, and now you'll live there until Judgment Day. Didn't I tell you, if you spared my life, Allah would spare yours? And, if you killed me, Allah would kill you? Even though I did say that, you spurned my speech. You only wanted to treat me terribly. But Allah threw you into my hands, and I'm more cunning than you are!"

The Genie slyly said, "Open the bottle, and I'll bring you wealth."

"You lie," said the Fisherman. "For this is just like it was for the Vizier of King Yunan, and the Sage Duban."

"Who were the Vizier and this Sage Duban?" asked the Genie. "What was their story?"

And so the Fisherman began to tell him. . . .

## *The Tale of the Vizier and the Sage Duban*

You should know, Genie, that in past years, a King named Yunan reigned over the cities of Persia in the Roman land. King Yunan was a powerful ruler, and quite wealthy. He had armies and guards and was allied with all nations. But he was afflicted with leprosy, and all the doctors in the world couldn't heal him. He drank potions, swallowed powders, and used lotions, but nothing would help; nobody could find him a cure.

Eventually, a mighty healer came to his city, called the Sage Duban. This aged wise man knew the works of the Greeks, Persians, Romans, Arabs, and Syrians; he had also studied astronomy and leechcraft. He knew everything, in theory and in practice, that could heal or harm a body. He knew the healing properties of every plant, grass, and herb, and he understood philosophy as well as medical science.

Now, this doctor Duban had only been in the city for a couple of days before he heard of the King's illness and suffering, with which Allah had afflicted him. Duban heard how all the doctors and wise men had failed to heal this King. And so, he sat up all during the night, deep in thought, until dawn broke through and the sun again greeted the world. Then Duban put on his best clothes, and went to see King Yunan. He kissed the ground before him, and prayed for the King's honor and life to prosper.

"Oh King," he said, "I've heard of your illness, and of how many doctors have failed to cure it. I can cure you, oh King, without having you drink another drop of medicine, and without having you use another drop of ointment!"

Surprised, King Yunan exclaimed, "But how will you do this? By Allah, if you do heal me, I'll give riches to you and all your sons. I'll give you lavish gifts—whatever you wish will be yours, and you'll be my closest companion." Then the King put a robe of honor on him, asking him graciously, "Can you really cure me of this illness without drug or ointment?"

"Yes," replied the Sage. "I'll heal you without the pains of medicines."

The King marvelled, and said, "Doctor, when should we start, and where, and how soon? Can it be soon?"

"Of course," answered Duban. "The cure will begin tomorrow."

Duban then left the palace, and rented a house nearby, arranging his books, scrolls, medicines and aromatic roots there. Then he set to work, choosing the best drugs and ointments. He carved two long sticks, making them hollow inside, and each one tapering into a flat handle, that could hit a ball. The next day, he would present both of these to the King. And so, after greeting the King and kissing the floor before him, Duban invited him to come play polo on the parade grounds.

The King came, accompanied by his Emirs, Chamberlains, Viziers, and Lords. Before he sat down, the Sage Duban approached him, handing him the stick and saying, "Take this stick and grip it like this." He guided the King's fingers around the instrument. "Good," Duban continued, as the King rested his hands on the polo stick. Then he explained, "Next, lean over your horse and drive the ball with all your strength, until your palm is sweaty and your whole body perspires. Then the medicine will penetrate through your palm and into your body. When you're done playing and you feel the effects of the medicine, return to your palace and make an ablution in the Hamman-bath. Lay down to sleep, and then peace will come upon you, and you'll be healed."

So King Yunan took the polo stick from Sage Duban and grasped it firmly. Mounting his horse, he drove the ball before him, galloping after it until he reached it. Once he came close to it, he struck it again with all his strength, his palm gripping the polo stick the whole time. He didn't stop playing until his palm was sweaty, and his whole body perspiring, so that he imbibed the medicines from the wood. In this way, the Sage Duban knew that the drugs had penetrated his body, and so he told the King to return to the palace and enter the Hamman-bath immediately. So King Yunan returned right away, and ordered that the bath be prepared for him. His subjects hurriedly spread the carpets, and brought the King a change of cloths. The King entered the bath, and made the ablution thoroughly. When he finished, he put on his clothes, lay down, and slept.

Meanwhile, the Sage Duban returned to his house, slept until morning, and then went to the palace to talk with the King. The King admitted him, and the Sage bowed down before him. As Duban rose, the King came towards him, embracing him. King Yunan ordered that Duban be clothed in luxurious robes—for after the King left the Hamman-bath, all traces of leprosy had vanished from his body. His skin was clean as pure silver. The King had never rejoiced more.

Later in the day, the King entered his audience-hall and seated himself on his throne. Chamberlains and Grandees came to see him, bringing the Sage Duban with them. The King rose to greet him, and seated him by his side; he ordered platters of food to be brought, spilling over with the daintiest morsels. The two men did not leave each other's side all day. At night, the King gave Duban two thousand gold pieces, as well as gifts and robes of honor, and sent him home on his own horse.

After Sage Duban left, the King exclaimed, "This man healed my body without even any ointments! By Allah, surely there's no one else with this skill! I'm bound to honor such a man with rewards and distinction, and to make him my companion and friend until the end of my days." And so King Yunan passed the night in joy and gladness, for his body had been made whole, without a trace of this horrible malady.

In the morning, the King sat on his throne again, with the Lords of Estate standing around him, and the Emirs and Viziers sitting at his right and left. He requested that the Sage Duban come. After he was brought, Duban again kissed the ground before the King. King Yunan rose to greet him, sat by his side, ate with him, and wished him a long life. Moreover, he gave Sage Duban more gifts, rich robes, and did not stop speaking with him until night approached. Then the King offered him a salary of one thousand dinars and five robes of honor. Sage Duban returned to his own house, full of gratitude to the King.

As the next morning dawned, the King went to his throne, again surrounded by Lords and Nobles, Chamberlains and Ministers. Now, the King had a Vizier among his nobles, who was spiteful, envious, and devoid of all generosity. His physical features were just as unpleasant, extremely unattractive to anyone's sight. When this Vizier saw the King place the healer Duban near him and give him all these gifts, his jealous nature consumed him. The Vizier instantly plotted to do harm to this Sage.

So the Vizier came before the King, kissing the ground before him and saying, "Oh King of this age and of all time, you who have helped me grow into manhood, I have advice to offer you. I can't withhold this information from you, or else I'd be a coward. If you permit me, I'll tell it to you."

The King grew troubled as he listened to his minister's words. "What is this advice?" he asked.

"Oh glorious monarch," the Vizier said, "wise men have said, 'Whoever does not regard the end is not Fortune's friend.' Indeed, lately I've seen the King taking the wrong path, for he bestows lavish gifts on his enemy—on one whose purpose is to destroy your reign! He shows this man ultimate favor, honoring him with every honor, and making him an intimate friend. For this reason, I fear for the King's life."

The color drained from the King's face, and the Vizier could see how intensely troubled he was. "Whom do you suspect?" he breathed.

"Oh King!" exclaimed the Vizier. "If you've been asleep, you must wake up! I mean the healer, Sage Duban."

"Cursed minister!" cried the King. "Duban is a true friend. I've favored him above all men, because he cured me with something I held in my hand. He healed my leprosy, which baffled all doctors! There's no one else in the whole world like him—from the far east to the far west! How could you accuse such a man? Today, I even granted him a salary and a gift—every month, one thousand gold pieces. And even if I shared my kingdom with him, it wouldn't matter to me! I think that it's your envy and jealousy that accuse him, just like that which accused King Sinbad."

*And Shahrazad again realized that dawn rose, and stopped her story. Dunyazad said, "Oh my sister, your tale is so beautiful, so pleasant!"*

*Shahrazad replied, "But this is nothing compared with what I could tell you tomorrow night, if the King would spare my life."*

*The King thought to himself, "By Allah, I won't kill her until I hear the rest of her tale, for she's a wonderful storyteller." So they all rested until dawn, and then the King went to his audience-hall, and the Vizier and the troops came in. The audience-hall thronged with people, and the King was busy giving orders, judgments, and appointments the rest of the day. Finally, after the long day, King Shahryar returned to his palace. And as this fifth night approached, Dunyazad said to her sister, "Shahrazad, if you're not sleepy, will you finish the story for us?" And so, she continued her tale. . . .*

## The Tale of King Sinbad and His Falcon

It is said that there was once a King of Persia who was especially fond of hunting. The King had raised a falcon, of which he was so fond that he carried it all night on his fist. Whenever he went hunting, he took the bird with him. He constructed a tiny gold cup for it, and hung it around its neck so the falcon could drink whenever it wanted.

One day, as the King sat quietly in his palace, the high falconer of his household suddenly said to him, "Oh King, this day is perfect for hunting."

And so the King gave orders accordingly and set out with the falcon on his fist. The hunting group all went along happily, reaching a ravine where they laid a circle of nets to trap their game. Suddenly, a gazelle came into sight, and the King cried out, "I'll kill whoever lets that gazelle jump over their head and escape!"

The huntsmen narrowed the nets around the gazelle as she drew near the place where the King crouched. As she approached, she sat on her hindquarters, and crossed her forehand over her breast, as if she were about to kiss the earth before the King! The gazelle was so reverent that the King also inclined his own head towards her, bowing in acknowledgement of her unique character. But just as he did, she bounced high over his head, vanishing into the forest.

The King's troops winked and pointed at him. Troubled, he turned to his Vizier. "What are my men saying?" he asked.

The Vizier answered, "They remind you that you did proclaim that any man who let the gazelle escape by jumping over his head should be put to death."

"Now, by the life of my head!" exclaimed the King. "I'll chase that gazelle until I bring her back!" So he set off, galloping on the gazelle's trail and tracking her until he reached the rambling foothills of a mountain chain, where he glimpsed her racing into a cave. The King released the falcon, watching it swoop down towards the gazelle and drive its talons into her eyes, bewildering and blinding her. Then the King drew his club, killing her with one blow. He dismounted, cut the gazelle's throat, and flayed the body, hanging it on the pommel of his saddle.

Now it reached the hottest part of the day, the time for afternoon siesta. No water could be found anywhere around the parched, dry land where the King stood. The King and his horse both grew extremely thirsty, and so he walked around searching for something to drink, until he found a tree whose branches dripped with a water so golden and promising it looked like melted butter. So the King, who wore a leather glove to protect his skin from poison, took the cup from the falcon's neck and filled it with some of the water. But as he set the cup before the falcon, the bird struck it with its talons, spilling it. Again, the King filled the cup with some water, thinking that the falcon must surely be thirsty; but a second time, the falcon upset the cup. Then the King became angry; he filled the cup again and offered it to the horse, instead. But for a third time, the falcon overturned the cup!

"By Allah, you're a horrible, unlucky bird!" cried the King. "You're keeping everyone from drinking, including yourself." He angrily struck the falcon with his sword, cutting off its wing. But the falcon raised his head, motioning for the King to look at the tree more closely.

The King lifted his eyebrows accordingly, and caught sight of a brood of vipers, whose poison-drops he had mistaken for water. As soon as he saw this, he repented having chopped off the falcon's wing. Mounting his horse, he moved on with the dead gazelle until he reached his camp, his starting-place. He threw the gazelle's body to the cook. "Take it, and broil it," he told him, as he sat down in his chair. He still carried the wounded falcon on his fist. But suddenly, the bird gasped, dying, and the King cried out in sorrow and remorse for having slain the very falcon that saved his life.

"Now this is what happened to King Sinbad; and I am certain, Vizier," said the King, "that if I were to do as you wish to Sage Duban, I should repent even more than the man who killed his parrot."

"And what happened to him?" asked the Vizier.

And so the King began to tell. . . .

## The Tale of the Husband and the Parrot

Once, a certain merchant had a beautiful, graceful, extraordinarily pretty wife. He was so suspicious and jealous of her that he wouldn't even leave the house to go on business trips. But one day, a certain business situation compelled him to leave her. Before going away, he went to the bird market, and bought a parrot for one hundred gold pieces. He took the parrot to his house to act as his wife's chaperon, expecting that when he returned, the bird would tell him everything that happened while he was away. The parrot, thought the husband, was cunning and never forgot what he saw or heard.

Now, this beautiful wife had fallen in love with a young Turkish man, who visited her as soon as her husband left. She gave him food all day, and lay in bed with him all night. When her husband came home, he asked for the parrot, and questioned it concerning his wife's behavior while he'd been away in foreign countries.

"Your wife had a male friend, who spent every night here with her during your absence," the parrot told him.

In a violent rage, the husband raced toward his wife, beating her until she nearly died. The woman suspected that one of the slave-girls had tattled to her husband, so she called them all together, to interrogate them. All of them swore they had kept her secret—but that the parrot had not. "We heard him with our own ears," the girls told her.

And so, the next night, the wife commanded one of the girls to grind a hand-mill underneath the parrot's cage. She ordered another girl to sprinkle water through the cage's roof, and a third girl to run around the cage, flashing a bright steel mirror all during the night.

The next morning, when the husband returned home after spending the night with friends, he began to talk with the parrot, asking what had happened while he was away.

"Pardon me, oh master," said the bird, "I couldn't see or hear anything last night, because of all that terrible lightning and thunder crashing through the murky night."

"But it's the middle of July!" the master cried, surprised. "There aren't any thunderstorms now."

"By Allah," declared the bird, "I saw it with my own eyes, just as I've told you."

The husband became extremely angry, not suspecting his wife's ploy. Instead, he started to think that he'd wrongly accused his wife. So he pulled the parrot from his cage, thrusting it upon the ground so furiously that he killed it on the spot.

Several days later, one of the slave-girls told him the whole story, but he still wouldn't believe it until he saw the young Turk, his wife's lover, coming out of her bedroom. As the Turk walked out, the husband drew his sword, killing him with a blow on the back of his neck. His wife rushed out of her room, and he instantly murdered her in the same way. The two of them, laden with mortal sin, went straight to the Eternal Fires of Hell.

So the merchant knew that the parrot had told him the truth all along. Though he mourned the bird, all his grief could not bring the parrot back.

The Vizier, hearing these words of King Yunan, said, "Oh Monarch, high in dignity, you must realize that I'm not contriving this man's execution. No, I'm only saying all this to be of service to you, for I do not think that if you accept my advice, you'll be saved—but if you reject it, you'll be destroyed just like that young Prince who was betrayed by the treacherous Vizier."

"What happened to them?" inquired the King.

And so, the minister began. . . .

## The Tale of the Prince and the Ogress

Once there was a King whose son enjoyed hunting so much that the King ordered one of his Viziers to accompany his son wherever he went. One day, the Prince and the Vizier went hunting, and as they paced through the fields together, a gigantic wild beast came in sight.

"Let's kill that beast!" cried the Vizier.

The Prince raced after the animal, soon disappearing out of everyone's sight. The beast disappeared from the Prince's own sight too, vanishing into the woods. The Prince, now lost in the forest, couldn't find his way out. He didn't even know which way to turn. Suddenly, a beautiful maiden appeared out of nowhere, her face streaming with tears.

"Who are you?" asked the Prince.

"I'm the daughter of a King among the Kings of the Hind," she said. "I was travelling with a caravan in the desert, when drowsiness suddenly spread through my body. As I fell asleep, I inadvertently fell from my horse. Now I can't find any of my people, and I'm so confused!"

The Prince pitied this unhappy girl, and helped her onto his horse. They travelled until they passed a ruined temple, where the maiden said, "Oh master, I need to obey a call of nature." So the Prince set her down, but she took so long that he thought she was wasting time. He crept towards her direction, and saw her—but she was transformed! She was not a fair damsel, but Ghulah, the wicked Ogress, telling her brood, "Oh my children, today I've got a fine, fat youth for dinner!"

"Bring him to us, mother!" they cried. "We can't wait to fill our stomachs with him!"

The Prince heard this whole conversation, and was sure he would die. All the muscles in his body quivered with fear. He turned around and was about to run, when Ghulah came out, seeing him trembling and afraid. "Why are you scared?" she asked.

"I've discovered a terrible enemy, whom I greatly fear," he replied.

"Aren't you a King's son?" asked the Ogress.

"I am."

"Then why don't you give him some money?" suggested Ghulah. "That would satisfy him."

"This enemy doesn't want my money," said the Prince, "only my life. That's why I dread him so much."

"If you're that distressed," said Ghulah, "ask Allah for protection. Surely Allah would protect you from the evils of this enemy."

So the Prince raised his eyes toward the heavens, calling, "Oh God who helps those in need—Oh God who dispels distress! Let me triumph over my enemy, and let him leave me. Protect me with your might, for you are strong above all else!"

When Ghulah heard this earnest prayer, she turned away from him, and let the Prince leave. The Prince then returned home to his father, and told him how the Vizier had left him lost in the woods while they were on the hunt. So the King summoned the Vizier, and executed him on the spot.

"Similarly, King," spoke the Vizier, "if you continue to trust this doctor, you'll die the worst sort of death. This Sage Duban that you've so admired and become intimate with, he'll bring about your destruction! You've seen how he healed your disease simply by something you grasped in your hand. He'll destroy you with something held in the same manner."

"You've spoken the truth, my Vizier," answered King Yunan thoughtfully. "It may indeed be as you've said. Perhaps this sage has come as a spy, figuring out the best way to kill me. For assuredly, if he cured me by something held in my hand, he can kill me by something given to me to smell. Vizier, what should I do with him?"

"Summon him here this very instant," replied the Vizier. "When he comes, have him beheaded; in this way, you'll be rid of him before he can harm you any more. Deceive him before he can deceive you!"

"You've again spoken the truth, Vizier," responded the King. He sent for the Sage Duban, who came joyfully to him, for he didn't know what the King intended. Duban praised and thanked the King for his compassion and generosity.

"Do you know why I've summoned you?" replied the King, coldly.

"Only Allah knows," said the Sage.

"I summoned you so that I could take your life, and destroy you," the King told him.

"Oh King," said Sage Duban wonderingly, his breath gasping in astonishment. "Why would you kill me? What harm have I done to you?"

"Men tell me that you're a spy, sent here to murder me," explained the King. "But I'll kill you before you kill me." He called to his executioner and said, "Behead this traitor and deliver us from his evil practices."

"If you spare my life, Allah will spare yours," Sage Duban replied. "If you don't kill me, Allah won't kill you."

The Fisherman paused in his story, and glanced towards the bottled Genie. "Yes, Genie, he repeated these very words that I said to you. You wouldn't let me go, you were so bent on killing me. Likewise, King Yunan did the same. . . ."

King Yunan only replied to Duban, "I won't be safe unless I kill you. For just as you healed me by something in my hand, you could kill me by something you give me to smell or to drink."

"You're returning evil for good," answered the Sage. "This is your reward?"

The King replied, "Nothing can help you now. You must die, without delay."

Now, when Sage Duban was certain that the King would kill him right away, he wept and regretted all the good he had done to such a bad man. The executioner stepped forward, tied a blindfold over the Sage Duban's eyes, and drew his sword. Turning to the King, he said, "Do I have your permission?"

Sage Duban wept and cried, "Spare me, that Allah might spare your own life. Don't kill me, or Allah will kill you! Is this the reward I deserve from you? It's nothing but crocodile-boon."

"What's this tale of the crocodile-boon?" inquired the King.

"It's impossible for me to tell it in this state right now," explained the doctor Duban. "May Allah bless you and spare your life if you spare mine."

He wept, tears streaming down his face until one of the King's favorite men stood up and said, "Oh King! Kill me, and not this Sage, for we've never seen him harm you. We've never seen him do anything but heal you from a disease that baffled every other scientist and doctor here."

"You don't know why I'm really putting him to death," explained the King. "If I spare his life, I'm condemning myself to his means of death. For the one who healed me of such a terrifying illness by something I held in my hand can surely kill me by something he holds to my nose. He may be killing me for a certain price. I fear that he might even be a spy, whose only purpose was to come here and plot my destruction. So there's no way out; he must die. Only then can I be sure that my own life is safe."

Again, Sage Duban cried, "Spare me and Allah will spare you! Kill me, and Allah will kill you." But this was all in vain.

"Now, Genie," interjected the Fisherman. "When the doctor Duban knew for certain that the King would kill him, he anxiously began to reason to him. . . ."

"Oh King," said Sage Duban. "If there is no help for me, if I indeed must die, let me just go to my house, release myself from my obligations, and tell my friends and neighbors where to bury me and how to distribute my medical books. Among these books there is one, extremely rare, which I would like to give you to keep as a treasure in your vaults."

"What's in this book?" asked the King.

"Things beyond your wildest dreams," said the Sage. "Astonishing secrets and mysteries—the best of which is, that after you behead me, you can open this book to the third page and read three lines from it, and then my head will speak to you and answer any question you wish."

The King shivered as Duban spoke, and delighted at such a novelty, exclaimed, "Oh Sage, do you really think that your head will speak to me after I cut it off?"

"Yes, King!" cried Duban.

"This is indeed a strange matter," mused the King. And so he sent Sage Duban, closely guarded, to his house; and there Duban settled all of his obligations. The next day, he went to the King's audience-hall, where Emirs and Viziers, Chamberlains and Nabobs, Grandees and Lords of Estate were gathered together, their robes making the room as colorful as a flower garden.

Sage Duban came up and stood before the King, holding a worn old volume of medical practices, and a little tin full of something resembling kohl, a dark powder for the eyes. He sat down, and requested a tray; then he poured the strange black powder onto it, spreading it around. "Oh King," he said, "take this book, but don't open it until my head falls; then, set my head on this tray, press it down upon the powder, and the blood will stop flowing. That is your cue to open the book."

So the King took the book and gave the sign to the executioner. The swordsman rose, striking off the doctor's head, placing it on the middle of the tray, and pressing it down on the powder. The blood stopped flowing, and Sage Duban opened his eyes, saying, "Now, oh King, open the book!"

The King opened the book, finding the pages stuck together; so he put his fingers to his mouth, moistening them so as to turn over the pages. He flipped through six pages, but found nothing written on them. "Oh doctor, there's no writing here!" said King Yunan.

"Turn over a few more pages," replied Duban faintly. And so, the King moistened his fingers again and turned over a few more pages in the same way. But the book was poisoned; and quickly, the deadly venom penetrated the King's body. He convulsed, crying out, "The poison has done its work!"

Duban's head ceased to speak as the King, too, rolled over dead.

"Now I would have you know, Genie," spoke the Fisherman, "that if the King Yunan had spared the Sage Duban, Allah would have spared him; but he refused to do so, and so Allah slew him. If you had spared me, Genie," said the Fisherman, "Allah would have spared you, too."

*Now Shahrazad saw the dim lights of dawn creeping into the room once more, and so she stopped her story. But Dunyazad again exclaimed, "Oh my sister, your tale is so beautiful, so pleasant!"*

*And again, Shahrazad responded, "But that was nothing compared to what I could tell you tomorrow night, if the King spares my life."*

*The King thought to himself, as he had during the past nights, "By Allah, I won't kill her until I hear the rest of her story, for it's truly wonderful!" And so they all slept until morning, when the King went to his audience-hall crowded with Viziers and troops. Again, the King gave orders and appointments and judgements all day long. When his duties were finally done, King Shahryar went back to his palace. The sixth night fell, and Dunyazad told Shahrazad, "Please finish your story!"*

*"I will, if the King lets me," she replied.*

*"Go on with your tale," said the King. And so, she continued. . . .*

It has reached me, Oh worthy King, that after the Fisherman told the Genie, "If you had spared my life, I would have spared yours—but you were so intent on killing me, I'm going to throw your jar into the sea," then the Genie shouted, "By Allah, Fisherman, don't do it! Spare me, and pardon my past actions. Return my tyrannical deeds with generous ones— for it's said, 'If one returns good for evil, then the evildoer will stop his evil deeds.' Don't deal with me as Umamah did to Atikah."

"What's their story?" asked the Fisherman.

"I don't have time for story-telling in this prison," said the Genie. "But if you set me free, I'll tell you my tale."

"Do be quiet," snapped the Fisherman. "There's no help left for you. I'm going to throw you so far into the sea that you'll never escape. When I humbled myself before you, weeping, you still only wanted to kill me. I'd never harmed you, never done any evil act against you. I only did you good when I released you from that jar. But now I know your truly evil nature; and so when I cast you back into the sea, I'll warn whoever catches you of what happened to me, and tell him to cast you back into the water again. You'll be trapped in this ocean until the End of Time!"

"No, set me free!" cried the Genie. "This is a perfect time to display your generosity. I swear to you, I'll never hurt you again in any way. In fact, I'll even help put an end to your poverty!"

The Fisherman considered the Genie's words, and accepted his promise—with the conditions that the Genie would never harm him, and would also go into his service, making him wealthy. After making the Genie swear a solemn oath by Allah the Most High, the Fisherman opened the lead seal to the jar. The pillar of smoke again snaked out from it, spiraling into the air. When all the smoke had trickled out, it condensed, once more forming the hideous presence of the Genie—who immediately kicked the bottle and sent it flying into the sea.

The Fisherman piddled in his pants as he saw how the Genie treated the bottle, certain that his own death would come next. "This does not seem to bode well for me," he murmured. But then he strengthened himself, shouting to the Genie, "Allah has said, keep your promises, for the performance of these things shall matter when you are judged! You've made a vow to me. You've sworn an oath not to deceive me, and if you don't follow this oath, then Allah will deceive you. For truly, He is a jealous God, who may give respite to sinners, but He doesn't let them ever actually escape. I say to you just as the Sage Duban said to King Yunan, 'Spare me so that Allah will spare you!'"

The Genie burst into laughter and stalked away, calling to the Fisherman, "Follow me." So the Fisherman followed at a safe distance, in case he needed to escape along the way. The Genie led him past the suburbs of the city, and deep into the wilderness. As they hiked through the uncultivated lands, they came to a still, cool mountain lake. Its steep, rocky banks sloped sharply downward, and tufts of willowy grass poked out from the calm, crystal pool. The Genie waded into the middle of its waters, again calling to the Fisherman, "Follow me."

As the Fisherman and the Genie both stood in the middle of the lake, the Genie told the Fisherman to cast his net and catch some fish. As the Fisherman looked into the water, astonishment rushed over him, for he saw the pond spilling over with multi-colored fish—white, red, blue, and yellow. He cast his net, and as he hauled it in he saw that it had trapped four fish, one of each color. He rejoiced when he saw these beautiful creatures, and became even happier as the Genie told him, "Carry these fish to the King and set them in his presence. When he sees them, he'll give you enough riches to make you a wealthy man. Now, please excuse me, for since I've lain in the sea for eighteen hundred years, I don't known any other way of helping you right now. Oh, but remember to only fish here once a day." The Genie departed, calling to the Fisherman, "May Allah be with you." Then the Genie struck the earth with one foot, cleaving the earth into two parts, so that it swallowed him whole.

The Fisherman marvelled at all that had happened with the Genie, and then he gathered the fish and walked back towards the city. As soon as he reached his home, he filled an earthen bowl with water and threw the struggling, writhing fish into it. He placed the bowl on his head, carrying it to the King's palace, just as the Genie had instructed him to do. Once the King welcomed him, the Fisherman laid the fish before the King.

As soon as the King saw these creatures, amazement and wonder swept over him, for he'd never seen any fish like these before. "Give these fish to the slave-girl, and have her cook them for me," he ordered. Now, the slave-girl who fixed the fish had been sent to the King only three days earlier, and had not learned much about cooking, or about the King's favorite dishes. As the Vizier handed these fish to her, he instructed her to fry them. Then he gently mentioned to her, "This dish is apparently a rare one, a present to the King. Hopefully he'll approve of your delicate handiwork and savory cooking."

After the Vizier had carefully prompted her, he returned to the King, who commanded the Vizier to give four hundred dinars to the Fisherman. After the Fisherman received these he ran home, stumbling and falling in excitement, imagining that the whole thing must be a dream. But it was all true, and as he burst indoors he rushed to his wife, full of joy since he'd thought he wouldn't see her again. Then he bought his family anything they wanted.

Meanwhile, the King's cook, the slave-girl, cleaned and fried the fish, basting them with oil. As she flipped them over in their pan, to baste their other side, the kitchen walls split open! A slender, gracefully beautiful young woman appeared from the rift in the wall, her eyes lined with heavy, black kohl. Large hoops dangled from her ears, and bracelets circled her wrists. Her blue, silk dress draped itself around her whole body, and her kerchief was edged with blue tassels. Thick rings, studded with expensive gems, rested on each finger; and in her hand, she held a long rattan cane, which she thrust into the frying pan saying, "Oh fish! Oh fish! Are you keeping your promise?"

The slave-girl fainted as she saw this apparition. The beautiful woman repeated her words several times, and finally the fish raised their heads from the pan, answering, "Yes! Yes!" And so the woman left the kitchen as she had entered, disappearing into the walls and letting them close in upon her. When the young girl woke up, she discovered the four fish charred black as charcoal, each one yelling, "His staff broke in his first bout," and so she immediately fainted again.

The Vizier came to gather the plate of fish, and seeing the young cook lying on the ground, nudged her with his foot and said, "Bring the fish to the King!"

She woke once again from her daze, weeping and informing the Vizier of all that had happened. Astonished, the Vizier exclaimed, "This is indeed a very strange matter." So he sent for the Fisherman, telling him, "You must catch four fish exactly like those you brought before." So the

Fisherman returned to the lake the next day, cast his net, and brought up four fish exactly like the others. He gave them to the Vizier, who brought them to the cooking-girl, saying, "Fry these fish right here in my presence, so that I can see this apparition for myself."

So the girl rose and cleaned the fish, and set them in a frying pan over the fire. Only minutes later, the walls cleaved open and the woman appeared. Again, she shoved her cane into the pan, crying out, "Oh fish! Have you really kept your promise?"

"Yes! Yes!" replied the fish, lifting their heads from the pan.

*And Shahrazad realized that dawn had risen, and so she stopped her story until the seventh night; then she continued. . . .*

It has reached me, O worthy King, that when these fish spoke, and the woman upset the frying pan with her rod and disappeared into the wall, the Vizier cried out, "This matter can't be kept secret from the King."

So the Vizier went and told the King what had happened, and the King replied, "I must see this with my own eyes." So he sent for the Fisherman, and commanded him to bring four more fish exactly like the first. He also sent three men with the Fisherman, as witnesses. The Fisherman immediately brought the fish, and the King repaid him with four hundred gold pieces. Then the King turned to the Vizier and ordered, "Fry these fish right here before me!"

"To hear is to obey," the minister replied, cleaning the fish and throwing them into the frying pan. Instantly, the walls split in half, and a black slave burst forth, carrying a green branch in each hand.

"Oh fish," he intoned, his terrifying voice rising through the palace, "Have you indeed kept your ancient pledge?"

"Yes! Yes!" cried the fish, lifting their heads from the frying pan. Then the man turned over the pan, and disappeared once more into the walls.

As he vanished, the King inspected the fish, finding them charred black as charcoal. Bewildered, he told the Vizier, "Truly, this matter can't be kept a secret any longer. Surely there's something marvelous connected to these fish." He turned to the Fisherman, demanding, "Where did these fish come from?"

"From a nearby mountain lake," he replied.

"How many day's journey from here?"

"Oh King, our Lord, only about half-an-hour's walk," answered the Fisherman.

Confused about the fish, and desperately hoping to unravel this mystery, the King ordered his troops to journey to the lake immediately. The Fisherman guided them, cursing the Genie under his breath. He led the troops over the mountain and through the desert valley, none of which the King's men had ever seen in their lives. The King and his troops rode in amazement, marvelling at the wildly beautiful, uncultivated nature surrounding them. Finally they reached the lake and its multi-colored fish of blue, red, yellow, and white. The King stood rooted to one spot near the edge of the water, asking everyone nearby, "Has anybody here ever seen this lake before?"

"Never, King," each one replied. Even the oldest men there had never heard of such a lake.

"Then, by Allah," declared the King, "I'm not going to return to my palace or sit on my throne until I learn the truth about the fish and this lake." So he ordered all his troops to dismount, and to set up camp near the mountains. After this, he summoned the Vizier, whom he regarded as an experienced, wise, and perceptive minister. "I must tell you about something," the King hurriedly informed him. "My heart is telling me to go forth alone tonight, to seek and uncover the mystery of this lake and its fish. You must help me by sitting at my tent-door and telling all the Emirs and Nabobs and Chamberlains that 'the King is ill, and you must not come in.' Be careful not to let anyone else know my plan."

The Vizier couldn't oppose the King, and so the King proceeded to change his clothes, sling his sword over his shoulder, and hike up a twisting mountain path, out of sight. The King hiked until dawn, and then well into the next day, despite the blazing heat. After only a short rest, he continued hiking through the second night until dawn, when he glimpsed a black point far in the distance. "Maybe there's somebody here who can tell me about the lake and the fish," the King said happily.

As he came closer to the dark object, he realized it was a stone palace, plated with iron. One side of the gate lay open, though the other was shut. The King's spirits rose as he stood before the gate, lightly rapping to be let inside. He knocked twice, then three times, and then a fourth time quite loudly, but nobody seemed to be home. "It must be empty," he thought to himself, and so he mustered up the courage to walk through the gates and into the main hall. "Hello, people of the palace," he called, his voice echoing through the room. "I'm a stranger, a traveller, in need of food. Is anybody here?" He repeated his words, but there was still no response. So he decided to explore the palace, and stalked through the hallways to its central rooms. Even there, he found no one. Still, even though nobody was present, the rooms were lavishly furnished with tapestries, and decorated with silken materials patterned with gold stars. In the middle of these rooms a spacious courtyard was laid out, with four open halls on each side. Canopies shaded the courtyard, and in the center stood a flowing fountain with four reddish-gold figures of lions. The water rushing from the fountain poured as clear as pearls, glittering like translucent gems. Birds flew freely around the palace, held inside by a net of golden wire. Really, thought the King, there was everything imaginable in this palace but human beings.

The King grew amazed at all this, but also became disappointed that there was nobody to explain the mystery of the lake and the fish — or to reveal the mystery of the palace itself. He sat between the palace doors, deep in thought, when he suddenly heard a mournful voice murmuring through the walls. The King sprang to his feet, following the sound to one chamber. Lifting the curtain over its door, he found a handsome young man there, sitting on a couch about three feet off the ground. His rosy cheeks shone brightly, and his forehead was white as a flower; on one cheek rested a tiny grey mole.

Rejoicing, the King greeted him, but the young man remained seated on his silken caftan, lined with Egyptian gold. The King could see that beneath his gem-studded crown, the young man's face was lined with sorrow. The man returned the King's salute, and said, "Oh my lord, your dignity demands that I rise to greet you, and I beg your pardon for not doing this."

"Certainly you have my pardon," replied the King. "Think of me as a guest who's here on a special mission. Please, tell me about this mysterious mountain lake and the fish there, and also about this lonely palace and why you're so unhappy."

When the young man heard the King's words, he wept so much his whole body became drenched with tears. This astounded the King, and he asked, "Why do you weep like this, young man?"

"How could I not weep, when I'm in this situation!" cried the man. Then he lifted the skirts of his garment, showing the King that his lower body, from his navel to his feet, had turned into stone, while the rest of his body remained human flesh. This moved the King to compassion, and he grieved for the lonely boy. "You heap sorrow upon my sorrow," the King explained. "I was going to ask you only about the mystery of the fish, but now I'm as interested in your story as in theirs." The King focused on the young man. "There is no majesty, no might, except Allah, the glorious and the great! Now, tell me your whole story."

"Lend me your ears, your sight, and your intuition," said the boy.

"All are at your service," replied the King.

"My situation is almost beyond imagination," began the young man. "It's as amazing as the fish themselves. I wish it could be engraved somewhere, warning all who see it."

"Why is that?" inquired the King.

And so the young man began to tell. . . .

## The Tale of the Enchanted Prince

My lord, you should know that my father was King Mahmud, ruler of this city and Lord of the Black Islands, as well as the owner of these four mountains. He ruled for seventy years before his death, and then I was appointed Sultan in his place. I married my cousin, the daughter of my paternal uncle; and her love for me was so abounding that she wouldn't eat or drink while I was away. We lived together for five years, until one day when she went to the Hamman-bath. I'd told the cook to prepare dinner for us, and then I came to lie on this bed and sleep, asking two servants to fan me as I waited for my wife to return. But I was restless and troubled because of her absence, and couldn't sleep. Even though my eyes were closed, my thoughts raced wildly in my head and kept me awake.

Suddenly, I heard the slave-girl fanning my head say to the other one, "Our poor master really must be miserable! His youth is wasted, and I pity that our mistress has betrayed him, that cursed whore!"

"Yes, indeed," the other replied. "May Allah curse all faithless, adulterous women. Our handsome, worthy master deserves someone better than this harlot who sleeps with other men every single night."

"Why is our master so foolish?" the first girl wondered. "I wish he would question her."

"Our master isn't foolish, don't say such a thing!" reprimanded the other girl. "He doesn't know what she's doing, so he doesn't have a choice whether to question her or not. What's more, she drugs his drink every night before he sleeps, so that he won't know where she goes or what she does. Only *we* know that after giving him that drugged wine, she slips into her richest clothes, puts on perfume, and leaves until daybreak. When she comes back, she burns a poultice under his nose, so that he'll finally wake up from that deathlike sleep."

Now, when I heard the slave-girls' words, I fumed with rage, anxiously waiting for night to fall. I thought it would never come. When my wife came home from the baths, we had dinner and drank some wine, as was our habit. She called for the particular wine I used to drink before sleeping, and poured me a cup. But instead of drinking it, that night I poured the contents down my shirt. I feigned sleep, waiting. Eventually she cried, "Sleep out the night, and never wake up! By Allah, I despise you and I loathe your whole body. My soul is disgusted every time I sleep with you, and I can't wait for the day when Allah ends your life!" Then she rose, putting on her prettiest dress, and perfume, and slinging my sword over her shoulder. Opening the palace gates, she went on her evil way.

I rose, following her out of the palace, and walking behind her as she threaded through the streets until she came to the city gate. There, she spoke some words I couldn't understand, and the padlocks to the gates dropped by themselves, as if they were broken. The gates actually swung open before her! I pursued her without her noticing, finally stopping when she reached the garbage-heaps. There was a reed fence built there around a mud-brick, round-roofed hut. As she entered the hut's door, I climbed on its roof to spy inside. And there I saw my wife, gone inside to an ugly black slave! He was also a leper and a paralytic, lying upon some matted, rotting sugar-cane and wrapped in tattered, ragged blankets. My wife kissed the ground before him, and he raised his head to see her saying, "Woe to you! Why have you been gone all this time? Some friends were here with me for a while, drinking wine with their young ladies, but I couldn't drink, because you were gone."

"Oh, my lord," she murmured. "My heart's love, don't you know that I'm married to my cousin, whose very looks I hate? I even despise my own self when I'm near him. If I wasn't afraid for your sake, I wouldn't let a single night pass before I turned this whole city into rubble—so that the ravens would croak, the owls hoot, and the jackals and wolves run around wildly! Indeed, I'd remove every stone of the city and throw it behind Mt. Caucasus!"

"You're lying, damn you!" cried the slave. "Now I'll swear an oath, by the honor of black men—and don't think our manliness is like the poor manliness of white men—that from this day forth, if you stay away from me for this length of time again, I'll reject you completely. I won't glue my body to yours again! Do you think you can play fast and loose with us, that we satisfy your dirty lusts, you stinking bitch? Vilest of the vile whites!"

As I heard his words, and saw with my own eyes what was happening between them, everything around me darkened, and my soul no longer knew where it was. My wife stood humbly before the slave, weeping and begging, "Oh my beloved, fruit of my heart, there is nobody who makes me happy like you. If you reject me, who will love me?" She didn't stop crying until he accepted her once more. When they reconciled, she became joyful again, slipping off her clothes and asking, "Oh my master, what is there for your handmaiden to eat?"

"Uncover that pot," he grumbled, "and at the bottom, you'll find some broiled bones of the rats we dined on. Pick at them, and then go to the slop-pot, where you'll find some leftover beer that you can drink."

So she ate and drank this, and washed her hands. Then she lay down beside the slave, stripping naked and creeping inside his foul, dirty blankets and rags. When I saw my wife, my cousin, the daughter of my uncle do this deed, I lost all my senses. Climbing down from the roof, I entered the hut and grabbed the sword she'd taken with her. I drew it, determined to kill both of them. I struck the slave's neck first, and thinking he'd died. . . .

*And Shahrazad saw that dawn crept into the room, and stopped her tale; on the eighth night, she continued. . . .*

It has reached me, Oh worthy King, that the young enchanted Prince said to the King: When I struck the slave, intending to chop off his head, I thought I'd killed him—for he'd uttered a loud, hissing groan. But really, I'd only cut his flesh and two arteries! His moans woke up my wife, so I sheathed the sword and hurried back inside the city. Entering the palace, I slept in my bed until morning. Later, my wife woke me up, and I saw that she'd cut off all her hair, and put on mourning garments.

"Oh son of my uncle," she said to me. "Don't blame me for this, for I've just heard that my mother is dead, my father's been killed in a holy war, one of my brothers has lost his life due to snake-sting, and another by falling off a cliff. I can do nothing but mourn for them."

When I heard her words, I didn't reproach her, but only said, "Do as you must. I won't stop you."

She continued grieving, weeping, and wailing for one whole year, and when this was done, she said to me, "I'd like to build a tomb with a cupola in your palace, which I'll set apart for mourning, and name the House of Lamentations."

"Do as you must," I told her again.

So she built this tomb where she could mourn, with a dome in its center, over the place where the body should rest. She carried the slave here, housing him. But due to his wound, he was exceedingly weak, and unable to make love to her. He could only drink wine, and since the day of his injury he hadn't spoken a single word. But he continued to live, because his appointed hour of death had not yet come. My wife tended to him every day, bringing him wines and strong soups, and weeping over him incessantly. She kept doing this for well over one more year. I patiently accepted it, not paying any attention to her.

However, one I day I approached her without her noticing, and I found her crying and slapping her face, hysterically shrieking, "Why are you absent from me, my heart's delight? Speak to me, my life! Talk to me, my love!"

When she paused in her tears and her weeping, I told her, "My cousin, stop this mourning. Your grief isn't going to change anything."

"Don't stop me," she demanded. "I have to do this, and if you stop me, I'll kill myself!"

So I kept my peace and let her go her own way, and she cried and indulged her affliction for a third year. At the end of this third year, I grew incredibly tired of all this mourning. One day—after already being annoyed and frustrated at something else—I passed near the tomb, hearing my wife say, "Oh my lord, I never hear you speak a single word to me! Why don't you answer me, my master?"

Rage tumbled through my body as I heard her, and I shrieked, "How long must this sorrow of yours last?"

When she heard my words, she sprang to her feet, screaming, "You wretched, foul cur! This is all your fault! You've wounded my heart's darling one, and wasted his youth. You've made him lie here for three years! He's lying here more dead than alive because of you! It's because of you that I've grieved all this time!"

"Foul harlot! Filthiest whore, hired to sleep with slaves!" I cried, my body rising with wrathful anger. "Yes, indeed, I'm the one who did this good deed to your heart's darling!" And without speaking another word, I snatched my sword, drawing it to cut her down.

But she laughed as I drew the blade, scornfully shouting, "Heel, you hound! Oh, yes, I grieve for the past that can't ever come back to life, and for the fact that nobody can raise the dead. But now Allah has placed into my hands the person who did this vile thing—this action that burned my heart with an undying fire, with a flame that will never be quenched!" She stood up, pronouncing some unintelligible words. Then she said, "By virtue of my magic you'll become half stone, half man."

And so I became what you see now: unable to rise or sit, neither dead nor alive. Moreover, she enchanted the whole city, every street and field, using her sorcery to transform the four islands into four mountains around the lake about which you've asked me. The citizens, who were of four different faiths—Muslim, Christian, Jewish, and Magian—she transformed into fish: Muslims as white fish; Christians as blue; Jews as yellow; and Magians as red. And every day she tortures me with one hundred lashes, each one cutting me so deeply it draws floods of blood, and scars my skin. Then she covers my upper body with a haircloth, and throws these robes over it.

As the Prince finished his story, shedding some tears, the King was moved by his situation. He turned toward the unfortunate Prince, saying, "You've removed one of my concerns, only to add another. Tell me, where is she? And where's the mausoleum with this wounded slave?"

"The slave's under that dome there," the Prince told him. "And my wife, she's sitting in that room across from the door. Every day at sunrise she comes in here. First she strips me naked, and then she beats me one hundred times with a leather whip. I shriek, I cry, but my body won't let me run away from her. After she finishes tormenting me she visits the slave, bringing him wine and boiled meat. Early tomorrow morning she'll be here."

"By Allah, young Prince," the King proclaimed, "I'll undoubtedly come then, and do you a good deed that the world won't ever forget. It'll be so daring, people will write about it long after I'm dead and gone." Then the King sat beside the young Prince, talking with him until night fell.

The King slept until the first lights of dawn began to gleam in the horizon. He hurriedly awakened, threw on his shirt and unsheathed his sword, hastening to the palace where the slave lay. He slipped quickly past the lighted candles and lamps, and followed scents of incense and ointments that led him to the slave. As the woman's lover lay in the tomb, the King struck him dead with one blow. Then he slung him over his shoulder, carrying him to a well in the palace and tossing him to the bottom. The King then moved back towards the tomb, putting on the slave's clothes and lying down in the mausoleum, with his sword drawn and ready at his side.

After an hour or so, the accursed, conniving wife arrived. First, she went to her husband, whipping him cruelly as he cried out, "Enough! Stop, and take pity on me, my cousin!"

"Did you ever take pity on me? Did you spare the life of my true love?" the woman replied. She drew the haircloth over his raw, bleeding skin and tossed the robe over his shoulders. Then she approached the slave with a goblet of wine and a bowl of meat-broth in her hands. She entered the dome weeping and wailing, "Oh my lord, my master! Speak just one word to me, talk just awhile with me!"

The King lowered his voice, twisted his tongue, and spoke in the slave's voice, saying, "There is no majesty, no might except Allah, the glorious, the great!"

As she heard these words, the wife shouted in joy and fainted, dropping to the floor. As her senses returned, she asked, "Oh my lord, is it true that you've regained the power of speech?"

"Cursed one," the King whispered in a small, faint voice. "Do you deserve me talking to you?"

"Why?" cried the wife worriedly.

"All day long you torment your husband," the King replied. "He keeps calling on heaven to help him so much that I can't sleep from evening to morning. He prays and curses both of us so much, and I'm truly disturbed by it! If this had been different, I would've become healthy long ago; I would've answered you and spoken with you long before."

"With your permission," replied the wife, "I'll release him from the spell I cast upon him."

"Release him, and let's have some rest," declared the King.

"To hear is to obey," the woman said, slipping out into the palace. She took a metal bowl, filling it with water and saying some words over it so that it started to bubble and boil, as if it were a cauldron on a fire. She sprinkled her husband with its waters, saying, "Because of the dreadful words I spoke, you became half-stone under my spells. Come forth from that form into your own original being."

Suddenly, the young Prince violently trembled, slowly rising to his feet. Still shaking, and rejoicing at his transformation, he shouted, "I testify that there is no God but *the* God, and Muhammad is His true apostle, Allah bless Him!"

The wife turned toward him, demanding, "Get out and don't come back. If you do return, I'll kill you."

So the Prince walked out from the palace, and the wife returned to the tomb, saying, "Oh lord, come to me so that I can look at you and your beauty!"

"Why?" answered the King faintly. "You've only gotten rid of the branch of my problems, but not the root."

"Oh my darling," she cried, "tell me the root."

"Cursed soul!" the King replied. "The people of this city, and the people of the four islands that you've turned into fish, all torment me. They lift their heads from the lake every night, crying out to heaven to come down in anger upon us. I can hear their cries of distress, and this is the reason why my body won't heal. Set them free at once. Then come to me, take my hand, and raise me up, for I have a little strength back within me."

When she heard the King's words, still supposing that he was the slave, she joyfully exclaimed, "Oh my master, every word you say is my command!" So she sprang to her feet, giddy with happiness, and ran down to the magical mountain lake. She cupped a bit of water in her hand. . . .

*And Shahrazad saw the gleaming lights of dawn pouring into the room, so she stopped her story. On the ninth night, she continued. . . .*

It has reached me, Oh worthy King, that when this young woman, the sorceress, cupped some water in her hand, she spoke more unintelligible words over it. Soon, the fish lifted their heads, stood up, and their bodies reshaped into human forms. The spell on all the people of the city was removed. The lake became a crowded city; the bazaars thronged with buyers and sellers; the four mountains again became islands; and each citizen became busy once more, as they had before the spell.

The young woman returned to the palace, approaching the King, whom she still thought was the slave. "Oh my love!" she murmured to him. "Stretch forth your honored hand, so I can help you to rise."

"Come nearer to me," the King urged.

She came close enough to embrace him, when he suddenly grasped the sword lying by his side, and stabbed her between the breasts, so that the sword's tip shone gleaming through her back. He struck her a second time, cutting her in two, and casting her halves on the ground.

He went outside the palace, finding the young Prince happily waiting for him. The Prince kissed the King's hand as the King told him what happened, and the Prince offered abundant thanks.

"Would you like to dwell here in this city, or come with me to my capital?" asked the King.

"How far is it between your capital and this city?" the Prince asked.

"Two-and-a-half days," answered the King.

Surprised, the Prince cried, "Oh, King, no! It must be at least a year's march. You must have only got here in two-and-a-half days because the city was under an enchanted spell. But, my King, I'll never part from you, not even for the twinkling of an eye!"

The King rejoiced as he heard these words, and cried, "Thanks be to Allah, who has brought us together. From this moment on, you're my son, my only son, for until now I've never been blessed with children." The two men embraced, full of gladness.

As they reached the palace, the Prince told his Lords and Grandees that he would go on a pilgrimage, and directed them to make everything ready for this. The preparations lasted ten days, and after this, he set out with the King.

The King's heart yearned to see the city from which he'd been separated for one whole year. An escort of servants carried all sorts of precious, rare gifts as they journeyed twelve months to reach the capital. As they reached the city, the Vizier and the whole army came to meet them. They rejoiced to see the King back safely, for they had all given up any hope of seeing him again. The troops kissed the ground before him, and the ministers led him to his throne. When everyone learned of what had happened to the young Prince, they congratulated the two men on their narrow escape.

After restoring order throughout his lands, the King gave gifts to numerous people, and then said to the Vizier, "Bring us the Fisherman who brought us those fish!"

So the Vizier sent for the man who had been the first cause of the citizens' release from enchantment. As the Fisherman came into the King's presence, he was bestowed a robe of honor, and asked if he had any children. The Fisherman replied that he had two daughters and a son. So the King sent for them, and took one of the daughters as his wife, and had the other daughter marry the young Prince. He made the Fisherman's son the country's head treasurer, and then he appointed his Vizier as Sultan of the City of the Black Islands, the Prince's previous home. He dispatched the Vizier with an escort of fifty armed slaves carrying robes of honor for all the nobles of that city.

The Vizier kissed the King's hands and went forth on his journey; and the King and the Prince dwelled at home, in solace and delight, content with their lives. The Fisherman became the richest man of his time, and his daughters lived as the kings' wives, until death came to them.

*"And yet, Oh King!" continued Shahrazad, immediately after finishing this tale, "This is not more wondrous than the story of the Porter, and the Three Ladies of Baghdad. . . ."*

## ■ Usamah ibn Munqidh (1095–1188) *Syria* (memoir)

TRANSLATED BY PHILLIP K. HITTI

Usamah ibn Munqidh's *The Book of Reflections* is a fascinating inversion of the Westerner's gaze at the Middle East. This book of memoirs was written (or dictated) when he was more than ninety years old and "too feeble to carry a pen," though his hand "had been strong enough to break a lance in a lion's breast." It describes a life begun at the start of the Crusades and has many passages that describe the Franks, Frankish medicine, and aspects of Frankish behavior that strike him as strange and outlandish. Usamah was born in 1095 to the family of a Syrian prince, in Shayzar, northern Syria. His family were lords of the Castle of Shayzar, a place of key strategic importance, located in the valley of the Orontes River. Invading armies from the north and south had to contend with it and with another key castle (Apamea), and so his life proved to be one of ongoing warfare with the Franks, the Ismailites, and other enemies. He was raised a gentleman and a warrior, with a literary and religious education, and the life he records in these memoirs is filled with dangerous encounters with lions, hyenas, and leopards, with stories of extraordinary bravery and remarkable cowardice, anecdotes of marvelous swordthrusts, trusty servants, captivity, redemption, holy men, and witches. His father was a deeply religious man who abdicated the sultanate in favor of his brother and led a life dedicated to hunting animals and to copying the Quran. Usamah was doted upon by his uncle, the Sultan, until the Sultan had his own sons, and jealousies developed that caused Usamah to leave the family castle. Usamah's son Murhaf was a friend and fellow-warrior to Saladin, the Kurdish warrior who founded a dynasty in Egypt, conquered much of the Middle East, and defeated the invading Crusaders. When Usamah was in his eighties, Saladin became his patron and established him first as governor of Beirut and then in Damascus, where he was a lecturer and the center of a literary salon.

He lived a life of close contact with the Frankish invaders, on the battlefield and in the town, and his stories of their peculiar medicine, strange attitudes, and system of justice are a valuable window onto a period otherwise scantily recorded. Throughout, they are replete with human interest and zest of narrative. The book is really a collection of anecdotes that are linked primarily by association, contrast, or whim. It is an old man's remembrances, and he is impatient with his longevity that "has left me no energy," and bemoans (in a poem) that though "I have always been the firebrand of battle," now "I have become like an idle maid who lies / On stuffed cushions behind screens and curtains. / I have almost become rotten from lying still so long, just as / The sword of Indian steel becomes rusty when kept long in its sheath." A lusty, grumbling, rambling storyteller, famed as a chivalric warrior, literary raconteur, and avid hunter, his personality is writ large in this book. As Philip K. Hitti notes, "More delectable stories can be had nowhere else in Arabic literature."

**FURTHER READING:** Hitti, Philip K., tr. *An Arab-Syrian Gentleman and Warrior in the Period of the Crusades: Memoirs of Usamah ibn-Munqidh (Kitab al-I'ti-bar)*, 1929.

## from *The Book of Reflections*

### A KURD CARRIES HIS BROTHER'S HEAD AS A TROPHY

One of the amazing things that happened in connection with the Franks in the course of that combat was the following: In the army of Hamāh were two Kurdish brothers, one named Badr and the other 'Annāz. The latter, 'Annāz, was feeble of sight. When the Franks were overpowered and massacred, their heads were cut off and tied to the belts of the horses. 'Annāz cut off one head and tied it to the belt of his horse. Seeing him, the army of Hamāh said to him, "O 'Annāz, what is this head with thee?" He replied, "Worthy of admiration is Allah because of what happened between me and him which resulted in my killing him!" They said to him. "Man, this is the head of thy brother, Badr!" 'Annāz looked at the head and investigated it, and behold! it was the head of his brother. He was so ashamed of himself before the men that he left Hamāh and we do not know where he went. In fact, we never heard a word about him since. It was, however, the Franks who killed his brother, Badr, in that battle.

## PREFERS TO BE A FRANKISH SHOEMAKER'S WIFE TO LIFE IN A MOSLEM CASTLE

A number of maids taken captive from the Franks were brought into the home of my father, may Allah's mercy rest upon his soul! The Franks (may Allah's curse be upon them!) are an accursed race, the members of which do not assimilate except with their own kin. My father saw among them a pretty maid who was in the prime of youth, and said to his housekeeper, "Introduce this woman into the bath, repair her clothing and prepare her for a journey." This she did. He then delivered the maid to a servant of his and sent her to al-Amīr Shihāb-al-Dīn Mālik ibn-Sālim, the lord of the Castle of Ja'bar, who was a friend of his. He also wrote him a letter, saying, "We have won some booty from the Franks, from which I am sending thee a share." The maid suited Shihāb-al-Dīn, and he was pleased with her. He took her to himself and she bore him a boy, whom he called Badrān.[1] [So] Badrān's father named him his heir apparent, and he became of age. On his father's death. Badrān became the governor of the town and its people, his mother being the real power. She entered into conspiracy with a band of men and let herself down from the castle by a rope. The band took her to Saruj,[2] which belonged at that time to the Franks. There she married a Frankish shoemaker, while her son was the lord of the Castle of Ja'bar.

## THEIR CURIOUS MEDICATION

A case illustrating [the Franks'] curious medicine is the following:

The lord of al-Munay{t}irah[1] wrote to my uncle asking him to dispatch a physician to treat certain sick persons among his people. My uncle sent him a Christian physician named Thābit. Thābit was absent but ten days when he returned. So we said to him, "How quickly hast thou healed thy patients!" He said:

> *They brought before me a knight in whose leg an abscess had grown; and a woman afflicted with imbecility.[2] To the knight I applied a small poultice until the abscess opened and became well; and the woman I put on diet and made her humor wet. Then a Frankish physician came to them and said, "This man knows nothing about treating them." He then said to the knight, "Which wouldst thou prefer, living with one leg or dying with two?" The latter replied, "Living with one leg." The physician said, "Bring me a strong knight and a sharp ax." A knight came with the ax. And I was standing by. Then the physician laid the leg of the*

---

1. Mentioned later by Kamāl-al-Dīn in *Recueil: historiens orientaux*, vol. III, p. 728.

2. In Mesopotamia, southwest of Edessa. Cf. ibn-al-Athīr in *Recueil: historiens orientaux*, vol. I, p. 207.

1. In Lebanon near Afqah, the source of Nahr-Ibrāhīm, i.e., ancient Adonis.

2. Ar. *nashāf;* "dryness," is not used as a name of a disease. I take the word therefore to be Persian *nishāf* = "imbecility."

*patient on a block of wood and bade the knight strike his leg with the ax and chop it off at one blow. Accordingly he struck it—while I was looking on—one blow, but the leg was not severed. He dealt another blow, upon which the marrow of the leg flowed out and the patient died on the spot. He then examined the woman and said, "This is a woman in whose head there is a devil which has possessed her. Shave off her hair." Accordingly they shaved it off and the woman began once more to eat their ordinary diet—garlic and mustard. Her imbecility took a turn for the worse. The physician then said, "The devil has penetrated through her head." He therefore took a razor, made a deep cruciform incision on it, peeled off the skin at the middle of the incision until the bone of the skull was exposed and rubbed it with salt. The woman also expired instantly. Thereupon I asked them whether my services were needed any longer, and when they replied in the negative I returned home, having learned of their medicine what I knew not before.*

I have, however, witnessed a case of their medicine which was quite different from that.

The king of the Franks[3] had for treasurer a knight named Bernard [*barnād*], who (may Allah's curse be upon him!) was one of the most accursed and wicked among the Franks. A horse kicked him in the leg, which was subsequently infected and which opened in fourteen different places. Every time one of these cuts would close in one place, another would open in another place. All this happened while I was praying for his perdition. Then came to him a Frankish physician and removed from the leg all the ointments which were on it and began to wash it with very strong vinegar. By this treatment all the cuts were healed and the man became well again. He was up again like a devil.

## NEWLY ARRIVED FRANKS ARE ESPECIALLY ROUGH: ONE INSISTS THAT USAMAH SHOULD PRAY EASTWARD

Everyone who is a fresh emigrant from the Frankish lands is ruder in character than those who have become acclimatized and have held long association with the Moslems. Here is an illustration of their rude character.

Whenever I visited Jerusalem I always entered the Aq{s}a Mosque, beside which stood a small mosque which the Franks had converted into a church. When I used to enter the Aq{s}a Mosque, which was occupied by the Templars [*al-dāwiyyah*], who were my friends, the Templars would evacuate the little adjoining mosque so that I might pray in it. One day[1] I entered this mosque, repeated the first formula, "Allah is great,' and stood up in the act of praying, upon which one of the Franks rushed on me, got hold of me and turned my face eastward saying, "This is the way thou shouldst pray!" A group of Templars hastened to him, seized him and re-

3. Fulk of Anjou, king of Jerusalem.

1. About 1140.

pelled him from me. I resumed my prayer. The same man, while the others were otherwise busy, rushed once more on me and turned my face eastward, saying, "This is the way thou shouldst pray!" The Templars again came in to him and expelled him. They apologized to me, saying, "This is a stranger who has only recently arrived from the land of the Franks and he has never before seen anyone praying except eastward." Thereupon I said to myself, "I have had enough prayer." So I went out and have ever been surprised at the conduct of this devil of a man, at the change in the color of his face, his trembling and his sentiment at the sight of one praying towards the *qiblah.*[2]

## FRANKS LACK JEALOUSY IN SEX AFFAIRS

The Franks are void of all zeal and jealousy. One of them may be walking along with his wife. He meets another man who takes the wife by the hand and steps aside to converse with her while the husband is standing on one side waiting for his wife to conclude the conversation. If she lingers too long for him, he leaves her alone with the conversant and goes away.

Here is an illustration which I myself witnessed:

When I used to visit Nāblus,[1] I always took lodging with a man named Mu'izz, whose home was a lodging house for the Moslems. The house had windows which opened to the road, and there stood opposite to it on the other side of the road a house belonging to a Frank who sold wine for the merchants. He would take some wine in a bottle and go around announcing it by shouting, "So and so, the merchant, has just opened a cask full of this wine. He who wants to buy some of it will find it in such and such a place." The Frank's pay for the announcement made would be the wine in that bottle. One day this Frank went home and found a man with his wife in the same bed. He asked him, "What could have made thee enter into my wife's room?" The man replied, "I was tired, so I went in to rest." "But how," asked he, "didst thou get into my bed?" The other replied, "I found a bed that was spread, so I slept in it." "But," said he, "my wife was sleeping together with thee!" The other replied, "Well, the bed is hers. How could I therefore have prevented her from using her own bed?"

"By the truth of my religion," said the husband, "if thou shouldst do it again, thou and I would have a quarrel." Such was for the Frank the entire expression of his disapproval and the limit of his jealousy.

Another illustration:

We had with us a bath-keeper named Sālim, originally an inhabitant of al-Ma'arrah,[2] who had charge of the bath of my father (may Allah's mercy rest upon his soul!). This man related the following story:

---

2. The direction of the Ka'bah in the holy city, Mecca.

1. Neapolis, ancient Shechem.

2. Ma'arrah-al-Nu'mān, between Hamāh and Aleppo.

*I once opened a bath in al-Ma'arrah in order to earn my living. To this bath there came a Frankish knight. The Franks disapprove of girding a cover around one's waist while in the bath. So this Frank stretched out his arm and pulled off my cover from my waist and threw it away. He looked and saw that I had recently shaved off my pubes. So he shouted, "Sālim!" As I drew near him he stretched his hand over my pubes and said, "Sālim, good! By the truth of my religion, do the same for me." Saying this, he lay on his back and I found that in that place the hair was like his beard. So I shaved it off. Then he passed his hand over the place and, finding it smooth, he said, "Sālim, by the truth of my religion, do the same to madame [al-dāma]" (al-dāma in their language means the lady), referring to his wife. He then said to a servant of his, "Tell madame to come here." Accordingly the servant went and brought her and made her enter the bath. She also lay on her back. The knight repeated, "Do what thou hast done to me." So I shaved all that hair while her husband was sitting looking at me. At last he thanked me and handed me the pay for my service.*

Consider now this great contradiction! They have neither jealousy nor zeal but they have great courage, although courage is nothing but the product of zeal and of ambition to be above ill repute.

## ORDEAL BY WATER

I once went in the company of al-Amīr Muīn-al-Dīn (may Allah's mercy rest upon his soul!) to Jerusalem. We stopped at Nāblus. There a blind man, a Moslem, who was still young and was well dressed, presented himself before al-amir carrying fruits for him and asked permission to be admitted into his service in Damascus. The amir consented. I inquired about this man and was informed that his mother had been married to a Frank whom she had killed. Her son used to practice ruses against the Frankish pilgrims and coöperate with his mother in assassinating them. They finally brought charges against him and tried his case according to the Frankish way of procedure.

They installed a huge cask and filled it with water. Across it they set a board of wood. They then bound the arms of the man charged with the act, tied a rope around his shoulders and dropped him into the cask, their idea being that in case he was innocent, he would sink in the water and they would then lift him up with the rope so that he might not die in the water; and in case he was guilty, he would not sink in the water. This man did his best to sink when they dropped him into the water, but he could not do it. So he had to submit to their sentence against him — may Allah's curse be upon them: They pierced his eyeballs with red-hot awls.

Later this same man arrived in Damascus. Al-Amīr Mu'īn-al-Dīn (may Allah's mercy rest upon his soul!) assigned him a stipend large enough to meet all his needs and said to a slave of his, "Conduct him to Burhān-al-Dīn al-Balkhi (may Allah's mercy rest upon his soul!) and ask him on my behalf to order somebody to teach this man the Koran and something of Moslem jurisprudence." Hearing that, the blind man remarked. "May triumph and victory be thine! But this was never my thought." "What didst thou think I was going to do for thee?" asked Mu'īn-al-Dīn. The blind man replied, "I thought thou wouldst give me a horse, a mule and a suit of armor and make me a knight." Mu'īn-al-Dīn then said, "I never thought that a blind man could become a knight."

## STRONG SPIRITS: A NEGRO SAWS HIS OWN LEG

Now for a contrary case.

Among our men of the banu-Kinānah was a black man named 'Ali ibn-Faraḥ,[1] in whose foot appeared a pustule. The pustule turned malignant. His toes fell off, and the whole leg began to rot. The surgeon said to him, "There is nothing to do for thy leg but amputation. Otherwise thou art lost." The man procured a saw and sawed his leg[2] until the flow of blood made him faint. On coming back to consciousness he would start sawing it again. This continued until he amputated it at the middle of the leg. After some treatment, it was cured.

This 'Ali (may Allah's mercy rest upon his soul!') was one of the most enduring and powerful of all men. He used to sit his saddle using one stirrup and putting his knee in a strap on the other side, and in this condition take part in combat and exchange lance thrusts with the Franks. I used to see him myself (may Allah's mercy rest upon his soul!): no man was able to stand a finger contest or come to grips with him. With all his strength and courage, he was a jovial and light-hearted fellow.

# Poems of Arab Andalusia

### Introduction (711–1492)[1]

In 711, Arab and Berber armies invaded Spain, and until 1492, the date of the Spanish reconquest, much of Spain was a multicultural, polyglot nation of Muslims, Christians, and Jews. The invasion occurred when most of Europe was living in darkness, between the fall of the Roman Empire and the high Middle Ages. The Arab world of the Near East,

---

1. Possibly "Faraj."

2. The pronouns and their antecedents are a little confused in this narrative and may be taken to mean that the surgeon did the sawing.

1. Poems of Arab Andalusia are from Arabic unless specifically noted to be from Hebrew. Frequently, little or nothing is known of the author's life. Hence, only a brief headnote appears when information is available.

Africa, and Spain was flourishing culturally. Aristotle, Plato and Neoplatonism, and Greek science and philosophy were preserved in Persian and Arabic translations and slowly made their way into Europe. Only in the eastern section of Europe was there an equivalent high culture: the empire of Byzantine Greece, with its magnificent capital of Constantinople. The cultural heritage of the Arab world, its law, academic disciplines, mathematics, medicine, architecture, and poetry, was transferred to Spain and especially to the great cities of the southern province of Andalusia—Granada, Córdoba, and Sevilla—as well as to Toledo, which eventually, under the Christian monarch Alfonso the Wise, with its school of translators, became the main crossroads for Spain and Europe of the diverse learning of the Iberian Peninsula. For at least four centuries after the conquest, Arabic civilization in this Spanish Eden was resplendent. Great libraries, mosques, and palaces made Andalusia as significant as Baghdad or Damascus. The royal courts in the cities attracted poets and scholars. Then, as the Christians began the reconquest of most of northern Spain and part of the south, in 1086, the ruler of Sevilla invited the fierce troops of the Amoravids to fight against the Christian armies. This fundamentalist militant sect of Muslim Berbers, strong in northwest Africa, fought well but disdained the arts and cared little about Arabic-language culture, since Berber, not Arabic, was their tongue. In 1145, the Almohads replaced the Amoravids and Arabic culture once again flourished. However, city after city fell to the Christians until in 1492 Granada, the last Muslim enclave, was overcome by the Catholic monarchs Fernando and Isabela.

Many arts and sciences claimed precedence in Andalusia. The thirteenth-century Córdoban Neoplatonic philosopher Averroës, in Arabic Ibn Rushd (1126–1198), was a renowned commentator on Aristotle when Aristotle was little more than a name in Western Europe. His erudition conquered not only Christian Spain and its philosophers, such as the Catalan mystic Ramon Llull, but Christian theologians in Paris, which was at one time divided between its Averroists and its anti-Averroist factions. Eventually Averroës' radical notions of the immortality of matter as well as the personal soul and his contention that truth is derived from reason, not faith, were condemned by Aquinas and the Catholic Church. Moses Maimonides, the greatest Jewish philosopher of the Middle Ages, practiced medicine in Córdoba, where he wrote his famous *Guide for the Perplexed* (1190). The city of Granada was graced with the gardens of the Alhambra Palace; Córdoba was a marvel of beautiful mosques and synagogues; and the whitewashed city of Sevilla, known as the poet's paradise, was then, as now, a city of architectural beauty, including its Alcazar tower.

Just as al-Andalus (Arab Andalusia) is still remembered as the Arab world's lost Garden of Eden, the poems of Andalusia are a rare fruit of Arabic poetry, sharing the qualities of the Arabic poem of the Near East and North Africa. These poems—and poetry was always an eminent Arab art—

contain all the classical poems, such as the mono-rhyming ode (*qasida*), the *rajaz* epic, and, most typical of Islamic Spain, the *muwashshaha*, a postclassical poem, which had a refrain called the *kharja* (*jarcha* in Spanish) composed in Spanish, though transliterated into Arabic script. The Jews of Arab Andalusia similarly wrote poems in Hebrew and composed the *jarcha* in Spanish transliterated into Hebrew script. The earliest examples of literature in the Spanish language, preceding the epic *Poem of the Cid* (1100–1140) by at least a century, are the *jarchas* written by Arabs and Jews in al-Andalus. Since the refrain is spoken in Spanish in a woman's colloquial voice and the main body of the *muwashshasha* is spoken in Arabic in a male voice, we find within the Arabic *muwashshaha* a dynamic dialogic scene of male and female, Arabic and Spanish, conveying essential oppositions in life and language in Islamic Spain. The most important volume of Arabic Andulasian writers was compiled by Ibn Said al-Maghribi (1213–1286) from Al-calâ de Real, outside Granada.

## ■ Ibn Shuhayd (992–1034) *Córdoba*

Ibn Shuhayd, born in Córdoba, was an aristocratic poet and close friend of the famous poet Ibn Hazm.

## *After the Orgy*

When he was completely drunk
and asleep and the eyes
of the watchmen also closed,

I came timidly toward her
like a friend staking out a secret
meeting on the sly, as if nothing

happened. I crawled toward her
inperceptibly as in dream. I rose
toward her softly like a breath.

I kissed the white brilliance
of her neck, drank her mouth's
eager redness.

I spent a delicious night with her
until darkness smiled,
revealing the dawn's white teeth.

TRANSLATED BY WILLIS BARNSTONE

## ■ Ibn Hazm (994–1064) *Córdoba*

Ibn Hazm of Córdoba is the outstanding poet of Islamic Spain. He wrote a long treatise on love, *The Ring of the Dove,* comparable to *The Book of Good Love* by Juan Ruiz, the Archpriest of Hita, who is medieval Spain's Chaucer. Ibn Hazm was also a philosopher, jurist, and vizier to the ruler of Córdoba.

## *My Love Comes*

You came to me just before
the Christians rang their bells,

when the half moon
was surging into the sky

like an old man's eyebrow                                                   5
covered almost wholly with white hairs

or like the delicate curve
of an instep.

Though it was still night,
when you came God's                                                          10

rainbow gleamed
on the horizon,

decked in all colors
like a peacock's tail.

TRANSLATED BY WILLIS BARNSTONE

## ■ Solomon ben Gabirol (1021/22–c. 1055) *Málaga* (Hebrew)

Born in Málaga, Solomon ben Gabirol ben Judah, poet and philosopher, spent most of his life in Saragossa. He died in Valencia. Orphaned as a child, his life was harsh. Gabirol seems to have suffered from angry rivals, and he may have been murdered. A poet from very young, he wrote secular poems about love and nature and also religious poems. He wrote in Hebrew, but, as other Jewish poets from Arab Spain, he followed the conventions of Hispano-Arabic poetry. His best known work is a long philosophical poem called "The Kingly Crown" in which he reveals his knowledge of Neoplatonic thought, the mysticism of the Midrash, and Islamic astronomy. He wrote his major prose work, *The Well of Life,* in Arabic and signed it Avicebron (an Arabic version of Gabirol); this treatise also was an extension of his strong Neoplatonic thought. Its Latin translation, *Fons vitae* (Fountain of Life), strongly influenced later Christian thought. His work is incorporated in Jewish liturgy.

## Dawn Storm

Fat clouds low like oxen.
Winter is annoyed and suddenly the sky

races like masts in a squall. A captain
grabs his horn and madly screams alarm.

Then the firmament is black mist
and morning stars babble with tiny light.

Sun carries the clouds on its wings
around the earth.

They burst and the earth bursts.
They were still, now eagles.

Wind blows rain into the abysses.
An infantry of clouds flattens out the earth,

cutting strange ridges for the sowing.
The harvest hides, is known

to only one. All winter the clouds
weep until the dead trees wake.

TRANSLATED BY WILLIS BARNSTONE

## Ibn Ammar (1030–1083) *Sevilla*

Ibn Ammar was born in Sevilla and lived his life in Sevilla and Córdoba. He was well known and a friend of the king, al-Mutamid. It is said that Ibn Ammar betrayed the king, and, consequently, the king killed him with his own hand.

## Reading

My pupil ransoms what the pages traps:
the white white and the black black.

TRANSLATED BY WILLIS BARNSTONE

## ■ Ibn Burd (d. 1053) *Córdoba*

## Moon

The moon is a mirror
whose metal is stained
by sighs of virgins.

Night clothes itself
with light from its lamp                                    5

as black ink
dresses up in white paper.

TRANSLATED BY WILLIS BARNSTONE

## ■ Judah Halevi (c. 1075–1141) *Tudela* (Hebrew)

Judah ben Samuel Halevi was a philosopher, poet, and rabbi from
Muslim Tudela, in Spain. He traveled and studied in the Jewish centers of
learning in Andalusia but settled in Toledo, another great city of learning
under Alfonso VI, which was then the capital of Castile. There, he practiced medicine and was apparently the king's doctor. But many of his com-
patriots, including his spiritual master, Solomon ben Ferrizuel, were murdered, and he moved to Muslim Spain, to Córdoba, also the city of the
great Jewish philosopher Maimonides (who wrote in Arabic). Halevi wrote
a famous book in Arabic, *The Book of Argument and Proof in Defence of the Despised Faith.* It was later translated into Hebrew and other languages. It became known as *The Book of the Kuzari* and contains a dialogue between a
Jewish scholar and the king of the Khazars, an eighth-century convert to
Judaism. This book continues to have a powerful effect on authors from
Jorge Luis Borges to Umberto Eco. Finally, he left Spain, which he loved,
for Zion, for which he longed. As he wrote, his heart was in the East. After
a difficult sea voyage, he reached Alexandria, where he was much appreciated, and where he continued writing at a great pace. He died six months
later. He is the great Hebrew poet of the diaspora. The modern Spanish
poet Rafael Alberti has a wonderful poem about Halevi in his *Book of Returns,* which he titles "Judah Halevi, first poet of Spain."

## My Heart Is in the East

My heart is in the East, and I live at the edge of the West.
I eat. I taste nothing. How can I enjoy it?
How can I fulfil my word to leave

while Zion is locked up in red Edom
and I stand in the ropes of Arabia?
Easily I could give up
all the good wonders of Spain.
Glory would be to see the dust of the Temple,
our ravaged shrine.

TRANSLATED BY WILLIS BARNSTONE

■ **Abu l-Hasan al-Husr (d. 1095)** *Eastern Andalusia*

## *Mourning in Andalusia*[1]

If white is the proper color
of mourning in Andalusia,
why not look at me?
I dress in white hair,
in mourning for my youth.

TRANSLATED BY WILLIS BARNSTONE

■ **Ibn Abi l-Haytham (uncertain period)**

## *Sun*

Look at the beautiful sun.
Rising it shows one gold eyebrow,
plays the miser with the other,

but we know it won't be
stingy. Soon it will splash its veil
of beauty everywhere.

---

1. This poem alludes to a poem by the famous Persian poet Rudaki (d. 940). Rudaki's poem (translated by Tony Barnstone) reads:
    I dye my hair black
    not to look young
    and act wild again.
    Black clothes are worn
    to mourn;
    I dyed my hair
    to mourn my youth.

A mirror of wonder
out of the East
hides again in dusk.

The horizon                                                              10
is desolate at its escape
and puts on mourning robes.

Falling stars
are tears
of iron.                                                                 15

TRANSLATED BY WILLIS BARNSTONE

■ **Ibn Iyad (1083–1149)** *Central Andalusia*

## Grainfield

Ripe wheat
is bending in the wind.

Horsemen flee defeated,
bleeding from
red wounds of the poppies.                                               5

TRANSLATED BY TONY BARNSTONE AND WILLIS BARNSTONE

■ **Abu l-Hasan ibn al-Qabturnuh (d. 1134)** *Badajoz*

Born in Badajoz, Abu l-Hasan ibn al-Qabturnuh wrote in the late
eleventh and twelfth centuries. He was secretary to the king.

## During the Battle

I remembered Sulayma
when the heat of battle
was like my body's fury
the night I left her.

I saw her slim waist                                                     5
among the spears
and as they bent toward me
I embraced them.

TRANSLATED BY WILLIS BARNSTONE

## Candle Light

The more you hurt me
the more I am patient.
When you cut its wick
the candle glows brighter.

TRANSLATED BY WILLIS BARNSTONE

■ **Abu l-Qasim al-Manisi (Twelfth Century)** *Sevilla*

## Rain over the River

The wind's hand
belongs to a silversmith who hammers
the river
into a thousand metal wrinkles.

The water is a delicate coat
of mail. When rain comes
the scales are riveted together
with tiny nails.

TRANSLATED BY TONY BARNSTONE AND WILLIS BARNSTONE

# Persian Literature

### Introduction

Around 1000 B.C., a nomadic Indo-European–speaking people related to the Aryans (who themselves migrated to India) left southern Russia and central Europe and joined with the prehistoric village cultures of Iran to become the Persians of the south and a related people of the north, the Medes. The Persians were conquered by the Medes in the eighth century B.C., who then proceeded in 612 B.C. to ally themselves with the Babylonians and conquer their common enemy, the brutal and warlike Assyrian Empire. The Medes in turn were overthrown by the first Persian empire, which emerged under the reign of Cyrus the Persian (550–530 B.C.), and his two successors, Cambyses and Darius I (522–486 B.C.). By 500 B.C., Achaemenid Persia, named in honor of an ancestor of Cyrus, had for the first time unified the greater Middle East under one imperial rule, which spanned from Egypt in the south to Greek Macedonia in the north and as far east over the Indus River as northwestern India. The Persian empire encompassed a wide range of conquered states and peoples—the Egyptians, Babylonians, Lydians, Greeks, Persians, Medes, Scythians, Parthians, and the Hindu Kush—and under the leadership of Darius I (also called Darius the Great) was organized into twenty-four provinces, each governed by an appointed satrap, creating a considerable administrative order. Darius resourcefully adapted the technological and governmental methods of his conquered subjects for the advancement and unification of his empire. He created a uniform legal system modeled upon the Mesopotamian legal code developed by the Babylonian king Hammurabi, adopted the practice of minting coins that was used in Lydia (modern-day Turkey), and borrowed from Egypt a common calendar. Darius unified his empire further with a series of royal roads that linked one end of Persia to the other and used horses for speedy communication and transportation across the empire. The empire was also linked through the ruling class religion of Zoroastrianism (though both Cyrus and Darius allowed conquered peoples to maintain their original faiths). In fact it was this tolerance, cosmopolitan attitude, and the peace assured by the protection of the powerful Persian empire that led many of its conquered peoples to accept its rule without significant dissent.

The literature of Persia begins with the writings of the Zoroastrian tradition, particularly the poems of the *Avesta,* said to be the words of the prophet Zoroaster (c. 628 B.C.–c. 551 B.C.), whose religion celebrated Ahura Mazda, the god of light and creator of all things. As Zoroastrianism developed, it incorporated a host of lesser beneficial deities, and also an antagonist deity, Ahriman, the god of darkness, and his host of evil spirits. The universe was the battleground for these opposing deities. Each person had to choose whether to be aligned with good or with evil. Humans were to be judged after their death and rewarded with an afterlife of everlasting bliss joined with Ahura Mazda or of everlasting punishment. Darius converted to Zoroastrianism, and the religion quickly spread through Persia. Though it has largely died out today, its concepts were a powerful contributor to Jewish thought and especially to the later Jewish thought that was to evolve into Christianity.

The Persians had periodic conflicts with the Ancient Greeks, culminating in the Persian wars of 500 B.C. to 449 B.C. Darius and his successor Xerxes were unsuccessful in conquering the Greek city-states, and about a hundred years later, in the fourth century B.C., Alexander the Great unified Greece and quickly conquered Persia. Although Alexander's empire fragmented after his death, Seleucus I, one of his successors, maintained control over much of Persia, and during his rule and that of his successors, the Seleucids, Persia was deeply Hellenized. The Greek occupation was replaced by Parthian occupation, and the Parthians were overthrown in A.D. 224 by the Sassanid dynasty. Although the Persian empire never regained the sweeping extent or glory of the Achaemenids, the Sassanids restored native rule for Persia and maintained it as a great empire during the Roman era.

The Sassanids were conquered around A.D. 640 by Arabic armies in a continuation of the holy war to spread Islam that Muhammad had initiated in the last years of his life. Persian administrators soon became essential to the effective management of the sprawling new empire, and Persian and Arabic culture became deeply intertwined. Arabic and Persian literatures were fused into an uneasy whole by the common religious tradition of Islam. The injunction against translating the Quran (though, in practice, generally ignored) caused Arabic to become the holy language of Islam, much as Latin was to Christianity until the Reformation. Therefore, educated Persians were pervasively influenced by the Arabic literary example, by an Arabic vocabulary that migrated into the Persian language, and by the position of the Quran as the supreme Muslim literary exemplar. Many great Arabic writers were in fact ethnic Persians who had adopted the conqueror's tongue. However, later Persian writers are celebrated in part because they strove to eliminate Arabic linguistic elements and to found a truly Persian national literature. Ferdowsi (c. 940–1020) is one such author, a major figure in the golden age of Persian literature, which began in the eleventh century in the court of Mahmud of Ghazna. Ferdowsi was the author of the Persian national epic *The Epic of the Kings*. Many of the great writers of the mystical literary tradition of Sufism were Persian, including such major figures as Attar (c. 1120–c. 1220), Rumi (1207–1273), Sadi (1193–1291), and Hafiz (c. 1320–1390). These great writers lived under the rule of the successors to the Arabs, the Seljuk Turk invaders, who had converted to Islam, and later of Genghis Khan's Mongols, who conquered Persia in the 1350s and ruled for a century. Surprisingly, Persian literature declined after native Persian rule was restored in 1500 under the Safavids, but great literature continued to be written in Persian and in Persian literary forms far from Baghdad—in India at the courts of the Islamic Mughal kings.

—Ayame Fukuda and the editors

## ■ Ferdowsi (Abul Qasim Hasan Ferdowsi) (c. 940–1020) *Persia* (epic poem)

TRANSLATED BY RUBEN LEVY, REVISED BY AMIN BANANI

*The Epic of the Kings* has always been the Persian national poem, and even today parts of it are recited on holidays in Iran, and it is taught to school children as are the Greek classics in parts of the West. It tells the history of Iran from the creation to the seventh century (when Iran was subjugated by Muslim Arabs) in a work of more than sixty-thousand couplets. Ferdowsi himself was born in Tus, in the province of Khorasan, to a

moderately wealthy landowning family, and he spent twenty-five years composing the poem, dying, according to legend, poor and embittered. The
original thousand lines of the poem were written by a young man named
Daqiqi, who was murdered by his Turkish slave in 980; at this point, Ferdowsi continued the epic, incorporating Daqiqi's lines. The heroic tales,
lyrics, and fairy tales that make up this history were drawn from a large
oral tradition and from earlier written sources. Like most epics, *The Epic of
the Kings* engages in exaggeration and repetition and portrays characters
in ideal types, and the poetry reflects the ornamentation, hyperbole, and
repetitive tropes that tend to characterize epic language. The sheer size of
the work, and the fact that Ferdowsi attempted to write a purely Persian
poem with as few words of Arabic as possible, had a decisive effect in establishing a separate Persian language and literature.

The great hero of the saga is Rustam, and the epic became widely
known in the West after Matthew Arnold reworked into English poetry the
episode in which he kills his son Suhrab. The episodes presented here
come before Rustam's introduction to the epic. They consist of an archetypal battle between good and evil, in which Eblis (the Devil) tempts a
young prince, Zahhak, into murdering his father and ruling through
witchcraft, until a young avenger named Kava rises among the people to
set them free. Kava creates a banner that becomes the royal banner of
Iranian kings, whereas Zahhak is of Arabic blood, so that the ethnic disputes of Ferdowsi's day, disputes that are still active today, take on mythic
dimensions in his poem.

**FURTHER READING:** Banani, Amin. "Ferdowsi and the Art of Tragic Epic" in *Persian
Literature.* Edited by Ehsan Yarshater, 1988. Davis, Dick, tr. *Ferdowsi: The Legend of Se-
vavash,* 1992. Levy, Reuben, tr. *The Epic of the Kings: Shah-Nama, the National Epic of
Persia by Ferdowsi.* Revised by Amin Banani, 1990.

## from *The Epic of the Kings (Shah-Nama)*

### The Reign of Jamshid

*[After Hushang came his son Tahmuras, who subjugated the demons and
earned the title of 'Demon-binder' and reigned for thirty years. He was followed
by his son Jamshid.]*

For a time Jamshid had respite from war, since all the demons, birds and
peris were subject to his command. 'I am,' he declared, 'endowed with the
divine *Farr*[1] and at the same time both king and priest. I shall stay the

---

1. A certain refulgence or 'nimbus', symbolizing Divine favour, and reserved for kings and other royal personages. It had almost a physical character, being as it were a palladium, talisman or mascot, which was
recognizable by beholders and implied infallible greatness and good fortune as long as its possessor held
the favour of the Divine Powers.

hand of the evil-doers from evil, and I shall guide the soul towards light.' He first devoted himself to the making of weapons of war, which he gave to valiant heroes eager for renown. By virtue of his kingly *Farr* he was able to mould iron into such equipment as helmets, chain-mail, and laminated armour as well as missile-proof vests, to swords and horse-armour, all of which he invented by his perspicuous intellect. He spent fifty years at this task, part of the time being devoted to the accumulation of stores.

For the next fifty years he gave his mind to the subject of apparel and such matters as the dress appropriate to feasting or to battle. Hence he contrived materials of linen, silk, wool and floss as well as rich brocades and satins. He taught men how to spin and weave and how to interlace the warp with the weft; then, when the weaving was completed, they learnt from him how to wash the materials and how to sew.

When that task was completed he turned to another employ, which was the bringing together of all the men engaged in each craft. Over that he spent fifty years. The class of men known as 'Katuzi', regarded as being specially charged with the rites of worship, was set apart from the common herd of mankind. As for the priests, the mountains were allotted to them as temples, where they were to devote themselves to worship and to supplication of their divine Master.

In contrast to them he established the caste whom men call 'Neysari'. They are lion-hearted warriors who shed lustre over the army and the whole land and because of whom the king sits securely on the throne. Through them the term 'manliness' was established.

The third group claiming recognition was that of the 'Nasudi' caste. They give homage to no man; tilling, sowing and themselves reaping. They heed no person's censure when the time comes for eating. Their heads refuse to bow to command; they are men of independence although clad in rags, and their ears are deaf to abuse. By them the earth is kept under cultivation and clear of strife and discord.

The fourth class is named 'Ahnukhwashi', who industriously spend themselves in all crafts. Their work is consummately skilled and their minds teem with ideas.

Over that task Jamshid consumed another fifty years, distributing benefits generously in every region. Thus he assigned to every living creature the right rank or station [proper to it] and directed [it on] its path, so that each might be aware of its place and understand the measure of it. Upon the demons he laid the duty of mingling earth with water, and when they understood what could be produced with clay they quickly fashioned moulds for bricks. With stone and mortar they built walls, upon which they were the first to erect works of masonry such as baths and lofty arches and castles which could provide refuge against attack.

For a length of time the king sought for gems amongst the rocks and by experiment discovered their lustre. Precious minerals of various kinds came into his hands. They included jacinth, yellow amber, silver and gold, which he extracted from the rock by magic art, the key to unloosening any bond of conglomeration. He also distilled sweet perfumes in whose fragrance men delight; essences like balsam, camphor, pure musk, aloes, ambergris and limpid rose-water. These are drugs and restoratives for those who suffer disease, and they are of use in health as well as during illness. All these hidden things he brought to light, there being no equal to him as a discoverer in the whole universe.

After that he went over the water in a ship, voyaging swiftly from one clime to another. In that way he spent another fifty years. And then he set foot even beyond greatness. With the aid of the royal *Farr*, he fashioned a marvellous throne, which at his bidding was lifted by demons into the air. He sat upon that throne like the sun in the firmament. To celebrate, that day was called a new day—the festival of Now-Ruz—the first day of the new year.

Thus another three hundred years went by and men never saw death, remaining unacquainted even with toil and hardship, for the demons waited ever ready to serve. All men were obedient to the king's command and the world was pervaded by the pleasant sounds of music. And so years went by until the royal *Farr* was wrested from him. The reason for it was that the king, who had always paid homage to God, now became filled with vanity and turned away from Him in forgetfulness of the gratitude he owed Him. He summoned those of his followers who were held in highest esteem and in these words addressed his nobles of long experience,

'I recognize no lord but myself. It was through me that skills appeared on earth, and no throne however famed has ever beheld a monarch like me. It was I who adorned the world with beauty and it is by my will that the earth has become what it now is. Sunshine, sleep and repose all come through me, and even your clothing and what enters your mouths originate from me. Power, crown and kingship are my prerogative. Who can claim that anyone but I am king? By means of drugs and other medicaments the world has been brought to such a level of health that sickness and death befall no one. Who but I have banished death from amongst mankind, although many kings have been upon the earth? It is because of me that you have minds and souls in your bodies. And now that you are aware that all this was accomplished by me, it is your duty to entitle me Creator of the World.'

The priests to a man remained with heads bowed low, none daring to ask 'Why?' or 'How?'. But as soon as he had made his speech the Farr departed from him and the world became full of discord. Men deserted his court and no one desiring repute would remain in his service, for when pride combines with power of action it brings ruin in its train and converts good fortune into bad. Jamshid's destiny was overcast with gloom and his world-illumining splendour disappeared.

# (i) The Story of Zahhak

In those days there lived a man who came from the deserts where men rode horses and brandished spears. He was a person much honoured for his generosity and one who in his fear of the Lord trembled as though shaken by a gale. The name of this noble man was Merdas. This true believer and prince had a son, whom he loved with a love beyond measure and who was called Zahhak, a youth of high courage, swift in action and bold. Of each day and night he spent two parts out of three in the saddle on noble enterprises, never for any unlawful purpose.

Now one day Eblis [the Devil] arrived on pretence of being a visitor who wished to pay him homage. The visitor's speeches fell agreeably on his ear, for he had no inkling of his character, and he surrendered to him with his whole mind, heart and pure soul, and humbled himself before him. Eblis, feeling that the prince had been completely won over by him, rejoiced beyond measure at his own cunning and said,

'I have many things to impart to you which no one knows but me.'

'Tell me then,' replied the youth, 'and hold nothing back. You are the man to give good advice. Instruct me.'

'First,' said he, 'I require an oath of you, and then I shall reveal such matters as I have to impart.'

The youth was innocent of heart. He gave his word, swearing an oath in which Eblis demanded that he would never disclose any part of his secret to anyone and would obey his every word. Eblis then said,

'Within this palace, my noble lord, what need for a being other than yourself? Why is a father necessary when a son like you exists? Listen to counsel. Over this aged nobleman long years have passed; he lingers on while you endure in wretchedness. Seize upon these riches and this palace; the high rank which he enjoys in the world is well suited to you. If you will have trust in what I say, you will be the only ruler in the world.'

As he heard this Zahhak became pensive, but his heart filled with pain at the thought of taking his father's life. 'It would conflict with all justice,' said he to Eblis. 'Suggest some other plan, for that is something which I cannot do.'

'If you fail in carrying out my advice,' replied Eblis, 'you will dishonour your pledge and the oath which you swore to me; that oath and your bond will lie heavily upon you. Moreover you will linger on as a person disregarded by all, while your father continues to command reverence.'

The head of the Arab Zahhak fell into the net and he was cowed into submission to the other's will. He asked what scheme he advised and declared he would not reject the slightest detail.

Now within the palace bounds the king had a garden which rejoiced his heart, and into it every night he went to prepare himself in privacy for the rites of worship by washing his head and body. The servants who accompanied him carried no lanterns, and on the path leading into the garden the vile demon, in pursuance of his evil plan, dug a deep pit, and covered it with straw. Night fell and the Arab chief [the king], that noble lord ever zealous for his good repute, arose to enter the garden. As he approached the abysmal pit, the royal fortunes sank heavily; down into it he fell and lay there broken. So departed that benevolent and God-fearing man.

Zahhak, despicable malefactor, seizing his opportunity, usurped his father's place and set on his head the crown of the Arabs, amongst whom he became the giver of good and evil.

Once Eblis understood that he had brought this matter to an end with success, he began to elaborate a further scheme. He said to Zahhak,

'When you turned to me for aid, you won all that you desired. If you will make another such compact with me, leaving nothing undone that I suggest and obeying my commands, the sovereignty of the whole world will be yours. Every living animal wild or tame, together with the birds and the fishes, shall be in submission to you.'

So saying he departed to further this scheme and to devise another strange artifice.

## (ii) Eblis Turns Cook

Having tricked himself out as a young man, glib-tongued, active and clean-limbed, Eblis found his way into the presence of Zahhak, whom he addressed in the language of flattery and said,

'If I am agreeable to your Majesty, I am myself a renowned and perfectly-trained cook.'

Zahhak accepted this with approval. He had a place got ready for him where he could prepare his viands, entrusted him with the key of the royal kitchens and gave him full oversight of all. In those days flocks were not plentiful, and living creatures were rarely killed for eating. Except for herbs men had nought to eat and it was the ground that produced all, until Ahriman, the Evil-doer, conceived and lodged in the minds of men the thought of killing animals. Out of every genus both of birds and quadrupeds he contrived eatables, making use of all. With their blood he fed Zahhak, as though it were milk, in order to make him stout of heart. And Zahhak obeyed every word that Eblis uttered, giving his mind in pledge to his command.

First Eblis gave Zahhak the yolk of an egg to eat and for a time kept his body in good health with it. Zahhak ate and, finding it agreeable to his palate, gave praise to Eblis. One day Eblis said to him,

'Proud monarch, may you live for ever! Tomorrow I will prepare a dish that will give you the perfection of sustenance.' Then he went to rest and all night long his mind was occupied with the thought of the wondrous dishes his cook would concoct on the morrow. Next day, when the azure vault [of heaven] raised aloft and displayed the yellow jacinth [of the sun], Eblis cooked a dish of partridge and white pheasant and brought it in with his mind full of expectation, and as the Arab king stretched out his hand to the tray of food, his foolish head betrayed him into a partiality for Eblis.

On the following day the tray was decked by Eblis with chicken and lamb as well as with other viands. On the next day again when he set his tray before the king, he had prepared a saddle of veal enriched with saffron and rose-water as well as with old wine and clarified musk. When Zahhak partook of this delicacy and savoured it, he was filled with admiration at the man's skill and said to him,

'Consider what you would most desire and then ask me for it.'

The cook replied.

'May your Majesty live happily for ever, endowed with all-powerful command! My heart is wholly devoted to love for you and from your countenance comes all that sustains my spirit. I have one petition to make of your Majesty, although I am not of the degree to aspire to it. It is, if your Majesty command, that I may be permitted to kiss your shoulders and rub them with my eyes and face.'

Zahhak heard the words and, little suspecting what lay behind all the doings of Eblis, replied,

'I grant your desire. Mayhap your fame will get advancement from it.'

And so he let him have his wish, as though he were his dearest friend, to kiss him on his shoulders. This Eblis did, and immediately vanished into the ground—a marvel such as no man in the world has ever seen.

From Zahhak's shoulders now two black serpents thrust their heads out, filling him with terror. On every hand he sought for a remedy and at last had recourse to cutting them off. But, just as branches sprout anew from trees, so those two black serpents grew again from the royal shoulders. Learned physicians crowded about him, each in turn advising what should be done; and every kind of wizardry was tried. Yet no remedy was found for the affliction.

And then Eblis appeared again, this time in the guise of a physician. Presenting himself gravely before Zahhak, he said,

'This is an occurrence predestined by fate. Leave all alone. Since they are there, you must not cut them off; rather let food be prepared and given them to eat so that they can be propitiated. That is the only proper expedient. For food let them have nothing but human brains, and it may be that given that kind of nurture they will die.' [And in this his secret intent was to empty the world of people.]

## (iii) Jamshid's Fortunes Decline

Days passed, and then, [God having withdrawn His favour from Jamshid] a mighty discontent arose throughout Iran. On every hand strife and turmoil erupted and glorious bright day was turned to darkness. Jamshid's allies broke away from him, his divine *Farr* became tarnished and he took to crooked paths and folly. On every hand new kings sprang up, on every frontier men sought a way to power. They gathered armies and made war, their hearts having been emptied of all affection for Jamshid. By ones and twos a host of men forsook Iran and went along the roads towards the Arabs, in whose land, they had heard, was an awe-inspiring king with a dragon's body.

Iranian knights, in search of a new king, turned their glances in unison towards Zahhak and, saluting him as sovereign, they proclaimed him king of Iran.

Swift as the wind the dragon-king journeyed to Iran, where he assumed the crown. In Iran and from amongst the Arabs he chose an army composed of the champions of every region. Then when fortune had withdrawn its face from Jamshid, the new king hemmed him in closely until he came and surrendered throne and crown, his high rank vanishing with his diadem, treasure and retinue. The world grew black in his sight, so that he hid himself away and no one saw him again for a hundred years. At last he, prince of besmirched faith, appeared in the sea of China. There Zahhak had him seized and, without granting him a moment's respite, had his body sawn in two, thus cleansing the world and ridding it of all fear of him.

After Zahhak had enthroned himself as emperor, a thousand years accumulated over him, an era during which the ways of rational men disappeared and the wishes of the devil-possessed everywhere prevailed. Virtue was humiliated and wizardry esteemed; truth hid itself and evil flourished openly. Now it became the practice that each night two young men, either humbly born or sons of noble families, were carried away to the royal palace by a cook, who out of them provided something for the solace of the king. He killed them and then drew out their brains, from which he made a dish with which to feed the dragon.

## Faridun

# (i) The Birth of Faridun

*[Zahhak dreamt one night that a hero named Faridun would appear to dethrone and slay him.]*

A long time went by, spent in anxiety by Zahhak, and then Faridun, blessed by fortune, came into the world. He grew up as beautiful as a slender cypress, and the royal *Farr* radiated from him. It had been inherited from Jamshid and he was refulgent as the sun that shines in the heavens, and as needful to the world as rain to the earth and as appropriate as knowledge to the mind. Over his head in affection for him the skies revolved in benignity.

[To discover Faridun's dwelling-place] Zahhak filled the world with hue and cry, hunting for him and searching in every direction. Faridun's father, Abtin, when the world narrowed about him, fled away in despair of his life but unsuspectingly fell into the lion's toils, for vile guards found him and carried him, bound like a tiger, into the presence of Zahhak, who put an end to his life.

*[Faranak, the hero's prudent mother, at that took flight with her child and after a number of adventures settled in a hiding place in the Alborz mountains.]*

## (ii) Zahhak and Kava the Blacksmith

Day and night the thoughts of Zahhak were occupied with Faridun, of whom he was constantly speaking. Fear of him caused his upright stature to become bowed and because of him his heart was ever pervaded with dread. One day, seated on his ivory throne and with his turquoise crown placed on his head, he summoned the princes charged with ruling over his provinces in order to secure from them their affirmation of his sovereignty. He then addressed his ministers, to whom he said,

'My revered and talented counsellors, I have a hidden enemy; a fact which is patent to men of understanding like yourselves. And, however despicable an enemy may be, I do not hold him in contempt, for I am ever doubtful of the malice of fate. I therefore stand in need of a large army, in which demons and peris shall be enrolled along with men, and such an army I am about to raise. Since I am unable to support the burden of it alone, you must ally yourselves with me in the project. And now I desire you to subscribe to a proclamation on my behalf that as commander in chief I have sown no seed but that of uprightness, that I have never spoken anything but the truth and that I would never fail to maintain justice.'

Being in awe of the monarch, those upright men allied themselves with him in his scheme and, old and young, willingly or unwillingly, wrote on the dragon's proclamation the assurance he desired. Just then an unexpected petitioner for justice entered the king's palace. He was a man who had been grievously wronged and, being summoned into the royal presence, was given a seat before those famous men. With an anxious countenance the monarch said to him,

'Tell me at whose hands it is that you have suffered wrong.'

Striking his head with his hand at seeing the king himself, the man cried out,

'Your Majesty, I am Kava, seeking for justice. Grant me justice! I have come here running and I implore you with grief in my soul. If you are active in doing justice, then the esteem in which you are held will be heightened to the extreme. Most of the wrong done to me comes from yourself. It is you who constantly thrust the lancet into my heart. If as you say you would not suffer an outrage upon me, why then do you inflict harm on my children? I had eighteen alive in the world, and now only one remains. Spare me this one child, or my spirit will everlastingly be tortured. My king, what crime have I committed? Tell me. If I am innocent, do not seek pretexts against me. Misfortune has bowed me down, as you see; it has left my heart devoid of hope and my mind full of misery. My youth is gone, and without children I will have no ties left in the world. There is a middle and a limit to injustice; even then it must have a pretext. If you have an accusation against me, present it, for you plan my destruction.

'I am a simple blacksmith, doing no wrong; yet fire descends on my head from your Majesty. Although you have a dragon's form, you are the king and it's your duty to let me have justice in this thing. You have sovereignty over the seven [planet-ruled] climes; why should the fate allotted to me be all grief and misery? You and I must come to a reckoning, and then the world will stand in amazement. Perhaps the reckoning with you will make clear how my last son's turn has come, how it was that from amongst all the people it was my son's brains which had to be sacrificed to your Majesty.'

The monarch at this speech opened his eyes wide and he was overcome with astonishment at the words. The man's son was restored to him and an effort was made with kindly treatment to win his support for the king. However, when the king commanded Kava to add his testimony to what was contained in the proclamation, Kava perused the document from end to end and then, turning swiftly to the elders of the land, he cried out,

'Henchmen of the Devil, you have cut off your hearts from fear of the Lord. All of you have turned your faces towards Hell and surrendered your hearts to obedience of the Devil. I will not lend my testimony to this proclamation, nor will I ever stand in awe of the king.'

With a cry he sprang up trembling, tore the proclamation into pieces, which he trampled underfoot. Out of the palace he went thundering into the street, his son ahead of him.

[In the audience-hall] the nobles made sychophantic speeches to the king.

'Most famous king of the world,' they said, 'even the cool winds of heaven do not venture to pass over your head on the day of battle. How then dare this crude-spoken Kava address you in anger as though he were your equal? He has destroyed our proclamation containing the covenant made with you and rejects your authority. His heart and head are swollen with wrath and he has gone as though to make common cause with Faridun. Never have we beheld viler conduct; we stand outraged by his actions.'

'Listen to a strange thing that has happened,' said the king in speedy reply. 'When Kava appeared in the audience-hall, as soon as my ears heard the sound of his voice there immediately arose between him and me in the chamber what seemed a mountain of iron, and then, when he struck his head with his hand, the thing fell, shattered in pieces. I do not know what will emerge from this portent; nobody knows Heaven's secrets.'

Meantime, when Kava came out after leaving the king's presence, the people crowded about him in the market-place. He called out, summoning men to come to his aid and urging the world to demand justice. On to the end of a spear he fastened a piece of leather, of the kind which blacksmiths wear in front of their legs when using their hammers, and as out of the market-place the dust rose high, with the spear held aloft he began to march, crying out as he went,

'Noble worshippers of God, let all who side with Faridun liberate their heads from the yoke of Zahhak! Let us go to Faridun and find refuge in the shelter of his *Farr*. Let us proclaim that this present king is Ahriman [the Maker of Evil], who is at heart the enemy of the Creator. By means of that leather, worth nothing and costing nothing, the voice of the enemy was distinguished from that of the friend.'

As the stout-hearted man marched onwards, an army of no small size rallied about him. He knew where Faridun lay and went directly towards the place, and as they at last approached the castle of the young prince they greeted him with a shout when they espied him in the distance. His eye caught the piece of leather attached to the spearhead and he beheld in it the foundation of prosperity to come. The leather he decorated with Greek brocade and as background to it had a golden figure outlined with jewels sewn on it. Ribands of red, yellow, and violet cloth were hung from it and it was given the title of 'The Kaviani Banner'. Since those days anyone who has assumed kingly rank and placed the crown of royalty on his head has added fresh jewels to that trifling thing of blacksmith's leather.

With him as his constant companions Faridun had two brothers, both older than himself, and to them he opened his heart, declaring that the skies revolved only to a benevolent purpose and the diadem of greatness would inevitably come to him.

'Get me cunning smiths to fashion me a heavy mace,' he bade them, and outlined in the dust a figure portraying the likeness of a buffalo's head.

## (iii) Faridun Makes War on Zahhak

Proudly Faridun raised his head sun-high and girt himself tightly to exact vengeance for his father's death. On an appointed day he eagerly began his undertaking beneath a happy star and with omens that brightened his day. At his palace, whose pinnacles reached the skies, troops massed about him with massive elephants, and buffaloes laden with the army's provender. In the forefront of the troops rode Kava, head on high, moving spiritedly from the halting-place and bearing aloft the the Kaviani Banner, regal emblem of majesty.

Faridun set his face towards the Arvand river as a man determined to find a crown. (If you are ignorant of the Pahlavi tongue, you call the Arvand by its Arabic name of Dijla [i.e. the Tigris].) When he reached the stream he sent salutations to its wardens and commanded them quickly to launch ships and other vessels.

'Ferry me and my soldiers across to the other bank,' he said, 'and leave no man behind on this side.'

The chief river-guard however, ignoring Faridun's command, brought no ships, but said in answer to him,

'The King of the World [Zahhak] secretly ordered me to launch no ship unless I had first obtained a permit from him, attested by his seal.'

Faridun was stirred to wrath by these words. Without fear of the deep flood, he fastened his royal girth tightly, sprang upon his lion-hearted steed and, with his mind sharply intent on vengeance and battle, spurred his rose-coloured horse into the torrent. His comrades, similarly girt for action, charged into the river with him, sinking on their swift-footed mounts as deep as the saddle. Coming to dry land on the opposite side they continued on their way to Jerusalem, which is now in Arabic called 'The Immaculate Abode', where Zahhak, you must know, had erected his palace.

From across the desert the warriors approached the city in high hopes of storming it. At the distance of a league Faridun observed it, and what caught his eye in the royal city was a palace whose pillared hail appeared to rise higher than the planet Saturn, so that you could have imagined it sweeping the stars out of the sky. There it shone against the heavens like Jupiter, as though it might be the abode of joy, peace and love. But he knew that it was the lair of the dragon and the seat of his power, a place filled with treasure. He said to his comrades,

'I am afraid that one who on the dark earth can build up so mighty an edifice, raising it out of the bowels of the ground, is in a conspiracy with the earth. Our best course in this campaign is to attack at once and permit no delay.'

With the words Faridun stretched out his hand to grasp his [bull-headed] mace and gave the rein to his swift-galloping courser. You would have said that fire burst forth of its own free will as he charged the men on guard. He raised his heavy club above the saddle, and, as the earth seemed to crash together in folds, he rode into the great palace—a youth inexperienced in the world, but stout of heart. Not a man of the sentinels had remained at the gates, and Faridun gave blessings to the Creator of the world.

# (iv) Faridun and the Deputy of Zahhak

At such times as the land was unoccupied by Zahhak's presence, there remained in his stead a certain worthy dignitary who occupied the throne, the treasury and the palace, since his master had great admiration of his trustiness. He was named 'Kondrow' ['Slow-mover'], because he walked with deliberate pace when in the presence of his tyrannical master. This Kondrow now came at a run into the palace and in the pillared hail saw a young man of princely stature at his ease in the place of honour, looking as beautiful as a tall cypress topped by the sphere of the moon. The citadel swarmed with his troops, every man ready for action, while others were arrayed in the portals. Kondrow showed no trepidation nor did he inquire the reason for this enigmatical occurrence, but approached uttering salutations and with blessings on his lips.

Faridun invited him to come forward and disclose to him the inner purpose of his arrival, then commanded them to set out the appurtenances of a royal banquet.

'Bring wine,' he bade, 'and call the musicians. Fill cups and let platters be decked. Let all who are able to provide me with music come to the feast and enliven my spirits. And invite to my dais such company as shall be in harmony with my good fortune.'

As he drank his wine and made his choice of music Faridun celebrated a night of feasting that accorded with his circumstances. At dawn, however, Kondrow swiftly withdrew from his new master and, mounted on a willing beast, rode off in search of Zahhak. When he had entered the royal presence he told of what he had seen and heard.

'King of the mighty,' he said, 'signs have appeared that your fortunes are in decline. Three great men with troops have arrived from a foreign land. The one that stands between the other two is the youngest, but he has the stature of a cypress and the visage of a king. Although he is youngest he is superior in dignity and it is he who stands forth amongst them. He wields a mace like a fragment of mountain and in any assembly he shines out. He rode on horseback into your Majesty's palace with those two mighty warriors, one on either side, and when he arrived at your Majesty's throne he sat on it, making nothing of your interceptors and your magic talisman. As for those stationed in your pillared hall, whether human beings or your own demons, he cut off all their heads as he sat on his horse, and mingled their brains with their blood.'

'Let him stay,' replied Zahhak, 'Perhaps he is a guest, and must be entertained.'

'A guest?' queried his steward. 'A person who boldly seats himself in the place where you yourself rest, who expunges your name from your crown and girdle and converts unfaithful creatures to his malpractices? If you wish to acknowledge such a one as your guest, do so!'

'Do not protest so loudly,' bade him Zahhak. 'An arrogant guest is an omen of the happiest kind.'

'I hear you,' retorted Kondrow. 'Now listen to what I have to say. If this renowned warrior is your guest, what business has he in your women's quarters? There he sits with Jamshid's sisters, discussing every kind of topic with them, with one hand fondling the cheeks of Shahrnaz, with the other the red lips of Arnavaz. When the night grows dark his conduct is even worse. Under his head he lays a pillow of musk, which is nothing other than the tresses of your two beauteous ones, who were ever your favourites.'

Zahhak was roused to fury like a wolf. At hearing this speech he cried aloud for death. With foul obloquy he raged in savage tones against the unfortunate steward.

'Never again,' said he, 'will you be my warden.' To that the steward replied,

'I believe now, my king, that you no longer enjoy fortune's favour. How then will you be able ever again to give me charge of the city? Since you are to be deprived of your office as ruler, how will you entrust to me the task of acting in your stead? You have been torn from the place of majesty as a hair is plucked out of dough. Now, my lord, make your plans and look to what needs to be done, for this is an occasion that has had no precedent.'

## (v) Faridun Takes Zahhak Prisoner

Zahhak boiled with rage at this exchange of talk and determined on speedy action. He commanded that his horse, swift of foot and of the keenest sight, should be saddled and at a breath-taking gallop he set off with a great army entirely composed of male demons inured to war. Moving by a devious way he reached the palace, whose gates and roof he occupied, with no thought in his head but that of exacting vengeance. Faridun's army received news of this and made by untrodden paths for the same goal, where, leaping in a spate from their war-horses, they attacked the closely guarded palace. On every roof and in every doorway stood the men of the city who had any strength to fight. But all sided with Faridun, for their hearts were sore at Zahhak's oppression, and although missiles rained down—bricks from the walls, stones from the roofs and, in the streets, javelins and poplar-wood arrows—in the city the youths, like their battle-hardened elders, deserted to Faridun's army in order to escape the wizardry of Zahhak.

He, meanwhile, cast about for a means of sating his venom. Leaving his troops he entered the palace clad in iron armour from head to foot in order to avoid recognition. In his hand he carried a lasso sixty cubits long, by the aid of which he quickly climbed to the top of the lofty building. From there he beheld that dark-eyed Shahrnaz, full of enchantment, in dalliance with Faridun, her cheeks bright as day and her tresses like night. He opened his mouth with curses, understanding that this was God's will and that he could not evade the clutch of evil. With the fires of jealousy searing his brain he flung the end of his lasso down into the portico and, reckless of throne and precious life, he climbed down from the palace roof. From its sheath he plucked his sharp dagger and, without a word that would reveal his secret, without calling on any name, and holding the tempered steel weapon in his clutch, he came forward athirst for the blood of the peri-cheeked woman. No sooner, however, had he set foot on the ground than Faridun advanced upon him with the speed of a storm-wind and dealt him a blow from his bull-headed mace that shattered his helmet. But at that instant an angel approached at speed and said,

'Do not strike him down; his time has not yet come. He is wounded; bind him firmly as a rock and carry him up to where two mountains close together will come in sight. Tie him securely inside one of them, where neither his kinsfolk nor his associates can have access to him.'

Faridun heard the words and with little hesitation carried out the behest. He got ready a noose of lion-skin and with it tied Zahhak's hands and waist so tightly together that a raging elephant could not have loosened the bond. Afterwards he seated himself on Zahhak's golden throne and cast down the symbols of his wicked rule, while at the palace gates a proclamation was by his command uttered in these words,

'You noble men of worth and good sense, it is not fitting that you should remain burdened with the weapons of war and be forced to seek fame and repute in this fashion. That soldiers and workmen should both win merit in one and the same way is not right; some are craftsmen, others wield the mace, and each man's occupation displays its worth in its own fashion. When, therefore, one group seeks to perform the other's task, the whole world becomes confused. That fellow who was so vile is now in fetters — that creature who kept the world in terror. As for you, may you live long and remain ever happy. Now depart to your tasks with song.'

In accordance with the advice which he had been given, Faridun, blessed by fortune, drove the tightly-bound Zahhak towards Shirkhan and into the mountains. There he would have stricken off the demon's head, but the benevolent angel appeared once again and gently spoke a quiet word in his ear, telling him to take the captive at the same good pace as before to Mount Damavand. No escort was to accompany them but one composed of men whose services were indispensable and who could be of assistance at a difficult moment. Accordingly, swift as a rumour, he brought Zahhak to Mount Damavand, where he left him in fetters. There he remained hanging, his heart's blood pouring down on to the earth.

■ **Omar Khayyam (c. 1048–1131)** *Persia* **(poems)**

TRANSLATED BY PETER AVERY AND JOHN HEATH-STUBBS

The fact that the astronomer and mathematician Omar Khayyam, a minor poet, has become the best known of all Persian poets in the West (though challenged in recent years by Rumi) is testimony to the lasting power of the fantastically altered version of his Rubaiyat rendered into English by Edward FitzGerald in 1859. His own biographers speak only of his achievements in science and seem unaware that he ever wrote poetry, as in fact were the majority of Khayyam's countrymen prior to FitzGerald's translation. The form of the poem is that of the *rubai*, or epigrammatic quatrain, many of which FitzGerald linked together with the work of other poets into a long connected poem, though in fact each should be understood as standing alone. The *rubai* is not a major form, and thus it is no surprise that one who only wrote in this form should not be considered a poet, at least professionally. But there is a wit, a pithiness, and a hard-edged materialism to the poems that seem to have been characteristic of Khayyam, the scientist, that make his work come across particularly well today. Seen as a whole, his *rubais* add up to a meditation on life and mortality (of the sort that FitzGerald intuited) as the same tropes return again and again. In this sense, his work is a constellation of isolate stars, the lines between which the reader is free to imagine.

Khayyam was an astronomer in the service of the Seljuk king of Malek-shah, for whom he constructed an observatory and compiled astronomical tables to construct a revised calendar that was many centuries ahead of anything of which Europe could boast. We also know that he wrote a pioneering work about algebra and in his forties went on an extensive journey to Mecca, Baghdad, and other places. He spent his last years in his hometown of Nishapur, teaching, and he died there in 1131, at around eighty-three years of age. Though there are those who say that Khayyam was a Sufi, there is more historical evidence that he was an early Persian scientific empiricist, a profound pessimist, doubting the afterlife, complaining about human helplessness in the hands of fate, and turning to a sensual *carpe diem* as consolation. In fact, he is chided for his materialism in a poem by mystical poet Farid ad-Din Attar, who presents Omar Khayyam in heaven, full of knowledge that does him no good when he is rejected by God.

**FURTHER READING:** Arberry, A. J. *Omar Khayyam: A New Version Based Upon Recent Discoveries,* 1952. Avery, Peter and John Heath-Stubbs, trs. *The Ruba'iyat of Omar Khayyam,* 1981. Elwell-Sutton, L. P. "Omar Khayyam" in *Persian Literature.* Edited by Ehsan Yarshater, 1988, pp. 147–160. FitzGerald, Edward. *Rubaiyat of Omar Khayyam,* undated.

## from *The Rubaiyat*

### 1

Although I have a handsome face and colour,
Cheek like the tulips, form like the cypress,
It is not clear why the Eternal Painter
Thus tricked me out for the dusty show-booth of earth.

### 4

Oh heart you will not arrive at the solving of the riddle,
You will not reach the goal the wise in their subtlety seek;
Make do here with wine and the cup of bliss,
For you may and you may not arrive at bliss hereafter.

### 33

The firmament secretly whispered in my heart,
'Do you know what sentence fate laid on me?
If my revolving were in my control,
I would release myself from this circling.'

### 34

The good and evil that are in man's heart,
The joy and sorrow that are our fortune and destiny,

Do not impute them to the wheel of heaven because, in the light of
    reason,
The wheel is a thousand times more helpless than you.

*41*

There was a water-drop, it joined the sea,
A speck of dust, it was fused with earth;
What of your entering and leaving this world?
A fly appeared, and disappeared.

*42*

You asked, 'What is this transient pattern?'
If we tell the truth of it, it will be a long story;
It is a pattern that came up out of an ocean
And in a moment returned to that ocean's depth.

*43*

It is a bowl the Creative Reason casts,
Pressing in tenderness a hundred kisses on its brim;
This cosmic potter makes such a rare bowl,
Then throws it back again to the ground.

*44*

The parts of a cup which are joined together
The drunkard does not hold it lawful to break:
So many delicate heads, legs, hands,
Through whose love were they joined, by whose hatred smashed?

*50*

We are the puppets and the firmament is the puppet-master,
In actual fact and not as a metaphor;
For a time we acted on this stage,
We went back one by one into the box of oblivion.

*51*

Oh what a long time we shall not be and the world will endure,
Neither name nor sign of us will exist;
Before this we were not and there was no deficiency,
After this, when we are not it will be the same as before.

*58*

Every particle of dust on a patch of earth
Was a sun-cheek or brow of the morning star;
Shake the dust off your sleeve carefully—
That too was a delicate, fair face.

*65*

I saw a man working on a building site,
He was stamping down the clay;

The clay protested,
'Stop it, you like me will be stamped on by many a foot.'

### 66

Oh heart-seeker raise the cup and the jug,
Go back to the meadows on the stream's verge:
This wheel has made many a radiant-cheeked, idol-form
Over and over again into cups and jugs.

### 71

I watched a potter in his work-place,
Saw the master, his foot on the wheel's treddle;
Unabashed, he was making a jug's lid and handle
From a king's head and a beggar's hand.

### 72

This jug was love-sick like me,
Tangled in a fair girl's locks;
This handle you now see on its neck
Was his hand on the neck of the girl.

### 80

I drink so much wine, its aroma
Will rise from the dust when I'm under it;
Should a toper come upon my dust,
The fragrance from my corpse will make him roaring drunk.

### 98

I need a jug of wine and a book of poetry,
Half a loaf for a bite to eat,
Then you and I, seated in a deserted spot,
Will have more wealth than a Sultan's realm.

### 104

I saw a waster sitting on a patch of ground,
Heedless of belief and unbelief, the world and the faith—
No God, no Truth, no Divine Law, no Certitude:
Who in either of the worlds has the courage of this man?

### 110

Nobody has known anything better than sparkling wine
Since the morning star and the moon graced the sky:
Wine-sellers astonish me because
What can they buy better than what they sell?

### 140

Khayyam, if you are drunk on wine, enjoy it,
If you are with the tulip-cheeked, enjoy her:

Since the world's business ends in nothing,
Think that you are not and, while you are, enjoy it.

*213*

Every now and then someone comes along saying, 'It is I.'
He arrives with favours, silver and gold, saying, 'It is I.'
When his little affair is sorted out for a day,
Death suddenly jumps out of ambush saying, 'It is I.'

*216*

Oh eye you are not blind, see the grave
And see this world full of distraction and bitterness;
Kings, heads and princes are under the clay,
See moon-bright faces in the jaws of ants.

*234*

If chance supplied a loaf of white bread,
Two casks of wine and a leg of mutton,
In the corner of a garden with a tulip-cheeked girl
There'd be enjoyment no Sultan could outdo.

## ■ Attar (Farid ad-Din Attar) (c. 1120 – c. 1220) *Persia* (poems)

### TRANSLATED BY AFKHAM DARBANDI AND DICK DAVIS

The Persian mystical poet Farid ad-Din Attar was born at Neishapour (located in northeast Iran) sometime during the twelfth century. There is considerable debate about when he was born, and estimates run from 1120 to 1157. He was educated at a religious school at the shrine of Imam Reza at Mashad and was said to have traveled to Rey, Egypt, Damascus, Mecca, Turkestan, and India in search of knowledge. Apparently, he was also seeking stories about the Islamic saints, which he collected and published in his prose work *Memorials of the Saints*. Attar's name suggests his profession, which seems to have been that of a perfume and drug seller, perhaps even that of a doctor, a profession he took up upon ending his travels and settling once again in Neishapour. The great Persian mystical poet Rumi was said to have played on Attar's knee, though this may be apocryphal. At some point in his life, Attar was tried and convicted of heresy, was banished, and was deprived of his property. He died sometime between 1193 and 1235.

Though he also wrote other important works, such as *The Book of the Divine, The Book of Secrets,* and *The Book of Affliction, The Conference of the Birds,* written in 1177, was his major effort. This epic collection of poems is a loosely bound depiction of the stages of religious experience as the Sufi seeks unity with God. Riddling teaching tales are set like gems within a framing narrative in which the hoopoe convinces the birds of the world to embark on a mystical Way to seek the ideal, spiritual king, the Simorgh. They must overcome their own weaknesses and attachments to the world, passing through the seven valleys (the Valleys of the Quest, of Love, of Insight into Mystery, of Detachment and Serenity, of Unity, of Awe, of Bewilderment, and of Poverty and Nothingness). They lose many questers on the way until a bedraggled group of thirty persevering birds finally meets the king. As translator Dick Davis notes, the birds at last find "that the Simorgh they have sought is none other than themselves. The moment depends on a pun—only thirty (*si*) birds (*morgh*) are left at the end of the Way, and the *si morgh* meet the Simorgh, the goal of their quest." The Sufism that the poem expounds often celebrates an ecstatic self-annihilation, in addition to celebrations of passionate love. Often this love causes its victims to break conventions, as beggars love kings, princesses love slaves, and men love men; the passionate commitment to the religious Way also demands that the mystic listen to the demands of spiritual love and ignore the world's judgment. In this poem we see that to the Sufi, the "world's bright surfaces" are illusion, a hall of mirrors hiding the supreme truth, a truth in which all disparate experiences are revealed to be the same when the mirror is broken: "The lovely forms and colours are undone, / And what seemed many things is only one. / All things are one—there isn't any two; It isn't me who speaks; it isn't you." As Rumi says, "I thought I knew who I was, but I was you."

In this version, Dick Davis and Afkham Darbandi translate the rhyming end-stopped *masnavi* form into an equivalent English form, heroic couplets, with remarkable grace and fluidity—a difficult task at best. For the most part, the chosen selections are from the self-contained teaching poems; the framing narrative that they illustrate has been eliminated, since these smaller jewels lend themselves more readily to excerption.

FURTHER READING: Attar, Farid ad-Din. *The Conference of the Birds.* Translated by A. Darbandi and D. Davis, 1984; *The Ilahi-Nama; or, Book of God of Farid al-Din 'Attar.* Translated by John A. Boyle, 1976; *Muslim Saints and Mystics: Episodes from the Tadhikirat Al-Auliya ("Memorial of the Saints").* Translated by A. J. Arberry, 1966; reprint, 1976. Rice, Cyprian. *The Persian Sufis,* 1964. Schimmel, Annemarie. *As Through a Veil: Mystical Poetry in Islam,* 1982.

## from *The Conference of the Birds*

### How Sheikh Abou Bakr's Self-satisfaction Was Reproved

Sheikh Abou Bakr of Neishapour one day
Led his disciples through a weary way.
His donkey carried him, aloof, apart—
And then the beast let out a monstrous fart!
The sheikh began to tear his clothes and cry                    5

Till one of his disciples asked him why.
The sheikh said: "When I looked I saw a sea
Of my disciples sworn to follow me;
They filled the roads and in my mind there slid
The thought: 'By God, I equal Bayazid![1]     *1*
So many praise me, can I doubt this sign
That heaven's boundless glories will be mine?'
Then as I triumphed in my inmost heart,
My donkey answered me—and with a fart;
My pompous, self-deceiving soul awoke,     *1*
And this is why I weep and tear my cloak."
How far away the truth remains while you
Are lost in praise for all you say and do—
Destroy your arrogance, and feed the fire
With that vain Self you foolishly admire.     *2*
You change your face each moment, but deep down
You are a Pharaoh and you wear his crown,
Whilst one small atom of this "you" survives
Hypocrisy enjoys a hundred lives.
If you put all your trust in "I" and "me"     *2*
You've chosen both worlds as your enemy—
But if you kill the Self, the darkest night
Will be illuminated with your light.
If you would flee from evil and its pain
Swear never to repeat this "I" again!     *3*

## A Drunkard Accuses a Drunkard

A sot became extremely drunk—his legs
And head sank listless, weighed by wine's thick dregs.
A sober neighbour put him in a sack
And took him homewards hoisted on his back.
Another drunk went stumbling by the first,
Who woke and stuck his head outside and cursed.
"Hey, you, you lousy dipsomaniac,"
He yelled as he was borne off in the sack,
"If you'd had fewer drinks, just two or three,
You would be walking now as well as me."     *1*
He saw the other's state but not his own,
And in this blindness he is not alone;
You cannot love, and this is why you seek
To find men vicious, or depraved, or weak—
If you could search for love and persevere     *1*
The sins of other men would disappear.

---

1. Bistami or Bayazid (Bistam, which was about halfway Rey and Neishapour, was his birthplace) was a famous ascetic associated with the "ecstatic" rather than the "sober" Sufi path. He died in 874 in Bistam.

## The Valley of Detachment

Next comes the Valley of Detachment; here
All claims, all lust for meaning disappear.
A wintry tempest blows with boisterous haste;
It scours the land and lays the valley waste —
The seven planets seem a fading spark,                                  5
The seven seas a pool, and heaven's arc
Is more like dust and death than paradise;
The seven burning hells freeze cold as ice.
More wonderful than this, a tiny ant
Is here far stronger than an elephant;                                 10
And, while a raven feeds, a caravan
Of countless souls will perish to a man.
A hundred thousand angels wept when light
Shone out in Adam and dispelled the night;
A hundred thousand drowning creatures died                            15
When Noah's ark rode out the rising tide;
For Abraham, as many gnats were sent
To humble Nimrod's vicious government;
As many children perished by the sword
Till Moses' sight was cleansed before the Lord;                       20
As many walked in wilful heresy
When Jesus saw Truth's hidden mystery;
As many souls endured their wretched fate
Before Mohammad rose to heaven's gate.
Here neither old nor new attempts prevail,                            25
And resolution is of no avail.
If you should see the world consumed in flame,
It is a dream compared to this, a game;
If thousands were to die here, they would be
One drop of dew absorbed within the sea;                              30
A hundred thousand fools would be as one
Brief atom's shadow in the blazing sun;
If all the stars and heavens came to grief,
They'd be the shedding of one withered leaf;
If all the worlds were swept away to hell,                            35
They'd be a crawling ant trapped down a well;
If earth and heaven were to pass away,
One grain of gravel would have gone astray;
If men and fiends were never seen again,
They'd vanish like a tiny splash of rain;                             40
And should they perish, broken by despair,
Think that some beast has lost a single hair;
If part and whole are wrecked and seen no more,
Think that the earth has lost a single straw;

And if the nine revolving heavens stop,                                    4
Think that the sea has lost a single drop.

## The Moths and the Flame

Moths gathered in a fluttering throng one night
To learn the truth about the candle's light,
And they decided one of them should go
To gather news of the elusive glow.
One flew till in the distance he discerned
A palace window where a candle burned—
And went no nearer; back again he flew
To tell the others what he thought he knew.
The mentor of the moths dismissed his claim,
Remarking: "He knows nothing of the flame."                                1(
A moth more eager than the one before
Set out and passed beyond the palace door.
He hovered in the aura of the fire,
A trembling blur of timorous desire,
Then headed back to say how far he'd been,                                 1
And how much he had undergone and seen.
The mentor said: "You do not bear the signs
Of one who's fathomed how the candle shines."
Another moth flew out—his dizzy flight
Turned to an ardent wooing of the light;                                   2(
He dipped and soared, and in his frenzied trance
Both Self and fire were mingled by his dance—
The flame engulfed his wing-tips, body, head;
His being glowed a fierce translucent red;
And when the mentor saw that sudden blaze,                                 2.
The moth's form lost within the glowing rays,
He said: "He knows, he knows the truth we seek,
That hidden truth of which we cannot speak."
To go beyond all knowledge is to find
That comprehension which eludes the mind,                                  3(
And you can never gain the longed-for goal
Until you first outsoar both flesh and soul;
But should one part remain, a single hair
Will drag you back and plunge you in despair—
No creature's Self can be admitted here,                                   3.
Where all identity must disappear.

## ■ Rumi (Jalal ad-Din Rumi) (1207–1273)
### *Persia/Turkey* (poems)

The *Mathnavi*, Rumi's epic-length verse collection of mystical stories
has been called the Quran of the Persians. His poetry was an inspiration

for Goethe, Gandhi recited his poems, and Hegel, who esteemed his poetry, also admired him as a major thinker. He was the founder of the Sufi sect called the Mavlavis, who are known as the Whirling Dervishes because of their ritual of ecstatic dance. Rumi's *Mathnavi* is the mystical Bible of the Sufis, which is itself the mystical branch of Islam. Sufism derives its name from *suf,* meaning wool, a material from which the robes of these mystics were woven. After Rabia the Mystic preached a doctrine of pure love, Sufism became a belief of transcendence in which stages of mysticism were delineated, and, through music, chanting, and dances, the subject sought self-abolition and an ecstatic union with God.

Jalal ad-Din Rumi was born in 1207 in Balkh in the Persian province of Khorasan, the son of a mystical theologian. His family was forced to flee during the Mongol invasion of central and western Asia and, after a decade of wandering through Persia, Iraq, Arabia, and Syria, settled in Anatolia, in Konya, the capital of the Seljuk empire. The region of Asia Minor, conquered from the Byzantines, was called Rum (Rome) in Turkish and Persian, and hence Jalal ad-Din became known as Rumi (literally, "the Roman"). "Jalal ad-Din" is an honorific meaning "majesty of religion." While in Konya, he married, took over his father's professorship, and became associated with a Sufi community. He became a sheik, or elder, and was given the title "Mevlana," meaning "our master," a name by which he is also known throughout the Middle East and India. It is also the etymological source of his sect, the Mavlavis.

In 1244, Rumi's life was changed when he met Shams ad-Din of Tabriz, who was destined to be the physical incarnation of his spiritual love and the specific source of much of his mystico-erotic poetry. After fifteen months, Shams disappeared and Rumi, heartbroken, wrote poems of desolate loss and abandonment by his God. Rumi traveled to Tabriz and Damascus, searching for his Sun (the meaning of Shams), but in vain. At last Rumi's son and Rumi's disciples went to Damascus and retrieved Shams, despite their disapproval of his master's attachment to him. A few months later, Shams disappeared again and was rumored to have been murdered, perhaps by Rumi's jealous disciples. Later, Rumi found mystical love for another man, a goldsmith named Salahoddin Zarkub, and his last lover was Hosamoddin Chelebi, who was his successor as leader of his Sufi sect. In addition to the *Mathnavi,* an epic of twenty-six thousand couplets, Rumi wrote a collection of lyrics entitled the *Divan of Shams of Tabriz,* containing about thirty thousand verses. Certainly, Rumi is one the world's major spiritual poets, a brother to the Spaniard Saint John of the Cross, the Indians Mirabai and Kabir, the Japanese Saigyo, and the Chinese Wang Wei. His poems wake us to a concealed union with each other and with God and, to use his words, open "a window . . . from one mind to another." At once ascetic and carnal, he celebrates drunkenness, erotic amazement, and disappearance into the mystical lover.

**FURTHER READING:** Arberry, A. J., tr. *Discourses of Rumi,* 1975; *More Tales from Masnavi,* 1963; *Mystical Poems of Rumi; First Selection, Poems 1–200,* 1968. Barks, Coleman, tr. *Delicious Laughter: Rambunctious Teaching Stories from the Mathnawi,* 1990. Barks, Coleman, and John Moyne, trs. *Open Secret: Versions of Rumi,* 1984; *This Longing: Poetry, Teaching Stories, and Selected Letters,* 1988. Bly, Robert, tr. *When Grapes Turn to Wine: Versions of Rumi,* 1986. Iqbal, Afzal. *The Life and Work of Muhammad Jalal-ud-Din Rumi,* 1974. Nicholson, Reynold A., tr. *Rumi, Poet and Mystic,* 1978; Chittick, William C., tr. *The Sufi Path of Love: The Spiritual Teachings of Rumi,* 1983.

## Love's Body

The moon and a batallion of stars came
and the sun, a lonely horseman, dissolved.

The moon lives beyond the night, beyond the day.
What eye can see him?

The sightless eye is a minaret.
How can it make out the bird on the minaret?

Sometimes the cloud in our heart is tight
because we love the moon.

Sometimes it falls away.
When you began to love your passion died

and though you had a thousand things to do,
you did nothing,

but since one day granite becomes a ruby,
it isn't lazy.

If in the market of love you see decapitated heads
hanging from butcher hooks,

don't run off. Come in. Look closely.
The dead are alive again.

TRANSLATED BY TONY BARNSTONE, WILLIS BARNSTONE,
AND REZA BARAHENI

## A New Promise

Last night I swore
my eyes
wouldn't leave your face
and I won't leave
though you hack me into chunks of meat
        with a sword.

No one else can cure me. I'm sick. You're gone.
Toss me into a bonfire.
If I let out one yelp I'm not a man.
I am dust. You raise me when you come.
When you've gone down the road, I collapse                    *10*
       again into dust.

TRANSLATED BY TONY BARNSTONE, WILLIS BARNSTONE,
AND REZA BARAHENI

## Caring for My Lover

Friends, last night I carefully watched my love
sleeping by a spring circled with eglantine.
The houris of paradise stood around him,
       their hands cupped together
between a tulip field and jasmines.
Wind tugged softly in his hair.                               *5*
His curls smelled of musk and ambergris.
Wind turned mad and tore the hair right off
       his face
like a flaming oil lamp in a gale.
From the beginning of this dream I told myself
       go slowly, wait
for the break into consciousness. Don't breathe.            *10*

TRANSLATED BY TONY BARNSTONE, WILLIS BARNSTONE,
AND REZA BARAHENI

## The New Rule

It's the old rule that drunks have to argue
and get into fights.
The lover is just as bad: He falls into a hole.
But down in that hole he finds something shining,
worth more than any amount of money or power.               *5*

Last night the moon came dropping its clothes in the street.
I took it as a sign to start singing,
falling up into the bowl of sky.
The bowl breaks. Everywhere is falling everywhere.
Nothing else to do.                                         *10*

Here's the new rule: Break the wineglass,
and fall toward the glassblower's breath.

TRANSLATED BY JOHN MOYNE AND COLEMAN BARKS

## The Clear Bead at the Center

The clear bead at the center changes everything.
There are no edges to my loving now.

I've heard it said there's a window that opens
from one mind to another,

but if there's no wall, there's no need
for fitting the window, or the latch.

TRANSLATED BY JOHN MOYNE AND COLEMAN BARKS

## Someone Who Goes with Half a Loaf of Bread

Someone who goes with half a loaf of bread
to a small place that fits like a nest around him,
someone who wants no more, who's not himself
longed for by anyone else,

He is a letter to everyone. You open it.
It says, *Live.*

TRANSLATED BY JOHN MOYNE AND COLEMAN BARKS

## Who Says Words with My Mouth

All day I think about it, then at night I say it.
Where did I come from, and what am I supposed to be doing?
I have no idea.
My soul is from elsewhere, I'm sure of that,
and I intend to end up there.

This drunkenness began in some other tavern.
When I get back around to that place,
I'll be completely sober. Meanwhile,
I'm like a bird from another continent, sitting in this aviary.

The day is coming when I fly off, 10
but who is it now in my ear, who hears my voice?
Who says words with my mouth?

Who looks out with my eyes? What is the soul?
I cannot stop asking.
If I could taste one sip of an answer, 15
I could break out of this prison for drunks.
I didn't come here of my own accord, and I can't leave that way.
Whoever brought me here will have to take me back.

This poetry. I never know what I'm going to say.
I don't plan it. 20
When I'm outside the saying of it,
I get very quiet and rarely speak at all.

TRANSLATED BY JOHN MOYNE AND COLEMAN BARKS

■ Sadi (1184–1292) *Persia* (prose and poems)

TRANSLATED BY PIERRE GRANGE

Sadi was born in Shiraz in 1184 and fled the Mongol invaders to Baghdad, where he studied at the Nizamiya college. After leaving college, he lived the life of a dervish, roving throughout the Middle East and making several pilgrimages to Mecca. In 1256, he returned to Shiraz and devoted himself to a literary life, achieving great fame in his own lifetime. He wrote many lyric *ghazals* and longer, laudatory *qasidas,* but he is best known for his *mathnavi* verse epic the *Bustan* or *The Scented Garden* and the mixed prose and poetry *Gulistan* or *The Rose Garden,* parts of which are presented here. He also wrote absurd and obscene verses, or *hazaliyat.* The moral lessons of his delightful teaching tales make him a "philosopher of common sense" whose work treats questions of overeating and flatulence, homosexual and heterosexual love, puberty, spitefulness, and ways to divide your enemies to conquer them. Yet, despite his profane subject matter, his work is infused with a deeper Islamic mysticism that teaches how to live and love in the world as an ethical person. His *Gulistan* has been translated into many languages, including Turkish as early as the fourteenth century, and it is the first book read in Persian classes throughout the Middle East. Emerson considered the *Gulistan* one of the world's bibles, and it has won the admiration of Voltaire, Benjamin Franklin, and Edwin Arnold, among other Western luminaries. In fact, Franklin successfully passed off one of its parables as a missing chapter of Genesis as a practical joke.

**FURTHER READING:** Arberry, A. J., tr. *Kings and Beggars: the First Two Chapters of Sa'di's Gulistan,* 1945. Clarke, H. Wilberforce, tr. *The Bustan by Shaikh Muslihu-d-din*

*Sa'di Shirazi: Translated for the First Time into Prose,* 1985. Levy, Reuben. *An Introduction to Persian Literature,* 1969. Nakosteen, Mehdi, tr. *The Maxims of Sa'di: Selected Translations,* 2nd ed., 1977. Rehatsek, Edward, tr. *The Gulistan, or Rose Garden, of Sa'di,* 1965. Wickens, G. M., tr. *Morals Pointed and Tales Adorned: The Bustan of Sa'di,* 1974.

## The Rose Garden

# Chapter I: The Manners of Kings

### STORY 2

One of the Kings of Khorasan, in Afghanistan, saw in a dream a vision of the Sultan Mahmud, one hundred years dead. Though his body had dissolved and become dust, the eyes still rotated in their sockets and gazed around him. None of the sultan's sages could interpret this vision, with the exception of one dervish, who bowed and stated, "His eyes still gaze about in amazement, to see his kingdom in the hands of others."

> Many famous kings are beneath the soil.
> Above ground, no trace of them remains.
> An old corpse given to earth
> is so eaten by soil that not even a bone is left.
> But the glorious name of Nushirvan survives untarnished
> though he's been dead so long.
> Do only good since life's a gift
> that will cease like a shout leaving the throat.

### STORY 7

Once a king and a Persian slave were seated in the same ship. The slave had never before seen the sea, nor experienced the troubles of sailing, and soon began to moan and weep and to tremble from head to foot. No one could calm him. The king was becoming increasingly irate at this disturbance, but no one could figure out what to do to bring the slave to his senses. There was, though, a philosopher on board who claimed to have the solution. The king responded, "I would consider it a great favor." The philosopher ordered the slave tossed into the salt sea, where he floundered and swallowed great mouthfuls of water. Then a crewmember grabbed him by the hair and dragged him back to the ship, whereupon the slave grabbed hold of the rudder and clung there until they pulled him aboard again. Once back in the ship, the slave sat meekly in a corner and stayed absolutely quiet. The king was amazed by the success of this experiment, and asked "What was the secret behind this thing?" The philosopher responded, "Before tasting the agony of being drowned, he didn't know the safety of the ship. In the same way, a man does not appreciate the value of freedom from misfortune until calamity hits."

> If you're gorged, you scorn barley bread;
> she who you think is ugly is my lover!
> To the houris of paradise, purgatory seems Hell;
> but those in hell would think purgatory Heaven.

> How different is the man who holds his lover
> from the one whose eyes rest expectantly on the door.

### from STORY 12

A cruel king asked a religious man what the best form of devotion would be. He replied, "For you to sleep till noon so you don't harm your people for a while."

### STORY 31

The vizers of Nushirvan were debating a matter of state, and each one gave his opinion based on what he knew. The king also gave his opinion, and Barzachumihr adopted the same point of view. Taking him aside in private, the vizers asked him "What did you discover in the king's opinion to judge it superior to that of so many sage men?" Barzachumihr replied, "Because the outcome of this affair remains unknown, and since it depends upon God's will whether our opinions will turn out to be right or wrong, it was better to conform to the king's opinion. That way, even if it turns out he is wrong, he cannot blame us without blaming himself!"

> Disagree with a king
> and you wash your hands in your own blood.
> Should he say in daylight, "It is night"
> you must shout "I can see the moon and the Pleiades!"

## Chapter II: The Morals of Dervishes

### from STORY 8

> To the world I appear beautiful
> but my inner sins bow my head with shame;
> people praise the peacock for his magnificent colors
> while he is ashamed of his ugly feet.

### from STORY 19

> When rust has bitten into steel
> no polishing will remove it.

Don't bother preaching to the corrupt;
an iron nail can't pierce a stone.

## STORY 31

There was a man who, afflicted by a powerful tempest in his belly, and lacking the strength to restrain it, allowed it to escape. He exclaimed, "O friends, forgive me! I had no choice in what has happened, and so no fault should fall upon me. Besides, I feel much better now."

Wind rustles in the dungeon of the belly
but no sage can keep the wind chained.
If wind whirls in your belly, let it free
because a storm in the belly afflicts the heart.

# Chapter III: The Fruits of Contentment

## STORY 6

It is said that King Ardeshir Babekan, first king of the Persian Sasanian dynasty (reigned A.D. 226-240), once asked an Arabic physician how much food he should eat each day. The physician answered, "A hundred dirhams of food would be enough." The king asked, "And what strength of body will this amount give me?" The doctor retorted, "This is enough to carry you, and if you eat any more you will have to carry it!"

We eat to live so we may praise God,
but you think we live to eat!

# Chapter IV: The Advantages of Holding Your Tongue

## from STORY 14

A fellow with an annoying voice was reading the Quran one day in a braying loud tone. A holy man passed by and inquired of him what his monthly wage happened to be for reading. The man replied, "Nothing at all." "Why, then," continued the sage, "do you take the trouble?" He replied, "I am reading for the sake of God." The holy man returned, "For God's sake, stop reading!"

# Chapter V: Love and Youth

## STORY 10

In the fire of my youth I had a lover with a sweet voice and a body beautiful as the moon just rising on the horizon.

To see his new beard is to live forever,
to see his sugar lips is to eat candy.

However, one day I found something unnatural in how he behaved, and
we had a fight. Now disapproving of my lover, I took my gown away from
him and abandoned the chess game of our friendship. I said to him:

Go do what you want.
You're not in my heart, so follow your own.

As he left me I heard him sing out,

If the bat doesn't want to join with the sun
the sun is no less beautiful.

After he left I fell into a deep despair.

The time of our union is gone, I knew nothing
of its value and delight until it had departed.

Come back! Kill me! Even to die with you
is better than living without you.

God is great, and through his mercy my lover came back to me after some
time. Now, however, my lover's sweet voice had gone harsh, his beauty
which had rivaled that of Joseph had dissipated, there was dust on the apple of his skin, and all of his marvelous grace had abandoned him. He
came up to me to take me in his arms and I let him, saying,

When you had your first wonderful growth of beard
you drove out of sight the one who lusted for that sight.
Today you are here to reconcile with him
but your beard shows straight I's and coiled S's,
you have turned yellow, and your fresh spring is exhausted.
Put away that kettle! There's no fire between us.
You strut about proudly
thinking of joys that have died.
Leave me! Go to someone who will buy your body,
flirt with someone who desires you.

It's said that green in a garden is pleasant
and I know this as I say these words
since the fresh grass of a moustache
mesmerizes lovers' hearts without end.
But your garden is a bed of weeds,
and the more you weed it, the more it grows.

You can pluck your beard all you want
but your happy youth is over.
If my life were as strong as your beard
I wouldn't die till resurrection day.
I asked, "What's happened to your beautiful face?
Ants are crawling on its moon."
He responded with a smile, "I don't know exactly.
Maybe it wears black to mourn my dead beauty."

## Chapter VI: Weakness and Decrepitude

*from* STORY 2

When a woman rises frustrated from bed
she'll raise no end of trouble
An old man can't arise without a stick,
so how can his stick arise?

Though you're quick tempered and beat me
I'll do anything for your beauty;
I'd rather be with you in Hell
than in a Heaven of old men.

## Chapter VII: Education

It is written in the compositions of the philosophers that scorpions are not born like other animals, but that they devour the entrails of their mothers, eat through the belly, and scatter into the desert. The skins that can be found in scorpion holes are the vestiges of this process. I told this story to a great man, who responded, "My heart can bear witness to the truth of this tale, for it couldn't be any other way: since they behave this way to their parents in infancy, they are loved and respected in the same way when they grow old."

## Chapter VIII: Society and Duty

**MAXIM 80**

What can an old whore do but give up sex, and a fired policeman do but give up oppression?

A young man who sits in the corner in prayer is a hero,
because an old man cannot even rise from his corner.

In youth it's difficult to squelch desire,
but when old it's more difficult to make your tool rise.

## *from* The Conclusion to the Book

All praise to God by whose grace this book is ended
before my own life has reached its conclusion.

## ■ Hafiz (Khajeh Shamsoddin Mohammad Hafez-e Shirazi) (c. 1320–1390) *Persia* (poems)

Hafiz is considered the finest lyric poet of the Persian language. He was born in great poverty in Shiraz around A.D. 1320. His pen name, Hafiz, is the epithet given to one who has learned the Quran by heart. He seems to have been familiar with the science of his day as well. Though he stayed in his native Shiraz, he became famous throughout Persia, the Near East, and India, and the Sultan of Baghdad and the Sultan of Bengal invited him to their courts. He specialized in the *ghazal,* or lyric ode, consisting of around six to fifteen rhymed couplets; in the final couplet, the poet usually addresses himself by name, in the third person.

After the death of his father, a merchant of moderate means from Isfahan, when Hafiz was young, the family seems to have lived a penurious existence. Until his poems won him fame and patronage, Hafiz lived as a scribe, a teacher, and perhaps a baker's apprentice. He was patronized by several shahs and wrote religious commentaries, but his poetry celebrates wine, women, and young men as much as mysticism. For some reason, he seems to have been banished from Shiraz for six years (1368–1374). Perhaps the Shah Shoja, who was his drinking companion, became jealous of Hafiz's superior poetry; perhaps the priesthood plotted against him as a famous freethinker and sensualist. While in exile, he met Dordane, the woman he celebrates in his poems, though no historical record of her remains. It is important to note, however, that the beloved in his poems is often male, the conventional figure of Beauty as a beautiful youth. Often the gender gets switched in the process of translation.

Hafiz's highly romantic, mystical poetry attracted an appreciative Western audience from the seventeenth century through the early twentieth century. He was a favorite of Goethe's and was translated into Latin, French, English, German, and Greek. However, he has been relatively ignored in the West for the past several decades. Emerson said of Hafiz, "He sees too far; he sees throughout; such is the only man I wish to see or be," while Goethe wrote, "Hafiz has no peer!" He was called the "Tongue of the Hidden," suggesting that his work gives vent to hidden mystical concepts, perhaps in hidden ways, but there is conflict between those who interpret his poems as Sufi mysticism, in which the Beloved stands for God, and those who see his work as sensual in nature, in which case the Beloved is a human lover. Perhaps, like William Blake, Hafiz discovered a marriage of these two opposites (Goethe has suggested as much). It is true that one critic believes him to have been part of the Malamatiyye Sufi sect, whose members behaved like beggars and drunkards. Certainly the Sufi trope of the worshiper annihilating him- or herself in God like a moth into a flame appears again and again in his verse. There is also evidence, in poems such as "The Body's Cup," that the drinking of wine is to be seen as a mystical intoxication, and that the tavern becomes a kind of temple. Peter Avery and John Health-Stubbs suggest that the imbibing of wine in Hafiz's poetry is to be understood as drinking from the magical cup of Jamshid, a hero of Ferdowsi's *Shahnama,* in which "His cup reflects the whole world in its depths, and confers all knowledge on him who drinks of it."[1]

FURTHER READING: Aryanpur, A., tr. *Poetical Horoscope or Odes,* 1965. Avery, Paul, and John Heath-Stubbs, trs. *Hafiz of Shiraz: Thirty Poems Translated,* 1952. Bell, G., tr. *Poems from the Divan,* 1928. Smith, Paul, tr. *Toyve of the Midden: Poems from the Divan,* 1986. Street, C. K., tr. *Hafiz in Quatrains,* 1946.

## The Body's Cup

Last night I saw angels knocking at the tavern door;
they shaped and cast a winecup from Adam's clay,

and I was drunk with potent wine poured
by ascetic angels who dwell behind the sacred veil.

The sky couldn't bear that burden of love alone,
so they cast the dice and my poor name came up.

Seventy-two sects bicker over fairy tales;
forgive them, they don't know the truth.

Thank you God for making peace with me;
the Sufis dance and raise their cups to you.

The candle laughs flame, but the true fire
harvests bodies of countless ecstatic moths.

The brides of poetry have combed my hair.
Only Hafiz has ripped the veil from wisdom's face.

TRANSLATED BY TONY BARNSTONE

## The Sickle

I see the new moon's sickle slicing
through the sky's green field
and think of what I've sown
and of the coming harvest.

---

1. Peter Avery, and John Heath-Stubbs. *Hafiz of Shiraz: Thirty Poems Translated* (London: Jon Murray, 1952), 7.

"Fortune, you've overslept," I say,                                          5
"the sun is already high."
But he replies "Don't worry
about the past;
if like the Messiah you rise
pure and bodiless into the sky,                                             10
your light will illuminate the sun.
Don't rely on that night thief the moon,
he stole Kay Kaus's crown and Kay Khusrau's belt;
though gold and rubies
hang from your ear,                                                         15
hear this advice
before your beauty passes.
May the evil eye
not gaze on your beauty mark,
for that mole like a pawn                                                   20
on heaven's chessboard
holds sun and moon in check.
Let the sky not boast
of its beautiful harvest
for a lover would trade the halo                                           25
of the moon for a barleycorn
and all the Pleiades for two.
As to the harvest of religion,
hypocrisy scorches it like wildfire.
So Hafiz, toss on your woolen cloak                                         30
and leave this place."

TRANSLATED BY TONY BARNSTONE

## Love's Journey

Boy, bring me a cup of wine and make it quick;
love seemed easy at first but trouble followed.
I can still smell his musky hair twisting
on the wind; it clots my heart.

In this caravansary I can't rest long;                                      5
the trader's bells are always calling me to move on.
Listen to the wise man even if he says to stain
        your prayer mat with wine;
that adept traveler understands the way.

My life is whirlpools, waves and tarry night;                              10
what do people on shore know of me? Nothing.

Yet my selfish lust has made me infamous;
my secrets are the latest juicy gossip.

Hafiz, don't renounce your lover's bed;
love him and forget the world instead.

TRANSLATED BY TONY BARNSTONE

# Modern Arabic, Hebrew, Turkish, Alexandrian Greek, and Persian Literatures

## INTRODUCTION

The modern period in the Near East and North Africa has been marked by European imperialism, the resistance to colonial power, revolutionary movements, and ethnic and religious conflicts within and between nations. At the turn of the nineteenth century, the French moved into Egypt, where they stayed until the British forced them out in the 1880s. Britain and Russia fought over Iran and Afghanistan, as the British strove to attain a secure land route to their colonial possessions in India. The French extended their economic influence into Lebanon and Syria, and the Germans created close economic and military ties with the Turkish Ottoman Empire. North Africa largely lost its independence in the imperialist frenzy of the late nineteenth century. Conflict between the European colonial powers over their African, North African, and Near Eastern holdings helped set the stage for World War I. The soldiers of the massive Ottoman Empire fought on the side of Germany against the British, who were aided by Arabic forces marshaled by Lawrence of Arabia. After World War I, anticolonial movements, nationalism, and at times armed resistance to European imperialism developed in North Africa, fueled by a widespread resurgence of Islamic culture and ideals, and by resistance to Christianity, which had become associated with the imperialist conquerors. Much of the Middle East had been under the dominion of the Ottoman Empire, which had spread rapidly from the fourteenth to the sixteenth centuries over Egypt, Persia, Mesopotamia, Arabia, Byzantium, Syria, Palestine, parts of North Africa, and large parts of southeastern Europe. After the late seventeenth century, however, the empire began to collapse in on itself and by the nineteenth century it was known as the "Sick Man of Europe." Its demise as an empire took place at the conclusion of World War I. The history of the modern Middle East and North Africa is in great part the history of the dissolution of the Ottoman Empire and the creation of newly independent states. The demise of the remnants of European colonial empires in the Middle East and North Africa took place in the years following World War II.

Egypt has been a marker of many of the essential political changes that the Bridge area has seen in our time. A brief look at its modern history will reflect a larger picture of the Near East and North Africa, the foreign occupations and humiliations, the revolutions and birth of new states. After dealing with French, Turkish, and British occupiers, an autonomous Egypt under Khedive Ismail Pasha built the Suez Canal. However, by 1875, in severe debt from overspending, the Egyptian leader was forced to sell the canal to the British and accept the establishment of a French-English Debt Commission. In 1881, Ismail's son rebelled against English interference, which prompted the landing of British troops and the country became a British protectorate. Egypt won back much of her independence from Britain in 1923, except for the Suez Canal, which remained in British hands. The Egyptians also were compelled to share with the British the Sudan, which had been a booty from an earlier Egyptian imperial conquest. In addition, Britain retained extraterritorial rights to station troops in parts of Egypt, a privilege that lasted until 1949. In the years following World War II, there was a substantial influx to Palestine of Jewish survivors of the Holocaust in Europe, which was a continuation of earlier immigration in the 1930s, with the purpose of realizing the late nineteenth-century Zionist movement to establish a Jewish homeland in the area. The Arabic population resisted this movement, leading to widespread violence and instability in the region. Concern over this conflict, and international sentiment over the massacre of approximately six million Jews by the Nazis, helped to catalyze a compromise settlement by the United Nations. In this 1947 settlement, the United Nations partitioned Palestine into a Jewish state, Israel (inhibited both by Jews and Arabs), and an Arabic state, Palestine, and ended the British mandate over the territory. Although there had always been a Jewish presence in the area (descendants from ancient communities in Israel, Iraq, Iran, Egypt, Yemen, and Libya), the Arab states did not accept what they saw as another European intrusion. As the British withdrew from the region in 1948, war broke out, and Israel was invaded by a coalition of surrounding Arab nations. As a result of the war, many Arabs were forced to leave Israel, and Jews were expelled from their homes in Arabic nations. The Arabic nations were defeated in the 1948 war, and the nascent Arab state of Palestine disappeared when Jordan (which had not recognized the validity of either Israel or Palestine) annexed East Jerusalem and the West Bank, and Egypt occupied the Gaza Strip. Israel also expanded as a result of the war, and it grew even more as a consequence of the later 1967 war. This history of frequent warfare (there have been five wars between Israel and its neighbors since Israel's founding), of dispute over territory, and of the dual diaspora of Arabs and Jews, has been the source of continuing embittered contention to this day. However, in 1977, Anwar Sadat, the president of Egypt, surprised the world with a peace initiative, and in 1979, Egypt and Israel formalized a peace treaty. Recent events have somewhat quieted the region with further rapprochement between Israel and Arab nations, and difficult negotiations between Israel and the Palestine Liberation Organization over the establishment of a Palestinian state.

Earlier in Egypt, under the military governments of General Muhammad Naguib, the monarchy was overthrown and abolished in 1953 and, under pressure from President Gamal Abdal Nasser, the English evacuated Suez in 1956. Egypt was finally free of foreign rule. That same year the huge Sudan announced its independence from Egyptian and British rule. Soon after, northern Muslim Sudan began an intermittent war with southern Christian Sudan, a terrible religious and ethnic battle that continues to this day.

Now, the process of overturning monarchies, which had begun in Turkey in the 1920s, spread and soon the monarchs and their retinues fled from Iraq, Iran, and Libya. In Saudi Arabia, Jordan, Morocco, and in small oil sheikdoms of the Arabian peninsula, they remained. After a devastating war of independence by Algerians against the French, Algeria achieved independence in 1962. The last of the imperialists went home, and colonial rule formally disappeared from this huge basis of ancient and modern civilization.

The political history of these regions has necessarily permeated the cultural life of each country. While Kemal Attaturk (1881–1938) was abolishing the Turkish sultanate (1922) and religious caliphate (1924), turning Turkey into a secular republic, social poets arose to add their word about further reform. The greatest poet of Turkey was Nazim Hikmet (1902–1963), a man who spent most of his adult life in prison as a Communist critic to each regime and a magnificent poet of solitude, prison, love, and everyday miseries and glories. In recent years, Turkey has produced many novelists and poets who are entering the world scene.

In Egypt are two great writers, the poet Constantine Cavafy (1873–1933), who wrote in Modern Greek, the language of his native Alexandria, and the novelist Naguib Mahfouz (1911– ), who has emerged as the foremost fiction writer in the Arabic language. In Syria, Iraq, Palestine, Jordan, Egypt, and Algeria, there have been remarkable new talents in poetry as well as the novel, and Israel has likewise seen a flourishing in the arts, including the fiction of Nobel Prize–winning novelist S. Y. Agnon. Other important modern writers of the Bridge area include Yashar Kemal (1922– ) in Turkey, and the extraordinary feminist poet Forugh Farokhzad (1935–1967) of Iran, who, like Sylvia Plath, died in her thirty-second year. After 1200 in Spain and 1300 in the East, there was a decline in Arabic writing, but in the nineteenth and twentieth centuries, there has been a resurgence of Arabic literatures exemplified by outstanding poets, like Adunis (1930– ) and Mahmud Darwish (1942– ), and novelists such as Naguib Mahfouz, winner of the 1988 Nobel Prize for Literature.

Similarly, Hebrew literature of the Bridge area—except for a flowering in Muslim Spain in poetry, philosophy, and mystical Kabbalah—was largely dormant after the biblical period. The diaspora Jews, spread around the world, usually wrote in the languages spoken in their adopted nations, and their work was assimilated into the literatures of their habitation. The Spanish-Portuguese philosopher Spinoza, living in Holland in safe exile from the Spanish Inquisition, wrote in Latin. Moses Mendelssohn, Karl Marx, Heinrich Heine, and Franz Kafka wrote in German, Primo Levi in Italian. Osip Mandelstam, Boris Pasternak, and Isaac Babel wrote in Russian. Sholom Aleichem and Isaac Bashevis Singer wrote in Yiddish, and Benjamin Disraeli, Saul Bellow, and many others wrote in English. But Hebrew took on new life as the diaspora Jews in Israel once again adopted biblical Hebrew as their literary language. Major Israeli writers include the poets Yehudah Amichai (1924– ) and Dan Pagis (1930–1986) and many outstanding novelists, who have been translated into the world's languages.

The English and French were the main colonial powers of the Near East and North Africa. By the second decade after World War II, Europe had withdrawn its political hegemony over the region, and so the English were gone from Iraq, Palestine, Jordan, Israel, the Arabian Peninsula, Egypt, and the Suez Canal, and the French from Lebanon, Tunisia, Libya, Algeria, and Morocco. But in many countries, English and French have remained not only as a *lingua franca* for purposes of commerce and travel, but as the literary language of writers in Lebanon and especially in Algeria. There, despite the intense war of independence against the French, many of the leading novelists have chosen to write in French in order to reach a global audience. But apart from the Algerians, Lebanese, and a few Egyptians who write in English or French, the writers of Asia Minor and North Africa largely continue to use their ancient tongues, Persian, Arabic, Turkish, Berber, and Hebrew, as the vehicle for verbal expression. They write in languages that still have an ancient memory and a modern historical vitality.

These modern writers often confront and absorb colonial experience and Western influence, as well as their own ancient traditions. The West itself, which owes so much of its philosophy, religion, and literature to western Asia and North Africa, has usually been an unacknowledging child, but our parents and their enormous surviving work continue to be read. With the increasing availability of fine translations, we are persuaded both to return to our historic and cultural progenitors and to hear the new voices that echo deeply today.

## ■ Traditional Song (from uncertain period) *Algeria*

### TRANSLATED BY WILLIS BARNSTONE

The old *haufi* traditional women's songs of Algeria were recorded in our century by Mostefa Lacheraf. They deal with many themes, including love, desert and garden landscapes of Algeria, and in this instance family social criticism, which is handled through the comic insult poem.

**FURTHER READING:** Lacheraf, Mostefa. *Écrits didactiques sur la culture, l'histoire et la societé en Algerie*, 1988.

## Be Happy

> Be happy for me, girls,
> my mother-in-law is dead!
> In the morning I found her
> stiff, her mouth shut.
> Yet I won't believe it                                   5
> till I see the grass
> waving over her tomb.

## ▣ Constantine Cavafy (1863–1933) *Alexandria, Egypt* (poems)

Constantine Cavafy was born in Alexandria, Egypt, to a family originally from Constantinople. From the age of nine to age sixteen, Cavafy was in England with his family, where he acquired English and a love for English literature. From 1882 to 1885, he lived in Constantinople and, thereafter, remained in Alexandria, where for thirty years he worked as a clerk and ultimately as assistant director in the irrigation section of the Ministry of Public Works. Alexandria, founded by Alexander the Great in 332 B.C., was a cosmopolitan city of Greek-speaking and Arabic-speaking inhabitants. Except for a few trips to Athens, Cavafy stayed in Alexandria, writing his poems, ordering them in an intended final canon, publishing a few of them privately, and gathering a secret major reputation in continental Greece and abroad. E. M. Forster was a great believer and carrier of his word.

Although he is considered the greatest modern poet in the Greek language—a language that has given us, among other poets, two Nobel Prize laureates, George Seferis and Odysseus Elytis—Cavafy did not formally publish a book during his lifetime. Rather, he had pamphlets printed, containing a few poems. Forster, who lived in Alexandria for five years, proclaimed his originality and quality in England, where T. S. Eliot published "Ithaka" in his magazine *Criterion*. Eschewing turn-of-the-century sentimentality, Cavafy was, before others, a modernist, whose work is characterized by a straightforwardness about homosexual themes, and by a deep interest in classical mythology. Cavafy's myth, in which his personal obsessions and ideals were realized, was Alexandria, the city of Neoplatonists and mystery religions, of geometers and grammarians—the diverse Hellenic world bound together by the Mouseion, an extraordinary library-university. His myth also included Roman settlements and Byzantine Greece of Asia Minor, as well as the color, shadows, intrigues, and anti-history of high and low life, of patriarchs and emperors and their jealous plotting relatives in Constantinople. When he wrote of everyday life in the Alexandria of his own period, it was of illicit, erotic encounters and their splendors, memories, and regrets; sordid and cheap rooms, where one heard voices from the workers playing cards in the suspect taverna downstairs, where in his plain bed he was drunk with love; of how a pencil sketch of a sensitive friend done on a ship evokes an afternoon on a ship, long ago, out of time, out of time, that his soul brings back to him. The pessimism, idealism, realism, historical recreations, and allegories in "Waiting for the Barbarians," "The City," "The God Abandons Antony," and "Ithaka" place these poems permanently in the world canon of literature. The South African novelist J. M. Coetzee chose "Waiting for the Barbarians" as the title for his great novel and effectively translated the poem into the mood and lesson of his entire work.

T. S. Eliot and Ezra Pound radically changed modern literature by their ventures into antiquity, and it is increasingly clear that their model was Cavafy. Yet, while Eliot and Pound explored history and myth through literature and anthropology and recreated a past that remained exotically remote, Cavafy was a participant in his histories and myths and created ancient history indistinguishable from the present—as would later Greek poets George Seferis and Yannis Ritsos in their distinguished imitations of his work. For Cavafy, Greece is all times, and he lives in them through his personal participatory creations. Cavafy, Pablo Neruda, and Rainer Maria Rilke are today probably the most translated poets in all languages. The obscure Alexandrian, a word-of-mouth myth during his lifetime, has become an icon for our century.

**FURTHER READING:** Bien, Peter. *Constantine Cavafy,* 1964. Cavafy, Constantine. *Collected Poems.* Translated by Edmund Keeley and Philip Sherrard, 1975; *The Complete Poems of Cavafy.* Translated by Rae Dalven, 1961. Keeley, Edmund. *Cavafy's Alexandria: A Study of Myth in Progress,* 1976.

## The Windows

In these shadowy rooms where I spend
boring days, I walk up down and around
to find the windows. When a window opens
it will be a consolation.
But the windows are unfindable or I can't                          5
find them. And perhaps it is better not to find them.
Perhaps the light will be a new tyranny.
Who knows what new things it will disclose?

TRANSLATED BY ALIKI BARNSTONE AND WILLIS BARNSTONE

## An Old Man

Back in a corner, alone in the clatter and babble
An old man sits with his head bent over a table
And his newspaper in front of him, in the cafe.

Sour with old age, he ponders a dreary truth—
How little he enjoyed the years when he had youth,
Good looks and strength and clever things to say.

He knows he's quite old now: he feels it, he sees it,
And yet the time when he was young seems—was it?
Yesterday. How quickly, how quickly it slipped away.

Now he sees how Discretion has betrayed him,
And how stupidly he let the liar persuade him
With phrases: *Tomorrow. There's plenty of time. Some day.*

He recalls the pull of impulses he suppressed,
The joy he sacrificed. Every chance he lost
Ridicules his brainless prudence a different way.

But all these thoughts and memories have made
The old man dizzy. He falls asleep, his head
Resting on the table in the noisy cafe.

TRANSLATED BY ROBERT PINSKY

## Walls

Without concern or pity or shame,
they have built wide and tall walls around me,

and now I sit here and despair,
thinking of nothing else. This fate eats me up.

I had so much to do outside.
When they were putting up the walls, how could I
 have been blind!

I never heard the noise. No sound of builders.
Imperceptibly they closed me off from the world.

TRANSLATED BY TONY BARNSTONE AND WILLIS BARNSTONE

## He Swears

He swears now and then to start a better life.
But when life comes with its own counsel,

its own compromises and promises,
when night comes with its own compulsion
of the body that wants and demands,                                    *5*
he returns, lost, to the same fatal joy.

TRANSLATED BY WILLIS BARNSTONE

## Desires

Like beautiful bodies that haven't aged
and were locked, with tears, in a brilliant mausoleum,
with roses at the head and jasmine at the feet,
that is what desires look like when they pass by
without having been fulfilled, without even                            *5*
a single night of passion, or a moon at dawn.

TRANSLATED BY ALIKI BARNSTONE AND WILLIS BARNSTONE

## The City

You said, "I will go to another city, go to another sea,
find another city better than this one.
Whatever I try to do is fated to go wrong
and my heart lies buried as if it were dead.
How long will my mind linger in this marasma?                          *5*
Wherever my eye wanders, wherever I look,
I see black ruins of my life, here
where I've spent so many years and wasted them
and destroyed them."

You won't find a new country, won't find another sea.                  *10*
The city will pursue you. You will walk
the same streets. In the same neighborhood you will grow old
and in the same houses you'll turn gray.
You will always end up in the same city.
Don't hope for things elsewhere.                                       *15*
There is no ship for you, there is no road.
As you have wasted your life here
in this small corner, you have destroyed it all over the earth.

TRANSLATED BY WILLIS BARNSTONE

## The Afternoon Sun

This room, how well I know it.
Now they're renting it and the one next door
as business offices. The whole house has become
an office building for agents, merchants, companies.

This room, how familiar it is.

Here near the door was the couch,
and a Turkish carpet in front of it.
Close by, the shelf with two yellow vases.
To the right—no, opposite—a wardrobe with a mirror.
In the middle the table where he wrote,                          *1*
and the three big wicker chairs.
Next to the window was the bed
where we made love so many times.

They must still be around somewhere, those other things.

Beside the window was the bed;                                   *1*
the afternoon sun fell half across it.

One afternoon at four o'clock we separated
for only a week . . . And then
that week became forever.

TRANSLATED BY WILLIS BARNSTONE

## Morning Sea

Let me stop here. Let me too look at nature awhile.
The glowing blue of the morning sea
and cloudless sky and yellow shore, all
beautiful and brightly lighted.

Let me stop here. Let me pretend I see this
(I really did see it for a second when I first stopped)
and not the usual daydreams here too,
my memories, the images of the body's pleasure.

TRANSLATED BY WILLIS BARNSTONE

## Manuel Komminós

One melancholy day in September
Emperor Manuel Komminós

felt his death was near. The astronomers
(paid off, of course) went on babbling                                    5
about how many years he still had to live.
But while they were talking, he
remembered an old religious custom
and ordered ecclesiastical vestments
to be brought from a monastery,
and he wore them, pleased to assume                                       10
the modest image of a priest or monk.

Happy are all those who believe,
and like Emperor Manuel leave this world
dressed modestly in their faith.

TRANSLATED BY WILLIS BARNSTONE

## Since Nine O'Clock

Half past twelve. Time has gone by quickly
from nine o'clock when I lit the lamp,
and sat down here. I've been sitting without reading
without speaking. Whom could I talk to
all alone in this house?                                                  5

Since nine when I lit the lamp
the image of my young body
came and took me and reminded me
of closed aromatic rooms
and past sensual pleasure—what daring pleasure!                           10
And it also brought back to my eyes
streets now unrecognizable,
bustling crowded night clubs closed down,
and theaters and cafes that once were.

The image of my young body                                                15
came and brought me the sad things too:
family grief, separations,
feelings of my own people, feelings
of the dead so little acknowledged.

Half past twelve. How time has gone by.                                   20
Half past twelve. How the years have gone by.

TRANSLATED BY WILLIS BARNSTONE

## *Waiting for the Barbarians*

What are we waiting for, assembled in the forum?

> The barbarians are coming today.

Why is nothing happening in the senate?
Why are senators sitting there without making laws?

> Because the barbarians are coming today.
> What laws can the senators make now?
> When the barbarians come, they make the laws.

Why did our emperor get up so early
and sit at the city's main gate,
on his throne, in state, wearing his crown?

> Because the barbarians are coming today
> and the emperor is waiting to receive
> their leader. Yes, he is preparing
> to give him a pergamon scroll. He has
> inscribed it with many titles and names.

Why have our two consuls and praetors come out
today in red robes, in embroidered togas?
Why have they put on bracelets with so many amethysts,
and rings glittering with magnificent emeralds?

Why today are they carrying elegant canes
exquisitely worked in silver and gold?

> Because the barbarians are coming today
> and such things dazzle the barbarians.

Why don't our distinguished orators come as usual
and whip out their speeches, and say their piece?

> Because the barbarians are coming today
> and they are fed up with rhetoric and public speaking.

Why are there these sudden signs of worry
and confusion? (How grave the faces have become.)
Why are the streets and squares quickly emptying
and everyone going home so lost in thought?

> Because it is night and the barbarians haven't come.
> And some have arrived from the borders
> and said there are no barbarians any longer.

And now what will happen without barbarians?
Those people were a kind of solution.

**TRANSLATED BY WILLIS BARNSTONE**

## Nero's Deadline

Nero wasn't troubled when he heard
the utterance of the Delfic oracle.
"Beware of the seventy-third year."
Plenty of time left for enjoyment.
He's thirty. The deadline the god                                    *5*
gave him is long enough
to confront his future dangers.

Now he'll go back to Rome, a little tired,
but wonderfully tired from that journey
whose days were all devoted to pleasure—                             *10*
the theaters, the gardens, friends, the stadiums,
evenings in the cities of Achaia,
and naked bodies and sweet lusts, especially . . .

So much for Nero. And in Spain Galba
secretly musters and drills his army,                                *15*
the old general in his seventy-third year.

TRANSLATED BY WILLIS BARNSTONE

## Ithaka[1]

When you set out on your journey to Ithaka,
pray that the road be long,
full of adventures, full of knowledge.
Don't be afraid of the Laistrygonians,
the Cyclops and angry Poseidon.                                      *5*
You'll never find such things on your way
if your thoughts remain high, if a rare
excitement touches your spirit and your body,
You will not encounter the Laistrygonians,
the Cyclops and angry Poseidon                                       *10*
if you do not harbor them inside your soul,
if your soul does not raise them up before you.

Pray that the road be long,
that there be many summer mornings
when with pleasure and joy                                           *15*
you enter ports seen for the first time;

---

1. In Homer's *Odyssey*, the protagonist Odysseus takes ten years to find his way back to Ithaka, his home island where he was king. The Cyclops and Laistrygonians are monster obstacles on his path.

may you stop at Phoenician market places
to buy fine merchandise,
mother of pearl and coral, amber and ebony,
sensual perfume of every kind,
as many sensual perfumes as you can;
may you walk through many Egyptian cities
to learn and to learn from their scholars.

Always keep Ithaka in your mind.
To arrive there is your destined vision.
But do not hurry the journey at all.
Better for it to last for years,
for you to be old when you reach the island,
rich with all you have gained on the way,
not expecting Ithaka to make you rich.

Ithaka gave you the beautiful voyage.
Without her you would not have taken the road.
But she has nothing else to give you.
And if you find her poor, Ithaka didn't fool you.
Wise as you've become, with so much experience,
but now you'll understand what Ithakas mean.

TRANSLATED BY WILLIS BARNSTONE

## The God Abandons Antony[2]

When suddenly at the hour of midnight
you hear the invisible troupe passing by
with beautiful music, with voices—
don't futilely mourn your luck giving out, your work
collapsing, the designs of your life
that have all proved to be illusions.
As if long time prepared, as if full of courage,
say goodbye to her, the Alexandria who is leaving.
Above all don't fool yourself, don't say how it was
a dream, how your ears tricked you.
Don't stoop to such empty hopes.
As if long time prepared, as if full of courage,

---

2. The title is a quotation from Plutarch's *Life of Antony*. In Cavafy's version the poet recounts that the night before Antony will fight and lose to Augustus Caesar for control of Alexandria, he hears a mysterious musical troupe passing through the streets under his window. He is urged to enjoy this last esthetic moment and also to confront, courageously, that this will be his last pleasure before defeat and death on the next day. In Plutarch this passing bacchanalia is interpreted as a sign that Bacchus, Antony's protector, had abandoned him, for the troupe is heading for the gates of the city nearest the enemy.

as is right for you who are worthy of such a city,
go and stand tall by the window
and listen with emotion, but not                                    15
with the pleas and whining of a coward,
hear the voices—your last pleasure—
the exquisite instruments of that secret troupe,
and say goodbye to her, the Alexandria you are losing.

—TRANSLATED BY ALIKI BARNSTONE AND WILLIS BARNSTONE

## One Night

The room was cheap and sordid,
hidden above the suspect tavern.
From the window you could see the alley
filthy and narrow. From below
came the voices of some workers                                    5
who were playing cards, having a good time.

And there on the plain, ordinary bed
I had love's body, I had the lips,
voluptuous and rosy lips of drunken ecstasy—
rosy lips of such ecstasy that now                                 10
as I write, after so many years
in my lonely house, I am drunk again.

TRANSLATED BY WILLIS BARNSTONE

## September, 1903

At least let me fool myself with illusions
so as not to feel the emptiness of my life.

And I came so close so many times.
And how paralyzed I was, and how cowardly;
Why did I keep my lips sealed                                      5
while the emptiness of my life wept inside me,
and my desires put on black clothes?

To have been so close so many times
to the eyes, to the voluptuous lips,
to the body I dreamed of, I loved.                                 10
To have been so close so many times.

TRANSLATED BY WILLIS BARNSTONE

## Of the Jews (A.D. 50)

Painter and poet, runner and discus thrower,
beautiful as Endymion: Ianthis, son of Antony,
from a family close to the synagogue.

"My noblest days are those
when I give up the search for sensation,
when I desert the bright and stark Hellenism,
with its masterly fixation
on perfectly shaped and perishable white limbs.
And become the man I would always
want to be: A son of the Jews, of the holy Jews."

His declaration was very fiery. "Be always
of the Jews, the holy Jews."

But he didn't stay that way at all.
The Hedonism and the Art of Alexandria
possessed him as their child.

TRANSLATED BY WILLIS BARNSTONE

## On the Ship

Of course it looks like him,
this little pencil drawing.

Quickly drawn on the deck of the ship,
on a magic afternoon,
the Ionian Sea around us.
It looks like him. But I remember him as handsomer.
He was sensitive to the point of suffering
and it illumined his expression.
He appears to me handsomer
now as my soul calls him back, out of Time.

Out of Time. All these things are very old—
the sketch, and the ship, and the afternoon.

TRANSLATED BY WILLIS BARNSTONE

## The Bandaged Shoulder

He said he'd banged into a wall or had fallen down.
But probably there was another reason
for the wounded and bandaged shoulder.

With a rather violent movement
as he was reaching for a shelf to take down                          5
some photographs he wanted to look at closely,
the bandage came loose and a little blood oozed out.

I did it up again, slowly, taking my time
with the binding. He wasn't in pain
and I liked looking at the blood. It was                             10
a thing of my love, that blood.

When he left I found in front of his chair
a bloody rag, from the dressing,
a rag to be thrown immediately into the garbage.

And I put it to my lips,                                             15
and kissed it a long time—
the blood of love against my lips.

TRANSLATED BY WILLIS BARNSTONE

## Hidden

From all I did and all I said,
let no one try to find out who I was.
An obstacle was there and it transformed
the actions and manner of my life.
An obstacle was there, and often it stopped me                      5
when I was about to speak.
From my most unobserved actions
and my most veiled writing—
from these alone I will be understood.
But maybe it isn't worth going through                              10
so much care and effort to discover who I am.
Later, in a more perfect society,
someone else made like me
is certain to appear and act freely.

TRANSLATED BY WILLIS BARNSTONE

■ **S. Y. Agnon (1888–1970)** *Israel* **(story)**

TRANSLATED BY ROBERT ALTER

Shmuel Yosef Agnon was born Samuel Josef Czaczkes in Buczacz, Galicia, at that time a part of the Austro-Hungarian Empire, now part of southern Poland. He adopted the pen name Agnon from the title of one of his stories, "Agunot" ("Deserted Wives"), after settling in Palestine in 1907. Often considered Israel's premier fiction writer, in 1966 he shared the Nobel Prize for Literature with the poet Nelly Sachs. He began writing in Yiddish when he was sixteen, and later on wrote prolifically in Hebrew, helping to form the modern language as a superbly rich vehicle for evoking modern and ancient Jewish traditions, from the biblical Song of Songs to the mystical Kabbalah to life in the East European Pale and Jerusalem. On one of his stays in Germany, early in the century, he collaborated with Martin Buber to co-edit a collection of Hasidic folklore. Some of his deepest, most ironic, and mysterious tales are dreamlike Kafkaesque allegories of men and women caught between ancient beliefs and modern despair. "The Doctor's Divorce," on the other hand, is a masterful psychological exploration of an obsessive personality destroyed by jealousy, set in Vienna, the city of Sigmund Freud.

**FURTHER READING:** Agnon, S. Y. *Forever More,* 1961; *Twenty-One Stories,* 1970; *Guest for the Night,* 1968; *Two Tales: Betrothed, & Edo and Enam,* 1966; *Tehilla and Other Israeli Tales,* 1956.

## The Doctor's Divorce

## 1̄

When I joined the staff of the hospital, I discovered there a blonde nurse who was loved by everyone and whose praise was on the lips of all the patients. As soon as they heard her footsteps, they would sit up in bed and stretch their arms out toward her as an only son reaches for his mother, and each one of them would call, "Nurse, nurse, come to me." Even the ill-tempered kind who find all the world provoking—as soon as she appeared, the frown-lines in their faces faded, their anger dissolved, and they were ready to do whatever she ordered. Not that it was her way to give orders: the smile that illuminated her face was enough to make patients obey her. In addition to her smile, there were her eyes, a kind of blue-black; everyone she looked at felt as if he were the most important thing in the world. Once I asked myself where such power comes from. From the moment I saw her eyes, I was just like the rest of the patients. And she had no special intentions toward me, nor toward anybody in particular. That smile on her lips, however, and that blue-black in her eyes had the further distinction of doing on their own more than their mistress intended.

One indication of the degree of affection in which she was generally held was the fact that even her fellow nurses liked her and were friendly toward her. And the head nurse, a woman of about forty, well born, thin and wan as vinegar, who hated everyone, patients and doctors alike, with the possible exception of black coffee and salted cakes and her lap dog— even she was favorably disposed in this case. Such a woman, who couldn't look at a girl without imagining her half wasted away, showed special kindness to this nurse. And one hardly need mention my fellow doctors. Every doctor with whom she happened to work thanked his stars. Even our professor, accustomed as he was to concern himself less with the suffering of the sick than with the orderliness of their beds, made no fuss if he found her sitting on a patient's bed. This old man, the master of so many disciples and the discoverer of cures for several diseases, died in a concentration camp where a Nazi trooper tormented him daily by forcing him to go through exercises. One day the trooper ordered him to lie flat on his belly with arms and legs outstretched, and as soon as he was down, he was commanded to get up. As he was not quick about it, the trooper trampled him with his cleated boots until the old man's thumbnails were mutilated. He contracted blood poisoning and died.

What more can I say? I took a liking to this girl just as everyone else did. But I can add that she also took a liking to me. And though any man could say as much, others did not dare while I dared, and so I married her.

## 2

This is how it came about. One afternoon, as I was leaving the dining hall, I ran into Dinah. I said to her, "Are you busy, nurse?"

"No, I'm not busy."

"What makes today so special?"

"Today is my day off from the hospital."

"And how are you celebrating your day off?"

"I haven't yet considered the matter."

"Would you allow me to give you some advice?"

"Please do, doctor."

"But only if I am paid for the advice. Nowadays you don't get something for nothing."

She looked at me and laughed. I continued, "I have one good piece of advice which is actually two—that we go to the Prater[1] and that we go to the opera. And if we hurry, we can stop first at a cafe. Do you agree, nurse?" She nodded yes good-humoredly.

---

1. Prater is a park in Vienna [Editor].

"When shall we go?" I asked.

"Whenever the doctor wants."

"I'll take care of what I have to as soon as possible and I'll be right over."

"Whenever you come, you'll find me ready."

She went to her room and I to my responsibilities. A little while later, when I arrived to pick her up, I discovered that she had changed clothes. All at once she seemed a new person to me, and with the metamorphosis her charm was doubled, for she had both the charm I felt in her when she was in uniform and that which was lent her by the new clothes. I sat in her room and looked at the flowers on the table and by the bed, and after asking her whether she knew their names, I recited the name of each flower, in German and in Latin. But I quickly became apprehensive that a serious patient might be brought in and I would be paged. I got up from my seat and urged that we leave at once. I saw she was disturbed.

"Is something bothering you?" I asked.

"I thought you'd have something to eat."

"Right now, let's go, and if you are still so kindly disposed toward me, I'll come back to enjoy everything you give me, and I'll even ask for more."

"May I count on that?"

"I've already given you my word. Not only that, but, as I said, I'll ask for more."

As we left the hospital court, I said to the doorman, "You see this nurse? I'm taking her away from here." The doorman looked at us benevolently and said, "More power to you, doctor. More power to you, nurse."

We walked to the trolley stop. A trolley came along, but turned out to be full. The next one that arrived we thought we would be able to take. Dinah got onto the car. When I tried to climb up after her, the conductor called out, "No more room." She came down and waited with me for another car. At that point I commented to myself, Some people say that one shouldn't worry about a trolley or a girl that has gone because others will soon come along. But those who think that are fools. As far as the girl is concerned, can one find another girl like Dinah? And as to the trolley, I regretted every delay.

Along came a suburban trolley. Since its cars were new and spacious and empty of passengers, we got on. Suddenly (or, according to the clock, after a while), the trolley reached the end of the line and we found ourselves standing in a lovely place filled with gardens, where the houses were few.

We crossed the street talking about the hospital and the patients and the head nurse and the professor, who had instituted a fast once a week for all patients with kidney ailments because someone with kidney pains had fasted on the Day of Atonement and afterward there was no albumen in his urine. Then we mentioned all the cripples the war had produced, and we were pleased by the setting for our walk because there were no cripples around. I threw up my arms suddenly and said, "Let's forget about the hospital and cripples and speak about more pleasant things." She agreed with me, even though from her expression one could tell she was concerned that we might not find any other subject for conversation.

Children were playing. They saw us and began to whisper to each other. "Do you know, Fräulein," I asked Dinah, "what the children are talking about? They are talking about us." — "Perhaps." "Do you know what they're saying?" I went on. "They're saying, 'The two of them are bride and groom.'" Her face reddened as she answered, "Perhaps that's what they are saying."

"You mean you don't object to it?"

"To what?"

"To what the children are saying."

"Why should I care?"

"And if it were true, what would you say?"

"If what were true?"

I summoned my courage and answered, "If what the children say were true, I mean, that you and I belong together." She laughed and looked at me. I took her hand and said, "Give me the other one, too." She gave me her hand. I bent over and kissed both her hands, then looked at her. Her face became still redder. "There is a proverb," I told her, "that truth is with children and fools. We've already heard what the children say, and now listen to what a fool has to say, I mean, myself, for I have been touched with wisdom."

I stuttered and went on, "Listen, Dinah . . . " I had hardly begun to say all that was in my heart before I found myself a man more fortunate than all others.

# 3

Never was there a better time in my life than the period of our engagement. If it had been my opinion that marriage exists only because a man needs a woman and a woman a man, I now came to realize that there is no higher need than that one. At the same time, I began to understand why the poets felt it necessary to write love poems, despite the fact that I would have no part of them or their poems, because they wrote about other women and not about Dinah. Often I would sit and wonder, How many nurses there are in the hospital; how many women in the world; and I am concerned with one girl alone, who absorbs all my thoughts. As soon as I saw her again, I would say to myself, The doctor must have lost his wits to put her in the same category as other women. And my feelings toward her were reciprocated. But that blue-black in her eyes darkened like a cloud about to burst.

Once I asked her. She fixed her eyes on me without answering. I repeated my question. She pressed against me and said, "You don't know how precious you are to me and how much I love you." And a smile spread across her melancholy lips, that smile which drove me wild with its sweetness and its sorrow.

I asked myself, If she loves me, what reason could there be for this sadness? Perhaps her family is poor. But she said they were well-to-do. Perhaps she had promised to marry someone else. But she told me she was completely free. I began to pester her about it. She showed me still more affection, and she remained silent.

Nevertheless, I began to investigate her relatives. Perhaps they were rich but had been impoverished and she felt bad about them. I discovered that some of them were industrialists and some were people of distinction in other fields, and they all made comfortable livings.

I grew proud. I, a poor boy, the son of a lowly tinsmith, became fastidious about my dress, even though she paid no attention to clothes, unless I asked her to look at them. My love for her grew still greater. This was beyond all logic, for, to begin with, I had given her all my love. And she, too, gave me all her love. But her love had a touch of sadness in it which injected into my happiness a drop of gall.

This drop worked its way into all my limbs. I would ponder, What is this sadness? Is that what love is supposed to be like? I continued to beleaguer her with questions. She promised an answer but persisted in her evasiveness. When I reminded her of her promise, she took my hand in hers and said, "Let's be happy, darling, let's be happy and not disturb our happiness." And she sighed in a way that broke my heart. I asked her, "Dinah, what are you sighing about?" She smiled and answered through her tears, "Please, darling, don't say anything more." I was silent and asked no more questions. But my mind was not at ease. And I still awaited the time when she would agree to tell me what it was all about.

# 4

One afternoon I stopped in to see her. At that hour she was free from her work with the patients and she was sitting in her room sewing a new dress. I took the dress by the hem and let my hand glide over it. Then I lifted my eyes toward her. She looked straight into my eyes and said, "I was once involved with somebody else." She saw that I didn't realize what she meant, so she made her meaning more explicit. A chill ran through me and I went weak inside. I sat without saying a word. After a few moments I told her, "Such a thing would have never even occurred to me." Once I had spoken, I sat wondering and amazed, wondering over my own calmness and amazed at her for having done a thing so much beneath her. Nevertheless, I treated her just as before, as though she had in no way fallen in esteem. And, in fact, at that moment she had not fallen in my esteem and was as dear to me as always. Once she saw that, a smile appeared on her lips again. But her eyes were veiled, like someone moving out of one darkness into another.

I asked her, "Who was this fellow who left you without marrying you?" She evaded the question. "Don't you see, Dinah," I pursued, "that I bear no ill feeling toward you. It's only curiosity that leads me to ask such a question. So tell me, darling, who was he?" "What difference does it make to you what his name is?" Dinah asked. "Even so," I persisted, "I would like to know." She told me his name. "Is he a lecturer or a professor?" I asked. Dinah said, "He is an official." I reflected silently that important officials worked for her relatives, men of knowledge and scholars and inventors. Undoubtedly it was to the most important of them that she gave her heart. Actually, it made no difference who the man was to whom this woman more dear to me than all the world gave her love, but to delude myself I imagined that he was a great man, superior to all his fellows. "He's an official?" I said to her. "What is his job?" Dinah answered. "He is a clerk in the legislature." "I'm amazed at you, Dinah," I told her, "that a minor official, a clerk, was able to sweep you off your feet like that. And, besides, he left you, which goes to show that he wasn't good enough for you in the first place." She lowered her eyes and was silent.

From then on I did not remind her of her past, just as I would not have reminded her what dress she had worn the day before. And if I thought of it, I banished the thought from my mind. And so we were married.

# 5

Our wedding was like most weddings in these times, private, without pomp and ceremony. For I had no family, with the possible exception of the relative who once hit my father in the eye. And Dinah, ever since she became close to me, had grown away from her relatives. During that period, moreover, it was not customary to have parties and public rejoicing. Governments came and governments went, and between one and the next there was panic and confusion, turmoil and dismay. People who one day were rulers the next day were chained in prisons or hiding in exile.

And so our wedding took place with neither relatives nor invited guests, except for a bare quorum summoned by the beadle, miserable creatures who an hour or two ago were called for a funeral and now were summoned for my wedding. How pitiful were their borrowed clothes, how comic their towering high hats, how audacious their greedy eyes that looked forward to the conclusion of the ceremony when they could go into a bar with the money they had gotten through my wedding. I was in high spirits, and as strange as the thing seemed to me, my joy was not diminished. Let others be led under the bridal canopy by renowned and wealthy wedding guests. I would be married in the presence of poor people who, with what they would earn for their trouble, could buy bread. The children we would have wouldn't ask me, "Father, who was at your wedding?" just as I never asked my father who was at his wedding.

I put my hand in my pocket and pulled out several shillings which I handed to the beadle to give to the men over and above the agreed price. The beadle took the money and said nothing. I was afraid they would overwhelm me with thanks and praise, and I prepared myself to demur modestly. But not one of them came up to me. Instead, one fellow bent over, leaning on his cane, another stretched himself in order to appear tall, and a third looked at the bride in a way that was not decent. I asked the beadle about him. "That one," the beadle replied, and he bore down emphatically on the "th"-sound, "that one was an official who got fired." I nodded and said, "Well, well," as though with two well's I had concluded all the fellow's affairs. Meanwhile, the beadle chose four of his quorum, put a pole in the hand of each of the four, stretched a canopy over the poles,[2] and, in doing that, pushed one man who bent forward and thus brought the canopy tumbling down.

Afterward, while standing under the bridal canopy, I recalled the story of a man whose mistress forced him to marry her. He went and gathered for the ceremony all her lovers who had lived with her before her marriage, both to remind her of her shame and to punish himself for agreeing to marry such a woman. What a contemptible fellow and what a contemptible act! Yet I found that man to my liking, and I thought well of what he had done. And when the rabbi stood and read the marriage contract, I looked at the wedding guests and tried to imagine what the woman was like and what her lovers were like at that moment. And in the same way, just before, when my wife put out her finger for the wedding ring and I said to her, "Behold thou art consecrated unto me," I knew without anyone's telling me what that man was like at that moment.

# $\overline{6}$

After the wedding we left for a certain village to spend our honeymoon. I won't tell you everything that happened to us on the way and in the station and on the train; and, accordingly, I won't describe every mountain and hill we saw, nor the brooks and springs in the valleys and mountains, as tellers of tales are accustomed to do when they set about describing the trip of a bride and groom. Undoubtedly there were mountains and hills and springs and brooks, and several things did happen to us on the way, but everything else has escaped me and been forgotten because of one incident which occurred on the first night. If you're not tired yet, I'll tell you about it.

We arrived at the village and registered at a little hotel situated among gardens and surrounded by mountains and rivers. We had supper and went up to the room that the hotel had set aside for us, for I had telegraphed our reservation before the wedding. Examining the room, my wife let her eyes dwell on the red roses that had been put there. "Who was so nice," I said jokingly, "to send us these lovely roses?" "Who?" asked my wife with genuine wonder, as though she thought there were someone here beside the hotel people who knew about us. "In any case," I said,

---

2. The bride, groom, their parents, and the Rabbi stand below this canopy in traditional Jewish weddings [Editor].

"I'm taking them away, because their fragrance will make it hard to sleep. Or perhaps we should leave them in honor of the occasion." "Oh yes," my wife answered after me in the voice of a person who speaks without hearing his own words. I said to her, "And don't you want to smell them?"—"Oh, yes, I want to." But she forgot to smell them. This forgetfulness was strange for Dinah, who loved flowers so much. I reminded her that she hadn't yet smelled the flowers. She bent her head over them. "Why are you bending down," I asked her, "when you can hold them up to you?" She looked at me as though she had just heard something novel. The blue-black in her eyes darkened, and she said, "You are very observant, my darling." I gave her a long kiss; then with closed eyes I said to her, "Now, Dinah, we are alone."

She stood up and took off her clothes with great deliberation, and began to fix her hair. As she was doing that, she sat down, bending her head over the table. I leaned over to see why she was taking so long, and I saw that she was reading a little pamphlet of the kind one finds in Catholic villages. The title was "Wait for Your Lord in Every Hour That He May Come."

I took her chin in my hand and said to her, "You don't have to wait, your lord has already come," and I pressed my mouth against hers. She lifted her eyes sadly and laid the pamphlet aside. I took her in my arms, put her in bed, and turned the lamp-wick down.

The flowers gave off their fragrance and sweet stillness surrounded me. Suddenly I heard the sound of footsteps in the room next to ours. I forced the sound out of my mind and refused to pay attention to it, for what difference did it make to me whether or not there was someone there. I didn't know him and he didn't know us. And if he did know us, we had a wedding and were properly married. I embraced my wife with great love and was happy beyond limit with her, for I knew she was entirely mine.

With Dinah still in my arms, I strained attentively to make out whether that fellow's footsteps had stopped, but I heard him still pacing back and forth. His footsteps drove me to distraction: a strange idea now occurred to me, that this was the clerk my wife had known before her marriage. I was horror-stricken at the thought, and I had to bite my lip to prevent myself from cursing out loud. My wife took notice.

"What's wrong, sweetheart?"

"Nothing, nothing."

"I see something's troubling you."

"I've already told you nothing is."

"Then I must have been mistaken."

I lost my head and said to her, "You were not mistaken."

"What is it, then?"

I told her.

She began to sob.

"Why are you crying?" I said.

She swallowed her tears and answered, "Open the door and the windows and tell the whole world of my depravity."

I was ashamed of what I had said, and I tried to mollify her. She listened to me and we made peace.

# $\overline{7}$

From then on that man was never out of my sight, whether my wife was present or not. If I sat by myself, I thought about him, and if I talked with my wife, I mentioned him. If I saw a flower, I was reminded of the red roses, and if I saw a red rose, I was reminded of him, suspecting that was the kind he used to give my wife. This, then, was the reason she refused to smell the roses on the first night, because she was ashamed in her husband's presence to smell the same kind of flowers that her lover used to bring her. When she cried, I would console her. But in the kiss of reconciliation I heard the echo of another kiss which someone else had given her. We are enlightened individuals, modern people, we seek freedom for ourselves and for all humanity, and in point of fact we are worse than the most diehard reactionaries.

Thus passed the first year. When I wanted to be happy with my wife, I would remember the one who had spoiled my happiness, and I would sink into gloom. If she was happy, I told myself, What makes her so happy? She must be thinking of that louse. As soon as I mentioned him to her, she would burst into tears. "What are you crying for?" I would say. "Is it so difficult for you to hear me talk against that louse?"

I knew that she had long since put all thought of him out of her mind, and if she thought of him at all, it was only negatively, for she had never really loved him. It was only his supreme audacity together with a transient moment of weakness in her that had led her to lose control and listen to his demands. But my understanding of the matter brought me no equanimity. I wanted to grasp his nature, what it was in him that had attracted this modest girl raised in a good family.

I began to search through her books in the hope of finding some sort of letter from him, for Dinah was in the habit of using her letters as bookmarks. I found nothing, however. Perhaps, I thought, she has deliberately hidden them somewhere else, inasmuch as I have already searched all her books and found nothing. I could not bring myself to examine her private things. And that made me still angrier, for I was pretending to be decent while my thoughts were contemptible. Since I had spoken with no one else about her past, I sought counsel in books and began to read love stories in order to understand the nature of women and their lovers. But the novels bored me, so I took to reading criminal documents. My friends noticed and jokingly asked me if I were planning to join the detective squad.

The second year brought no mitigation or relief. If a day passed without my mentioning him, I spoke about him twice as much on the following day. From all the anguish I caused her, my wife fell sick. I healed her with medicines and battered her heart with words. I would tell her, "All your illness comes to you only because of the man who ruined your life. Right now he's playing around with other women, and me he has left with an invalid wife to take care of." A thousand kinds of remorse would sting me for every single word, and a thousand times I repeated those words.

At that time I began visiting my wife's relatives together with her. And here a strange thing occurred. I've already mentioned that Dinah came of good family and that her relatives were distinguished people. In consequence, they and their homes gratified me, and I began to show favor to my wife because of her relatives. These people, the grandchildren of ghetto[3] dwellers, had achieved wealth and honor: their wealth was an ornament to their honor and their honor an ornament to their wealth. For even during the war, when the great figures of the nation made money out of people's hunger, they kept their hands clean of all money coming from an evil source, and, accordingly, they refused to stuff themselves with food and accepted only their legitimate rations. Among their number were the kind of imposing men we used to imagine but never really saw with our own eyes. And then there were the women. You don't know Vienna, and if you know it, you know the sort of Jewish women the gentiles wag their tongues over. If they could only see the women I saw, they would stop up their own mouths. Not that I care what the non-Jewish peoples say about us, for there is no hope that we'll ever please them, but inasmuch as I have mentioned their censure of us, I also mention their praise, because there is no higher praise for a brother than that which he receives from his sisters, through whom he is commended and extolled.

Before long I thought of my wife's relatives without connecting them with her, as though I and not she were their relation. I would think to myself, If they only knew how miserable I make her. And I was just about ready to unlock my lips and to open my heart to them. When I realized that my heart was urging me to talk, I stayed away from them, and they quite naturally stayed away from me. It's a big city and people are busy. If someone avoids his friends, they don't go hunting after him.

The third year my wife adopted a new mode of behavior. If I mentioned him, she ignored what I said, and if I connected his name with hers, she kept silent and didn't answer me, as though I weren't speaking about her. Infuriated, I would comment to myself, What a miserable woman not to take notice!

# 8̄

One summer day at twilight she and I were sitting at supper. It hadn't rained for a number of days, and the city was seething with heat. The water of the Danube[4] showed green, and a dull odor floated over the city.

---

3. The city area where the Jews lived [Editor].

4. River in Vienna [Editor].

The windows in our glass-enclosed porch gave off a sultry heat that exhausted body and soul. Since the day before, my shoulders had been aching, and now the pain was more intense. My head was heavy, my hair was dry. I ran my hand over my head and said to myself, I need a haircut. I looked across at my wife and saw that she was letting her hair grow long. Yet ever since women adopted men's haircuts, she always wore her hair close-cropped. I said to myself, My own head can't bear the weight of the little hair it has, and she's growing herself plumes like a peacock without even asking me if it looks nice that way. As a matter of fact, her hair looked lovely, but there was nothing lovely about my state of mind. I shoved my chair back from the table as though it were pushing against my stomach, and I ripped a piece of bread from the middle of the loaf and chewed it. It had been several days since I last mentioned him to her, and I hardly have to say that she made no mention of him to me. At that time, I was accustomed to saying very little to her, and when I did speak to her, I spoke without anger.

All at once I said to her, "There's something I've been thinking about."

She nodded her head. "Oh, yes," she said, "I feel the same way."

"So you know what is in the secret corners of my heart. Then, go ahead, tell me what I was thinking of."

In a whisper, she said, "Divorce."

As she spoke, she lifted her face to me and looked at me sadly. My heart was torn from its moorings, and I felt weak inside. I thought to myself, What a pitiful creature you are to treat your wife this way and cause her such pain. I lowered my voice and asked, "How do you know what is in my heart?"

"And what do you think I do with all my time? I sit and think about you, my dear."

The words leaped out of my mouth: I said to her, "Then you agree?"

She lifted her eyes to me. "You mean the divorce?"

I lowered my eyes and nodded in affirmation.

"Whether I want to or not," she said, "I agree to do whatever you ask, if it will only relieve your suffering."

"Even a divorce?"

"Even a divorce."

I was aware of all that I was losing. But the statement had already been made, and the desire to turn my wrath against myself drove me beyond reason. I clenched both hands and said angrily, "Well and good."

Several days passed, and I mentioned to her neither the divorce nor the one who had brought down ruin upon us. I told myself, Three years have passed since she became my wife. Perhaps the time has come to wipe out the memory of that affair. If she had been a widow or a divorcee when I married her, would there be anything I could have held against her? As things are, then, let me consider her as though she were a widow or a divorcee when I took her to be my wife.

And having reached this conclusion, I upbraided myself for every single day I had tormented her, and I resolved to be good to my wife. During that period I became a completely new person, and I began to feel an awakening of love as on the day I first met her. I was soon ready to conclude that everything is the result of man's will and desire: if he so wills it, he can introduce anger and hatred into his heart; if he wills it, he can live in peace with everyone. If this is so, I reasoned, what cause is there to stir up anger and bring evil upon ourselves when we are capable of doing good for ourselves and being happy? So I reasoned, that is, until something happened to me which set things back right where they were before.

# 9

What happened was this. One day a patient was brought to the hospital. I examined him and left him with the nurses to be washed and put to bed. In the evening I entered the ward to make my rounds. When I came to his bed, I saw his name on the card over his head, and I realized who he was.

What could I do? I'm a doctor, and I treated him. As a matter of fact, I gave him an extraordinary amount of care, so that all the other patients grew jealous of him and called him doctor's pet. And he really deserved the name, for whether he needed it or not, I treated him. I told the nurses that I had discovered in him a disease which hadn't been adequately studied yet, and that I wanted to investigate it myself. I left instructions for them to give him good food, and sometimes to add a glass of wine, so that he would get a little enjoyment out of his hospital stay. Further, I asked the nurses not to be too strict with him if he took certain liberties and didn't follow all the hospital regulations.

He lay in his hospital bed eating and drinking and enjoying all sorts of luxuries. And I came in to visit him and examine him again and again, asking him if he had a good night's sleep and if he was given all the food he wanted. I would order medication for him and praise his body to him, telling him that it would in all probability last to a ripe old age. He on his part listened with enjoyment and basked in pleasure before me like a worm. I told him, "If you're used to smoking, go ahead and smoke. I myself don't smoke, and if you ask me whether smoking is a good thing, I'll tell you it's bad and harmful to the body. But if you're used to smoking, I won't stop you." And in this way I gave him various special privileges, just so he would feel completely comfortable. At the same time I reflected, Over a man for whom I wouldn't waste so much as a word I am going to all this trouble, and it's all because of that business which is difficult to speak of and difficult to forget. Not only that, but I watch him and study him as though I could learn what rubbed off on him from Dinah and what rubbed off on her from him—and from devoting so much attention to him, I was acquiring some of his gestures.

At first I kept the whole matter secret from my wife. But it burst forth when I tried to suppress it, and it told itself. My wife listened without the slightest sign of interest. On the surface, one would have thought that this was just what I wanted, but I was not satisfied, even though I realized that if she had responded differently I would certainly not have been pleased.

After some while he was cured and had recuperated, and it was high time for him to leave the hospital. I kept him day after day and ordered the nurses to give him the best of treatment, so that he would not be anxious to leave. And that was the period right after the war, when it was hard to get provisions for the sick, not to speak of the convalescent, and certainly not to speak of the healthy, so I gave him from my own food which the farmers used to bring me. He sat in the hospital eating and drinking and gladdening his heart, reading newspapers and strolling in the garden, playing with the patients and laughing with the nurses. He put on some weight and was healthier than the people who took care of him, so that it became impossible to keep him any longer in the hospital. I gave instructions that a proper final dinner be prepared for him, and I discharged him.

After the dinner, he came to say goodbye to me. I looked at the double chin he had developed. His eyes were embedded in fat, like those of a woman who has given up everything for the sake of eating and drinking. I stood by my desk rummaging through the papers on it as though I were looking for something I had lost. Then I took a stethoscope to examine him. As I was trying to appear busy, two nurses came in, one to ask me something and one to say goodbye to the doctor's pet. I pulled my head back suddenly, as though I had been reminded that someone was waiting for me, and I let out a brief exclamation of surprise, the way Dinah does when she sees that someone has been waiting for her. As I did that, I looked at the healthy patient with his double chin and I said to myself, You don't know who I am, but I know who you are. You are the man who brought ruin down on me and wrecked my wife's life. Anger surged within me, and I became so furious that my eyes ached.

He extended his hand to me in special deference and began to stutter words of thanks about my saving him from death and restoring him to life. I offered him my fingertips to shake, in an impolite and deprecatory manner, and immediately I wiped them on my white coat, as though I had touched a dead reptile. Then I turned my face away from him as from some disgusting thing, and I walked away. I sensed that the nurses were looking at me and knew the reason for my behavior, even though there were no grounds for such apprehension.

After a little while I went back to work, but my head and heart were not with me. I went up to the doctors' lounge and looked for a friend to take my place. I told him that I had been summoned to court to give testimony about a certain criminal, and that it was impossible to postpone the case. A nurse came and asked whether she should order a cab. "Certainly, nurse, certainly," I answered. While she went to the switchboard to telephone, I ran out of the hospital like someone who had gone berserk.

I passed by a bar and considered going in to drown my sorrows in drink, as embittered men are accustomed to say. I grew a bit calmer and told myself, Troubles come and go, your troubles will also pass. But I had only grown calm temporarily, and only to lose control again. I began walking. After an hour or so, I stopped and saw that I had gone all around myself and completed a circle around the same spot.

# 10

I came home and told my wife. She listened and said nothing. I was infuriated that she should sit there in silence, as if she had heard nothing of significance. I bowed my head over my chest the way he did when he stood before me to thank me, and, imitating his voice, I said, "I wish to thank you, doctor, for saving me from death and restoring me to life." And I told my wife, "That's the way his voice sounds and that's the way he stands," in order to show her how low he was, what a pitiful creature was the man whom she had preferred to me and to whom she had given her love before she knew me. My wife looked up at me as though the whole thing were not worth her while to care about. Rising, I scrutinized her face in the hope of finding some indication of joy over that good-for-nothing's recovery, but just as I had seen no signs of sorrow when I told her he was sick, I saw now not the slightest sign of joy over his recovery.

After two or three days, the experience lost its sting and no longer disturbed me. I treated patients, talked much with the nurses, and immediately after work went home to my wife. Sometimes I would ask her to read to me from one of her books, and she would agree. She read while I sat looking at her, thinking, This is the face that had the power to drive away the frowns and dissipate the anger of whoever saw it. And I would run my hand over my face in gratification as I continued to look at her. Sometimes we had a friend over for coffee or for supper. And once again we talked about everything people talk about, and once again I realized that there were things in the world other than woman-trouble. Often now I climbed into bed at night with a feeling of contentment and gratification.

One night this fellow came to me in a dream: his face was sickly and yet just a little—just a little—likable. I was ashamed of myself for thinking evil of him, and I resolved to put an end to my anger against him. He bent down and said, "What do you want from me? Is the fact that she raped me any reason for you to have it in for me?"

The next night we had as dinner guests two of our friends, a married couple, whom we both particularly liked—him because of his admirable qualities, her because of her blue eyes filled with radiance, and because of her high forehead which deceived the eye into thinking that she was unusually intelligent, and because of the golden curls trembling on her head, and also because of her voice, the voice of a woman who suppresses her longings within her. We sat together some three hours without being aware of the time. He discussed the questions of the day, and she helped him with the radiance from her eyes.

After they left, I said to my wife, "Let me tell you a dream."

"A dream?" cried my wife in surprise, and fixed her eyes on me sorrowfully and repeated in a whisper, "A dream." For it was not my way to tell dreams, and it seems to me that all those years I had not dreamed at all.

"I had a dream," I told her. And as I said it, my heart suddenly quaked.

My wife sat down and looked into my face intently. I proceeded to tell her my dream. Her shoulders shook and her body began to tremble. She stretched out her arms all of a sudden and, placing them around my neck, she embraced me. I returned her embrace and we stood clinging together in love and affection and pity, while all that time, this fellow never left my sight, and I could hear him saying, "Is the fact that she raped me any reason for you to have it in for me?"

I pushed my wife's arms away from my neck, and a terrible sadness welled up within me. I got into bed and thought over the whole affair quietly and calmly until I fell asleep.

The next day we got up and ate breakfast together. I looked over at my wife and saw that her face was the same as always. I thanked her in my heart for bearing no grudge against me over the night before. At that moment, I recalled all the trouble and suffering I had caused her since the day she married me, how time after time I drained her lifeblood and insulted her in every possible way, while she took everything in silence. My heart swelled with love and tenderness for this miserable soul whom I had tortured so much, and I resolved to be good to her. And so I was for one day, for two days, for three days.

# 11

And I was quite prepared to conclude that everything was being set right. In point of fact, nothing had been set right. From the very day I made peace with myself, that peace was robbed from me through another means. My wife treated me as though I had become a stranger to her. Yet all the efforts I was making with her were for her sake. How this woman failed to take notice! But she did notice.

One day she said to me, "What a good thing it would be if I were dead!"

"Why do you say that?"

"Why, you ask?" And in the wrinkles around her lips there was visible a sort of smile which made my heart jump.

"Don't be a fool," I scolded her.

She sighed. "Ah, my dear, I am not a fool."

"Then I am a fool."

"No, you're not a fool either."

I raised my voice and challenged her. "Then what do you want from me?"

"What do I want?" she answered. "I want the same thing you want."

I brushed one palm off with the other and said, "There's nothing at all I want."

She looked into my face intently. "There's nothing at all you want. Then everything must be all right."

"All right?" I laughed scornfully.

"You see, my dear," she said, "that laugh does not sit well with me."

"What am I supposed to do, then?"

"Do what you've been wanting to do."

"Namely?"

"Namely, why should I repeat something you yourself know?"

"I'm afraid I don't know what that something is. But since you know, you can tell me."

She pronounced in a whisper, "Divorce."

I raised my voice as I answered. "You want to force me into giving you a divorce."

She nodded. "If you think it's proper for you to put it that way and say that I want to force you, then I agree."

"Meaning what?" I asked.

"Why do we have to repeat things when there's no call for it? Let us do what is written for us above."

In anger, I mocked her. "Even Heaven is an open book for you, as you know what's written there. I am a doctor and I can only go by what my eyes see, while you, madam, you know what is written on high. Where did you pick up such knowledge, maybe from that louse?"

"Be still!" Dinah cried. "Please, be still!"

"You don't have to get so angry," I told her. "After all, what did I say?"

She rose, went to her room, and locked the door behind her.

I came to the door and asked her to open it for me, but she refused. "Look, I'm leaving," I said to her. "The whole house is yours, and you don't have to lock the door." When she still did not answer, I began to be afraid that she had taken sleeping pills and, God forbid, committed suicide. I began to beg and plead for her to open the door, but still she did not open. I peeked through the keyhole, my heart pounding me blow after blow, as though I were a murderer. Thus I stood before the locked door until evening came on and the walls darkened.

With darkness, she came out of her room, pale as a corpse. When I took her hands in mine, a deathly chill flowed out of them that made my own hands cold. She made no effort to pull her hands away from me, as though she had no feeling left in them.

I laid her down on her bed and calmed her with sedatives, nor did I move from her until she had dozed off. I looked at her face, a face innocent of any flaw, without the slightest blemish, and I said to myself, What a lovely world in which such a woman exists, and what difficult lives we have to live! I bent down in order to kiss her. She turned her head in sign of refusal. "Did you say something?" I asked. "No," she said, and I couldn't tell whether she was conscious of me or simply was talking in her sleep. Thoroughly disconcerted, I kept my distance from her. But I sat there all night long.

The next day I went to work and came back at noon. Whether out of prudence or for some other reason, I made no mention to her of what had happened the day before. She on her part did not speak of it either. So it was on the second day, so again on the third day. I was ready to conclude that matters were returning to their previous state. Yet I knew that though I might try to forget, she would not forget.

During that period her appearance became more vigorous and she changed some of her habits. Where she was accustomed to greet me as I came in the door, she no longer greeted me. Sometimes she would leave me and go off somewhere, and there were times when I came home and did not find her.

The anniversary of our engagement fell at that time. I said to her, "Let's celebrate and take a trip to the place we went to when we were first married."

"That's impossible."

"Why?"

"Because I have to go somewhere else."

"Pardon me, but where is it you are going?"

"There's a patient I'm taking care of."

"Why this all of a sudden?"

"Not everything a person does is all of a sudden. For a long time now I've felt that I ought to work and do something."

"And isn't it enough for you that I am working and doing something?"

"Once that was enough for me. Now it's not enough."

"Why not?"

"Why not? If you yourself don't know, I can't explain it to you."

"Is it such a complicated issue that it's difficult to explain?"

"It's not hard to explain, but I doubt if you would want to understand."

"Why are you doing it?"

"Because I want to earn my own living."

"Do you think you're not supported adequately in your own home, that you have to go look for a living elsewhere."

"Right now I'm being supported. Who knows what will be tomorrow?"

"Why all of a sudden such ideas?"

"I already told you that nothing happens all of a sudden."

"I don't know what you're talking about."

"You understand, all right, but you prefer to say, 'I don't understand.'"

I nodded my head in despair and said, "That's how it is, then."

"Really, that's how it is."

"This whole dialectic is beyond me."

"It's beyond you, and it's not particularly close to me. So it would be better if we kept still. You do what you have to do, and I'll do what I have to."

"What I do, I know. But I have no idea what it is you want to do."

"If you don't know now, you'll soon find out."

But her efforts did not succeed. And however they may have succeeded, she failed to make a penny out of them. She was caring for a paralyzed girl, the daughter of a poor widow, and she received no payment for her work. On the contrary, she helped the widow financially, and she even brought her flowers. At that time Dinah's strength drained from her as though she were sick, and she herself needed someone to take care of her instead of her caring for others. Once I asked her, "How long are you going to continue working with that sick girl?" She fixed her eyes on me and said, "Are you asking me as a doctor?"

"What difference does it make whether I ask as a doctor or as your husband?"

"If you ask as a doctor, I don't know what to tell you, and if you ask for other reasons, I see no need to answer."

I tried to act as if she were joking with me, so I laughed. She averted her face from me, and, leaving me where I was, went off. The laughter immediately died on my lips, nor has it yet returned.

It's just a mood, I told myself, and I can put up with it. Yet I knew that all my optimism was completely baseless. I recalled the first time she spoke to me about a divorce, and I remembered what she said: "Whether I want it or not, I am prepared to do whatever you ask, if only it will relieve your suffering—even a divorce." Now I thought, However you look at it, there's no way out for us except a divorce. As soon as this idea occurred to me, I dismissed it, as a man will dismiss something painful from his thoughts. But Dinah was right when she said we had to do what was written for us above. Before long I saw with my own eyes and I grasped with my own understanding what at first I had not seen and I had not grasped. At once I decided that I would grant Dinah the divorce. We had no children, for I had been apprehensive about begetting children for fear they would look like him. I arranged our affairs and gave her the divorce.

And so we parted from one another, the way people will part outwardly. But in my heart, my friend, the smile on her lips is still locked up, and that blue-black in her eyes, as on the day I first saw her. Sometimes at night I sit up in bed like those patients she used to take care of, and I stretch out both hands and call, "Nurse, nurse, come to me."

## ■ Nazim Hikmet (1902–1963) *Turkey* (poem)

### TRANSLATED BY RANDY BLASING AND MUTLA KONUK

Nazim Hikmet was born in Salonica, Greece, in 1902, when it was part of the Ottoman Empire. He was the grandson of Nazim Pasha, a poet and critic who introduced him to the Turkish literary heritage; his mother introduced him to the music and literature of the West. He studied at Istanbul's Heybeli Naval Academy in 1917 but was expelled for participating in a student strike. He went into hiding and became a Communist, moving to Moscow, where he studied at the University of the East (in 1922). On his return to Turkey, he quickly found himself in jail, serving a fifteen-year sentence for his political poetry. He was released early, but in 1937 he was sentenced to 28 years in jail for writing an anti-Fascist tract. International pressure brought about his release in 1951, and he emigrated to the Soviet Union, living in a number of socialist countries before taking Polish citizenship. His work celebrated the poor people of Anatolia, who became his heroes, and moved more and more toward simple melodic poetry based on folk songs. He also wrote plays and novels. He died in Moscow in 1963.

**FURTHER READING:** Hikmet, Nazim. *The Day Before Tomorrow: Poems.* Translated by Taner Baybars, 1972; *The Epic of Sheik Bedreddin and Other Poems.* Translated by Randy Blasing ad Mutlu Konuk, 1977; *Landscapes.* Translated by Randy Blasing and Mutlu Konuk, 1982; *The Moscow Symphony and Other Poems.* Translated by Taner Baybars, 1970; *Poems.* Translated by Ali Yunus, 1954; *Poems of Nazim Hikmet.* Translated from the Turkish by Randy Blasing and Mutlu Konuk, 1994; *A Sad State of Freedom.* Translated by Taner Baybars and Richard McKane, 1990; *Things I Didn't Know I Loved: Selected Poems of Nazim Hikmet.* Translated by Randy Blasing and Mutlu Konuk, 1975.

## Since I Was Thrown Inside

Since I was thrown inside
    the earth has gone around the sun ten times.
If you ask it:
    "Not worth mentioning—
    a microscopic span."
If you ask me:
    "Ten years of my life."

I had a pencil
    the year I was thrown inside.
It was used up after a week of writing.
If you ask it:
    "A whole lifetime."
If you ask me:
    "What's a week."

Since I've been inside,
    Osman, who was in for murder,
      did his seven-and-a-half and left,
      knocked around on the outside for a while,
      then landed back inside for smuggling,

served six months and was out again;
yesterday we got a letter—he's married,
with a kid coming in the spring.                                    *20*

They're ten-years-old now,
    the children who were conceived
        the year I was thrown inside.                               *25*
And that year's foals—shaky on their long, spindly legs—
    have been wide-rumped, contented mares for some time
    now.

But the olive seedlings are still saplings,
        still children.                                             *30*
New squares have opened in my faraway city
        since I was thrown inside.
And my family now lives
    on a street I don't know,
        in a house I haven't seen.                                  *35*

Bread was like cotton—soft and white—
        the year I was thrown inside.
Then it was rationed,
and here inside people killed each other
        over a black loaf the size of a fist.                      *40*
Now it's free again,
but it's dark and has no taste.

The year I was thrown inside
        the SECOND hadn't started yet.
The ovens at Dachau hadn't been lit,                                *45*
the atom bomb hadn't been dropped on Hiroshima.

Time flowed like blood from the slit throat of a child.
Then that chapter was officially closed—
now the American dollar is talking of a THIRD.
But in spite of everything the day has gotten lighter               *50*
        since I was thrown inside.
And "at the edge of darkness,
    pushing against the earth with their heavy hands.
        THEY've risen up" halfway.

Since I was thrown inside                                           *55*
        the earth has gone around the sun ten times.
And I repeat once more with the same passion
        what I wrote about Them
        the year I was thrown inside:
"They who are numberless like ants in the earth.                    *60*
        fish in the sea,
            birds in the air,

who are cowardly, brave,
    ignorant, wise,
        and childlike,
and who destroy
    and create, they—

     6

our songs tell only of their adventures."
    And anything else,
        such as my ten years here,
        is just so much talk.

     7

## ◼ Naguib Mahfouz (1911– ) *Egypt* (story)

### TRANSLATED BY DENYS JOHNSON-DAVIES

In October 1988, the world learned that an Egyptian novelist, Naguib Mahfouz (also transliterated as Najib Mahfuz), highly esteemed in his country, but a secret beyond the borders of Arabic letters, had won the Nobel Prize for Literature. Mahfouz, an author concerned with family generations, had been read by millions in the Arab world, and his short stories and novels were also known through film and television adaptations. More than any writer, he had established a demotic Arabic literary speech, which made the language of Egypt the standard. With his greater recognition, the readers of many nations would soon, by way of multiple translations, follow the generations of ordinary middle-class life in Egypt as it changed with the social and political climates of our century.

Mahfouz was born in Cairo on December 12, 1911. His father was a civil servant, and he was one of seven children. After attending public schools, he went to the University of Cairo in 1934 and four years later received a degree in philosophy. He grew up in a turbulent period that saw England alter its occupation of Egypt into a protectorate in 1914. A constitutional monarchy was established in 1923. The momentous year of 1952 saw Gamal Abdel-Nasser overthrow the monarchy and institute a republic. At first optimistic, later disappointed with the promised reforms, Mahfouz became an open critic of the Nasser regime. After graduation from the university, Mahfouz began to publish short stories, including his first book *Whispers of Madness* (1938). To earn a living, he wrote for magazines and the newspaper *Al-Ahram.* He also worked for the Ministry of Culture, adapted fiction for film and television, and became director of the government Cinema Organization, where he worked until his retirement in the early 1970s. Although Mahfouz has rarely traveled abroad—once to Yemen and once to Yugoslavia—and even sent his two daughters to receive his Nobel honors in Stockholm, he learned the craft of the novel from the European and American masters, including Tolstoy, Chekhov, Balzac, Mann, Hemingway, and Faulkner. Because of his frequent focus on everyday reality in generations of merchant families, he has been called, perhaps too simply, the Balzac of the Arab world. Whether it was Balzac, Zola, or, as he claims, their disciples who helped him find his way, the thematic sources of his early novels were ancient and contemporary Egypt. He is obsessed with time, with glamorous dancing girls and their shattered ambitions, with life in the coffee houses and tyranny in the home as fathers enslave, with those around him, and, especially, with women. His masterpiece is usually said to be his Cairo trilogy (1956–1957), *Palace Walk, Palace of Desire,* and *Sugar Street,* which traces generations of a Cairo merchant family. The fierce patriarch reflects the desires, aspirations, debauchery, and social ills of the period between 1917 and 1944. Mahfouz brings into his fiction an almost journalistic, and sometimes surreal, view of love, death, and despair, in his depictions of picaresque Cairo types and political prisoners and men and women with broken dreams. He has stood alone, unafraid to criticize and praise, and has spread his gaze from extreme left to extreme right, from kind to cruel, from idealists to the corrupt. Independent of his awards, he is generally esteemed as the leading author in the Arabic language.

**FURTHER READING:** Mahfouz, Naguib. *Children of Gebelawi,* 1981; *Autumn Quail,* 1985; *Wedding Song,* 1984; *Thief and the Dogs,* 1984; *Beggar,* 1986; *Day the Leader Was Killed,* 1989; *Palace Walk,* 1989; *Time and the Place and Other Stories,* 1991; *Desire,* 1991; *Sugar Street: The Cairo Trilogy,* 1992; *Adrift on the Nile,* 1993.

# Zaabalawi

Finally I became convinced that I had to find Sheikh Zaabalawi.
   The first time I had heard his name had been in a song:

Oh what's become of the world, Zaabalawi?
They've turned it upside down and taken away its taste.

   It had been a popular song in my childhood, and one day it had occurred to me to demand of my father, in the way children have of asking endless questions:
   "Who is Zaabalawi?"
   He had looked at me hesitantly as though doubting my ability to understand the answer. However, he had replied, "May his blessing descend upon you, he's a true saint of God, a remover of worries and troubles. Were it not for him I would have died miserably—"
   In the years that followed, I heard my father many a time sing the praises of this good saint and speak of the miracles he performed. The days passed and brought with them many illnesses, for each one of which I was able, without too much trouble and at a cost I could afford, to find a cure, until I be-

came afflicted with that illness for which no one possesses a remedy. When I had tried everything in vain and was overcome by despair, I remembered by chance what I had heard in my childhood: Why, I asked myself, should I not seek out Sheikh Zaabalawi? I recollected my father saying that he had made his acquaintance in Khan Gaafar at the house of Sheikh Qamar, one of those sheikhs who practiced law in the religious courts, and so I took myself off to his house. Wishing to make sure that he was still living there, I made inquiries of a vendor of beans whom I found in the lower part of the house.

"Sheikh Qamar!" he said, looking at me in amazement. "He left the quarter ages ago. They say he's now living in Garden City and has his office in al-Azhar Square."

I looked up the office address in the telephone book and immediately set off to the Chamber of Commerce Building, where it was located. On asking to see Sheikh Qamar, I was ushered into a room just as a beautiful woman with a most intoxicating perfume was leaving it. The man received me with a smile and motioned me toward a fine leather-upholstered chair. Despite the thick soles of my shoes, my feet were conscious of the lushness of the costly carpet. The man wore a lounge suit and was smoking a cigar; his manner of sitting was that of someone well satisfied both with himself and with his worldly possessions. The look of warm welcome he gave me left no doubt in my mind that he thought me a prospective client, and I felt acutely embarrassed at encroaching upon his valuable time.

"Welcome!" he said, prompting me to speak.

"I am the son of your old friend Sheikh Ali al-Tatawi," I answered so as to put an end to my equivocal position.

A certain languor was apparent in the glance he cast at me; the languor was not total in that he had not as yet lost all hope in me.

"God rest his soul," he said. "He was a fine man."

The very pain that had driven me to go there now prevailed upon me to stay.

"He told me," I continued, "of a devout saint named Zaabalawi whom he met at Your Honor's. I am in need of him, sir, if he be still in the land of the living."

The languor became firmly entrenched in his eyes, and it would have come as no surprise if he had shown the door to both me and my father's memory.

"That," he said in the tone of one who has made up his mind to terminate the conversation, "was a very long time ago and I scarcely recall him now."

Rising to my feet so as to put his mind at rest regarding my intention of going, I asked, "Was he really a saint?"

"We used to regard him as a man of miracles."

"And where could I find him today?" I asked, making another move toward the door.

"To the best of my knowledge he was living in the Birgawi Residence in al-Azhar," and he applied himself to some papers on his desk with a resolute movement that indicated he would not open his mouth again. I bowed my head in thanks, apologized several times for disturbing him, and left the office, my head so buzzing with embarrassment that I was oblivious to all sounds around me.

I went to the Birgawi Residence, which was situated in a thickly populated quarter. I found that time had so eaten away at the building that nothing was left of it save an antiquated façade and a courtyard that, despite being supposedly in the charge of a caretaker, was being used as a rubbish dump. A small, insignificant fellow, a mere prologue to a man, was using the covered entrance as a place for the sale of old books on theology and mysticism.

When I asked him about Zaabalawi, he peered at me through narrow, inflamed eyes and said in amazement, "Zaabalawi! Good heavens, what a time ago that was! Certainly he used to live in this house when it was habitable. Many were the times he would sit with me talking of bygone days, and I would be blessed by his holy presence. Where, though, is Zaabalawi today?"

He shrugged his shoulders sorrowfully and soon left me, to attend to an approaching customer. I proceeded to make inquiries of many shopkeepers in the district. While I found that a large number of them had never even heard of Zaabalawi, some, though recalling nostalgically the pleasant times they had spent with him, were ignorant of his present whereabouts, while others openly made fun of him, labeled him a charlatan, and advised me to put myself in the hands of a doctor—as though I had not already done so. I therefore had no alternative but to return disconsolately home.

With the passing of days like motes in the air, my pains grew so severe that I was sure I would not be able to hold out much longer. Once again I fell to wondering about Zaabalawi and clutching at the hope his venerable name stirred within me. Then it occurred to me to seek the help of the local sheikh of the district; in fact, I was surprised I had not thought of this to begin with. His office was in the nature of a small shop, except that it contained a desk and a telephone, and I found him sitting at his desk, wearing a jacket over his striped galabeya. As he did not interrupt his conversation with a man sitting beside him, I stood waiting till the man had gone. The sheikh then looked up at me coldly. I told myself that I should win him over by the usual methods, and it was not long before I had him cheerfully inviting me to sit down.

"I'm in need of Sheikh Zaabalawi," I answered his inquiry as to the purpose of my visit.

He gazed at me with the same astonishment as that shown by those I had previously encountered.

"At least," he said, giving me a smile that revealed his gold teeth, "he is still alive. The devil of it is, though, he has no fixed abode. You might well bump into him as you go out of here, on the other hand you might spend days and months in fruitless searching."

"Even you can't find him!"

"Even I! He's a baffling man, but I thank the Lord that he's still alive!"

He gazed at me intently, and murmured, "It seems your condition is serious."

"Very."

"May God come to your aid! But why don't you go about it systematically?" He spread out a sheet of paper on the desk and drew on it with unexpected speed and skill until he had made a full plan of the district, showing all the various quarters, lanes, alleyways, and squares. He looked at it admiringly and said, "These are dwelling-houses, here is the Quarter of the Perfumers, here the Quarter of the Coppersmiths, the Mouski, the police and fire stations. The drawing is your best guide. Look carefully in the cafés, the places where the dervishes perform their rites, the mosques and prayer-rooms, and the Green Gate, for he may well be concealed among the beggars and be indistinguishable from them. Actually, I myself haven't seen him for years, having been somewhat preoccupied with the cares of the world, and was only brought back by your inquiry to those most exquisite times of my youth."

I gazed at the map in bewilderment. The telephone rang, and he took up the receiver.

"Take it," he told me, generously. "We're at your service."

Folding up the map, I left and wandered off through the quarter, from square to street to alleyway, making inquiries of everyone I felt was familiar with the place. At last the owner of a small establishment for ironing clothes told me, "Go to the calligrapher Hassanein in Umm al-Ghulam — they were friends."

I went to Umm al-Ghulam, where I found old Hassanein working in a deep, narrow shop full of signboards and jars of color. A strange smell, a mixture of glue and perfume, permeated its every corner. Old Hassanein was squatting on a sheepskin rug in front of a board propped against the wall; in the middle of it he had inscribed the word "Allah" in silver lettering. He was engrossed in embellishing the letters with prodigious care. I stood behind him, fearful of disturbing him or breaking the inspiration that flowed to his masterly hand. When my concern at not interrupting him had lasted some time, he suddenly inquired with unaffected gentleness, "Yes?"

Realizing that he was aware of my presence, I introduced myself. "I've been told that Sheikh Zaabalawi is your friend; I'm looking for him," I said.

His hand came to a stop. He scrutinized me in astonishment. "Zaabalawi! God be praised!" he said with a sigh.

"He *is* a friend of yours, isn't he?" I asked eagerly.

"He was, once upon a time. A real man of mystery: he'd visit you so often that people would imagine he was your nearest and dearest, then would disappear as though he'd never existed. Yet saints are not to be blamed."

The spark of hope went out with the suddenness of a lamp snuffed by a power-cut.

"He was so constantly with me," said the man, "that I felt him to be a part of everything I drew. But where is he today?"

"Perhaps he is still alive?"

"He's alive, without a doubt. . . . He had impeccable taste, and it was due to him that I made my most beautiful drawings."

"God knows," I said, in a voice almost stifled by the dead ashes of hope, "how dire my need for him is, and no one knows better than you of the ailments in respect to which he is sought."

"Yes, yes. May God restore you to health. He is in truth, as is said of him, a man, and more . . . ."

Smiling broadly, he added, "And his face possesses an unforgettable beauty. But where is he?"

Reluctantly I rose to my feet, shook hands, and left. I continued wandering eastward and westward through the quarter, inquiring about Zaabalawi from everyone who, by reason of age or experience, I felt might be likely to help me. Eventually I was informed by a vendor of lupine that he had met him a short while ago at the house of Sheikh Gad, the well-known composer. I went to the musician's house in Tabakshiyya, where I found him in a room tastefully furnished in the old style, its walls redolent with history. He was seated on a divan, his famous lute beside him, concealing within itself the most beautiful melodies of our age, while somewhere from within the house came the sound of pestle and mortar and the clamor of children. I immediately greeted him and introduced myself, and was put at my ease by the unaffected way in which he received me. He did not ask, either in words or gesture, what had brought me, and I did not feel that he even harbored any such curiosity. Amazed at his understanding and kindness, which boded well, I said, "O Sheikh Gad, I am an admirer of yours, having long been enchanted by the renderings of your songs."

"Thank you," he said with a smile.

"Please excuse my disturbing you," I continued timidly, "but I was told that Zaabalawi was your friend, and I am in urgent need of him."

"Zaabalawi!" he said, frowning in concentration. "You need him? God be with you, for who knows, O Zaabalawi, where you are."

"Doesn't he visit you?" I asked eagerly.

"He visited me some time ago. He might well come right now; on the other hand I mightn't see him till death!"

I gave an audible sigh and asked, "What made him like that?"

The musician took up his lute. "Such are saints or they would not be saints," he said, laughing.

"Do those who need him suffer as I do?"

"Such suffering is part of the cure!"

He took up the plectrum and began plucking soft strains from the strings. Lost in thought, I followed his movements. Then, as though addressing myself, I said, "So my visit has been in vain."

He smiled, laying his cheek against the side of the lute. "God forgive you," he said, "for saying such a thing of a visit that has caused me to know you and you me!"

I was much embarrassed and said apologetically, "Please forgive me; my feelings of defeat made me forget my manners."

"Do not give in to defeat. This extraordinary man brings fatigue to all who seek him. It was easy enough with him in the old days, when his place of abode was known. Today, though, the world has changed, and after having enjoyed a position attained only by potentates, he is now pursued by the police on a charge of false pretenses. It is therefore no longer an easy matter to reach him, but have patience and be sure that you will do so."

He raised his head from the lute and skillfully fingered the opening bars of a melody. Then he sang:

"I make lavish mention, even though I blame myself, of those I love,
For the stories of the beloved are my wine."

With a heart that was weary and listless, I followed the beauty of the melody and the singing.

"I composed the music to this poem in a single night," he told me when he had finished. "I remember that it was the eve of the Lesser Bairam. Zaabalawi was my guest for the whole of that night, and the poem was of his choosing. He would sit for a while just where you are, then would get up and play with my children as though he were one of them. Whenever I was overcome by weariness or my inspiration failed me, he would punch me playfully in the chest and joke with me, and I would bubble over with melodies, and thus I continued working till I finished the most beautiful piece I have ever composed."

"Does he know anything about music?"

"He is the epitome of things musical. He has an extremely beautiful speaking voice, and you have only to hear him to want to burst into song and to be inspired to creativity. . . ."

"How was it that he cured those diseases before which men are powerless?"

"That is his secret. Maybe you will learn it when you meet him."

But when would that meeting occur? We relapsed into silence, and the hubbub of children once more filled the room.

Again the sheikh began to sing. He went on repeating the words "and I have a memory of her" in different and beautiful variations until the very walls danced in ecstasy. I expressed my wholehearted admiration, and he gave me a smile of thanks. I then got up and asked permission to leave, and he accompanied me to the front door. As I shook him by the hand, he said, "I hear that nowadays he frequents the house of Hagg Wanas al-Damanhouri. Do you know him?"

I shook my head, though a modicum of renewed hope crept into my heart.

"He is a man of private means," the sheikh told me, "who from time to time visits Cairo, putting up at some hotel or other. Every evening, though, he spends at the Negma Bar in Alfi Street."

I waited for nightfall and went to the Negma Bar. I asked a waiter about Hagg Wanas, and he pointed to a corner that was semisecluded because of its position behind a large pillar with mirrors on all four sides. There I saw a man seated alone at a table with two bottles in front of him, one empty, the other two-thirds empty. There were no snacks or food to be seen, and I was sure that I was in the presence of a hardened drinker. He was wearing a loosely flowing silk galabeya and a carefully wound turban; his legs were stretched out toward the base of the pillar, and as he gazed into the mirror in rapt contentment, the sides of his face, rounded and handsome despite the fact that he was approaching old age, were flushed with wine. I approached quietly till I stood but a few feet away from him. He did not turn toward me or give any indication that he was aware of my presence.

"Good evening, Mr. Wanas," I greeted him cordially.

He turned toward me abruptly, as though my voice had roused him from slumber, and glared at me in disapproval. I was about to explain what had brought me when he interrupted in an almost imperative tone of voice that was nonetheless not devoid of an extraordinary gentleness, "First, please sit down, and second, please get drunk!"

I opened my mouth to make my excuses, but, stopping up his ears with his fingers, he said, "Not a word till you do what I say."

I realized I was in the presence of a capricious drunkard and told myself that I should at least humor him a bit. "Would you permit me to ask one question?" I said with a smile, sitting down.

Without removing his hands from his ears he indicated the bottle. "When engaged in a drinking bout like this, I do not allow any conversation between myself and another unless, like me, he is drunk, otherwise all propriety is lost and mutual comprehension is rendered impossible."

I made a sign indicating that I did not drink.

"That's your lookout," he said offhandedly. "And that's my condition!"

He filled me a glass, which I meekly took and drank. No sooner had the wine settled in my stomach than it seemed to ignite. I waited patiently till I had grown used to its ferocity, and said, "It's very strong, and I think the time has come for me to ask you about—"

Once again, however, he put his fingers in his ears. "I shan't listen to you until you're drunk!"

He filled up my glass for the second time. I glanced at it in trepidation; then, overcoming my inherent objection, I drank it down at a gulp. No sooner had the wine come to rest inside me than I lost all willpower. With the third glass, I lost my memory, and with the fourth the future vanished. The world turned round about me, and I forgot why I had gone there. The man leaned toward me attentively, but I saw him—saw everything—as a mere meaningless series of colored planes. I don't know how long it was before my head sank down onto the arm of the chair and I plunged into deep sleep. During it, I had a beautiful dream the like of which I had never experienced. I dreamed that I was in an immense garden surrounded on all sides by luxuriant trees, and the sky was nothing but stars seen between the entwined branches, all enfolded in an atmosphere like that of sunset or a sky overcast with cloud. I was lying on a small hummock of jasmine petals, more of which fell upon me like rain, while the lucent spray of a fountain unceasingly sprinkled the crown of my head and my temples. I was in a state of deep contentedness, of ecstatic serenity. An orchestra of warbling and cooing played in my ear. There was an extraordinary sense of harmony between me and my inner self, and between the two of us and the world, everything being in its rightful place, without discord or distortion. In the whole world there was no single reason for speech or movement, for the universe moved in a rapture of ecstasy. This lasted but a short while. When I opened my eyes, consciousness struck at me like a policeman's fist, and I saw Wanas al-Damanhouri peering at me with concern. Only a few drowsy customers were left in the bar.

"You have slept deeply," said my companion. "You were obviously hungry for sleep."

I rested my heavy head in the palms of my hands. When I took them away in astonishment and looked down at them, I found that they glistened with drops of water.

"My head's wet," I protested.

"Yes, my friend tried to rouse you," he answered quietly.

"Somebody saw me in this state?"

"Don't worry, he is a good man. Have you not heard of Sheikh Zaabalawi?"

"Zaabalawi!" I exclaimed, jumping to my feet.

"Yes," he answered in surprise. "What's wrong?"

"Where is he?"

"I don't know where he is now. He was here and then he left."

I was about to run off in pursuit but found I was more exhausted than I had imagined. Collapsed over the table, I cried out in despair, "My sole reason for coming to you was to meet him! Help me to catch up with him or send someone after him."

The man called a vendor of prawns and asked him to seek out the sheikh and bring him back. Then he turned to me. "I didn't realize you were afflicted. I'm very sorry. . . ."

"You wouldn't let me speak," I said irritably.

"What a pity! He was sitting on this chair beside you the whole time. He was playing with a string of jasmine petals he had around his neck, a gift from one of his admirers, then, taking pity on you, he began to sprinkle some water on your head to bring you around."

"Does he meet you here every night?" I asked, my eyes not leaving the doorway through which the vendor of prawns had left.

"He was with me tonight, last night, and the night before that, but before that I hadn't seen him for a month."

"Perhaps he will come tomorrow," I answered with a sigh.

"Perhaps."

"I am willing to give him any money he wants."

Wanas answered sympathetically, "The strange thing is that he is not open to such temptations, yet he will cure you if you meet him."

"Without charge?"

"Merely on sensing that you love him."

The vendor of prawns returned, having failed in his mission.

I recovered some of my energy and left the bar, albeit unsteadily. At every street corner I called out "Zaabalawi!" in the vague hope that I would be rewarded with an answering shout. The street boys turned contemptuous eyes on me till I sought refuge in the first available taxi.

The following evening I stayed up with Wanas al-Damanhouri till dawn, but the sheikh did not put in an appearance. Wanas informed me that he would be going away to the country and would not be returning to Cairo until he had sold the cotton crop.

I must wait, I told myself; I must train myself to be patient. Let me content myself with having made certain of the existence of Zaabalawi, and even of his affection for me, which encourages me to think that he will be prepared to cure me if a meeting takes place between us.

Sometimes, however, the long delay wearied me. I would become beset by despair and would try to persuade myself to dismiss him from my mind completely. How many weary people in this life know him not or regard him as a mere myth! Why, then, should I torture myself about him in this way?

No sooner, however, did my pains force themselves upon me than I would again begin to think about him, asking myself when I would be fortunate enough to meet him. The fact that I ceased to have any news of Wanas and was told he had gone to live abroad did not deflect me from my purpose; the truth of the matter was that I had become fully convinced that I had to find Zaabalawi.

Yes, I have to find Zaabalawi.


■ **Mririda Naït Attik (1919– )** *Morocco* **(Berber) (poems)**

TRANSLATED BY DANIEL HALPERN AND PAULA PALEY

Little is known of the life of Mririda except that she was a courtesan of the *souk* (the market) of Azilal in the Atlas Mountains of Morocco and sang her poems in Tachelhait, a Berber dialect. The poem songs were rescued from anonymity by René Euloge, a French soldier, who translated them into French and published them. Although the poems have a defiant individualism, they also partake of an oral tradition. Her clients,

French soldiers or local truck drivers and merchants, evidently paid no attention to her songs, but this did not dissuade her from composing or singing them. Euloge describes her voice as "a bouquet of thistles and wild oats, not a sumptuous carnation with a sweet perfume."[1] As a creative courtesan, she reflects a universal role, found in small and great civilizations, from the educated and high class *hetaerae* (companions) of Greece to the *geishas* of Japan and the Tang and Song dynasty concubine poets of China. These women, literate in societies in which few men and fewer women could read and write, often came from the educated entertainment and companion class. Mririda's poems were translated from their French translation by two gifted American poets, Daniel Halpern and Paula Paley.

**FURTHER READING:** Attik, Mririda n'Aït. *Songs of Mririda: Courtesan of the High Atlas.* Translated from the French of René Euloge by Daniel Halpern and Paula Paley, 1974.

## Mririda

They nicknamed me Mririda.
Mririda, nimble tree-frog of the meadow.
I don't have her gold eyes,
I don't have her white throat
Or green tunic.
But what I have, like Mririda,
Is my *zezarit*, my call
That carries up to the sheepfolds—
The whole valley
And the other side of the mountain
Speak of it. . . .
My call, which brings astonishment and envy.

They named me Mririda
Because the first time I walked in the fields
I gently took a tree-frog,
Afraid and trembling in my hands,
And pressed her white throat
To my lips of a child,
And then of a girl.

---

1. Mririda n'Aït Attik, *Songs of Mririda: Courtesan of the High Atlas.* Translated from the French at René Euloge by Daniel Halpern and Paula Paley (Greensboro, NC: Unicorn Press, 1924), 10.

And so I was given the *baraka,*                                    20
The magic that gives them their song
Which fills the summer nights,
A song clear as glass,
Sharp as the sound of an anvil
In the vibrating air before rain. . . .                             25
Because of this gift
They call me Mririda,
And he who will come for me
Will feel my heart beat in his hand
As I have felt the racing hearts of frogs                           30
Beneath my fingertips.

In the nights bathed in moonlight
He will call me, *Mririda, Mririda,*
Sweet nickname that I love,
And for him I will release my piercing call,                        35
Shrill and drawn-out,
Bringing wonder from men
And jealousy from women,
Nothing like it ever heard in this valley.

## The Bad Lover

Leave me, soldier without sense or manners!
I can see that you are full of contempt,
Your hand raised, insults on your lips,
Now that you've had what you want from me.
And you leave, calling me a dog!                                    5
Sated with my pleasures,
You'd have me blush for my trade,
But you, were you ashamed
When you pushed gently at my door,
Up like a bull?                                                     10
Were you coming to play cards?
You turned yourself into something humble,
Agreeing right off to my demands,
To losing all your pay in advance.
And the more your eyes undressed me,                                15
The more your rough desire put you in my power.

When you finally took off my clothes
I could have had your soul for the asking!
I could have cursed your mother
And your father, and their ancestors!                               20
Toward what paradise were you flying?

But now that you've calmed down,
You're back on earth,
Arrogant, rough and coarse as your *djellaba*.

Guest of mine for the moment, my slave,                                            2
Don't you feel my disgust and hate?
One of these days
The memory of tonight will bring you back to me
Conquered and submissive again.
You'll leave your pride at the door                                               3(
And I'll laugh at your glances and your wishes.
But you'll have to pay three times the price next time!
This will be the cost of your insults and pride.

I'll no more notice your clutching
Than the river notices a drop of rain.                                             3

## ■ Yashar Kemal (1922– ) *Turkey* (story)

TRANSLATED BY THILDA KEMAL

Yashar Kemal is Turkey's finest living writer, a candidate for the Nobel
Prize in Literature. He was born Yashar Kemal Gokceli in 1922 in Hemite, a
small village in Southern Anatolia, to a family that blended his father's line
of feudal lords with his mother's line of thieves. When he was five, his father
was murdered before his eyes in a mosque, and he developed a stammer
from the shock that left him only when he sang. He walked long distances
to a secondary school to learn to read and write, but after several years had
to go to work in the cotton fields and later as a factory worker. He was a tireless defender of the poor workers and peasants, which cost him jobs and
eventually led to his arrest in 1950 on allegations, later disproved, of involvement with Communist propaganda. He worked as a public letter writer and
later as a reporter in Istanbul, where he dropped his surname. He published his first book of short stories in 1952. His novel *Ince Memed* appeared
in 1955 and was translated into English in two parts as *Memed My Hawk*
(1961) and *They Burn the Thistles* (1977). He was a member of the Central
Committee of the Turkish Worker's Party until it was banned. Other books
available in English are *Anatolian Tales, Wind from the Plain, The Legend of
Ararat, The Legend of the Thousand Bulls, The Undying Grass, The Lords of
Akchasaz, Murder in the Ironsmiths,* and *Iron Earth, Copper Sky.*

## A Dirty Story

The three of them were sitting on the damp earth, their backs against the
dung-daubed brush wall and their knees drawn up to their chests, when
another man walked up and crouched beside them.

"Have you heard?" said one of them excitedly. "Broken-Nose Jabbar's done it again! You know Jabbar, the fellow who brings all those women from the mountain villages and sells them in the plain? Well, this time he's come down with a couple of real beauties. The lads of Misdik have got together and bought one of them on the spot, and now they're having fun and making her dance and all that . . . It's unbelievable! Where does the fellow find so many women? How does he get them to come with him? He's the devil's own son, he is . . ."

"Well, that's how he makes a living," commented one of the men. "Ever since I can remember, this Jabbar's been peddling women for the villagers of the Chukurova plain. Allah provides for all and sundry . . ."

"He's still got the other one," said the newcomer, "and he's ready to give her away for a hundred liras."

"He'll find a customer soon enough," put in another man whose head was hunched between his shoulders. "A good woman's worth more than a team of oxen, at least, in the Chukurova plain she is. You can always put her to the plow and, come summer, she'll bind and carry the sheaves, hoe, do anything. What's a hundred liras? Why, a woman brings in that much in one single summer. In the fields, at home, in bed. There's nothing like a woman. What's a hundred liras?"

Just then, Hollow Osman came up mumbling to himself and flopped down beside them without a word of greeting. He was a tall, broad-shouldered man with a rather shapeless potbellied body. His lips drooped foolishly and his eyes had an odd squintlike gaze.

"Hey, Osman," the man who had been talking addressed him. "Broken Nose Jabbar's got a woman for sale again. Only a hundred liras. Tell Mistress Huru to buy her for you and have done with living alone and sleeping in barns like a dog."

Osman shrugged his shoulders doubtfully.

"Look here, man," pursued the other, "this is a chance in a million. What's a hundred liras? You've been slaving for that Huru since you dropped out of your mother's womb and she's never paid you a lira. She owes you this. And anyway she'll get back her money's worth in just one summer. A woman's good for everything, in the house, in the fields, in bed . . ."

Osman rose abruptly.

"I'll ask the Mistress," he said. "How should I know? . . ."

A couple of days later, a short, broad-hipped girl with blue beads strung into her plaited hair was seen at the door of Huru's barn in which Hollow Osman always slept. She was staring out with huge wondering eyes.

A month passed. Two months . . . And passersby grew familiar with the sight of the strange wide-eyed girl at the barn door.

One day, a small dark boy with a face the size of a hand was seen pelting through the village. He rushed up to his mother where she sat on the threshold of her hut gossiping with Seedy Doneh.

"Mother," he screeched, "I've seen them! It's the truth, I swear it is. Uncle Osman's wife with . . . May my eyes drop out right here if I'm telling a lie."

Seedy Doneh turned to him sharply.

"What?" she cried. "Say it again. What's that about Fadik?"

"She was with the Agha's son. I saw them with my own eyes. He went into the barn with her. They couldn't see me where I was hiding. Then he took off his boots, you know the shiny yellow boots he wears . . . And then they lay down and . . . Let my two eyes drop out if . . ."

"I knew it!" crowed Seedy Doneh. "I knew it would turn out this way."

"Hollow Osman never had any manhood in him anyway," said the child's mother. "Always under that viper-tongued Huru's petticoats . . ."

"Didn't I tell you, Ansha, the very first day she came here that this would happen?" said Doneh. "I said this girl's ready to play around. Pretending she was too bashful to speak to anyone. Ah, still waters run deep . . ."

She rose quickly and hurried off to spread the news.

"Have you heard? Just as I foretold . . . Still waters . . . The Agha's son . . . Fadik . . ."

In a trice all the neighboring women had crowded at Ansha's door, trying to squeeze the last drop of information out of the child.

"Come on, tell us," urged one of the women for perhaps the hundredth time. "How did you see them?"

"Let my two eyes drop out right here if I'm lying," the child repeated again and again with unabated excitement. "The Agha's son came in, and then they lay down, both of them, and did things . . . I was watching through a chink in the wall. Uncle Osman's wife, you know, was crying. I can't do it, she was saying, and she was sobbing away all the time. Then the Agha's son pulled off those shiny yellow boots of his . . . Then I ran right here to tell Mother."

The news spread through the village like wildfire. People could talk about nothing else. Seedy Doneh, for one, seemed to have made it her job to leave no man or woman uninformed. As she scoured the village for new listeners, she chanced upon Osman himself.

"Haven't you heard what's come upon you?" she said, drawing him aside behind the wall of a hut. "You're disgraced, you jackass. The Agha's son has got his fingers up your wife's skirt. Try and clear your good name now if you can!"

Osman did not seem to understand.

"I don't know . . ." he murmured, shrugging his shoulders. "I'll have to ask the Mistress. What would the Agha's son want with my wife?"

Doneh was incensed.

"What would he want with her, blockhead?" she screamed. "Damn you, your wife's become a whore, that's what! She's turned your home into a brothel. Anyone can come in and have her." She flounced off still screaming. "I spit on you! I spit on your manhood . . ."

Osman was upset.

"What are you shouting for, woman?" he called after her. "People will think something's wrong. I have to ask the Mistress. She knows everything. How should I know?"

He started walking home, his long arms dangling at his sides as though they had been hitched to his shoulders as an afterthought, his fingers sticking out wide apart as was his habit. This time he was waylaid by their next-door neighbor, Zeynep, who planted herself before him and tackled him at the top of her voice.

"Ah Osman! You'd be better off dead! Why don't you go and bury yourself! The whole village knows about it. Your wife . . . The Agha's son . . . Ah Osman, how could you have brought such a woman into your home? Where's your honor now? Disgraced . . . Ah Osman!"

He stared at her in bewilderment.

"How should I know?" he stammered, his huge hands opening out like pitchforks. "The Mistress knows all about such things. I'll go and ask her."

Zeynep turned her back on him in exasperation, her large skirt ballooning about her legs.

"Go bury yourself, Osman! I hope I see you dead after this."

A group of children were playing tipcat nearby. Suddenly one of them broke into a chant.

"Go bury yourself, Osman . . . See you dead, Osman . . ."

The other children joined in mechanically without interrupting their game.

Osman stared at them and turned away.

"How should I know?" he muttered. "I must go to the Mistress."

He found Huru sitting at her spinning wheel. Fadik was there too, squatting near the hearth and listlessly chewing mastic gum.

"Mistress," said Osman, "have you heard what Seedy Doneh's saying? She's saying I'm disgraced . . ."

Huru stepped on the pedal forcefully and brought the wheel to a stop.

"What's that?" she said. "What about Seedy Doneh?"

"I don't know . . . She said Fadik . . ."

"Look here," said Huru, "you mustn't believe those lying bitches. You've got a good wife. Where would you find such a woman?"

"I don't know. Go bury yourself, they said. The children too . . ."

"Shut up," cried Huru, annoyed. "People always gossip about a beautiful woman. They go looking for the mote in their neighbor's eye without seeing the beam in their own. They'd better hold their peace because I've got a tongue in my head too . . ."

Osman smiled with relief.

"How could I know?" he said.

Down in the villages of the Chukurova plain, a sure sign of oncoming spring is when the women are seen with their heads on one another's lap, picking the lice out of one another's hair. So it was, on one of the first warm days of the year. A balmy sun shone caressingly down on the fields and village, and not a leaf stirred. A group of women were sitting before their huts on the dusty ground, busy with the lice and wagging their tongues for all they were worth. An acrid odor of sweat hung about the group. Seedy Doneh was rummaging in the hair of a large woman who was stretched full length on the ground. She decided that she had been silent long enough.

"No," she declared suddenly, "it's not as you say, sister! He didn't force her or any such thing. She simply fell for him the minute she saw those shiny yellow boots. If you're going to believe Huru! . . . She's got to deny it, of course."

"That Huru was born with a silver spoon in her mouth," said white-haired, toothless old Zala, wiping her bloodstained fingers on her ragged skirt. "Hollow Osman's been slaving for her like twenty men ever since she took him in, a kid the size of your hand! And all for a mere pittance of food. And now there's the woman too. Tell me, what's there left for Huru to do?"

"Ah," sighed another woman, "fortune has smiled on Huru, she has indeed! She's got two people serving her now."

"And both for nothing," old Zala reminded her.

"What it amounts to," said Seedy Doneh spitefully, "is that Huru used to have one wife and now she's got two. Osman was always a woman, and as for Fadik she's a real woman. He-he!"

"That she is, a real woman!" the others agreed.

"Huru says the Agha's son took her by force," pursued Doneh. "All right, but what about the others? What about those lining up at her door all through the night, eh? She never says no to any one of them, does she? She takes in everyone, young and old."

"The Lady Bountiful, that's what she is," said Elif. "And do you know something? Now that Fadik's here, the young men are leaving Omarja's yellow bitch in peace . . ."

"They've got somewhere better to go!" cackled the others.

Omarja's dumpy wife jumped up from where she was sitting on the edge of the group.

"Now look here, Elif!" she cried. "What's all this about our yellow dog? Stop blackening people's characters, will you?"

"Well, it's no lie, is it?" Doneh challenged her. "When was that bitch ever at your door where she should be all night? No, instead, there she came trotting up a-mornings with a rope dangling from her neck!"

"Don't go slandering our dog," protested Omarja's wife. "Why, if Omarja hears this, he'll kill the poor creature. Upon my word he will!"

"Go on!" said Doneh derisively. "Don't you come telling me that Omarja doesn't know his yellow bitch is the paramour of all the village youths! What about that time when Stumpy Veli caught some of them down by the river, all taking it in turns over her? Is there anyone in this village who didn't hear of that? It's no use trying to whitewash your bitch to us!"

Omarja's wife was alarmed.

"Don't, sister," she pleaded. "Omarja'll shoot the dog, that's sure . . ."

"Well, I'm not to blame for that, sister," retorted Doneh tartly. "Anyway, the bitch'll be all right now that Fadik's around. And so will Kurdish Velo's donkey . . ."

Kurdish Velo's wife began to fidget nervously.

"Not our fault," she blurted out in her broken Turkish. "We lock our donkey in, but they come and break the door! Velo furious. Velo say people round here savage. He say, with an animal deadly sin! He say he kill someone. Then he complain to the Headman. Velo going sell this donkey."

"You know what I think?" interposed Seedy Doneh. "They're going to make it hot for her in this village. Yes, they'll do what they did to Esheh."

"Poor Esheh," sighed old Zala. "What a woman she was before her man got thrown into prison! She would never have come to that, but she had no one to protect her. May they rot in hell, those that forced her into it! But she is dead and gone, poor thing."

"Eh!" said Doneh. "How could she be otherwise after the youths of five villages had done with her?" She straightened up. "Look here, sister," she said to the woman whose head was on her lap, "I couldn't get through your lice in days! They say the Government's invented some medicine for lice which they call Dee-Dee. Ah, if only we had a spoonful of that . . . Do you know, women, that Huru keeps watch over Fadik at night? She tells the youths when to come in and then drives them out with a stick. Ha-ha, and she wants us to believe in Fadik's virtue . . ."

"That's because it suits her. Where will she find people who'll work for nothing like those two?"

"Well, the lads are well provided for this year," snickered Doneh. "Who knows but that Huru may hop in and help Fadik out!"

Just then, Huru loomed up from behind a hut. She was a large woman with a sharp chin and a wrinkled face. Her graying hair was always carefully dyed with henna.

"Whores!" she shouted at the top of her voice, as she bore down upon them with arms akimbo. "City trollops! You get hold of a poor fellow's wife and let your tongues go wagging away. Tell me, are you any better than she? What do you want of this harmless mountain girl?" She pounced on Doneh who cringed back. "As for you, you filthy shitty-assed bitch, you'll shut your mouth or I'll start telling the truth about you and that husband of yours who pretends he's a man. You know me, don't you?"

Doneh blenched.

"Me, sister?" she stammered. "Me? I never . . . Other people's good name . . ."

The women were dispersing hastily. Only Kurdish Velo's wife, unaware of what was going on, continued picking lice out of her companion's hair.

"Velo says in our country women like this burnt alive. He says there no virtue in this Chukurova. No honor . . ."

The eastern sky had only just begun to pale as, with a great hullabaloo and calls and cries, the women and children drove the cattle out to pasture. Before their houses, red-aproned matrons were busy at the churns beating yogurt. The damp air smelled of spring.

Osman had long ago yoked the oxen and was waiting at Huru's door. She appeared in the doorway.

"Osman, my lion," she said, "you're not to come back until you've plowed through the whole field. The girl Aysheh will look after your food and get you some bedding. Mind you do the sowing properly, my child. Husneh's hard pressed this year. And there's your wife to feed too now . . ."

Husneh was Huru's only child, whom in a moment of aberration she had given in marriage to Ali Efendi, a low-salaried tax collector. All the product of her land, everything Huru had, was for this daughter.

Osman did not move or say a word. He stood there in the half-light, a large black shadow near the yoked oxen whose tails were flapping their legs in slow rhythm.

Huru stepped up to him.

"What's the matter with you, Osman, my child," she said anxiously. "Is anything wrong?"

"Mistress," whispered Osman, "it's what Seedy Doneh's saying. And Zeynep too . . . That my house . . . I don't know . . ."

Huru flared up.

"Shut up, you spineless dolt," she cried. "Don't you come babbling to me about the filthy inventions of those city trollops. I paid that broken-nosed thief a hundred good bank notes for the girl, didn't I? Did I ask you for as much as a lira? You listen to me. You can find fault with pure gold, but not with Fadik. Don't let me hear such nonsense from you again!"

Osman hesitated.

"I don't know . . ." he murmured, as he turned at last and drove the oxen off before him.

It was midmorning. A bright sun glowed over the sparkling fields.

Osman was struggling with the lean, emaciated oxen, which after plowing through only one acre had stretched themselves on the ground and simply refused to budge. Flushed and breathless, he let himself drop onto a mound and took his head in his hands. After a while, he rose and tried pulling the animals up by the tail.

"Accursed beasts," he muttered. "The Mistress says Husneh's in need this year. Get up this minute, accursed beasts!"

He pushed and heaved, but to no avail. Suddenly in a burst of fury, he flung himself on the black ox, dug his teeth into its nose, and shook it with all his might. Then he straightened up and looked about him sheepishly.

"If anyone saw me . . ." He swore as he spat out blood. "What can I do? Husneh's in need and there's Fadik to feed too. And now these heathen beasts . . . I don't know."

It was in this state of perplexity that Stumpy Veli found him when he strolled over from a neighboring field.

"So the team's collapsed eh?" he commented. "Well, it was to be expected. Look at how their ribs are sticking out. You won't be able to get anything out of them."

"I don't know," muttered Osman faintly. "Husneh's in a bad way and I got married . . ."

"And a fine mess that's landed you in," burst out Veli angrily. "You'd have been better off dead!"

"I don't know," said Osman. "The Mistress paid a hundred liras for her . . ."

Stumpy Veli took hold of his arm and made him sit down.

"Look, Osman," he said, "the villagers told me to talk to you. They say you're giving the village a bad name. Ever since the Agha's son took up with your wife, all the other youths have followed suit and your house is just like a brothel now. The villagers say you've got to repudiate her. If you don't, they'll drive you both out. The honor of the whole village is at stake, and you know honor doesn't grow on trees . . ."

Osman, his head hanging down, was as still as a statue. A stray ant had caught his eye.

What's this ant doing around here at this time of day, he wondered to himself. Where can its nest be?

Veli nudged him sharply.

"Damn you, man!" he cried. "Think what'll happen if the police get wind of this. She hasn't got any papers. Why, if the gendarmes once lay their hands on her, you know how it'll be. They'll play around with her for months, poor creature."

Osman started as though an electric current had been sent through his large frame.

"I haven't got any papers either," he whispered.

Veli drew nearer. Their shoulders touched. Osman's were trembling fitfully.

"Papers are the business of the Government," Veli said. "You and me, we can't understand such things. If we did, then what would we need a Government for? Now, listen to me. If the gendarmes get hold of her, we'll be the laughingstock of villages for miles around. We'll never be able to hold up our heads again in the Chukurova. You mustn't trifle with the honor of the whole village. Get rid of her before she drags you into more trouble."

"But where will I be without her?" protested Osman. "I'll die, that's all. Who'll do my washing? Who'll cook bulgur pilaf for me? I'll starve to death if I have to eat gruel again every day. I just can't do without her."

"The villagers will buy you another woman," said Veli. "We'll collect the money among us. A better woman, an honorable one, and beautiful too . . . I'll go up into the mountain villages and pick one for you myself. Just you pack this one off quickly . . ."

"I don't know," said Osman. "It's the Mistress knows about these things."

Veli was exasperated.

"Damn the Mistress!" he shouted. "It's up to you, you idiot!"

Then he softened. He tried persuasion again. He talked and talked. He talked himself hoarse, but Osman sat there immovable as a rock, his mouth clamped tight. Finally Veli spat in his face and stalked off.

It was well on in the afternoon when it occurred to Osman to unyoke the team. He had not stirred since Veli's departure. As for the oxen, they had just lain there placidly chewing the cud. He managed to get them to their feet and let them wander about the field, while he walked back to the village. He made straight for the Agha's house and waited in the yard, not speaking to anyone, until he saw the Agha's son riding in, the bridle of his horse lathered with sweat.

The Agha's son was taken aback. He dismounted quickly, but Osman waylaid him.

"Listen," he pleaded, "you're the son of our all-powerful Agha. What do you want with my wife?"

The Agha's son became the color of his famous boots. He hastily pulled a five-lira note out of his pocket and thrust it into Osman's hand.

"Take this," he mumbled and hurried away.

"But you're a great big Agha's son!" cried Osman after him. "Why do you want to drive her away? What harm has she done you? You're a great big . . ."

He was crushed. He stumbled away towards Huru's house, the five-lira note still in his hand.

At the sight of Osman, Huru blew her top.

"What are you doing here, you feebleminded ass?" she shouted. "Didn't I tell you not to come back until you'd finished all the plowing? Do you want to ruin me, you idiot?"

"Wait, Mistress," stammered Osman. "Listen . . ."

"Listen, he says! Damn the fool!"

"Mistress," he pleaded, "let me explain . . ."

Huru glared at him.

"Mistress, you haven't heard. You don't know what the villagers are going to do to me. They're going to throw me out of this village. Stumpy Veli said so. He said the police . . . He said papers . . . We haven't got any papers. Fadik hasn't and I haven't either. He said the gendarmes would carry Fadik away and do things to her. He said I must repudiate her because my house is a brothel. That's what he said. I said the Mistress knows these things . . . She paid the hundred liras . . ."

Huru was dancing with fury. She rushed out into the village square and began howling at the top of her voice.

"Bastards! So she's a thorn in your flesh, this poor fellow's wife! If you want to drive whores out of this village why don't you start with your own wives and daughters? You'd better look for whores in your own homes, pimps that you are, all of you! And tell your sons to leave poor folks' women alone . . ."

Then she turned to Osman and gave him a push.

"Off you go! To the fields! No one's going to do anything to your wife. Not while I'm alive."

The villagers had gathered in the square and had heard Huru out in profound silence. As soon as she was gone, though, they started muttering among themselves.

"Who does that bitch think she is, abusing the whole village like that? . . ."

The Agha, Wolf Mahmut, had heard her too.

"You just wait, Huru," he said grinding his teeth. "If you think you're going to get away with this . . ."

The night was dark, a thick damp darkness that seemed to cling to the face and hands. Huru had been waiting for some time now, concealed in the blackest shadow of the barn, when suddenly she perceived a stirring in the darkness, and a voice was calling softly at the door.

"Fadik! Open up, girl. It's me . . ."

The door creaked open and a shadow glided in. An uncontrollable trembling seized Huru. She gripped her stick and flung herself on the door. It was unbolted and went crashing back against the wall. As she stood there trying to pierce the darkness, a few vague figures hustled by and made their escape. Taken by surprise, she hurled out a vitriolic oath and started groping about until she discovered Fadik crouching in a corner. She seized her by the hair and began to beat her with the stick.

"Bitch!" she hissed. "To think I was standing up for you . . ."

Fadik did not utter a sound as the blows rained down on her. At last Huru, exhausted, let go of her.

"Get up," she ordered, "and light some kindling."

Fadik raked out the dying embers and with much puffing and blowing managed to light a stick of torchwood. A pale honeyed light fell dimly over the stacked hay. There was an old pallet in one corner and a few kitchen utensils, but nothing else to show that the place was lived in.

Huru took Fadik's hand and looked at her sternly.

"Didn't you promise me, girl, that you'd never do it again?"

Fadik's head hung low.

"Do you know, you bitch," continued Huru, "what the villagers are going to do? They're going to kick you out of the village. Do you hear me?"

Fadik stirred a little. "Mistress, I swear I didn't go after them! They just came in spite of everything."

"Listen to me, girl," said Huru. "Do you know what happened to Esheh? That's what you'll come to if you're not careful. They're like ravening wolves, these men. If you fall into their clutches, they'll tear you to shreds. To shreds, I tell you!"

"But Mistress, I swear I never did anything to—"

"You must bolt your door because they'll be after you whether you do anything or not, and their pimps of fathers will put the blame on me. It's my hundred liras they can't swallow. They're dying to see it go to pot . . . Just like Esheh you'll be. They had no one in the world, she and her man, and when Ali was thrown into jail she was left all alone. He'd lifted a sheep from the Agha's flock and bought clothes and shoes for their son. A lovely child he was, three years old . . . Ali doted on him. But there he was in jail, and that yellow-booted good-for-nothing was soon after Esheh like the plague. She kept him at arm's length for as long as she could, poor Esheh, but he got what he wanted in the end. Then he turned her over to those ravening wolves . . . They dragged her about from village to village, from mountain to mountain. Twenty, thirty good-for-nothings . . . Her child was left among strangers, the little boy she had loved so. He died . . . Those who saw her said she was like a consumptive, thin and gray, but still they wouldn't let her go, those scoundrels. Then one day the village dogs came in all smeared with blood, and an eagle was circling over the plain. So the men went to look, and they found Esheh, her body half devoured by the dogs . . . They'd made her dance naked for them . . . They'd done all sorts of things to her. Yes, they as good as killed her. That's what the police said when they came up from the town. And when Ali heard of it, he died of grief in jail. Yes, my girl, you've got Esheh's fate before you. It isn't my hundred liras that I care for, it's you. As for Osman, I can always find another woman for him. Now I've warned you. Just call me if they come again. Esheh was all alone in the world. You've got me, at least. Do you swear to do as I'm telling you?"

"I swear it, Mistress," said Fadik.

Huru was suddenly very tired.

"Well, I'm going. You'll call me, won't you?"

As soon as she was gone, the youths crept out of the darkness and sneaked into the barn again.

"Hey, Fadik," they whispered. "Huru was lying to you, girl. Esheh just killed herself . . ."

There was a stretch of grass in front of the Agha's house, and on one side of it dung had been heaped to the size of a small hillock. The dung steamed in the early morning sun and not a breath stirred the warm air. A cock climbed to the top of the heap. It scraped the dung, stretched its neck, and crowed triumphantly, flapping its wings.

The group of villagers squatting about on the grass silently eyed the angry Agha. Wolf Mahmut was a huge man whose shadow when he was sitting was as large as that of an average man standing up. He was never seen without a frayed, checked overcoat, the only one in the village, that he had been wearing for years now.

He was toying irritably with his metal-framed glasses when Stumpy Veli, who had been sent for a while ago, made his appearance. The Agha glared at him.

"Is this the way you get things done, you fraud?" he expostulated. "So you'd have Hollow Osman eating out of your hand in no time, eh?"

Stumpy Veli seemed to shrink to half his size.

"Agha," he said, "I tried everything. I talked and talked. I told him the villagers would drive them both out. I warned him of the gendarmes. All right, he said, I'll send her away. And then he didn't . . . If you ask me, Huru's at the bottom of it all."

The others stirred. "That she is!" they agreed.

Mahmut Agha jumped up. "I'll get even with her," he growled.

"That, you will, Agha," they assented. "But . . ."

"We've put up with that old whore long enough," continued the Agha, sitting down again.

"Yes, Agha," said Stumpy Veli, "but, you see, she relies on her son-in-law Ali, the tax collector. They'd better stop treading on my toes, she said, or I'll have Ali strip this village bare . . ."

"He can't do anything," said the Agha. "I don't owe the Government a bean."

"But we do, Agha," interposed one of the men. "He can come here and take away our blankets and rugs, whatever we have . . ."

"It's because of Huru that he hasn't fleeced this village up to now," said another. "We owe a lot of money, Agha."

"Well, what are we to do then?" cried Mahmut Agha angrily. "All our youths have left the plow and the fields and are after the woman night and day like rutting bulls. At this rate, the whole village'll starve this year."

An old man spoke up in a tremulous voice. "I'm dead, for one," he wailed. "That woman's ruined my hearth. High morning it is already. Go to the plow, my son, I beg the boy. We'll starve if you don't plow. But he won't listen. He's always after that woman. I've lost my son because of that whore. I'm too old to plow any more. I'll starve this year. I'll go and throw myself at Huru's feet. There's nothing else to do . . ."

The Agha rose abruptly. "That Huru!" He gritted his teeth. "I'll settle her account."

He strode away.

The villagers looked up hopefully. "Mahmut Agha'll settle her account," they muttered. "He'll find a way . . ."

The Agha heard them and swelled with pride. "Yes, Mahmut Agha'll settle her account," he repeated grimly to himself.

He stopped before a hut and called out.

"Hatije Woman! Hatije!"

A middle-aged woman rushed out wiping her hands on her apron.

"Mahmut Agha!" she cried. "Welcome to our home. You never visit us these days." Then she whirled back. "Get up, you damned lazybones," she shouted angrily. "It's high morning, and look who's here."

Mahmut Agha followed her inside.

"Look, Agha," she complained, pointing to her son, "it's high morning and Halil still abed!"

Startled at the sight of the Agha, Halil sprang up and drew on his black shalvar trousers shamefacedly, while his mother continued with her lamentations.

"Ah, Mahmut Agha, you don't know what's befallen us! You don't know, may I kiss your feet, my Agha, or you wouldn't have us on your land any longer . . . Ah, Mahmut Agha! This accursed son of mine . . . I would have seen him dead and buried, yes, buried in this black earth before . . ."

"What are you cursing the lad for?" Mahmut Agha interrupted her. "Wait, just tell me first."

"Ah, Agha, if you knew! It was full day when he came home this night. And it's the same every night, the same ever since Hollow Osman's woman came to the village. He lies abed all through the livelong day. Who'll do the plowing, I ask you? We'll starve this year. Ah, Mahmut Agha, do something! Please do something . . ."

"You go outside a little, will you, Hatije," said the Agha. Then he turned to Halil, stretching out his long, wrinkled neck which had become as red as a turkey's. "Listen to me, my boy, this has got to end. You must get this whore out of our village and give her to the youths of another village, any village. She's got to go and you'll do it. It's an order. Do you hear me?"

"Why, Agha!" Halil said ingratiatingly. "Is that what's worrying you? I'll get hold of her this very night and turn her over to Jelil from Ortakli village. You can count on me."

The Agha's spirits rose.

"Hatije," he called out, "come in here. See how I'm getting you out of this mess? And all the village too . . . Let that Huru know who she's dealing with in the future. They call me Wolf Mahmut and I know how to put her nose out of joint."

Long before dawn, piercing shrieks startled the echoes in the village.

"Bastards! Pimps!" Huru was howling. "You won't get away with this, not on your life you won't. My hundred liras were too much for you to swallow, eh, you fiends? You were jealous of this poor fellow's wife, eh? But you just wait and see, Wolf Mahmut! I'll set the tax collector after you all in no time. I'll get even with you if I have to spend my last penny! I'll bribe the Mudir, the Kaymakam, all the officials. I'll send telegrams to Ankara, to Ismet Pasha, to the head of the Democrats. I'll have you all dragged into court, rotting away in police stations. I'll get my own back on you for Fadik's sake."

She paused to get her breath and was off again even louder than before.

Fadik had disappeared, that was the long and the short of it. Huru soon found out that someone else was missing too. Huseyin's half-witted son, The Tick.

"Impossible," she said. "The Tick ravishing women? Not to save his life, he couldn't! This is just another trick of those good-for-nothings . . ."

"But really, Huru," the villagers tried to persuade her, "he was after her all the time. Don't you know he gathered white snails in the hills, threaded them into a necklace, and offered it to Fadik, and she hung it up on her wall as a keepsake? That's the plain truth, Huru."

"I don't believe it," Huru said stubbornly. "I wouldn't even if I saw them together with my own eyes . . ."

The next day it started raining, that sheer, plumb-line torrent which sets in over the Chukurova for days. The minute the bad news had reached him, Osman had abandoned his plow and had rushed back to the village. He was standing now motionless at Huru's door, the peak of his cap drooping over his eyes. His wet clothes clung to his flesh, glistening darkly, and his rawhide boots were clogged with mud.

"Come in out of the rain, Osman, do!" Huru kept urging him.

"I can't. I don't know . . ." was all he could say.

"Now, look here, Osman," said Huru. "She's gone, so what? Let them have that bitch. I'll find you a good woman, my Osman. Never mind the money. I'll spend twice as much on a new wife for you. Just you come in out of the rain."

Osman never moved.

"Listen, Osman. I've sent word to Ali. Come and levy the taxes at once, I said. Have no mercy on these ungrateful wretches. If you don't fleece them to their last rag, I said, you needn't count on me as a mother again. You'll see what I'm going to do to them, my Osman. You just come inside . . ."

The rain poured down straight and thick as the warp in a loom, and Osman still stood there, his chin resting on his staff, like a thick tree whose branches have been lopped off.

Huru appealed to the neighbors. Two men came and pulled and pushed, but he seemed nailed to the ground. It was well in the afternoon when he stirred and began to pace the village from one end to the other, his head sunk between his shoulders and the rain streaming down his body.

"Poor fellow, he's gone mad," opined the villagers.

A few strong men finally carried him home. They undressed him and put him to bed.

Huru sat down beside him. "Look, Osman, I'll get you a new woman even if it costs me a thousand liras. You mustn't distress yourself so. Just for a woman . . ."

The next morning he was more his normal self, but no amount of reasoning or pleading from Huru could induce him to go back to the field. He left the house and resumed his pacing up and down.

The villagers had really begun to feel sorry for him now.

"Alas, poor Osman!" they murmured as he passed between the huts.

Osman heard them and heaved deep, heartrending sighs. And still he roamed aimlessly round and round.

Wolf Mahmut should have known better. Why, the whole village saw with half an eye what a rascal Halil was! How could he be trusted to give up a woman once he had got her into his hands? He had indeed got Fadik out of the way, but what he had done was to shut her up in one of the empty sheep pens in the hills beyond the village, and there he had posted The Tick to guard her.

"Play around with her if you like," he had told him contemptuously. "But if you let her give you the slip— " and he had seized The Tick's wrist and squeezed it until it hurt—"you're as good as dead."

Though twenty years old, The Tick was so scraggy and undersized that at first glance people would take him to be only ten. His arms and legs were as thin as matchsticks and he walked sideways like a crab. He had always had a way of clinging tenaciously to people or objects he took a fancy to, which even as a child had earned him his nickname. No one had ever called him by his real name and it looked as though his own mother had forgotten it too . . .

Halil would come every evening bringing food for Fadik and The Tick, and he would leave again just before dawn. But it was not three days before the village youths found out what was going on. After that there was a long queue every night outside the sheep pen. They would take it in turns, heedless of Fadik's tears and howls, and at daybreak, singing and firing their guns as though in a wedding procession, they would make their way back to the village.

Night was falling and Fadik began to tremble like a leaf. They would not be long now. They would come again and torture her. She was weak with fear and exhaustion. For the past two days, her gorge had risen at the very sight of food, and she lay there on the dirt floor, hardly able to move, her whole body covered with bruises and wounds.

The Tick was dozing away near the door of the pen.

Fadik tried to plead with him. "Let me go, brother," she begged. "I'll die if I have to bear another night of this."

The Tick half-opened his eyes. "I can't," he replied.

"But if I die, it'll be your fault. Before God it will . . . Please let me go."

"Why should it be my fault?" said The Tick. "I didn't bring you here, did I?"

"They'll never know. You'll say you fell asleep. I'll go off and hide somewhere. I'll go back to my mother . . ."

"I can't," said The Tick. "Halil would kill me if I let you go."

"But I want to go to my mother," she cried desperately. "You must let me go. Please let me go . . ."

It was dark now and the sound of singing drifted up from the village.

Fadik was seized with a violent fit of trembling. "They're coming," she said. "Let me get away now, brother. Save me! If you save me, I'll be your woman. I'll do anything . . ."

But The Tick had not been nicknamed for nothing.

"They'd kill me," he said. "Why should I die because of you? And Halil's promised to buy me a pair of shoes, too. I'm not going to go without shoes because of you."

Fadik broke into wild sobbing. There was no hope now.

"Oh, God," she wept, "what shall I do now? Oh, Mother, why was I ever born?"

They lined up as usual at the entrance to the pen. The first one went in and a nerve-racking scream rose from Fadik, a scream that would have moved the most hardened of hearts. But the youths were deaf to everything. In they went, one after the other, and soon Fadik's screams died down. Not even a moan came out of her.

There were traces of blood on the ground at the back of the sheep pen. Halil and the Agha's son had had a fight the night before and the Agha's son had split open Halil's head.

"The woman's mine," Halil had insisted. "I've a right to go in first."

"No, you haven't," the Agha's son had contended. "I'm going to be the first."

The other youths had taken sides and joined the fray which had lasted most of the night, and it was a bedraggled band that wended back to the village that night.

Bowed down with grief, Hatije Woman came weeping to the Muhtar.

"My son is dying," she cried. "He's at his last gasp, my poor Halil, and it's the Agha's son who did it, all because of that whore of Huru's. Ah, Muhtar, if my son dies what's to become of me? There he lies struggling for life, the only hope of my hearth. But I won't let the Agha get away with this. I'll go to the Government. An old woman's only prop, I'll say . . ."

The Muhtar had great difficulty in talking Hatije out of her purpose.

"You go back home, Hatije Woman," he said when she had calmed down a little, "and don't worry. I'll deal with this business."

He summoned the Agha and the elders, and a long discussion ensued. It would not do to hand over the woman to the police station. These rapacious gendarmes! . . . The honor of the whole village was at stake. And if they passed her on to the youths of another village, Huru was sure to find out and bring her back. She would not rest until she did.

After long deliberation, they came to a decision at last. The woman would be returned to Osman, but on one condition. He would take himself off with her to some distant place and never appear in the village again. They had no doubt that Osman, grateful to have Fadik back to himself, would accept. And that would cook Huru's goose too. She would lose both the woman and Osman. It would teach her to insult a whole village!

A couple of men went to find Osman and brought him back with them to the Muhtar's house.

"Sit down," they urged him, but he just stood there grasping his staff, staring about him with bloodshot eyes. His clothes hung down torn and crumpled and stained yellow from his lying all wet on the hay. His hair was a tangled, clotted mass and bits of straw clung to the stubble on his chin.

Wolf Mahmut took off his glasses and fidgeted with them.

"Osman, my lad," he remonstrated, "what's this state you're in? And all for a woman! Does a man let himself break down like this just for a woman? You'll die if you go on like this . . ."

"I don't know," said Osman. "I'll die . . ."

"See here, Osman," said the Agha. "We're here to help you. We'll get your woman back for you from out of those rascals' hands. Then you'll take her and go. You'll both get away from here, as far as possible. But you're not to tell Huru. She mustn't know where you are."

"You see, Osman," said Stumpy Veli, "how good the Agha's being to you. Your own father wouldn't have done more."

"But you're not to tell Huru," the Agha insisted. "If you do, she'll never let you go away. And then the youths will come and take your woman away from you again. And how will you ever get yourself another woman?"

"And who'll wash your clothes then?" added Stumpy Veli. "Who'll cook your bulgur pilaf for you? You mustn't breathe a word to Huru. Just take Fadik and go off to the villages around Antep. Once there, you'll be sure to get a job on a farm. You'll be much better off than you ever were with Huru, and you'll have your woman with you too . . ."

"But how can I do that?" protested Osman. "The Mistress paid a hundred liras for Fadik."

"We'll collect that much among us," the Agha assured him. "Don't you worry about that. We'll see that Huru gets her money back. You just take the woman and go."

"I don't know," said Osman. His eyes filled with tears and he swallowed. "The Mistress has always been so good to me . . . How can I . . . Just for a woman . . ."

"If you tell Huru, you're lost," said the Agha. "Is Huru the only mistress in the world? Aren't there other villages in this country? Take the woman and go. You'll never find another woman like Fadik. Listen, Veli'll tell you where she is and tomorrow you'll take her and go."

Osman bowed his head. He thought for a long time. Then he looked up at them.

"I won't tell her," he said at last. "Why should I want to stay here? There are other villages . . ."

Before dawn the next day, he set out for the sheep pen which Stumpy Veli had indicated.

"I don't know . . ." he hesitated at the door. "I don't know . . ." Then he called out softly, "Fadik? Fadik, girl . . ."

There was no answer. Trembling with hope and fear, he stepped in, then stopped aghast. Fadik was lying there on the dirt floor with only a few tatters left to cover her naked body. Her huge eyes were fixed vacantly on the branches that roofed the pen.

He stood frozen, his eyes filling with tears. Then he bent his large body over her.

"Fadik," he whispered, "are you all right?"

Her answering moan shook him to the core. He slipped off his shirt and helped her into it. Then he noticed The Tick who had shrunk back into a corner, trying to make himself invisible. Osman moved on him threateningly.

"Uncle Osman," cried The Tick shaking with fear, "I didn't do it. It was Halil. He said he'd buy me a pair of shoes . . . And Fadik would have died if I hadn't been here . . ."

Osman turned away, heaved Fadik onto his back swiftly, and threw himself out of the pen.

The mountain peaks were pale and the sun was about to rise. A few white clouds floated in the sky and a cool breeze caressed his face. The earth was wet with dew.

The Tick was scurrying off towards the village.

"Brother," Osman called after him, "go to the Mistress and tell her I thank her for all she's done for me, but I have to go. Tell her to forgive me . . ."

He set out in the opposite direction with Fadik on his back. He walked without a break until the sun was up the height of two minarets. Then he lowered Fadik to the ground and sat down opposite her. They looked at each other for a long while without speaking.

"Tell me," said Osman. "Where shall we go now? I don't know . . ."

Fadik moaned.

The air smelled of spring and the earth steamed under the sun.

## ■ Nizar Qabbani (1923– ) *Syria* (poem)

TRANSLATED BY BEN BENNANI

Syrian poet Nizar Qabbani studied law at the Syrian University, graduating in 1945, and embarked on a career in the Syrian diplomatic corps, which has taken him to China, Europe, and across the Arab world. His early work tends to be about women and his later work focuses more on social and political questions. He published his first of twenty-five collections of poetry at age nineteen and is considered the most popular living Arab poet. When the poem "Bread, Hashish, and Moon" appeared, Qabbani was threatened with prosecution for its anti-Arab and Moslem sentiments, but he left Syria before the government acted and settled in Beirut, where he started his own publishing firm.

**FURTHER READING:** Al-Udhari, Abdullah, tr. and ed. *Modern Poetry of the Arab World,* 1986. Bennani, Ben, ed. and tr. *Bread Hashish and Moon: Four Modern Arab Poets,* 1982. Khouri, Mounhah A., and Hamid Algar, eds. and trs. *An Anthology of Modern Arabic Poetry,* 1974.

## Bread, Hashish, and Moon

When the moon rises in the East
The white roofs fall asleep
Beneath a heap of flowers
And people leave their shops and walk in groups
To meet the moon
Carrying bread, hashish, and phonographs to mountain tops
To sell and buy delusions
To die so the moon may live.

What does a disc of light do
To my country?
To a country of prophets
A country of simple people
Tobacco chewers and dope peddlers?
What does the moon do to us
To make us lose pride
And spend our lives imploring heaven?
What does heaven have
For the stuporous and weak
Who choose to die so the moon may live
Who shake the tombs of saints
Begging for rice and children
Who spread out carpets of delicate embroideries
And flirt with a drug we call fate
And divine decree?

In my country, in the country of simple people
What weakness and decay
Overcome us when light flows everywhere
And carpets and thousands of baskets
Teacups and children take the hills?
In my country
Where people live without eyes
Where the innocent weep
And pray
And fornicate
And live on fatalism
(they have always lived on fatalism)
Calling to the moon:

O, moon!
Spring of diamonds
Hashish and slumber                                           40
O, suspended marble god
You are unbelievable!
Live for the East
A cluster of diamonds!
Live for the millions who are senseless . . .                45

At night in the East when
The moon is full
The East strips off all dignity
And resistance
The millions who run off without shoes                       50
And who believe in four wives
And the Day of Judgment,
The millions who never find bread
Except in dreams
Who spend their nights in houses                             55
Made of coughs
Never having medicine to take
Become corpses under the moonlight
In my country
Where the imbeciles weep                                     60
And die weeping
Whenever the moon's face rises over them
And go on weeping
Whenever a tender lute moves them to amorous chants
That death we call in the East                              65
*Layali*,[1] and to songs
In my country
In the country of simple people
Where we regurgitate Andalusian chants
A disease that ravishes the East                            70
The long *tawashih*[2]
Our East that regurgitates its history
Lazy dreams
And ancient superstitions
Our East that seeks all kinds of heroism                    75
In Abu-Zayd al-Hilali.[3]

---

1. *Layali* [sing, *layl*, night] are equivalent to evening concerts in the West.

2. *Tawashih* [sing, *muwashshah*] are stanzaic and lyrical poems dealing exclusively with love and nature, invented and perfected by the Arabs in the 11th century.

3. Abu Zayd al-Hilali is a fictional character supposedly endowed with supernatural and heroic qualities.

## ■ Yehuda Amichai (1924– ) *Israel* (poems)

TRANSLATED BY CHANA BLOCH

Yehuda Amichai is the leading poet in Israel and has gained widespread international fame. He was born in Würzburg, Germany, in 1924, and he immigrated to Palestine in 1936. During World War II, he fought in the British army and later in the Israeli army during the War of Independence and two later wars. He went to Hebrew University and gained fame as a poet and as a novelist and short story writer. He has also won first prize for a radio script in a national competition. He lives in Israel and until recently was a teacher and a sergeant-major in the Israeli army. Among his fiction publications are *The World Is a Room and Other Stories* (a collection of short stories) and *Not of This Time, Not of This Place* (a novel); *Selected Poetry of Yehuda Amichai* and *Travels* (a long autobiographical poem) both appeared in English in 1986. Earlier collections in English translation include *Selected Poems* (1969), *Poems* (1971), and *Songs of Jerusalem and Myself* (1973). He is a poet who has experienced a lifetime of war and who writes of searching for the possibility of love and peace (as in his poem "Wildpeace"). Bombs and shrapnel and a lush, elegiac humanism inform the work of this self-ironic dreamer, and his words open doors to the Bible and to hidden rooms of consciousness.

## *The Sweet Breakdowns of Abigail*

Everyone whacks her with tiny blows
the way you peel an egg.

With desperate bursts of perfume
she strikes back at the world.

With sharp giggles she gets even
for all the sadness,

and with quick little fallings-in-love,
like burps and hiccups of feeling.

A terrorist of sweetness,
she stuffs bombshells with despair and cinnamon,
with cloves, with shrapnel of love.

At night when she tears off her jewelry,
there's a danger she won't know when to stop
and will go on tearing and slashing away at her whole life.

## The Diameter of the Bomb

The diameter of the bomb was thirty centimeters
and the diameter of its effective range about seven meters,
with four dead and eleven wounded.
And around these, in a larger circle
of pain and time, two hospitals are scattered                                   5
and one graveyard. But the young woman
who was buried in the city she came from,
at a distance of more than a hundred kilometers,
enlarges the circle considerably,
and the solitary man mourning her death                                        10
at the distant shores of a country far across the sea
includes the entire world in the circle.
And I won't even mention the crying of orphans
that reaches up to the throne of God and
beyond, making                                                                 15
a circle with no end and no God.

## When I Banged My Head on the Door

When I banged my head on the door, I screamed,
"My head, my head," and I screamed, "Door, door,"
and I didn't scream "Mama" and I didn't scream "God."
And I didn't prophesy a world at the End of Days
where there will be no more heads and doors.                                    5

When you stroked my head, I whispered,
"My head, my head," and I whispered, "Your hand, your hand,"
and I didn't whisper "Mama" or "God."
And I didn't have miraculous visions
of hands stroking heads in the heavens                                         10
as they split wide open.
Whatever I scream or say or whisper is only
to console myself: My head, my head.
Door, door. Your hand, your hand.

## You Carry the Weight of Heavy Buttocks

You carry the weight of heavy buttocks,
but your eyes are clear.
Around your waist a wide belt that won't protect you.

You're made of the kind of materials that slow down
the process of joy
and its pain.

I've already taught my penis
to say your name
like a trained parakeet.

And you're not even impressed. As if
you didn't hear.
What else should I have done for you?

All I have left now is your name,
completely independent,
like an animal:

it eats out of my hand
and lies down at night
curled up in my dark brain.

## Wildpeace

Not that of a cease-fire,
let alone the vision
of the wolf and the lamb,
but rather
as in the heart after a surge of emotion:
to speak only about a great weariness.
I know that I know how
to kill: that's why I'm an adult.
And my son plays with a toy gun that knows
how to open and close its eyes and say Mama.
A peace
without the big noise of beating swords into plowshares,
without words, without
the heavy thud of the rubber stamp; I want it
gentle over us, like lazy white foam.
A little rest for the wounds—
who speaks of healing?
(And the orphans' outcry is passed from one generation
to the next, as in a relay race:
the baton never falls.)

I want it to come
like wildflowers,
suddenly, because the field
needs it: wildpeace.

# ■ Badr Shakir Al-Sayyab (1926–1964) *Iraq* (poem)

## TRANSLATED BY LENA JAYYUSI AND CHRISTOPHER MIDDLETON

Badr Shakir al-Sayyab was born in southern Iraq in 1926 in the village of Jaikur and was educated in Basra and later at the Teacher's Training College of Baghdad. He was a schoolteacher, a journalist, and a civil servant. Early on he was a Communist, but then he moved toward mainstream Arab nationalism, rejecting the Communists for not supporting Palestinian autonomy. Ironically, he was persecuted both by Arab nationalists and by the Communists and died destitute and in shattered health. He was influenced in his work by English-language poets, first the Romantics, Shelley and Keats, and later T. S. Eliot, and he was one of the innovators who introduced free verse to Arabic. His books of poems include *Faded Flowers* (1947), *Legends* (1950), *Song of Rain* (1960), *The Drowned Shrine* (1962), *The House of Slaves* (1963), *The Oriel Window of the Nobleman's Daughter* (1964), and *Iqbal* (1965).

## *Song in August*

Tammuz dies on the skyline,[1]
His blood seeps away with twilight
In the dim cavern. Darkness
Is a black ambulance,
Night a flock of women:                                              5
Kohl, black cloaks.
Night, an enormous tent.
Night, a blocked day.

I called to my negro maid:
"Murjana, it's dark now,                                            10
Switch the light on. You know what? I'm hungry.
There's a song, I forgot, some sort of a song.
What's this chatter on the radio?
From London, Murjana, a
Jazz concert so                                                     15
Find it, I'm happy, jazz,
Blood rhythm."

Tammuz dies and Murjana
Crouches cold like the forest.

---

1. Tammuz was an ancient Babylonian nature god, a god of agriculture. He was the lover of the fertility goddess Ishtar, who, according to one legend, killed him and then restored his life for part of the year. When he lived, spring came; when he died, it was winter. His Sumerian name was Dumuzi [Editor].

She says, breathless:
"The night, wild pig,
How miserable the night is."
"Murjana, was that the doorbell?"
So she says, breathless:
"There are women at the door."
And Murjana makes the coffee.

Fur over white shoulders:
Wolf covers woman.
On her breasts a whole sheen of tiger skin
Filling the forest, stealing from the trees.
Night stretches,
Distraction, night
An earth-oven, radiant from ghosts,
Bread inhaling the night fires,
And the visitor eats, famished.
Murjana crouches
Cold like the forest.

The visitor laughs, she says: "Su'ad's boyfriend,
Been giving her a bad time, broke the engagement,
The dog disowned the bitch . . ."
Tammuz dies, never to return.
Coldness drips from the moon,
The visitor huddles at the fire gossiping, sharp-tongued.
Night has extinguished the coasts,
The visitor crouches, cold, robed
With wolf fur.
The fire she lit with bloody talk
Goes out.

Night and ice,
Across them a sound falls, clank of iron
Muffled by wolf howls.
Distant sound,
The visitor, like me, is cold.
So come on over and share my cold,
Come by God,
Husband, I'm alone here,
The visitor is cold as I am—
So come on over,
Only with you can I talk about everyone.
And there are so many people to be talked about.
The dark is a hearse, the driver blind
And your heart is a burial ground.

# ■ Yusuf Idris (1927–1990) *Egypt* (story)

## TRANSLATED BY DENYS JOHNSON-DAVIES

Yusuf Idris was born in a village in Egypt in 1927. He was trained as a physician and worked for a period as a government health inspector. Like other great doctor writers, such as Anton Chekov and William Carlos Williams, Idris's fiction shows a great interest in the common people his profession brought him in contact with. And like the lush lines of "The Ode to a Nightingale" by John Keats (a surgeon by profession) —

> I cannot see what flowers are at my feet,
> Nor what soft incense hangs upon the boughs,
> But, in embalmèd darkness, guess each sweet,

—Idris's story "House of Flesh" hinges upon a sensual encounter in blind darkness. Idris published novels, plays, and short story collections and was considered among the finest short fiction masters in the Arab world. His work has been translated into Russian and other East European tongues, and it is available in several good English-language editions.

**FURTHER READING:** Idris, Yusuf. *In the Eye of the Beholder: Tales of Egyptian Life from the Writings of Yusuf Idris,* 1978; *The Cheapest Nights: Short Stories.* Translated by Wadida Wassef, 1991; *Rings of Burnished Brass and Other Stories.* Translated by Catherine Cobham, 1992.

## *House of Flesh*

The ring is beside the lamp. Silence reigns and ears are blinded. In the silence the finger slides along and slips on the ring. In silence too, the lamp is put out. Darkness is all around. In the darkness eyes too are blinded.

The widow and her three daughters. The house is a room. The beginning is silence.

\* \* \*

The widow is tall, fair-skinned, slender, thirty-five years of age. Her daughters too are tall and full of life. They never take off their flowing clothes which, whether they be in or out of mourning, are black. The youngest is sixteen, the eldest twenty. They are ugly, having inherited their father's dark-skinned body, full of bulges and curves wrongly disposed; from their mother they have taken hardly anything but her height.

Despite its small size, the room is large enough for them during the daytime; despite the poverty of it, it is neat and tidy, homely with the touches given to it by four females. At night their bodies are scattered about like large heaps of warm, living flesh, some on the bed, some around it, their breathing rising up warm and restless, sometimes deeply drawn.

Silence has reigned ever since the man died. Two years ago the man died after a long illness. Mourning ended but the habits of the mourners stayed on, and of these silence was the most marked, a silence long and interminable, for it was in truth the silence of waiting. The girls grew up and for long they waited expectantly, but the bridegrooms did not come. What madman will knock at the door of the poor and the ugly, particularly if they happen to be orphans? But hope, of course, is present, for—as the proverb says—even a rotten bean finds some blind person to weigh it out, and every girl can find her better half. Be there poverty, there is always someone who is poorer; be there ugliness, there is always someone uglier. Hopes come true, sometimes come true, with patience.

A silence broken only by the sound of reciting from the Koran; the sound rises up, with dull, unimpassioned monotony. It is being given by a Koranic reciter and the reciter is blind. It is for the soul of the deceased and the appointed time for it never changes: Friday afternoons he comes, raps at the door with his stick, gives himself over to the hand stretched out to him, and squats down on the mat. When he finishes he feels around for his sandals, gives a greeting which no one troubles to answer, and takes himself off. By habit he recites, by habit he takes himself off, and so no one is aware of him.

The silence is permanent. Even the breaking of it by the Friday afternoon recital has become like silence broken by silence. It is permanent like the waiting, like hope, a hope that is meager yet permanent, which is at least hope. However little a thing may be, there is always something less, and they are not on the look-out for anything more; never do they do so.

Silence goes on till something happens. Friday afternoon comes and the reciter does not come, for to every agreement however long it may last there is an end—and the agreement has come to an end.

Only now the widow and her daughters realize what has occurred: it was not merely that his was the only voice that broke the silence but that he was the only man, be it only once a week, who knocked at the door. Other things too they realized: while it was true that he was poor like them, his clothes were always clean, his sandals always polished, his turban always wound with a precision of which people with sound eyesight were incapable, while his voice was strong, deep and resonant.

The suggestion is broached: Why not renew the agreement, right away? Why not send for him this very moment? If he's busy, so what—waiting's nothing new? Towards sunset he comes and recites, and it is as if he recites for the first time. The suggestion evolves: Why doesn't one of us marry a man who fills the house for us with his voice? He is a bachelor, has never married, has sprouted a sparse moustache and is still young. One word leads to another—after all he too is no doubt looking for some nice girl to marry.

The girls make suggestions and the mother looks into their faces so as to determine to whose lot he shall fall, but the faces turn away, suggesting, merely suggesting, saying things without being explicit. Shall we fast and break that fast with a blind man? They are still dreaming of bridegrooms—and normally bridegrooms are men endowed with sight. Poor things, they do not yet know the world of men; it is impossible for them to understand that eyes do not make a man.

"You marry him, Mother. You marry him,"

"I? Shame on you! And what will people say?"

"Let them say what they like. Whatever they say is better than a house in which there is not the sound of men's voices."

"Marry before you do? Impossible."

"Is it not better that you marry before us so that men's feet may know the way to our house and that we may marry after you. Marry him. Marry him, Mother."

She married him. Their number increased by one and their income increased slightly—and a bigger problem came into being.

It is true that the first night passed with the two of them in their bed, but they did not dare, even accidentally, to draw close to one another. The three girls were asleep but from each one of them was focused a pair of searchlights, aimed unerringly across the space between them; searchlights made up of eyes, of ears, of senses. The girls are grown up; they know; they are aware of things, and by their wakeful presence it is as if the room has been changed into broad daylight. During the day, however, there is no reason for them to stay there, and one after the other they sneak out and do not return till around sunset. They return shy and hesitant, moving a step forward, a step back, until, coming closer, they are amazed, thrown into confusion, are made to hasten their steps by the laughter and guffaws of a man interspersed by the giggling of a woman. It must be their mother who is laughing, also laughing is the man whom previously they had always heard behaving so correctly, so properly. Still laughing, she met them with open arms, her head bared, her hair wet and combed out, and still laughing. Her face, which they had instinctively perceived as nothing but a dead lantern where spiders, like wrinkles, had made their nest, had suddenly filled with light; there it was in front of them as bright as an electric bulb. Her eyes were sparkling; they had come forth and shown themselves, bright with tears of laughter; eyes that had previously sought shelter deep down in their sockets.

The silence vanished, completely disappeared. During dinner, before dinner, and after dinner, there are plenty of jokes and stories, also singing, for he has a beautiful voice when he sings and imitates Umm Kulthoum and Abdul Wahhab; his voice is loud and booming, raucous with happiness.

You have done well, Mother. Tomorrow the laughter will attract men, for men are bait for men.

Yes, daughters. Tomorrow men will come, bridegrooms will make their appearance. Yet the fact is that what most occupied her was not men or bridegrooms but that young man—albeit he was blind, for how often are we blind to people just because they are blind—that strong young man full of robust health and life who had made up for her the years of sickness and failure and premature old age.

The silence vanished as though never to return and the clamour of life pervaded the place. The husband was hers, her legitimate right in accordance with the law of God and His Prophet. What, then, was there to be ashamed about when everything he does is lawful? No longer does she even worry about hiding her secrets or being discreet, and even as night comes and they are all together and bodies and souls are set loose, even as the girls are scattered far apart about the room, knowing and understanding, as though nailed to where they are sleeping, all sounds and breathing aquiver, controlling movements and coughs, suddenly deep sighs issue forth and are themselves stifled by more sighs.

She spent her day doing the washing at the houses of the rich, he his day reciting the Koran at the houses of the poor. At first he did not make it a practice to return to the house at midday, but when the nights grew longer and his hours of sleep less, he began to return at midday to rest his body for a while from the toil of the night that had passed and to prepare himself for the night to come. Once, after they had had their fill of the night, he suddenly asked her what had been the matter with her at midday; why was she talking unrestrainedly now and had maintained such complete silence then, why was she now wearing the ring that was so dear to him, it being the only thing by way of bridal money and gifts the marriage had cost him, while she had not been wearing it then?

She could have risen up in horror and screamed, could have gone mad. He could be killed for this, for what he is saying has only one meaning—and what a strange and repulsive meaning.

A choking lump in the throat stifled all this, stifled her very breathing. She kept silent. With ears that had turned into nostrils, tactile sense and eyes, she began listening, her sole concern being to discover the culprit. For some reason she is sure it is the middle one: in her eyes there is a boldness that even bullets cannot kill. She listens. The breathing of the three girls rises up, deep and warm as if fevered; it groans with yearning, hesitates, is broken, as sinful dreams interrupt it. The disturbed breathing changes to a hissing sound, a hissing like the scorching heat that is spat out by thirsty earth. The lump in the throat sinks down deeper, becomes stuck. What she hears is the breathing of the famished. However much she sharpens her senses she is unable to distinguish between one warm, muffled heap of living flesh and another. All are famished; all scream and groan, and the moaning breathes not with breathing but perhaps with shouts for help, perhaps with entreaties, perhaps with something that is even more.

She immersed herself in her second legitimate pursuit and forgot her first, her daughters. Patience became bitter-tasting, even the mirage of bridegrooms no longer made its appearance. Like someone awakened in terror to some mysterious call, she is suddenly stung into attention: the girls are famished. It is true that food is sinful, but hunger is even more so. There is nothing more sinful than hunger. She knows it. Hunger had known her, had dried up her soul, had sucked at her bones; she knows it, and however sated she is, it is impossible for her to forget its taste.

They are famished, and it was she who used to take the piece of food out of her own mouth in order to feed them; she, the mother, whose sole concern it was feed them even if she herself went hungry. Has she forgotten?

Despite his pressing her to speak, the feeling of choking turned into silence. The mother kept silent and from that moment silence was ever with her.

At breakfast, exactly as she had expected, the middle one was silent— and continued in her silence.

Dinner-time came with the young man happy and blind and enjoying himself, still joking and singing and laughing, and with no one sharing his laughter but the youngest and the eldest.

Patience is protracted, its bitter taste turns to sickness—and still no one shows up.

One day, the eldest one looks at her mother's ring on her finger, ex-presses her delight in it. The mother's heart beats fast—and beats yet faster as she asks her if she might wear it for a day, just for one single day. In silence she draws it off her finger; in silence the eldest puts it on her own same finger.

At the next dinner-time the eldest one is silent, refuses to utter.

The blind youth is noisy; he sings and he laughs, and only the youngest one joins in with him.

But the youngest one, through patience, through worry, through lack of luck, grows older and begins asking about when her turn will come in the ring game. In silence she achieves her turn.

The ring lies beside the lamp. Silence descends and ears are blinded. In silence the finger whose turn it is stealthily slips on the ring. The lamp is put out: darkness is all-embracing and in the darkness eyes are blinded.

No one remains who is noisy, who tells jokes, who sings, except for the blind young man.

Behind his noisy boisterousness there lurks a desire that almost makes him rebel against the silence and break it to pieces. He too wants to know, wants to know for certain. At first he used to tell himself that it was the na-ture of women to refuse to stay the same, sometimes radiantly fresh as drops of dew, at other times spent and stale as water in a puddle; some-times as soft as the touch of rose petals, at other times rough as cactus plants. True, the ring was always there, but it was as if the finger wearing it were a different finger. He all but knows, while they all know for certain, so why does the silence not speak, why does it not utter?

One dinner-time the question sneaks in upon him unawares: What if the silence should utter? What if it should talk?

The mere posing of the question halted the morsel of food in his throat.

From that moment onwards he sought refuge in silence and refused to relinquish it.

In fact it was he who became frightened that sometime by ill chance the silence might be scratched; maybe a word might slip out and the whole edifice of silence come tumbling down—and woe to him should the edifice of silence tumble down!

The strange, different silence in which they all sought refuge.

Intentional silence this time, of which neither poverty nor ugliness nor patient waiting nor despair is the cause.

It is, though, the deepest form of silence, for it is silence agreed upon by the strongest form of agreement—that which is concluded without any agreement.

$$* \quad * \quad *$$

The widow and her three daughters.

And the house is a room.
And the new silence.
And the Koran reciter who brought that silence with him, and who with silence set about assuring for himself that she who shared his bed was always his wife, all proper and legitimate, the wearer of his ring. Sometimes she grows younger or older, she is softskinned or rough, slender or fat—it is solely her concern, the concern of those with sight, it is their responsibility alone in that they possess the boon of knowing things for certain; it is they who are capable of distinguishing while the most he can do is to doubt, a doubt which cannot become certainty without the boon of sight and so long as he is deprived of it just so long will he remain deprived of certainty, for he is blind and no moral responsibility attaches to a blind man.

Or does it?

## ■ Joyce Mansour (1928–1988) *Egypt/England/France* (poems)

TRANSLATED BY MOLLY BENDALL

Of Egyptian origin, Joyce Mansour was born in Bowden, England, in 1928. She was educated in Egypt, England, and Switzerland. Her work, imbued with imagery of diverse backgrounds—the Egypt of the Pharaonic mummies and desert landscape blended with her adopted Paris cityscape—she was early championed by André Breton, the leader of the French surreal movement. Mansour's first collection, *Cris* (*Cries*), was published by Seghers in 1953, and it brought her instant recognition. Subsequently, she published numerous collections of poetry and prose. She died in Paris in 1988. Her poems are filled with an unabashed sexuality and provocative wit. Egypt, eroticism, and French surrealism come together in her book *Phallus and Mummies* (1969). Like Derek Walcott (Saint Lucia), Khaled Mattawa (Libya), and Bharati Mukherjee (India), she is a writer who has crossed borders and language, yet carries the wealth of her background language and culture, which she infuses into the intensely personal, erotic poetry of her adopted France. Her collected works were published posthumously, *Prose & Poésie: Oeuvre Complète* (1991). Her poems have been superbly rendered into English by Molly Bendall.

**FURTHER READING:** Mansour, Joyce. *Cris* (*Cries*), 1953; *Les Gisants satisfaits*, 1958; *Rapaces*, 1960; *Carré Blanc*, 1965; *Phallus et momies*, 1969; *Faire signe au machiniste*, 1977; *Ça*, 1970; *Prose & Poésie: Oeuvre Complète*, 1991.

## In the Gloom on the Left

Why my legs
Around your neck
Tight neck-tie puffed dark blue
Same old entrance of the laughing crack
White olives of Christianity    5
Why should I wait in front of the closed door
Shy and beseeching passionate cello
Have children
Soak your gums with rare vinegars
The most delicate white is tainted with black    10
Your cock is smoother
Than a virgin's complexion
More provoking than pity
Feathered tool of incredible hubbub
Goodbye see you again it's done adieu    15
The longing for abundant blossoms is exhausted
Will come back
More vivid more violent
These mauve bonbons with their devoted swoons
Anxious and tetanus-like    20
The fervid nightmares of afternoon
Without you

## A Mango

I long for a mango
I detest men who don't know how to eat

Without bestowing their wisdom in quick sputters
You cry
Alone wounded and healed by my friendly lip
Do you see a phallus eaten by the hand
I'm hungry for dust
There's no accommodation spacious enough
Not a century nor beach empty enough for my taste
The sleepy vigil by Caesar's descendents                      1(
I lose my hair without a shudder too sad to resist
My heart needs a mango
It's not necessary to kill anyone
Today someone says be careful
The eyes of love are dry                                       1⁵
Oil stains replace the Corn Festival on our walls
The heavy carts of dawn
Pass interminably
Behind the teddy bear
The intoxicated look of the serpent                            2(
And my mother who dreams in English far far
Far the mango and its odor of night


## ▪ Adunis (Ali Ahmed Said) (1930– ) *Syria/Lebanon* (poem)

### TRANSLATED BY ABDULLAH AL-UDHARI

Best known by his pen name "Adunis" or "Adonis," Ali Ahmed Said was born in the Syrian village of Qassabin and attended Damascus University, where he studied philosophy and literature. Later he earned a doctorate from St. Joseph's University in Beirut. Because his work questioned Syrian society and political organization, he found himself imprisoned and later exiled to Beirut in 1956. That same year, he became a citizen of Lebanon, where he settled. He founded and edited first *Shi'r* magazine and then, in 1968, the journal of experimental poetry *Mawagif*. He is considered the foremost poet of the Arab world and is a critic, philosopher, and translator as well. He works as a literary journalist. In addition to many books of poetry, he has published several books of literary criticism and a three-volume anthology of classical Arabic poetry.

**FURTHER READING:** Al-Udhari, Abdullah, ed. and tr. *Modern Poetry of the Arab World*, 1986. Bennani, Ben, ed. and tr. *Bread Hashish and Moon: Four Modern Arab Poets*, 1982. Khouri, Mounhah A., and Hamid Algar, eds. and trs. *An Anthology of Modern Arabic Poetry*, 1974.

# from *The Desert*

*The Diary of Beirut under Siege, 1982*

The cities break up
The land is a train of dust
Only poetry knows how to marry this space.

\*   \*   \*

No road to his house—the siege.
And the streets are graveyards:
  Far away a stunned moon
  Hangs on threads of dust
  Over his house.       5

\*   \*   \*

I said: This street leads to our house. He said: No.
  You won't pass. And pointed his bullets at me.

Fine, in every street
  I have homes and friends.

\*   \*   \*

They found people in sacks:
  One without a head
  One without a tongue or hands
  One strangled
  The rest without shape or names.   5
Have you gone mad? Please,
  Don't write about these things.

\*   \*   \*

In a page of a book
Bombs see themselves,
Prophetic sayings and ancient wisdom see themselves,
Niches see themselves.
The thread of carpet words      5
Go through memory's needle
Over the city's face.

\*   \*   \*

From the palm wine to the calmness of the desert  .  .  . etc.
From the morning that smuggles its stomach and sleeps on the corpses
  of the refugees  .  .  . etc.
From the streets, army vehicles, concentration of troops  .  .  . etc.
From the shadows, men, women  .  .  . etc.     5
From the bombs stuffed with the prayers of Muslims and infidels  .  .  .
  etc.

From the flesh of iron that bleeds and sweats pus . . . etc.
From the fields that long for the wheat, the green and the workers . . .
    etc.
From the castles walling our bodies and bombarding us with darkness
    . . . etc.
From the myths of the dead which speak of life, express life . . . etc.
From the speech which is the slaughter, the slaughtered and the
    slaughterers . . . etc.
From the dark dark dark
I breathe, feel my body, search for you and him, myself and others.
And hang my death
Between my face and these bleeding words . . . etc.

*   *   *

Seeds are scattered in our land.
So keep the secret of this blood,
Fields that nourish our myths—
    I'm talking about the zest of the seasons
    About the lightning in space.

*   *   *

My era tells me bluntly:
You do not belong.
I answer bluntly:
I do not belong,
I try to understand you
Now I am a shadow
Lost in the desert
And shelter in the tent of a skull.

*   *   *

The door of my house is closed.
Darkness is a blanket:
    A pale moon comes with
    A handful of light
    My words fail
    To convey my gratitude.

*   *   *

He shuts the door
Not to trap his joy
. . . But to free his grief.

*   *   *

The night descends (these are the papers he gave to the ink—
    morning's ink that never came)

The night descends on the bed (the bed of the lover who never came)
The night descends/not a sound (clouds, smoke)
The night descends (someone has in his hands rabbits? Ants?)
The night descends (the wall of the building shakes. All the curtains     5
    are transparent)
The night descends, listens (the stars as the night knows are dumb,
    and the last trees at the end of the wall remember nothing of
    what the air said to their branches)
The night descends (the wind whispers to the windows)
The night descends (the light penetrates. A neighbour lies in his
    nakedness)
The night descends (two people. A dress holding a dress—and the
    windows are transparent)
The night descends (this is a whim: the moon complains to its     10
    trousers
    about what the lovers have always complained of)
The night descends (he relaxes in a pitcher filled with wine. No friends
    just one man turning in his glass)
The night descends (carries a few spiders, feels at ease with insects
    which are a pest only to houses/signs of light: an angel coming,
    missiles or invitations? Our women neighbours have gone on
    pilgrimage/come back less slim and more coquettish)
The night descends (he enters between the breasts of the days/our
    women neighbours are my days)
The night descends (that sofa/that pillow: this is an alleyway, this is a
    place)
The night descends (what shall we prepare? Wine? Meat, soup and     15
    bread? The night hides from us its appetite)
The night descends (he plays for a short while with his snails, with
    strange doves which came from an unknown land, and with the
    insects not mentioned in the chapters of the book about
    reproduction among different animal species)
The night descends (thunder—or is it the noise of angels coming on
    their horses?)
The night descends (he mumbles, turning in his glass . . . )

*   *   *

The flower
    That tempted the wind to carry its perfume
Died yesterday.

*   *   *

A bat
    Claims the light is dark.
    And the sun a road to the grave.
Then babbles on.

The bat didn't fall,
Only the child asleep in dawn's lap fell off.

\* \* \*

A creator devoured by his creatures, a country
      Hiding in the blood running from his remains.
This is the beginning of a new era.

\* \* \*

Whenever I say: my country is within reach
      And bears fruit in a reachable language
Another language kicks me
To another language.

\* \* \*

Trees bow to say goodbye
Flowers open, glow, lower their leaves to say goodbye,
Reads like pauses between the breathing and the words say goodbye,
A body wears sand, falls in a wilderness to say goodbye.
The papers that love ink.
      The alphabet, the poets say goodbye.
And the poem says goodbye.

\* \* \*

All the certainty I have lived slips away
All the torches of my desire slip away
All that was between the faces that lit my exile and me slips away
I have to start from the beginning
To teach my limbs to reach the future.
To talk, to climb, to descend from the beginning
In the sky of beginnings, in the abyss of the alphabet.

\* \* \*

They are falling, the land is a thread of smoke
      Time a train
      Travelling along a track of smoke . . .
My obsession is here now, loss.
My concern is the end
      Is not over.
They are falling, I am not looking for a new beginning.

# ◼ Dan Pagis (1930–1986) *Israel* (poems)

## TRANSLATED BY STEPHEN MITCHELL

Dan Pagis was born in Bukovina, now a part of Russia, though it had formerly been part of Austria, and then Romania. During World War II, he survived three years in a Nazi concentration camp and moved to Israel in 1946, where he learned Hebrew and taught in a kibbutz. In 1956, he moved to Jerusalem, where he received a doctorate from the Hebrew University and was a professor of Medieval Hebrew literature. He wrote his poems in Hebrew, and though he was not limited to poems about the Holocaust, his poems on that subject are among the most powerful written anywhere. He died on July 29, 1986. His books of poems are *The Shadow Dial* (1959), *Late Leisure* (1964), *Transformation* (1970), *Brain* (1975, 1977), *Twelve Faces* (1981), *Double Exposure* (1983), and *Last Poems* (1987). He also wrote a number of scholarly books.

**FURTHER READING:** Mitchell, Stephen, tr. *Variable Directions: The Selected Poetry of Dan Pagis,* 1989.

## *End of the Questionnaire*

Housing conditions: number of galaxy and star,
number of grave.
Are you alone or not.
What grass grows on top of you,
and from where (e.g., from your stomach, eyes, mouth, etc.).          5

You have the right to appeal.

In the blank space below, state
how long you have been awake and why you are surprised.

## *Written in Pencil in the Sealed Railway-Car*

here in this carload
i am eve
with abel my son
if you see my other son
cain son of man                                                      5
tell him that i

■ **Nawal al-Saadawi (1931– )** *Egypt* **(story, memoir)**

TRANSLATED BY J. RYDER

Born in Egypt in 1931, Nawal al-Saadawi is a prominent feminist, physician, and prolific writer, publishing in many genres including short stories, essays, and novels. Receiving her medical degree in 1955, al-Saadawi has practiced psychiatry, surgery, family medicine, and gynecology. In the field of gynecology, she has strongly criticized the conservative Islamic practice of clitoridectomy and the general suppression of female sexuality. Much of her writing examines femaleness—both femininity and being a female—in Arab cultures. Her experience as a doctor has given her special access and insight into a society she wishes to comment on and explore. Over the years, she has traveled extensively and is a familiar and passionate speaker at international literary and political forums. She has also taught at various universities, including Duke University, where she was a visiting professor. Her *Memoirs of a Female Physician* has been superbly rendered into English by Fedwa Malti-Douglas. Nawal al-Saadawi is one of the most forceful and accomplished writers in Arabic, and her influential books have been translated into the languages of the world.

**FURTHER READING:** al-Saadawi, Nawal. *The Hidden Face of Eve: Women in the Arab World.* Translated and edited by Sherif Hetata, 1980; *Memoirs from the Women's Prison.* Translated by Marilyn Booth, 1986; *Memoirs of a Woman Doctor.* Translated by Catherine Cobham, 1988; *The Well of Life and the Thread: Two Short Novels.* Translated by Sherif Hetata, 1993; *Woman at Point Zero.* Translated by Sherif Hetata, 1983.

## The Thirst

The fierce heat of the noonday sun made the cement pavement soft under her feet, burning her like a piece of molten iron. She jumped here and there, stumbling about like a little moth that collides unawares with the walls of a burning lamp. She could have turned toward the shade at the roadside and sat awhile on the moist ground, but the vegetable basket was hanging on her arm and her right hand was closed upon a ragged 50-piaster note as she repeated to herself the things she would buy at the market so that she'd remember them . . . ½ a kilo of meat for 35 piasters, a kilo of zucchini for 5 piasters, a kilo of tomatoes for 7 piasters, and 3 piasters change; ½ a kilo of meat for 35 piasters, a kilo of zucchini for 5 piasters, a kilo of tomatoes for 7 piasters, and 3 piasters change; ½ a kilo of meat for . . .

She could have continued the enumeration as she did every day until reaching the market, but her eyes suddenly spotted something strange, something she never would have dreamed of, and her surprise prevailed over the heat of the ground and she stopped and stared, her eyes wide and her mouth open; there was Hamida, in the flesh, standing before the kiosk with a bottle of ice-cold soda-pop in her hand, lifting it up to her mouth and drinking from it.

For the first instant she wasn't aware that it was Hamida; she saw her from behind as she stood in front of the kiosk, but it didn't occur to her that it was Hamida. It might have been one of the girls she used to see every day in front of the kiosk drinking soda-pop . . . the middle-class girls like Suad and Muna and Amal and Mirvat, all her young mistress Sahir's friends.

She had thought it was one of those girls, and she was going to continue along her way, but she spotted the vegetable basket; she spotted it hanging from her arm as she stood in front of the kiosk, and she couldn't believe her eyes, so she looked closer and saw her curly locks of hair hanging down upon the nape of her neck from under a white scarf. This was Hamida's head scarf, and this was her arm on which the vegetable basket hung, but was it possible that this was, in fact, Hamida?

She began to examine her closely from behind, and she saw her cracked heels protruding from her green plastic slippers; these were Hamida's green slippers and her heels. But in spite of all that, she couldn't believe it, and she began to scrutinize her from every angle—from the left and from the right—and every time, she saw something that could only belong to the Hamida she knew: the yellow linen galabiyya with a little split on the side above her left thigh, the rusted earring in her right ear, and the old deep wound on her right temple. It was Hamida before her eyes, in the flesh, and not under any circumstances another girl, and she stood looking at her even more closely.

Hamida was standing in front of the kiosk and in her right hand was a soda-pop bottle with those transparent watery drops on its outer surface. She wasn't drinking quickly like the other girls; she drank with extreme slowness, moving her fingers down around the bottle and feeling its coldness with delight. She continued to hold the bottle for a moment, then she lifted it slowly to her mouth and touched the edge of her lips to the bottle mouth and licked it, gathering up all the droplets around it with her tongue; then she raised her arm a bit higher to tilt the bottle up to her mouth slightly, only allowing herself a single sip of the rosy, ice-cold liquid. Here she closed her lips with great control, keeping the sip in her mouth for a while without swallowing it all at once; she swallowed it slowly until the last drop of it disappeared from her mouth, enjoying herself tremendously, tossing her head back a bit, her back muscles going limp, leaning in relaxation against the wooden wall of the kiosk.

Now she couldn't resist, for bit by bit she had drawn closer to the kiosk without noticing, and she stood seeking shelter from the sun in its shade. She sat upon the ground and put the vegetable basket down beside her, her eyes riveted, observing the passionate meeting between Hamida's lips and the bottle mouth, then the sip and the slow sucking process and the enjoyment and relaxation which followed it. The ground was hot and burned her lean buttocks through her threadbare calico galabiyya, but she paid it no heed; all that interested her was to continue watching, to continue following Hamida's movements one by one with her eyes and her limbs. She inclined her head backwards whenever Hamida bent her head backwards, and she opened her lips whenever Hamida opened her lips, and she moved her tongue around inside her mouth whenever Hamida moved her tongue. But her throat was dry, without so much as a single drop of saliva, and her tongue was stiff, moving back and forth and striking the walls of her mouth like a wooden stick. The dryness stretched from her palate to her throat and even plunged down into her stomach . . . a strange, horrible dryness she hadn't felt before, as if the water had suddenly evaporated from every cell in her body . . . from her eyes and her nose and from the skin that covered every part of her. The dryness reached her veins and the blood which flowed in them, and it dried up too. She felt burning pains inside, and she ran her hand over her skin and it felt thick, dry and wrinkled, like the skin of a dried sardine. She noticed a salty taste in her mouth, bitter like colocynth, acrid, burning, and she tried to search for the saliva to moisten her salty lips, but the tip of her tongue caught fire without stumbling upon so much as a single drop, and all the while Hamida remained before her, encircling the icy bottle mouth with her lips, the cells of her body sucking in the soda-pop one cell at a time. Hamida carried a vegetable basket, like hers, on her arm, and she had slippers, like hers, on her feet, and she had a cheap, torn galabiyya, like hers, on her body, and she worked, as she did, in houses.

The muscles of her fingers which clasped the dirty 50-piaster note twitched slightly, and she returned to the litany she was memorizing . . . ½ a kilo of meat for 35 piasters, a kilo of zucchini for 5 piasters, a kilo of tomatoes for 7 piasters, and 3 piasters change, and the price of a bottle of soda-pop is 3 piasters. Very expensive! It was only 1½ piasters last year. If this had happened last year it would have been possible to consider buying a bottle. One and a half piasters wasn't cheap, but it might be possible to sort things out. Sometimes zucchini cost 5½ and tomatoes 7½; as for the meat, it couldn't possibly cost more than ½ a piaster extra because it had a fixed price, and her mistress knew the prices by heart, and nothing could possibly escape her. Even as regarded the vegetables, whose price changed every day, going up or down by ½ a piaster, she knew of the increase or decrease day by day as well, as if she dreamt of the price list every night. And supposing that she were able to cheat her out of ½ a piaster on the zucchini and ½ a piaster on the tomatoes, where would she get the third ½ a piaster? It wouldn't be easy to claim that she had lost them, for that was a ploy which her honest mistress with the hard slaps wouldn't believe, even if she were to resort to lying for all this. Lying was akin to stealing, and as her mother had told her: "Beware, Fatima, of stretching out your hands for a piaster; theft, my daughter, is forbidden, and our Lord will burn you in hell."

She was afraid of hell; how could the fire burn in her hair and her head and her body? The sting of a matchstick caused her pain, but hellfire consuming her entire body was inconceivable. She couldn't imagine this fire; she neither knew it nor felt it. What she did feel was this other fire which burned inside her . . . the fire of dryness and thirst, a fire which nothing other than some sips from a bottle of soda-pop would extinguish. She could touch the walls of the kiosk beside her with the palm of her hand, and Hamida was in front of her, drinking a bottle of soda-pop . . . but how would she get the 3 piasters? The easiest thing would be for her to allot it equally to the meat and the zucchini and tomatoes, to add a piaster to all of them. Her mother's words had no meaning now. She didn't know the hell her mother threatened her with; she didn't see anyone burning in it before her. Perhaps this hell didn't exist. If it did exist it was very far away from her, far away after death. She didn't know when she would die, but she didn't imagine that she would die today.

She got up from where she was sitting and shook the dust off her galabiyya and stood staring at Hamida as she emptied the last mouthful of soda-pop into her mouth and closed her lips around the bottle mouth, not wanting to part with it. But the man grabbed the bottle from her hand and she left the mark of a long good-bye kiss upon it before removing it forever from between her lips. Then she opened her left hand in desire and counted 3 whole piasters . . .

She trembled a bit as she stood before the kiosk in the very place where Hamida had stood. A cool breeze bearing the aroma of soda-pop drifted out of the kiosk. Let what happens happen after this . . . the hard slaps could no longer cause her pain, for she had become used to them, and the hellfire that burned could no longer frighten her because it was far away, and the world with all its pains and fears was not equal to a single sip of an ice-cold soda-pop.

## ■ Forugh Farrokhzad (1935–1967) *Iran* (poems)

### TRANSLATED BY LEORA BAUDE AND ALI SHASHAANI

Forugh Farrokhzad was born in Teheran and educated in the public schools, though she did not graduate from high school. She was a prodigy, composing *ghazals* (short lyrics) by age thirteen. At sixteen, she married Parviz Shapur, and she published her first book of poems, *The Captive,* in 1952, a volume that created a great controversy because of its sexual candor. She had a son in 1953, but in the divorce that soon followed she lost custody of him. Her other books of poems include *The Wall* (1956), *Rebellion* (1957), *Rebirth* (1961), and a book of selected poems published in 1964. She was a filmmaker, and she studied film production in England in 1959. Both Bernardo Bertolucci and UNESCO produced film biographies about her in 1965. At the peak of her mature creativity, she died tragically, in 1967, in an automobile accident. Farrokhzad's poems move from an early formalism to free verse and are characterized by fierce passion, melancholy, ironic belligerence, and a modern original diction. Her stark and simple poems of love shift easily into a surreal nightmare of modern existence suffused with Quranic apocalypse. Her fearless intelligence and disdain for the inferior role dictated socially for Iranian women and the sheer brilliance of her poems make her a sister of Sylvia Plath—to whom she is often compared. She was the leading poet of Iran and one of Asia's outstanding twentieth-century poets.

## *Window*

a window for seeing
a window for hearing
like a well shaft reaches to the core
of the earth and turns its eye
to a landscape of kindness
blue, the color of water
a window filled each night
with mercy and the fragrance of stars
by the little hands of loneliness
and there you could invite the sun
to join the red geraniums
in exile
one window is enough for me

I come from toyland
from under the shade of cardboard trees
from a storybook garden
I come from drought stricken fields of love
the dust bowl of innocence
from desks at the tuberculosis school
where alphabet letters grow wan with age
from that moment when children first print "stone" on the board
and a flock of starlings quit their ancient tree
I come from the roots of flesh eating plants
and my brain is braced
for the butterfly's scream
of anguish, pinned to a page
a textbook crucifixion

when my faith was hanging
by fraying righteousness
my lamp smashed
and scattered city wide

when the infant eyes of my love
were gouged by justice
and my temples
spewed blood                                           35
when my life made no noise
but tick tock tick tock tick tock
I learned I must love
insanely

one window is enough for me                            40
one window for seeing for knowing
for silence
look, the walnut sapling
now is grown so big
it teaches its leaves                                  45
the meaning of "wall"
ask for the name
the savior's name
isn't the earth that has rotted under your feet
lonelier than you?                                     50

prophets handed down to us
the tablets of destruction
do the poisonous clouds
the unceasing explosions
shine in the holy mirrors?                             55
my friend, my brother, flesh of my flesh
when you take the moon, remember
and record the genocide of flowers

all dreams die
thrown from the peak of their folly                    60
four leaf clovers root
and suck up sap
through the mounded grave of meaning
is it me
the woman wrapped in the winding sheet                 65
of chastity?
will I ever climb again
on the steps of curiosity
to meet god on the roof
I sense the time has passed                            70
I sense my day is torn from the calendar
I sense a distance the width of a table
between my hair and these sad, strange hands
Say something to me
Say something to me                                    75

What do I ask when I offer you my body
but to know I am alive?
Say something to me
Say something to me
I am safe at my window
I am coupled with the sun

## The Windup Doll

More than this—yes,
you can be more still than this

You can stare long hours
with a look of the dead, still
stare, eyes trapped by your cigarette's smoke
stare into the vortex of a teacup
a blanched flower, a faded rug
a possible crack in the plaster
You can pull aside the curtain
with your dried up paw
to see in the street sheets of rain
slamming down
A child and its colorful kites
take shelter in an archway
as an old cart rolls from the unpeopled square
raucous and fast

You can stay put
behind the curtain
but blind
but deaf

You can cry
estranged, the liar's strident cry:
I love—
You can seem fine, unblemished stuff
in his strapping arms
your skin a leather table cloth
topped by two big cones
your breasts
You can lie
in sheets clean as love
with a slobbering drunk
an idiot, a tramp
You can make fun of
any puzzle without answers
You can work a crossword

all by yourself
You can make up
an answer all by yourself
an answer in five or six letters

You can kneel and nod 40
at a mausoleum
You can see God
in an unmarked grave
You can find faith
in a collection plate 45
You can rot
with the pious
in a mosque

You can cipher like zero
a constant sum 50
You can pop your eye
from its petulant lid
replace it with a button
from an antique boot
You can dry up 55
and vacate your gutter

You can hide the moment
in a box, with shame;
an awkward shot from a photo booth
You can hang 60
in the empty frame of your day
an icon of the damned one, defeated one
the crucified
You can cover the cracks with faces
and other such vacant designs 65

You can be a windup doll
with two glass eyes to see your sphere
You can sleep and sleep in your cloth lined box
sleep in your tulle and confetti
your body stuffed with straw 70
For every squeeze, every groping hand
you can scream and mechanically say:
Oh yes I am so happy!

■ **Reza Baraheni (1935– )** *Iran* **(poem)**

Reza Baraheni, born in Tabriz, a Turkish-speaking city in Iran, is an Iranian Turk who writes in Persian, the national language. The author of some forty-five volumes in Persian, he is a leading novelist, essayist, and poet in Iran. In the sixties he was a professor of American and English literature at the University of Teheran and was also a visiting professor at the universities of Maryland and Indiana and at Bard College. Under the Shah he was tortured and imprisoned. After the Shah's fall, he returned to Iran, resumed his position at the university, and frequently broadcast news and commentary for NPR's "All Things Considered." With the rise of the Islamic Republic he was fired from his university post and again imprisoned. Under the mullahs he has managed to publish many novels, which have been immediate best-sellers, censored and withdrawn from circulation, followed by legal appeals for republication. In his introduction to Baraheni's *The Crowned Cannibals* (1971), E. L. Doctorow called him "the chronicler of his nation's torture industry." For thirty-five years Reza Baraheni has been in the forefront of the struggle for democracy and human rights in Iran. Once more in exile, he lives in Toronto, Canada.

**FURTHER READING:** Baraheni, Reza. *God's Shadow: Prison Poems,* 1976; *The Crowned Cannibal.* Introduction by E. L. Doctorow, 1977.

## *Autumn in Tehran*

At first   A strange whisper   Began in the wind
    and the leaves
then carefree kids of the street came down
    with colds that sent them to bed
defining how such people use their eyes suits only
    minds in love with music
when the wind blew it whirled tears deep within
    weary eyes of retired men in the parks
as if an eternal grief had rained on their cheeks
the women hurried   The queue grew restless   they
    were shivering
in the wind the leaves on the surface young and
    green watched them   eyeless and wet
in fragments they consoled the women in love
    leaned their shoulders against their lovers' chests
—I'm cold! It suddenly got cold! Aren't you cold?
—no, perhaps from your kisses I still feel warm   still
then a blatant crow flew in the horizon   drew
    its dagger at the swallows   with the convex
    dagger of its beak the crow savaged the air

the crow screamed: here comes the season of sphere
    in flames   I'm your emperor!
The looting of the branches began in the evening
as though there was no end to it
it poured down in the sparkling of rain and wind         *15*
    in the street lights
millions of small, wet, and coloured balancing
    scales landed from the sky
men with bare heads, having no umbrellas, walked
    with newspapers over their heads
the night drove freshets from the bright north
    down in the dark south
and the next day   The world's streets were full
and the fresh perfume of the season's opium came     *20*
    from the piles of leaves
a strange siesta took hold of the world and bore it
    away
in the dull hour   the haggard autumn man thrust
    his wooden spear into death's leafy food

# ■ Dahlia Ravikovitch (1936– ) *Israel* (poem)

## TRANSLATED BY CHANA BLOCH AND ARIEL BLOCH

Dahlia Ravikovitch is Israel's finest woman poet. She was born in 1936 in Ramat Gan, a suburb of Tel Aviv. She studied at Jerusalem's Hebrew University and has worked as a journalist and a teacher. In addition to her poems, she has written two books of children's verse, a book of short stories, and many television reviews. She has won Israel's top literary awards. Her poetry has moved from rhyming high diction, archaic and biblical, to unrhymed colloquial free verse. After the Israeli invasion of Lebanon in June 1982, she joined other Israeli antiwar intellectuals, writing protest poems about the waste of life. Her ironic poem "Clockwork Doll," like Forugh Farrokhzad's "The Windup Doll," portrays a woman as an automaton valued for her graceful exterior and programmed interior. The poems often treat the roles, the powers, and the oppressions of women. In a *New Republic* review, Irving Howe noted that her poetry

    deals overwhelmingly with extreme states of personal life: desolation, loss, estrangement, breakdown. . . . Landscape, history, the Bible, and best of all a caustic mother wit: all figure behind the shaken self. . . . To read these poems is to see the whole world pressed into one imperiled being, and then, through the calming maneuvers of imagination, to watch that being glide past its own squalor and smallness.

Her five volumes of poetry are *The Love of an Orange, A Hard Winter, The Third Book, Deep Calleth Unto Deep,* and *Real Love.* Her book of selected poems is entitled *All Thy Breakers and Waves.*

**FURTHER READING:** Ravikovitch, Dahlia. *The Window: Poems by Dahlia Ravikovitch.* Translated by Chana Bloch and Ariel Bloch, 1989.


## Clockwork Doll

That night, I was a clockwork doll
and I whirled around, this way and that,
and I fell on my face and shattered to bits
and they tried to fix me with all their skill.

Then I was a proper doll once again
and I did what they told me, poised and polite.
But I was a doll of a different sort,
an injured twig that dangles from a stem.

And then I went to dance at the ball,
but they left me alone with the dogs and cats
though my steps were measured and rhythmical.

And I had blue eyes and golden hair
and a dress all the colors of garden flowers,
and a trimming of cherries on my straw hat.


## ▪ Haydar Haydar (1936– ) *Syria* (story)

TRANSLATED BY MICHAEL G. AZRAK, REVISED BY M. J. L. YOUNG

Haydar Haydar was born in Tartous in 1936. He worked in Algeria for many years and was employed as a schoolteacher until 1962. In addition to short stories, he published a novel (*Savage Time*) in 1974.


## The Ants and the Qat

As the first ant crawled over the toe of Mahmud ibn Abdullah al-Zubayri as he lay beneath the tree, he gazed at it for a moment; an idle chuckle overcame him as he watched the diminutive creature climb over his giant body. In a sweetly languorous state he chewed a mouthful of qat,[1] moving it about in his mouth with relish, like a man caressing a woman's breast.

Mahmud ibn Abdullah al-Zubayri said to himself: "What a pity these poor mites are deprived of this pleasure!"

The sunlight, piercing through the leaves of the tree, combined with the delicious taste of the qat to produce a refreshing torpor in the body of the man, lying half in the sun and half in the shade. From a nearby cafe wafted the voice of an eastern singer, bearing him away to an ineffable tranquility.

Just as he was sucking the morsel of qat and greedily squeezing the last drop from it, another ant, followed by a companion, began to scale the toes of his supine body. The ascent of the third ant tickled him. Then the ant nipped him with its tiny jaws, and it felt as though a small thorn had pricked him. Mahmud ibn Abdullah said, "How stupid ants are!" and with a drowsy movement stirred his toes to shake the ant off or crush it. The ant, however, was more deft than this movement: it abandoned his toe and descended to the sole of his foot.

Torpor oozed into every cell of the man's recumbent body. He gave himself up to the sun, the qat, and the sweet soothing voice of the Star of the East.[2] The sleepy daze gave rise to visions and variegated daydreams, like a rainbow. He saw himself flying above the fields and mountains until he had reached the stars in their courses. As he looked on the stars they changed to flowers. He plucked them and put them in his buttonhole, proudly displaying himself like a peacock. Then he noticed that the stars had been transformed into golden globes. He took them to sell in the market place, and with the money bought guns and horses and falcons and hunting dogs.

When he was weary of the stars and the gold and the guns and the falcons, he dreamed of white-skinned women the color of snow, their hair like ears of corn, and their eyes the color of the sea.

Then he imagined himself a knight riding into the wind, with a sword and a lance in his hand, and he was the unchallenged monarch of the world; and lo! Here was the world at his feet, with him issuing commands as he pleased, while around him serfs, slave-girls and soldiers obeyed his every whim. He married several wives, and allotted a palace and a night to each one.

At length, when his rule was firmly established, he considered it a good idea to eliminate his enemies—beginning with his neighbor of long standing, she of the sharp tongue, whom he had desired, but who had rebuffed him. He summoned her and condemned her, ordering her to kneel naked at his feet and to acknowledge that he was a king without

---

1. A shrub native to Arabia, the leaves of which are chewed to produce a pleasant state of drugged elation.

2. Umm Kulthum, the famous Arab woman singer.

peer in manliness and courage. Then he ordered his executioner to cut out her tongue, and passed her over to his slaves, for each of them to have, one after the other.

The happy king Mahmud ibn Abdullah al-Zubayri then commanded that a certain man should be brought to him who had once comprehensively described him as impotent, an ignoramus and a fool. He ordered his two hangmen to flog him until the blood flowed. Then they emasculated him and threw the remains to the dogs in front of the assembled people.

Then Mahmud ibn Abdullah al-Zubayri, recumbent upon his throne, began to avenge himself upon his enemies one after another, while the tiny insignificant ants climbed over the body swimming in its dreamy stupor. Now they were slowly making their way in throngs over it, attacking it with confidence.

The man's eyelids began to grow heavy; the visions and the fantasies began to dance, and jump from mountaintop to mountaintop, from city to city, as he was borne aloft on a gentle breeze and one imaginary voice melted into another, from star to star, from the sweet-voiced eastern songstress. The overpowering qat coursed through his thirsty veins.

Mahmud ibn Abdullah al-Zubayri slept as the sun began to decline toward the horizon. Deep sleep carried him to remote islands filled with mermaids and buried treasures: treasures of rubies, diamonds and qat. Then he noticed that all these islands with all their treasures and rocks and trees had become a forest of qat trees. He embraced it with open arms and went on chewing with savage ecstasy.

The ants had now become armies. They swarmed from all directions, invading the body of the dreaming man; they pried all over him without let or hindrance. When the ants with their formic instinct had made sure that the man was beyond the sphere of consciousness and that the chewing had ceased, they peered at the fixed wide stupid smile, and began their relentless work on their prey, which had now become transformed into a corpse.

## ■ Mohamed el-Bisatie (1938– ) *Egypt* (story)

### TRANSLATED BY DENYS JOHNSON-DAVIES

Mohamed el-Bisatie was born in Egypt and has worked as an Egyptian government official. His well-received volumes of short stories describe quotidian Egyptian society with deep compassion. In "A Conversation from the Third Floor," el-Bisatie illustrates the complicated interactions of a woman visiting her prisoner husband, the lewd chorus of fellow prisoners, and the stoic and mutely sympathetic policeman. His lucid prose records every tiny perception and event, sketching out with cinematic patience the scorched prison landscape and the slightest motion of shadow and emotion. El-Bisatie has also published a novel that has yet to be translated from Arabic.

# A Conversation from the Third Floor

She came to the place for the second time. The policeman stared down at her from his horse.

The time was afternoon. The yellow-coloured wall stretched right along the road. Inside the wall was a large rectangular three-storey building; its small identical windows looked more like dark apertures. The woman stood a few paces away from the horse. The policeman looked behind him at the windows, then at the woman. He placed both hands on the pommel of the saddle and closed his eyes. After a while the horse moved. It was standing halfway down the street. Then, a moment later, it made a half-turn and once again stood itself at the top of the street.

The woman came two steps forward. The horse bent one of its forelegs, then gently lowered it.

'Sergeant, please, just let me say two words to him.'

His eyes remained closed, his hands motionless on the pommel.

Above the wall stretched a fencing of barbed wire at the end of which was a wooden tower. Inside there stood an armed soldier.

The woman took another step forward.

'You see, he's been transferred. . . .'

The sun had passed beyond the central point in the sky. Despite this the weather was still hot. A narrow patch of shade lay at the bottom of the wall.

The woman transferred the child to her shoulder.

When she again looked at the policeman's face, she noticed thin lines of sweat on his forehead.

Quietly she moved away from in front of the horse and walked beside the wall. About halfway along it she sat down on a heap of stones opposite the building.

The prisoners' washing, hung by the arms and legs, could be seen outside the bars of the windows. Mostly it was completely motionless, even with the breeze that blew from time to time.

The woman whispered to herself: 'They must be wet.'

She placed the child in her lap. For a moment her eyes fastened on a djellaba that gently swayed to the movement of the wind. She stretched out her leg and gazed at her toes and the dried mud that clung to them. She rubbed her feet together, then gazed at them once again.

Putting back her head, she looked up at the windows of the third floor with half-closed eyes.

The soldier in the tower took a step forward. He rested his against the edge of the wooden wall.

He looked at the sky, at the roofs of the houses, at the street, then at the head of the white horse.

Suddenly a shout broke the silence. The woman quickly drew back her leg. She caught sight of a bare arm waving from between the bars of a window on the third floor.

'Aziza! Aziza! It's Ashour.'

She moved a step nearer to the wall and stared in silence at the window.

'It's Ashour, Aziza. Ashour.'

She saw his other arm stretching out through the window. She searched with her eyes for something between the two arms and succeeded in making out a face pressed between the two bars. Other faces could be seen above and alongside him.

'Aziza, I've been transferred. Did you get my letter? In four days I'll be transferred. Did you prune the two date palms? Where are Hamid and Saniyya? Why didn't you bring them with you? I'm being transferred. Where's Hamid?'

He turned round suddenly, shouting:

'Stop it, you bastards!'

She heard him shouting and saw the faces disappear from the window. After a while his face was again looking out through the bars, then the other faces looked out above his.

'Aziza!'

She looked at the policeman on the horse, then at the soldier in the tower.

'Who are you holding? Shakir? Aziza!' She shook her head twice.

'Lift him up. Lift him up high.'

She took the child between her hands and lifted him above her head.

She noticed his arms suddenly being withdrawn inside and his hands gripping the iron bars of the window. Then his face disappeared from view. For a while she searched for him among the faces that looked down. She lowered her arms a little and heard shouts of laughter from the window. She spotted his arm once again stretching outwards, then his face appeared clearly in the middle.

'Up, Aziza. Up. Face him towards the sun so I can see him.' She lowered her arms for a moment, then raised him up again, turning his face towards the sun. The child closed his eyes and burst out crying.

'He's crying.'

He turned round, laughing.

'The boy's crying! The little so-and-so! Aziza, woman, keep him crying!'

He cupped his hand round his mouth and shouted: 'Let him cry!'

Again he laughed. A few shouts went up around him. She heard their words and shoutings. Then she saw his large nose poking out through the bars.

'Woman! Don't be silly, that's enough! Cover the boy—he'll get sunstroke!'

She hugged the child to her chest and saw the soldier withdrawing inside the tower.

'Did you prune the two date palms?'

She shook her head.

'Why not? Why don't you talk? I'm being transferred. Pass by Abu Is-mail and tell him I send him my best wishes—he'll do it as a favour and prune the trees, then you can bring along a few dates. Did you bring the cigarettes?'

She made a sign with her hand.

'Talk. What are you saying?'

'You've got 'em.'

'Louder, woman.'

'You've got 'em, I sent them to you.'

'When?'

'Just now.'

'Just now? Here, hang on—don't move.'

He disappeared suddenly. Two faces remained at the window. One of them stretched out his arm; he made an obscene movement in the air with his hand. She lowered her eyes, then went back to the pile of stones.

'Aziza!'

Though she did not recognise the voice, she looked up at the window. She saw the man was smiling, his arm still moving about. The second man was kneeling, having raised his djellaba above his thighs. She heard him call out:

'Aziza, look!'

She smiled. The policeman was still sitting on his horse as though asleep. From the side window of the tower she had a partial view of the sol-dier's head. He had taken off his helmet.

She heard several voices calling her. She listened attentively, concen-trating her gaze on the soldier's head as he moved within the opening of the window. The calls were repeated, interspersed with abuse. The soldier put on his helmet, but remained inside the tower.

Suddenly the voices were silent and some moments later there came to her the breathless voice of her husband:

'Aziza? I said five—didn't I tell you five packets?' She stared up to-wards him in silence.

'Woman, what's the use of three packets?' She gestured to him with her hand.

'What are you saying?'

'Five—I sent five.'

'Five?' he shouted fiercely. 'The bastards!'

He disappeared suddenly, then leant out again shouting:

'Wait! Don't go!'

She turned her face towards the window of the tower. He was away for a while, then he returned.

'It's all right, Aziza. Never mind. Five—yes, there were five. Never mind, a couple got taken, it doesn't matter. Listen—what was I going to say?' Silence. She saw him staring out in silence from the window. She shook out her black djellaba and walked forward towards the wall. He smiled.

'Aziza, I was thinking of saying something to you.'

Again there was silence. She turned away her head so that part of her face was against the sun. She shifted her head-veil slightly from her head.

'They took a couple of packets. Never mind, Aziza. Never mind.'

He laughed. His voice had become calm. The other faces disappeared from above him, only a single face remaining alongside his.

'Did you build the wall?'

'Not yet.'

'Why not?'

'When Uncle Ahmed lights the furnace, I'll get some bricks from him.'

'All right. Be careful on the tram. Look after the boy.'

She remained standing.

'Anything you want?'

'No.'

She gazed at his face, his large nose, his bare arms. She smiled. The face next to his smiled back.

Suddenly he shouted. 'Did you get the letter? I'm being transferred.'

'Where to?'

'I don't know.'

'When?'

'You see, they're pulling down the prison.'

'Where will you go?'

'God knows—anywhere. No one knows.'

'When?'

'In two or three days. Don't come here again. I'll let you know when I'm transferred. Has the boy gone to sleep?'

'No, he's awake.'

He stared back for a while in silence.

'Aziza!'

Again there was silence. The face alongside his smiled, then slowly slid back inside and disappeared. Her husband remained silent, his arms around the bars.

Suddenly he glanced behind him and quickly drew in his arms. He signalled to her to move away, then disappeared from the window.

She stepped back, though she remained standing looking up at the window.

After a while she seated herself on the stones and stretched out her leg. Taking out her breasts, she suckled her child.

The shadow advanced halfway across the street. She saw that its fringe was touching her foot. She drew her foot back a little. The place was quiet and the washing that had been hung out gently swayed in the breeze.

When she looked at her foot again; she saw that the shadow clothed the tips of her toes. She stood up.

The soldier was still inside the tower; the toe of his boot could be seen at the edge of the wooden platform. Before reaching where the horse stood she glanced behind her, but the window was empty.

She looked quietly at the policeman: his eyes were closed, his hands on the pommel of the saddle. The horse stood motionless.

She walked down the narrow passageway towards the main street.

## ■ Amos Oz (1939– ) *Israel* (story)

TRANSLATED BY AMOS OZ

Amos Oz is among Israel's finest writers, a prolific novelist and short story and essay writer. He was born Amos Khausner to a strict Zionist family in Jerusalem but moved to a kibbutz and changed his name in rebellion. He has served in the military in two wars, and the conflict between Arab and Jew, and between ideals and realities, is a central concern of his work. "Nomad and Viper" is a representative story in this sense, and it is a good example of his ability as a masterful prose stylist. He continues living on the kibbutz today. His books in English translation are *Black Box* (1988); *Elsewhere, Perhaps* (1973), his fine novel about kibbutz life; *The Hill of Evil Counsel: Three Stories* (1978); *In the Land of Israel* (1983); *My Michael* (1972); *A Perfect Peace* (1985); *The Slopes of Lebanon* (1989); *Soumchi* (1980); *To Know a Woman* (1991); *Touch the Water, Touch the Wind* (1974); *Unto Death* (1975); *Where the Jackals Howl, and Other Stories* (1981); and *Until Daybreak: Stories from the Kibbutz* (1984).

## Nomad and Viper

### 1

The famine brought them.

They fled north from the horrors of famine, together with their dusty flocks. From September to April the desert had not known a moment's relief from drought. The loess was pounded to dust. Famine had spread through the nomads' encampments and wrought havoc among their flocks.

The military authorities gave the situation their urgent attention. Despite certain hesitations, they decided to open the roads leading north to the Bedouins. A whole population—men, women, and children—could not simply be abandoned to the horrors of starvation.

Dark, sinuous, and wiry, the desert tribesmen trickled along the dirt paths, and with them came their emaciated flocks. They meandered along gullies hidden from town dwellers' eyes. A persistent stream pressed northward, circling the scattered settlements, staring wide-eyed at the sights of the settled land. The dark flocks spread into the fields of golden stubble, tearing and chewing with strong, vengeful teeth. The nomads' bearing was stealthy and subdued; they shrank from watchful eyes. They took pains to avoid encounters. Tried to conceal their presence.

If you passed them on a noisy tractor and set billows of dust loose on them, they would courteously gather their scattered flocks and give you a wide passage, wider by far than was necessary. They stared at you from a distance, frozen like statues. The scorching atmosphere blurred their appearance and gave a uniform look to their features: a shepherd with his staff, a woman with her babes, an old man with his eyes sunk deep in their sockets. Some were half-blind, or perhaps feigned half-blindness from some vague alms-gathering motive. Inscrutable to the likes of you.

How unlike our well-tended sheep were their miserable specimens: knots of small, skinny beasts huddling into a dark, seething mass, silent and subdued, humble as their dumb keepers.

The camels alone spurn meekness. From atop tall necks they fix you with tired eyes brimming with scornful sorrow. The wisdom of age seems to lurk in their eyes, and a nameless tremor runs often through their skin.

Sometimes you manage to catch them unawares. Crossing a field on foot, you may suddenly happen on an indolent flock standing motionless, noon-struck, their feet apparently rooted in the parched soil. Among them lies the shepherd, fast asleep, dark as a block of basalt. You approach and cover him with a harsh shadow. You are startled to find his eyes wide open. He bares most of his teeth in a placatory smile. Some of them are gleaming, others decayed. His smell hits you. You grimace. Your grimace hits him like a punch in the face. Daintily he picks himself up, trunk erect, shoulders hunched. You fix him with a cold blue eye. He broadens his smile and utters a guttural syllable. His garb is a compromise: a short, patched European jacket over a white desert robe. He cocks his head to one side. An appeased gleam crosses his face. If you do not upbraid him, he suddenly extends his left hand and asks for a cigarette in rapid Hebrew. His voice has a silken quality, like that of a shy woman. If your mood is generous, you put a cigarette to your lips and toss another into his wrinkled palm. To your surprise, he snatches a gilt lighter from the recesses of his robe and offers a furtive flame. The smile never leaves his lips. His smile lasts too long, is unconvincing. A flash of sunlight darts off the thick gold ring adorning his finger and pierces your squinting eyes.

Eventually you turn your back on the nomad and continue on your way. After a hundred, two hundred paces, you may turn your head and see him standing just as he was, his gaze stabbing your back. You could swear that he is still smiling, that he will go on smiling for a long while to come.

\* \* \*

And then, their singing in the night. A long-drawn-out, dolorous wail drifts on the night air from sunset until the early hours. The voices penetrate to the gardens and pathways of the kibbutz and charge our nights with an uneasy heaviness. No sooner have you settled down to sleep than a distant drumbeat sets the rhythm of your slumber like the pounding of an obdurate heart. Hot are the nights, and vapor-laden. Stray clouds caress the moon like a train of gentle camels, camels without any bells.

The nomads' tents are made up of dark drapes. Stray women drift around at night, barefoot and noiseless. Lean, vicious nomad hounds dart out of the camp to challenge the moon all night long. Their barking drives our kibbutz dogs insane. Our finest dog went mad one night, broke into the henhouse, and massacred the young chicks. It was not out of savagery that the watchmen shot him. There was no alternative. Any reasonable man would justify the action.

# 2

You might imagine that the nomad incursion enriched our heat-prostrated nights with a dimension of poetry. This may have been the case for some of our unattached girls. But we cannot refrain from mentioning a whole string of prosaic, indeed unaesthetic disturbances, such as foot-and-mouth disease, crop damage, and an epidemic of petty thefts.

The foot-and-mouth disease came out of the desert, carried by their livestock, which had never been subjected to any proper medical inspection. Although we took various early precautions, the virus infected our sheep and cattle, severely reducing the milk yield and killing off a number of animals.

As for the damage to the crops, we had to admit that we had never managed to catch one of the nomads in the act. All we ever found were the tracks of men and animals among the rows of vegetables, in the hayfields, and deep inside the carefully fenced orchards. And wrecked irrigation pipes, plot markers, farming implements left out in the fields, and other objects.

We are not the kind to take such things lying down. We are no believers in forbearance or vegetarianism. This is especially true of our younger men. Among the veteran founders there are a few adherents of Tolstoyan ideas and such like. Decency constrains me not to dwell in detail on certain isolated and exceptional acts of reprisal conducted by some of the youngsters whose patience had expired, such as cattle rustling, stoning a nomad boy, or beating one of the shepherds senseless. In defense of the perpetrators of the last-mentioned act of retaliation I must state clearly that the shepherd in question had an infuriatingly sly face. He was blind in one eye, broken-nosed, drooling; and his mouth—on this men responsible were unanimous—was set with long, curved fangs like a fox's. A man with such an appearance was capable of anything. And the Bedouins would certainly not forget this lesson.

The pilfering was the most worrisome aspect of all. They laid hands on the unripe fruit in our orchards, pocketed the faucets, whittled away piles of empty sacks in the fields, stole into the henhouses, and even made away with the modest valuables from our little houses.

The very darkness was their accomplice. Elusive as the wind, they passed through the settlement, evading both the guards we had posted and the extra guards we had added. Sometimes you would set out on a tractor or a battered jeep toward midnight to turn off the irrigation faucets in an outlying field and your headlights would trap fleeting shadows, a man or a night beast. An irritable guard decided one night to open fire, and in the dark he managed to kill a stray jackal.

Needless to say, the kibbutz secretariat did not remain silent. Several times Etkin, the secretary, called in the police, but their tracking dogs betrayed or failed them. Having led their handlers a few paces outside the kibbutz fence, they raised their black noses, uttered a savage howl, and stared foolishly ahead.

Spot raids on the tattered tents revealed nothing. It was as if the very earth had decided to cover up the plunder and brazenly outstare the victims. Eventually the elder of the tribe was brought to the kibbutz office, flanked by a pair of inscrutable nomads. The short-tempered policemen pushed them forward with repeated cries of "Yallah, yallah."

We, the members of the secretariat, received the elder and his men politely and respectfully. We invited them to sit down on the bench, smiled at them, and offered them steaming coffee prepared by Geula at Etkin's special request. The old man responded with elaborate courtesies, favoring us with a smile which he kept up from the beginning of the interview till its conclusion. He phrased his remarks in careful, formal Hebrew.

It was true that some of the youngsters of his tribe had laid hands on our property. Why should he deny it. Boys would be boys, and the world was getting steadily worse. He had the honor of begging our pardon and restoring the stolen property. Stolen property fastens its teeth in the flesh of the thief, as the proverb says. That was the way of it. What could one do about the hotheadedness of youth? He deeply regretted the trouble and distress we had been caused.

So saying, he put his hand into the folds of his robe and drew out a few screws, some gleaming, some rusty, a pair of pruning hooks, a stray knife-blade, a pocket flashlight, a broken hammer, and three grubby bank notes, as a recompense for our loss and worry.

Etkin spread his hands in embarrassment. For reasons best known to himself, he chose to ignore our guest's Hebrew and to reply in broken Arabic, the residue of his studies during the time of the riots and the siege. He opened his remarks with a frank and clear statement about the brotherhood of nations—the cornerstone of our ideology—and about the quality of neighborliness of which the peoples of the East had long been justly proud, and never more so than in these days of bloodshed and groundless hatred.

To Etkin's credit, let it be said that he did not shrink in the slightest from reciting a full and detailed list of the acts of theft, damage, and sabotage that our guest—as the result of oversight, no doubt—had refrained from mentioning in his apology. If all the stolen property were returned and the vandalism stopped once and for all, we would be wholeheartedly willing to open a new page in the relations of our two neighboring communities. Our children would doubtless enjoy and profit from an educational courtesy visit to the Bedouin encampment, the kind of visit that broadens horizons. And it went without saying that the tribe's children would pay a return visit to our kibbutz home, in the interest of deepening mutual understanding.

The old man neither relaxed nor broadened his smile, but kept it sternly at its former level as he remarked with an abundance of polite phrases that the gentlemen of the kibbutz would be able to prove no further thefts beyond those he had already admitted and for which he had sought our forgiveness.

He concluded with elaborate benedictions, wished us health and long life, posterity and plenty, then took his leave and departed, accompanied by his two barefooted companions wrapped in their dark robes. They were soon swallowed up by the wadi that lay outside the kibbutz fence.

Since the police had proved ineffectual—and had indeed abandoned the investigation—some of our young men suggested making an excursion one night to teach the savages a lesson in a language they would really understand.

Etkin rejected their suggestion with disgust and with reasonable arguments. The young men, in turn, applied to Etkin a number of epithets that decency obliges me to pass over in silence. Strangely enough, Etkin ignored their insults and reluctantly agreed to put their suggestion before the kibbutz secretariat. Perhaps he was afraid that they might take matters into their own hands.

Toward evening, Etkin went around from room to room and invited the committee to an urgent meeting at eight-thirty. When he came to Geula, he told her about the young men's ideas and the undemocratic pressure to which he was being subjected, and asked her to bring along to the meeting a pot of black coffee and a lot of good will. Geula responded with an acid smile. Her eyes were bleary because Etkin had awakened her from a troubled sleep. As she changed her clothes, the night fell, damp and hot and close.

# 3

Damp and close and hot the night fell on the kibbutz, tangled in the dust-laden cypresses, oppressed the lawns and ornamental shrubs. Sprinklers scattered water onto the thirsty lawn, but it was swallowed up at once: perhaps it evaporated even before it touched the grass. An irritable phone rang vainly in the locked office. The walls of the houses gave out a damp vapor. From the kitchen chimney a stiff column of smoke rose like an arrow into the heart of the sky, because there was no breeze. From the greasy sinks came a shout. A dish had been broken and somebody was bleeding. A fat house-cat had killed a lizard or a snake and dragged its prey onto the baking concrete path to toy with it lazily in the dense evening sunlight. An ancient tractor started to rumble in one of the sheds, choked, belched a stench of oil, roared, spluttered, and finally managed to set out to deliver an evening meal to the second shift, who were toiling in an outlying field. Near the Persian lilac Geula saw a bottle dirty with the remnants of a greasy liquid. She kicked at it repeatedly, but instead of shattering, the bottle rolled heavily among the rosebushes. She picked up a big stone. She tried to hit the bottle. She longed to smash it. The stone missed. The girl began to whistle a vague tune.

Geula was a short, energetic girl of twenty-nine or so. Although she had not yet found a husband, none of us would deny her good qualities, such as the dedication she lavished on local social and cultural activities. Her face was pale and thin. No one could rival her in brewing strong coffee—coffee to raise the dead, we called it. A pair of bitter lines were etched at the corners of her mouth.

On summer evenings, when the rest of us would lounge in a group on a rug spread on one of the lawns and launch jokes and bursts of cheerful song heavenward, accompanied by clouds of cigarette smoke, Geula would shut herself up in her room and not join us until she had prepared the pot of scalding, strong coffee. She it was, too, who always took pains to ensure that there was no shortage of biscuits.

What had passed between Geula and me is not relevant here, and I shall make do with a hint or two. Long ago we used to stroll together to the orchards in the evening and talk. It was all a long time ago, and it is a long time since it ended. We would exchange unconventional political ideas or argue about the latest books. Geula was a stern and sometimes merciless critic: I was covered in confusion. She did not like my stories, because of the extreme polarity of situations, scenery, and characters, with no intermediate shades between black and white. I would utter an apology or a denial, but Geula always had ready proofs and she was a very methodical thinker. Sometimes I would dare to rest a conciliatory hand on her neck, and wait for her to calm down. But she never relaxed completely. If once or twice she leaned against me, she always blamed her broken sandal or her aching head. And so we drifted apart. To this day she still cuts my stories out of the periodicals, and arranges them in a cardboard box kept in a special drawer devoted to them alone.

I always buy her a new book of poems for her birthday. I creep into her room when she is out and leave the book on her table, without any inscription or dedication. Sometimes we happen to sit together in the dining hall. I avoid her glance, so as not to have to face her mocking sadness. On hot days, when faces are covered in sweat, the acne on her cheeks reddens and she seems to have no hope. When the cool of autumn comes, I sometimes find her pretty and attractive from a distance. On such days Geula likes to walk to the orchards in the early evening. She goes alone and comes back alone. Some of the youngsters come and ask me what she is looking for there, and they have a malicious snicker on their faces. I tell them that I don't know. And I really don't.

# 4

Viciously Geula picked up another stone to hurl at the bottle. This time she did not miss, but she still failed to hear the shattering sound she craved. The stone grazed the bottle, which tinkled faintly and disappeared under one of the bushes. A third stone, bigger and heavier than the other two, was launched from ridiculously close range: the girl trampled on the loose soil of the flower bed and stood right over the bottle. This time there was a harsh, dry explosion, which brought no relief. Must get out.

Damp and close and hot the night fell, its heat prickling the skin like broken glass. Geula retraced her steps, passed the balcony of her room, tossed her sandals inside, and walked down barefoot onto the dirt path.

The clods of earth tickled the soles of her feet. There was a rough friction, and her nerve endings quivered with flickers of vague excitement. Beyond the rocky hill the shadows were waiting for her: the orchard in the last of the light. With determined hands she widened the gap in the fence and slipped through. At that moment a slight evening breeze began to stir. It was a warmish summer breeze with no definite direction. An old sun rolled westward, trying to be sucked up by the dusty horizon. A last tractor climbed back to the depot, panting along the dirt road from the outlying plots. No doubt it was the tractor that had taken the second-shift workers their supper. It seemed shrouded in smoke or summer haze.

Geula bent down and picked some pebbles out of the dust. Absently she began to throw them back again, one by one. There were lines of poetry on her lips, some by the young poets she was fond of, others her own. By the irrigation pipe she paused, bent down, and drank as though kissing the faucet. But the faucet was rusty, the pipe was still hot, and the water was tepid and foul. Nevertheless she bent her head and let the water pour over her face and neck and into her shirt. A sharp taste of rust and wet dust filled her throat. She closed her eyes and stood in silence. No relief. Perhaps a cup of coffee. But only after the orchard. Must go now.

# 5

The orchards were heavily laden and fragrant. The branches intertwined, converging above the rows of trunks to form a shadowy dome. Underfoot the irrigated soil retained a hidden dampness. Shadows upon shadows at the foot of those gnarled trunks. Geula picked a plum, sniffed and crushed it. Sticky juice dripped from it. The sight made her feel dizzy. And the smell. She crushed a second plum. She picked another and rubbed it on her cheek till she was spattered with juice. Then, on her knees, she picked up a dry stick and scratched shapes in the dust. Aimless lines and curves. Sharp angles. Domes. A distant bleating invaded the orchard. Dimly she became aware of a sound of bells. She was far away. The nomad stopped behind Geula's back, as silent as a phantom. He dug at the dust with his big toe, and his shadow fell in front of him. But the girl was blinded by a flood of sounds. She saw and heard nothing. For a long time she continued to kneel on the ground and draw shapes in the dust with her twig. The nomad waited patiently in total silence. From time to time he closed his good eye and stared ahead of him with the other, the blind one. Finally he reached out and bestowed a long caress on the air. His obedient shadow moved in the dust. Geula stared, leapt to her feet, and leaned against the nearest tree, letting out a low sound. The nomad let his shoulders drop and put on a faint smile. Geula raised her arm and stabbed the air with her twig. The nomad continued to smile. His gaze dropped to her bare feet. His voice was hushed, and the Hebrew he spoke exuded a rare gentleness:

"What time is it?"

Geula inhaled to her lungs' full capacity. Her features grew sharp, her glance cold. Clearly and dryly she replied:

"It is half past six. Precisely."

The Arab broadened his smile and bowed slightly, as if to acknowledge a great kindness.

"Thank you very much, miss."

His bare toe had dug deep into the damp soil, and the clods of earth crawled at his feet as if there were a startled mole burrowing underneath them.

Geula fastened the top button of her blouse. There were large perspiration stains on her shirt, drawing attention to her armpits. She could smell the sweat on her body, and her nostrils widened. The nomad closed his blind eye and looked up. His good eye blinked. His skin was very dark; it was alive and warm. Creases were etched in his cheeks. He was unlike any man Geula had ever known, and his smell and color and breathing were also strange. His nose was long and narrow, and a shadow of a mustache showed beneath it. His cheeks seemed to be sunk into his mouth cavity. His lips were thin and fine, much finer than her own. But the chin was strong, almost expressing contempt or rebellion.

The man was repulsively handsome, Geula decided to herself. Unconsciously she responded with a mocking half-smile to the nomad's persistent grin. The Bedouin drew two crumpled cigarettes from a hidden pocket in his belt, laid them on his dark, outstretched palm, and held them out to her as though proffering crumbs to a sparrow. Geula dropped her smile, nodded twice, and accepted one. She ran the cigarette through her fingers, slowly, dreamily, ironing out the creases, straightening it, and only then did she put it to her lips. Quick as lightning, before she realized the purpose of the man's sudden movement, a tiny flame was dancing in front of her. Geula shielded the lighter with her hand even though there was no breeze in the orchard, sucked in the flame, closed her eyes. The nomad lit his own cigarette and bowed politely.

"Thank you very much," he said in his velvety voice.

"Thanks," Geula replied. "Thank you."

"You from the kibbutz?"

Geula nodded.

"Goo-d." An elongated syllable escaped from between his gleaming teeth. "That's goo-d."

The girl eyed his desert robe.

"Aren't you hot in that thing?"

The man gave an embarrassed, guilty smile, as if he had been caught red-handed. He took a slight step backward.

"Heaven forbid, it's not hot. Really not. Why? There's air, there's water. . . ." And he fell silent.

The treetops were already growing darker. A first jackal sniffed the on-coming night and let out a tired howl. The orchard filled with a scurry of small, busy feet. All of a sudden Geula became aware of the throngs of black goats intruding in search of their master. They swirled silently in and out of the fruit trees. Geula pursed her lips and let out a short whistle of surprise.

"What are you doing here, anyway? Stealing?"

The nomad cowered as though a stone had been thrown at him. His hand beat a hollow tattoo on his chest.

"No, not stealing, heaven forbid, really not." He added a lengthy oath in his own language and resumed his silent smile. His blind eye winked nervously. Meanwhile an emaciated goat darted forward and rubbed against his leg. He kicked it away and continued to swear with passion:

"Not steal, truly, by Allah not steal. Forbidden to steal."

"Forbidden in the Bible," Geula replied with a dry, cruel smile. "For-bidden to steal, forbidden to kill, forbidden to covet, and forbidden to commit adultery. The righteous are above suspicion."

The Arab cowered before the onslaught of words and looked down at the ground. Shamefaced. Guilty. His foot continued to kick restlessly at the loose earth. He was trying to ingratiate himself. His blind eye nar-rowed. Geula was momentarily alarmed: surely it was a wink. The smile left his lips. He spoke in a soft, drawn-out whisper, as though uttering a prayer.

"Beautiful girl, truly very beautiful girl. Me, I got no girl yet. Me still young. No girl yet. Yaaa," he concluded with a guttural yell directed at an impudent goat that had rested its forelegs against a tree trunk and was munching hungrily at the foliage. The animal cast a pensive, skeptical glance at its master, shook its beard, and solemnly resumed its munching.

Without warning, and with amazing agility, the shepherd leapt through the air and seized the beast by the hindquarters, lifted it above his head, let out a terrifying, savage screech, and flung it ruthlessly to the ground. Then he spat and turned to the girl.

"Beast," he apologized. "Beast. What to do. No brains. No manners."

The girl let go of the tree trunk against which she had been resting and leaned toward the nomad. A sweet shudder ran down her back. Her voice was still firm and cool.

"Another cigarette?" she asked. "Have you got another cigarette?"

The Bedouin replied with a look of anguish, almost of despair. He apologized. He explained at length that he had no more cigarettes, not even one, not even a little one. No more. All gone. What a pity. He would gladly, very gladly, have given her one. None left. All gone.

The beaten goat was getting shakily to its feet. Treading circumspectly, it returned to the tree trunk, disingenuously observing its master out of the corner of its eye. The shepherd watched it without moving. The goat reached up, rested its front hoofs on the tree, and calmly continued munching. The Arab picked up a heavy stone and swung his arm wildly. Geula seized his arm and restrained him.

"Leave it. Why. Let it be. It doesn't understand. It's only a beast. No brains, no manners."

The nomad obeyed. In total submission he let the stone drop. Then Geula let go of his arm. Once again the man drew the lighter out of his belt. With thin, pensive fingers he toyed with it. He accidentally lit a small flame, and hastily blew at it. The flame widened slightly, slanted, and died. Nearby a jackal broke into a loud, piercing wail. The rest of the goats, meanwhile, had followed the example of the first and were absorbed in rapid, almost angry munching.

A vague wail came from the nomad encampment away to the south, the dim drum beating time to its languorous call. The dusky men were sitting around their campfires, sending skyward their single-noted song. The night took up the strain and answered with dismal cricket-chirp. Last glimmers of light were dying away in the far west. The orchard stood in darkness. Sounds gathered all around, the wind's whispering, the goats' sniffing, the rustle of ravished leaves. Geula pursed her lips and whistled an old tune. The nomad listened to her with rapt attention, his head cocked to one side in surprise, his mouth hanging slightly open. She glanced at her watch. The hands winked back at her with a malign, phosphorescent glint, but said nothing. Night.

The Arab turned his back on Geula, dropped to his knees, touched his forehead on the ground, and began mumbling fervently.

"You've got no girl yet," Geula broke into his prayer. "You're still too young." Her voice was loud and strange. Her hands were on her lips, her breathing still even. The man stopped praying, turned his dark face toward her, and muttered a phrase in Arabic. He was still crouched on all fours, but his pose suggested a certain suppressed joy.

"You're still young," Geula repeated, "very young. Perhaps twenty. Perhaps thirty. Young. No girl for you. Too young."

The man replied with a very long and solemn remark in his own language. She laughed nervously, her hands embracing her hips.

"What's the matter with you?" she inquired, laughing still. "Why are you talking to me in Arabic all of a sudden? What do you think I am? What do you want here, anyway?"

Again the nomad replied in his own language. Now a note of terror filled his voice. With soft, silent steps he recoiled and withdrew as though from a dying creature. She was breathing heavily now, panting, trembling. A single wild syllable escaped from the shepherd's mouth: a sign between him and his goats. The goats responded and thronged around him, their feet pattering on the carpet of dead leaves like cloth ripping. The crickets fell silent. The goats huddled in the dark, a terrified, quivering mass, and disappeared into the darkness, the shepherd vanishing in their midst.

Afterward, alone and trembling, she watched an airplane passing in the dark sky above the treetops, rumbling dully, its lights blinking alternately with a rhythm as precise as that of the drums: red, green, red, green, red. The night covered over the traces. There was a smell of bonfires on the air and a smell of dust borne on the breeze. Only a slight breeze among the fruit trees. Then panic struck her and her blood froze. Her mouth opened to scream but she did not scream, she started to run and she ran barefoot with all her strength for home and stumbled and rose and ran as though pursued, but only the sawing of the crickets chased after her.

## 6

She returned to her room and made coffee for all the members of the secretariat, because she remembered her promise to Etkin. Outside the cool of evening had set in, but inside her room the walls were hot and her body was also on fire. Her clothes stuck to her body because she had been running, and her armpits disgusted her. The spots on her face were glowing. She stood and counted the number of times the coffee boiled—seven successive boilings, as she had learned to do it from her brother Ehud before he was killed in a reprisal raid in the desert. With pursed lips she counted as the black liquid rose and subsided, rose and subsided, bubbling fiercely as it reached its climax.

That's enough, now. Take clean clothes for the evening. Go to the showers.

What can that Etkin understand about savages. A great socialist. What does he know about Bedouins. A nomad sniffs out weakness from a distance. Give him a kind word, or a smile, and he pounces on you like a wild beast and tries to rape you. It was just as well I ran away from him.

In the showers the drain was clogged and the bench was greasy. Geula put her clean clothes on the stone ledge. I'm not shivering because the water's cold. I'm shivering with disgust. Those black fingers, and how he went straight for my throat. And his teeth. And the goats. Small and skinny like a child, but so strong. It was only by biting and kicking that I managed to escape. Soap my belly and everything, soap it again and again. Yes, let the boys go right away tonight to their camp and smash their black bones because of what they did to me. Now I must get outside.

## 7

She left the shower and started back toward her room, to pick up the coffee and take it to the secretariat. But on the way she heard crickets and laughter, and she remembered him bent down on all fours, and she was alarmed and stood still in the dark. Suddenly she vomited among the flowering shrubs. And she began to cry. Then her knees gave way. She sat down to rest on the dark earth. She stopped crying. But her teeth continued to chatter, from the cold or from pity. Suddenly she was not in a hurry any more, even the coffee no longer seemed important, and she thought to herself: There's still time. There's still time.

Those planes sweeping the sky tonight were probably on a night-bombing exercise. Repeatedly they roared among the stars, keeping up a constant flashing, red, green, red, green, red. In counterpoint came the singing of the nomads and their drums, a persistent heartbeat in the distance: One, one, two. One, one, two. And silence.

# $\overline{8}$

From eight-thirty until nearly nine o'clock we waited for Geula. At five to nine Etkin said that he could not imagine what had happened; he could not recall her ever having missed a meeting or been late before; at all events, we must now begin the meeting and turn to the business on the agenda.

He began with a summary of the facts. He gave details of the damage that had apparently been caused by the Bedouins, although there was no formal proof, and enumerated the steps that had been taken on the committee's initiative. The appeal to good will. Calling in the police. Strengthening the guard around the settlement. Tracking dogs. The meeting with the elder of the tribe. He had to admit, Etkin said, that we had now reached an impasse. Nevertheless, he believed that we had to maintain a sense of balance and not give way to extremism, because hatred always gave rise to further hatred. It was essential to break the vicious circle of hostility. He therefore opposed with all the moral force at his disposal the approach—and particularly the intentions—of certain of the younger members. He wished to remind us, by way of conclusion, that the conflict between herdsmen and tillers of the soil was as old as human civilization, as seemed to be evidenced by the story of Cain, who rose up against Abel, his brother. It was fitting, in view of the social gospel we had adopted, that we should put an end to this ancient feud, too, just as we had put an end to other ugly phenomena. It was up to us, and everything depended on our moral strength.

The room was full of tension, even unpleasantness. Rami twice interrupted Etkin and on one occasion went so far as to use the ugly word "rubbish." Etkin took offense, accused the younger members of planning terrorist activities, and said in conclusion, "We're not going to have that sort of thing here."

Geula had not arrived, and that was why there was no one to cool down the temper of the meeting. And no coffee. A heated exchange broke out between me and Rami. Although in age I belonged with the younger men, I did not agree with their proposals. Like Etkin, I was absolutely opposed to answering the nomads with violence—for two reasons, and when I was given permission to speak I mentioned them both. In the first place, nothing really serious had happened so far. A little stealing perhaps, but even that was not certain: every faucet or pair of pliers that a tractor driver left in a field or lost in the garage or took home with him was immediately blamed on the Bedouins. Secondly, there had been no rape or murder. Hereupon Rami broke in excitedly and asked what I was waiting for. Was I perhaps waiting for some small incident of rape that Geula could write poems about and I could make into a short story? I flushed and cast around in my mind for a telling retort.

But Etkin, upset by our rudeness, immediately deprived us both of the right to speak and began to explain his position all over again. He asked us how it would look if the papers reported that a kibbutz had sent out a lynch mob to settle scores with its Arab neighbors. As Etkin uttered the phrase "lynch mob," Rami made a gesture to his young friends that is commonly used by basketball players. At this signal they rose in a body and walked out in disgust, leaving Etkin to lecture to his heart's content to three elderly women and a long-retired member of Parliament.

After a moment's hesitation I rose and followed them. True, I did not share their views, but I, too, had been deprived of the right to speak in an arbitrary and insulting manner.

# 9

If only Geula had come to the meeting and brought her famous coffee with her, it is possible that tempers might have been soothed. Perhaps, too, her understanding might have achieved some sort of compromise between the conflicting points of view. But the coffee was standing, cold by now, on the table in her room. And Geula herself was lying among the bushes behind the Memorial Hall, watching the lights of the planes and listening to the sounds of the night. How she longed to make her peace and to forgive. Not to hate him and wish him dead. Perhaps to get up and go to him, to find him among the wadis and forgive him and never come back. Even to sing to him. The sharp slivers piercing her skin and drawing blood were the fragments of the bottle she had smashed here with a big stone at the beginning of the evening. And the living thing slithering among the slivers of glass among the clods of earth was a snake, perhaps a venomous snake, perhaps a viper. It stuck out a forked tongue, and its triangular head was cold and erect. Its eyes were dark glass. It could never close them, because it had no eyelids. A thorn in her flesh, perhaps a sliver of glass. She was very tired. And the pain was vague, almost pleasant. A distant ringing in her ears. To sleep now. Wearily, through the thickening film, she watched the gang of youngsters crossing the lawn on their way to the fields and the wadi to even the score with the nomads. We were carrying short, thick sticks. Excitement was dilating our pupils. And the blood was drumming in our temples.

Far away in the darkened orchards stood somber, dust-laden cypresses, swaying to and fro with a gentle, religious fervor. She felt tired, and that was why she did not come to see us off. But her fingers caressed the dust, and her face was very calm and almost beautiful.

■ **Mohammed Mrabet (1940– )** *Morocco* **(story)**

TRANSLATED BY PAUL BOWLES

Mohammed Mrabet was born in Tangiers in 1940 when it was an international tax-free city. Mrabet still lives in Tangiers, but his tales often concern the Moghrebi region. In his book *M'Hashish* (1988), he speaks about hashish and the uncertain pleasures of being a habitual user of the drug. He is also concerned with the plight of Muslim women and their virtual imprisonment in the houses of their husbands. In fact, Mrabet's grandfather murdered one of his wives because she was standing in the doorway of his house, gazing into the street. Mrabet is a gripping storyteller. His translator is the American writer Paul Bowles, famed friend of the Beat writers, who has spent most of his life in Morocco. We owe Mrabet's own recognition to Bowles's excellent translations.

**FURTHER READING:** Mrabet, Mohammed. *M'Hashish*. Taped and translated from Moghrebi by Paul Bowles, 1988; *The Boy Who Set the Fire and Other Stories*. Taped and translated from Moghrebi by Paul Bowles, 1974; *Chocolate Cream and Dollars*. Taped and translated from Moghrebi by Paul Bowles, 1992.

## The Canebrake

Kacem and Stito met every afternoon at a café. They were old friends. Kacem drank, and he had a wife whom he never allowed to go out of the house. No matter how much she entreated him and argued with him, he would not even let her go to the hammam to bathe. Stito had no troubles because he was a bachelor, and only smoked kif.

Kacem would come into the café with a bottle in his shopping bag, and soon both of them would go on to Kacem's house. On the way they would stop at the market to buy food, since Kacem would not permit his wife to go to market, either. Stito had no one to cook for him, and so he ate each night at Kacem's house, and always paid his share.

They would carry the food to Kacem's wife so she could prepare it. First, however, she would make tapas for Kacem's drinks, and tea for Stito's kif. Later when the food was cooking she would go in and sit with the two men.

Once when they were all sitting there together, Stito turned to Kacem and said: Sometimes I wonder how you can drink so much. Where do you store it all?

Kacem laughed. And you? You don't get anything but smoke out of your pipe. I get the alcohol right inside me, and it feels wonderful.

That's an empty idea you have, said Stito. Kif gives me more pleasure than alcohol could ever give anybody. And it makes me think straighter and talk better.

Kacem's wife decided that this was a good moment to say to her husband: Your friend's right. You drink too much.

Kacem was annoyed. Go and look at the food, he told her. It ought to be ready. We want to eat.

She brought the dinner in, and they set to work eating it. After they had finished, they talked for a half hour or so, and then Stito stood up. Until tomorrow, he told Kacem.

Yes, yes. Until tomorrow, said Kacem, who was drunk.

If Allah wills, Stito added.

Kacem's wife got up and opened the door for him.

Good night.

She shut the door, and then she and Kacem went to bed. Feeling full of love, she began to kiss her husband. But he only lay there, too drunk to notice her.

Soon she sat up and began to complain. From the day of our wedding you've never loved me, she said. You never pay me any attention at all unless you want to eat.

Go to sleep, woman, he told her.

She had started to cry, and it was a long time before she slept.

The next afternoon when he finished work, Kacem went to the café to meet Stito. They did the marketing and carried the food back to Kacem's house. The evening passed the same as always. Kacem was very drunk by the time Stito was ready to go home.

Kacem's wife opened the door for Stito and stepped outside. As he went through the doorway she whispered: Try and come alone tomorrow. Let him come by himself.

What do you mean? he said.

She pointed at the canebrake behind the garden. Hide there, she said.

Stito understood. But he'll be here, he whispered.

That's all right. Don't worry, she told him. Good night.

Good night.

The woman shut the door. Kacem was still sitting there drinking. She left him there and went to bed.

Again the following afternoon the two friends met in the café. Stito put away his pipe. How are you? he said.

Let's go, said Kacem. He was eager to get home and open his bottle.

I can't go right now, Stito told him. I've got to wait here and see somebody. I'll come later. Here's the money for the food.

Yes, said Kacem. I'll go on to the market, then.

Sit down with me a minute, said Stito.

No, no. I'll be going.

I'll see you later, Stito said.

Stito sat there in the café until dusk, and then he got up and went to the street where Kacem's house was. He waited until no one was passing by before he began to make his way through the canebrake. He was invisible in here. He peered between the canes and saw Kacem sitting in his room with a bottle on the table beside him, and a glass in his hand. And he saw the woman bring in the tailor.

Then she came outside carrying a large basin, and walked straight to the edge of the canebrake. She set the basin down and bent over it as if she were working. She was facing her husband and talking with him, and her garments reached to the ground in front of her. In the back, however, she was completely uncovered, and Stito saw everything he wanted to see. While she pretended to be washing something in the basin, she pushed her bare haunches back against the canes, and he pressed forward and began to enjoy himself with her.

When you're ready, she whispered, pull it out and let me catch it all in my hand.

That's no way, he said. How can I do that?

The woman moved forward suddenly and made it slip out, so that Stito understood that if he were to have anything at all with her, he would have to do as she wanted.

You can do it again afterwards and finish inside, if you like, she whispered.

She backed against the canes again, and he started once more. When he was almost ready he warned her, and she reached back with her hand, and got what she wanted. Keeping her fist shut, she waited so he could do it again the way he enjoyed it. He finished and went out of the canebrake into the street. No one saw him.

The woman walked into the house. She stood by the chair where Kacem sat, looking down at him. Can't I go to the hammam tomorrow? she said.

Are you starting that all over again? cried Kacem. I've told you no a thousand times. No! You can't leave this house.

She reached out her hand, opened it, and let what she had been holding drip into the taifor beside Kacem's glass.

Kacem stared. He had been drunk a moment before, and now he was no longer drunk. He did not even ask her from whom she had got it, or how. He stood up, leaving the bottle and glass, and went to bed without his dinner.

In the morning when he went out to work, Kacem left the door of his house wide open. All day he thought about his wife. When he had finished work, he went to the café to meet Stito.

His face was sad as he sat down. Fill me a pipe, he said.

What? Stito cried.

Yes.

Stito gave him his pipe. What's happened? It's the first time you've ever asked for kif.

I'm through with drinking, Kacem told him. I'm going to start smoking kif.

But why?

Kacem did not reply, and Stito did not ask again.

That evening the two friends arrived at Kacem's house laughing and joking, with their heads full of kif. Kacem was in a fine humor all evening. After Stito had gone, he said to his wife: You went to the hammam?

Yes, she said. Thank you for leaving the door open. I thought you'd forgotten to shut it when you went out.

I'm not going to lock it any more, he told her.

She kissed him and they went to bed. It was the first time in many nights that Kacem was not too drunk to play games with his wife. They made one another very happy, and finally they fell into a perfect sleep.

## ■ Mahmud Darwish (1942– ) *Palestine/Lebanon* (poems)

Mahmud Darwish was born in the village of al-Barwa in Palestine and grew up under Israeli rule, writing resistance poems and experiencing prison and house arrest. In 1948, when he was six, his village was attacked and obliterated by Israeli forces, and his family fled to Lebanon where they lived as refugees for a year. He worked as a journalist in Haifa until 1971, when he left for Beirut, where he lived until 1982. He currently resides in Paris and is the editor of the journal *Al-Karmal.* He has been awarded the Lotus Prize (1969) and the Lenin Prize (1983). He has published more than a dozen books of poetry and an autobiographical novel. He is probably the world's most celebrated Palestinian poet.

**FURTHER READING:** Al-Udhari, Abdullah, tr. and ed. *Modern Poetry of the Arab World,* 1986. Bennani, Ben, ed. and tr. *Bread Hashish and Moon: Four Modern Arab Poets,* 1982. Wedde, Ian, and Fawwaz Tuqan, trs. *Selected Poems: Mahmoud Darwish,* 1973.

## *The Prison Cell*

It is possible . . .
It is possible at least sometimes . . .
It is possible especially now
To ride a horse
Inside a prison cell                                                                5
And run away . . .

It is possible for prison walls
To disappear,
For the cell to become a distant land
Without frontiers:

—What did you do with the walls?
—I gave them back to the rocks.
—And what did you do with the ceiling?
—I turned it into a saddle.
—And your chain?
—I turned it into a pencil.

The prison guard got angry:
He put an end to the dialogue.
He said he didn't care for poetry,
And bolted the door of my cell.

He came back to see me
In the morning;
He shouted at me:

—Where did all this water come from?
—I brought it from the Nile.
—And the trees?
—From the orchards of Damascus.
—And the music?
—From my heartbeat.

The prison guard got mad;
He put an end to the dialogue.
He said he didn't like poetry,
And bolted the door of my cell.

But he returned in the evening:
—Where did this moon come from?
—From the nights of Bagdad.
—And the wine?
—From the vineyards of Algiers.
—And this freedom?
—From the chain you tied me with last night.

The prison guard grew so sad . . .
He begged me to give him back
His freedom.

TRANSLATED BY BEN BENNANI

## *Victim No. 48*

He was lying dead on a stone.
They found in his chest the moon and a rose lantern,
They found in his pocket a few coins,
A box of matches and a travel permit.
      He had tattoos on his arms.            *5*

His mother kissed him
And cried for a year.
Boxthorn tangled in his eyes.
      And it was dark.

His brother grew up            *10*
And went to town looking for work.
He was put in prison
Because he had no travel permit;
He was carrying a dustbin
      And boxes down the street.            *15*

Children of my country,
      That's how the moon died.

TRANSLATED BY ABDULLAH AL-UDHARI

## Hatif Janabi (1955– ) *Iraq/Poland* (poem)

TRANSLATED BY KHALED MATTAWA

Hatif Janabi was born in Iraq and has lived in Poland since 1976. He writes mainly in Arabic, but also in Polish. He has published five bilingual volumes of poetry and has won many Polish poetry prizes. He earned a Ph.D. in drama from Warsaw University, where he currently teaches Arabic literature and world drama. His poems, essays, and translations have appeared in many Arab literary magazines and he has been a visiting professor in the United States. His poems have a deep philosophical and historical resonance and can be gnomic and evocative or broad, surreal, fantastic, and Whitmanian in scope. They have a dramatic fullness, and a poem such as "Questions and Their Retinue" veers widely through Arabic history and literature with postmodern humor, elegaic wistfulness, and sardonic commentary.

## Questions and Their Retinue

( . . . These are the questions
and their retinue of poetry and prose.
There is no difference between one testicle and another
except for swelling. Now I ask all
those who differentiate between one finger and another
a catastrophe and another, a woman and another.
They give birth and were born on the banks of paralysis and weeping.
They have pointed hooves. Before they emerge they kick the wombs
    and the midwives' caves collapse. Afterwards everywhere
    becomes a barren place.
They are born in a quilt that quickly turns into a street,
a neighborhood, a lavish yacht, an expensive harem, etc. etc.                    *1*
Thank you, it was you, from the beginning, who forced us
to start writing verse, and because the old meters have calcified
we now are trying a new form of expression
for the violets of failure,
for the swings of despair,                                                       *1*
for the crumbs of white tombs
(white in wartime)
for the chirping of a bedouin as he leans over a prostitute,
soft and marble-like,
for the garbage heaps of plenty procreating and flying                           *2*
in the air of strange coasts,
always fleeing the holy books and their prohibitions.

This then is the bludgeon of civilization
that forced us to bring prohibited animals to our lands,
pigs to plow our fields, grasshoppers in clinics                                 *2*
grasshoppers slapping widows
who give birth now (and forever)
in a landfill-museum . . .
This is our heritage.
Let us return to its chains and spears,                                          *3*
its freedom and licentiousness.
What a marvelous indigenous cocktail
fortified with promiscuity,
blessed by the computers of friendly allies!
*Danke! ça va!* Good!                                                            *3*
Once again we feel our bodies,
our fingers touching and listening attentively
for things, minerals, ores, and stones.
What a blessed magical return to the stone ages! It is
the miracle of our offspring that we now bless with verse:                       *4*
    As they plough our steps

as they crack open the horizon
  a grass blade of speech
and Babylon weeping in refugee camps to a stone
flung at us by witches                         45
and our feet have yet to reach the Black Stone[1]
  but the winds were generous
  giving us an arm with which we struck
the archipelago of the dark.
Blackness smears the fingernails                  50
with burns of light and a querulous wound.
Naked we danced
wiping off the dust of the night.
To the river in the outfit of willows
we moved.                                 55
Fishermen began throwing clubs and dictionaries
and heavy boots into the river
and an idea began to glow—
The naked ones screamed:
Hang her! Hang her!                     60
For centuries the ropes have been ready
to be used in various ways
in these arid, ravished cities.
—"And now Ibn Munif you must write
the last chapter of your salt mine,"[2]          65
said a speaker with obvious contempt!
Everyone laughed then
and a child began
hammering the forehead of a poet
with a stone—the miracle of stone.        70
"Now say what you will,"
the child said as though drunk.
Nothing except stone can subdue this metal.
. . . A flurry of stabs
  and behind the crooked statues a woman     75
  fell
  (the poet said . . . )
I said lift your arms and kiss
her coat, O body
her lacquered chest—                80
her knees, a violin
her limbs, reeds.
Now she twists her fingers into a song.
Released from the noose of stabs,

---

1. A holy stone in the Ka'aba shrine in Mecca.

2. A reference to novelist Abdulrahman Munif and his novel *Cities of Salt*.

she proudly plants her nails in the dirt. 8
These are the questions
and their retinues are funerals
that stretch from door to door.
These are the questions,
stone and childhood, 9
and the retinues are a herd
of impoverished streets.
A wide horizon.
No window to shut us from it, no veil.

## ■ Khaled Mattawa (1964– ) *Libya* (poems, written in English)

Khaled Mattawa, born in Benghazi, Libya, came to America in his late teens, took his M.A. in English and Creative Writing at Indiana University, has taught at California State University at Northridge, and has received a Guggenheim Fellowship. He has translated and published the poetry of the Syrian-Lebanese poet Adunis and the exiled Iraqi poet Hatif Janabi. Mattawa's own poems, like the writings of the Indian novelist Bharati Mukherjee and many writers living outside their native country, are composed in English and have been published widely in American literary magazines, including *The Kenyon Review, The Iowa Review,* and *The Michigan Quarterly.* He is one of the most vigorous and sophisticated painters of modern Arab life. His lush, ironic, moving poem, "Watermelon Tales," concerning family and neighbors in Benghazi, Libya, was selected for publication in *The Pushcart Prize Anthology.*

**FURTHER READING:** Mattawa, Khaled. *Ismailia Eclipse,* 1995.

## *History of My Face*

My lips came with a caravan of slaves
That belonged to the Grand Sanussi.
In Al-Jaghbub he freed them.
They still live in the poor section of Benghazi
Near the hospital where I was born.

They never meant to settle
In Tokara, those Greeks
Whose eyebrows I wear.
Then they smelled the wild sage
And declared my country their birthplace. 1

The Knights of St. John invaded Tripoli.
The residents of the city
Sought help from Istanbul. In 1531
The Turks brought along my nose.

My hair stretches back                                          15
To a concubine of Septimius Severus.
She made his breakfast,
Bore four of his sons.

Uqba took my city
In the name of God.                                             20
We sit by his grave
And I sing to you:
        Sweet lashes, arrow sharp
        Is that my face I see
        Reflected in your eyes?                                25

## Watermelon Tales

January. Snow. For days I have craved
        watermelons, wanted
        to freckle the ground with seeds,
to perform a ritual:
        Noon time, an early                                     5
        summer Sunday, the village
chief faces north, spits seven mouthfuls,
        fingers a circle
around the galaxy of seeds.

                ✳   ✳   ✳
                                                                10
Maimoon the bedouin visited in
        summer, always with
        a gift: a pick-up truck load
of watermelons. "Something for the
        children," he explained.
        Neighbors brought wheelbarrows to              15
fetch their share. Our chickens ate the rest.

                ✳   ✳   ✳

        His right ear pricked up
        close, my father taps on a
watermelon, strokes as though it were
        a thigh. A light slap.                                 20
        "If it doesn't sound like your hands
clapping at a wedding, it's not yours."

                ✳   ✳   ✳

        Men shake the chief's hand,
        children kiss it. Everyone files
behind him when he walks back. No one                          25
        talks until the tomb

of the local saint. The rich
place coin sacks at his feet, the poor leave
        cups of melon seeds.

*  *  *

        Maimoon also brought us meat,
gazelles he rammed with his truck.
        His daughter, Selima,
            said he once swerved off the road
suddenly, drove for an hour until
            he spotted six. He hadn't
            hit any when the truck ran out
of gas. Thirty yards away the gazelles
            stood panting, and he
            ran to catch one with bare hands.

*  *  *

Two choices, my father's doctor tells us:
            transplant or six months
        of pain. Outside the office,
I point to a fruit stall, the seller
            waving off flies with
            a feather fan. My father
strokes, slaps, and when I lift the melon
            to my shoulder, says
            "Eleven years in America
and you carry a watermelon
            like a damn peasant!"

*  *  *

        Uncle Abdallah buries
a watermelon underneath the
            approach of the waves—
        "Like a refrigerator
down there." It's July, a picnic at
            Tokara Beach. We're
            kicking a ball when
my brother trips hard on the hole. He's
            told to eat what he'd
            broken too soon. I watched him
swallow pulp, seed, salt, and sand.

*  *  *

        Her shadow twice her
        height, the village sorceress
walks to where the chief spat. She reveals
            size of the harvest,

chance of drought, whose sons will wed
whose daughters, and names of elders whose
    ailments will not cease.

✳   ✳   ✳

    Selima told the gazelle
story sitting in a tub. With soap,                    70
      my mother scrubbed the girl's scalp,
tossing handfuls of foam against
      the white tile. She then
      poured kerosene on Selima's
hair, rubbed till lice slid down her face,      75
      combed till the tines
      filled with the dead.

✳   ✳   ✳

Selima married. My mother sent her
    a silver anklet,
    a green silk shawl, and decided          80
against an ivory comb. My father paid
    the sheikh to perform
    the wedding. A week later
at his door, the sheikh found three watermelons and a gazelle-    85
    skin prayer rug, a tire mark
across the spot where he would have rested his
    head in prostration.

✳   ✳   ✳

    I cut the melon we bought
into cubes, strawberry red. But they were    90
    dry, almost bitter.
    After the third taste, my father
dropped his fork. He gazed at the window
    for a while, and spent
    the rest of his days in bed.          95

# 3

# Sub-Sahara
# Africa

## INTRODUCTION

Africa is the second largest continent in the world, superseded only by
Asia. It includes both a northern Saharan culture that was conquered by
the Greeks, the Romans, and the Muslim empires, and a sub-Saharan
region inhabited largely by dark-skinned Bantus, but also by the light-
skinned Khoikhoi and the San (also known in the West as the Hottentots
and the Bushmen, respectively), and more recently by European colonial
expatriates, as well as populations of Indians and Arabs. Cultural, linguistic, and geographical differences make the division of North Africa and
sub-Sahara Africa a useful, if flawed, model. For reasons elaborated in the
General Introduction and the Introduction to Sumerian, Akkadian, and
Ancient Egyptian Literatures, we have placed North Africa and Muslim
Spain with the Near East in a section entitled The Bridge and considered
the sub-Sahara as a single entity. Of course, there are also many lines of
cultural connection: sub-Sahara Africa was conquered by later imperial

empires; its largely animistic religions were replaced in areas by Islam, Christianity, and Judaism; and trade through the Sahara and from its coasts facilitated contact with Europe, the Middle East, and India. Even the term *sub-Sahara* is not very satisfactory, since the Sudan is both Sahara and sub-Sahara.

Sub-Sahara Africa has some eight hundred languages. These major linguistic families are the Hamito-Semitic, Nilo-Saharan, and Niger-Kordofanian (including Niger-Congo). These units are in turn broken up into many important branches, such as the hundreds of Bantu languages in central Africa. In addition, there are the colonial languages of old Africa, which have become the main vehicle for modern literature in sub-Sahara Africa: French, English, Portuguese, Afrikaans, and pidgin or creole versions of these European tongues. Then, there is widespread Swahili, a Bantu language with many lone words from Arabic, which is not only broadly spoken in Kenya, Zaire, Tanzania, Burundi, and Uganda, but also serves as a lingua franca in these East African countries formed out of many ethnicities and languages.

Generally speaking, these languages were not written until modern times. Important exceptions are Swahili, which was written before the European conquest; the Niger-Congo language Vai that developed a script in the nineteenth century; Nubian in Southern Egypt and Sudan, of which there are eighth-century documents; and the Hamito-Semitic tongues of Ethiopia that go back to earliest Christian times and in which noncanonical apocrypha, including an Ethiopic infancy gospel of the life of the child Jesus, have been preserved. Muslim religious books were written in both Swahili and Arabic in premodern times in sub-Sahara Africa, and there is a tradition of Swahili poetry written first in Arabic letters and later in the Roman alphabet going back several hundred years. Africans from the sub-Sahara who were transplanted through the slave trade to Spain, Portugal, the Caribbean, and the Americas, also have a written tradition of verse and slave narratives. Phyllis Wheatley (c. 1754–1784), for example, was brought to Boston from either Senegal or Gambia at age seven or eight and quickly learned English and later Latin. She admired Alexander Pope and John Milton and published a volume of poems while still in her teens, written largely in English heroic couplets. In the sub-Sahara itself, however, creative expression in ancient and modern times has most often taken the expression of story, myth, history, song, riddle, and proverbial wisdom as passed down from generation to generation in an extensive oral tradition.

# The Premodern Period

■

## INTRODUCTION

Current anthropological research suggests that the earliest hominids evolved in Africa into *Homo sapiens*. For much of the ancient period, the peoples of sub-Sahara Africa subsisted through a hunter-gatherer economy, but agricultural methods began to permeate the sub-Sahara several thousand years before Christ. With agriculture came a fixed lifestyle; the development of settled extended families; village life; and more extensive collectives, kingdoms, and empires, all linked by the great carrier of goods and culture—trade. Great Saharan and sub-Saharan empires included the Egyptian-influenced Sudanese kingdom of Kush, which flourished independently of Egypt from the eighth century B.C. through the first centuries A.D.; the West African kingdom of Ghana (c. 900–1100), which flourished by straddling the trans-Saharan caravan routes in modern-day Mali, Mauritania, and Senegal; the successor kingdoms to Ghana, the ancient empire of Mali (c. 1200–1450) and the Songhay empire (fifteenth to sixteenth centuries), with the great center of Muslim scholarship at Timbuktu; the southern Zimbabwean kingdom of Great Zimbabwe (first millennium A.D. to the fifteenth century); and the kingdom of Ethiopia at Axum, which adopted Coptic Christianity in the fourth century A.D., and whose mercantile, political, and military power declined after the spread of Islam in the eighth century.

With the explosive spread of Islam across North Africa and the Middle East in the centuries after the death of Muhammad came a great increase in the long-distance trade between North Africa and the sub-Sahara. Much of this trade consisted of gold and ivory, but the great caravan routes through the Sahara also were the primary means of supplying the Muslim kingdoms of the north with slaves to tend their houses, work in their mines, and fight in their armies. Some four and a quarter million black Africans were enslaved in the eight and a half centuries after the death of Muhammad in 632 on the trans-Saharan trade routes alone. However, black Africans were also captured and enslaved by Muslim traders in the East African coastal trade to the Middle East and India, and the trade sometimes went both ways—a smaller number of Caucasians were enslaved by Muslims or sold to West African monarchs as household slaves.

African states, which were often founded and dependent upon trade, were politically unstable and thus were inherently vulnerable economically and politically to the new European demand for gold, raw materials, and especially slaves in the seventeenth and eighteenth centuries. During these centuries, as many as nine or ten million black Africans were shipped to the Americas to work as slave laborers on agricultural plantations in the New World. The practice of slavery was not limited to what was to become the United States. Slaves toiled in horrific conditions throughout the colonies of the English, Spanish, French, Dutch, and Portuguese, in South America, Central America, and the Caribbean. Slave traders were a diverse group. There were Europeans; Arabs, who had been in the trade for a millennium; as well as black Africans, whose tribal rivalries were exploited by the European traders. Often, members of coastal African kingdoms would collaborate with the slave traders, using modern European armaments to conquer and enslave their inland enemies. One East African slave trader, Tippu Tip, even carved out his own inland kingdom in what was to become the Belgian Congo based on his soldiery, exploitation of tribal conflict, and use of the slave trade to dispose of his enemies.

The first extended literary work by a known author from sub-Sahara Africa is a slave autobiography, an immensely important historical document, by the Nigerian memoirist Olaudah Equiano (1745/6–1797), who, in recording his life on sea and land, graphically depicts the work and drama of an African black on three continents. In his memoir, Equiano details the horrific slave trade in Africa, survival on board slave and commercial ships, and the existence of a writer and politically active African in eighteenth-century London. As a slave sailor, Equiano eventually earned enough to buy his freedom; he became a merchant seaman and quartermaster and later settled in London where he married an English woman. In England, he worked in various government offices, all with intense dedication to the abolitionist cause.

Prior to Equiano, African literature below the Sahara consisted largely of an oral tradition of myth, histories, stories, songs, poems, and proverbs, a body of ancient wisdom that was recorded in modern times. The creation myths, with which we begin this section, are probably the most inspired and marvelous oral literature of sub-Sahara Africa. The creation myths of peoples of every continent are the foundation of their religions. In practice, however, "myth," from the beautiful Greek work *mythos,* is inevitably applied to stories in other people's religions, not one's own. One's own "myths" are history, truth, holy Scripture, and definitely not myth, which implies imaginative fiction rather than chronicle. So, in dealing with ancient tales, we speak of Greek and Akkadian myths, yet Jewish or Christian Scriptures. What may be considered "history" or "truth" within a community, to the outsider is myth, legend, and story. However, whatever we wish to call the oral creation stories of sub-Sahara Africa, be it myth, legend, story, or religious history of a people, they are universal in their essential concerns, profound, and wondrously imaginative. Traditional myths have been extremely influential in the development of a contemporary African tradition. We see this for example in the work of Nigerian novelist Amos Tutuola (1920–1997), whose novel *The Palm-Wine Drinkard* is imbued with the richness of the African creation tale.

The human repository for the oral tradition of wisdom and literature was termed the *griot* (praise singer), who usually told folktales with musical accompaniment. The stories in the tradition are grave, frightening, funny, and fascinating. The questions of existence, God, gods, demons, beasts, death, eternity, the fantastic, reality and appearance, and salvation are all there, distinctively elaborated through each tribal tradition. Every rhetorical device is found in them, although symbolism, allegory, and extended metaphor prevail. What is thrilling in myth, as in Franz Kafka's parables or any of the major writers of the fantastic, is the realistic elaboration of the impossible. These African primal myths read, as Homer and Genesis or the Gospel of John, as pleasurable and significant literature. In them, the unconscious and conscious meet, and we overhear the history of diverse people's creations and extraordinary vision. In their transcendental notions of creation, sub-Sahara Africa has its enormous literary beginnings. The tales are presented here in plain, excellent translations.

—Ayame Fukuda and the editors

FURTHER READING: Feldman, Susan. *African Myths and Tales,* 1963. Leach, Maria. *The Beginning,* 1956. Sproul, Barbara C. *Primal Myths: Creation Myths Around the World,* 1979.

# Oral Creation Myths

## (uncertain period)

### ▪ Bumba Vomits the World, Bushongo (Bantu) *Zaire*

TRANSLATED BY E. TORDAY AND T. A. JOYCE,
ADAPTED BY MARIA LEACH

The Bushongo or Bakuba, a Bantu people of the Congo River region in Zaire, describe creation in generative terms. Alone in the dark and watery chaos, without a mate, Bumba vomited forth the powers of the world. The structural similarities between this and more common birth metaphors (mouth–womb; vomit–baby; pain of delivery in both cases) are clear and serve to underscore Bumba's extraordinary fertility.

Bumba first vomited the sun, whose heat caused the primordial waters to recede and land to form. Next he vomited forth nine prototypical creatures, each of which made others of his own kind. Only lightning proved obstreperous and had to be banished from earth. Lastly, Bumba created men, one of whom was white like himself (signifying light or purity? the influence of Christianity and European domination?) and in the role of culture hero taught the people to make fire.

Awe before the power and beauty of nature, often obscured in the pessimistic overtones of African myths more concerned with man's sins, is stated here simply in Bumba's benediction: "Behold these wonders. They belong to you."

The Bushongo kingdom was the oldest and most advanced of the Bantu realms in the Congo area. Its oral tradition traces some 120 rulers since its founding in the fifth century A.D.

—Barbara C. Sproul

In the beginning, in the dark, there was nothing but water. And Bumba was alone.

One day Bumba was in terrible pain. He retched and strained and vomited up the sun. After that light spread over everything. The heat of the sun dried up the water until the black edges of the world began to show. Black sandbanks and reefs could be seen. But there were no living things.

Bumba vomited up the moon and then the stars, and after that the night had its own light also.

Still Bumba was in pain. He strained again and nine living creatures came forth: the leopard named Koy Bumba, and Pongo Bumba the crested eagle, the crocodile, Ganda Bumba, and one little fish named Yo; next, old Kono Bumba, the tortoise, and Tsetse, the lightning, swift, deadly, beautiful like the leopard, then the white heron, Nyanyi Bumba, also one beetle, and the goat named Budi.

Last of all came forth men. There were many men, but only one was white like Bumba. His name was Loko Yima.

The creatures themselves then created all the creatures. The heron created all the birds of the air except the kite. He did not make the kite. The crocodile made serpents and the iguana. The goat produced every beast with horns. Yo, the small fish, brought forth all the fish of all the seas and waters. The beetle created insects.

Then the serpents in their turn made grasshoppers, and the iguana made the creatures without horns.

Then the three sons of Bumba said they would finish the world. The first, Nyonye Ngana, made the white ants; but he was not equal to the task, and died of it. The ants, however, thankful for life and being, went searching for black earth in the depths of the world and covered the barren sands to bury and honor their creator.

Chonganda, the second son, brought forth a marvelous living plant from which all the trees and grasses and flowers and plants in the world have sprung. The third son, Chedi Bumba, wanted something different, but for all his trying made only the bird called the kite.

Of all the creatures, Tsetse, lightning, was the only troublemaker. She stirred up so much trouble that Bumba chased her into the sky. Then mankind was without fire until Bumba showed the people how to draw fire out of trees. "There is fire in every tree," he told them, and showed them how to make the firedrill and liberate it. Sometimes today Tsetse still leaps down and strikes the earth and causes damage.

When at last the work of creation was finished, Bumba walked through the peaceful villages and said to the people, "Behold these wonders. They belong to you." Thus from Bumba, the Creator, the First Ancestor, came forth all the wonders that we see and hold and use, and all the brotherhood of beasts and man.

## ■ Cagn Orders the World, Bushman *Southern Africa*

TRANSLATED BY J. M. ORPEN

The Bushmen of Southern Africa are related to the Pygmies and Hottentots in their short stature, complex languages, and rich mythology. As nomadic hunters, their social groupings were necessarily small, rendering them vulnerable to the Bantu and white settlers who moved into their territory south of the Zambezi River. Those who survived with their culture intact moved to the more remote desert regions of Namibia, South Africa, and southern Angola.

The Bushmen believe not only in a good creator god (Kaang, Khu, or Thora, depending on the specific tribe) but also in an evil deity (Gauna or Gawa, god of the dead and of wicked spirits), the source of all trouble in the world. Some scholars have argued, however, that these high gods reflect Bantu influence. All agree that the main feature of the Bushmen's religion is belief in animal spirits, the most prominent of which (Cagn) is the hero of this myth.

Sometimes confused with Kaang, as he is here, Cagn is a perfunctory creator at best. His real interest lies on earth, where he reigns as the great magician and organizer. Ordering the world, enjoying endless adventures, and even slaying monsters, Cagn himself finally dies and is reborn — a sacred event whose story is repeated during the initiation of young men so that they may die to their youth and be reconstituted in a similar manner.

—Barbara C. Sproul

A daughter of Cagn became cross because her father had scolded her and she ran away to destroy herself by throwing herself among the snakes (*qabu*). The snakes were also men, and their chief married her and they ate snake's meat, but they gave her eland's meat to eat, because the child of Cagn must eat no evil thing. Cagn used to know things that were far off, and he sent his son Cogaz to bring her back, so Cogaz went with his young men, and Cagn lent him his tooth to make him strong. When the snakes saw Cogaz approaching with his party, they became angry and began to hide their heads, but their chief said, "You must not get angry, they are coming to their child," so the snakes went away to hunt, and his sister gave him meat, and they told her to tell her husband they were come to fetch her and she prepared food for the road and they went with her next morning, and they prepared themselves by binding rushes round their limbs and bodies, and three snakes followed them. These tried to bite them, but they only bit the rushes; they tried to beat them with reins, but they only beat rushes, and they tried throwing sand at them to cause wind to drive them into the water, not knowing he had the tooth of Cagn, and they failed. The children at home, the young men with the chief of the snakes, knew that when those snakes came back they would fill the country with water. So they commenced to build a high stage with willow poles, and the female snakes took their husbands on their return and threw them into the water, and it rose about the mountains, but the chief and his young men were saved on the high stage; and Cagn sent Cogaz for them to come and turn from being snakes, and he told them to lie down, and he struck them with his stick, and as he struck each the body of a person came out, and the skin of a snake was left on the ground, and he sprinkled the skins with canna, and the snakes turned from being snakes, and they became his people. . . .

Cagn sent Cogaz to cut sticks to make bows. When Cogaz came to the bush, the baboons (*cogn*) caught him. They called all the other baboons together to hear him, and they asked him who sent him there. He said his father sent him to cut sticks to make bows. So they said—"Your father thinks himself more clever than we are, he wants those bows to kill us, so we'll kill you," and they killed Cogaz, and tied him up in the top of a tree, and they danced around the tree singing (an untranscribable baboon song), with a chorus saying, "Cagn thinks he is clever." Cagn was asleep when Cogaz was killed, but when he awoke he told Coti to give him his charms, and he put some on his nose, and said the baboons have hung Cogaz. So he went to where the baboons were, and when they saw him coming close by, they changed their song so as to omit the words about Cagn, but a little baboon girl said, "Don't sing that way; sing the way you were singing before." And Cagn said, "Sing as the little girl wishes," and they sang and danced away as before. And Cagn said, "That is the song I heard, that is what I wanted, go on dancing till I return"; and he went and fetched a bag full of pegs, and he went behind each of them as they were dancing and making a great dust, and he drove a peg into each one's back, and gave it a crack, and sent them off to the mountains to live on roots, beetles and scorpions, as a punishment. Before that baboons were men, but since that they have tails, and their tails hang crooked. Then Cagn took Cogaz down, and gave him canna and made him alive again.

Cagn found an eagle getting honey from a precipice, and said, "My friend, give me some too," and it said, "Wait a bit," and it took a comb and put it down, and went back and took more, and told Cagn to take the rest, and he climbed up and licked only what remained on the rock, and when he tried to come down he found he could not. Presently he thought of his charms, and took some from his belt, and caused them to go to Cogaz to ask advice; and Cogaz sent word back by means of the charms that he was to make water to run down the rock, and he would find himself able to come down; and he did so, and when he got down, he descended into the ground and came up again, and he did this three times, and the third time he came up near the eagle, in the form of a huge bull eland; and the eagle said, "What a big eland," and went to kill it, and it threw an assegai, which passed it on the right side, and then another, which missed it, to the left, and a third, which passed between its legs, and the eagle trampled on it, and immediately hail fell and stunned the eagle, and Cagn killed it, and took some of the honey home to Cogaz, and told him he had killed the eagle which had acted treacherously to him, and Cogaz said, "You will get harm some day by these fightings." And Cagn found a woman named Cgorioinsi, who eats men, and she had made a big fire and was dancing round it, and she used to seize men and throw them into the fire, and Cagn began to roast roots at the fire, and at last she came and pitched him in, but he slipped through at the other side, and went on roasting and eating his roots, and she pitched him in again and again, and he only said "Wait a bit until I have finished my roots and I'll show you what I am." And when he had done he threw her into the fire as a punishment for killing people. Then Cagn went back to the mountain, where he had left some of the honey he took from the eagle, and he left his sticks there, and went down to the river, and there was a person in the river named Quuisi, who had been standing there a long time, something having caught him by the foot, and held him there since the winter, and he called to Cagn to come and help him, and Cagn went to help him, and put his hand down into the water to loosen his leg, and the thing let go the man's leg, and seized Cagn's arm. And the man ran stumbling out of the water, for his leg was stiffened by his being so long held fast, and he called out, "Now you will be held there till the winter," and he went to the honey, and threw Cagn's sticks away; and Cagn began to bethink him of his charms, and he sent to ask Cogaz for advice through his charms, and Cogaz sent word and told him to let down a piece of his garment into the water alongside his hand, and he did so, and the thing let go his hand and seized his garment, and he cut off the end of his garment, and ran and collected his sticks, and pursued the man and killed him, and took the honey to Cogaz.

The thorns (*dobbletjes*) were people—they are called Cagn-cagn—they were dwarfs, and Cagn found them fighting together, and he went to separate them, and they all turned upon him and killed him, and the biting ants helped them, and they ate Cagn up; but after a time they and the dwarfs collected his bones, and put them together and tied his head on, and these went stumbling home, and Cogaz cured him and made him all right again, and asked what had happened to him, and he told him; and Cogaz gave him advice and power, telling him how to fight them, that he was to make feints and strike as if at their legs, and then hit them on the head, and he went and killed many, and drove the rest into the mountains.

## ■ The Separation of God from Man (Krachi) *Togo*

### RETOLD BY PAUL RADIN FROM MATERIAL IN S. W. CARINALL

This fragment of a tale from the Krachi people of Togo envisages a primordial unity between sky and earth, god and man. Because of people's disrespect, the god Wulbari eventually retreated from earth and rose to the sky "where one can admire him but not reach him."

—Barbara C. Sproul

In the beginning of days Wulbari and man lived close together and Wulbari lay on top of Mother Earth, Asase Ya. Thus it happened that, as there was so little space to move about in, man annoyed the divinity, who in disgust went away and rose up to the present place where one can admire him but not reach him.

He was annoyed for a number of reasons. An old woman, while making her *fufu* outside her hut, kept on knocking Wulbari with her pestle. This hurt him and, as she persisted, he was forced to go higher out of her reach. Besides, the smoke of the cooking fires got into his eyes so that he had to go farther way. According to others, however, Wulbari, being so close to men, made a convenient sort of towel, and the people used to wipe their dirty fingers on him. This naturally annoyed him. Yet this was not so bad a grievance as that which caused We, the Wulbari of the Kassena people, to remove himself out of the reach of man. He did so because an old woman, anxious to make a good soup, used to cut off a bit of him at each mealtime, and We, being pained at this treatment, went higher.

# Oral Epics, Stories, Songs

## (diverse periods)

■ **Sundiata: An Epic of Old Mali (uncertain period)**
*Mali/Guinea, Mandingo* **(verse epic)**
**Djeli Mamoudou Kouyate, the "Griot" or oral**
**transmitter of the epic**

TRANSCRIBED AND TRANSLATED INTO FRENCH BY D. T. NIANE;
TRANSLATED INTO ENGLISH BY G. D. PICKETT

This section of an epic of old Mali is given to us by Djeli Mamoudou
Kouyate, a "griot," an oral transmitter from the Mandingo village of
Djeliba Koro in Siguiri, Mali/Guinea. The work was transcribed by D. T.
Niane, who also translated it into French. The English translation was
done by G. D. Pickett. The translation tradition has imitated the oral tradition, going from one figure to another. In modern times the word *griot*
refers to a professional itinerant musician. Formerly the griot was a counselor of rich families and of kings, the tutor of wealthy children, and pre-
server of tribal traditions. Today in Mali, away from urban areas, the griots
still operate, preserving folklore and recalling historical tradition. Like
their city counterparts, they earn their way as living archives of old tales.
They are, as D. T. Niane calls them, "speaking documents." With all the incarnations these legends have gone through, the English version of the
birth, childhood, and maturation of Sundiata is a significant English document of a heroic African past. We see, in the most vivid language, surely
helped by the griot, family life, court intrigue, warfare, and resolution.
Epic is heroic by definition, romantic-realist by practice, and narratively
intriguing when good. This short epic is a jewel in the treasury of early
African literature.

**FURTHER READING:** Kouyate, Djeli Mamoudou. *Sundiata: An Epic of Old Mali.* Transcribed by D. T. Niane, 1969.

## The Lion's Awakening

A short while after this interview between Naré Maghan and his son the
king died. Sogolon's son was no more than seven years old. The council of
elders met in the king's palace. It was no use Doua's defending the king's
will which reserved the throne for Mari Djata, for the council took no account of Naré Maghan's wish. With the help of Sassouma Bérété's in-

trigues, Dankaran Touman was proclaimed king and a regency council was formed in which the queen mother was all-powerful. A short time after, Doua died.

As men have short memories, Sogolon's son was spoken of with nothing but irony and scorn. People had seen one-eyed kings, one-armed kings, and lame kings, but a stiff-legged king had never been heard tell of. No matter how great the destiny promised for Mari Djata might be, the throne could not be given to someone who had no power in his legs; if the jinn loved him, let them begin by giving him the use of his legs. Such were the remarks that Sogolon heard every day. The queen mother, Sassouma Bérété, was the source of all this gossip.

Having become all-powerful, Sassouma Bérété persecuted Sogolon because the late Naré Maghan had preferred her. She banished Sogolon and her son to a back yard of the palace. Mari Djata's mother now occupied an old hut which had served as a lumber-room of Sassouma's.

The wicked queen mother allowed free passage to all those inquisitive people who wanted to see the child that still crawled at the age of seven. Nearly all the inhabitants of Niani filed into the palace and the poor Sogolon wept to see herself thus given over to public ridicule. Mari Djata took on a ferocious look in front of the crowd of sightseers. Sogolon found a little consolation only in the love of her eldest daughter, Kolonkan. She was four and she could walk. She seemed to understand all her mother's miseries and already she helped her with the housework. Sometimes, when Sogolon was attending to the chores, it was she who stayed beside her sister Djamarou, quite small as yet.

Sogolon Kedjou and her children lived on the queen mother's leftovers, but she kept a little garden in the open ground behind the village. It was there that she passed her brightest moments looking after her onions and gnougous. One day she happened to be short of condiments and went to the queen mother to beg a little baobab leaf.

'Look you,' said the malicious Sassouma, 'I have a calabash full. Help yourself, you poor woman. As for me, my son knew how to walk at seven and it was he who went and picked these baobab leaves. Take them then, since your son is unequal to mine.' Then she laughed derisively with that fierce laughter which cuts through your flesh and penetrates right to the bone.

Sogolon Kedjou was dumbfounded. She had never imagined that hate could be so strong in a human being. With a lump in her throat she left Sassouma's. Outside her hut Mari Djata, sitting on his useless legs, was blandly eating out of a calabash. Unable to contain herself any longer, Sogolon burst into sobs and seizing a piece of wood, hit her son.

'Oh son of misfortune, will you never walk? Through your fault I have just suffered the greatest affront of my life! What have I done, God, for you to punish me in this way?'

Mari Djata seized the piece of wood and, looking at his mother, said, 'Mother, what's the matter?'

'Shut up, nothing can ever wash me clean of this insult.'

'But what then?'

'Sassouma has just humiliated me over a matter of a baobab leaf. At your age her own son could walk and used to bring his mother baobab leaves.'

'Cheer up, Mother, cheer up.'

'No. It's too much. I can't.'

'Very well then, I am going to walk today,' said Mari Djata. 'Go and tell my father's smiths to make me the heaviest possible iron rod. Mother, do you want just the leaves of the baobab or would you rather I brought you the whole tree?'

'Ah, my son, to wipe out this insult I want the tree and its roots at my feet outside my hut.'

Balla Fasséké, who was present, ran to the master smith, Farakourou, to order an iron rod.

Sogolon had sat down in front of her hut. She was weeping softly and holding her head between her two hands. Mari Djata went calmly back to his calabash of rice and began eating again as if nothing had happened. From time to time he looked up discreetly at his mother who was murmuring in a low voice, 'I want the whole tree, in front of my hut, the whole tree.'

All of a sudden a voice burst into laughter behind the hut. It was the wicked Sassouma telling one of her serving women about the scene of humiliation and she was laughing loudly so that Sogolon could hear. Sogolon fled into the hut and hid her face under the blankets so as not to have before her eyes this heedless boy, who was more preoccupied with eating than with anything else. With her head buried in the bed-clothes Sogolon wept and her body shook violently. Her daughter, Sogolon Djamarou, had come and sat down beside her and she said, 'Mother, Mother, don't cry. Why are you crying?'

Mari Djata had finished eating and, dragging himself along on his legs, he came and sat under the wall of the hut for the sun was scorching. What was he thinking about? He alone knew.

The royal forges were situated outside the walls and over a hundred smiths worked there. The bows, spears, arrows and shields of Niani's warriors came from there. When Balla Fasséké came to order the iron rod, Farakourou said to him, 'The great day has arrived then?'

'Yes. Today is a day like any other, but it will see what no other day has seen.'

The master of the forges, Farakourou, was the son of the old Nounfaïri, and he was a soothsayer like his father. In his workshops there was an enormous iron bar wrought by his father Nounfaïri. Everybody wondered what this bar was destined to be used for. Farakourou called six of his apprentices and told them to carry the iron bar to Sogolon's house.

When the smiths put the gigantic iron bar down in front of the hut the noise was so frightening that Sogolon, who was lying down, jumped up with a start. Then Balla Fasséké, son of Gnankouman Doua, spoke.

'Here is the great day, Mari Djata. I am speaking to you, Maghan, son of Sogolon. The waters of the Niger can efface the stain from the body, but they cannot wipe out an insult. Arise, young lion, roar, and may the bush know that from henceforth it has a master.'

The apprentice smiths were still there, Sogolon had come out and everyone was watching Mari Djata. He crept on all-fours and came to the iron bar. Supporting himself on his knees and one hand, with the other hand he picked up the iron bar without any effort and stood it up vertically. Now he was resting on nothing but his knees and held the bar with both his hands. A deathly silence had gripped all those present. Sogolon Djata closed his eyes, held tight, the muscles in his arms tensed. With a violent jerk he threw his weight on to it and his knees left the ground. Sogolon Kedjou was all eyes and watched her son's legs which were trembling as though from an electric shock. Djata was sweating and the sweat ran from his brow. In a great effort he straightened up and was on his feet at one go—but the great bar of iron was twisted and had taken the form of a bow!

Then Balla Fasséké sang out the 'Hymn to the Bow', striking up with his powerful voice:

'Take your bow, Simbon,
Take your bow and let us go.
Take your bow, Sogolon Djata.'

When Sogolon saw her son standing she stood dumb for a moment, then suddenly she sang these words of thanks to God who had given her son the use of his legs:

'Oh day, what a beautiful day,
Oh day, day of joy;
Allah Almighty, you never created a finer day.
So my son is going to walk!'

Standing in the position of a soldier at ease, Sogolon Djata, supported by his enormous rod, was sweating great beads of sweat. Balla Fasséké's song had alerted the whole palace and people came running from all over to see what had happened, and each stood bewildered before Sogolon's son. The queen mother had rushed there and when she saw Mari Djata standing up she trembled from head to foot. After recovering his breath Sogolon's son dropped the bar and the crowd stood to one side. His first steps were those of a giant. Balla Fasséké fell into step and pointing his finger at Djata, he cried:

'Room, room, make room!
The lion has walked;
Hide antelopes,
Get out of his way.'

Behind Niani there was a young baobab tree and it was there that the children of the town came to pick leaves for their mothers. With all his might the son of Sogolon tore up the tree and put it on his shoulders and went back to his mother. He threw the tree in front of the hut and said, 'Mother, here are some baobab leaves for you. From henceforth it will be outside your hut that the women of Niani will come to stock up.'

Sogolon Djata walked. From that day forward the queen mother had no more peace of mind. But what can one do against destiny? Nothing. Man, under the influence of certain illusions, thinks he can alter the course which God has mapped out, but everything he does falls into a higher order which he barely understands. That is why Sassouma's efforts were vain against Sogolon's son, everything she did lay in the child's destiny. Scorned the day before and the object of public ridicule, now Sogolon's son was as popular as he had been despised. The multitude loves and fears strength. All Niani talked of nothing but Djata; the mothers urged their sons to become hunting companions of Djata and to share his games, as if they wanted their offspring to profit from the nascent glory of the buffalo-woman's son. The words of Doua on the name-giving day came back to men's minds and Sogolon was now surrounded with much respect; in conversation people were fond of contrasting Sogolon's modesty with the pride and malice of Soussouma Bérété. It was because the former had been an exemplary wife and mother that God had granted strength to her son's legs for, it was said, the more a wife loves and respects her husband and the more she suffers for her child, the more valorous will the child be one day. Each is the child of his mother; the child is worth no more than the mother is worth. It was not astonishing that the king Dankaran Touman was so colourless, for his mother had never shown the slightest respect to her husband and never, in the presence of the late king, did she show that humility which every wife should show before her husband. People recalled her scenes of jealousy and the spiteful remarks she circulated about her co-wife and her child. And people would conclude gravely, 'Nobody knows God's mystery. The snake has no legs yet it is as swift as any other animal that has four.'

Sogolon Djata's popularity grew from day to day and he was surrounded by a gang of children of the same age as himself. These were Fran Kamara, son of the king of Tabon; Kamandjan, son of the king of Sibi; and other princes whose fathers had sent them to the court of Niani. The son of Namandjé, Manding Bory, was already joining in their games. Balla Fasséké followed Sogolon Djata all the time. He was past twenty and it was he who gave the child education and instruction according to Mandingo rules of conduct. Whether in town or at the hunt, he missed no opportunity of instructing his pupil. Many young boys of Niani came to join in the games of the royal child.

He liked hunting best of all. Farakourou, master of the forges, had made Djata a fine bow, and he proved himself to be a good shot with the bow. He made frequent hunting trips with his troops, and in the evening all Niani would be in the square to be present at the entry of the young hunters. The crowd would sing the 'Hymn to the Bow' which Balla Fasséké had composed, and Sogolon Djata was quite young when he received the title of Simbon, or master hunter, which is only conferred on great hunters who have proved themselves.

Every evening Sogolon Kedjou would gather Djata and his companions outside her hut. She would tell them stories about the beasts of the bush, the dumb brothers of man. Sogolon Djata learnt to distinguish between the animals; he knew why the buffalo was his mother's wraith and also why the lion was the protector of his father's family. He also listened to the history of the kings which Balla Fasséké told him; enraptured by the story of Alexander the Great, the mighty king of gold and silver, whose sun shone over quite half the world. Sogolon initiated her son into certain secrets and revealed to him the names of the medicinal plants which every hunter should know. Thus, between his mother and his griot, the child got to know all that needed to be known.

Sogolon's son was now ten. The name Sogolon Djata in the rapid Mandingo language became Sundiata or Sondjata. He was a lad full of strength; his arms had the strength of ten and his biceps inspired fear in his companions. He had already that authoritative way of speaking which belongs to those who are destined to command. His brother, Manding Bory, became his best friend, and whenever Djata was seen, Manding Bory appeared too. They were like a man and his shadow. Fran Kamara and Kamandjan were the closest friends of the young princes, while Balla Fasséké followed them all like a guardian angel.

But Sundiata's popularity was so great that the queen mother became apprehensive for her son's throne. Dankaran Touman was the most retiring of men. At the age of eighteen he was still under the influence of his mother and a handful of old schemers. It was Sassouma Bérété who really reigned in his name. The queen mother wanted to put an end to this popularity by killing Sundiata and it was thus that one night she received the nine great witches of Mali. They were all old women. The eldest, and the most dangerous too, was called Soumosso Konkomba. When the nine old hags had seated themselves in a semi-circle around her bed the queen mother said:

'You who rule supreme at night, nocturnal powers, oh you who hold the secret of life, you who can put an end to one life, can you help me?'

'The night is potent,' said Soumosso Konkomba, 'Oh queen, tell us what is to be done, on whom must we turn the fatal blade?'

'I want to kill Sundiata,' said Sassouma. 'His destiny runs counter to my son's and he must be killed while there is still time. If you succeed, I promise you the finest rewards. First of all I bestow on each of you a cow and her calf and from tomorrow go to the royal granaries and each of you will receive a hundred measures of rice and a hundred measures of hay on my authority.'

'Mother of the king,' rejoined Soumosso Konkomba, 'life hangs by nothing but a very fine thread, but all is interwoven here below. Life has a cause, and death as well. The one comes from the other. Your hate has a cause and your action must have a cause. Mother of the king, everything holds together, our action will have no effect unless we are ourselves implicated, but Mari Djata has done us no wrong. It is, then, difficult for us to compass his death.'

'But you are also concerned,' replied the queen mother, 'for the son of Sogolon will be a scourge to us all.'

'The snake seldom bites the foot that does not walk,' said one of the witches.

'Yes, but there are snakes that attack everybody. Allow Sundiata to grow up and we will all repent of it. Tomorrow go to Sogolon's vegetable patch and make a show of picking a few gnougou leaves. Mari Djata stands guard there and you will see how vicious the boy is. He won't have any respect for your age, he'll give you a good thrashing.'

'That's a clever idea,' said one of the old hags.

'But the cause of our discomfiture will be ourselves, for having touched something which did not belong to us.'

'We could repeat the offence,' said another, 'and then if he beats us again we would be able to reproach him with being unkind, heartless. In that case we would be concerned, I think.'

'The idea is ingenious,' said Soumosso Konkomba. 'Tomorrow we shall go to Sogolon's vegetable patch.'

'Now there's a happy thought,' concluded the queen mother, laughing for joy. 'Go to the vegetable patch tomorrow and you will see that Sogolon's son is mean. Beforehand, present yourselves at the royal granaries where you will receive the grain I promised you; the cows and calves are already yours.'

The old hags bowed and disappeared into the black night. The queen mother was now alone and gloated over her anticipated victory. But her daughter, Nana Triban, woke up.

'Mother, who were you talking to? I thought I heard voices.'

'Sleep, my daughter, it is nothing. You didn't hear anything.'

In the morning, as usual, Sundiata got his companions together in front of his mother's hut and said, 'What animal are we going to hunt today?'

Kamandjan said, 'I wouldn't mind if we attacked some elephants right now.'

'Yes, I am of this opinion too,' said Fran Kamara. 'That will allow us to go far into the bush.'

And the young band left after Sogolon had filled the hunting bags with eatables. Sundiata and his companions came back late to the village, but first Djata wanted to take a look at his mother's vegetable patch as was his custom. It was dusk. There he found the nine witches stealing gnougou leaves. They made a show of running away like thieves caught red-handed.

'Stop, stop, poor old women,' said Sundiata, 'what is the matter with you to run away like this. This garden belongs to all.'

Straight away his companions and he filled the gourds of the old hags with leaves, aubergines and onions.

'Each time that you run short of condiments come to stock up here without fear.'

'You disarm us,' said one of the old crones, and another added, 'And you confound us with your bounty.'

'Listen, Djata,' said Soumosso Konkomba, 'we had come here to test you. We have no need of condiments but your generosity disarms us. We were sent here by the queen mother to provoke you and draw the anger of the nocturnal powers upon you. But nothing can be done against a heart full of kindness. And to think that we have already drawn a hundred measures of rice and a hundred measures of millet—and the queen promises us each a cow and her calf in addition. Forgive us, son of Sogolon.'

'I bear you no ill-will,' said Djata. 'Here, I am returning from the hunt with my companions and we have killed ten elephants, so I will give you an elephant each and there you have some meat!'

'Thank you, son of Sogolon.'

'Thank you, child of Justice.'

'Henceforth,' concluded Soumosso Konkomba, 'we will watch over you.' And the nine witches disappeared into the night. Sundiata and his companions continued on their way to Niani and got back after dark.

'You were really frightened; those nine witches really scared you, eh?' said Sogolon Kolonkan, Djata's young sister.

'How do you know,' retorted Sundiata, astonished.

'I saw them at night hatching their scheme, but I knew there was no danger for you.' Kolonkan was well versed in the art of witchcraft and watched over her brother without his suspecting it.

## Niani

After this great assembly Sundiata stayed a few more days at Ka-ba. For the people these were days of festivity. For them Djata caused hundreds of oxen, taken from Soumaoro's immense exchequer, to be slaughtered every day. In the main square of Ka-ba the girls of the town came and laid big calabashes of rice and meat at the foot of the observation platforms. Anybody could come and eat his fill and go away. Soon Ka-ba was full of people who had come from all directions attracted by the opulence. A year of war had emptied all the granaries so each came to take his share of the king of Sosso's reserves. It is even said that certain people had set up their household gods on that very spot during Djata's stay at Ka-ba. These were the summer months so these people slept on the observation platforms during the night and on awakening found calabashes of rice at their feet. That was the time when people sang the 'Hymn to Abundance' in Sundiata's honour:

He has come
And happiness has come
Sundiata is here
And happiness is here.

But it was time to return to his native Mali. Sundiata assembled his army in the plain and each people provided a contingent to accompany the Mansa to Niani. At Ka-ba all the peoples separated in friendship and in joy at their new-found peace.

Sundiata and his men had to cross the Niger in order to enter old Mali. One might have thought that all the dug-out canoes in the world had arranged to meet at the port of Ka-ba. It was the dry season and there was not much water in the river. The fishing tribe of Somono, to whom Djata had given the monopoly of the water, were bent on expressing their thanks to the son of Sogolon. They put all their dug-outs side by side across the Niger so that Sundiata's sofas could cross without wetting their feet.

When the whole army was on the other side of the river, Sundiata ordered great sacrifices. A hundred oxen and a hundred rams were sacrificed. It was thus that Sundiata thanked God on returning to Mali.

The villages of Mali gave Maghan Sundiata an unprecedented welcome. At normal times a traveller on foot can cover the distance from Ka-ba to Niani with only two halts, but Sogolon's son with his army took three days. The road to Mali from the river was flanked by a double human hedge. Flocking from every corner of Mali, all the inhabitants were resolved to see their saviour from close up. The women of Mali tried to create a sensation and they did not fail. At the entrance to each village they had carpeted the road with their multi-coloured pagnes so that Sundiata's horse would not so much as dirty its feet on entering their village. At the village exits the children, holding leafy branches in their hands, greeted Djata with cries of 'Wassa, Wassa, Ayé.'

Sundiata was leading the van. He had donned his costume of a hunter king—a plain smock, skin-tight trousers and his bow slung across his back. At his side Balla Fasséké was still wearing his festive garments gleaming with gold. Between Djata's general staff and the army Sosso Balla had been placed, amid his father's fetishes. But his hands were no longer tied. As at Ka-ba, abuse was everywhere heaped upon him and the prisoner did not dare look up at the hostile crowd. Some people, always ready to feel sympathy, were saying among themselves:

'How few things good fortune prizes!'

'Yes, the day you are fortunate is also the day when you are the most unfortunate, for in good fortune you cannot imagine what suffering is.'

The troops were marching along singing the 'Hymn to the Bow,' which the crowd took up. New songs flew from mouth to mouth. Young women offered the soldiers cool water and cola nuts. And so the triumphal march across Mali ended outside Niani, Sundiata's city.

It was a ruined town which was beginning to be rebuilt by its inhabitants. A part of the ramparts had been destroyed and the charred walls still bore the marks of the fire. From the top of the hill Djata looked on Niani, which looked like a dead city. He saw the plain of Sounkarani, and he also saw the site of the young baobab tree. The survivors of the catastrophe were standing in rows on the Mali road. The children were waving branches, a few young women were singing, but the adults were mute.

'Rejoice,' said Balla Fasséké to Sundiata, 'for your part you will have the bliss of rebuilding Niani, the city of your fathers, but nevermore will anyone rebuild Sosso out of its ruins. Men will lose recollection of the very site of Soumaoro's city.'

With Sundiata peace and happiness entered Niani. Lovingly Sogolon's son had his native city rebuilt. He restored in the ancient style his father's old enclosure where he had grown up. People came from all the villages of Mali to settle in Niani. The walls had to be destroyed to enlarge the town, and new quarters were built for each kin group in the enormous army.

Sundiata had left his brother Manding Bory at Bagadou-Djeliba on the river. He was Sundiata's Kankoro Sigui, that is to say, viceroy. Manding Bory had looked after all the conquered countries. When reconstruction of the capital was finished he went to wage war in the south in order to frighten the forest peoples. He received an embassy from the country of Sangaran where a few Kondé clans had settled, and although these latter had not been represented at Kouroukan Fougan, Sundiata granted his alliance and they were placed on the same footing as the Kondés of the land of Do.

After a year Sundiata held a new assembly at Niani, but this one was the assembly of dignitaries and kings of the empire. The kings and notables of all the tribes came to Niani. The kings spoke of their administration and the dignitaries talked of their kings. Fakoli, the nephew of Soumaoro, having proved himself too independent, had to flee to evade the Mansa's anger. His lands were confiscated and the taxes of Sosso were payed directly into the granaries of Niani. In this way, every year, Sundiata gathered about him all the kings and notables; so justice prevailed everywhere, for the kings were afraid of being denounced at Niani.

Djata's justice spared nobody. He followed the very word of God. He protected the weak against the strong and people would make journeys lasting several days to come and demand justice of him. Under his sun the upright man was rewarded and the wicked one punished.

In their new-found peace the villages knew prosperity again, for with Sundiata happiness had come into everyone's home. Vast fields of millet, rice, cotton, indigo and fonio surrounded the villages. Whoever worked always had something to live on. Each year long caravans carried the taxes in kind to Niani. You could go from village to village without fearing brigands. A thief would have his right hand chopped off and if he stole again he would be put to the sword.

New villages and new towns sprang up in Mali and elsewhere. 'Dyulas,' or traders, became numerous and during the reign of Sundiata the world knew happiness.

There are some kings who are powerful through their military strength. Everybody trembles before them, but when they die nothing but ill is spoken of them. Others do neither good nor ill and when they die they are forgotten. Others are feared because they have power, but they know how to use it and they are loved because they love justice. Sundiata belonged to this group. He was feared, but loved as well. He was the father of Mali and gave the world peace. After him the world has not seen a greater conqueror, for he was the seventh and last conqueror. He had made the capital of an empire out of his father's village, and Niani became the navel of the earth. In the most distant lands Niani was talked of and foreigners said, 'Travellers from Mali can tell lies with impunity,' for Mali was a remote country for many peoples.

The griots, fine talkers that they were, used to boast of Niani and Mali saying: 'If you want salt, go to Niani, for Niani is the camping place of the Sahel caravans. If you want gold, go to Niani, for Bouré, Bambougou and Wagadou work for Niani. If you want fine cloth, go to Niani, for the Mecca road passes by Niani. If you want fish, go to Niani, for it is there that the fishermen of Maouti and Djenné come to sell their catches. If you want meat, go to Niani, the country of the great hunters, and the land of the ox and the sheep. If you want to see an army, go to Niani, for it is there that the united forces of Mali are to be found. If you want to see a great king, go to Niani, for it is there that the son of Sogolon lives, the man with two names.'

This is what the masters of the spoken word used to sing.

I must mention Kita among the great cities of the empire, the city of holy water which became the second capital of the Keitas. I shall mention vanished Tabon, the iron-gated city. I shall not forget Do, nor Kri, the motherland of Sogolon, the buffalo woman. I shall also cite Koukouba, Batamba and Kambasiga, towns of the sofas. I shall mention the town of Diaghan, Mema, the town of hospitality, and Wagadou, where the descendants of Alexander the Great used to reign. How many heaped-up ruins, how many vanished cities! How many wildernesses peopled by the spirits of great kings! The silk-cotton trees and baobabs that you see in Mali are the only traces of extinct cities.

## ■ Emperor Shaka the Great: A Zulu Epic (Twentieth Century) *South Africa* (nineteenth-century oral poetic tradition)

### TRANSCRIBED AND TRANSLATED BY MAZISI KUNENE

*Emperor Shaka the Great* is a transcription, translation, and reconstruction of an oral nineteenth-century Zulu epic by Mazisi Kunene. Kunene is a poet, professor, and translator of Zulu oral tradition. Through his scholarship and re-creation, he gave us two long epic poems, *Emperor Shaka the Great* (1979) and *Anthem of the Decades* (1981), that extol and dignify Zulu history and culture. Born in Durban, South Africa, Kunene graduated from the University of Natal and later specialized in Zulu literature at the School of Oriental and African Studies of the University of London. He has been a professor of African literature at the University College of Lesotho and has held posts at diverse places outside South Africa, including the University of California at Los Angeles. His major work is *Emperor Shaka the Great,* which he calls a Zulu epic. Gathered from Zulu folklore and recorded in Zulu, he translated his own compilation into English. The work traces a heroic past of Zulu emperors, and specifically Emperor Shaka, born in 1795, who organized a well-disciplined devastating army that conquered powerful Zulu kings and generals. At the age of twenty-three, he defeated a powerful rival general. He was assassinated in 1828.

Kunene's work is difficult to access because it is massive in scope and uneven in quality. His scholarly and national research has been prodigious. He is the most ambitious poet in Africa, similar to Nikos Kazantzakis in modern Greek, who in his *The Odyssey, a Modern Sequel* wrote a continuation of Homer's epic, or Zakarias Topelius and Elias Lönnrot, who in the early nineteenth century reconstructed the medieval Finnish epic *Kaleva,* which has become the Finnish national epic. Kunene has created a national epic in his native Zulu. However, his romantic English version suffers from a tone of relentless heroism and praise as he records the battles. As a work to reveal a recreated historical dignity of Zulu warriors, it is of immense importance. As literature it is, among the works by many distinguished contemporary writers, a fascinating document.

**FURTHER READING:** Kunene, Mazisi. *Emperor Shaka the Great: A Zulu Epic,* 1979.

## from *The Campaign or Cleansing*

After a long and tiring march
The Zulu army now halted near the sea.
It was here that Shaka began to seethe with ideas.
No sooner had he rested than he began to talk fervently,
Pointing to the ocean, he commented to his generals:
'Such are the battle movements the Zulu army shall adopt.'
They were all puzzled by these words.
But he continued, somewhat absent-mindedly, and said:
'Like the approach of each giant wave to the seashore,
Like a succession of angry waves—
So must be the measured sequence of our troops.
Those ahead must fight in the thick of battle,
Reinforced by the thought of immediate relief;

For no battle is fought spiritedly without hope of reinforcements.
There should be no in-between ground for enemy troops.                    *15*
Those in front must fight and give way to those who follow.
Indeed, such an army can never tire.'
The generals stared at each other, elated at this battle plan.
Though this idea did not differ from their experience
By this illustration they saw the whole strategy clearly.                 *20*
Thus the poet commented on Shaka and said:
'My lord is like a pile of ruined cities.
He rears high like the waves of a stormy sea.
All night long the waves tumble over each other.'
Re-enacting the Mpondo campaign, the poet said:                           *25*
'You burst open a giant hole in the land of the Mpondo.
Even today that region is still a yawning crater.
You seized the prized beasts of Faku among the Mpondos!
You took those of Ngubowencuge among the Mpondos!
You confiscated those of Ncokazi among the Mpondos!                       *30*
You took those of Ncasana of Majola clan!
You seized those of Macingwane of Ngonyameni!
You confiscated those of Bhugane of a thousand honours!
You took those of the Sothos who wear a dhoti!
You seized the beasts of the people of little honour,                     *35*
Whose hair is plaited in fringes!
The thunderclap that flashed in the land of the Mpondo
Over the great House of Faku, the son of Ngqungqushe—
It flashed and cindered the shields of the Mpondos.
The lightning forked and stood at the pass of Nyoka.                      *40*
He wheeled back only when he reached the maBomyana clan.
Morning star of long rays, the star of Mjokwane—
It stands on its tail, hanging on the dome of the sky.
Two morning stars emerged from heaven;
They made danger signals to each other!                                   *45*
Great fierce flame, whose explosions face each other:
One is of Queen Ntombazi; the other is of Queen Nandi.
Oh, my lord, how terrible of you!
You did not spare even those of your maternal uncle,
Unforgiving even to your relative Bhebhe, the son of Ncumela!             *50*
Many shields come close to each other and embrace.
They are of Gwagaza and Dlakudla of Ntotheleni regiment.
Staff of shining brass of Mjokwane,
That struck the water and it opened into the mud.'
The great poet's words reverberated to the heavens.                       *55*
The uFasimba regiment, elated, began to sing their anthem.
They shouted their slogans calling for greater wars.

Early, at dawn, Shaka summoned his regiments.
All the generals reluctantly responded to this call

Except the great General Mdlaka, the son of Ncidi,
Who never once hesitated at a call to battle.
He still yearned for a decisive war.
When Shaka arrived at the arena he angrily addressed the regiments:
'Never did I have a wink of sleep.
All night I listened to the discontented voices of our army
And heard the high boasts of the Mpondo army
Claiming: "The Zulus did not dislodge us.
We have never been conquered."
Though many bandit nations have been tamed,
There still remain those who would cause disorder
And violate custom and bully the smaller nations.
There are those like Soshangane who still boast their power.
Constantly my trusted messengers report
His armies harass the peaceful nations of the north.
The Thongas of the coastal region have had no peace from him.
These disturbances violate the order of our region.
Greater nations may yet be led to endless wars,
Bringing back the chaos once experienced in Nguniland.
Soshangane's army is not unlike that of Zwide.
Like Sikhunyana who dared invade our borders,
Disturbing us at our peaceful festivals,
So could he by his bravado seek to enhance his reputation.
Because of this we must act swiftly.
We must pluck the wings of the little eagle before it flies,
Before he, too, comes to search for his family's old capitals,
Hoping to revive the rule once held by Zwide.
Soshangane shall always be restless,
Like a bird that never builds its nest in one place.
We must strike him and stop his rampage on smaller nations.
Here, too, is an order I want you to observe:
The "little carrier boys" are carrier boys no more.
They now shall fight in battle like men.
Each man from now on shall carry his own baggage.
Even food you will find in plenty wherever you fight.
You must depend on your own resources.
If our Forefathers could survive in their own battles,
Why can't we, whose life is eased by theirs?'
He spoke these words in anger,
Still remembering the episodes of the Mzinkhulu river.

Though the generals were alarmed at these changes
They did not oppose him.
They simply said: 'Son of Ndaba, you know best.
You founded the nation; you opened these paths,
So shall by your vision close and open the new directions.'
Shaka was irritated by these words. He said:

'No one builds a nation.
Such words betray some secret plots.
Flattery constantly hides some deeper motive.'
Shot by suspicion and their reluctance to proceed to battle,
He stared directly at each one of them.                                    *110*
But the whole concourse of commanders
Vowed their loyalty to the king and country.
Each sought to applaud the king's words louder than others.
The great gathering of regiments shouted the royal salute,
Demanding that Soshangane and the Mtshali clan be punished.               *115*
For like the Mpondos they, too, had not joined in the mourning.
Prince Hlangabeza of the Mtshalis had spit saliva on the ground
As news of Queen Nandi's death was told:
'I shall never mourn for Nandi,' he said.
'Did Shaka ever mourn for my father, Khondlo, when he died?'             *120*
It was because of these words that the army attacked him,
Taking the supplies they needed for their war against
        Soshangane.

It is said Prince Dingane and Prince Mhlangane met together.
Through a trusted messenger they sent a word to Mbopha,
Telling him of their resentment towards this new campaign.               *125*
Said Prince Dingane: 'It would not matter if others went to war,
But we are the children of the king.
We must not endlessly be exposed to danger
Indeed, as of late we shall travel like commoners,
Deprived as we shall be of a retinue of baggage carriers.                *130*
Even food we shall scavenge, wherever we are, like dogs.'
He spoke these words to Mhlangane hurriedly,
As though Mhlangane himself had not known them.
Prince Mhlangane replied to him softly and said:
'I agree with your words, my brother.                                    *135*
I, too, was alarmed at these things.
I almost confronted Shaka personally
But restrained myself until our moment of consultation.
What frustrates most is his ever-growing reputation.'
Prince Dingane quietly assured him and said:                             *140*
'The regiments are composed of ordinary people.
They applaud whoever is king of the day.
Today they praise the man they shall denounce tomorrow.
People, my brother, are like water; they follow the gulleys.
If one digs a tunnel the water goes that way.                            *145*
We, too, must open the lips of those who are silent;
Then we shall hear a volume of protests.
But, above all, keep your own lips sealed.
For if we fail to strike at this moment only death awaits us.
We shall either die in foreign lands or in our homes.                    *150*

Even if Shaka does not by his own hand kill us,
We may yet be killed in the cause of his many campaigns.
If we die in battle it shall only enhance his rule;
Indeed, he shall say: "Even my brothers died in battle."
But then the greatness of a man depends on whether he lives or            *1*
         not—
It shall not benefit us to earn fame
While the proud vultures pick on our flesh.
I am truly tired of wars; I want to be a family man.
If you still hesitate and still follow his commands,
Then, my brother, you shall have only yourself to blame.                  *1*
Shaka shall never change from his love of wars.
Besides, his mother's death has broken his supporting pillar.
Indeed, his tears have already undermined the nation.'
Prince Dingane spoke these words with great vehemence,
Knowing Prince Mhlangane was weak and often had doubts.                   *1*
He hoped by these words he would entrap him.
As he spoke his eyes were directed at Mhlangane.
Hesitatingly, Mhlangane commented on these words:
'I hear your words, my brother.
They bite deep by their meaningfulness.                                   *1*
I only promise this; by my honour as a man,
I shall never tell of things we discuss together.
Even when I am overwhelmed by doubts,
I shall come back to you.'
Prince Dingane did not answer but just laughed.                          *1*
He knew Mhlangane always depended on him.
He laughed at the childishness of Mhlangane.
Nothing is sacred to the struggles of power;
Not even the bonds of families and friendships.
Close relations, in madness, slaughter their own clansmen.                *1*


Like a huge cloud of locusts the army followed the northward
         direction.
Eastwards and westwards it whirled and turned
Like a cluster of winter leaves blown by the wind,
Like a dark cloud of hurrying vultures,
Like a whirlwind carrying pillars and roofs of villages.                  *1*
Thus it departed from the region of the Mngeni river.
The river flows clear and beautiful.
Touched by the lips of the ancient warrior,
It sings the song inherited from the sea.
To this very day Mngeni river sings the song of the Sacred               *1*
         Circle.
Sometimes it bursts open to feed a new generation,
Making their song the first anthem of the season

And bringing back the story of the ancient hero.
Listen to the echoes of song as the king approaches Dukuza.
Listen to the royal poets reciting to each other the epics.          *195*
Listen to their voices as they carry the message everywhere.
The poets sing for the return of plenty at the royal city of
    Dukuza.
To the horizon spread the large herds of captured cattle.
They bellow, turning their heads towards Faku's territory.
Many sang the great anthems learnt from Mpondoland.                  *200*
Then was heard the round ringing sound of the Mbelebele
    regiment.
It meandered, following the direction of the Ndosi settlements.
There, people compete with each other in song.
Of the Mpondo campaign Princess Mkhabayi constantly asked,
Probing on all issues of the southern strategy.                      *205*
When she heard of the army that went to attack Soshangane,
She said: 'It is clear Shaka knows the truth of plots against him.
How else could he risk his brothers' lives in two wars?
I fear this child; he possesses diabolical powers.'
She spoke these words to her sister, Princess Mawa.                  *210*
Princess Mkhabayi, said continuing:
It seems we must think in new directions,
For, indeed, we do not know what our brother's son could do;
Nor would it surprise me if he mobilized an old woman's
    regiment.
Shaka's cleverness is of evil power.                                 *215*
Even when threatened by danger he takes his own time.
He simply sings his own song, believing himself the wisest of
    men.
Of late he seems to toss people around
As though they were some branches loaded with decaying fruit.
No longer is there anyone who can restrain him.'                     *220*
These words alarmed Princess Mawa. She said:
'Do not exaggerate his power.
In this world it is not courage alone that wins,
But a mind that patiently waits for an error.
The nation shall rise against all his wars.                          *225*
We, too, possess the power to cut short his knot of authority.
Our position is unique:
We are not suspects in any game of power;
Whatever we do shall only be for the nation's welfare.'
Princess Mkhabayi merely shook her head and said:                    *230*
'What one does for the nation is not always applauded;
Only time steadily raises its voices for the dead.
That is why our Ancestors have said:
"No one reaps fame in his own lifetime."

As long as one lives, life multiplies the race of enemies.
Even by this act they will claim we were hungry for power:
We chose him who would give us authority.
For this reason whatever we do must be carefully thought out.'
She spoke these words, ending their conversation
As though she detected some listener.

How beautiful was that time
When the great ruler, Shaka of Senzangakhona, returned.
While the army proceeded to Soshangane
He, the Great One, stayed initiating new changes.
The preservers of our ancient legends tell us
He now revealed his plan to re-organize the far-flung regions.
In his discussions with the Assembly
He often said: 'The nation must now have a new order.
The Zulu nation must live a full life.
It must enjoy the fruits of its achievements.
When the army returns from Soshangane
We must proclaim a new law for all young men to marry.
I shall send messengers to all neighbouring nations
To tell them: the Palm Race must eat from the same bowl.
I shall yet heal the wounds of the Mpondo nation,
Reminding them our quarrels are only of brothers.
We, the nations of the Palm Race,
Shall outwit and stop the vermin of over-the-seas nations.
Their fanatical love for the land threatens the very life of
    humankind.
Should there be time, I shall patiently teach them these lessons.'
The old wise men who heard him shook their heads, and said:
'How baffling is the son of Senzangakhona.
He is the ruler who rules with strength and wisdom.
But his mind changes like the strange colours of a chameleon.'
Those present knew also there were complaints of families about
    wars;
Some counted many relatives who had been killed in battle.
Our Forefathers say each person is precious to his own family.
Many spoke openly: 'Let our nation enjoy a period of peace,
Or else let a new king be born to rule without war.
Such was the mood among the families of the land.

At this period news came of the arrival of King George's
    messengers.
It was followed with yet another piece of startling news:
King, who of all the White Strangers was Shaka's favourite,
Suffered a strange and weakening illness.
He lay ailing in the settlement near the Ngcobo region.
Shaka spoke to his friend, Prince Zihlandlo, saying:

'I feel a deep sadness about King, the man I like.
He is the most humane of all the overseas wanderers.
People often comment on him and say:
"The heart of King overflows with kindness.
He possesses the generosity of the Palm Race."                    *280*
He is still young but his mind is of a mature man.
I had hoped one day he would return to his home
And tell his people bout the life in our world.
His early death would only deprive us of his inspired words.
I shall make a sacrifice of two of my best bulls              *285*
And plead for his life to the Ancestors.
Through him the lives of others may yet be fulfilled.'
Prince Zihlandlo warmly welcomed these words and said:
'I, too, found him full of generosity and humanity.
Often he abandons his group of foreigners                     *290*
And is heard laughing loud with the young men of our nation.
When he was made commander-in-chief of Gabangaye regiment
There was general rejoicing throughout the army.
I applaud your words, my lord.
People are the same throughout the earth;                     *295*
Indeed, should he die many of his relatives would mourn for
     him.
Yet it is true no mountain is without a grave.
May he overcome the power of the earth
May he praise the hand that lifted him from the ground!'
Shaka was quiet, as though his mind dwelt on the thought of   *300*
     death,
For often the very word made him pensive.
Raising his head he finally said to Zihlandlo,
'I hear your kind words, you of the Mkhize clan.
Yet I believe he shall not live.
It seems whatever I treasure withers suddenly.'               *305*
He spoke as though he no longer doubted his words.
Prince Zihlandlo himself made jokes about this,
Eager to dispel these convictions with friendly thoughts;
Yet he himself felt the ominous truth of these words.
Unable to bear the pain, he spoke of lighter subjects.        *310*
Shaka continued and said: 'I have sent a messenger to the
     Ngcobo region,
Ordering that I be told immediately of his fate.
Meanwhile I await reports from the war against the Soshangane.
I told Mdlaka to send all the former carrier boys.
They shall now comprise the iziNyosi regiment.               *315*
By a speedy transmission of this message
These young boys shall be here in the arena tomorrow.
Mdlaka's view tallies with mine;

But Mdlaka is not like you. His mind is that of a solider.
Besides, when I uttered these decisions I was angry,
Having seen how the regiments abuse their power.
Then the punishment fitted the crime.
Yet when I thought of the hardships, these decisions imposed on
   the army,
I chastised myself, thinking how rashly I may have acted.'
Prince Zihlandlo smiled slightly and said:
'My lord, I follow all the directions of your thoughts;
I appreciate each of their meanings.
I saw you as you stood in the middle of the river
And thought to myself how different our nation would be
If all people had the same quick grasp of things as you.
I agree, my lord, to deprive the army of carrier boys
Creates problems for each fighting man;
Yet these hardships will be forgotten
And in aftertimes only praise shall be heard.
For, indeed, my lord, you must not build a nation of soldiers,
But one that shall live by the codes of its humanity;
It is its songs of life that must be heard.
Our nation must not evolve the habit of rulers,
Making one a special nation, the other a serving nation.
Then our army shall no longer be different from that of
   Matiwane,
Whose sweat is often washed with the tears of others.
For these reasons, my lord, I accept your decision.
There is only one comment I would like to make.
It is wrong to speak in anger.
You, the wisest of men, must advise and teach patiently,
For not all peoples are gifted with the same insights.
Besides, through haste you violated the authority of the
   Assembly.
Had this decision come from the Assembly
It would have been we who bore the pains of doubt.
Indeed, the errors of the Assembly are forgiven, but not those of
   rulers.
Our Forefathers have rightfully said:
A great ruler rules only through the approval of his people.
For people detest the laws that are sprung on them.
To this very day we applaud the great King Ndaba,
Who said: "I am no king; I am only the nation's mouthpiece.
My thoughts can only be enriched by argument."
I know, too, a ruler who rules in fear does not have long to live.'
Shaka listened intently to Zihlandlo;
He was like a man who had travelled far for wisdom.
He said: 'Son of Ghubela, these are profound thoughts.

Great ideas are those that are nourished by others:
They fulfil their truths only in their timely season.
I have sometimes felt contempt for the actions of people,
Which often are cowardly and self-centered.
Images of my youth rush back and I decide:                                    *365*
People must be controlled until they learn the higher truth.
But people like you hold me back.
Then I think: it is better to listen to these great men,
To be nourished by them beyond the night.
I know now I shall not run this distance alone.                               *370*
We who are loved by the Ancestors shall nourish our nation;
We shall be the stepping stones for our children.
There is not much time ahead of us, Ghubela.
The races of over-the-ocean have come:
Over our heads they have cast their shadows.                                  *375*
If we do not hurry, if we do not block the passages,
Their wiliness shall endanger the whole Palm Race.
In years to come they shall invade the whole region,
Recruiting even old women for their wars.
We must paralyse the young of the locust,                                     *380*
Driving them back before they learn to fly.
Because of this we must conquer the Soshangane utterly,
Making the route to our north wide and unhindered,
Enabling our army to move freely against the overseas invaders.
We should be the rallying point for all the children of the Palm             *385*
    Race.
If we are weak it is through us the region shall finally be
    conquered.
These over-the-ocean people trust only in their guns;
For this reason we must increase and strengthen our power.
Indeed, wars are ultimately won through people:
It is through collective actions that enemies are repelled.                   *390*
People shall break the gun with their hands.'
After Shaka spoke these words, he sighed loudly,
As though he had emptied himself of deep harrowing thoughts.
Prince Zihlandlo, the son of Gowabe, said:
'I repeat my words, my lord:                                                  *395*
Your speed of thought excels all in our generation,
Making us seem dull and foolish and lacking in vision.
Then you yourself see us only as children.
The words you speak penetrate deep into my mind,
Yet even I had not seen the extent of these truths.'                         *400*
Shaka did not let him finish these words.
He said: 'It is not wise for one to undermine oneself.
It is not true that those who judge look beyond the consequence.
Our task is to strengthen our nation, not to see this truth.'

Prince Zihlandlo tailed onto these words and said:
'The builder, my lord, knows where to find his materials.
To his house often comes many petitions.
The man of wisdom seals the lips of those who doubt
    themselves;
His laughter creates new visions for his listeners.
If our nation continues to follow your wisdom, it shall prosper.
It is clear that the crowd shall always be limited;
Thus it must constantly be fed with new visions.
People are not always the ones who fail;
Rather, it is the oracles
Who must drink in the farthest springs of future times.
From your truths all peoples of Zululand shall learn.
They shall dig the ground with their own hoes.'
Shaka shook his head and said: 'I understand your thoughts,
Even though I may not share their truth.
For many years I shouldered
Those who must grow and live by their own vision.
I have lived to see great men;
Some I have accompanied into great battles.
Many men and women have widened my horizons of thought.
No, Ghubela, great heroes breed their own greatness
At the beginning of eras their truth is manifest,
They do not wait for large arenas for their battles,
Theirs is not a war of weapons but a war of ideas.
They are like a vast field on which new plants must grow.
Yet they should die to fertilize the ground.'
Zihlandlo then said: 'Ahead of us are challenging times.
For us to win totally we must act in concert.
For this reason I ask that we strengthen all aspects of our lives.
Let nothing take us by surprise.'
When this discussion was concluded
The great heroes drank quietly from one large beer pot.
Each let his mind wander in its own direction.

## ■ Damara Folktale (Nineteenth Century) *Namibia*

TRANSLATED BY W. H. I. BLEEK

In the mid-nineteenth century, Wilhelm H. I. Bleek (1827–1875) sailed for southwest Africa to record and study indigenous languages. "The Unreasonable Child to Whom the Dog Gave Its Deserts," transcribed during this trip with help from Breakwater prisoners, was probably the first story to be recorded in its original Damara, one of many Khoikhoian languages spoken by Bushmen in southern Africa. A forefather in modern linguistics, Bleek was the first to research and approach the indigenous languages in an exacting and scientific manner, systematically recording their grammar for later study.

**FURTHER READING:** Bleek, W. H. I. *The Mantis and His Friends*, 1924; *Reynard the Fox in South Africa; or, Hottentot Fables and Tales*, 1864.

## The Unreasonable Child to Whom the Dog Gave Its Deserts; or, A Receipt for Putting Anyone to Sleep

There was a little girl who had an eïngi (pronounced 'a-inghi', some kind of fruit). She said to her Mother, 'Mother, why is it that you do not say, "My first-born, give me the eïngi"? Do I refuse it?'

Her Mother said, 'My first-born, give me the eïngi.' She gave it to her and went away, and her Mother ate eïngi.

When the child came back, she said, 'Mother, give me my eïngi,' but her Mother answered, 'I have eaten the eïngi!'

The child said, 'Mother, how is it that you have eaten my eïngi, which I plucked from our tree?' The Mother then (to appease her) gave her a needle.

The little girl went away and found her Father sewing thongs with thorns; so she said, 'Father, how is it that you sew with thorns? Why do not you say, "My first-born, give me your needle"? Do I refuse?' So her Father said, 'My first-born, give me your needle.' She gave it to him and went away for a while. Her Father commenced sewing, but the needle broke; when, therefore, the child came back and said, 'Father, give me my needle,' he answered, 'The needle is broken;' but she complained about it, saying, 'Father, how is it that you break my needle, which I got from Mother, who ate my eïngi, which I had plucked from our tree?' Her Father then gave her an axe.

Going farther on she met the lads who were in charge of the cattle. They were busy taking out honey, and in order to get at it they were obliged to cut down the trees with stones. She addressed them: 'Our sons, how is it that you use stones in order to get at the honey? Why do not you say, "Our first-born, give us the axe"? Do I refuse, or what do I?' They said, 'Our first-born, give us the axe.' So she gave it them, and went away for some time. The axe broke entirely. When she came back she asked, 'Where is the axe? Please give it me.' They answered, 'The axe is broken.' She then said, 'How is it that you break my axe, which I had received from Father who had broken my needle, which I got from Mother who had eaten my eïngi, which I had plucked from our tree?' But they gave her some honey (to comfort her).

She went her way again, and met a little old woman eating insects, to whom she said, 'Little old woman, how is it that you eat insects? Why don't you say, "My first-born, give me honey"? Do I refuse or not?' Then the little old woman asked, 'My first-born, give me honey.' She gave it her and went away; but presently returning said, 'Little old woman, let me have my honey!' Now the old woman had managed to eat it all during her absence, so she answered, 'Oh! I have eaten the honey!' So the child complained, saying, 'How is it that you eat my honey, which I received from the lads of our cattle, from our children who had broken my axe, which had been given me by Father who had broken my needle, which was a present from my Mother who had eaten up my eïngi, that I had plucked from our tree?'

The little old woman gave her food, and she went away. This time she came to the pheasants, who scratched the ground; and she said, 'Pheasants! how is it that you scratch the ground? Why do not you say, "First-born, give us food"? Do I refuse, or what do I?' They said, 'First-born, give.' So she gave to them, and went away. When she came back and demanded her food again, they said, 'We have eaten the food.' She asked, 'How is it that you eat my food, which I had received from a little old woman who had eaten up my honey, that I had got from the lads of our cattle who had broken my axe, which had been given me by my Father who had broken my needle, which was a present from my Mother who had eaten my eïngi, which I had plucked from our tree?' The pheasants, flying up, pulled out each one a feather and threw them down to the little girl.

She then, walking along, met the children who watched the sheep. They were plucking out hairs from the sheep-skins. So she asked them, 'How is it that you pull at these skins? Why do not you say, "First-born, give us the feathers"? Do I refuse, or what do I?' They said, 'First-born, give us the feathers.' She gave them and went away, but all the feathers broke. When she returned and said, 'Give me my feathers,' they answered, 'The feathers are broken.' Then she complained, 'Do you break my feathers which I received from the pheasants who had eaten my food, which had been given me by a little old woman?' They gave her some milk.

She went again on her way, and found their own handsome dog gnawing bones. She said, 'Our dog, how is it that you gnaw these bones?' The dog answered, 'Give me milk.' She gave it him, and he drank it all. Then she said to the dog, 'Give me back my milk.' He said, 'I drank it.' She then repeats the same words which she had spoken so often before; but the dog ran away and when she pursued him, he scampered up a tree. She climbed up after him but the dog jumped down again on the other side. She wanted to do the same but could not. Then she said, 'Our dog, please help me down.' He answered 'Why did you pursue me?' and ran away, leaving her up the tree.

'That is enough,' say the Damara.

## ■ Traditional Songs of Africa (diverse early periods)

In the past, the traditional songs and poems of Africa were compiled by anthropologists, sociologists, and members of the clergy, whose purpose for recording the oral tradition of the tribes was not aesthetic. The results of their labors in Africa, as elsewhere in the world, were dreary and trivialized the soul of popular culture. Social scientists and men and women of the cloth have usually had neither the interest nor the ability to render traditional songs into good poetry in English. The distinguished literary translator Willard Trask published a small book of startlingly beautiful poems, all translated from African languages. His versions and some recent renditions have the universal qualities of the best oral poetry, some of them indistinguishable from the most ancient Egyptian traditional poems that have survived in hieroglyphic texts. Popular song, like African myth and legend, has been a major source for contemporary writers. The Nigerian Amos Tutuola based his great novel *The Palm-Tree Drinkard* on local mythology and his compatriot Wole Soyinka, one of Africa's premier poets, saw in popular song his precursors, which he included in poetry anthologies and mined for his own verse.

**FURTHER READING:** Barnstone, Aliki, and Willis Barnstone. *A Book of Women Poets from Antiquity to Now,* 1980. Beier, Ulli. *An Anthology of Traditional African Poems,* 1966. Soyinka, Wole. *Poems of Black Africa,* 1975. Trask, Willard. *Classical Black African Poems,* 1971.

## Mugala's Song
## (Sung while Hoeing)

*from Bosumbwa, Tanzania*

We were born under an evil star, we poets,
When the jackal howls!
We were given a thankless trade.
They who are marked with python's excrement,
They are born lucky,                                                    5
They are the rich.
God created me ill. I had a desire.
I do not know, but if I had stayed
In my mother's belly, it would be over and done with.
Crafts are dealt out.                                                   10
I was sound asleep,
I woke—someone calls me:
"You're asleep, Mugala!
Come out here and see
How the ground is ringing!"                                             15

TRANSLATED BY WILLARD R. TRASK

## In Praise of Bow and Arrow

*from Dahomean (Fon), Dahomey*

> The sword does not run the elephant through,
> Fire does not devour the King's house,
> A wind does not pass through stones, through stones;
> A reed cartridge-pouch drops:
> A bow sends an arrow,
> The game falls in a heap;
> It is like a pearl on a manure pile.
>
> Few men try to grasp iron red-hot from the fire;
> The earth does not bring forth the crocodiles of the lagoon;
> Until a beast is dead, it has not done dying;
> Cities that are too great perish;
> A horse does not travel in a reed boat;
> The wind does not pass through stones, through stones;
> A reed cartridge-pouch drops:
> An arrow . . . and the game falls in a heap;
> It is like a pearl on a manure pile.

TRANSLATED BY WILLARD R. TRASK

## Caravaners

*from Galla, Southern Ethiopia*

> In summer they even make the dust rise;
> In winter they even trample the mud!
> If they talk with the dark maiden,
> And smile upon the red maiden,
> Poverty will never leave them.
> Poverty is a terrible disease;
> It penetrates the sides,
> It bends the vertebrae,
> It dresses one in rags,
> It makes people stupid;
> It makes every desire remain in the breast;
> Those who are long, it shortens;
> Those who are short it destroys wholly.
> Not even the mother that has borne [the poor man]
>      loves him any longer!
> Not even the father who has begotten him any longer
>      esteems him!

TRANSLATED BY WILLARD R. TRASK

## Three Friends

*from Yoruba, Nigeria*

I had three friends.
One asked me to sleep on the mat.
One asked me to sleep on the ground.
One asked me to sleep on his breast.
I decided to sleep on his breast.                                     5
I saw myself carried on a river.
I saw the king of the river and the king of the sun.
There in that country I saw palm trees
so weighed down with fruit
that the trees bent under the fruit,                                  10
and the fruit killed it.

TRANSLATED BY ULLI BEIER

## Song to a Lover

*from Amharic, Ethiopia*

His trousers are wind,
his buttons hail.

He's a lump of Shoa earth,
at Gonda he is nothing.

A hyena with meat in its mouth,                                       5
dragged by a piece of leather.

Water in a glass, by the fire,
thrown into the heat.

A horse untouchable as mist,
a flooding brook.                                                     10

No good for anything,
for anyone.

Why am I in love
with him?

TRANSLATED BY WILLIS BARNSTONE

# Slave Narrative

■ **Olaudah Equiano (1745/6–1797)**
*Nigeria/England* (memoir)

The literary progenitor of African writers, their achetypal model and ancestor, is Olaudah Equiano. He achieved this status not because he is the first African writer whom we know by name and of whom we have truly substantive work, but because he is a major writer, who has been imitated and revered as the source. Chinua Achebe in Africa, Caryl Phillips in the Caribbean, Toni Morrison and Alex Haley in America all have found their ancestor in Equiano's great autobiography, *The Interesting Narrative of Olaudah Equiano, or Gustavus Vassa, the African, Written by Himself* (1789). To the twentieth-century reader, the baroque title is intriguing and patronizingly informative. The "Written by Himself" postscript was typically appended to titles of works by slaves. We read *Narrative of the Life of Frederick Douglass, An American Slave, Written by Himself* (1845) and Harriet Jacobs's *Life of a Slave Girl, Written by Herself* (1861). The addendum assures a skeptical nineteenth-century reader that this slave author (unlike the normal illiterate slave incapable of serious authorship) composed the autobiography all by him- or herself.

Equiano was born perhaps as early as 1745 in an Igbo village called Isseke. When he was eleven or twelve, he was kidnapped by African slave traders and sold to white slave traders whom he describes as having "horrible looks, red faces, and loose hair." He was then shipped to Barbados in the West Indies and later to Virginia, where he was bought by Lt. Michael Henry Pascal, an English naval officer, who give him the name Gustavus Vassa. He served Pascal for years on his ship, during which time his master had him educated both on sea and on shore. Despite this good treatment, Pascal eventually sold him to an American Quaker from Philadelphia, Robert King. Equiano worked on King's merchant ships and earned enough money to buy back his freedom. Thereafter, he had many adventurous voyages: he went to Central America where he spent six months with the Miskito Indians, to the Arctic as a surgeon's assistant, and around the Mediterranean as a companion to an Englishman. After visiting Smyrna, he accumulated a knowledge of Islam and the black Muslim movement, which entered his writings and informed his antislavery work.

In London, which became his permanent domicile, Equiano was the leading spokesman for its African population, and he made speeches all over England both to sell his book and to decry slavery. In 1790, he submitted a petition to Parliament calling for the abolishment of slavery. He worked closely with white abolitionists, especially with Granville Sharp, whom he alerted to the murder in 1783 of more than a hundred slaves on the Zong, a slave ship. Meanwhile he was writing and in 1789 published his *The Life of Olaudah Equiano,* which was extremely popular in his time, going through eight English editions. In 1791, his narration was published in America and was subsequently translated into German and Dutch. Through the nineteenth century, his book was frequently reprinted.

In 1792, Equiano married Susan Cullen, an Englishwoman, with whom he had two daughters. Three years after their marriage, his wife died. Equiano was to die at fifty-two in 1797.

In his *Interesting Narrative,* Olaudah Equiano deals extensively with his Igbo childhood. In lucid, understated speech, he writes: "I still look back with pleasure on the first scenes of my life, though that pleasure has been for the most part mingled with sorrow." After the initial shock of slavery, he was especially traumatized by the fact that his first master, Pascal, whom he loved as a father, ultimately resold him into slavery. Always sensitive, a man of reason, even nominally a Christian, and allied with white abolitionists, he never forgot his essential fate and task, which was to end slavery and to improve the treatment of blacks in American and European societies. He suffered brutalities and indignities, experienced deep friendships with other Europeans, and without overt irony he could write: "I consider myself an European," and indeed he thought himself predestined to have a favored life. As proof of his luck we may remember that his Igbo name, Olaudah, means "favored by heaven." He dedicated his years to the cause of Africans and, for our immense benefit, to the art of autobiography. In doing so, he bequeathed an essential history and ethics and a uniquely profound volume of literature.

**FURTHER READING:** Equiano, Olaudah. *Travels: The Interesting Narrative of the Life of Olaudah Equiano, or Gustavus Vassa, the African, Written by Himself,* 1967.

## *from The Life of Olaudah Equiano*

### Life in Guinea and a Slave's Fate

I believe it is difficult for those who publish their own memoirs to escape the imputation of vanity. Nor is this the only disadvantage under which they labour: it is also their misfortune that whatever is uncommon is rarely, if ever, believed, and from what is obvious we are apt to turn with disgust, and to charge the writer of it with impertinence.

People generally think those memoirs only worthy to be read or remembered which abound in great or striking events, those, in short, which in a high degree excite either admiration or pity: all others they consign to contempt and oblivion. It is therefore, I confess, not a little hazardous in a private and obscure individual, and a stranger too, thus to solicit the indulgent attention of the public; especially when I own I offer here the history of neither a saint, a hero, nor a tyrant. I believe there are few events in my life, which have not happened to many: it is true the incidents of it are numerous; and, did I consider myself an European, I might say my sufferings were great: but when I compare my lot with that of most of my countrymen, I regard myself as a *particular favourite of Heaven,* and acknowledge the mercies of Providence in every occurrence of my life. If then the following narrative does not appear sufficiently interesting to engage general attention, let my motive be some excuse for its publication. I am not so foolishly vain as to expect from it either immortality or literary reputation. If it affords any satisfaction to my numerous friends, at whose request it has been written, or in the smallest degree promotes the interests of humanity, the ends for which it was undertaken will be fully attained, and every wish of my heart gratified. Let it therefore be remembered, that, in wishing to avoid censure, I do not aspire to praise.

That part of Africa, known by the name of Guinea, to which the trade for slaves is carried on, extends along the coast above 3400 miles, from Senegal to Angola, and includes a variety of kingdoms. Of these the most considerable is the kingdom of Benin, both as to extent and wealth, the richness and cultivation of the soil, the power of its king, and the number and warlike disposition of the inhabitants. It is situated nearly under the line, and extends along the coast about 170 miles, but runs back into the interior part of Africa to a distance hitherto I believe unexplored by any traveller: and seems only terminated at length by the empire of Abyssinia, near 1500 miles from its beginning. This kingdom is divided into many provinces or districts: in one of the most remote and fertile of which, called Eboe, I was born, in the year 1745, in a charming fruitful vale, named Essaka. The distance of the province from the capital of Benin and the sea coast must be very considerable; for I had never heard of white men or Europeans, nor of the sea: and our subjection to the king of Benin was little more than nominal; for every transaction of the government, as far as my slender observation extended, was conducted by the chiefs or elders of the place. The manners and government of a people who have little commerce with other countries are generally very simple; and the history of what passes in one family or village may serve as a specimen of a nation. My father was one of those elders or chiefs I have spoken of, and was styled Embrenche; a term, as I remember, importing the highest distinction, and signifying in our language a *mark* of grandeur. This mark is conferred on the person entitled to it, by cutting the skin across at the top of the forehead, and drawing it down to the eye-brows; and while it is in this situation applying a warm hand, and rubbing it until it shrinks up into a thick *weal* across the lower part of the forehead. Most of the judges and senators were thus marked; my father had long born it: I had seen it conferred on one of my brothers, and I was also *destined* to receive it by my parents. Those Embrenche, or chief men, decided disputes and punished crimes; for which purpose they always assembled together. The proceedings were generally short; and in most cases the law of retaliation prevailed. I remember a man was brought before my father, and the other judges, for kidnapping a boy; and, although he was the son of a chief or senator, he was condemned to make recompense by a man or woman slave. Adultery, however, was sometimes punished with slavery or death; a punishment which I believe is inflicted on it throughout most of the nations of Africa[1]: so sacred among them is the honour of the marriage bed, and so jealous are they of the fidelity of their wives. Of this I recollect an instance:—a woman was convicted before the judges of adultery, and delivered over, as the custom was, to her husband to be punished. Accordingly he determined to put her to death: but it being found, just before her execution, that she had an infant at her breast; and no woman being prevailed on to perform the part of a nurse, she was spared on account of the child. The men, however, do not preserve the same constancy to their wives, which they expect from them; for they indulge in a plurality, though seldom in more than two. Their mode of marriage is thus:—both parties are usually betrothed when young by their parents, (though I have known the males to betroth themselves). On this occasion a feast is prepared, and the bride and bridegroom stand up in the midst of all their friends, who are assembled for the purpose, while he declares she is thenceforth to be looked upon as his wife, and that no other person is to pay any addresses to her. This is also immediately proclaimed in the vicinity, on which the bride retires from the assembly. Some time after she is brought home to her husband, and then another feast is made, to which the relations of both parties are invited: her parents then deliver her to the bridegroom, accompanied with a number of blessings, and at the same time they tie round her waist a cotton string of the thickness of a goose-quill, which none but married women are permitted to wear: she is now considered as completely his wife; and at this time the dowry is given to the new married pair, which generally consists of portions of land, slaves, and cattle, household goods, and implements of husbandry. These are offered by the friends of both parties; besides which the parents of the bridegroom present gifts to those of the bride, whose property she is looked upon before marriage; but after it she is esteemed the sole property of her husband. The ceremony being now ended the festival begins, which is celebrated with bonfires, and loud acclamations of joy, accompanied by music and dancing.

We are almost a nation of dancers, musicians, and poets. Thus every great event, such as a triumphant return from battle, or other cause of public rejoicing is celebrated in public dances, which are accompanied with songs and music suited to the occasion. The assembly is separated into four divisions, which dance either apart or in succession, and each with a character peculiar to itself. The first division contains the married men, who in their dances frequently exhibit feats of arms, and the repre-

1. See Benezet's *Account of Guinea* throughout.

sentation of a battle. To these succeed the married women, who dance in the second division. The young men occupy the third; and the maidens the fourth. Each represents some interesting scene of real life, such as a great achievement, domestic employment, a pathetic story, or some rural sport; and as the subject is generally founded on some recent event, it is therefore ever new. This gives our dances a spirit and variety which I have scarcely seen elsewhere.[2] We have many musical instruments, particularly drums of different kinds, a piece of music which resembles a guitar, and another much like a stickado. These last are chiefly used by betrothed virgins, who play on them on all grand festivals.

As our manners are simple, our luxuries are few. The dress of both sexes is nearly the same. It generally consists of a long piece of calico, or muslin, wrapped loosely round the body, somewhat in the form of a highland plaid. This is usually dyed blue, which is our favourite colour. It is extracted from a berry, and is brighter and richer than any I have seen in Europe. Besides this, our women of distinction wear golden ornaments; which they dispose with some profusion on their arms and legs. When our women are not employed with the men in tillage, their usual occupation is spinning and weaving cotton, which they afterwards dye and make it into garments. They also manufacture earthen vessels, of which we have many kinds. Among the rest tobacco pipes, made after the same fashion, and used in the same manner, as those in Turkey.[3]

Our manner of living is entirely plain; for as yet the natives are unacquainted with those refinements in cookery which debauch the taste: bullocks, goats, and poultry, supply the greatest part of their food. These constitute likewise the principal wealth of the country, and the chief articles of its commerce. The flesh is usually stewed in a pan; to make it savoury we sometimes use also pepper, and other spices, and we have salt made of wood ashes. Our vegetables are mostly plantains, eadas, yams, beans, and Indian corn. The head of the family usually eats alone; his wives and slaves have also their separate tables. Before we taste food we always wash our hands: indeed our cleanliness on all occasions is extreme; but on this it is an indispensable ceremony. After washing, libation is made, by pouring out a small portion of the food, in a certain place, for the spirits of departed relations, which the natives suppose to preside over their conduct, and guard them from evil. They are totally unacquainted with strong or spirituous liquours; and their principal beverage is palm wine. This is gotten from a tree of that name by tapping it at the top, and fastening a large gourd to it; and sometimes one tree will yield three or four gallons in a night. When just drawn it is of a most delicious sweetness; but in a few days it acquires a tartish and more spirituous flavour: though I never saw any one intoxicated by it. The same tree also produces nuts and oil. Our prin-

---

2. When I was in Smyrna I have frequently seen the Greeks dance after this manner.

3. The bowl is earthen, curiously figured, to which a long reed is fixed as a tube. This tube is sometimes so long as to be born by one, and frequently out of grandeur by two boys.

cipal luxury is in perfumes; one sort of these is an odoriferous wood of delicious fragrance: the other a kind of earth; a small portion of which thrown into the fire diffuses a most powerful odour.[4] We beat this wood into powder, and mix it with palm oil; with which both men and women perfume themselves.

In our buildings we study convenience rather than ornament. Each master of a family has a large square piece of ground, surrounded with a moat or fence, or enclosed with a wall made of red earth tempered; which, when dry, is as hard as brick. Within this are his houses to accommodate his family and slaves; which, if numerous, frequently present the appearance of a village. In the middle stands the principal building, appropriated to the sole use of the master, and consisting of two apartments; in one of which he sits in the day with his family, the other is left apart for the reception of his friends. He has besides these a distinct apartment in which he sleeps, together with his male children. On each side are the apartments of his wives, who have also their separate day and night houses. The habitations of the slaves and their families are distributed throughout the rest of the enclosure. These houses never exceed one story in height: they are always built of wood, or stakes driven into the ground, crossed with wattles, and neatly plastered within, and without. The roof is thatched with reeds. Our day-houses are left open at the sides; but those in which we sleep are always covered, and plastered in the inside, with a composition mixed with cow-dung, to keep off the different insects, which annoy us during the night. The walls and floors also of these are generally covered with mats. Our beds consist of a platform, raised three or four feet from the ground, on which are laid skins, and different parts of a spongy tree called plaintain. Our covering is calico or muslin, the same as our dress. The usual seats are a few logs of wood; but we have benches, which are generally perfumed, to accommodate strangers: these compose the greater part of our household furniture. Houses so constructed and furnished require but little skill to erect them. Every man is a sufficient architect for the purpose. The whole neighbourhood afford their unanimous assistance in building them and in return receive, and expect no other recompense than a feast.

As we live in a country where nature is prodigal of her favours, our wants are few and easily supplied; of course we have few manufactures. They consist for the most part of calicoes, earthen ware, ornaments, and instruments of war and husbandry. But these make no part of our commerce, the principal articles of which, as I have observed, are provisions. In such a state money is of little use; however we have some small pieces of coin, if I may call them such. They are made something like an anchor; but I do not remember either their value or denomination. We have also markets, at which I have been frequently with my mother. These are some-

---

4. When I was in Smyrna I saw the same kind of earth, and brought some of it with me to England; it resembles musk in strength, but is more delicious in scent, and is not unlike the smell of a rose.

times visited by stout mahogany-coloured men from the south west of us: we call them Oye-Eboe, which term signifies red men living at a distance. They generally bring us fire-arms, gunpowder, hats, beads, and dried fish. The last we esteemed a great rarity, as our waters were only brooks and springs. These articles they barter with us for odoriferous woods and earth, and our salt of wood ashes. They always carry slaves through our land; but the strictest account is exacted of their manner of procuring them before they are suffered to pass. Sometimes indeed we sold slaves to them, but they were only prisoners of war, or such among us as had been convicted of kidnapping, or adultery, and some other crimes, which we esteemed heinous. This practice of kidnapping induces me to think, that, notwithstanding all our strictness, their principal business among us was to trepan our people. I remember too they carried great sacks along with them, which not long after I had an opportunity of fatally seeing applied to that infamous purpose.

Our land is uncommonly rich and fruitful, and produces all kinds of vegetables in great abundance. We have plenty of Indian corn, and vast quantities of cotton and tobacco. Our pine apples grow without culture; they are about the size of the largest sugar-loaf, and finely flavoured. We have also spices of different kinds, particularly pepper; and a variety of delicious fruits which I have never seen in Europe; together with gums of various kinds, and honey in abundance. All our industry is exerted to improve those blessings of nature. Agriculture is our chief employment; and every one, even the children and women, are engaged in it. Thus we are all habituated to labour from our earliest years. Every one contributes something to the common stock; and as we are unacquainted with idleness, we have no beggars. The benefits of such a mode of living are obvious. The West India planters prefer the slaves of Benin or Eboe to those of any other part of Guinea, for their hardiness, intelligence, integrity, and zeal. Those benefits are felt by us in the general healthiness of the people, and in their vigour and activity; I might have added too in their comeliness. Deformity is indeed unknown amongst us, I mean that of shape. Numbers of the natives of Eboe now in London might be brought in support of this assertion: for, in regard to complexion, ideas of beauty are wholly relative. I remember while in Africa to have seen three negro children, who were tawny, and another quite white, who were universally regarded by myself, and the natives in general, as far as related to their complexions, as deformed. Our women too were in my eyes at least uncommonly graceful, alert, and modest to a degree of bashfulness; nor do I remember to have ever heard of an instance of incontinence amongst them before marriage. They are also remarkably cheerful. Indeed cheerfulness and affability are two of the leading characteristics of our nation.

Our tillage is exercised in a large plain or common, some hours walk from our dwellings, and all the neighbours resort thither in a body. They use no beasts of husbandry; and their only instruments are hoes, axes, shovels, and beaks, or pointed iron to dig with. Sometimes we are visited by locusts, which come in large clouds, so as to darken the air, and destroy our harvest. This however happens rarely, but when it does, a famine is produced by it. I remember an instance or two wherein this happened. This common is often the theatre of war; and therefore when our people go out to till their land, they not only go in a body, but generally take arms with them for fear of a surprise; and when they apprehend an invasion they guard the avenues to their dwellings, by driving sticks into the ground, which are so sharp at one end as to pierce the foot, and are generally dipt in poison. From what I can recollect of these battles, they appear to have been irruptions of one little state or district on the other, to obtain prisoners or booty. Perhaps they were incited to this by those traders who brought the European goods I mentioned amongst us. Such a mode of obtaining slaves in Africa is common; and I believe more are procured this way, and by kidnapping, than any other.[5] When a trader wants slaves, he applies to a chief for them, and tempts him with his wares. It is not extraordinary, if on this occasion he yields to the temptation with as little firmness, and accepts the price of his fellow creature's liberty with as little reluctance as the enlightened merchant. Accordingly he falls on his neighbours, and a desperate battle ensues. If he prevails and takes prisoners, he gratifies his avarice by selling them; but, if his party be vanquished, and he falls into the hands of the enemy, he is put to death: for, as he has been known to foment their quarrels, it is thought dangerous to let him survive, and no ransom can save him, though all other prisoners may be redeemed. We have firearms, bows and arrows, broad two-edged swords and javelins: we have shields also which cover a man from head to foot. All are taught the use of these weapons: even our women are warriors, and march boldy out to fight along with the men. Our whole district is a kind of militia: on a certain signal given, such as the firing of a gun at night, they all rise in arms and rush upon their enemy. It is perhaps something remarkable, that when our people march to the field a red flag or banner is borne before them. I was once a witness to a battle in our common. We had been all at work in it one day as usual, when our people were suddenly attacked. I climbed a tree at some distance, from which I beheld the fight. There were many women as well as men on both sides; among others my mother was there, and armed with a broad sword. After fighting for a considerable time with great fury, and after many had been killed our people obtained the victory, and took their enemy's Chief prisoner. He was carried off in great triumph, and, though he offered a large ransom for his life, he was put to death. A virgin of note among our enemies had been slain in the battle, and her arm was exposed in our market-place, where our trophies were always exhibited. The spoils were divided according to the merit of the warriors. Those prisoners which were not sold or redeemed we kept as slaves: but how different was their condition from

---

5. See Benezet's *Account of Africa* throughout.

that of the slaves in the West Indies! With us they do no more work than other members of the community, even their masters; their food, clothing and lodging were nearly the same as theirs, (except that they were not permitted to eat with those who were free-born); and there was scarce any other difference between them, than a superior degree of importance which the head of a family possesses in our state, and that authority which, as such, he exercises over every part of his household. Some of these slaves have even slaves under them as their own property, and for their own use.

As to religion, the natives believe that there is one Creator of all things, and that he lives in the sun, and is girted round with a belt that he may never eat or drink; but, according to some, he smokes a pipe, which is our own favourite luxury. They believe he governs events, especially our deaths or captivity; but, as for the doctrine of eternity, I do not remember to have ever heard of it: some however believe in the transmigration of souls in a certain degree. Those spirits, which are not transmigrated, such as our dear friends or relations, they believe always attend them, and guard them from the bad spirits or their foes. For this reason they always before eating, as I have observed, put some small portion of the meat, and pour some of their drink, on the ground for them; and they often make oblations of the blood of beasts or fowls at their graves. I was very fond of my mother, and almost constantly with her. When she went to make these oblations at her mother's tomb, which was a kind of small solitary thatched house, I sometimes attended her. There she made her libations, and spent most of the night in cries and lamentations. I have been often extremely terrified on these occasions. The loneliness of the place, the darkness of the night, and the ceremony of libation, naturally awful and gloomy, were heightened by my mother's lamentations; and these, concuring with the cries of doleful birds, by which these places were frequented, gave an inexpressible terror to the scene.

We compute the year from the day on which the sun crosses the line, and on its setting that evening there is a general shout throughout the land; at least I can speak from my own knowledge throughout our vicinity. The people at the same time make a great noise with rattles, not unlike the basket rattles used by children here, though much larger, and hold up their hands to heaven for a blessing. It is then the greatest offerings are made; and those children whom our wise men foretell will be fortunate are then presented to different people. I remember many used to come to see me, and I was carried about to others for that purpose. They have many offerings, particularly at full moons; generally two at harvest before the fruits are taken out of the ground: and when any young animals are killed, sometimes they offer up part of them as a sacrifice. These offerings, when made by one of the heads of a family, serve for the whole, I remember we often had them at my father's and my uncle's, and their families have been present. Some of our offerings are eaten with bitter herbs. We had a saying among us to any one of a cross temper, 'That if they were to be eaten, they should be eaten with bitter herbs.'

We practised circumcision like the Jews, and made offerings and feasts on that occasion in the same manner as they did. Like them also, our children were named from some event, some circumstance, or fancied foreboding at the time of their birth. I was named *Olaudah,* which, in our language, signifies vicissitude or fortune also; one favoured, and having a loud voice and well spoken. I remember we never polluted the name of the object of our adoration; on the contrary, it was always mentioned with the greatest reverence; and we were totally unacquainted with swearing, and all those terms of abuse and reproach which find their way so readily and copiously into the languages of more civilised people. The only expressions of that kind I remember were 'May you rot, or may you swell, or may a beast take you.'

I have before remarked that the natives of this part of Africa are extremely cleanly. This necessary habit of decency was with us a part of religion, and therefore we had many purifications and washings; indeed almost as many, and used on the same occasions, if my recollection does not fail me, as the Jews. Those that touched the dead at any time were obliged to wash and purify themselves before they could enter a dwelling-house. Every woman too, at certain times, was forbidden to come into a dwelling-house, or touch any person, or any thing we ate. I was so fond of my mother I could not keep from her, or avoid touching her at some of those periods, in consequence of which I was obliged to be kept out with her, in a little house made for that purpose, till offering was made, and then we were purified.

Though we had no places of public worship, we had priests and magicians, or wise men. I do not remember whether they had different offices, or whether they were united in the same persons, but they were held in great reverence by the people. They calculated our time, and foretold events, as their name imported, for we called them *Ah-affoe-way-cah,* which signifies calculators or yearly men, our year being called *Ah-affoe.* They wore their beards, and when they died they were succeeded by their sons. Most of their implements and things of value were interred along with them. Pipes and tobacco were also put into the grave with the corpse, which was always perfumed and ornamented, and animals were offered in sacrifice to them. None accompanied their funerals but those of the same profession or tribe. These buried them after sunset, and always returned from the grave by a different way from that which they went.

These magicians were also our doctors or physicians. They practised bleeding by cupping; and were very successful in healing wounds and expelling poisons. They had likewise some extraordinary method of discovering jealousy, theft, and poisoning; the success of which no doubt they derived from their unbounded influence over the credulity and superstition of the people. I do not remember what those methods were, except that as to poisoning: I recollect an instance or two, which I hope it will not be deemed impertinent here to insert, as it may serve as a kind of specimen of the rest, and is still used by the negroes in the West Indies. A virgin had been poisoned, but it was not known by whom; the doctors ordered the corpse to be taken up by some persons, and carried to the grave. As soon as the bearers had raised it on their shoulders, they seemed seized with some sudden impulse, and ran to and fro unable to stop themselves. At last, after having passed through a number of thorns and prickly bushes unhurt, the corpse fell from them close to a house, and defaced it in the fall; and, the owner being taken up, he immediately confessed the poisoning.[6]

An instance of this kind happened at Montserrat in the West Indies in the year 1763. I then belonged to the Charming Sally, Capt. Doran.—The chief mate, Mr. Mansfield, and some of the crew being one day on shore, were present at the burying of a poisoned negro girl. Though they had often heard of the circumstance of the running in such cases, and had even seen it, they imagined it to be a trick of the corpse-bearers. The mate therefore desired two of the sailors to take up the coffin, and carry it to the grave. The sailors, who were all of the same opinion, readily obeyed; but they had scarcely raised it to their shoulders, before they began to run furiously about, quite unable to direct themselves, till, at last, without intention, they came to the hut of him who had poisoned the girl. The coffin then immediately fell from their shoulders against the hut, and damaged part of the wall. The owner of the hut was taken into custody on this, and confessed the poisoning—I give this story as it was related by the mate and crew on their return to the ship. The credit which is due to it I leave with the reader.

The natives are extremely cautious about poison. When they buy any eatable the seller kisses it all round before the buyer, to shew him it is not poisoned; and the same is done when any meat or drink is presented, particularly to a stranger. We have serpents of different kinds, some of which are esteemed ominous when they appear in our houses, and these we never molest. I remember two of those ominous snakes, each of which was as thick as the calf of a man's leg, and in colour resembling a dolphin in the water, crept at different times into my mother's night-house, where I always lay with her, and coiled themselves into folds, and each time they crowed like a cock. I was desired by some of our wise men to touch these, that I might be interested in the good omens, which I did, for they were quite harmless, and would tamely suffer themselves to be handled; and then they were put into a large open earthen pan, and set to one side of the highway. Some of our snakes, however, were poisonous: one of them crossed the road one day when I was standing on it, and passed between my feet without offering to touch me, to the great surprise of many who saw it; and these incidents were accounted by the wise men, and therefore by my mother and the rest of the people, as remarkable omens in my favour.

Such is the imperfect sketch my memory has furnished me with of the manners and customs of a people among whom I first drew my breath.

---

6. See also Leut. Matthew's Voyage, p. 123.

*At this point Equiano draws a comparison between 'the manners and customs of my countrymen and those of the Jews, before they reached the Land of Promise, and particularly the patriarchs while they were yet in the pastoral state which is described in Genesis'. This kind of analogy with the release of Israel from bondage is to become a commonplace of black literature, particularly in the American slave narratives, and of black song. Equiano goes so far as to suggest that his 'Eboe' people may have been originally Hebrew, and proposes interbreeding as the reason for their darker complexion.*

These instances, and a great many more which might be adduced, while they shew how the complexions of the same persons vary in different climates, it is hoped may tend also to remove the prejudice that some conceive against the natives of Africa on account of their colour. Surely the minds of the Spaniards did not change with their complexions! Are there not causes enough to which the apparent inferiority of an African may be ascribed, without limiting the goodness of God, and supposing he forbore to stamp understanding on certainly his own image, because 'carved in ebony.' Might it not naturally be ascribed to their situation? When they come among Europeans, they are ignorant of their language, religion, manners, and customs. Are any pains taken to teach them these? Are they treated as men? Does not slavery itself depress the mind, and extinguish all its fire and every noble sentiment? But, above all, what advantages do not a refined people possess over those who are rude and uncultivated. Let the polished and haughty European recollect that his ancestors were once, like the Africans, uncivilised, and even barbarous. Did Nature make *them* inferior to their sons? and should *they too* have been made slaves? Every rational mind answers, No. Let such reflections as these melt the pride of their superiority into sympathy for the wants and miseries of their sable brethren, and compel them to acknowledge, that understanding is not confined to feature or colour. If, when they look round the world, they feel exultation, let it be tempered with benevolence to others, and gratitude to God, 'who hath made of one blood all nations of men for to dwell on all the face of the earth;[7] and whose wisdom is not our wisdom, neither are our ways his ways.'

## Despair of Being Sold as a Slave by a Sea Captain

In pursuance of our orders we sailed from Portsmouth for the Thames, and arrived at Deptford the 10th of December, where we cast anchor just as it was high water. The ship was up about half an hour, when my master ordered the barge to be manned; and all in an instant, without having before given me the least reason to suspect any thing of the matter, he forced me into the barge; saying, I was going to leave him, but he would take care I should not. I was so struck with the unexpectedness of this proceeding, that for some time I did not make a reply, only I made an offer to

---

7. Acts, c. xvii, v. 26.

go for my books and chest of clothes, but he swore I should not move out of his sight; and if I did he would cut my throat, at the same time taking his hanger. I began, however, to collect myself; and, plucking up courage, I told him I was free, and he could not by law serve me so. But this only enraged him the more; and he continued to swear, and said he would soon let me know whether he would or not, and at that instant sprung himself into the barge from the ship, to the astonishment and sorrow of all on board. The tide, rather unluckily for me, had just turned downward, so that we quickly fell down the river along with it, till we came among some outward-bound West Indiamen; for he was resolved to put me on board the first vessel he could get to receive me. The boat's crew, who pulled against their will, became quite faint different times, and would have gone ashore; but he would not let them. Some of them strove then to cheer me, and told me he could not sell me, and that they would stand by me, which revived me a little; and I still entertained hopes; for as they pulled along he asked some vessels to receive me, but they could not. But, just as we had got a little below Gravesend, we came alongside of a ship which was going away the next tide for the West Indies; her name was the *Charming Sally,* Captain James Doran; and my master went on board and agreed with him for me; and in a little time I was sent for into the cabin. When I came there Captain Doran asked me if I knew him; I answered that I did not; 'Then,' said he, 'you are now my slave.' I told him my master could not sell me to him nor to any one else. 'Why,' said he, 'did not your master buy you?' I confessed he did. 'But I have served him,' said I, 'many years, and he has taken all my wages and prize-money, for I only got one sixpence during the war; besides this I have been baptised; and by the laws of the land no man has a right to sell me.' And I added, that I had heard a lawyer and others at different times tell my master so. They both then said that those people who told me so were not my friends; but I replied—it was very extraordinary that other people did not know the law as well as they. Upon this Captain Doran said I talked too much English; and if I did not behave myself well, and be quiet, he had a method on board to make me. I was too well convinced of his power over me to doubt what he said; and my former sufferings in the slaveship presenting themselves to my mind, the recollection of them made me shudder. However, before I retired I told them that as I could not get any right among men here I hoped I should hereafter in Heaven; and I immediately left the cabin, filled with resentment and sorrow. The only coat I had with me my master took away with him, and said if my prize-money had been £10,000, he had a right to it all, and would have taken it. I had about nine guineas, which, during my long sea-faring life, I had scraped together from trifling perquisites and little ventures; and I hid it that instant, lest my master should take that from me likewise, still hoping that by some means or other I should make my escape to the shore; and indeed some of my old shipmates told me not to despair, for they would get me back again; and that, as soon as they could get their pay, they would immediately come to

Portsmouth to me, where this ship was going: but alas! all my hopes were baffled, and the hour of my deliverance was yet far off. My master, having soon concluded his bargain with the captain, came out of the cabin, and he and his people got into the boat and put off; I followed them with aching eyes as long as I could, and when they were out of sight I threw myself on the deck, while my heart was ready to burst with sorrow and anguish.

Thus, at the moment I expected all my toils to end, was I plunged, as I supposed, in a new slavery; in comparison of which all my service hitherto had been 'perfect freedom'; and whose horrors, always present to my mind, now rushed on it with tenfold aggravation. I wept bitterly for some time: and began to think that I must have done something to displease the Lord, that he thus punished me so severely. This filled me with painful reflections on my past conduct; I recollected that on the morning of our arrival at Deptford I had rashly sworn that as soon as we reached London I would spend the day in rambling and sport. My conscience smote me for this unguarded expression: I felt that the Lord was able to disappoint me in all things, and immediately considered my present situation as a judgement of Heaven on account of my presumption in swearing: I therefore, with contrition of heart, acknowledged my transgression to God, and poured out my soul before him with unfeigned repentance, and with earnest supplications I besought him not to abandon me in my distress, nor cast me from his mercy for ever. In a little time my grief, spent with its own violence, began to subside; and after the first confusion of my thoughts was over I reflected with more calmness on my present condition: I considered that trials and disappointments are sometimes for our good, and I thought God might perhaps have permitted this in order to teach me wisdom and resignation; for he had hitherto shadowed me with the wings of his mercy, and by his invisible but powerful hand brought me the way I knew not. These reflections gave me a little comfort, and I rose at last from the deck with dejection and sorrow in my countenance, yet mixed with some faint hope that the *Lord would appear* for my deliverance.

Soon afterwards, as my new master was going ashore, he called me to him, and told me to behave myself well, and do the business of the ship the same as any of the rest of the boys, and that I should fare better for it; but I made him no answer. I was then asked if I could swim, and I said, No. However I was made to go under the deck, and was well watched. The next tide the ship got under way, and soon after arrived at the Mother Bank, Portsmouth; where she waited a few days for some of the West India convoy. While I was here I tried every means I could devise amongst the people of the ship to get me a boat from the shore, as there was none suffered to come alongside of the ship; and their own, whenever it was used, was hoisted in again immediately. A sailor on board took a guinea from me on pretence of getting me a boat; and promised me, time after time, that it was hourly to come off. When he had the watch upon deck I watched also; and looked long enough, but all in vain; I could never see either the boat or my guinea again. And what I thought was still the worst of all, the fellow gave information, as I afterwards found, all the while to the mates, of my intention to go off, if I could in any way do it; but, rogue like, he never told them he had got a guinea from me to procure my escape. However, after we had sailed, and his trick was made known to the ship's crew, I had some satisfaction in seeing him detested and despised by them all for his behaviour to me. I was still in hopes that my old shipmates would not forget their promise to come for me to Portsmouth: and, indeed, at last, but not till the day before we sailed, some of them did come there, and sent me off some oranges, and other tokens of their regard. They also sent me word they would come off to me themselves the next day or the day after; and a lady also, who lived in Gosport, wrote to me that she would come and take me out of the ship at the same time. This lady had been once very intimate with my former master: I used to sell and take care of a great deal of property for her, in different ships; and in return she always shewed great friendship for me, and used to tell my master that she would take me away to live with her: but, unfortunately for me, a disagreement soon afterwards took place between them; and she was succeeded in my master's good graces by another lady, who appeared sole mistress of the *Ætna,* and mostly lodged on board. I was not so great a favourite with this lady as with the former; she had conceived a pique against me on some occasion when she was on board, and she did not fail to instigate my master to treat me in the manner he did.[8]

However, the next morning, the 30th of December, the wind being brisk and easterly, the *Œolus* frigate, which was to escort the convoy, made a signal for sailing. All the ships then got up their anchors; and, before any of my friends had an opportunity to come off to my relief, to my inexpressible anguish our ship had got under way. What tumultuous emotions agitated my soul when the convoy got under sail, and I a prisoner on board, now without hope! I kept my swimming eyes upon the land in a state of unutterable grief; not knowing what to do, and despairing how to help myself. While my mind was in this situation the fleet sailed on, and in one day's time I lost sight of the wished-for land. In the first expressions of my grief I reproached my fate, and wished I had never been born. I was ready to curse the tide that bore us, the gale that wasted my prison, and even the ship that conducted us; and I called on death to relieve me from the horrors I felt and dreaded, that I might be in that place

---

8. Thus was I sacrificed to the envy and resentment of this woman for knowing that the lady whom she had succeeded in my master's good graces designed to take me into her service; which, had I once got on shore, she would not have been able to prevent. She felt her pride alarmed at the superiority of her rival in being attended by a black servant: it was not less to prevent this than to be revenged on me, that she caused the captain to treat me thus cruelly.

Where slaves are free, and men oppress no more.
Fool that I was, inur'd so long to pain,
To trust to hope, or dream of joy again.

\*　\*　\*

While I was thus employed by my master I was often a witness to cruelties of every kind, which were exercised on my unhappy fellow slaves. I used frequently to have different cargoes of new negroes in my care for sale: and it was almost a constant practice with our clerks, and other whites, to commit violent depredations on the chastity of the female slaves: and there I was, though with reluctance, obliged to submit to at all times, being unable to help them. When we have had some of these slaves on board my master's vessels to carry them to other islands, or to America, I have known our mates to commit these acts most shamefully, to the disgrace, not of Christians only, but of men. I have even known them to gratify their brutal passion with females not ten years old; and these abominations some of them practised to such scandalous excess, that one of our captains discharged the mate and others on that account. And yet in Montserrat I have seen a negro man staked to the ground, and cut most shockingly, and then his ears cut off bit by bit, because he had been connected with a white woman who was a common prostitute: as if it were no crime in the whites to rob an innocent African girl of her virtue; but most heinous in a black man only to gratify a passion of nature, where the temptation was offered by one of a different colour, though the most abandoned woman of her species. Another negro man was half hanged, and then burnt, for attempting to poison a cruel overseer. Thus by repeated cruelties are the wretched first urged to despair, and then murdered, because they still retain so much of human nature about them as to wish to put an end to their misery, and retaliate on their tyrants! These overseers are indeed for the most part persons of the worst character of any denomination of men in the West Indies. Unfortunately, many humane gentlemen, by not residing on their estates, are obliged to leave the management of them in the hands of these human butchers, who cut and mangle the slaves in a shocking manner on the most trifling occasions, and altogether treat them in every respect like brutes. They pay no regard to the situation of pregnant women, nor the least attention to the lodging of the field negroes. Their huts, which ought to be well covered, and the place dry where they take their little repose, are often open sheds, built in damp places; so that, when the poor creatures return tired from the toils of the field, they contract many disorders, from being exposed to the damp air in this uncomfortable state, while they are heated, and their pores are open. This neglect certainly conspires with many others to cause a decrease in the births as well as in the lives of the grown negroes. I can quote many instances of gentlemen who reside on their estates in the West Indies, and then the scene is quite changed; the negroes are treated with lenity and proper care, by which their lives are prolonged, and their masters are profited. To the honour of humanity, I knew several gentlemen who managed their estates in this manner; and they found that benevolence was their true interest. And, among many I could mention in several of the islands, I knew one in Montserrat[9] whose slaves looked remarkably well, and never needed any fresh supplies of negroes; and there are many other estates, especially in Barbados, which, from such judicious treatment, need no fresh stock of negroes at any time. I have the honour of knowing a most worthy and humane gentleman, who is a native of Barbados, and has estates there.[10] This gentleman has written a treatise on the usage of his own slaves. He allows them two hours for refreshment at midday; and many other indulgencies and comforts, particularly in their lying; and, besides this, he raises more provisions on his estate than they can destroy; so that by these attentions he saves the lives of his negroes, and keeps them healthy, and as happy as the condition of slavery can admit. I myself, as shall appear in the sequel, managed an estate, where, by those attentions, the negroes were uncommonly cheerful and healthy, and did more work by half than by the common mode of treatment they usually do. For want, therefore, of such care and attention to the poor negroes, and otherwise oppressed as they are, it is no wonder that the decrease should require 20,000 new negroes annually to fill up the vacant places of the dead.

Even in Barbados, notwithstanding those humane exceptions which I have mentioned, and others I am acquainted with, which justly make it quoted as a place where slaves meet with the best treatment, and need fewest recruits of any in the West Indies, yet this island requires 1000 negroes annually to keep up the original stock, which is only 80,000. So that the whole term of a negro's life may be said to be there but sixteen years![11] And yet the climate here is in every respect the same as that from which they are taken, except in being more wholesome. Do the British colonies decrease in this manner? And yet what a prodigious difference is there between an English and West India climate?

While I was in Montserrat I knew a negro man, named Emanuel Sankey, who endeavoured to escape from his miserable bondage, by concealing himself on board of a London ship: but fate did not favour the poor oppressed man; for, being discovered when the vessel was under sail, he was delivered up again to his master. This *Christian master* immediately pinned the wretch down to the ground at each wrist and ankle, and then took some sticks of sealing wax, and lighted them, and dropped it all over his back. There was another master who was noted for cruelty; and I believe he had not a slave but what had been cut, and had pieces fairly taken out of the flesh: and, after they had been punished thus, he used to make

---

9. Mr. Dubury, and many others, Montserrat.

10. Sir Philip Gibbe, Baronet, Barbados.

11. Benezet's *Account of Guinea.*

them get into a long wooden box or case he had for that purpose, in which he shut them up during pleasure. It was just about the height and breadth of a man; and the poor wretches had no room, when in the case, to move.

It was very common in several of the islands, particularly in St. Kitt's, for the slaves to be branded with the initial letters of their master's name; and a load of heavy iron hooks hung about their necks. Indeed on the most trifling occasions they were loaded with chains; and often instruments of torture were added. The iron muzzle, thumb-screws, &c. are so well known, as not to need a description, and were sometimes applied for the slightest faults. I have seen a negro beaten till some of his bones were broken, for even letting a pot boil over. Is it surprising that usage like this should drive the poor creatures to despair, and make them seek a refuge in death from those evils which render their lives intolerable—while,

> With shudd'ring horror pale, and eyes aghast.
> They view their lamentable lot, and find
> No rest!

This they frequently do. A negro-man on board a vessel of my master, while I belonged to her, having been put in irons for some trifling misdemeanor, and kept in that state for some days, being weary of life, took an opportunity of jumping overboard into the sea; however, he was picked up without being drowned. Another, whose life was also a burden to him resolved to starve himself to death, and refused to eat any victuals; this procured him a severe flogging: and he also, on the first occasion which offered, jumped overboard at Charles Town, but was saved.

Nor is there any greater regard shewn to the little property than there is to the persons and lives of the negroes. I have already related an instance or two of particular oppression out of many which I have witnessed; but the following is frequent in all the islands. The wretched field-slaves, after toiling all the day for an unfeeling owner, who gives them but little victuals, steal sometimes a few moments from rest or refreshment to gather some small portion of grass, according as their time will admit. This they commonly tie up in a parcel; (either a bit, worth six pence; or half a bit's-worth) and bring it to town, or to the market, to sell. Nothing is more common than for the white people on this occasion to take the grass from them without paying for it; and not only so, but too often also, to my knowledge, our clerks, and many others, at the same time have committed acts of violence on the poor, wretched, and helpless females; whom I have seen for hours stand crying to no purpose, and get no redress or pay of any kind. Is not this one common and crying sin enough to bring down God's judgement on the islands? He tells us the oppressor and the oppressed are both in his hands; and if these are not the poor, the broken-hearted, the blind, the captive, the bruised, which our Saviour speaks of, who are they? One of these depredators once, in St. Eustatia, came on board of our vessel, and brought some fowls and pigs of me; and a whole day after his departure with the things he returned again and wanted his money back: I refused to give it; and, not seeing my captain on board, he began the common pranks with me; and swore he would even break open my chest and take my money. I therefore expected, as my captain was absent, that he would be as good as his word: and he was just proceeding to strike me, when fortunately a British seaman on board, whose heart had not been debauched by a West India climate, interposed and prevented him. But had the cruel man struck me I certainly should have defended myself at the hazard of my life; for what is life to a man thus oppressed? He went away, however, swearing; and threatened that whenever he caught me on shore he would shoot me, and pay for me afterwards.

The small account in which the life of a negro is held in the West Indies is so universally known, that it might seem impertinent to quote the following extract, if some people had not been hardy enough of late to assert that negroes are on the same footing in that respect as Europeans. By the 329th Act. page 125, of the Assembly of Barbados, it is enacted 'That if any negro, or other slave, under punishment by his master, or his order, for running away, or any other crime or misdemeanor towards his said master, unfortunately shall suffer in life or member, no person whatsoever shall be liable to a fine; but if any man shall out of *wantonness, or only of bloody-mindedness, or cruel intention, wilfully kill a negro, or other slave, of his own, he shall pay into the public treasury fifteen pounds sterling.'* And it is the same in most, if not all, of the West India islands. Is not this one of the many acts of the islands which call loudly for redress? And do not the assembly which enacted it deserve the appellation of savages and brutes rather than of Christians and men? It is an act at once unmerciful, unjust, and unwise; which for cruelty would disgrace an assembly of those who are called barbarians; and for its injustice and *insanity* would shock the morality and common sense of a Samoyed or a Hottentot.

Shocking as this and many more acts of the bloody West India code at first view appear, how is the iniquity of it heightened when we consider to whom it may be extended! Mr. James Tobin, a zealous labourer in the vineyard of slavery, gives an account of a French planter of his acquaintance, in the island of Martinique, who shewed him many mulattoes working in the fields like beasts of burden: and he told Mr. Tobin these were all the produce of his own loins! And I myself have known similar instances. Pray, reader, are these sons and daughters of the French planter less his children by being begotten on a black woman? And what must be the virtue of those legislators, and the feelings of those fathers, who estimate the lives of their sons, however begotten, at no more than fifteen pounds; though they should be murdered, as the act says, *out of wantonness and bloody-mindedness!* But is not the slave trade entirely a war with the heart of man? And surely that which is begun by breaking down the barriers of virtue involves in its continuance destruction to every principle, and buries all sentiments in ruin!

I have often seen slaves, particularly those who were meagre, in different islands, put into scales and weighed; and then sold from three pence to six pence or nine pence a pound. My master, however, whose humanity was shocked at this mode, used to sell such by the lump. And at or after a sale it was not uncommon to see negroes taken from their wives, wives taken from their husbands, and children from their parents, and sent off to other islands, and wherever else their merciless lords chose; and probably never more during life to see each other! Oftentimes my heart has bled at these partings; when the friends of the departed have been at the water side, and, with sighs and tears, have kept their eyes fixed on the vessel till it went out of sight.

A poor Creole negro I knew well, who, after having been often thus transported from island to island, at last resided in Montserrat. This man used to tell me many melancholy tales of himself. Generally, after he had done working for his master, he used to employ his few leisure moments to go a fishing. When he had caught any fish, his master would frequently take them from him without paying him; and at other times some other white people would serve him in the same manner. One day he said to me, very movingly, 'Sometimes when a white man take away my fish I go to my master, and he get me my right; and when my master by strength take away my fishes, what me must do? I can't go to any body to be righted: then,' said the poor man, looking up above, 'I must look up to God Mighty in the top for right.' This artless tale moved me much, and I could not help feeling the just cause Moses had in redressing his brother against the Egyptian. I exhorted the man to look up still to the God on the top, since there was no redress below. Though I little thought then that I myself should more than once experience such imposition, and read the same exhortation hereafter, in my own transactions in the islands; and that even this poor man and I should some time after suffer together in the same manner, as shall be related hereafter.

Nor was such usage as this confined to particular places or individuals; for, in all the different islands in which I have been (and I have visited no less than fifteen) the treatment of the slaves was nearly the same; so nearly indeed, that the history of an island, or even a plantation, with a few such exceptions as I have mentioned, might serve for a history of the whole. Such a tendency has the slave-trade to debauch men's minds, and harden them to every feeling of humanity! For I will not suppose that the dealers in slaves are born worse than other men—No; it is the fatality of this mistaken avarice, that it corrupts the milk of human kindness and turns it into gall. And, had the pursuits of those men been different, they might have been as generous, as tender-hearted and just, as they are unfeeling, rapacious and cruel. Surely this traffic cannot be good, which spreads like a pestilence, and taints what it touches! which violates that first natural right of mankind, equality and independency, and gives one man a dominion over his fellows which God could never intend! For it raises the owner to a state as far above man as it depresses the slave below it; and, with all the presumption of human pride, sets a distinction between them, immeasurable in extent, and endless in duration! Yet how mistaken is the avarice even of the planters? Are slaves more useful by being thus humbled to the condition of brutes, than they would be if suffered to enjoy the privileges of men? The freedom which diffuses health and prosperity throughout Britain answers you—No. When you make men slaves you deprive them of half their virtue, you set them in your own conduct an example of fraud, rapine, and cruelty, and compel them to live with you in a state of war; and yet you complain that they are not honest or faithful! You stupify them with stripes, and think it necessary to keep them in a state of ignorance; and yet you assert that they are incapable of learning; that their minds are such a barren soil or moor, that culture would be lost on them; and that they come from a climate, where nature, though prodigal of her bounties in a degree unknown to yourselves, has left man alone scant and unfinished, and incapable of enjoying the treasures she has poured out for him!—An assertion at once impious and absurd. Why do you use those instruments of torture? Are they fit to be applied by one rational being to another? And are ye not struck with shame and mortification, to see the partakers of your nature reduced so low? But, above all, are there no dangers attending this mode of treatment? Are you not hourly in dread of an insurrection? Nor would it be surprising: for when:

> —No peace is given
> To us enslav'd, but custody severe;
> And stripes and arbitrary punishment
> Inflicted—What peace can we return?
> But to our power, hostility and hate;
> Untam'd reluctance, and revenge, though slow,
> Yet ever plotting how the conqueror least
> May reap his conquest, and may least rejoice
> In doing what we most in suffering feel.

But by changing your conduct, and treating your slaves as men, every cause of fear would be banished. They would be faithful, honest, intelligent and vigorous; and peace, prosperity, and happiness, would attend you.

\* \* \*

## London Respectability and Struggle for My People

*Equiano next quotes a letter he wrote to the Queen 'on behalf of my African brethren'. He then continues:*

The negro consolidated act, made by the assembly of Jamaica last year, and the new act of amendment now in agitation there, contain a proof of the existence of those charges that have been made against the planters relative to the treatment of their slaves.

I hope to have the satisfaction of seeing the renovation of liberty and justice resting on the British government, to vindicate the honour of our common nature. These are concerns which do not perhaps belong to any particular office; but, to speak more seriously to every man of sentiment, actions like these are the just and sure foundation of future fame; a revision, though remote, is coveted by some noble minds as a substantial good. It is upon these grounds that I hope and expect the attention of gentlemen in power. These are designs consonant to the elevation of their rank, and the dignity of their stations: they are ends suitable to the nature of a free and generous government; and, connected with views of empire and dominion, suited to the benevolence and solid merit of the legislature. It is a pursuit of substantial greatness. — May the time come — at least the speculation to me is pleasing — when the sable people shall gratefully commemorate the auspicious era of extensive freedom. Then shall those persons[12] particularly be named with praise and honour, who generously proposed and stood forth in the cause of humanity, liberty, and good policy; and brought to the ear of the legislature designs worthy of royal patronage and adoption. May Heaven make the British senators the dispersers of light, liberty, and science, to the uttermost parts of the earth: then will be glory to God on the highest, on earth peace, and good-will to men: — Glory, honour, peace, &c. to every soul of man that worketh good, to the Britons first, (because to them the Gospel is preached) and also to the nations. 'Those that honour their Maker have mercy on the poor.' 'It is righteousness exalteth a nation; but sin is a reproach to any people; destruction shall be to the workers of iniquity, and the wicked shall fall by their own wickedness.' May the blessings of the Lord be upon the heads of all those who commiserated the cases of the oppressed negroes, and the fear of God prolong their days; and may their expectations be filled with gladness! 'The liberal devise liberal things, and by liberal things shall stand,' Isaiah xxxii 8. They can say with pious Job, 'Did not I weep for him that was in trouble? was not my soul grieved for the poor?' Job xxx 25.

As the inhuman traffic of slavery is to be taken into the consideration of the British legislature, I doubt not, if a system of commerce was established in Africa, the demand for manufactures would most rapidly augment, as the native inhabitants will insensibly adopt the British fashions, manners, customs, &c. In proportion to the civilisation, so will be the consumption of British manufactures.

The wear and tear of a continent, nearly twice as large as Europe, and rich in vegetable and mineral productions, is much easier conceived than calculated.

A case in point. — It cost the Aborigines of Britain little or nothing in clothing, &c. The difference between their forefathers and the present

---

12. Granville Sharp, Esq; the Reverend Thomas Clarkson; the Reverend James Ramsay; our approved friends, men of virtue, are an honour to their country, ornamental to human nature, happy in themselves, and benefactors to mankind!

generation, in point of consumption, is literally infinite. The supposition is most obvious. It will be equally immense in Africa—the same cause, viz. civilisation, will ever have the same effect.

It is trading upon safe grounds. A commercial intercourse with Africa opens an inexhaustible source of wealth to the manufacturing interests of Great Britain, and to all which the slave trade is an objection.

If I am not misinformed, the manufacturing interest is equal, if not superior, to the landed interest, as to the value, for reasons which will soon appear. The abolition of slavery, so diabolical, will give a most rapid extension of manufactures, which is totally and diametrically opposite to what some interested people assert.

The manufacturers of this country must and will, in the nature and reason of things, have a full and constant employ by supplying the African markets.

Population, the bowels and surface of Africa, abound in valuable and useful returns; the hidden treasures of centuries will be brought to light and into circulation. Industry, enterprize, and mining, will have their full scope, proportionably as they civilise. In a word, it lays open an endless field of commerce to the British manufactures and merchant adventurer. The manufacturing interest and the general interests are synonymous. The abolition of slavery would be in reality an universal good.

Tortures, murder, and every other imaginable barbarity and iniquity, are practised upon the poor slaves with impunity. I hope the slave trade will be abolished. I pray it may be an event at hand. The great body of manufacturers, uniting in the cause, will considerably facilitate and expedite it; and, as I have already stated, it is most substantially their interest and advantage, and as such the nation's at large, (except those persons concerned in the manufacturing neck-yokes, collars, chains, hand-cuffs, leg-bolts, drags, thumb-screws, iron muzzles, and coffins; cats, scourges, and other instruments of torture used in the slave trade). In a short time one sentiment alone will prevail, from motives of interest as well as justice and humanity. Europe contains one hundred and twenty millions of inhabitants. Query— How many millions doth Africa contain? Supposing the Africans, collectively and individually, to expend £5 a head in raiment and furniture yearly when civilised, &c. an immensity beyond the reach of imagination!

This I conceive to be a theory founded upon facts, and therefore an infallible one. If the blacks were permitted to remain in their own country, they would double themselves every fifteen years. In proportion to such increase will be the demand for manufactures. Cotton and indigo grow spontaneously in most parts of Africa; a consideration this of no small consequence to the manufacturing towns of Great Britain. It opens a most immense, glorious, and happy prospect—the clothing, &c. of a continent ten thousand miles in circumference, and immensely rich in productions of every denomination in return for manufactures.

I have only therefore to request the reader's indulgence and conclude. I am far from the vanity of thinking there is any merit in this narrative: I hope censure will be suspended, when it is considered that it was written by one who was as unwilling as unable to adorn the plainness of truth by the colouring of imagination. My life and fortune have been extremely chequered, and my adventures various. Even those I have related are considerably abridged. If any incident in this little work should appear uninteresting and trifling to most readers, I can only say, as my excuse for mentioning it, that almost every event of my life made an impression on my mind and influenced my conduct. I early accustomed myself to look for the hand of God in the minutest occurrence, and to learn from it a lesson of morality and religion; and in this light every circumstance I have related was to me of importance. After all, what makes any event important, unless by its observation we become better and wiser, and learn 'to do justly, to love mercy, and to walk humbly before God?' To those who are possessed of this spirit, there is scarcely any book or incident so trifling that does not afford some profit, while to others the experience of ages seems of no use; and even to pour out to them the treasures of wisdom is throwing the jewels of instruction away.

# The Modern Period

■

## INTRODUCTION

The slave trade of the seventeenth and eighteenth centuries laid the groundwork for the colonial conquest of Africa by the European powers, but for most of this period actual settlement of Africa was limited to coastal trading stations, such as Zanzibar, in East Africa, and many others along the west coast of the continent. European expansionism in Africa started with the Portuguese, who were interested in the lucrative gold trade, and established trading posts along the eastern, southern, and western coasts of Africa as early as the fifteenth century. Most of the center of Africa remained unknown to the Europeans. However, the reports of great wealth in the interior by flamboyant explorers and missionaries such as John Speke and David Livingstone sparked colonial fervor and economic interest. Between 1880 and 1912, there was a great rush to carve up the continent of Africa among European imperialist powers— England, France, Germany, Belgium, Portugal, and Italy. Despite African resistance, European conquest was swift, facilitated by modern weapons of war, such as the machine gun. Soon, all of this massive continent was under colonial rule, with the exceptions of Liberia and of Ethiopia, which defeated the Italian army in a great battle at Adowa.

In the decades following the close of World War II, global sentiment turned against the holding of colonial territories and imperial rule over conquered peoples. In the mid- to late twentieth century, grassroots independence movements developed, organized and spurred by charismatic African figures educated in the West, such as Kwame Nkrumah of the British Gold Coast colony (present-day Ghana), Léopold Senghor of French West Africa, and Jomo Kenyatta and Julius Nyerere of British East Africa. Independence movements utilized strikes, boycotts, public critique, and in some cases violent revolt—such as in the Mau Mau revolution in Kenya—to pressure the colonial administrations and turn public feeling against continued foreign rule. Beginning in the 1950s, independence was granted to many colonies by their European rulers, often without violent struggle, though there were notable exceptions, such as the bloody fight for independence in French Algeria. The African struggle for independence continued through the 1970s and culminated in the achievement of majority rule in South Africa in 1993, after many years of apartheid and repression by British and Boer colonials.

In the nineteenth century, African journalists in western Africa expressed their anticolonialist feelings in their own newspapers. These journalistic essays preceded the literary movements of the early twentieth century. The first literature started out closely tied to the sociopolitical fate and aspirations of the African abroad and at home. African identity, colonialism, political change, and socialism were primary concerns. In the 1930s, Léopold Senghor (1906– ), poet, politician, and later president of the Republic of Senegal (1960–1980), founded the first major literary movement, which he called Négritude. Senghor wrote in French, drawing upon both the rich tradition of African folklore and a knowledge of European writing, but his central aim was to break down colonialist imperatives and to assert suppressed or concealed perspectives on African life. In short, Négritude sought to define a specific politico-literary identity for the African writer; more, it established rules of literary behavior that should not be transgressed. The African writer should show pride and feel dignity in being African; esteem the beauty of African person, place, and traditions; emulate African and third-world literary models; and reject white colonial models, values, and stereotyping of Africa.

Aimé Césaire (1913– ), the Martinique poet, and Léon Damas (1912–1978), from Guiana, were early exponents of Négritude. Césaire, by far the most talented of the early members, was to develop diverse styles throughout his life and became one of the giants of modern French poetry. Négritude, which denounced colonialism, preceded the independence of most African nations. Eventually, leading writers like the Nigerians Wole Soyinka (1934– ) and Chinua Achebe (1930– ), who in their theater, poetry, and novels were deeply influenced by folklore, myth, and African life, were to free themselves of Négritude's limiting edicts. Thereafter, in a period of resurgent literary vitality, the literary scene has witnessed intense debate, recriminations, and declarations about what constitutes proper writing by an African. These preoccupations of literary correctness have been mostly, though not entirely, the work of critics rather than of the novelists and poets.

Although virtually all writing that has gained publication nationally and internationally was and remains in French, English, Afrikaans, or Portuguese, in recent years there has been a spirited growth of writing in African languages. Ngugi wa Thiong¢o was even jailed for producing a play in Kikuyu that lashed out against the Kenyan government. Beginning in the late forties and fifties (coinciding with successful independence movements), the number of serious writers multipled decisively in most parts of Africa. Indeed, there has been an explosion of creativity in all the arts, particularly in the novel and the theater. Now many novels are filmed and music tracks are written for them. African music, in film, concert, or bar, varies from polyrhythmic drums and xylophones of folkloric origin to classical European instrumentation, jazz, and widespread Afro-pop.

Among outstanding writers in the modern period are Amos Tutuola, Wole Soyinka (Nobel Prize, 1986), Chinua Achebe, Tchicaya U Tam¢si,

Camera Laye, and Ben Okri in western Africa, Nygui wa Thion¢o in Kenya, Doris Lessing from Zimbabwe (Southern Rhodesia when she first wrote), and many writers from South Africa, including Alan Paton, Bessie Head, Nadine Gordimer (Nobel Prize, 1991), Dennis Brutus, J. M. Coetzee, Breyten Breytenbach, Peter Abrams, Richard Rive, and Arthur Nortje. Each year, and each new anthology, reveals fascinating new authors.

One of the characteristics in the work of many authors is the theme of exile, since so many work and write in Paris, London, Canada, and American cities and universities. Exile complicates the already complex contentions of Africa with the West, native traditions with modern life, and personal identity with surrounding society. In counterpoint to the displaced writings by African writers in exile are the texts of immigrant Europeans who have adopted Africa as their homeland. Africa has also given us much prison literature. In Breyten Breytenbach's memoirs, his seven years in a South African jail yield a fiercely realistic picture of physical and mental survival in confinement. The stunning personal poems of South African exile and suicide Arthur Nortje reveal the private and public forces that make and crush an artist.

With ever increasing international recognition, African novelists, much like the innovative and famous Latin American "boom" novelists and authors from India, China, and Japan, have begun to win major international literary prizes and to find their works sold in original or translation everywhere. The themes have in part shifted from colonial preoccupation to criticism of internal social and political corruption and, without apologies, to the politics of the single unaffiliated person. As with the embattled "Misty Writers" movement in China of the last decades, so in Africa the right to write about oneself, metaphorically or in detailed confession, is also a desirable privilege worth risking one's life for.

African literature promises a very full, eclectic future—where anything that makes good literature goes—where the best work will be taken up internationally as the information superhighway shrinks the planet into communicating villages of writers and readers, and all the literary genres and media mix in unforeseen confusion and brilliance. When early in the century, Walter Benjamin wrote, "To an ever greater extent the work of art reproduced becomes the work of art designed for reproducibility"[1] in his now famous "The Work of Art in the Age of Mechanical Reproduction," he could not possibly have known how prophetic his essay would be; how from all continents, the national literatures and arts are mixing and reproducing, making, for example, a new popular African novel the window feature in a Nairobi, Paris, or Cambridge bookstore or a

---

1. Benjamin, Walter. *Illuminations and Reflections.* Edited and with an introduction by Hannah Arendt; translated by Harry Zohn. New York: Schocken Books, 1969, p. 224.

short story by a writer from Ghana or South Africa the assigned reading at any university, college, or high school in the world.

—Ayame Fukuda and the editors

## ◼ Alan Paton (1903–1988) *South Africa* (novel)

Alan Paton wrote the first novel to attract worldwide attention to apartheid and the division of blacks and whites in South Africa. The novel, *Cry the Beloved Country,* published in 1948, is a lyrical and moving document of the tragedy of segregation that became an international classic. Paton was born in Pietermaritzburg. After studying at the University of Natal, he became a schoolmaster and then a principal at the Diepkloof Reformatory near Johannesburg, a model facility for young blacks. The success of *Cry the Beloved Country* made it possible for him to give up teaching and turn completely to writing and political reform. He was a founder of the South African Liberal Party in 1953 and its president from 1963 to 1968. The party advocated a multinational democracy to be achieved through nonviolence. The party was outlawed in 1968.

In his first novel, Paton, a master in lucid description of person and place, portrays an idealized rural black clergyman and the abominable conditions of blacks in the city ghetto. He stirred the conscience of the world. In 1953, he wrote *Too Late the Phalarope,* in which he explores the tragic consequences of Afrikaner racial politics. *Tales from a Troubled Land* (1961), a volume of stories, again concerns justice and relations between the races in his country. In 1981, he turned to personal history, giving us the autobiographical *Towards the Mountain.* His writings focus largely on the calamitous problems of South Africa. In them, he found his subject and, quietly passionate, produced two novels that eternalize the historical and social period and at the same time transcend the moment through their humanity and artistry.

**FURTHER READING:** Paton, Alan. *Cry the Beloved Country,* 1948; *Too Late the Phalarope,* 1953; *Tales from a Troubled Land,* 1965 (first published in South Africa as *Debbie Go Home,* 1961); *Towards the Mountain,* 1981.

## *from* Cry the Beloved Country

# Chapter 35

There is ploughing in Ndotsheni, and indeed on all the farms around it. But the ploughing goes slowly, because the young demonstrator, and behind him the chief, tell the men they must no longer go up and down.

They throw up walls of earth, and plough round the hills, so that the fields look no longer as they used to look in the old days of ploughing. Women and boys collect the dung, but it looks so little on the land that the chief has ordered a kraal to be built, where the cattle can stay and the dung be easily collected; but that is a hard thing, because there will be nothing to eat in the kraal. The young demonstrator shakes his head over the dung, but next year he says it will be better. The wattle seed is boiled, and no one has heard of such a thing before in this valley, but those that have worked for the white farmers say it is right, and so they boil it. For this seed one or two desolate places have been chosen, but the young demonstrator shakes his head over them, there is so little food in the soil. And the demonstrator has told the people they can throw away the maize they have kept for planting, because it is inferior and he has better seed from uJarvis. But they do not throw it away, they keep it for eating.

But all this was not done by magic. There have been meetings, and much silence, and much sullenness. It was only the fear of the chief that made anything come out of these meetings. No one was more dissatisfied than those who had to give up their fields. Kuluse's brother was silent for days because the dam was to eat up his land, and he was dissatisfied with the poor piece of land they gave him. Indeed the umfundisi had to persuade him, and it was hard to refuse the umfundisi, because it was through him that had come the milk that had saved his brother's child.

The chief had hinted that there were still harder things he would ask, and indeed the young demonstrator was dissatisfied that they had not been asked at once. But it would be hard to get these people to agree to everything at once. Even this year he hoped, said the young demonstrator, that the people would see something with their eyes, though he shook his head sadly over the poverty-stricken soil.

There was talk that the Government would give a bull to the chief, and the young demonstrator explained to Kumalo that they would get rid of the cows that gave the smallest yield, but he did not talk thus in the meeting, for that was one of the hard things for a people who counted their wealth in cattle, even these miserable cattle.

But the greatest wonder of all is the great machine, that was fighting in the war, they said, and pushes the earth of Kuluse's brother's land over to the line of the sticks, and leaves it there, growing ever higher and higher. And even Kuluse's brother, watching it sullenly, breaks out into unwilling laughter, but remembers again and is sullen. But there is some satisfaction for him, for next year, when the dam is full, Zuma and his brother must both give up their land that lies below the dam, for white man's grass is to be planted there, to be watered from the dam, to be cut and thrown into the kraal where the cattle will be kept. And both Zuma and his brother laughed at him, because he was sullen about the dam; so in some measure he is satisfied.

Indeed, there is something new in this valley, some spirit and some life, and much to talk about in the huts. Although nothing has come yet, something is here already.

*    *    *

—There was another Napoleon, said Kumalo, who was also a man who did many things. So many things did he do that many books were written about him.

The young demonstrator laughed, but he cast his eyes on the ground, and rubbed his one boot against the other.

—You can be proud, said Kumalo. For there is a new life in this valley. I have been here for many years, but I have never seen ploughing with such spirit.

—There is a new thing happening here, he said. It is not only these rains, though they too refresh the spirit. There is hope here, such as I have never seen before.

—You must not expect too much, said the young man anxiously. I do not expect much this year. The maize will be a little higher, and the harvest a little bigger, but the soil is poor indeed.

—But next year there will be the kraal.

—Yes, said the young man eagerly. We will save much dung in the kraal. They say to me, umfundisi, that even if the winter is cold, they will not burn the dung.

—How long will it be before the trees are ready?

—Many years, said the demonstrator gloomily. Tell me, umfundisi, he said anxiously, do you think they will bear the winter for seven years?

—Have courage, young man. Both the chief and I are working for you.

—I am impatient for the dam, said the demonstrator. When the dam is made, there will be water for the pastures. I tell you, umfundisi, he said excitedly, there will be milk in this valley. It will not be necessary to take the white man's milk.

Kumalo looked at him. Where would we be without the white man's milk? he asked. Where would we be without all that this white man has done for us? Where would you be also? Would you be working for him here?

—It is true I am paid by him, said the young man stubbornly. I am not ungrateful.

—Then you should not speak so, said Kumalo coldly.

There fell a constraint between them, until the young demonstrator said quietly, umfundisi, I work here with all my heart, is it not so?

—That is true indeed.

—I work so because I work for my country and my people. You must see that, umfundisi. I could not work so for any master.

—If you had no master, you would not be here at all.

—I understand you, said the young man. This man is a good man, and I respect him. But it is not the way it should be done, that is all.

—And what way should it be done?

—Not this way, said the young man doggedly.

—What way then?

—Umfundisi, it was the white man who gave us so little land, it was the white man who took us away from the land to go to work. And we were ignorant also. It is all these things together that have made this valley desolate. Therefore, what this good white man does is only a repayment.

—I do not like this talk.

—I understand you, umfundisi, I understand you completely. But let me ask one thing of you.

—Ask it then.

—If this valley were restored, as you are always asking in your prayers, do you think it would hold all the people of this tribe if they all returned?

—I do not know indeed.

—But I know, umfundisi. We can restore this valley for those who are here, but when the children grow up, there will again be too many. Some will have to go still.

And Kumalo was silent, having no answer. He sighed. You are too clever for me, he said.

—I am sorry, umfundisi.

—You need not be sorry. I see you have a love for truth.

—I was taught that, umfundisi. It was a white man who taught me. There is not even good farming, he said, without the truth.

—This man was wise.

—It was he also who taught me that we do not work for men, that we work for the land and the people. We do not even work for money, he said.

Kumalo was touched, and he said to the young man, Are there many who think as you do?

—I do not know, umfundisi. I do not know if there are many. But there are some.

He grew excited. We work for Africa, he said, not for this man or that man. Not for a white man or a black man, but for Africa.

—Why do you not say South Africa?

—We would if we could, said the young man soberly.

He reflected for a moment. We speak as we sing, he said, for we sing *Nkosi Sikelel' iAfrika.*

—It is getting dark, said Kumalo, and it is time for us to wash.

—You must not misunderstand me, umfundisi, said the young man earnestly. I am not a man for politics. I am not a man to make trouble in your valley. I desire to restore it, that is all.

—May God give you your desire, said Kumalo with equal earnestness. My son, one word.

—Yes, umfundisi.

—I cannot stop you from thinking your thoughts. It is good that a young man has such deep thoughts. But hate no man, and desire power over no man. For I have a friend who taught me that power corrupts.

—I hate no man, umfundisi. I desire power over none.

—That is well. For there is enough hating in our land already.

The young man went into the house to wash, and Kumalo stood for a moment in the dark, where the stars were coming out over the valley that was to be restored. And that for him was enough, for his life was nearly finished. He was too old for new and disturbing thoughts and they hurt him also, for they struck at many things. Yes, they struck at the grave silent man at High Place, who after such deep hurt, had shown such deep compassion. He was too old for new and disturbing thoughts. A white man's dog, that is what they called him and his kind. Well, that was the way his life had been lived, that was the way he would die.

He turned and followed the young man into the house.

# Chapter 36

This was the fourteenth day. Kumalo said to his wife, I am going up into the mountain. And she said, I understand you. For twice before he had done it, once when the small boy Absalom was sick unto death, and once when he had thought of giving up the ministry to run a native store at Donnybrook for a white man named Baxter, for more money than the church could ever pay. And there was a third time, but that was without her knowledge, for she was away, and he had been sorely tempted to commit adultery with one of the teachers at Ndotsheni, who was weak and lonely.

—Would you come with me, he said, for I do not like to leave you alone.

She was touched and she said, I cannot come, for the girl is near her time, and who knows when it will be. But you must certainly go.

She made him a bottle of tea, of the kind that is made by boiling the leaves, and she wrapped up a few heavy cakes of maize. He took his coat and his stick and walked up the path that went to the place of the chief. But at the first fork you go to the side of the hand that you eat with, and you climb another hill to other huts that lie beneath the mountain itself. There you turn and walk under the mountain to the east, as though you were going to the far valley of Empayeni, which is another valley where the fields are red and bare, a valley of old men and women, and mothers and children. But when you reach the end of the level path, where it begins to fall to this other valley, you strike upwards into the mountain itself. This mountain is called Emoyeni, which means, in the winds, and it stands high above Carisbrooke and the tops, and higher still above the valleys of Ndotsheni and Empayeni. Indeed it is a rampart of the great valley itself, the valley of the Umzimkulu, and from it you look down on one of the fairest scenes of Africa.

Now it was almost dark, and he was alone in the dusk; which was well, for one did not go publicly on a journey of this nature. But even as he started to climb the path that ran through the great stones, a man on a horse was there, and a voice said to him, It is you, *umfundisi?*

—It is I, *umnumzana.*

—Then we are well met, *umfundisi.* For here in my pocket I have a letter for the people of your church. He paused for a moment, and then he said, The flowers were of great beauty, *umfundisi.*

—I thank you, *umnumzana.*

—And the church, *umfundisi.* Do you desire a new church?

Kumalo could only smile and shake his head, there were no words in him. And though he shook his head as if it were No, Jarvis understood him.

—The plans will shortly come to you, and you must say if they are what you desire.

—I shall send them to the Bishop, *umnumzana.*

—You will know what to do. But I am anxious to do it quickly, for I shall be leaving this place.

Kumalo stood shocked at the frightening and desolating words. And although it was dark, Jarvis understood him, for he said swiftly, I shall be often here. You know I have a work in Ndotsheni. Tell me, how is the young man?

—He works night and day. There is no quietness in him.

The white man laughed softly. That is good, he said. Then he said gravely, I am alone in my house, so I am going to Johannesburg to live with my daughter and her children. You know the small boy?

—Indeed, *umnumzana,* I know him.

—Is he like him?

—He is like him, *umnumzana.*

And then Kumalo said, Indeed, I have never seen such a child as he is.

Jarvis turned on his horse, and in the dark the grave silent man was eager. What do you mean? he asked.

— *Umnumzana,* there is a brightness inside him.

—Yes, yes, that is true. The other was even so.

And then he said, like a man with hunger, do you remember?

And because this man was hungry, Kumalo, though he did not well remember, said, I remember.

They stayed there in silence till Jarvis said, *umfundisi,* I must go. But he did not go. Instead he said, Where are you going at this hour?

Kumalo was embarrassed, and the words fell about on his tongue, but he answered, I am going into the mountain.

Because Jarvis made no answer he sought for words to explain it, but before he had spoken a word, the other had already spoken. I understand you, he said, I understand completely.

And because he spoke with compassion, the old man wept, and Jarvis sat embarrassed on his horse. Indeed he might have come down from it, but such a thing is not lightly done. But he stretched his hand over the darkening valley, and he said, One thing is about to be finished, but here is something that is only begun. And while I live it will continue. *Umfundisi,* go well.

—*Umnumzana!*

—Yes.

—Do not go before I have thanked you. For the young man, and the milk. And now for the church.

—I have seen a man, said Jarvis with a kind of grim gaiety, who was in darkness till you found him. If that is what you do, I give it willingly.

Perhaps it was something deep that was here, or perhaps the darkness gives courage, but Kumalo said, truly, of all the white men that I have ever known—

—I am no saintly man, said Jarvis fiercely.

—Of that I cannot speak, but God put His hands on you.

And Jarvis said, That may be, that may be. He turned suddenly to Kumalo. Go well, *umfundisi.* Throughout this night, stay well.

And Kumalo cried after him, Go well, go well.

Indeed there were other things, deep things, that he could have cried, but such a thing is not lightly done. He waited till the sounds of the horse had died away, then started to climb heavily, holding onto the greatest stones, for he was young no longer. He was tired and panting when he reached the summit, and he sat down on a stone to rest, looking out over the great valley, to the mountains of Ingeli and East Griqualand, dark against the sky. Then recovered, he walked a short distance and found the place that he had used before on these occasions. It was an angle in the rock, sheltered from the winds, with a place for a man to sit on, his legs at ease over the edge. The first of these occasions he remembered clearly, perhaps because it was the first, perhaps because he had come to pray for the child that no prayer could save any more. The child could not write then, but here were three letters from him now, and in all of them he said, If I could come back to Ndotsheni, I would not leave it any more. And in a day or two they would receive the last he would ever write. His heart went out in a great compassion for the boy that must die, who promised now, when there was no more mercy, to sin no more. If he had got to him sooner, perhaps. He knitted his brows at the memory of that terrible and useless questioning, the terrible and useless answering, it is as my father wishes, it is as my father says. What would it have helped if he had said, My father, I do not know?

He turned aside from such fruitless remembering, and set himself to the order of his vigil. He confessed his sins, remembering them as well as he could since the last time he had been in this mountain. There were some he remembered easily, the lie in the train, the lie to his brother, when John had barred the door against him and shut him out in the street; his loss of faith in Johannesburg, and his desire to hurt the girl, the sinning and innocent child. All this he did as fully as he could, and prayed for absolution.

Then he turned to thanksgiving, and remembered, with profound awareness, that he had great cause for thanksgiving, and that for many things. He took them one by one, giving thanks for each, and praying for each person that he remembered. There was above all the beloved Msimangu and his generous gift. There was the young man from the reformatory saying with angry brows, I am sorry, umfundisi, that I spoke such angry words. There was Mrs. Lithebe, who said so often, Why else were we born? And Father Vincent, holding both his hands and saying. Anything, anything, you have only to ask, I shall do anything. And the lawyer that took the case for God, and had written to say there was no mercy in such kind and gentle words.

Then there was the return to Ndotsheni, with his wife and his friend to meet him. And the woman who threw her apron over her head. And the women waiting at the church. And the great joy of the return, so that pain was forgotten.

He pondered long over this, for might not another man, returning to another valley, have found none of these things? Why was it given to one man to have his pain transmuted into gladness? Why was it given to one man to have such an awareness of God? And might not another, having no such awareness, live with pain that never ended? Why was there a compulsion upon him to pray for the restoration of Ndotsheni, and why was there a white man there on the tops, to do in this valley what no other could have done? And why of all men, the father of the man who had been murdered by his son? And might not another feel also a compulsion, and pray night and day without ceasing, for the restoration of some other valley that would never be restored?

But his mind would contain it no longer. It was not for man's knowing. He put it from his mind, for it was a secret.

And then the white man Jarvis, and the inkosikazi that was dead, and the small boy with the brightness inside him. As his mind could not contain that other, neither could this be contained. But here were thanks that a man could render till the end of his days. And some of them he strove now to render.

He woke with a start. It was cold, but not so cold. He had never slept before on these vigils, but he was old, not quite finished, but nearly finished. He thought of all those that were suffering, of Gertrude the weak and foolish one, of the people of Shanty Town and Alexandra, of his wife now at this moment. But above all of his son, Absalom. Would he be awake, would he be able to sleep, this night before the morning? He cried out, My son, my son, my son.

With his crying he was now fully awake, and he looked at his watch and saw that it was one o'clock. The sun would rise soon after five, and it was then it was done, they said. If the boy was asleep, then let him sleep, it was better. But if he was awake, then oh Christ of the abundant mercy, be with him. Over this he prayed long and earnestly.

Would his wife be awake, and thinking of it? She would have come with him, were it not for the girl. And the girl, why, he had forgotten her. But she was no doubt asleep; she was loving enough, but this husband had given her so little, no more than her others had done.

And there was Jarvis, bereaved of his wife and his son, and his daughter-in-law bereaved of her husband, and her children bereaved of their father, especially the small boy, the bright laughing boy. The small boy stood there before his eyes, and he said to Kumalo, When I go, something bright will go out of Ndotsheni. Yes, I see, he said. Yes, I see. He was not shy or ashamed, but he said, Yes, I see, and laughed with his pleasure.

And now for all the people of Africa, the beloved country. *Nkosi Sikelel' iAfrika*, God save Africa. But he would not see that salvation. It lay afar off, because men were afraid of it. Because, to tell the truth, they were afraid of him, and his wife, and Msimangu, and the young demonstrator. And what was there evil in their desires, in their hunger? That men should walk upright in the land where they were born, and be free to use the fruits of the earth, what was there evil in it? Yet men were afraid, with a fear that was deep, deep in the heart, a fear so deep that they hid their kindness, or brought it out with fierceness and anger, and hid it behind fierce and frowning eyes. They were afraid because they were so few. And such fear could not be cast out, but by love.

It was Msimangu who had said, Msimangu who had no hate for any man, I have one great fear in my heart, that one day when they turn to loving they will find we are turned to hating.

Oh, the grave and the sombre words.

$$* \quad * \quad *$$

When he woke again there was a faint change in the east, and he looked at his watch almost with a panic. But it was four o'clock and he was reassured. And now it was time to be awake, for it might be they had wakened his son, and called him to make ready. He left his place and could hardly stand, for his feet were cold and numb. He found another place where he could look to the east, and if it was true what men said, when the sun came up over the rim, it would be done.

He had heard that they could eat what they wished on a morning like this. Strange that a man should ask for food at such a time. Did the body hunger, driven by some deep dark power that did not know it must die? Is the boy quiet, and does he dress quietly, and does he think of Ndotsheni now? Do tears come into his eyes, and does he wipe them away, and stand up like a man? Does he say, I will not eat any food, I will pray? Is Msimangu there with him, or Father Vincent, or some other priest whose duty it is, to comfort and strengthen him, for he is afraid of the hanging? Does he repent him, or is there only room for his fear? Is there nothing that can be done now, is there not an angel that comes there and cries, This is for God not for man, come child, come with me?

He looked out of his clouded eyes at the faint steady lightening in the east. But he calmed himself, and took out the heavy maize cakes and the tea, and put them upon a stone. And he gave thanks, and broke the cakes and ate them, and drank of the tea. Then he gave himself over to deep and earnest prayer, and after each petition he raised his eyes and looked to the east. And the east lightened and lightened, till he knew that the time was not far off. And when he expected it, he rose to his feet and took off his hat and laid it down on the earth, and clasped his hands before him. And while he stood there the sun rose in the east.

\*   \*   \*

Yes, it is the dawn that has come. The titihoya wakes from sleep, and goes about its work of forlorn crying. The sun tips with light the mountains of Ingeli and East Griqualand. The great valley of the Umzimkulu is still in darkness, but the light will come there. Ndotsheni is still in darkness, but the light will come there also. For it is the dawn that has come, as it has come for a thousand centuries, never failing. But when that dawn will come, of our emancipation, from the fear of bondage and the bondage of fear, why, that is a secret.

## ■ Léopold Sedar Senghor (1906– ) *Senegal* (poem)

### TRANSLATED BY NORMAN SHAPIRO

Léopold Senghor was born into a prosperous Catholic family in a predominantly Muslim community in the town of Joal, south of the capital city of Dakar. He attended a Catholic mission school and then a French lycée in Dakar. A brilliant student, he went on to study in Paris, eventually receiving the prestigious aggregation degree from the Sorbonne, the first black African to do so. He went on to earn higher degrees in both French literature and African languages, the latter at the École des Hautes Études. Significant for his own poetry was his doctoral thesis on "Exoticism in Baudelaire." In the poems of Charles Baudelaire, he found the sensual and "foreign" model he was later to transform into his ideal African woman. Africa was also the paradise of his childhood; his memories of that time would haunt him during his European years and he would extoll them throughout his literary career. Senghor taught Latin and Greek in a French lycée near Paris until World War II when he entered the French army as an officer. He fought at the front, was captured, and was a prisoner-of-war for two years. He was eventually released shortly before the war's end and taught again in a French lycée.

As a student in Paris, Senghor was already a poet. His friends were Aimé Césaire of Martinique and Léon Gontran Damas of French Guiana. Together they started the Négritude movement—the term was Césaire's invention—which was to become historically the single most acclaimed movement in Africa. Through Négritude, the founders strove to discover and redeem the cultural heritage of Africa, infuse it with pride and ethnic value, and prescribe it for their fellow artists. It had an immense following among African writers as well as black writers in the Americas and the Caribbean. Its greatest appeal was initially in France among African students and writers using French as their idiom. In the early 1950s, Négritude was intimately linked with the independence movements for French African colonies. In the end, the most gifted practitioner was Aimé Césaire of Martinique. Having served its purpose, the movement itself became a collar to throw off, notably by leading writers like Wole Solinka, who refused to submit their talent to any obligatory rules and purpose. While Senghor was busy with literature, teaching, and founding the politico-literary journals, *Condition Humaine* and *Présence Africaine,* he also found himself at the center of African politics. He became a leader, founding a political party, and in 1951 he was elected to the French national parliament as one of two members representing Senegal. In 1959, Senghor became president of Mali, the union of Senegal with the former French Soudan. Senegal broke away, and, in 1960, Senghor was elected president of Senegal, a position he retained, despite domestic revolts, until his retirement in 1981.

Senghor's center has been his poetry, his many collections, and his famous French black African anthology, *Anthologie de la nouvelle poésie nègre et magache de langue française* (1948), was the single most important book of the Négritude movement. Its preface by Jean Paul Sartre was later published separately as *Orphée Noir.* Senghor has been championed by literary critics and politicians from Sartre to presidents of nations. Given his enormous prestige and the appearance of his publications in many fields in distinguished French journals, such as *Les Temps Modernes, Les Lettres Française,* and *Présence Africaine,* and books with the major French publishers Seuil, Seghers, and Presses Universitaires de Frances, Senghor was for some years a perennial candidate for the Nobel Prize for Literature. In his Négritude poems, Africa is often symbolized as a sensual African woman, with Baudelairean erotic descriptive language. He has enormous power and enthusiasm in his poems, although they suffer from his role of "great poet," meaning that they fall into predictable and banal rhetoric. Ultimately, his poems in French, adequately translated into English by John Reed and Clive Wake and superbly rendered by Norman Shapiro, only occasionally have enduring qualities. He is a hero of African ethnicities and historically paramount as an initiator in literature. His work fares poorly in comparison with the major career of his original partner Aimé Césaire or with that of later generations which he helped generate.

**FURTHER READING:** Senghor, Léopold. *Anthologie de la nouvelle poésie nègre et magache de langue française,* 1948; *Senghor: Prose and Poetry.* Translated by John Reed and Clive Wake, 1965; *Selected Poems of Léopold Sedar Senghor.* Edited by Abiola Irele, 1977; *Collected Poetry.* Translated by Melvin Dixon, 1991.

## Black Woman

Nude woman, black woman
Clothed in your color which is life itself, in your form which is beauty!
I grew in your shadow, and the softness of your hands covered my
    eyes.
Then, in the heat of Summer and Noon, suddenly I discover you,
    Promised Land, from the top of a high parched hill
And your beauty strikes me to the heart, like the flash of an eagle.

Nude woman, dark woman
Ripe fruit firm of flesh, somber ecstasies of black wine, mouth that
    moves my mouth to poetry
Prairie of pure horizons, prairie trembling in the East wind's
    passionate caress
Tom-tom taut over sculptured frame, groaning beneath the
    Conqueror's fingers
Your deep contralto voice is the sacred melody of the Beloved.

Nude woman, dark woman
Oil not ruffled by the slightest breath, oil smooth on the athlete's
    flanks, the flanks of the princes of Mali
Heaven-limbed gazelle, the moist drops are stars on the night of your
    skin
Delights of mind's caprice, reflections of red gold on your rippling
    skin
In the dark shadow of your hair, my anguish brightens with the
    dawning sun of your eyes.

Nude woman, black woman
I sing your disappearing beauty, fixing it in an Eternal shape,
Before an envious Destiny transforms you into ashes to nourish the
    roots of life.

## ■ Bernard Binlin Dadié (1916–1989) *Ivory Coast* (poems)

TRANSLATED BY JOHN REED AND CLIVE WAKE

Dadié was part of the first generation of Francophone African writers. Born in Assinie, Côte d'Ivoire, at age six he was sent to live with his uncle in Grand Bassam. His mother feared that her one bad eye was an "evil eye" and had been responsible for the deaths of her first three children. She wanted Dadié to survive. He attended the local Catholic school and became involved in the drama and folklore movement when he attended the École William Ponty. Upon graduation and until 1947, he worked in

Dakar, Senegal, at the French Institute of Black Africa. He then returned to the Côte d'Ivoire and worked for the newspaper of the nationalist party, the Parti Démocratique de Côte d'Ivoire.

Dadié's first collection of poetry, *Afrique debout,* was published in 1950. Later, with the publishing of his novel *Une nègre à Paris* in 1959, Dadié was one of the first writers to place the African hero outside Africa and its colonialist restraints. A profuse writer in all genres, he was most successful with his drama and also published short stories and essays—both political and critical. Dadié continued to write creatively even as he held the high position of Minister of Culture and Information in Côte d'Ivoire.

The excerpt here is from a much anthologized poem, "Leaf in the Wind," with its incantatory repetition reminiscent of Robert's Frost "Acquainted with the Night." Preceding the present generation of accomplished writers (which he helped generate), Dadié's heroic writing, with its daring rhetorical qualities, remains historically significant.

**FURTHER READING:** Dadié, Bernard Binlin. *Afrique debout (Africa Upright),* 1950; *Une nègre à Paris (A black in Paris),* 1959.

# I Thank You God

I thank you God for creating me black,
For making of me
Porter of all sorrows,
Setting on my head
The World.                                                          5
I wear the Centaur's hide
And I have carried the World since the first morning.

White is a colour for special occasions
Black the colour for every day
And I have carried the World since the first evening.       10

I am glad
Of the shape of my head
Made to carry the World,
Content
With the shape of my nose                                     15
That must snuff every wind of the World
Pleased
With the shape of my legs
Ready to run all the heats of the World.

I thank you God for creating me black                         20
For making of me
Porter of all sorrows.

Thirty-six swords have pierced my heart.
Thirty-six fires have burnt my body.
And my blood on all calvaries has reddened the snow,          2
And my blood at every dawn has reddened all nature.

Still I am
Glad to carry the World,
Glad of my short arms
    of my long arms                                        3
       of the thickness of my lips.

I thank you God for creating me black.
White is a colour for special occasions
Black the colour for every day
And I have carried the World since the dawn of time.          3
And my laugh over the World, through the night, creates the Day.

I thank you God for creating me black.


## *from* **Leaf in the Wind**

I am the man the colour of Night
Leaf in the wind, I go at the drift of my dreams.

I am the tree budding in spring
The dew that hums in the baobab's hollow.

Leaf in the wind, I go at the drift of my dreams.

I am the man they complain of
Because opposed to formality
The man they laugh at
Because opposed to barriers.

Leaf in the wind, I go at the drift of my dreams.              1

I am the man they talk about:
    "Oh him!"
Him you cannot hold
The breeze that touches you and is gone

Leaf in the wind, I go at the drift of my dreams.             1

# ■ Birago Diop (1906– ) *Senegal* (story)

## TRANSLATED BY EILEEN JULIEN AND EUNICE C. SMITH

Born in Ouakam, a suburb of Dakar, Diop received his early education in rural community schools and his high school education in Dakar where he stayed until he was fifteen. Diop was awarded a scholarship and transfered to the Lycée Faidherbe in Saint-Louis, Senegal. After earning a French baccalauréat in philosophy and winning the Brevet de Capacité in 1925, Diop left for France to study veterinary medicine. He received his doctorate from the University of Toulouse in 1933 and stayed in Paris where he collaborated with a fellow Senegalese, Léopold Senghor. Together they edited and published the first and only issue of the journal *L'etudiant noir,* which would prove to be groundbreaking in its efforts to establish a voice and an outlet for independent African writers.

Diop and his French wife returned to Africa in 1937 when he accepted a veterinarian position in the Sudan. He eventually traveled and worked in many areas of the French empire. It was during this time in Mali that Diop met the griot, or folksinger, Amadou Koumba N'Gom. Diop retold his stories in two books, *Les contes d'Amadou Koumba* (*The Stories of Amadou Koumba;* 1947), and *Les nouveaux contes d'Amadou Koumba* (*The New Stories of Amadou Koumba;* 1958), with a long preface by Senghor. The first collection was instantly awarded the Grand Prix Littéraire de l'Afrique Occidentale Française. The book was then edited by Joyce Hutchinson, who added thoughtful discussions on oral African traditions and superb English notes for use as a textbook.

Assigned to Paris during wartime, Diop did not return to Africa again until 1945 when he was commissioned as head of the Zoological Technical Services in Côte D'Ivoire. In 1955, Diop worked in Senegal and, five years later when Senegal achieved its independence, he was appointed its first ambassador to Tunis by President Senghor. That same year saw the publication of his only, though often anthologized, collection of poetry *Leurres et lueurs.* Three years later another collection of legends, *Contes et lavanes,* was published, winning the Prix d'Afrique Noire in 1964. From his first collection of tales, three stories have been successfully adapted for stage presentation. His stories have been praised for wedding the oral and written traditions without the loss of vigor or stamina. The story of Mawdo and the fart is a version of a joke tale that appeared much earlier in *The Thousand and One Nights.*

**FURTHER READING:** Diop, Birago. *Les contes d'Amadou Koumba (The Stories of Amadou Koumba),* 1948; *Les nouveaux contes d'Amadou Koumba (The New Stories of Amadou Koumba),* 1958; *Contes et lavanes,* 1964.

## N'Gor Niébé

N'Gor Sène was pure-blooded Serer, black as coal, a Serer from Diakaw. If in the course of his life he had once gone as far as the reef of Sangomar, on the shore of the Great Sea, N'Gor Sène had never been up North nor East. Consequently, he had never heard of the misfortunes of Mawdo, the old Peulh who, years and years ago, over in Macina, had forgotten himself to such a degree one evening during a palaver, that there before everyone he made an inappropriate sound. Everyone, old and young alike, exchanged glances and stared him down. So Mawdo got up and, going off into the night, disappeared towards the South. He walked night and day, he walked for moons and moons, he crossed the country of the Markas, the lands of the Bambaras, the villages of the Miniankas and the bumpy fields of the Senefos which, during the dry season, look like immense cemeteries. He stayed seven times seven years in the forest, the land of Naked Men. Then, slowly, with the steps of an old man, weary and worn out, he turned towards Macina, his poor heart withering with homesickness for the vast expanses. He walked again for moons and moons. Finally one evening he reached the shores of the Niger. Huge flocks had crossed the swollen and swift river that day. The shepherds, dead tired, chatted around a small fire, blazing high. Mawdo came up to the fire to warm his numb and crippled limbs when he heard:

— I tell you it wasn't so long ago as all that.

— I'm sure it was longer ago. Listen, my father told me it was "the year of the fart."

Hearing this, old Mawdo turned around, disappeared into the night and went to finish his last days far, far to the South . . .

N'Gor Sène had never heard of the misfortunes of Mawdo, the poor old Peulh; however, from the time he could tell his right hand from his left, he had always refused to eat beans.

In whatever way they were prepared, with whatever sauce they were dressed, peppery peanut sauce or sour sorrel sauce, whatever meat accompanied them: goat chops or mutton necks, slices of beef or of antelope, N'Gor had never touched a *niébé*. Never had a single bean entered his mouth.

Everyone knew that N'Gor was "the one who eats no beans." But, explain it as you will, no one ever called him any longer by his given name. For everyone he had become N'Gor Niébé, for the people in his village and for those in the whole country.

Annoyed by seeing him always refuse to crouch down beside a calabash where the black nose of a niébé appeared, his friends pledged to each other one day to make him eat some.

N'Dèné was a fine-looking young woman with firm breasts and a taut, rounded bottom, with a body as supple as a creeper. N'Dèné was N'Gor Sène's sweetheart. It was she whom N'Gor's friends sought out. They said to her:

"N'Dèné, we'll give you whatever you want: boubous, pagnes, silver and necklaces, if you succeed in getting N'Gor to eat niébés. He's really beginning to amaze us, his brothers, because he won't even tell us the reasons for his refusal. There's no injunction against beans for his family."

Promise pagnes and jewels to a pretty young woman, a charmer! What wouldn't she do to earn them? How far wouldn't she go? To get someone to eat a dish which no tradition forbids him to touch, someone who says he loves you and who proves it every evening? Doubtless, nothing could be easier, and N'Dèné promised in her turn.

For three nights, after the griots, musicians and singers (who had entertained the young lovers) took their leave, N'Dèné showed herself more thoughtful and more tender than usual. Without sleeping a single instant, she massaged, she fanned, she caressed N'Gor, singing him sweet songs, and uttering tender words. The morning of the third night N'Gor asked her:

—N'Dèné, my sister, my darling, what do you want of me?

—N'Gor, my uncle, said the young woman, my love, everyone claims that you won't eat beans, even when prepared by your mother. I'd like you to eat some prepared by me, if only a handful. If you really love me as you say you do, you'll do it and I'll be the only one to know.

—Is that all? That's your greatest desire? Well, my love, tomorrow you'll cook some beans and, when the earth has grown cool, I shall eat them, if that's the proof you need of my great love.

That evening N'Dèné cooked some beans, seasoned them with peanut sauce, added hot pepper, cloves, and so many other spices that they no longer smelled or tasted like beans.

When N'Gor turned over in his second sleep, N'Dèné woke him gently by stroking his head and offered him the appetizing calabash.

N'Gor got up, washed his right hand, sat down on the mat near the calabash, and said to his sweetheart:

—N'Dèné, is there a person in Diakaw to whom you'd give your nose to save her life, if she had just lost hers, a person whose heart is one with yours, a friend for whom you have no secrets, a single person in whom you confide openly?

—Yes, said N'Dèné.

—Who is it?

—It's Thioro.

—Go fetch her.

N'Dèné went to bring her closest friend. When Thioro arrived, N'Gor asked her:

—Thioro, have you a close friend, the only person in the world to whom you open your heart?

—Yes, said Thioro, it's N'Goné.

—Go tell N'Goné to come.

Thioro went to fetch N'Goné, her closer-than-sister.

When N'Goné arrived, N'Gor asked her:

—N'Goné, do you have one person in the whole world for whom your tongue hides no secret, for whom your heart is as clear as the day?

—Yes, it's Djégane, said the young woman.

Djégane came and responded to N'Gor's question that it was with Sira that she shared her secrets. N'Gor told her to bring Sira, her close friend. Sira came and then went to fetch the only confidante of her life, Khary. Khary went off and brought back the friend with whom she shared her most intimate secrets. So it went on until N'Gor, squatting before the calabash of beans in his hut, found himself surrounded by twelve women who had come, each one called by another.

—N'Dèné, my sister, he then said, I shall never eat beans. If I had eaten the beans you prepared this evening, tomorrow all these women would have known it, and from close friend to close friend, from wife to husband, from husband to relatives, from relatives to neighbors, from neighbors to acquaintances, the whole village and the whole country would have learned it.

And N'Gor Sèné went back to his own hut in the night, thinking it was Kotje Barma's first quip that was right: "give your love to a woman but not your trust."

■ **A. C. Jordan (1906–1968)**
*South Africa* (story)

TRANSLATED AND RETOLD BY AUTHOR FROM XHOSA

A[rchibald] C[ambell] Jordan, like many South African writers, though thoroughly South African in birth, education, and native language, chose exile in the last years of his life rather than contend with the oppressions of apartheid. Jordan was born at Mbokothwana Mission in Cape Province and educated at the University of South Africa in Fort Hare and finally at the University of Cape Town, where he took his Ph.D. in 1956. During these long years, he taught in high schools and wrote a novel in his native Xhosa, *Inggoumvo yeminyanya* (*The Wrath of the Ancestral Spirits;* 1940). After first being denied a passport to leave South Africa, eventually he was able to leave in 1961; he went to UCLA for two years and, in 1963, attended the University of Wisconsin, first as a visiting fellow and in 1964 as a professor of African languages and literature. Jordan's major contribution lies in that wondrously confused gray area between originality and creation: translation. He interpreted and retold in English a fantastic Xhosa legend, "The King of Waters," and to the extent that his graceful shaping of the myth entered the English language, he expanded the linguistic contours of English and also revealed an African territory previously inaccessible to most English readers.

FURTHER READING: Jordan, A. C. *Inggoumvo yeminyanya (The Wrath of the Ancestral Spirits),* 1940.

## The King of the Waters

It came about, according to some tale, that Tfulako, renowned hunter and son of a great chief, was returning home with his youthful comrades after a hunt that had lasted many days. On a misty night, they lost their way in the forests, and when the next day dawned, they found they were travelling on a wide plain of bare, barren land that they had never seen before. As the day strengthened towards midday, it became very hot. The youths had plenty of baggage—skins and skulls of big game, carcasses of smaller game as well as their clothes and hunting equipment. They felt hungry and thirsty, but there was no point in camping where there were no trees, no firewood, and no water. So they walked on wearily, their baggage becoming heavier and heavier, their stomachs feeling emptier, their lips dry, and their throats burning hot with thirst.

At last, just as the sun was beginning to slant towards the west, they suddenly came upon a fertile stretch of low land lying between two mountains. At the foot of the mountains there was a grove of big tall trees surrounding a beautiful fountain of icy-cold water. With shouts of joy the youthful hunters laid down their baggage on the green grass in the shade and made for the fountain. They took turns stooping and drinking in groups. Tfulako was in the last group, together with his immediate subordinates. When he knelt and bent down to drink, the fountain suddenly dried up, and so did the stream flowing from the fountain. All the youths fell back, startled. They exchanged glances but said nothing. Tfulako stood a little while gazing at the fountain, and then he motioned his subordinates to come forward, kneel and bend down again. They obeyed his order, and the fountain filled and the water began to flow as before. Tfulako stepped forward, knelt beside them, but as soon as he bent down to drink, the water vanished. He withdrew, and the water appeared again, and his comrades drank their fill. Tfulako walked silently back to his place in the shade, and from there he gave a signal that all must draw near.

'Comrades,' he said, 'you all saw what happened just now. I assure you I don't know what it means. You all know me well. I've never practised sorcery. I don't remember doing any evil before or during or after this hunt. Therefore I've nothing to confess to you, my comrades. It looks as if this matter has its own depth, a depth that cannot be known to any of our age-group here. However, I charge you to go about your duties in preparation for our day's feast—wood-gathering, lighting of fires, flaying of carcasses, and roasting—as if nothing had happened. We'll feast and enjoy ourselves, but before I leave this fountain, I must drink, for we don't know where and when we'll find water again in this strange land.'

The youths went about their assigned duties, some flaying the wild game, some collecting wood, some kindling the fires, some cutting off titbits from the half-flayed carcasses and roasting them, so that while the main feast was preparing the company could remove the immediate hunger from their eyes, and stop their mouths watering. Tfulako tried to eat some titbits too, but this aggravated his thirst. So he went to stand some distance away from his comrades and watched the fountain. It had filled again, and the water was streaming down the valley as it had been doing when they first came upon this strange place.

When the main feast was ready, he joined his comrades as he had promised, but found it impossible to eat because of his burning throat. So he just sat there and joined in the chat, trying to share in all the youthful jokes that accompanied feasting. The meat naturally made all of them thirsty again. So once more they took turns drinking from the fountain. Once more Tfulako came forward with his own group, but once more the fountain dried up as soon as he bent down to drink.

There could be no doubt now. It was he and he alone who must not drink, he alone who must die of thirst and hunger, he, son of the great chief. But what power was it that controlled this fountain? He moved away from the fountain and thought deeply. He had heard tales of the King of the Waters who could make rivers flow or dry at will. He concluded that the King of the Waters, whoever he was and whatever he looked like, must be in this fountain, that this King must have recognized him as the son of the great chief, that this King must have resolved that the son of the great chief must either pay a great price for the water from this fountain or die of thirst. What price was he expected to pay? Then suddenly he turned about, walked up to the brink of the fountain and, in sheer desperation, called out aloud: 'King of the Waters! I die of thirst. Allow me to drink, and I will give you the most beautiful of my sisters to be your wife.'

At once the fountain filled, and Tfulako bent down and quenched his thirst while all his comrades looked on in silence. Then he had his share of meat.

After this the whole company felt relaxed, and the youths stripped and bathed in the cool stream to refresh themselves for the long journey before them. Tfulako took part in all this and enjoyed himself as if he had forgotten what had just happened. Towards sunset, they filled their gourds with water from the fountain, picked up their baggage and resumed their journey home. On the afternoon of the fourth day, they were within the domain of their great chief and, to announce their approach, they chanted their favourite hunting-song:

> Ye ha he! Ye ha he!
> A mighty whirlwind, the buffalo!
> Make for your homes, ye who fear him.
> They chase them far! They chase them near!
> As for us, we smite the lively ones

And we leave the wounded alone.
Ye ha he! Ye ha he!
A mighty whirlwind, the buffalo!

So Tfulako and his comrades entered the gates of the Royal Place, amid the praises of the bards and the cheering of the women.

Tfulako took the first opportunity, when the excitement over the return of the hunters had died down, to report to his people what had happened at the fountain. No one, not even the oldest councillors, had any idea what the King of the Waters looked like. Most of them thought that since he lived in the water, he might look like a giant otter or giant reptile, while others expressed the hope that he was a man-like spirit. But everybody, including the beautiful princess, felt that this was the only offer Tfulako could have made in the circumstances. So they awaited the coming of the King of the Waters.

One afternoon, after many moons had died, a terrible cyclone approached the Royal Place. On seeing it, the people ran quickly into their huts and fastened the doors. As it drew nearer, the cyclone narrowed itself and made straight for the girls' hut where the beautiful princess and the other girls were but instead of sweeping the hut before it, as cyclones usually do, this one folded itself and vanished at the door.

When calm was restored, the girls discovered that they were in the company of a snake of enormous length. Its girth was greater than the thigh of a very big man. They had never seen a snake of such size before. This then, they concluded, must be Nkanyamba, King of the Waters, come to claim his bride. One by one the girls left the hut, until the princess was left alone with the bridegroom. She decided to follow the other girls, but as soon as she rose to go the King of the Waters unfolded quickly, coiled himself round her body, rested his head on her breasts and gazed hungrily into her eyes.

The princess ran out of the hut with her burden round her body and, without stopping to speak to anybody at the Royal Place, she set out on a long, long journey to her mother's people, far over the mountains. As she went, she sang in a high-pitched, wailing voice:

> *Ndingatsi ndihumntfan' abo Tfulako,*
> *Ndingatsi ndihumntfan' abo Tfulako,*
> *Ndilale nesibitwa ngokutsiwa hinyoka, nyoka?*

> Can I, a daughter of Tfulako's people,
> Can I, a daughter of Tfulako's people,
> Sleep with that which is called a snake, snake?

I reply, the King of the Waters sang in a deep voice:

> *Ndingatsi ndimlelelele ndinje, ndinje,*
> *Ndingatsi ndimlelelele ndinje, ndinje,*
> *Ndingalali nesibitwa ngokutsiwa humfati, fati lo?*

> Long and graceful that I am, so graceful,
> Long and graceful that I am, so graceful,
> May I not sleep with that which is called a woman, a mere woman?

And so they travelled through forest and ravine, the whole night and the following day, singing pride at each other.

At nightfall they reached the home of the princess's mother's people. But the princess decided to wait in the shadows for a while. When she was sure that there was no one in the girls' hut, she entered there unnoticed and closed the door. Then for the first time she addressed herself directly to her burden:

> King of the Waters, mighty one!
> Sole possessor of the staff of life!
> Thou that makest the rivers flow or dry at will!
> Saviour of the lives of thirsty hunters!
> Thou that comest borne on the wings of mighty storms!
> Thou of many coils, long and graceful!

By this time, the King of the Waters had raised his head from its pillowed position and was listening. So the princess went on: 'I am tired, covered with the dust of the road and ugly. I pray you, undo yourself and rest here while I go announce the great news of your royal visit to my mother's people. Then I shall also take a little time to wash and dress myself in a manner befitting the hostess of the greatest of kings, Nkanyamba the Mighty, Nkanyamba the King of the Waters.'

Without a word, the King of the Waters unwound himself and slithered to the far end of the hut where he coiled himself into a great heap that almost reached the thatch roof.

The princess went straight to the Great Hut and there, weeping, she told the whole story to her uncle and his wife. They comforted her and assured her that they would rid her of the Nkanyamba that same night, if only she would be brave and intelligent. She brushed away her tears immediately and assured them that she would be brave and determined. Thereupon her mother's brother told his wife to give orders that large quantities of water be boiled so that the princess could have a bath. While these preparations were going on, he took out some ointment and mixed it with some powders that the princess had never seen before. These he gave to his wife and instructed her to anoint the whole of the princess's body as soon as she had had her bath. Then the princess and her aunt disappeared, leaving the head of the family sitting there alone, grim and determined.

When they returned, the princess looked fresh and lovely in her *nkciyo*. She had stripped herself of most of her ornaments. All she had were her glittering brass headring, a necklace whose pendant hung delicately between her breasts, a pair of armlets, and a pair of anklets.

'Your aunt has told you everything you are to do when you get there?' asked her mother's brother, rising to his feet, as they came in.

'Everything, malume,' replied the princess, smiling brightly.

'You're sure you will not make any mistake — doing things too hastily and so on?'

'I'm quite cool now, malume. You can be sure that I'll do everything at the right moment.'

Then the head of the family produced a beautiful kaross, all made of leopard-skins, unfolded it, and covered his sister's daughter with it. 'Go now my sister's child. I'm sure you'll be more than a match for this — this snake!'

The princess walked briskly back to the girls' hut. Once inside, she threw off the kaross and addressed the King of the Waters: 'King of the Waters, Here I stand, I, daughter of the people of Tfulako, ready for the embrace of Nkanyamba, the tall and graceful.'

As she said these words, she stretched out her beautiful arms invitingly to the King of the Waters.

This invitation was accepted eagerly, but when the King of the Waters tried to hold her in his coils, he slipped down and fell with a thud on the floor. Smiling and chiding him, the princess once more stretched out her arms and invited him to have another try. He tried again, but again he fell on the floor with a thud. Once again the princess stretched out her arms encouragingly, but again the King of the Waters found her body so slippery that for all his coils and scales he could not hold her. This time he slipped down and fell with such a heavy thud on the floor that he seemed to have lost all strength. He could hardly move his body, and all he could do in response to the princess's invitation was to feast his eyes on her beautiful body.

'It's my mistake, graceful one,' said the princess, lowering her arms. 'In my eagerness to make myself beautiful for the King of the Waters, I put too much ointment on my body. I'll go back to the Great Hut and remove it immediately, then I shall return and claim the embrace I so desire.'

With these words, she picked up her kaross, stepped over the threshold, and fastened the door securely from outside. Her uncle and aunt were ready with a blazing firebrand, and as soon as she had fastened the door, they handed it to her without saying a word. She grabbed it and ran round the hut, setting the grass thatch alight at many points, and finally she thrust the firebrand into the thatch just above the door. The grass caught fire at once, and the flames lit the entire homestead.

No sound of any struggle on the part of the King of the Waters in the burning hut. He had lost all power. No power to lift his body from the ground. No power to summon the wings of mighty storms to bear him away from the scorching flames. The King of the Waters was burned to death.

Everything happened so quickly that by the time the neighbours came, nothing was left except the crackling wood.

'What happened? What happened?' asked one neighbour after another.

'It's only one of those things that happen because we are in this world.'

'Is everybody safe in your household?' they asked.

'Everybody is safe. It's a pleasant event, my neighbours. Go and sleep in peace. When the present moon dies, I'll invite you all to a great feast in honour of my sister's beautiful daughter here. Then will I tell you all there is to tell about the evil we've just destroyed.'

The following morning the head of the family rose up early and went to examine the scene of the fire very carefully. He found that although the body of the Nkanyamba had been reduced to ashes, bones and all, the skull was intact. He picked it up and examined it. Then he collected some wood, piled it on the ashes and set fire to it. He then picked out the brains of the Nkanyamba from every little cranny, and let them fall on the fire. Then he scraped the inside of the skull, removing every little projection and making it as smooth as a clay pot. All the matter removed fell on to the fire and burned out completely. He took the skull indoors and washed it thoroughly with boiling-hot water, and then rubbed it thoroughly with the remnants of the grease and powder that had been used by the princess on the previous night.

Meanwhile the princess was in a deep sleep, nor did she wake up at all until the early afternoon. Her aunt had given orders that no one was to go into the hut where she was sleeping, except herself, for a whole day and night. So, after putting the Nkanyamba's skull away, the head of the family went about his daily duties and kept away from his niece's hut. But on the following morning, as soon as he knew that the princess was awake, he went to see her, taking the skull with him. The princess shuddered a little when she saw it.

'Touch it, child of my sister,' said her uncle. 'Touch it, and all fear of it will go.'

The princess touched it, but noticing that she still shuddered, her uncle withdrew it, sat beside her and chatted a little.

Later in the day, the head and mistress of the house discussed the condition of the princess. They agreed that her cousins could enter her hut and sit and chat with her as long as they wished, but that she must remain in bed until all signs of fear had disappeared. So every morning her uncle took the skull to her and made her handle it. When he was quite satisfied that she did not shudder any more, he told his wife that the princess was now ready to get up and live normally with the rest of the family.

One day the head and mistress of the family were sitting and chatting with the princess in the Great Hut when the princess casually rose and walked across the floor, took the Nkanyamba's skull down from its place on the wall and turned it over and over in her hands, while all the time she carried on with the conversation as if not thinking about the skull at all. The two elderly people exchanged glances, nodded to each other and smiled.

'Now I can see she's ready to go back to her parents,' said the head of the family as soon as he and his wife were alone. 'She doesn't fear that skull any more now. It's just like any other vessel in the house. So we can proceed with the preparations.'

Two—three days passed, and a great feast was held in honour of the princess. All the neighbours came, and the head of the family told them the whole story of Tfulako's promise to the King of the Waters, and what happened thereafter. The neighbours praised the princess for her bravery and thanked their neighbour on behalf of the parents and brother of the girl. The uncle then pointed out five head of cattle that he was giving to his sister's child to take home. Then one after another his well-to-do friends and neighbours rose to make little speeches, thanking him for the gift to his sister's child, and adding their own 'little calves to accompany their neighbour's gift', until there were well over two tens of cattle in all. After each gift of a 'little calf', the princess kissed the right hand of the giver. Then it was the uncle's turn to thank his neighbours for making him a somebody by enriching so much the gift that his sister's child would take home with her.

The village mothers had withdrawn to a separate part of the homestead, and while the men were making gifts in cattle, the women were making a joint present consisting of mats, pots, bowls and ornaments of all kinds. When these had been collected, the head of the family was asked to accompany the princess to come and see them. Some of the elderly mothers made little speeches, presented the 'small gift' to the princess on behalf of the whole motherhood, and wished her a happy journey back home. Both the head and the mistress of the family thanked the mothers.

Before the festivities came to an end, the young men of the village sent spokesmen to their fathers, reminding them that the princess would need an escort.

'We know that very well,' said one of the elderly men with a smile. 'But you can't all go. And let me remind you that those of you who are going will have not only to drive the cattle but also to carry all those pots and other things that your mothers have loaded the princess with.'

'We understand, father,' replied the chief spokesman. 'We are ready to carry everything. We have already agreed too that it would be fitting that the princess be escorted by those of the age-group of her brother, Tfulako.'

'You've done well,' murmured some of the men.

A few days later, while the princess was being helped by her aunt to pack her belongings, the head of the family brought the beautiful kaross that the princess had worn on the night of the killing of the Nkanyamba. The princess accepted it very gratefully and embraced her uncle for the wonderful gift. Then he produced the Nkanyamba's skull and would hand it over to her.

'What am I to do with this thing, malume?' asked the princess, much surprised.

'It's yours,' replied her uncle. 'It was you who carried the King of the Waters all the way from your home village so that you could destroy him here.'

The princess received the skull with both hands, thanked her uncle, looked at it for a little while and smiled.

'I know what I'll do with this,' she said as she packed it away.

'Aren't we going to be told this great secret?' asked her uncle.

'In truth it's no secret to you two,' replied the princess. 'Some day, some day when my brother Tfulako becomes the chief of our people, I'll give this to him to use as a vessel for washing.'

'You have a mind, child of my sister,' remarked her uncle.

'Why do you say that, malume?'

'Because that was exactly what I hoped you would do with it.'

It was a pleasant journey for the princess and her male cousins and other young men of her brother's age-group. They did not take their journey hurriedly, for they must allow the cattle to graze as they went along. They themselves camped and rested whenever they came to a particularly beautiful place. They sang as they travelled and, among other songs, the princess taught them the songs that she and the King of the Waters had sung to each other in these same forests and ravines. She sang her high-pitched song, and the young men sang the song of the King of the Waters in a chorus.

When they approached the Royal Place on the afternoon of the third day of their journey, they started to sing this song aloud. The song was heard and immediately recognized by all those villagers who had heard it on the day of the cyclone. The princess's voice was recognized as hers, but the many deep voices remained a puzzle.

No one had seen Tfulako run into his hut to grab his spears and shield, but there he was, standing alone near the gate, shading his eyes in order to have the first glimpse of the singers who were about to appear on the horizon.

When the singers and the herd of cattle came in sight, he concluded that his sister was in the company of the Nkanyamba she loathed, together with a whole troop of followers driving the customary bride-tribute of cattle.

'What!' he exclaimed, blazing with anger. 'Does this mean that my sister has been burdened with this hateful snake all this time? I'm going to get my sister free!' And he took one leap over the closed gate.

'Wait, Son of the Beautiful!' shouted the councillors. 'You're going into danger. Wait until they get here.'

'I'll never allow those snakes to enter this gate. I don't want any of their cattle in the folds of my fathers. If no one will come with me, I'll fight them alone. Let him bring all the nkanyambas in the world, I'll die fighting for my sister.'

And he ran to meet the singers.

Before he had reached them, however, all the hunters of his age-group were with him. For the women of the Royal Place had raised the alarm, and it had been taken up by other women throughout the village, and from one village to another, so that in no time all the youths had grabbed their spears and shields and followed the direction indicated by the cries of the womenfolk.

The singing suddenly stopped, and there were bursts of laughter from the princess's escort.

'Withhold your spears!' shouted one of them. 'The enemy you're looking for is not here. That which was he is now ashes at Tfulako's mother's people. Here's Tfulako's sister, beautiful as the rising sun.'

And the princess stepped forward to meet her brother who had already leapt forward to meet her. They embraced with affection.

'Forgive me, my father's child,' said Tfulako, deeply moved.

But the princess would not allow her brother to shed a tear in the presence of other young men. She laughed, disengaged herself and stepped away from him.

'Forgive you what?' she asked. 'Forgive you for giving me a chance to prove that I am the worthy sister of Tfulako, killer of buffaloes?'

Before Tfulako could reply, she started to sing his favourite hunting-song, altering the words to suit the event. By this time, the youths of the two groups had mingled together in a friendly manner. As soon as they took up the song, she pulled out the Nkanyamba's skull and, holding it high, she led the march into the village and through the gates of the Royal Place:

Ye ha he! Ye ha he!
A mighty whirlwind, the Nkanyamba!
Fasten your doors, ye who fear him.
They chase them far! They chase them near!
As for us, we scorch the cyclone-borne
And we carry their skulls aloft.
Ye ha he! Ye ha he!
A mighty whirlwind, the Nkanyamba!

## ■ Doris Lessing (1919– ), *Zimbabwe/London* (story)

Doris Lessing was born in Kermansha, Iran (Persia). At five her family moved to Zimbabwe (then, Southern Rhodesia) where her father, formerly a banker, became a farmer. At age fifteen, she left school, took diverse ordinary jobs, became a political activist, and for a while a member of the Communist Party. She gave herself to the cause of justice for black Africans. At thirty, she was forced into political exile. Thereafter, except for visits to Africa, she has spent her life in London. In England, she completed her experiences in Africa by turning her novel manuscript into her first published novel, *The Grass Is Singing* (1950), and the following year, she published a book of stories, *This Was the Old Chief's Country*. Her

*African Stories* first appeared in 1963. It carries a preface that reveals her poignant addiction to the African continent:

> I believe that the chief gift from Africa to writers, white and black, is the continent itself, its presence which for some people is like an old fever, latent always in their blood; or like an old wound throbbing in the bones as the air changes. That is not a place to visit unless one chooses to be an exile ever afterwards from an inexplicable majestic silence lying just over the border of memory or of thought. Africa gives you the knowledge that man is a small creature, among other creatures, in a large landscape.[1]

A masterful and worldwide artist, dedicated to socialism and to exploring the traumas of the mind, Lessing has championed women and the economic plight of black Africans. As a radical in politics and a strong feminist, she traces the breakdown of the individual—sometimes the singular artist—in a restrictive and coercive society. Prolific, didactic, sometimes realistic, frequently experimental, she changes her art and passions with each new volume. Her most famous book has been *The Golden Notebook* (1962), a novel in part realistically conventional, in part lyrically experimental, that describes a woman writer's experience as revealed in her notebook. In the end, the segments of the work come triumphantly together in the *Golden Notebook*. Of her many novels, those that deal more distinctly with madness, neurosis, and destructive relations between man and women are *Briefing for a Descent into Hell* (1971) and *The Summer before the Dark* (1973). She also has an allegorical, messianic side in visionary novels of the future, including *Shikasta* (1979), *The Marriages between Zones Three, Four, and Five* (1980), and *The Sirian Experiments* (1981). More recently, she has published the provocative books *The Good Terrorists* (1985) and *Prisons We Choose to Live By* (1987).

**FURTHER READING:** Lessing, Doris. *The Grass is Singing*, 1950; *This Was the Old Chief's Country*, 1951; *The Habit of Loving*, 1958; *The Golden Notebook*, 1962; *African Stories*, 1963; *Shikasta*, 1979; *The Marriages between Zones Three, Four, and Five*, 1980; *The Sirian Experiments*, 1981; *Briefing for a Descent into Hell*, 1971; *The Summer before the Dark*, 1973; *The Good Terrorist*, 1985; *Prisons We Choose to Live By*, 1987.

## Out of the Fountain

I could begin, There was once a man called Ephraim who lived in . . . but for me this story begins with a fog. Fog in Paris delayed a flight to London by a couple of hours, and so a group of travellers sat around a table drinking coffee and entertaining each other.

---

1. Doris Lessing, *African Stories* (New York: Simon & Schuster, 1961), 10.

A woman from Texas joked that a week before she had thrown coins into the fountain in Rome for luck—and had been dogged by minor ill-fortune ever since. A Canadian said she had spent far too much money on a holiday and at the same fountain three days ago had been tempted to lift coins out with a magnet when no one was looking. Someone said that in a Berlin theatre last night there had been a scene where a girl flung money all about the stage in a magnificently scornful gesture. Which led us on to where money is trampled on, burned, flung about or otherwise ritually scorned; which is odd, since such gestures never take place in life. Not at all, said a matron from New York—she had seen with her own eyes some Flower Children burning money on a sidewalk to show their con-tempt for it; but for her part what it showed was that they must have rich parents. (This dates the story, or at least the fog.)

All the same, considering the role money plays in all our lives, it is odd how often authors cause characters to insult dollar bills, roubles, pound notes. Which enables audience, readers, to go home, or to shut the book, feeling cleansed of the stuff? Above it?

Whereas we are told that in less surly days sultans on feast days flung gold coins into crowds happy to scramble for it; that kings caused showers of gold to descend on loved ministers; and that if jewels fell in showers from the sky no one would dream of asking suspicious questions.

The nearest any one of us could remember to this kingly stuff was a certain newspaper mogul in London who would reward a promising young journalist for an article which he (the mogul) liked, with an enve-lope stuffed full of five-pound notes sent around by special messenger—but this kind of thing is only too open to unkind interpretation; and the amount of ill-feeling aroused in the bosoms of fellow journalists, and the terror in that of the recipient for fear the thing might be talked about, is probably why we stage such scenes as it were in reverse, and why, on the edge of a magic fountain, we slide in a single coin, like a love letter into an envelope during an affair which one's better sense entirely deplores. Sym-pathetic magic—but a small magic, a mini-magic, a most furtive summon-ing of the Gods of Gold. And, if a hand rose from the fountain to throw us coins and jewels, it is more than likely that, schooled as we are by recent literature, we'd sneer and throw them back in its teeth—so to speak.

And now a man who had not spoken at all said that he knew of a case where jewels had been flung into the dust of a public square in Italy. No one had thrown them back. He took from his pocket a wallet, and from the wallet a fold of paper such as jewellers use, and on the paper lay a sin-gle spark or gleam of light. It was a slice of milk-and-rainbow opal. Yes, he said, he had been there. He had picked up the fragment and kept it. It wasn't valuable, of course. He would tell us the story if he thought there was time, but for some reason it was a tale so precious to him that he didn't want to bungle it through having to hurry. Here there was another swirl of silkily gleaming fog beyond the glass of the restaurant wall, and an-other announcement of unavoidable delay.

So he told the story. One day someone will introduce me to a young man called Nikki (perhaps, or what you will) who was born during the Second World War in Italy. His father was a hero, and his mother now the wife of the Ambassador to . . . Or perhaps in a bus, or at a dinner party, there will be a girl who has a pearl hanging around her neck on a chain, and when asked about it she will say: Imagine, my mother was given this pearl by a man who was practically a stranger, and when she gave it to me she said . . . Something like that will happen: and then this story will have a different beginning, not a fog at all . . .

There was a man called Ephraim who lived in Johannesburg. His father was to do with diamonds, as had been his father. The family were immigrants. This is still true of all people from Johannesburg, a city a century old. Ephraim was a middle son, not brilliant or stupid, not good or bad. He was nothing in particular. His brothers became diamond merchants, but Ephraim was not cut out for anything immediately obvious, and so at last he was apprenticed to an uncle to learn the trade of diamond-cutting.

To cut a diamond perfectly is an act like a samurai's sword-thrust, or a master archer's centred arrow. When an important diamond is shaped a man may spend a week, or even weeks, studying it, accumulating powers of attention, memory, intuition, till he has reached that moment when he finally knows that a tap, no more, at just *that* point of tension in the stone will split it exactly *so*.

While Ephraim learned to do this, he lived at home in a Johannesburg suburb; and his brothers and sisters married and had families. He was the son who took his time about getting married, and about whom the family first joked, saying that he was choosy; and then they remained silent when others talked of him with that edge on their voices, irritated, a little malicious, even frightened, which is caused by those men and women who refuse to fulfil the ordinary purposes of nature. The kind ones said he was a good son, working nicely under his uncle Ben, and living respectably at home, and on Sunday nights playing poker with bachelor friends. He was twenty-five, then thirty, thirty-five, forty. His parents became old and died, and he lived alone in the family house. People stopped noticing him. Nothing was expected of him.

Then a senior person became ill, and Ephraim was asked to fly in his stead to Alexandria for a special job. A certain rich merchant of Alexandria had purchased an uncut diamond as a present for his daughter, who was to be married shortly. He wished only the best for the diamond. Ephraim, revealed by this happening as one of the world's master diamond-cutters, flew to Egypt, spent some days in communion with the stone in a quiet room in the merchant's house, and then caused it to fall apart into three lovely pieces. These were for a ring and earrings.

Now he should have flown home again; but the merchant asked him to dinner. An odd chance that—unusual. Not many people got inside that rich closed world. But perhaps the merchant had become infected by the week of rising tension while Ephraim became one with the diamond in a quiet room.

At dinner Ephraim met the girl for whom the jewels were destined.

And now—but what can be said about the fortnight that followed? Certainly not that Ephraim, the little artisan from Johannesburg, fell in love with Mihrène, daughter of a modern merchant prince. Nothing so simple. And that the affair had about it a quality out of the ordinary was shown by the reaction of the merchant himself, Mihrène's conventional papa.

Conventional, commonplace, banal—these are the words for the members of the set, or class, to which Mihrène Kantannis belonged. In all the cities about the Mediterranean they live in a scattered community, very rich, but tastefully so, following international fashions, approving Paris when they should and London when they should, making trips to New York or Rome, summering on whichever shore they have chosen, by a kind of group instinct, to be the right one for the year, and sharing comfortably tolerant opinions. They were people, are people, with nothing remarkable about them but their wealth, and the enchanting Mihrène, whom Ephraim first saw in a mist of white embroidered muslin standing by a fountain, was a girl neither more pretty nor more gifted than, let's say, a dozen that evening in Alexandria, a thousand or so in Egypt, hundreds of thousands in the countries round about, all of which produce so plentifully her particular type—her beautiful type: small-boned, black-haired, black-eyed, apricot-skinned, lithe.

She had lived for twenty years in this atmosphere of well-chosen luxury; loved and bickered with her mother and her sisters; respected her papa; and was intending to marry Paulo, a young man from South America with whom she would continue to live exactly the same kind of life, only in Buenos Aires.

For her it was an ordinary evening, a family dinner at which a friend of Papa's was present. She did not know about the diamonds: they were to be a surprise. She was wearing last year's dress and a choker of false pearls: that season it was smart to wear 'costume' pearls, and to leave one's real pearls in a box on one's dressing-table.

Ephraim, son of jewellers, saw the false pearls around that neck and suffered.

Why, though? Johannesburg is full of pretty girls. But he had not travelled much, and Johannesburg, rough, built on gold, as it were breathing by the power of gold, a city waxing and waning with the fortunes of gold (as befits this story), may be exciting, violent, vibrant, but it has no mystery, nothing for the imagination, no invisible dimensions. Whereas Alexandria . . . This house, for instance, with its discreetly blank outer walls that might conceal anything, crime, or the hidden court of an exiled king, held inner gardens and fountains, and Mihrène, dressed appropriately in moonwhite and who . . . well, perhaps she wasn't entirely at her best that evening. There were those who said she had an ugly laugh.

Sometimes the family joked that it was lucky she would never have to earn a living. At one point during dinner, perhaps feeling that she ought to contribute to the entertainment, she told a rather flat and slightly bitchy story about a friend. She was certainly bored, yawned once or twice, and did not try too hard to hide the yawns. The diamond-cutter from Johannesburg gazed at her, forgot to eat, and asked twice why she wore false pearls in a voice rough with complaint. He was gauche, she decided—and forgot him.

He did not return home, but wired for money. He had never spent any, and so had a great deal available for the single perfect pearl which he spent days looking for, and which he found at last in a back room in Cairo, where he sat bargaining over coffee cups for some days with an old Persian dealer who knew as much about gems as he did, and who would not trade in anything but the best.

With this jewel he arrived at the house of Mihrène's father, and when he was seated in a room opening on to an inner court where jasmine clothed a wall, and lily pads a pool, he asked permission to give the pearl to the young girl.

It had been strange that Papa had invited this tradesman to dinner. It was strange that now Papa did not get angry. He was shrewd: it was his life to be shrewd. There was no nuance of commercial implication in a glance, a tone of voice, a turn of phrase, that he was not certain to assess rightly. Opposite this fabulously rich man into whose house only the rich came as guests, sat a little diamond-cutter who proposed to give his daughter a small fortune in the shape of a pearl, and who wanted nothing in return for it.

They drank coffee, and then they drank whisky, and they talked of the world's jewels and of the forthcoming wedding, until for the second time Ephraim was asked to dinner.

At dinner Mihrène sat opposite the elderly gentleman (he was forty-five or so) who was Papa's business friend, and was ordinarily polite: then slightly more polite, because of a look from Papa. The party was Mihrène, her father, her fiancé Paulo, and Ephraim. The mother and sisters were visiting elsewhere. Nothing happened during the meal. The young couple were rather inattentive to the older pair. At the end, Ephraim took a screw of paper from his pocket, and emptied from it a single perfect pearl that had a gleam like the flesh of a rose, or of a twenty-year-old girl. This pearl he offered to Mihrène, with the remark that she oughtn't to wear false pearls. Again it was harshly inflected; a complaint, or a reproach for imperfect perfection.

The pearl lay on white damask in candlelight. Into the light above the pearl was thrust the face of Ephraim, whose features she could reconstruct from the last time she had seen him a couple of weeks before only with the greatest of difficulty.

It was, of course, an extraordinary moment. But not dramatic—no, it lacked that high apex of decisiveness as when Ephraim tapped a diamond, or an archer lets loose his bow. Mihrène looked at her father for an explanation. So, of course, did her fiancé. Her father did not look confused, or embarrassed, so much as that he wore the air of somebody standing on one side because here is a situation which he has never professed himself competent to judge. And Mihrène had probably never before in her life been left free to make a decision.

She picked up the pearl from the damask, and let it lie in her palm. She, her fiancé, and her father, looked at the pearl whose value they were all well equipped to assess, and Ephraim looked sternly at the girl. Then she lifted long, feathery black lashes and looked at him—in inquiry? An appeal to be let off? His eyes were judging, disappointed; they said what his words had said: Why are you content with the second-rate?

Preposterous . . .

Impossible . . .

Finally Mihrène gave the slightest shrug of shoulders, tonight covered in pink organza, and said to Ephraim, 'Thank you, thank you very much.'

They rose from the table. The four drank coffee on the terrace over which rose a wildly evocative Alexandrian moon, two nights away from the full, a moon quite unlike any that might shine over strident Johannesburg. Mihrène let the pearl lie on her palm and reflect moonrays, while from time to time her black eyes engaged with Ephraim's—but what colour his were had never been, would never be, of interest to anyone—and, there was no doubt of it, he was like someone warning, or reminding, or even threatening.

Next day he went back to Johannesburg, and on Mihrène's dressing-table lay a small silver box in which was a single perfect pearl.

She was to marry in three weeks.

Immediately the incident became in the family: 'That crazy little Jew who fell for Mihrène . . .' Her acceptance of the pearl was talked of as an act of delicacy on her part, of kindness. 'Mihrène was so kind to the poor old thing . . .' Thus they smoothed over what had happened, made acceptable an incident which could have no place in their life, their thinking. But they knew, of course, and most particularly did Mihrène know, that something else had happened.

When she refused to marry Paulo, quite prettily and nicely, Papa and Mamma Kantannis made ritual remarks about her folly, her ingratitude, and so forth, but in engagements like these no hearts are expected to be broken, for the marriages are like the arranged marriages of dynasties. If she did not marry Paulo, she would marry someone like him—and she was very young.

They remarked that she had not been herself since the affair of the pearl. Papa said to himself that he would see to it no more fly-by-nights arrived at his dinner-table. They arranged for Mihrène a visit to cousins in Istanbul.

Meanwhile in Johannesburg a diamond-cutter worked at his trade, cutting diamonds for engagement rings, dress rings, tie pins, necklaces, bracelets. He imagined a flat bowl of crystal, which glittered like diamonds, in which were massed roses. But the roses were all white, shades of white. He saw roses which were cold marble white, white verging on coffee colour, greenish white, like the wings of certain butterflies, white that blushed, a creamy white, white that was nearly beige, white that was almost yellow. He imagined a hundred shades of white in rose shapes. These he pressed together, filled a crystal dish with them and gave them to— Mihrène? It is possible that already he scarcely thought of her. He imagined how he would collect stones in shades of white, and create a perfect jewel, bracelet, necklet, or crescent for the hair, and present this jewel to—Mihrène? Does it matter whom it was for? He bought opals, like mist held behind glass on which lights moved and faded, like milk where fire lay buried, like the congealed breath of a girl on a frosty night. He bought pearls, each one separately, each one perfect. He bought fragments of mother-of-pearl. He bought moonstones like clouded diamonds. He even bought lumps of glass that someone had shaped to reflect light perfectly. He bought white jade and crystals and collected chips of diamond to make the suppressed fires in pearl and opal flash out in reply to their glittering frost. These jewels he had in folded flat paper, and they were kept first in a small cigarette box, and then were transferred to a larger box that had been for throat lozenges, and then to an even larger box that had held cigars. He played with these gems, dreamed over them, arranged them in his mind in a thousand ways. Sometimes he remembered an exquisite girl dressed in moonmist: the memory was becoming more and more like a sentimental postcard or an old-fashioned calendar.

In Istanbul Mihrène married, without her family's approval, a young Italian engineer whom normally she would never have met. Her uncle was engaged in reconstructing a certain yacht; the engineer was in the uncle's office to discuss the reconstruction when Mihrène came in. It was she who made the first move: it would have to be. He was twenty-seven, with nothing but his salary, and no particular prospects. His name was Carlos. He was political. That is, precisely, he was revolutionary, a conspirator. Politics did not enter the world of Mihrène. Or rather, it could be said that such families are politics, politics in their aspect of wealth, but this becomes evident only when deals are made that are so vast that they have international cachet, and repute, like the alliances or rifts between countries.

Carlos called Mihrène 'a white goose' when she tried to impress him with her seriousness. He called her 'a little rich bitch'. He made a favour of taking her to meetings where desperately serious young men and women discussed the forthcoming war—the year was 1939. It was an affair absolutely within the traditions of such romances: her family were bound to think she was throwing herself away; he and his friends on the whole considered that it was he who was conferring the benefits.

To give herself courage in her determination to be worthy of this young hero, she would open a tiny silver box where a pearl lay on silk, and say to herself: *He* thought I was worth something . . .

She married her Carlos in the week Paulo married a girl from a French dynasty. Mihrène went to Rome and lived in a small villa without servants, and with nothing to fall back on but the memory of a nondescript elderly man who had sat opposite her throughout two long, dull dinners and who had given her a pearl as if he were giving her a lesson. She thought that in all her life no one else had ever demanded anything of her, ever asked anything, ever taken her seriously.

The war began. In Buenos Aires the bride who had taken her place lived in luxury. Mihrène, a poor housewife, saw her husband who was a conspirator against the fascist Mussolini become a conscript in Mussolini's armies, then saw him go away to fight, while she waited for the birth of her first child.

The war swallowed her. When she was heard of again, her hero was dead, and her first child was dead, and her second, conceived on Carlos's final leave, was due to be born in a couple of months. She was in a small town in the centre of Italy with no resources at all but her pride: she had sworn she would not earn the approval of her parents on any terms but her own. The family she had married into had suffered badly: she had a room in the house of an aunt.

The Germans were retreating through Italy: after them chased the victorious armies of the Allies . . . but that sounds like an official war history.

To try again: over a peninsula that was shattered, ruinous, starved by war, two armies of men foreign to the natives of the place were in movement; one in retreat up towards the body of Europe, the other following it. There were places where these opposing bodies were geographically so intermingled that only uniforms distinguished them. Both armies were warm, well clothed, well fed, supplied with alcohol and cigarettes. The native inhabitants had no heat, no warm clothes, little food, no cigarettes. They had, however, a great deal of alcohol.

In one army was a man called Ephraim who, being elderly, was not a combatant, but part of the machinery which supplied it with food and goods. He was a sergeant, and as unremarkable in the army as he was in civilian life. For the four years he had been a soldier, for the most part in North Africa, he had pursued a private interest, or obsession, which was, when he arrived anywhere at all, to seek out the people and places that could add yet another fragment of iridescent or gleaming substance to the mass which he carried around in a flat tin in his pack.

The men he served with found him and his preoccupation mildly humorous. He was not disliked or liked enough to make a target for that concentration of unease caused by people who alarm others. They did not laugh at him, or call him madman. Perhaps he was more like that dog who is a regiment's pet. Once he mislaid his tin of loot and a couple of men went into a moderate danger to get it back: sometimes a comrade would bring him a bit of something or other picked up in a bazaar-amber, an amulet, a jade. He advised them how to make bargains; he went on expeditions with them to buy stones for wives and girls back home.

He was in Italy that week when — *everything disintegrated.* Anyone who has been in, or near, war (which means, by now, everyone, or at least everyone in Europe and Asia) knows that time — a week, days, sometimes hours — when everything falls apart, when all forms of order dissolve, including those which mark the difference between enemy and enemy.

During this time old scores of all kinds are settled. It is when unpopular officers get killed by 'accident'. It is when a man who has an antipathy for another will kill him, or beat him up. A man who wants a woman will rape her, if she is around, or rape another in her stead if she is not. Women get raped; and those who want to be will make sure they are where the raping is. A woman who hates another will harm her. In short, it is a time of anarchy, of looting, of arson and destruction for destruction's sake. There are those who believe that this time out of ordinary order is the reason of war, its hidden justification, its purpose and law, another pattern behind the one we see. Afterwards there are no records of what has happened. There is no one to keep records: everyone is engaged in participating, or in protecting himself.

Ephraim was in a small town near Florence when his war reached that phase. There was a certain corporal, also from Johannesburg, who always had a glitter in his look when they talked of Ephraim's tin full of jewels. On an evening when every human being in the place was hunter or hunted, manoeuvred for advantage, or followed scents of gain, this man, in civilian life a storekeeper, looked across a room at Ephraim and grinned. Ephraim knew what to expect. Everyone knew what to expect — at such moments much older knowledges come to the surface together with old instincts. Ephraim quietly left a schoolroom for that week converted into a mess, and went out into the early dark of streets emptied by fear, where walls still shook and dust fell in clouds because of near gunfire. But it was also very quiet. Terror's cold nausea silences, places invisible hands across mouths . . . The occasional person hurrying through those streets kept his eyes in front, and his mouth tight. Two such people meeting did not look at each other except for a moment when their eyes violently encountered in a hard clash of inquiry. Behind every shutter or pane or door people stood, or sat or crouched, waiting for the time out of order to end, and guns and sharp instruments stood near their hands.

Through these streets went Ephraim. The Corporal had not seen him go, but by now would certainly have found the scent. At any moment he would catch up with Ephraim who carried in his hand a flat tin, and who as he walked looked into holes in walls and in pavements, peered into a church half filled with rubble, investigated torn earth where bomb fragments had fallen and even looked up into the branches of trees as he passed and at the plants growing at doorways. Finally, as he passed a fountain clogged with debris, he knelt for a moment and slid his tin down into the mud. He walked away, fast, not looking back to see if he had been seen, and around the corner of the church he met Corporal Van der Merwe. As Ephraim came up to his enemy he held out empty hands and stood still. The Corporal was a big man and twenty years younger. Van der Merwe gave him a frowning look, indicative of his powers of shrewd assessment, rather like Mihrène's father's look when he heard how this little nonentity proposed to give his daughter a valuable pearl for no reason at all, and when Ephraim saw it, he at once raised his hands above his head like a prisoner surrendering, while Van der Merwe frisked him. There was a moment when Ephraim might very well have been killed: it hung in the balance. But down the street a rabble of soldiers were looting pictures and valuables from another church, and Van der Merwe, his attention caught by them, simply watched Ephraim walk away, and then ran off himself to join the looters.

By the time that season of anarchy had finished, Ephraim was a couple of hundred miles north. Six months later, in a town ten miles from the one where he had nearly been murdered by a man once again his military subordinate (but that incident had disappeared, had become buried in the foreign texture of another time, or dimension), Ephraim asked for an evening's leave and travelled as he could to V—, where he imagined, perhaps, that he would walk through deserted streets to a rubble-filled fountain and beside this fountain would kneel, and slide his hand into dirty water to retrieve his treasure.

But the square was full of people, and though this was not a time when a café served more than a cup of bad coffee or water flavoured with chemicals, the two cafés had people in them who were half starved but already inhabiting the forms of ordinary life. They served, of course, unlimited quantities of cheap wine. Everyone was drunken, or tipsy. In a wine country, when there is no food, wine becomes a kind of food, craved like food. Ephraim walked past the fountain and saw that the water was filthy, too dirty to let anyone see what was in it, or whether it had been cleared of rubble, and, with the rubble, his treasure.

He sat on the pavement under a torn awning, by a cracked wood table, and ordered coffee. He was the only soldier there; or at least, the only uniform. The main tide of soldiery was washing back and forth to one side of this little town. Uniforms meant barter, meant food, clothing, cigarettes. In a moment half a dozen little boys were at his elbow offering him girls. Women of all ages were sauntering past or making themselves visible, or trying to catch his eye, since the female population of the town were for the most part in that condition for which in our debased time we have the shorthand term: being prepared to sell themselves for a cigarette. Old women, old men, cripples, all kinds of person, stretched in front of him hands displaying various more or less useless objects—lighters, watches, old buckles or bottles or brooches—hoping to get chocolate or food in return. Ephraim sat on, sad with himself because he had not brought eggs or tinned stuffs or chocolate. He had not thought of it. He sat while hungry people with sharp faces that glittered with a winy fever pressed about him and the bodies of a dozen or so women arranged themselves in this or that pose for his inspection. He felt sick. He was almost ready to go away and forget his tin full of gems. Then a tired-looking woman in a much-washed print dress lifted high in front because of pregnancy came to sit at his table. He thought she was there to sell herself, and hardly looked at her, unable to bear it that a pregnant woman was brought to such a pass.

She said: 'Don't you remember me?'

And now he searched her face, and she searched his. He looked for Mihrène; and she tried to see in him what it was that changed her life, to find what it was that that pearl embodied which she carried with her in a bit of cloth sewn into her slip.

They sat trying to exchange news; but these two people had so little in common they could not even say: And how is so and so? What has happened to him, or to her?

The hungry inhabitants of the town withdrew a little way, because this soldier had become a person, a man who was a friend of Mihrène, who was their friend.

The two were there for a couple of hours. They were on the whole more embarrassed than anything. It was clear to both by now that whatever events had taken place between them, momentous or not (they were not equipped to say), these events were in some realm or on a level where their daylight selves were strangers. It was certainly not the point that she, the unforgettable girl of Alexandria, had become a rather drab young woman waiting to give birth in a war-shattered town; not the point that for her he had carried with him for four years of war a treasury of gems, some precious, some mildly valuable, some worthless, bits of substance with one thing in common: their value related to some other good which had had, arbitrarily and for a short time, the name *Mihrène*.

It had become intolerable to sit there, over coffee made of burned grain, while all round great hungry eyes focused on him, the soldier, who had come so cruelly to their starving town with empty hands. He had soon to leave. He had reached this town on the back boards of a peasant's cart, there being no other transport; and if he did not get another lift of the same kind, he would have to walk ten miles before midnight.

Over the square was rising a famished watery moon, unlike the moons of his own city, unlike the wild moons of Egypt. At last he simply got up and walked to the edge of the evil-smelling fountain. He kneeled down on its edge, plunged in his hand, encountered all sorts of slimy things, probably dead rats or cats or even bits of dead people, and, after some groping, felt the familiar shape of his tin. He pulled it out, wiped it dry on some old newspaper that had blown there, went back to the table, sat down, opened the tin. Pearls are fed on light and air. Opals don't like being shut away from light which makes their depths come alive. But no water had got in, and he emptied the glittering, gleaming heap on to the cracked wood of the table top.

All round pressed the hungry people who looked at the gems and thought of food.

She took from her breast a bit of cloth and untwisted her pearl. She held it out to him.

'I never sold it,' she said.

And now he looked at her—sternly, as he had done before.

She said, in the pretty English of those who have learned it from governesses: 'I have sometimes needed food, I've been hungry, you know! I've had no servants . . .'

He looked at her. Oh, how she knew that look, how she had studied it in memory! Irritation, annoyance, grief. All these, but above all disappointment. And more than these, a warning, or reminder. It said, she felt: Silly white goose! Rich little bitch! Poor little nothing! Why do you always get it wrong? Why are you stupid? What is a pearl compared with what it stands for? If you are hungry and need money, sell it, of course!

She sat in that sudden stillness that says a person is fighting not to weep. Her beautiful eyes brimmed. Then she said stubbornly: 'I'll never sell it. Never!'

As for him he was muttering: I should have brought food. I was a dummkopf. What's the use of these things . . .

But in the hungry eyes around him he read that they were thinking how even in times of famine there are always men and women who have food hidden away to be bought by gold or jewels.

'Take them,' he said to the children, to the women, to the old people.

They did not understand him, did not believe him.

He said again: 'Go on. Take them!'

No one moved. Then he stood up and began flinging into the air pearls, opals, moonstones, gems of all kinds, to fall as they would. For a few moments there was a mad scene of people bobbing and scrambling, and the square emptied as people raced back to the corners they lived in with what they had picked up out of the dust. It was not yet time for the myth to start, the story of how a soldier had walked into the town, and inexplicably pulled treasure out of the fountain which he flung into the air like a king or a sultan—treasure that was ambiguous and fertile like a king's, since one man might pick up the glitter of a diamond that later turned out to be worthless glass, and another be left with a smallish pearl that had nevertheless been so carefully chosen it was worth months of food, or even a house or small farm.

'I must go,' said Ephraim to his companion.

She inclined her head in farewell, as to an acquaintance re-encountered. She watched a greying, dumpy little man walk away past a fountain, past a church, then out of sight.

Later that night she took out the pearl and held it in her hand. If she sold it, she would remain comfortably independent of her own family. Here, in the circle of the family of her dead husband, she would marry again, another engineer or civil servant: she would be worth marrying, even as a widow with a child. Of course if she returned to her own family, she would also remarry, as a rich young widow with a small child from that dreadful war, luckily now over.

Such thoughts went through her head: at last she thought that it didn't make any difference what she did. Whatever function Ephraim's intervention had performed in her life was over when she refused to marry Paulo, had married Carlos, had come to Italy and given birth to two children, one dead from an unimportant children's disease that had been fatal only because of the quality of war-food, war-warmth. She had been wrenched out of her pattern, had been stamped, or claimed, by the pearl—by something else. Nothing she could do now would put her back where she had been. It did not matter whether she stayed in Italy or returned to the circles she had been born in.

As for Ephraim, he went back to Johannesburg when the war finished, and continued to cut diamonds and to play poker on Sunday nights.

This story ended more or less with the calling of the flight number. As we went to the tarmac where illuminated wisps of fog still lingered, the lady from Texas asked the man who had told the story if perhaps he was Ephraim?

'No,' said Dr Rosen, a man of sixty or so from Johannesburg, a brisk, well-dressed man with nothing much to notice about him—like most of the world's citizens.

No, he was most emphatically not Ephraim.

Then how did he know all this? Perhaps he was there?

Yes, he was there. But if he was to tell us how he came to be a hundred miles from where he should have been, in that chaotic, horrible week—it was horrible, horrible!—and in civvies, then that story would be even longer than the one he had already told us.

Couldn't he tell us why he was there?

Perhaps he was after that tin of Ephraim's too! We could think so if we liked. It would be excusable of us to think so. There was a fortune in that tin, and everyone in the regiment knew it.

He was a friend of Ephraim's then? He knew Ephraim?

Yes, he could say that. He had known Ephraim for, let's see, nearly fifty years. Yes, he thought he could say he was Ephraim's friend.

In the aircraft Dr Rosen sat reading, with nothing more to tell us.

But one day I'll meet a young man called Nikki, or Raffele; or a girl wearing a single pearl around her neck on a gold chain; or perhaps a middle-aged woman who says she thinks pearls are unlucky, she would never touch them herself: a man once gave her younger sister a pearl and it ruined her entire life. Something like that will happen, and this story will have a different shape.

■ **Peter Abrahams (1919– )** *South Africa* **(story)**

Peter Abrahams was the first self-exiled South African writer and a pioneer African figure in English letters. Born in a Johannesburg slum,

Abrahams was still illiterate at age ten, working as a tinsmith's helper, when he was discovered by a young Jewish South African who read him the English classics and encouraged him to start school. His family's poverty forced him to interrupt his schooling to work as a dishwasher, porter, clerk, and whatever other job he could find. At sixteen, he left school for good. Then he began years of wandering on land and sea; yet, by the time he was thirty, he was writing articles for *The London Observer*, which were reprinted in the Paris *Herald Tribune*. Thereafter, he entered English literary life, writing for the BBC Third Programme in the fifties. Eventually, the English government asked him to go to Jamaica to do a book on the island, which resulted in *Jamaica: An Island Mosaic* (1967).

Abrahams has written short stories, novels, poetry, and, of course, journalism. *Mine Boy* (1946), his second novel, is a brutal and moving narration of the life of a child worker in the mines. His third novel, *The Path of Thunder* (1948), details the impossible love of a white Afrikaaner woman and a Coloured. The novel was eventually translated into thirty foreign languages. Perhaps his best book is the historical novel *Wild Conquest* (1951). In addressing the politics of racial inequality, he often wrote with great foresight about the problems African leaders would face as they recovered from colonialism. In the opening passages of his story "Lonesome," the speaker enters the conflicts of race, politics, and sex. Soon, alone and gone mad, he falls into a torrential monologue in which the fears, passions, and ideas of his life dramatically impinge on him, and he has no refuge. Peter Abrahams is one of Africa's most compelling and powerful writers of fiction.

**FURTHER READING:** Abrahams, Peter. *A Blackman Speaks of Freedom!*, 1941; *Mine Boy*, 1946; *The Paths of Thunder*, 1948; *Wild Conquest*, 1951; *Tell Freedom*, 1954; *Jamaica: An Island Mosaic; This Island Now*, 1967; *The View from Coyaba*, 1985.

# Lonesome

I had just arrived in Cape Town when I met her. But that's going too fast. See, on my way down I was happy till I came to the spot. It was a strange spot. I have often wondered since then why the train had to stop there. See, it had so much to do with me afterwards. I could not sleep for nights on end. I kept on thinking about it.

When I thought, I saw everything again. The few houses where the railway siding was. Deep in a valley . . . The earth was green when the train passed there. Beautiful and green. Little grass fingers stretched out to touch the sun. Just like human beings stretching out to touch something they don't know. Funny how people want things they don't know. But that's why it's so good to live . . . I hate philosophers sometimes. I know my friends will say, 'Oh, don't!' You see it's a crime. But I love crimes sometimes. That kind of crime. It's a crime to know so much, and to understand so much, like the philosophers.

What I mean is this. The doctor who delivers the woman of her child is doing a job. Just a job. If he's a new one, there is some excitement in it. But it's still just a job . . . But with you and me it's so different. It's the earth. Generations of earth. Centuries of earth. Timeless earth. It's the earth bursting loose slowly. Coming up and breaking up. Opening up. You know, like a ball of damp earth falling apart. And you see inside it. You see nothing. But it's beautiful to see it, although it's nothing . . . That is what philosophers miss. That's why I hate them sometimes.

The deep valley without the sun. It was early morning. The steward had brought a cup of coffee that was like muddy water. See, I travelled in the coloured carriage, and that is very far from the dining car. So it was muddy and cold . . . But I had had some worse things to drink in my life, and it was all right. I didn't even blame him for charging me a tickey for the cup of cold muddy water. I said, 'Thank you,' very decently, and smiled at him. He just looked at me and took the tickey and went out. I didn't even blame him for that. See, he was white. And you're everything in this country if you are white. Bishop, king, steward, bum, office boy, all of them. You are God's chosen child. Even Mrs Millin says it. She says we coloureds are 'God's step-children', and all the papers review her and say, 'Yea, yea.' So what do I say? Well, just nothing.

But it was beautiful in that little place. After the steward took the tickey and went out I sat down and gulped down the muddy water so I should not get bilious looking at it. It was better inside than out. My insides didn't have eyes, and so could not look at it . . . Then I looked out of the window . . . I should have looked at the houses of the railway officials living at that siding. I know what the houses of the Natives are without looking. I just know. I should have looked at the homes of the officials, but I did not. I looked at the houses of the Native workers who are workers. I say this because in this country you have WORKERS and Workers and workers. The one with the small w is the working-class worker. The one with the big W gets his orders from the one with all the big letters, and passes them on to those with all the small letters. So it's WORKERS and Workers and workers.

If you are fortunate enough to have a sickly-looking fowl-run you will know what I mean . . . Only your fowl-run is usually very well ventilated. These houses were not. Half a dozen or so pieces of corrugated iron. A pole. Usually a rotting tree-trunk. Wire. Rope. String. Rotting planks. Every type of junk . . . Nail these together and you have the houses I saw . . . But I wasn't shocked at all. I just wanted to refresh my memory.

See, it's like this everywhere in this country. You start off at Louis Trichardt or Pietersburg and you go down to Cape Town or Natal. And if you don't travel first, and pull down your blind to flirt with the young lady who got on at the last station, and look around you, and say, 'Poor black things,' and throw a penny when you see little native boys begging at the sidings, and pull down your blind again . . . Mostly you do these things. But if you do not do these things, you will see that everywhere things are like this. Dirt, Death stinking, squalor shouting at you. And you will wonder.

All the people in this country are so used to it all that they do the things I have said. Pull down their blinds. Flirt with the young girl who got on at the last station. Murmur, 'Poor black things.' Throw a tickey and laugh to see the little bags of skin and bone fighting for it.

Poor black things!

This is South Africa. The land of the white man. Stolen from the black man. He says so. I don't. I don't say anything of my own. I have no brain. Niggers are not supposed to have any brain here. It is a crime. Again, my friends say, 'No, you should not say such things. We are white, but we respect your brain. We treat you as our equal, don't we? You must not be a defeatist. Things will come out right. The whites in the country are learning to know that the blacks are as good as they are. You must do your share in educating them.'

Yes. But what am I? Am I a superman? Always understanding? Always doing the right thing? Always the perfect and understanding person? I am human, too. I want to live a sane and rational life. I do not want to work for things that will come when I perhaps am not here. Why should I work for a brave new world that I will not see? I think of the simple things of life, too.

These are the things I spoke to her about when I met her in Cape Town when I had just arrived.

She was good to look at. I think I was a little in love with her. Not really. Just because of the awful loneliness, I think. Somebody to sit with quietly. Somebody to talk to. Somebody to look at. I guess that made me imagine I was a little in love with her. Human sympathy. Understanding, and somebody to share a bit of myself with . . . But, comrade, you are a defeatist. You must not think of such things. You know that there is companionship in the Movement as far as that is possible.

As far as that is possible.

How far?

Again, I told her about the siding where the train stopped, and what the steward did, and how I looked at the shacks of the native workers, and I told her about the three types of workers.

She did not understand. I know she thought I was a little mad. That I was a defeatist. That I had sold out the Movement. Funny, huh? Well, it's true. The Movement. People living in shacks. People begging for a living.

Young intellectuals feeling utterly impotent.

They don't see. And they say, 'Don't, comrade; that's defeatism.' What do I care about defeatism when I am feeling lonesome? What do I care about anything when I need human companionship and sympathy and am told that all will be well after the . . .

What about a bit of now?

Nigger with a brain? Nigger thinking? No. I'm sorry to disappoint you. I'm scared to think. I will go mad if I think. Those others who are mad are thinking these things. They have passed them on to me. I told her these things. A little companionship. Not to discuss anything. Not to hear that I am a promising young writer for the Movement. Not to be told that they think my book is going to be good. Not these things. Not to be told that there is going to be a Mass Meeting and that I must give the crowd of my best.

What about a little bit of warmth? Someone to hold in my arms? Someone to love and lie down with when I am tired?

Young intellectual? Young fool would be better.

I told her these things. Sitting in a non-European café where we went so that it would be all right.

I was a little bit in love with her; or rather, with her company. She could understand, and could give me sympathy, and then interest me in the Mass Meeting. But I guess she wanted to get away to go to a show. So we rushed through the tea, and again she told me the Movement was doomed if young, intellectual leaders like myself were becoming defeatist. What did the comrades in the other countries do?

They at least had someone to talk to. Some woman to understand. Sex can be got in the street. But companionship is something like a religion. A God.

The green valley at the little siding where the train stopped . . .

The little hovels that refreshed my memory of my people . . .

The steward . . .

The nights spent in reading. Talking aloud to myself to hear some voice. Any voice. Even my own. Just not to be mad by morning.

Young intellectual!

God and the Movement. Must do something.

Do you know what it is to be a nigger in body? Sub-human. And in mind a person? That is what I call loneliness. But don't forget, I am not thinking. That is reserved for Europeans only. Niggers go to jail.

That spot . . . little niggers asking for a penny . . .

White man flirting with girl who got on at the last station.

Steward. Muddy water. Oh, God!

She was talking. What is the position like up north? How is work? To hell with work, and the position, and everything! Be a comrade! See, I am lonely. See, I have not spoken to a person for years. Either it's all about the Movement or all about nothing. Talk about something, for God's sake. Any bloody old thing.

That spot. Green valley in the mountains at a siding where the train stopped.

Years of utter loneliness.

The Movement.

A woman to talk to. A woman with brains who can talk; instead, she babbles silence.

Jesus. Nigger body. Animal body.

Human mind.

That spot. Muddy water. God and the nigger bodies with nigger brains. Wish I was like them!

Damned fool to have gone to college.

Not me speaking.
Do you know what I have been saying? Do you understand?
Don't be ashamed to say so if you do not. Millions have failed to.
It would be too good to be true, for you to understand.
Don't hide your smile of pity.
I understand . . .
Loneliness taught me.
The spot . . .
GOD!

## ▩ Ezekiel (Es'Ka) Mphahlele (1919–1983)
*South Africa* (story)

The fiction writer Ezekiel Mphahlele was born in Pretoria, South Africa, in 1919, was educated in local schools, and was awarded a Teacher's Certificate from Adams' College in 1940. He was one generation away from a village in Sekhukhuneland where his father was born and where his ancestors were chiefs and headmen. From ages five to twelve, he lived in the countryside in Maupaneng, a place of great beauty, which he would later describe with nostalgia and terror. At thirteen, he was back in Pretoria, living on Second Avenue, which gave him the title of his autobiography, *Down Second Avenue* (1959). From 1941 to 1945, he worked as a typist for an institute for the blind. Then for seven years he taught English and Afrikaans in Johannesburg until his dismissal for participating in a demonstration against the Bantu Education Act—the law that began apartheid as it was to be known. Banned from teaching, he edited the important literary journal, *The Drum* and, in 1957, he and his family left for Nigeria. There he taught, wrote, and, as of 1960, edited the journal *Black Orpheus*. He wrote his only novel *The Wanderers* (1971) in Nigeria. Mphahlele, like Wole Soyinka and many African writers, opposed the Négritude movement. Reflecting on his early writing, Mphahlele has spoken of moving away from his short-fused impulse to record anger and observations in the short story, an atmosphere that enveloped him during his years in South Africa, to diverse and more complex forms, culminating in the novel and many essays. The story included reveals an urgency to act in defiance of authority and the fearful consequences that confrontation brings.

FURTHER READING: Mphahlele, Ezekiel. *Down Second Avenue*, 1959; *The Living and the Dead, and Other Stories*, 1961; *The Wanderers*, 1971.

## The Master of Doornvlei

The early summer rain was pouring fiercely.

In the mud-and-grass church house a bird flitted from one rafter to another, trapped. All was silent in the church except for a cough now and again that punctuated the preacher's sermon. Now and then, to relieve the gravity of the devotional moment, a few members of the congregation allowed themselves to be ensnared by the circling movements of the bird.

But only a few of them. Most of the people had their eyes fixed on the elderly preacher, as if they were following the motion of every line on each lip as he gave his sermon. In any case, he did not have a booming voice, like his deacon's (a point on which the old man was often plagued by a feeling of inferiority). So his listeners always watched his lips. One or two older women at the back screwed up their faces to see him better.

A nine-year-old boy was particularly charmed by the lost bird, and his eyes roved with it. Then he felt pity for it and wished he could catch it and let it out through the window which it missed several times. But the preacher went on, and his listeners soared on the wings of his sermon to regions where there was no labour or sweat and care.

Suddenly the boy saw the bird make straight for a closed window and hit against the glass and flutter to the floor. It tried to fly but could not. He went to pick it up. He hugged it and stroked it. He looked about, but the people's faces looked ahead, like stolid clay figures. Why are they so cold and quiet when a bird is in pain? he asked himself.

It lay quiet in his hand, and he could feel the slight beat of the heart in the little feathered form.

'And so, brothers and sisters,' the preacher concluded, 'the Holy Word bids us love one another, and do to others as we would that they do to us. Amen.' He asked his flock to kneel for prayer.

At this time Mfukeri, the foreman of Doornvlei Farm on which the makeshift church was built, came in. He looked around and spotted his target—a puny wisp of a boy with scraggy legs, the boy with the bird in his hand.

When he took the boy out the people continued to kneel, unperturbed, except for the raising of a head here and there; perhaps just to make sure who the victim was this time. As the two went out the boy's rather big waistcoast that dangled loosely from his shoulders, flapped about.

It was common for Mfukeri to butt in at a prayer session to fetch a man or woman or child for a job that needed urgent attention. The congregants were labour tenants, who in return for their work earned the few square yards of earth on which they lived, and a ration of mealie-meal, sugar, and an occasional piece of meat.

When they complained about such disturbances to the farmer, Sarel Britz, he said: 'I'm just to my labourers. I favour nobody above the rest. Farm work is farm work; I often have to give up my church service myself.'

The boy tried to protect the bird. He could not keep it on his person, so he put in under a tin in the fowlrun before he went about the work Mfukeri had directed him to do. The rain continued to pour.

The following day the boy took ill with pneumonia. He had got soaked in the rain. On such days the little mud-and-grass houses of the labourers looked wretched: as if they might cave in any time under some unseen load. The nearest hospital was fifty miles away, and if the workers wanted to see the district surgeon, they would have to travel 25 miles there and back. The district surgeon could only be seen once a week.

The boy ran a high temperature. When he was able to speak he asked his mother to go and see how his bird fared in the fowlrun. She came back to tell him that the bird had been found under a tin, dead. That same night the boy died.

When the news went round, the workers seemed to run beserk.

'It has happened before . . .'

'My child—not even ten yet . . . !'

'Come, let's go to Sarel Britz . . . !'

'No, wait, he'll be angry with us, very angry . . . '

'Yes, but the White man is very powerful . . . '

'And truly so—where do we get work if he drives us off the farm . . . ?'

'He wants our hands and our sweat—he cannot do that . . .'

'He beats us, and now he wants to kill us . . .'

'Send him back to Rhodesia—this Mfukeri . . . !'

'Yes, we don't do such things on this farm . . .'

'By the spirits, we don't work tomorrow until we see this thing out . . . !'

'Give us our trek-passes . . . ! Save our children . . . !'

'Ho friends! I am not going with you. I have children to look after . . . !'

'That is why we are going to Sarel Britz . . . !'

'Come, friends, let's talk first before we march to the master of Doorn-vlei.'

Tau Rathebe, who could read and write, rallied the workers to an open spot not far from the main gate. Grim and rugged farm workers; shaggy; none with extra flesh on him; young and old; with tough sinewy limbs. Those who were too scared to join the march kept in the bushes nearby to watch. Women remained behind.

The men were angry and impatient. 'We want Mfukeri away from Doornvlei, or we go, trek-pass or none!' was the general cry, echoed and re-echoed.

And they marched, as they had never done before, to the master's house.

Britz and Mfukeri were standing on the front verandah, waiting. It was to be expected: the foreman had already gone to warn Britz. Apart from what knowledge he had about Tau Rathebe, it was plain from the early morning that the workers were not prepared to work.

'What is it, men?'

'The people want Mfukeri sent away,' said Tau. 'He has been using his sjambok on some workers, and now old Petrus Sechele's son is dead, because Mfukeri took him out in the rain. I've warned him about this before.'

'I'll think about it. You're asking me to do a difficult thing; you must give me time to think.'

'How long?' asked Tau.

Sarel Britz felt annoyed at the implied ultimatum and Tau's insolent manner; but he restrained himself.

'Till noon today. Just now I want you to go to your work. I'm just, and to show it, Mfukeri is not going to the fields until I've decided.'

They dispersed, each to his work, discontented and surly. When Mfukeri left Sarel Britz in conference with his mother, the usually smooth and slippery texture on the foreman's face, peculiar to Rhodesian Africans, looked flabby.

'I've told him not to use the *sjambok,* but he insists on doing it, just because I forbid it,' said Britz when he had gone.

'Reason?' Marta Britz asked.

'Just to make me feel I depend on him.'

'He never behaved like this when your father was alive. Once he was told he must do a thing or mustn't he obeyed.'

There was a pause during which mother and son almost heard each other's thoughts.

'You know, Mamma, when I was at university—on the experimental farm—I knew many Black and Coloured folk. Thinking back on the time, now, makes me feel Pa was wrong.'

'Wrong about what?'

'About Kaffirs being children.'

'But they are, my son. Your father himself said so.'

'No, one has to be on the alert with them. One can't afford to take things for granted.'

'How are they grown up?'

Sarel went and stood right in front of her. 'Yes, Ma, they're fully grown up; some of them are cleverer and wiser than a lot of us Whites. Their damned patience makes them all the more dangerous. Maybe Mfukeri's still somewhat of a child. But certainly not the others. Take today, for instance. A coming together like this has never been heard of on a White man's farm. And they've left everything in the hands of their leader. No disorder. They're serpent's eggs, and I'm going to crush them.' He paused.

'I didn't tell you that Mfukeri has been keeping an eye on this Tau Rathebe. We've found out he was deported from Johannesburg. Somehow slipped into this farm. And now he's been having secret meetings with three or four of our Kaffirs at a time, to teach them what to do—like today.'

'So! Hemel!'

'So you see, Ma, Papa was wrong. I'm going to keep a sharp eye on the black swine. But first thing, I'm ready now to drive Rathebe away; out with him tomorrow.'

At noon the master of Doornvlei made his double decision known: that Tau Rathebe was to leave the farm the following morning, and that Mfukeri had been warned and would be given another chance—the last.

This caused a stir among the labourers, but Tau Rathebe asked them to keep calm.

They wanted to leave with him.

'No. The police will take you as soon as you leave here. You can't go from one farm to another without a trek-pass,' he reminded them.

He left Doornvlei . . .

Sarel Britz felt confused. He kept repeating to himself what he had said to his mother earlier. These are no children, no children . . . they are men . . . I'm dealing with the minds of men . . . My father was wrong . . . All my boyhood he led me to believe that black people were children . . . O Hemel, they aren't . . . !

He had begun to see the weakness of his father's theory during his university years, but it was the incident with Rathebe that had stamped that weakness on his mind.

Harvest time came, and Doornvlei became a little world of intense life and work. The maize triangle of South Africa was buzzing with talk of a surplus crop and the threat of low prices.

'A big crop again, Mfukeri, what do you say?' said Britz.

'Yes, baas,' he grinned consent, 'little bit better than last year.'

'You know you're a good worker and foreman, Mfukeri. Without you I don't know how I'd run this farm.'

'Yes, baas. If baas is happy I'm happy.'

'Since Rathebe left there's peace here, not so.'

'Yes, baas, he makes too much trouble. Long time I tell baas he always meet the men by the valley. They talk a long time there. Sometime one man tell me they want more money and food. I'm happy for you baas. The old baas he say I must help you all the time because I work for him fifteen years. I want him to rest in peace in his grave.'

Britz nodded several times.

The Rhodesian foreman worked as hard as ever to retain the master's praise. He did not spare himself; and the other workers had to keep up with his almost inhuman pace.

'Hey you!' Mfukeri shouted often. 'You there, you're not working fast enough.' He drove them on, and some worked in panic, breaking off mealie cobs and throwing them with the dexterity of a juggler into sacks hanging from the shoulder. Mfukeri did not beat the workers any more. On this Sarel Britz had put his foot down. 'Beat your workers and you lose them,' his father had often said. But every servant felt the foreman's presence and became jittery. And the army of black sweating labourers spread out among the mealie stalks after the systematic fashion of a battle strategy.

Sometimes they sang their songs of grief and hope while reaping in the autumn sun. Sometimes they were too tired even to sing of grief; then they just went on sweating and thinking; then there was a Sunday afternoon to look forward to, when they would go to the village for a drink and song and dance and lovemaking.

Sarel Britz became sterner and more exacting. And his moods and attitude were always reflected in his trusty Mfukeri. Britz kept reminding his tenants that he was just; he favoured no one above the others; he repeated it often to Mfukeri and to his mother. He leant more and more on his foreman, who realized it and made the most of it.

Back at university the students had had endless talks about the Blacks. Britz had discussed with them his father's theory about allowing the Black man a few rungs to climb up at a time; because he was still a child. Most of his colleagues had laughed at this. Gradually he accepted their line of thinking: the White man must be vigilant.

Often when he did his accounts and books, Sarel Britz would stop in the middle of his work, thinking and wondering what he would do if he lost much of his labour, like the other farmers. What if the towns continued to attract the Black labourer by offering him jobs once preserved for the White man. Would the Black workers continue to flow into the towns, or would the law come to the farmer's rescue by stopping the influx?

Sarel Britz lived in this fear. At the same time, he thought, it would break him if he paid his workers more than forty shillings a month in order to keep them. A mighty heap of troubles rose before his eyes, and he could almost hear the shouts and yells of labour tenants from all the farms rising against their masters . . .

The threat became more and more real to Britz. But Mfukeri consoled him. Britz had lately been inviting him to the house quite often for a chat about doings on the farm. If only that Kaffir didn't know so much about the farm so that he, Britz, had to depend on him more than he cared to . . . 'Come to the house tonight, Mfukeri, and let's talk,' he said, one afternoon in late autumn.

'All right, baas.'

Mfukeri went to see his master. He wondered what the master had to say. He found him reclining comfortably on his chair. Mfukeri could not dare to take a chair before he was told to sit down — in the same chair he always sat on.

'Thank you, baas.'

After a moment of silence, 'What do you think of me, Mfukeri?'

'Why do you ask me, baas?' — after looking about.

'Don't be afraid to say your mind.'

'You're all right, baas.'

'Sure?'

'Yes, baas.' They smoked silently.

'You still like this farm?'

'Very much baas.'

'I'm glad. You're a good foreman — the only man I trust here.'

Mfukeri understood Britz. He wanted to assure his master that he would never desert him, that he was capable of keeping the tenants together. Hadn't he spied cleverly on Tau Rathebe and avoided an upheaval?

The foreman felt triumphant. He had never in his life dreamt he would work his way into a White man's trust. He had always felt so inferior before a White man that he despised himself. The more he despised himself the sterner and more ruthless he became towards his fellow-workers. At least he could retain a certain amount of self-respect and the feeling that he was a man, now that his master looked so helpless.

As the foreman sat smoking his pipe, he thought: 'How pitiable they look when they're at a Black man's mercy . . . I wonder now . . .'

'All right, Mfukeri,' said the master. The Rhodesian rose and stood erect, like a bluegum tree, over the White man; and the White man thought how indifferent his servant looked; just like a tree. To assert his authority once more Britz gave a few orders.

'Attend to that compost manure first thing tomorrow morning. And also the cleaning up of the chicken hospital; see to that fanbelt in the threshing machine.'

'Yes, baas, goodnight.'

He was moving towards the door when Britz said, 'Before I forget, be careful about Donker mixing with the cows. It wasn't your fault, of course, but you'll take care, won't you?'

'Yes.' He knew his master regarded his bull Donker as inferior stock, and felt hurt.

It was a bewildered Britz the foreman left behind. The farmer thought how overwhelming his servant was when he stood before him. Something in him quaked. He was sensitive enough to catch the tone of the last 'baas' when Mfukeri left: it was such an indifferent echo of what 'baas' sounded like years before.

Mfukeri kept a bull with a squatter family on a farm adjoining Doorn-vlei. Labour tenants were not allowed to keep livestock on the farm on which they themselves worked, because they were paid and received food rations. Mfukeri's friend agreed to keep Donker, the bull, for him. It was a good bull, though scrub.

Two days later Sarel Britz was roused from his lunch hour sleep by noise outside. He ran out and saw workers hurrying towards a common point. In a few moments he found himself standing near Mfukeri and a group of workers. In front of the barn Britz's pedigree stallion, Kasper, was kicking out at Donker, Mfukeri's bull. Donker had the horse against the barn wall, and was roaring and pawing the earth.

Kasper kicked, a quick barrage of hoofs landing a square on the bull's forehead. But the stocky Donker kept coming in and slashing out with his short horns. Normally, there would be ecstatic shouting from the workers. They stood in silence weaving and ducking to follow the movements of the fighters. They couldn't express their attitude towards either side, because they hated both Britz and Mfukeri; and yet the foreman was one of them.

The stallion tried to turn round, which was almost fatal; for Donker charged and unleashed more furious lightning kicks. Master and foreman watched, each feeling that he was entangled in this strife between their animals; more so than they dared to show outwardly. Sarel Britz bit his lower lip as he watched the rage of the bull. He seemed to see scalding fury in the very slime that came from the mouth of the bull to mix with the earth.

He didn't like the slime mixing with the sand: it looked as if Donker were invoking a mystic power in the earth to keep his fore-hoofs from slipping. Once the hoofs were planted in the ground the bull found an opening and gored Kasper in the stomach, ripping the skin with the upward motion of the horn.

Sarel Britz gave a shout, and walked away hurriedly.

When Mfukeri saw Kasper tottering, and his beloved bull drawing back, an overwhelming feeling of victory shot through every nerve in him. What he had been suppressing all through the fight came out in a gasp and, with tears in his eyes, he shouted: 'Donker! Donker!'

There was a murmur among some of the onlookers who said what a pity it was the horse's hoofs weren't shod; otherwise the ending would have been different.

Kasper was giving his last dying kicks when Britz came back with a rifle in his hand. His face was set. The workers stood aside. Two shots from the rifle finished off the stallion.

'Here, destroy the bull!' he ordered Mfukeri, handing him the gun. The foreman hesitated. 'I said shoot that bull!'

'Why do you want me to shoot my bull, baas?'

'If you don't want to do it, then you must leave this farm, at once!'

Mfukeri did not answer. They both knew the moment had come. He stood still and looked at Britz. Then he walked off, and coaxed his bull out of the premises.

'I gave him a choice,' Sarel said to his mother, telling her the whole story.

'You shouldn't have, Sarel. He has worked for us these fifteen years.'

Sarel knew he had been right. As he looked out of the window to the empty paddock, he was stricken with grief. And then he was glad. He had got rid of yet another threat to his authority.

But the fear remained.

## ■ Amos Tutuola (1920–1997) *Nigeria* (novel)

There is magic in the fact that the first African writer to achieve international fame was himself the author of a book of relentlessly magical prose. Amos Tutuola's short epic, *The Palm-Wine Drinkard and His Dead Palm-Wine Tapster in the Dead's Town* (1952), is a picaresque story of ambition, quest, endurance, and family furies. In thirty episodes, Tutuola imaginatively adapts Yoruba myths to his own purpose, just as in Latin America Gabriel García Márquez found the tale and mood of his famous brand of magic realism in local legends of his native Colombia. Tutuola's work has qualities of the village teller of tales. His English speech, sometimes ungrammatical, is immensely rich in plot and metaphysical excursions into consciousness outside the body, in beasts and forest, in monsters, and in death itself, which takes on many allegorical trappings. Amos Tutuola is not only a fantastic storyteller, but a describer of fierce, terrifying dangers, strange deaths, and sufferings, where bitter wisdoms derive from family and tribal customs and traditions. Every harsh aspect of life in village and jungle comes out in the life/death ventures of the hero and his lady. Transcending rhetorical means and genre, in his profoundly lyrical, wild, fearful epic novella, Tutuola has written a unique classic for our century.

Born in Abeokuta, Nigeria, Tutuola had very little schooling. He exploited his academic ignorance to achieve an expressive and inimitably authentic voice. Even in the words "Drinkard" and "Dead's Town," which he included in the baroquely long title of his great work, we see his inventive use of the English language. He carries us into the Yoruba imagination and reveals a whole culture, impossible to have invented, which Africa bequeathed him and, through him, the world. This blacksmith, farmer, office-messenger-turned-writer adapted African myths, as Homer adapted Greek myths, for his special literary and spiritual purposes. Tutuola has a special genius of recognition and re-creation, which resulted in his masterpiece *The Palm-Wine Drinkard.* He wrote many novels following his haunting classic, but his first published work remains his great creation.

**FURTHER READING:** Tutuola, Amos. *The Palm-Wine Drinkard and His Dead Palm Wine Tapster in the Dead's Town,* 1952; *My Life in the Bush of Ghosts,* 1954; *Simbi and the Satyr of the Dark Jungle,* 1958; *The Brave African Huntress,* 1958; *Feather Woman of the Jungle,* 1981; *The Witch Herbalist of the Remote Town,* 1981; and *The Wild Hunter in the Bush of Ghosts,* 1982.

## *from* The Palm-Wine Drinkard

### How I Got a Wife

I was a palm-wine drinkard since I was a boy of ten years of age. I had no other work more than to drink palm-wine in my life. In those days we did not know other money, except COWRIES, so that everything was very cheap, and my father was the richest man in our town.

My father got eight children and I was the eldest among them, all of the rest were hard workers, but I myself was an expert palm-wine drinkard. I was drinking palm-wine from morning till night and from night till morning. By that time I could not drink ordinary water at all except palm-wine.

But when my father noticed that I could not do any work more than to drink, he engaged an expert palm-wine tapster for me; he had no other work more than to tap palm-wine every day.

So my father gave me a palm-tree farm which was nine miles square and it contained 560,000 palm-trees, and this palm-wine tapster was tapping one hundred and fifty kegs of palm-wine every morning, but before 2 o'clock p.m., I would have drunk all of it; after that he would go and tap another 75 kegs in the evening which I would be drinking till morning. So my friends were uncountable by that time and they were drinking palm-wine with me from morning till a late hour in the night. But when my palm-wine tapster completed the period of 15 years that he was tapping the palm-wine for me, then my father died suddenly, and when it was the 6th month after my father had died, the tapster went to the palm-tree farm on a Sunday evening to tap palm-wine for me. When he reached the farm, he climbed one of the tallest palm-trees in the farm to tap palm-wine but as he was tapping on, he fell down unexpectedly and died at the foot of the palm-tree as a result of injuries. As I was waiting for him to bring the palm-wine, when I saw that he did not return in time, because he was not keeping me long like that before, then I called two of my friends to accompany me to the farm. When we reached the farm, we began to look at every palm-tree, after a while we found him under the palm-tree, where he fell down and died.

But what I did first when we saw him dead there, was that I climbed another palm-tree which was near the spot, after that I tapped palm-wine and drank it to my satisfaction before I came back to the spot. Then both my friends who accompanied me to the farm and I dug a pit under the palm-tree that he fell down as a grave and buried him there, after that we came back to the town.

When it was early in the morning of the next day, I had no palm-wine to drink at all, and throughout that day I felt not so happy as before; I was seriously sat down in my parlour, but when it was the third day that I had no palm-wine at all, all my friends did not come to my house again, they left me there alone, because there was no palm-wine for them to drink.

But when I completed a week in my house without palm-wine, then I went out and, I saw one of them in the town, so I saluted him, he answered but he did not approach me at all, he hastily went away.

Then I started to find out another expert palm-wine tapster, but I could not get me one who could tap the palm-wine to my requirement. When there was no palm-wine for me to drink I started to drink ordinary water which I was unable to taste before, but I did not satisfy with it as palm-wine.

When I saw that there was no palm-wine for me again, and nobody could tap it for me, then I thought within myself that old people were saying that the whole people who had died in this world, did not go to heaven directly, but they were living in one place somewhere in this world. So that I said that I would find out where my palm-wine tapster who had died was.

One fine morning, I took all my native *juju* and also my father's juju with me and I left my father's hometown to find out whereabouts was my tapster who had died.

But in those days, there were many wild animals and every place was covered by thick bushes and forests; again, towns and villages were not near each other as nowadays, and as I was travelling from bushes to bushes and from forests to forests and sleeping inside it for many days and months, I was sleeping on the branches of trees, because spirits etc. were just like partners, and to save my life from them; and again I could spend two or three months before reaching a town or a village. Whenever I reached a town or a village, I would spend almost four months there, to find out my palm-wine tapster from the inhabitants of that town or village and if he did not reach there, then I would leave there and continue my journey to another town or village. After the seventh month that I had left my home town, I reached a town and went to an old man, this old man was not a really man, he was a god and he was eating with his wife when I reached there. When I entered the house I saluted both of them, they answered me well, although nobody should enter his house like that as he was a god, but I myself was a god and juju-man. Then I told the old man (god) that I am looking for my palm-wine tapster who had died in my town some time ago, he did not answer to my question but asked me first what was my name? I replied that my name was "Father of gods" who could do everything in this world, then he said: "was that true" and I said yes; after that he told me to go to his native black-smith in an unknown place, or who was living in another town, and bring the right thing that he had told the black-smith to make for him. He said that if I could bring the right thing that he told the black-smith to make for him, then he would believe that I was the "Father of gods who could do everything in this world" and he would tell me where my tapster was.

Immediately this old man told or promised me so, I went away, but after I had travelled about one mile away then I used one of my *juju* and at once I changed into a very big bird and flew back to the roof of the old man's house; but as I stood on the roof of his house, many people saw me there. They came nearer and looked at me on the roof, so when the old man noticed that many had surrounded his house and were looking at the roof, he and his wife came out from the house and when he saw me (bird) on the roof, he told his wife that if he had not sent me to his native black-smith to bring the bell that he told the black-smith to make for him, he would tell me to mention the name of the bird. But at the same time that he said so, I knew what he wanted from the black-smith and I flew away to his black-smith, then when I reached there I told the black-smith that the old man (god) told me to bring his bell which he had told him to make for him. So the black-smith gave me the bell; after that, I returned to the old man with the bell and when he saw me with the bell, he and his wife were surprised and also shocked at that moment.

After that he told his wife to give me food, but after I had eaten the food, he told me again, that there remained another wonderful work to do for him, before he would tell me whereabouts my tapster was. When it was 6.30 a.m. of the following morning, he (god) woke me up, and gave me a wide and strong net which was the same in colour as the ground of that town. He told me to go and bring "Death" from his house with the net.

When I left his house or the town about a mile, there I saw a junction of roads and I was doubtful when I reached the junction, I did not know which was Death's road among these roads, and when I thought within myself that as it was the market day, and all the market goers would soon be returning from the market—I lied down on the middle of the roads, I put my head to one of the roads, my left hand to one, right hand to another one, and my both feet to the rest, after that I pretended as I had slept there. But when all the market goers were returning from the market, they saw me lied down there and shouted thus:—"Who was the mother of this fine boy, he slept on the roads and put his head towards Death's road."

Then I began to travel on Death's road, and I spent about eight hours to reach there, but to my surprise I did not meet anybody on this road until I reached there and I was afraid because of that. When I reached his (Death's) house, he was not at home by that time, he was in his yam garden which was very close to his house, and I met a small rolling drum in his verandah, then I beat it to Death as a sign of salutation. But when he (Death) heard the sound of the drum, he said thus:—"Is that man still alive or dead?" Then I replied "I am still alive and I am not a dead man."

But at the same time that he heard so from me, he was greatly annoyed and he commanded the drum with a kind of voice that the strings of the drum should tight me there; as a matter of fact, the strings of the drum tighted me so that I was hardly breathing.

When I felt that these strings did not allow me to breathe and again every part of my body was bleeding too much, then I myself commanded the ropes of the yams in his garden to tight him there, and the yams in his garden to tight him there, and the yam stakes should begin to beat him also. After I had said so and at the same time, all the ropes of the yams in his garden tighted him hardly, and all the yam stakes were beating him repeatedly, so when he (Death) saw that these stakes were beating him repeatedly, then he commanded the strings of the drum which tighted me to release me, and I was released at the same time. But when I saw that I was released, then I myself commanded the ropes of the yams to release him and the yam stakes to stop beating him, and he was released at once. After he was released by the ropes of yams and yam stakes, he came to his house and met me at his verandah, then we shook hands together, and he told me to enter the house, he put me to one of his rooms, and after a while, he brought food to me and we ate it together, after that we started conversations which went thus:—He (Death) asked me from where did I come? I replied that I came from a certain town which was not so far from his place. Then he asked what did I come to do? I told him that I had been hearing about him in my town and all over the world and I thought within myself that one day I should come and visit or to know him personally. After that he replied that his work was only to kill the people of the world, after that he got up and told me to follow him and I did so.

He took me around his house and his yam garden too, he showed me the skeleton bones of human-beings which he had killed since a century ago and showed me many other things also, but there I saw that he was using skeleton bones of human-beings as fuel woods and skull heads of human-beings as his basins, plates and tumblers etc.

Nobody was living near or with him there, he was living lonely, even bush animals and birds were very far away from his house. So when I wanted to sleep at night, he gave me a wide black cover cloth and then gave me a separate room to sleep inside, but when I entered the room, I met a bed which was made with bones of human-beings; but as this bed was terrible to look at or to sleep on it, I slept under it instead, because I knew his trick already. Even as this bed was very terrible, I was unable to sleep under as I lied down there because of fear of the bones of human-beings, but I lied down there awoke. To my surprise was that when it was about two o'clock in the mid-night, there I saw somebody enter into the room cautiously with a heavy club in his hands, he came nearer to the bed on which he had told me to sleep, then he clubbed the bed with all his power, he clubbed the centre of the bed thrice and he returned cautiously, he thought that I slept on that bed and he thought also that he had killed me.

But when it was 6 o'clock early in the morning, I first woke up and went to the room in which he slept, I woke him up, so when he heard my voice, he was frightened, even he could not salute me at all when he got up from his bed, because he thought that he had killed me last night.

But the second day that I slept there, he did not attempt to do anything again, but I woke up by two o'clock of that night, and went to the road which I should follow to the town and I travelled about a quarter of a mile to his house, then I stopped and dug a pit of his (Death's) size on the centre of that road, after that I spread the net which the old man gave me to bring him (Death) with on that pit, then I returned to his house, but he did not wake up as I was playing this trick.

When it was 6 o'clock in the morning, I went to his door and woke him up as usual, then I told him that I wanted to return to my town this morning, so that I wanted him to lead me a short distance; then he got up from his bed and he began to lead me as I told him, but when he led me to the place that I had dug, I told him to sit down, so I myself sat down on the road side, but as he sat down on the net, he fell into the pit, and without any ado I rolled up the net with him and put him on my head and I kept going to the old man's house who told me to go and bring him Death.

As I was carrying him along the road, he was trying all his efforts to escape or to kill me, but I did not give him a chance to do that. When I had travelled about eight hours, then I reached the town and went straight to the old man's house who told me to go and bring Death from his house. When I reached the old man's house, he was inside his room, then I called him and told him that I had brought Death that he told me to go and bring. But immediately he heard from me that I had brought Death and when he saw him on my head, he was greatly terrified and raised alarm that he thought nobody could go and bring Death from his house, then he told me to carry him (Death) back to his house at once, and he (old man) hastily went back to his room and started to close all his doors and windows, but before he could close two or three of his windows, I threw down Death before his door and at the same time that I threw him down, the net cut into pieces and Death found his way out.

Then the old man and his wife escaped through the windows and also the whole people in that town ran away for their lives and left their properties there. (The old man had thought that Death would kill me if I went to his house, because nobody could reach Death's house and return, but I had known the old man's trick already.)

So that since the day that I had brought Death out from his house, he has no permanent place to dwell or stay, and we are hearing his name about in the world. This was how I brought out Death to the old man who told me to go and bring him before he (old man) would tell me whereabouts my palm-wine tapster was that I was looking for before I reached that town and went to the old man.

But the old man who had promised me that if I could go to Death's house and bring him, he would tell me whereabouts my palm-wine tapster was, could not wait and fulfil his promise because he himself and his wife were narrowly escaped from that town.

Then I left the town without knowing where my tapster was, and I started another fresh journey.

When it was the fifth month since I had left that town, then I reached another town which was not so big, although there was a large and famous market. At the same time that I entered the town, I went to the house of the head of the town who received me with kindness into his house; after a little while he told one of his wives to give me food and after I had eaten the food, he told his wife to give me palm-wine too; I drank the palm-wine to excess as when I was in my town or as when my tapster was alive. But when I tasted the palm-wine given to me there, I said that I got what I wanted here. After I had eaten the food and drunk the palm-wine to my satisfaction, the head of the town who received me as his guest asked for my name, I told him that my name was called "Father of gods who could do anything in this world." As he heard this from me, he was soon faint with fear. After that he asked me what I came to him for. I replied that I was looking for my palm-wine tapster who had died in my town some time ago. Then he told me that he knew where the tapster was.

After that he told me that if I could help him to find out his daughter who was captured by a curious creature from the market which was in that town, and bring her to him, then he would tell me whereabouts my tapster was.

He said furthermore that as I called myself "Father of gods who could do anything in this world," this would be very easy for me to do; he said so.

I did not know that his daughter was taken away by a curious creature from the market.

I was about to refuse to go and find out his daughter who was taken away from the market by a curious creature, but when I remembered my name I was ashamed to refuse. So I agreed to find out his daughter. There was a big market in this town from where the daughter was captured, and the market-day was fixed for every 5th day and the whole people of that town and from all the villages around the town and also spirits and curious creatures from various bushes and forests were coming to this market every 5th day to sell or buy articles. By 4 o'clock in the evening, the market would close for that day and then everybody would be returning to his or her destination or to where he or she came from. But the daughter of the head of that town was a petty trader and she was due to be married before she was taken away from the market. Before that time, her father was telling her to marry a man but she did not listen to her father; when her father saw that she did not care to marry anybody, he gave her to a man for himself, but this lady refused totally to marry that man who was introduced to her by her father. So that her father left her to herself.

This lady was very beautiful as an angel but no man could convince her for marriage. So, one day she went to the market on a market-day as she was doing before, or to sell her articles as usual; on that market-day, she saw a curious creature in the market, but she did not know where the man came from and never knew him before.

## The Description of the Curious Creature: —

He was a beautiful "complete" gentleman, he dressed with the finest and most costly clothes, all the parts of his body were completed, he was a tall man but stout. As this gentleman came to the market on that day, if he had been an article or animal for sale, he would be sold at least for £2000 (two thousand pounds). As this complete gentleman came to the market on that day, and at the same time that this lady saw him in the market, she did nothing more than to ask him where he was living, but this fine gentleman did not answer her or approach her at all. But when she noticed that the fine or complete gentleman did not listen to her, she left her articles and began to watch the movements of the complete gentleman about in the market and left her articles unsold.

By and by the market closed for that day then the whole people in the market were returning to their destinations etc., and the complete gentleman was returning to his own too, but as this lady was following him about in the market all the while, she saw him when he was returning to his destination as others did, then she was following him (complete gentleman) to an unknown place. But as she was following the complete gentleman along the road, he was telling her to go back or not to follow him, but the lady did not listen to what he was telling her, and when the complete gentleman had tired of telling her not to follow him or to go back to her town, he left her to follow him.

## "Do Not Follow Unknown Man's Beauty"

But when they had travelled about twelve miles away from that market, they left the road on which they were travelling and started to travel inside an endless forest in which only all the terrible creatures were living.

## "Return the Parts of Body to the Owners; or Hired Parts of the Complete Gentleman's Body to Be Returned"

As they were travelling along in this endless forest then the complete gentleman in the market that the lady was following, began to return the hired parts of his body to the owners and he was paying them the rentage money. When he reached where he hired the left foot, he pulled it out, he gave it to the owner and paid him, and they kept going; when they reached the place where he hired the right foot, he pulled it out and gave it to the owner and paid for the rentage. Now both feet had returned to the owners, so he began to crawl along on the ground, by that time, that lady wanted to go back to her town or her father, but the terrible and curious creature or the complete gentleman did not allow her to return or go back to her town or her father again and the complete gentleman said thus:—"I had told you not to follow me before we branched into this endless forest which belongs to only terrible and curious creatures, but when I became a half-bodied incomplete gentleman you wanted to go back, now that cannot be done, you have failed. Even you have never seen anything yet, just follow me."

When they went furthermore, then they reached where he hired the belly, ribs, chest etc., then he pulled them out and gave them to the owner and paid for the rentage.

Now to this gentleman or terrible creature remained only the head and both arms with neck, by that time he could not crawl as before but only went jumping on as a bull-frog and now this lady was soon faint for this fearful creature whom she was following. But when the lady saw every part of this complete gentleman in the market was spared or hired and he was returning them to the owners, then she began to try all her efforts to return to her father's town, but she was not allowed by this fearful creature at all.

When they reached where he hired both arms, he pulled them out and gave them to the owner, he paid for them; and they were still going on in this endless forest, they reached the place where he hired the neck, he pulled it out and gave it to the owner and paid for it as well.

## "A Full-Bodied Gentleman Reduced to Head"

Now this complete gentleman was reduced to head and when they reached where he hired the skin and flesh which covered the head, he returned them, and paid to the owner, now the complete gentleman in the market reduced to a "SKULL" and this lady remained with only "Skull." When the lady saw that she remained with only Skull, she began to say that her father had been telling her to marry a man, but she did not listen to or believe him.

When the lady saw that the gentleman became a Skull, she began to faint, but the Skull told her if she would die she would die and she would follow him to his house. But by the time that he was saying so, he was humming with a terrible voice and also grew very wild and even if there was a person two miles away he would not have to listen before hearing him, so this lady began to run away in that forest for her life, but the Skull chased her and within a few yards, he caught her, because he was very clever and smart as he was only Skull and he could jump a mile to the second before coming down. He caught the lady in this way: so when the lady was running away for her life, he hastily ran to her front and stopped her as a log of wood.

By and by, this lady followed the Skull to his house, and the house was a hole which was under the ground. When they reached there both of them entered the hole. But there were only Skulls living in that hole. At the same time that they entered the hole, he tied a single cowrie on the neck of this lady with a kind of rope, after that, he gave her a large frog on which she sat as a stool, then he gave a whistle to a Skull of his kind to keep watch on this lady whenever she wanted to run away. Because the Skull knew already that the lady would attempt to run away from the hole. Then he went to the back-yard to where his family were staying in the day time till night.

But one day, the lady attempted to escape from the hole, and at the same time that the Skull who was watching her whistled to the rest of the Skulls that were in the back-yard, the whole of them rushed out to the place where the lady sat on the bull-frog, so they caught her, but as all of them were rushing out, they were rolling on the ground as if a thousand petrol drums were pushing along a hard road. After she was caught, then they brought her back to sit on the same frog as usual. If the Skull who was watching her fell asleep, and if the lady wanted to escape, the cowrie that was tied on her neck would raise up the alarm with a terrible noise, so that the Skull who was watching her would wake up at once and then the rest of the Skull's family would rush out from the back in thousands to the lady and ask her what she wanted to do with a curious and terrible voice.

But the lady could not talk at all, because as the cowrie had been tied on her neck, she became dumb at the same moment.

## "The Father of Gods Should Find Out Whereabouts the Daughter of the Head of the Town Was"

Now as the father of the lady first asked for my name and I told him that my name was "Father of gods who could do anything in this world," then he told me that if I could find out where his daughter was and bring her to him, then he would tell me where my palm-wine tapster was. But when he said so, I was jumping up with gladness that he should promise me that he would tell me where my tapster was. I agreed to what he said; the father and parent of this lady never knew whereabouts their daughter was, but they had information that the lady followed a complete gentleman in the market. As I was the "Father of gods who could do anything in this world," when it was at night I sacrificed to my juju with a goat.

And when it was early in the morning, I sent for forty kegs of palm-wine, after I had drunk it all, I started to investigate whereabouts was the lady. As it was the market-day, I started the investigation from the market. But as I was a juju-man, I knew all the kinds of people in that market. When it was exactly 9 o'clock a.m., the very complete gentleman whom the lady followed came to the market again, and at the same time that I saw him, I knew that he was a curious and terrible creature.

## "The Lady Was Not to Be Blamed for Following the Skull as a Complete Gentleman"

I could not blame the lady for following the Skull as a complete gentleman to his house at all. Because if I were a lady, no doubt I would follow him to wherever he would go, and still as I was a man I would jealous him more than that, because if this gentleman went to the battle field, surely, enemy would not kill him or capture him and if bombers saw him in a town which was to be bombed, they would not throw bombs on his presence, and if they did throw it, the bomb itself would not explode until this gentleman would leave that town, because of his beauty. At the same time that I saw this gentleman in the market on that day, what I was doing was only to follow him about in the market. After I looked at him for so many hours, then I ran to a corner of the market and I cried for a few minutes because I thought within myself why was I not created with beauty as this gentleman, but when I remembered that he was only a Skull, then I thanked God that He had created me without beauty, so I went back to him in the market, but I was still attracted by his beauty. So when the market closed for that day, and when everybody was returning to his or her destination, this gentleman was returning to his own too and I followed him to know where he was living.

## "Investigation to the Skull's Family's House"

When I travelled with him a distance of about twelve miles away to that market, the gentleman left the really road on which we were travelling and branched into an endless forest and I was following him, but as I did not want him to see that I was following him, then I used one of my juju which changed me into a lizard and followed him. But after I had travelled with him a distance of about twenty-five miles away in this endless forest, he began to pull out all the parts of his body and return them to the owners, and paid them.

After I had travelled with him for another fifty miles in this forest, then he reached his house and entered it, but I entered it also with him, as I was a lizard. The first thing that he did when he entered the hole (house) he went straight to the place where the lady was, and I saw the lady sat on a bull-frog with a single cowrie tied on her neck and a Skull who was watching her stood behind her. After he (gentleman) had seen that the lady was there, he went to the back-yard where all his family were working.

## "The Investigator's Wonderful Work in the Skull's Family's House"

When I saw this lady and when the Skull who brought her to that hole or whom I followed from the market to that hole went to the back-yard, then I changed myself to a man as before, then I talked to the lady but she could not answer me at all, she only showed that she was in a serious condition. The Skull who was guarding her with a whistle fell asleep at that time.

To my surprise, when I helped the lady to stand up from the frog on which she sat, the cowrie that was tied on her neck made a curious noise at once, and when the Skull who was watching her heard the noise, he woke up and blew the whistle to the rest, then the whole of them rushed to the place and surrounded the lady and me, but at the same time that they saw me there, one of them ran to a pit which was not so far from that spot, the pit was filled with cowries. He picked one cowrie out of the pit, after that he was running towards me, and the whole crowd wanted to tie the cowrie on my neck too. But before they could do that, I had changed myself into air, they could not trace me out again, but I was looking at them. I believed that the cowries in that pit were their power and to reduce the power of any human being whenever tied on his or her neck and also to make a person dumb.

Over one hour after I had dissolved into air, these Skulls went back to the back-yard, but there remained the Skull who was watching her.

After they had returned to the back-yard, I changed to a man as usual, then I took the lady from the frog, but at the same time that I touched her, the cowrie which was tied on her neck began to shout; even if a person was four miles away he would not have to listen before hearing, but immediately the Skull who was watching her heard the noise and saw me when I took her from that frog, he blew the whistle to the rest of them who were in the back-yard.

Immediately the whole Skull family heard the whistle when blew to them, they were rushing out to the place and before they could reach there, I had left their hole for the forest, but before I could travel about one hundred yards in the forest, they had rushed out from their hole to inside the forest and I was still running away with the lady. As these Skulls were chasing me about in the forest, they were rolling on the ground like large stones and also humming with terrible noise, but when I saw that they had nearly caught me or if I continued to run away like that, no doubt, they would catch me sooner, then I changed the lady to a kitten and put her inside my pocket and changed myself to a very small bird which I could describe as a "sparrow" in English language.

After that I flew away, but as I was flying in the sky, the cowrie which was tied on that lady's neck was still making a noise and I tried all my best to stop the noise, but all were in vain. When I reached home with the lady, I changed her to a lady as she was before and also myself changed to man as well. When her father saw that I brought his daughter back home, he was exceedingly glad and said thus:—"You are the 'Father of gods' as you had told me before."

But as the lady was now at home, the cowrie on her neck did not stop making a terrible noise once, and she could not talk to anybody; she showed only that she was very glad she was at home. Now I had brought the lady but she could not talk, eat or loose away the cowrie on her neck, because the terrible noise of the cowrie did not allow anybody to rest or sleep at all.

## "There Remain Greater Tasks Ahead"

Now I began to cut the rope of the cowrie from her neck and to make her talk and eat, but all my efforts were in vain. At last I tried my best to cut off the rope of the cowrie; it only stopped the noise, but I was unable to loose it away from her neck.

When her father saw all my trouble, he thanked me greatly and repeated again that as I called myself "Father of gods who could do anything in this world" I ought to do the rest of the work. But when he said so, I was very ashamed and thought within myself that if I return to the Skulls' hole or house, they might kill me and the forest was very dangerous travel always, again I could not go directly to the Skulls in their hole and ask them how to loose away the cowrie which was tied on the lady's neck and to make her talk and eat.

## "Back to the Skull's Family's House"

On the third day after I had brought the lady to her father's house, I returned to the endless forest for further investigation. When there remained about one mile to reach the hole of these Skulls, there I saw the very Skull who the lady had followed from the market as a complete gentleman to the hole of Skull's family's house, and at the same time that I saw him like that, I changed into a lizard and climbed a tree which was near him.

He stood before two plants, then he cut a single opposite leaf from the opposite plant; he held the leaf with his right hand and he was saying thus: — "As this lady was taken from me, if this opposite leaf is not given her to eat, she will not talk for ever," after that he threw the leaf down on the ground. Then he cut another single compound leaf from the compound plant which was in the same place with the opposite plant, he held the compound leaf with his left hand and said that if this single compound is not given to this lady, to eat, the cowrie on her neck could not be loosened away for ever and it would be making a terrible noise for ever."

After he said so, he threw the leaf down at the same spot, then he jumped away. So after he had jumped very far away, (luckily, I was there when he was doing all these things, and I saw the place that he threw both leaves separately), then I changed myself to a man as before, I went to the place that he threw both leaves, then I picked them up and I went home at once.

But at the same time that I reached home, I cooked both leaves separately and gave her to eat; to my surprise the lady began to talk at once. After that, I gave her the compound leaf to eat for the second time and immediately she ate that too, the cowrie which was tied on her neck by the Skull, loosened away by itself, but it disappeared at the same time. So when the father and mother saw the wonderful work which I had done for them, they brought fifty kegs of palm-wine for me, they gave me the lady as wife and two rooms in that house in which to live with them. So, I saved the lady from the complete gentleman in the market who afterwards reduced to a "Skull" and the lady became my wife since that day. This was how I got a wife.

# ■ Agostinho Neto (1922–1979) *Angola* (poems)

TRANSLATED BY W. S. MERWIN

Agostinho Neto was born in Angola in the village of Kaxikane, about forty miles from the capital city of Luanda. He studied medicine in Lisbon and returned to Angola where he practiced. He was very early associated with a movement, led by Viriato Cruz, for the rediscovery of Angola's indigenous culture. He was a leader in the resistance to the Portuguese, for many years heading the People's Liberation Movement of Angola (MPLA), was arrested three times, and was taken to Portugal in 1962 where he was imprisoned. He escaped later that year. When Angola achieved independence, he became its first president. Some of his poems written in prison were widely known. He died in Moscow where his books were published in diverse languages, including English, for distribution especially in the formerly socialist nations of Eastern Europe. Eventually, his work appeared in many languages, and it is highly regarded in Portugal. A few of his poems have been admirably translated into English by W. S. Merwin, and Neto comes through as one of Africa's most skilled and effective poets.

**FURTHER READING:** Neto, Agostinho. *Sacred Hope.* Translated by Marga Holness, 1974.

## Kinaxixi

I liked to sit down
on a bench in Kinaxixi
at six o'clock of a hot evening
and just sit there  . . .

Someone would come
maybe
to sit beside me

And I would see the black faces of the people
going uptown
in no hurry
expressing absence in the jumbled Kimbundu
they conversed in.

I would see the tired footsteps
of the servants whose fathers also are servants
looking for love here, glory there, wanting
something more than drunkeness in every alcohol

Neither happiness nor hate

After the sun had set
lights would be turned on and I
would wander off
thinking that our life after all is simple
too simple
for anyone who is tired and still has to walk.

## ■ Nadine Gordimer (1923– ) *South Africa* (story)

Born in Springs, Transvaal, South Africa, of Jewish immigrant parents from Eastern Europe, Nadine Gordimer is one of several South African fiction writers who has spent her artistic life fighting apartheid through her word and her political activities. She graduated from the University of Witwatersrand in Johannesburg where she lives today. She has been a frequent world traveler, promoting, more than her own work, the cause of racial integration in her native land. Her cumulative collection of story, novel, and essay has not gone unrecognized, however. She was the recipient of the French International Literary Prize in 1975 and also shared the prestigious United Kingdom Booker Prize. In 1991, she was awarded the Nobel Prize for Literature.

Gordimer's consummate gifts are the precise word and the slanting psychological trait by which she builds up powerful characters in dramatic situations that often reveal the chasms between white and black in South Africa. Her first two volumes of stories, *Face to Face* (1949) and *The Soft Voice of the Serpent* (1952), established her distinguished reputation. The malaise and enigmas of South Africa trouble her characters. The stories capture moments of intense illumination. The novels give a larger picture, but perhaps her highest literary achievement lies in the surprise, profundity, and precision of the story. At the core of her message is her description of society's moral corruption and of those who awaken to the knowledge of that corruption.

Nadine Gordimer's many outspoken and daring public appearances on behalf of racial equality and justice, which took place for decades before South Africa finally and admirably elected a multiracial government, were all given at personal risk. She was viciously attacked by opponents, but they did not silence her. Gordimer is a world author, and her public speech and numerous articles in newspapers and journals authenticate the private creative task of drawing psychological and ethical portraits of her people, black, white, East Indian, and Coloured, which she has done with unique and lucid eloquence. Her spoken word, logical and passionate, has been an art in itself in a world in great need of hearing her courageous intelligence.

**FURTHER READING:** Gordimer, Nadine. *Face to Face*, 1949; *The Soft Voice of the Serpent*, 1952; *Feet of the Country*, 1952; *The Late Bourgeois World*, 1966; *A Guest of Honour*, 1971; *July's People*, 1981; *A Sport of Nature*, 1987; *Something Out There*, 1984.

## Amnesty

When we heard he was released I ran all over the farm and through the fence to our people on the next farm to tell everybody. I only saw afterwards I'd torn my dress on the barbed wire, and there was a scratch, with blood, on my shoulder.

He went away from this place eight years ago, signed up to work in town with what they call a construction company—building glass walls up to the sky. For the first two years he came home for the weekend once a month and two weeks at Christmas; that was when he asked my father for me. And he began to pay. He and I thought that in three years he would have paid enough for us to get married. But then he started wearing that T-shirt, he told us he'd joined the union, he told us about the strike, how he was one of the men who went to talk to the bosses because some others had been laid off after the strike. He's always been good at talking, even in English—he was the best at the farm school, he used to read the newspapers the Indian wraps soap and sugar in when you buy at the store.

There was trouble at the hostel where he had a bed, and riots over paying rent in the townships and he told me—just me, not the old ones—that wherever people were fighting against the way we are treated they were doing it for all of us, on the farms as well as the towns, and the unions were with them, he was with them, making speeches, marching. The third year, we heard he was in prison. Instead of getting married. We didn't know where to find him, until he went on trial. The case was heard in a town far away. I couldn't go often to the court because by that time I had passed my Standard 8 and I was working in the farm school. Also my parents were short of money. Two of my brothers who had gone away to work in town didn't send home; I suppose they lived with girlfriends and had to buy things for them. My father and other brother work here for the Boer and the pay is very small, we have two goats, a few cows we're allowed to graze, and a patch of land where my mother can grow vegetables. No cash from that.

When I saw him in the court he looked beautiful in a blue suit with a striped shirt and brown tie. All the accused—his comrades, he said—were well dressed. The union bought the clothes so that the judge and the prosecutor would know they weren't dealing with stupid yes-baas black men who didn't know their rights. These things and everything else about the court and trial he explained to me when I was allowed to visit him in jail. Our little girl was born while the trial went on and when I brought the baby to court the first time to show him, his comrades hugged him and then hugged me across the barrier of the prisoners' dock and they had clubbed together to give me some money as a present for the baby. He chose the name for her, Inkululeko.

Then the trial was over and he got six years. He was sent to the Island. We all knew about the Island. Our leaders had been there so long. But I have never seen the sea except to colour it in blue at school, and I couldn't imagine a piece of earth surrounded by it. I could only think of a cake of dung, dropped by the cattle, floating in a pool of rainwater they'd crossed, the water showing the sky like a looking-glass, blue. I was ashamed only to think that. He had told me how the glass walls showed the pavement trees and the other buildings in the street and the colours of the cars and the clouds as the crane lifted him on a platform higher and higher through the sky to work at the top of a building.

He was allowed one letter a month. It was my letter because his parents didn't know how to write. I used to go to them where they worked on another farm to ask what message they wanted to send. The mother always cried and put her hands on her head and said nothing, and the old man, who preached to us in the veld every Sunday, said tell my son we are praying, God will make everything all right for him. Once he wrote back, That's the trouble—our people on the farms, they're told God will decide what's good for them so that they won't find the force to do anything to change their lives.

After two years had passed, we—his parents and I—had saved up enough money to go to Cape Town to visit him. We went by train and slept on the floor at the station and asked the way, next day, to the ferry. People were kind; they all knew that if you wanted the ferry it was because you had somebody of yours on the Island.

And there it was—there was the sea. It was green and blue, climbing and falling, bursting white, all the way to the sky. A terrible wind was slapping it this way and that; it hid the Island, but people like us, also waiting for the ferry, pointed where the Island must be, far out in the sea that I never thought would be like it really was.

There were other boats, and ships as big as buildings that go to other places, all over the world, but the ferry is only for the Island, it doesn't go anywhere else in the world, only to the Island. So everybody waiting there was waiting for the Island, there could be no mistake we were not in the right place. We had sweets and biscuits, trousers and a warm coat for him (a woman standing with us said we wouldn't be allowed to give him the clothes) and I wasn't wearing, any more, the old beret pulled down over my head that farm girls wear, I had bought relaxer cream from the man who comes round the farms selling things out of a box on his bicycle, and my hair was combed up thick under a flowered scarf that didn't cover the gold-coloured rings in my ears. His mother had her blanket tied round her waist over her dress, a farm woman, but I looked just as good as any of the other girls there. When the ferry was ready to take us, we stood all pressed together and quiet like the cattle waiting to be let through a gate. One man kept looking round with his chin moving up and down, he was counting, he must have been afraid there were too many to get on and he didn't want to be left behind. We all moved up to the policeman in charge and everyone ahead of us went on to the boat. But when our turn came and he put out his hand for something, I didn't know what.

We didn't have a permit. We didn't know that before you come to Cape Town, before you come to the ferry for the Island, you have to have a police permit to visit a prisoner on the Island. I tried to ask him nicely. The wind blew the voice out of my mouth.

We were turned away. We saw the ferry rock, bumping the landing where we stood, moving, lifted and dropped by all that water, getting smaller and smaller until we didn't know if we were really seeing it or one of the birds that looked black, dipping up and down, out there.

The only good thing was one of the other people took the sweets and biscuits for him. He wrote and said he got them. But it wasn't a good letter. Of course not. He was cross with me; I should have found out, I should have known about the permit. He was right—I bought the train tickets, I asked where to go for the ferry, I should have known about the permit. I have passed Standard 8. There was an advice office to go to in town, the churches ran it, he wrote. But the farm is so far from town, we on the farms don't know about these things. It was as he said; our ignorance is the way we are kept down, this ignorance must go.

We took the train back and we never went to the Island—never saw him in the three more years he was there. Not once. We couldn't find the money for the train. His father died and I had to help his mother from my pay. For our people the worry is always money, I wrote. When will we ever have money? Then he sent such a good letter. That's what I'm on the Island for, far away from you, I'm here so that one day our people will have the things they need, land, food, the end of ignorance. There was something else—I could just read the word 'power' the prison had blacked out. All his letters were not just for me; the prison officer read them before I could.

\* \* \*

He was coming home after only five years!

That's what it seemed to me, when I heard—the five years was suddenly disappeared—nothing!—there was no whole year still to wait. I showed my—our—little girl his photo again. That's your daddy, he's coming, you're going to see him. She told the other children at school, I've got a daddy, just as she showed off about the kid goat she had at home.

We wanted him to come at once, and at the same time we wanted time to prepare. His mother lived with one of his uncles; now that his father was dead there was no house of his father for him to take me to as soon as we married. If there had been time, my father would have cut poles, my mother and I would have baked bricks, cut thatch, and built a house for him and me and the child.

We were not sure what day he would arrive. We only heard on my radio his name and the names of some others who were released. Then at the Indian's store I noticed the newspaper, *The Nation,* written by black people, and on the front a picture of a lot of people dancing and waving—I saw at once it was at that ferry. Some men were being carried on other men's shoulders. I couldn't see which one was him. We were waiting. The ferry had brought him from the Island but we remembered Cape Town is a long way from us. Then he did come. On a Saturday, no school, so I was working with my mother, hoeing and weeding round the pumpkins and mealies, my hair, that I meant to keep nice, tied in an old *doek.* A combi came over the veld and his comrades had brought him. I wanted to run away and wash but he stood there stretching his legs, calling, hey! hey! with his comrades making a noise around him, and my mother started shrieking in the old style aie! aie! and my father was clapping and stamping towards him. He held his arms open to us, this big man in town clothes, polished shoes, and all the time while he hugged me I was holding my dirty hands, full of mud, away from him behind his back. His teeth hit me hard through his lips, he grabbed at my mother and she struggled to hold the child up to him. I thought we would all fall down! Then everyone was quiet. The child hid behind my mother. He picked her up but she turned her head away to her shoulder. He spoke to her gently but she wouldn't speak to him. She's nearly six years old! I told her not to be a baby. She said, That's not him.

The comrades all laughed, we laughed, she ran off and he said, She has to have time to get used to me.

He has put on weight, yes; a lot. You couldn't believe it. He used to be so thin his feet looked too big for him. I used to feel his bones but now—that night—when he lay on me he was so heavy, I didn't remember it was like that. Such a long time. It's strange to get stronger in prison; I thought he wouldn't have enough to eat and would come out weak. Everyone said, Look at him!—he's a man, now. He laughed and banged his fist on his chest, told them how the comrades exercised in their cells, he would run three miles a day, stepping up and down on one place on the floor of that small cell where he was kept. After we were together at night we used to whisper a long time but now I can feel he's thinking of some things I don't know and I can't worry him with talk. Also I don't know what to say. To ask him what it was like, five years shut away there; or to tell him something about school or about the child. What else has happened, here? Nothing. Just waiting. Sometimes in the daytime I do try to tell him what it was like for me, here at home on the farm, five years. He listens, he's interested, just like he's interested when people from the other farms come to visit and talk to him about little things that happened to them while he was away all that time on the Island. He smiles and nods, asks a couple of questions and then stands up and stretches. I see it's to show them it's enough, his mind is going back to something he was busy with before they came. And we farm people are very slow; we tell things slowly, he used to, too.

He hasn't signed on for another job. But he can't stay at home with us; we thought, after five years over there in the middle of that green and blue sea, so far, he would rest with us a little while. The combi or some car comes to fetch him and he says don't worry, I don't know what day I'll be back. At first I asked, what week, next week? He tried to explain to me: in the Movement it's not like it was in the union, where you do your work every day and after that you are busy with meetings; in the Movement you never know where you will have to go and what is going to come up next. And the same with money. In the Movement, it's not like a job, with regular pay—I know that, he doesn't have to tell me—it's like it was going to the Island, you do it for all our people who suffer because we haven't got money, we haven't got land—look, he said, speaking of my parents', my home, the home that has been waiting for him, with his child: look at this place where the white man owns the ground and lets you squat in mud and tin huts here only as long as you work for him—*Baba* and your brother planting his crops and looking after his cattle, Mama cleaning his house and you in the school without even having the chance to train properly as a teacher. The farmer owns us, he says. I've been thinking we haven't got a home because there wasn't time to build a house before he came from the Island; but we haven't got a home at all. Now I've understood that.

I'm not stupid. When the comrades come to this place in the combi to talk to him here I don't go away with my mother after we've brought them tea or (if she's made it for the weekend) beer. They like her beer, they talk about our culture and there's one of them who makes a point of putting his arm around my mother, calling her the mama of all of them, the mama of Africa. Sometimes they please her very much by telling her how they used to sing on the Island and getting her to sing an old song we all know from our grandmothers. Then they join in with their strong voices. My father doesn't like this noise travelling across the veld; he's afraid that if the Boer finds out my man is a political, from the Island, and he's holding meetings on the Boer's land, he'll tell my father to go, and take his family with him. But my brother says if the Boer asks anything just tell him it's a prayer meeting. Then the singing is over; my mother knows she must go away into the house.

I stay, and listen. He forgets I'm there when he's talking and arguing about something I can see is important, more important than anything we could ever have to say to each other when we're alone. But now and then, when one of the other comrades is speaking I see him look at me for a moment the way I will look up at one of my favourite children in school to encourage the child to understand. The men don't speak to me and I don't speak. One of the things they talk about is organising the people on the farms — the workers, like my father and brother, and like his parents used to be. I learn what all these things are: minimum wage, limitation of working hours, the right to strike, annual leave, accident compensation, pensions, sick and even maternity leave. I am pregnant, at last I have another child inside me, but that's women's business. When they talk about the Big Man, the Old Men, I know who these are: our leaders are also back from prison. I told him about the child coming; he said, And this one belongs to a new country, he'll build the freedom we've fought for! I know he wants to get married but there's no time for that at present. There was hardly time for him to make the child. He comes to me just like he comes here to eat a meal or put on clean clothes. He picks up the little girl and swings her round and there! — it's done, he's getting into the combi, he's already turning to his comrade that face of his that knows only what's inside his head, those eyes that move quickly as if he's chasing something you can't see. The little girl hasn't had time to get used to this man. But I know she'll be proud of him, one day!

How can you tell that to a child six years old? But I tell her about the Big Man and the Old Men, our leaders, so she'll know that her father was with them on the Island, this man is a great man, too.

On Saturday, no school and I plant and weed with my mother, she sings but I don't; I think. On Sunday there's no work, only prayer meetings out of the farmer's way under the trees, and beer drinks at the mud and tin huts where the farmers allow us to squat on their land. I go off on my own as I used to do when I was a child, making up games and talking to myself where no one would hear me or look for me. I sit on a warm stone in the late afternoon, high up, and the whole valley is a path between the hills, leading away from my feet. It's the Boer's farm but that's not true, it belongs to nobody. The cattle don't know that anyone says he owns it, the sheep — they are grey stones, and then they become a thick grey snake moving—don't know. Our huts and the old mulberry tree and the little brown mat of earth that my mother dug over yesterday, way down there, and way over there the clump of trees round the chimneys and the shiny thing that is the TV mast of the farmhouse—they are nothing, on the back of this earth. It could twitch them away like a dog does a fly.

I am up with the clouds. The sun behind me is changing the colours of the sky and the clouds are changing themselves, slowly, slowly. Some are white, blowing themselves up like bubbles. Underneath is a bar of grey, not enough to make rain. It gets longer and darker while the other clouds are all pink, it grows a thin snout and long body and then the end of it is a tail. There's a huge grey rat moving across the sky, eating the sky.

The child remembered the photo; she said, That's not him. I'm sitting here where I came often when he was on the Island. I came to get away from the others, to wait by myself.

I'm watching the rat, it's losing itself, it's shape, eating the sky, and I'm waiting. Waiting for him to come back.

Waiting. I'm waiting to come back home.

## ■ Dennis Brutus (1924– ) *Zimbabwe/South Africa/United States* (poem)

Dennis Brutus was born in Harare, Zimbabwe, but he grew up in Port Elizabeth in South Africa. He went to Fort Hare University College and, for fourteen years, taught English and Afrikaans in high school. He was dismissed from teaching for political activities and went on to study law at the University of Witwaterstrand in Johannesburg. Brutus had a truly brutal life in South Africa. He was arrested, shot, and banned from publishing. In 1966, he was finally able to leave the country, first, going to London, and, then, to the United States where he was a professor at Northwestern University. His strongest poems recall his time in prison.

FURTHER READING: Brutus, Dennis. *Letters to Martha and Other Poems,* 1968; *Poems from Algiers,* 1970; *China Poems,* 1975; *Strains,* 1975; *Stubborn Hope: New Poems, and Selections from China Poems and Strains,* 1983; *African Literature,* 1988; *New Masks,* 1990.

## *Letter #18*

I remember rising one night
after midnight
and moving
through an impulse of loneliness
to try and find the stars.

And through the haze
the battens of fluorescents made
I saw pinpricks of white
I thought were stars.

Greatly daring
I thrust my arm through the bars
and easing the switch in the corridor
plunged my cell in darkness

I scampered to the window
and saw the splashes of light
where the stars flowered.

But through my delight
thudded the anxious boots
and a warning barked
from the machine-gun post
on the catwalk.

And it is the brusque inquiry
and threat
that I remember of that night
rather than the stars.

## ■ Alex La Guma (1925–1985) *South Africa* (story)

Alex La Guma's rebellion was his legacy. His father, Jimmy La Guma, had been a leader in South Africa's nonwhite liberation movement. La Guma followed, forgoing his education in favor of politics. Interested in seeing combat in World War II, he tried to join the British Army, but he was rejected because he was too young and underweight. Rather than return to school, he went to work in a furniture company and then at the Metal Box Company. There, La Guma was fired because of his union activities. He joined the Communist Party in 1947 and was a member of the Cape Town District Committee until it was banned by the government in 1950.

In 1956, La Guma and 156 other people were arrested in the famous Treason Trial. For the next eleven years, he would spend most of his time in jail or under house arrest for his political activities. During this period, La Guma joined *New Age*, a progressive newspaper, where he worked until August 1962. That same year, the publishers Mbari released his controversial first novel *A Walk in the Night*. The following year began a five-year house arrest sentence during which nothing La Guma said or wrote could be published in South Africa.

Alex La Guma established his literary career as a short story writer when he published two stories in early editions of *Black Orpheus*. His complex characters are people on the fringe of society—prostitutes, anti-apartheid activists, and thieves—who have an uncanny ability to understand the human plight and to raise their position to heroic. Their environment, laden with cruel and startling images ("a rubbed smear of lipstick like a half-healed wound" and "a torn undergarment hanging from a brass knob was a specter in the room") only sustains their shadowed situation. They cannot escape their social position, yet they survive. His social-realist heroes transcend inclement situations, becoming moral and honorable in their heightened sensitivity. La Guma utilizes sophisticated and subtle techniques to evoke chaos and uncertainty in his writing. In "Blankets," he repeats a key passage, effectively creating a bewildering environment for his main character, Choker, who is stabbed by his lover's husband. During his ride in the ambulance, though in a state of delirium, Choker is able to survive by having a clean warm blanket instead of the vile blankets of his lover. In the reality and symbol of a blanket, Choker discerns both violence and salvation.

In 1966, La Guma left South Africa with his family, and they settled in Great Britain the following year. There, he continued to write about Africa until his death in 1985.

FURTHER READING: La Guma, Alex. *A Walk in the Night,* 1962; *And a Threefold Cord,* 1964; *In the Fog of the Seasons' End,* 1972; *Time of the Butcherbird,* 1979; *Memories of Home: The Writings of Alex La Guma,* 1991.

# Blankets

Choker woke up. The woman's wiry hair got into his mouth and tasted of stale brilliantine. The old double bed sagged and wobbled when he shifted his weight, and there were dark stains made by heads on the crumpled gray-white pillows, and a rubbed smear of lipstick like a half-healed wound. His mouth felt parched from the drinking of the night before, and he had a headache.

The woman was saying, half asleep, "No, man. No, man." Her body was moist and sweaty under the blanket, and the bed smelled of a mixture of cheap perfume, spilled powder and human bodies mixed with infant urine. The faded curtain over the room window beckoned to him in the hot breeze. In the early, slum-colored light, a torn undergarment hanging from a brass knob was a specter in the room.

Choker felt ill and angry. The unwashed, worn blanket brushed his face and he smelled it with the other smells, and thought vaguely that he had slept under such blankets all his life. He wished he could sleep in a bed in some posh hotel, under fresh-laundered bedding. Then this thought was displaced by desire for a drink of cold beer, even water. He felt irritable, and thrust the bedding from him.

The woman turned beside him under the blanket, protesting in her half-sleep, and Choker sat up, cursing. The agonized sounds of the bedspring woke up the baby who lay in a bathtub on the floor, and it began to cry, its toothless voice rising in a high-pitched wail.

Choker sat on the edge of the bed and cursed the baby and the woman in his mind. He wondered why the hell he had crept in with somebody else's woman in the first place. And she with a bloody baby, too. The child in the tin tub kept on wailing.

"Ah — " he snapped angrily at the infant.

The woman woke up and looked at him, disheveled, from the soiled pillow. "You made such a noise. You woke the child," she chided.

"Ah, hold your mouth," Choker told her angrily. "Get up and see to your damn kid."

He stood up and walked around the bed to find his shirt and trousers. The woman asked, "You going?"

"Of course, yes. You reckon I want to listen to this blerry noise?"

"Well," the woman said crossly, "can I help it? You knew *mos* I had the child."

The baby kept on wailing. Choker looked at it as he pulled on his trousers and buttoned his shirt. "Babies, dammit."

She asked, in a humbler tone, "You coming back?"

"Maybe. Maybe not. I don't know."

"Listen," she said. "Careful when you come, hey? I don't want my man to see you come here. He got an idea you been coming here. He'll may be do something to you."

Choker sneered: "Him? Jesus, I'll break him in two with my bare hands."

He laughed, standing hugely in the room. He was a big man, with muscles like bulges of steel wire, and great hands. He was brutal and vicious, and used the thick, ropy, grimed hands for hurting rather than for working.

She said, "Awright, man. But even though he left me, he don't like 'nother man coming here. He may be watching out for you."

"The hell with him," Choker growled. "His mother."

The woman said nothing, and climbed out of the jangling bed to attend to the baby. She sat on the edge of the bed in her limp petticoat and suckled it.

She said, "If you wait a little I'll make a little tea."

"Forget it."

Choker looked at her, sneered and shook his head, and then went out.

He walked along the corridor of the house, past the other rooms, frowning irritably against the nagging ache in his head, and the brittle feeling in his mouth and throat. There were holes in the boards of the floor, and he walked as carefully as his heavy body allowed.

In the morning sunlight, outside the smelly house, he headed for the tap in the dry, hollowed-out area which had once been a garden. He drank thirstily for a few moments, and then splashed his face, drying it on the sleeve of his shirt. He thought, To hell with her, I'll be boggered if I go back to that lot.

Around him were the rows of old, crammed houses and tumble-down boxboard-and-tin shanties of the suburban slum. Chickens and dogs picked their way around among the weeds. He made his way idly through the broken streets and pathways. People avoided him, or gave him a casual greeting and passed on quickly, knowing his reputation. He was a drifting hulk, an accursed ship moving through a rotting sargasso.

Choker was passing a walled-in yard when the three men stepped quickly from a gateway behind him. One of them cried, "That's him," and then, before he could turn, pain speared him with red-hot blades. He felt the pain in his head and the pain in his body almost simultaneously, and he fell, cursing. They didn't even wait to examine him, or to try again, but fled swiftly from the reach of the grappling-iron hands, leaving him to bleed in the roadway.

Choker lay in the road and felt the pain and the trickling of blood against his skin. He wanted to get up, but his legs were suddenly useless, and his arms would not lift his body. He lay there, his throbbing mind stubbornly cursing his attackers, while a crowd gathered, everybody talking excitedly.

Somebody said, "Better carry him off the road."

"I don't want nothing to do with it, hey."

"Well, he can't *mos* just lie about there."

"Better go over to the shop and phone for the am'ulance."

"Okay. Did you see them?"

"Look, pally, I didn't see nothing, man."

"Well, pick him up. Look, Freddy, you take his feet. Sampie, you he'p him. Me and Points can take his arms."

Lying there, bleeding and feeling ill, Choker thought—you all, and then he felt himself being lifted roughly. He thought it was a hell of a thing to be so weak all of a sudden. They were bundling him about and he cursed them, and one of them laughed, "Jesus, he's a real tough guy."

Choker lay on the floor of the lean-to in the backyard where they had carried him. It was cooler under the sagging roof, with the pile of assorted junk in one corner: an ancient motor tire, sundry split and warped boxes, and an old enamel display sign with patches like maps of continents on another planet, where the paintwork had worn away, and the dusty footboard of a bed. There was also the smell of dust and chicken droppings in the lean-to.

From outside, beyond a chrome-colored rhomboid of sun, came a clatter of voices. In the yard they were discussing him. Choker opened his eyes, and peering down the length of his body, past the bare, grimy toes, he could see several pairs of legs, male and female, in tattered trousers and laddered stockings.

A man was saying, " . . . that was coward . . . from behind, *mos*."

*"Ja.* But look what he done to others, don't I say?"

Choker thought, To hell with those baskets. To hell with them all.

Somebody had thrown an old blanket over him. It smelled of sweat and dust and having been slept in unwashed, and it was torn and threadbare and stained. He touched the exhausted blanket with thick, grubby fingers. The texture was rough in parts and shiny thin where it had worn away. He was used to blankets like this.

Choker had been stabbed three times, each from behind. Once in the head, then between the shoulder blades, and again in the right side. The bleeding had stopped and there was not much pain. He had been knifed before, admittedly not as badly as this, and he thought, through the faraway pain. The baskets couldn't even do a decent job. He lay there and waited for the ambulance. Blood was drying slowly on the side of his hammered-copper face, and he also had a bad headache.

The voices, now and then raised in laughter, crackled outside, somewhere far away. Feet moved on the rough floor of the yard and a face not unlike that of a brown dog wearing an expired cloth cap, peered in.

"You still awright, Choker? Am'ulance is coming just now, hey."

"— off," Choker said. His voice croaked.

The voice withdrew, laughing: "*Ou* Choker. *Ou* Choker."

Another voice said: "That burg was waiting for him a long time awready."

*"Ja.* But Choker wasn't no good with a knife. Always used his hands, man."

"That was bad enough, I reckon."

The hell with them, Choker thought. He was feeling tired now. The hard grubby fingers, like corroded iron clamps, strayed over the parched field of the blanket. . . . He was being taken down a wet, tarred yard with tough wire netting over the barred windows looking into it. The place smelled of carbolic disinfectant, and the bunch of heavy keys clink-clinked as it swung from the hooked finger of the guard.

They reached a room fitted with shelving which was stacked here and there with piled blankets. "Take two, *jong,*" the guard said, and Choker began to rummage through the piles, searching for the thickest and warmest. But the guard, who somehow had a doggish face and wore a disintegrating cloth cap, laughed and jerked him aside, and seizing the nearest blankets, found two at random and flung them at Choker. They were filthy and smelly, and within their folds vermin waited like irregular troops in ambush.

"Come on. Come on. You think I got time to waste?"

"Is cold *mos,* man," Choker said.

But it was not the guard to whom he was talking. He was six years old and his brother, Willie, a year his senior, twisted and turned in the narrow, cramped, sagging bedstead which they shared, dragging the thin cotton blanket from Choker's body. Outside, the rain slapped against the cardboard-patched window, and the wind wheezed through the cracks and corners like an asthmatic old man.

"No, man, Willie, man. You got all the blanket, *jong.*"

"Well, I can't he'p it, *mos,* man. Is cold."

"What about me?" Choker whined. "What about me? I'm also cold, *mos.*"

Huddled under the blanket, fitted against each other like two pieces of a jigsaw puzzle. . . . The woman's wiry hair got into his mouth and smelled of stale hair oil. There were dark stains made by heads on the gray-white pillow, and a rubbed smear of lipstick like a half-healed wound.

The woman was saying, half-asleep, "You see? You see? What did I tell you?" Her body was moist and sweaty under the blanket; and the blanket and bed smelled of cheap perfume, spilled powder, urine and chicken droppings. The faded curtain beckoned to him in the hot breeze. The woman turned from him under the blanket, muttering, and Choker sat up. The agonized sounds of the bedspring woke the baby in the tin bathtub on the floor, and it began to cry in a high-pitched metallic wail that grew louder and louder. . . .

Choker woke up as the wail grew to a crescendo and then faded quickly as the siren was switched off. Voices still excitedly shattered the sunlight in the yard. Choker saw the skirts of white coats and then the ambulance men were in the lean-to. His head was aching badly, and his wounds were throbbing. His face perspired like a squeezed-out washcloth.

Hands searched his body. One of the ambulance attendants asked: "Do you feel any pain?"

Choker looked at the pink-white face above him, scowling. "No, sir."

The layer of old newspapers on which he was lying was soaked with his blood. "Knife wounds," one of the attendants said. "He isn't bleeding much outside," the other said. "Put on a couple of pressure pads."

He was in midair, carried on a stretcher flanked by a procession of onlookers. Rubber sheeting was cool against his back. The stretcher rumbled into the ambulance and the doors slammed shut, sealing off the spectators. Then the siren whined and rose, clearing a path through the crowd.

Choker felt the vibration of the ambulance through his body as it sped away. His murderous fingers touched the folded edge of the bedding. The sheet over him was white as cocaine, and the blanket was thick and new and warm. He lay still, listening to the siren.

# ■ Camara Laye (1928–1980) *Guinea* (novel)

## TRANSLATED BY JAMES KIRKUP AND ERNEST JONES

One of the first African writers to gain worldwide recognition, Camara Laye spent his childhood in upper Guinea in the village of Kouroussa, where both his maternal and paternal ancestors were goldsmiths. Though Muslim, his family still held the traditional belief that goldsmiths possessed magical powers and supernatural gifts and were to be revered as powerful figures in the village. Laye was educated at the local quranic school and then the Government Primary School. He left Kouroussa for Conakry to attend the technical college, École Poiret, where he received a scholarship to study in France. Laye left Guinea to study engineering in Argenteuil near Paris. Once his scholarship was exhausted, he went to work for the Simca car factory and attended night classes at the Conservatoire des Arts et Métiers.

It was during these lonely times that Laye decided he should record, in French, his memories and longings for his family and country, lest they be forgotten. These accounts were published in Paris in 1953 as *L'Enfant Noir* (*The Dark Child*) and won the Prix Charles Veillon. Laye also wrote about his country's political problems but believed that writers need not address specific governmental dilemmas to be political. In his third and last novel, *A Dream of Africa,* he did not romanticize "mother Africa" like many exiled authors. He saw a corrupted regime for what it was, whether as a colony or under the sway of a local tyrant.

In 1965, under the pretext of needing urgent medical care, Laye left Guinea for Paris and never returned home. He later moved back to Africa, living first in Côte D'Ivoire, and eventually settling permanently in Senegal. He worked in Dakar at the French Institute of Black Africa as a researcher in the oral traditions of the Malinke people (from his region of Africa). His death in 1980 was hastened by the hardships, physical and financial, endured in exile.

FURTHER READING: Laye, Camara. *The Dark Child,* 1954; *The Radiance of the King,* 1956; *A Dream of Africa.* Translated by James Kirkup and Ernest Jones, 1968; *The Autobiography of an African Boy.* Translated by Philippe Thoby-Marcellin, 1989.

## from *The Dark Child*

I was a little boy playing around my father's hut. How old would I have been at that time? I can not remember exactly. I must still have been very young: five, maybe six years old. My mother was in the workshop with my father, and I could just hear their familiar voices above the noise of the anvil and the conversation of the customers.

Suddenly I stopped playing, my whole attention fixed on a snake that was creeping around the hut. After a moment I went over to him. I had taken in my hand a reed that was lying in the yard—there were always some lying around; they used to get broken off the fence of plaited reeds that marked the boundary of our concession—and I thrust it into his mouth. The snake did not try to get away: he was beginning to enjoy our little game; he was slowly swallowing the reed; he was devouring it, I thought, as if it were some delicious prey, his eyes glittering with voluptuous bliss; and inch by inch his head was drawing nearer to my hand. At last the reed was almost entirely swallowed, and the snake's jaws were terribly close to my fingers.

I was laughing. I had not the slightest fear, and I feel sure that the snake would not have hesitated much longer before burying his fangs in my fingers if, at that moment, Damany, one of the apprentices, had not come out of the workshop. He called my father, and almost at once I felt myself lifted off my feet: I was safe in the arms of one of my father's friends.

Around me there was a great commotion. My mother was shouting hardest of all, and she gave me a few sharp slaps. I wept, more upset by the sudden uproar than by the blows. A little later, when I was somewhat calmer and the shouting had ceased, my mother solemnly warned me never to play that game again. I promised, although the game still didn't seem dangerous to me.

My father's hut was near the workshop, and I often played beneath the veranda that ran around the outside. It was his private hut, and like all our huts built of mud bricks that had been pounded and moulded with water; it was round, and proudly helmeted with thatch. It was entered by a rectangular doorway. Inside, a tiny window let in a thin shaft of daylight. On the right was the bed, made of beaten earth like the bricks, and spread with a simple wicker-work mat on which lay a pillow stuffed with kapok. At the rear, right under the window where the light was strongest, were the toolboxes. On the left were the *boubous* and the prayer-rugs. At the head of the bed, hanging over the pillow and watching over my father's slumber, stood a row of pots that contained extracts from plants and the bark of trees. These pots all had metal lids and were profusely and curiously garlanded with chaplets of cowry shells; it did not take me long to discover that they were the most important things in the hut; they contained magic charms—those mysterious liquids that keep the evil spirits at bay, and, if smeared on the body, make it invulnerable to every kind of black magic. My father, before going to bed, never failed to smear his body with a little of each liquid, first one, then another, for each charm had its own particular property: but exactly *what* property I did not know: I had left my father's house too soon.

From the veranda under which I played I could keep an eye on the workshop opposite, and the adults for their part could keep an eye on me. This workshop was the main building in our concession, and my father was generally to be found there, looking after the work, forging the most important items himself, or repairing delicate mechanisms; there he received his friends and his customers, and the place resounded with noise from morning to night. Moreover, everyone who entered or left our concession had to cross the workshop. There was a perpetual coming and going, though no one seemed to be in any particular hurry; each had his bit of gossip; each lingered at the forge to watch. Sometimes I came near the door, but I rarely went in; everyone there frightened me, and I would run away as soon as anyone tried to touch me. It was not until very much later that I got into the habit of crouching in a corner of the workshop to watch the fire blazing in the forge.

My private domain at that time was the veranda that encircled my father's hut, my mother's hut, and the orange tree that grew in the middle of the concession.

As soon as you crossed the workshop and went through the door at the back, you would see the orange tree. Compared with the giants of our native forests, the tree was not very big, but its mass of glossy leaves cast a dense shade that kept the heat at bay. When it was in flower a heady perfume pervaded the entire concession. When the fruit first appeared we were only allowed to look: we had to wait patiently until it was ripe. Then my father, who as head of the family—and a very large family it was—governed the concession, gave the order to pick the fruit. The men who did the picking brought their baskets one by one to my father, who portioned them out among the people who lived in the concession and among his neighbors and customers. After that we were permitted to help ourselves from the baskets and we were allowed as much as we liked! My father was open-handed; in fact, a lavish giver. Any visitor, no matter who he was, shared our meals; since I could never keep up with the speed at which such guests ate I might have remained forever hungry if my mother had not taken the precaution of putting my share aside.

"Sit here," she would say, "and eat, for your father's mad."

She did not look upon such guests with a kindly eye. There were too many for her liking, all bent on filling their bellies at her expense. My father, for his part, ate very little; he was an extremely temperate man.

We lived beside a railroad. The trains skirted the reed fence of the concession so closely that sparks thrown off from the locomotive set fire to it every now and then which had to be quickly extinguished so that the whole concession would not go up in smoke. These alarms, frightening yet exciting, made me aware of the passing trains. And even where there were no trains—for in those days the railroad was dependent on a most irregular water traffic—much of my time was spent watching the iron rails. They glistened cruelly in a light which nothing in that place could relieve. Baking since dawn, the roadbed was so hot that oil which dropped from the locomotives evaporated immediately, leaving no trace. Was it the oven-like heat or the smell of oil—for the smell remained in spite of everything—which attracted the snakes? I do not know. But often I came upon them crawling in that hot roadbed. It would have been fatal if they had gotten into the concession.

Ever since the day when I had been forbidden by my mother to play with snakes I ran to her as soon as I saw one.

"There's a snake!" I would cry.

"What? Another?"

And she would come running to see what sort of snake it was. If it was just a snake like any other snake—actually they were all quite different—she would immediately beat it to death; and, like all the women of our country, she would work herself into a frenzy, beating the snake to a pulp. The men contented themselves with a single hard blow, neatly struck.

One day, however, I noticed a little black snake with a strikingly marked body. He was proceeding slowly in the direction of the workshop. I ran to warn my mother, as usual. But as soon as she saw the black snake she said to me gravely:

"My son, this one must not be killed: he is not like other snakes, and he will not harm you; you must never interfere with him."

Everyone in our concession knew that this snake must not be killed— everyone except myself, and, I suppose, my little playmates, who were still ignorant children.

"This snake," my mother added, "is your father's guiding spirit."

I gazed dumbfounded at the little snake. He was proceeding calmly toward the workshop, gracefully, very sure of himself, and almost as if conscious of his immunity; his body, black and brilliant, glittered in the harsh light of the sun. When he reached the workshop, I noticed for the first time a small hole in the wall, cut out level with the ground. The snake disappeared through this hole.

"Look," said my mother, "the snake is going to pay your father a visit."

Although I was familiar with the supernatural, this sight filled me with such astonishment that I was struck dumb. What business would a snake have with my father? And why this particular snake? No one was to kill him because he was my father's guiding spirit! At any rate, that was the explanation my mother had given me. But what exactly was a "guiding spirit"? What were these guiding spirits that I encountered almost everywhere, forbidding one thing, commanding another to be done? I could not understand it at all, though their presences surrounded me as I grew to manhood. There were good spirits, and there were evil ones; and more evil than good ones, it seemed. And how was I to know that this snake was harmless? He was a snake like the others: black, to be sure, with extraordinary markings—but for all that a snake. I was completely perplexed, but I did not question my mother: I had decided that I must ask my father about it, as if this were a mystery to be discussed only between men, a mystery in which women had no part. I decided to wait until evening to speak to him.

Immediately after the evening meal, when the palavers were over, my father bade his friends farewell and sat under the veranda of his hut; I seated myself near him. I began questioning him in a dilatory manner, as all children do, regarding every subject under the sun. Actually I was no more talkative than on other evenings. Only this evening I withheld what troubled me, waiting for the opportunity when—my face betraying nothing—I might ask the question which had worried me so deeply from the moment when I first saw the black snake going toward the workshop. Finally, unable to restrain myself any longer, I asked:

"My father, what is that little snake that comes to visit you?"

"What snake do you mean?"

"Why the little black snake that my mother forbids us to kill."

"Ah!" he said.

He gazed at me for a long while. He seemed to be considering whether to answer or not. Perhaps he was thinking about how old I was, perhaps he was wondering if it was not a little too soon to confide such a secret to a twelve-year-old boy. Then suddenly he made up his mind.

"That snake," he said, "is the guiding spirit of our race. Can you understand that?"

"Yes," I answered, although I did not understand very well.

"That snake," he went on, "has always been with us; he has always made himself known to one of us. In our time, it is to me that he has made himself known."

"Yes," I said.

And I said it with all my heart, for it seemed obvious to me that the snake could have made himself known to no one but my father. Was not my father the head man in our concession? Was it not my father who had authority over all the blacksmiths in our district? Was he not the most skilled? Was he not, after all, my father?

"How did he make himself known?" I asked.

"First of all, he made himself known in the semblance of a dream. He appeared to me several times in sleep and told me the day on which he would appear to me in reality: he gave me the precise time and place. But when I really saw him for the first time, I was filled with fear. I took him for a snake like any other snake, and I had to keep myself under control or I would have tried to kill him. When he saw that I did not receive him kindly, he turned away and departed the way he had come. And there I stood, watching him depart, wondering all the time if I should not simply have killed him there and then; but a power greater than I stayed my hand and prevented me from pursuing him. I stood watching him disappear. And even then, at that very moment, I could easily have overtaken him; a few swift strides would have been enough; but I was struck motionless by a kind of paralysis. Such was my first encounter with the little black snake."

He was silent a moment, then went on:

"The following night, I saw the snake again in my dream. 'I came as I foretold,' he said, 'but thou didst not receive me kindly; nay, rather I did perceive that thou didst intend to receive me unkindly: I did read it thus in thine eyes. Wherefore dost thou reject me? Lo, I am the guiding spirit of thy race, and it is even as the guiding spirit of thy race that I make myself known to thee, as to the most worthy. Therefore forbear to look with fear upon me, and beware that thou dost not reject me, for behold, I bring thee good fortune.' After that, I received the snake kindly when he made himself known to me a second time; I received him without fear, I received him with loving kindness, and he brought me nothing but good."

My father again was silent for a moment, then he said:

"You can see for yourself that I am not more gifted than other men, that I have nothing which other men have not also, and even that I have less than others, since I give everything away, and would even give away the last thing I had, the shirt on my back. Nevertheless I am better known. My name is on everyone's tongue, and it is I who have authority over all the blacksmiths in the five cantons. If these things are so, it is by virtue of this snake alone, who is the guiding spirit of our race. It is to this snake that I owe everything; it is he who gives me warning of all that is to happen. Thus I am never surprised, when I awake, to see this or that person waiting for me outside my workshop: I already know that he will be there. No more am I surprised when this or that motorcycle or bicycle breaks down, or when an accident happens to a clock: because I have had fore-knowledge of what would come to pass. Everything is transmitted to me in the course of the night, together with an account of all the work I shall have to perform, so that from the start, without having to cast about in my mind, I know how to repair whatever is brought to me. These things have established my renown as a craftsman. But all this—let it never be forgotten—I owe to the snake, I owe it to the guiding spirit of our race."

He was silent; and then I understood why, when my father came back from a walk he would enter the workshop and say to the apprentices: "During my absence, this or that person has been here, he was dressed in such and such a way, he came from such and such a place and he brought with him such and such a piece of work to be done." And all marveled at this curious knowledge. When I raised my eyes, I saw that my father was watching me.

"I have told you all these things, little one, because you are my son, the eldest of my sons, and because I have nothing to hide from you. There is a certain form of behavior to observe, and certain ways of acting in order that the guiding spirit of our race may approach you also. I, your father, was observing that form of behavior which persuades our guiding spirit to visit us. Oh, perhaps not consciously: but nevertheless it is true that if you desire the guiding spirit of our race to visit you one day, if you desire to inherit it in your turn, you will have to conduct yourself in the selfsame manner; from now on, it will be necessary for you to be more and more in my company."

He gazed at me with burning eyes, then suddenly he heaved a sigh.

"I fear, I very much fear, little one, that you are not often enough in my company. You are all day at school, and one day you will depart from that school for a greater one. You will leave me, little one. . . ."

And again he heaved a sigh. I saw that his heart was heavy within him. The hurricane-lamp hanging on the veranda cast a harsh glare on his face. He suddenly seemed to me an old man.

"Father!" I cried.

"Son . . ." he whispered.

And I was no longer sure whether I ought to continue to attend school or whether I ought to remain in the workshop: I felt unutterably confused.

"Go now," said my father.

I went to my mother's hut. The night was full of sparkling stars; an owl was hooting nearby. Ah! what was the right path for me? Did I know yet where that path lay? My perplexity was boundless as the sky, and mine was a sky, alas, without any stars. . . . I entered my mother's hut, which at that time was mine also, and went to bed at once. But sleep did not come and I tossed restlessly on my bed.

"What's the matter with you?" asked my mother.

"Nothing."

No. I couldn't find anything to say.

"Why don't you go to sleep?" my mother continued.

"I don't know."

"Go to sleep!" she said.

"Yes," I said.

"Sleep . . . Nothing can resist sleep," she said sadly.

Why did she, too, appear so sad? Had she divined my distress? Anything that concerned me she sensed very deeply. I was trying to sleep, but I shut my eyes and lay still in vain: the image of my father under the hurricane-lamp would not leave me: my father who had suddenly seemed so old and who was so young, so lively—younger and livelier than the rest of us, a man no one could outrun, who was swifter of limb than any of us. . . . "Father! . . . Father! . . . !" I kept repeating. "What must I do if I am to do the right thing?" And I wept silently and fell asleep still weeping.

After that we never mentioned the little black snake again: my father had spoken to me about him for the first and last time. But from that time on, as soon as I saw the little snake, I would run and sit in the workshop. I would watch him glide through the little hole in the wall. As if informed of his presence, my father at that very instant would turn his eyes to the hole and smile. The snake would go straight to him, opening his jaws. When he was within reach my father would stroke him and the snake would accept the caress with a quivering of his whole body. I never saw the little snake attempt to do the slightest harm to my father. That caress and the answering tremor—but I ought to say: that appealing caress and that answering tremor—threw me each time into an inexpressible confusion. I imagined I know not what mysterious conversations: the hand inquired and the tremor replied. . . .

Yes. It was like a conversation. Would I too converse that way some day? No. I would continue to attend school. Yet I should have liked so much to place my hand, my own hand, on that snake, and to understand and listen to that tremor too; but I did not know whether the snake would have accepted my hand, and I felt now that he would have nothing to tell me. I was afraid that he would never have anything to tell me.

When my father felt that he had stroked the snake enough he left him alone. Then the snake coiled himself under the edge of one of the sheepskins on which my father, facing his anvil, was seated. . . .

# ■ Ferdinand Oyono (1929– ) *Cameroon* (novel)

## TRANSLATED BY JOHN REED

One of Africa's most celebrated satirical writers, Ferdinand Oyono was born in French Cameroon. He was educated and worked in a missionary school in the small village of N'goulemakong after his Catholic mother left her polygamous husband, unwilling to share him with his other legal wife. Working as a seamstress, she managed to get him through the local lycée and eventually his father sent him to the Faculté de Droit (law school) and the National School of Administration in Paris. He chose a diplomatic life and has served at various levels in the Cameroon embassies, including that of ambassador stationed in important capitals, including Rome and Brussels. He has also been Cameroon's representative to the United Nations. Ferdinand Oyono had written his first two novels by the time he was twenty-seven, including his most famous volume, *Une vie de boy* (*Houseboy*). At first his works were ignored, but eventually *Houseboy* would become an African classic. Brilliant, swift, skillfully wrought, his comic bitter prose inevitably has a playful undercurrent of tragic force.

**FURTHER READING:** Oyono, Ferdinand. *Houseboy; Old Man and the Medal,* 1969; *Road and Europe,* 1989.

# *from Houseboy*

'I knew it, I recognized you were, brother, by your face. . . . Some arki, I want some arki.'

A woman passed me a cup full of a kind of rum smelling of smoke. I poured it into his mouth. He was a connoisseur. In spite of his pain he gave me a wink. He seemed to have gathered strength again. Even before he had called out to me to help him sit up he had begun to lift himself on his elbow. I put my arm round his shoulders and drew him up so that he could lean his back against the wall. His vacant eyes suddenly shone. They never left me.

'Brother,' he said. 'Brother, what are we? What are we blackmen who are called French?'

His voice grew bitter. I had never asked myself the question. I was young then and thoughtless. I felt myself grow stupid.

'You see, brother,' he went on, 'I'm finished . . . they've got me . . .' He showed me his shoulder. 'Still I'm glad I'm dying well away from where they are. My mother always used to say what my greediness would bring me to in the end . . . If I had known it would bring me to my grave . . . She was right, my poor mother.'

A hiccup shook him and his head dropped on to his shoulder. He cleared his throat.

'I am from the Cameroons, my friend, I am a Makake. I'd have made old bones if I'd been good and stayed at home in the village.'

His mind began to wander. He was interrupted by a fit of coughing, then once more his breathing grew normal. I helped him to lie down again. He drew his wasted arms on to his breast and crossed them. We were soon forgotten as he contemplated the mats of the roof, blackened by soot. I turned up the wick of the lamp where the flame had begun to flicker. It lit up the side of the bamboo bed on which the dying man lay. His shadow was thrown on to the cracked wall of the aba. Two spiders were running over it. Their enormously exaggerated shadows looked like two octopuses whose tentacles hung down like the branches of a willow tree weeping over the ape-like shadow of the dying man's head. Spasms seized him. He shuddered and expired. He could not be kept till morning and they buried him directly, that night. He was already rotten before he died.

I learnt that they had found him unconscious close to the frontier in the Spanish zone. A khaki bundle was handed over to me.

The man who had found it said gravely, 'He must have been *uno alumno.*'

I opened the packet. Inside there were two worn exercise books, a toothbrush, a stub of pencil and a large native comb made of ivory.

That was how I came to read Toundi's diary. It was written in Ewondo which is one of the main languages of the Cameroons. In the translation which I have made and which you are about to read, I have tried to keep the richness of the original language without letting it get in the way of the story itself.

# First Exercise Book

## AUGUST

Father Gilbert says I can read and write fluently. Now I can keep a diary like he does. Keeping a diary is a white man's custom and what pleasure there is in it I do not know. But I shall try it out.

While my master and benefactor was hearing confessions, I had a look into his diary. Ah, it is a grain-store for memories. These white men can preserve everything. In Father Gilbert's diary I found the kick he gave me when he caught me mimicking him in the sacristy. I felt my bottom burning all over again. It is strange, I thought I had forgotten all about it. . . .

\*　\*　\*

My name is Toundi Ondoua. I am the son of Toundi and of Zama. When the Father baptized me he gave me the name of Joseph. I am Maka by my mother and Ndjem by my father. My ancestors were cannibals. Since the white men came we have learnt other men must not be looked upon as animals.

They say in the village that I was the cause of my father's death because I ran away to a white priest on the day before my initiation when I should have met the famous serpent who watches over all the men of my race. Father Gilbert believes it was the Holy Spirit that led me to him. In fact I just wanted to get close to the white man with hair like the beard on a maize cob who dressed in woman's clothes and gave little black boys sugar lumps. I was in a gang of heathen boys who followed the missionary about as he went from hut to hut trying to make converts to the new religion. He knew a few words of Ndjem but his pronunciation was so bad that the way he said them, they all had obscene meanings. This amused everybody and his success was assured. He threw the little lumps of sugar to us like throwing corn to chickens. What a battle to get hold of one of those little white lumps! They were worth all the scraped knees, swollen eyes and painful cuts. Sometimes these distributions of sugar turned into brawls between our parents. One day my mother got into a fight with the mother of my friend Tinati because he had twisted my arm to make me let go of two lumps of sugar which I had won at the cost of a bleeding nose. That battle nearly came to bloodshed. My father had to be restrained by the neighbours from splitting open the head of Tinati's father, while Tinati's father was threatening to put his assegai through my father's stomach. When they had both been calmed down, my father, armed with a cane, invited me to follow him behind the house.

'You, Toundi, are the cause of this whole business. Your greediness will be the ruin of us. Anyone would think you don't have enough to eat at home. So on the day before your initiation you have to cross a stream to go begging lumps of sugar from some white man-woman who is a complete stranger to you.'

My father however was not a stranger and I was well acquainted with what he could do with a stick. Whenever he went for either my mother or me, it always took us a week to recover. I was a good way from his stick. He swished it in the air and came towards me. I edged backwards.

'Are you going to stop? I've not got legs to go chasing you. You know if I don't get you now I will wait for you for a hundred years to give you your punishment. Now come here and get it over with.'

'I haven't done anything to be beaten for, father,' I protested.

'Aaaaaaaaaaakiaaaaay!' he roared. 'You dare to say you haven't done anything? If you weren't such a glutton, if you hadn't the blood of the gluttons that flows through your mother's veins you wouldn't have been in Fia to fight like the little rat you are over the bits of sugar that cursed white man gives you. You wouldn't have got your arm twisted, your mother wouldn't have had a fight and I wouldn't have wanted to split open Tinati's old father's head. . . . I warn you, you had better stop. If you go one more step backwards, that will be an insult to me. I will take it as a sign that you are capable of taking your mother to bed.'

I stopped. He flung himself on me and the cane swished down on to my bare shoulders. I twisted like a worm in the sun.

'Turn round and put up your arms. I don't want to knock your eye out.'

'Let me off, father,' I begged, 'I won't do it again.'

'You always say that when I start to give you a thrashing. But today I'm going to go on thrashing and thrashing until I'm not angry any more.'

I couldn't cry out because that might have attracted the neighbours. My friends would have thought me a girl. I would have lost my place in the group of 'boys-who-are-soon-to-be-men'. My father gave me another blow that I dodged neatly.

'If you dodge again it means you are capable of taking my mother, your grandmother, to bed.'

My father always used this blackmail to stop me from getting away and to make me submit to his blows.

'I have not insulted you and I am not capable of taking my mother to bed or yours and I won't be beaten any more, so there.'

'How dare you speak to me like that! A drop of my own liquid speaking to me like that! Unless you stand still at once, I shall curse you.'

My father was choking. I had never seen him so furious. I went on backing away from him. He came on after me, down behind the huts, for a good hundred yards.

'Very well then,' he said. 'We'll see where you spend the night. I will tell your mother you have insulted us both. Your way back into the house will pass through my anus.'

With that he turned his back. I did not know where I could go. I had an uncle I did not like because of his scabies. His wife smelt of bad fish and so did he. I hated going into their house. It was growing dark. You could begin to see the flashing light of the fireflies. The thud of mortars announced the preparation of the evening meal. I went back softly behind our house and peered through the cracks in the mud wall. My father had his back to me. My unpleasant uncle was facing him. They were eating. . . . The aroma of porcupine made my mouth water. It had been caught in one of my father's traps and we had found it half eaten by ants two days later. My mother was famous in the village for her cooking of porcupine.

'The very first of the season,' said my uncle with his mouth full.

My father did not speak but pointed with his finger above his head to where the skulls of the animals he had taken in his traps were hung up in a row.

'You can eat it all up,' said my mother, 'I've kept some for Toundi in the pot.'

My father leapt up, stammering with rage. I saw there would be a storm.

'Bring Toundi's share here,' he shouted. 'He's not to have any of this porcupine. I will teach him to disobey me.'

'But he hasn't had anything since this morning. What will he eat when he gets in?'

'Nothing at all,' said my father.

'If you want to make him obedient,' added my uncle, 'take away his food . . . this porcupine is really delicious.'

My mother got up and fetched the pot. I saw my father's hand and my uncle's hand go in. Then I heard my mother crying. For the first time in my life I thought of killing my father.

I went back to Fia . . . and after hesitating for a long while I knocked at the white priest's door. I found him in the middle of his dinner. He was very surprised. I tried to explain through signs that I wanted to go away with him. He laughed with all his teeth so his mouth looked like a crescent moon. I stood shyly by the door. He made signs that I should come closer and he offered me what was left of his meal. I found it strange and delicious. We continued a conversation by signs. I knew I had been accepted.

That is how I became Father Gilbert's boy.

My father heard the news next day. I was afraid of how angry he would be . . . I explained to the priest, still using signs. He was amused. He gave me a friendly pat on the shoulder. I felt protected.

In the afternoon my father came. All he said to me was that I was still his son, the drop of his liquid and that he bore me no grudge. If I came home, everything would be forgotten. I knew just how much trust I could put in a speech like this made in front of the white man. I put my tongue out at him. The look came into his eye that always came when he was going to 'teach me how to behave.' But I was not afraid while Father Gilbert was there. Father Gilbert's eyes seemed to cast a spell over my father. He lowered his head and went out crestfallen.

My mother came to see me that night. She was crying. We cried together. She told me I had done well to leave my father's house and that my father did not love me as a father ought to love his son. She said that she gave me her blessing and that if ever I fell ill I had only to bathe in a stream and I would be cured.

Father Gilbert gave me a pair of khaki shorts and a red jersey. All the boys in Fia were so impressed by these that they came to ask Father Gilbert to take them on as well.

Two days later Father Gilbert took me on his motor cycle. We spread panic through the villages by the noise we made. His tour had lasted a fortnight and now we were on our way back to the Saint Peter's Catholic Mission at Dangan. I was happy. The speed intoxicated me. I was going to learn about the city and white men and live like them. I caught myself thinking I was like one of the wild parrots we used to attract in the village with grains of maize. They were captured through their greediness. My mother often used to say, laughing, 'Toundi, what will your greediness bring you to . . . ?'

My parents are dead. I have never been back to the village.

\* \* \*

Now I am at the Saint Peter's Catholic Mission at Dangan. I wake up every morning at five o'clock and even earlier sometimes when all the priests are at the Mission. I ring the little bell hung at the entrance to the sacristy, then I wait for the first father to come for Mass. I serve up to three or four Masses every day. The skin on my knees is now as hard as crocodile skin. When I kneel down I seem to be kneeling on cushions.

I like the distribution of Communion on Sundays best of all. All the faithful come up to the altar rail with their eyes shut, and their mouths open and their tongues stuck out as if they were pulling a face. The Europeans receive Communion separately. They haven't got nice teeth. I like stroking the white girls under the chin with the paten I am holding for them while the priest pops the host into their mouths. The houseboy of a priest from Yaoundé taught me that trick. It's the only chance we'll ever get of stroking them. . . .

An old woman from the Sixa[1] gets our food. We prefer the leavings from the priests' meals. Sometimes we find scraps of meat there.

\*　\*　\*

Everything I am I owe to Father Gilbert. He is my benefactor and I am very fond of him. He is cheerful and pleasant and when I was small he treated me like a pet animal. He loved to pull my ears and all the time I have been getting my education he has loved to watch my constant amazement at everything.

He presents me to the whites who visit the Mission as his masterpiece. I am his boy, a boy who can read and write, serve Mass, lay a table, sweep out his room and make his bed. I don't earn any money. Now and then he gives me an old shirt or an old pair of trousers. Father Gilbert knew me when I was stark naked, he taught me to read and write. . . . Nothing can be more precious than that, even if I have to go badly dressed.

\*　\*　\*

Today Father Vandermayer came back from the bush. He has brought five women with him. It seems they are Christians that he has taken away from their polygamous husband. Five more boarders for the Sixa. If they knew the work there is waiting for them here, they would have stayed behind with their husband.

Father Vandermayer is Father Gilbert's assistant. He has the best voice in the Mission so he sings Mass at the major feasts. But he is rather a funny person, Father Vandermayer. On a Sunday when he isn't singing the High Mass he won't let anyone else take the collection. One day when I had taken it he made me come to his room. Then he undressed me and searched me. He made one of the catechists stay with me all through the day in case I had swallowed any of the coins.

---

1. A kind of boarding house for women who are intending to become Christians and for Christian women who have left their pagan families.

He is censor for the houseboys and the faithful of the parish. He has never managed to catch me out. I could never stand what he does to people who have misbehaved. He loves to beat the Christians who have committed adultery—native Christians of course. . . . He makes them undress in his office while he repeats in bad Ndjem, 'When you were kissing, weren't you ashamed before God?' Sunday after Mass has become a terrible time for everyone who has Father Vandermayer as spiritual director.

\* \* \*

I saw a very pretty girl at the blacks' communion. I stroked her under the chin with the paten like we do the white girls. She opened one eye, then she shut it again. She really must come to Communion again.

\* \* \*

Father Vandermayer has been down with a bout of malaria. He shouted obscenities all night. Father Gilbert has told us not to hang about near his room.

\* \* \*

My father, my benefactor, Father Gilbert is dead. They found him bloody and crushed on his motor cycle by the side of a branch from the giant cotton tree that the natives call the 'Hammer of the whites.' They say two white men, Greeks, had already suffered the same fate as Father Gilbert. On a windless day the cotton tree dropped one of its branches like a gigantic club on the Greek's car just at the moment it was passing underneath. All they found afterwards were two pulpy masses in drill suits amongst the twisted metal. The Commandant who was at Dangan at that time talked about having the cotton tree cut down. But after the Greeks were buried the whole thing was forgotten . . . until this morning.

Every Thursday Father Gilbert used to go into Dangan so that he could collect the mail for the Mission personally. How pleased he used to be at the thought of a letter from home. As soon as we had finished the main service he would rush to the garage to get out the motor cycle. Then he would call to me to hold it while he tucked his cassock up to his waist, showing his hairy legs and khaki shorts. When he was ready he would take the machine and drop heavily into the saddle. I would push it till the noise of the engine became steady. Then he would disappear at high speed leaving behind a cloud of fumes and dust and a smell of petrol that turned my stomach over.

This morning, the motor cycle was more difficult than ever to get started. Father Gilbert got off several times and fiddled with something in the engine. I was bathed in sweat from pushing him. He was cursing and swearing and calling the motor cycle names. I had never seen him so on edge. At last after one or two sudden starts and then a thunderous noise, he burst away and I caught a glimpse of him through the dust, his body bent slightly forward disappearing at speed like a thing bewitched. . . . Who could have told me then that was to be my last image of Father Gilbert?

It was about ten o'clock when the head catechist, the one Father Vandermayer had set to watch me, came howling up to the gate of the priests' villa. He rolled about on the ground shouting 'Father . . . Father . . .' Out rushed Father Vandermayer with such a stream of abuse as only he could produce. I thought Martin must be drunk. They said he rolled about like that in his hut when he had been drinking. Father Vandermayer opened the gate swearing and grabbed Martin by the coat.

'Father . . . Father . . . is . . . is . . . dead,' stammered Martin, '. . . in . . . in . . .'

Father Vandermayer stopped him short. He gave him a kick and pointed to the path leading to the Mission workers' compound.

'Go and get drunk somewhere else! Go and get drunk at home!' roared Father Vandermayer giving him a push in the back.

At that moment the hospital ambulance appeared in the courtyard of the church, followed closely by all the cars in Dangan. My blood drained away, my knees buckled. . . .

No, it could not be true that Father Gilbert was dead. . . .

I ran towards the ambulance, towards the stretcher. The white man who had been everything in the world to me lay there. I collided with a white man with a long neck, then with another, a hulking yellowish man. They pushed me back, one with the whip he always carried, the other feinted a kick. . . .

The whole of Saint Peter's Mission was there. The Sixa women had pushed their way through the old catechists and surrounded the group of whites, weeping. Everybody who wanted to show how attached he had been to the dead Father was there. Workers forcing out their tears. You could see from their contorted faces the difficulty they were having to make their eyes wet. Stupid-looking catechists uncertainly stroking their rosaries, starry-eyed catechumens hoping that perhaps they would be lucky enough to be present at a miracle. Labourers who looked so miserable that Father Vandermayer would hardly have the heart to stop them the day's pay. But most of the crowd was there because they had never had a chance before to see a white man's corpse—still less the corpse of a white priest. All these people kept up a squealing round the group of white men. The long-necked white man spoke to one of the constables who was in his car. The constable counted out ten paces walking against the crowd and the crowd fell back at each step, once, twice, three times . . . up to ten. Two orderlies carried Father Gilbert's body into his room. The Europeans followed it in. Father Vandermayer led them into the sitting-room. A few moments later he came out again, down the steps. He spoke to the crowd.

'The Father of us all,' he began, rubbing his fingers together, 'the Father of us all is dead. Pray for him, my brothers, pray for him, for God is just, he gives to every man his due. . . .'

He stroked his hair, then went on to give his orders.

'Go to the church . . . Pray for him, my brothers. Pray for him, the

Father of all of us who will rest in this Mission, among you all that he loved so much . . .'

He rubbed his eyes. The howls redoubled.

'God is just,' he went on. 'He is everlasting. His will be done.'

He made the sign of the cross and the crowd copied him. He went up the steps. At the top step his hands came down to his thighs and straightened his cassock.

Martin, the head catechist, was crying at my side. I do not know why he was there instead of leading the other catechists in their prayers. He had unbuttoned his old coat and his tears ran down his wrinkled belly underneath the knot he had tied in his loin-cloth over his grizzled pubic hairs.

'There is nothing left for me but to go away,' he intoned. 'There is nothing left except to die. . . . I knew someone was going to die, the chimpanzees howled all night. There is nothing left for me but to go away, nothing except to die. . . .'

The crowd was swallowed up in the church. The Europeans went away. One stayed behind to supervise the carpenters who came across the courtyard with planks and sheet-iron. Two constables with fixed bayonets marched up and down the veranda outside the room where the body lay.

The funeral will be at four tomorrow. Twice the constables have made me move off. Father Vandermayer has not said anything. . . .

## AFTER THE FUNERAL

My benefactor was buried in the corner of the cemetery reserved for Europeans. The grave of Father Gilbert lies next to the grave of M. Diamond's daughter—the one he had by his mistress and acknowledged. Father Vandermayer said the burial service. All the Europeans in Dangan were there, even the Americans from the Protestant Mission.

It is only now that I realize that Father Gilbert is dead. I have not heard his voice since yesterday. The Catholic Mission is in mourning. But for me, it is more than mourning. I have died my first death. . . .

I saw the girl from communion at the funeral. She shut her eyes again. She is stupid.

*   *   *

The new Commandant needs a boy. Father Vandermayer told me to report to the Residence tomorrow. I am glad because I have not been able to bear life at the Mission since Father Gilbert died. Of course it is a good riddance for Father Vandermayer as well. . . .

I shall be the Chief European's boy. The dog of the King is the King of dogs.

I shall leave the Mission this evening. From now on I shall live with my brother-in-law in the location. A new life is starting for me.

O Lord, Thy will be done . . .

*   *   *

At last it has happened. The Commandant has definitely taken me into his service. It was midnight, I had finished my work and was getting ready to go back to the location when the Commandant told me to follow him into his office. It was a terrible moment for me.

After he had looked at me for a long while, he asked me point-blank if I were a thief.

'No, Sir,' I answered.

'Why aren't you a thief?'

'Because I do not want to go to hell.'

He seemed taken aback by my answer. He tossed his head in disbelief.

'Where did you learn that?'

'I am a Christian, Sir,' I told him, and proudly showed him the St Christopher medal I wear round my neck.

'So, you are not a thief because you don't want to go to hell?'

'Yes, Sir.'

'What is it like, hell?'

'Well, Sir, it is flames and snakes and the Devil with horns. There is a picture of hell in my prayer book . . . I . . . I . . . can show it to you.'

I was going to pull the little prayer book out of the back pocket of my shorts but the Commandant made a sign to stop me. He watched me for a minute through the wreathes of smoke he was puffing into my face. He sat down. I bowed my head. I could feel his eyes on me. He crossed his legs and uncrossed them. He signalled me to a chair opposite to him. He leant towards me and lifted up my chin. He gazed into my eyes and went on.

'Good, good, Joseph, we shall be friends.'

'Yes, Sir. Thank you, Sir.'

'But if you steal, I shan't wait till you go to hell. It's too far . . .'

'Yes, sir. It's . . . Where is it, sir?'

I had never asked myself the question. My master was amused to see my puzzlement. He shrugged and leant against the back of his chair.

'So you don't know where this hell is where you're afraid you'll go and burn?'

'It's next to Purgatory, Sir. It's . . . It's . . . in the sky.'

My master smothered a laugh. Then, serious again, he pierced me with his panther eyes.

'Well done! There we are then. I think you see why I can't wait till "small Joseph go burn in hell".'

The Commandant imitated the pidgin used by native soldiers. He put on a strange voice. I thought he was very funny. I coughed hard so as not to laugh. He went on, not noticing.

'If you steal from me I shall skin you alive.'

'Yes, Sir. I know, Sir. I didn't say that just now, Sir, because I took that for granted, Sir . . .'

'All right, all right,' said the Commandant, impatiently.

He got up and began to walk round me.

'You're a clean lad,' he said, looking me over carefully. 'No jiggers. Your shirt is clean, No scabies.'

He stepped back and looked me up and down again.

'You're intelligent. The priests speak very well of you. So I can count on little Joseph, eh?'

'Yes, Sir,' I said. My eyes shone with pleasure and pride.

'You may go. Be here every morning at six o'clock. You understand?'

When I was outside on the veranda I felt I had just come through a hard battle. The end of my nose was perspiring.

My master is thickset. His legs have great muscles like the legs of a pedlar. He is the kind of man we call 'mahogany-trunk' because the trunk of the mahogany tree is so strong that it never bends in a storm. I am not a storm. I am the thing that obeys.

■ **Chinua Achebe (1930– )** *Nigeria* **(story)**

Born in Nigeria, Chinua Achebe grew up in the small village of Agidi in the eastern part of the country. His father, an Ibo mission teacher and one of the first Nigerians to embrace Christianity, sent him to a school of the Church Missionary Society. He then studied at Government College in Umuahia, a town he would later write about, and he earned a scholarship to study medicine at the University College of Ibadan. After completing his first year, Achebe decided to study literature and received his B.A. in 1953.

After teaching for a few months, Achebe began a career at the Nigerian Broadcasting Company (NBC) in Lagos. A few years later, in 1961, he became the first director of external broadcasting for NBC, but he left the post in 1966 to concentrate on his writing, for which he had achieved early and startling success. During the Nigerian Civil War (1967–1970), Achebe served as a Biafran diplomat and wrote letters to international papers, including the *London Sunday Times,* on the atrocities of war, the reasons behind the Biafran struggle for independence, and his own ideas about the Federal Government of Nigeria. During these days of national strife, he found little time for his own work.

In 1958, he published *Things Fall Apart,* a novel depicting generations of the life of the Ibo people in precolonial times as well as during the British colonial period. His book about tropical Africa became a classic and gained him international fame. In 1964, he published his even more famous work, *Arrow of God.* His more recent novel, *Anthills of the Savannah* (1987), whose setting is modern Nigeria, has added to his reputation.

In the 1970s, Achebe devoted himself to establishing a forum through which Nigerian writers could publish. Consistent with his theory of history and politics, Achebe took an extremist nationalist view that for an authentic Nigerian tradition of literature to develop, not only must the writers come from Nigeria, but so too its publishers, editors, and printers. As he achieved international fame and became a pan-African writer, editing anthologies containing authors from all parts of Africa, whether of black, Arabic, or European origin, he modified his earlier doctrine of Nigerian purity.

Achebe has worked as a teacher and a professional writer, giving us novels, poems, short stories, and essays. Much of his writing is confessional, drawing on autobiographical experience. He evokes his grandparents' generation, an era that encompasses precolonial days. His own village was a meeting of the past and present, where non-Christians and Christians kept their distance. As a young adult, he was energetically immersed in Nigerian independence, which came in 1960, and, of course, in the Biafran struggle that was to tear Africa's most populous country apart. His pen has many turns, including a satiric twist when, as in *A Man of the People* (1966), he exposes the corruption of African politicians. Chinua Achebe edited the literary journal *Okike* and taught at the University of Nigeria in Nsukka. With the advent of extreme repression and the execution of protestors, Achebe has gone into exile in the United States, where he is a visiting professor.

**FURTHER READING:** Achebe, Chinua. *Things Fall Apart,* 1958; *Arrow of God,* 1964; *Beware, Soul Brother, and Other Poems,* 1971; *Girls at War and Other Stories,* 1972; *Morning Yet on Creation Day: Essays,* 1975; *Anthills of the Savannah,* 1988; *Hopes and Impediments: Selected Essays, 1965–1987,* 1988; *A Tribute to James Baldwin,* 1989.

## The Madman

He was drawn to markets and straight roads. Not any tiny neighborhood market where a handful of garrulous women might gather at sunset to gossip and buy ogili for the evening's soup, but a huge, engulfing bazaar beckoning people familiar and strange from far and near. And not any dusty, old footpath beginning in this village, and ending in that stream, but broad, black, mysterious highways without beginning or end. After much wandering he had discovered two such markets linked together by such a highway; and so ended his wandering. One market was, Af̲o̲, the other Eke. The two days between them suited him very well: before setting out for Eke he had ample time to wind up his business properly at Af̲o̲. He passed the night there putting right again his hut after a day of defilement by two fat-bottomed market women who said it was their market stall. At first he had put up a fight but the women had gone and brought their menfolk—four hefty beasts of the bush—to whip him out of the hut. After that he always avoided them, moving out on the morning of the market and back in at dusk to pass the night. Then in the morning he rounded off his affairs swiftly and set out on that long, beautiful boa constrictor of a road to Eke in the distant town of Ogbu. He held his staff and cudgel at the ready in his right hand, and with the left he steadied the basket of his belongings on his head. He had got himself this cudgel lately to deal with little beasts on the way who threw stones at him and made fun of their mothers' nakedness, not his own.

He used to walk in the middle of the road, holding it in conversation. But one day the driver of a mammy-wagon and his mate came down on him shouting, pushing and slapping his face. They said their lorry very nearly ran over their mother, not him. After that he avoided those noisy lorries too, with the vagabonds inside them.

Having walked one day and one night he was now close to the Eke market-place. From every little sideroad, crowds of market people poured into the big highway to join the enormous flow to Eke. Then he saw some young ladies with water pots on their heads coming toward him, unlike all the rest, away from the market. This surprised him. Then he saw two more water pots rise out of a sloping footpath leading off his side of the highway. He felt thirsty then and stopped to think it over. Then he set down his basket on the roadside and turned into the sloping footpath. But first he begged his highway not to be offended or continue the journey without him. "I'll get some for you too," he said coaxingly with a tender backward glance. "I know you are thirsty."

Nwibe was a man of high standing in Ogbu and was rising higher; a man of wealth and integrity. He had just given notice to all the ozo men of the town that he proposed to seek admission into their honored hierarchy in the coming initiation sendseason.

"Your proposal is excellent," said the men of title. "When we see we shall believe." Which was their dignified way of telling you to think it over once again and make sure you have the means to go through with it. For ozo is not a child's naming ceremony; and where is the man to hide his face who begins the ozo dance and then is foot-stuck to the arena? But in this instance the caution of the elders was no more than a formality for Nwibe was such a sensible man that no one could think of him beginning something he was not sure to finish.

On that Eke day Nwibe had risen early so as to visit his farm beyond the stream and do some light work before going to the market at midday to drink a horn or two of palm wine with his peers and perhaps buy that bundle of roofing thatch for the repairs of his wives' huts. As for his own hut he had a couple of years back settled it finally by changing his thatch roof to zinc. Sooner or later he would do the same for his wives. He could have done Mgboye's hut right away but decided to wait until he could do the two together, or else Udenkwo would set the entire compound on fire. Udenkwo was the junior wife, by three years, but she never let that worry her. Happily, Mgboye was a woman of peace who rarely demanded the respect due to her from the other. She would suffer Udenkwo's provoking tongue sometimes for a whole day without offering a word in reply. And when she did reply at all her words were always few and her voice very low.

That very morning Udenkwo had accused her of spite and all kinds of wickedness on account of a little dog.

"What has a little dog done to you?" she screamed loud enough for half the village to hear. "I ask you, Mgboye, what is the offense of a puppy this early in the day?"

"What your puppy did this early in the day," replied Mgboye, "is that he put his shit-mouth into my soup pot."

"And then?"

"And then I smacked him."

"You smacked him! Why don't you cover your soup pot? Is it easier to hit a dog than cover a pot? Is a small puppy to have more sense than a woman who leaves her soup pot about . . . ?"

"Enough from you, Udenkwo."

"It is not enough, Mgboye, it is not enough. If that dog owes you any debt I want to know. Everything I have, even a little dog I bought to eat my infant's excrement keeps you awake at nights. You are a bad woman, Mgboye, you are a very bad woman!"

Nwibe had listened to all of this in silence in his hut. He knew from the vigor in Udenkwo's voice that she could go on like this till market time. So he intervened, in his characteristic manner by calling out to his senior wife.

"Mgboye! Let me have peace this early morning!"

"Don't you hear all the abuses Udenkwo . . ."

"I hear nothing at all from Udenkwo and I want peace in my compound. If Udenkwo is crazy must everybody else go crazy with her? Is one crazy woman not enough in my compound so early in the day?"

"The great judge has spoken," sang Udenkwo in a sneering sing-song. "Thank you, great judge. Udenkwo is mad. Udenkwo is always mad, but those of you who are sane let . . ."

"Shut your mouth, shameless woman, or a wild beast will lick your eyes for you this morning. When will you learn to keep your badness within this compound instead of shouting it to all Ogbu to hear? I say shut your mouth!"

There was silence then except for Udenkwo's infant whose yelling had up till then been swallowed up by the larger noise of the adults.

"Don't cry, my father," said Udenkwo to him. "They want to kill your dog, but our people say the man who decides to chase after a chicken, for him is the fall . . ."

By the middle of the morning Nwibe had done all the work he had to do on his farm and was on his way again to prepare for market. At the little stream he decided as he always did to wash off the sweat of work. So he put his cloth on a huge boulder by the men's bathing section and waded in. There was nobody else around because of the time of day and because it was market day. But from instinctive modesty he turned to face the forest away from the approaches.

The madman watched him for quite a while. Each time he bent down to carry water in cupped hands from the shallow stream to his head and body the madman smiled at his parted behind. And then remembered. This was the same hefty man who brought three others like him and whipped me out of my hut in the Af<u>o</u> market. He nodded to himself. And he remembered again: this was the same vagabond who descended on me from the lorry in the middle of my highway. He nodded once more. And then he remembered yet again: this was the same fellow who set his children to throw stones at me and make remarks about their mothers' buttocks, not mine. Then he laughed.

Nwibe turned sharply round and saw the naked man laughing, the deep grove of the stream amplifying his laughter. Then he stopped as suddenly as he had begun; the merriment vanished from his face.

"I have caught you naked," he said.

Nwibe ran a hand swiftly down his face to clear his eyes of water.

"I say I have caught you naked, with your thing dangling about."

"I can see you are hungry for a whipping," said Nwibe with quiet menace in his voice, for a madman is said to be easily scared away by the very mention of a whip. "Wait till I get up there. . . . What are you doing? Drop it at once . . . I say drop it!"

The madman had picked up Nwibe's cloth and wrapped it round his own waist. He looked down at himself and began to laugh again.

"I will kill you," screamed Nwibe as he splashed toward the bank, maddened by anger. "I will whip that madness out of you today!"

They ran all the way up the steep and rocky footpath hedged in by the shadowy green forest. A mist gathered and hung over Nwibe's vision as he ran, stumbled, fell, pulled himself up again and stumbled on, shouting and cursing. The other, despite his unaccustomed encumbrance, steadily increased his lead, for he was spare and wiry, a thing made for speed. Furthermore, he did not waste his breath shouting and cursing; he just ran. Two girls going down to the stream saw a man running up the slope toward them pursued by a stark-naked madman. They threw down their pots and fled, screaming.

When Nwibe emerged into the full glare of the highway he could not see his cloth clearly anymore and his chest was on the point of exploding from the fire and torment within. But he kept running. He was only vaguely aware of crowds of people on all sides and he appealed to them tearfully without stopping: "Hold the madman, he's got my cloth!" By this time the man with the cloth was practically lost among the much denser crowds far in front so that the link between him and the naked man was no longer clear.

Now Nwibe continually bumped against people's backs and then laid flat a frail old man struggling with a stubborn goat on a leash. "Stop the madman," he shouted hoarsely, his heart tearing to shreds, "he's got my cloth!" Everyone looked at him first in surprise and then less surprise because strange sights are common in a great market. Some of them even laughed.

"They've got his cloth he says."

"That's a new one I'm sure. He hardly looks mad yet. Doesn't he have people, I wonder."

"People are so careless these days. Why can't they keep proper watch over their sick relation, especially on the day of the market?"

Farther up the road on the very brink of the marketplace two men from Nwibe's village recognized him and, throwing down the one his long basket of yams, the other his calabash of palm wine held on a loop, gave desperate chase, to stop him setting foot irrevocably within the occult territory of the powers of the market. But it was in vain. When finally they caught him it was well inside the crowded square. Udenkwo in tears tore off her top-cloth which they draped on him and led him home by the hand. He spoke just once about a madman who took his cloth in the stream.

"It is all right," said one of the men in the tone of a father to a crying child. They led and he followed blindly, his heavy chest heaving up and down in silent weeping. Many more people from his village, a few of his in-laws and one or two others from his mother's place had joined the grief-stricken party. One man whispered to another that it was the worst kind of madness, deep and tongue-tied.

"May it end ill for him who did this," prayed the other.

The first medicine man his relatives consulted refused to take him on, out of some kind of integrity.

"I could say yes to you and take your money," he said. "But that is not my way. My powers of cure are known throughout Olu and Igbo but never have I professed to bring back to life a man who has sipped the spirit-waters of ani-mmo. It is the same with a madman who of his own accord delivers himself to the divinities of the marketplace. You should have kept better watch over him."

"Don't blame us too much," said Nwibe's relative. "When he left home that morning his senses were as complete as yours and mine now. Don't blame us too much."

"Yes, I know. It happens that way sometimes. And they are the ones that medicine will not reach. I know."

"Can you do nothing at all then, not even to untie his tongue?"

"Nothing can be done. They have already embraced him. It is like a man who runs away from the oppression of his fellows to the grove of an alusi and says to him: Take me, oh spirit, I am your osu. No man can touch him thereafter. He is free and yet no power can break his bondage. He is free of men but bonded to a god."

The second doctor was not as famous as the first and not so strict. He said the case was bad, very bad indeed, but no one folds his arms because the condition of his child is beyond hope. He must still grope around and do his best. His hearers nodded in eager agreement. And then he muttered into his own inward ear: If doctors were to send away every patient whose cure they were uncertain of, how many of them would eat one meal in a whole week from their practice?

Nwibe was cured of his madness. That humble practitioner who did the miracle became overnight the most celebrated mad-doctor of his generation. They called him Sojourner to the Land of the Spirits. Even so it remains true that madness may indeed sometimes depart but never with all his clamorous train. Some of these always remain — the trailers of madness you might call them — to haunt the doorway of the eyes. For how could a man be the same again of whom witnesses from all the lands of Olu and Igbo have once reported that they saw today a fine, hefty man in his prime, stark naked, tearing through the crowds to answer the call of the marketplace? Such a man is marked for ever.

Nwibe became a quiet, withdrawn man avoiding whenever he could the boisterous side of the life of his people. Two years later, before another initiation season, he made a new inquiry about joining the community of titled men in his town. Had they received him perhaps he might have become at least partially restored, but those ozo men, dignified and polite as ever, deftly steered the conversation away to other matters.

## ■ Richard Rive (1931–1989) *South Africa* (story)

An immediately engaging writer, Richard Rive was born in Cape Town, son of an African American father and a South African Coloured mother. He took a B.A. degree from the University of Cape Town. He taught English and Latin in a high school and later went to New York's Columbia University (M.A., 1966) and in 1974 took his Ph.D. in English from Oxford. Unlike most of his contemporary writers who went into exile, especially in the 1950s and 1960s, Rive spent most of his life in South Africa. He taught at Hewat College of Education, where he had also studied. He became head of its English Department in 1988. The following year, on June 4, 1989, he was murdered in his home in his native Cape Town. Two weeks before his murder, he had completed his third novel, *Emergency Continued* (1990), which, like his first novel, *Emergency* (1964), describes conditions in South Africa under its "temporary" state of emergency laws.

Rive's first published book was *African Songs* (1963), a collection of short stories that appeared in East Germany. As in all his writing, he combines humor with social observation. Because of its criticism of the prevailing racial oppression, the book was immediately banned in South Africa. His second book, the novel *Emergency*, published in England by Faber and Faber, was similarly banned from his country. Its success abroad, however, established his early reputation. In *Emergency*, he describes the chaotic times after the Sharpeville massacre in March 1960 of students and teachers by the security police. Rive follows the fate of his characters, those who leave the country, and those who remain and struggle for change.

In the same period, Richard Rive also edited and contributed to anthologies of African fiction, containing work of then emerging writers such as Chinua Achebe, Alex La Guma, and Ngugi wa Thiongo: *Quartet* (1963) and *Modern African Prose* (1964). After some years of limited production, Rive reached his peak in the mid-eighties when he published a book of stories, *Advance, Retreat,* (1983) and the novel *"Buckingham Palace," District Six* (1986), perhaps his best work, which he was also to adapt into a play that was performed after his death. *Emergency Continued* (1980) was published posthumously. In all his work, Rive is foremost an attractive and exciting stylist, committed, enlightened, and amused by the diverse impossibilities of existence.

**FURTHER READING:** Rive, Richard. *Advance, Retreat,* 1983; *Quartet,* 1963; *Modern African Prose,* 1964; *Emergency,* 1964; *Advance, Retreat,* 1983; *"Buckingham Palace," District Six,* 1986; *Emergency Continued,* 1990.

# *Rain*

Rain pouring down and blotting out all sound with its sharp and vibrant tattoo. Dripping neon signs reflecting lurid reds and yellows in mirror-wet streets. Swollen gutters. Water overflowing and squelching onto pavements. Gurgling and sucking at storm-water drains. Table Mountain cut off by a grey film of mist and rain. A lost City Hall clock trying manfully to chime nine over an indifferent Cape Town. Baleful reverberations through a spluttering all-consuming drizzle.

Yellow light filtering through from Solly's 'Grand Fish and Chips Palace.' Door tightshut against the weather. Inside stuffy with heat, hot bodies, steaming clothes, and the nauseating smell of stale fish oil. Misty patterns on the plate-glass windows and a messy pool where rain has filtered beneath the door and mixed with the sawdust.

Solly himself in shirt sleeves and apron, sweating, vulgar and moody. Bellowing at a dripping woman who has just come in.

"Shut 'e damn door. You live in a tent?"

"Ag, Solly."

"Don't ag me. You coloured people never shut blarry doors."

"Don't you bloomingwell swear at me!"

"I bloomingwell swear at you, yes."

"Come. Gimme two pieces o' fish. Tail cut."

"Two pieces o' fish."

"Raining like hell outside," the woman said to no one.

"Mmmmmm. Raining like hell," a thin befezzed Muslim cut in.

"One an' six. Thank you. An' close 'e door behin' you."

"Thanks. Think you got 'e on'y door in Hanover Street?"

"Go to hell!" Solly cut the interchange short and turned to another customer.

The north-wester sobbed heavy rain squalls against the windowpanes. The Hanover Street bus screeched to a slithery stop and passengers darted for shelter in a cinema entrance. The street lamps shone blurredly.

Solly sweated as he wrapped parcels of fish and chips in a newspaper. Fish and Chips. Vinegar? Wrap. One an' six please. Thank you! Next. Fish an' chips. No? Two fish. No chips? Salt? Vinegar? One an' six please. Thank you! Next. Fish an' chips?

"Close 'e blarry door!" Solly glared at a woman who had just come in. She half-smiled apologetically at him.

"You also live in a blarry tent?"

She struggled with the door and then stood dripping in a pool of wet sawdust. Solly left the counter to add two logs to the furnace. She moved out of the way. Another customer showed indignation at Solly's remarks.

"Fish an' chips. Vinegar? Salt? One an' six. Thank you. Yes, madam?"

"Could you tell me when the bioscope comes out?"

"Am I the blooming manager?"

"Please."

"Half pas' ten, tonight," the Muslim offered helpfully.

"Thank you. Can I stay here till then? It's raining outside."

"I know it's blarrywell raining, but this is not a Salvation Army."

"Please, baas!"

This caught Solly unaware. He had had his shop in that corner of Hanover Street since most could remember and had been called a great many unsavoury things in the years. Solly didn't mind. But this caught him unaware. Please, baas. This felt good. His imagination adjusted a black bow-tie to an evening suit. Please, baas.

"O.K. You stay for a short while. But when 'e rain stops you go!"

She nodded dumbly and tried to make out the blurred name of the cinema opposite, through the misted windows.

"Waiting fer somebody?" Solly asked. No response.

"I ask if yer waiting fer somebody?" The figure continued to stare. "Oh, go to hell," said Solly, turning to another customer.

Through the rain blur Siena stared at nothing in particular. Dim visions of slippery wet cars. Honking and wheezing in the rain. Spluttering buses. Heavy, drowsy voices in the Grand Fish and Chips Palace. Her eyes travelled beyond the street and the water cascades of Table Mountain, beyond the winter of Cape Town to the summer of the Boland. Past the green grapelands of Stellenbosch and Paarl and the stuffy wheat district of Malmesbury to the lazy sun and laughter of Teslaarsdal.

Inside the gabled nineteenth-century mission church she had first met Joseph. The church is quiet and beautiful and the ivy climbs over it and makes it more beautiful. Huge silver oil lamps suspended from the roof, polished and shining. It was in the flicker of the lamps that she had first become aware of him. He was visiting from Cape Town. She sang that night as she had never sung before.

"Al ging ik ook in een dal der schaduw des doods . . . " Though I walk through the valley of the shadow of death . . . "der schaduw des doods." And then he had looked at her. She felt as if everyone was looking at her.

"Ik zoude geen kwaad vreezen . . . " I will fear no evil. And she had not feared but loved. Had loved him. Had sung for him. For the wide eyes, the yellow skin, the high cheekbones. She had sung for a creator who could create a man like Joseph. "Want gij zijt met mij; Uw stok en Uw staf, die vertroosten mij."

Those were black-and-white polka-dot nights when the moon did a golliwog cakewalk across a banjo-strung sky. Nights of sweet remembrances when he had whispered love to her and told her of Cape Town. She had giggled coyly at his obscenities. It was fashionable, she hoped, to giggle coyly at obscenities. He lived in one of those streets off District Six, it sounded like Horsburg Lane, and was, he boasted, quite a one with the girls. She heard of Molly and Miena and Sophia and a sophisticated Charmaine who was almost a schoolteacher and always spoke English. But he told her that he had only found love in Teslaarsdal. She wasn't sure whether to believe him. And then he felt her richness, and the moon darted behind a cloud.

The loud screeching of the train to Cape Town. Screeching loud enough to drown the protests of her family. The wrath of her father. The icy stares of Teslaarsdal matrons. Loud and confused screechings to drown her hysteria, her ecstasy. Drowned and confused in the roar of a thousand cars and a hundred thousand lights and a summer of carnival evenings that are Cape Town.

And the agony of the nights when he came home later and later and sometimes not at all. The waning of his passion and whispered names of others. Molly and Miena and Sophia, Charmaine. The helpless knowledge that he was slipping from her. Faster and faster. Gathering momentum.

Not that I'm saying so but I only heard. Why don't you go to bioscope one night and see for yourself? Marian's man is searching for Joseph. Searching for Joseph. Looking for Joseph. Knifing for Joseph. Joseph. Joseph! *Joseph!* Molly! Miena! Sophia! Names! Names! Names! Gossip. One-sided desire. Go to bioscope and see. See what? See why? When? Where?

And after he had been away a week she decided to see. Decided to go through the rain and stand in a sweating fish-and-chips shop owned by a blaspheming and vulgar man. And wait for the cinema to come out.

The rain had stopped sobbing against the plate-glass window. A skin-soaking drizzle now set in. Continuous. Unending. Filming everything with dark depression. A shivering, weeping neon sign flickering convulsively on and off. A tired Solly shooting a quick glance at a cheap alarm clock.

"Half pas' ten, bioscope out soon."

Siena looked more intently through the misty screen. No movement whatsoever in the deserted cinema foyer.

"Time it was bloomingwell out." Solly braced himself for the wave of after-show customers who would invade the Palace.

"Comin' out late tonight, missus."

"Thank you, baas."

Solly rubbed sweat out of his eyes and took in her neat and plain fig-ure. Tired face but good legs. A few late stragglers catching colds in the streets. Wet and squally outside.

"Your man in bioscope?"

She was intent on a khaki-uniformed usher struggling to open the door.

"Man in bioscope, missus?"

The cinema had to come out some time or other. An usher opening the door. Adusting the outside gate. Preparing for the crowds to pour out. To vomit and spill out.

"Man in bioscope?"

No response.

"Oh, go to hell!"

They would be out now. Joseph would be out. She rushed for the door, throwing words of thanks to Solly.

"Close 'e blarry door!"

She never heard him. The drizzle had stopped. An unnatural calm hung over the empty foyer, over the deserted street. She took up her stand on the bottom step. Expectantly. Her heart pounding.

Then they came. Pouring, laughing, pushing, jostling. She stared with fierce intensity, but faces passed too fast. Laughing, roaring, gay. Wide-eyed, yellow-skinned, high-cheekboned. Black, brown, ivory, yel-low. Black-eyed, laughing-eyed, bouncing. No Joseph. Palpitating heart that felt like bursting into a thousand pieces. If she should miss him. She found herself searching for the wrong face. Solly's face. Ridicu-lously searching for hard blue eyes and a sharp white chin in a sea of ebony and brown. Solly's face. Missing half a hundred faces and then again searching for the familiar high cheekbones. Solly. Joseph. Molly. Miena. Charmaine.

The drizzle resumed. Studying overcoats instead of faces. Longing for the pale-blue shirt she had seen in the shop at Solitaire. A bargain for one pound five shillings. She had scraped and scrounged to buy it for him. A week's wages. Collecting her thoughts and continuing the search for Joseph. And then the thinning out of the crowd and the last few strag-glers. The ushers shutting the iron gate. They might be shutting Joseph in. Herself out. Only ushers left.

"Please, is Joseph inside?"

"Who's Joseph?"

"Is Joseph still inside?"

"Joseph who?"

They were teasing her. Laughing behind her back. Preventing her from finding him.

"Joseph is inside!" she shouted frenziedly.

"Look, it's raining cats and dogs. Go home."

Go home. To whom. To what? An empty room? An empty bed?

And then she was aware of the crowd on the corner. Maybe he was there. Running and peering into every face. Joseph. The crowd in the drizzle. Two battling figures. Joseph. Figures locked in struggle slithering in the wet gutter. Muck streaking down clothes through which wet bodies were silhouetted. Joseph. A blue shirt. And then she wiped the rain out of her eyes and saw him. Fighting for his life. Desperately kicking in the gutter. Joseph. The blast of a police whistle. A pick-up van screeching to a stop.

"Please, sir, it wasn't him. They all ran away. Please, sir, he's Joseph. He done nothing. He done nothing, my baas. Please, sir, he's my Joseph. Please, baas!"

"Maak dat jy wegkom. Get away. Voetsak!"

"Please, sir, it wasn't him. They ran away!"

Solly's Grand Fish and Chips Palace crowded out. People milling inside. Rain once more squalling and sobbing against the door and windows. Swollen gutters unable to cope with the giddy rush of water. Solly sweating to deal with the after-cinema rush.

Fish an' chips. Vinegar? Salt? One an' six. Thank you. Sorry, no fish yet. Wait five minutes. Chips on'y. Vinegar? Ninepence. Tickey change. Thank you. Sorry, no fish. Five minutes time. Chips? Ninepence. Thank you. Solly paused for breath and stirred the fish.

"What's 'e trouble outside?"

"Real bioscope, Solly."

"No man, outside!"

"I say, real bioscope."

"What were 'e police doing? Sorry, no fish yet, sir. Five minutes time. What were 'e police doin'?"

"A fight in 'e blooming rain."

"Jesus, in 'e rain."

"Ja."

"Who was fighting?"

"Joseph an' somebody."

"Joseph?"

"Ja, fellow in Horsburg Lane."

"Yes, I know Joseph. Always in trouble. Chucked him outta here a'reddy."

"Well, that chap."

"An' who?"

"Dinno."

"Police got them?"

"Got Joseph."

"Why were 'ey fighting? Fish in a minute sir."

"Over a dame."

"Who?"

"You know Marian who works by Patel? Now she. Her boyfriend caught 'em."

"In bioscope?"

"Ja."

Solly chuckled suggestively.

"See that woman an' 'e police."

"What woman?" Solly asked.

"One crying' to 'e police. They say it's Joseph's girl from 'e country."

"Joseph always got plenty dames from 'e town an' country. F-I-S-H R-E-A-D-Y! Two pieces for you, sir? One an' six. Shilling change. Fish an' chips? One an' six. Thank you. Fish on'y? Vinegar? Salt? Ninepence. Tickey change. Thank you! What you say about 'e woman?"

"They say Joseph's girl was crying to 'e police."

"Oh, he got plenty o' girls."

"This one was living with him."

"Oh, what she look like? Fish, sir?"

"Like 'e country. O.K. Nice legs."

"Hmmmmm," said Solly. "Hey, close 'e damn door. Oh, you again." Siena came in. A momentary silence. Then a buzzing and whispering.

"Oh," said Solly, nodding as someone whispered over the counter to him. "I see. She was waiting here. Musta been waiting for him."

A young girl in jeans giggled.

"Fish an' chips costs one an' six, madam."

"Wasn't it one an' three before?"

"Before the Boer War, madam. Price of fish go up. Potatoes go up an' you expect me to charge one an' three?"

"Why not?"

"Oh, go to hell! Next please!"

"Yes, that's 'e one, Solly."

"Mmmmm. Excuse me, madam,"—turning to Siena—"like some fish an' chips? Free of charge, never min' 'e money."

"Thank you, my baas."

The rain now sobbed wildly as the shop emptied, and Solly counted the cash in his till. Thousands of watery horses charging down the street. Rain drilling into cobbles and pavings. Miniature waterfalls down the sides of buildings. Blurred lights through unending streams. Siena listlessly holding the newspaper parcel of fish and chips.

"You can stay here till it clears up," said Solly.

She looked up tearfully.

Solly grinned showing his yellow teeth. "It's O.K."

A smile flickered across her face for a second.

"It's quite O.K. by me."

She looked down and hesitated for a moment. Then she struggled against the door. It yielded with a crash and the north-wester howled into Solly's Palace.

"Close 'e blarry door!" he said grinning.

"Thank you, my baas," she said as she shivered out into the rain.

## ■ Tchicaya U Tam'si (1931–1988) *Congo* (poems)

Born in the Moyen-Congo (now the Congo), Félix Tchicaya left his native land to go to France at the age of fifteen, accompanying his father who was an official in the French National Assembly. He studied at lycées in Orléans and Paris where he later became a producer of French radio programs based on African legends. He changed his name from Félix Tchicaya to Tchicaya Gérard-Félix U Tam'si and published under Tchicaya U Tam'si. He returned to Africa in 1960, choosing to live in Zaire (formerly the Belgian Congo) where he worked in Léopoldville as the managing editor for *Congo,* the party newspaper of Patrice Lumumba. That same year, he went back to Paris where from 1965 to 1985 he worked for UNESCO; thereafter, he spent all his time on his writing. Tchicaya died suddenly of a heart attack in 1988.

A leading voice of Francophone African poetry, U Tam'si wrote with shocking originality as he chose common themes and described them with hauntingly poignant images as in "The Flight of the Vampires," where evoking death, he writes, "the soul is losing / all of its fragrant water / pissed out drop by drop" and, speaking of childbirth, he says, "the ochre moon / was split in two / by cries of woman giving birth."

In his marvelous fiction, he plays with time and reality, expressing in poetic and richly rural element speech the traditional life of the Congo. He uses aphorisms, folk tales, ghosts, and transcendental figures to convey his stories. As Eric Sellin writes, in his brilliant introduction to the equally brilliant translation of *The Madman and the Medusa* by Sonja Haussmann Smith and William Jay Smith, "There are pages where sublime poetry and the banal phrase abut without transition."

**FURTHER READING:** U Tam'si, Tchicaya. *Le mauvais sang* (*Bad Blood*), 1955; *Feu de brousse* (*Brush Fire*), 1957; *A triche-coeur* (*The Tricky Heart*), 1958; *Epitomé,* 1962; *Le ventre* (*The Belly*), 1964.

## *The Flight of the Vampires*

in the morning we found the brush was scorched
and the sun smoked over
as usual we ate
boiled squash
then went to see
the swallower of fire
to help along the difficult digestion
in that dog-day heat
over fish-remains were straying
cockroaches, ants

1

and buffaloes black and hornless
hyenas whimpered behind our beds

the ochre moon
was split in two
by cries of woman giving birth                                          *15*

and look a mother had her child
one with two heads
the mother herself had two round breasts
banded about by cactus-root

the baby had a single leg                                               *20*

the trees in the fire-scorched brush
took hold of the woman and her child
she scratched at the ground
the winds had teeth sharp as a dog's
and now the winds                                                       *25*
those selfsame winds have brought
new leaves to the trees
feathered the parrots
scented the jackals
waiting                                                                 *30*
until some mother later
gives birth
to a child
with three heads
and maybe no legs at all                                                *35*
spreading more devastation
over the grassy plain

here are the vampires
the sky is still blue
the soul is losing                                                      *40*
all of its fragrant water
pissed out drop by drop

TRANSLATED BY NORMAN SHAPIRO

## *Agony*

there is no better key to dreams
than my name sang a bird
in a lake of blood
the sea danced alongside
dressed in blue-jeans                                                   *5*
blowing the squalling gulls to bits

a black boatman
who claimed to know the stars
said he could cure with the mud of his sad eyes
the lepers of their leprosy                                          1
if a tonic love would unloose his arms

my name is key to dreams
I am not leprous
take me across this river before you speak my name
and your arms will be unloosed                                       1

I hold the singing oar
where is this river I must cross
is it that lake of blood

follow me
close your eyes                                                      2
think of the moon
contemplate my river
and let us cross

the man and the bird sang
steered three days three nights to cross                             2
the dirty bed of a river

listen
the wave rocks the boatman
he sleeps
he dreams                                                            3
a charnel house offers a feast
where his bowels are eaten first
then his arms then his memory

where the putrid bodies eat each other
by the glimmer of fire-flies                                         3
which each carries at his temples
striving to resemble the christian god

there where they drink the slow song of the nightingale
one innocent pities his legs
scrapes from the bowl of ebony-wood                                  4
the last scrap of his memory
rope dancer on the thread
of low-water mark

He knows the love which opposes his pain
the nightmares of the boatman in his troubled sleep                  4
the wings of the birds who float their anthem
and who row too happily over the singing water

on the far bank the plain comes to drink

with its troops of wild grasses
bellowing their thirst in a tropical rhythm                              *50*
while the peevish sun stabs at them

the sun pricks the side of the fisherman
his swords all newly forged

all newly tempered
with blood                                                               *55*
and this blood oozes from the earth
and trickles from the sky
on a night of yellow rain

the boatman tells his name to the quail
no my name is key to dreams                                              *60*
I am not leprous
quail is not my name
do not die awaiting me

I am your soul farewell
my dark body farewell                                                    *65*
your arms will unloose themselves
I am not leprous

do not die awaiting me
arms opened in a cross

TRANSLATED BY GERALD MOORE

## ■ Ingrid Jonker (1933–1965) *South Africa* (poem)

### TRANSLATED BY JACK COPE AND WILLIAM PLOMER

Ingrid Jonker was born in South Africa. She traveled extensively in Europe—some of her haunting poems take place in Amsterdam—and, in South Africa, she espoused the cause of the poor and the black population. Her social convictions pitted her against the government and her own family. She also was a feminist and open about sexuality. Her disappointments come through poignantly in the lines: "And please forget / about justice it doesn't exist / about brotherhood / it's deceit / about love/ it has no right."[1] Her poems were translated into English by Jack Cope and William Plomer; otherwise, we should have nothing today in English, and even now we have only a small part of her writings. She died by suicide. The dates of her life almost coincide with those of Sylvia Plath, with whom she has many qualities in common, including stark, well-

---

1. Ingrid Jonker, "I Am with Those." In *Selected Poems*. Translated by Jack Cope and William Plomer (London: Jonathan Cape, 1968), 50.

chosen language, intensity, and the drama of a short, extremely talented dramatic life. In addition to her feminism, Jonker took on her government and the cause of racism, without diminishing the quality and passion of her solitary poems.

**FURTHER READING:** Jonker, Ingrid. *Selected Poems.* Translated from the Afrikaans by Jack Cope and William Plomer, 1968.

## I Am with Those

I am with those
who abuse sex
because the individual doesn't count
with those who get drunk
against the abyss of the brain
against the illusion that life
once was good or had beauty or sense
against the garden parties of falsehood
against the silence that beats into the temples
with those who poor and old                                    10
race against death the atom-bomb of the days
and in shacks count the last
flies on the walls
with those stupefied in institutions
shocked with electric currents                                 15
through the cataracts of the senses
with those who have been deprived of their hearts
like the light out of the robot of safety
with those coloured, african dispossessed
with those who murder                                          20
because every death confirms anew
the lie of life

And please forget
about justice it doesn't exist
about brotherhood it's deceit                                  25
about love it has no right

## ■ Wole Soyinka (1934– ) Nigeria (play)

Wole Soyinka was the first African to win the Nobel Prize, in 1986. In its award statement, the committee portrayed Soyinka as one who "with wide cultural perspective and with poetic overtones, fashions the drama of existence." Poet, essayist, editor, anthologist, novelist, and above all playwright, Wole Soyinka (pen name Akinwande Oluwole) was born in 1934 in Abeokuta in western Nigeria. He is from the Yoruba tribe, and traditional Yoruba culture has strongly affected his person and letters. His father, a headmaster in a Christian grammar school, introduced him to European culture. After schooling in Nigeria, he went to the University of Leeds in England (1954–1957). There he took honors in English. He remained in England for another three years where he was connected with the English Stage Company and especially with the Royal Court Theatre. In 1955, the Royal Court produced his first play, *The Invention*. Back in Nigeria, he formed a national theater and taught drama at the universities of Ibadan, Ife, and Lagos. During the Nigerian civil war, he supported the secessionist province of Biafra, was arrested, and spent twenty-two months in solitary confinement. When he was freed, he returned to Europe for five years and then went to Ghana. By 1976, he was back in Nigeria and became a professor of comparative literature and drama at the University of Ife.

Soyinka's dramas draw on the conflict and tension between rural Yoruba culture and European values. He finds good and greed, idealism and evil in all quarters, including precolonial African regimes. Early on he establishes a comedic and poetic drama, rich in its verbal range, always with a concern for justice, humanity, and revolution. He satirizes the abuses of religion and colonialism and the enemies of his idealism. In his poetry of protest, he has iterated caustic anti-semitism, associating Israeli agents and other Jews with right-wing conspiracies, though in reality he has been assailed from the left for his attacks on the abuses of what he calls the "leftocracy" and from the right for his "revolutionary individualism." He has also made many enemies by denouncing Négritude. The term *Négritude*, reflecting a political and aesthetic view invented by Aimé Césaire, popularized by Léopold Senghor, and espoused by French-speaking African authors, upholds pride in black heritage. Feeling limited by any stereotypes of people, Soyinka is said to have punned on Négritude that a tiger does not have to go around proclaiming his tigritude.

A prolific author, in *A Dance of Thieves*, 1960, he draws on folk motifs. Elsewhere, though never far from his Yoruba roots, he is also a modernist, and his *The Interpreter* (1965) was reviewed with superlatives in the *New York Review of Books* as a book whose mentor was James Joyce. His powerful novel *Season of Anomaly* (1973) examined the violence of civil war with special reference to his Yoruba beliefs. *Myth, Literature and the African World* (1980) collects some of his important essays. The energy of the young would-be author is revealed in his autobiography *Aké: The Years of Childhood* (1981). Among his most famous works are the farces *The Trials of Brother Jero* (1963) and its dark sequel *Jero's Metamorphosis* (1973).

The center of this diverse author's career is the international performances of his dramatic theater. His plays have received acclaim in the capitals of the world. In 1963, Mbari published three of his best-known plays, *The Swamp Dwellers, The Trials of Brother Jero,* and *The Strong Breed*. In 1965, his play *The Road* was performed in London. The next year, Oxford published the collection, *Five Plays*. Each year, in Africa, in Europe, or in America, has seen the writing and production of new plays. In 1981, he was a visiting professor at Yale University, which had awarded him an honorary doctorate. There he worked on a new work, *A Play of Giants*, a play that not only condemns Adi Amin in Uganda but censors military leadership in general throughout Africa. In 1991, the BBC was broadcasting his play *A Scourge of Hyacinths*, and a year later he was directing *From Zia, with Love* at a festival in Sienna, Italy. Soyinka is Africa's major black writer. The Nobel Prize for Literature has come to Wole Soyinka, a Nigerian; Naguib Mafouz, an Egyptian; and Nadine Gordimer, a South African; three writers whose diversity, artistry, and humanity display Africa's rich contemporary genius.

FURTHER READING: Soyinka, Wole. *A Dance of Thieves*, 1960; *Idanre and Other Poems*, 1967; *Poems from Prison*, 1969; *Season of Anomaly*, 1973; *Myth, Literature and the African World*, 1980; *Aké: The Years of Childhood*, 1981; *Requiem for a Futurologist*, 1985.

# The Trials of Brother Jero

CHARACTERS

JEROBOAM, a Beach Divine
OLD PROPHET, his mentor
CHUME, assistant to Jeroboam
AMOPE, his wife
A TRADER
MEMBER OF PARLIAMENT
DRUMMER BOY
PENITENT
NEIGHBOURS
WORSHIPPERS
A TOUGH MAMMA
A YOUNG GIRL

## SCENE I

*The stage is completely dark. A spotlight reveals the Prophet, a heavily but neatly bearded man; his hair is thick and high, but well-combed, unlike that of most prophets. Suave is the word for him. He carries a canvas pouch and a divine rod.[1] He speaks directly and with his accustomed loftiness to the audience.*

JEROBOAM. I am a Prophet. A prophet by birth and by inclination. You
have probably seen many of us on the streets, many with their own

---

1. A metal rod carried as a symbol of authority.

churches, many inland, many on the coast, many leading processions, many looking for processions to lead, many curing the deaf, many raising the dead. In fact, there are eggs and there are eggs. Same thing with prophets. I was born a Prophet. I think my parents found that I was born with rather thick and long hair. It was said to come right down to my eyes and down to my neck. For them, this was a certain sign that I was born a natural prophet. And I grew to love the trade. It used to be a very respectable one in those days and competition was dignified. But in the last few years, the beach has become fashionable, and the struggle for land has turned the profession into a thing of ridicule. Some prophets I could name gained their present beaches by getting women penitents to shake their bosoms in spiritual ecstasy. This prejudiced the councilors who came to divide the beach among us.

Yes, it did come to the point where it became necessary for the Town Council to come to the beach and settle the Prophets' territorial warfare once and for all. My Master, the same one who brought me up in prophetic ways, staked his claim and won a grant of land. . . . I helped him, with a campaign led by six dancing girls from the French territory, all dressed as Jehovah's Witnesses.[2] What my old Master did not realize was that I was really helping myself.

Mind you, the beach is hardly worth having these days. The worshippers have dwindled to a mere trickle and we really have to fight for every new convert. They all prefer High Life to the rhythm of celestial hymns. And television too is keeping our wealthier patrons at home. They used to come in the evening when they would not easily be recognized. Now they stay at home and watch television. However, my whole purpose in coming here is to show you one rather eventful day in my life, a day when I thought for a moment that the curse of my old Master was about to be fulfilled. It shook me quite a bit, but . . . the Lord protects his own. . . .

*[Enter* OLD PROPHET *shaking his fist.]*

OLD PROPHET. Ungrateful wretch! Is this how you repay the long years of training I have given you? To drive me, your old Tutor, off my piece of land . . . telling me I have lived beyond my time. Ha! May you be rewarded in the same manner. May the Wheel[3] come right round and find you just as helpless as you make me now. . . .

*[He continues to mouth curses, but inaudibly.]*

2. A proselytizing Christian sect founded by Charles T. Russell (1852–1916).

3. The Wheel of Fortune.

JEROBOAM [*ignoring him*]. He didn't move me one bit. The old dodderer had been foolish enough to imagine that when I organized the campaign to acquire his land in competition with [*ticking them off on his fingers*] — The Brotherhood of Jehu, the Cherubims and Seraphims, the Sisters of Judgement Day, the Heavenly Cowboys,[4] not to mention the Jehovah's Witnesses whom the French girls impersonated — well, he must have been pretty conceited to think that I did it all for him.

OLD PROPHET. Ingrate! Monster! I curse you with the curse of the Daughters of Discord. May they be your downfall. May the Daughters of Eve bring ruin down on your head!

*[OLD PROPHET goes off, shaking his fist.]*

JEROBOAM. Actually that was a very cheap curse. He knew very well that I had one weakness — women. Not my fault, mind you. You must admit that I am rather good-looking . . . no, don't be misled, I am not at all vain. Nevertheless, I decided to be on my guard. The call of Prophecy is in my blood and I would not risk my calling with the fickleness of women. So I kept away from them. I am still single and since that day when I came into my own, no scandal has ever touched my name. And it was a sad day indeed when I woke up one morning and the first thing to meet my eyes was a Daughter of Eve. You may compare that feeling with waking up and finding a vulture crouched on your bedpost.

BLACKOUT

# Scene II

*Early morning. A few poles with nets and other litter denote a fishing village. Downstage right is the corner of a hut, window on one side, door on the other.*

*A cycle bell is heard ringing. Seconds after, a cycle is ridden on stage towards the hut. The rider is a shortish man; his feet barely touch the pedals. On the crossbar is a woman; the cross-bar itself is wound round with a mat, and on the carrier is a large travelling sack, with a woman's household stool hanging from a corner of it.*

AMOPE. Stop here. Stop here. That's his house.

*[The man applies the brakes too suddenly. The weight leans towards the woman's side, with the result that she props up the bicycle with her feet, rather jerkily. It is in fact no worse than any ordinary landing, but it is enough to bring out her sense of aggrievement.]*

---

4. Invented sects.

AMOPE [*Her tone of martyrdom is easy, accustomed to use.*]. I suppose we all do our best, but after all these years one would think you could set me down a little more gently.

CHUME. You didn't give me much notice. I had to brake suddenly.

AMOPE. The way you complain—anybody who didn't see what happened would think you were the one who broke an ankle. [*She has already begun to limp.*]

CHUME. Don't tell me that was enough to break your ankle.

AMOPE. Break? You didn't hear me complain. You did your best, but if my toes are to be broken one by one just because I have to monkey on your bicycle, you must admit it's a tough life for a woman.

CHUME. I did my . . .

AMOPE. Yes, you did your best. I know. Didn't I admit it? Please . . . give me that stool . . . You know yourself that I'm not one to make much of a little thing like that, but I haven't been too well. If anyone knows that, it's you. Thank you. [*Taking the stool.*] . . . I haven't been well, that's all, otherwise I wouldn't have said a thing.

[*She sits down near the door of the hut, sighing heavily, and begins to nurse her feet.*]

CHUME. Do you want me to bandage it for you?

AMOPE. No, no. What for?

[CHUME *hesitates, then begins to unload the bundle.*]

CHUME. You're sure you don't want me to take you back? If it swells after I've gone . . .

AMOPE. I can look after myself. I've always done, and looked after you too. Just help me unload the things and place them against the wall . . . you know I wouldn't ask if it wasn't for the ankle.

[CHUME *had placed the bag next to her, thinking that was all. He returns now to untie the bundle. Brings out a small brazier covered with paper which is tied down, two small saucepans . . .*]

AMOPE. You haven't let the soup pour out, have you?

CHUME [*with some show of exasperation*]. Do you see oil on the wrapper? [*Throws down the wrapper.*]

AMOPE. Abuse me. All right, go on, begin to abuse me. You know that all I asked was if the soup had poured away, and it isn't as if that was something no one ever asked before. I would do it all myself if it wasn't for my ankle—anyone would think it was my fault . . . careful . . . careful now . . . the cork nearly came off that bottle. You know how difficult it is to get any clean water in this place . . .

*[*CHUME *unloads two bottles filled with water, two little parcels wrapped in paper, another tied in a knot, a box of matches, a piece of yam, two tins, one probably an Ovaltine tin but containing something else of course, a cheap breakable spoon, a knife, while* AMOPE *keeps up her patient monologue, spoken almost with indifference.]*

AMOPE. Do, I beg you, take better care of that jar. . . . I know you didn't want to bring me, but it wasn't the fault of the jar, was it?

CHUME. Who said I didn't want to bring you?

AMOPE. You said it was too far away for you to bring me on your bicycle. . . . I suppose you really wanted me to walk. . . .

CHUME. I . . .

AMOPE. And after you'd broken my foot, the first thing you asked was if you should take me home. You were only too glad it happened . . . in fact if I wasn't the kind of person who would never think evil of anyone—even you—I would have said that you did it on purpose.

*[The unloading is over.* CHUME *shakes out the bag.]*

AMOPE. Just leave the bag here. I can use it for a pillow.

CHUME. Is there anything else before I go?

AMOPE. You've forgotten the mat. I know it's not much, but I would like something to sleep on. There are women who sleep in beds of course, but I'm not complaining. They are just lucky with their husbands, and we can't all be lucky I suppose.

CHUME. You've got a bed at home.

*[He unties the mat which is wound round the cross-bar.]*

AMOPE. And so I'm to leave my work undone. My trade is to suffer because I have a bed at home? Thank God I am not the kind of woman who . . .

CHUME. I am nearly late for work.

AMOPE. I know you can't wait to get away. You only use your work as an excuse. A Chief Messenger in the Local Government Office—do you call that work? Your old school friends are now Ministers, riding in long cars. . . .

*[CHUME gets on his bike and flees. AMOPE shouts after him, craning her neck in his direction.]*

AMOPE. Don't forget to bring some more water when you're returning from work. *[She relapses and sighs heavily.]* He doesn't realize it is all for his own good. He's no worse than other men, but he won't make the effort to become something in life. A Chief Messenger. Am I to go to my grave as the wife of a Chief Messenger?

*[She is seated so that the Prophet does not immediately see her when he opens the window to breathe some fresh air. He stares straight out for a few moments, then shuts his eyes tightly, clasps his hands together above his chest, chin uplifted for a few moments' meditation. He relaxes and is about to go in when he sees AMOPE's back. He leans out to try to take in the rest of her but this proves impossible. Puzzled, he leaves the window and goes round to the door which is then seen to open about a foot and shut rapidly. AMOPE is calmly chewing cola.⁵ As the door shuts she takes out a notebook and a pencil and checks some figures.*

BROTHER JEROBOAM, *known to his congregation as* BROTHER JERO, *is seen again at the window, this time with his canvas pouch and divine stick. He lowers the bag to the ground, eases one leg over the window.]*

AMOPE. *[without looking back].* Where do you think you're going?

*[BROTHER JERO practically flings himself back into the house.]*

AMOPE. One pound, eight shillings, and ninepence for three months. And he calls himself a man of God.

*[She puts the notebook away, unwraps the brazier, and proceeds to light it preparatory to getting breakfast. The door opens another foot.]*

JERO *[Coughs].* Sister . . . my dear sister in Christ . . .

AMOPE. I hope you slept well, Brother Jero. . . .

JERO. Yes, thanks be to God. *[Hems and coughs.]* I—er—I hope you have not come to stand in the way of Christ and his work.

AMOPE. If Christ doesn't stand in the way of me and my work.

JERO. Beware of pride, sister. That was a sinful way to talk.

AMOPE. Listen, you bearded debtor. You owe me one pound, eight and nine. You promised you would pay me three months ago but of course you have been too busy doing the work of God. Well, let me tell you that you are not going anywhere until you do a bit of my own work.

---

5. Seeds of the Kola tree.

JERO. But the money is not in the house. I must get it from the post office before I can pay you.

AMOPE *[fanning the brazier]*. You'll have to think of something else before you call me a fool.

*[BROTHER JEROBOAM shuts the door. A woman TRADER goes past with a deep calabash bowl[6] on her head.]*

AMOPE. Ei, what are you selling?

*[The TRADER hesitates, decides to continue on her way.]*

AMOPE. Isn't it you I'm calling? What have you got there?

TRADER *[stops, without turning round]*. Are you buying for trade or just for yourself?

AMOPE. It might help if you first told me what you have.

TRADER. Smoked fish.

AMOPE. Well, let's see it.

TRADER *[hesitates]*. All right, help me to set it down. But I don't usually stop on the way.

AMOPE. Isn't it money you are going to the market for, and isn't it money I'm going to pay you?

TRADER *[as AMOPE gets up and unloads her]*. Well, just remember it is early in the morning. Don't start me off wrong by haggling.

AMOPE. All right, all right. *[Looks at the fish.]* How much a dozen?

TRADER. One and three, and I'm not taking a penny less.

AMOPE. It is last week's, isn't it?

TRADER. I've told you, you're my first customer, so don't ruin my trade with the ill-luck of the morning.

AMOPE *[holding one up to her nose]*. Well, it does smell a bit, doesn't it?

TRADER *[putting back the wrappings]*. Maybe it is you who haven't had a bath for a week.

AMOPE. Yeh! All right, go on. Abuse me. Go on and abuse me when all I wanted was a few of your miserable fish. I deserve it for trying to be neighbourly with a cross-eyed wretch, pauper that you are . . .

---

6. A container made from a gourd.

TRADER. It is early in the morning. I am not going to let you infect my luck with your foul tongue by answering you back. And just you keep your cursed fingers from my goods because that is where you'll meet with the father of all devils if you don't.

*[She lifts the load to her head all by herself.]*

AMOPE. Yes, go on. Carry the burden of your crimes and take your beggar's rags out of my sight. . . .

TRADER. I leave you in the hands of your flatulent belly, you barren sinner. May you never do good in all your life.

AMOPE. You're cursing me now, are you?

*[She leaps up just in time to see BROTHER JERO escape through the window.]*

Help! Thief! Thief! You bearded rogue. Call yourself a prophet? But you'll find it easier to get out than to get in. You'll find that out or my name isn't Amope. . . .

*[She turns on the TRADER who has already disappeared.]*

Do you see what you have done, you spindle-leg toad? Receiver of stolen goods, just wait until the police catch up with you. . . .

*[Towards the end of this speech the sound of "gangan" drums is heard, coming from the side opposite the hut. A BOY enters carrying a drum on each shoulder. He walks towards her, drumming. She turns almost at once.]*

AMOPE. Take yourself off, you dirty beggar. Do you think my money is for the likes of you?

*[The BOY flees, turns suddenly, and beats a parting abuse on the drums.]*

AMOPE. I don't know what the world is coming to. A thief of a Prophet, a swindler of a fish-seller and now that thing with lice on his head comes begging for money. He and the Prophet ought to get together with the fish-seller their mother.

LIGHTS FADE

# Scene III

*A short while later. The beach. A few stakes and palm leaves denote the territory of BROTHER JEROBOAM'S church. To one side is a palm tree, and in the centre is a heap of sand with assorted empty bottles, a small mirror, and hanging from one of the bottles is a rosary[7] and cross.* BROTHER JERO *is standing as he was last seen when he made his escape—white flowing gown and a very fine velvet cape, white also. Stands upright, divine rod in hand, while the other caresses the velvet cape.*

JERO. I don't know how she found out my house. When I bought the goods off her, she did not even ask any questions. My calling was enough to guarantee payment. It is not as if this was a well-paid job. And it is not what I would call a luxury, this velvet cape which I bought from her. It would not have been necessary if one were not forced to distinguish himself more and more from these scum who degrade the calling of the Prophet. It becomes important to stand out, to be distinctive. I have set my heart after a particular name. They will look at my velvet cape and they will think of my goodness. Inevitably they must begin to call me . . . the Velvet-hearted Jeroboam. *[Straightens himself.]* Immaculate Jero, Articulate Hero of Christ's Crusade. . . .

   Well, it is out. I have not breathed it to a single soul, but that has been my ambition. You've got to have a name that appeals to the imagination—because the imagination is a thing of the spirit—it must catch the imagination of the crowd. Yes, one must move with modern times. Lack of colour gets one nowhere even in the Prophet's business. *[Looks all round him.]* Charlatans! If only I had this beach to myself. *[With sudden violence.]* But how does one maintain his dignity when the daughter of Eve forces him to leave his own house through a window? God curse that woman! I never thought she would dare affront the presence of a man of God. One pound eight for this little cape. It is sheer robbery.

*[He surveys the scene again. A young girl passes, sleepily, clothed only in her wrapper.]*

JERO. She passes here every morning, on her way to take a swim. Dirty-looking thing.

*[He yawns.]*

   I am glad I got here before any customers—I mean worshippers—well, customers if you like. I always get that feeling every morning that I am a shopkeeper waiting for customers. The regular ones come at definite times. Strange, dissatisfied people. I know they are dissatisfied because I keep them dissatisfied. Once they are full, they won't come again. Like my good apprentice, Brother Chume. He wants to beat his wife, but I won't let him. If I do, he will become contented, and then that's another of my flock gone for ever. As long as he doesn't beat

---

7. A string of beads used to keep count when saying prayers.

her, he comes here feeling helpless, and so there is no chance of his rebelling against me. Everything, in fact, is planned.

*[The young girl crosses the stage again. She has just had her swim and the difference is remarkable. Clean, wet, shiny face and hair. She continues to wipe herself with her wrapper as she walks.]*

JERO *[following her all the way with his eyes].* Every morning, every day I witness this divine transformation, O Lord.

*[He shakes his head suddenly and bellows.]*

Pray Brother Jeroboam, pray! Pray for strength against temptation.

*[He falls on his knees, face squeezed in agony and hands clasped. CHUME enters, wheeling his bike. He leans it against the palm tree.]*

JERO *[not opening his eyes].* Pray with me brother. Pray with me. Pray for me against this one weakness . . . against this one weakness, O Lord . . .

CHUME *[falling down at once].* Help him, Lord. Help him, Lord.

JERO. Against this one weakness, this weakness, O Abraham[8] . . .

CHUME. Help him, Lord. Help him, Lord.

JERO. Against this one weakness, David, David, Samuel, Samuel.[9]

CHUME. Help him. Help him. Help am. Help am.

JERO. Job Job, Elijah Elijah.[10]

CHUME *[getting more worked up].* Help am God. Help am God. I say make you help am. Help am quick quick.

JERO. Tear the image from my heart. Tear this love for the daughters of Eve . . .

CHUME. Adam, help am. Na[11] your son, help am. Help this your son.

JERO. Burn out this lust for the daughters of Eve.

CHUME. Je-e-esu, J-e-esu, Je-e-esu. Help am one time Je-e-e-e-su.

JERO. Abraka, Abraka, Abraka.

---

8. In the Bible, the first patriarch and ancestor of the Jewish people.

9. Biblical figures. David was the second king of Israel, father of Solomon, and the reputed author of the Psalms. Samuel was a Jewish judge and prophet.

10. Job was a Biblical figure who endured much suffering, but retained his faith in God. Elijah was a ninth century B.C. Israeli prophet.

11. Now.

[CHUME *joins in.*]

Abraka, Abraka, Hebra, Hebra, Hebra, Hebra, Hebra, Hebra, Hebra, Hebra. . . .

JERO [*rising*]. God bless you, brother. [*Turns around.*] Chume!

CHUME. Good morning, Brother Jeroboam.

JERO. Chume, you are not at work. You've never come before in the morning.

CHUME. No. I went to work but I had to report sick.

JERO. Why, are you unwell, brother?

CHUME. No, Brother Jero . . . I . . .

JERO. A-ah, you have troubles and you could not wait to get them to God. We shall pray together.

CHUME. Brother Jero . . . I . . . I [*He stops altogether.*]

JERO. Is it difficult? Then let us commune silently for a while.

[CHUME *folds his arms, raises his eyes to heaven.*]

JERO. I wonder what is the matter with him. Actually I knew it was he the moment he opened his mouth. Only Brother Chume reverts to that animal jabber when he gets his spiritual excitement. And that is much too often for my liking. He is too crude, but then that is to my advantage. It means he would think of setting himself up as my equal.

[*He joins* CHUME *in his meditative attitude, but almost immediately discards it, as if he has just remembered something.*]

Christ my Protector! It is a good job I got away from that wretched woman as soon as I did. My disciple believes that I sleep on the beach, that is, if he thinks I sleep at all. Most of them believe the same but, for myself, I prefer my bed. Much more comfortable. And it gets rather cold on the beach at nights. Still, it does them good to believe that I am something of an ascetic. . . .

[*He resumes his meditative pose for a couple of moments.*]

[*Gently.*] Open your mind to God, brother. This is the tabernacle of Christ. Open your mind to God.

[CHUME *is silent for a while, then bursts out suddenly.*]

CHUME. Brother Jero, you must let me beat her!

JERO. What!

CHUME [*desperately*]. Just once, Prophet. Just once.

JERO. Brother Chume!

CHUME. Just once. Just one sound beating, and I swear not to ask again.

JERO. Apostate. Have I not told you the will of God in this matter?

CHUME. But I've got to beat her, Prophet. You must save me from madness.

JERO. I will. But only if you obey me.

CHUME. In anything else, Prophet. But for this one, make you let me just beat am once.

JERO. Apostate!

CHUME. I n' go beat am too hard. Jus' once small small.

JERO. Traitor!

CHUME. Jus' this one time. I no' go ask again. Jus' do me this one favour, make a beat am today.

JERO. Brother Chume, what were you before you came to me?

CHUME. Prophet . . .

JERO [*sternly*]. What were you before the grace of God?

CHUME. A labourer, Prophet. A common labourer.

JERO. And did I not prophesy you would become an office boy?

CHUME. You do am, brother. Na so.

JERO. And then a messenger?

CHUME. Na you do am, brother. Na you.

JERO. And then quick promotion? Did I not prophesy it?

CHUME. Na true, prophet. Na true.

JERO. And what are you now? What are you?

CHUME. Chief Messenger.

JERO. By the grace of God! And by the grace of God, have I not seen you at the table of the Chief Clerk? And you behind the desk, giving orders?

CHUME. Yes, Prophet . . . but . . .

JERO. With a telephone and a table bell for calling the Messenger?

CHUME. Very true, Prophet, but . . .

JERO. But? But? Kneel! *[pointing to the ground]* Kneel!

CHUME *[wringing his hands].* Prophet!

JERO. Kneel, sinner, kneel. Hardener of heart, harbourer of Ashtoreth, Protector of Baal,[12] kneel, kneel.

*[CHUME falls on his knees.]*

CHUME. My life is a hell . . .

JERO. Forgive him, Father, forgive him.

CHUME. This woman will kill me . . .

JERO. Forgive him, Father, forgive him.

CHUME. Only this morning I . . .

JERO. Forgive him, Father, forgive him.

CHUME. All the way on my bicycle . . .

JERO. Forgive . . .

CHUME. And not a word of thanks . . .

JERO. Out Ashtoreth. Out Baal . . .

CHUME. All she gave me was abuse, abuse, abuse . . .

JERO. Hardener of the . . .

CHUME. Nothing but abuse . . .

JERO. Petrifier of the soul . . .

CHUME. If I could only beat her once, only once . . .

JERO *[shouting him down].* Forgive this sinner, Father. Forgive him by day, forgive him by night, forgive him in the morning, forgive him at noon . . .

*[A man enters. Kneels at once and begins to chorus "Amen," or "Forgive him, Lord," or "In the name of Jesus (pronounced Je-e-e-sus)." Those who follow later do the same.]*

. . . This is the son whom you appointed to follow in my footsteps. Soften his heart. Brother Chume, this woman whom you so desire to beat is your cross—bear it well. She is your heaven-sent trial—lay not

---

12. Ashtoreth was the Syrian and Phonecian goddess of love and fertility, akin to the Greek goddess Aphrodite and the Babylonian and Assyrian goddess Ishtar. Baal was an ancient Semitic Stoem god, whose worship was opposed by the Prophets, as it diminished the authority of Yahweh (Jehovah). Later, Baal was demonized and, under the name Baal-zebub, associated with Satan.

your hands on her. I command you to speak no harsh word to her. Pray, Brother Chume, for strength in this hour of your trial. Pray for strength and fortitude.

[JEROBOAM *leaves them to continue their chorus,* CHUME *chanting, "Mercy, Mercy" while he makes his next remarks.*]

They begin to arrive. As usual in the same order. This one who always comes earliest, I have prophesied that he will be made a chief in his home town. That is a very safe prophecy. As safe as our most popular prophecy, that a man will live to be eighty. If it doesn't come true,

[*Enter an old couple, joining chorus as before.*]

that man doesn't find out until he's on the other side. So everybody is quite happy. One of my most faithful adherents—unfortunately, he can only be present at week-ends—firmly believes that he is going to be the first Prime Minister of the new Mid-North-East-State—when it is created. That was a risky prophecy of mine, but I badly needed more worshippers around that time.

[*He looks at his watch.*]

The next one to arrive is my most faithful penitent. She wants children, so she is quite a sad case. Or you would think so. But even in the midst of her most self-abasing convulsions, she manages to notice everything that goes on around her. In fact, I had better get back to the service. She is always the one to tell me that my mind is not on the service. . . .

[*Altering his manner—*]

Rise, Brother Chume. Rise and let the Lord enter into you. Apprentice of the Lord, are you not he upon whose shoulders my mantle must descend?

[*A woman (the* PENITENT) *enters and kneels at once in an attitude of prayer.*]

CHUME. It is so, Brother Jero.

JERO. Then why do you harden your heart? The Lord says that you may not beat the good woman whom he has chosen to be your wife, to be your cross in your period of trial, and will you disobey him?

CHUME. No, Brother Jero.

JERO. Will you?

CHUME. No, Brother Jero.

JERO. Praise be to God.

CONGREGATION. Praise be to God.

JERO. Allelu . . .

CONGREGATION. Alleluia.

*[To the clapping of hands, they sing "I will follow Jesus," swaying and then dancing as they get warmer.*

*BROTHER JERO, as the singing starts, hands two empty bottles to* CHUME *who goes to fill them with water from the sea.* CHUME *has hardly gone out when the drummer boy enters from upstage, running. He is rather weighed down by two "gangan" drums, and darts fearful glances back in mortal terror of whatever it is that is chasing him. This turns out, some ten or so yards later, to be a woman, sash tightened around her waist, wrapper pulled so high up that half the length of her thigh is exposed. Her sleeves are rolled above the shoulder and she is striding after the* DRUMMER *in no unmistakable manner.* JEROBOAM, *who has followed the woman's exposed limbs with quite distressed concentration, comes suddenly to himself and kneels sharply, muttering.*

*Again the* DRUMMER *appears, going across the stage in a different direction, running still. The woman follows, distance undiminished, the same set pace.* JEROBOAM *calls to him.]*

JERO. What did you do to her?

DRUMMER *[without stopping].* Nothing. I was only drumming and then she said I was using it to abuse her father.

JERO *[as the woman comes into sight].* Woman!

*[She continues out.* CHUME *enters with filled bottles.]*

JERO *[shaking his head].* I know her very well. She's my neighbour. But she ignored me. . . .

*[JEROBOAM prepares to bless the water when once again the procession appears,* DRUMMER *first and the woman after.]*

JERO. Come here. She wouldn't dare touch you.

DRUMMER *[increasing his pace].* You don't know her . . .

*[The woman comes in sight.]*

JERO. Neighbour, neighbour. My dear sister in Moses[13] . . .

---

13. Biblical prophet who led the Israelites out of captivity in Egypt.

*[She continues her pursuit offstage. JERO hesitates, then hands over his rod to* CHUME *and goes after them.]*

CHUME *[suddenly remembering].* You haven't blessed the water, Brother Jeroboam.

*[JERO is already out of hearing.* CHUME *is obviously bewildered by the new responsibility. He fiddles around with the rod and eventually uses it to conduct the singing, which has gone on all this time, flagging when the two contestants came in view, and reviving again after they had passed.*

*CHUME has hardly begun to conduct his band when a woman detaches herself from the crowd in the expected PENINTENT's paroxysm.]*

PENITENT.  Echa, echa, echa, echa, echa  . . . eei, eei, eei, eei.

CHUME *[taken aback].*  Ngh? What's the matter?

PENITENT.  Efie, efie, efie, efie, enh, enh, enh, enh  . . .

CHUME *[dashing off].*  Brother Jeroboam, Brother Jeroboam  . . .

*[CHUME shouts in all directions, returning confusedly each time in an attempt to minister to the PENITENT. As JEROBOAM is not forthcoming, he begins, very uncertainly, to sprinkle some of the water on the PENITENT, crossing her on the forehead. This has to be achieved very rapidly in the brief moment when the PENITEN I 's head is lifted from beating on the ground.]*

CHUME *[stammering].*  Father . . . forgive her.

CONGREGATION *[strongly].*  Amen.

*[The unexpectedness of the response nearly throws CHUME, but then it also serves to bolster him up, receiving such support.]*

CHUME.  Father, forgive her.

CONGREGATION.  Amen.

*[The PENITENT continues to moan.]*

CHUME.  Father forgive her.

CONGREGATION.  Amen.

CHUME.  Father forgive am.

CONGREGATION.  Amen.

CHUME *[warming up to the task].*  Make you forgive am. Father.

CONGREGATION.  Amen.

*[They rapidly gain pace,* CHUME *getting quite carried away.]*

CHUME. I say make you forgive am.

CONGREGATION. Amen.

CHUME. Forgive am one time.

CONGREGATION. Amen.

CHUME. Forgive am quick quick.

CONGREGATION. Amen.

CHUME. Forgive am, Father.

CONGREGATION. Amen.

CHUME. Forgive us all.

CONGREGATION. Amen.

CHUME. Forgive us all.

*[And then, punctuated regularly with Amens. . . .]*

Yes, Father, make you forgive us all. Make you save us from palaver. Save us from trouble at home. Tell our wives not to give us trouble . . .

*[The* PENITENT *has become placid. She is stretched out flat on the ground.]*

. . . Tell our wives not to give us trouble. And give us money to have a happy home. Give us money to satisfy our daily necessities. Make you no forget those of us who dey struggle daily. Those who be clerk today, make them Chief Clerk tomorrow. Those who are Messenger today, make them Senior Service tomorrow. Yes Father, those who are Messenger today, make them Senior Service tomorrow.

*[The Amens grow more and more ecstatic.]*

Those who are petty trader today, make them big contractor tomorrow. Those who dey sweep street today, give them their own big office tomorrow. If we dey walka today, give us our own bicycle tomorrow. I say those who dey walka today, give them their own bicycle tomorrow. Those who have bicycle today, they will ride their own car tomorrow.

*[The enthusiasm of the response, becomes, at this point, quite overpowering.]*

I say those who dey push bicycle, give them big car tomorrow. Give them big car tomorrow. Give them big car tomorrow, give them big car tomorrow.

*[The angry woman comes again in view, striding with the same gait as before, but now in possession of the drums. A few yards behind, the* DRUMMER *jog-trots wretchedly, pleading.]*

DRUMMER. I beg you, give me my drums. I take God's name beg you, I was not abusing your father. . . . For God's sake I beg you . . . I was not abusing your father. I was only drumming . . . I swear to God I was only drumming. . . .

*[They pass through.]*

PENITENT *[who has become much alive from the latter part of the prayers, pointing].* Brother Jeroboam!

*[*BROTHER JERO *has just come in view. They all rush to help him back into the circle. He is a much altered man, his clothes torn and his face bleeding.]*

JERO *[slowly and painfully].* Thank you, brother, sisters. Brother Chume, kindly tell these friends to leave me. I must pray for the soul of that sinful woman. I must say a personal prayer for her.

*[*CHUME *ushers them off. They go reluctantly, chattering excitedly.]*

JERO. Prayers this evening, as usual. Late afternoon.

CHUME *[shouting after].* Prayers late afternoon as always. Brother Jeroboam says God keep you till then. Are you all right, Brother Jero?

JERO. Who would have thought that she would dare lift her hand against a prophet of God!

CHUME. Women are a plague, brother.

JERO. I had a premonition this morning that women would be my downfall today. But I thought of it only in the spiritual sense.

CHUME. Now you see how it is, Brother Jero.

JERO. From the moment I looked out of my window this morning, I have been tormented one way or another by the Daughters of Discord.

CHUME *[eagerly].* That is how it is with me, Brother. Every day. Every morning and night. Only this morning she made me take her to the house of some poor man, whom she says owes her money. She loaded enough on my bicycle to lay a siege for a week, and all the thanks I got was abuse.

JERO. Indeed, it must be a trial, Brother Chume . . . and it requires great . . .

*[He becomes suddenly suspicious.]*

Brother Chume, did you say that your wife went to make camp only this morning at the house of a . . . of someone who owes her money?

CHUME. Yes, I took her there myself.

JERO. Er . . . indeed, indeed. *[Coughs.]* Is . . . your wife a trader?

CHUME. Yes, Petty trading, you know. Wool, silk, cloth, and all that stuff.

JERO. Indeed. Quite an enterprising woman. *[Hems.]* Er . . . where was the house of this man . . . I mean, this man who owes her money?

CHUME. Not very far from here. Ajete settlement, a mile or so from here. I did not even know the place existed until today.

JERO *[to himself]*. So that is your wife . . .

CHUME. Did you speak, prophet?

JERO. No, no. I was only thinking how little women have changed since Eve, since Delilah, since Jezebel.[14] But we must be strong of heart. I have my own cross too, Brother Chume. This morning alone I have been thrice in conflict with the Daughters of Discord. First there was . . . no, never mind that. There is another who crosses my path every day. Goes to swim just over there and then waits for me to be in the midst of my meditation before she swings her hips across here, flaunting her near nakedness before my eyes. . . .

CHUME *[to himself, with deep feeling]*. I'd willingly change crosses with you.

JERO. What, Brother Chume?

CHUME. I was only praying.

JERO. Ah. That is the only way. But er . . . I wonder really what the will of God would be in this matter. After all, Christ himself was not averse to using the whip when occasion demanded it.

CHUME *[eagerly]*. No, he did not hesitate.

JERO. In that case, since, Brother Chume, your wife seems such a wicked, wilful sinner, I think . . .

CHUME. Yes, Holy One. . . ?

JERO. You must take her home tonight. . . .

CHUME. Yes. . . .

---

14. Three Biblical women who represent the mysogynist tradition in Judeo-Christianity.

JERO. And beat her.

CHUME *[kneeling, clasps JERO's hand in his]*. Prophet!

JERO. Remember, it must be done in your own house. Never show the discord within your family to the world. Take her home and beat her.

*[CHUME leaps up and gets his bike.]*

JERO. And Brother Chume . . .

CHUME. Yes, Prophet . . .

JERO. The Son of God appeared to me again this morning, robed just as he was when he named you my successor. And he placed his burning sword on my shoulder and called me his knight. He gave me a new title . . . but you must tell it to no one—yet.

CHUME. I swear, Brother Jero.

JERO *[staring into space]*. He named me the Immaculate Jero, Articulate Hero of Christ's Crusade.

*[Pauses, then, with a regal dismissal—]* You may go, Brother Chume.

CHUME. God keep you, Brother Jero—the Immaculate.

JERO. God keep you, brother. *[He sadly fingers the velvet cape.]*

LIGHTS FADE

## Scene IV

*As Scene II, i.e., in front of the Prophet's home. Later that day. CHUME is just wiping off the last crumbs of yams on his plate. AMOPE watches him.*

AMOPE. You can't say I don't try. Hounded out of house by debtors, I still manage to make you a meal.

CHUME *[sucking his fingers, sets down his plate]*. It was a good meal too.

AMOPE. I do my share as I've always done. I cooked you your meal. But when I ask you to bring me some clean water, you forget.

CHUME. I did not forget.

AMOPE. You keep saying that. Where is it then? Or perhaps the bottles fell off your bicycle on the way and got broken.

CHUME. That's a child's lie, Amope. You are talking to a man.

AMOPE. A fine man you are then, when you can't remember a simple thing like a bottle of clean water.

CHUME. I remembered. I just did not bring it. So that is that. And now pack up your things because we're going home.

[AMOPE *stares at him unbelieving.*]

CHUME. Pack up your things; you heard what I said.

AMOPE [*scrutinizing*]. I thought you were a bit early to get back. You haven't been to work at all. You've been drinking all day.

CHUME. You may think what suits you. You know I never touch any liquor.

AMOPE. You needn't say it as if it was a virtue. You don't drink only because you cannot afford to. That is all the reason there is.

CHUME. Hurry. I have certain work to do when I get home and I don't want you delaying me.

AMOPE. Go then. I am not budging from here till I get my money.

[CHUME *leaps up, begins to throw her things into the bag.* BROTHER JERO *enters, hides, and observes them.*]

AMOPE [*quietly*]. I hope you have ropes to tie me on the bicycle, because I don't intend to leave this place unless I am carried out. One pound eight shillings is no child's play. And it is my money not yours.

[CHUME *has finished packing the bag and is now tying it on to the carrier.*]

AMOPE. A messenger's pay isn't that much you know—just in case you've forgotten you're not drawing a minister's pay. So you better think again if you think I am letting my hard-earned money stay in the hands of that good-for-nothing. Just think, only this morning while I sat here, a Sanitary Inspector came along. He looked me all over and he made some notes in his book. Then he said, I suppose, woman, you realize that this place is marked down for slum clearance. This to me, as if I lived here. But you sit down and let your wife be exposed to such insults. And the Sanitary Inspector had a motor-cycle too, which is one better than a bicycle.

CHUME. You'd better be ready soon.

AMOPE. A Sanitary Inspector is a better job anyway. You can make something of yourself one way or another. They all do. A little here and a little there, call it bribery if you like, but see where you've got even though you don't drink or smoke or take bribes. He's got a motor-bike . . . anyway, who would want to offer cola to a Chief Messenger?

CHUME. Shut your big mouth!

AMOPE [*aghast*]. What did you say?

CHUME. I said shut your big mouth.

AMOPE. To me?

CHUME. Shut your big mouth before I shut it for you. *[Ties the mat round the cross-bar.]* And you'd better start to watch your step from now on. My period of abstinence is over. My cross has been lifted off my shoulders by the Prophet.

AMOPE *[genuinely distressed].* He's mad.

CHUME *[viciously tying up the mat].* My period of trial is over. *[Practically strangling the mat.]* If you so much as open your mouth now . . . *[Gives a further twist to the string.]*

AMOPE. God help me. He's gone mad.

CHUME *[imperiously].* Get on the bike.

AMOPE *[backing away].* I'm not coming with you.

CHUME. I said get on the bike!

AMOPE. Not with you. I'll find my own way home.

*[CHUME advances on her. AMOPE screams for help. BROTHER JERO crosses himself. CHUME catches her by the arm but she escapes, runs to the side of the house and beats on the door.]*

AMOPE. Help! Open the door for God's sake. Let me in. Let me in . . .

*[BROTHER JERO grimaces.]*

Is anyone in? Let me in for God's sake! Let me in or God will punish you!

JERO *[sticking his fingers in his ears].* Blasphemy!

AMOPE. Prophet! Where's the Prophet?

*[CHUME lifts her bodily.]*

AMOPE. Let me down! Police! Police!

CHUME *[setting her down].* If you shout just once more I'll . . . *[He raises a huge fist.]*

*[BROTHER JERO gasps in mock-horror, tut-tuts, covers his eyes with both hands, and departs.]*

AMOPE. Ho! You're mad. You're mad.

CHUME. Get on the bike.

Sub-Sahara Africa / The Modern Period

AMOPE. Kill me! Kill me!

CHUME. Don't tempt me, woman!

AMOPE. I won't get on that thing unless you kill me first.

CHUME. Woman!

[Two or three neighbours arrive, but keep a respectful distance.]

AMOPE. Kill me. You'll have to kill me. Everybody come and bear witness.
He's going to kill me so come and bear witness. I forgive everyone
who has ever done me evil. I forgive all my debtors especially the
Prophet who has got me into all this trouble. Prophet Jeroboam, I
hope you will pray for my soul in heaven. . . .

CHUME. You have no soul, wicked woman.

AMOPE. Brother Jeroboam, curse this man for me. You may keep the velvet
cape if you curse this foolish man. I forgive you your debt. Go on,
foolish man, kill me. If you don't kill me you won't do well in life.

CHUME [suddenly]. Shut up!

AMOPE [warming up as more people arrive]. Bear witness all of you. Tell the
Prophet I forgive him his debt but he must curse this foolish man to
hell. Go on, kill me!

CHUME [who has turned away, forehead knotted in confusion]. Can't you shut
up, woman!

AMOPE. No, you must kill me . . .

[The crowd hub-bubs all the time, scared as always at the prospect of interfering in
man-wife palaver, but throwing in half-hearted tokens of concern—]

"What's the matter, eh?" "You two keep quiet." "Who are they?"
"Where is Brother Jero?" "Do you think we ought to send for the
Prophet?" "These women are so troublesome! Somebody go and call
Brother Jero."

CHUME [lifting up AMOPE's head. She has, in the tradition of the "Kill me" woman,
shut her eyes tightly and continued to beat her fists on the Prophet's
doorstep.]. Shut up and listen. Did I hear you say Prophet Jeroboam?

AMOPE. See him now. Let you bear witness. He's going to kill me. . . .

CHUME. I'm not touching you but I will if you don't answer my question.

AMOPE. Kill me . . . Kill me . . .

CHUME. Woman, did you say it was the Prophet who owed you money?

AMOPE. Kill me . . .

CHUME. Is this his house? *[Gives her head a shake.]* Does he live here. . . ?

AMOPE. Kill me . . . Kill me . . .

CHUME *[pushing her away in disgust and turning to the crowd. They retreat instinctively.].* Is Brother Jeroboam. . . ?

NEAREST ONE *[hastily].* No, no. I'm not Brother Jero. It's not me.

CHUME. Who said you were? Does the Prophet live here?

SAME MAN. Yes. Over there. That house.

CHUME *[Turns round and stands stock still. Stares at the house for quite some time.].* So . . . so . . . so . . . so . . .

*[The crowd is puzzled over his change of mood. Even AMOPE looks up wonderingly. CHUME walks towards his bicycle, muttering to himself.]*

So . . . so . . . Suddenly he decides I may beat my wife, eh? For his own convenience. At his own convenience.

*[He releases the bundle from the carrier, pushing it down carelessly. He unties the mat also.]*

BYSTANDER. What next is he doing now?

CHUME *[mounting his bicycle].* You stay here and don't move. If I don't find you here when I get back . . .

*[He rides off. They all stare at him in bewilderment.]*

AMOPE. He is quite mad. I have never seen him behave like that.

BYSTANDER. You are sure?

AMOPE. Am I sure? I'm his wife, so I ought to know, shouldn't I?

A WOMAN BYSTANDER. Then you ought to let the Prophet see to him. I had a brother once who had the fits and foamed at the mouth every other week. But the Prophet cured him. Drove the devils out of him, he did.

AMOPE. This one can't do anything. He's a debtor and that's all he knows. How to dodge his creditors.

*[She prepares to unpack her bundle.]*

LIGHTS FADE

## Scene V

*The beach. Nightfall.*

*A man in an elaborate "agbada" outfit, with long train and a cap is standing right, downstage, with a sheaf of notes in his hand. He is obviously delivering a speech, but we don't hear it. It is undoubtedly a fire-breathing speech.*

*The PROPHET JEROBOAM stands bolt upright as always, surveying him with lofty compassion.*

JERO. I could teach him a trick or two about speech-making. He's a member of the Federal House, a back-bencher but with one eye on a ministerial post. Comes here every day to rehearse his speeches. But he never makes them. Too scared.

*[Pause. The Prophet continues to study the MEMBER.]*

Poor fish. *[Chuckles and looks away.]* Oho, I had almost forgotten Brother Chume. By now he ought to have beaten his wife senseless. Pity! That means I've lost him. He is fulfilled and no longer needs me. True, he still has to become a Chief Clerk. But I have lost him as the one who was most dependent on me. . . . Never mind, it was a good price to pay for getting rid of my creditor. . . .

*[Goes back to the MEMBER.]*

Now he . . . he is already a member of my flock. He does not know it of course, but he is a follower. All I need do is claim him. Call him and say to him, My dear Member of the House, your place awaits you . . . Or do you doubt it? Watch me go to work on him. *[Raises his voice.]* My dear brother in Jesus!

*[The MEMBER stops, looks round, resumes his speech.]*

Dear brother, do I not know you?

*[MEMBER stops, looks round again.]*

Yes, you. In God's name, do I not know you?

*[MEMBER approaches slowly.]*

Yes indeed. It is you. And you come as it was predicted. Do you not perhaps remember me?

*[MEMBER looks at him scornfully.]*

Then you cannot be of the Lord. In another world, in another body, we met, and my message was for you . . .

*[The* MEMBER *turns his back impatiently.]*

MEMBER *[with great pomposity].* Go and practise your fraudulences on another person of greater gullibility.

JERO *[very kindly, smiling].* Indeed the matter is quite plain. You are not of the Lord. And yet such is the mystery of God's ways that his favour has lighted upon you . . . Minister . . . Minister by the grace of God . . .

*[The* MEMBER *stops dead.]*

Yes, brother, we have met. I saw this country plunged into strife. I saw the mustering of men, gathered in the name of peace through strength. And at a desk, in a large gilt room, great men of the land awaited your decision. Emissaries of foreign nations hung on your word, and on the door leading into your office, I read the words, Minister for War. . . .

*[The* MEMBER *turns round slowly.]*

. . . It is a position of power. But are you of the Lord? Are you in fact worthy? Must I, when I have looked into your soul, as the Lord has commanded me to do, must I pray to the Lord to remove this mantle from your shoulders and place it on a more God-fearing man?

*[The* MEMBER *moves forward unconsciously. The Prophet gestures him to stay where he is. Slowly—]*

Yes . . . I think I see Satan in your eyes. I see him entrenched in your eyes . . .

*[The* MEMBER *grows fearful, raises his arms in half-supplication.]*

The Minister for War would be the most powerful position in the Land. The Lord knows best, but he has empowered his lieutenants on earth to intercede where necessary. We can reach him by fasting and by prayer . . . we can make recommendations. . . . Brother, are you of God or are you ranged among his enemies. . . ?

*[*JEROBOAM's *face fades away and the light also dims on him as another voice—* CHUME's*—is heard long before he is seen.* CHUME *enters from left, downstage, agitated, and talking to himself.]*

CHUME . . . . What for . . . why, why, why, why 'e do am? For two years 'e no let me beat that woman. Why? No because God no like am. That one no fool me any more. 'E no be man of God. 'E say 'in sleep for beach whether 'e rain or cold but that one too na big lie. The man get house and 'e sleep there every night. But 'in get peace for 'in house, why 'en no let me get peace for mine? Wetin I do for am? Anyway, how they come meet? Where? When? What time 'e know say na my wife? Why 'e dey protect am from me? Perhaps na my woman dey give am chop[15] and in return he promise to see say 'in husband no beat am. A-a-a-ah, give am clothes, give am food and all comforts and necessities, and for exchange, 'in go see that 'in husband no beat am . . . Mmmmmm.

*[He shakes his head.]*

No, is not possible. I no believe that. If na so, how they come quarrel then. Why she go sit for front of 'in house demand all 'in money. I no beat am yet . . .

*[He stops suddenly. His eyes slowly distend.]*

Almighty! Chume, fool! O God, my life done spoil. My life done spoil finish. O God a no' get eyes for my head. Na lie. Na big lie. Na pretence 'e de pretend that wicked woman! She no' go collect nutin! She no' mean to sleep for outside house. The Prophet na 'in lover. As soon as 'e dark, she go in go meet 'in man. O God, wetin a do for you wey you go spoil my life so? Wetin make you vex for me so? I offend you? Chume, foolish man, your life done spoil. Your life done spoil. Yeah, ye . . . ah ah, ye-e-ah, they done ruin Chume for life . . . ye-e-ah, ye-e-ah, . . .

*[He goes off, his cries dying offstage.*
*Light up slowly on* JERO. *The* MEMBER *is seen kneeling now at* BROTHER JERO'S *feet, hands clasped, and shut eyes raised to heaven. . . .]*

JERO *[his voice gaining volume].* Protect him therefore. Protect him when he must lead this country as his great ancestors have done. He comes from the great warriors of the land. In his innocence he was not aware of this heritage. But you know everything and you plan it all. There is no end, no beginning. . . .

*[CHUME rushes in, brandishing a cutlass.]*

---

15. Bargains.

CHUME. Adulterer! Woman-thief! Na today a go finish you!

*[JERO looks round.]*

JERO. God save us! *[Flees.]*

MEMBER *[unaware of what is happening].* Amen.

*[CHUME follows out JERO, murder-bent.]*

MEMBER. Amen. Amen. *[Opens his eyes.]* Thank you, Proph . . .

*[He looks right, left, back, front, but he finds the PROPHET has really disappeared.]*

> Prophet! Prophet! *[Turns sharply and rapidly in every direction, shouting.]* Prophet, where are you? Where have you gone? Prophet! Don't leave me, Prophet, don't leave me!

*[He looks up slowly, with awe.]*

> Vanished. Transported. Utterly transmuted. I knew it. I knew I stood in the presence of God. . . .

*[He bows his head, standing. JEROBOAM enters quite collected, and points to the convert.]*

JEROBOAM. You heard him. With your own ears you heard him. By tomorrow, the whole town will have heard about the miraculous disappearance of Brother Jeroboam. Testified to and witnessed by no less a person than one of the elected Rulers of the country. . . .

MEMBER *[goes to sit on the mound].* I must await his return. If I show faith, he will show himself again to me. . . . *[Leaps up as he is about to sit.]* This is holy ground. *[Takes off his shoes and sits. Gets up again.]* I must hear further from him. Perhaps he has gone to learn more about this ministerial post. . . . *[Sits.]*

JEROBOAM. I have already sent for the police. It is a pity about Chume. But he has given me a fright, and no prophet likes to be frightened. With the influence of that nincompoop I should succeed in getting him certified with ease. A year in the lunatic asylum would do him good anyway.

*[The MEMBER is already nodding.]*

> Good . . . He is falling asleep. When I appear again to him he'll think I have just fallen from the sky. Then I'll tell him that Satan just sent one of his emissaries into the world under the name of Chume,

and that he had better put him in a strait-jacket at once . . . And so the day is saved. The police will call on me here as soon as they catch Chume. And it looks as if it is not quite time for the fulfilment of that spiteful man's prophecy.

*[He picks up a pebble and throws it at the* MEMBER *. At the same time a ring of red on some equally startling colour plays on his head, forming a sort of halo. The* MEMBER *wakes with a start, stares open-mouthed, and falls flat on his face, whispering in rapt awe—]*

"Master!"

BLACKOUT

## ■ José Luandino Vieira (1935– ) *Portugal/Angola* (poem)

TRANSLATED BY MICHAEL WOLFERS

Born in 1935 in Portugal, Vieira moved as a child to Luanda, Angola. A white Angolan citizen, he worked for his country's independence as did white writers Alan Paton, Nadine Gordimer, and Breiten Breitenbach in South Africa, who worked for the end of apartheid and for majority rule. Vieira was a member of the Popular Movement for the Liberation of Angola (MPLA) and was arrested in 1961. He was sentenced to fourteen years in prison, which he spent in Luanda and in the Cape Verde Islands; after 1972, he lived under restricted residence but could work for a publisher. In 1974, he returned, free, to Angola, became a television director, and continued his work in revolutionary politics. In Portugal, Brazil, and Angola, he has been well known as a novelist and short story writer. He is also one of Africa's most interesting poets.

**FURTHER READING:** Vieira, José Luandino. *The Real Life of Domingos Xavier,* 1971; *The Loves of Joao Vencio,* 1991.

## *Song for Luanda*

The question in the air
on the shore
on the tongue of everyone
          —Luanda, where are you?
Silence in the streets
Silence on the tongues
Silence in the eyes

5

—Hey
sister Rose the fishwife
can you tell?                                          10

—Brother
I can't tell
have to sell
rush around the city
if you want to eat!                                    15

"Lu-u-nch, choose your lu-u-u-nch
sprats or mackerel
fine fish, fine fi-i-i-sh"
—You then
Mary, market mammy                                     20
selling wild orange
breasts of wild orange
shouting
bouncing
your feet skipping                                     25
on rust red roads
all day long?
"Wild orange fine wild orange
sweeter than sweet"

—Brother                                               30
I can't tell you
time is running short
if I want to make a sale!

Half-caste Zefa
body up for sale                                       35
rouge on her lips
earrings of brass
and that brass's smile
offering her body
—built like a house!                                   40
Her body's up for sale
it's been around
by night and day.
          —Luanda, where are you?

                                                       45
Half-caste Zefa
built like a house
earrings of brass
she's good for a lay
with someone who'll pay
—a girl's gotter eat!                                  50

—Newspaper fellow
Luanda, where are you?
The ancient houses
the rust-red clay
even our ballads                                                5
bulldozed away?

Nippers in the streets
children's forfeits
"now you're caught"
tricks and treats                                               60
swallowed by asphalt?

—All the sisters
fishwife Rose
market mammy Mary
not forgetting you                                              6
half-caste Zefa
and your earrings of brass
          —Luanda, where are you?

With a smile
punnets on the ground                                           70
fruit and fish
sweet wild orange
hope-filled eyes
sure touch of hands
sister Rose the fishwife                                        75
market mammy Mary
Zefa the half-caste
—whether your clothes be shoddy
or gaudy
or bawdy                                                        80
they give away your heart:
—Luanda, you are here!

## ■ Bessie Head (1937–1986) *South Africa/Botswana (stories)*

Born in a Pietermritzburg (South Africa) mental institution to a white mother and a black father, Bessie Head lived with black foster parents until the age of thirteen. Although her birth mother had been committed to the institution for her interracial affair, she was able to provide for Head's education. Head attended a mission school until she was eighteen where she trained to become a teacher. Upon graduation, she taught for four years and then went to work as a journalist for the magazine *Drum*. Wanting to end an unhappy marriage and knowing that apartheid would soon be institutionalized, she left the newly independent Republic of South Africa for Botswana in 1964.

When she left South Africa, she was given a canceled exit visa, depriving her of citizenship and making her a refugee. Unlike most exiles who fled to the United States or Western Europe, Head stayed in Botswana. Fifteen years later, her limbo status ended when she was granted Botswana citizenship and made Serowe her home. During this precarious time, Head wrote many novels and short stories that dealt with exile, confronted black on black racism, and examined Africa's past without sentimentality. Eventually, she attempted to alter her focus from the struggle of the individual to the larger movement of society to maintain and define a cultural and historical heritage. Nevertheless, the individual figures who populate her stories stand out for their often heroic fortitude or their simple humanity.

Bessie Head died of hepatitis in 1986, leaving behind a collection of writings rich in geographical descriptions and characters like Keaja and Tselane in "The Lovers," who are not hesitant to protest their role in society in order to ameliorate their position.

FURTHER READING: Head, Bessie. *When Rain Clouds Gather*, 1968; *Maru*, 1971; *A Question of Power*, 1973; *The Collector of Treasures, and Other Botswana Tales*, 1977; *A Bewitched Crossroad: An African Saga*, 1984; *Tales of Tenderness and Power*, 1989.

## Looking for a Rain God

It is lonely at the lands where the people go to plow. These lands are vast clearings in the bush, and the wild bush is lonely too. Nearly all the lands are within walking distance from the village. In some parts of the bush where the underground water is very near the surface, people made little rest camps for themselves and dug shallow wells to quench their thirst while on their journey to their own lands. They experienced all kinds of things once they left the village. They could rest at shady watering places full of lush, tangled trees with delicate pale-gold and purple wildflowers springing up between soft green moss and the children could hunt around for wild figs and any berries that might be in season. But from 1958, a seven-year drought fell upon the land and even the watering places began to look as dismal as the dry open thornbush country; the leaves of the trees curled up and withered; the moss became dry and hard and, under the shade of the tangled trees, the ground turned a powdery black and white, because there was no rain. People said rather humorously that if you tried to catch the rain in a cup it would only fill a teaspoon. Toward the beginning of the seventh year of drought, the summer had become an anguish to live through. The air was so dry and moisture-free that it burned the skin. No one knew what to do to escape the heat and tragedy was in the air. At the beginning of that summer, a number of men just went out of their homes and hung themselves to death from trees. The majority of the people had lived off crops, but for two years past they had all returned from the lands with only their rolled-up skin blankets and cooking utensils. Only the charlatans, incanters, and witch doctors made a pile of money during this time because people were always turning to them in desperation for little talismans and herbs to rub on the plow for the crops to grow and the rain to fall.

The rains were late that year. They came in early November, with a promise of good rain. It wasn't the full, steady downpour of the years of good rain, but thin, scanty, misty rain. It softened the earth and a rich growth of green things sprang up everywhere for the animals to eat. People were called to the village *kgotla* to hear the proclamation of the beginning of the plowing season; they stirred themselves and whole families began to move off to the lands to plow.

The family of the old man, Mokgobja, were among those who left early for the lands. They had a donkey cart and piled everything onto it, Mokgobja—who was over seventy years old; two little girls, Neo and Boseyong; their mother Tiro and an unmarried sister, Nesta; and the father and supporter of the family, Ramadi, who drove the donkey cart. In the rush of the first hope of rain, the man, Ramadi, and the two women, cleared the land of thornbush and then hedged their vast plowing area with this same thornbush to protect the future crop from the goats they had brought along for milk. They cleared out and deepened the old well with its pool of muddy water and still in this light, misty rain, Ramadi inspanned two oxen and turned the earth over with a hand plow.

The land was ready and plowed, waiting for the crops. At night, the earth was alive with insects singing and rustling about in search of food. But suddenly, by mid-November, the rain fled away; the rainclouds fled away and left the sky bare. The sun danced dizzily in the sky, with a strange cruelty. Each day the land was covered in a haze of mist as the sun sucked up the last drop of moisture out of the earth. The family sat down in despair, waiting and waiting. Their hopes had run so high; the goats had started producing milk, which they had eagerly poured on their porridge; now they ate plain porridge with no milk. It was impossible to plant the corn, maize, pumpkin and water-melon seeds in the dry earth. They sat the whole day in the shadow of the huts and even stopped thinking, for the rain had fled away. Only the children, Neo and Boseyong, were quite happy in their little-girl world. They carried on with their game of making house like their mother and chattered to each other in light, soft tones. They made children from sticks around which they tied rags, and scolded them severely in an exact imitation of their own mother. Their voices could be heard scolding the day long: "You stupid thing, when I send you to draw water, why do you spill half of it out of the bucket!" "You stupid thing! Can't you mind the porridge pot without letting the porridge burn!" And then they would beat the ragdolls on their bottoms with severe expressions.

The adults paid no attention to this; they did not even hear the funny chatter; they sat waiting for rain; their nerves were stretched to breaking point willing the rain to fall out of the sky. Nothing was important, beyond that. All their animals had been sold during the bad years to purchase food, and of all their herd only two goats were left. It was the women of the family who finally broke down under the strain of waiting for rain. It was really the two women who caused the death of the little girls. Each night they started a weird, high-pitched wailing that began on a low, mournful note and whipped up to a frenzy. Then they would stamp their feet and shout as though they had lost their heads. The men sat quiet and self-controlled; it was important for men to maintain their self-control at all times but their nerve was breaking too. They knew the women were haunted by the starvation of the coming year.

Finally, an ancient memory stirred in the old man, Mokgobja. When he was very young and the customs of the ancestors still ruled the land, he had been witness to a rainmaking ceremony. And he came alive a little, struggling to recall the details which had been buried by years and years of prayer in a Christian church. As soon as the mists cleared a little, he began consulting in whispers with his youngest son, Ramadi. There was, he said, a certain rain god who accepted only the sacrifice of the bodies of children. Then the rain would fall; then the crops would grow, he said. He explained the ritual and as he talked, his memory became a conviction and he began to talk with unshakable authority. Ramadi's nerves were smashed by the nightly wailing of the women and soon the two men began whispering with the two women. The children continued their game: "You stupid thing! How could you have lost the money on the way to the shop! You must have been playing again!"

After it was all over and the bodies of the two little girls had been spread across the land, the rain did not fall. Instead, there was a deathly silence at night and the devouring heat of the sun by day. A terror, extreme and deep, overwhelmed the whole family. They packed, rolling up their skin blankets and pots, and fled back to the village.

People in the village soon noted the absence of the two little girls. They had died at the lands and were buried there, the family said. But people noted their ashen, terror-stricken faces and a murmur arose. What had killed the children, they wanted to know? And the family replied that they had just died. And people said amongst themselves that it was strange that the two deaths had occurred at the same time. And there was a feeling of great unease at the unnatural looks of the family. Soon the police came around. The family told them the same story of death and burial at the lands. They did not know what the children had died of. So the police asked to see the graves. At this, the mother of the children broke down and told everything.

Throughout that terrible summer the story of the children hung like a dark cloud of sorrow over the village, and the sorrow was not assuaged when the old man and Ramadi were sentenced to death for ritual murder.

All they had on the statute books was that ritual murder was against the law and must be stamped out with the death penalty. The subtle story of strain and starvation and breakdown was inadmissible evidence at court; but all the people who lived off crops knew in their hearts that only a hair's breadth had saved them from sharing a fate similar to that of the Mokgobja family. They could have killed something to make the rain fall.

## The Lovers

The love affair began in the summer. The love affair began in those dim dark days when young men and women did not have love affairs. It was one of those summers when it rained in torrents. Almost every afternoon towards sunset the low-hanging, rain-filled clouds would sweep across the sky in packed masses and suddenly, with barely a warning, the rain would pour down in blinding sheets.

The young women and little girls were still out in the forest gathering wood that afternoon when the first warning signs of rain appeared in the sky. They hastily gathered up their bundles of wood and began running home to escape the approaching storm. Suddenly, one of the young women halted painfully. In her haste she had trodden on a large thorn.

"Hurry on home, Monosi!" she cried to a little girl panting behind her. "I have to get this thorn out of my foot. If the rain catches me I shall find some shelter and come home once it is over."

Without a backward glance the little girl sped on after the hard-running group of wood gatherers. The young woman was quite alone with the approaching storm. The thorn proved difficult to extract. It had broken off and embedded itself deeply in her heel. A few drops of rain beat down on her back. The sky darkened.

Anxiously she looked around for the nearest shelter and saw a cavern in some rocks at the base of a hill nearby. She picked up her bundle of wood and limped hastily towards it, with the drops of rain pounding down faster and faster. She had barely entered the cavern when the torrent unleashed itself in a violent downpour. Her immediate concern was to seek its sanctuary but a moment later her heart lurched in fear as she realized that she was not alone. The warmth of another human filled the interior. She swung around swiftly and found herself almost face to face with a young man.

"We can shelter here together from the storm" he said with a quiet authority.

His face was as kind and protective as his words. Reassured, the young woman set down her bundle of sticks in the roomy interior of the cavern and together they seated themselves near its entrance. The roar of the rain was deafening so that even the thunder and lightning was muffled by its intensity. With quiet, harmonious movements the young man undid a leather pouch tied at his waist. He spent all his time cattle-herding and to while away the long hours he busied himself with all kinds of leather work, assembling skins into all kinds of clothes and blankets. He had a large number of sharpened implements in his pouch. He indicated to the young woman that he wished to extract the thorn. She extended her foot towards him and for some time he busied himself with this task, gently whittling away the skin around the thorn until he had exposed it sufficiently enough to extract it.

The young woman looked at his face with interest and marvelled at the ease and comfort she felt in his presence. In their world men and women lived strictly apart, especially the young and unmarried. This sense of apartness and separateness continued even throughout married life and marriage itself seemed to have no significance beyond a union for the production of children. This wide gap between the sexes created embarrassment on the level of personal contact; the young men often slid their eyes away uneasily or giggled at the sight of a woman. The young man did none of this. He had stared her directly in the eyes; all his movements were natural and unaffected. He was also very pleasing to look at. She thanked him with a smile once he had extracted the thorn and folded her extended foot beneath her. The violence of the storm abated a little but the heavily-laden sky continued to pour forth a steady downpour.

She had seen the young man around the village; she could vaguely place his family connections.

"Aren't you the son of Rra-Keaja?" she asked. She had a light chatty voice with an undertone of laughter in it, very expressive of her personality. She liked above all to be happy.

"I am the very Keaja he is named after," the young man replied with a smile. "I am the first-born in the family."

"I am the first born in the family, too," she said. "I am Tselane, the daughter of Mma-Tselane."

His family ramifications were more complicated than hers. His father had three wives. All the first born of the first, second and third house were boys. The children totalled eight in number, three boys and five girls, he explained. It was only when the conversation moved into deep water that Tselane realized that a whole area of the young man's speech had eluded her. He was the extreme opposite of her light chatty tone. He talked from deep rhythms within himself as though he had specifically invented language for his own use. He had an immense range of expression and feeling at his command; now his eyes lit up with humour, then they were absolutely serious and in earnest. He swayed almost imperceptibly as he talked. He talked like no one she had ever heard talking before, yet all his utterances were direct, simple and forthright. She bent forward and listened more attentively to his peculiar manner of speech.

"I don't like my mother," he said, shocking her. "I am her only son simply because my father stopped cohabiting with her after I was born. My father and I are alike. We don't like to be controlled by anyone and she made his life a misery when they were newly married. It was as if she had been born with a worm eating at her heart because she is satisfied with nothing. The only way my father could control the situation was to ignore her completely . . ."

He remained silent a while, concentrating on his own thoughts. "I don't think I approve of all the arranged marriages we have here," he said finally. "My father would never have married her had he had his own choice. He was merely presented with her one day by his family and told that they were to be married and there was nothing he could do about it."

He kept silent about the torture he endured from his mother. She hated him deeply and bitterly. She had hurled stones at him and scratched him on the arms and legs in her wild frustration. Like his father he eluded her. He rarely spent time at home but kept the cattle-post as his permanent residence. When he approached home it was always with some gift of clothes or blankets. On that particular day he had an enormous gourd filled with milk.

The young woman, Tselane, floundered out of her depth in the face of such stark revelations. They lived the strictest of traditional ways of life; all children were under the control of their parents until they married, therefore it was taboo to discuss their elders. In her impulsive chatty way and partly out of embarrassment, it had been on the tip of her tongue to say that she liked her mother, that her mother was very kind-hearted. But there was a disturbing undertone in her household too. Her mother and father—and she was sure of it due to her detailed knowledge of her mother's way of life—had not cohabited for years either. A few years ago her father had taken another wife. She was her mother's only child. Oh, the surface of their household was polite and harmonious but her father was rarely at home. He was always irritable and morose when he was home.

"I am sorry about all the trouble in your home," she said at last, in a softer, more thoughtful tone. She was shaken at having been abruptly jolted into completely new ways of thought.

The young man smiled and then quite deliberately turned and stared at her. She stared back at him with friendly interest. She did not mind his close scrutiny of her person; he was easy to associate with, comfortable, truthful and open in his every gesture.

"Do you approve of arranged marriages?" he asked, still smiling.

"I have not thought of anything," she replied truthfully.

The dark was approaching rapidly. The rain had trickled down to a fine drizzle. Tselane stood up and picked up her bundle of wood. The young man picked up his gourd of milk. They were barely visible as they walked home together in the dark. Tselane's home was not too far from the hill. She lived on the extreme western side of the village, he on the extreme eastern side.

A bright fire burned in the hut they used as a cooking place on rainy days. Tselane's mother was sitting bent forward on her low stool, listening attentively to a visitor's tale. It was always like this—her mother was permanently surrounded by women who confided in her. The whole story of life unfolded daily around her stool: the ailments of children, women who had just had miscarriages, women undergoing treatment for barren wombs—the story was endless. It was the great pleasure of Tselane to seat herself quietly behind her mother's stool and listen with fascinated ears to this endless tale of woe. Her mother's visitor that evening was on the tail-end of a description of one of her children's ailments; chronic epilepsy, which seemed beyond cure. The child seemed in her death throes and the mother was just at the point of demonstrating the violent seizures when Tselane entered. Tselane quietly set her bundle of wood down in a corner and the conversation continued uninterrupted. She took her favoured place behind her mother's stool. Her father's second wife, Mma-Monosi, was seated on the opposite side of the fire, her face composed and serious. Her child, the little girl, Monosi, fed and attended to, lay fast asleep on a sleeping mat in one corner of the hut.

Tselane loved the two women of the household equally. They were both powerful independent women but with sharply differing personalities. Mma-Tselane was a queen who vaguely surveyed the kingdom she ruled with an abstracted, absent-minded air. Over the years of her married life she had built up a way of life for herself that filled her with content. She was reputed to be very delicate in health as after the birth of Tselane she had suffered a number of miscarriages and seemed incapable of bearing any more children. Her delicate health was a source of extreme irritation to her husband and at some stage he had abandoned her completely and taken Mma-Monosi as his second wife, intending to perpetuate his line and name through her healthy body. The arrangement suited Mma-Tselane. She was big-hearted and broadminded and yet, conversely, she prided herself in being the meticulous upholder of all the traditions the community adhered to. Once Mma-Monosi became a part of the household, Mma-Tselane did no work but entertained and paid calls the day long. Mma-Monosi ran the entire household.

The two women complemented each other, for, if Mma-Tselane was a queen, then Mma-Monosi was a humble worker. On the surface, Mma-Monosi appeared as sane and balanced as Mma-Tselane, but there was another side of her personality that was very precariously balanced. Mma-Monosi took her trembling way through life. If all was stable and peaceful, then Mma-Monosi was stable and peaceful. If there was any disruption or disorder, Mma-Monosi's precarious inner balance registered every wave and upheaval. She hungered for approval of her every action and could be upset for days if criticized or reprimanded.

So, between them, the two women achieved a very harmonious household. Both were entirely absorbed in their full busy daily round; both were unconcerned that they received scant attention from the man of the household for Rra-Tselane was entirely concerned with his own affairs. He was a prominent member of the chief's court and he divided his time between the chief's court and his cattle-post. He was rich in cattle and his herds were taken care of by servants. He was away at his cattle-post at that time.

It was with Mma-Monosi that the young girl, Tselane, enjoyed a free and happy relationship. They treated each other as equals, they both enjoyed hard work and whenever they were alone together, they laughed and joked all the time. Her own mother regarded Tselane as an object to whom she lowered her voice and issued commands between clenched teeth. Very soon Mma-Tselane stirred in her chair and said in that lowered voice: "Tselane, fetch me my bag of herbs."

Tselane obediently stood up and hurried to her mother's living-quarters for the bag of herbs. Then another interval followed during which her mother and the visitor discussed the medicinal properties of the herbs. Then Mma-Monosi served the evening meal. Then the visitor departed with assurances that Mma-Tselane would call on her the following day. Then they sat for a while in companionable silence. At one stage, seeing that the fire was burning low, Mma-Tselane arose and selected a few pieces of wood from Tselane's bundle to stoke up the fire.

"Er, Tselane," she said. "Your wood is quite dry. Did you shelter from the storm?"

"There is a cave in the hill not far from here, mother," Tselane replied. "And I sheltered there." She did not think it wise to add that she had shared the shelter with a young man; a lot of awkward questions of the wrong kind might have followed.

The mother cast her eyes vaguely over her daughter as if to say all was in order in her world; she always established simple facts about any matter and turned peacefully to the next task at hand. She suddenly decided that she was tired and would retire. Tselane and Mma-Monosi were left alone seated near the fire. Tselane was still elated by her encounter with the young man; so many pleasant thoughts were flying through her head.

"I want to ask you some questions, Mma-Monosi," she said eagerly.

"What is it you want to say, my child?" Mma-Monosi said, stirring out of a reverie.

"Do you approve of arranged marriages, Mma-Monosi?" she asked earnestly.

Mma-Monosi drew in her breath between her teeth with a sharp, hissing sound, then she lowered her voice in horror and said: "Tselane, you know quite well that I am your friend but if anyone else heard you talking like that you would be in trouble! Such things are never discussed here! What put that idea into your head because it is totally unknown to me?"

"But you question life when you begin to grow up," Tselane said defensively.

"That is what you never, never do," Mma-Monosi said severely. "If you question life you will upset it. Life is always in order." She looked thoroughly startled and agitated. "I know of something terrible that once happened to someone who questioned life," she added grimly.

"Who was it? What terrible thing happened?" Tselane asked, in her turn agitated.

"I can't tell you," Mma-Monosi said firmly. "It is too terrible to mention."

Tselane subsided into silence with a speculative look in her eye. She understood Mma-Monosi well. She couldn't keep a secret. She could always be tempted into telling a secret, if not today then on some other day. She decided to find out the terrible story.

When Keaja arrived home his family was eating the evening meal. He first approached the women's quarters and offered them the gourd of milk.

"The cows are calving heavily," he explained. "There is a lot of milk and I can bring some home every day."

He was greeted joyously by the second and third wife of his father who anxiously inquired after their sons who lived with him at the cattle-post.

"They are quite well," he said politely. "I settled them and the cattle before I left. I shall return again in the early morning because I am worried about the young calves."

He avoided his mother's baleful stare and tight, deprived mouth. She never had anything to say to him, although, on his approach to the women's quarters, he had heard her voice, shrill and harsh, dominating the conversation. His meal was handed to him and he retreated to his father's quarters. He ate alone and apart from the women. A bright fire burned in his father's living quarters.

"Hello, Father-Of-Me," his father greeted him, making affectionate play on the name Keaja. Keaja meant: I am eating now because I have a son to take care of me.

His father doted on him. In his eyes there was no greater son than Keaja. After an exchange of greetings his father asked: "And what is your news?"

He gave his father the same information about the cows calving heavily and the rich supply of milk; that his other two sons were quite well. They ate for a while in companionable silence. His mother's voice rose shrill and penetrating in the silent night. Quite unexpectedly his father looked up with a twinkle in his eye and said: "Those extra calves will stand us in good stead, Father-Of-Me. I have just started negotiations about your marriage."

A spasm of chill, cold fear almost constricted Keaja's heart. "Who am I to marry, father?" he asked, alarmed.

"I cannot mention the family name just yet," his father replied carefully, not sensing his son's alarm. "The negotiations are still at a very delicate stage."

"Have you committed yourself in this matter, father?" he asked, a sharp angry note in his voice.

"Oh, yes," his father replied. "I have given my honour in this matter. It is just that these things take a long time to arrange as there are many courtesies to be observed."

"How long?" the son asked.

"About six new moons may have to pass," his father replied. "It may even be longer than that. I cannot say at this stage."

"I could choose a wife for myself," the son said with deadly quietude. "I could choose my own wife and then inform you of my choice."

His father stared at him in surprise.

"You cannot be different from everyone else," he said. "I must be a parent with a weakness that you can talk to me so."

His father knew that he indulged his son, that they had free and easy exchanges beyond what was socially permissible; even that brief exchange was more than most parents allowed their children. They arranged all details of their children's future and on the fatal day merely informed them that they were to be married to so-and-so. There was no point in saying: "I might not be able to live with so-and-so. She might be unsuited to me," so that when Keaja lapsed into silence, his father merely smiled indulgently and engaged him in small talk.

Keaja was certainly of a marriageable age. The previous year he had gone through his initiation ceremony. Apart from other trials endured during the ceremony, detailed instruction had been given to the young men of his age group about sexual relations between men and women. They were hardly private and personal but affected by a large number of social regulations and taboos. If he broke the taboos at a personal and private level, death, sickness and great misfortune would fall upon his family. If he broke the taboos at a social level, death and disaster would fall upon the community. There were many periods in a man's life when abstinence from sexual relations was required; often this abstinence had to be practised communally, as in the period preceding the harvest of crops and only broken on the day of the harvest thanksgiving ceremony.

These regulations and taboos applied to men and women alike but the initiation ceremony for women, which Tselane had also experienced the previous year, was much more complex in their instruction. A delicate balance had to be preserved between a woman's reproductive cycle and the safety of the community; at almost every stage in her life a woman was a potential source of danger to the community. All women were given careful instruction in precautions to be observed during times of menstruation, childbirth and accidental miscarriages. Failure to observe the taboos could bring harm to animal life, crops and the community.

It could be seen then that the community held no place for people wildly carried away by their passions, that there was a logic and order in the carefully arranged sterile emotional and physical relationships between men and women. There was no one to challenge the established order of things; if people felt any personal unhappiness it was smothered and subdued and so life for the community proceeded from day to day in peace and harmony.

As all lovers do, they began a personal and emotional dialogue that excluded all life around them. Perhaps its pattern and direction was the same for all lovers, painful and maddening by turns in its initial insecurity. Who looked for who? They could not say, except that the far-western unpolluted end of the river where women drew water and the forests where they gathered firewood became Keaja's favoured hunting grounds. Their work periods coincided at that time. The corn had just been sowed and the women were idling in the village until the heavy soaking rains raised the weeds in their fields, then their next busy period would follow when they hoed out the weeds between their corn.

Keaja returned every day to the village with gourds of milk for his family and it did not take Tselane long to note that he delayed and lingered in her work areas until he had caught some glimpse of her. She was always in a crowd of gaily chattering young women. The memory of their first encounter had been so fresh and stimulating, so full of unexpected surprises in dialogue that she longed to approach him. One afternoon, while out wood gathering with her companions, she noticed him among the distant bushes and contrived to remove herself from her companions. As she walked towards him, he quite directly approached her and took hold of her hand. She made no effort to pull her hand free. It rested in his as though it belonged there. They walked on some distance, then he paused, and turning to face her told her all he had on his mind in his direct, simple way. This time he did not smile at all.

"My father will arrange a marriage for me after about six new moons have passed," he said. "I do not want that, I want a wife of my own choosing but all the things I want can only cause trouble."

She looked away into the distance, not immediately knowing what she ought to say. Her own parents had given her no clue of their plans for her future; indeed she had not had cause to think about it but she did not like most of the young men of the village. They had a hang-dog air as though the society and its oppressive ways had broken their will. She liked everything about Keaja and she felt safe with him as on that stormy afternoon in the cavern when he had said: "We can shelter here together from the storm . . ."

"My own thoughts are not complicated," he went on, still holding on to her hand. "I thought I would find out how you felt about this matter. I thought I would like to choose you as my wife. If you do not want to choose me in turn, I shall not pursue my own wants any longer. I might even marry the wife my father chooses for me."

She turned around and faced him and spoke with a clarity of thought that startled her.

"I am afraid of nothing," she said. "Not even trouble or death but I need some time to find out what I am thinking."

Of his own accord, he let go of her hand and so they parted and went their separate ways. From that point onwards right until the following day, she lived in a state of high elation. Her thought processes were not all coherent; indeed she had not a thought in her head. Then the illogic of love took over. Just as she was about to pick up the pitcher in the late afternoon, she suddenly felt desperately ill, so ill that she was almost brought to the point of death. She experienced a paralysing lameness in her arms and legs. The weight of the pitcher with which she was to draw water was too heavy for her to endure.

She appealed to Mma-Monosi.

"I feel faint and ill today," she said. "I cannot draw water."

Mma-Monosi was only too happy to take over her chores but at the same time consulted anxiously with her mother about this sudden illness. Mma-Tselane, after some deliberation, decided that it was the illness young girls get in the limbs when they are growing too rapidly. She spent a happy three days doctoring her daughter with warm herb drinks, for Mma-Tselane liked nothing better than to concentrate on illness. Still, the physical turmoil the young girl felt continued unabated; at night she trembled violently from head to toe. It was so shocking and new that for two days she succumbed completely to the blow. It wasn't any coherent thought processes that made her struggle desperately to her feet on the third day but a need to quieten the anguish. She convinced her mother and Mma-Monosi that she felt well enough to perform her wood gathering chores. Towards the afternoon she hurried to the forest area, carefully avoiding her gathering companions.

She was relieved, on meeting Keaja, to see that his face bore the same anguished look that she felt. He spoke first.

"I felt so ill and disturbed," he said. "I could do nothing but wait for your appearance."

They sat down on the ground together. She was so exhausted by her two-day struggle that for a moment she leaned forward and rested her head on his knees. Her thought processes seemed to awaken once more because she smiled peacefully and said: "I want to think."

Eventually, she raised herself and looked at the young man with shining eyes.

"I felt so ill," she said. "My mother kept on giving me herb drinks. She said it was normal to feel faint and dizzy when one is growing. I know now what made me feel so ill. I was fighting my training. My training has told me that people are not important in themselves but you so suddenly became important to me, as a person. I did not know how to tell my mother all this. I did not know how to tell her anything yet she was kind and took care of me. Eventually I thought I would lose my mind so I came here to find you . . ."

It was as if, from that moment onwards, they quietly and of their own willing, married each other. They began to plan together how they should meet and when they should meet. The young man was full of forethought and planning. He knew that, in the terms of his own society, he was starting a terrible mess, but then his society only calculated along the lines of human helplessness in the face of overwhelming odds. It did not calculate for human inventiveness and initiative. He only needed the young girl's pledge and from then onwards he took the initiative in all things. He was to startle and please her from that very day with his forethought. It was as if he knew that she would come at some time, that they would linger in joy with their love-making, so that when Tselane eventually expressed agitation at the lateness of the hour, he, with a superior smile, indicated a large bundle of wood nearby that he had collected for her to take home.

A peaceful interlude followed and the community innocently lived out its day-by-day life, unaware of the disruption and upheaval that would soon fall upon it. The women were soon out in the fields, hoeing weeds and tending their crops, Tselane among them, working side by side with Mma-Monosi, as she had always done. There was not even a ripple of the secret life she now lived; if anything, she worked harder and with greater contentment. She laughed and joked as usual with Mma-Monosi but sound instinct made her keep her private affair to herself.

When the corn was already high in the fields and about to ripen, Tselane realized that she was expecting a child. A matter that had been secret could be a secret no longer. When she confided this news to Keaja, he quite happily accepted it as a part of all the plans he had made, for as he said to her at that time: "I am not planning for death when we are so happy. I want it that we should live."

He had only one part of all his planning secure, a safe escape route outside the village and on to a new and unknown life they would make for themselves. They had made themselves outcasts from the acceptable order of village life and he presented her with two alternatives from which she could choose. The one alternative was simpler for them. They could leave the village at any moment and without informing anyone of their intentions. The world was very wide for a man. He had travelled great distances, both alone and in the company of other men, while on his hunting and herding duties. The area was safe for travel for some distance. He had sat around firesides and heard stories about wars and fugitives and other hospitable tribes who lived distances away and whose customs differed from theirs. Keaja had not been idle all this while. He had prepared all they would need for their journey and hidden their provisions in a secret place.

The alternative was more difficult for the lovers. They could inform their parents of their love and ask that they be married. He was not sure of the outcome but it was to invite death or worse. It might still lead to the escape route out of the village as he was not planning for death.

So after some thought Tselane decided to tell her parents because as she pointed out the first plan would be too heartbreaking for their parents. They therefore decided on that very day to inform their parents of their love and name the date on which they wished to marry.

It was nearing dusk when Tselane arrived home with her bundle of wood. Her mother and Mma-Monosi were seated out in the courtyard, engaged in some quiet conversation of their own. Tselane set down her bundle, approached the two women and knelt down quietly by her mother's side. Her mother turned towards her, expecting some request or message from a friend. There was no other way except for Tselane to convey her own message in the most direct way possible.

"Mother," she said. "I am expecting a child by the son of Rra-Keaja. We wish to be married by the next moon. We love each other . . . ."

For a moment her mother frowned as though her child's words did not make sense. Mma-Monosi's body shuddered several times as though she were cold but she maintained a deathly silence. Eventually Tselane's mother lowered her voice and said between clenched teeth: "You are to go to your hut and remain there. On no account are you to leave it without the supervision of Mma-Monosi."

For a time Mma-Tselane sat looking into the distance, a broken woman. Her social prestige, her kingdom, her self-esteem crumbled around her.

A short while later her husband entered the yard. He had spent an enjoyable day at the chief's court with other men. He now wished for his evening meal and retirement for the night. The last thing he wanted was conversation with women, so he looked up irritably as his wife appeared without his evening meal. She explained herself with as much dignity as she could muster. She was almost collapsing with shock. He listened in disbelief and gave a sharp exclamation of anger.

Just at this moment Keaja's father announced himself in the yard. "Rra-Tselane, I have just heard from my own son the offence he has committed against your house, but he desires nothing more than to marry your child. If this would remove some of the offence, then I am agreeable to it."

"Rra-Keaja," Tselane's father replied. "You know as well as I that this marriage isn't in the interests of your family or mine." He stood up and walked violently into the night.

Brokenly, Keaja's father also stood up and walked out of the yard.

It was her husband's words that shook Mma-Tselane out of her stupor of self-pity. She hurried to her living quarters for her skin shawl, whispered a few words to Mma-Monosi about her mission. Mma-Monosi too sped off into the night after Rra-Keaja. On catching up with him she whispered urgently: "Rra-Keaja! You may not know me. I approach you because we now share this trouble which has come upon us. This matter will never be secret. Tomorrow it will be a public affair. I therefore urge you to do as Mma-Tselane has done and make an appeal for your child at once. She has gone to the woman's compound of the chief's house as she has many friends there."

Her words lightened the old man's heavy heart. With a promise to send her his news, he turned and walked in the direction of the chief's yard.

Mma-Monosi sped back to her own yard.

"Tselane," she said, earnestly. "It is no light matter to break custom. You pay for it with your life. I should have told you the story that night we discussed custom. When I was a young girl we had a case such as this but not such a deep mess. The young man had taken a fancy to a girl and she to him. He therefore refused the girl his parents had chosen for him.

They could not break him and so they killed him. They killed even though he had not touched the girl. But there is one thing I want you to know. I am your friend and I will die for you. No one will injure you while I am alive."

Their easy, affectionate relationship returned to them. They talked for some time about the love affair, Mma-Monosi absorbing every word with delight. A while later Mma-Tselane re-entered the yard. She was still too angry to talk to her own child but she called Mma-Monosi to one side and informed her that she had won an assurance in high places that no harm would come to her child.

And so began a week of raging storms and wild irrational deliberations. It was a family affair. It was a public affair. As a public affair, it would bring ruin and disaster upon the community and public anger was high. Two parents showed themselves up in a bad light, the father of Tselane and the mother of Keaja. Rra-Tselane was adamant that the marriage would never take place. He preferred to sound death warnings all the time. The worm that had been eating at the heart of Keaja's mother all this while finally arose and devoured her heart. She too could be heard to sound death warnings. Then a curious and temporary solution was handed down from high places. It was said that if the lovers removed themselves from the community for a certain number of days, it would make allowance for public anger to die down. Then the marriage of the lovers would be considered.

So appalling was the drama to the community that on the day Keaja was released from his home and allowed to approach the home of Tselane, all the people withdrew to their own homes so as not to witness the fearful sight. Only Mma-Monosi, who had supervised the last details of the departure, stood openly watching the direction in which the young lovers left the village. She saw them begin to ascend the hill not far from the home of Tselane. As darkness was approaching, she turned and walked back to her yard. To Mma-Tselane, who lay in a state of nervous collapse in her hut, Mma-Monosi made her last, sane pronouncement on the whole affair.

"The young man is no fool," she said. "They have taken the direction of the hill. He knows that the hilltop is superior to any other. People are angry and someone might think of attacking them. An attacker will find it a difficult task as the young man will hurtle stones down on him before he ever gets near. Our child is quite safe with him."

Then the story took a horrible turn. Tension built up towards the day the lovers were supposed to return to community life. Days went by and they did not return. Eventually search parties were sent out to look for them but they had disappeared. Not even their footmarks were visible on the bare rock faces and tufts of grass on the hillside. At first the searchers returned and did not report having seen any abnormal phenomena, only a baffled surprise. Then Mma-Monosi's precarious imaginative balance tipped over into chaos. She was seen walking grief-stricken towards the hill. As she reached its base she stood still and the whole drama of the disappearance of the lovers was re-created before her eyes. She first heard loud groans of anguish that made her blood run cold. She saw that as soon as Tselane and Keaja set foot on the hill, the rocks parted and a gaping hole appeared. The lovers sank into its depths and the rocks closed over them. As she called, "Tselane! Keaja!" their spirits arose and floated soundlessly with unseeing eyes to the top of the hill.

Mma-Monosi returned to the village and told a solemn and convincing story of all the phenomena she had seen. People only had to be informed that such phenomena existed and they all began seeing them too. Then Mma-Tselane, maddened and distraught by the loss her daughter, slowly made her way to the hill. With sorrowful eyes she watched the drama re-create itself before her. She returned home and died. The hill from then onwards became an unpleasant embodiment of sinister forces which destroy life. It was no longer considered a safe dwelling place for the tribe. They packed up their belongings on the backs of their animals, destroyed the village and migrated to a safer area.

The deserted area remained unoccupied from then onwards until 1875 when people of the Bamalete tribe settled there. Although strangers to the area, they saw the same phenomena, they heard the load groans of anguish and saw the silent floating spirits of the lovers. The legend was kept alive from generation unto generation and so the hill stands until this day in the village of Otse in southern Botswana as an eternal legend of love. Letswe La Baratani, The Hill of the Lovers, it is called.

## ■ Ngugi wa Thiong'o (James Ngugi) (1938– ) *Kenya* (story)

Son of a Kenyan squatter farmer, James Ngugi was born in Limuru. He was one of some twenty-eight children in a polygamous household, fifth child from the third of his father's four wives. The family was impoverished. In his book *Homecoming* (1976), he writes, "Harvests were often poor. Sweetened tea with milk at any time of day was a luxury. We had one meal a day—late in the evening." His first schooling was in 1946 at a missionary primary school near his home; two years later, he was placed in a school run by tribal nationalists. An excellent student, he went to the prestigious Alliance colonial high school at Kikuyu. There Ngugi read widely in English literature. The Mau-Mau uprising from 1952–1956, with all its violence and bloodshed, profoundly affected the young student. One of his brothers participated in the rebellion for land and liberation. Ngugi went to Makerere University College in Uganda from 1959 to 1964, where he took his degree. After three years at the University of Leeds, during which time he worked furiously on his fiction, he returned to Africa to become a lecturer at University College in Nairobi. Thereafter, he was a lecturer at Northwestern University in Evanston, Illinois, from 1970 to 1971, and later a professor and chairman of the Literature Department at the University of Nairobi.

During his career as writer and professor, Ngugi was jailed from 1977 to 1978 at the Kamiti Maximum Security Prison near Nairobi specifically because of the production of a play in his native Kikuyu, but probably because of his passionate dissidence. His political ideas also caused him to be sent into exile. At the center of his life, however, the vehicle for personal and political ideas has primarily been his writings and publications. Working in the short story, fiction, prison diary, drama, and essay, Ngugi's primary strength has been the novel in which he remains perhaps the most significant figure in East Africa.

While still a student at Leeds, he completed and published *Weep Not, Child* (1964) with Heinemann in London, which gave him an early reputation. He achieved maturity in *A Grain of Wheat* (1967). His many essays, speeches, and reviews were gathered together in *Homecoming*, which not only includes essays on Chinua Achebe, Wole Soyinka, and other leading African writers, but on Caribbean authors; it also records his own experiences as a developing artist.

Ngugi deals with the problems that preoccupy most African writers: colonialism's residue, contemporary corruption, and family structures. He carries with him the markings of his own closeness to Christianity, Islam, and African religions and shows how they control the lives of his characters in the stories "The Wedding at the Cross" and "The Blackbird." While the spirit of Christian ethics haunts, at the same time it leads to refutation. Using elements of recurrent fantasy, he empathizes with the dignity of women from all classes who want to lead their own lives and men who are stalked by the actions of their fathers. Performing his magic through vivid writing and the persistence of important symbols such as the recurring blackbird in the story of the same name, Ngugi also ties a thread of didactic idealism into his extraordinary artistry.

**FURTHER READING:** Ngugi, wa Thiong'o. *Weep Not, Child,* 1967; *The River Between,* 1965; *A Grain of Wheat,* 1967; *Homecoming: Essays on African and Caribbean Literature, Culture and Politics,* 1972; *Secret Lives and Other Stories,* 1975; *Detained: A Writer's Prison Diary,* 1981; *Decolonizing the Mind: The Politics of Language in African Literature,* 1986.

## Minutes of Glory

Her name was Wanjiru. But she liked better her Christian one, Beatrice. It sounded more pure and more beautiful. Not that she was ugly; but she could not be called beautiful either. Her body, dark and full fleshed, had the form, yes, but it was as if it waited to be filled by the spirit. She worked in beer-halls where sons of women came to drown their inner lives in beer cans and froth. Nobody seemed to notice her. Except, perhaps, when a proprietor or an impatient customer called out her name, Beatrice; then other customers would raise their heads briefly, a few seconds, as if to behold the bearer of such a beautiful name, but not finding anybody there, they would resume their drinking, their ribald jokes, their laughter and play with the other serving girls. She was like a wounded bird in flight: a forced landing now and then but nevertheless wobbling from place to place so that she would variously be found in Alaska, Paradise, The Modern, Thome and other beer-halls all over Limuru. Sometimes it was because an irate proprietor found she was not attracting enough customers; he would sack her without notice and without a salary. She would wobble to the next bar. But sometimes she was simply tired of nesting in one place, a daily witness of familiar scenes; girls even more decidedly ugly than she were fought over by numerous claimants at closing hours. What do they have that I don't have? she would ask herself, depressed. She longed for a bar-kingdom where she would be at least one of the rulers, where petitioners would bring their gifts of beer, frustrated smiles and often curses that hid more lust and love than hate.

She left Limuru town proper and tried the mushrooming townlets around. She worked at Ngarariga, Kamiritho, Rironi and even Tiekunu and everywhere the story was the same. Oh, yes, occasionally she would get a client; but none cared for her as she would have liked, none really wanted her enough to fight over her. She was always a hard-up customer's last resort. No make-believe even, not for her that sweet pretence that men indulged in after their fifth bottle of Tusker. The following night or during a pay-day, the same client would pretend not to know her; he would be trying his money-power over girls who already had more than a fair share of admirers.

She resented this. She saw in every girl a rival and adopted a sullen attitude. Nyagūthū especially was the thorn that always pricked her wounded flesh. Nyagūthū arrogant and aloof, but men always in her courtyard; Nyagūthū fighting with men, and to her they would bring propitiating gifts which she accepted as of right. Nyagūthū could look bored, impatient, or downright contemptuous and still men would cling to her as if they enjoyed being whipped with biting words, curled lips and the indifferent eyes of a free woman. Nyagūthū was also a bird in flight, never really able to settle in one place, but in her case it was because she hungered for change and excitement: new faces and new territories for her conquest. Beatrice resented her very shadow. She saw in her the girl she would have liked to be, a girl who was both totally immersed in and yet completely above the underworld of bar violence and sex. Wherever Beatrice went the long shadow of Nyagūthū would sooner or later follow her.

She fled Limuru for Ilmorog in Chiri District. Ilmorog had once been a ghost village, but had been resurrected to life by that legendary woman,

Nyang'endo, to whom every pop group had paid their tribute. It was of her that the young dancing Muthuu and Muchun g'wa sang:

When I left Nairobi for Ilmorog
Never did I know
I would bear this wonder-child mine
Nyang'endo.

As a result, Ilmorog was always seen as a town of hope where the weary and the down-trodden would find their rest and fresh water. But again Nyagūthū followed her.

She found that Ilmorog, despite the legend, despite the songs and dances, was not different from Limuru. She tried various tricks. Clothes? But even here she never earned enough to buy herself glittering robes. What was seventy-five shillings a month without house allowance, posho, without salaried boy-friends? By that time, Ambi had reached Ilmorog, and Beatrice thought that this would be the answer. Had she not, in Limuru, seen girls blacker than herself transformed overnight from ugly sins into white stars by a touch of skin-lightening creams? And men would ogle them, would even talk with exaggerated pride of their newborn girl friends. Men were strange creatures, Beatrice thought in moments of searching analysis. They talked heatedly against Ambi, Butone, Firesnow, Moonsnow, wigs, straightened hair; but they always went for a girl with an Ambi-lightened skin and head covered with a wig made in imitation of European or Indian hair. Beatrice never tried to find the root cause of this black self-hatred, she simply accepted the contradiction and applied herself to Ambi with a vengeance. She had to rub out her black shame. But even Ambi she could not afford in abundance; she could only apply it to her face and her arms so that her legs and neck retained their blackness. Besides there were parts of her face she could not readily reach—behind the ears and above the eyelashes, for instance—and these were a constant source of shame and irritation for her Ambi-self.

She would always remember this Ambi period as one of her deepest humiliation before her later minutes of glory. She worked in Ilmorog Starlight Bar and Lodging. Nyagūthū with her bangled hands, her huge earrings, served behind the counter. The owner was a good Christian soul who regularly went to church and paid all his dues to Harambee projects. Pot-belly. Grey hairs. Soft-spoken. A respectable family man, well known in Ilmorog. Hardworking even, for he would not leave the bar until the closing hours, or more precisely, until Nyagūthū left. He had no eyes for any other girl; he hung around her, and surreptitiously brought her gifts of clothes without receiving gratitude in kind. Only the promise. Only the hope for tomorrow. Other girls he gave eighty shillings a month. Nyagūthū had a room to herself. Nyagūthū woke up whenever she liked to take the stock. But Beatrice and the other girls had to wake up at five or so, make tea for the lodgers, clean up the bar and wash dishes and glasses.

Then they would hang around the bar and in shifts until two o'clock when they would go for a small break. At five o'clock, they had to be in again, ready for customers whom they would now serve with frothy beers and smiles until twelve o'clock or for as long as there were customers thirsty for more Tuskers and Pilsners. What often galled Beatrice, although in her case it did not matter one way or another, was the owner's insistence that the girls should sleep in Starlight. They would otherwise be late for work, he said. But what he really wanted was for the girls to use their bodies to attract more lodgers in Starlight. Most of the girls, led by Nyagūthū defied the rule and bribed the watchman to let them out and in. They wanted to meet their regular or one-night boy-friends in places where they would be free and where they would be treated as not just barmaids. Beatrice always slept in. Her occasional one-night patrons wanted to spend the minimum. Came a night when the owner, refused by Nyagūthū, approached her. He started by finding fault with her work; he called her names, then as suddenly he started praising her, although in a grudging almost contemptuous manner. He grabbed her, struggled with her, potbelly, grey hairs, and everything. Beatrice felt an unusual revulsion for the man. She could not, she would not bring herself to accept that which had so recently been cast aside by Nyagūthū. My God, she wept inside, what does Nyagūthū have that I don't have? The man now humiliated himself before her. He implored. He promised her gifts. But she would not yield. That night she too defied the rule. She jumped through a window; she sought a bed in another bar and only came back at six. The proprietor called her in front of all the others and dismissed her. But Beatrice was rather surprised at herself.

She stayed a month without a job. She lived from room to room at the capricious mercy of the other girls. She did not have the heart to leave Ilmorog and start all over again in a new town. The wound hurt. She was tired of wandering. She stopped using Ambi. No money. She looked at herself in the mirror. She had so aged, hardly a year after she had fallen from grace. Why then was she scrupulous, she would ask herself. But somehow she had a horror of soliciting lovers or directly bartering her body for hard cash. What she wanted was decent work and a man or several men who cared for her. Perhaps she took that need for a man, for a home and for a child with her to bed. Perhaps it was this genuine need that scared off men who wanted other things from barmaids. She wept late at nights and remembered home. At such moments, her mother's village in Nyeri seemed the sweetest place on God's earth. She would invest the life of her peasant mother and father with romantic illusions of immeasurable peace and harmony. She longed to go back home to see them. But how could she go back with empty hands? In any case the place was now a distant landscape in the memory. Her life was here in the bar among this crowd of lost strangers. Fallen from grace, fallen from grace. She was part of a generation which would never again be one with the soil, the crops, the wind and the moon. Not for them that whispering in dark hedges, not for her that dance and love-making under the glare of the moon, with the hills of Tumu Tumu rising to touch the sky. She remembered that girl from her home village who, despite a life of apparent glamour being the kept mistress of one rich man after another in Limuru, had gassed herself to death. This generation was now awed by the mystery of death, just as it was callous to the mystery of life; for how many unmarried mothers had thrown their babies into latrines rather than lose that glamour? The girl's death became the subject of jokes. She had gone metric—without pains, they said. Thereafter, for a week, Beatrice thought of going metric. But she could not bring herself to do it.

She wanted love; she wanted life.

A new bar was opened in Ilmorog. Treetop Bar, Lodging and Restaurant. Why Treetop, Beatrice could not understand unless because it was a storied building: tea-shop on the ground floor and beer-shop in a room at the top. The rest were rooms for five-minute or one-night lodgers. The owner was a retired civil servant but one who still played at politics. He was enormously wealthy with business sites and enterprises in every major town in Kenya. Big shots from all over the country came to his bar. Big men in Mercedes. Big men in their Bentleys. Big men in their Jaguars and Daimlers. Big men with uniformed chauffeurs drowsing with boredom in cars waiting outside. There were others not so big who came to pay respects to the great. They talked politics mostly. And about their work. Gossip was rife. Didn't you know? Indeed so and so has been promoted. Really? And so and so has been sacked. Embezzlement of public funds. So foolish you know. Not clever about it at all. They argued, they quarrelled, sometimes they fought it out with fists, especially during the elections campaign. The only point on which they were all agreed was that the Luo community was the root cause of all the trouble in Kenya; that intellectuals and University students were living in an ivory tower of privilege and arrogance; that Kiambu had more than a lion's share of developments; that men from Nyeri and Muranga had acquired all the big business in Nairobi and were even encroaching on Chiri District; that African workers, especially those on the farms, were lazy and jealous of 'us' who had sweated ourselves to sudden prosperity. Otherwise each would hymn his own praises or return compliments. Occasionally in moments of drunken ebullience and self-praise, one would order two rounds of beer for each man present in the bar. Even the poor from Ilmorog would come to Treetop to dine at the gates of the nouveaux riches.

Here Beatrice got a job as a sweeper and bedmaker. Here for a few weeks she felt closer to greatness. Now she made beds for men she had previously known as names. She watched how even the poor tried to drink and act big in front of the big. But soon fate caught up with her. Girls flocked to Treetop from other bars. Girls she had known at Limuru, girls she had known at Ilmorog. And most had attached themselves to one or several big men, often playing a hide-and-not-to-be found game with their numerous lovers. And Nyagũthũ was there behind the counter, with the eyes of the rich and the poor fixed on her. And she, with her big eyes, bangled hands and earrings maintained the same air of bored indifference. Beatrice as a sweeper and bedmaker became even more invisible. Girls who had fallen into good fortune looked down upon her.

She fought life with dreams. In between putting clean sheets on beds that had just witnessed a five-minute struggle that ended in a half-strangled cry and a pool, she would stand by the window and watch the cars and the chauffeurs, so that soon she knew all the owners by the number plates of their cars and the uniforms of their chauffeurs. She dreamt of lovers who would come for her in sleek Mercedes sports cars made for two. She saw herself linking hands with such a lover, walking in the streets of Nairobi and Mombasa, tapping the ground with high heels, quick, quick short steps. And suddenly she would stop in front of a display glass window, exclaiming at the same time, Oh darling, won't you buy me those . . . ? Those what? he would ask, affecting anger. Those stockings, darling. It was as an owner of several stockings, ladderless and holeless, that she thought of her well-being. Never again would she mend torn things. Never, never, never. Do you understand? Never. She was next the proud owner of different coloured wigs, blonde wigs, brunette wigs, redhead wigs, Afro wigs, wigs, wigs, all the wigs in the world. Only then would the whole earth sing hallelujah to the one Beatrice. At such moments, she would feel exalted, lifted out of her murky self, no longer a floor sweeper and bedmaker for a five-minute instant love, but Beatrice, descendant of Wangu Makeri who made men tremble with desire at her naked body bathed in moonlight, daughter of Nyang'endo, the founder of modern Ilmorog, of whom they often sang that she had worked several lovers into impotence.

Then she noticed him and he was the opposite of the lover of her dreams. He came one Saturday afternoon driving a big five-ton lorry. He carefully parked it beside the Benzes, the Jaguars and the Daimlers, not as a lorry, but as one of those sleek cream-bodied frames, so proud of it he seemed to be. He dressed in a baggy grey suit over which he wore a heavy khaki military overcoat. He removed the overcoat, folded it with care, and put it in the front seat. He locked all the doors, dusted himself a little, then walked round the lorry as if inspecting it for damage. A few steps before he entered Treetop, he turned round for a final glance at his lorry dwarfing the other things. At Treetops he sat in a corner and, with a rather loud defiant voice, ordered a Kenya one. He drank it with relish, looking around at the same time for a face he might recognize. He indeed did recognize one of the big ones and he immediately ordered for him a quarter bottle of Vat 69. This was accepted with a bare nod of the head and a patronising smile; but when he tried to follow his generosity with a conversation, he was firmly ignored. He froze, sank into his Muratina. But only for a time. He tried again: he was met with frowning faces. More pathetic were his attempts to join in jokes; he would laugh rather too loudly, which would make the big ones stop, leaving him in the air alone. Later in the evening he stood up, counted several crisp hundred shilling notes and handed them to Nyagūthū behind the counter ostensibly for safekeeping. People whispered; murmured; a few laughed, rather derisively, though they were rather impressed. But this act did not win him immediate recognition. He staggered towards room no. 7 which he had hired. Beatrice brought him the keys. He glanced at her, briefly, then lost all interest.

Thereafter he came every Saturday. At five when most of the big shots were already seated. He repeated the same ritual, except the money act, and always met with defeat. He nearly always sat in the same corner and always rented room 7. Beatrice grew to anticipate his visits and, without being conscious of it, kept the room ready for him. Often after he had been badly humiliated by the big company, he would detain Beatrice and talk to her, or rather he talked to himself in her presence. For him, it had been a life of struggles. He had never been to school although getting an education had been his ambition. He never had a chance. His father was a squatter in the European settled area in the Rift Valley. That meant a lot in those colonial days. It meant among other things a man and his children were doomed to a future of sweat and toil for the white devils and their children. He had joined the freedom struggle and like the others had been sent to detention. He came from detention the same as his mother had brought him to this world. Nothing. With independence he found he did not possess the kind of education which would have placed him in one of the vacancies at the top. He started as a charcoal burner, then a butcher, gradually working his own way to become a big transporter of vegetables and potatoes from the Rift Valley and Chiri districts to Nairobi. He was proud of his achievement. But he resented that others, who had climbed to their present wealth through loans and a subsidized education, would not recognize his like. He would rumble on like this, dwelling on education he would never have, and talking of better chances for his children. Then he would carefully count the money, put it under the pillow, and then dismiss Beatrice. Occasionally he would buy her a beer but he was clearly suspicious of women whom he saw as money-eaters of men. He had not yet married.

One night he slept with her. In the morning he scratched for a twenty shilling note and gave it to her. She accepted the money with an odd feeling of guilt. He did this for several weeks. She did not mind the money. It was useful. But he paid for her body as he would pay for a bag of potatoes or a sack of cabbages. With the one pound, he had paid for her services as a listener, a vessel of his complaints against those above, and as a one-night receptacle of his man's burden. She was becoming bored with his ego, with his stories that never varied in content, but somehow, in him, deep inside, she felt that something had been there, a fire, a seed, a flower which was being smothered. In him she saw a fellow victim and looked forward to his visits. She too longed to talk to someone. She too longed to confide in a human being who would understand.

And she did it one Saturday night, suddenly interrupting the story of his difficult climb to the top. She did not know why she did it. Maybe it was the rain outside. It was softly drumming the corrugated iron sheets, bringing with the drumming a warm and drowsy indifference. He would listen. He had to listen. She came from Karatina in Nyeri. Her two brothers had been gunned down by the British soldiers. Another one had died in detention. She was, so to speak, an only child. Her parents were poor. But they worked hard on their bare strip of land and managed to pay her fees in primary school. For the first six years she had worked hard. In the seventh year, she must have relaxed a little. She did not pass with a good grade. Of course she knew many with similar grades who had been called to good government secondary schools. She knew a few others with lesser grades who had gone to very top schools on the strength of their connections. But she was not called to any high school with reasonable fees. Her parents could not afford fees in a Harambee school. And she would not hear of repeating standard seven. She stayed at home with her parents. Occasionally she would help them in the shamba and with house chores. But imagine: for the past six years she had led a life with a different rhythm from that of her parents. Life in the village was dull. She would often go to Karatina and to Nyeri in search of work. In every office, they would ask her the same questions: what work do you want? What do you know? Can you type? Can you take shorthand? She was desperate. It was in Nyeri, drinking Fanta in a shop, tears in her eyes, that she met a young man in a dark suit and sun-glasses. He saw her plight and talked to her. He came from Nairobi. Looking for work? That's easy; in a big city there would be no difficulty with jobs. He would certainly help. Transport? He had a car—a cream-white Peugeot. Heaven. It was a beautiful ride, with the promise of dawn. Nairobi. He drove her to Terrace Bar. They drank beer and talked about Nairobi. Through the window she could see the neon-lit city and knew that here was hope. That night she gave herself to him, with the promise of dawn making her feel light and gay. She had a very deep sleep. When she woke in the morning, the man in the cream-white Peugeot was not there. She never saw him again. That's how she had started the life of a barmaid. And for one and a half years now she had not been once to see her parents. Beatrice started weeping. Huge sobs of self-pity. Her humiliation and constant flight were fresh in her mind. She had never been able to take to bar culture, she always thought that something better would come her way. But she was trapped, it was the only life she now knew, although she had never really learnt all its laws and norms. Again she heaved out and in, tears tossing out with every sob. Then suddenly she froze. Her sobbing was arrested in the air. The man had long covered himself. His snores were huge and unmistakable.

She felt a strange hollowness. Then a bile of bitterness spilt inside her. She wanted to cry at her new failure. She had met several men who had treated her cruelly, who had laughed at her scruples, at what they thought was an ill-disguised attempt at innocence. She had accepted. But not this, Lord, not this. Was this man not a fellow victim? Had he not, Saturday after Saturday, unburdened himself to her? He had paid for her human services; he had paid away his responsibility with his bottle of Tuskers and hard cash in the morning. Her innermost turmoil had been his lullaby. And suddenly something in her snapped. All the anger of a year and a half, all the bitterness against her humiliation were now directed at this man.

What she did later had the mechanical precision of an experienced hand.

She touched his eyes. He was sound asleep. She raised his head. She let it fall. Her tearless eyes were now cold and set. She removed the pillow from under him. She rummaged through it. She took out his money. She counted five crisp pink notes. She put the money inside her brassiere.

She went out of room no. 7. Outside it was still raining. She did not want to go to her usual place. She could not now stand the tiny cupboard room or the superior chatter of her roommate. She walked through mud and rain. She found herself walking towards Nyagūthū's room. She knocked at the door. At first she had no response. Then she heard Nyagūthū's sleepy voice above the drumming rain.

'Who is that?'

'It is me. Please open.'

'Who?'

'Beatrice.'

'At this hour of the night?'

'Please.'

Lights were put on. Bolts unfastened. The door opened. Beatrice stepped inside. She and Nyagūthū stood there face to face. Nyagūthū was in a see-through nightdress: on her shoulders she had a green pullover.

'Beatrice, is there anything wrong?' She at last asked, a note of concern in her voice.

'Can I rest here for a while? I am tired. And I want to talk to you.' Beatrice's voice carried assurance and power.

'But what has happened?'

'I only want to ask you a question, Nyagūthū.'

They were still standing. Then, without a word, they both sat on the bed.

'Why did you leave home, Nyagūthū?' Beatrice asked. Another silent moment. Nyagūthū seemed to be thinking about the question. Beatrice waited. Nyagūthū's voice when at last it came was slightly tremulous, unsteady.

'It is a long story, Beatrice. My father and mother were fairly wealthy. They were also good Christians. We lived under regulations. You must never walk with the heathen. You must not attend their pagan customs — dances and circumcision rites, for instance. There were rules about what, how and when to eat. You must even walk like a Christian lady. You must never be seen with boys. Rules, rules all the way. One day instead of returning home from school, I and another girl from a similar home ran away to Eastleigh. I have never been home once this last four years. That's all.'

Another silence. Then they looked at one another in mutual recognition.

'One more question, Nyagũthũ. You need not answer it. But I have always thought that you hated me, you despised me.'

'No, no, Beatrice, I have never hated you. I have never hated anybody. It is just that nothing interests me. Even men do not move me now. Yet I want, I need instant excitement. I need the attention of those false flattering eyes to make me feel myself, myself. But you, you seemed above all this—somehow you had something inside you that I did not have.'

Beatrice tried to hold her tears with difficulty.

Early the next day, she boarded a bus bound for Nairobi. She walked down Bazaar Street looking at the shops. Then down Government Road, right into Kenyatta Avenue, and Kimathi Street. She went into a shop near Hussein Suleman's Street and bought several stockings. She put on a pair. She next bought herself a new dress. Again she changed into it. In a Bata Shoeshop, she bought high heeled shoes, put them on and discarded her old flat ones. On to an Akamba kiosk, and she fitted herself with earrings. She went to a mirror and looked at her new self. Suddenly she felt enormous hunger as if she had been hungry all her life. She hesitated in front of Moti Mahal. Then she walked on, eventually entering Fransae. There was a glint in her eyes that made men's eyes turn to her. This thrilled her. She chose a table in a corner and ordered Indian curry. A man left his table and joined her. She looked at him. Her eyes were merry. He was dressed in a dark suit and his eyes spoke of lust. He bought her a drink. He tried to engage her in conversation. But she ate in silence. He put his hand under the table and felt her knees. She let him do it. The hand went up and up her thigh. Then suddenly she left her unfinished food and her untouched drink and walked out. She felt good. He followed her. She knew this without once turning her eyes. He walked beside her for a few yards. She smiled at herself but did not look at him. He lost his confidence. She left him standing sheepishly looking at a glass window outside Gino's. In the bus back to Ilmorog, men gave her seats. She accepted this as of right. At Treetops bar she went straight to the counter. The usual crowd of big men were there. Their conversations stopped for a few seconds at her entry. Their lascivious eyes were turned to her. The girls stared at her. Even Nyagũthũ could not maintain her bored indifference. Beatrice bought them drinks. The manager came to her, rather unsure. He tried a conversation. Why had she left work? Where had she been? Would she like to work in the bar, helping Nyagũthũ behind the counter? Now and then? A barmaid brought her a note. A certain big shot wanted to know if she would join their table. More notes came from different big quarters with the one question; would she be free tonight? A trip to Nairobi even. She did not leave her place at the counter. But she accepted their drinks as of right. She felt a new power, confidence even.

She took out a shilling, put it in the slot and the juke box boomed with the voice of Robinson Mwangi singing *Hũnyũ wa Mashambani*. He sang of those despised girls who worked on farms and contrasted them with urban girls. Then she played a Kamaru and a D. K. Men wanted to dance with her. She ignored them, but enjoyed their flutter around her. She twisted her hips to the sound of yet another D. K. Her body was free. She was free. She sucked in the excitement and tension in the air.

Then suddenly at around six, the man with the five-ton lorry stormed into the bar. This time he had on his military overcoat. Behind him was a policeman. He looked around. Everybody's eyes were raised to him. But Beatrice went on swaying her hips. At first he could not recognize Beatrice in the girl celebrating her few minutes of glory by the juke box. Then he shouted in triumph. 'That is the girl! Thief! Thief!'

People melted back to their seats. The policeman went and handcuffed her. She did not resist. Only at the door she turned her head and spat. Then she went out followed by the policeman.

In the bar the stunned silence broke into hilarious laughter when someone made a joke about sweetened robbery without violence. They discussed her. Some said she should have been beaten. Others talked contemptuously about 'these bar girls'. Yet others talked with a concern noticeable in unbelieving shakes of their heads about the rising rate of crime. Shouldn't the Hanging Bill be extended to all thefts of property? And without anybody being aware of it the man with the five-ton lorry had become a hero. They now surrounded him with questions and demanded the whole story. Some even bought him drinks. More remarkable, they listened, their attentive silence punctuated by appreciative laughter. The averted threat to property had temporarily knit them into one family. And the man, accepted for the first time, told the story with relish.

But behind the counter Nyagūthū wept.

## ■ Breyten Breytenbach (1939– ) *South Africa* (memoir)

Breyten Breytenbach has been called South Africa's Solzhenitsyn for his opposition to the regime that condemned him to seven years in prison. A white Afrikaner by birth, multilingual, writing in English, Afrikaans (Taal), and French, he has, like Nadine Gordimer and Alan Paton, been a champion in the anti-apartheid movement. His years of brutal imprisonment, including two years of solitary confinement in a miniscule cell, have elected him to that solitary class of writers—including Saint John of the Cross and Miguel Hernández in Spain, Jean Genet in France, Nazim Hikmet in Turkey, Jacobo Timerman in Argentina, Aleksandr Solzhenitsyn in Russia, and Wang Meng in China—who have made prison the source and subject of their books. A prolific writer of fiction, poetry, and essays, Breytenbach's poetry, well translated from Afrikaans into English, is eclectically European and African, peppered with French phrases, reflecting his present Paris residence and literary affinity, and an energetic speech of city, prison, and nature. *Confessions of an Albino Terrorist,* his masterpiece, is a memoir-reportage of his years of confinement, dramatically recounted in some five hundred pages, which he recorded on tape in Paris in the months following his release. The pages selected here record the first moments of arrest and of foretold gloom.

**FURTHER READING:** Breytenbach, Breyten. *In Africa Even the Flies Are Happy: Selected Poems,* 1978; *Confessions of an Albino Terrorist,* 1983; *Memory of Snow and of Dust,* 1989; *All One Horse: Fiction and Images,* 1990.

## *from* Confessions of an Albino Terrorist

The name you will see under this document is Breyten Breytenbach. That is my name. It's not the only one; after all, what is a name? I used to be called Dick; sometimes I was called Antoine; some knew me as Hervé; others as Jan Blom; at one point I was called Christian Jean-Marc Galaska; then I was the Professor; later I was Mr Bird: all these different names with different meanings being the labels attached to different people. Because, Mr Investigator, if there is one thing that has become amply clear to me over the years, it is exactly that there is no one person that can be named and in the process of naming be fixed for all eternity.

What did your face look like before you were born? What did *you* look like before you or your father or your mother were born? Where were you then? In fact, where do you come from? And will it be possible one day to know where you come from, and therefore where you are, and therefore where you're heading, and therefore what you are, in which case you should be able to attach a name to it? Isn't that the whole process of our being, this looking for a name?

And then, this same process is an open-ended one; I can hear the echoes. As it continues — this jumble-talk, this trial — I can go on searching, and I can hear the reverberation of my own voice. I'm sitting here — I have this little instrument in my hand; I have the earphones on my head and I speak to you and I listen to the voice coming back. And I learn from these words the reality as it is being presented at the moment of emitting the sounds. That is perhaps as close as I can come to what the identity is considered to be. That is as close as I come to the truth. Here I am. Here the truth is also.

I hope, Mr Investigator, that that is what you expect of me. Because, you know, you could force me to deny whatever I say immediately after having said it; and you could probably force me to start all over again. I can tell you in advance that if I were to do that it would come out differently; it would be different; I'd no longer be there; I'd be somebody else — as sincere, as keen to help, as obsessed by the necessity to confess.

But let us push him back into the darkness of non-existence and let us go forward with what we have in hand at the moment. May I be your humble servant, Mr Investigator? Listen to me. I shall confess.

## HERE I WAS

It's dark outside. Against the slanted window set into the roof there is this very soft rustling of rain coming down. I can look at it and I can see the wet tracks on the dusty surface. Across a dark space beyond the building there are windows alight and if one looks long enough you can see people moving behind the curtains, intent upon their nightly tasks and fancies, each living in his own little cocoon of fantasy and desire and ritual and habit.

When they finally identified me that other night, more than seven years ago now, it was dark too, though it was not winter then, at least it was not winter in Europe and it's never really winter in Africa, not on the Highveld. It was in August 1975. I had arrived earlier that evening at Jan Smuts Airport on my way back to France. I had known even as I arrived that I was blown, that they knew about me and rather in the fashion of a small child closing its eyes hoping that in so doing the hideousness will go away, I'd hoped against hope that I'd be able to slip through the net which had been closing around me for some time.

As I booked in at the departure counter I noticed a man, young, rather well dressed, looking at me. He then turned around, walked to the telephone, picked it up, talked to someone. You know how it is when you get that tingling feeling down your back. In later years I'd get to recognize that sensation and respect it far more clearly, in the same way as one develops in due time a heightened sense of smell: being able to sniff out these policemen from quite a long way away.

I booked in. I reserved a seat by the window. I spoke to the counter girl in Italian, which I was rather proud of, and then I moved through customs and the customs official looked at my passport, stared at me for a few seconds, did something else with his hands below the counter where I couldn't see, flipped my passport back at me, and I continued. In the departure hall I became intensely aware of several men sitting there, moving around, watching me. One is never so obvious as when you're trying to integrate with your surroundings. In fact, I became so paranoid that I went downstairs to the gents' toilets with one of them dogging my footsteps, and there, unzipping my pants, hunching my shoulders, I managed to swallow a few lines of paper with names on it. Not everything, unfortunately, could be disposed of in that way. If only I had been more rational I might have been able to get rid of more incriminating evidence. I then went back upstairs and suddenly over the intercom system an announcement came asking for Monsieur Galaska to present himself at counter so and so. I didn't budge. The soothing voice with the airport accent called again. I realized that there was no way out: I couldn't go back the way I'd come in—that would have meant going through customs again—and there was no other exit. I therefore went up to the counter where a girl from South African Airways was talking to various passengers and before I could even address her a gentleman at my elbow put his hand on my shoulder and said, 'Are you Mr Galaska?' I said, 'Yes.' He said, 'Would you mind following me please?' and he led me off into a little office giving on to this departure hall. He then asked me for my passport, my ticket—which I gave to him—and with these he disappeared, leaving me in the care of a young man loitering behind a big table.

Just so one is delivered into the hands of one's enemies . . . Well, it was obvious that the game was up. My plane hadn't departed yet. I enquired after the reason for my hold up and was told by the young man that he didn't know any more than I did, but surely it was just a matter of checking my identity and that everything should be all right in a few minutes when I would be allowed to proceed. In any event, he said, I needn't worry about my luggage or anything like that—they'll take care of those little mundane matters. At one stage during this interval a young Black girl came in, very distraught: she was due to have left on the same flight and she now suddenly found that she had lost her passport somewhere in the departure hall and was therefore prevented from going. A big search was started and the passport wasn't found. Time passed. The young man asked me if I'd like to smoke. I said I'd rather have one of my own cigarettes and took out a packet of Gauloises and my body was cold. The door then opened and in walked the man who had originally asked me to follow him, now accompanied by two others, one of whom was very familiar to me indeed. Colonel, I believe he had the rank of colonel, Jan Snaaks. With him a man younger than he was, medium height, very athletically built, very sharp blue eyes, the obligatory civil service moustache; and in a very friendly, even quite polite way, they started asking me questions. They meticulously searched my hand luggage which I had with me. They then asked me to strip and went through all my clothing and came up among other things with a strip of paper which I had unfortunately not destroyed, upon which was marked, 'La révolution est un art d'exécution'—which, I think, one can translate as 'Revolution is a practice.' As in a hallucination I saw on the table the small personal belongings, inconsequential as these things always are, being an element or an indication of the stranger's identity, of the foreigner, the I.

I was subsequently asked to write briefly my *curriculum vitae.* One did so. I remember that it was with a feeling somewhat akin to having a high. It came right off the top of my head. I had to invent on the spur of the moment thirty years of life, starting with where I was born, which I knew from the passport; going on to primary school, to secondary school, to my studies after school, to the work I did; including references to friends, to the area in which I lived, to the bank where I was supposed to work; and I remember that I had parading in front of my mind's eye the faces of my mates and I included them in this picture that I was asked to draw up. In fact, I borrowed heavily from what I remembered, knew or surmised of their young years in France. One stole from life in a derisory attempt to stave off death. I think that my interrogator was quite impressed by my effort. Much later he would tell me that he remained convinced that I'd been given this cover and that I'd memorized it carefully. He did not deem it possible to invent a life at the drop of a hat. But you would understand that, Mr Investigator. *You* know that we're always inventing our lives. *You* know that what I'm confessing now is also the instantaneous invention of what might have happened.

'You are a Russian agent!' Snaaks snarled, his eyes close to his nose. He has the strawberry nose of a toper. What could I answer? The man was so desperately and bravely living for the *big* catch.

It became obvious that they weren't going to let me go. I asked for permission to make contact with my Ambassador and this was refused. Sarcastically. As the night wore on it more and more happened that the various officers—I cannot call them gentlemen—spoke to one another in Afrikaans within my hearing, watching for the reaction that it might have on me. I remember Blue Eyes saying to Snaaks, 'Look, his knees are trembling, he must be scared shitless'; and I tried to control my knees. At a later stage Snaaks would look very keenly at me several times. Again he left this holding area. Apparently went to phone. Came back. Asked me to take hold of the pipe which he'd found in my luggage. And then pointed to the little wart smack between my eyes and said in Afrikaans, 'Come on, Breyten, the game's up, we know who you are. Do you want us to go and fetch one of your brothers and confront you with him?' And knowing that he could do so I said in Afrikaans too, 'No, it won't be necessary.' I learned later that I had had rather bad luck—as I was preparing to leave from Jan Smuts Airport the plane bearing John Vorster, then Prime Minister of South Africa, and his entourage, on return from a visit to South America, landed. One of my brothers happened to be in the party accompanying Big Chief Sitting Bull and of course there was a large number of security officials both arriving with him and awaiting him at the airport, so that the place was literally crawling with lice. (And flushed with excitement they were, having just cemented ties with staunch fellow democrats like Stroessner and Pinochet.)

Snaaks and Blue Eyes were BOSS agents.[1] Not only did Snaaks insist, foaming at the mouth, that I'm a KGB man, but that I'm one of an ultrasecret section of killers led by a certain Colonel Unpronounceable. In the following days, as the interrogation unfolded, 'Uncle Jan' Snaaks would drop away—Blue Eyes would be BOSS's man with the Security Police proper—and I, after having been successively (unsuccessfully) a French, British and Israeli agent, would end up being accused of working for the CIA. How Blue Eyes stumbled over my glorious career in the CIA I shall describe later . . .

---

1. BOSS—the Bureau for State Security; after the so-called 'Information Scandal', the demise of General van den Berg, and the coming to national power of P. W. Botha (by means of a camouflaged *coup d'état* in fact), BOSS became the DNS—Department of National Security.

After this undramatic revelation of my true identity I was allowed to take hold of my hand luggage, pocket my half-empty packet of Gauloises, and told to follow a young man who had turned up in the meantime. This young man escorted me to a car, one of the very typical broad, comfortable security vehicles, parked in an underground parking lot. Another man came up out of the dark dressed incongruously in a battle jacket, and took the wheel. I was told to sit in the back next to the young man in his little navy-blue blazer. He was tough, with a modish haircut. He sat in his corner and never let me stray from his eyesight. The he-man in front drove at a comfortable pace from Johannesburg, at least from the airport, to Pretoria, all the while shooting questions at me, wanting to know why, why, why do you people do this? *What* is it that motivates you? He said, 'I'm not interested in the small facts, the petty crimes, the little political actions. I want to know what *causes* you to do something like this? *What* is the ideology line behind it? I want you to tell me all about socialism, I want you to tell me about Marxism, I want you to get to the gist of the matter.' He sounded very much like the university professor he probably was in real life, which he probably still is. Because, Mr Investigator, I don't know if I need tell you this; surely you must know that so many of the agents working for BOSS are very respectable, well-to-do bourgeois professionals holding down positions at university, or at law firms, or as insurance agents or whatever. Some of them are even, quite improbably, disguised as policemen. BOSS/DNS constitute a *political* force in the country, both as a decision-making organ and a controlling agent. They are in fact deeply involved in internal mind-control. The demarcation of territories isn't very clear, and there's much strife and jealousy among the various intelligence groups. The SP (Security Police or Special Branch) have their own agents abroad—witness the Williamson incident.[2]

Koos Bruin, smooth and rather likable BOSS operator, once told me of how he was involved, as a student representative, in organizing a staff/student protest meeting on the campus of Witwatersrand University. The lady professor chairing the meeting expressed to him, her confidant, concern because she knew for a fact that there must be three 'government spies' present. He had to laugh in his sleeve, he told me, as he was one of the seven undercover agents in the hall that day.

Maybe it was all a farce. Maybe the spooks and the controllers only feigned surprise at coming across a mask called Breytenbach under a mask named Galaska. Their being at the airport had nothing to do with the arrival of Sitting Bull. And they were loath to turn me over to the SP. Blue Eyes later explained to me that they would have preferred to whisk me off to 'The Farm' without anyone (ever) knowing. ('The Farm', as far

---

2. Craig Williamson, an officer in the Special Branch (as opposed to BOSS) infiltrated opposition forces— starting with the National Union of South African Students when he was still a student, and eventually the International University Exchange Fund based in Geneva, from where he reported on the Liberation Movement and Anti-Apartheid groups. When finally unmasked in the late 1970s, General Johan Coetzee (his 'handler' later to be head of the SP) went to Switzerland to retrieve his agent.

as I could make out, is indeed a farm where the BOSS/DNS people prepare their 'dirty tricks' in all impunity, and where they can work over their suspects in absolute secrecy—without the intervention of the Prisons Department or the Department of Justice.) Had it not been for crossed lines and inter-agency rivalry I might never have been here to whisper to you, dear Investigator. Blue Eyes—he's still there—fancies himself as a psychologist, an experimenter, a washer of brains.

It was unreal: going for a quiet spin to Pretoria in a big limousine with a phosphorescent-green dashboard—being chauffeured by a ranting political scientist who believes himself to be in the Bush, facing clever ideologues.

We arrived in Pretoria. My two accompanies, if that's the right word, handed me over into the care of two gentlemen from the Security Police proper. I was introduced into the masher. I was delivered at the Compol Buildings which served as the headquarters of the political police in that area. It's an old building, claimed to have been built during the time of Paul Kruger. The walls are very thick. In the daytime, because over the next month I got to know the building rather well, in daytime there will be quite a lot of people moving through the corridors, mumbling away behind doors. At the back they had a cell where I was to spend a lot of time; it had a barred window giving onto the street level outside. Upstairs they had a police museum. In due time I believe my passport, my beautifully crafted false passport, would figure there amongst the exhibits honouring the grand exploits of the South African Police, probably tucked in between a bloodied axe and a few sticks of dynamite.

But that night the place was quiet; not even the blind lift attendant whom I would get to know later on and who knew his way around the building so well—what a horrible thing it must be to spend one's blindness in a place like that—not even he was there then. As far as I could hear and see we were the only ones present in the caverns of the night. They took me into an office, cold, giving off the smell and the presence and the colour of brownness: the kind of chocolate station waiting room brownness; and stale, dusty, impersonal walls having witnessed many breakdowns. Walls which in the way of all walls will never say anything about it. On one such wall behind one of the tables there hung a framed picture of C. R. Swarts who had been, a long time before, the Minister of Justice. I don't know whether this was out of particular loyalty to whatever he stood for or whether time hadn't moved since the period of his tenure as minister.

My hosts weren't violent in any way. Why should they be? I was dead. All they had to do was to process the dead, to pick over the bones. They weren't particularly interested. Again I had to go through the procedure of stripping and then I was counted: that is, all my possessions were itemized and these were then carefully noted in red ink on a large sheet of paper. Night was ticking away like an unsatiable beast.

Mr Investigator, as we arrive at the end of this first talk, permit me to give you a brief extract of what I consisted of as written down on this sheet of paper. I have it here in my hand. The paper's called P21: i.e., it is a lined single sheet of folio paper. I translate:

1 bed ticket
1 SAA ticket No. 710902 dated 6/8/75
1 red handbag with the following items therein:
3 ballpoint pens: 2 green, 1 silver
3 keys
Scissors and keyholder
1 book *A Universal History of Infamy*
1 blue notebook
14 envelopes and Hotel Elizabeth writing paper
1 Hotel Elizabeth receipt No. 39110 for R41.25
1 500 lire note, Italian
1 silver coin, 100 lire
3 glass bangles
1 necklace of beads, yellow, black and white
1 French matchbox
1 blue toothbrush
1 tube of toothpaste
Receipt No. 3570, some sum (I can't make out the writing there), Berg resort
1 Banca Nazionale del Lavoro statement
1 Alitalia boarding pass
1 Alitalia passenger ticket and baggage check
1 piece of paper with *'L'art de la révolution'* etc. written on it
1 strip of paper with Bergville code 03647/1801 written on it
1 Johannesburg street map
1 shorthand notebook
1 piece of paper with 433236 written on it
1 bottle of brandy Oudemeester
1 paper bag with the following therein:
A packet of protea seeds
1 gramophone record
1 small clay flute
1 light brown envelope marked 'Dollars $370', with the following notes in it:
five $10 = $50
eleven $20 = $220
one $100 = $100
seventeen notes altogether $370
(On the back is written, according to the writing of the police scribe):
'W 430730' (scratched out)
'W 930430/km 877314'

1 tie black with blue dots

1 pair of glasses

1 glass bangle

1 match folder 'Berg Holiday Resort Bergville' written on it

1 box of matches, Lion matches

1 brown portfolio with the following contents:

R15 (fifteen Rands) in notes equalling R15

R4.70 (four Rands seventy cents in silver equalling R4.70)

15 1/2 (fifteen and a half cents copper equalling 15 1/2 cents) the to-
     tal being R19.85 1/2 cents

7 silver French coins

1 $50 note equalling $50

4 dix francs notes equalling F10

3 cent francs notes (F100)
     (I can't imagine how they got those totals.)

4 Banca d'Italia Lire Mille

1 Banca d'Italia Lire Cinque Milla

2 Volkskas cash receipts for R69.93 (a little bit further on they've writ-
     ten $100)

1 Barclays Bank receipt for R70.14 (again it's written $100)[3]

And 6 *metro-autobus* tickets

1 pipe

1 tobacco pouch

And finally one inoculation certificate in the name of C. Galaska,
     672774.

There you see me, Mr Investigator, in all my naked glory, with all my possessions around me, as I stand that first evening. *Ecce homo.*

I was quite rich, wasn't I? There was something for them to work on, something to keep them busy. What a beautiful collection of clues! But of
course, that was not what they were interested in. Maybe that's not even
what would interest *you.* (Am I reading the signals correctly?) They would
much rather want to know the whole history and all the schemes and all
the dreams that I was carrying around with me. You see, I was a travelling
salesman in dreams and illusions.

     And even more than that—they must have been dying to use me to
get hold of all manner of other people, to sniff out the dark secrets threatening the State, to bring to light all the evil conspiracies; particularly to
prove that this was only one more manifestation of the worldwide onslaught against this small, embattled nation of pure and upright, Godfear-
ing, chosen ones.

     So, perhaps, once and for all, I should tell you about those dreams,
about where I came from and where I thought I was heading.

---

3. The Japanese tourist, complaining on the third day about the jumping exchange rate, is told by the
cashier it is due to 'Fluctuations'. 'Fluctuations?' the Japanese splutters. 'Well, fluck the Eulopeans tool'.

**INSERT**

Where did I know Colonel Jan Snaaks from and where does the pipe and the tobacco pouch fit into the story? You remember, Mr Investigator, I am sure, that I tried to describe how, when we visited No Man's Land in 1973 and spent one season in that paradise, I was followed all over the country by certain security agents, and how towards the end of our stay, one night in Paarl, thanks to the intervention of one of my brothers who is certainly a close friend and colleague of these people, I was confronted by two grey eminences chomping at the bit, and this was exactly then Jan Snaaks and another big, bulky fellow called 'Kleintjie' (the little one) Heiden, I believe, with the head of a dog and a long history as hunter of political dissidents. (In a totalitarian state the political police operate quite openly, à visage découvert, although they always have their underground activities also of course. The point is: to fulfil their function of intimidating and terrorizing the population they also have to be visible to some extent. They can be affable people to meet, real Afrikaner gentlemen, good drinking companions, opening doors for ladies. What distinguishes them will be the way they look at one, something around the eyes, and the brutal power they exude.) During the ensuing evening they tried to impress upon me the extent of their knowledge of my activities and contacts, and tried frightening me into giving them information. That was my first mask to mask confrontation with the Greyshit, the BOSS people, and as my luck would have it, it had to be the same Jan Snaaks at the airport that specific night. Was it coincidence? Wasn't he on my tracks the whole time of my passage in South Africa? Since I was known to be a pipe smoker I deliberately took no pipe or tobacco with me into the country, but started smoking cigarettes—hence the packet of Gauloises. Then, whilst passing through Cape Town, I remember going to Greenmarket Square where, years before, many, many years ago when I lived and dreamed around the corner, in Long Street, I used to buy my supply of tobacco. One could have it mixed on the spot to one's taste and I couldn't resist the temptation of walking in there again, into old times' youth, sniffing the beautiful aroma of freshly prepared tobacco. (I was on the run then: perhaps I was looking for some form of innocence.) Having bought some tobacco I obviously also had to acquire a pipe. I thought I'd be clever, I thought I'd leave it in my suitcase to smoke it only in the secret of my hotel room. And of course they dug it up at the airport and they had me hold it and they recognized my way of fondling the pipe as someone else might have recognized my way of handling a pen or my way of stuttering into a tape recorder. These are the indelible finger prints of the fugacious identity. There is no 'I', there is no name, there is no identity. But there are unchanging manifestations, habits, a hulk, a carcass, recognizable. There is a sore thumb. The cause has disappeared, the symptoms remain.

What fastidious workers they are, how obsessed they must be! Look how they dig into one's past, how they project one's future, how they alter one's present. I have no private lives: it's all in their hands; they know the I better than I do, they are far more interested in it than I am. They have the files, they have the computer. Or they know all about my ways, my preferences, my accretions, my little secrets—my gardens—be they political or sexual. And they are fascinated by it. They smell it like freshly mixed tobacco. They knead it. They manipulate it, they slobber over it. It justifies their lives . . .

## INSERT

Home. Home, James, and don't spare the horses. Screaming down the tunnels of darkness, careening down the passages, going deeper ever deeper into the labyrinth; but I'm home now, maimed, diminished, splayed, with my vision impaired, my horizon narrowed, my reference points vague, obscure; and yet there is this total clarity even if it's only at the level of language, which is the surface, which is the superficial, which, by the definition of language must disappear to be allowed to exist.

When first I came out of prison I was thrown into emptiness and I found all space around me cluttered. For so long had I been conditioned to the simplification of four walls, the square of a barred window, a double square door, a square bed, emptiness, nowhere to hide the smallest illegal object, nowhere to hide the crust of bread to which you were not entitled, nowhere to efface yourself, or tuck away the soul or to protect your three dreams from prying eyes and acquisitive fingers, nowhere to hide your anguish: all these had been erased by being made apparent. It just became language. So that when I found myself ejected into what *you* would consider to be the normal world, I found it terribly confusing. Why are there so many people moving through the theatre décor of streets? How come the air is so bloated with useless words? Why on earth do people have so many objects in their houses? Why do they have to hang things on the wall, or have to have more than one set of clothes? Why do they collect possessions? You should know by now that one can never possess anything, and when The Law strikes you will lose everything anyway. And I remember, because now it is passing, that whenever I entered a new space I lifted my feet very high and I pulled my head down between my shoulders from fear of the unexpected step or beam.

What else must I describe? Do you really want to know what it's like to be free?

Freedom is not knowing where to stop. It is a gargantuan appetite; it is a need to burn clean, with whatever is spicy and hot, the taste of dullness which has encrusted your memory and your appetite; it is the unquenchable thirst; it's the need to absorb, to take, to grasp, to experience, to renew and to drink, because it is simultaneously the necessity to deaden the nerve ends. I have not the slightest measure of what ought and ought not to be done and when and how. I should eat whatever you put before me. I read on the wall 'Mangez-vous les uns les autres', and I discover all kinds of lusts: a yearning for seafood; I must have mustards; I must have pickles. I must exercise the regrets and the shame and the guilt.

Ah, Mr Investigator, don't you think I'm guilty? Yes, I have the guilt of the survivor. All my friends are dead because they are still alive, locked in the cleanliness of asexual and dehumanized space. And I, I'm outside alive in the deadness of my surroundings.

I'm the Lazarus. I came back from that paradoxical paradise and have no life left. I have lived it. What remains is gratuitous, free, no attachments, no importance. I have no affairs. I have no interests. These too have been scorched clean.

Now I must get rid of the unreality. I must vomit. I must eject this darkness. I must plead with you, Mr Investigator, to not stop asking me questions. Do not desist, do not turn away from me.

The people? What about the people? Yes, I know, I'm the man who went down to the corner to buy cigarettes and who came back eight years later. Of course my return was a shock to my friends. I'm the 'happening' in the slur of their daily existence which gives it a different colouring. I'm the horse in the soup. And then very quickly I'm the invisible ghost, because their lives must continue as their lives had continued for seven years and had changed and had grown finally around the absence or the arsehole which I must have been for them, the way a tree grows around a knot in its fibres.

Which is why I turn back to you, Mr Investigator, Mr I, and I talk because you must give me sounds. You must allow me to regurgitate all the words, like the arabesques of a blind mind. I am the man on the corner, with dark glasses, waiting for your coin. I am the lift attendant in Security Headquarters. Don't ask me any questions. You don't have to. You will not be able to stop the answers in any event. The black vomit must be spewed out. See here, I hold it in my hands. I have the black gloves. Feel it. Feel the gloves. Look at the glasses. I know. I know what it is like to be black in a white country.

Freedom is the minotaur outside the walls.


## ■ J. M. Coetzee (1940– ) *South Africa* (novel)

There is a sadness, an excitement, an almost solipsistic intellect at work in the adventures, allegories, and political messages of J[ohn] M[ichael] Coetzee's novels. In his magnificent allegorical novel *Waiting for the Barbarians* (1980), Coetzee centers on the predicament of a magistrate in charge of a frontier settlement, whose complicity with a despicable regime conflicts with his sense of just and decent behavior. In the end, he rebels, uncertain of the meaning of his act or its consequences. The book title comes from the allegorical poem of the same title by the Alexandrian Greek poet, Constantine Cavafy (1863–1933).

Coetzee was born in Cape Town. He was educated in South Africa and the United States as a computer scientist and a linguist. Coetzee has not written short stories; his entire fiction effort has gone into the novel. His first work was a powerful novella about Vietnam, *Dusklands* (1974) and his second, *In the Heart of the Country* (1977), is a book about an eighteenth-century Boer pioneer who exercised brutal power over a native population. In *Waiting for the Barbarians,* as in Cavafy's poem, the unseen mythical enemy justifies everything and is perceived as some kind of solution. Its unreality and its Robinson Crusoe footprints everywhere leaving fear and insecurity create a twilight zone atmosphere. The magistrate fetishizes the barbarian woman's feet, converting the symbol of fear into love, and also making himself vulnerable to the torture and repression of the government he had locally represented. Who are the real barbarians? In the end there are no answers, no solution to the right use of power.

Coetzee's *Life & Times of Michael K* (1983), with its Kafkian "K" title, treats the uncertain survival of an obsessed intellectual. It won him the esteemed Booker Prize in 1983. Coetzee was also awarded the Jerusalem Prize in 1987. The passage given here is the rich concluding chapter of *Waiting for the Barbarians.*

FURTHER READING: Coetzee, J. M. *Dusklands,* 1974; *In the Heart of the Country,* 1977; *Waiting for the Barbarians,* 1980; *Life & Times of Michael K,* 1983.

## from *Waiting for the Barbarians*

## VI

Sometimes in the mornings there are fresh hoofprints in the fields. Among the straggling bushes that mark the far limit of the ploughed land the watchman sees a shape which he swears was not there the day before and which has vanished a day later. The fisherfolk will not venture out before sunrise. Their catch has dropped so low that they barely subsist.

In two days of co-operative effort in which we laboured with our weapons at our sides, we have harvested the far fields, all that was left after the flooding. The yield is less than four cups a day for each family, but better than nothing.

Although the blind horse continues to turn the wheel that fills the tank by the lakeshore that irrigates the gardens of the town, we know that the pipe can be cut at any time and have already begun with the digging of new wells within the walls.

I have urged my fellow-citizens to cultivate their kitchen gardens, to plant root vegetables that will withstand the winter frosts. "Above all we must find ways of surviving the winter," I tell them. "In the spring they will send relief, there is no doubt of that. After the first thaw we can plant sixty-day millet."

The school has been closed and the children are employed in trawling the salty southern fingers of the lake for the tiny red crustaceans that abound in the shallows. These we smoke and pack in one-pound slabs. They have a vile oily taste; normally only the fisherfolk eat them; but before the winter is out I suspect we will all be happy to have rats and insects to devour.

Along the north rampart we have propped a row of helmets with spears upright beside them. Every half-hour a child passes along the row moving each helmet slightly. Thus do we hope to deceive the keen eyes of the barbarians.

The garrison that Mandel bequeathed us consists of three men. They take turns in standing guard at the locked courthouse door, ignored by the rest of the town, keeping to themselves.

In all measures for our preservation I have taken the lead. No one has challenged me. My beard is trimmed, I wear clean clothes, I have in effect resumed the legal administration that was interrupted a year ago by the arrival of the Civil Guard.

We ought to be cutting and storing firewood; but no one can be found who will venture into the charred woods along the river, where the fisherfolk swear they have seen fresh signs of barbarian encampments.

\* \* \*

I am woken by a pounding on the door of my apartment. It is a man with a lantern, windburnt, gaunt, out of breath, in a soldier's greatcoat too large for him. He stares at me in bewilderment.

"Who are you?" I say.

"Where is the Warrant Officer?" he replies, panting, trying to look over my shoulder.

It is two o'clock in the morning. The gates have been opened to let in Colonel Joll's carriage, which stands with its shaft resting on the ground in the middle of the square. Several men shelter in its lee against the bitter wind. From the wall the men of the watch peer down.

"We need food, fresh horses, fodder," my visitor is saying. He trots ahead of me, opens the door of the carriage, speaks: "The Warrant Officer is not here, sir, he has left." At the window, in the moonlight, I catch a glimpse of Joll himself. He sees me too: the door is slammed shut, I hear the click of the bolt inside. Peering through the glass I can make him out sitting in the dim far corner, rigidly averting his face. I rap on the glass but he pays no attention. Then his underlings shoulder me away.

Thrown out of the darkness, a stone lands on the roof of the carriage.

Another of Joll's escort comes running up. "There is nothing," he pants. "The stables are empty, they have taken every single one." The man who has unharnessed the sweating horses begins to curse. A second stone misses the carriage and nearly hits me. They are being thrown from the walls.

"Listen to me," I say. "You are cold and tired. Stable the horses, come inside, have something to eat, tell us your story. We have had no news since you left. If that madman wants to sit in his carriage all night, let him sit."

They barely listen to me: famished, exhausted men who have done more than their duty in hauling this policeman to safety out of the clutches of the barbarians, they whisper together, already re-harnessing a pair of their weary horses.

I stare through the window at the faint blur against the blackness that is Colonel Joll. My cloak flaps, I shiver from the cold, but also from the tension of suppressed anger. An urge runs through me to smash the glass, to reach in and drag the man out through the jagged hole, to feel his flesh catch and tear on the edges, to hurl him to the ground and kick his body to pulp.

As though touched by this murderous current he reluctantly turns his face towards me. Then he sidles across the seat until he is looking at me through the glass. His face is naked, washed clean, perhaps by the blue moonlight, perhaps by physical exhaustion. I stare at his pale high temples. Memories of his mother's soft breast, of the tug in his hand of the first kite he ever flew, as well as of those intimate cruelties for which I abhor him, shelter in that beehive.

He looks out at me, his eyes searching my face. The dark lenses are gone. Must he too suppress an urge to reach out, claw me, blind me with splinters?

I have a lesson for him that I have long meditated. I mouth the words and watch him read them on my lips: "The crime that is latent in us we must inflict on ourselves," I say. I nod and nod, driving the message home. "Not on others," I say. I repeat the words, pointing at my chest, pointing at his. He watches my lips, his thin lips move in imitation, or perhaps in derision, I do not know. Another stone, heavier, perhaps a brick, hits the carriage with a thunderous clatter. He starts, the horses jerk in their traces.

Someone comes running up. "Go!" he shouts. He pushes past me, beats at the door of the carriage. His arms are full of loaves. "We must go!" he shouts. Colonel Joll slips the bolt and he tumbles the loaves in. The door slams shut. "Hurry!" he shouts. The carriage heaves into motion, its springs groaning.

I grip the man's arm. "Wait!" I cry. "I will not let you go until I know what has happened!"

"Can't you see?" he shouts, beating at my grasp. My hands are still weak; to hold him I have to clasp him in a hug. "Tell me and you can go!" I pant.

The carriage is nearing the gates. The two mounted men have already passed through; the other men run behind. Stones clatter against the carriage out of the darkness, shouts and curses rain down.

"What do you want to know?" he says, struggling vainly.

"Where is everyone else?"

"Gone. Scattered. All over the place. I don't know where they are. We had to find our own way. It was impossible to keep together." As his comrades disappear into the night he wrestles harder. "Let me go!" he sobs. He is no stronger than a child.

"In a minute. How could it be that the barbarians did this to you?"

"We froze in the mountains! We starved in the desert! Why did no one tell us it would be like that? We were not beaten—they led us out into the desert and then they vanished!"

"Who led you?"

"They—the barbarians! They lured us on and on, we could never catch them. They picked off the stragglers, they cut our horses loose in the night, they would not stand up to us!"

"So you gave up and came home?"

"Yes!"

"Do you expect me to believe that?"

He glares desperately back at me. "Why should I lie?" he shouts. "I don't want to be left behind, that is all!" He tears himself loose. Shielding his head with his hands, he races through the gate and into the darkness.

*   *   *

Digging has ceased at the third well-site. Some of the diggers have already gone home, others stand around waiting for orders.

"What is the trouble?" I say.

They point to the bones lying on a heap of fresh earth: a child's bones.

"There must have been a grave here," I say. "A strange place for a grave." We are on the vacant plot behind the barracks, between the barracks and the south wall. The bones are old, they have absorbed the colour of the red clay. "What do you want to do? We can start digging again nearer the wall if you like."

They help me to climb into the pit. Standing chest-deep I scratch away the earth around the side of a jawbone embedded in the wall. "Here is the skull," I say. But no, the skull has already been dug up, they show it to me.

"Look under your feet," says the foreman.

It is too dark to see, but when I chop lightly with the mattock I strike something hard; my fingers tell me it is bone.

"They aren't buried properly," he says. He squats at the lip of the pit. "They are lying just any old how, on top of each other."

"Yes," I say. "We can't dig here, can we?"

"No," he says.

"We must fill it in and start again nearer the wall."

He is silent. He reaches out a hand and helps me clamber out. The bystanders say nothing either. I have to toss the bones back in and shovel the first earth before they will pick up their spades.

*   *   *

In the dream I stand again in the pit. The earth is damp, dark water seeps up, my feet squelch, it costs me a slow effort to lift them.

I feel under the surface, searching for the bones. My hand comes up with the corner of a jute sack, black, rotten, which crumbles away between my fingers. I dip back into the ooze. A fork, bent and tarnished. A dead bird, a parrot: I hold it by the tail, its bedraggled feathers hang down, its soggy wings droop, its eye sockets are empty. When I release it, it falls through the surface without a splash. "Poisoned water," I think. "I must be careful not to drink here. I must not touch my right hand to my mouth."

\* \* \*

I have not slept with a woman since I returned from the desert. Now at this most inappropriate of times my sex begins to reassert itself. I sleep badly and wake up in the mornings with a sullen erection growing like a branch out of my groin. It has nothing to do with desire. Lying in my rumpled bed I wait in vain for it go away. I try to invoke images of the girl who night after night slept here with me. I see her standing barelegged in her shift, one foot in the basin, waiting for me to wash her, her hand pressing down on my shoulder. I lather the stocky calf. She slips the shift up over her head. I lather her thighs; then I put the soap aside, embrace her hips, rub my face in her belly. I can smell the soap, feel the warmth of the water, the pressure of her hands. From the depths of that memory I reach out to touch myself. There is no leap of response. It is like touching my own wrist: part of myself, but hard, dull, a limb with no life of its own. I try to bring it off: futile, for there is no feeling. "I am tired," I tell myself.

For an hour I sit in an armchair waiting for this rod of blood to dwindle. In its own good time it does. Then I dress and go out.

In the night it comes back: an arrow growing out of me, pointing nowhere. Again I try to feed it on images, but detect no answering life.

"Try bread mould and milkroot," the herbalist says. "It may work. If it does not, come back to me. Here is some milkroot. You grind it and mix it to a paste with the mould and a little warm water. Take two spoonfuls after each meal. It is very unpleasant, very bitter, but be assured it will not do you any harm."

I pay him in silver. No one but children will take copper coins any more.

"But tell me," he says: "why should a fine healthy man like yourself want to kill off his desires?"

"It has nothing to do with desire, father. It is simply an irritation. A stiffening. Like rheumatism."

He smiles. I smile back.

"This must be the only shop in town they did not loot," I say. It is not a shop, just a recess and a front under an awning, with racks of dusty jars and, hanging from hooks on the wall, roots and bunches of dried leaves, the medicines with which he has dosed the town for fifty years.

"Yes, they did not trouble me. They suggested that I leave for my own good. 'The barbarians will fry your balls and eat them' — that was what they said, those were their words. I said, 'I was born here, I'll die here, I'm not leaving.' Now they are gone, and it's better without them, I say."

"Yes."

"Try the milkroot. If it doesn't work, come back."

I drink the bitter concoction and eat as much lettuce as I can, since people say that lettuce takes away one's potency. But I do all this half-heartedly, aware that I am misinterpreting the signs.

I also call on Mai. The inn had closed down, there being too little custom; now she comes in to help her mother in the barracks. I find her in the kitchen putting her baby to sleep in its cot near the stove. "I love the big old stove you have here," she says. "It keeps its warmth for hours. Such a gentle warmth." She brews tea; we sit at the table watching the glowing coals through the grate. "I wish I had something nice to offer you," she says, "but the soldiers cleaned out the storeroom, there is hardly anything left."

"I want you to come upstairs with me," I say. "Can you leave the child here?"

We are old friends. Years ago, before she married the second time, she used to visit me in my apartment in the afternoons.

"I'd rather not leave him," she says, "in case he wakes up alone." So I wait while she wraps the child, and then follow her up the stairs: a young woman still, with a heavy body and shapeless spreading thighs. I try to recall what it was like with her, but cannot. In those days all women pleased me.

She settles the child on cushions in a corner, murmuring to it till it falls asleep again.

"It is just for a night or two," I say. "Everything is coming to an end. We must live as we can." She drops her drawers, trampling on them like a horse, and comes to me in her smock. I blow out the lamp. My words have left me dispirited.

As I enter her she sighs. I rub my cheek against hers. My hand finds her breast; her own hand closes over it, caresses it, pushes it aside. "I am a bit sore," she whispers. "From the baby."

I am still searching for something I want to say when I feel the climax come, far-off, slight, like an earth-tremor in another part of the world.

"This is your fourth child, isn't it?" We lie side by side under the covers.

"Yes, the fourth. One died."

"And the father? Does he help?"

"He left some money behind. He was with the army."

"I am sure he will come back."

I feel her placid weight against my side. "I have grown very fond of your eldest boy," I say. "He used to bring me my meals while I was locked up." We lie for a while in silence. Then my head begins to spin. I re-emerge from sleep in time to hear the tail-end of a rattle from my throat, an old man's snore.

J. M. Coetzee **1473**

She sits up. "I will have to go," she says. "I can't sleep in such bare rooms, I hear creaking all night." I watch her dim shape move as she dresses and picks up the child. "Can I light the lamp?" she says. "I'm afraid of falling on the stairs. Go to sleep. I will bring you breakfast in the morning, if you don't mind millet porridge."

\* \* \*

"I liked her very much," she says. "We all did. She never complained, she always did what she was asked, though I know her feet gave her pain. She was friendly. There was always something to laugh about when she was around."

Again I am as dull as wood. She labours with me: her big hands stroke my back, grip my buttocks. The climax comes: like a spark struck far away over the sea and lost at once.

The baby begins to whimper. She eases herself away from me and gets up. Big and naked, she walks back and forth across the patch of moonlight with the baby over her shoulder, patting it, crooning. "He will be asleep in a minute," she whispers. I am half asleep myself when I feel her cool body settle down again beside me, her lips nuzzle my arm.

\* \* \*

"I don't want to think about the barbarians," she says. "Life is too short to spend worrying about the future."

I have nothing to say.

"I don't make you happy," she says. "I know you don't enjoy it with me. You are always somewhere else."

I wait for her next words.

"She told me the same thing. She said you were somewhere else. She could not understand you. She did not know what you wanted from her."

"I didn't know you and she were intimate."

"I was often here, downstairs. We talked to each other about what was on our minds. Sometimes she would cry and cry and cry. You made her very unhappy. Did you know that?"

She is opening a door through which a wind of utter desolation blows on me.

"You don't understand," I say huskily. She shrugs. I go on: "There is a whole side to the story you don't know, that she could not have told you because she did not know it herself. Which I don't want to talk about now."

"It is none of my business."

We are silent, thinking our own thoughts about the girl who tonight sleeps far away under the stars.

"Perhaps when the barbarians come riding in," I say, "she will come riding with them." I imagine her trotting through the open gateway at the head of a troop of horsemen, erect in the saddle, her eyes shining, a forerunner, a guide, pointing out to her comrades the lay of this foreign town where she once lived. "Then everything will be on a new footing."

We lie in the dark thinking.

"I am terrified," she says. "I am terrified to think what is going to become of us. I try to hope for the best and live from day to day. But sometimes all of a sudden I find myself imagining what might happen and I am paralyzed with fear. I don't know what to do any more. I can only think of the children. What is going to become of the children?" She sits up in the bed. "What is going to become of the children?" she demands vehemently.

"They won't harm the children," I tell her. "They won't harm anyone." I stroke her hair, calm her, hold her tight, till it is time again to feed the baby.

\* \* \*

She sleeps better downstairs in the kitchen, she says. She feels more secure when she can wake up and see the glow of coals in the grate. Also she likes to have the child with her in the bed. Also it is better if her mother does not find out where she spends the nights.

I too feel it was a mistake and do not visit her again. Sleeping alone, I miss the scent of thyme and onion on her fingertips. For an evening or two I experience a quiet, fickle sadness, before I begin to forget.

\* \* \*

I stand out in the open watching the coming of the storm. The sky has been fading till now it is bone-white with tones of pink rippling in the north. The ochre rooftiles glisten, the air grows luminous, the town shines out shadowless, mysteriously beautiful in these last moments.

I climb the wall. Among the armed dummies stand people staring out towards the horizon where a great cloud of dust and sand already boils up. No one speaks.

The sun turns coppery. The boats have all left the lake, the birds have stopped singing. There is an interval of utter silence. Then the wind strikes.

In the shelter of our homes, with the windows bolted and bolsters pushed against the doors, with fine grey dust already sifting through roof and ceiling to settle on every uncovered surface, film the drinking water, grate on our teeth, we sit thinking of our fellow-creatures out in the open who at times like this have no recourse but to turn their backs to the wind and endure.

\* \* \*

In the evenings, in the hour or two I can afford at the fireplace before my ration of wood gives out and I must creep into bed, I occupy myself in my old hobbies, repairing as best I can the cases of stones I found smashed and tossed away in the courthouse gardens, toying again with the decipherment of the archaic writing on the poplar slips.

It seems right that, as a gesture to the people who inhabited the ruins in the desert, we too ought to set down a record of settlement to be left for posterity buried under the walls of our town; and to write such a history no one would seem to be better fitted than our last magistrate. But when I sit down at my writing-table, wrapped against the cold in my great old bearskin, with a single candle (for tallow too is rationed) and a pile of yellowed documents at my elbow, what I find myself beginning to write is not the annals of an imperial outpost or an account of how the people of that outpost spent their last year composing their souls as they waited for the barbarians.

"No one who paid a visit to this oasis," I write, "failed to be struck by the charm of life here. We lived in the time of the seasons, of the harvests, of the migrations of the waterbirds. We lived with nothing between us and the stars. We would have made any concession, had we only known what, to go on living here. This was paradise on earth."

For a long while I stare at the plea I have written. It would be disappointing to know that the poplar slips I have spent so much time on contain a message as devious, as equivocal, as reprehensible as this.

"Perhaps by the end of the winter," I think, "when hunger truly bites us, when we are cold and starving, or when the barbarian is truly at the gate, perhaps then I will abandon the locutions of a civil servant with literary ambitions and begin to tell the truth."

I think: "I wanted to live outside history. I wanted to live outside the history that Empire imposes on its subjects, even its lost subjects. I never wished it for the barbarians that they should have the history of Empire laid upon them. How can I believe that that is cause for shame?"

I think: "I have lived through an eventful year, yet understand no more of it than a babe in arms. Of all the people of this town I am the one least fitted to write a memorial. Better the blacksmith with his cries of rage and woe."

I think: "But when the barbarians taste bread, new bread and mulberry jam, bread and gooseberry jam, they will be won over to our ways. They will find that they are unable to live without the skills of men who know how to rear the pacific grains, without the arts of women who know how to use the benign fruits."

I think: "When one day people come scratching around in the ruins, they will be more interested in the relics from the desert than in anything I may leave behind. And rightly so." (Thus I spend an evening coating the slips one by one in linseed oil and wrapping them in an oilcloth. When the wind lets up, I promise myself, I will go out and bury them where I found them.)

I think: "There has been something staring me in the face, and still I do not see it."

\*　\*　\*

The wind has dropped, and now the snowflakes come floating down, the first fall of the year, flecking the rooftiles with white. All morning I stand at my window watching the snow fall. When I cross the barracks yard it is already inches deep and my footsteps crunch with an eerie lightness.

In the middle of the square there are children at play building a snow-man. Anxious not to alarm them, but inexplicably joyful, I approach them across the snow.

They are not alarmed, they are too busy to cast me a glance. They have completed the great round body, now they are rolling a ball for the head.

"Someone fetch things for the mouth and nose and eyes," says the child who is their leader.

It strikes me that the snowman will need arms too, but I do not want to interfere.

They settle the head on the shoulders and fill it out with pebbles for eyes, ears, nose and mouth. One of them crowns it with his cap.

It is not a bad snowman.

This is not the scene I dreamed of. Like much else nowadays I leave it feeling stupid, like a man who lost his way long ago but presses on along a road that may lead nowhere.

## ■ Arthur Nortje (1942–1970)
### *South Africa* (poems)

Born in South Africa in 1942, (Kenneth) Arthur Nortje died of an apparent suicide when he overdosed on sleeping pills in England only days away from his twenty-eighth birthday. He leaves behind a collection of sensual poems that hypnotizes and carries one to a place of exiles and misfits. Seldom anthologized, his voluptuous free verse, as in the closing of "Immigrant," found in *Dead Roots,* reads like literary erotica: "Maybe she is like you, maybe most women / deeply resemble you, all of them are / all things to all poets: the cigarette girl / in velvet with mink nipples, fishnet thighs, / whose womb is full of tobacco / Have a B.C. apple in the A.D. city of the savior, / and sing the centennial song."[1]

The good and bad in Arthur Nortje's brief life formed him as a writer and, in this instance, contributed to his death. The illegitimate son of mixed Jewish and Khoikhoi ancestry, a Coloured by South African appellation, he was raised speaking Afrikaans but then moved into an English-speaking milieu in Port Elizabeth. He would speak of himself in his early poems as a "dogsbody halfbreed," a self-title he invented from his experience of apartheid. The immediate effect of apartheid on this talent was exile, which he found in England and later in British Columbia and Toronto where he taught. His wandering gave a cast to his poems, authenticated them, and made them deeper. Appropriately his best work, published posthumously, is contained in a book with the chilling and perfectly right title, *Dead Roots* (1973). In his last work, he also brought in many formulations: African oral tradition, politics, and distressing pessimism.

---

1. Arthur Nortje, *Dead Roots: Poems* (London: Heinemann, 1973), 92.

A good high school student, Nortje had to attend a segregated college, Belleville College of the Western Cape, and, after graduation in 1963, he taught in high schools for two years until in 1965 he won a scholarship to enroll in Jesus College, Oxford, which he attended for two years. Before leaving South Africa, he won recognition for his poetry and became friends with leading writers, including Richard Rive. Back in England, he found himself at the center of South Africa's best writers in exile. The freedom was at times intoxicating; it was also disturbing. It made the realities of his South African past an imperfect memory, and a personal bleakness took over. He was close to breakdown, which infected his poems in the most powerful and terrifying way: "You lie like an assassin in wait for the moon: / but your jugular swells, your wrist can stain razors." When he left for British Columbia to take a job in the town of Hope, a new desolation overcame him. He found appropriate substances—alcohol and uppers and downers—that matched his mood of discovery and his personal and political anger.

After two years, he found a position in Toronto, was further on the road of alcohol, drugs, and despair, but also was writing many of his best poems. Some of the political work suffers from generalizations in contrast with the personal cry, where political and existential merge in his singular voice. In July 1970, he was in England where he earned his B. Phil. degree at Oxford. In December, he overdosed on barbiturates. Living in an atmosphere of powerful prescription for the committed writer, Nortje was criticized for a lack of commitment, for too much commitment, and finally for being South Africa's Charles Baudelaire, the despairing poet who lived and saw the city underworld as did no poet of the nineteenth century. One could do worse than to be accused as being the incarnation of Charles Baudelaire.

FURTHER READING: Nortje, Arthur. *Lonely Against the Light,* 1973; *Dead Roots,* 1973.

## Up Late

Night here, the owners asleep upstairs
the room's eyes shut, its voices dead,
though I admire it when its mirrors
oblige me with my presence. Looking ahead
needs glancing back to what I once                                5
was, the time that mischance
borrowed my body to break it by terror.

Now the cameras rest in their elegant
leather coffins, having caught
the whirl of streets before the wheels go silent.              10
Rain trickles as the red biro writes my heart:

time demands no attention of the will,
the clock is yellow with black numerals.
The icebox resumes its purring descant.

This picture opens on the past. I rise
to study a calendar scene from what was home:
an old white mill, sentimental, South African Airways
(the blue lithe buck), peaceful, implausible. Some
fugitive sense holds back the bruising wave:
that gift to spend, my song where I arrive,
didn't I take it from the first dispiriting wilderness?

My mind burned and I shackled it
with squalid love, the violence of the flesh.
The quiet scars over my veins bit
less deep now than the knife or lash
could feel content about:
no longer need I shout
freedom in the house. I sit in light

here, the refugee's privilege. Nor do I want
fruit in a bowl, banana pleasure, the skin
that slides from my fingers, spent
because the soft heart only must be eaten.
Give me the whole experience to savour
who have known waste and also favour:
time to come may find me eloquent

in other rooms, that reminisce
of this one so composed in silence. Love,
the necessary pain, has spurred a search.
Moving from place to place I always have
come some way closer to knowing
the final sequence of song that's going
to master the solitudes that night can teach.

## London Impressions

*I*

Out of the Whitehall shadows I pass
into a blaze of sun as sudden as fountains.
Between the bronze paws of a lion
a beatnik stretches his slack indifferent muscles.

Nelson's patina of pigeon shit
hardly oppresses that plucky sailor. Cloudbanks

lazily roll in the blue heavens beyond.
The birds home in on seas of seed.

Foil tins float on the dusty water.
The walls are full of faces and thighs.                                    10
I smoke a Gold Leaf close to the filter,
viewing dimly the circles of traffic.

The isle is full of Foreign Noises
that jangle in trafalgar square,
England expects every tourist                                              15
to do his duty now the Pound is sick

## II

A girl plays games with mirrors
in Hyde Park while I'm half-suggestive
with the dolly scanning a volume idly.
In the flare of an instant it takes to light
a cigarette:                                                               5
against her treetrunk comes to lean
the ugliest bloke that you have ever seen.
Predictably they disappear
through the distance of August green.

The nymph on the grass behind                                              10
proves her point by blinding my return look.
She picks her black bag up and drifts on further,
not helpful as to whether I should follow.
Meanwhile a huge Alsatian sniffs my loose boots,
the gentleman with the leash exchanges gossip.                             15

Sun, you are all I have:
the grass already welcomes the brown leaves.
I do not want to cross the road again,
having learnt the value of other faces,
acquired the pace and tone of other voices.                               20

And big red buses; I thought I would never catch
sight of the gentle monsters
When I was young and shackled for my sharpness
in the Union of South Africa.

# Letter from Pretoria Central Prison

The bell wakes me at 6 in the pale spring dawn
with the familiar rumble of the guts negotiating
murky corridors that smell of bodies. My eyes

find salutary the insurgent light of distances.
Waterdrops rain crystal cold, my wet
face in ascent from an iron basin
greets its rifled shadow in the doorway.

They walk us to the workshop. I am eminent,
the blacksmith of the block: these active hours
fly like sparks in the furnace, I hammer metals
with zest letting the sweating muscles
forge a forgetfulness of worlds more magnetic.
The heart, being at rest, life peaceable,
your words filter softly through my fibres.

Taken care of, in no way am I unhappy,
being changed to neutral. You must decide
today, tomorrow, bear responsibility,
take gaps in pavement crowds, refine ideas.
Our food we get on time. Most evenings
I read books, Jane Austen
for elegance, agreeableness (Persuasion).

Trees are green beyond the wall, leaves through the mesh
are cool in sunshine
among the monastic white flowers of spring that floats
prematurely across the exercise yard, a square
of the cleanest stone I have ever walked on.
Sentinels smoke in their boxes, the wisps
curling lovely through the barbed wire.

Also music and cinema, yesterday double feature.
At 4 pm it's back to the cell, don't laugh
to hear how accustomed one becomes. You spoke
of hospital treatment—I see the smart nurses
bringing you grapefruit and tea—good
luck to the troublesome kidney.
Sorry there's no more space. But date your reply.

## Stephen Watson (1940– ) *South Africa* (poems)

Stephen Watson, a white South African, has published extensive literary criticism and numerous books of poetry, including his recent *The Song of the Broken String / Poems of the Lost Oral Tradition of the Xam Bushman* (1995). His poems are infused with the South African landscape and sounds of early tribal inhabitants. He makes use of neglected oral traditions, especially those of the Bushmen, as in the poem "The Rain-Sorcerer," in which we hear the click sound, signified by the double forward slash (//) before the name Kunn. The click is a characteristic of the Khoisan, or Click, linguistic family of which Xam (San) Bushman is one. Watson teaches in the English department at the University of Capetown. His latest book is *A Writer's Diary* (1997).

**FURTHER READING:** Watson, Stephen. *Presence of the Earth,* 1995; *The Song of the Broken String / Poems of the Lost Oral Tradition of the Xam Bushman,* 1995; *A Writer's Diary,* 1997.

## The Rain-Sorcerer

He was of our family, the man we called //Kunn.
He was a rain's man; he used to make rain.
He made the rain's hair, the kind falling softly.
He made the rain's legs, falling only in columns.
He would summon the cloud, this sorcerer of rain.                5

//Kunn could make rain come out of the west.
When he lived to the north, a mountain Bushman,
the rain from the west would always turn north.
//Kunn could make rain, he could move rain
to the place where he lived, in the mountain.                   10

He was one of us, this sorcerer of rain.
But he lived to the north, we to the east.
Both his father, his mother, were unknown to me.
//Kunn was old even then, when I was a child.
He was very old then. He is long since dead.                    15

He no longer dances, catching the rain-animal.
His heart no longer falls down, into the water-pit,
fetching the rain-bull, the rain in its wake.
He no longer leads it across the parched flats,
scattering its meat, its blood and milk become rain.            20

He was the last that I knew, this rain-sorcerer.
He was the very last, the man we called//Kunn—
this maker of rain, and the scent of the rain,
this sorcerer of water, of the fragrance of grass,
sorcerer of rain's hair, summoner of clouds.                    25

## A Farewell

Port city, selfsame city, in all the promiscuity of summer,
with that scruffness in your wind, salty on the leaves of shrubs,

with that sadness in your light once more, returning in the wind—
each year I add another word to the elements I've named before:
I call the light, last year windblown, now a laminate of salt;
each year I conjure colours—of amber, burnt sienna, earthy umber—
just to return to you your coastline, the khaki of a summer's day;
and the mountain by now afflicted as the moon has been by epithets,
the drab liturgy of suburbs that still eludes me like the dawns
when inland, against the light, far hills approach the harbour          1
and all along the skylines pines stand unaided, wordless, clear—
I've tried to name them all, and all the while in the good hope
that I could finally say goodbye at last, and not just learn again
thought this love of love's frustration, the futility of words,
the unattainable peninsula that is this small corner of the world.          1

## ■ Ben Okri (1951– ) *Nigeria* (novel)

In 1992, the reputation of the Nigerian novelist Ben Okri was confirmed when he was awarded the coveted international award of the
Booker Prize for his novel *The Famished Road* (1991). Born in Lagos, he
was educated at Urhobo College, in Warri, and later at the University of
Essex, in England. Unlike Chinua Achebe, leader of the preceding generation of Nigerian writers, Okri has not conformed to the moral charge
that writers focus on the corruption of national political leaders. He
touched lightly on historical themes in order to create a personal, meditative narration. His work is urban, the language standard as opposed to
"Africanized" English, the subject largely autobiographical. In 1980, he
published *Flowers and Shadows* and, in 1981, *The Landscapes Within,* whose
very title suggests the introspective meadows he wishes to describe. His
collected short stories are *Incidents at the Shrine,* 1986. With all his sophistication, Okri can summon up an elemental, mysterious quality that specifically relates his work to Latin American magic realists who slip into the
fantastic and mythological. In evoking the fantastic, he shares the mystery
of Amos Tutuola, who exploits the terror, beauty, and morality of African
tribal life. We see Okri's *African Genesis* in the wondrous opening lines of
his novel *The Famished Road:*

> In the beginning there was a river. The river became a road and the road
> branched out to the whole world. And because the road was once a river it
> was always hungry. In that land of beginnings spirits mingled with the unborn.
> We could assume numerous forms. Many of us were birds. We knew no
> boundaries. There was much feasting, playing, and sorrowing. We feasted
> much because of the beautiful terrors of eternity.

**FURTHER READING:** Okri, Ben. *Flowers and Shadows,* 1980; *The Landscapes Within,*
1981; *Incidents at the Shrine,* 1986; *The Famished Road,* 1991.

# *from* Converging City

When Agodi woke up in the morning it seemed that the spirit was still with him. Sunbeams came through the window and played on his face. The first flash of light he saw when he opened his eyes made him think of Saul's blinding. He remembered that he should pray.

He knelt by the bed in the single room and prayed through his mouth's staleness, but without his usual passion. He felt cheated of an audience. His wife had gone to the market where she sold garri. His two children were at school. When he finished his prayer he made his way over the disorder of empty sacks and blackened cooking utensils and fetched a cup of water from the earthenware pot. He washed out his mouth through the window while thinking about his financial crisis. He spat a mouthful of water down on to the street and the water fell on a girl who had just detached herself from the crowd. The girl stopped and immediately proceeded to abuse him. Her lips were painted red and she wore red earrings. Her high-heeled shoes made her legs look very thin. Agodi mimed an apology, but the girl was unappeased.

'God hammer your head,' she shouted up at him.

'Who? Me?'

'Yes, you, your very wretched self!' she said, relaxing into an impregnable posture of derision. 'It is you I am talking to, you who spits water down at people. You are a goat. You are not a man. You are a shameless fool with nothing better to do but spit water at people. You will die spitting.'

Benevolently, Agodi said: 'Is it because of a small thing like this that you're shouting, eh? If you have so many problems, I will pray for you . . .'

Interrupting, the girl said: 'Pray for your wretched self! I don't blame you. I blame your mother for allowing your father to touch her.'

Agodi was half-way through his invocation on her behalf when he heard the reference to his father. He stammered. Then thunderously he shouted: *'The devil block your anus.'*

And he tore downstairs after her.

He had rushed down one flight of stairs when he realised that all he had on was a wrapper. He stopped. He started to go back up. But the combination of sunlight on the filthy staircase and the magnitude of her insult aroused in him a peculiar humility. He decided to preach to her; there seemed no telling where a conversion might occur. He ran down the remaining flight of stairs and burst out into the street. Startled by the blasts of music pouring from the record shops, he soon found himself entangled in the hectic crowd.

He looked for the girl and saw her a little way up the road. She made furious insulting signs at him. He ran after her, shouting: 'You, this girl: the word of God is calling you today! I accept the sacrifice of your sinful life. You abuse my father, I pray for your mother. Why are you running? The word of God is calling you and you are running.'

The crowd cleared a path for him. The girl was already in full flight; she ran awkwardly in her high-heels. Agodi raged after her. Voices in the crowd asked if that was his wife fleeing from his insane desires or if she was a prostitute who had infected him with gonorrhoea. Agodi ignored the voices. Anxious to keep the girl in view, he pushed past a man who had been waddling along like a monstrous duck. Agodi's fingers were soon caught in the man's *agbada* sleeve.

'Are you mad?' The man asked, as he tripped Agodi with a wedged foot. Agodi fell, struggled back up, and found himself confronting a short man whose face was lit up with an expansive, demented smile. The man looked like an abnormally developed midget. He gathered the folds of his *agbada* on his shoulder and Agodi saw his glistening muscles and the veins bunched along his short arms.

'You want to fight?' the man asked with polite relish. He had incredible face marks. He looked as though he had been reluctantly rescued from a fire. Agodi backed away and looked regretfully at the girl, who was disappearing in the crowd.

'If you don't want to fight, then you must hapologisc now.'

Agodi apologised in the name of the Almighty. Playing with his *agbada* and slowly flexing his muscles, the man said that he found the apology unsatisfactory. Spinning up the interest of the crowd, he said that the god he worshipped accepted only dog-meat as sacrifice. Agodi stammered. With great deliberation, for a few girls had appeared in their midst, the man asked Agodi to repeat his apology. Agodi didn't hear what the man said because he became aware of everyone spitting. He grew conscious of the smell of a rotting body. Sweating and confused, Agodi wondered if the smell came from his antagonist. Then he located the corpse of an upturned and bloated cow at the side of the road. Exulting flies formed a buzzing black cloud above the swollen body. Agodi had barely recovered from the surprise when the man tapped him twice on the head. Angered by the short man's audacity, Agodi held his fists before him. He hopped and goaded the man and at the same time made pleading insinuations about the fires of hell, the agony of sinners. The man found his cue. He made a strange noise and held Agodi in a curious grip and then tossed him into the air. When Agodi landed it was with a squelchy explosion as he scattered the flies and was immediately covered in a burst of foul-smelling liquids. Beyond the wild sounds, and the jubilant flies, he saw the world pointing at him. He pulled himself out, using the horn as a lever. When he had extricated himself from the belly of the cow he found his wrapper irredeemably soaked.

The city followed him as he shambled back to the house. A contingent of flies followed him as well. The children jeered at him. The man who had hurled him into shame was meanwhile busily distributing his business cards. His gestures were magnanimous and he had a disconcerting smile for everyone. His card read: COACH IN ACTION, PROFESSIONAL EX-WRESTLER. I OFFER PROTECTION OF PROPERTY, PETROL STATIONS, COMPOUNDS AND STREETS.

AVAILABLE FOR ALL OPERATIONS. TRAINED ROUND THE WORLD. His name was Ajasco Atlas.

When he finished distributing the cards he shook hands with several people. He told them that he had just come from India. They were impressed. The girls had gathered round him. He was seen leaving with them.

\* \* \*

Agodi hid himself in the bathroom. He thought how every single person in the world had witnessed his shame. The news would certainly reach the Church of Eternal Hope. He was due to get a small loan from the church. He had been with them, as a faithful servant and crusader, for five years now. The Head Minister had explained how a church should also be a bank that keeps its members safe. The funds were controlled by a strict inner circle of elders. They gave out loans only in times of absolute need and on the strength of conduct glorifying the church. Agodi thought about all this while he washed the suppurating liquids from his body. Out of the corner of his eye, he saw a millipede crawling along the rotted plank wall. He saw three earthworms stretching their way through the wet sand that flowed out with the water. He blew his nose and his snot landed on the back of the millipede. He blamed himself severely for not having turned the other cheek; at the same time he knew that he wouldn't be alive now if he had. The ways of the world, he thought, were wickedly unjust. He dried himself and went back upstairs.

Agodi anointed himself with coconut oil. Then he lit three candles and a stick of incense and prayed for thirty minutes. The prayer consisted of one long sentence, breathlessly articulated. Wrestling with the demons of language, he asked for peace and prosperity, he begged that the news of his disgrace should not reach the church, and he wished havoc on all his enemies.

When he finished with his prayer he felt sufficiently charged. He felt that he could now possess the day. He was almost sure that the city would concede what the fervour of his prayer had sanctioned. His body ached all over. He got dressed. He wore a thread-loose French suit which conferred on him a hint of suffering dignity.

He went downstairs to his little shop, which was situated in front of the house. It was a slanted wooden shed with rusted zinc roofing. It was painted blue and it had a padlock.

He sold items of clothing: shirts, trousers, Italian shoes and fabrics, sunshades and wigs. Most of the goods had been smuggled into the country with the collaboration of officials at the docks. His signboard read: J. J. AGODI AND SONS. GENERAL CONTRACTORS. IMPORTING AND EXPORTING. TRY US FOR SIZE. A TRIAL WILL CONVICT YOU. When Agodi went in he repossessed the spirit of the shed in prayer. It was stuffy inside. The available space had been shrunken with wooden chairs and unsold goods. Old newspapers, which he had never read, were in disarray about the floor. He didn't notice the letter that had been sent to him. He tried to open the window, but found that it had got stuck. He tried to force it open, but a splinter caught in his flesh. He banged his fist against the window, half-expecting the wooden frame to disintegrate. Nothing happened. He tried the window again and it opened without fuss.

He compiled his accounts for the week. He had made very little money. No one showed much interest in his goods. Enquiries were few, buyers were even fewer. He hoped that the small consignment at the wharf would change all that. He played around with his accounts as though, by applying some mathematical trick, he could effect a multiplication. His armpits became wet. The month's rent was overdue. There was a hunger in his calculations that made him aware of the city outside the shed. He heard the scrapings of a rat. A chafer fanned past his face. A lizard scuttled half-way up the wall. Agodi caught the lizard in a gaze and was surprised that it stared back at him. He looked for an object and was lost in the multiplicity of things which could come in handy. The lizard nodded. Agodi surreptitiously eased off a shoe, threw it, and missed by several feet. The lizard nodded. Agodi grabbed a handful of newspapers and before he threw them he discovered that the lizard had gone. Only its tail writhed on the floor.

He thought about his money problems. He looked at his watch. It had stopped. He shook it and it started ticking again. He gave it an hour. He put his shoe back on. It was time for him to go out into the city.

When he stood up he saw the letter on the floor. It was addressed to the owner of the shed. He opened it and the letter read: 'To the owners of dis shop, We are coming to rub you tonite. If you like call the police. Anytime is good for us.'

Agodi read the letter three times. He creaked his neck and twisted his head. There had always been stories of people receiving letters like this. He could not remember one person who was finally robbed. If thieves are going to pay you a visit, he thought, they don't write you a letter first. But he started to pray. His voice, quivering, turned into a complaint. And the sight of the lizard's tail made him see the city beyond: he saw people lying at street corners, scratching themselves; he saw the youths who grow angrier and then sooner or later turn to armed robbery; he saw those who are executed at the beach; and he saw the children who put a piece of wood into their mouths and die four days later, poisoned by their own innocent hunger. It all came to him in the form of shapeless waves of dizziness. He believed he had just witnessed a revelation. Again he thought of Saul. The real trouble was that he had not yet eaten. He swayed with a minor fit of vertigo. He surmounted the shapes by rallying the powers of the prophets, the Head Minister of his church, and Jesu Christi.

At that moment he might have collapsed if someone hadn't pushed open the door. Saved by the prospect of business and the immediate resolve to charge more than normal, Agodi was surprised that the man who had come in didn't have on a pair of trousers; and his underpants were in very bad condition. The man was very thin and his face was angular. His hair looked as if it had never been intended to be combed. He was so wretched that Agodi screamed. Then he dived for a spanner beneath the table. The man stood staring. Then Agodi flung the spanner, the man tore out of the shed. Agodi pursued him.

The man fled across the street. He ran, blindly flailing out against the heat and the noise and the dust. He crossed the full width of the street without being hit by a vehicle. He stopped. Puzzled, he ran back. He paused in the middle of the street and looked both ways. He saw nothing, except for an old woman cycling towards him. When he saw that there were no vehicles along one of the busiest streets in the world he laughed. He also laughed at Agodi, who had rushed out of the shed, brandishing the spanner, shouting that he had single-handedly routed the thieves of the city.

The man in the street revelled in his safety. He marvelled. He rolled over on his back. Cars and buses swerved round him. Drivers abused him. Motorcyclists missed him by the narrowest of inches. Then an intractable traffic jam resulted. Streets and main roads were blocked. Cars and lorries stood bumper to bumper. The whole traffic jam soon resembled a long and obscenely metallic millipede.

The Head of State was being driven home after a hectic morning at a trade conference, when his escorts found themselves trapped in the traffic jam. The soldiers and mobile policemen thrashed out in every direction. They kicked the metalwork of cars, pounced on lorry drivers, and beat up people who seemed to be obstructing the traffic in any visible or invisible way. The heat was a tonic and the official escorts were completely in their element.

But the Head of State was furious. He felt that the traffic jam was a particularly perverse way for his people to show how much they wanted him out of office. When he stared at the congestion all around him he experienced a sudden panic. He phoned through to Intelligence and demanded an immediate unwinding of the traffic jam by any means possible. When he looked up he saw, in the shape of an earthworm moving across the tinted window, the shadow of his executioner. Watching the earthworm out of the corner of his eye, he scribbled down notes about a new decree for the swift reduction of traffic jams.

Suddenly a shot was fired, which cracked the glass, and missed his head. He fell forward, a trained, if flaccid, soldier. He heard a further volley of shots. He had heard them every night for the past five years. He clutched the notes. He waited. He heard nothing. Minutes later he was told that he was out of danger. The plotters had been killed. Then the traffic jam eased, and vehicles started to move.

The Head of State decided to change his country. He wrote down a list of decrees to be discussed as soon as possible with the Supreme Military Council. He wrote down a very long list and soon ran out of paper. As the official vehicle eased back fully into motion, the Head of State looked over his jottings. Listening to the wailing sirens, he decided that the decrees were impractical and designed only to create martyrs. He had to think of his own safety as well as the entangled safety of his embezzlements. He knew that there would be even more attempts on his life if one word got out of his new efforts to clean up the stables. For the first time, he realised that he didn't really rule the country. He had no idea who did. Hot air blew at him from the shattered window and he tore up the notes with more energy than was necessary. When his motorcade turned into his barracks, when he saw the clean stretch of tree-lined road ahead, he immediately decided that the civilians had better return. Let them carry the cross of the country. He was going where the earthworms go.

\*    \*    \*

The man in the street, who had started the traffic jam in the first place, attempted to get up. He was starving. He staggered and fell. People rushed over and picked him up. They dumped him at the side of the street. They asked him what was wrong with him and he said: sardines and Fanta. They left him in a hurry.

The man in the street lay there all through the day. He watched the dust rise. He watched the air saturate with smoke and he heard the desperate music that rode over the area. He saw arguments that led to fights. He saw the rich and how they created the poor. He saw the mice and how they fed on the poor. It amused him. He heard those with invisibly splayed feet, who were stalked all day and all night. He heard those that did the stalking. They were legion. He also heard Agodi start his Vespa and saw him ride out into the city. When Agodi was gone, the man in the street found the serenity to sleep. He nodded in his dreams.

\*    \*    \*

As Agodi rode into the city he saw people at bus stops fighting to get on the buses: and he was glad that he had maintained his Vespa. At the Iddo garage he saw two women wrestling. They tore at one another's clothes till they were both nearly naked. Agodi parked. Soon many people gathered to watch the staged fight. Three soldiers circled the barricade beside the road. A man clambered on top of a trailer and delivered himself of a lengthy speech, which few people heard, on why destruction must fall on soldiers, thieves and prostitutes. He denounced the regime. He said fire was coming; and before he finished, one of the women was thrown. Suddenly the soldiers found that their money and identity cards had been stolen. They went berserk and cracked their new horsewhips on the gathered crowd. Agodi rejoiced that he was a man of God. And rode on.

Being a man of God didn't help him at the wharf. He had to sit in a hot outshed and wait for his contact man. He waited till he began to feel dizzy with the heat. Then he went out and got himself a snack and a soft drink. When he came back he found that his contact man had been impatiently waiting for him. The contact man told Agodi straightaway that his smuggled goods had been seized.

He said: 'My friend, the Inspector is very angry with what you offered. He says it's a mere pittance. Birdshit.'

Agodi stammered.

The contact man said: 'That's the way things go.'

Agodi knew what he had to do. But he tried conversation first. He told the contact man about the wonders of God; about how a man might be one thing one day, and the exact opposite the next. Agodi preached till sweat poured into his mouth.

The contact man was neither moved nor intimidated by God's reversals. He said: 'Save your saliva, my friend. Money na hand, back na ground.'

Agodi calculated that he could spare another fifty naira. He offered. The contact man took it as an insult. He walked away slowly. Agodi swallowed.

The man said: 'They will just burn your things for nothing. You can't be serious. If you are serious you will know what to say. You have the money, my friend.'

Agodi fought his tears. He pleaded. The man ignored him. Then Agodi tried to abase himself to the point where, out of shame and human feeling, the contact man just might relent. He listed his problems.

But the contact man's face was so unforgivingly impassive it might have been made of stone. He said: 'You are wasting my time. I didn't come here to listen to your problems. I have my own *wahala*, you hear? Either you want to collect or you don't want to collect. Which one you dey, eh? Tell me, make I hear.'

Agodi made promises. The man yawned. Agodi asked for a day's grace. The contact man chewed on the idea for almost a day before he finally consented. Agodi climbed on his Vespa, feeling that he had salvaged something from a really desperate situation.

He needed money. The church was completely out of it. He had not only slackened in attendance, but there was also the business of the cow. His wife was also out of it. He owed her too much money already. Every night, when she returned from the market, she looked more burnt and punished. Her eyes were now permanently red from the dust and pepper at the market. Her cheekbones stood out in relief and her spirit had hardened. She was definitely out of it. Besides, she was paying for the children's school uniforms.

Agodi rode around the city casting for ways of getting money to save his goods. He visited friends and relatives in their offices and in their homes. They were not particularly pleased to see him. They gave him food, but they had no money to lend him. He owed most of them enough as it was. Night fell and Agodi rode back home.

* * *

The man in the street had seen a whole day pass and had learnt nothing. He had settled himself near a gutter. He covered himself with unread newspapers. He lay down as if dead, though he jerked in delirium now and again. He watched Ajasco Atlas, who had gone past a few times, shouting about his feats in India. Ajasco Atlas had been intimidating people into accepting his business cards. He told everyone that he was an ex-world champion. He told them that he was a businessman as well. All-weather. He said he participated in the capture of two cities during the war and that he had done business with even the Head of State. All day he had warned people that if they were robbed it was entirely their own fault. He considered that he had done his best in offering cheap protection. Ajasco Atlas had, in fact, opened a small office along the street and was seen doing the most astonishing exercises in public.

The man in the street also watched the shed of J. J. Agodi with special zeal. He was the only person who saw the road move. He saw the henchmen of Ajasco Atlas move. Then he saw the shed as it moved gently. He saw it raised high as if lifted by a mighty and erratic hand. Then the shed disappeared into the darkness of the street.

\* \* \*

Agodi rode into the compound and meticulously locked the Vespa. He thought about doing some very serious calculations. One hundred naira. The birds of the air feed, he thought. He had arrived at the conclusion that he would have to double his prices. He looked for his shed and he could not find it. The birds of the naira. He wandered around the compound, he went to the backyard. And still he couldn't find his shed. Saul's blindness. He called to his compound people, he called to the great wide world to come and see the extent of his suffering. Saul's one hundred naira. The world came and stared at the empty space where a battered little shed had once stood. They saw nothing except for the carcass of a lizard. They stared at the lizard and stared at Agodi. One by one they left.

Agodi sat out all night watching the space where the shed had been. He waited for his act of repossession. He abused the city. He grew hoarse. He gathered his wife and two children together. His wife was exhausted to the point of sleepwalking. He asked them to pray for the return of the shed. He started to cry and his wife severely rebuked him. The children cried and she joined them.

The man in the street, who nodded in his dreams, learned something. A very small thing. He learned where the earthworms go.

Agodi stayed up all night staring at the dead lizard. When dawn broke he fetched some holy water and poured the whole bottle on the lizard. Nothing happened. Agodi prayed and prayed. He felt the spirit leaving him. Then he called for kerosene and fire.

\* \* \*

A week later Agodi rebuilt the shed. It did not have its former glory. He did not use it. Nobody wanted to rent it either. His consignment was sold off at the wharf. Then one morning his wife took the children and fled home to her village.

Agodi suddenly disappeared. Nobody saw him for a month. When Agodi reappeared he was seen wearing a purple-and-yellow robe. He had grown a reddish beard and his hair was in tiny braids. He announced that in the forests of the city he had achieved blindness and had seen God. He declared that he was now a true prophet. God and money, he said, were inseparable. He founded a new church and had several business cards printed. His new signboards sprang up along the busy street. Ajasco Atlas was sometimes seen around the premises. Everyone has problems.

\* \* \*

While things improved, Agodi became aware of the man in the street, who had obsessively taken to watching him. Sometimes Agodi was sure that the man was making curious faces at him from across the street. And sometimes Agodi remembered the lizard that he had burned on that terrible morning. It had simply turned into air.

## ■ Mia Couto (1955– ) *Mozambique* (story)

### TRANSLATED BY DAVID BROOKSHAW

Mia Couto was born in Beira, Mozambique, in 1955. He has worked as director of the Mozambique Information Agency and written for the magazine *Tempo* and the newspaper *Noticias*. He writes in Portuguese. His first book of poetry, *Raíz de orvalho* (*Root of Dew*), came out in 1983, followed by *Voces anoitecidas* (*Voices Made Night*) (1990). He is one of the brilliant new voices of Africa.

## *The Birds of God*

Begging your pardon, I don't know anything more like a pilgrim than the river. The waves pass by on a journey which has no end. For how long has it been water's job to do that? Alone in his old dugout, Ernesto Timba measured his life. At the age of twelve he had entered the school of pulling fish from the water. Ever in the waft of the current, his shadow had reflected the laws of the river dweller for the last thirty years. And what was it all for? Drought had exhausted the earth, the seeds were not fulfilling their promise. When he returned from fishing, he had nothing to defend himself from his wife and children, who impaled him with their eyes. Eyes like those of a dog, he was loath to admit, but the truth is that hunger makes men like animals.

While he contemplated his suffering, Timba made his craft glide slowly along. Under the *mafurreira* tree, there on the bank where the river narrows, he brought the boat to rest so that he might drive away his sad thoughts. He allowed his paddle to nibble the water and the dugout clung to the stillness. But he could not stop his thoughts:

*'What life have I lived? Water, water, just nothing else.'*

As it rocked to and fro, the dugout caused his anguish to multiply.

*'One day they'll fish me out of the water, swallowed up by the river.'*

He foresaw his wife and children watching him being pulled from the mud, and it was as if the roots of the water were being torn up.

Overhead, the *mafurreira* retained the sun's fierce dispatch. But Timba wasn't listening to the tree, his eyes were peeping into his soul. And it was as if they were blind, for pain is a dust which drains light away. Still higher above, morning called and he caught the smell of the intense blue.

*'If only I belonged to the sky,'* he sighed.

And he felt the burden of thirty years of tiredness upon his life. He remembered the words of his father, uttered to teach him courage:

*'See the hunter there, what he does? He prepares his spear the moment he sees the gazelle. But the fisherman can't see the fish inside the river. The fisherman believes in something he can't see.'*

That was the lesson of the bound-to-be of life and he now recalled those wise words. It was getting late and hunger told him it was time to go home. He began to move his arm while casting a last glance upwards, beyond the clouds. It was then that a huge bird passed over the sky. It was like a king, pleased with its own majesty. The creature, high on the wing, held his eyes and an uncanny anxiety took root within him. He thought:

*'If that bird were to fall on my canoe now!'*

He uttered these words aloud. Hardly had he finished speaking than the bird shook its huge wings and quickly flew in a downward spiral towards the boat. It fell as if expelled from life. Timba picked up the damaged bird and holding it in his hands, saw that the blood had not yet unbuttoned its body. In the boat, the animal gradually recovered, until it stood up and climbed onto the prow to take stock of its survival. Timba grabbed it, and weighed its flesh in order to work out how many meals it would provide. He put the idea out of his mind, and with a shove, helped the bird to take off.

*'Be off with you, bird, go back from where you came!'*

But the bird turned round and headed back to the boat. The fisherman once again drove it away. Yet again it returned. Ernesto Timba began to despair.

*'Get back to your life, you bloody bird.'*

Nothing. The bird didn't move. It was then that the fisherman began to wonder: that thing wasn't a bird, it was a sign from God. The warning from heaven would destroy his peace of mind for ever.

Accompanied by the animal, he returned to the village. His wife celebrated his homecoming:

*'Let's have the bird for lunch!'*

Delighted, she called the children:

*'Little ones, come and see the dicky-bird.'*

Without answering, Timba placed the bird on the mat and went to the back of the house to fetch some wooden boards, wire and reeds. Then he set to work to build a cage so large that even a man could fit inside standing up straight. He put the animal inside and fed it the fish he had caught.

His wife was flabbergasted: the man was mad. Time passed and Timba only cared about the bird.

His wife would ask, pointing at the bird:

'Seeing as how hunger is pinching us, don't you want to kill it?'

Timba would raise his arm, emphatically. 'Never! Whoever touched the bird would be punished by God, would be marked down for life.'

And so the days passed by, while the fisherman awaited fresh signs of divine intentions. Countless times he lingered in the moist afternoon heat while the river sat there in front of him. When the sun went down, he would go and check the cage where the animal was growing ever fatter. Little by little, he began to notice a shadow of sadness fall over the sacred bird. He realised the creature was suffering because it was lonely. One night he asked God to send the solitary fowl a companion. The following day, the cage had a new inmate, a female. Timba silently thanked the heavens for this new gift. At the same time, anxiety took root in him: why had God entrusted him to keep these animals? What might be the message they brought?

He thought and thought. That sign, that lightning flash of white plumage, could only mean that heaven's humour was about to change. If men would agree to dispense their kindness to those messengers from heaven, then the drought would end and the season of rains would begin. It had befallen him, a poor fisherman of the river, to play host to God's envoys. It was his task to show that men could still be good. Yes, that true goodness cannot be measured in times of abundance but when hunger dances in the bodies of men.

His wife, who had returned from the *machamba*, interrupted his thoughts:

'So there are two of them now, are there?'

She came over, sat down on the same mat and looking long and hard into her companion's eyes, said:

'Husband, the pot's on the fire. I'm asking you for the neck of one of them, just one.'

It was a waste of time. Timba promised severe punishment to whoever mistreated the divine birds.

In time, the couple had chicks. There were three of them, clumsy and ugly, their gullets ever open: enough appetite to empty the river. Timba toiled on behalf of their parents. The household provisions, already so scarce, were diverted to feed the coop.

In the village, the rumour went around: Ernesto Timba was stark raving mad. His own wife, after many a threat, left home taking with her all the children. Timba didn't even seem to notice his family's absence. He was more concerned with ensuring his poultry's protection. He detected a spirit of envy around him, vengeance hatching itself. Was it his fault that he had been chosen? They said he had gone crazy. But he who is chosen by God always wanders off his path.

Then, one afternoon when he had finished his work on the river, a feeling of uncertainty set his mind aflame: the birds! He set off home at a rush. When he got near, he saw a pall of smoke rising through the trees around his house. He paddled his dugout towards the river bank, jumped out without even tying it up, and began to run towards the scene of the tragedy. When he arrived, all he saw was wreckage and ashes. The wood and wire had been chewed up by the flames. From between the boards a wing, untouched by the fire, sought to save itself. The bird must have hurled itself against the wall of flames and the wing had got away, an arrow ominously pointing towards disaster. It was not swaying to and fro, as is the obsession of dead things. It was rigid, full of certainty.

Timba stepped back, appalled. He shouted for his wife, for his children, and then, on discovering that there was nobody else to shout for, he wept such copious tears of rage that his eyes hurt.

Why? Why had they harmed those birds, pretty as they were? And there and then, amidst all the ash and the smoke, he addressed himself to God:

*'You're going to be angry, I know. You're going to punish your children. But look: I'm asking you to forgive them. Let me be the one to die, me. Leave the others to suffer what they are already suffering. You can forget the rain even, you can leave the dust lying on the ground, but please don't punish the men of this land.'*

The following day, they found Ernesto hugging the current of the river, chilled by the early morning mist. When they tried to raise him, they found him heavy and impossible to separate from the water. The strongest men were brought to the task, but their efforts were in vain. The body was stuck to the surface of the river. A strange feeling of dread spread among those present. To hide their fear, someone said:

*'Go and tell his wife. Tell the others that the village madman has died.'*

And they withdrew. As they were climbing the bank, the clouds clashed, the sky seemed to cough sullenly as if it were sick. In different circumstances, they would have celebrated the coming of the rain. Not now. For the first time, their faiths joined together pleading that it might not rain.

Impassive, the river flowed on into the distance, laughing at the ignorance of men. Ernesto Timba, gently lulled by the current, was carried downstream, and shown the by-ways he had only glimpsed in dreams.

### ■ Dambudzo Marechera (1955–1987)
### *Zimbabwe* (story)

Dambudzo Marechera had a brief productive life, dying in his thirty-second year. He attended Rhodesia University, was expelled, and obtained a fellowship at Oxford University. His collection of stories, *The House of Hunger* (1978), appeared in England in his twenty-third year, with Heinemann Publishers, the company responsible for publishing much of the brilliant writing from central and south Africa. His book was extremely well received critically, winning the Guardian Fiction Prize in 1979. It was reprinted in Zimbabwe in 1980. His two subsequent novels, *Black Sunlight* (1980) and *Mindblast* (1984), were similarly well received. In the story "Black Skin, White Mask," Marechera writes movingly and bitterly about black skin in the white world. It begins, "My skin sticks out a mile in all the crowds around here." In the tale selected here, "The Slow Sound of His Feet," Marechera creates a learned, even scholarly, nightmare, which he elaborates in a first person dramatic meditation on death in an African family. Inevitably, the remarkable story reads as a premonition of his own young death.

**FURTHER READING:** Marechera, Dambudzo. *The House of Hunger*, 1978; *Black Sunlight*, 1980; *Mindblast*, 1984.

## The Slow Sound of His Feet

> *But someday if I sit*
> *Quietly at this corner listening, there*
> *May come this way the slow sound of his feet.*
>
> —*J. D. C. Pellow*

I dreamt last night that the Prussian surgeon Johann Friedrich Dieffenbach had decided that I stuttered because my tongue was too large; and he cut my large organ down to size by snipping of chunks from the tip and the sides. Mother woke me up to tell me that father had been struck down by a speeding car at the roundabout; I went to the mortuary to see him, and they had sewn back his head to the trunk and his eyes were open. I tried to close them but they would not shut, and later we buried him with his eyes still staring upwards.

It was raining when we buried him.

It was raining when I woke up looking for him. His pipe lay where it had always been, on the mantelpiece. When I looked at it the rain came down strongly and rattled the tin roof of my memories of him. His leatherbound books were upright and very still in the bookcase. One of them was Oliver Bloodstein's *A Handbook on Stuttering*. There was also a cuneiform tablet—a replica of the original—on which was written, several centuries before Christ, an earnest prayer for release from the anguish of stuttering. He had told me that Moses, Demosthenes and Aristotle also had a speech impediment; that Prince Battus, advised by the oracle, cured himself of stuttering by conquering the North Africans; and that Demosthenes taught himself to speak without blocks by outshouting the surf through a mouthful of pebbles.

It was still raining when I lay down and closed my eyes, and I could see him stretched out in the sodden grave and trying to move his mandibles. When I woke up I could feel him inside me; and he was trying to speak, but I could not. Aristotle muttered something about my tongue being abnormally thick and hard. Hippocrates then forced my mouth open and stuck blistering substances to my tongue to drain away the dark fluid. Celsus shook his head and said: 'All that the tongue needs is a good gargle and a massage.' But Galen, who would not be left out, said my tongue was merely too cold and wet. And Francis Bacon suggested a glass of hot wine.

As I walked down to the beerhall I saw a long line of troop-carriers drawn up at the gates of the township. They were all white soldiers. One of them jumped down and prodded me with his rifle and demanded to see my papers. I had only my University student card. He scrutinized it for such a long time that I wondered what was wrong with it.

'Why are you sweating?' he asked.

I took out my paper and pencil and wrote something and showed it to him.

'Dumb, eh?'

I nodded.

'And you think I'm dumb too, eh?'

I shook my head. But before I could finish shaking my head, his hand came up fast and smacked my jaw. I brought up my hand to wipe away the blood, but he blocked it and hit me again. My false teeth cracked and I was afraid I would swallow the jagged fragments. I spat them out without bringing up my hand to my mouth.

'False teeth too, eh?'

My eyes were stinging. I couldn't see him clearly. But I nodded.

'False identity too, eh?'

I had an overwhelming desire to move my jaws and force my tongue to repeat what my student card had told him. But I only managed to croak out unintelligible sounds. I pointed to my paper and pencil which had fallen to the ground.

He nodded.

But as I bent down to pick them up, he brought up his knee suddenly and almost broke my neck.

'Looking for a stone, were you, eh?'

I shook my head and it hurt so much I couldn't stop shaking my head any more. There were running feet behind me; my mother's and my sister's voices. There was the sharp report of firing. Mother, struck in midstride, her body held rigid by the acrid air, was staring straight through her eyes. A second later, something broke inside her and she toppled over. My sister's outstretched hand, coming up to touch my face, flew to her opening mouth and I could see her straining her vocal muscles to scream through my mouth.

Mother died in the ambulance.

The sun was screaming soundlessly when I buried her. There were hot and cold rings around its wet brightness. My sister and I, we walked the four miles back home, passing the Africans Only hospital, the Europeans Only hospital, the British South Africa Police camp, the Post Office, the railway station, and walked across the mile-wide green belt, and walked into the black township.

The room was so silent I could feel it trying to move its tongue and its mandibles, trying to speak to me. I was staring up at the wooden beams of the roof. I could hear my sister pacing up and down in her room which was next to mine. I could feel her strongly inside me. My room contained nothing but my iron bed, my desk, my books, and the canvases upon which I had for so long tried to paint the feeling of the silent but desperate voices inside me. I stung back the tears and felt her so strongly inside me I could not bear it. But the door mercifully opened and they came in leading her by the hand. She was dressed in pure white. A pale blue light was emanating from her. On her slender feet were the sandals of gleaming white leather. But the magnet of her fleshless face, the two empty eye-sockets, the sharp grinning teeth (one of her teeth was slightly chipped), and high cheekbones, and the cruelly missing nose—the magnet of them held my gaze until, it seemed, my straining eyes were abruptly sucked into her rigid stillness.

He was dressed in black. Her fleshless hand lay still in his fleshless fingers. His head had not been sewn back properly; it was precariously leaning to one side and it seemed as if it would fall off any moment. His skull had a jagged crack running down from the centre of the forehead to the tip of the lower jaw; the skull had been crudely welded back into shape, so much so it looked as though it would fall apart any moment.

The pain in my eyes was unbearable. I blinked. When I opened my eyes they had gone. My sister was standing in their place. She was breathing heavily and that made my chest ache. I held out my hand and touched her: she was warm and alive and her very breath was painfully anxious in my voice. I had to speak! but before I could utter a single sound she bent down over me and kissed me. The hot flush of it shook us in each other's arms. Outside, the night was making a muffled gibberish upon the roof and the wind had tightened its hold upon the windows. We could hear, in the distance, the brass and strings of a distant military band.

# 4

# Precolumbian America, Latin America, and Caribbean

■

## INTRODUCTION

In 1839, two explorers, John Lloyd Stephens, an American archeologist, and Frederick Catherwood, an English architect and archeological artist, were in the almost impenetrable jungles of Honduras, looking for the fabled Mayan ruins of Copán. The nineteenth-century explorer Charles Gallenkamp describes their moment of encounter when they found themselves

> *in the midst of wonders exceeding their wildest expectations. Scattered about were gigantic sculptured monoliths and altars, some standing erect, others fallen over broken, their surfaces richly carved with masks, animals, human figures, and inscriptions. Huge pyramid-shaped structures reached up through the trees, scarcely visible under a thick mantle of rubble and vegetation. . . . Grotesque heads of jaguars, serpents, and mythical creatures had fallen from their facades — images of unknown gods in whose veneration the once-magnificent temples had been erected . . . wherever Stephens and Catherwood looked they saw miracles frozen in its crumbled monuments.*[1]

An earlier traveler remarked, "The genii who attended on King Solomon seem to have been the artists."[2] Three centuries earlier, the Spanish chronicler Bernal Díaz del Castillo described Cortés's first view of Tenochtitlán, the Aztec capital in Mexico (now Mexico City), stating that Cortés and his men also marveled before the splendor of temples, towers, crowded bridges, and great causeways and wondered whether it was all a dream.

The Maya city of Cobán, along with magnificent Tikal, Palenque, Uxmal, and Chichén Itzá, had actually disappeared into the concealing safety yet slow decay of the jungle four centuries before the Spanish conquerors reached Mesoamerica. But even in a period of decline, there was still much Indian culture to dazzle the Spaniards, particularly in Mexico City where Montezuma and the Aztecs were at the pinnacle of their power. The Spanish mission was to seize the material wealth of the empire, to convert the natives from their "devilish idolatry" to the "true faith" of Catholicism, and to build new cities throughout Spanish America, which the Spaniards did with enormous energy. Since the temples and written documents that preserved the Maya past were perceived as the greatest obstacles to the imposition of Christianity, temples were razed throughout "New Spain" and the great Maya and Aztec codices were burned wherever they could be discovered. The most ardent destroyer was a young Franciscan monk, Diego de Landa (1524–1579). At the age of twenty-five, he traveled the Yucatán, cleansing the pagans of their native religion by means of fire and torture. In Maní, southeast of Mérida, he discovered the greatest repository of ancient hieroglyphic books. He burned it. One of the few surviving Maya works to escape the Inquisitional fires of the Church, the epic *Popol Vuh* from the Guatemalan highlands, is a genesis and cosmology of the Quiché Maya and a monument of world literature. Paradoxically, the same ardent friar was to become the Bishop of Yucatán and write *The Relation of Things in the Yucatán*, the most important ethnological account of the area from the colonial period.

---

1. Charles Gullenkamp, *Maya: The Riddle and Rediscovery of a Lost Civilization* (3rd rev. ed.) (New York: Viking, 1985), 28.

2. Ibid.

Despite the angry flames of religious arrogance and bigotry, diverse writings from the Precolumbian periods survived, many of them oral narrations and songs recorded by churchmen in native tongue—as was the *Popol Vuh*—or in Spanish translation in the early days after the conquest. In recent decades, most of the obstacles to deciphering Maya hieroglyphs have been overcome, and the stones and remaining fragments of codices have revealed their secrets. Moreover, works in Native American languages have continued to be written in the Americas. Despite tribal and linguistic differences, we have seen Native American writings as part of a larger phenomenon of civilization in the Americas prior to and contemporaneous with the European presence.

With the conquest complete, Spanish became the tongue of chronicle and literature. New World literature begins with the discoverers and first historians, and so Columbus and Amerigo Vespucci, the geographer whose name gave us the unifying word America, were among the first authors. In his *The Royal Commentaries of Peru,* Garcilaso de la Vega Inca (1539–1695), the son of a Spanish father and Inca princess mother, was the perfect writer to transform oral memory into a history of the Incas. Living the latter part of his life in Spain, Garcilaso published his *Commentaries* there and introduced Europe to the history and fable of one of the great Precolumbian cultures. The foremost literary writer of the Spanish Americas was the Mexican nun Sor Juana Inés de la Cruz (1648/51–1695). Sor Juana's "First Dream" is the single most important and extended metaphysical poem in all Europe or the Americas.

In the nineteenth century, two Argentine writers emerged, the statesman Domingo Faustino Sarmiento (1811–1888) and the epic poet José Hernández (1834–1886), who made the gaucho the symbol of the wild outlaw hero. Two decades later, the Cuban journalist and poet José Martí (1853–1895) wrote revolutionary lyrics for the common man and woman. But the major nineteenth-century author was the Brazilian Machado de Assis (1867–1907), who in dramatic, ironic novelas captured the drama and absurdity of Brazilian middle-class lives.

Latin American writing reached its zenith, however, with the publications of the Argentine parabalist, fiction writer, and poet, Jorge Luis Borges (1899–1986). Along with Kafka and Joyce, Borges is one of the masters, innovators, and highly imitated writers of twentieth-century world literature. His younger counterparts, authors of the Latin American novel who developed and extended Borges's fantasy and magic realism, have taken over modern world literature. As the epithet the "boom novel" suggests, there was (and continues to be) an explosion of interest around the globe when the great men and women fiction writers from Latin America appeared on the scene. Beginning with Borges, who is their "fantastic" father, Julio Cortázar and Manuel Puig from Argentina, Gabriel García Márquez from Colombia, José Donoso and Isabel de Allende from Chile, Mario Vargas Llosa from Peru, Juan Rulfo and Carlos Fuentes from Mexico, Alejo Carpentier, Guillermo Cabrera Infante, and Reinaldo Arenas from Cuba have made the novel from Latin America the most translated work in the world. The bestselling novel *Like Water for Chocolate* by the Mexican novelist Laura Esquivel is the latest artistic wonder to come out of Latin America. In her engaging, experimental, historical, and enthralling novel, she has given us, in concise and specific speech, a drama of women and men in the panorama of the early twentieth century.

There have been great poets from Latin America—the Chileans Gabriela Mistral and Pablo Neruda, Octavio Paz from Mexico (all three Nobel Prize laureates), the Peruvian César Vallejo and the Brazilian Carlos Drummond de Andrade. These poets have been abundantly and excellently translated by the best poets in the English language and consequently have had a profound effect on the development of poetry in English. Before World War II, it was to France that American and British poets went for models. So T. S. Eliot found Jules Laforgue and Tristan Corbiere when he wanted to introduce a waste land city life into American poetry; Wallace Stevens went to the French symbolist poets, especially Mallarmé; and the humor and typographical trickery of e. e. cummings is inconceivable without the earlier *Calligrammes* of the French poet Guillaume Apollinaire. But after World War II, it was the Russian, Greek, Spanish, and Spanish American poets who replaced the French. Since Spanish is a language accessible to many English-speaking readers (unlike Russian and Modern Greek), our leading poets, W. S. Merwin, Robert Bly, Denise Levertov, Robert Lowell, Richard Wilbur, and Mark Strand have translated from the Spanish. Elizabeth Bishop, the leading woman poet of her generation, lived for more than a decade in Brazil. She not only translated Drumond de Andrade (1902– ) and Joao Cabral de Melo Neto (1920– ) but coedited with Mark Strand an anthology of very important contemporary Brazilian poets with magnificent translations by American poets.

From the Caribbean, we also have many world-famous authors, such as the French-writing poet Aimé Césaire (1913– ), whose surreal writings link Caribbean Martinique with Paris and Africa; the East Indian Trinidadian V. S. Naipaul (1932– ), whose novels and reportage link his island with London, India, and Africa; and the 1992 Nobel poet Derek Walcott (1924– ) from Saint Lucia, whose epic poem *Omeros* owes its sources to Homeric Greek, to Africa, and to his Carib islands.

The twentieth century ends with the dissolution of cultural borders. As Asia and Africa have become part of our reading habit, so too have Latin America and the Caribbean. From Boston and New York all the way down to Borges's gaucho pampas and Pablo Neruda's southernmost Chilean mountains near the Arctic circle, we now witness the reality of the writers in all the Americas.

# Native American Literature of Precolumbian and Later Periods

EDITED BY GORDON BROTHERSTON AND WILLIS BARNSTONE

## INTRODUCTION

B efore Columbus set sail, literature had been evolving in the Americas for thousands of years, along with agriculture (plant genetics), medicine, mathematics, astronomy, architecture, weaving, metallurgy, and many other orders of knowledge. This great endeavor, which is largely unrivaled anywhere, was the work of peoples whose survivors are today commonly referred to as American Indians or Native Americans. Modern analysis of their languages, as of their blood, confirms their long occupation of America, north and south, and that they were and are the true authors of culture in their continent.

In 1492, the Old World from which Columbus set sail was customarily thought of as threefold, with Asia, Europe, and Africa respectively in first, second, and third positions. America came to be perceived as the "fourth part of the world" *(quarta orbis pars),* or simply the "Fourth World." In recent decades, this term has been adopted by George Manuel and other Native Americans. It helps to establish a comparability among all four worlds, in terms of their "cumulative history," when in practice, America has been more thoroughly dispossessed than the other three. For, despite native resistance that continues even today, Columbus announced a destruction of people and culture so violent and cynical as to defy belief.

Fourth-World texts, Native Americans' accounts of themselves and their place, constitute a great neglected chapter of world literature. Based on and transcribed in part from scripts and recording systems developed in the first millennium B.C. or earlier, these texts range from cosmogony—the story of the world ages and the epic of human emergence told from one end of the continent to the other—to history and annals, from poetry to law. Yet throughout we find the same literary recurrence to the guardian mountains of creation, the bird messengers, and the revered plants that sustain humankind—manioc, maize or corn in all its colors, beans, squash, potatoes, quinoa, to mention but a few. Paramount among these texts stands the *Popol Vuh,* written by the Quiche-Maya in the sixteenth century in what is now Guatemala. Its ingenuity as a text and the scale of the knowledge it encodes as a genesis make it a classic not just of the Fourth World but of world literature. In turn, this literary wealth has become an ever more immediate source for Americans writing in imported languages like Portuguese, Spanish, French, and English. An exemplary case is that of the Guatemalan Miguel Angel Asturias, who won the Nobel Prize thanks to *Hombres de maíz* (1949; *Men of Maize*), a novel that draws profoundly on the *Popol Vuh.*

Encompassing no more than a fraction of major Fourth-World texts, the selections here focus on seven language traditions, which range geographically over the Andes and the rainforest of South America, then Mexico and Mesoamerica. Each of these traditions lives today along with a wealth of texts that lead us back to the great American story of genesis. As the language of the former Inca empire, Tahuantinsuyu, Quechua has had a continuous visible presence for us since the sixteenth century, when it was first transcribed into the alphabet. The same is true of the languages that survived from the empires of Mesoamerica, Nahuatl (the language of the Aztecs and their Toltec forebears), and lowland and highland Maya.

Generally Fourth-World texts first entered the Western tradition already in translation, through the reports of missionaries and conquistadors and the works of early historians, native and European. From the start, there was an appreciation of their literary qualities, as in Ixtlilxochitl's commentary in Spanish on the lyrics of his ancestor Nezahualcoyotl, or Montaigne's famous remark on the "Anacreontic" style of a poem in Tupi-Guarani (a major South American language not represented here). J. G. Herder's *Stimmen der Völkern in Liedern* (1797), one of the first attempts to anthologize world literature, included Quechua hymns and poems, and in the following century D. G. Brinton published a range of texts in the nine volumes of his remarkable *Library of Aboriginal American Literature* (1882–1890). Yet only in the last three or four decades have many key works been edited and translated adequately for the first time, especially into English, which had lagged notably behind German, French, and Spanish. In the process, anthropology and literature have intelligently conjoined, as will be apparent from many of the more recent translations included here by Edmonson, Rothenberg, Tarn, Tedlock, Guss, Burns, and several others. At the same time, the verse tradition of both Nahuatl and Quechua, once the languages of Aztec and Inca, have repeatedly attracted the attentions of translators who are poets in their own right.

Within each language section, the arrangement is broadly chronological and ends with work of recent years that often bears an author's name. The longer Quechua and Nahuatl sections draw on a wealth of sixteenth-century texts transcribed from Inca and Aztec antecedents, where dates of transcription or publication are often unhelpful, and a more thematic sequence has been preferred. Here, the opening pieces are chosen to reflect the moment of encounter with Europe.

—Gordon Brotherston

# Quechua Language

Known in various dialects, for example the northern Quichua, Quechua is the major American language to have survived from precolumbian times. It was the common tongue *(runasimi)* of the Inca empire Tahuantinsuyu or "Four Districts" that centered on Cuzco. Today, it is spoken by more than ten million people in the Andean countries that once made up Tahuantinsuyu (Peru, Bolivia, northern Argentina, Ecuador, southern Colombia), and it has been declared a second official language in Peru and Ecuador. Native and Spanish historians mention several Quechua texts, for example, hymns to the deity Viracocha, that in the sixteenth century were transcribed from the Inca recording medium, the knotted-string *quipu,* whole libraries of which were burnt by the European invaders. Quechua is also renowned for its vigorous tradition in drama and music, a cycle of Inca kingship plays, and a rich repertoire of poetry and song that continues into this century and affirms resistance to modern assaults on native lands, economy, and language.

Only a few Quechua poems have found their way to literary translation into English, which presumably reproduces the quality and beauty of the original version. Just as the Spanish Arabist Juan García Gómez translated poetry of Arabic Spain into Spanish and thereby for the first time gave Spanish writers (particularly Federico García Lorca) a real awareness of their Moorish past, so the translation of even a few Native American poems into Spanish brings alive the silent literature of the Americas. From the Spanish, two of America's best and most skillful poets and poet translators, Mark Strand and W. S. Merwin, have given us a taste of Quechuan lyrics. Those familiar with popular song of many civilizations in all continents will easily recognize common thematic and prosodic elements that appear and reappear in the world's oral and written poetry.

**FURTHER READING:** *18 Poems from the Quechua.* Translated by Mark Strand, 1971. W. S. Merwin. *Selected Translations: 1948–1968,* 1968.

—Gordon Brotherston and editors

■ **Apu Inca Atawallpaman (Sixteenth Century)**
*Peru* **(poem)**

TRANSLATED BY W. S. MERWIN

Although he satisfied Pizarro's inordinate demands for gold as ransom, the Inca emperor Atahuallpa was nonetheless murdered by the conquistadors in Cajamarca in 1533. The shock was felt throughout the four districts of Tahuantinsuyu, as numerous native texts testify, including dramas that continued the Inca kingship cycle and are still performed in the Andes today. This lament closely resembles speeches made in those dramas yet has a strong elegiac quality of its own.

## from *The Elegy for the Great Inca Atawallpa*

> . . . You all by yourself fulfilled
>        Their malignant demands,
> But your life was snuffed out
>        In Cajamarca.
>
> Already the blood has curdled
>        In your veins,
> And under your eyelids your sight
>        Has withered.
> Your glance is hiding in the brilliance
>        Of some star.
>
> Only your dove suffers and moans
>        And drifts here and there.
> Lost in sorrow, she weeps, who had her nest
>        In your heart.
>
> The heart, with the pain of this catastrophe,
>        Shatters.
> They have robbed you of your golden litter
>        And your palace.
> All of your treasures which they have found
>        They have divided among them.
>
> Condemned to perpetual suffering,
>        And brought to ruin,
> Muttering, with thoughts that are elusive
>        And far away from this world,
> Finding ourselves without refuge or help,
>        We are weeping,

And not knowing to whom we can turn our eyes,
    We are lost.

Oh sovereign king,
    Will your heart permit us                                  *30*
To live scattered, far from each other,
    Drifting here and there,
Subject to an alien power,
    Trodden upon?

Discover to us your eyes which can wound                          *35*
    Like a noble arrow;
Extend to us your hand which grants
    More than we ask,
And when we are comforted with this blessing
    Tell us to depart.                                              *40*

## ▪ The Huarochiri Manuscript (1608) *Peru* (prose narration)

### TRANSLATED BY FRANK SALOMON AND GEORGE URIOSTE

Often referred to as the "Popol Vuh of the Andes," this remarkable text comes from Huarochiri, which lies between the old Inca capital Cuzco and the coastal capital Lima established by the Spanish. It threads through its thirty-one chapters the story of the American world ages that end in flood, eclipse, volcanic fire, and hurricane. It was recorded as part of the Jesuit-trained Francisco de Avila's efforts to extirpate native religion, and it deals explicitly with the relative status of Viracocha, the deity imposed by Cuzco, and local gods like Paria Caca, who features in the world age story and becomes the principal *huaca* or shrine mountain of the region. This accounts for the rather irreverent account of Viracocha's behavior in which he adopts undignified subterfuge in order to impregnate a woman at the same time that he raises the structures of civilization.

Only a few native documents deal with the forty-year Spanish invasion of the vast Inca empire. Among the most valuable of these is the sixteenth-century Quechua text known as the Huarochiri Narrative. It consists of oral and written reports gathered by Francisco de Avila in the area around Huarochiri, Checa, and Yauyos (on the road from Lima to Cuzco). In chapter 2, we hear a version of parthenogenesis that is closely related to the origins of the Inca state. In the early heroic days of the gods, it is said, Viracocha both founded the towns of the state and established himself as superior to other gods who represented only local interests. At first, less prepossessing than they, he nonetheless ousts them "in his wisdom" and reveals himself as nothing less than a solar father, "enlightening the earth," like his later representative, the Sapa Inca.

The tale is filled with humorous ironies that humanize the gods and universalize them as the insecure yet arrogant gods of every civilization. Clearly, the mother is ashamed of the godman who claims to be the father, and she feels pity for her child. Viracocha, liked a spurned Zeus, attempts to impress the virgin mother with his potential magnificence. While the other gods tremble, he dons a golden suit (Zeus resorted to golden rain in his seduction); then (like the sungod Apollo who was spurned by Daphne), he uses his power to light up the world.

FURTHER READING: *The Huarochiri Manuscripts: A Testament of Ancient and Colonial Andean Religion*. Translated by Frank Salomon, 1991.

# Chapter 1

## HOW THE IDOLS OF OLD WERE, AND HOW THEY WARRED AMONG THEMSELVES, AND HOW THE NATIVES EXISTED AT THAT TIME

In ancient times, there were *huacas* named Yana Namca and Tuta Namca.
   Later, another *huaca* named Huallallo Caruincho defeated them.
   After he defeated them, he ordered the people to bear two children and no more.
   He would eat one of them himself.
   The parents would raise the other, whichever one was loved best.

Although people did die in those times, they came back to life exactly on the fifth day.
   And as for their foodstuffs, they ripened exactly five days after being planted.
   These villages and all the others like them were full of Yunca.

When a great number of people had filled the land, they lived miserably, scratching and digging the rock faces and ledges to make terraced fields.
   These fields, some small, others large, are still visible today on all the rocky heights.
   And all the birds of that age were perfectly beautiful, parrots and toucans all yellow and red.

Later, at the time when another huaca named Paria Caca appeared, these beings and all their works were cast out to the hot Anti lands by Paria Caca's actions.
   Further on we'll speak of Paria Caca's emergence and of his victories.

There was another *huaca* named Cuni Raya.
   Regarding him, we're not sure whether he existed before Paria Caca or maybe after him.

However, Cuni Raya's essential nature almost matches Vira Cocha's,[1] for when people worshiped this *huaca*, they would invoke him, saying,

"Cuni Raya Vira Cocha,

You who animate mankind,

Who charge the world with being,

All things are yours!

Yours the fields and yours the people."

And so long ago, when beginning anything difficult, though they couldn't see Vira Cocha, the ancients used to throw coca leaves to the ground, talk to him, and worship him before all others, saying,

"Help me remember how,

Help me work it out,

Cuni Raya Vira Cocha!"

And the master weaver would worship and call on him whenever it was hard for him to weave.

For that reason, we'll write first about this *huaca* and about his life, and later on about Paria Caca.

# Chapter 2

## HOW CUNI RAYA VIRA COCHA ACTED IN HIS OWN AGE. THE LIFE OF CUNI RAYA VIRA COCHA. HOW CAUI LLACA GAVE BIRTH TO HIS CHILD, AND WHAT FOLLOWED

A long, long time ago, Cuni Raya Vira Cocha used to go around posing as a miserably poor and friendless man, with his cloak and tunic all ripped and tattered. Some people who didn't recognize him yelled, "You poor lousy[2] wretch!"

Yet it was this man who fashioned all the villages. Simply by speaking he made the fields, and finished the terraces with walls of fine masonry. As for the irrigation canals, he channeled them out from their sources simply by tossing down the flower of a reed called *pupuna*.

---

1. Because of his alleged importance as a supreme deity, comparable to the Christian God, Vira Cocha has become the subject of a large and frequently misleading literature. Here, however, this deity's role has little to do with the Christian concept of God and a lot in common with the pan-New World concept of a Trickster, whose buffoonery is at the same time a force making and remaking the world.

2. Lice have a peculiar double meaning; Marie-France Souffez (1986), relying partly on findings by Christopher Donnan and Maria Rostworowski, notes that in Mochica imagery of shamanism the lice growing on a shaman's body emblematize the many people her or his power can sustain. Latent wealth hidden in apparent squalor is a common attribute of Huarochiri protagonists.

After that, he went around performing all kinds of wonders, putting some of the local *huacas* to shame with his cleverness.

Once there was a female *huaca* named Caui Llaca.

Caui Llaca had remained a virgin.

Since she was very beautiful, every one of the *huacas* and *villcas*[3] longed for her. "I've got to sleep with her!" they thought.

But she never consented.

Once this woman, who had not allowed any male to fondle[4] her, was weaving beneath a *lúcuma* tree.

Cuni Raya, in his cleverness, turned himself into a bird and climbed into the *lúcuma.*

He put his semen into a ripened fruit and dropped it next to the woman.

The woman swallowed it down delightedly.

Thus she got pregnant even though she remained untouched by man.

In her ninth month, still a virgin, she gave birth just as other women give birth.

And for one year she nursed her child at her breast, wondering, "Whose child could this be?"

In the fullness of the year, when the youngster was crawling around on all fours, she summoned all the *huacas* and *villcas* to find out who was the child's father.

When the *huacas* heard the message, they were overjoyed, and they came dressed in their best clothes, each saying to himself, "It's me!" "It's me she'll love!"

This gathering took place at Anchi Cocha, where the woman lived.

When the *huacas* and *villcas* had taken their seats there, that woman addressed them:

"Behold, gentlemen and lords. Acknowledge this child. Who made me pregnant?"[5] One by one she asked them:

"Was it you?"

"Was it you?"

But nobody answered, "The child is mine."

The one called Cuni Raya Vira Cocha had taken his seat at the edge of the gathering. Since he looked like a friendless beggar, and since so many

---

3. Internal evidence (chap. 31, sec. 417) suggests that in the Huarochirí context it means a person who has entered into the society of *huacas* by achievement or marriage. In the *Tratado* (Arguedas and Duviols 1966: 209), the word *villca* is translated "a very important *cacique*" (*cacique muy principal;* see also Zuidema 1973: 19). In Huánchor village in 1621, the founding hero Huánchor was mummified and housed underneath a *huaca* called Huanchorvilca (Arguedas and Duviols 1966: 264). Overall, the implication seems to be that a *villca* is a human being who partakes of a *huaca*'s status.

4. *chancaycochicuspa* "fondle": González Holguín ([1608] 1952:94) glosses related verbs as meaning "to stroke or touch lightly." Similar verbs in modern Quechua usually sound sexually piquant.

5. *yumahuarcanquichic* "made me pregnant": The root is yumay "sperm." "The literal sense is "inseminated me."

handsome men were present, she spurned him and didn't question him. She thought, "How could my baby possibly be the child of that beggar?"

Since no one had said, "The child is mine," she first warned the *huacas*, "If the baby is yours, it'll crawl up to you," and then addressed the child:

"Go, identify your father yourself!"

The child began at one end of the group and crawled along on all fours without climbing up on anyone, until reaching the other end, where its father sat.

On reaching him the baby instantly brightened up and climbed onto its father's knee.

When its mother saw this, she was indignant: "Atatay, what a disgrace! How could I have given birth to the child of a beggar?" she said. And taking only her child, she headed straight for the ocean.

Then, while all the local *huacas* stood in awe, Cuni Raya Vira Cocha put on his golden garment. He started to chase her at once, thinking, "She'll be overcome by sudden desire for me."

"Sister Caui Llaca!" he called after her. "Here, look at me! Now I'm really beautiful!" he said, and he stood making his garment glitter.[6]

Caui Llaca didn't even turn her face back to him.

"Because I've given birth to the child of such a ruffian, such a mangy beggar, I'll just disappear into the ocean," she said. She headed straight out into the deep sea near Pacha Camac, where even now two stones that clearly look like people stand.

And when she arrived at what is today her dwelling, she turned to stone.

Yet Cuni Raya Vira Cocha thought, "She'll see me anyway, she'll come to look at me!" He followed her at a distance, shouting and calling out to her.

First, he met a condor.

"Brother, where did you see that woman?" he asked him.

"Right near here. Soon you'll find her," replied the condor.

Cuni Raya Vira Cocha said to him,

"You'll live a long life. You alone will eat any dead animal from the wild mountain slopes, both guanacos and vicuñas, of any kind and in any number. And if anybody should kill you, he'll die himself."

Farther on, he met a skunk.

"Sister, where did you meet that woman?" he asked.

"You'll never find her now. She's gone far away," replied the skunk.

When she said this, he cursed her hatefully, saying,

---

6. If Cuni Raya is indeed a water deity, as Rostworowski (1977) persuasively argues, his glittering garment may be a metaphor for water sparkling in sunlight.

"Because of what you've told me, you'll never go around in the daytime. You'll only walk at night, stinking disgustingly. People will be revolted by you."

Next he met a puma.

"She just passed this way. She's still nearby. You'll soon reach her," the puma told him.

Cuni Raya Vira Cocha spoke to him, saying,

"You'll be well beloved. You'll eat llamas, especially the llamas of people who bear guilt. Although people may kill you, they'll wear you on their heads during a great festival and set you to dancing. And then when they bring you out annually they'll sacrifice a llama first and then set you to dancing."

Then he met a fox.

"She's already gone way far away. You'll never find her now," that fox told him.

When the fox said this, he replied,

"As for you, even when you skulk around keeping your distance, people will thoroughly despise you and say, 'That fox is a sneak thief.' When they kill you, they'll carelessly throw you away and your skin, too."

Likewise he met a falcon.

"She's just passed this way. You'll soon find her," said the falcon.

He replied.

"You're greatly blessed. When you eat, you'll eat the hummingbird first, then all other birds. When people kill you, the man who has slain you will have you mourned with the sacrifice of a llama. And when they dance, they'll put you on their heads so you can sit there shining with beauty."

And then he met some parakeets.

"She's already gone far away. You'll never find her now," the parakeets told him.

"As for you, you'll travel around shrieking raucously," replied Cuni Raya Vira Cocha. "Although you may say, 'I'll spoil your crops!' when people hear your screaming they'll chase you away at once. You'll live in great misery amidst the hatred of humans."

And so he traveled on. Whenever he met anyone who gave him good news, he conferred on him good fortune. But he went along viciously cursing those who gave him bad news.

When he reached the seashore, he went straight over it. Today people say, "He was headed for Castile," but in the old days people said, "He went to another land, another world," and he turned back toward Pacha Camac.

He arrived at the place where Pacha Camac's two daughters lived, guarded by a snake.

Just before this, the two girls' mother had gone into the deep sea to visit Caui Llaca. Her name was Urpay Huachac.

While Urpay Huachac was away, Cuni Raya Vira Cocha seduced one girl, her older daughter.

When he sought to sleep with the other sister, she turned into a dove and darted away.

That's why her mother's name means 'Gives Birth to Doves'.

At that time there wasn't a single fish in the ocean.

Only Urpay Huachac used to breed them, at her home, in a small pond.

It was these fish, all of them, that Cuni Raya angrily scattered into the ocean, saying, "Why did she visit Caui Llaca, the woman of the ocean depths?"

Ever since, fish have filled the sea.

Then Cuni Raya Vira Cocha fled along the seashore.

When Urpay Huachac's daughters told her how he'd seduced them, she got furious and chased him.

As she followed him, calling him again and again, he waited for her and said, "Yes?"

"Cuni, I'm just going to remove your lice," she said, and she picked them off.

While she picked his lice, she caused a huge abyss.

# Chapter 4

## HOW THE SUN DISAPPEARED FOR FIVE DAYS. IN WHAT FOLLOWS WE SHALL TELL A STORY ABOUT THE DEATH OF THE SUN

In ancient times the sun died.[7]

Because of his death it was night for five days.

Rocks banged against each other.

Mortars and grinding stones began to eat people.

Buck llamas started to drive men.

Here's what we Christians think about it: We think these stories tell of the darkness following the death of our Lord Jesus Christ.

Maybe that's what it was.

Afterward, man began to multiply once more.

---

7. Like various New World mythologies, Andean myths both ancient and modern include a motif of successive deaths and replacements of suns. Juan Ossio believes this chapter and Guaman Poma's scheme of "ages" are related to Montesinos' mid-seventeenth-century account of an Andean myth about successive suns equated to millennia (Ossio 1973: 188). Many modern Andeans interpret precolumbian structures as the houses of people who lived before the current sun arose.

That's the reason there are people until today.

Regarding this story, we Christians believe it refers to the time of the Flood.

But they believe it was Villca Coto mountain that saved them.

# Chapter 5

## HOW IN ANCIENT TIMES PARIA CACA APPEARED ON A MOUNTAIN NAMED CONDOR COTO IN THE FORM OF FIVE EGGS, AND WHAT FOLLOWED. HERE WILL BEGIN THE ACCOUNT OF PARIA CACA'S EMERGENCE

In preceding chapters we have recounted the lives lived in ancient times.
Nevertheless, we don't know the origins of the people of those days.

These people, who lived in that era, spent their lives warring and conquering each other. For their leaders, they recognized only the strong and the rich.

We speak of them as the Purum Runa, 'people of desolation.'

It was at this time that the one called Paria Caca was born in the form of five eggs on Condor Coto mountain.

A certain man, and a poor friendless one at that, was the first to see and know the fact of his birth; he was called Huatya Curi, but was also known as Paria Caca's son.

Now we'll speak of his discovery, and of the many wonders he performed.

They say that fellow called Huatya Curi subsisted by baking potatoes in earth pits, eating the way a poor man does, and people named him the "Baked Potato Gleaner."

At that time there was another man named Tamta Ñamca, a very rich and powerful lord.

Both his own house and all his other houses looked like *cassa* and *cancho* feather-weavings, for they were thatched with wings of birds. His llamas were yellow llamas, red and blue llamas; he owned llamas of every hue.

Seeing that this man lived so well, people who came from all the villages paid him homage and worshiped him.

For his part, he pretended to be very wise and spent his life deceiving a lot of people with the little he really knew.

Then this man called Tamta Ñamca, who pretended to be so wise, even to be a god, contracted a really horrible disease.

His illness went on for a great many years, and in time people talked. "How can a man who knows so much, who's so powerful, be so sick?" they said.

Just like the Spaniards who, on such occasions, summon experts and doctors, Tamta Ñamca, hoping to recover, summoned all sorts of shamans and wise men.

But no one could diagnose his disease.

Just then Huatya Curi was coming from the vicinity of Ura Cocha, and he went to sleep on the mountain by which we descend to Sieneguella.

While he was sleeping, a fox who'd come from down below and one who'd come from up above met face to face there. One fox asked the other, "Brother, how are things in Upper Villca?"

"What's good is good. But a lord in Anchi Cocha, a *villca* as a matter of fact, one who claims to know a lot, to be a god himself, is terribly ill. All the wise men who found their way to him are wondering, 'Why's he so ill?' No one can identify his sickness. But his disease is this: while his wife was toasting maize, a grain of muro maize popped from the griddle and got into her private part.

"She picked it out and served it to a man to eat. Because of having served it, she became a sinner in relation to the man who ate it." (Nowadays they reckon that act tantamount to being an adulteress.)

"As a result of this fault," he told the fox who'd come from down below, "a snake has made its dwelling on top of that magnificent house and is eating them up. What's more, a toad, a two-headed one, lives under their grinding stone. And nobody is aware of these devouring animals."

Then he asked, "And how are people doing in Lower Villca, brother?"

The other fox answered similarly, saying, "There's a woman, the offspring of a great lord and a *villca*, who almost died because of a penis."

As the foxes were telling each other these tidings, the man called Huatya Curi heard that the great lord who pretended to be a god was ill.

This great man had two daughters.

He had joined the elder daughter to a fellow *ayllu* member who was very rich. [He married her.]

The poor man called Huatya Curi came to that lord while he was still ill.

When he arrived, he went around asking surreptitiously, "Isn't someone sick in this town?"

"It's my father who's sick," replied the younger daughter.

Huatya Curi answered, "Let's get together. For your sake I'll cure your father."

The young woman didn't agree right away.

She told her father, "Father, there's a poor man here. He came and said to me, 'I'll cure your father.'"

All the wise men who were sitting there burst into laughter when they heard these words, and said, "If we ourselves can't cure him, how can this nobody make him well?"

But that lord wanted a cure so badly that he called for Huatya Curi. "Let him come, never mind what sort of man he is," he said.

When the great lord summoned him, Huatya Curi entered and said, "Father, if you want to get well, I'll make you well. But you have to give me your daughter."

Overjoyed, Tamta Ñamca replied, "Very well then!"

But when his older daughter's husband heard this proposition he flew into a rage. "How dare he join her, the sister-in-law of such a powerful man as me, to a nobody like that?"

Huatya Curi began his cure by saying, "Father, your wife is an adulteress. Because she's an adulteress, a sinner, she's made you ill. As for what's eating you, it's the two snakes that dwell on top of this magnificent house of yours. And there's a toad, too, a two-headed one, that lives under your grinding stone.

"Now we'll kill them all. Then you'll get well. After you recover, you must worship my father above all things. He'll be born tomorrow or the day after. And as for you, you're not such a powerful man. If you were really powerful, you wouldn't be sick."

The rich man was astonished when Huatya Curi said this.

And when Huatya Curi said, "Now I'll take apart this gorgeous house of his," he became distraught.

And his wife started yelling, "This nobody, this crook, is slandering me! I'm no adulteress!"

Nonetheless the sick man wanted his health back very badly, and he let his house be dismantled.

Then Huatya Curi removed the two snakes and killed them. Next he clearly explained the facts to the rich man's wife: just how a grain of muro maize had popped out and gotten in her private part, and how she, after picking it out, had served it to a man.

After that, the woman confessed everything. "It's all true," she said.

Next he had the grinding stone lifted.

A toad, a two-headed one, came out from under it and fled to Anchi Cocha ravine.

It exists in a spring there to this day.

When people come to that spring, it either makes them disappear or else drives them crazy.

Once Huatya Curi finished all these deeds, the ailing man got well.

After Tamta Ñamca's recovery, on the day that had been foretold, Huatya Curi went for the first time to Condor Coto mountain.

It was there that the one called Paria Caca dwelled in the form of five eggs.

All around him a wind rose up and began to blow.

In earlier times no wind had been observed.

Just before he went there on the appointed day, the man who'd recovered his health gave him his unmarried daughter.

While the two of them were traveling in the vicinity of that mountain they sinned together.[8]

As soon as that elder brother-in-law heard they'd sinned together he set out to compete against Huatya Curi.

"I'll bring deep shame on that beggarman," he muttered.

And so one day that man challenged him, saying, "Brother, let's have it out in a contest, whatever kind. How dare a nobody like you marry the sister-in-law of a powerful man like me?"

That poor man agreed, and went to inform his father Paria Caca.

"Very well then. Whatever he tells you, come to me right away," his father replied.

The contest between them was like this.

One day the challenger said, "Let's have a drinking and dancing contest."

So that poor man Huatya Curi went to inform his father.

His father Paria Caca advised him, "Go to that mountain over there. There you'll pretend to be a guanaco and lie down as if dead. Early in the morning a fox with his skunk wife will come there to see me."

"They'll bring their maize beer in a small long-necked jar and they'll also bring along their drum. When they spot you, a dead guanaco, they'll set their things on the ground, and as soon as the fox puts down his panpipes, they'll start to eat you. Then turn back into a man, scream so loud it hurts their ears, and run away. When they scamper off forgetting their possessions, you'll take them and go to the contest."

The poor man did as he was told.

The rich man was the first to dance in the contest.

His wives, who numbered almost two hundred, danced along with him, and after they were done the poor man entered by himself, with only his wife, just the two of them.

As they entered through the doorway, as they danced to the skunk's drum he'd brought along, the earth of that whole region quaked.

With this, he beat them all.

Next, they began drinking.

Huatya Curi went with just his wife to sit at the head of the group, exactly as guests do until today.

---

8. *hochallicorcan* "they sinned together": *hochalliy*, like *pincay* "private part" (literally, "shame"), is a shame-oriented term of Quechua lexicon and Christian mentality. The verb root employed seems to have meant a ceremonial debt or obligation (it is still used in this sense), but Christian missionaries chose it as the translation for "sin."

And all of those people who were sitting there served him drink after drink without giving him a break.

Even though he drank every bit of it he sat there with no problem.

Then it was his turn. He began to serve the maize beer he'd brought in that little long-necked jar, and everybody ridiculed him. "How could he possibly fill so many people from such a tiny jar?" they said.

But when he began to serve, starting from the head of the gathering, they dropped down drunk in no time, one after another.

The next day, since Huatya Curi had won, the other man wanted a different contest.

This contest was all about outdoing each other in splendid costumes decorated with the exquisite feather-weavings called *cassa* and *cancho*.

So Huatya Curi again went to his father.

His father gave him a snow garment.

In that garment he dazzled all the people's eyes and won the contest.

Then the challenger said, "Let's compete in putting on puma skins."

That man wanted to win by wearing the puma skins he had.

The poor man, following his father's advice, went to a spring early in the morning and brought back a red puma skin.

He danced. And while he was dancing in that red puma, a rainbow appeared in the sky, like the rainbow that appears in the sky today.

Next the rich man wanted to compete at house-building.

Since that man had access to many people, he almost finished a large house in a single day.

The poor man just laid down the foundations and then strolled around all day long with his wife.

That night all kinds of birds, snakes, and other animals of the land walled the house.

The next day, seeing it already finished, the challenger was awestruck.

Likewise Huatya Curi won at roofing the house. All the guanacos and vicuñas brought his thatching straw.

As for the other man, while his materials were being transported on llamas, Huatya Curi availed himself of a bobcat's help. He lay in ambush for them by a cliff, stampeded them, and destroyed them by making them fall over it.

By this trick he won again.

After winning all these contests, the poor man spoke just as his father had advised: "Brother, we've competed so many times now, always agreeing to your rules. Now you agree to my rules."

"Very well then," the rich man agreed.

Huatya Curi said, "Now, with blue tunics! And let our breechclouts be of white cotton! That's how we'll dance!"

"Very well then," the rich man agreed.

The rich man, since he'd danced first from the beginning, went ahead and danced first.

As he was dancing, Huatya Curi charged down on him from outside screaming. That man panicked, turned into a brocket deer, and ran away.

And his wife followed him, saying, "I'll die with my own old man!"

Then that poor man flew into a rage: "Go, idiot! You two have victimized me so much, I'll kill you!" he said, and he chased after them.

Chasing them, he caught the wife on the road to Anchi Cocha and stood her upside down on her head. "People coming from up above and those coming from down below will gape at your private parts as they pass by," he said.

And right then and there she turned to stone instantly.

This stone, just like a woman's legs with thighs and a vagina, stands there until today.

Even now people put coca on top of it when they undertake something.

But the man who'd turned into a brocket deer climbed up a mountain and disappeared.

(Now, in ancient times, brocket deer used to eat human beings.

Later on, when brocket deer were very numerous, they danced, ritually chanting, "How shall we eat people?"

Then one of their little fawns made a mistake and said, "How shall people eat us?"

When the brocket deer heard this they scattered.

From then on brocket deer became food for humans.)

After Huatya Curi finished all these deeds, Paria Caca flew forth from the five eggs in the shape of five falcons.

These five falcons turned into humans and they began to roam around.

And at that time, hearing all about the things people had done, about how that man called Tamta Ñamca had said, "I am a god," and about how the man had himself worshiped, Paria Caca went into a rage over all these sins of theirs. Rising up as rain, he flushed them all away to the ocean, together with all their houses and their llamas, sparing not a single one.

At that time, too, there was something called the Pullao, which bridged like an arch Llantapa mountain[9] and another mountain called Vichoca.[10]

---

9. Llantapa mountain today is 14 km southwest of Llacsa Tambo (if the latter is modern Llaquistambo) (IGM 1970–1971).

10. Modern Guichuca peak, 4,000 m above sea level, 14 km southwest of Llantapa.

That thing called the Pullao was a gigantic tree.
Monkeys, toucans, and birds of all colors used to live on it.
These animals, too, all of their kind, he swept to the sea.
After he finished these feats, Paria Caca ascended to the place that's
known today as Upper Paria Caca.

## ■ Zithuwa Hymns (1575?) *Peru*

The Zithuwa Hymns to the gods and divine powers were performed in
Cuzco as part of the Inca "cleansing" ritual. Urban and hierarchic, they recall the Twenty Sacred Hymns in Nahuatl performed at the Aztec capital
in Tenochtitlan. There is an important difference here, however: all
events are subject to the overarching power of the patriarchal deity Viracocha, the herder who protects his flock, his llama-people. In the Americas, this pastoral scheme, like the economy that underpinned it, was in
fact particular to the Andes.

## *Harvest*

Viracocha, ancient Viracocha,
skilled creator,
who makes and establishes:
Below on earth
may they eat
may they drink,
you say.
For those you set in place,
those you made,
may food be plentiful.
May there be
potatoes, maize,
all kinds of food,
you say, who command and increase.
They shall not suffer,
and not suffering, do your will.
May there be no frost, no hail.
Keep them in peace.

TRANSLATED BY J. H. ROWE

## Sister Rain

Fair princess,
your brother has broken your jar.
That is why
it thunders and lightens.

So princess,                                                    5
you give us falling rain
or hail and snow.

Viracocha,
earth-establisher, earth maker,
for this duty                                                   10
has established and made you.

TRANSLATED BY GORDON BROTHERSTON, AFTER TRANSLATION BY
GARCILASO DE LA VEGA INCA

## ■ Afu Ollantay (1770) *Peru* (song)

TRANSLATED BY MARK STRAND

Known in several late eighteenth-century copies, *Afu Ollantay* deals with the unsuccessful rebellion of Ollantay, a prince from the District (Suyu) of Anti, against the authority of the Inca in Cuzco. It is also the story of Ollantay's love for an Inca princess, thwarted by the edict that the royal family may marry only among themselves. In celebrating Inca power and statesmanship, the play belongs to the cycle of Inca kingship drama that lives on still in parts of the Andes and which, at the time of Tupac Amaru's rising against the Spanish (1780), was fiercely suppressed. The first of these extracts is a song of the type that was sung in the fields to scare birds away from the crops and was then adapted to the taste of the Cuzco court—and of numerous writers since (it appears, for example, in Peter Shaffer's *The Royal Hunt of the Sun*). It is a small play within a play that warns Ollantay away from the princess. The second extract, from the Edwardian translation of Sir Clements Markham, tells how the Inca agent Rumi Ñaui ("Stone Eye") enters Ollantay's camp, a maneuver that leads to the latter's downfall.

## Song

Stop, don't eat now,
my little dove,

on the princess's land,
my little dove.
Don't try to eat,
my little dove,
the tempting corn,
my little dove.
The kernels are white,
my little dove,                                                    1(
the ears are still thin,
my little dove.
You won't be nourished,
my little dove,
the leaves are still tender,                                       1
my little dove.
Gluttons get caught,
my little dove,
and so will you,
my little dove.                                                    2(
I'm picking a quarrel,
my little dove,
for your own good,
my little dove.
Look at the quail,                                                 2
my little dove,
there he hangs,
my little dove.
Ask your heart,
my little dove,                                                    3(
consult your feathers,
my little dove.
He was destroyed,
my little dove,
for pecking grain,                                                 3
my little dove.
And that's what happens,
my little dove,
to careless birds,
my little dove.                                                    4(

## ◼ Folk Songs and Poems (Sixteenth to Twentieth Centuries) *Peru, Bolivia, Ecuador*

In communal life throughout Bolivia, Peru, and Ecuador, Quechua continues to be the medium of songs, a point aptly illustrated at the start of this century in *Tarmpa Pacha Huaray* (1905), edited in Peru by dissident quechuans, proud of their language and its literary tradition. Their effort was followed by the D'Harcourts's monumental study of Inca music (1925) and by the major anthologies of Basadre (1938), Arguedas (1938, 1949), Lara (1947), and others. Many of the pieces in these collections are in pre-Hispanic modes—that directly recall antecedents recorded in the sixteenth century by Guaman Poma, Garcilaso El Inca, and other historians. Found in Guaman Poma, "War Song," for example, is still sung today; the knotted rope in "Pastoral" is the Inca quipu; and the strength invoked in "A Woman Goes to the Fields" is that of the ancient demon-spirit zupay.

## Like a Feather in the Air

My mother gave me my being,
    Ay!
In the middle of a rain cloud,
    Ay!
So that I would weep like rain,       5
    Ay!
So that I would go round like a cloud,
    Ay!
Wandering from door to door
    Ay!      10
Like a feather in the air,
    Ay!

TRANSLATED BY W. S. MERWIN (ARAWI)

## I Have Lost My Dove

    I have lost my dove.
Wandering, I call to her in a loud voice.
Everyone who finds me says,
"Why did you love her?"
    Where have you flown?      5
Who have you left here to console me?
Like a dove whose wings have been cut off
I will die walking back and forth.
    Come back, dove whom I cherished.
How long must I wait for you?      10
In the nest, where we should be,
Now the birds of night raise their moans.

TRANSLATED BY W. S. MERWIN (ARAWI)

## Where Are You

Where are you where are you going
they say
and we still have to go on

sun and moon go past
      and go past
      six months to get from Cuzco to Quito
at the foot of Tayo we'll rest

fear nothing
lord Inca fear nothing
we're going with you we'll get there together

TRANSLATED BY W. S. MERWIN (INCA) (1979; AFTER BASADRE 1938)

## War Song

We shall drink from the traitor's skull,
we shall wear his teeth as a necklace,
of his bones we shall make flutes,
of his skin we shall make a drum;
later, we'll dance.

TRANSLATED BY MARK STRAND (CUZCO)

## To This Song

To this song
you will sleep.
At midnight
I shall come.

TRANSLATED BY MARK STRAND

## Song

*Prince*
Because you're a star
      yes

you shine at night
      yes                             5
under the sun's fire
      yes
I'll never see you
      yes

*Princess*                                   10
If I'm a star
      no
open your heart
      no
and under the sun's fire               15
      no
half-close your eyes
      no

*Prince*
You seem to call                         20
      yes
only in moonlight
      yes
and when I come near
      yes                             25
you change into snow
      yes

*Princess*
If I seem to call
      no                             30
please come quickly
      no
if I change into snow
      no
toss me your fire                           35
      no

*Prince*
When my fire burns you
      yes
you change into dew                   40
      yes
are you the wind
      yes
or are you a dream
      yes                             45

*Princess*
If you think I am dew

```
        no
bring your lips near
        no                                                      5
though I may be a dream
        no
don't ever lose me
        no
```

TRANSLATED BY MARK STRAND

## I Am Raising a Fly

I am raising a fly
with wings of gold,
I am raising a fly
with burning eyes.

It brings death
in its eyes of fire,
brings death
in its hair of gold,
in its beautiful wings.

I am raising it
in a green bottle;                                              10
nobody knows
if it drinks,
nobody knows
if it eats.                                                     15

It wanders at night
like a star,
and wounds to death
with its glowing red,
with its eyes of fire.                                          20

In its eyes of fire
it brings love,
its blood
shines in the night,
the love it brings                                              25
in its heart.

Insect of night,
fly of death,
loving it so,
I am raising it                                                 30
in a green bottle.

And that is all,
that is all.
Nobody knows
if I give it                                                             *35*
something to drink,
if I give it
something to eat.

TRANSLATED BY MARK STRAND

## Doesn't Your Heart Hurt

doesn't your heart hurt
don't you want to cry
you, my precious flower
you, my queen,
you, my princess                                                        *5*
see how justice takes me off in spate
and imprisons me
when I glimpse your mantle
when I see your dress
the day does not exist for me                                           *10*
in this night I awake to know
it will never dawn;
I think that you,
my queen, my señora,
don't remember me                                                       *15*
I'm eaten up
by the puma and the fox of the zancay
I'm alone,
disheartened and lost, my lady.

TRANSLATED BY GORDON BROTHERSTON (AFTER BASADRE,
FROM *GUAMAN POMA*)

## Poems for a Carnival

*1*
That's the big
boss's house
shining with the money

studded in it
rolls of bank notes
papered on it
his cows even
shit gold

2

The carnival was
a sad old man it was
under the bridge
sniffing around he was
I saw him with his
*such'i* fish moustache
in his bag
two eggs there were
I tried to grab them
but hollow they were

3

The politicians from the valley
have no mouths
being without mouths
they peck with their nails

TRANSLATED BY GORDON BROTHERSTON (AFTER LARA)

## ■ Folk Tales (Twentieth Century) *Peru*

Like songs, tales continue to be told in Quechua throughout the former Tahuantinsuyu, many of them strongly reminiscent of those told in classic texts like the Huarochiri Manuscript. Basadre (1938) and Arguedas (1949) are prominent among their collectors.

## *Ichi the Dwarf*

TRANSLATED BY W. S. MERWIN

In Qjelle Huanca the earth opened and a dwarf popped out. He was naked and his hair was bright red like a fire. He sat down on a stone, and for the fun of it he brandished his lighted hair. His little lively eyes, like small coals, stared at the landscape in wonder, and because it was cold he began to cry like a sucking pig.

Then that little dwarf began to leap around among the rocks and crags and his scarlet hair caught in the thick leaves and fig branches and tangled him. At midnight he beat his belly like a drum and the raw sound rebounded from hill to hill. In the quiet afternoons he blew on his pipe and the flute warbled and trilled, but what he liked best of all was to frighten the men working in the fields. Whenever he found them gathering wood he would growl, he would give a low growl.

He sang, too, under the ground, and his songs went up into the air in the same way that the water of the marshes turns into clouds. When dawn rose into the heavens the far away songs of the little dwarf Ichi woke the children, and the calves lowed sweetly.

# Carib Languages

In its several varieties, Cariban speech belongs to the sea named for it—the Caribbean—where it is all but extinct, and to northern South America, where is it still strong, especially in the Guyana highlands that stand between the Orinoco and Amazon river systems. Found in the uppermost reaches of the Orinoco in southern Venezuela is Makiritare or Yekuana Carib, which names itself *Soto* ("the people"). Through contacts made over the last half century or so, this Soto tradition has provided texts that superbly exemplify rainforest teaching about the creation of the world and human perception. Chief among them are *Watunna,* a cosmogony and history, and its companion piece *Medatia.*

■ **Watunna: An Orinoco Creation Cycle (1950)**
*Venezuela* **(oral creation myth)**

TRANSLATED BY DAVID M. GUSS

Only recently published in translation, *Watunna* stands as one of the great cosmogonies of the rainforest, indeed of the Fourth World as a whole, and readily bears comparison with the *Popol Vuh* in the scope and the subtlety of its construction. It takes us from the beginnings of time, the ages of great floods and repeated metamorphosis, up to the invasion of the rainforest that is occurring today. The flight of the watersnake Huiio reveals the origins of the "plumed serpent" motif integral to American accounts of evolution; and, at the first harvest, it confirms the summit of human achievement to have been agriculture, focused in this case on manioc, the staple crop in the conuco or field-garden of the tropical forest.

The *Watunna* is a sacred oral tradition that unites a Cariban-speaking tribe called Makiritare, who live along the rivers in the Guyana highlands of southern Venezuela. This Venzuelan creation cycle, transcribed by Marc de Civrieux, is an account of the earth's genesis, with all the imagination, symbolism, and moral authority of the world's great creation and fertility myths. However, it is not the tale of magnificent gods who are uniquely chosen and powerful and rule the entire earth. Rather, it is the moving story of the miracle creation work of poor Native American gods in an impoverished isolated basin area of the Orinoco River. The birds, like angel instructors, come to a dry earth, bring knowledge and hope, and at the same time establish social proprieties for living the good life in a region that they cause to be generated with abundant trees, fruit, and crops. After the miracles of huge mountains, enormous yucca trees, and great new rivers, there appears the outlaw Jaguar, who robs food and stores his loot in a cave for his private use. Jaguar must be punished so that the people can live with food and in peace. Jaguar, who robs, is not forgiven, unlike the young demigod Kuchi, who originally stole fruit and the seed of trees to bring them to earth for the benefit of humanity. The humble, skinned-alive Kuchi, a Promethean and Eve-like figure, will have his body restored to its former condition and be forgiven—unlike Prometheus, who suffers eternal physical dismemberment for bringing fire to the earth, and Eve, who forever bears the sin of offending Heaven for having brought knowledge to humanity.

FURTHER READING: *Watunna: An Orinoco Creation Cycle.* Translated and edited by David M. Guss (1950), transcribed by Marc de Civrieux.

## *Kuchi, Who Brought Trees and Fruit to the Dirt Earth*

Those old people were very poor now. They had no food. There weren't any trees on the Earth. They had no *conucos*. They ate dirt and nothing else. They sent their children out to gather it in *tudi*. They just ate dirt. There was no water.

It had been different in the beginning. Iamankave, the Yuca Mistress, the food keeper, she lived in the highest part of the Sky. She always sent a *damodede* with armfuls of cassava for them.

"Where do you come from?" they would ask.

"From far away," he'd say. And he gave them the cassava and left.

Iyako, the veinticuatro ant, used to come down to Earth all the time. He brought them water. "Where do you come from?" they would ask. He didn't answer. He just gave them the water and went on his way.

Then Odosha came. When he came, he ruined everything. He brought evil and sickness. Now that cassava man didn't come back anymore. Neither did that ant with the water. Hunger and thirst came.

One day, a man said: "I know the ant's road. I'm going to find water again."

That man was named Dariche. He turned into a swift. He flew off. He grew smaller and smaller in the clouds. He disappeared. Then he came back with the water. They say that he went to Akuenaña in the highest Sky, that he stole the water from Lake Akuena.

He brought it to the Kashishare (Casiquiare). He made a great pool there. They call it the Old Water. There was no water on the Earth before that. The Orinoco and the Ventuari didn't exist yet. There weren't any rivers.

Now there was just that water by the Casiquiare far away from here. It didn't run. It was all in one place, still. Dariche brought the Old Water. The old people went off to look for it. They walked and walked. When they got there they were tired. They didn't find anything but a smelly old pond.

Then another man said: "I know the cassava road. I'll go look for it again."

His name was Kuchi. Now we'll tell the story of that man.

"I know," he said. "I know the way."

He knew it. He was wise. "Once I dreamed I went to Iamankave's house in Heaven." That's what he said.

That man turned into Kuchi, the kinkajou. Then he went to Heaven. He left his body on Earth for the kinkajous of today. He was the first one, the grandfather of them all. Now that man went up to the Sky, climbing and climbing. He grew very small. You couldn't see him at all anymore. He arrived at Iamankave's house at the top of Heaven. He saw a huge *kanawa* full of *mañoco* hanging in the doorway. Near the house, in the garden, he saw the giant food tree surrounded by a fence. It was Iamankave's garden. Now he hid so Iamankave wouldn't see him.

A boy named Wedama came out of the house. He was Iamankave's son, Kuchi's friend.

Kuchi called him. "I came to find food," he said.

"You're here. Okay. Let's hide. Come with me." That's what the boy said.

He turned into a swallow. He flew over the fence, up to the top of the branches. Kuchi turned into a kinkajou. He jumped over the fence. He climbed up the trunk. They flew, they climbed up to the fruit. There was every kind of fruit up on that tree. It was the Yuca Mother. Each branch was different and filled with another kind of food.

As they ate, they shook up the wasps. They had their nest there. They guarded the tree. They were flying around now, screaming: "Someone's here! Someone's stealing the food!"

Now the Yuca Mistress knew. She came running out to see what was happening.

She came up there. The swallow hid. Kuchi ran. As he ran, he hid a little piece of that tree beneath his nail. He went on running. He couldn't get away. The Yuca Mistress caught him. She skinned him. Then she hung him on the fence without a skin.

"I'm going to die," Kuchi thought. He had a powerful, wise sister. She lived in the Sky Place. He called and called, asking her for help. The sister came. Her name is Iumakawa.

When she came, she said to him: "You stole the food. That's why you're hanging here without any skin. You got what you deserved."

"We're hungry on Earth. That's why I stole it," he said. "Help me. I'm going to die here without any skin."

His sister helped him. She asked the Yuca Mistress to forgive him.

"He was hungry," she said. "He came from the Earth. There's no food there. He's my brother. That's why I'm asking you."

First the Mistress said: "He robbed the food. His punishment is fair." Then she said: "Okay. I'll forgive him." And she gave Iumakawa Kuchi's skin back. She healed her brother. She made him like new again. Now he jumped up. He ran. He went back down to Earth. He had a splinter of the tree hidden beneath his nail.

When he returned, he was like a man again. He sat down on his shaman's bench, without speaking, without doing anything, just thinking and nothing else. He waited until night. When night came, he pulled the splinter out from under his nail and planted it.

That was far away in Dodoima (Mount Roraima). During the night, the yuca began to sprout. You couldn't see it. When dawn came, there was a tall, tall tree with many branches and all sorts of fruit. "It's done," said Kuchi. He ate. He was happy when the dawn came. That was the beginning of our food, the Dodoima tree, when the people were hungry.

Dodoima was the first tree. Now we see it as a very tall mountain. Many wild fruits still grow there. No one plants them. They just grow as reminders.

Kamaso heard about it. That man lived in Kamaso wochi (Kamaso's Savanna). "Good," he said. "Kuchi has planted food in Dodoima. That's too far away. The people there can eat now. We don't have anything to eat but dirt. All we have are stories."

Kamaso sent a messenger to Roraima. She was a woman named Edenawadi. She walked for days and came to the East. She spoke with Kuchi. She asked for a yuca shoot to plant here. "Okay," said Kuchi. He gave her the shoot.

Then Edenawadi headed back toward the sunset. On her way, night fell. The night found her in a place called Uaiante (Auyan Tepui). When she arrived there, Edenawadi sat down. She planted the shoot. She dreamed of yuca, food, different fruits. When the sun came up, there was a shoot, just one little shoot. Three little green yuca leaves and nothing else. It didn't grow like a tree. It didn't have different fruits. That soil was no good.

Edenawadi picked up her shoot. She started walking toward the sunset again. When night came, she planted the yuca, in Kuntinama. Nothing. The next night in Metakuni. Nothing. The next night in Arahame. Nothing. Now she came to her house in Kamaso wochi. She gave the shoot to Kamaso. Many people came to see. They were shouting with joy:

"Our food's arrived!" Kamaso planted it during the night. He sang and sang. When the sun came up, there was just one shoot. There wasn't any fruit. "This soil's no good," he said. They all went away, sad, like before, looking for dirt to eat.

There was Madunawe. She was a woman too. She lived in Wade's house in Truma achaka. She was kin to Wade.

When the news came, Wade shook with joy: "Kuchi, yuca, Dodoima, Kamaso, Edenawadi!" When the news came, he called the woman named Madunawe.

"We have good soil here," he said. "Let's ask for the shoot."

"Good," answered Madunawe. "We'll plant it."

It was nighttime when the woman planted the shoot in the black soil. All the fruits, palms, trees, vines, every green thing there is on the Earth today, was born in one night, when that woman planted the yuca.

When day came, the tree was tallllll. They called it Marahuaka. The branches, the leaves, the fruits of Marahuaka covered the entire Earth. It was like a roof. Each branch was budding and sprouting and bearing fruit, turning into another and another and another, and every one with a different food. It was all the yuca. All the plants, all the fruits we know today began there. It was just one tree with many branches. It wouldn't stop sprouting. Every time it was something different.

The people came to look at Marahuaka. When they came, they were hungry. They were sick and thin. Now they shouted: "Marahuaka! Our food has come!"

Some were laughing. Others wept as the tree went on sprouting. There wasn't anything else. There was no food, no water, nothing on the Earth. That's what the old ones say. I didn't see it.

First they were happy, then sad. With empty stomachs, they opened up their arms, their mouths, their eyes. They just looked at the fruit. It was up there in the sky. "What'll we do now? How can we get it?" asked one after another with their arms and mouths and eyes open. They were really sad as they stood there and looked.

Now a branch full of *cucurito* came crashing down.

"Ahhhhhhh!" they shouted. "Here comes our food."

When the branch fell, it killed someone. It fell on the head of a boy, Wade's son.

Now a branch full of *pijiguao* fell.

"Ahhhh!" they shouted. "Our food!"

When it fell, it landed right on the nose of Odoma, the paca. He ran off screaming and yelling. He had his face crushed. The pacas are still that way today, with flat faces. That's the reason why. You can see them.

Then another branch fell, and another and another. They were falling all over. The people got crushed, killed.

They just ran, terrified. They didn't know where to go. The whole Earth covered. Wherever they went, fruit was falling, crushing them.

That's what they say.

## Semenia, the Bird Who Showed How to Plant

Wanadi was still living here on Earth, in Wade's house. They gathered around him, weeping, asking for help.

Wanadi said: "Okay. Now I'll make new people. I'll make birds to help you. They'll have wings to fly up to the branches. They'll get the fruit."

At that time there were no birds. That was in the beginning.

Wanadi stuck a few rows of sticks in the earth and looked at them. He sat down in front of them, smoking. He played his maraca. He sang. He thought.

That's the way he made his new people for the harvest, his new people called birds. When they wanted to, they turned into birds and flew. Then they changed back into people like us again.

Now the birds made ladders out of vines. Some went climbing up them like people. They climbed up the vines. Others flew up to the branches like birds. Now they started gathering the fruit. The old people watched them from the ground. They wove *tudi*. The birds began to come. They were carrying the fruit. It was heavy. It started to slip and fall. It killed people like before.

"That's no good," said one of the birds. "We'll plant. We'll cultivate the earth. We can help. We're strong, us birds. Let's stop this gathering and cut down the tree. Then we'll plant in the earth."

That was the chief of the birds. His name is Semenia. He was wise. He showed us how to plant. They cut the trees down. That's how they make *conucos*. That's how they plant. The old people didn't know that. They only knew how to gather wild fruit, like monkeys. When Semenia came, he showed them how to cut down trees to make *conucos*. When they cut down the Marahuaka tree, they fed the earth. Semenia showed them how to work to get their food.

There were two who didn't want to obey. They didn't want to work. They were called Mado, the jaguar, and Wachedi, the tapir.

"Who's that giving orders now?" they asked. "Everyone's obeying. Well, we don't want to work or obey. When we're hungry, we just find our food and eat it, that's all. We're not going to have anything to do with those people."

They went looking for fallen fruit. They ate. They gorged themselves. What was left they were going to hide. They thought: "We two are the biggest ones on Earth. The others are so small. Semenia is tiny. How can we obey him? How can we share?"

They hid the food in caves. They went back to get more. They weren't thinking of the others. They were their own chiefs. They worked alone. They didn't want to share because they were so hungry. They didn't listen to Semenia when he said: "First we work together; then we celebrate. We'll divide the food later."

In the old days Semenia was our chief. They said: "Why's he chief?"

The people watched them. Semenia watched them. "That's no good," he said. "Those two are hiding food. They don't want to live with us. They've forgotten we're here. They're making fun of us. Now we'll punish them."

Then he called for them. At first they didn't want to come. Then everyone circled around them, staring at them. They were afraid. Then they went to see Semenia.

"You're working?" he asked.

"Oh, yeh. We're working," they answered.

"Good. That's why I called. We all work together. Now we're thirsty. There's no water here. You're going to go to the Casiquiare to get water for us."

"Okay," they said. They were scared now. The others were watching them.

Semenia gave them a strainer to carry the water in. It was a trick. You can't carry water in a strainer. They were both idiots. They didn't catch on.

"Okay," they said. They went walking and walking, far off there on the Casiquiare trail to get water with a strainer.

Semenia wanted hunger and misery to stop. That's why he came with his new people, with the birds. Wanadi made them. The people were living in hunger and misery because of Odosha. They were listening to Odosha. They weren't together. There was no order, no justice. They were all selfish. They had no chiefs. Each one just found his own dirt and ate it. They didn't worry about anyone else. They never thought about the others.

Semenia made himself chief to teach us. He showed us how to work. He punished the ones that didn't want to live like people, like brothers. He brought food, rain, fertility and obedience for everyone. He showed them what to do. Now we have food again. We're happy despite Odosha. Semenia was Wanadi's messenger, our first chief in the beginning.

When Jaguar and Tapir left, Semenia said: "Now we'll cut it down."

Four toucans came up. They were like people in the beginning. They brought some good axes to cut down Marahuaka. They hit the trunk. Their axes bounced off. The tree was thick. The wood was hard. The tree wouldn't go down. The axes couldn't cut it. Now they turned into birds, toucans with long, hard beaks. They were their axes now. They tried to peck the tree down. Nothing. They couldn't do it. The first toucan broke the edge of his beak. That's the way the toucans are now, with beaks like saws. Then another toucan came up, and another and another. Nothing. Then the woodpeckers came. Wanadi came up to peck like Wanadi tonoro. Semenia came as a Semenia bird. Waraihai and Sumunuadi came too. They went at the tree with their beaks. They cut all day. At night, they rested. They slept. When the sun rose, they got up. The tree was intact again as if nothing had happened.

"What are we going to do?" they asked. "We can't go to sleep. Our cuts just close up. We're just wasting our time. We'll never finish."

Semenia said: "We won't cut this way anymore, all at the same time. We'll take turns now. One will cut and the others will rest."

So that's what they did. There was always one cutting, day and night. The cut didn't close. They kept on cutting deeper and deeper, first one, then the other. They just kept on cutting. They slept too, first one, then the other. They didn't get tired. Peck . . . peck . . . peck . . . peck. They pecked like that for days.

Now one of them came up. He gave the last blow. It was Wanadi. He was happy. "It's done!" he shouted.

It really was done. It was completely cut.

They all turned to look. They were frightened. "It's going to fall now. Which way is it going to fall? Which way should we run?"

Marahuaka didn't fall. It just stood there, hanging from the Sky in silence. It was just there. It wouldn't budge.

They all stood there looking.

"What was all that work for?" That tree just wouldn't fall. They couldn't understand it.

Now they called Kadiio, the squirrel. "Run up there and see what's happening."

"Okay," said Kadiio. And he went running up to see. Then he came back down. "It's tangled up there in the Sky," he said. "The branches are caught. They look like roots up there. That's why it's hanging. It's stuck."

Semenia gave him an axe. "Go up and cut it."

Kadiio cut Marahuaka. He cut it up there in Heaven. It was an upside down tree, with its roots on top.

Then the great Marahuaka tree finally fell. The entire Earth shook. Branches, fruit, palms, seeds, everything fell. It felt like the sky was falling. It was like the end of the world.

They hid in caves. They huddled together. They shut their eyes. They were afraid.

Then they came out. When they came out it was raining everywhere. They didn't know what it was. It was the first rain. It fell from Heaven in waterfalls and rapids. It poured down from Heaven out of Marahuaka's cut roots.

"Rain," said Semenia. "Now we can plant."

The water looked for a way through the Earth. Now new paths, the rivers, were born. The Orinoco, Fhadamu, Kunukunuma, Antawari, Merewari, Metakuni, Kuntinama, and others, many others. All the rivers were born. They called them the New Water. They ran like snakes across the Earth.

The earth became very soft for planting. Now the women gathered cuttings, shoots, sprouts, seeds. They gathered them in the rain to plant.

Now four waterfalls came down from the top of Marahuaka, from the cliffs: Motasha, Iamo, Namanama, and Kuhuaka. They were born on the green Earth and they opened beautiful ways.

In Kushamakari, three waterfalls were searching for paths, Auakosho, Iukati, and Matuhushi. They ran along pulling up stones and shooting out foam. You couldn't recognize the Earth anymore from the beginning.

Now there were buds everywhere. The Earth became green. The forest bloomed, our *conucos* blossomed. The forest filled with trees. Our *conucos* filled with yuca.

Marahuaka's trunk broke into three pieces. We call them Marahuaka huha, Marahuaka huih and Atawashiho. They turned into stone when they fell. Now they're mountains, the three parts of the highest mountain on Earth. They're there as reminders. It was that day that our food came.

Kadiio fell down too, onto one of the Duida's peaks. Now he lives there, hidden. He's the master of that peak they call Kadiio ewiti.

The people were happy; happy together in their *conuco*. The yuca grew quickly. All of a sudden it was there. Now the men rested. That's what Semenia told them. Now the women worked. That's how we still do it. We don't forget that way. The men clear the *conuco,* like Marahuaka in the beginning. The women plant and harvest and prepare it.

Now they came carrying *wuwa* filled with yuca. Then the men worked again. They wove baskets, strainers, trays, presses. They carved graters and *kanawa.* Those are their jobs. The women harvest, carry, grate, press, cook the cassava. They make *iarake* in the *kanawa.*

"That's good," said Semenia. Then he said: "Let's dance. Let's sing and eat and drink. Now we'll remember."

It was the first harvest festival. The Conuco Song, that's what they call it, *Adahe ademi hidi,* that's its name.

Now they played the momi bark horns and Semenia sang. Wanadi and Wade sang too. They remembered everything. They didn't forget anything: Kuchi, Dodoima, Kamaso, Marahuaka, how they planted, how they cleared. *Watunna,* that's what we call the memory of our beginning.

Just as they sang, we sing now.

The *aichudiaha,* the old ones of today, they know the ancient ways. They sing and teach the young ones what Semenia did. They teach us how to work so that our food returns. They sing about how Jaguar and Tapir were punished.

It's always the same, now as before. The way we ate once, we do over and over again. We obey. We remember. The old ones sing beautifully. We just repeat.

Now those people who came to help in the beginning, those people that Wanadi made to cut down Marahuaka, said goodby.

As they were dancing and singing, they turned into birds of every color. They flew off. The air was filled with feathers, all red and green and yellow and blue. It was beautiful. Now the Water Mother, Huiio, the Great Snake, came leaping out of the water and shot into the air.

"I want my crown," she said, looking for birds and feathers for her crown. Huiio threw her great body into the sky. Many birds came. She covered herself with feathers. She was the rainbow. They called it *wasudi*

"Good. It's done," the birds said. "Let's leave now."

Then they disappeared. They went to Heaven. They just left their bodies on the Earth for the birds of today. You couldn't see the rainbow anymore. It went to live in Lake Akuena.

Semenia went off as a bird too. He looked like the Wanadi bird. He was kin to Wanadi. Now he's the master of the Earth's food.

Okay. That's it.

## Glossary

*Adekato*   The *akato's* journey, which is recounted to its body in the form of dreams. The *adekato* is a dangerous journey, for whenever it leaves the body, the *akato* may be captured by Odosha.

*Aichuriaha*   The "aichuri," or "song man," referring to the keeper of the *Watunna*. Neither a hereditary nor paid position, there is in every village a small group of elders who guard and perpetuate this tradition.

*Aiuku*   A hallucinogenic snuff made from the seeds of a large, leguminous tree *(Anadenanthera peregrina)*, aiuku is found throughout the South American rain forest and is variously known as ñopo, yopo, and vilca.

*Akato*   The body's companion spirit or double, which descends from heaven to occupy it upon birth. All *akato* are eternal and upon the body's death return to live in heaven once again.

*Akene*   The water of Lake Akuena, which has the power of immortality, derived in part from the *kaahi* plant that grows along its shores.

*Chakara*   The shaman's medicine pouch in which he stores a variety of magic herbs, power stones and tobacco.

*Conuco*   The large slash and burn gardens found throughout the greater Amazon region.

*Ennemadi*   The fifth house of heaven, where the masters of the *wiriki* crystals dwell.

*Hadewa*   The master of the seventh house of heaven, Hadewa is identified as a fish and is very likely the father-in-law of Wanadi, the culture hero who married the daughter of the master of fish.

*Höhöttu*   The ferruginous pygmy owl, *Glaucidium brasilianum phalaenoides,* who lives in the sixth house of heaven with Mudo and Tawadi and forms, along with them, the great trinity of shaman's helpers.

*Huhai*   (pronounced fhufhai) Shaman.

*Huiio*   A supernatural anaconda with a feathered crown who lives in the rapids with her mawadi people, Huiio is the mistress of all water and the mother of everything in it.

*Iarake*   The most important alcoholic beverage of the Makiritare, made with fermented yuca.

*Iukuta*   The principal Makiritare beverage made from cassava and water and drunk in great quantities at every meal.

*Kaahi*   A hallucinogenic made from a *Banisteriopsis* vine, *kaahi* among the Makiritare is restricted to the *huhai* who uses it to travel to heaven to make contact with the invisible world. One of the most wide-spread hallucinogens in native South America, it is also known as caapi, yage, and ayahuasca, the "dead man's vine."

*Koiohiña*   The dark, cavelike region of the universe where Odosha and his Odoshankomo dwell.

*Maraka*   The shaman's gourd rattle, whose great magical properties are attributed to the *wiriki* crystals inside of it.

*Mawadi*   Supernatural anaconda, extremely feared for their custom of kidnapping women, overturning canoes, and causing floods.

*Motadewa*   The shamanic or secret name of heaven.

*Mudo*   The great potoo, *Nyctibius grandis,* who is Wanadi's brother and one of the three great bird spirits living in the sixth heaven.

*Nuna*   The moon, who is an evil cannibal spirit that spends all its time searching for *akato* and *huhai* travelling between earth and heaven.

*Odosha*   The master of evil and the incarnation of all negative forces in the universe, Odosha lives with his people, the Odoshankomo, in dark caves in a land called Koiohiña and is involved in a constant struggle to dominate the earth.

*Setawa Kaliana*   The "*huhai's* masters," who dwell in ladekuna hana, the second house of heaven, these spirits are said to be related to the Kaliana, or Sape Indians, of the Paragua River. It is the image of the Setawa Kaliana shamans, seated back to back in meditation, which is carved at the top of every maraca.

*Shiriche*   The stars, both those we see in our own sky and the invisible ones dwelling in Shiriche Kumenadi at the top of heaven.

*So'to*   A human being or person, defined as any member of the Makiritare tribe or one who speaks its language.

*Tawadi*   The nacunda nighthawk, *Podager nacunda,* who dwells with Mudo and Höhöttu in the sixth heaven, Matawahuña.

*Wanadi*   God, culture hero and proto-shaman all in one, Wanadi is the unknowable, unseen force ("light") in heaven, who since his farewell has taken no part in the affairs of humans. Created by Shi, the sun, it was Wanadi who established order as it is known today.

*Watuma*   The complete, sacred narrative tradition of the Makiritare.

*Wiriki*   Small quartz crystals (by which Wanadi himself was created); all shamans, upon initiation, must travel to heaven to find these "power stones," which are then put in their maraca along with the roots of the shaman's drugs, *aiuku* and *kaahi.* The Makiritare claim that a long time ago, all people were created from *wiriki.*

# Maya Language

Maya is the name used by speakers themselves, a million or so in number, to denote the language of the lowlands that include Peten and the Yucatan peninsula. This is the domain of the great cities of the Classic Period (300–900), like Copan, Tikal, and Palenque, whose hieroglyphic inscriptions record the Maya language phonetically. Today, these Maya are divided by the national frontiers of Mexico, Guatemala, Belize, Honduras, and El Salvador. Transcribed in part from hieroglyphic script, the corpus of Maya texts is dominated by the tradition of the Chilam Balam books, which has been kept alive into this century in Chumayel and several Yucatecan towns and which defends the old calendar against the conventions and values imported by foreigners (*dzulob*).

## ■ The Chilam Balam Book of Chumayel (1780)
### *Mexico* (religious narration)

The core of these books is the calendrical cycle known as the *kahlay katunob,* or Katun Count, which corresponds to a period of 260 years (of 360 days each). The Katun Count texts have a direct antecedent in the Maya hieroglyphic books and inscriptions, and they went on to regulate life after the Spanish invasion in a system that rotated political power among the Yucatecan towns after which these Chilam Books are named, like Chumayel, Mani, Tizimin, Kaua, Oxcutzcab, and Ixil. Here the count of thirteen named katuns (e.g., 2 Ahau, or 13 Ahau) is the model for history and prognosis, for cosmogony, and for the prophecies of individual "speakers" or priests (*chilam*). Even riddles were incorporated into this corpus, as the means of examining pretenders to office in the katun system of government.

## The Interrogation of the Chiefs

This is the examination which takes place in the katun which ends today. The time has arrived for examining the knowledge of the chiefs of the towns, to see whether they know how the ruling men came, whether they have explained the coming of the chiefs, of the head-chiefs, whether they are of the lineage of rulers, whether they are of the lineage of chiefs, that they may prove it.

This is the first question which will be asked of them: he shall ask them for his food "Bring the sun." This is the word of the head-chief to the chiefs. "Bring the sun, my son, bear it on the palm of your hand to my plate. A lance is planted, a lofty cross, in the middle of its heart. A green jaguar is seated over the sun to drink its blood." Of Zuyua is the wisdom. This is what the sun is which is demanded of them: a very large fried egg. This is the lance and the lofty cross planted in its heart of which he speaks: it is the benediction. This is what the green jaguar is which is set over it to drink its blood: it is a green chile-pepper, is the jaguar. This is the language of Zuyua.

This is the second question that will be asked of them: let them go and get the brains of the sky, so the head-chief may see how large they are. "It is my desire to see them; let me see them." This is what he would say to them. This is what the brains of the sky are: it is copal gum.[1]

This is the third question which will be asked of them: let them construct a large house. Six *thils* is its length: one such measure is that of its upright timbers. This is what the large house is: it is a very large hat set on the floor. He shall be told to mount a very large white horse. White shall be his mantle and his cape, and he shall grasp a white rattle in his hand, while he rattles it at his horse. There is coagulated blood on the rosette of his rattle, which comes out of it. This is what the white horse is: it is a stirrup of henequen fiber. This is the white rattle mentioned, and the white cape: they are a Plumeria flower and a white wreath. This is the coagulated blood on the rosette of the rattle, which is demanded of them: it is the gold in the middle, because it is blood which comes from the veins of the fatherless and motherless orphan.

---

1. The gum of the copal (*Protium copal* Engl.) was the principal incense used by the Maya. The thick clouds of smoke may have suggested the convolutions of the brain.

This is the fourth question which will be asked of them: Let them go to his house and then they shall be told: "When you come, you shall be visible at midday. You shall be children again, you shall creep again. When you arrive, your little dog shall be just behind you. This little dog of yours carries with its teeth the soul of our holy mistress,[2] when you come with it." This is what the second childhood at midday is, which is mentioned to him. He shall go where he casts a shadow, this is what is called creeping. Then he shall come to the house of the head-chief. This is what his little dog is which is demanded of him: it is his wife. This is what the soul of our holy mistress is: it is an enormous thick wax candle.

This is the fifth question which will be asked of them. They shall be told to go and get the heart of God the Father in heaven. "Then you shall bring me thirteen layers[3] wrapped up in a coarse white fabric." This is the heart of God the Father, of which they are told: it is a bead of precious stone. This is what the covering of thirteen layers is, which is mentioned. It is an enormous tortilla. Thirteen layers of beans are in it. This is what the coarse white fabric is, it is a white mantle. This shall be demanded of them, as signified in the language of Zuyua.

This is the sixth question which will be asked of them: to go and get the branch of the *pochote* tree, and a cord of three strands, and a living liana. This he will relish. "My food for tomorrow. It is my desire to eat it." It is not bad to gnaw the trunk of the *pochote* tree, so they are told. This is what the trunk of the *pochote* tree is: it is a lizard. This is the cord of three strands, the tail of an iguana. This is the living liana, it is the entrails of a pig. This is the trunk of the *pochote* tree, the base of the tail of a lizard.

This is the seventh question which will be asked of them. They shall be told: "Go and gather for me those things which plug the bottom of the cenote, two white ones, two yellow ones. I desire to eat them." These are the things which plug the bottom of the cenote, which are demanded of them. They are two white and two yellow jícamas.[4] These are the things to be understood in order to become chiefs of the town, when they are brought before the ruler, the first head-chief.

These are the words. If they are not understood by the chiefs of the towns, ill-omened is the star adorning the night. Frightful is its house. Sad is the havoc[5] in the courtyards of the nobles. Those who die are those who do not understand; those who live will understand it. This competitive test shall hang over the chiefs of the towns; it has been copied so that the severity may be known in which the reign is to end.

TRANSLATED BY RALPH ROYS

---

2. Our holy mistress (*ca cilich colel*) is a term usually applied to the Holy Virgin.

3. Probably a reference to the thirteen heavens of the Maya cosmos.

4. *Pachyrhizus erosus* (L.) Urban. The Maya name, *chicam*, appears to be derived from the Nahuatl jícama, and this edible root may have been introduced by the Toltecs.

5. *Bulcum*, a misfortune frequently associated in these pages with swarming flies.

## ■ How Human Time Begins

It was set out this way by the first
        sage Melchisedek, the first
        prophet Napuctum, sacerdote,
        the first priest.
This is the song of how the *uinal*
        was realized, before the world
        was.
He started up from his inherent
        motion alone.
His mother's mother and her
        mother, his mother's sister and
        his sister-in-law, they all said:
How shall we say, how shall we
        see, that man is on the road?
These are the words they spoke as
        they moved along, where there
        was no man.
When they arrived in the east they
        began to say:
Who has been here? These are
        footprints. Get the rhythm of
        his step.
So said the Lady of the world,
and our Father, Dios, measured his
        step.
This is why the count by footstep
        of the whole world, *xoc lah cab*
        *oc,* was called *lahca oc* "12 Oc."
This was the order born through 13
        Oc,
when the one foot joined its
        counter print to make the
        moment of the eastern
        horizon.
Then he spoke its name when the
        day had no name
as he moved along with his
        mother's mother and her
        mother, his mother's sister and
        his sister-in-law.
The *uinal* born, the day so named,
        the sky and earth,
the stairway of water, earth, stone,
        and wood, the things of sea

and earth realized.                                45
Chuen, the day he rose to be a
        day-ity and made the sky and
        earth.
Eb, he made the first stairway. It
        ebbs from heaven's heart,          50
the heart of water, before there was
        earth, stone, and wood.
Ben, the day for making
        everything, all there is,
the things of the air, of the sea, of   55
        the earth.
Ix, he fixed the tilt of the sky and
        earth.
Men, he made everything.
Cib, he made the number one              60
        candle
and there was light in the absence
        of sun and moon.
Caban, honey was conceived
        when we had not a caban.          65
Etznab, his hands and feet were
        set, he sorted minutiae on the
        ground.
Cauac, the first deliberation of
        hell.                              70
Ahau, evil men were assigned to
        hell out of respect for Ds.
that they need not be noticed.
Imix, he construed stone and
        wood;                              75
he did this within the face of the
        day.
Ik, occurred the first breath;
it was named Ik because there was
        no death in it.                    80
Akbal, he poured water on the
        ground;
this he worked into man.
Kan, he "canned" the first anger
        because of the evil he had        85
        created.
Chicchan, he uncovered the evil
        he saw within the town.

Cimi, he invented death;
as it happened the father Ds.            90

invented the first death

Lamat, he invented the seven
    great seas.
Muluc, came the deluge and the
    submersion of everything
before the dawning. Then the
    father Ds. invented the word
when there was no word in heaven,
    when there was neither stone
    nor wood.
Then the twenty deities came to
    consider themselves in
    summation and said:
Thirteen units plus seven units
    equals one.
So said the *uinal* when the word
    came in, when there had been
    no word,
and this led to the question by the
    day Ahau, ruler,
Why was the meaning of the word
    not opened to them
so that they could declare
    themselves?
Then they went to heaven's heart
    and joined hands.

TRANSLATED BY GORDON BROTHERSTON AND ED DORN

## The Three Invasions

They didn't want to join the foreigners
Christianity was not their desire
they didn't want another tax

Those with their sign in the bird
those with their sign in the stone, flat worked stone
those with their sign in the jaguar — three emblems —:
four times four hundred *hab* was the period of their lives
plus fifteen score *hab* before that period ended
because they knew the rhythm of the days in themselves.

Whole the moon whole the *hab*
whole the day whole the night

whole the breath when it moved too whole the blood too
when they came to their beds their mats their thrones;
rhythm in their reading of the good hours
rhythm in their search for the good days                                        *15*
as they observed the good stars enter their reign
as they watched the reign of the good stars begin
Everything was good.

For they kept sound reason
there was no sin in the holy faith of their lives                               *20*
there was no sickness they had no aching bones
they had no high fever they had no smallpox
they had no burning chest they had no bellyache
they had no chest disease they had no headache
The course of mankind was ciphered clearly.                                     *25*

Not what the foreigners arranged when they came here
Then shame and terror were preferred
carnal sophistication in the flowers of Nacxit Xuchit and his circle
no more good days were shown to us
this was the start of the two-day chair, the two-day rule                       *30*
this was the start of our sickness also
there were no good days for us, no more sound reason.
At the end of the loss of our vision and of our shame
everything will be revealed.
There was no great priest no lord speaker no lord priest                        *35*
with the change of rulers when the foreigners came
The priests they set down here were lewd
they left their sons here at Mayapan
These in turn received their affliction from the foreigners called the
     Itza.
The saying is: since foreigners came three times                               *40*
three score *hab* is the age to get us exempted from tax
The trouble was the aggression of those men the Itza
we didn't do it we pay for it today
But there is an agreement at last to make us and the foreigners
     unanimous
Failing that we have no alternative to war                                      *45*

TRANSLATED BY GORDON BROTHERSTON AND ED DORN

## Last Words

This alone is the word
I, Chilam Balam, have interpreted the word

of the true god of all places in the world
in every part of the world it is heard, oh father
of sky and earth. Splendid indeed is his word in heaven
oh father, his rule over us, over our souls.
Yet as thrice the offspring of animals are the old men
of the younger brothers of the land. Snarled minds, hearts dead
in carnal sophistication, who too often turn back, who
propagate Nacxit Xuchit through the sophistication of his circle          1(
the two-day rulers, lustful on their thrones
lustful in their sophistication. Two-day men, their words
two-day their seats, their bowls, their hats
the day crime, the night crime, hoods of the world.
They turn back their necks, they wink their eyes, they drool          1!
          at the mouth
before our own representatives, oh father. See,
when they come the foreigners bring no truth.
Yet great secrets are told by the sons of the men
and the women of seven ruined houses          2(
          Who is the prophet
who is the priest who shall read
the word of this book

TRANSLATED BY GORDON BROTHERSTON AND ED DORN

## ■ Ritual of the Bacabs (1650) *Mesoamerica* (shaman cure)

TRANSLATED BY GORDON BROTHERSTON

Containing cures in the mainstream tradition of American shamanism, the texts in this manuscript originate entirely in the pre-Hispanic period and were written down in the alphabet around 1600. In addition to the usual shamanic appeal to birds, fourfold sky-bearers (bacabs), colors and winds, we find a peculiarly Maya emphasis on calendar dates, strikingly the "4 Ahau" date with which the current Mesoamerican era began in 3114 B.C.

## *This Is to Cool Burning Fever and to Cool Fire, the Ailment Fire*

My foot's coolness, my hand's coolness,
   as I cooled this fire.
Fivefold my white hail, my black hail, yellow hail,
   as I cool the fire.

Thirteenfold my red cloth, my white cloth, black cloth,       *5*
    yellow cloth,
    when I answered the strength of this fire.
A black fan my emblem,
    as I answered the strength of this fire.
With me comes the white water maize,       *10*
    and I answered the strength of this fire.
With me comes the white water lily,
    and I have answered the strength of this fire.
Just now I settled my foot's coolness, my hand's coolness.
    Amen.       *15*

## ■ X-Kolom-Che (Eighteenth Century) *Mexico* (song)

TRANSLATED BY ANN LONDON

Originally from the village of Dzitbalche in Campeche, this manu-script was found in Merida in 1942; it contains fifteen songs (*kay*) and its orthography (e.g., z for c) is eighteenth century. The thirteenth song (*X'okoot-kay h'ppum-t-huul*), translated here, directly invokes pre-Hispanic ritual through the prowess of the archer.

## *The Archer's Dance Song*

Look,
    stalker, mountain hunter,
once,
      twice
we're going to dance/hunt       *5*
    up to where the trees begin
three times in all.

Keep your head up
    look around
      don't make any mistakes that       *10*
      will lose you the game.

Were you careful to?
    1. file down your arrowhead
    2. stretch your bowstring tight
    3. resin the feathers with *catzim*       *15*
      down to the endknob of your arrowshaft
    4. smear the fat from a stag in rut
      on the power of your arm
      on the power of your foot
      on your knees       *20*

on your balls
on your ribs
on your chest
over your heart

NOW

    dance three times around
    the painted stone shaft

THERE

    where the young man is
    lashed
    virile, virgin, perfect

first time around

second time around

    take your bow
    fit the arrow
    aim at his chest
        but don't shoot with all your strength
        or tear into his flesh too deep

    let him suffer a little while

because this is the way

    Lord God
    wanted it.

The next time
    you dance around the (painted blue) shaft
    shoot him
again

        you must do this thing without
        a break in the dance because
        that is how the good fighters,
        the ones with shields, do it
        men who were chosen
        to please
        the eyes of
        Lord God

        As soon as the sun looks out
        over the eastern woods
    comes
the song of the archer

They do it all
        the shieldbearers
        the fighters

# Quiche-Maya Language

One of the several highland Maya languages spoken by majority populations in Chiapas and Guatemala, Quiche also names a kingdom whose western frontier with the Aztec tribute empire coincides with that between Guatemala and Mexico today. The term *Qui-che* means people of the trees or woods and as such approximates the Nahuatl Cuauh-temellan from which the very name Guatemala derives. The object of murderous military suppression in recent years, the town and province of Quiche remain unsubdued. Written alphabetically by native scribes soon after the European invasion, Quiche-Maya has the distinction of being the language of the *Popol Vuh*, by common consent the greatest work of early American literature.

## ■ Popol Vuh (1558) *Guatemala, Mexico* (religious narration)

As the book (*vuh*) of counsel, community, or the woven mat (*pop*), this text offers the fullest known American account of the world ages and the birth of humankind. Though written in the alphabet and "within Christianity," in the interests of a particular clan of the Quiche, it is grand enough to deserve the title "bible of America," and it builds on the deepest foundations in geology and biology in affirming its political claim. At the very start, energy switches between the feather-snake, iridescent in the water below, and Sky Heart, the "hurricane" One Leg above, and then moves through four "sproutings and humiliations" in time and space. It reveals the world ages and their endings. The mud men of the first age were too sloppy and reverted to fish in the flood water; those of the second were too stiff and perished when the "face of the earth was darkened" in eclipse. Next, under the protection of hairy mammal ancestors, the Twins defeat the egg-laying bird-reptile family of Seven Parrot, whose saurian sons play like volcanoes with the earth's crust. Consequently, the Twins are able to usurp their elder half brothers, who become monkeys and whose mother Alligator Macaw lacked the genetic advantage given to the Twins by their mother Blood Woman, daughter of the boney lord of the underworld Xibalba. Finally, Xibalba itself is overcome through the Twins' epic defeat of its rulers, and after they have walked into the sky as sun and moon, the people of this era are created from maize.

## Preamble: Silence of Sea and Sky

And now we shall name the name of the father of Hunahpu and Xbalanque. Let's drink to him, and let's just drink to the telling and accounting of the begetting of Hunahpu and Xbalanque. We shall tell just half of it, just a part of the account of their father. Here follows the account.

These are the names: One Hunahpu and Seven Hunahpu, as they are called.

And these are their parents: Xpiyacoc, Xmucane. In the blackness, in the night, One Hunahpu and Seven Hunahpu were born to Xpiyacoc and Xmucane.

And this One Hunahpu had two children, and the two were sons, the firstborn named One Monkey and the second named One Artisan.

And this is the name of their mother: she is called Xbaquiyalo, the wife of One Hunahpu. As for Seven Hunahpu, he has no wife. He's just a partner and just secondary; he just remains a boy.

They are great thinkers and great is their knowledge. They are the midmost seers, here on the face of the earth. There is only good in their being and their birthright. They taught skills to One Monkey and One Artisan, the sons of One Hunahpu. One Monkey and One Artisan became flautists, singers, and writers; carvers, jewelers, metalworkers as well.

And as for One and Seven Hunahpu, all they did was throw dice and play ball, every day. They would play each other in pairs, the four of them together. When they gathered in the ball court for entertainment a falcon would come to watch them, the messenger of Hurricane, Newborn Thunderbolt, Raw Thunderbolt. And for this falcon it wasn't far to the earth here, nor was it far to Xibalba; he could get back to the sky, to Hurricane, in an instant.

The four ballplayers remained here on the face of the earth after the mother of One Monkey and One Artisan had died. Since it was on the road to Xibalba that they played, they were heard by One Death and Seven Death, the lords of Xibalba:

"What's happening on the face of the earth? They're just stomping and shouting. They should be summoned to come play ball here. We'll defeat them, since we simply get no deference from them. They show no respect, nor do they have any shame. They're really determined to run right over us!" said all of Xibalba, when they all shared their thoughts, the ones named One and Seven Death. They are great lawgivers.

And these are the Lords over Everything, each lord with a commission and a domain assigned by One and Seven Death:

There are the lords named House Corner and Blood Gatherer. And this is their commission: to draw blood from people.

Next are the lordships of Pus Master and Jaundice Master. And this is their domain: to make people swell up, to make pus come out of their legs, to make their faces yellow, to cause jaundice, as it is called. Such is the domain of Pus Master and Jaundice Master.

Next are the lords Bone Scepter and Skull Scepter, the staff bearers of Xibalba; their staffs are just bones. And this is their staff-bearing: to reduce people to bones, right down to the bones and skulls, until they die from emaciation and edema. This is the commission of the ones named Bone Scepter and Skull Scepter.

Next are the lords named Trash Master and Stab Master. This is their commission: just to catch up with people whenever they have filth or grime in the doorway of the house, the patio of the house. Then they're struck, they're just punctured until they crawl on the ground, then die. And this is the domain of Trash Master and Stab Master, as they are called.

Next are the lords named Wing and Packstrap. This is their domain: that people should die in the road, just "sudden death," as it is called. Blood comes to the mouth, then there is death from vomiting blood. So to each of them his burden, the load on his shoulders: just to strike people on the neck and chest. Then there is death in the road, and then they just go on causing suffering, whether one is coming or going. And this is the domain of Wing and Packstrap.

Such are those who shared their thoughts when they were piqued and driven by One and Seven Hunahpu. What Xibalba desired was the gaming equipment of One and Seven Hunahpu: their kilts, their yokes, their arm guards, their panaches and headbands, the costumes of One and Seven Hunahpu.

And this is where we shall continue telling of their trip to Xibalba. One Monkey and One Artisan, the sons of One Hunahpu, stayed behind. Their mother died—and, what is more, they were to be defeated by Hunahpu and Xbalanque.

And now for the messengers of One and Seven Death: "You're going, you Military Keepers of the Mat, to summon One and Seven Hunahpu. You'll tell them, when you arrive:

"'They must come,' the lords say to you. "Would that they might come to play ball with us here. Then we could have some excitement with them. We are truly amazed at them. Therefore they should come," say the lords, "and they should bring their playthings, their yokes and arm guards should come, along with their rubber ball," say the lords,' you will say when you arrive," the messengers were told.

And these messengers of theirs are owls: Shooting Owl, One-legged Owl, Macaw Owl, Skull Owl, as the messengers of Xibalba are called.

There is Shooting Owl, like a point, just piercing.

And there is One-legged Owl, with just one leg; he has wings.

And there is Macaw Owl, with a red back; he has wings.

And there is also Skull Owl, with only a head alone; he has no legs, but he does have wings.

There are four messengers, Military Keepers of the Mat in rank.

And when they came out of Xibalba they arrived quickly, alighting above the ball court where One and Seven Hunahpu were playing, at the ball court called Great Abyss at Carchah. The owls, arriving in a flurry over the ball court, now repeated their words, reciting the exact words of One Death, Seven Death, Pus Master, Jaundice Master, Bone Scepter, Skull Scepter, House Corner, Blood Gatherer, Trash Master, Stab Master, Wing, Packstrap, as all the lords are named. Their words were repeated by the owls.

"Don't the lords One and Seven Death speak truly?"

"Truly indeed," the owls replied. "We'll accompany you. 'They're to bring along all their gaming equipment,' say the lords."

"Very well, but wait for us while we notify our mother," they replied.

And when they went to their house, they spoke to their mother; their father had died:

"We're going, our dear mother, even though we've just arrived. The messengers of the lord have come to get us:

"'They should come,' he says,' they say, giving us orders. We'll leave our rubber ball behind here," they said, then they went to tie it up under the roof of the house. "Until we return — then we'll put it in play again."

They told One Monkey and One Artisan:

"As for you, just play and just sing, write and carve to warm our house and to warm the heart of your grandmother." When they had been given their instructions, their grandmother Xmucane sobbed, she had to weep.

"We're going, we're not dying. Don't be sad," said One and Seven Hunahpu, then they left.

After that One and Seven Hunahpu left, guided down the road by the messengers.

And then they descended the road to Xibalba, going down a steep cliff, and they descended until they came out where the rapids cut through, the roaring canyon narrows named Neck Canyon. They passed through there, then they passed on into the River of Churning Spikes. They passed through countless spikes but they were not stabbed.

And then they came to water again, to blood: Blood River. They crossed but did not drink. They came to a river, but a river filled with pus. Still they were not defeated, but passed through again.

And then they came to the Crossroads, but here they were defeated, at the Crossroads:

Red Road was one and Black Road another.

White Road was one and Yellow Road another.

There were four roads, and Black Road spoke:

"I am the one you are taking. I am the lord's road," said the road. And they were defeated there: this was the Road of Xibalba.

And then they came to the council place of the lords of Xibalba, and they were defeated again there. The ones seated first there are just manikins, just woodcarvings dressed up by Xibalba. And they greeted the first ones:

"Morning, One Death," they said to the manikin. "Morning, Seven Death," they said to the woodcarving in turn.

So they did not win out, and the lords of Xibalba shouted out with laughter over this. All the lords just shouted with laughter because they had triumphed; in their hearts they had beaten One and Seven Hunahpu. They laughed on until One and Seven Death spoke:

"It's good that you've come. Tomorrow you must put your yokes and arm guards into action," they were told.

"Sit here on our bench," they were told, but the only bench they were offered was a burning-hot rock.

So now they were burned on the bench; they really jumped around on the bench now, but they got no relief. They really got up fast, having burned their butts. At this the Xibalbans laughed again, they began to shriek with laughter, the laughter rose up like a serpent in their very cores, all the lords of Xibalba laughed themselves down to their blood and bones.

"Just go in the house. Your torch and cigars will be brought to your sleeping quarters," the boys were told.

After that they came to the Dark House, a house with darkness alone inside. Meanwhile the Xibalbans shared their thoughts:

"Let's just sacrifice them tomorrow. It can only turn out to be quick; they'll die quickly because of our playing equipment, our gaming things," the Xibalbans are saying among themselves.

This ball of theirs is just a spherical knife. White Dagger is the name of the ball, the ball of Xibalba. Their ball is just ground down to make it smooth; the ball of Xibalba is just surfaced with crushed bone to make it firm.

And One and Seven Hunahpu went inside Dark House. And then their torch was brought, only one torch, already lit, sent by One and Seven Death, along with a cigar for each of them, also already lit, sent by the lords. When these were brought to One and Seven Hunahpu they were cowering, here in the dark. When the bearer of their torch and cigars arrived, the torch was bright as it entered; their torch and both of their cigars were burning. The bearer spoke:

"'They must be sure to return them in the morning—not finished, but just as they look now. They must return them intact,' the lords say to you," they were told, and they were defeated. They finished the torch and they finished the cigars that had been brought to them.

And Xibalba is packed with tests, heaps and piles of tests.

This is the first one: the Dark House, with darkness alone inside.

And the second is named Rattling House, heavy with cold inside, whistling with drafts, clattering with hail. A deep chill comes inside here.

And the third is named Jaguar House, with jaguars alone inside, jostling one another, crowding together, with gnashing teeth. They're scratching around; these jaguars are shut inside the house.

Bat House is the name of the fourth test, with bats alone inside the house, squeaking, shrieking, darting through the house. The bats are shut inside; they can't get out.

And the fifth is named Razor House, with blades alone inside. The blades are moving back and forth, ripping, slashing through the house.

These are the first tests of Xibalba, but One and Seven Hunahpu never entered into them, except for the one named earlier, the specified test house.

And when One and Seven Hunahpu went back before One and Seven Death, they were asked:

"Where are my cigars? What of my torch? They were brought to you last night!"

"We finished them, your lordship."

"Very well. This very day, your day is finished, you will die, you will disappear, and we shall break you off. Here you will hide your faces: you are to be sacrificed!" said One and Seven Death.

And then they were sacrificed and buried. They were buried at the Place of Ball Game Sacrifice, as it is called. The head of One Hunahpu was cut off; only his body was buried with his younger brother.

"Put his head in the fork of the tree that stands by the road," said One and Seven Death.

And when his head was put in the fork of the tree, the tree bore fruit. It would not have had any fruit, had not the head of One Hunahpu been put in the fork of the tree.

This is the calabash tree, as we call it today, or "the head of One Hunahpu," as it is said.

And then One and Seven Death were amazed at the fruit of the tree. The fruit grows out everywhere, and it isn't clear where the head of One Hunahpu is; now it looks just the way the calabashes look. All the Xibalbans see this, when they come to look.

The state of the tree loomed large in their thoughts, because it came about at the same time the head of One Hunahpu was put in the fork. The Xibalbans said among themselves:

"No one is to pick the fruit, nor is anyone to go beneath the tree," they said. They restricted themselves; all of Xibalba held back.

It isn't clear which is the head of One Hunahpu; now it's exactly the same as the fruit of the tree. Calabash tree came to be its name, and much was said about it. A maiden heard about it, and here we shall tell of her arrival.

And here is the account of a maiden, the daughter of a lord named Blood Gatherer.

And this is when a maiden heard of it, the daughter of a lord. Blood Gatherer is the name of her father, and Blood Woman is the name of the maiden.

And when he heard the account of the fruit of the tree, her father retold it. And she was amazed at the account:

"I'm not acquainted with that tree they talk about. '"Its fruit is truly sweet!" they say,' I hear," she said.

Next, she went all alone and arrived where the tree stood. It stood at the Place of Ball Game Sacrifice:

"What? Well! What's the fruit of this tree? Shouldn't this tree bear something sweet? They shouldn't die, they shouldn't be wasted. Should I pick one?" said the maiden.

And then the bone spoke; it was here in the fork of the tree:

"Why do you want a mere bone, a round thing in the branches of a tree?" said the head of One Hunahpu when it spoke to the maiden. "You don't want it," she was told.

"I do want it," said the maiden.

"Very well. Stretch out your right hand here, so I can see it," said the bone.

"Yes," said the maiden. She stretched out her right hand, up there in front of the bone.

And then the bone spit out its saliva, which landed squarely in the hand of the maiden.

And then she looked in her hand, she inspected it right away, but the bone's saliva wasn't in her hand.

"It is just a sign I have given you, my saliva, my spittle. This, my head, has nothing on it—just bone, nothing of meat. It's just the same with the head of a great lord: it's just the flesh that makes his face look good. And when he dies, people get frightened by his bones. After that, his son is like his saliva, his spittle, in his being, whether it be the son of a lord or the son of a craftsman, an orator. The father does not disappear, but goes on being fulfilled. Neither dimmed nor destroyed is the face of a lord, a warrior, craftsman, orator. Rather, he will leave his daughters and sons. So it is that I have done likewise through you. Now go up there on the face of the earth; you will not die. Keep the word. So be it," said the head of One and Seven Hunahpu—they were of one mind when they did it.

This was the word Hurricane, Newborn Thunderbolt, Raw Thunderbolt had given them. In the same way, by the time the maiden returned to her home, she had been given many instructions. Right away something was generated in her belly, from the saliva alone, and this was the generation of Hunahpu and Xbalanque.

And when the maiden got home and six months had passed, she was found out by her father. Blood Gatherer is the name of her father.

And after the maiden was noticed by her father, when he saw that she was now with child, all the lords then shared their thoughts—One and Seven Death, along with Blood Gatherer:

"This daughter of mine is with child, lords. It's just a bastard," Blood Gatherer said when he joined the lords.

"Very well. Get her to open her mouth. If she doesn't tell, then sacrifice her. Go far away and sacrifice her."

"Very well, your lordships," he replied. After that, he questioned his daughter:

"Who is responsible for the child in your belly, my daughter?" he said.

"There is no child, my father, sir; there is no man whose face I've known," she replied.

"Very well. It really is a bastard you carry! Take her away for sacrifice, you Military Keepers of the Mat. Bring back her heart in a bowl, so the lords can take it in their hands this very day," the owls were told, the four of them.

Then they left, carrying the bowl. When they left they took the maiden by the hand, bringing along the White Dagger, the instrument of sacrifice.

"It would not turn out well if you sacrificed me, messengers, because it is not a bastard that's in my belly. What's in my belly generated all by itself when I went to marvel at the head of One Hunahpu, which is there at the Place of Ball Game Sacrifice. So please stop: don't do your sacrifice, messengers," said the maiden. Then they talked:

"What are we going to use in place of her heart? We were told by her father:

'Bring back her heart. The lords will take it in their hands, they will satisfy themselves, they will make themselves familiar with its composition. Hurry, bring it back in a bowl, put her heart in the bowl.' Isn't that what we've been told? What shall we deliver in the bowl? What we want above all is that you should not die," said the messengers.

"Very well. My heart must not be theirs, nor will your homes be here. Nor will you simply force people to die, but hereafter, what will be truly yours will be the true bearers of bastards. And hereafter, as for One and Seven Death, only blood, only nodules of sap, will be theirs. So be it that these things are presented before them, and not that hearts are burned before them. So be it: use the fruit of a tree," said the maiden. And it was red tree sap she went out to gather in the bowl.

After it congealed, the substitute for her heart became round. When the sap of the croton tree was tapped, tree sap like blood, it became the substitute for her blood. When she rolled the blood around inside there, the sap of the croton tree, it formed a surface like blood, glistening red now, round inside the bowl. When the tree was cut open by the maiden, the so-called cochineal croton, the sap is what she called blood, and so there is talk of "nodules of blood."

"So you have been blessed with the face of the earth. It shall be yours," she told the owls.

"Very well, maiden. We'll show you the way up there. You just walk on ahead; we have yet to deliver this apparent duplicate of your heart before the lords," said the messengers.

And when they came before the lords, they were all watching closely:

"Hasn't it turned out well?" said One Death.

"It has turned out well, your lordships, and this is her heart. It's in the bowl."

"Very well. So I'll look," said One Death, and when he lifted it up with his fingers, its surface was soaked with gore, its surface glistened red with blood.

"Good. Stir up the fire, put it over the fire," said One Death.

After that they dried it over the fire, and the Xibalbans savored the aroma. They all ended up standing here, they leaned over it intently. They found the smoke of the blood to be truly sweet!

And while they stayed at their cooking, the owls went to show the maiden the way out. They sent her up through a hole onto the earth, and then the guides returned below.

In this way the lords of Xibalba were defeated by a maiden; all of them were blinded.

And here, where the mother of One Monkey and One Artisan lived, was where the woman named Blood Woman arrived.

And when the Blood Woman came to the mother of One Monkey and One Artisan, her children were still in her belly, but it wasn't very long before the birth of Hunahpu and Xbalanque, as they are called.

And when the woman came to the grandmother, the woman said to the grandmother:

"I've come, mother, madam. I'm your daughter-in-law and I'm your child, mother, madam," she said when she came here to the grandmother.

"Where do you come from? As for my last born children, didn't they die in Xibalba? And these two remain as their sign and their word: One Monkey and One Artisan are their names. So if you've come to see my children, get out of here!" the maiden was told by the grandmother.

"Even so, I really am your daughter-in-law. I am already his, I belong to One Hunahpu. What I carry is his. One Hunahpu and Seven Hunahpu are alive, they are not dead. They have merely made a way for the light to show itself, madam mother-in-law, as you will see when you look at the faces of what I carry," the grandmother was told.

And One Monkey and One Artisan have been keeping their grandmother entertained: all they do is play and sing, all they work at is writing and carving, every day, and this cheers the heart of their grandmother.

And then the grandmother said:

"I don't want you, no thanks, my daughter-in-law. It's just a bastard in your belly, you trickster! These children of mine who are named by you are dead," said the grandmother.

"Truly, what I say to you is so!"

"Very well, my daughter-in-law, I hear you. So get going, get their food so they can eat. Go pick a big netful of corn, then come back—since you are already my daughter-in-law, as I understand it," the maiden was told.

"Very well," she replied.

After that, she went to the garden; One Monkey and One Artisan had a garden. The maiden followed the path they had cleared and arrived there in the garden, but there was only one clump, there was no other plant, no second or third. That one clump had borne its ears. So then the maiden's heart stopped:

"It looks like I'm a sinner, a debtor! Where will I get the netful of food she asked for?" she said. And then the guardians of food were called upon by her:

"Come thou, rise up, come thou, stand up:
Generous Woman, Harvest Woman,
Cacao Woman, Cornmeal Woman,
    thou guardian of the food of One Monkey, One Artisan,"
said the maiden.

And then she took hold of the silk, the bunch of silk at the top of the ear. She pulled it straight out, she didn't pick the ear, and the ear reproduced itself to make food for the net. It filled the big net.

And then the maiden came back, but animals carried her net. When she got back she went to put the pack frame in the corner of the house, so it would look to the grandmother as if she had arrived with a load.

And then, when the grandmother saw the food, a big netful:

"Where did that food of yours come from? You've leveled the place! I'm going to see if you've brought back our whole garden!" said the grandmother.

And then she went off, she went to look at the garden, but the one clump was still there, and the place where the net had been put at the foot of it was still obvious.

And the grandmother came back in a hurry, and she got back home, and she said to the maiden:

"The sign is still there. You really are my daughter-in-law! I'll have to keep watching what you do. These grandchildren of mine are already showing genius," the maiden was told.

Now this is where we shall speak of the birth of Hunahpu and Xbalanque.

And this is their birth; we shall tell of it here.

Then it came to the day of their birth, and the maiden named Blood Woman gave birth. The grandmother was not present when they were born; they were born suddenly. Two of them were born, named Hunahpu and Xbalanque. They were born in the mountains, and then they came into the house. Since they weren't sleeping:

"Throw them out of here! They're really loudmouths!" said the grandmother.

After that, when they put them on an anthill, they slept soundly there. And when they removed them from there, they put them in brambles next.

And this is what One Monkey and One Artisan wanted: that they should die on the anthill and die in the brambles. One Monkey and One Artisan wanted this because they were rowdyish and flushed with jealousy. They didn't allow their younger brothers in the house at first, as if they didn't even know them, but even so they flourished in the mountains.

And One Monkey and One Artisan were great flautists and singers, and as they grew up they went through great suffering and pain. It had cost them suffering to become great knowers. Through it all they became flautists, singers, and writers, carvers. They did everything well. They simply knew it when they were born, they simply had genius. And they were the successors of their fathers who had gone to Xibalba, their dead fathers.

Since One Monkey and One Artisan were great knowers, in their hearts they already realized everything when their younger brothers came into being, but they didn't reveal their insight because of their jealousy. The anger in their hearts came down on their own heads; no great harm was done. They were decoyed by Hunahpu and Xbalanque, who merely went out shooting every day. These two got no love from the grandmother, or from One Monkey and One Artisan. They weren't given their meals; the meals had been prepared and One Monkey and One Artisan had already eaten them before they got there.

But Hunahpu and Xbalanque aren't turning red with anger; rather, they just let it go, even though they know their proper place, which they see as clear as day. So they bring birds when they arrive each day, and One Monkey and One Artisan eat them. Nothing whatsoever is given to Hunahpu and Xbalanque, either one of them. All One Monkey and One Artisan do is play and sing.

And then Hunahpu and Xbalanque arrived again, but now they came in here without bringing their birds, so the grandmother turned red:

"What's your reason for not bringing birds?" Hunahpu and Xbalanque were asked.

"There are some, our dear grandmother, but our birds just got hung up in a tree," they said, "and there's no way to get up the tree after them, our dear grandmother, and so we'd like our elder brothers to please go with us, to please go get the birds down," they said.

"Very well. We'll go with you at dawn," the elder brothers replied.

Now they had won, and they gathered their thoughts, the two of them, about the fall of One Monkey and One Artisan:

"We'll just turn their very being around with our words. So be it, since they have caused us great suffering. They wished that we might die and disappear—we, their younger brothers. Just as they wished us to be slaves here, so we shall defeat them there. We shall simply make a sign of it," they said to one another.

And then they went there beneath a tree, the kind named yellowwood, together with the elder brothers. When they got there they started shooting. There were countless birds up in the tree, chittering, and the elder brothers were amazed when they saw the birds. And not one of these birds fell down beneath the tree:

"Those birds of ours don't fall down; just go throw them down," they told their elder brothers.

"Very well," they replied.

And then they climbed up the tree, and the tree began to grow, its trunk got thicker.

After that, they wanted to get down, but now One Monkey and One Artisan couldn't make it down from the tree. So they said, from up in the tree:

"How can we grab hold? You, our younger brothers, take pity on us! Now this tree looks frightening to us, dear younger brothers," they said from up in the tree. Then Hunahpu and Xbalanque told them:

"Undo your pants, tie them around your hips, with the long end trailing like a tail behind you, and then you'll be better able to move," they were told by their younger brothers.

"All right," they said.

And then they left the ends of their loincloths trailing, and all at once these became tails. Now they looked like mere monkeys.

After that they went along in the trees of the mountains, small and great. They went through the forests, now howling, now keeping quiet in the branches of trees.

Such was the defeat of One Monkey and One Artisan by Hunahpu and Xbalanque. They did it by means of their genius alone.

And when they got home they said, when they came to their grandmother and mother:

"Our dear grandmother, something has happened to our elder brothers. They've become simply shameless, they're like animals now," they said.

"If you've done something to your elder brothers, you've knocked me down and stood me on my head. Please don't do anything to your elder brothers, my dear grandchildren," the grandmother said to Hunahpu and Xbalanque. And they told their grandmother:

"Don't be sad, our dear grandmother. You will see the faces of our elder brothers again. They'll come, but this will be a test for you, our dear grandmother. Will you please not laugh while we test their destiny?" they said.

And then they began playing. They played "Hunahpu Monkey."

And then they sang, they played, they drummed. When they took up their flutes and drums, their grandmother sat down with them, then they played, they sounded out the tune, the song that got its name then. "Hunahpu Monkey" is the name of the tune.

And then One Monkey and One Artisan came back, dancing when they arrived.

And then, when the grandmother looked, it was their ugly faces the grandmother saw. Then she laughed, the grandmother could not hold back her laughter, so they just left right away, out of her sight again, they went up and away in the forest.

"Why are you doing that, our dear grandmother? We'll only try four times; only three times are left. We'll call them with the flute, with song. Please hold back your laughter. We'll try again," said Hunahpu and Xbalanque.

Next they played again, then they came back, dancing again, they arrived again, in the middle of the patio of the house. As before, what they did was delightful; as before, they tempted their grandmother to laugh. Their grandmother laughed at them soon enough. The monkeys looked truly ridiculous, with the skinny little things below their bellies and their tails wiggling in front of their breasts. When they came back the grandmother had to laugh at them, and they went back into the mountains.

"Please, why are you doing that, our dear grandmother? Even so, we'll try it a third time now," said Hunahpu and Xbalanque.

Again they played, again they came dancing, but their grandmother held back her laughter. Then they climbed up here, cutting right across the building, with thin red lips, with faces blank, puckering their lips, wiping their mouths and faces, suddenly scratching themselves. And when the grandmother saw them again, the grandmother burst out laughing again, and again they went out of sight because of the grandmother's laughter.

"Even so, our dear grandmother, we'll get their attention."

So for the fourth time they called on the flute, but they didn't come back again. The fourth time they went straight into the forest. So they told their grandmother:

"Well, we've tried, our dear grandmother. They came at first, and we've tried calling them again. So don't be sad. We're here—we, your grandchildren. Just love our mother, dear grandmother. Our elder brothers will be remembered. So be it: they have lived here and they have been named; they are to be called One Monkey and One Artisan," said Hunahpu and Xbalanque.

So they were prayed to by the flautists and singers among the ancient people, and the writers and carvers prayed to them. In ancient times they turned into animals, they became monkeys, because they just magnified themselves, they abused their younger brothers. Just as they wished them to be slaves, so they themselves were brought low. One Monkey and One Artisan were lost then, they became animals, and this is now their place forever.

Even so, they were flautists and singers; they did great things while they lived with their grandmother and mother.

\* \* \*

And here is the beginning of the conception of humans, and of the search for the ingredients of the human body. So they spoke, the Bearer, Begetter, the Makers, Modelers named Sovereign Plumed Serpent:

"The dawn has approached, preparations have been made, and morning has come for the provider, nurturer, born in the light, begotten in the light. Morning has come for humankind, for the people of the face of the earth," they said. It all came together as they went on thinking in the darkness, in the night, as they searched and they sifted, they thought and they wondered.

And here their thoughts came out in clear light. They sought and discovered what was needed for human flesh. It was only a short while before the sun, moon, and stars were to appear above the Makers and Modelers. Broken Place, Bitter Water Place is the name: the yellow corn, white corn came from there.

And these are the names of the animals who brought the food: fox, coyote, parrot, crow. There were four animals who brought the news of the ears of yellow corn and white corn. They were coming from over there at Broken Place, they showed the way to the break.

And this was when they found the staple foods.

And these were the ingredients for the flesh of the human work, the human design, and the water was for the blood. It became human blood, and corn was also used by the Bearer, Begetter.

And so they were happy over the provisions of the good mountain, filled with sweet things, thick with yellow corn, white corn, and thick with pataxte and cacao, countless zapotes, anonas, jocotes, nances, matasanos, sweets—the rich foods filling up the citadel named Broken Place, Bitter Water Place. All the edible fruits were there: small staples, great staples, small plants, great plants. The way was shown by the animals.

And then the yellow corn and white corn were ground, and Xmucane did the grinding nine times. Corn was used, along with the water she rinsed her hands with, for the creation of grease; it became human fat when it was worked by the Bearer, Begetter, Sovereign Plumed Serpent, as they are called.

After that, they put it into words:

the making, the modeling of our first mother-father,
with yellow corn, white corn alone for the flesh,
food alone for the human legs and arms,
for our first fathers, the four human works.

It was staples alone that made up their flesh.

These are the names of the first people who were made and modeled.
This is the first person: Jaguar Quitze.
And now the second: Jaguar Night.
And now the third: Mahucutah.
And the fourth: True Jaguar.

And these are the names of our first mother-fathers. They were simply made and modeled, it is said; they had no mother and no father. We have named the men by themselves. No woman gave birth to them, nor were they begotten by the builder, sculptor, Bearer, Begetter. By sacrifice alone, by genius alone they were made, they were modeled by the Maker, Modeler, Bearer, Begetter, Sovereign Plumed Serpent. And when they came to fruition, they came out human:

They talked and they made words.
They looked and they listened.
They walked, they worked.

They were good people, handsome, with looks of the male kind. Thoughts came into existence and they gazed; their vision came all at once. Perfectly they saw, perfectly they knew everything under the sky, whenever they looked. The moment they turned around and looked around in the sky, on the earth, everything was seen without any obstruction. They didn't have to walk around before they could see what was under the sky; they just stayed where they were.

As they looked, their knowledge became intense. Their sight passed through trees, through rocks, through lakes, through seas, through mountains, through plains. Jaguar Quitze, Jaguar Night, Mahucutah, and True Jaguar were truly gifted people.

And then they were asked by the builder and mason:

"What do you know about your being? Don't you look, don't you listen? Isn't your speech good, and your walk? So you must look, to see out under the sky. Don't you see the mountain-plain clearly? So try it," they were told.

And then they saw everything under the sky perfectly. After that, they thanked the Maker, Modeler:

"Truly now,
double thanks, triple thanks
that we've been formed, we've been given
our mouths, our faces,
we speak, we listen,
we wonder, we move,
our knowledge is good, we've understood
what is far and near,
and we've seen what is great and small
under the sky, on the earth.
Thanks to you we've been formed,
we've come to be made and modeled,
our grandmother, our grandfather,"

they said when they gave thanks for having been made and modeled. They understood everything perfectly, they sighted the four sides, the four corners in the sky, on the earth, and this didn't sound good to the builder and sculptor:

"What our works and designs have said is no good:

'We have understood everything, great and small,' they say." And so the Bearer, Begetter took back their knowledge:

"What should we do with them now? Their vision should at least reach nearby, they should see at least a small part of the face of the earth, but what they're saying isn't good. Aren't they merely 'works' and 'designs' in their very names? Yet they'll become as great as gods, unless they procreate, proliferate at the sowing, the dawning, unless they increase."

"Let it be this way: now we'll take them apart just a little, that's what we need. What we've found out isn't good. Their deeds would become equal to ours, just because their knowledge reaches so far. They see everything," so said

the Heart of Sky, Hurricane,
Newborn Thunderbolt, Raw Thunderbolt,

Sovereign Plumed Serpent,
Bearer, Begetter,
Xpiyacoc, Xmucane,
Maker, Modeler,

as they are called. And when they changed the nature of their works, their designs, it was enough that the eyes be marred by the Heart of Sky. They were blinded as the face of a mirror is breathed upon. Their eyes were weakened. Now it was only when they looked nearby that things were clear.

And such was the loss of the means of understanding, along with the means of knowing everything, by the four humans. The root was implanted.

And such was the making, modeling of our first grandfather, our father, by the Heart of Sky, Heart of Earth.

And then their wives and women came into being. Again, the same gods thought of it. It was as if they were asleep when they received them, truly beautiful women were there with Jaguar Quitze, Jaguar Night, Mahucutah, and True Jaguar. With their women there they became wider awake. Right away they were happy at heart again, because of their wives.

Celebrated Seahouse is the name of the wife of Jaguar Quitze.
Prawn House is the name of the wife of Jaguar Night.
Hummingbird House is the name of the wife of Mahucutah.
Macaw House is the name of the wife of True Jaguar.
So these are the names of their wives, who became ladies of rank, giving birth to the people of the tribes, small and great.

TRANSLATED BY DENNIS TEDLOCK

## The End of the Doll People

This is the root of the former word.
　　Here is Quiche by name.
Here we shall write then,
　　We shall start out then, the former words,
The beginnings
　　And the taproots
Of everything done in the Quiche town,
　　The tribe of the Quiche people.
So this is what we shall collect then,
　　The decipherment,
The clarification,
　　And the explanation

*1*

Of the mysteries
  And the illumination
By Former,             15
  And Shaper;
Bearer
  And Engenderer are their names,

Hunter Possum
  And Hunter Coyote,        20
Great White Pig
  And Coati,
Majesty
  And Quetzal Serpent,
The Heart of the Lake         25
  And the Heart of the Sea,
Green Plate Spirit
  And Blue Bowl Spirit, as it is said,
Who are likewise called,
  Who are likewise spoken of     30
As the Woman with Grandchildren
  And Man with Grandchildren,
Xpiacoc
  And Xmucane by name,
Shelterer             35
  And Protector,
Great-Grandmother
  And Great-Grandfather,
As it is said
  In Quiche words.         40
Then they said everything
  And did it furthermore,
In the bright existence
  And bright words.
This we shall write already within the word of God,  45

  Already in Christianity.
We shall save it
  Because there is no longer
A sight of the Book of Counsel,
  A sight of the bright things come    50
    from beside the sea,
The description of our shadows,
  A sight of the bright life, as it is called.
There was once the manuscript of it,
  And it was written long ago,      55
Only hiding his face is the reader of it,
  The meditator of it.

Great was its account
    And its description
Of when there was finished 60
    The birth
Of all of heaven
    And earth:
    The four humiliations,
The knowledge 6_
    Of the four punishments,
The rope of tying together,
    The line of tying together,
The womb of heaven,
    The womb of earth. 7(
Four creations,
    Four humiliations, it was told,

By the Former
    And Shaper,
The Mother 7⁵
    And Father
Of Life
    And Mankind,
The Inspirer
    And Heartener, 8(
Bearer
    And Heartener
Light
    And the Race,
Children of the Mother of Light, 8⁵
    Sons of the Father of Light,
The Meditator,
    The Thinker
Of everything,
    Whatever exists: 9(
Heaven,
    Earth,
Lake,
    And Sea

*II*

Here is the description
    Of these things:
Truly it was yet quiet,
    Truly it was yet stilled.
It was quiet.
    Truly it was calm.

Truly it was solitary
    And it was also still empty, the womb of heaven.

*III*

These are truly then the first words,
    The first utterances.
There was not one person yet,
    One animal,
(Deer,)                              *5*
    Bird,
Fish,
    Crab,
Tree,
    Rock,                           *10*
Hole,
    Canyon,
Meadow
    Or forest.
All by itself the sky existed.                *15*
    The face of the earth was not yet visible.
All by itself the sea lay dammed,
    And the womb of heaven,
Everything.
    There was nothing whatever         *20*
Silenced
    Or at rest.
Each thing was made silent,
    Each thing was made calm,
Was made invisible,                  *25*

    Was made to rest in heaven.
There was not, then, anything in fact
    That was standing there.
Only the pooled water,
    Only the flat sea.                *30*
All by itself it lay dammed.
    There was not, then, anything in fact that might have existed.
It was just still.
    It was quiet
In the darkness,                   *35*
    In the night.
All alone the Former
    And Shaper,
Majesty,
    And Quetzal Serpent,          *40*
The Mothers
    And Fathers

Were in the water.
    Brilliant they were then,
And wrapped in quetzal
    And dove feathers.
Thence came the name
    Of Quetzal Serpent.
Great sages they were
    And great thinkers in their essence,
For indeed there is Heaven
    And there is also the Heart of Heaven.
That is the name
    Of the deity, it is said.

*IV*

So then came his word here.
    It reached
To Majesty
    And Quetzal Serpent
There in the obscurity,
    In the nighttime.
It spoke to Majesty
    And Quetzal Serpent, and they spoke.
Then they thought;
    Then they pondered.
Then they found themselves;
    They assembled
Their words,
    Their thoughts.
Then they gave birth—
    Then they heartened themselves.
Then they caused to be created
    And they bore men.
Then they thought about the birth,
    The creation
Of trees
And the birth of life
    And humanity
In the obscurity,
    In the nighttime
Through him who is the Heart of Heaven,
    Leg by name.
Leg Lightning is the first,
    And the second is Dwarf Lightning.
Third then is Green Lightning,
    So that the three of them are the Heart of Hearts
Then they came to Majesty

And Quetzal Serpent, and then was the invention
Of light
  And life.               *35*
"What if it were planted?
  Then something would brighten —
A supporter,
  A nourisher.
So be it.                 *40*
  You must decide on it.
There is the water to get rid of,
  To be emptied out,
To create this,
  The earth             *45*
And have it surfaced
  And levelled
When it is planted,
  When it is brightened —
Heaven              *50*
  And earth.
But there can be no adoration
  Or glorification
Of what we have formed,
  What we have shaped.        *55*
Until we have created a human form,
  A human shape," so they said.
So then this the earth was created by them.
  Only their word was the creation of it.
To create the earth, "Earth," they said.    *60*
  Immediately it was created.
It was just like a cloud,
  Like a mist then,
The creation then,
  The whirlwind.          *65*
Then the mountain was asked to come from the water.
  Straightaway there were great mountains.
Just their power,
  Just their magic
Caused the making then,        *70*
  The invention
Of mountains
  And valleys.
At a stroke there were also created cedar groves on them
  And pine forests on them.      *75*
So Quetzal Serpent then rejoiced,
  "It is good that you have come,
Oh Heart of Heaven,

       Oh Leg,
And you, Dwarf Lightning
       And Green Lightning.
Our forming is successful,
       And our shaping," they said.
And once they had created
       The earth,
The mountains
       And valleys,
The paths of the waters were unravelled
       And they proceeded to twist along among the hills.
So the rivers then became more divided
       As the great mountains were appearing.
And thus was the creation of the earth
       When it was created by him
Who is the Heart of Heaven,
       The Heart of Earth,
As they are called.
       And they were the first to think of it.
The sky was rounded out there
       And the earth was rounded out in the water,

And thus it was invented as they thought,
       As they reflected
On its perfection,
       Its being made by them.


    *V*

Then they thought further
       Of the wild animals,
Guardians of the forest,
       And all the population of the wild:
Deer,
       Birds,
Panthers,
       Jaguars,
Serpents,
       Rattlers,
Yellowmouths,
       Guardians of plants.
The Mother said this,
       And the Father:
"Should it only be still,
       Or should it not be silent
Under the trees
       And shrubs?

Indeed, it would be good if there were
          Guardians for them," they said,                                    *20*
And when they thought
          And talked,
At a stroke there came to be
          And were created
Deer                                                                        *25*
          And birds.
Then they awarded homes also to the deer
          And birds.
"You, Deer, on the rivers
          And in the canyons                                                 *30*
Will you sleep then.
          There will you be then,
In the grass,
          In the fruits.
In the wilderness                                                            *35*
          Will you multiply yourselves then.
On all fours your walk,
          Your gait will be,"
They were told,
          And then they designated                                           *40*
The homes of the little birds
          And the big birds.
"You, oh Birds, in the trees,
          In the bushes
Make your homes then,                                                        *45*
          Make your houses then.
Multiply there then,
          Increase then
On the branches of trees,
          On the branches of shrubs,"                                        *50*
The deer were told,
          And the birds.
When they had done
          Their creating,
They gave them everything: their nests                                       *55*
          And lairs.
And so the homes
          Of the animals were the earth.
They gave it, the Mother
          And Father.                                                        *60*
There was completed
          The assignment
Of all the deer
          And birds.

VI
Then also they were told, the deer
    And birds
By Former
    And Shaper,
The Mother
    And Father,
"Talk, then,
    Call, then.
Don't warble;
    Don't cry.
Make yourselves understood
    To each other
In each species,
    In each grouping,"
The deer were told,
    And the birds,
Panthers,
    Jaguars,
Serpents,
    (And snakes).
"Now then, pronounce
    Our names.
Worship us, your Mother
    And your Father.
Now then, say this:
    *Leg,*
*Dwarf Lightning,*
    *Green Lightning,*
*The Heart of Heaven,*
    *The Heart of Earth,*
*Former,*
    *Shaper,*
*Mother*
    *And Father.*
Talk then,
    And call to us.
Worship us,"
    They were told.
But they did not succeed in talking like men.
    They just pretended to.
They just rattled;
    And they just croaked.
The form of their speech did not emerge.
    Differently they made cries, each one apart.
When Former heard it

And Shaper,
"It is not yet arranged
        So they can talk,"
They repeated

        To each other.                                          50
"They do not succeed in pronouncing
        Our names,
Although we are their Former
        And we are their Shaper.
It isn't good," they repeated                                    55
        To each other,
They the Mother
        And Father.
And they were told,
        "Just change yourselves,                                 60
Because it is not yet successful
        Since you do not speak.
We shall therefore change
        Our word.
Your food,                                                       65
        Your nourishment,
Your sleeping places,
        Your lairs,
What has been yours
        Has now become                                          70
The canyons
        And the wilderness,
Because our worship has not been achieved;
        You do not yet call upon us.
Indeed there is,                                                 75
        Or there should be
A worshipper,
        A praiser whom we shall yet make
Who will just take your places,

        And your flesh will just be eaten.                       80
So be it then,
        And there may you serve,"
They were told.
        So they were commanded—
The little animals                                               85
        And big animals who are upon the earth.
And then it was necessary for them to try their luck again.
It was necessary for them to make another attempt,
And it was necessary for them to arrange again for worship.
For they couldn't catch their speech among themselves.           90

For it couldn't be understood,
    As it wasn't made that way.
And so their flesh was humbled.
    They served.
They were eaten.
    They were killed,
The animals that were here on the face of the earth.
    And so there was another effort
To form man,
    To shape man
By the Former
    And Shaper,
The Mother
    And Father.
"Let us just try again.
    Already it has approached
The planting,
    The brightening.
Let us make a supporter for us,
    A nourisher for us.
How then can we be called upon
    And be remembered upon the earth?
We have already tried with the first of our formings
    Our shapings.
We did not attain our being worshipped
    And being glorified by them.
And so let us try now
    To make
A praiser,
    A worshipper,
A supporter,
    A nourisher," they said.
For then there was the forming
    And the working
Of earth
    And mud.
Its body they made,
    But it didn't look good to them.
It just kept coming apart.
    It was just absorbent.
It was just soggy;
    It was just damp.
It was just crumbling
    And it was just dissolving.
Its head wasn't rounded.

Its face was just one sided.
Its eyes were just veiled
    And couldn't be looked into.
As soon as it spoke
    It made no sense.                   *140*
Just all at once it dissolved in the water.
    "It wasn't strong," they said then,
Former
    And Shaper.
"It looks wet.                         *145*
    If it should just get wet
It couldn't walk
    And it couldn't be made to multiply.
So be it.
    Its mind is dark there," they said.        *150*
And so they destroyed it.
    They overthrew again
What they had formed,
    They had shaped.
And they said again,                  *155*
    "What are there that we can make
That may succeed then,
    That may be intelligent then,
Worshipping us,
    And calling upon us?" they said.         *160*
Then they thought further
    And just called upon
Xpiacoc
    And Xmucane,
Hunter Possum                  *165*
    And Hunter Coyote.
"They can try again their divination,
    Their creation," they told each other—
The Former
    And Shaper.                    *170*
And so they spoke to Xpiacoc
    And Xmucane.
And indeed it was proposed to them,
    The far seers,
The Grandmother of Day,           *175*
    The Grandmother of Light.
They were addressed by the Former
    And Shaper.
These are the names of Xpiacoc
    And Xmucane.                *180*

*VII*

And there spoke also
    Leg
With Majesty
    And Quetzal Serpent.
Then they spoke to the Sun Priest
    And the Shaper, the far seers,
"It must be sought
    And it will just be found
So that then again we can shape man,
    So that we can form man again then,        1
As a supporter
    And nourisher.
We shall be called upon,
    And we shall be remembered.
Then there may be support        1
    In words,
Ancestress of Grandchildren,
    Ancestor of Grandchildren,
Our Grandmother,
    Our Grandfather,        2
Xpiacoc
    And Xmucane.
If you plow it
    And it is then planted
Then it will brighten into        2
    Our being called upon,
Our being supported,
    Our being remembered
By the formed people,
    The shaped people,        3
The doll people.
    The made up people.
Do it then.
    So be it.
Manifest you        3
    Your names,
Hunter Possum,
    Hunter Coyote,
Grandmother,
    Grandfather,        4
Great Pig,
    Great Coati,
Gemcutter,
    Jeweller,

Carver,                                                          *45*
    Sculptor,
Green Plate Spirit,
    Blue Bowl Spirit,
Incense Maker,
    Craftsman,                                 *50*
Grandmother of Day,
    Grandmother of Light.
Be called upon by what we form,
    What we shape.
Cast with the corn;                                              *55*
    With the tz'ite beans operate,
And it will just come
    To pass
That we elaborate
    And that we chisel out                     *60*
His mouth
    And his face for him,"
They declared
    To the Sun Priests.
And then indeed was their throwing,                              *65*
    Their divining,
That they cast with corn
    And with tz'ite —
The Sun
    And Shaper.                                *70*
And then spoke a Grandmother
    And a Grandfather to them.
There was the Grandfather:
    He was the tz'ite man.
Xpiacoc was his name.                                            *75*
    There was the Grandmother,
Sun Priest,
    The Shaper,
At his feet,
    Xmucane was her name.                      *80*
And they said
    As they began to divine,
*"Just look around*
    *And just find it,*
You say.                                                         *85*
    Our ear hears
Your speaking
    What may have been said.
*Just find the wood to be worked*
    *And to be carved*                         *90*

*By the Former*
  *And Shaper.*
*Indeed this will be a nourisher*
  *And supporter*
*When it is planted then,*
  *When it brightens then.*
Oh, Corn,
  Oh, Tz'ite,
Oh, Sun,
  Oh, Shaper,
Join now
  And be coupled"

TRANSLATED BY MUNRO EDMUNSON

# Nahuatl Language

Once the lingua franca of the area known as Mesoamerica, Nahuatl names most of its present-day states, like Mexico, Guatemala, Cuzcatlan (the old name of El Salvador), and Nicaragua. It was inherited from Toltec and other predecessors by the Aztecs or Mexica, the major political power in the area when Cortes arrived in 1519. Based initially on folding books written in the iconic script of Mesoamerica, the literature in Nahuatl is vast and includes annals, histories, cosmogonies, epics, poems, hymns, prayers, letters, and petitions. Spoken by a million or more people in Mexico, it has recently undergone a literary renaissance.

## ■ Tlatelolco Annals (1528) *Mexico* (chronicles)

The annals of Tlatelolco, the twin city of the Aztec capital Tenochtitlan, span the twelfth century to 1528. In them, local historians tell how the Spaniards were at first welcomed there in the year 1 Reed (1519), before being expelled on account of their barbaric behavior. In the year 3 Reed (1521), the Spaniards and their Tlaxcalan allies returned, built a fleet to control the lake that surrounded the capital, and besieged it. At the very end, the battle shifted from Tenochtitlan to Tlatelolco, where the emperor Cuauhtemoc finally surrendered to Hernan Cortes.

## All This Happened among Us

### TRANSLATED BY GORDON BROTHERSTON

And all this happened among us. We saw it. We lived through it with
     an astonishment worthy of tears
and of pity for the pain we suffered.
On the roads lie broken shafts and torn hair,
houses are roofless, homes are stained red,
worms swarm in the streets, walls are spattered with brains.
The water is reddish, like dyed water;
we drink it so, we even drink brine;
the water we drink is full of saltpetre.
The wells are crammed with adobe bricks.

Whatever was still alive was kept between shields, like precious treasure,
between shields, until it was eaten.

We chewed on hard tzompantli wood, brackish *zacatl* fodder, chunks of
adobe, lizards, vermin, dust and worms.

We eat what was on the fire, as soon as it is done we eat it together right by
the fire.

We had a single price; there was a standard price for a youth, a priest, a
boy and a young girl. The maximum price for a slave amounted to only
two handfuls of maize, to only ten tortillas. Only twenty bundles of brackish fodder was the price of gold, jade, mantles, quetzal plumes; all valuables fetched the same low price. It went down further when the
Spaniards set up their battering engine in the market place.

Now, Cuauhtemoc orders the prisoners to be brought out; the guards
don't miss any. The elders and chiefs grab them by their extremities and
Cuauhtemoc slits open their bellies with his own hand.

■ ### The Aztec Priests' Speech (1524) *Mexico* (poem)

### TRANSLATED BY GORDON BROTHERSTON AND EDWARD DORN

In 1524, twelve Franciscan missionaries were sent from Rome to urge
the Aztec priesthood to convert to Christianity. Their efforts provoked this
considered reply, the record of which was revised and polished in 1564 by
Nahuatl scribes from Tlatelolco and other centers. It opens on a note of
humility and courtesy, like the welcome first offered by Moctezuma to

Cortes in 1519. The speaker then rehearses the claims made by the Christians on their own behalf, which gives them an ironic air. Yet his concern is professional: the Aztecs no more want to demolish the friars than they themselves wish to be demolished. Knowing that both parties have been "cast in a corner" by the secular authority Cortes ("our sovereign here"), they say they prefer not to unsettle things "with what we say amongst ourselves." What they reveal of their own religion is imaged as three "gifts," proper to the priesthood itself, the maize farmer, and the warrior. This last statement defends a political tradition older than Teotihuacan, which reaches back to the start of the era and the first named city of Mesoamerica, the lowland Tula of Quetzalcoatl, and the ancient Toltecs.

What we say here is for its own reason
beyond response and against our future.

Our revered lords, sirs, dear ones,
take rest from the toil of the road,
you are now in your house and in your nature.
Here we are before you, subjected,
in the mirror of yourselves.
Our sovereign here has let you come,
you have come to rule
as you must in your own place.
Where is it you come from,
how is it that your gods have been scattered
from their municipal centres?
Out of the clouds, out of the mist,
out of ocean's midst you have appeared.
The Alldeity takes form in you,
in your eye, in your ear, in your lips.
So, as we stand here,
we see, we address,
the one through whom everything lives,
the night, the Wind,
whose representatives you are.

And we have felt the breath, the word
of our lord the Alldeity
which you have brought with you.
The speaker of the world sent you because of us.
Here we are, amazed by this.
You brought his book with you, his script,
heaven's word, the word of god.

And now what? How is it,
what are we supposed to say,
what shall we present to your ears?

Can it be said we are anything at all?
We are small subjects.

We are just dirt,                                                        *35*
no good,
pressed, reduced to want;
furthermore our sovereign here
mistook us consistently
and has cast us into a corner.                                          *40*

But we refute the logo of the Alldeity.

We are down to our skulls in this and we fall over
into the river, into the abyss.
Anger and wrath
will be attracted to our behaviour.                                     *45*
Maybe this is our moment; perhaps this is ruin.
In any case, we shall be dispirited.
Where do we go from here
in our subjection,
reduced, mortalized?                                                    *50*
Cut us loose,
because the gods have died.
But you don't have to feel any of this.

Our dear lords,
we share some of it all.                                                *55*
Now we open a little
the store, the treasure casket,
for our sovereign here.

You say
we don't know                                                          *60*
the Alldeity of heaven and earth.
You say our gods are not original.
That's news to us
and it drives us crazy.
It's a shock and a scandal.                                             *65*
Our ancestors came to earth
and spoke quite differently.

They gave us
their law
and they believed,                                                     *70*
they served, and they taught honour among gods;
they taught the whole service.
That's why we eat earth before them;
that's why we draw our blood and do penance;
and why we burn copal and kill the living.                              *75*

They were the Lifelord
and they became our only subject.
When and where? — In the eldest Darkness.

They gave us
our supper and our breakfast,
all things to drink and eat,
maize and beans, purslane and sage.
And we beg them
for thunder rain and water
on which the earth thrives.
They are the rich ones
and they have more than simply what it takes;
they are the ones with the stuff,
all ways and all means, forever,
the greenness of growth.
Where and how? — In Tlalocan
hunger is not their experience,
nor sickness, and not poverty.

They also gave
inner manliness, kingly valour
and the acquisitions of the hunt:
the insignia of the lip, the knotting of the mantle,
loin-cloth and mantle,
Flower and aromatic leaf, jade,
quetzal plumes, and the godshit you call gold.
When and where? It is a long tradition.
Do you know
when the emplacement of Tula came, of Uapalcalco,
of Xuchatlappan, of Tamoanchan
of Yoalli ichan, of Teotihuacan?
They were the world-makers who founded
the mat of power, the seat of rule.
They gave
authority and entity,
fame and honour.
And should we now destroy the old law,
Toltec law, Chichimec law,
Colhua law,
Tepanec law,
on which the heart of being flows,
from which we animate our selves,
through which we pass to adulthood,
from which flows our cosmology
and the manner of our prayer?

Oooh! Señores Nuestros,                                                      *120*
do nothing;
don't do anything to your population.
It can only bring more ruin,
it can only bring more ruin to the old ones,
our elders, from whom man and woman have grown.                              *125*

Let us not
anger the gods;
let us not invite their hunger.
Do not unsettle this population.
Why should we agitate them                                                   *130*
with what we say among us?
If you want peace
don't force the people
to see we are put aside.

Let's think about this.                                                      *135*
We don't believe. We don't mock.
We may offend you,
for here stand
the citizens,
the officials,                                                               *140*
the chiefs,
the trustees and rulers of this entire world.

It is enough that we have done penance,
that we are ruined,
that we are forbidden and stripped of power.                                 *145*
To remain here is to be imprisoned.
Make of us
the thing that most suits you.
This is all we have to reply,
Señores.                                                                     *150*

## ■ Twenty Sacred Hymns (1554) *Mexico*

The highest form of Nahuatl poetry, these hymns were recorded by
the Franciscan friar Bernardino de Sahagun around 1559 just north of
Tenochtitlan. He attached them to the Florentine Codex but left them un-
translated for fear of their demonic power. Their subjects include the
Mexica or Aztec war god Huitzilopochtli, who was "born on his shield,"
and whose temple stood atop the main pyramid in Tenochtitlan, alongside
that of the raingod Tlaloc; the Mother of the Gods Tonantzin, the proto-

type of the Virgin of Guadalupe; the Chichimec patron Mixcoatl or "Cloud-Snake"; the guardians of childbirth; and Cinteotl and other maize deities. An idea of the complex language of these hymns can be gleaned from the term *jaguar-snake* (oceló-coatl) that is applied to Tlaloc. In the visual language of the ancient books, this name evokes his thunder and lightning, as the roar of the jaguar and the strike of the snake. Moreover, in ritual arithmetic Tlaloc's mask is Sign XIX, the sum of the Signs Jaguar (XIV) and Snake (V).

## Tlaloc (Hymn 3)

CHORUS In Mexico the god is being asked for a loan
    among the paper banners in four directions
    now is the time for weeping

PRIEST I am prepared    I take to the courtyard
    the bundles of bloodthorns of my god
    you are my commander magic prince
    and you are the one who makes our flesh
    you are the very first one    the offerings
    can only cause you shame

TLALOC But if someone causes me shame
    it is because he didn't know me
    you are my fathers my elder priesthood
    the Jaguar Snake
    the Jaguar Snake

PRIEST From Tlalocan in a jade boat
    Acatonal comes out
    extend yourself in Poyauhtlan
    with rattles of mist he is taken to Tlalocan

VICTIM *My brother, Tozcuecuexi,*
    *I am going forever it's the time of weeping*
    *send me to wherever it is*
    *under his command*    *I have already said*
    *to the frightening prince I am going forever*
    *it is time for weeping*
    *over four years me shall be carried on the wind*
    *unknown to others by you it is told*
    *to the place of the unfleshed*
    *In the house of Quetzal plumes*
    *transformation is effected*
    *it is the due of the one who vivifies men*

CHORUS Extend yourself in Poyauhtlan
　　　with rattles of mist he is taken to Tlalocan

TRANSLATED BY GORDON BROTHERSTON AND EDWARD DORN

## To the Mother of the Gods (Hymn 4)

Oh, golden flower opened up
　　　she is our mother
whose thighs are holy
　　　whose face is a dark mask.
She came from Tamoanchan,                          5
　　　the first place
where all descended
　　　where all was born.
Oh, golden flower flowered
　　　she is our mother                              10
whose thighs are holy
　　　whose face is a dark mask.
She came from Tamoanchan
Oh, white flower opened up
　　　she is our mother                              15
whose thighs are holy
　　　whose face is a dark mask.
She came from Tamoanchan,
　　　the first place
where all descended                                20
　　　where all was born.
Oh, white flower flowered
　　　she is our mother
whose thighs are holy
　　　whose face is a dark mask.                     25
She came from Tamoanchan.

　　　　　　　*　*　*

She lights on the round cactus,
　　　she is our mother
the dark obsidian butterfly.
　　　Oh, we saw her as we wandered                 30
across the Nine Plains,
　　　she fed herself with deers' hearts.
She is our mother,
　　　the goddess earth.
　　　She is dressed                                35
in plumes

she is smeared with clay.
In all four directions of wind
    the arrows are broken.
They saw you as a deer
    in the barren land.
those two men, Xiuhnel and Mimich.

4

TRANSLATED BY EDWARD KISSAM


## To Ease Birth (Hymn 12)

in the house with the tortoise chair
    she will give birth to the pearl
        to the beautiful feather

in the house of the goddess who sits on a tortoise
    she will give birth to the necklace of pearls
        to the beautiful feathers we are

there she sits on the tortoise
    swelling to give us birth

on your way on your way
    child be on your way to me here
        you whom I made new

come here child   come be pearl
    be beautiful feather

1

TRANSLATED BY ANSELM HOLLO


## For Eating Unleavened Tamales (Hymn 14)

*1*

the flower
    my heart
        it opened
at midnight
    that lordly hour

she has arrived
        Tlaçolteotl
           our mother
               goddess desire

*2*

in the birth house
in the flower place
on the day called 'one flower'
    the maize god is born

in the vapor and rain place               *5*
    where we go angling for jewel-fish

    where we too make our young

*3*

soon day   red sky
quechol-birds in the flowers

*4*

down here on earth
    you rise in the market place and say
I am the lord Quetzalcoatl

let there be gladness among the flowering trees
    and the quechol-bird tribes           *5*
who are the souls of the brave

may they rejoice
    hear the word of our lord
the quechol-bird's word

'your brother whom we mourn           *10*
    will never be killed again
never again will the poison dart strike him'

*5*

maize flowers
    white and yellow
I have brought from the flower place

see there is the lord of the jewel land
    playing ball in his holy field           *5*

there he is the old dog god
            Xolotl

*6*

now go look if Piltzintecutli
    lord fertility himself
has yet lain down in the dark house
        in the house where it grows dark

o Piltzintli Piltzintli           *5*
    yellow feathers
you glue all over yourself

on the ball-playing field you lie down
    and in the dark house where it grows dark

*7*

here comes a merchant

a vassal of Xochiquetzal
    mistress of Cholula

(heart o heart
    I fear the maize god is still on his way)        5

a merchant a man from Chacalla
    sells turquoise spikes for your ears
and turquoise bands for your arms

*8*

the sleeper the sleeper he sleeps

with my hand I have rolled him to sleep

*9*

here
        the woman
here
        am I
here
            asleep

TRANSLATED BY ANSELM HOLLO, AFTER EDWARD SELER

## ■ Legend of the Suns (1558) *Mexico* (epic poem)

Completed in the last year of Tenochtitian's fifty-two-year calendar cycle, this manuscript prefaces its history of highland Tula with a long account of the world ages or "Suns" that inhere in our present Era Four-Ollin (*Ollin* means rubber, elasticity, movement, earthquake; and from it is derived the name Olmec, the "rubber people" of Mesoamerica's earliest civilization). In the bridging epic sequence, Quetzalcoatl the traveler in the council of the gods makes the great descent to the underworld, like the Quiche Twins, and enters the Food mountain as an ant in order that the people of this era may be created and fed. For his part, the invalid Nanahuatl sacrifices himself so that the sun and moon (both male) may be set in motion.

## *Quetzalcoatl Descends to Mictlan*

And then Quetzalcoatl goes to Mictlan, the Dead Land.
He approached the Lord and Lady of Mictlan and said:
"What I have come for is the precious bones which you possess;

I have come to fetch them."
And he was asked: 5
"What do you want to do with them, Quetzalcoatl!"
And he answered:
"What worries the gods is who shall live on earth."
And the Lord of Mictlan then said:
"All right. Blow this conch and carry the bones four times round my 10
    jade circle."
But the conch is totally blocked up.
Quetzalcoatl summons the worms, they hollow it out.

The large and the small bees force their way through.
He blows it; the sound reaches the Lord of Mictlan.

And the Lord of Mictlan next said to him: 15
"All right, take them."
But to his vassals, the Micteca, he said:
"Tell him, o gods, he should leave them here."
But Quetzalcoatl answered:
"No, I'm taking them with me." 20
And then his nahual said to him:
"Just tell them: 'I've left them here.'"
And so he said, he shouted to them:
"I have left them here."
But then he really went back up, clutching the precious bones, 25
male bones on one side, female on the other.
He took them and wrapped them up, and took them with him.
And the Lord of Mictlan again spoke to his vassals:
"O gods, is Quetzalcoatl really taking the bones? Dig him a pit."
They dug him one; he stumbled and fell in. 30
And Quails menaced him and he fainted.
He dropped the precious bones and the Quails tore and pecked at them.
And then Quetzalcoatl came to and weeps and says to his nahual:
"O my nahual, what now?"
And the reply came: 35
"What now? Things went badly; let it be."

When he had brought it there it was ground up
by the woman named Quilaztli, by Cihuacoatl.
Then she placed the meal in a jade bowl and Quetzalcoatl dropped blood
on it by piercing his member. 40
Then all the gods named here did penance like
the Bridger, the Tiller,
the Emerger, the Earth-firmer,
the Plunger, the Shooter:
Quetzalcoatl. 45
And they said:
"The servants of the gods are born." For indeed they did penance for us.

Then they said: "What shall they eat? The gods must find food";
and the ant fetched the maize kernels
from the heart of the Food Mountain.                                           5
Quetzalcoatl met the ant and said:
"Tell me where you went to find them?"
He asked repeatedly but it didn't answer.
Then it said: "Over there, pointing."
And he accompanied it,                                                         5
becoming a black ant himself.
They both went in
and carried off the maize to Tamoanchan.
The gods chewed it
and put it in our mouths to strengthen us.                                     6

TRANSLATED BY GORDON BROTHERSTON

## The Fifth Sun

This sun is named 4 Movement. We who live today have this one, it's our sun, though what's here is merely its signification, because the sun fell into the fire, the spirit oven, at Teotihuacan.

It's the same as the sun of Topiltzin, Quetzalcoatl of Tollan. And before it was the sun, its name was Nanahuatl, whose home was yonder in Tamoanchan.

Eagle, jaguar, falcon, wolf. 6 Wind, 6 Flower: both are names of the sun.

Now, here is what is called the spirit oven. For four years it burned.

Well then, Tonacateuctli and Xiuhteuctli summoned Nanahuatl. They said to him, "You are the one who must keep the sky and the earth."

And then he was very sad. He said, "What are they saying? There are gods, and I am a worthless invalid!"

They also summoned 4 Flint, the moon. The ones who summoned him were Tlalocanteuctli and Nappateuctli.

And so Nanahuatl fasts. He takes his spines and his needles. Then he gives thorns to the moon, and they do penance.

Then Nanahuatl bathes first. Afterward the moon bathes.

His needles are plumes, his spines are jade. He uses jade as incense.

And when four days have gone by, they feather Nanahuatl, and they chalk him. Then he goes off to fall in the fire, and 4 Flint meanwhile sings and dances for him like a woman.

So Nanahuatl went off to fall in the fire. But the moon only went to fall in the ashes.

And so he went off. And he was able to grab the eagle and carry it along.

But he could not carry the jaguar. It just stood next to the fire and jumped over it. That's how it became spotted. At that time the falcon became smoke-colored. At that time the wolf was singed. These three were unable to go with him.

Well, when he got to the sky, Tonacateuctli and Tonacacihuatl bathed him. Then they sat him in a *quechol* chair. Then they adorned his head with a red border.

Then he tarries in the sky for four days. And then he appears on 4 Movement.

But he spent four days without moving, just staying in place.

Then the gods say, "Why doesn't he move?" Then they send the blade falcon, who goes and tells the sun that it has come to question him. It tells him, "The gods are saying, 'Ask him why he doesn't move.'"

Then the sun said, "Why? Because I'm asking for their blood, their color, their precious substance."

Then the gods hold council. And then Tlahuizcalpanteuctli grows angry. He says, "Well, why is this? I'll shoot him! He must not stay put!"

Then he shoots him. But he failed to hit him.

Meanwhile the sun is shooting at Tlahuizcalpanteuctli, and he succeeds in hitting him because his arrows are like shafts of flame. And then the nine layers covered up his face.

This Tlahuizcalpanteuctli is the frost.

Then all the gods get together. Titlacahuan, Huitzilopochtli, and the women Xochiquetzal, Yapalliicue, Nochpalliicue. And there in Teotihuacan they all died a sacrificial death. So then the sun went into the sky.

And then goes the moon, who had fallen only in the ashes. And when he got to the edge of the sky, Papaztac came and broke his face with a rabbit pot.

And then at a crossroads he met the *tzitzimime,* the *coleletin,* and they said to him, "Come here." They detained him for a long while, dressing him all in rags.

And so it was the sun of 4 Movement that appeared at that time. And at that time, too, he established nightfall.

TRANSLATED BY JOHN BIERHORST

## ■ Cuauhtitlan Annals (1570) *Mexico* (chronicles)

TRANSLATED BY GORDON BROTHERSTON

The annals of Cuauhtitlan, a town just north of Tenochtitlan give an unbroken count of years from the seventh century, when the Chichimecs first began to emerge from their homeland Seven Caves (Chicomoztoc, some distance to the northwest), up to the arrival of the Spaniards nine centuries later. In its early stages, the authors insert flashbacks that recall how the era itself began millennia ago, having emerged from the cataclysms of the world ages: these correspond exactly to the ones depicted on the giant Sunstone carving of Tenochtitlan and also match the sequence given in the *Popol Vuh*. We also learn in detail about the rise and fall of highland Tula around the tenth century, and how its ruler One Reed was driven out and finally burned himself in the east. Of outstanding brilliance (D. H. Lawrence drew on it in *The Plumed Serpent*), this last passage was made to echo the flight of Quetzalcoatl told in the Florentine Codex, and Jerome Rothenberg, in fact, added it to his translation of that source.

## The Five Suns

The first Sun to be founded
has the Sign Four Water.
it is called Water Sun.
Then it happened
that water carried everything away                               5
everything vanished
the people were changed into fish.

The second Sun to be founded
has the Sign Four Jaguar.
it is called Jaguar Sun.                                         10
Then it happened
that the sky collapsed
the Sun did not follow its course at midday
immediately it was night
and when it grew dark                                            15
the people were torn to pieces.
In this Sun giants lived.
The old ones said
the giants greeted each other thus:
"Don't fall over," for whoever fell,                             20
fell forever.

The third Sun to be founded
has the Sign Four Rain.
it is called Rain Sun.
It happened then that fire rained down.                          25
those who lived there were burned.
And they say that then tiny stones rained down and spread
the fine stones that we can see
the *tezontli* boiled into stone
and the reddish rocks were twisted up.                           30

The fourth Sun.
Sign Four Wind,
is called Wind Sun.
Then the wind carried everything away.
The people all turned into monkeys                                    *35*
and went to live in the forests.

The fifth Sun.
Sign Four Ollin.
is called Earthquake Sun
because it started into motion.                                       *40*
The old ones said
in this Sun there will be earthquakes and general hunger
from which we shall perish.

## ■ Florentine Codex (1579) *Mexico* (poetry, prose)

The many diverse texts gathered in the Codex served as source material for Bernardino de Sahagún's *History of the Things of New Spain* (ca. 1580). Arranged in twelve books, they offer an encyclopedic range of information about ancient Mexico, in such matters as the origins of the gods and the story of Tula (Book 3), rulers and administration (Book 6), and human types and professions (Book 10).

## *The Toltecs Were Certainly Rich (Book III)*

the toltecs were certainly rich
food was not scarce enough to sell
their vegetables were large
melons for example mostly too fat to get your arms round
maize ears millstone size                                            *5*
and they actually *climbed*
        their amaranth plants
cotton came ready dyed
in colours like crimson saffron pink violet leaf-green azure
        verdigris orange umbra grey rose-red and coyote yellow      *10*
it all just grew that way

they had all kinds of valuable birds
blue cotingas quetzals turpials red-spoonbills
which could talk and sang in tune
jade and gold were low-priced popular possessions                    *15*
they had chocolate too, fine cocoa flowers everywhere

the toltecs did not in fact lack anything
no one was poor or had a shabby house
and the smaller maize ears they used as fuel
to heat their steam baths with                                             2

TRANSLATED BY GORDON BROTHERSTON AND EDWARD DORN

## The Deadly Dance (Book III)

That shaman, owl man,
    dressed himself in shining yellow feathers
once he had won.
    Then he planned that the people
should come together and dance.
    So the cryer went to the hill
and announced it,
    and called to all the people.
Everyone in the country around heard him
    and left quickly for                                    1
Texcalapa, that place in the rocky country.
    They all came,
both nobles and the people,
    young men and young women,
so many they could not be counted,                                          1
    there were so many.
And then he began his song.
    He beats his drum,
again and again.
    They begin to join in the dance.                        2
They leap into the air,
    they join hands weaving themselves together,
whirling around, and there is great happiness.
The chant wavers
    up and breaks into the air,                             2
returns as an echo from the distant hills
    and sustains itself.
He sang it, he thought of it,
    and they answered him.
As he planned, they took it from his lips.                                  3
It began at dusk
    and went on halfway to midnight.
And when the dance
    they all did together
reached its climax,                                                         3
    numbers of them hurled themselves from the cliffs

into the gulleys.
      They all died and became stones.
Others, who were on the bridge over the canyon,
      the shaman broke it                                 *40*
under them
      though it was stone.
They fell in the rapids
      and became stones.
The Toltecs                                             *45*
      never understood what happened there,
they were drunk with it,
      blind,
and afterwards gathered many times there to dance.
Each time,                                            *50*
      there were more dead,
      more had fallen from the heights
into the rubble,
      and the Toltecs destroyed themselves.

TRANSLATED BY EDWARD KISSAM

## The Artist (Book X)

The artist: disciple, abundant, multiple, restless.
The true artist: capable, practicing, skillful;
maintains dialogue with his heart, meets things with his mind.
The true artist: draws out all from his heart,
works with delight, makes things with calm, with sagacity,       *5*
works like a true Toltec, composes his objects, works dexterously,
      invents;
arranges materials, adorns them, makes them adjust.

The carrion artist: works at random, sneers at the people,
makes things opaque, brushes across the surface of the face of things,
works without care, defrauds people, is a thief.       *10*

TRANSLATED BY DENISE LEVERTOV

■ **Cantares Mexicanos (Sixteenth Century)**
*Mexico* (songs)

## Orphan Song

where is the dios
for whom we live?

where are you?
your sad friends await you
with songs they are grieving
with flowers they seek you
they feel pain
searching for your soul
strength, honour, ay!

I say and think                                                    1
if this is orphanhood
what will console my heart
what will ease my sorrow
I who am from Huexotzinco
if my father is gone                                               1.
if my mother is gone
let them be waiting for me
to ease my heart
and the great pain of orphanhood, ay

I note that others here                                            2
are happy and make merry
they have their capes and jewels
and I suffer
what will make me happy
what will give me pleasure                                         2
leaving the others here

the lords intertwine
friendship intertwines
the nobility, ay
will come from here, from there                                    3
yet I want and wish for earthly things
what will make me happy
what will give me pleasure
leaving the others here

you who are the tloque                                             3
you who are the nahuaque
we here amuse you
and what is to be had from you
who is being served
if you consider us as flowers                                      4
if we your friends wither?

like precious obsidian you splinter us
like painted script you erase us
everything here goes to the place of the dead
the place where we all disappear                                   4

as what do you, one god, consider us
that we are born
and die like this?
where shall we disappear to
we the common people? 50
where shall we really go?

hence I weep
for you refuse to act
ypalnemohuani
the jade breaks 55
the quetzal plumes rip
you poke fun
as what, how do you consider us
blotting us out here
destroying us 60

ay what mischance
ypalnemohuani is poking fun
it is a dream to say he is our brother
our hearts convert to the faith
really dios pokes fun 65

hence I weep and grieve
for I was left an orphan
among strangers here on earth
what does your heart desire ypalnemohuani?
let your anger cease 70
let orphanhood be glorious
beside you
who are dios and want me dead

TRANSLATED BY LUIS REYES AND GORDON BROTHERSTON

## Could It Be True We Live on Earth?

by Nezahualcoyotl

Could it be true we live on earth?
On earth forever?

Just one brief instant here.

Even the finest stones begin to split,
even gold is tarnished, 5

even precious bird-plumes
shrivel like a cough.

Just one brief instant here.

TRANSLATED BY EDWARD KISSAM

## Death and Rebirth of Tula

At Tula stood the beamed sanctuary,
only the snake columns still stand,
our prince Nacxitl has gone, has moved away.
    Our vanguard is wept for with conches;
    he is going to his destruction in Tlapallan.

He was there in Cholula,
made an end at Mount Poyauhtecatitlan,
crossed the water at Acallan.
    Our vanguard is wept for with conches;
    he is going to his destruction in Tlapallan.

I come to the frontier with winged finery,
the lord who pierces and the victim.
    My fine-plumed lord has gone away
    has left me, 10-Flower, an orphan.

The pyramid burst apart hence my tears
the sacred sand whirled up hence my desolation.
    My fine-plumed lord has gone away
    has left me, 10-Flower, an orphan.
Tlapallan is where you are expected
is where you are destined to rest;
you are moving on, my fine-plumed lord,
destined for Xicalanco.
Still yet, still yet. . . .
    Your house will always be there, your gates
    your palace will always be there.
    You left them orphaned here at the Tula frontier.

You wept endlessly, great lord;
    your house will always be there, your gates
    your palace will always be there.
    You left them orphaned here at the Tula frontier.
Stone and wood, you painted them
in the city of Tula.
    Where you ruled, our prince Nacxitl,

your name will never be destroyed;
your people will always cry for you.                                    35

The turquoise house and the snake house, you built them
in the city of Tula.
Where you ruled, our prince Nacxitl,
your name will never be destroyed;
your people will always cry for you.                                    40
As white and yellow maize I am born,
The many-coloured flower of living flesh rises up
and opens its glistening seeds before the face of our mother.
In the moisture of Tlalocan, the quetzal water-plants open their
corollas.
I am the work of the only god, his creation.                            45

Your heart lives in the painted page,
you sing the royal fibres of the book,
you make the princes dance,
there you command by the water's discourse.
He created you,                                                         50
he uttered you like a flower,
he painted you like a song:
a Toltec artist.
The book has come to the end:
your heart is now complete.                                             55

Here through art I shall live for ever.
Who will take me, who will go with me?
Here I stand, my friends.
A singer, from my heart I strew my songs,
my fragrant songs before the face of others.                            60
I carve a great stone, I paint thick wood
my song is in them.

It will be spoken of when I have gone.
I shall leave my song-image on earth.
My heart shall live, it will come back,                                 65
my memory will live and my fame.
I cry as I speak and discourse with my heart.
Let me see the root of song,
let me implant it here on earth so it may be realized.
My heart shall live, it will come back,                                 70
my memory will live and my fame.
The Prince Flower gently breathes his aroma,
our flowers are uniting.
My song is heard and flourishes.
My implanted word is sprouting,                                         75
our flowers stand up in the rain.

The Cocoa flower gently opens his aroma,
the gentle Peyote falls like rain.
    My song is heard and flourishes.
    My implanted word is sprouting,                   8(
    our flowers stand up in the rain.

TRANSLATED BY GORDON BROTHERSTON

## Three Nahuatl Poems

One by one I proclaim your songs:
    I bind them on, gold crabs, as if they were anklets:
    like emeralds I gather them.
Clothe yourself in them: they are your riches.
    Bathe in feathers of the quetzal,                     5
your treasury of birds, plumes, black and yellow,
the red feathers of the macaw
beat your drums about the world:
deck yourself out in them: they are your riches.

TRANSLATED BY WILLIAM CARLOS WILLIAMS

Where am I to go, whither?
    The road's there, the road to Two-Gods.
    Well, who checks men here,
here where all lack a body,                            5
at the bottom of the sky?
Or, maybe, it is only on Earth
that we lose the body?
    Cleaned out, rid of it completely,
His House: there remains none on this earth!            1(
Who is it that said:
Where find them? our friends no longer exist!

TRANSLATED BY WILLIAM CARLOS WILLIAMS

Will he return will Prince Cuautli ever return?
Will Ayocuan, the one who drove an arrow into the sky?
Shall these two yet gladden you?
    Events don't recur: we vanish once only.

Hence the cause of my weeping:                                                                 5
Prince Ayocuan, warrior chief
governed us harshly.
His pride waxed more, he grew haughty
here among men.
      But his time is finished . . .                                                          10
he can no longer come to bow down before Father and Mother. . . .
This is the reason for my weeping:
He has fled to the place where all lack a body.

TRANSLATED BY WILLIAM CARLOS WILLIAMS

## ■ Yancuic Tlahtolli: The New Word (1990)
## *Mexico* (poem)

TRANSLATED BY GORDON BROTHERSTON

J. Fausto Hernández Hernández's poem appeared in Martínez Hernández's monolingual anthology of Nahuatl poetry published in Tlaxcala (1987). The person addressed could be either father or mother; hardship has driven both sexes to find work in the cities, especially in the northern Veracruz area from which this poem comes.

## *Bird*

J. Fausto Hernández Hernández

Bird, you went, and lost your head
Why did you not return to your nest?
Where in truth are you?
Where, my fellow bird?
Where shall I find you?                                                                        5
Then towards evening I find you
they hurt you and now you are ill
it's a sin what they did to you precious bird
now you will no longer be able to return, fellow of mine
and now what will there be in your nest?                                                       10
the babies await you
they await since they are hungry and cold
they cry and endlessly await you

# Discovery, Conquest, and the Colonies

∎

## INTRODUCTION

For Europe, the discovery of the New World was, as "New World" implies, an astonishing encounter with oceans, many populated islands, and two new continents. No discovery of place, even of a second moon or alternate solar system, could have rivaled the significance of those enormous unexplored Americas, which made the last years of the fifteenth and the entire sixteenth century the age of discovery for the seagoing nations of Europe. The old restrictive circles of knowledge were broken. The English poet John Donne (1572–1631) woke as a young man in his bedroom, looked out the window to the ports across the seas to an amazing light, presence, and mystery; he called out to his America as if addressing a new lover who would bequeath him youth, life, and hope: "Oh my America, my new found lande / . . . How blest am I in this discovering thee" ("Elegie: To his Mistris Going to Bed"). Curiosity, enthusiasm, dreams, religious mission, and greed led adventurers, colonizers, and missionary priests to risk the waters between old Europe and the virgin terrains of the Native American (whose civilizations were actually as old as Athens and Rome). The discoverers, who were Italian, Spanish, Portuguese, Dutch, and English, eventually brought their languages to the far lands they would conquer and inhabit. The colonizers would also bring slaves from Africa to augment their work force of conscripted Indians, thereby introducing new peoples, languages, and cultures into the ethnic mix of the new-found continents, now consisting of West Europeans, Native Americans, and Africans.

The first to record the New World was its discoverer, Christopher Columbus (1451–1506), an Italian, in the hire of the Spanish monarchy. Columbus, as revealed in his ship's log, was a fabulist and a dreamer who first cast the Americas into the mold of a "New World," a virgin territory, an undiscovered and unexplored land inhabited by a gentle and innocent people. These romantic terms are undermined by the other motives revealed in his log—warlike imperialism, missionary zeal, and hunger for gold. The cost of discovery to the Native Americans, however, was the vast destruction of their writings, cultural integrity, and independence. The preceding section is a selection from what has survived.

In this next section, we cover the writings of the discoverers, conquistadors, and people of the colonies. After Columbus came the chroniclers, who walked with the conquerors and recorded the adventures and tragedies, followed by critics of the conquerors, like the Spanish missionary Bartolomé de las Casas (1474–1566), who in his monumental *History of the Indies* decried Native American slavery. Then followed the ethnographers, historians, poets, and fabulists of the New World literatures, including the Inca Garcilaso de la Vega (1539–1616), son of a Spanish conquistador and an Inca princess, who through oral sources preserved an Inca version of his people's history and religion. Garcilaso's extensive and elegant writings clarified the fact that while the New World was new to Europe (as China and Japan once seemed new to the West), to Native American inhabitants the New World was their own, their very old and familiar, world, with complex and diverse cultures, each of which implied a long prehistory prior to the conquest. Finally come the writers of Latin America and the Caribbean.

## Christopher Columbus (1451?–1506)
### *Italy/Spain/Española* (ship's log)

TRANSLATED BY ROBERT H. FUSON

The Italian explorer Christopher Columbus, in the service of the Catholic monarchs Queen Isabella and King Ferdinand of Spain, set out in 1492 from Spain for China and Japan by sailing to the west. Convinced that the world was round—as was any literate seaman of his age—he hoped thereby to find a shorter route to Asia. Columbus proposed that the traditional slow wagons of the Silk Road, carrying valuable spices, silks, and other goods from central and eastern Asia to Europe, be replaced by ships sailing directly to Asia's eastern shores, which he calculated lay about three thousand miles west of Lisbon. He promised his royal patrons great economic gains. So in 1492, the same year that saw Spain's reconquest of Andalusia from the Moors, the expulsion or forced conversion of Spanish Jews, and the unification of Spain, the Spanish monarchs backed Columbus's wild venture of sailing west to find the East. Between Columbus and Asia, however, was a continent, soon to be called America in honor of Amerigo Vespucci, Columbus's fellow Italian cartographer and explorer. On landing in Hispaniola, Columbus thought, or wished to think, that he was indeed in Asia, on islands off the subcontinent of India: hence the West Indies, Indians, and many related misnomers, which trace their etymological origin to the Hindus River from which India also took its name.

It is said that Columbus was born Cristofero Colombo in Genoa, Italy, in 1451. Yet the date and place of his birth remain in doubt. Columbus (or

Cristóbal Colón, the Spanish name he went by most of his life) concealed and confused his personal background. Many places claim him, including the Greek island of Chios, a former Genoese colony; Catalan Mallorca, which satisfies those Spanish historians who claim a concealed Spanish-Jewish or convert background; and even Galicia, a Portuguese-speaking part of Spain. As a young man, the talented navigator attempted to convince John II of Portugal and later the Spanish and English courts to finance his venture. After the capture of Granada from the Moors, Isabella agreed to commission Columbus to organize a voyage in the name of Spain, and on August 3, 1492, he sailed from Palos de la Frontera in Andalusian Spain, with three small ships under his command—the *Santa María*, the *Pinta*, and the *Niña*. After landing on a small island in the Bahamas and exploring Cuba, he reached Hispaniola on December 5. Soon, his flagship Santa María was wrecked, and after taking captives and some cultural objects from his discovered world, he hurried back to Spain on the Niña. He left behind a colony of some forty crew members (who, he found on his second voyage, had been killed). In Spain, he was welcomed as a hero and his royal patrons declared him to be "Admiral of the Ocean Sea" and "Governor of All Territories Discovered and To Be Discovered."

In his writings about the discovery, Columbus reflects an idylic point of view, although in them we may surmise, and elsewhere learn, that the discovery and conquest also were to bring extermination to the Arawak Indian population of Hispaniola. With and after Columbus came a radical alteration of the discovered world. Although Columbus himself never encountered the highly developed societies that Cortés was to meet and demolish, his initial explorations, the goal of which was to acquire wealth and slaves, all in the name of nation and religion, set in motion the world's ancient and modern habit of conquest and destruction. In the Spain of his day, while the Holy Inquisition was busy cleansing the country of heresy by burning both "converts" and old Christians suspected of religious insincerity, its monarchs were dispatching captains and priests to spread the Christian faith to peoples it considered pagan and idolatrous. The lustful dream of gold and the entry of armies of conquistador and inquisitor into the New World ultimately led to the virtual obliteration of the architectural, sculptural, and written records of past and contemporaneous civilizations of the Americas. While the Incas and Aztecs were at a high point, the Olmec and Maya city states had long since been abandoned by the time Spain set foot in Mesoamerica. But past and present were annihilated wherever they were found. William Prescott's famed histories of the conquests of Peru and Mexico, albeit written in the nineteenth century, describe in great detail the extinction of the foremost New World civilizations.

As in the chronicles recorded by later conquistadors and their scribes, Columbus's initial response to the newly sighted lands was amazement. His word pictures of the Indies were noble and beautiful just as medieval depictions sanctified the cruel and devastating Crusades as courageous and noble pilgrimages to the Holy Land. Those green islands that Columbus came upon—the Bahamas, Cuba, and Hispaniola (Española)—the explorer romantically perceived as new Gardens of Eden. Their description in his journal and letters evokes the marvelous, not unlike Pliny's *Natural Histories,* Marco Polo's wonders along the Silk Road to Asia, and the chivalric novels of the late Middle Ages and early Renaissance that, a century later, were to madden and illumine the mind of Spain's famous internal explorer, Don Quijote de la Mancha. And like Quijote, who saw windmills as monsters in Spain's heartland, Columbus found sirens singing in the Caribbean, guardian Amazons armored with plates of copper in Martinique; he told of men with tails and heard nightingales singing across the islands where no nightingales were. Closer to reality, he found naked "timid" Indians (he was the first to use the term *indios* from which English "Indian" derives); quick huge canoes; gum mastic (*chicle*) that reminded him of the lake of gum on the Greek island of Chios (Homer's reputed birthplace); and bears, fabrics, rhubarb, cinnamon, and golden jewelry. The gold, with its specific wonders, did not disinterest him or his royal sponsors. In exchange for help, he promised his highnesses as much gold as they would want and as much cotton, spice, and slaves as they would command.

In October 1493, fitted out with a fleet of seventeen ships and some fifteen hundred colonists, Columbus sailed from Cádiz on his second voyage to what he called the "other world." He made landfall on the Lesser Antilles, the Leeward Islands, and Puerto Rico; surveyed Cuba; and colonized Hispaniola, leaving his brother Bartolomew in charge. After some three years, he returned to Spain, with few possessions to justify his dream and promise of great wealth and with a sickly crew disgruntled by their meager earnings. His third voyage in 1498 was personally calamitous. He was obliged to carry convicts aboard his ships as the new colonists. He reached the mouth of the Orinoco River in present-day Venezuela. In 1500, after reports of terrible conditions in the colonies, Isabella and Ferdinand sent an independent governor to arrest Governor Columbus, who was accordingly brought back to Spain in chains.

On arrival, Columbus was quickly freed, but by then, with other navigators having explored the coasts of South America, including Amerigo Vespucci, Columbus's name had lost its currency. With difficulty, he convinced the court to support a fourth voyage. Anxious to redeem his reputation by finding Asia, or at least a quick passage to it beyond those islands he had discovered, in 1502 Columbus set out on his fourth voyage into the western seas. He reached his Indies where, through trade, he obtained many gold masks and gold pendants. Continuing his discoveries, enduring storms, swarms of mosquitoes, and more disease, he finally struck the coast of Honduras, where he coasted south, experiencing further terrible hardships, until he reached the Gulf of Darien. He attempted to sail to the colony at Hispaniola, but he was marooned for about a year in Jamaica. His rescue was delayed by Governor Ovando of Hispaniola, who feared that Columbus might seize his post. During his time on Jamaica, by look-ing at his almanac he was able to predict an eclipse on February 29, 1504; when the eclipse occurred, he told the Indians he would intercede to re-store the dying sun in exchange for desperately needed food, which was thereupon provided him and his mutinous crew. After waiting about a year for his reluctant rescue, he returned to Spain in 1504, his greater hopes all but abandoned.

In his last few years of poverty and failing health, the former Admiral of the Ocean Sea requested the king to restore his name and a fair share of trade profits. He failed in his solicitations. For his epoch and continent, Christopher Columbus, with what scholars have shown to be an unsur-passed skill in dead reckoning, had indeed charted a way to the "other world." He left us the fact of exploration—with all its positive and nega-tive implications—and his writings. The navigator died in his modest dwelling in Valladolid, Spain, in 1506.

In his writing, Columbus described his version of what Jean Jacques Rousseau was to call the "noble savage" and his work was a model for later utopias. In reality, he and those who followed were to bring abundant Old World distopias to the New World—destruction, disease, death, and slav-ery to native inhabitants of Columbus's America, along with Western civi-lization, its financial and social hierarchies, and its imposed religions. From a literary point of view, Columbus was an innovator; and in his jour-nal and his significant writings, he was a living and courageous Odysseus, recording his voyages, explorations, and ventures into the geography of the unknown.

FURTHER READING: Columbus, Christopher. *Journals and Other Documents on the Life and Voyages of Christopher Columbus,* 1963; *The Four Voyages of Columbus to the New World: Letters.* Edited and translated by J. M. Cohen, 1969; *The Log of Christopher Columbus.* Translated by Robert H. Fuson, 1992; *The Four Voyages of Columbus: A Doc-umentary History.* Translated and edited by Cecil Jane, 1988; *Book of the Wonders of the World,* 1988. Bradford, Ernle Dusgate Selby. *Christopher Columbus,* 1973. Mori-son, Samuel Eliot. *Admiral of the Ocean: Christopher Columbus,* 1942. Sable, Martin Howard. *Columbus, Marrano Discoverer from Mallorca,* 1992.

# from *The Log of Christopher Columbus*

## The Outward Voyage 3 August to 10 October 1492

### *In the Name of Our Lord Jesus Christ*

Most Christian, exalted, excellent, and powerful princes, King and Queen of the Spains and of the islands of the sea, our Sovereigns: It was in this year of 1492 that Your Highnesses concluded the war with the Moors who reigned in Europe. On the second day of January, in the great city of Granada, I saw the royal banners of Your Highnesses placed by force of arms on the towers of the Alhambra, which is the fortress of the city. And I saw the Moorish king come to the city gates and kiss the royal hands of Your Highnesses, and those of the Prince, my Lord. Afterwards, in that same month, based on the information that I had given Your Highnesses about the land of India and about a Prince who is called the Great Khan, which in our language means "King of Kings," Your Highnesses decided to send me, Christopher Columbus,[1] to the regions of India, to see the Princes there and the peoples and the lands, and to learn of their disposition, and of everything, and the measures which could be taken for their conversion to our Holy Faith.

I informed Your Highnesses how this Great Khan and his predecessors had sent to Rome many times to beg for men learned in our Holy Faith so that his people might be instructed therein, and that the Holy Father had never furnished them, and therefore, many peoples believing in idolatries and receiving among themselves sects of perdition were lost.

Your Highnesses, as Catholic Christians and Princes devoted to the Holy Christian faith and to the spreading of it, and as enemies of the Muslim sect and of all idolatries and heresies, ordered that I should go to the east, but not by land as is customary. I was to go by way of the west, whence until today we do not know with certainty that anyone has gone.

Therefore, after having banished all the Jews[2] from all your Kingdoms and realms, during this same month of January Your Highnesses ordered me to go with a sufficient fleet to the said regions of India. For that purpose I was granted great favors and ennobled; from then henceforward I might entitle myself *Don* and be High Admiral of the Ocean Sea and Viceroy and perpetual Governor of all the islands and continental land that I might discover and acquire, as well as any other future discoveries in the Ocean Sea. Further, my eldest son shall succeed to the same position, and so on from generation to generation for ever after.

I left Granada on Saturday, the 12th day of the month of May in the same year of 1492 and went to the town of Palos, which is a seaport. There I fitted out three vessels, very suited to such an undertaking. I left the said port well supplied with a large quantity of provisions and with many seamen on the third day of the month of August in the said year, on a Friday, half an hour before sunrise. I set my course for the Canary Islands of Your Highnesses, which are in the Ocean Sea, from there to embark on a voyage that will last until I arrive in the Indies and deliver the letter of Your Highnesses to those Princes, and do all that Your Highnesses have commanded me to do.

---

1. The transcription reads, "*pensaro de embiarme a mi xpoual Colon.*" ("You thought of sending me, Cristóval Colón"). Inasmuch as Columbus never signed his name in this conventional form, some believe that the entire Prologue was written by Las Casas. It is more reasonable to assume that Las Casas inserted the name when he made his abstract.

2. The General Edict on the expulsion of the Jews from Spain was actually issued on March 31, 1492. This complicated situation, which evolved over the course of many years, is carefully analyzed by Simon Wiesenthal in *The Secret Mission of Christopher Columbus*.

To this end I decided to write down everything I might do and see and experience on this voyage, from day to day, and very carefully. Also, Sovereign Princes, besides describing each night what takes place during the day, and during the day the sailings of the night, I propose to make a new chart for navigation, on which I will set down all the sea and lands of the Ocean Sea, in their correct locations and with their correct bearings. Further, I shall compile a book and shall map everything by latitude and longitude. And above all, it is fitting that I forget about sleeping and devote much attention to navigation in order to accomplish this. And these things will be a great task.

### Sunday, 2 September 1492

I arrived this morning in Gomera without incident. There are many fine Spaniards on this island, including Doña Beatriz de Pedraza y Bobadilla, the mistress of the island. These Spaniards swear under oath that every year they see land to the west, where the sun sets. I remember that when I was in Portugal, in 1484, a man came from the island of Madeira to ask the King for a caravel to go to the land that he had seen in the west. Also, people in the Azores say that they see land to the west every year. All these people see this land to the west under the same conditions and report it to be about the same size.

### Monday, 3 September 1492

When I went to Grand Canary to help Martín Alonso with his rudder, I left a dozen men on Gomera under the command of Pedro Gutiérrez. As an officer of the royal household, he is most experienced in obtaining supplies and is well qualified in the areas of food acquisition and storage.

Gutiérrez has already acquired all the wood and water necessary for the voyage, which I estimate will last 21 days. However, to be on the safe side, in case of contrary winds or currents, I ordered Gutiérrez to prepare for a voyage of 28 days. I anticipate no problem in replenishing our supplies when we reach the Indies.

### Wednesday, 5 September 1492

The ships have been loaded, and all is ready for the voyage. Tonight I shall order a special service of thanksgiving; at sunrise I will lift anchors to begin the journey westward.

### Thursday, 6 September 1492

Shortly before noon I sailed from the harbor at Gomera and set my course to the west. I am somewhat disturbed by word I received this morning from the captain of a caravel that came to Gomera from the island of Hierro.[3] He reported that a Portuguese squadron of three caravels is in the vicinity of Hierro, apparently with orders to prevent me from departing the Canaries. There could be some truth in this, for King John[4] must be angry that I went over to Castile.

### Sunday, 9 September 1492

*(Most of this entry [except for course, speed and distance notations] has been interpolated from Fernando's Historie.)*

This day we completely lost sight of land, and many men sighed and wept for fear they would not see it again for a long time. I comforted them with great promises of lands and riches. To sustain their hope and dispel their fears of a long voyage, I decided to reckon fewer leagues than we actually made. I did this that they might not think themselves so great a distance from Spain as they really were. For myself I will keep a confidential accurate reckoning.

### Monday, 10 September 1492

Today I made 180 miles at a speed of 7½ knots. I recorded only 144 miles in order not to alarm the sailors if the voyage is lengthy.

### Saturday, 15 September 1492

I sailed to the west day and night for 81 miles, or more. Early this morning I saw a marvelous meteorite fall into the sea 12 or 15 miles away to the SW. This was taken by some people to be a bad omen, but I calmed them by telling of the numerous occasions that I have witnessed such events. I have to confess that this is the closest that a falling star has ever come to my ship.

### Sunday, 16 September 1492

The weather is like April in Andalucia, with mild breezes, and the mornings are a delight. The only thing lacking is the call of the nightingales. We have begun to see large patches of yellowish-green weed, which seems to have been torn away from some island or reef. I know that the weed has not come from the mainland because I make the mainland to be farther on.

---

3. *Hierro* ("iron") is the Spanish name, but the Portuguese *Ferro* is more often used on charts today. Columbus always used *Hierro*.

4. King John II of Portugal (João II). Spain and Portugal were at peace, but the Portuguese would have been concerned with a Spanish expedition to their West African claims. This may have been the reason why there was a Portuguese squadron in the area.

*Monday, 17 September 1492*

I held my course to the west and made, day and night, 150 miles or more, but I only logged 141 miles. I have a favorable current. I saw a great deal of weed[5] today—weed from rocks that lie to the west. I take this to mean that we are near land. The weed resembles stargrass, except that it has long stalks and shoots and is loaded with fruit like the mastic tree. Some of this weed looks like river grass, and the crew found a live crab in a patch of it. This is a sure sign of land, for crabs are not found even 240 miles from shore.

The sea is less salty by half[6] than it is in the Canaries, and the breezes are more gentle. Everyone is cheerful, and the *Pinta,* the fastest sailing vessel, went ahead as fast as it could in order to sight land.

*Tuesday, 18 September 1492*

I sailed day and night more than 165 miles, but I recorded only 144 miles. The sea has been as smooth as the river at Sevilla. Martín Alonso Pinzón, who had sailed ahead yesterday in the *Pinta,* a very fast sailer, lay-to for me to come up. He told me that he saw a great flight of birds moving westward. He hoped to sight land last night; that is why he was going so fast. He is a fine captain and very resourceful, but his independence disturbs me somewhat. I trust that this tendency to strike out on his own does not continue, for we can ill afford to become separated this far from home.

*Thursday, 20 September 1492*

The sailors caught a little fish, and we saw much weed of the kind I have already mentioned, even more than before, stretching to the north as far as you can see. In a way this weed comforted the men, since they have concluded that it must come from some nearby land. But at the same time, it caused some of them great apprehension because in some places it was so thick that it actually held back the ships. Since fear evokes imaginary terrors, the men thought that the weed might become so thick and matted that there might happen to them what is supposed to have happened to St. Amador, when he was trapped in a frozen sea that held his ship fast.

*Sunday, 23 September 1492*

The crew is still grumbling about the wind. When I get a wind from the sw or west it is inconstant, and that, along with a flat sea, has led the men to believe that we will never get home. I told them that we are near land and that is what is keeping the sea smooth. Later, when the sea made up con-

---

5. Columbus was entering the Sargasso Sea; any weed of the genus *Sargassum* is called "sargasso weed" or simply "sargassum."

6. There is no basis for this comment.

siderably without wind, they were astonished. I saw this as a sign from God, and it was very helpful to me. Such a sign has not appeared since Moses led the Jews out of Egypt, and they dared not lay violent hands on him because of the miracle that God had wrought. As with Moses when he led his people out of captivity, my people were humbled by this act of the Almighty.

## Monday, 24 September 1492

I returned to my westerly course and made about 43½ miles, logging only 36. A tern came to the ship, and I saw many petrels.

I am having serious trouble with the crew, despite the signs of land that we have and those given to us by Almighty God. In fact, the more God shows the men manifest signs that we are near land, the more their impatience and inconstancy increases, and the more indignant they become against me. All day long and all night long those who are awake and able to get together never cease to talk to each other in circles, complaining that they will never be able to return home. They have said that it is insanity and suicidal on their part to risk their lives following the madness of a foreigner. They have said that not only am I willing to risk my life just to become a great Lord, but that I have deceived them to further my ambition. They have also said that because my proposition has been contradicted by so many wise and lettered men who considered it vain and foolish, they may be excused for whatever might be done in the matter. Some feel that they have already arrived where men have never dared to sail and that they are not obliged to go to the end of the world, especially if they are delayed anymore and will not have sufficient provisions to return. I am told by a few trusted men (and these are few in number!) that if I persist in going onward, the best course of action will be to throw me into the sea some night. They will then affirm that I fell overboard while taking the position of the North Star with my quadrant.[7] Since I am a foreigner, little or no account will be asked of the matter, but rather, there will be a great many who will swear that God had given me my just desserts on account of my rashness. I know that the men are taking these complaints to the Pinzóns and that the Pinzóns have sided with them.

Inasmuch as most of these people are from Palos and the surrounding area, they stick together, and I know that Martín Alonso cannot be trusted. He is a skilled mariner, but he wants the rewards and honors of this enterprise for himself. He is always running ahead of the fleet, seeking to be the first to sight land. But I am fully aware that I must use him, for his support is too great among the men. I am also confident that if I lose command, the fleet will never reach the Indies and will probably never get back to Spain. With God's help I shall persevere.

---

7. An "improved," lightweight mariner's astrolabe.

## The Discovery of the Bahamas 11 to 27 October 1492

*Thursday, 11 October 1492*

I sailed to the WSW, and we took more water aboard than at any other time on the voyage. I saw several things that were indications of land. At one time a large flock of sea birds flew overhead, and a green reed was found floating near the ship. The crew of the *Pinta* spotted some of the same reeds and some other plants; they also saw what looked like a small board or plank. A stick was recovered that looks manmade, perhaps carved with an iron tool. Those on the *Niña* saw a little stick covered with barnacles. I am certain that many things were overlooked because of the heavy sea, but even these few made the crew breathe easier; in fact, the men have even become cheerful. I sailed 81 miles from sunset yesterday to sunset today. As is our custom, vespers were said in the late afternoon, and a special thanksgiving was offered to God for giving us renewed hope through the many signs of land He has provided.

After sunset I ordered the pilot to return to my original westerly course, and I urged the crew to be ever-vigilant. I took the added precaution of doubling the number of lookouts, and I reminded the men that the first to sight land would be given a silk doublet as a personal token from me. Further, he would be given an annuity of 10,000 maravedíes from the Sovereigns.

About 10 o'clock at night, while standing on the sterncastle, I thought I saw a light to the west. It looked like a little wax candle bobbing up and down. It had the same appearance as a light or torch belonging to fishermen or travellers who alternately raised and lowered it, or perhaps were going from house to house. I am the first to admit that I was so eager to find land that I did not trust my own senses, so I called for Pedro Gutiérrez, the representative of the King's household, and asked him to watch for the light. After a few moments, he too saw it. I then summoned Rodrigo Sánchez of Segovia, the comptroller of the fleet, and asked him to watch for the light. He saw nothing, nor did any other member of the crew. It was such an uncertain thing that I did not feel it was adequate proof of land.

The moon, in its third quarter, rose in the east shortly before midnight. I estimate that we were making about 9 knots and had gone some 67½ miles between the beginning of night and 2 o'clock in the morning. Then, at two hours after midnight, the *Pinta* fired a cannon, my prearranged signal for the sighting of land.

I now believe that the light I saw earlier was a sign from God and that it was truly the first positive indication of land. When we caught up with the *Pinta*, which was always running ahead because she was a swift sailer, I learned that the first man to sight land was Rodrigo de Triana, a seaman from Lepe.

I hauled in all sails but the mainsail and lay-to till daylight. The land is about 6 miles to the west.

## Friday, 12 October 1492

*(Log entry for 12 October is combined with that of 11 October.)*

At dawn we saw naked people, and I went ashore in the ship's boat, armed, followed by Martín Alonso Pinzón, captain of the *Pinta,* and his brother, Vincente Yáñez Pinzón, captain of the *Niña.* I unfurled the royal banner and the captains brought the flags which displayed a large green cross with the letters F and Y at the left and right side of the cross. Over each letter was the appropriate crown of that Sovereign. These flags were carried as a standard on all of the ships. After a prayer of thanksgiving I ordered the captains of the *Pinta* and *Niña,* together with Rodrigo de Escobedo (secretary of the fleet), and Rodrigo Sánchez of Segovia (comptroller of the fleet) to bear faith and witness that I was taking possession of this island for the King and Queen. I made all the necessary declarations and had these testimonies carefully written down by the secretary. In addition to those named above, the entire company of the fleet bore witness to this act. To this island I gave the name *San Salvador,*[8] in honor of our Blessed Lord.

No sooner had we concluded the formalities of taking possession of the island than people began to come to the beach, all as naked as their mothers bore them, and the women also, although I did not see more than one very young girl. All those that I saw were young people, none of whom was over 30 years old. They are very well-built people, with handsome bodies and very fine faces, though their appearance is marred somewhat by very broad heads and foreheads, more so than I have ever seen in any other race. Their eyes are large and very pretty, and their skin is the color of Canary Islanders or of sunburned peasants, not at all black, as would be expected because we are on an east-west line with Hierro in the Canaries. These are tall people and their legs, with no exceptions, are quite straight, and none of them has a paunch. They are, in fact, well proportioned. Their hair is not kinky, but straight, and coarse like horsehair. They wear it short over the eyebrows, but they have a long hank in the back that they never cut. Many of the natives paint their faces; others paint their whole bodies; some, only the eyes or nose. Some are painted black, some white, some red; others are of different colors.

The people here called this island *Guanahaní* in their language, and their speech is very fluent, although I do not understand any of it. They are friendly and well-dispositioned people who bare no arms except for small spears, and they have no iron. I showed one my sword, and through ignorance he grabbed it by the blade and cut himself. Their spears are made

---

8. Samana Cay. For a more extensive discussion of the various landfall theories, see Epilogue.

of wood, to which they attach a fish tooth at one end, or some other sharp thing.

I want the natives to develop a friendly attitude toward us because I know that they are a people who can be made free and converted to our Holy Faith more by love than by force. I therefore gave red caps to some and glass beads to others. They hung the beads around their necks, along with some other things of slight value that I gave them. And they took great pleasure in this and became so friendly that it was a marvel. They traded and gave everything they had with good will, but it seems to me that they have very little and are poor in everything. I warned my men to take nothing from the people without giving something in exchange.

This afternoon the people of San Salvador came swimming to our ships and in boats made from one log. They brought us parrots, balls of cotton thread, spears, and many other things, including a kind of dry leaf[9] that they hold in great esteem. For these items we swapped them little glass beads and hawks' bells.

Many of the men I have seen have scars on their bodies, and when I made signs to them to find out how this happened, they indicated that people from other nearby islands come to San Salvador to capture them; they defend themselves the best they can. I believe that people from the mainland come here to take them as slaves. They ought to make good and skilled servants, for they repeat very quickly whatever we say to them. I think they can easily be made Christians, for they seem to have no religion. If it pleases Our Lord, I will take six of them to Your Highnesses when I depart, in order that they may learn our language.

### Saturday, 13 October 1492

I have been very attentive and have tried very hard to find out if there is any gold here. I have seen a few natives who wear a little piece of gold hanging from a hole made in the nose. By signs, if I interpret them correctly, I have learned that by going to the south, or rounding the island to the south, I can find a king who possesses a lot of gold and has great containers of it. I have tried to find some natives who will take me to this great king, but none seems inclined to make the journey.

### Sunday, 14 October 1492

At daybreak I ordered the small boats to be made ready, that is, put in tow behind, and I went along the island to the NNE, to see the other part of the east and the villages. Soon I saw two or three of them, and the people came to the beach, shouting and praising God. Some brought us water;

---

9. The "dry leaves" are not actually mentioned until the October 15 entry. At that time Columbus tells us that these highly prized dry leaves were offered to him on 12 October. It is reasonable, then, that the tobacco was part of "the many other things" cited in the Log entry.

others, things to eat. Others, seeing that I did not care to go ashore, jumped into the sea and swam out to us. By the signs they made I think they were asking if we came from Heaven. One old man even climbed into the boat we were towing, and others shouted in loud voices to everyone on the beach, saying, "Come see the men from Heaven; bring them food and drink." Many men and women came, each one with something. They threw themselves on the sand and raised their hands to the sky, shouting for us to come ashore, while giving thanks to God. I kept going this morning despite the pleas of the people to come ashore, for I was alarmed at seeing that the entire island is surrounded by a large reef. . . .

Also, I wanted to see if I could find a suitable place to build a fort. I saw a piece of land that looked like an island, even though it is not, with six houses on it. I believe that it could be cut through and made into an island in two days. I do not think this is necessary, however, for these people are very unskilled in arms. Your Highnesses will see this for yourselves when I bring to you the seven that I have taken. After they learn our language I shall return them, unless Your Highnesses order that the entire population be taken to Castile, or held captive here. With 50 men you could subject everyone and make them do what you wished.

### Tuesday, 16 October 1492

At daybreak I went ashore in the small boat. People met us on the beach. There were many people, and they went naked and in the same condition as those of San Salvador. They let us go anywhere we desired and gave us anything we asked.

I decided not to linger very long at Santa María de al Concepción, for I saw that there was no gold there and the wind freshened to a SE crosswind. . . .

Not only was there a shifting wind and no gold here, I was also afraid that all the men from San Salvador would escape if I did not move on and get farther away. I wanted to go to another large island that I determined lay to the west.

Judging by the clouds and the signs made by the men from San Salvador, this large island to the west was about 27 miles distant. They said that there is a lot of gold there and that the people wear it on their arms, legs, ears, noses, and necks. I do not know if this is another ruse of theirs or not, for I am beginning to believe that all they want to do is escape and they will tell me anything I want to hear.

### Sunday, 21 October 1492

At 10 o'clock in the morning I arrived at *Cabo del Isleo* and anchored, as did the other two ships. After having eaten, I went ashore and found no settlement except one house. I found no one; the inhabitants must have fled in fear, for all their housewares were left behind. I did not permit my men to touch a thing, and I went with my captains to see the island. If the other islands are very green and beautiful and fertile, this is much more, with great and green groves of trees. There are some large lakes and above and around them is the most wonderful wooded area. The woods and vegetation are as green as in April in Andalucía, and the song of the little birds might make a man wish never to leave here. The flocks of parrots that darken the sun and the large and small birds of so many species are so different from our own that it is a wonder. In addition, there are trees of a thousand kinds, all with fruit according to their kind, and they all give off a marvelous fragrance. I am the saddest man in the world for not knowing what kind of things these are because I am very sure that they are valuable. I am bringing a sample of everything I can.

## Wednesday, 24 October 1492

At midnight I weighed anchors from the island of Isabela, from *Cabo del Isleo* which is in the north part, in order to go to the island of Cuba, which the Indians tell me is very large and has much commerce; gold, spices, ships, and merchants.

The Indians indicated that I should sail to the SW to get to Cuba, and I believe them because all my globes and world maps seem to indicate that the island of Japan is in this vicinity and I am sure that Cuba and Japan are one and the same.

## The Discovery of Cuba
## 28 October to 5 December 1492

### Tuesday, 30 October 1492

I departed Río de Mares to the NW, and after having gone 45 miles, I saw a cape covered with palms and named it the *Cabo de Palmas*.[10] The Indians who were in the *Pinta* said that behind that cape was a river, from which it was four days' journey to Cuba. The captain of the *Pinta* understood that Cuba was a city, and that it was on the mainland, a very large land that extends far to the north. He also understood that the king of Cuba was at war with the Great Khan, whom they call *Cami* and whose country or city they call *Faba* and many other names. . . .

I must try to go to the Great Khan, for he is in the vicinity or at the city of Cathay, which is the city of the Great Khan. This is a very great city, according to what I was told before leaving Spain.

This entire country is low and beautiful, and the sea is very deep.

---

10. Palm Cape (Cape of Palms); now known as *Punta Uvero*.

*Sunday, 4 November 1492*

I also understand that, a long distance from here, there are men with one eye and others with dogs' snouts who eat men. On taking a man they behead him and drink his blood and cut off his genitals.

*Tuesday, 6 November 1492*

Last night the two men I had sent inland to see the country returned and told me how they had gone 36 miles, to a village of 50 houses where there were a thousand inhabitants, as a great many live in one house. These houses are like very large pavilions.

The Spaniards said that the Indians received them with great solemnity, according to Indian custom, and all the men and women came to see them and lodged them in the best houses. The Indians touched them and kissed their hands and feet in wonderment, believing that we Spaniards came from Heaven, and so my men led them to understand. The Indians gave them to eat what they had.

The men said that on their arrival, the most distinguished persons in the village took them on their shoulders and carried them to the principal house and gave them two chairs in which to sit, and all the Indians seated themselves on the floor around them. These were most peculiar chairs. Each was made in one piece and in a strange shape, resembling a short-legged animal[11] with a tail as broad as the seat. This tail lifted up to make a back to lean against. These seats are called *dujos* or *duchos* in their language.

The Indians who had gone with my men, that is, the one from Guanahaní and the one from here, told the people how the Christians lived and how we were good people. Afterwards the men left, and the women seated themselves in the same manner around them, kissing their hands and feet, trying to see if they were of flesh and bone like themselves. The women pleaded with them to stay there longer, at least for five days.

My men showed the Indians the cinnamon and pepper and other spices I had given them, and they were told by signs that there were many such spices nearby to the SE, but that they did not know if they had those things there in their own village. Having seen that there were no rich cities, my men returned to *Puerto de Mares*. . . .

All that these people have they will give for a very ridiculous price; they gave one great basket of cotton for the end of a leather strap. These people are very free from evil and war. All the men and women are as naked as their mothers bore them. It is true that the women wear a cotton swatch only large enough to cover their private parts and no more. They are modest, nevertheless, and are not as dark as the people of the Canaries.

---

11. The animal chair was the *dujo*. Several excellent ones are on display in the Museo del Hombre Dominicano, Santo Domingo, Dominican Republic.

I have to say, Most Serene Princes, that if devout religious persons knew the Indian language well, all these people would soon become Christians. Thus I pray to Our Lord that Your Highnesses will appoint persons of great diligence in order to bring to the Church such great numbers of peoples, and that they will convert these peoples, just as they have destroyed those[12] who would not confess the Father, Son, and Holy Spirit. And after your days, for we are all mortal, you will leave your realms in a very tranquil state, free from heresy and wickedness, and you will be well received before the Eternal Creator, Whom may it please to grant you a long life and a great increase of larger realms and dominions, and the will and disposition to spread the Holy Christian religion, as you have done up until this time. Amen.

Today I will launch the ship and prepare to depart Thursday, in the name of God, to go to the SE and seek gold and spices and discover land.

## Sunday, 11 November 1492

It appears to me that it would be well to take some of these people dwelling by this river to the Sovereigns, in order that they might learn our language and we might learn what there is in this country. Upon return they may speak the language of the Christians and take our customs and Faith to their people. I see and know that these people have no religion whatever, nor are they idolaters, but rather, they are very meek and know no evil. They do not kill or capture others and are without weapons. They are so timid that a hundred of them flee from one of us, even if we are merely teasing. They are very trusting; they believe that there is a God in Heaven, and they firmly believe that we come from Heaven. They learn very quickly any prayer we tell them to say, and they make the sign of the cross. Therefore, Your Highnesses must resolve to make them Christians. I believe that if this effort commences, in a short time a multitude of peoples will be converted to our Holy Faith, and Spain will acquire great domains and riches and all of their villages. Beyond doubt there is a very great amount of gold in this country. These Indians I am bringing say, not without cause, that there are places in these islands where they dig gold and wear it around the neck, in the ears, and on the arms and the legs—and these are very heavy bracelets. Also, there are precious stones and pearls, and an infinite quantity of spices.

## Wednesday, 14 November 1492

Your Highnesses will have to pardon me for repeating myself concerning the beauty and fertility of this land, but I can assure you that I have not told a hundredth part. Some of the mountains appear to reach Heaven and are like points of diamonds; others of great height seem to have a

---

12. Columbus is referring to the defeat of the Moors, not to the expulsion of the Jews.

table on top; and the sea is so deep that a ship can approach some of them right up to the base. They are all covered with forests and are without rocks.

### Thursday, 22 November 1492

Last night I sailed south by east, with the wind east and almost calm. About 3 in the morning it blew NNE. I was still going to the south in order to see the country that lay in that direction, but when the sun rose I found myself as far away as yesterday because of the contrary currents; The land was a distance of 30 miles from me.

Last night, after Martín Alonso departed for the east and the island of Babeque, I could see him for a long time, until he was 12 miles away. I sailed all night toward the land, but took in some of the sails and even showed a light because it seemed that Pinzón was coming toward me. The night was very clear and the light wind favorable for him to sail in my direction if he had so chosen.

### Friday, 23 November 1492

I sailed all this day toward the land to the south, always with light wind, and the current never letting me reach land. At sunset I was as far away from land as I was in the morning. The wind was ENE and favorable to sail south, but it was almost calm. Beyond the cape, visible in the distance, is another land or cape that extends to the east. The Indians aboard call this Bohío and say it is very large and has people there with one eye in the forehead, as well as others they call cannibals,[13] of whom they show great fear. When they saw I was taking that course, they were too afraid to talk. They say that the cannibals eat people and are well armed. I believe there is some truth in this, although if they are armed they must be an intelligent people. Perhaps these people may have captured some of the other Indians; when the captives did not return to their own country, it was said that they were eaten. The Indians we have encountered believed the same thing at first about us Christians.

### Monday, 26 November 1492

All the people I have encountered up until this time greatly fear the people of Caniba or Canima, whom they say live on this island of Bohío. This island appears to be very large, and I believe that the people on it go and take the other Indians and their lands and houses, because the ones I have seen are very cowardly and know nothing about arms. It is for these reasons that I think the Indians I am taking with me are not accustomed to settling on the coast. The Indians with me continued to show great fear

---

13. *Canibales*, the people of *Caniba* who eat other people. This is the first recorded usage of this term, which is a Taino Indian word.

because of the course I was taking and kept insisting that the people of Bohío had only one eye and the face of a dog, and they fear being eaten. I do not believe any of this. I feel that the Indians they fear belong to the domain of the Great Khan.

### Tuesday, 27 November 1492

Yesterday at sunset I arrived in the vicinity of Cabo de Campana, but did not anchor even though the sky was clear and the wind light and there were five or six wonderful harbors to the leeward. Whenever I enter one of these harbors, I am detained by sheer pleasure and delight as I see and marvel at the beauty and freshness of these countries, and I do not want to be delayed in pursuing what I am engaged upon. For all these reasons, I stood off the coast last night and beat about until day. . . .

After sailing 1½ miles along the same bay, I saw to the south a very remarkable harbor, and to the SE some incredibly beautiful land, similar to a rolling valley surrounded by mountains. There was a lot of smoke and a number of large villages there, and the land was intensely cultivated. Because of this I decided to enter this harbor and see if I could communicate with these people. If I have praised other harbors, then this one deserves more, along with the land and surroundings and the temperate climate and the population. It is a beautiful place, with pines and palms and a rolling plain extending to the SSE. There are low, smooth mountains on the plain and many streams flowing from the mountains. It is the most beautiful thing in the world.

I anchored the ship and jumped into the boat in order to take soundings in the harbor, which is shaped like a small hammer. When I was facing the entrance to the south, I found the mouth of a river that was wide enough for a galley to enter and so situated that it could not be seen until it was reached. Within a boat's length of the entrance it was 5 fathoms and 8 fathoms in depth.

As I went along the river it was marvelous to see the forests and greenery, the very clear water, the birds, and the fine situation, and I almost did not want to leave this place. I told the men with me that, in order to make a report to the Sovereigns of the things they saw, a thousand tongues would not be sufficient to tell it, nor my hand to write it, for it looks like an enchanted land. I want many other persons who are prudent and have the proper credentials to see this, so as to be certain that they do not praise these things less than I do.

I do not need to write how great the benefits will be from here. It is certain, Lords and Princes, that where there are such lands there must be an infinite quantity of profitable things.

And I certify to Your Highnesses that it does not seem to me that there can be more fertile countries under the sun, or any more temperate in heat and cold, with a greater abundance of good, pure water—unlike those rivers of Guinea, which are all pestilent. Praise be to Our Lord, so far there has not been a single one of my people who has had a headache or who has been in bed because of sickness, except for one old man through pain from kidney stones, from which he has suffered all his life— and even he became well at the end of two days. I say this in regard to all three ships. So may it please God that Your Highnesses may send learned men here, or that they shall come, and they will see that everything I say is true.

I say that Christendom will enter into negotiations, but most of all with Spain, to which all these lands should be subject. And I say that Your Highnesses must not allow any foreigner to set foot here or trade, except Catholic Christians, since it was the beginning and the end of this enterprise that it should be for the increase and the glory of the Christian religion. No one should come to these regions who is not a good Christian.

## The Discovery of Española 6 December 1492 to 15 January 1493

*Sunday, 16 December 1492*

Coming from the coast of the Isla Española, I sailed close to the wind, because later, by 9 o'clock the next morning, the wind blew from the east. In the middle of that bay I found a canoe with a solitary Indian in it. I wondered how he was able to keep himself afloat when there was such a high wind. I brought him and his canoe on board and pleased him greatly by giving him glass beads, hawks' bells, and brass rings. I took him in the ship to a coastal village 12 miles distant. I found a good anchorage there next to the village, which appeared to be newly constructed, for all the houses were new. I let the Indian go ashore in his canoe and trusted that he would spread the word that we Christians are good people. They already knew this, however, from information they had received where my six men had gone before; soon more than 500 men came to the beach, where they gathered near the ships, for we were anchored very near to the shore. After a little while, their King came.

One by one, and in small groups, they came to the ship without bringing anything with them, although some of them wore grains of very fine gold in their ears and noses, which they gave away willingly. I ordered that everyone be treated honorably because they are the best and gentlest people in the world, and above all because I have great hope in Our Lord that Your Highnesses will convert all of them to Christianity and they will all belong to you, for I regard them as yours now.

I saw that they all showed respect for the King, who was on the beach. I sent him a gift, which he received with much ceremony. He is a young man, about 21 years of age. He had an old governor or advisor and other counselors who advised him and spoke for him. He himself said very few words. One of the Indians with me spoke with the King and told him how we had come from Heaven, and that we were searching for gold and wished to see the island of Babeque. He replied that this was good, and that there was a great deal of gold on that island. He showed my master-at-arms who had delivered my gift, the course that must be followed to reach Babeque and said that it could be reached in two days' time from where we were anchored. He also said that if we needed anything in his country, he would give it to us willingly.

The King and all the others went about as naked as they were born, and the women, too, without any shyness, and they are the handsomest men and women I have found up until now. They are exceedingly white, and if they wore clothing and were protected from the sun and the air they would be almost as white as the people in Spain. . . .

Your Highnesses may rest assured that these lands are so extensive and good and fertile, and especially these of this Isla Española, that there is no one who can describe it, and no one who can believe it if he does not see it. And Your Highnesses may believe that this island and all the others are as much yours as is Castile, and all that is needed here is to build a town and order the Indians to do your bidding. I, with the people I have with me, who are not many in number, could go through all these islands without any opposition. I have already seen three of my sailors go ashore where there is a great number of Indians, and the Indians have all fled without anyone wishing to do them any harm. They have no arms and are naked, and have no knowledge of arms and are very timid. A thousand of them would not face three Christians, and so they are suitable to be governed and made to work and sow and do everything else that shall be necessary, to build villages and be taught to wear clothing and to observe our customs.

### Tuesday, 18 December 1492

Today I traded for only a small quantity of gold, but I learned from an old man that there were many islands in the vicinity—at a distance of 300 miles or more, according to what I was able to make out—in which a lot of gold is found. I was told that on some of these islands there is so much gold that the whole island is gold. On others they gather it and sift it with sieves and melt it to make bars, and work it in a thousand ways. I was shown, by signs, how this is done. The old man indicated to me the course to take to get to those islands and the place where they may be found. I decided to go there, and if the old man had not been one of the principal persons belonging to the king, I would have taken him along. If I had known the language, I would have begged him to accompany me, and I believe that we are on such good terms that he would have gone along of his own free will. But since I already consider that these people belong to the Sovereigns of Castile, it is not right to offend them. So I decided to leave him alone.

I placed a very large cross in the center of the plaza of that village, and the Indians assisted me greatly in this work. They said prayers and worshipped it, and from their actions I trust in the Lord that all these islands are to be Christianized.

## Tuesday, 25 December 1492—Christmas Day

I sailed in a light wind yesterday from La Mar de Santo Tomás to Punta Santa, and at the passing of the first watch, 11 o'clock at night, I was 3 miles east of the point. I decided to lie down to sleep because I had not slept for two days[14] and one night. Since it was calm, the sailor who was steering the ship also decided to catch a few winks and left the steering to a young ship's boy, a thing which I have always expressly prohibited throughout the voyage. It made no difference whether there was a wind or calm; the ships were not to be steered by young boys.

I felt secure from shoals and rocks because on Sunday, when I had sent the boats to that King, they had gone a good 10 miles to the east of Punta Santa, and the sailors had seen this entire coast and the shoals that extend from Punta Santa a good 9 miles to the ESE, and they saw where we could pass. This is something I had not done before on this voyage.

Our Lord willed that at midnight, when the crew saw me lie down to rest and also saw that there was a dead calm and the sea was as in a bowl, they all lay down to sleep and left the helm to that boy. The currents carried the ship upon one of these banks. Although it was night, the sea breaking on them made so much noise that they could be heard and seen at a 3-mile distance. The ship went upon the bank so quietly that it was hardly noticeable.[15] When the boy felt the rudder ground and heard the noise of the sea, he cried out. I jumped up instantly; no one else had yet felt that we were aground. Then the master of the ship, Juan de la Cosa,[16] who was

---

14. Columbus had been extremely busy with the multitude of Indians coming and going, and he probably did a little celebrating on Christmas Eve, just before the grounding. Too much "partying" may be the simple explanation of the accident that was to follow.

15. Columbus used the term *banco* (bank), where the *Santa María* grounded, not his term for coral reef (*restinga de piedras*). The ship appears to have missed the reef, where the waves made the noise Columbus heard, and gently eased into a sand bank. The ship was not really damaged very much, merely hopelessly stuck.

16. Juan de la Cosa, owner of the *Santa María*, was the same man who made (or compiled) the famous chart of the New World in 1500. He sailed again with Columbus on the second voyage; made an expedition to South America with Alonso de Ojeda and Amerigo Vespucci (1499); and was the pilot for Rodrigo de Bastidas in 1500–1501 (when Vasco Nuñez de Balboa was aboard and the coast between Cartagena, Colombia, and Porto Belo, Panama, was first explored). In 1504 he returned to Santo Domingo to serve as Ojeda's lieutenant in the colonization of what is now Colombia (called *Nueva Andalucía*). In 1509, in a fight with the Caribs, Juan de la Cosa died from a poisoned arrow.

on watch, came out. I ordered him to rouse the crew, to launch the small boat we carry on our stern, and to take an anchor and cast it at the stern. The master and many others jumped into the small boat, and I assumed they were going to follow my orders. Instead, their only thoughts were to escape to the *Niña*, which was 1½ miles to the windward. The crew of the *Niña* would not receive them, which was correct, and therefore they returned to the ship. But the boat from the Niña reached the ship before my own boat did!

When I saw that some of my own crew were fleeing and that the sea was becoming more shallow, with my ship broadside to it, I did the only thing I could. I ordered the mast cut and the ship lightened as much as possible, to see if it could be refloated. But the water became even more shallow, and the ship settled more and more to one side. Although there was little or no sea, I could not save her. Then the seams opened, though she remained in one piece.

I took my crew to the *Niña* for their safety, and as there was a light land breeze and still half the night ahead of us, and since I did not know how far the banks extended, I beat about till daybreak and then went inside the bank to the ship. I also dispatched Diego de Arana, master-at-arms of the fleet, and Pedro Gutiérrez, representative of the Royal Household, to take the small boat and go directly to the King that had last Saturday invited me to his village. I instructed them to beg the King to come to this harbor with his boats.

The village of this King is about 5 miles beyond this bank. My men told me that the King wept when he heard of the disaster. He sent all his people from the village with many large canoes to help us unload the ship.

### Wednesday, 26 December 1492

Today at sunrise the King of this country came to the *Niña*, where I was, and almost in tears told me not to be dismayed because he would give me whatever he had. He had already given two very large houses to my men, and he would give us more if we needed them. And yesterday he gave us as many canoes as we needed and the labor to unload the ship, and not even a breadcrumb was taken. They are so loyal and so respectful of the property of others, and this King is even more honest than the others. . . .

The King dined with me on the *Niña* and afterwards went ashore with me, where he paid me great honor. Later we had a meal with two or three kinds of ajes, served with shrimp, game, and other foods they have, including their bread; which they call *cazabe*.[17] Then the King took me to see some groves of trees near the houses, and fully 1,000 people, all naked,

---

17. Manioc bread. For a more extensive discussion of roots and breads, see Epilogue.

went with us. The King was already wearing a shirt and a pair of gloves which I had given him, and he was more excited about the gloves than anything else that had been given him.

By his manner of eating, his decent behavior, and his exceptional cleanliness, he showed himself to be of good birth.

After the meal we remained at the table for some time, and we were brought some herbs with which to rub our hands—I believe they use these to soften the skin. We were also given water for our hands. Later, after we had eaten, the Indians took me to the beach, and I sent for a Turkish bow and a handful of arrows. I had a man from my company who was a skilled archer shoot the arrows. Inasmuch as the King did not know what arms are, since his people neither possess nor use them, the demonstration impressed him very much. This all came about because we had had a conversation about the people of Caniba, whom they call *Caribes*,[18] who come to seize them and who carry bows and arrows without iron tips. Nowhere in these lands is there knowledge of iron or steel, nor of any other metal except gold and copper, and I have seen very little of the latter. I told the King by signs that the Sovereigns of Castile would order the destruction of the Caribes, commanding the Caribes to be brought before them with their hands tied.

I ordered that a lombard and a musket be fired, and the King was spellbound when he saw the effect of their force and what they penetrated. When the people heard the shots, they fell to their knees. They brought me a large mask, which had large pieces of gold in the ears and eyes and in other places, which the King himself presented to me. He placed this, along with other jewels of gold, on my head and around my neck. They also gave many things to the men with me. I derived a great deal of pleasure and consolation from these things, and when I realized that this mitigated the trouble and affliction I had experienced by losing the ship, I recognized that Our Lord had caused me to run aground at this place so that I might establish a settlement here. And so many things came to hand here that the disaster was a blessing in disguise. Certainly, if I had not run aground here, I would have kept out to sea without anchoring at this place because it is situated inside a large bay containing two or three banks of shoals. Neither would I have left any of my people here on this voyage; even if I had desired to leave them, I could not have outfitted them well enough, nor given them enough ammunition, provisions, and materials for a fort. It is quite true that many of the people with me have pleaded with me to permit them to remain here.

Now I have ordered that a tower and a fortress be constructed, very well built, with a large moat. This is not because I believe this to be necessary

---

18. First mention of these feared cannibals using the name by which they are known today. Native to South America, they had followed the Taino migrations northward through the Lesser Antilles to Puerto Rico. By 1492 they were raiding Española. Their name also survives in the name Caribbean Sea.

with these Indians, for I am sure that I could subjugate the entire island—which I believe is larger than Portugal with twice the population—with the men that I have in my company. These Indians are naked, unarmed, and cowardly beyond help. But it is right that this tower be built, and what must be, must be. Since these Indians are so far from Your Highnesses, it is necessary that the people here know your people and what they can do, in order that the Indians may obey Your Highnesses with love and fear.

The men remaining have timbers with which to construct the fortress and provisions of bread and wine for more than a year, as well as seeds for sowing, and the ship's boat. I am leaving a caulker, a carpenter, a gunner, and a caskmaker among the many men who desire zealously to serve Your Highnesses and who will please me greatly if they find the mine where the gold comes from. Thus, everything that has happened was for this purpose, that this beginning may be made.

All this was the will of God: the ship's running aground so easily that it could not be felt, with neither wind nor wave; the cowardice of the ship's master and some of the crew (who were mostly from his part of Spain), who refused my order to cast the stern anchor to draw the ship off and save it; the discovery of this country.

I hope to God that when I come back here from Castile, which I intend on doing, that I will find a barrel of gold, for which these people I am leaving will have traded, and that they will have found the gold mine, and the spices, and in such quantities *that within three years*[19] *the Sovereigns will prepare for and undertake the conquest of the Holy Land. I have already petitioned Your Highnesses to see that all the profits of this, my enterprise, should be spent on the conquest of Jerusalem, and Your Highnesses smiled and said that the idea pleased them, and that even without this expedition they had the inclination to do it.*

### Sunday, 6 January 1493

After midday the wind blew strongly from the east, and I ordered a sailor to climb to the top of the mast to look out for shoals. He saw the *Pinta* approaching from the east,[20] and she came up to me. Because the water was so shallow, I was afraid to anchor, so I retraced my course 30 miles to Monte Cristi, and the *Pinta* went with me.

Martín Alonso Pinzón came aboard the *Niña* to apologize, saying that he had become separated against his will. He gave many reasons for his departure, but they are all false. Pinzón acted with greed and arrogance that night when he sailed off and left me, and I do not know why he has been so disloyal and untrustworthy toward me on this voyage. Even so, I am go-

---

19. Author's italics. According to John Boyd Thacher, this is Columbus' Grand Design: the conquest of the Holy Land, financed by the wealth obtained from the enterprise.

20. Since departing the fleet on 21 November, the *Pinta* had sailed to Babeque (Great Inagua Island) and thence to a location east of Monte Cristi on the island of Española.

ing to ignore these actions in order to prevent Satan from hindering this voyage, as he has done up until now.

An Indian, among those I had commended to Pinzón, told Pinzón that on the island of Babeque there was a great quantity of gold; since the *Pinta* was light and swift, he wished to withdraw and go by himself, leaving me.

*Wednesday, 9 January 1493*

At midnight I raised sails with the wind SE and sailed to the ENE. I reached a point I named *Punta Roja*,[21] which is exactly east of Monte Cristi some 45 miles. In the shelter of this point I anchored at 3 o'clock in the afternoon. I dared not depart from there at night because of the many reefs.

In this country there are many tortoises; the sailors captured some of them that had come ashore to lay their eggs at Monte Cristi. They are very large, like great wooden shields. Yesterday, when I was going to the Río del Oro, I saw three sirens[22] that came up very high out of the sea. They are not as beautiful as they are painted, since in some ways they have a face like a man. I have seen them on other occasions in Guinea on the coast of Manegueta.[23] Tonight, in the name of Our Lord, I will start on my journey without further delay for any reason, since I have found what I have sought. Also, I do not wish to have more trouble with this Martín Alonso until Your Highnesses learn the news of this voyage and what he has done. Then I will not suffer from the evil actions of persons without virtue, who, with little regard, presume to follow their own wills in opposition to those who did them honor.

## The Homeward Voyage 16 January to 15 March 1493

*Wednesday, 16 January 1493*

Three hours before dawn I departed the gulf, which I have named the *Golfo de las Flechas*,[24] first with a land breeze and then with a west wind. I turned the prow to the east by north, in order to go to the Isla de Caribe, where the people are whom the inhabitants of all these islands and countries fear so greatly. This is because the Caribes cross all these seas in their countless canoes and eat the men they are able to capture. One of the four Indians I took yesterday in the Puerto de las Flechas[25] has shown me

---

21. Red Point; now known as *Punta Cabo Isabela*.

22. The common manatee, known in Spanish as *sirena* until the Taino word *manatí* came into use after Columbus, thence into English.

23. Malagueta Coast of Liberia and Sierra Leone.

24. Gulf of the Arrows; now known as *Puerto Rincón*. See note for Sunday, 13 January.

25. Port of the Arrows; an unspecified anchorage, probably on the north shore of the Gulf.

the course. After we had gone about 48 miles, the Indians indicated to me that the island lay to the SE. I wanted to follow that course and ordered the sails trimmed, but after we had gone 6 miles the wind again blew very favorably for going to Spain. I noted that the crew were becoming dismayed because we had departed from a direct course for home; and as both ships were taking in a great deal of water, they had no help save that of God. I was compelled to abandon the course that I believe was taking me to the island; I returned to the direct course for Spain, NE by east, and held it until sunset, 36 miles. The Indians told me that on this course I would find the island of Matinino, which is inhabited only by women. I would like to carry five or six of them to the Sovereigns, but I doubt if the Indians know the course well, and I am not able to delay because of the danger with the leaking caravels. I am certain that there is such an island, and that at a certain time of year men come to these women from the Isla de Caribe, which is 30 or 36 miles from us; if the women give birth to a boy they send him to the island of the men, and if a girl they keep her with them.

*Thursday, 21 February 1493*

*(Part of this entry is under the Log entry of 22 February.)*

The sacred theologians and learned philosophers were quite correct when they said that the earthly Paradise is at the end of the Orient, because it is a most temperate place. Those lands which I have now discovered are at the end of the Orient.

## ■ Bartolomé de las Casas (1474–1566)
### *Spain/Mexico* (history)

The Spanish missionary and historian Bartolomé de las Casas has been called the Apostle of the Indies. His role was to awaken the Spanish authorities to the genocide of the *indios* in New Spain. Las Casas arrived in Hispaniola in 1492, only ten years after Christopher Columbus landed there on his first voyage. He became a priest in 1510 and shortly thereafter worked the rest of his life to improve the conditions of the Indian. He did so within the confines of the Catholic church, which is to say, he accepted that pagan "idols" had to be eliminated, both physically and in the hearts of the Indian and did not object to the zealous destruction of religious art objects and documents. His enormous contributions lay in his efforts to provide a better life for the forced native converts to the church. To that end, Las Casas labored against slavery as practiced under the *encomienda*, a food-for-work economic system first used to obtain cheap labor from the Moors in reconquered Spain and then transplanted to the New World.

Theoretically, the encomienda obliged the landowner to protect the Indians, instructing them in the Christian faith in return for which the Indian laborers paid tribute. In practice, it was a form of economic slavery and quickly led to the decimation of the Indians in the West Indies. The encomienda was also the law in continental America, especially in Mexico and Guatemala—then called New Spain. Although the crown and the Dominican order of monks made some efforts to suppress it, the encomienda persisted until 1542, when the "New Laws," promulgated by Las Casas, outlawed forced labor and debt peonage. But encomienda died slowly and was ultimately replaced by the *repartimiento,* another system of distributing land on which Indians worked under forced labor conditions. In reality, though the words changed, the practice of economic serfdom continued in Mexico and Central America well into the twentieth century. Formal slavery itself was not outlawed in Portuguese-settled Brazil until 1888.

Bartolomé de las Casas was the leading figure in all the colonial period in creating awareness of and change in the conditions of the Indian. He spent his life writing and petitioning the Spanish government in Spain, Mexico, and Peru to abolish the virtual slavery of the Indians, who had become forced laborers on the estates of Spanish landholders. He also published descriptions of massacres and maltreatment in his *Very Brief Account of the Destruction of the Indies,* a book that was translated into many languages and countered the Black Legend. The Black Legend was at once a detailed description of massacres and maltreatment and, in the eyes of the deniers of these events, a phrase to indicate a false "legendary" accusation. Las Casas came to the defense of the Native Americans, arguing that Indians are rational beings with souls, and he campaigned against their forced labor in gold and silver mines, where they were dying in droves. He suggested that they be replaced by bringing in African slaves who he thought had no souls and whose death would be of less consequence. He quickly withdrew his suggestion with regard to Africans. Las Casas spent his life battling all parties for better treatment of the Indian population, and he succeeded in bringing into being the New Laws. These laws to protect the Indians were altered and ignored, but at the very least they kept alive the question of the plight of the Indian serf. As an observer of the societies of Indians and an early anthropologist, he spent many years writing his monumental *Historia de las Indias* (History of the Indies).

FURTHER READING: Las Casas, Bartolomé de. *Very Brief Account of the Destruction of the Indies,* 1522; *Devastation of the Indies,* 1974; *Historia de las Indias (The History of the Indies),* 1875–1876; *Tears of the Indians: Selected Works of Bartolomé de las Casas.* Edited by John Phillips, 1953; *Bartolomé de las Casas: A Selection of His Writings,* 1971.

## from *The Horrors of the Conquest*

### The Conquest of Cuba

At this time, when it was known in the island of Jamaica that Diego Velázquez had gone to settle and pacify . . . the island of Cuba, Juan de

Esquivel, the deputy in Jamaica, agreed to send one Pánfilo de Narváez, a native of Valladolid . . . with thirty Spaniards, to aid Diego Velázquez— or else they bestirred themselves and asked permission to go there. All were archers, with their bows and arrows, in the use of which they were more practiced than the Indians.

This Pánfilo de Narváez was a man with an air of authority, tall of stature, and rather fair-haired, tending toward red. He was honorable and wise, but not very prudent; good company, with good habits, valiant in fighting against the Indians and would perhaps have been valiant against other peoples—but above all he had this defect, that he was very careless. . . .

With his band of bowmen he was well received by Diego Velázquez. . . . Velázquez promptly gave them shares of Indians, as if these were heads of cattle, so that the Indians would serve them, although they had brought some Jamaican Indians to do that wherever they went. Diego Velázquez made this Narváez his chief captain and always honored him in such a way that, after Velázquez, Narváez held first place in that island.

A few days later I went there, the said Diego Velázquez having sent for me because of our past friendship in this island of Hispaniola. We went together, Narváez and I, for about two years, and secured the rest of that island, to the detriment of all of it, as will be seen.

[*Las Casas tells how Velázquez terrorized the natives of eastern Cuba, near Cape Maisi, executed the chieftain Hatuey, and went on to Baracoa. Narváez landed at the Gulf of Guacayanabo, on the south coast near Maisi, and, on orders from Velázquez, invaded the province of Camagüey, in central Cuba.*]

The Spaniards entered the province of Camagüey, which is large and densely populated . . . and when they reached the villages, the inhabitants had prepared as well as they could cassava bread from their food; what they called *guaminiquinajes* from their hunting; and also fish, if they had caught any.

Immediately upon arriving at a village, the cleric Casas would have all the little children band together; taking two or three Spaniards to help him, along with some sagacious Indians of this island of Hispaniola, whom he had brought with him, and a certain servant of his, he would baptize the children he found in the village. He did this throughout the island . . . and there were many for whom God provided holy baptism because He had predestined them to glory. God provided it at a fitting time, for none or almost none of those children remained alive after a few months. . . .

When the Spaniards arrived at a village and found the Indians at peace in their houses, they did not fail to injure and scandalize them. Not content with what the Indians freely gave, they took their wretched subsistence from them, and some, going further, chased after their wives and daughters, for this is and always has been the Spaniards' common custom in these Indies. Because of this and at the urging of the said father, Captain Narváez ordered that after the father had separated all the inhabitants of the village in half the houses, leaving the other half empty for the Spaniards' lodging, no one should dare go to the Indians' section. For this purpose, the father would go ahead with three or four men and reach a village early; by the time the Spaniards came, he had already gathered the Indians in one part and cleared the other.

Thus, because the Indians saw that the father did things for them, defending and comforting them, and also baptizing their children, in which affairs he seemed to have more command and authority than others, he received much respect and credit throughout the island among the Indians. Further, they honored him as they did their priests, magicians, prophets, or physicians, who were all one and the same.

Because of this . . . it became unnecessary to go ahead of the Spaniards. He had only to send an Indian with an old piece of paper on a stick, informing them through the messenger that those letters said thus and so. That is, that they should all be calm, that no one should absent himself because he would do them no harm, that they should have food prepared for the Christians and their children ready for baptism, or that they should gather in one part of the village, and anything else that it seemed good to counsel them—and that if they did not carry these things out, the father would be angry, which was the greatest threat that could be sent them.

They performed everything with a very good will, to the best of their ability. And great was the reverence and fear which they had for the letters, for they saw that through these what was being done in other, distant regions was known. It seemed more than a miracle to them. . . .

The Spaniards thus passed through certain villages of that province on the road they were taking. And because the folk of the villages . . . were eager to see such a new people and especially to see the three or four mares being taken there, at which the whole land was frightened—news of them flew through the island—many came to look at them in a large town called Caonao, the penultimate syllable long. And the Spaniards, on the morning of the day they arrived at the town, stopped to breakfast in a riverbed that was dry but for a few small pools. This riverbed was full of whetstones, and all longed to sharpen their swords on them [and did]. When they had finished their breakfast, they continued on the road to Caonao.

Along the road for two or three leagues there was an arid plain, where one found oneself thirsty after any work; and there certain Indians from the villages brought them some gourds of water and some things to eat.

They arrived at the town of Caonao in the evening. Here they found many people, who had prepared a great deal of food consisting of cassava bread and fish, because they had a large river close by and also were near the sea. In a little square were 2,000 Indians, all squatting because they have this custom, all staring, frightened, at the mares. Nearby was a large *bohío,* or large house, in which were more than 500 other Indians, close-packed and fearful, who did not dare come out.

When some of the domestic Indians the Spaniards were taking with them as servants (who were more than 1,000 souls . . . ) wished to enter the large house, the Cuban Indians had chickens ready and said to them: "Take these—do not enter here." For they already knew that the Indians who served the Spaniards were not apt to perform any other deeds than those of their masters.

There was a custom among the Spaniards that one person, appointed by the captain, should be in charge of distributing to each Spaniard the food and other things the Indians gave. And while the captain was thus on his mare and the others mounted on theirs, and the father himself was observing how the bread and fish were distributed, a Spaniard, in whom the devil is thought to have clothed himself, suddenly drew his sword. Then the whole hundred drew theirs and began to rip open the bellies, to cut and kill those lambs—men, women, children, and old folk, all of whom were seated, off guard and frightened, watching the mares and the Spaniards. And within two credos, not a man of all of them there remains alive.

The Spaniards enter the large house nearby, for this was happening at its door, and in the same way, with cuts and stabs, begin to kill as many as they found there, so that a stream of blood was running, as if a great number of cows had perished. Some of the Indians who could make haste climbed up the poles and woodwork of the house to the top, and thus escaped.

The cleric had withdrawn shortly before this massacre to where another small square of the town was formed, near where they had lodged him. This was in a large house where all the Spaniards also had to stay, and here about forty of the Indians who had carried the Spaniards' baggage from the provinces farther back were stretched out on the ground, resting. And five Spaniards chanced to be with the cleric. When these heard the blows of the swords and knew that the Spaniards were killing the Indians—without seeing anything, because there were certain houses between—they put hands to their swords and are about to kill the forty Indians . . . to pay them their commission.

The cleric, moved to wrath, opposes and rebukes them harshly to prevent them, and having some respect for him, they stopped what they were going to do, so the forty were left alive. The five go to kill where the others were killing. And as the cleric had been detained in hindering the slaying of the forty carriers, when he went he found a heap of dead, which the Spaniards had made among the Indians, which was certainly a horrible sight.

When Narváez, the captain, saw him he said: "How does Your Honor like what these our Spaniards have done?"

Seeing so many cut to pieces before him, and very upset at such a cruel event, the cleric replied: "That I commend you and them to the devil!"

The heedless Narváez remained, still watching the slaughter as it took place, without speaking, acting, or moving any more than if he had been marble. For if he had wished, being on horseback and with a lance in his hands, he could have prevented the Spaniards from killing even ten persons.

Then the cleric leaves him, and goes elsewhere through some groves seeking Spaniards to stop them from killing. For they were passing through the groves looking for someone to kill, sparing neither boy, child, woman, nor old person. And they did more, in that certain Spaniards went to the road to the river, which was nearby. Then all the Indians who had escaped with wounds, stabs, and cuts—all who could flee to throw themselves into the river to save themselves—met with the Spaniards who finished them.

Another outrage occurred which should not be left untold, so that the deeds of our Christians in these regions may be observed. When the cleric entered the large house where I said there were about 500 souls—or whatever the number, which was great—and saw with horror the dead there and those who had escaped above by the poles or woodwork, he said to them:

"No more, no more. Do not be afraid. There will be no more, there will be no more."

With this assurance, believing that it would be thus, an Indian descended, a well-disposed young man of twenty-five or thirty years, weeping. And as the cleric did not rest but went everywhere to stop the killing, the cleric then left the house. And just as the young man came down, a Spaniard who was there drew a cutlass or half sword and gives him a cut through the loins, so that his intestines fall out. . . .

The Indian, moaning, takes his intestines in his hands and comes fleeing out of the house. He encounters the cleric . . . and the cleric tells him some things about the faith, as much as the time and anguish permitted, explaining to him that if he wished to be baptized he would go to heaven to live with God. The sad one, weeping and showing pain as if he were burning in flames, said yes, and with this the cleric baptized him. He then fell dead on the ground. . . .

Of all that has been said, I am a witness. I was present and saw it; and I omit many other particulars in order to shorten the account.

TRANSLATED BY GEORGE SANDERLIN

## "Are Not the Indians Men?"

When Sunday and the hour to preach arrived . . . Father Fray Antonio de Montesinos ascended the pulpit and took as the text and foundation of his sermon, which he carried written out and signed by the other friars: "I am the voice of one crying in the desert." After he completed his introduction and said something concerning the subject of Advent, he began to emphasize the aridity in the desert of Spanish consciences in this island, and the ignorance in which they lived; also, in what danger of eternal damnation they were, from taking no notice of the grave sins in which, with such apathy, they were immersed and dying.

Then he returns to his text, speaking thus: "I have ascended here to cause you to know those sins, I who am the voice of Christ in the desert of this island. Therefore it is fitting that you listen to this voice, not with careless attention, but with all your heart and senses. For this voice will be the strangest you ever heard, the harshest and hardest, most fearful and most dangerous you ever thought to hear."

This voice cried out for some time, with very combative and terrible words, so that it made their flesh tremble, and they seemed already standing before the divine judgment. Then, in a grand manner, the voice . . . declared what it was, or what that divine inspiration consisted of: "This voice," he said, "declares that you are all in mortal sin, and live and die in it, because of the cruelty and tyranny you practice among these innocent peoples.

"Tell me, by what right or justice do you hold these Indians in such a cruel and horrible servitude? On what authority have you waged such detestable wars against these peoples, who dwelt quietly and peacefully on their own land? Wars in which you have destroyed such infinite numbers of them by homicides and slaughters never before heard of? Why do you keep them so oppressed and exhausted, without giving them enough to eat or curing them of the sicknesses they incur from the excessive labor you give them, and they die, or rather, you kill them, in order to extract and acquire gold every day?

"And what care do you take that they should be instructed in religion, so that they may know their God and creator, may be baptized, may hear Mass, and may keep Sundays and feast days? Are these not men? Do they not have rational souls? Are you not bound to love them as you love yourselves? Don't you understand this? Don't you feel this? Why are you sleeping in such a profound and lethargic slumber? Be assured that in your present state you can no more be saved than the Moors or Turks, who lack the faith of Jesus Christ and do not desire it."

TRANSLATED BY GEORGE SANDERLIN

■ **Bernal Díaz del Castillo (1496–1560)**
*Spain/Mexico* (chronicle)

TRANSLATED BY J. M. COHEN

The soldier chronicler Bernal Díaz del Castillo recorded Cortés's entry into Tenochtitlán, the fabled Aztec capital of Mexico, and the meeting of Hernán Cortés with the Aztec king Montezuma, whom Cortés ultimately executed in his conquest of Mexico. Díaz, like Columbus, was mesmerized by the almost dreamlike vision that moments of discovery of the New World gave to its Old World viewers. So, when he caught sight of gigantic Tenochtitlán (today's Mexico City), he too wondered whether it was not a dream or some enchanted place recounted in the same chivalric novel, *Amadís de Gaula,* that had addled the brains of the poor burgher Alonso Quijano to make him believe that he was a great knight called Don Quijote. The more normal tone of Castillo's great chronicle is, however, neither that of the dreamer nor of Cortés and his high officers, but of the common soldier. He had been there and experienced the marches, battles, and astonishments of the ordinary soldier. In his old age, retired to what is now Guatemala, he wrote his *Natural History of the Indies.* Emir Rodríguez Monegal writes, "The freshness of his style make[s] his book one of the greatest historical narratives of the Renaissance." Monegal goes on to characterize it as an oral history, put together like a novel. Of the many chronicles and histories of the invasion into the New World, the "true history of the conquest" by Bernal is foremost for its clarity, vigor, and narrative fervor.

**FURTHER READING:** *True History of the Conquest of New Spain,* 1632.

## from *True History of the Conquest of New Spain*

### The Entrance into Mexico

Early next day we left Iztapalapa with a large escort of these great Caciques, and followed the causeway, which is eight yard wide and goes so straight to the city of Mexico that I do not think it curves at all. Wide though it was, it was so crowded with people that there was hardly room for them all. Some were going to Mexico and others coming away, besides those who had come out to see us, and we could hardly get through the crowds that were there. For the towers and the cues were full, and then came in canoes from all parts of the lake. No wonder, since they had never seen horses or men like us before!

With such wonderful sights to gaze on we did not know what to say, or if this was real that we saw before our eyes. On the land side there were great cities, and on the lake many more. The lake was crowded with canoes. At intervals along the causeway there were many bridges, and before us was the great city of Mexico. As for us, we were scarcely four hundred strong and we well remembered the words and warnings of the people. Huexotzinco and Tlascala and Tlamanalco, and the many other warnings we had received to beware of entering the city of Mexico, since they would kill us as soon as they had us inside. Let the interested reader consider whether there is not much to ponder in this narrative of mine. What men in all the world have shown such daring? But let us go on.

We marched along our causeway to a point where another small causeway branches off to another city called Coyoacan and there, beside some towerlike buildings, which were the shrines, we were met by many more *Caciques* and dignity in very rich cloaks. The different chieftains wore different brilliant liveries, and the causeways were full of them. Montezuma had sent these great *Caciques* in advance to receive us, and as soon as they came before Cortes they told him in their language that we were welcome, and as a sign of peace they touched the ground with their hands and kissed it.

There we halted for some time while Cacamatzin, the lord of Texcoco, and the lords of Iztapalapa, Tacuba, and Coyoacan went ahead to meet the great Montezuma, who approached in a rich litter, accompanied by other great lords and feudal *Caciques* who owned vassals. When we came near to Mexico, at a place where there were some other small towers, the great Montezuma descended from his litter, and these other great *Caciques* supported him beneath a marvelously rich canopy of green feathers, decorated with gold work, silver, pearls, and *chalchihuites,* which hung from a sort of border. It was a marvellous sight. The great Montezuma was magnificently clad, in their fashion, and wore sandals of a kind for which their name is *cotaras,*[1] the soles of which are of gold and the upper parts ornamented with precious stones. And the four lords who supported him were richly clad also in garments that seem to have been kept ready for them on the road so that they could accompany their master. For they had not worn clothes like this when they came out to receive us. There were four other great *Caciques* who carried the canopy above their heads, and many more lords who walked before the great Montezuma, sweeping the ground on which he was to tread, and laying down cloaks so that his feet should not touch the earth. Not one of these chieftains dared to look him in the face. All kept their eyes lowered most reverently except those four lords, his nephews, who were supporting him.

When Cortes saw, heard, and was told that the great Montezuma was approaching, he dismounted from his horse, and when he came near to Montezuma each bowed deeply to the other. Montezuma welcomed our Captain, and Cortes, speaking through Doña Marina, answered by wishing him very good health. Cortes, I think, offered Montezuma his right hand, but Montezuma refused it and extended his own. Then Cortes brought out a necklace which he had been holding. It was made of those elaborately worked and coloured glass beads called *margaritas,* of which I have spoken, and was strung on a gold cord and dipped in musk to give it a good odour. This he hung around the great Montezuma's neck, and as he did so attempted to embrace him. But the great princes who stood round Montezuma grasped Cortes' arm to prevent him, for they considered this an indignity.

---

1. Actually a Cuban word: the Mexican word was *cactli.*

Then Cortes told Montezuma that it rejoiced his heart to have seen such a great prince, and that he took his coming in person to receive him and the repeated favours he had done him as a high honour. After this Montezuma made him another complimentary speech, and ordered two of his nephews who were supporting him, the lords of Texcoco and Coyoacan, to go with us and show us our quarters. Montezuma returned to the city with the other two kinsmen of his escort, the lords of Cuitlahuac and Tacuba; and all those grand companies of *Caciques* and dignitaries who had come with him returned also in his train. And as they accompanied their lord we observed them marching with their eyes downcast so that they should not see him, and keeping close to the wall as they followed him with great reverence. Thus space was made for us to enter the streets of Mexico without being pressed by the crowd.

Who could now count the multitude of men, women, and boys in the streets, on the roof-tops and in canoes on the waterways, who had come out to see us? It was a wonderful sight and, as I write, it all comes before my eyes as if it had happened only yesterday.

They led us to our quarters, which were in some large houses capable of accommodating us all and had formerly belonged to the great Montezuma's father, who was called Axayacatl. Here Montezuma now kept the great shrines of his gods, and a secret chamber containing gold bars and jewels. This was the treasure he had inherited from his father, which he never touched. Perhaps their reason for lodging us here was that, since they called us *Teules* and considered us as such, they wished to have us near their idols. In any case they took us to this place, where there were many great halls, and a dais hung with the cloth of their country for our Captain, and matting beds with canopies over them for each of us.

On our arrival we entered the large court, where the great Montezuma was awaiting our Captain. Taking him by the hand, the prince led him to his apartment in the hall where he was to lodge, which was very richly furnished in their manner. Montezuma had ready for him a very rich necklace, made of golden crabs, a marvellous piece of work, which he hung round Cortes' neck. His captains were greatly astonished at this sign of honour.

After this ceremony, for which Cortes thanked him through our interpreters, Montezuma said: 'Malinche, you and your brothers are in your own house. Rest awhile.' He then returned to his palace, which was not far off.

We divided our lodgings by companies, and placed our artillery in a convenient spot. Then the order we were to keep was clearly explained to us, and we were warned to be very much on the alert, both the horsemen and the rest of us soldiers. We then ate a sumptuous dinner which they had prepared for us in their native style.

So, with luck on our side, we boldly entered the city of Tenochtitlan or Mexico on 8 November in the year of our Lord 1519.

## The Stay in Mexico

When the great Montezuma had dined and was told that our Captain and all of us had finished our meal some time ago, he came to our quarters in the grandest state with a great number of princes, all of them his kinsmen. On being told of his approach, Cortes came into the middle of the hall to receive him. Montezuma then took him by the hand, and they brought chairs made in their fashion and very richly decorated in various ways with gold. Montezuma requested our Captain to sit down, and both of them sat, each on his own chair.

Then Montezuma began a very good speech, saying that he was delighted to have such valiant gentlemen as Cortes and the rest of us in his house and his kingdom. That two years ago he had received news of a Captain who had come to Champoton, and that last year also he had received a report of another Captain who had come with four ships. Each time he had wished to see them, and now that he had us with him he was not only at our service but would share all that he possessed with us. He ended by saying that we must truly be the men about whom his ancestors had long ago prophesied, saying that they would come from the direction of the sunrise to rule over these lands, and that he was confirmed in this belief by the valour with which we had fought at Champoton and Tabasco and against the Tlascalans, for lifelike pictures of these battles had been brought to him.

Cortes replied through our interpreters that we did not know how to repay the daily favours we received from him, and that indeed we did come from the direction of the sunrise, and were vassals and servants of a great king called the Emperor Charles, who was ruler over many great princes. Having heard news of Montezuma and what a great prince he was, the Emperor, he said, had sent us to this country to visit him, and to beg them to become Christians, like our Emperor and all of us, so that his soul and those of all his vassals might be saved. Cortes promised to explain to him later how this could be, and how we worship the one true God and who He is, also many other good things which he had already communicated to his ambassadors Tendile, Pitalpitoque, and Quintalbor.

The great Montezuma had some fine gold jewels of various shapes in readiness which he gave to Cortes after this conversation. And to each of our captains he presented small gold objects and three loads of cloaks of rich feather work; and to us soldiers he gave two loads of cloaks each, all with a princely air. For in every way he was like a great prince. After the distribution of presents, he asked Cortes if we were all brothers and vassals of our great Emperor; and Cortes answered that we were brothers in love and friendship, persons of great distinction, and servants of our great king and lord. Further polite speeches passed between Montezuma and Cortes, but as this was the first time he had visited us and we did not want to tire him, the conversation ended.

Montezuma had ordered his stewards to provide us with everything we needed for our way of living: maize, grindstones, women to make our bread, fowls, fruit, and plenty of fodder for the horses. He then took leave of us all with the greatest courtesy, and we accompanied him to the street. However, Cortes ordered us not to go far from our quarters for the present until we knew better what conduct to observe.

Next day Cortes decided to go to Montezuma's palace. But first he sent to know whether the prince was busy and to inform him of our coming. He took four captains with him: Pedro de Alvarado, Juan Velazquez de Leon, Diego de Ordaz, and Gonzalo de Sandoval, and five of us soldiers.

When Montezuma was informed of our coming, he advanced into the middle of the hall to receive us, closely surrounded by his nephews, for no other chiefs were allowed to enter his palace or communicate with him except upon important business. Cortes and Montezuma exchanged bows, and clasped hands. Then Montezuma led Cortes to his own dais, and setting him down on his right, called for more seats, on which he ordered us all to sit also.

Cortes began to make a speech through our interpreters, saying that we were all now rested, and that in coming to see and speak with such a great prince we had fulfilled the purpose of our voyage and the orders of our lord the King. The principal things he had come to say on behalf of our Lord God had already been communicated to Montezuma through his three ambassadors, on that occasion in the sandhills when he did us the favour of sending us the golden moon and sun. We had then told him that we were Christians and worshipped one God alone, named Jesus Christ, who had suffered His passion and death to save us; and that what they worshipped as gods were not gods but devils, which were evil things, and if they were ugly to look at, their deeds were uglier. But he had proved to them how evil and ineffectual their gods were, as both the prince and his people would observe in the course of time, since where we had put up crosses such as their ambassadors had seen, they had been too frightened to appear before them.

The favour he now begged of the great Montezuma was that he should listen to the words he now wished to speak. Then he very carefully expounded the creation of the world, how we are all brothers, the children of one mother and father called Adam and Eve; and how such a brother as our great Emperor, grieving for the perdition of so many souls as their idols were leading to hell, where they burnt in living flame, had sent us to tell him this, so that he might put a stop to it, and so that they might give up the worship of idols and make no more human sacrifices— for all men are brothers—and commit no more robbery or sodomy. He also promised that in the course of time the King would send some men who lead holy lives among us, much better than our own, to explain this more fully, for we had only come to give them warning. Therefore he begged Montezuma to do as he was asked.

As Montezuma seemed about to reply, Cortes broke off his speech, saying to those of us who were with him: 'Since this is only the first attempt, we have now done our duty.'

'My lord Malinche,' Montezuma replied, 'these arguments of yours have been familiar to me for some time. I understand what you said to my ambassadors on the sandhills about the three gods and the cross, also what you preached in the various towns through which you passed. We have given you no answer, since we have worshipped our own gods here from the beginning and know them to be good. No doubt yours are good also, but do not trouble to tell us any more about them at present. Regarding the creation of the world, we have held the same belief for many ages, and for this reason are certain that you are those who our ancestors predicted would come from the direction of the sunrise. As for your great King, I am in his debt and will give him of what I possess. For, as I have already said, two years ago I had news of the Captains who came in ships, by the road that you came, and said they were servants of this great king of yours. I should like to know if you are all the same people.'

Cortes answered that we were all brothers and servants of the Emperor, and that they had come to discover a route and explore the seas and ports, so that when they knew them well we could follow, as we had done. Montezuma was referring to the expeditions of Francisco Hernandez de Cordoba and of Grijalva, the first voyages of discovery. He said that ever since that time he had wanted to invite some of these men to visit the cities of his kingdom, where he would receive them and do them honour, and that now his gods had fulfilled his desire, for we were in his house, which we might call our own. Here we might rest and enjoy ourselves, for we should receive good treatment. If on other occasions he had sent to forbid our entrance into his city, it was not of his own free will, but because his vassals were afraid. For they told him we shot out flashes of lightning, and killed many Indians with our horses, and that we were angry *Teules,* and other such childish stories. But now that he had seen us, he knew that we were of flesh and blood and very intelligent, also very brave. Therefore he had a far greater esteem for us than these reports had given him, and would share with us what he had.

We all thanked him heartily for his signal good will, and Montezuma replied with a laugh, because in his princely manner he spoke very gaily: 'Malinche, I know that these people of Tlascala with whom you are so friendly have told you that I am a sort of god or *Teule,* and keep nothing in any of my houses that is not made of silver and gold and precious stones. But I know very well that you are too intelligent to believe this and will take it as a joke. See now, Malinche, my body is made of flesh and blood like yours, and my houses and palaces are of stone, wood, and plaster. It is true that I am a great king, and have inherited the riches of my ancestors, but the lies and nonsense you have heard of us are not true. You must take them as a joke, as I take the story of your thunders and lightnings.'

Cortes answered also with a laugh that enemies always speak evil and tell lies about the people they hate, but he knew he could not hope to find a more magnificent prince in that land, and there was good reason why his fame should have reached our Emperor.

While this conversation was going on, Montezuma quietly sent one of his nephews, a great *Cacique*, to order his stewards to bring certain pieces of gold, which had apparently been set aside as a gift for Cortes, and ten loads of fine cloaks which he divided: the gold and cloaks between Cortes and the four captains, and for each of us soldiers two gold necklaces, each worth ten pesos, and two loads of cloaks. The gold that he then gave us was worth in all more than a thousand pesos, and he gave it all cheerfully, like a great and valiant prince.

As it was now past midday and he did not wish to be importunate, Cortes said to Montezuma: 'My lord, the favours you do us increase, load by load, every day, and it is now the hour of your dinner.' Montezuma answered that he thanked us for visiting him. We then took our leave with the greatest courtesy, and returned to our quarters, talking as we went of the prince's fine breeding and manners and deciding to show him the greatest respect in every way, and to remove our quilted caps in his presence, which we always did.

The great Montezuma was about forty years old, of good height, well proportioned, spare and slight, and not very dark, though of the usual Indian complexion. He did not wear his hair long but just over his ears, and he had a short black beard, well-shaped and thin. His face was rather long and cheerful, he had fine eyes, and in his appearance and manner could express geniality or, when necessary, a serious composure. He was very neat and clean, and took a bath every afternoon. He had many women as his mistresses, the daughters of chieftains, but two legitimate wives who were *Caciques* in their own right, and when he had intercourse with any of them it was so secret that only some of his servants knew of it. He was quite free from sodomy. The clothes he wore one day he did not wear again till three or four days later. He had a guard of two hundred chieftains lodged in rooms beside his own, only some of whom were permitted to speak to him. When they entered his presence they were compelled to take off their rich cloaks and put on others of little value. They had to be clean and walk barefoot, with their eyes downcast, for they were not allowed to look him in the face, and as they approached they had to make three obeisances, saying as they did so, 'Lord, my lord, my great lord!' Then, when they had said what they had come to say, he would dismiss them with a few words. They did not turn their backs on him as they went out, but kept their faces towards him and their eyes downcast, only turning round when they had left the room. Another thing I noticed was that when other great chiefs came from distant lands about disputes or on business, they too had to take off their shoes and put on poor cloaks before entering Montezuma's apartments; and they were not allowed to enter the palace immediately but had to linger for a while near the door, since to enter hurriedly was considered disrespectful.

For each meal his servants prepared him more than thirty dishes cooked in their native style, which they put over small earthenware braziers to prevent them from getting cold. They cooked more than three hundred plates of the food the great Montezuma was going to eat, and more than a thousand more for the guard. I have heard that they used to cook him the flesh of young boys. But as he had such a variety of dishes, made of so many different ingredients, we could not tell whether a dish was of human flesh or anything else, since every day they cooked fowls, turkeys, pheasants, local partridges, quail, tame and wild duck, venison, wild boar, marsh birds, pigeons, hares and rabbits, also many other kinds of birds and beasts native to their country, so numerous that I cannot quickly name them all. I know for certain, however, that after our Captain spoke against the sacrifice of human beings and the eating of their flesh, Montezuma ordered that it should no longer be served to him.

Let us now turn to the way his meals were served, which was like this. If it was cold, they built a large fire of live coals made by burning the bark of a tree which gave off no smoke. The smell of the bark from which they made these coals was very sweet. In order that he should get no more heat than he wanted, they placed a sort of screen in front of it adorned with the figures of idols worked in gold. He would sit on a soft low stool, which was richly worked. His table, which was also low and decorated in the same way, was covered with white tablecloths and rather long napkins of the same material. Then four very clean and beautiful girls brought water for his hands in one of those deep basins that they call *xicales*.[1] They held others like plates beneath it to catch the water, and brought him towels. Two other women brought him maize-cakes.

When he began his meal they placed in front of him a sort of wooden screen, richly decorated with gold, so that no one should see him eat. Then the four women retired, and four great chieftains, all old men, stood beside him. He talked with them every now and then and asked them questions, and as a great favour he would sometimes offer one of them a dish of whatever tasted best. They say that these were his closest relations and advisers and judges of lawsuits, and if he gave them anything to eat they ate it standing, with deep reverence and without looking in his face.

Montezuma's food was served on Cholula ware, some red and some black. While he was dining, the guards in the adjoining rooms did not dare to speak or make a noise above a whisper. His servants brought him some of every kind of fruit that grew in the country, but he ate very little of it. Sometimes they brought him in cups of pure gold a drink made from the cocoaplant, which they said he took before visiting his wives. We did not take much notice of this at the time, though I saw them bring in a good fifty large jugs of this chocolate, all frothed up, of which he would drink a little. They always served it with great reverence. Sometimes some little humpbacked dwarfs would be present at his meals, whose bodies seemed almost to be broken in the middle. These were his jesters. There were other Indians who told him jokes and must have been his clowns,

---

1. Gourds.

and others who sang and danced, for Montezuma was very fond of music and entertainment and would reward his entertainers with the leavings of the food and chocolate. The same four women removed the tablecloths and again most reverently brought him water for his hands. Then Montezuma would talk to these four old chieftains about matters that interested him, and they would take their leave with great ceremony. He stayed behind to rest.

As soon as the great Montezuma had dined, all the guards and many more of his household servants ate in their turn. I think more than a thousand plates of food must have been brought in for them, and more than two thousand jugs of chocolate frothed up in the Mexican style, and infinite quantities of fruit, so that with his women and serving-maids and breadmakers and chocolate-makers his expenses must have been considerable.

One thing I had forgotten to say is that two more very handsome women served Montezuma when he was at table with maize-cakes kneaded with eggs and other nourishing ingredients. These maize-cakes were very white, and were brought in on plates covered with clean napkins. They brought him a different kind of bread also, in a long ball kneaded with other kinds of nourishing food, and *pachol* cake, as they call it in that country, which is a kind of wafer. They also placed on the table three tubes, much painted and gilded, in which they put liquidamber[2] mixed with some herbs which are called tobacco. When Montezuma had finished his dinner, and the singing and dancing were over and the cloths had been removed, he would inhale the smoke from one of these tubes. He took very little of it, and then fell asleep.

I remember that at that time his steward was a great *Cacique* whom we nicknamed Tapia, and he kept an account of all the revenue that was brought to Montezuma in his books, which were made of paper—their name for which is *amal*—and he had a great house full of these books. But they have nothing to do with our story.

Montezuma had two houses stocked with every sort of weapon: many of them were richly adorned with gold and precious stones. There were shields large and small, and a sort of broadsword, and two-handed swords set with flint blades that cut much better than our swords, and lances longer than ours, with five-foot blades consisting of many knives. Even when these are driven at a buckler or a shield they are not deflected. In fact they cut like razors, and the Indians can shave their heads with them. They had very good bows and arrows, and double and single-pointed javelins as well as their throwing-sticks and many slings and round stones shaped by hand, and another sort of shield that can be rolled up when they are not fighting, so that it does not get in the way, but which can be opened when they need it in battle and covers their bodies from head to foot. There was also a great deal of cotton armour richly worked on the

2. The gum of a native tree.

outside with different coloured feathers, which they used as devices and distinguishing marks, and they had casques and helmets made of wood and bone which were also highly decorated with feathers on the outside. They had other arms of different kinds which I will not mention through fear of prolixity, and workmen skilled in the manufacture of such things, and stewards who were in charge of these arms.

Let us pass on to the aviary. I cannot possibly enumerate every kind of bird that was in it or describe its characteristics. There was everything from the royal eagle, smaller kinds of eagles, and other large birds, down to multi-coloured little birds, and those from which they take the fine green feathers they use in their feather-work. These last birds are about the size of our magpies, and here they are called *quetzals*. There were other birds too which have feathers of five colours: green, red, white, yellow, and blue, but I do not know what they are called. Then there were parrots with different coloured plumage, so many of them that I have forgotten their names. There were also beautifully marked ducks, and bigger ones like them. At the proper season they plucked the feathers of all these birds, which then grew again. All of them were bred in this aviary, and at hatching time the men and women who looked after them would place them on their eggs and clean their nests and feed them, giving each breed of birds its proper food.

In the aviary there was a large tank of fresh water, and in it was another type of bird on long stilt-like legs with a red body, wings, and tail. I do not know its name, but in Cuba birds rather like them are called *ypiris*. Also in this tank there were many other kinds of water birds.

Let us go on to another large house where they kept many idols whom they called their fierce gods, and with them all kinds of beasts of prey, tigers and two sorts of lion, and beasts rather like wolves which they call *adives*,[3] and foxes and other small animals, all of them carnivores, and most of them bred there. They were fed on deer, fowls, little dogs, and other creatures which they hunt and also on the bodies of the Indians they sacrificed, as I was told.

I have already described the manner of their sacrifices. They strike open the wretched Indian's chest with flint knives and hastily tear out the palpitating heart which, with the blood, they present to the idols in whose name they have performed the sacrifice. Then they cut off the arms, thighs, and head, eating the arms and thighs at their ceremonial banquets. The head they hang up on a beam, and the body of the sacrificed man is not eaten but given to the beasts of prey. They also had many vipers in this accursed house, and poisonous snakes which have something that sounds like a bell in their tails. These, which are the deadliest snakes of all, they kept in jars and great pottery vessels full of feathers, in which they laid their eggs and reared their young. They were fed on the bodies

---

3. Bernal Díaz is mistaken here. This is an Arabic word for jackal, quite commonly used in Spain.

of sacrificed Indians and the flesh of the dogs that they bred. We know for certain, too, that when they drove us out of Mexico and killed over eight hundred and fifty of our soldiers, they fed those beasts and snakes on their bodies for many days, as I shall relate in due course. These snakes and wild beasts were dedicated to their fierce idols, and kept them company. As for the horrible noise when the lions and tigers roared, and the jackals and foxes howled, and the serpents hissed, it was so appalling that one seemed to be in hell.

I must now speak of the skilled workmen whom Montezuma employed in all the crafts they practised, beginning with the jewellers and workers in silver and gold and various kinds of hollowed objects, which excited the admiration of our great silversmiths at home. Many of the best of them lived in a town called Atzcapotzalco, three miles from Mexico. There were other skilled craftsmen who worked with precious stones and *chalchihuites*, and specialists in feather-work, and very fine painters and carvers. We can form some judgement of what they did then from what we can see of their work today. There are three Indians now living in the city of Mexico, named Marcos de Aquino, Juan de la Cruz, and El Crespillo, who are such magnificent painters and carvers that, had they lived in the age of the Apelles of old, or of Michael Angelo, or Berruguete in our own day, they would be counted in the same rank.

Let us go on to the women, the weavers and sempstresses, who made such a huge quantity of fine robes with very elaborate feather designs. These things were generally brought from some towns in the province of Cotaxtla, which is on the north coast, quite near San Juan de Ulua. In Montezuma's own palaces very fine cloths were woven by those chieftains' daughters whom he kept as mistresses; and the daughters of other dignitaries, who lived in a kind of retirement like nuns in some houses close to the great cue of Huichilobos, wore robes entirely of featherwork. Out of devotion for that god and a female deity who was said to preside over marriage, their fathers would place them in religious retirement until they found husbands. They would then take them out to be married.

Now to speak of the great number of performers whom Montezuma kept to entertain him. There were dancers and stilt-walkers, and some who seemed to fly as they leapt through the air, and men rather like clowns to make him laugh. There was a whole quarter full of these people who had no other occupation. He had as many workmen as he needed, too, stonecutters, masons, and carpenters, to keep his houses in repair.

We must not forget the gardens with their many varieties of flowers and sweet-scented trees planted in order, and their ponds and tanks of fresh water into which a stream flowed at one end and out of which it flowed at the other, and the baths he had there, and the variety of small birds that nested in the branches, and the medicinal and useful herbs that grew there. His gardens were a wonderful sight, and required many gardeners to take care of them. Everything was built of stone and plastered; baths and walks and closets and rooms like summerhouses where they danced and sang. There was so much to see in these gardens, as everywhere else, that we could not tire of contemplating his great riches and the large number of skilled Indians employed in the many crafts they practised.

When we had already been in Mexico for four days, and neither our Captain nor anyone else had left our quarters except to visit these houses and gardens, Cortes said it would be a good thing to visit the large square of Tlatelolco and see the great *cue* of Huichilobos. So he sent Aguilar, Doña Marina, and his own young page Orteguilla, who by now knew something of the language, to ask for Montezuma's approval of this plan. On receiving his request, the prince replied that we were welcome to go, but for fear that we might offer some offence to his idols he would himself accompany us with many of his chieftains. Leaving the palace in his fine litter, when he had gone about half way, he dismounted beside some shrines, since he considered it an insult to his gods to visit their dwelling in a litter. Some of the great chieftains then supported him by the arms, and his principal vassals walked before him, carrying two staves, like sceptres raised on high as a sign that the great Montezuma was approaching. When riding in his litter he had carried a rod, partly of gold and partly of wood, held up like a wand of justice. The prince now climbed the steps of the great *cue*, escorted by many *papas*, and began to burn incense and perform other ceremonies for Huichilobos.

Let us leave Montezuma, who had gone ahead as I have said, and return to Cortes and our soldiers. We carried our weapons, as was our custom, both by night and day. Indeed, Montezuma was so used to our visiting him armed that he did not think it strange. I say this because our Captain and those of us who had horses went to Tlatelolco mounted, and the majority of our men were fully equipped. On reaching the market-place, escorted by the many *Caciques* whom Montezuma had assigned to us, we were astounded at the great number of people and the quantities of merchandise, and at the orderliness and good arrangements that prevailed, for we had never seen such a thing before. The chieftains who accompanied us pointed everything out. Every kind of merchandise was kept separate and had its fixed place marked for it.

Let us begin with the dealers in gold, silver, and precious stones, feathers, cloaks, and embroidered goods, and male and female slaves who are also sold there. They bring as many slaves to be sold in that market as the Portuguese bring Negroes from Guinea. Some are brought there attached to long poles by means of collars round their necks to prevent them from escaping, but others are left loose. Next there were those who sold coarser cloth, and cotton goods and fabrics made of twisted thread, and there were chocolate merchants with their chocolate. In this way you could see every kind of merchandise to be found anywhere in New Spain, laid out in the same way as goods are laid out in my own district of Medina del Campo, a centre for fairs, where each line of stalls has its own particular sort. So it was in this great market. There were those who sold sisal cloth and ropes and the sandals they wear on their feet, which are made from the same plant. All these were kept in one part of the market, in the place assigned to them, and in another part were skins of tigers and lions, otters, jackals, and deer, badgers, mountain cats, and other wild animals, some tanned and some untanned, and other classes of merchandise.

There were sellers of kidney-beans and sage and other vegetables and herbs in another place, and in yet another they were selling fowls, and birds with great dewlaps,[4] also rabbits, hares, deer, young ducks, little dogs, and other such creatures. Then there were the fruiterers; and the women who sold cooked food, flour and honey cake, and tripe, had their part of the market. Then came pottery of all kinds, from big water-jars to little jugs, displayed in its own place, also honey, honey-paste, and other sweets like nougat. Elsewhere they sold timber too, boards, cradles, beams, blocks, and benches, all in a quarter of their own.

Then there were the sellers of pitch-pine for torches, and other things of that kind, and I must also mention, with all apologies, that they sold many canoe-loads of human excrement, which they kept in the creeks near the market. This was for the manufacture of salt and the curing of skins, which they say cannot be done without it. I know that many gentlemen will laugh at this, but I assure them it is true. I may add that on all the roads they have shelters made of reeds or straw or grass so that they can retire when they wish to do so, and purge their bowels unseen by passersby, and also in order that their excrement shall not be lost.

But why waste so many words on the goods in their great market? If I describe everything in detail I shall never be done. Paper, which in Mexico they call *amal,* and some reeds that smell of liquidamber, and are full of tobacco, and yellow ointments and other such things, are sold in a separate part. Much cochineal is for sale too, under the arcades of that market, and there are many sellers of herbs and other such things. They have a building there also in which three judges sit, and there are officials like constables who examine the merchandise. I am forgetting the sellers of salt and the makers of flint knives, and how they split them off the stone itself, and the fisherwomen and the men who sell small cakes made from a sort of weed which they get out of the great lake, which curdles and forms a kind of bread which tastes rather like cheese. They sell axes too, made of bronze and copper and tin, and gourds and brightly painted wooden jars.

We went on to the great *cue,* and as we approached its wide courts, before leaving the market-place itself, we saw many more merchants who, so I was told, brought gold to sell in grains, just as they extract it from the mines. This gold is placed in the thin quills of the large geese of that country, which are so white as to be transparent. They used to reckon their accounts with one another by the length and thickness of these little quills, how much so many cloaks or so many gourds of chocolate or so many slaves were worth, or anything else they were bartering.

---

4. Turkeys.

Now let us leave the market, having given it a final glance, and come to the courts and enclosures in which their great *cue* stood. Before reaching it you passed through a series of large courts, bigger I think than the Plaza at Salamanca. These courts were surrounded by a double masonry wall and paved, like the whole place, with very large smooth white flagstones. Where these stones were absent everything was whitened and polished, indeed the whole place was so clean that there was not a straw or a grain of dust to be found there.

When we arrived near the great temple and before we had climbed a single step, the great Montezuma sent six *papas* and two chieftains down from the top, where he was making his sacrifices, to escort our Captain; and as he climbed the steps, of which there were one hundred and fourteen, they tried to take him by the arms to help him up in the same way as they helped Montezuma, thinking he might be tired, but he would not let them near him.

The top of the *cue* formed an open square on which stood something like a platform, and it was here that the great stones stood on which they placed the poor Indians for sacrifice. Here also was a massive image like a dragon, and other hideous figures, and a great deal of blood that had been spilled that day. Emerging in the company of two *papas* from the shrine which houses his accursed images, Montezuma made a deep bow to us all and said: 'My lord Malinche, you must be tired after climbing this great *cue* of ours.' And Cortes replied that none of us was ever exhausted by anything. Then Montezuma took him by the hand, and told him to look at his great city and all the other cities standing in the water, and the many others on the land round the lake; and he said that if Cortes had not had a good view of the great market-place he could see it better from where he now was. So we stood there looking, because that huge accursed *cue* stood so high that it dominated everything. We saw the three causeways that led into Mexico: the causeway of Iztapalapa by which we had entered four days before, and that of Tacuba along which we were afterwards to flee on the night of our great defeat, when the new prince Cuitlahuac drove us out of the city (as I shall tell in due course), and that of Tepeaquilla.[5] We saw the fresh water which came from Chapultepec to supply the city, and the bridges that were constructed at intervals on the causeways so that the water could flow in and out from one part of the lake to another. We saw a great number of canoes, some coming with provisions and others returning with cargo and merchandise; and we saw too that one could not pass from one house to another of that great city and the other cities that were built on the water except over wooden drawbridges or by canoe. We saw *cues* and shrines in these cities that looked like gleaming white towers and castles: a marvelous sight. All the houses had flat roofs, and on the causeways were other small towers and shrines built like fortresses.

---

5. Guadalupe.

Having examined and considered all that we had seen, we turned back to the great market and the swarm of people buying and selling. The mere murmur of their voices talking was loud enough to be heard more than three miles away. Some of our soldiers who had been in many parts of the world, in Constantinople, in Rome, and all over Italy, said that they had never seen a market so well laid out, so large, so orderly, and so full of people.

But to return to our Captain, he observed to Father Bartolome de Olmedo, whom I have often mentioned and who happened to be standing near him: 'It would be a good thing, I think, Father, if we were to sound Montezuma as to whether he would let us build our church here.' Father Bartolome answered that it would be a good thing if it were successful, but he did not think this a proper time to speak of it, for Montezuma did not look as if he would allow such a thing.

Cortes, however, addressed Montezuma through Doña Marina: 'Your lordship is a great prince and worthy of even greater things. We have enjoyed the sight of your cities, and since we are now here in your temple, I beg of you to show us your gods and *Teules*.' Montezuma answered that first he would consult his chief *papas;* and when he had spoken to them he said that we might enter a small tower, an apartment like a sort of hall, in which there were two altars with very rich wooden carvings over the roof. On each altar was a giant figure, very tall and very fat. They said that the one on the right was Huichilobos, their war-god. He had a very broad face and huge terrible eyes. And there were so many precious stones, so much gold, so many pearls and seed-pearls stuck to him with a paste which the natives made from a sort of root, that his whole body and head were covered with them. He was girdled with huge snakes made of gold and precious stones, and in one hand he held a bow, in the other some arrows. Another smaller idol beside him, which they said was his page, carried a short lance and a very rich shield of gold and precious stones. Around Huichilobos' neck hung some Indian faces and other objects in the shape of hearts, the former made of gold and the latter of silver, with many precious blue stones.

There were some smoking braziers of their incense, which they call copal, in which they were burning the hearts of three Indians whom they had sacrificed that day; and all the walls of that shrine were so splashed and caked with blood that they and the floor too were black. Indeed, the whole place stank abominably. We then looked to the left and saw another great image of the same height as Huichilobos, with a face like a bear and eyes that glittered, being made of their mirror-glass, which they call *tezcat*. Its body, like that of Huichilobos, was encrusted with precious stones, for they said that the two were brothers. This Tezcatlipoca, the god of hell, had charge of the Mexicans' souls, and his body was surrounded by figures of little devils with snakes' tails. The walls of this shrine also were so caked with blood and the floor so bathed in it that the stench was worse than that of any slaughter-house in Spain. They had offered that idol five hearts from the day's sacrifices.

At the very top of the *cue* there was another alcove, the woodwork of which was very finely carved, and here there was another image, half man and half lizard, encrusted with precious stones, with half its body covered in a cloak. They said that the body of this creature contained all the seeds in the world, and that he was the god of seedtime and harvest. I do not remember his name.[6] Here too all was covered with blood, both walls and altar, and the stench was such that we could hardly wait to get out. They kept a very large drum there, and when they beat it the sound was most dismal, like some music from the infernal regions, as you might say, and it could be heard six miles away. This drum was said to be covered with the skins of huge serpents. In that small platform were many more diabolical objects, trumpets great and small, and large knives, and many hearts that had been burnt with incense before their idols; and everything was caked with blood. The stench here too was like a slaughter-house, and we could scarcely stay in the place.

Our Captain said to Montezuma, through our interpreters, with something like a laugh: 'Lord Montezuma, I cannot imagine how a prince as great and wise as your Majesty can have failed to realize that these idols of yours are not gods but evil things, the proper name for which is devils. But so that I may prove this to you, and make it clear to all your *papas,* grant me one favour. Allow us to erect a cross here on the top of this tower, and let us divide off a part of this sanctuary where your Huichilobos and Tezcatlipoca stand, as a place where we can put an image of Our Lady'— which image Montezuma had already seen—'and then you will see, by the fear that your idols have of her, how grievously they have deceived you.'

Montezuma, however, replied in some temper (and the two *papas* beside him showed real anger): 'Lord Malinche, if I had known that you were going to utter these insults I should not have shown you my gods. We hold them to be very good. They give us health and rain and crops and weather, and all the victories we desire. So we are bound to worship them and sacrifice to them, and I beg you to say nothing more against them.'

On hearing this and seeing Montezuma's fury, our Captain said no more on the subject but observed cheerfully: 'It is time for your Majesty and ourselves to depart.' Montezuma replied that this was so, but that he had to pray and offer certain sacrifices on account of the great *tatacul*— that is to say sin—which he had committed in allowing us to climb his great *cue* and in being instrumental in letting us see his gods and in the dishonour we had done them by our abuse. Therefore before he left he must pray and worship.

'If that is so, my lord,' Cortes answered, 'I ask your pardon.' And we went down the steps, of which there were a hundred and fourteen, as I said. As some of our soldiers were suffering from pustules or running sores, their thighs pained them as they went down.

---

6. This was probably Tlaltecuhtli.

I will now give my impression of the *cue's* surroundings. Do not be surprised, however, if I do not describe them as accurately as I might, for I had other thoughts in my head at the time than that of telling a story. I was more concerned with my military duties and the orders my Captain had given me. But to come to the facts, I think the site of the great *cue* was equal to the plots of six large town houses at home. It tapered from the base to the top of the small tower where they kept their idols. Between the middle of this tall *cue* and its highest point there were five holes like loopholes for cannon, but open and unprotected. But as there are many *cues* painted on the banners of the conquerors, including my own, anyone who has seen them can gather what a *cue* looked like from the outside. I heard a report that, at the time when this great *cue* was built, all the inhabitants of that mighty city placed offerings of gold and silver and pearls and precious stones in the foundations, and bathed them in the blood of prisoners of war whom they had sacrificed. They also put there every kind of seed that grew in their country, so that their idols should give them victories and riches and great crops. Some curious readers may ask how we came to know that they had thrown gold and silver and precious *chalchihuites* and seeds into the foundation of the *cue*, and watered them with the blood of Indian victims, seeing that the building was erected a thousand years ago. My answer is that after we conquered that great and strong city and divided the ground we decided to build a church to our patron and guide St James in place of Huichilobos' *cue*, and a great part of the site was taken for the purpose. When the ground was excavated to lay a foundation, gold and silver and *chalchihuites*, and pearls, seed-pearls, and other precious stones were found in great quantities; and a settler in Mexico who built on another part of the site found the same. The officers of His Majesty's Treasury demanded this find as rightfully belonging to the King, and there was a lawsuit about it. I do not remember what the outcome was, only that they asked for information from the *Caciques* and dignitaries of Mexico, and from Guatemoc who was then alive, and they affirmed that all the inhabitants of Mexico had thrown jewels and other things into the foundations, as was recorded in their pictures and records of ancient times. The treasure was therefore preserved for the building of St James's church.

Let me go on to describe the great and splendid courts in front of Huichilobos, on the site where that church now stands, which was called at that time Tlatelolco. I have already said that there were two masonry walls before the entrance to the *cue*, and the court was paved with white stones like flagstones, and all was whitened, burnished and clean. A little apart from the *cue* stood another small tower which was also an idol-house or true hell, for one of its doors was in the shape of a terrible mouth, such as they paint to depict the jaws of hell. This mouth was open and contained great fangs to devour souls. Beside this door were groups of devils and the shapes of serpents, and a little way off was a place of sacrifice, all bloodstained and black with smoke. There were many great pots and jars and pitchers in this house, full of water. For it was here that they cooked the flesh of the wretched Indians who were sacrificed and eaten by the *papas*. Near this place of sacrifice there were many large knives and chopping-blocks like those on which men cut up meat in slaughter-houses; and behind that dreadful house, some distance away, were great piles of brushwood, beside which was a tank of water that was filled and emptied through a pipe from the covered channel that comes into the city from Chapultepec. I always called that building Hell.

Crossing the court you came to another *cue*, where the great Mexican princes were buried. This also contained many idols and was full of blood and smoke. It too had doorways with hellish figures; and beside it was another *cue*, full of skulls and large bones arranged in an orderly pattern, and so numerous that you could not count them however long you looked. The skulls were in one place and the bones in separate piles. Here there were more idols, and in every building or *cue* or shrine were *papas* in long black cloth robes and long hoods.

To proceed, there were other *cues*, a short distance away from that of the skulls, which contained other idols and sacrificial altars decorated with horrible paintings. These idols were said to preside over the marriages of men. But I will waste no more time on the subject of idols. I will only say that all round that great court there were many low houses, used and occupied by the *papas* and other Indians who were in charge of them. On one side of the great *cue* there was another, much bigger pond or tank of very clean water which was solely devoted to the service of Huichilobos and Tezcatlipoca, and the water for this tank was also supplied by covered pipes that came from Chapultepec. Near by were the large buildings of a kind of nunnery where many of the daughters of the inhabitants of Mexico dwelt in retirement until the time of their marriage. Here there were two massive female idols who presided over the marriages of women, and to which they offered sacrifices and feasts in order that they should get good husbands.

I have spent a long time talking about the great *cue* of Tlatelolco and its courts. I will conclude by saying that it was the biggest temple in Mexico, though there were many other fine ones, for every four or five parishes or districts supported a shrine with idols: and since there were many districts I cannot keep a count of them all. I must say, however, that the great *cue* in Cholula was higher than that in Mexico, for it had a hundred and twenty steps. The idol at Cholula, as I heard, had a great reputation, and people made pilgrimages to it from all over New Spain to obtain pardons. This was the reason why they had built it such a magnificent *cue*. It was differently planned from that of Mexico, but also had great courts and a double wall. The *cue* of the city of Texcoco was very high too, having a hundred and seventeen steps, and fine wide courtyards, again of a different shape from the others. Absurd though it was, every province had its own idols, and those of one province or city were of no help in another. Therefore they had infinite numbers of idols and sacrificed to them all.

When we were all tired of walking about and seeing such a diversity of idols and sacrifices, we returned to our quarters, still accompanied by the many *Caciques* and dignitaries whom Montezuma had sent with us.

When our Captain and the Mercedarian friar realized that Montezuma would not allow us to set up a cross at Huichilobos' *cue* or build a church there, it was decided that we should ask his stewards for masons so that we could put up a church in our own quarters. For every time we had said mass since entering the city of Mexico we had had to erect an altar on tables and dismantle it again.

The stewards promised to tell Montezuma of our wishes, and Cortes also sent our interpreters to ask him in person. Montezuma granted our request and ordered that we should be supplied with all the necessary material. We had our church finished in two days, and a cross erected in front of our lodgings, and mass was said there each day until the wine gave out. For as Cortes and some other captains and a friar had been ill during the Tlascalan campaign, there had been a run on the wine that we kept for mass. Still, though it was finished, we still went to church every day and prayed on our knees before the altar and images, firstly because it was our obligation as Christians and a good habit, and secondly so that Montezuma and all his captains should observe us and, seeing us worshipping on our knees before the cross—especially when we intoned the Ave Maria—might be inclined to imitate us.

It being our habit to examine and inquire into everything, when we were all assembled in our lodging and considering which was the best place for an altar, two of our men, one of whom was the carpenter Alonso Yañez, called attention to some marks on one of the walls which showed that there had once been a door, though it had been well plastered up and painted. Now as we had heard that Montezuma kept his father's treasure in this building, we immediately suspected that it must be in this room, which had been closed up only a few days before. Yañez made the suggestion to Juan Velazquez de Leon and Francisco de Lugo, both relatives of mine, to whom he had attached himself as a servant; and they mentioned the matter to Cortes. So the door was secretly opened, and Cortes went in first with certain captains. When they saw the quantity of golden objects—jewels and plates and ingots—which lay in that chamber they were quite transported. They did not know what to think of such riches. The news soon spread to the other captains and soldiers, and very secretly we all went in to see. The sight of all that wealth dumbfounded me. Being only a youth at the time and never having seen such riches before, I felt certain that there could not be a store like it in the whole world. We unanimously decided that we could not think of touching a particle of it, and that the stones should immediately be replaced in the doorway, which should be blocked again and cemented just as we had found it. We resolved also that not a word should be said about this until times changed, for fear Montezuma might hear of our discovery.

Let us leave this subject of the treasure and tell how four of our most valiant captains took Cortes aside in the church, with a dozen soldiers who were in his trust and confidence, myself among them, and asked him to consider the net or trap in which we were caught, to look at the great strength of the city and observe the causeways and bridges, and remember the warnings we had received in every town we had passed through that Huichilobos had counselled Montezuma to let us into the city and kill us there. We reminded him that the hearts of men are very fickle, especially among the Indians, and begged him not to trust the good will and affection that Montezuma was showing us, because from one hour to another it might change. If he should take it into his head to attack us, we said, the stoppage of our supplies of food and water, or the raising of any of the bridges, would render us helpless. Then, considering the vast army of warriors he possessed, we should be incapable of attacking or defending ourselves. And since all the houses stood in the water, how could our Tlascalan allies come in to help us? We asked him to think over all that we had said, for if we wanted to preserve our lives we must seize Montezuma immediately, without even a day's delay. We pointed out that all the gold Montezuma had given us, and all that we had seen in the treasury of his father Axayacatl, and all the food we ate was turning to poison in our bodies, for we could not sleep by night or day or take any rest while these thoughts were in our minds. If any of our soldiers gave him less drastic advice, we concluded, they would be senseless beasts charmed by the gold and incapable of looking death in the eye.

When he had heard our opinion, Cortes answered: 'Do not imagine, gentlemen, that I am asleep or that I do not share your anxiety. You must have seen that I do. But what strength have we got for so bold a course as to take this great lord in his own palace, surrounded as he is by warriors and guards? What scheme or trick can we devise to prevent him from summoning his soldiers to attack us at once?'

Our captains (Juan Velazquez de Leon, Diego de Ordaz, Gonzalo de Sandoval, and Pedro de Alvarado) replied that Montezuma must be got out of his palace by smooth words and brought to our quarters. Once there, he must be told that he must remain as a prisoner, and that if he called out or made any disturbance he would pay for it with his life. If Cortes was unwilling to take this course at once, they begged him for permission to do it themselves. With two very dangerous alternatives before us, the better and more profitable thing, they said, would be to seize Montezuma rather than wait for him to attack us. Once he did so, what chance would we have? Some of us soldiers also remarked that Montezuma's stewards who brought us our food seemed to be growing insolent, and did not serve us as politely as they had at first. Two of our Tlascalan allies had, moreover, secretly observed to Jeronimo de Aguilar that for the last two days the Mexicans had appeared less well disposed to us. We spent a good hour discussing whether or not to take Montezuma prisoner, and how it should be done. But our final advice, that at all costs we should take him prisoner, was approved by our Captain, and we then left the matter till next day. All night we prayed God to direct events in the interests of His holy service.

Next morning two Tlascalan Indians arrived very secretly with letters from Villa Rica containing the news of an attack by the Mexicans at a place called Almeria, in which one of our men and the Constable's horse had been killed, as well as many Totonacs. Moreover the Constable Escalante himself and six more men had died of their wounds after returning to Villa Rica. Now all the hill towns and Cempoala and its dependencies were in revolt. They refused to bring food or serve in the fort; whereas hitherto our men had been respected as *Teules,* now after this disaster Mexicans and Totonacs alike were behaving like wild beasts. They could not control the Indians in any way, and did not know what measures to take.

God knows the distress this news caused us. It was the first defeat we had suffered in New Spain, and misfortunes, as the reader will see, were now descending upon us.

## ◼ The Inca Garcilaso de la Vega (1539–1616)
## *Peru/Spain* (history)

TRANSLATED BY HAROLD V. LIVERMORE

The illegitimate son of a conquistador and an Inca princess, the Inca Garcilaso is the first American-born writer of distinction in the New World. With him begins American letters in its most profoundly ethnic and literary modes. With Garcilaso, a child of Europe and America, begins the indigious literature in Spanish of the New World. Garcilaso was born in the high Andes city of Cuzco, the ancient capital of the Inca kingdom. Because he was a "half-caste" and illegitimate, he was denied his father's name and was baptized Gómez Suárez de Figueroa. His father was Sebastián de Garcilaso, of the family of Garcilaso de la Vega, the great Spanish Renaissance poet. For the literatures of the Americas, Garcilaso Inca was the perfect interpreter and stylist for the postconquest period, carrying with him a knowledge of Spain and its language as well as his more favored knowledge of Inca reality, history, and legend, which he gave to us in elegant Spanish prose.

Schooled in Peru, in 1560 he went to Spain to complete his education. In Andalusia, he was protected by his paternal uncle and assumed his family name, adding Inca to it to display his Inca heritage. He was unable, however, to assume control of his father's confiscated estate and fortune. In Spain, he led a full literary life and produced three significant books. He edited and compiled *La Florida* (1605), the work of the explorer Hernando de Soto. He translated from Italian into Spanish *Dialoghi d'Amore,* a key Neoplatonic work by the exiled Spanish Jew León Hebreo. Hebreo's original dialogues, early in the sixteenth century, with their mystical lexicon for spiritual love, were, along with the Song of Songs, the principal source for the poetry and commentaries of the Spanish mystical poet Saint John of the Cross. His third book was his literary treasure, *The Royal Commentaries* (1609 and 1617).

In the *Commentaries,* Garcilaso used all the available sources of an educated, well-connected exile in Spain. Schooled in Quechua as a young man, he wrote to his royal Inca relatives for information. He also preserved his own memory of an oral tradition of narration, which had been essential to his Peruvian youth. In the "histories," he recreated Inca glory. He could not know then that the Incas, whose recorded culture dated back to the twelfth century, were not the first Indian civilization in Peru, but, rather, the last in a series of civilizations, and that, for example, the famous, beautiful Peruvian textiles long preceded the Inca period. He did preserve the Inca version of his people's history and religion, reminding Spain that Peru had been ruled by the Sons of the Sun, *los Hijos del Sol.* In later years, the Spanish censors held the book hostage; and when it was permitted publication, the word "Royalty" was removed from the title. The volume was retitled *General History of Peru*—in the manner of the Spanish chronicles of conquest. The grand interior, however, remained untouched, and the majestic quality shone on virtually every page.

**FURTHER READING:** The Inca Garcilaso de la Vega. *The Dialogues of Love,* 1590; *The Royal Commentaries,* 1609, II, 1617.

## from *The Royal Commentaries of Peru*

### The Idolatry of the Indians and the Gods They Worshipped before the Incas

For the better understanding of the idolatry, way of life, and customs of the Indians of Peru, it will be necessary for us to divide those times into two periods. First we shall say how they lived before the Incas, and then how the Inca kings governed, so as not to confuse the one thing with the other, and so that the customs and gods of one period are not attributed to the other. It must therefore be realized that in the first age of primitive heathendom there were Indians who were little better than tame beasts and others much worse than wild beasts. To begin with their gods, we may say that they were of a piece with the simplicity and stupidity of the times, as regards the multiplicity of gods and the vileness and crudity of the things the people worshipped. Each province, each tribe, each village, each quarter, each clan, each house had gods different from the rest, for they considered that other people's gods, being busy with other people's affairs, could not help them, but they must have their own. Thus they came to have so great a variety of gods, which were too numerous to count. They did not understand, as the gentile Romans did, how to create abstract gods such as Hope, Victory, Peace, and so on, for their thoughts did not rise to invisible things, and they worshipped what they saw some in one way and others in another. They did not consider whether the things they worshipped were worthy of their worship and they had no self-respect, in the sense of refraining from worshipping things inferior to themselves. They only thought of distinguishing themselves from one another, and each from all the rest. Thus they worshipped grasses, plants, flowers, trees of all kinds, high hills, great rocks and nooks in them, deep caves, pebbles, and little pieces of stone of various colors found in rivers and streams, such as jasper. They worshipped the emerald, especially in the province now called Puerto Viejo. They did not worship diamonds or rubies because these stones did not exist there. Instead they worshipped various animals, some for their ferocity, such as the tiger, lion, and bear: and consequently, regarding them as gods, if they chanced to meet them, they did not flee but fell down and worshipped them and let themselves be killed and eaten without escaping or making any defence at all. They also worshipped other animals for their cunning, such as the fox and monkeys. They worshipped the dog for its faithfulness and nobility, the wild cat for its quickness, and the bird they call *cuntur* for its size; and some natives worshipped eagles, because they boast of descending from them and also from the *cuntur*. Other peoples adored hawks for their quickness and ability in winning their food. They adored the owl for the beauty of its eyes and head; the bat for the keenness of its sight—it caused them much wonder that it could see at night. They also adored many other birds according to their whims. They adored great snakes for their monstrous size and fierceness (some of those in the Antis are about twenty-five or thirty feet long and as thick round as a man's thigh). They also considered other smaller snakes—where there were none so big as in the Antis—to be gods, and they adored lizards, toads, and frogs. In a word, there was no beast too vile and filthy for them to worship as a god, merely in order to differ from one another in their choice of gods, without adoring any real god or being able to expect any benefit from them. They were very simple in everything, like sheep without a shepherd. But we need not be surprised that such unlettered and untaught people should have fallen into these follies, for it is well known that the Greeks and Romans, who prided themselves so greatly on their learning, had thirty thousand gods when their empire was at its height.

## The Great Variety of Other Gods They Had

There were many other Indians of various nations in this first period who chose their gods with rather more discrimination than these. They worshipped certain objects that were beneficial, such as streaming fountains and great rivers, which they argued gave them water to irrigate their crops.

Others adored the earth and called it "mother," because it gave them its fruits. Others the air they breathed, saying that men lived by it; others fire, because it warmed them and they cooked their food with it. Others worshipped a ram, because of the great flocks reared in their region; others the great chain of the Sierra Nevada, because of its height and wonderful grandeur and because many rivers used for irrigation flow from it; others maize or *sara*, as they call it, because it was their usual bread; others other cereals or legumes, according to what grew most abundantly in their provinces.

The coastal Indians, in addition to an infinity of other gods they had, even including those already mentioned, generally worshipped the sea, which they called *Mamacocha*, or "Mother Sea," implying that it was like a mother to them in sustaining them with its fish. They also worshipped the whale on account of its monstrous greatness. Besides these cults, which were common to the whole coast, various provinces and regions worshipped the fish most commonly caught there, holding that the first fish that was in the upper world (their word for heaven) was the origin of all other fish of the kind they ate and that it took care to send them plenty of its children to sustain their tribe. Thus in some provinces they worshipped the sardine, which they killed in greater quantity than any other fish, in others the skate, in others the dogfish, in others the goldfish for its beauty, in others the crab and other shellfish for lack of anything better in their waters or because they could not catch or kill anything else. In short, they worshipped and considered gods any fish that was more beneficial to them than the rest. So they had for gods not only the four elements, each separately, but also the compounds and forms of them, however vile and squalid. Other tribes, such as the Chirihuanas and the people of Cape Passau (that is, the southernmost and northernmost provinces of Peru) felt no inclination to worship anything, high or low, either from interest or fear, but lived and still live exactly like beasts, because the doctrine and teaching of the Inca kings did not reach them.

## The Kinds of Sacrifices They Made

The cruelty and barbarity of the sacrifices of that ancient idolatry were of a piece with the vileness and crudity of its gods. For in addition to ordinary things such as animals and the fruits of the earth, they sacrificed men and women of all ages taken captive in the wars they waged on one another. Among some tribes their inhuman cruelty exceeded that of wild beasts. Not satisfied with sacrificing their captured foes, in case of need they offered up their own children. They performed these sacrifices of men and women, lads and children by opening their breasts while they were still alive and plucking out their hearts and lungs. The idol that had bidden the sacrifice was then sprinkled with still-warm blood, after which the same heart and lungs were examined for omens to show if the sacrifice had been acceptable or not. In either case the heart and lungs were burnt as an offering before the idol until they were consumed, and the victim of the sacrifice was eaten with the greatest pleasure and relish, and not the less merrymaking and rejoicing, even though it might have been their own child.

Padre Blas Valera, as appears from many parts of his torn papers, had the same design as we have in much of what he wrote. He divided the periods, ages, and provinces so as to show clearly the customs of each tribe. Thus in one of his mutilated notebooks he writes as follows, using the present tense, for the people he speaks of still practice these inhumanities:

*Those who live in the Antis eat human flesh: they are fiercer than tigers, have neither god nor law, nor know what virtue is. They have no idols nor likenesses of them. They worship the Devil when he represents himself in the form of some animal or serpent and speaks to them. If they make a prisoner in war or otherwise and know that he is a plebeian of low rank, they quarter him and give the quarters to their friends and servants to eat or to sell in the meat market. But if he is of noble rank, the chiefs foregather with their wives and children, and, like ministers of the devil, strip him, tie him alive to a stake, and cut him to pieces with flint knives and razors, not so as to dismember him, but to remove the meat from the fleshiest parts, the calves, thighs, buttocks, and fleshy parts of the arms. Men, women, and children sprinkle themselves with the blood, and they all devour the flesh very rapidly, without cooking it or roasting it thoroughly or even chewing it. They swallow it in mouthfuls so that the wretched victim sees himself eaten alive by others and buried in their bellies. The women, crueller than the men, anoint the nipples of their breasts with the unfortunate victim's blood so that their babies may suck it and drink it with their milk. This is all done in a place of sacrifice with great rejoicing and lightheartedness until the man dies. They then finish eating the flesh together with all his inner parts, no longer as hitherto as a feast or delight, but as a matter of the greatest divinity. Thenceforward they regard the flesh with great veneration and eat it as a sacred thing. If while they were tormenting the unfortunate fellow he showed any signs of suffering in his face or body or gave any groan or sigh, they break his bones to pieces after having eaten the flesh, entrails, and tripes, and throw them scornfully into the fields or river. But if he has shown himself firm, composed, and fierce under torture, when they have eaten the flesh and inner parts they dry the bones and sinews in the sun and set them on the top of hills and hold them and worship them as gods, and offer sacrifices to them. These are the idols of these savages. The empire of the Incas did not reach them, nor so far has that of the Spaniards, so they remain in this state to this day. This race of terrible and cruel men came from the Mexican area and peopled Panama and Darien and all the great forests that stretch to the kingdom of New Granada and in the other direction to Santa Marta.*

This is all quoted from Padre Blas Valera, who vividly describes such devilries and assists us to give an idea of what happened in those primitive times, and still endures.

There were other Indians less cruel in their sacrifices, who, though they used human blood, did not kill victims, but obtained it by bleeding their arms and legs, according to the importance of the sacrifice: for the most solemn occasions they extracted it from the root of the nose between the eyebrows. This bleeding was common among the Indians of Peru, even after the Incas came, both for their sacrifices (and one kind especially which we shall presently describe), and in case of illness attended by serious headache. Other types of sacrifice were common to all the Indians (those mentioned above were practiced in some provinces and not in others). Those generally used were of animals such as sheep, ewes, lambs, rabbits, partridges and other birds, tallow, the herb they value so highly called *cuca* [coca], maize and other seeds, and vegetables, and scented woods, and similar things, according to what each tribe produced and thought would please its gods, and taking into account the nature of the latter, whether they were animals or birds, and carnivorous or not. They offered up what they usually saw them eat and what seemed to be most agreeable to their taste. This shall suffice so far as our account of the sacrifices of that ancient heathendom is concerned.

## The Life and Government of the Ancient Indians, and the Things They Ate

These gentiles were as barbarous in the style of their houses and villages as in their gods and sacrifices. The more civilized had villages without squares or any order in their streets and houses, but rather after the fashion of a den of wild beasts. Others, because of the wars they waged on one another, dwelt on ridges or high rocks, like fortresses, where they would be least molested by their enemies; others in huts scattered over the fields, valleys, and river bottoms as each happened to find convenient for food and dwellings. Others lived in underground caves, in nooks in the rocks, in hollow trees, each as he happened to find a home, since he was not able to make one. Some of them, like those of Cape Passau and the Chirihuanas and other tribes not conquered by the Inca kings, remain in that state of primitive savagery. They are the most difficult to reduce both to the service of the Spaniards and to Christianity, for as they never had any doctrine, they are irrational beings, who only had a language to make themselves understood within their own tribe, and so live like animals of different kinds which do not meet or deal or communicate between one another.

In these villages and dwelling places the ruler was whoever was boldest and had the will to govern the rest. As soon as he became master, he treated his vassals tyrannically and cruelly, using them as slaves, taking their wives and daughters at will, and making war on his rivals. In some areas they flayed captives and used their skins to cover drums and to terrify their enemies, who, they said, would fly at once on hearing the skins of their relatives. They led a life of banditry, stealing, killing, and burning villages. Thus there arose a multiplicity of chiefs and petty kings, of whom some were good and treated their people well, maintaining peace and justice. The Indians in their simplicity worshipped these as gods for their goodness and nobility, realizing that they were different from and opposed to the horde of tyrants. Elsewhere they lived without rulers or governors, and were unable to form a republic of their own to settle and regulate their lives. They lived in great simplicity like sheep, doing neither good nor harm, though this was due more to ignorance and lack of malice, than to excess of virtue.

In many areas the Indians were so simple and stupid in their way of dressing and covering their bodies that their attempts at dress were laughable. Elsewhere they were astonishingly savage and barbarous in their food and eating; and in many places the two things were found together. In the hottest and consequently most fertile areas they sowed little or nothing, but lived on herbs, roots, wild fruit, and other vegetables that the earth yielded spontaneously or with little improvement from them. As none of them desired more than to sustain their natural lives, they were satisfied with little. In many parts they were extremely fond of human flesh and so greedy that, when they were killing an Indian, they would drink his blood through the wound they had given him before he died: they did the same if they were quartering him, sucking his blood and licking their hands so as not to lose a drop. They had public markets for human flesh, and in order not to waste it they made sausages and polonies of gut which they filled with meat. Pedro de Cieza (ch. xxvi) confirms this and saw it with his own eyes. The passion reached such a pitch with them that they did not spare their own sons by foreign captives taken in war whom they took as concubines. Their children by these women were carefully brought up to the age of twelve or thirteen, and then eaten, and the mothers too, when they were past childbearing. Furthermore, they would spare the lives of many male Indian captives, give them wives from their tribe—the tribe of the victors—bring up the children as their own, and, when they were youths, eat them. It was in fact a cannibals' seminary. They spared none on account of parentage or upbringing, which usually breed affection even among animals of quite various and opposite kinds, as we can affirm from some we have seen and others we have heard about. But among these savages neither the one nor the other availed: they killed the children they had begotten, and the relatives they had reared for the purpose of eating them, treating the parents the same when they no longer served to breed children, without any regard for their close relationship. There was a tribe so strongly addicted to devouring human flesh that they buried their dead in their stomachs. As soon as the deceased had breathed his last, his relatives gathered round and ate him roasted or boiled, according to the amount of flesh he still had: if little, boiled, if much, roasted. Afterwards they assembled the bones and gave them a funeral with great mourning, burying them in crannies in rocks or hollow trees. They had no gods and no conception of worshipping, and are still in the same state. The consumption of human flesh is commoner among Indians of the hot regions than among those of the cold.

In cold and sterile regions where the earth did not bear fruit, roots, and herbs spontaneously, they sowed maize and vegetables, obliged by necessity; but they did this without regard to time or season. They fished and hunted with the same primitive savagery as they displayed in other things.

## How They Dressed in Those Ancient Times

Their dress was so indecent that it is rather a subject for silence and secrecy than for discussion and description. But as history obliges one to set down the whole truth, I must beg the modest to turn a deaf ear to this part, and if they censure me in this way, I shall consider their disfavor justified. In this first period the Indians dressed like animals, for they wore no more clothing than the skin nature had given them. Many of them, out of ingenuity or for love of adornment, had a thick string girded round their bodies. They thought that was clothing enough, and we must not go beyond, for it is improper. In 1560, on my way to Spain, I met five Indians in the street in Cartagena without any clothes at all, and they did not walk abreast but one behind the other like cranes, although they had mingled with Spaniards for so many years.

The women went in the same dress, naked. When married they wore a string round the body with a cotton rag about a yard square hanging like an apron from it. Where they could not or would not spin or weave, they made it of the barks or leaves of trees. This covered their modesty. Maidens also wore a string girdle, and instead of the apron they wore something else to show they were maidens. But out of proper respect for our hearers, we had better keep to ourselves what remains to be said. Suffice it to say that this was the dress and costume of the hot regions, so that as regards decency, they resembled irrational beasts, and it can be imagined from this bestiality in adorning their persons alone how brutal they would be in everything else—these Indians of heathen times before the empire of the Incas.

In cold regions they were more decently clad, not indeed out of decency, but obliged by the cold. They covered themselves with skins of animals and a sort of blanket they made of wild hemp and a long, pliable, soft straw that grows in the fields. With these contrivances they covered their nakedness as well as they could. Other tribes had a greater sense of propriety and wore clumsily made cloaks, ill-spun and worse-woven, of wool or wild hemp called cháhuar. They wore them fastened about the neck and girded to the body, and were thus adequately covered. The dress we have mentioned used in primitive times in the hot lands—that is going naked—was found by the Spaniards in many regions never conquered by the Incas, and is still today found in many places conquered by the Spaniards, where the Indians are such brutes that they will not dress, except for those who have close intercourse with Spaniards in their houses and wear clothes more because the Spaniards insist on it than from any choice or modesty of their own. The women refuse just as much as the men, and Spaniards often chaff them about their indecency and unwillingness to spin, and ask if they don't dress because they won't spin, or if they don't spin because they won't dress.

## The Origin of the Inca Kings of Peru

While these peoples were living or dying in the manner we have seen, it pleased our Lord God that from their midst there should appear a morning star to give them in the dense darkness in which they dwelt some glimmerings of natural law, of civilization, and of the respect men owe to one another. The descendants of this leader should thus tame those savages and convert them into men, made capable of reason and of receiving good doctrine, so that when God, who is the sun of justice, saw fit to send forth the light of His divine rays upon those idolaters, it might find them no longer in their first savagery, but rendered more docile to receive the Catholic faith and the teaching and doctrine of our Holy Mother the Roman Church, as indeed they have received it—all of which will be seen in the course of this history. It has been observed by clear experience how much prompter and quicker to receive the Gospel were the Indians subdued, governed, and taught by the Inca kings than the other neighboring peoples unreached by the Incas' teachings, many of which are still today as savage and brutish as before, despite the fact that the Spaniards have been in Peru seventy years. And since we stand on the threshold of this great maze, we had better enter and say what lay within.

After having prepared many schemes and taken many ways to begin to give an account of the origin and establishment of the native Inca kings of Peru, it seemed to me that the best scheme and simplest and easiest way was to recount what I often heard as a child from the lips of my mother and her brothers and uncles and other elders about these beginnings. For everything said about them from other sources comes down to the same story as we shall relate, and it will be better to have it as told in the very words of the Incas than in those of foreign authors. My mother dwelt in Cuzco, her native place, and was visited there every week by the few relatives, both male and female, who escaped the cruelty and tyranny of Atahuallpa (which we shall describe in our account of his life). On these visits the ordinary subject of conversation was always the origin of the Inca kings, their greatness, the grandeur of their empire, their deeds and conquests, their government in peace and war, and the laws they ordained so greatly to the advantage of their vassals. In short, there was nothing concerning the most flourishing period of their history that they did not bring up in their conversations.

From the greatness and prosperity of the past they turned to the present, mourning their dead kings, their lost empire, and their fallen state, etc. These and similar topics were broached by the Incas and Pallas on their visits, and on recalling their departed happiness, they always ended these conversations with tears and mourning, saying: "Our rule is turned to bondage" etc. During these talks, I, as a boy, often came in and went out of the place where they were, and I loved to hear them, as boys always do like to hear stories. Days, months, and years went by, until I was sixteen or seventeen. Then it happened that one day when my family was talking in this fashion about their kings and the olden times, I remarked to the senior of them, who usually related these things: "Inca, my uncle, though you have no writings to preserve the memory of past events, what information have you of the origin and beginnings of our kings? For the Spaniards and the other peoples who live on their borders have divine and human histories from which they know when their own kings and their neighbors' kings began to reign and when one empire gave way to another. They even know how many thousand years it is since God created heaven and earth. All this and much more they know through their books. But you, who have no books, what memory have you preserved of your antiquity? Who was the first of our Incas? What was he called? What was the origin of his line? How did he begin to reign? With what men and arms did he conquer this great empire? How did our heroic deeds begin?"

The Inca was delighted to hear these questions, since it gave him great pleasure to reply to them, and turned to me (who had already often heard him tell the tale, but had never paid as much attention as then) saying:

"Nephew, I will tell you these things with pleasure: indeed it is right that you should hear them and keep them in your heart (this is their phrase for 'in the memory'). You should know that in olden times the whole of this region before you was covered with brush and heath, and people lived in those times like wild beasts, with no religion or government and no towns or houses, and without tilling or sowing the soil, or clothing or covering their flesh, for they did not know how to weave cotton or wool to make clothes. They lived in twos and threes as chance brought them together in caves and crannies in rocks and underground caverns. Like wild beasts they ate the herbs of the field and roots of trees and fruits growing wild and also human flesh. They covered their bodies with leaves and the bark of trees and animals' skins. Others went naked. In short, they lived like deer or other game, and even in their intercourse with women they behaved like beasts, for they knew nothing of having separate wives."

I must remark, in order to avoid many repetitions of the words "our father the Sun," that the phrase was used by the Incas to express respect whenever they mentioned the sun, for they boasted of descending from it, and none but Incas were allowed to utter the words: it would have been blasphemy and the speaker would have been stoned. The Inca said:

"Our father the Sun, seeing men in the state I have mentioned, took pity and was sorry for them, and sent from heaven to earth a son and a daughter of his to indoctrinate them in the knowledge of our father the Sun that they might worship him and adopt him as their god, and to give them precepts and laws by which they would live as reasonable and civilized men, and dwell in houses and settled towns, and learn to till the soil, and grow plants and crops, and breed flocks, and use the fruits of the earth like rational beings and not like beasts. With this order and mandate our father the Sun set these two children of his in Lake Titicaca, eighty leagues from here, and bade them go where they would, and wherever they stopped to eat or sleep to try to thrust into the ground a golden wand half a yard long and two fingers in thickness which he gave them as a sign and token: when this wand should sink into the ground at a single thrust, there our father the Sun wished them to stop and set up their court.

"Finally he told them: 'When you have reduced these people to our service, you shall maintain them in reason and justice, showing mercy, clemency, and mildness, and always treating them as a merciful father treats his beloved and tender children. Imitate my example in this. I do good to all the world. I give them my light and brightness that they may see and go about their business; I warm them when they are cold; and I grow their pastures and crops, and bring fruit to their trees, and multiply their flocks. I bring rain and calm weather in turn, and I take care to go round the world once a day to observe the wants that exist in the world and to fill and supply them as the sustainer and benefactor of men. I wish you as children of mine to follow this example sent down to earth to teach and benefit those men who live like beasts. And henceforward I establish and nominate you as kings and lords over all the people you may thus instruct with your reason, government, and good works.'

"When our father the Sun had thus made manifest his will to his two children he bade them farewell. They left Titicaca and travelled northwards, and wherever they stopped on the way they thrust the golden wand into the earth, but it never sank in. Thus they reached a small inn or resthouse seven or eight leagues south of this city. Today it is called Pacárec Tampu, 'inn or resthouse of the dawn.' The Inca gave it this name because he set out from it about daybreak. It is one of the towns the prince later ordered to be founded, and its inhabitants to this day boast greatly of its name because our first Inca bestowed it. From this place he and his wife, our queen, reached the valley of Cuzco which was then a wilderness."

## ■ Sor Juana Inés de la Cruz (1651–1691) *Mexico* (poems, letter)

Scholar, intellectual, poet, and playwright, the Mexican nun Juana Inés de la Cruz is the outstanding writer of the long colonial period. Juana Ramírez de Asbaje was born on a hacienda in a village southeast of the

Mexico City, called San Miguel de Nepantla. Nepantla in Nahuatl signifies "land in the middle," and her village lay between the great volcanoes of Popocatépatl and Ixtacíhuatal. Juana was a "daughter of the Church"—a euphemism of the day meaning that she was illegitimate. As a young child, she was precocious and has popularly been called a genius. She learned to read at three, she tells us in her largely autobiographical *Response to Sor Filotea,* and from very early was concerned with laws of the physical universe: "Once in my presence two young girls were spinning a top, and scarcely had I seen the motion and the figure described when I began, out of this madness of mine, to meditate on the effortless *motus* of the spherical form, and how the impulse persisted even when free and independent of its cause." Juana Inés's brief and acute observation about force and inertia anticipate contemporary laws of gravity and energy and precede Sir Isaac Newton's four laws of inertia elaborated in *Principia Mathematica.*

Juana Inés went to Mexico City as a child and there, in the house of an uncle who possessed a good library, she immersed herself in her readings and early literary writings. She was an avid autodidact. One delightful story, probably true, recounted by her contemporary biographer, the Jesuit father Diego Callejas, has the twelve-year-old Juana taken to the University of Mexico where, to test her knowledge and wisdom, the child is asked questions by the forty leading theologians, philosophers, and historians at the university. She outwitted them all, as Callejas states, "in the manner of a royal galleon fending off the attacks of a few canoes." But for all her knowledge and pleasure in accumulating it, she lacked companionship and the stimulation of fellow students. There were few choices for a talented young woman who wished to pursue artistic and intellectual aspirations: there was the court, the church, and marriage. Each had its price. Her first choice was the court, and at sixteen Juana Inés entered the court where she became a lady-in-waiting to the viceroy's wife, the countess of Paredes, who cared for literature and was to encourage and facilitate Juana throughout her life.

At the worldly court, Juana was a brilliant figure and there was much elegant conversation and courting, *galaneo,* by would-be suitors who tended to be already well-married. From her autobiographical letter, we learn that amid the glamor and glitter of court activities, she possessed a gravity and determination of iron. But the wooing undoubtedly served, in disguised and invented form, as the basis of her love poems. With all her charm and brilliance, however, Juana Ramírez de Asbaje was still a fatherless orphan, without a dowry to obtain, through marriage, a life in which she might practice her literary pursuits. With no real future in the court or society, in 1669, at age twenty-one, at the height of her admiration by the literati and court society, Juana Inés took the veil in the relatively permissive Convent of Santa Paula of the Hieronymite order (the order of Saint Jerome).

In her quarters, she wrote poems that found publication and wrote her plays, including the extraordinary *The Divine Narcissus* that was published in 1689 in Madrid. Her convent was her library, work place, literary salon, and *tertulia* (a literary discussion usually held in a cafe). As in the first- and second-century Hermetic and apocalyptic traditions, her great long poem "First Dream" describes the voyage of a soul soaring among superlunary spheres, while the harborer of the soul remains behind in deep bodily sleep. As such, it is a poem concerning ecstasy in its strictly etymological sense of "being outside oneself" or "being elsewhere." In her daring metaphysical meditation—the great extended poem of the Spanish baroque period—she attempts to find some philosophical explanation for this world of deceptive appearances and dream.

In reply to an oblique yet devastating letter from the Bishop of Puebla, who wrote her under the pseudonym of Sor Filotea, urging her to cease her creative work, she wrote her defiant *Response*. Her answer contains her threat of silence, which was to be executed, but the threat is not the essence of the *carta*. The letter is a biography of her life and mind, an assertion of her intellectual and creative freedom, and a refutation of censorial intrusion. It is also probably the world's first and extensive declaration of a woman's artistic and intellectual right to study, teach, write, and publish freely. Though she did not write anything new while under the constraints of the bishop, she did not order her works into silence. Indeed, Sor Juana oversaw and assiduously corrected the publication of the volumes of her collected works, which began a few years earlier in 1689 when her friend the countess of Paredes published the first volume of her poems in Spain. Four years later, after laying down her pen and selling off her library, she died on April 17, 1694, while nursing her sister nuns during an epidemic. The last high moment of poetry of the Spanish Golden Age was found in the first poetic figure of the New World.

**FURTHER READING:** Sor Juana Inés de la Cruz. *Sor Juana Inés de la Cruz, 1651–1691.* Bilingual. Translated by Margaret Sayers Peden, 1985; *A Sor Juana Anthology.* Translated by Alan S. Trueblood. Foreword by Octavio Paz, 1988. Paz, Octavio. *Sor Juana, or the Traps of Faith,* 1988.

## To Her Self-Portrait

What you see here is colorful illusion,
an art boasting of beauty and its skill,
which in false reasoning of color will
pervert the mind in delicate delusion.
Here where the flatteries of paint engage                    5
to vitiate the horrors of the years,
where softening the rust of time appears
to triumph over oblivion and age,
all is a vain, careful disguise of clothing,
it is a slender blossom in the gale,                          10

it is a futile port for doom reserved,
it is a foolish labor that can only fail:
it is a wasting zeal and, well observed,
is corpse, is dust, is shadow, and is nothing.

TRANSLATED BY WILLIS BARNSTONE

## To Hope

A green beguilement in our natural life,
mad hope and frenzy wrapped about with gold,
a dream by those awake, yet thinly cold
like dreams and treasures: mere gossip and rife.
Soul of the world, exuberant old age,
decrepit greenness of pure fantasy,
the now for which the happy ones rampage,
the future where the pitiful agree.
Clutching your name, seeking your day as real,
they stick green lenses in their glasses, and
the world they see is painted by command.
But I, much saner in my state of mind,
keep both eyes focused on my hands. Not blind,
I only see what I can touch and feel.

TRANSLATED BY WILLIS BARNSTONE

## She Complains about Her Fate: She Asserts Her Aversion to Vices and Justifies Her Pleasure in the Muses

Why persecute me, world? To what effect?
Tell me how I offend. My sole intent
is to fix beauty to my intellect,
not hang my intellect in beauty's tent.
I do not care for emeralds or for gold,
and so I feel a happier effect
by fixing emeralds to my intellect
than to affix my intellect to gold.
I do not care for beauty that the knife
of age cuts into booty for the public hall,
nor can perfidious wealth please me at all.
The best I find of all my verities
is to consume my vanities in life
and not consume my life in vanities.

TRANSLATED BY WILLIS BARNSTONE

## In Which She Morally Censures a Rose, and through the Rose Her Peers

Holy rose, who in genteel cultivation
you show in all your redolent finesse
a magisterial beauty in your station,
a snowy discourse in your loveliness,
a fearful sign to human architecture,                               *5*
emblem of the vanity in grace's bloom,
whose being unites through trickery of nature
the joyous cradle and the sorrowing tomb.
How haughty in your pomp, how arrogant,
sovereign, while you disdain the risk of death;                     *10*
and then, collapsing, shrinking, you are plucked
in feebleness of being, a withered plant!
And so through stupid life and dying breath,
in life you fool, in dying you instruct.

TRANSLATED BY ALIKI BARNSTONE AND WILLIS BARNSTONE

## A Good Face One Should Choose before Dying Rather Than to Expose Oneself to the Outrages of Old Age

Celia looked at a rose proud in the field,
happily showing off its futile grace,
and, while adorned in rouge fully revealed,
it cheerfully was bathing its white face;
Courageously enjoy your destiny,                                    *5*
the brief migration of your fertile age;
then death that comes tomorrow will not be
in place to rob you of a joy, your wage
today. And though persistent death comes now
and your delicious life moves far from you,                         *10*
and youth and beauty mix with death and fears,
see what experience informs, and how
it's best to die with youth and beauty too
than to observe the outrage of the years.

TRANSLATED BY WILLIS BARNSTONE

## She Suspects That the Relief That Hope Gives Is Dissimulated Cruelty

With my one daily malady of hope
you plot to entertain my graying years
and in the scheme of goods and hangman's rope
you keep the scale in balance for all spheres;
and always hanging there (in the delay
before it tilts one way), your trickery
you won't let dominate to a degree
of posing crude belief or grave dismay.
Who stole the name from you of homicide?
You're it—severely so, if well observed—
and in the air you hang my laughing soul.
While between losing and your lucky side,
you do not work to keep a life preserved
but to give tolling death a lingering toll.

TRANSLATED BY WILLIS BARNSTONE

## In Which She Satisfies a Fear with the Rhetoric of Tears

This afternoon, my love, speaking to you
since I could see that in your face and walk
I failed in coming close to you with talk,
I wanted you to see my heart. Love, who
supported me in what I longed to do,
conquered what is impossible to gain.
Amid my tears that were poured out in pain,
my heart became distilled and broken through.
Enough, my love. Don't be so stiff. Don't let
these maddening jealousies and arrogance
haunt you or let your quiet be upset
by foolish shadows: false signs of a man's
presence; and as you see my heart which met
your touch—now it is liquid in your hands.

TRANSLATED BY WILLIS BARNSTONE

## In Which Her Fantasy Is Contented with Decent Love

Don't leave me, shadow of my love, elusive
and obsessed image which I care for most,

handsome deceit for whom I'd be a ghost,
sweet fiction for which pain is not abusive.
If my own body of obedient steel                                    *5*
serves as a magnet fated to your grace,
why flatter me with lover's commonplace,
only to drop me, run, while I congeal?
And yet you cannot brag of anything,
of any triumph through your tyranny.                                *10*
If you elude the narrow noose I've set
to capture your fantastic form, and spring
out of my arms, who cares? You flee, and yet
I've got you locked up in my fantasy.

TRANSLATED BY WILLIS BARNSTONE

## Concerning a Sage Reflection That Mitigates a Passion

With the affliction of a mortal wound
I brooded on a sore offense of love;
to see if death would drag me underground
I tried to make it grow and loom above.
The separated soul in clouds of pain,                               *5*
counted its anguish one hurt at a time,
and with each second it was darkly plain
a thousand deaths dug one life into grime.
And after blows of battering a skull,
the ruptured heart discerned a maddening sign                       *10*
that it had come to its last hopeless sigh—
and yet by some prodigious destiny
I woke, sensing: Am I not wonderful,
and who in love has happiness like mine?

TRANSLATED BY WILLIS BARNSTONE

## She Continues with the Same Matter and Ends with Reason Prevailing over Pleasure

The ingrate dumping me I seek as lover,
seek me as lover, I'll throw him away.
I always worship one who runs for cover;
who worships me I bump out of my way.
Whom I beseech with love is hard as steel,                          *5*

I'm hard as steel to you beseeching me.
Triumphant I want you who murder me,
I murder you who want my triumph real.
If someone wants me, my desire is gone.
If I want you, I crush my dignity;
and either way I end up feeling bashed.
So I choose as the better course to be
a violent curse on you who make me yawn,
than be for you who dump me vilely trashed.

TRANSLATED BY WILLIS BARNSTONE

## Inés

When they revile you as sly and obscene,
you have no problem getting off the hook,
you launch into your gobbledygook,
knowing just how to wipe your asshole clean,
and when you grab the word, no magpie can
dish out such bad-year garbage from its throat:
you thunder and the clatter fills a moat,
stunning the world like pounding on a can.
That rumble jumbles all, one tumbling turd,
a con game making you a sweet Rebecca.
Though you, Inés, a wanton cuckoo bird,
must know my love and how to spot a sin;
your bumbling passion stumbles, fails to win,
though you're a holy saint and I'm from Mecca.

TRANSLATED BY WILLIS BARNSTONE

## She Proves the Inconsistency of the Desires and Criticism of Men Who Accuse Women of What They Themselves Cause

Foolish men who accuse
women unreasonably,
you blame yet never see
you cause what you abuse

You crawl before her, sad,
begging for a quick cure;

why ask her to be pure
when you have made her bad?

You combat her resistance
and then with gravity,                                        10
you call frivolity
the fruit of your intents.

In one heroic breath
your reason fails, like a wild
bogeyman made up by a child                                   15
who then is scared to death.

With idiotic pride
you hope to find your prize:
a regal whore like Thaïs
and Lucretia for a bride.                                     20

Has anyone ever seen
a stranger moral fervor:
you who dirty the mirror
regret it is not clean?

You treat favor and disdain                                   25
with the same shallow mocking
voice: love you and you squawk,
demur and you complain.

No answer at her door
will be a proper part:                                        30
say no—she has no heart,
say yes—and she's a whore.

Two levels to your game
in which you are the fool:
one you blame as cruel,                                       35
one who yields, you shame.

How can one not be bad
the way your love pretends
to be? Say no and she offends.
Consent and you are mad.                                      40

With all the fury and pain
your whims cause her, it's good
for her who has withstood
you. Now go and complain!

You let her grief take flight                                 45
and free her with new wings.
Then after sordid things
you say she's not upright.

Who is at fault in all
this errant passion? She                                                    5(
who falls for his pleas, or he
who pleads for her to fall?

Whose guilt is greater in
this raw erotic play?
The girl who sins for pay                                                    5.
or man who pays for sin?

So why be shocked or taunt
her for the steps you take?
Care for her as you make
her, or shape her as you want,                                              6(

but do not come with pleas
and later throw them in
her face, screaming of sin
when you were at her knees.

You fight us from our birth                                                  6
with weapons of arrogance.
Between promise and pleading stance,
you are the devil, flesh, and earth.

TRANSLATED BY ALIKI BARNSTONE AND WILLIS BARNSTONE

## from *First Dream*

But Venus first
with her fair gentle morning-star
shone through the dayspring,
and old Tithonus' beauteous spouse
—Amazon in radiance clad—
armed against the night,
fair though martial
and though plaintive brave,
showed her lovely brow
crowned with morning glimmers,                                               1
tender yet intrepid harbinger
of the fierce luminary
that came, mustering his van
of tiro gleams
and his rearward                                                            1
of stouter veteran lights
against her, usurping tyrant

of day's empire, who,
girt with gloom's black bays
sways with dread nocturnal sceptre                                          *20*
the shades,
herself by them appalled.
But the fair forerunner,
herald of the bright sun,
scarce flew her banner in the orient sky,                                   *25*
calling all the sweet if warlike
clarions of the birds to arms,
their featly artless
sonorous bugles,
when the doomed tyrant, trembling,                                          *30*
distraught with dread misgiving,
striving the while
to launch her vaunted might, opposing
the shield of her funereal cloak
in vain to the unerring                                                     *35*
shafts of light
with the rash unavailing
valiance of despair,
sensible of her faintness to withstand,
prone already to commit to flight,                                          *40*
more than to might, the means of her salvation,
wound her raucous horn,
summoning her black battalions
to orderly retreat.
Forthwith she was assailed                                                  *45*
with nearer plenitude of rays
that streaked the highest pitch
of the world's lofty towers.
The sun in truth, its circuit closed, drew near,
limning with gold on sapphire blue a thousand                              *50*
times a thousand points and gleaming scarves,
and from its luminous circumference
innumerable rays of pure light streamed,
scoring the sky's cerulean plain,
and serried fell on her who was but now                                     *55*
the baneful tyrant of their empire.
She, flying in headlong rout,
mid her own horrors stumbling,
trampling on her shade,
strove, with her now blindly fleeing host                                   *60*
of shadows harried by the overtaking light,
to gain the western verge which loomed at last
before her impetuous course.

Then, by her very downfall vivified,
plunging in ever more precipitant ruin,                                    6⁵
with renewed rebellion she resolves,
in that part of the globe
forsaken by the day,
to wear the crown,
what time upon our hemisphere the sun                                      7⁰
the radiance of his fair golden tresses shed,
with equable diffusion of just light
apportioning to visible things their colours
and still restoring
to outward sense its full efficacy,                                        7.
committing to surer light
the world illuminated and myself awake.

TRANSLATED BY SAMUEL BECKETT

Sor Juana Inés de la Cruz's Response to Sor Filotea begins with a bit-terly ironic humility, in which she states that she will open her heart to the bishop who has criticized her. Then she proceeds to tell her life and her struggle for intellectual and creative freedom. Here are excerpts from the Mexican nun's defense of her life as a student of books and a poet of un-restricted personal expression.

## from *Response to Sor Filotea*

I have never written by my own choice but at the urgency of others to whom I can say truthfully: You have compelled me. What is true, and I will not deny the truth (first, because it is known publicly, and second, though it may be held against me God has granted me the mercy of a great love for the truth), which is that from the moment I was pierced with the first rays of reason, my inclination to letters has been so vehement and power-ful that neither external reprimands, of which I have had many, nor my own meditations, and they have not been few, have been strong enough to make me abandon this natural impulse that God placed in me. The Lord's Majesty knows why and for what purpose, and he knows that I have prayed that he extinguish the light of my reason, leaving only what is necessary in me to obey his Law, for according to some there is too much reason in a woman. And there are even those who say that such knowledge does in-jury.

And his Majesty also knows that not being able to do this, I have tried to bury my knowledge along with my name, and to sacrifice it to him alone who gave it to me; and for no other reason I entered into religion, although the spiritual exercises and the company of a community were repugnant to the freedom and quiet that my intention to study required. Thereupon, and the Lord and only he in the world must know it, I *did* try to conceal my name, but they did not allow this, saying that my work was a temptation. And no doubt it was. If I could pay you what I owe you, my lady, I might do so by relating these matters to you, which earlier never escaped from my lips except to those who had to hear them. But in having thrown wide open the doors of my heart by making patent to you my most deeply hidden secrets, I want you to know that you must not disdain the belief I have in your venerable person and excessive favors toward me.

Continuing the narration of my inclinations, about which I wish to inform you fully, I was not yet three years old when my mother sent my sister, older than I was, to learn to read in one of those schools we call *Amigas*. Affection and mischief led me to follow her. And seeing that they were giving her lessons I was inflamed with desire to learn to read, and so by tricking the teacher, or so I thought, I told her that my mother had directed her to give me lessons. She did not believe it, because it was not believable, but to go along with my trick she gave me lessons. I continued to go there and she continued to teach me, but now no longer as a joke because the experience alerted her. And I learned to read in such a short time that I already knew how by the time my mother found out. The teacher had kept it from her in order to surprise her and receive a reward all at once. I kept still, thinking I would be whipped for having acted without her permission. The woman who taught me (God preserve her) is still alive and can attest to this.

I remember that in those days my love for eating being the same as children of my age, I abstained from eating cheese because I had heard that it made you stupid, and my desire to know was stronger than to eat. When I was six or seven, already knowing how to read and write along with all the other skills of sewing and needlework that women learn, I discovered that the University had schools in Mexico City where one studied the sciences. The moment I heard this, I began to batter my mother with constant and urgent pleas to change my manner of dress and send me to Mexico City, to the house of some relatives she had there, to study and be tutored at the University. She did not want to do so (and rightly so) but I satisfied my longings by reading many and diverse books in my grandfather's library, and there were not enough punishments or reprimands to stop me. Hence, when I came to the city of Mexico, people marveled, not so much at my intelligence as at my memory and store of knowledge I had at an age where it seemed that I had hardly had time to learn to speak.

I began to study Latin grammar, in which I think I did not have twenty lessons in all. So intense was my concern that although among women, and especially those in the flower of their youth, the natural adornment of one's hair is so highly esteemed, I cut four or five finger's width from mine, measuring the place it had reached before, and imposed a rule on myself that by the time it had grown back to its former length, if I had not learned such and such a thing that I had set out to learn while the hair was growing back, I would cut it again as punishment for my stupidity. It turned out that it grew out and I was learning slowly, and in fact I did cut it as a punishment for my dullness, for it did not seem to me right that the head should be dressed with hair when it was so naked of knowledge, which was the more desirable adornment.

I entered a religious order. Although I knew that the way of life had things about it (I speak of its secondary not its most formal qualities) many of them repugnant to my nature, but, given the total antipathy I had for marriage, it was the least unreasonable and most decent choice I could make to insure my salvation. To this first and finally most important end, all the trivial things that had dominated my nature I gave up: my desire to live alone—to have no duties that would interfere with the freedom of my studies, nor have the sounds of a community that would intrude upon the peaceful silence of my books. This made me hesitate in my determination until some learned persons enlightened me, explaining that my inclination was temptation; I overcame it with divine favor, and assumed the state which now I so unworthily hold. I thought that I was fleeing from myself, but, miserable person that I am, I brought to me and with me my worst enemy, which is this inclination to study and write—and I do not know whether this was a gift or punishment from Heaven—for though for a while it was dimmed and encumbered by the many duties of religious life, it exploded like gunpowder, proving that privation is the source of appetite.

I went back (I said it wrong, since I never stopped), I went on with my studious tasks (which for me were a respite in those moments not occupied by my religious duties) to reading and more reading, to studying and more studying, with no other master than the books themselves. And one can see how hard it is to study those soulless letters, lacking a live voice and the explanation of the teacher. But all this work I suffered with great pleasure for the love of letters. O had it been for the love God, which was the right way, how worthy it would have been! While I strove to elevate it as best I could and direct it to his service, since the goal I aspired to was to study Theology, and it seemed to me a diminishment for me as Catholic not to know all, through natural means, that this life in its divine mysteries can dissipate before us. Since I was a nun and not a lay person, it seemed right that I should profess my learning through ecclesiastical channels. Moreover, being a daughter of Saint Jerome and Saint Paula, it would be shameless for the daughter of such learned parents to be an idiot.[1] This is what I proposed for myself and it appeared reasonable, unless it was (and surely it was) that all these invented guides were to flatter and approve my own inclination and to enjoy what I offered as an obligation.

---

1. Paula (d. 414) was a Roman lady who became attached to Jerome. She and her daughters went with Jerome to Bethlehem, and she established and presided over the first nunneries of the Hieronymite order. Sor Juana's convent was Hieronymite and Paula was one of its patron saints.

In this way I want on, directing as always, as I have said, the course of my studies toward the peak of Sacred Theology, and, in order to arrive there, it seemed necessary for me to climb the steps of human sciences and arts, since how can one understand the style of the queen of sciences if one does not also know the ancillary branches? How, without Logic, could I understand the general and specific ways in which the Holy Scripture is written? How, without Rhetoric, could I understand its figures, tropes, and locutions? How could I survive without Physics and so many natural questions concerning the nature of sacrificial animals, where many things are symbolized, many already explained, and others are waiting for explanation? How should I know whether Saul's being refreshed by the sound of David's harp was due to the virtue and natural force of music or to the supernatural powers that God wished to place in David? How without Arithmetic could one understand so many computations of years, of days, of months, of hours, of weeks, mysterious like those of Daniel, and others for the intelligence of which one must know the natures, concordances, and properties of numbers? How without Geometry could one measure the Holy Arc of the Covenant and the Holy City of Jerusalem, whose mysterious numbers form a cube in all its dimensions along with the marvelous proportions in the distribution of its parts? How without Architecture, could the great Temple of Solomon, where God himself was the artificer providing both the layout and design and the wise king Solomon, could only the overseer have carried it all out? No base was without its mystery, column without its symbol, cornice without its allusion, architrave without its significance, and so on with the other parts. . . . How without an expertise in music could one understand those delightful fine points of musical proportions that are in so many places, especially in Abraham's petitions to God for the cities, asking whether he would forgive them if they had fifty just men? And from this number he reduced it to forty-five, which is a ninth and goes from Mi to Re; then to forty, which is a tone and goes from Re to Mi; from forty to thirty, which is a diastesseron; then to twenty, which is the perfect fifth and from twenty to ten, which is the octave, the diapason. And since there are no more harmonic proportions it stopped there. Now how can one understand this without a knowledge of music?

\* \* \*

I confess that I find myself very distant from the borders of wisdom and that I wish to follow her, even from far off. But everything has brought me into the fire of persecution, to the crucible of torture, and to such a degree that they have forbidden me my studies. At one time they managed to do so through the offices of a very saintly and ingenuous Abbess who believed that study was a matter for the Inquisition, and she commanded me to give up studying. I obeyed her (for some three months her power to command me endured) for I did not take up a book. But as for not studying at all that was not within my powers to satisfy, for while I did not study books, I studied all the things that God created, which served as my letters and as the book of the universal machine. I looked on nothing without reflecting on it. I heard nothing without considering it, even the tiniest material thing. For there is no creature, however lowly, in which one does not recognize that *God made me.* There is nothing that does not astonish reason, if one stops to observe it.

So, I repeat, I looked and admired all things. Thus even the people with whom I spoke, and what they were telling me, evoked a thousand meditations. Since we are from one species, where did that variety of geniuses and wit come from? What temperaments and hidden qualities brought this about? If I saw a figure, I was forever combining the proportion of its lines and measuring it with my reason and reducing it to new proportions. Sometimes I would walk back and forth along the far wall of our dormitory (which is a very large room) and noticed that though the lines of both sides were parallel and its ceiling level, one's vision made it appear that the lines sloped in toward each other and that the ceilings were lower at the far end, from which I inferred that visual lines run straight, but not parallel, and that they form a pyramidal figure. And I pondered whether this might be the reason that caused the ancients to question whether the world was spherical or not. Although straight lines appear to be bent, this could be a deception of vision,[2] showing concavities where none might have been.

This type of observation would occur to me about everything, and as it always occurs, without my being in control of it, I am constantly annoyed because this activity tires my mind. And I thought the same thing happened to everyone, also with regard to writing verse, until experience taught me otherwise. So it has become a habit that I can look at nothing without reflecting on it. Once in my presence, two young girls were playing with a top. As soon as I saw the motion and form, I began, with this madness of mine, to contemplate the easy motion of the spherical form, and how the impulse once given it persisted independent of the cause, since at a distance from the girl's hand, which was the causal force, the top went on dancing. And not content with this, I had flour brought in and spread so that one could know whether what described its movement were perfect circles. And I found that they were not, but were spiral lines that were losing their circular form as the impulse slowed down.

Other girls were playing with pins (surely childhood's most frivolous game). I came near to observe the figures they formed, and seeing that by chance three were placed in a triangle I began to connect one to the other, recalling that this was the shape that Solomon's mysterious ring was said to have and on which there were distant lights and depictions of the Most Holy Trinity by virtue of which it worked so many prodigies and marvels.[3] The same shape was said to form David's harp and that is why Saul

---

2. An optical illusion.

3. There is no reference to such in incident in the Bible. It derives from a tradition of anecdotal commentary in which Old Testament Scripture is anachronistically given a level of Christian meaning.

was said to have been cured by its sound. And harps today conserve almost the same shape.

What shall I tell you, my lady, of the natural secrets that I have discovered while cooking? That an egg holds together and fries in butter or oil, but, by contrast, it comes apart in syrup. That in order to keep sugar liquid one need only add a few drops of water in which a quince or some other bitter fruit has been soaked. That the yolk and the white of the same egg are so different in nature that when eggs are used with sugar, it works when using one (the yolk or the white), but not when using both. But I should not weary you with such trivia, which I relate only to give you a full idea of my nature and because I think that they might make you laugh. But, lady, what can women know other than philosophies of the kitchen? Lupercio Leonardo spoke well when he said how well one can philosophize while preparing the supper.[4]

I like to say, when seeing these small details: If Aristotle had been a cook, he would have written much more.

And going on with my cogitations, I say that this goes on so constantly in me that I do not need books. On one occasion, as a result of a gravely troubled stomach, the doctors forbade me from studying. I passed some days in this manner, and then I proposed that permitting me my books was less harmful and they conceded, for my meditations were so strong and vigorous that they consumed my spirit more in a quarter of an hour than four days of studying books. Moreover, my lady, not even my dreams have been freed from this ceaseless movement of my imagination. In fact, it seems to go on more openly and unimpeded, conferring a greater clarity and peace on the images that I have conserved from the day. I argue and make verses, of which I could offer you an extensive catalogue, including thoughts and subtleties that I have better achieved in sleep than when awake. I leave this matter now so as not to bore you, but the above is enough to allow your discretion and transcendent understanding to perceive and be perfectly informed about the nature, principle, means, and present state of my studies.

∗ ∗ ∗

Oh, how much injury might have been avoided in our land if our old women were as learned as Laeta, and knew how to teach in the manner of Saint Paul and my Father Saint Jerome. And if this is not the case, if fathers wish to educate their daughters in a way beyond what is customary, because of the absence of wise older women, they are forced to bring in men teachers to teach reading, writing, calculating, the playing of musical instruments, and other skills. No little harm is done by this, as we witness every day in doleful examples of perilous association. Because of the immediate ease of contact and close company over a period of time, there

---

4. The saying comes not from Lupercio Leonardo but from his brother, the Aragonese poet Bartolomé de Argensola (1562–1631).

come about things not thought possible. As a result many fathers prefer to leave their daughters barbaric and uncultivated rather than to expose them to the notorious danger that familiarity with men breeds. All of this would be eliminated if there were older women of learning, as Saint Paul wished, and if the teaching were handed down from one to another, as is the practice with needlework and other traditional skills.

\* \* \*

If I turn my eyes to my habit of writing verses, which has been so chastised and persecuted, which in me is so natural that I must do violence to myself to keep this letter from turning into verse, I might cite that line from Ovid, "All I wished to say took the form of verse."[5] I see that my poetry is condemned and criticized by so many and I have attempted to find what harm there is in it, and I have found none. Rather, I see verse applauded on the lips of the Sybils, sanctified in the pens of the Prophets, and especially in King David of whom my great expositor and beloved Father Jerome, in explaining its metrical patterns, says, "in the manner of Horace and Pindar now it runs in iambs, now in alcaics, now it swells in sapphics, then it moves in half-feet.[6]

\* \* \*

In the end, if the wrong in me is that I a woman compose poems, since clearly many have done so and to great praise, what evil is there in my being a woman poet?

TRANSLATED BY WILLIS BARNSTONE

---

5. From Ovid's *Tristia* 4.10.26.

6. The application of Greek prosody, which is the later basis of Latin and most modern formal verse, to Hebrew poetry, such as the Psalms of David or Job, is wrong. Hebrew prosody, based on parallelism and closer to its imitators in William Blake and Walt Whitman, has nothing to do with Greek meter and prosody. Sor Juana gives a long list of those who have practiced verse, including passages in the books of Moses, the saints, and also the "Magnificat," a Greek poem of praise, which appears in Luke 1:46–55, and which is attributed to "Our Lady," meaning the Virgin Mary. The attribution to Mary is widely considered false in that Jesus' Aramaic-speaking mother was not likely to have been trained in writing Greek verse. The poem may have been a translation from a lost Hebrew or Aramaic source.

# Nineteenth and Twentieth Centuries

■

## INTRODUCTION

In Spain as well as Latin America, there is an artistic chasm between the sixteenth and seventeenth centuries (the *Siglo de Oro* or "Golden Age" of literature spanning the Renaissance and Baroque periods) and the nineteenth and twentieth centuries. The eighteenth century—the age of reason, encyclopedias, neoclassical imitations, and birth of modern democracy in document and practice—did not produce major literary figures in Spain or in its colonies. The great exception in the arts is the painter Francisco Goya (1748–1828). With the nineteenth century came Romanticism, Realism, the beginnings of what we now call Modernism as found in the great Brazilian fiction writer Machado de Assis (1839–1908), and the notion of political engagement as in the popular poet/journalist José Martí (1867–1916) from Cuba. Latin American literature reaches its present zenith, however, after the first decades of the twentieth century with the explosion of major fiction writers in a group that has been called the "Boom" authors, ranging from Argentina and Chile to Mexico and Cuba, from Jorge Luis Borges to Carlos Fuentes. This astonishing group of authors has dominated fiction in Spanish in our century and, along with equally important poets, including Pablo Neruda (1904–1974) and Octavio Paz (1904– ), has been awarded five Nobel Prizes in literature. Among Caribbean authors we have a sixth Nobel Prize winner, poet Derek Walcott (1924– ) from Saint Lucia, and other outstanding writers, including Aimé Césaire (1913– ) and V. S. Naipaul (1932– ). Between the older recognized giants and more recent dazzling writers from Latin America and the Caribbean, the twentieth century has given us a new Golden Age in literature.

# ▪ Domingo Faustino Sarmiento (1811–1888)
## *Argentina* (biography)

TRANSLATED BY MRS. HORACE MANN

Journalist, professor, and later president of Argentina, Domingo Faustino Sarmiento drew a portrait of an evil, barbarous though secretly admired gaucho, the cowboy of the Argentine pampas, whom he called Facundo. Facundo was Sarmiento's vaguely disguised portrait of Juan Manuel Rosas, the more sinister Argentine dictator whom Sarmiento helped to overthrow. As a good, imaginative writer, Sarmiento depicted a gaucho more attractive than the figure he probably wished to portray, which paradoxically may explain why his writing has lived beyond the didactic purpose of the historical and political moment. Indeed, his fictious Facundo survives in the Spanish-reading public more distinctly than the political leader and dictator Rosas.

Sarmiento is one of many statesman writers whom Latin America has produced. In our day, Pablo Neruda, Octavio Paz, Carlos Fuentes, and Rosario Castellanos, former ambassadors to France, India, France, and Israel, continue that tradition. Sarmiento, however, went further. He not only became president (1864–1874) and participated in the defeat of the tyrant dictator Rosas, but his portrait of the gaucho leader Juan Facundo Quiroga became a force in shaping political and literary thought in Latin America.

Sarmiento's Facundo is a gaucho outsider and leader, ruthless yet with moments of Solomonic wisdom. Like Milton's Satan, this antihero did not lack appealingly romantic qualities. But for Sarmiento the gaucho was, as a wild force tearing up Argentina, an essential outlaw to be defeated militarily and crushed in the struggle of urban civilization against the wild and uncontrolled natural barbarian. Soon after the publication of *Facundo,* José Hernández's epic *Martín Fierro* would portray the gaucho with full sympathy in a literary masterpiece. But Sarmiento, who had a political motive in describing the gaucho, made his Facundo crude and cruel to better reflect the tyrant Rosas who was destroying the nation.

Sarmiento was born in the far province of San Juan where, too poor to obtain a good formal education, he taught himself. He read everything of value he could find, from Spanish classics and Ben Franklin to French eighteenth-century encyclopedists and early nineteenth-century romantics. He taught elementary school and later worked as a political journalist. After his political journal *El Zonda* was closed by authorities in 1831, he went into exile in democratic Chile. In Chile, he found companionship and taught at the university. He returned to Argentina in 1837, only to be exiled again in 1840. During his second exile, he founded a newspaper *El Progreso,* in Santiago and, most important, wrote *Facundo* (1845), which had an enormous national and international impact. Sarmiento spent three years in Europe and the United States (1845–1848), where *Facundo* was translated into English and made famous internationally by Mrs. Horace Mann. In 1851, he returned to participate in the national struggle, joining General Urquiza in the march from Entre Ríos to Buenos Aires and was present when the dictator Rosas was defeated at the battle of Caseros in 1852. Thereafter, he was a congressman, ambassador to the United States, and eventually president of the Argentine Republic (1868–1874), whereupon he undertook a massive building program to modernize his nation. As elsewhere in North and South America, Sarmiento worked for "civilization" by supporting the suppression and killing of the Indian. Sarmiento was fascinated with the gaucho and the countryside, but ultimately he lacked sympathy for whatever was nonurban.

Facundo is a fierce, gripping portrait, as romantic as it is political. In its totality, it is naive, uneven, and brilliantly engaging and goes beyond its obvious message. The story of Facundo and the tiger has the parabolic ring of A Thousand and One Nights. It anticipates one of Sarmiento's later readers, Borges, lover of the tiger and portrayer of the gaucho. The gaucho to Argentina is comparable in many ways to the outsider, independent American cowboy. In each case, the figure is normally romanticized, seen as brave, tough, generous, or cruel; free of middle-class urban restraints; close to the land but not obedient to place or convention as is the farmer; and often beyond the law. Sarmiento was the first in Latin America to recognize this colorful and essential figure in a growing pioneer country and to convert the image into reportage and literature.

**FURTHER READING:** Sarmiento, Domingo Faustino. *Life in the Argentine Republic in the Days of the Tyrant,* 1868.

## from *Life in the Argentine Republic in the Days of the Tyrants*

### The Gaucho Outlaw

The example of this type of character, to be found in certain places, is an outlaw, a squatter, a kind of misanthrope. He is Cooper's Hawkeye or Trapper, with all the knowledge of the wilderness possessed by the latter; and with all his aversion to the settlements of the whites, but without his natural morality or his friendly relations with the savages. The name of gaucho outlaw is not applied to him wholly as an uncomplimentary epithet. The law has been for many years in pursuit of him. His name is dreaded—spoken under the breath, but not in hate, and almost respectfully. He is a mysterious personage; his abode is the pampa; his lodgings are the thistle fields; he lives on partridges and hedgehogs, and whenever he is disposed to regale himself upon a tongue, he lassos a cow, throws her without assistance, kills her, takes his favorite morsel, and leaves the rest for the carrion birds. The gaucho outlaw will make his appearance in a place just left by soldiers, will talk in a friendly way with the admiring group of good gauchos around him; provide himself with tobacco, yerba maté, which makes a refreshing beverage, and if he discovers the soldiers, he mounts his horse quietly and directs his steps leisurely to the wilderness, not even deigning to look back. He is seldom pursued; that would be killing horses to no purpose, for the beast of the gaucho outlaw is a bay courser, as noted in his own way as his master. If he ever happens to fall unawares into the hands of the soldiers, he sets upon the densest masses of his assailants, and breaks through them, with the help of a few slashes left by his knife upon the faces or bodies of his opponents; and lying along the ridge of his horse's back to avoid the bullets sent after him, he hastens towards the wilderness, until, having left his pursuers at a convenient distance, he pulls up and travels at his ease. The poets of the vicinity add this new exploit to the biography of the desert hero, and his renown flies through all the vast region around. Sometimes he appears before the scene of a rustic festival with a young woman whom he has carried off, and takes a place in the dance with his partner, goes through the figures of the *cielito,* and disappears, unnoticed. Another day he brings the girl he has seduced, to the house of her offended family, sets her down from his horse's croup, and reckless of the parents' curses by which he is followed, quietly betakes himself to his boundless abode.

This white-skinned savage, at war with society and proscribed by the laws, is no more depraved at heart than the inhabitants of the settlements. The reckless outlaw who attacks a whole troop, does no harm to the traveller. The gaucho outlaw is no bandit, or highwayman; murderous assaults do not suit his temper, as robbery would not suit the character of the *churriador* (sheep-stealer). To be sure, he steals; but this is his profession, his trade, his science. He steals horses. He arrives, for instance, at the camp of a train from the interior; its master offers to buy of him a horse of some unusual color, of a particular shape and quality, with a white star on the shoulder. The gaucho collects his thoughts, considers a moment, and replies, after a short silence: "There is no such horse alive." What thoughts have been passing through the gaucho's mind? In that moment his memory has traversed a thousand estates upon the pampa; has seen and examined every horse in the province, with its marks, color, and special traits, and he has convinced himself that not one of them has a star on its shoulder; some have one on their foreheads, others have white spots on their haunches. Is this power of memory amazing? No! Napoleon knew two hundred thousand soldiers by name, and remembered, when he saw any one of them, all the facts relating to him. Therefore, if nothing impossible is required of him, the gaucho will deliver upon a designated day and spot, just such a horse as has been asked for, and with no less punctuality if he has been paid in advance. His honor is as sensitive upon this point as that of a gambler about his debts.

Sometimes he travels to the country about Cordova or Santa Fé. Then he may be seen crossing the pampa behind a small body of horses; if any one meets him, he follows his course without approaching the new comer unless he is requested to do so.

## A Portrait of Facundo

Between the cities of San Luis and San Juan lies an extensive desert, called the Travesia, a word that signifies *want of water*. The aspect of that waste is mostly gloomy and unpromising, and the traveler coming from the east does not fail to provide his *chifles* with a sufficient quantity of water at the last cistern that he passes as he approaches it. This Travesia once witnessed the following strange scene. The consequences of some of the encounters with knives so common among our gauchos had driven one of them in haste from the city of San Luis and forced him to escape to the Travesia on foot, and with his riding gear on his shoulder, in order to avoid the pursuit of the law. Two comrades were to join him as soon as they could steal horses for all three. Hunger and thirst were not the only dangers which at that time awaited him in the desert; in these regions, where man must contend with the tiger for dominion over nature, the former sometimes falls a victim, upon which the tiger begins to acquire a preference for the taste of human flesh, and when it has once devoted itself to this novel form of chase, the pursuit of mankind, it gets the name of *man-eater*. The provincial justice nearest the scene of his depredations calls out the huntsmen of his district, who join, under his authority and guidance, in the pursuit of the beast, which seldom escapes the consequences of its outlawry.

When our fugitive had proceeded some six leagues, he thought he heard the distant roar of the animal, and a shudder ran through him. The roar of the tiger resembles the screech of the hog, but is prolonged, sharp, and piercing, and even when there is no occasion for fear, causes an involuntary tremor of the nerves as if the flesh shuddered consciously at the menace of death. The roaring was heard clearer and nearer. The tiger was already upon the trail of the man, who saw no refuge but a small carob tree at a great distance. He had to quicken his pace, and finally to run, for the roars behind him began to follow each other more rapidly, and each was clearer and more ringing than the last. At length, flinging his riding gear to one side of the path, the gaucho turned to the tree which he had noticed, and in spite of the weakness of its trunk, happily quite a tall one, he succeeded in clambering to its top and keeping himself half concealed among its boughs, which oscillated violently. Thence he could see the swift approach of the tiger, sniffing the soil and roaring more frequently in proportion to its increasing perception of the nearness of its prey. Passing beyond the spot where our traveler had left the path, it lost the track and, becoming enraged, rapidly circled about until it discovered the riding gear, which it dashed to fragments by a single blow. Still more furious from this failure, it resumed its search for the trail, and at last found out the direction in which it led. It soon discerned its prey, under whose weight the slight tree was swaying like a reed upon the summit of which a bird has alighted. The tiger now sprang forward, and in the twinkling of an eye its monstrous forepaws were resting on the slender trunk two yards from the ground, and were imparting to the tree a convulsive trembling calculated to act upon the nerves of the gaucho, whose position was far from secure. The beast exerted its strength in an ineffectual leap; it circled around the tree, measuring the elevation with eyes reddened by the thirst for blood, and at length, roaring with rage, it crouched down, beating the ground frantically with its tail, its eyes fixed on its prey, its parched mouth half open. This horrible scene had lasted for nearly two mortal hours; the gaucho's constrained attitude, and the fearful fascination exercised over him by the fixed and bloodthirsty stare of the tiger, which irresistibly attracted and retained his own glances, had begun to diminish his strength, and he already perceived that the moment was at hand when his exhausted body would fall into the capacious mouth of his pursuer. But at this moment the distant sound of the feet of horses on a rapid gallop gave him hope of rescue. His friends had indeed seen the tiger's footprints and were hastening on, though without hope of saving him. The scattered fragments of the saddle directed them to the scene of action, and it was the work of a moment for them to reach it, to uncoil their lassos, and to fling them over the tiger, now blinded by rage. The beast, drawn in opposite directions by the two lassos, could not evade the swift stabs by which its destined victim took his revenge for his prolonged torments. "On that occasion I knew what it was to be afraid," was the expression of Don Juan Facundo Quiroga, as he related this incident to a group of officers.

And here ends the private life of Quiroga, in which I have omitted a long series of deeds which only show his evil nature, his bad education, and his fierce and bloody instincts. . . . The fault is not his that thus he was born. In order to contend with, rule, and control the power of the city, and the judicial authority, he is willing to descend to anything. If he is offered a place in the army, he disdains it, because his impatience cannot wait for promotion. Such a position demands submission, and places fetters upon individual independence; the soldier's coat oppresses his body, and military tactics control his steps, all of which are insufferable! His equestrian life, a life of danger and of strong excitements, has steeled his spirit and hardened his heart. He feels an unconquerable and instinctive hatred for the laws which have pursued him, for the judges who have condemned him, and for the whole society and organism from which he has felt himself withdrawn from his childhood, and which regards him with suspicion and contempt. With these remarks is connected by imperceptible links the motto of this chapter, "He is the natural man, as yet unused either to repress or disguise his passions; he does not restrain their energy, but gives free rein to their impetuosity. This is the character of the human race." And thus it appears in the rural districts of the Argentine Republic. Facundo is a type of primitive barbarism. He recognized no form of subjection. His rage was that of a wild beast. The locks of his crisp black hair, which fell in meshes over his brow and eyes, resembled the snakes of

Medusa's head. Anger made his voice hoarse, and turned his glances into dragons. In a fit of passion he kicked out the brains of a man with whom he had quarreled at play. He tore off both the ears of a woman he had lived with, and had promised to marry, upon her asking him for thirty dollars for the celebration of the wedding; and laid open his son John's head with an axe, because he could not make him hold his tongue. He violently beat a beautiful young lady at Tucuman, whom he had failed either to seduce or to subdue, and exhibited in all his actions a low and brutal yet not a stupid nature, or one wholly without lofty aims. Incapable of commanding noble admiration, he delighted in exciting fear; and this pleasure was exclusive and dominant with him to the arranging all his actions so as to produce terror in those around him, whether it was society in general, the victim on his way to execution, or his own wife and children. Wanting ability to manage the machinery of civil government, he substituted terror for patriotism and self-sacrifice. Destitute of learning, he surrounded himself with mysteries, and pretended to a foreknowledge of events which gave him prestige and reputation among the commonalty, supporting his claims by an air of impenetrability, by natural sagacity, an uncommon power of observation, and the advantage he derived from vulgar credulity.

The repertory of anecdotes relating to Quiroga, and with which the popular memory is replete, is inexhaustible; his sayings, his expedients, bear the stamp of an originality which gives them a certain Eastern aspect, a certain tint of Solomonic wisdom in the conception of the vulgar. Indeed, how does Solomon's advice for discovering the true mother of the disputed child differ from Facundo's method of detecting a thief in the following instances:

An article had been stolen from a band, and all endeavors to discover the thief had proved fruitless. Quiroga drew up the troops and gave orders for the cutting of as many small wands of equal length as there were soldiers; then, having had these wands distributed one to each man, he said in a confident voice, "The man whose wand will be longer than the others tomorrow morning is the thief." Next day the troops were again paraded, and Quiroga proceeded to inspect the wands. There was one whose wand was, not *longer*, but *shorter* than the others. "Wretch!" cried Facundo, in a voice which overpowered the man with dismay, "it is thou!" And so it was; the culprit's confusion was proof of the fact. The expedient was a simple one; the credulous gaucho, fearing that his wand would really grow, had cut off a piece of it. But to avail oneself of such means, a man must be superior in intellect to those about him, and must at least have some knowledge of human nature.

Some portions of a soldier's accounterments having been stolen and all inquiries having failed to detect the thief, Quiroga had the troops paraded and marched past him as he stood with crossed arms and a fixed, piercing, and terrible gaze. He had previously said, "I know the man," with an air of assurance not to be questioned. The review began; many men had passed, and Quiroga still remained motionless, like the statue of

Jupiter Tonans or the God of the Last Judgment. All at once he descended upon one man and said in a curt and dry voice, "Where is the saddle?" "Yonder, sir," replied the other, pointing to a thicket. "Ho! Four fusiliers!" cried Quiroga. What revelation was this? That of terror and guilt made to a man of sagacity.

On another occasion, when a gaucho was answering to charges of theft which had been brought against him, Facundo interrupted him with the words, "This rogue has begun to lie. Ho, there! A hundred lashes!" When the criminal had been taken away, Quiroga said to someone present, "Look you, my master, when a gaucho moves his foot while talking, it is a sign he is telling lies." The lashes extorted from the gaucho the confession that he had stolen a yoke of oxen.

At another time he was in need of a man of resolution and boldness to whom he could entrust a dangerous mission. When a man was brought to him for this purpose, Quiroga was writing; he raised his head after the man's presence had been repeatedly announced, looked at him, and returned to his writing with the remark, "Pooh! That is a wretched creature. I want a brave man and a venturesome one!" It turned out to be true that the fellow was actually good for nothing.

Hundreds of such stories of Facundo's life, which show the man of superior ability, served effectually to give him a mysterious fame among the vulgar, who even attribute superior powers to him.

### ■ Ricardo Palma (1833–1919) *Peru* (tale)

A Peruvian historian of eighteenth-century life, Ricardo Palma wrote historical fictions based on research and the elegance of his imagination. His sources were libraries, archives, and monasteries; his means were re-creation and characterization, often through Goyaesque satire. Palma began his career as naval officer, journalist, and politician and, in 1863, published a significant historical volume on the Inquisition in Lima, Peru. After the War of the Pacific (1879–1884), he dedicated his time to rebuilding the destroyed national library. For many years he was its director. Palma converted a ruined structure into one of the finest libraries in South America. The library also served him perfectly for his research into a national past, which, through the invention of a new literary genre, the *tradición* (a historical anecdote), he converted into volumes of brief tales about colonial Peru. The *tradición* is historical, invented, fantastic, funny, and above all charmingly satiric. A favorite subject was Micaela Luján, La Perricholi (the bitch), concubine of the Viceroy in eighteenth-century Lima. She later appears in Thornton Wilder's *The Bridge of San Luis Rey*. In the historical re-creation "Of the Agony of Christ," Palma states in a deadpan, perhaps intentionally naive, manner, the grotesquely perverse morality of a painter who murders for art. "Margarita's Nightgown," which like many stories derides the colonial obsession with class and status, follows the psychological realism in Guy de Maupassant, with its classic epiphany. Ricardo Palma remains one of the most read earlier writers of Latin America.

**FURTHER READING:** Palma, Ricardo. *Peruvian Traditions*, 1872; *The Knights of the Cape*. Edited by Harriet de Onis, 1945.

# Margarita's Chemise

## TRANSLATED BY WILLIS BARNSTONE

Some of my readers may have heard of old women in Lima, speaking about the high prices of things, commenting: "Good lord, it costs more than Margarita Pareja's chemise."

Margarita's chemise was on everybody's tongue and my curiosity about it would surely never have been satisfied if I had not happened on an article in *La América* of Madrid, signed by Don Ildefonso Antonio Bermejo (author of an excellent book on Paraguay). Although Bermejo merely alluded to the young woman in the chemise, it gave me the clue I needed to find the story you are about to read.

# I

Around 1765 Margarita Pareja was the pampered darling of her father, Don Raimundo Pareja, Knight of Santiago and a tax collector at the port of Callao.

The woman was one of those beauties Lima in famous for. She could have enchanted the Devil and made him cross himself and turn somersaults. Her black eyes were like dynamite charges that explode in the inner corners of the soul of the gallant men of her day.

Around this time a dashing young man from Spain turned up, a son of the royal villa of Madrid, whose name was Don Luis Alcázar. In Lima he had a rich bachelor uncle, of old Aragonese stock, escutcheons and all, and prouder than the sons of King Fruela.

Of course, until he became his uncle's heir, he was poorer than a church mouse. When I tell you that even his amorous escapes were on credit, I don't have to say more.

In a procession in honor of Santa Rosa, Alcázar met the lovely Margarita. The arrows of her eyes flew right into his heart. He poured compliments on her, and though she did not affirm or reject him, with all the other weapons in her feminine arsenal she made it clear that the young man was a dish exactly to her taste. The fact is they had fallen in love up to their eyelashes. I know it as if they themselves had told me.

Since lovers never remember there is something called arithmetic, Don Luis never imagined that his poverty could be an impediment to their desires. He went to Margarita's father, and, without any diversions, asked for her hand.

Don Raimundo didn't like the petition at all, and he politely dismissed the suitor, saying that Margarita was still very young to be choosing a husband, and that despite her eighteen summers she still played with dolls.

But this was not the real obstacle. Don Raimundo's refusal was because he did not want to be the father-in-law to a pauper, a fact that he confided in his friends, one of whom repeated the story to Don Honorato, the uncle from Aragon. When the uncle heard it, being prouder than the Cid, he fumed with rage, and said, "Who ever heard of something like this! Snubbing my nephew. There are many who would be out of their mind with joy to marry him. There is not a more elegant young man in all Lima. What insolence! I'll put this money-counting collector in his place."

Margarita, very much ahead of her time, was a high-strung young modern woman. She wept and tore her hair and fainted. And if she didn't threaten to poison herself, it was because matches with phosphorus tips had not yet been invented.

She lost weight and color. She began to fade, and spoke of entering a convent. Nobody could do anything with her.

"Luis or God," she cried every time her nerves overcame her, and this happened on the hour.

The Knight of Santiago, her adoring father, was alarmed and called in doctors and the curanderas. They all declared that the young woman was declining, that she looked consumptive, and the medicine she needed could not be found in a pharmacy.

They offered him his choice. Either he let her marry the man she desired or he would soon lay her out in her coffin. This was the doctor's ultimatum.

Don Raimundo—a father is always a father—raced out of the house like a lunatic, in such haste that he forgot his cape and cane, and came to Don Honorato's home where he said to the gentleman, "I have come to ask you to give your consent for your nephew to marry Margarita tomorrow. Otherwise we are going to lose her, and very quickly."

"That's impossible," the uncle replied, sneering. "My nephew is just a pauper, and you need someone with his pockets full of gold for your daughter."

It was a stormy interview. The more Don Raimundo pleaded, the more stubborn the Aragonese became. Finally, as the father was about to give everything up as lost, Don Luis took a hand in the affair. He said, "Uncle, it's not Christian to kill a person who has done nothing wrong."

"Are you willing to have her?"

"O yes! With all my heart, my lord and uncle."

"Very well. I'll give my consent to make you happy, but on one condition. Don Raimundo must swear that he will not give his daughter a peseta or leave her five pesetas of his money."

Then an even more agitated argument took place.

"But, sir," Don Raimundo, countered, my daughter has a dowry of twenty thousand duros."

"We don't care for the dowry. The young woman will come to her husband with nothing but what she has on her back."

At least let me provide the furnishings for her house and a trousseau."

"Not a pin. If this doesn't meet with your approval, we can call it all off and let the young woman die."

"Don Honorato, be reasonable. My daughter at least needs to take along a change of chemise."

"Very well. I'll agree to that so you can't accuse me of being difficult. You may offer her a bridal chemise, but nothing else."

The following day Don Raimundo and Don Honorato went to the Church of San Francisco early in the morning, where they knelt to hear mass. Then, as they agreed the day before, when the priest raised the holy wafer, Margarita's father said, "I swear to give my daughter nothing but her bridal chemise. An may God damn my soul if I don't keep my word."

## II

And Don Raimundo Pareja kept his oath to the letter. In his life and after his death he gave his daughter nothing.

The Brussels lace that trimmed the chemise cost 2,700 duros, according to Bermejo, who evidently gathered this information from *Secret Relations* by Ulloa and Don Jorge Juan. Moreover, the drawstring at the neck was a chain of diamonds worth 30,000 morlacas.

The newlyweds led the Aragonese uncle to believe that the chemise was worth a doubloon, since Don Honorato was so stubborn that if he found out the truth, he would have forced his nephew to get a divorce.

I am sure you will agree with me that Margarita Pareja's bridal chemise merited its widespread and enduring fame.

## ■ José Hernández (1834–1886) *Argentina* (epic verse)

TRANSLATED BY WALTER OWEN

Argentine soldier, journalist, and legislator, José Hernández is author of an epic of the pampas, *Martín Fierro* (1872) that redeems and glorifies the heroic outlaw gaucho at a moment when the gaucho was vanishing. The gaucho was disappearing because the rich soil of the pampas attracted industrious immigrant farmers who fenced off *estancias* (vast estates) with newly invented barbed wire. Hernández painted a golden age of the gauchos living free on their horses. His hero's name "Fierro" is an older spelling of "hierro," meaning "iron," a reference not lost to the Spanish reader. Fierro's iron will and body sum up the indomitable and adventurous qualities of the gaucho. The hero tells his own story as a *payador* (an improvising popular singer) as he moves from gaucho to badly treated military conscript to deserter and killer outlaw. Ultimately, to avoid persecution, he joins and becomes one with the Indians. In 1879, the sequel, *La vuelta de Martín Fierro (The Return of Fierro)*, was published, by which time life had become more tolerable and conscription less arbitrary and cruel. Fierro, who had lost everything, returns to find his family, reclaim his property, and begin a new life.

In the beginning, the epic had a popular following. It was printed in thin pamphlets, sold for pennies, and read aloud in country taverns. In its time, it was much appreciated, perhaps more by gauchos than by literary critics. Near the end of the century, the Spanish writer and philosopher Miguel de Unamuno discovered it as major literature and later the Argentines Leopoldo Lugones and Jorge Luis Borges declared it the national epic. It has become a Latin American classic. Unfortunately, the text, in colorful Argentine dialect, has not found a translation that transfers its literary qualities into English. The most successful version, tainted with archaisms, is by Walter Owen, which at its best, as in the selection here, has the rough darkness and simplicity of a Robert Frost narration.

**FURTHER READING:** Hernández, José. *Martín Fierro*, 1872; *The Gaucho Martín Fierro*. Translated by Walter Owen, 1936.

## from *The Gaucho Martín Fierro*

### Martín Fierro Relates His Meeting with Two of His Sons

Now pass me the crock and I'll take a swig
To cool my warmed-up throat;
And while my youngster tunes his strings
And finds his opening note,
I'll tell you how in my wanderings
I found my two lads once more.

     For many a day I roamed around
And stopped at many a door,
I wanted to know how matters went
In the pickle they call the Government,
But everything I very soon found
Was much as it was before.
So I just lay low and spied the land
And opened my eyes and ears;

It wasn't a bit of good I guessed                                    *15*
To meddle too much with a hornet's nest.
If you've been in trouble you'll understand
The law always holds the winning hand;
And whether it's weeks or months or years
If you're poor they get you in the end.                              *20*
          But my luck held good — I found one day
A trusty old-time friend,
That put me wise how matters lay,
I was wasting my fears, he said;
For the judge whose nose had been on my trail                        *25*
These many years was dead.
I had him to thank for ten long years
Of trials and sufferings sore,
And ten's a heap for a man like me
That hasn't got many more.                                           *30*
And this is the way I count my tale
Of trouble and misery;
Three years I lost at the frontier post,
Two years from the law I fled,
And five I spent in our little tent                                  *35*
In the hands of the infidel.
If I'm right, that's ten. And my friend said then,
I could put my mind at ease
That the Government had long forgot
All about my private row,                                            *40*
And none round there ever gave a thought
To the death of that nigger now.
          Though I snuffed his light, it's only right
To say he was part to blame;
I was middling tight — I picked the fight,                           *45*
And he lost; but all the same
The brute got mad and he forced my hand
For he cut me first I'll swear,
He marked my face, — and you'll understand
That that's no light affair.                                         *50*
          The friend I'm telling of, told me more;
There was no more talk about
The gaucho killer that in a store
I had tumbled insides-out;
There was only one to blame for that                                 *55*
And that one wasn't me;
He dropped in there to look for a brawl
He got what was coming to him — that's all;
He thought I'd be good to practise on
And if I'd been slow, or a simpleton                                 *60*

It would have been him that hit the trail
And me that messed the floor.
      My old friend told me furthermore
That none even told the tale
Of the ding-dong fight I had the night
I met Cruz, with the police-patrol.
There's nothing in that to worry my soul,
To fight for his life is a man's first right;
They were out for my hide, and they sent a band
By night in the open, arms in hand;
They didn't arrest me in proper form,
But just came on in a yelling swarm,
And shouted out threats to have my life;
Was it any wonder I peeled my knife?
A gaucho outlaw I was, they said,
They were going to get me alive or dead
And it wasn't the Captain that told me that,
Although there was one commanding,
But the first that came up just barked at me,
And whatever I'd done, you'll all agree,
A man's got his rights, and that's no way
To come to an understanding.
      When I got such news I'm bound to say
I was pretty well content,
I felt I could show my face again,
And wherever I liked I went.
Of the little lads that long ago
From their mother and me were riven,
I've found but two; and thanks I owe
For that to the grace of heaven.
Though far and wide round the countryside
I hunted to find their trail,
Though I spared no dint I could get no hint
Of where they might hap to be,
And my hopes at last began to fail
When chance brought them back to me.
For not far off from this very spot
They were holding a racing-meet
And there I went though not a cent
To bless myself with, I'd got;
There were gauchos came from far and near
And many an 'estanciero'
And you'll guess no doubt there were lots about
That had heard of Martín Fierro.
There two of the sons I had thought were lost

Were dressing some mounts by the starting post,
When they heard my name, like a flash they came
And soon were at my side,
They shied a bit as they looked at me,
They had some excuse to stare;                                                   110
I was tanned like a hide by the desert sun,
And was somewhat the worse for wear;
You can guess we didn't make any show
In front of crowd. Few words we spoke,
For kisses and hugs are for women folk,                                          115
That are built that way; yet all men know
Though a man on his sleeve doesn't wear his heart,
There's a bit of a woman inside of him,
And he often sighs though his face be grim,
And his tears in secret start.                                                   120
The only thing they've told me yet
Is that my poor wife is dead;
To look for her littlest lamb of all
She went to the town, they said.
And she who was prairie-born and bred                                            125
Must have suffered there full sore;
For all she was well set-up and strong,
She was in the hospital ere long,
And in that pen of pains and ills
Lay down to rise no more.                                                        130
          There's not a thing in the whole wide earth
That will fill the gap she's left,
When they told me of her I was now bereft
I haven't cried bitterer since my birth;
But it's time to leave sadnesses aside,                                          135
Though my life doesn't hold for me much joy
It seems to me that my eldest boy
Is ready to sing us a stave or two;
Let's see how he handles the instrument
And the capers and paces he puts it through.                                     140
          Though both lads are strange to you,
Their father here's quite confident;
It's not because they bear my blood
That I think they've got their father's vein,
But because since they teethed they've chewed the cud                            145
Of sorrow and suffering, want and pain;
They've both got spirit and like to play
With fire, more or less in their father's way,
Let them show us their paces, and if they're lame,
On their old crocked sire you can lay the blame.                                 150

## ■ Machado de Assis (1839–1908) *Brazil* (novels)

Many speak of Joaquin Maria Machado de Assis as Latin America's most significant novelist. He was born in Rio de Janeiro, his mother a Portuguese, his father a Brazilian mulatto. The family was poor and literate and provided the future writer with conditions to encourage early expression. His early education was from a priest. Subsequently, he became a typesetter, proofreader, journalist, and accountant. He published his first poem at fifteen and wrote prolifically all his life—some two hundred short stories, nine novels, translations, journalism, plays, literary criticism—while working for thirty-four years as an accountant and finally director accountant at the Ministry of Agriculture, Commerce, and Public Works. He also became the first president of the Brazilian Academy of Letters. As he rose in the literary world, he always seemed to carry with him the psychological and social awareness of the insider/outsider looking in, with a clear and thorough knowledge of the social scene. During his lifetime, his stories were increasingly popular. His novels make him one of the nineteenth century's main fiction writers. Initially, it was the shocking realism and irony of his fiction—in contrast to contemporary romantic prose—that gained him his reputation. With the years, his innovative, sophisticated reader/narrator voice has caught our attention. Sharp and satiric as Goya, Machado de Assis anticipates Jorge Luis Borges and Italo Calvino in using metaliterary devices in an urbane fiction that self-consciously draws both reader and narrator into the text to speak about the activity of writing the novel. He became known internationally quite suddenly in 1952 when his novel *Epitaph of a Small Winner (Memórias póstumas de Braz Cubas,* 1881) was published in English (seventy-one years after its publication in Brazil). His popular fiction masterpiece *Dom Casmurro* appeared in 1900, but other works, such as *Philosopher or Dog* (translated in 1954) and *Quincas Borba* (1891), are distinctive and equally important. He must be considered one of the great fiction writers from any country in the nineteenth century. Susan Sontag speaks of him as the greatest writer ever produced by Latin America. *Epitaph of a Small Winner* is an imaginary autobiography, which might have been written in our postmodern era, more than a century after its publication. In the opening lines of this amusing, profound, and thoroughly ironic novel, the imaginary writer establishes the contours of his story: "I am a deceased writer not in the sense of one who has written and is now deceased, but in the sense of one who has died and is now writing." On the page before, in his "To the Reader," he also sets his mysteriously implausible tone, saying, "The work of a man already dead. I wrote it with the pen of Mirth and the ink of Melancholy, and no one can readily foresee what may come of such a union."

FURTHER READING: Machado de Assis, Joaquin Maria. *Dom Casmurro,* 1900 (tr. 1966); *The Psychiatrist and Other Stories; Devils Church and Other Stories,* 1977; *Epitaph of a Small Winner.* Foreword by Susan Sontag, 1990.

# *from* **Epitaph of a Small Winner**

TRANSLATED BY WILLIAM L. GROSSMAN

## To the Reader

When we learn from Stendhal that he wrote one of his books for only a hundred readers, we are both astonished and disturbed. The world will be neither astonished nor, probably, disturbed if the present book has not one hundred readers like Stendhal's, nor fifty, nor twenty, nor even ten. Ten? Maybe five. It is, in truth, a diffuse work, in which I, Braz Cubas, if indeed I have adopted the free form of a Sterne or of a Xavier de Maistre, have possibly added a certain peevish pessimism of my own. Quite possibly. The work of a man already dead. I wrote it with the pen of Mirth and the ink of Melancholy, and no one can readily foresee what may come of such a union. Moreover, solemn people will find in the book an aspect of pure romance, while frivolous folk will not find in it the sort of romance to which they have become accustomed; thus it is and will remain, disrespected by the solemn and unloved by the frivolous, the two great pillars of public opinion.

But I still entertain at least the hope of winning public favor, and the first step in that direction is to avoid a long and detailed prologue. The best prologue is the one that has the least matter or that presents it most briefly, even to the point of obscurity. Hence I shall not relate the extraordinary method that I used in the composition of these memoirs, written here in the world beyond. It is a most curious method, but its relation would require an excessive amount of space and, moreover, is unnecessary to an understanding of the work. The book must suffice in itself: if it please you, excellent reader, I shall be rewarded for my labor; if it please you not, I shall reward you with a snap of my fingers, and good riddance to you.

## The Death of the Author

I hesitated some time, not knowing whether to open these memoirs at the beginning or at the end, i. e., whether to start with my birth or with my death. Granted, the usual practice is to begin with one's birth, but two considerations led me to adopt a different method: the first is that, properly speaking, I am a deceased writer not in the sense of one who has written and is now deceased, but in the sense of one who has died and is now writing, a writer for whom the grave was really a new cradle; the second is that the book would thus gain in merriment and novelty. Moses, who also related his own death, placed it not at the beginning but at the end: a radical difference between this book and the Pentateuch.

Accordingly: I expired at two o'clock of a Friday afternoon in the month of August, 1869, at my lovely suburban home in Catumby. I was sixty-four, sturdy, prosperous, and single, was worth about three hundred contos, and was accompanied to the cemetery by eleven friends. Only eleven! True, there had been no invitations and no notices in the newspapers. Moreover, there was a fine drizzle, steady and sad, so steady and so sad, in fact, that it led one of those faithful friends of my last hour to work this ingenious thought into the discourse that he offered at the edge of my grave: "You who knew him may well affirm with me that Nature herself appears to be weeping her lamentation over her irreparable loss, one of the most beautiful characters that ever honored humanity by his presence in our poor world. This sombre air, these drops from heaven, those dark clouds covering the blue like a crepe of mourning, all manifest the harsh and cruel grief that gnaws at her deepest entrails and the praise that heaven itself bestows upon our great and dear departed." Good and faithful friend! I shall never regret the legacy of twenty government bonds that I left him.

And thus I arrived at the end of my days; thus I started on the road to Hamlet's "undiscovered country," with neither the anxiety nor the doubts of the young prince, but slow and halting, like a person who has lingered in the theatre long after the end of the performance. Tardy and jaded. Some nine or ten people saw me go, among them three ladies: my sister Sabina, who was married to Cotrim; her daughter, a real lily of the valley; and . . . Have patience! In a little while I shall reveal the identity of the third lady. Be content for the moment to know that this anonymous lady, although not a relative of mine, suffered more than the relatives. You must believe me: she really suffered more. I do not say that she tore her hair, nor that she rolled on the floor in convulsions. For there was nothing dramatic about my passing. The death of a bachelor at the age of sixty-four does not take on the proportions of high tragedy. And even if it did, nothing could have been more improper than that this anonymous lady display the intensity of her sorrow. Standing at the head of the bed, eyes glazed and mouth half open, she could hardly believe I had gone.

"Dead! Dead!" she repeated to herself.

And her imagination—like the storks that a famous traveler saw setting out in flight from the Ilissus to the African shores, heedless of the times and of the ruins—her imagination flew above the desolation of the moment to the shores of an ever youthful Africa.

Let her go; we shall go there later. We shall go there when I return to my early years. At present, I wish to die calmly, methodically, hearing the sobs of the ladies, the soft words of the men, the rain drumming on the taro leaves, and the piercing noise of a razor being sharpened by a knife-grinder outside in front of the door of a leather craftsman. I assure you that the music of this orchestra of death was much less sad than may appear. After a certain time, it was actually pleasurable. Life was shaking my body with the force of a great wave, my consciousness was fading away, I was descending to a physical and mental state of utter immobility, and my body was becoming a plant, a stone, clay, nothing at all.

I died of pneumonia; but, if I were to tell the reader that the cause of my death was less the pneumonia than a great and useful idea, possibly he would not believe me, yet it would be true. I am going to explain the matter to him briefly. Let him judge for himself.

# On That Day

On that day, the Cubas tree brought forth a lovely flower: I was born. I was received in the arms of Paschoela, famous midwife from Minho, Portugal, who boasted that she had opened the doors to the world for a whole generation of noblemen. Quite possibly my father had heard her say this; I believe, however, that it was paternal sentiment that induced him to gratify her with two half-dobras. Washed and diapered, I immediately became the hero of the house. Everyone predicted for me what best suited his taste. Uncle João, the old infantry officer, found that I had a certain facial expression like Bonaparte's, a thing that my father could not hear without nausea. Uncle Ildefonso, then a plain priest, scented a future canon in me.

"He will most surely be a canon, and I shall say no more for fear of appearing prideful; but I should not be surprised in the least if God has destined him for a bishopric . . . Yes, a bishopric; it is by no means impossible. What is your opinion, brother Bento?"

My father replied to everyone that I would be what God desired. Then he would lift me high in the air, as if he wanted to show me to the whole city and, indeed, to the whole world. He asked everyone whether I looked like him, whether I was intelligent, pretty . . .

I relate these things briefly, just as I heard them related years later; I am uninformed about most of the details of that great day. I know that the neighbors came or sent their compliments to the new-born, and that during the first few weeks we had many visitors. There was no chair or stool that escaped service. Many Sunday coats and fine breeches put in an appearance. If I do not relate the caresses, the kisses, the admiration, the blessings, it is because, if I did so, I should never finish the chapter, and finish it I must.

Item: I can tell nothing about my baptism, for they told me nothing about it, except that it was the occasion for one of the jolliest parties of the following year, 1806. I was baptized in the church of Saint Dominic on a Tuesday in March, a fine, pure, clear day, with Colonel Rodrigues de Mattos and his wife as godparents. They were both descended from old families of the North, and did real honor to the blood that ran in their veins, blood that had once been spilled in the war against Holland. I believe that their names were among the first things that I learned; and surely I could repeat them with great charm, or I revealed a precocious talent in doing so, for I was obliged to recite them before every visitor.

"Nhonhô, tell these gentlemen the name of your godfather."

"My godfather? He is the Most Excellent Senhor Colonel Paulo Vaz Lobo Cesar de Andrade e Souza Rodrigues de Mattos. My godmother is the Most Excellent Senhora Dona Maria Luiza de Macedo Rezende e Souza Rodrigues de Mattos."

"Your little boy is so clever!" exclaimed the listeners.

"Very clever," my father agreed. His eyes spilled over with gratification, and, placing the palm of his hand on my head, he gazed at me a long time, lovingly, proudly.

Item: I began to walk—I do not know exactly when, but ahead of time. Perhaps to hurry nature, they had me hold on to chairs while they supported me by the diaper and promised me little wooden wagons as a reward. "There we go, Nhonhô, all alone now!" my Negro nurse would say to me. And I, attracted by the tin rattle that my mother shook in front of me, started forward, fell, arose, fell again; and walked, doubtless badly, but walked, and I have been walking ever since.

## The First Kiss

I was seventeen; I was trying to convince the world and myself that the down on my upper lip was a mustache. My eyes, lively and resolute, were my most genuinely masculine feature. As I conducted myself with a certain arrogance, it was hard to know whether I was a child with manly ways or a man with childish ways. At all events, I was a handsome lad, handsome and bold, and I galloped into life in my boots and spurs, a whip in my hand and blood in my veins, riding a nervous, strong, high-spirited courser like the horse in the old ballads, which Romanticism found in the medieval castle and left in the streets of our own century. The Romanticists rode the poor beast until he was so nearly dead that he finally lay down in the gutter, where the realists found him, his flesh eaten away by sores and worms, and, out of pity, carried him away to their books.

Yes, I was good-looking, elegant, rich; and you may well believe that more ladies than one lowered before me a pensive brow or raised to me a pair of covetous eyes. Of all of them, however, the one who captivated me was a . . . a . . . I do not know whether to say it; this book is chaste, at least in intention; in intention, it is super-chaste. But come, I must tell either all or nothing. She who captivated me was a Spanish woman, Marcella, "the gorgeous Marcella," as the young blades used to call her. And the young blades were in the right. She was the daughter of an Asturian vegetable farmer; she told me this herself in a moment of sincerity, for the accepted belief was that she had been born to a Madrid lawyer, a victim of the French invasion, who had been wounded, imprisoned, and shot by a firing squad when she was only twelve years old. *Cosas de España.*

But whether her father was a vegetable farmer or a lawyer, the fact is that Marcella was wholly wanting in rustic innocence, and indeed it is doubtful whether she accepted even the modest ethics of the legal code. She was a beautifully built young lady, gay, without moral scruple, but inhibited a little by the austerity of the times, which did not permit her to parade her extravagances through the streets; luxurious, impatient, a lover of money and of young men. In that year, she was dying of love for a certain Xavier, a fellow who was both rich and consumptive—a gem.

I saw her for the first time in the Rocio Grande on the night of the fireworks after the announcement of the declaration of independence, a celebration of spring, of the awakening of the public soul. We were two young men, the people and I; we were fresh from childhood, with all the eagerness and fervor of youth. I saw her get out of a sedan chair; graceful and bewitching, she had a slim, undulating body, with a sauciness that I have never observed in chaste women. "Follow me," she said to her manservant. And I followed her, as much her servant as the other; I followed her lovingly, vibrantly, full of the first dawns. I heard someone say "the gorgeous Marcella," I remembered what I had heard about her from Uncle João, and I became, I confess it, actually dizzy.

Three days later, my uncle asked me in private whether I wished to go to a supper party in Cajueiros, with women. We went; it was in Marcella's house. Xavier, for all his tuberculosis, was presiding at the supper, of which I ate little or nothing, for I could take neither my eyes nor my thoughts away from the lady of the house. How lovely was this Spanish girl! There were seven or eight other women—all more or less loose—and they were pretty and charming, but the Spanish beauty . . . My ecstasy, several draughts of wine, my imperious, impulsive nature, all led me to do an unheard-of thing: as we were leaving, at the street door, I asked my uncle to wait a moment and went back up the stairs.

"Did you forget something?" asked Marcella, standing at the head of the stairway.

"My handkerchief."

She got out of my way so that I could return to the salon; I seized her hands, drew her to me, and kissed her. I do not know whether she said something, whether she shouted, whether she called anyone; I know only that I rushed down the stairs, fast as a whirlwind and stumbling like a drunk.

## Vision in the Hallway

In the dark hallway at the bottom of the stairs, I stopped a minute to catch my breath, to compose myself, to collect my scattered thoughts—in short, to regain my self-possession after such deep and contrary emotional experiences. I decided that I was happy. Certainly the diamonds tainted my happiness a little; but it is certain also that a pretty woman can very well love both the Greeks and their gifts. Moreover, I had confidence in my Marcella; she may have had faults, but she loved me . . .

"An angel!" I murmured, looking at the ceiling of the hallway.

And there, mocking me, I saw Marcella's eyes, with the expression that had given me, a few minutes earlier, a shudder of distrust, and they were sparkling above a nose that was at once Bakbarah's nose and my own. Poor infatuated fool of *The Thousand and One Nights!* I saw you running the length of the gallery after the vizier's wife, she beckoning you to possess her and you running, running, running, until you came to the garden path and out into the street, where the leather venders laughed at you and beat you. Then it seemed to me that Marcella's hallway was the garden path and that the street outside was the one in Bagdad. Indeed, as I looked toward the street door, I saw three of the leather venders, one in a cassock, another in livery, and the third in ordinary clothes, come into the hallway; they seized me by the arms, put me in a chaise—my father on my right, my uncle, the canon, on my left, and the man in livery on the driver's box—and took me to the house of the local police captain, from which I was transported to a galleon that was to sail for Lisbon. You can imagine how I resisted; but all resistance was in vain.

Three days later, downcast and silent, I crossed the bar. I did not even cry; I had a fixed idea. Accursed fixed ideas! On this occasion, my idea was to repeat the name Marcella as I leaped into the ocean.

## from *Dom Casmurro*

TRANSLATED BY HELEN CAULDWELL

### Othello

I dined out; went to the theater in the evening. They happened to be playing *Othello*, which I had never seen or read. I was familiar only with its theme, and rejoiced at the coincidence. I watched the Moor rage because of a handkerchief—a simple handkerchief!—and here I furnish material to be considered by psychologists of this and other continents, since I could not escape the observation that a handkerchief was enough to kindle the jealousy of Othello and fashion the most sublime tragedy of this world. Handkerchiefs have passed out of use; today one must have nothing less than sheets, at times it is not sheets but only shirts that matter. These were the vague and muddled ideas that passed through my mind as the Moor rolled convulsively and Iago distilled his calumny. During the intervals between the acts I did not leave my seat. I did not wish to risk meeting someone I knew. Most of the ladies remained in the boxes, while the men went out to smoke. Then I asked myself if one of these women might not have loved someone who now lay quiet in the cemetery; and there came to me other incoherencies, until the curtain rose and the play went on. The last act showed me that not I, but Capitú ought to die. I heard the prayers of Desdemona, her pure and loving words, the fury of the Moor, and the death he meted out to her amid the frantic applause of the audience.

"And she was innocent!" I kept saying to myself all the way down the street. "What would the audience do if she were really guilty, as guilty as Capitú? And what death would the Moor mete out to her then? A bolster would not suffice; there would be need of blood and fire, a vast, intense fire to consume her wholly, and reduce her to dust, and the dust tossed to the wind, in eternal extinction. . . ."

I roamed through the streets the rest of the night. I had supper, it is true, a trifle, but enough to live on till morning. I saw the last hours of night and the first hours of day. I saw the late strollers and the first sweepers, the first carts, the first noises, the first white streaks of day, a day that came after the other and would see me depart never to return. The streets I roamed seemed to flee from me of themselves. I would never again contemplate the sea beyond Gloria, nor the Serra dos Orgãos, nor the fortress of Santa Cruz, and the rest. There were not so many people on the street as on weekdays but there were quite a number off to tasks they would do again; but I would never do anything again.

I reached home, opened the door very slowly, climbed the stairs on tiptoe, and let myself into my study. It was almost six. I took the poison out of my pocket, sat in my shirt sleeves and wrote one more letter, the last, directed to Capitú. None of the others were for her. I felt the necessity of writing some word which would leave her remorseful for my death. I wrote two versions. I burned the first, thinking it too long and diffuse. The second contained only what was necessary, clear and brief. It did not remind her of our past, nor of the struggles we had had, nor of any joy: it spoke only of Escobar and of the necessity of dying.

# ■ José Martí (1853–1895) *Cuba* (poems)

## TRANSLATED BY WILLIS BARNSTONE

Journalist, essayist, poet, and leader of the Cuban Revolutionary Party, which sought independence for Cuba from Spain (it came in 1898), José Martí was killed in a landing in Cuba in the last major battle against Spain. Politically active from an early age, at sixteen Martí was arrested and sent into exile. Thereafter, he lived in Mexico, Spain, Guatemala, Venezuela, and mainly, for a period of fourteen years, in the United States. In New York, where he had his longest residence, he earned his living as a newspaperman, writing for the *New York Sun* and foreign papers. He wrote about literary, social, and political matters in the United States and Latin America. Among the memorable writings in his *Chronicles* are pages on the life of Ulysses Grant and on the first exhibition of French impressionist paintings in New York. He admired and wrote about Whitman, whom he met in Camden, New Jersey, and he painted a vivid picture of the celebration of Whitman's seventieth birthday. In his last residence in New York (1891–1895), he founded the Cuban Revolutionary Party and led the liberation movement until his death, during an invasion attempt at Dos Ríos in 1895, the same year as the liberation. He is Cuba's national hero.

As a poet, he was schooled in Spanish and French classics. Like the Argentine writer and leader Sarmiento, Martí was a political journalist and in his fine essays and newspaper columns, he combined social ardor with a sure aesthetic hand. Because he rejected the stilted rhetoric of the past in favor of straightforward prose, he is usually credited with being one of the precursors of the *modernismo* movement. Yet only in that the modernistas, including their leader, the Nicaraguan poet Rubén Darío, were also interested in revolutionary politics, might he be included under the loose and ill-defined rubric of *modernismo*. He had none of the French Parnassian escapist aestheticism that permeated the work of Leopoldo Lugones or Darío; no symbolic peacocks, swans, delicate princesses in glass towers enter his writing. On the contrary, in his best poetry, Martí is elegantly simple as in the brief lyrics of *Simple Lyrics,* the title of his best-known volume of verse. The revolutionary song "Guantanamera," made popular by Joan Baez in the 1960s, incorporates the famous line "I am a sincere man" from one of his "simple lyrics."

**FURTHER READING:** Martí, José. *Simple Lyrics,* 1891; *Free Lyrics,* c. 1882, published 1913; *The America of José Martí: Selected Writings.* Translated by Juan de Onís, 1953.

## I Am a Sincere Man

I am a sincere man
from where the palms grow,
and before I die I want
to spread my soul poems.

I come from everywhere
and to everywhere I go.
I am art among the arts.
In the hills I am a hill.

I know the exotic names
of grasses and flowers,
of fatal betrayals
and sublime sorrows.

In dark night I have seen
rays of pure fire
and holy beauty
rain upon my head.

I have seen wings born
in beautiful women's shoulders,
and butterflies flying
out of piles of rubble.

I have seen a man living
with a dagger in his side,
who will never say the name
of the woman who killed him.

Swiftly like a reflection
twice I saw the soul, twice:

when the old poor man died,
when she told me goodbye.

I shivered once on the grating
at the entrance to the vineyard                                    *30*
when I saw a barbarous bee
scratch a girl's forehead.

I enjoyed my fate
like never before when
the mayor weeping                                                  *35*
read my sentence of death.

I hear a sigh across
the lands and the sea:
it is not a sigh. It is
my son about to wake                                               *40*

If they say I got the best
jewel from the jewelers,
I take on a sincere friend
and put love aside.

I have seen the wounded eagle                                      *45*
fly into a serene blue,
and a poisonous viper
die in its den.

I'm aware that when the world
yields lividly to rest,                                            *50*
a tame stream murmurs
over a profound silence.

I put a daring hand
stiff with horror and jubilation
over an extinct star                                               *55*
that fell before my door.

I conceal in my brave chest
a pain that wounds me:
the son of an enslaved people
lives for it, hushes and dies.                                     *60*

All is beautiful and constant,
all is music and reason,
and all, like the diamond,
before light is carbon.

I know that a fool is buried                                       *65*
with grand wealth and wailing,
and there is no earthly fruit
like the fruit of a peasant.

I shut up, catch on, and get rid
of a rhymer's pomp,
and hang my doctor's hood
on a withered tree.

## ■ Rubén Darío (1867–1916) *Nicaragua* (poems)

The Nicaraguan poet Rubén Darío was the founder and leader of the
modernismo movement and, by his example, profoundly altered Spanish
poetry in the Americas. Darío looked to France and particularly to the
French poet Paul Verlaine in whose purity, perfection, ineffable sadness,
and "music above all," he found a model for his own verse. He brought a
Spanish form of French symbolism and Parnassian aestheticism to a worn
out, dispirited poetry of Latin America and Spain, renovating its diction
with exotic, clear imagery and sonorous rhythms. A prodigy, Darío was
eighteen when he published *Blue* (1888), which made him famous. His
next major work was *Profane Proses* (1896), a volume of poems that moved
from "purity" of content and form to graceful exoticism. Yet artificiality
and art-for-art's sake prevailed. In his later books, *Songs of Life and Hope*
(1905), he initiated an anti–North American polemic, calling for the political, religious, and cultural independence of the Hispanic world. In
Spanish America and Spain, early poets of our century initially embraced
him for his fresh beauty and magic and later for his political word. The
Spanish poet Antonio Machado and the Argentine Leopoldo Lugones
were at first in debt to the Nicaraguan modernist, but soon, searching for
their own voice, they rejected him as an Hispanic equivalent of *fin de siècle*
French preciosity. Darío spent his later years in Nicaragua, Madrid, and
Paris. Like his mentor Paul Verlaine, he embraced a bohemian lifestyle
and in his last years was often sick from severe alcoholism. He died at age
forty-nine. No poet in the Spanish language, on either side of the Atlantic,
has so thoroughly changed the poetry of the Spanish language. His political poems have been rewritten by fellow Nicaraguan Ernesto Cardenal in
his own modern idiom.

**FURTHER READING:** Darío, Rubén. *Blue*, 1888; *Profane Proses and Other Poems*, 1896;
*Songs of Life and Hope*, 1905; *Selected Poems*. Translated by Lysander Kemp, 1965.

## Symphony in Gray Major

The sea, great mercury mirror,
reflects the zinc sheet of sky;
stain of faraway birds
on pale burnished gray.

Opaque round window, the sun                                               5
at a sick pace totters to the zenith;
a sea wind stretches
in shade, pillowed on its black
trumpet.

Under the pier the waves                                                   10
groan, twitching leaden bellies.
A sailor sits on a coil of rope,
smoking, remembering
distant landfalls, a misty country.

This sea dog is old. Fiery rays                                            15
of Brazilian sun have scorched his face;
vicious Chinese typhoons have seen him
tilting his gin bottle.

Foam infused with saltpeter and iodine
has long been familiar with his red nose,                                  20
his crisp curls and athlete's biceps,
his canvas cap and drill shirt.

In the tobacco smoke he sees
that far-off misty land for which,
one golden, hot afternoon,                                                 25
his brig set out in full sail.

Tropical siesta. The old man sleeps.
The scale of gray major envelops him.
It's as if an enormous
soft charcoal had been rubbed                                              30
over where the horizon used to curve.

Tropical siesta. An old cigala
tries out her obsolete, hoarse guitar;
a grasshopper begins
a monotone on his one-stringed fiddle.                                     35

TRANSLATED BY DENISE LEVERTOV


## To Roosevelt

The voice that would reach you, Hunter, must speak
in Biblical tones, or in the poetry of Walt Whitman.
You are primitive and modern, simple and complex;
you are one part George Washington and one part Nimrod.
        You are the United States,                                         5
future invader of our naïve America

with its Indian blood, an America
that still prays to Christ and still speaks Spanish.

You are a strong, proud model of your race;
you are cultured and able; you oppose Tolstoy.
You are an Alexander-Nebuchadnezzar,
breaking horses and murdering tigers.
(You are a Professor of Energy,
as the current lunatics say.)

You think that life is a fire,
that progress is an irruption,
that the future is wherever
your bullet strikes.
        No.

The United States is grand and powerful.
Whenever it trembles, a profound shudder
runs down the enormous backbone of the Andes.
If it shouts, the sound is like the roar of a lion.
And Hugo said to Grant: "The stars are yours."
(The dawning sun of the Argentine barely shines;
the star of Chile is rising . . . ) A wealthy country,
joining the cult of Mammon to the cult of Hercules;
while Liberty, lighting the path
to easy conquest, raises her torch in New York.

But our own America, which has had poets
since the ancient times of Nezahualcóyotl;
which preserved the footprints of great Bacchus,
and learned the Panic alphabet once,
and consulted the stars; which also knew Atlantis
(whose name comes ringing down to us in Plato)
and has lived, since the earliest moments of its life,
in light, in fire, in fragrance, and in love—
the America of Moctezuma and Atahualpa,
the aromatic America of Columbus,
Catholic America, Spanish America,
the America where noble Cuauhtémoc said:
"I am not on a bed of roses"—our America,
trembling with hurricanes, trembling with Love:
O men with Saxon eyes and barbarous souls,
our America lives. And dreams. And loves.
And it is the daughter of the Sun. Be careful.
Long live Spanish America!
A thousand cubs of the Spanish lion are roaming free.
Roosevelt, you must become, by God's own will,
the deadly Rifleman and the dreadful Hunter

before you can clutch us in your iron claws.

And though you have everything, you are lacking one thing:
God!

TRANSLATED BY LYSANDER KEMP

# ■ Ramón López Velarde (1880–1921)
## *Mexico* (poem)

TRANSLATED BY WILLIS BARNSTONE

Ramón López Velarde was born in a Mexican town, and though he moved to Mexico City, he never lost his feeling for the landscape and villages of his youth, and they remain the main references in his poems. He received a law degree from the University of San Luis Potosí. In 1919, he published *Zozobra* (*Worries*), which gave him an immediate reputation. *El son del corazón* (*Heartbeat*) appeared posthumously in 1932. Although influenced by Lugones and Latin American modernism, his natural affinity is with the Spanish nature poet Antonio Machado or the village poems about place, family, and friends in César Vallejo's compassionate early poems. López Velarde's poems are free of modernista preciosity. On the contrary, a grave simplicity and an elemental humanity run through them. A poet far ahead of his time, he has enduring qualities of ordinary, sensitive speech that have enhanced his readership and reputation and have made him today one of Latin America's most esteemed writers from the early part of the century.

**FURTHER READING:** López Velarde, Ramón. *Devoted Blood,* 1916; *Worries,* 1919; *Heartbeat,* 1932.

## *Our Lives Are Pendulums*

Where is that girl, I wonder,
who one night at a dance
in a forsaken town
revealed how she had to
get out, to travel, and told me
her boredom?

The waltz was groaning for her,
and she was a languid artist's
plaster model: two amber

5

drop earrings, and a jasmine
in her hair.

Girl who told me
your secrets of boredom
one night at a dance
in that forsaken town,
wherever you're exhaling
your discreet sigh,
our lives are pendulums.

Two far off pendulums
swinging and parallel
in the same fog
of winter.

## ■ Ricardo Güiraldes (1886–1927) *Argentina* (novel)

TRANSLATED BY HARRIET DE ONÍS

An Argentine aristocrat who spent his life between Buenos Aires and Paris, Ricardo Güiraldes also traveled to the Far East, but in his writing he was perfectly at home in the pampas. Like José Hernández, the author of *Martin Fierro,* Güiraldes created a gaucho after the gaucho had effectively vanished, publishing his masterpiece of the gauchoesque novel in 1926, a year before his death. The hero Don Segundo Sombra, who is a "second shadow" of a disappeared gaucho reality, comes through as a poetically described hero of integrity, adventure, and sporadic epic qualities. Don Segundo is perceived largely through the eyes of the young boy Fabio Cáceres, who idealizes and mythologizes Don Segundo Sombra. At the same time, the boy is also a myth created by Güiraldes. The novel *Don Segundo Sombra* is an elaborate, beautifully crafted anachronism, a fairy tale for all ages like Antoine de Saint-Exupéry's *The Little Prince;* and, like Exupéry's fable or a tale from *A Thousand and One Nights,* it remains alive for each generation. Provided one does not look for fiction to replace history or chronicle, *Don Segundo* works as a finely wrought adventure story.

**FURTHER READING:** Güiraldes, Ricardo. *Don Segundo Sombra,* 1926. Translated by Harriet de Onís, 1935.

## *from* **Don Segundo Sombra**

Slowly, with my fishing rod over my shoulder and dangling my small victims heartlessly at my side, I made my way toward town. The street still was flooded by a recent thundershower, and I had to walk carefully to keep from sinking in the mud that clung to my sandals and almost sucked them off my feet. My mind was a blank as I took the narrow path that crept along the hedges of prickly pear, thorn, myrrh, following the rise of the ground, like hares seeking a level place to run.

The lane ahead of me stretched dark. The sky, still blue with twilight, lay in reflected shards in the puddles or in the deep wagon ruts, where it looked like strips of carefully trimmed steel.

I had reached the first houses, where the hour put the dogs on the alert. Fear twitched in my legs as I heard the growl of a dangerous mastiff not far off, but without a mistake I called all the brutes by name: Sentinel, Captain, Watcher. When some mutt set up a barking as swift as it was inoffensive, I disdainfully shied a clod at it.

I passed the graveyard and a familiar tremor ran down my spine, radiating its pallid chill to my calves and forearms. The dead, will-o'-the-wisps, ghosts, scared me far more than any encounter I might have with mortals in that neighborhood. What could the greediest robber hope for from me? I was on good terms with the slyest of them; and if one was so careless as to hold me up, he would be the loser by a cigarette.

The lane became a street, the outlying farms thickened into blocks of houses; and neither walls nor bead-tree hedges held any secrets for me. Here was a stand of alfalfa, there a patch of corn, a barn lot, or just brush. Now I could make out the first shanties, silent in their squalor and illumined only by the frail glow of a candle or stinking kerosene lamps. As I crossed a street I frightened a horse whose step had sounded farther off than it was; and as fear is catching, even from animal to man, I stood stock-still in the mud without daring to move. The rider, who seemed to me enormous in his light poncho, urged the horse on, whirling the whiplash past its left eye; but as soon as I tried to take a step the scared beast snorted like a mule and reared. A puddle cracked beneath his hoof with the sound of breaking glass. A high-pitched voice spoke calmly, "Steady, boy. Steady, boy."

Then trot and gallop splashed through the sleek mud.

I stood still and watched the silhouette of horse and rider disappear strangely magnified against the glowing sky. It was as if I had seen a vision, a shade, a something that passes and is more a thought than a living thing, a something that drew me as a pool swallows the current of a river into its depths.

Filled with my vision, I reached the first sidewalks, where I could make better time. Stronger than ever was the need I felt to get away, to leave this paltry town forever. I had glimpsed a new life, a life of motion and space.

In a whirl of dreams and doubts I kept on through the town and down the blackness of another alley to La Blanqueada. As I entered, the light made me pucker up my eyes. Behind the counter, as usual, stood the owner, and in front of him the half-breed Burgos was just finishing off a brandy.

"Good evening, gentlemen."

"Evening," mumbled Burgos.

"What you got?" asked the owner.

"There you are, Don Pedro." I showed him my string of catfish.

"All right. Want some rock candy?"

"No, Don Pedro."

"Couple packages of La Popular?"

"No, Don Pedro. Remember the last money you gave me?"

"Sure."

"It was round."

"And you made it roll?"

"You said it."

"All right. Here you are." He clinked several nickel coins down on the counter.

"Gonna set up the drinks?" grinned the half-breed.

"Sure — in the *Wouldn't You Like It* café."

"Anything new?" asked Don Pedro, for whom I was a kind of reporter.

"Yes, sir; a stranger."

"Where'd you see him?"

"At the crossing, as I was coming in from the river."

"And you don't know who he is?"

"I know he's not from here. There's no man as big as him in this town."

Don Pedro frowned, as if trying to concentrate on some half-forgotten memory. "Tell me, was he very dark?"

"I think so—yes, sir. And strong!"

As though talking of something extraordinary, the saloonkeeper muttered, "Who knows if it isn't Don Segundo Sombra!"

"It is!" I said, without knowing why, and I felt the same thrill as when at nightfall I had stood motionless before the portentous vision of that gaucho stamped black on the horizon.

"You know him?" Don Pedro asked the half-breed, paying no attention to my exclamation.

"Only what I've heard tell of him. The devil, I reckon, ain't as fierce as he's painted. How about serving me another drink?"

"Hm," went on Don Pedro. "I've seen him more than once. He used to come in here, afternoons. He's a man you want to watch your step with. He's from San Pedro. Had a run in, they say, with the police some time ago."

"I suppose he butchered somebody else's steer."

"Yes. But, if I remember rightly, the steer was a Christian."

Burgos kept his stolid eyes on the glass, and a frown wrinkled his narrow forehead of a pampas Indian half-breed. The fame of another man seemed to lessen his own as an expert with the knife.

We heard a gallop stop short at the door, then the soft hiss with which the country folk quiet a horse, and Don Segundo's silent figure stood framed in the doorway.

"Good evening," came the high-pitched voice, and it was easy to recognize. "How's Don Pedro?"

"Good. And you, Don Segundo?"

"I can't complain, thank God."

As they greeted each other with the customary courtesies, I looked the man over. He was not really so big. What made him seem so, as he appears to me even today, was the sense of power flowing from his body. His chest was enormous and his joints big-boned like those of a horse. His feet were short and high-arched; his hands thick and leathery like the scales of an armadillo. His skin was copper-hued and his eyes slanted slightly toward his temples. To talk more at ease he pushed his narrow-brimmed hat back from his forehead showing bangs cut like a horse's, level with his eyebrows. His attire was that of a poor gaucho. A plain pigskin belt girded his waist. The short blouse was caught up by the bone-handled knife from which swung a rough, plaited quirt, dark with use. His chiripá was long and coarse, and a plain black kerchief was knotted around his neck with the ends across his shoulders. He had split his *alpargatas* at the instep to make room for the fleshy foot.

When I had looked my fill at him, I listened to the talk. Don Segundo was looking for work, and Don Pedro was telling him where to find it; his constant business with the country people made him know everything that was going on at the ranches.

"At Galván's there are some mares they want broke. A few days ago Valerio was here and asked me if there was anyone I could recommend. I told him about Mosco Pereira, but if it suits you—"

"Seems to me it might."

"Good. I'll tell the boy they send to town every day. He generally drops in."

"I'd rather you said nothing. If I can, I'll go by the ranch myself."

"All right. Like a drink?"

"Well, I don't mind," said Don Segundo, sitting down at a nearby table. "Give me a glass of brandy, and thanks for the invitation."

Everything that had to be said was said. A calm silence filled the place. Burgos poured out his fourth glass. His eyes were bleary and his face expressionless. Suddenly, and for no apparent reason, he said to me, "If I was a fisher like you, I'd want to haul in a great big mud-bottom catfish." A sarcastic giggle underlined his words, and he kept looking at Don Segundo out of the corner of his eye. "They seem tough because they flop around and make such a fuss. But what can they do when they're nothing but niggers."

Don Pedro gave the half-breed a sharp look. Both of us knew what Burgos was like and that nothing could hold him when he turned ugly. The only one of the four of us who didn't understand the drift of things was Don Segundo, who went on sipping his liquor, his thoughts far away. The half-breed giggled again; he was proud of the comparison he had hit on. I longed to do something—something terrible if need be—to break the strain. Don Pedro was humming to himself. And the air was tense for us all, except for the stranger, who seemed to have neither understood nor felt the chill of our silence.

"A big mud-bottom catfish," repeated the drunk again. "But nothing but a catfish, for all it's got whiskers and walks on two legs like Christians. . . . I've heard there's a lot of 'em in San Pedro. That's why they say:

> 'Anyone from San Pedro
> Is either a chink or a mulatto.'"

Twice he repeated the rhyme in a voice that grew thicker and more insolent.

Don Segundo looked up and, as if just realizing that the half-breed's words were meant for him, said calmly, "Come, friend, I'll soon begin to think you're trying to start something."

So unexpected were the words, so amusing the expression of surprise on his face, that we had to smile despite the ugly turn the talk was taking. The drunk himself was nonplussed, but only for a moment.

"Yeah? I was beginning to think everybody around here was deaf."

"How could a catfish be deaf, with the big ears they got? But me? I'm a busy man and I can't take care of you now. When you want to fight with me, let me know at least three days in advance."

We burst out laughing, in spite of the amazement this calm that verged on foolhardiness aroused in us. Again he began to grow in my imagination. He was the "masked man," the "mystery man," the man of silence, who inspires a wondering admiration in the pampas.

The half-breed Burgos paid for his drinks, muttering threats. I followed him to the door and saw him hide in the shadow. Don Segundo got up and took his leave of Don Pedro, who was pale with fear. The drunk was going to kill this man to whom my heart went out! As if speaking to Don Pedro, I warned Don Segundo, "Watch out!"

And then I sat down on the doorsill, my heart in my mouth, waiting for the fight that was sure to come.

Don Segundo stood on the threshold, looking from side to side. I understood that he was getting his eyes used to the dark, so as not to be taken by surprise. Then, keeping to the wall, he started toward his horse.

The half-breed stepped from the shadow feeling sure of his man and let loose his knife aimed straight at the heart. I saw the blade cut the night like the flash of a gun. With incredible swiftness Don Segundo dodged, and the knife shattered against the brick wall with the clang of a bell. Burgos stepped back two paces and waited for what must be his death. The triangular blade of a small knife glittered in Don Segundo's fist. But the attack did not come. Don Segundo bent calmly over, picked the broken steel from the ground, and said in his ironic voice, "Here you are, friend. Better get it fixed. This way, it's no good even to skin a sheep."

The attacker kept his distance. Don Segundo put away his own little knife and again held out the fragments of the blade.

"Take it, friend."

The bully came forward, his head low, moved by a force stronger than his fear. His clumsy fist took the hilt of the knife, now harmless as a broken cross. Don Segundo shrugged and walked toward his horse. And Burgos followed him. Don Segundo mounted and made ready to move into the night. The drunk came close, seeming to have recovered the gift of speech.

"Listen, friend," he said and raised his sullen face, in which only the eyes were alive. "I'm gonna have this knife fixed for whenever you need me." The dull bully's mind could think of only one act of thanks: to offer his life to the other. "Now, shake."

"Sure thing," agreed Don Segundo, as calm as ever. "Put it there, brother."

And without further ado he went down the narrow street, while the half-breed stood seeming to struggle with a thought too great and radiant for him.

I went striding along beside Don Segundo, who kept his horse at a walk.

"You know that fellow?" he asked, muffling himself in his voluminous poncho with a leisurely gesture.

"Yes, sir. I know him well."

"Seems sort of foolish, don't he?"


# ■ Manuel Bandeira (1886–1968) *Brazil* (poems)

Manuel Bandeira was born in the north of Brazil, in Recife. His family moved to Rio de Janeiro when he was ten. In Rio, he attended a collegio and the Polytechnical School in São Paulo, where he studied architecture. Sick with turberculosis, in 1913 he went to Switzerland to a sanatorium near Davos-Platz. There he met the poet Paul Eluard, who was a patient in the same clinic. His early work was French Parnassian and symbolist—as were the poems of most of his Latin American and Iberian contemporaries. He found his own style in *The Dissolute Rhythm* (1924) and *Libertinism* (1930). The later ironic and semisurreal spirit of Apollinaire was now in his poems, which became a model for later Brazilian masters. In *Territory*, he returned to the landscapes, people, and myths of rural northern Brazil. Eventually, he also moved to a more socially committed poetry.


## *Silence*

In the complicit darkness of the room,
In the contact of my slow hands

with the substance of your flesh,
It was the same as silence.

It was a roaring of musical silence,
A grave feeling of enigma.
I was wounded by a grace
That came mortally sharp, and soft.

Ah, so soft and sharp!
It seemed to rise from death.
Silence was saying all
That before I could poorly guess.

Silence was your flesh,
Amber and naked body.
It is better to live in the mind
Than wait for tenderness.

TRANSLATED BY WILLIS BARNSTONE

## Brazilian Tragedy

Misael, civil servant in the Ministry of Labor, 63 years old,
    Knew Maria Elvira of the Grotto: prostitute, syphilitic, with ulcerated fingers, a pawned wedding ring and teeth in the last stages of decay.
    Misael took Maria out of "the life," installed her in a two-storey house in Junction City, paid for the doctor, dentist, manicurist. . . . He gave her everything she wanted.
    When Maria Elvira discovered she had a pretty mouth, she immediately took a boy-friend.
    Misael didn't want a scandal. He could have beaten her, shot her, or stabbed her. He did none of these: they moved.
    They lived like that for three years.
    Each time Maria Elvira took a new boy-friend, they moved.
    The lovers lived in Junction City. Boulder. On General Pedra Street, The Sties. The Brickyards. Glendale. Pay Dirt. On Marquês de Sapucaí Street in Villa Isabel. Niterói. Euphoria. In Junction City again, on Clapp Street. All Saints. Carousel. Edgewood. The Mines. Soldiers Home . . .
    Finally, in Constitution Street, where Misael, bereft of sense and reason, killed her with six shots, and the police found her stretched out, supine, dressed in blue organdy.

TRANSLATED BY ELIZABETH BISHOP

# ■ Gabriela Mistral (1889–1957) *Chile* (poems)

## TRANSLATED BY CHRISTIANE JACOX KYLE

Born in Chile as Lucila Godoy Alcayaga, the poet adopted the more euphonious name Gabriela Mistral. She took Gabriela from the Archangel Gabriel and Mistral from the mistral wind that blows over the south of France. In 1914, while a provincial schoolteacher in Chile, she issued her first poems, *Sonetos de la muerte* (The Sonnets of Death), which won her the Chilean National Prize for Poetry. These sonnets, along with some fifty stories and poems published in 1917, established her as an important national writer. Her lullabies and despairing love lyrics became extremely popular in her time. The poet speaks of elemental things—of nature, death, childbirth. Although she had no children of her own, maternity is an obsessive preoccupation in her poetry. Her best poems have a taut strength in their brevity and clarity. Yet, it is her very early series of the sonnets of death, included in *Desolación* (*Desolation*, 1992) that contains her most enduring poetry. She lived her later years in Long Island, New York, with her companion translator. For her educational labors on behalf of Indian adults and children in rural areas, she became known as the "Citizen of the Americas." In her lifetime, Gabriela Mistral received every external form of recognition a poet can have. In 1945, she was awarded the Nobel Prize for Literature. Her *Selected Poems* (1957) were translated by Langston Hughes.

**FURTHER READING:** Mistral, Gabriela. *Desolation*, 1922; *Tenderness*, 1924; *Feeling*, 1938; *Wine Press*, 1954; *Selected Poems*. Translated by Langston Hughes, 1957; *Complete Poems*, 1958.

## *Poems of the Saddest Mother*

### Cast Out

My father said he would throw me
out; he shouted at my mother that he
would cast me out this very night.

    The night is warm; by the clear light
of the stars, I could walk to the next                                    5
village; but what if he's born during
these hours? Maybe my sobs have
called him; maybe he would want to
come out to see my face. And he would
shiver in the raw wind, even though I                                     10
would cover him.

## ■ César Vallejo (1892–1938) *Peru* (poems)

Born in Santiago de Chuco, a remote mining town in Northern Peru, César Vallejo came from Spanish and Indian ancestors. Like the French poet Guillaume Apollinaire whom he admired and who claimed the pope as his father, Vallejo could claim at least one Spanish priest as a grandfather. He studied at the University of San Marcos in Lima (the oldest university in the Americas) and the University of Trujillo. After graduation, he taught elementary school and worked on his poems. In 1918, he published *Los heraldos negros* (*The Black Heralds*) in Lima, probably the first major book of truly modern poetry in the Spanish language in the Americas. This extraordinary volume of classically modeled poems, avant-garde in their lexicon, treats everyday life of family and the abused poor; Vallejo observes the black iron handiwork of a dispassionate God who distributes misery along the black coffin edges of the earth. The American poet Robert Bly, who, with another poet James Wright, translated and introduced Vallejo into English, writes about the book: "It is a staggering book, sensual, prophetic, affectionate, wild. It has a kind of compassion for God, and compassion for death, who has so many problems, and it moves with incredible leaps of imagination. I think it is the greatest single collection of poems I have ever read. The first two lines of *The Black Heralds* in the poem "There Are Blows in Life" sets the powerful tone: "There are blows in life, so strong—I don't know!/Blows like the hatred of God."

On a visit in 1920 to the city of Trujillo, where he had studied, there was political turmoil. Vallejo was arrested on false charges (for which he was later exonerated) and spent nearly four months in jail. There, he wrote poems included in *Trilce* (1922), a radically experimental, surreal, humorous, and, at the same time, dark and tragic volume. The poems are direct, often difficult, and as powerful as any poems written in our century. (Only the Spanish poet Miguel Hernández, who died in 1942 in a Spanish prison at age thirty-two, composed verse of comparable strength in their surreal imagination, black-and-white imagery, immediacy, and searing humanity.) *Trilce,* despite its Joycean delight in creating outrageous neologisms and its obscurities that recall Paul Celan's last books of poems, elaborates the essential themes of family remembrances, poverty, and the great ideas of time and death, all with wit and depth. The next year, Vallejo lost his teaching job in Lima. In 1923, fearful and angry about his life in Peru, he obtained a job as a stringer in Paris for a Trujillo newspaper and left Peru, never to return.

In Paris, he married, was poor, even hungry, became a Communist, and twice visited the U.S.S.R., in 1928 and 1930. On the second visit, he interviewed the Russian poet Vladimir Mayakovsky in Moscow. On returning from Russia, he and his wife Georgette were deported from France. They spent two years (1930–1932) in Spain, during the furiously good days of the early thirties when the poets Federico García Lorca, Rafael Alberti, Miguel Hernández, Vicente Aleixandre, Luis Cernuda, Jorge Guillén, and Pedro Salinas were creating the greatest flowering in Spanish poetry since the Golden Age. Soon, the Chilean Pablo Neruda would spend crucial years of his life in Madrid, writing his *Residencias* (*Residences*) and befriending Lorca, Aleixandre, and Hernández. With Vallejo, Neruda, and the Mexican poet Octavio Paz in Spain during those vital years, the best poets of Spain and Hispanic America came together in person and in poetic conspiracy. Vallejo wrote prolifically in Spain, completing, in addition to poems, a novel, *Tungsteno,* a play, *Lockout,* and a travel book about the Soviet Union, *Rusia.*

Back in Paris, César Vallejo wrote most of the poems for *Poemas humanos* (*Human Poems*), which, like all his poems after he left Peru in 1923, were to remain unpublished in book form until after his death. *Human Poems* contains verse interspersed with some prose poems. It has less experimentation than his earlier *Trilce,* which is a singular phenomenon among all books of poetry, but the same humanity and unsentimental sorrow persist. All the pathos and eloquent poignancy of the French nineteenth-century poet Charles Baudelaire (1821–1867), who wrote about the poor, the drunk, the prostitutes, the miserable of Paris, reappear in the Spanish poems of the Peruvian master. Like Baudelaire, who also led a bohemian life with little glamor and much sorrow, physical suffering, and sickness, Vallejo wrote himself out in Paris. When the Spanish Civil War began in 1936, he threw himself into the Republican cause. In the second year of the war (1936–1939), he went to Spain and wrote *Spain, Let This Cup Pass from Me,* which, with *Human Poems,* was published posthumously in 1938, shortly after his death in the Parisian Clinique Aragon. Vallejo wrote a sonnet in Paris, "White Stone over a White Stone," in which he states that he will die one day in Paris, in the rain, on a day he can already remember. When death came, it took him, as it did Baudelaire, in his forty-sixth year. Vallejo, the poet of his generation of piercing compassion, caustic candor, and startling and original experimentation, died of undiagnosed causes in Paris on Holy Friday, April 15, 1938, during a rainfall.

**FURTHER READING:** Vallejo, César. *Black Heralds,* 1918; *Trilce,* 1922; *Human Poems,* 1938; *Spain, Let This Cup Pass from Me,* 1938; *Trilce.* Translated by David Smith, 1973; *Neruda and Vallejo: Selected Poems.* Translated by Robert Bly, John Knoepfle, and James Wright, 1971; *Spain, Take This Cup from Me.* Translated by Clayton Eshleman and José Rubia Barcia, 1974; *Spain, Take This Cup from Me.* Translated by Alvaro Cardona-Hine, 1972; *The Complete Posthumous Poetry.* Translated by Clayton Eshleman and José Rubia Barcia, 1978; *Selected Poems of César Vallejo.* Translated by E. Dorn and Gordon Brotherston, 1978; *Selected Poems.* Translated by H. R. Hays, 1981; *Black Heralds.* Translated by Kathleen Ross and Richard Schaaf, 1990; *Trilce.* Translated by Rebecca Seiferle, 1992.

## There Are Blows in Life

There are blows in life, so strong . . . I don't know!
Blows like the hatred of God, as if before them
the undertow of everything suffered
puddled up in the soul . . . I don't know!

Just a few; but they are . . . They open dark trenches
on the fiercest face and on the strongest back.
Maybe they are the colts of barbarous Attilas
or the black heralds sent to us by Death.

They are deep plunges of the Christs in the soul,
of some worshipable faith that Destiny blasphemes.                          1
Those bloody blows are the crackling sounds
of some bread burning up on us at the oven door.

And the man . . . poor . . . poor! He turns his eyes as
when over a shoulder a clapping of hands call us.
He turns his crazy eyes, and everything lived                               1
puddles up like a pool of guilt in that glance.

There are blows in life, so strong . . . I don't know!

TRANSLATED BY WILLIS BARNSTONE

## Agape[1]

Today no one has come to question me;
nor asked anything from me this evening.

I haven't seen even one cemetery flower
in so cheerful a procession of lights.
Forgive me, Lord, how little I have died!

This evening everyone, everyone passes me by
and no one begs or asks me for a thing.

I don't know what they're forgetting but it sits
wrong in my hands, like something alien.

---

1. Agape is Greek for spiritual love.

I come to the door                                                              *10*
and would like to scream at all of them:
If you're missing something, here it is!

Because through all the evenings of this life,
I don't know what doors have slammed in a face
and my soul seizes on something alien.                                          *15*

Nobody came today;
and today how little I've died on this evening!

TRANSLATED BY TONY BARNSTONE AND WILLIS BARNSTONE

## The Black Cup

The night is a cup of evil. A watchman's stinging
whistle pierces through it like a vibrating pin.
Listen, you little slut, how come, if you're already gone,
the wave is still black and still burning me up.

The Earth spreads coffin edges in its shadow.                                   *5*
Listen, you little tramp, don't come back.

My flesh swims, swims
in the cup of shadow that keeps on hurting me;
my flesh swims in it
as in the swampy heart of a woman.                                              *10*

Star coal . . . I've felt
the dry frictions of clay
fall across my diaphanous lotus.
Ah, woman! For you
this flesh of instinct exists. Ah, woman!                                       *15*

So, oh black chalice, even now with you gone
I choke on dust;
and more desires to drink paw inside my flesh.

TRANSLATED BY TONY BARNSTONE AND WILLIS BARNSTONE

## In That Corner Where We Slept Together

In that corner where we slept together
so many nights, now I sit down

to take a walk. The bedstead of the dead lovers
was taken away, or something must have happened.

You came early for other matters
and now you're gone. It's the corner
where beside you I read one night
between your tender nipples
a story by Daudet. It is our lovers'
corner. Don't mistake it.                                                    1

I've begun to remember the lost days
of summers, your coming and going,
small and fed up and pale in the rooms.

On this rainy night,
already far from them both, suddenly I jump up . . .                         1.
They are two doors coming open, shutting,
two doors that come and go with the wind
shadow          to          shadow.

TRANSLATED BY TONY BARNSTONE AND WILLIS BARNSTONE

## Oh the Four Walls of the Cell

Oh the four walls of the cell,
the four whitening walls
inescapably facing themselves.

Hothouse of nerves, of terrible cracks,
my daily shackled limbs
drag from corner to corner.

Sweet keeper of unnumbered keys,
if you were here you'd see the time
of these four walls striking four.
We two would stand against them together,                                    1
more two than ever, and you wouldn't sob,
I swear it, my savior!

Ah the four walls of the cell.
I pity them and especially tonight
the two long ones somehow shaped                                             1.
like mothers already dead
leading a child by the hand
down a slope of corrosive bromine.

And only I stay on here,
waving my right hand high (my only                                           2

working hand), seeking a third arm
to teach—between my where and my when—
the impotent majority of men.

TRANSLATED BY TONY BARNSTONE AND WILLIS BARNSTONE

## White Stone over a White Stone

I will die in Paris during a heavy rain,
a day whose being already I recall.
I will die in Paris—and I won't escape—
perhaps a Thursday like today in fall.

It must be Thursday, since today, Thursday,          5
that I prose this verse, I've put my shoulder bones
on wrong, and turn—and never like today—
with all my road to see myself alone.

César Vallejo is dead. And everyone
beat him, though he never hurt anyone.          10
They clobbered him hard with a stick, also

hard with a rope. Among the witnesses
are the days Thursdays and the shoulder bones,
the rain, the roads, the loneliness . . .

TRANSLATED BY WILLIS BARNSTONE

## Hat, Coat, Gloves

Before the Comédie Française is the Café
de la Regénce; in it behind the stair
there is a hidden room, a table and armchair.
When I come in, the lifeless dust stands up to play.
Between my lips turned rubbery, the smoldering tip          5
of a cigarette fumes. In the smoke lies the way
of two intense smokes, the thorax of the Café,
and in the thorax a rust deep with sorrow's lip.
It is important that the fall is caught in fall.
It is important the the fall consists of all          10
it shoots—clouds, months, its cheekbone and its wrinkle.
It is important to smell madly and guess then
how hot is the snow, how evasive the turtle,
the how so simple, lightning struck the when!

TRANSLATED BY WILLIS BARNSTONE

## Our Daily Bread

I drink my breakfast . . . Damp earth
of the cemetery freezes the precious blood.
City of winter . . . the biting crusade
of a wheelbarrow appears, hauling
a feeling of starvation in chains.

I wish I could beat on all the doors,
and ask for somebody; and then
look at the poor, and, while they wept softly,
give bits of fresh bread to them.
And plunder the rich of their vineyards                                    1
with my two blessed hands
which, with one blow of light,
could blast nails from the Cross!

Eyelash of morning, Thou wilt not rise!
Give us our daily bread,                                                    1
Lord . . . !
Every bone in me belongs to others;
and maybe I robbed them.

I came to take something for myself that maybe
was meant for some other man;                                              2
and so I start thinking that, if I had not been born,
another poor man could have drunk this coffee.
I feel like a dirty sneak-thief . . . Wherever I go!

And in this frigid hour, when the earth
transcends human dust and is so sorrowful,                                 2
I wish I could beat on all the doors
and beg pardon from someone,
and make bits of fresh bread with it
here, in the oven of my heart . . . !

TRANSLATED BY JAMES WRIGHT

## Masses

When the battle ended
and the combatant was dead, a man came toward him
and said to him "Don't die, I love you too much!"
But the corpse, ay!, went on dying.

Two came up to him and repeated                                                    5
"Don't leave us! Courage! Come back to life!
But the corpse, ay!, went on dying.

Twenty came up to him, a hundred, a thousand, a hundred thousand,
clamoring, "So much love, and not able to do anything against death!"
But the corpse, ay!, went on dying.                                                10

Millions of people came around him,
with one common plea; the corpse gazed at them sadly, emotionally;
slowly he pulled his body up,
embraced the first man; and broke into a walk.

TRANSLATED BY TONY BARNSTONE AND WILLIS BARNSTONE

## ■ Alfonsina Storni (1892–1938)
### *Switzerland/Argentina* (poems)

TRANSLATED BY ALIKI BARNSTONE AND WILLIS BARNSTONE

Born in Sala Capriasca, Switzerland, of Italian-Swiss parents, Alfonsina
Storni lived in Argentina from the age of four. After the death of her father, she had various jobs to help support her family and worked as an actress, touring Argentina for a year. Then in 1910, she began to teach elementary school in San Juan, Argentina. During this same year, she
published her first poems and moved to Buenos Aires. In 1912, her illegitimate son was born. She supported herself and her son in Buenos Aires as a
journalist and held teaching positions in state schools. She was awarded
various prizes and, in 1923, was named professor of literature at the Normal School of Modern Languages. Then came disease. In 1935, she underwent cancer surgery for a breast tumor. In 1938, the cancer recurred and
on October 25 Alfonsina Storni walked into the ocean at Mar del Plata and
drowned. Storni's work developed from commonplace sentimental poems
with expected clichés to a poetry of surprise, ironic strength, and gloomy
vision. Indeed, she has the qualities of the Russian poet Anna Akhmatova
in combining extreme sensitivity with terrible power. Like Vladimir
Mayakovsky, she left a suicide poem that captures her various moods and
strengths. Not to be deprived of savage humor even in the midst of death,
she writes: ". . . Thank you. Oh, one request:/if he telephones again/tell
him not to keep trying for I have left. . . . "

**FURTHER READING:** Storni, Alfonsina. *The Disquiet of the Rosebush,* 1916; *Selected Poems,* 1940; *Poetry,* 1948.

## My Sister

It's ten. Evening. The room is in half light.
My sister's sleeping, her hand on her chest; although
her face is very white, her bed entirely white,
the light, as if knowing, almost doesn't show.

She sinks into the bed the way pinkish fruit
does, into the deep mattress of soft grass.
Wind brushes her breasts, lifts them resolutely
chaste, measuring seconds as they pass.

I cover her tenderly with the white spread
and keep her lovely hands safe from the air.                           1
On tiptoes I close all the doors near her bed,
leave the windows open, pull the curtain, prepare

for night. A lot of noise outside. Enough to drown
in: quarreling men, women with the juiciest
gossip. Hatred drifting upward, storekeepers shouting down    1
below. O voices, stop! Don't touch her nest.

Now my sister is weaving her silk cocoon
like a skillful worm. Her cocoon is a dream.
She weaves a pod with threads of a gold gleam.
Her life is spring. I am the summer afternoon.                          2

She has only fifteen Octobers in her eyes
and so the eyes are bright, clear, and clean.
She thinks that storks from strange lands fly unseen,
leaving blond children with small red feet. Who tries

to come in? Is it you, now, the good wind?                              2
You want to see her? Come in. But first cool
my forehead a second. Don't freeze the pool
of unwild dreams I sense in her. Undisciplined

they want to flood in and stay here, like you,
staring at that whiteness, at those tidy cheeks,                        3
those fine circles under her eyes that speak
simplicity. Wind, you would see them and, falling to

your knees, cry. If you love her at all, be good
to her, for she will flee from wounding light.
Watch your word and intention. Her soul like wood                      3
or wax is shaped, but rubbing makes a blight.

Be like that star which in the night stares at
her, whose eye is filtered through glassy thread.
That star rubs her eyelashes, turning like a cat
quiet in the sky, not to wake her in her bed.                          4

Fly, if you can, among her snowy trees.
Pity her soul! She is immaculate.
Pity her soul! I know everything, but she's
like heaven and knows nothing. Which is her fate.

## Lighthouse in the Night

The sky a black sphere,
the sea a black disk.

The lighthouse opens
its solar fan on the coast.

Spinning endlessly at night,                                    5
whom is it searching for

when the mortal heart
looks for me in my chest?

Look at the black rock
where it is nailed down.                                        10

A crow digs endlessly
but no longer bleeds.

## I Am Going to Sleep (Suicide Poem)

Teeth of flowers, hairnet of dew,
hands of herbs, you, perfect wet nurse,
prepare the earthly sheets for me
and the down quilt of weeded moss.

I am going to sleep, my nurse, put me to bed.                   5
Set a lamp at my headboard;
a constellation; whatever you like;
all are good: lower it a bit.

Leave me alone: you hear the buds breaking through . . .
a celestial foot rocks you from above                           10
and a bird traces a pattern for you

so you'll forget . . . Thank you. Oh, one request:
if he telephones again
tell him not to keep trying, for I have left . . .

# ■ Vicente Huidobro (1893–1948) *Chile* (poems)

## TRANSLATED BY PAUL BLACKBURN

Poet and theoretician of the Dada-like experimental literary movement called *Creationism,* Vicente Huidobro changed modern poetry in Spanish. Unlike Rubén Darío, who gave Spanish letters a sugary taste of "purist" French Parnassian poetry under the misnomer of modernismo, Vicente Huidobro, in the Poundian sense, gave us the new, and went further than Pound—as did the European avant-garde generally in rejecting the immediate past and turning poetic practice upside down. Octavio Paz speaks of Huidobro as the "magnificent bird," commenting: "He is everywhere and nowhere. He is the invisible oxygen of our poetry."

Huidobro was born García Fernández in Santiago, Chile. (Like his fellow Chilean poets Gabriela Mistral and Pablo Neruda, he assumed a more glamorous poetic name.) In 1916, he went to Europe and became one of the Paris school of writers, writing in both French and Spanish. He wrote poetry, plays, and novels, and even collaborated on a novel with the French avant-garde sculptor and painter Hans Arp. He was painted by the great modern painters Pablo Picasso, Robert Delaunay, and Juan Gris, who were, along with Guillaume Apollinaire, Jacques Lipchitz, Max Jacob, and Pierre Reverdy, his friends. He invented, or claimed to invent, Creationism and spent much of his latter life writing manifestos about and lecturing on Creationism. He also feuded with fellow writers about his doctrine in Europe, and, on his triumphant return to Chile in 1933, he feuded with the Chilean poet Pablo Neruda.

In Creationism, words radically create their own realities, which then clash and interact with other realities. Huidobro's Creationism—with its revolutionary, spoofing, radically unreferential symbolism and unpunctuated typography borrowed from Apollinaire—lies somewhere in the frame of the many similar experimental movements of Dadaism, Spanish *ultraísmo,* and surrealism. The poet in parachutes, as he describes himself in *Altazor,* goes to every extreme, breaks every rule and convention, and attempts a visionary transcendence in his parachute, which falls and rises at the same time. His literary monument is the book *Altazor.* In his very last years of seclusion near Cartegena on the coast of Chile, he wrote simple and moving verses—one might say wisdom poems about death—but always with the humor, irony, and outrageous imagery that pervade his poetry.

Huidobro's American editor David Guss describes the poet as the "animist, looking for God in trees and waves. The 'magician' imploring us to fly with him. The 'antipoet' giving us a new language. The one of the endless hunger 'to be the first free man, the first to break all the chains.'" The notion of chance, experiment, and buoyant faith in futurity is all contained in one line from Vicente Huidobro's 1925 *Manifestos,* "The wind points my flute toward the future."

**FURTHER READING:** Huidobro, Vincente. *Altazor,* 1931; *Complete Works,* 1964; *The Selected Poetry of Vicente Huidobro.* Translated by David M. Guss, 1981.

## Glances and Souvenirs

      The sea
raising the sighs of travellers
runs in behind its waves swept by the wind
Infinity looks for a gull to hold aloft
one point of support, smooth and logical.        *5*
As we shall do

The sky clacks full of the wings it loves
        while I
look for my poem on foot
A star crunches like the wheel of        *10*
a car carrying away
the last souvenirs.

      Nothing will be encountered
The well of things lost will never be filled, never
with the glances and the echoes        *15*
      which move away
      above the fog
        and its great beasts.

## ▪ Miguel Angel Asturias (1899–1974)
### Guatemala (story)

TRANSLATED BY HARDIE ST. MARTIN

    Born in Guatemala and raised in the nightmarish times of dictator Estrada Cabrera, Miguel Angel Asturias went to London and Paris to study and there discovered Maya literature. He translated the Maya *Popol Vuh* into Spanish; Paul Valéry wrote the preface for his *Legends of Guatemala* (1930). He worked as a journalist, joined the diplomatic corps, and eventually was ambassador to El Salvador and to France. *El Señor Presidente* (1946), his grand uneven work, published in Mexico, depicts the prototypical Latin American dictatorship. It initiated a series of books on the perennial Latin American dictator, including Gabriel García Márquez's *Autumn of the Patriarch* (1975). Asturias's master political novel was eventually translated widely and gained him world fame. In his highly praised second novel, *Man of Maize* (1949), Asturias brings Maya myths into a contemporary social setting. As such, he established a literary practice of resurrecting dramatic tales of Indian culture; years later, his Mexican neighbor, Carlos Fuentes, elaborated a tale of fearful mystery of the Maya rain-god in his story "Chac-Mool." A prolific writer in many genres, including children's books, for many years Miguel Angel Asturias was a dominant figure in Latin American fiction. One of his last works was *The Bejeweled Boy* (tr. 1972), an allusive novel, mystical and rich in Guatemalan legend. His short stories appear in *A Week-end in Guatemala* (1956). He was awarded the Nobel Prize in 1967. He died in Madrid in 1974.

**FURTHER READING:** Asturias, Miguel Angel. *El Señor Presidente,* 1946, tr. 1963; *Man of Maize,* 1949; *Strong Wind,* 1950, tr. 1968; *The Green Pope,* 1954, tr. 1971; *The Eyes of the Interred,* 1955, tr. 1973; *A Week-end in Guatemala,* 1956; *The Bejeweled Boy,* tr. 1972.

# Legend of "El Cadejo"

*And El Cadejo, who steals girls with long braids and knots the manes of horses, makes his appearance in the valley.*

In the course of time, Mother Elvira of St. Francis, abbess of the monastery of St. Catherine, would be the novice who cut out the hosts in the convent of the Conception, a girl noted for her beauty and manner of speaking, so ingenuous that on her lips the word was a flower of gentleness and love.

From a large window without glass, the novice used to watch the flights of leaves dried by the summer's heat, the trees putting on their flowers and ripe fruit dropping in the orchards next to the convent, through the part that was in ruins, where the foliage, hiding the wounded walls and the open roofs, transformed the cells and the cloisters into paradises filled with the scent of *búcaro* clay and wild roses; bowers of feasting, as the chroniclers recorded, where nuns were replaced by pigeons with pink feet and their canticles by the warble of the cimarron mockingbird.

Outside her window, in the collapsed rooms, the warm shade, where butterflies worked the dust of their wings into silk, joined the silence of the courtyard, interrupted by the coming and going of the lizards, and the soft aroma of the leaves that multiplied the tender feelings of the trees whose roots were coiled into the very ancient walls.

And inside, in the sweet company of God, trimming the peel from the fruit of angels to disclose the meat and seed that is the Body of Christ, long as the orange's medulla—*vere tu es Deus absconditus!*—, Elvira of St. Francis reunited her spirit and her flesh to the house of her childhood, with its heavy locks and its light roses, its doors that split sobs into the loose seams of the wind, its walls reflected in the troughs of the fountains like clouds of breath on clean glass.

The voices of the city broke the peace of her window: last-minute blues of the passenger that hears the movement of the port at sailing time; a man's laughter as he brings his galloping horse to a stop, a cart wheeling by, or a child crying.

Horse, cart, man, child passed before her eyes, evoked in country settings, under skies whose tranquil appearance put under a spell the wise eyes of the fountain troughs sitting around the water with the long-suffering air of old women servants.

And the images were accompanied by odors. The sky smelled like a sky, the child like a child, the fields like fields, the cart like hay, the horse like an old rosebush, the man like a saint, the troughs like shadows, the shadows like Sunday rest and the Lord's day of rest like fresh washing. . . .

Dark was coming on. The shadows erased their thought, luminous mixture of dust particles swimming in a shaft of sunlight. The bells drew their lips towards the cup of evening without a sound. Who talks of kisses? The wind shook up the heliotropes. Heliotropes or hippocampi? And the hummingbirds quenched their desire for God in streams of flowers. Who talks of kisses?

The tap of heels hurrying brought her to herself. Their sound frilled along the corridor like drumsticks.

Could she be hearing right? Could it be the man with the long eyelashes who came by late on Fridays for the hosts to take them nine towns away from there, to the Valley of the Virgin, where a pleasant hermitage rested on a hill's top?

They called him the poppy-man. The wind moved in his feet. When the sound of his goat's footsteps stopped, there he would be, like a ghost: hat in hand, tiny boots, a goldish color, wrapped in his blue greatcoat; and he waited for the wafer boxes in the doorway.

Yes, it was he; but this time he rushed in looking very frightened, as if to prevent some catastrophe.

"Miss, oh miss!" he came in shouting, "they're going to cut off your hair! They're going to cut it off!"

When she saw him coming in, livid and elastic, the novice sprang to her feet intending to reach the door. But, wearing shoes she had charitably inherited from a paralytic nun who had worn them in life, when she heard his shout, she felt as if the nun who had spent her life motionless had stepped on her feet, and she couldn't move a step. . . .

. . . A sob, like a star, trembled in her throat. Birds scissored the twilight among the grey, crippled ruins. Two giant eucalyptus trees were saying prayers of penance.

Bound to the feet of a corpse, unable to move, she wept disconsolately, swallowing her tears silently as sick people whose organs begin to dry up and turn cold, bit by bit. She felt as if she were dead, covered with dirt; she felt that in her grave—her orphan's dress being filled with clay—rosebushes of white words bloomed and, little by little, her dismay changed into a quiet sort of happiness. Walking rosebushes, the nuns were cutting off one another's roses to dress the altars of the Virgin and the roses became the month of May, a spider web of fragrances that trapped Our Lady like a fly of light.

But the sensation of her body's flowering after death was a shortlived happiness.

Like a kite that suddenly runs out of string among the clouds, the weight of her braid pulled her headlong, with all her clothes, into hell. The mystery was in her braid. Sum of anguished instants. She lost consciousness for as long as a couple of her sighs lasted and felt herself back on earth only when she had almost reached the boiling pit where devils bubble. A fan of possible realities opened around her: the night sweetened with puff paste, pine trees that smell like altars, the pollen of life in the hair of the air, formless, colorless cat that scratches the waters of the fountain troughs and unsettles old papers.

The window and she herself became filled with heaven. . . .

"Miss, when I receive Holy Communion, God tastes like your hands!" the one in the greatcoat whispered, laying the grille of his lashes over the coals of his eyes.

The novice pulled her hands away from the hosts when she heard the blasphemy. No, it wasn't a dream! Then she touched her arms, her shoulders, her neck, her face, her braid. She held her breath one moment, long as a century, when she felt her braid. No, it wasn't a dream! Under the warm handful of hair she came alive, aware of her womanly charms, accompanied in her diabolic nuptials by the poppy-man and a candle burning at the end of the room, oblong as a coffin. The light supported the impossible reality of the lover, who stretched out his arms like a Christ who had turned into a bat in a viaticum, and this was her own flesh! She closed her eyes to escape, wrapped in her blindness, from that vision from hell, from the man who caressed her down to where she was a woman, simply by being a man—the most abominable of conscupiscences!—; but as soon as she lowered her round pale eyelids the paralytic nun seemed to step from her shoes, soaked in tears, and she quickly opened them. She tore through the darkness, opened her eyes, left their deep interior with their pupils restless as mice in a trap, wild, insensible, the color drained out of her cheeks, caught between the stertor of a strange agony she carried in her feet and her braid's stream of live coals twisted like an invisible flame on her back.

And that's the last she knew about it. Like someone under a spell that can't be broken, with a sob on her tongue which seemed to be filled with poison, like her heart, she broke away from the presence of the corpse and the man, half mad, spilling the wafers about, in search of her scissors and, finding them, she cut off the braid and, free of the spell, she fled in search of the sure refuge of the Mother Superior, no longer feeling the nun's feet on hers. . . .

But when the braid fell it was no longer a braid: it moved, undulated over the tiny mattress of hosts scattered on the floor.

The poppy-man turned to look for light. Tears quivered on his eyelashes like the last little flames on the black of the match that is about to go out. He slid along the side of the wall with bated breath, without disturbing the shadows, without making a sound, desperate to reach the flame he believed would be his salvation. But his measured step soon dissolved into a flight of fear. The headless reptile was moving past the sacred leaf-pile of hosts and filing towards him. It dragged itself right under his feet like the black blood of a dead animal and suddenly, as he was about to take hold of the light, leaped with the speed of water that runs free and light to coil itself like a whip around the candle which it caused to weep until it consumed itself for the soul of him who was being extinguished, along with it, forever. And so the poppy-man, for whom cactus plants still weep white tears, reached eternity.

The devil had passed like a breath through the braid which fell lifeless on the floor when the candle's flame went out.

And at midnight, changed into a long animal—twice as long as a ram by full moon, big as a weeping willow by new moon—with goat's hoofs, rabbit's ears and a bat's face, the poppy-man dragged down to hell the black braid of the novice who, in the course of time, would be Mother Elvira of St. Francis—that's how "El Cadejo" was born—while, on her knees in her cell, smiling like an angel, she dreamed of the lily and the mystic lamb.

## ■ Jorge Luis Borges (1899–1986) *Argentina* (parables, stories, poems)

Author of stories, poems, and essays, the great writer Jorge Luis Borges was born in Buenos Aires into a family whose ancestors included military heroes of Argentina's independence. His father Jorge Guillermo Borges, however, was a gentle academic and the young boy grew up in the "paradise" of his father's ample personal library. He learned English natively from his paternal grandmother Fanny Haslin, who was from Northumberland in England. As a child, he knew he was to be a writer, and at seven and eight he was rewriting Greek mythology in English and composing his own stories; at nine he published a translation of Oscar Wilde's fairy tale "The Happy Prince." His father retired from teaching because of failing eyesight (a problem his son was to inherit), and, in 1914, he moved the family to Geneva where the younger Borges learned French and eventually German. His first publication was in French. In Geneva, Borges discovered "modern poetry" through Walt Whitman, whom he first encountered in German translation; Whitman, whom he later translated into Spanish, was to be a decisive influence in his poetry. He also developed his lifelong passion for the writings of the German philosopher Schopenhauer (1788–1860); Borges's metaphysical orientation and his meditations on time, being, and the "other" are related to his readings of

Schopenhauer as well as to other philosophers, such as Baruch Spinoza (1632–1677), the reading of whose works became, to use his words, "his habit."

In 1919, the family moved to Spain where Borges, now twenty-one, became an active initiator of the avant-garde poetic movement of *ultraismo*. When he returned to Argentina two years later, after seven formative years in Europe, he left *ultraismo* and discovered his native city of Buenos Aires, which he documents in the poems of *Fervor of Buenos Aires* (1923). During the next decade, he met and collaborated with Victoria Ocampo, who had founded the famous literary review *Sur* (*South*), and for which he wrote book and film reviews and poems, edited manuscripts, and did translations. Borges was the first to translate into Spanish a volume of the stories of Franz Kafka, with whom he had a spiritual and literary affinity. He wrote seminal essays, which often read like philosophical fables or erudite stories, that he eventually gathered in *Other Inquisitions* (1937–1952) and in the fascinating and outrageous volume concerning "fictional historic figures," which he entitled *A Universal History of Infamy*. In 1930, he met Adolfo Bioy Casares, who would be his lifelong friend and literary partner. With Bioy Casares, he compiled original anthologies of the fantastic and also coauthored a series of comic detective books under the pseudonymn of H. Bustos Domecq.

When his father died in 1938, to earn his living, Borges became an assistant librarian in a modest public library. The same year, after hitting his head against an open stairway window and falling down the stairs, he nearly died from the subsequent septicemia that set in after a botched operation. On recovering, he wrote his first story, "El sur" ("The South"), which takes place either in the hospital under a surgeon's knife, or in the pampas during a knife fight among gauchos, or in a dream. His years in the library left him free to increase his learning, to write such stories as "The Library at Babylon," and, in the next decade, to compose most of the erudite, fantastic, and outlaw stories in *Ficciones* (1944) and *The Aleph* (1949), which were to revolutionize the Latin American and world short story.

A strong opponent of the Nazis during World War II, which was not a popular stance in the Argentina of those years, he equally opposed Juan Perón, who brought in a dictatorship (1946–1955) modeled after Mussolini's fascist blackshirts. Borges was dismissed from his library post and, by necessity, began a new career as public speaker in Buenos Aires and other cities, lecturing on his favorite ideas and literary and philosophical figures. Some of these essential talks would appear in *Seven Nights* (1977). They represent the oral or spoken Borges, who figures in the many brilliant *charlas* (chats) or dialogues, which have been gathered in books of interviews. After the fall of Perón, Borges, now virtually blind, was appointed director of the National Library and began his study of Anglo-Saxon. Then, for nearly twenty years he taught Old English at the University of Buenos Aires, traveled frequently abroad, lectured, and was in residence at various American universities, including the University of Texas, Indiana University, and Michigan State. He received honorary degrees from the leading universities of Europe and the United States. In 1961, Borges shared the First Formentor Prize with Samuel Becket, and prizes came plentifully, including the Cervantes Prize bestowed on him by Juan Carlos of Spain and knighthood from the English monarchy. He died in Geneva, Switzerland, where on his deathbed he married María Kodama, his friend and collaborator for many years.

Along with the great modernists Kafka, Joyce, and Beckett, Borges transcends academic categories. He is one of the century's most profound and influential thinkers and writers. His themes and intellectual fancy have had a deep influence on a younger generation of experimental writers and filmmakers. Julio Cortázar's experimental novel *Hopscotch* was structured on Borges's notions in "The Garden of Bifurcating Paths" of the labyrinths of language and time that go off on infinitely tangential paths. Umberto Eco's internationally best-selling novel *The Name of the Rose* shares Borges's interest in obscure religious sects, creates its own version of the labyrinthine library in Borges's "The Library of Babylon," and even models the murderer of the novel, a blind librarian, on Borges himself. Borges was more than one person, as he suggests in his famous parable "Borges and I." He is the gentle, endlessly erudite academic and jeweler of language, a narrator named Borges trapped in his own stories, the author as maker and god, and, for generations of readers and artists, a Protean figure inhabiting the labyrinths of dream.

**FURTHER READING:** Borges, Jorge Luis. *Fervor of Buenos Aires*, 1923; *Ficciones*, 1944; *The Aleph*, 1949; *Other Inquisitions*, 1960, tr. 1964; *Labyrinths*, 1960; *A Personal Anthology*, 1961. Translated by Anthony Kerrigan, 1967; *The Book of Imaginary Beings*, 1967; *In Praise of Darkness*, 1969. Translated by Norman Thomas Di Giovanni, 1973; *Selected Poems*, 1923–1967. Translated by Norman Thomas Di Giovanni, 1981; *Dr. Brodie's Report*, tr. 1972; *The Gold of the Tigers: Selected Later Poems*, 1972; *The Book of Sand*, 1975. Burgin, Richard. *Conversations with Borges*, 1969. Barnstone, Willis. *Borges at Eighty: Conversations*, 1982; *With Borges on an Ordinary Evening in Buenos Aires*, 1993. Barrenechea, A. M. *Jorge Luis Borges*, 1965. Christ, Ronald. *Jorge Luis Borges*, 1969. Alazraki, Jaime. *Jorge Luis Borges*, 1971.

## Borges and I

It's to the other man, to Borges, that things happen. I walk along the streets of Buenos Aires, stopping now and then—perhaps out of habit—to look at the arch of an old entranceway or a grillwork gate; of Borges I get news through the mail and glimpse his name among a committee of professors or in a dictionary of biography. I have a taste for hourglasses, maps, eighteenth-century typography, the roots of words, the smell of coffee, and Stevenson's prose; the other man shares these likes, but in a showy way that turns them into stagy mannerisms. It would be an exaggeration to say that we are on bad terms; I live, I let myself live, so that Borges can weave his tales and poems, and those tales and poems are my justification. It is not hard for me to admit that he has managed to write a few worthwhile pages, but these pages cannot save me, perhaps because what is good no longer belongs to anyone—not even the other man—but rather to speech or tradition. In any case, I am fated to become lost once and for all, and only some moment of myself will survive in the other man. Little by little, I have been surrendering everything to him, even though I have evidence of his stubborn habit of falsification and exaggerating. Spinoza held that all things try to keep on being themselves; a stone wants to be a stone and the tiger, a tiger. I shall remain in Borges, not in myself (if it is so that I am someone), but I recognize myself less in his books than in those of others or than in the laborious tuning of a guitar. Years ago, I tried ridding myself of him and I went from myths of the outlying slums of the city to games with time and infinity, but those games are now part of Borges and I will have to turn to other things. And so, my life is a running away, and I lose everything and everything is left to oblivion or to the other man.

Which of us is writing this page I don't know.

TRANSLATED BY ANTHONY KERRIGAN

## Kafka and His Precursors

Once I planned to make a survey of Kafka's precursors. At first I thought he was as singular as the fabulous phoenix; when I knew him better I thought I recognized his voice, or his habits, in the texts of various literatures and various ages. I shall record a few of them here, in chronological order.

The first is Zeno's paradox against movement. A moving body at A (declares Aristotle) will not be able to reach point B, because before it does, it must cover half of the distance between the two, and before that, half of the half, and before that, half of the half of the half, and so on to infinity; the formula of this famous problem is, exactly, that of *The Castle;* and the moving body and the arrow and Achilles are the first Kafkian characters in literature.

In the second text that happened to come to my attention, the affinity is not of form but rather of tone. It is an apologue by Han Yu, a prose writer of the ninth century, and it is included in the admirable *Anthologie raisonnée de la littérature chinoise* by Margouliès (1948). This is the paragraph I marked, a mysterious and tranquil one:

> It is universally admitted that the unicorn is a supernatural being and one of
> good omen; this is declared in the odes, in the annals, in the biographies of il-

*lustrious men, and in other texts of unquestioned authority. Even the women and children of the populace know that the unicorn constitutes a favorable presage. But this animal is not one of the domestic animals, it is not always easy to find, it does not lend itself to classification. It is not like the horse or the bull, the wolf or the deer. And therefore we could be in the presence of the unicorn and we would not know for certain that it was one. We know that a certain animal with a mane is a horse, and that one with horns is a bull. We do not know what the unicorn is like.*[1]

The third text proceeds from a more foreseeable source: the writings of Kierkegaard. The mental affinity of both writers is known to almost everyone; what has not yet been brought out, as far as I know, is that Kierkegaard, like Kafka, abounded in religious parables on contemporary and middle-class themes. Lowrie, in his *Kierkegaard* (Oxford University Press, 1938), mentions two. One is the story of a forger who examines Bank of England notes while under constant surveillance; in the same way, God must have been suspicious of Kierkegaard and must have entrusted him with a mission simply because He knew that he was accustomed to evil. Expeditions to the North Pole are the subject of the other. Danish clergymen had announced from their pulpits that to participate in those expeditions would be beneficial for the eternal salvation of the soul. However, they admitted that it was difficult and perhaps impossible to reach the Pole, and that not everyone could undertake such an adventure. Finally, they announced that any journey—from Denmark to London, say, by ship—or a Sunday outing in a hackney coach, was in fact a real expedition to the North Pole.

The fourth prefiguration I found is the poem "Fears and Scruples," by Browning, which was published in 1876. A man has, or thinks he has, a famous friend. He has never seen this friend, and the latter has not yet been able to help him, but he is reputed to have very noble qualities, and letters he has written are circulated. Some question his good qualities, and handwriting experts assert that the letters are apocryphal. In the last verse the man asks: "What if this friend happens to be—God?"

My notes also include two short stories. One is from the *Histoires désobligeantes*, by Léon Bloy, and tells of people who have a collection of atlases, globes, train schedules, and trunks, and then die without ever having left the town where they were born. The other is entitled "Carcassonne" and is by Lord Dunsany. An invincible army of warriors departs from an enormous castle, subjugates kingdoms, sees monsters, conquers deserts and mountains, but never arrives at Carcassonne, although the men catch sight of the city once from afar. (This story is the exact opposite of the other one; in the first story, a city is never departed from; in the second, a city is never reached.)

---

1. The failure to recognize the sacred animal and its opprobrious or casual death at the hands of the populace are traditional themes in Chinese literature. See the last chapter of Jung's *Psychologie und Alchemie* (Zurich, 1944), which includes two curious illustrations.

If I am not mistaken, the heterogeneous selections I have mentioned resemble Kafka's work: if I am not mistaken, not all of them resemble each other, and this fact is the significant one. Kafka's idiosyncrasy, in greater or lesser degree, is present in each of these writings, but if Kafka had not written we would not perceive it; that is to say, it would not exist. The poem "Fears and Scruples" by Robert Browning is like a prophecy of Kafka's stories, but our reading of Kafka refines and changes our reading of the poem perceptibly. Browning did not read it as we read it now. The word "precursor" is indispensable in the vocabulary of criticism, but one should try to purify it from every connotation of polemic or rivalry. The fact is that each writer *creates* his precursors. His work modifies our conception of the past, as it will modify the future.[2] In this correlation the identity or plurality of men matters not at all. The first Kafka of *Betrachtung* is less a precursor of the Kafka of the shadowy myths and atrocious institutions than is Browning or Lord Dunsany.

TRANSLATED BY RUTH L. C. SIMMS

## *The South*

The man who landed in Buenos Aires in 1871 bore the name of Johannes Dahlmann and he was a minister in the Evangelical Church. In 1939, one of his grandchildren, Juan Dahlmann, was secretary of a municipal library on Calle Córdoba, and he considered himself profoundly Argentinian. His maternal grandfather had been that Francisco Flores, of the Second Line-Infantry Division, who had died on the frontier of Buenos Aires, run through with a lance by Indians from Catriel; in the discord inherent between his two lines of descent, Juan Dahlmann (perhaps driven to it by his Germanic blood) chose the line represented by his romantic ancestor, his ancestor of the romantic death. An old sword, a leather frame containing the daguerreotype of a blank-faced man with a beard, the dash and grace of certain music, the familiar strophes of *Martín Fierro*, the passing years, boredom and solitude, all went to foster this voluntary, but never ostentatious nationalism. At the cost of numerous small privations, Dahlmann had managed to save the empty shell of a ranch in the South which had belonged to the Flores family; he continually recalled the image of the balsamic eucalyptus trees and the great rose-colored house which had once been crimson. His duties, perhaps even indolence, kept him in the city. Summer after summer he contented himself with the abstract idea of possession and with the certitude that his ranch was waiting for him on a precise site in the middle of the plain. Late in February, 1939, something happened to him.

---

2. See T. S. Eliot, *Points of View* (1941), pages 25–26.

Blind to all fault, destiny can be ruthless at one's slightest distraction. Dahlmann had succeeded in acquiring, on that very afternoon, an imperfect copy of Weil's edition of *The Thousand and One Nights*. Avid to examine this find, he did not wait for the elevator but hurried up the stairs. In the obscurity, something brushed by his forehead: a bat, a bird? On the face of the woman who opened the door to him he saw horror engraved, and the hand he wiped across his face came away red with blood. The edge of a recently painted door which someone had forgotten to close had caused this wound. Dahlmann was able to fall asleep, but from the moment he awoke at dawn the savor of all things was atrociously poignant. Fever wasted him and the pictures in *The Thousand and One Nights* served to illustrate nightmares. Friends and relatives paid him visits and, with exaggerated smiles, assured him that they thought he looked fine. Dahlmann listened to them with a kind of feeble stupor and he marveled at their not knowing that he was in hell. A week, eight days passed, and they were like eight centuries. One afternoon, the usual doctor appeared, accompanied by a new doctor, and they carried him off to a sanitarium on the Calle Ecuador, for it was necessary to X-ray him. Dahlmann, in the hackney coach which bore them away, thought that he would, at last, be able to sleep in a room different from his own. He felt happy and communicative. When he arrived at his destination, they undressed him, shaved his head, bound him with metal fastenings to a stretcher; they shone bright lights on him until he was blind and dizzy, auscultated him, and a masked man stuck a needle into his arm. He awoke with a feeling of nausea, covered with a bandage, in a cell with something of a well about it; in the days and nights which followed the operation he came to realize that he had merely been, up until then, in a suburb of hell. Ice in his mouth did not leave the least trace of freshness. During these days Dahlmann hated himself in minute detail: he hated his identity, his bodily necessities, his humiliation, the beard which bristled upon his face. He stoically endured the curative measures, which were painful, but when the surgeon told him he had been on the point of death from septicemia, Dahlmann dissolved in tears of self-pity for his fate. Physical wretchedness and the incessant anticipation of horrible nights had not allowed him time to think of anything so abstract as death. On another day, the surgeon told him he was healing and that, very soon, he would be able to go to his ranch for convalescence. Incredibly enough, the promised day arrived.

Reality favors symmetries and slight anachronisms: Dahlmann had arrived at the sanitarium in a hackney coach and now a hackney coach was to take him to the Constitución station. The first fresh tang of autumn, after the summer's oppressiveness, seemed like a symbol in nature of his rescue and release from fever and death. The city, at seven in the morning, had not lost that air of an old house lent it by the night; the streets seemed like long vestibules, the plazas were like patios. Dahlmann recognized the city with joy on the edge of vertigo: a second before his eyes registered the phenomena themselves, he recalled the corners, the billboards, the modest variety of Buenos Aires. In the yellow light of the new day, all things returned to him.

Every Argentine knows that the South begins at the other side of Rivadavia. Dahlmann was in the habit of saying that this was no mere convention, that whoever crosses this street enters a more ancient and sterner world. From inside the carriage he sought out, among the new buildings, the iron grille window, the brass knocker, the arched door, the entranceway, the intimate patio.

At the railroad station he noted that he still had thirty minutes. He quickly recalled that in a café on the Calle Brazil (a few dozen feet from Yrigoyen's house) there was an enormous cat which allowed itself to be caressed as if it were a disdainful divinity. He entered the café. There was the cat, asleep. He ordered a cup of coffee, slowly stirred the sugar, sipped it (this pleasure had been denied him in the clinic), and thought, as he smoothed the cat's black coat, that this contact was an illusion and that the two beings, man and cat, were as good as separated by a glass, for man lives in time, in succession, while the magical animal lives in the present, in the eternity of the instant.

Along the next to the last platform the train lay waiting. Dahlmann walked through the coaches until he found one almost empty. He arranged his baggage in the network rack. When the train started off, he took down his valise and extracted, after some hesitation, the first volume of *The Thousand and One Nights*. To travel with this book, which was so much a part of the history of his ill-fortune, was a kind of affirmation that his ill-fortune had been annulled; it was a joyous and secret defiance of the frustrated forces of evil.

Along both sides of the train the city dissipated into suburbs; this sight, and then a view of the gardens and villas, delayed the beginning of his reading. The truth was that Dahlmann read very little. The magnetized mountain and the genie who swore to kill his benefactor are—who would deny it?—marvelous, but not so much more than the morning itself and the mere fact of being. The joy of life distracted him from paying attention to Scheherazade and her superfluous miracles. Dahlmann closed his book and allowed himself to live.

Lunch—the bouillon served in shining metal bowls, as in the remote summers of childhood—was one more peaceful and rewarding delight.

*Tomorrow I'll wake up at the ranch,* he thought, and it was as if he was two men at a time: the man who traveled through the autumn day and across the geography of the fatherland, and the other one, locked up in a sanitarium and subject to methodical servitude. He saw unplastered brick houses, long and angled, timelessly watching the trains go by; he saw horsemen along the dirt roads; he saw gullies and lagoons and ranches; he saw great luminous clouds that resembled marble; and all these things were accidental, casual, like dreams of the plain. He also thought he recognized trees and crop fields; but he would not have been able to name them, for his actual knowledge of the countryside was quite inferior to his nostalgic and literary knowledge.

From time to time he slept, and his dreams were animated by the impetus of the train. The intolerable white sun of high noon had already become the yellow sun which precedes nightfall, and it would not be long before it would turn red. The railroad car was now also different; it was not the same as the one which had quit the station siding at Constitución; the plain and the hours had transfigured it. Outside, the moving shadow of the railroad car stretched toward the horizon. The elemental earth was not perturbed either by settlements or other signs of humanity. The country was vast but at the same time intimate and, in some measure, secret. The limitless country sometimes contained only a solitary bull. The solitude was perfect, perhaps hostile, and it might have occurred to Dahlmann that he was traveling into the past and not merely south. He was distracted from these considerations by the railroad inspector who, on reading his ticket, advised him that the train would not let him off at the regular station but at another: an earlier stop, one scarcely known to Dahlmann. (The man added an explanation which Dahlmann did not attempt to understand, and which he hardly heard, for the mechanism of events did not concern him.)

The train laboriously ground to a halt, practically in the middle of the plain. The station lay on the other side of the tracks; it was not much more than a siding and a shed. There was no means of conveyance to be seen, but the station chief supposed that the traveler might secure a vehicle from a general store and inn to be found some ten or twelve blocks away.

Dahlmann accepted the walk as a small adventure. The sun had already disappeared from view, but a final splendor exalted the vivid and silent plain, before the night erased its color. Less to avoid fatigue than to draw out his enjoyment of these sights, Dahlmann walked slowly, breathing in the odor of clover with sumptuous joy.

The general store at one time had been painted a deep scarlet, but the years had tempered this violent color for its own good. Something in its poor architecture recalled a steel engraving, perhaps one from an old edition of *Paul et Virginie*. A number of horses were hitched up to the paling. Once inside, Dahlmann thought he recognized the shopkeeper. Then he realized that he had been deceived by the man's resemblance to one of the male nurses in the sanitarium. When the shopkeeper heard Dahlmann's request, he said he would have the shay made up. In order to add one more event to that day and to kill time, Dahlmann decided to eat at the general store.

Some country louts, to whom Dahlmann did not at first pay any attention, were eating and drinking at one of the tables. On the floor, and hanging on to the bar, squatted an old man, immobile as an object. His years had reduced and polished him as water does a stone or the generations of men do a sentence. He was dark, dried up, diminutive, and seemed outside time, situated in eternity. Dahlmann noted with satisfaction the kerchief, the thick poncho, the long *chiripá*, and the colt boots, and told himself, as he recalled futile discussions with people from the Northern counties or from the province of Entre Rios, that gauchos like this no longer existed outside the South.

Dahlmann sat down next to the window. The darkness began overcoming the plain, but the odor and sound of the earth penetrated the iron bars of the window. The shop owner brought him sardines, followed by some roast meat. Dahlmann washed the meal down with several glasses of red wine. Idling, he relished the tart savor of the wine, and let his gaze, now grown somewhat drowsy, wander over the shop. A kerosene lamp hung from a beam. There were three customers at the other table: two of them appeared to be farm workers; the third man, whose features hinted at Chinese blood, was drinking with his hat on. Of a sudden, Dahlmann felt something brush lightly against his face. Next to the heavy glass of turbid wine, upon one of the stripes in the tablecloth, lay a spit ball of breadcrumb. That was all: but someone had thrown it there.

The men at the other table seemed totally cut off from him. Perplexed, Dahlmann decided that nothing had happened, and he opened the volume of *The Thousand and One Nights*, by way of suppressing reality. After a few moments another little ball landed on his table, and now the peones laughed outright. Dahlmann said to himself that he was not frightened, but he reasoned that it would be a major blunder if he, a convalescent, were to allow himself to be dragged by strangers into some chaotic quarrel. He determined to leave, and had already gotten to his feet when the owner came up and exhorted him in an alarmed voice:

"*Señor* Dahlmann, don't pay any attention to those lads; they're half high."

Dahlmann was not surprised to learn that the other man, now, knew his name. But he felt that these conciliatory words served only to aggravate the situation. Previously to this moment, the *peones'* provocation was directed against an unknown face, against no one in particular, almost against no one at all. Now it was an attack against him, against his name, and his neighbors knew it. Dahlmann pushed the owner aside, confronted the *peones,* and demanded to know what they wanted of him.

The tough with the Chinese look staggered heavily to his feet. Almost in Juan Dahlmann's face he shouted insults, as if he had been a long way off. His game was to exaggerate his drunkenness, and this extravagance constituted a ferocious mockery. Between curses and obscenities, he threw a long knife into the air, followed it with his eyes, caught and juggled it, and challenged Dahlmann to a knife fight. The owner objected in a tremulous voice, pointing out that Dahlmann was unarmed. At this point, something unforeseeable occurred.

From a corner of the room, the old ecstatic gaucho—in whom Dahlmann saw a summary and cipher of the South (his South)—threw him a naked dagger, which landed at his feet. It was as if the South had resolved that Dahlmann should accept the duel. Dahlmann bent over to pick up the dagger, and felt two things. The first, that this almost instinctive act bound him to fight. The second, that the weapon, in his torpid hand, was no defense at all, but would merely serve to justify his murder. He had once played with a poniard, like all men, but his idea of fencing and knife-play did not go further than the notion that all strokes should be directed upward, with the cutting edge held inward. *They would not have allowed such things to happen to me in the sanitarium,* he thought.

"Let's get on our way," said the other man.

They went out and if Dahlmann was without hope, he was also without fear. As he crossed the threshold, he felt that to die in a knife fight, under the open sky, and going forward to the attack, would have been a liberation, a joy, and a festive occasion, on the first night in the sanitarium, when they stuck him with the needle. He felt that if he had been able to choose, then, or to dream his death, this would have been the death he would have chosen or dreamt.

Firmly clutching his knife, which he perhaps would not know how to wield, Dahlmann went out into the plain.

TRANSLATED BY ANTHONY KERRIGAN

## Death and the Compass

*To Mandie Molina Vedia*

Of the many problems which exercised the daring perspicacity of Lönnrot none was so strange—so harshly strange, we may say—as the staggered series of bloody acts which culminated at the villa of Triste-le-Roy, amid the boundless odor of the eucalypti. It is true that Erik Lönnrot did not succeed in preventing the last crime, but it is indisputable that he foresaw it. Nor did he, of course, guess the identity of Yarmolinsky's unfortunate assassin, but he did divine the secrete morphology of the vicious series as well as the participation of Red Scharlach, whose alias is Scharlach the Dandy. This criminal (as so many others) had sworn on his honor to kill Lönnrot, but the latter had never allowed himself to be intimidated. Lönnrot thought of himself as a pure thinker, an Auguste Dupin, but there was something of the adventurer in him, and even of the gamester.

The first crime occurred at the Hôtel du Nord—that high prism that dominates the estuary whose waters are the colors of the desert. To this tower (which most manifestly unites the hateful whiteness of a sanitorium, the numbered divisibility of a prison, and the general appearance of a bawdy house) on the third day of December came the delegate from Podolsk to the Third Talmudic Congress, Doctor Marcel Yarmolinsky, a man of gray beard and gray eyes. We shall never know whether the Hôtel du Nord pleased him: he accepted it with the ancient resignation which had allowed him to endure three years of war in the Carpathians and three thousand years of oppression and pogroms. He was given a sleeping room on floor R, in front of the suite which the Tetrarch of Galilee occupied not without some splendor. Yarmolinsky supped, postponed until the following day an investigation of the unknown city, arranged upon a cupboard his many books and his few possessions, and before midnight turned off the light. (Thus declared the Tetrarch's chauffeur, who slept in an adjoining room.) On the fourth, at 11:03 A.M., there was a telephone call for him from the editor of the *Yiddische Zeitung;* Doctor Yarmolinsky did not reply; he was found in his room, his face already a little dark, and his body, almost nude, beneath a large anachronistic cape. He was lying not far from the door which gave onto the corridor; a deep stab wound had split open his breast. In the same room, a couple of hours later, in the midst of journalists, photographers, and police, Commissioner Treviranus and Lönnrot were discussing the problem with equanimity.

"There's no need to look for a Chimera, or a cat with three legs," Treviranus was saying as he brandished an imperious cigar. "We all know that the Tetrarch of Galilee is the possessor of the finest sapphires in the world. Someone, intending to steal them, came in here by mistake. Yarmolinsky got up; the robber had to kill him. What do you think?"

"It's possible, but not interesting," Lönnrot answered. "You will reply that reality hasn't the slightest need to be of interest. And I'll answer you that reality may avoid the obligation to be interesting, but that hypotheses may not. In the hypothesis you have postulated, chance intervenes largely. Here lies a dead rabbi; I should prefer a purely rabbinical explanation; not the imaginary mischances of an imaginary robber."

Treviranus answered ill-humoredly:

"I am not interested in rabbinical explanations; I am interested in the capture of the man who stabbed this unknown person."

"Not so unknown," corrected Lönnrot. "Here are his complete works." He indicated a line of tall volumes: *A Vindication of the Cabala; An Examination of the Philosophy of Robert Fludd;* a literal translation of the *Sepher Yezirah; a Biography of the Baal Shem;* a *History of the Sect of the Hasidim;* a monograph (in German) on the Tetragrammaton; another, on the divine nomenclature of the Pentateuch. The Commissioner gazed at them with suspicion, almost with revulsion. Then he fell to laughing.

"I'm only a poor Christian," he replied. "Carry off all these moth-eaten classics if you like; I haven't got time to lose in Jewish superstitions."

"Maybe this crime belongs to the history of Jewish superstitions," murmured Lönnrot.

"Like Christianity," the editor of the *Yiddische Zeitung* dared to put in. He was a myope, an atheist, and very timid.

No one answered him. One of the agents had found inserted in the small typewriter a piece of paper on which was written the following inconclusive sentence.

*The first letter of the Name has been spoken*

Lönnrot abstained from smiling. Suddenly becoming a bibliophile—or Hebraist—he directed that the dead man's books be made into a parcel, and he carried them to his office. Indifferent to the police investigation, he dedicated himself to studying them. A large octavo volume revealed to him the teachings of Israel Baal Shem-Tob, founder of the sect of the Pious; another volume, the virtues and terrors of the Tetragrammaton, which is the ineffable name of God; another, the thesis that God has a secret name, in which is epitomized (as in the crystal sphere which the Persians attribute to Alexander of Macedon) his ninth attribute, eternity—that is to say, the immediate knowledge of everything that will exist, exists, and has existed in the universe. Tradition numbers ninety-nine names of God; the Hebraists attribute this imperfect number to the magical fear of even numbers; the Hasidim reason that this hiatus indicates a hundredth name—the Absolute Name.

From this erudition he was distracted, within a few days, by the appearance of the editor of the *Yiddische Zeitung*. This man wished to talk of the assassination; Lönnrot preferred to speak of the diverse names of God. The journalist declared, in three columns, that the investigator Erik Lönnrot had dedicated himself to studying the names of God in order to "come up with" the name of the assassin. Lönnrot, habituated to the simplifications of journalism, did not become indignant. One of those shopkeepers who have found that there are buyers for every book came out with a popular edition of the *History of the Sect of the Hasidim*.

The second crime occurred on the night of the third of January, in the most deserted and empty corner of the capital's western suburbs. Toward dawn, one of the gendarmes who patrol these lonely places on horseback detected a man in a cape, lying prone in the shadow of an ancient paint shop. The hard visage seemed bathed in blood; a deep stab wound had split open his breast. On the wall, upon the yellow and red rhombs, there were some words written in chalk. The gendarme spelled them out. . . .

That afternoon Treviranus and Lönnrot made their way toward the remote scene of the crime. To the left and right of the automobile, the city disintegrated; the firmament grew larger and the houses meant less and less and a brick kiln or a poplar grove more and more. They reached their miserable destination: a final alley of rose-colored mud walls which in some way seemed to reflect the disordered setting of the sun. The dead man had already been identified. He was Daniel Simon Azevedo, a man of some fame in the ancient northern suburbs, who had risen from wagoner to political tough, only to degenerate later into a thief and even an informer. (The singular style of his death struck them as appropriate: Azevedo was the last representative of a generation of bandits who knew how to handle a dagger, but not a revolver.) The words in chalk were the following:

*The second letter of the Name has been spoken*

The third crime occurred on the night of the third of February. A little before one o'clock, the telephone rang in the office of Commissioner Treviranus. In avid secretiveness a man with a guttural voice spoke: he said his name was Ginzberg (or Ginsburg) and that he was disposed to communicate, for a reasonable remuneration, an explanation of the two sacrifices of Azevedo and Yarmolinsky. The discordant sound of whistles and horns drowned out the voice of the informer. Then the connection was cut off. Without rejecting the possibility of a hoax (it was carnival time), Treviranus checked and found he had been called from Liverpool House, a tavern on the Rue de Toulon—that dirty street where cheek by jowl are the peepshow and the milk store, the bordello and the women selling Bibles. Treviranus called back and spoke to the owner. This personage (Black Finnegan by name, an old Irish criminal who was crushed, annihilated almost, by respectability) told him that the last person to use the establishment's phone had been a lodger, a certain Gryphius, who had just gone out with some friends. Treviranus immediately went to Liverpool House, where Finnegan related the following facts. Eight days previously, Gryphius had taken a room above the saloon. He was a man of sharp features, a nebulous gray beard, shabbily clothed in black; Finnegan (who put the room to a use which Treviranus guessed) demanded a rent which was undoubtedly excessive; Gryphius immediately paid the stipulated sum. He scarcely ever went out; he dined and lunched in his room; his face was hardly known in the bar. On this particular night, he came down to telephone from Finnegan's office. A closed coupe stopped in front of the tavern. The driver did not move from his seat; several of the patrons recalled that he was wearing a bear mask. Two harlequins descended from the coupe; they were short in stature, and no one could fail to observe that they were very drunk. With a tooting of horns they burst into Finnegan's office; they embraced Gryphius, who seemed to recognize them but who replied to them coldly; they exchanged a few words in Yiddish—he, in a low guttural voice; they, in shrill, falsetto tones—and then the party climbed to the upstairs room. Within a quarter hour the three descended, very joyous; Gryphius, staggering, seemed as drunk as the others. He walked—tall, dazed—in the middle, between the masked harlequins. (One of the women in the bar remembered the yellow, red and green rhombs, the diamond designs.) Twice he stumbled; twice he was held up by the harlequins. Alongside the adjoining dock basin, whose water was rectangular, the trio got into the coupe and disappeared. From the running board, the last of the harlequins had scrawled an obscene figure and a sentence on one of the slates of the outdoor shed.

Treviranus gazed upon the sentence. It was nearly foreknowable. It read:

*The last of the letters of the Name has been spoken*

He examined, then, the small room of Gryphius-Ginzberg. On the floor was a violent star of blood; in the corners, the remains of some Hungarian-brand cigarettes; in a cabinet, a book in Latin—the *Philologus Hebraeo-Grae-cus* (1739) of Leusden—along with various manuscript notes. Treviranus studied the book with indignation and had Lönnrot summoned. The latter, without taking off his hat, began to read while the Commissioner questioned the contradictory witnesses to the possible kidnapping. At four in the morning they came out. In the tortuous Rue de Toulon, as they stepped on the dead serpentines of the dawn, Treviranus said:

"And supposing the story of this night were a sham?"

Erik Lönnrot smiled and read him with due gravity a passage (underlined) of the thirty-third dissertation of the *Philologus:*

Dies Judaeorum incipit a solis occasu
usque ad solis occasum diei sequentis.

"This means," he added, "that *the Hebrew day begins at sundown and lasts until the following sundown.*"

Treviranus attempted an irony.

"Is this fact the most worthwhile you've picked up tonight?"

"No. Of even greater value is a word Ginzberg used."

The afternoon dailies did not neglect this series of disappearances. *The Cross and the Sword* contrasted them with the admirable discipline and order of the last Eremitical Congress; Ernest Palast, writing in *The Martyr,* spoke out against "the intolerable delays in this clandestine and frugal pogrom, which has taken three months to liquidate three Jews", the *Yiddische Zeitung* rejected the terrible hypothesis of an anti-Semitic plot, "even though many discerning intellects do not admit of any other solution to the triple mystery"; the most illustrious gunman in the South, Dandy Red Scharlach, swore that in his district such crimes as these would never occur, and he accused Commissioner Franz Treviranus of criminal negligence.

On the night of March first, the Commissioner received an imposing-looking, sealed envelope. He opened it: the envelope contained a letter signed Baruj Spinoza, and a detailed plan of the city, obviously torn from a Baedeker. The letter prophesied that on the third of March there would not be a fourth crime, inasmuch as the paint shop in the West, the Tavern on the Rue de Toulon and the Hôtel du Nord were the "perfect vertices of an equilateral and mystic triangle"; the regularity of this triangle was made clear on the map with red ink. This argument, *more geometrico,* Treviranus read with resignation, and sent the letter and map on to Lönnrot—who deserved such a piece of insanity.

Erik Lönnrot studied the documents. The three sites were in fact equidistant. Symmetry in time (the third of December, the third of January, the third of February); symmetry in space as well. . . . Of a sudden he sensed he was about to decipher the mystery. A set of calipers and a compass completed his sudden intuition. He smiled, pronounced the word "Tetragrammaton" (of recent acquisition), and called the Commissioner on the telephone. He told him:

"Thank you for the equilateral triangle you sent me last night. It has enabled me to solve the problem. Tomorrow, Friday, the criminals will be in jail, we can rest assured."

"In that case, they're not planning a fourth crime?"

"Precisely because they *are* planning a fourth crime can we rest assured."

Lönnrot hung up. An hour later he was traveling in one of the trains of the Southern Railways, en route to the abandoned villa of Triste-le-Roy. South of the city of our story there flows a blind little river filled with muddy water made disgraceful by floating scraps and garbage. On the further side is a manufacturing suburb where, under the protection of a chief from Barcelona, gunmen flourish. Lönnrot smiled to himself to think that the most famous of them—Red Scharlach—would have given anything to know of this clandestine visit. Azevedo had been a comrade of Scharlach's; Lönnrot considered the remote possibility that the fourth victim might be Scharlach himself. Then, he put aside the thought. . . . He had virtually deciphered the problem; the mere circumstances, or the reality (names, prison records, faces, judicial and penal proceedings), scarcely interested him now. Most of all he wanted to take a stroll, to relax from three months of sedentary investigation. He reflected on how the explanation of the crimes lay in an anonymous triangle and a dust-laden Greek word. The mystery seemed to him almost crystalline now; he was mortified to have dedicated a hundred days to it.

The train stopped at a silent loading platform. Lönnrot descended. It was one of those deserted afternoons which seem like dawn. The air over the muddy plain was damp and cold. Lönnrot set off across the fields. He saw dogs, he saw a wagon on a dead road, he saw the horizon, he saw a silvery horse drinking the crapulous water of a puddle. Dusk was falling when he saw the rectangular belvedere of the villa of Triste-le-Roy, almost as tall as the black eucalypti which surrounded it. He thought of the fact that only one more dawn and one more nightfall (an ancient splendor in the east, and another in the west) separated him from the hour so much desired by the seekers of the Name.

A rust colored wrought-iron fence defined the irregular perimeter of the villa. The main gate was closed. Without much expectation of entering, Lönnrot made a complete circuit. In front of the insurmountable gate once again, he put his hand between the bars almost mechanically and chanced upon the bolt. The creaking of the iron surprised him. With laborious passivity the entire gate gave way.

Lönnrot advanced among the eucalypti, stepping amidst confused generations of rigid, broken leaves. Close up, the house on the estate of Triste-le-Roy was seen to abound in superfluous symmetries and in maniacal repetitions: a glacial Diana in one lugubrious niche was complemented by another Diana in another niche; one balcony was repeated by another balcony; double steps of stairs opened into a double balustrade. A two-faced Hermes cast a monstrous shadow. Lönnrot circled the house as he had the estate. He examined everything; beneath the level of the terrace he noticed a narrow shutter door.

He pushed against it: some marble steps descended to a vault. Versed now in the architect's preferences, Lönnrot divined that there would be a set of stairs on the opposite wall. He found them, ascended, raised his hands, and pushed up a trap door.

The diffusion of light guided him to a window. He opened it: a round, yellow moon outlined two stopped-up fountains in the melancholy garden. Lönnrot explored the house. He traveled through antechambers and galleries to emerge upon duplicate patios; several times he emerged upon the same patio. He ascended dust-covered stairways and came out into circular antechambers; he was infinitely reflected in opposing mirrors; he grew weary of opening or half-opening windows which revealed the same desolate garden outside, from various heights and various angles; inside, the furniture was wrapped in yellow covers and the chandeliers bound up with cretonne. A bedroom detained him; in the bedroom, a single rose in a porcelain vase—at the first touch the ancient petals fell apart. On the second floor, on the top story, the house seemed to be infinite and growing. *The house is not this large,* he thought. *It is only made larger by the penumbra, the symmetry, the mirrors, the years, my ignorance, the solitude.*

Going up a spiral staircase he arrived at the observatory. The evening moon shone through the rhomboid diamonds of the windows, which were yellow, red and green. He was brought to a halt by a stunning and dizzying recollection.

Two men of short stature, ferocious and stocky, hurled themselves upon him and took his weapon. Another man, very tall, saluted him gravely, and said:

"You are very thoughtful. You've saved us a night and a day."

It was Red Scharlach. His men manacled Lönnrot's hands. Lönnrot at length found his voice.

"Are you looking for the Secret Name, Scharlach?"

Scharlach remained standing, indifferent. He had not participated in the short struggle; he scarcely stretched out his hand to receive Lönnrot's revolver. He spoke; in his voice Lönnrot detected a fatigued triumph, a hatred the size of the universe, a sadness no smaller than that hatred.

"No," answered Scharlach. "I am looking for something more ephemeral and slippery, I am looking for Erik Lönnrot. Three years ago, in a gambling house on the Rue de Toulon, you arrested my brother and had him sent to prison. In the exchange of shots that night my men got me away in a coupe, with a police bullet in my chest. Nine days and nine nights I lay dying in this desolate, symmetrical villa; I was racked with fever, and the odious double-faced Janus who gazes toward the twilights of dusk and dawn terrorized my dreams and my waking. I learned to abominate my body, I came to feel that two eyes, two hands, two lungs are as monstrous as two faces. An Irishman attempted to convert me to the faith of Jesus; he repeated to me that famous axiom of the *goyim:* All roads lead to Rome. At night, my delirium nurtured itself on this metaphor: I sensed that the world was a labyrinth, from which it was impossible to flee, for all paths, whether they seemed to lead north or south, actually led to Rome, which was also the quadrilateral jail where my brother was dying and the villa of Triste-le-Roy. During those nights I swore by the god who sees from two faces, and by all the gods of fever and of mirrors, to weave a labyrinth around the man who had imprisoned my brother. I have woven it, and it holds: the materials are a dead writer on heresies, a compass, an eighteenth-century sect, a Greek word, a dagger, the rhombs of a paint shop.

"The first objective in the sequence was given me by chance. I had made plans with some colleagues—among them, Daniel Azevedo—to take the Tetrarch's sapphires. Azevedo betrayed us; with the money we advanced him he got himself inebriated and started on the job a day early. In the vastness of the hotel he got lost; at two in the morning he blundered into Yarmolinsky's room. The latter, harassed by insomnia, had set himself to writing. He was editing some notes, apparently, or writing an article on the Name of God; he had just written the words *The first letter of the Name has been spoken.* Azevedo enjoined him to be quiet; Yarmolinsky reached out his hand for the bell which would arouse all the hotel's forces; Azevedo at once stabbed him in the chest. It was almost a reflex action: half a century of violence had taught him that it was easiest and surest to kill. . . . Ten days later, I learned through the *Yiddische Zeitung* that you were perusing the writings of Yarmolinsky for the key to his death. For my part I read the *History of the Sect of the Hasidim;* I learned that the reverent fear of pronouncing the Name of God had given rise to the doctrine that this Name is all-powerful and mystic. I learned that some Hasidim, in search of this secret Name, had gone as far as to offer human sacrifices. . . . I knew you would conjecture that the Hasidim had sacrificed the rabbi; I set myself to justifying this conjecture.

"Marcel Yarmolinsky died on the night of December third; for the second sacrifice I selected the night of January third. Yarmolinsky died in the North; for the second sacrifice a place in the West was preferable. Daniel Azevedo was the inevitable victim. He deserved death: he was an impulsive person, a traitor; his capture could destroy the entire plan. One of our men stabbed him; in order to link his corpse to the other one I wrote on the paint shop diamonds *The second letter of the Name has been spoken.*

"The third 'crime' was produced on the third of February. It was as Treviranus must have guessed, a mere mockery, a simulacrum. I am Gryphius-Ginzberg-Ginsburg; I endured an interminable week (filled out with a tenuous false beard) in that perverse cubicle on the Rue de Toulon, until my friends spirited me away. From the running board one of them wrote on a pillar *The last of the letters of the Name has been spoken.* This sentence revealed that the series of crimes was *triple.* And the public thus understood it; nevertheless, I interspersed repeated signs that would allow you, Erik Lönnrot, the reasoner, to understand that it is *quadruple.* A portent in the North, others in the East and West, demand a fourth portent in the South; the Tetragrammaton—the name of God, JHVH—is made up of four letters; the harlequins and the paint shop sign suggested *four* points. In the manual of Leusden I underlined a certain passage: it manifested that the Hebrews calculate a day counting from dusk to dusk and that therefore the deaths occurred on the *fourth* day of each month. To Trevi-ranus I sent the equilateral triangle. I sensed that you would supply the missing point. The point which would form a perfect rhomb, the point which fixes where death, exactly, awaits you. In order to attract you I have premeditated everything, Erik Lönnrot, so as to draw you to the solitude of Triste-le-Roy."

Lönnrot avoided Scharlach's eyes. He was looking at the trees and the sky divided into rhombs of turbid yellow, green and red. He felt a little cold, and felt, too, an impersonal, almost anonymous sadness. It was al-ready night; from the dusty garden arose the useless cry of a bird. For the last time, Lönnrot considered the problem of symmetrical and periodic death.

"In your labyrinth there are three lines too many," he said at last. "I know of a Greek labyrinth which is a single straight line. Along this line so many philosophers have lost themselves that a mere detective might well do so too. Scharlach, when, in some other incarnation you hunt me, feign to commit (or do commit) a crime at A, then a second crime at B, eight kilometers from A, then a third crime at C, four kilometers from A and B, halfway enroute between the two. Wait for me later at D, two kilometers from A and C, halfway, once again, between both. Kill me at D, as you are now going to kill me at Triste-le-Roy."

"The next time I kill you," said Scharlach, "I promise you the labyrinth made of the single straight line which is invisible and everlasting."

He stepped back a few paces. Then, very carefully, he fired.

TRANSLATED BY ANTHONY KERRIGAN

## Poem of the Gifts

*To María Esther Vásquez*

Let no one with tears or disapproval slight
This declaration of the majesty
Of God, who with magnificent irony
Granted me books and, at the same time, night.

He made this set of lightless eyes the lord          5
In this city of books, and they can only read
In the library of dreams where the dawns cede
These senseless paragraphs to unexplored.

Wishful longings. Futilely the day
Squanders its infinite books on them in scripts
Elusive like the elusive manuscripts
Of Alexandria, which burned away.

A king among his fountains and greenery
Is dying of hunger and thirst (the Greek relates).
I lurch from side to side, lost in the straits
Of this towering, profound, blind library.

The encyclopedia, atlas, the Orient
And the West, centuries, the dynasties,
Symbols, cosmos, the cosmogonies
Salute the walls, yet all is impotent.

Slow in my darkness, I am exploring the
Thread of twilight with my faltering cane,
I who imagined Paradise was the domain
Under the heading of a library.

Something, which surely cannot be defined
By the word *chance*, presides over these things;
Some other man controlled, in shadowy evenings,
The multitude of books. He too was blind.

Straying through the slowness of these galleries
I often feel with unclear, holy dread
That I am the other, the dead man who tread
The same steps on the same days. Which of these

Two beings, which of us is writing this poem
Of a plural I and one lone shadow? I came
To ask: what difference if one name is my name
When our curse is indivisible, a single gloom?

Groussac[1] or Borges, now I look upon
A dear world coming apart like smoldering trash,
Formless, burning to a vague, pale ash
That looks like sleep and like oblivion.

TRANSLATED BY WILLIS BARNSTONE

## The Labyrinth

Zeus, Zeus himself could not undo these nets
Of stone encircling me. My mind forgets

---

1. Groussac was the former director of the National Library and was, like Borges, blind.

The persons I have been along the way,
The hated way of monotonous walls,
Which is my fate. The galleries seem straight                    *5*
But curve furtively, forming secret circles
At the terminus of years; and the parapets
Have been worn smooth by the passage of days.
Here, in the tepid alabaster dust,
Are tracks that frighten me. The hollow air                      *10*
Of evening sometimes brings a bellowing,
Or the echo, desolate, of bellowing.
I know that hidden in the shadows there
Lurks another, whose task is to exhaust
The loneliness that braids and weaves this hell,                 *15*
To crave my blood, and to fatten on my death.
We seek each other. Oh, if only this
Were the last day of our antithesis!

TRANSLATED BY JOHN UPDIKE


## In Praise of Shadow

Old age (this is the name that others give it)
may be the time of our happiness.
The animal is dead or nearly dead.
Man and his soul remain.
I live among vague and luminous forms                            *5*
that are not yet darkness.
Buenos Aires,
which once was torn into far suburbs
facing the endless plain,
is now the cemetery of the Recoleta, the Retiro square,          *10*
the dingy streets of the Eleventh district,
and the precarious old houses
that we still call the South.
Always there were too many things in my life;
Demokritos of Abdera tore out his eyes to think;                 *15*
time has been my Demokritos.
This penumbra is slow and brings no pain;
it flows down a gentle slope
and resembles eternity.
My friends have no faces,                                        *20*
women are what they were so many years ago,
one street corner might be another,
there are no letters on the pages of books.

All this ought to unnerve me,
but it is a sweetness, a return.                                      2⁵
From the generations of texts on the earth
I have read only a few,
the ones I keep reading in memory,
reading and distorting.
From the South, the East, the West, the North,                       3(
roads converge that have led me
to my secret center.
Those roads were echoes and footsteps,
women, men, agonies, resurrections,
days and nights,                                                     3⁵
half-dreams and dreams,
every obscure instant of yesterday
and of the world's yesterdays,
the firm sword of the Dane and the moon of the Persian,
the deeds of the dead,                                               4(
shared love, words,
Emerson and snow and so many things.
Now I can forget them. I reach my center,
my algebra and my key,
my mirror,                                                           4⁵
Soon I will know who I am.

TRANSLATED BY TONY BARNSTONE AND WILLIS BARNSTONE

## The Other Tiger

I think of a tiger. Half-light exalts
The vast busy Library
And seems to set the bookshelves back;
Strong, innocent, bloodstained, fresh,
It wanders through its jungle and its morning
And prints its tracks on the muddy
Banks of a river whose name it doesn't know
(In its world there are no names or past
Or future, only a certain now)
And slips through barbaric distances,                                1(
Sniffing smells in the braided labyrinth
Out of the smell of dawn
And the delicious smell of deer;
Among the stripes of the bamboo tree
I decipher the tiger's stripes and feel                              1⁵
Its bony frame under the splendid quivering hide.

The curving seas and deserts of the planet
Futilely intervene;
From this house in a remote port
In South America I track you and dream you,                    *20*
O tiger of the Ganges's banks.

As evening fills my soul I think
The tiger addressed in my poem
Is a tiger of symbols and shadows,
A string of literary tropes                                    *25*
And scraps from the encyclopedia
And not the fatal tiger, the deadly jewel
That under the sun or changing moon
Goes on in Sumatra or Bengal fulfilling
Its rounds of love, indolence and death.                       *30*
To the tiger of symbols I oppose
The real one, with hot blood,
Decimating a herd of buffalos,
And today, August 3rd. 1959,
A deliberate shadow spreads over the grass                     *35*
Yet in the act of naming it
And conjecturing its word, it becomes
A fiction, art, and not a living beast
Among beasts roaming the earth.
We will seek a third tiger. Like                               *40*
The others it will be a shape
From my dream, a system of human words,
And not the vertebrate tiger
Which beyond mythologies
Paces the earth. I know all this,                              *45*
Yet something drives me to this vague,
Insane and ancient adventure, and I go on,
Searching through the hours of the afternoon
For the other tiger, not in the poem.

TRANSLATED BY WILLIS BARNSTONE

## A Blindman

I do not know what face looks back at me
When I look at the mirrored face, nor know
What aged man conspires in the glow
Of the glass, silent and with tired fury.
Slow in my shadow, with my hand I explore                      *5*

My invisible features. A sparkling ray
Reaches me. Glimmers of your hair are gray
Or some still gold. I say I've lost no more
Than just the useless surfaces of things.
This consolation is of great import,                    1(
A comfort had by Milton. I resort
To letters and the rose — my wonderings.
I think if I could see my face I'd soon
Know who I am on this rare afternoon.

TRANSLATED BY WILLIS BARNSTONE


## Remorse

I have committed the worst sin of all
That a man can commit. I have not been
Happy. Let the glaciers of oblivion
Drag me and mercilessly let me fall.
My parents bred and bore me for a higher
Faith in the human game of nights and days;
For earth, for air, for water, and for fire.
I let them down. I wasn't happy. My ways
Have not fulfilled their youthful hope. I gave      1(
My mind to the symmetric stubbornness
Of art, and all its webs of pettiness.
They willed me bravery. I wasn't brave.
It never leaves my side, since I began:
This shadow of having been a brooding man.

TRANSLATED BY WILLIS BARNSTONE


## Spinoza

Here in the twilight the translucent hands
Of the Jew polishing the crystal glass.
The dying afternoon is cold with bands
Of fear. Each day the afternoons all pass
The same. The hands and space of hyacinth
Paling in the confines of the ghetto walls
Barely exists for the quiet man who stalls
There, dreaming up a brilliant labyrinth.
Fame doesn't trouble him (that reflection of

Dreams in the dream of another mirror), nor love,                    *10*
The timid love women. Gone the bars,
He's free, from metaphor and myth, to sit
Polishing a stubborn lens: the infinite
Map of the One who now is all His stars.

TRANSLATED BY WILLIS BARNSTONE


## Camden, 1892

The smell of coffee and of newspapers.
Sunday and its monotony. The morning,
Some allegoric verses are adorning
The glimpsed at page, the vain pentameters
Of a contented colleague. The old man lies                    *5*
Stretched out and white in his respectable
Poor man's room. Then lazily he fills
The weary mirror with his gaze. His eyes
See a face. Unsurprised he thinks: That face
Is me. With fumbling hand he reaches out                    *10*
To touch the tangled beard and ravaged mouth.
The end is not far off. His voice declares:
I'm almost gone and yet my verses scan
Life and its splendor. I was Walt Whitman.

TRANSLATED BY WILLIS BARNSTONE


## Proteus

Before the oarsmen of Odysseus
had strained their arms against the wine dark sea,
I can divine the physiognomy
of that strange god whose name was Proteus.
He was the herdsman tending to the seas                    *5*
and had the gift of reading omens too,
but he preferred to hide the things he knew
and wove odd things into his auguries.
When urged by people he would take upon
himself a lion's shape, be a huge blaze,                    *10*
grow treelike on the shore and give out shade,

or blend—water in a wave—and be gone.
Don't shrink from Proteus the Egyptian.
You too are one, and yet are many men.

TRANSLATED BY TONY BARNSTONE

## I Am

I am a man who knows he's no less vain
than the observer on the mirror's other
side: crystal, silent, following his brother's
body or reflection (it is the same).
No other pardon and no other vengeance
than oblivion is what I see,
my silent friends. A god gave this strange key
to men to solve their hate of other men.
Time belongs to me as it does to all
and yet, in spite of wandering so far,
its labyrinth remains as singular,
as plural, harsh, distinct, as hard to solve.
No man of war, I am oblivion,
an echo, just a zero. I am no one.

TRANSLATED BY TONY BARNSTONE

## To the Mirror

Why is it you persist, incessant mirror?
Why copy me, down to the smallest gesture of my hand? Why suddenly reflect
there in the shadows? You, uncanny brother,
you are the other me that ancient Greek
spoke of. You've watched forever. From a glaze
of old and watery crystal do you gaze
at me? It's useless to be blind. You seek
me and it's worse that I can't see, can't tell;
that really is your horror, magic thing
who multiplies the cipher of our being
then sucks our blessings into your strange well.
And when I'm dead, you'll duplicate another,
another, then another, and another . . .

TRANSLATED BY TONY BARNSTONE

# ■ Cecília Meireles (1901–1964) *Brazil* (poem)

TRANSLATED BY JAMES MERRILL

Born in Rio de Janeiro, Cecília Meireles worked as a primary school teacher, librarian, journalist, and professor of comparative literature. A playwright, translator of European and Indian writers into Portuguese, and a specialist in Brazilian folklore, she was once considered one of Brazil's major poets. Unlike Bandeira and Drumond de Andrade, she never fully altered her turn-of-the-century aesthetic of romanticism and beauty into a speech of modernity. In her best poems, however, she is very good and strong, and a social or metaphysical irony underlies the work. She has been favored in English with masterful translations by Elizabeth Bishop and James Merrill.

FURTHER READING: Meireles, Cecília. *Spectres*, 1919; *Collected Works*, 1958.

## *Ballad of the Ten Casino Dancers*

Ten dancers glide
across a mirror floor.
They have thin gilt plaques on Egyptian bodies,
fingertips reddened, blue lids painted,
lift white veils naively scented,                                      5
bend yellow knees.

The ten dancers go
voiceless among customers,
hands above knives, teeth above roses,
little lamps befuddled by cigars.                                      10
Between the music and the movement flows
depravity, a flight of silken stairs.

The dancers now advance
like ten lost grasshoppers,
advance, recoil, avoiding glances                                      15
in the close room, and plucking at the din
they are so naked, you imagine
them clothed in the stuff of tears.

The ten dancers screen
their pupils under great green lashes.                                 20
Death passes tranquil as a belt around
their phosphorescent waists.
As who should bear a dead child to the ground
each bears her flesh that moves and scintillates.

Fat men watch in massive tedium
those cold, cold dancers,
pitiful serpents without appetite
who are children by daylight.
Ten anemic angles made of hollows,
melancholy embalms them.

Ten mummies in a band,
back and forth go the tired dancers.
Branch whose fragrant blossoms bend
blue, green, gold, white.
Ten mothers would weep at the sight
of those dancers hand in hand.

## ▪ Carlos Drummond de Andrade (1902– ) *Brazil* (poems)

The Brazilian poet Carlos Drummond de Andrade was brought up in
the mining district of Minas Gerais, was educated in Belo Horizonte, studied pharmacy, but earned his living as a teacher and journalist. In 1930, he
settled in Rio de Janeiro where he spent his life. A poet always with a social
eye, he is at the same time personal both in voice and interest. Understated and subtle, his difficult, elusive poems have been splendidly translated by Mark Strand and Elizabeth Bishop. In his lifetime, he was Brazil's
outstanding poet. Over the years, his reputation has continued to grow
and now, like his counterpart Fernando Pessoa in Portugal, he is esteemed
as one of the twentieth century's major poetic voices.

FURTHER READING: Drummond de Andrade, Carlos. *The People's Rose,* 1945; *Lessons
in Things,* 1962.

## *Seven-Sided Poem*

When I was born, one of the crooked
angels who live in shadow, said:
Carlos, go on! Be *gauche* in life.

The houses watch the men,
men who run after women.
If the afternoon had been blue,
there might have been less desire.

The trolley goes by full of legs:
white legs, black legs, yellow legs.

My God, why all the legs?                                        *10*
my heart asks. But my eyes
ask nothing at all.

The man behind the moustache
is serious, simple, and strong.
He hardly ever speaks.                                           *15*
He has a few, choice friends,
the man behind the spectacles and the moustache.

My God, why hast Thou forsaken me
if Thou knew'st I was not God,
if Thou knew'st that I was weak?                                 *20*

Universe, vast universe,
if I had been named Eugene
that would not be what I mean
but it would go into verse
faster.                                                          *25*

Universe, vast universe,
my heart is vaster.

I oughtn't to tell you,
but this moon
and this brandy                                                  *30*
play the devil with one's emotions.

TRANSLATED BY ELIZABETH BISHOP

## Widower's Song

At night the agony
Overtakes my soul.
I see a shadow coming,
Coming. She hugs me.

The shadow of my love                                            *5*
Who died long ago.

She hugs me gingerly
yet chains me with fire,
kisses and consoles me.

I grin. Slowly she                                               *10*
nods goodbye and walks
through the wall. I shut

the door, hearing her
clacking on the stairs.
Then nothing. Curtain.

TRANSLATED BY WILLIS BARNSTONE

## Souvenir of the Ancient World

Clara strolled in the garden with the children.
The sky was green over the grass,
the water was golden under the bridges,
other elements were blue and rose and orange,
a policeman smiled, bicycles passed,
a girl stepped onto the lawn to catch a bird,
the whole world—Germany, China—
      all was quiet around Clara.

The children looked at the sky: it was not forbidden.
Mouth, nose, eyes were open. There was no danger.
What Clara feared were the flu, the heat, the insects.
Clara feared missing the eleven o'clock trolley:
She waited for letters slow to arrive,
She couldn't always wear a new dress. But
      she strolled in the garden, in the morning!
They had gardens, they had mornings in those days!

TRANSLATED BY MARK STRAND

## Family Portrait

Yes, this family portrait
is a little dusty.
The father's face doesn't show
how much money he earned.

The uncles' hands don't reveal
the voyages both of them made.
The grandmother's smoothed and yellowed;
she's forgotten the monarchy.

The children, how they've changed.
Peter's face is tranquil,
that wore the best dreams.
And John's no longer a liar.

The garden's become fantastic.
The flowers are gray badges.

And the sand, beneath dead feet,                    *15*
is an ocean of fog.

In the semicircle of armchairs
a certain movement is noticed.
The children are changing places,
but noiselessly! it's a picture.                    *20*

Twenty years is a long time.
It can form any image.
If one face starts to wither,
another presents itself, smiling.

All these seated strangers,                          *25*
my relations? I don't believe it.
They're guests amusing themselves
in a rarely-opened parlor.

Family features remain
lost in the play of bodies.                          *30*
But there's enough to suggest
that a body is full of surprises.

The frame of this family portrait
holds its personages in vain.
They're there voluntarily,                           *35*
they'd know how—if need be—to fly.

They could refine themselves
in the room's chiaroscuro,
live inside the furniture
or the pockets of old waistcoats.                    *40*

The house has many drawers,
papers, long staircases.
When matter becomes annoyed,
who knows the malice of things?

The portrait does not reply,                         *45*
it stares; in my dusty eyes
it contemplates itself.
The living and dead relations

multiply in the glass.
I don't distinguish those                            *50*
that went away from those
that stay. I only perceive
the strange idea of family

travelling through the flesh.

TRANSLATED BY ELIZABETH BISHOP

## Song for a Young Girl's Album

Good morning: I said to the girl
who smiled from far away.
Good morning: but she didn't
respond from the distance.
Eye contact was pointless
so I waved my arms
good morning to the girl who,
day or night,
was far out of my range,
far from my poor good morning.                                    1
Good morning forever: maybe
the answer will come cold
or come late, yet
I shall wait
for her good morning.                                             1
And over the rows of houses,
over the hills and valleys,
I shall lamely repeat
at whatever hour: good morning.
Maybe the time is wrong                                           2
and my sadness too great
to warrant
this absurd good morning.
The girl does not know,
or sense, or suspect                                              2
the tenderness within
the heart of my good morning.
Good morning: I repeat
in the afternoon;
at midnight: good morning.                                        3
And at dawn
I color my day
blue and pink:
so the girl can find it!
good morning.                                                     3
Good morning: only an echo
in the bushes (but who can say)
makes out my message
or wishes me good morning.
Smiling from far away,                                            4
the girl in her joy
does not feel the violence
in the radiance of this
good morning.

Night that had betrayed                                                         *45*
sadness, trouble, confusion,
wanders without fire
in the wildest nostalgia.
If only she would say
good morning to my good morning,                                               *50*
the night would change
to the clearest of days!

TRANSLATED BY MARK STRAND

# ▪ Alejo Carpentier (1904–1980) *Cuba* (story)

TRANSLATED BY FRANCES PARTRIDGE

Born in Havana of a French father and Russian mother, in 1914, Alejo Carpentier and his family returned to Europe. In the early 1920s, he returned to Cuba to study architecture and music and threw himself into literary and political activities. While in Cuba, he helped form the Cuban Communist Party. He was arrested in 1927, and in early 1928, after forty days in jail for opposition to the Machado dictatorship, he fled to Paris, posing as the French surrealist poet who had lent him his passport. In Paris, he was immersed in French and Latin American literary ventures and ideological struggles, meeting André Breton and other surrealists through his friend Robert Desnos. He also came to know the Guatemalan political novelist Miguel Angel Asturias (who was to win the Nobel Prize in Literature in 1967). Like Asturias, who gave life to Maya legends, Carpentier discovered the Precolumbian world and determined to revivify it in avant-garde fiction. He returned to Cuba at the start of World War II where he wrote his second novel, *The Kingdom of This World* (1949), which mythologizes the times of the Haitian King Henri Christoph (reigned 1811–1820), a former slave who helped secure independence from France and used compulsary labor to build the fabulous palace of Sans Souci and the gigantic mountain-top citadel of La Ferrière. Carpentier also began writing the stories that would later be published as *The War of Time* (1958). As a professor of music at the National Conservatory, he wrote a volume on Cuban music, *La música en Cuba* (1946). He moved to Venezuela in 1946, where he wrote two more novels, and after Fidel Castro's victory in 1959, he returned to Cuba where he wrote *Explosion in a Cathedral* (1962) while working at the State Publishing House. He was posted in 1966 as cultural attaché to the Cuban embassy in Paris where he stayed until his death in 1980. An author of impeccable and imaginative craft, whose historical re-creations live between dream and brutal reality,

Carpentier is one of the most original and accomplished twentieth-century writers of fiction.

**FURTHER READING:** Carpentier, Alejo. *The Kingdom of This World,* 1949; *The Lost Steps,* 1953; *The Chase,* 1956; *The War of Time (Stories)* 1958; *Reasons of State,* 1974; *The Harp and the Shadow,* 1979.

## Like the Night

> *And he traveled like the night.*
>
> —Iliad, *Book I.*

### I

Although the headlands still lay in shadow, the sea between them was beginning to turn green when the lookout blew his conch to announce that the fifty black ships sent us by King Agamemnon had arrived. Hearing the signal, those who had been waiting for so many days on the dung-covered threshing floors began carrying the wheat toward the shore, where rollers were already being made ready so that the vessels could be brought right up to the walls of the fortress. When the keels touched the sand, there was a certain amount of wrangling with the steersmen, because the Mycenaeans had so often been told about our complete ignorance of nautical matters that they tried to keep us at a distance with their poles. Moreover, the beach was now crowded with children, who got between the soldiers' legs, hindered their movements, and scrambled up the sides of the ships to steal nuts from under the oarsmen's benches. The transparent waves of dawn were breaking amid cries, insults, tussles, and blows, and our leading citizens could not make their speeches of welcome in the middle of such pandemonium. I had been expecting something more solemn, more ceremonious, from our meeting with these men who had come to fetch us to fight for them, and I walked off, feeling somewhat disillusioned, toward the fig tree on whose thickest branch I often sat astride, gripping the wood with my knees, because it reminded me somewhat of a woman's body.

As the ships were drawn out of the water and the tops of the mountains behind began to catch the sun, my first bad impression gradually faded; it had clearly been the result of a sleepless night of waiting, and also of my having drunk too heavily the day before with the young men recently arrived on the coast from inland, who were to embark with us soon after dawn. As I watched the procession of men carrying jars, black wineskins, and baskets moving toward the ships, a warm pride swelled within me, and a sense of my superiority as a soldier. That oil, that resinated wine, and above all that wheat from which biscuits would be cooked under the cinders at night while we slept in the shelter of the wet prows in some mysterious and unknown bay on the way to the Great City of Ships—the grain that I had helped to winnow with my shovel—all these things were being put on board for me; nor need I tire my long, muscular limbs, and arms designed for handling an ashwood pile, with tasks fit only for men who knew nothing but the smell of the soil, men who looked at the earth over the sweating backs of their animals or spent their lives crouched over it, weeding, uprooting, and raking, in almost the same attitudes as their own browsing cattle. These men would never pass under the clouds that at this time of day darken the distant green islands, whence the acrid-scented silphium was brought. They would never know the wide streets of the Trojans' city, the city we were now going to surround, attack, and destroy.

For days and days, the messengers sent us by the Mycenaean king had been telling us about Priam's insolence and the sufferings that threatened our people because of the arrogant behavior of his subjects. They had been jeering at our manly way of life; and, trembling with rage, we had heard of the challenges hurled at us long-haired Achaeans by the men of Ilium although our courage is unmatched by any other race. Cries of rage were heard, fists clenched and shaken, oaths sworn with the hands palm upward, and shields thrown against the walls, when we heard of the abduction of Helen of Sparta. While wine flowed from skins into helmets, in loud voices the emissaries told us of her marvelous beauty, her noble bearing, and adorable way of walking, and described the cruelties she had endured in her miserable captivity. That same evening, when the whole town was seething with indignation, we were told that the fifty black ships were being sent. Fires were lighted in the bronze foundries while old women brought wood from the mountains.

And now, several days later, here I was gazing at the vessels drawn up at my feet, with their powerful keels and their masts at rest between the bulwarks like a man's virility between his thighs; I felt as if in some sense I was the owner of those timbers, transformed by some portentous carpentry unknown to our people into racehorses of the ocean, ready to carry us where the greatest adventure of all time was now unfolding like an epic. And I, son of a harness maker and grandson of a castrator of bulls, was to have the good fortune to go where those deeds were being done whose luster reached us in sailors' stories; I was to have the honor of seeing the walls of Troy, of following noble leaders and contributing my energy and strength to the cause of rescuing Helen of Sparta—a manly undertaking and the supreme triumph of a war that would give us prosperity, happiness, and pride in ourselves forever. I took a deep breath of the breeze blowing from the olive-covered hillside and thought how splendid it would be to die in such a just conflict, for the cause of Reason itself. But the idea of being pierced by an enemy lance made me think of my mother's grief and also of another, perhaps even profounder grief, though in this case the news would have to be heard with dry eyes because the hearer was head of the family. I walked slowly down to the town by the shepherds' path. Three kids were gamboling in the thyme-scented air. Down on the beach the loading of wheat was still going on.

# II

The impending departure of the ships was being celebrated on all sides with thrumming of guitars and clashing of cymbals. The sailors from *La Gallarda* were dancing the zarambeque with enfranchised Negresses, and singing familiar *coplas*—like the song of the *Moza del Retoño,* wherein groping hands supplied the blanks left in the words. Meanwhile the loading of wine, oil, and grain was still going on, with the help of the overseer's Indian servants, who were impatient to return to their native land. Our future chaplain was on his way to the harbor, driving before him two mules loaded with the bellows and pipes of a wooden organ. Whenever I met any of the men from the ships, there were noisy embraces, exaggerated gestures, and enough laughter and boasting to bring the women to their windows. We seemed to be men of a different race, expressly created to carry out exploits beyond the ken of the baker, the wool carder, and the merchant who hawked holland shirts embroidered by parties of nuns in their patios. In the middle of the square, their brass instruments flashing in the sun, the Captain's six trumpeters were playing popular airs while the Burgundian drummers thundered on their instruments, and a sackbut with a mouthpiece like a dragon was bellowing as if it wanted to bite.

In his shop, smelling of calfskin and Cordovan leather, my father was driving his awl into a stirrup strap with the half-heartedness of someone whose mind is elsewhere. When he saw me, he took me in his arms with serene sadness, perhaps remembering the horrible death of Cristobalillo, the companion of my youthful escapades, whom the Indians of the Dragon's Mouth had pierced with their arrows. But he knew that everyone was wild to embark for the Indies then—although most men in possession of their senses were already realizing that it was the "madness of many for the gain of a few." He spoke in praise of good craftsmanship and told me that a man could gain as much respect by carrying the harness maker's standard in the Corpus Christi procession as from dangerous exploits. He pointed out the advantages of a well-provided table, a full coffer, and a peaceful old age. But, probably having realized that the excitement in the town was steadily increasing and that my mood was not attuned to such sensible reasoning, he gently led me to the door of my mother's room.

This was the moment I had most dreaded, and I could hardly restrain my own tears when I saw hers, for we had put off telling her of my departure until everyone knew that my name had been entered in the books of the Casa de la Contratación. I thanked her for the vows she had made to the Virgin of Navigators in exchange for my speedy return, and promised her everything she asked of me, such as to have no sinful dealings with the women of those far-off countries, whom the Devil kept in a state of paradisiac nakedness in order to confuse and mislead unwary Christians, even if they were not actually corrupted by the sight of such a careless display of flesh. Then, realizing that it was useless to make demands of someone who was already dreaming of what lay beyond the horizon, my mother began asking me anxiously about the safety of the ships and the skill of their pilots. I exaggerated the solidity and seaworthiness of *La Gallarda,* declaring that her pilot was a veteran of the Indies and a comrade of Nuño García. And to distract her from her fears, I told her about the wonders of the New World, where all diseases could be cured by the Claw of the Great Beast and by bezoar stones; I told her, too, that in the country of the Omeguas there was a city built entirely of gold, so large that it would take a good walker a night and two days to cross it, and that we should surely go there unless we found our fortune in some not-yet-discovered regions inhabited by rich tribes for us to conquer. Gently shaking her head, my mother then said that travelers returned from the Indies told lying, boastful stories, and spoke of Amazons and anthropophagi, of terrible Bermudan tempests and poisoned spears that transformed into a statue anyone they pierced.

Seeing that she confronted all my hopeful remarks with unpleasant facts, I talked to her of our high-minded aims and tried to make her see the plight of all the poor idol worshippers who did not even know the sign of the Cross. We should win thousands of souls to our holy religion and carry out Christ's commandments to the Apostles. We were soldiers of God as well as soldiers of the King, and by baptizing the Indians and freeing them from their barbarous superstitions our nation would win imperishable glory and greater happiness, prosperity, and power than all the kingdoms of Europe. Soothed by my remarks, my mother hung a scapulary around my neck and gave me various ointments against the bites of poisonous creatures, at the same time making me promise that I would never go to sleep without wearing some woolen socks she had made for me herself. And as the cathedral bells began to peal, she went to look for an embroidered shawl that she wore only on very important occasions. On the way to church I noticed that in spite of everything my parents had, as it were, grown in stature because of their pride in having a son in the Captain's fleet, and that they greeted people more often and more demonstratively than usual. It is always gratifying to have a brave son on his way to fight for a splendid and just cause. I looked toward the harbor. Grain was still being carried onto the ships.

# III

I used to call her my sweetheart, although no one yet knew that we were in love. When I saw her father near the ships, I realized that she would be alone, so I followed the dreary jetty battered by the winds, splashed with green water, and edged with chains and rings green with slime until I reached the last house, the one with green shutters that were always closed. Hardly had I sounded the tarnished knocker when the door opened, and I entered the house along with a gust of wind full of sea spray. The lamps had already been lighted because of the mist. My sweetheart sat down beside me in a deep armchair covered in old brocade and rested her head on my shoulder with such a sad air of resignation that I did not dare question those beloved eyes, which seemed to be gazing at nothing, but with an air of amazement. The strange objects that filled the room now took on a new significance for me. Some link bound me to the astrolabe, the compass, and the wind rose, as well as to the sawfish hanging from the beams of the ceiling and the charts by Mercator and Ortelius spread out on either side of the fireplace among maps of the heavens populated by Bears, Dogs, and Archers.

Above the whistling of the wind as it crept under the doors, I heard the voice of my sweetheart asking how our preparations were going. Reassured to find that it was possible to talk of something other than ourselves, I told her about the Sulpicians and Recollects who were to embark with us, and praised the piety of the gentlemen and farmers chosen by the man who would take possession of these far-off countries in the name of the King of France. I told her what I knew of the great River Colbert, bordered with ancient trees draped in silvery moss, its red waters flowing majestically beneath a sky white with herons. We were taking provisions for six months. The lowest decks of the *Belle* and the *Amiable* were full of corn. We were undertaking the important task of civilizing the vast areas of forest lying between the burning Gulf of Mexico and Chicagua, and we would teach new skills to the inhabitants.

Just when I thought my sweetheart was listening most attentively to what I was saying, she suddenly sat up, and said with unexpected vehemence that there was nothing glorious about the enterprise that had set all the town bells ringing since dawn. Last night, with her eyes inflamed with weeping, her anxiety to know something about the world across the sea to which I was going had driven her to pick up Montaigne's *Essais* and read everything to do with America in the chapter on Coaches. There she had learned about the treachery of the Spaniards, and how they had succeeded in passing themselves off as gods, with their horses and bombards. Aflame with virginal indignation, my sweetheart showed me the passage in which the skeptical Bordelais says of the Indians that "we have made use of their ignorance and inexperience to draw them more easily into fraud, luxury, avarice, and all manner of inhumanity and cruelty by the example of our life and pattern of our customs." Blinded by her distress at such perfidy, this devout young woman who always wore a gold cross on her bosom actually approved of a writer who could impiously declare that the savages of the New World had no reason to exchange their religion for ours, their own having served them very well for a long time.

I realized that these errors came only from the resentment of a girl in love—and a very charming girl—against the man who was forcing her to wait for him so long merely because he wanted to make his fortune quickly in a much-proclaimed undertaking. But although I understood this, I felt deeply wounded by her scorn for my courage and her lack of interest in an adventure that would make my name famous; for the news of some exploit of mine, or of some region I had pacified, might well lead to the King's conferring a title on me, even though it might involve a few Indians dying by my hand. No great deed is achieved without a struggle, and as for our holy faith, the Word must be imposed with blood. But it was jealousy that made my sweetheart paint such an ugly picture of the island of Santo Domingo, where we were to make a landing, describing it in adorably unsuitable words as "a paradise of wicked women." It was obvious that in spite of her chastity, she knew what sort of women they were who often embarked for Cap Français from a jetty nearby under the supervision of the police and amid shouts of laughter and coarse jokes from the sailors. Someone, perhaps one of the servants, may have told her that a certain sort of abstinence is not healthy for a man, and she was imagining me beset by greater perils than the floods, storms, and water dragons that abound in American rivers, in some Eden of nudity and demoralizing heat.

In the end I began to be annoyed that we should be having this wrangle instead of the tender farewells I had expected at such a moment. I started abusing the cowardice of women, their incapacity for heroism, the way their philosophy was bounded by baby linen and workboxes, when a loud knocking announced the untimely return of her father. I jumped out of a back window, unnoticed by anyone in the marketplace, for passersby, fishermen, and drunkards—already numerous even so early in the evening—had gathered around a table on which a man stood shouting. I took him at first for a hawker trying to sell Orvieto elixir, but he turned out to be a hermit demanding the liberation of the holy places, I shrugged my shoulder and went on my way. Some time ago I had been on the point of enlisting in Foulque de Neuilly's crusade. A malignant fever—cured thanks to God and my sainted mother's ointments—most opportunely kept me shivering in bed on the day of departure: that adventure ended, as everyone knows, in a war between Christians and Christians. The crusades had fallen into disrepute. Besides, I had other things to think about.

# IV

The wind had died down. Still annoyed by my stupid quarrel with my betrothed, I went off to the harbor to look at the ships. They were all moored to the jetty, side by side, with hatches open, receiving thousands of sacks of wheat flour between their brightly camouflaged sides. The infantry regiments were slowly going up the gangways amid the shouts of stevedores, blasts from the boatswain's whistle, and signals tearing through the mist to set the cranes in motion. On the decks, shapeless objects and menacing machines were being heaped together under tarpaulins. From time to time an aluminum wing revolved slowly above the bulwarks before disappearing into the darkness of the hold. The generals' horses, suspended from webbing bands, traveled over the roofs of the shops like the horses of the Valkyries. I was standing on a high iron gangway watching the final preparations, when suddenly I became agonizingly aware that there were only a few hours left—scarcely thirteen—before I too should have to board one of those ships now being loaded with weapons for my use. Then I thought of women; of the days of abstinence lying ahead; of the sadness of dying without having once more taken my pleasure from another warm body.

Full of impatience, and still angry because I had not got even a kiss from my sweetheart, I struck off toward the house where the dancers lived. Christopher, very drunk, was already shut into his girl's room. My girl embraced me, laughing and crying, saying that she was proud of me, that I looked very handsome in my uniform, and that a fortuneteller had read the cards and told her that no harm would come to me during the Great Landing. She more than once called me a "hero," as if she knew how cruelly her flattery contrasted with my sweetheart's unjust remarks. I went out onto the roof. The lights were coming on in the town, outlining the gigantic geometry of the buildings in luminous points. Below, in the streets, was a confused swarm of heads and hats.

At this distance, it was impossible to tell women from men in the evening mist. Yet it was in order that this crowd of unknown human beings should go on existing, that I was due to make my way to the ships soon after dawn. I should plow the stormy ocean during the winter months and land on a remote shore under attack from steel and fire, in defense of my countrymen's principles. It was the last time a sword would be brandished over the maps of the West. This time we should finish off the new Teutonic Order for good and all, and advance as victors into that longed-for future when man would be reconciled with man. My mistress laid her trembling hand on my head, perhaps guessing at the nobility of my thoughts. She was naked under the half-open flaps of her dressing gown.

# V̄

I returned home a few hours before dawn, walking unsteadily from the wine with which I had tried to cheat the fatigue of a body surfeited with enjoyment of another body. I was hungry and sleepy, and at the same time deeply disturbed by the thought of my approaching departure. I laid my weapons and belt on a stool and threw myself on my bed. Then I realized, with a start of surprise, that someone was lying under the thick woolen blanket; and I was just stretching out my hand for my knife when I found myself embraced by two burning-hot arms, which clasped me around the neck like the arms of a drowning man while two inexpressibly smooth legs twined themselves between mine. I was struck dumb with astonishment when I saw that the person who had slipped into my bed was my sweetheart. Between her sobs, she told me how she had escaped in the darkness, had run away in terror from barking dogs and crept furtively through my father's garden to the window of my room. Here she had waited for me in terror and impatience. After our stupid quarrel that afternoon, she had thought of the dangers and sufferings lying in wait for me, with that sense of impotent longing to lighten a soldier's hazardous lot which women so often express by offering their own bodies, as if the sacrifice of their jealously guarded virginity at the moment of departure and without hope of enjoyment, this reckless abandonment to another's pleasure, could have the propitiatory power of ritual oblation.

There is a unique and special freshness in an encounter with a chaste body never touched by a lover's hands, a felicitious clumsiness of response, an intuitive candor that, responding to some obscure promptings, divines and adopts the attitudes that favor the closest possible physical union. As I lay in my sweetheart's arms and felt the little fleece that timidly brushed against one of my thighs, I grew more and more angry at having exhausted my strength in all-too-familiar coupling, in the absurd belief that I was ensuring my future serenity by means of present excesses. And now that I was being offered this so desirable compliance, I lay almost insensible beneath my sweetheart's tremulous and impatient body. I would not say that my youth was incapable of catching fire once again that night under the stimulus of this new pleasure. But the idea that it was a virgin who was offering herself to me, and that her closed and intact flesh would require a slow and sustained effort on my part, filled me with an obsessive fear of failure.

I pushed my sweetheart to one side, kissing her gently on the shoulders, and began telling her with assumed sincerity what a mistake it would be for our nuptial joys to be marred by the hurry of departure; how ashamed she would be if she became pregnant and how sad it was for children to grow up with no father to teach them how to get green honey out of hollow tree trunks and look for cuttlefish under stones. She listened, her large bright eyes burning in the darkness, and I was aware that she was in the grip of a resentment drawn from the underworld of the instincts and felt nothing but scorn for a man who, when offered such an opportunity, invoked reason and prudence instead of taking her by force, leaving her bleeding on the bed like a trophy of the chase, defiled, with breasts bitten, but having become a woman in her hour of defeat.

Just then we heard the lowing of cattle going to be sacrificed on the shore and the watchmen blowing their conchs. With scorn showing clearly in her face, my sweetheart got quickly out of bed without letting me touch her, and with a gesture not so much of modesty as of someone taking back what he had been on the point of selling too cheap, she covered those charms which had suddenly begun to enflame my desire. Before I could stop her, she had jumped out of the window. I saw her running away as fast as she could among the olives, and I realized in that instant that it would be easier for me to enter the city of Troy without a scratch than to regain what I had lost.

When I went down to the ships with my parents, my soldier's pride had been replaced by an intolerable sense of disgust, of inner emptiness and self-depreciation. And when the steersmen pushed the ships away from the shore with their strong poles, and the masts stood erect between the row of oarsmen, I realized that the display, excesses, and feasting that precede the departure of soldiers to the battlefield were now over. There was no time now for garlands, laurel wreaths, wine drinking in every house, envious glances from weaklings, and favors from women. Instead, our lot would consist of bugle calls, mud, rainsoaked bread, the arrogance of our leaders, blood spilled in error, the sickly, tainted smell of gangrene. I already felt less confident that my courage would contribute to the power and happiness of the long-haired Achaeans. A veteran soldier, going to war because it was his profession and with no more enthusiasm than a sheep shearer on his way to the pen, was telling anyone prepared to listen that Helen of Sparta was very happy to be in Troy, and that when she disported herself in Paris' bed, her hoarse cries of enjoyment brought blushes to the cheeks of the virgins who lived in Priam's palace. It was said that the whole story of the unhappy captivity of Leda's daughter, and of the insults and humiliations the Trojans had subjected her to, was simply war propaganda, inspired by Agamemnon with the consent of Menelaus. In fact, behind this enterprise and the noble ideals it had set up as a screen, a great many aims were concealed which would not benefit the combatants in the very least: above all, so the old soldier said, to sell more pottery, more cloth, more vases decorated with scenes from chariot races, and to open new ways of access to Asia, whose peoples had a passion for barter, and so put an end once and for all to Trojan competition.

Too heavily loaded with flour and men, the ship responded slowly to the oars. I gazed for a long time at the sunlit houses of my native town. I was nearly in tears, I took off my helmet and hid my eyes behind its crest; I had taken great trouble to make it round and smooth, like the magnificent crests of the men who could order their accouterments of war from the most highly skilled craftsmen and who were voyaging on the swiftest and longest ship.

■ **João Guimarães Rosa (1908–1967)** *Brazil* **(story)**

TRANSLATED BY BARBARA SHELBY MERELLO

A Brazilian doctor from the Minas Girais plateau, in his native state João Guimarães Rosa accumulated a knowledge of regional legends from working in libraries and long conversations with local storytellers. He transformed this material into his first collections of tales. Rosa entered the diplomatic service and was stationed in Germany, Colombia, Paris, and Rio. In 1942, while serving as the counsular attaché in Hamburg, he was interned by the Nazis after Brazil broke diplomatic relations with Germany. He was eventually released in an exchange of diplomatics. He was an extraordinary polyglot, with a fine knowledge of Russian, Japanese,

English, German, French, Latin, and Greek. He published his first collection of short stories in 1946, a difficult, extremely successful book, which effectively changed fiction writing in Brazil. The "saga" in *Sagarana* (1946) is an explicit reference to oral legendary saga, suggesting the mythical, magical yet historical basis for these interrelated tales. Guimarães's great novel is *Grande Sertão* (1956), a hypnotic narration, in the exquisite lucid language of his best tales. The Mexican novelist Juan Rulfo considered him the finest author produced by the Americas in our century. In his stories he plays with time and existence. The title of his most famous story, "The Third Bank of the River," is fascinatingly mysterious. It has many meanings as it describes the narrator's father in midstream, holding steady against the allegorical current. What is the third shore? Time, death, the planks of the boat, redemption after a new flood? The story ends, as great art often does, with an ending that is open and continuing like the river.

**FURTHER READING:** Rosa, João Guimarães. *Sagarana*, 1946; *Grande Sertao: Veredas* (*The Devil to Pay in the Backlands*), 1956; *First Tales*, 1962 (tr. as *The Third Bank of the River and Other Stories*); *Tutaméia*, 1967; *These Tales*, 1969.

## The Third Bank of the River

Father was a reliable, law-abiding, practical man, and had been ever since he was a boy, as various people of good sense testified when I asked them about him. I don't remember that he seemed any crazier or even any moodier than anyone else we knew. He just didn't talk much. It was our mother who gave the orders and scolded us every day—my sister, my brother, and me. Then one day my father ordered a canoe for himself.

He took the matter very seriously. He had the canoe made to his specifications of fine *vinhático* wood; a small one, with a narrow board in the stern as though to leave only enough room for the oarsman. Every bit of it was hand-hewn of special strong wood carefully shaped, fit to last in the water for twenty or thirty years. Mother railed at the idea. How could a man who had never fiddled away his time on such tricks propose to go fishing and hunting now, at his time of life? Father said nothing. Our house was closer to the river then than it is now, less than a quarter of a league away: there rolled the river, great, deep, and silent, always silent. It was so wide that you could hardly see the bank on the other side. I can never forget the day the canoe was ready.

Neither happy nor excited nor downcast, Father pulled his hat well down on his head and said one firm goodbye. He spoke not another word, took neither food nor other supplies, gave no parting advice. We thought Mother would have a fit, but she only blanched white, bit her lip, and said bitterly: "Go or stay; but if you go, don't you ever come back!" Father left his answer in suspense. He gave me a mild look and motioned me to go aside with him a few steps. I was afraid of Mother's anger, but I obeyed anyway, that time. The turn things had taken gave me the courage to ask: "Father, will you take me with you in that canoe?" But he just gave me a long look in return: gave me his blessing and motioned me to go back. I pretended to go, but instead turned off into a deep woodsy hollow to watch. Father stepped into the canoe, untied it, and began to paddle off. The canoe slipped away, a straight, even shadow like an alligator, slithery, long.

Our father never came back. He hadn't gone anywhere. He stuck to that stretch of the river, staying halfway across, always in the canoe, never to spring out of it, ever again. The strangeness of that truth was enough to dismay us all. What had never been before, was. Our relatives, the neighbors, and all our acquaintances met and took counsel together.

Mother, though, behaved very reasonably, with the result that everybody believed what no one wanted to put into words about our father: that he was mad. Only a few of them thought he might be keeping a vow, or — who could tell — maybe he was sick with some hideous disease like leprosy, and that was what had made him desert us to live out another life, close to his family and yet far enough away. The news spread by word of mouth, carried by people like travelers and those who lived along the banks of the river, who said of Father that he never landed at spit or cove, by day or by night, but always stuck to the river, lonely and outside human society. Finally, Mother and our relatives realized that the provisions he had hidden in the canoe must be getting low and thought that he would have to either land somewhere and go away from us for good — that seemed the most likely — or repent once and for all and come back home.

But they were wrong. I had made myself responsible for stealing a bit of food for him every day, an idea that had come to me the very first night, when the family had lighted bonfires on the riverbank and in their glare prayed and called out to Father. Every day from then on I went back to the river with a lump of hard brown sugar, some corn bread, or a bunch of bananas. Once, at the end of an hour of waiting that had dragged on and on, I caught sight of Father; he was way off, sitting in the bottom of the canoe as if suspended in the mirror smoothness of the river. He saw me, but he did not paddle over or make any sign. I held up the things to eat and then laid them in a hollowed-out rock in the river bluff, safe from any animals who might nose around and where they would be kept dry in rain or dew. Time after time, day after day, I did the same thing. Much later I had a surprise: Mother knew about my mission but, saying nothing and pretending she didn't, made it easier for me by putting out leftovers where I was sure to find them. Mother almost never showed what she was thinking.

Finally she sent for an uncle of ours, her brother, to help with the farm and with money matters, and she got a tutor for us children. She also arranged for the priest to come in his vestments to the river edge to exorcise Father and call upon him to desist from his sad obsession. Another time, she tried to scare Father by getting two soldiers to come. But none of it was any use. Father passed by at a distance, discernible only dimly through the river haze, going by in the canoe without ever letting anyone go close enough to touch him or even talk to him. The reporters who went out in a launch and tried to take his picture not long ago failed just like everybody else; Father crossed over to the other bank and steered the canoe into the thick swamp that goes on for miles, part reeds and part brush. Only he knew every hand's breadth of its blackness.

We just had to try to get used to it. But it was hard, and we never really managed. I'm judging by myself, of course. Whether I wanted to or not, my thoughts kept circling back and I found myself thinking of Father. The hard nub of it was that I couldn't begin to understand how he could hold out. Day and night, in bright sunshine or in rainstorms, in muggy heat or in the terrible cold spells in the middle of the year, without shelter or any protection but the old hat on his head, all through the weeks, and months, and years—he marked in no way the passing of his life. Father never landed, never put in at either shore or stopped at any part of the river islands or sandbars; and he never again stepped onto grass or solid earth. It was true that in order to catch a little sleep he may have tied up the canoe at some concealed islet-spit. But he never lighted a fire on shore, had no lamp or candle, never struck a match again. He did no more than taste food; even the morsels he took from what we left for him along the roots of the fig tree or in the hollow stone at the foot of the cliff could not have been enough to keep him alive. Wasn't he ever sick? And what constant strength he must have had in his arms to maintain himself and the canoe ready for the piling up of the floodwaters where danger rolls on the great current, sweeping the bodies of dead animals and tree trunks downstream—frightening, threatening, crashing into him. And he never spoke another word to a living soul. We never talked about him, either. We only thought of him. Father could never be forgotten; and if, for short periods of time, we pretended to ourselves that we had forgotten, it was only to find ourselves roused suddenly by his memory, startled by it again and again.

My sister married; but Mother would have no festivities. He came into our minds whenever we ate something especially tasty, and when we were wrapped up snugly at night we thought of those bare unsheltered nights of cold, heavy rain, and Father with only his hand and maybe a calabash to bail the storm water out of the canoe. Every so often someone who knew us would remark that I was getting to look more and more like my father. But I knew that now he must be bushy-haired and bearded, his nails long, his body cadaverous and gaunt, burnt black by the sun, hairy as a beast and almost as naked, even with the pieces of clothing we left for him at intervals.

He never felt the need to know anything about us; had he no family affection? But out of love, love and respect, whenever I was praised for something good I had done, I would say: "It was Father who taught me how to do it that way." It wasn't true, exactly, but it was a truthful kind of lie. If he didn't remember us any more and didn't want to know how we were, why didn't he go farther up the river or down it, away to landing places where he would never be found? Only he knew. When my sister had a baby boy, she got it into her head that she must show Father his grandson. All of us went and stood on the bluff. The day was fine and my sister was wearing the white dress she had worn at her wedding. She lifted the baby up in her arms and her husband held a parasol over the two of them. We called and we waited. Our father didn't come. My sister wept; we all cried and hugged one another as we stood there.

After that my sister moved far away with her husband, and my brother decided to go live in the city. Times changed, with the slow swiftness of time. Mother went away too in the end, to live with my sister because she was growing old. I stayed on here, the only one of the family who was left. I could never think of marriage. I stayed where I was, burdened down with all life's cumbrous baggage. I knew Father needed me, as he wandered up and down on the river in the wilderness, even though he never gave a reason for what he had done. When at last I made up my mind that I had to know and finally made a firm attempt to find out, people told me rumor had it that Father might have given some explanation to the man who made the canoe for him. But now the builder was dead; and no one really knew or could recollect any more except that there had been some silly talk in the beginning, when the river was first swollen by such endless torrents of rain that everyone was afraid the world was coming to an end; then they had said that Father might have received a warning, like Noah, and so prepared the canoe ahead of time. I could half-recall the story. I could not even blame my father. And a few first white hairs began to appear on my head.

I was a man whose words were all sorrowful. Why did I feel so guilty, so guilty? Was it because of my father, who made his absence felt always, and because of the river-river-river, the river-flowing forever? I was suffering the onset of old age—this life of mine only postponed the inevitable. I had bad spells, pains in the belly, dizziness, twinges of rheumatism. And he? Why, oh why must he do what he did? He must suffer terribly. Old as he was, was he not bound to weaken in vigor sooner or later and let the canoe overturn or, when the river rose, let it drift unguided for hours downstream, until it finally went over the brink of the loud rushing fall of the cataract, with its wild boiling and death? My heart shrank. He was out there, with none of my easy security. I was guilty of I knew not what, filled with boundless sorrow in the deepest part of me. If I only knew—if only things were otherwise. And then, little by little, the idea came to me.

I could not even wait until next day. Was I *crazy*? No. In our house, the word crazy was not spoken, had never been spoken again in all those years; no one was condemned as crazy. Either no one is crazy, or everyone is. I just went, taking along a sheet to wave with. I was very much in my right mind. I waited. After a long time he appeared; his indistinct bulk took form. He was there, sitting in the stern. He was there, a shout away. I called out several times. And I said the words which were making me say them, the sworn promise, the declaration. I had to force my voice to say: "Father, you're getting old, you've done your part. . . . You can come back now, you don't have to stay any longer. . . . You come back, and I'll do it, right now or whenever you want me to; it's what we both want. I'll take your place in the canoe!" And as I said it my heart beat to the rhythm of what was truest and best in me.

He heard me. He got to his feet. He dipped the paddle in the water, the bow pointed toward me; he had agreed. And suddenly I shuddered deeply, because he had lifted his arm and gestured a greeting—the first, after so many years. And I could not. . . . Panic-stricken, my hair standing on end, I ran, I fled, I left the place behind me in a mad headlong rush. For he seemed to be coming from the hereafter. And I am pleading, pleading, pleading for forgiveness.

I was struck by the solemn ice of fear, and I fell ill. I knew that no one ever heard of him again. Can I be a man, after having thus failed him? I am what never was—the unspeakable. I know it is too late for salvation now, but I am afraid to cut life short in the shallows of the world. At least, when death comes to the body, let them take me and put me in a wretched little canoe, and on the water that flows forever past its unending banks, let me go—down the river, away from the river, into the river— the river.

## ■ Juan Carlos Onetti (1909–1994) *Uruguay* (story)

TRANSLATED BY ANDREW HURLEY

Writer of novels and stories, Juan Carlos Onetti was born in Montevideo and divided most of his literary life between that city and Buenos Aires. As a child, he was a reader of popular novelists, including Jules Verne and, later, Knut Hamsun. He did not finish high school. In Montevideo and Buenos Aires, he did odd jobs, and when he returned to Montevideo in 1939, he worked as literary editor and contributor for *Marcha*, a weekly news magazine; at the same time, he wrote and published his first novel, *El pozo* (*The Pit*), which brought him limited acclaim in Uruguay. He spent most of his life as a journalist. As with many writers of his generation, he was clearly influenced by William Faulkner's *Sanctuary* and Louis Ferdinand Céline's *Voyage to the End of the Night*. In 1941, he moved back to Buenos Aires where he published *Tierra de nadie* (*No Man's Land*, 1941), a book about Buenos Aires immigrant lowlife modeled on the American novelist John Dos Passos's *Manhattan Transfer,* which was a pivotal experimental book about street life, squalor, crime, and social conflict. Onetti absorbed the cinematic techniques, obscenities, and tough observor glance of *Manhattan Transfer,* a book that internationally established a tone among socially committed writers of France, Germany, Italy, and

Spain, guiding, among others, the Spanish Nobel laureate novelist Camilo José Cela. Onetti's fiction has also led critics to speak of early Jean Paul Sartre and Dostoyevsky, because of their dark themes of nihilistic loneliness, sexual obsession, humor, despair, and existential dream fantasy. In three novels written in Buenos Aires, Onetti created an imaginary town of Santa María for his distopian scenes in *A Brief Life* (1950), *The Shipyard* (1961), and *Juntacadáveres* (*Corpse Gatherers*, 1964). He returned to Montevideo in 1954, and, in 1957, he became the director of municipal libraries in the capital city. He was arrested in Uruguay in 1974 for his participation in a jury that awarded a prize for a novel that suggested sexual misadventures by a member of the ruling military junta. There was an international protest against his arrest organized by the Argentine novelist Adolfo Bioy Casares, and Onetti, in poor health, was released. He then retired to Spain in 1976 where he continued writing. In 1980, Onetti received the Cervantes Award, Spain's highest literary honor. He died in Madrid in 1994, a grand master of the Latin American narrative.

**FURTHER READING:** Onetti, Juan Carlos. *A Brief Life*, 1950, *The Shipyard*, 1961; *Juntacadáveres* (*Corpse Gatherers*, 1964); *Goodbye and Stories*, 1990.

## The Dog Will Have Its Day

*For my teacher, Enrico Cicogna*

The overseer, his head bared in respect, was handling the pieces of bloody meat one by one to the man in the bowler hat and frock coat. At afternoon's end, in silence. The man in the bowler waved his arms in a circle above the kennel, and immediately there arose the dark hot wind of the four Dobermans, thin, almost skin and bone, and the blind avidity of their muzzles, their innumerable teeth.

The man in the bowler stood for a few moments watching them eat, swallow, then watched them beg for more meat.

"All right," he said to the overseer, "as I ordered. All the water they want, but no food. Today is Thursday. Let them out on Saturday at this same time, more or less—when the sun sets. And tell everyone to go to bed. Saturday I want everyone deaf even if you can hear it all the way from the peons' quarters."

"Sir," nodded the overseer.

Then the man in the bowler handed the overseer a few meat-colored bills, refusing to hear his words of thanks. He settled his gray bowler lower on his forehead and spoke as he continued to watch the dogs. The four Dobermans were kept separate by wire-mesh fences; the four Dobermans were male.

"I'll be up to the house in a half-hour or so. Have the coach ready. I'm going to Buenos Aires. Business. I don't know how long I'll be there. And don't forget. All his clothes have to be changed afterward. Burn the papers. The money is yours, and anything else you want—rings, cufflinks, watch. But don't wear anything for several months. I'll let you know when. The money is yours," he repeated. "City men always have plenty of money. And his hands—don't forget about his hands."

Then he was small and strong, dressed now in a gray embroidered shirt, a wide belt heavy with silver medallions, a dark poncho, and a black necktie. The color had been imposed on him when he was thirteen, and by now he had forgotten why or by whom. There was a big silver knife, sometimes, for show or for decoration, and the hat with the brim turned back. His eyes, like his moustache, were the color of new wire, and they had the same stiffness.

He gazed at the world without real hatred or pain, looked invariably to other men as though he were sure that life, his life, would unfold in pleasant routine until the last. But he was lying. Leaning on the mantelpiece, he saw the room lie: the silk-and-gilt armchairs he had never allowed himself to sit in, the cabinets and "curios" with their twisted, elaborate legs, their glass doors, their shelves full of tea services, coffee services, chocolate services which probably had never been used, the enormous birdcage with its dreadful cacophony, the curves of the loveseat, the low fragile tables of no known purpose. The heavy wine-colored drapes shut out the calm afternoon: all that existed was suffocating bric-a-brac.

"I'm going to Buenos Aires," the man was saying again, as he did every Friday afternoon, in his slow, solemn, deep voice. "The boat leaves at ten. Business, that swindle they're trying to pull on me with those lands of yours up north."

He looked at the bonbons, the thin slices of ham, the little triangles of cheese, the woman pouring tea: she was young, blond, forever pale, quite mistaken now about her immediate future.

He looked at the six-year-old child, nervous, speechless, whiter than its mother, always dressed by her in feminine clothes, profusions of velvet and lace. He said nothing, because everything had been said long before. The woman's repugnance, the man's growing hatred had both been born on that same extravagant wedding night they had conceived the girl-boy that now leaned open-mouthed against its mother's thigh, its restless fingers twirling the thick yellow curls that fell to its neck, to its necklace of little holy medals.

The coach was a shining black; it gleamed as though it were new—varnished every day. It bore two great carriage-lamps which years later would be disputed over by the wealthy of Santa María, who would want them (with lightbulbs now, instead of candles) to grace their front porches. The coach was drawn by a dapple-gray horse that could have been forged of silver, or of pewter. And the coach itself had not been made by Daglio; it had been brought from England.

Sometimes with envy, even almost with hate, he marked the speed, the blind youth of the animal; sometimes he imagined himself infected with its youth, its ignorance of its own future.

But once again that Friday—that Friday especially—he did not go to Buenos Aires. He wasn't even in Santa María, in fact; because as he came to the first houses outside Enduro he pulled the young dapple's head to the left, and the barouche swung around, its wheels kicking up clods as it spun down a dry-clay road that led through fields of burned hay and past a distant, solitary tree here and there, and that continued on toward the dirty beach which many years later would be a resort that bore his name, with beach houses and shops and summering people, another humble stone in the edifice of the achievement of his ambitions.

Farther on, through enormous flatlands, the horse trotted along a road flanked by the peaceableness of wheat fields, of seemingly deserted farms, all timidly washed-out, bleached, immersed in the growing heat of the afternoon.

He halted the coach in front of the largest building in the ramshackle settlement. He did not reply to the murmured words that greeted his arrival; into the hand of the dark man who emerged to meet him he counted out ten bills. He was paying for the animal's feed, the stable in the barn, the secret, the silence which both men knew was a lie.

Then he walked over to a new-looking, whitewashed shack. It was surrounded by pigweed, and a huge, straight pine planted by no one half a century before seemed to be what was keeping it upright.

As always, he knocked imperiously, coolly three times with the handle of the whip at the flimsy door. Perhaps that too was an implicit part of the ritual: the woman silent, maybe not even at home, taking her time. The man did not knock again. He waited there unmoving, drinking in, with his heavy breaths, this first dose of the weekly suffering that she, Josephine, obediently and generously served him up.

Submissive, the girl opened the door; hiding the revulsion and disgust that once had been pity, she unbuttoned her robe, let it fall to the floor, and turned and walked naked to the bed.

One Friday long ago, uneasy because she was afraid of another man, she had looked at her little clock: she knew, then, that this ritual took two hours. He took off his coat, laid it next to the whip and the hat, and then, trembling, went on folding things across a chair. Then he walked over to her and, as always, began at the girl's feet, sobbing in a hoarse, broken voice, begging forgiveness with incomprehensible moans for some old, old sin still unpardoned, his tears and saliva wetting the girl's red toenails.

For almost three whole days the girl had him underfoot about the place, rolling cigarettes, silent, emptying with no hurry, no drunkenness the big bottles of gin, getting up to go to the bathroom or to come back, furious and docile, to the torture of the bed.

Carried by the seeds wrapped in filaments of white silk, flying on the wings of the capricious air, the news reached Santa María, reached Enduro, reached the little white house on the coast. When the man got it—the horse's caretaker stirred himself to scratch at the door and tell him the news, his eyes averted, his strangled cap in his huge dark hands—he realized that, incredibly, the naked woman imprisoned in the bed already knew it.

Standing there outside the door, his head still bowed from trying to catch the servile, less and less understandable words, the man with the wire-colored moustache, with the gleaming black barouche, with the pewter horse, with more than half the property in the settlement, spoke slowly and spoke too much:

"Fruit thieves. It's for them I've got the best dogs, the most murderous dogs there are. They don't attack. They defend." He looked an instant at the impassive sky, not smiling, not sad; he took more bills from his waist. "But I don't know anything, don't forget. I'm in Buenos Aires."

It was Sunday noon, but the man didn't leave the house until Monday morning. Now the little dappled horse was held back to a trot; it didn't need to be guided; it was trotting back home so rhythmically it had something of a wind-up animal, something of a toy about it.

"A soldier-boy," unconcernedly thought the man when he saw a bored young policeman leaning on the wall beside the great black wrought-iron gate with its ornate doubling swirls of a J overlaid with a P. The young man's uniform had once been blue; it had once belonged to a heavier, taller man.

"The first soldier-boy," the man thought almost smiling, feeling himself fill slowly with excitement, with something like the beginnings of amusement.

"Pardon, sir," said the uniformed young man, looking younger and shyer the closer the older man came, almost a boy at last. "Commissioner Medina told me to ask you to stop by the Station. I, I mean at your convenience."

"Another soldier-boy," murmured the man, his senses entangled in the steam and the smell of the horse. "But it's no fault of yours. Tell Medina that I'm home. I'll be in my house. All day. If he wants to see me."

He ticked the reins imperceptibly and the animal jubilantly drew him past the garden and the arbor out to the half-moon of dry earth and the coach house.

The men who came over to meet him and take charge of the carriage were glum yet experienced; none of them spoke of Saturday night or of Sunday morning.

Petrus didn't smile, because he had discharged his mockery years before, and perhaps forever, into the moustache the color of iron filings. He had a blurred memory of reaching fifty; he knew everything that he still had to do or try to do in that strange spot in the world not yet on any map; it was his opinion that he would never meet any obstacle more stubborn, more viscous and sticky, than the stupidity and incomprehension of other people, of all the other people he'd be obliged to come up against.

And so, that afternoon, when the suffocating heat began to soften a little under the trees, there came Medina, the Commissioner, a man timeless, heavy, and slothful, driving the first Model T Henry Ford had managed to sell in the country in 1907.

The overseer greeted him with a salute too slow and exaggerated. Medina measured him with a wry smile and spoke to him mildly.

"I expect you at the Station at seven, Petrus or no Petrus. It'll be to your advantage to come. I promise you it will not be to your advantage if you make me send somebody to get you."

The man dropped his arm and consented, nodding. He was not intimidated.

"The master said that if you came he was in the house."

Medina walked deliberately, planting his heels in the dried-out earth at each step, swaggering a little, and he went up the granite steps, too wide, too high. "A palace; this foreigner thinks he can live in a palace here. In Santa María."

All the doors were closed against the heat. Medina brushed off his hands as a kind of notice and he stepped into the large parlor with all the glass, all the fans, all the flowers. In a different suit from the morning's, and as neatly dressed as though he were about to go for an evening spin in his barouche, even wearing a hat, sitting with a cigarette in the only chair that looked able to support the weight of a man, Jeremías Petrus dropped onto the carpet the book he had been reading and raised two fingers in a kind of salute, a welcome.

"Take a seat, please, Commissioner."

"Thank you. Last time we saw each other my name was Medina."

"But today I promoted you. I already know what brought you here."

Medina looked doubtfully at the profusion of little gilt chairs.

"Any chair, any chair," Petrus insisted. "If you break it, you'll be doing me a favor. But first, what'll we drink? I'm sick of gin."

"I didn't come for a drink."

"Or to tell me no alcohol while you're on duty, either. No bottles from France have been delivered in months. Some little soldierboy must be drinking my Moët Chandon in some cathouse somewhere. But I've got some bitters—Campari—that I think would be about right for this time of day."

He rang a little bell, and the servant who had been waiting behind a curtain came. He was young, dark-skinned, his hair greased down on his skull. Medina knew him; he was reformatory fodder, a messenger-boy for secretive whores—and what woman isn't one?—a petty thief when the opportunity presented itself. He remembered, looking without triumph into the boy's eyes, the classic, if now butchered, phrase, "I know you, Mirabelles." The boy looked comical in his white waiter's jacket and black bow tie. "He brought furniture, a wife, a whore, and a little horse and buggy from Europe. But I guess he couldn't find an exportable servant. He had to pick one out of the garbage in Santa María."

A parade of memories had filed by—of ruined harvests, staggering harvests, rises and falls in the price of cattle; they had reminded each other of long-gone summers and winters, so worn and polished by time as to have become unreal, when the bottle showed only two glasses left of the red liquid as soft as sweet water. Neither of the two men had changed, neither showed a trace of mockery or of dominance.

"My wife and the boy went to Santa María. They may go on farther. I mean, you never know with women," Petrus said.

"I beg your pardon, I didn't ask how your wife was getting along," Medina replied.

"No matter. You aren't a doctor, anyway; you came because my dogs killed a chicken thief."

"No, don Jeremías, with respect. I came for two reasons. The corpse we carried away had been disguised. Your peons muddied his face and his hands, they dressed the body in the overseer's clothes, they stole his belongings. Rings—you could see the marks on the fingers. Wash off the mud, and you saw he'd been clean and sweet when he came; just out of the bath. They forgot the cologne, good cologne, as sweet and sissified as the cologne your own wife wears, don Jeremías. A clumsy trick, typical of these peons. But that's enough of that—I know the man's name now. It's very possible that you don't know who he was, or it's possible that you'll place him when I tell you the name or when you see—if you want to be troubled to come to the Station, of course—when you see the file. The dogs mangled his throat, his hands, half his face. But the dead man didn't come to steal your chickens. He came from Buenos Aires, and you didn't go to Buenos Aires on Friday."

A pause chewed over by both men, a shared apprehension.

Petrus smelled danger, but no fear. His peons had been stupid, clumsy, and so had he—he had trusted in them and this grotesque charade.

"Medina. Or Commissioner. I went to Buenos Aires on Friday. I go almost every Friday. I paid a lot of money so that everyone would swear to that."

"Which they did, don Jeremías. No one double-crossed you, no one cheated you out of so much as a single peso. They swore on their fear, on the Bible, on the ashes of their whoring mothers. Although not all of them were orphans. But anyway, and flattery aside, I felt like they were swearing out of some other respect, don Jeremías, something besides money."

"Thank you," Petrus said without moving his head, a slight line of dry amusement trying to push at his moustache. "The end, story over, case closed, then. I was in Buenos Aires."

"Case closed because the dead man was inside your house, your land, your sacred private property. And because it wasn't you that murdered him. It was the dogs. And I tried, don Jeremías, but your dogs refuse to testify."

"Dobermans," Petrus nodded. "Intelligent breed. Very refined. They don't talk to police dogs."

"Hah. Maybe not out of scorn for them, though. Discretion, maybe. Anyway—case closed. But there are some things I'd like clear. You weren't around here on Saturday night. But you weren't in Buenos Aires, either. You weren't anywhere, you weren't alive, you didn't exist from Friday to Monday. Curious. A story about a ghost, vanished. No one ever wrote that story, and nobody ever told it to me."

At that Jeremías Petrus left his chair and stood motionless, looking straight and hard at Medina's face, the useless riding-quirt dangling from his wrist.

"I have been patient," he said slowly, as though talking to himself, as though he were murmuring into the magnifying mirror he shaved at every morning. "All this bores me, it befuddles me, it makes me slow, it wastes my time. I want, I *have* to do so many things—there may not be room for them all in one man's life. Because in this work, I'm all alone . . ." He broke off. He stood unmoving for a long time in the enormous parlor filled with things—objects born of and imposed by the never-defeated female sex. His voice had sounded, a little, like a prayer and a confession. Now it turned cold; he returned to everyday stupidity to ask without curiosity, without insult, "How much?"

Medina chuckled softly, making his poor hilarity fit the atmosphere of unbearable vitrines, japanned tables, fans, gilt settees, and dead butterflies under domes of crystal.

"Money? Nothing for me. If you want to pay off the mortgage, that's another thing, don Jeremías. It's the Bank's, or nobody's. I always have my cot at the Station."

"Done," Petrus said.

"As you like. In payment, I want to tell you something that will upset you maybe at first, tonight or tomorrow, say . . ."

"You always hated to waste time. Me too. Maybe that's why we put up with each other for so many years. Maybe that's why I'm listening to you this minute. Say what you have to say."

"As you wish. I thought a little prologue, between two gentlemen whose hands are clean . . . But as you wish. Mam'selle Josefina refused to say or listen to a single word. I beg your pardon, she did say one thing, I didn't quite catch it, just one thing, something like 'say petty car song.' I'm not sure . . . She cried a little. Then she scattered a bagful of silver coins all over the bed. They're at the Station, with the file, waiting for the judge. He went to a horse race; he may stop by here on his way back."

"That's fine," Petrus said. "She was heard to say that—no matter. The money, a little under a hundred and thirty-seven—that's no matter, either, and it's got nothing to do with the case."

"I beg your pardon again," Medina said, trying to sweeten his voice. "Less than fifty."

"I understand. There are always expenses."

"Exactly. Especially for a trip. Because Mam'selle was using the telephone in the train station. You know poor old Masiota, you know how poor old Masiota treats all the women, as long as it's not his, of course, as we all know—all you have to do is look at his left eye on Monday after the conjugal spree every Saturday night. All the women except the one he puts up with and the one that was lucky enough to find him half awake this Monday morning at the train station, when you reappeared. A coin, a smile, a kind word was all it took for him to put all the telephone lines, all the freight cars full of bags and cows waiting on the siding, all the miles of rails going who knows where, the left ones and the right ones both—put all of it at her service."

"And so?" Petrus interrupted him, lashing at his boot with the whip impatiently.

"I was taking my time getting there because I thought we were gentlemen. I apologize. I know we don't like to waste time. So: Mam'selle must have worn out our station-master's batteries. But in an hour or two she got what she'd wanted. Train, hotel, ship for Europe. I learned all this a few minutes ago. There's never a want of a drunk or some layabout on a train-station bench."

Petrus had been nibbling at the whip-handle, pensive, all desire to lash out at something now gone, as Medina, not at ease, not entirely inattentive, rubbed his thumb over the trigger of the pistol at his waist. Without prior agreement, his mouth and his thumb, both slow, drew out the pause: it was too long at last to fit this story. At last it was Petrus who spoke; his voice was slow and hoarse, the voice of a woman about to be overtaken by menopause. He was too proud to ask.

"Josephine knew his name. She knew the name of the chicken thief and I'm sure much more besides. I see no other reason for her to have gone away."

"That may be, don Jeremías," Medina said syllable by syllable, watchful of the whip's verticality. "Why *would* she have gone?"

It had been so long since Petrus had laughed that his wide-open, black mouth began first with a long mooing sound and then tapered off into the bleat of a lost calf.

"Why explain, Commissioner? Women are whores. Every one of them. Worse than us. Mares, even better. Not even real whores. I've known a few I'd take my hat off to, I suppose. They were ladies. A long time ago. But women today are little whores, no better than that. Sad little whores."

"True, don Jeremías," Medina recoiled at the memory of Petrus's señora offering him tea and cake in that very parlor. "Almost all, anyway. Poor things, that's what they're born for. You fight to make a lumberyard. Fight against the whole world. I fight—Saturdays to go to bed drunk, sometimes to find out who the owner of the stolen sheep is. And I need time to paint. Paint the river, paint you."

"I bought two of your paintings," Petrus said. "Two or three."

"Yes, you did, don Jeremías, and you paid well for them. But they aren't here in the parlor. They're out in the peons' quarters. That's neither here nor there. You're right, what you were saying. They don't have an ounce of brain to be anything more than what you said they were."

The whip fell, tilted into the man's legs, then lay lengthwise on the floor. Petrus, sitting down, opened his hand:

"What do you say we have a drink, Commissioner?"

When he left, Medina saw one of the animals in the shade, out of the sun, taking a long siesta.

# ▓ Jorge Amado (1912– ) *Brazil* (novel)

## TRANSLATED BY BARBARA SHELBY MERELLO

Jorge Amado, one of the most successful writers in Latin America, a precursor to the Boom novelists, has been translated into the main languages of the world. His fame rests on his literary qualities as well as on his immensely popular and colorful Brazilian love novels. His mother was part Indian, his father a backwoodsman landowner, whose authority rested on his rifle. The family was made destitute first by the great flood of 1914 and later by the stock market crash of 1929; yet, Amado managed to attend a Jesuit boarding school, complete law school, and become an active journalist. He began his career as a journalist and was early interested in politics. He was arrested by the Getulio Vargas regime in 1936, and many times thereafter, because of his proletarian novels about life in the slums and shanty towns of Brazil. His books were banned, confiscated, and burned; and in 1942, he was arrested again for his participation in anti-Axis activities. In 1946, he was elected a Communist deputy to the Brazilian Congress, but he went into exile when the Communist Party was banned in 1948. After a few years in Paris, he was expelled from France and fled to Czechoslovakia. He won the Stalin Peace Prize in 1952; but in 1954 he spoke out in Moscow against the confines of socialist-realism, and, in 1955, he broke definitively with the party and Communism. He returned to Brazil, disillusioned with the Soviet Union.

Amado has many voices: the conscience of and sharp eye for the city poor, the storytelling fabulist of popular love novels, a graceful allegorist in children's books. In the excerpts from *The Two Deaths of Quincas Wateryell*, we have a coherent picaresque novel, with full Cervantes-like exuberance, wildness, and existential absurdity, as Quincas, like a picaresque ruffian of individualist survival, chooses his own death, an appropriate one for his beliefs and condition.

**FURTHER READING:** Amado, Jorge. *Jubiabá*, 1935; *The Sea of Death*, 1936; *Captains of the Sands*, 1937; *The Violent Land*, 1943; *Gabriela, Clove and Cinnamon*, 1958; *Home is the Sailor; Dona Flor and Her Two Husbands; The Two Deaths of Quincas Wateryell*, 1959;

Shepherds of the Night, 1964; The Tent of Miracles, 1969; Tereza Batista Home from the Wars, 1972; Pen Sword Camisole, 1980; Showdown, 1985; The War of the Saints: a Tale of Sorcery, 1988.

## from The Two Deaths of Quincas Wateryell

### A Certain Amount of Confusion

A certain amount of confusion about the death of Quincas Wateryell persists even today. There are doubts to be explained away, ridiculous details, contradictory testimony from witnesses, divers gaps in the story. Time, place, and last words are uncertain. The family, backed up by neighbors and acquaintances, sticks to its version of a quiet death in the morning—with no witnesses, no fuss, and no last words—occurring almost twenty hours before that other, notorious death just before dawn, when the moon faded into the ocean and mysterious things took place on the docks of Bahia. Quincas's last words were sworn to nevertheless by reliable witnesses and passed on by word of mouth through steep streets and back alleys, and they meant far more to those who repeated them than a mere farewell to the world. They were a prophetic pronouncement, a message of deep significance (as one of our young contemporary authors would put it).

With so many reliable witnesses around—including Cap'n Manuel and Wide-Eyed Quitéria, a woman of her word—there are still those who deny any and all authenticity not only to the much-admired last words but also to everything that happened on that memorable night when, at an uncertain hour and in ambiguous circumstances, Quincas Wateryell dived into the gulf of Bahia and set off on his last journey, never to return. That's the world for you—swarming with doubters and skeptics who are yoked like oxen to law and order, due process, and notarized documents. These good people triumphantly display the death certificate signed by the doctor just before noon, and with that one scrap of paper—for no other reason than that it has printing and stamps on it—try to blot out the last few hours lived so intensely by Quincas Wateryell before he departed of his own free will, or so he proclaimed loud and clear to his friends and the others who were present.

The dead man's family—his respectable daughter and conventional son-in-law, a civil servant with a promising career; Aunt Marocas and her younger brother, a businessman with a modest bank account—stoutly asserts that the whole story is nothing but a gross falsehood concocted by inveterate drunkards, scoundrels on the fringes of lawful society, crooks who ought to be seeing the world from behind bars instead of enjoying the free run of the streets, the port of Bahia, the white sandy beaches, the vast friendly night. They unjustly lay at the door of these pals of Quincas all responsibility for the ill-fated life he had been leading during the past few years, to the grief and shame of his family. In fact, his name was never uttered and his deeds never were mentioned in the presence of the innocent children. As far as they were concerned, their Grandfather Joaquim, of fond memory, had decently passed away long ago, esteemed and respected by all who knew him. All of which leads us to deduce a first death, moral if not physical, dating from years back and bringing the total to three—thus making Quincas a record-holder for dying, and, justifying us in thinking that the events that took place afterward, from the signing of the death certificate to his dive into the ocean, were a farce acted out with the sole aim of mortifying his relatives one last time by turning their lives upside down, covering them with shame, and exposing them to malicious gossip. He was not a man to earn respect or keep up appearances, in spite of his gambling partners' respect for the lucky gambler and the fine-talking tippler.

I honestly don't know whether the mystery of Quincas Wateryell's death (or deaths) can ever be cleared up. But I am going to try my best, for as Quincas said himself, the important thing is to attempt even the impossible.

## In the Opinion of the Family

In the opinion of the family, the rapscallions who reported Quincas's last moments in the streets and alleys, in front of the Trade Mart and in the open-air market of Água dos Meninos,[1] showed an appalling lack of respect for the dead. Furthermore, a leaflet containing doggerel verses composed by Cuica de Santo Amaro, the improviser, was enjoying a brisk sale. A dead man's memory is, as we all know, sacred and not meant to be bandied about in the dirty mouths of drunken sots, gamblers, and marijuana smugglers. Nor should it be turned into a subject for uninspired rhyming by folk singers at the entrance to the Lacerda Elevator, where so many of the best people pass by every day, including co-workers of Leonardo Barreto, Quincas's humiliated son-in-law. When a man dies, he is automatically restored to genuine respectability, no matter what sort of folly he may have indulged in when he was alive. Death wipes out the black marks of the past with an absentminded hand, and the memory of the dear departed shines flawless as a diamond. This at any rate was the family's theory, and it was applauded by their friends and neighbors. According to this theory, Quincas Wateryell, when he died, became once again the former respectable, well-born Joaquim Soares de Cunha, exemplary employee of the State Rent Board, with his measured step, his close-shaved beard, his black alpaca coat, and his briefcase under his arm; listened to respectfully by the neighbors when he chose to express his opinions on weather and politics; never seen in a bar; a temperate, home-

---

1. Salvador's most famous open-air market for generations, the Feira Água dos Meninos, was totally destroyed by fire in 1964.

loving drinker. The family had in fact, by dint of extremely praiseworthy efforts, succeeded in making Quincas's memory shine unimpaired for several years after declaring him dead to society. They spoke of him in the past tense when obliged by circumstances to speak of him at all. Unfortunately, every so often a neighbor, or some colleague of Leonardo, or a busybody friend of Vanda (the disgraced daughter), ran into Quincas or heard about him from someone else. Then it was as though the dead man had risen from his grave to defile his own memory—lying dead drunk in broad daylight in the marketplace; or, dirty and disheveled, hunched over a pack of greasy cards in the courtyard of the Church of the Pillar; or even singing in a hoarse voice in São Miguel Alley, chummily embracing Negro and mulatto women of doubtful virtue. It was simply dreadful!

When at last, on that particular morning, a man who sold religious articles on Tabuão Street hurried in distress to the Barretos' house, which was small but neat, and told daughter Vanda and son-in-law Leonardo that Quincas had definitely departed this life in the wretched pigsty he had been occupying, the couple let out a simultaneous sigh of relief. Never again would the memory of the retired employee of the State Rent Board be dragged in the mud by the wild, thoughtless behavior of the bum he had turned into at the end of his life. Their well-earned rest had come at last. Now they could talk freely about Joaquim Soares da Cunha, praise his conduct as an employee, as a husband and father, and as a citizen, point out his virtues as an example to the children, and teach them to honor their grandfather's memory without fear of contradiction.

The saint-seller, a skinny old man with a white woolly pate, expatiated on details of his story: a Negro woman who sold cornmeal mush, beancakes wrapped in banana leaves, and other delicacies, had had an important matter to bring up with Quincas that morning. He had promised to get hold of certain herbs for her that were hard to find but absolutely necessary for her voodoo devotions. She had come for the herbs; she just had to have them; the time for Xangô's sacred rites was at hand. The door of his room at the top of the steep flight of stairs was open as usual; Quincas had lost the big hundred-year-old key a long time before. It was believed that he had actually sold it to some tourists on a lean day when he had had no luck at cards, adding into the bargain a grand story, lavishly embellished with dates and details, of its being a blessed church key. The Negro woman called, got no answer, thought he was still asleep, and pushed the door open. The sheet black with dirt, a torn bedspread over his legs, Quincas was lying on the cot and smiling his usual welcoming smile. She didn't notice anything wrong. When she asked him about the herbs, he smiled and didn't answer. His right big toe stuck out through a hole in his sock, and his shabby shoes were on the floor. The woman, who knew Quincas well and was used to his jokes, sat down on the bed and told him she was in a hurry. She was surprised that he didn't put out his shameless hand, which never missed a chance to pinch and feel around. She had another look at his right big toe; it looked funny. She touched Quincas's body, jumped up in alarm, and felt his cold hand. Then she ran down the stairs and spread the news.

Daughter and son-in-law listened without relish to this detailed narration of Negro women and herbs, voodoo, and feeling around. They shook their heads impatiently, trying to get him to cut it short; but the saint-seller was a deliberate man and liked to tell a story with all the details. He was the only one who knew about Quincas's relatives, whose identity had been revealed one night during a monumental binge; that was why he had come. He composed his face into a suitably contrite expression to present "his heartfelt condolences."

It was time for Leonardo to go to work. He said to his wife: "You go on, I'll stop at the office. I have to sign in and explain to the boss."

They told the saint-seller to come in and showed him to a chair in the living room. Vanda went to change her clothes, and the old man told Leonardo about Quincas, about how there wasn't anybody on Tabuão Street who didn't like him. Why had a man from a good background, a man of means (the saint-seller could see he had been one, now that he had had the pleasure of making the acquaintance of his daughter and son-in-law), decided to live the life of a tramp? Had something happened at home to make him unhappy? That must be it. Maybe his wife had put horns on him; that happened pretty often. The saint-seller placed his forefingers on his forehead in sly interrogation. Had he guessed right?

"Dona Otacília, my mother-in-law, was a saintly woman!"

The saint-seller scratched his chin: why had he done it then? But instead of replying, Leonardo got up to join Vanda, who was calling him from the bedroom.

"We'll have to let people know."

"Let who know? What for?"

"Aunt Marocas and Uncle Eduardo and the neighbors. We'll have to invite them to the funeral."

"Why should we tell the neighbors right away? We can tell them later. Otherwise they'll talk their damned heads off."

"But what about Aunt Marocas?"

"I'll talk to her and Eduardo after I stop by the office. Hurry up. Otherwise that old guy'll be running around telling everybody he sees."

"Who would ever have thought he would die that way, all alone?"

"It was his own fault, the crazy screwball."

In the living room, the saint-seller was admiring a colored portrait of Quincas painted about ten years before. It showed him as a fine-looking gentleman with a high collar, a black necktie, pointed mustaches, slicked-down hair, and rosy cheeks. Next to him in an identical frame was Dona Otacília in a black lace dress, her eyes accusing, her mouth hard. The saint-seller examined her sour visage.

"She doesn't have a husband-cheating face, but she sure looks like a hard bone to gnaw on . . . saintly woman, my foot!"

## Only a Few Friends from Tabuão Street

Only a few friends from Tabuão Street were keeping Quincas's body company when Vanda entered the room. The saint-seller explained to them in a low voice: "That's his daughter. And he had a son-in-law and a brother and sister, too, all high-class people. The son-in-law's a clerk and lives in Itapagipe, in a very fine house."

They made way for Vanda to pass, waiting expectantly for her to fling herself on the corpse and embrace it, to dissolve into tears, or to burst out sobbing. Quincas Wateryell, lying on the cot in his patched old trousers, tattered shirt, and enormous greasy vest, smiled as though enjoying himself hugely. Vanda stood stock still and stared at his unshaved face and dirty hands, and at the big toe sticking out through the hole in his sock. She had no tears left to shed, no sobs to fill the room with. All her tears and sobs had been used up long ago, when she had tried again and again to persuade Quincas to come back to the home he had abandoned. Now she could only stare at him, her face flushed with shame.

He made a most unpresentable corpse—the corpse of a bum who had died accidentally and indecently, laughing cynically at her, and no doubt at Leonardo and the rest of the family. That corpse belonged in a morgue; it should have been dumped into a police wagon to be cut up by the medical students and buried in a shallow grave, with no cross and no inscription. It was the body of Quincas Wateryell, rum-swiller, debauchee, and gambler, who had no family, no home, no flowers, and no one to pray for him. It was certainly not Joaquim Soares da Cunha, respectable functionary of the State Rent Board who had retired after twenty-five years of loyal service, or the model husband to whom people had tipped their hats and whose hand everyone had been proud to shake. How could a fifty-year-old man leave his home, his family, his life-long habits, and his old acquaintances to wander the streets, drink in cheap bars, visit whorehouses, go around dirty and unshaved, live in a filthy hole in the worst part of town, and sleep on an old cot that was falling to pieces? Vanda racked her brains for a valid explanation. Often at night, after Otacília's death (not even on that solemn occasion had Quincas consented to return to the fold), she had talked it over with her husband. He wasn't crazy, at least not crazy enough to be put away; the doctors had been unanimous on that point. How on earth, then, could such behavior be accounted for?

Now it was all over at last—the nightmare that had dragged on for years, the blot on the family escutcheon. Vanda had inherited a good deal of her mother's practical common sense and was capable of making rapid decisions and carrying them out. As she gazed at the dead man, a disgusting caricature of what her father had been, she made up her mind what to do. First she would call in a doctor to write out the death certificate. Then she would have him dressed in decent clothes, take him home, and bury him next to Otacília. It would have to be a very modest funeral—times were hard—but good enough so they would not lose face in the eyes of their friends and neighbors and Leonardo's colleagues. Aunt Marocas and Uncle Eduardo would help. At this thought, Vanda, her eyes fixed on Quincas's smiling face, wondered what would become of the money from her father's retirement fund. Would they inherit it, or would they get only the life insurance? Maybe Leonardo would know.

She turned to the curious eyes gazing at her. It was that scruffy riffraff from Tabuão Street whose company Quincas had enjoyed so much. What on earth were they doing there? Didn't they realize that when Quincas Wateryell had breathed his last, that had been the end of him? That Quincas Wateryell had been an invention of the devil, a bad dream, a nightmare? Joaquim Soares da Cunha would come back now and stay for a little while with his own people in the comfort of a decent house, his respectability restored. It was time for him to come home. And this time Quincas couldn't laugh at his daughter and son-in-law, tell them to go jump in the lake, wave them an ironic farewell, and walk out whistling. He was lying on the cot, not making a move. Quincas Wateryell was gone for good.

Vanda lifted her head, scanned the faces before her defiantly, and gave an order in Otacília's voice: "Do you want anything? If not, you can leave." Then she addressed the saint-seller: "Would you kindly call a doctor to sign the death certificate?"

The saint-seller nodded, impressed; and the others filed slowly out. Vanda remained alone with the corpse. Quincas Wateryell was smiling, and his big right toe seemed to grow bigger through the hole in his sock.

## ■ Léon Damas (1912–1978) *French Guiana* (poem)

### TRANSLATED BY ROBERT BAGG

With Léopold Senghor and Aimé Césaire, Léon Damas was a founder of the Négritude movement, the important midcentury literary movement that emphasized black consciousness, pride, and the achievement of black culture in Africa and the Antilles. The three poets—each one was also to be a statesman—produced a magazine called *L'Étudiant noir* (*The Black Student*, 1934). Damas wrote an experimental syncopated verse in which he attempted to reproduce the musical sounds of his culture in such books as *Pigments* (1937) and *Graffiti* (1951). It is energetic and intense, like the persona of the poet. His *African Songs of Love, Grief, War, and Abuse* (1961) reveals life in an African village.

**FURTHER READING:** Damas, Léon. *Pigments*, 1937; *Graffiti*, 1951; *African Songs of Love, Grief, War, and Abuse*, 1961.

## *Position Paper*

The days
shape themselves: African masks
aloof
from the quick-lime obscenities
enraging                                                                    5
a piano pounding with the same old wheeze—
Breathless Moonlight
in the shrubbery
in the gondolas
etc.                                                                        10

■ ## Vinícius De Morães (1913– ) *Brazil* (poem)

TRANSLATED BY RICHARD WILBUR

Vinícius de Morães, born in Rio, studied law at the University of Brazil and English literature at Oxford University. In England, he later worked for the Brazilian program of the BBC. In 1943, he entered the diplomatic service, serving in Los Angeles, Paris, and Montevideo. A versatile writer of poetry, popular song, and filmscripts, he was at one time called the "Pope of the Bossa Nova." He wrote the script for Marcel Camus's famous film *Black Orpheus.*

## *Song*

Never take her away,
The daughter whom you gave me,
The gentle, moist, untroubled
Small daughter whom you gave me;
O let her heavenly babbling                                                  5
Beset me and enslave me.
Don't take her; let her stay,
Beset my heart, and win me,
That I may put away
The firstborn child within me,                                              10
That cold, petrific, dry
Daughter whom death once gave,
Whose life is a long cry

For milk she may not have,
And who, in the night-time, calls me                                    *1*
In the saddest voice that can be
Father, Father, and tells me
Of the love she feels for me.
Don't let her go away,
Her whom you gave — my daughter —                                     *2*
Lest I should come to favor
That wilder one, that other
Who does not leave me ever.

■ ## Aimé Césaire (1913– ) *Martinique* (poems)

### TRANSLATED BY CLAYTON ESHLEMAN AND ANNETTE SMITH

Aimeé Césaire was born in Martinique in the West Indies. After an early career in politics in his native island, he has given himself to the writing and politics of literature. A poet above all, but also an essayist and playwright, very early in his career he was a surrealist following in the footsteps of the French poet Guillaume Apollinaire (1880–1918) and appropriately entitled his first famous book of poems *Soleil cou coupé* (*Sun Its Neck Cut Off*), taking the title from the last words of Apollinaire's surreal poem "Zone." When Césaire was a student in Paris, he was mortified by the colonial tradition, which denied a black heritage. Together with Léopold Senghor and Léon Damas he developed the notion of Négritude, which resisted assimilation and vaunted the accomplishments of black culture, especially in Africa, but also elsewhere in the world, as in Martinique where there were large communities. Among Aimé Césaires writings are *Return to My Native Land,* 1969; *A Season in the Congo,* 1969; *Discourse on Colonialism,* 1972; and his very important *Collected Poetry,* 1984. Césaire remains one of the most important twentieth-century French poets.

**FURTHER READING:** Césaire, Aimé, *Return to My Native Land,* 1969; *A Season in the Congo,* 1969; *Discourse on Colonialism,* 1972; *Collected Poetry.* Translated by Clayton Eshleman and Annette Smith, 1984.

## *zaffer sun*

at the foot of stammering volcanoes
earlier than the little violet fog arising from my fever
i am sitting in the middle of a courtyard
a horologer of three centuries accumulated in bat droppings
under the false hope of sweet grigris

already howling from a bitch soul
and carrying the true shackles
i have exchanged a thousand of my hearts
for the one today that
powerfully 10
rises in our throat
parakinesized by lofty bitter kingdoms
i
zaffer sun

## *abyss*

he pondered the logic of the swamp's teeth
he pondered the molten lead in the Chimera's throat
he pondered a morgue of beaks in the coral dump for the dying
he pondered the boundless extension
of the century-old quarrel 5
across the beaches of time
(in the time it took a soul to vanish there went
through me the passion of a piton)
he pondered a mouse pitter-pattering through the palace of a royal
soul
he pondered the voice of a galley slave strangled by a song 10
then by the soulless halt of a herd
an isolate of sea slugs coiffed with venom helmets

thus
all nostalgia
rolls 15
into the abyss

## ■ Julia de Burgos (1914–1953) *Puerto Rico* (poem)

### TRANSLATED BY ALIKI BARNSTONE AND WILLIS BARNSTONE

Born in Carolina, Puerto Rico, the eldest of thirteen children, Julia de Burgos attended the University of Puerto Rico and taught school in Naranjito. After the publication of her first book in 1938, she taught at the University of Havana and then, in 1940, moved to New York where she spent her remaining years. Her short life was tormented and chaotic, fraught with poverty and alcoholism. The harsh tone of her often self-demeaning verses reveals unusual force. Her nihilism, sometimes obscured by her rhetoric, breaks through the masks, even through the words, to reveal devastating humor and nothingness.

FURTHER READING: Burgos, Julia de. *Poems in Twenty Furrows,* 1938; *Collected Works,* 1961; *Collected Poems,* 1979.

## Nothing

Since life is nothing in your philosophy,
let's drink to the fact of not being our bodies.

Let's drink to the nothing of your sensual lips,
which are sensual zeros in your blue kisses:
like all blue a chimerical lie
of white oceans and white firmaments.

Let's drink to the touchable decoy bird
sinking and rising in your carnal desire:
like all flesh, lightning, spark,
in the truth, unending lie of the universe.

Let's drink to nothing, the perfect nothing
of your soul, that races its lie on a wild colt:
like all nothing, perfect nothing, it's not even
seen for a second in sudden dazzle.

Let's drink to us, to them, to no one;
to our always nothing of our never bodies;
to everyone at least; to everyone so much nothing,
to bodiless shadows of the living who are dead.

We come from not being and march toward not being:
nothing between two nothings, zero between two zeros,
and since between two nothings nothing can be,
let's drink to the splendor of not being our bodies.

## ■ Julio Cortázar (1914–1988) *Argentina* (story)

TRANSLATED BY PAUL BLACKBURN

Julio Cortázar was born in Brussels, but his Argentine parents moved back to Buenos Aires when he was four. After his parents' divorce, he was brought up by his mother. Fluent in French and English, he took a degree in literature and eventually became a teacher of French in Buenos Aires high schools. He began to translate literature, including the complete prose short stories of Edgar Allan Poe—a task Baudelaire performed as his livelihood in the mid–nineteenth century. Jorge Luis Borges published Cortázar's first story in the magazine *Sur,* which he was editing. In the late forties, unhappy with the Perón dictatorship and its oppression of intellectuals, he quit teaching and trained as an interpreter. He went to Paris in 1951 and began to work as a translator for UNESCO, a position he kept most of his life. Cortázar's first book of stories, *Bestiary,* came out that same year, but, since he was removed from Argentine letters, the book found no immediate resonance, and it disappeared into neglect. Then came two volumes of stories: *The End of the Game and Other Stories* (1956), including the story "Blow-Up" (Spanish title *Las babas del diablo*) on which the Italian film director Michelangelo Antonioni based his film *Blow-up* (1966), and *Secret Weapons* (1959). He wrote an allegorical novel, *The Winners* (1961), which satirized the regime of the dictator Juan Perón. By now, the American poet and translator Paul Blackburn was translating Cortázar into English and publishing his stories widely. His world fame, however, was established by the experimental, ingenious novel *Rayhuela* (1963, translated as *Hopscotch* in 1965). The story, which takes place simultaneously in Paris and Buenos Aires, was inspired by Borges's story "The Garden of the Forking Paths." *Hopscotch* was followed by another experimental novel, *62: A Model Kit* (1968). His last book, which he wrote in English with his young Canadian wife, is a collage of travel journals, *Around the Day in Eighty Worlds* (1967).

Despite the notoriety and praise for *Hopscotch* and his more Dadaist and nutty experimental tales as in *Cronopios and Famas* (1969), it is in the straight short story that his combination of Borgesian intellectual fantasy and his own grotesques and sexual obsessions makes him unique and one of the world's important storytellers. Julio Cortázar was for his works and person among the most appreciated authors. The Chilean poet Pablo Neruda said of him, "Anyone who doesn't read Cortázar is doomed. Not to read him is a serious invisible disease, which in time can have terrible consequences. Something similar to a man who has never tasted peaches. He would quietly become sadder, noticeably paler, and probably, little by little, he would lose his hair."

**FURTHER READING:** Cortázar, Julio. *Bestiary,* 1951; *The End of the Game and Other Stories,* 1956; *Secret Weapons,* 1959; *The Winners,* 1961; *Rayhuela,* 1963, tr. *Hopscotch; 62: A Model Kit,* 1968, tr. 1972; *Cronopios and Famas,* 1969; *All Fires the Fire and Other Stories,* 1966, tr. 1973; *A Manual for Manuel,* 1973; *A Change of Light and Other Stories,* 1977; *We Love Glenda So Much and Other Stories,* 1981.

## Axolotl

There was a time when I thought a great deal about the axolotls. I went to see them in the aquarium at the Jardin des Plantes and stayed for hours watching them, observing their immobility, their faint movements. Now I am an axolotl.

I got to them by chance one spring morning when Paris was spreading its peacock tail after a wintry Lent. I was heading down the boulevard Port-Royal, then I took Saint-Marcel and L'Hôpital and saw green among all that grey and remembered the lions. I was friend of the lions and panthers, but had never gone into the dark, humid building that was the aquarium. I left my bike against the gratings and went to look at the tulips. The lions were sad and ugly and my panther was asleep. I decided on the aquarium, looked obliquely at banal fish until, unexpectedly, I hit it off with the axolotls. I stayed watching them for an hour and left, unable to think of anything else.

In the library at Sainte-Geneivève, I consulted a dictionary and learned that axolotls are the larval stage (provided with gills) of a species of salamander of the genus Ambystoma. That they were Mexican I knew already by looking at them and their little pink Aztec faces and the placard at the top of the tank. I read that specimens of them had been found in Africa capable of living on dry land during the periods of drought, and continuing their life under water when the rainy season came. I found their Spanish name, *ajolote*, and the mention that they were edible, and that their oil was used (no longer used, it said) like cod-liver oil.

I didn't care to look up any of the specialized works, but the next day I went back to the Jardin des Plantes. I began to go every morning, morning and afternoon some days. The aquarium guard smiled perplexedly taking my ticket. I would lean up against the iron bar in front of the tanks and set to watching them. There's nothing strange in this, because after the first minute I knew that we were linked, that something infinitely lost and distant kept pulling us together. It had been enough to detain me that first morning in front of the sheet of glass where some bubbles rose through the water. The axolotls huddled on the wretched narrow (only I can know how narrow and wretched) floor of moss and stone in the tank. There were nine specimens, and the majority pressed their heads against the glass looking with their eyes of gold at whoever came near them. Disconcerted, almost ashamed, I felt it a lewdness to be peering at these silent and immobile figures heaped at the bottom of the tank. Mentally I isolated one, situated on the right and somewhat apart from the others, to study it better. I saw a rosy little body, translucent (I thought of those Chinese figurines of milky glass), looking like a small lizard about six inches long, ending in a fish's tail of extraordinary delicacy, the most sensitive part of our body. Along the back ran a transparent fin which joined with the tail, but what obsessed me was the feet, of the slenderest nicety, ending in tiny fingers with minutely human nails. And then I discovered its eyes, its face. Inexpressive features, with no other trait save the eyes, two orifices, like brooches, wholly of transparent gold, lacking any life but looking, letting themselves be penetrated by my look, which seemed to travel past the golden level and lose itself in a diaphanous interior mystery. A very slender black halo ringed the eye and etched it onto the pink flesh, onto the rosy stone of the head, vaguely triangular, but with curved and irregular sides which gave it a total likeness to a statuette corroded by time. The mouth was masked by the triangular plane of the face, its considerable size would be guessed only in profile; in front a delicate crevice barely slit the lifeless stone. On both sides of the head where the ears should have been, there grew three tiny sprigs red as coral, a vegetal outgrowth, the gills, I suppose. And they were the only thing quick about it; every ten or fifteen seconds the sprigs pricked up stiffly and again subsided. Once in a while a foot would barely move, I saw the diminutive toes poise mildly on the moss. It's that we don't enjoy moving a lot, and the tank is so cramped—we barely move in any direction and we're hitting one of the others with our tail or our head—difficulties arise, fights, tiredness. The time feels like it's less if we stay quietly.

It was their quietness that made me lean toward them fascinated the first time I saw the axolotls. Obscurely I seemed to understand their secret will, to abolish space and time with an indifferent immobility. I knew better later; the gill contraction, the tentative reckoning of the delicate feet on the stones, the abrupt swimming (some of them swim with a simple undulation of the body) proved to me that they were capable of escaping that mineral lethargy in which they spent whole hours. Above all else, their eyes obsessed me. In the standing tanks on either side of them, different fishes showed me the simple stupidity of their handsome eyes so similar to our own. The eyes of the axolotls spoke to me of the presence of a different life, of another way of seeing. Glueing my face to the glass (the guard would cough fussily once in a while), I tried to see better those diminutive golden points, that entrance to the infinitely slow and remote world of these rosy creatures. It was useless to tap with one finger on the glass directly in front of their faces; they never gave the least reaction. The golden eyes continued burning with their soft, terrible light; they continued looking at me from an unfathomable depth which made me dizzy.

And nevertheless they were close. I knew it before this, before being an axolotl. I learned it the day I came near them for the first time. The anthropomorphic features of a monkey reveal the reverse of what most people believe, the distance that is traveled from them to us. The absolute lack of similarity between axolotls and human beings proved to me that my recognition was valid, that I was not propping myself up with easy analogies. Only the little hands . . . But an eft, the common newt, has such hands also, and we are not at all alike. I think it was the axolotls' heads, that triangular pink shape with the tiny eyes of gold. That looked and knew. That laid the claim. They were not *animals*.

It would seem easy, almost obvious, to fall into mythology. I began seeing in the axolotls a metamorphosis which did not succeed in revoking a mysterious humanity. I imagined them aware, slaves of their bodies, condemned infinitely to the silence of the abyss, to a hopeless meditation. Their blind gaze, the diminutive gold disc without expression and nonetheless terribly shining, went through me like a message: "Save us, save us." I caught myself mumbling words of advice, conveying childish hopes. They continued to look at me, immobile; from time to time the rosy branches of the gills stiffened. In that instant I felt a muted pain; perhaps they were seeing me, attracting my strength to penetrate into the impenetrable thing of their lives. They were not human beings, but I had found in no animal such a profound relation with myself. The axolotls were like witnesses of something, and at times like horrible judges. I felt ignoble in front of them; there was such a terrifying purity in those transparent eyes. They were larvas, but larva means disguise and also phantom. Behind those Aztec faces, without expression but of an implacable cruelty, what semblance was awaiting its hour?

I was afraid of them. I think that had it not been for feeling the proximity of other visitors and the guard, I would not have been bold enough to remain alone with them. "You eat them alive with your eyes, hey," the guard said, laughing; he likely thought I was a little cracked. What he didn't notice was that it was they devouring me slowly with their eyes, in a cannibalism of gold. At any distance from the aquarium, I had only to think of them, it was as though I were being affected from a distance. It got to the point that I was going every day, and at night I thought of them immobile in the darkness, slowly putting a hand out which immediately encountered another. Perhaps their eyes could see in the dead of night, and for them the day continued indefinitely. The eyes of axolotls have no lids.

I know now that there was nothing strange, that that had to occur. Leaning over in front of the tank each morning, the recognition was greater. They were suffering, every fiber of my body reached toward that stifled pain, that stiff torment at the bottom of the tank. They were lying in wait for something, a remote dominion destroyed, an age of liberty when the world had been that of the axolotls. Not possible that such a terrible expression which was attaining the overthrow of that forced blankness on their stone faces should carry any message other than one of pain, proof of that eternal sentence, of that liquid hell they were undergoing. Hopelessly, I wanted to prove to myself that my own sensibility was projecting a nonexistent consciousness upon the axolotls. They and I knew. So there was nothing strange in what happened. My face was pressed against the glass of the aquarium, my eyes were attempting once more to penetrate the mystery of those eyes of gold without iris, without pupil. I saw from very close up the face of an axolotl immobile next to the glass. No transition and no surprise, I saw my face against the glass, I saw it on the outside of the tank, I saw it on the other side of the glass. Then my face drew back and I understood.

Only one thing was strange: to go on thinking as usual, to know. To realize that was, for the first moment, like the horror of a man buried alive awaking to his fate. Outside, my face came close to the glass again, I saw my mouth, the lips compressed with the effort of understanding the axolotls. I was an axolotl and now I knew instantly that no understanding was possible. He was outside the aquarium, his thinking was a thinking outside the tank. Recognizing him, being him himself, I was an axolotl and in my world. The horror began—I learned in the same moment—of believing myself prisoner in the body of an axolotl, metamorphosed into him with my human mind intact, buried alive in an axolotl, condemned to move lucidly among unconscious creatures. But that stopped when a foot just grazed my face, when I moved just a little to one side and saw an ax-olotl next to me who was looking at me, and understood that he knew also, no communication possible, but very clearly. Or I was also in him, or all of us were thinking humanlike, incapable of expression, limited to the golden splendor of our eyes looking at the face of the man pressed against the aquarium.

He returned many times, but he comes less often now. Weeks pass without his showing up. I saw him yesterday, he looked at me for a long time and left briskly. It seemed to me that he was not so much interested in us any more, that he was coming out of habit. Since the only thing I do is think, I would think about him a lot. It occurs to me that at the begin-ning we continued to communicate, that he felt more than ever one with the mystery which was claiming him. But the bridges were broken between him and me, because what was his obsession is now an axolotl, alien to his human life. I think that at the beginning I was capable of returning to him in a certain way—ah, only in a certain way— and of keeping awake his de-sire to know us better. I am an axolotl for good now, and if I think like a man it's only because every axolotl thinks like a man inside his rosy stone semblance. I believe that all this succeeded in communicating something to him in those first days, when I was still he. And in this final solitude to which he no longer comes, I console myself by thinking that perhaps he is going to write a story about us, that, believing he's making up a story, he's going to write all this about axolotls.

## ■ Octavio Paz (1914–1998) *Mexico* (poems)

Octavio Paz was born in Mexico City. His father was from Jalisco and had Spanish and Indian blood. His paternal grandfather was a well-known journalist who fought against the French-imposed emperor Maximilian. His father, a lawyer, took part in the Mexican revolution and represented the Zapotec revolutionary leader Emiliano Zapata and was also an archi-tect of agrarian reform. In 1937, Octavio Paz went to Spain for the Second International Conference of Anti-Fascist Writers and traveled around the war-ravaged country. Initially a participant in activities of Marxist writers, the Nazi-Soviet pact led him to break with the Stalinists—and, like the late painter Rufino Tamayo, he was often criticized for turning away from Communist orthodoxy and the doctrine of socialist-realism. Paz began a life of long journeys—to the United States on a Guggenheim (1944–1945); to Paris in 1945 where he met the surrealist poet André Breton; and, a year later, he entered the Mexican diplomatic corps. In the next decades, he worked in Paris, New York, San Francisco, Geneva, and New Delhi where he was the Mexican ambassador to India. There he met and married Marie-José Tramini and wrote *Eastern Rampart* (1968). He resigned his post to protest the 1968 slaughter by the Mexican government of student demonstrators. For some years after 1968, he spent part of each year as professor of comparative literature at Harvard University. On his permanent return to Mexico City, he founded the literary journal *Plural* and published *Salamander* (1962) and other books. Octavio Paz, like Borges, was a poet and essayist, and like Borges, though the areas are different, he had a global knowledge of diverse Eastern and Western literature, religion, and philosophy. He was particularly affected by Buddhism, including Buddhist art and religion. In addition to his poetry, he published many books of essays, notably *The Labyrinth of Solitude* and *Sor Juana Inés de la Cruz, or the Traps of Faith* (1988), important anthologies of Spanish and Mexican verse, and translations of William Carlos Williams, Pessoa, Apollinaire, and others. He founded many literary journals and collaborated with a number of artists such as Robert Motherwell, Henri Michaux, Robert Rauchenberg, and Rufino Tamayo. His books and essays represent the many aspects of a life devoted to the arts. In 1990, when he was in New York to open a great exhibition of ancient and contemporary Mexican art at the Metropolitan Museum of Art, he received word that he had been awarded the Nobel Prize for Literature.

FURTHER READING: Paz, Octavio. *The Labyrinth of Solitude* (essays), 1950. Translated by Lysander Kemp, 1961; *Sunstone.* Translated by Muriel Rukeyser, 1962; *Blanco, The Violent Season,* 1958; *Marcel Duchamp or the Castle of Purity,* 1966; *The Bow and the Lyre* (essays), 1967; *Eastern Rampart,* 1968; *Alternating Current.* Translated by Helen Lane, 1973; *The Grammatical Monkey* (essays), 1974; *Children of the Mire* (essays). Translated by Rachel Phillips, 1974; *A Draft of Shadows and Other Poems,* 1979; *On Poets and Others.* Translated by Michael Schmidt, 1986; *Convergences: Selected Essays on Art and Literature.* Translated by Helen Lane, 1987; *The Collected Poems of Octavio Paz: 1957–1987.* Edited by Eliot Weinberger, 1987; *Sor Juana Inés de la Cruz, or the Traps of Faith,* 1988; *The Other Voice, Essays on Modern Poetry.* Translated by Helen Lane, 1992.

## Sight, Touch

*For Balthus*

Light holds between its hands
the white hill and black oaks,
the path that goes on,
the tree that stays;

light is a stone that breathes                                    5
by the sleepwalking river,
light: a girl stretching,
a dark bundle dawning;

light shapes the breeze in the curtains,
makes a living body from each hour,          *10*
enters the room and slips out,
barefoot, on the edge of a knife;

light is born a woman in a mirror,
naked under diaphanous leaves,
chained by a look,          *15*
dissolved in a wink;

it touches the fruit and the unbodied,
it is a pitcher from which the eye drinks clarities,
a flame cut in blossom, a candle watching
where the blackwinged butterfly burns;          *20*

light opens the folds of the sheets
and the creases of puberty,
glows in the fireplace, its flames become shadows
that climb the walls, yearning ivy;

light does not absolve or condemn,          *25*
is neither just or unjust,
light with impalpable hands raises
the buildings of symmetry;

light escapes through a passage of mirrors
and returns to light:          *30*
is a hand that invents itself,
an eye that sees itself in its own inventions.

Light is time reflecting on time.

TRANSLATED BY MARK STRAND

## The Key of Water

After Rishikesh
the Ganges is still green.
The glass horizon
breaks among the peaks.
We walk upon crystals.          *5*
Above and below
great gulfs of calm.
In the blue spaces

white rocks, black clouds.
You said:                                                                        1
     *Le pays est plein de sources.*[1]
That night I dipped my hands in your breasts.

TRANSLATED BY ELIZABETH BISHOP

## Wind from All Compass Points

The present is motionless
The mountains are of bone and of snow
they have been here since the beginning
The wind has just been born
     ageless                                             5
as the light and the dust
     A windmill of sounds
the bazaar spins its colors
     bells   motors   radios
the stony trot of dark donkeys                                                   10
songs and complaints entangled
among the beards of the merchants
the tall light chiselled with hammer-strokes
In the clearings of silence
     boys' cries                                          15
     explode
Princes in tattered clothes
on the banks of the tortured river
pray     pee     meditate
     The present is motionless                            20
The floodgates of the year open
     day flashes out
    agate
    The fallen bird
between rue Montalambert and rue de Bac                                          25
is a girl
     held back
at the edge of a precipice of looks
If water is fire
     flame                                                30
     dazzled
in the center of the spherical hour
     a sorrel filly

---

1. The countryside is full of springs.

A marching battalion of sparks
      a real girl                              *35*
among wraithlike houses and people
Presence a fountain of reality
I looked out through my own unrealities
I took her hand
      together we crossed                     *40*
the four quadrants the three times
floating tribes of reflections
and we returned to the day of beginning
The present is motionless

      June 21st                            *45*
today is the beginning of summer
      Two or three birds
invent a garden
      You read and eat a peach
on the red couch                         *50*
      naked
like the wine in the glass pitcher
      A great flock of crows
Our brothers are dying in Santo Domingo
If we had the munitions                     *55*
      You people would not be here
      We chew our nails down to the elbow
In the gardens of this summer fortress
Tipoo Sultan planted the Jacobin tree
then distributed glass shards among         *60*
the imprisoned English officers
and ordered them to cut their foreskins
and eat them
      The century
has set fire to itself in our lands              *65*
Will the builders of cathedrals and pyramids
charred hands
      raise their transparent houses
by its light?

      The present is motionless           *70*
The sun has fallen asleep between your breasts
The red covering is black and heaves
Not planet and not jewel
      fruit
you are named                             *75*
      date
      Datia

castle of Leave-If-You-Can
     scarlet stain
upon the obdurate stone
Corridors
     terraces
     stairways
dismantled nuptial chambers
of the scorpion
     Echoes repetitions
the intricate and erotic works of a watch
     beyond time
      You
taciturn patios under the pitiless afternoon
a cloak of needles on your untouched shoulders
If fire is water
     you are a diaphanous drop
the real girl
     transparency of the world
The present is motionless
     The mountains
     quartered suns
petrified storm earth-yellow
     The wind whips
      it hurts to see
The sky is another deeper abyss
     Gorge of the Salang Pass
black cloud over black rock
Fist of blood strikes
     gates of stone
Only the water is human
in these precipitous solitudes
Only your eyes of human water
     Down there
in the cleft
desire covers you with its two black wings
Your eyes flash open and close
     phosphorescent animals
Down there
     the hot canyon
the wave that stretches and breaks
     your legs apart
the plunging whiteness
the foam of our bodies abandoned

     The present is motionless
The hermit watered the saint's tomb

his beard was whiter than the clouds
Facing the mulberry
      on the flank of the rushing stream                *125*
you repeat my name
      dispersion of syllables
A young man with green eyes presented you
with a pomegranate
      On the other bank of the Amu-Darya             *130*
smoke rose from Russian cottages
The sound of an Usbek flute
was another river invisible clearer
The boatman
      on the barge was strangling chickens          *135*
The countryside is an open hand
      its lines
      marks of a broken alphabet
Cow skeletons on the prairie
Bactria                                         *140*
      a shattered statue
I scraped a few names out of the dust
By these fallen syllables
seeds of a charred pomegranate
I swear to be earth and wind                   *145*
      whirling
over your bones
      The present is motionless
Night comes down with its trees
night of electric insects and silken beasts      *150*
night of grasses which cover the dead
meeting of waters which come from far off
rustlings
      universes are strewn about
a world falls                            *155*
      a seed flares up
each word beats
      I hear you throb in the shadow
a riddle shaped like an hour-glass
      woman asleep                    *160*
Space living spaces
Anima mundi
      maternal substance
always torn from itself
always falling into your empty womb          *165*
      Anima mundi
mother of the nomadic tribes
      of suns and men

The spaces turn
        the present is motionless
At the top of the world
Shiva and Parvati caress
            Each caress lasts a century
for the god and for the man
            an identical time
an equivalent hurling headlong
            Lahore
                red river black boats
a barefoot girl
            between two tamarinds
and her timeless gaze
            An identical throbbing
death and birth
A group of poplars
suspended between sky and earth
they are a quiver of light more than a trembling of leaves
            Do they rise
            or fall?
The present is motionless
            It rains on my childhood
it rains on the feverish garden
flint flowers trees of smoke
In a fig-leaf you sail
            on my brow
The rain does not wet you
you are flame of water
            the diaphanous drop of fire
spilling upon my eyelids
I look out through my own unrealities
the same day is beginning
            Space wheels
the world wrenches up its roots
Our bodies
        stretched out
            weigh no more than dawn

TRANSLATED BY PAUL BLACKBURN


## The Grove

Enormous and solid
        but swaying,

beaten by the winds
  but chained
to the soil,              5
  murmur of millions of leaves
against the window:
  the inextricable
mass
  woven dark green branches       10
and dazzling spaces.
   Fallen
into these nets
  there's a material
violent, resplendent,            15
  an animal
wrathful and swift,
  now immobile,
light that lights itself
  to extinguish itself.         20
To the left, above the wall,
  more idea than color,
the blue blue of a basin
 edged round by large rod
crumbling,              25
  sand silently precipitated
into the funnel of the grove.
  In the central
part
  thick drops of ink         30
  spattered
on a sheet of paper inflamed by the west,
  black
there, almost entirely,
  in the far southeast,        35
where the horizon breaks down.
  The grove
turns copper, shines.
  Three blackbirds
pass through the blaze and reappear,    40
  unharmed,
in an emptiness: neither light nor shade.
  Vegetation
on fire for its dissolution.
  In the houses         45
lights are lit.
  In the window
the sky gathers.

                    In its walls of tile
the patio                                                                        5
            grows more and more
secluded:
            it perfects
its reality.
            And now                                                              5
on the opaque cement
            nothing but
sackfuls of shadow
            the trash-can,
the empty flower-pot.                                                            6
            Space closes
over itself:
            inhuman.
Little by little, the names petrify.

TRANSLATED BY ELIZABETH BISHOP

## The River

The restless city circles in my blood like a bee.
And the plane that traces a querulous moan in a long S, the trams
            that break down on remote corners,
that tree weighted with affronts that someone shakes at midnight in
            the plaza,
the noises that rise and shatter and those that fade away and whisper a
            secret that wriggles in the ear,
they open the darkness, precipices of a's and o's, tunnels of taciturn
            vowels,
galleries I run down blindfolded, the drowsy alphabet falls in the pit
            like a river of ink,
and the city goes and comes and its stone body shatters as it arrives at
            my temple,
all night, one by one, statue by statue, fountain by fountain, stone by
            stone, the whole night long
its shards seek one another in my forehead, all night long the city
            talks in its sleep through my mouth,
a gasping discourse, a stammering of waters and arguing stone, its
            story.                                                                1

To stop still an instant, to still my blood which goes and comes, goes
            and comes and says nothing,
seated on top of me like a yogi in the shadow of a fig tree, like
            Buddha on the river's edge, to stop the instant,

a single instant, seated on the edge of time, to strike out my image of the
 river that talks in its sleep and says nothing and carries me with it,
seated on the bank to stop the river, to unlock the instant, to
 penetrate its astonished rooms reaching the center of water,
to drink at the fountain, to be the cascade of blue syllables falling
 from stone lips,     *15*
seated on the edge of night like Buddha on his self's edge, to be the
 flicker of the lidded instant,
the conflagration and the destruction and the birth of the instant, the
 breathing of night rushing enormous at the edge of time,
to say what the river says, a long word resembling lips, a long word
 that never ends,
to say what time says in hard sentences of stone, in vast gestures of sea
 covering worlds.

In mid-poem a great helplessness overtakes me, everything abandons
 me,     *20*
there is no one beside me, not even those eyes that gaze from behind
 me at what I write,
no one behind or in front of me, the pen mutinies, there is neither
 beginning nor end nor even a wall to leap,
the poem is a deserted esplanade, what's said is not said, the unsaid is
 unsayable,
towers, devastated terraces, Babylons, a sea of black salt, a blind
 kingdom,
    No,     *25*
to stop myself, to keep quiet, to close my eyes until a green spike
 sprouts from my eyelids, a spurt of suns,
and the alphabet wavers long under the wind of the vision and the
 tide rolls into one wave and the wave breaks the dike,
to wait until the paper is covered with stars and the poem a forest of
 tangled words,
    No,
I have nothing to say, no one has anything to say, nothing and nobody
 except the blood,     *30*
nothing except this coming and going of the blood, this writing over
 the written, the repetition of the same word in mid-poem,
syllables of time, broken letters, splotches of ink, blood that goes and
 comes and says nothing and carries me with it.

And I speak, my beak bent over the paper and someone beside me
 writes while the blood goes and comes,
and the city goes and comes through his blood, wants to say
 something, time wants to say something, the night wants to speak,
all night long the man wants to say one single word, to speak his
 discourse at last, made up of moldered stones,     *35*

and I whet my hearing, I want to hear what the man says, to repeat
    what the drifting city says,
all night the broken stones seek one another, groping in my forehead,
    all night the water fights the stone,
the words against the night, the night against the night, nothing lights
    up the opaque combat,
the shock of arms does not wrench away a single gleam to the stone,
    one spark to the night, no one grants a respite,
it is a fight to the death between immortals to offer retreat, to stop the
    river of blood, the river of ink,                         40
to stop the river of words, to go back upstream, and that the night
    turn upon itself display its bowels of flaming gold,
and that the water show its heart, a cluster of drowned mirrors, a glass
    tree that the wind uproots
(and every leaf of the tree flutters and glints and is lost in a cruel
    light, as the words of the poet's image are lost),
may time thicken and its wound be an invisible scar, scarcely a delicate
    line upon the skin of the world,
let the words lay down their arms and the poem be one single
    interwoven word, an implacable radiance that advances         45
and may the soul be the blackened grass after fire, the lunar breast of
    a sea that's turned to stone and reflects nothing
except splayed dimension, expansion, space lying down upon itself,
    spread wings immense,
and may everything be like flame that cuts itself into and freezes into
    the rock of diaphanous bowels,
hard blazing resolved now in crystal, peaceable clarity.

And the river goes back upstream, strikes its sails, picks up its images
    and coils within itself.                                  50

TRANSLATED BY PAUL BLACKBURN

## ■ Nicanor Parra (1914– ) *Chile* (poems)

    Born to a poor family in southern Chile, Nicanor Parra used to play
with his brothers and sisters in a cemetery. Later, he studied mathematics
and astrophysics in Santiago and went abroad to study at Brown and Oxford Universities. At Oxford, he discovered the poems of John Donne;
and after reading the line "Death be not proud," he claims he could do no
less than devote his life to poetry. Nevertheless, he continued in his science studies and became a professor of astrophysics at the University of
Santiago. While at Oxford, he studied with A. A. Milne, the author of *Win-
nie-the-Pooh*. His first book of poems was *Songbook without a Name* (1937),
and it would be seventeen years before he published his next book, *Poems*

*and Antipoems* (1954), which won several national prizes, much acclaim, and denunciation for its shocking, funny, deep irreverence. It also catapulted him into world fame. His sister was the famous Chilean folk singer Violeta Parra, whose song "Gracias a la vida" ("Thanks to Life") was made popular in the United States by Joan Baez. Later books were *Parlor Verses* (1962), *Russian Songs* (1967), and *Emergency Poems* (1972). On Sundays during the long Pinochet dictatorship, which began in 1973 with the overthrow of Salvador Allende, the poet would sit outside the entrance to the main cathedral in Santiago, with a hat for contributions, under a sign that said he was reading poems to collect money for the oppressed intellectuals of Chile. Nicanor Parra was perhaps the only Chilean intellectual who could do this with impunity. His most recent books *reflect* his opposition to the Pinochet regime or any overbearing police state: *Sermons and Homiles of the Christ of Elqui* (1984) and *Jokes for Disorienting Police about Poetry*.

Nicanor Parra has always written under the shadow of Neruda, with whom and about whom he wrote a fine critical book, *Discourses with Pablo Neruda* (1960). His poems, thoroughly framed in colloquial irony, social satire, and fantasy, mirror the humor of the great English modernists. His poems are antirhetorical; so he will not write with Nerudian prophetic ardor, yet he shares Neruda's wild and wicket wit and humor. His experimentation is not surrealist imagery or syntactic contortions or outrageous neologisms. Rather, he turns the absurdly prosaic, the folly, loneliness, and cruelty of ordinary life to his own mocking vision of humanity.

**FURTHER READING:** Parra, Nicanor. *Songbook without Title*, 1937; *Poems and Antipoems*. Translated by Miller Williams, 1954; *Discourses with Pablo Neruda*, 1960; *Parlor Verses*, 1962; *Russian Songs*, 1967; *Emergency Poems*. Translated by Miller Williams, 1972; *Sermons and Homilies of the Christ of Elqui*. Translated Sandra Reyes, 1984; *Jokes for Disorienting Police about Poetry*.

## Viva Stalin

those motherfuckers
wouldn't give me time to get my overcoat
with no warning at all
they grabbed me and knocked me around
one got me in the chest with his gun butt          5
another son of a bitch spat on me
but I never lost patience

then they took me in a patrol car
to an abandoned street
close to the railroad station                     10
they said ok now you can go free

I knew exactly what they meant by that

murderers!
    that's what I ought to have screamed
but I died screaming Viva Stalin.

TRANSLATED BY MILLER WILLIAMS

## Warnings

No praying allowed, no sneezing.
No spitting, eulogizing, kneeling
worshipping, howling, expectorating.

No sleeping permitted in this precinct
No inoculating, talking, excommunicating
Harmonizing, escaping, catching.

Running is absolutely forbidden.

No smoking. No fucking.

TRANSLATED BY MILLER WILLIAMS

## ■ Juan Rulfo (1918–1986) *Mexico* (story)

TRANSLATED BY GEORGE D. SCHADE

Juan Rulfo, a child of the Mexican revolution, was born and brought up in the village of San Gabriel near Jaslisco. His father was murdered when he was seven. In the chaos of his orphan youth, he attended school in his village and then in Guadalajara. At fifteen, he went to Mexico City where eventually he obtained a bureaucratic job. Later, he worked as an archivist at the Indian Institute in Mexico City. In 1953, he published a book of short stories, *The Burning Plain*. He received a Rockefeller grant to write a novel and three years later, in 1956, he came out with *Pedro Páramo,* which gained him national and very soon international acclaim. After the publication of these two volumes, a few short stories appeared, but during the last three decades of his life he drank heavily and never resumed his career as a writer of fiction. He did write a novel in the forties that he destroyed. His two books, however, are classics of contemporary Latin American fiction. In the burning plains and harsh rocks and tragically macabre atmosphere of his stories and novel, we discover that we are overhearing the confessions of a ghost speaking in a time of murder and personal and political corruption. Rulfo is a writer of great depth and burning accuracy. His modernist ruminations owe much to William Faulkner's *As I Lay Dying*, but his world is a Mexican wasteland of feudal landowners, desperate peasants, and bitterly furious personal conflicts. A master of the word, a writer of immense strength, one is in awe before his two volumes and wishes there had been more.

**FURTHER READING:** Rulfo, Juan. *The Burning Plain,* 1953; *Pedro Páramo,* 1956.

## Talpa

Natalia threw herself into her mother's arms, crying on and on with a quiet sobbing. She'd bottled it up for many days, until we got back to Zenzontla today and she saw her mother and began feeling like she needed consolation.

But during those days when we had so many difficult things to do—when we had to bury Tanilo in a grave at Talpa without anyone to help us, when she and I, just the two of us alone, joined forces and began to dig the grave, pulling out the clods of earth with our hands, hurrying to hide Tanilo in the grave so he wouldn't keep on scaring people with his smell so full of death—then she didn't cry.

Not afterward either, on the way back, when we were traveling at night without getting any rest, groping our way as if asleep and trudging along the steps that seemed like blows on Tanilo's grave. At that time Natalia seemed to have hardened and steeled her heart so she wouldn't feel it boiling inside her. Not a single tear did she shed.

She came here, near her mother, to cry, just to upset her, so she'd know she was suffering, upsetting all the rest of us besides. I felt that weeping of hers inside me too as if she was wringing out the cloth of our sins.

Because what happened is that Natalia and I killed Tanilo Santos between the two of us. We got him to go with us to Talpa so he'd die. And he died. We knew he couldn't stand all that traveling; but just the same, we pushed him along between us, thinking we'd finished him off forever. That's what we did.

The idea of going to Talpa came from my brother Tanilo. It was his idea before anyone else's. For years he'd been asking us to take him. For years. From the day when he woke up with some purple blisters scattered about on his arms and legs. And later on the blisters became wounds that didn't bleed—just a yellow gummy thing like thick distilled water came out of them. From that time I remember very well he told us how afraid he was that there was no cure for him any more. That's why he wanted to go see the Virgin of Talpa, so she'd cure him with her look. Although he knew Talpa was far away and we'd have to walk a lot under the sun in the daytime and in the cold March nights, he wanted to go anyway. The blessed Virgin would give him the cure to get rid of that stuff that never dried up. She knew how to do that, by washing them, making everything fresh and new like a recently rained-on field. Once he was there before Her, his troubles would be over; nothing would hurt him then or hurt him ever again. That's what he thought.

And that's what Natalia and I latched on to so we could take him. I had to go with Tanilo because he was my brother. Natalia would have to go too, of course, because she was his wife. She had to help him, taking him by the arm, bearing his weight on her shoulders on the trip there and perhaps on the way back, while he dragged along on his hope.

I already knew what Natalia was feeling inside. I knew something about her. I knew, for example, that her round legs, firm and hot like stones in the noonday sun, had been alone for a long time. I knew that. We'd been together many times, but always Tanilo's shadow separated us; we felt that his scabby hands got between us and took Natalia away so she'd go on taking care of him. And that's the way it'd be as long as he was alive.

I know now that Natalia is sorry for what happened. And I am too; but that won't save us from feeling guilty or give us any peace ever again. It won't make us feel any better to know that Tanilo would've died anyway because his time was coming, and that it hadn't done any good to go to Talpa, so far away, for it's almost sure he would've died just as well here as there, maybe a little afterward, because of all he suffered on the road, and the blood he lost besides, and the anger and everything—all those things together were what killed him off quicker. What's bad about it is that Natalia and I pushed him when he didn't want to go on anymore, when he felt it was useless to go on and he asked us to take him back. We jerked him up from the ground so he'd keep on walking, telling him we couldn't go back now.

"Talpa is closer now than Zenzontla." That's what we told him. But Talpa was still far away then, many days away.

We wanted him to die. It's no exaggeration to say that's what we wanted before we left Zenzontla and each night that we spent on the road to Talpa. It's something we can't understand now, but it was what we wanted. I remember very well.

I remember those nights very well. First we had some light from a wood fire. Afterward we'd let the fire die down, then Natalia and I would search out the shadows to hide from the light of the sky, taking shelter in the loneliness of the countryside, away from Tanilo's eyes, and we disappeared into the night. And that loneliness pushed us toward each other, thrusting Natalia's body into my arms, giving her a release. She felt as if she was resting; she forgot many things and then she'd go to sleep with her body feeling a great relief.

It always happened that the ground on which we slept was hot. And Natalia's flesh, the flesh of my brother Tanilo's wife, immediately became hot with the heat of the earth. Then those two heats burned together and made one wake up from one's dreams. Then my hands groped for her; they ran over her red-hot body, first lightly, but then they tightened on her as if they wanted to squeeze her blood out. This happened again and again, night after night, until dawn came and the cold wind put out the fire of our bodies. That's what Natalia and I did along the roadside to Talpa when we took Tanilo so the Virgin would relieve his suffering.

Now it's all over. Even from the pain of living Tanilo found relief. He won't talk any more about how hard it was for him to keep on living, with his body poisoned like it was, full of rotting water inside that came out in each crack of his legs or arms. Wounds this big, that opened up slow, real slow, and then let out bubbles of stinking air that had us all scared.

But now that he's dead things are different. Now Natalia weeps for him, maybe so he'll see, from where he is, how full of remorse her soul is. She says she's seen Tanilo's face these last days. It was the only part of him she cared about—Tanilo's face, always wet with the sweat which the effort to bear his pain left him in. She felt it approaching her mouth, hiding in her hair, begging her, in a voice she could scarcely hear, to help him. She says he told her he was finally cured, that he no longer had any pain. "Now I can be with you, Natalia. Help me to be with you," she says he said to her.

We'd just left Talpa, just left him buried there deep down in that ditch we dug to bury him.

Since then Natalia has forgotten about me. I know how her eyes used to shine like pools lit up by the moon. But suddenly they faded, that look of hers was wiped away as if it'd been stamped into the earth. And she didn't seem to see anything any more. All that existed for her was her Tanilo, whom she'd taken care of while he was alive and had buried when his time came to die.

It took us twenty days to get to the main road to Talpa. Up to then the three of us had been alone. At that point people coming from all over began to join us, people like us who turned onto that wide road, like the current of a river, making us fall behind, pushed from all sides as if we were tied to them by threads of dust. Because from the ground a white dust rose up with the swarm of people like corn fuzz that swirled up high and then came down again; all the feet scuffling against it made it rise again, so that dust was above and below us all the time. And above this land was the empty sky, without any clouds, just the dust, and the dust didn't give any shade.

We had to wait until nighttime to rest from the sun and that white light from the road.

Then the days began to get longer. We'd left Zenzontla about the middle of February, and now that we were in the first part of March it got light very early. We hardly got our eyes closed at night when the sun woke us up again, the same sun that'd gone down just a little while ago.

I'd never felt life so slow and violent as when we were trudging along with so many people, just like we were a swarm of worms all balled together under the sun, wriggling through the cloud of dust that closed us all in on the same path and had us corralled. Our eyes followed the dust cloud and struck the dust as if stumbling against something they could not pass through. And the sky was always gray, like a heavy gray spot crushing us all from above. Only at times, when we crossed a river, did the dust clear up a bit. We'd plunge our feverish and blackened heads into the green water, and for a moment a blue smoke, like the steam that comes out of your mouth when it's cold, would come from all of us. But a little while afterward we'd disappear again, mixed in with the dust, sheltering each other from the sun, from that heat of the sun we all had to endure.

Eventually night will come. That's what we thought about. Night will come and we'll get some rest. Now we have to get through the day, get through it somehow to escape from the heat and the sun. Then we'll stop—afterward. What we've got to do now is keep plugging right along behind so many others just like us and in front of many others. That's what we have to do. We'll really only rest well when we're dead.

That's what Natalia and I thought about, and maybe Tanilo too, when we were walking along the main road to Talpa among the procession, wanting to be the first to reach the Virgin, before she ran out of miracles.

But Tanilo began to get worse. The time came when he didn't want to go any farther. The flesh on his feet had burst open and begun to bleed. We took care of him until he got better. But, he'd decided not to go any farther.

"I'll sit here for a day or two and then I'll go back to Zenzontla." That's what he said to us.

But Natalia and I didn't want him to. Something inside us wouldn't let us feel any pity for Tanilo. We wanted to get to Talpa with him, for at that point he still had life left in him. That's why Natalia encouraged him while she rubbed his feet with alcohol so the swelling would go down. She told him that only the Virgin of Talpa would cure him. She was the only one who could make him well forever. She and no one else. There were lots of other Virgins, but none like the Virgin of Talpa. That's what Natalia told him.

Then Tanilo began to cry, and his tears made streaks down his sweaty face, and he cursed himself for having been bad. Natalia wiped away the streaky tears with her shawl, and between us we lifted him off the ground so he'd walk on a little further before night fell.

So, dragging him along was how we got to Talpa with him.

The last few days we started getting tired too. Natalia and I felt that our bodies were being bent double. It was as if something was holding us and placing a heavy load on top of us. Tanilo fell down more often and we had to pick him up and sometimes carry him on our backs. Maybe that's why we felt the way we did, with our bodies slack and with no desire to keep on walking. But the people who were going along by us made us walk faster.

At night that frantic world calmed down. Scattered everywhere the bonfires shone, and around the fire the pilgrims said their rosaries, with their arms crossed, gazing toward the sky in the direction of Talpa. And you could hear how the wind picked up and carried that noise, mixing it together until it was all one roaring sound. A little bit afterward everything would get quiet. About midnight you could hear someone singing far away. Then you closed your eyes and waited for the dawn to come without getting any sleep.

We entered Talpa singing the hymn praising Our Lord.

We'd left around the middle of February and we got to Talpa the last days of March, when a lot of people were already on their way back. All because Tanilo took it into his head to do penance. As soon as he saw himself surrounded by men wearing cactus leaves hanging down like scapularies, he decided to do something like that too. He tied his feet together with his shirt sleeves so his steps became more desperate. Then he wanted to wear a crown of thorns. A little later he bandaged his eyes, and still later, during the last part of the way, he knelt on the ground and shuffled along on his knees with his hands crossed behind him; so that thing that was my brother Tanilo Santos reached Talpa, that thing so covered with plasters and dried streaks of blood that it left in the air a sour smell like a dead animal when he passed by.

When we least expected it we saw him there among the dancers. We hardly realized it and there he was with a long rattle in his hand, stomping hard on the ground with his bare bruised feet. He seemed to be in a fury, as if he was shaking out all the anger he'd been carrying inside him for such a long time, or making a last effort to try to live a little longer.

Maybe when he saw the dances he remembered going every year to Tolimán during the novena of Our Lord and dancing all night long until his bones limbered up without getting tired. Maybe that's what he remembered and he wanted to get back the strength he used to have.

Natalia and I saw him like that for a moment. Right afterward we saw him raise his arms and slump to the ground with the rattle still sounding in his bloodspeckled hands. We dragged him out so he wouldn't be tromped on by the dancers, away from the fury of those feet that slipped on stones and leaped about stomping the earth without knowing that something had fallen among them.

Holding him up between us as if he was crippled, we went into the church with him. Natalia had him kneel down next to her before that little golden figure of the Virgin of Talpa. And Tanilo started to pray and let a huge tear fall, from way down inside him, snuffing out the candle Natalia had placed in his hands. But he didn't realize this; the light from so many lit candles kept him from realizing what was happening right there. He went on praying with his candle snuffed out. Shouting his prayers so he could hear himself praying.

But it didn't do him any good. He died just the same.

"... *from our hearts filled with pain we all send her the same plea. Many laments mixed with hope. Her tenderness is not deaf to laments nor tears, for She suffers with us. She knows how to take away that stain and to leave the heart soft and pure to receive her mercy and charity. Our Virgin, our mother, who wants to know nothing of our sins, who blames herself for our sins, who wanted to bear us in her arms so life wouldn't hurt us, is right here by us, relieving our tiredness and the sicknesses of our souls and our bodies filled with thorns, wounded and supplicant. She knows that each day our faith is greater because it is made up of sacrifices ...*"

That's what the priest said from up in the pulpit. And after he quit talking the people started praying all at once with a noise just like a lot of wasps frightened by smoke.

But Tanilo no longer heard what the priest was saying. He'd become still, with his head resting on his knees. And when Natalia moved him so he'd get up he was already dead.

Outside you could hear the noise of the dancing, the drums and the hornpipes, the ringing of bells. That's when I got sad. To see so many living things, to see the Virgin there, right in front of us with a smile on her face, and to see Tanilo on the other hand as if he was in the way. It made me sad.

But we took him there so he'd die, and that's what I can't forget.

Now the two of us are in Zenzontla. We've come back without him. And Natalia's mother hasn't asked me anything, what I did with my brother Tanilo, or anything. Natalia started crying on her shoulder and poured out the whole story to her.

I'm beginning to feel as if we hadn't reached any place; that we're only here in passing, just to rest, and that then we'll keep on traveling. I don't know where to, but we'll have to go on, because here we're very close to our guild and the memory of Tanilo.

Maybe until we begin to be afraid of each other. Not saying anything to each other since we left Talpa may mean that. Maybe Tanilo's body is too close to us, the way it was stretched out on the rolled petate, filled inside and out with a swarm of blue flies that buzzed like a big snore coming from his mouth, that mouth we couldn't shut in spite of everything we did and that seemed to want to go on breathing without finding any breath. That Tanilo, who didn't feel pain any more but who looked like he was still in pain with his hands and feet twisted and his eyes wide open like he was looking at his own death. And here and there all his wounds dripping a yellow water, full of that smell that spread everywhere and that you could taste in your mouth, like it was a thick and bitter honey melting into your blood with each mouthful of air you took.

I guess that's what we remember here most often—that Tanilo we buried in the Talpa graveyard, that Tanilo Natalia and I threw earth and stones on so the wild animals wouldn't come dig him up.

# ■ Juan José Arreola (1918– ) *Mexico* (fable)

## TRANSLATED BY GEORGE D. SCHADE

Juan José Arreola was born in Ciudad Guzmán in Jalisco. Despite his worldliness, his years in Europe, the life in the province of Jalisco remains at the center of his work. In the 1940s, he went to Guadalajara where he began to work for journals. He met the famous actor Louis Jouvet, who took him to Paris. He returned to Mexico City to found a publishing house, *Los Presentes,* to introduce the new writers, including Carlos Fuentes. He also began to publish his own inimitable stories and to work actively in the theater. *Various Inventions,* a book of stories, came out in 1949, followed by *Silvertip* in 1958. These stories and other writings were incorporated in *Confabulario and Other Inventions,* which appeared in English in 1964. Arreola is funny, savagely witty, a bit fantastically crazy in his satires and always reveals an immense grace. Like the contemporary playwright Eugène Ionesco, who invented the theater of the absurd in Paris, Arreola invented and has been a master of the absurd, often in miniature. As his fellow Mexican writer Juan Rulfo was fantastic and grave, Arreola beams with mischievous life. *The Fair* was published in 1977.

**FURTHER READING:** Arreola, Juan José. *Various Inventions,* 1949; *Silvertip,* 1958; *Confabulario and other Inventions.* Translated by George D. Schade, 1964; *The Fair.* Translated by John Upton, 1977.

## *I'm Telling You the Truth*

Everybody who is interested in seeing a camel pass through the eye of the needle should inscribe his name on the list of patrons for the Niklaus Experiment.

Disassociated from a group of death-dealing scientists, the kind who manipulate uranium, cobalt, and hydrogen, Arpad Niklaus is guiding his present research toward a charitable and radically humanitarian end: the salvation of the souls of the rich.

He proposes a scientific plan to disintegrate a camel and make it pass in a stream of electrons through a needle's eye. A receiving apparatus (very similar to the television screen) will organize the electrons into atoms, the atoms into molecules, and the molecules into cells, immediately reconstructing the camel according to its original scheme. Niklaus has already managed to make a drop of heavy water change its position without touching it. He has also been able to evaluate, up to the point where the discretion of the material permits, the quantum energy discharged by a camel's hoof. It seems pointless here to burden the reader with that astronomical figure.

The only serious difficulty Professor Niklaus has run into is the lack of his own atomic plant. Such installations, extensive as cities, are incredibly expensive. But a special committee is already busy solving the problem by means of a world-wide subscription drive. The first contributions, still rather anemic, are serving to defray the cost of thousands of pamphlets, bonds, and explanatory prospectuses, as well as to assure Professor Niklaus the modest salary permitting him to continue with his calculations and theoretical investigations while the immense laboratories are being built.

At present, the committee can count only on the camel and the needle. As the societies for the prevention of cruelty to animals approve the project, which is inoffensive and even healthful for any camel (Niklaus speaks of a probable regeneration of all the cells), the country's zoos have offered a veritable caravan. New York City has not hesitated to risk its very famous white dromedary.

As for the needle, Arpad Niklaus is very proud of it and considers it the keystone of the experiment. It is not just any needle, but a marvelous object discovered by his assiduous talent. At first glance, it might be confused with a common ordinary needle. Mrs. Niklaus, displaying a fine sense of humor, takes pleasure in mending her husband's clothes with it. But its value is infinite. It is made from an extraordinary, as yet unclassified, metal, whose chemical formula, scarcely hinted at by Niklaus, seems to indicate that it involves a base composed exclusively of isotopes of nickel. This mysterious substance has made scientists ponder a great deal. There was even one who sustained the laughable hypothesis of a synthetic osmium or an abnormal molybdenum, or still another who dared to proclaim in public the words of an envious professor who was sure he had recognized Niklaus metal in the form of tiny crystalline clusters encysted in dense masses of siderite. What is known with certainty is that Niklaus' needle can resist the friction of a stream of electrons flowing at ultrasonic speed.

In one of those explanations so pleasing to abstain mathematicians, Professor Niklaus compares the camel in its transit to a spider's thread. He tells us that if we were to use that thread to weave a fabric, we would need all of sidereal space to stretch it out in, and that the visible and invisible stars would be caught in it like sprays of dew. The skein in question measures millions of light years, and Niklaus is offering to wind it up in about three-fifths of a second.

As can be seen, the project is completely viable, and we might even say, overly scientific. It can already count on the sympathy and moral support (not officially confirmed yet) of the Interplanetary League, presided over in London by the eminent Olaf Stapledon.

In view of the natural expectation and anxiety that Niklaus' project has provoked everywhere, the committee is manifesting a special interest by calling the world powers' attention to it, so they will not let themselves be surprised by charlatans who are passing dead camels through subtle orifices. These individuals, who do not hesitate to call themselves scientists, are simply swindlers on the lookout for imprudent optimists. They proceed by an extremely vulgar method, dissolving the camel in sulphuric acid solutions each time lighter than the last. Then they distill the liquid through the needle's eye, using a steam clepsydra, believing that they have performed the miracle. As one can see, the experiment is useless, and there is no reason to finance it. The camel must be alive before and after the impossible transfer.

Instead of melting down tons of candle wax and spending money on indecipherable works of charity, persons interested in the eternal life who have more capital than they know what to do with should subsidize the disintegration of the camel, which is scientific, colorful, and, ultimately, lucrative. To speak of generosity in such a case is totally unnecessary. One must shut one's eyes and open one's purse generously, knowing full well that all expenses will be met pro rata. The reward for all the contributors will be the same; what is urgent is to hasten the date of payment as much as possible.

The total capital necessary cannot be known until the unpredictable end, and Professor Niklaus, in all honesty, refuses to work with a budget that is not fundamentally elastic. The subscribers should pay out their investment quotas patiently over the years. It is necessary to contract for thousands of technicians, managers, and workers. Regional and national subcommittees must be established. And the statute founding a school of successors for Professor Niklaus must not only be foreseen, but budgeted for in detail, since the experiment might reasonably extend over several generations. In this respect, it is not beside the point to indicate the ripe old age of the learned Niklaus.

Like all human plans, Experiment Niklaus offers two probable results: failure and success. Besides simplifying the problem of personal salvation, a success by Niklaus will convert the promoters of such a mystical experience into stockholders of a fabulous transport company. It will be very easy to develop the disintegration of human beings in a practical and economical way. The men of tomorrow will travel great distances in an instant and without danger, dissolved in electronic flashes.

But the possibility of a failure is even more attractive. If Arpad Niklaus is a maker of chimeras and is followed at his death by a whole line of impostors, his humanitarian work will only have increased in grandeur, like a geometric progression or the texture of a chicken bread by Carib. Nothing will keep him from passing into history as the glorious innovator of the universal disintegration of capital. And the rich, impoverished en masse by the draining investments, will easily enter the kingdom of heaven by the narrow gate (the eye of the needle), though the camel may not pass through.

## ■ João Cabral de Melo Neto (1920– ) *Brazil* (poems)

João Cabral de Melo Neto was born in Recife, to a wealthy family, and as a young man he entered the diplomatic service. He served largely in

Europe. While in Spain, he became closely connected to Spanish poets. In 1950, he published a long poem, "The Dog without Feathers." Since the appearance of his *Complete Poems* in 1968, he has become his generation's natural heir to Carlos Drummond de Andrade, a social critic with modernist ways and strong, brilliant verse, often framed in traditional ballad form. A major poetic voice in Latin America, he has, Elizabeth Bishop writes, "striking visual imagery and an insistent use of concrete, tactile nouns. He is 'difficult': but at the present time his work displays the highest development and the greatest coherency of style of any Brazilian poet."[1]

**FURTHER READING:** Cabral de Melo Neto, João. *Poems,* 1968.

## Poem

My eyes have telescopes
trained on the street
trained on my soul
a mile away.

Women come and go swimming
in invisible rivers.
Cars like blind fish
compose my mechanical visions.

For twenty years I've not said the word
I always expect from me.
I'll go on indefinitely gazing
at the portrait of me, dead.

TRANSLATED BY W. S. MERWIN

## The End of the World

At the end of a melancholy world
men read the newspapers.
Men indifferent to eating oranges
that flame like the sun.

---

1. Elizabeth Bishop, ed., *An Anthology of Twentieth-century Brazilian Poetry* (Middletown, CT: Wesleyan University Press, 1972), xxi.

They gave me an apple to remind me                                              5
of death. I know that cities telegraph
asking for kerosene. The veil I saw flying fell in the desert.

No one will write the final poem
about this particular twelve o'clock world.
Instead of the last judgment, what worries me                                  10
is the final dream.

TRANSLATED BY JAMES WRIGHT

## ■ Derek Walcott (1930– ) *Saint Lucia/United States* (epic poem)

The only American-born poet to win the Nobel Prize in Poetry is T. S.
Eliot, although Eliot was by then an English citizen, who from graduate
student days before World War I had lived in London. Three foreign-born
poets, however (Josef Brodsky, a Russian; Czelaw Milosz, a Pole; and
Derek Walcott, a Saint Lucian), each a Nobel laureate, have lived in the
United States. Unlike Eliot, who after "Prufock" scarcely alludes to the
United States, Brodsky, Milosz, and Walcott write frequently about American life. To add another level of sophisticated, international complication
to literatures without borders, Walcott's most impressive poem—which
won the Swedish literary award—is *Omeros,* an epic in Dante-flowing tercets, tracing the life and adventures of a fisherman on a Caribbean island,
based on Homer's *Odysseus.*

Derek Walcott was born in Castries, Saint Lucia. A poet and playwright
from his undergraduate days, he published his first book, *25 Poems,* in 1948
when he was eighteen and two years later his first play, *Henri Christophe,* was
staged. He obtained his B.A. from the University College of the West Indies
in Jamaica. In 1958, he went to New York on a Rockefeller Foundation Fellowship to study theater. Then, in Port of Spain, Trinidad, he founded and
ran the Little Carib Theatre Workshop from 1959 to 1976. In his back-and-
forth life between Trinidad and the United States, he wrote his early masterpiece, *Dream on Monkey Mountain* (1967), whose West Indian hero Makak has
South Africa in his mind. Its 1971 version won an Obie Award. Walcott's first
important volume of poems is *In a Green Night: Poems, 1948–1962* (1962),
published in England by Cape. Two years later, Farrar Straus published his
*Selected Poems in America. Another Life* (1973), also with Farrar Straus, continues the autobiographical search for identity through a sequence of poems.
His next two plays, *The Joker of Seville* and *O Babylon!,* came out together as a
book of the same name. *The Joker,* with calypso music, retells the Spanish playwright Tirso de Molina's sixteenth-century play, *The Trickster of Seville* as a
modern version of the notorious Don Juan Tenorio in which both men and
women are victimized by their socially imposed roles. *O Babylon!,* with music

by Galt MacDermot, is, Walcott states, his first real musical; it dramatizes the Rastafarian cult in Jamaica. His plays prospered. *Pantomine* (1978) was premiered at Joseph Papp's Shakespeare Festival. In 1979, he was named an honorary member of the American Academy of Arts and Letters, and he began to teach at American universities: New York University, Yale, Columbia, and, ultimately, Boston University where he accepted a permanent post.

Derek Walcott continued publishing volumes of poems, *Sea Grapes* (1976), *The Star-Apple Kingdom* (1979), and *The Fortunate Traveller* (1981). The latter, suggesting the traveler between United States urban centers and the Caribbean, feels increasingly like work by Josef Brodsky, to whom his work is dedicated. Both authors are cosmopolitan world travelers and commentators. A certain formal stiffness often characterizes their city and nature pictures. After *Collected Poems* in 1986, Derek Walcott turned to the two great epics of the West, Homer's *Odyssey* and Dante's *Comedy*, to find a Homeric narrative pitch and a version of Dante's flowing tercets to compose his New World epic, *Omeros* (1990), about a black Helen from Saint Lucia and the life of its dispossessed descendants of African slaves. As Gabriel García Márquez wrote the prose book of the Americas, so Walcott has given us the epic poem of the Americas in wondrously beautiful speech, with extraordinary local detail, and a masterly humane story engaging to the last page. Recognition of his multiple talents, which climax in *Omeros*, came with his 1991 Nobel Prize for Literature.

**FURTHER READING:** Walcott, Derek. *25 Poems*, 1948; *Henri Christophe*, 1950; *Dream on Monkey Mountain*, 1967; *In a Green Night: Poems, 1948–1962*, 1962; *Selected Poems*, 1964; *Another Life*, 1973; *The Joker of Seville and O Babylon!*, 1978; *Sea Grapes*, 1976; *The Star-Apple Kingdom*, 1979; *The Fortunate Traveller*, 1981; *Collected Poems*, 1986; *Omeros*, 1990.

## from *Omeros*

### Chapter XXXVII

I

I crossed my meridian. Rust terraces, olive trees,
the grey horns of a port. Then, from a cobbled corner
of this mud-caked settlement founded by Ulysses—

swifts, launched from the nesting sills of Ulissibona,
their cries modulated to "Lisbon" as the Mediterranean
aged into the white Atlantic, their flight, in reverse,                    5

repeating the X of an hourglass, every twitter an aeon
from which a horizon climbed in the upturned vase.
A church clock spun back its helm. Turtleback alleys

crawled from the sea, not towards it, to resettle                                    *10*
in the courtyard under the olives, and a breeze
turned over the leaves to show their silvery metal.

Here, clouds read backwards, muffling the clash
of church bells in cotton. There, on an opposite wharf,
Sunday in a cream suit, with a grey horned moustache,                      *15*

strolled past wooden crates, and the long-shadowed Sabbath
was no longer Lisbon but Port of Spain. There, time sifts
like grain from a jute sack under the crooning pigeons.

Sunday clicks open a gold watch, startling the swifts
from the opening eye of a tower, closes it, then slips the sun's         *20*
pendulum back into its fob, patting it with a nod.

Sunday strolls past a warehouse whose iron-ringed door
exhales an odour of coffee as a reek of salt cod
slithers through the railings. Sunday is a widower

in an ice-cream suit, and a straw with a mourning band,               *25*
an old Portugee leathery as Portugal, via Madeira,
with a stalled watch for a compass. When he rewinds its hand

it raises an uproar of docks, mulatto clerks cowed
by jets of abuse from wine-barrelled wholesalers.
winches and cranes, black drivers cursing black loaders,              *30*

and gold-manacled vendors teasing the Vincentian sailors
folded over the hulls. Then not a single word, as Saturday went home
        at one, except from the pigeons

and a boy rattling his stick along the rusted staves
of a railing, its bars caging him as he runs.
After that arpeggio, Sunday hears his own footsteps,                    *35*

making centuries recede, the ebbing market in slaves
and sugar declining below the horizon. Then Sunday stops
to hear schooners thudding on overlapping wharves.

## II

Across the meridian, I try seeing the other side,
past rusty containers, waves like welts from the lash
in a light as clear as oil from the olive seed.

Once the world's green gourd was split like a calabash
by Pope Alexander's decree. Spices, vanilla
sweetened this wharf; the grain of swifts would scatter

in their unchanging pattern, their cries no shriller
than they are now over the past, or ours, for that matter,
if our roles were reversed, and the sand in one half

replicated the sand in the other. Now I had come
to a place I felt I had known, an antipodal wharf
where my forked shadow swayed to the same brass pendulum.

Yes, but not as one of those pilgrims whose veneration carried
the salt of their eyes up the grooves of a column
to the blue where forked swifts navigated. Far from it; instead,

I saw how my shadow detached itself from them
when it disembarked on the wharf through a golden haze
of corn from another coast. My throat was scarred

from a horizon that linked me to others, when our eyes
lowered to the cobbles that climbed to the castle yard,
when the coins of the olives showed us their sovereign's face.

My shadow had preceded me. How else could it recognize
that light to which it was attached, this port where Europe
rose with its terrors and terraces, slope after slope?

# III

A bronze horseman halts at a wharf, his green-bronze
cloak flecked with white droppings, his wedged visor
shading the sockets' hyphenating horizons,

his stare fixed like a helm. We had no such erections
above our colonial wharves, our erogenous zones
were not drawn to power, our squares shrank the directions

of the Empire's plazas. Above us, no stallions paw
the sky's pavement to strike stars from the stones,
no sword is pointed to recapture the port of Genoa.

There the past is an infinite Sunday. It's hot, or it rains;
the sun lifts the sheets of the rain, and the gutters
run out. For those to whom history is the presence

of ruins, there is a green nothing. No bell tower utters
its flotilla of swallows memorizing an alphabet,
no cobbles crawl towards the sea. We think of the past          *15*

as better forgotten than fixed with stony regret.
Here, a castle in the olives rises over the tiered roofs
of crusted tile but, like the stone Don in the opera,

is the ghost of itself. Over the flagstones, hooves
clop down from the courtyard, stuttering pennons appear          *20*
from the mouths of arches, and the past dryly grieves

from the O's of a Roman aqueduct; silver cuirasses
flash in the reversible olives, their silvery leaves,
and twilight ripens the municipal canvases,

where, one knee folded, like a drinking deer, an admiral          *25*
with a grey horned moustache and foam collar proffers a gift
of plumed Indians and slaves. The wharves of Portugal

were empty as those of the islands. The slate pigeons lift
from the roof of a Levantine warehouse, the castle in the trees
is its own headstone. Yet, once, Alexander's meridian          *30*

gave half a gourd to Lisbon, the seeds of its races,
and half to Imperial Spain. Now Sunday afternoon passes
the empty cafés, their beads hanging like rosaries,

as shawled fado singers sob in turn to their mandolins
while a cobbled lane climbs like a tortoise, and tiredly raises          *35*
its head of a pope at the limp sails on washing lines.

## Chapter XXXVIII

I

In scorched summer light, from the circle of Charing Cross,
he arose with the Underground's grit and its embers of sparrows
in a bargeman's black greatcoat, clutching in one scrofulous

claw his brown paper manuscript. The nose, like a pharos,
bulbed from his cragged face, and the beard under it was          *5*
foam that exploded into the spray burst of eyebrows.

On the verge of collapse, the fallen sails of his trousers
were upheld by a rope. In the barges of different shoes
he flapped towards the National. The winch of his voice,

a fog still in its throat, barged through the queues                                  1(
at the newspaper kiosks, then changed gears with the noise
of red double-deckers embarking on chartered views

from pigeon-stirred Trafalgar; it broke off the icing
from wedding-cake London. Gryphons on their ridge
of sandstone snarled because it had carried the cries in                              1'

the Isle of Dogs running over Westminster Bridge.
Today it would anchor in the stone waves of the entrance
of St. Martin-in-the-Fields. There, in tiered sunshine,

the black sail collapsed, face sunward with both hands
crossed over the shop-paper volume bound with grey twine.                            2(
He looked like a heap of slag-coal crusting the tiers

with their summering tourists. Eyes shut, the frayed lips
chewed the breeze, the beard curled like the dog's ears
of his turned-down Odyssey, but Omeros was naming the ships

whose oars spidered soundlessly over the sun-webbed calm                             2.
behind his own lashes. Then, suddenly, a raging sparrow
of a church-warden bobbed down the steps. It picked one arm.

The bargeman huddled. It screeched. It yanked an elbow,
then kicked him with polished pumps, and a curse as
Greek to the choleric cleric as one might imagine                                    3(

sprayed the spluttering soutane. It showed him the verses
framed at the entrance announcing this Sunday's lesson
in charity, etc. Then, like a dromedary, over the sands

of the scorching pavement, the hump began to press on
back to the river. The sparrow, rubbing both hands,                                  3.
nodded, and chirruped up the steps back to its sanctuary,

where, dipping one claw in the font, it vanished inside
the webbed stone. The bargeman tacked toward his estuary
of light. It was summer. London rustled with pride.

## II

He curled up on a bench underneath the Embankment wall.
He saw London gliding with the Thames around its neck
like a barge which an old brown horse draws up a canal

if its yoke is Time. From here he could see the dreck
under the scrolled skirts of statues, the grit in the stone lions'     5
eyes; he saw under everything an underlying grime

that itched in the balls of rearing bronze stallions,
how the stare of somnolent sphinxes closed in time
to the swaying bells of "cities all the floure"

petalling the spear-railed park where a couple suns     10
near the angled shade of All-Hallows by the Tower,
as the tinkling Thames drags by in its ankle-irons,

while the ginkgo's leaves flexed their fingers overhead.
He mutters its fluent alphabet, the peaked A of a spire,
the half-vowels of bridges, down to the crumpled Z     15

of his overcoat draping a bench in midsummer's fire.
He read the inverted names of boats in their element,
he saw the tugs chirring up a devalued empire

as the coins of their wake passed the Houses of Parliament.
But the shadows keep multiplying from the Outer     20
Provinces, their dialects light as the ginkgo's leaf, their

fingers plucking their saris as wind picks at water,
and the statues raising objections; he sees a wide river
with its landing of pier-stakes flooding Westminster's

flagstones, and traces the wake of dugouts in the frieze     25
of a bank's running cornice, and whenever the ginkgo stirs
the wash of far navies settles in the bargeman's eyes.

A statue swims upside down, one hand up in response
to a question raised in the House, and applause rises
from the clapping Thames, from benches in the leaves.     30

And the sunflower sets after all, retracting its irises
with the bargeman's own, then buds on black, iron trees
as a gliding fog hides the empires: London, Rome, Greece.

## III

Who decrees a great epoch? The meridian of Greenwich.
Who doles out our zeal, and in which way lies our
hope? In the cobbles of sinister Shoreditch,

in the widening rings of Big Ben's iron flower,
in the barges chained like our islands to the Thames.
Where is the alchemical corn and the light it yields?

Where, in which stones of the Abbey, are incised our names?
Who defines our delight? St. Martin-in-the-Fields.
After every Michaelmas, its piercing soprano steeple

defines our delight. Within whose palatable vault                    1
will echo the Saints' litany of our island people?
St. Paul's salt shaker, when we are worth their salt.

Stand by the tilted crosses of well-quiet Glen-da-Lough.
Follow the rook's crook'd finger to the ivied grange.
As black as the rook is, it comes from a higher stock.               1.

Who screams out our price? The crows of the Corn Exchange.
Where are the pleasant pastures? A green baize-table.
Who invests in our happiness? The Chartered Tour.

Who will teach us a history of which we too are capable?
The red double-decker's view of the Bloody Tower.                    2
When are our brood, like the sparrows, a public nuisance?

When they screech at the sinuous swans on the Serpentine.
The swans are royally protected, but in whose hands
are the black crusts of our children? In the pointing sign

under the harps of the willows, to the litter of Margate Sands.      2
What has all this to do with the price of fish, our salary
tidally scanned with the bank-rate by waxworks tellers?

Where is the light of the world? In the National Gallery.
In Palladian Wren. In the City that can buy and sell us
the packets of tea stirred with our crystals of sweat.               3

Where is our sublunar peace? In that sickle sovereign
peeling the gilt from St. Paul's onion silhouette.
There is our lunar peace: in the glittering grain

of the coined estuary, our moonlit, immortal wheat,
its white sail cresting the gradual swell of the Downs,              3
startling the hare from the pillars on Salisbury Plain,

sharpening the grimaces of thin-lipped market towns,
whitewashing the walls of Brixton, darkening the grain
when coal-shadows cross it. Dark future down darker street.

## Chapter LXIV

I

I sang of quiet Achille, Afolabe's son,
who never ascended in an elevator,
who had no passport, since the horizon needs none,

never begged nor borrowed, was nobody's waiter,
whose end, when it comes, will be a death by water        5
(which is not for this book, which will remain unknown

and unread by him). I sang the only slaughter
that brought him delight, and that from necessity—
of fish, sang the channels of his back in the sun.

I sang our wide country, the Caribbean Sea.        10
Who hated shoes, whose soles were as cracked as a stone,
who was gentle with ropes, who had one suit alone,

whom no man dared insult and who insulted no one,
whose grin was a white breaker cresting, but whose frown
was a growing thunderhead, whose fist of iron        15

would do me a greater honour if it held on
to my casket's oarlocks than mine lifting his own
when both anchors are lowered in the one island,

but now the idyll dies, the goblet is broken,
and rainwater trickles down the brown cheek of a jar        20
from the clay of Choiseul. So much left unspoken

by my chirping nib! And my earth-door lies ajar.
I lie wrapped in a flour-sack sail. The clods thud
on my rope-lowered canoe. Rasping shovels scrape

a dry rain of dirt on its hold, but turn your head        25
when the sea-almond rattles or the rust-leaved grape
from the shells of my unpharaonic pyramid

towards paper shredded by the wind and scattered
like white gulls that separate their names from the foam
and nod to a fisherman with his khaki dog        30

that skitters from the wave-crash, then frown at his form
for one swift second. In its earth-trough, my pirogue
with its brass-handled oarlocks is sailing. Not from

but with them, with Hector, with Maud in the rhythm
of her beds trowelled over, with a swirling log                                    3
lifting its mossed head from the swell; let the deep hymn

of the Caribbean continue my epilogue;
may waves remove their shawls as my mourners walk home
to their rusted villages, good shoes in one hand,

passing a boy who walked through the ignorant foam,                                4
and saw a sail going out or else coming in,
and watched asterisks of rain puckering the sand.

## II

You can see Helen at the Halcyon. She is dressed
in the national costume: white, low-cut bodice,
with frilled lace at the collar, just a cleft of a breast

for the customers when she places their orders
on the shields of the tables. They can guess the rest
under the madras skirt with its golden borders

and the flirtatious knot of the madras head-tie.
She pauses between the tables, holding a tray
over her stomach to hide the wave-rounded sigh

of her pregnancy. There is something too remote                                    1
about her stillness. Women study her beauty,
but turn their faces away if their eyes should meet,

like an ebony carving. But if she should swerve
that silhouette hammered out of the sea's metal
like a profile on a shield, its sinuous neck                                       1

longing like a palm's, you might recall that battle
for which they named an island or the heaving wreck
of the *Ville de Paris* in her foam-frilled bodice,

or just think, "What a fine local woman!" and her
head will turn when you snap your fingers, the slow eyes                           2
approaching you with the leisure of a panther

through white tables with palm-green iron umbrellas,
past children wading with water-wings in the pool;
and Africa strides, not alabaster Hellas,

and half the world lies open to show its black pearl.                    *25*
She waits for your order and you lower your eyes
away from hers that have never carried the spoil

of Troy, that never betrayed horned Menelaus
or netted Agamemnon in their irises.
But the name Helen had gripped my wrist in its vise          *30*

to plunge it into the foaming page. For three years,
phantom hearer, I kept wandering to a voice
hoarse as winter's echo in the throat of a vase!

Like Philoctete's wound, this language carries its cure,
its radiant affliction; reluctantly now,                           *35*
like Achille's, my craft slips the chain of its anchor,

moored to its cross as I leave it; its nodding prow
lettered as simply, ribbed in our native timber,
riding these last worried lines; its rhythm agrees

that all it forgot a swift made it remember                       *40*
since that green sunrise of axes and laurel-trees,
till the sunset chars it, slowly, to an ember.

And Achille himself had been one of those children
whose voices are surf under a galvanized roof;
sheep bleating in the schoolyard; a Caribbean            *45*

whose woolly crests were the backs of the Cyclops's flock,
with the smart man under one's belly. Blue stories
we recited as children lifted with the rock

of Polyphemus. From a plaster Omeros
the smoke and the scarves of mare's tails, continually        *50*
chalked associate phantoms across our own sky.

## III

Out of their element, the thrashing mackerel
thudded, silver, then leaden. The vermilion scales
of snappers faded like sunset. The wet, mossed coral

sea-fans that winnowed weeds in the wiry water
stiffened to bony lace, and the dripping tendrils                  *5*
of an octopus wrung its hands at the slaughter

from the gutting knives. Achille unstitched the entrails
and hurled them on the sand for the palm-ribbed mongrels
and the sawing flies. As skittish as hyenas

the dogs trotted, then paused, angling their muzzles                          1(
sideways to gnaw on trembling legs, then lift a nose
at more scavengers. A triumphant Achilles,

his hands gloved in blood, moved to the other canoes
whose hulls were thumping with fishes. In the spread seine
the silvery mackerel multiplied the noise                                     1:

of coins in a basin. The copper scales, swaying,
were balanced by one iron tear; then there was peace.
They washed their short knives, they wrapped the flour-bag sails,

then they helped him haul *In God We Trust* back in place,
jamming logs under its keel. He felt his muscles                              2(
unknotting like rope. The nets were closing their eyes,

sagging on bamboo poles near the concrete depot.
In the standpipe's sandy trough aching Achilles
washed sand from his heels, then tightened the brass spigot

to its last drop. An immense lilac emptiness                                  2:
settled the sea. He sniffed his name in one armpit.
He scraped dry scales off his hands. He liked the odours

of the sea in him. Night was fanning its coalpot
from one catching star. The No Pain lit its doors
in the village. Achille put the wedge of dolphin                              3(

that he'd saved for Helen in Hector's rusty tin.
A full moon shone like a slice of raw onion.
When he left the beach the sea was still going on.

## ■ Clarice Lispector (1925–1977) *Brazil* (stories)

Born of Ukranian Jews, Clarice Lispector and her family emigrated to
Recife, Brazil, when she was only two months old. She grew up in poverty.
When she was nine, her mother died after two difficult childbirths. The
family moved to Rio de Janeiro in 1937, where she completed secondary
school and where, still a schoolgirl, she published her first short story. She
did her law studies in Rio, where she married a fellow law student, who became a diplomat. In 1944, the year of her graduation, she published her

first novel, *Near to the Wild Heart*. Soon thereafter, her husband was assigned to foreign posts, and she spent many years living abroad, in Switzerland, England, Italy, and the United States. After her marriage ended, she returned to Rio in 1959, where she supported herself and her two children on what she earned as a journalist and author. Although she received much national and international recognition, she had financial and health problems during her difficult last years, finally dying of cancer in a public hospital.

Clarice Lispector seems equally indebted to Katherine Mansfield, Virginia Woolf, and the experimental New Wave French antinovel of Nathalie Sarraute. A splendid concise stylist and an outstanding short story writer in the Portuguese language, she creates lonely characters who sometimes even attempt to escape from the page into their own fictions. In the introduction to Alexis Levitin's masterful English translation of Lispector's stories in Soulstorm, Grace Paley writes:

> Lispector was lucky enough to have begun to think about all these lives, men's lives as well as women's, in the early years of the women's movement—that is, at a time when she found herself working among the scrabbly low tides of that movement in the ignorance which is often essential to later understanding. That historical fact is what has kept her language crooked and clean.[1]

In her "Explanation" that precedes the thirteen stories in *Soulstorm*, we have a short story in which the author herself writes a tale about writing her "bruising stories" and about her enigmatic and unresponsive encounters with would-be characters in her tales.

**FURTHER READING:** Lispector, Clarice. *Near to the Wild Heart*, 1944; *Besieged City*, 1949; *Family Links*, 1960; *The Foreign Legion*, 1964; *The Passion According to G. H.*, 1964; *The Apple in the Dark*, 1967; *Soulstorm*, 1989.

## Marmosets

The first time we had a marmoset was just before New Year's. We were without water and without a maid, people were lining up to buy meat, the hot weather had suddenly begun—when, dumbfounded, I saw the present enter the house, already eating a banana, examining everything with great rapidity, and with a long tail. It looked like a monkey not yet grown; its potentialities were tremendous. It climbed up the drying clothes to the clothesline, where it swore like a sailor, and the banana peelings fell where they would. I was exhausted already. Every time I forgot and absent-

---

1. Clarice Lispector, *Soulstorm: Stories*. Translated by Alexis Levitin; introduction by Grace Paley (New York: New Directions, 1989), x.

mindedly went out on the back terrace, I gave a start: there was that happy
man. My younger son knew, before I did, that I would get rid of this gorilla: "If I promise that sometime the monkey will get sick and die, will you
let him stay? Or if you knew that sometime he'd fall out the window, somehow, and die down there?" My feelings would glance aside. The filthiness
and blithe unconsciousness of the little monkey made me responsible for
his fate, since he himself would not take any blame. A friend understood
how bitterly I had resigned myself, what dark deeds were being nourished
beneath my dreaminess, and rudely saved me: a delighted gang of little
boys appeared from the hill and carried off the laughing man. The new
year was devitalized but at least monkeyless.

A year later, at a time of happiness, suddenly there in Copacabana I
saw the small crowd. I thought of my children, the joys they gave me, free,
unconnected with the worries they also gave me, free, and I thought of a
chain of joy: "Will the person receiving this pass it along to someone else,"
one to another, like a spark along a train of powder. Then and there I
bought the one who would be called Lisette.

She could almost fit in one hand. She was wearing a skirt, and earrings, necklace, and bracelet of glass beads. The air of an immigrant just
disembarking in her native costume. Like an immigrant's, too, her round
eyes.

This one was a woman in miniature. She lived with us three days. She
had such delicate bones. She was of such a sweetness. More than her eyes,
her look was rounded. With every movement, the earrings shook; the skirt
was always neat, the red necklace glinted. She slept a lot, but, as to eating,
she was discreet and languid. Her rare caress was only a light bite that left
no mark.

On the third day we were out on the back terrace admiring Lisette
and the way she was ours. "A little too gentle," I thought, missing the gorilla. And suddenly my heart said harshly: "But this isn't sweetness. This is
death." The dryness of the message left me calm. I said to the children:
"Lisette is dying." Looking at her, I realized the stage of love we had already reached. I rolled her up in a napkin and went with the children to
the nearest first-aid station, where the doctor couldn't attend to her because he was performing an emergency operation on a dog. Another
taxi—"Lisette thinks she's out for a drive, Mama"—another hospital.
There they gave her oxygen.

And with the breath of life, a Lisette we hadn't known was revealed.
The eyes less round, more secretive, more laughing, and in the prog-
nathous and ordinary face a certain ironic haughtiness. A little more oxygen and she wanted to speak so badly she couldn't bear being a monkey;
she was, and she would have had much to tell. More oxygen, and then an
injection of salt solution; she reacted to the prick with an angry slap, her
bracelet glittering. The male nurse smiled; "Lisette! Gently, my dear!"

The diagnosis: she wouldn't live unless there was oxygen at hand, and
even then it was unlikely. "Don't buy monkeys in the street," he scolded

me; "sometimes they're already sick." No, one must buy dependable monkeys, and know where they came from, to ensure at least five years of love, and know what they had or hadn't done, like getting married. I discussed it with the children a minute. Then I said to the nurse: "You seem to like Lisette very much. So if you let her stay a few days, near the oxygen, you can have her." He was thinking. "Lisette is pretty!" I implored.

"She's beautiful!" he agreed, thoughtfully. Then he sighed and said, "If I cure Lisette, she's yours." We went away with our empty napkin.

The next day they telephoned, and I informed the children that Lisette had died. The younger one asked me, "Do you think she died wearing her earrings?" I said yes. A week later the older one told me, "You look so much like Lisette!"

I replied, "I like you, too."

TRANSLATED BY ELIZABETH BISHOP

## *Explanation*

My editor commissioned me to write three stories which, said he, had really happened. The facts I had, only imagination was missing. And the subject was dangerous. I told him that I didn't know how to write commissioned stories. But—even as he talked to me over the phone—I began to feel inspiration growing in me. The phone conversation was on Friday. I began on Saturday. Sunday morning the three stories were ready: "Miss Algrave," "The Body," and "The Way of the Cross." I myself, amazed. All the stories in this book are bruising stories. And the one who suffered most was me myself. I was shocked by reality. If there are indecencies in these stories, the fault is not mine. It's useless to say they didn't happen to me, my own family, and my friends. How do I know? I know. Artists know things. I just want to tell you that I don't write for money, but rather on impulse. They will throw stones at me. It hardly matters. I'm not playing games, I'm a serious woman. Besides, it was a challenge.

Today is the twelfth of May, Mother's Day. It wouldn't make sense to write stories on this day that I wouldn't want my children to read because I'd be ashamed. So I said to my editor: I'll only publish these under a pseudonym. I had, in fact, already chosen a very nice name: Cláudio Lemos. But he refused. He said that I ought to have the freedom to write whatever I wanted. I gave in. What could I do but be my own victim? I just pray to God that no one ever commissions anything from me again. For it looks as if I'm likely to rebelliously obey, I the unliberated one.

Someone read my stories and said that that wasn't literature, it was trash. I agree. But there's a time for everything. There's also a time for trash. This book is a bit sad because I discovered, like a foolish child, that it's a dog's world.

This is a book of thirteen stories. It could have been fourteen. But I didn't want it to be. It would have shown disrespect for the trust of a simple man who told me his life. He drives the cart on a farm. And he said to me: "In order not to spill blood, I separated from my woman. She had gone astray and had led my sixteen-year-old daughter astray." He has an eighteen-year-old son who doesn't even want to hear the sound of his own mother's name. And that's how things are.

P. S.—"The Man Who Appeared" and "For the Time Being" were also written on that same damned Sunday. Today, the thirteenth of May, Monday, the day of freedom for the slaves—therefore for me, too—I wrote "Day by Day," "Pig Latin," and "Plaza Mauá." "Footsteps" was written a few days later on a farm, in the darkness of the great night.

I've tried to look closely into someone else's face—a cashier at the movies. In order to learn the secret of her life. Useless. The other person is an enigma. And with eyes that are those of a statue: blind.

> "My soul breaketh for longing of Thee."
> *Psalms* 119:20
> "I, who understand the body. And its cruel exigencies. I've always known the body. Its dizzying vortex. The solemn body."
>
> *One of my characters*
> *still without a name*
>
> "Therefore do I weep, and my eyes run down with water."
> *Lamentations of Jeremiah*
> "And let all flesh bless his holy name for ever and ever."
> *Psalm of David*
> "Who has ever seen a love life and not seen it drown in tears of disaster or remorse?"
>
> *I don't know whose this is*

TRANSLATED BY ALEXIS LEVITIN

# ■ José Donoso (1924–1996) *Chile* (novel)

TRANSLATED BY HARDIE ST. MARTIN

José Donoso was born in Chile into a family of doctors and lawyers, and he studied at an English school in Santiago. In 1949, he went to Princeton University where he studied English literature for two years. In 1974, he returned to Princeton as a visiting professor. During his two years at the Writers' Workshop in Iowa, he taught American students how to write and publish novels in English. Although his first stories were written and published in English, he never strayed from the Spanish language or his native Chile as his lifelong focus—even when living in Mexico, the

United States, or Barcelona where he wrote most of *The Obscene Bird of the Night* (1969). Donoso's first novel, *Coronation* (1957, translated in 1962), was awarded the 1962 Faulkner Foundation Prize for the best Latin American novel of the year. With *Coronation,* an "Upstairs/Downstairs" story contrasting a decaying aristocratic family with its vigorous servants, Donoso emerged as the breakthrough novelist of his generation. Donoso worked as a shepherd in southern Chile and a dock worker in Buenos Aires; these varied experiences are reflected in his books *Summer Vacation* (1955) and *Charleston* (1960). Donoso has many voices, all showing artistic mastery, as we hear in one of his most telling books, *Hell Has No Limits* (1966), an ironic, powerful tale of love in a small-town brothel. Of the generation of new novelists, all highly educated and rich in diverse cultures, Donoso may have the most subtle and intellectually inquisitive pen.

**FURTHER READING:** Donoso, José. *Summer Vacation,* 1955; *Coronation,* 1957, tr. 1962; *Charleston and Other Stories,* 1960; *Hell Has No Limits,* 1966; *The Obscene Bird of Night,* 1969, tr. 1973; *A House in the Country,* 1978, tr. 1984.

## from *The Obscene Bird of Night*

Misiá Raquel Ruiz (Mistress Raquel Ruiz, that is) shed many tears when Mother Benita called up to tell her that Brígida had died in her sleep. Then she calmed down a little and asked for more details.

"Amalia, the little one-eyed woman who was a sort of servant to her, I don't know if you remember her . . ."

"Why, yes, Amalia . . ."

"Well, as I was saying, Amalia brewed Brígida her cup of tea, very strong, the way she liked it at night, and Amalia says that Brígida went right off to sleep, as peacefully as ever. It seems that before she went to bed she'd been darning a lovely nightgown, cream satin . . ."

"Oh, my God! It's a good thing you mentioned it, Mother! I've been so upset, it slipped my mind. Have them wrap it for me and tell Rita to hold it in the vestibule. It's my granddaughter Malú's bridal nightgown, she just got married, you remember how I was telling you all about it. The nightgown got caught in the zipper of her suitcase during the honeymoon. I used to like to take Brígida a little needlework, to give her something to do and make her still feel like part of the family. There was no one like Brígida for delicate work like that. How good she was at it! . . ."

Misiá Raquel took over the funeral arrangements. A wake in the chapel of the Casa de Ejercicios Espirituales de la Encarnación, the retreat house at La Chimba where Brígida spent the last fifteen years of her life, with High Mass for its forty women inmates, three nuns, and five young orphans, as well as Misiá Raquel's own children, daughters-in-law and granddaughters who attended the service. Since it was to be the last Mass celebrated in the chapel before it was deconsecrated by the Archbishop and the Casa was torn down, it was sung by Father Azócar. Then, burial in the Ruiz family's mausoleum, as she'd always promised her. Unfortunately, the mausoleum was very crowded. But, with a few phone calls, Misiá Raquel arranged things so that, by hook or by crook, they'd make room for Brígida. The blind faith the poor old woman had had in Misiá Raquel's promise to let her too rest under that marble enabled her to live out her last years in peace: in Mother Benita's archaic but still touching rhetoric, her death became a little flame that flickered out. One of these days, of course, they'd have to see to the weeding out of some of the remains interred in the mausoleum—all those babies from a time when they hadn't even found a cure for diphtheria, some French governess who died far from her own country, old bachelor uncles whose identities were fading—in order to store that miscellany of bones in a small box that would take up only a little space.

Everything went according to Misiá Raquel's plans. The inmates spent the entire afternoon helping me put up the black hangings in the chapel. Other old women, close friends of the deceased, washed the corpse, combed her hair, inserted her dentures, got her up in her finest under-clothes and, lamenting and whimpering as they tried to decide the best way to dress her for the last time, finally chose her Oxford gray jersey dress and her pink shawl, the one Brígida kept folded in tissue paper and wore only on Sundays. We arranged the wreaths, sent by the Ruiz family, around the bier. We lit the candles . . . It's really worthwhile being a servant like that, with an employer like Misiá Raquel. Such a good lady! But how many of us women have Brígida's luck? None. Look at Mercedes Barroso, only last week. A public welfare truck came to carry off poor Menche, and we ourselves, yes, it's hard to believe that we ourselves had to pick a few red geraniums from the vestibule court to dress up her coffin, and her former employers, who, over the phone, kept promising poor Menche the sun, the moon and the stars . . . wait, woman, wait, have patience, better wait till summer, no, better still when we get back from the summer holidays since you don't like the beach, remember how the sea air always gives you a windburn, when we come back that's when, you'll see, you'll love the new chalet with its garden, it has a room over the garage that's ideal for you . . . and, you see, Menche's employers didn't even show up at the Casa when she died. Poor Menche! What hard luck! And she was so good at telling dirty jokes, and she knew so many of them. Who knows where she used to dig them up. But Brígida's funeral was something else again: she had real wreaths, with white flowers and all, the way funeral flowers ought to be, and with calling cards too. The first thing Rita did when they brought the coffin was to run her hand under it to check if that part of the box was well polished like first-class coffins in the old days. I watched her purse her lips and nod approval. Such a fine job was done on Brígida's cof-fin! Misiá Raquel even kept her word about that. Nothing disappointed us. Neither the hearse drawn by four black horses bedecked with caparison and tufts of feathers nor the Ruiz family's gleaming cars lined up along the sidewalk, waiting for the funeral procession to start.

But it can't start yet. Misiá Raquel remembers, at the very last minute, that she has a bicycle that's a bit damaged but, with a little fixing here and there, will make a perfect gift for her gardener on the feast day of St. Peter and Paul . . . go Mudito (I was *Mudito* to everyone because I was mute), take your cart and fetch it for me, my chauffeur can put it in the back of the station wagon and save an extra trip.

"Aren't you coming back to see us any more, Misiá Raquel?"

"I've have to come when Inés gets back from Rome."

"Have you had any news from Misiá Inés?"

"Not a word. She hates writing letters. And now that the famous business of the beatification fell through and Jerónimo signed the chaplaincy of the Azcoitías over to the Archbishopric, she must be hiding her head and she's not even going to send postcards. If she stays in Rome much longer, it'll be a miracle if she finds the Casa still standing."

"Father Azócar's been showing me the plans for his Children's Village. They're lovely! You should see all the glass windows! The drawings made me feel a little better about . . . this being the last Mass in the chapel."

"One of Father Azócar's tall stories, Mother Benita. Don't be so naïve! He's the worst kind of scheming priest. This property Jerónimo signed over to the Archbishop is very, yes, very very valuable. Children's Village! I'll bet anything they divide all this into lots after they tear the Casa down and sell it, and the money will evaporate in smoke. Mudito's taking long, Mother, and with Brígida waiting for us to bury her! What can be holding him up? Of course the Casa's so big it takes all day to make your way through all the passageways and corridors that lead to the cell where I keep my stuff, and Mudito's so thin and sickly. But I'm tired, I want to go bury Brígida, I want to get away, this whole business is too much for me, I'm burying a whole life, poor Brígida, only a couple of years older than I, my God, and, to keep my word, I gave up my vault in the mausoleum for her to start rotting in my place, keeping it warm for me with her remains so that when they take them out mine won't get numb, won't be afraid, giving up my vault to her for the time being was the only way to keep my word, now that even relatives I haven't so much as said hello to in years come around claiming—I don't know what makes them think they have a leg to stand on—that they must be buried in the mausoleum, but I'm not afraid that they'll steal my place now, she'll be there, holding it for me, heating it with her body like in the days when she used to turn down the covers and slip a good hot water bottle under them, for me to go to bed early when I came in exhausted from running around on business errands in winter. But when I die she'll have to move out of my vault. What can I do? Yes, Brígida, yes, I'm going to hire lawyers to strip those relatives of their rights, but I doubt that we'll win the lawsuits . . . you'll have to get out. It won't be my fault. I won't have to answer for it anymore, Brígida, no one knows what they'll do after I'm gone. You can't say I haven't been good to you, I've done everything you told me, but I'm afraid because when they take you out I don't know what they're going to do with your bones, nobody will give a rap . . . who knows how many years from now I'll die, fortunately I'm in very good health, imagine, I haven't spent a single day in bed this winter, not even a chill, Mother Benita, not a thing, half of my grandchildren down with the flu and my daughters calling me up to please go over and help them because even their servants are sick . . ."

"How lucky! Almost all the orphans here came down with it. But then, the Casa's so cold, and coal is so expensive . . ."

"Imagine! It's the last straw! All this talk about a Children's Village, and look at the miserable conditions they keep them in. I'm going to send you a little contribution next time I go out to the farm. I have no idea what's left over from this year's crops, but I'll send you something so that you'll all remember poor Brígida. Were you able to get the bicycle in, Jenaro?"

The chauffeur sits next to Misiá Raquel. They can get under way now. The coachman climbs into the driver's seat of the hearse, Misiá Raquel's daughter-in-law puts on her perforated driving gloves, the black horses stamp, tears fill the eyes of the old women who go out on the sidewalk muffled up, shivering, coughing, to see the procession off. Before Misiá Raquel gives the order to get under way, I go over to her window and hand her the package.

"What's this?"

I wait.

"Malú's nightgown! My God! If this poor little man hadn't thought of it, I'd have forgotten, and he'd have had to pull the cart back here again for me . . . Thanks, Mudito . . . no, no, wait . . . have him wait, Mother . . . here, Mudito, for cigarettes, for your little vices, go on, take it . . . Blow the horn, Jenaro, get the procession started . . . Well, goodbye, Mother Benita . . ."

"Goodbye, Misiá Raquel . . ."

"Goodbye, Brígida . . ."

"Goodbye . . ."

When the last car disappears around the corner, we go in—Mother Benita, I, the old women who mumble as they slowly scatter to their courts. I bolt and lock the outside door. Rita closes the inner one with its rattly glass panes. Straggling behind, one of the old women picks up a white rose from the tile floor of the vestibule and, yawning and tuckered out from all the excitement, pins it on her bun before disappearing into the passageways to look for her friends, her bowl of watery soup, her shawl, her bed.

In a nook in one of the corridors, they stopped before the door I sealed off with two boards nailed crosswise. I'd loosened the nails, to make it easy for them to pry off the boards and go up to the next floor. The orphans pulled out the nails, took the boards off and helped Iris Mateluna go up . . . Get a move on, chubby, I'm scared, these stairs don't have a railing, some of the steps are gone . . . hey, fatso's so heavy everything's creaking under her . . . They take their time going up, studying where to take each step so the whole works won't collapse, looking for solid places so as to get Iris to the next floor. Ten years ago Mother Benita had me board up those doors so as to forget about that section of the Casa once and for all and not have to think about cleaning and keeping it neat, because we just don't have the strength to do it anymore . . . Mudito, better let it go to pot and not lose any sleep over it . . . Until the five little girls, bored with wandering about the Casa with nothing to do, discovered that they could open this door and go up to the cloistered galleries on the next floor that surround the courts . . . let's go up, kids, don't be scared . . . scared of what, when it's still light out, let's go see what's there . . . like what, nothing, filth, same as all over the Casa, but at least it's fun because no one's allowed to roam there because they say it might cave in . . . Eliana warns them to watch their step and make sure nobody sees them from downstairs but it's not too risky today because they're at the doorkeeper's, seeing Brígida off. Still, they'd better not take chances, Mother Benita's in a nasty mood . . . make yourselves useful, you little pests, pick that up, help with this pile of spoons and plates, they have to be left clean, now that they're going to hold an auction, fold the napkins, count them, sweep, get some washing done, wash your own things at least, you've been going around filthy as pigs, don't spend all your time playing . . . shshshshshsh, kids, shshshshshsh . . . careful, or we'll get punished . . .

They round one court and then another, until they come to a door Eliana pushes open. A room with twenty rusty iron bedsteads, disassembled, others crippled—missing rollers, patched-up springs—but set up in two rows against the walls, like beds in a boarding school. Twin windows: high, narrow, deeply recessed, their glass painted a chocolate brown up to a person's height so that no one can see anything outside except the dark clouds veiled by chicken wire and iron bars. I also loosened the nails with which I myself sealed the two windows. The orphans already know how to open them and they did it in time to wave goodbye to Brígida's hearse led by the four plumed horses followed by nine automobiles. Eliana counts eight, Mirella nine . . . no, eight . . . no, nine . . . and when the procession disappears the little neighborhood children take over the middle of the street again, scrambling after the soccer ball . . . Good pass, Ricardo! Kick, Mito! Quick, after it, Lucho, pass it, now, kick, there, goal, goooooal . . . a shrill scream from Mirella, who cheers her friends' *goooooooooooal* and applauds and waves to them.

Iris has stayed behind, at the back of the dormitory, sitting sleepily on an innerspring. She yawns. She leafs through a magazine. The orphans make faces at people going by, talk in shouts to their friends, sit in the window recess, laugh at a woman passing by, yawn. When it begins to get dark Iris calls Eliana.

"What do you want?"

"You promised to read me this one with Pluto the dog and Popeye the sailor man."

"No. You owe me for two readings."

"I'm going to get together with the Giant this evening and play yumyum. I'll pay you tomorrow."

"Then I'll read for you tomorrow."

Eliana presses up against the window bars again. The street lamps begin to go on. A woman in the house across the street opens her balcony window. As she combs her long jet-black hair, looking into the street, she turns on a radio . . . ta-ra-tat-tat-tatatat-tat-tatat . . . syncopated piercing sounds from electric guitars and twanging voices pour into the dormitory, the orphans rouse Iris from the bedsprings and get her to stand up in the aisle between the two rows of beds when they hear *babalú, babalú ayé* . . . hey, do a little dance for us, Gina, they urge her, come on, do your stuff . . . tossing her neck back like a mare, she twirls her long wavy hair, swaggering down the aisle, a look of ecstasy in her eyes half-closed like those of actresses in cheap illustrated love stories . . . I don't feel lazy anymore, I'm not yawning, I want to get out and dance like Gina, the actress who lived in a convent run by bad nuns in the love story Eliana read to me . . . Iris stops. She digs in her pockets. She smears her lips with a purplish lipstick, the horrible dark color turns to unbaked dough . . . Come on, Gina, do your stuff, dance down the aisle for us, shake it, that's it, that's it, more, more . . . At the window, Eliana's lighting two candles she stole from the chapel where Brígida lay in state; all she can do is set the stage, she's too young, the youngsters in the street don't call up to her, they want Iris, Eliana doesn't have breasts to show off or thighs to put on display. She shoos the other orphans over to the farther window and helps Iris climb up on the window recess.

"Look, Gina, the Giant's here."

"Yell down to them that I'll go out as soon as the old ladies are in bed."

"The guys want you to dance for them."

She's the only one left at the lighted window. She grinds her hips. Sticking out her breasts, she smooths her sweater with a long caress that runs the whole length of her body and ends with her hiking her skirt to show her heavy thighs that are a quivering mass, while her other hand piles up her hair and she puckers her lips as if she were about to give someone a madly passionate kiss. The group gathering under the streetlight cheers her on. The woman combing her hair in the window across the way turns up the music, resting her elbows on the railing to get a good look. Iris begins to move very slowly, only rubbing her thighs together at first, then shaking her whole body to the wild beat of *babalú,* whirling, hair flying, arms outstretched, hands open as if searching for something or someone, whirling again, again, bending, stretching; she tosses back her head and lets all her hair spill forward, her gyrating body moving to the rhythm of rock, the frug, anything, as long as she can rotate and show her thighs and her filthy panties and her bouncing breasts, her tongue hot and searching like her hands, as she dances at the window so that the people in the street will applaud and egg her on and yell up to her . . . come on, give, Gina baby, give it all you've got, good-lookin', shake those tits, shake your ass off, burn down the Casa, burn us all . . . And the Giant, with his enormous papier-mâché head, steps into the middle of the street and dances as if he were dancing with Iris, Iris sways, grinds her hips, gyrates, shakes and screams from her candlelit cage that seems to hang from the side of the Casa as she dances like a Virgin Mary gone berserk in her niche. The Giant stands on the sidewalk in front and calls to her: "Gina, Gina, come on down so we can play yumyum, hey kid, yell up at her, she can't hear me because I'm shut up inside this stinking head."

"He says for you to come down, Gina!"

"Hey, Eliana, ask him what kind of present he's brought me today. Otherwise I won't go down."

"Not money, he says, but he's got five love story magazines for you and a lipstick that's not new but's real good and comes in a gold case."

"It must be gold-plated, gold ones are very expensive."

"Don't accept any of his crappy stuff, Iris, don't be stupid. You gotta get money out of him so you can pay me for the readings."

"If you don't read to me Mirella will, so who cares."

"But you like how I read because I explain the story, otherwise you don't understand a thing. I've got you where I want you, Iris Mateluna, right where I want you, because if I don't read and explain the love stories and Donald Duck you get bored to death here in this shithouse . . ."

Iris hangs on to the bars to get a look at him . . . it's him with his eyes that are as big and round as saucers and his laugh that's always the same because he never gets mad, he's good, we play yumyum real nice and when he calls me Gina he raises his eyebrow and the wrinkles on his forehead hold up his silly little hat . . . it's him, he wants to marry me because he likes the way I play yumyum, he's going to take me to see movies that show real live actresses so that pain-in-the-ass Eliana won't have to read anything to me, the Giant's going to take me to one of those tall buildings downtown so I can dance in a contest and win the prize, and makeup kit they say they give to the girl who dances best, and afterwards her picture comes out in the love story magazines and that moron Eliana and Miss Rita and Mudito and Mother Benita and the girls and all the old bags will see my picture in the magazines.

"What are you gonna pay me with if the Giant doesn't give you money today?"

Iris shrugs.

"Because you've got to pay me before you get married, you hear, or else I'll get the cops after you, the same ones who carried off your old man, to make you pay up, and if you don't pay they'll drag you off to jail too. I'll settle for the lipstick and two of the magazines the Giant's going to give you today."

"Do you think I'm stupid? One magazine and you can use the lipstick twice, and that's it . . ."

"It's a deal. But you'll have to give me the lipstick case when it's all used up."

"It's a deal."

Mother Benita remains very still for a second in the vestibule, her hands together and her eyes closed. Rita and I wait for her to move, to open her eyes, and she opens them and motions me to follow her. I know very well that, stopped and rickety or not, I have to pull my little cart as if I were her idiot son pulling a toy. I know why she wants me to follow her. We've done it so many times: to clean up what the dead woman left behind. Misiá Raquel told her to divide Brígida's things among her friends. No, among her mates is what she said, as if this were a finishing school. I don't want to look at Brígida's room, Mother, for God's sake, I don't want to, I don't want to go over anything or look at anything, no, there can't be anything of value so I don't want to look at anything, I tell you, you can do what you like with her things, Mother Benita, give them away, these old women are so poor they'll be happy with anything they can remember Brígida by, she was so well liked here at the Casa.

I follow her down the corridors, pulling the platform on four wheels. I put brooms, buckets, rags, father dusters on. In the court where the kitchen is, a group of old women forming a circle around Mother Anselma peel potatoes into a huge pot . . . what a lovely funeral Brígida had! . . . Misiá Raquel's princesse overcoat, they say they're coming back . . . the coachman had a mustache, I'm not sure it's right to let coachmen who drive first-class hearses wear a mustache, it's a sort of lack of respect . . . the funeral would keep tongues wagging for months . . . another group of old women farther over have already forgotten about it, they've forgotten Brígida, they're playing cards on a sugar bin . . . Watch out for that step, Mother, it's a step, not a shadow, and we come out into still another court that's not the one where Brígida lived, so we have to go down other passageways . . . One, then a second empty room, rows of vacant rooms, more doors, some open, some closed, because it's all the same if they're open or closed, more rooms to cross, shattered windowpanes coated with dust, the semidarkness sticking to the dried-up walls where a hen pecks at the centuries-old adobe, hunting for specks of grain. Another court. The laundry court where no laundry's done anymore because only three of them are left now, the court with the palm tree, the one with the linden, this court without a name, Ernestina Gómez's court, the refectory court no one uses because the old women prefer to eat in the kitchen, endless courts and cloisters connected by corridors that never end, rooms we'll never try to clean again even if up until a short time ago you used to say, yes, Mudito, one of these days, the first chance we have, we're going to clean everything out with brooms and dusters and rags and pails and soap powder because it's such a filthy mess . . . Watch out, Mother, I'll give you a hand, let's step around this rubble, better walk down this corridor that leads into still another court that's on a different level because of the now-forgotten purposes it once served, and opens onto rooms where sounds are softened by cobwebs and onto galleries where the echoes of forgotten comings and goings linger, or perhaps it's mice and cats and chickens and pigeons chasing one another among the ruins of this wall no one ever finished tearing down.

I walk ahead of Mother Benita. I stop next to a cluster of shacks made of tin, boards, cardboards, branches—shacks as flimsy and gray as though they were build with the well-worn cards the old women use for playing their age-old games . . . You've tried so many times to convince them to sleep in the rooms. There are hundreds and hundreds of them, good, spacious, all vacant . . . pick the ones you like in whatever court you like, Mudito and I will make them comfortable for you . . . no, Mother, we're afraid they're much too big and the ceilings are too high and the walls too thick and someone may have died or spent her life praying in those rooms and that's enough to scare anybody, they're damp, bad for rheumatism, they're enormous and gloomy, all that space when we're not used to living in rooms with so much space because we're servants used to living in cubbyholes crammed with all kinds of things, in the back part of our employers' houses, no, no, Mother Benita, thanks just the same, we prefer these rickety shacks that are sheltered by the long balconies, because we want to be as close to one another as possible so as to hear someone else breathing in the shack next door and smell stale tea leaves and listen to another sleepless body like our own tossing and turning on the other side of the thin wall, and the coughing and farts and intestinal rumblings and nightmares; who cares about the cold coming in through the cracks in the badly fitted boards as long as we're all together, in spite of the envy and greed or the terror that shrivels our toothless mouths and makes our gummy eyes squint, we're together and toward evening can go to the chapel in groups, because it's terrifying to go all by yourself, we can cling to one another's rags, through the cloisters, down passageways like tunnels that never end, through unlit galleries where a moth may brush against my face and make me scream because I get frightened if anyone touches me in the dark when I don't know who it is, we're together and can drive off any shadows that drops from the beams and stretch out toward us when it begins to get dark . . . Here comes the crotchety old woman who lines her eyebrows with black crayon. And here's Amalia . . . good afternoon Amalia, cheer up, wait for me here, I want to talk to you when I've tidied up Brígida's cell . . . no, no thanks, Mudito will help me as usual, look he's opening the padlock on Brígida's door . . . And Rosa Pérez, who can stir up a courtyard full of women with her gossip . . . Good afternoon, Carmela . . . yes, yes, they'll come for you, wait, woman . . . but you've been waiting for ten years and nobody comes . . . they say Rafaelito rented a house with an extra room . . . this little lock of hair I keep here, look, Mother Benita, it's one of his as a little boy when I was bringing him up, blond as a corn tassel and none of that drugstore-blond stuff like other kids, that's what his hair used to be like before it started turning darker, what a pity he's bald now, so they say, I called him on the phone the other day but that new wife of his said to me, call him some other time . . . wait Carmela . . . but Carmela is waiting for what all of them are waiting for with their hands crossed in their laps, staring through the secretions that have collected in their eyes, to see if they can make out what's creeping up on them and growing and beginning to cover up the light, at little at first, not quite all the light, and then all of it, all, all, all, all, all, total darkness suddenly in which you can't cry out because in the dark you can't find your voice to call for help, and one fine night you sink and you're lost in the sudden darkness like Brígida night before last. And, while they wait, the old women sweep a little as they've done all their lives or darn or do their laundry or peel potatoes or whatever there is to peel or wash, as long as it doesn't require much strength because there's no strength left, one day exactly like the next, one morning repeating the one before, one afternoon the same as all the others, sunning themselves as they sit by the cloister's drainage ditch and drive away the flies that feast on their slobber or their sores, their elbows digging into their knees and their faces buried in their hands, tired of waiting for the moment none of them believes she's waiting for, waiting as they've always waited, in other courtyards, beside other pilasters, behind other windowpanes, or else whiling away their time picking red geraniums with which to decorate the wooden box in which they carted off Mercedes Barroso, so that poor Menche wouldn't leave this earth without so much as a single flower even if they could provide only those dusty geraniums . . . she was a scream when she did the dances Iris Mateluna taught her, the frug, rock, with the rest of the orphans and even we keeping time by clapping so that they could dance together, Iris and Menche . . . poor Menche . . . Mercedes Barroso must of died of sheer fatness on a night exactly like this one that's beginning to fall.

I step back a little so you can go in. The dresser with its mirror and the brass bed barely fit in here. The sheets are rumpled so little that no one would guess a woman passed away between them forty-eight hours ago. Brígida's still alive here. This place is still here, it keeps another Brígida alive while the body of the dead one is beginning to feed the worms: this peculiar arrangement, these objects she gradually wore out with her attachment to them and with her pursuits, this attempt at elegance . . . look, Mother Benita, at the way she attached the Easter palms to a corner of the print showing the Annunciation, how she used Christmas wrapping paper to cover the Coca-Cola bottle she turned into a vase. Photographs of the Ruiz family. Holy pictures. She was so painstaking at her needlework that she was able to restore the embroidery on some chasubles Father Azócar took away because, he said, they were eighteenth-century ones and were too precious to let go to ruin here at the Casa. They were the only things of any value here, Mother Benita, everything else is trash, it's hard to believe that this country's ruling families haven't been able to collect anything but filthy junk in this place. And, without disturbing anything on the dresser, you run your fingertips over the perfect row formed by the thimble, pincushion, nail file, small scissors, tweezers, buffer—everything neatly arranged on the fresh, starched white runner. Mother Benita, you and I have come here to carve up this Brígida who's still alive, to divide her up, to burn her, to throw her out, to eradicate the Brígida who hoped to live on in the orderliness of her possessions. To wipe out all traces of her so that tomorrow or the next day they can send us another old woman who can start leaving the particular imprint of her dying hour on this place, an imprint that's not much different but is unmistakably her own. She'll replace Brígida as Brígida replaced . . . I can't think of the name of the quiet old woman with hands disfigured by warts who lived in this shack before Brígida came here.

The news that Mother Benita's started cleaning out Brígida's hovel travels through the Casa. Old women come from other courts to snoop. Mother Benita never favors any of the beggars and that's why, at first, none of them comes too close, they maraud silently or muttering under their breaths, they go past the door for a second: she smiles at you sweetly, she winks at me, and I wink my Mudito's eye back at her. They go past the door, slowing down more gradually until they barely stir, darkening the doorway like flies glued to a drop of syrup, whispering, shuffling, shouting, till you finally beg me to chase them off . . . get them out of here, Mudito . . . get out, for God's sake, let us get our work done in peace, we'll call you later. Once more they fall back a little. They sit down on the side of the corridor, at the foot of the pilasters, their hands fidgeting in their laps . . . look at Brígida's blue satin quilt, I hear it's all down, I wonder who they're going to give it to, I think the one who'll get the good things like that is Misiá Raquel, she'll take them for her house . . . look at the radio, Zunilda, I'll bet they're going to send it to some auction, radios are expensive, I'd love to own a radio like Brígida did, because she used to stay in bed on Sunday and listen to the Mass sung in the cathedral, and I'd love to hear Mass in bed some Sunday when it's cold. And that black shawl, take a look, Clemencia, I tell you it's the black shawl I was telling you about the other day, see, the one Miss Malú gave her on her birthday and she never wore because, you see, Brígida didn't care for black . . . it must be like new . . .

You roll up her sheets along with the stains and odors of her final moment, a moment no one was there to witness . . . straight to the wash! I take up the two layers of the mattress to air them out in the passageway. You strip off the ticking that protects the mattress from the rust on the spring—a wire cage that's a den where flat, long, soft, square, shapeless creatures crouch: dozens, hundreds, of packages, cartons tied with strips of cloth, balls of string or wool, a broken soap dish, an odd shoe, a bottle, a dented lampshade, a raspberry-colored bathing cap. All of them are velvety to the touch, homogeneous, motionless under the soft dust that covers everything with the silky, delicate fuzz that the slightest movement, like the flicker of an eye or someone's breathing, could scatter through the room, choking and blinding us and causing all those creatures that are resting quietly in the momentarily gentle shapes of small bundles of rags, sheaves of old magazines, umbrella ribs, boxes, box tops, pieces of box tops, to spring to life and pounce on us. More and more packages under the bed, and . . . look, Mother Benita, under the dresser too, between it and the wall and behind the curtain in the corner . . . and everything hidden just below or beyond eye level.

Don't stand there dangling your arms. Don't you know this Brígida who tamed the dust and tamed uselessness itself? Does this Brígida disturb you? Ah, Mother, you don't know it but that old woman had more secret recesses in her than the Casa. The pincushion, the scissors, the buffer, the white thread—yes, to the eye, everything was in order on the runner. Very touching. But now, suddenly, you have to face this other unofficial Brígida, the one who didn't leave herself open to view on the starched runner, the one who was queen of the inmates, who had a queen's funeral, who, from the pulchritude of her embroidered sheets, with her perfect hands and pleasant look, passed judgment by simply dropping a hint, gave orders with a moan or a sigh, changed the course of other people's lives with the flick of a finger . . . no, you didn't know her and you could never have known her, Mother Benita's eyes don't reach under the beds or into the hiding places, it's preferable to feel sorry for people, to serve them, to stick to this, even if it means working yourself to the bone as you've done for years among these decrepit old ladies in this condemned place, surrounded by imbeciles, by the sick, by the wretched, by the abandoned, by executioner and victim you can't tell apart—all of them complaining and suffering from the cold and hunger you try desperately to relieve; they drive you crazy with the anarchy of old age, which has first call on everything . . . poor old things, something must be done for them, yes, you've worked yourself to death in order to ignore Brígida's other side.

She sighs as she bends over to fish out a square package, done up in manila paper and string, from under the bedspring. I dust it with my rag and we have to wrinkle our noses because the tiny room fills up with fuzz. You begin undoing the package; it contains one of those cardboard mats on which they used to mount studio photographs with raised garlands and the photographer's signature embossed in gold in one corner, but there's no photograph. I take the paper and the cardboard out to the middle of the court and start the pile of trash that will turn into a pyre. The old women move in to rummage and grab anything they can find, but there's little, very little. Nothing. Anyhow, this is only the beginning. And it's going to be something! Because Brígida was rich. A millionaire, they say. All they have to do is wait a bit longer. The old women who've stationed themselves in the corridor or mill around never take their eyes off us.

Everything you find is tied, packaged, wrapped in something, inside something else—tattered clothing wrapped in itself, broken objects that crumble as you unwrap them, the porcelain handle of a demitasse, ribbons from a First Communion sash, things saved for the sake of saving, packing, tying, preserving this static, reiterative community that never lets you in on its secret, Mother Benita, because it's too cruel for you to bear the notion that you and I and the old women who are still alive and those who are dead, and all of us, are tied up in these packages you want to force a meaning from because you respect human beings, and if poor Brígida made up all these little packages, Mother Benita muses, carried away by her feelings, it was in order to raise a banner reading, "I want to protect, I want to rescue, I want to preserve, I want to survive." But I can assure you, Mother, that Brígida had more complex methods to make sure of her survival . . . little packages, oh yes, all old women make little packages and stow them away under their beds.

Let's open the packages, Mudito, there may be something important here, something that . . . you can't finish what you started to say because you're afraid to tie it to an incoherent idea, and instead you begin to play the game of supposing that by undoing knots, unwrapping rags, opening envelopes and cartons, you're going to discover something worth saving. No, everything into the trash pile! Rags and more rags. Papers. Cotton brown with blood from some past wound. Bundle after bundle. Don't you see, Mother Benita, that the act of wrapping, and not what's inside the wrappings, is the important thing? I go on heaping up trash in the court. A steady hum swells from the hive of old women who, as they rummage, fight over a cork, a brass knob, buttons kept inside a tea tin, an insole, the top of a pen. Sometimes, when we clean out the hovel of an inmate who just died, some familiar object turns up among her things; this black wooden curtain ring, for instance, is the very one we threw in the trash last week when Mercedes Barroso died, and she, in turn, had salvaged it, for no particular reason, from another dead woman's belongings and that one from still another's, and another's . . .

The toothless crone who winked at me tries on the raspberry-colored bathing cap and struts to the applause of the others. Dora unravels the remains of a moth-eaten cardigan, rolling the curly wool into a ball and piecing it together so that she can wash and then knit it into a little sweater for the baby that's going to be born. This package: this one. You're becoming tense, impatient, it has to be the package with the key to what Brígida was trying to say. This one. Do you want to open it? All right. Yes, Mudito, open it with respect, because Brígida wrapped it so that I would understand . . . no, Mother Benita, no, don't be fooled, Brígida made this package and the others because she was afraid. She was queen, scourge, dictator, judge, but she tied things and saved them the same as the rest of the old women. I know you're praying for this package to have something other than junk in it. You strip off the brown paper and throw it out. There's more paper, finer stuff, all wrinkled up, you tear it and drop it on the floor. Why go on opening and tearing wrappings—this apple-green taffeta one with a piece of newspaper underneath showing Roosevelt and Fala and Stalin's smile on board a ship—if you surely know you won't find a thing? This gray cotton shoulder pad is what made the parcel soft and bulky. You search, your anxious fingernails pull the shoulder pad apart and let the padding fall to the floor. There's still another hard little package you hold between your forefinger and your thumb. You peel off the layer of rusty homespun and press gently . . . yes, yes, dear God, there's something inside, something solid, with a definite shape— this object I finger anxiously. Your fingers get all tangled up undoing the homespun, only to discover a ball of silver foil. You rip it to shreds that remain in the open palm of your trembling hand. I'm about to blow on those shreds and scatter them but you snap your fist shut just in time, grabbing it away from my breath, and your fingers reconstruct the silver ball in a second. You look at it and glance toward me, inviting me to accept the wholeness of this thing you've restored. You move to the door. The old women stop, quiet down, their eyes trace the swoop of your arm and then the arc of the shining little sphere as it falls. They run toward the trash pile and pounce on the silvery thing that streaked through the air. Don't worry, we'll find it again among some other dead old woman's things.

Why do you cover your face with your hands, Mother? You rush down the passages, the galleries, across the courts, the cloisters, with the old women tagging after you with their gnarled faces and pleading gummy eyes as they ask for things—one of the women in a voice that's muffled because of the shawl she wears to protect her mouth from some imaginary chill or some imaginary contagion, another in a voice that's harsh from smoking too much and drinking too much scalding-hot tea to warm her body that's stiff from the cold. They reach out to touch your habit, to hold you fast, to hang on to your denim apron, to your sleeve . . . don't go away, Mother, I want the brass bedstead . . . and me the glasses she sometimes let me wear because I don't have any and I like to read the papers even if they're old . . . a blanket for me because I can't stand the cold at night even in the summer, I was her friend, she liked me better, I was her neighbor to the right . . . I was to her left, I used to trim her nails, even her toenails and her corns too because I used to be a manicurist when I was young, she liked me much better than Amalia, who used to charge her too much to wash her clothes . . . hands like tongs with wooden claws grab me by the arms, wrinkled mouths claim things I don't know anything about . . . I'm a widow, the little scissors were mine . . . look at Rafaelito's lock of hair, Mother Benita, what a pity the boy's bald now, and they even say he's gotten fat . . . a needle I lent her just the other day, and me a piece of crochet work . . . and me some buttons . . . These withered hands are stronger than mine, their fingers shoot out like branches to hold me back, their pleas and litanies bind me . . . for me, for me, Mother Benita . . . I want, I need . . . why don't you give me the tea Brígida left, you know how poor I am . . . no, not to her, me, give it to me, everybody knows she's a thief, keep an eye on the things because she's liable to steal them . . . give it to me, to me . . . old women in a corner, whose voices are as soft as balls of fluff, are stirred up by want or greed, chipped fingernails, filthy rags that fall apart on their bodies, bodies with the stench of old age that back me against this vestibule door with broken panes. The key! I open, I slip out and shut the door. I turn the key from the outside. I take it out and put it in my apron pocket. At last, dear God! They remain on the other side of the door like prisoners, collecting dust. Their arms, their faces twisted by grimaces, stick out through the broken panes . . . the wail of their pleading voices dies out.

## ▪ Jaime Sabines (1925– ) *Mexico* (poems)

Born in Tuxtla Gutiérrez in the southern province of Chiapas, Jaime Sabines is a businessman in Mexico City. His encantatory poems combine surreal images, nature, and the everyday life of city people and their surroundings, including God, whom he has snoring outside his grandmother's house. The poems treat serious themes, whether love, death, or the Deity, with humor and piercing irony, yet within the fantasy he uses a highly lyrical language. Like a traditional poet from India, such as Mirabai, who addresses her god at the end of each poem, Sabines, inventing his own universal tradition, addresses his mock god Tarumba. His tone is grave, ironic, amusing; his sympathy is with the Indian, displaced in a society that cannot handle the outsider.

**FURTHER READING:** Sabines, Jaime. *Collection of Poems*, 1962; *Bad Times*, 1972; *Nuevo New Collection of Poems*, 1972; *Tarumba: The Selected Poems of Jaime Sabines*. Translated by Philip Levine and Ernesto Trejo, 1987.

## *Tarumba*

Tarumba.
I go with the ants
among the feet of the flies.
I go with the ground, through the wind,
in the shoes of men,                                          5
in the cloven hooves, the leaves, the papers;
I go where you go, Tarumba,
where you come from, I'm coming.
I know the spider.
I know what you know of yourself                              10
and what your father knew.
I know what you've told me of me.
I'm afraid not to know,
to be here like my grandmother
looking at the wall, good and dead.                           15
I want to go out and piss in the moonlight.
Tarumba, it looks like rain.

TRANSLATED BY W. S. MERWIN

## In the House of the Day

People and things enter the house of the day,
stinkweeds,
the horses of insomnia,
catchy tunes,
window dummies that are girls;
you and I enter, Tarumba.
The dance enters. The sun enters.
An insurance agent enters
and a poet.
A cop.
We're all going to sell ourselves, Tarumba.

TRANSLATED BY PHILIP LEVINE

■ **Ernesto Cardenal (1925– )** *Nicaragua* **(poems)**

TRANSLATED BY JONATHAN COHEN

Poet, Catholic priest, former ruling member of the Sandinista government in Nicaragua, Ernesto Cardenal has become the best-known Marxist social poet in Latin America after Pablo Neruda. His work has been translated
into many languages, including English where New Directions has published
his books of fabled and social expression. Born in Nicaragua, as a young man
he stayed with Thomas Merton in his seminary in Kentucky and considered
becoming a Trappist monk. But he returned to Nicaragua to struggle against
the dictatorship of Anastasio Samoza. Cardenal was, in the Andy Warhol time
sense, famous worldwide for those minutes when international television
flashed clips of Pope John Paul rebuking the kneeling but unrepentant
priest for his Liberation Catholicism, a branch of Latin American Catholicism in which the priests and their churches are socially committed and usually in sympathy with Marxist or revolutionary movements. Cardenal borrows
from many traditions: surrealism, socialist realism, and fantasy literature —
and continues as a leader of committed poetry in modernist dress.

**FURTHER READING:** Cardenal, Ernesto. *Apocalypse and Other Poems,* 1977; *Zero Hour
and Other Documentary Poems,* 1980; *With Walker in Nicaragua,* 1984; *From Nicaragua
with Love: Poems,* 1986; *Golden UFOs: The Indian Poems,* 1992.

## 19th-Century Traveler on the Río San Juan

The silent bungo was oared up the river
bordered by water lilies and rushes

(as wide as the Seine in front of the Louvre).
The birds quit singing,
and all was quietness and endless verdure and echoless retreats.                5
At 6 o'clock night came without twilight.
Only the splash of oars in the river was heard . . .
And my thoughts filled with shadows,
      and I fell asleep.

When I awoke the bungo was motionless in the dark.                10
We were tied up to the trunk of a tree.
Thousands of fireflies in the black foliage
and the Southern Cross
      deep in the black sky . . .
And there was a clamor in the air:                15
the cry perhaps of a strange bird,
answering another cry like it farther off.
*Sarapiquí!:*
The water so clear
it was invisible.                20
Two green riverbanks
      and the riverbanks upside down.
Blue sky above
      and sky below
And the water in between, invisible.                25

## León

I used to live in a big house by the Church of St. Francis
which had an inscription in the entrance hall saying
    AVE MARIA
and red corridors of brick,
and old red-tiled roof,                5
      and windows with rusty iron grilles,
and a large courtyard just unbearable on stuffy afternoons
with a sad clock bird singing out the hours,
and someone's pale aunt in the courtyard reciting the rosary.
In the evenings I'd hear that angelus bell                10
    (*"The Angel of the Lord declared unto Mary . . . ."*)
the hand of a distant little girl playing a note on the piano,
      and the bugle from some barracks.
At night a huge red moon rose above Calvary
They told me stories of souls in purgatory and ghosts.                15
    At midnight
the shade of General Arechabala rode a horse through the streets.

And the noise of a door closing . . . A black coach . . .
An empty cart rattling as it rolled through the Calle Real.
And then all the roosters in the neighborhood crowing,       2(
and the song of the clock bird,
and my aunt who'd leave each morning for mass at 4
with the bells ringing in St. Francis,
    ringing
in Calvary       2:
    and in St. John's Hospital
and the jars of the milkmen clattering on the stone pavement
and a bread vendor knocking on a front door
and crying
    BREAD       3(
      BREAD

## ■ Rosario Castellanos (1925–1974) *Mexico* (poems)

### TRANSLATED BY WILLIS BARNSTONE

Born in Mexico City, Castellanos was raised in Comitán, a small town in the province of Chiapas on the Guatemalan border, where much of the population was Indian. It is a region of great natural beauty—mountains, ruins of Maya civilizations, Indians in white pajamas, ox-bulls in rice paddies. Thus Indians are a main subject of her novels. She attended the University of Mexico, where she later taught; she also taught at Indiana University. But Rosario Castellanos supported herself mainly from her novels and other writings, the first Mexican woman to do so. Her best-known novel, *Labors of Darkness* (1962), was awarded the Sor Juana Inés de la Cruz Prize in the year of its publication. She began her literary career as a poet and her lyrics explore the "geography of women." Her novels partake of both the social and the fantastic, yet in depicting the plight of the Indians she has strictly avoided sentimentalizing or romanticizing her subject; rather, she observes with a sharp and critical eye the tedium, the cruelty, as well as the diverse harshness and drama of Indian life. In the tradition that saw Octavio Paz ambassador to India and Carlos Fuentes ambassador to France, Rosario Castellanos was appointed Mexican ambassador to Israel. In a freak accident recalling the death of the American monk poet Thomas Merton in Burma, she was killed in Jerusalem from a faulty electrical connection in her hotel room. Rosario Castellanos is one of the few writers in Latin America who is equally known as poet and novelist.

**FURTHER READING:** Castellanos, Rosario. *Balún-Canán*, 1951; *The Nine Guardians*, 1959; *Ciudad Real* (stories), 1960; *Labors of Darkness*, 1962; *A Rosario Castellanos*

*Reader: An Anthology of Her Poetry, Short Fiction, Essays, and Drama.* Translated by Maureen Ahern, 1988; *The Selected Poems of Rosario Castellanos.* Translated by Magda Bogin, 1988; *Presentation in the Temple. Another Way to Be: Selections.* Translated by Marylyn F. Allgood, 1990.

## Three Poems

### I

What is weaker than a god? It groans hungry and smells out
its victim's blood,
eating sacrifices, and looks for the entrails
of what it created in order to sink
its hundred rapacious teeth in them.                                                           5

(A god. Or certain men who have a destiny.)

Each morning it wakes
and the world is newly freshly devoured.

### II

The great fish's eyes never shut.
It doesn't sleep. It always stares (at whom? where?)
in its bright and soundless universe.

Once its heart, beating
near a thorn, says: I want.                                                                      5

And the great devouring fish,
weighs down and dyes the water with its rage,
and moves with nerves of lightning,
can do nothing, not even shut its eyes.

It stares beyond the glass.                                                                     10

### III

O cloud that wants to be the sky's arrow
or God's halo or lightning's fist!

Each wind alters its form and it vanishes,
and each gust drags it about and tricks it.

Unraveling rag, dirty fleece,                                                                   5
with no entrails, no force, nothing, cloud.

■ **René Dépestre (1926– )** *Haiti* **(poem)**

TRANSLATED BY JAMES SCULLY

René Dépestre is a Haitian poet from the town of Jacmel on the southern coast of the island. His first book of poems was titled *Sparks* and was published when he was nineteen. He was co-founder of a Marxist magazine, *The Beehive*, which was closed down by the government, and in 1946 he went to Paris and Africa, in exile. He returned to Haiti in 1958 but soon went to Cuba where his views were more welcome. He has published many books. His work is vibrantly influenced by French surrealism and political poetry. His strength lies in wild, in-your-face imagery, the depth of his political and racial anger, and his ability to sustain long and powerful poems.

**FURTHER READING:** Dépestre, René. *Sparks,* 1945; *Vegetations of Clarity,* 1951; *Black Ore,* 1956; *A Rainbow for the Christian West,* 1967.

## Black Ore

When the sun, and it was abrupt, had dried up the sweat of the Indian
When gold fever had drained the last drop of Indian blood into the
     marketplace
So that, on the grounds of the gold mines, there wasn't an Indian left
They looked then to the muscular African river
Sure to be relieved of their despair
Then began the rush on the inexhaustible
Treasure of black flesh
Began then the mad scramble
Into the gleaming black tropical body
And throughout the earth echoed the clamor of picks
In packed black ore
Which would have been all wrong, if chemists hadn't thought up
Ways to make some precious alloy
With black metal, all wrong if ladies hadn't
Dreamed of a battery of cooks
In negrony from Senegal, of a tea service
In hulking niggerboy from the West Indies
All wrong if some priest
Hadn't promised his parish
A bell surging with the resonance of black blood
Or, again, if an irreproachable Santa Claus hadn't considered
For his annual visit

Little soldiers in black lead
Or if some brave captain
Hadn't sharpened his sword in the petrified ebony                                    *25*
And throughout the earth quivered with drills
In the bowels of my race
In the muscular strata of the black man
And so many centuries gone on quarrying
Marvels from this race                                                               *30*
O metallic seams, veins of my people
Inexhaustible ore of human dew
How many pirates have forced
The dark depths of your flesh
How many marauders hacked a road                                                     *35*
Through the lush vegetation of lights on your body
Strewing your years with dead stalks
Small pools of tears
A people plundered, a people turned over top to bottom
Like a laboring land                                                                 *40*
A people broken up to enrich
The great fair grounds of the world
Brood, deep in your flesh-and-blood night, on what will erupt
No one will dare cast cannon or pieces of gold
From the black metal of your wrath pouring out                                       *45*

## ▪ Carlos Fuentes (1928– ) *Mexico* (story)

### TRANSLATED BY MARGARET SAYERS PEDEN

Carlos Fuentes was born in Panama City into a wealthy Mexican family. His father was a diplomat and, consequently, Fuentes spent his childhood in Mexico, Chile (where he was in school with José Donoso), Buenos Aires, Washington, and Geneva (where he completed a law degree). He returned to Mexico in the fifties and headed the cultural division of the Ministry of Foreign Affairs. He also entered diplomacy and was the Mexican ambassador to France until the massacre of students in Mexico City led him, as it did Octavio Paz when he was ambassador to India, to resign his post. He has also been a professor at Cambridge, Princeton, and Harvard and is a frequent lecturer. As a result of his career as one of the most prolific and major authors of the Latin American "boom" novelists—a term applied to the phenomenon of the great international success and sale of Latin American novelists—he has been a candidate for the Nobel Prize. At the Frankfort International Book Fair and by the measure of world publication, Fuentes and his fellow novelists have been the most valuable commercial property of the last two decades. Among these ambitious and innovative writers, Fuentes has been among the most daring, following many masters—especially American, English, and French ones. His subject has always been Mexico. His characters range from postrevolutionary heroes, like Artemio Cruz in the novel *The Death of Artemio Cruz* (1962), in which we see, through experimental splitting of voices and time, a figure move from revolutionary to the exploiting cacique (a local political boss), to the jaded international couples who populate *A Change of Skin* (1968). His monumental work is *Terra Nostra* (1975), in which the world, in a Cervantine and almost magically Borgesian way, is his domain. Not always easy to read, he moves on every level of intellect. His recent volume, *The Old Gringo,* based on the life of Ambrose Bierce, concerns a stubbornly individualist old American gringo living in Mexico during its revolution and a Mexican leader who yields to personal temptations at the expense of the revolution. His response to 1992, the five hundredth anniversary of Columbus's voyage to America was his illuminating television historical-cultural series on Spain and the New World, *The Burnt Mirror,* which has since appeared in book form. His most famous short story, "Chac-Mool," takes its title from the Maya god of rain, who is depicted as a reclining figure in Maya statuary.

FURTHER READING: Fuentes, Carlos. *The Masked Days; Where the Air Is Clear,* 1960; *The Death of Artemio Cruz,* 1964; *A Change of Skin,* 1968; *Terra Nostra,* 1975; *Hydra Head,* 1978; *Burnt Water,* 1980; *Distant Relations,* 1981; *The Old Gringo,* 1985; *Christopher Unborn,* 1988; *Constancia and Other Stories for Virgins,* 1989; *The Burnt Mirror,* 1993.

## Chac-Mool

It was only recently that Filiberto drowned in Acapulco. It happened during Easter Week. Even though he'd been fired from his government job, Filiberto couldn't resist the bureaucratic temptation to make his annual pilgrimage to the small German hotel, to eat sauerkraut sweetened by the sweat of the tropical cuisine, dance away Holy Saturday on La Quebrada, and feel he was one of the "beautiful people" in the dim anonymity of dusk on Hornos Beach. Of course we all knew he'd been a good swimmer when he was young, but now, at forty, and the shape he was in, to try to swim that distance, at midnight! Frau Müller wouldn't allow a wake in her hotel—steady client or not; just the opposite, she held a dance on her stifling little terrace while Filiberto, very pale in his coffin, awaited the departure of the first morning bus from the terminal, spending the first night of his new life surrounded by crates and parcels. When I arrived, early in the morning, to supervise the loading of the casket, I found Filiberto buried beneath a mound of coconuts; the driver wanted to get him in the luggage compartment as quickly as possible, covered with canvas in order not to upset the passengers and to avoid bad luck on the trip.

When we left Acapulco there was still a good breeze. Near Tierra Colorada it began to get hot and bright. As I was eating my breakfast eggs and sausage, I had opened Filiberto's satchel, collected the day before along with his other personal belongings from the Müllers' hotel. Two hundred pesos. An old newspaper; expired lottery tickets; a one-way ticket to Acapulco—one way?—and a cheap notebook with graph-paper pages and marbleized-paper binding.

On the bus I ventured to read it, in spite of the sharp curves, the stench of vomit, and a certain natural feeling of respect for the private life of a deceased friend. It should be a record—yes, it began that way—of our daily office routine; maybe I'd find out what caused him to neglect his duties, why he'd written memoranda without rhyme or reason or any authorization. The reasons, in short, for his being fired, his seniority ignored and his pension lost.

"Today I went to see about my pension. Lawyer extremely pleasant. I was so happy when I left that I decided to blow five pesos at a café. The same café we used to go to when we were young and where I never go now because it reminds me that I lived better at twenty than I do at forty. We were all equals then, energetically discouraging any unfavorable remarks about our classmates. In fact, we'd open fire on anyone in the house who so much as mentioned inferior background or lack of elegance. I knew that many of us (perhaps those of most humble origin) would go far, and that here in school we were forging lasting friendships; together we would brave the stormy seas of life. But it didn't work out that way. Someone didn't follow the rules. Many of the lowly were left behind, though some climbed higher even than we could have predicted in those high-spirited, affable get-togethers. Some who seemed to have the most promise got stuck somewhere along the way, cut down in some extracurricular activity, isolated by an invisible chasm from those who'd triumphed and those who'd gone nowhere at all. Today, after all this time, I again sat in the chairs—remodeled, as well as the soda fountain, a kind of barricade against invasion—and pretended to read some business papers. I saw many of the old faces, amnesiac, changed in the neon light, prosperous. Like the café, which I barely recognized, along with the city itself, they'd been chipping away at a pace different from my own. No, they didn't recognize me now, or didn't want to. At most, one or two clapped a quick, fat hand on my shoulder. So long, old friend, how's it been going? Between us stretched the eighteen holes of the Country Club. I buried myself in my papers. The years of my dreams, the optimistic predictions, filed before my eyes, along with the obstacles that had kept me from achieving them. I felt frustrated that I couldn't dig my fingers into the past and put together the pieces of some long-forgotten puzzle. But one's toy chest is a part of the past, and when all's said and done, who knows where his lead soldiers went, his helmets and wooden swords. The make-believe we loved so much was only that, make-believe. Still, I'd been diligent, disciplined, devoted to duty. Wasn't that enough? Was it too much? Often, I was assaulted by the recollection of Rilke: the great reward for the adventure of youth in death; we should die young, taking all our secrets with us. Today I wouldn't be looking back at a city of salt. Five pesos? Two pesos tip."

"In addition to his passion for corporation law, Pepe likes to theorize. He saw me coming out of the Cathedral, and we walked together toward the National Palace. He's not a believer, but he's not content to stop at that: within half a block he had to propose a theory. If I weren't a Mexican, I wouldn't worship Christ, and . . . No, look, it's obvious. The Spanish arrive and say, Adore this God who died a bloody death nailed to a cross with a bleeding wound in his side. Sacrificed. Made an offering. What could be more natural than to accept something so close to your own ritual, your own life . . . ? Imagine, on the other hand, if Mexico had been conquered by Buddhists or Moslems. It's not conceivable that our Indians would have worshipped some person who died of indigestion. But a God that's not only sacrificed for you but has his heart torn out, God Almighty, checkmate to Huitzilopochtli! Christianity, with its emotion, its bloody sacrifice and ritual, becomes a natural and novel extension of the native religion. The qualities of charity, love, and turn-the-other-cheek, however, are rejected. And that's what Mexico is all about: you have to kill a man in order to believe in him.

"Pepe knew that ever since I was young I've been mad for certain pieces of Mexican Indian art. I collect small statues, idols, pots. I spend my weekends in Tlaxcala, or in Teotihuacan. That may be why he likes to relate to indigenous themes all the theories he concocts for me. Pepe knows that I've been looking for a reasonable replica of the Chac-Mool for a long time, and today he told me about a little shop in the flea market of La Lagunilla where they're selling one, apparently at a good price. I'll go Sunday.

"A joker put red coloring in the office water cooler, naturally interrupting our duties. I had to report him to the director, who simply thought it was funny. So all day the bastard's been going around making fun of me, with cracks about water. Motherfu . . ."

"Today, Sunday, I had time to go out to La Lagunilla. I found the Chac-Mool in the cheap little shop Pepe had told me about. It's a marvelous piece, life-size, and though the dealer assures me it's an original, I question it. The stone is nothing out of the ordinary, but that doesn't diminish the elegance of the composition, or its massiveness. The rascal has smeared tomato ketchup on the belly to convince the tourists of its bloody authenticity.

"Moving the piece to my house cost more than the purchase price. But it's here now, temporarily in the cellar while I reorganize my collection to make room for it. These figures demand a vertical and burning-hot sun; that was their natural element. The effect is lost in the darkness of the cellar, where it's simply another lifeless mass and its grimace seems to reproach me for denying it light. The dealer had a spotlight focused directly on the sculpture, highlighting all the planes and lending a more amiable expression to my Chac-Mool. I must follow his example."

"I awoke to find the pipes had burst. Somehow, I'd carelessly left the water running in the kitchen; it flooded the floor and poured into the cellar before I'd noticed it. The dampness didn't damage the Chac-Mool, but my suitcases suffered; everything has to happen on a weekday. I was late to work."

"At last they came to fix the plumbing. Suitcases ruined. There's slime on the base of the Chac-Mool."

"I awakened at one; I'd heard a terrible moan. I thought it might be burglars. Purely imaginary."

"The moaning at night continues. I don't know where it's coming from, but it makes me nervous. To top it all off, the pipes burst again, and the rains have seeped through the foundation and flooded the cellar."

"Plumber still hasn't come; I'm desperate. As far as the City Water Department's concerned, the less said the better. This is the first time the runoff from the rains has drained into my cellar instead of the storm sewers. The moaning's stopped. An even trade?"

"They pumped out the cellar. The Chac-Mool is covered with slime. It makes him look grotesque; the whole sculpture seems to be suffering from a kind of green erysipelas, with the exception of the eyes. I'll scrape off the moss Sunday. Pepe suggested I move to an apartment on an upper floor, to prevent any more of these aquatic tragedies. But I can't leave my house; it's obviously more than I need, a little gloomy in its turn-of-the-century style, but it's the only inheritance, the only memory, I have left of my parents. I don't know how I'd feel if I saw a soda fountain with a juke-box in the cellar and an interior decorator's shop on the ground floor."

"Used a trowel to scrape the Chac-Mool. The moss now seemed almost a part of the stone; it took more than an hour and it was six in the evening before I finished. I couldn't see anything in the darkness, but I ran my hand over the outlines of the stone. With every stroke, the stone seemed to become softer. I couldn't believe it; it felt like dough. That dealer in La Lagunilla has really swindled me. His 'pre-Columbian sculpture' is nothing but plaster, and the dampness is ruining it. I've covered it with some rags and will bring it upstairs tomorrow before it dissolves completely."

"The rags are on the floor. Incredible. Again I felt the Chac-Mool. It's firm, but not stone. I don't want to write this: the texture of the torso feels a little like flesh; I press it like rubber, and feel something coursing through that recumbent figure . . . I went down again later at night. No doubt about it: the Chac-Mool has hair on its arms."

"This kind of thing has never happened to me before. I fouled up my work in the office: I sent out a payment that hadn't been authorized, and the director had to call it to my attention. I think I may even have been rude to my coworkers, I'm going to have to see a doctor, find out whether it's my imagination, whether I'm delirious, or what . . . and get rid of that damned Chac-Mool."

Up to this point I recognized Filiberto's hand, the large, rounded letters I'd seen on so many memoranda and forms. The entry for August 25 seemed to have been written by a different person. At times it was the writing of a child, each letter laboriously separated; other times, nervous, trailing into illegibility. Three days are blank, and then the narrative continues:

"It's all so natural, though normally we believe only in what's real . . . but this is real, more real than anything I've ever known. A water cooler is real, more than real, because we fully realize its existence, or being, when some joker puts something in the water to turn it red . . . An ephemeral smoke ring is real, a grotesque image in a fun-house mirror is real; aren't all deaths, present and forgotten, real . . . ? If a man passes through paradise in a dream, and is handed a flower as proof of having been there, and if when he awakens he finds this flower in his hand . . . then . . . ? Reality: one day it was shattered into a thousand pieces, its head rolled in one direction and its tail in another, and all we have is one of the pieces from the gigantic body. A free and fictitious ocean, real only when it is imprisoned in a seashell. Until three days ago, my reality was of such a degree it would be erased today; it was reflex action, routine, memory, carapace. And then, like the earth that one day trembles to remind us of its power, of the death to come, recriminating against me for having turned my back on life, an orphaned reality we always knew was there presents itself, jolting us in order to become living present. Again I believed it to be imagination: the Chac-Mool, soft and elegant, had changed color overnight; yellow, almost golden, it seemed to suggest it was a god, at ease now, the knees more relaxed than before, the smile more benevolent. And yesterday, finally, I awakened with a start, with the frightening certainty that two creatures are breathing in the night, that in the darkness there beats a pulse in addition to one's own. Yes, I heard footsteps on the stairway. Nightmare. Go back to sleep. I don't know how long I feigned sleep. When I opened my eyes again, it still was not dawn. The room smelled of horror, of incense and blood. In the darkness, I gazed about the bedroom until my eyes found two points of flickering, cruel yellow light.

"Scarcely breathing, I turned on the light. There was the Chac-Mool, standing erect, smiling, ocher-colored except for the flesh-red belly. I was paralyzed by the two tiny, almost crossed eyes set close to the wedge-shaped nose. The lower teeth closed tightly on the upper lip; only the glimmer from the squarish helmet on the abnormally large head betrayed any sign of life. Chac-Mool moved toward my bed; then it began to rain."

I remember that it was at the end of August that Filiberto had been fired from his job, with a public condemnation by the director, amid rumors of madness and even theft. I didn't believe it. I did see some wild memoranda, one asking the Secretary of the Department whether water had an odor; another, offering his services to the Department of Water Resources to make it rain in the desert. I couldn't explain it. I thought the exceptionally heavy rains of that summer had affected him. Or that living in that ancient mansion with half the rooms locked and thick with dust, without any servants or family life, had finally deranged him. The following entries are for the end of September.

"Chac-Mool can be pleasant enough when he wishes . . . the gurgling of enchanted water . . . He knows wonderful stories about the monsoons, the equatorial rains, the scourge of the deserts; the genealogy of every plant engendered by his mythic paternity: the willow, his wayward daughter; the lotus, his favorite child; the cactus, his mother-in-law. What I can't bear is the odor, the nonhuman odor, emanating from flesh that isn't flesh, from sandals that shriek their antiquity. Laughing stridently, the Chac-Mool recounts how he was discovered by Le Plongeon and brought into physical contact with men of other gods. His spirit had survived quite peacefully in water vessels and storms; his stone was another matter, and to have dragged him from his hiding place was unnatural and cruel. I think the Chac-Mool will never forgive that. He savors the imminence of the aesthetic.

"I've had to provide him with pumice stone to clean the belly the dealer smeared with ketchup when he thought he was Aztec. He didn't seem to like my question about his relation to Tlaloc, and when he becomes angry his teeth, repulsive enough in themselves, glitter and grow pointed. The first days he slept in the cellar; since yesterday, in my bed."

"The dry season has begun. Last night, from the living room where I'm sleeping now, I heard the same hoarse moans I'd heard in the beginning, followed by a terrible racket. I went upstairs and peered into the bedroom: the Chac-Mool was breaking the lamps and furniture; he sprang toward the door with outstretched bleeding hands, and I was barely able to slam the door and run to hide in the bathroom. Later he came downstairs, panting and begging for water. He leaves the faucets running all day; there's not a dry spot in the house. I have to sleep wrapped in blankets, and I've asked him please to let the living room dry out."[1]

---

1. Filiberto does not say in what language he communicated with the Chac-Mool.

"The Chac-Mool flooded the living room today. Exasperated, I told him I was going to return him to La Lagunilla. His laughter—so frighteningly different from the laugh of any man or animal—was as terrible as the blow from that heavily braceleted arm. I have to admit it: I am his prisoner. My original plan was quite different. I was going to play with the Chac-Mool the way you play with a toy; this may have been an extension of the security of childhood. But—who said it?—the fruit of childhood is consumed by the years, and I hadn't seen that. He's taken my clothes, and when the green moss begins to sprout, he covers himself in my bathrobes. The Chac-Mool is accustomed to obedience, always; I, who have never had cause to command, can only submit. Until it rains—what happened to his magic power?—he will be choleric and irritable."

"Today I discovered that the Chac-Mool leaves the house at night. Always, as it grows dark, he sings a shrill and ancient tune, older than song itself. Then everything is quiet. I knocked several times at the door, and when he didn't answer I dared enter. The bedroom, which I hadn't seen since the day the statue tried to attack me, is a ruin; the odor of incense and blood that permeates the entire house is particularly concentrated here. And I discovered bones behind the door, dog and rat and cat bones. This is what the Chac-Mool steals in the night for nourishment. This explains the hideous barking every morning."

"February, dry. Chac-Mool watches every move I make; he made me telephone a restaurant and ask them to deliver chicken and rice every day. But what I took from the office is about to run out. So the inevitable happened: on the first they cut off the water and lights for nonpayment. But Chac has discovered a public fountain two blocks from the house; I make ten or twelve trips a day for water while he watches me from the roof. He says that if I try to run away he will strike me dead in my tracks; he is also the God of Lightning. What he doesn't realize is that I know about his nighttime forays. Since we don't have any electricity, I have to go to bed about eight. I should be used to the Chac-Mool by now, but just a moment ago, when I ran into him on the stairway, I touched his icy arms, the scales of his renewed skin, and I wanted to scream.

"If it doesn't rain soon, the Chac-Mool will return to stone. I've noticed his recent difficulty in moving; sometimes he lies for hours, paralyzed, and almost seems an idol again. But this repose merely gives him new strength to abuse me, to claw at me as if he could extract liquid from my flesh. We don't have the amiable intervals any more, when he used to tell me old tales; instead, I seem to notice a heightened resentment. There have been other indications that set me thinking: my wine cellar is diminishing; he likes to stroke the silk of my bathrobes; he wants me to bring a servant girl to the house; he has made me teach him how to use soap and lotions. I believe the Chac-Mool is falling into human temptations; now I see in the face that once seemed eternal something that is merely old.

This may be my salvation: if the Chac becomes human, it's possible that all the centuries of his life will accumulate in an instant and he will die in a flash of lightning. But this might also cause my death: the Chac won't want me to witness his downfall; he may decide to kill me.

"I plan to take advantage tonight of Chac's nightly excursion to flee. I will go to Acapulco; I'll see if I can't find a job, and await the death of the Chac-Mool. Yes, it will be soon; his hair is gray, his face bloated. I need to get some sun, to swim, to regain my strength. I have four hundred pesos left. I'll go to the Müllers' hotel, it's cheap and comfortable. Let Chac-Mool take over the whole place; we'll see how long he lasts without my pails of water."

Filiberto's diary ends here. I didn't want to think about what he'd written; I slept as far as Cuernavaca. From there to Mexico City I tried to make some sense out of the account, to attribute it to overwork, or some psychological disturbance. By the time we reached the terminal at nine in the evening, I still hadn't accepted the fact of my friend's madness. I hired a truck to carry the coffin to Filiberto's house, where I would arrange for his burial.

Before I could insert the key in the lock, the door opened. A yellow-skinned Indian in a smoking jacket and ascot stood in the doorway. He couldn't have been more repulsive; he smelled of cheap cologne; he'd tried to cover his wrinkles with thick powder, his mouth was clumsily smeared with lipstick, and his hair appeared to be dyed.

"I'm sorry . . . I didn't know that Filiberto had . . ."

"No matter. I know all about it. Tell the men to carry the body down to the cellar."

■ ## Gabriel García Márquez (1928– ) *Colombia* (novel, story)

Born in Azacataca on the Caribbean coast of Colombia, Gabriel García Márquez became a journalist and remains a productive one in Latin America and Spain, despite his highly successful novels and short stories and a Nobel Prize in Literature. After living and writing many years in Spain, he now makes his home in Mexico. When in 1967 he published *One Hundred Years of Solitude,* García Márquez had written the "great American novel," that is, of all the Americas. Only John Dos Passos's *U.S.A.* equals its scope and linguistic and thematic achievement. In addition to the instant international sensation of *One Hundred Years of Solitude* that his narration created, like Melville's *Moby Dick,* it is a monumental achievement. Combining Rabelaisian grotesque and hyperbole and a cyclical Borgesian manipulation of time and mythical storytelling, the author uses his extraordinary skills and magical fantasy to paint a fabulous one hundred years of adventures and misadventures in Macondo, his invented tropical town in Colombia. García Márquez had already written superb books prior to *One Hundred Years of Solitude,* his fourth novel, notably, the haunting novela, *No One Writes to the Colonel,* a movingly fantastic story of a colonel decaying with age and revolutionary memories as he waits for a long delayed government pension. *The Autumn of the Patriarch* (1967) is one long sentence, an experimental novel about a Latin American dictator. It is brilliant. *The Autumn of the Patriarch* is a document of the essential problems of power, corruption, and the perennial strongman leader in Latin American politics. There followed wonderful short stories, a riveting confession of crime in the novela *Chronicle of a Death Foretold* (1981, tr. 1983), and the continuation of *One Hundred Years* in *Love in the Time of Cholera* (1988). This generational book reveals all the old graces, archaic habits, personal passions, and societal bigotries. It centers upon two separated lovers who must wait through most of the novel to attain—in their very last years when age has reduced most of their physical forces and their handsome façades—a full and complete passion of love, intensified by the lifelong delay and seeming impossibilities of its realization. It is another tour de force. And as with few authors of his sophistication, García Márquez has retained the writer's cunning to trap the reader and not allow escape until the last page. García Márquez's books, despite his profound view of society and history (including a novel based on the life of Simon Bolivar) do not pretend the intellectual dimensions of a Borges, Donoso, Cortázar, or Fuentes. His books operate always as story and as a complete and entrancing original world. He is an extraordinarily skilled natural writer, and ambience, intuition, spirit, and life-and-death attitudes overtake the more recognizably conceptual writing of his contemporaries. His magic is in his fabulous imagination. Gabriel García Márquez is a fabulist and there is none like him. His very title, *One Hundred Years of Solitude,* initiates the mystery and metaphysical wonder of life in Macondo.

**FURTHER READING:** García Márquez, Gabriel. *The Leaf Storm,* 1955; *No One Writes to the Colonel,* 1962, tr. 1968; *An Evil Hour,* 1962; *Big Mama's Funeral* (stories), 1962; *One Hundred Years of Solitude,* 1967. Translated by Gregory Rabassa, 1970; *The Autumn of the Patriarch,* 1975; *Chronicle of a Death Foretold,* 1981, tr. 1983; *Love in the Time of Cholera,* 1985, tr. 1988.

# *from* One Hundred Years of Solitude

## The Founding of Macondo

Many years later, as he faced the firing squad, Colonel Aureliano Buendía was to remember that distant afternoon when his father took him to discover ice. At that time Macondo was a village of twenty adobe houses, built on the bank of a river of clear water that ran along a bed of polished stones, which were white and enormous, like prehistoric eggs. The world was so recent that many things lacked names, and in order to indicate them it was necessary to point. Every year during the month of March a family of ragged gypsies would set up their tents near the village, and with a great uproar of pipes and kettledrums they would display new inventions. First they brought the magnet. A heavy gypsy with an untamed beard and sparrow hands, who introduced himself as Melquíades, put on a bold public demonstration of what he himself called the eighth wonder of the learned alchemists of Macedonia. He went from house to house dragging two metal ingots and everybody was amazed to see pots, pans, tongs, and braziers tumble down from their places and beams creak from the desperation of nails and screws trying to emerge, and even objects that had been lost for a long time appeared from where they had been searched for most and went dragging along in turbulent confusion behind Melquíades' magical irons. "Things have a life of their own," the gypsy proclaimed with a harsh accent. "It's simply a matter of waking up their souls." José Arcadio Buendía, whose unbridled imagination always went beyond the genius of nature and even beyond miracles and magic, thought that it would be possible to make use of that useless invention to extract gold from the bowels of the earth. Melquíades, who was an honest man, warned him: "It won't work for that." But José Arcadio Buendía at that time did not believe in the honesty of gypsies, so he traded his mule and a pair of goats for the two magnetized ingots. Úrsula Iguarán, his wife, who relied on those animals to increase their poor domestic holdings, was unable to dissuade him. "Very soon we'll have gold enough and more to pave the floors of the house," her husband replied. For several months he worked hard to demonstrate the truth of his idea. He explored every inch of the region, even the riverbed, dragging the two iron ingots along and reciting Melquíades' incantation aloud. The only thing he succeeded in doing was to unearth a suit of fifteenth-century armor which had all of its pieces soldered together with rust and inside of which there was the hollow resonance of an enormous stone-filled gourd. When José Arcadio Buendía and the four men of his expedition managed to take the armor apart, they found inside a calcified skeleton with a copper locket containing a woman's hair around its neck.

In March the gypsies returned. This time they brought a telescope and a magnifying glass the size of a drum, which they exhibited as the latest discovery of the Jews of Amsterdam. They placed a gypsy woman at one end of the village and set up the telescope at the entrance to the tent. For the price of five reales, people could look into the telescope and see the gypsy woman an arm's length away. "Science has eliminated distance," Melquíades proclaimed. "In a short time, man will be able to see what is happening in any place in the world without leaving his own house." A burning noonday sun brought out a startling demonstration with the gigantic magnifying glass: they put a pile of dry hay in the middle of the street and set it on fire by concentrating the sun's rays. José Arcadio Buendía, who had still not been consoled for the failure of his magnets, conceived the idea of using that invention as a weapon of war. Again Melquíades tried to dissuade him, but he finally accepted the two magnetized ingots and three colonial coins in exchange for the magnifying glass. Úrsula wept in consternation. That money was from a chest of gold coins that her father had put together over an entire life of privation and that she had buried underneath her bed in hopes of a proper occasion to make use of it. José Arcadio Buendía made no attempt to console her, completely absorbed in his tactical experiments with the abnegation of a scientist and even at the risk of his own life. In an attempt to show the effects of the glass on enemy troops, he exposed himself to the concentration of the sun's rays and suffered burns which turned into sores that took a long time to heal. Over the protests of his wife, who was alarmed at such a dangerous invention, at one point he was ready to set the house on fire. He would spend hours on end in his room, calculating the strategic possibilities of his novel weapon until he succeeded in putting together a manual of startling instructional clarity and an irresistible power of conviction. He sent it to the government, accompanied by numerous descriptions of his experiments and several pages of explanatory sketches, by a messenger who crossed the mountains, got lost in measureless swamps, forded stormy rivers, and was on the point of perishing under the lash of despair, plague, and wild beasts until he found a route that joined the one used by the mules that carried the mail. In spite of the fact that a trip to the capital was little less than impossible at that time, José Arcadio Buendía promised to undertake it as soon as the government ordered him to so that he could put on some practical demonstrations of his invention for the military authorities and could train them himself in the complicated art of solar war. For several years he waited for an answer. Finally, tired of waiting, he bemoaned to Melquíades the failure of his project and the gypsy then gave him a convincing proof of his honesty: he gave him back the doubloons in exchange for the magnifying glass, and he left him in addition some Portuguese maps and several instruments of navigation. In his own handwriting he set down a concise synthesis of the studies by Monk Hermann, which he left José Arcadio so that he would be able to make use of the astrolabe, the compass, and the sextant. José Arcadio Buendía spent the long months of the rainy season shut up in a small room that he had built in the rear of the house so that no one would disturb his experiments. Having completely abandoned his domestic obligations, he spent entire nights in the courtyard watching the course of the stars and he almost contracted sunstroke from trying to establish an exact method to ascertain noon. When he became an expert in the use and manipulation of his instruments, he conceived a notion of space that allowed him to navigate across unknown seas, to visit uninhabited territories, and to establish relations with splendid beings without having to leave his study. That was the period in which he acquired the habit of talking to himself, of walking through the house without paying attention to anyone, as Úrsula and the children broke their backs in the garden, growing banana and caladium, cassava and yams, ahuyama roots and eggplants. Suddenly, without warning, his feverish activity was interrupted and was replaced by a kind of fascination. He spent several days as if he were bewitched, softly repeating to himself a string of fearful conjectures without giving credit to his own understanding. Finally, one Tuesday in December, at lunchtime, all at once he released the whole weight of his torment. The children would remember for the rest of their lives the august solemnity with which their father, devastated by his prolonged vigil and by the wrath of his imagination, revealed his discovery to them:

"The earth is round, like an orange."

Úrsula lost her patience. "If you have to go crazy, please go crazy all by yourself!" she shouted. "But don't try to put your gypsy ideas into the heads of the children." José Arcadio Buendía, impassive, did not let himself be frightened by the desperation of his wife, who, in a seizure of rage, smashed the astrolabe against the floor. He built another one, he gathered the men of the village in his little room, and he demonstrated to them, with theories that none of them could understand, the possibility of returning to where one had set out by consistently sailing east. The whole village was convinced that José Arcadio Buendía had lost his reason, when Melquíades returned to set things straight. He gave public praise to the intelligence of a man who from pure astronomical speculation had evolved a theory that had already been provided in practice, although unknown in Macondo, until then, and as a proof of his admiration he made him a gift that was to have a profound influence on the future of the village: the laboratory of an alchemist.

By then Melquíades had aged with surprising rapidity. On his first trips he seemed to be the same age as José Arcadio Buendía. But while the latter had preserved his extraordinary strength, which permitted him to pull down a horse by grabbing its ears, the gypsy seemed to have been worn down by some tenacious illness. It was, in reality, the result of multiple and rare diseases contracted on his innumerable trips around the world. According to what he himself said as he spoke to José Arcadio Buendía while helping him set up the laboratory, death followed him everywhere, sniffing at the cuff of his pants, but never deciding to give him the final clutch of its claws. He was a fugitive from all the plagues and catastrophes that had ever lashed mankind. He had survived pellagra in Persia, scurvy in the Malayan archipelago, leprosy in Alexandria, beriberi in Japan, bubonic plague in Madagascar, an earthquake in Sicily, and a disastrous shipwreck in the Strait of Magellan. That prodigious creature, said to possess the keys of Nostradamus, was a gloomy man, enveloped in a sad aura, with an Asiatic look that seemed to know what there was on the other side of things. He wore a large black hat that looked like a raven with widespread wings, and a velvet vest across which the patina of the centuries had skated. But in spite of his immense wisdom and his mysterious breadth, he had a human burden, an earthly condition that kept him involved in the small problems of daily life. He would complain of the ailments of old age, he suffered from the most insignificant economic difficulties, and he had stopped laughing a long time back because scurvy had made his teeth drop out. On that suffocating noontime when the gypsy revealed his secrets, José Arcadio Buendía had the certainty that it was the beginning of a great friendship. The children were startled by his fantastic stories. Aureliano, who could not have been more than five at the time, would remember him for the rest of his life as he saw him that afternoon, sitting against the metallic and quivering light from the window, lighting up with his deep organ voice the darkest reaches of the imagination, while down over his temples there flowed the grease that was being melted by the heat. José Arcadio, his older brother, would pass on that wonderful image as a hereditary memory to all of his descendants. Úrsula, on the other hand, held a bad memory of that visit, for she had entered the room just as Melquíades had carelessly broken a flask of bichloride of mercury.

"It's the smell of the devil," she said.

"Not at all," Melquíades corrected her. "It has been proven that the devil has sulphuric properties and this is just a little corrosive sublimate."

Always didactic, he went into a learned exposition of the diabolical properties of cinnabar, but Úrsula paid no attention to him, although she took the children off to pray. That biting odor would stay forever in her mind linked to the memory of Melquíades.

The rudimentary laboratory—in addition to a profusion of pots, funnels, retorts, filters, and sieves—was made up of a primitive water pipe, a glass beaker with a long, thin neck, a reproduction of the philosopher's egg, and a still the gypsies themselves had built in accordance with modern descriptions of the three-armed alembic of Mary the Jew. Along with those items, Melquíades left samples of the seven metals that corresponded to the seven planets, the formulas of Moses and Zosimus for doubling the quantity of gold, and a set of notes and sketches concerning the processes of the Great Teaching that would permit those who could interpret them to undertake the manufacture of the philosopher's stone. Seduced by the simplicity of the formulas to double the quantity of gold, José Arcadio Buendía paid court to Úrsula for several weeks so that she would let him dig up her colonial coins and increase them by as many times as it was possible to subdivide mercury. Úrsula gave in, as always, to her husband's unyielding obstinacy. Then José Arcadio Buendía threw three doubloons into a pan and fused them with copper filings, orpiment, brimstone, and lead. He put it all to boil in a pot of castor oil until he got a thick and pestilential syrup which was more like common caramel than valuable gold. In risky and desperate processes of distillation, melted with the seven planetary metals, mixed with hermetic mercury and vitriol of Cyprus, and put back to cook in hog fat for lack of any radish oil, Úrsula's precious inheritance was reduced to a large piece of burnt hog cracklings that was firmly stuck to the bottom of the pot.

When the gypsies came back, Úrsula had turned the whole population of the village against them. But curiosity was greater than fear, for that time the gypsies went about the town making a deafening noise with all manner of musical instruments while a hawker announced the exhibition of the most fabulous discovery of the Naciancenes. So that everyone went to the tent and by paying one cent they saw a youthful Melquíades, recovered, unwrinkled, with a new and flashing set of teeth. Those who remembered his gums that had been destroyed by scurvy, his flaccid cheeks, and his withered lips trembled with fear at the final proof of the gypsy's supernatural power. The fear turned into panic when Melquíades took out his teeth, intact, encased in their gums, and showed them to the audience for an instant—a fleeting instant in which he went back to being the same decrepit man of years past—and put them back again and smiled once more with the full control of his restored youth. Even José Arcadio Buendía considered that Melquíades knowledge had reached unbearable extremes, but he felt a healthy excitement when the gypsy explained to him alone the workings of his false teeth. It seemed so simple and so prodigious at the same time that overnight he lost all interest in his experiments in alchemy. He underwent a new crisis of bad humor. He did not go back to eating regularly, and he would spend the day walking through the house. "Incredible things are happening in the world," he said to Úrsula. "Right there across the river there are all kinds of magical instruments while we keep on living like donkeys." Those who had known him since the foundation of Macondo were startled at how much he had changed under Melquíades' influence.

At first José Arcadio Buendía had been a kind of youthful patriarch who would give instructions for planting and advice for the raising of children and animals, and who collaborated with everyone, even in the physical work, for the welfare of the community. Since his house from the very first had been the best in the village, the others had been built in its image and likeness. It had a small, well-lighted living room, a dining room in the shape of a terrace with gaily colored flowers, two bedrooms, a courtyard with a gigantic chestnut tree, a well-kept garden, and a corral where goats, pigs, and hens lived in peaceful communion. The only animals that were prohibited, not just in his house but in the entire settlement, were fighting cocks.

Úrsula's capacity for work was the same as that of her husband. Active, small, severe, that woman of unbreakable nerves who at no moment in her life had been heard to sing seemed to be everywhere, from dawn until quite late at night, always pursued by the soft whispering of her stiff, starched petticoats. Thanks to her the floors of tamped earth, the unwhitewashed mud walls, the rustic, wooden furniture they had built themselves were always clean, and the old chests where they kept their clothes exhaled the warm smell of basil.

José Arcadio Buendía, who was the most enterprising man ever to be seen in the village, had set up the placement of the houses in such a way that from all of them one could reach the river and draw water with the same effort, and he had lined up the streets with such good sense that no house got more sun than another during the hot time of day. Within a few years Macondo was a village that was more orderly and hard-working than any known until then by its three hundred inhabitants. It was a truly happy village where no one was over thirty years of age and where no one had died.

Since the time of its founding, José Arcadio Buendía had built traps and cages. In a short time he filled not only his own house but all of those in the village with troupials, canaries, bee eaters, and redbreasts. The concert of so many different birds became so disturbing that Úrsula would plug her ears with beeswax so as not to lose her sense of reality. The first time that Melquíades' tribe arrived, selling glass balls for headaches, everyone was surprised that they had been able to find that village lost in the drowsiness of the swamp, and the gypsies confessed that they had found their way by the song of the birds.

That spirit of social initiative disappeared in a short time, pulled away by the fever of the magnets, the astronomical calculations, the dreams of transmutation, and the urge to discover the wonders of the world. From a clean and active man, José Arcadio Buendía changed into a man lazy in appearance, careless in his dress, with a wild beard that Úrsula managed to trim with great effort and a kitchen knife. There were many who considered him the victim of some strange spell. But even those most convinced of his madness left work and family to follow him when he brought out his tools to clear the land and asked the assembled group to open a way that would put Macondo in contact with the great inventions.

José Arcadio Buendía was completely ignorant of the geography of the region. He knew that to the east there lay an impenetrable mountain chain and that on the other side of the mountains there was the ancient city of Riohacha, where in times past—according to what he had been told by the first Aureliano Buendía, his grandfather—Sir Francis Drake had gone crocodile hunting with cannons and that he repaired them and stuffed them with straw to bring to Queen Elizabeth. In his youth, José Arcadio Buendía and his men, with wives and children, animals and all kinds of domestic implements, had crossed the mountains in search of an outlet to the sea, and after twenty-six months they gave up the expedition and founded Macondo, so they would not have to go back. It was, therefore, a route that did not interest him, for it could lead only to the past. To the south lay the swamps, covered with an eternal vegetable scum, and the whole vast universe of the great swamp, which, according to what the gypsies said, had no limits. The great swamp in the west mingled with a boundless extension of water where there were soft-skinned cetaceans that had the head and torso of a woman, causing the ruination of sailors with the charm of their extraordinary breasts. The gypsies sailed along that route for six months before they reached the strip of land over which the mules that carried the mail passed. According to José Arcadio Buendía's calculations, the only possibility of contact with civilization lay along the northern route. So he handed out clearing tools and hunting weapons to the same men who had been with him during the founding of Macondo.

He threw his directional instruments and his maps into a knapsack, and he undertook the reckless adventure.

During the first days they did not come across any appreciable obstacle. They went down along the stony bank of the river to the place where years before they had found the soldier's armor, and from there they went into the woods along a path between wild orange trees. At the end of the first week they killed and roasted a deer, but they agreed to eat only half of it and salt the rest for the days that lay ahead. With that precaution they tried to postpone the necessity of having to eat macaws, whose blue flesh had a harsh and musky taste. Then, for more than ten days, they did not see the sun again. The ground became soft and damp, like volcanic ash, and the vegetation was thicker and thicker, and the cries of the birds and the uproar of the monkeys became more and more remote, and the world became eternally sad. The men on the expedition felt overwhelmed by their most ancient memories in that paradise of dampness and silence, going back to before original sin, as their boots sank into pools of steaming oil and their machetes destroyed bloody lilies and golden salamanders. For a week, almost without speaking, they went ahead like sleepwalkers through a universe of grief, lighted only by the tenuous reflection of luminous insects, and their lungs were overwhelmed by a suffocating smell of blood. They could not return because the strip that they were opening as they went along would soon close up with a new vegetation that almost seemed to grow before their eyes. "It's all right," José Arcadio Buendía would say. "The main thing is not to lose our bearings." Always following his compass, he kept on guiding his men toward the invisible north so that they would be able to get out of that enchanted region. It was a thick night, starless, but the darkness was becoming impregnated with a fresh and clear air. Exhausted by the long crossing, they hung up their hammocks and slept deeply for the first time in two weeks. When they woke up, with the sun already high in the sky, they were speechless with fascination. Before them, surrounded by ferns and palm trees, white and powdery in the silent morning light, was an enormous Spanish galleon. Tilted slightly to the starboard, it had hanging from its intact masts the dirty rags of its sails in the midst of its rigging, which was adorned with orchids. The hull, covered with an armor of petrified barnacles and soft moss, was firmly fastened into a surface of stones. The whole structure seemed to occupy its own space, one of solitude and oblivion, protected from the vices of time and the habits of the birds. Inside, where the expeditionaries explored with careful intent, there was nothing but a thick forest of flowers.

The discovery of the galleon, an indication of the proximity of the sea, broke José Arcadio Buendía's drive. He considered it a trick of his whimsical fate to have searched for the sea without finding it, at the cost of countless sacrifices and suffering, and to have found it all of a sudden without looking for it, as if it lay across his path like an insurmountable object. Many years later Colonel Aureliano Buendía crossed the region again, when it was already a regular mail route, and the only part of the ship he found was its burned-out frame in the midst of a field of poppies. Only then, convinced that the story had not been some product of his father's imagination, did he wonder how the galleon had been able to get inland to that spot. But José Arcadio Buendía did not concern himself with that when he found the sea after another four days' journey from the galleon. His dreams ended as he faced that ashen, foamy, dirty sea, which had not merited the risks and sacrifices of the adventure.

"God damn it!" he shouted. "Macondo is surrounded by water on all sides."

The idea of a peninsular Macondo prevailed for a long time, inspired by the arbitrary map that José Arcadio Buendía sketched on his return from the expedition. He drew it in rage, evilly, exaggerating the difficulties of communication, as if to punish himself for the absolute lack of sense with which he had chosen the place. "We'll never get anywhere," he lamented to Úrsula. "We're going to rot our lives away here without receiving the benefits of science." That certainty, mulled over for several months in the small room he used as his laboratory, brought him to the conception of the plan to move Macondo to a better place. But that time Úrsula had anticipated his feverish designs. With the secret and implacable labor of a small ant she predisposed the women of the village against the flightiness of their husbands, who were already preparing for the move. José Arcadio Buendía did not know at what moment or because of what adverse forces his plan had become enveloped in a web of pretexts, disappointments, and evasions until it turned into nothing but an illusion. Úrsula watched him with innocent attention and even felt some pity for him on the morning when she found him in the back room muttering about his plans for moving as he placed his laboratory pieces in their original boxes. She let him finish. She let him nail up the boxes and put his initials on them with an inked brush, without reproaching him, but knowing now that he knew (because she had heard him say so in his soft monologues) that the men of the village would not back him up in his undertaking. Only when he began to take down the door of the room did Úrsula dare ask him what he was doing, and he answered with a certain bitterness. "Since no one wants to leave, we'll leave all by ourselves." Úrsula did not become upset.

"We will not leave," she said. "We will stay here, because we have had a son here."

"We have still not had a death," he said. "A person does not belong to a place until there is someone dead under the ground."

Úrsula replied with a soft firmness:

"If I have to die for the rest of you to stay here, I will die."

José Arcadio Buendía had not thought that his wife's will was so firm. He tried to seduce her with the charm of his fantasy, with the promise of a prodigious world where all one had to do was sprinkle some magic liquid on the ground and the plants would bear fruit whenever a man wished, and where all manner of instruments against pain were sold at bargain prices. But Úrsula was insensible to his clairvoyance.

"Instead of going around thinking about your crazy inventions, you should be worrying about your sons," she replied. "Look at the state they're in, running wild just like donkeys."

José Arcadio Buendía took his wife's words literally. He looked out the window and saw the barefoot children in the sunny garden and he had the impression that only at that instant had they begun to exist, conceived by Úrsula's spell. Something occurred inside of him then, something mysterious and definitive that uprooted him from his own time and carried him adrift through an unexplored region of his memory. While Úrsula continued sweeping the house, which was safe now from being abandoned for the rest of her life, he stood there with an absorbed look, contemplating the children until his eyes became moist and he dried them with the back of his hand, exhaling a deep sigh of resignation.

"All right," he said. "Tell them to come help me take the things out of the boxes."

José Arcadio, the older of the children, was fourteen. He had a square head, thick hair, and his father's character. Although he had the same impulse for growth and physical strength, it was early evident that he lacked imagination. He had been conceived and born during the difficult crossing of the mountains, before the founding of Macondo, and his parents gave thanks to heaven when they saw he had no animal features. Aureliano, the first human being to be born in Macondo, would be six years old in March. He was silent and withdrawn. He had wept in his mother's womb and had been born with his eyes open. As they were cutting the umbilical cord, he moved his head from side to side, taking in the things in the room and examining the faces of the people with a fearless curiosity. Then, indifferent to those who came close to look at him, he kept his attention concentrated on the palm roof, which looked as if it were about to collapse under the tremendous pressure of the rain. Úrsula did not remember the intensity of that look again until one day when little Aureliano, at the age of three, went into the kitchen at the moment she was taking a pot of boiling soup from the stove and putting it on the table. The child, perplexed, said from the doorway, "It's going to spill." The pot was firmly placed in the center of the table, but just as soon as the child made his announcement, it began an unmistakable movement toward the edge, as if impelled by some inner dynamism, and it fell and broke on the floor. Úrsula, alarmed, told her husband about the episode, but he interpreted it as natural phenomenon. That was the way he always was alien to the existence of his sons, partly because he considered childhood as a period of mental insufficiency, and partly because he was always too absorbed in his fantastic speculations.

But since the afternoon when he called the children in to help him unpack the things in the laboratory, he gave them his best hours. In the small separate room, where the walls were gradually being covered by strange maps and fabulous drawings, he taught them to read and write and do sums, and he spoke to them about the wonders of the world, not

only where his learning had extended, but forcing the limits of his imagination to extremes. It was in that way that the boys ended up learning that
in the southern extremes of Africa there were men so intelligent and
peaceful that their only pastime was to sit and think, and that it was possible to cross the Aegean Sea on foot by jumping from island to island all
the way to the port of Salonika. Those hallucinating sessions remained
printed on the memories of the boys in such a way that many years later, a
second before the regular army officer gave the firing squad the command to fire, Colonal Aureliano Buendía saw once more that warm March
afternoon on which his father had interrupted the lesson in physics and
stood fascinated, with his hand in the air and his eyes motionless, listening
to the distant pipes, drums, and jingles of the gypsies, who were coming to
the village once more, announcing the latest and most startling discovery
of the sages of Memphis.

They were new gypsies, young men and women who knew only their
own language, handsome specimens with oily skins and intelligent hands,
whose dances and music sowed a panic of uproarious joy through the
streets, with parrots painted all colors reciting Italian arias, and a hen who
laid a hundred golden eggs to the sound of a tambourine, and a trained
monkey who read minds, and the multiple-use machine that could be
used at the same time to sew on buttons and reduce fevers, and the apparatus to make a person forget his bad memories, and a poultice to lose
time, and a thousand more inventions so ingenious and unusual that José
Arcadio Buendía must have wanted to invent a memory machine so that
he could remember them all. In an instant they transformed the village.
The inhabitants of Macondo found themselves lost in their own streets,
confused by the crowded fair.

Holding a child by each hand so as not to lose them in the tumult,
bumping into acrobats with gold-capped teeth and jugglers with six arms,
suffocated by the mingled breath of manure and sandals that the crowd
exhaled, José Arcadio Buendía went about everywhere like a madman,
looking for Melquíades so that he could reveal to him the infinite secrets
of that fabulous nightmare. He asked several gypsies, who did not understand his language. Finally he reached the place where Melquíades used
to set up his tent and he found a taciturn Armenian who in Spanish was
hawking a syrup to make oneself invisible. He had drunk down a glass of
the amber substance in one gulp as José Arcadio Buendía elbowed his way
through the absorbed group that was witnessing the spectacle, and was
able to ask his question. The gypsy wrapped him in the frightful climate of
his look before he turned into a puddle of pestilential and smoking pitch
over which the echo of his reply still floated: "Melquíades is dead." Upset
by the news, José Arcadio Buendía stood motionless, trying to rise above
his affliction, until the group dispersed, called away by other artifices, and
the puddle of the taciturn Armenian evaporated completely. Other gypsies confirmed later on that Melquíades had in fact succumbed to the
fever on the beach at Singapore and that his body had been thrown into

the deepest part of the Java Sea. The children had no interest in the news. They insisted that their father take them to see the overwhelming novelty of the sages of Memphis that was being advertised at the entrance of a tent that, according to what was said, had belonged to King Solomon. They insisted so much that José Arcadio Buendía paid the thirty reales and led them into the center of the tent, where there was a giant with a hairy torso and a shaved head, with a copper ring in his nose and a heavy iron chain on his ankle, watching over a pirate chest. When it was opened by the giant, the chest gave off a glacial exhalation. Inside there was only an enormous, transparent block with infinite internal needles in which the light of the sunset was broken up into colored stars. Disconcerted, knowing that the children were waiting for an immediate explanation, José Arcadio Buendía ventured a murmur:

"It's the largest diamond in the world."

"No," the gypsy countered. "It's ice."

José Arcadio Buendía, without understanding, stretched out his hand toward the cake, but the giant moved it away. "Five reales more to touch it," he said. José Arcadio Buendía paid them and put his hand on the ice and held it there for several minutes as his heart filled with fear and jubilation at the contact with mystery. Without knowing what to say, he paid ten reales more so that his sons could have that prodigious experience. Little José Arcadio refused to touch it. Aureliano, on the other hand, took a step forward and put his hand on it, withdrawing it immediately. "It's boiling," he exclaimed, startled. But his father paid no attention to him. Intoxicated by the evidence of the miracle, he forgot at that moment about the frustration of his delirious undertakings and Melquíades's body, abandoned to the appetite of the squids. He paid another five reales and with his hand on the cake, as if giving testimony on the holy scriptures, he exclaimed:

"This is the great invention of our time."

TRANSLATED BY GREGORY RABASSA

## A Very Old Man with Enormous Wings

### A Tale for Children

On the third day of rain they had killed so many crabs inside the house that Pelayo had to cross his drenched courtyard and throw them into the sea, because the newborn child had a temperature all night and they thought it was due to the stench. The world had been sad since Tuesday. Sea and sky were a single ash-gray thing and the sands of the beach, which on March nights glimmered like powdered light, had become a stew of mud and rotten shellfish. The light was so weak at noon that when Pelayo was coming back to the house after throwing away the crabs, it was hard for him to see what it was that was moving and groaning in the rear of the courtyard. He had to go very close to see that it was an old man, a very old man, lying face down in the mud, who, in spite of his tremendous efforts, couldn't get up, impeded by his enormous wings.

Frightened by that nightmare, Pelayo ran to get Elisenda, his wife, who was putting compresses on the sick child, and he took her to the rear of the courtyard. They both looked at the fallen body with mute stupor. He was dressed like a ragpicker. There were only a few faded hairs left on his bald skull and very few teeth in his mouth, and his pitiful condition of a drenched great-grandfather had taken away any sense of grandeur he might have had. His huge buzzard wings, dirty and half-plucked, were forever entangled in the mud. They looked at him so long and so closely that Pelayo and Elisenda very soon overcame their surprise and in the end found him familiar. Then they dared speak to him, and he answered in an incomprehensible dialect with a strong sailor's voice. That was how they skipped over the inconvenience of the wings and quite intelligently concluded that he was a lonely castaway from some foreign ship wrecked by the storm. And yet, they called in a neighbor woman who knew everything about life and death to see him, and all she needed was one look to show them their mistake.

"He's an angel," she told them. "He must have been coming for the child, but the poor fellow is so old that the rain knocked him down."

On the following day everyone knew that a flesh-and-blood angel was held captive in Pelayo's house. Against the judgment of the wise neighbor woman, for whom angels in those times were the fugitive survivors of a celestial conspiracy, they did not have the heart to club him to death. Pelayo watched over him all afternoon from the kitchen, armed with his bailiff's club, and before going to bed he dragged him out of the mud and locked him up with the hens in the wire chicken coop. In the middle of the night, when the rain stopped, Pelayo and Elisenda were still killing crabs. A short time afterward the child woke up without a fever and with a desire to eat. Then they felt magnanimous and decided to put the angel on a raft with fresh water and provisions for three days and leave him to his fate on the high seas. But when they went out into the courtyard with the first light of dawn, they found the whole neighborhood in front of the chicken coop having fun with the angel, without the slightest reverence, tossing him things to eat through the openings in the wire as if he weren't a supernatural creature but a circus animal.

Father Gonzaga arrived before seven o'clock, alarmed at the strange news. By that time onlookers less frivolous than those at dawn had already arrived and they were making all kinds of conjectures concerning the captive's future. The simplest among them thought that he should be named mayor of the world. Others of sterner mind felt that he should be promoted to the rank of five-star general in order to win all wars. Some visionaries hoped that he could be put to stud in order to implant on earth a race of winged wise men who could take charge of the universe. But Father Gonzaga, before becoming a priest, had been a robust woodcutter. Standing by the wire, he reviewed his catechism in an instant and asked them to open the door so that he could take a close look at that pitiful man who looked more like a huge decrepit hen among the fascinated chickens. He was lying in a corner drying his open wings in the sunlight among the fruit peels and breakfast leftovers that the early risers had thrown him. Alien to the impertinences of the world, he only lifted his antiquarian eyes and murmured something in his dialect when Father Gonzaga went into the chicken coop and said good morning to him in Latin. The parish priest had his first suspicion of an impostor when he saw that he did not understand the language of God or know how to greet His ministers. Then he noticed that seen close up he was much too human: he had an unbearable smell of the outdoors, the back side of his wings was strewn with parasites and his main feathers had been mistreated by terrestrial winds, and nothing about him measured up to the proud dignity of angels. Then he came out of the chicken coop and in a brief sermon warned the curious against the risks of being ingenuous. He reminded them that the devil had the bad habit of making use of carnival tricks in order to confuse the unwary. He argued that if wings were not the essential element in determining the difference between a hawk and an airplane, they were even less so in the recognition of angels. Nevertheless, he promised to write a letter to his bishop so that the latter would write to his primate so that the latter would write to the Supreme Pontiff in order to get the final verdict from the highest courts.

His prudence fell on sterile hearts. The news of the captive angel spread with such rapidity that after a few hours the courtyard had the bustle of a marketplace and they had to call in troops with fixed bayonets to disperse the mob that was about to knock the house down. Elisenda, her spine all twisted from sweeping up so much marketplace trash, then got the idea of fencing in the yard and charging five cents admission to see the angel.

The curious came from far away. A traveling carnival arrived with a flying acrobat who buzzed over the crowd several times, but no one paid any attention to him because his wings were not those of an angel but, rather, those of a sidereal bat. The most unfortunate invalids on earth came in search of health: a poor woman who since childhood had been counting her heartbeats and had run out of numbers; a Portuguese man who couldn't sleep because the noise of the stars disturbed him; a sleepwalker who got up at night to undo the things he had done while awake; and many others with less serious ailments. In the midst of that shipwreck disorder that made the earth tremble, Pelayo and Elisenda were happy with fatigue, for in less than a week they had crammed their rooms with money and the line of pilgrims waiting their turn to enter still reached beyond the horizon.

The angel was the only one who took no part in his own act. He spent his time trying to get comfortable in his borrowed nest, befuddled by the hellish heat of the oil lamps and sacramental candles that had been placed along the wire. At first they tried to make him eat some mothballs, which, according to the wisdom of the wise neighbor woman, were the food prescribed for angels. But he turned them down, just as he turned down the papal lunches that the penitents brought him, and they never found out whether it was because he was an angel or because he was an old man that in the end he ate nothing but eggplant mush. His only supernatural virtue seemed to be patience. Especially during the first days, when the hens pecked at him, searching for the stellar parasites that proliferated in his wings, and the cripples pulled out feathers to touch their defective parts with, and even the most merciful threw stones at him, trying to get him to rise so they could see him standing. The only time they succeeded in arousing him was when they burned his side with an iron for branding steers, for he had been motionless for so many hours that they thought he was dead. He awoke with a start, ranting in his hermetic language and with tears in his eyes, and he flapped his wings a couple of times, which brought on a whirlwind of chicken dung and lunar dust and a gale of panic that did not seem to be of this world. Although many thought that his reaction had been one not of rage but of pain, from then on they were careful not to annoy him, because the majority understood that his passivity was not that of a hero taking his ease but that of a cataclysm in repose.

Father Gonzaga held back the crowd's frivolity with formulas of maidservant inspiration while awaiting the arrival of a final judgment on the nature of the captive. But the mail from Rome showed no sense of urgency. They spent their time finding out if the prisoner had a navel, if his dialect had any connection with Aramaic, how many times he could fit on the head of a pin, or whether he wasn't just a Norwegian with wings. Those meager letters might have come and gone until the end of time if a providential event had not put an end to the priest's tribulations.

It so happened that during those days, among so many other carnival attractions, there arrived in town the traveling show of the woman who had been changed into a spider for having disobeyed her parents. The admission to see her was not only less than the admission to see the angel, but people were permitted to ask her all manner of questions about her absurd state and to examine her up and down so that no one would ever doubt the truth of her horror. She was a frightful tarantula the size of a ram and with the head of a sad maiden. What was most heartrending, however, was not her outlandish shape but the sincere affliction with which she recounted the details of her misfortune. While still practically a child she had sneaked out of her parents' house to go to a dance, and while she was coming back through the woods after having danced all night without permission, a fearful thunderclap rent the sky in two and through the crack came the lightning bolt of brimstone that changed her into a spider. He only nourishment came from the meatballs that charitable souls chose to toss into her mouth. A spectacle like that, full of so much human truth and with such a fearful lesson, was bound to defeat without even trying that of a haughty angel who scarcely designed to look at mortals. Besides, the few miracles attributed to the angel showed a certain mental disorder, like the blind man who didn't recover his sight but grew three new teeth, or the paralytic who didn't get to walk but almost won the lottery, and the leper whose sores sprouted sunflowers. Those consolation miracles, which were more like mocking fun, had already ruined the angel's reputation when the woman who had been changed into a spider finally crushed him completely. That was how Father Gonzaga was cured forever of his insomnia and Pelayo's courtyard went back to being as empty as during the time it had rained for three days and crabs walked through the bedrooms.

The owners of the house had no reason to lament. With the money they saved they build a two-story mansion with balconies and gardens and high netting so that crabs wouldn't get in during the winter, and with iron bars on the windows so that angels wouldn't get in. Pelayo also set up a rabbit warren close to town and gave up his job as bailiff for good, and Elisenda bought some satin pumps with high heels and many dresses of iridescent silk, the kind worn on Sunday by the most desirable women in those times. The chicken coop was the only thing that didn't receive any attention. If they washed it down with creolin and burned tears of myrrh inside it every so often, it was not in homage to the angel but to drive away the dungheap stench that still hung everywhere like a ghost and was turning the new house into an old one. At first, when the child learned to walk, they were careful that he not get too close to the chicken coop. But then they began to lose their fears and got used to the smell, and before the child got his second teeth he'd gone inside the chicken coop to play, where the wires were falling apart. The angel was no less standoffish with him than with other mortals, but he tolerated the most ingenious infamies with the patience of a dog who had no illusions. They both came down with chicken pox at the same time. The doctor who took care of the child couldn't resist the temptation to listen to the angel's heart, and he found so much whistling in the heart and so many sounds in his kidneys that it seemed impossible for him to be alive. What surprised him most, however, was the logic of his wings. They seemed so natural on that completely human organism that he couldn't understand why other men didn't have them too.

When the child began school it had been some time since the sun and rain had caused the collapse of the chicken coop. The angel went dragging himself about here and there like a stray dying man. They would drive him out of the bedroom with a broom and a moment later find him in the kitchen. He seemed to be in so many places at the same time that they grew to think that he'd been duplicated, that he was reproducing himself all through the house, and the exasperated and unhinged Elisenda shouted that it was awful living in that hell full of angels. He could scarcely eat and his antiquarian eyes had also become so foggy that he went about bumping into posts. All he had left were the bare cannulae of his last feathers. Pelayo threw a blanket over him and extended him the charity of letting him sleep in the shed, and only then did they notice that he had a temperature at night, and was delirious with the tongue twisters of an old Norwegian. That was one of the few times they became alarmed, for they thought he was going to die and not even the wise neighbor woman had been able to tell them what to do with dead angels.

And yet he not only survived his worst winter, but seemed improved with the first sunny days. He remained motionless for several days in the farthest corner of the courtyard, where no one would see him, and at the beginning of December some large, stiff feathers began to grow on his wings, the feathers of a scarecrow, which looked more like another misfortune of decrepitude. But he must have known the reason for those changes, for he was quite careful that no one should notice them, that no one should hear the sea chanteys that he sometimes sang under the stars. One morning Elisenda was cutting some bunches of onions for lunch when a wind that seemed to come from the high seas blew into the kitchen. Then she went to the window and caught the angel in his first attempts at flight. They were so clumsy that his fingernails opened a furrow in the vegetable patch and he was on the point of knocking the shed down with the ungainly flapping that slipped on the light and couldn't get a grip on the air. But he did manage to gain altitude. Elisenda let out a sigh of relief, for herself and for him, when she saw him pass over the last houses, holding himself up in some way with the risky flapping of a senile vulture. She kept watching him even when she was through cutting the onions and she kept on watching until it was no longer possible for her to see him, because then he was no longer an annoyance in her life but an imaginary dot on the horizon of the sea.

TRANSLATED BY GREGORY RABASSA AND J. S. BERNSTEIN

## ■ Guillermo Cabrera Infante (1929– ) *Cuba* (novel)

TRANSLATED BY DONALD GARDNER AND SUZANNE JILL LEVINE

Cabrera Infante came from the correct proletarian family background to justify a place for the young intellectual novelist in postrevolutionary Cuba. His parents were Communists, and they had worked for the overthrow of the Batista regime. With Castro's triumph, Cabrera was appointed director of the nation's most prestigious literary magazine buoyed by the large circulation of the newspaper *Revolucion,* in which it appeared as the weekly literary supplement. But as Cabrera Infante's writing, with its Joycean flow and pure love of the word as word and his retelling of the eve of the Cuban revolution, became less tolerated, the magazine lacked paper and was killed. Cabrera Infante was then appointed cultural attaché in

Brussels. Soon the mutual disenchantment between author and regime was reached as the writer's acerbic pen sharpened and he went from non-person to enemy of the state. The Cuban writer—one of five major boom novelists from Cuba: the others are Alejo Carpentier, José Lezama Lima, Reinaldo Arenas, and Severo Sarduy—likened the writer to a translator. In a larger sense all writing is translation of experience and imagination into text, of tradition into one's originality; in Cabrera Infante's instance, the epithet "translator" is specifically appropriate for his transformation (the essential activity of translating or "carrying over") of Latin, English, American, and Latin American authors into his authors, who are, as Rodriguez Monegal and others have suggested, Petronius, Sterne, Joyce, Mark Twain, Lewis Carroll, and Borges. If two writers were to be chosen from these as the master source of Cabrera Infante's translations, they would have to be Joyce and Borges, along with the slick, slangy, overheard talk of contemporary fiction. When into all this we add Spanish and Cuban tropical rhythmic black speech, we have the inimitable voices of this Fellini of the Cuban *La dolce vita,* transformed into English masterfully by the author and Jill Levine.

Author of many books, short stories, film reviews, political and social essays, Guillermo Cabrera Infante's masterpiece is the tongue-twister titled novel *Tres tristes tigres* (1967; *Three Trapped Tigers,* 1971), which in Spanish means literally "three sad tigers," containing a multitude of puns, associations, and the obvious alliterative, childlike, mocking wordplay of the three *t*'s and *s*'s in *tres tristes tigres.* The book uses every Joycean and Cabrera Infante trick of the trade in the way of monologue, collage, and extraneous documentation. The word *deconstruction* as it applies to architecture and narration is perhaps rarely apt in his case—not as a critic's tool but the author's. Yet, as in all his mixtures of fact, fiction, and metafiction, there is a sensual and exciting engagement between interesting characters and sharp dialogue, and the novel never descends into mere tour de force tedium.

**FURTHER READING:** Cabrera Infante, Guillermo. *Así en la paz como en la guerra (In Peace as in War)* (short stories), 1961; *Vista del amanecer en el trópico (A View of Dawn in the Tropics),* 1965; *A Twentieth Century Job* (film reviews), 1963; *Tres tristes tigres,* 1967 *(Three Trapped Tigers,* 1971); *Habana para un infante difunto,* 1979; *Infante's Inferno.* Translated by Suzanne Jill Levine with author, 1984.

## from *Three Trapped Tigers*

### I Heard Her Sing

I dreamed I was an old man who'd gone out on a skiff into the Gulf Stream of the night and had gone 68 days now without catching any fish, not even a damselfish or a sardine. Silvestre had been with me for the first 66 days. After 67 days without a single fish Bustrófedon and Eribó and Arsenio Cué had told Silvestre that I was now definitely and finally *salao,* which is the worst form of salty. But on day number 69 (which is a lucky number in Havana-by-night: Bustrófedon says that it's because it's a capicúa, that's Cuban for a palindrome number, Arsenio Cué for a thing or two he knows about it and Rine for other reasons: it's the number of his house) on day or rather on night number 69 I was really at sea and all alone, when through the deep blue, violet, ultraviolet waters a phosphorescent fish came swimming. It was very large and bosomy and it looked like Cuba and then it became small and toothy and it was Irenita and then it got dark, blackish, pitch black and lissome and it was Magalena and when it bit my line and I caught it, it began to grow and grow and grow and it fought the line as it grew and it was as big as the boat now and it stayed there floating with strange sounds coming from its liver-lipped mouth, purring, groaning beside the boat, gaping, palpitating, making funny noises, noises more weird than funny like somebody choking as he swallows, and then the big fish was quite still, and then predatory fish began to arrive, sharks and barracudas and piranhas, all of them with faces I could recognize, in fact one of them looked very much like Gianni Boutade and another like the Emcee and it had a star on its mouth and yet another fish was Vítor Perla and I knew it was him because it had a throat like a tie made of blood and a pearl pinned on it, and I pulled the line quickly and fastened it to the side and, funny thing, I started talking to it, to the fish, Big fish, I said, fish that you are, fish, Nobel fish, I have lampooned you, harpooned I mean, it's true I caught you but I'm not going to let them eat you, and I began to haul it into the boat in a slow frenzy and I managed to get its tail into the boat and it was a radiant white now, the fish tail only, the rest of it being jet black, and suddenly I began to struggle with its soft, sticky, gelatin-flanks, gelatin because that side of it wasn't a fish but a jellyfish, an *aguamala,* but all the same I kept on pulling and suddenly I lost my balance and fell back into the boat, still pulling at its jelly side and the whole whale of a fish fell on top of me and the boat was too small for both of us and it, the fish not the boat, gave me no room to breathe and I was suffocating because its gills had landed on my face and over my mouth and nostrils and as this fish was all blubber it was spreading over me, smothering me as it sucked in my air, all the air, not only the air for breathing, the air outside but the already breathed air, the air *inside* as well, the air from my nostrils and from my mouth and from my lungs, and it left me with no air to breathe and I was suffocating badly, choking, asphyxiated. I was about to drown or choke when I woke up.

I stopped fighting the noble fish that was in my dream to begin another struggle, kicking and wrestling with a villainous sperm whale in real life which was lying on top of me and *kissing me* with its immense lunglike lips, kissing me all over my face, kissing my eyes and nose and mouth and who was now chewing my ear and biting my neck and sucking my breast and La Estrella kept sliding off my body and climbing back onto it again making unbelievably weird noises, as if she were singing and snoring at the same time and in between her groans she was speaking to me, whispering, gasping in her rasping baritone *mi amor* please kiss me *ni negro* please kill me *mi chino* come come come, things which would have made me die laughing if I'd been able to breathe and I pushed her with what strength I had left, using a half-crushed leg as a fulcrum and making a springboard not of the bed but of the wall (because I'd been driven back against the wall by that expansion wave of fat, flattened, almost obliterated by that black universe that was expanding in my direction at the speed of love), I managed to give her a final big push and succeeded in putting her off balance and out of bed, *my* bed. She fell on the floor and there she stayed puffing and panting and sobbing but I leaped out of bed and switched on the light and then I *saw* her. She was stark naked and her breasts were as fat as her arms and twice as large as my head, and one of them fell over on one side and touched the floor and the other jutted out over the central breaker of the three great rollers that separated her legs from what would have been her neck if she had had one and the first roller above her thighs was a sort of canopied extension of her mons veneris and I could see how right Alex Bayer was when he said that "she depilated herself completely" because there wasn't a single trace of hair, pubic or otherwise, on her whole body and that couldn't have been natural, but then nothing was natural about La Estrella. It was then that I began to wonder whether she came from outer space.

If the dreams of reason beget monsters, what do the dreams of unreason beget? I dreamed (because I had fallen asleep again: sleep can be as stubborn as insomnia) that UFOs were invading the earth, not as Oscar Hurtado threatened in ships that touched down noiselessly on the rooftops or like Arsenio Cué's creatures quote hurld headlong flaming from th'Ethereal Skie/ with hideous ruin and combustion down unquote or as Silvestre feared infiltrating our lives in the form of microbes reproducing silently, but with definitely Martian shapes, creatures with suckers that could create total suction, as Rine would say, and adhere to walls made of air and then descend or ascend invisible steps and with majestic footfall could spread terror like an overflow of their black, brilliant, silent presences. In another dream or perhaps another form of the same dream these alien beings were sound waves which mingled with us and haunted us and enchanted us, like unseen sirens: from every corner a music gushed out that made men stupid, a paralysing song ray which nobody could resist and nobody could in fact do anything to fight this invasion from outer space because nobody knew that music could be the secret and final weapon, so nobody was going to stop his ears with wax or even with his fingers and at the end of that dream I was the only man on earth who could realize what was actually happening and I tried to lift my hands to my ears and I couldn't because my hands were tied and even my neck and shoulders were tied to the ground by some invisible menders and it happened that I must have fallen off the bed because I woke in a pool of sweat on the floor. I remembered then that I'd dragged myself right across the floor to the opposite end of the room and had gone to sleep right there near the door. Did I wake up with a motorman's glove in my mouth? I can't tell but I can tell that I had a taste of bile on my lips, and was terribly thirsty, and I didn't even drink so much as a cup of coffee because I felt like vomiting, but I thought twice before getting up. I wasn't at all keen to see La Estrella whether she was freak or foe, sleeping in my bed, snoring with her mouth open and half-closed eyes, rolling from side to side: nobody ever wants to meet the nightmare of the night before when he wakes up. So I began to work out how I could get to the bathroom to wash and return to look for my clothes and put them on and go out into the street without disturbing her. When I'd done all this in my mind I began to write a mental note to La Estrella to ask her more or less when she got up to do me the favor of leaving without letting anyone see her, no that was no good: of leaving everything as she'd found it, no that was no good either: of closing the door behind her: shit, all this was childish and besides it was quite useless because La Estrella might not know how to read, O.K. I'd write it in big bold caps with my grease pencil but who told me she couldn't read? Racial segregation, that's who, I said to myself as I was making up my mind to get up and wake her up and talk to her openly. Of course I had to get dressed first. I staggered to my feet and looked at the Castro convertible and she wasn't there and I didn't have to look for her very far because I could see that empty kitchen right in front of me and the bathroom door was open so I could see the bath was empty as well: she wasn't here, she'd gone. I looked at my watch which I had forgotten to take off last night and it was two o'clock (in the afternoon?) and I thought she must have gotten up early and left without making any noise. Very considerate of her. I went to the bathroom and as I was sitting on the can, reading those instructions that come with every roll of Kodak film which had been left on the floor I don't know by whom, reading this conveniently simple division of life into Sunny, Cloudy, Shade, Beach or Snow (snow in Cuba, they must be joking!) and finally Clear Well-lighted Indoors, reading these instructions without understanding them, I heard the doorbell ringing and if I'd been able to jump up without foul consequences, I'd have done so because I was sure it was La Estrella's triumphal comeback, so I let the bell ring and ring and ring and I managed to silence my gut and my lungs and the rest of my body so I became the Silent ???Doni. But a Cuban friend is more adhesive than a Scotch tape and someone shouted my name through the airshaft between the kitchen and bathroom, not a difficult operation for someone who knows the building, has the physique of a trapeze artiste, the chest of an opera singer, the persistence of memory and a stunt man's daring to risk his neck by sticking his head through the corridor window. It wasn't the voice of a Martian. I opened the door after performing some hygienic rituals and Silvestre burst through the doorway like a white tornado, livid, shouting excitedly that Bustro was sick, seriously ill. Who? I said, picking up the debris of my hair after the wind of his entry had scattered it over a radius of my face, and he said, Bustrófedon, I left him in his house early this morning because he was feeling sick, throwing up and all that and I laughed at him because I thought he was able to take his drink better than that but he told me to leave him alone and take him to his place and not disturb him but this morning when I went to look for him to go to the beach the maid told me there was nobody at home neither the señor nor the señora nor Bustrófedon because they'd taken him to the hospital so Silvestre told me all in one breath without a comma. And the maid called him Bustrófedon, just like that? A question that was my token gift of shit to this morning already brimming with drowsiness, hangover and diarrhea. No, you cunt, she didn't say Bustrófedon but of course it was Bustrófedon, who else. Did they tell you what was wrong with him? I said on my way to the kitchen to drink a glass of milk, that oasis well in the morning-after desert of us nomad drinkers. I didn't know, Silvestre said, I don't believe it's serious but I don't think he's at all well either. I don't like the sound of his symptoms, it could very well be aneurysm. A new *rhythm?* I asked in mock disbelief. No, hell no! Cerebral *aneurysm,* an embolism of the brain arteries, I don't know, and I laughed at his words just before he said I don't know. What the fuck are you laughing at now? Silvestre said. You're on your way to becoming a famous diagnostician, *viejito,* I said. Why, he shouted and I could see he was getting angry, why did you say that? Forget it, I said. So you think I'm a hypochondriac too? he said and I said I didn't, I was merely laughing at his vocabulary but admiringly, dazzled by his instant diagnosis and stunned by his scientific knowledge. He smiled but didn't say anything and I narrowly missed hearing yet again his story of how he'd already started or was about to start studying medicine when he'd gone with a classmate of his to the faculty and straight into the dissection room and had seen the corpses and smelled the smell of formaldehyde and dead flesh and heard the ghastly sound of bones creaking when a professor cut them up with a saw, a *common* saw for chrissake! And so on and so forth. I offered him a grateful glass of milk and he said, No thank you I've already had breakfast and from the word breakfast he went on to what comes before breakfast—which is not the morning after but the night before.

What happened to you last night? he asked and I've never known anyone to ask more questions than Silvestre: Why should be his middle name. I went out, I said. For a walk. Where? Nowhere special I said. Are you sure? What do you mean, am I sure? Of cures I'm sure! At least nobody else was in my shoes, or were they? Ah! he said, making a guttural noise to show he understood what I meant, how interesting! I didn't want to ask him any questions and he took advantage of my disadvantage to ask me some more. So you don't know what happened last night? Here, I said, trying not to make it sound like a question. No, not here, he said, in the street. We were the last to leave, I believe. Yes, the last because Sebastián Morán left before you returned with La Estrella as he still had to do his show (I thought I heard a musical note of sarcasm in his voice) and then Gianni and Franemilio left and we stayed and by we I mean Eribó and Cué and

Bustrófedon and me, talking, shouting rather above La Estrella's snores and Eribó and Cué and Piloto & Vera left together and Rine had gone earlier with Jesse and Juan Blanco, I think, I'm not sure, so Bustrófedon and I took Ingrid and Edith with us. I mean, what happened was that after closing up shop in your place Bustro and I picked up Ingrid and Edith as we planned to go to the Chori and on our way to La Playa Bustrófedon was in true form, you should have heard him, but we were already on the heavy side of the river when he began to feel ill and we had to go back and Edith finally told the driver to stop on the corner and she went to bed all by herself, Silvestre said.

In the room I come and go talking to my guardian angelo as I look for my socks which only last night came in pairs and have now all managed to become single specimens. When I got tired of searching for them through the universe of my studio I returned to my own private galaxy and went to the closet and pulled out a new pair and put them on while Silvestre went on talking, telling me his story, and I was working out what do with the rest of that Sunday. The thing is, he said, that I was making out with Ingrid (and now I should explain that Ingrid is Ingrid Bergamo but that's not her name, that's her nickname, we gave it to her because that's how she pronounces the name Ingrid Bergman: she's a *mulata adelantada,* as she herself puts it when she's in a good mood, meaning she can easily pass for white, and she dyes her hair ash blond and puts on lots of makeup and wears the tightest skirts of anyone in this island where the women don't wear dresses in any case but body gloves, and she's a very easy lay, which didn't do anything to diminish Silvestre's pleasure because no woman is easy on the eve of her bedding), so I picked her up and took her to the *posada* on 84th Street, he said, and after we were already inside the patio she started saying no, no and no, and I had to tell the driver to please drive on. But, he said, when we were back in El Vedado and the taxi had gone through the tunnel for the fourth or fifth time, we started kissing and all that and she let me take her to the *posada* on 11th and 24th Street and the same thing happened there except that the driver said he was a cab driver not a pimp and that I should pay him there and then so he could go away and then Ingrid started arguing with him for not taking her home and the guy was so cut up that I paid him quickly and he shot off. Of kosher, he said, Silvestre said, I took Ingrid with me and there in the intimate darkness she staged a big row and we went out onto the street again arguing with each other or rather she was doing all the arguing as I was trying to calm her down, as reasonable and cool as George Sanders in *All About Eve* (Silvestre always talks like that in filmese: once he had a frame with his hands playing the photographer, and he said to me, Whoa! Budge an inch and you go out of frame! and another time I arrived at his house, which was dark, with the doors of the balcony closed because the evening sun hit them hard and I inadvertently opened the balcony and he said, You've just exploded twenty thousand full candles in my face! and the time he and Cué and I were talking about jazz and then Cué said something pedantic about its origins in New Orleans and Silvestre told him, Don't cut in with that flashback now, viejito! and other things I forget or can't remember now), and there we were walking and quarreling and crossing El Vedado from north to south, you know where we finally ended up? he asked but didn't wait for my answer. We arrived at the posada on 31st Street and went in as though there was nothing to it. I believe, he told me, I won the game by default but this was only the first round and inside, once we were in the room there was a wrestling match between a heroine from Griffith and a Von Stroheim villain to get her to sit down, are you listening? just to get her to sit down and not even on the bed but in a chair! After she'd sat down she didn't want to let go of her handbag. Finally, he said, I got her to calm down and sit quietly, almost relaxed and I go and take off my jacket and she's up like a shot and runs to open the door to leave the room and I zoom in on the door and see her hand in big close-up on the bolt and I put my jacket back on and calm her down once more but in calming her down she gets so nervous she makes a mistake and sits on the bed and no sooner is she sitting than she leaps up as though it was a fakir's bed of nails and I, playing the part of a man of the world, very much a la Cary Grant, I manage to persuade her not to be frightened, there's nothing to be afraid of, sitting on the bed is only sitting, and the bed is just like any other bit of furniture, namely a chair, and like a chair the bed could just as well be a seat and she's much quieter now, so she gets up and leaves her handbag on the table and sits back on the bed again. I don't know why, Silvestre told me, but I guessed I could now take my jacket off, so I took it off and sat beside her and began to caress and kiss her and having got this far I push her back, so she would lie down, and she lies down only a second because up she pops like on a spring again and I go on pushing her down and she goes on sitting up and I insist she lie down until something's got to give and this time she lies down and stays down for good, very quiet and very much the ingenue in a romantic-but-risqué scene, so I decide to take a chance and begin telling her how hot it is and that it's a pity she's going to fuck—pardon—to wreck her dress and how it's getting all rumpled and how elegant it indeed is and she says, It's cute, isn't it? And with no heralding effect whatsoever she tells me she's going to take it off so as not to crease it, but that she won't take off anything more, that she will definitely keep her slip on, and then she takes her dress off. She gets back on the bed again and I've already taken my shoes off and I forget the Hays code, I start working on her body in medium shot, and I plead with her, I beg her, and I almost go down on my knees on the bed, asking her to take off her slip and I tell her I want to see her beautiful starlet's body, that she needn't wear more than just panties and bra, that it's only the same as a swimsuit except she's in bed not on the beach and I succeed in convincing her with this argument, viejito, and she takes her slip off though first she tells me that's all, she's not taking off anything more. But nothing. So then we start kissing and caressing and I tell her I'm going to get my pants rumpled unless I take them off so I take them off and I take my shirt off too and now I've got nothing on but my shorts and when I scramble back on the bed again she starts getting angry or pretends she's angry already and she won't let me caress her like before. But a minute later I'm touching her hand with a finger and then the finger climbs on top of her hand and then climbs up her arm not only one finger but two and then my hand climbs up the south face of her tit because it's there, and then I caress her body and we start feeling and fondling each other again and then I ask her, beginning in a whisper, almost in voice off, telling her, pleading with her to take off the rest of her clothes, or just her bra so I can see her marvelous breasts but she won't let me convince her and then just when I'm on the point of losing my cool, she says, O.K. and suddenly she's taken her bra off and what do you guess I'm seeing in the dim red light in the bedroom? That was the subject of another public debate: switching off the overhead light and switching on the bedside lamp. What I'm seeing is the eighth wonder of the world, the eighth and the ninth because there are *two* of them! And I start going crazy over them, and she starts going crazy and the whole atmosphere switches from suspense to euphoria like in a Hitchcock movie. The end of the sequence was, so as not to bore you with any more detail shots, that with the same or similar arguments that had become standard treatment by now I succeeded in persuading her to take off her pants, *but*, BUT, where old Hitch would have cut to insert an intercut of fireworks, I'll give it to you straight—I didn't get any further than that. Not even the Great Cary would have been able to persuade this poor man's Ingrid to do a love scene, torrid or horrid, and I came to the conclusion that rape is one of the labors of Hercules and that really there's no such thing as rape, because it can't be called a crime if the victim is conscious and only one person commits the act. No, that's quite impossible, dear De Sad.

I begin to laugh seismically but Silvestre interrupts me. Wait a moment, hang on a sec, as Ingrid says, that's not the end of the film. We spent the night, Silvestre tells me, or the bit of the night that was left on the best of terms and succored by her expert hands, satisfied more or less and in *Ecstasy,* a state of, I fell asleep and when I wake up it's already light and I look for my loved one and I see my costar has changed with the night, that sleep has transformed her and like poor Franz Kafka I call it a metamorphosis and even though it's not Gregor Samsa whom I find beside me it sure is another woman: night and kisses and sleep have removed not only her lipstick but the whole of her makeup, the lot: the once perfect eyebrows, the large thick lovely black lashes, the phosphorescent and pale complexion that was so kissable the night before are no more, and, wait a moment, don't laugh please: you ain't heard nothing yet, so hold on, I'll be rocking the boat: there, by my side, between her and me like an abyss of falsyhood, there's a yellowish object, round more or less and silky in appearance but not in texture, and as I touch it I almost leap out of bed: it's hairy! I pick it up, he says, in my hands, very cautiously, and hold it up to the morning light to see it better and it is, a last tremolo of strings attached plus a clash of cymbals, yes, a wig: my leading lady becomes the American eagle because she is hairless or, he said, bald, bald, bald, bald! Well, not *completely* bald, which is even wore because she has a few bits of colorless fuzz here and there, quite disgusting I must say. So there I was, Ionesco Malgré Louis, Silvestre said, in bed with the bald soprano. I must have been thinking this so hard I said it out loud, because she began to stir and then woke up. In the immediately preceding shot I'd left the wig where it was, had lain down again and feigned sleep, and as she wakes up now the first thing she does is to put a hand to her head and in a frenzy she frisks around, she leaps around, looking for her hairpiece everywhere and she finds it and puts it on—but *upside down, chico,* upside down! Then she gets up, goes to the bathroom, closes the door and turns on the light and when she opens it again everything's in its place. She looks at me and then she does a double take because she was so worried about losing her hair she forgot I existed and it's only now she remembers she's in a posada and with me. She looks at me twice, Silvestre said, to make sure I'm sleeping, but she looks at me from a distance and there I am fast asleep with my eyes half opened, seeing everything: I'm a film camera. She picks up her handbag and her clothes and goes into the bathroom again. When she comes out she's another woman. Or rather she's the same woman you and I and everybody else know and who gave me such a hard time last night before she consented to let me be present at her unveiling, at her total striptease, *au dépouillement à la Allais.*

All this time I couldn't contain my laughter and Silvestre had to narrate his *Odyssey* above my guffaws and now the two of us laughed together. But then he signaled me to stop and said, But don't you laugh at Barnum, old Bailey, because we're both partners of Browning in Freaks. What do you mean, I say. Yes sirce, you've been making love with the Negro nation's answer to Oliver Hardy. What do you mean, I repeat. Yes, yes. Listen, after I'd left the lie-detector chamber I took that delectable little blonde back to where she once belonged in an early taxi and after I'd seen her safely home I went off toward the sunrise and beyond, where my house is, and as I was passing here, it must have been about 5 o'clock A.M., there was La Estrella walking along the sidewalk up 23rd Street, looking real cross, and I don't mean her hair but her looks. So I called her and picked her up and took her home but along the way, my friend and lighting cameraman, she told me that a horrible thing happened to her on her way to stardom and she proceeded to tell me that she'd fallen asleep in your camera obscura and that you came back drunk and had tried to sodomize her, and she ended by swearing to me that she'd never never never put a foot inside your house again, and I'm telling you, she was really mad at you. So you see one freak equals another and a farce mirrors a fiasco or *fracaso,* failure's saddest form. Did she actually say that? I asked. No, not her but probably Carlos or Ernesto. Come on! Is that what she told you, is that what she said? Well, said Silvestre, she said you tried to bugger her, that's what she told me but I'm not keeping to the text. I'm giving you a fair film copy instead.

As I had no more laughter left in my body, I left Silvestre sitting on the bed or the sofa and went to brush my teeth. From the bathroom I asked him which hospital Bustrófedon was in and he told me he was in Antomarchi. I asked him if he was going to see him in the evening and he shook his head and said that at four o'clock he had a date with Ingrid the woman from Bergamo and he thought that today he shouldn't put off till tomorrow what he should have done yesterday. I smiled but without conviction now and Silvestre told me I shouldn't smile like that because it wasn't her body he was after but only that naked soul of hers and that I should also bear in mind her antecedents in film myth: Jean Harlow also wore a wig. Made by Max Factor of Hollywood.

## ■ V. S. Naipaul (1932– ) *Trinidad* (novel)

The novelist, essayist, and memoirist Surajprasad Naipaul was born in Chaguanas, Trinidad, to which his grandfather had come. He was educated at Queen's Royal College in Trinidad and later at University College, Oxford, where he was an outstanding student, praised by one of his famed examiners, J. R. Tolkien. For some years, he worked for the BBC's Caribbean Voices. Naipaul has traveled extensively in the Americas, Europe, Africa, and Asia but has lived in Britain since 1950. Given his dispersed background, of East Indian ancestry, born in the West Indies, and living in London, he has the ambivalent sensibility of the exile, whose insight and sardonic humor inform his work and take him from the Indies to India and down to the back streets of Buenos Aires where he scorns the pretentious Catholic city's big red light district and the corrupt politicians who rob and degrade the culture. He is a magnificent stylist, and few people and places escape his irony and satire. Nothing is sacred—particularly the sacred mysteries of Hinduism—before his pen, although a more compassionate Naipaul at times emerges when he explores his own troubled, complex cultural identity. He attacks the deeds of the colonial British Empire as well as its present or former subjects, beginning with his fellow Trinidadians whom he seems to dismiss as the "Third World's third world," yet Trinidad enriched him with the material for his early novels.

His first three novels, *The Mystic Masseur* (1957), *The Suffrage of Elvira* (1958), and *Miguel Street* (1958) (the following self-contained segments about an antihero trickster are taken from *Miguel Street*), comically and genially describe personal and political life in Trinidad and the Caribbean, showing the cultural provincialism and economic ruin of the area, and the survival of the trickster. His *A House for Mr. Biswas* (1961), also set in the Caribbean, is his longest novel and his early masterpiece, establishing his world reputation. He turns his moralistic eye and ear to Africa in *In a Free State* (1971), a book of short fiction. The superb style and polished narrations of *In a Free State* won him the Booker Prize. He wrote about Africa again in *A Bend in the River* (1979), a political satire about the messes and contradictions of revolutionary politics. Less than a decade later in 1983, he was awarded the prestigious Jerusalem Prize. He was knighted in 1990. While Naipaul has been criticized for his acid pen, he has, in fiction, travel book, or essay, followed the ways of virtually all leading authors of Asia, Africa, and Latin America in the severity of his criticism. He does not sentimentalize and aggrandize revolutionary folk heroes; rather, he attacks their fraudulent offspring. V. S. Naipaul, a figure ever displaced, rooted in his rootlessness, has taken the world as his subject and is of the handful of truly major twentieth-century novelists. He provides cunning, often devastating observations of mythical or real nations caught in their chaos and pathos.

**FURTHER READING:** Naipaul, V. S. *The Mystic Masseur,* 1957; *The Suffrage of Elvira,* 1958; *A House for Mr. Biswas,* 1961; *In a Free State,* 1971; *Guerrillas,* 1975; *India: A Wounded Civilization,* 1977; *A Bend in the River,* 1979; *The Return of Eva Peron,* 1980; *Among the Believers: An Islamic Journey,* 1981; *The Loss of El Dorado: A History,* 1984; *Mr. Stone and The Knight's Companion,* 1985; *The Enigma of Arrival: a Novel,* 1987; *Finding the Center: Two Narratives,* 1984; *A Turn in the South,* 1989; *India: A Million Mutinies Now,* 1990; *A Way in the World: A Novel,* 1994.

# *from* Miguel Street

## The Thing without a Name

The only thing that Popo, who called himself a carpenter, ever built was the little galvanized-iron workshop under the mango tree at the back of his yard. And even that he didn't quite finish. He couldn't be bothered to nail on the sheets of galvanized-iron for the root, and kept them weighted down with huge stones. Whenever there was a high wind the roof made a frightening banging noise and seemed ready to fly away.

And yet Popo was never idle. He was always busy hammering and sawing and planing. I liked watching him work. I liked the smell of the woods—cyp and cedar and crapaud. I liked the colour of the shavings, and I liked the way the sawdust powdered Popo's kinky hair.

'What you making, Mr Popo?' I asked.

Popo would always say, 'Ha, boy! That's the question. I making the thing without a name.'

I liked Popo for that. I thought he was a poetic man.

One day I said to Popo, 'Give me something to make.'

'What you want to make?' he said.

It was hard to think of something I really wanted.

'You see,' Popo said. 'You thinking about the thing without a name.'

Eventually I decided on an egg-stand.

'Who you making it for?' Popo asked.

'Ma.'

He laughed. 'Think she going use it?'

My mother was pleased with the egg-stand, and used it for about a week. Then she seemed to forget all about it; and began putting the eggs in bowls or plates, just as she did before.

And Popo laughed when I told him. He said, 'Boy, the only thing to make is the thing without a name.'

After I painted the tailoring sign for Bogart, Popo made me do one for him as well.

He took the little red stump of a pencil he had stuck over his ear and puzzled over the words. At first he wanted to announce himself as an architect; but I managed to dissuade him. He wasn't sure about the spelling. The finished sign said:

BUILDER AND CONTRACTOR
Carpenter
And Cabinet-Maker

And I signed my name, as sign-writer, in the bottom right-hand corner.

Popo liked standing up in front of the sign. But he had a little panic when people who didn't know about him came to inquire.

'The carpenter fellow?' Popo would say. 'He don't live here again.'

I thought Popo was a much nicer man than Bogart. Bogart said little to me; but Popo was always ready to talk. He talked about serious things, like life and death and work, and I felt he really liked talking to me.

Yet Popo was not a popular man in the street. They didn't think he was mad or stupid. Hat used to say, 'Popo too conceited, you hear.'

It was an unreasonable thing to say. Popo had the habit of taking a glass of rum to the pavement every morning. He never sipped the rum. But whenever he saw someone he knew he dipped his middle finger in the rum, licked it, and then waved to the man.

'We could buy rum too,' Hat used to say. 'But we don't show off like Popo.'

I myself never thought about it in that way, and one day I asked Popo about it.

Popo said, 'Boy, in the morning, when the sun shining and it still cool, and you just get up, it make you feel good to know that you could go out and stand up in the sun and have some rum.'

Popo never made any money. His wife used to go out and work, and this was easy, because they had no children. Popo said, 'Women and them like work. Man not make for work.'

Hat said, 'Popo is a man-woman. Not a proper man.'

Popo's wife had a job as a cook in a big house near my school. She used to wait for me in the afternoons and take me into the big kitchen and give me a lot of nice things to eat. The only thing I didn't like was the way she sat and watched me while I ate. It was as though I was eating for her. She asked me to call her Auntie.

She introduced me to the gardener of the big house. He was a good-looking brown man, and he loved his flowers. I liked the gardens he looked after. The flower-beds were always black and wet; and the grass green and damp and always cut. Sometimes he let me water the flower-beds. And he used to gather the cut grass into little bags which he gave me to take home to my mother. Grass was good for the hens.

One day I missed Popo's wife. She wasn't waiting for me.

Next morning I didn't see Popo dipping his finger in the glass of rum on the pavement.

And that evening I didn't see Popo's wife.

I found Popo sad in his workshop. He was sitting on a plank and twisting a bit of shaving around his fingers.

Popo said, 'Your auntie gone, boy.'

'Where, Mr Popo?'

'Ha, boy! That's the question,' and he pulled himself up there.

Popo found himself then a popular man. The news got around very quickly. And when Eddoes said one day, 'I wonder what happen to Popo. Like he got no more rum,' Hat jumped up and almost cuffed him. And then all the men began to gather in Popo's workshop, and they would talk about cricket and football and pictures—everything except women—just to try to cheer Popo up.

Popo's workshop no longer sounded with hammering and sawing. The sawdust no longer smelled fresh, and became black, almost like dirt. Popo began drinking a lot, and I didn't like him when he was drunk. He smelled of rum, and he used to cry and then grow angry and want to beat up everybody. That made him an accepted member of the gang.

Hat said, 'We was wrong about Popo. He is a man, like any of we.'

Popo liked the new companionship. He was at heart a loquacious man, and always wanted to be friendly with the men of the street and he was always surprised that he was not liked. So it looked as though he had got what he wanted. But Popo was not really happy. The friendship had come a little too late, and he found he didn't like it as much as he'd expected. Hat tried to get Popo interested in other women, but Popo wasn't interested.

Popo didn't think I was too young to be told anything.

'Boy, when you grow old as me,' he said once, 'you find that you don't care for the things you thought you woulda like if you coulda afford them.'

That was his way of talking, in riddles.

Then one day Popo left us.

Hat said, 'He don't have to tell me where he gone. He gone looking for he wife.'

Edward said, 'Think she going come back with he?'

Hat said, 'Let we wait and see.'

We didn't have to wait long. It came out in the papers. Hat said it was just what he expected. Popo had beaten up a man in Arima, the man had taken his wife away. It was the gardener who used to give me bags of grass.

Nothing much happened to Popo. He had to pay a fine, but they let him off otherwise. The magistrate said that Popo had better not molest his wife again.

They made a calypso about Popo that was the rage that year. It was the road-march for the Carnival, and the Andrews Sisters sang it for an American recording company:

> A certain carpenter feller went to Arima
> Looking for a mopsy called Emelda.

It was a great thing for the street.

At school, I used to say, 'The carpenter feller was a good, good friend of mine.'

And, at cricket matches, and at the races, Hat used to say, 'Know him? God, I used to drink with that man night and day. Boy, he could carry his liquor.'

Popo wasn't the same man when he came back to us. He growled at me when I tried to talk to him, and he drove out Hat and the others when they brought a bottle of rum to the workshop.

Hat said, 'Woman send that man mad, you hear.'

But the old noises began to be heard once more from Popo's workshop. He was working hard, and I wondered whether he was still making the thing without a name. But I was too afraid to ask.

He ran an electric light to the workshop and began working in the night-time. Vans stopped outside his house and were always depositing and taking away things. Then Popo began painting his house. He used a bright green, and he painted the roof a bright red. Hat said, 'The man really mad.'

And added, 'Like he getting married again.'

Hat wasn't too far wrong. One day, about two weeks later, Popo returned, and he brought a woman with him. It was his wife. My auntie.

'You see the sort of thing woman is,' Hat commented. 'You see the sort of thing they like. Not the man. But the new house paint up, and all the new furniture inside it. I bet you if the man in Arima had a new house and new furnitures, she wouldnta come back with Popo.'

But I didn't mind. I was glad. It was good to see Popo standing outside with his glass of rum in the mornings and dipping his finger into the rum and waving at his friends; and it was good to ask him again, 'What you making, Mr Popo?' and to get the old answer, 'Ha, boy! That's the question. I making the thing without a name.'

Popo returned very quickly to his old way of living, and he was still devoting his time to making the thing without a name. He had stopped working, and his wife got her job with the same people near my school.

People in the street were almost angry with Popo when his wife came back. They felt that all their sympathy had been mocked and wasted. And again Hat was saying, 'That blasted Popo too conceited, you hear.'

But this time Popo didn't mind.

He used to tell me, 'Boy, go home and pray tonight that you get happy like me.'

What happened afterwards happened so suddenly that we didn't even know it had happened. Even Hat didn't know about it until he read it in the papers. Hat always read the papers. He read them from about ten in the morning until about six in the evening.

Hat shouted out, 'But what is this I seeing?' and he showed us the headlines: CALYPSO CARPENTER JAILED

It was a fantastic story. Popo had been stealing things left and right. All the new furnitures, as Hat called them, hadn't been made by Popo. He had stolen things and simply remodelled them. He had stolen too much as a matter of fact, and had had to sell the things he didn't want. That was how he had been caught. And we understood now why the vans were always outside Popo's house. Even the paint and the brushes with which he had redecorated the house had been stolen.

Hat spoke for all of us when he said, 'That man too foolish. Why he had to sell what he thief? Just tell me that. Why?'

We agreed it was a stupid thing to do. But we felt deep inside ourselves that Popo was really a man, perhaps a bigger man than any of us.

And as for my auntie . . .

Hat said, 'How much jail he get? A year? With three months off for good behaviour, that's nine months in all. And I give she three months good behaviour too. And after that, it ain't going to have no more Emelda in Miguel Street, you hear.'

But Emelda never left Miguel Street. She not only kept her job as cook, but she started taking in washing and ironing as well. No one in the street felt sorry that Popo had gone to jail because of the shame; after all that was a thing that could happen to any of us. They felt sorry only that Emelda was going to be left alone for so long.

He came back as a hero. He was one of the boys. He was a better man than either Hat or Bogart.

But for me, he had changed. And the change made me sad.

For Popo began working.

He began making morris chairs and tables and wardrobes for people.

And when I asked him, 'Mr Popo, when you going start making the thing without a name again?' he growled at me.

'You too troublesome,' he said. 'Go away quick, before I lay my hand on you.'

## George and The Pink House

I was much more afraid of George than I was of Big Foot, although Big Foot was the biggest and the strongest man in the street. George was short and fat. He had a grey moustache and a big belly. He looked harmless enough but he was always muttering to himself and cursing and I never tried to become friendly with him.

He was like the donkey he had tied in the front of his yard, grey and old and silent except when it brayed loudly. You felt that George was never really in touch with what was going on around him all the time, and I found it strange that no one should have said that George was mad, while everybody said that Man-man, whom I liked, was mad.

George's house also made me feel afraid. It was a brokendown wooden building, painted pink on the outside, and the galvanized-iron roof was brown from rust. One door, the one to the right, was always left open. The inside walls had never been painted, and were grey and black with age. There was a dirty bed in one corner and in another there was a table and a stool. That was all. No curtains, no pictures on the wall. Even Bogart had a picture of Lauren Bacall in his room.

I found it hard to believe that George had a wife and a son and a daughter.

Like Popo, George was happy to let his wife do all the work in the house and the yard. They kept cows, and again I hated George for that. Because the water from his pens made the gutters stink, and when we were playing cricket on the pavement the ball often got wet in the gutter. Boyee and Errol used to wet the ball deliberately in the stinking gutter. They wanted to make it shoot.

George's wife was never a proper person. I always thought of her just as George's wife, and that was all. And I always thought, too, that George's wife was nearly always in the cow-pen.

And while George sat on the front concrete step outside the open door of his house, his wife was busy.

George never became one of the gang in Miguel Street. He didn't seem to mind. He had his wife and his daughter and his son. He beat them all. And when the boy Elias grew too big, George beat his daughter and his wife more than ever. The blows didn't appear to do the mother any good. She just grew thinner and thinner; but the daughter, Dolly, thrived on it. She grew fatter and fatter, and giggled more and more every year. Elias, the son, grew more and more stern, but he never spoke a hard word to his father.

Hat said, 'That boy Elias have too much good mind.'

One day Bogart, of all people, said, 'Ha! I mad to break old George tail up, you hear.'

And the few times when Elias joined the crowd, Hat would say, 'Boy, I too sorry for you. Why you don't fix the old man up good?'

Elias would say, 'It is all God work.'

Elias was only fourteen or so at the time. But that was the sort of boy he was. He was serious and he had big ambitions.

I began to be terrified of George, particularly when he bought two great Alsatian dogs and tied them to pickets at the foot of the concrete steps.

Every morning and afternoon when I passed his house, he would say to the dogs, 'Shook him!'

And the dogs would bound and leap and bark; and I could see their ropes stretched tight and I always felt that the ropes would break at the next leap. Now, when Hat had an Alsatian, he made it like me. And Hat had said to me then, 'Never fraid dog. Go brave. Don't run.'

And so I used to walk slowly past George's house, lengthening out my torture.

I don't know whether George disliked me personally, or whether he simply had no use for people in general. I never discussed it with the other boys in the street, because I was too ashamed to say I was afraid of barking dogs.

Presently, though, I grew used to the dogs. And even George's laughter when I passed the house didn't worry me very much.

One day George was on the pavement as I was passing; I heard him mumbling. I heard him mumble again that afternoon and again the following day. He was saying, 'Horse-face!'

Sometimes he said, 'Like it only have horse-face people living in this place.'

Sometimes he said, 'Short-arse'

And, 'But how it have people so short-arse in the world?'

I pretended not to hear, of course, but after a week or so I was almost in tears whenever George mumbled these things.

One evening, when we had stopped playing cricket on the pavement because Boyee had hit the ball into Miss Hilton's yard, and that was a lost ball (it counted six and out) — that evening, I asked Elias, 'but what your father have with me so? Why he does keep on calling me names?'

Hat laughed, and Elias looked a little solemn.

Hat said, 'What sort of names?'

I said, 'The fat old man does call me horse-face.' I couldn't bring myself to say the other name.

Hat began laughing.

Elias said, 'Boy, my father is a funny man. But you must forgive him. What he say don't matter. He old. He have life hard. He not educated like we here. He have a soul just like any of we, too besides.'

And he was so serious that Hat didn't laugh and whenever I walked past George's house, I kept on saying to myself, 'I must forgive him. He ain't know what he doing.'

And then Elias's mother died, and had the shabbiest and the saddest and the loneliest funeral Miguel Street had ever seen.

That empty front room became sadder and more frightening for me.

The strange thing was that I felt a little sorry for George. The Miguel Street men held a post-mortem outside Hat's house. Hat said, 'He did beat she too bad.'

Bogart nodded and drew a circle on the pavement with his right index finger.

Edward said, 'I think he kill she, you know. Boyee tell me that the evening before she dead he hear George giving the woman licks like fire.'

Hat said, 'What you think they have doctors and magistrates in this place for? For fun?'

'But I telling you,' Edward said. 'It's really true. Boyee wouldn't lie about a thing like that. The woman dead from blows. I telling you. London can take it; but not George wife.'

Not one of the men said a word for George.

Boyee said something I didn't expect him to say. He said, 'The person I really feel sorry for is Dolly. You suppose he going to beat she still?'

Hat said wisely. 'Let we wait and see.'

Elias dropped out of our circle.

George was very sad for the first few days after the funeral. He drank a lot of rum and went about crying in the streets, beating his chest and asking everybody to forgive him, and to take pity on him, a poor widower.

He kept up the drinking into the following weeks, and he was still running up and down the street, making everyone feel foolish when he asked for forgiveness. 'My son Elias,' George used to say, 'my son Elias forgive me, and he is a educated boy.'

When he came to Hat, Hat said, 'What happening to your cows? You milking them? You feeding them? You want to kill your cows now too?'

George sold all his cows to Hat.

'God will say is robbery,' Hat laughed. 'I say is a bargain.'

Edward said, 'It good for George. He beginning to pay for his sins.'

'Well, I look at it this way,' Hat said, 'I give him enough money to remain drunk for two whole months.'

George was away from Miguel Street for a week. During that time we saw more of Dolly. She swept out the front room and begged flowers of the neighbours and put them in the room. She giggled more than ever.

Someone in the street (not me) poisoned the two Alsatians.

We hoped that George had gone away for good.

He did come back, however, still drunk, but no longer crying or helpless, and he had a woman with him. She was a very Indian woman, a little old, but she looked strong enough to handle George.

'She look like a drinker sheself,' Hat said.

This woman took control of George's house, and once more Dolly retreated into the back, where the empty cowpens were.

We heard stories of beatings and everybody said he was sorry for Dolly and the new woman.

My heart went out to the woman and Dolly. I couldn't understand how anybody in the world would want to live with George, and I wasn't surprised when one day, about two weeks later, Popo told me, 'George new wife leave him, you ain't hear?'

Hat said, 'I wonder what he going do when the money I give him finish.'

We soon saw.

The pink house, almost overnight, became a full and noisy place. There were many women about, talking loudly and not paying too much attention to the way they dressed. And whenever I passed the pink house, these women shouted abusive remarks at me; and some of them did things with their mouths, inviting me to 'come to mooma'. And there were not only these new women. Many American soldiers drove up in jeeps, and Miguel Street became full of laughter and shrieks.

Hat said, 'That man George giving the street a bad name, you know.'

It was as though Miguel Street belonged to these new people. Hat and the rest of the boys were no longer assured of privacy when they sat down to talk things over on the pavement.

But Bogart became friendly with the new people and spent two or three evenings a week with them. He pretended he was disgusted at what he saw, but I didn't believe him because he was always going back.

'What happening to Dolly?' Hat asked him one day.

'She dey,' Bogart said, meaning that she was all right.

'Ah know she dey,' Hat said. 'But how she dey?'

'Well, she cleaning and cooking.'

'For everybody?'

'Everybody.'

Elias had a room of his own which he never left whenever he came home. He ate his meals outside. He was trying to study for some important exam. He had lost interest in his family, Bogart said, or rather, implied.

George was still drinking a lot; but he was prospering. He was wearing a suit now, and a tie.

Hat said, 'He must be making a lot of money, if he have to bribe all the policemen and them.'

What I couldn't understand at all, though, was the way these new women behaved to George. They all appeared to like him as well as respect him. And George wasn't attempting to be nice in return either. He remained himself.

One day he said to everyone, 'Dolly ain't have no mooma now. I have to be father and mother to the child. And I say is high time Dolly get married.'

His choice fell on a man called Razor. It was hard to think of a more suitable name for this man. He was small. He was thin. He had a neat, sharp moustache above neat, tiny lips. The creases on his trousers were always sharp and clean and straight. And he was supposed to carry a knife.

Hat didn't like Dolly marrying Razor. 'He too sharp for we,' he said. 'He is the sort of man who wouldn't think anything about forgetting a knife in your back, you know.'

But Dolly still giggled.

Razor and Dolly were married at church, and they came back to a reception in the pink house. The women were all dressed up, and there were lots of American soldiers and sailors drinking and laughing and congratulating George. The women and the Americans made Dolly and Razor kiss and kiss, and they cheered. Dolly giggled.

Hat said, 'She ain't giggling, you know. She crying really.'

Elias wasn't at home that day.

The women and the Americans sang *Sweet Sixteen* and *As Time Goes By*. Then they made Dolly and Razor kiss again. Someone shouted, 'Speech' and everybody laughed and shouted, 'Speech! Speech!'

Razor left Dolly standing by herself giggling.

'Speech! Speech' the wedding guests called.

Dolly only giggled more.

Then George spoke out. 'Dolly, you married, it true. But don't think you too big for me to put you across my lap and cut your tail.' He said it in a jocular manner, and the guests laughed.

Then Dolly stopped giggling and looked stupidly at the people.

For a moment so brief you could scarcely measure it there was absolute silence; then an American sailor waved his hands drunkenly and shouted. 'You could put this girl to better work, George.' And everybody laughed.

Dolly picked up a handful of gravel from the yard and was making as if to throw it at the sailor. But she stopped suddenly, and burst into tears.

There was much laughing and cheering and shouting.

I never knew what happened to Dolly. Edward said one day that she was living in Sangre Grande. Hat said he saw her selling in the George Street Market. But she had left the street, left it for good.

As the months went by, the women began to disappear and the numbers of jeeps that stopped outside George's house grew smaller.

'You gotta be organized,' Hat said.

Bogart nodded.

Hat added, 'And they have lots of nice places all over the place in Port of Spain these days. The trouble with George is that he too stupid for a big man.'

Hat was a prophet. Within six months. George was living alone in his pink house. I used to see him then, sitting on the steps, but he never looked at me any more. He looked old and weary and very sad.

He died soon afterwards. Hat and the boys got some money together and we buried him at Lapeyrouse Cemetery. Elias turned up for the funeral.

# ■ Luisa Valenzuela (1938– ) *Argentina* (story)

## TRANSLATED BY MARGARET SAYERS PEDEN

Born in Argentina, Luisa Valenzuela became a writer at an early age. Her mother, Luisa Mercedes Levinson, was a well-known Argentine novelist. As a teenager, Valenzuela worked with Jorge Luis Borges when he was director of the National Library and also for the newspaper *La Nación*. She has traveled widely and lived in Paris, New York, and Mexico City. She published her first novel, *You Have to Laugh* (1969), in her twenties. Her world fame came with the publication in English and other languages of a series of novels and books of short stories, including *Clara: Thirteen Short Stories and a Novel* (1976), *Other Weapons* (1985), *Open Door Stories* (1988), and *The Lizard's Tail*. Like Isabel Allende, the political events of her country during the "Dirty War" led her to work and write abroad, and she has become an extremely well-known contemporary woman writer, translated by Helen Lane and Gregory Rabassa among others. Her skilled narrative techniques and her use of multiple voices, elusive time, and always a metaphysical thread have contributed to winning her both critical and popular acclaim. She has taught at Columbia University and lives mainly in the United States.

**FURTHER READING:** Valenzuela, Luisa. *Clara: Thirteen Short Stories and a Novel.* Translated by Hortense Carpentier and J. Jorge Castello, 1976; *Strange Things Happen Here: Twenty-six Short Stories and a Novel.* Translated by Helen Lane, 1979; *The Lizard's Tail.* Translated by Gregory Rabassa, 1983; *Other Weapons.* Translated by Deborah Bonner, 1985; *Open Door.* Translated by Hortense Carpentier et al., 1988.

## *Up among the Eagles*

You're going to find it hard to believe what I tell you because these days who knows anything about life in the country? And up there, life on the mountain, up among the eagles? But you get used to it. Oh, yes. I can say that, I who never knew anything but the city, see how I am now, the color of earth, carrying my pails of water from the public fountain. Water for myself and water for others. I do it to eke out a living; I've done it ever since the day I made the foolish mistake of climbing the path that borders the cliff. I climbed up, and when I looked down and saw the green dot of the valley far below, I decided to stay here forever. It wasn't that I was afraid, I was just being prudent, as they say: threatening cliffs, beyond imagination; impossible even to consider returning. I traded everything I had for food; my shoes, my wrist watch, my key chain with all my keys (I wouldn't be needing them now), a fountain pen that was almost out of ink.

The only thing of any value I have left is my polaroid camera; no one wanted it. Up here they don't believe in preserving images; just the opposite: every day they strive to create new images, they invent new images only for the moment. Often they get together to tell one another about the incorporeal images they've been entertaining. They sit in a circle on the dirt floor in the darkness of their communal building—a kind of hut—and concentrate on making the vision appear. One day, out of nothing, they materialized a tapestry of non-existent colors and ineffable design, but they decided that it was but a pale reflection of the mental image, and they broke the circle in order to return the tapestry to the nothingness from which it had come.

They are strange creatures; normally they speak a language whose meaning they themselves have forgotten. They communicate by interpreting pauses, intonations, facial expressions, and sighs. I tried to learn this language of silences, but it seems that my tongue is not meant for such subtleties. At any rate, they speak our language when they refer to trivial matters, the daily needs that have nothing to do with their images. Even so, some words are missing from their vocabulary. For example, they have no word for yesterday or tomorrow, before and after, or one of these days. Here everything is now, and always. An unsatisfactory imitation of eternity, like the tapestry I've already mentioned. Have mentioned? Oh, yes, I'm the only one that uses that verb tense; I may also be the only one who has any notion of conjugations. A vice left over from the world down there, knowledge I can't trade anyone, because no one wants it.

"Will you trade me a few beans for a notion of time?" I went around asking the women in the marketplace, but they shook their heads emphatically. (A notion of time? They were incredulous; a way of being, of moving on a different plane? That has nothing to do with the knowledge we're after.)

Who dares speak of the passage of time to the inhabitants of this high place where everything endures? Even their bodies endure. Death neither decays nor obliterates them; it merely stops them in their path. Then the others, with exquisite delicacy—a delicacy I've seen only in connection with newly dropped kids or certain mushrooms—carry the body beyond the rushing stream and with precise symmetry arrange it in the exact place it had in life. With infinite patience they have succeeded in creating, on the other side, a second population, one that obliterates time, an unmoving reflection of themselves that is secure because it is mummified, unmodifiable.

The only change they permit themselves is with their images. They grow, yes, they grow, and reach adulthood with a suspicion of implicit old age, and they stay that way until they die. In contrast, I note with horror that I have a sprinkling of gray hairs, and wrinkles are lining my face, premature, of course, but who could keep her youth in this dry air, beneath skies like these? What will become of me when they discover that time passes in my life, and is leaving its mark?

They are absorbed in other concerns, in trying to retain visions seemingly of jewelled palaces and splendors unknown on this earth. They glide through their astounding worlds while it is all I can do—very infrequently and with extreme stealth—to take a photograph of myself. I crawl along at ground level, in spite of the fact that I am in an elevated land floating in clouds. They say that the altitude deranges those of us who come here from sea level. But it is my belief, my fear, that they are the ones who are deranged, that it's something ancestral, inexplicable—especially when I see them sitting on their haunches, as they almost always are, looking inward in contemplation. I'm always looking outward, I search every path, almost nonchalantly nourishing my fear, something silent and my own. They watch me go by carrying water, with the pole across my shoulders and the two pails dangling from the pole, and I would like to think they do not suspect my fear. This is twinned, it has two faces, not at all like the fear that kept me from returning after I had climbed the mountain. No, this is not simple fear; it reflects others, and becomes voracious.

On the one hand, I am here, now. A now that grows and changes and expands with time and, if I am lucky, will continue to evolve. I do not want them to be aware of this evolving, as I have already said, and even less do I want to be like them, exempt from time. For what would become of me if I kept this face forever, as if surprised between two ages? I think about the mummies in the mirror city, oh yes, absolutely, only mummies are unchanged by time. Time does not pass for the dead. I told myself one day, and on a different day (because I, if not they, am very careful to relate question to calendar) I added: nor does it pass for those who have no concept of death. Death is a milestone.

The inhabitants here, with their language of silence, could teach me the secrets of immobility that so closely resemble immortality, but I am not eager to learn. Life is a movement toward death; to be static is already to be dead.

"Stay here, little lady, nice and quiet here with us," is one of the few things they consent to say to me in my own language, and I shake my head energetically (one more way of insuring movement), and as soon as I am out of their vision, I begin to run like a madwoman along the neglected paths. More often than not I run up, not down, but either way, I don't want to get too far from the town, I don't want to stumble into the still city and find myself face to face with the mummies.

The secret city. I don't know its exact location, but I know everything about it—or maybe I only suspect. I know it has to be identical to this humble little clump of huts where we live, a faithful replica with the exact same number of bodies, for when one of them dies the oldest mummy is thrown into the void. It's noisy in the secret city. The noise announces its proximity, but it also serves a basic purpose: scraps of tin, of every size and shape, hang from the rafters of the huts to scare away the buzzards. They are all that moves in the secret city, those scraps of tin to scare away the vultures, the only thing that moves or makes a sound, and on certain limpid nights the wind carries the sound to where we the living dwell, and on those nights they gather in the plaza, and dance.

They dance, but oh so slowly, almost without moving their feet, more as if they were undulating, submerged in the dense water of sound. This happens only rarely, and when it does I feel an almost uncontrollable urge to join in the dance—the need to dance soaks into my bones, sways me—but I resist with all my power to resist. I am afraid that nothing could be more paralyzing than to yield to this music that comes from death. So that I won't be paralyzed, I don't dance. I don't dance and I don't share their visions.

I have not witnessed a birth since I have been here. I know they couple, but they don't reproduce. They do nothing to avoid it, simply the stillness of the air, the immobility, prevents it. As for me, at this point, I don't even go near men. It must be admitted that men don't come near me either, and there must be a reason, considering how often and how closely they approach almost everything else. Something in my expression must drive them away, but I've no way of knowing what it is. There are no mirrors here. No reflections. Water is either glaucous or torrential white. I despair. And every so often in the privacy of my cave, sparingly and with extreme caution, I take a new photograph.

I do this when I can't stand things any longer, when I have an overwhelming need to know about myself, and then no fear, no caution, can hold me back. One problem is that I am running out of film. In addition, I know perfectly well that if they find my photographs, if they place them in chronological order, two things can happen: they will either abominate or adore me. And neither possibility is to be desired, both are too much like being stone. There are no alternatives. If they put the photographs in order and draw the conclusions. If they see that when I arrived, my face was smoother, my hair brighter, my bearing more alert. If they discover the marks of time, they will know that I have not controlled time even for a moment. And so if they find I am growing older, they will not want me to continue to live among them, and they will stone me from the town and I will have to face the terrifying cliffs.

I don't even want to think about the other possibility. That they will adore me because I have so efficiently and so concretely materialized these images of myself. I would then be like stone to them, like a statue forever captive and contained.

Either of these two quite lapidary prospects should be sufficient reason to restrain my suicidal impulse to take yet another photograph, but it isn't. Each time, I succumb, hoping against hope that they will not be alerted by the glare of the flash. Sometimes I choose stormy nights; perhaps I conjure the lightning with the pale simulacrum of its rays. Other times I seek the protection of the radiance of dawn, which at this altitude can be incendiary.

Elaborate preparations for each of my secret snapshots, preparations charged with hope and danger. That is, with life. The resulting picture does not always please me but the emotion of seeing myself—no matter how horrible or haggard I appear—is immeasurable. This is I, changing, in a static world that imitates death. And I feel safe. Then I am able to stop and speak of simple things with the women in the market and even understand their silences, and answer them. I can live a little longer without love, without anyone's touch.

Until another relapse, a new photo. And this will be the last. On a day with the sound of death, when the minimal activity of the town has come to a halt and they have all congregated to dance in the market plaza. That deliberate dancing that is like praying with their feet, a quiet prayer. They will never admit it, but I suspect that they count to themselves, that their dance is an intricate web of steps like stitches, one up, two stitches backward, one to the right. All to the tinkling of the faroff tin scraps: the wind in the house of the dead. A day like any other; a very special day for them because of the sound that they would call music; if they were interested in making such distinctions. But all that interests them is the dance, or believing they are dancing, or thinking of the dance, which is the same thing. To the pulse of the sound that floods over us, whose origins I cannot locate, though I know it comes from the city of the dead. A sound that threatens to engulf me.

They do not call to me, they don't even see me. It's as if I didn't exist. Maybe they're right, maybe I don't exist. Maybe I am my own invention, or a peculiar materialization of an image they have evoked. That sound is joyful, and yet the most mournful ever heard. I seem to be alive, and yet . . .

I hid in my cave trying not to think about these things, trying not to hear the tinkling; I don't know from where it comes, but I fear toward what it may lead me. With the hope of setting these fears to rest, I begin my preparations for the last photo. A desperate attempt to recover my being, to return to myself, which is all I have.

Anxiously, I await the perfect instant, while outside, darkness is weaving its blackest threads. Suddenly, an unexpected radiance causes me to trip the shutter before I am ready. No photograph emerges, only a dark rectangle which gradually reveals a blurred image of a wall of stone. And that's all. I have no more film so I may as well throw away the camera. A cause for weeping were it not for the fact the radiance is not fading. A cause for uneasiness, then, because when I peer out I see that the blazing light is originating from the very place I wanted not to know about, from the very heart of the sound, from a peak just below our feet, and that now the radiance comes from millions of glittering scraps of tin in the moonlight. The city of the dead.

Spontaneously, I set forth with all my stupid photos, responding to an unfathomable impulse that may be a response to a summons from the sonorous radiance. They are calling me from down there, over to the left, and I answer, and at first I run along the treacherous path and when the path ends I continue on. I stumble, I climb and descend, I trip and hurt myself; to avoid hurtling into the ravine I try to imitate the goats, leaping across the rocks; I lose my footing, I slip and slide, I try to check my fall, thorns rake my skin but at the same time save me. Rashly, I rush ahead, because I must, I will reach the city of the mummies, I will give my faces to them, I will place my successive faces on the mummies and then at last I will be free to take the path to the valley without fearing stone, because I will take the last photograph with me and I am myself in that photograph and I am stone.

## ■ José Emilio Pacheco (1939– ) *Mexico* (poems)

Mexican poet, novelist, and short story writer, José Emilio Pacheco has earned his living as journalist and professor. His early novel, *The Principle of Pleasure,* contains the craft, painful and ecstatic emotion, and sun-cut imagery that will show in his poems. A poet of poets and place, he experiences the work of the poets he loves as a personal document of experience, and so we hear poets from Cavafy to Vallejo and accompany the poet's eyes as he moves from the Mexican tropics to New Orleans, Paris, Rio, and the Canadian northwest.

FURTHER READING: Pacheco, José Emilio. *Principio del placer* (novel) (*The Principle of Pleasure*), 1972; *No me preguntes como pasa el tiempo* (*Don't Ask Me How the Time Goes By*), 1977, Translated by Alastair Reid, 1978; *Selected Poems,* 1987.

## *from Some Time to This Place*

### I

It's the sun with its single eye, the fire-spitting mouth that never tires of charring eternity. Like a broken king who looks from his throne at the rout of his vassals.

Sometimes, the poor sun, the herald of the day who insults and slanders you, settled on your body, adorning with light all you loved.

Today it limits itself to coming in through the window and letting you know that it's already seven o'clock and you still have your sentence to serve: the papers floating in the office, the smiles that others spit on you, hope, memory . . . and the word: your enemy, your death, your origin.

### II

The day of your ninth birthday you built a sand castle at the beach. Its moats connected with the sea, its patios lodged the shimmer of the sun, its turrets were incrustations of coral and reflected light.

An army of strangers gathered around to admire your work. You saw their potbellies chewed by curls, the legs of the women gnawed by bloody nights and by desires.

Stuffed with hearing about your perfect castle, you returned home, ripe with conceit. Twelve years have passed since then, and often you return to the beach and try to find the ruins of the castle.

The ebb and flow are blamed for wearing it away. But the tides aren't guilty: you know that someone stamped it down to nothing—and one day the sea will build it again.

### III

On the last day of the world—when there is no longer hell, time, or tomorrow—you will say her name uncontaminated by ashes, pardons, and fear. Her name, high and pure, like that split second that brought her to your side.

### IV

The sea sounds. The old lamp of dawn fires the breast of the dark islands. The great ship founders and drowns in solitude. On the breakwater, wounded by the hours and standing like an open minute, the night takes its time.

The creatures of the shore weaved labyrinths in the eye of the shipwrecked one, on his way to becoming a surge of waves, a flock faithful to time. Algae, green shore, ruined girl who dances and gleams when the sun visits her.

### V

From some time to this place, things have for you the sour taste of the dying or beginning. Hard triumph of your own defeat, you lived each day in an armor of illusion. The sick year left as hostages days that enclose and humiliate you, hours that won't come back but still live their confusion in your memory.

You began to die and to realize that the mystery will never be easier. Awakening is a forest of findings, a miracle that finds the lost and destroys the found. And that future day, a misery that finds you alone: inventing and burnishing your words.

Come, chase after and enter your own past. Look at yourself, strange and alone, from some time to this place.

TRANSLATED BY PHILIP LEVINE

## Whistler's London

Unreal in the water
the *unreal city* is duplicated[1]

---

1. An allusion to section III. The fire sermon in T. S. Eliot's *The Waste Land.*

Stacked shadows overflow the wharves
    The river
bears them along on a quivering shaft of air

Like a ghost on the other bank .
    you observe
blurred lights in the gray mass
of buildings and warehouses

    The night too
is gray
The darkness thinned out
The moon burns deep down in the water.

TRANSLATED BY GEORGE MCWHIRTER

## ■ Gustavo Sainz (1940– ) *Mexico* (novel)

TRANSLATED BY ANDREW HURLEY

After studying law and humanities at the National University and film at the University Center of Cultural Studies, where film became one of his literary instruments, Gustavo Sainz published his first novel, *Gazapo* (1965). He found himself, at the age of twenty-five, the leader of the younger experimental novelists and a new star in Latin American fiction. In *Gazapo,* he is a parodic painter of ordinary people in all stratas of Mexico City society. The film, James Joyce, and European vanguardist fiction all leave their traces in his work, which plays with narrative voices and includes, as its material, tape-recorded events, diaries, and overheard phone conversations. He focuses on con games, small conspiracies, sex, and multiple seduction, which he records with fascinating bravura. The novel was not only an instant local success but was quickly translated into English, Italian, German, French, and Portuguese.

**FURTHER READING:** Sainz, Gustavo. *Gazapo,* 1965; *The Princess in the Glass Cage.* Translated by Helen Lane, 1987.

## *from* The Princess of the Iron Palace

### He Had a Chivas Regal Face

Gabriel Infante had been such a drunk, he'd been so drunk for so long that he even had a face like a bottle. And he started getting attached to me, you know, like hanging on me, he conceived this deep attachment for me, there was this whole dependence thing. Maybe because I'd listen to him . . .

Like this one time he was going to commit suicide. He called me on the telephone, and he told me to get a pencil and paper, he had something for me to write down. He was crying like crazy, right?, and it was raining cats and dogs outside. You know who was there visiting me for the first time? That was the first day Alexis Stamatis ever came to visit me. He came to visit me for the first time that night, and there was this rainstorm you wouldn't believe—torrents!—and what happened was, that the Jalisco Monk had called me to tell me all about how the maître d' with those gorilla hands didn't work in the restaurant anymore, that he'd gone over there to tell him where to stick it, and he wasn't there, he'd run off or escaped or something with one of the whores, did you ever hear such a story?, but I didn't want to hear about it, although at the same time I was sort of interested, you know? But anyway, we got cut off. It was a terrible storm, like one of those ones in the Bible or something, so we got cut off, and then in about two seconds the telephone rings again, and I say to the other people, Oh, come with me, because on top of everything else, the lights had gone out. So I say to Alexis, to the maids, to everybody, Oh, come with me to answer the telephone. And Gabriel starts talking, I mean, it was Gabriel.

With him, well, there were a lot of things that kept us together. Not love, of course, not really love, but sort of the fact that he talked to me. Was it you that said that love is the wordiest of all passions? Because if that's true, then it was love. I let him talk to me when he was high as a kite on drugs, right? He talked and talked and talked. I even had problems because of that. I got into big trouble, because see he lived with these two women, these two women shared him, you might say. He was real in love with one of them, and he got a lot of money out of the other one. Anyway, the one he was so in love with—how can I put this delicately? She was a whore. I mean she was the biggest whore you could ever imagine in all your wildest dreams of whoredom. And he was madly in love with her, right?, but she told him, one day she said this wouldn't work, she couldn't live just for him, she liked to go out with other men. Other men . . . He suffered something awful. Just like the hairy maître d' I was telling you about, right?, that later on I found out his name was Tarcisio and he had run off with Carmelita Longlegs. He'd kidnapped her. And they lived together in hiding, from the gang, I mean, and since he couldn't go back to the restaurant he became a taxi driver. Anyway, that's what I heard, because they were hunting for him like he was Pancho Villa or somebody. Seems he had stolen a lot of money or some papers or something that was worth a lot of money to somebody. And whoever it was that told me also said that this guy wanted to marry Carmelita, but she said 'Fraid not, I'm a whore through and through, from my hormones to the tip of my lower lips, man, woman, or tableleg, it's all the same to me, I'll run around on you, and you won't be able to take it. She had a tarantula tatooed on the inside of one of her thighs as big as your hand. And Handsome to the Maximum told me once that whenever he went out with her, he put on spiked underwear, on top of a chastity belt, because she'd eat you alive, a devow, devowsomethingess, with teeth in her vagina and prehensile lips . . . Uh . . .

So anyway, Gabriel was telling me that this woman that gave him all this money, that they had had this big terrible scene, and he'd hit her and practically blinded her in one eye. So she'd gone to her mother and told her. This woman had run home and told her mother, and her mother it turns out is the lover of some big bigshot. Anyway, on and on like that. But I couldn't believe it was Gabriel on the phone, because the last time he had called me, I made him promise, he promised he'd never ever call me on the telephone again, because I was like tortured by all these telephone calls, you know? So I had decided to cut him off, right? I mean all the things he'd tell me about were making me sick, literally . . . Anyway, so this day with all the rain and the storm to beat all storms, terrible, terrible rain and then on top of everything the blackout, who should call but him, and he just starts talking. But meanwhile, my mother is on the phone upstairs, right?, waiting for me to pick up the telephone downstairs for her to hang up. So I answer the phone and it's him, so I go Gabriel, you said you weren't going to call me anymore. So he goes Yes, but listen, I've got to talk to you, I just had this big fight with what's-her-name, do you know what what's-her-name did. And then he told me all the gory details. And of course, my mother is listening to all this stuff on the extension absolutely appalled, and just about then my father comes home, and he yells Come up here right this minute. So I went upstairs, right? My father had barely taken off his raincoat, and he says to me, You tell me right now who this Gabriel is. What Gabriel?, I say. The person that just called you, he says, because I'm going to kill him. What do you mean you're going to kill him? I mean just what I said—I'm going to go find him and I'm going to kill him. Now, I'm going to kill him right now, this instant, because you know as well as I do that stained honor can only be washed in blood. It was just that simple, right? . . . He was good as gold, really he was, but he always swore he had Sicilian blood. So that's why stained honor had to be washed in blood, because that's the way his ancestors washed it, right?

What Gabriel was telling me was how this girl had run to her mother and told her he was a drug addict, he was always on something, plus all this other stuff, right? Like that she kept him, she worked in a house of ill repute so she could keep him, so she could give him the money he needed. And she's standing there telling her mother all this with her face all banged up to boot, from the beating he had given her. Terrible, right? So imagine what this girl's family thought about all this—I mean it was a big-deal family. Not to mention what my family thought. When they heard all this stuff you can picture the fit they threw. So anyway, he had called me to tell me all this stuff, right?, but also to leave a message in case something happened to his other woman. But mostly he called me to tell me all this stuff because his brain was . . . He took cocaine and marijuana. He was this very, very intelligent boy, too. Not to mention very handsome — he had this great body, I mean has, and one time he won the national auto racing championship. He won I don't know how much money. But he was one of those Viva México! types, you know, he drove down the road with his nose sucking up the white line. If he'd been Japanese, he'd have been a kamikaze pilot, right? Couldn't care less. I mean he'd say he'd rather live for five days on drugs than twenty years as a jerk. He was just a drug addict at heart, that's all there was to it. So anyway, my father, as soon as he found out about Gabriel, my father swore he was going to kill him. Wildwigged urologists!

You know the type — as far as my father was concerned there were two kinds of women, two count 'em two, kinds or classes or types or categories — good girls and prostitutes. A good girl, like me for example, could never have friends her family didn't know, she had to go out solely and exclusively with one guy, from whom she had to remain aloof and, as the maids and one or another of my squarer friends would say, not get hot. They had to get to know my boyfriends in all these family gettogethers and stuff, and I was never supposed to go to the movies or bars or parties by myself. That's what my brother was for. To chaperone me? Even when I went on a date with a guy, my brother went with me, can you imagine? My father liked to listen to music like Agustín Lara, you know, Mexico's own Lawrence Welk, and before that he used to like to go out dancing with my mother to Ciro's. He also liked the idea of quote, purely masculine pursuits, unquote; so there'd be these nights, it didn't have to be Friday but it helped, when he'd take a night out with the boys, just whoosh! and he'd be gone, to some boxing match or a real Friday bash with some of his noisy friends — The Bad Boys . . . And then he has the gall to tell me he's going to go out and kill Gabriel. He swore up and down that he was going to kill him. So of course, I got real depressed, and really disappointed in my mother and father, right?, because on top of everything I never told who it was. They'd seen him a couple of times, we'd even gone out together, but they were so forgetful about names, they could never seem to get faces and names together or anything, so these guys would always be my anonymous "friends," and that was that. So anyway, Alexis left and I never told. They knew his name was Gabriel Infante, but they had no idea where to find him, right? But by this time I felt so awful, so awful, I mean so depressed and awful, that I ran to my room and slammed the door and started to cry. I cried so hard, I cried so hard my tears were actually splashing, like this, I was crying with my breasts and my throat, torrents were running out my nose — tears even came out my navel. I kid you not. And nobody came in to check on me, so I just cried all night.

So then the next day, in the afternoon, I still didn't come out of my room or eat, all I did was cry, right? The floodgates of tears had opened, and I hadn't been able to go to sleep all night. So when I saw that everybody in my family had left the house, I decided to take a sleeping pill. . . . What I'm going to tell you I swear to God happened just like I'm going to tell you, okay? I'm not trying to hide anything or change anything around, I swear. This is how it was. . . . I took a phenobarbitol about three o'clock in the afternoon. Actually I took two, because I figured two of them would put me out till the next day, right? To just get some rest, to sleep. But then about two hours later this girlfriend of mine came by to bring me an invitation to her wedding. She came over, she gave it to me, and we cried for a while. Because this girl was, well I'd practically been sisters with her for years and years and years, and we'd lost touch with each other because we'd made all these new friends. When I became friends with Handsome to the Maximum and Tito Caruso and those people, she lost touch with me, right? So when she left, I thought the effect had worn off, I decided the effect of the phenobarbitol had worn off, so I popped in two more and went back to bed. . . .

In fact . . . I'll tell you, this girl, you know who it was? Mercedes, the one that had been my brother's girlfriend . . . And one day she was driving up the Acapulco highway, coming to Mexico City, right? She had two beautiful little twin boys, about five years old, all smiling and pretty, right?, with little rabbit teeth. And all of a sudden, a trailer truck is coming the wrong, this big huge truck comes down the highway the wrong way and there's no way to get out of its way. It runs right over them and it doesn't even slow down. She had this sports car, a little tiny thing, about this high off the ground, you know?, I don't know the name of it, and their heads were cut off. Decapitated? Decapitated, her and the two little boys. It was tragic. I didn't want to go to the funeral or the funeral home or anything. It was so horrible that they buried all three of them in the same coffin and welded the coffin shut. They screwed on the top, they closed up the coffin, and then on top of that they welded it closed. . . . Why do people like to look at dead people? Why do they leave this hole in their memory, this peephole in their memory? . . .

So anyway, a little while later I woke up. I felt great, I was happy, I felt fine. It was like everything was over, the problem had passed, Gabriel Infante was behind me, Alexis Stamatis was behind me, Handsome to the Maximum was behind me. So I got in the shower, took a shower, put on a new nightgown, I put on the best nightgown I owned. Of course, also always thinking, thinking, thinking, about all these things that were happening. But I wanted to snap out of it completely, be just fine. When my parents came home I planned for everything to be okeydokey, hunky-dory, terrific, because I thought No problem, right? What's the problem? But then I saw these four pills lying beside the bottle. There were four of them. And I didn't even give it a second thought, didn't bat an eye, I just picked them up and popped them in my mouth and swallowed them. Like you're walking by and you see this piece of candy, and you pick it up and pop it in your mouth and eat it, and you never think it might be bad for you, you know? I mean, later I found out about a lot of stuff there was no way I could know back then, right? But anyway, I took these pills and just went on as happy and calm as anybody could be . . . And I went back to sleep.

While I was asleep, then, one of the Jalisco Sisters called, and they told her I was asleep. But she knew that if I was asleep, all you had to do was scratch at the door and I'd wake up, right? I mean I was an *extremely* light sleeper. So the maid goes and tells her The señorita is asleep, she must be very tired, because I knocked on the door and she didn't answer. So she figures, I mean by intuition, that something's wrong, right? So she went and got this guy she was going out with at the time. He was a doctor, a pediatrician I think. Anyway, he was hilarious because he kept trying to brainwash my girlfriend. You're not the kind to go out with just one man, he'd tell her, no, not you, you have to go out with lots of men, that's in your personality. And he'd make her dates with other men himself, so she'd go out with two men at the same time. I mean even with one of his brothers, right? But Big Jalisco was a real bitch, I'm telling you, and I'm not real sure what happened exactly, but she'd do very weird things to these people. For example, she tried to get all these relationships to turn out so the guy would ask her to marry him. Then when he did, she'd calmly tell the guy to go screw himself. It was like a bet she had with herself, right? Well, so in those days she was going out with this doctor and with this friend of Handsome to the Maximum's named Andrés. . . . While you were having one drink, he'd have three. Or anyway that's what she said all the time. . . .

So, uh . . . Where was I? Oh yeah, so she ran to get these two guys, and they all came to my house. The first thing I knew about them being there, we were all in the living room, and they were trying to wake me up. They'd tried to get into the bedroom through this big window, they thought they could get in from the pool, the garden side, you know?, but they finally gave up and broke in the door. Andrés and this doctor dragged me out of the bedroom, holding me up like this, and they walked me past my parents' bedroom, who were watching some program on television and hadn't even realized that any of this was going on. They were dragging me out of my bedroom and everything, breaking down the door. So then Alberto, or whatever his name was, started giving me coffee and helping me walk. He'd ask me my name and all, right? So then he started trying to find out, with me dead asleep, find out how many pills I'd taken. Big Jalisco was terribly worried and she kept shrieking like a bluejay, Aiee baby, you're soooo asleep. That's the way they were treating me, right, like a lost cause or something, right? How many pills did you take? And I'd say One. Then they'd say Oh no, we think you took more than one. So then I went Two. So then a little time went by, and finally they said Listen sweetheart, listen kiddo, we think you probably took quite a few more than that . . . Three, at least, you must have taken. And I shook my finger at them, like this, right?, saying No, more than three, more than four. Then things sort of started making sense to me, right?, and it turned out I'd taken I don't know how many, but a lot. They were really scared now, because, or anyway that's what I remember, the mortal or lethal or whatever it is dosage is ten pills. *Ten* is the number that poisons you, and I'd taken I think eight. So then they made me swear that when they left I'd go get into bed and not get out again till the next day. They said I had to stay as calm as possible, and rest, and I ought to read something. So of course, I said Okay, right? So I went right to my bedroom. I was pretty sleepy anyway . . . As you can imagine . . .

So now I'd been in my room for two days already, two days, and all of a sudden my mother comes. She hadn't noticed that I'd been in my room or that Andrés, Alberto, and Big Jalisco had come over. Incredible, but she hadn't noticed a thing. So she comes into my bedroom. It was strange as everything for her, because she was so tough, so hard-hearted I mean that, for example, when she saw the headless corpses of my friend and her little boys and all, all she said was Look how innocent they look. And I mean they were still a little burned-looking, right?, but How nice that they'll all go to heaven together, my mother says. And the corpses without any heads, okay? . . . She was so hard-hearted she could see you lying there in the middle of the street and not blink an eyelash. A strong character, horrible, *cold*, right? So anyway, I was lying there in my room, and she comes in to tell me I should have a glass of milk. Well, she wasn't quite so hardhearted in those days, right? The lights were off, and I said No, Mama, listen, I don't, . . . no, thanks. So then she says Why are you talking like that? And I go How? I'm talking all right, I say to her . . . in the dark . . . She says No you aren't . . . So she flips on the light, and she yells, in horror, I mean she lets out such a scream—AAAAAGGGGGHHHHH! Like that, more or less, and she shoots out of the room in absolute terror. So I got scared myself, then, you know?, I got really really scared. . . .

Am I dragging this out too long?

So instead of staying in bed I went downstairs. I thought I'd watch television, see my father and mother, be a little sociable, you know? That'll cheer me up, I said to myself. So I walked in the TV room, and the two of them were sitting there, sitting there like . . . I mean they just sat there like a ghost had walked in. My own mother and father. So I say Well, okay, hey, everything's okay, don't get upset, I'm going to go lie down, I'm real sleepy. And my mother walks along behind me and helps me get into bed, right? And so then she told me about the glass of milk again. And I go No thanks again. So then she starts crying and moaning. Oh please drink a glass of milk! Just one glass of milk, for all you hold dearest! I mean there was my mother kneeling beside the bed crying and begging me to drink just a little something, if I loved her. I beg you, as you love me! She was so *servile* about the whole thing, you know, and this was such an old-fashioned way to . . . well. Drink a glass of milk! Please! So finally to make her happy I said Okay, and in less than three minutes she was back with the glass of milk. I drank it slowly, until she finally gave this sigh of relief, because while I was drinking the milk she had been holding her breath. You don't know how much I thank you, she said, reaching for the glass automatically. Now sleep.

As soon as she was out of the room, I got up and looked at myself in the mirror, first just to see why they were all so shocked, but second to splash a little water on my face. Because they'd looked at me, and like that!, they'd started screaming to high heaven and acting like I was this horrible-looking monster or something, and that worried me, you know? So I'm standing there looking at myself, and I see these spots on my face. Because I'd gotten poisoned, right? My face was practically completely deformed, all swollen up, like this, and there were these huge blotches like bruises, purple and white and all different colors. I was a rainbow all to myself. I looked like I'd bumped into a clown. . . . You could hear the voices from the television 'way off, so I went to bed, right? I just went to bed and nobody ever mentioned the subject again. . . .

But all the razor blades disappeared from my house, all the kitchen knives disappeared, all the sleeping pills, the bottles of strychnine, everything. *Every*thing. Because I think they thought I'd tried to commit suicide, which was not what it was at all, right? I was just trying to get some sleep and forget some of the things I was going through, you know, forget your troubles. But mostly just sleep. Afterwards this doctor guy explained it all to me. He said I got a little under the influence, you know, from those first phenobarbitols, and then I got so drunk it was like I'd drunk a whole bottle of whisky all by myself. So what happened to me then was, that I lost consciousness. It was like *snap!*, and I was out. So then you don't know what's good for you and what's not. They say when I got up and took those four phenobarbitols, when I got out of bed to take a shower, when I tell you I felt like a million dollars, well . . . They say that when I went to the bathroom I had to hold on to the walls, that I must have had to work myself along like this, against the wall?, because I'd taken such a bunch of pills that I must have been completely, completely drunk, right? So anyway, that went away. I was okay in no time . . . I was sort of stupid and blah for two or three days, but I didn't have any trouble, I mean I don't have any complexes or anything or any psychological hang-ups or frustrations or maladjustments because I wanted to kill myself and didn't—no, none of that stuff, forget it. I mean, I didn't want to poison myself at all, right? All I wanted to do was sleep it off, rest, just sleep for a while. . . .

(*"From that moment on, even the most remote figures suggested the idea of death so violently, so urgently, that a can of sardines—for example—brought up the memory of the lining of a coffin, or the stones in a sidewalk, noticed for the first time, revealed their kinship to the marble markers of a vault. In the thrall of this macabre vision, one's eyes simply saw that the plaster of façades was of the very color and texture of bones, and at last, just as stepping into a bath, sinking into the waters of a bath inescapably led to the posture one would adopt in a coffin, likewise not a person buried his body between the sheets without brooding on the pattern which the folds and creases of his shroud would take."*)

## ■ Isabel Allende (1942– ) *Chile* (story)

### TRANSLATED BY MARGARET SAYERS REDEN

Isabel Allende, daughter of Chilean diplomats and niece of President Salvador Allende, was born in Lima, Peru. She was taken back to Chile at three to live with her mother and grandparents after her parents divorced. After her mother's marriage to another diplomat, she spent part of her childhood in Europe and the Middle East. She left school at sixteen to work. She had a job with the United Nations Food and Agricultural Organization in Santiago and later as a journalist, a talk show host, and a newscaster. She married at twenty and became an author of children's tales. After her uncle Salvador Allende was murdered during the coup led by General Pinochet in 1973, she has lived abroad, for a long time in Venezuela, and presently in the San Francisco Bay area. She is one of Latin America's most important younger writers, which became internationally apparent with the publication of her best-known novel, *The House of Spirits* (1982), which appeared in more than twenty languages. She is a feminist who brings political concerns to her work. *The House of Spirits* was followed by *Of Love and Shadows* (1984, tr. 1987) and the novel *Eva Luna* (1987, tr. 1988). Her short story collection is called *The Stories of Eva Luna* (1991). She has also been a spokesperson for the political novel in her *Paths of Resistance and the Art and Craft of the Political Novel* (1989). Isabel Allende, a magical writer, is a frequent lecturer in classrooms and on public radio. She is one of the most popular women novelists Latin America has ever had, and, presently, she ranks among the most translated and enjoyed writers in the world.

**FURTHER READING:** Allende, Isabel. *The House of Spirits,* 1982, tr. 1985; *Of Love and Shadows,* 1984; *Eva Luna,* 1987, tr. 1988; *Paths of Resistance and the Art and Craft of the Political Novel,* 1989; *The Stories of Eva Luna,* 1991.

## *Gift for a Sweetheart*

Horacio Fortunato was forty-six when the languid Jewish woman who was to change his roguish ways and deflate his fanfaronade entered his life. Fortunato came from a long line of circus people, the kind who are born with rubber bones and a natural gift for somersaults, people who at an age when other infants are crawling around like worms are hanging upside down from a trapeze and brushing the lion's teeth. Before his father made it into a serious enterprise, rather than the idle fancy it had been, the Fortunato Circus experienced more difficulty than glory. At different times of catastrophe and turmoil the company was reduced to two or three members of the clan who wandered the byways in a broken-down gypsy wagon with a threadbare tent they set up in godforsaken little towns. For years Horacio's grandfather bore the sole responsibility for the spectacle: he walked the tightrope, juggled with lighted torches, swallowed Toledo swords, extracted oranges and serpents from a top hat, and danced a graceful minuet with his only companion, a female monkey decked out in ruffles and a plumed hat. His grandfather, however, managed somehow to survive bad times, and while many other circuses succumbed, obliterated by more modern diversions, he saved his circus and, at the end of his life, was able to retire to the south of the continent and cultivate his garden of asparagus and strawberries, leaving a debt-free enterprise to his son Fortunato II. The scion lacked his father's humility, nor was he disposed to perform a balancing act on a tightrope or do pirouettes with a chimpanzee; on the other hand, he was gifted with the unshakable prudence of a born businessman. Under his direction the circus grew in size and prestige until it was the largest in the nation. Three colossal striped tents replaced the modest tarp of the earlier hard times; various cages sheltered a traveling zoo of tamed wild animals; and other fanciful vehicles transported the artists, who included the only hermaphroditic and ventriloquist dwarf in history. An exact, wheeled replica of Christopher Columbus's caravel completed the Fortunato Family Famous International Circus. This enormous caravan no longer drifted aimlessly, as it had in his father's day, but steamed purposefully along the principal highways from the Rio Grande to the Straits of Magellan, stopping only in major cities, where it made an entrance with such a clamor of drums, elephants, and clowns — the caravel at the lead, like a miraculous reenactment of the Conquest — that no man, woman, or child could escape knowing the circus had come to town.

Fortunato II married a trapeze artist, and they had a son they named Horacio. But one day wife-and-mother stayed behind, determined to be independent of her husband and support herself through her somewhat precarious calling, leaving the boy in his father's care. Her son held a rather dim picture of her in his memory, never completely separating the image of his mother from that of the many acrobats he had known. When he was ten, his father married another circus artist, this time an equestrienne able to stand on her head on a galloping steed or leap from one croup to another with eyes blindfolded. She was very beautiful. No matter how much soap, water, and perfume she used, she could not erase the last trace of the essence of horse, a sharp aroma of sweat and effort. In her magnificent bosom the young Horacio, enveloped in that unique odor, found consolation for his mother's absence. But with time the horsewoman also decamped without a farewell. In the ripeness of his years, Fortunato II entered into matrimony, for the third and final time, with a Swiss woman he met on a tour bus in America. He was weary of his Bedouin-like existence and felt too old for new alarms, so when his Swiss bride requested it, he had not the slightest difficulty in giving up the circus for a sedentary life, and ended his days on a small farm in the Alps amid bucolic hills and woods. His son Horacio, who was a little over twenty, took charge of the family business.

Horacio had grown up with the instability of moving every few days, of sleeping on wheels and living beneath a canvas roof, but he was very content with his fate. He had never envied other little boys who wore gray uniforms to school and who had their destinies mapped out before they were born. By contrast, he felt powerful and free. He knew all the secrets of the circus, and with the same confidence and ease he mucked out the animal cages or balanced fifty meters above the ground dressed as a hussar and charming the audience with his dolphin smile. If at any moment he longed for stability, he did not admit it, even in his sleep. The experience of having been abandoned first by his mother and then by his stepmother had left him slightly insecure, especially with women, but it had not made him a cynic, because he had inherited his grandfather's sentimental heart. He had an enormous flair for the circus, but he was fascinated by the commercial aspect of the business even more than by the art. He had intended to be rich from the time he was a young boy, with the naïve conviction that money would bring the security he had not received from his family. He increased the number of tentacles spreading from the family enterprise by buying a chain of boxing arenas in several capital cities. From boxing he moved naturally to wrestling, and as he was a man of inventive imagination he transformed that gross sport into a dramatic spectacle. Among his initiatives were the Mummy, who appeared at ringside in an Egyptian sarcophagus; Tarzan, who covered his privates with a tiger skin so tiny that with every lunge the audience held its breath, expecting some major revelation; and the Angel, who every night bet his golden hair and lost it to the scissors of the ferocious Kuramoto—a Mapuche Indian disguised as a Samurai—but then appeared the following day with curls intact, irrefutable proof of his divine condition. These and other commercial ventures, along with public appearances with a pair of bodyguards whose role it was to intimidate his competitors and pique the ladies' curiosity, had earned him a reputation of being a shady character, a distinction he reveled in. He lived a good life, traveled through the world closing deals and looking for monsters, frequented clubs and casinos, owned a glass mansion in California and a retreat in the Yucatán, but lived most of the year in luxury hotels. He bought the temporary company of a series of blondes. He liked them soft, with ample bosoms, in homage to the memory of his stepmother, but he wasted very little energy on amorous affairs, and when his grandfather urged him to marry and bring sons into the world so the Fortunato name would not vanish without an heir, he replied that not even out of his mind would he ascend the matrimonial gallows. He was a dark-skinned, hefty man with thick hair slicked back with brilliantine, shrewd eyes, and an authoritative voice that accentuated his self-satisfied vulgarity. He was obsessed with elegance and he bought clothes befitting a duke—but his suits were a little too shiny, his ties verging on the audacious, the ruby in his ring too ostentatious, his cologne too penetrating.

He had the heart of a lion tamer, and no English tailor alive would ever disguise that fact.

This man, who had spent a good part of his existence cutting a wide swath with his lavish lifestyle, met Patricia Zimmerman on a Tuesday in March, and on the spot lost both unpredictability of spirit and clarity of thought. He was sitting in the only restaurant in the city that still refused to serve blacks, with four cohorts and a diva whom he was planning to take to the Bahamas for a week, when Patricia entered the room on her husband's arm, dressed in silk and adorned with some of the diamonds that had made the Zimmerman firm famous. Nothing could have been further from the unforgettable stepmother smelling of horses, or the complacent blondes, than this woman. He watched her advance, small, refined, her chest bones bared by her décolletage and her chestnut-colored hair drawn back into a severe bun, and he felt his knees grow heavy and an insufferable burning in his breast. He preferred uncomplicated women ready for a good time, whereas this was a woman who would have to be studied carefully if her worth was to be known, and even then her virtues would be visible only to an eye trained in appreciating subtleties—which had never been the case with Horacio Fortunato. If the fortune-teller in his circus had consulted her crystal ball and predicted that Fortunato would fall in love at first sight with a fortyish and haughty aristocrat, he would have had a good laugh. But that is exactly what happened as he watched Patricia walk toward him like the shade of a nineteenth-century widow-empress in her dark gown with the glitter of all those diamonds shooting fire at her neck. As Patricia walked past, she paused for an instant before that giant with the napkin tucked into his waistcoat and a trace of gravy at the corner of his mouth. Horacio Fortunato caught a whiff of her perfume and the full impact of her aquiline profile and completely forgot the diva, the bodyguards, his business affairs, everything that interested him in life, and decided with absolute seriousness to steal this woman from her jeweler and love her to the best of his ability. He turned his chair to one side and, ignoring his guests, measured the distance that separated her from him, while Patricia Zimmerman wondered whether that stranger was examining her jewels with some evil design.

That same night an extravagant bouquet of orchids was delivered to the Zimmerman residence. Patricia looked at the card, a sepia-colored rectangle with a name from a novel written in golden arabesques. What ghastly taste, she muttered, divining immediately it had come from the man with the plastered-down hair she had seen in the restaurant, and she ordered the gift to be tossed into the street, with the hope that the sender would be circling the house and thus learn the fate of his flowers. The following day a crystal box arrived bearing a single perfect rose, without a card. The majordomo also placed this offering in the trash. Different bouquets followed for the rest of the week: a basket of wild flowers on a bed of lavender, a pyramid of white carnations in a silver goblet, a dozen black tulips imported from Holland, and other varieties impossible to find in this hot climate. Each suffered the fate of the first, but this did not discourage the gallant, whose siege was becoming so unbearable that Patricia Zimmerman did not dare answer the telephone for fear of hearing his voice whispering indecent proposals, as had happened the previous Tuesday at two in the morning. She returned his letters unopened. She stopped going out, because she ran into Fortunato in the most unexpected places: observing her from the adjoining box at the opera; in the street, waiting to open the door of her car before the chauffeur could reach it; materializing like an illusion in an elevator or on some stairway. She was a prisoner in her own home, and frightened. He'll get over it, he'll get over it, she kept telling herself, but Fortunato did not evaporate like a bad dream; he was always there, on the other side of the wall, breathing heavily. She thought of calling the police, or telling her husband, but her horror of scandal prevented her. One morning she was attending to her correspondence when the majordomo announced the visit of the president of Fortunato and Sons.

"In my own house, how dare he!" Patricia muttered, her heart racing. She had to call on the implacable discipline she had acquired in years of small dramas played in salons to disguise the trembling of her hands and voice. For an instant she was tempted to confront this madman once and for all, but she realized that her strength would fail her; she felt defeated even before she saw him.

"Tell him I'm not in. Show him the door, and inform the servants that the gentleman is not welcome in this house," she ordered.

The next day there were no exotic flowers at breakfast, and Patricia thought with a sigh of relief, or dejection, that the man must finally have understood her message. That morning she felt free for the first time in a week, and she went out for a game of tennis and a trip to the beauty salon. She returned home at two in the afternoon with a new haircut and a bad headache. On the hall table she saw a royal purple velvet jewel box with the name Zimmerman printed in gold letters. She opened it rather absently, thinking that her husband had left it there, but found a necklace of emeralds accompanied by one of those pretentious sepia cards she had come to know and detest. Her headache turned to panic. This adventurer seemed prepared to ruin her life; as if it wasn't enough to buy a necklace from her own husband, he then had the gall to send it to her house. She could not throw this gift into the trash, as she had done with the flowers. With the case clutched to her bosom, she locked herself in her writing room. A half-hour later, she called the chauffeur and ordered him to deliver a package to the same address to which he had returned several letters. As she handed him the jewels she felt no relief; to the contrary, she had the impression that she was sinking into a quagmire.

At the same time, Fortunato was slogging through his own swamp, getting nowhere, feeling his way blindly. He had never spent so much money and time to court a woman, although it was true, he admitted, that all his women had been quite different from this one. For the first time in his life as a showman, he felt ridiculous. He could not go on this way; always strong as an ox, his health was suffering, he slept only a few hours at a time, he was short of breath, he had heart palpitations, he felt fire in his stomach and ringing in his temples. His business was similarly suffering the impact of his love fever; he was making hasty decisions, and losing money. Good Christ, I don't know who I am or what I'm doing here; damn it all, he grumbled, sweating, but not for a minute did he consider abandoning the chase.

Slumped in an armchair in the hotel where he was staying, the purple jewel box back in his hands, Fortunato remembered his grandfather. He rarely thought of his father, but his memory often dwelt on that formidable ancestor who at ninety-some years was still cultivating his garden. He picked up the telephone and asked for long distance.

The elder Fortunato was nearly deaf and, in addition, unable to adapt to the mechanism of that devilish apparatus that carried voices halfway around the planet, but the years had not affected his lucidity. He listened carefully to his grandson's sorrowful tale, speaking only at the end.

"So, the sly vixen is giving herself the luxury of snubbing my boy, is that it, eh?"

"She won't even look at me, Nono. She's rich, she's beautiful, she's classy. . . . She has everything."

"Ummm . . . including a husband."

"Yes, but that's not important. If I could only speak to her."

"Speak to her? What about? You have nothing to say to a woman like that, son."

"I gave her a necklace fit for a queen and she returned it without a word."

"Well, give her something she doesn't have."

"What, for example?"

"A good excuse to laugh, that always gets 'em." And his grandfather nodded off with the receiver in his hand, dreaming of the pretty things who had given him their hearts as he performed his death-defying acrobatics on the trapeze or danced with his monkey.

The next day in his office the jeweler Zimmerman received a splendid young woman, a manicurist by trade, she said; she had come, she explained, to sell back at half price the very emerald necklace he had sold only forty-eight hours before. The jeweler remembered the purchase very well; impossible to forget such a conceited boor.

"I need something that will crumble the defenses of a haughty lady," he had said.

Zimmerman had studied him a moment, and decided he must be one of those new oil or cocaine millionaires. He could not tolerate vulgarity; he was accustomed to a different class of customer. He rarely served clients himself, but this man had insisted on speaking to him and seemed prepared to spend an unlimited amount of money.

"What do you recommend?" the man had asked before the tray where the most valuable jewels sparkled.

"It depends upon the lady. Rubies and pearls look good on dark skin; emeralds on someone fairer; and diamonds are perfect for anyone."

"She has too many diamonds. Her husband gives them to her as if they were candy."

Zimmerman coughed. He disliked this kind of confidence. The man picked up a necklace, held it to the light with no respect, shook it like a sleigh bell, and the air filled with tinkling and green sparks as the jeweler's ulcer twitched within him.

"Do you think emeralds bring good luck?"

"I suppose that all precious stones fit that description, sir, but I am not superstitious."

"This is a very special woman. I don't want to make any mistake with the gift, you understand?"

"Perfectly."

But apparently that was precisely what had happened, Zimmerman told himself, unable to restrain a scornful smirk when the girl returned the necklace. No, there was nothing wrong with the jewels, the mistake was the girl. He had imagined a more refined woman, certainly not a manicurist carrying a plastic handbag and wearing a cheap blouse. He was, nonetheless, intrigued by the girl, there was something vulnerable and pathetic about her, poor child; she would not fare well in the hands of that bandit, he thought.

"Why don't you tell me the whole story, my dear," said Zimmerman finally.

The girl spun him the tale she had memorized, and an hour later left the shop with a light step. According to plan, the jeweler had not only bought back the necklace, he had invited her to dinner as well. It was plain to her that Zimmerman was one of those men who are astute and suspicious in business dealings but naïve in every other regard; she would have no difficulty distracting him the amount of time Horacio Fortunato needed and was prepared to pay for.

That was a memorable night for Zimmerman; he had planned on dinner but found himself in the grip of an unexpected passion. The next day he saw his new friend again and by the end of the week he was stammering to Patricia something about going to New York for a few days to attend a sale of Russian jewels saved from the massacre of Ekaterinburg. His wife was totally unmoved.

\*   \*   \*

Alone in her house, too listless to go out and suffering that headache that came and went without respite, Patricia decided to devote her Saturday to recouping her strength. She settled on the terrace to leaf through some fashion magazines. It had not rained for a week and the air was still and hot. She read awhile, until the sun made her drowsy; her body grew heavy, her eyes closed, and the magazine slipped from her hands. At that moment she heard a sound from deep in the garden; she thought it must be the gardener, a headstrong old man who in less than a year had transformed her property into a tropical jungle, ripping out pots of chrysanthemums to make way for an efflorescence gone wild. She opened her eyes, stared half-seeing against the sun, and saw something unusually large moving in the top of the avocado tree. She removed her dark glasses and sat up. No doubt about it, a shadow was moving up there, and it was not part of the foliage.

Patricia Zimmerman rose from her chair and walked forward a step or two; then she saw it clearly: a ghostly blue-clad figure with a golden cape flew several meters over her head, turned a somersault in the air and, for an instant, seemed to freeze at the moment of waving to her from the sky. She choked back a scream, sure that the apparition would plummet like a stone and be pulverized on contact with the ground, but the cape filled with air and that gleaming coleopteran stretched out its arms and swung into a nearby medlar tree. Immediately, a second blue figure appeared, hanging by its legs in the top branches of another tree, swinging by the wrists a young girl wearing a flower crown. The first gave a signal and the holder released the girl, who scattered a rain of paper butterflies before being caught by the ankles. Patricia did not dare move while those silent, gold-caped birds flew through the air.

Suddenly a whoop filled the garden, a long, barbaric yowl that tore Patricia's attention from the trapeze artists. She saw a thick rope fall from the rear wall of the property and, climbing down it, Tarzan, in person, the same Tarzan of the matinées and comic books of her childhood, with his skimpy loincloth and live monkey on his hip. The King of the Jungle leapt gracefully to earth, thumped his chest with his fists, and repeated the visceral bellow, attracting all the servants, who rushed out to the terrace. With a wave of the hand, Patricia gestured to them to stay where they were, while the voice of Tarzan gave way to a lugubrious drumroll announcing a retinue of four Egyptian dancers who advanced as if trapped in a frieze, head and feet at right angles to their bodies; they were followed by a hunchback wearing a striped hooded cape and leading a black panther at the end of a chain. Then came two monks carrying a sarcophagus and, behind them, an angel with long golden locks and then, bringing up the rear, an Indian disguised as a Japanese wearing a dressing gown and wooden clogs. All of them paused behind the swimming pool. The monks deposited the coffin on the grass and, while the Egyptian maidens chanted softly in some dead tongue and the Angel and Kuramoto rippled their prodigious muscles, the lid of the sarcophagus swung open and a nightmarish creature emerged from inside. Once revealed, swathed in gauze, it was obvious that this was a mummy in perfect health. At this moment, Tarzan yodeled another cry and, with absolutely no provocation, began hopping around the Egyptians, brandishing the simian. The Mummy lost its millenary patience, lifted one rigid arm and let it swing like a cudgel against the nape of the savage's neck, who fell to the ground, his face buried in the lawn. The monkey screamed and scrambled up a tree. Before the embalmed pharaoh could deliver a second blow, Tarzan leapt to his feet and fell upon the Mummy with a roar. Locked in legendary combat, their rolling and thrashing freed the panther; the characters in the parade ran to hide in the garden and all the servants flew back to the safety of the kitchen. Patricia was about to jump into the pool when, as if by magic, an individual in tails and a top hat appeared and with one snap of his whip stopped the cat, who fell to the ground purring like a pussycat, with all four paws in the air; the hunchback recaptured the chain, as the ringmaster swept off his hat and pulled from it a meringue torte that he carried to the terrace and deposited at the feet of the lady of the house.

This was the signal for the remainder of the cast to march in from the rear of the garden: musicians playing military marches, clowns assaulting one another with slapsticks, dwarfs from medieval courts, an equestrienne standing on her mount, a bearded lady, dogs on bicycles, an ostrich costumed as Columbine and, finally, a team of boxers in satin trunks and boxing gloves pushing a wheeled platform crowned by a painted cardboard arch. And there, on the dais of a stage-set emperor, sat Horacio Fortunato, his mane slicked down with brilliantine, grinning his irrepressible gallant's grin, pompous beneath his triumphal dome, surrounded by his outrageous circus, acclaimed by the trumpets and cymbals of his own orchestra, the most conceited, most lovesick, and most entertaining man in the world. Patricia laughed, and walked forward to meet him.

## ■ Reinaldo Arenas (1943–1990) *Cuba* (novel)

### TRANSLATED BY ANDREW HURLEY

Born in Oriente province, as a youth Reinaldo Arenas joined Fidel Castro's revolutionary movement. He worked as a researcher for some years in Havana, and in 1966 his first novel, *The Pit,* was published and sold out in a week. It is the story of a poor family during the Batista period as told by the idiot son. His postmodernist second novel, *Hallucinations* (1968), is a parodic treatment of a monk's hallucinatory life in Spain, London, and elsewhere. The monk on whose life his novel is based was two centuries earlier imprisoned in the same El Morro prison where Arenas was held a few years after having written his semifictitious story. Although he could not publish it in Cuba (where it remains unpublished), it was translated into most European languages, and, in 1969, it won the Prix Medici in France for the best foreign novel of the year. His impressive later novels, which won him international recognition, are *Farewell to the Sea* (1982, tr. 1986), *The Palace of the White Skunks* (1980, tr. 1990), and *The Doorman* (1987, tr. 1991).

Although Arenas's manuscripts were often seized by the police, he managed to smuggle most of his writing out of the country. In 1970, he spent time in a forced labor camp, where, as in China during the Cultural Revolution, intellectuals were sent for moral and political re-education. Despite increasing world fame, from 1974 to 1976 he was sent to the harsh El Morro prison. By luck and a bureaucratic mistake, he managed to leave Cuba in 1980 during the Mariel exodus. Greatly esteemed by writers of all political sides while in Cuba, even while in prison, once he went abroad as an exile he found his works and person deemed controversial and his books often dropped from the curriculum in Latin American and U.S. universities. He moved to France where he was well received. He worked with great difficulty to finish his last novels and memoir, and in December 1990, suffering from AIDS, he committed suicide. Since his death, several new volumes have appeared, and his reputation has soared.

**FURTHER READING:** Arenas, Reinaldo. *The Pit*, 1966; *Hallucinations*, 1968; *Farewell to the Sea*, 1982; *The Palace of the White Skunks*, 1980; *The Doorman*, 1987.

## from *Singing from the Well*

There went my mother, she just went running out the door. She was screaming like a crazy woman that she was going to jump down the well. I see my mother at the bottom of the well. I see her floating in the greenish water choked with leaves. So I run for the yard, out to where the well is, that's fenced around with a wellhead of naked-boy saplings so rickety it's almost falling in.

I run up and peek over. But just like always—the only one down there is me. Me being reflected from way down there up to me above. Me—and I disappear if you so much as spit into the oozy green water.

Madre mía, Mama! This is not the first time you've tricked me—every day you say you're going to jump headfirst down the well, but ha! You never do it. You think you're going to drive me crazy, making me run these wild-goose chases from the house to the well and the well to the house. Well, no. I'm getting tired of this. If you're not going to jump, it's all right with me. But don't say you're going to jump and then not do it.

We're out here crying, behind the old thicket of prickly wild pineapples. My mother and I, we're crying. The lizards are so big in this pineapple thicket! You ought to see them! The lizards here are in all different shapes. I just saw one with two heads. Two heads on that lizard slithering along.

Most of these lizards know me, and they hate me. I know they hate me, and they're just waiting for the day . . . Bastards!, I say to them, and I dry my eyes. And then I pick up a stick and go for them. But they know a lot more than you'd give them credit for, and the second they see me stop crying they run into the thicket, and they disappear. What really makes me mad is that I know that all the time I can't see them and I'm thrashing around looking for them, to try to catch them, they're watching me. They're probably laughing at me.

Finally I catch one. I whack him with the stick and break him in half. But he's still alive, and one half runs off while the other piece jumps up and down in front of me like it was saying, You little crybaby, don't think you can kill me *that* easy . . .

"You beast!" says my mother to me, and she throws a rock at me and hits me in the head. "Let those poor lizards live in peace!" My head has split into two halves and one of them has run off. The other half, though, stays there in front of my mother. Dancing. Dancing. Dancing.

Now all of us are dancing, up here on the roof of the house. What a lot of people on the roof! I love to climb up onto the palm branches of the thatch, and I always find one or two nests of shiny little green-and-purple blackbirds up here. I don't eat the blackbirds' eggs, because people say they're always rotten, so what I do is throw them at my grandfather's head, because every time he sees me up on top of the house he picks up the long pole he uses to cut off palm leaves way up on the tree and he starts poking at me like I was a bunch of coconuts. One of the eggs has splattered in my grandfather's eye, and I'm not sure, but it looks to me like it put his eye out. One-eyed Grandpa. But no—you'd have to poke that old coot's eyes out with a spear, because his eyeballs are tougher than the bottom of a bucket.

Dancing all by myself on the roof. I made my cousins get down, and now they're asleep under the pine trees. Inside the white brick wall. And the crosses.

"What are there so many crosses for?" I asked Mama the day we went to see my cousins.

"It's so they'll rest in peace and go to heaven," my mother told me, while she cried her eyes out and stole a fresh wreath off one of the crosses a little way away. So I pulled up seven crosses and carried them home with me under my arm. And I kept them in bed with me, so that way I could sleep when I went to bed and not even feel the mosquitoes, and mosquitoes here have worse stingers than scorpions.

"These crosses are so I can sleep," I told my grandmother when she came into my room. My grandmother is an old, old woman, I thought, while I squatted under the bed. "Take these crosses for you," I told Grandma, handing her the crosses. But she carried them *all* off. "We've got a shortage of firewood today," she said. And when she got to the cookstove she chopped them into kindling and threw them in the fire.

"What have you done with my crosses, you old nanny goat!" I said, and I grabbed a piece of smoking cross and went at her. I was going to poke out her eyes. But that old biddy wasn't born yesterday, and when I picked up the burning stick she grabbed the pot of scalding water that was on top of the cookstove and threw it on me. If I hadn't jumped back I'd have been cooked alive. "Don't fool with me," said Grandma, and then she gave me a roasted sweet potato to eat. I took the half-eaten sweet potato out to the bileweed plant and I dug a hole there and I put it in the ground. Then I made a cross out of a dry bileweed plant and put it in the ground, too, next to the dead sweet potato.

But now I better stop thinking about those things and see about getting down off the roof without Grandpa running me through with the pole. I know—I'll slip down the zinc rain gutters like I was a cat, and when he's not looking I'll jump out of the rain gutter and run off. Oh, I wish I could jump on top of my grandfather and squash him! Everything is all *his* fault. His fault. That's why I and all my cousins all meet here. Up here on the roof of the house. Like we've done so many times—we have to plan a way to have Grandpa die before his time.

This house has always been a hell. Even before everybody died all anybody ever talked about was dead people. And more dead people. And Grandma outprayed everybody, crossing herself in every corner of the house. But when things got really bad was when Celestino took it into his head to write poems. Poor Celestino! I can see him now—sitting on the parlor doorsill beam and pulling off his arms.

Poor Celestino! Writing. Writing and writing and writing, and never stopping, even on the spines of the account books where Grandpa writes down the dates the cows got pregnant. On yucca leaves and even on the hard round husks of the palm trees the horses didn't get there soon enough to eat.

Writing. Writing. And when not a single yucca leaf is left to mess up— or a single palm leaf husk, or Grandpa's ledger books—Celestino starts writing on the trunks of the trees.

"That's what girls do," said my mother, when she found out Celestino had got it into his head to start writing. And that was the first time she jumped down the well.

\* \* \*

"I'd rather die than have a son like that," and the water level in the well rose.

Mama was so fat in those days! Really really fat. So when she dived into the water it came way up. You ought to have seen it! I ran out to the well and I could wash my hands in the water and I got a drink almost without bending over. I just stretched out my neck a little. And then I started drinking, using my two hands like they were dippers. The water was so cool and clear! I love drinking out of my hands and getting them all wet. Like birds do. But of course, since birds don't have hands, they drink with their beaks . . . What if they did have hands, though, and we were the ones that were mixed up? . . . I don't even know what to say. In this house things have gone from bad to worse—I don't even know, really and truly, what to think. But I still think anyway. And worry. And think. And worry . . . And now Celestino comes up to me again with all the palm branches under his arms and the carpenter's pencils sticking out the middle of his stomach.

"Celestino! Celestino!"

"Carmelina's child has gone crazy!"

"He's gone crazy! He's gone crazy!"

"He's scribbling on the trunks of the trees!"

"He's batty as a loon!"

"What a disgrace! My God! This kind of thing could only happen to me!"

"What a disgrace!"

We went down to the river. The boys' voices kept getting louder and louder, and finally they were yelling. They pushed Celestino out of the water and told him to go swim with the women. I got out of the water too, right behind Celestino, and then the boys caught me and kicked my behind eight times—four on each side. I felt like I wanted to cry. But he cried for me too.

*    *    *

And night caught us in the middle of the pasture. Boom, just like that, night falls around here. Just when you'd least expect it, here it comes. It wraps all around us and then it won't go away. The sun almost never comes up here. Oh, of course a lot of people say the sun comes up, or morning comes. I say the same thing once in a while.

"When we get to the house, don't let them find out what the boys did," Celestino said, and he dried his eyes with a guava leaf. But when we got to the house they were already waiting for us at the door. Nobody said a word. Not a peep. We came to the house, went into the dining room, and at that, she ran out through the kitchen door. She gave a shriek behind the cookstove and started running all over the yard, and finally she jumped down the well again . . . When I was littler, Grandma gave me a hen and told me, "Follow her till you find her nest, and don't come back to this house till your pockets are full of eggs." I turned the hen loose in the middle of the yard. She took off. She flapped her wings and flew three circles in the air. And she disappeared, cackling through the thicket of wild pineapples.

"The hen got away from me, Grandma."

"Son of a bitch! We'd all be better off if you just died!"

Celestino came up to me and put his hand on my head. I was so sad. It was the first time anybody had ever cursed at me. I was so sad I started crying. Celestino lifted me up in the air, and he said to me, "What foolishness, but you might as well get used to it." I looked at Celestino, and I realized that he was crying too, but he was trying not to show it. So that made me realize that he still hadn't got used to it either. I stopped crying a second. And the two of us went out into the yard. It was still daylight.

It was still daylight.

*    *    *

There had been a rainstorm. But the lightning bolts hadn't been satisfied with just that, so they kept on winking and flashing behind the clouds and way up in the highest leaves of the shower-of-gold bushes. What a nice smell there is after it rains . . . I had never noticed things like that before. Now I did. So I took air in through my nose and mouth, both. And then I filled my stomach up again with the smell and the air. The sun wasn't going to come back out anymore now, there were too many clouds. But it was still light out. We walked along under the sugar apple trees, and I could feel the mud with leaves all mixed up in it coming up through the holes in my shoes. The mud was cold, and all of a sudden I got the idea of playing like I was walking through snow and that the sugar apple trees were Christmas trees and pines and evergreens and that the whole family was in the house buzzing and clattering and laughing, which up to then I'd never heard before. "What a shame there's no snow here where we live," I said to Celestino. But he wasn't with me anymore. "Celestino! Celestino!" I called, very very softly, trying not to wake myself up and find myself in the middle of a mud puddle.

Celestino! Celestino!

The lightning bolts came back again. My mother ran across the snow and hugged me tight. And she said "son" to me. I smiled at my mother, and then I jumped and hugged her around the neck. And the two of us started to dance on the ground, all dressed in white. At that, the noise of the people singing and making such a hubbub in the house got closer and closer to us; they were coming towards us with a whole roast pig on a spit, and they were singing all the way. All my cousins made a chorus and danced around us in a ring. Mama lifted me way up in the air. As high as her arms could reach. And from up there I could see the sky getting darker and darker, and a shower bigger and whiter than the one that had come down before starting to work its way out of the clouds. So I wiggled out of my mother's arms and ran over to where my cousins were, and we started jumping up and down in the snow as high as we could and we sang and sang and sang, and little by little we turned transparent—as transparent as the snow that didn't get mixed up with the mud, it just spread out white and pure and clean no matter how much we jumped around.

For one second there was a great big loud clap of thunder. I saw the lightning melt every bit of the snow as quick as you could snap your fingers. And before I could yell and close my eyes, I saw myself—walking through a big mud puddle—and saw Celestino writing poems on the sugar apple trees, and their bark is as hard as iron. And my grandfather came out of the kitchen with a hatchet and started cutting down all the trees Celestino had written on, even if it was just one word.

I watched him swinging his hatchet, whacking away at the tree trunks, and I said to myself, "The time has come. I'm going to break his back with a rock." But I didn't. What if I miss and it doesn't kill him? If the rock doesn't hit him just right, then I'm done for, because Grandpa will jump on me like a mad dog and make mincemeat out of me with the hatchet.

There's not a thing I can do all by myself. Sometimes there are a whole lot of things I wish I could do. But I don't do a single solitary thing. One day I told myself I was going to set the house on fire. I climbed up one of the forked props for the wall, up to the roof, and I had already struck the match and all I had to do was hold it to the palm thatch for the whole house and everything to go up like gunpowder, and not a black smudge of what had been the house be left, and all of a sudden I remembered the baby blackbirds. They had just pecked out of their shells and they were asleep all nice and still in the nest over by the rain gutters. I remembered them and that made me feel so sad. So I didn't do it. I didn't do a thing. I got down off the roof saying to myself, "Well, when the baby blackbirds grow up and fly away from the nest I'll set fire to the house, and there won't be any problem with doing it then at all." And when I got to the ground I felt the hard crack of a big thick switch that rattled my ribs and almost broke my back.

"Son of a bitch! I told you not to climb up on the roof of the house — it stops raining faster outside than it does inside these days, with you climbing all over the thatch and shinnying down the rain gutters all the time and punching holes in the roof. You goose! Get to work!"

And another crack. And another. And another. Grandpa had been waiting for me, just biding his time, under the rainspout, and he had taken such good aim when I was climbing down that there was no way I could duck the switch cracking and then cracking again, going "psssst-ch!" through the air from the mad blind rage Grandpa was taking out on my back. The stinking old coot! He caught me by surprise, and I didn't know what to do when I saw that switch coming at me. Something just came over me, and I really felt like crying. But then I started getting so mad, so mad inside that I bet I even turned all different colors and everything. So at that I gave a great big huge scream and ran for the meadow on the mountainside as fast as I could go, with the old coot after me, cursing and muttering and stumbling over the tree stumps he had cut down his own evil self. The high meadow is so beautiful! I love it.

When I got there I jumped into the first clump of tall grass I could find. And I didn't even feel the chiggers biting me, or even the ticks there are on the mountain. I lay on my back and made myself as comfortable as I could and watched the clouds. And I started eating some little wild persimmons I could just reach and pull off from a persimmon tree. Two great big clouds ran into each other and smashed into a million pieces.

The pieces fell on my house and squashed it, right down to the ground. I never thought pieces of cloud would be so big and heavy. They're sharp as a knife, too. One of them just sliced my grandfather's head right off. My cousins were down at the river, so they managed to escape. Not hide nor hair of my grandmother has been found, so I guess the clouds broke her to smithereens and ants came and carried off the pieces. I run down from the high meadow to the house, buried under the rubble of clouds, and when I get there all I can see is one of my mother's arms and one of Celestino's. My mother's arm is moving a little in the rubble and soot and ashes. (Because in this house the smoke from the cookstove has no place to go, because there's just one window and it's in the dining room, so that's why the house is always as black as the bottom of a kettle.)

"Get me out of here, I'm suffocating!" the voice of my mother tells me, and her arm waves around and jumps and twitches.

I can't hear Celestino say a word. Not a peep. His arm is barely sticking out of the soot and ashes and palm branches, and it's moving so very very slow and still that it's almost like his hand is petting the beams and the pieces of black thatch that have buried him alive.

"Get me out of here, goddammit! I'm your mother!"

"I'll be right there. I'll be right there!"

And I smile as I go over to where Celestino's still, cold hand is, and I start lifting up the big boulders of cloud from on top of him. Until finally, at just about nightfall, I've finally got him free.

The storm of clouds has let up a little, and a fine fine shower is little by little turning everything an almost transparent white white color. Out of that mist of water just barely barely falling I see my mother coming towards me carrying the ox prod in her hands. Sharpened to a fine point.

The chiggers have almost eaten my whole back, but I didn't feel them biting me, I was in such a daze. My mother walks right across the top of the wild pineapple thicket, not even watching out for thorns, and then she takes off flying.

Now she's right in front of me. In the middle of the high meadow, and pointing the prod straight at my throat.

"Why didn't you save me? You jackass!"

Mama grips the prod tighter, and I can feel a cold tickle that starts going right through the skin of my throat.

"I am your mother."

My cousin Eulogia got lost in this meadow one time. Poor Eulogia! She went out to get firewood and she never came back to the house again. With or without the firewood.

"Answer me—why didn't you save me, if I'm the woman that brought you into the world!"

Something must have happened to my cousin Eulogia that she still hasn't come back. We all waited for her in the dining room, not saying a word to one another. Looking at the floor or out the only window. But not saying a single word to one another.

Eulogia!

Eulogia!

Grandma cries because she says she knows that if Eulogia's lost Grandpa will hang himself. I feel sorry for Eulogia. But if it's true about Grandpa then I'd be very happy if she were to get lost.

"You're no son of mine! What you are is a beast!"

Hail Mary, full of grace. Blessed be the fruit of thy womb. Virgin Mary, please let Eulogia show up, because if she doesn't I'll pitch you into that cookstove . . .

Our Father, Who art in heaven . . .

✳  ✳  ✳

"You beast! You beast! Instead of saving your own mother, you'd let her suffocate in that ash heap."

Poor Eulogia . . . When she went off to the mountain I saw that she was crying. She had just come out of Grandpa's room. Poor Eulogia! If she wasn't the goose she is she wouldn't have let Grandpa get up on top of her like he did. But she's the slave for this whole house and everybody gets on top of her. And does whatever they want to her. Even me. One afternoon I tripped her and pulled her down out behind the bileweed patch and got up on top of her. She didn't make the slightest peep. She brayed like a mule when you give it three or four slaps with a stick of wood, and she broke out in big drops of sweat.

Poor Eulogia! She left the house crying while Grandma was throwing the biggest fit you ever saw. As soon as she turned her back Mama slushed the dirty dishwater on her head.

"Goddamn you! My only son, and he's turned out to be as thick as a mule! Was there ever a sadder fate than mine! I knew I should've died before I came into the world!"

It's as plain as day that Eulogia didn't really get lost on the mountain, like my whole family would like me to think. And if she didn't, then they'll see—one day we'll find her hanging from a tree with a vine around her neck, hanging almost as high as the parson birds, and they *never* come down to the ground, except to get a drink of water, maybe, when they can't find a drop on the leaves of the trees and they're so thirsty they can't even fly. If it weren't for that, they'd never *ever* come down!

What I wouldn't give to be a parson bird! I wouldn't drink water even if my throat got as dry as a rock.

✳  ✳  ✳

The point of the prod goes in very very cool right through my throat. I hang on to the rocks and grass for dear life and I can feel that coolness all the way to my tonsils.

I wish I could escape.

Except really, I'm not so sure I do. And I think, If they let me go I'd tell Mama to stab me again with the stick. I would—I'd even get down on my knees to her and beg her to do it, and tell her to make the stick sharper, too.

"Goddamn you! Goddamn you!"

As the cool feeling fills my whole throat I gradually realize that my mother isn't mean. I look at her, standing over me, and she looks like a giant, or like a great big huge crepe myrtle bush like the ones people tie animals to. Never noticing that the crepe myrtle is all dried up from so many reins and ropes being tied around it.

My mother gets prettier and prettier and prettier. How beautiful! She's so pretty in her burlapbag skirt and the big blouse she stole from Eulogia. I love my mother and I know she's good and that she loves me. I have never seen my mother. But I always picture her like she is now—crying and running her fingers over my throat in the coolest, nicest tickling way you can imagine.

I should picture her like that, not the other way.

"You miserable child! What I really ought to do is hang myself this very instant!"

I feel like getting up and hugging her. Telling her I'm sorry and carrying her off far away where neither Grandma nor Grandpa could ever bother us anymore. I feel like saying, *"Madre mía! Madre mía, Mama!* You're so pretty today with that honeysuckle in your hair! You look like one of those women that you only see on Christmas cards. Let's get out of here, let's leave right this second. Let's get our things together and just take off. Let's not stay another minute in this horrible horrible house that looks like the bottom of a kettle. Let's leave now, before that jackass of a grandfather wakes up and makes us get out of bed and milk the cows."

"Let's leave right this minute, because in the daytime we won't be able to get away."

*"Madre mia! Madre mia!"*

But I don't say another single word. What I was planning to say got stuck in my throat. It hit the point of the stick that ran all the way through me now. And it didn't come out my mouth. For a second my mother stood there paralyzed—listening to me. The whole high meadow knows now that I said my mother. The whole hill knows it too, and now it repeats it in a very very strange echo that's almost as close as my own voice.

Mama just stands there with her mouth open. She pulls the prod out of my throat. She throws it into the grass. She puts her hands to her face and lets out a huge huge wail.

Huge.

And she takes off flying, across the old thicket of wild pineapples and into the house, through those big holes in the roof that I've made climbing up and down looking for baby blackbirds or meeting my dead cousins.

I don't know what to do. My throat stings like the dickens. I run my hand over it and it turns out it's nothing. Not even a scratch. The fire ants have eaten my whole back away and the chiggers are starting to get on my face. My mother has disappeared and it's getting to be almost night now. I wish I could make it to the house without anybody seeing me and without her starting to poke me with the prod again or Grandma throwing scalding water on my back.

"You can, you can. Tonight you can," a band of blackbirds tells me, flying over way up high, all in rows, one after another. But how in the world could those blackbirds have been talking to me! I don't believe it. I look up at the sky again, and the black line of their wings is as straight and perfect as could be—the birds' trip has just gone right on and I'll never find out the truth.

Then I start crying.

I like to walk at night, when nobody can see me. I do. I like to because that's when I can hop on just one foot. Get up on a tree stump and spread out my arms and let myself go and dance on it, with my arms out to keep my balance. Do all kinds of somersaults and tricks, and all of them different. Roll around on the ground and take off running again, until I disappear into the fog and in the branches of the Indian laurel tree, which is still standing. I like to be by myself and just break out singing. Celestino has come up to me and asked me for a drink of water. Where from. "Where from," I ask him, and I hold out my empty hands. But the real truth is that I have a terrible memory and I can never remember a song. And so that's why I make them up. I almost like making them up better than learning them by heart.

I'm making one up now.

I hope nobody hears me, because I don't know if this song is any good. I hope nobody hears me, because I'd hate for them to hear me. How embarrassing if my cousins were to surprise me singing made-up songs and hopping through the tree stumps! How embarrassing it would be if somebody heard me!

## ■ Jamaica Kincaid (1949– ) *Antigua/United States* (story)

Jamaica Kincaid was born in St. John's on the Caribbean island of Antigua. She came to the United States when she was sixteen to go to school and later had success as a freelance writer, a staff writer for the *New Yorker*, and a novelist. Her stories have appeared in *Rolling Stone* and *The Paris Review*. In addition to her highly successful book of short stories, *At the Bottom of the River* (1983), she has written two novels, *Annie John* (1983) and *Lucy* (1990), as well as a prose piece about Antigua titled *A Small Place* (1988). She is an extraordinary writer, peculiar, experimental, magical, and postmodern. Her stories dissect themselves as they speak to us. Or they exist in a dreamscape where anything can and does happen. Each of her brief tales surprises, perplexes, and acrobatically saves itself from its own narrative plunge.

**FURTHER READING:** Kincaid, Jamaica. *Annie John*, 1983; *At the Bottom of the River*, 1983; *A Small Place*, 1988; *Lucy*, 1990.

# Girl

Wash the white clothes on Monday and put them on the stone heap; wash the color clothes on Tuesday and put them on the clothesline to dry; don't walk barehead in the hot sun; cook pumpkin fritters in very hot sweet oil; soak your little cloths right after you take them off; when buying cotton to make yourself a nice blouse, be sure that it doesn't have gum on it, because that way it won't hold up well after a wash; soak salt fish overnight before you cook it; is it true that you sing benna in Sunday school?; always eat your food in such a way that it won't turn someone else's stomach; on Sundays try to walk like a lady and not like the slut you are so bent on becoming; don't sing benna in Sunday school; you mustn't speak to wharf-rat boys, not even to give directions; don't eat fruits on the street—flies will follow you; *but I don't sing benna on Sundays at all and never in Sunday school;* this is how to sew on a button; this is how to make a button-hole for the button you have just sewed on; this is how to hem a dress when you see the hem coming down and so to prevent yourself from looking like the slut I know you are so bent on becoming; this is how you iron your father's khaki shirt so that it doesn't have a crease; this is how you iron your father's khaki pants so that they don't have a crease; this is how you grow okra—far from the house, because okra tree harbors red ants; when you are growing dasheen, make sure it gets plenty of water or else it makes your throat itch when you are eating it; this is how you sweep a corner; this is how you sweep a whole house; this is how you sweep a yard; this is how you smile to someone you don't like too much; this is how you smile to someone you don't like at all; this is how you smile to someone you like completely; this is how you set a table for tea; this is how you set a table for dinner; this is how you set a table for dinner with an important guest; this is how you set a table for lunch; this is how you set a table for breakfast; this is how to be-have in the presence of men who don't know you very well, and this way they won't recognize immediately the slut I have warned you against be-coming; be sure to wash every day, even if it is with your own spit; don't squat down to play marbles—you are not a boy, you know; don't pick peo-ple's flowers—you might catch something; don't throw stones at black-birds, because it might not be a blackbird at all; this is how to make a bread pudding; this is how to make doukona; this is how to make pepper pot; this is how to make a good medicine for a cold; this is how to make a good medicine to throw away a child before it even becomes a child; this is how to catch a fish; this is how to throw back a fish you don't like, and that way something bad won't fall on you; this is how to bully a man; this is how a man bullies you; this is how to love a man, and if this doesn't work there are other ways, and if they don't work don't feel too bad about giving up; this is how to spit up in the air if you feel like it, and this is how to move quick so that it doesn't fall on you; this is how to make ends meet; always squeeze bread to make sure it's fresh; *but what if the baker won't let me feel the bread?;* you mean to say that after all you are really going to be the kind of woman who the baker won't let near the bread?

## ■ Laura Esquivel (1950– ) *Mexico* (novel)

### TRANSLATED BY CAROL CHRISTIANSEN AND THOMAS CHRISTIANSEN

Laura Esquivel was originally a screenwriter and her screenplay *Chido One* was nominated for the highest award from the Mexican Academy of Motion Pictures. Her film version of *Like Water for Chocolate* won awards in all categories, ten altogether, including one for Esquivel's screenplay, which was based on her best-selling international novel. The frame of Laura Esquivel's novel is cooking, and she precedes each month of the year with a recipe. So January's recipe is Christmas Rolls. There is a curious tradition of cooking, food, and literature of which a fine example is the Byzantine volume *Doctors at Dinner.* In it, the author gathered gems of Ancient Greek lyric poetry containing references to food and cooking. As a result, we possess many poems by Alkman and Sappho that would otherwise have been lost. Had Laura Esquivel composed her novel in Byzantine or Classical Greek times, *Doctors at Dinner* would be replete with Mexican spices and sauces.

Esquivel's story is more fantastic than her recipes. In the first pages, we read about Tita, whose mother was cutting onions in the kitchen, which brought on early labor and caused Tita to be "literally washed into this world on a great tide of tears that spilled over the edge of the table and flooded across the kitchen floor." We learn that when the tears dried and were swept up there was enough salt to fill a ten-pound sack. Esquivel's magic realism gives a mythic quality to the book, which scintillates with family drama, stupidity, and anger born of a traditionally tyrannical mother and a sickly farting sister who marries Pedro whom Tita is mad about. The book flows, like Tita's salt tears at her birth. Esquivel, in lucid, spare language, re-creates a historic rural Mexico during its revolution, and with humor and pain she fuels the domestic love tragedies to the story's burning climax. With a single spellbinding novel, her first, Laura Esquivel has taken her place as a writer read all over the world.

**FURTHER READING:** Esquivel, Laura, *Like Water for Chocolate,* 1992.

## *from Like Water for Chocolate*

### January

*Christmas Rolls*
   INGREDIENTS:
   *1 can of sardines*
   *½ chorizo sausage*

*1 onion*
*oregano*
*1 can of chiles serranos*
*10 hard rolls*

## PREPARATION

Take care to chop the onion fine. To keep from crying when you chop it (which is so annoying!), I suggest you place a little bit on your head. The trouble with crying over an onion is that once the chopping gets you started and the tears begin to well up, the next thing you know you just can't stop. I don't know whether that's ever happened to you, but I have to confess it's happened to me, many times. Mama used to say it was because I was especially sensitive to onions, like my great-aunt, Tita.

Tita was so sensitive to onions, any time they were being chopped, they say she would just cry and cry; when she was still in my great-grandmother's belly her sobs were so loud that even Nacha, the cook, who was half-deaf, could hear them easily. Once her wailing got so violent that it brought on an early labor. And before my great-grandmother could let out a word or even a whimper, Tita made her entrance into this world, prematurely, right there on the kitchen table amid the smells of simmering noodle soup, thyme, bay leaves, and cilantro, steamed milk, garlic, and, of course, onion. Tita had no need for the usual slap on the bottom, because she was already crying as she emerged; maybe that was because she knew then that it would be her lot in life to be denied marriage. The way Nacha told it, Tita was literally washed into this world on a great tide of tears that spilled over the edge of the table and flooded across the kitchen floor.

That afternoon, when the uproar had subsided and the water had been dried up by the sun, Nacha swept up the residue the tears had left on the red stone floor. There was enough salt to fill a ten-pound sack—it was used for cooking and lasted a long time. Thanks to her unusual birth, Tita felt a deep love for the kitchen, where she spent most of her life from the day she was born.

When she was only two days old, Tita's father, my great-grandfather, died of a heart attack and Mama Elena's milk dried up from the shock. Since there was no such thing as powdered milk in those days, and they couldn't find a wet nurse anywhere, they were in a panic to satisfy the infant's hunger. Nacha, who knew everything about cooking—and much more that doesn't enter the picture until later—offered to take charge of feeding Tita. She felt she had the best chance of "educating the innocent child's stomach," even though she had never married or had children. Though she didn't know how to read or write, when it came to cooking she knew everything there was to know. Mama Elena accepted her offer gratefully; she had enough to do between her mourning and the enormous responsibility of running the ranch—and it was the ranch that would provide her children the food and education they deserved—without having to worry about feeding a newborn baby on top of everything else.

From that day on, Tita's domain was the kitchen, where she grew vigorous and healthy on a diet of teas and thin corn gruels. This explains the sixth sense Tita developed about everything concerning food. Her eating habits, for example, were attuned to the kitchen routine: in the morning, when she could smell that the beans were ready; at midday, when she sensed the water was ready for plucking the chickens; and in the afternoon, when the dinner bread was baking, Tita knew it was time for her to be fed.

Sometimes she would cry for no reason at all, like when Nacha chopped onions, but since they both knew the cause of those tears, they didn't pay them much mind. They made them a source of entertainment, so that during her childhood Tita didn't distinguish between tears of laughter and tears of sorrow. For her laughing was a form of crying.

Likewise for Tita the joy of living was wrapped up in the delights of food. It wasn't easy for a person whose knowledge of life was based on the kitchen to comprehend the outside world. That world was an endless expanse that began at the door between the kitchen and the rest of the house, whereas everything on the kitchen side of that door, on through the door leading to the patio and the kitchen and herb gardens was completely hers—it was Tita's realm.

Her sisters were just the opposite: to them, Tita's world seemed full of unknown dangers, and they were terrified of it. They felt that playing in the kitchen was foolish and dangerous. But once, Tita managed to convince them to join her in watching the dazzling display made by dancing water drops dribbled on a red hot griddle.

While Tita was singing and waving her wet hands in time, showering drops of water down on the griddle so they would "dance," Rosaura was cowering in the corner, stunned by the display. Gertrudis, on the other hand, found this game enticing, and she threw herself into it with the enthusiasm she always showed where rhythm, movement, or music were involved. Then Rosaura had tried to join them—but since she barely moistened her hands and then shook them gingerly, her efforts didn't have the desired effect. So Tita tried to move her hands closer to the griddle. Rosaura resisted, and they struggled for control until Tita became annoyed and let go, so that momentum carried Rosaura's hands onto it. Tita got a terrible spanking for that, and she was forbidden to play with her sisters in her own world. Nacha became her playmate then. Together they made up all sorts of games and activities having to do with cooking. Like the day they saw a man in the village plaza twisting long thin balloons into animal shapes, and they decided to do it with sausages. They didn't just make real animals, they also made up some of their own, creatures with the neck of a swan, the legs of a dog, the tail of a horse, and on and on.

Then there was trouble, however, when the animals had to be taken apart to fry the sausage. Tita refused to do it. The only time she was willing to take them apart was when the sausage was intended for the Christmas rolls she loved so much. Then she not only allowed her animals to be dismantled, she watched them fry with glee.

The sausage for the rolls must be fried over very low heat, so that it cooks thoroughly without getting too brown. When done, remove from the heat and add the sardines, which have been deboned ahead of time. Any black spots on the skin should also have been scraped off with a knife. Combine the onions, chopped chiles, and the ground oregano with the sardines. Let the mixture stand before filling the rolls.

Tita enjoyed this step enormously; while the filling was resting, it was very pleasant to savor its aroma, for smells have the power to evoke the past, bringing back sounds and even other smells that have no match in the present. Tita liked to take a deep breath and let the characteristic smoke and smell transport her through the recesses of her memory.

It was useless to try to recall the first time she had smelled one of those rolls—she couldn't, possibly because it had been before she was born. It might have been the unusual combination of sardines and sausages that had called to her and made her decide to trade the peace of ethereal existence in Mama Elena's belly for life as her daughter, in order to enter the De la Garza family and share their delicious meals and wonderful sausage.

On Mama Elena's ranch, sausage making was a real ritual. The day before, they started peeling garlic, cleaning chiles, and grinding spices. All the women in the family had to participate: Mama Elena, her daughters, Gertrudis, Rosaura, and Tita; Nacha, the cook; and Chencha, the maid. They gathered around the dining-room table in the afternoon, and between the talking and the joking the time flew by until it started to get dark. Then Mama Elena would say:

"That's it for today."

For a good listener, it is said, a single word will suffice, so when they heard that, they all sprang into action. First they had to clear the table; then they had to assign tasks: one collected the chickens, another drew water for breakfast from the well, a third was in charge of wood for the stove. There would be no ironing, no embroidery, no sewing that day. When it was all finished, they went to their bedrooms to read, say their prayers, and go to sleep. One afternoon, before Mama Elena told them they could leave the table, Tita, who was then fifteen, announced in a trembling voice that Pedro Muzquiz would like to come and speak with her. . . .

After an endless silence during which Tita's soul shrank, Mama Elena asked:

"And why should this gentleman want to come talk to me?"

Tita's answer could barely be heard:

"I don't know."

Mama Elena threw her a look that seemed to Tita to contain all the years of repression that had flowed over the family, and said:

"If he intends to ask for your hand, tell him not to bother. He'll be wasting his time and mine too. You know perfectly well that being the youngest daughter means you have to take care of me until the day I die."

With that Mama Elena got slowly to her feet, put her glasses in her apron, and said in a tone of final command:

"That's it for today."

Tita knew that discussion was not one of the forms of communication permitted in Mama Elena's household, but even so, for the first time in her life, she intended to protest her mother's ruling.

"But in my opinion . . . "

"You don't have an opinion, and that's all I want to hear about it. For generations, not a single person in my family has ever questioned this tradition, and no daughter of mine is going to be the one to start."

Tita lowered her head, and the realization of her fate struck her as forcibly as her tears struck the table. From then on they knew, she and the table, that they could never have even the slightest voice in the unknown forces that fated Tita to bow before her mother's absurd decision, and the table to continue to receive the bitter tears that she had first shed on the day of her birth.

Still Tita did not submit. Doubts and anxieties sprang to her mind. For one thing, she wanted to know who started this family tradition. It would be nice if she could let that genius know about one little flaw in this perfect plan for taking care of women in their old age. If Tita couldn't marry and have children, who would take care of her when she got old? Was there a solution in a case like that? Or are daughters who stay home and take care of their mothers not expected to survive too long after the parent's death? And what about women who marry and can't have children, who will take care of them? And besides, she'd like to know what kind of studies had established that the youngest daughter and not the eldest is best suited to care for their mother. Had the opinion of the daughter affected by the plan ever been taken into account? If she couldn't marry, was she at least allowed to experience love? Or not even that?

Tita knew perfectly well that all these questions would have to be buried forever in the archive of questions that have no answers. In the De la Garza family, one obeyed—immediately. Ignoring Tita completely, a very angry Mama Elena left the kitchen, and for the next week she didn't speak a single word to her.

What passed for communication between them resumed when Mama Elena, who was inspecting the clothes each of the women had been sewing, discovered that Tita's creation, which was the most perfect, had not been basted before it was sewed.

"Congratulations," she said, "your stitches are perfect—but you didn't baste it, did you?"

"No," answered Tita, astonished that the sentence of silence had been revoked.

"Then go and rip it out. Baste it and sew it again and then come and show it to me. And remember that the lazy man and the stingy man end up walking their road twice."

"But that's if a person makes a mistake, and you yourself said a moment ago that my sewing was . . ."

"Are you starting up with your rebelliousness again? It's enough that you have the audacity to break the rules in your sewing."

"I'm sorry, Mami. I won't ever do it again."

With that Tita succeeded in calming Mama Elena's anger. For once she had been very careful; she had called her "Mami" in the correct tone of voice. Mama Elena felt that the word *Mama* had a disrespectful sound to it, and so, from the time they were little, she had ordered her daughters to use the word *Mami* when speaking to her. The only one who resisted, the only one who said the word without the proper deference was Tita, which had earned her plenty of slaps. But how perfectly she had said it this time! Mama Elena took comfort in the hope that she had finally managed to subdue her youngest daughter.

Unfortunately her hope was short-lived, for the very next day Pedro Muzquiz appeared at the house, his esteemed father at his side, to ask for Tita's hand in marriage. His arrival caused a huge uproar, as his visit was completely unexpected. Several days earlier Tita had sent Pedro a message via Nacha's brother asking him to abandon his suit. The brother swore he had delivered the message to Pedro, and yet, there they were, in the house. Mama Elena received them in the living room; she was extremely polite and explained why it was impossible for Tita to marry.

"But if you really want Pedro to get married, allow me to suggest my daughter Rosaura, who's just two years older than Tita. *She* is one hundred percent available, and ready for marriage. . . . "

At that Chencha almost dropped right onto Mama Elena the tray containing coffee and cookies, which she had carried into the living room to offer don Pascual and his son. Excusing herself, she rushed back to the kitchen, where Tita, Rosaura, and Gertrudis were waiting for her to fill them in on every detail about what was going on in the living room. She burst headlong into the room, and they all immediately stopped what they were doing, so as not to miss a word she said.

They were together in the kitchen making Christmas Rolls. As the name implies, these rolls are usually prepared around Christmas, but today they were being prepared in honor of Tita's birthday. She would soon be sixteen years old, and she wanted to celebrate with one of her favorite dishes.

"Isn't that something? Your ma talks about being ready for marriage like she was dishing up a plate of enchiladas! And the worse thing is, they're completely different! You can't just switch tacos and enchiladas like that!"

Chencha kept up this kind of running commentary as she told the others—in her own way, of course—about the scene she had just witnessed. Tita knew Chencha sometimes exaggerated and distorted things, so she held her aching heart in check. She would not accept what she had just heard. Feigning calm, she continued cutting the rolls for her sisters and Nacha to fill.

It is best to use homemade rolls. Hard rolls can easily be obtained from a bakery, but they should be small; the larger ones are unsuited for this recipe. After filling the rolls, bake for ten minutes and serve hot. For best results, leave the rolls out overnight, wrapped in a cloth, so that the grease from the sausage soaks into the bread.

When Tita was finishing wrapping the next day's rolls, Mama Elena came into the kitchen and informed them that she had agreed to Pedro's marriage—to Rosaura.

Hearing Chencha's story confirmed, Tita felt her body fill with a wintry chill: in one sharp, quick blast she was so cold and dry her cheeks burned and turned red, red as the apples beside her. That overpowering chill lasted a long time, and she could find no respite, not even when Nacha told her that she had overheard as she escorted don Pascual Muzquiz and his son to the ranch's gate. Nacha followed them, walking as quietly as she could in order to hear the conversation between father and son. Don Pascual and Pedro were walking slowly, speaking in low, controlled, angry voices.

"Why did you do that, Pedro? It will look ridiculous, your agreeing to marry Rosaura. What happened to the eternal love you swore to Tita? Aren't you going to keep that vow?"

"Of course I'll keep it. When you're told there's no way you can marry the woman you love and your only hope of being near her is to marry her sister, wouldn't you do the same?"

Nacha didn't manage to hear the answer; Pulque, the ranch dog, went running by, barking at a rabbit he mistook for a cat.

"So you intend to marry without love?"

"No, Papa, I am going to marry with a great love for Tita that will never die."

Their voices grew less and less audible, drowned out by the crackling of dried leaves beneath their feet. How strange that Nacha, who was quite hard of hearing by that time, should have claimed to have heard this conversation. Still, Tita thanked Nacha for telling her—but that did not alter the icy feelings she began to have for Pedro. It is said that the deaf can't hear but can understand. Perhaps Nacha only heard what everyone else was afraid to say. Tita could not get to sleep that night; she could not find the words for what she was feeling. How unfortunate that black holes in space had not yet been discovered, for then she might have understood the black hole in the center of her chest, infinite coldness flowing through it.

Whenever she closed her eyes she saw scenes from last Christmas, the first time Pedro and his family had been invited to dinner; the scenes grew more and more vivid, and the cold within her grew sharper. Despite the time that had passed since that evening, she remembered it perfectly: the sounds, the smells, the way her new dress had grazed the freshly waxed floor, the look Pedro gave her . . . That look! She had been walking to the table carrying a tray of egg-yolk candies when she first felt his hot gaze burning her skin. She turned her head, and her eyes met Pedro's. It was then she understood how dough feels when it is plunged into boiling oil. The heat that invaded her body was so real she was afraid she would start to bubble—her face, her stomach, her heart, her breasts—like batter, and unable to endure his gaze she lowered her eyes and hastily crossed the room, to where Gertrudis was pedaling the player piano, playing a waltz called "The Eyes of Youth." She set her tray on a little table in the middle of the room, picked up a glass of Noyo liquor that was in front of her, hardly aware of what she was doing, and sat down next to Paquita Lobo, the De la Garzas' neighbor. But even that distance between herself and Pedro was not enough; she felt her blood pulsing, searing her veins. A deep flush suffused her face and no matter how she tried she could not find a place for her eyes to rest. Paquita saw that something was bothering her, and with a look of great concern, she asked:

"That liquor is pretty strong, isn't it?"

"Pardon me?"

"You look a little woozy, Tita. Are you feeling all right?"

"Yes, thank you."

"You're old enough to have a little drink on a special occasion, but tell me, you little devil, did your mama say it was okay? I can see you're excited—you're shaking—and I'm sorry but I must say you'd better not have any more. You wouldn't want to make a fool of yourself."

That was the last straw! To have Paquita Lobo think she was drunk. She couldn't allow the tiniest suspicion to remain in Paquita's mind or she might tell her mother. Tita's fear of her mother was enough to make her forget Pedro for a moment, and she applied herself to convincing Paquita, any way she could, that she was thinking clearly, that her mind was alert. She chatted with her, she gossiped, she made small talk. She even told her the recipe for this Noyo liquor which was supposed to have had such an effect on her. The liquor is made by soaking four ounces of peaches and a half pound of apricots in water for twenty-four hours to loosen the skin; next, they are peeled, crushed, and steeped in hot water for fifteen days. Then the liquor is distilled. After two and a half pounds of sugar have been completely dissolved in the water, four ounces of orange-flower water are added, and the mixture is stirred and strained. And so there would be no lingering doubts about her mental and physical well-being, she reminded Paquita, as if it were just an aside, that the water containers held 2.016 liters, no more and no less.

So when Mama Elena came over to ask Paquita if she was being properly entertained, she replied enthusiastically.

"Oh yes, perfectly! You have such wonderful daughters. Such fascinating conversation!"

Mama Elena sent Tita to the kitchen to get something for the guests. Pedro "happened" to be walking by at that moment and he offered his help. Tita rushed off to the kitchen without a word. His presence made her extremely uncomfortable. He followed her in, and she quickly sent him off with one of the trays of delicious snacks that had been waiting on the kitchen table.

She would never forget the moment their hands accidentally touched as they both slowly bent down to pick up the same tray.

That was when Pedro confessed his love.

"Señorita Tita, I would like to take advantage of this opportunity to be alone with you to tell you that I am deeply in love with you. I know this declaration is presumptuous, and that it's quite sudden, but it's so hard to get near you that I decided to tell you tonight. All I ask is that you tell me whether I can hope to win your love."

"I don't know what to say . . . give me time to think."

"No, no, I can't! I need an answer now: you don't have to think about love; you either feel it or you don't. I am a man of few words, but my word is my pledge. I swear that my love for you will last forever. What about you? Do you feel the same way about me?"

"Yes!"

Yes, a thousand times. From that night on she would love him forever. And now she had to give him up. It wasn't decent to desire your sister's future husband. She had to try to put him out of her mind somehow, so she could get to sleep. She started to eat the Christmas Roll Nacha had left out on her bureau, along with a glass of milk; this remedy had proven effective many times. Nacha, with all her experience, knew that for Tita there was no pain that wouldn't disappear if she ate a delicious Christmas Roll. But this time it didn't work. She felt no relief from the hollow sensation in her stomach. Just the opposite, a wave of nausea flowed over her. She realized that the hollow sensation was not hunger but an icy feeling of grief. She had to get rid of that terrible sensation of cold. First she put on a wool robe and a heavy cloak. The cold still gripped her. Then she put on felt slippers and another two shawls. No good. Finally she went to her sewing box and pulled out the bedspread she had started the day Pedro first spoke of marriage. A bedspread like that, a crocheted one, takes about a year to complete. Exactly the length of time Pedro and Tita had planned to wait before getting married. She decided to use the yarn, not to let it go to waste, and so she worked on the bedspread and wept furiously, weeping and working until dawn, and threw it over herself. It didn't help at all. Not that night, nor many others, for as long as she lived, could she free herself from that cold.

■ **Giannina Braschi (1953– )** *Puerto Rico/New York* **(prose poem)**

TRANSLATED BY TESS O'DWYER

Giannina Braschi's collected poems, an epic-length sequence of prose poems, *The Empire of Dreams (El imperio de los sueños),* was published to acclaim in Barcelona in 1988. In 1994, Yale University Press, which usually publishes no poets other than those in the yearly Yale Younger Poets Series, chose to bring out *Empire of Dreams*. Alicia Ostriker wrote an illuminating introduction. In substantial ways, Braschi is the brightest new voice in her generation in the Spanish language. She was born in Puerto Rico and has lived in New York since 1977. She took her Ph.D. from State University of New York at Stony Brook and presently teaches at Queens College and John Jay College, City University of New York. She published a critical volume on the poetry of the nineteenth-century Spanish poet Gustavo Bécquer, *La poesía de Bécquer: el tiempo de los objetos o los espacious de la luz* (1982). Her focus now is her poetry and drama.

Braschi is a Spanish Arthur Rimbaud, re-inventing surrealism, creating a maze of characters—clowns, shepherds, magicians madmen, witches, and artists who perform their fantasies in city streets. The shepherds spread straw over New York and enter triumphantly with their herds. Her language is erotic, linguistically innovative, sexually ambiguous, postmodern, fluid, inevitable. She gives meaning to the meaningless as she creates, identifies, and slides between them. She is cosmopolitan— of the great cities of Europe and the Americas—and above all magical. *The Empire of Dreams* has been called a modern classic.

**FURTHER READING:** Giannina Braschi. *La poesía de Bécquer: el tiempo de los objetos o los espacios de la luz,* 1982; *El imperio de los sueños,* 1988; *Empire of Dreams,* 1994.

## *from* Empire of Dreams

Behind the word is silence. Behind what sounds is the door. There is a back and a fold hiding in everything. And what was approaching fell and stopped far away in proximity. An expression falls asleep and rises. And what was over there returns. It's a way to put the world back in its place. And something comes back when it should remain remembering.

But if I ring the bell, water jumps and a river falls out of the water again. And the body rises and shakes. And the rock wakes and says, I'm singing. And a hand turns into a kerchief. And twilight and wind are companions. And this twilight appears amidst lightning. Outside there is a bird and a branch and a tree and that lightning. Above all, there is noon without form. And suddenly everything acquires movement. Two travelers meet and their shoes dance. And breeze and morning clash. And the seagull runs and the rabbit flies. And runs and runs, and the current ran. Behind what runs is life. Behind that silence is the door.

\*　\*　\*

I want to be rid of this corpse that murders my soul. I have other things to say. Get away from me. Leave me alone. I request another name, another clown. Too many buffoons, too many dead dwarves. I want a giant. Get out of my body. Don't take the corpse away from me, let it walk. Swing with the trapeze, glide. Make me a shoe or dig the sole into me. Become a stocking and fill me. I have a nickel for the dance and the comedy. You see, that's just what I was telling you. I have no comedies. Kill me if you want. But do for me the black, the white, the void. Absence, as though it were the death of absence. As though absence could drop dead, dead. Of course, the corpse is a stick that walks. Of course, the stick gives you a blow on the head. Of course, you should never play with death.

\* \* \*

On the top floor of the Empire State a shepherd has stood up to sing and dance. What a wonderful thing. That New York City has been invaded by so many shepherds. That work has stopped and there is only singing and dancing. And that the newspapers — the *New York Times,* in headlines, and the *Daily News* — call out: New York. New York. New York. Listen to it. Hear it on the radio. And on television. Listen to the loudspeakers. Listen to it. The buffoons have died. And the little lead soldier. Shepherds have invaded New York. They have conquered New York. They have colonized New York. The special of the day in New York's most expensive restaurant is golden acorns. It's an egg. It's an apple. It's a bird. Fish. Melody. Poetry. And epigram. Now there is only song. Now there is only dance. Now we do whatever we please. Whatever we please. Whatever we damn well please.

\* \* \*

I love hiccups and I love sneezes and I love blinks and I love belches and I love gluttons. I love hair. I love bears. For me, the round. For me, the world. Round is the happy face. And round is the midday. And when the moon is most beautiful is when it's round. Sex is round. And the heart also. The hand is round. The mouth also. Sneezes are round. And hiccups also. The milk from the breast of Lady Macbeth was also round. I would have liked to be like her and be bad. I am good. I am shepherd. I am sex. And I am hiccup. And I am sneeze. And I am cough. Hoarse. Hoarse. Hoarse. I am thunder. I am voice. I am Obscene. Obscene. Obscene. I am pure like the tit or the milk. I am water, sea, or fish, or tadpole. I am round.

\* \* \*

I'm really sorry, folks, but the shepherds are also farting in New York. I'm sorry. But they're gross. And the cops are chiming in. And they're farting too. And they're competing to see who can fart the loudest. So there's fart traffic. And burps. Traffic of bulls and cows and ambrosia and water. And bulls are pissing on buildings. And cows are shitting in shops. And all the shops are filled with shepherds. And all the mannequins are shepherds. I'm really sorry, folks, but shepherds are gross. Dirt. Dirt. Everything is dirty. Everything is disgusting. Everything is full of crap. Cow crap. Worm crap. Lizard crap. Santa Claus crap. Vulture crap. Beetle crap. The streets are full of crap. And the food too. I'm sorry, folks, but these New Yorkers are pigs. Pigs. Pigs.

\* \* \*

Memories walk around dressed up as old men. But they're not old. They're hypocrites and gossipers. I love gossip. But I hate memories and sorrows. I like the he told me and I told him, and we fell in love, and rode off into the sunset, and lived happily ever after. I like the sun and the beach. I like sidewalks. And soup and beets. I like men and women. And I like mountains and seas. I like fire and water. I like trashy movies and novels. I like tackiness and gossip. Most of all, I like to forget everything. Especially memories. I am forgetfulness. And nothingness. I am joy, well-being, and happiness. I am laughter, gossip, and pantomime. I am the idiot and the prince. I am the grain of rice and the bean. I am the chickpea and the casserole. I am the red apple. And salt and pepper. I am the shepherd of life. I am the shepherd of memories, which I love despite everything. Affirming is everything I love and everything I hate. Affirming. And living. And denying. Affirming everything.

\* \* \*

A little while longer. Ten days repeated. I'm looking at the moon. The highest star. The solution to the same math problem. On a pile of conjectures. Polysynchronized colors. And the answer ten kilometers from my house. Proof for a theorem. I'll supply you with all the necessary material. I'll give you a certificate. A science diploma. Some goggles. From the time before iguanas and the world. A frog croaks. A cricket sings. I love bird nests from the time before life. I love frog dreams. Toad interpretations. I come whenever I hear iguana concerts. My orgasm is an organ. An organism. A simple tadpole that becomes a frog. A mouse has his own way of fighting a cat. He takes him out of context. The cat's text meows. Mice want cheese. Cows eat lots of meat. Polychromatic urban cows. Green. Orange. Or yellow. The piano, softly. Or the C in E-flat. In A minor. Still listening to the symphony. Still. Allegretto. Fugue. Scherzo. Or andante con moto, or andante con brio, or rondo burlesco. In the rondo of the minuet or the waltz. A C in E-flat. Ten days of fugue. Music vacations. An ironic fit of laughter rules over the sea. And a stupid drool.

# ACKNOWLEDGMENTS

## SECTION 1: ASIA

### INDIA, PAKISTAN, AND BANGLADESH

Excerpts from *The Upanishads,* tr. Juan Mascaró (Penguin Classics, 1965). Copyright © Juan Mascaró, 1965. Reproduced by permission of Penguin Books Ltd.

Excerpts from Theravada Buddhist Texts: *Visuddhi-Magga, Sainyutta-Nikaya, Milindapaiiha,* and *Maha-Vagga,* tr. Henry Clarke Warren from *Buddhism in Translation.* Copyright © 1896 by Harvard University. Reprinted by permission of Harvard University Press.

From *The Dhammapada: The Path of Perfection,* tr. Juan Mascaró (Penguin Classics, 1973). Copyright © Juan Mascaró, 1973. Reproduced by permission of Penguin Books Ltd.

"The Parable of the Burning House," tr. Burton Watson from *The Lotus Sutra,* edited by Burton Watson. Copyright © 1993. Reprinted by permission of Columbia University Press.

Excerpts from Volume II, Aranya Kanda, Chapters 17–18, 32–35, 46–48; and Volume III, Yuddha Kanda, Chapters 100–102, 110. Translated by Hari Prasad Shastri, 1957, from *The Ramayana of Valmiki,* in three volumes. Available from the publishers, Shanti Sadan, 29 Chepstow Villas, London W11 3DR, U.K.

Poems of Love and War, *Akam Poems,* "What She Said," by Kaccipettu Nannakaiyer, "What Her Friend Said to Him," by Kannan, "What She Said" by Kalporu Cirunuraiyar, tr. A.K. Ramanujan; *Puram Poems,* "Harvest of War," by Kappiyarrukkappiyanar; "A King's Last Words, in Jail, before He Takes His Life," by Ceraman Kanaikkal Irumporai; "A Woman and Her Dying Warrior," by Vanparanar, tr. A.K. Ramanujan, from *Poems of Love and War,* edited by A.K. Ramanujan. Copyright © 1985. Reprinted by permission of Columbia University Press.

*The Gatha Saptashati,* "Nineteen quatrains," tr. David Ray from *Not Far from the River: Poems from the Gatha-Saptasati.* Translation copyright © 1993 by David Ray. Reprinted by permission of Copper Canyon Press, P.O. Box 271, Port Townsend, WA 98368.

Vijjika, "Friends," tr. Willis Barnstone from *A Book of Women Poets from Antiquity to Now,* edited by Willis and Aliki Barnstone. Copyright © 1980 by Schocken Books Inc. Reprinted by permission of Schocken Books, published by Pantheon Books, a division of Random House, Inc.

Vijjika, "Ominous Clouds" and "To Her Daughter," tr. Andrew Schelling. Reprinted by permission of the translator.

Amaru, "Ingenue" and "Finesse," tr. V.N. Misra, L. Nathan, and S.H. Vatsyayan from *The Indian Poetic Tradition: An Anthology of Poetry from the Vedic Period to the Seventeenth Century,* edited by S.H. Vatsyayan, V.N. Misra, and L. Nathan. Reprinted by permission of Y.K. Publishers, Agra, India.

Amaru, "Somehow She Got," tr. Andrew Schelling. Reprinted by permission of the translator.

Basavanna, "The Pot Is a God," tr. A.K. Ramanujan from *Speaking of Siva* (Penguin Classics, 1973). Copyright © A.K. Ramanujam, 1973. Reproduced by permission of Penguin Books Ltd.

Excerpts from *Speaking of Siva,* tr. A.K. Ramanujan (Penguin Classics, 1973). Copyright © A.K. Ramanujan, 1973. Reproduced by permission of Penguin Books Ltd.

Jayadeva, excerpts from *The Gitagovinda,* tr. Barbara Stoler Miller from *Love Song of the Dark Lord,* edited by Barbara Stoller Miller. Copyright © 1977. Reprinted by permission of Columbia University Press.

Lalla, "Dance, Lalla, with Nothing On," "Whatever Your Name, Shiva, Vishnu," and "The Soul, Like the Moon," tr. Coleman Barks. Reprinted by permission of the translator.

Kabir, "Between the Conscious and the Unconscious," "I Have Been Thinking of the Difference," and "Are You Looking for Me?" tr. Robert Bly from *The Kabir Book* by Robert Bly. Copyright © 1971, 1977 by Robert Bly. Reprinted by permission of Beacon Press and Robert Bly.

Excerpts from Mirabai, tr. Willis Barnstone and Usha Nilsson from *A Book of Women Poets from Antiquity to Now,* edited by Willis and Aliki Barnstone. Copyright © 1980 by Schocken Books Inc. Reprinted by permission of Schocken Books, published by Pantheon Books, a division of Random House, Inc.

Rabindranath Tagore, "The Sick-Bed," "Recovery," and "On My Birthday," tr. William Radice from *Selected Poems* by Rabindranath Tagore (Penguin Books, 1985). Copyright © William Radice, 1985. Reproduced by permission of Penguin Books Ltd.

Mahatma Gandhi, "Passive Resistance" (*Indian Home Rule*) from *The Gandhi Reader: A Sourcebook of His Life and Writings,* edited by Homer Jack. Reprinted courtesy of Alex Jack.

Sarat Chandra Chatterjee, "Drought," tr. S. Sinha from *Profiles in Faith* (Indus/HarperCollins India, 1997). Reprinted by permission of the publisher.

Premchand, "The Shroud," from *Deliverance and Other Stories,* translated from the Hindi by David Rubin. Reprinted by permission of Penguin Books India Pvt. Ltd. and the translator.

Jibanananda Das, "Grass," tr. Chidananda Das Gupta. Reprinted by permission of Donald Junkins.

R.K. Narayan, "Forty-Five a Month," from *Malgudi Days.* Copyright © 1972, 1975, 1978, 1980, 1981, 1982 by R.K. Narayan. Used by permission of Viking Penguin, a division of Penguin Books USA Inc.

Faiz Ahmed Faiz, "Before You Came" and "Prison Meeting," tr. Naomi Lazard from *The True Subject: Selected Poems of Faiz Ahmed Faiz.* Copyright © 1988 by Princeton University Press. Reprinted by permission of Princeton University Press.

Ruth Prawer Jhabvala, "Picnic with Moonlight and Mangoes" from *How I Became a Holy Mother and Other Stories.* © Ruth Prawer Jhabvala 1976, 1984. Used by permission of Harriet Wasserman Literary Agency, Inc., as agent for author.

Bharati Mukherjee, "Buried Lives" from *The Middleman and Other Stories.* Copyright © 1988 by Bharati Mukherjee. Reprinted by permission of Grove/Atlantic, Inc. and the author.

Salman Rushdie, "The Perforated Sheet" from *Midnight's Children* by Salman Rushdie. Copyright © 1981 by Salman Rushdie. Reprinted by permission of Alfred A. Knopf, Inc. and The Wylie Agency, Inc.

## CHINA

Excerpts from *The Book of Songs,* tr. Tony Barnstone and Chou Ping. Reprinted by permission of the translators.

Confucius, "The Analects," tr. Raymond Dawson from *Confucius: The Analects* (World's Classic, 1993). © Raymond Dawson 1993. Reprinted by permission of Oxford University Press.

Laozi, "The Dao De Jing," tr. Gia-fu Feng and Jane English from *Tao Te Ching: A New Translation* by Lao Tsu. Copyright © 1972 by Gia-fu Feng and Jane English. Reprinted by permission of Alfred A. Knopf, Inc.

Zhuangzi, "The Zhuangzi," tr. Burton Watson from *Chuang Tzu.* Copyright © 1964. Reprinted by permission of Columbia University Press.

Qu Yuan, "The Fisherman," tr. David Hawkes from *The Songs of the South: An Anthology of Ancient Chinese Poems by Qu Yuan and Other Poets* (Penguin Classics, 1985). Copyright © David Hawkes, 1985. Reproduced by permission of Penguin Books Ltd.

Liu Xijun, "Lament," tr. Tony Barnstone and Chou Ping. Reprinted by permission of the translators.

Anonymous Folk Songs from the Music Bureau, "The East Gate" and "A Sad Tune," tr. Tony Barnstone and Chou Ping. Reprinted by permission of the translators.

Lu Ji, "The Art of Writing," tr. Tony Barnstone and Chou Ping. Reprinted by permission of the translators.

Tao Qian, "Return to My Country Home" and poem from the Series "Drinking Wine," tr. Tony Barnstone and Chou Ping. Reprinted by permission of the translators.

Tao Qian, "Preface to the Poem on the Peach Blossom Spring," tr. Burton Watson from *The Columbia Book of Chinese Poetry*. Copyright © 1984. Reprinted by permission of Columbia University Press.

Excerpts from Wang Wei, tr. Tony Barnstone, Willis Barnstone, and Xu Haixin from *Laughing Lost in the Mountains: Poems of Wang Wei*. © 1992 University Press of New England. Reprinted by permission of the publisher.

Excerpts from Li Bai, tr. Willis Barnstone, Tony Barnstone, and Chou Ping. Reprinted by permission of the translators.

Excerpts from Du Fu, tr. Tony Barnstone and Chou Ping. Reprinted by permission of the translators.

Du Fu, "P'eng-ya Road," tr. Sam Hamill from *Facing the Snow: Visions of Tu Fu* (White Pine Press, 1988). Reprinted by permission of Sam Hamill.

Du Fu, "Broken Boat," tr. Stephen Owen from *Traditional Chinese Poetry and Poetics: Omen of the World*. © 1985. Reprinted by permission of The University of Wisconsin Press.

Meng Jiao, "Autumn Meditations," tr. James A. Wilson. Cf. *Shanti: Chinese and Chinese-American Poetry*, Vol. 10, No. 1 (Winter-Spring 1995), edited by Tony Barnstone and Ayame Fukuda. Reprinted by permission of James A. Wilson.

Han Yu, "Mountain Rocks," tr. Tony Barnstone and Chou Ping. Reprinted by permission of the translators.

Xue Tao, "Spring-Gazing Song," tr. Carolyn Kizer from *A Book of Women Poets from Antiquity to Now*, edited by Willis and Aliki Barnstone. Copyright © 1980 by Schocken Books Inc. Reprinted by permission of Schocken Books, published by Pantheon Books, a division of Random House, Inc.

Xue Tao, "Seeing a Friend Off," tr. Tony Barnstone and Chou Ping. Reprinted by permission of the translators.

Li Gongzuo, "The Governor of Southern-Bough," tr. Chou Ping. Reprinted by permission of the translator.

Excerpts from Bo Juyi, tr. Tony Barnstone and Chou Ping. Reprinted by permission of the translators.

Bo Juyi, "At the End of Spring" and "On His Baldness," tr. Arthur Waley from Po Chu-i, *Translations from the Chinese* (1919, 1941). Copyright secured by Alfred A. Knopf. Reprinted by permission of John Robinson for the Arthur Waley Estate.

Bo Juyi, "Light Furs, Fat Horses," tr. Burton Watson from *The Columbia Book of Chinese Poetry*. Copyright © 1984. Reprinted with permission of Columbia University Press.

Excerpts from Liu Zongyuan, tr. Tony Barnstone and Chou Ping. Reprinted by permission of the translators.

Liu Zongyuan, "The Donkey of Guizhou" and "The Snake-Catcher," tr. Chou Ping. Reprinted by permission of the translator.

Yuan Zhen, "When Told Bai Juyi Was Demoted and Sent to Jiangzhou," tr. Tony Barnstone and Chou Ping. Reprinted by permission of the translators.

Sikong Tu, excerpts from *The Twenty-Four Modes of Poetry*, tr. Tony Barnstone and Chou Ping. Reprinted by permission of the translators.

Yu Xuanji, "To Tzu-an" and "Letting My Feelings Out," tr. Geoffrey Waters from *A Book of Women Poets from Antiquity to Now,* edited by Willis and Aliki Barnstone. Copyright © 1980 by Schocken Books Inc. Reprinted by permission of Schocken Books, published by Pantheon Books, a division of Random House, Inc.

Excerpts from Li Yu, tr. Tony Barnstone and Chou Ping. Reprinted by permission of the translators.

Li Yu, "To the Tune of 'Crows Cawing at Night'" and "To the Tune of 'Encountering Joy,'" tr. Brendan Connell and Marty Jiang. Reprinted by permission of the translators.

Mei Yaochen, "Sorrow," tr. Kenneth Rexroth from *One Hundred Poems from the Chinese.* Copyright © 1971 by Kenneth Rexroth. Reprinted by permission of New Directions Publishing Corp.

Ouyang Xiu, "You Cannot Hold It," tr. J.P Seaton from *Love and Time: The Poems of Ou-Yang Hsiu.* Translation © 1989 by J.P. Seaton. Reprinted by permission of Copper Canyon Press, P.O. Box 271, Port Townsend, WA 98368.

Ouyang Xiu, "The Autumn Sound," tr. Ch'u Chai and Winberg Chai from *A Treasury of Chinese Literature: A New Prose Anthology Including Fiction and Drama* (New York: Appleton-Century, 1965). Reprinted by permission of Winberg Chai.

Excerpts from Su Dongpo, tr. Tony Barnstone and Chou Ping. Reprinted by permission of the translators.

Excerpts from Li Qingzhao, tr. Tony Barnstone and Chou Ping. Reprinted by permission of the translators.

Excerpts from *Poets' Jade Dust,* tr. Tony Barnstone and Chou Ping. Reprinted by permission of the translators.

Excerpts from Ma Zhiyuan, tr. Tony Barnstone and Chou Ping. Reprinted by permission of the translators.

Ma Zhiyuan "Autumn Moon on the Tung T'ing Lake," tr. Gary Gachard and C.H. Kwock from *Renditions* Nos. 21 & 22 (Spring & Autumn 1984). Hong Kong: Research Centre for Translation of the Chinese University of Hong Kong, p. 222. Reprinted by permission.

Shi Naian and Luo Guanzhong, excerpt from *Outlaws of the Marsh,* tr. Sidney Shapiro from *Outlaws of the Marsh.* Reprinted by permission of Indiana University Press.

Wu Chengen, excerpt tr. Arthur Waley from *Monkey: A Folk Novel of China* by Wu Ch'eng-en. Copyright © 1943 by John Day Company. Used by permission of Grove/Atlantic, Inc.

Pu Songling, "The Cricket," tr. Yang Xianyi and Gladys Yang from *Selected Tales of Liao Zhai* by Pu Songling. Reprinted by permission of China Books and Periodicals, Inc., 2929 24th Street, San Francisco, CA 94110, Phone: 415/282-2994, Fax: 415/282-0994. Catalog available.

Yuan Mei, Four Zen Poems, tr. J.P. Seaton from *I Don't Bow to Buddhas,* © 1997 by J.P. Seaton, reprinted by permission of Copper Canyon Press, P.O. Box 271, Port Townsend, WA 98368.

Li Ruzhen, excerpt tr. Lin Tai-yi from *Flowers in the Mirror* by Li Ju-chen. Reprinted by permission of Peter Owen Ltd., Publishers.

Cao Xueqin, excerpt from Chapter 82, tr. John Minford from *Dream of the Red Chamber:* Vol. 4: "The Debt of Tears" (Penguin Classics, 1982). Copyright © John Minford, 1982. Reprinted by permission of Penguin Books Ltd.

Excerpts from Mao Zedong, tr. Willis Barnstone and Ko Ching-Po. Copyright Willis Barnstone. Reprinted by permission.

Wen Yiduo, "Miracle," tr. Arthur Sze; first appeared in *Two Ravens* (Tooth of Time Books, 1984). Copyright © Arthur Sze, 1984. Reprinted by permission of the translator.

Lao She, "Filling a Prescription," tr. Don J. Cohn from *Selected Tales of Liao Zhai* by Pu Songling, translated by Yang Xianyi and Gladys Yang. Reprinted by permission of China

Books and Periodicals, Inc., 2929 24th Street, San Francisco, CA 94110, Phone: 415/282-2994, Fax: 415/282-0994. Catalog available.

Wang Meng, "Anecdotes of Minister Maimaiti: A Uygur Man's Black Humor," tr. Qinyun Wu from *Return Trip Tango* by Frank MacShane and Lori M. Carlson. Copyright © 1992. Reprinted by permission of Columbia University Press.

Chen Rong, "Regarding the Problem of Newborn Piglets in Winter," tr. Chun-Ye Shih from *The Rose Colored Dinner* (Hong Kong: Joint Publishing [H.K.] Co. Ltd., 1988). Copyright © by the publisher, transferred to Shen Rong. Reprinted by permission of Shen Rong.

Bei Dao, "Sweet Tangerines," tr. James A. Wilson from *August Sleepwalker.* Copyright © 1988 by Bei Dao. Reprinted by permission of New Directions Publishing Corp.

Bei Dao, "Coming Home at Night," tr. Bonnie McDougall and Chen Maiping from *Old Snow.* Copyright © 1991 by Bei Dao. Reprinted by permission of New Directions Publishing Corp.

Bei Dao, "Night: Theme and Variations," tr. Tony Barnstone and Newton Liu from *Old Snow.* Copyright © 1991 by Bei Dao. Reprinted by permission of New Directions Publishing Corp.

Bei Dao, "Beyond," tr. Donald Finkel and Xueliang Chen from *Old Snow.* Copyright © 1991 by Bei Dao. Reprinted by permission of New Directions Publishing Corp.

Shu Ting, "Two or Three Incidents Recollected," tr. Chou Ping from *Out of the Howling Storm: The New Chinese Poetry,* edited by Tony Barnstone. © 1993 by Wesleyan University, used by permission of University Press of New England.

Liang Heng and Judith Shapiro, excerpts from *Son of the Revolution.* Copyright © 1983 by Liang Heng and Judith Shapiro. Reprinted by permission of Alfred A. Knopf, Inc.

Yang Lian, "An Ancient Children's Tale," tr. Tony Barnstone and Newton Liu from *Out of the Howling Storm: The New Chinese Poetry,* edited by Tony Barnstone. © 1993 by Wesleyan University, used by permission of University Press of New England.

Ha Jin, "My Best Soldier," published in *Ocean of Words: Army Stories* by Ha Jin (Zoland Books, 1996). Reprinted by permission of Ha Jin.

Chou Ping, "Ways of Looking at a Poet," from *Out of the Howling Storm: The New Chinese Poetry,* edited by Tony Barnstone. © 1993 by Wesleyan University, used by permission of University Press of New England.

Tang Yaping, excerpt from *Black Desert Suite,* tr. Tony Barnstone and Newton Liu from *Out of the Howling Storm: The New Chinese Poetry,* edited by Tony Barnstone. © 1993 by Wesleyan University, used by permission of University Press of New England.

## JAPAN

Empress Iwanohime, excerpts from *Missing Emperor Nintoku,* tr. Ayame Fukuda. Reprinted by permission of the translator.

Empress Jito, "On the Death of the Emperor Temmu," tr. Kenneth Rexroth and Ikuko Atsumi, from *Women Poets of Japan.* Copyright © 1977 by Kenneth Rexroth and Ikuko Atsumi. Reprinted by permission of New Directions Publishing Corp.

Kakinomoto Hitomaro, "Poem by Kakinomoto Hitomaro as He Shed Tears of Blood in His Grief following the Death of His Wife" and "Poem by Kakinomoto Hitomaro at the Time of the Temporary Enshrinement of Prince Takechi at Kinoe," tr. Ian Hideo Levy from *Ten Thousand Leaves.* Copyright © 1981 by Princeton University Press. Reprinted by permission of Princeton University Press.

The Priest Mansei, "What Shall I Compare," tr. Ayame Fukuda. Reprinted by permission of the translator.

Lady Ki, "Poem Sent to a Friend with a Gift" and "Poem Sent by Lady Ki to Otomo Yakamochi in Response to His," tr. Ayame Fukuda. Reprinted by permission of the translator.

Otomo Yakamochi, "In a Dream" and "Wild Geese Cry," tr. Ayame Fukuda. Reprinted by permission of the translator.

Lady Kasa, *Poems Sent to Otomo Yakamochi by Lady Kasa,* "My Keepsake," tr. Burton Watson from *The Country of Eight Islands* by Hiroaki Sato and Burton Watson. Copyright © 1981 by Hiroaki Sato and Burton Watson. Used by permission of Doubleday, a division of Bantam Doubleday Dell Publishing Group, Inc.

Ki no Tsurayuki, from *Preface to the Kokinshu,* "Five Tanka," tr. Burton Watson from *The Country of Eight Islands* by Hiroaki Sato and Burton Watson. Copyright © 1981 by Hiroaki Sato and Burton Watson. Used by permission of Doubleday, a division of Bantam Doubleday Dell Publishing Group, Inc.

Ono no Komachi, "Doesn't He Realize," "I Fell Asleep Thinking of Him," and "He Does Not Come," tr. Kenneth Rexroth and Ikuko Atsumi, from *Women Poets of Japan.* Copyright © 1977 by Kenneth Rexroth and Ikuko Atsumi. Reprinted by permission of New Directions Publishing Corp.

Ono no Komachi, "I Am So Lonely," tr. Ayame Fukuda and Tony Barnstone. Reprinted by permission of the translators.

Ono no Komachi, "The Autumn Night" and "How Invisibly," tr. Jane Hirshfield and Mariko Aratani from *The Ink Dark Moon* by Jane Hirshfield and Mariko Aratani. Copyright © 1990 by Jane Hirshfield and Mariko Aratani. Reprinted by permission of Vintage Books, a division of Random House, Inc.

Lady Ise, "Like a Ravaged Sea," tr. Etsuko Terasaki and Irma Brandies from *A Book of Women Poets from Antiquity to Now,* edited by Willis and Aliki Barnstone. Copyright © 1980 by Schocken Books Inc. Reprinted by permission of Schocken Books, published by Pantheon Books, a division of Random House, Inc.

*The Tales of Ise,* tr. Helen Craig McCullough from *The Tales of Ise,* translated, with an Introduction and Notes, by Helen Craig McCullough. © 1986 by the Board of Trustees of the Leland Stanford Junior University. Reprinted by permission of Stanford University Press.

Sei Shonagon, excerpts from *The Pillow Book of Sei Shonagon,* tr. Ivan Morris. Copyright © 1991 by Columbia University Press. Reprinted by permission of the publisher.

Izumi Shikibu, "In This World," "I Cannot Say," "This Heart," and "Mourning Naishi," tr. Jane Hirshfield and Mariko Aratani from *The Ink Dark Moon* by Jane Hirshfield and Mariko Aratani. Copyright © 1990 by Jane Hirshfield and Mariko Aratani. Reprinted by permission of Vintage, Books, a division of Random House, Inc.

Izumi Shikibu, "On Nights When Hail," "Since That Night," "You Wear the Face," "When You Broke from Me," "If You Have No Time," "If You Love Me," "On This Winter Night," and "Here in This World," tr. Willis Barnstone from *A Book of Women Poets from Antiquity to Now,* edited by Willis and Aliki Barnstone. Copyright © 1980 by Schocken Books Inc. Reprinted by permission of Schocken Books, published by Pantheon Books, a division of Random House, Inc.

Murasaki Shikibu, "The Broom-Tree" from *The Tale of Genji* by Lady Murasaki, tr. Arthur Waley (Tokyo: Charles C. Tuttle, 1971). Copyright Alison Waley. Reprinted by permission of John Robinson for the Estate of Arthur Waley.

Saigyo, excerpts from *Poems of a Mountain Home* by Saigyo, tr. Burton Watson. Copyright © 1991. Reprinted by permission of Columbia University Press.

The Middle Councilor of the Riverbank, "The Lady Who Admired Vermin" from *The Riverside Counselor's Stories: Vernacular Fiction of Late Heian Japan,* translated, with an Introduction and Notes, by Robert L. Backus. © 1985 by the Board of Trustees of the Leland Stanford Junior University. Reprinted by permission of Stanford University Press.

"How an Invisible Man Regained Corporeal Form through Kannon's Aid," tr. Marian Ury from *Tales of Time Now Past: Sixty-Two Stories from a Medieval Japanese Collection* (Berkeley: University of California Press, 1979). Reprinted by permission of Marian Ury.

Excerpts from *The Tale of the Heike,* translated, with an Introduction, by Helen Craig McCullough. © 1988 by the Board of Trustees of the Leland Stanford Junior University. Reprinted by permission of Stanford University Press.

Kamo no Chomei, "An Account of My Hermitage" tr. Helen Craig McCullough from *Classical Japanese Prose: An Anthology,* compiled and edited by Helen Craig McCullough. © 1990 by the Board of Trustees of the Leland Stanford Junior University. Reprinted by permission of Stanford University Press.

Dogen, tr. Brian Unger and Kazuaki Tanahashi, excerpts from *Moon in a Dewdrop: Writings of Zen Master Dogen,* edited by Kazuaki Tanahashi. Translation copyright © 1985 by the San Francisco Zen Center. Reprinted by permission of North Point Press, a division of Farrar, Straus & Giroux, Inc.

Zen stories from *Sand and Pebbles,* from *Zen Flesh, Zen Bones* by Nyogen Senzaki and Paul Reps, translated by Paul Reps. © 1989. Reprinted by permission of Charles E. Tuttle Co., Inc., Rutland, Vermont and Tokyo, Japan.

Muso Soseki, tr. W.S. Merwin and Soiku Shigematsu from *Muso Soseki (1275–1351).* Reprinted by permission of the translators.

Kenko, excerpt from *Essays in Idleness; the Tsurezuregusa of Kenko,* tr. Donald Keene. Copyright © 1967. Reprinted by permission of Columbia University Press.

Zeami Motokiyo, "Semimaru," tr. Susan Matisoff from *Twenty Plays of the No Theatre,* translated by Donald Keene. Copyright © 1970. Reprinted by permission of Columbia University Press.

Zeami Motokiyo, "The One Mind Linking All Powers," tr. Donald Keene from *Anthology of Japanese Literature,* edited by Donald Keene. Copyright © 1955 by Grove Press, Inc. Reprinted by permission of Grove/Atlantic, Inc.

Ihara Saikaku, "A Beauty of Easy Virtue," tr. Ivan Morris from *The Life of an Amorous Woman* in *The Life of an Amorous Woman and Other Writings.* Copyright © 1963 by New Directions Publishing Corp. Reprinted by permission of New Directions Publishing Corp.

Matsuo Basho, excerpt from *Narrow Road to the Interior,* tr. Sam Hamill. © 1991. Reprinted by arrangement with Shambhala Publications, Inc., 300 Massachusetts Ave., Boston, MA 02115.

Matsuo Basho and His School, from "Throughout the Town," tr. Earl Miner and Hiroko Odagiri from *The Monkey's Straw Raincoat* by Earl Miner and Hiroko Odagiri. Reprinted by permission of Earl Miner.

Chikamatsu Monzaemon, "The Love Suicides at Amijima" and "Chikamatsu on the Art of the Puppet Stage," tr. Donald Keene from *Four Major Plays of Chikamatsu.* Copyright © 1961. Reprinted by permission of Columbia University Press.

Yosa Buson, "Three Haiku," tr. Ayame Fukuda. Reprinted by permission of the translator.

Ryokan, "Who Says My Poem Is a Poem?," "The New Pond," and "For an Old Man, a Dream Is Easily Broken," tr. Dennis Maloney and Hide Oshiro from *Between the Floating Mist: Poems of Ryokan* (Buffalo, NY: Springhouse Editions, an imprint of White Pine Press, Fredonia, NY, 1992). Reprinted by permission of White Pine Press.

Ryokan, "Shaggy Hair Past the Ears" and "The Thief Left It Behind," tr. John Stevens from *One Robe One Bowl: The Zen Poetry of Ryokan,* translated by John Stevens. Reprinted by permission of Weatherill, Publishers.

Issa, "Three Haiku," tr. Ayame Fukuda. Reprinted by permission of the translator.

Natsume Soseki, "The Seventh Night," tr. Aiko Ito and Graeme Wilson from *Ten Nights of Dream, Hearing Things, the Heredity of Taste* by Natsume Soseki. © 1974. Published by Charles E. Tuttle Co., Inc., Rutland, Vermont and Tokyo, Japan.

Shiki, "Thirteen Haiku," tr. Burton Watson from *The Country of Eight Islands* by Hiroaki Sato and Burton Watson. Copyright © 1981 by Hiroaki Sato and Burton Watson. Used by permission of Doubleday, a division of Bantam Doubleday Dell Publishing Group, Inc.

Yosano Akiko, excerpts from *Tangled Hair,* tr. Sanford Goldstein and Seishi Shinoda. Reprinted by permission of Charles E. Tuttle Co., Inc., Tokyo.

Tanizaki Junichiro, "The Tattooer," tr. Howard Hibbet from *Seven Japanese Tales.* Copyright © 1963 and renewed 1991 by Alfred A. Knopf, Inc. Reprinted by permission of Alfred A. Knopf, Inc.

Akutagawa Ryunosuke, "Rashomon," tr. Takashi Kojima from *Rashomon and Other Stories.* Copyright 1952 by Charles E. Tuttle Co. English translation copyright 1952 by Liveright Publishing Corporation. Reprinted by permission of Liveright Publishing Corporation.

Kawabata Yasunari, "The Mole," tr. Edward Seidensticker from *Modern Japanese Literature,* edited by Donald Keene. Copyirght © 1956 by Grove Press, Inc. Used by permission of Grove/Atlantic, Inc.

Kawabata Yasunari, "Eggs," tr. J. Martin Holman from *Palm-of-the-Hand Stories.* Translation copyright © 1988 by Lane Dunlop and J. Martin Holman. Reprinted by permission of North Point Press, a division of Farrar, Straus & Giroux, Inc.

Nakamoto Takako, "The Female Bell-Cricket," tr. Yukiko Tanaka from *To Live and To Write: Selections by Japanese Women Writers, 1913–1938,* edited by Yukiko Tanaka. Reprinted by permission of Seal Press.

Sakaki Nanao, "Future Knows" and "Small People," tr. Sakaki Nanao. © Nanao Sakaki, 1989. Reprinted by permission.

Tamura Ryuichi, "Green Conceptual Body" and "Human House," tr. Christopher Drake from *A Play of Mirrors: Eight Major Poets of Modern Japan* (Rochester, MI: Katydid Books, 1987). Reprinted by permission of Thomas Fitzsimmons.

Abe Kobo, "The Magic Chalk," tr. Alison Kibrick from *Other Voices, Other Vistas: Short Stories from Africa, China, India, Japan and Latin America,* edited by Barbara Solomon. Copyright © 1950 by Kobo Abe in Japan. Copyright © 1982 in English translation by Alison Kibrick. Reprinted by permission of International Creative Management, Inc.

Mishima Yukio, "Martyrdom (*Junkyo*)," tr. John Bester. © 1948 Iichiro Hiraoka, from *Acts of Worship: Seven Stories* by Yukio Mishima. Published by Kodansha International Ltd. The anthology copyright © 1989 by Kodansha International Ltd. Reprinted by permission. All rights reserved.

Shiraishi Kazuko, "The Man Root," from *Women Poets of Japan.* Copyright © 1977 by Kenneth Rexroth and Ikuko Atsumi. Reprinted by permission of New Directions Publishing Corp.

Tanikawa Shuntaro, "Museum," "Growth," and "Ten Yen Coin," tr. Harold Wright. Reprinted by permission of Bonnie R. Crown.

Oe Kenzaburo, "Aghwee the Sky Monster," tr. John Nathan from *Teach Us to Outgrow Our Madness.* Copyright © 1977 by John Nathan. Used by permission of Grove/Atlantic, Inc.

Murakami Haruki, from *Hard-Boiled Wonderland and the End of the World,* "Elevator, Silence, Overweight," tr. Alfred Birnbaum. Published by Kodansha International Ltd. Copyright © 1991 by Kodansha International Ltd. Reprinted by permission. All rights reserved.

## SECTION 2: NEAR EAST AND NORTH AFRICA (THE BRIDGE)

Enheduanna, tr. Aliki Barnstone and Willis Barnstone, excerpts from *A Book of Women Poets from Antiquity to Now,* edited by Willis and Aliki Barnstone. Copyright © 1980 by Schocken Books Inc. Reprinted by permission of Schocken Books, published by Pantheon Books, a division of Random House, Inc.

"Adapa the Man," tr. N. K. Sandars, from *Poems of Heaven and Hell from Ancient Mesopotamia,* translated by N. K. Sandars (Penguin Classics, 1971). Copyright © N. K. Sandars, 1971. Reproduced by permission of Penguin Books Ltd.

"The Shipwrecked Sailor" and "The Tale of the Doomed Prince," tr. Edward F. Wente, Jr., from *The Literature of Ancient Egypt: An Anthology of Stories, Instructions, and Poetry,* edited with an Introduction by William Kelly Simpson, pp. 50–55, 85–91. Copyright 1972. Reprinted by permission of Yale University Press.

*The Book of the Dead,* "Spell 26" and "Spell 53," tr. Raymond O. Faulkner, from *Ancient Egyptian Book of the Dead,* edited by Carol Andrews. Copyright the Trustees of the British Museum, British Museum Press. Reprinted by permission of British Museum Press.

From "Pleasant Songs of the Sweetheart Who Meets You in the Fields," from "Garden Songs," and "Love Lyrics," tr. Ezra Pound and Noel Stock. By anonymous, from *Love Poems of Ancient Egypt,* translated by Noel Stock. Copyright © 1962 by Noel Stock. Reprinted by permission of New Directions Publishing Corp.

From Job, *Revised Standard Version of the Bible,* Old Testament Section. Copyright 1952 by Division of Christian Education of the National Council of Churches of Christ in the USA. Used by permission. All rights reserved.

"Ecclesiastes, or the Preacher," from *Revised Standard Version of the Bible,* Old Testament Section. Copyright 1952 by Division of Christian Education of the National Council of Churches of Christ in the USA. Used by permission. All rights reserved.

From Isaiah, *Revised Standard Version of the Bible,* Old Testament Section. Copyright 1952 by Division of Christian Education of the National Council of Churches of Christ in the USA. Used by permission. All rights reserved.

From Daniel, *Revised Standard Version of the Bible,* Old Testament Section. Copyright 1952 by Division of Christian Education of the National Council of Churches of Christ in the USA. Used by permission. All rights reserved.

*Jewish Apocrypha,* "Susanna" and "Bel and the Dragon," from *New Revised Standard Version Apocryphal/Deuterocanonical Books.* Copyright 1989 by Division of Christian Education of the National Council of the Churches of Christ in the USA. Used by permission. All rights reserved.

From Paul, *First Letter to the Corinthians, New Revised Standard Version of the Bible.* Copyright 1989 by Division of Christian Education of the National Council of the Churches of Christ in the USA. Used by permission. All rights reserved.

Intertestament from *The Book of Jubilees,* tr. R. H. Charles, adapted by Willis Barnstone from "The Book of Jubilees," translated by R. H. Charles, in *The Other Bible* by Willis Barnstone, editor. Copyright © 1984 by Willis Barnstone. Used by permission of Bantam Books, a division of Bantam Doubleday Dell Publishing Group, Inc.

*The Gospel of Thomas,* tr. Helmut Koester from *The Nag Hammadi Library in English,* 3rd, completely revised edition by James M. Robinson, Gen. Ed. Copyright © 1988 by E. J. Brill, Leiden, The Netherlands. Reprinted by permission of HarperCollins Publishers, Inc.

*On the Origin of the World,* "The Raising of Adam from Mud by Eve" and "The Rape of Eve by the Prime Ruler (God) and by His Angels," tr. Hans-Gebhard Bethge and Orval S. Wintermute from *The Nag Hammadi Library in English,* 3rd, completely revised edition by James M. Robinson, Gen. Ed. Copyright © 1988 by E. J. Brill, Leiden, The Netherlands. Reprinted by permission of HarperCollins Publishers, Inc.

Plotinus, "The Ascent to Union with the One" from "The Enneads" tr. A. H. Armstrong from *Plotinus* by A. H. Armstrong. Copyright 1953. Reprinted by permission of Routledge, London.

Al-Khansa, "Elegy for Her Brother Sakhr" and "Sleepless," tr. Willis Barnstone from *A Book of Women Poets from Antiquity to Now,* edited by Willis and Aliki Barnstone. Copyright © 1980 by Schocken Books Inc. Reprinted by permission of Schocken Books, published by Pantheon Books, a division of Random House, Inc.

Muallaqat, from "The Ode of Tarafa" and from "The Ode of Imru al-Quays," tr. Tony Barnstone and Beatrice Gruendler. Reprinted by permission of the translators.

Excerpts from the Quran, translated by N. J. Dawood (Penguin Classics 1956, Fifth revised edition 1990). Copyright © N. J. Dawood 1956, 1959, 1965, 1968, 1974, 1990. Reprinted by permission of Penguin Books Ltd.

Rabia the Mystic, "O My Lord, the Stars Glitter and the Eyes of Men Are Closed," tr. Willis Barnstone from *A Book of Women Poets from Antiquity to Now,* edited by Willis and Aliki Barnstone. Copyright © 1980 by Schocken Books Inc. Reprinted by permission of Schocken Books, published by Pantheon Books, a division of Random House, Inc.

Rabia the Mystic, "Miracle Story" and "How Long Will You Keep Pounding," tr. Charles Upton from *Doorkeeper of the Heart*. Reprinted by permission of Threshold Books, 139 Main St., Brattleboro, VT 05301.

Abu Nuwas, "Drunkenness after Drunkenness," tr. Richard Serrano. Reprinted by permission of the translator.

From *The Thousand and One Nights*, "The Tale of the Fisherman and the Genie," "The Tale of the Vizier and the Sage Duban," "The Tale of King Sinbad and His Falcon," "The Tale of the Husband and the Parrot," "The Tale of the Prince and the Ogress," and "The Tale of the Enchanted Prince," tr. Richard Burton, adapted by Emma Varesio. Reprinted by permission of Emma Varesio.

Usamah ibn Munqidh, from "The Book of Reflections," tr. Phillip K. Hitti from *An Arab-Syrian Gentleman and Warrior in the Period of the Crusades: Memoirs of Usamah Ibn-Munqidh*, translated by Phillip K. Hitti. Copyirght © 1987 by Princeton University Press. Reprinted by permission of Princeton University Press.

Ferdowsi, from *The Epic of the Kings*, "The Reign of Jamshid" and "Faridun," tr. Ruben Levy, revised by Amin Banani from *The Epic of the Kings* by Ferdowsi, translated by Reuben Levy, Persian Heritage Series, Ehsan Yarshater, General Editor (University of Chicago Press, 1967), pp. 9–16, 17–25. Reprinted by permission of Ehsan Yarshater.

Omar Khayyam, *The Rubaiyat*, tr. Peter Avery and John Heath-Stubbs from *The Ruba'iyat of Omar Khayyam*, translated by Peter Avery and John Heath-Stubbs (Allen Lane, 1979). Translation copyright © Peter Avery and John Heath-Stubbs, 1979. Reprinted by permission of Penguin Books Ltd.

Attar, excerpts from *The Conference of the Birds*, tr. Afkham Darbandi and Dick Davis from *The Conference of the Birds* by Farid ud-Din Attar, translated by Afkham Darbandi and Dick Davis (Penguin Classics, 1984). Copyright © Afkham Darbandi and Dick Davis, 1984. Reproduced by permission of Penguin Books Ltd.

Rumi, "Love's Body," "A New Promise," and "Caring for My Lover," tr. Tony Barnstone, Willis Barnstone, and Reza Baraheni. Reprinted by permission of the translators.

Rumi, "The New Rule," "The Clear Bead at the Center," "Someone Who Goes with Half a Loaf of Bread," and "Who Says Words with My Mouth," tr. John Moyne and Coleman Barks from *Open Secret*. Reprinted by permission of Threshold Books, 139 Main St., Brattleboro, VT 05301.

Sadi, from *The Rose Garden* (The Gulistan), tr. Edward Rehatsek, adapted Tony Barnstone. Reprinted by permission of Pierre Grange.

Traditional Song, "Be Happy," tr. Willis Barnstone from *A Book of Women Poets from Antiquity to Now*, edited by Willis and Aliki Barnstone. Copyright © 1980 by Schocken Books Inc. Reprinted by permission of Schocken Books, published by Pantheon Books, a division of Random House, Inc.

Constantine Cavafy, "The Window," "Desires," and "The God Abandons Antony," tr. Aliki Barnstone and Willis Barnstone. Reprinted by permission of the translators.

S. Y. Agnon, "The Doctor's Divorce," tr. Robert Alter from *Twenty-One Stories* by S. Y. Agnon, edited by Nahum N. Glatzer. Coyright © 1970 by Schocken Books Inc. Reprinted by permission of Schocken Books, distributed by Pantheon Books, a division of Random House, Inc.

Nazim Hikmet, "Since I Was Thrown Inside," tr. Randy Blasing and Mutla Konuk from *New Writing from the Middle East*, edited with an Introduction and Commentary by Leo Hamalian and John D. Yohannan (New American Library, 1978). Reprinted by permission of Balkin Agency, agent for the editors.

Naguib Mahfouz, "Zaabalawi," tr. Denys Johnson-Davies from *The Time and the Place and Other Stories*, translated by Denys Johnson-Davies. Translation copyright © 1967 by Denys Johnson-Davies. Used by permission of Doubleday, a division of Bantam Doubleday Dell Publishing Group, Inc.

Mririda Naït Attik, "Mririda," and "The Bad Lover," tr. Daniel Halpern and Paula Paley from *The Songs of Mririda: Courtesan of the High Atlas,* translated by Daniel Halpern and Paula Paley. Copyright 1974. Reprinted by permission of Unicorn Press, Inc.

Yashar Kemal, "A Dirty Story," from *Anatolian Tales,* translated by Thilda Kemal. Reprinted by permission of Writers and Readers.

Nizar Qabbani, "Bread, Hashish, and Moon," from *Bread, Hashish, and Moon: Four Modern Arab Poets,* translated by Ben Bennani. Copyright 1982. Reprinted by permission of Unicorn Press, Inc.

Yehuda Amichai, excerpts from *The Selected Poetry of Yehuda Amichai* (revised and expanded edition), edited and translated by Chana Bloch and Stephen Mitchell (Berkeley: University of California Press, 1996).

Badr Shakir Al-Sayyab, "Song in August," tr. Lena Jayyusi and Christopher Middleton from *Modern Arabic Poetry: An Anthology* by S. Jayyusi. Copyright © 1987. Reprinted by permission of Columbia University Press.

Yusuf Idris, "House of Flesh," tr. Denys Johnson-Davies from *Egyptian Short Stories,* selected and edited by Denys Johnson-Davies. Copyright © 1996 by Lynne Rienner Publishers, Inc. Copyright © in selection and translation by Denys Johnson-Davies 1978. Reprinted by permission of Lynne Rienner Publishers, Inc.

Joyce Mansour, "In the Gloom on the Left" and "A Mango," from *Prose & Poésie: Oeuvre Complète* (Arles: Actes Sud, 1991). English translation of "In the Gloom on the Left" published in *APR,* Vol. 123.4, 1994, © 1992 Molly Bendall. English translation of "A Mango" published in *Volt,* No. 1, 1993, © 1993 Molly Bendall. Reprinted by permission of Molly Bendall and Samir Mansour.

Adunis, from "The Desert: The Diary of Beirut under Siege," 1982, by Aldonis (Ali Ahmed Sa'id), in *Modern Poetry of the Arab World,* translated and edited by Abdullah al-Udhari (Penguin Books, 1986). Copyright © Abdullah al-Udhari, 1986. Reprinted by permission of Penguin Books Ltd.

Dan Pagis, "End of the Questionnaire" and "Written in Pencil in the Sealed Railway-Car" from *Variable Directions: The Selected Poetry of Dan Pagis,* translated by Stephen Mitchell (San Francisco: North Point Press, 1989). Reprinted by permission of Stephen Mitchell.

Nawal Al-Saadawi, "The Thirst," tr. J. Ryder, published in *Translation,* Vol. XI (Fall 1983). Reprinted by permission of Nawal Al-Saadawi.

Forough Farokhzad, "Window" and "The Windup Doll," tr. Leora Baude and Ali Shashaani. Reprinted by permission of the translators.

Reza Baraheni, "Autumn in Tehran." Reprinted by permission of Reza Baraheni.

Dahlia Ravikovitch, "Clockwork Doll," from *The Window: New and Selected Poems by Dahlia Ravikovitch,* translated and edited by Chana Bloch and Ariel Bloch (Sheep Meadow Press, 1989). Reprinted by permission of Chana Bloch.

Haydar Haydar, "The Ants and the Qat," tr. Michel G. Azrak, revised by M. J. L. Young from *Modern Syrian Short Stories* (Three Continents Press, 1988). Reprinted by permission of the publisher.

Mohamed el-Bisatie, "A Conversation from the Third Floor," tr. Denys Johnson-Davies from *A Last Glass of Tea and Other Stories,* translated by Denys Johnson-Davies. English-language translation copyright © 1994, 1998 by Denys Johnson-Davies. Arabic text copyright © 1970, 1979, 1988, 1992, 1993 by Mohamed El-Bisatie. Used by permission of Lynne Rienner Publishers, Inc.

Amos Oz, "Nomad and Viper," tr. Amos Oz from *Where the Jackals Howl and Other Stories.* English translation copyright © 1973 by Amos Oz. Reprinted by permission of Harcourt Brace & Company.

Mohammed Mrabet, "The Canebrake," from *M'Hashish,* translated by Paul Bowles. Copyright © 1969 by Paul Bowles. Reprinted by permission of City Lights Books.

## SECTION 3: SUB-SAHARA AFRICA

### THE PREMODERN PERIOD

### THE MODERN PERIOD

*Black Africa,* edited by Wole Soyinka, Secker & Warburg, 1975). Reprinted by permission of Clive Wake and John Reed.

Birago Diop, "N'Gor Niébé," tr. Eileen Julien and Eunice C. Smith from *Les Contes d'Amadou Koumba* by Birago Diop (Paris: Présence Africaine, 1961). Reprinted by permission of Présence Africaine Editions and Eileen Julien.

A. C. Jordan, "The King of Waters," tr. and retold by author from Xhosa in *Tales from Southern Africa* by A. C. Jordan. © 1973 Regents of the University of California. Reprinted by permission of University of California Press.

Doris Lessing, "Out of the Fountain" from *The Story of a Non-Marrying Man.* Coypright © 1972 Doris Lessing. Reproduced by kind permission of Jonathan Clowes Ltd., London, on behalf of Peter Lessing.

Peter Abrahams, "Lonesome," from *Dark Testament* by Peter Abrahams. Copyright 1942. Reprinted by permission of HarperCollins Ltd.

Es'kia Mphahlele, "The Master of Doorvlei," from *African Short Stories* by J. De Grandsaigne. Copyright © J. De Grandsaigne. Reprinted by permission of St. Martin's Press, Inc. and Es'kia Mphahlele.

Amos Tutuola, "How I Got a Wife," from *The Palm-Wine Drinkard and His Dead Palm-Wine Tapster in the Dead's Town.* Copyright © 1952, 1953 by George Braziller. Used by permission of Grove / Atlantic, Inc. and Faber & Faber Ltd.

Agostinho Neto, "Kinaxixi," tr. W. S. Merwin from *Selected Translations 1948–1968* (New York: Atheneum, 1968). Copyright 1948, 1949, 1950, 1954, © 1956, 1957, 1958, 1959, 1960, 1961, 1962, 1965, 1966, 1967, 1968 by W. S. Merwin. Reprinted by permission of Georges Borchardt, Inc. for W. S. Merwin.

Nadine Gordimer, "Amnesty," from *Jump and Other Stories* by Nadine Gordimer. Copyright © 1991 by Felix Licensing, B.V. Reprinted by permission of Farrar, Straus & Giroux, Inc. and Penguin Books Canada Ltd.

Dennis Brutus, "Letter #18," from *Letters to Martha and Other Poems from a South African Prison, 1968.* Reprinted by permission of Dennis Brutus.

Alex La Guma, "Blankets," from *Walk in the Night.* Reprinted by permission of Northwestern University Press.

Camara Laye, from *The Dark Child,* tr. James Kirkup and Ernest Jones. Copyright © 1954 and copyright renewed © 1982 by Camara Laye. Reprinted by permission of Hill and Wang, a division of Farrar, Straus & Giroux, Inc.

From *Houseboy* by Ferdinand Oyono; translated by John Reed. © Julliard, 1969. Reprinted by permission of Heinemann Publishers (Oxford) Ltd. and Editions Julliard, Paris.

Chinua Achebe, "The Madman." Reprinted by permission of Chinua Achebe.

Richard Rive, "Rain," from *Advance, Retreat.* Copyright © Richard Rive. Reprinted by permission of St. Martin's Press, Inc.

Tchicaya U Tam'si, "The Flight of the Vampire," from *Negritude: Black Poetry from Africa and the Caribbean,* edited and translated by Norman R. Shapiro. Copyright © 1970 by Norman R. Shapiro. Reprinted by permission of October House, Publishers, and Norman R. Shapiro.

Tchicaya U Tam'si, "Agony," from *Selected Poems of Tchicaya U Tam'si,* translated by Gerald Moore (Heinemann Educational Books, 1970). Selection and translation © Gerald Moore 1970. Reprinted by permission of Gerald Moore.

Ingrid Jonker, "I Am with Those," from *Selected Poems,* translated by Jack Cope and William Plomer. Copyright 1968 by the Ingrid Jonker Trust. Reprinted by permission of Human & Rousseau, Publishers.

Wole Soyinka, "The Trials of Brother Jero," from *Collected Plays 2* by Wole Soyinka. © Oxford University Press 1964. Reprinted by permission of Oxford University Press.

José Luandino Vieira, "Song for Luanda," from *Poems from Angola,* translated by Michael Wolfers (Heinemann Educational Books, 1979). Translation copyright Michael Wolfers. Reprinted by permission of Michael Wolfers.

# SECTION 4: PRECOLUMBIAN AMERICA, LATIN AMERICA, AND CARIBBEAN

## NATIVE AMERICAN LITERATURE OF PRECOLUMBIAN AND LATER PERIODS

*1968–1978* (New York: Atheneum, 1980). Copyright © 1979 by W. S. Merwin. Reprinted by permission of Georges Borchardt, Inc. for W. S. Merwin.

"War Song" (Cuzco), "To This Song," "Song," and "I Am Raising a Fly," tr. Mark Strand from *Eighteen Poems from the Quechua.* Copyright 1971. Reprinted by permission of Mark Strand.

"Ichi the Dwarf" (Anonymous, Quechua, Peru), tr. W. S. Merwin from *Selected Translations 1968–1978* (New York: Atheneum, 1980). Copyright © 1979 by W. S. Merwin. Reprinted by permission of Georges Borchardt, Inc. for W. S. Merwin.

"Kuchi, Who Brought Trees and Fruit to the Dirt Earth" and "Semenia, the Bird Who Showed How to Plant," from *Watunna: An Orinoco Creation Cycle* by Marc de Civrieux, edited and translated by David M. Guss. Copyirght © 1980. Reprinted by permission of the University of Texas Press.

"The Interrogation of the Chiefs," tr. Ralph Roys from *The Book of Chilam Balam of Chumayel* by Ralph L. Roys. New edition copyright © 1967 by the University of Oklahoma Press, reproduced from the first edition published by the Carnegie Institution of Washington in 1933.

Chilam Balam, *Book of Chumayel,* "How Human Time Begins" and "Last Words," tr. Gordon Brotherston and Ed Dorn. Reprinted by permission of the translators.

Ritual of the Bacabs, "This Is to Cool Burning Fever," tr. Gordon Brotherston. Reprinted by permission of Gordon Brotherston.

X-Kolom-che, "The Archer's Dance Song," tr. Ann London, published in *Shaking the Pumpkin,* edited by Jerome Rothenberg (Doubleday, 1972 and University of New Mexico Press, 1991). Compiled, commented and translated from Maya by Alfredo Barrera Vásquez. © 1965 Instituto Nacional de Antropología e Historia, México. The Ann London Scott papers are located at Schlesinger Library, Radcliffe College. Translation reprinted by permission of Thomas Scott.

"Preamble: Silence of Sea and Sky," from *Popol Vuh,* translated by Dennis Tedlock. Copyright © 1985 by Dennis Tedlock. Reprinted by permission of Simon & Schuster.

Popol Vuh, "The End of the Doll People," tr. Munro Edmunson. Reprinted by permission of Munro Edmundson.

Tlatelolco Annals, "All This Happened among Us," tr. Gordon Brotherston. Reprinted by permission of Gordon Brotherston.

The Aztec Priests' Speech, tr. Gordon Brotherston and Edward Dorn. Reprinted by permission of the translators.

Twenty Sacred Hymns, "Tlaloc (Hymn 3)," tr. Gordon Brotherston and Edward Dorn. Reprinted by permission of the translators.

Twenty Sacred Hymns, "To the Mother of the Gods (Hymn 4)," tr. Edward Kissam from *Poems of the Aztec Peoples,* translated by Edward Kissam and Michael Schmidt. Copyright 1983. Reprinted by permission of Bilingual Press / Editorial Bilingue, Arizona State University, Tempe, AZ.

Twenty Sacred Hymns, "To Ease Birth (Hymn 12)" and "For Eating Unleavened Tamales (Hymn 14)," tr. Anselm Hollo after Edward Seler, published in *Shaking the Pumpkin,* edited by Jerome Rothenberg (Doubleday, 1972). Translations © 1972, 1998 by Anselm Hollo. Reprinted by permission of Anselm Hollo.

Legend of the Suns, "Quetzalcoatl Descends to Mictlan," tr. Gordon Brotherston. Reprinted by permission of Gordon Brotherston.

Legend of the Suns, "The Fifth Sun," tr. John Bierhorst from *History and Mythology of the Aztecs: The Codex Chimalpopoca,* translated from the Nahuatl by John Bierhorst. Copyright © 1992 by John Bierhorst. Reprinted by permission of the University of Arizona Press.

Cuauhtitlan Annals, "The Five Suns," tr. Gordon Brotherston. Reprinted by permission of Gordon Brotherston.

Florentine Codex, "The Toltecs Were Certainly Rich (Book III)" tr. Gordon Brotherston and Edward Dorn. Reprinted by permission of the translators.

Florentine Codex, "The Deadly Dance (Book III)," tr. Edward Kissam from *Poems of the Aztec*

*Peoples,* translated by Edward Kissam and Michael Schmidt. Copyright 1983. Reprinted by permission of Bilingual Press / Editorial Bilingue, Arizona State University, Tempe, AZ.

Florentine Codex, "The Artist (Book X)," tr. Denise Levertov from *Collected Earlier Poems 1940–1960.* Copyright © 1949, 1979 by Denise Levertov. Reprinted by permission of New Directions Publishing Corp.

Cantares Mexicanos, "Orphan Song," tr. Luis Reyes and Gordon Brotherston. Reprinted by permission of the translators.

Cantares Mexicanos, "Could It Be True We Live on Earth?," tr. Edward Kissam from *Poems of the Aztec Peoples,* translated by Edward Kissam and Michael Schmidt. Copyright 1983. Reprinted by permission of Bilingual Press / Editorial Bilingue, Arizona State University, Tempe, AZ.

Cantares Mexicanos, "Death and Rebirth of Tula," tr. Gordon Brotherston. Reprinted by permission of Gordon Brotherston.

Cantares Mexicanos, "Three Nahuatl Poems," tr. William Carlos Williams from *Collected Poems: 1909–1939,* Vol. 1. Copyright © 1938 by New Directions Publishing Corp. Reprinted by permission of New Directions Publishing Corp.

*Yancuic Tlahtolli: The New Word,* "Bird," by J. Fausto Hernández Hernández, tr. Gordon Brotherston. Reprinted by permission of Gordon Brotherston.

## DISCOVERY, CONQUEST, AND THE COLONIES

Christopher Columbus, excerpts from *The Log of Christopher Columbus,* tr. Robert H. Fuson (Camden, ME: International Marine Publishing, a Division of The McGraw-Hill Companies). Reprinted by permission of The McGraw-Hill Companies.

"The Conquest of Cuba" and "Are Not the Indians Men?," tr. George Sanderlin from *Bartolomé de las Casas: A Selection of His Writings* by Bartolomé de las Casas, translated by George Sanderlin. Copyright © 1971 by Alfred A. Knopf Inc. Reprinted by permission of the publisher.

"The Entrance into Mexico" and "The Stay in Mexico," tr. J. M. Cohen from *The Conquest of New Spain* by Bernal Díaz, translated by J. M. Cohen (Penguin Classics, 1963). Copyright © J. M. Cohen, 1963. Reprinted by permission of Penguin Books Ltd.

Excerpts from *Royal Commentaries of the Incas and General History of Peru,* Part One, by Garcilaso de la Vega, translated by Harold V. Livermore. Copyright © 1996. Reprinted by permission of University of Texas Press.

Sor Juana Ines Cruz "In Which She Morally Censures a Rose, and through the Rose Her Peers," tr. Aliki Barnstone and Willis Barnstone. Reprinted by permission of Aliki Barnstone.

Sor Juana Ines de la Cruz, "She Proves the Inconsistency of the Desires and Criticism of Men Who Accuse Women of What They Themselves Cause," tr. Aliki Barnstone and Willis Barnstone. Reprinted by permission of Aliki Barnstone.

Sor Juana Ines Cruz, from "First Dream," tr. Samuel Beckett from *An Anthology of Mexican Poetry* by Octavio Paz. © Samuel Beckett and Octavio Paz 1958, 1986. Reprinted by permission of Indiana University Press.

## NINETEENTH AND TWENTIETH CENTURIES

José Hernández, from *The Gaucho Martín Fierro,* "Martín Fierro Relates His Meeting with Two of His Sons," tr. Walter Owen. Copyright 1936, © 1964 by Henry Holt & Company, Inc. Reprinted by permission of Henry Holt & Company, Inc.

Excerpts from *Epitaph of a Small Winner* by Machado de Assis, translated by William L. Grossman. Translation copyright © 1952 by William Leonard Grossman. Translation copyright renewed © 1980 by Mignon S. Grossman. Reprinted by permission of Farrar, Straus & Giroux, Inc.

Machado De Assis, from *Dom Casmurro*, "Othello," tr. Helen Cauldwell. Translation copyright © 1953 and translation copyright renewed © 1981 by Helen Caldwell. Reprinted by permission of Farrar, Straus & Giroux, Inc.

Rubén Darío, "Symphony in Gray Major," tr. Denise Levertov from reverted rights of Levertov's translations. Copyright © 1961 by Denise Levertov. Reprinted by permission of New Directions Publishing Corp. Also from *An Anthology of Spanish Poetry from Garcilaso to García Lorca*, edited by Angel Flores. Copyright © 1961 by Angel Flores. All Rights Reserved. Reprinted by permission of the Estate of Angel Flores.

"To Roosevelt," by Rubén Darío, translated by Lysander Kemp. In *An Anthology of Spanish Poetry from Garcilaso to García Lorca*, edited by Angel Flores. Copyright © 1961 by Angel Flores. All Rights Reserved. Reprinted by permission of the Estate of Angel Flores. And in *Selected Poems of Rubén Darío*. Copyright © 1965, renewed 1993. Reprinted by permission of the University of Texas Press.

From *Don Segundo Sombra (Shadows on the Pampas)* by Ricardo Güiraldes, translated by Harriet de Onís. Copyright 1935, © 1963 by Henry Holt & Co., Inc. Reprinted by permission of Henry Holt & Co., Inc.

Manuel Bandeira, "Brazilian Tragedy," tr. Elizabeth Bishop from *An Anthology of Twentieth-Century Brazilian Poetry* edited by Elizabeth Bishop and Emanuel Brasil. © 1972 by Wesleyan University. Reprinted by permission of University Press of New England.

"Poems of the Saddest Mother: Cast Out" from *The Mothers' Poems/Poemas de las Madres* by Gabriela Mistral, edited by Margaret Sayers Peden, translated by Christiane Jacox Kyle. English translation copyright 1996 by Christiane Jacox Kyle. Reprinted by permission of Eastern Washington University Press.

Cesar Vallejo, "Our Daily Bread," tr. James Wright from *Above the River: The Complete Poems* by César Vallejo, translated by James Wright. © 1990 by Anne Wright, Wesleyan University Press. Reprinted by permission of University Press of New England.

Alfonsina Storni, "My Sister," "Lighthouse in the Night," and "I Am Going to Sleep," tr. Aliki Barnstone and Willis Barnstone. Reprinted by permission of Aliki Barnstone.

Vincente Huidobro, "Glances and Souvenirs" tr. Paul Blackburn from *Modern European Poetry*, edited by Willis Barnstone. Copyright © 1966 by Bantam Books, a division of Bantam Doubleday Dell Publishing Group, Inc. Used by permission of Bantam Books, a division of Bantam Doubleday Dell Publishing Group, Inc.

Miguel Angel Asturias, "Legend of 'El Cadejo,'" tr. Hardie St. Martin. Reprinted by permission of Hardie St. Martin.

"Borges and I" from *A Personal Anthology* by Jorge Luís Borges, translated by Anthony Kerrigan. Copyright © 1967 by Grove Press, Inc. Used by permission of Grove/Atlantic, Inc.

"Kafka and His Precursors," from *Other Inquisitions: 1937–1952* by Jorge Luís Borges, translated by Ruth L. C. Simms. Copyright © 1964, renewed 1993. Reprinted by permission of the University of Texas Press.

"The South" and "Death and the Compass," from *Ficciones* by Jorge Luís Borges, translated by Anthony Kerrigan. Copyright © 1962 by Grove Press, Inc. Used by permission of Grove/Atlantic, Inc.

"Poem of the Gifts," tr. Willis Barnstone from *The Collected Works of Jorge Luís Borges*, 3 Vols., by Jorge Luís Borges. Translation copyright © 1967 by Willis Barnstone. Used by permission of Viking Penguin, a division of Penguin Putnam Inc.

Jorge Luís Borges, "The Labyrinth," tr. John Updike. Copyright © 1972 by Emece Editores, S.A. and Norman Thomas di Giovanni, English translation. Used by permission of Viking Penguin, a division of Penguin Putnam Inc.

"In Praise of Shadow," tr. Tony Barnstone and Willis Barnstone from *The Collected Works of Jorge Luís Borges*, 3 Vols., by Jorge Luís Borges. Translation copyright © 1998 by Willis and Tony Barnstone. Used by permission of Viking Penguin, a division of Penguin Putnam Inc.

Jorge Luís Borges, "The Other Tiger," "A Blind Man," and "Remorse," tr. Willis Barnstone. Copyright © 1998 by Willis Barnstone. Used by permission of Viking Penguin, a division of Penguin Putnam Inc.

"Spinoza," tr. Willis Barnstone from *The Collected Works of Jorge Luís Borges,* 3 Vols., by Jorge Luís Borges. Translation copyright © 1998 by Willis and Tony Barnstone. Used by permission of Viking Penguin, a division of Penguin Putnam Inc

Jorge Luís Borges, "Camden," tr. Willis Barnstone. Copyright © 1998 by Willis and Tony Barnstone. Used by permission of Viking Penguin, a division of Penguin Putnam Inc.

Jorge Luís Borges, "Proteus," "I Am," "To the Mirror," tr. Tony Barnstone. Copyright © 1998 by Tony and Willis Barnstone. Used by permission of Viking Penguin, a division of Penguin Putnam Inc.

Cecilia Meireles, "Ballad of the Ten Casino Dancers," tr. James Merrill from *An Anthology of Twentieth-Century Brazilian Poetry* edited by Elizabeth Bishop and Emanuel Brasil. © 1972 by Wesleyan University. Reprinted by permission of University Press of New England.

Carlos Drummond de Andrade, "Seven-Sided Poem," tr. Elizabeth Bishop; "Widower's Song," tr. Willis Barnstone; "Souvenir of the Ancient World," tr. Mark Strand; "Family Portrait," tr. Elizabeth Bishop; and "Song for a Young Girl's Album," tr. Mark Strand from *Travelling in the Family* by Carlos Drummond de Andrade (various translators). Copyright © 1986 by Carlos Drummond de Andrade and Thomas Colchie. Reprinted by permission of Random House Inc.

Alejo Carpentier, "Like the Night," tr. Frances Partridge. Reprinted by permission of Fundación Alejo Carpentier, Havana.

João Guimarães Rosa, "The Third Bank of the River," tr. Barbara Shelby Merello from *The Third Bank of the River and Other Stories* by João Guimarães Rosa, translated by B. Shelby. Copyright © 1968 by Alfred A. Knopf Inc. Reprinted by permission of the publisher.

Juan Carlos Onetti, "The Dog Will Have Its Day," tr. Andrew Hurley. In *Tan triste como ella y otros cuentos,* by Juan Carlos Onetti, translated by Andrew Hurley. Reprinted by permission of Agencia Literaria Carmen Balcells, agent for the estate of Juan Carlos Onetti. And in *A Hammock Beneath the Mangoes,* edited by Thomas Colchie. Copyright 1992. Reprinted by permission of Andrew Hurley.

Jorge Amado, from *The Two Deaths of Quincas Wateryell,* "A Certain Amount of Confusion," tr. Barbara Shelby Merello. Copyright © 1965 by Alfred A. Knopf, Inc. Reprinted by permission of Alfred A. Knopf, Inc.

Leon Damas, "Position Paper," tr. Robert Bagg from *The Contemporary World of Poetry,* edited by Donald Junkins. Reprinted by permission of Donald Junkins.

Vincius de Moraes, "Song," tr. Richard Wilbur from *An Anthology of Twentieth-Century Brazilian Poetry* edited by Elizabeth Bishop and Emanuel Brasil. © 1972 by Wesleyan University. Reprinted by permission of University Press of New England.

Aimé Cesaire, "zaffer sun" and "abyss," tr. Clayton Eshelman and Annette Smith from *Lyric and Dramatic Poetry, 1946–82 (moi, luminaire...).* Copyright © Editions du Seuil, 1982. Reprinted by permission of Georges Borchardt, Inc.

Julia de Burgos, "Nothing," tr. Aliki Barnstone and Willis Barnstone. Reprinted by permission of Aliki Barnstone.

Julio Cortázar, "Axolotl," tr. Paul Blackburn from *End of the Game and Other Stories* by Julio Cortázar, translated by P. Blackburn. Copyright © 1967, 1963 by Random House Inc. Reprinted by permission of Pantheon Books, a Division of Random House Inc.

Octavio Paz, "Sight, Touch," tr. Mark Strand from *Selected Poems* by Octavio Paz, translated by Mark Strand. Copyright © 1979 by Octavio Paz and Mark Strand. Reprinted by permission of New Directions Publishing Corp.

Octavio Paz, "The Key of Water," tr. Elizabeth Bishop from *Collected Poems 1957–1987.* Copyright © 1972, 1975 by Octavio Paz and Elizabeth Bishop. Used by permission of Farrar, Straus & Giroux. Reprinted by permission of New Directions Publishing Corp.

"I Heard Her Sing," tr. Donald Gardner and Suzanne Jill Levine, from *Three Trapped Tigers* by Guillermo Cabrera Infante. English translation copyright © 1971 by Harper & Row, Publishers, Inc. Reprinted bypermission of HarperCollins Publishers, Inc.

V. S. Naipaul, from *Miguel Street,* "The Thing without a Name" and "George and the Pink House." Copyright © 1959 by V. S. Naipaul. Used by permission of Viking Penguin, a division of Penguin Books USA Inc., and Wylie, Aitken & Stone.

"Up among the Eagles," from *Open Door: Stories* by Luisa Valenzuela, translated by Margaret Sayers Peden (San Francisco: North Point Press). Copyright 1988. Reprinted by permission of Rosario Santos, agent for Luisa Valenzuela.

José Emilio Pacheco, "From Some Time to This Place," tr. Philip Levine from *New Poetry of Mexico,* edited by Mark Strand (Farrar, Straus & Giroux, 1970). © Philip Levine. Reprinted by permission of Philip Levine.

José Emilio Pacheco, "Whistler's London," tr. George McWhirter from *Selected Poems.* Copyright © 1975, 1987 by George McWhirter. Reprinted by permission of New Directions Publishing Corp.

Gustavo Sainz, from *The Princess of Iron Palace,* "He Had a Chivas Regal Face," tr. Andrew Hurley. English translation copyright © 1987 by Andrew Hurley. Used by permission of Grove/Atlantic, Inc.

"Gift for a Sweetheart," from *The Stories of Eva Luna* by Isabel Allende, translated from Spanish by Margaret Sayers Peden. Copyright © 1989 by Isabel Allende, English translation copyright 1991 by Macmillan Publishing Company. Reprinted by permission of Scribner, a Division of Simon & Schuster.

From *Singing from the Well,* by Reinaldo Arenas, translated by Andrew Hurley. Translation copyright © 1987 by Andrew Hurley and Reinaldo Arenas, English translation. Used by permission of Viking Penguin, a division of Penguin Books USA Inc.

Jamaica Kincaid, "Girl," from *At the Bottom of the River.* Copyright © 1983 by Jamaica Kincaid. Reprinted by permission of Farrar, Straus & Giroux, Inc.

Laura Esquivel, from *Like Water for Chocolate,* tr. Carol Christiansen and Thomas Christiansen. Translation copyright © 1992 by Doubleday, a div. of Bantam, Doubleday, Dell Publishing Group Inc. Used by permission of Doubleday, a division of Bantam Doubleday Dell Publishing Group, Inc.

Giannina Braschi, from *Empire of Dreams,* tr. Tess O'Dwyer. Copyright 1994 by Yale University. Reprinted by permission of Yale University Press.

# INDEX